Official 2007
National Football League

Record
& Fact Book

NATIONAL FOOTBALL LEAGUE
280 Park Avenue, New York, N.Y. 10017 (212) 450-2000. NFL Internet Address: http://www.NFL.com

Printed in the United States of America.

A National Football League Book.

Compiled by the NFL Communications Department and Seymour Siwoff, Elias Sports Bureau.
Statistics by Elias Sports Bureau.

Edited by Jon Zimmer and Randall Liu, NFL Communications Department, and Matt Marini. Layout by William Tham. Cover design by NFL Creative.
Produced by NFL Communications Department.

Cover photograph of Peyton Manning of the Super Bowl XLI champion Indianapolis Colts by Jonathan Daniel/GETTY IMAGES.

Time Inc. Home Entertainment
1271 Avenue of the Americas, New York, N.Y. 10020
Manufactured in the United States of America.
First printing, July 2007.
10 9 8 7 6 5 4 3 2 1

A National Football League Book
Time Inc. Home Entertainment

TABLE OF CONTENTS

All times local. Dates and times subject to change.
Nationally televised games indicated by network in parentheses.

Sunday, August 5	Hall of Fame Game at Canton, Ohio	
	New Orleans _____ vs. Pittsburgh _____	(NFLN) 8:00

PRESEASON/WEEK 1

Thursday, August 9	Indianapolis _____ at Dallas _____	(FOX) 7:00
	Cincinnati _____ at Detroit _____	7:30
Friday, August 10	Buffalo _____ at New Orleans _____	(CBS) 7:00
	Atlanta _____ at New York Jets _____	7:00
	New England _____ at Tampa Bay _____	7:30
	St. Louis _____ at Minnesota _____	7:00
Saturday, August 11	Washington _____ at Tennessee _____	(NFLN) 7:00
	Green Bay _____ at Pittsburgh _____	7:30
	Jacksonville _____ at Miami _____	7:30
	Kansas City _____ at Cleveland _____	7:30
	Carolina _____ at New York Giants _____	8:00
	Chicago _____ at Houston _____	7:00
	Arizona _____ at Oakland _____	7:00
Sunday, August 12	Seattle _____ at San Diego _____	(NBC) 5:00
Monday, August 13	Denver _____ at San Francisco _____	(ESPN) 5:00
	Philadelphia _____ at Baltimore _____	7:00

PRESEASON/WEEK 2

Thursday, August 16	Miami _____ at Kansas City _____	(ESPN) 7:00
Friday, August 17	Minnesota _____ at New York Jets _____	(FOX) 8:00
	Atlanta _____ at Buffalo _____	7:00
	Carolina _____ at Philadelphia _____	7:00
	Tennessee _____ at New England _____	8:00
Saturday, August 18	San Diego _____ at St. Louis _____	(CBS) 7:00
	Houston _____ at Arizona _____	1:00
	Detroit _____ at Cleveland _____	7:00
	New Orleans _____ at Cincinnati _____	7:30
	Tampa Bay _____ at Jacksonville _____	7:30
	Denver _____ at Dallas _____	7:00
	Pittsburgh _____ at Washington _____	8:00
	Seattle _____ at Green Bay _____	7:00
	Oakland _____ at San Francisco _____	7:00
Sunday, August 19	New York Giants _____ at Baltimore _____	(NBC) 8:00
Monday, August 20	Chicago _____ at Indianapolis _____	(ESPN) 8:00

PRESEASON/WEEK 3

Thursday, August 23	Jacksonville _____ at Green Bay _____	(FOX) 7:00
	New Orleans _____ at Kansas City _____	7:30
Friday, August 24	New England _____ at Carolina _____	(CBS) 8:00
	Tennessee _____ at Buffalo _____	7:00
	St. Louis _____ at Oakland _____	7:00
Saturday, August 25	Detroit _____ at Indianapolis _____	7:00
	Tampa Bay _____ at Miami _____	7:30
	Baltimore _____ at Washington _____	8:00
	Dallas _____ at Houston _____	7:00
	New York Jets _____ at New York Giants _____	8:00
	San Francisco _____ at Chicago _____	7:00
	Cleveland _____ at Denver _____	7:00
	Minnesota _____ at Seattle _____	6:00
	San Diego _____ at Arizona _____	7:00
Sunday, August 26	Philadelphia _____ at Pittsburgh _____	(NBC) 8:00
Monday, August 27	Cincinnati _____ at Atlanta _____	(ESPN) 8:00

PRESEASON/WEEK 4

Thursday, August 30
Buffalo _____ at Detroit _____	7:00
New York Giants _____ at New England _____	7:30
New York Jets _____ at Philadelphia _____	7:30
Washington _____ at Jacksonville _____	7:30
Cleveland _____ at Chicago _____	7:00
Dallas _____ at Minnesota _____	7:00
Green Bay _____ at Tennessee _____	7:00
Houston _____ at Tampa Bay _____	8:00
Kansas City _____ at St. Louis _____	7:00
Miami _____ at New Orleans _____	7:00
Pittsburgh _____ at Carolina _____	8:00
Arizona _____ at Denver _____	7:00
Oakland _____ at Seattle _____	7:00
San Francisco _____ at San Diego _____	7:00

Friday, August 31
Baltimore _____ at Atlanta _____	7:30
Indianapolis _____ at Cincinnati _____	7:30

KICKOFF WEEKEND

Thursday, September 6
New Orleans _____ at Indianapolis _____	8:30

Sunday, September 9
Denver _____ at Buffalo _____	1:00
Pittsburgh _____ at Cleveland _____	1:00
Philadelphia _____ at Green Bay _____	12:00
Kansas City _____ at Houston _____	12:00
Tennessee _____ at Jacksonville _____	1:00
Atlanta _____ at Minnesota _____	12:00
New England _____ at N.Y. Jets _____	1:00
Carolina _____ at St. Louis _____	12:00
Miami _____ at Washington _____	1:00
Detroit _____ at Oakland _____	1:15
Chicago _____ at San Diego _____	1:15
Tampa Bay _____ at Seattle _____	1:15
N.Y. Giants _____ at Dallas _____	7:15

Monday, September 10
Baltimore _____ at Cincinnati _____	7:00
Arizona _____ at San Francisco _____	7:15

SECOND WEEKEND

Sunday, September 16
Houston _____ at Carolina _____	1:00
Cincinnati _____ at Cleveland _____	1:00
Atlanta _____ at Jacksonville _____	1:00
Green Bay _____ at N.Y. Giants _____	1:00
Buffalo _____ at Pittsburgh _____	1:00
San Francisco _____ at St. Louis _____	12:00
New Orleans _____ at Tampa Bay _____	1:00
Indianapolis _____ at Tennessee _____	12:00
Seattle _____ at Arizona _____	1:05
Minnesota _____ at Detroit _____	4:05
Dallas _____ at Miami _____	4:05
N.Y. Jets _____ at Baltimore _____	4:15
Kansas City _____ at Chicago _____	3:15
Oakland _____ at Denver _____	2:15
San Diego _____ at New England _____	8:15

Monday, September 17
Washington _____ at Philadelphia _____	8:30

THIRD WEEKEND

Sunday, September 23
Arizona _____ at Baltimore _____	1:00
San Diego _____ at Green Bay _____	12:00
Indianapolis _____ at Houston _____	12:00
Minnesota _____ at Kansas City _____	12:00
Buffalo _____ at New England _____	1:00
Miami _____ at N.Y. Jets _____	1:00
Detroit _____ at Philadelphia _____	1:00
San Francisco _____ at Pittsburgh _____	1:00
St. Louis _____ at Tampa Bay _____	1:00
Jacksonville _____ at Denver _____	2:05
Cleveland _____ at Oakland _____	1:05
Cincinnati _____ at Seattle _____	1:05
Carolina _____ at Atlanta _____	4:15
N.Y. Giants _____ at Washington _____	4:15
Dallas _____ at Chicago _____	7:15

Monday, September 24
Tennessee _____ at New Orleans _____	7:30

FOURTH WEEKEND
Open Dates:
Jacksonville, New Orleans, Tennessee, Washington

Sunday, September 30	Houston _____ at Atlanta _____	1:00
	N.Y. Jets _____ at Buffalo _____	1:00
	Baltimore _____ at Cleveland _____	1:00
	St. Louis _____ at Dallas _____	12:00
	Chicago _____ at Detroit _____	1:00
	Oakland _____ at Miami _____	1:00
	Green Bay _____ at Minnesota _____	12:00
	Tampa Bay _____ at Carolina _____	4:05
	Seattle _____ at San Francisco _____	1:05
	Pittsburgh _____ at Arizona _____	1:15
	Denver _____ at Indianapolis _____	4:15
	Kansas City _____ at San Diego _____	1:15
	Philadelphia _____ at N.Y. Giants _____	8:15
Monday, October 1	New England _____ at Cincinnati _____	8:30

FIFTH WEEKEND
Open Dates:
Cincinnati, Minnesota, Oakland, Philadelphia

Sunday, October 7	Miami _____ at Houston _____	12:00
	Jacksonville _____ at Kansas City _____	12:00
	Cleveland _____ at New England _____	1:00
	Carolina _____ at New Orleans _____	12:00
	N.Y. Jets _____ at N.Y. Giants _____	1:00
	Seattle _____ at Pittsburgh _____	1:00
	Arizona _____ at St. Louis _____	12:00
	Atlanta _____ at Tennessee _____	12:00
	Detroit _____ at Washington _____	1:00
	Tampa Bay _____ at Indianapolis _____	4:05
	San Diego _____ at Denver _____	2:15
	Baltimore _____ at San Francisco _____	1:15
	Chicago _____ at Green Bay _____	7:15
Monday, October 8	Dallas _____ at Buffalo _____	8:30

SIXTH WEEKEND
Open Dates:
Buffalo, Denver, Detroit,
Indianapolis, Pittsburgh, San Francisco

Sunday, October 14	St. Louis _____ at Baltimore _____	1:00
	Minnesota _____ at Chicago _____	12:00
	Miami _____ at Cleveland _____	1:00
	Washington _____ at Green Bay _____	12:00
	Houston _____ at Jacksonville _____	1:00
	Cincinnati _____ at Kansas City _____	12:00
	Philadelphia _____ at N.Y. Jets _____	1:00
	Tennessee _____ at Tampa Bay _____	1:00
	Carolina _____ at Arizona _____	1:05
	New England _____ at Dallas _____	3:15
	Oakland _____ at San Diego _____	1:15
	New Orleans _____ at Seattle _____	5:15
Monday, October 15	N.Y. Giants _____ at Atlanta _____	8:30

SEVENTH WEEKEND
Open Dates:
Carolina, Cleveland, Green Bay, San Diego

Sunday, October 21	Baltimore _____ at Buffalo _____	1:00
	Minnesota _____ at Dallas _____	12:00
	Tampa Bay _____ at Detroit _____	1:00
	Tennessee _____ at Houston _____	12:00
	New England _____ at Miami _____	1:00
	San Francisco _____ at N.Y. Giants _____	1:00
	Atlanta _____ at New Orleans _____	12:00
	Arizona _____ at Washington _____	1:00
	N.Y. Jets _____ at Cincinnati _____	4:05
	Kansas City _____ at Oakland _____	1:05
	Chicago _____ at Philadelphia _____	4:15
	St. Louis _____ at Seattle _____	1:15
	Pittsburgh _____ at Denver _____	6:15
Monday, October 22	Indianapolis _____ at Jacksonville _____	8:30

EIGHTH WEEKEND
Open Dates:
Arizona, Atlanta, Baltimore, Dallas, Kansas City, Seattle

NFL INTERNATIONAL SERIES
◄ LONDON ►

Sunday, October 28	Indianapolis _____ at Carolina _____	1:00
	Detroit _____ at Chicago _____	12:00
	Pittsburgh _____ at Cincinnati _____	1:00
	N.Y. Giants _____ at Miami (London) _____	5:00
	Philadelphia _____ at Minnesota _____	12:00
	Cleveland _____ at St. Louis _____	12:00
	Oakland _____ at Tennessee _____	12:00
	Buffalo _____ at N.Y. Jets _____	4:05
	Houston _____ at San Diego _____	1:05
	Jacksonville _____ at Tampa Bay _____	4:05
	Washington _____ at New England _____	4:15
	New Orleans _____ at San Francisco _____	1:15
Monday, October 29	Green Bay _____ at Denver _____	6:30

NINTH WEEKEND
Open Dates:
Chicago, Miami, N.Y. Giants, St. Louis

Sunday, November 4	San Francisco _____ at Atlanta _____	1:00
	Cincinnati _____ at Buffalo _____	1:00
	Denver _____ at Detroit _____	1:00
	Green Bay _____ at Kansas City _____	12:00
	San Diego _____ at Minnesota _____	12:00
	Jacksonville _____ at New Orleans _____	12:00
	Washington _____ at N.Y. Jets _____	1:00
	Arizona _____ at Tampa Bay _____	1:00
	Carolina _____ at Tennessee _____	12:00
	Seattle _____ at Cleveland _____	4:05
	New England _____ at Indianapolis _____	4:15
	Houston _____ at Oakland _____	1:15
	Dallas _____ at Philadelphia _____	8:15
Monday, November 5	Baltimore _____ at Pittsburgh _____	8:30

TENTH WEEKEND
Open Dates:
Houston, New England, N.Y. Jets, Tampa Bay

Sunday, November 11	Atlanta _____ at Carolina _____	1:00
	Minnesota _____ at Green Bay _____	12:00
	Denver _____ at Kansas City _____	12:00
	Buffalo _____ at Miami _____	1:00
	St. Louis _____ at New Orleans _____	12:00
	Cleveland _____ at Pittsburgh _____	1:00
	Jacksonville _____ at Tennessee _____	12:00
	Philadelphia _____ at Washington _____	1:00
	Cincinnati _____ at Baltimore _____	4:05
	Detroit _____ at Arizona _____	2:15
	Dallas _____ at N.Y. Giants _____	4:15
	Chicago _____ at Oakland _____	1:15
	Indianapolis _____ at San Diego _____	5:15
Monday, November 12	San Francisco _____ at Seattle _____	5:30

ELEVENTH WEEKEND

Sunday, November 18	Tampa Bay _____ at Atlanta _____	1:00
	Cleveland _____ at Baltimore _____	1:00
	New England _____ at Buffalo _____	1:00
	Arizona _____ at Cincinnati _____	1:00
	Washington _____ at Dallas _____	12:00
	Carolina _____ at Green Bay _____	12:00
	New Orleans _____ at Houston _____	12:00
	Kansas City _____ at Indianapolis _____	1:00
	San Diego _____ at Jacksonville _____	1:00
	Oakland _____ at Minnesota _____	12:00
	Pittsburgh _____ at N.Y. Jets _____	1:00
	Miami _____ at Philadelphia _____	1:00
	N.Y. Giants _____ at Detroit _____	4:15
	St. Louis _____ at San Francisco _____	1:15
	Chicago _____ at Seattle _____	*5:15
Monday, November 19	Tennessee _____ at Denver _____	6:30

*-Sunday Night Games In Weeks 11-17 Subject To Change

TWELFTH WEEKEND

NFL THANKSGIVING 2007

Thursday, November 22	Green Bay _____ at Detroit _____	12:30
	N.Y. Jets _____ at Dallas _____	3:15
	Indianapolis _____ at Atlanta _____	8:15
Sunday, November 25	New Orleans _____ at Carolina _____	1:00
	Denver _____ at Chicago _____	12:00
	Tennessee _____ at Cincinnati _____	1:00
	Houston _____ at Cleveland _____	1:00
	Buffalo _____ at Jacksonville _____	1:00
	Oakland _____ at Kansas City _____	12:00
	Minnesota _____ at N.Y. Giants _____	1:00
	Seattle _____ at St. Louis _____	12:00
	Washington _____ at Tampa Bay _____	1:00
	San Francisco _____ at Arizona _____	2:05
	Baltimore _____ at San Diego _____	1:15
	Philadelphia _____ at New England _____	*8:15
Monday, November 26	Miami _____ at Pittsburgh _____	8:30

*-Sunday Night Games In Weeks 11-17 Subject To Change

THIRTEENTH WEEKEND

Thursday, November 29	Green Bay _____ at Dallas _____	7:15
Sunday, December 2	San Francisco _____ at Carolina _____	1:00
	Jacksonville _____ at Indianapolis _____	1:00
	San Diego _____ at Kansas City _____	12:00
	N.Y. Jets _____ at Miami _____	1:00
	Detroit _____ at Minnesota _____	12:00
	Tampa Bay _____ at New Orleans _____	12:00
	Seattle _____ at Philadelphia _____	1:00
	Atlanta _____ at St. Louis _____	12:00
	Houston _____ at Tennessee _____	12:00
	Buffalo _____ at Washington _____	1:00
	Cleveland _____ at Arizona _____	2:05
	Denver _____ at Oakland _____	1:05
	N.Y. Giants _____ at Chicago _____	3:15
	Cincinnati _____ at Pittsburgh _____	*8:15
Monday, December 3	New England _____ at Baltimore _____	8:30

*-Sunday Night Games In Weeks 11-17 Subject To Change

FOURTEENTH WEEKEND

Thursday, December 6	Chicago _____ at Washington _____	8:15
Sunday, December 9	Miami _____ at Buffalo _____	1:00
	St. Louis _____ at Cincinnati _____	1:00
	Dallas _____ at Detroit _____	1:00
	Oakland _____ at Green Bay _____	12:00
	Tampa Bay _____ at Houston _____	12:00
	Carolina _____ at Jacksonville _____	1:00
	Pittsburgh _____ at New England _____	1:00
	N.Y. Giants _____ at Philadelphia _____	1:00
	San Diego _____ at Tennessee _____	12:00
	Minnesota _____ at San Francisco _____	1:05
	Arizona _____ at Seattle _____	1:05
	Kansas City _____ at Denver _____	2:15
	Cleveland _____ at N.Y. Jets _____	4:15
	Indianapolis _____ at Baltimore _____	*8:15
Monday, December 10	New Orleans _____ at Atlanta _____	8:30

*-Sunday Night Games In Weeks 11-17 Subject To Change

FIFTEENTH WEEKEND

Thursday, December 13	Denver _____ at Houston _____	7:15
Saturday, December 15	Cincinnati _____ at San Francisco _____	5:15
Sunday, December 16	Seattle _____ at Carolina _____	1:00
	Buffalo _____ at Cleveland _____	1:00
	Tennessee _____ at Kansas City _____	12:00
	Baltimore _____ at Miami _____	1:00
	N.Y. Jets _____ at New England _____	1:00
	Arizona _____ at New Orleans _____	12:00
	Jacksonville _____ at Pittsburgh _____	1:00
	Green Bay _____ at St. Louis _____	12:00
	Atlanta _____ at Tampa Bay _____	1:00
	Indianapolis _____ at Oakland _____	1:05
	Philadelphia _____ at Dallas _____	3:15
	Detroit _____ at San Diego _____	1:15
	Washington _____ at N.Y. Giants _____	*8:15
Monday, December 17	Chicago _____ at Minnesota _____	7:30

-Sunday Night Games In Weeks 11-17 Subject To Change

SIXTEENTH WEEKEND

Thursday, December 20	Pittsburgh _____ at St. Louis _____	7:15
Saturday, December 22	Dallas _____ at Carolina _____	8:15
Sunday, December 23	N.Y. Giants _____ at Buffalo _____	1:00
	Green Bay _____ at Chicago _____	12:00
	Cleveland _____ at Cincinnati _____	1:00
	Kansas City _____ at Detroit _____	1:00
	Houston _____ at Indianapolis _____	1:00
	Oakland _____ at Jacksonville _____	1:00
	Washington _____ at Minnesota _____	12:00
	Miami _____ at New England _____	1:00
	Philadelphia _____ at New Orleans _____	12:00
	Atlanta _____ at Arizona _____	2:05
	Baltimore _____ at Seattle _____	1:15
	N.Y. Jets _____ at Tennessee _____	3:15
	Tampa Bay _____ at San Francisco _____	*5:15
Monday, December 24	Denver _____ at San Diego _____	5:00

-Sunday Night Games In Weeks 11-17 Subject To Change

SEVENTEENTH WEEKEND

Saturday, December 29	New England _____ at N.Y. Giants _____	8:15
Sunday, December 30	Seattle _____ at Atlanta _____	1:00
	Pittsburgh _____ at Baltimore _____	1:00
	New Orleans _____ at Chicago _____	12:00
	San Francisco _____ at Cleveland _____	1:00
	Detroit _____ at Green Bay _____	12:00
	Jacksonville _____ at Houston _____	12:00
	Tennessee _____ at Indianapolis _____	1:00
	Cincinnati _____ at Miami _____	1:00
	Buffalo _____ at Philadelphia _____	1:00
	Carolina _____ at Tampa Bay _____	1:00
	Dallas _____ at Washington _____	1:00
	St. Louis _____ at Arizona _____	2:15
	Minnesota _____ at Denver _____	2:15
	San Diego _____ at Oakland _____	1:15
	Kansas City _____ at N.Y. Jets _____	*8:15

-Sunday Night Games In Weeks 11-17 Subject To Change

PLAYOFFS

Wild Card Playoff Games
Site Priorities
Two Wild Card teams (division non-champions with best two records) from each conference and the division champions with the third and fourth-best record in each conference will enter the first round of the playoffs. The division champion with the third-best record will play host to the Wild Card team with the second-best record. The division champion with the fourth-best record will play host to the Wild Card team with the best record. There are no restrictions on intra-division games.

Saturday, January 5, 2008   American Football Conference

_____ at _____ (NBC)

National Football Conference

_____ at _____ (NBC)

Sunday, January 6, 2008   American Football Conference

_____ at _____ (CBS)

National Football Conference

_____ at _____ (FOX)

Divisional Playoff Games
Site Priorities
In each conference, the two division champions with the highest won-lost-tied percentage during the regular season will play host to the Wild Card winners. The division champion with the best record in each conference is assured of playing the lowest seeded Wild Card survivor. There are no restrictions on intra-division games.

Saturday, January 12, 2008   American Football Conference

_____ at _____ (CBS)

National Football Conference

_____ at _____ (FOX)

Sunday, January 13, 2008   American Football Conference

_____ at _____ (CBS)

National Football Conference

_____ at _____ (FOX)

Championship Games
Site Priorities for
Championship Games
The home teams will be the surviving playoff winners with the highest seeds. A Wild Card team cannot play host unless two Wild Card teams are in the game, in which case the Wild Card team that was seeded highest in the first round of the playoffs will be the home team.

Sunday, January 20, 2008   American Football Conference

_____ at _____ (CBS)

National Football Conference

_____ at _____ (FOX)

Super Bowl XLII

Sunday, February 3, 2008   Super Bowl XLII at University of Phoenix Stadium, Glendale, Arizona

_____ vs. _____ (FOX)

AFC-NFC Pro Bowl

Sunday, February 10, 2008   AFC-NFC Pro Bowl at Aloha Stadium, Honolulu, Hawaii

AFC_____ vs. NFC _____ (FOX)

2007 NATIONALLY TELEVISED GAMES AT A GLANCE

All times ET.

Thursday, Sept. 6	New Orleans at Indianapolis (NBC)	8:30 P.M.
Sunday, Sept. 9	N.Y. Giants at Dallas (NBC)	8:15 P.M.
Monday, Sept. 10	Baltimore at Cincinnati (ESPN)	7:00 P.M.
	Arizona at San Francisco (ESPN)	10:15 P.M.
Sunday, Sept. 16	San Diego at New England (NBC)	8:15 P.M.
Monday, Sept. 17	Washington at Philadelphia (ESPN)	8:30 P.M.
Sunday, Sept. 23	Dallas at Chicago (NBC)	8:15 P.M.
Monday, Sept. 24	Tennessee at New Orleans (ESPN)	8:30 P.M.
Sunday, Sept. 30	Philadelphia at N.Y. Giants (NBC)	8:15 P.M.
Monday, Oct. 1	New England at Cincinnati (ESPN)	8:30 P.M.
Sunday, Oct. 7	Chicago at Green Bay (NBC)	8:15 P.M.
Monday, Oct. 8	Dallas at Buffalo (ESPN)	8:30 P.M.
Sunday, Oct. 14	New Orleans at Seattle (NBC)	8:15 P.M.
Monday, Oct. 15	N.Y. Giants at Atlanta (ESPN)	8:30 P.M.
Sunday, Oct. 21	Pittsburgh at Denver (NBC)	8:15 P.M.
Monday, Oct. 22	Indianapolis at Jacksonville (ESPN)	8:30 P.M.
Monday, Oct. 29	Green Bay at Denver (ESPN)	8:30 P.M.
Sunday, Nov. 4	Dallas at Philadelphia (NBC)	8:15 P.M.
Monday, Nov. 5	Baltimore at Pittsburgh (ESPN)	8:30 P.M.
Sunday, Nov. 11	Indianapolis at San Diego (NBC)	8:15 P.M.
Monday, Nov. 12	San Francisco at Seattle (ESPN)	8:30 P.M.
Sunday, Nov. 18	Chicago at Seattle (NBC)*	8:15 P.M.
Monday, Nov. 19	Tennessee at Denver (ESPN)	8:30 P.M.
Thursday, Nov. 22	Green Bay at Detroit (CBS)	12:30 P.M.
	N.Y. Jets at Dallas (FOX)	4:15 P.M.
	Indianapolis at Atlanta (NFL Network)	8:15 P.M.
Sunday, Nov. 25	Philadelphia at New England (NBC)*	8:15 P.M.
Monday, Nov. 26	Miami at Pittsburgh (ESPN)	8:30 P.M.
Thursday, Nov. 30	Green Bay at Dallas (NFL Network)	8:00 P.M.
Sunday, Dec. 2	Cincinnati at Pittsburgh (NBC)*	8:15 P.M.
Monday, Dec. 3	New England at Baltimore (ESPN)	8:30 P.M.
Thursday, Dec. 6	Chicago at Washington (NFL Network)	8:15 P.M.
Sunday, Dec. 9	Indianapolis at Baltimore (NBC)*	8:15 P.M.
Monday, Dec. 10	New Orleans at Atlanta (ESPN)	8:30 P.M.
Thursday, Dec. 13	Denver at Houston (NFL Network)	8:15 P.M.
Saturday, Dec. 15	Cincinnati at San Francisco (NFL Network)	8:15 P.M.
Sunday, Dec. 16	Washington at N.Y. Giants (NBC)*	8:15 P.M.
Monday, Dec. 17	Chicago at Minnesota (ESPN)	8:30 P.M.
Thursday, Dec. 20	Pittsburgh at St. Louis (NFL Network)	8:15 P.M.
Saturday, Dec. 22	Dallas at Carolina (NFL Network)	8:15 P.M.
Sunday, Dec. 23	Tampa Bay at San Francisco (NBC)*	8:15 P.M.
Monday, Dec. 24	Denver at San Diego (ESPN)	8:00 P.M.
Saturday, Dec. 29	New England at N.Y. Giants (NFL Network)	8:15 P.M.
Sunday, Dec. 30	Kansas City at N.Y. Jets (NBC)*	8:15 P.M.

POSTSEASON GAMES

Saturday, January 5	AFC and NFC Wild Card Playoffs (NBC)
Sunday, January 6	AFC and NFC Wild Card Playoffs (CBS and FOX)
Saturday, January 12	AFC and NFC Divisional Playoffs (CBS and FOX)
Sunday, January 13	AFC and NFC Divisional Playoffs (CBS and FOX)
Sunday, January 20	AFC and NFC Championship Games (CBS and FOX)
Sunday, February 3	Super Bowl XLII at University of Phoenix Stadium, Glendale, Arizona (FOX)
Sunday, February 10	AFC-NFC Pro Bowl in Honolulu, Hawaii (FOX)

The NFL again will utilize "flexible scheduling" in 2007.

In the final seven weeks of the season (Weeks 11-17), the schedule lists the games tentatively set for Sunday night on NBC. Only Sunday afternoon games are eligible to be moved to Sunday night, in which case the tentatively scheduled Sunday night game will be moved to an afternoon start time.

A flexible scheduling move will be announced at least 12 days before the game. For Week 17, the change may be announced six days before the game. Flexible scheduling will ensure quality matchups on Sunday night in those weeks and give "surprise" teams a chance to play their way onto primetime.

2007

July 5 Claiming period of 24 hours begins in waiver system.

Mid-July Preseason training camps open. Clubs not permitted to open official preseason camp earlier than July 5. Veteran players cannot be required to report earlier than 15 days prior to club's first preseason game.

July 16 Deadline at 4 P.M., New York time, for any club that designated a Franchise Player to sign such player to a multi-year contract or extension. After this date, the player may sign only a one-year ctonract with the designating club for the 2007 season, and such contract cannot be extended until after the Club's last regular season game.

July 22 Signing period ends at 4 P.M., New York time, for Transition Players with outstanding tenders. After this date and through 4 P.M., New York time, on the Tuesday after the 10th regular season weekend, Old Club has exclusive negotiating rights to these players.

July 22# Signing period ends at 4 P.M., New York time, for Unrestricted Free Agents to whom a June 1 tender was made by Old Club. After this date and through 4 P.M., New York time, on the Tuesday after the 10th regular season weekend, Old Club has exclusive negotiating rights to these players.

#or the first scheduled day of the first NFL training camp, whichever is later.

August 3-5 Hall of Fame Weekend.

August 5 Pro Football Hall of Fame Game, Canton, Ohio: New Orleans vs. Pittsburgh

August 7 Deadline for players under contract to report to earn a season of free-agency credit.

August 10 If a Drafted Rookie has not signed with his club by this date, he may not be traded to any other club in 2007.

August 9-13 First Preseason Weekend.

August 11-15 Deadline for club to provide written notice to certain unsigned players and the NFLPA of its intent to place them on the Exempt List if they fail to report no later than one day prior to the club's second preseason game. Any player who fails to report prior to the deadline will be ineligible to play or receive compensation for at least three games (preseason or regular season) from the time that he reports.

August 28 Roster cut-down to maximum of 75 players on Active List by 4 P.M., New York time.

August 29 All tryouts on this date and for the remainder of the season must be reported to the League office.

September 1 Roster cut-down to maximum of 53 players on Active/Inactive List by 4 P.M., New York time. Clubs may dress minimum of 42 and maximum of 45 players and Third Quarterback for each regular-season and postseason game.

September 1 Simultaneously with the cut-down to 53, clubs that have players in the categories of Active/Physically Unable to Perform or Active/Non-Football Injury or Illness must take one of the following options: place player on Reserve/Physically Unable to Perform or Reserve/Non-Football Injury or Illness, whichever is applicable; ask waivers; terminate; trade; or continue to count him on Active List.

September 2 After 12 noon, New York time, clubs may establish a Practice Squad of eight players by signing free agents who do not have an accrued season of free-agency credit or who were on the 45-player Active List for less than nine regular-season games during their only Accrued Season(s). A player cannot participate on the Practice Squad for more than three seasons.

September 5 All clubs are required to file a personnel (injury) report with their conference information manager by 4:00 p.m., New York time. Reports are to be filed every Wednesday, Thursday and Friday before a regular-season game by 4:00 p.m., New York time (or as soon as possible after the completion of practice). An update must also be reported if there is any change in a player's condition after Friday.

September 5 Beginning at 4 P.M., New York time, Team Salary includes all players receiving compensation under their 2007 contracts. Top 51 rule is no longer in effect.

September 6-10 Regular Season opens.

September 6-10 Beginning on these dates vested veterans terminated from the Active List or Inactive List (and from Reserve/Injured if the player is placed on Reserve/Injured after the beginning of the regular season) are entitled to receive, after the end of the regular-season schedule, Termination Pay pursuant to the terms of the CBA.

September 25 Priority on multiple waiver claims is now based on the current season's standing.

October 16 Beginning the day after the conclusion of the sixth regular-season weekend and continuing through the day after the conclusion of the ninth regular-season weekend, clubs are permitted to begin practicing players on Reserve/Physically Unable to Perform and Reserve/Non-Football Injury or Illness for a period not to exceed 21 days. Players may be activated during the 21-day practice period or until 4 P.M., New York time, on the day after the conclusion of the 21-day period.

October 16 All trading ends at 4 P.M., New York time.

October 17 Players with at least four previous pension-credited seasons are subject to the waiver system for the remainder of the regular season and postseason.

November 5	Deadline at 4 P.M., New York time, for an increase in a player's 2007 Salary to be counted as Salary for the current year. Any notice of an increase in a player's 2007 Salary received by the NFLMC after this deadline will be treated as a Signing Bonus.
November 13	Signing period ends at 4 P.M., New York time, for Franchise Players who are eligible to receive Offer Sheets.
November 13	Deadline for clubs to sign by 4 P.M., New York time, their unsigned Franchise and Transition Players, including Franchise Players who were eligible to receive Offer Sheets until this date. If still unsigned after this date, such players are prohibited from playing in NFL in 2007.
November 13	Deadline for clubs to sign by 4 P.M., New York time, their Unrestricted Free Agents to whom June 1 tender was made. If still unsigned after this date, such players are prohibited from playing in NFL in 2007.
November 13	Deadline for clubs to sign by 4 P.M., New York time, their Restricted Free Agents to whom June 1 tender was made. If such players remain unsigned, they are prohibited from playing in NFL in 2007.
November 13	Deadline for clubs to sign Drafted players by 4 P.M., New York time. If such players remain unsigned, they are prohibited from playing in NFL in 2007.
November 30	Deadline for reinstatement of players in Reserve List categories of Retired, Did Not Report, and Exclusive Rights, and of players who were placed on Reserve/Left Squad in a previous season.
December 28	Deadline for waiver requests in 2007, except for "special waiver requests," which have a 10-day claiming period, with termination or assignment delayed until after the Super Bowl.
December 31	Clubs may begin signing free-agent players for the 2008 season.

2008

January 5-6	Wild Card Playoff Games.
January 12-13	Divisional Playoff Games.
January 20	AFC and NFC Championship Games.
February 3	Super Bowl XLII, University of Phoenix Stadium, Arizona.
February 10	AFC-NFC Pro Bowl, Honolulu, Hawaii.

2009

February 1	Super Bowl XLIII, Raymond James Stadium, Tampa, Florida.

2010

February 7	Super Bowl XLIV, Dolphin Stadium, South Florida.

2011

February 6	Super Bowl XLV, Dallas Cowboys New Stadium, North Texas.

The NFL is online to provide fans and media quick and easy access to all the latest professional football information.

NFL.COM—(http://NFL.com or AOL Keyword: NFL.com)

NFL.com, the league's year-round home page on the Internet, enters its 11th season in cyberspace. The site provides NFL information during the regular season, postseason, and offseason, including:

NEWS/STATS: Up-to-the-minute news from around the league, plus game previews, injury reports, and player and team stats.

GAMEDAY COVERAGE: Live game coverage with play-by-play, scores, and statistics, including graphical drive charts and comprehensive scoreboard that reloads automatically with the latest information.

VIDEO HIGHLIGHTS: The site showcases NFL Films video highlights of the previous week's games as well as upcoming matchups. Video also supports feature stories and team highlight clips from every game last season. In addition, exclusive NFL Network programming is featured.

TEAM AREAS: Customized areas for all 32 clubs, featuring updated rosters, depth carts, and all the latest news from the teams.

SUPERBOWL.COM—(http://SuperBowl.com)

Look for SuperBowl.com in late December for complete coverage of the playoffs and Super Bowl XLII. The multimedia site follows all postseason action and features audio and video clips of past Super Bowls.

During the week leading up to Super Bowl XLII, the site will go "live" from Arizona, providing coverage of events, press conferences, and chats with Super Bowl players and coaches. On Super Bowl Sunday, SuperBowl.com will showcase a live Internet cybercast, complete with online commentators calling the action. The site also features digital photos from the game, live public address audio and press-box announcements, and live audio from foreign broadcasts.

NFLEUROPE.COM—(http://NFLEurope.com)

The official site of NFL Europa provides in-depth information on the six teams and their players, with weekly video highlights of game action. In addition, the site includes weekly player diaries from NFL-allocated players, as well as a complete league stats package.

NFLYOUTHFOOTBALL.COM—(http://nflyouthfootball.com)

NFLyouthfootball.com is the NFL's official youth football website. Boys and girls ages 6-18 can be a part of something big by getting involved nationwide with one of the NFL's Youth Football programs. Coaches, parents, and youth organizations can learn how to host their own local NFL Punt, Pass, and Kick event and can learn how to get children involved with an NFL FLAG league in their local community. Our website is also a resource for coaches and parents to help them promote a positive experience for all youth participants. The NFL's youth football programs follow our Seven Guiding Principles, which are posted on our website, and were developed from feedback from kids, parents, and coaches.

NFLRUSH.COM—(http://www.NFLRUSH.com)

NFLRush.com offers an NFL experience solely for kids, with unique content, games, contests, fun daily features on NFL players, and football basics for the young fan and player. Kids can customize the site based on their favorite team and select their own mix of music to listen to while surfing the site through NFLRush Radio. The site also includes a special section for parents with information about NFL participatory youth programs and initiatives.

NFLHS.COM—(http://nflhs.com)

The League's Website dedicated to high school football. NFLHS.com covers high school football on a nation-wide basis and also looks into the high school careers of current and former NFL players and coaches. NFLHS.com goes behind the scenes at major NFL events, such as the Super Bowl and the Draft, and provides coverage from a high school perspective. The site is packed with tips and drills, health and safety information, academic tips and news on the NFL's and its teams' efforts in the community. Whatever you are looking for regarding high school football, we've got it!

JOINTHETEAM.COM—(http://JoinTheTeam.com)

JointheTeam.com is the official Website dedicated to the off-the field community work of the NFL and the member clubs. The site provides news and information regarding how the NFL gives back and serves as a useful tool for individuals who are looking for a way to make a difference in their communities. As part of the NFL's Join The Team platform, the site encourages people to unite with NFL teams, players and partners to give back to communities across America. Join The Team is a "call to action" —a way for everyone to come together and make a difference through community involvement.

PROFOOTBALLHOF.COM—(http://profootballhof.com)

Profootballhof.com is the official site of the Pro Football Hall of Fame in Canton, Ohio. In addition to a complete visitor's guide to the Hall, the site features bios, stories and Q & A's with Hall of Fame inductees, a detailed archive of football history, and information on appearances by members of the Hall.

OFFICIAL NFL TEAM SITES

In addition to a dedicated area on NFL.com, all 32 teams have their own Websites, which have separate URLs, and are linked from NFL.com.

Arizona Cardinals (www.azcardinals.com)
Atlanta Falcons (www.atlantafalcons.com)
Baltimore Ravens (www.baltimoreravens.com)
Buffalo Bills (www.buffalobills.com)
Carolina Panthers (www.panthers.com)
Chicago Bears (www.chicagobears.com)
Cincinnati Bengals (www.bengals.com)
Cleveland Browns (www.clevelandbrowns.com)
Dallas Cowboys (www.dallascowboys.com)
Denver Broncos (www.denverbroncos.com)
Detroit Lions (www.detroitlions.com)
Green Bay Packers (www.packers.com)
Houston Texans (www.houstontexans.com)
Indianapolis Colts (www.colts.com)
Jacksonville Jaguars (www.jaguars.com)
Kansas City Chiefs (www.kcchiefs.com)
Miami Dolphins (www.miamidolphins.com)
Minnesota Vikings (www.vikings.com)
New England Patriots (www.patriots.com)
New Orleans Saints (www.neworleanssaints.com)
New York Giants (www.giants.com)
New York Jets (www.newyorkjets.com)
Oakland Raiders (www.raiders.com)
Philadelphia Eagles (www.philadelphiaeagles.com)
Pittsburgh Steelers (www.steelers.com)
St. Louis Rams (www.stlouisrams.com)
San Diego Chargers (www.chargers.com)
San Francisco 49ers (www.sf49ers.com)
Seattle Seahawks (www.seahawks.com)
Tampa Bay Buccaneers (www.buccaneers.com)
Tennessee Titans (www.titansonline.com)
Washington Redskins (www.redskins.com)

NFL Network provides fans with a network to call their own. Seven days a week, 24 hours a day, 365 days a year, fans turn to NFL Network to receive information and insight straight from team headquarters, league offices and wherever else the NFL is making news.

NFL Network gives fans unprecedented year-round access to all NFL events, including the preseason, regular season, Playoffs, Super Bowl, Pro Bowl, Scouting Combine, Pro Football Hall of Fame Game and induction weekend, Senior Bowl, Insight Bowl, Texas Bowl, league meetings, the playing schedule, NFL Draft, minicamps, and training camps.

In addition, NFL Network is the only place on television for fans to view NFL games outside their initial live airings. From original broadcast versions of past Super Bowls, in-week replays of current games, original network telecasts of classic NFL regular season and postseason games, to live telecasts of preseason games, NFL Europa games, regular season NFL games and college bowl games— NFL Network is truly the year-round destination for football fans.

NFL Network is available on cable and satellite television through your local service provider. If your provider doesn't currently offer NFL Network, please call (866) NFL-NETWORK to make them aware of your interest in receiving it.

KEY PROGRAMMING

EXCLUSIVE LIVE PRIMETIME GAMES
NFL Network's "Run to the Playoffs" eight-game Thursday-Saturday night package kicks off in high definition on Thanksgiving night with award-winning broadcasters Bryant Gumbel and Cris Collinsworth calling the games. Collinsworth won a 2006 Sports Emmy for his analysis of NFL Network games. Each game, at 8:15 PM ET, will be preceded by a two-hour onsite pregame show and followed by a live post-game show from the field.

NFL TOTAL ACCESS
NFL Network's signature show is THE football show of record. *NFL Total Access* is uniquely structured to see the game through the participants' eyes, airing at 6:00 PM ET every Monday and 7:00 PM ET each Tuesday through Saturday and hosted by Rich Eisen.

Covering all 32 teams, *NFL Total Access* features interviews with players, coaches and other key league personnel. Using the most advanced technology, *NFL Total Access* has the ability to go live to any NFL team headquarters at any time.

NFL GAMEDAY
After each Sunday's final game, the 90-minute *NFL GameDay* delivers comprehensive coverage of the day's action. Host Rich Eisen is joined by Steve Mariucci and Deion Sanders. *NFL Game-Day* kicks off at 11:30 PM ET and features highlights, post-game press conferences, on-field interviews, analysis and more in wrapping up each NFL Sunday. GameDay runs in a continuous loop until 1:00 PM ET each Monday.

NFL REPLAY
NFL games will be re-aired with the original television announcers and cameras. This offering features the five most exciting games each week in a 90-minute format (eliminating halftime and other non-critical elements) at 7:00 PM ET on Mondays and 8:00 PM ET and 10:30 PM ET each Tuesday and Wednesday.

Enhancements to each broadcast include additional camera angles, sideline sound and post-game interviews.

POINT AFTER
NFL Network brings you inside the interview rooms of the NFL and top college teams each weekday afternoon with *Point After*. Jamie Dukes, Adam Schefter, and former NFL head coach Jim Mora provide analysis for *Point After* which airs at 2:30 PM ET on Mondays and Wednesdays and 3:00 PM ET on Tuesdays, Thursdays and Fridays.

NFL SCOREBOARD
After Sunday's early games conclude, *NFL Scoreboard* takes viewers around the league for post-game press conferences and game highlights. *NFL Scoreboard* airs at 4:30 PM ET on Sundays and continues through the Sunday evening game.

RED ZONE
NFL Network provides the best place on television to get up-to-the-minute scores, statistics and news each game day during the season. Airing at 1:00 PM ET on Sundays, *Red Zone* features continuously scrolling real-time game statistics with audio from Sirius NFL Radio's *Around the League* program.

NFL's TOP 10
Putting a fresh twist on the countdown genre, *NFL's Top 10* is a fast-paced weekly series. *NFL's Top 10* provides an irreverent look at some of the most intriguing subjects in the NFL, creating and debating a top ten list for each category. Each 60-minute episode counts down from No. 10 to the top ranking in each category.

NFL NETWORK GAME OF THE WEEK
Every Saturday at 12:00 noon ET *NFL Network Game of the Week*, a 60-minute condensed version of a current NFL game, takes fans inside the game in a way they do not see on a traditional broadcast. Using unique NFL Films camera angles, microphones on the field and in the locker room, *GOTW* tells the story of the game from the inside out. This show is available in high definition.

PRESEASON GAMES
NFL Network kicks off the preseason with exclusive coverage of the Pro Football Hall of Fame Game from Canton, Ohio. NFL Network is the only place on television where fans can view the majority of NFL preseason games. NFL Network televises every game that does not appear on the four NFL broadcast partners (CBS, FOX, NBC, and ESPN) during the preseason, more than 50 games each summer.

Log on to www.NFL.com/NFLnetwork for more information on NFL Network.

SCHEDULING FORMULA

The NFL expanded to 32 teams in 2002 with the addition of the Houston Texans. In addition, the NFL realigned for the first time since 1970—into eight divisions of four teams each—and the scheduling formula that was introduced guarantees for the first time that all teams play each other on a regular, rotating basis. Although the number of teams has increased to 32, the number of playoff teams remains the same at 12.

Under the NFL scheduling formula, every team within a division plays 16 games as follows:

- Home and away against its three division opponents (6 games).
- The four teams from another division within its conference on a rotating three-year cycle (4 games).
- The four teams from a division in the other conference on a rotating four-year cycle (4 games).
- Two intraconference games based on the prior year's standings (2 games). These games will match a first-place team against the first-place teams in the two same-conference divisions the team is not scheduled to play that season. The second-place, third-place, and fourth-place teams in a conference will be matched in the same way each year.

The schedule format takes each team through a cycle of games—home and away—against every other team in the league. From 2002-2009, every team will play every other team at least twice—once home and once away. After the 2009 season, a decision will be made on whether to continue with the same rotation or modify it.

In determining how to begin the divisional rotation in 2002, the displacement of teams from their old divisions in the new alignment was taken into account. Preference was given to scheduling games with former division rivals and other regional opponents for clubs realigned from otherwise intact divisions.

FUTURE SCHEDULING ROTATION

		2007	2008	2009
AFC EAST	Intraconference	AFCN	AFCW	AFCS
	Interconference	NFCE	NFCW	NFCS
AFC NORTH	Intraconference	AFCE	AFCS	AFCW
	Interconference	NFCW	NFCE	NFCN
AFC SOUTH	Intraconference	AFCW	AFCN	AFCE
	Interconference	NFCS	NFCN	NFCW
AFC WEST	Intraconference	AFCS	AFCE	AFCN
	Interconference	NFCN	NFCS	NFCE
NFC EAST	Intraconference	NFCN	NFCW	NFCS
	Interconference	AFCE	AFCN	AFCW
NFC NORTH	Intraconference	NFCE	NFCS	NFCW
	Interconference	AFCW	AFCS	AFCN
NFC SOUTH	Intraconference	NFCW	NFCN	NFCE
	Interconference	AFCS	AFCW	AFCE
NFC WEST	Intraconference	NFCS	NFCE	NFCN
	Interconference	AFCN	AFCE	AFCS

AFC EAST NON-DIVISIONAL OPPONENTS 2007-2009

BUFFALO BILLS

	2007 Home	Away	2008 Home	Away	2009 Home	Away
Intraconference by Division	BALT	CLE	OAK	DEN	HOU	JAX
	CIN	PITT	SD	KC	IND	TENN
Interconference by Division	DALL	PHIL	SF	ARIZ	NO	ATL
	NYG	WASH	SEA	STL	TB	CAR
Intraconference by Position	AFCW	AFCS	AFCN	AFCS	AFCN	AFCW

MIAMI DOLPHINS

	2007 Home	Away	2008 Home	Away	2009 Home	Away
Intraconference by Division	BALT	CLE	OAK	DEN	HOU	JAX
	CIN	PITT	SD	KC	IND	TENN
Interconference by Division	DALL	PHIL	SF	ARIZ	NO	ATL
	NYG	WASH	SEA	STL	TB	CAR
Intraconference by Position	AFCW	AFCS	AFCN	AFCS	AFCN	AFCW

NEW ENGLAND PATRIOTS

	2007 Home	Away	2008 Home	Away	2009 Home	Away
Intraconference by Division	CLE	BALT	DEN	OAK	JAX	HOU
	PITT	CIN	KC	SD	TENN	IND
Interconference by Division	PHIL	DALL	ARIZ	SF	ATL	NO
	WASH	NYG	STL	SEA	CAR	TB
Intraconference by Position	AFCW	AFCS	AFCN	AFCS	AFCN	AFCW

NEW YORK JETS

	2007 Home	Away	2008 Home	Away	2009 Home	Away
Intraconference by Division	CLE	BALT	DEN	OAK	JAX	HOU
	PITT	CIN	KC	SD	TENN	IND
Interconference by Division	PHIL	DALL	ARIZ	SF	ATL	NO
	WASH	NYG	STL	SEA	CAR	TB
Intraconference by Position	AFCW	AFCS	AFCN	AFCS	AFCN	AFCW

AFC NORTH NON-DIVISIONAL OPPONENTS 2007-2009

BALTIMORE RAVENS

	2007 Home	Away	2008 Home	Away	2009 Home	Away
Intraconference by Division	NE	BUFF	JAX	HOU	DEN	OAK
	NYJ	MIA	TENN	IND	KC	SD
Interconference by Division	ARIZ	SF	PHIL	DALL	CHI	GB
	STL	SEA	WASH	NYG	DET	MINN
Intraconference by Position	AFCS	AFCW	AFCW	AFCE	AFCS	AFCE

CINCINNATI BENGALS

	2007 Home	Away	2008 Home	Away	2009 Home	Away
Intraconference by Division	NE	BUFF	JAX	HOU	DEN	OAK
	NYJ	MIA	TENN	IND	KC	SD
Interconference by Division	ARIZ	SF	PHIL	DALL	CHI	GB
	STL	SEA	WASH	NYG	DET	MINN
Intraconference by Position	AFCS	AFCW	AFCW	AFCE	AFCS	AFCE

CLEVELAND BROWNS

	2007 Home	Away	2008 Home	Away	2009 Home	Away
Intraconference by Division	BUFF	NE	HOU	JAX	OAK	DEN
	MIA	NYJ	IND	TENN	SD	KC
Interconference by Division	SF	ARIZ	DALL	PHIL	GB	CHI
	SEA	STL	NYG	WASH	MINN	DET
Intraconference by Position	AFCS	AFCW	AFCW	AFCE	AFCS	AFCE

PITTSBURGH STEELERS

	2007 Home	Away	2008 Home	Away	2009 Home	Away
Intraconference by Division	BUFF	NE	HOU	JAX	OAK	DEN
	MIA	NYJ	IND	TENN	SD	KC
Interconference by Division	SF	ARIZ	DALL	PHIL	GB	CHI
	SEA	STL	NYG	WASH	MINN	DET
Intraconference by Position	AFCS	AFCW	AFCW	AFCE	AFCS	AFCE

AFC SOUTH NON-DIVISIONAL OPPONENTS 2007-2009

HOUSTON TEXANS

	2007 Home	Away	2008 Home	Away	2009 Home	Away
Intraconference by Division	DEN	OAK	BALT	CLE	NE	BUFF
	KC	SD	CIN	PITT	NYJ	MIA
Interconference by Division	NO	ATL	CHI	GB	SF	ARIZ
	TB	CAR	DET	MINN	SEA	STL
Intraconference by Position	AFCE	AFCN	AFCE	AFCW	AFCW	AFCN

INDIANAPOLIS COLTS

	2007 Home	Away	2008 Home	Away	2009 Home	Away
Intraconference by Division	DEN	OAK	BALT	CLE	NE	BUFF
	KC	SD	CIN	PITT	NYJ	MIA
Interconference by Division	NO	ATL	CHI	GB	SF	ARIZ
	TB	CAR	DET	MINN	SEA	STL
Intraconference by Position	AFCE	AFCN	AFCE	AFCW	AFCW	AFCN

JACKSONVILLE JAGUARS

	2007 Home	Away	2008 Home	Away	2009 Home	Away
Intraconference by Division	OAK	DEN	CLE	BALT	BUFF	NE
	SD	KC	PITT	CIN	MIA	NYJ
Interconference by Division	ATL	NO	GB	CHI	ARIZ	SF
	CAR	TB	MINN	DET	STL	SEA
Intraconference by Position	AFCE	AFCN	AFCE	AFCW	AFCW	AFCN

TENNESSEE TITANS

	2007 Home	Away	2008 Home	Away	2009 Home	Away
Intraconference by Division	OAK	DEN	CLE	BALT	BUFF	NE
	SD	KC	PITT	CIN	MIA	NYJ
Interconference by Division	ATL	NO	GB	CHI	ARIZ	SF
	CAR	TB	MINN	DET	STL	SEA
Intraconference by Position	AFCE	AFCN	AFCE	AFCW	AFCW	AFCN

AFC WEST NON-DIVISIONAL OPPONENTS 2007-2009

DENVER BRONCOS

	2007 Home	Away	2008 Home	Away	2009 Home	Away
Intraconference by Division	JAX	HOU	BUFF	NE	CLE	BALT
	TENN	IND	MIA	NYJ	PITT	CIN
Interconference by Division	GB	CHI	NO	ATL	DALL	PHIL
	MINN	DET	TB	CAR	NYG	WASH
Intraconference by Position	AFCN	AFCE	AFCS	AFCN	AFCE	AFCS

KANSAS CITY CHIEFS

	2007 Home	Away	2008 Home	Away	2009 Home	Away
Intraconference by Division	JAX	HOU	BUFF	NE	CLE	BALT
	TENN	IND	MIA	NYJ	PITT	CIN
Interconference by Division	GB	CHI	NO	ATL	DALL	PHIL
	MINN	DET	TB	CAR	NYG	WASH
Intraconference by Position	AFCN	AFCE	AFCS	AFCN	AFCE	AFCS

OAKLAND RAIDERS

	2007 Home	Away	2008 Home	Away	2009 Home	Away
Intraconference by Division	HOU	JAX	NE	BUFF	BALT	CLE
	IND	TENN	NYJ	MIA	CIN	PITT
Interconference by Division	CHI	GB	ATL	NO	PHIL	DALL
	DET	MINN	CAR	TB	WASH	NYG
Intraconference by Position	AFCN	AFCE	AFCS	AFCN	AFCE	AFCS

SAN DIEGO CHARGERS

	2007 Home	Away	2008 Home	Away	2009 Home	Away
Intraconference by Division	HOU	JAX	NE	BUFF	BALT	CLE
	IND	TENN	NYJ	MIA	CIN	PITT
Interconference by Division	CHI	GB	ATL	NO	PHIL	DALL
	DET	MINN	CAR	TB	WASH	NYG
Intraconference by Position	AFCN	AFCE	AFCS	AFCN	AFCE	AFCS

NFC EAST NON-DIVISIONAL OPPONENTS 2007-2009

DALLAS COWBOYS

	2007 Home	Away	2008 Home	Away	2009 Home	Away
Intraconference by Division	GB	CHI	SF	ARIZ	ATL	NO
	MINN	DET	SEA	STL	CAR	TB
Interconference by Division	NE	BUFF	BALT	CLE	OAK	DEN
	NYJ	MIA	CIN	PITT	SD	KC
Intraconference by Position	NFCW	NFCS	NFCS	NFCN	NFCW	NFCN

NEW YORK GIANTS

	2007 Home	Away	2008 Home	Away	2009 Home	Away
Intraconference by Division	GB	CHI	SF	ARIZ	ATL	NO
	MINN	DET	SEA	STL	CAR	TB
Interconference by Division	NE	BUFF	BALT	CLE	OAK	DEN
	NYJ	MIA	CIN	PITT	SD	KC
Intraconference by Position	NFCW	NFCS	NFCS	NFCN	NFCW	NFCN

PHILADELPHIA EAGLES

	2007 Home	Away	2008 Home	Away	2009 Home	Away
Intraconference by Division	CHI	GB	ARIZ	SF	NO	ATL
	DET	MINN	STL	SEA	TB	CAR
Interconference by Division	BUFF	NE	CLE	BALT	DEN	OAK
	MIA	NYJ	PITT	CIN	KC	SD
Intraconference by Position	NFCW	NFCS	NFCS	NFCN	NFCW	NFCN

WASHINGTON REDSKINS

	2007 Home	Away	2008 Home	Away	2009 Home	Away
Intraconference by Division	CHI	GB	ARIZ	SF	NO	ATL
	DET	MINN	STL	SEA	TB	CAR
Interconference by Division	BUFF	NE	CLE	BALT	DEN	OAK
	MIA	NYJ	PITT	CIN	KC	SD
Intraconference by Position	NFCW	NFCS	NFCS	NFCN	NFCW	NFCN

NFC NORTH NON-DIVISIONAL OPPONENTS 2007-2009

CHICAGO BEARS

	2007 Home	Away	2008 Home	Away	2009 Home	Away
Intraconference by Division	DALL	PHIL	NO	ATL	ARIZ	SF
	NYG	WASH	TB	CAR	STL	SEA
Interconference by Division	DEN	OAK	JAX	HOU	CLE	BALT
	KC	SD	TENN	IND	PITT	CIN
Intraconference by Position	NFCS	NFCW	NFCE	NFCW	NFCE	NFCS

DETROIT LIONS

	2007 Home	Away	2008 Home	Away	2009 Home	Away
Intraconference by Division	DALL	PHIL	NO	ATL	ARIZ	SF
	NYG	WASH	TB	CAR	STL	SEA
Interconference by Division	DEN	OAK	JAX	HOU	CLE	BALT
	KC	SD	TENN	IND	PITT	CIN
Intraconference by Position	NFCS	NFCW	NFCE	NFCW	NFCE	NFCS

GREEN BAY PACKERS

	2007 Home	Away	2008 Home	Away	2009 Home	Away
Intraconference by Division	PHIL	DALL	ATL	NO	SF	ARIZ
	WASH	NYG	CAR	TB	SEA	STL
Interconference by Division	OAK	DEN	HOU	JAX	BALT	CLE
	SD	KC	IND	TENN	CIN	PITT
Intraconference by Position	NFCS	NFCW	NFCE	NFCW	NFCE	NFCS

MINNESOTA VIKINGS

	2007 Home	Away	2008 Home	Away	2009 Home	Away
Intraconference by Division	PHIL	DALL	ATL	NO	SF	ARIZ
	WASH	NYG	CAR	TB	SEA	STL
Interconference by Division	OAK	DEN	HOU	JAX	BALT	CLE
	SD	KC	IND	TENN	CIN	PITT
Intraconference by Position	NFCS	NFCW	NFCE	NFCW	NFCE	NFCS

NFC SOUTH NON-DIVISIONAL OPPONENTS 2007-2009

ATLANTA FALCONS

	2007 Home	2007 Away	2008 Home	2008 Away	2009 Home	2009 Away
Intraconference by Division	SF	ARIZ	CHI	GB	PHIL	DALL
	SEA	STL	DET	MINN	WASH	NYG
Interconference by Division	HOU	JAX	DEN	OAK	BUFF	NE
	IND	TENN	KC	SD	MIA	NYJ
Intraconference by Position	NFCE	NFCN	NFCW	NFCE	NFCN	NFCW

CAROLINA PANTHERS

	2007 Home	2007 Away	2008 Home	2008 Away	2009 Home	2009 Away
Intraconference by Division	SF	ARIZ	CHI	GB	PHIL	DALL
	SEA	STL	DET	MINN	WASH	NYG
Interconference by Division	HOU	JAX	DEN	OAK	BUFF	NE
	IND	TENN	KC	SD	MIA	NYJ
Intraconference by Position	NFCE	NFCN	NFCW	NFCE	NFCN	NFCW

NEW ORLEANS SAINTS

	2007 Home	2007 Away	2008 Home	2008 Away	2009 Home	2009 Away
Intraconference by Division	ARIZ	SF	GB	CHI	DALL	PHIL
	STL	SEA	MINN	DET	NYG	WASH
Interconference by Division	JAX	HOU	OAK	DEN	NE	BUFF
	TENN	IND	SD	KC	NYJ	MIA
Intraconference by Position	NFCE	NFCN	NFCW	NFCE	NFCN	NFCW

TAMPA BAY BUCCANEERS

	2007 Home	2007 Away	2008 Home	2008 Away	2009 Home	2009 Away
Intraconference by Division	ARIZ	SF	GB	CHI	DALL	PHIL
	STL	SEA	MINN	DET	NYG	WASH
Interconference by Division	JAX	HOU	OAK	DEN	NE	BUFF
	TENN	IND	SD	KC	NYJ	MIA
Intraconference by Position	NFCE	NFCN	NFCW	NFCE	NFCN	NFCW

NFC WEST NON-DIVISIONAL OPPONENTS 2007-2009

ARIZONA CARDINALS

	2007 Home	2007 Away	2008 Home	2008 Away	2009 Home	2009 Away
Intraconference by Division	ATL	NO	DALL	PHIL	GB	CHI
	CAR	TB	NYG	WASH	MINN	DET
Interconference by Division	CLE	BALT	BUFF	NE	HOU	JAX
	PITT	CIN	MIA	NYJ	IND	TENN
Intraconference by Position	NFCN	NFCE	NFCN	NFCS	NFCS	NFCE

ST. LOUIS RAMS

	2007 Home	2007 Away	2008 Home	2008 Away	2009 Home	2009 Away
Intraconference by Division	ATL	NO	DALL	PHIL	GB	CHI
	CAR	TB	NYG	WASH	MINN	DET
Interconference by Division	CLE	BALT	BUFF	NE	HOU	JAX
	PITT	CIN	MIA	NYJ	IND	TENN
Intraconference by Position	NFCN	NFCE	NFCN	NFCS	NFCS	NFCE

SAN FRANCISCO 49ERS

	2007 Home	2007 Away	2008 Home	2008 Away	2009 Home	2009 Away
Intraconference by Division	NO	ATL	PHIL	DALL	CHI	GB
	TB	CAR	WASH	NYG	DET	MINN
Interconference by Division	BALT	CLE	NE	BUFF	JAX	HOU
	CIN	PITT	NYJ	MIA	TENN	IND
Intraconference by Position	NFCN	NFCE	NFCN	NFCS	NFCS	NFCE

SEATTLE SEAHAWKS

	2007 Home	2007 Away	2008 Home	2008 Away	2009 Home	2009 Away
Intraconference by Division	NO	ATL	PHIL	DALL	CHI	GB
	TB	CAR	WASH	NYG	DET	MINN
Interconference by Division	BALT	CLE	NE	BUFF	JAX	HOU
	CIN	PITT	NYJ	MIA	TENN	IND
Intraconference by Position	NFCN	NFCE	NFCN	NFCS	NFCS	NFCE

TOP ACTIVE PASSERS
1,000 or more attempts

		Yrs.	Att.	Comp.	Pct. Comp.	Yards	TD	Pct. TD	Had Int.	Pct. Int.	Ratings Pts.
1.	Peyton Manning, Ind.	9	4,890	3,131	64.0	37,586	275	5.6	139	2.8	94.4
2.	Kurt Warner, Ari.	9	2,508	1,645	65.6	20,591	125	5.0	83	3.3	93.8
3.	Carson Palmer, Cin.	3	1,461	932	63.8	10,768	78	5.3	43	2.9	91.5
4.	Marc Bulger, St.L.	5	2,106	1,357	64.4	16,233	95	4.5	59	2.8	91.3
5.	Daunte Culpepper, Mia.	8	2,741	1,759	64.2	21,091	137	5.0	89	3.2	90.8
6.	Chad Pennington, NYJ	7	1,659	1,080	65.1	11,973	72	4.3	46	2.8	89.3
7.	Tom Brady, N.E.	7	3,064	1,896	61.9	21,564	147	4.8	78	2.5	88.4
8.	Ben Roethlisberger, Pit.	3	1,032	644	62.4	8,519	52	5.0	43	4.2	87.9
9.	Drew Brees, N.O.	6	2,363	1,481	62.7	16,766	106	4.5	64	2.7	87.5
10.	Trent Green, K.C.	9	3,527	2,143	60.8	26,963	157	4.5	101	2.9	87.5
11.	Jeff Garcia, T.B.	8	2,973	1,811	60.9	20,385	136	4.6	73	2.5	86.4
12.	Donovan McNabb, Phi.	8	3,259	1,898	58.2	22,080	152	4.7	72	2.2	85.2
13.	Matt Hasselbeck, Sea.	8	2,576	1,552	60.3	18,367	114	4.4	72	2.8	85.1
14.	Brett Favre, G.B.	16	8,223	5,021	61.1	57,500	414	5.0	273	3.3	85.1
15.	Brian Griese, Chi.	9	2,350	1,481	63.0	16,564	104	4.4	80	3.4	84.5
16.	Mark Brunell, Was.	13	4,594	2,738	59.6	31,826	182	4.0	106	2.3	84.2
17.	Jake Delhomme, Car.	6	1,934	1,151	59.5	13,965	92	4.8	63	3.3	84.0
18.	Steve McNair, Bal.	12	4,339	2,600	59.9	30,191	172	4.0	115	2.7	83.2
19.	Brad Johnson, Dal.	13	4,237	2,620	61.8	28,548	164	3.9	117	2.8	83.1
20.	Byron Leftwich, Jax.	4	1,344	789	58.7	9,042	51	3.8	36	2.7	80.5
21.	Charlie Batch, Pit.	9	1,423	801	56.3	9,801	55	3.9	41	2.9	78.6
22.	Aaron Brooks, *	7	2,963	1,673	56.5	20,261	123	4.2	92	3.1	78.5
23.	Jon Kitna, Det.	10	3,433	2,039	59.4	22,467	129	3.8	126	3.7	76.1
24.	Michael Vick, Atl.	6	1,730	930	53.8	11,505	71	4.1	52	3.0	75.7
25.	David Carr, Car.	5	2,070	1,243	60.1	13,391	59	2.9	65	3.1	75.5

TOP ACTIVE SCORERS
(number in parantheses represents 2-point conversions scored)

		Yrs.	TD	FG	PAT	TP
1.	Morten Andersen, *	24	0	540	825	2,445
2.	John Carney, *	19	0	413	510	1,749
3.	Matt Stover, Bal.	16	0	408	491	1,715
4.	Jason Elam, Den.	14	0	368	568	1,672
5.	Jason Hanson, Det.	15	0	356	469	1,537
6.	John Kasay, Car.	16	0	334	403	1,405
7.	Jeff Wilkins, St.L.	13	0	283	470	1,319
8.	Adam Vinatieri, Ind.	11	0	288	405(1)	1,271
9.	Ryan Longwell, Min.	10	0	247	403	1,144
10.	Olindo Mare, N.O.	10	0	245	313	1,048
11.	John Hall, *	10	0	203	280	889
12.	David Akers, Phi.	9	0	173	272	791
13.	Joe Nedney, S.F.	11	0	182	239	785
14.	Kris Brown, Hou.	8	0	177	227	758
15.	Marvin Harrison, Ind.	11	122	0	0(5)	742
16.	Sebastian Janikowski, Oak.	7	0	156	243	711
17.	Terrell Owens, Dal.	11	116	0	0(3)	702
18.	Jay Feely, Mia.	6	0	156	223	691
19.	Rian Lindell, Buf.	7	0	151	224	677
20.	Phil Dawson, Cle.	8	1	156	195	669
21.	LaDainian Tomlinson, S.D.	6	111	0	0	666
22.	Shaun Alexander, Sea.	7	107	0	0	642
23.	Martin Gramatica, Dal.	7	0	144	204	636
24.	Randy Moss, N.E.	9	102	0	0(3)	618
25.	Neil Rackers, Ari.	7	0	143	162	591

TOP ACTIVE RUSHERS

		Yrs.	Att.	Yards	TD
1.	Corey Dillon, *	10	2,618	11,241	82
2.	Edgerrin James, Ari.	8	2,525	10,385	70
3.	Fred Taylor, Jax.	9	2,062	9,513	56
4.	Warrick Dunn, Atl.	10	2,256	9,461	43
5.	LaDainian Tomlinson, S.D.	6	2,050	9,176	100
6.	Shaun Alexander, Sea.	7	1,969	8,713	96
7.	Ahman Green, Hou.	9	1,871	8,491	54
8.	Stephen Davis, *	11	1,945	8,052	65
9.	Priest Holmes, K.C.	10	1,734	8,035	86
10.	Jamal Lewis, Cle.	6	1,822	7,801	45
11.	Clinton Portis, Was.	5	1,385	6,453	52
12.	Deuce McAllister, N.O.	6	1,298	5,586	44
13.	Travis Henry, Den.	6	1,321	5,395	34
14.	Thomas Jones, NYJ	7	1,349	5,384	34
15.	Rudi Johnson, Cin.	6	1,271	5,245	45
16.	Mike Alstott, T.B.	11	1,359	5,088	58
17.	Michael Pittman, T.B.	9	1,248	5,021	21
18.	Larry Johnson, K.C.	4	892	4,205	47
19.	Mike Anderson, Bal.	6	904	4,005	37
20.	Kevan Barlow, Pit.	6	1,022	3,984	30
21.	Michael Vick, Atl.	6	529	3,859	21
22.	Anthony Thomas, Buf.	6	1,008	3,802	2
23.	Steve McNair, Bal.	12	659	3,558	37
24.	Brian Westbrook, Phi.	5	736	3,452	20
25.	Michael Bennett, K.C.	6	749	3,374	12

Free agent; subject to developments.

TOP ACTIVE PASS RECEIVERS

	Yrs.	No.	Yards	TD
1. Marvin Harrison, Ind.	11	1,022	13,697	122
2. Isaac Bruce, St.L.	13	887	13,376	80
3. Keenan McCardell, *	15	861	11,117	62
4. Rod Smith, Den.	12	849	11,389	68
5. Keyshawn Johnson, Car.	11	814	10,571	64
6. Terrell Owens, Dal.	11	801	11,715	114
7. Eric Moulds, *	10	732	9,653	49
8. Tony Gonzalez, K.C.	10	721	8,710	61
9. Torry Holt, St.L.	8	712	10,675	64
10. Muhsin Muhammad, Chi.	11	702	9,364	53
11. Randy Moss, N.E.	9	676	10,700	101
12. Ricky Proehl, *	17	669	8,878	54
13. Hines Ward, Pit.	9	648	8,005	58
14. Joey Galloway, T.B.	12	612	9,558	71
15. Derrick Mason, Bal.	10	607	7,937	42
16. Terry Glenn, Dal.	11	593	8,823	44
17. Joe Horn, Atl.	11	576	8,501	57
18. Amani Toomer, NYG	11	561	8,157	47
19. Troy Brown, *	14	557	6,366	31
20. Eddie Kennison, K.C.	11	535	8,244	42
21. Laveranues Coles, NYJ	7	506	6,599	31
22. Bobby Engram, Sea.	11	504	6,054	29
23. Chad Johnson, Cin.	6	466	6,925	41
24. Marty Booker, Mia.	8	459	5,755	33
25. Darrell Jackson, S.F.	7	441	6,445	47

TOP ACTIVE INTERCEPTORS

	Yrs.	No.	Yards	TD
1. Ty Law, K.C.	12	50	789	7
2. Darren Sharper, Min.	10	49	963	7
3. Troy Vincent, *	15	47	711	3
4. Aaron Glenn, Dal.	13	40	532	5
5. Champ Bailey, Den.	8	39	425	4
Tory James, *	10	39	377	0
7. Sammy Knight, *	10	38	633	4
8. Patrick Surtain, K.C.	9	34	355	2
9. Dre' Bly, Den.	8	33	510	5
Sam Madison, NYG	10	33	515	2
11. Brian Dawkins, Phi.	11	32	489	2
Rodney Harrison, N.E.	13	32	359	2
13. Ronde Barber, T.B.	10	31	552	5
Dexter McCleon, Hou.	10	31	179	0
15. Deltha O'Neal, Cin.	7	30	396	3
Tony Parrish, *	9	30	670	2
17. Greg Wesley, K.C.	7	29	542	0
18. Walt Harris, S.F.	11	28	265	4
19. Donnie Edwards, K.C.	11	27	329	4
Robert Griffith, *	13	27	230	0
Ed Reed, Bal.	5	27	750	3
Samari Rolle, Bal.	9	27	420	1
Shawn Springs, Was.	10	27	358	2
24. John Lynch, Den.	14	26	204	0
25. Duane Starks, Oak.	9	25	245	2
Charles Woodson, G.B.	9	25	389	3

TOP ACTIVE PUNT RETURNERS
40 or more punt returns

	Yrs.	No.	Yards	Avg.	TD
1. Devin Hester, Chi.	1	47	600	12.8	3
2. Rod Smith, Den.	12	53	647	12.2	1
3. Roscoe Parrish, Buf.	2	46	550	12.0	1
4. Santana Moss, Was.	6	95	1,092	11.5	2
5. B.J. Sams, Bal.	3	117	1,283	11.0	2
6. Az-Zahir Hakim, Mia.	9	165	1,773	10.7	3
7. Dennis Northcutt, Cin.	7	202	2,149	10.6	3
8. Mewelde Moore, Min.	3	61	638	10.5	2
9. Troy Brown, *	14	246	2,570	10.4	3
10. Michael Lewis, N.O.	6	142	1,482	10.4	1
11. Bobby Engram, Sea.	11	101	1,053	10.4	2
12. Allen Rossum, Atl.	9	244	2,517	10.3	3
13. Hank Poteat, NYJ	6	77	788	10.2	1
14. Phillip Buchanon, T.B.	5	98	986	10.1	3
15. Deltha O'Neal, Cin.	7	136	1,368	10.1	2
16. Dante Hall, St.L.	7	188	1,882	10.0	5
17. Eddie Kennison, K.C.	11	145	1,448	10.0	3
18. Eddie Drummond, Det.	5	108	1,058	9.8	4
19. Tim Dwight, NYJ	9	176	1,719	9.8	3
20. Amani Toomer, NYG	11	109	1,060	9.7	3
21. Wes Welker, N.E.	3	127	1,232	9.7	0
22. Joey Galloway, T.B.	12	138	1,335	9.7	5
23. Nate Clements, S.F.	6	65	617	9.5	2
24. Reno Mahe, *	4	64	602	9.4	0
25. Steve Smith, Car.	6	169	1,589	9.4	4

TOP ACTIVE KICKOFF RETURNERS
40 or more kickoff returns

	Yrs.	No.	Yards	Avg.	TD
1. Jerome Mathis, Hou.	2	61	1,734	28.4	2
2. Justin Miller, NYJ	2	106	2,881	27.2	3
3. Terrence McGee, Buf.	4	158	4,276	27.1	4
4. Willie Ponder, *	4	122	3,064	25.1	2
5. Koren Robinson, G.B.	6	59	1,474	25.0	1
6. Quincy Morgan, Den.	6	51	1,273	25.0	0
7. Reuben Droughns, NYG	6	51	1,272	24.9	0
8. Tyson Thompson, Dal.	2	78	1,945	24.9	0
9. Chris Carr, Oak.	2	142	3,514	24.7	0
10. Bethel Johnson, Phi.	4	147	3,611	24.6	2
11. Josh Cribbs, Cle.	2	106	2,588	24.4	2
12. Michael Lewis, N.O.	6	243	5,903	24.3	3
13. Kevin Kasper, Det.	6	77	1,869	24.3	0
14. Darren Sproles, S.D.	2	63	1,528	24.3	0
15. Deuce McAllister, N.O.	6	45	1,091	24.2	0
16. Steve Smith, Car.	6	98	2,371	24.2	2
17. Derrick Wimbush, Jax.	2	47	1,136	24.2	1
18. Ladell Betts, Was.	5	80	1,925	24.1	1
19. Dante Hall, St.L.	7	360	8,644	24.0	6
20. Tab Perry, Cin.	2	68	1,631	24.0	0
21. Bobby Wade, Min.	4	50	1,194	23.9	0
22. Kevin Mathis, *	9	51	1,216	23.8	0
23. Dominic Rhodes, Oak.	5	119	2,810	23.6	2
24. Eddie Drummond, Det.	5	213	5,026	23.6	2
25. Chad Morton, *	7	229	5,401	23.6	3

TOP ACTIVE PUNTERS
50 or more punts

	Yrs.	No.	Avg.	LG
1. Shane Lechler, Oak.	7	519	46.1	73
2. Ryan Plackemeier, Sea.	1	84	45.0	72
3. Jon Ryan, G.B.	1	84	44.5	66
4. Mat McBriar, Dal.	3	212	44.0	75
5. Todd Sauerbrun, Den.	12	842	44.0	73
6. Ben Graham, NYJ	2	146	43.9	69
7. Steven Weatherford, N.O.	1	77	43.8	59
8. Brian Moorman, Buf.	6	471	43.5	84
9. Hunter Smith, Ind.	8	472	43.5	69
10. Kyle Larson, Cin.	3	220	43.3	75
11. Mitch Berger, N.O.	12	710	43.2	75
12. Josh Miller, N.E.	11	747	43.1	75
13. Chris Kluwe, Min.	2	164	43.1	68
14. Scott Player, Ari.	9	714	43.1	67
15. Sam Koch, Bal.	1	86	43.0	61
16. Mike Scifres, S.D.	4	209	42.9	71
17. Craig Hentrich, Ten.	13	984	42.9	78
18. Chris Hanson, Jax.	7	428	42.9	74
19. Chris Gardocki, Pit.	16	1177	42.8	72
20. Donnie Jones, St.L.	3	199	42.5	64
21. Andy Lee, S.F.	3	284	42.5	81
22. Matt Turk, *	11	862	42.5	77
23. Josh Bidwell, T.B.	7	573	42.4	68
24. Brad Maynard, Chi.	10	914	42.2	75
25. Michael Koenen, Atl.	2	154	42.2	67

TOP ACTIVE QUARTERBACK SACKERS

	Yrs.	No.
1. Michael Strahan, NYG	14	132.5
2. Simeon Rice, T.B.	11	121.0
3. Jason Taylor, Mia.	10	106.0
4. Kevin Carter, T.B.	12	97.5
5. Warren Sapp, Oak.	12	94.5
6. Bryant Young, S.F.	13	83.0
7. Willie McGinest, Cle.	13	82.0
8. Chad Brown, *	14	79.0
9. La'Roi Glover, St.L.	11	77.0
Trevor Pryce, Bal.	10	77.0
11. Leonard Little, St.L.	9	74.0
12. Lance Johnstone, *	11	72.0
13. Jevon Kearse, Phi.	8	66.0
14. Kabeer Gbaja-Biamila, G.B.	7	64.5
15. Aaron Schobel, Buf.	6	60.5
16. Joey Porter, Mia.	8	60.0
17. Patrick Kerney, Sea.	8	58.0
18. John Abraham, Atl.	7	57.5
19. Rod Coleman, Atl.	8	56.5
Phillip Daniels, Was.	11	56.5
Greg Ellis, Dal.	9	56.5
Dwight Freeney, Ind.	5	56.5
23. Dan Wilkinson, Mia.	13	54.5
24. Julius Peppers, Car.	5	53.5
25. Junior Seau, *	17	53.0
Grant Wistrom, *	9	53.0

ACTIVE COACHES' CAREER RECORDS (Order Based on Career Victories)
Start of 2007 Season

Coach	Team(s)	Yrs.	Regular Season				Postseason			Career			
			Won	Lost	Tied	Pct.	Won	Lost	Pct.	Won	Lost	Tied	Pct.
Joe Gibbs	Washington Redskins	15	145	87	0	.625	17	6	.739	162	93	0	.635
Mike Holmgren	Green Bay Packers, Seattle Seahawks	15	147	93	0	.613	12	10	.545	159	103	0	.607
Mike Shanahan	Los Angeles Raiders, Denver Broncos	14	131	81	0	.618	8	5	.615	139	86	0	.618
Bill Belichick	Cleveland Browns, New England Patriots	12	111	81	0	.578	13	3	.813	124	84	0	.596
Tony Dungy	Tampa Bay Buccaneers, Indianapolis Colts	11	114	62	0	.648	9	8	.529	123	70	0	.637
Jeff Fisher	Tennessee Titans	12	105	93	0	.530	5	4	.556	110	97	0	.531
Tom Coughlin	Jacksonville Jaguars, New York Giants	11	93	83	0	.528	4	6	.400	97	89	0	.522
Andy Reid	Philadelphia Eagles	8	80	48	0	.625	8	6	.571	88	54	0	.620
Jon Gruden	Oakland Raiders, Tampa Bay Buccaneers	9	77	67	0	.535	5	3	.625	82	70	0	.539
Brian Billick	Baltimore Ravens	8	75	53	0	.586	5	3	.625	80	56	0	.588
Norv Turner	Washington Redskins, Oakland Raiders, San Diego Chargers	9	58	82	1	.414	1	1	.500	59	83	1	.416
Herm Edwards	New York Jets, Kansas City Chiefs	6	48	48	0	.500	2	4	.333	50	52	0	.490
John Fox	Carolina Panthers	5	44	36	0	.550	5	2	.714	49	38	0	.563
Wade Phillips	New Orleans Saints, Denver Broncos, Buffalo Bills, Atlanta Falcons, Dallas Cowboys	7	48	39	0	.552	0	3	.000	48	42	0	.533
Dick Jauron	Chicago Bears, Detroit Lions, Buffalo Bills	7	43	58	0	.426	0	1	.000	43	59	0	.422
Marvin Lewis	Cincinnati Bengals	4	35	29	0	.547	0	1	.000	35	30	0	.538
Jack Del Rio	Jacksonville Jaguars	4	34	30	0	.531	0	1	.000	34	31	0	.523
Lovie Smith	Chicago Bears	3	29	19	0	.604	2	2	.500	31	21	0	.596
Sean Payton	New Orleans Saints	1	10	6	0	.625	1	1	.500	11	7	0	.611
Mike Nolan	San Francisco 49ers	2	11	21	0	.344	0	0	—	11	21	0	.344
Eric Mangini	New York Jets	1	10	6	0	.625	0	1	.000	10	7	0	.588
Romeo Crennel	Cleveland Browns	2	10	22	0	.313	0	0	—	10	22	0	.313
Scott Linehan	St. Louis Rams	1	8	8	0	.500	0	0	—	8	8	0	.500
Mike McCarthy	Green Bay Packers	1	8	8	0	.500	0	0	—	8	8	0	.500
Brad Childress	Minnesota Vikings	1	6	10	0	.375	0	0	—	6	10	0	.375
Gary Kubiak	Houston Texans	1	6	10	0	.375	0	0	—	6	10	0	.375
Rod Marinelli	Detroit Lions	1	3	13	0	.188	0	0	—	3	13	0	.188
Cam Cameron	Miami Dolphins	0	0	0	0	—	0	0	—	0	0	0	—
Lane Kiffin	Oakland Raiders	0	0	0	0	—	0	0	—	0	0	0	—
Bobby Petrino	Atlanta Falcons	0	0	0	0	—	0	0	—	0	0	0	—
Mike Tomlin	Pittsburgh Steelers	0	0	0	0	—	0	0	—	0	0	0	—
Ken Whisenhunt	Arizona Cardinals	0	0	0	0	—	0	0	—	0	0	0	—

COACHES WITH 100 CAREER VICTORIES (Order Based on Career Victories)
Start of 2007 Season

Coach	Team(s)	Regular Season				Postseason			Career			
		Yrs.	Won	Lost	Tied	Pct.	Won	Lost	Pct.	Won	Lost	Tied	Pct.
Don Shula	Baltimore Colts, Miami Dolphins	33	328	156	6	.677	19	17	.528	347	173	6	.666
George Halas	Chicago Bears	40	318	148	31	.682	6	3	.667	324	151	31	.682
Tom Landry	Dallas Cowboys	29	250	162	6	.607	20	16	.556	270	178	6	.603
Earl (Curly) Lambeau	Green Bay Packers, Chicago Cardinals, Washington Redskins	33	226	132	22	.631	3	2	.600	229	134	22	.631
Chuck Noll	Pittsburgh Steelers	23	193	148	1	.566	16	8	.667	209	156	1	.572
Marty Schottenheimer	Cleveland Browns, Kansas City Chiefs, Washington Redskins, San Diego Chargers	21	200	126	1	.613	5	13	.278	205	139	1	.596
Dan Reeves	Denver Broncos, New York Giants, Atlanta Falcons	23	190	165	2	.535	11	9	.550	201	174	2	.536
Chuck Knox	Los Angeles Rams, Buffalo Bills, Seattle Seahawks	22	186	147	1	.558	7	11	.389	193	158	1	.550
Bill Parcells	New York Giants, New England Patriots, New York Jets, Dallas Cowboys	19	172	130	1	.569	11	8	.579	183	138	1	.570
Paul Brown	Cleveland Browns, Cincinnati Bengals	21	166	100	6	.624	4	8	.333	170	108	6	.612
Bud Grant	Minnesota Vikings	18	158	96	5	.621	10	12	.455	168	108	5	.608
Joe Gibbs	Washington Redskins	15	145	87	0	.625	17	6	.739	162	93	0	.635
Bill Cowher	Pittsburgh Steelers	15	149	90	1	.598	12	9	.571	161	99	1	.619
Mike Holmgren	Green Bay Packers, Seattle Seahawks	15	147	93	0	.613	12	10	.545	159	103	0	.607
Marv Levy	Kansas City Chiefs, Buffalo Bills	17	143	112	0	.561	11	8	.579	154	120	0	.562
Steve Owen	New York Giants	23	151	100	17	.602	2	8	.200	153	108	17	.586
Mike Shanahan	Los Angeles Raiders, Denver Broncos	14	131	81	0	.618	8	5	.615	139	86	0	.618
Hank Stram	Kansas City Chiefs, New Orleans Saints	17	131	97	10	.574	5	3	.625	136	100	10	.576
Weeb Ewbank	Baltimore Colts, New York Jets	20	130	129	7	.502	4	1	.800	134	130	7	.508
Mike Ditka	Chicago Bears, New Orleans Saints	14	121	95	0	.560	6	6	.500	127	101	0	.557
Dick Vermeil	Philadelphia Eagles, St. Louis Rams, Kansas City Chiefs	15	120	109	0	.524	6	5	.545	126	114	0	.525
Jim Mora	New Orleans Saints, Indianapolis Colts	15	125	106	0	.541	0	6	.000	125	112	0	.527
George Seifert	San Francisco 49ers, Carolina Panthers	11	114	62	0	.648	10	5	.667	124	67	0	.649
Bill Belichick	Cleveland Browns, New England Patriots	12	111	81	0	.578	13	3	.813	124	84	0	.596
Tony Dungy	Tampa Bay Buccaneers, Indianapolis Colts	11	114	62	0	.648	9	8	.529	123	70	0	.637
Sid Gillman	Los Angeles Rams, Los Angeles-San Diego Chargers, Houston Oilers	18	122	99	7	.552	1	5	.167	123	104	7	.542
George Allen	Los Angeles Rams, Washington Redskins	12	116	47	5	.712	2	7	.222	118	54	5	.686
Dennis Green	Minnesota Vikings, Arizona Cardinals	13	113	94	0	.546	4	8	.333	117	102	0	.534
Don Coryell	St. Louis Cardinals, San Diego Chargers	14	111	83	1	.572	3	6	.333	114	89	1	.561
John Madden	Oakland Raiders	10	103	32	7	.759	9	7	.563	112	39	7	.739
Jeff Fisher	Tennessee Titans	12	105	93	0	.530	5	4	.556	110	97	0	.531
Ray (Buddy) Parker	Chicago Cardinals, Detroit Lions, Pittsburgh Steelers	15	104	75	9	.581	3	1	.750	107	76	9	.585
Vince Lombardi	Green Bay Packers, Washington Redskins	10	96	34	6	.739	9	1	.900	105	35	6	.750
Tom Flores	Oakland-Los Angeles Raiders, Seattle Seahawks	12	97	87	0	.527	8	3	.727	105	90	0	.538
Bill Walsh	San Francisco 49ers	10	92	59	1	.609	10	4	.714	102	63	1	.617

Active coaches in bold.
From 1920-71, tie games were not included in winning percentage.

The **Baltimore Ravens** need four victories to reach 100 total victories. Baltimore's all-time record is 96-87-1.

The **Carolina Panthers** need four victories to reach 100 total victories. Carolina's all-time record is 96-105-0.

The **Denver Broncos** need 12 victories to reach 400 total victories. Denver's all-time record is (388-342-10).

The **Green Bay Packers** need two victories to become the second team (Chicago Bears, 686) with 650 total victories. Green Bay's all-time record is 648-514-36.

The **Indianapolis Colts** need 12 regular-season wins to become the first team in NFL history with five consecutive 12-win regular seasons. Indianapolis (2003-06) and Dallas (1992-95) are the only two teams with four consecutive seasons with 12 regular-season wins.

The **New York Giants** need four regular-season victories to become the third team (Chicago Bears, 670 and Green Bay Packers, 624) with 600 regular-season victories. New York's all-time regular-season record is 596-500-33.

The **Pittsburgh Steelers** need two regular-season victories to become the first AFC team to reach 500 regular-season victories. Pittsburgh's all-time regular-season record is 498-478-20.

The **St. Louis Rams** need two regular-season victories to reach 500 regular-season victories. St. Louis' all-time regular-season record is 498-441-20.

The **Oakland Raiders** need four regular-season victories to reach 400 regular-season victories. Oakland's all-time regular-season record is 396-301-11.

Joe Gibbs, Washington, needs nine victories to pass Bud Grant (168) and Chuck Knox (170) to move into tenth place all-time in career victories (see Holmgren note) and needs five regular-season victories to reach 150 regular-season victories. In 15 seasons, Gibbs has 162 career victories and 145 regular-season victories.

Mike Holmgren, Seattle, needs 12 victories to pass Bill Cowher (161), Joe Gibbs (162), Bud Grant (168) and Chuck Knox (170) to move into tenth place all-time in career victories (see Gibbs note) and needs three regular-season victories to reach 150 regular-season victories. In 15 seasons, Holmgren has 159 career victories and 147 regular-season victories.

Mike Shanahan, Denver, needs 11 victories to reach 150 regular-season victories. In 15 seasons, Shanahan has 139 regular-season victories.

Tom Coughlin, New York Giants, needs three victories to reach 100 career victories and seven regular-season victories to reach 100 regular-season victories. In 11 seasons, Coughlin has 97 career victories and 93 regular-season victories.

Andy Reid, Philadelphia Eagles, needs 12 victories to reach 100 career victories. In eight seasons, Reid has 88 career victories.

Brett Favre, Green Bay, needs seven touchdown passes to pass Dan Marino (420) for the most touchdown passes in NFL history. In his 16-year career, Favre has 414 touchdown passes.

Favre needs 3,862 passing yards to pass Dan Marino (61,361) for the most passing yards in NFL history. In 16 seasons, Favre has passed for 57,500 yards.

Favre needs two wins to pass John Elway (148) for the most wins by a quarterback. In 16 seasons, Favre has won 147 games.

Favre has passed for 3,000 yards in a season 15 times in his 16-year career and can extend his NFL-record streak with another 3,000-yard season. Favre also holds the record for the most consecutive seasons with 3,000 passing yards with 15 (active).

Favre has led the league in touchdown passes four times in his 15-year career and can pass Johnny Unitas, Len Dawson and Steve Young (4) for the most seasons leading the league in touchdown passes.

In his 16-year career, Favre has passed for four touchdowns in a game 19 times. Favre needs three more four-touchdown games to pass Dan Marino (21) for the most games with four touchdown passes in NFL history.

Peyton Manning, Indianapolis, needs 4,000 passing yards to become the first quarterback in NFL history with eight 4,000-yard seasons. Manning is the only quarterback to accomplish the feat in seven seasons.

Manning needs 25 touchdown passes to become the first player in NFL history to throw 25 touchdown passes in 10 consecutive seasons. Manning is the only player to have nine consecutive seasons with 25 touchdown passes.

Manning has passed for 3,000 yards in each of the past nine seasons and can surpass Dan Marino (9) for the second-longest streak of consecutive 3,000-yard seasons. Manning is the only player in NFL history to start a career with nine consecutive 3,000-yard seasons.

Manning has led the league in touchdown passes three times in his nine-year career and can tie Brett Favre, Johnny Unitas, Len Dawson and Steve Young (4) for the most seasons leading the league in touchdown passes (see Favre note).

Manning has passed for 400 yards in a game seven times in his nine-year NFL career. Manning needs one 400-yard passing game to surpass Joe Montana and Warren Moon (7) for the second-most games with 400 yards passing in NFL history.

Manning needs 26 touchdown passes to surpass John Unitas (290), Warren Moon (291) and John Elway (300) to move into fourth place all-time. In nine seasons, Manning has thrown 275 touchdown passes.

Manning needs 2,966 passing yards to surpass Boomer Esiason (37,920), Dave Krieg (38,147), John Unitas (40,239) and Joe Montana (40,551) to move into eight place all-time. In nine seasons, Manning has passed for 37,586 yards.

Daunte Culpepper, Miami, needs 3,000 passing yards and 400 rushing yards this season to become the first quarterback in NFL history with five seasons with 3,000 passing yards and 400 rushing yards. Culpepper is the only player to accomplish the feat in four seasons.

LaDainian Tomlinson, San Diego, needs 10 rushing touchdowns to extend his NFL-record streak of consecutive seasons to begin a career with 10 rushing touchdowns to seven.

Tomlinson needs 1,200 rushing yards to join Eric Dickerson (1983-89) as the only players in NFL history to begin a career with seven 1,200-yard rushing seasons.

Tomlinson needs 16 touchdowns to pass Lenny Moore (111), Terrell Owens (116), John Riggins (116), Marvin Harrison (122), Walter Payton (125), Jim Brown (126) and Cris Carter (130) to move into sixth place all-time (see M. Harrison and Owens notes). In six seasons, Tomlinson has scored 111 touchdowns.

Edgerrin James, Arizona, has gained 2,000 scrimmage yards three times in his eight-year career. With one more 2,000-scrimmage yard season, James will tie Eric Dickerson, Marshall Faulk and Walter Payton (4) for the most all-time.

James has gained 2,000 combined yards three times in his career. James needs one more season with 2,000 combined yards to tie Eric Dickerson, Marshall Faulk, Dante Hall, Brian Mitchell and Walter Payton (4) for the most all-time (see Hall note).

Shaun Alexander, Seattle, needs four rushing touchdowns to become the eighth player in NFL history to rush for 100 touchdowns. In seven seasons, Alexander has rushed for 96 touchdowns.

Marvin Harrison, Indianapolis, needs 10 receiving touchdowns to become the first player in NFL history with nine consecutive seasons with at least 10 receiving touchdowns. Harrison is the only player to accomplish the feat in eight straight seasons.

Harrison needs 80 receptions to become the first player in NFL history with nine consecutive 80-reception seasons. He is currently tied with Jerry Rice (8) for the most such consecutive seasons.

Harrison needs 100 receptions to pass Jerry Rice (4) to become the first player in NFL history with five 100-catch seasons. In 11 seasons, Harrison has four seasons with 100 receptions.

Harrison needs 81 receptions to surpass Tim Brown (1,094) and Cris Carter (1,101) to move into second place all-time. In 11 seasons, Harrison has 1,021 receptions.

Harrison needs 1,238 receiving yards to surpass Henry Ellard (13,777), Cris Carter (13,899), James Lofton (14,004) and Tim Brown (14,934) to move into second place all-time (see Bruce note). In 11 seasons, Harrison has 13,697 receiving yards.

Harrison has three 1,500-receiving yard seasons in his 11-year career and needs 1,500 receiving yards to tie Jerry Rice (4) for the most 1,500-receiving yard seasons.

Harrison needs 1,000 receiving yards to pass Cris Carter, Steve Largent and Rod Smith (8) to move into a second place tie with Tim Brown and Jimmy Smith in 1,000-yard receiving seasons. In 11 seasons, Harrison has eight 1,000-yard seasons (see Smith note).

Harrison has 122 career touchdowns and needs 15 to pass Walter Payton (125), Jim Brown (126), Cris Carter (130) and Marshall Faulk (136) to move into fourth place all-time (see Tomlinson and Owens note).

Terrell Owens, Dallas, needs 15 touchdowns to pass John Riggins (116), Marvin Harrison (122), Walter Payton (125), Jim Brown (126) and Cris Carter (130) to move into fifth place all-time (see Tomlinson and M. Harrison notes). In 11 seasons, Owens has 116 touchdowns.

Isaac Bruce, St. Louis, needs 629 receiving yards to surpass Marvin Harrison (13,697), Henry Ellard (13,777), Cris Carter (13,899) and James Lofton (14,004) to move into third place all-time (see M. Harrison note). In 13 seasons, Bruce has 13,376 receiving yards.

Bruce needs 13 receptions to become the seventh player in NFL history with 900 career receptions. In 13 seasons, Bruce has 887 receptions.

Rod Smith, Denver, needs 1,000 receiving yards to pass Cris Carter, Steve Largent and Marvin Harrison (8) to move into a second place tie with Tim Brown and Jimmy Smith in 1,000-yard receiving seasons. In 13 seasons, Smith has eight 1,000-yard seasons (see M. Harrison note).

Smith has recorded 100 receptions in a season two times in his 12-year NFL career. Smith can join Marvin Harrison and Jerry Rice (4) as the only players in NFL history with three seasons with 100 receptions (see Boldin, Holt and Moss notes).

Randy Moss, New England, has recorded 100 receptions in a season two times in his nine-year NFL career. Moss can join Marvin Harrison and Jerry Rice (4) as the only players in NFL history with three seasons with 100 receptions (see Boldin, Holt and Smith notes).

Torry Holt, St. Louis, has recorded 100 receptions in a season two times in his eight-year NFL career. Holt can join Marvin Harrison and Jerry Rice (4) as the only players in NFL history with three seasons with 100 receptions (see Boldin, Moss and Smith notes).

Anquan Boldin, Arizona, has recorded 100 receptions in a season two times in his four-year NFL career. Boldin can join Marvin Harrison and Jerry Rice (4) as the only players in NFL history with three seasons with 100 receptions (see Holt, Moss and Smith notes).

Tony Gonzalez, Kansas City, needs two touchdowns to pass Shannon Sharpe (62) to become the all-time leader in touchdowns by a tight end in NFL history. In 10 seasons, Gonzalez has 61 touchdown receptions.

Gonzalez needs 50 receptions to become the first tight end in NFL history with 10 consecutive 50-reception seasons. Gonzalez is the only tight end with nine consecutive 50-reception seasons.

Dante Hall, St. Louis, has six kickoff-return touchdowns in his seven-year career, tied for the most all-time. Hall needs one kickoff-return touchdown to pass Mel Gray, Ollie Matson, Gale Sayers and Travis Williams (6) for sole possession of first place in NFL history.

Hall has gained 2,000 combined yards four times in his seven-year career, tied for the most in NFL history. Hall needs one more season with 2,000 combined yards to pass Eric Dickerson, Marshall Faulk, Brian Mitchell and Walter Payton (4) for the most all-time.

Michael Strahan, New York Giants, needs 5.5 sacks to pass Leslie O'Neal (132.5), Lawrence Taylor (132.5), Richard Dent (137.5) and John Randle (137.5) to move into fifth place all-time. In 14 seasons, Strahan has 132.5 sacks.

Rodney Harrison, New England, needs 1.5 sacks to become the first player in NFL history with 30 interceptions and 30.0 sacks. In his 13-year career, Harrison has 32 interceptions and 28.5 sacks.

Jason Elam, Denver, has scored 100 points in each of his first 14 seasons, the longest streak of all-time. Elam needs 100 points to tie Morten Andersen and Gary Anderson (14) for the most seasons with 100 points in NFL history.

Adam Vinatieri, Indianapolis, has scored 100 points in each of his first 11 seasons and needs 100 points to become the second player (Jason Elam, 14) in NFL history with 100 points in each of his first 12 seasons.

Jeff Wilkins, St. Louis, has successfully kicked 346 consecutive points after touchdowns, the second-longest streak in NFL history. Wilkins needs to convert 26 in a row to pass Jason Elam (371) for the longest streak all-time.

Matt Stover, Baltimore, needs 26 points to pass Norm Johnson (1,736) to move into fifth place on the NFL's all-time scoring list. Stover is currently sixth with 1,711 career points.

72nd Annual NFL Draft, April 28-29, 2007
+Denotes Compensatory Selection
#Denotes Underclassman Selection

ARIZONA CARDINALS
1. Levi Brown—5, T, Penn State
2.# Alan Branch—33, DT, Michigan, from Oakland.
3. Buster Davis—69, LB, Florida State
5. Steve Breaston—142, WR, Michigan
7. Ben Patrick—215, TE, Delaware

ATLANTA FALCONS
1.# Jamaal Anderson—8, DE, Arkansas, from Houston
2. Justin Blalock—39, G, Texas, from Houston
   # Chris Houston—41, DB, Arkansas, from Minnesota
3. Laurent Robinson—75, WR, Illinois State
4. Stephen Nicholas—109, LB, South Florida
   + Martrez Milner—133, TE, Georgia
6. Trey Lewis—185, DT, Washburn
   David Irons—194, DB, Auburn, from Jacksonville
   Doug Datish—198, C, Ohio State, from Denver through Jacksonville
   Daren Stone—203, DB, Maine, from Baltimore through Jacksonville
7.+ Jason Snelling—244, RB, Virginia

BALTIMORE RAVENS
1. Ben Grubbs—29, G, Auburn
3. Yamon Figurs—74, WR, Kansas State
   from Buffalo through Detroit
3. Marshal Yanda—86, T, Iowa
   from Denver through Jacksonville
4.+ Antwan Barnes—134, LB, Florida International
   + Le'Ron McClain—137, RB, Alabama
5.+ Troy Smith—174, QB, Ohio State
6.+ Prescott Burgess—207, LB, Michigan

BUFFALO BILLS
1.# Marshawn Lynch—12, RB, California
2. Paul Posluszny—34, LB, Penn State from Detroit
3. Trent Edwards—92, QB, Stanford from Baltimore
4. Dwayne Wright—111, RB, Fresno State
6. John Wendling—184, DB, Wyoming
7. Derek Schouman—222, TE, Boise State
   C.J. Ah You—239, DE, Oklahoma from Baltimore

CAROLINA PANTHERS
1.# Jon Beason—25, LB, Miami from New York Jets
2.# Dwayne Jarrett—45, WR, Southern California
   Ryan Kalil—59, C, Southern California, from New York Jets
3.# Charles Johnson—83, DE, Georgia
4. Ryne Robinson—118, WR, Miami,O.
5. Dante Rosario—155, TE, Oregon
   Tim Shaw—164, LB, Penn State, from New York Jets
7 C.J. Wilson—226, DB, Baylor

CHICAGO BEARS
1.# Greg Olsen—31, TE, Miami
2. Dan Bazuin—62, DE, Central Michigan from San Diego
3. Garrett Wolfe—93, RB, Northern Illinois from San Diego
   Michael Okwo—94, LB, Stanford
4. Josh Beekman—130, G, Boston College
5. Kevin Payne—167, DB, Louisiana-Monroe from San Diego
   Corey Graham—168, DB, New Hampshire
7. Trumaine McBride—221, DB, Mississippi from San Francisco through Cleveland
   Aaron Brant—241, T, Iowa State

CINCINNATI BENGALS
1. Leon Hall—18, DB, Michigan
2. Kenny Irons—49, RB, Auburn
3.# Choice Exercised in 2006 Supplemental Draft for Ahmad Brooks—LB, Virginia
4. Marvin White—114, DB, Texas Christian
5. Jeff Rowe—151, QB, Nevada
6. Matt Toeaina—187, DT, Oregon
7. Dan Santucci—230, C, Notre Dame
   + Chinedum Ndukwe—253, DB, Notre Dame

CLEVELAND BROWNS
1. Joe Thomas—3, T, Wisconsin
   Brady Quinn—22, QB, Notre Dame, from Dallas
2.# Eric Wright—53, DB, Nevada-Las Vegas, from Dallas
5. Brandon McDonald—140, DB, Memphis
6. Melila Purcell—200, DE, Hawaii, from New York Jets through Dallas
7. Chase Pittman—213, DE, Louisiana State
   Syndric Steptoe—234, WR, Arizona, from Dallas

DALLAS COWBOYS
1. Anthony Spencer—26, LB, Purdue, from Philadelphia
3. James Marten—67, T, Boston College, from Cleveland
4. Isaiah Stanback—103, QB, Washington, from Cleveland
   Doug Free—122, T, Northern Illinois
6. Nick Folk—178, K, Arizona from Cleveland
   Deon Anderson—195, RB, Connecticut, Reacquired Cleveland
7. Courtney Brown—212, DB, Cal Poly-SLO, from Detroit through New York Jets
   Alan Ball—237, DB, Illinois from New Orleans

DENVER BRONCOS
1.# Jarvis Moss—17, DE, Florida, from Jacksonville
2. Tim Crowder—56, DE, Texas
3. Ryan Harris—70, T, Notre Dame, from Washington
4. Marcus Thomas—121, DT, Florida, Reacquired Atlanta and Minnesota

DETROIT LIONS
1.# Calvin Johnson—2, WR, Georgia Tech
2. Drew Stanton—43, QB, Michigan State, from Buffalo
   Ikaika Alama-Francis—58, DE, Hawaii, from New Orleans
   Gerald Alexander—61, DB, Boise State, from Baltimore
4. A.J. Davis—105, DB, North Carolina State, from Arizona through Oakland
   Manuel Ramirez—117, G, Texas Tech, from St. Louis
5. Johnny Baldwin—158, LB, Alabama A&M, from Denver
7.+ Ramzee Robinson—255, DB, Alabama

GREEN BAY PACKERS
1. Justin Harrell—16, DT, Tennessee
2.# Brandon Jackson—63, RB, Nebraska, from Chicago through New York Jets
3. James Jones—78, WR, San Jose State
   Aaron Rouse—89, DB, Virginia Tech, from New York Jets
4. Allen Barbre—119, T, Missouri Southern, from Pittsburgh
5. David Clowney—157, WR, Virginia Tech
6. Korey Hall—191, LB, Boise State, from Carolina through New York Jets
   Desmond Bishop—192, LB, California, from Pittsburgh
   Mason Crosby—193, K, Colorado
7. DeShawn Wynn—228, RB, Florida
   + Clark Harris—243, TE, Rutgers

HOUSTON TEXANS
1. Amobi Okoye—10, DT, Louisville, from Atlanta
3. Jacoby Jones—73, WR, Lane
4. Fred Bennett—123, DB, South Carolina, from Kansas City through New Orleans
5. Brandon Harrison—144, DB, Stanford
   Brandon Frye—163, T, Virginia Tech, from New Orleans
6. Kasey Studdard—183, G, Texas
7. Zac Diles—218, LB, Kansas State

INDIANAPOLIS COLTS
1.# Anthony Gonzalez—32, WR, Ohio State
2. Tony Ugoh—42, T, Arkansas, from San Francisco
3. Daymeion Hughes—95, DB, California
 + Quinn Pitcock—98, DT, Ohio State
4. Brannon Condren—131, DB, Troy
 + Clint Session—136, LB, Pittsburgh
5. Roy Hall—169, WR, Ohio State
 + Michael Coe—131
7. Keyunta Dawson—242, DE, Texas Tech

JACKSONVILLE JAGUARS
1.# Reggie Nelson—21, DB, Florida, from Denver
2. Justin Durant—48, LB, Hampton
3. Mike Walker—79, WR, Central Florida
4. Adam Podlesh—101, P, Maryland,
   from Detroit through Baltimore
   Brian Smith—113, DE, Missouri
5. Uche Nwaneri—149, G, Purdue, from Atlanta
   Josh Gattis—150, DB, Wake Forest
   Derek Landri—166, DT, Notre Dame, from Baltimore
7. John Broussard—229, WR, San Jose State
   Chad Nkang—251, LB, Elon
 + Andrew Carnahan—252, T, Arizona State

KANSAS CITY CHIEFS
1. Dwayne Bowe—23, WR, Louisiana State
2. Turk McBride—54, DT, Tennessee
3. DeMarcus Tyler—82, DT, North Carolina State, from St. Louis
5. Kolby Smith—148, RB, Louisville
   from Buffalo through St. Louis
   Justin Medlock—160, K, UCLA
6. Herbert Taylor—196, G, Texas Christian
7. Michael Allan—231, TE, Whitworth

MIAMI DOLPHINS
1. Ted Ginn—9, WR, Ohio State
2. John Beck—40, QB, Brigham Young
   Samson Satele—60, G, Hawaii, from New England
3. Lorenzo Booker—71, RB, Florida State
4. Paul Soliai—108, NT, Utah
6. Reagan Mauia—181, RB, Hawaii
   Drew Mormino—199,C, Central Michigan, from New Orleans
7. Kelvin Smith—219, LB, Syracuse
   Brandon Fields—225, P, Michigan State, from St. Louis
   Abraham Wright—238, DE, Colorado, from New England

MINNESOTA VIKINGS
1.# Adrian Peterson—7, RB, Oklahoma
2.# Sidney Rice—44, WR, South Carolina, from Atlanta
3. Marcus McCauley—72, DB, Fresno State
4. Brian Robison—102, DE, Texas, from Tampa Bay
5. Aundrae Allison—146, WR, East Carolina
6. Rufus Alexander—176, LB, Oklahoma
7. Tyler Thigpen—217, QB, Coastal Carolina
   Chandler Williams—233, WR, Florida International

NEW ENGLAND PATRIOTS
1. Brandon Meriweather—24, DB, Miami, from Seattle
4. Kareem Brown—127, DT, Miami
5.+ Clint Oldenburg—171, T, Colorado State
6. Justin Rogers—180, LB, Southern Methodist, from Arizona
   Mike Richardson—202, DB, Notre Dame
 + Justise Hairston—208, RB, Central Connecticut
 + Corey Hilliard—209, T, Oklahoma State
7. Oscar Lua—211, LB, Southern California, from Oakland
 + Mike Elgin—247, G, Iowa

NEW ORLEANS SAINTS
1.# Robert Meachem—27, WR, Tennessee
3. Usama Young—66, DB, Kent State, from Detroit
   Andy Alleman—88, G, Akron
4.# Antonio Pittman—107, RB, Ohio State, from Houston
   Jermon Bushrod—125, T, Towson, from Philadelphia
5. David Jones—145, DB, Wingate, N.C., from Miami through Detroit
7. Marvin Mitchell—220, LB, Tennessee, from Atlanta

NEW YORK GIANTS
1. Aaron Ross—20, DB, Texas
2. Steve Smith—51, WR, Southern California
3. Jay Alford—81, DT, Penn State
4. Zak DeOssie—116, LB, Brown
5. Kevin Boss—153, TE, Western Oregon
6. Adam Koets—189, T, Oregon State
7. Michael Johnson—224, DB, Arizona
 + Ahmad Bradshaw—250, RB, Marshall

NEW YORK JETS
1.# Darrelle Revis—14, DB, Pittsburgh from Carolina
2. David Harris—47, LB, Michigan from Green Bay
6. Jacob Bender—177, T, Nicholls State from Tampa Bay
7. Chansi Stuckey—235, WR, Clemson
   Reacquired Green Bay

OAKLAND RAIDERS
1.# JaMarcus Russell—1, QB, Louisiana State
2.# Zach Miller—38, TE, Arizona State. from Arizona
3. Quentin Moses—65, DE, Georgia
   Mario Henderson—91, T, Florida State, from New England
 + Johnnie Lee Higgins—99, WR, Texas-El Paso
4.# Michael Bush—100, RB, Louisville
   John Bowie—110, DB, Cincinnati,
   from San Francisco through New England
5. Jay Richardson—138, DE, Ohio State
   Eric Frampton—165, DB, Washington State, from New England
6. Oren O'Neal—175, RB, Arkansas State
7.+ Johnathan Holland—254, WR, Louisiana Tech

PHILADELPHIA EAGLES
2. Kevin Kolb—36, QB, Houston,
   from Cleveland through Dallas
   Victor Abiamiri—57, DE, Notre Dame
3. Stewart Bradley—87, LB, Nebraska, from Dallas
   Tony Hunt—90, RB, Penn State
5.# C.J. Gaddis—159, DB, Clemson, from Dallas
   Brent Celek—162, TE, Cincinnati
6. Rashad Barksdale—201, DB, Albany,N.Y.
7. Nate Ilaoa—236, RB, Hawaii

PITTSBURGH STEELERS
1.# Lawrence Timmons—15, LB, Florida State
2. LaMarr Woodley—46, LB, Michigan
3. Matt Spaeth—77, TE, Minnesota
4. Daniel Sepulveda—112, P, Baylor, from Green Bay
 + Ryan McBean—132, DE, Oklahoma State
5. Cameron Stephenson—156, G, Rutgers
 + William Gay—170, DB, Louisville
7. Dallas Baker—227, WR, Florida

ST. LOUIS RAMS
1. Adam Carriker—13, DE, Nebraska
2. Brian Leonard—52, RB, Rutgers
3. Jonathan Wade—84, DB, Tennessee, from Kansas City
5. Dustin Fry—139, C, Clemson, from Detroit
 Clifton Ryan—154, DT, Michigan Staet
6. Ken Shackleford—190, T, Georgia
7.+ Keith Jackson—248, DT, Arkansas
 + Derek Stanley—249, WR, Wisconsin-Whitewater

SAN DIEGO CHARGERS
1. Craig Davis—30, WR, Louisiana State
2. Eric Weddle—37, DB, Utah
 from Washington through New York Jets and Chicago
3.+ Anthony Waters—96, LB, Clemson
4. Scott Chandler—129, TE, Iowa
5.+ Legedu Naanee—172, WR, Boise State
7.# Brandon Siler—240, LB, Florida

SAN FRANCISCO 49ERS
1. Patrick Willis—11, LB, Mississippi
 Joe Staley—28, T, Central Michigan, from New England
3. Jason Hill—76, WR, Washington State
 + Ray McDonald—97, DE, Florida
4. Jay Moore—104, LB, Nebraska, from Washington
 Dashon Goldson—126, DB, Washington,
 from New Orleans through Indianapolis
 + Joe Cohen—135, DT, Florida
5. Tarell Brown—147, DB, Texas
6. Thomas Clayton—186, RB, Kansas State

SEATTLE SEAHAWKS
2. Josh Wilson—55, DB, Maryland
3. Brandon Mebane—85, DT, California
4. Baraka Atkins—120, DE, Miami
 Mansfield Wrotto—124, G, Georgia Tech,
 from New York Jets through San Francisco
5. Will Herring—161, LB, Auburn
6. Courtney Taylor—197, WR, Auburn
 + Jordan Kent—210, WR, Oregon
7. Steve Vallos—232, G, Wake Forest

TAMPA BAY BUCCANEERS
1. Gaines Adams—4, DE, Clemson
2. Arron Sears—35, G, Tennessee
 Sabby Piscitelli—64, DB, Oregon State, from Indianapolis
3. Quincy Black—68, LB, New Mexico
4. Tanard Jackson—106, DB, Syracuse, from Minnesota
5. Greg Peterson—141, DT, N. Carolina Central
6. Adam Hayward—182, LB, Portland State, from Minnesota
7. Chris Denman—214, T, Fresno State
 + Marcus Hamilton—245, DB, Virginia
 + Kenneth Darby—246, RB, Alabama

TENNESSEE TITANS
1. Michael Griffin—19, DB, Texas
2. Chris Henry—50, RB, Rutgers
3. Paul Williams—80, WR, Fresno State
4. Leroy Harris—115, C, North Carolina State
 Chris Davis—128, DT, Floida State, from Baltimore
5. Antoino Johnson—152, DT, Mississippi State
6. Joel Filani—188, WR, Texas Tech
 # Jacob Ford—204, DE, Central Arkansas
 Ryan Smith—206, DB, Floida, from Indianapolis
7. Mike Otto—223, T, Purdue

WASHINGTON REDSKINS
1. LaRon Landry—6, DB, Louisiana State
5. Dallas Sartz—143, LB, Southern California
6. H.B. Blades—179, LB, Pittsburgh
 Jordan Palmer—205, QB, Texas-El Paso, from Chicago
7. Tyler Ecker—216, TE, Michigan

NUMBER OF PLAYERS DRAFTED—2007

BY POSITION:

Defensive Backs	50
Linebackers	35
Wide Receivers	34
Running Backs	24
Defensive Ends	22
Tackles	21
Defensive Tackles	18
Guards	14
Tight Ends	13
Quarterbacks	11
Centers	6
Kickers	3
Punters	3
Nose Tackle	1

BY COLLEGE:

Florida	9
Ohio State	8
Michigan	7
Notre Dame	7
Texas	7
Tennessee	6
Auburn	5
Clemson	5
Florida Sate	5
Hawaii	5
Miami	5
Louisiana State	5
Penn State	5
Southern California	5
Arizona	4
Arkansas	4
Boise State	4
California	4
Fresno State	4
Georgia	4
Louisville	4
Nebraska	4
Alabama	3
Central Michigan	3
Iowa	3
Kansas State	3
Michigan State	3
North Carolina State	3
Oklahoma	3
Oregon	3
Pittsburgh	3
Purdue	3
Rutgers	3
Stanford	3
Texas Tech	3
Virginia Tech	3
Arizona State	2
Baylor	2
Boston College	2
Cincinnati	2
Colorado	2
Florida International	2
Georgia Tech	2
Maryland	2
Mississippi	2
Northern Illinois	2
Oklahoma State	2
Oregon State	2
San Jose State	2
South Carolina	2
Syracuse	2

Texas Christian	2
Texas-El Paso	2
Utah	2
Virignia	2
Wake Forest	2
Washington	2
Washington State	2
Akron	1
Alabama A&M	1
Alabama State	1
Albany (N.Y.)	1
Arkansas State	1
Brigham Young	1
Brown	1
Cal Poly-San Lius Obispo	1
Central Arkansas	1
Central Connecticut	1
Central Florida	1
Coastal Carolina	1
Colorado State	1
Connecticut	1
Delaware	1
East Carolina	1
Elon	1
Hampton	1
Houston	1
Illinois	1
Illinois State	1
Iowa State	1
Kent State	1
Lane	1
Louisiana Tech	1
Louisiana-Monroe	1
Maine	1
Marshall	1
Memphis	1
Miami (Ohio)	1
Mississippi State	1
Missouri	1
Missouri Southern	1
Minnesota	1
Nevada	1
Nevada-Las Vegas	1
New Hampshire	1
New Mexico	1
Nicholls State	1
North Carolina Central	1
Portland State	1
South Florida	1
Southern Methodist	1
Towson	1
Troy	1
UCLA	1
Washburn	1
Western Oregon	1
Whitworth	1
Wingate	1
Wisconsin	1
Wisconsin-Whitewater	1
Wyoming	1

BY CONFERENCE:

Southeastern	41
Big Ten	32
Atlantic Coast	31
Pacific 10	28
Big 12	28
Western Athletic	17
Big East	16
Independent	9
Mountain West	9
Conference USA	8
Mid-American	8
Sun Belt	5
Atlantic 10	4
Mid-America Intercollegiate Athletic	2
Northeast	2
Southwestern Athletic	2
Big Sky	1
Big South	1
Central Intercollegiate Athletic	1
Great West Football	1
Gateway Football	1
Ivy League	1
Mid-Eastern Athletic	1
Northwest	1
South Atlantic	1
Southern	1
Southern Intercollegiate Athletic	1
Southland	1
Wisconsin Intercollegiate Athletic	1

UNDERCLASSMEN IN THE DRAFT

Year	Entered	Drafted	In Top 10
1989	25	12	3
1990	38	18	5
1991	33	22	2
1992	48	25	5
1993	46	24	5
1994	43	26	6
1995	42	22	2
1996	46	21	4
1997	44	27	7
1998	41	20	3
1999	42	27	5
2000	31	20	4
2001	54	31	5
2002	43	26	5
2003	54	32	5
2004	44	35	5
2005	57	38	4
2006	62	34	6
2007	40	29	4

WAIVERS

The waiver system is a procedure by which player contracts or NFL rights to players are made available by a club to other clubs in the League. During the procedure, the 31 other clubs either file claims to obtain the players or waive the opportunity to do so—thus the term "waiver." Claiming clubs are assigned players on a priority based on the inverse of won-and-lost standing. The claiming period is 24 hours from the first business day after the Pro Bowl through the last business day prior to June 1. From June 1 through the last business day prior to July 4, the claiming period is three days. From the first business day after July 4 through the conclusion of the regular season, the claiming period is 24 hours. If a player passes through waivers unclaimed, he becomes a free agent. All waivers are no recall and no withdrawal. Under the Collective Bargaining Agreement, from the beginning of the waiver system each year through the trading deadline (October 16, 2007), any veteran who has acquired four years of pension credit is not subject to the waiver system if the club desires to release him. After the trading deadline, such players are subject to the waiver system.

ACTIVE/INACTIVE LIST

The Active/Inactive List is the principal status for players participating for a club. It consists of all players under contract who are eligible for preseason, regular-season, and postseason games. Teams are permitted to open training camp with no more than 80 players under contract and thereafter must meet two mandatory roster reductions prior to the season opener. Teams will be permitted an Active List of 45 players and an Inactive List of eight players for each regular-season and postseason game. Provided that a club has two quarterbacks on its 45-player Active List, a third quarterback from its Inactive List is permitted to dress for the game, but if he enters the game during the first three quarters, the other two quarterbacks are thereafter prohibited from playing. Teams also are permitted to establish Practice Squads of up to eight players who are eligible to participate in practice, but these players remain free agents and are eligible to sign with any other team in the league.

August 28	Roster reduction to 75 players
September 1	Roster reduction to 53 players
September 2	Teams establish a Practice Squad of up to eight players

In addition to the squad limits described above, the overall roster limit of 80 players remains in effect throughout the regular season and postseason. The overall limit is applicable to players on a team's Active, Inactive, and certain Exempt Lists, players on the Practice Squad, and players on the Reserve List as Injured, Physically Unable to Perform, Non-Football Illness/Injury, and Suspended by Club.

RESERVE LIST

The Reserve List is a status for players who, for reasons of injury, retirement, military service, or other circumstances, are not immediately available for participation with a club. Players on Reserve/Injured are not eligible to practice or return to the Active/Inactive List in the same season that they are placed on Reserve. Players in the category of Reserve/Retired, Reserve/Did Not Report, Reserve/Exclusive Rights, and players who were placed in the category of Reserve/Left Squad in a previous season may not be reinstated during the period from 30 days before the end of the regular season through the postseason.

TRADES

Unrestricted trading between the AFC and NFC is allowed in 2007 through October 16, after which trading will end until 2008.

ANNUAL ACTIVE PLAYER LIMITS

NFL

Year(s)	Limit
1991-2007	45**
1985-90	45
1983-84	49
1982	45†-49
1978-81	45
1975-77	43
1974	47
1964-73	40
1963	37
1961-62	36
1960	38
1959	36
1957-58	35
1951-56	33
1949-50	32
1948	35
1947	35*-34
1945-46	33
1943-44	28
1940-42	33
1938-39	30
1936-37	25
1935	24
1930-34	20
1926-29	18
1925	16

** 45 plus a third quarterback
† 45 for first two games
* 35 for first three games

AFL

Year(s)	Limit
1966-69	40
1965	38
1964	34
1962-63	33
1960-61	35

NFL FREE AGENCY MOVEMENT

The following chart details veteran free agents who signed with new teams:

	Unrestricted	Restricted	Transition	Franchise	TOTALS
1993	108	8	4	1	121
1994	121	7	4	0	132
1995	171	6	2	0	179
1996	100	4	2	0	106
1997	86	2	2	0	90
1998	112	4	1	2	119
1999	115	2	1	0	118
2000	107	4	0	0	111
2001	93	4	0	0	97
2002	130	1	0	0	131
2003	111	5	1	0	117
2004	124	1	1	0	126
2005	104	3	0	0	107
2006	149	4	1	0	154

The following procedures will be used to break standings ties for postseason playoffs and to determine regular-season schedules.

Note: Tie games count as one-half win and one-half loss for both clubs.

TO BREAK A TIE WITHIN A DIVISION

If, at the end of the regular season, two or more clubs in the same division finish with the best won-lost-tied percentage, the following steps will be taken until a champion is determined:

TWO CLUBS

1. Head-to-head (best won-lost-tied percentage in games between the clubs.)
2. Best won-lost-tied percentage in games played within the division.
3. Best won-lost-tied percentage in common games.
4. Best won-lost-tied percentage in games played within the conference.
5. Strength of victory.
6. Strength of schedule.
7. Best combined ranking among conference teams in points scored and points allowed.
8. Best combined ranking among all teams in points scored and points allowed.
9. Best net points in common games.
10. Best net points in all games.
11. Best net touchdowns in all games
12. Coin toss.

THREE OR MORE CLUBS

(Note: If two clubs remain tied after a third club is eliminated during any step, tie-breaker reverts to Step 1 of the two-club format.)

1. Head-to-head (best won-lost-tied percentage in games among the clubs.)
2. Best won-lost-tied percentage in games played within the division.
3. Best won-lost-tied percentage in common games.
4. Best won-lost-tied percentage in games played within the conference.
5. Strength of victory.
6. Strength of schedule.
7. Best combined ranking among conference teams in points scored and points allowed.
8. Best combined ranking among all teams in points scored and points allowed.
9. Best net points in common games.
10. Best net points in all games.
11. Best net touchdowns in all games.
12. Coin toss.

TO BREAK A TIE FOR THE WILD-CARD TEAM

If it is necessary to break ties to determine the two Wild Card clubs from each conference, the following steps will be taken:

A. If all the tied clubs are from the same division, apply division tie-breaker.

B. If the tied clubs are from different divisions, apply the following steps:

TWO CLUBS

1. Head-to-head, if applicable.
2. Best won-lost-tied percentage in the games played within the conference.
3. Best won-lost-tied percentage in common games, minimum of four.
4. Strength of victory.
5. Strength of schedule.
6. Best combined ranking among conference teams in points scored and points allowed.
7. Best combined ranking among all teams in points scored and points allowed.
8. Best net points in conference games.
9. Best net points in all games.
10. Best net touchdowns in all games.
11. Coin toss.

THREE OR MORE CLUBS

1. Apply division tie-breaker to eliminate all but highest ranked club in each division prior to proceeding to Step 2. The original seeding within a division upon application of the division tie-breaker remains the same for all subsequent applications of the procedure that are necessary to identify the Wild Card participants.
2. Head-to-head sweep (apply only if one club has defeated each of the others or one club has lost to each of the others).
3. Best won-lost-tied percentage in games played within the conference.
4. Best won-lost-tied percentage in common games, minimum of four.
5. Strength of victory.
6. Strength of schedule.
7. Best combined ranking among conference teams in points scored and points allowed.
8. Best combined ranking among all teams in points scored and points allowed.
9. Best net points in conference games.
10. Best net points in all games.
11. Best net touchdowns in all games.
12. Coin toss.

When the first Wild Card team has been identified, the procedure is repeated to name the second Wild Card (i.e., eliminate all but the highest ranked club in each division prior to proceeding to Step 2.) In situations where three teams from the same division are involved in the procedure, the original seeding of the teams remains the same for subsequent applications of the tie-breaker if the top-ranked team in that division qualifies for a Wild Card berth.

OTHER TIE-BREAKING PROCEDURES

1. Only one club advances to the playoffs in any tie-breaking step. Remaining tied clubs revert to the first step of the applicable division or Wild Card tie-breakers. As an

example, if two clubs remain tied in any tie-breaker step after all other clubs have been eliminated, the procedure reverts to Step 1 of the two-club format to determine the winner. When one club wins the tie-breaker, all other clubs revert to Step 1 of the applicable two-club or three-club format.

2. In comparing records against common opponents among tied teams, the best won-lost-tied percentage is the deciding factor since teams may have played an unequal number of games.

3. To determine home-field priority among division-titlists, apply Wild Card tie-breakers.

4. To determine home-field priority for Wild Card qualifiers, apply division tie-breakers (if teams are from the same division) or Wild Card tie-breakers (if teams are from different divisions).

TIE-BREAKING PROCEDURE FOR SELECTION MEETING

If two or more clubs are tied in the selection order, the strength-of-schedule tie-breaker is applied, subject to the following exceptions for playoff clubs:

1. The Super Bowl winner is last and the Super Bowl loser next-to-last.

2. Any non-Super Bowl playoff club involved in a tie shall be assigned priority within its segment below that of non-playoff clubs and in the order that the playoff club exited from the playoffs. Thus, within a tied segment a playoff club that loses in the Wild Card game will have priority over a playoff club that loses in the Divisional playoff game, which in turn will have priority over a club that loses in the Conference Championship game. If two tied clubs exited the playoffs in the same round, the tie is broken by strength of schedule.

If any ties cannot be broken by strength of schedule, the divisional or conference tie-breakers, whichever are applicable, are applied. Any ties that still exist are broken by a coin flip.

The NFL utilizes a system of Referee Replay Review to aid officiating.

Prior to the two-minute warning of each half, a Coaches' Challenge System will be in effect. After the two-minute warning, and throughout any overtime period, a Referee Review will be initiated by a Replay Assistant from a Replay Booth.

The following procedures will be used:

Reviews by Referee: All Replay Reviews will be conducted by the Referee on a field-level monitor after consultation with the other covering official(s), prior to review. A decision will be reversed only when the Referee has *indisputable visual evidence* available to him that warrants the change.

Coaches' Challenge: In each game, a team will be permitted two challenges that will initiate Referee Replay reviews. Each challenge will require the use of a team time out. If a challenge is upheld, the time out will be restored to the challenging team. If both challenges are upheld, a third challenge will be awarded to the challenging team. No challenges will be recognized from a team that has exhausted its time outs.

Replay Assistant's Request for Review: After the two-minute warning of each half, and throughout any overtime period, any review will be initiated by a Replay Assistant. There is no limit to the number of reviews that may be initiated by the Replay Assistant. His ability to initiate a review will be unrelated to the number of time outs that either team has remaining, and no time out will be charged for any review initiated by the Replay Assistant.

Time Limit: Each review will be a maximum of 60 seconds in length, timed from when the Referee begins his review of the replay at the field-level monitor.

Reviewable Plays: The Replay System will cover the following play situations only:

A) **Plays Governed by Sideline, Goal Line, End Zone, and End Line:**
1. Scoring plays, including a runner breaking the plane of the goal line.
2. Pass complete/incomplete/intercepted at sideline, goal line, end zone, and end line.
3. Runner/receiver in or out of bounds.
4. Recovery of loose ball in or out of bounds.

B) **Passing Plays:**
1. Pass ruled complete/incomplete/intercepted in the field of play.
2. Touching of a forward pass by an ineligible receiver.
3. Touching of a forward pass by a defensive player.

4. Quarterback (Passer) forward pass or fumble.
5. Illegal forward pass beyond line of scrimmage.
6. Illegal forward pass after change of possession.
7. Forward or backward pass thrown from behind line of scrimmage.

C) **Other Detectable Infractions:**
1. Runner ruled not down by defensive contact.
2. Runner ruled down by defensive contact and there is a recovery by defense.
3. Forward progress with respect to first down.
4. Touching of a kick.
5. Number of players on the field.
6. Recovery of loose ball in the field of play.

INSTANT REPLAY HISTORY

From 1986-1991, a limited system of Instant Replay was used on a year-by-year basis. Replay also was experimented with during the 1996 and 1998 preseasons. For the 1999 season, the NFL introduced a system of Referee Replay Review to aid officiating. That system was extended on a one-year basis for the 2000 season and then approved for the next three years through 2003. The system was extended on a five-year basis in March 2004 and was later installed permanently in March 2007.

Following are the results of the different systems:

REGULAR SEASON, 1986-1991

Year	Games	Plays Closely Reviewed	Reversals
1986	224	374	38
1987	210	490	57
1988	224	537	53
1989	224	492	65
1990	224	504	73
1991	224	570	90
TOTAL	1,330	2,967	376

PRESEASON, 1996, 1998

Year	Games	Challenges	Reversals
1996	10	13	3
1998	10	10	3
TOTAL	20	23	6

REGULAR SEASON, 1999-2006

Year	Games	Total Replay Reviews	Challenges	Reversals
1999	248	195	133	57
2000	248	247	179	84
2001	248	258	191	89
2002	256	294	208	94
2003	256	255	184	66
2004	256	283	233	88
2005	256	295	223	92
2006	256	311	237	107
TOTAL	2,024	2,138	1,588	677

The AFC

American Football Conference
North Division
Team Colors: Black, Purple, and Metallic Gold
1 Winning Drive
Owings Mills, Maryland 21117
Telephone: (410) 701-4000

2007 SCHEDULE
PRESEASON
Aug. 13 **Philadelphia** 7:00
Aug. 19 **N.Y. Giants** 8:00
Aug. 25 at Washington 8:00
Aug. 31 at Atlanta...........................7:30

REGULAR SEASON
Sep. 10 at Cincinnati (Mon.)............7:00
Sep. 16 **N.Y. Jets** 4:15
Sep. 23 **Arizona** 1:00
Sep. 30 at Cleveland 1:00
Oct. 7   at San Francisco 1:15
Oct. 14 **St. Louis** 1:00
Oct. 21 at Buffalo 1:00
Oct. 28 Open Date
Nov. 5   at Pittsburgh (Mon.) 8:30
Nov. 11 **Cincinnati** 4:05
Nov. 18 **Cleveland** 1:00
Nov. 25 at San Diego 1:15
Dec. 3   **New England** (Mon.).........8:30
Dec. 9   **Indianapolis** *8:15
Dec. 16 at Miami 1:00
Dec. 23 at Seattle 1:15
Dec. 30 **Pittsburgh** 1:00
Sunday night games in Weeks 11-17 subject to change

Stadium: M&T Bank Stadium
            (opened in 1998)
          •**Capacity:** 70,107
            1101 Russell Street
            Baltimore, Maryland 21230
Playing Surface: Sportexe Momentum
Training Camp: McDaniel College
                  2 College Hill
                  Westminster, MD 21157

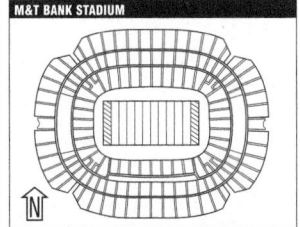

M&T BANK STADIUM

CLUB OFFICIALS
Owner: Steve Bisciotti
President: Dick Cass
Executive Vice President/General
  Manager: Ozzie Newsome
Senior Vice President/Public and
  Community Relations: Kevin Byrne
Senior Vice President/Business Ventures:
  Dennis Mannion
Vice President of Football Administration:
  Pat Moriarty
Chief Financial Officer: Jeff Goering
Vice President of Medical Services/
  Head Athletic Trainer: Bill Tessendorf
Senior Director of Operations: Bob Eller
Senior Director of Publications:
  Francine Lubera
Director of Pro Personnel: George Kokinis
Director of College Scouting:
  Eric DeCosta
Director of Player Development:
  O.J. Brigance
Director of Media Relations:
  Chad Steele
Assistant Director of Pro Personnel:
  Vince Newsome
Scouts: Chad Alexander, Joe Douglas,
  Joe Hortiz, Daniel Jeremiah,
  Lionel Vital, Jeremiah Washburn,
  Andrew Weidl
Equipment Manager: Ed Carroll
Video Director: Jon Dubé
Senior Director, Media Sales and
  Business Development: Mark Burdett
Senior Director, Marketing:
  Gabrielle Dow
Senior Director, Information Technology:
  Bill Jankowski
Senior Director, Ticket Sales and
  Operations: Baker Koppelman
Senior Director, Stadium Operations:
  Roy Sommerhof
Senior Director of Broadcasting:
  Larry Rosen
Director of Premium Services/Suites:
  Theresa Abato
Director, Community Relations:
  Kenny Abrams
Director, Corporate Partnerships:
  Ed Burchell
Director, Information Technology:
  Nick Fusee
Director, Corporate Sales: Kevin Rochlitz
Director, Security: Darren Sanders
Director, Corporate Sales Administration:
  Erin Howland

COACHING HISTORY
(96-87-1)
Records include postseason games
1996-98   Ted Marchibroda 16-31-1
1999-2006 Brian Billick...............80-56-0

PAID ATTENDANCE
Home 557,707   Away 548,953
Total 1,106,660
Single-game home record,
  70,946 (11/26/06)
Single-season home record, 557,707
  (2006)

2007 DRAFT CHOICES

Round	Name	Pos.	College
1	Ben Grubbs	G	Auburn
3	Yamon Figurs	WR	Kansas State
	Marshal Yanda	T	Iowa
4	Antwan Barnes	LB	Florida International
	Le'Ron McClain	RB	Alabama
5	Troy Smith	QB	Ohio State
6	Prescott Burgess	LB	Michigan

2006 TEAM RECORD

PRESEASON (2-2)

Date	Result	Opponent
8/11	L 16-17	N.Y. Giants
8/17	W 20-10	Philadelphia
8/25	L 7-30	at Minnesota
8/31	W 17-10	at Washington

REGULAR SEASON (13-3)

Date	Result	Opponent	Att.
9/10	W 27-0	at Tampa Bay	65,087
9/17	W 28-6	Oakland	70,744
9/24	W 15-14	at Cleveland	72,474
10/1	W 16-13	San Diego	70,743
10/9	L 3-13	at Denver	76,355
10/15	L 21-23	Carolina	70,762
10/29	W 35-22	at New Orleans	69,152
11/5	W 26-20	Cincinnati	70,792
11/12	W 27-26	at Tennessee	69,143
11/19	W 24-10	Atlanta	70,790
11/26	W 27-0	Pittsburgh	70,946
11/30	L 7-13	at Cincinnati	65,973
12/10	W 20-10	at Kansas City	77,232
12/17	W 27-17	Cleveland	70,857
12/24	W 31-7	at Pittsburgh	63,224
12/31	W 19-7	Buffalo	70,913

POSTSEASON (0-1)

1/13	L 6-15	Indianapolis	71,162

SCORE BY PERIODS

Ravens	84	91	73	105	0	—	353
Opponents	32	84	30	55	0	—	201

2006 TEAM STATISTICS

	Ravens	Opp.
Total First Downs	282	236
Rushing	86	59
Passing	179	151
Penalty	17	26
3rd Down: Made/Att	96/233	60/208
3rd Down Pct.	41.2	28.8
4th Down: Made/Att	8/11	9/23
4th Down Pct.	72.7	39.1
Possession Avg.	32:49	27:12
Total Net Yards	5072	4225
Avg. Per Game	317.0	264.1
Total Plays	1017	936
Avg. Per Play	5.0	4.5
Net Yards Rushing	1637	1214
Avg. Per Game	102.3	75.9
Total Rushes	476	367
Net Yards Passing	3435	3011
Avg. Per Game	214.7	188.2
Sacked/Yards Lost	17/100	60/418
Gross Yards	3535	3429
Att./Completions	524/328	509/279
Completion Pct.	62.6	54.8
Had Intercepted	14	28
Punts/Average	86/43.0	86/44.9
Net Punting Avg.	86/37.6	86/38.3
Penalties/Yards	109/878	79/580
Fumbles/Ball Lost	21/9	24/12
Touchdowns	38	21
Rushing	11	5
Passing	21	16
Returns	6	0

2006 INDIVIDUAL STATISTICS

PASSING	Att.	Comp.	Yds.	Pct.	TD	Int.	Tkld.	Rate
McNair	468	295	3,050	63.0	16	12	14/84	82.5
Boller	55	33	485	60.0	5	2	3/16	104.0
Clayton	1	0	—	0.0	0	0	0/0	39.6
Ravens	524	328	3,535	62.6	21	14	17/100	84.6
Opponents	509	279	3,429	54.8	16	28	60/418	63.4

	TD	TD	TD					
SCORING	R	P	Rt	PAT	FG	Saf	PTS
Stover	0	0	0	37/37	28/30	0	121
J. Lewis	9	0	0	0/0	0/0	0	54
Heap	0	6	0	0/0	0/0	0	36
Clayton	0	5	0	0/0	0/0	0	30
Wilcox	0	3	0	0/0	0/0	0	18
Mason	0	2	0	0/0	0/0	0	12
McAlister	0	0	2	0/0	0/0	0	12
Mughelli	0	2	0	0/0	0/0	0	12
Williams	0	2	0	0/0	0/0	0	12
Reed	0	0	1	0/0	0/0	1	8
Thomas	0	0	1	0/0	0/0	1	8
Anderson	1	0	0	0/0	0/0	0	6
Landry	0	0	1	0/0	0/0	0	6
McNair	1	0	0	0/0	0/0	0	6
Moore	0	1	0	0/0	0/0	0	6
Prude	0	0	1	0/0	0/0	0	6
Ravens	11	21	6	37/37	28/30	2	353
Opponents	5	16	0	20/20	17/23	1	201

2-Pt. Conversions:
Ravens 0-1, Opponents 1-1

RUSHING	Att.	Yds.	Avg.	LG	TD
J. Lewis	314	1132	3.6	52	9
Anderson	39	183	4.7	34t	1
Mu. Smith	36	153	4.3	30	0
McNair	45	119	2.6	19	1
Mughelli	12	50	4.2	12	0
Boller	22	34	1.5	10	0
Mason	1	-4	-4.0	-4	0
Clayton	7	-30	-4.3	3	0
Ravens	476	1637	3.4	52	11
Opponents	367	1214	3.3	47	5

RECEIVING	No.	Yds.	Avg.	LG	TD
Heap	73	765	10.5	30	6
Mason	68	750	11.0	38	2
Clayton	67	939	14.0	87t	5
Williams	22	396	18.0	77t	2
Mu. Smith	22	135	6.1	30	0
Mughelli	21	182	8.7	30t	2
Wilcox	20	166	8.3	35	3
J. Lewis	18	115	6.4	15	0
Anderson	9	54	6.0	13	0
Green	4	17	4.3	12	0
Sypniewski	2	15	7.5	9	0
Moore	2	1	0.5	4t	1
Ravens	328	3535	10.8	87t	21
Opponents	279	3429	12.3	72t	16

INTERCEPTIONS	No.	Yds.	Avg.	LG	TD
McAlister	6	121	20.2	60t	2
Landry	5	101	20.2	37	1
Reed	5	70	14.0	37	1
Rolle	3	60	20.0	44	0
Prude	2	66	33.0	54	1
Scott	2	31	15.5	24	0
R. Lewis	2	27	13.5	27	0
Ngata	1	60	60.0	60	0
Thomas	1	7	7.0	7	0
Ivy	1	0	0.0	0	0
Sapp	0	1	—	1	0
Ravens	28	544	19.4	60t	5
Opponents	14	142	10.1	45	0

PUNTING	No.	Yds.	Avg.	In 20	LG
Koch	86	3,695	43.0	30	61
Ravens	86	3,695	43.0	30	61
Opponents	86	3,864	44.9	26	71

PUNT RETURNS	No.	FC	Yds.	Avg.	LG	TD
Sams	29	4	307	10.6	65	0
Ross	13	3	37	2.8	9	0
Ivy	2	0	7	3.5	7	0
Oglesby	1	0	0	0.0	0	0
Ravens	45	7	351	7.8	65	0
Opponents	44	16	404	9.2	38	0

KICKOFF RETURNS	No.	Yds	Avg	LG	TD
Sams	30	772	25.7	72	0
Ross	9	194	21.6	28	0
J. Johnson	3	28	9.3	14	0
Ivy	1	14	14.0	14	0
Mu. Smith	1	27	27.0	27	0
Sypniewski	1	11	11.0	11	0
Ravens	45	1046	23.2	72	0
Opponents	75	1636	21.8	46	0

FIELD GOALS	1-19	20-29	30-39	40-49	50+
Stover	0/0	12/13	9/9	6/7	1/1
Ravens	0/0	12/13	9/9	6/7	1/1
Opponents	0/0	6/6	4/5	3/8	4/4

SACKS	No.
Pryce	13.0
Thomas	11.0
Scott	9.5
Suggs	9.5
R. Lewis	5.0
Gregg	3.5
Landry	3.0
Ivy	2.0
J. Johnson	1.5
Ngata	1.0
Rolle	1.0
Ravens	60.0
Opponents	17.0

RECORD HOLDERS
INDIVIDUAL RECORDS—CAREER

Category	Name	Performance
Rushing (Yds.)	Jamal Lewis, 2000-06	7,801
Passing (Yds.)	Vinny Testaverde, 1996-97	7,148
Passing (TDs)	Vinny Testaverde, 1996-97	51
Receiving (No.)	Todd Heap, 2001-06	316
Receiving (Yds.)	Todd Heap, 2001-06	3,658
Interceptions	Ed Reed, 2002-06	27
Punting (Avg.)	Greg Montgomery, 1996-97	43.2
Punt Return (Avg.)	Jermaine Lewis, 1996-2001	11.8
Kickoff Return (Avg.)	Corey Harris, 1998-2001	24.0
Field Goals	Matt Stover, 1996-2006	300
Touchdowns (Tot.)	Jamal Lewis, 2000-06	47
Points	Matt Stover, 1996-2006	1,235

INDIVIDUAL RECORDS—SINGLE SEASON

Category	Name	Performance
Rushing (Yds.)	Jamal Lewis, 2003	2,066
Passing (Yds.)	Vinny Testaverde, 1996	4,177
Passing (TDs)	Vinny Testaverde, 1996	33
Receiving (No.)	Derrick Mason, 2005	86
Receiving (Yds.)	Michael Jackson, 1996	1,201
Interceptions	Ed Reed, 2004	9
Punting (Avg.)	Kyle Richardson, 1998	43.9
Punt Return (Avg.)	Jermaine Lewis, 2000	16.1
Kickoff Return (Avg.)	Corey Harris, 1998	27.6
Field Goals	Matt Stover, 2000	35
Touchdowns (Tot.)	Michael Jackson, 1996	14
	Jamal Lewis, 2003	14
Points	Matt Stover, 2000	135

INDIVIDUAL RECORDS—SINGLE GAME

Category	Name	Performance
Rushing (Yds.)	Jamal Lewis, 9-14-03	*295
Passing (Yds.)	Vinny Testaverde, 10-27-96	429
Passing (TDs)	Tony Banks, 9-10-00	5
Receiving (No.)	Priest Holmes, 10-11-98	13
Receiving (Yds.)	Qadry Ismail, 12-12-99	268
Interceptions	Many times	2
	Last time by Ed Reed, 12-10-06	
Field Goals	Matt Stover, 9-21-97, 12-26-99, 10-28-00	5
Touchdowns (Tot.)	Marcus Robinson, 11-23-03	4
Points	Marcus Robinson, 11-23-03	24

*NFL Record

BALTIMORE RAVENS

2007 VETERAN ROSTER

No.	Name	Pos.	Ht.	Wt.	Birthdate	NFL Exp.	College	Hometown	How Acq.	'06 Games/ Starts
38	Anderson, Mike	RB	6-0	230	9/21/73	8	Utah	Fairfield, S.C.	FA-'06	16/0
94	Bannan, Justin	DT	6-3	310	4/18/79	6	Colorado	Orangerale, Calif.	UFA(Buff)-'06	12/1
7	Boller, Kyle	QB	6-3	220	6/17/81	5	California	Newhall, Calif.	D1b-'03	5/0
60	Brown, Jason	G/C	6-3	320	5/5/83	3	North Carolina	Henderson, N.C.	D4-'05	16/12
65	Chester, Chris	G/C	6-3	305	1/12/83	2	Oklahoma	Tustin, Calif.	D2-'06	11/4
89	Clayton, Mark	WR	5-10	195	7/2/82	3	Oklahoma	Arlington, Texas	D1-'05	16/12
53	Cody, Dan	LB	6-5	255	12/1/81	3	Oklahoma	Ada, Okla.	D2a-'05	2/0
30	Daniels, P.J.	RB	5-10	214	12/21/82	2	Georgia Tech	Houston, Texas	D4b-'06	0*
81	Darling, Devard	WR	6-1	215	4/16/82	4	Washington State	Houston, Texas	D3-'04	1/0
93	Edwards, Dwan	DT	6-3	315	5/16/81	4	Oregon State	Columbus, Mont.	D2-'04	8/0
98	Ellison, Atiyyah	DT	6-3	318	9/29/81	3	Missouri	St. Louis, Mo.	FA-'06	0*
62	Flynn, Mike	C	6-3	305	6/15/74	10	Maine	Springfield, Mass.	FA-'97	16/16
33	Green, Justin	FB	5-11	251	4/30/82	3	Montana	San Diego, Calif.	D5-'05	12/3
97	Gregg, Kelly	DT	6-0	310	11/1/76	8	Oklahoma	Edmond, Okla.	FA-'00	16/16
58	Haley, Dennis	ILB	6-1	247	2/18/82	2	Virginia	Salem, Va.	FA-'05	9/0
86	Heap, Todd	TE	6-5	252	3/16/80	7	Arizona State	Mesa, Ariz.	D1-'01	16/16
35	Ivy, Corey	CB	5-9	188	3/29/77	7	Oklahoma	Moore, Okla.	UFA(StL)-'06	13/0
95	Johnson, Jarret	DE	6-3	270	8/14/81	5	Alabama	Cedar Key, Fla.	D5a-'03	16/2
70	Katula, Matt	LS	6-6	272	8/22/82	3	Wisconsin	Brookfield, Wis.	FA-'05	16/0
71	King, Kenny	DT	6-4	284	4/23/81	4	Alabama	Daphne, Ala.	FA-'07	0*
4	Koch, Sam	P	6-1	230	8/13/82	2	Nebraska	Seward, Neb.	D6a-'06	16/0
26	Landry, Dawan	S	6-0	220	12/30/82	2	Georgia Tech	Ama, La.	D5a-'06	16/14
52	Lewis, Ray	LB	6-1	250	5/15/75	12	Miami	Lakeland, Fla.	D1b-'96	14/14
29	Martin, Derrick	CB	5-10	202	5/16/85	2	Wyoming	Denver, Colo.	D6b-'06	9/0
85	Mason, Derrick	WR	5-10	192	1/17/74	11	Michigan State	Detroit, Mich.	FA-'05	16/15
21	McAlister, Chris	CB	6-1	206	6/14/77	9	Arizona	Pasadena, Calif.	D1 '99	16/16
23 t-	McGahee, Willis	RB	6-0	232	10/21/81	5	Miami	Miami, Fla.	T(Buff)-'07	14/14*
9	McNair, Steve	QB	6-2	230	2/14/73	13	Alcorn State	Mount Olive, MS	T(Tenn)-'06	16/16
84	Moore, Clarence	WR	6-6	220	9/24/82	4	Northern Arizona	Buena Park, Calif.	D6-'04	10/1
63	Ndukwe, Ikechuku	G	6-4	338	7/17/82	2	Northwestern	Powell, Ohio	FA-'06	5/0
92	Ngata, Haloti	NT	6-4	340	1/21/84	2	Oregon	Salt Lake City, Utah	D1-'06	16/16
75	Ogden, Jonathan	T	6-9	345	7/31/74	12	UCLA	Washington, D.C.	D1a-'96	14/14
25	Oglesby, Evan	CB	5-10	185	12/18/81	2	North Alabama	Tocca, Ga.	FA-'05	16/0
24	Pittman, David	CB	5-11	182	10/14/83	2	Northwestern State	Gramercy, La.	D3-'06	0*
27	Prude, Ronnie	CB	5-11	178	6/4/82	2	Louisiana State	Shreveport, La.	FA-'06	15/0
90	Pryce, Trevor	DT	6-5	286	8/3/75	11	Clemson	Winter Park, Fla.	FA-'06	16/16
20	Reed, Ed	S	5-11	200	9/11/78	6	Miami	St. Rose, La.	D1-'02	16/16
69	Rimpf, Brian	G	6-5	319	2/11/81	4	East Carolina	Raleigh, N.C.	D7b-'04	0*
22	Rolle, Samari	CB	6-0	175	8/10/76	10	Florida State	Miami, Fla.	FA-'05	16/16
34	Ross, Cory	RB	5-6	201	9/22/82	2	Nebraska	Denver, Colo.	FA-'06	4/0
36	Sams, B.J.	DB/RS	5-10	185	10/29/80	4	McNeese State	Mandeville, La.	FA-'04	12/0
42	Sapp, Gerome	S	6-1	216	2/8/81	5	Notre Dame	Houtson, Texas	T(Ind)-'06	15/1
57	Scott, Bart	LB	6-2	240	8/18/80	6	Southern Illinois	Detroit, Mich.	FA-'02	16/16
51	Smith, Mike	LB	6-1	235	9/2/81	3	Texas Tech	Lubbock, Texas	D7-'05	8/1
32	Smith, Musa	RB	6-0	232	5/31/82	5	Georgia	West Perry, Pa.	D3-'03	12/0
56	Stills, Gary	LB	6-2	250	7/11/74	9	West Virginia	Trenton, N.J.	FA-'06	16/0
3	Stover, Matt	K	5-11	178	1/27/68	18	Louisiana Tech	Dallas, Texas	PB(NYG)-'91	16/0
55	Suggs, Terrell	LB	6-3	260	10/11/82	5	Arizona State	Chandler, Ariz.	D1a-'03	16/15
88	Sypniewski, Quinn	TE	6-6	270	4/14/82	2	Colorado	Johnston, Iowa	D5b-'06	16/3
78	Terry, Adam	T	6-8	330	9/1/82	3	Syracuse	Queensbury, N.Y.	D2b-'05	15/2
68	Vincent, Keydrick	G	6-5	325	4/13/78	7	Mississippi	Bartow, Fla.	UFA(Pitt)-'05	12/12
83	Wilcox, Daniel	TE	6-1	245	3/23/77	5	Appalachian State	Atlanta, Ga.	FA- '04	14/6
87	Williams, Demetrius	WR	6-2	197	3/28/83	2	Oregon	Concord, Calif.	D4a-'06	16/0
28	Winborne, Jamaine	DB	5-10	202	12/26/80	3	Virginia	Chesapeake, Va.	FA-'05	1/0

* Daniels inactive 16 games; Ellison inactive 3 games; King inactive 1 game with Arizona in '06; McGahee played 14 games with Buffalo in '06; Pittman inactive for 16 games; Rimpf missed '06 season because of injury.

t- Ravens traded for McGahee (Buff).

Players lost through free agency (4): DT Aubrayo Franklin (SF; 14 games in '06), FB Ovie Mughelli (Atl; 16), T Tony Pashos (Jax; 16), LB Adalius Thomas (NE; 16).

Also played with Ravens in '06—WR Alex Bannister (2), LB Tim Johnson (4), RB Jamal Lewis (16), G Edwin Mulitalo (4).

2007 FIRST-YEAR ROSTER

Name	Pos.	Ht.	Wt.	Birthdate	College	Hometown	How Acq.
Ballantyne, Kendrick	TE	6-4	243	7/7/83	Northeastern	Gorham, Maine	FA
Barnes, Antwan	LB	6-1	240	10/19/84	Florida International	Miami, Fla.	D4a
Bryant, Romby (1)	WR	6-1	181	12/21/79	Tulsa	Oklahoma City, Okla.	FA-'05
Burgess, Prescott	LB	6-3	240	3/6/84	Michigan	Warren, Ohio	D6
Carney, Brendan	P	6-4	203	12/23/82	Syracuse	Valley Forge, Pa.	FA
Cottrell, Jim (1)	LB	6-2	257	1/13/83	New Mexico State	Castle Rock, Colo.	FA-'06
Figurs, Yamon	WR-RS	5-11	175	1/10/83	Kansas State	Fort Pierce, Fla.	D3a
Freeman, Marcus	TE	6-2	246	10/24/83	Notre Dame	St. Paul, Minn.	FA
Gaston, Willie	CB	5-10	187	12/15/82	Houston	Houston, Texas	FA
Grubbs, Ben	G	6-3	315	3/10/84	Auburn	Eclectic, Ala.	D1
Johnson, Donnie	S	6-0	209	6/13/83	Penn State	Cincinnati, Ohio	FA
Jones, Edgar	DE	6-3	263	12/1/84	Southeast Missouri	Rayville, La.	FA
Kracalik, Mike (1)	T	6-8	337	9/9/82	San Diego State	San Diego, Calif.	FA-'05
Leeson, Nick	LS	6-1	255	10/29/82	Virginia Tech	Abington, Va.	FA
Leitko, Travis	DE	6-6	273	8/9/83	Notre Dame	The Woodlands, Texas	FA
Linson, Damien	WR	5-10	186	1/23/85	Central Michigan	Plymouth, N.C.	FA
Martin, Joe	LB	6-1	229	10/25/83	San Diego State	Palmdale, Calif.	FA
Maze, Terrell	CB	5-10	171	3/13/84	San Diego State	Santa Monica, Calif.	FA
McClain, Le'Ron	FB	6-0	260	12/27/84	Alabama	Northport, Ala.	D4b
Olson, Drew (1)	QB	6-2	222	6/6/83	UCLA	Piedmont, Calif.	FA-'06
Pino, Chris (1)	G	6-5	315	8/18/82	San Diego State	Oceanside, Calif.	FA-'06
Powell, Andrew	DT	6-0	317	11/18/83	Mississippi State	Clewiston, Fla.	FA
Pruitt, Jr., Greg	RB	5-9	210	12/14/83	North Carolina Central	Cleveland, Ohio	FA
Smith, Troy	QB	6-0	225	7/20/84	Ohio State	Cleveland, Ohio	D5
Wilhoit, James	K	5-10	200	6/30/83	Tennessee	Hendersonville, Tenn.	FA
Willis, Matt	WR	5-11	185	4/13/84	UCLA	La Palma, Calif.	FA
Wilson, Lawrence	DT	6-0	296	5/12/84	Hawaii	Honolulu, Hawaii	FA
Yanda, Marshal	G-T	6-3	310	9/15/84	Iowa	Anamosa, Iowa	D3b

The term NFL Rookie is defined as a player who is in his first season of professional football and has not been on the roster of another professional football team for any regular-season or postseason games. A Rookie is designated by an "R" on NFL rosters. Players who have been active in another professional football league or players who have NFL experience, including either preseason training camp or being on an Active List or Inactive List, or on Reserve/Injured or Reserve/Physically Unable to Perform for fewer than six regular-season games, are termed NFL First-Year Players. An NFL First-Year Player is designated by a "1" on NFL rosters. Thereafter, a player is credited with an additional year of experience for each season in which he accumulates six games on the Active List or Inactive List, or on Reserve/Injured or Reserve/Physically Unable to Perform.

Log on to www.baltimoreravens.com for an up-to-date roster.

COACHING STAFF

Head Coach,
Brian Billick

Pro Career: Entering his ninth season with the Baltimore Ravens, Brian Billick is tied for third in longevity with one team in the NFL. Billick, Philadelphia's Andy Reid and Seattle's Mike Holmgren trail only Tennessee's Jeff Fisher (13) and Denver's Mike Shanahan (12). For the second time in their history, the Ravens won the AFC North in 2006 with a franchise-best 13-3 record. Baltimore's elite defense was No. 1 in the NFL and boasted six Pro Bowl players (team had seven total). Billick led the Ravens to the Super Bowl XXXV title in 2000. Baltimore defeated the New York Giants, 34-7, on January 28, 2001. During that season, Billick's Ravens allowed the fewest points in NFL history (165) in a 16-game season and also became the first team since 1978 to allow fewer than 1,000 rushing yards (970) in a regular season. His teams made the play-offs in 2000 (Super Bowl XXXV champions), 2001 (lost in Divisional playoff to the AFC champion Steelers) and 2003 (lost to Titans in Wild Card playoff). Prior to becoming the Ravens' head coach, Billick spent five years as Minnesota's offensive coordinator, where in 1998, the Vikings' offense scored an NFL single-season record 556 points. Billick was named the second head coach in Ravens history on January 19, 1999. Career record: 80-56.

Background: Billick was an honorable mention All-America tight end in 1976 at Brigham Young. Played linebacker at Air Force as a freshman before transferring to BYU. Drafted by the 49ers in the eleventh round of the 1977 draft, was released, and had a brief stint with the Dallas Cowboys, but did not play. Coached collegiately at Redlands (1977), Brigham Young (1978), San Diego State (1981-85), Utah State (1986-88), and Stanford (1989-1991). From 1979-1980 Billick was the San Francisco 49ers' assistant director of public relations.

Personal: Born February 28, 1954 in Fairborn, Ohio. He and his wife, Kim, have two daughters—Aubree and Keegan. Billick has co-authored two books: *Competitive Leadership: Twelve Principles for Success* (with Dr. James A. Peterson) and *Finding the Winning Edge* with Pro Football Hall of Fame coach Bill Walsh.

ASSISTANT COACHES

Clarence Brooks, defensive line; born May 20, 1951, New York, N.Y. Guard Massachusetts 1970-73. No pro playing experience. College coach: Massachusetts 1976-1980, Syracuse 1981-89, Arizona 1990-92. Pro coach: Chicago Bears 1993-98, Cleveland Browns 1999, Miami Dolphins 2000-04, joined Ravens in 2005.
Mark Carrier, secondary; born April 28, 1968, Lake Charles, La. Cornerback Southern California 1987-89. Pro cornerback Chicago Bears, 1990-96, Detroit Lions 1997-99, Washington Redskins 2000. College coach: Arizona State 2004-05. Pro coach: Joined Ravens in 2006.
Vic Fangio, asst. to the head coach/defense; born August 22, 1958, Dunmore, Pa. Attended East Stroudsburg State. No pro playing experience. College coach: North Carolina 1983. Pro coach: Philadelphia/Baltimore Stars (USFL) 1984-85, New Orleans Saints 1986-1994, Carolina Panthers 1995-98, Indianapolis Colts 1999-2001, Houston Texans 2002-2005, joined Ravens in 2006.
John Fassel, special teams assistant; born January 10, 1974, Anaheim, Calif. Wide receiver/quarterback Pacific 1994-95, Weber State 1996-98. No pro playing experience. College coach: Bucknell 1999, 2001, Idaho State 2000, New Mexico Highlands 2002-03. Pro coach: Amsterdam Admirals (NFLE) 2000, joined Ravens in 2005.
Jedd Fisch, asst. quarterbacks; born May 5, 1976, Livingston, N.J. Attended Florida. No college or pro playing experience. College coach: Florida 1999-2000. Pro coach: Houston Texans 2001-2003, joined Ravens in 2004.
Jeff FitzGerald, linebackers; born April 18, 1960, Burbank, Calif. Linebacker Oregon State 1980. No pro playing experience. College coach: Cincinnati 1985-86, Alabama 1987-89, San Diego State 1994-97. Pro coach: Tampa Bay Buccaneers 1990-93, Washington Redskins 1998-99, Arizona Cardinals 2000-2003, joined Ravens in 2004.
Chris Foerster, offensive line/asst. head coach; born October 12, 1961, Milwaukee, Wis. Center Colorado State 1979-1982. No pro playing experience. College coach: Colorado State 1983-87, Stanford 1988-1991, Minnesota 1992. Pro coach: Minnesota Vikings 1993-95, Tampa Bay Buccaneers 1996-2001, Indianapolis Colts 2002-03, Miami Dolphins 2004, joined Ravens in 2005.
Jeff Friday, strength and conditioning; born October 11, 1966, Milwaukee, Wis. Attended Wisconsin-Milwaukee. No college or pro playing experience. College coach: Illinois State 1991-92, Northwestern 1992-95. Pro coach: Minnesota Vikings 1996-98, joined Ravens in 1999.
Frank Gansz, Jr., special teams coordinator; born August 8, 1962, Greenville, S.C. Defensive back The Citadel 1981-84. No pro playing experience. College coach: Kansas 1987, Pittsburgh 1988-89, Army 1990-91, Houston 1993-97. Pro coach: New York/New Jersey Knights (WLAF) 1992, Oakland Raiders 1998-99, Kansas City Chiefs 2001-2005, joined Ravens in 2006.
Wade Harman, tight ends/asst. offensive line; born October 1, 1963, Corydon, Iowa. Linebacker Drake 1985, Utah State 1986. No pro playing experience. College coach: Utah State 1987-1991, Pacific 1992-95, Morningside 1996. Pro coach: Minnesota Vikings 1997-98, joined Ravens in 1999.
Mike Johnson, wide receivers; born May 2, 1967, Los Angeles. Quarterback Arizona State 1985-86, Akron 1988-89. Pro quarterback Arizona Cardinals 1990, San Antonio Riders (World League) 1991-92, British Columbia Lions (CFL) 1992-93, Shreveport Pirates (CFL) 1994-95. College coach: Oregon State 1997-99. Pro coach: San Diego Chargers 2000-01, Atlanta Falcons 2002-2005, joined Ravens in 2006.
Tony Nathan, running backs; born December 14, 1956, Birmingham, Ala. Running back Alabama 1975-78. Pro running back Miami Dolphins 1979-1987. College coach: Florida International 2003-05. Pro coach: Miami Dolphins 1988-1995, Tampa Bay Buccaneers 1996-2001, joined Ravens in 2006.
Rick Neuheisel, offensive coordinator/quarterbacks; born February 7, 1961, Madison, Wis. Quarterback UCLA 1979-1983. Pro quarterback San Antonio Gunslingers (USFL) 1984-85, San Diego Chargers 1987, Tampa Bay Buccaneers 1987. College coach: UCLA 1988-1994, Colorado 1995-98 (head coach), Washington 1999-2002 (head coach). Pro coach: Joined Ravens in 2005.
Mike Pettine, outside linebackers; born September 25, 1966, Doylestown, Pa. Safety Virginia 1984-87. No pro playing experience. College coach: Pittsburgh 1993-94. Pro coach: Joined Ravens in 2002.
Paul Ricci, asst. strength and conditioning; born November 15, 1969, Elmer, N.J. Offensive lineman Penn State 1988-89. Pro coach: Seattle Seahawks 1993, Philadelphia Eagles 1995-96, Arizona Cardinals 1996-97, joined Ravens in 2002.
Greg Roman, asst. offensive line; born August 19, 1972, Atlantic City, N.J. Defensive line/linebacker John Carroll 1990-94. No pro playing experience. Pro coach: Carolina Panthers 1995-2001, Houston Texans 2002-2005, joined Ravens in 2006.
Rex Ryan, defensive coordinator; born December 13, 1962, Ardmore, Okla. Defensive end Southwest Oklahoma State 1983-86. No pro playing experience. College coach: Eastern Kentucky 1987-88, New Mexico Highlands 1989, Morehead State 1990-93, Cincinnati 1996-97, Oklahoma 1998. Pro coach: Arizona Cardinals 1994-95, joined Ravens in 1999.
Dennis Thurman, secondary; born April 13, 1956, Santa Monica, Calif. Safety Southern California 1974-77. Pro defensive back Dallas Cowboys 1978-1985, St. Louis Cardinals 1986. College coach: Southern California 1993-2000. Pro coach: Phoenix Cardinals 1988-89, joined Ravens in 2002.

**American Football Conference
East Division
Team Colors:** Dark Navy, Red, Royal,
and Nickel
**One Bills Drive
Orchard Park, New York 14127-2296
Telephone:** (716) 648-1800

2007 SCHEDULE
PRESEASON

Aug. 10	at New Orleans	7:00
Aug. 17	**Atlanta**	7:00
Aug. 24	**Tennessee**	7:00
Aug. 30	at Detroit	7:00

REGULAR SEASON

Sep. 9	**Denver**	1:00
Sep. 16	at Pittsburgh	1:00
Sep. 23	at New England	1:00
Sep. 30	**N.Y. Jets**	1:00
Oct. 8	**Dallas** (Mon.)	8:30
Oct. 14	Open Date	
Oct. 21	**Baltimore**	1:00
Oct. 28	at N.Y. Jets	4:05
Nov. 4	**Cincinnati**	1:00
Nov. 11	at Miami	1:00
Nov. 18	**New England**	1:00
Nov. 25	at Jacksonville	1:00
Dec. 2	at Washington	1:00
Dec. 9	**Miami**	1:00
Dec. 16	at Cleveland	1:00
Dec. 23	**N.Y. Giants**	1:00
Dec. 30	at Philadelphia	1:00

Stadium: Ralph Wilson Stadium
(opened in 1973)
• **Capacity:** 73,967
One Bills Drive
Orchard Park, New York
14127-2296
Playing Surface: AstroPlay
Training Camp: St. John Fisher College
Rochester, New York
14618

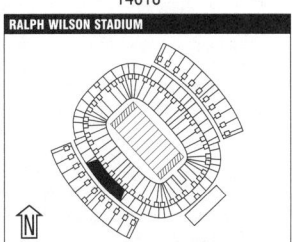

RALPH WILSON STADIUM

CLUB OFFICIALS
Owner and President:
Ralph C. Wilson, Jr.
General Manager/Football Operations:
Marv Levy
Assistant General Manager: Tom Modrak
Vice President/Assistant Director of
College and Pro Scouting:
Linda Bogdan
Treasurer: Jeffrey C. Littmann
Executive Vice President of Business
Operations: Russ Brandon
Vice President of Communications:
Scott Berchtold
Vice President of Stadium Operations:
Joe Frandina
Vice President of Business Development:
Pete Guelli
Vice President of Marketing and
Broadcasting: Marc Honan
Vice President of Public Affairs:
Bill Munson
Vice President of Football Administration:
Jim Overdorf
Vice President of Strategic Planning:
Mary Owen
Vice President of Business Operations
and Ticketing: Dave Wheat
Director of Pro Personnel: John Guy
Consultant: Christy Wilson Hofmann
Executive Director of Community
Relations: Gretchen Geitter
Executive Director of Information
Technology: Dan Evans
Director of Football Administration:
Don Purdy
Director of Merchandise: Tim Kehoe
Director of Player Programs:
Paul Lancaster
Director of Security: Chris Clark
Controller: Frank Wojnicki
Strength and Conditioning Assistant:
Kenne Pitts
Equipment Manager: Dave Hojnowski
Assistant Equipment Managers:
Randy Ribbeck, Jeff Mazurek
Head Athletic Trainer: Bud Carpenter
Athletic Trainers: Chris Fischetti,
Shone Gipson, Greg McMillen
Video Director: Henry Kunttu
Assistant Video Director: Greg Estes
Video Assistant: Kevin Shearer
Scouts: Brad Forsyth, Joe Haering,
Shawn Heilen, Doug Majeski,
Marc Ross, Tom Roth,
(emeritus) Bob Ryan,
(emeritus) David G. Smith,
(emeritus) David W. Smith,
Terry Wooden

COACHING HISTORY
(348-381-8)
Records include postseason games

1960-61	Buster Ramsey	11-16-1
1962-65	Lou Saban	38-18-3
1966-68	Joe Collier*	13-17-1
1968	Harvey Johnson	1-10-1
1969-1970	John Rauch	7-20-1
1971	Harvey Johnson	1-13-0
1972-76	Lou Saban**	32-29-1
1976-77	Jim Ringo	3-20-0
1978-1982	Chuck Knox	38-38-0
1983-85	Kay Stephenson***	10-26-0
1985-86	Hank Bullough****	4-17-0
1986-1997	Marv Levy	123-78-0
1998-2000	Wade Phillips	29-21-0
2001-03	Gregg Williams	17-31-0
2004-05	Mike Mularkey	14-18-0
2006	Dick Jauron	7-9-0

*Released after two games in 1968
**Resigned after five games in 1976
***Released after four games in 1985
****Released after nine games in 1986

PAID ATTENDANCE
Home 529,695   Away 537,354
Total 1,067,049
Single-game home record,
80,368 (10/4/92)
Single-season home record,
635,889 (1991)

2007 DRAFT CHOICES

Round	Name	Pos.	College
1	Marshawn Lynch	RB	California
2	Paul Posluszny	LB	Penn State
3	Trent Edwards	QB	Stanford
4	Dwayne Wright	RB	Fresno State
6	John Wendling	DB	Wyoming
7	Derek Schouman	TE	Boise State
	C.J. Ah You	DE	Oklahoma

BUFFALO BILLS

2006 TEAM RECORD
PRESEASON (1-3)

Date	Result	Opponent
8/12	L 13-14	at Carolina
8/18	L 31-44	Cincinnati
8/26	L 17-20	Cleveland
8/31	W 20-13	at Detroit

REGULAR SEASON (7-9)

Date	Result	Opponent	Att.
9/10	L 17-19	at New England	68,756
9/17	W 16-6	at Miami	72,797
9/24	L 20-28	N.Y. Jets	72,067
10/1	W 17-12	Minnesota	71,972
10/8	L 7-40	at Chicago	62,206
10/15	L 17-20	at Detroit	60,704
10/22	L 6-28	New England	72,180
11/5	W 24-10	Green Bay	72,205
11/12	L 16-17	at Indianapolis	57,306
11/19	W 24-21	at Houston	70,125
11/26	W 27-24	Jacksonville	63,608
12/3	L 21-24	San Diego	63,361
12/10	W 31-13	at N.Y. Jets	77,131
12/17	W 21-0	Miami	71,011
12/24	L 29-30	Tennessee	54,765
12/31	L 7-19	at Baltimore	70,913

SCORE BY PERIODS

Bills	67	84	75	74	0 —	300
Opponents	74	105	55	77	0 —	311

2006 TEAM STATISTICS

	Bills	Opp.
Total First Downs	234	298
Rushing	82	117
Passing	132	168
Penalty	20	13
3rd Down: Made/Att	63/199	79/216
3rd Down Pct.	31.7	36.6
4th Down: Made/Att	5/11	11/17
4th Down Pct.	45.5	64.7
Possession Avg.	28:04	31:56
Total Net Yards	4271	5273
Avg. Per Game	266.9	329.6
Total Plays	898	1029
Avg. Per Play	4.8	5.1
Net Yards Rushing	1552	2254
Avg. Per Game	97.0	140.9
Total Rushes	420	476
Net Yards Passing	2719	3019
Avg. Per Game	169.9	188.7
Sacked/Yards Lost	47/332	40/265
Gross Yards	3051	3284
Att./Completions	431/268	513/324
Completion Pct.	62.2	63.2
Had Intercepted	14	13
Punts/Average	92/43.6	86/41.6
Net Punting Avg.	92/39.2	86/34.8
Penalties/Yards	87/629	90/709
Fumbles/Ball Lost	28/15	28/11
Touchdowns	33	35
Rushing	9	14
Passing	19	18
Returns	5	3

2006 INDIVIDUAL STATISTICS

PASSING

	Att.	Comp.	Yds.	Pct.	TD	Int.	Tkld.	Rate
Losman	429	268	3,051	62.5	19	14	47/332	84.9
Evans	1	0	—	0.0	0	0	0/0	39.6
Moorman	1	0	—	0.0	0	0	0/0	39.6
Bills	431	268	3,051	62.2	19	14	47/332	84.6
Opponents	513	324	3,284	63.2	18	13	40/265	82.5

SCORING

	TD R	TD P	TD Rt	PAT	FG	Saf	PTS
Lindell	0	0	0	33/33	23/25	0	102
Evans	0	8	0	0/0	0/0	0	48
McGahee	6	0	0	0/0	0/0	0	36
Parrish	0	2	1	0/0	0/0	0	18
Price	0	3	0	0/0	0/0	0	18
Royal	0	3	0	0/0	0/0	0	18
Fletcher-Baker	0	0	2	0/0	0/0	0	12
Reed	0	2	0	0/0	0/0	0	12
A. Thomas	2	0	0	0/0	0/0	0	12
Clements	0	0	1	0/0	0/0	0	6
Losman	1	0	0	0/0	0/0	0	6
McGee	0	0	1	0/0	0/0	0	6
Neufeld	0	1	0	0/0	0/0	0	6
Bills	39	19	5	33/33	23/25	0	300
Opponents	14	18	3	33/33	22/26	1	311

2-Pt. Conversions: Bills 0-0, Opponents 0-2

RUSHING

	Att.	Yds.	Avg.	LG	TD
McGahee	259	990	3.8	57t	6
A. Thomas	107	378	3.5	19	2
Losman	38	140	3.7	15	1
Parrish	2	18	9.0	11	0
Price	5	18	3.6	9	0
Reed	4	13	3.3	15	0
Moorman	2	2	1.0	2	0
S. Williams	2	2	1.0	2	0
Royal	1	-9	-9.0	-9	0
Bills	420	1552	3.7	57t	9
Opponents	476	2254	4.7	52	14

RECEIVING

	No.	Yds.	Avg.	LG	TD
Evans	82	1292	15.8	83t	8
Price	49	402	8.2	25	3
Reed	34	410	12.1	52	2
Parrish	23	320	13.9	51t	2
Royal	23	233	10.1	33t	3
A. Thomas	22	139	6.3	18	0
McGahee	18	156	8.7	56	0
Shelton	7	35	5.0	14	0
Cieslak	6	46	7.7	13	0
Davis	2	13	6.5	8	0
Neufeld	1	4	4.0	4t	1
Everett	1	1	1.0	1	0
Bills	268	3051	11.4	83t	19
Opponents	324	3284	10.1	62	18

INTERCEPTIONS

	No.	Yds.	Avg.	LG	TD
Fletcher-Baker	4	30	7.5	17t	1
Clements	3	80	26.7	58t	1
Simpson	2	76	38.0	76	0
Crowell	2	0	0.0	0	0
Whitner	1	10	10.0	10	0
Ellison	1	7	7.0	7	0
Bills	13	203	15.6	76	2
Opponents	14	198	14.1	44	2

PUNTING

	No.	Yds.	Avg.	In 20	LG
Moorman	92	4,012	43.6	33	66
Bills	92	4,012	43.6	33	66
Opponents	86	3,578	41.6	31	64

PUNT RETURNS

	No.	FC	Yds.	Avg.	LG	TD
Parrish	32	9	364	11.4	82t	1
Leonhard	7	1	58	8.3	32	0
Bills	39	10	422	10.8	82t	1
Opponents	36	20	265	7.4	25	0

KICKOFF RETURNS

	No.	Yds.	Avg.	LG	TD
McGee	52	1,355	26.1	88	0
Davis	6	99	16.5	27	0
Preston	2	10	5.0	9	0
Haggan	2	4	2.0	5	0
S. Williams	1	17	17.0	17	0
Leonhard	0	18	—	18	0
Bills	63	1,503	23.9	88	0
Opponents	60	1,279	21.3	74	0

FIELD GOALS

	1-19	20-29	30-39	40-49	50+
Lindell	0/0	8/8	5/5	8/10	2/2
Bills	0/0	8/8	5/5	8/10	2/2
Opponents	0/0	5/5	9/10	8/9	0/2

SACKS

	No.
Schobel	14.0
Denney	6.0
Kelsay	5.5
(group)	4.0
Tripplett	2.5
Crowell	2.0
Fletcher-Baker	2.0
Hargrove	1.0
Ellison	1.0
Simpson	1.0
Spikes	1.0
Bills	40.0
Opponents	47.0

RECORD HOLDERS
INDIVIDUAL RECORDS—CAREER

Category	Name	Performance
Rushing (Yds.)	Thurman Thomas, 1988-1999	11,938
Passing (Yds.)	Jim Kelly, 1986-1996	35,467
Passing (TDs)	Jim Kelly, 1986-1996	237
Receiving (No.)	Andre Reed, 1985-1999	941
Receiving (Yds.)	Andre Reed, 1985-1999	13,095
Interceptions	George (Butch) Byrd, 1964-1970	40
Punting (Avg.)	Brian Moorman, 2001-05	43.4
Punt Return (Avg.)	Clifford Hicks, 1990-92	12.2
Kickoff Return (Avg.)	O.J. Simpson, 1969-1977	30.0
Field Goals	Steve Christie, 1992-2000	234
Touchdowns (Tot.)	Andre Reed, 1985-1999	87
	Thurman Thomas, 1988-1999	87
Points	Steve Christie, 1992-2000	1,011

INDIVIDUAL RECORDS—SINGLE SEASON

Category	Name	Performance
Rushing (Yds.)	O.J. Simpson, 1973	2,003
Passing (Yds.)	Drew Bledsoe, 2002	4,359
Passing (TDs)	Jim Kelly, 1991	33
Receiving (No.)	Eric Moulds, 2002	100
Receiving (Yds.)	Eric Moulds, 1998	1,368
Interceptions	Billy Atkins, 1961	10
	Tom Janik, 1967	10
Punting (Avg.)	Brian Moorman, 2005	45.7
Punt Return (Avg.)	Keith Moody, 1977	13.1
Kickoff Return (Avg.)	Terrence McGee, 2005	30.24
Field Goals	Steve Christie, 1998	33
Touchdowns (Tot.)	O.J. Simpson, 1975	23
Points	Steve Christie, 1998	140

INDIVIDUAL RECORDS—SINGLE GAME

Category	Name	Performance
Rushing (Yds.)	O.J. Simpson, 11-25-76	273
Passing (Yds.)	Drew Bledsoe, 9-15-02	463
Passing (TDs)	Jim Kelly, 9-8-91	6
Receiving (No.)	Andre Reed, 11-20-94	15
Receiving (Yds.)	Lee Evans, 11-19-06	265
Interceptions	Many times	3
	Last time by Nate Clements, 10-20-02	
Field Goals	Steve Christie, 10-20-96	6
Touchdowns (Tot.)	Cookie Gilchrist, 12-8-63	5
Points	Cookie Gilchrist, 12-8-63	30

2007 VETERAN ROSTER

No.	Name	Pos.	Ht.	Wt.	Birthdate	NFL Exp.	College	Hometown	How Acq.	'06 Games/ Starts
89	Aiken, Sam	WR	6-2	215	12/14/80	5	North Carolina	Kenansville, N.C.	D4b-'03	15/0
77	Anderson, Tim	DT	6-3	328	11/22/80	4	Ohio State	Clyde, Ohio	D3-'04	15/5
60	Butler, Brad	G/T	6-7	315	9/18/83	2	Virginia	Lynchburg, Va.	D5b-'06	2/0
73	Chambers, Kirk	G/T	6-7	315	3/19/79	3	Stanford	Provo, Utah	FA-'07	0*
86	Cieslak, Brad	TE	6-3	253	7/1/82	3	Northern Illinois	Long Grove, Ill.	FA-'05	7/2
55	Crowell, Angelo	LB	6-1	246	8/16/81	5	Virginia	Winston-Salem, N.C.	D3-'03	12/12
92	Denney, Ryan	DE	6-7	264	6/15/77	6	Brigham Young	Thornton, Colo.	D2b-'02	16/0
52	DiGiorgio, John	LB	6-2	229	6/29/82	2	Saginaw Valley State	Shelby Township, Mich.	FA-'06	12/0
66	Dockery, Derrick	G/T	6-6	330	9/7/80	5	Texas	Lakeview, Texas	UFA(Wash)-'07	16/16*
56	Ellison, Keith	LB	6-0	229	2/6/84	2	Oregon State	Redondo Beach, Calif.	D6-'06	14/7
83	Evans, Lee	WR	5-10	197	3/11/81	4	Wisconsin	Bedford, Ohio	D1a-'04	16/15
85	Everett, Kevin	TE	6-4	253	2/5/82	2	Miami	Kilgore, Texas	D3-'05	16/4
67	Fowler, Melvin	C/T	6-3	310	3/31/79	6	Maryland	Wheatley Heights, N.Y.	UFA(Minn)-'06	16/16
33	Greer, Jabari	CB	5-11	175	2/11/82	4	Tennessee	Jackson, Tenn.	FA-'04	16/0
53	Haggan, Mario	LB	6-3	263	3/3/80	5	Mississippi State	Clarksdale, Miss.	D7-'03	16/0
93	Hargrove, Anthony	DE	6-3	271	7/20/83	4	Georgia Tech	Punta Gorda, Fla.	T(StL)-'06	14/2*
99	Jefferson, Jason	DT	6-1	295	12/20/81	3	Wisconsin	Chicago, Ill.	FA-'05	4/0
90	Kelsay, Chris	DE	6-4	261	10/31/79	5	Nebraska	Auburn, Neb.	D2-'03	16/16
42	Leonhard, Jim	S	5-8	185	10/27/82	3	Wisconsin	Tony, Wis.	FA-'05	15/1
9	Lindell, Rian	K	6-3	233	1/20/77	8	Washington State	Vancouver, Wash.	FA-'03	16/0
7	Losman, J.P.	QB	6-2	212	3/12/81	4	Tulane	Venice, Calif.	D1b-'04	16/16
58	Manning, Roy	LB	6-2	245	12/4/81	3	Michigan	Saginaw, Mich.	FA-'06	0*
97	McCargo, John	DT	6-2	307	8/19/83	2	North Carolina State	Drakes Branch, Va.	D1b-'06	5/0
24	McGee, Terrence	CB	5-9	198	10/14/80	5	Northwestern State	Athens, Texas	D4a-'03	15/14
62	Merz, Aaron	G/T	6-4	325	8/27/83	2	California	Wasco, Calif.	D7b-'06	7/1
8	Moorman, Brian	P	6-0	172	2/5/76	7	Pittsburg State	Sedgwick, Kan.	FA-'01	16/0
87	Murphy, Matt	TE	6-5	277	2/23/80	6	Maryland	New Haven, Mich.	FA-'06	2/0
16	Nall, Craig	QB	6-3	245	4/21/79	7	Northwestern State	Alexandria, La.	UFA(GB)-'06	0*
88	Neufeld, Ryan	TE	6-4	245	11/22/75	7	UCLA	Morgan Hill, Calif.	FA-'03	9/0
11	Parrish, Roscoe	WR	5-9	171	7/16/82	3	Miami	Miami, Fla.	D2-'05	16/1
79	Pennington, Terrance	T/G	6-7	331	9/25/83	2	New Mexico	Compton, Calif.	D7a-'06	11/9
71	Peters, Jason	T/G	6-4	340	1/22/82	4	Arkansas	Queen City, Texas	FA-'04	16/16
91	Powell, Eric	DE/DT	6-3	284	11/16/79	2	Florida State	Orlando, Fla.	FA-'05	0*
75	Preston, Duke	G/T	6-5	326	6/12/82	3	Illinois	San Diego, Calif.	D4-'05	16/8
81	Price, Peerless	WR	5-11	194	9/27/76	9	Tennessee	Dayton, Ohio	FA-'06	16/15
82	Reed, Josh	WR	5-10	210	5/1/80	6	Louisiana State	Rayne, La.	D2a-'02	13/1
84	Royal, Robert	TE	6-4	255	5/15/78	6	Louisiana State	New Orleans, La.	UFA(Wash)-'06	16/15
54	Schneck, Mike	LS	6-1	233	8/4/77	9	Wisconsin	Whitefish Bay, Wis.	FA-'05	16/0
94	Schobel, Aaron	DE	6-4	243	9/1/77	7	Texas Christian	Columbus, Texas	D2-'01	15/14
35	Scobey, Josh	RB	6-0	220	12/11/79	5	Kansas State	Oklahoma City, Okla.	UFA(Sea)-'07	12/0*
30	Simpson, Ko	S	6-1	202	11/9/83	2	South Carolina	Rock Hill, S.C.	D4-'06	16/15
57	Stamer, Josh	LB	6-2	236	10/11/77	5	South Dakota	Sutherland, Iowa	FA-'03	6/0
28	Thomas, Anthony	RB	6-2	221	11/7/77	7	Michigan	Winnfield, La.	UFA(NO)-'06	16/2
25	Thomas, Kiwaukee	DB	5-11	188	6/19/77	8	Georgia Southern	Perry, Ga.	UFA(Mia)-'06	16/3
98	Tripplett, Larry	DT	6-2	293	1/18/79	6	Washington	Los Angeles, Calif.	UFA(Ind)-'06	16/16
96	t- Walker, Darwin	DT	6-3	294	6/15/77	8	Tennessee	Walterboro, S.C.	T(Phil)-'07	16/15*
68	Walker, Langston	T/G	6-8	366	9/3/79	6	California	Oakland, Calif.	UFA(Oak)-'07	16/16*
20	Whitner, Donte	S	5-10	208	7/24/85	2	Ohio State	Cleveland, Ohio	D1-'06	15/14
65	Whittle, Jason	G/T	6-4	279	3/7/75	9	Southwest Missouri State	Camdenton, Mo.	UFA(Minn)-'07	16/2*
95	Williams, Kyle	DT	6-1	306	6/10/83	2	Louisiana State	Ruston, La.	D5a-'06	16/11
36	Williams, Shaud	RB	5-7	193	10/02/80	4	Alabama	Andrews, Texas	FA-'04	5/0
15	Wilson, George	WR	6-0	212	3/14/81	2	Arkansas	Paducah, Ky.	FA-'04	0*
27	Wire, Coy	S	6-0	220	11/7/78	6	Stanford	Camp Hill, Pa.	D3-'02	16/1
26	Youboty, Ashton	CB	5-11	189	7/7/84	2	Ohio State	Klein, Texas	D3-'06	3/1

* Chambers last active with Cleveland in '05; Dockery played 16 games with Washington in '06; Hargrove played 4 games with St. Louis and 10 games with Buffalo; Manning inactive for 4 games; Nall inactive as third quarterback for 16 games; Powell inactive for 16 games; Scobey played 12 games with Seattle; D. Walker played 16 games with Philadelphia; L. Walker played 16 games with Oakland; Whittle played 16 games with Minnesota; Wilson inactive for 1 game.

t- Bills traded for D. Walker (Phil).

Traded—QB Kelly Holcomb (Phil; 0 games in '06), RB Willis McGahee (Balt; 14), LB Takeo Spikes (Phil; 12).

Players lost through free agency (4): CB Nate Clements (SF; 16 games in '06); WR Andre Davis (Hou; 16), LB London Fletcher (Wash; 16), T/G Mike Gandy (Ariz; 16).

Also played with Bills in '06—S Matt Bowen (5 games), G/T Tutan Reyes (6), FB Daimon Shelton (14), G/T Chris Villarrial (8), S Troy Vincent (1).

2007 FIRST-YEAR ROSTER

Name	Pos.	Ht.	Wt.	Birthdate	College	Hometown	How Acq.
Ah You, C.J.	DE	6-4	275	7/7/82	Oklahoma	Highland, Utah	D7b
Bassey, Eric (1)	CB	6-1	203	1/23/83	Oklahoma	Garland, Texas	FA-'06
Brown, Aaron	WR	6-3	210	11/27/85	New Hampshire	Central Square, N.Y.	FA
Coleman, Duane	CB	5-11	195	12/23/82	Clemson	Naples, Fla.	FA
Cornelius, Jemalle	WR	5-11	185	8/10/84	Florida	Fort Meade, Fla.	FA
Davis, Corey	G/T	6-4	325	7/14/85	James Madison	Hampton, Va.	FA
Denney, Chris (1)	WR	6-3	219	1/25/83	Nebraska-Omaha	Norfolk, Neb.	FA
Eakin, Kevin (1)	QB	6-0	205	7/22/81	Fordham	Coral Springs, Fla.	FA
Edwards, Trent	QB	6-4	231	10/30/83	Stanford	Los Gatos, Calif.	D3
Gaddis, Christian	G/T	6-1	300	10/5/84	Villanova	North Miami Beach, Fla.	FA
Hand, Randy (1)	T	6-6	324	1/19/84	Florida	Fort Myers, Fla.	FA-'06
Harrison, Kevin	LB	6-0	250	12/24/81	Eastern Michigan	Belleville, Mich.	FA-'06
Hooper, Trevor	S	6-1	205	2/8/84	Stanford	Mountain View, Calif.	FA
Jackson, Fred (1)	RB	6-1	215	2/20/81	Coe College	Fort Worth, Texas	FA-'06
Jackson, Chris	P/K	6-0	172	12/13/83	Louisiana State	Metairie, La.	FA
Lewis, Reggie	CB	5-10	195	5/30/84	Florida	Jacksonville, Fla.	FA
Lynch, Marshawn	RB	5-11	215	4/22/86	California	Oakland, Calif.	D1
Mace, Corey	DE	6-3	287	12/22/85	Wyoming	Port Moody, B.C., Canada	FA
Mayle, Scott	WR	6-1	175	10/14/83	Ohio	Philippi, W. Va.	FA
Neill, Ryan (1)	DT/DE	6-3	253	12/12/82	Rutgers	Wayne Hills, N.J.	FA-'06
Peterson, Daunta (1)	WR	5-11	200	1/2/83	Dubuque (Iowa)	Tampa, Fla.	FA
Posluszny, Paul	LB	6-1	238	10/10/84	Penn State	Aliquippa, Pa.	D2
Quinn, Johnny	WR	6-0	202	11/6/83	North Texas	Harrisburg, Pa.	FA
Schouman, Derek	TE	6-2	223	3/11/85	Boise State	Eagle, Idaho	D7a
Stith, Walter (1)	T	6-9	295	1/2/83	North Carolina A & T	Atlanta, Ga.	FA-'06
Swanson, Riley	CB/S	5-11	188	4/20/84	Wake Forest	Atlanta, Ga.	FA
Thomas, Stacey	S	6-0	200	12/4/84	Texas Southern	New Orleans, La.	FA
Tubbs, Zach	G/T	6-6	335	5/14/84	Arkansas	Cullman, Ala.	FA
Washington, Thaddaeus	LB	5-11	245	11/10/83	Colorado	New Orleans, La.	FA
Wendling, John	S	6-1	222	6/4/83	Wyoming	Cody, Wyo.	D6
Wright, Dwayne	RB	5-11	228	6/2/83	Fresno State	San Diego, Calif.	D4

The term NFL Rookie is defined as a player who is in his first season of professional football and has not been on the roster of another professional football team for any regular-season or postseason games. A Rookie is designated by an "R" on NFL rosters. Players who have been active in another professional football league or players who have NFL experience, including either preseason training camp or being on an Active List or Inactive List, or on Reserve/Injured or Reserve/Physically Unable to Perform for fewer than six regular-season games, are termed NFL First-Year Players. An NFL First-Year Player is designated by a "1" on NFL rosters. Thereafter, a player is credited with an additional year of experience for each season in which he accumulates six games on the Active List or Inactive List, or on Reserve/Injured or Reserve/Physically Unable to Perform.

Log on to www.buffalobills.com for an up-to-date roster.

BUFFALO BILLS

COACHING STAFF
Head Coach,
Dick Jauron
Pro Career: Finished his first season as Buffalo's fourteenth head coach with a 7-9 record. The Bills seem to be heading in the right direction under Dick Jauron after improving by two games over the previous season's record. Jauron is in his third stint as an NFL head coach after serving as the head coach of the Chicago Bears (1999-2003) and as interim head coach of the Detroit Lions for the final five games of 2005. The highlight of his Bears' tenure career came in 2001 when Chicago finished 13-3 and claim its first division championship since 1990. Under Jauron's leadership, the 2001 Bears were 8-0 in games decided by seven points or less, and engineered five second half, come-from-behind victories. The Bears defense ranked first in the NFL in points allowed and second in rushing yards allowed. For his efforts, Jauron was selected as the *Associated Press* NFL Coach of the Year. He was just the third coach in team history to win 13 games in a season. The 2001 season marked the greatest single-season turnaround in team history improving from 5-11 in 2000 to 13-3. In his five seasons in Chicago, Jauron accumulated a 35-46 (.432) record. He became the first Bears coach to defeat the Green Bay Packers in Lambeau Field on his first two trips. Jauron began his coaching career with the Buffalo Bills (1985, defensive backs), Green Bay Packers (1986-1994, defensive backs), and Jacksonville Jaguars (1995-98, defensive coordinator). As Jacksonville's inaugural defensive coordinator, he was instrumental in the early success of the franchise which included three playoff berths in the franchise's first four seasons and a run to the 1996 AFC Championship game. He served as the Lions' defensive coordinator from 2004-05. Career record: 43-59.
Background: A three-sport (football, basketball, and baseball) standout at Swampscott (Mass.) High School. Named one of the top 10 prep athletes of the 20th Century in the state of Massachusetts by the *Boston Globe*. Played running back at Yale (1970-72) where, for 27 years, he held the school's career rushing mark with 2,947 yards. Drafted by the Detroit Lions in the fourth round of the 1973 draft. Played defensive back for Detroit (1973-77) and was named to the Pro Bowl following the 1974 season after leading the NFC in punt return average (16.8). He finished his career with the Cincinnati Bengals (1978-1980).
Personal: Born October 7, 1950, Peoria, Ill. Dick and his wife Gail have two daughters—Kacy and Amy.

ASSISTANT COACHES
John Allaire, strength and conditioning; born December 3, 1970, Woonsocket, R.I. Attended Springfield College. No college or pro playing experience. College coach: Boston College 1992, Clemson 1993-95, Tulsa 1996-2001. Pro coach: Joined Bills in 2002.
Bobby April, asst. head coach/special teams; born April 15, 1963, New Orleans. Linebacker/defensive end Nicholls State 1972-75. No pro playing experience. College coach: Southern Mississippi 1978, Tulane 1979, Arizona 1980-86, Southern California 1987-1990. Pro coach: Atlanta Falcons 1991-93, Pittsburgh Steelers 1994-95, New Orleans Saints 1996-99, St. Louis Rams 2001-02, joined Bills in 2004.
George Catavolos, defensive backs; born May 8, 1945, Chicago. Defensive back Purdue 1964-67. No pro playing experience. College coach: Purdue 1967-68, 1971-76, Middle Tennessee State 1969, Louisville 1970, Kentucky 1977-81, Tennessee 1982-83. Pro coach: Indianapolis Colts 1984-1994, 1998-2001, Carolina Panthers 1995-97, Washington Redskins 2002-03, Detroit Lions 2004-05, joined Bills in 2006.
Charlie Coiner, tight ends; born April 24, 1960, Wayensboro, Va. Attended Catawba College, Appalachian State. No college or pro playing experience. College coach: Appalachian State 1983-86, Minnesota 1987, Louisville 1995-97, Tennessee-Chattanooga 1998, Louisiana State 1999, Texas Southern 2000. Pro coach: Chicago Bears 2001-05, joined Bills in 2006.
DeMontie Cross, defensive/special teams assistant; born February 26, 1974, St. Louis, Mo. Free safety Missouri 1994-96. No pro playing experience. College coach: Missouri 1998-99, Sam Houston State 2000, Iowa State 2001-05. Pro coach: Joined Bills in 2006.
Steve Fairchild, offensive coordinator; born June 21, 1958, Decatur, Ill. Quarterback San Diego Mesa C.C. 1978-79, Colorado State 1980-81. No pro playing experience. College coach: San Diego Mesa C.C. 1982-83, Ferris State 1984-85, San Diego State 1991-92, Colorado State 1997-2000. Pro coach: Buffalo Bills 2001-02, St. Louis Rams 2003-05, rejoined Bills in 2006.
Perry Fewell, defensive coordinator; born September 7, 1962, Gastonia, N.C. Defensive back Lenoir-Rhyne 1981-84. No pro playing experience. College coach: North Carolina 1985-86, Army 1987, 1992-94, Kent State 1988-1991, Vanderbilt 1995-97. Pro coach: Jacksonville Jaguars 1998-2002, St. Louis Rams 2003-04, Chicago Bears 2005, joined Bills in 2006.
Sean Hayes, asst. strength and conditioning; born October 25, 1975, Peabody, Mass. No college or pro playing experience. College coach: Springfield College 1997-98, Tulsa 1999-2000, Harvard 2001-03, Clemson 2004-05. Pro coach: Joined Bills in 2006.
Bill Kollar, defensive line; born November 27, 1952, Warren, Ohio. Defensive end Montana State 1971-74. Pro defensive end Cincinnati Bengals 1974-76, Tampa Bay Buccaneers 1977-1981. College coach: Illinois 1985-87, Purdue 1988-89. Pro coach: Tampa Bay Buccaneers 1984, Atlanta Falcons 1990-2000, St. Louis Rams 2001-2005, joined Bills in 2006.
Sean Kugler, asst. offensive line; born August 9, 1966, Lockport, N.Y. Offensive line Texas-El Paso 1985-89. No pro playing experience. College coach: Texas-El Paso 1993-2000, Boise State 2006. Pro coach: Detroit Lions 2001-05, joined Bills in 2007.
Chuck Lester, asst. to the head coach/defensive assistant; born May 18, 1955, Chicago. Linebacker Oklahoma 1974. No pro playing experience. College coach: Iowa State 1980-81, Oklahoma 1982-84. Pro coach: Kansas City Chiefs 1984-86 (scout), joined Bills in 1987.
Jim McNally, offensive line; born December 13, 1943, Buffalo. Guard Buffalo 1961-65. No pro playing experience. College coach: Buffalo 1966-1970, Marshall 1971-74, Boston College 1975-77, Wake Forest 1978-79. Pro coach: Cincinnati Bengals 1980-1994, Carolina Panthers 1995-98, New York Giants 1999-2003, joined Bills in 2004.
Turk Schonert, quarterbacks; born January 15, 1957, Torrance, Calif. Quarterback Stanford 1975-79. Pro quarterback Cincinnati Bengals 1980-85, 1987-89, Atlanta Falcons 1986. Pro coach: Tampa Bay Buccaneers 1992-95, Buffalo Bills 1998-2000, Carolina Panthers 2001, New York Giants 2003, New Orleans Saints 2005, rejoined Bills in 2006.
Matt Sheldon, linebackers; born February 26, 1969, Berwyn, Ill. Cornerback Minnesota 1987-1991. No pro playing experience. College coach: Wisconsin 1997-99. Pro coach: St. Louis Rams 2001-05, joined Bills in 2006.
Eric Studesville, running backs; born May 29, 1967, Madison, Wis. Defensive back Wisconsin-Whitewater 1985-88. No pro playing experience. College coach: Wingate 1994, Kent State 1995-96. Pro coach: Chicago Bears 1997-2000, New York Giants 2001-03, joined Bills in 2004.
Tyke Tolbert, wide receivers; born September 15, 1967, Conroe, Texas. Wide receiver Louisiana State 1988-1990. No pro playing experience. College coach: Louisiana-Monroe 1994-97, Auburn 1998, Louisiana-Lafayette 1999-2001, Florida 2002. Pro coach: Arizona Cardinals 2003, joined Bills in 2004.
Alex Van Pelt, offensive quality control; born May 1, 1970, Pittsburgh. Quarterback Pittsburgh 1990-94. Pro quarterback Buffalo Bills 1995-2003. College coach: Buffalo 2005. Pro coach: Frankfurt Galaxy (NFLE) 2005, joined Bills in 2006.

**American Football Conference
North Division**
Team Colors: Black, Orange, and White
One Paul Brown Stadium
Cincinnati, Ohio 45202-3492
Telephone: (513) 621-3550
Ticket Office (513) 621-TDTD (8383)

2007 SCHEDULE
PRESEASON
Aug. 9 at Detroit 7:30
Aug. 18 **New Orleans**.....................7:30
Aug. 27 at Atlanta............................8:00
Aug. 31 **Indianapolis**.......................7:30

REGULAR SEASON
Sep. 10 **Baltimore** (Mon.) 7:00
Sep. 16 at Cleveland 1:00
Sep. 23 at Seattle 1:05
Oct. 1 **New England** (Mon.)..........8:30
Oct. 7 Open Date
Oct. 14 at Kansas City 12:00
Oct. 21 **N.Y. Jets** 4:05
Oct. 28 **Pittsburgh** 1:00
Nov. 4 at Buffalo 1:00
Nov. 11 at Baltimore 4:05
Nov. 18 **Arizona** 1:00
Nov. 25 **Tennessee** 1:00
Dec. 2 at Pittsburgh *8:15
Dec. 9 **St. Louis** 1:00
Dec. 15 at San Francisco (Sat.) 5:15
Dec. 23 **Cleveland** 1:00
Dec. 30 at Miami 1:00
Sunday night games in Weeks 11-17 subject to change

Stadium: Paul Brown Stadium
(opened in 2000)
•**Capacity:** 65,515
One Paul Brown Stadium
Cincinnati, Ohio 45202-3492
Playing Surface: Synthetic
Training Camp: Georgetown College
Georgetown, KY 40324

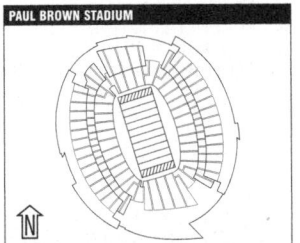

PAUL BROWN STADIUM

CLUB OFFICIALS
President: Mike Brown
Senior Vice President: Pete Brown
Executive Vice President: Katie Blackburn
Vice President: Paul Brown
Vice President: John Sawyer
Vice President: Troy Blackburn
Business Manager: Bill Connelly
Chief Financial Officer: Bill Scanlon
Director of Development—Paul Brown
 Stadium: Bob Bedinghaus
Managing Director of Paul Brown
 Stadium: Eric Brown
Directors of Technology: Michael Kayes,
 Jo Ann Ralstin
Bengals.com Editor: Geoff Hobson
Director of Sales and Public Affairs:
 Jeff Berding
Director of Corporate Sales and
 Marketing: Vince Cicero
Ticket Manager: Tim Kelly
Director of Ticket Sales: Kevin Lane
Director of Player Relations: Eric Ball
Director of Football Operations:
 Jim Lippincott
Director of Player Personnel: Duke Tobin
Public Relations Director: Jack Brennan
Athletic Trainer: Paul Sparling
Equipment Manager: Rob Recker
Video Director: Travis Brammer

COACHING HISTORY
(266-342-1)
Records include postseason games
1968-1975	Paul Brown	55-59-1
1976-78	Bill Johnson*	18-15-0
1978-79	Homer Rice	8-19-0
1980-83	Forrest Gregg	34-27-0
1984-1991	Sam Wyche	64-68-0
1992-96	Dave Shula**	19-52-0
1996-2000	Bruce Coslet***	21-39-0
2000-02	Dick LeBeau	12-33-0
2003-06	Marvin Lewis	35-30-0

* Resigned after five games in 1978
** Released after seven games in 1996
*** Resigned after three games in 2000

PAID ATTENDANCE
Home 516,154   Away 542,450
Total 1,058,604
Single-game home record,
 65,362 (12/28/03)
Single-season home record, 516,154
 (2006)

2007 DRAFT CHOICES
Round	Name	Pos.	College
1	Leon Hall	DB	Michigan
2	Kenny Irons	RB	Auburn
4	Marvin White	DB	Texas Christian
5	Jeff Rowe	QB	Nevada
6	Matt Toeaina	DT	Oregon
7	Dan Santucci	C	Notre Dame
	Chinedum Ndukwe	DB	Notre Dame

2006 TEAM RECORD
PRESEASON (4-0)

Date	Result	Opponent
8/13	W 19-3	Washington
8/18	W 44-31	at Buffalo
8/28	W 48-17	Green Bay
9/1	W 20-3	at Indianapolis

REGULAR SEASON (8-8)

Date	Result	Opponent	Att.
9/10	W 23-10	at Kansas City	77,956
9/17	W 34-17	Cleveland	66,072
9/24	W 28-20	at Pittsburgh	64,922
10/1	L 13-38	New England	66,035
10/15	L 13-14	at Tampa Bay	65,732
10/22	W 17-14	Carolina	65,964
10/29	L 27-29	Atlanta	65,978
11/5	L 20-26	at Baltimore	70,792
11/12	L 41-49	San Diego	65,917
11/19	W 31-16	at New Orleans	68,001
11/26	W 30-0	at Cleveland	72,926
11/30	W 13-7	Baltimore	65,973
12/10	W 27-10	Oakland	65,882
12/18	L 16-34	at Indianapolis	57,292
12/24	L 23-24	at Denver	75,759
12/31	L 17-23	Pittsburgh (OT)	66,049

SCORE BY PERIODS

Bengals	86	111	58	118	0	— 373
Opponents	50	76	85	114	6	— 331

2006 TEAM STATISTICS

	Bengals	Opp.
Total First Downs	313	337
Rushing	88	109
Passing	200	206
Penalty	25	22
3rd Down: Made/Att	72/201	88/211
3rd Down Pct.	35.8	41.7
4th Down: Made/Att	6/9	11/21
4th Down Pct.	66.7	52.4
Possession Avg.	28:34	31:26
Total Net Yards	5462	5681
Avg. Per Game	341.4	355.1
Total Plays	994	1038
Avg. Per Play	5.5	5.5
Net Yards Rushing	1629	1863
Avg. Per Game	101.8	116.4
Total Rushes	435	448
Net Yards Passing	3833	3818
Avg. Per Game	239.6	238.6
Sacked/Yards Lost	36/233	35/211
Gross Yards	4066	4029
Att./Completions	523/327	555/349
Completion Pct.	62.5	62.9
Had Intercepted	13	19
Punts/Average	77/44.5	72/43.5
Net Punting Avg.	77/38.6	72/37.4
Penalties/Yards	92/717	97/836
Fumbles/Ball Lost	25/11	24/12
Touchdowns	43	40
Rushing	14	15
Passing	28	24
Returns	1	1

2006 INDIVIDUAL STATISTICS

PASSING	Att.	Comp.	Yds.	Pct.	TD	Int.	Tkld.	Rate
Palmer	520	324	4,035	62.3	28	13	36/233	93.9
Wright	3	3	31	100.0	0	0	0/0	109.7
Bengals	523	327	4,066	62.5	28	13	36/233	94.1
Opponents	555	349	4,029	62.9	24	19	35/211	84.9

SCORING	TD R	TD P	TD Rt	PAT	FG	Saf	PTS
Graham	0	0	0	40/42	25/30	0	115
R. Johnson	12	0	0	0/0	0/0	0	72
Henry	0	9	0	0/0	0/0	0	54
Houshmandzadeh	0	9	0	0/0	0/0	0	54
C. Johnson	0	7	0	0/0	0/0	0	42
J. Johnson	1	0	0	0/0	0/0	0	6
Kelly	0	1	0	0/0	0/0	0	6
Kilmer	0	0	1	0/0	0/0	0	6
Stewart	0	1	0	0/0	0/0	0	6
Washington	0	1	0	0/0	0/0	0	6
Watson	1	0	0	0/0	0/0	0	6
Bengals	14	28	1	40/42	25/30	0	373
Opponents	15	24	1	37/38	18/25	0	331

2-Pt. Conversions:
Bengals 0-1, Opponents 0-1.

RUSHING	No.	Yds	Avg	LG	TD
R. Johnson	341	1309	3.8	22t	12
Watson	25	138	5.5	18	1
C. Perry	10	57	5.7	18	0
J.Johnson	15	56	3.7	15	1
Palmer	26	37	1.4	11	0
C. Johnson	6	24	4.0	8	0
McNeal	1	8	8.0	8	0
Houshmandzadeh	3	6	2.0	13	0
T. Perry	2	4	2.0	2	0
Wilson	2	2	1.0	5	0
Wright	4	-12	-3.0	-1	0
Bengals	435	1629	3.7	22t	14
Opponents	448	1863	4.2	41	15

RECEIVING	No.	Yds	Avg	LG	TD
Houshmandzadeh	90	1081	12.0	40t	9
C. Johnson	87	1369	15.7	74t	7
Henry	36	605	16.8	71	9
Watson	23	213	9.3	46	0
R. Johnson	23	124	5.4	18	0
Kelly	21	254	12.1	32	1
Stewart	14	120	8.6	26	1
Washington	9	115	12.8	22t	1
C. Perry	9	42	4.7	12	0
J. Johnson	6	37	6.2	17	0
T. Perry	5	81	16.2	30	0
Chatman	3	22	7.3	10	0
Holt	1	3	3.0	3	0
Bengals	327	4066	12.4	74t	28
Opponents	349	4029	11.5	75	24

INTERCEPTIONS	No.	Yds	Avg	LG	TD
Kaesviharn	6	24	4.0	22	0
James	4	44	11.0	28	0
M. Williams	3	33	11.0	25	0
Simmons	2	5	2.5	5	0
Kilmer	1	52	52.0	52t	1
Jackson	1	46	46.0	46	0
O'Neal	1	42	42.0	42	0
L. Johnson	1	2	2.0	2	0
Bengals	19	248	13.1	52t	1
Opponents	13	180	13.8	49t	1

PUNTING	No.	Yds.	Avg.	In 20	LG
Larson	77	3428	44.5	26	67
Bengals	77	3428	44.5	26	67
Opponents	72	3131	43.5	22	65

PUNT RETURNS	Ret	FC	Yds	Avg	LG	TD
Ratliff	27	9	176	6.5	38	0
Chatman	8	3	53	6.6	19	0
O'Neal	1	2	10	10.0	10	0
Bengals	36	14	239	6.6	38	0
Opponents	42	9	236	5.6	43	0

KICKOFF RETURNS	No.	Yds	Avg	LG	TD
C. Perry	21	412	19.6	36	0
Holt	17	419	24.6	38	0
Watson	10	198	19.8	34	0
Chatman	4	93	23.3	31	0
T. Perry	4	69	17.3	34	0
Kelly	2	8	4.0	8	0
Stewart	1	10	10.0	10	0
Bengals	59	1209	20.5	38	0
Opponents	70	1472	21.0	49	0

FIELD GOALS	1-19	20-29	30-39	40-49	50+
Graham	0/0	9/9	8/9	6/8	2/4
Bengals	0/0	9/9	8/9	6/8	2/4
Opponents	0/0	5/6	9/9	4/8	0/2

SACKS	No.
Geathers	10.5
J. Smith	7.5
Kaesviharn	4.0
Robinson	3.0
Peko	2.5
Adams	2.0
Thornton	2.0
A. Brooks	1.0
Jackson	1.0
Miller	1.0
L. Johnson	0.5
Bengals	35.0
Opponents	36.0

RECORD HOLDERS
INDIVIDUAL RECORDS—CAREER

Category	Name	Performance
Rushing (Yds.)	Corey Dillon, 1997-2003	8,061
Passing (Yds.)	Ken Anderson, 1971-1986	32,838
Passing (TDs)	Ken Anderson, 1971-1986	197
Receiving (No.)	Carl Pickens, 1992-99	530
Receiving (Yds.)	Isaac Curtis, 1973-1984	7,101
Interceptions	Ken Riley, 1969-1983	65
Punting (Avg.)	Dave Lewis, 1970-73	43.8
Punt Return (Avg.)	Mike Martin, 1983-89	9.9
Kickoff Return (Avg.)	Lemar Parrish, 1970-77	24.7
Field Goals	Jim Breech, 1980-1992	225
Touchdowns (Tot.)	Pete Johnson, 1977-1983	70
Points	Jim Breech, 1980-1992	1,151

INDIVIDUAL RECORDS—SINGLE SEASON

Category	Name	Performance
Rushing (Yds.)	Rudi Johnson, 2005	1,458
Passing (Yds.)	Carson Palmer, 2006	4,035
Passing (TDs)	Carson Palmer, 2005	32
Receiving (No.)	Carl Pickens, 1996	100
Receiving (Yds.)	Chad Johnson, 2005	1,432
Interceptions	Deltha O'Neal, 2005	10
Punting (Avg.)	Dave Lewis, 1970	46.2
Punt Return (Avg.)	Lemar Parrish, 1974	18.8
Kickoff Return (Avg.)	Tremain Mack, 1999	27.1
Field Goals	Doug Pelfrey, 1995	29
Touchdowns (Tot.)	Carl Pickens, 1995	17
Points	Shayne Graham, 2005	131

INDIVIDUAL RECORDS—SINGLE GAME

Category	Name	Performance
Rushing (Yds.)	Corey Dillon, 10-22-00	278
Passing (Yds.)	Boomer Esiason, 10-7-90	490
Passing (TDs)	Boomer Esiason, 12-21-86, 10-29-89	5
Receiving (No.)	Carl Pickens, 10-11-98	13
Receiving (Yds.)	Chad Johnson, 11-12-06	260
Interceptions	Many times	3
	Last time by Deltha O'Neal, 9-18-05	
Field Goals	Doug Pelfrey, 11-6-94	6
Touchdowns (Tot.)	Larry Kinnebrew, 10-28-84	4
	Corey Dillon, 12-4-97	4
Points	Larry Kinnebrew, 10-28-84	24
	Corey Dillon, 12-4-97	24

2007 VETERAN ROSTER

No.	Name	Pos.	Ht.	Wt.	Birthdate	NFL Exp.	College	Hometown	How Acq.	'06 Games/ Starts
67	Allen, Kenderick	DT	6-5	328	9/14/78	5	Louisiana State	Bogalusa, La.	UFA(GB)-'07	2/0*
71	Anderson, Willie	T	6-5	340	7/11/75	12	Auburn	Whistler, Ala.	D1-'96	16/16
79	Andrews, Stacy	G	6-7	342	6/2/81	4	Mississippi	Camden, Ark.	D4c-'04	16/3
21#	Bauman, Rashad	CB	5-8	184	5/7/79	6	Oregon	Phoenix, Ariz.	W(Wash)-'04	0*
81	Brazell, Bennie	WR	6-0	176	6/2/82	2	Louisiana State	Houston, Texas	D7b-'06	0*
50	Brooks, Ahmad	LB	6-3	259	3/14/84	2	Virginia	Woodbridge, Va.	SD3-'06	11/5
27	Brooks, Greg	CB	5-11	182	12/16/80	4	Southern Mississippi	New Orleans, La.	D6-'04	5/0
36	Busing, John	S	6-2	221	9/1/83	2	Miami (Ohio)	Johns Creek, Ga.	FA-'06	7/0
83	Chatman, Antonio	WR	5-8	182	2/12/79	5	Cincinnati	Los Angeles, Calif.	FA-'06	3/0
68	Fanene, Jonathan	DE	6-4	295	3/19/82	3	Utah	Pago Pago, American Samoa	D7-'05	4/0
57	Frazier, Andre	LB	6-5	234	6/29/82	3	Cincinnati	Cincinnati, Ohio	FA-'06	11/0
91	Geathers, Robert	DE	6-3	265	8/11/83	4	Georgia	Georgetown, S.C.	D4b-'04	16/0
53	Ghiaciuc, Eric	C	6-4	302	5/28/81	3	Central Michigan	Oxford, Mich.	D4-'05	15/13
17	Graham, Shayne	K	6-0	200	12/9/77	7	Virginia Tech	Dublin, Va.	W(Car)-'03	16/0
18	Green, Skyler	WR	5-9	190	9/12/84	2	Louisiana State	Harvey, La.	W(Dall)-'06	2/0*
89	Guenther, Gregg	TE	6-8	255	1/29/82	2	Southern California	Van Nuys, Calif.	FA-'06	0*
56	Hartwell, Edgerton	LB	6-1	250	5/27/78	7	Western Illinois	Las Vegas, Nev.	FA-'07	8/6*
15	Henry, Chris	WR	6-4	200	5/17/83	3	West Virginia	Belle Chasse, La.	D3-'05	13/4
16	Holt, Glenn	WR	6-1	193	7/31/84	2	Kentucky	Miami, Fla.	FA-'06	11/0
84	Houshmandzadeh, T.J.	WR	6-1	199	9/26/77	7	Oregon State	Barstow, Calif.	D7-'01	14/13
28	Jackson, Dexter	S	6-0	210	7/28/77	9	Florida State	Quincy, Fla.	UFA(TB)-'06	12/11
93	Jeanty, Rashad	LB	6-2	245	4/17/83	2	Central Florida	Miami, Fla.	FA-'06	12/9
85	Johnson, Chad	WR	6-1	192	1/9/78	7	Oregon State	Miami, Fla.	D2-'01	16/16
11	Johnson, Doug	QB	6-2	218	10/27/77	7	Florida	Gainesville, Fla.	FA-'06	0*
31	Johnson, Jeremi	FB	5-11	260	9/4/80	5	Western Kentucky	Louisville, Ky.	D4b-'03	16/11
59	Johnson, Landon	LB	6-2	228	3/13/81	4	Purdue	Lubbock, Texas	D3b-'04	16/16
32	Johnson, Rudi	HB	5-10	214	10/1/79	7	Auburn	Ettrick, Va.	D4-'01	16/15
44	Jones, Herana-Daze	S	5-11	205	4/15/82	2	Indiana	Louisville, Ky.	FA-'05	16/0
76	Jones, Levi	T	6-5	307	8/24/79	6	Arizona State	Eloy, Ariz.	D1-'02	6/5
22	Joseph, Johnathan	CB	5-11	193	4/16/84	2	South Carolina	Rock Hill, S.C.	D1-'06	16/9
82	Kelly, Reggie	TE	6-4	255	2/22/77	9	Mississippi State	Aberdeen, Miss.	UFA(Atl)-'03	16/16
70	Kieft, Adam	T	6-7	328	8/21/82	3	Central Michigan	Rockford, Mich.	D5-'05	0*
43	Kilmer, Ethan	S	6-0	204	1/31/83	2	Penn State	Wyalusing, Pa.	D7a-'06	16/0
75	Kooistra, Scott	T	6-6	320	10/14/80	5	North Carolina State	Cary, N.C.	D7a-'03	15/0
19	Larson, Kyle	P	6-1	204	9/2/80	4	Nebraska	Funk, Neb.	FA-'04	16/0
10	McNeal, Reggie	WR	6-2	205	9/20/83	2	Texas A&M	Lufkin, Texas	D6-'06	7/0
58	Miller, Caleb	LB	6-2	225	9/3/80	4	Arkansas	Sulphur Springs, Texas	D3a-'04	16/7
42#	Mitchell, Anthony	S	6-1	220	12/13/74	8	Tuskegee	Atlanta, Ga.	FA-'04	0*
96	Myers, Michael	DT	6-2	300	1/20/76	10	Alabama	Vicksburg, Miss.	UFA(Den)-'07	16/16*
52	Nicholson, A.J.	LB	6-1	240	6/25/83	2	Florida State	Winston-Salem, N.C.	D5-'06	2/0
24	O'Neal, Deltha	CB	5-11	194	1/30/77	8	California	Milpitas, Calif.	T(Den)-'04	12/7
9	Palmer, Carson	QB	6-5	230	12/27/79	5	Southern California	Mission Viejo, Calif.	D1-'03	16/16
94	Peko, Domata	DT	6-3	319	11/27/84	2	Michigan State	Pago Pago, American Samoa	D4-'06	16/1
23	Perry, Chris	HB	6-0	224	12/27/81	4	Michigan	Advance, N.C.	D1-'04	6/1
88	Perry, Tab	WR	6-3	208	1/20/82	3	UCLA	Milpitas, Calif.	D6-'05	2/0
99	Pollack, David	LB	6-2	255	6/19/82	3	Georgia	Snellville, Ga.	D1-'05	2/1
25	Ratliff, Keiwan	CB	5-11	188	4/19/81	4	Florida	Columbus, Ohio	D2a-'04	16/0
73	Reuber, Alan	T	6-6	307	1/26/81	2	Texas A&M	Plano, Texas	FA-'06	0*
98	Robinson, Bryan	DE	6-4	304	6/22/74	11	Fresno State	Toledo, Ohio	UFA(Mia)-'05	16/16
92	Rucker, Frostee	DE	6-3	267	9/14/83	2	Southern California	Tustin, Calif.	D3-'06	0*
48	St. Louis, Brad	LS-TE	6-3	243	8/19/76	8	Southwest Missouri State	Belton, Mo.	D7-'00	16/0
90	Smith, Justin	DE	6-4	275	9/30/79	7	Missouri	Holts Summit, Mo.	D1-'01	16/16
69	Stepanovich, Alex	C	6-4	312	9/25/81	4	Ohio State	Berea, Ohio	FA-'07	5/5*
97	Thornton, John	DT	6-3	297	10/2/76	9	West Virginia	Philadelphia, Pa.	UFA(Tenn)-'03	15/15
33	Watson, Kenny	HB	6-0	218	3/13/78	6	Penn State	Harrisburg, Pa.	FA-'03	16/0
20	Whitehead, Terrence	HB	5-10	215	5/31/83	2	Oregon	Los Angeles, Calif.	FA-'06	0*
77	Whitworth, Andrew	G-T	6-7	339	12/12/81	2	Louisiana State	West Monroe, La.	D2-'06	16/12
64	Wilkerson, Ben	C	6-4	305	11/22/82	2	Louisiana State	Hemphill, Texas	FA-'05	3/0
63	Williams, Bobbie	G	6-4	345	9/25/76	8	Arkansas	Jefferson, Texas	UFA(Phil)-'04	13/13
40	Williams, Madieu	S	6-1	203	10/18/81	4	Maryland	Lanham, Md.	D2b-'04	16/16
35	Wilson, Quincy	HB	5-9	220	4/26/81	2	West Virginia	Weirton, W.Va.	PS(Atl)-'04	3/0

* Allen played 2 games with Green Bay in '06; Bauman missed '06 season because of injury; Brazell missed '06 season because of injury; Green played 2 games with Dallas; Guenther last active with Tennessee in '05; Hartwell played 8 games with Atlanta; D. Johnson did not play in 3 games; Kieft missed '06 season because of injury; Mitchell missed '06 season because of injury; Myers played 16 games with Denver; Reuber last active with Arizona in '04; Rucker inactive for 3 games; Stepanovich played 5 games with Arizona; Whitehead missed '06 season because of injury.

\# Unrestricted Free Agent; subject to developments.

Players lost through free agency (8): CB Tory James (NE; 16 games in '06), S Kevin Kaesviharn (NO; 14), DT Shaun Smith (Cle; 13), G Eric Steinbach (Cle; 16), TE Tony Stewart (Oak; 16), WR Kelley Washington (NE; 5), LB Marcus Wilkins (Atl; 16), QB Anthony Wright (NYG; 4).

Also played with Bengals in '06—DT Sam Adams (16 games), C Rich Braham (2), LB Brian Simmons (11).

2007 FIRST-YEAR ROSTER

Name	Pos.	Ht.	Wt.	Birthdate	College	Hometown	How Acq.
Andrews, Bryan	DE	6-5	266	5/5/83	Wake Forest	Lima, Ohio	FA
Coats, Daniel	TE	6-3	255	4/16/84	Brigham Young	Layton, Utah	FA
Day, Tim (1)	TE	6-3	255	9/3/83	Oregon	Las Vegas, Nev.	FA-'06
Everett, Earl	LB	6-3	231	12/10/84	Florida	Webster, Fla.	FA
Ghent, Ronnie (1)	TE	6-2	253	1/5/80	Louisville	Lakeland, Fla.	FA-'04
Hall, Leon	CB	5-11	199	12/9/84	Michigan	Vista, Calif.	D1
Henderson, Eric (1)	LB	6-2	263	1/8/83	Georgia Tech	New Orleans, La.	FA-'06
Holley, Jesse	WR	6-2	213	1/8/84	North Carolina	Roselle, N.J.	FA
Irons, Kenny	HB	5-11	200	9/15/83	Auburn	Dacula, Ga.	D2
Jackson, Xzavie	DE	6-3	287	9/21/84	Missouri	Vacaville, Calif.	FA
Kays, Tony	WR	6-0	189	3/6/84	California-Davis	Elk Grove, Calif.	FA
Livings, Nate (1)	G	6-5	335	3/16/82	Louisiana State	Lake Charles, La.	FA-'06
Manderino, Chris (1)	FB	6-0	239	12/22/82	California	Newport Beach, Calif.	FA-'06
Mulcahy, Sean (1)	TE	6-5	260	2/14/82	Connecticut	Westport, Conn.	FA
Muncy, Matt	LB	6-1	238	7/6/83	Ohio	Miamisburg, Ohio	FA
Ndukwe, Chinedum	S	6-2	218	3/4/85	Notre Dame	Powell, Ohio	D7b
Nikolao, Harrison	G	6-3	310	9/5/84	Eastern Washington	Tacoma, Wash.	FA
Rowe, Jeff	QB	6-5	221	3/21/84	Nevada	Reno, Nev.	D5
Santucci, Dan	C	6-4	304	9/6/83	Notre Dame	Harwood Heights, Ill.	D7a
Seifert, Elliot	T	6-7	312	12/16/83	Temple	Reading, Pa.	FA
Siskowic, Cameron	LB	6-1	227	4/10/84	Illinois State	San Diego, Calif.	FA
Smith, Jeff	QB	6-5	235	4/27/84	Georgetown (Ky.) College	Fort Thomas, Ky.	FA
Toeaina, Matt	DT	6-2	311	10/9/84	Oregon	Pago Pago, American Samoa	D6
Uperesa, Dane	T	6-5	315	1/25/84	Hawaii	Hauula, Oahu, Hawaii	FA
Verdon, Jimmy (1)	DE	6-3	280	11/4/81	Arizona State	Pomona, Calif.	FA
White, Marvin	S	6-1	199	12/5/83	Texas Christian	Port Barre, La.	D4
White, Stan	FB	6-1	255	9/4/83	Ohio State	Baltimore, Md.	FA
Williams, Brandon (1)	CB	5-11	186	11/17/80	Michigan	Omaha, Neb.	FA-'06
Wright, T.J.	CB	5-10	176	11/29/83	Ohio	Beaumont, Texas	FA

The term NFL Rookie is defined as a player who is in his first season of professional football and has not been on the roster of another professional football team for any regular-season or postseason games. A Rookie is designated by an "R" on NFL rosters. Players who have been active in another professional football league or players who have NFL experience, including either preseason training camp or being on an Active List or Inactive List, or on Reserve/Injured or Reserve/Physically Unable to Perform for fewer than six regular-season games, are termed NFL First-Year Players. An NFL First-Year Player is designated by a "1" on NFL rosters. Thereafter, a player is credited with an additional year of experience for each season in which he accumulates six games on the Active List or Inactive List, or on Reserve/Injured or Reserve/Physically Unable to Perform.

Log on to www.bengals.com for an up-to-date roster.

CINCINNATI BENGALS

COACHING STAFF

Head Coach,
Marvin Lewis
Pro Career: After establishing himself as a record-setting NFL defensive coordinator, Lewis was named the ninth head coach in Bengals history on January 14, 2003. He is now in his fifth season. He enters 2007 with a 35-29 regular-season record, good for the second-best regular-season winning percentage (.547) in franchise history. He trails only Forrest Gregg (.561, 32-25 record). Lewis is the only Bengals head coach never to experience a losing season, and in 2005 he guided the team to the AFC North Division title. The 2005 Bengals gained the No. 3 seed in the AFC playoffs with an 11-5 record before losing to Pittsburgh, the eventual Super Bowl winner, in the Wild Card round. In 2003, the Bengals were the NFL's most improved team (six-game increase), and Lewis finished second in *Associated Press* voting for NFL Coach of the Year while also being named Rookie Coach of the Year by *Football Digest*. Prior to his arrival, Lewis was the Washington Redskins' defensive coordinator (2002), serving as assistant head coach in addition to his coordinator's role. He spent six seasons (1996-2001) as defensive coordinator with the Baltimore Ravens, a tenure that included a Super Bowl victory following the 2000 season. In the 2000 regular season, Lewis' Baltimore defense set the NFL record for fewest points allowed in a 16-game campaign (165). Lewis' 2000 defensive unit has been widely considered as one of the best NFL defenses of all time. The 970 rushing yards allowed was the fewest in NFL history for a 16-game season. The Ravens' four shutouts were the most in the NFL since 1976. Prior to joining Baltimore, he spent four seasons (1992-95) with Pittsburgh as linebackers coach. Career record: 35-30.
Background: Earned All-Big Sky Conference honors as a linebacker at Idaho State for three years (1978-1980), and saw action at quarterback and free safety. Received his bachelor's degree in physical education from Idaho State in 1981, and earned his Master's degree in athletic administration from the school in 1982. Inducted into Idaho State's Hall of Fame in 2001. Began his coaching career at Idaho State (1981-84). The team finished 12-1 during his first season and won the NCAA Division I-AA championship. Was also the linebackers coach at Long Beach State (1985-86), New Mexico (1987-89), and Pittsburgh (1990-91).
Personal: Born September 23, 1958, McDonald, Pa. Lewis and his wife, Peggy, have two children—Whitney and Marcus.

ASSISTANT COACHES

Paul Alexander, asst. head coach/offensive line; born February 12, 1960, Rochester, N.Y. Tackle Cortland State 1979-1981. No pro playing experience.

College coach: Penn State 1982-84, Michigan 1985-86, Central Michigan 1987-1991. Pro coach: New York Jets 1992-93, joined Bengals in 1994.
Jim Anderson, running backs; born March 27, 1948, Harrisburg, Pa. Linebacker/defensive end California Western 1967-69. No pro playing experience. College coach: California Western 1970-71, Scottsdale (Ariz.) C.C. 1973, Nevada-Las Vegas 1974-75, Southern Methodist 1976-1980, Stanford 1981-83. Pro coach: Joined Bengals in 1984.
Bob Bratkowski, offensive coordinator; born December 2, 1955, San Angelo, Texas. Wide receiver Washington State 1975-77. No pro playing experience. College coach: Missouri 1978-1980, Weber State 1981-85, Wyoming 1986, Washington State 1987-88, Miami 1989-1991. Pro coach: Seattle Seahawks 1992-98, Pittsburgh Steelers 1999-2000, joined Bengals in 2001.
Chuck Bresnahan, defensive coordinator; born September 8, 1960, Springfield, Mass. Linebacker Navy 1979-1982. No pro playing experience. College coach: Navy 1983, 1986, Georgia Tech 1987-1991, Maine 1992-93. Pro coach: Cleveland Browns 1994-95, Indianapolis Colts 1996-97, Oakland Raiders 1998-2003, joined Bengals in 2004.
Louie Cioffi, asst. defensive backs; born September 21, 1973, Greenlawn, N.Y. Attended SUNY-Stony Brook. No college or pro playing experience. College coach: C.W. Post 1995-96. Pro coach: New York Jets 1993-94, joined Bengals in 1997.
Kevin Coyle, defensive backs; born January 14, 1956, Staten Island, N.Y. Defensive back Massachusetts 1975-77. No pro playing experience. College coach: Cincinnati 1978-79, Arkansas 1980, U.S. Merchant Marine Academy 1981, Holy Cross 1982-1990, Syracuse 1991-93, Maryland 1994-96, Fresno State 1997-2000. Pro coach: Joined Bengals in 2001.
Paul Guenther, staff assistant; born Nov. 22, 1971, Richboro, Pa. Linebacker Ursinus College 1990-93. No pro playing experience. College coach: Western Maryland 1994-95, Ursinus College 1996, 1997-2001 (head coach 1997-2001), Jacksonville 1997. Pro coach: Washington Redskins 2002-03, joined Bengals in 2005.
Jay Hayes, defensive line; born March 3, 1960, South Fayette, Pa. Defensive end Idaho 1978-1981. Pro defensive end/linebacker Michigan Panthers (USFL) 1984, Memphis Showboats (USFL) 1985. College coach: Notre Dame 1988-1991, California 1992-94, Wisconsin 1995-98. Pro coach: Pittsburgh Steelers 1999-2001, Minnesota Vikings 2002, joined Bengals in 2003.
Jonathan Hayes, tight ends; born Aug. 11, 1962, South Fayette, Pa. Linebacker/tight end Iowa 1981-84. Pro tight end Kansas City Chiefs 1985-1993,

Pittsburgh Steelers 1994-96. College coach: Oklahoma 1999-2002. Pro coach: Joined Bengals in 2003.
Ricky Hunley, linebackers; born November 11, 1961, Petersburg, Va. Linebacker Arizona 1980-83. Pro linebacker Denver Broncos 1984-87, Los Angeles Raiders 1989-1990. College coach: Southern California 1992-93, Missouri 1994-2000, Florida 2001. Pro coach: Washington Redskins 2002, joined Bengals in 2003.
Chip Morton, strength and conditioning; born November 27, 1962, Hamden, Conn. Attended North Carolina. No college or pro playing experience. College coach: Ohio State 1985-86, Penn State 1987-1991. Pro coach: San Diego Chargers 1992-94, Carolina Panthers 1995-98, Baltimore Ravens 1999-2001, Washington Redskins 2002, joined Bengals in 2003.
Ray Oliver, asst. strength and conditioning; born June 6, 1961, Cincinnati. Defensive back Ohio State 1980-81. College coach: Pittsburgh 1985-88, Kentucky 1989-1991, South Carolina 1993-95, Memphis 2001-03. Pro coach: Tampa Bay Buccaneers 1992, New Jersey Nets (NBA) 1996-97, joined Bengals in 2004.
Mike Sheppard, wide receivers; born October 29, 1951, Tulsa, Okla. Wide receiver Cal Lutheran 1969-1972. No pro playing experience. College coach: Cal Lutheran 1974-76, Brigham Young 1977-78, U.S. International 1979, Idaho State 1980-81, Long Beach State 1982, 1984-86, Kansas 1983, New Mexico 1987-1991, California 1992. Pro coach: Cleveland Browns 1993-95, Baltimore Ravens 1996, San Diego Chargers 1997-98, Seattle Seahawks 1999-2000, Buffalo Bills 2001, New Orleans Saints 2002-05, joined Bengals in 2007.
Darrin Simmons, special teams; born April 9, 1973, Elkhart, Kan. Punter Kansas 1993-95. No pro playing experience. College coach: Kansas 1996, Minnesota 1997. Pro coach: Baltimore Ravens 1998, Carolina Panthers 1999-2002, joined Bengals in 2003.
Bob Surace, offensive assistant; born April 25, 1968, Harrisburg, Pa. Center Princeton 1987-89. No pro playing experience. College coach: Springfield College 1990-91, Maine Maritime Academy 1992-93, Rensselaer Polytechnic Institute 1995, Western Connecticut State 1996-2001 (head coach 2000-01). Pro coach: Shreveport Pirates (CFL) 1994, joined Bengals in 2002.
Ken Zampese, quarterbacks; born July 19, 1967, Santa Maria, Calif. Wide receiver San Diego 1985-88. No pro playing experience. College coach: San Diego 1989, Southern California 1990-91, Northern Arizona 1992-95, Miami (Ohio) 1996-97. Pro coach: Philadelphia Eagles 1998, Green Bay Packers 1999, St. Louis Rams 2000-02, joined Bengals in 2003.

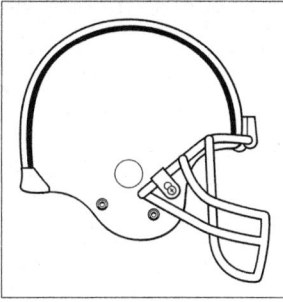

**American Football Conference
North Division
Team Colors:** Brown, Orange, and White
**76 Lou Groza Blvd.
Berea, Ohio 44017
Telephone:** (440) 891-5000

2007 SCHEDULE
PRESEASON
Aug. 11 **Kansas City** 7:30
Aug. 18 **Detroit** 7:00
Aug. 25 at Denver 7:00
Aug. 30 at Chicago...........................7:00

REGULAR SEASON
Sep. 9   **Pittsburgh** 1:00
Sep. 16 **Cincinnati** 1:00
Sep. 23 at Oakland 1:05
Sep. 30 **Baltimore** 1:00
Oct. 7   at New England 1:00
Oct. 14 **Miami** 1:00
Oct. 21 Open Date
Oct. 28 at St. Louis 12:00
Nov. 4   **Seattle** 4:05
Nov. 11 at Pittsburgh 1:00
Nov. 18 at Baltimore........................1:00
Nov. 25 **Houston** 1:00
Dec. 2   at Arizona 2:05
Dec. 9   at N.Y. Jets.........................4:15
Dec. 16 **Buffalo** 1:00
Dec. 23 at Cincinnati 1:00
Dec. 30 **San Francisco** 1:00

Stadium: Cleveland Browns Stadium
      (opened in 1999)
      •Capacity: 73,300
      100 Alfred Lerner Way
      Cleveland, Ohio 44114
Playing Surface: Grass
Headquarters/Training Camp:
      76 Lou Groza Boulevard
      Berea, Ohio 44017

CLEVELAND BROWNS STADIUM

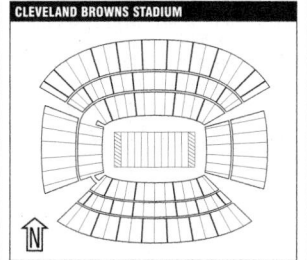

CLUB OFFICIALS
Owner: Randy Lerner
Vice Chairman: Bob Kain
Senior Vice President and General
  Manager: Phil Savage
Head Coach: Romeo Crennel
Chief Adminstrative Officer: Lew Merletti
Chief Financial Officer: Mike Keenan
Vice President, Communications:
  Bill Bonsiewicz
Vice President, Administration:
  Diane Downing
Vice President, Security, Logistics and
  Information Technology: Carl Meyer
Director, Business Development:
  Lorne Novick
Director, Corporate Sales and Partnership
  Marketing: Brett Reynolds
Director, Direct Marketing and Customer
  Service: John Schulze
Director, Finance: David Jenkins
Director, Marketing Services:
  George Muller
Director, Media Information: Ken Mather
Director, Team Operations: Brendan Rowe
Head Athletic Trainer: Marty Lauzon
Equipment Manager: Brad Melland
Video Director: Pat Dolan
Head Groundskeeper: Chris Powell

COACHING HISTORY
(425-374-10)
Records include postseason games
1950-1962	Paul Brown	115-49-5
1963-1970	Blanton Collier	79-38-2
1971-74	Nick Skorich	30-26-2
1975-77	Forrest Gregg*	18-23-0
1977	Dick Modzelewski	0-1-0
1978-1984	Sam Rutigliano**	47-52-0
1984-88	Marty Schottenheimer	..46-31-0
1989-1990	Bud Carson***	12-14-1
1990	Jim Shofner	1-6-0
1991-95	Bill Belichick	37-45-0
1999-2000	Chris Palmer	5-27-0
2001-04	Butch Davis****	24-36-0
2004	Terry Robiskie	1-4-0
2005-06	Romeo Crennel	10-22-0

     *Resigned after 13 games in 1977
    **Released after eight games in 1984
   ***Released after nine games in 1990
  ****Resigned after 11 games in 2004

PAID ATTENDANCE
Home 563,827   Away 536,694
Total 1,100,521
Single-game home record,
  85,073 (9/21/70)
Single-season home record, 620,496
  (1980)

2007 DRAFT CHOICES
Round	Name	Pos.	College
1	Joe Thomas	T	Wisconsin
	Brady Quinn	QB	Notre Dame
2	Eric Wright	DB	Nevada-Las Vegas
5	Brandon McDonald	DB	Memphis
6	Melila Purcell	DE	Hawaii
	Chase Pittman	DE	Louisiana State
7	Syndric Steptoe	WR	Arizona

CLEVELAND BROWNS

2006 TEAM RECORD

PRESEASON (2-2)

Date	Result		Opponent
8/10	L	7-20	at Philadelphia
8/18	W	20-16	Detroit
8/26	W	20-17	at Buffalo
8/31	L	7-20	Chicago

REGULAR SEASON (4-12)

Date	Result		Opponent	Att.
9/10	L	14-19	New Orleans	72,915
9/17	L	17-34	at Cincinnati	66,072
9/24	L	14-15	Baltimore	72,474
10/1	W	24-21	at Oakland	61,426
10/8	L	12-20	at Carolina	73,520
10/22	L	7-17	Denver	73,024
10/29	W	20-13	N.Y. Jets	72,507
11/5	L	25-32	at San Diego	65,558
11/12	W	17-13	at Atlanta	70,793
11/19	L	20-24	Pittsburgh	73,296
11/26	L	0-30	Cincinnati	72,926
12/3	W	31-28	Kansas City (OT)	71,927
12/7	L	7-27	at Pittsburgh	55,246
12/17	L	17-27	at Baltimore	70,857
12/24	L	7-22	Tampa Bay	69,603
12/31	L	6-14	at Houston	70,097
(OT) Overtime				

SCORE BY PERIODS

Browns	29	74	41	91	3	—	238
Opponents	64	90	95	107	0	—	356

2006 TEAM STATISTICS

	Browns	Opp.
Total First Downs	250	303
Rushing	72	107
Passing	153	178
Penalty	25	18
3rd Down: Made/Att	70/209	100/228
3rd Down Pct.	33.5	43.9
4th Down: Made/Att	6/15	4/10
4th Down Pct.	40.0	40.0
Possession Avg.	29:21	30:39
Total Net Yards	4233	5517
Avg. Per Game	264.6	344.8
Total Plays	938	1041
Avg. Per Play	4.5	5.3
Net Yards Rushing	1335	2275
Avg. Per Game	83.4	142.2
Total Rushes	372	514
Net Yards Passing	2898	3242
Avg. Per Game	181.1	202.6
Sacked/Yards Lost	54/349	28/137
Gross Yards	3247	3379
Att./Completions	512/318	499/283
Completion Pct.	62.1	56.7
Had Intercepted	25	18
Punts/Average	83/43.6	77/43.0
Net Punting Avg.	83/37.9	77/36.9
Penalties/Yards	74/687	84/678
Fumbles/Ball Lost	23/17	13/9
Touchdowns	25	40
Rushing	7	14
Passing	15	20
Returns	3	6

2006 INDIVIDUAL STATISTICS

PASSING

PASSING	Att.	Comp.	Yds.	Pct.	TD	Int.	Tkld.	Rate
Frye	393	252	2,454	64.1	10	17	44/262	72.0
Anderson	117	66	793	56.4	5	8	8/66	63.1
Cribbs	1	0	—	0.0	0	0	0/0	39.6
K. Dorsey	1	0	—	0.0	0	0	1/7	39.6
Winslow	0	0	—	—	0	0	1/14	—
Browns	512	318	3,247	62.1	15	25	54/349	69.7
Opponents	499	283	3,379	56.7	20	18	28/137	75.9

SCORING

SCORING	TD R	TD P	TD Rt	PAT	FG	Saf	PTS
Dawson	0	0	0	25/25	21/29	0	88
Edwards	0	6	0	0/0	0/0	0	36
Droughns	4	0	0	0/0	0/0	0	24
Frye	3	0	0	0/0	0/0	0	18
Jurevicius	0	3	0	0/0	0/0	0	18
Winslow	0	3	0	0/0	0/0	0	18
Heiden	2	2	0	0/0	0/0	0	12
Holly	2	0	2	0/0	0/0	0	12
Cribbs	1	0	1	0/0	0/0	0	6
Dinkins	0	1	0	0/0	0/0	0	6
Browns	7	15	3	25/25	21/29	0	238
Opponents	14	20	6	36/38	26/31	0	356

2-Pt. Conversions:
Browns 0-0, Opponents 1-2.

RUSHING

RUSHING	No.	Yds	Avg	LG	TD
Droughns	220	758	3.4	22	4
Frye	47	215	4.6	17	3
Wright	62	189	3.0	18	0
Harrison	20	60	3.0	15	0
Anderson	4	47	11.8	33	0
Northcutt	3	32	10.7	16	0
T. Smith	8	14	1.8	3	0
Cribbs	2	11	5.5	9	0
Edwards	3	7	2.3	8	0
Vickers	3	2	0.7	2	0
Browns	372	1335	3.6	33	7
Opponents	514	2275	4.4	59t	14

RECEIVING

RECEIVING	No.	Yds	Avg	LG	TD
Winslow	89	875	9.8	40	3
Edwards	61	884	14.5	75	6
Jurevicius	40	495	12.4	52	3
Heiden	36	249	6.9	13	2
Droughns	27	169	6.3	24	0
Northcutt	22	228	10.4	43	0
Cribbs	10	91	9.1	14	0
Harrison	9	47	5.2	12	0
T. Smith	8	21	2.6	7	0
Wright	6	82	13.7	54	0
Vickers	6	60	10.0	29	0
Wilson	2	32	16.0	16	0
Dinkins	2	14	7.0	11	1
Browns	318	3247	10.2	75	15
Opponents	283	3379	11.9	77t	20

INTERCEPTIONS

INTERCEPTIONS	No.	Yds	Avg	LG	TD
Holly	5	127	25.4	57t	1
Jones	5	46	9.2	19	0
Bodden	2	48	24.0	35	0
Davis	2	19	9.5	19	0
Baxter	1	10	10.0	10	0
Russell	1	6	6.0	6	0
McGinest	1	0	0.0	0	0
Pool	1	0	0.0	0	0
Browns	18	256	14.2	57t	1
Opponents	25	273	10.9	37	2

PUNTING

PUNTING	No.	Yds	Avg	In 20	LG
Zastudil	81	3,563	44.0	28	61
Dawson	2	58	29.0	1	31
Browns	83	3,621	43.6	29	61
Opponents	77	3,309	43.0	21	69

PUNT RETURNS

PUNT RETURNS	Ret	FC	Yds	Avg	LG	TD
Northcutt	28	13	312	11.1	81	0
Cribbs	6	3	51	8.5	34	0
Jones	1	0	8	8.0	8	0
Unck	1	0	0	0.0	0	0
Browns	36	16	371	10.3	81	0
Opponents	43	11	312	7.3	37	0

KICKOFF RETURNS

KICKOFF RETURNS	No.	Yds	Avg	LG	TD
Cribbs	61	1494	24.5	92t	1
Vickers	5	84	16.8	22	0
Dinkins	3	44	14.7	20	0
Heiden	1	11	11.0	11	0
Friedman	1	2	2.0	2	0
Browns	71	1635	23.0	92t	1
Opponents	48	1053	21.9	99t	1

FIELD GOALS

FIELD GOALS	1-19	20-29	30-39	40-49	50+
Dawson	0/0	5/6	9/10	6/12	1/1
Browns	0/0	5/6	9/10	6/12	1/1
Opponents	1/1	12/12	6/7	6/8	1/3

SACKS

SACKS	No.
Wimbley	11.0
Fraser	4.5
McGinest	4.0
Thompson	2.0
Davis	1.0
McKinley	1.0
Pool	1.0
Roye	1.0
Stewart	1.0
Williams	1.0
Jones	0.5
Browns	28.0
Opponents	54.0

RECORD HOLDERS
INDIVIDUAL RECORDS—CAREER

Category	Name	Performance
Rushing (Yds.)	Jim Brown, 1957-1965	12,312
Passing (Yds.)	Brian Sipe, 1974-1983	23,713
Passing (TDs)	Brian Sipe, 1974-1983	154
Receiving (No.)	Ozzie Newsome, 1978-1990	662
Receiving (Yds.)	Ozzie Newsome, 1978-1990	7,980
Interceptions	Thom Darden, 1972-74, 1976-1981	45
Punting (Avg.)	Dave Zastudil, 2006	44.0
Punt Return (Avg.)	Greg Pruitt, 1973-1981	11.8
Kickoff Return (Avg.)	Greg Pruitt, 1973-1981	26.3
Field Goals	Lou Groza, 1950-59, 1961-67	234
Touchdowns (Tot.)	Jim Brown, 1957-1965	126
Points	Lou Groza, 1950-59, 1961-67	1,349

INDIVIDUAL RECORDS—SINGLE SEASON

Category	Name	Performance
Rushing (Yds.)	Jim Brown, 1963	1,863
Passing (Yds.)	Brian Sipe, 1980	4,132
Passing (TDs)	Brian Sipe, 1980	30
Receiving (No.)	Ozzie Newsome, 1983	89
	Ozzie Newsome, 1984	89
	Kellen Winslow, 2006	89
Receiving (Yds.)	Webster Slaughter, 1989	1,236
Interceptions	Thom Darden, 1978	10
	Anthony Henry, 2001	10
Punting (Avg.)	Gary Collins, 1965	46.7
Punt Return (Avg.)	Leroy Kelly, 1965	15.6
Kickoff Return (Avg.)	Billy Lefear, 1975	31.7
Field Goals	Matt Stover, 1995	29
Touchdowns (Tot.)	Jim Brown, 1965	21
Points	Jim Brown, 1965	126

INDIVIDUAL RECORDS—SINGLE GAME

Category	Name	Performance
Rushing (Yds.)	Jim Brown, 11-24-57	237
	Jim Brown, 11-19-61	237
Passing (Yds.)	Brian Sipe, 10-25-81	444
Passing (TDs)	Frank Ryan, 12-12-64	5
	Bill Nelsen, 11-2-69	5
	Brian Sipe, 10-7-79	5
	Kelly Holcomb, 11-28-04	5
Receiving (No.)	Ozzie Newsome, 10-14-84	14
Receiving (Yds.)	Ozzie Newsome, 10-14-84	191
Interceptions	Many times	3
	Last time by Anthony Henry, 11-18-01	
Field Goals	Phil Dawson, 11-5-06	6
Touchdowns (Tot.)	Dub Jones, 11-25-51	*6
Points	Dub Jones, 11-25-51	36

*NFL Record

2007 VETERAN ROSTER

No.	Name	Pos.	Ht.	Wt.	Birthdate	NFL Exp.	College	Hometown	How Acq.	'06 Games/ Starts
20	Adams, Mike	S	5-11	195	3/24/81	4	Delaware	Paterson, N.J.	FA-'07	16/8*
3	Anderson, Derek	QB	6-6	229	6/15/83	3	Oregon State	Portland, Ore.	W(Balt)-'05	5/3
23	Baxter, Gary	DB	6-2	210	11/24/78	7	Baylor	Tyler, Texas	UFA(Balt)-'05	3/3
57	Bentley, LeCharles	OL	6-2	309	11/7/79	6	Ohio State	Cleveland, Ohio	UFA(NO)-'06	0*
28	Bodden, Leigh	DB	6-1	192	9/24/81	5	Duquesne	Upper Marlborough, Md.	FA-'03	9/9
71	Butler, Kelly	OL	6-7	330	7/24/82	4	Purdue	Grand Rapids, Mich.	W(Det)-'06	6/5
86 t-	Carter, Tim	WR	6-0	200	9/21/79	6	Auburn	Atlanta, Ga.	T(NYG)-'07	16/8*
16	Cribbs, Joshua	WR	6-1	192	6/9/83	3	Kent State	Washington, D.C.	FA-'05	16/1
54	Davis, Andra	LB	6-2	254	12/23/78	6	Florida	Live Oak, Fla.	D5-'02	14/14
4	Dawson, Phil	K	5-11	201	1/23/75	9	Texas	Dallas, Texas	FA-'99	16/0
87	Dinkins, Darnell	TE	6-4	259	1/20/77	6	Pittsburgh	Pittsburgh, Pa.	UFA(Balt)-'06	14/2
11	Dorsey, Ken	QB	6-4	211	4/22/81	5	Miami	Orinda, Calif.	T(SF)-'06	1/0
70	Dorsey, Nat	OL	6-7	345	9/9/83	4	Georgia Tech	New Orleans, La.	T(Minn)-'05	13/2
17	Edwards, Braylon	WR	6-3	212	2/21/83	3	Michigan	Detroit, Mich.	D1-'05	16/15
36	Emanuel, Ben	DB	6-2	220	6/18/82	2	UCLA	Texas City, Texas	FA-'06	0*
66	Fraley, Hank	OL	6-2	300	9/21/77	8	Robert Morris	Gaithersburg, Md.	T(Phil)-'06	16/16
75	Fraser, Simon	DL	6-6	295	3/27/83	3	Ohio State	Upper Arlington, Ohio	FA-'05	16/5
62	Friedman, Lennie	OL	6-3	295	8/13/76	9	Duke	Milford, N.J.	T(Chi)-'05	16/2
9	Frye, Charlie	QB	6-4	218	8/28/81	3	Akron	Willard, Ohio	D3-'05	13/13
27	Hamilton, Justin	DB	6-3	217	9/17/82	2	Virginia Tech	Norton, Va.	D7-'06	10/0
35	Harrison, Jerome	RB	5-9	199	2/26/83	2	Washington State	Kalamazoo, Mich	D5a-'06	10/1
82	Heiden, Steve	TE	6-5	267	9/21/76	9	South Dakota State	Rushford, Minn.	T(SD)-'02	16/16
39	Holly, Daven	DB	5-10	192	8/8/82	3	Cincinnati	Clairton, Pa.	FA-'06	14/2
58	Jackson, D'Qwell	LB	6-0	228	9/26/83	2	Maryland	Largo, Fla.	D2-'06	13/13
26	Jones, Sean	DB	6-1	215	3/2/82	4	Georgia	Atlanta, Ga.	D2-'04	16/16
84	Jurevicius, Joe	WR	6-5	232	12/23/74	10	Penn State	Mentor, Ohio	UFA(Sea)-'06	13/8
78	Kelley, Ethan	DL	6-2	320	2/12/80	3	Baylor	Sugarland, Texas	W(NE)-'05	11/1
89	Krause, Ryan	TE	6-3	256	6/16/81	4	Nebraska-Omaha	Omaha, Neb.	FA-'07	0*
41	Lesueur, Jeremy	DB	6-0	204	10/5/80	4	Michigan	Holly Springs, Miss.	FA-'07	0*
31	Lewis, Jamal	RB	5-11	245	8/26/79	8	Tennessee	Atlanta, Ga.	FA-'07	16/16*
67	Matua, Fred	OL	6-2	305	1/14/84	2	Southern California	Lakewood, Calif.	FA-'06	0*
55	McGinest, Willie	LB	6-5	268	12/11/71	14	Southern California	Long Beach, Calif.	UFA(NE)-'06	14/13
68	McKinney, Seth	OL	6-3	310	6/12/79	6	Texas A&M	Buffalo, Texas	FA-'07	0*
90	McMillan, David	LB	6-3	250	9/20/81	3	Kansas	Killeen, Texas	D5-'05	10/0
22	Minter, DeMario	DB	5-11	190	2/20/84	2	Georgia	Stone Mountain, Ga.	D5b-'06	0*
69	Parker, J'Vonne	DL	6-4	323	6/7/82	2	Rutgers	Newark, N.J.	FA-'06	4/0
56	Peek, Antwan	LB	6-3	258	10/29/79	5	Cincinnati	Cincinnati, Ohio	UFA(Hou)-'07	11/2*
30	Perkins, Antonio	DB	5-11	194	1/9/82	3	Oklahoma	Lawton, Okla.	D4-'05	5/0
33	Perry, Jereme	DB	6-0	190	12/15/81	2	Eastern Michigan	Saginaw, Mich.	FA-'06	12/0
64	Pontbriand, Ryan	LS	6-2	250	10/1/79	5	Rice	Houston, Texas	D5a-'03	16/0
21	Pool, Brodney	DB	6-2	208	5/24/84	3	Oklahoma	Houston, Texas	D2-'05	16/8
34	Ricard, Alan	FB	5-11	237	1/17/77	6	Northeast Louisiana	Independence, Mo.	FA-'07	0*
99	Roye, Orpheus	DL	6-4	315	1/21/73	12	Florida State	Carrol City, Fla.	UFA(Pitt)-'00	9/9
37	Sandy, Justin	DB	6-0	214	2/22/82	2	Northern Iowa	Wayne, Neb.	FA-'06	0*
77	Shaffer, Kevin	G/T	6-5	320	3/2/80	6	Tulsa	Salisbury, Md.	UFA(Atl)-'06	16/16
50	Short, Jason	LB	6-4	254	7/15/78	4	Eastern Michigan	Painesville, Ohio	FA-'07	12/0
98	Smith, Robaire	DT/DE	6-4	314	11/15/77	8	Michigan State	Flint, Mich.	UFA(Tenn)-'07	15/12*
91	Smith, Shaun	DT/DE	6-2	325	8/19/81	4	South Carolina	Lewisville, Texas	RFA(Cin)-'07	13/0*
45	Smith, Terrelle	FB	6-0	246	3/12/78	8	Arizona State	West Covina, Calif.	UFA(NO)-'04	16/8
61	Sowells, Isaac	T/G	6-3	324	5/4/82	2	Indiana	Louisville, Ky.	D4b-'06	1/0
65	Steinbach, Eric	T/G	6-6	290	4/4/80	5	Iowa	Lockport, Ill.	UFA(Cin)-'07	16/16*
52	Stewart, Matt	LB	6-3	236	8/31/79	7	Vanderbilt	Columbus, Ohio	UFA(Atl)-'05	16/4
51	Thompson, Chaun	LB	6-2	249	5/22/80	5	West Texas A&M	Mt. Pleasant, Texas	D2-'03	16/2
72	Tucker, Ryan	T/G	6-6	318	6/12/75	11	Texas Christian	Midland, Texas	UFA(StL)-'02	9/9
53	Unck, Mason	LB	6-3	238	3/30/80	4	Arizona State	Ogden, Utah	FA-'04	16/0
47	Vickers, Lawrence	FB	6-0	233	5/8/83	2	Colorado	Beaumont, Texas	D6a-'06	16/1
92	Washington, Ted	DT	6-5	365	4/13/68	17	Louisville	Tampa, Fla.	UFA(Oak)-'06	16/16
94	Williams, Leon	LB	6-2	238	7/30/83	2	Miami	Brooklyn, N.Y.	D4a-'06	16/3
81	Wilson, Travis	WR	6-1	213	2/11/84	2	Oklahoma	Carrollton, Texas	D3-'06	4/1
95	Wimbley, Kamerion	LB	6-3	245	10/13/83	2	Florida State	Wichita, Kan.	D1-'06	16/15
80	Winslow, Kellen	TE	6-4	248	7/21/83	4	Miami	San Diego, Calif.	D1-04	16/16
29	Wright, Jason	RB	5-10	210	7/12/82	3	Northwestern	Diamond Bar, Calif.	FA-'05	13/3
25	Wright, Kenny	S/CB	6-1	207	9/14/77	9	Northwestern State	Ruston, La.	UFA(Wash)-'07	16/9*
15	Zastudil, Dave	P	6-3	220	10/26/78	6	Ohio University	Bay Village, Ohio	UFA(Balt)-'06	16/0

* Adams played 16 games with San Francisco in '06; Bentley missed '06 season because of injury; Carter played 16 games with N.Y. Giants; Emanuel inactive for 3 games; Krause inactive for 16 games with San Diego; Lesueur missed '06 season because of injury; Lewis played 16 games with Baltimore; Matua did not play in 1 game; McKinney missed '06 season with Miami because of injury; Minter spent '06 season on PUP list; Peek played 11 games with Houston; Ricard last active with Baltimore in '05; Sandy last active with Tennessee in '05; Short played 12 games with Philadelphia; R. Smith played 15 games with Tennessee; S. Smith played 13 games with Cincinnati; Steinbach played 16 games with Cincinnati; K. Wright played 16 games with Washington.

t- Browns traded for T. Carter (NYG).

Traded—RB Reuben Droughns (14 games in '06) to N.Y. Giants.

Players lost through free agency (6): DB Ralph Brown (Ariz; 16 games in '06), DE Nick Eason (Pitt; 13), DE Alvin McKinley (Den; 14), WR Dennis Northcutt (Jax; 13), S Brian Russell (Sea; 12), FB Terrelle Smith (Ariz; 16).

Also played with Browns in '06—T Joe Andruzzi (14 games), G Cosey Coleman (15), CB/S Mike Hawkins (7).

2007 FIRST-YEAR ROSTER

Name	Pos.	Ht.	Wt.	Birthdate	College	Hometown	How Acq.
Ainsworth, Jesse	K	6-2	218	6/2/85	Arizona State	Thousand Oaks, Calif.	FA
Ali, Charles	FB	6-2	260	8/23/84	Arkansas-Pine Bluff	St. Louis, Mo.	FA
Alston, Mike	LB	6-2	212	8/28/85	Toledo	Columbus, Ohio	FA
Barclay, Chris (1)	RB	5-10	180	10/15/83	Wake Forest	Louisville, Ky.	FA-'06
Basler, Kyle	P	6-3	238	12/27/82	Washington State	Olympia, Wash.	FA
Fontenot, Therrian (1)	DB	5-10	187	6/20/82	Fresno State	Pineville, La.	FA-'06
Harris, Orien (1)	DL	6-3	302	6/3/83	Miami	Newark Del.	FA-'06
Hoffman, Andrew (1)	OL	6-4	300	2/15/82	Virginia	Fairfax, Va.	D6b-'05
Jackson, Jerome	RB	5-11	206	5/15/84	Michigan	Saginaw, Mich.	FA
Lougheed, Pete (1)	OL	6-5	300	11/5/79	Purdue	Fort Wayne, Ind.	FA-'06
Louis, Cliff	OL	6-8	300	8/24/84	Morgan State	Stanford, Ct.	FA
Mason, Mike	WR	5-11	190	2/28/85	Tennessee State	Rocky Mount, N.C.	FA
McDonald, Brandon	DB	5-10	181	8/26/85	Memphis	Collins, Miss.	D5
Mosley, Kendrick (1)	WR	6-2	207	7/21/81	Western Michigan	Pahokee, Fla.	FA-'06
Ortega, Buck (1)	TE	6-4	227	11/22/81	Miami	Miami, Fla.	FA-'06
Oshinowo, Babatunde (1)	DL	6-1	305	1/14/83	Stanford	Naperville, Ill.	D6b-'06
Pittman, Chase	DE	6-5	273	5/15/83	Louisiana State	Minden, La.	D6b
Pousson, Brent	OL	6-4	305	9/22/84	McNeese State	Iota, La.	FA
Purcell, Melila	DE	6-5	266	2/5/84	Hawaii	Leone, American Samoa	D6a
Quinn, Brady	QB	6-3	232	10/27/84	Notre Dame	Dublin, Ohio	D1b
Sanders, Steve (1)	WR	6-3	201	12/23/82	Bowling Green	Cleveland, Ohio	FA-'06
Sears, Kevin	LB	6-5	237	7/1/83	Auburn	Russellville, Ala.	FA
Smith, Alvin (1)	DL	6-2	307	6/16/82	Oregon State	Dallas, Texas	FA-'06
Smith, Clifton (1)	LB	6-3	253	7/21/80	Syracuse	Freeport, N.Y.	FA-'06
Smith, Rob (1)	OL	6-4	306	3/8/84	Tennessee	Ft. Thomas, Ky.	FA-'06
Stephenson, Scott	OL	6-4	305	10/26/83	Iowa State	St. Paul, Minn.	FA
Steptoe, Syndric	WR	5-9	170	12/6/84	Arizona	Bryan, Texas	D7
Thomas, Joe	OL	6-6	311	12/4/84	Wisconsin	Brookfield, Wisc.	D1a
Wright, Eric	DB	5-10	192	7/24/85	Nevada-Las Vegas	San Francisco, Calif.	D2

The term NFL Rookie is defined as a player who is in his first season of professional football and has not been on the roster of another professional football team for any regular-season or postseason games. A Rookie is designated by an "R" on NFL rosters. Players who have been active in another professional football league or players who have NFL experience, including either preseason training camp or being on an Active List or Inactive List, or on Reserve/Injured or Reserve/Physically Unable to Perform for fewer than six regular-season games, are termed NFL First-Year Players. An NFL First-Year Player is designated by a "1" on NFL rosters. Thereafter, a player is credited with an additional year of experience for each season in which he accumulates six games on the Active List or Inactive List, or on Reserve/Injured or Reserve/Physically Unable to Perform.

Log on to www.clevelandbrowns.com for an up-to-date roster.

COACHING STAFF
Head Coach,
Romeo Crennel
Pro Career: Romeo Crennel was named head coach of the Cleveland Browns on Feb. 8, 2005, the eleventh full-time head coach in team history. Crennel led the Browns to a 6-10 record in 2005 and posted a 4-12 mark in 2006. His resumé includes 37 years of coaching experience, including 26 years in the NFL, and has appeared in six Super Bowls, including five Super Bowl rings. Crennel crafted the defense for the New England Patriots and helped the Patriots win three Super Bowl's (2001, 2003-04). In 2003, he was recognized by the Pro Football Writers of America as the NFL's Assistant Coach of the Year. Crennel had previously coached in the NFL with Cleveland (2000), the Jets (1997-99), New England (1993-96), and the Giants (1981-1992), where he was the defensive line coach for the Giants' Super Bowl XXV title. Career record: 10-22.
Background: Crennel was a four-year starter (1966-69) as a defensive lineman at Western Kentucky. He earned team MVP honors as a senior. Earned his bachelor's degree in physical education from Western Kentucky, and then earned his master's degree while serving as a graduate assistant. Crennel coached collegiately at Western Kentucky (1970-74), Texas Tech (1975-77), Mississippi (1978-79), and Georgia Tech (1980).
Personal: Born June 18, 1947 in Lynchburg, Va. He and his wife, Rosemary, have three daughters, Lisa Tulley, Tiffany Crennel and Kristin Cullinane.

ASSISTANT COACHES
Dave Atkins, senior offensive assistant; born May 18, 1949, Victoria, Texas. Running back Texas El-Paso 1970-72. Pro running back San Francisco 49ers 1973, Honolulu Hawaiians (WFL) 1974, San Diego Chargers 1975. College coach: Texas El-Paso 1978-1980, San Diego State 1981-85. Pro coach: Philadelphia Eagles 1986-1992, New England Patriots 1993, Arizona Cardinals 1994-95, New Orleans Saints 1996, 2000-04, Minnesota Vikings 1997-99, joined Browns in 2005.
Wes Chandler, wide receivers; born Aug. 22, 1956, New Smyrna Beach, Fla. Wide receiver Florida 1974-77. Pro wide receiver New Orleans 1978-1981, San Diego 1981-87. College coach: Central Florida 1994-95. Pro coach: Orlando Thunder (WL) 1991-92, Rhein Fire (NFLE) 1995-97, Frankfurt Galaxy (NFLE) 1998, Berlin Thunder (NFLE) 1999, Dallas Cowboys 2000-02, Minnesota Vikings 2005, joined Browns in 2007.
Rob Chudzinski, offensive coordinator; born May 12, 1968, Toledo, Ohio. Tight end Miami 1986-1990. No pro playing experience. College coach: Miami 1994-2003. Pro coach: Cleveland Browns 2004, San Diego Chargers 2005-06, re-joined

Browns in 2007.
Ted Daisher, special teams coordinator; born Feb. 2, 1955, Taylor, Mich. College experience: Wide receiver/defensive back Western Michigan 1975-77. No pro playing experience. College coach: Illinois 1980-84, Eastern Michigan 1985-88, Cincinnati 1989-1992, Army 1995-97, Indiana 1998-2000, East Carolina 2001-02. Pro coach: Philadelphia Eagles 2004-05, Oakland Raiders 2006, joined Browns in 2007.
Alan DeGennaro, asst. strength and conditioning coach; born Jan. 21, 1977, Altoona, Pa. Attended Pittsburgh. No college or pro playing experience. Pro coach: Joined Browns in 2007.
Todd Grantham, defensive coordinator; born Sept. 13, 1966, Pulaski, Va. Offensive lineman Virginia Tech 1984-88. No pro playing experience. College coach: Virginia Tech 1990-95, Michigan State 1996-98. Pro coach: Indianapolis Colts 1999-2001, Houston Texans 2002-04, joined Browns in 2005.
Mike Haluchak, linebackers; born Nov. 28, 1949, Concord, Calif. Linebacker Southern California 1967-1970. No pro playing experience. College coach: Southern California 1976-77, Cal State-Fullerton 1978, Pacific 1979-1980, California 1981, North Carolina State 1982. Pro coach: Oakland Invaders (USFL) 1983-85, San Diego Chargers 1986-1991, Cincinnati Bengals 1992-93, Washington Redskins 1994-96, New York Giants 1997-99, St. Louis Rams 2000-02, Jacksonville Jaguars 2003-04, joined Browns in 2005.
Umberto Leone, defensive quality control; born Jan. 20, 1983, Garfield Heights, Ohio. Attended Ohio State. No college or pro playing experience. Pro coach: Joined Browns in 2005.
Anthony Lynn, running backs; born Dec. 21, 1968, McKinney, Texas. Running back Texas Tech 1987-1990. Pro fullback Denver Broncos 1993, 1997-99, San Francisco 49ers 1995-96. Pro coach: Denver Broncos 2000-02, Jacksonville Jaguars 2003-04, Dallas Cowboys 2005-06, joined Browns in 2007.
Steve Marshall, offensive line; born June 20, 1956, Hartford, Conn. Guard/tight end Louisville 1976-78. No pro playing experience. College coach: Plymouth State 1979, Tennessee 1980-81, Marshall 1982-83, Louisville 1984, Murray State 1985-86, Virginia Tech 1987-1992, Tennessee 1993-95, UCLA 1996, Texas A&M 1997, North Carolina 1998-99, Colorado 2000-01, Alabama 2007. Pro coach: Houston Texans 2002-05, joined Browns in 2007.
Randy Melvin, defensive line; born April 3, 1959, Aurora, Ill. Defensive line Eastern Illinois 1978-1981. No pro playing experience. College coach: Eastern Illinois 1988-1994, Wyoming 1995-96, Purdue 1997-99, Rutgers 2002-04, Illinois 2005. Pro coach: New England 2000-01, joined Browns in 2005.
Tom Myslinski, strength and conditioning;

born Dec. 7, 1968, Rome, N.Y. Guard Tennessee 1989-1992. Pro guard Chicago Bears 1993-94, Pittsburgh Steelers 1996-97, 2000, Indianapolis Colts 1998. College coach: North Florida 1996, Pittsburgh 1998-2001, 2007, Robert Morris 2005-06. Pro coach: Cleveland Browns 2001-04, re-joined Browns in 2007.
Alfredo Roberts, tight ends; born March 17, 1965, Ft. Lauderdale, Fla. Tight end Miami 1983-87. Pro playing experience: Kansas City Chiefs 1988-1990, Dallas Cowboys 1991-93. College coach: Florida Atlantic 1999-2002. Pro coach: Jacksonville Jaguars 2003-06, joined Browns in 2007.
Rip Scherer, asst. head coach/quarterbacks; born Aug. 3, 1952. Quarterback William & Mary 1970-74. No pro playing experience. College coach: Penn State 1974-75, North Carolina State 1976, Hawaii 1977-78, Virginia 1979, Georgia Tech 1980-86, Alabama 1987, Arizona 1988-1990, James Madison 1991-94, Memphis 1995-2000, Kansas 2001, Southern Mississippi 2003-04. Pro coach: Joined Browns in 2005.
Mike Sullivan, asst. offensive line; born Dec. 22, 1967, Chicago. Offensive lineman Miami 1986-1990. Pro offensive lineman Dallas Cowboys 1991, Tampa Bay Buccaneers 1992-95. College coach: Miami 2000, Western Michigan 2005-06. Pro coach: Cleveland Browns 2001-04, re-joined Browns in 2007.
Bob Trott, defensive assistant; born March 19, 1954, Concord, N.C. College safety North Carolina 1973-75. No pro playing experience. College coach: North Carolina 1976-77, Air Force 1978-1983, Arkansas 1984-89, Clemson 1990, Duke 1996-2001, Baylor 2002, Louisiana-Monroe 2003-04. Pro coach: New York Giants 1991-92, New England Patriots 1993-95, joined Browns in 2005.
Mel Tucker, secondary; born Jan. 4, 1972, Cleveland. College defensive back Wisconsin 1992-95. No pro playing experience. College coach: Michigan State 1997, Miami (Ohio) 1998-99, Louisiana State 2000, Ohio State 2001-04. Pro coach: Joined Browns in 2005.
Cory Undlin, secondary/asst. special teams; born June 29, 1971, St. Cloud, Minn. Safety California Lutheran 1990-94. No pro playing experience. College coach: California Lutheran 1998-2002, Fresno State 2002-03. Pro coach: New England 2004, joined Browns in 2005.
Frank Verducci, offensive assistant; born March 17, 1957, Glen Ridge, N.J. Tight end/fullback U.S. Merchant Marine Academy-Kings Point 1975. No pro playing experience. College coach: Colorado State 1980, Maryland 1981-83, Northern Illinois 1984, Iowa 1985-86, 1989-1998, Northwestern 1987-88. Pro coach: Cincinnati Bengals 1999-2001, Dallas Cowboys 2002, Buffalo Bills 2004-05, joined Browns in 2007.

**American Football Conference
West Division**
Team Colors: Orange,
Broncos Navy Blue, and White
13655 Broncos Parkway
Englewood, Colorado 80112
Telephone: (303) 649-9000

2007 SCHEDULE
PRESEASON
Aug. 13 at San Francisco 5:00
Aug. 18 at Dallas..........................7:00
Aug. 25 **Cleveland** 7:00
Aug. 30 **Houston**..........................7:00

REGULAR SEASON
Sep. 9   at Buffalo 1:00
Sep. 16 **Oakland** 2:15
Sep. 23 **Jacksonville** 2:05
Sep. 30 at Indianapolis 4:15
Oct. 7   **San Diego** 2:15
Oct. 14 Open Date
Oct. 21 **Pittsburgh** 6:15
Oct. 29 **Green Bay** (Mon.)............6:30
Nov. 4   at Detroit 1:00
Nov. 11 at Kansas City 12:00
Nov. 19 **Tennessee** (Mon.)............6:30
Nov. 25 at Chicago 12:00
Dec. 2   at Oakland 1:05
Dec. 9   **Kansas City** 2:15
Dec. 13 at Houston (Thu.).............7:15
Dec. 24 at San Diego (Mon.)........5:00
Dec. 30 **Minnesota** 2:15

Stadium: INVESCO Field at Mile High
        (opened in 2001)
        • Capacity: 76,125
        1701 Bryant Street
        Denver, Colorado 80204
Playing Surface: DDGrassmaster
Training Camp: 13655 Broncos Parkway
        Englewood, Colorado
        80112

INVESCO FIELD AT MILE HIGH

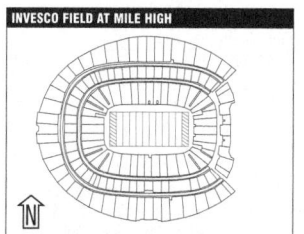

CLUB OFFICIALS
President-Chief Executive Officer:
  Pat Bowlen
Executive Vice President of Football
  Operations/ Head Coach:
  Mike Shanahan
Executive Vice President of Business
  Operations: Joe Ellis
FOOTBALL STAFF
General Manager: Ted Sundquist
Assistant General Manager: Rick Smith
Director of Player Personnel:
  Jim Goodman
Coordinator of Football Administration:
  Mike Bluem
Trainer: Steve Antonopulos
Equipment Manager: Chris Valenti
Video Director: Kent Erickson
BUSINESS STAFF
General Counsel/Senior Vice President of
  Administration: Rich Slivka
Vice President of Public Relations:
  Jim Saccomano
Vice President of Marketing: Greg Carney
Vice President of Finance: Jim Barlow
Vice President of Community
  Development: Cindy Galloway-Kellogg
STADIUM MANAGEMENT COMPANY
Vice President and General Manager:
  Mac Freeman

COACHING HISTORY
(388-342-10)
Records include postseason games
1960-61	Frank Filchock	7-20-1
1962-61	Jack Faulkner*	9-22-1
1964-66	Mac Speedie**	6-19-1
1966	Ray Malavasi	4-8-0
1967-1971	Lou Saban***	20-42-3
1971	Jerry Smith	2-3-0
1972-76	John Ralston	34-33-3
1977-1980	Robert (Red) Miller	42-25-0
1981-1992	Dan Reeves	117-79-1
1993-94	Wade Phillips	16-17-0
1995-2006	Mike Shanahan	131-74-0

  *Released after four games in 1964
  **Resigned after two games in 1966
***Resigned after nine games in 1971

PAID ATTENDANCE
Home 596,550   Away 543,020
Total 1,139,570
Single-game home record,
  76,643 (11/11/00)
Single-season home record, 596,550
  (2006)

2007 DRAFT CHOICES
Round	Name	Pos.	College
1	Jarvis Moss	DE	Florida
2	Tim Crowder	DE	Texsa
3	Ryan Harris	T	Notre Dame
4	Marcus Thomas	DT	Florida

2006 TEAM RECORD
PRESEASON (3-1)

Date	Result	Opponent
8/11	L 13-20	at Detroit
8/19	W 35-10	Tennessee
8/27	W 17-14	Houston
8/31	W 29-23	at Arizona

REGULAR SEASON (9-7)

Date	Result		Opponent	Att.
9/10	L	10-18	at St. Louis	65,577
9/17	W	9-6	Kansas City (OT)	76,786
9/24	W	17-7	at New England	68,756
10/9	W	13-3	Baltimore	76,355
10/15	W	13-3	Oakland	76,691
10/22	W	17-7	at Cleveland	73,024
10/29	L	31-34	Indianapolis	76,767
11/5	W	31-20	at Pittsburgh	64,661
11/12	W	17-13	at Oakland	62,094
11/19	L	27-35	San Diego	76,723
11/23	L	10-19	at Kansas City	79,484
12/3	L	20-23	Seattle	76,146
12/10	L	20-48	at San Diego	67,514
12/17	W	37-20	at Arizona	63,845
12/24	W	24-23	Cincinnati	75,759
12/31	L	23-26	San Francisco (OT)	75,555

(OT) Overtime

SCORE BY PERIODS

Broncos	44	110	75	87	3	—	319
Opponents	47	82	64	109	3	—	305

2006 TEAM STATISTICS

	Broncos	Opp.
Total First Downs	285	291
Rushing	106	97
Passing	151	183
Penalty	28	11
3rd Down: Made/Att	78/211	81/221
3rd Down Pct.	37.0	36.7
4th Down: Made/Att	7/13	5/14
4th Down Pct.	53.8	35.7
Possession Avg.	29:50	30:10
Total Net Yards	4951	5223
Avg. Per Game	309.4	326.4
Total Plays	973	1020
Avg. Per Play	5.1	5.1
Net Yards Rushing	2152	1813
Avg. Per Game	134.5	113.3
Total Rushes	488	447
Net Yards Passing	2799	3410
Avg. Per Game	174.9	213.1
Sacked/Yards Lost	31/196	35/202
Gross Yards	2995	3612
Att./Completions	454/256	538/327
Completion Pct.	56.4	60.8
Had Intercepted	18	17
Punts/Average	80/41.7	74/43.8
Net Punting Avg.	80/36.6	74/37.9
Penalties/Yards	67/478	97/785
Fumbles/Ball Lost	29/12	28/13
Touchdowns	34	29
Rushing	12	13
Passing	20	13
Returns	2	3

2006 INDIVIDUAL STATISTICS

PASSING

	Att.	Comp.	Yds.	Pct.	TD	Int.	Tkld.	Rate
Plummer	317	175	1,994	55.2	11	13	18/111	68.8
Cutler	137	81	1,001	59.1	9	5	13/85	88.5
Broncos	454	256	2,995	56.4	20	18	31/196	74.7
Opponents	538	327	3,612	60.8	13	17	35/202	75.6

SCORING

	TD R	TD P	TD Rt	PAT	FG	Saf	PTS
Elam	0	0	0	34/34	27/29	0	115
Walker	1	8	0	0/0	0/0	0	54
M. Bell	8	0	0	0/0	0/0	0	48
Scheffler	0	4	0	0/0	0/0	0	24
Smith	0	3	0	0/0	0/0	0	18
Alexander	0	2	0	0/0	0/0	0	12
T. Bell	2	0	0	0/0	0/0	0	12
Marshall	0	2	0	0/0	0/0	0	12
Bailey	0	0	1	0/0	0/0	0	6
Johnson	0	1	0	0/0	0/0	0	6
Plummer	1	0	0	0/0	0/0	0	6
Da. Williams	0	0	1	0/0	0/0	0	6
Broncos	12	20	2	34/34	27/29	0	319
Opponents	13	13	3	27/27	34/42	0	305

2-Pt. Conversions:
Broncos 0-0, Opponents 1-2.

RUSHING

	No.	Yds	Avg	LG	TD
T. Bell	233	1025	4.4	51	2
M. Bell	157	677	4.3	48	8
Walker	9	123	13.7	72t	1
Plummer	36	112	3.1	19	1
Sapp	10	80	8.0	28	0
Nash	18	66	3.7	26	0
Johnson	5	30	6.0	15	0
Cutler	12	18	1.5	9	0
Marshall	2	12	6.0	6	0
Cobbs	3	9	3.0	5	0
Scheffler	1	3	3.0	3	0
Elam	1	2	2.0	2	0
Smith	1	-5	-5.0	-5	0
Broncos	488	2152	4.4	72t	12
Opponents	447	1813	4.1	41	13

RECEIVING

	No.	Yds	Avg	LG	TD
Walker	69	1084	15.7	83t	8
Smith	52	512	9.8	20	3
T. Bell	24	115	4.8	16	0
Marshall	20	309	15.5	71t	2
M. Bell	20	158	7.9	24	0
Scheffler	18	286	15.9	29	4
Alexander	18	160	8.9	24	2
Kircus	9	187	20.8	45	0
Sapp	8	34	4.3	9	0
Johnson	7	37	5.3	20	1
Jackson	5	49	9.8	24	0
Nash	4	41	10.3	13	0
Mustard	2	23	11.5	14	0
Broncos	256	2995	11.7	83t	20
Opponents	327	3612	11.0	63	13

INTERCEPTIONS

	No.	Yds	Avg	LG	TD
Bailey	10	162	16.2	70t	1
Da. Williams	4	37	9.3	31t	1
Foxworth	1	45	45.0	45	0
Cox	1	0	0.0	0	0
Ferguson	1	0	0.0	0	0
Broncos	17	244	14.4	70t	2
Opponents	18	292	16.2	46	2

PUNTING

	No.	Yds.	Avg.	In 20	LG
Ernster	80	3,338	41.7	23	61
Broncos	80	3,338	41.7	23	61
Opponents	74	3,240	43.8	33	67

PUNT RETURNS

	Ret	FC	Yds	Avg	LG	TD
Da. Williams	25	12	206	8.2	34	0
Kircus	6	4	86	14.3	42	0
Smith	1	0	2	2.0	2	0
Broncos	32	16	294	9.2	42	0
Opponents	39	16	268	6.9	21	0

KICKOFF RETURNS

	No.	Yds	Avg	LG	TD
Clark	23	512	22.3	36	0
Morgan	17	423	24.9	64	0
M. Bell	5	97	19.4	22	0
Sapp	4	95	23.8	53	0
Kircus	2	38	19.0	20	0
Johnson	1	14	14.0	14	0
Mustard	1	2	2.0	2	0
Cobbs	1	0	0.0	0	0
Da. Williams	0	6	—	6	0
Broncos	54	1187	22.0	64	0
Opponents	55	1480	26.9	60	0

FIELD GOALS

	1-19	20-29	30-39	40-49	50+
Elam	0/0	10/10	10/10	6/8	1/1
Broncos	0/0	10/10	10/10	6/8	1/1
Opponents	0/0	12/12	8/9	11/14	3/7

SACKS

	No.
Dumervil	8.5
Ekuban	7.0
Lang	6.0
Chukwurah	4.5
Warren	2.5
M. Myers	2.0
Veal	1.5
Engelberger	1.0
D.J. Williams	1.0
Wilson	1.0
Broncos	35.0
Opponents	31.0

RECORD HOLDERS
INDIVIDUAL RECORDS—CAREER

Category	Name	Performance
Rushing (Yds.)	Terrell Davis, 1995-2001	7,607
Passing (Yds.)	John Elway, 1983-1998	51,475
Passing (TDs)	John Elway, 1983-1998	300
Receiving (No.)	Rod Smith, 1995-2006	849
Receiving (Yds.)	Rod Smith, 1995-2006	11,389
Interceptions	Steve Foley, 1976-1986	44
Punting (Avg.)	Jim Fraser, 1962-64	45.2
Punt Return (Avg.)	Darrien Gordon, 1997-98	12.5
Kickoff Return (Avg.)	Abner Haynes, 1965-66	26.3
Field Goals	Jason Elam, 1993-2006	368
Touchdowns (Tot.)	Rod Smith, 1995-2006	69
Points	Jason Elam, 1993-2006	1,672

INDIVIDUAL RECORDS—SINGLE SEASON

Category	Name	Performance
Rushing (Yds.)	Terrell Davis, 1998	2,008
Passing (Yds.)	Jake Plummer, 2004	4,089
Passing (TDs)	John Elway, 1997	27
	Jake Plummer, 2004	27
Receiving (No.)	Rod Smith, 2001	113
Receiving (Yds.)	Rod Smith, 2000	1,602
Interceptions	Goose Gonsoulin, 1960	11
Punting (Avg.)	Tom Rouen, 1998	46.9
Punt Return (Avg.)	Floyd Little, 1967	16.9
Kickoff Return (Avg.)	Bill Thompson, 1969	28.5
Field Goals	Jason Elam, 1995, 2001	31
Touchdowns (Tot.)	Terrell Davis, 1998	23
Points	Terrell Davis, 1998	138

INDIVIDUAL RECORDS—SINGLE GAME

Category	Name	Performance
Rushing (Yds.)	Mike Anderson, 12-3-00	251
Passing (Yds.)	Jake Plummer, 10-31-04	499
Passing (TDs)	Frank Tripucka, 10-28-62	5
	John Elway, 11-18-84	5
	Gus Frerotte, 11-19-00	5
Receiving (No.)	Rod Smith, 9-23-01	14
Receiving (Yds.)	Shannon Sharpe, 10-20-02	214
Interceptions	Goose Gonsoulin, 9-18-60	*4
	Willie Brown, 11-15-64	*4
	Deltha O'Neal, 10-7-01	*4
Field Goals	Gene Mingo, 10-6-63	5
	Rich Karlis, 11-20-83	5
	Jason Elam, 9-3-95, 10-13-02	5
Touchdowns (Tot.)	Clinton Portis, 12-7-03	5
Points	Clinton Portis, 12-7-03	30

*NFL Record

2007 VETERAN ROSTER

No.	Name	Pos.	Ht.	Wt.	Birthdate	NFL Exp.	College	Hometown	How Acq.	'06 Games/ Starts
21	Abdullah, Hamza	S	6-2	216	8/19/79	3	Washington State	Pomona, Calif.	PS(TB)-'05	11/0
82	Alexander, Stephen	TE	6-4	250	11/6/71	10	Oklahoma	Chickasha, Okla.	UFA(Det)-'05	16/14
24	Bailey, Champ	CB	6-0	192	6/21/74	9	Georgia	Folkston, Ga.	T(Wash)-'04	16/16
30	Bell, Mike	RB	6-0	220	4/22/79	2	Arizona	Tolleson, Ariz.	FA-'06	15/0
33	Belton, Thump	FB	6-0	232	5/31/77	3	Syracuse	Charlotte, N.C.	FA-'06	0*
32	t-Bly, Dré	CB	5-10	188	5/21/73	9	North Carolina	Chesapeake, Va.	T(Det)-'07	16/16*
42	Brandon, Sam	S	6-2	200	7/4/75	6	Nevada-Las Vegas	Riverside, Calif.	D4-'02	8/0
93	Burton, Antwon	DT	6-2	318	6/10/79	2	Temple	Cheektowaga, N.Y.	FA-'06	1/0
38	Cargile, Steve	S	6-2	210	6/1/78	3	Columbia	Bedford, Ohio	FA-'06	3/0
19	Clark, Brian	WR	6-2	204	12/25/79	2	North Carolina State	Tampa, Fla.	FA-'06	6/0
40	Cox, Curome	S	6-1	204	2/27/77	3	Maryland	Washington, D.C.	FA-'04	16/4
6	Cutler, Jay	QB	6-3	233	4/28/79	2	Vanderbilt	Lincoln City, Ind.	D1-'06	5/5
92	Dumervil, Elvis	DL	5-11	250	1/18/80	2	Louisville	Miami, Fla.	D4b-'06	13/0
91	Ekuban, Ebenezer	DE	6-4	275	5/28/72	9	North Carolina	Bladensburg, Md.	T(Cle)-'05	15/15
1	Elam, Jason	K	5-11	200	3/7/66	15	Hawaii	Ft. Walton Beach, Fla.	D3b-'93	16/0
60	Engelberger, John	DE	6-4	252	10/17/72	8	Virginia Tech	Springfield, Va.	T(SF)-'05	16/1
3	Ernster, Paul	P/K	6-0	217	1/25/78	3	Northern Arizona	Glendale, Ariz.	D7-'05	16/0
	Eslinger, Greg	C	6-3	290	4/22/79	2	Minnesota	Bismarck, N.D.	D6-'06	0*
25	Ferguson, Nick	S	5-11	201	11/26/70	8	Georgia Tech	Miami, Fla.	FA-'03	10/10
34	Fleming, Troy	FB	6-0	245	9/30/76	3	Tennessee	Franklin, Tenn.	FA-'07	0*
22	Foxworth, Domonique	CB	5-11	180	3/26/79	3	Maryland	Catonsville, Md.	D3b-'05	16/5
52	Gold, Ian	LB	6-0	223	8/22/74	8	Michigan	Belleville, Mich.	FA-'05	15/15
94	Gordon, Amon	DL	6-2	305	10/12/77	3	Stanford	San Diego, Calif.	FA-'07	0*
89	Graham, Daniel	TE	6-3	257	11/15/74	6	Colorado	Denver, Colo.	UFA(NE)-'07	12/11*
53	Green, Louis	LB	6-2	228	9/22/75	4	Alcorn State	Fayette, Miss.	FA-'03	16/0
98	Hall, Carlos	DE	6-4	259	1/15/75	5	Arkansas	Marianna, Ark.	FA-'07	0*
50	Hamilton, Ben	G/C	6-4	283	8/17/73	7	Minnesota	Minneapolis, Minn.	D4a-'01	16/16
31	Harris, Quentin	S	6-1	213	1/25/73	6	Syracuse	Kingston, Pa.	FA-'06	6/0
20	Henry, Travis	RB	5-9	215	10/28/74	7	Tennessee	Frostproof, Fla.	FA-'07	14/13*
12	Hixon, Domenik	WR	6-2	185	10/7/80	2	Akron	Columbus, Ohio	D4c-'06	0*
56	Holdman, Warrick	LB	6-1	243	11/21/71	9	Texas A&M	Alief, Texas	UFA(Wash)-'07	16/16*
70	Holland, Montrae	G	6-2	322	5/20/76	5	Florida State	Ore City, Texas	UFA(NO)-'07	8/0*
57	Hollowell, T.J.	LB	6-0	235	4/7/77	3	Nebraska	Copperas Cove, Texas	FA-'07	0*
81	Jackson, Nate	TE	6-3	235	6/3/75	5	Menlo	San Jose, Calif.	T(SF)-'03	11/0
39	Johnson, Kyle	FB	6-0	242	12/14/74	5	Syracuse	Woodbridge, N.J.	FA-'03	14/7
	Johnson, Teyo	TE	6-6	245	11/28/77	4	Stanford	San Diego, Calif.	FA-'07	0*
87	Kircus, David	WR	6-2	192	2/18/76	4	Grand Valley State	Imlay City, Mich.	FA-'06	16/0
73	Kuper, Chris	G	6-4	302	12/18/78	2	North Dakota	Anchorage, Alaska	D5-'06	1/0
76	Lang, Kenard	DE	6-3	264	1/30/71	11	Miami	Orlando, Fla.	FA-'06	16/16
83	Leach, Mike	TE/LS	6-2	245	10/17/72	8	William & Mary	Jefferson Township, N.J.	FA-'02	16/0
78	Lepsis, Matt	T	6-4	290	1/12/70	11	Colorado	Conroe, Texas	FA-'97	6/6
54	Lewis, D.D.	LB	6-1	241	1/7/75	6	Texas	Houston, Texas	UFA(Sea)-'07	5/1*
47	Lynch, John	S	6-2	220	9/24/67	15	Stanford	Del Mar, Calif.	FA-'04	16/16
15	Marshall, Brandon	WR	6-4	222	3/22/80	2	Central Florida	Lake Howell, Fla.	D4a-'06	16/1
99	McKinley, Alvin	DT/DE	6-2	294	6/8/74	8	Mississippi State	Weir, Miss.	UFA(Cle)-'07	14/14*
75	Meadows, Adam	T	6-5	290	1/24/70	9	Georgia	Powder Springs, Ga.	FA-'06	3/3
51	Moore, Eddie	LB	6-1	235	7/4/76	4	Tennessee	South Pittsburg, Tenn.	FA-'07	0*
11	Morgan, Quincy	WR	6-1	215	9/22/73	7	Kansas State	South Garland, Texas	UFA(Den)-'07	7/0
85	Mustard, Chad	TE	6-6	277	10/7/73	4	North Dakota	Columbus, Neb.	FA-'06	12/4
62	Myers, Chris	C/G	6-4	300	9/14/77	3	Miami	Miami, Fla.	D6-'05	16/0
66	Nalen, Tom	C	6-3	286	5/12/67	14	Boston College	Foxboro, Mass.	D7c-'94	16/16
71	Nienhuis, Doug	T	6-6	307	2/15/78	2	Oregon State	Irvine, Calif.	FA-'06	0*
5	Parsons, Preston	QB	6-4	235	2/18/75	3	Northern Arizona	Portland, Ore.	FA-'06	0*
41	Paymah, Karl	CB	6-0	200	11/28/78	3	Washington State	Culver City, Calif.	D3a-'05	16/0
64	Pears, Erik	T	6-8	305	6/24/78	2	Colorado State	Denver, Colo.	FA-'05	16/10
90	Peterson, Kenny	DE	6-3	285	11/20/74	5	Ohio State	Canton, Ohio	UFA(Den)-'07	3/0
8	Ramsey, Patrick	QB	6-2	227	2/13/75	6	Tulane	Ruston, La.	FA-'07	1/0
	Reid, Lamont	CB	5-11	195	5/3/78	2	North Carolina State	Concord, N.C.	FA-'07	0*
69	Rogers, Jacob	T	6-6	312	8/16/77	3	Southern California	Oxnard, Calif.	FA-'07	0*
37	Sapp, Cecil	RB	5-11	229	12/22/74	5	Colorado State	Miami, Fla.	FA-'03	11/1
10	Sauerbrun, Todd	P	5-11	215	1/3/69	13	West Virginia	East Setauket, N.Y.	UFA(NE)-'07	2/0*
88	Scheffler, Tony	TE	6-5	250	2/14/79	2	Western Michigan	Morenci, Mich.	D2-'06	13/5
28	Shoate, Jeff	CB	5-10	180	3/22/77	3	San Diego State	San Diego, Calif.	D5-'04	0*
26	Smith, Paul	RB	5-11	237	1/30/74	8	Texas-El Paso	El Paso, Texas	UFA(StL)-'07	10/3*
80	Smith, Rod	WR	6-0	200	5/14/66	13	Missouri Southern	Texarkana, Ark.	FA-'94	16/16
14	Stokley, Brandon	WR	5-11	197	6/22/72	9	Southwestern Louisiana	Lafayette, La.	FA-'07	4/1*

13	Terrell, David	WR	6-3	213	3/12/75	6	Michigan	Richmond, Va.	FA-'05	0*
86	Trusty, Landon	TE	6-7	266	10/8/77	3	Central Arkansas	Hot Springs, Ark.	FA-'06	0*
97	Veal, Demetrin	DT	6-2	288	8/10/77	5	Tennessee	Paramount, Calif.	FA-'04	16/1
84	Walker, Javon	WR	6-3	209	10/13/74	6	Florida State	Lafayette, La.	T(GB)-'06	16/16
61	Warren, Gerard	DT	6-4	325	7/24/74	7	Florida	Raiford, Fla.	T(Cle)-'05	15/15
58	Webster, Nate	LB	6-0	237	11/28/73	8	Miami	Miami, Fla.	UFA(Cin)-'06	3/2
55	Williams, D.J.	LB	6-1	242	7/19/78	4	Miami	Concord, Calif.	D1-'04	16/15

* Belton last active with Chicago in '04; Eslinger missed '06 season because of injury; Fleming last active with Tennessee in '05; Gordon spent '06 season on Denver's practice squad; Hall last active with Kansas City in '05; Hixon spent '06 season on reserve non-football injury; Hollowell last active with Miami in '05; T. Johnson last active with Arizona in '05; Moore last active with Miami in '05; Nienhuis last active with N.Y. Jets in '05; Parsons last active with Arizona in '03; Reid last active with Arizona in '05; Rogers missed the '05 season with Dallas because of injury; Shoate missed '05 season because of injury; Stokley played 4 games with Indianapolis; Terrell last active with Denver in '05; Trusty missed '06 season because of injury.

t- Broncos traded for Bly (Det).

Traded—RB Tatum Bell (13 games in '06) to Detroit, QB Jake Plummer (16) to Tampa Bay.

Players lost through free agency (3): G Cooper Carlisle (Oak; 16 games in '06), LB Patrick Chukwurah (TB; 14), DT Michael Myers (Cin; 16).

Also played with Broncos in '06—LB Keith Burns (15 games), RB Cedric Cobbs (2), WR Todd Devoe (1), T George Foster (16), CB Darrent Williams (15), LB Al Wilson (15).

2007 FIRST-YEAR ROSTER

Name	Pos.	Ht.	Wt.	Birthdate	College	Hometown	How Acq.
Crowder, Tim	DE	6-4	270	6/29/81	Texas	Tyler, Texas	D2
Fenton, Mark	C	6-4	295	11/13/79	Colorado	Los Angeles, Calif.	FA
Hackney, Darrell (1)	QB	6-0	240	8/6/79	Alabama-Birmingham	Atlanta, Ga.	FA
Hall, Andre (1)	RB	5-10	205	8/19/78	South Florida	St. Petersburg, Fla.	FA-'06
Harris, Ryan	T	6-5	292	3/10/81	Notre Dame	St. Paul, Minn.	D3
Harris, Steven	DT	6-5	285	8/13/80	Florida	Coral Gables, Fla.	FA
Hill, Eric (1)	CB	6-0	190	5/21/76	Colorado State	Denver, Colo.	FA
Martinez, Glenn (1)	WR	6-1	183	11/29/77	Saginaw Valley State	Auburndale, Fla.	FA
McAlmont, Kevin (1)	G	6-1	320	7/23/80	Western Carolina	Union City, Ga.	FA
McDaniel, Marquay	WR	5-10	205	4/19/80	Hampton	Virginia Beach, Va.	FA
Moss, Jarvis	DE	6-6	251	8/2/80	Florida	Denton, Texas	D1
Pace, Brandon	K	5-10	194	11/10/79	Virginia Tech	Virginia Beach, Va.	FA
Rogers, Roderick	S	6-2	287	9/6/80	Wisconsin	Stone Mountain, Ga.	FA
Thomas, Marcus	DT	6-3	296	9/22/81	Florida	Jacksonville, Fla.	D4
Vaughn, Cameron (1)	LB	6-4	241	2/26/80	Louisiana State	Marrero, La.	FA-'06
Young, Selvin	RB	5-11	207	9/30/79	Texas	Jersey City Village, Texas	FA

The term NFL Rookie is defined as a player who is in his first season of professional football and has not been on the roster of another professional football team for any regular-season or postseason games. A Rookie is designated by an "R" on NFL rosters. Players who have been active in another professional football league or players who have NFL experience, including either preseason training camp or being on an Active List or Inactive List, or on Reserve/Injured or Reserve/Physically Unable to Perform for fewer than six regular-season games, are termed NFL First-Year Players. An NFL First-Year Player is designated by a "1" on NFL rosters. Thereafter, a player is credited with an additional year of experience for each season in which he accumulates six games on the Active List or Inactive List, or on Reserve/Injured or Reserve/Physically Unable to Perform.

Log on to www.denverbroncos.com for an up-to-date roster.

COACHING STAFF

Head Coach,
Mike Shanahan
Pro Career: Became the eleventh head coach in Broncos history on January 31, 1995. Mike Shanahan led the Broncos to back-to-back Super Bowl championships in 1997 and 1998, becoming just the fifth head coach to accomplish that feat, and is the only coach to win seven consecutive postseason games in a two-year period. No NFL head coach has won more game than Mike Shanahan's 139 victories since the start of the 1995 season. During his NFL career, Shanahan has been a part of teams that have played in nine conference championship games and six Super Bowls. In 28 seasons as a pro and college coach, Shanahan's teams have participated in postseason or bowl games 22 times. Under Shanahan's guidance, Denver has set and NFL record by posting the most victories in both a two-year (33, 1997-98) and three-year (46, 1996-98) period. In the last thirteen years (ten with Denver and three as offensive coordinator with the San Francisco 49ers), Shanahan's offenses have finished number one in the NFL four times, second twice, and third twice. Shanahan was an assistant with Denver (1984-87, 1989-1991) and San Francisco (1992-94). Returned to Denver as quarterbacks coach on October 16, 1989, after posting 8-12 record as the Los Angeles Raiders' head coach. Career record: 139-86.
Background: Shanahan coached at Oklahoma (1975-76), Northern Arizona (1977), Eastern Illinois (1978), Minnesota (1979), and Florida (1980-83).
Personal: Born in Oak Park, Illinois, on August 24, 1952. He was a wishbone quarterback-defensive back at Eastern Illinois. Mike and his wife, Peggy, have two children—Kyle and Krystal.

ASSISTANT COACHES

Joe Baker, linebackers; born June 29, 1969, Glen Ridge, N.J. Wide receiver Princeton 1987-1990. No pro playing experience. College coach: East Stroudsburg 1991, Samford 1993, Wisconsin 1999. Pro coach: Birmingham Fire (WLAF) 1992, Jacksonville Jaguars 1994-98, New Orleans Saints 2000-04, Green Bay Packers 2005, St. Louis Rams 2006, joined Broncos in 2007.
Jeremy Bates, wide receivers/quarterbacks; born August 27, 1976, Manhattan, Kan. Quarterback Tennessee 1995, Rick 1996-99. No pro playing experience. Pro coach: Tampa Bay Buccaneers 2002-04, New York Jets 2005, joined Broncos in 2006.
Jim Bates, asst. head coach; born May 31, 1946, Pontiac, Mich. Linebacker Tennessee 1964-67. No pro playing experience. College coach: Tennessee 1968, Southern Mississippi 1972, Villanova 1973-74, Kansas State 1975-76, West

Virginia 1977, Texas Tech 1978-1983, Tennessee 1989, Florida 1990. Pro coach: San Antonio Gunslingers (USFL) 1984-85 (head coach 1985), Arizona Outlaws (USFL) 1986, Detroit Drive (AFL) 1988, Cleveland Browns 1991-93, 1995, Atlanta Falcons 1994, Dallas Cowboys 1996-99, Miami Dolphins 2000-04 (interim head coach 2004), Green Bay Packers 2005, joined Broncos in 2007.
Ronnie Bradford, asst. defensive backs; born October 1, 1970, Minot, N.D. Defensive back Colorado 1989-1992. Pro defensive back Denver Broncos 1993-95, Arizona Cardinals 1996, Atlanta Falcons 1997-2001, Minnesota Vikings 2002. Pro coach: Joined Broncos in 2003.
Jacob Burney, defensive line; born January 24, 1959, Chattanooga, Tenn. Defensive tackle Tennessee-Chattanooga 1977-1980. No pro playing experience. College coach: New Mexico 1983-86, Tulsa 1987, Mississippi State 1988, Wisconsin 1989, UCLA 1990-92, Tennessee 1993. Pro coach: Cleveland Browns/Baltimore Ravens 1994-98, Carolina Panthers 1999-2001, joined Broncos in 2002.
Dwayne Chandler, asst. strength & conditioning; born March 11, 1973, Aberdeen, Miss. Fullback Oklahoma 1991-1995. No pro playing experience. College coach: Oklahoma 1999, Minnesota 2001-2006. Pro coach: Dallas Cowboys 2000, joined Broncos in 2007.
Rick Dennison, offensive coordinator/offensive line; born June 22, 1958, Kalispell, Mont. Tight end Colorado State 1976-79. Pro linebacker Denver Broncos 1982-1990. Pro coach: Joined Broncos in 1995.
Mike Heimerdinger, asst. head coach/quarterbacks; born October 13, 1952, DeKalb, Ill. Wide receiver Eastern Illinois 1970-1974. No pro playing experience. College coach: Florida 1980, Air Force 1981, North Texas State 1982, Florida 1983-87, Cal State-Fullerton 1988, Rice 1989-1993, Duke 1994. Pro coach: Denver Broncos 1995-99, Tennessee Titans 2000-04, New York Jets 2005, re-joined Broncos in 2006.
Charlie Jackson, defensive assistant; born November 4, 1976, Vienna, Ga. Defensive back Air Force Academy 1997-99. No pro playing experience. College coach: UCLA 2002-03, Air Force Academy 2004. Pro coach: Green Bay Packers 2005, joined Broncos in 2007.
Bill Johnson, defensive line; born June 23, 1955, Monroe, La. Defensive lineman Northwestern (La.) State 1976-79. No pro playing experience. College coach: Northwestern (La.) State 1980-81, McNeese State 1985-86, Miami 1987, Louisiana Tech 1988-89, Arkansas 1990-91, 2000, Texas A&M 1992-99. Pro coach: Atlanta Falcons 2001-06, joined Broncos in 2007.
Pat McPherson, tight ends; born April 15, 1969, Santa Clara, Calif. Linebacker Santa

Clara 1991-92. No pro playing experience. Pro coach: Joined Broncos in 1998.
Scott O'Brien, special teams coordinator; born June 25, 1957, Superior, Wis. Linebacker Wisconsin-Superior 1975-78. No pro playing experience. College coach: Wisconsin-Superior 1980-82, Nevada-Las Vegas 1983-85, Rice 1986, Pittsburgh 1987-1990. Pro coach: Cleveland Browns 1991-95, Baltimore Ravens 1996-98, Carolina Panthers 1999-2004, Miami Dolphins 2005-06, joined Broncos in 2007.
Jim Ryan, offensive assistant; born May 18, 1957, Bellmawr, N.J.. Linebacker William & Mary 1974-1978. Linebacker Denver Broncos 1979-1988. Pro coach: Joined Broncos in 2005.
Greg Saporta, asst. strength and conditioning; born February 2, 1957, New York, N.Y. Wide receiver Buffalo State 1977-79. No pro playing experience. College coach: Florida 1981-88, 1993-94, North Carolina 1989-1992. Pro coach: Joined Broncos in 1995.
Bob Slowik, defensive coordinator/defensive backs; born May 16, 1954, Pittsburgh. Defensive back Delaware 1973-76. No pro playing experience. College coach: Delaware 1977-78, Florida 1979-1982, Drake 1983, Rutgers 1984-89, East Carolina 1990-91. Pro coach: Dallas Cowboys 1992, Chicago Bears 1993-98, Cleveland Browns 1999, Green Bay Packers 2000-04, joined Broncos in 2005.
Ryan Slowik, special teams assistant; born Dec. 27, 1980, Chicago. Safety Wisconsin-Oshkosh 2002-03. No pro playing experience. College coach: Wisconsin-Oshkosh 2004. Pro coach: Joined Broncos in 2005.
Jimmy Spencer, special teams assistant; born March 29, 1969, Manning, S.C. Cornerback Florida 1988-1990. Pro cornerback Washington Redskins 1991, New Orleans Saints 1992-95, Cincinnati Bengals 1996-97, San Diego Chargers 1998-99, Denver Broncos 2000-current. Pro coach: Joined Broncos in 2003.
Bobby Turner, running backs; born May 6, 1949, East Chicago, Ind. Defensive back Indiana State 1968-1971. No pro playing experience. College coach: Indiana State 1975-1982, Fresno State 1983-88, Ohio State 1989-1990, Purdue 1991-94. Pro coach: Joined Broncos in 1995.
Rich Tuten, strength and conditioning; born December 30, 1953, Columbia, S.C. Nose guard Clemson 1976-78. No pro playing experience. College coach: Florida 1979-1988, 1993-94, North Carolina 1989-1992. Pro coach: Joined Broncos in 1995.
Steve Watson, associate head coach; born May 28, 1957, Baltimore. Wide receiver Temple 1975-78. Pro wide receiver Denver 1979-1987. Pro coach: Joined Broncos in 2001.

**American Football Conference
South Division**
Team Colors: Deep Steel Blue, Battle
Red, and Liberty White
Two Reliant Park
Houston, Texas 77054
Telephone: (832) 667-2000

2007 SCHEDULE
PRESEASON
Aug. 11	**Chicago**	7:00
Aug. 18	at Arizona	1:00
Aug. 25	**Dallas**	7:00
Aug. 30	at Tampa Bay	8:00

REGULAR SEASON
Sep. 9	**Kansas City**	12:00
Sep. 16	at Carolina	1:00
Sep. 23	**Indianapolis**	12:00
Sep. 30	at Atlanta	1:00
Oct. 7	**Miami**	12:00
Oct. 14	at Jacksonville	1:00
Oct. 21	**Tennessee**	12:00
Oct. 28	at San Diego	1:05
Nov. 4	at Oakland	1:15
Nov. 11	Open Date	
Nov. 18	**New Orleans**	12:00
Nov. 25	at Cleveland	1:00
Dec. 2	at Tennessee	12:00
Dec. 9	**Tampa Bay**	12:00
Dec. 13	**Denver** (Thu.)	7:15
Dec. 23	at Indianapolis	1:00
Dec. 30	**Jacksonville**	12:00

Stadium: Reliant Stadium
(opened in 2002)
• **Capacity:** 71,054
Houston, Texas 77054
Playing Surface: Grass
Training Camp: Methodist Training
Center

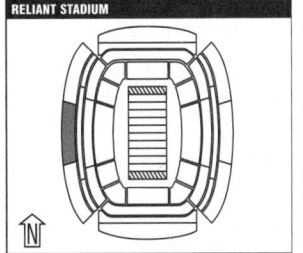

RELIANT STADIUM

CLUB OFFICIALS
Chairman and CEO: Robert C. McNair
Vice Chairman: Philip J. Burguieres
General Manager: Rick Smith
President: Jamey Rootes
Senior Vice President, Treasurer and
CFO: Scott Schwinger
Senior Vice President, General Counsel
and CAO: Suzie Thomas
Vice President and Controller:
Marilan Logan
Vice President, Ticketing and Event
Management: John Schriever
Vice President, Sales and Marketing:
John Vidalin
Vice President, Finance: Greg Watson
Vice President, Communications:
Tony Wyllie
Director of Football Administration:
Chris Olsen
Director of Football Operations:
Lloyd Richards
Director of Security: Ryan Reichert
Director of Player Development:
Sean Washington
Director of College Scouting:
Dale Strahm
Associate Director of Pro Scouting:
Bobby Grier, Miller McCalmon
Coordinator of College Scouting:
Mike Maccagnan
College Scouts: Larry Bryan,
Brian Hudspeth, Dave Sears
Head Athletic Trainer: Kevin Bastin
Coordinator of Rehabilitation: Tom Colt
Assistant Athletic Trainer: Jon Ishop
Director of Equipment Services:
Jay Brunetti
Assistant Director of Equipment Services:
Matt Grupp
Equipment Services Assistant:
Christian Snell
Director of Video Operations:
Ken Sparacino
Assistant Director of Video Operations:
Joe Malota
Video Operations Assistant: Robert Wells
Director of Media Relations:
Kevin Cooper
Director of Corporate Development:
Greg Grissom
Director of Information Technology:
Nick Ignatiev
Corporate Counsel: Greg Kondritz
Director Human Resources:
Glenda Morrison
Director of Media Products:
Nick Schenck
Director of Community Relations:
Regina Woolfolk
Risk Manager: Jan Kelly
Assistant Treasurer: Jon Southern

COACHING HISTORY
(24-56-0)
2002-05	Dom Capers	18-46-0
2006	Gary Kubiak	6-10-0

PAID ATTENDANCE
Home 547,875   Away 515,398
Total 1,063,273
Single-game home record,
70,758 (12/21/03)
Single-season home record,
555,421 (2004)

2007 DRAFT CHOICES
Round	Name	Pos.	College
1	Amobi Okoye	DT	Louisville
3	Jacoby Jones	WR	Lane
4	Fred Bennett	DB	South Carolina
5	Brandon Harrison	DB	Stanford
	Brandon Frye	T	Virginia Tech
6	Kasey Studdard	G	Texas
7	Zach Diles	LB	Kansas State

2006 TEAM RECORD
PRESEASON (3-1)

Date	Result	Opponent
8/12	W 24-14	Kansas City
8/19	W 27-20	at St. Louis
8/27	L 14-17	at Denver
8/31	W 16-13	Tampa Bay

REGULAR SEASON (6-10)

Date	Result	Opponent	Att.
9/10	L 10-24	Philadelphia	70,180
9/17	L 24-43	at Indianapolis	56,614
9/24	L 15-31	Washington	70,069
10/1	W 17-15	Miami	70,071
10/15	L 6-34	at Dallas	63,186
10/22	W 27-7	Jacksonville	70,035
10/29	L 22-28	at Tennessee	69,143
11/5	L 10-14	at N.Y. Giants	78,485
11/12	W 13-10	at Jacksonville	65,918
11/19	L 21-24	Buffalo	70,125
11/26	L 11-26	at N.Y. Jets	76,596
12/3	W 23-14	at Oakland	46,276
12/10	L 20-26	Tennessee (OT)	70,760
12/17	L 7-40	at New England	68,756
12/24	W 27-24	Indianapolis	70,132
12/31	W 14-6	Cleveland	70,097

(OT) Overtime

SCORE BY PERIODS

Texans	55	52	59	101	0	—	267
Opponents	72	103	86	99	6	—	366

2006 TEAM STATISTICS

	Texans	Opp.
Total First Downs	282	312
Rushing	106	115
Passing	156	174
Penalty	20	23
3rd Down: Made/Att	77/198	88/198
3rd Down Pct.	38.9	44.4
4th Down: Made/Att	9/13	5/11
4th Down Pct.	69.2	45.5
Possession Avg.	29:14	30:46
Total Net Yards	4465	5400
Avg. Per Game	279.1	337.5
Total Plays	955	979
Avg. Per Play	4.7	5.5
Net Yards Rushing	1687	1956
Avg. Per Game	105.4	122.3
Total Rushes	431	446
Net Yards Passing	2778	3444
Avg. Per Game	173.6	215.3
Sacked/Yards Lost	43/254	28/191
Gross Yards	3032	3635
Att./Completions	481/329	505/328
Completion Pct.	68.4	65.0
Had Intercepted	13	11
Punts/Average	76/41.6	65/45.4
Net Punting Avg.	76/36.7	65/37.6
Penalties/Yards	90/761	96/792
Fumbles/Ball Lost	28/12	16/11
Touchdowns	30	42
Rushing	13	16
Passing	14	22
Returns	3	4

2006 INDIVIDUAL STATISTICS

PASSING

	Att.	Comp.	Yds.	Pct.	TD	Int.	Tkld.	Rate
Carr	442	302	2,767	68.3	11	12	41/240	82.1
Rosenfels	39	27	265	69.2	3	1	1/5	103.0
Lundy	0	0	—	—	0	0	1/9	—
Texans	481	329	3,032	68.4	14	13	43/254	83.8
Opponents	505	328	3,635	65.0	22	11	28/191	91.6

SCORING

	TD R	TD P	TD Rt	PAT	FG	Saf	PTS
K. Brown	0	0	0	26/27	19/25	0	83
Dayne	5	0	0	0/0	0/0	0	32
Daniels	0	5	0	0/0	0/0	0	30
A. Johnson	0	5	0	0/0	0/0	0	30
Lundy	4	0	0	0/0	0/0	0	26
Bruener	0	2	0	0/0	0/0	0	12
Carr	2	0	0	0/0	0/0	0	12
Faggins	0	0	1	0/0	0/0	0	6
Gado	1	0	0	0/0	0/0	0	6
Leach	0	1	0	0/0	0/0	0	6
Maddox	0	0	1	0/0	0/0	0	6
Moulds	0	1	0	0/0	0/0	0	6
Robinson	0	0	1	0/0	0/0	0	6
Taylor	1	0	0	0/0	0/0	0	6
Texans	13	14	3	26/27	19/25	0	267
Opponents	16	22	4	39/40	25/29	0	366

2-Pt. Conversions: Dayne, Lundy, Texans 2-3, Opponents 0-1.

RUSHING

	No.	Yds	Avg	LG	TD
Dayne	151	612	4.1	19	5
Lundy	124	476	3.8	35	4
Gado	54	217	4.0	34	1
Carr	53	195	3.7	16	2
Taylor	28	123	4.4	17	1
Cook	3	18	6.0	14	0
A. Johnson	3	14	4.7	18	0
Morency	5	13	2.6	12	0
Moulds	1	6	6.0	6	0
Rosenfels	4	5	1.3	7	0
Shepherd	2	5	2.5	6	0
Walter	1	3	3.0	3	0
Simmons	1	0	0.0	0	0
Stanley	1	0	0.0	0	0
Texans	431	1,687	3.9	35	13
Opponents	446	1,956	4.4	39t	16

RECEIVING

	No.	Yds	Avg	LG	TD
A. Johnson	103	1,147	11.1	53	5
Moulds	57	557	9.8	29	1
Daniels	34	352	10.4	33t	5
Lundy	33	204	6.2	15	0
Cook	18	107	5.9	15	0
Walter	17	160	9.4	15	0
Gado	16	80	5.0	19	0
Dayne	14	77	5.5	13	0
Putzier	13	125	9.6	26	0
Bruener	9	62	6.9	25	2
Leach	6	61	10.2	19	1
Taylor	3	40	13.3	24	0
Shepherd	3	22	7.3	8	0
D. Anderson	1	27	27.0	27	0
Morency	1	6	6.0	6	0
Lewis	1	5	5.0	5	0
Texans	329	3032	9.2	53	14
Opponents	328	3635	11.1	83t	22

INTERCEPTIONS

	No.	Yds	Avg	LG	TD
Robinson	2	9	4.5	9t	1
Faggins	2	0	0.0	0	0
Weaver	1	21	21.0	21	0
McCleon	1	19	19.0	19	0
Ryans	1	16	16.0	16	0
Simmons	1	11	11.0	11	0
Earl	1	2	2.0	2	0
C. Brown	1	0	0.0	0	0
Greenwood	1	0	0.0	0	0
Texans	11	78	7.1	21	1
Opponents	13	174	13.4	41	0

PUNTING

	No.	Yds.	Avg.	In 20	LG
Stanley	76	3,161	41.6	15	62
Texans	76	3,161	41.6	15	62
Opponents	65	2,949	45.4	25	75

PUNT RETURNS

	Ret	FC	Yds	Avg	LG	TD
Wynn	12	9	139	11.6	58	0
Buchanan	8	2	79	9.9	45	0
Shepherd	3	2	24	8.0	14	0
Lewis	0	2	0	—	—	0
Texans	23	15	242	10.5	58	0
Opponents	36	24	275	7.6	53t	1

KICKOFF RETURNS

	No.	Yds	Avg	LG	TD
Wynn	30	670	22.3	38	0
Shepherd	17	395	23.2	42	0
Mathis	7	192	27.4	87	0
Buchanan	5	106	21.2	28	0
Lundy	4	67	16.8	23	0
D. Anderson	3	90	30.0	38	0
Lewis	1	27	27.0	27	0
Alexander	1	18	18.0	18	0
Tr. Johnson	1	17	17.0	17	0
Bruener	1	8	8.0	8	0
Cook	1	2	2.0	2	0
Wong	0	17	—	17	0
Texans	71	1,609	22.7	87	0
Opponents	52	1,215	23.4	93t	1

FIELD GOALS

	1-19	20-29	30-39	40-49	50+
K. Brown	1/1	4/4	3/5	11/13	0/2
Texans	1/1	4/4	3/5	11/13	0/2
Opponents	0/0	6/7	9/10	8/9	2/3

SACKS

	No.
Babin	5.0
M. Williams	4.5
Ryans	3.5
Earl, Kalu, Maddox	2.0
Orr	1.5
C. Brown, Dalton, Faggins	1.0
Greenwood, Payne, Peek, Weaver	1.0
Malone	0.5
Texans	28.0
Opponents	43.0

RECORD HOLDERS
INDIVIDUAL RECORDS—CAREER

Category	Name	Performance
Rushing (Yds.)	Domanick Williams, 2003-06	3,195
Passing (Yds.)	David Carr, 2002-06	13,391
Passing (TDs)	David Carr, 2002-06	59
Receiving (No.)	Andre Johnson, 2003-06	311
Receiving (Yds.)	Andre Johnson, 2003-06	3,953
Interceptions	Marcus Coleman, 2002-06	11
	Aaron Glenn, 2002-04	11
Punting (Avg.)	Chad Stanley, 2002-06	41.0
Punt Return (Avg.)	Avion Black, 2002	13.4
Kickoff Return (Avg.)	Jerome Mathis, 2005-06	28.4
Field Goals	Kris Brown, 2002-06	97
Touchdowns (Tot.)	Domanick Williams, 2003-06	28
Points	Kris Brown, 2002-06	422

INDIVIDUAL RECORDS—SINGLE SEASON

Category	Name	Performance
Rushing (Yds.)	Domanick Williams, 2004	1,188
Passing (Yds.)	David Carr, 2004	3,531
Passing (TDs)	David Carr, 2004	16
Receiving (No.)	Andre Johnson, 2006	103
Receiving (Yds.)	Andre Johnson, 2006	1,147
Interceptions	Marcus Coleman, 2003	7
Punting (Avg.)	Chad Stanley, 2006	41.6
Punt Return (Avg.)	Avion Black, 2002	13.4
Kickoff Return (Avg.)	Jerome Mathis, 2005	28.6
Field Goals	Kris Brown, 2005	26
Touchdowns (Tot.)	Domanick Williams, 2004	14
Points	Kris Brown, 2005	102

INDIVIDUAL RECORDS—SINGLE GAME

Category	Name	Performance
Rushing (Yds.)	Domanick Williams, 12-26-04	158
Passing (Yds.)	David Carr, 10-10-04	372
Passing (TDs)	David Carr, 10-10-04, 11-27-05, 9-17-06	3
	Sage Rosenfels, 10-29-06	3
Receiving (No.)	Andre Johnson, 10-10-04	12
	Andre Johnson, 11-27-05	12
Receiving (Yds.)	Andre Johnson, 10-10-04	170
Interceptions	Aaron Glenn, 12-8-02	2
	Marcus Coleman, 9-7-03	2
	Kenny Wright, 9-28-03	2
	Dunta Robinson, 10-3-04	2
Field Goals	Kris Brown, 9-7-03, 12-4-05	5
Touchdowns (Tot.)	Many times	2
	Last time by Ron Dayne, 12-24-06	
Points	Kris Brown, 9-7-03, 12-4-05	15

2007 VETERAN ROSTER

No.	Name	Pos.	Ht.	Wt.	Birthdate	NFL Exp.	College	Hometown	How Acq.	'05 Games/ Starts
19	Adams, Charlie	WR	6-2	210	10/23/79	4	Hofstra	Mechanicsburg, Pa.	FA-'06	0*
28	Alexander, Roc	CB	5-10	190	9/23/81	4	Washington	Colorado Springs, Co.	W(Den)-'06	1/0
50	Anderson, Charlie	LB	6-4	245	12/8/81	4	Mississippi	Jackson, Miss.	D6c-'04	13/0
89	Anderson, David	WR	5-10	197	7/28/83	2	Colorado State	Thousand Oaks, Calif.	D7-'06	9/0
93	Babin, Jason	DE	6-2	267	5/24/80	4	Western Michigan	Kalamazoo. Mich.	D1b-'04	15/3
51	Barber, Shawn	LB	6-2	240	1/14/75	10	Richmond	Richmond, Va.	UFA(Phil)-'07	13/1*
68#	Bedell, Brad	T	6-4	307	2/12/77	6	Colorado	Arcadia, Calif.	FA-'06	9/0
72	Black, Jordan	T	6-5	310	1/28/80	4	Notre Dame	Dallas, Texas	UFA(KC)-'07	16/15*
24	Brown, C.C.	S	6-0	204	1/27/83	3	Louisiana-Lafayette	Greenwood, Miss.	D6-'05	15/15
3	Brown, Kris	PK	5-11	208	12/23/76	9	Nebraska	Southlake, Texas	RFA(Pitt)-'02	16/0
87	Bruener, Mark	TE	6-4	256	9/16/72	13	Washington	Olympia, Wash.	UFA(Pitt)-'04	15/4
79	Bulman, Tim	DT	6-4	292	10/31/82	3	Boston College	Dorchester, Mass.	FA-'06	0*
55	Clark, Danny	LB	6-2	245	5/9/77	8	Illinois	Blue Island, Ill.	UFA(NO)-'07	16/0*
60	Cochran, Earl	DE	6-5	272	4/19/81	3	Alabama State	Bessemer, Ala.	FA-'06	1/0
43	Cook, Jameel	FB	5-10	237	2/8/79	6	Illinois	Miami, Fla.	UFA(TB)-'06	11/6
75#	Dalton, Lional	DT	6-1	315	2/21/75	10	Eastern Michigan	Detroit, Mich.	FA-'06	10/2
81	Daniels, Owen	TE	6-3	246	11/9/82	2	Wisconsin	Naperville, Ill.	D4-'06	14/12
11	Davis, Andre'	WR	6-1	195	6/12/79	6	Virginia Tech	Niskayuna, N.Y.	UFA(Buff)-'07	16/1*
36	Dayne, Ron	RB	5-10	245	3/14/78	8	Wisconsin	Berlin, N.J.	FA-'06	11/6
85	Dreessen, Joel	TE	6-4	260	7/26/82	3	Colorado State	Ida Grove, Ia.	FA-'07	0*
26	Earl, Glenn	S	6-1	213	6/10/81	4	Notre Dame	Naperville, Ill.	D4-'04	15/15
38	Faggins, Demarcus	CB	5-10	179	6/13/79	6	Kansas State	Irving, Texas	D6a-'02	11/10
58	Flanagan, Mike	C	6-5	303	11/10/73	12	UCLA	Sacramento, Calif.	UFA(GB)-'06	9/9
21	Fletcher, Jamar	CB	5-10	186	8/28/79	7	Wisconsin	St. Louis, Mo.	UFA(Det)-'07	13/2*
35	Gado, Samkon	RB	5-10	226	11/13/82	3	Liberty	Columbia, S.C.	T(GB)-'06	9/1*
30	Green, Ahman	RB	6-0	218	2/16/77	10	Nebraska	Omaha, Neb.	UFA(GB)-'07	14/14*
56	Greenwood, Morlon	LB	6-0	234	7/17/78	7	Syracuse	Freeport, N.Y.	UFA(Mia)-'05	16/16
57	Hodgdon, Drew	C	6-3	291	11/15/81	3	Arizona State	Palo Alto, Calif.	D5-'05	9/5
29	Horton, Jason	CB	6-0	190	2/16/80	4	North Carolina A&T	Ahoskie, N.C.	FA-'07	0*
34	Hutchins, Von	CB	5-10	180	2/14/81	4	Mississippi	Natchez, Miss.	FA-'06	3/0
62	Jackson, Scott	T	6-4	302	1/19/79	3	Brigham Young	Rancho Palos Verdes, Calif.	FA-'06	0*
80	Johnson, Andre	WR	6-3	222	7/11/81	5	Miami	Miami, Fla.	D1-'03	16/16
96	Johnson, Thomas	DT	6-2	302	6/24/81	3	Middle Tennessee State	Hamilton, Tenn.	FA-'06	10/3
99	Johnson, Travis	DT	6-3	315	4/26/82	3	Florida State	Sherman Oaks, Calif.	D1-'05	9/8
94	Kalu, N.D.	DE	6-3	265	8/3/75	11	Rice	San Antonio, Texas	UFA(Phil)-'06	15/3
78	Killings, Cedric	DT	6-3	310	12/14/77	5	Carson-Newman	Miami, Fla.	FA-'06	4/0
44	Leach, Vonta	FB	6-0	250	11/6/81	4	East Carolina	Rowland, N.C.	FA-'06	12/4
33	Lundy, Wali	RB	5-10	211	9/8/83	2	Virginia	Delran, N.J.	D6-'06	14/8
95	Maddox, Anthony	DT	6-1	295	11/22/78	4	Delta State	Albany, Ga.	FA-'06	12/9
97	Malone, Alfred	DT	6-5	308	2/21/82	2	Troy	Frisco City, Ala.	FA-'05	2/0
13	Mathis, Jerome	WR	5-11	184	7/26/83	3	Hampton	Petersburg, Va.	D4-'05	2/0
20	McCleon, Dexter	CB	5-10	195	10/9/73	11	Clemson	Meridian, Miss.	FA-'06	16/5
28+	McKenzie, Chris	CB	5-8	177	3/17/82	4	Arizona State	Queens, N.Y.	FA-'05	0*
76	McKinney, Steve	G	6-4	305	10/15/75	10	Texas A&M	Friendswood, Texas	UFA(Ind)-'02	16/6
53	Orr, Shantee	LB	6-0	246	5/28/81	5	Michigan	Detroit, Mich.	FA-'03	16/11
48	Pittman, Bryan	LS	6-3	282	1/20/77	5	Washington	Auburn, Wash.	FA-'03	16/0
69	Pitts, Chester	G	6-4	322	6/26/79	6	San Diego State	Inglewood, Calif.	D2-'02	16/16
51#	Polk, DaShon	LB	6-2	245	3/13/77	8	Arizona	Pacoima, Calif.	UFA(Buff)-'04	10/0
88	Putzier, Jeb	TE	6-4	251	1/20/79	6	Boise State	Eagle, Idaho	UFA(Den)-'06	14/5
96#	Rainer, Wali	LB	6-2	237	4/19/77	9	Virginia	Charlotte, N.C.	UFA(Det)-'06	0*
23	Robinson, Dunta	CB	5-10	180	4/11/82	4	South Carolina	Athens, Ga.	D1a-'04	16/16
18	Rosenfels, Sage	QB	6-2	224	3/6/78	7	Iowa State	Maquoketa, Ia.	UFA(Mia)-'06	4/0
59	Ryans, DeMeco	LB	6-1	239	7/28/84	2	Alabama	Bessemer, Ala.	D2-'06	16/16
74	Salaam, Ephraim	T	6-7	302	6/19/76	10	San Diego State	Sacramento, Calif.	UFA(Jax)-'06	15/14
8 t-	Schaub, Matt	QB	6-5	237	6/25/81	4	Virginia	West Chester, Pa.	T(Atl)-'07	16/0*
22	Simmons, Jason	FS	5-9	204	3/30/76	10	Arizona State	Lawndale, Calif.	UFA(Pitt)-'02	16/2
77	Spencer, Charles	T	6-4	337	3/17/82	2	Pittsburgh	Poughkeepsie, N.Y.	D3a-'06	2/2
7	Stanley, Chad	P	6-3	209	1/29/76	8	Stephen F. Austin	Ore City, Texas	FA-'02	16/0
82	Steele, Ben	TE	6-5	245	5/27/78	4	Mesa College	Denver, Colo.	FA-'06	0*
10	Van Pelt, Bradlee	QB	6-2	220	7/3/80	2	Colorado State	Santa Barbara, Calif.	FA-'06	0*
83	Walter, Kevin	WR	6-3	215	8/4/81	5	Eastern Michigan	Vernon Hills, Ill.	RFA(Cin)-'06	16/2
70	Weary, Fred	G	6-4	307	9/30/77	6	Tennessee	Montgomery, Ala.	D3a-'02	15/12
98	Weaver, Anthony	DE	6-3	286	7/28/80	6	Notre Dame	Saratoga, N.Y.	UFA(Balt)-'06	15/15
63	White, Chris	C	6-2	293	2/28/83	3	Southern Mississippi	Winona, Miss.	FA-'06	0*
86	Williams, Harry	WR	6-2	187	8/10/82	2	Tuskegee	Birmingham, Ala.	FA-'06	0*
90	Williams, Mario	DE	6-6	293	1/31/85	2	North Carolina State	Richlands, N.C.	D1-'06	16/16

73	Winston, Eric	T	6-5	307	11/17/83	2	Miami	Midland, Texas	D3b-'06	12/7
52	Wong, Kailee	LB	6-2	244	5/23/76	9	Stanford	Eugene, Ore.	UFA(Minn)-'02	10/0
25	Wynn, Dexter	CB	5-9	177	2/25/81	4	Colorado State	Colorado Springs, Colo.	FA-'06	15/0
92	Zgonina, Jeff	DT	6-2	290	5/24/70	15	Purdue	Chicago, Ill.	UFA(Mia)-'07	14/2*

* Adams inactive for 2 games in '06; Barber played 13 games with Philadelphia in '06; Black played 16 games with Kansas City; Bulman inactive for 2 games; Clark played 16 games with New Orleans; Davis played 16 games with Buffalo; Dreessen last active with N.Y. Jets in '05; Fletcher played 13 games with Detroit; Gado played 1 game with Green Bay and 8 games with Houston; Green played 14 games with Green Bay; Horton last active with Green Bay in '05; Jackson inactive for 10 games; McKenzie missed '06 season because of injury; Rainer missed '06 season because of injury; Schaub played 16 games with Atlanta; Steele missed '06 season because of injury; Van Pelt inactive for 5 games; White last active with Green Bay in '05; H. Williams last active with N.Y. Jets in '05; Zgonina played 14 games with Miami.

\+ Exclusive rights player; subject to developments.

\# Unrestricted free agent; subject to developments.

t- Texans traded for Schaub (Atl).

Players lost through free agency (4): LB Troy Evans (NO; 16 games in '06), DE Antwan Peek (Cle; 11), CB Lewis Sanders (Atl; 9), S Michael Stone (NYG; 2).

Also played with Texans in '06—CB Phillip Buchanon (4 games), QB David Carr (16), CB Kevin Garrett (1), CB Derrick Johnson (3), WR Derrick Lewis (5), LB Roy Manning (1), RB Vernand Morency (1), WR Eric Moulds (16), DT Seth Payne (5), S Guss Scott (5), WR Edell Shepherd (7), T Zach Wiegert (9).

2007 FIRST-YEAR ROSTER

Name	Pos.	Ht.	Wt.	Birthdate	College	Hometown	How Acq.
Abbate, Jon	LB	5-11	245	6/18/85	Wake Forest	Powder Springs, Ga.	FA
Anderson, Cory	FB	6-3	255	9/10/83	Tennessee	Knoxville, Tenn.	FA
Bennett, Fred	CB	6-1	199	12/31/83	South Carolina	Manning, S.C.	D4
Bray, Trent (1)	LB	6-0	227	9/28/82	Oregon State	Pullman, Wash.	FA
Brisiel, Mike (1)	G	6-5	310	3/14/83	Colorado State	Fayetteville, Ark.	FA-'06
Degrate, Victor	DE	6-3	250	2/8/85	Oklahoma State	DeSoto, Texas	FA
Diles, Zac	LB	6-2	230	6/11/85	Kansas State	Tulare, Calif.	D7
Frye, Brandon	T	6-4	300	1/23/83	Virginia Tech	Myrtle Beach, S.C.	D5b
Harrison, Brandon	S	6-2	215	4/29/84	Stanford	Baton Rouge, La.	D5a
Herrion, Atlas (1)	G	6-4	305	12/3/80	Alabama	Daphne, Ala.	FA-'06
Jones, Jacoby	WR	6-2	210	7/11/84	Lane College	New Orleans, La.	D3
Jones, Onrea	WR	6-2	203	12/22/83	Hampton	Williamsburg, Va.	FA
Lucas, Enoka	C	6-4	299	4/29/84	Oregon	Honolulu, Hawaii	FA
Mitchell, Brandon	S	6-3	205	10/26/83	Ohio State	Atlanta, Ga.	FA
Okoye, Amobi	DT	6-2	302	6/10/87	Louisville	Huntsville, Ala.	D1
Porter, Quinton (1)	QB	6-5	228	12/28/82	Boston College	Portland, Maine	FA-'06
Richardson, Terry	WR	6-1	188	12/12/84	Arizona State	Corona, Calif.	FA
Roberson, Derrick	CB	5-10	175	3/12/85	Rutgers	Oakland Park, Fla.	FA
Robinson, DelJuan	DE	6-3	296	7/1/84	Mississippi State	Hernando, Miss.	FA
Smith-Anderson, Luke	TE	6-5	253	4/25/83	Idaho	Couer d'Alene, Idaho	FA
Studdard, Kasey	G	6-3	310	7/1/84	Texas	Lone Tree, Colo.	D6
Taylor, Chris (1)	RB	6-0	224	11/7/83	Indiana	Memphis, Tenn.	FA-'06
Tupola, Tavo	T	6-4	311	12/23/80	Utah	Kahuku, Hawaii	FA
Walker, Darius	RB	5-11	205	10/21/85	Notre Dame	Buford, Ga.	FA
Walker, John (1)	CB	6-1	204	4/25/83	Southern California	North Hills, Calif.	FA-'06
Wilbur, Eric	P	6-2	200	12/12/84	Florida	Orlando, Fla.	FA
Zabransky, Jared	QB	6-2	203	12/4/83	Boise State	Hermiston, Ore.	FA

The term NFL Rookie is defined as a player who is in his first season of professional football and has not been on the roster of another professional football team for any regular-season or postseason games. A Rookie is designated by an "R" on NFL rosters. Players who have been active in another professional football league or players who have NFL experience, including either preseason training camp or being on an Active List or Inactive List, or on Reserve/Injured or Reserve/Physically Unable to Perform for fewer than six regular-season games, are termed NFL First-Year Players. An NFL First-Year Player is designated by a "1" on NFL rosters. Thereafter, a player is credited with an additional year of experience for each season in which he accumulates six games on the Active List or Inactive List, or on Reserve/Injured or Reserve/Physically Unable to Perform.

Log on to www.houstontexans.com for an up-to-date roster.

COACHING STAFF

Head Coach,
Gary Kubiak

Pro Career: Gary Kubiak was introduced as the second head coach in Houston Texans history on January 26, 2006. Kubiak returned to Houston after spending 20 of the previous 23 years in the Denver area. In his first season, Kubiak guided the Texans to a 6-10 record, tripling the team's win total from 2005, including the club's first-ever win over Indianapolis. The Texans also posted club records for conference victories (6) and home victories (4). From 1995-2005, Kubiak served as Denver's offensive coordinator, coaching John Elway and Terrell Davis and helping guide the Broncos to back-to-back Super Bowl titles (XXXII and XXXIII) and three AFC West Division titles. In Kubiak's 11 years in Denver, the Broncos had 28 Pro Bowl players on the offensive side of the ball. Kubiak began his coaching career as the running backs coach at Texas A&M (1992-93). Kubiak started his NFL coaching career with the San Francisco 49ers as the quarterbacks coach. In his lone season in San Francisco (1994), he guided Hall of Fame quarterback Steve Young to league MVP honors as the 49ers won Super Bowl XXIX. Kubiak is a veteran of six Super Bowls as a player and three as a coach. Career record: 6-10.

Background: Kubiak starred at quarterback for Texas A&M from 1979-1982, earning all-Southwest Conference honors as a senior. He played for the Broncos from 1983-1991 as the backup to Elway. Kubiak played in 119 career games, tossed 14 touchdowns, and was a part of three teams that reached the Super Bowl.

Personal: Born August 15, 1961 in Houston. He and his wife, Rhonda, have three sons—Klint, Klay, and Klein.

ASSISTANT COACHES

Martin Bayless, asst. defensive backs; born October 11, 1962, Dayton, Ohio. Defensive back Bowling Green 1981-83. Pro defensive back St. Louis Cardinals 1984, Buffalo Bills 1984-86, San Diego Chargers 1987-1991, Kansas City Chiefs 1992-93, 1995-96, Washington Redskins 1994. College coach: North Carolina 2001. Pro coach: Amsterdam Admirals (NFLEL) 2002-03, Carolina Panthers 2003, Oakland Raiders 2004-05, joined Texans in 2006.

Tim Bender, offensive assistant; born December 8, 1980, Pittsburgh, Pa. Attended Clarion, California Univ. (Penn.). No college or pro playing experience. Pro coach: Joined Texans in 2006.

John Benton, offensive line; born December 13, 1963, Los Angeles. Offensive lineman Colorado State 1986-1990. No pro playing experience. College coach: California University (Pa.) 1990-94, Colorado State 1996-2003. Pro coach: St. Louis Rams 2004-05, joined Texans in 2006.

Frank Bush, Sr., defensive assistant; born January 10, 1963, Athens, Ga. Linebacker North Carolina State 1981-84. Pro linebacker Houston Oilers 1985-86. Pro coach: Houston Oilers 1987-1991 (scout) 1992-94, Denver Broncos 1995-2003, Arizona Cardinals 2004-06, joined Texans in 2007.

Perry Carter, defensive assistant; born August 15, 1971, McComb, Miss. Defensive back Southern Mississippi 1989-1993. Pro defensive back Arizona Cardinals 1994, Kansas City Chiefs 1995, Oakland Raiders 1996-98, Edmonton Eskimos (CFL) 2000-01, Montreal Alouettes (CFL) 2002, British Columbia Lions (CFL) 2003-04. College coach: Texas A&M-Commerce 2004. Pro coach: Hamburg Sea Devils (NFLEL) 2006, joined Texans in 2006.

Jethro Franklin, defensive line; born October 25, 1965, St. Lazaire, France. Defensive lineman San Jose (Calif.) Community College 1984-85, Fresno State 1986-87. Pro defensive lineman Houston Oilers 1988-1990. College coach: Fresno State 1991-98, UCLA 1999, Southern California 2005. Pro coach: Green Bay Packers 2000-04, Tampa Bay Buccaneers 2006, joined Texans in 2007.

Chick Harris, running backs; born September 21, 1945, Durham, N.C. Running back Northern Arizona 1966-69. No pro playing experience. College coach: Colorado State 1970-71, Long Beach State 1972-73, Washington 1975-1980. Pro coach: Detroit Wheels (WFL) 1974, Buffalo Bills 1981-82, Seattle Seahawks 1983-1991, Los Angeles Rams 1992-94, Carolina Panthers 1995-2001, joined Texans in 2002.

Richard Hightower, defensive assistant; born September 15, 1980, Houston. Wide receiver/defensive back Texas 1998-2002. No pro playing experience. Pro coach: Joined Texans in 2006.

Jon Hoke, defensive backs; born January 24, 1957, Kettering, Ohio. Defensive back Ball State 1976-1979. Pro defensive back Chicago Bears 1980. College coach: Bowling Green 1983-86, San Diego State 1987-88, Kent State 1989-1993, Missouri 1994-98, Florida 1999-2001. Pro coach: Joined Texans in 2002.

Johnny Holland, linebackers; born March 11, 1965, Belleville, Texas. Linebacker Texas A&M 1983-86. Pro linebacker Green Bay Packers 1987-1993. Pro coach: Green Bay Packers 1995-99, Seattle Seahawks 2000-02, Detroit Lions 2003-05, joined Texans in 2006.

Larry Kirksey, wide receivers; born January 6, 1951, Harlan, Ky. Wide receiver Eastern Kentucky 1970-73. No pro playing experience. College coach: Miami (Ohio) 1974-76, Kentucky 1977-1981, Kansas 1982, Kentucky State 1983 (head coach), Florida 1984-88, Pittsburgh

1989, Alabama 1990-93, Texas A&M 2000, Middle Tennessee State 2006. Pro coach: San Francisco 49ers 1994-99, Detroit Lions 2001-02, Jacksonville Jaguars 2003, Denver Broncos 2004, joined Texans in 2007.

Joe Marciano, special teams coordinator; born February 10, 1954, Dunmore, Pa. Quarterback Temple 1972-75. No pro playing experience. College coach: East Stroudsburg State 1977, Rhode Island 1978-79, Villanova 1980, Penn State 1981, Temple 1982. Pro coach: Philadelphia/Baltimore Stars (USFL) 1983-85, New Orleans Saints 1986-1995, Tampa Bay Buccaneers 1996-2001, joined Texans in 2002.

Mike McDaniel, offensive quality control; born March 6, 1983, Greeley, Colo. Wide receiver Yale 2001-04. No pro playing experience. Pro coach: Joined Texans in 2006.

Brian Pariani, tight ends; born July 2, 1965, San Francisco. No college or pro playing experience. College coach: UCLA 1989, Syracuse 2005. Pro coach: San Francisco 49ers 1991-94, Denver Broncos 1994-2004, joined Texans in 2006.

Frank Pollack, asst. offensive line; born November 5, 1967, Camp Springs, Md. Offensive lineman Northern Arizona 1985-1989. Pro offensive lineman San Francisco 49ers 1990-97. College coach: Northern Arizona 2005-06. Pro coach: Joined Texans in 2007.

Robert Saleh, defensive quality control; born January 31, 1979, Dearborn, Mich. Tight end Northern Michigan 1997-2000. No pro playing experience. College coach: Michigan State 2002-03, Central Michigan 2004. Pro coach: Joined Texans in 2005.

Kyle Shanahan, quarterbacks; born December 14, 1979, Minneapolis. Wide receiver Duke 1998-99, Texas 2000-02. No pro playing experience. College coach: UCLA 2003. Pro coach: Tampa Bay Buccaneers 2004-05, joined Texans in 2006.

Mike Sherman, asst. head coach/offensive coordinator; born December 19, 1954, Norwood, Mass. Guard/tackle/linebacker Central Connecticut State 1974, 1976-77. No pro playing experience. College coach: Pittsburgh 1981-82, Tulane 1983-84, Holy Cross 1985-88, Texas A&M 1989-1993, 1995-96, UCLA 1994. Pro coach: Green Bay 1995-96, 2000-05 (head coach 2000-05), joined Texans in 2006.

Richard Smith, defensive coordinator; born October 17, 1955, Los Angeles. Offensive lineman Rio Hondo (Calif.) J.C. 1975-76, Fresno State 1977-78. No pro playing experience. College coach: Rio Hondo (Calif.) J.C. 1979-1980, Cal State-Fullerton 1981-83, California 1984-86, Arizona 1987. Pro coach: Houston Oilers 1988-1992, Denver Broncos 1993-96, San Francisco 49ers 1997-2002, Detroit Lions 2003-04, Miami Dolphins 2005, joined Texans in 2006.

**American Football Conference
South Division**
Team Colors: Royal Blue and White
P.O. Box 535000
Indianapolis, Indiana 46253
Telephone: (317) 297-2658

2007 SCHEDULE
PRESEASON
Aug. 9	at Dallas	7:00
Aug. 20	Chicago	8:00
Aug. 25	Detroit	7:00
Aug. 31	at Cincinnati	7:30

REGULAR SEASON
Sep. 6	New Orleans (Thu.)	8:30
Sep. 16	at Tennessee	12:00
Sep. 23	at Houston	12:00
Sep. 30	Denver	4:15
Oct. 7	Tampa Bay	4:05
Oct. 14	Open Date	
Oct. 22	at Jacksonville (Mon.)	8:30
Oct. 28	at Carolina	1:00
Nov. 4	New England	4:15
Nov. 11	at San Diego	5:15
Nov. 18	Kansas City	1:00
Nov. 22	at Atlanta (Thu.)	8:15
Dec. 2	Jacksonville	1:00
Dec. 9	at Baltimore	*8:15
Dec. 16	at Oakland	1:05
Dec. 23	Houston	1:00
Dec. 30	Tennessee	1:00

* Sunday night games in Weeks 11-17 subject to change

Stadium: RCA Dome (opened in 1983)
 • **Capacity:** 55,531
  100 South Capitol Avenue
  Indianapolis, Indiana 46225
Playing Surface: FieldTurf
Training Camp: Rose-Hulman Institute
  5500 Wabash Avenue
  Terre Haute, IN 47803

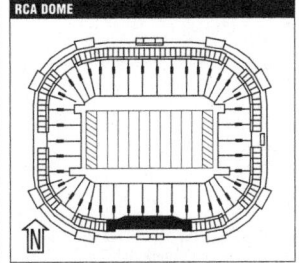

RCA DOME

CLUB OFFICIALS
Owner and CEO: James Irsay
President: Bill Polian
Head Coach: Tony Dungy
Senior Executive Vice President:
 Pete Ward
Executive Vice President: Bob Terpening
Senior Vice President of Sales and
 Marketing: Tom Zupancic
Vice President of Football Operations:
 Chris Polian
Vice President-Finance: Kurt Humphrey
Vice President-Ticket Operations/Guest
 Relations: Larry Hall
Vice President-Public Relations:
 Craig Kelley
Vice President of Sponsorship Sales:
 Jay Souers
Vice President of Premium Seating and
 Ticket Sales: Greg Hylton
Director of Football Administration:
 Steve Champlin
Director of Pro Player Personnel:
 Clyde Powers
Executive Director of Administration:
 Bill Brooks
Executive Director of Community
 Relations: Nicole Duncan
Equipment Manager: Jon Scott
Video Director: Marty Heckscher
Head Trainer: Hunter Smith
Assistant Director of Public Relations:
 Vernon Cheek
Assistant Equipment Managers:
 Mike Mays, Sean Sullivan,
 Brian Seabrooks
Head Athletic Trainer: Hunter Smith
Associate Head Athletic Trainer:
 Dave Hammer
Assistant Trainers: Dave Walston,
 Bryant Baugh
Assistant Video Director: John Starliper
Purchasing Administrator: Dave Filar

COACHING HISTORY
Baltimore 1953-1983
(419-397-7)
Records include postseason games
1953	Keith Molesworth	3-9-0
1954-1962	Weeb Ewbank	61-52-1
1963-69	Don Shula	73-26-4
1970-72	Don McCafferty*	26-11-1
1972	John Sandusky	4-5-0
1973-74	Howard Schnellenberger**	4-13-0
1974	Joe Thomas	2-9-0
1975-79	Ted Marchibroda	41-36-0
1980-81	Mike McCormack	9-23-0
1982-84	Frank Kush***	11-28-1
1984	Hal Hunter	0-1-0
1985-86	Rod Dowhower****	5-24-0
1986-1991	Ron Meyer#	36-36-0
1991	Rick Venturi	1-10-0
1992-95	Ted Marchibroda	32-35-0
1996-97	Lindy Infante	12-21-0
1998-2001	Jim Mora	32-34-0
2002-06	Tony Dungy	67-24-0

*Released after five games in 1972
**Released after three games in 1974
***Resigned after 15 games in 1984
****Released after 13 games in 1986
#Released after five games in 1991

PAID ATTENDANCE
Home 443,322   Away 563,087
Total 1,006,409
Single-game home record,
 61,139 (10/20/97)
Single-season home record, 481,305
 (1984)

2007 DRAFT CHOICES
Round	Name	Pos.	College
1	Anthony Gonzalez	WR	Ohio State
2	Tony Ugoh	T	Arkansas
3	Daymeion Hughes	DB	California
	Quinn Pitcock	DT	Ohio State
4	Brannon Condren	DB	Troy
	Clint Session	LB	Pittsburgh
5	Roy Hall	WR	Ohio State
	Michael Coe	DB	Alabama State
7	Keyunta Dawson	DE	Texas Tech

INDIANAPOLIS COLTS

2006 TEAM RECORD

PRESEASON (1-3)

Date	Result	Opponent
8/10	L 17-19	at St. Louis
8/20	L 17-30	Seattle
8/26	W 27-14	at New Orleans
9/1	L 3-20	Cincinnati

REGULAR SEASON (12-4)

Date	Result	Opponent	Att.
9/10	W 26-21	at N.Y. Giants	78,622
9/17	W 43-24	Houston	56,614
9/24	W 21-14	Jacksonville	57,041
10/1	W 31-28	at N.Y. Jets	77,190
10/8	W 14-13	Tennessee	57,021
10/22	W 36-22	Washington	57,274
10/29	W 34-31	at Denver	76,767
11/5	W 27-20	at New England	68,756
11/12	W 17-16	Buffalo	57,306
11/19	L 14-21	at Dallas	63,706
11/26	W 45-21	Philadelphia	57,296
12/3	L 17-20	at Tennessee	69,143
12/10	L 17-44	at Jacksonville	67,164
12/18	W 34-16	Cincinnati	57,292
12/24	L 24-27	at Houston	70,132
12/31	W 27-22	Miami	57,310

POSTSEASON (4-0)

1/6	W 23-8	Kansas City	57,215
1/13	W 15-6	at Baltimore	71,162
1/21	W 38-34	New England	57,433
2/4	W 29-17	vs. Chicago, South Florida	74,512

SCORE BY PERIODS

Colts	68	138	106	115	0	— 427
Opponents	44	127	59	130	0	— 360

2006 TEAM STATISTICS

	Colts	Opp.
Total First Downs	376	325
Rushing	112	150
Passing	241	150
Penalty	23	25
3rd Down: Made/Att	105/187	90/191
3rd Down Pct.	56.1	47.1
4th Down: Made/Att	0/4	11/14
4th Down Pct.	0.0	78.6
Possession Avg.	29:32	30:28
Total Net Yards	6070	5316
Avg. Per Game	379.4	332.3
Total Plays	1011	959
Avg. Per Play	6.0	5.5
Net Yards Rushing	1762	2768
Avg. Per Game	110.1	173.0
Total Rushes	439	519
Net Yards Passing	4308	2548
Avg. Per Game	269.3	159.3
Sacked/Yards Lost	15/89	25/157
Gross Yards	4397	2705
Att./Completions	557/362	415/266
Completion Pct.	65.0	64.1
Had Intercepted	9	15
Punts/Average	48/43.4	47/43.3
Net Punting Avg.	48/34.5	47/36.8
Penalties/Yards	86/718	86/667
Fumbles/Ball Lost	13/10	28/11
Touchdowns	50	41
Rushing	17	20
Passing	31	16
Returns	2	5

2006 INDIVIDUAL STATISTICS

PASSING	Att.	Comp.	Yds.	Pct.	TD	Int.	Tkld.	Rate
Manning	557	362	4,397	65.0	31	9	14/86	101.0
Addai	0	0	—	—	0	0	1/3	—
Colts	557	362	4,397	65.0	31	9	15/89	101.0
Opponents	415	266	2,705	64.1	16	15	25/157	80.4

SCORING	TD R	TD P	TD Rt	PAT	FG	Saf	PTS
Vinatieri	0	0	0	38/38	25/28	0	113
Harrison	0	12	0	0/0	0/0	0	72
Wayne	0	9	0	0/0	0/0	0	56
Addai	7	1	0	0/0	0/0	0	48
Rhodes	5	0	0	0/0	0/0	0	30
Clark	0	4	0	0/0	0/0	0	24
Manning	4	0	0	0/0	0/0	0	24
Fletcher	0	2	0	0/0	0/0	0	12
Gramatica	0	0	0	9/9	1/1	0	12
Carthon	1	0	0	0/0	0/0	0	6
Hayden	0	0	1	0/0	0/0	0	6
Klecko	0	1	0	0/0	0/0	0	6
Moorehead	0	1	0	0/0	0/0	0	6
Stokley	0	1	0	0/0	0/0	0	6
Wilkins	0	0	1	0/0	0/0	0	6
Smith	0	0	0	0/1	0/0	0	0
Colts	17	31	2	47/48	26/29	0	427
Opponents	20	16	5	40/40	24/35	0	360

2-Pt. Conversions: Wayne, Colts 1-2, Opponents 1-1.

RUSHING	No.	Yds	Avg	LG	TD
Addai	226	1081	4.8	41	7
Rhodes	187	641	3.4	17	5
Manning	23	36	1.6	12	4
Carthon	3	4	1.3	3t	1
Colts	439	1762	4.0	41	17
Opponents	519	2768	5.3	76	20

RECEIVING	No.	Yds	Avg	LG	TD
Harrison	95	1366	14.4	68t	12
Wayne	86	1310	15.2	51t	9
Addai	40	325	8.1	21t	1
Utecht	37	377	10.2	26	0
Rhodes	36	251	7.0	27	0
Clark	30	367	12.2	40	4
Fletcher	18	202	11.2	26	2
Stokley	8	85	10.6	23	1
Moorehead	8	82	10.3	36	1
Proehl	3	30	10.0	13	0
Klecko	1	2	2.0	2t	1
Colts	362	4397	12.1	68t	31
Opponents	266	2705	10.2	46	16

INTERCEPTIONS	No.	Yds	Avg	LG	TD
Harper	3	18	6.0	19	0
June	3	14	4.7	8	0
Doss	2	47	23.5	31	0
David	2	16	8.0	16	0
Bethea	1	38	38.0	38	0
Jackson	1	24	24.0	24	0
Boiman	1	0	0.0	0	0
Giordano	1	0	0.0	0	0
Sanders	1	0	0.0	0	0
Colts	15	157	10.5	38	0
Opponents	9	136	15.1	39t	1

PUNTING	No.	Yds.	Avg.	In 20	LG
Smith	47	2085	44.4	14	61
Colts	48	2085	43.4	14	61
Opponents	47	2036	43.3	17	63

PUNT RETURNS	Ret	FC	Yds	Avg	LG	TD
Wilkins	21	13	193	9.2	82t	1
Rushing	2	2	14	7.0	8	0
Colts	23	15	207	9.0	82t	1
Opponents	25	9	327	13.1	87t	1

KICKOFF RETURNS	No.	Yds	Avg	LG	TD
Wilkins	52	1,272	24.5	70	0
Carthon	2	21	10.5	21	0
Rushing	2	67	33.5	47	0
Da. Reid	1	3	3.0	3	0
Hayden	1	1	1.0	1	0
Dorsey	0	4	—	4	0
Colts	58	1,368	23.6	70	0
Opponents	78	2,029	26.0	103t	2

FIELD GOALS	1-19	20-29	30-39	40-49	50+
Vinatieri	1/1	3/3	12/13	9/10	0/1
Gramatica	0/0	1/1	0/0	0/0	0/0
Colts	1/1	4/4	12/13	9/10	0/1
Opponents	0/0	8/9	5/8	10/17	1/1

SACKS	No.
Mathis	9.5
Freeney	5.5
Brock	3.0
McFarland	2.5
June	1.0
Reagor	1.0
Thomas	1.0
(group)	1.0
Schobel	0.5
Colts	25.0
Opponents	15.0

RECORD HOLDERS
INDIVIDUAL RECORDS—CAREER

Category	Name	Performance
Rushing (Yds.)	Edgerrin James, 1999-2005	9,226
Passing (Yds.)	Johnny Unitas, 1956-1972	39,768
Passing (TDs)	Johnny Unitas, 1956-1972	287
Receiving (No.)	Marvin Harrison, 1996-2006	1,022
Receiving (Yds.)	Marvin Harrison, 1996-2006	13,697
Interceptions	Bob Boyd, 1960-68	57
Punting (Avg.)	Chris Gardocki, 1995-98	44.8
Punt Return (Avg.)	Ron Gardin, 1970-71	13.5
Kickoff Return (Avg.)	Jim Duncan, 1969-1971	32.6
Field Goals	Mike Vanderjagt, 1998-2005	217
Touchdowns (Tot.)	Marvin Harrison, 1996-2006	122
Points	Mike Vanderjagt, 1998-2005	995

INDIVIDUAL RECORDS—SINGLE SEASON

Category	Name	Performance
Rushing (Yds.)	Edgerrin James, 2000	1,709
Passing (Yds.)	Peyton Manning, 2004	4,557
Passing (TDs)	Peyton Manning, 2004	*49
Receiving (No.)	Marvin Harrison, 2002	*143
Receiving (Yds.)	Marvin Harrison, 2002	1,722
Interceptions	Tom Keane, 1953	11
Punting (Avg.)	Rohn Stark, 1985	45.9
Punt Return (Avg.)	Clarence Verdin, 1989	12.9
Kickoff Return (Avg.)	Jim Duncan, 1970	35.4
Field Goals	Mike Vanderjagt, 2003	37
Touchdowns (Tot.)	Lenny Moore, 1964	20
Points	Mike Vanderjagt, 2003	157

INDIVIDUAL RECORDS—SINGLE GAME

Category	Name	Performance
Rushing (Yds.)	Edgerrin James, 10-15-00	219
Passing (Yds.)	Peyton Manning, 10-31-04	472
Passing (TDs)	Peyton Manning, 9-28-03, 11-25-04	6
Receiving (No.)	Marvin Harrison, 12-26-99, 11-17-02	14
Receiving (Yds.)	Raymond Berry, 11-10-57	224
Interceptions	Many times	3
	Last time by Mike Prior, 12-20-92	
Field Goals	Many times	5
	Last time by Mike Vanderjagt, 12-7-03	
Touchdowns (Tot.)	Many times	4
	Last time by Joseph Addai, 11-26-06	
Points	Many times	24
	Last time by Joseph Addai, 11-26-06	

*NFL Record

2007 VETERAN ROSTER

No.	Name	Pos.	Ht.	Wt.	Birthdate	NFL Exp.	College	Hometown	How Acq.	'06 Games/ Starts
29	Addai, Joseph	RB	5-11	214	5/3/83	2	Louisiana State	Houston, Texas	D1-'06	16/0
41	Bethea, Antoine	S/CB	5-11	203	7/7/84	2	Howard	Newport News, Va.	D6b-'06	14/14
50	Boiman, Rocky	LB	6-4	236	1/24/80	6	Notre Dame	Cincinnati, Ohio	FA-'06	16/1
58	Brackett, Gary	LB	5-11	235	5/23/80	5	Rutgers	Glassboro, N.J.	FA-'03	14/14
79	Brock, Raheem	DE	6-4	274	6/10/78	6	Temple	Philadelphia, Pa.	FA-'02	16/16
44	Clark, Dallas	TE/FB	6-3	252	6/12/79	5	Iowa	Livermore, Iowa	D1-'03	12/12
64	DeMulling, Rick	G	6-4	310	7/21/77	7	Idaho	Cheney, Wash.	UFA(Det)-'07	14/7*
71	Diem, Ryan	T	6-6	331	7/1/79	7	Northern Illinois	Carol Stream, Ill.	D4-'01	15/15
25	Dorsey, Dede	RB	5-11	196	8/1/84	2	Lindenwood	Broken Arrow, Okla.	W(Cin)-'06	13/0
76	Federkeil, Dan	T	6-6	290	11/9/83	2	Calgary	Medicine Hat, Alberta,Canada	FA-'06	2/0
81	Fletcher, Bryan	TE	6-5	230	3/23/79	3	UCLA	St. Louis, Mo.	FA-'05	15/3
93	Freeney, Dwight	DE	6-1	268	2/19/80	6	Syracuse	Hartford, Conn.	D1-'02	16/16
57	Gandy, Dylan	G	6-3	302	3/8/82	3	Texas Tech	Harlingen, Texas	D4a-'05	16/11
51	Gardner, Gilbert	LB	6-1	228	5/9/82	4	Purdue	Angleton, Texas	D3b-'04	15/12
43	Giordano, Matt	S/CB	5-11	192	10/16/82	3	California	Fresno, Calif.	D4b-'05	12/1
78	Glenn, Tarik	T	6-5	332	5/25/76	11	California	Oakland, Calif.	D1-'97	16/16
56	Hagler, Tyjuan	LB	6-0	236	12/3/81	2	Cincinnati	Kankakee, Ill.	D5c-'05	9/0
88	Harrison, Marvin	WR	6-0	175	8/25/72	12	Syracuse	Philadelphia, Pa.	D1-'96	16/16
26	Hayden, Kelvin	S/CB	6-0	195	7/23/83	3	Illinois	Chicago, Ill.	D2-'05	15/1
6	Hodges, Reggie	P	6-0	226	1/26/82	3	Ball State	Champaign, Ill.	FA-'07	0*
28	Jackson, Marlin	S/CB	6-0	196	6/30/83	3	Michigan	Sharon, Pa.	D1-'05	14/8
27	Jennings, Tim	S/CB	5-8	185	12/24/83	2	Georgia	Orangeburg, S.C.	D2-'06	11/0
74	Johnson, Charlie	T	6-4	305	5/2/84	2	Oklahoma State	Sherman, Texas	D6a-'06	16/1
54	Keiaho, Freddy	LB	5-11	226	12/18/82	2	San Diego State	Ventura, Calif.	D3-'06	14/0
90	Klecko, Dan	DT	5-11	275	1/12/81	5	Temple	Colts Neck, N.J.	W(NE)-'06	12/0
52	Labinjo, Mike	LB	6-1	255	7/8/80	2	Michigan State	Toronto, Ontario, Canada	FA-'07	0*
99	Lacasse, Ryan	DE	6-2	257	2/6/83	2	Syracuse	Stoughton, Mass.	T(Balt)-'06	12/0
45	Lawton, Luke	RB	6-0	245	8/26/80	2	McNeese State	New Iberia, La.	FA-'07	1/0
40	Lejeune, Norman	S/CB	6-0	210	5/10/80	2	Louisiana State	Brusly, La.	W(Mia)-'07	2/0*
65	Lilja, Ryan	G	6-2	285	10/15/81	4	Kansas State	Shawnee, Kan.	W(KC)-04	11/5
18	Manning, Peyton	QB	6-5	230	3/24/76	10	Tennessee	New Orleans, La.	D1-'98	16/16
98	Mathis, Robert	DE	6-2	235	2/26/81	5	Alabama A&M	Atlanta, Ga.	D5a-'03	16/16
92	McFarland, Anthony	DT	6-0	300	12/18/77	9	Louisiana State	Winnsboro, La.	T(TB)-'06	16/16
85	Moorehead, Aaron	WR	6-3	200	11/5/80	5	Illinois	Deerfield, Ill.	FA-'03	12/0
94	Morris, Rob	LB	6-2	243	1/18/75	8	Brigham Young	Nampa, Idaho	D1-'00	15/5
16	Navarre, John	QB	6-6	241	9/9/80	4	Michigan	Cudahy, Wis.	FA-'07	0*
53	O'Neil, Keith	LB	6-0	240	8/26/80	5	Northern Arizona	Amherst, N.Y.	W(Dall)-'05	10/0
95	Reid, Darrell	DT	6-2	288	6/20/82	3	Minnesota	Freehold, N.J.	FA-'05	15/0
34	Rushing, T.J.	S/CB	5-9	186	6/8/83	2	Stanford	Pauls Valley, Okla.	D7-'06	6/0
21	Sanders, Bob	S	5-8	206	2/24/81	4	Iowa	Erie, Pa.	D2b-'04	4/4
63	Saturday, Jeff	C	6-2	295	6/8/75	9	North Carolina	Tucker, Ga.	FA-'99	16/16
96	Schobel, Bo	DE	6-5	264	3/24/81	4	Texas Christian	Columbus, Texas	FA-'06	14/0
73	Scott, Jake	G	6-5	280	4/16/81	4	Idaho	Lewiston, Idaho	D5a-'04	16/16
42	Seidman, Mike	TE	6-4	261	2/11/81	5	UCLA	Westlake Village, Calif.	UFA(Car)-'07	3/3*
97	Simon, Corey	DT	6-2	293	3/2/77	8	Florida State	Pompano Beach, Fla.	UFA(Phil)-'05	0*
17	Smith, Hunter	P	6-2	209	8/9/77	9	Notre Dame	Sherman, Texas	D7a-'99	16/0
48	Snow, Justin	TE	6-3	240	12/21/76	8	Baylor	Abilene, Texas	FA-'00	16/0
12	Sorgi, Jim	QB	6-5	196	12/3/80	4	Wisconsin	Fraser, Mich.	D6b-'04	1/0
84	Standeford, John	WR	6-4	206	4/15/82	2	Purdue	Monrovia, Ind.	FA-'06	0*
91	Thomas, Josh	DE	6-5	271	6/26/81	4	Syracuse	Orchard Park, N.Y.	FA-'04	14/0
69	Ulrich, Matt	G/T	6-2	309	12/30/81	3	Northwestern	Streamwood, Ill.	FA-'05	5/0
86	Utecht, Ben	TE	6-6	251	6/30/81	4	Minnesota	Hastings, Minn.	FA-'04	15/15
4	Vinatieri, Adam	K	6-0	202	12/28/72	12	South Dakota State	Rapid City, S.D.	UFA(NE)-'06	13/0
87	Wayne, Reggie	WR	6-0	198	11/17/78	7	Miami	New Orleans, La.	D1b-'01	16/16

DeMuling played 14 games with Detroit in '06; Hodges last active with Philadelphia in '05; Labinjo last active with Miami in '05; Lejeune played 2 games with Miami; McFarland played 5 games with Tampa Bay and 11 games with Indianapolis; Mungro missed '06 season because of injury; Navarre did not play in 1 game with Arizona; Simon missed '06 season because of injury; Standeford did not play in 2 games.

Players lost through free agency (5): DB Jason David (NO; 16 games in '06); S Mike Doss (Minn; 5), DB Nick Harper (Tenn; 15), LB Cato June (TB; 16), RB Dominic Rhodes (Oak; 16)).

Also played with Colts in '06—RB Ran Carthon (3), K Martin Gramatica (3), WR Ricky Proehl (3), DT Montae Reagor (16), WR Brandon Stokley (4), G Matt Ulrich (5), WR Terrence Wilkins (15).

2007 FIRST-YEAR ROSTER

Name	Pos.	Ht.	Wt.	Birthdate	College	Hometown	How Acq.
Archer, Brandon	LB	6-0	239	10/30/83	Kansas State	Minneapolis, Minn.	FA
Aromashodu, Devin (1)	WR	6-2	200	5/23/84	Auburn	Miami, Fla,	FA
Betts, Josh (1)	QB	6-2	217	8/25/82	Miami (Ohio)	Vandalia, Ohio	FA
Bimper, Albert (1)	G	6-0	300	7/26/83	Colorado State	Arlington, Texas	FA
Bullitt, Melvin	CB/S	6-1	201	11/13/84	Texas A&M	Bryan, Texas	FA
Charleston, Jeff (1)	DE	6-4	265	1/19/83	Idaho State	Oregon City, Ore.	FA
Coe, Michael	CB/S	6-0	190	12/17/83	Alabama State	Memphis, Tenn.	D5b
Coley, Trevis (1)	CB/S	6-2	217	6/23/82	Southern Mississippi	Palatka, Fla,	FA
Condren, Brannon	CB/S	6-1	205	8/19/83	Troy State	Ft.Walton Beach, Fla.	D4b
David, Tanard (1)	CB/S	5-9	184	1/27/83	Miami	Miami, Fla.	FA
Dawson, Clifton	RB	5-10	212	10/8/83	Harvard	Scarborough, Ontario, Canada	FA
Dawson, Keyunta	DE	6-3	254	9/13/85	Texas Tech	Shreveport, La	D7
DePriest, Michael	WR	6-0	185	7/2/84	Texas Christian	Keller, Texas	FA
Echols, Quintin	DT	6-1	313	7/8/84	Kansas State	Ft. Worth, Texas	FA
Gonzalez, Anthony	WR	6-0	193	9/18/84	Ohio State	Cleveland, Ohio	D1
Guzman, Ramon	LB	6-2	232	9/29/82	Buffalo	Bronx, N.Y.	FA
Hall, Kamichael	LB	6-0	219	1/22/85	Georgia Tech	Houston, Texas	FA
Hall, Roy	WR	6-3	240	12/8/83	Ohio State	Lyndhurst, Ohio	D5a
Hare, Brian (1)	WR	6-2	192	8/18/83	Purdue	Arlington Hgts., Ill.	FA
Harline, Jonny	TE	6-4	245	11/6/82	Brigham Young	New Brunswick, N.J.	FA
Hoyte, Brandon (1)	LB	5-11	246	9/26/83	Notre Dame	Parlin, N.J.	FA
Hughes, Daymeion	CB/S	5-10	190	8/21/85	California	Los Angeles, Calif.	D3a
Johnson, Tom (1)	DT	6-2	286	8/30/84	Southern Mississippi	Moss Point, Miss.	FA
Keith, Kenton (1)	RB	5-11	198	7/14/80	New Mexico State	Lincoln, Neb.	FA
Lobdell, Joe	T	6-6	288	5/20/83	Northern Iowa	Monroe, Wis.	FA
McGann, Mike (1)	QB	6-5	225	9/15/82	Temple	Lansdowne, Pa.	FA
McMahan, Kevin (1)	WR	6-3	193	3/2/83	Maine	Rochester, N.Y.	FA
Meekins, Ramel	DT	5-11	284	8/6/85	Rutgers	Westwood, N.J.	FA
Pitcock, Quinn	DT	6-2	299	9/14/83	Ohio State	Piqua, Ohio	D3b
Robinson, Gijon	TE	6-1	255	10/12/84	Missouri West State	Waynesville, Mo.	FA
Sele, Taylor	WR	6-0	204	7/28/83	Boston College	Monrovia, Liberia	W(Wash)
Session, Clint	LB	6-0	235	9/9/84	Pittsburgh	Pompano Beach, Fla.	D4c
Shelton, Trent	WR	6-0	202	9/21/84	Baylor	Little Rock, Ark.	FA
Smith, Antonio	CB/S	5-9	192	6/12/84	Ohio State	Columbus, Ohio	FA
Thorpe, Craphonso (1)	WR	6-0	187	6/27/83	Florida State	Tallahassee, Fla.	W(Det)
Toudouze, Michael (1)	T	6-6	303	4/27/83	Texas Christian	San Antonio, Texas	FA
Ugoh, Tony	T	6-5	301	11/17/83	Arkansas	Houston, Texas	D2a
Ware, Scott (1)	CB/S	6-2	215	5/5/83	Southern California	Santa Rosa, Calif.	FA
Wilder, Sam (1)	G	6-5	300	1/10/82	Colorado	Dallas, Texas	FA
Worsley, Victor	LB	6-1	234	4/24/84	North Carolina	Battleboro, Ncb.	FA

The term NFL Rookie is defined as a player who is in his first season of professional football and has not been on the roster of another professional football team for any regular-season or postseason games. A Rookie is designated by an "R" on NFL rosters. Players who have been active in another professional football league or players who have NFL experience, including either preseason training camp or being on an Active List or Inactive List, or on Reserve/Injured or Reserve/Physically Unable to Perform for fewer than six regular-season games, are termed NFL First-Year Players. An NFL First-Year Player is designated by a "1" on NFL rosters. Thereafter, a player is credited with an additional year of experience for each season in which he accumulates six games on the Active List or Inactive List, or on Reserve/Injured or Reserve/Physically Unable to Perform.

Log on to www.colts.com for an up-to-date roster.

INDIANAPOLIS COLTS

COACHING STAFF

Head Coach,
Tony Dungy
Pro Career: Tony Dungy was named head coach of the club on January 22, 2002. This season marks Dungy's sixth with the Colts and twelfth as an NFL head coach. Dungy is 60-20 at the Colts' helm. Dungy's career record is 123-70. Dungy directed the Colts to a 29-17 win over Chicago in Super Bowl XLI on February 4, 2007, the fourth championship in club history. Dungy joined Tom Flores and Mike Ditka as the only people to earn Super Bowl titles as a player and a head coach. In 2005, Dungy became only the sixth head coach to win 100-plus regular-season games in the first 10 years. He is the NFL's winningest head coach from 1999-2006 with a mark of 90-38 (30-18 with Tampa Bay, 60-20 with Colts), and his .648 winning percentage ranks first among active head coaches. In 2006, Dungy led the club to its fourth consecutive division title, and the Colts are the only team to qualify for postseason play seven times in the last eight seasons. The Colts (14-2, 2005; 12-4, 2003, 2004 and 2006) joined Dallas (1992-95) as the only NFL teams with four consecutive 12-plus win seasons. Dungy was the first coach to defeat all 32 NFL teams. Dungy held a 54-42 record as head coach with Tampa Bay (1996-2001), with four playoff appearances. At 25, Dungy was the NFL's youngest assistant coach with Pittsburgh in 1981. In 1982, he was promoted from defensive assistant to defensive backs coach, before becoming the league's youngest defensive coordinator in 1984 at age 28. He served as defensive backs coach at Kansas City (1989-1991) and as defensive coordinator at Minnesota (1992-95). Dungy signed with Pittsburgh as a free agent in 1977 and played safety for two seasons. He had 9 interceptions in 30 games for Pittsburgh and played in the club's Super Bowl XIII victory over Dallas. He was traded to San Francisco in 1979. Career record: 123-70.
Background: Starred as a quarterback at University of Minnesota from 1973-76. Finished career as school's all-time leader in attempts, completions, passing yards and touchdown passes. Two-time team most valuable player, played in Hula Bowl, East-West Shrine Game and Japan Bowl.
Personal: Born October 6, 1955, in Jackson, Mich. Tony and his wife, Lauren, are the parents of six children, daughters Tiara and Jade, and sons Eric, Jordan, and Justin, and the late James Dungy.

ASSISTANT COACHES

Jim Caldwell, asst. head coach/quarterbacks; born January 16, 1955, Beloit, Wis. Defensive back Iowa 1973-76. No pro playing experience. College coach: Iowa 1977, Southern Illinois 1978-1980, Northwestern 1981, Colorado 1982-84, Louisville 1985, Penn State 1986-1992, Wake Forest 1993-2000 (head coach). Pro coach: Tampa Bay Buccaneers 2001, joined Colts in 2002.
Clyde Christensen, wide receivers; born January 28, 1956, Covina, Calif. Quarterback Fresno City College 1975, North Carolina 1976-78. No pro playing experience. College coach: Mississippi 1979, East Tennessee State 1980-82, Temple 1983-85, East Carolina 1986-88, Holy Cross 1989-1990, South Carolina 1991, Maryland 1992-93, Clemson 1994-95. Pro coach: Tampa Bay Buccaneers 1996-2001, joined Colts in 2002.
Richard Howell, asst. strength and conditioning; born February 19, 1972, Bladenboro, N.C. Quarterback Davidson 1990-93. No pro playing experience. College coach: Davidson 1994-98, North Carolina 1998-99. Pro coach: Barcelona Dragons (NFLE) 1999, joined Colts in 2000.
Gene Huey, running backs; born July 20, 1947, Uniontown, Pa. Defensive back-wide receiver Wyoming 1965-68. Pro running back San Diego Chargers 1969. College coach: Wyoming 1970-73, New Mexico 1974-76, Nebraska 1977-1986, Arizona State 1987, Ohio State 1988-1991. Pro coach: Joined Colts in 1992.
Ron Meeks, defensive coordinator; born August 27, 1954, Jacksonville. Defensive back Arkansas State 1972-76. Pro defensive back Hamilton Tiger-Cats (CFL) 1977-79, Ottawa Rough Riders (CFL) 1979, Toronto Argonauts (CFL) 1980-81. College coach: Arkansas State 1984-85, Miami 1986-87, New Mexico State 1988, Fresno State 1989-1990. Pro coach: Dallas Cowboys 1991, Cincinnati Bengals 1992-96, Atlanta Falcons 1997-99, Washington Redskins 2000, St. Louis Rams 2001, joined Colts in 2002.
Pete Metzelaars, offensive quality control; born May 24, 1960, Three Rivers, Mich. Tight end Wabash College 1978-1981. Pro tight end Seattle Seahawks 1982-84, Buffalo Bills 1985-1994, Carolina Panthers 1995, Detroit Lions 1996-97. College coach: Wingate 2003. Pro coach: Barcelona Dragons (NFLE) 2003, joined Colts in 2004.
Tom Moore, offensive coordinator; born November 7, 1938, Owatanna, Minn. Quarterback Iowa 1957-1960. No pro playing experience. College coach: Iowa 1961-62, Dayton 1965-68, Wake Forest 1969, Georgia Tech 1970-71, Minnesota 1972-73, 1975-76. Pro coach: New York Stars (WFL) 1974, Pittsburgh Steelers 1977-1989, Minnesota Vikings 1990-93, Detroit Lions 1994-96, New Orleans Saints 1997, joined Colts in 1998.
Howard Mudd, offensive line; born February 10, 1942, Midland, Mich. Guard Hillsdale (Mich.) College 1960-63. Pro offensive lineman San Francisco 49ers 1964-69, Chicago Bears 1969-1971. College coach: California 1972-73. Pro coach: San Diego Chargers 1974-76, San Francisco 49ers 1977, Seattle Seahawks 1978-1982, 1993-97, Cleveland Browns 1983-88, Kansas City Chiefs 1989-1992, joined Colts in 1998.
Mike Murphy, linebackers; born September 25, 1944, New York, N.Y. Guard/linebacker Huron (S.D.) 1963-66. No pro playing experience. College coach: Vermont 1970-73, Idaho State 1974-76, Western Illinois 1977-78. Pro coach: Saskatchewan Roughriders (CFL) 1979-1983, Chicago Blitz (USFL) 1984, Detroit Lions 1985-89, Arizona Cardinals 1990-93, Seattle Seahawks 1995-97, joined Colts in 1998.
Rod Perry, secondary; born September 11, 1953, Fresno, Calif. Defensive back Colorado 1972-74. Pro cornerback Los Angeles Rams 1975-1982, Cleveland Browns 1983-84. College coach: Columbia 1985, Fresno City College 1986, Fresno State 1987-88. Pro coach: Seattle Seahawks 1989-1991, Los Angeles Rams 1992-94, Houston Oilers 1995-96, San Diego Chargers 1997-2001, Carolina Panthers 2002-06, joined Colts in 2007.
Russ Purnell, special teams; born June 12, 1948, Chicago. Center Orange Coast (Calif.) J.C. 1966-67, Whittier College 1968-69. No pro playing experience. College coach: Whittier College 1970-71, Southern California 1982-85. Pro coach: Seattle Seahawks 1986-1994, Tennessee Oilers/Titans 1995-98, Baltimore Ravens 1999-2001, joined Colts in 2002.
John Teerlinck, defensive line; born April 9, 1951, Rochester, N.Y. Defensive lineman Western Illinois 1970-73. Pro defensive tackle San Diego Chargers 1974-77. College coach: Iowa Lakes J.C. 1977, Eastern Illinois 1978-79, Illinois 1980-82. Pro coach: Chicago Blitz (USFL) 1983-84, Arizona Wranglers/Outlaws (USFL) 1985-86, Cleveland Browns 1989-1990, Los Angeles Rams 1991, Minnesota Vikings 1992-94, Detroit Lions 1995-96, Denver Broncos 1997-2001, joined Colts in 2002.
Ricky Thomas, tight ends; born March 29, 1965, London, England. Safety Alabama 1983-86. No pro playing experience. College coach: Kentucky 1996, Gardner-Webb 1997. Pro coach: Tampa Bay Buccaneers 1997-2001, joined Colts in 2002.
Jon Torine, strength and conditioning; born November 16, 1973, Livingston, N.J. Linebacker Springfield (Mass.) College 1991. No pro playing experience. Pro coach: Buffalo Bills 1995-97, joined Colts in 1998.
Alan Williams, defensive backs; born November 4, 1969, Norfolk, Va. Running back William & Mary 1988-1991. No pro playing experience. College coach: William & Mary 1996-2000. Pro coach: Tampa Bay Buccaneers 2001, joined Colts in 2002.
Carlos Woods, defensive quality control; born April 21, 1980, Virginia Beach, Va. Linebacker/defensive end Delaware State 1998-2002. No pro playing experience. College coach: Penn State 2004-05. Pro coach: Joined Colts in 2007.

**American Football Conference
South Division
Team Colors:** Teal, Black, and Gold
**Jacksonville Municipal Stadium
One Stadium Place
Jacksonville, Florida 32202
Telephone:** (904) 633-6000

**2007 SCHEDULE
PRESEASON**
Aug. 11 at Miami.............................7:30
Aug. 18 **Tampa Bay**.........................7:30
Aug. 23 at Green Bay 7:00
Aug. 30 **Washington** 7:30

REGULAR SEASON
Sep. 9   **Tennessee** 1:00
Sep. 16 **Atlanta** 1:00
Sep. 23 at Denver 2:05
Sep. 30 Open Date
Oct. 7   at Kansas City 12:00
Oct. 14 **Houston** 1:00
Oct. 22 **Indianapolis** (Mon.) 8:30
Oct. 28 at Tampa Bay 4:05
Nov. 4   at New Orleans 12:00
Nov. 11 at Tennessee 12:00
Nov. 18 **San Diego** 1:00
Nov. 25 **Buffalo** 1:00
Dec. 2   at Indianapolis 1:00
Dec. 9   **Carolina** 1:00
Dec. 16 at Pittsburgh 1:00
Dec. 23 **Oakland** 1:00
Dec. 30 at Houston 12:00

Stadium: Jacksonville Municipal Stadium
(opened in 1995)
•**Capacity:** 67,164
One Stadium Place
Jacksonville, Florida 32202
Playing Surface: Grass
Training Camp: Jacksonville Municipal Stadium
One Stadium Place
Jacksonville, Florida 32202

JACKSONVILLE MUNICIPAL STADIUM

CLUB OFFICIALS
Chairman and Chief Executive Officer:
Wayne Weaver
Senior Vice President/Football
Operations: Paul Vance
Senior Vice President/Chief Financial
Officer: Bill Prescott
Senior Vice President/Business
Development: Tim Connolly
Vice President/Player Personnel:
James Harris
Vice President/Communications and
Media: Dan Edwards
Executive Director of Ticket Sales and
Marketing: Scott Loft
Executive Director of Corporate
Sponsorship: Macky Weaver
Executive Director of Football Operations:
Skip Richardson
Executive Director of Information
Technology: Bruce Swindell
Director of Pro Personnel: Charles Bailey
Director of College Scouting: Gene Smith
Director of Ticket Operations: Tim Bishko
Director of Marketing: Jennifer Perkins
Associate General Counsel: Sashi Brown
Head Athletic Trainer: Michael Ryan
Video Director: Mike Perkins
Equipment Manager: Drew Hampton
Assistant Director of Pro Personnel:
Louis Clark
Executive Scouts: Terry McDonough,
Tim Mingey
Regional Scouts: Andy Dengler,
Chris Driggers, Art Perkins
BLESTO Representative: Kadar Hamilton
Scouts: Marty Miller, Larry Wright
Scouting Assistant: Chris Prescott
Coordinator, Communications:
Hunter Robinson
Coordinator, Communications:
Ryan Robinson
Executive Assistant to VP,
Communications and Media:
Alisa Abbott
Chair & Chief Executive Officer, Jaguars
Foundation: Delores Barr Weaver
Executive Director: Peter Racine

**COACHING HISTORY
(106-95-0)**
Records include postseason games
1995-2002 Tom Coughlin 72-64-0
2003-06   Jack Del Rio 34-31-0

PAID ATTENDANCE
Home 486,957   Away 559,607
Total 1,046,564
Single-game home record,
74,143 (12/28/98)
Single-season home record, 561,472
(1998)

2007 DRAFT CHOICES

Round	Name	Pos.	College
1	Reggie Nelson	DB	Florida
2	Justin Durant	LB	Hampton
3	Mike Walker	WR	Central Florida
4	Adam Podlesh	P	Maryland
	Brian Smith	DE	Missouri
5	Uche Nwaneri	G	Purdue
	Josh Gattis	DB	Wake Forest
	Derek Landri	DT	Notre Dame
7	John Broussard	WR	San Jose State
	Chad Nkang	LB	Elon
	Andrew Carnahan	T	Arizona State

JACKSONVILLE JAGUARS

2006 TEAM RECORD

PRESEASON (1-3)

Date	Result	Opponent
8/12	W 31-26	at Miami
8/19	L 10-17	Carolina
8/26	W 29-18	Tampa Bay
8/31	W 20-17	at Atlanta

REGULAR SEASON (8-8)

Date	Result	Opponent	Att.
9/10	W 24-17	Dallas	67,164
9/18	W 9-0	Pittsburgh	67,164
9/24	L 14-21	at Indianapolis	57,041
10/1	L 30-36	at Washington (OT)	89,450
10/8	W 41-0	N.Y. Jets	66,604
10/22	L 7-27	at Houston	70,035
10/29	W 13-6	at Philadelphia	69,249
11/5	W 37-7	Tennessee	66,524
11/12	L 10-13	Houston	65,918
11/20	W 26-10	N.Y. Giants	67,164
11/26	L 24-27	at Buffalo	63,608
12/3	W 24-10	at Miami	73,160
12/10	W 44-17	Indianapolis	67,164
12/17	L 17-24	at Tennessee	69,143
12/24	L 21-24	New England	67,164
12/31	L 30-35	at Kansas City	77,500

(OT) Overtime

SCORE BY PERIODS

Jaguars	72	112	80	107	0 —	371
Opponents	61	64	72	71	6 —	274

2006 TEAM STATISTICS

	Jaguars	Opp.
Total First Downs	293	259
Rushing	127	94
Passing	147	143
Penalty	19	22
3rd Down: Made/Att	85/217	83/227
3rd Down Pct.	39.2	36.6
4th Down: Made/Att	7/14	4/14
4th Down Pct.	50.0	28.6
Possession Avg.	32:11	27:49
Total Net Yards	5423	4538
Avg. Per Game	338.9	283.6
Total Plays	989	978
Avg. Per Play	5.5	4.6
Net Yards Rushing	2541	1460
Avg. Per Game	158.8	91.3
Total Rushes	513	420
Net Yards Passing	2882	3078
Avg. Per Game	180.1	192.4
Sacked/Yards Lost	30/178	35/200
Gross Yards	3060	3278
Att./Completions	446/266	523/294
Completion Pct.	59.6	56.2
Had Intercepted	14	20
Punts/Average	73/40.0	90/41.4
Net Punting Avg.	73/33.4	90/35.8
Penalties/Yards	97/806	80/684
Fumbles/Ball Lost	16/9	12/4
Touchdowns	42	32
Rushing	23	14
Passing	17	12
Returns	2	6

2006 INDIVIDUAL STATISTICS

PASSING	Att.	Comp.	Yds.	Pct.	TD	Int.	Tkld.	Rate
Garrard	241	145	1,735	60.2	10	9	20/119	80.5
Leftwich	183	108	1,159	59.0	7	5	9/48	79.0
Gray	22	13	166	59.1	0	0	1/11	82.8
Jaguars	446	266	3,060	59.6	17	14	30/178	80.0
Opponents	523	294	3,278	56.2	12	20	35/200	66.8

SCORING	TD R	TD P	TD Rt	PAT	FG	Saf	PTS
Scobee	0	0	0	41/41	26/32	0	119
Jones-Drew	13	2	1	0/0	0/0	0	96
Taylor	5	1	0	0/0	0/0	0	36
M. Jones	0	4	0	0/0	0/0	0	24
R. Williams	0	4	0	0/0	0/0	0	24
Wrighster	0	3	0	0/0	0/0	0	18
Gray	2	0	0	0/0	0/0	0	12
Leftwich	2	0	0	0/0	0/0	0	12
Wilford	0	2	0	0/0	0/0	0	12
Lewis	0	1	0	0/0	0/0	0	6
Pearman	1	0	0	0/0	0/0	0	6
Starks	0	0	1	0/0	0/0	0	6
Jaguars	23	17	2	41/41	26/32	0	371
Opponents	14	12	6	31/31	17/24	0	274

2-Pt. Conversions: Jaguars 0-1, Opponents 0-0

RUSHING	No.	Yds	Avg	LG	TD
Taylor	231	1146	5.0	76	5
Jones-Drew	166	941	5.7	74t	13
Garrard	47	250	5.3	20	0
Pearman	19	89	4.7	12	1
Leftwich	25	41	1.6	7	2
R. Williams	7	33	4.7	10	0
Gray	2	26	13.0	17t	2
Toefield	10	22	2.2	12	0
Alexis	3	5	1.7	3	0
Wimbush	1	3	3.0	3	0
M. Jones	2	-15	-7.5	-6	0
Jaguars	513	2541	5.0	76	23
Opponents	420	1460	3.5	40	14

RECEIVING	No.	Yds	Avg	LG	TD
R. Williams	52	616	11.8	48	4
Jones-Drew	46	436	9.5	51t	2
M. Jones	41	643	15.7	49	4
Wrighster	39	353	9.1	23	3
Wilford	36	524	14.6	41	2
Taylor	23	242	10.5	36	1
Lewis	13	126	9.7	31	1
Hankton	5	48	9.6	15	0
Brady	5	37	7.4	13	0
Wimbush	4	23	5.8	9	0
Pearman	2	12	6.0	7	0
Jaguars	266	3060	11.5	51t	17
Opponents	294	3278	11.1	68t	12

INTERCEPTIONS	No.	Yds	Avg	LG	TD
Mathis	8	146	18.3	55	0
Grant	2	25	12.5	24	0
Sensabaugh	2	8	4.0	8	0
Starks	1	55	55.0	55t	1
Cousin	1	16	16.0	16	0
Peterson	1	15	15.0	15	0
Greisen	1	6	6.0	6	0
Smith	1	4	4.0	4	0
B. Williams	1	4	4.0	4	0
Webb	1	1	1.0	1	0
Ingram	1	0	0.0	0	0
Jaguars	20	280	14.0	55t	1
Opponents	14	222	15.9	83t	2

PUNTING	No.	Yds.	Avg.	In 20	LG
Hanson	72	2920	40.6	20	58
Jaguars	73	2920	40.0	20	58
Opponents	90	3724	41.4	25	73

PUNT RETURNS	Ret	FC	Yds	Avg	LG	TD
Pearman	32	16	283	8.8	29	0
C. Owens	9	5	56	6.2	13	0
Mathis	2	1	9	4.5	9	0
Jones-Drew	1	0	13	13.0	13	0
Toefield	1	0	0	0.0	0	0
Jaguars	45	22	361	8.0	29	0
Opponents	29	16	343	11.8	82t	2

KICKOFF RETURNS	No.	Yds	Avg	LG	TD
Jones-Drew	31	860	27.7	93t	1
Wimbush	8	181	22.6	33	0
Brady	4	18	4.5	9	0
Pearman	3	56	18.7	22	0
Toefield	1	9	9.0	9	0
Collier	1	8	8.0	8	0
M. Owens	1	4	4.0	4	0
Jaguars	49	1136	23.2	93t	1
Opponents	60	1262	21.0	70	0

FIELD GOALS	1-19	20-29	30-39	40-49	50+
Scobee	0/0	5/6	7/7	14/18	0/1
Jaguars	0/0	5/6	7/7	14/18	0/1
Opponents	0/0	7/7	3/6	7/10	0/1

SACKS	No.
McCray	10.0
Meier	5.0
Henderson	3.5
Smith	3.0
Spicer	3.0
Stroud	2.5
Hawkins	2.0
Pettway	2.0
Ingram	1.5
Gilbert	1.0
McDaniel	1.0
Stanley	0.0
Jaguars	35.0
Opponents	30.0

RECORD HOLDERS
INDIVIDUAL RECORDS—CAREER

Category	Name	Performance
Rushing (Yds.)	Fred Taylor, 1998-2006	9,513
Passing (Yds.)	Mark Brunell, 1995-2003	25,698
Passing (TDs)	Mark Brunell, 1995-2003	144
Receiving (No.)	Jimmy Smith, 1995-2005	862
Receiving (Yds.)	Jimmy Smith, 1995-2005	12,287
Interceptions	Rashean Mathis, 2003-06	20
Punting (Avg.)	Bryan Barker, 1995-2000	43.5
Punt Return (Avg.)	Chris Hudson, 1995-98	10.9
Kickoff Return (Avg.)	Maurice Jones-Drew, 2006	27.7
Field Goals	Mike Hollis, 1995-2001	175
Touchdowns (Tot.)	Jimmy Smith, 1995-2005	69
Points	Mike Hollis, 1995-2001	764

INDIVIDUAL RECORDS—SINGLE SEASON

Category	Name	Performance
Rushing (Yds.)	Fred Taylor, 2003	1,572
Passing (Yds.)	Mark Brunell, 1996	4,367
Passing (TDs)	Mark Brunell, 1998	20
Receiving (No.)	Jimmy Smith, 1999	116
Receiving (Yds.)	Jimmy Smith, 1999	1,636
Interceptions	Rashean Mathis, 2006	8
Punting (Avg.)	Bryan Barker, 1998	45.0
Punt Return (Avg.)	Reggie Barlow, 1998	12.9
Kickoff Return (Avg.)	Maurice Jones-Drew, 2006	27.7
Field Goals	Mike Hollis, 1997, 1999	31
Touchdowns (Tot.)	Fred Taylor, 1998	17
Points	Mike Hollis, 1997	134

INDIVIDUAL RECORDS—SINGLE GAME

Category	Name	Performance
Rushing (Yds.)	Fred Taylor, 11-19-00	234
Passing (Yds.)	Mark Brunell, 9-22-96	432
Passing (TDs)	Mark Brunell, 11-29-98	4
Receiving (No.)	Keenan McCardell, 10-20-96	16
Receiving (Yds.)	Jimmy Smith, 9-10-00	291
Interceptions	Many times	2
	Last time by Rashean Mathis, 11-5-06	
Field Goals	Mike Hollis, 12-1-96, 11-30-97, 9-10-00	5
Touchdowns (Tot.)	James Stewart, 10-12-97	5
Points	James Stewart, 10-12-97	30

2007 VETERAN ROSTER

No.	Name	Pos.	Ht.	Wt.	Birthdate	NFL Exp.	College	Hometown	How Acq.	'06 Games/ Starts
69	Barnes, Khalif	T	6-5	325	4/21/82	3	Washington	Spring Valley, Calif.	D2 '05	15/15
76	Collier, Richard	T	6-7	358	10/23/81	2	Valdosta State	Shreveport, La.	FA-'06	5/0
61	Connolly, Dan	G	6-4	318	9/2/82	3	Southeast Missouri State	St. Louis, Mo.	FA-'05	0*
58	Cordova, Jorge	LB/DE	6-1	241	9/25/81	4	Nevada	Murrieta, Calif.	D3-'04	13/0
21	Cousin, Terry	CB	5-9	185	4/11/75	11	South Carolina	Miami, Fla.	FA '05	10/4
20	Darius, Donovin	S	6-1	225	8/12/75	10	Syracuse	Camden, N.J.	D1b '98	10/10
84	Farris, Jimmy	WR	6-0	200	4/13/78	4	Montana	Lewiston, Idaho	FA-'07	0*
42	Fudge, Jamaal	S	5-9	196	5/17/83	2	Clemson	Jacksonville, Fla.	FA-'06	6/0
9	Garrard, David	QB	6-1	240	2/14/78	6	East Carolina	Durham, N.C.	D4-'02	11/10
50	Gilbert, Tony	LB	6-0	239	10/16/79	5	Georgia	Macon, Ga.	W(Ariz)-'03	16/0
5	Gray, Quinn	QB	6-3	246	5/21/79	4	Florida A&M	Ft. Lauderdale, Fla.	FA-'03	2/0
55	Greisen, Nick	LB	6-1	245	8/10/79	6	Wisconsin	Sturgeon Bay, Wis.	UFA(NYG)-'06	16/10
57	Hawkins, Brent	DE	6-2	245	9/1/83	2	Illinois State	Godfrey, Ill.	D5-'06	6/0
97	Hayward, Reggie	DE	6-5	285	3/14/79	7	Iowa State	Dolton, Ill.	UFA(Den)-'05	1/1
98	Henderson, John	DT	6-7	325	1/9/79	6	Tennessee	Nashville, Tenn.	D1-'02	16/16
51	Ingram, Clint	LB	6-2	245	3/21/83	2	Oklahoma	Hallsville, Texas	D3-'06	14/11
59	Iwuh, Brian	LB	6-0	235	3/8/84	2	Colorado	Houston, Texas	FA-'06	12/0
33	Jones, Greg	FB/RB	6-1	255	5/9/81	4	Florida State	Beaufort, S.C.	D2b-'04	0*
18	Jones, Matt	WR	6-6	238	4/22/83	3	Arkansas	Fort Smith, Ark.	D1-'05	14/4
32	Jones-Drew, Maurice	RB/KR	5-7	212	3/23/85	2	UCLA	Antioch, Calif.	D2-'06	16/1
7	Leftwich, Byron	QB	6-5	242	1/14/80	5	Marshall	Washington, D.C.	D1-'03	6/6
89	Lewis, Marcedes	TE	6-6	265	5/19/84	2	UCLA	Lakewood, Calif.	D1 '06	15/3
67	Manuwai, Vince	G	6-2	325	7/12/80	5	Hawaii	Honolulu, Hawaii	D3-'03	16/16
27	Mathis, Rashean	CB	6-1	195	8/27/80	5	Bethune-Cookman	Jacksonville, Fla.	D2-'03	16/16
26	McCadam, Kevin	S	6-1	215	3/6/79	6	Virginia Tech	Lakeside, Calif.	FA-'07	16/0*
93	+McCray, Bobby	DE	6-6	261	8/8/81	4	Florida	Miami, Fla.	D7-'04	15/12
96	McDaniel, Tony	DT	6-7	295	1/20/85	2	Tennessee	Columbia, S.C.	FA-'06	11/0
73	McDougle, Stockar	G/T	6-6	348	1/11/77	8	Oklahoma	Deerfield Beach, Fla.	UFA(Mia)-'06	11/0
63	Meester, Brad	C	6-3	300	3/23/77	8	Northern Iowa	Parkersburg, Iowa	D2-'00	16/16
92	Meier, Rob	DE/DT	6-5	298	8/29/77	8	Washington State	West Vancouver, B.C., Canada	D7b-'00	16/8
65	Naeole, Chris	G	6-3	330	12/25/74	11	Colorado	Kaava, Hawaii	UFA(NO)-'02	16/16
62	Norman, Dennis	C/G	6-5	323	1/26/80	6	Princeton	Marlton, N.J.	FA-'04	16/1
86	Northcutt, Dennis	WR/KR	5-11	171	12/22/77	8	Arizona	Los Angeles, Calif.	UFA(Cle)-'07	13/6*
24	Owens, Montell	RB	5-10	219	5/4/84	2	Maine	Wilmington, Del.	FA-'06	14/0
79	Pashos, Tony	T	6-6	320	8/3/80	5	Illinois	Lock Port, Ill.	UFA(Balt)-'07	16/16*
34	Pearman, Alvin	RB/KR	5-10	206	8/10/82	3	Virginia	Charlotte, N.C.	D4-'05	13/0
54	Peterson, Mike	LB	6-1	235	6/17/76	9	Florida	Gainesville, Fla.	UFA(Ind)-'03	5/5
91	Pettway, Kenny	DE	6-4	238	11/13/82	3	Grambling State	Gilmer, Texas	FA-'06	7/0
38	Roberson, Chris	CB	5-11	185	6/3/83	3	Eastern Michigan	Farmington Hills, Mich.	D7-'05	0*
10	Scobee, Josh	K	6-1	190	6/23/82	4	Louisiana Tech	Longview, Texas	D5a-'04	16/0
43	Sensabaugh, Gerald	S	6-0	218	6/13/83	3	North Carolina	Kingsport, Tenn.	D5-'05	16/7
17	Sharon, Charles	WR	6-0	184	4/4/83	2	Bowling Green	Palatka, Fla.	FA-'06	0*
52	Smith, Daryl	LB	6-2	244	3/14/82	4	Georgia Tech	Albany, Ga.	D2a-'04	16/16
41	Sorensen, Nick	S	6-3	210	7/31/78	7	Virginia Tech	Vienna, Va.	FA-'03	12/0
95	Spicer, Paul	DE	6-4	296	8/18/75	8	Saginaw Valley State	Indianapolis, Ind.	FA-'00	16/16
31	Starks, Scott	CB	5-9	176	6/27/83	3	Wisconsin	St. Louis, Mo.	D3-'05	16/1
99	Stroud, Marcus	DT	6-6	306	6/25/78	7	Georgia	Barney, Ga.	D1-'01	11/11
28	Taylor, Fred	RB	6-1	226	1/27/76	10	Florida	Belle Glade, Fla.	D1a-'98	15/15
53	Thomas, Pat	LB	6-2	246	1/26/83	3	North Carolina State	Miami, Fla.	D6b-'05	2/0
37	Thornton, Bruce	CB	5-10	195	1/31/80	3	Georgia	Atlanta, Ga.	FA-'07	0*
22	Toefield, LaBrandon	RB	5-11	232	9/24/80	5	Louisiana State	Independence, La.	D4b-'03	4/0
23	Webb, Dee	CB	5-11	186	12/8/84	2	Florida	Jacksonville, Fla.	D7b-'06	11/1
85	Wiggins, Jermaine	TE	6-2	260	1/8/75	8	Georgia	Boston, Mass.	FA-'07	16/3*
19	Wilford, Ernest	WR	6-4	218	1/14/79	4	Virginia Tech	Richmond, Va.	D4b-'04	16/12
29	Williams, Brian	CB	5-11	198	7/2/79	6	North Carolina State	High Point, N.C.	UFA(Minn)-'06	15/15
74	Williams, Maurice	T	6-5	315	6/29/79	7	Michigan	Detroit, Mich.	D2-'01	16/16
11	Williams, Reggie	WR	6-4	214	5/17/83	4	Washington	Tacoma, Wash.	D1-'04	16/14
36	Wimbush, Derrick	RB/KR	6-1	233	8/26/80	3	Fort Valley State	Mauk, Ga.	FA-'05	12/6
87	Wrighster, George	TE	6-3	257	4/1/81	5	Oregon	Van Nuys, Calif.	D4a-'03	16/10
90	Wyche, James	DE	6-5	271	4/19/82	2	Syracuse	Roosevelt, N.Y.	D7a-'06	0*
88	Zelenka, Joe	LS/TE	6-3	265	3/9/76	9	Wake Forest	Cleveland, Ohio	FA-'01	16/0

* Connolly missed '06 season because of injury; Farris last active with Washington in '05; G. Jones missed '06 season because of injury; McCadam played 16 games with Carolina in '06; Northcutt played 13 games with Cleveland; Pashos played 16 games with Baltimore; Roberson missed '06 season because of injury; Sharon did not play in 1 game; Thornton last active with San Francisco in '05; Wiggins played 16 games with Minnesota; Wyche inactive for 7 games.

+ Restricted Free Agent; subject to developments.

Players lost through free agency (3): TE Kyle Brady (NE; 16 games in '06), S Deon Grant (Sea; 16), WR Cortez Hankton (Minn; 12).

Also played with Jaguars in '06—RB Rich Alexis (1 game), P Chris Hanson (16), T Wayne Hunter (1), WR Chad Owens (4), DT Montavious Stanley (3), DE Marcellus Wiley (12).

2007 FIRST-YEAR ROSTER

Name	Pos.	Ht.	Wt.	Birthdate	College	Hometown	How Acq.
Broussard, John	WR	6-1	172	12/18/83	San Jose State	Kingwood, Texas	D7a
Carnahan, Andrew	T	6-7	307	9/8/83	Arizona State	Hereford, Texas	D7c
Curry, Walter (1)	DT/DE	6-4	275	6/18/81	Albany State	Daytona Beach, Fla.	FA-'06
Durant, Justin	LB	6-1	230	9/21/85	Hampton	Florence, S.C.	D2
Estandia, Greg (1)	TE	6-8	240	11/18/82	Nevada-Las Vegas	Moorpark, Calif.	FA-'06
Gattis, Josh	S	6-1	206	1/15/84	Wake Forest	Durham, N.C.	D5b
Gibbons, Ryan (1)	T	6-6	318	3/13/83	Northeastern	Marshfield, Mass.	FA-'06
Goode, Brett	LS	6-1	244	11/2/84	Arkansas	Fort Smith, Ark.	FA
Kiser, Roosevelt	WR	5-8	169	5/30/85	Florida A&M	Ft. Lauderdale, Fla.	FA
Landri, Derek	DT	6-2	288	9/21/83	Notre Dame	Huntington Beach, Calif.	D5c
Landrom, Jamar (1)	DB	6-3	215	2/16/84	Tennessee State	Pontiac, Mich.	FA-'06
McMahon, Pete (1)	G	6-8	330	10/15/81	Iowa	Dubuque, Iowa	FA-'06
Mincey, Jeremy (1)	DE	6-3	260	12/14/83	Florida	Statesboro, Ga.	FA-'06
Moulton, Rashod	CB	5-11	190	11/6/80	Fort Valley State	St. Petersburg, Fla.	FA
Murray, Dan	TE	6-5	256	8/18/83	Connecticut	Glouchester, Mass.	FA
Nelson, Reggie	S	5-11	198	9/21/83	Florida	Melbourne, Fla.	D1
Nkang, Chad	LB	5-11	220	7/1/85	Elon	Hyattsville, Mary.	D7b
Nwaneri, Uche	G	6-3	325	3/20/84	Purdue	Garland, Texas	D5a
Parrish, Dan	T	6-6	348	7/4/83	Florida A&M	Tallahassee, Fla.	FA
Podlesh, Adam	P	5-11	202	8/11/83	Maryland	Pittsford, N.Y.	D4a
Pudewell, Anthony	TE	6-4	252	4/6/83	Nevada	El Dorado Hills, Calif.	FA
Ricard, Lester	QB	6-4	232	12/11/83	Tulane	Denham Springs, La.	FA
Smith, Brian	DE	6-3	230	9/16/83	Missouri	Denton, Texas	D4b
Terry, D.D.	RB	6-1	190	9/9/83	Sam Houston	Willis, Texas	FA
Walker, Mike	WR	6-2	209	11/21/84	Central Florida	Orlando, Fla.	D3
Woods, D'Juan	WR	6-1	207	6/11/84	Oklahoma State	Oklahoma City, Okla.	FA
Yelk, Tony (1)	P	6-1	205	9/29/81	Iowa State	Madison, Wis.	FA

The term NFL Rookie is defined as a player who is in his first season of professional football and has not been on the roster of another professional football team for any regular-season or postseason games. A Rookie is designated by an "R" on NFL rosters. Players who have been active in another professional football league or players who have NFL experience, including either preseason training camp or being on an Active List or Inactive List, or on Reserve/Injured or Reserve/Physically Unable to Perform for fewer than six regular-season games, are termed NFL First-Year Players. An NFL First-Year Player is designated by a "1" on NFL rosters. Thereafter, a player is credited with an additional year of experience for each season in which he accumulates six games on the Active List or Inactive List, or on Reserve/Injured or Reserve/Physically Unable to Perform.

Log on to www.jaguars.com for an up-to-date roster.

COACHING STAFF

Head Coach,
Jack Del Rio

Pro Career: Jack Del Rio was named head coach of the Jaguars on January 17, 2003, becoming the second head coach in franchise history. In 2006, the Jaguars finished second in the NFL in total defense and third in rushing offense but fell just shy of the playoffs with an 8-8 record. Jacksonville finished with a 12-4 record in 2005 and Del Rio guided the franchise to its first postseason appearance since 1999. In 2004, the Jaguars registered a 9-7 record for the franchise's first winning season since 1999. In 2003, six of the Jaguars' eleven losses were by seven points or less. Del Rio was the defensive coordinator for the Carolina Panthers in 2002, and the team's defense ranked second in the league after finishing thirty-first in 2001. From 1999-2001, he was the linebackers coach for the Baltimore Ravens, helping the team win Super Bowl XXXV. Del Rio previously coached in New Orleans (1997-98). He previously played 11 years as an NFL linebacker. In 1985, he was a third-round choice of the New Orleans Saints and was named to the NFL's All-Rookie team. Del Rio also played for the Kansas City Chiefs (1987-88), Dallas Cowboys (1989-1991), and Minnesota Vikings (1992-95). He played in the Pro Bowl following the 1994 season. Career record: 34-31.

Background: Four-year starter at linebacker from 1981-84 at Southern California, where he earned consensus All-America honors as a senior and was runner-up for the Lombardi Award. He was co-MVP of the 1985 Rose Bowl. Drafted by baseball's Toronto Blue Jays in 1981, Del Rio batted .340 while playing catcher on USC's baseball team. He has a political science degree from Kansas.

Personal: Born April 4, 1963 in Castro Valley, Calif. Jack and his wife, Linda, live in Jacksonville, and have three daughters, Lauren, Hope, and Aubrey, and a son, Luke.

ASSISTANT COACHES

Mark Asanovich, strength and conditioning; born May 20, 1959, Duluth, Minn. Attended St. Cloud State. No college or pro playing experience. College coach: Ohio State 1984-85, The Citadel 1986. Pro coach: Minnesota Vikings 1995, Tampa Bay Buccaneers 1996-2001, Baltimore Ravens 2002, joined Jaguars in 2003.

Dave Campo, asst. head coach/secondary; born July 18, 1947, Groton, Conn. Defensive back Central Connecticut State 1967-1970. No pro playing experience. College coach: Central Connecticut State 1971-72, Albany 1973, Bridgeport 1974, Pittsburgh 1975, Washington State 1976, Boise State 1977-79, Oregon State 1980, Weber State 1981-82, Iowa State 1983, Syracuse 1984-86, Miami 1987-88. Pro coach: Dallas Cowboys 1989-2002 (head

coach 2000-2002), Cleveland Browns 2003-2004, joined Jaguars in 2005.

Joe DeCamillis, special teams coordinator; born June 29, 1965, Arvada, Colo. Attended Wyoming. No college or pro playing experience. College coach: Wyoming 1988. Pro coach: Denver Broncos 1989, Miami Dolphins 1990, New York Giants 1993-96, Atlanta Falcons 1997-2006, joined Jaguars in 2007.

Mark Duffner, linebackers; born July 19, 1953, Annadale, Va. Defensive lineman William & Mary 1972-74. No pro playing experience. College coach: Ohio State 1975-76, Cincinnati 1977-1980, Holy Cross 1981-1991 (head coach 1986-1991), Maryland 1992-1996 (head coach). Pro coach: Cincinnati Bengals 1997-2002, Green Bay Packers 2003-2005, joined Jaguars in 2006.

Les Ebert, asst. strength and conditioning; born October 1, 1972, Brainerd, Minn. Attended Minnesota-Duluth. No college or pro playing experience. Pro coach: Tampa Bay Buccaneers 1999-2002, joined Jaguars in 2003.

Ray Hamilton, defensive line; born January 20, 1951, Omaha, Neb. Nose tackle Oklahoma 1969-1972. Pro defensive lineman New England Patriots 1973-1981. College coach: Tennessee 1992. Pro coach: New England Patriots 1985-89, Tampa Bay Buccaneers 1991, Los Angeles Raiders 1993-94, New York Jets 1994-96, 2000, New England Patriots 1997-99, Cleveland Browns 2001-02, joined Jaguars in 2003.

Andy Heck, offensive line; born January 1, 1967, Fargo, N.D. Tackle Notre Dame 1985-88. Pro tackle Seattle 1989-1993, Chicago 1994-98, Washington 1999-2000. College coach: Virginia 2001-03. Pro coach: Joined Jaguars in 2004.

Dirk Koetter, offensive coordinator; born February 5, 1959, Pocatello, Idaho. Quarterback Idaho State 1978-1981. No pro playing experience. College coach: San Francisco State 1985, Texas El-Paso 1986-88, Missouri 1989-1993, Boston College 1994-95, Oregon 1996-97, Boise State 1998-2000 (head coach), Arizona State 2001-06 (head coach). Joined Jaguars in 2007.

Ted Monachino, asst. defensive line; born October 15, 1966, Council Bluffs, Iowa. Defensive lineman Missouri 1988-1990. No pro playing experience. College coach: Texas Christian 1998, Southwest Missouri State 1999, Boise State 2000, Arizona State 2001-2005. Pro coach: Joined Jaguars in 2006.

Todd Monken, wide receivers; born February 2, 1966, Wheaton, Ill. Quarterback Knox College 1987-1989. No pro playing experience. College coach: Grand Valley State 1989-1990, Notre Dame 1991-92, Eastern Michigan 1993-99, Louisiana Tech 2000-01, Oklahoma State 2002-04, Louisiana State 2005-06. Pro coach: Joined Jaguars in 2007.

Kennedy Pola, running backs; born November 22, 1963, Pago, Pago, American Samoa. Fullback Southern California 1982-85. No pro playing experience. College coach: UCLA 1992-93, San Diego State 1994-96, Colorado 1997-98, San Diego State 1999, Southern California 2000-2003. Pro coach: Cleveland Browns 2004, joined Jaguars in 2005.

Robert Prince, asst. wide receivers; born May 8, 1965, Okinawa, Japan. Wide receiver Humbolt State 1985-86. No pro playing experience. College coach: Humbolt State 1989-1990, Montana State 1991, Sacramento State 1992-93, Fort Lewis College 1994-95, Recruit Seagulls (Japan) 1996-97, Portland State 1998-2000, Boise State 2001-03. Pro coach: Atlanta Falcons, 2004-06, joined Jaguars in 2007.

Alvin Reynolds, defensive backs; born June 24, 1959, Pineville, La. Safety Indiana State 1978-1981. No pro playing experience. College coach: Indiana State 1982-1992. Pro coach: Denver Broncos 1993-95, Baltimore Ravens 1996-98, Carolina Panthers 1999-2002, joined Jaguars in 2003.

Mike Shula, quarterbacks; born June 3, 1965, Baltimore. Quarterback Alabama 1984-86. No pro playing experience. College coach: Alabama 2003-06 (head coach). Pro coach: Miami Dolphins 1991-92, Chicago Bears 1993-95, Tampa Bay Buccaneers 1996-99, Miami Dolphins 2000-02, joined Jaguars in 2007.

Mike Smith, defensive coordinator; born November 30, 1959, Chicago. Linebacker East Tennessee 1977-1981. Pro linebacker Winnipeg Blue Bombers (CFL) 1982. College coach: San Diego State 1982-85, Morehead State (Ky.) 1986, Tennessee Tech 1987-1998. Pro coach: Baltimore Ravens 1999-2002, joined Jaguars in 2003.

Mike Tice, asst. head coach/offense; born February 2, 1959, Bayshore, N.Y. Quarterback Maryland 1977-1980. Pro tight end Seattle Seahawks 1981-1988, 1990-91, Washington Redskins 1989, Minnesota Vikings 1992-1993, 1995. Pro coach: Minnesota Vikings 1996-2005 (head coach 2001-2005), joined Jaguars in 2006.

Tom Williams, asst. special teams; born December 22, 1969, Fort Worth, Texas. Linebacker Stanford 1989-1992. No pro playing experience. College coach: Hawaii 1996-98, Washington 1999-2001, Stanford 2002-04, San Jose State 2005-06. Pro coach: Joined Jaguars in 2007.

American Football Conference
West Division
Team Colors: Red, Gold, and White
One Arrowhead Drive
Kansas City, Missouri 64129
Telephone: (816) 920-9300

2007 SCHEDULE
PRESEASON
Aug. 11 at Cleveland 7:30
Aug. 16 **Miami**...............................7:00
Aug. 23 **New Orleans**.....................7:30
Aug. 30 at St. Louis..........................7:00

REGULAR SEASON
Sep. 9   at Houston 12:00
Sep. 16 at Chicago 3:15
Sep. 23 **Minnesota** 12:00
Sep. 30 at San Diego 1:15
Oct. 7   **Jacksonville** 12:00
Oct. 14 **Cincinnati** 12:00
Oct. 21 at Oakland 1:05
Oct. 28 Open Date
Nov. 4   **Green Bay** 12:00
Nov. 11 **Denver** 12:00
Nov. 18 at Indianapolis 1:00
Nov. 25 **Oakland** 12:00
Dec. 2   **San Diego** 12:00
Dec. 9   at Denver 2:15
Dec. 16 **Tennessee** 12:00
Dec. 23 at Detroit 1:00
Dec. 30 at N.Y. Jets *8:15
Sunday night games in Weeks 11-17 subject to change

Stadium: Arrowhead Stadium
(opened in 1972)
•**Capacity:** 79,451
One Arrowhead Drive
Kansas City, Missouri 64129
Playing Surface: Grass
Training Camp: University of
Wisconsin-River Falls
River Falls, WI 54022

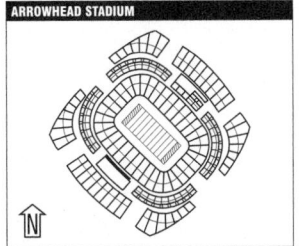
ARROWHEAD STADIUM

CLUB OFFICIALS
Chairman of the Board: Clark Hunt
President: Carl Peterson
Executive Vice President/Chief Operating
Officer: Denny Thum
Vice President of Player Personnel:
Bill Kuharich
Vice President of Football Operations:
Lynn Stiles
Senior Vice President of Administration:
Bill Newman
Secretary: Jim Seigfreid
Director of Finance/Treasurer: Dale Young
Vice President of Sales and Marketing:
Tammy Fruits
Director of College Scouting: Chuck Cook
Director of Public Relations: Bob Moore
Associate Director of Public Relations:
Pete Moris
Director of Stadium Operations:
Steve Schneider
Director of Development: Ken Blume
Director of Corporate Sponsorship Sales:
Anita Bailey
Director of Ticket and Event Marketing:
Gary Spani
Director of Player Development:
Lamonte Winston
Director of Community Relations:
Brenda Sniezek
Director of Ticket Operations:
Doug Hopkins
Equipment Manager: Mike Davidson
Asst. Equipment Managers: Allen Wright,
Chris Shropshire
Head Athletic Trainer: David Price
Assistant Athletic Trainers: David Glover,
Jimmy Ntelekos, Owen Stanley
Director of Video Operations: Pat Brazil
Assistant Director Video Operations:
Ken Radino
Video Assistant: Josh Schmitt

COACHING HISTORY
Dallas Texans 1960-62
(383-334-12)
Records include postseason games
1960-1974 Hank Stram 129-79-10
1975-77   Paul Wiggin* 11-24-0
1977   Tom Bettis 1-6-0
1978-1982 Marv Levy 31-42-0
1983-86   John Mackovic 30-35-0
1987-88   Frank Gansz.................8-22-1
1989-1998 Marty Schottenheimer...104-65-1
1999-2000 Gunther Cunningham ...16-16-0
2001-05   Dick Vermeil.................44-37-0
2006   Herm Edwards.................9-8-0
*Released after seven games in 1977

PAID ATTENDANCE
Home 624,171   Away 530,045
Total 1,154,216
Single-game home record,
82,893* (10/2/00)
Single-season home record,
629,569 (1999)
*Arrowhead Stadium attendance: 78,502;
Kauffman Stadium attendance: 4,391

2007 DRAFT CHOICES
Round	Name	Pos.	College
1	Dwayne Bowe	WR	Louisiana State
2	Claude McBride	DE	Tennessee
3	DeMarcus Tyler	DT	North Carolina St.
5	Kolby Smith	RB	Louisville
	Justin Medlock	K	UCLA
6	Herb Taylor	T	TCU
7	Michael Allan	TE	Whitworth

KANSAS CITY CHIEFS

2006 TEAM RECORD

PRESEASON (2-2)

Date	Result	Opponent
8/12	L 14-24	at Houston
8/17	L 0-17	at N.Y. Giants
8/26	W 16-12	St. Louis
8/31	W 10-9	New Orleans

REGULAR SEASON (9-7)

Date	Result	Opponent	Att.
9/10	L 10-23	Cincinnati	77,956
9/17	L 6-9	at Denver (OT)	76,786
10/1	W 41-0	San Francisco	77,609
10/8	W 23-20	at Arizona	63,445
10/15	L 7-45	at Pittsburgh	64,727
10/22	W 30-27	San Diego	77,752
10/29	W 35-28	Seattle	77,645
11/5	W 31-17	at St. Louis	66,191
11/12	L 10-13	at Miami	73,132
11/19	W 17-13	Oakland	78,097
11/23	W 19-10	Denver	79,484
12/3	L 28-31	at Cleveland (OT)	71,927
12/10	L 10-20	Baltimore	77,232
12/17	L 9-20	at San Diego	66,583
12/23	W 20-9	at Oakland	61,446
12/31	W 35-30	Jacksonville	77,500

POSTSEASON (0-1)

Date	Result	Opponent	Att.
1/6	L 8-23	at Indianapolis	57,215

SCORE BY PERIODS

Chiefs	71	105	60	95	0	—	331
Opponents	61	113	58	77	6	—	315

2006 TEAM STATISTICS

	Chiefs	Opp.
Total First Downs	310	298
Rushing	105	109
Passing	184	171
Penalty	21	18
3rd Down: Made/Att	89/219	83/212
3rd Down Pct.	40.6	39.2
4th Down: Made/Att	9/15	8/13
4th Down Pct.	60.0	61.5
Possession Avg.	30:06	29:54
Total Net Yards	5143	5262
Avg. Per Game	321.4	328.9
Total Plays	1004	999
Avg. Per Play	5.1	5.3
Net Yards Rushing	2143	1928
Avg. Per Game	133.9	120.5
Total Rushes	513	461
Net Yards Passing	3000	3334
Avg. Per Game	187.5	208.4
Sacked/Yards Lost	41/243	32/190
Gross Yards	3243	3524
Att./Completions	450/272	506/314
Completion Pct.	60.4	62.1
Had Intercepted	12	15
Punts/Average	72/44.1	75/40.8
Net Punting Avg.	72/39.2	75/34.4
Penalties/Yards	76/577	85/709
Fumbles/Ball Lost	25/14	29/15
Touchdowns	37	34
Rushing	17	14
Passing	18	18
Returns	2	2

2006 INDIVIDUAL STATISTICS

PASSING

PASSING	Att.	Comp.	Yds.	Pct.	TD	Int.	Tkld.	Rate
Huard	244	148	1,878	60.7	11	1	16/106	98.0
Green	198	121	1,342	61.1	7	9	24/127	74.1
Croyle	7	3	23	42.9	0	2	1/10	11.9
L. Johnson	1	0	—	0.0	0	0	0/0	39.6
Chiefs	450	272	3,243	60.4	18	12	41/243	84.7
Opponents	506	314	3,524	62.1	18	15	32/190	82.3

SCORING

SCORING	TD R	TD P	TD Rt	PAT	FG	Saf	PTS
L. Johnson	17	2	0	0/0	0/0	0	114
Tynes	0	0	0	35/36	24/31	0	107
Gonzalez	0	5	0	0/0	0/0	0	32
Kennison	0	5	0	0/0	0/0	0	30
Hall	0	2	1	0/0	0/0	0	18
Wilson	0	3	0	0/0	0/0	0	18
Parker	0	1	0	0/0	0/0	0	6
Pollard	0	0	1	0/0	0/0	0	6
Chiefs	17	18	2	35/36	24/31	0	331
Opponents	14	18	2	33/33	26/32	0	315

2-Pt. Conversions:
Gonzalez, Chiefs 1-1, Opponents 0-1.

RUSHING

RUSHING	No.	Yds	Avg	LG	TD
L. Johnson	416	1789	4.3	47	17
Bennett	36	200	5.6	41	0
Green	19	59	3.1	10	0
D. Brown	10	24	2.4	7	0
Cruz	5	19	3.8	7	0
Kennison	4	16	4.0	9	0
Hall	3	11	3.7	9	0
Huard	9	9	1.0	8	0
Ross	3	8	2.7	4	0
Parker	3	7	2.3	5	0
Page	1	4	4.0	4	0
Colquitt	1	0	0.0	0	0
Croyle	3	-3	-1.0	-1	0
Chiefs	513	2143	4.2	47	17
Opponents	461	1928	4.2	85t	14

RECEIVING

RECEIVING	No.	Yds	Avg	LG	TD
Gonzalez	73	900	12.3	57	5
Kennison	53	860	16.2	51	5
Parker	41	561	13.7	43	1
L. Johnson	41	410	10.0	78	2
Hall	26	204	7.8	19	2
Wilson	15	132	8.8	19	3
Bennett	9	77	8.6	14	0
Dunn	4	40	10.0	15	0
Webb	3	23	7.7	11	0
Cruz	2	20	10.0	11	0
Gardner	2	17	8.5	13	0
Huard	2	-6	-3.0	-2	0
D. Brown	1	5	5.0	5	0
Chiefs	272	3243	11.9	78	18
Opponents	314	3524	11.2	87t	18

INTERCEPTIONS

INTERCEPTIONS	No.	Yds	Avg	LG	TD
Law	4	11	2.8	16	0
Wesley	3	39	13.0	29	0
Page	3	30	10.0	30	0
Knight	1	27	27.0	27	0
K. Mitchell	1	23	23.0	23	0
Allen	1	3	3.0	3	0
Surtain	1	0	0.0	0	0
Hali	1	-9	-9.0	-9	0
Chiefs	15	124	8.3	30	0
Opponents	12	146	12.2	49	1

PUNTING

PUNTING	No.	Yds.	Avg.	In 20	LG
Colquitt	71	3145	44.3	23	72
Tynes	1	33	33.0	1	33
Chiefs	72	3178	44.1	24	72
Opponents	75	3063	40.8	23	61

PUNT RETURNS

PUNT RETURNS	Ret	FC	Yds	Avg	LG	TD
Hall	27	6	240	8.9	60t	1
Kennison	3	1	18	6.0	11	0
Walls	2	0	6	3.0	6	0
Ross	1	0	0	0.0	0	0
Chiefs	33	7	264	8.0	60t	1
Opponents	32	19	254	7.9	50	0

KICKOFF RETURNS

KICKOFF RETURNS	No.	Yds	Avg	LG	TD
Hall	53	1207	22.8	60	0
Webb	7	169	24.1	50	0
Sapp	1	21	21.0	21	0
Cruz	1	7	7.0	7	0
D. Brown	1	0	0.0	0	0
Pollard	1	0	0.0	0	0
Chiefs	64	1404	21.9	60	0
Opponents	71	1646	23.2	58	0

FIELD GOALS

FIELD GOALS	1-19	20-29	30-39	40-49	50+
Tynes	1/1	10/10	4/6	7/10	2/4
Chiefs	1/1	10/10	4/6	7/10	2/4
Opponents	0/0	6/7	12/12	7/9	1/4

SACKS

SACKS	No.
Hali	8.0
Allen	7.5
D Johnson	4.5
Edwards	2.5
Knight	2.0
K Mitchell	1.5
Bell	1.0
Fox	1.0
Law	1.0
Page	1.0
Reed	1.0
Surtain	1.0
Chiefs	32.0
Opponents	41.0

RECORD HOLDERS
INDIVIDUAL RECORDS—CAREER

Category	Name	Performance
Rushing (Yds.)	Priest Holmes, 2001-06	5,933
Passing (Yds.)	Len Dawson, 1962-1975	28,507
Passing (TDs)	Len Dawson, 1962-1975	237
Receiving (No.)	Tony Gonzalez, 1997-2006	721
Receiving (Yds.)	Tony Gonzalez, 1997-2006	8,710
Interceptions	Emmitt Thomas, 1966-1978	58
Punting (Avg.)	Jerrel Wilson, 1963-1977	43.4
Punt Return (Avg.)	Noland Smith, 1967-69	11.1
Kickoff Return (Avg.)	Noland Smith, 1967-69	26.8
Field Goals	Nick Lowery, 1980-1993	329
Touchdowns (Tot.)	Priest Holmes, 2001-06	83
Points	Nick Lowery, 1980-1993	1,466

INDIVIDUAL RECORDS—SINGLE SEASON

Category	Name	Performance
Rushing (Yds.)	Larry Johnson, 2006	1,789
Passing (Yds.)	Trent Green, 2004	4,591
Passing (TDs)	Len Dawson, 1964	30
Receiving (No.)	Tony Gonzalez, 2004	102
Receiving (Yds.)	Derrick Alexander, 2000	1,391
Interceptions	Emmitt Thomas, 1974	12
Punting (Avg.)	Jerrel Wilson, 1965	45.4
Punt Return (Avg.)	Dante Hall, 2003	16.3
Kickoff Return (Avg.)	Dave Grayson, 1962	29.7
Field Goals	Nick Lowery, 1990	34
Touchdowns (Tot.)	Priest Holmes, 2003	27
Points	Priest Holmes, 2003	162

INDIVIDUAL RECORDS—SINGLE GAME

Category	Name	Performance
Rushing (Yds.)	Larry Johnson, 11-20-05	211
Passing (Yds.)	Elvis Grbac, 11-5-00	504
Passing (TDs)	Len Dawson, 11-1-64	6
Receiving (No.)	Tony Gonzalez, 1-2-05	14
Receiving (Yds.)	Stephone Paige, 12-22-85	309
Interceptions	Bobby Ply, 12-16-62	*5
	Bobby Hunt, 10-4-64	*5
	Deron Cherry, 9-29-85	*4
Field Goals	Many times	5
	Last time by Nick Lowery, 9-20-93	
Touchdowns (Tot.)	Abner Haynes, 11-26-61	5
Points	Abner Haynes, 11-26-61	30

*NFL Record

2007 VETERAN ROSTER

No.	Name	Pos.	Ht.	Wt.	Birthdate	NFL Exp.	College	Hometown	How Acq.	'06 Games/ Starts
69	Allen, Jared	DE	6-6	270	4/3/82	4	Idaho State	Los Gatos, Calif.	D4b-'04	16/16
99	Bell, Kendrell	LB	6-1	245	7/2/78	7	Georgia	Augusta, Ga.	UFA(Pitt)-'05	16/14
26	Bennett, Michael	RB	5-9	207	8/13/78	7	Wisconsin	Milwaukee, Wis.	T(NO)-'06	11/0
67	Bober, Chris	G	6-5	310	12/24/76	8	Nebraska-Omaha	Omaha, Neb.	UFA(NYG)-'04	16/2
70	Boone, Alfonso	DT	6-3	305	1/11/76	7	Mt. San Antonio (Calif.) J.C.	Saginaw, Mich.	UFA(Chi)-'07	12/4*
2	Colquitt, Dustin	P	6-3	210	5/6/82	3	Tennessee	Knoxville, Tenn.	D3-'05	16/0
12	Croyle, Brodie	QB	6-2	206	2/6/83	2	Alabama	Rainbow City, Ala.	D3-'06	2/0
51	Darche, Jean-Philippe	LS	6-0	242	2/28/75	8	McGill	Montreal, Quebec, Canada	UFA(Sea)-'07	1/0*
89	Dunn, Jason	TE	6-6	274	11/15/73	11	Eastern Kentucky	Harrodsburg, Ky.	FA-'00	15/5
59	Edwards, Donnie	LB	6-2	224	4/6/73	12	UCLA	Chula Vista, Calif.	UFA(SD)-'07	16/16*
95	Edwards, Ron	DT	6-3	315	7/12/79	7	Texas A&M	Houston, Texas	UFA(Buff)-'06	16/16
97	Fox, Keyaron	LB	6-3	235	1/31/82	4	Georgia Tech	Atlanta, Ga.	D3-'04	16/4
85	Gardner, Rod	WR	6-2	219	10/26/77	7	Clemson	Jacksonville, Fla.	FA-'06	14/0
88	Gonzalez, Tony	TE	6-5	251	2/27/76	11	California	Huntington Beach, Calif.	D1-97	15/15
10	Green, Trent	QB	6-3	217	7/9/70	14	Indiana	St. Louis, Mo.	T(StL)-'01	8/8
53	Griffin, Kris	LB	6-3	240	5/27/81	3	Indiana (Pa.)	Rochester, Pa.	FA-'05	16/0
46	Grigsby, Boomer	FB	5-11	249	11/15/81	3	Illinois State	Canton, Ill.	D5a-'05	15/0
91	Hali, Tamba	DE	6-3	275	11/3/83	2	Penn State	Teaneck, N.J.	D1-'06	16/16
50	Harris, Napoleon	LB	6-3	253	2/25/79	6	Northwestern	Harvey, Ill.	UFA(Minn)-'07	14/14*
31	Holmes, Priest	RB	5-9	213	10/7/73	11	Texas	San Antonio, Texas	UFA(Balt)-'01	0*
11	Huard, Damon	QB	6-3	218	7/9/73	11	Washington	Puyallup, Wash.	FA-'04	10/8
56	Johnson, Derrick	LB	6-3	242	11/22/82	3	Texas	Waco, Texas	D1-'05	13/12
27	Johnson, Larry	RB	6-1	230	11/19/79	5	Penn State	State College, Pa.	D1-'03	16/16
87	Kennison, Eddie	WR	6-1	201	1/20/73	12	Louisiana State	Lake Charles, La.	FA-'01	16/16
24	Law, Ty	CB	5-11	200	2/10/74	13	Michigan	Aliquippa, Pa.	FA-'06	16/16
45	Maxey, Marcus	CB	6-0	192	2/2/83	2	Miami	Navasota, Texas	D5-'06	1/0
47	McGraw, Jon	S	6-3	208	4/2/79	6	Kansas State	Manhattan, Kan.	UFA(Det)-'07	16/3*
77	McIntosh, Damion	T	6-4	320	3/25/77	8	Kansas State	Hollywood, Fla.	UFA(Mia)-'07	13/13*
64	Niswanger, Rudy	C	6-5	301	11/9/82	2	Louisiana State	Monroe, La.	FA-'06	4/0
44	Page, Jarrad	S	6-0	225	10/19/84	2	UCLA	San Leandro, Calif.	D7-'06	16/2
18	Parker, Samie	WR	5-11	190	3/25/81	4	Oregon	Long Beach, Calif.	D4a-'04	16/15
39	Patterson, Dimitri	CB	5-10	190	6/18/83	2	Tuskegee	Orlando, Fla.	FA-'07	0*
49	Pollard, Bernard	S	6-1	224	12/23/84	2	Purdue	Ft. Wayne, Ind.	D2-'06	16/0
92	Reed, James	DT	6-0	286	2/3/77	7	Iowa State	Saginaw, Mich.	FA-'06	15/15
39	Ross, Derrick	RB	5-10	226	12/29/83	2	Tarleton State	Huntsville, Texas	FA-'06	7/0
79	Sampson, Kevin	T	6-4	312	6/19/81	4	Syracuse	Westwood, N.J.	D7-'04	6/6
20	Sapp, Benny	CB	5-9	190	1/20/81	4	Northern Iowa	Ft. Lauderdale, Fla.	FA-'04	11/0
55	Scanlon, Rich	LB	6-2	249	12/23/80	2	Syracuse	Oradell, N.J.	FA-'04	9/0
61	Stallings, Tre	G	6-3	315	1/8/83	2	Mississippi	Magnolia, Miss.	D6a-'06	0*
23	Surtain, Patrick	CB	5-11	195	6/19/76	10	Southern Mississippi	New Orleans, La.	T(Mia)-'05	16/16
71	Svitek, Will	T	6-6	300	1/8/82	3	Stanford	Newbury, Calif.	D6a-'05	2/0
60	Terry, Chris	T	6-5	295	8/8/75	8	Georgia	Jacksonville, Fla.	FA-'06	7/0
1	Tynes, Lawrence	K	6-1	202	5/3/78	4	Troy State	Milton, Fla.	FA-'04	16/0
54	Waters, Brian	G	6-3	320	2/18/77	8	North Texas	Waxahachie, Texas	FA-'00	14/14
80	Webb, Jeff	WR	6-2	211	1/31/82	2	San Diego State	La Quinta, Calif.	D6b-'06	10/0
76	Welbourn, John	G	6-5	310	3/30/76	9	California	Rolling Hills, Calif.	T(Phil)-'04	9/4
25	Wesley, Greg	S	6-2	206	3/19/78	8	Arkansas-Pine Bluff	England, Ark.	D3-'00	14/14
62	Wiegmann, Casey	C	6-2	285	7/20/73	12	Iowa	Parkersburg, Iowa	UFA(Chi)-'01	16/16
96	Wilkerson, Jimmy	DE	6-2	290	1/4/81	5	Oklahoma	Omaha, Texas	D6-'03	13/1
84	Wilson, Kris	TE	6-2	251	8/22/81	4	Pittsburgh	Lancaster, Pa.	D2b-'04	16/10

* Boone played 12 games with Chicago in '06; Darche played 1 game with Seattle, D. Edwards played 16 games with San Diego; Harris played 14 games with Minnesota; Holmes missed '06 season because of injury; McGraw played 16 games with Detroit; McIntosh played 13 games with Miami; Patterson last active with Washington in '05; Stallings inactive for 16 games.

Traded—KR Dante Hall (15 games in '06) to St. Louis, DT Ryan Sims (16) to Tampa Bay.

Players lost through free agency (3): T Jordan Black (Hou; 16), LB Kawika Mitchell (NYG; 16), CB Lenny Walls (StL; 16).

Also played with Chiefs in '06 —FB Ronnie Cruz (5 games), DT Lional Dalton (2), DE Eric Hicks (16), S Sammy Knight (16), DT Stephen Williams (11).

2007 FIRST-YEAR ROSTER

Name	Pos.	Ht.	Wt.	Birthdate	College	Hometown	How Acq.
Allan, Michael	TE	6-6	254	9/8/83	Whitworth	Bellevue, Wash.	D7
Barret, Aaron (1)	K	5-10	175	5/14/82	New Mexico	Temecula, Calif.	FA
Batiste, George	T	6-4	289	11/28/84	Southern Mississippi	Avondale, La.	FA
Bowe, Dwayne	WR	6-2	221	9/21/84	Louisiana State	Miami, Fla.	D1
Brackenridge, Tyron	CB	5-11	189	6/30/84	Washington State	Ontario, Calif.	FA
Bragg, Michael (1)	CB	6-1	190	12/31/81	Texas A&M-Kingsville	Los Angeles, Calif.	FA-'06
Butler, Robb (1)	S	6-0	200	9/14/81	Robert Morris	Pittsburgh, Pa.	FA
Crum, Brian	LB	6-2	233	12/17/83	Florida	Kingsland, Ga.	FA
Doughty, Stanley	DT	6-1	330	1/18/84	South Carolina	Greensburg, La.	FA
Ekwrekwu, Brad	WR	6-3	216	10/3/85	Missouri	Arlington, Texas	FA
Fair, Marlon	S	5-10	204	5/29/85	Hampton	Knightdale, N.C.	FA
Franklin, Tony	CB	5-10	180	9/1/84	Virginia	Cleveland, Ohio	FA
Hannon, Chris (1)	WR	6-3	205	2/18/84	Tennessee	Sarasota, Fla.	FA-'06
Hanoian, Greg (1)	FB	6-2	263	12/9/81	Syracuse	Providence, R.I.	FA
Harris, Chris	DE	6-5	257	12/14/83	Alabama	Tuscaloosa, Ala.	FA
Harris, Gilbert	FB	6-2	235	6/18/84	Arizona	San Antonio, Texas	FA
Harris, Nate	LB	6-0	230	3/8/83	Louisville	Miami, Fla.	FA
Heard, Michael	DE	6-1	253	5/24/84	Mississippi State	Atlanta, Ga.	FA
Hicks, David	LB	6-2	236	8/7/84	Grambling State	El Dorado, Ark.	FA
Hunt, Rob (1)	G	6-4	301	3/3/81	North Dakota State	Cavalier, N.D.	FA
Jacobs, Omar (1)	QB	6-4	232	3/3/84	Bowling Green	Delray Beach, Fla.	FA
Kershaw, William (1)	LB	6-3	240	12/15/83	Maryland	Raeford, N.C.	FA-'06
McBride, Claude	DE	6-2	278	5/30/85	Tennessee	Camden, N.J.	D2
McGlothlin, Matt	DT	5-11	300	2/17/83	Tennessee	Pounding Mill, Va.	FA
Medlock, Justin	K	5-11	201	10/23/83	UCLA	Fremont, Calif.	D5b
Murphy, Montez (1)	DE	6-6	256	1/6/82	Baylor	St. Louis, Ill.	FA
Murphy, Wes	TE	6-3	268	6/16/83	Arkansas	Cuthbert, Ga.	FA
Newby, James	T	6-5	294	11/18/83	North Carolina State	Athens, Ala.	FA
O'Keith, Marcus	RB	5-11	198	10/15/83	California	Carson, Calif.	FA
Phinisee, Justin (1)	CB	5-11	199	4/10/83	Oregon	Long Beach, Calif.	FA
Price, Maurice	WR	6-0	197	9/11/85	Charleston Southern	Orlando, Fla.	FA
Printers, Casey (1)	QB	6-2	222	5/16/81	Florida A&M	DeSoto, Texas	FA-'06
Pruneda, Ramiro (1)	T	6-6	317	1/25/83	Monterrey Tech	Monterrey, Mexico	FA
Randolph, Ean	WR	5-8	173	11/14/85	South Florida	Plant City, Fla.	FA
Reid, Nick (1)	LB	6-3	234	11/18/83	Kansas	Derby, Kan.	FA
Ryan, Titus	WR	6-0	193	5/19/84	Concordia	Tuscaloosa, Ala.	FA
Smith, Kolby	RB	5-11	219	12/15/84	Louisville	Tallahassee, Fla.	D5a
Taylor, Herb	T	6-3	295	9/22/84	Texas Christian	Houston, Texas	D6
Terrell, Jeff	QB	6-1	220	1/24/85	Princeton	Chagrin Falls, Ohio	FA
Tyler, DeMarcus	DT	6-2	306	2/14/85	North Carolina State	Fayetteville, N.C.	D3
Willis, Keith (1)	TE	6-6	260	12/14/80	Virginia Tech	Norfolk, Va.	FA
Wusu, Timi (1)	LB	6-2	219	6/10/83	Stanford	St. Thomas, Virgin Island	FA

The term NFL Rookie is defined as a player who is in his first season of professional football and has not been on the roster of another professional football team for any regular-season or postseason games. A Rookie is designated by an "R" on NFL rosters. Players who have been active in another professional football league or players who have NFL experience, including either preseason training camp or being on an Active List or Inactive List, or on Reserve/Injured or Reserve/Physically Unable to Perform for fewer than six regular-season games, are termed NFL First-Year Players. An NFL First-Year Player is designated by a "1" on NFL rosters. Thereafter, a player is credited with an additional year of experience for each season in which he accumulates six games on the Active List or Inactive List, or on Reserve/Injured or Reserve/Physically Unable to Perform.

Log on to www.kcchiefs.com for an up-to-date roster.

COACHING STAFF
Head Coach,
Herm Edwards

Pro Career: Herm Edwards was named the tenth head coach in Chiefs franchise history on January 9, 2006. He enters his seventh season as an NFL head coach and his twenty-eighth season in the league. He rejoined the Chiefs in 2006 after spending six seasons with Kansas City as a scout (1990-91), defensive backs coach (1992-94), and pro personnel scout (1995). Last season, he became the first head coach in franchise history to guide the Chiefs to the playoffs in his initial season with the club. His 9-7 record tied for the most victories by a first-year coach in franchise annals as the Chiefs became just the fifth team since 2000 to bounce back from an 0-2 start and still earn a spot in the postseason. After leading the Chiefs to the playoffs in 2006, Edwards became one of just five coaches in NFL history to guide two different squads (Chiefs 2006, Jets 2001) to a playoff berth in their debut campaign with those teams. He began his pro coaching career as a participant in the NFL's Minority Coaching Fellowship program with Kansas City in 1989 and is the first graduate of the program to go on to become the head coach of the franchise for which he served his fellowship. Edwards was an assistant coach with Tampa Bay (1996-2000), and then enjoyed a five-year stint as the head coach of the N.Y. Jets (2001-05). He led the Jets to 41 wins, and was on the sideline for a Jets-best five postseason games. He joined the NFL as a rookie free agent cornerback with Philadelphia in 1977. He started 135 consecutive games, had a franchise-record 38 combined interceptions in regular and postseason action. He also played in Super Bowl XV, and finished his career with the Rams and Atlanta in 1986. Career record: 50-52.

Background: Edwards played cornerback collegiately for California (1972, 1974), Monterey Peninsula (Calif.) J.C. (1973), and San Diego State (1976). He played 10 NFL seasons with Philadelphia (1977-85), the L.A. Rams (1986) and Atlanta Falcons (1986). Collegiately, he was the defensive backs coach at San Jose State (1987-89).

Personal: Born April 27, 1954 in Fort Monmouth, N.J. He and his wife Lia have a son, Marcus and two daughters, Gabrielle and Vivian.

ASSISTANT COACHES

Bob Bicknell, asst. offensive line; born November 13, 1969, Holliston, Mass. Tight end Boston College 1988-1991. No pro playing experience. College coach: Boston 1993-97, Temple 2006. Pro coach: Frankfurt Galaxy (NFLEL) 1998-99, Berlin Thunder (NFLEL) 2000-03, Cologne Centurions (NFLEL) 2004-05, joined Chiefs in 2007.

Don Blackmon, linebackers; born March 14, 1958, Pompano Beach, Fla. Linebacker Tulsa 1976-1980. Pro linebacker New England Patriots 1981-87. Pro coach: New England Patriots 1988-1990, Cleveland Browns 1991, N.Y. Giants 1993-96, Atlanta Falcons 1997-2001, Buffalo Bills 2003-05, joined Chiefs in 2006.

Gunther Cunningham, defensive coordinator; born June 19, 1946, Munich, Germany. Linebacker/placekicker Oregon 1966-68. No pro playing experience. College coach: Oregon 1969-1971, Arkansas 1972, Stanford 1973-76, California 1977-1980. Pro coach: Hamilton Tiger-Cats (CFL) 1981, Baltimore/Indianapolis Colts 1982-84, San Diego Chargers 1985-1990, L.A. Raiders 1991-94, Kansas City Chiefs 1995-2000 (head coach 1999-2000), Tennessee Titans 2001-03, rejoined Chiefs in 2004.

Dick Curl, asst. head coach/quarterbacks; born May 4, 1940, Chester, Pa. Quarterback Richmond 1958-1962. No pro playing experience. College coach: Trenton State 1973-74 (head coach 1974), Rutgers 1975-1980, 1983-89, Virginia 1981-82, Boston College 1990. Pro coach: Barcelona Dragons (NFLEL) 1991-97, Frankfurt Galaxy (NFLEL) 1998-2000 (head coach), New York Jets 2003-05, joined Chiefs in 2006.

Jon Embree, tight ends; born October 15, 1965, Los Angeles. Tight end Colorado 1983-86. Pro tight end Los Angeles Rams 1987-88. College coach: Colorado 1991, 1993-2002, UCLA 2003-05. Pro coach: Joined Chiefs in 2006.

David Gibbs, defensive backs; born January 10, 1968, Mount Airy, N.C. Defensive back Colorado 1987-1990. No pro playing experience. College coach: Oklahoma 1991-92, Colorado 1993-94, Kansas 1995-96, Minnesota 1997-2000, Auburn 2005. Pro coach: Denver Broncos 2001-04, joined Chiefs in 2006.

Charlie Joiner, receivers; born October 14, 1947, Many, La. Wide receiver Grambling State 1965-68. Pro defensive back/wide receiver Houston Oilers 1969-1972, Cincinnati Bengals 1972-75, San Diego Chargers 1976-1986. Inducted into Pro Football Hall of Fame 1996. Pro coach: San Diego Chargers 1987-1991, Buffalo Bills 1992-2000, joined Chiefs in 2001.

Mike Ketchum, defensive assistant; born July 2, 1977, Ft. Benning, Ga. Offensive/defensive lineman University of the South 1995-98. College coach: Cumberland 1999-2000, Vanderbilt 2001-02, Iowa 2003-05. Pro coach: Joined Chiefs in 2006.

Tim Krumrie, defensive line; born May 20, 1960, Menomonie, Wis. Defensive tackle Wisconsin 1979-1982, Pro defensive tackle Cincinnati Bengals 1983-1994, Pro coach: Cincinnati Bengals 1995-2002, Buffalo Bills 2003-05, joined Chiefs in 2006.

John Matsko, offensive line; born February 2, 1951, Cleveland. Fullback Kent State 1970-73. No pro playing expe-

rience. College coach: Kent State 1973, Miami (Ohio) 1974-75, 1977, North Carolina 1978-1984, Navy 1985, Arizona 1986, Southern California 1987-1991. Pro coach: Phoenix Cardinals 1992-93, New Orleans Saints 1994-96, N.Y. Giants 1997-98, St. Louis Rams 1999-2005, joined Chiefs in 2006.

Kevin Patullo, offensive assistant/quality control; born July 14, 1981, Hillsborough, N.J. Quarterback/wide receiver South Florida 1999-2001. College coach: South Florida 2002-03, Arizona 2004-06. Pro coach: Joined Chiefs in 2007.

Mike Priefer, special teams; born August 21, 1966, Cleveland. Attended U.S. Naval Academy. No college or pro playing experience. College coach: Navy 1994-96, Youngstown State 1997-98, Virginia Military Institute 1999, Northern Illinois 2000-01. Pro coach: Jacksonville Jaguars 2002, New York Giants 2003-05, joined Chiefs in 2006.

Brent Salazar, asst. strength and conditioning; born May 22, 1980, Denver. Attended New Mexico. No college or pro playing experience. College coach: New Mexico 2002-03, Nevada-Las Vegas 2004, Pacific 2006. Pro coach: Joined Chiefs in 2007.

James Saxon, running backs; born March 23, 1966, Beaufort, S.C. Running back American River (Calif.) J.C. 1984-85, San Jose State 1986-87. Pro running back Kansas City Chiefs 1988-1991, Miami Dolphins 1992-94, Philadelphia Eagles 1995. College coach: Rutgers 1997-98, Menlo College 1999. Pro coach: Buffalo Bills 2000, joined Chiefs in 2001.

Cedric Smith, strength and conditioning; born May 27, 1968, Enterprise, Alabama. Fullback Florida 1986-89. Pro fullback Minnesota Vikings 1990, New Orleans Saints 1991, Washington Redskins 1994-95, Arizona Cardinals 1996-98. Pro coach: Denver Broncos 2001-06, joined Chiefs in 2007.

Mike Solari, offensive coordinator; born January 16, 1955, Daly City, Calif. Offensive lineman San Diego State 1972-75. No pro playing experience. College coach: Mira Vista (Calif.) J.C. 1978, U.S. International 1979, Boise State 1980, Cincinnati 1981-82, Kansas 1983-85, Pittsburgh 1986, Alabama 1990-91. Pro coach: Dallas Cowboys 1987-88, Phoenix Cardinals 1989, San Francisco 49ers 1992-96, joined Chiefs in 1997.

Nate Wainwright, manager of football administration; born July 28, 1975, Wilton, Iowa. Attended Iowa. No college or pro playing experience. Pro coach: N.Y. Jets 2001-05, joined Chiefs in 2006.

Darvin Wallis, defensive assistant/quality control; born February 14, 1949, Ft. Branch, Ind. Defensive end Arizona 1970-71. No pro playing experience. College coach: Adams State 1976-77, Tulane 1978-79, Mississippi 1980-81. Pro coach: Cleveland Browns 1982-88, joined Chiefs in 1989.

**American Football Conference
East Division**
Team Colors: Aqua, Coral, Blue, and
White
7500 S.W. 30th Street
Davie, Florida 33314
Telephone: (954) 452-7000

2007 SCHEDULE
PRESEASON
Aug. 11 **Jacksonville**........................7:30
Aug. 16 at Kansas City 7:00
Aug. 25 **Tampa Bay**........................7:30
Aug. 30 at New Orleans..................7:00

REGULAR SEASON
Sep. 9   at Washington 1:00
Sep. 16 **Dallas** 4:05
Sep. 23 at N.Y. Jets 1:00
Sep. 30 **Oakland** 1:00
Oct. 7   at Houston 12:00
Oct. 14 at Cleveland 1:00
Oct. 21 **New England** 1:00
Oct. 28 **N.Y. Giants (London)**..........5:00
Nov. 4   Open Date
Nov. 11 **Buffalo** 1:00
Nov. 18 at Philadelphia 1:00
Nov. 26 at Pittsburgh (Mon.) 8:30
Dec. 2   **N.Y. Jets** 1:00
Dec. 9   at Buffalo 1:00
Dec. 16 **Baltimore** 1:00
Dec. 23 at New England 1:00
Dec. 30 **Cincinnati** 1:00

Stadium: Dolphin Stadium
(opened in 1987)
•**Capacity:** 75,192
2269 Dan Marino Blvd.
Miami Gardens, Florida 33056
Playing Surface: Grass (PAT)
Training Camp: Nova Southeastern Univ.
7500 S.W. 30th Street
Davie, Florida 33314

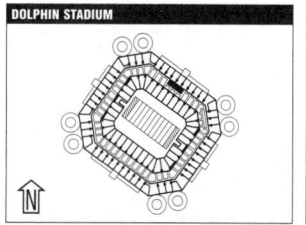

CLUB OFFICIALS
Owner/Chairman of the Board:
H. Wayne Huizenga
Chief Executive Officer, Dolphins
Enterprises: Joe Bailey
President & Chief Operating Officer:
Bryan Wiedmeier
General Manager: Randy Mueller
Head Coach: Cam Cameron
Senior Vice President-Finance &
Administration: Jill R. Strafaci
Senior Vice President-Operations:
Bill Galante
Senior Vice President-Media Relations:
Harvey Greene
Director of Pro Personnel: George Paton
Director of College Scouting:
Ron Labadie
Assistant Director of Player Personnel:
Mike Baugh
Head Strength & Conditioning:
Matt Schiotz
Asst. Strength & Conditioning: Brad Ohrt
Special Assistant to the Head Coach:
Tony Egues
Director of Player Development:
John Gamble
Staff Counsel: Matt Thomas
Director of Ticket Operations:
Greg Menzel
Senior Director of Internet & Publications:
Scott Stone
Alumni, Youth & Special Projects:
Nat Moore
Youth Programs Coordinator:
Twan Russell
Director of Media Relations: Neal Gulkis
Director of Information Technology:
Tery Howard
Director of Event Entertainment:
Dorie Grogan
Director of Programming & Production:
Jeff Griffith
Director of Cheerleaders: Heather Fraga
Director of Records & Archives:
Kristin Hingston
Director of Community Relations:
Ilona Wolpin
Head Athletic Trainer: Kevin O'Neill
Equipment Manager: Joe Cimino
Video Director: Dave Hack
Team Security Investigator:
Stuart Weinstein

COACHING HISTORY
(388-271-4)
Records include postseason games
1966-69   George Wilson.............15-39-2
1970-1995 Don Shula 274-147-2
1996-99   Jimmy Johnson...........38-31-0
2000-04   Dave Wannstedt* 43-33-0
2004   Jim Bates.........................3-4-0
2005-06   Nick Saban.................15-17-0
*Resigned after nine games in 2004

PAID ATTENDANCE
Home 585,973   Away 530,106
Total 1,116,079
Single-game home record,
75,283 (10/27/96)
Single-season home record, 592,161
(1999)

2007 DRAFT CHOICES
Round	Name	Pos.	College
1	Ted Ginn	WR	Ohio State
2	John Beck	QB	Brigham Young
	Samson Satele	G	Hawaii
3	Lorenzo Booker	RB	Florida State
4	Paul Soliai	NT	Utah
6	Reagan Mauia	RB	Hawaii
	Drew Mormino	C	Central Michigan
7	Kelvin Smith	LB	Syracuse
	Brandon Fields	P	Michigan State
	Abraham Wright	DE	Colorado

2006 TEAM RECORD
PRESEASON (2-2)

Date	Result	Opponent
8/12	L 26-31	Jacksonville
8/19	W 13-10	at Tampa Bay
8/24	L 10-19	at Carolina
8/31	W 29-9	St, Louis

REGULAR SEASON (6-10)

Date	Result	Opponent	Att.
9/7	L 17-28	at Pittsburgh	64,927
9/17	L 6-16	Buffalo	72,797
9/24	W 13-10	Tennessee	72,733
10/1	L 15-17	at Houston	70,071
10/8	L 10-20	at New England	68,756
10/15	L 17-20	at N.Y. Jets	77,439
10/22	L 24-34	Green Bay	73,548
11/5	W 31-13	at Chicago	62,206
11/12	W 13-10	Kansas City	73,132
11/19	W 24-20	Minnesota	73,070
11/23	W 27-10	at Detroit	61,562
12/3	L 10-24	Jacksonville	73,160
12/10	W 21-0	New England	74,033
12/17	L 0-21	at Buffalo	71,011
12/25	L 10-13	N.Y. Jets	73,500
12/31	L 22-27	at Indianapolis	57,310

SCORE BY PERIODS

Dolphins	33	73	53	101	0 —	260
Opponents	32	85	59	107	0 —	283

2006 TEAM STATISTICS

	Dolphins	Opp.
Total First Downs	281	267
Rushing	82	72
Passing	180	166
Penalty	19	29
3rd Down: Made/Att	88/234	89/234
3rd Down Pct.	37.6	38.0
4th Down: Made/Att	7/14	9/16
4th Down Pct.	50.0	56.3
Possession Avg.	30:01	29:59
Total Net Yards	4960	4625
Avg. Per Game	310.0	289.1
Total Plays	1034	1005
Avg. Per Play	4.8	4.6
Net Yards Rushing	1673	1618
Avg. Per Game	104.6	101.1
Total Rushes	402	461
Net Yards Passing	3287	3007
Avg. Per Game	205.4	187.9
Sacked/Yards Lost	41/290	47/268
Gross Yards	3577	3275
Att./Completions	591/342	497/279
Completion Pct.	57.9	56.1
Had Intercepted	19	8
Punts/Average	86/42.3	91/41.6
Net Punting Avg.	86/35.7	91/36.3
Penalties/Yards	90/789	91/720
Fumbles/Ball Lost	19/6	35/19
Touchdowns	26	31
Rushing	7	7
Passing	16	22
Returns	3	2

2006 INDIVIDUAL STATISTICS

PASSING

	Att.	Comp.	Yds.	Pct.	TD	Int.	Tkld.	Rate
Harrington	388	223	2,236	57.5	12	15	15/116	68.2
Culpepper	134	81	929	60.4	2	3	21/150	77.0
Lemon	68	38	412	55.9	2	1	5/24	77.6
Brown	1	0	—	0.0	0	0	0/0	39.6
Dolphins	591	342	3,577	57.9	16	19	41/290	71.2
Opponents	497	279	3,275	56.1	22	8	47/268	84.4

SCORING

	TD R	TD P	TD Rt	PAT	FG	Saf	PTS
Mare	0	0	0	22/22	26/36	0	100
Booker	0	6	0	0/0	0/0	0	40
Brown	5	0	0	0/0	0/0	0	30
Chambers	0	4	0	0/0	0/0	0	24
McMichael	0	3	0	0/0	0/0	0	18
Taylor	0	0	2	0/0	0/0	0	12
Culpepper	1	0	0	0/0	0/0	0	6
Hagan	0	1	0	0/0	0/0	0	6
Hill	0	0	1	0/0	0/0	0	6
Morris	1	0	0	0/0	0/0	0	6
Peelle	0	1	0	0/0	0/0	0	6
Welker	0	1	0	0/0	0/0	0	6
Dolphins	7	16	3	22/22	26/36	0	260
Opponents	7	22	2	31/31	22/25	0	283

2-Pt. Conversions: Booker 2, Dolphins 2-4, Opponents 0-0

RUSHING

	No.	Yds	Avg	LG	TD
Brown	241	1,008	4.2	47	5
Morris	92	400	4.3	55	1
Chambers	8	95	11.9	39	0
Minor	19	74	3.9	9	0
Suggs	6	26	4.3	7	0
Harrington	19	24	1.3	7	0
Culpepper	10	20	2.0	7	1
Booker	3	19	6.3	18	0
Lemon	3	7	2.3	6	0
Jones	1	0	0.0	0	0
Dolphins	402	1,673	4.2	55	7
Opponents	461	1,618	3.5	70t	7

RECEIVING

	No.	Yds	Avg	LG	TD
Welker	67	687	10.3	38	1
McMichael	62	640	10.3	24	3
Chambers	59	677	11.5	46	4
Booker	55	747	13.6	52	6
Brown	33	276	8.4	24	0
Hagan	21	221	10.5	24	1
Morris	21	162	7.7	44	0
Peelle	16	116	7.3	25	1
Barnes	3	22	7.3	13	0
Minor	3	2	0.7	4	0
Russell	2	14	7.0	9	0
Suggs	0	13	—	13	0
Dolphins	342	3577	10.5	52	16
Opponents	279	3275	11.7	87t	22

INTERCEPTIONS

	No.	Yds	Avg	LG	TD
Taylor	2	71	35.5	51t	2
Hill	2	33	16.5	21	0
W. Allen	1	11	11.0	11	0
J. Allen	1	7	7.0	7	0
Daniels	1	-2	-2.0	-2	0
Thomas	1	-4	-4.0	-4	0
Dolphins	8	116	14.5	51t	2
Opponents	19	207	10.9	42t	2

PUNTING

	No.	Yds.	Avg.	In 20	LG
Jones	85	3,640	42.8	28	64
Dolphins	86	3,640	42.3	28	64
Opponents	91	3,785	41.6	27	62

PUNT RETURNS

	Ret	FC	Yds	Avg	LG	TD
Welker	41	29	378	9.2	47	0
Dolphins	41	29	378	9.2	47	0
Opponents	49	10	367	7.5	28	0

KICKOFF RETURNS

	No.	Yds	Avg	LG	TD
Welker	48	1064	22.2	46	0
Bowens	2	21	10.5	11	0
Minor	2	17	8.5	17	0
Dolphins	52	1,102	21.2	46	0
Opponents	40	981	24.5	51	0

FIELD GOALS

	1-19	20-29	30-39	40-49	50+
Mare	0/0	10/10	6/8	9/12	1/6
Dolphins	0/0	10/10	6/8	9/12	1/6
Opponents	1/1	3/3	12/12	5/7	1/2

SACKS

	No.
Taylor	13.5
Holliday	7.0
Carter	5.5
Bowens	5.0
Traylor	4.0
Roth	3.5
Thomas	3.0
Bell	2.0
Spragan	1.5
W Allen	1.0
Crowder	1.0
Dolphins	47.0
Opponents	41.0

RECORD HOLDERS
INDIVIDUAL RECORDS—CAREER

Category	Name	Performance
Rushing (Yds.)	Larry Csonka, 1968-1974, 1979	6,737
Passing (Yds.)	Dan Marino, 1983-1999	*61,361
Passing (TDs)	Dan Marino, 1983-1999	*420
Receiving (No.)	Mark Clayton, 1983-1992	550
Receiving (Yds.)	Mark Duper, 1982-1992	8,869
Interceptions	Jake Scott, 1970-75	35
Punting (Avg.)	John Kidd, 1994-97	44.2
Punt Return (Avg.)	Jeff Ogden, 2000-01	13.7
Kickoff Return (Avg.)	Mercury Morris, 1969-1975	26.5
Field Goals	Olindo Mare, 1997-2006	245
Touchdowns (Tot.)	Mark Clayton, 1983-1992	82
Points	Olindo Mare, 1997-2006	1,048

INDIVIDUAL RECORDS—SINGLE SEASON

Category	Name	Performance
Rushing (Yds.)	Ricky Williams, 2002	1,853
Passing (Yds.)	Dan Marino, 1984	*5,084
Passing (TDs)	Dan Marino, 1984	48
Receiving (No.)	O.J. McDuffie, 1998	90
Receiving (Yds.)	Mark Clayton, 1984	1,389
Interceptions	Dick Westmoreland, 1967	10
Punting (Avg.)	John Kidd, 1996	46.3
Punt Return (Avg.)	Jeff Ogden, 2000	17.0
Kickoff Return (Avg.)	Duriel Harris, 1976	32.9
Field Goals	Olindo Mare, 1999	39
Touchdowns (Tot.)	Mark Clayton, 1984	18
Points	Olindo Mare, 1999	144

INDIVIDUAL RECORDS—SINGLE GAME

Category	Name	Performance
Rushing (Yds.)	Ricky Williams, 12-1-02	228
Passing (Yds.)	Dan Marino, 10-23-88	521
Passing (TDs)	Bob Griese, 11-24-77	6
	Dan Marino, 9-21-86	6
Receiving (No.)	Chris Chambers, 12-4-05	15
Receiving (Yds.)	Chris Chambers, 12-4-05	238
Interceptions	Dick Anderson, 12-3-73	*4
Field Goals	Olindo Mare, 10-17-99	6
Touchdowns (Tot.)	Paul Warfield, 12-15-73	4
	Mark Ingram, 11-27-94	4
Points	Paul Warfield, 12-15-73	24
	Mark Ingram, 11-27-94	24

*NFL Record

2007 VETERAN ROSTER

No.	Name	Pos.	Ht.	Wt.	Birthdate	NFL Exp.	College	Hometown	How Acq.	'06 Games/ Starts
	Adams, Keith	LB	5-11	240	11/22/79	7	Clemson	Atlanta, Ga.	FA-'06	15/0
79	Alabi, Anthony	T	6-5	315	2/16/81	3	Texas Christian	San Antonio, Texas	D5-'05	6/0
32	Allen, Jason	CB	6-1	213	7/5/83	2	Tennessee	Muscle Shoals, Ala.	D1-'06	16/0
25	Allen, Will	CB	5-10	196	8/5/78	7	Syracuse	Syracuse, N.Y.	UFA(NYG)-'06	15/15
37	+Bell, Yeremiah	S	6-0	200	3/3/78	4	Eastern Kentucky	Winchester, Ky.	D6-03	16/10
86	Booker, Marty	WR	6-0	210	7/31/76	9	Louisiana-Monroe	Jonesboro, La.	T(Chi)-'04	14/13
23	Brown, Ronnie	RB	6-0	232	12/12/81	3	Auburn	Cartersville, Ga.	D1-'05	13/12
80	Campbell, Kelly	WR	5-10	175	7/23/80	4	Georgia Tech	Atlanta, Ga.	FA-'06	0*
72	Carey, Vernon	T	6-5	335	7/31/81	4	Miami	Miami, Fla.	D1-'04	16/16
84	Chambers, Chris	WR	5-11	210	8/12/78	7	Wisconsin	Cleveland, Ohio	D2-'01	16/16
28	Chatman, Jesse	RB	5-8	223	9/22/79	5	Eastern Washington	Seattle, Wash.	FA-'07	0*
38	Cobbs, Patrick	RB	5-8	210	1/31/83	2	North Texas	Tecumseh, Okla.	FA-'06	3/0
52	Crowder, Channing	LB	6-2	245	12/2/83	3	Florida	Atlanta, Ga.	D3-'05	16/14
8	Culpepper, Daunte	QB	6-4	265	1/28/77	9	Central Florida	Ocala, Fla.	T(Minn)-'06	4/4
29	Daniels, Travis	CB	6-1	192	9/8/82	3	Louisiana State	Hollywood, Fla.	D4-'05	12/6
97	Denney, John	LS	6-5	270	12/13/78	3	Brigham Young	Thornton, Colo.	FA-'05	16/0
40	Eckel, Kyle	FB	5-11	237	12/30/81	2	Navy	Harverford, Pa.	W(NE)-'05	0*
62	Evans, Fred	DT	6-4	305	11/6/83	2	Texas State	Morgan Park, Ill.	D7a-'06	1/0
3	Feely, Jay	K	5-10	210	5/26/76	7	Michigan	Tampa, Fla.	UFA(NYG)-'07	16/0
93	Gbaja-Biamila, Akbar	DE	6-5	263	5/6/79	3	San Diego State	Los Angeles, Calif.	FA-'07	3/0*
21	Goodman, Andre	CB	5-10	185	8/11/78	6	South Carolina	Greenville, S.C.	UFA(Det)-'06	15/14
66	Hadnot, Rex	C	6-2	325	1/28/82	4	Houston	Lufkin, Texas	D6-04	16/16
82	Hagan, Derek	WR	6-2	203	9/21/84	2	Arizona State	Palmdale, Calif.	D3-'06	16/0
81	Hakim, Az-Zahir	WR	5-10	190	6/3/77	10	San Diego State	Los Angeles, Calif.	UFA(SD)-'07	6/0*
24	Hill, Renaldo	S	5-11	190	11/12/78	7	Michigan State	Detroit, Mich.	UFA(Oak)-'06	16/16
91	Holliday, Vonnie	DT	6-5	288	12/11/75	10	North Carolina	Camden, S.C.	FA-'05	16/16
68	Ingram, Johnathan	C	6-2	290	9/20/80	2	San Diego State	La Quinta, Calif.	FA-'07	0*
	#Jacox, Kendyl	G	6-2	325	6/10/75	10	Kansas State	Dallas, Texas	FA-'06	16/8
30	Lehan, Michael	CB	6-0	190	11/25/79	5	Minnesota	Hopkins, Minn.	FA-'06	15/2
17	+Lemon, Cleo	QB	6-2	215	8/16/79	4	Arkansas State	Greenwood, Miss.	T(SD)-'05	4/1
76	Liwienski, Chris	G	6-5	325	8/2/75	9	Indiana	Sterling Heights, Mich.	UFA(Ariz)-'07	16/6*
88	Martin, David	TE	6-4	265	3/13/79	7	Tennessee	Norfolk, Va.	UFA(GB)-'07	11/4
89	Massaquoi, Tim	TE	6-3	255	7/8/82	2	Michigan	Allentown, Pa.	W(TB)-'07	7/0
	#Matthews, Shane	QB	6-3	199	6/1/70	13	Florida	Pascagoula, Miss.	FA-'06	0*
57	Maxwell, Jim	LB	6-4	240	8/8/81	4	Gardner-Webb	Jacksonville, S.C.	FA-'06	8/0
51	McCune, Robert	LB	6-0	240	3/9/79	2	Louisville	Mobile, Ala.	FA-'06	0*
87	Peelle, Justin	TE	6-4	255	3/15/79	6	Oregon	Dublin, Calif.	UFA(SD)-'06	15/10
27	Poole, Will	CB	5-10	192	7/24/81	3	Southern California	Queens, N.Y.	D4-'04	0*
56	Pope, Derrick	LB	6-0	232	5/4/82	4	Alabama	Galveston, Texas	D7b-'04	11/0
55	Porter, Joey	LB	6-3	250	3/22/77	9	Colorado State	Bakersfield, Calif.	FA-'07	16/16
85	Rader, Jason	TE	6-4	260	4/12/81	2	Marshall	St. Albans, W. Va.	FA-'05	5/1
78	Rosenthal, Mike	T	6-7	318	6/10/77	9	Notre Dame	Mishawaka, Ind.	FA-'07	15/6*
98	Roth, Matt	DE	6-4	272	10/14/82	3	Iowa	Villa Park, Ill.	D2-'05	16/0
14	Sam, P.K.	WR	6-3	210	2/26/83	2	Florida State	Buford, Ga.	FA-'07	0*
30	Schlesinger, Cory	FB	6-1	246	6/23/72	13	Nebraska	Duncan, Neb.	UFA(Det)-'07	14/5
70	Shelton, L.J.	G/T	6-6	345	3/21/76	9	Eastern Michigan	Rochester, Mich.	UFA(Cle)-'06	16/16
59	Spragan, Donnie	LB	6-3	242	7/12/76	7	Stanford	Union City, Calif.	UFA(Den)-'05	16/9
99	Taylor, Jason	DE	6-6	255	9/1/74	11	Akron	Woodland Hills, Pa.	D3a-97	16/16
54	Thomas, Zach	LB	5-11	228	9/1/73	12	Texas Tech	Pampa, Texas	D5c-96	16/16
26	Tillman, Travares	S	6-1	205	10/8/77	7	Georgia Tech	Lyons, Ga.	UFA(Car)-'05	14/7
67	Toledo, Joe	G	6-6	330	10/20/82	2	Washington	Carlsbad, Calif.	D4-'06	0*
94	Traylor, Keith	DT	6-2	337	9/3/69	16	Central State (Okla.)	Malvern, Ark.	FA-'05	14/14
92	Vickerson, Kevin	DT	6-5	305	1/8/83	3	Michigan State	Detroit, Mich.	D7-'05	0*
	Wilkinson, Dan	DT	6-4	340	3/13/73	14	Ohio State	Dayton, Ohio	FA-'06	10/0
44	Worrell, Cameron	S	5-11	194	12/14/79	5	Fresno State	Chowcilla, Calif.	UFA(Chi)-'07	16/0*

* Campbell last active with Minnesota in '04; Chatman last active with San Diego in '04; Eckel on NFL Exempt List in '06; Feely played 16 games with N.Y. Giants in '06; Gbaja-Biamila played 3 games with San Diego; Hakim played 6 games with Detroit; Ingram last active with Kansas City in '05; Liwienski played 16 games with Arizona; Martin played 11 games with Green Bay; Matthews inactive for 3 games; McCune inactive for 3 games; Poole missed '06 season because of injury; Porter played 16 games with Pittsburgh; Rosenthal played 15 games with Minnesota; Sam last active with New England in '04; Schlesinger played 14 games with Detroit; Toledo missed '06 season because of injury; Vickerson inactive for 16 games; Worrell played 16 games with Chicago.

\# Unrestricted Free Agent; subject to developments.

+ Restricted Free Agent; subject to developments.

Traded—WR Wes Welker (16 games in '06) to New England.

Players lost through free agency (8): FB Darian Barnes (NYJ; 16 games in '06), DE David Bowens (NYJ; 16), G Toniu Fonoti (Atl; 6), P Donnie Jones (StL; 16), T Damion McIntosh (KC; 13), RB Travis Minor (StL; 16), RB Sammy Morris (NE; 12), DT Jeff Zgonina (Hou; 14).

Also played with Dolphins in '06—G Bennie Anderson (2 games), DE Kevin Carter (16), QB Joey Harrington (11), S Jack Hunt (1), CB Eddie Jackson (14), G Jeno James (9), S Norman LeJeune (2), K Olindo Mare (16), TE Randy McMichael (16), LB Keith Newman (11), WR Cliff Russell (3), RB Lee Suggs (5), WR Marcus Vick (1).

2007 FIRST-YEAR ROSTER

Name	Pos.	Ht.	Wt.	Birthdate	College	Hometown	How Acq.
Beck, John	QB	6-2	216	8/12/81	Brigham Young	Mesa, Ariz.	D2a
Booker, Lorenzo	RB	5-10	191	6/14/84	Florida State	Ventura, Calif.	D3
Bruce, Mkristo	DE	6-6	260	10/16/84	Washington State	Renton, Wash.	FA
Bryan, Courtney	S	6-0	202	10/2/84	New Mexico State	San Jose, Calif.	FA
Dukes, Marion	TE	6-3	319	11/22/84	Clemson	Pickens, S.C.	FA
Esera, Tala	G	6-3	310	6/15/84	Hawaii	Honolulu, Hawaii	FA
Fields, Brandon	P	6-5	235	5/21/84	Michigan State	Toledo, Ohio	D7b
Fifita, Steve (1)	DT	6-0	312	5/17/86	Utah	Fountain Valley, Calif.	FA
Flinn, Ryan (1)	P	6-5	210	2/15/84	Central Florida	Ft. Myers, Fla.	FA
Ginn, Ted Jr.	WR	5-11	178	4/12/85	Ohio State	Cleveland, Ohio	D1
Halterman, Aaron (1)	TE	6-5	255	4/1/85	Indiana	Greenwood, Ind.	FA
Hamdan, Gibran (1)	QB	6-4	220	2/9/85	Indiana	Potomac, Md.	FA
Harris, Tuff	CB	6-0	198	1/23/83	Montana	Colstrip, Mont.	FA
Hatchett, Gabe	WR	6-2	216	1/19/83	Southern Oregon	Minden, Nev.	FA
Love, Marquay	DT	6-0	307	7/20/85	Houston	Fort Worth, Texas	FA
Mauia, Reagan	FB	6-0	270	7/6/84	Hawaii	Stockton, Calif.	D6a
Miles, Edmond	LB	6-0	230	7/6/84	Iowa	Tallahassee, Fla.	FA
Mitchell, Shirdonya (1)	CB	5-11	183	5/17/86	Missouri	Arlington, Texas	FA-'05
Mormino, Drew	C	6-3	299	11/21/87	Central Michigan	Buffalo Grove, Ill.	D6b
Page, Chase (1)	DT	6-4	295	5/3/87	North Carolina	Mt. Pleasant, S.C.	FA-'06
Parker, Stephen	G	6-4	303	8/2/84	Arkansas	Mandeville, La.	FA
Perkins, Ray (1)	RB	5-10	205	11/7/86	Southeastern Louisiana	Ft. Lauderdale, Fla.	FA
Pope, Geoffrey	CB	6-0	186	6/21/84	Howard	Detroit, Mich.	FA
Prater, Matt (1)	K	5-10	180	8/11/88	Central Florida	Estero, Fla.	FA
Reed, Kerry	WR	6-1	201	12/24/84	Michigan State	Homestead, Fla.	FA
Satele, Samson	G/C	6-2	310	11/29/84	Hawaii	Kailua, Hawaii	D2b
Smith, Kelvin	LB	6-2	240	3/20/84	Syracuse	Spring Valley, N.Y.	D7a
Soliai, Paul	DT	6-4	345	12/30/83	Utah	Pago Pago, American Samoa	D4
Stevenson, Dan (1)	G	6-5	300	10/5/86	Notre Dame	Barrington, Ill.	FA-'06
Sutton, David	WR	6-6	222	5/30/84	Texas El-Paso	Long Beach, Calif.	FA
Vedder, Chris	S	5-11	210	9/4/85	San Jose State	San Jose, Calif.	FA
Wilson, Julius	T	6-4	327	10/17/83	Alabama-Birmingham	Bradenton, Fla.	FA
Wright, Abraham	LB	6-2	245	10/15/84	Colorado	Oklahoma City, Okla.	D7c
Wright, Rodrique (1)	DT	6-5	300	8/1/88	Texas	Houston, Texas	D7b-'06

The term NFL Rookie is defined as a player who is in his first season of professional football and has not been on the roster of another professional football team for any regular-season or postseason games. A Rookie is designated by an "R" on NFL rosters. Players who have been active in another professional football league or players who have NFL experience, including either preseason training camp or being on an Active List or Inactive List, or on Reserve/Injured or Reserve/Physically Unable to Perform for fewer than six regular-season games, are termed NFL First-Year Players. An NFL First-Year Player is designated by a "1" on NFL rosters. Thereafter, a player is credited with an additional year of experience for each season in which he accumulates six games on the Active List or Inactive List, or on Reserve/Injured or Reserve/Physically Unable to Perform.

Log on to www.miamidolphins.com for an up-to-date roster.

COACHING STAFF

Head Coach,
Cam Cameron

Pro Career: Became the seventh head coach in Dolphins history on January 19, 2007. Had spent the previous five seasons (2002-06) as the offensive coordinator with the San Diego Chargers. With Cameron as offensive coordinator, San Diego led the National Football League in scoring last season and finished third and fifth in that category in 2004 and 2005, respectively. Prior to joining the Chargers, Cameron had a five-year reign (1997-2001) as the head coach at Indiana University, his alma mater. Before that, he was the quarterbacks coach with the Washington Redskins for three seasons (1994-96). Career record: 0-0.

Background: Cameron was a two-sport letterman, in football and basketball, at Indiana, where he graduated with a degree in business in 1983. He earned two letters as a quarterback for Lee Corso (1982) and Sam Wyche (1983) and two (1981-82, 1982-83) playing basketball for Bobby Knight before a knee injury in his senior year ended his playing career. He was an assistant at the University of Michigan from 1984-1993, serving the first six of those years under the late Bo Schembechler.

Personal: Born February 6, 1961 in Chapel Hill, N.C. Grew up in Terre Haute, Indiana. He and his wife, Missy, have three sons, Tommy, Danny and Christopher, and one daughter, Elizabeth.

ASSISTANT COACHES

Keith Armstrong, special teams coordinator; born December 15, 1963, Trenton, N.J. Running back/defensive back Temple 1983-86. No pro playing experience. College coach: Temple 1987, Miami 1988, Akron 1989, Oklahoma State 1990-92, Notre Dame 1993. Pro coach: Atlanta Falcons 1994-96, Chicago Bears 1997-2000, joined Dolphins in 2001.

Dom Capers, defensive coordinator; born August 5, 1950, Cambridge, Ohio. Defensive back Mount Union College 1968-1971. No pro playing experience. College coach: Kent State 1972-74, Hawaii 1975-76, San Jose State 1977, California 1978-79, Tennessee 1980-81, Ohio State 1982-83. Pro coach: Philadelphia/Baltimore Stars (USFL) 1984-85, New Orleans Saints 1986-1991, Pittsburgh Steelers 1992-94, Carolina Panthers 1995-98 (head coach), Jacksonville Jaguars 1999-2000, Houston Texans 2001-05 (head coach), joined Dolphins in 2005.

Tim Davis, asst. offensive line; born June 17, 1958. Tackle Utah 1978-1980. No pro playing experience. College coach: Wisconsin 1983-86, Arizona 1987, Walla Walla (Wash.) C.C. 1988, Idaho State 1989, Utah 1990-96, Wisconsin 1997-2001, Southern California 2002-04. Pro coach: Joined Dolphins in 2005.

Mike Dumas, defensive secondary coaches' assistant; born March 18, 1969, Grand Rapids, Mich. Defensive back Indiana University 1987-91. Pro defensive back Houston Oilers 1991-93, Buffalo Bills 1994, Jacksonville Jaguars 1995, San Diego Chargers 1997-2000. Pro coach: Joined Dolphins in 2005.

George Edwards, linebackers; born January 16, 1967, Siler City, N.C. Linebacker Duke 1985-89. No pro playing experience. College coach: Florida 1990-91, Appalachian State 1992-95, Duke 1996, Georgia 1997. Pro coach: Dallas Cowboys 1998-2001, Washington Redskins 2002-03, Cleveland Browns 2004, joined Dolphins in 2005.

Steve Hoffman, asst. special teams; born September 8, 1958, Camden, N.J. Quarterback/running back/wide receiver Dickinson College 1977-1980. Pro punter Washington Federals (USFL) 1983. College coach: Miami 1985-87. Pro coach: Dallas Cowboys 1989-2004, Atlanta Falcons 2006, joined Dolphins in 2007.

Hudson Houck, offensive line; born January 7, 1943, Los Angeles. Center Southern California 1962-64. No pro playing experience. College coach: Southern California 1970-72, 1976-1982, Stanford 1973-75. Pro coach: Los Angeles Rams 1983-1991, Seattle Seahawks 1992, Dallas Cowboys 1993-2001, San Diego Chargers 2002-04, joined Dolphins in 2005.

Bobby Jackson, running backs; born February 16, 1940, Forsyth, Ga. Linebacker/running back Samford 1959-1962. No pro playing experience. College coach:Florida State 1965-69, Kansas State 1970-74, Louisville 1975-76, Tennessee 1977-1982. Pro coach: Atlanta Falcons 1983-86, San Diego Chargers 1987-1991, Phoenix Cardinals 1992-93, Washington Redskins 1994-99, St. Louis Rams 2000-02, joined Dolphins in 2007.

Travis Jones, defensive line (ends); born June 6, 1972, Milledgville, Ga. Linebacker Georgia 1991-94. Pro linebacker Baltimore Stallions (CFL) 1995. College coach: Georgia 1997, Appalachian State 1998-2000, Kansas 2001-02, Louisiana State 2003-04. Pro coach: Joined Dolphins in 2005.

Marvin Marshall, offensive quality control; born June 21, 1972, Aschaffenburg, Germany. Quarterback South Carolina State 1992-94. Pro wide receiver Tampa Bay Buccaneers 1996-97. Pro coach: New Orleans Saints 2005, San Diego Chargers 2006, joined Dolphins in 2007.

Brett Maxie, secondary (safeties); born January 13, 1962, Dallas. Safety Texas Southern 1982-84. Pro safety New Orleans Saints 1985-1993, Atlanta Falcons 1994, Carolina Panthers 1995-96, San Francisco 49ers 1997. Pro coach: Joined Dolphins in 2005.

Mike Dumas, defensive secondary coaches' assistant; born March 18, 1969, Grand Rapids, Mich. Defensive back Indiana University 1987-91. Pro defensive back Houston Oilers 1991-93, Buffalo Bills 1994, Jacksonville Jaguars 1995, San Diego Chargers 1997-2000. Pro coach: Joined Dolphins in 2005.

coach: Carolina Panthers 1998, San Francisco 49ers 1999-2003, Atlanta Falcons 2004-06, joined Dolphins in 2007.

Mike Mularkey, tight ends; born November 19, 1961, Ft. Lauderdale, Fla. Tight end Florida 1979-1982. Pro tight end Minnesota Vikings 1983-88, Pittsburgh Steelers 1989-1991. College coach: Concordia 1993. Pro coach: Tampa Bay Buccaneers 1994-95, Pittsburgh Steelers, 1996-2003, Buffalo Bills 2004-05 (head coach), joined Dolphins in 2006.

Mel Phillips, secondary (cornerbacks); born January 6, 1942, Shelby, N.C. Defensive back/running back North Carolina A&T 1964-65. Pro defensive back San Francisco 49ers 1966-1977. Pro coach: Detroit Lions 1980-84, joined Dolphins in 1985.

Glenn Pires, asst. linebackers; born September 13, 1958, New Bedford, Mass. Offensive lineman Springfield College 1976-79. No pro playing experience. College coach: Dartmouth 1985-88, Syracuse 1989-1994, Michigan State 1995. Pro coach: Arizona Cardinals 1996-2000, Detroit Lions 2001-02, joined Dolphins in 2003.

Diron Reynolds, defensive line (tackles); born February 23, 1971, Aiken, S.C. Linebacker Wake Forest 1989-1993. No pro playing experience. College coach: Wake Forest 1997-2000, Indiana 2001. Pro coach: Indianapolis Colts 2002-06, joined Dolphins in 2007.

Terry Robiskie, wide receivers; born November 12, 1954, New Orleans. Running back Louisiana State 1973-76. Pro running back Oakland Raiders 1977-79, Miami Dolphins 1980-81. Pro coach: Los Angeles Raiders 1982-93, Washington Redskins 1994-2000 (interim head coach 2000), Cleveland Browns 2001-06 (interim head coach 2004), joined Dolphins in 2007.

Terry Shea, quarterbacks; born June 12, 1946, San Mateo, Calif. Quarterback Oregon 1965-67. No pro playing experience. College coach: Oregon 1968-69, Mt. Hood (Ore.) J.C. 1970-75, Utah State 1976-1983, San Jose State 1984-86, 1990-91 (head coach 1990-91), California 1987-89, Stanford 1992-94, Rutgers 1996-2000 (head coach). Pro coach: British Columbia Lions (CFL) 1995, Kansas City Chiefs 2001-03, 2005-06, Chicago Bears 2004, joined Dolphins in 2007.

Chad Walker, defensive quality control; born September 2, 1976, New Orleans. No college or pro playing experience. College coach: West Virginia 2001, Louisiana-Monroe 2002, Louisiana State 2003-04. Pro coach: Joined Dolphins in 2005.

American Football Conference
East Division
Team Colors: Blue, Red, Silver, and White
Gillette Stadium
One Patriot Place
Foxborough, Massachusetts 02035
Telephone: (508) 543-8200

2007 SCHEDULE
PRESEASON
Aug. 10   at Tampa Bay 7:30
Aug. 17   **Tennessee** 8:00
Aug. 24   at Carolina..........................8:00
Aug. 30   **New York Giants**...............7:30

REGULAR SEASON
Sep. 9   at N.Y. Jets 1:00
Sep. 16   **San Diego** 8:15
Sep. 23   **Buffalo** 1:00
Oct. 1   at Cincinnati (Mon.)..............8:30
Oct. 7   **Cleveland** 1:00
Oct. 14   at Dallas 3:15
Oct. 21   at Miami 1:00
Oct. 28   **Washington** 4:15
Nov. 4   at Indianapolis 4:15
Nov. 11   Open Date
Nov. 18   at Buffalo 1:00
Nov. 25   **Philadelphia** *8:15
Dec. 3   at Baltimore (Mon.) 8:30
Dec. 9   **Pittsburgh** 1:00
Dec. 16   **N.Y. Jets** 1:00
Dec. 23   **Miami** 1:00
Dec. 29   at N.Y. Giants (Sat.) 8:15
Sunday night games in Weeks 11-17 subject to change

Stadium: Gillette Stadium
 (opened in 2002)
 •**Capacity:** 68,756
 One Patriot Place
 Foxborough, Massachusetts 02035
Playing Surface: FieldTurf
Training Camp: Gillette Stadium
 Foxborough, MA 02035

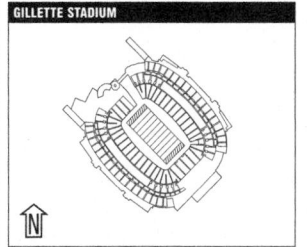
GILLETTE STADIUM

CLUB OFFICIALS
Chairman and CEO: Robert K. Kraft
President: Jonathan A. Kraft
Vice President, Player Personnel:
 Scott Pioli
Chief Administrative Officer:
 Jim Hausmann
Chief Financial Officer: John Mitchell
General Counsel-Player Personnel:
 Jack Mula
Vice President, Human Resources:
 Robin Boudreau
Vice President, Marketing Operations:
 Jennifer Ferron
Vice President, Media Relations:
 Stacey James
Executive Director of Sales: Murray Kohl
Executive Director of Corporate
 Development: David Pearlstein
Publisher/Editor-in-Chief and Director of
 Interactive Media: Fred Kirsch
Director of Football/Head Coach
 Administration: Berj Najarian
Equipment Manager: Don Brocher
Video Director: Jimmy Dee
Head Athletic Trainer: Jim Whalen
Director of College Scouting:
 Thomas Dimitroff
Director of Premium Seating:
 Melissa Aghjayian
Director of Strategic Initiatives and Retail
 Operations: Brian Bilello
Director of Supply Chain Management:
 Ken Flanders
Director of Business Development:
 Jessica Gelman
Director of Entertainment and Broadcast
 Production: Gary Grodecki
Director of Ticketing: Maryruth Hughey
Director of Sales: Jon Levy
Director of Sales: Joe Mariani
Director of Research: Richard Miller
Director of Corporate Relationships:
 Bill Nelsen
Director of Cheerleaders: Tracy Sormanti
Director of Football Development and
 Promotions for Community Affairs:
 Andre Tippett
Director of Customer and Sponsor
 Services: Gail Titus
Director of Finance: Jim Wilson
Kraft Group, Vice President of
 Information Technology: Pat Curley
Chief Operating Officer of Team Ops:
 Mark Briggs
Gillette Stadium, Vice President of
 Business Development and External
 Affairs: Dan Murphy
Gillette Stadium, Vice President of
 Operations: Jim Nolan

COACHING HISTORY
Boston 1960-1970
(369-361-9)
Records include postseason games
1960-61   Lou Saban*....................7-12-0
1961-68   Mike Holovak 53-47-9
1969-1970 Clive Rush**..................5-16-0
1970-72   John Mazur***.............9-21-0
1972   Phil Bengtson....................1-4-0
1973-78   Chuck Fairbanks****....46-41-0
1978   Hank Bullough-Ron Erhardt#...0-1-0
1979-1981 Ron Erhardt 21-27-0
1982-84   Ron Meyer##.............18-16-0
1984-89   Raymond Berry 51-41-0
1990   Rod Rust.........................1-15-0
1991-92   Dick MacPherson 8-24-0
1993-96   Bill Parcells 34-34-0
1997-99   Pete Carroll..................28-23-0
2000-06   Bill Belichick.................87-39-0
Records include postseason games
  *Released after five games in 1961
 **Released after seven games in 1970
 ***Resigned after nine games in 1972
****Suspended for final regular-season game in 1978
 #Co-coaches
 ##Released after eight games in 1984

PAID ATTENDANCE
Home 578,661   Away 548,597
Total 1,127,258
Single-game home record,
 70,262 (12/12/04)
Single-season home record,
 578,661 (2006)

2007 DRAFT CHOICES

Round	Name	Pos.	College
1	Brandon Meriweather	DB	Miami
4	Kareem Brown	DT	Miami
5	Clint Oldenburg	T	Colorado State
6	Justin Rogers	LB	So. Methodist
	Mike Richardson	DB	Notre Dame
	Justise Hairston	RB	Cent. Connecticut St.
	Corey Hilliard	T	Oklahoma State
7	Oscar Lua	LB	So. California
	Mike Elgin	G	Iowa

2006 TEAM RECORD

PRESEASON (2-2)

Date	Result	Opponent
8/11	L 23-26	at Atlanta
8/19	W 30-3	Arizona
8/26	W 41-0	Washington
8/31	L 23-31	at N.Y. Giants

REGULAR SEASON (12-4)

Date	Result	Opponent	Att.
9/10	W 19-17	Buffalo	68,756
9/17	W 24-17	at N.Y. Jets	77,595
9/24	L 7-17	Denver	68,756
10/1	W 38-13	at Cincinnati	66,035
10/8	W 20-10	Miami	68,756
10/22	W 28-6	at Buffalo	72,180
10/30	W 31-7	at Minnesota	63,819
11/5	L 20-27	Indianapolis	68,756
11/12	L 14-17	N.Y. Jets	68,756
11/19	W 35-0	at Green Bay	70,753
11/26	W 17-13	Chicago	68,756
12/3	W 28-21	Detroit	68,756
12/10	L 0-21	at Miami	74,033
12/17	W 40-7	Houston	68,756
12/24	W 24-21	at Jacksonville	67,164
12/31	W 40-23	at Tennessee	69,143

POSTSEASON (2-1)

Date	Result	Opponent	
1/7	W 37-16	New York Jets	68,756
1/14	W 24-21	at San Diego	68,810
1/21	L 34-38	at Indianapolis	57,433

SCORE BY PERIODS

Patriots	74	128	73	110	0	—	385
Opponents	32	74	80	51	0	—	237

2006 TEAM STATISTICS

	Patriots	Opp.
Total First Downs	330	264
Rushing	121	67
Passing	181	164
Penalty	28	33
3rd Down: Made/Att	96/226	75/209
3rd Down Pct.	42.5	35.9
4th Down: Made/Att	16/20	3/11
4th Down Pct.	80.0	27.3
Possession Avg.	31:35	28:25
Total Net Yards	5369	4710
Avg. Per Game	335.6	294.4
Total Plays	1055	950
Avg. Per Play	5.1	5.0
Net Yards Rushing	1969	1507
Avg. Per Game	123.1	94.2
Total Rushes	499	388
Net Yards Passing	3400	3203
Avg. Per Game	212.5	200.2
Sacked/Yards Lost	29/190	44/281
Gross Yards	3590	3484
Att./Completions	527/326	518/294
Completion Pct.	61.9	56.8
Had Intercepted	12	22
Punts/Average	69/41.3	79/41.6
Net Punting Avg.	69/34.6	79/34.4
Penalties/Yards	98/940	102/918
Fumbles/Ball Lost	27/15	24/13
Touchdowns	46	24
Rushing	20	11
Passing	25	10
Returns	1	3

2006 INDIVIDUAL STATISTICS

PASSING

	Att.	Comp.	Yds.	Pct.	TD	Int.	Tkld.	Rate
Brady	516	319	3,529	61.8	24	12	26/175	87.9
Cassel	8	5	32	62.5	0	0	3/15	70.8
Testaverde	3	2	29	66.7	1	0	0/0	137.5
Patriots	527	326	3,590	61.9	25	12	29/190	88.3
Opponents	518	294	3,484	56.8	10	22	44/281	66.1

SCORING

	TD R	TD P	TD Rt	PAT	FG	Saf	PTS
Gostkowski	0	0	0	43/44	20/26	0	103
Dillon	13	0	0	0/0	0/0	0	78
Maroney	6	1	0	0/0	0/0	0	42
Brown	0	4	0	0/0	0/0	0	26
Caldwell	0	4	0	0/0	0/0	0	26
Faulk	1	2	0	0/0	0/0	0	18
Gabriel	0	3	0	0/0	0/0	0	18
Jackson	0	3	0	0/0	0/0	0	18
Watson	0	3	0	0/0	0/0	0	18
Graham	0	2	0	0/0	0/0	0	12
Evans	0	1	0	0/0	0/0	0	6
Gaffney	0	1	0	0/0	0/0	0	6
Hobbs	0	0	1	0/0	0/0	0	6
D. Thomas	0	1	0	0/0	0/0	0	6
Warren	0	0	0	0/0	0/0	1	2
Patriots	20	25	1	43/44	20/26	1	385
Opponents	11	10	3	23/23	22/30	1	237

2-Pt. Conversions: Brown, Caldwell,
Patriots 2-2, Opponents 1-1

RUSHING

	No.	Yds	Avg	LG	TD
Dillon	199	812	4.1	50	13
Maroney	175	745	4.3	41	6
Faulk	25	123	4.9	11t	1
Evans	27	117	4.3	35	0
Brady	49	102	2.1	22	0
Jackson	4	22	5.5	14	0
Pass	6	21	3.5	6	0
Brown	2	18	9.0	16	0
Kight	1	8	8.0	8	0
Caldwell	1	5	5.0	5	0
Cassel	2	4	2.0	5	0
Testaverde	8	-8	-1.0	-1	0
Patriots	499	1,969	3.9	50	20
Opponents	388	1,507	3.9	74t	11

RECEIVING

	No.	Yds	Avg	LG	TD
Caldwell	61	760	12.5	62t	4
Watson	49	643	13.1	40	3
Brown	43	384	8.9	23	4
Faulk	43	356	8.3	43t	2
Gabriel	25	344	13.8	45	3
Maroney	22	194	8.8	31	1
Graham	21	235	11.2	29	2
Dillon	15	147	9.8	52	0
Jackson	13	152	11.7	35t	0
D. Thomas	11	159	14.5	36	1
Gaffney	11	142	12.9	33	1
Evans	7	34	4.9	11	1
Pass	2	24	12.0	16	0
Childress	2	7	3.5	5	0
Kight	1	9	9.0	9	0
Patriots	326	3,590	11.0	62t	25
Opponents	294	3,484	11.9	83t	10

INTERCEPTIONS

	No.	Yds	Avg	LG	TD
Samuel	10	120	12.0	33	0
Vrabel	3	0	0.0	2	0
Hobbs	2	79	39.5	70	0
C. Scott	2	32	16.0	32	0
Sanders	1	21	21.0	21	0
Bruschi	1	8	8.0	8	0
Harrison	1	2	2.0	2	0
Hawkins	1	0	0.0	0	0
Seymour	1	0	0.0	0	0
Patriots	22	262	11.9	70	0
Opponents	12	72	6.0	38	0

PUNTING

	No.	Yds.	Avg.	In 20	LG
Miller	43	1848	43.0	12	62
Walter	16	591	36.9	5	47
Sauerbrun	10	408	40.8	2	58
Patriots	69	2847	41.3	19	62
Opponents	79	3283	41.6	27	61

PUNT RETURNS

	Ret	FC	Yds	Avg	LG	TD
Faulk	31	5	330	10.6	43	0
Jackson	3	0	76	25.3	39	0
Brown	2	9	16	8.0	12	0
Patriots	36	14	422	11.7	43	0
Opponents	29	15	322	11.1	81t	2

KICKOFF RETURNS

	No.	Yds	Avg	LG	TD
Maroney	28	783	28.0	77	0
Faulk	17	364	21.4	31	0
Hobbs	10	360	36.0	93t	1
Banta-Cain	2	25	12.5	16	0
Jackson	1	21	21.0	21	0
Patriots	58	1,553	26.8	93t	1
Opponents	68	1,547	22.8	70	0

FIELD GOALS

	1-19	20-29	30-39	40-49	50+
Gostkowski	0/0	10/11	7/10	2/4	1/1
Patriots	0/0	10/11	7/10	2/4	1/1
Opponents	0/0	7/8	6/7	8/12	1/3

SACKS

	No.
Colvin	8.5
Green	7.5
Warren	7.5
Banta-Cain	5.5
Vrabel	4.5
Seymour	4.0
Bruschi	1.5
Harrison	1.0
Sanders	1.0
Seau	1.0
Wilfork	1.0
Wright	1.0
Patriots	44.0
Opponents	29.0

RECORD HOLDERS
INDIVIDUAL RECORDS—CAREER

Category	Name	Performance
Rushing (Yds.)	Sam Cunningham, 1973-79, 1981-82	5,453
Passing (Yds.)	Drew Bledsoe, 1993-2001	29,657
Passing (TDs)	Steve Grogan, 1975-1990	182
Receiving (No.)	Troy Brown, 1993-2006	557
Receiving (Yds.)	Stanley Morgan, 1977-1989	10,352
Interceptions	Raymond Clayborn, 1977-1989	36
	Ty Law, 1995-2004	36
Punting (Avg.)	Tom Tupa, 1996-98	44.7
Punt Return (Avg.)	Mack Herron, 1973-75	12.0
Kickoff Return (Avg.)	Allen Carter, 1975-76	27.2
Field Goals	Adam Vinatieri, 1996-2005	263
Touchdowns (Tot.)	Stanley Morgan, 1977-1989	68
Points	Adam Vinatieri, 1996-2005	1,158

INDIVIDUAL RECORDS—SINGLE SEASON

Category	Name	Performance
Rushing (Yds.)	Corey Dillon, 2004	1,635
Passing (Yds.)	Drew Bledsoe, 1994	4,555
Passing (TDs)	Vito (Babe) Parilli, 1964	31
Receiving (No.)	Troy Brown, 2001	101
Receiving (Yds.)	Stanley Morgan, 1986	1,491
Interceptions	Ron Hall, 1964	11
Punting (Avg.)	Tom Tupa, 1997	45.8
Punt Return (Avg.)	Mack Herron, 1974	14.8
Kickoff Return (Avg.)	Raymond Clayborn, 1977	31.0
Field Goals	Tony Franklin, 1986	32
Touchdowns (Tot.)	Curtis Martin, 1996	17
Points	Gino Cappelletti, 1964	155

INDIVIDUAL RECORDS—SINGLE GAME

Category	Name	Performance
Rushing (Yds.)	Tony Collins, 9-18-83	212
Passing (Yds.)	Drew Bledsoe, 11-13-94	426
Passing (TDs)	Vito (Babe) Parilli, 11-15-64	5
	Vito (Babe) Parilli, 10-15-67	5
	Steve Grogan, 9-9-79	5
Receiving (No.)	Troy Brown, 9-22-02	16
Receiving (Yds.)	Terry Glenn, 10-3-99	214
Interceptions	Many times	3
	Last time by Asante Samuel, 11-26-06	
Field Goals	Gino Cappelletti, 10-4-64	6
Touchdowns (Tot.)	Many times	3
	Last time by Corey Dillon, 12-3-06	
Points	Gino Cappelletti, 12-18-65	28

2007 VETERAN ROSTER

No.	Name	Pos.	Ht.	Wt.	Birthdate	NFL Exp.	College	Hometown	How Acq.	'06 Games/ Starts
52	Alexander, Eric	LB	6-2	240	2/8/82	3	Louisiana State	Port Arthur, Texas	FA-'04	14/0
23	Andrews, Willie	DB	5-10	195	11/2/83	2	Baylor	Longview, Texas	D7-'06	15/0
32	Baker, Rashad	S	5-10	198	2/22/82	4	Tennessee	Camden, N.J.	W(Minn)-'06	5/0
88	Brady, Kyle	TE	6-6	280	1/14/72	13	Penn State	Camp Hill, Pa.	UFA(Jax)-'07	16/14*
12	Brady, Tom	QB	6-4	225	8/3/77	8	Michigan	San Mateo, Calif.	D6b-'00	16/16
65	Britt, Wesley	T	6-8	320	11/21/81	2	Alabama	Cullman, Ala.	FA-'06	10/1
54	Bruschi, Tedy	LB	6-1	247	6/9/73	12	Arizona	Roseville, Calif.	D3-'96	15/14
80#	Brown, Troy	WR	5-10	196	7/2/71	15	Marshall	Blackville, S.C.	D8-'93	16/9
87	Caldwell, Reche	WR	6-0	210	3/28/79	6	Florida	Tampa, Fla.	UFA(SD)-'06	16/14
16	Cassel, Matt	QB	6-4	225	5/17/82	3	Southern California	Northridge, Calif.	D7a-'05	6/0
13	Childress, Bam	WR	5-10	185	3/31/82	2	Ohio State	Warrensville Heights, Ohio	FA-'05	2/1
59	Colvin, Rosevelt	LB	6-3	250	9/5/77	9	Purdue	Indianapolis, Ind.	UFA(Chi)-'03	16/15
44	Evans, Heath	RB	6-0	250	12/30/78	7	Auburn	West Palm Beach, Fla.	FA-'05	16/3
33	Faulk, Kevin	RB	5-8	202	6/5/76	9	Louisiana State	Carencro, La.	D2-'99	15/1
10	Gaffney, Jabar	WR	6-1	205	12/1/80	6	Florida	Jacksonville, Fla.	FA-'06	11/6
47#	Gardner, Barry	LB	6-1	245	12/13/76	9	Northwestern	Harvey, Ill.	FA-'06	0*
21	Gay, Randall	CB	5-11	190	5/5/82	4	Louisiana State	Brusly, La.	FA-'04	3/0
3	Gostkowski, Stephen	K	6-1	210	1/28/84	2	Memphis	Madison, Miss.	D4b-'06	16/0
97	Green, Jarvis	DL	6-3	285	1/12/79	6	Louisiana State	Donaldsonville, La.	D4b-'02	16/4
37	Harrison, Rodney	S	6-1	220	12/15/72	14	Western Illinois	Chicago, Ill.	FA-'03	10/10
25	Hawkins, Artrell	DB	5-10	195	11/24/76	10	Cincinnati	Johnstown, Pa.	FA-'05	14/12
27	Hobbs, Ellis	CB	5-9	190	5/16/83	3	Iowa State	DeSoto, Texas	D3a-'05	15/9
71	Hochstein, Russ	G/C	6-4	305	10/7/77	7	Nebraska	Hartington, Neb.	FA-'03	13/0
53	Izzo, Larry	LB	5-10	228	9/26/74	12	Rice	Houston, Texas	UFA(Mia)-'01	16/0
17	Jackson, Chad	WR	6-1	215	3/6/85	2	Florida	Hoover, Ala.	D2-'06	12/1
29	Jackson, Eddie	CB	6-0	200	12/19/80	4	Arkansas	Richardson, Texas	FA-'07	14/2*
28	James, Tory	CB	6-2	192	5/18/73	12	Louisiana State	Marrero, La.	UFA(Cin)-'07	16/16*
77	Kaczur, Nick	T	6-4	315	7/28/79	3	Toledo	Brantford, Ontario, Canada	D3b-'05	11/9
19	Kight, Kelvin	WR	6-0	213	7/2/82	2	Florida	Decatur, Ga.	FA-'06	4/1
67	Koppen, Dan	C	6-2	296	9/12/79	5	Boston College	Whitehall, Pa.	D5-'03	16/16
85	Kranchick, Matt	TE	6-7	260	12/13/79	2	Penn State	Mercersburg, Pa.	FA-'06	0*
72	Light, Matt	T	6-4	305	6/23/78	7	Purdue	Greenville, Ohio	D2-'01	16/16
70	Mankins, Logan	G	6-4	310	3/10/82	3	Fresno State	Catheys Valley, Calif.	D1-'05	16/16
39	Maroney, Laurence	RB	5-11	220	2/5/85	2	Minnesota	St. Louis, Mo.	D1-'06	14/0
46	Mays, Corey	LB	6-1	245	11/27/83	2	Notre Dame	Chicago, Ill.	FA-'06	8/0
38#	Mickens, Ray	CB	5-8	180	1/4/73	12	Texas A&M	Andress, Texas	FA-'06	4/0
8	Miller, Josh	P	6-4	225	7/14/70	12	Arizona	Rockaway, N.Y.	FA-'04	10/0
45	Mills, Garrett	TE	6-1	235	10/12/83	2	Tulsa	Jenks, Okla.	D4a-'06	0*
24	Mitchell, Mel	S	6-1	225	2/10/79	6	Western Kentucky	Rockledge, Fla.	UFA(NO)-'06	0*
34	Morris, Sammy	RB	6-0	218	3/23/77	8	Texas Tech	San Antonio, Texas	UFA(Mia)-'07	12/4*
t-	Moss, Randy	WR	6-4	210	2/13/77	10	Marshall	Rand, W. Va.	T(Oak)-'07	13/13*
64	Mruczkowski, Gene	G/C	6-2	305	6/6/80	4	Purdue	Cleveland, Ohio	FA-'03	1/0
61	Neal, Stephen	G	6-4	305	10/9/76	6	Cal State-Bakersfield	San Diego, Calif.	FA-'01	13/13
68	O'Callaghan, Ryan	T	6-7	330	7/19/83	2	California	Redding, Calif.	D5-'06	11/6
35#	Pass, Patrick	RB	5-10	217	12/31/77	8	Georgia	Tucker, Ga.	D7b-'00	3/0
66	Paxton, Lonie	LS	6-2	260	3/13/78	8	Sacramento State	Corona, Calif.	FA-'00	16/0
22	Samuel, Asante	CB	5-10	185	1/6/81	5	Central Florida	Ft. Lauderdale, Fla.	D4b-'03	15/15
36	Sanders, James	S	5-10	210	11/11/83	3	Fresno State	Porterville, Calif.	D4-'05	16/5
30	Scott, Chad	DB	6-1	205	9/6/74	11	Maryland	Suitland, Md.	FA-'05	14/9
55#	Seau, Junior	LB	6-3	248	1/19/69	18	Southern California	San Diego, Calif.	FA-'06	11/10
93	Seymour, Richard	DL	6-6	310	10/6/79	7	Georgia	Gadsden, S.C.	D1-'01	16/15
81	Smith, Jonathan	WR	5-10	194	11/28/81	3	Georgia Tech	Homerville, Ala.	FA-'06	2/0
90	Smith, Le Kevin	DL	6-1	308	7/21/82	2	Nebraska	Macon, Ga.	D6c-'06	3/0
31	Spann, Antwain	CB	6-0	190	2/22/83	2	Louisiana-Lafayette	El Camino, Calif.	FA-'06	8/0
18	Stallworth, Donté	WR	6-0	196	11/10/80	6	Tennessee	Sacramento, Calif.	UFA(Phil)-'07	12/11*
14#	Testaverde, Vinny	QB	6-5	235	11/13/63	21	Miami	Brooklyn, N.Y.	FA-'06	2/0
96	Thomas, Adalius	LB	6-2	270	8/18/77	8	Southern Mississippi	Equality, Ala.	UFA(Balt)-'07	16/16*
86	Thomas, David	TE	6-3	248	7/5/83	2	Texas	Wolfforth, Texas	D3-'06	16/3
50	Vrabel, Mike	LB	6-4	261	8/14/75	11	Ohio State	Akron, Ohio	UFA(Pitt)-'01	16/16
15#	Walter, Ken	P	6-1	207	8/15/72	10	Kent State	Cleveland, Ohio	FA-'06	4/0
94	Warren, Ty	DL	6-5	300	2/6/81	5	Texas A&M	Bryan, Texas	D1-'03	15/15
15	Washington, Kelley	WR	6-3	216	8/21/79	5	Tennessee	Stephens City, Va.	UFA(Cin)-'07	5/1*
84	Watson, Benjamin	TE	6-3	255	12/18/80	4	Georgia	Rock Hill, S.C.	D1b-'04	13/13
83	t- Welker, Wes	WR	5-9	185	5/1/81	4	Texas Tech	Oklahoma City, Okla.	T(Mia)-'07	16/2*
75	Wilfork, Vince	DL	6-2	325	11/4/81	4	Miami	Boynton Beach, Fla.	D1a-'04	13/13

42	Williams, Gemara	CB	5-8	180	4/30/83	2	Buffalo	Oak Park, Mich.	FA-'06	0*
26	Wilson, Eugene	DB	5-10	195	8/17/80	5	Illinois	Merrillville, Ind.	D2a-'03	4/4
58	Woods, Pierre	LB	6-5	250	1/6/82	2	Michigan	Cleveland, Ohio	FA-'06	8/0
99	Wright, Mike	DL	6-4	295	3/1/82	3	Cincinnati	Cincinnati, Ohio	FA-'05	16/3
74	Yates, Billy	G	6-2	305	4/15/80	4	Texas A&M	Fort Worth, Texas	FA-'05	4/3

* K. Brady played 16 games with Jacksonville in '06; Gardner missed '06 season because of injury; E. Jackson played 12 games with Miami; James played 16 games with Cincinnati; Kranchick last active with N.Y. Giants in '05; Mills inactive for 9 games; Mitchell missed '06 season because of injury; Morris played 12 games with Miami; Moss played 13 games with Oakland; Stallworth played 12 games with Philadelphia; A. Thomas played 16 games with Baltimore; Washington played 5 games with Cincinnati; Welker played 16 games with Miami; Williams missed '06 season because of injury.

t- Patriots traded for Moss (Oak) and Welker (Mia).

#Unrestricted Free Agent; subject to developments.

Retired—Don Davis, 11-year linebacker, 12 games in '06.

Players lost through free agency (3): LB Tully Banta-Cain (SF; 16 games in '06), TE Daniel Graham (Den; 12), P Todd Sauerbrun (Den; 2).

Also played with Patriots in '06—WR Doug Gabriel (12 games), DL Marquise Hill (4), CB Chidi Iwouma (3), CB Hank Poteat (2), S Guss Scott (1).

2007 FIRST-YEAR ROSTER

Name	Pos.	Ht.	Wt.	Birthdate	College	Hometown	How Acq.
Anam, Larry	CB	5-11	197	10/29/83	Boston College	Hialeah, Fla.	FA
Barthelmes, Brian (1)	C	6-6	300	1/28/83	Virginia	Parkman, Ohio	FA-'06
Bissinger, Kyle	LB	6-3	255	8/20/83	Alabama-Birmingham	Kennesaw, Ga.	FA
Brown, Kareem	DL	6-4	290	1/30/84	Miami	Miami, Fla.	D4
Case, Tony (1)	LS	6-2	285	7/10/82	Adams State	Colorado Springs, Colo.	FA
Dunlap, Chris	WR	5-11	200	11/16/85	Georgia Tech	Miramar, Fla.	FA
Elgin, Mike	G/C	6-4	277	10/15/83	Iowa	Bankston, Iowa	D7b
Gutierrez, Matt	QB	6-4	231	6/9/84	Idaho State	Concord, Calif.	FA
Hairston, Justise	RB	6-1	210	6/27/83	Central Connecticut	New Britain, Conn.	D6c
Hill, Quadtrine (1)	RB	6-2	228	11/18/82	Miami	Sunrise, Fla.	FA-'06
Hilliard, Corey	T	6-6	315	4/26/85	Oklahoma State	New Orleans, La.	D6d
Lua, Oscar	LB	6-1	240	5/9/84	Southern California	Indio, Calif.	D7a
Meriweather, Brandon	S	5-11	195	1/14/84	Miami	Apopka, Fla.	D1
Nordin, Jake	TE	6-3	262	7/8/84	Northern Illinois	Grove City, Minn.	FA
Oldenburg, Clint	T	6-5	297	9/9/83	Colorado State	Gillette, Wyo.	D5
Poland, Denny	S	6-1	227	3/17/83	Air Force	Pittsburgh, Pa.	FA
Richardson, Mike	CB	5-11	188	2/18/84	Notre Dame	Warner Robins, Ga.	D6b
Rogers, Justin	LB	6-4	250	8/31/83	Southern Methodist	Greenville, Texas	D6a
Smith, Quinton	RB	5-11	195	1/14/84	Rice	Cedar Park, Texas	FA
Thomas, Santonio (1)	DE	6-4	305	7/2/81	Miami	Belle Glade, Fla.	FA-'05
Warren, Justin	LB	6-3	237	4/10/85	Texas A&M	Tyler, Texas	FA
West, Zach	DT	6-5	295	4/27/84	Texas-El Paso	Ocala, Fla.	FA

The term NFL Rookie is defined as a player who is in his first season of professional football and has not been on the roster of another professional football team for any regular-season or postseason games. A Rookie is designated by an "R" on NFL rosters. Players who have been active in another professional football league or players who have NFL experience, including either preseason training camp or being on an Active List or Inactive List, or on Reserve/Injured or Reserve/Physically Unable to Perform for fewer than six regular-season games, are termed NFL First-Year Players. An NFL First-Year Player is designated by a "1" on NFL rosters. Thereafter, a player is credited with an additional year of experience for each season in which he accumulates six games on the Active List or Inactive List, or on Reserve/Injured or Reserve/Physically Unable to Perform.

Log on to www.patriots.com for an up-to-date roster.

COACHING STAFF
Head Coach,
Bill Belichick

Pro Career: Bill Belichick is in his 33rd season as an NFL coach. He is the only head coach in league history to win three Super Bowl championships in a four-year span and has more years of NFL experience than any of the other 31 head coaches. Hired by Chairman and CEO Robert Kraft on January 27, 2000, Belichick is in his eighth season as New England's head coach. In 2001, just his second season at the helm, Belichick guided the Patriots to their first league title with a dramatic victory in Super Bowl XXXVI. In the seasons since then, he has directed New England to sustained on-field success through an instilled philosophy of maintaining short-term focus to deliver long-term goals. Belichick directed the Patriots to victories in Super Bowls XXXVI (2001), XXXVIII (2003) and XXXIX (2004), and New England's 12 playoff victories since 2001 mark the second highest playoff win total for any six-year period in NFL history. Belichick's teams have won the AFC East title in each of the last four seasons (2003-06) and advanced in the playoffs in each of those years. The Patriots' four straight years of playoff advancement mark the longest current streak in the NFL, while their string of four consecutive division crowns is a team record and is tied for the longest current streak in the league. Belichick's accomplishments have placed him among the NFL's elite coaches. His Patriots teams own all of the major winning streaks in NFL history: consecutive overall wins (21 from 2003-04), consecutive regular season wins (18 from 2003-04) and consecutive playoff wins (10 from 2001-05). Only one coach (Pittsburgh's Chuck Noll, 4) has won more Super Bowls than Belichick, and his three Super Bowl titles tie Washington's Joe Gibbs and San Francisco's Bill Walsh for second place on the NFL's all-time list. Belichick's 13 career playoff victories rank fifth among all head coaches on the NFL's all-time list. Including regular season and playoff games, Belichick enters 2007 as the winningest head coach in the NFL over the last six seasons and is also the Patriots' all-time leader in victories (87) and winning percentage (.690). Since 2001, Belichick has directed the Patriots to an 82-28 (.745) record – the most successful run in franchise history – including a 12-2 postseason mark. Belichick owns a career playoff record of 13-3, a winning percentage that ranks second in NFL history behind only the legendary Vince Lombardi (9-1). From 2003-04, Belichick directed the Patriots through the most prosperous two-year period for any team in NFL history, netting back-to-back Super Bowl victories and consecutive 17-2 campaigns. The team's 34 victories in 2003-04 mark the highest two-year win total in the NFL's 87-year history. Belichick has helped produce five Super Bowl titles, six conference championships and 12 division titles since entering the NFL in 1975. He won his first two Super Bowls as the defensive coordinator for the New York Giants in 1986 and 1990. George Seifert is the only other man to have won multiple Super Bowls both as a head coach and as an assistant coach. Belichick began as an assistant coach with the Baltimore Colts (1975), Detroit (1976-77), Denver (1978), and the New York Giants (1979-1990) in which he contributed to two Super Bowl championships as the defensive coordinator. Belichick was named head coach of the Cleveland Browns in 1991, becoming the NFL's youngest head coach at age 37. By 1994, Belichick guided the Browns to the second round of the playoffs, while allowing a league-low 204 total points. In 1996, Belichick joined New England and was a key contributor to the team's rebound from a 6-10 season in 1995 to an 11-5 season and the team's first division title in 10 years en route to the Patriots' appearance in Super Bowl XXXI. Belichick then spent three seasons with the New York Jets (1997-1999), helping New York improve from a 1-15 season in 1996 to an appearance in the AFC Championship Game in 1998. Career record: 124-84.

Background: Belichick was a center/tight end at Wesleyan 1971-74.

Personal: Born April 16, 1952, Nashville.

ASSISTANT COACHES

Nick Caserio, wide receivers; born December 27, 1975, Westlake, Ohio. Quarterback John Carroll 1995-98. No pro playing experience. College coach: Saginaw Valley State 1999-2000. Pro coach: Joined Patriots in 2001.

Joel Collier, secondary; born December 25, 1963, Buffalo. Linebacker Northern Colorado 1984-87. No pro playing experience. College coach: Syracuse 1988-89. Pro coach: Tampa Bay Buccaneers 1990, New England Patriots 1991-93, Miami Dolphins 1994-2004, rejoined Patriots in 2005.

Ivan Fears, running backs; born November 15, 1954, Portsmouth, Va. Running back William & Mary 1973-75. No pro playing experience. College coach: William & Mary 1977-79, Syracuse 1980-1990. Pro coach: New England Patriots 1991-92, Chicago Bears 1993-98, rejoined Patriots in 1999.

Pepper Johnson, defensive line; born July 29, 1964, Detroit. Linebacker Ohio State 1982-85. Pro linebacker New York Giants 1986-1992, Cleveland Browns 1993-95, Detroit Lions 1996, New York Jets 1997-98. Pro coach: Joined Patriots in 2001.

Pete Mangurian, tight ends; born June 17, 1955, Los Angeles. Defensive lineman Louisiana State. No pro playing experience. College coach: Southern Methodist 1979-1980, New Mexico State 1981, Stanford 1982-83, Louisiana State 1984-87, Cornell 1998-2000 (head coach). Pro coach: Denver Broncos 1988-1992, New York Giants 1993-96, Atlanta Falcons 1997, 2001-03, joined Patriots in 2005.

Josh McDaniels, offensive coordinator/quarterbacks; born April 22, 1976, Canton, Ohio. Wide receiver John Carroll 1995-98. No pro playing experience. College coach: Michigan State 1999. Pro coach: Joined Patriots in 2001.

Harold Nash, asst. strength and conditioning; born May 5, 1970, New Orleans. Defensive back Louisiana-Lafayette 1988-1993. Pro defensive back Shreveport Pirates (CFL) 1994-95, Montreal Alouettes (CFL) 1996-99, Winnipeg Blue Bombers (CFL) 1999-2003, Edmonton Eskimos (CFL) 2004. Pro coach: Joined Patriots in 2005.

Bill O'Brien, offensive assistant; born October 23, 1969, Andover, Mass. Linebacker/defensive end Brown 1990-92. College coach: Brown 1993-94, Georgia Tech 1995-2002, Maryland 2003-04, Duke 2005-06. Pro coach: Joined Patriots in 2007.

Matt Patricia, linebackers; born Sept. 13, 1974. Center-guard Rensselaer 1992-96. No pro playing experience. College coach: Rensselaer 1996, Amherst 1999-2000, Syracuse 2001-03. Pro coach: Joined Patriots in 2004.

Dean Pees, defensive coordinator; born September 4, 1949, Dunkirk, Ohio. Attended Bowling Green. No college or pro playing experience. College coach: Findlay 1979-1982, Miami (Ohio) 1983-86, Navy 1987-89, Toledo 1990-93, Notre Dame 1994, Michigan State 1995-97, Kent State 1998-2003. Pro coach: Joined Patriots in 2004.

Dante Scarnecchia, asst. head coach/offensive line; born February 15, 1948, Los Angeles. Center/guard California Western 1968-1970. No pro playing experience. College coach: California Western 1970-72, Iowa State 1973-74, Southern Methodist 1975-76, 1980-81, Pacific 1977-78, Northern Arizona 1979. Pro coach: New England Patriots 1982-88, Indianapolis Colts 1989-1990, rejoined Patriots in 1991.

Brad Seely, special teams; born September 6, 1956, Vinton, Iowa. Tackle-guard South Dakota State 1974-77. No pro playing experience. College coach: Colorado State 1980, Southern Methodist 1981, North Carolina State 1982, Pacific 1983, Oklahoma State 1984-88. Pro coach: Indianapolis Colts 1989-1993, New York Jets 1994, Carolina Panthers 1995-98, joined Patriots in 1999.

Mike Woicik, strength and conditioning; born September 26, 1956, Baltimore. Attended Boston College. No college or pro playing experience. College coach: Springfield College 1978-79, Syracuse 1980-89. Pro coach: Dallas Cowboys 1990-96, New Orleans Saints 1997-99, joined Patriots in 2000.

**American Football Conference
East Division**
Team Colors: Green and White
1000 Fulton Avenue
Hempstead, New York 11550
Telephone: (516) 560-8100

2007 SCHEDULE
PRESEASON
Aug. 10	**Atlanta**	7:00
Aug. 17	**Minnesota**	8:00
Aug. 25	at N.Y. Giants	8:00
Aug. 30	at Philadelphia	7:30

REGULAR SEASON
Sep. 9	**New England**	1:00
Sep. 16	at Baltimore	4:15
Sep. 23	**Miami**	1:00
Sep. 30	at Buffalo	1:00
Oct. 7	at N.Y. Giants	1:00
Oct. 14	**Philadelphia**	1:00
Oct. 21	at Cincinnati	4:05
Oct. 28	**Buffalo**	4:05
Nov. 4	**Washington**	1:00
Nov. 11	Open Date	
Nov. 18	**Pittsburgh**	1:00
Nov. 22	at Dallas (Thu.)	3:15
Dec. 2	at Miami	1:00
Dec. 9	**Cleveland**	4:15
Dec. 16	at New England	1:00
Dec. 23	at Tennessee	3:15
Dec. 30	**Kansas City**	*8:15

Sunday night games in Weeks 11-17 subject to change

Stadium: Meadowlands
(opened in 1976)
•**Capacity:** 80,062
East Rutherford, New Jersey
07073
Playing Surface: FieldTurf
Training Camp: 1000 Fulton Avenue
Hempstead, NY 11550

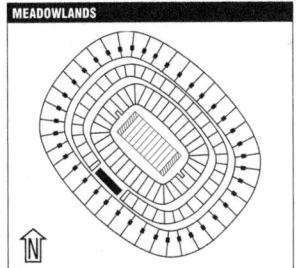

MEADOWLANDS

CLUB OFFICIALS
Chairman and CEO:
  Robert Wood Johnson IV
President: Jay Cross
General Manager: Mike Tannenbaum
Senior V.P. for Public Affairs:
  Matt Higgins
Senior V.P. for New Meadowlands
  Stadium Project: Bill Senn
Senior V.P. for Finance: Thad Sheely
V.P., Sales: Marc Riccio
Director, Player Personnel: Terry Bradway
Director, Pro Personnel: JoJo Wooden
Assistant Director, Pro Personnel:
  Brendan Prophett
Senior Director, Football Administration:
  David Socie
Manager, Football Administration:
  Ari Nissim
Pro Scout: Tom Frawley
Pro Personnel Assistant: Cole Hufnagel
Director, College Scouting:
  Joey Clinckscales
National Scout: Joe Bammarito,
  Jim Cochran, Michael Davis
Coordinator, College Scouting:
  Jay Mandolesi
Personnel Scouts: Jeff Bauer,
  Matt Bazirgan, Denny Marcin,
  Gary Smith, Marvin Sutherland,
  Kirwin Watson
Senior Personnel Consultant: Jesse Kaye
Assistant, Player Personnel: Keri Stork
Head Athletic Trainer: John Mellody
Assistant Athletic Trainer: Josh Koch,
  Dave Zuffelato
Manager, Equipment: Gus Granneman
V.P., Media Relations: TBD
Director, Media Relations: David Tratner
Senior Director, Information Technology:
  Tom Murphy
Senior Director, Operations:
  Clay Hampton
Senior Director, Security: Steve Yarnell
Director, Video: Steve Scarnecchia
Director, Player Development:
  Jerome Henderson
Director, Ticket Sales: John Buschhorn
Director, Community Relations:
  Jesse Linder
Manager, Equipment: Gus Granneman
Assistant Manager, Equipment:
  Vito Contento
Assistant, Equipment: Cortez Robinson

COACHING HISTORY
**New York Titans 1960-62
(326-393-8)**
Records include postseason games
1960-61	Sammy Baugh	14-14-0
1962	Clyde (Bulldog) Turner	5-9-0
1963-1973	Weeb Ewbank	73-78-6
1974-75	Charley Winner*	9-14-0
1975	Ken Shipp	1-4-0
1976	Lou Holtz**	3-10-0
1976	Mike Holovak	0-1-0
1977-1982	Walt Michaels	41-49-1
1983-89	Joe Walton	54-59-1
1990-93	Bruce Coslet	26-39-0
1994	Pete Carroll	6-10-0
1995-96	Rich Kotite	4-28-0
1997-99	Bill Parcells	30-20-0
2000	Al Groh	9-7-0
2001-05	Herman Edwards	41-44-0
2006	Eric Mangini	10-7-0

*Released after nine games in 1975
**Resigned after 13 games in 1976

PAID ATTENDANCE
Home 618,563   Away 546,796
Total 1,165,359
Single-game home record,
  79,572 (11/19/06)
Single-season home record,
  628,773 (2002)

2007 DRAFT CHOICES
Round	Name	Pos.	College
1	Darrelle Revis	DB	Pittsburgh
2	David Harris	LB	Michigan
6	Jacob Bender	T	Nicholls State
7	Chansi Stuckey	WR	Clemson

2006 TEAM RECORD
PRESEASON (2-2)

Date	Result	Opponent
8/11	L 3-16	at Tampa Bay
8/19	W 27-14	at Washington
8/25	L 7-13	N.Y. Giants
9/1	W 20-17	Philadelphia

REGULAR SEASON (10-6)

Date	Result	Opponent	Att.
9/10	W 23-16	at Tennessee	69,143
9/17	L 17-24	New England	77,595
9/24	W 28-20	at Buffalo	72,067
10/1	L 28-31	Indianapolis	77,190
10/8	L 0-41	at Jacksonville	66,604
10/15	W 20-17	Miami	77,439
10/22	W 31-24	Detroit	76,953
10/29	L 13-20	at Cleveland	72,507
11/12	W 17-14	at New England	68,756
11/19	L 0-10	Chicago	77,632
11/26	W 26-11	Houston	76,596
12/3	W 38-10	at Green Bay	70,527
12/10	L 13-31	Buffalo	77,131
12/17	W 26-13	at Minnesota	63,677
12/25	W 13-10	at Miami	73,500
12/31	W 23-3	Oakland	78,039

POSTSEASON (0-1)

1/7	L 16-37	at New England	68,756

SCORE BY PERIODS

Jets	54	107	67	88	0	—	316
Opponents	52	74	53	116	0	—	295

2006 TEAM STATISTICS

	Jets	Opp.
Total First Downs	289	312
Rushing	99	111
Passing	161	181
Penalty	29	20
3rd Down: Made/Att	99/226	76/208
3rd Down Pct.	43.8	36.5
4th Down: Made/Att	5/16	12/23
4th Down Pct.	31.3	52.2
Possession Avg.	31:03	28:57
Total Net Yards	4,891	5,306
Avg. Per Game	305.7	331.6
Total Plays	1013	1020
Avg. Per Play	4.8	5.2
Net Yards Rushing	1,738	2,084
Avg. Per Game	108.6	130.3
Total Rushes	491	453
Net Yards Passing	3,153	3,222
Avg. Per Game	197.1	201.4
Sacked/Yards Lost	34/199	35/230
Gross Yards	3,352	3,452
Att./Completions	488/313	532/316
Completion Pct.	64.1	59.4
Had Intercepted	16	16
Punts/Average	74/43.4	74/44.1
Net Punting Avg.	74/37.6	74/36.8
Penalties/Yards	70/560	105/843
Fumbles/Ball Lost	21/9	17/9
Touchdowns	35	34
Rushing	15	14
Passing	17	19
Returns	3	1

2006 INDIVIDUAL STATISTICS

PASSING

	Att.	Comp.	Yds.	Pct.	TD	Int.	Tkld.	Rate
Pennington	485	313	3,352	64.5	17	16	30/172	82.6
Clemens	1	0	—	0.0	0	0	4/27	39.6
Graham	1	0	—	0.0	0	0	0/0	39.6
Ramsey	1	0	—	0.0	0	0	0/0	39.6
Jets	488	313	3,352	64.1	17	16	34/199	82.1
Opponents	532	316	3,452	59.4	19	16	35/230	78.0

SCORING

	TD R	TD P	TD Rt	PAT	FG	Saf	PTS
Nugent	0	0	0	34/35	24/27	0	106
Barlow	6	0	0	0/0	0/0	0	36
Coles	0	6	0	0/0	0/0	0	36
Cotchery	0	6	0	0/0	0/0	0	36
Houston	5	0	0	0/0	0/0	0	30
Baker	0	4	0	0/0	0/0	0	24
L. Washington	4	0	0	0/0	0/0	0	24
Miller	0	0	2	0/0	0/0	0	12
Hobson	0	0	1	0/0	0/0	0	6
McCareins	0	1	0	0/0	0/0	0	6
Jets	15	17	3	34/35	24/27	0	316
Opponents	14	19	1	29/29	18/24	0	295

2-Pt. Conversions: Jets 0-0, Opponents 4-5.

RUSHING

	No.	Yds	Avg	LG	TD
L. Washington	151	650	4.3	23	4
Houston	113	374	3.3	31	5
Barlow	131	370	2.8	12	6
Pennington	35	109	3.1	15	0
B. Smith	18	103	5.7	32	0
Blaylock	25	44	1.8	6	0
Dwight	2	28	14.0	28	0
Cotchery	5	25	5.0	10	0
Coles	2	14	7.0	15	0
Askew	6	11	1.8	5	0
Clemens	2	10	5.0	8	0
Graham	1	0	0.0	0	0
Jets	491	1738	3.5	32	15
Opponents	453	2084	4.6	57t	14

RECEIVING

	No.	Yds	Avg	LG	TD
Coles	91	1098	12.1	58t	6
Cotchery	82	961	11.7	71t	6
Baker	31	300	9.7	28	4
L. Washington	25	270	10.8	64	0
McCareins	23	347	15.1	50	1
Dwight	16	112	7.0	15	0
B. Smith	9	61	6.8	19	0
Askew	9	50	5.6	12	0
Houston	7	43	6.1	11	0
Barlow	7	21	3.0	8	0
Ryan	6	44	7.3	10	0
Blaylock	5	29	5.8	9	0
Hodgins	2	9	4.5	6	0
Pennington	0	7	—	7	0
Jets	313	3352	10.7	71t	17
Opponents	316	3452	10.9	77t	19

INTERCEPTIONS

	No.	Yds	Avg	LG	TD
Rhodes	4	46	11.5	25	0
Dyson	4	-3	-.8	0	0
Barrett	3	0	0.0	0	0
E. Smith	2	1	0.5	1	0
Hobson	1	9	9.0	9	0
E. Coleman	1	3	3.0	3	0
Vilma	1	0	0.0	0	0
Jets	16	56	3.5	25	0
Opponents	16	148	9.3	58t	1

PUNTING

	No.	Yds	Avg.	In 20	LG
Graham	72	3182	44.2	26	69
Pennington	1	29	29.0	1	29
Jets	74	3211	43.4	27	69
Opponents	74	3266	44.1	18	68

PUNT RETURNS

	Ret	FC	Yds	Avg	LG	TD
Dwight	14	9	146	10.4	18	0
L. Washington	13	6	97	7.5	38	0
Kassell	1	0	0	0.0	0	0
Poteat	1	0	0	0.0	0	0
Cotchery	0	2	0	—	0	0
Jets	29	17	243	8.4	38	0
Opponents	28	15	205	7.3	18	0

KICKOFF RETURNS

	No.	Yds	Avg	LG	TD
Miller	46	1304	28.3	103t	2
L. Washington	6	79	13.2	23	0
Baker	2	15	7.5	11	0
Chatham	2	26	13.0	20	0
Hodgins	1	17	17.0	17	0
B. Smith	1	4	4.0	4	0
Coles	1	0	0.0	0	0
Rhodes	1	0	0.0	0	0
Jets	60	1445	24.1	103t	2
Opponents	69	1462	21.2	39	0

FIELD GOALS

	1-19	20-29	30-39	40-49	50+
Nugent	1/1	7/7	10/12	4/4	2/3
Jets	1/1	7/7	10/12	4/4	2/3
Opponents	0/0	9/11	5/5	4/6	0/2

SACKS

	No.
B. Thomas	8.5
Hobson	6.0
Ellis	5.0
Rhodes	5.0
Barton	4.5
Robertson	2.5
D. Coleman	1.0
Mosley	1.0
Von Oelhoffen	1.0
R. Washington	0.5
Jets	35.0
Opponents	34.0

RECORD HOLDERS
INDIVIDUAL RECORDS—CAREER

Category	Name	Performance
Rushing (Yds.)	Curtis Martin, 1998-2005	10,302
Passing (Yds.)	Joe Namath, 1965-1976	27,057
Passing (TDs)	Joe Namath, 1965-1976	170
Receiving (No.)	Don Maynard, 1960-1972	627
Receiving (Yds.)	Don Maynard, 1960-1972	11,732
Interceptions	Bill Baird, 1963-69	34
Punting (Avg.)	Ben Graham, 2005-06	43.9
Punt Return (Avg.)	Dick Christy, 1961-63	16.2
Kickoff Return (Avg.)	Justin Miller, 2005-06	27.2
Field Goals	Pat Leahy, 1974-1991	304
Touchdowns (Tot.)	Don Maynard, 1960-1972	88
Points	Pat Leahy, 1974-1991	1,470

INDIVIDUAL RECORDS—SINGLE SEASON

Category	Name	Performance
Rushing (Yds.)	Curtis Martin, 2004	1,697
Passing (Yds.)	Joe Namath, 1967	4,007
Passing (TDs)	Vinny Testaverde, 1998	29
Receiving (No.)	Al Toon, 1988	93
Receiving (Yds.)	Don Maynard, 1967	1,434
Interceptions	Dainard Paulson, 1964	12
Punting (Avg.)	Curley Johnson, 1965	45.3
Punt Return (Avg.)	Dick Christy, 1961	21.3
Kickoff Return (Avg.)	Bobby Humphrey, 1984	30.7
Field Goals	Jim Turner, 1968	34
Touchdowns (Tot.)	Art Powell, 1960	14
	Don Maynard, 1965	14
	Emerson Boozer, 1972	14
	Curtis Martin, 2004	14
Points	Jim Turner, 1968	145

INDIVIDUAL RECORDS—SINGLE GAME

Category	Name	Performance
Rushing (Yds.)	Curtis Martin, 12-3-00	203
Passing (Yds.)	Joe Namath, 9-24-72	496
Passing (TDs)	Joe Namath, 9-24-72	6
Receiving (No.)	Clark Gaines, 9-21-80	17
Receiving (Yds.)	Don Maynard, 11-17-68	228
Interceptions	Many times	3
	Last time by Ty Law, 1-1-06	
Field Goals	Jim Turner, 11-3-68	5
	Bobby Howfield, 12-3-72	6
Touchdowns (Tot.)	Wesley Walker, 9-21-86	4
Points	Wesley Walker, 9-21-86	24

2007 VETERAN ROSTER

No.	Name	Pos.	Ht.	Wt.	Birthdate	NFL Exp.	College	Hometown	How Acq.	'06 Games/ Starts
86	Baker, Chris	TE	6-3	258	11/19/83	6	Michigan State	Queens, N.Y.	D3-'02	16/14
37	Barnes, Darian	FB	6-2	240	3/1/84	6	Hampton	Toms River, N.J.	UFA(Mia)-'07	15/6*
36	Barrett, David	CB	5-10	195	12/23/81	8	Arkansas	Osceola, Ark.	UFA(Ariz)-'04	13/3
50	Barton, Eric	LB	6-2	245	9/30/81	9	Maryland	Alexandria, Va.	UFA(Oak)-'04	16/15
96	Bowens, David	DE	6-3	265	7/4/81	9	Western Illinois	Detroit, Mich.	UFA(Mia)-'07	16/0*
58	Chatham, Matt	LB	6-4	250	6/29/81	8	South Dakota	Sioux City, Iowa	UFA(NE)-'06	16/0
61	Clarke, Adrien	G	6-5	330	3/27/85	2	Ohio State	Shaker Heights, Ohio	FA-'07	0*
11	Clemens, Kellen	QB	6-2	223	6/8/87	2	Oregon	Burns, Ore.	D2-'06	2/0
68	Clement, Anthony	T	6-8	320	4/11/80	10	Louisiana-Lafayette	Lafayette, La.	UFA(SF)-'06	16/16
30	Coleman, Drew	CB	5-9	175	4/23/87	2	Texas Christian	Henderson, Texas	D6-'06	16/3
26	Coleman, Erik	S	5-10	200	5/7/86	4	Washington State	Spokane, Wash.	D5-'04	16/14
93	Coleman, Kenyon	DE	6-5	295	4/11/83	5	UCLA	Alta Loma, Calif.	UFA(Dall)-'07	16/0*
87	Coles, Laveranues	WR	5-11	193	12/30/81	8	Florida State	Jacksonville, Fla.	T(Wash)-'05	16/16
89	Cotchery, Jerricho	WR/KR	6-0	207	6/17/86	4	North Carolina State	Birmingham, Ala.	D4a-'04	16/16
85	Dearth, James	TE/LS	6-4	270	1/23/80	7	Tarleton State	Scurry, Texas	FA-'01	16/0
17	Dwight, Tim	WR/KR	5-8	180	7/14/79	10	Iowa	Iowa City, Iowa	UFA(NE)-'06	9/2
21	Dyson, Andre	CB	5-10	183	5/26/83	7	Utah	Clearfield, Utah	UFA(Sea)-'06	15/15
92	Ellis, Shaun	DE	6-5	285	6/25/81	8	Tennessee	Anderson, S.C.	D1a-'00	16/16
60	Ferguson, D'Brickashaw	T	6-6	312	12/11/87	2	Virginia	Freeport, N.Y.	D1a-'06	16/16
76	Goddard, Na'Shan	T/G	6-5	315	4/24/87	2	South Carolina	Dayton, Ohio	FA-'06	0*
7	Graham, Ben	P	6-5	220	11/3/77	3	Deakin (Australia)	Geelong, Victoria, Australia	FA-'05	16/0
98	Hamilton, Bobby	DE	6-5	285	7/2/75	13	Southern Mississippi	Columbia, Miss.	T-'06	16/1
94	Haynes, Michael	DE	6-4	283	9/14/84	4	Penn State	Columbus, N.J.	FA-'07	0*
54	Hobson, Victor	LB	6-0	252	2/4/84	5	Michigan	Mt. Laurel, N.J.	D2-'03	16/16
32	Houston, Cedric	RB	6-0	220	6/29/86	3	Tennessee	Clarendon, Ark.	D6a-'05	8/1
18	Jackson, Frisman	WR	6-3	217	6/13/83	5	Western Illinois	Chicago, Ill.	FA-'07	0*
79	Jones, Adrian	T	6-4	296	6/11/85	4	Kansas	Dallas, Texas	D4b-'04	9/0
20 t-	Jones, Thomas	RB	5-10	215	8/20/82	8	Virginia	Big Stone Gap, Va.	T(Chi)-'07	16/16*
55	Kassell, Brad	LB	6-3	242	1/8/84	6	North Texas	Llano, Texas	UFA(Tenn)-'06	16/0
66	Kendall, Pete	G	6-5	292	7/10/77	12	Boston College	Weymouth, Mass.	UFA-'04	14/14
74	Mangold, Nick	C	6-4	300	1/14/88	2	Ohio State	Kettering, Ohio	D1b-'06	16/16
28	Martin, Curtis	RB	5-11	210	5/2/77	13	Pittsburgh	Pittsburgh, Pa.	RFA(NE)-'98	0*
81	McCareins, Justin	WR	6-2	215	12/12/82	7	Northern Illinois	Naperville, Ill.	T(Tenn)-'04	16/7
62	McChesney, Matt	DT	6-4	307	11/7/85	2	Colorado	Santa Cruz, Calif.	UFA-'05	0*
22	Miller, Justin	CB/KR	5-10	196	2/15/88	3	Clemson	Owensboro, Ky.	D2b-'05	16/5
65	Moore, Brandon	G	6-3	295	6/4/84	5	Illinois	Gary, Ind.	FA-'03	16/16
95	Mosley, C.J.	DT	6-2	312	8/7/87	3	Missouri	Fort Knox, Ky.	T(Minn)-'06	6/0
1	Nugent, Mike	K	5-9	182	3/3/86	3	Ohio State	Centerville, Ohio	D2a-'05	16/0
10	Pennington, Chad	QB	6-3	225	6/27/80	8	Marshall	Knoxville, Tenn.	D1c-'00	16/16
82	Pociask, Jason	TE	6-2	259	2/10/87	2	Wisconsin	Plainfield, Ind.	D5-'06	0*
31	Poteat, Hank	CB	5-10	195	8/31/81	7	Pittsburgh	Harrisburg, Pa.	FA-'06	11/6
91	Pouha, Sione	DT	6-3	325	2/4/83	3	Utah	Salt Lake City, Utah	D3-'05	0*
25	Rhodes, Kerry	S	6-3	210	8/3/86	3	Louisville	Bessemer, Ala.	D4-'05	16/16
63	Robertson, Dewayne	DT	6-1	317	10/17/85	5	Kentucky	Memphis, Tenn.	D1-'03	16/16
88	Ryan, Sean	TE	6-5	265	12/23/85	4	Boston College	Buffalo, N.Y.	T(Dall)-'06	16/3
56	Schlegel, Anthony	LB	6-1	251	3/2/85	2	Ohio State	Dallas, Texas	D3a-'06	4/0
16	Smith, Brad	WR/QB/RB	6-2	210	12/13/87	2	Missouri	Liberty, Ohio	D4a-'06	16/3
33	Smith, Eric	S	6-1	209	3/18/87	2	Michigan State	Groveton, Ohio	D3b-'06	15/0
71	Smith, Wade	G/T	6-4	318	4/27/85	5	Memphis	Dallas, Texas	FA-'06	7/0
53	Spencer, Cody	LB	6-2	245	6/2/85	4	North Texas	Grapevine, Texas	FA-'06	12/1
99	Thomas, Bryan	DE/LB	6-4	266	6/8/83	6	Alabama-Birmingham	Birmingham, Ala.	D1-'02	16/16
8	Tuiasosopo, Marques	QB	6-1	220	3/23/83	7	Washington	Woodinville, Wash.	UFA(Oak)-'07	2/0*
41	Ventrone, Raymond	S	5-10	200	10/22/86	2	Villanova	Pittsburgh, Pa..	FA-'07	0*
51	Vilma, Jonathan	LB	6-1	230	4/17/86	4	Miami	South Miami, Fla.	D1-'04	16/16
67	von Oelhoffen, Kimo	DT/DE	6-4	299	1/31/75	14	Boise State	Kaunakakai, Hawaii	UFA(Pitt)-'06	16/16
57	Wadsworth, Andre	LB	6-4	272	10/20/78	4	Florida State	Miami, Fla.	FA-'07	0/0*
29	Washington, Leon	RB/KR	5-8	202	8/30/86	2	Florida State	Jacksonville, Fla.	D4b-'06	16/8
42	Washington, Rashad	S	6-1	217	3/16/84	4	Kansas State	Wichita, Kan.	D7d-'04	16/0
15	Wright, Wallace	WR	6-0	191	2/2/88	2	North Carolina	Fayetteville, N.C.	FA-'06	5/0

* Barnes played 15 games with Miami in '06; Bowens played 16 games with Miami; Clarke last active with Philadelphia in '05; K. Coleman played 16 games with Dallas; Goodard did not play in 1 game; Haynes inactive for 2 games with Chicago; Jackson last active with Cleveland in '05; T. Jones played 16 games with Chicago; Martin missed '06 season on PUP list; McChesney last active with N.Y. Jets in '05; Pociask missed '06 season because of injury; Pouha missed '06 season because of injury; Tuiasosopo played 2 games with Oakland; Ventrone missed '06 season on PUP list with New England, Wadsworth last active with Arizona in '00.

t-   Jets traded for T. Jones (Chi).

Players lost through free agency (1): RB B.J. Askew (TB; 13 games in '06).

Also played with Jets in '06—DE Dave Ball (10 games), RB Kevan Barlow (12), RB Derrick Blaylock (4), RB James Hodgins (6), G Norm Katnik (2), RB Jamar Martin (2), DT Rashad Moore (13), LB Ryan Myers (3), QB Patrick Ramsey (1), LB Ryan Riddle (5), S Derrick Strait (5), S Jamie Thompson (3), RB Stacy Tutt (2).

2007 FIRST-YEAR ROSTER

Name	Pos.	Ht.	Wt.	Birthdate	College	Hometown	How Acq.
Adams, Darrell (1)	DE	6-5	282	9/16/83	Villanova	Bay Shore, N.Y.	FA-'06
Allen, Jesse	FB	6-0	247	10/22/83	Virginia Tech	Monson, Mass.	FA
Banks, Alvin	RB	5-10	225	8/25/84	James Madison	Hampton, Va.	FA
Bender, Jacob	T/G	6-6	315	4/25/85	Nicholls State	Mayo, Md.	D6
Blanton, Ed (1)	T	6-9	330	10/23/82	UCLA	Winfield, Ill.	FA-'06
Costanzo, Blake (1)	LB	6-2	235	4/14/84	Lafayette	Franklin Lakes, N.J.	FA-'06
DeVito, Mike	DE	6-3	298	6/10/84	Maine	Wellfleet, Mass.	FA
Fitch, Zarnell (1)	DT	6-3	320	7/6/83	Texas Christian	Spencer, Okla.	FA-'06
Harris, David	LB	6-2	243	1/21/84	Michigan	Grand Rapids, Mich.	D2
Hendrix, Caleb	DB	5-10	185	2/28/85	Southern Miss	Ensley, Ala.	FA
Hodge, Alphonso (1)	CB	5-10	203	5/30/82	Miami (Ohio)	Cleveland, Ohio	FA-'06
King, Matt	LB	6-3	242	7/13/83	Maine	Stoughton, Mass.	FA
Kowalewski, Joe (1)	TE	6-4	250	11/15/82	Syracuse	Warners, N.Y.	FA-'06
Marshall, Keyonta (1)	DT	6-1	325	8/13/81	Grand Valley State	Saginaw, Mich.	FA-'06
Moran, Dominic	T/G	6-5	303	3/3/84	Western Michigan	Rochester Hills, Mich.	FA
Osborn, Dustin	WR	5-11	194	3/26/84	Colorado State	Junta, Colo.	FA
Peters, Leonard	S	6-1	199	12/26/81	Hawai'i	La'ie, O'ahu, Hawaii	FA
Ratliff, Brett	QB	6-4	224	8/8/85	Utah	Chico, Calif.	FA
Revis, Darrelle	DB/PR	6-0	204	7/14/85	Pittsburgh	Aliquippa, Pa.	D1
Smith, Nick	G/T	6-6	320	7/22/84	San Diego State	Orinda, Calif.	FA
Steffes, Kyle	RB	5-11	209	6/28/83	North Dakota State	Dickinson, N.D.	FA
Stuckey, Chansi	WR	6-0	185	10/4/83	Clemson	Warner Robins, Ga.	D7
Thompson, Jamie (1)	S	6-0	192	5/25/83	Oklahoma State	Sparr, Fla.	FA-'06
Trusnik, Jason	LB	6-5	250	6/6/84	Ohio Northern	Macedonia, Ohio	FA
Tutt, Stacy (1)	FB	6-1	233	8/8/82	Richmond	Fredricksburg, Va.	FA-'06
Wicker, Andrew	G/T	6-5	295	9/20/83	Mississippi	Zachary, La.	FA
Zalewski, Mark	LB	6-2	234	3/15/84	Wisconsin	Wausau, Wis.	FA

The term NFL Rookie is defined as a player who is in his first season of professional football and has not been on the roster of another professional football team for any regular-season or postseason games. A Rookie is designated by an "R" on NFL rosters. Players who have been active in another professional football league or players who have NFL experience, including either preseason training camp or being on an Active List or Inactive List, or on Reserve/Injured or Reserve/Physically Unable to Perform for fewer than six regular-season games, are termed NFL First-Year Players. An NFL First-Year Player is designated by a "1" on NFL rosters. Thereafter, a player is credited with an additional year of experience for each season in which he accumulates six games on the Active List or Inactive List, or on Reserve/Injured or Reserve/Physically Unable to Perform.

Log on to www.newyorkjets.com for an up-to-date roster.

COACHING STAFF

Head Coach,
Eric Mangini

Pro Career: Eric Mangini was named the fourteenth full-time head coach of the New York Jets on January 17, 2006. Last season, Mangini guided the Jets to a record of 10-6 and their 12th postseason berth in franchise history. The 10-6 record tied him with the Saints' Sean Payton for the best record among first-year head coaches in 2006. He joined the Jets following six seasons with the New England Patriots (2000-05), the first five of which he served as the defensive backs coach before earning a promotion to defensive coordinator. Mangini is entering his thirteenth season in the NFL and his second as a head coach. He has been a part of five division titles and three Super Bowl championships in his career. Prior to joining the Patriots, Mangini served as an assistant on Bill Parcells' coaching staff with the Jets (1997-1999), where he worked primarily as the defensive assistant/quality control coach. In 1996, he served as a quality control/offensive assistant on Ted Marchibroda's coaching staff with the Baltimore Ravens. Mangini's first NFL coaching opportunity came in 1995 as an assistant on Belichick's Cleveland Browns staff. While completing his Wesleyan degree in Melbourne, Australia, Mangini served as the head coach and defensive coordinator for the Kew Colts, a semi-professional football team, and led them to back-to-back titles. Career record: 10-7.

Background: Mangini set a school record with 36.5 sacks as a nose tackle in college for Wesleyan (Conn.) from 1989-1990, 1992-93. He was voted a first-team all-star by NESCAC and ECAC New England Division III.

Personal: Born January 19, 1971, Hartford, Conn. Mangini and his wife, Julie, have two sons, Jake and Luke.

ASSISTANT COACHES

Sal Alosi, head strength and conditioning; born May 11, 1977, Massapequa, N.Y. Linebacker Hofstra 1996-2000. No pro playing experience. College coach: Hofstra 2001. Pro coach: New York Jets 2002-05, Atlanta Falcons 2006, re-joined Jets in 2007.

Mike Bloomgren, quality control/offense; born January 25, 1977, Tallahassee, Fl.a Attended Florida State. No college or pro playing experience. College coach: Florida State 1997-98 Alabama 1999-2001, Catawba College 2002-04, Delta State 2005-06. Pro coach: Joined Jets in 2007.

Bryan Cox, asst. defensive line; born February 17, 1968, East St. Louis, Ill. Linebacker Western Illinois 1987-1990. Pro linebacker Miami Dolphins 1991-95, Chicago Bears 1996-97, New York Jets 1998-2000, New England Patriots 2001, New Orleans Saints 2002. Pro coach:

Joined Jets in 2006.

Brian Daboll, quarterbacks; born April 14, 1975, Welland, Ontario, Canada. Safety Rochester 1994-96. No pro playing experience. College coach: William & Mary 1997, Michigan State 1998-99. Pro coach: New England Patriots 2000-2006, joined Jets in 2007.

Mike Devlin, tight ends/asst. offensive line; born November 16, 1969, Blacksburg, Va. Offensive line Iowa 1989-1992. Pro offensive lineman Buffalo Bills 1993-95, Arizona Cardinals 1996-99. College coach: Toledo 2004-05. Pro coach: Arizona Cardinals 2000-03, joined Jets in 2006.

Andy Dickerson, quality control/defense; born January 29, 1982, Wilmington, Del. Offensive lineman Tufts 1999-2002. No pro playing experience. College coach: Tufts 2003. Pro coach: Joined Jets in 2006.

Jerome Henderson; asst. secondary; born August 8, 1969, Portsmouth, Va. Defensive back Clemson 1987-1990. Pro cornerback New England Patriots 1991-93, 1996, Buffalo Bills 1993-94, Philadelphia Eagles 1995, New York Jets 1997-98. Pro coach: Joined Jets in 2006.

Jim Herrmann, linebackers; born December 8, 1960, Hollywood, Calif. Linebacker Michigan 1979-1982. No pro playing experience. College coach: Michigan 1983, 1986-2005. Pro coach: Joined Jets in 2006.

Mike Jones, asst. strength and conditioning; August, 16, 1971, Thomasville, Ga. Safety Georgia 1989-1992. No pro experience. College coach: Arizona State 2006. Pro coach: Joined Jets in 2007.

Ben Kotwica, quality control/special teams and defense; born December 8, 1974, Tinley Park, Ill. Linebacker Army 1995-97. No pro playing experience. Pro coach: Joined Jets in 2007.

Rick Lyle, asst. strength and conditioning; born February 26, 1971, Monroe, La. Defensive lineman Missouri 1989-1993. Pro defensive lineman Cleveland Browns 1994-95, Baltimore Ravens 1996, New York Jets 1997-2001, New England Patriots 2002-03. Pro coach: Joined Jets in 2006.

Mike MacIntyre, defensive backs; born March 14, 1965, Nashville, Tenn. Safety Vanderbilt 1984-85, Georgia Tech 1986-88. No pro playing experience. College coach: Georgia 1990-91, Davidson 1992, Tennessee-Martin 1993-96, Mississippi 1999-2002. Pro coach: Dallas Cowboys 2003-06, joined Jets in 2007.

Noel Mazzone, wide receivers; born March 21, 1957, Mt. Vernon, Wash. Quarterback New Mexico 1975-79. No pro playing experience. College coach: New Mexico 1980-81, Colorado State 1982-86, Texas Christian 1987-1991, Minnesota 1992-94, Mississippi 1994-98, Auburn 1999-2001, Oregon State 2002, North Carolina State 2003-05. Pro coach: Joined Jets in 2006.

Jason Michael, offensive assistant; born October 15, 1978, Portsmouth, Ohio. Quarterback Western Kentucky 1999-

2002. No pro playing experience. College coach: Tennessee 2003-04. Pro coach: Oakland Raiders 2005, joined Jets in 2006.

Dan Quinn, defensive line; born September 11, 1970, Orange, N.J. Defensive lineman Salisbury State 1990-93. No pro playing experience. College coach: William & Mary 1994, Virginia Military Institute 1995, Hofstra 1997-2000. Pro coach: San Francisco 49ers 2001-04, Miami Dolphins 2005-06, joined Jets in 2007.

Jimmy Raye, running backs; born March 26, 1946, Fayetteville, N.C. Quarterback Michigan State 1964-68. Pro defensive back Philadelphia Eagles 1969. College coach: Michigan State 1971-75, Wyoming 1976. Pro coach: San Francisco 49ers 1977, Detroit Lions 1978-79, Atlanta Falcons 1980-82, 1987-89, Los Angeles Rams 1983-84, 1991, Tampa Bay Buccaneers 1985-86, New England Patriots 1990, Kansas City Chiefs 1992-2000, Washington Redskins 2001, New York Jets 2002-03, Oakland Raiders 2004-2005, re-joined Jets in 2006.

Brian Schottenheimer, offensive coordinator; born October 16, 1973, Denver. Quarterback Kansas 1992, Florida 1993-96. No pro playing experience. College coach: Syracuse 1999, Southern California 2000. Pro coach: St. Louis Rams 1997, Kansas City Chiefs 1998, Washington Redskins 2001, San Diego Chargers 2002-05, joined Jets in 2006.

Bob Sutton, defensive coordinator; born January 28, 1951, Ypsilanti, Mich. Attended Eastern Michigan. No college or pro playing experience. College coach: Michigan 1972-73, Syracuse 1974, Western Michigan 1975-76, 1980-81, Illinois 1977-79, North Carolina State 1982, Army 1983-1999 (head coach 1991-99). Pro coach: Joined Jets in 2000.

Brian Smith, quality control/offense; born July 15, 1979, Wilmington, Del. Defensive back Massachusetts 1997-2000. No pro playing experience. College coach: Massachusetts 2004-06. Pro coach: Joined Jets in 2007.

Mike Westhoff, special teams coordinator; born January 10, 1948, Pittsburgh. Center/linebacker Wichita State 1967-69. No pro playing experience. College coach: Indiana 1974-75, Dayton 1976, Indiana State 1977, Northwestern 1978-1980, Texas Christian 1981. Pro coach: Baltimore/Indianapolis Colts 1982-84, Arizona Outlaws (USFL) 1985, Miami Dolphins 1986-2000, joined Jets in 2001.

Tony Wise, offensive line; born December 28, 1951, Albany, N.Y. Offensive lineman Ithaca College 1969-1972. No pro playing experience. College coach: Albany State 1973, Bridgeport 1974, Central Connecticut State 1975, Washington State 1976, Pittsburgh 1977-78, Oklahoma State 1979-1983, Syracuse 1984, Miami 1985-88. Pro coach: Dallas Cowboys 1989-1992, Chicago Bears 1993-98, Carolina Panthers 1999-2000, Miami Dolphins 2001-04, joined Jets in 2006.

**American Football Conference
West Division
Team Colors:** Silver and Black
1220 Harbor Bay Parkway
Alameda, California 94502
Telephone: (510) 864-5000

2007 SCHEDULE
PRESEASON
Aug. 11 **Arizona**. 7:00
Aug. 18 at San Francisco. 7:00
Aug. 24 **St. Louis**. 7:00
Aug. 30 at Seattle. 7:00

REGULAR SEASON
Sep. 9 **Detroit** 1:15
Sep. 16 at Denver 2:15
Sep. 23 **Cleveland** 1:05
Sep. 30 at Miami 1:00
Oct. 7 Open Date
Oct. 14 at San Diego 1:15
Oct. 21 **Kansas City** 1:05
Oct. 28 at Tennessee 12:00
Nov. 4 **Houston** 1:15
Nov. 11 **Chicago** 1:15
Nov. 18 at Minnesota 12:00
Nov. 25 at Kansas City 12:00
Dec. 2 **Denver** 1:05
Dec. 9 at Green Bay 12:00
Dec. 16 **Indianapolis** 1:05
Dec. 23 at Jacksonville 1:00
Dec. 30 **San Diego** 1:15

Stadium: McAfee Coliseum
(opened in 1966)
• **Capacity:** 63,132
7000 Coliseum Way
Oakland, CA 94621-1917
Playing Surface: Grass
Training Camp: Napa Valley Marriott
Napa, California 94558

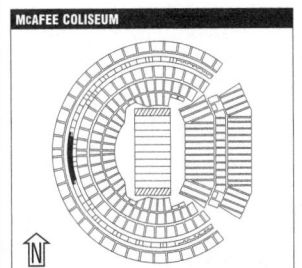

McAFEE COLISEUM

CLUB OFFICIALS
Owner: Al Davis
Chief Executive: Amy Trask
Legal: Jeff Birren, Dan Ventrelle
Finance: Marc Badain, Tom Blanda,
Ed Villanueva, Derek Person
Special Projects: Jim Otto
Senior Executive: John Herrera
Public Relations: Mike Taylor
Tickets, Suites & Premium Seats:
Rob Sullivan
Multi-Cultural Initiatives: Patty Herrera,
Elena Valenzuela
Internet: Jerry Knaak
Marketing: Craig Purcell
Community Relations: Scott Fink
Youth Initiatives: Rosie Bone
Raiderettes: Karen Kovac
Trainers: H. Rod Martin, Scott Touchet
Equipment: Bob Romanski,
Richard Romanski, Danny Molina
Video Operations: Dave Nash, Jim Otten,
John Otten
Broadcasting: Chris Gargano,
Vittorio DeBartolo
Computer Operations: Matt Pasco

COACHING HISTORY
Oakland 1960-1981
Los Angeles 1982-1994
(421-319-11)
Records include postseason games

1960-61	Eddie Erdelatz*	6-10-0
1961-62	Marty Feldman**	2-15-0
1962	Red Conkright	1-8-0
1963-65	Al Davis	23-16-3
1966-68	John Rauch	35-10-1
1969-1978	John Madden	112-39-7
1979-1987	Tom Flores	91-56-0
1988-89	Mike Shanahan***	8-12-0
1989-1994	Art Shell	56-41-0
1995-96	Mike White	15-17-0
1997	Joe Bugel	4-12-0
1998-2001	Jon Gruden	40-28-0
2002-03	Bill Callahan	17-18-0
2004-05	Norv Turner	9-23-0
2006	Art Shell	2-14-0

*Released after two games in 1961
**Released after five games in 1962
***Released after four games in 1989

PAID ATTENDANCE
Home 445,549   Away 567,386
Total 1,012,935
Single-game home record,
62,660 (11/3/02)
Single-season home record,
471,151 (2002)

2007 DRAFT CHOICES
Round	Name	Pos.	College
1	JaMarcus Russell	QB	Louisiana State
2	Zach Miller	TE	Arizona State
3	Quentin Moses	DE	Georgia
	Mario Henderson	T	Florida State
	Johnnie Lee Higgins	WR	Texas-El Paso
4	Michael Bush	RB	Louisville
	John Bowie	DB	Cincinnati
5	Jay Richardson	DE	Ohjio State
	Eric Frampton	DB	Washington St.
6	Oren O'Neal	RB	Arkansas State
7	Johnathan Holland	WR	Louisiana Tech

2006 TEAM RECORD

PRESEASON (4-1)

Date	Result	Opponent
8/6	W 16-10	vs. Philadelphia, at Canton, OH
8/14	W 16-13	at Minnesota
8/20	W 23-7	San Francisco
8/25	W 21-3	Detroit
8/31	L 7-30	at Seattle

REGULAR SEASON (2-14)

Date	Result	Opponent	Att.
9/11	L 0-27	San Diego	62,578
9/17	L 6-28	at Baltimore	70,744
10/1	L 21-24	Cleveland	61,426
10/8	L 20-34	at San Francisco	68,368
10/15	L 3-13	at Denver	76,691
10/22	W 22-9	Arizona	61,595
10/29	W 20-13	Pittsburgh	62,385
11/6	L 0-16	at Seattle	67,816
11/12	L 13-17	Denver	62,094
11/19	L 13-17	at Kansas City	78,097
11/26	L 14-21	at San Diego	66,105
12/3	L 14-23	Houston	46,276
12/10	L 10-27	at Cincinnati	65,882
12/17	L 0-20	St. Louis	50,164
12/23	L 9-20	Kansas City	61,446
12/31	L 3-23	at N.Y. Jets	78,039

SCORE BY PERIODS

Raiders	44	79	21	24	0 —	168
Opponents	88	68	66	110	0 —	332

2006 TEAM STATISTICS

	Raiders	Opp.
Total First Downs	243	267
Rushing	73	107
Passing	144	137
Penalty	26	23
3rd Down: Made/Att	77/212	79/221
3rd Down Pct.	36.3	35.7
4th Down: Made/Att	7/21	10/19
4th Down Pct.	33.3	52.6
Possession Avg.	28:13	31:47
Total Net Yards	3,939	4,557
Avg. Per Game	246.2	284.8
Total Plays	949	986
Avg. Per Play	4.2	4.6
Net Yards Rushing	1,519	2,144
Avg. Per Game	94.9	134.0
Total Rushes	394	542
Net Yards Passing	2,420	2,413
Avg. Per Game	151.3	150.8
Sacked/Yards Lost	72/430	34/218
Gross Yards	2,850	2,631
Att./Completions	483/263	410/245
Completion Pct.	54.5	59.8
Had Intercepted	24	18
Punts/Average	78/46.9	68/41.5
Net Punting Avg.	78/36.4	68/37.4
Penalties/Yards	111/847	85/665
Fumbles/Ball Lost	32/22	16/5
Touchdowns	16	34
Rushing	5	15
Passing	7	17
Returns	4	2

2006 INDIVIDUAL STATISTICS

PASSING	Att.	Comp.	Yds.	Pct.	TD	Int.	Tkld.	Rate
Walter	276	147	1,677	53.3	3	13	46/256	55.8
Brooks	192	110	1,105	57.3	3	8	26/174	61.7
M. Tuiasosopo	13	6	68	46.2	1	2	0/0	48.4
Curry	2	0	—	0.0	0	1	0/0	0.0
Raiders	483	263	2,850	54.5	7	24	72/430	56.2
Opponents	410	245	2,631	59.8	17	18	34/218	74.1

SCORING	TD R	TD P	TD Rt	PAT	FG	Saf	PTS
Janikowski	0	0	0	16/16	18/25	0	70
Moss	0	3	0	0/0	0/0	0	18
Anderson	0	2	0	0/0	0/0	0	12
Jordan	2	0	0	0/0	0/0	0	12
Lee	2	0	0	0/0	0/0	0	12
Asomugha	0	0	1	0/0	0/0	0	6
Carr	0	0	1	0/0	0/0	0	6
Curry	0	1	0	0/0	0/0	0	6
Fargas	1	0	0	0/0	0/0	0	6
Madsen	0	1	0	0/0	0/0	0	6
Morrison	0	0	1	0/0	0/0	0	6
S. Williams	0	0	1	0/0	0/0	0	6
Huff	0	0	0	0/0	0/0	1	2
Raiders	5	7	4	16/16	18/25	1	168
Opponents	15	17	2	33/34	31/37	1	332

2-Pt. Conversions:
Raiders 0-0, Opponents 0-0.

RUSHING	No.	Yds	Avg	LG	TD
Fargas	178	659	3.7	48	1
Jordan	114	434	3.8	59t	2
Crockett	39	163	4.2	17	0
Brooks	22	124	5.6	23	0
Lee	21	72	3.4	13	2
Walter	14	30	2.1	12	0
M. Tuiasosopo	4	29	7.3	11	0
Curry	1	4	4.0	4	0
Whitted	1	4	4.0	4	0
Raiders	394	1,519	3.9	59t	5
Opponents	542	2,144	4.0	58	15

RECEIVING	No.	Yds	Avg	LG	TD
Curry	62	727	11.7	39	1
Moss	42	553	13.2	51	3
R. Williams	28	293	10.5	28	0
Whitted	27	299	11.1	33	0
Anderson	25	285	11.4	35	2
Lee	20	138	6.9	15	0
Fargas	13	91	7.0	21	0
Madsen	11	146	13.3	57	1
Jordan	10	74	7.4	21	0
Crockett	10	53	5.3	14	0
Morant	7	70	10.0	18	0
Gabriel	5	84	16.8	28	0
Porter	1	19	19.0	19	0
Adkisson	1	9	9.0	9	0
Buchanon	1	9	9.0	9	0
Raiders	263	2,850	10.8	57	7
Opponents	245	2,631	10.7	58	17

INTERCEPTIONS	No.	Yds	Avg	LG	TD
Asomugha	8	59	7.4	24t	1
Washington	4	4	1.0	7	0
Morrison	2	32	16.0	31	0
Carr	1	100	100.0	100t	1
Routt	1	6	6.0	6	0
Sands	1	5	5.0	5	0
Poole	1	0	0.0	0	0
Raiders	18	206	11.4	100t	2
Opponents	24	286	11.9	54	0

PUNTING	No.	Yds.	Avg.	In 20	LG
Lechler	77	3660	47.5	19	67
Raiders	78	3660	46.9	19	67
Opponents	68	2822	41.5	23	74

PUNT RETURNS	Ret	FC	Yds	Avg	LG	TD
Carr	35	12	216	6.2	35	0
Raiders	35	12	216	6.2	35	0
Opponents	34	10	437	12.9	58	0

KICKOFF RETURNS	No.	Yds	Avg	LG	TD
Carr	69	1762	25.5	50	0
Lee	4	49	12.3	17	0
Raiders	73	1811	24.8	50	0
Opponents	42	1200	28.6	91	0

FIELD GOALS	1-19	20-29	30-39	40-49	50+
Janikowski	1/1	2/3	9/11	3/3	3/7
Raiders	1/1	2/3	9/11	3/3	3/7
Opponents	1/1	15/15	10/11	4/9	1/1

SACKS	No.
Burgess	11.0
Sapp	10.0
Kelly	3.5
Huntley	2.5
Johnstone	2.0
Asomugha	1.0
Morrison	1.0
Poole	1.0
Sands	1.0
S. Williams	1.0
Raiders	34.0
Opponents	72.0

RECORD HOLDERS
INDIVIDUAL RECORDS—CAREER

Category	Name	Performance
Rushing (Yds.)	Marcus Allen, 1982-1992	8,545
Passing (Yds.)	Ken Stabler, 1970-79	19,078
Passing (TDs)	Ken Stabler, 1970-79	150
Receiving (No.)	Tim Brown, 1988-2003	1,070
Receiving (Yds.)	Tim Brown, 1988-2003	14,734
Interceptions	Willie Brown, 1967-1978	39
	Lester Hayes, 1977-1986	39
Punting (Avg.)	Shane Lechler, 2000-05	*45.9
Punt Return (Avg.)	Claude Gibson, 1963-65	12.6
Kickoff Return (Avg.)	Jack Larscheid, 1960-61	28.4
Field Goals	Chris Bahr, 1980-88	162
Touchdowns (Tot.)	Tim Brown, 1988-2003	104
Points	George Blanda, 1967-1975	863

INDIVIDUAL RECORDS—SINGLE SEASON

Category	Name	Performance
Rushing (Yds.)	Marcus Allen, 1985	1,759
Passing (Yds.)	Rich Gannon, 2002	4,689
Passing (TDs)	Daryle Lamonica, 1969	34
Receiving (No.)	Tim Brown 1997	104
Receiving (Yds.)	Tim Brown, 1997	1,408
Interceptions	Lester Hayes, 1980	13
Punting (Avg.)	Shane Lechler, 2003	46.9
Punt Return (Avg.)	Claude Gibson, 1964	14.4
Kickoff Return (Avg.)	Harold Hart, 1975	30.5
Field Goals	Jeff Jaeger, 1993	35
Touchdowns (Tot.)	Marcus Allen, 1984	18
Points	Jeff Jaeger, 1993	132

INDIVIDUAL RECORDS—SINGLE GAME

Category	Name	Performance
Rushing (Yds.)	Napoleon Kaufman, 10-19-97	227
Passing (Yds.)	Cotton Davidson, 10-25-64	427
Passing (TDs)	Tom Flores, 12-22-63	6
	Daryle Lamonica, 10-19-69	6
Receiving (No.)	Tim Brown, 12-21-97	14
Receiving (Yds.)	Art Powell, 12-22-63	247
Interceptions	Many times	3
	Last time by Rod Woodson, 9-29-02	
Field Goals	Jeff Jaeger, 12-11-94	5
	Sebastian Janikowski, 10-29-00	5
Touchdowns (Tot.)	Art Powell, 12-22-63	4
	Marcus Allen, 9-24-84	4
	Harvey Williams, 11-16-97	4
Points	Art Powell, 12-22-63	24
	Marcus Allen, 9-24-84	24
	Harvey Williams, 11-16-97	24

*NFL Record

2007 VETERAN ROSTER

No.	Name	Pos.	Ht.	Wt.	Birthdate	NFL Exp.	College	Hometown	How Acq.	'06 Games/ Starts
88	Adkisson, James	TE	6-5	230	1/11/80	2	South Carolina	St. Louis, Mo.	FA-'03	2/0
83	Anderson, Courtney	TE	6-6	270	11/19/80	4	San Jose State	Richmond, Calif.	D7-'04	16/11
21	Asomugha, Nnamdi	CB	6-2	210	7/6/81	5	California	Los Angeles, Calif.	D1-'03	15/15
29	Bing, Darnell	S	6-2	230	9/10/84	2	Southern California	Long Beach, Calif.	D4-'06	0*
67	Boothe, Kevin	G	6-5	315	7/5/83	2	Cornell	Plantation, Fla.	D6-'06	16/14
10	Booty, Josh	QB	6-3	220	4/29/75	4	Louisiana State	Shreveport, La.	FA-'07	0*
91	Brayton, Tyler	DE	6-6	280	11/20/79	5	Colorado	Pasco, Wash.	D1-'03	16/13
57	Brown, Ricky	LB	6-2	235	12/27/83	2	Boston College	Cincinnati, Ohio	FA--06	13/0
13	Buchanon, Will	WR	6-3	190	4/5/83	2	Southern California	Oceanside, Calif.	FA-'06	1/0
56	Burgess, Derrick	DE	6-2	260	8/12/78	7	Mississippi	Greenbelt, Md.	UFA(Phil)-'05	16/16
44	Campbell, Kurt	LB	6-1	240	7/30/82	2	SUNY-Albany	Kingston, Jamaica	FA-'07	0*
66	Carlisle, Cooper	G	6-5	295	8/11/77	8	Florida	McComb, Miss.	UFA(Den)-'07	16/16*
23	Carr, Chris	CB	5-10	180	4/30/83	3	Boise State	Reno, Nev.	FA-'05	16/2
69	Claxton, Ben	G/T	6-2	300	7/30/80	3	Mississippi	Dublin, Ga.	W(Atl)-'07	0*
48	Clemons, Chris	LB	6-3	240	10/30/81	4	Georgia	Griffin, Ga.	FA-'07	0*
40	Cooper, Jarrod	S	6-1	215	3/31/78	7	Kansas State	Pearland, Texas	FA-'04	16/0
32	Crockett, Zack	RB	6-2	240	12/2/72	13	Florida State	Pompano Beach, Fla.	UFA(Jax)-'99	16/9
89	Curry, Ronald	WR	6-2	210	5/28/79	6	North Carolina	Hampton, Va.	D7-'02	16/4
20	Echemandu, Adimchinobe	RB	5-10	225	11/20/80	4	California	Hawthorne, Calif.	FA-'06	4/0
50	Ekejiuba, Isaiah	LB	6-4	240	10/5/81	3	Virginia	Somerset, N.J.	FA-'05	12/0
25	Fargas, Justin	RB	6-1	220	1/25/80	5	Southern California	Sherman Oaks, Calif.	D3-'03	16/6
82	Francis, Carlos	WR	5-10	190	1/3/81	4	Texas Tech	Fort Worth, Texas	D4-'04	0*
80	Gabriel, Doug	WR	6-2	215	8/27/80	5	Central Florida	Miami, Fla.	D5-'03	15/5*
76	Gallery, Robert	T	6-7	325	7/26/80	4	Iowa	Masonville, Iowa	D1-'04	10/10
36	#Gibson, Derrick	S	6-2	215	3/22/79	7	Florida State	Miami, Fla.	D1-'01	16/1
74	Green, Cornell	T	6-6	315	8/25/76	9	Central Florida	St. Petersburg, Fla.	UFA(TB)-'07	14/0*
36	Griffith, Justin	FB	6-0	235	7/21/80	5	Mississippi State	Magee, Miss.	UFA(Atl)-'07	16/11*
64	Grove, Jake	C	6-4	300	1/22/80	4	Virginia Tech	Forest, Va.	D2-'04	16/16
77	Hawthorne, Anttaj	DT	6-3	310	11/15/81	3	Wisconsin	New Haven, Conn.	D6a-'05	16/0
53	Howard, Thomas	LB	6-3	240	7/14/83	2	Texas-El Paso	Lubbock, Texas	D2-'06	16/15
24	Huff, Michael	S	6-1	205	3/6/83	2	Texas	Irving, Texas	D1-'06	16/16
71	#Hulsey , Corey	G	6-4	325	7/26/77	6	Clemson	Gainesville, Ga.	FA-'03	5/5
94	Huntley, Kevin	DE	6-7	270	4/8/82	3	Kansas State	Washington, D.C.	FA-'06	6/0
96	#Irons, Grant	LB	6-6	285	7/7/79	6	Notre Dame	The Woodlands, Texas	FA-'03	2/1
11	Janikowski, Sebastian	K	6-2	250	3/2/78	8	Florida State	Daytona Beach, Fla.	D1-'00	16/0
37	Johnson, Chris	CB	6-1	200	9/25/79	5	Louisville	Longview, Texas	FA-'07	0*
34	Jordan, LaMont	RB	5-10	230	11/11/78	7	Maryland	Suitland, Md.	UFA(NYJ)-'05	9/8
93	Kelly, Tommy	DT	6-6	300	12/27/80	4	Mississippi State	Jackson, Miss.	FA-'04	16/16
9	Lechler, Shane	P	6-2	225	8/7/76	8	Texas A&M	Sealy, Texas	D5-'00	16/0
42	Lee, ReShard	RB	5-10	220	10/12/80	4	Middle Tennessee State	Brunswick, Ga.	FA-'06	16/3
85	Madsen, John	TE	6-5	235	5/9/83	2	Utah	West Valley City, Utah	FA-'06	15/1
12	t-McCown, Josh	QB	6-4	215	7/4/79	6	Sam Houston State	Jacksonville, Texas	T(Det)-'07	2/0*
92	McNeal, Bryant	DE	6-4	250	7/13/79	3	Clemson	Swansea, S.C.	FA-'06	0*
79	McQuistan, Paul	G	6-6	315	4/30/83	2	Weber State	Lebanon, Ore.	D3-'06	15/6
19	Morant, Johnnie	WR	6-4	220	12/7/81	4	Syracuse	Parsippany, N.J.	D5-'04	10/2
61	Morris, Chris	C	6-4	305	2/2/83	2	Michigan State	Temperance, Mich.	D7-'06	5/0
52	Morrison, Kirk	LB	6-2	240	2/19/82	3	San Diego State	Oakland, Calif.	D3b-'05	16/16
60	Newberry, Jeremy	C	6-5	315	3/23/76	10	California	Antioch, Calif.	UFA(SF)-'07	0*
	Parson, Rich	WR	5-10	185	11/11/81	3	Maryland	Dewark, Del.	FA-'07	0*
81	Porter, Jerry	WR	6-2	220	7/14/78	8	West Virginia	Washington, D.C.	D2-'00	4/0
33	Rhodes, Dominic	RB	5-9	205	1/17/79	7	Midwestern State	Abilene, Texas	UFA(Ind)-'07	16/16*
38	Richard, Kris	CB	5-11	190	10/28/78	5	Southern California	Gardena, Calif.	FA-'07	0*
26	Routt, Stanford	CB	6-1	195	7/26/83	3	Houston	Austin, Texas	D2-'05	16/2
90	Sands, Terdell	DT	6-7	335	10/31/79	5	Tennessee-Chattanooga	Chattanooga, Tenn.	FA-'03	16/2
99	Sapp, Warren	DT	6-2	300	12/19/72	13	Miami	Apopka, Fla.	UFA(TB)-'04	16/16
30	Schweigert, Stuart	S	6-2	210	6/21/81	4	Purdue	Saginaw, Mich.	D3-'04	16/16
95	Shaw, Josh	DT	6-3	305	9/7/79	3	Michigan State	Ft. Lauderdale, Fla.	FA-'07	0*
65	Sims, Barry	G	6-5	300	12/1/74	9	Utah	Park City, Utah	FA-'99	10/7
78	Slaughter, Chad	T	6-8	340	6/4/78	7	Alcorn State	Dallas, Texas	FA-'02	15/6
22	Starks, Duane	CB	5-10	175	5/23/74	10	Miami	Miami, Fla.	FA-'06	3/0
84	Stewart, Tony	TE	6-5	260	8/9/79	7	Penn State	Allentown, Pa.	UFA(Cin)-'07	16/3*
55	Thomas, Robert	LB	6-0	235	7/17/80	6	UCLA	El Centro, Calif.	FA-'06	16/0
62	Treu, Adam	C	6-5	300	6/24/74	11	Nebraska	Lincoln, Neb.	D3-'97	11/0
47	Wakefield, Fred	TE	6-7	295	9/17/78	7	Illinois	Tuscola, Ill.	UFA(Ariz)-'07	16/9*
16	Walter, Andrew	QB	6-6	230	5/11/82	3	Arizona State	Grand Junction, Colo.	D3a-'05	12/8

28	Ward, B.J.	S	6-3	210	11/4/81	2	Florida State	Dallas, Texas	FA-'07	0*
27	Washington, Fabian	CB	5-11	185	6/9/83	3	Nebraska	Bradenton, Fla.	D1-'05	14/14
87	Whitted, Alvis	WR	6-0	185	9/4/74	10	North Carolina State	Hillsborough, N.C.	FA-'02	14/13
17	t-Williams, Mike	WR	6-5	230	1/4/84	3	Southern California	Tampa, Fla.	T(Det)-'07	8/2*
86	Williams, Randal	TE	6-3	235	5/21/78	7	New Hampshire	Bronx, N.Y.	FA-'05	16/10
54	Williams, Sam	LB	6-5	260	7/28/80	5	Fresno State	Clayton, Calif.	D3-'03	15/12
63	Wilson, Mark	T	6-7	320	11/11/80	3	California	McArthur, Calif.	FA-'06	0*

* Bing missed '06 season because of injury; Booty last active with Cleveland in '03; Campbell missed '06 season with Green Bay because of injury; Carlisle played 16 games with Denver in '06; Claxton missed '06 season with Atlanta because of injury; Clemons last active with Washington in '05; Francis missed '06 season because of injury; Gabriel played 12 games with New England and 3 games with Oakland; Green played 14 games with Tampa Bay; Griffith played 16 games with Atlanta; C. Johnson last active with St. Louis in '05; McCown played 2 games with Detroit; McNeal inactive for 2 games with Tampa Bay in '04; Newberry missed '06 season with San Francisco because of injury; Parson last active with Washington in '05; Rhodes played 16 games with Indianapolis; Richard missed '06 season with San Francisco because of injury; Shaw inactive for 5 games with Miami in '05; Stewart played 16 games with Cincinnati; Wakefield played 16 games with Arizona; Ward last active with Baltimore in '05; M. Williams played 8 games with Detroit; Wilson last active with Washington in '04.

\# Unrestricted Free Agent; subject to developments.

t- Raiders traded for McCown (Det) and M. Williams (Det).

Traded—WR Randy Moss (13 games in '06) to New England.

Players lost through free agency (2): QB Marques Tuiasosopo (NYJ; 2 games in '06), T Langston Walker (Buff; 16).

Also played with Raiders in '06—G Brad Badger (7 games), QB Aaron Brooks (8), RB John Paul Foschi (1), DE Lance Johnstone (11), CB Tyrone Poole (12).

2007 FIRST-YEAR ROSTER

Name	Pos.	Ht.	Wt.	Birthdate	College	Hometown	How Acq.
Bowie, John	CB	5-11	190	5/11/84	Cincinnati	Columbus, Ohio	D4
Brown, Larry	DT	6-3	295	10/15/84	Oklahoma State	Spatranburg, S.C.	FA
Bush, Michael	RB	6-1	245	6/16/84	Louisville	Louisville, Ky.	D4
Cole, Marquice	CB	5-10	190	11/13/83	Northwestern	Hazel Crest, Ill.	FA
Condo, Jon (1)	LS	6-3	250	1/3/82	Maryland	Philipsburg, Pa.	FA-'06
Dickerson, Ricardo (1)	LB	6-1	250	7/10/82	Maryland	Hyattsville, N.D.	FA
Eugene, Hiram (1)	S	6-2	200	11/24/80	Louisiana Tech	Jeanerette, La.	FA-'06
Frampton, Eric	S	5-11	205	2/6/84	Washington State	San Jose, Calif.	D5
Henderson, Mario	T	6-7	300	10/29/84	Florida State	Lehigh Acres, Fla.	D3
Higgins, Johnnie Lee	WR	5-11	185	9/8/83	Texas-El Paso	Sweeny, Texas	D3
Holland , Jonathan	WR	6-1	195	2/18/85	Louisiana Tech	Archibald, La.	D7
Jackson, Tony (1)	RB	6-2	255	7/5/82	Iowa	Ypsilanti, Mich.	FA-'06
Keele, Eddie	T	6-6	305	7/6/81	Brigham Young	Othello, Wash.	FA
Keith, Charlton (1)	LB	6-5	240	5/4/83	Kansas	Akron, Ohio	FA
McFoy, Chris	WR	6-1	200	8/14/83	Southern California	Chino, Calif.	FA
Milan, J.J.	LB	6-5	265	8/11/84	Nevada	Reno, Nev.	FA
Miller, Zach	TE	6-5	255	12/11/85	Arizona State	Phoenix, Ariz.	D2
Moses, Quentin	DE	6-5	260	11/18/83	Georgia	Athens, Ga.	D3
O'Neal, Oren	RB	5-11	245	9/8/83	Arkansas State	Stuttgart, Ark.	D6
Otis, Jeff (1)	QB	6-1	210	1/30/83	Columbia	St. Louis, Mo.	FA
Patton, Kenny	CB	6-0	185	1/31/84	Hawaii	La Canada, Calif.	FA
Richardson, Jay	DE	6-6	280	1/27/84	Ohio State	Washington, D.C.	D5
Rowan, Levonne (1)	DB	6-1	190	11/2/82	Wisconsin	Erie, Pa.	FA
Russell, JaMarcus	QB	6-6	255	8/9/85	Louisiana State	Mobile, Ala.	D1
Shotwell, Kyle	LB	6-1	240	3/29/84	Cal Poly-San Luis Obispo	Santa Barbara, Calif.	FA
Tolleefson, Dave (1)	DE	6-4	265	5/19/81	Northwest Missouri State	Concord, Calif.	FA
Williams, Lauren (1)	WR	6-3	195	4/19/83	Liberty	Upper Marlboro, Md.	FA

The term NFL Rookie is defined as a player who is in his first season of professional football and has not been on the roster of another professional football team for any regular-season or postseason games. A Rookie is designated by an "R" on NFL rosters. Players who have been active in another professional football league or players who have NFL experience, including either preseason training camp or being on an Active List or Inactive List, or on Reserve/Injured or Reserve/Physically Unable to Perform for fewer than six regular-season games, are termed NFL First-Year Players. An NFL First-Year Player is designated by a "1" on NFL rosters. Thereafter, a player is credited with an additional year of experience for each season in which he accumulates six games on the Active List or Inactive List, or on Reserve/Injured or Reserve/Physically Unable to Perform.

Log on to www.raiders.com for an up-to-date roster.

COACHING STAFF

Head Coach,

Lane Kiffin

Pro Career: Named the sixteenth head coach in Raiders history. At 31, he is the youngest head coach in the NFL modern era. He was an assistant for the Jacksonville Jaguars in 2000. No pro playing experience.

Background: Lettered three seasons at quarterback for Fresno State (1994-96). Coached at Fresno State (1997-98), Colorado State (1999), and the University of Southern California (2001-06). He was offensive coordinator and recruiting coordinator in addition to coaching wide receivers at Southern California from 2005-06; was receivers coach/passing game coordinator in 2004; wide receivers coach from 2002-03 and was the Trojans' tight ends coach in 2001. Kiffin's play-calling, structure, and offensive design helped the Trojans produce two Heisman Trophy winners—Matt Leinart in 2004 and Reggie Bush in 2005—and two national championships (2003 and 2004).

Personal: Born May 9, 1975, in Bloomington, Minn. Lane and his wife Layla have two daughters, Landry and Pressley. Father, Monte, is currently Tampa Bay's defensive coordinator.

ASSISTANT COACHES

Willie Brown, squad development, defensive backs; born December 2, 1940, Yazoo City, Miss. Defensive back Grambling State 1959-1962. Pro defensive back Denver Broncos 1963-66, Oakland Raiders 1967-1978. Inducted into Pro Football Hall of Fame in 1984. College coach: Long Beach State 1990-91 (head coach 1991). Pro coach: Oakland/Los Angeles Raiders 1979-1988, rejoined Raiders in 1995.

Tom Cable, offensive line; born November 26, 1964, Merced, Calif. Offensive lineman Idaho 1982-86. Pro offensive lineman Indianapolis Colts 1987. College coach: Idaho 1987-88, San Diego State 1989, Cal State-Fullerton 1990, Nevada-Las Vegas 1991, California 1992-97, Colorado 1998-99, Idaho 2000-03, UCLA 2004-05. Pro coach: Atlanta Falcons 2006, joined Raiders in 2007.

Charles Coe, wide receivers; born October 31, 1948, St. Louis. Defensive back Kansas State 1968-1971. Pro defensive back St. Louis Cardinals 1974. College coach: Iowa 1976, Cincinnati 1977-79, Ball State 1982, Louisville 1983-84, Missouri 1985-88, Kansas State 1989, Tennessee 1990-92, Pittsburgh 1993-97, Memphis 1997-02, Alabama State 2003-06 (head coach). Pro coach: Joined Raiders in 2007.

James Cregg, asst. offensive line; born August, 18, 1973, Syracuse, N.Y. Offensive lineman Colorado State 1992-95. No pro playing experience. College coach: Colorado State 1997-99, Colgate 2000-03, Idaho

2004-06. Pro coach: Joined Raiders in 2007.

John DeFilippo, quarterbacks; born April 12, 1978, Youngstown, Ohio. Quarterback James Madison 1996-99. No pro playing experience. College coach: Fordham 2000, Notre Dame 2001-02, Columbia 2003-04. Pro coach: New York Giants 2005-06, joined Raiders in 2007.

Jeff Fish, strength & conditioning; born June 6, 1966, Ithaca, N.Y. Wide receiver Western Carolina 1986-88. No pro playing experience. College coach: Clemson 1991-92, Kent State 1993-94, Tulsa 1995-96, Missouri 2001-02. Pro coach: Tampa Bay Buccaneers 1997, Kansas City Chiefs 1998-2000, joined Raiders in 2004.

Curtis Fuller, quality control, special teams; born July 25, 1978, Fort Worth, Texas. Defensive back Texas Christian 1997-2000. Pro defensive back Seattle Seahawks 2001-02, Green Bay Packers 2003, Jacksonville Jaguars 2004-05. Pro coach: Joined Raiders in 2007.

Randy Hanson, asst. defensive backs; born January 17, 1968, Burlington, Wash. Quarterback Delta (Calif.) J.C. 1987, Walla Walla (Wash.) 1988-89, Pacific University (Ore.) 1990-91. No pro playing experience. College coach: Eastern Washington 1993-95, Washington 1996-97, Eastern Washington 1998-99, Portland State 2000-02. Pro coach: Minnesota Vikings 2003-05, St. Louis Rams 2006, joined Raiders in 2007.

Adam Henry, quality control, offense; born April 27, 1972, Beaumont, Texas. Wide receiver McNeese State 1992-93. Pro receiver New Orleans Saints 1995. College coach: McNeese State 1996-2006. Pro coach: joined Raiders in 2007.

Mark Jackson, director of football development; born September 14, 1972, Boston, Mass. Defensive back Colby (Maine) 1991-1994. No pro playing experience. College coach: Trinity 1995-96, Southern California 2001-2005. Pro coach: New England Patriots 1998-2000, joined Raiders in 2007.

Don Johnson, asst. defensive line; born November 3, 1954, Newark, N.J. Linebacker Jersey City State 1973-76. College coach: Jersey City State 1984-85. Riverside (Calif.) C.C. 1987-1990, Cal State-Fullerton 1991-92, Nevada 1995-98, UCLA 1999-2004. Pro coach: Chicago Bears 2005-06, joined Raiders in 2007.

Greg Knapp, offensive coordinator; born March 5, 1963, Long Beach, Calif. Quarterback Sacramento State 1982-85. No pro playing experience. College coach: Sacramento State 1986-1994. Pro coach: San Francisco 49ers 1995-2003, Atlanta Falcons 2004-06, joined Raiders in 2007.

Sanjay Lal, quality control, offense; born July 23, 1969, London, England. Wide receiver UCLA 1989, Washington, 1990-92. Pro wide receiver St. Louis Rams 1998, Scottish Claymores (World League) 1999. College coach: Los Medanos (Calif.) College 2003, Saint Mary's

College 2004, California 2005-06, joined Raiders in 2007.

Don Martindale, linebackers; born May 19, 1963, Dayton, Ohio. Linebacker Defiance College 1984-86. No pro playing experience. College coach: Defiance College 1987, Notre Dame 1994-95, Cincinnati 1996-98, Western Illinois 1999, Western Kentucky 2000-02. Pro coach: Joined Raiders in 2007.

George Martinez, quality control, defense; born August 5, 1951, Fort Bragg, N.C. Quarterback Northwestern Oklahoma State 1969-1972. No pro playing experience. College coach: East Central (Okla.) 1981-87, Panhandle State 1988. New Mexico Highlands 1989-1991 (head coach). Pro coach: Arizona Cardinals 1993-94, joined Raiders in 2006.

Keith Millard, defensive line; born March 18, 1962, Pleasanton, Calif. Defensive lineman Washington State 1980-84. Pro defensive lineman Minnesota Vikings 1985-1991, Seattle Seahawks 1992, Green Bay Packers 1992, Philadelphia Eagles 1993. College coach: Fort Lewis 1996, Menlo College 1997-2000. Pro coach: San Francisco Demons (XFL) 2001, Denver Broncos 2002-04, joined Raiders in 2005.

Darren Perry, defensive backs; born December 29, 1968, Norfolk, Va. Safety Penn State 1989-1991. Pro safety Pittsburgh Steelers 1992-98, San Diego Chargers 1999, New Orleans Saints 2000. Pro coach: Cincinnati Bengals 2002, Pittsburgh Steelers 2003-06, joined Raiders in 2007.

Tom Rathman, running backs; born October 7, 1962, Grand Island, Neb. Running back Nebraska 1983-85. Pro running back San Francisco 49ers 1986-1993, Los Angeles Raiders 1994. College coach: Menlo College (Calif.) 1996. Pro coach: San Francisco 1997-2002, Detroit Lions 2003-05, joined Raiders in 2007.

Rob Ryan, defensive coordinator; born December 13, 1962, Ardmore, Okla. Linebacker Oklahoma State 1984-86. Southwestern Oklahoma State 1985-86. No pro playing experience. College coach: Western Kentucky 1987, Ohio State 1988, Tennessee State 1989-1993, Hutchinson (Kan.) C.C. 1996, Oklahoma State 1997-99. Pro coach: Arizona Cardinals 1994-95, New England Patriots 2000-03, joined Raiders in 2004.

Brian Schneider, special teams; born May 16, 1971, San Diego. Linebacker Colorado State 1989-1993. No pro playing experience. College coach: Colorado State 1994-2002, UCLA 2003-05, Iowa State 2006, Air Force 2007. Pro coach: Joined Raiders in 2007.

Kelly Skipper, tight ends; born July 25, 1967, Brawley, Calif. Running back Fresno State 1985-88. No pro playing experience. College coach: Fresno State 1989-1997, UCLA 1998-2002, Washington State 2003-06. Pro coach: Joined Raiders in 2007.

**American Football Conference
North Division
Team Colors:** Black and Gold
3400 South Water Street
Pittsburgh, Pennsylvania 15203
Telephone: (412) 432-7800

2007 SCHEDULE
PRESEASON
Aug. 5	vs. New Orleans at Canton, OH	8:00
Aug. 11	**Green Bay**	7:30
Aug. 18	at Washington	8:00
Aug. 26	**Philadelphia**	8:00
Aug. 30	at Carolina	8:00

REGULAR SEASON
Sep. 9	at Cleveland	1:00
Sep. 16	**Buffalo**	1:00
Sep. 23	**San Francisco**	1:00
Sep. 30	at Arizona	1:15
Oct. 7	**Seattle**	1:00
Oct. 14	Open Date	
Oct. 21	at Denver	6:15
Oct. 28	at Cincinnati	1:00
Nov. 5	**Baltimore** (Mon.)	8:30
Nov. 11	**Cleveland**	1:00
Nov. 18	at N.Y. Jets	1:00
Nov. 26	**Miami** (Mon.)	8:30
Dec. 2	**Cincinnati**	*8:15
Dec. 9	at New England	1:00
Dec. 16	**Jacksonville**	1:00
Dec. 20	at St. Louis (Thu.)	7:15
Dec. 30	at Baltimore	1:00

Sunday night games in Weeks 11-17 subject to change
Stadium: Heinz Field (opened in 2001)
 • **Capacity:** 65,050
 100 Art Rooney Avenue
 Pittsburgh, Pennsylvania 15212
Playing Surface: DD GrassMaster
Training Camp: St. Vincent College
 Latrobe, PA 15650

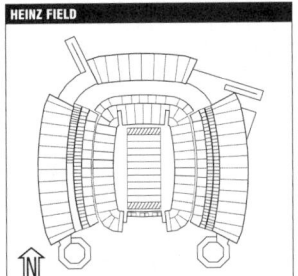

HEINZ FIELD

CLUB OFFICIALS
Chairman: Daniel M. Rooney
President: Arthur J. Rooney II
Vice President: John R. McGinley
Vice President: Arthur J. Rooney Jr.
Administration Advisor: Charles H. Noll
Director of Business: Mark Hart
Business Operations: Omar Khan
Director of Football Operations:
 Kevin Colbert
College Scouting Coordinator:
 Ron Hughes
Pro Scouting Coordinator: Doug Whaley
Head Athletic Trainer: John Norwig
Director of Marketing: Tony Quatrini
Communications Coordinator:
 Dave Lockett
Public Relations/Media Manager:
 Burt Lauten
Director of Stadium Management:
 Jim Sacco
Video Coordinator: Bob McCartney
Human Relations/Office Coordinator:
 Geraldine Glenn
Ticket Manager: Ben Lentz

COACHING HISTORY
**Pittsburgh Pirates 1933-39
(531-510-21)**
Records include postseason games
1933	Forrest (Jap) Douds	3-6-2
1934	Luby DiMelio	2-10-0
1935-36	Joe Bach	10-14-0
1937-39	Johnny (Blood) McNally*	6-19-0
1939-1940	Walt Kiesling	3-13-3
1941	Bert Bell**	0-2-0
	Aldo (Buff) Donelli***	0-5-0
1941-44	Walt Kiesling****	13-20-2
1945	Jim Leonard	2-8-0
1946-47	Jock Sutherland	13-10-1
1948-1951	Johnny Michelosen	20-26-2
1952-53	Joe Bach	11-13-0
1954-56	Walt Kiesling	14-22-0
1957-1964	Raymond (Buddy) Parker	51-47-6
1965	Mike Nixon	2-12-0
1966-68	Bill Austin	11-28-3
1969-1991	Chuck Noll	209-156-1
1992-2006	Bill Cowher	169-107-1

 *Released after three games in 1939
 **Resigned after two games in 1941
 ***Released after five games in 1941
 ****Co-coach with Earle (Greasy) Neale in
 Philadelphia-Pittsburgh merger in 1943 and
 with Phil Handler in Chicago Cardinals-
 Pittsburgh merger in 1944

PAID ATTENDANCE
Home 514,151   Away 539,091
Total 1,053,242
Single-game home record,
 64,046 (12/26/04)
Single-season home record,
 514,151 (2006)

2007 DRAFT CHOICES
Round	Name	Pos.	College
1	Lawrence Timmons	LB	Florida State
2	LaMarr Woodley	LB	Michigan
3	Matt Spaeth	TE	Minnesota
4	Daniel Sepulveda	P	Baylor
	Ryan McBean	DE	Oklahoma State
5	Cameron Stephenson	G	Rutgers
	William Gay	DB	Louisville
7	Dallas Baker	WR	Florida

2006 TEAM RECORD

PRESEASON (0-4)

Date	Result	Opponent
8/12	L 13-21	at Arizona
8/19	L 10-17	Minnesota
8/25	L 7-16	at Philadelphia
8/31	L 13-15	Carolina

REGULAR SEASON (8-8)

Date	Result	Opponent	Att.
9/7	W 28-17	Miami	64,927
9/18	L 0-9	at Jacksonville	67,164
9/24	L 20-28	Cincinnati	64,922
10/8	L 13-23	at San Diego	67,837
10/15	W 45-7	Kansas City	64,727
10/22	L 38-41	at Atlanta (OT)	71,151
10/29	L 13-20	at Oakland	62,385
11/5	L 20-31	Denver	64,661
11/12	W 38-31	New Orleans	61,911
11/19	W 24-20	at Cleveland	73,296
11/26	L 0-27	at Baltimore	70,946
12/3	W 20-3	Tampa Bay	59,843
12/7	W 27-7	Cleveland	55,246
12/17	W 37-3	at Carolina	73,798
12/24	L 7-31	Baltimore	63,224
12/31	W 23-17	at Cincinnati (OT)	66,049

(OT) Overtime

SCORE BY PERIODS

Steelers	66	107	58	116	6	—	353
Opponents	49	98	65	100	3	—	315

2006 TEAM STATISTICS

	Steelers	Opp.
Total First Downs	327	269
Rushing	100	72
Passing	201	176
Penalty	26	21
3rd Down: Made/Att	93/217	86/219
3rd Down Pct.	42.9	39.3
4th Down: Made/Att	10/21	6/12
4th Down Pct.	47.6	50.0
Possession Avg.	31:13	28:47
Total Net Yards	5,725	4,805
Avg. Per Game	357.8	300.3
Total Plays	1,041	976
Avg. Per Play	5.5	4.9
Net Yards Rushing	1,992	1,412
Avg. Per Game	124.5	88.3
Total Rushes	469	408
Net Yards Passing	3,733	3,393
Avg. Per Game	233.3	212.1
Sacked/Yards Lost	49/293	39/226
Gross Yards	4,026	3,619
Att./Completions	523/312	529/319
Completion Pct.	59.7	60.3
Had Intercepted	23	20
Punts/Average	65/41.3	86/43.8
Net Punting Avg.	65/36.7	86/38.0
Penalties/Yards	69/611	104/862
Fumbles/Ball Lost	27/14	16/9
Touchdowns	42	36
Rushing	16	9
Passing	23	21
Returns	3	6

2006 INDIVIDUAL STATISTICS

PASSING	Att.	Comp.	Yds.	Pct.	TD	Int.	Tkld.	Rate
Roethlisberger	469	280	3,513	59.7	18	23	46/280	75.4
Batch	53	31	492	58.5	5	0	3/13	121.0
Wilson	1	1	21	100.0	0	0	0/0	118.8
Steelers	523	312	4,026	59.7	23	23	49/293	80.2
Opponents	529	319	3,619	60.3	21	20	39/226	78.3

SCORING	TD R	TD P	TD Rt	PAT	FG	Saf	PTS
Reed	0	0	0	41/41	20/27	0	101
Parker	13	3	0	0/0	0/0	0	96
Ward	0	6	0	0/0	0/0	0	36
Miller	0	5	0	0/0	0/0	0	30
Washington	0	4	0	0/0	0/0	0	24
Holmes	0	2	1	0/0	0/0	0	18
Davenport	1	1	0	0/0	0/0	0	12
Roethlisberger	2	0	0	0/0	0/0	0	12
Porter	0	0	1	0/0	0/0	0	6
Tuman	0	1	0	0/0	0/0	0	6
Wallace	0	0	1	0/0	0/0	0	6
Wilson	0	1	0	0/0	0/0	0	6
Steelers	16	23	3	41/41	20/27	0	353
Opponents	9	21	6	36/36	21/27	0	315

2-Pt. Conversions:
Steelers 0-0, Opponents 0-0.

RUSHING	No.	Yds	Avg	LG	TD
Parker	337	1,494	4.4	76	13
Davenport	60	221	3.7	48	1
Roethlisberger	32	98	3.1	20	2
Haynes	15	78	5.2	13	0
Ward	2	30	15.0	21	0
Kuhn	2	18	9.0	16	0
Batch	13	15	1.2	12	0
Wilson	2	14	7.0	14	0
Holmes	1	13	13.0	13	0
Washington	3	8	2.7	8	0
Kreider	1	5	5.0	5	0
McFadden	1	-2	-2.0	-2	0
Steelers	469	1,992	4.2	76	16
Opponents	408	1,412	3.5	72t	9

RECEIVING	No.	Yds	Avg	LG	TD
Ward	74	975	13.2	70t	6
Holmes	49	824	16.8	67t	2
Wilson	37	504	13.6	38t	1
Washington	35	624	17.8	49t	4
Miller	34	393	11.6	87t	5
Parker	31	222	7.2	25t	3
Haynes	18	95	5.3	16	0
Davenport	15	193	12.9	32	1
Kreider	8	62	7.8	15	0
Tuman	7	73	10.4	21	1
Morey	2	29	14.5	19	0
Young	1	17	17.0	17	0
Kuhn	1	15	15.0	15	0
Steelers	312	4,026	12.9	87t	23
Opponents	319	3,619	11.3	66t	21

PUNTING	No.	Yds	Avg	In 20	Lg
Gardocki	65	2,687	41.3	11	56
Steelers	65	2,687	41.3	11	56
Opponents	86	3,769	43.8	31	67

INTERCEPTIONS	No.	Yds	Avg	LG	TD
Polamalu	3	51	17.0	49	0
McFadden	3	39	13.0	39	0
Porter	2	49	24.5	42t	1
An. Smith	2	40	20.0	20	0
Taylor	2	34	17.0	34	0
Townsend	2	6	3.0	6	0
Wallace	1	30	30.0	30t	1
Kriewaldt	1	12	12.0	12	0
Foote	1	11	11.0	11	0
Farrior	1	1	1.0	1	0
Haggans	1	0	0.0	0	0
Clark	1	-1	-1.0	-1	0
Steelers	20	272	13.6	49	2
Opponents	23	441	19.2	100t	3

PUNT RETURNS	Ret	FC	Yds	Avg	LG	TD
Holmes	26	21	264	10.2	65t	1
Colclough	4	0	6	1.5	3	0
Wilson	2	1	4	2.0	3	0
Reid	1	0	11	11.0	11	0
Taylor	1	0	0	0.0	0	0
Steelers	34	22	285	8.4	65t	1
Opponents	38	10	219	5.8	47	0

KICKOFF RETURNS	No.	Yds	Avg	LG	TD
Davenport	21	448	21.3	40	0
Holmes	18	436	24.2	42	0
Morey	8	202	25.3	76	0
Taylor	4	72	18.0	23	0
Colclough	1	26	26.0	26	0
Reid	1	19	19.0	19	0
Wilson	1	11	11.0	11	0
Kirschke	1	0	0.0	0	0
Steelers	55	1,214	22.1	76	0
Opponents	70	1,570	22.4	92t	1

FIELD GOALS	1-19	20-29	30-39	40-49	50+
Reed	1/1	6/7	8/11	4/7	1/1
Steelers	1/1	6/7	8/11	4/7	1/1
Opponents	1/1	8/8	9/11	3/5	0/2

SACKS	No.
Porter	7.0
Haggans	6.0
Keisel	5.5
Aa. Smith	4.5
Farrior	4.0
Foote	4.0
Carter	2.0
Kirschke	2.0
Townsend	2.0
Brown	1.0
Polamalu	1.0
Steelers	39.0
Opponents	49.0

RECORD HOLDERS

INDIVIDUAL RECORDS—CAREER

Category	Name	Performance
Rushing (Yds.)	Franco Harris, 1972-1983	11,950
Passing (Yds.)	Terry Bradshaw, 1970-1983	27,989
Passing (TDs)	Terry Bradshaw, 1970-1983	212
Receiving (No.)	Hines Ward, 1998-2006	648
Receiving (Yds.)	John Stallworth, 1974-1987	8,723
Interceptions	Mel Blount, 1970-1983	57
Punting (Avg.)	Bobby Joe Green, 1960-61	45.7
Punt Return (Avg.)	Bobby Gage, 1949-1950	14.9
Kickoff Return (Avg.)	Lynn Chandnois, 1950-56	29.6
Field Goals	Gary Anderson, 1982-1994	309
Touchdowns (Tot.)	Franco Harris, 1972-1983	100
Points	Gary Anderson, 1982-1994	1,343

INDIVIDUAL RECORDS—SINGLE SEASON

Category	Name	Performance
Rushing (Yds.)	Barry Foster, 1992	1,690
Passing (Yds.)	Terry Bradshaw, 1979	3,724
Passing (TDs)	Terry Bradshaw, 1978	28
Receiving (No.)	Hines Ward, 2002	112
Receiving (Yds.)	Yancey Thigpen, 1997	1,398
Interceptions	Mel Blount, 1975	11
Punting (Avg.)	Bobby Joe Green, 1961	47.0
Punt Return (Avg.)	Bobby Gage, 1949	16.0
Kickoff Return (Avg.)	Lynn Chandnois, 1952	35.2
Field Goals	Norm Johnson, 1995	34
Touchdowns (Tot.)	Willie Parker, 2006	16
Points	Norm Johnson, 1995	141

INDIVIDUAL RECORDS—SINGLE GAME

Category	Name	Performance
Rushing (Yds.)	Willie Parker, 12-7-06	223
Passing (Yds.)	Tommy Maddox, 11-10-02	473
Passing (TDs)	Terry Bradshaw, 11-15-81	5
	Mark Malone, 9-8-85	5
Receiving (No.)	Courtney Hawkins, 11-1-98	14
Receiving (Yds.)	Plaxico Burress, 11-10-02	253
Interceptions	Jack Butler, 12-13-53	*4
Field Goals	Gary Anderson, 10-23-88	6
	Jeff Reed, 12-1-02	6
Touchdowns (Tot.)	Ray Mathews, 10-17-54	4
	Roy Jefferson, 11-3-68	4
Points	Ray Mathews, 10-17-54	24
	Roy Jefferson, 11-3-68	24

*NFL Record

2007 VETERAN ROSTER

No.	Name	Pos.	Ht.	Wt.	Birthdate	NFL Exp.	College	Hometown	How Acq.	'06 Games/ Starts
	Barlow, Kevan	RB	6-1	234	1/7/79	7	Pittsburgh	Pittsburgh, Pa.	FA-'07	12/3*
16	Batch, Charlie	QB	6-2	216	12/4/70	10	Eastern Michigan	Homestead, Pa.	FA-'02	8/1
23	Carter, Tyrone	S	5-8	195	3/30/72	8	Minnesota	Pompano Beach, Fla.	FA-'04	16/3
25	Clark, Ryan	S	5-11	205	10/11/75	6	Louisiana State	Merraro, La.	UFA(Wash)-'06	13/12
21	Colclough, Ricardo	CB	5-11	195	4/17/78	4	Tusculum	Sumter, S.C.	D2-'04	3/0
74	Colon, Willie	T	6-3	315	4/8/79	2	Hofstra	Bronx, N.Y.	D4a-'06	2/0
44	Davenport, Najeh	RB	6-1	247	2/7/75	6	Miami	Raleigh, N.C.	FA-'06	13/0
93	Eason, Nick	DE	6-3	305	5/28/76	5	Clemson	Lyons, Ga.	UFA(Cle)-'07	13/3*
79	Essex, Trai	T	6-4	324	12/4/78	3	Northwestern	Fort Wayne, Ind.	D3-'05	15/0
66	Faneca, Alan	G	6-5	307	12/6/72	10	Louisiana State	New Orleans, La.	D1-'98	16/16
51	Farrior, James	LB	6-2	243	1/5/71	11	Virginia	Ettrick, Va.	UFA(NYJ)-'02	16/16
50	Foote, Larry	LB	6-1	239	6/11/76	6	Michigan	Detroit, Mich.	D4-'02	16/16
17	Gardocki, Chris	P	6-1	192	2/6/66	17	Clemson	Stone Mountain, Ga.	UFA-'04	16/0
53	Haggans, Clark	LB	6-4	243	1/9/73	8	Colorado State	Torrance, Calif.	D5a-'00	15/15
98	Hampton, Casey	DT	6-1	325	9/2/73	7	Texas	Galveston, Texas	D1-'01	15/15
97	Harrison, Arnold	LB	6-3	241	9/19/78	2	Georgia	Augusta, Ga.	FA-'05	7/2
92	Harrison, James	LB	6-0	242	5/3/74	4	Kent State	Akron, Ohio	FA-'04	11/1
76	Hoke, Chris	DT	6-2	305	4/5/72	7	Brigham Young	Long Beach, Calif.	FA-'02	16/1
10	Holmes, Santonio	WR	5-11	189	3/2/80	2	Ohio State	Belle Glade, Fla.	D1-'06	16/4
29	Iwuoma, Chidi	CB	5-9	184	2/18/74	7	California	Los Angeles, Calif.	FA-'07	5/0*
28	Johnson, Jovon	CB	5-9	177	12/1/79	2	Iowa	Erie, Pa.	FA-'06	2/0
99	Keisel, Brett	DE	6-5	285	9/18/74	6	Brigham Young	Greybull, Fla.	D7b-'02	16/16
68	Kemoeatu, Chris	G	6-3	344	1/3/79	3	Utah	Kahuka, Hawaii	D6-'05	3/2
90	Kirschke, Travis	DE	6-3	298	9/5/70	11	UCLA	Highland Ranch, Colo.	UFA(SF)-'04	16/0
35	Kreider, Dan	FB	5-11	255	3/10/73	8	New Hampshire	Lancaster, Pa.	FA-'00	16/12
57	Kriewaldt, Clint	LB	6-1	248	3/15/72	9	Wisconsin-Stevens Point	Shiocton, Wis.	UFA(Det)-'03	14/0
42	Kuhn, John	RB	6-0	255	9/8/78	2	Shippensburg	York, Pa.	FA-'05	9/0
37	Madison, Anthony	CB	5-9	180	10/7/77	2	Alabama	Thomasville, Ala.	FA-'06	16/0
61	Mahan, Sean	G/T	6-3	301	5/27/76	5	Notre Dame	Jenks, Okla.	UFA(TB)-'07	16/12*
11	Marshall, Rasheed	WR	6-1	188	7/10/77	2	West Virginia	Pittsburgh, Pa.	FA-'07	0*
20	McFadden, Bryant	CB	6-0	190	11/20/77	3	Florida State	Hollywood, Fla.	D2-'05	16/9
83	Miller, Heath	TE	6-5	256	10/21/78	3	Virginia	Swords Creek, Va.	D1-'05	16/16
56	Okobi, Chukky	C	6-1	305	11/17/74	7	Purdue	Pittsburgh, Pa.	D5-'01	15/2
39	Parker, Willie	RB	5-10	209	11/10/76	4	North Carolina	Clinton, N.C.	FA-'04	16/16
62	Philip, Marvin	C	6-1	307	2/2/78	2	California	Redwood City, Calif.	D6-'06	0*
43	Polamalu, Troy	S	5-10	207	4/18/77	5	Southern California	Tenmile, Ore.	D1-'03	13/13
3	Reed, Jeff	K	5-11	225	4/8/75	6	North Carolina	Charlotte, N.C.	FA-'02	16/0
15	Reid, Willie	WR	5-10	186	9/18/78	2	Florida State	Kathleen, Ga.	D3b-'06	1/0
7	Roethlisberger, Ben	QB	6-5	241	3/1/78	4	Miami (Ohio)	Findlay, Ohio	D1-'04	15/15
2	St. Pierre, Brian	QB	6-3	230	11/27/75	5	Boston College	Salem, Mass.	FA-'06	0*
73	Simmons, Kendall	G	6-3	315	3/10/75	6	Auburn	Ripley, Miss.	D1-'02	14/14
91	Smith, Aaron	DE	6-5	298	4/8/72	9	Northern Colorado	Colorado Springs, Colo.	D4-'99	16/16
27	Smith, Anthony	S	5-11	192	9/19/79	2	Syracuse	Hubbard, Ohio	D3a-'06	16/4
77	Smith, Marvel	T	6-5	321	8/5/74	8	Arizona State	Oakland, Calif.	D2-'00	16/16
47	Stanley, Ron	LB	6-0	244	3/5/79	2	Michigan State	Saginaw, Mich.	FA-'06	1/0
78	Starks, Max	T	6-8	337	1/9/78	4	Florida	Orlando, Fla.	D3-'04	14/14
24	Taylor, Ike	CB	6-1	191	5/4/76	5	Louisiana-Lafayette	Gretna, La.	D4-'03	16/11
26	Townsend, Deshea	CB	5-10	190	9/7/71	10	Alabama	Batesville, Miss.	D4a-'98	16/12
84	Tuman, Jerame	TE	6-4	253	3/23/72	9	Michigan	Liberal, Kan.	D5-'99	15/4
54	Wallace, Rian	LB	6-3	243	5/23/78	3	Temple	Pottstown, Pa.	D5-'05	12/0
86	Ward, Hines	WR	6-0	205	3/7/72	10	Georgia	Forest Park, Ga.	D3b-'98	14/14
60	Warren, Greg	LS	6-3	252	10/17/77	3	North Carolina	Goldsboro, N.C.	FA-'05	16/0
85	Washington, Nate	WR	6-1	185	8/27/79	3	Tiffin	Toledo, Ohio	FA-'05	16/2
80	Wilson, Cedrick	WR	5-10	183	12/16/74	7	Tennessee	Memphis, Tenn.	UFA(SF)-'05	15/12
18	Young, Walter	WR	6-4	220	12/6/75	3	Illinois	Park Forest, Ill.	FA-'06	2/0

* Barlow played 12 games with N.Y. Jets in '06; Eason played 13 games with Cleveland; Iwuoma played 3 games with New England and 2 games with Pittsburgh; Mahan played 16 games with Tampa Bay; Marshall last active with San Francisco in '05; Philip did not play in 2 games; St. Pierre did not play in 1 game.

Players lost through free agency (2): DE Rodney Bailey (Ariz; 12 games in '06), WR Sean Morey (Ariz; 16).

Also played with Steelers in '06—TE Tim Euhus (1 game), C Jeff Hartings (14)), LB Richard Seigler (2).

2007 FIRST-YEAR ROSTER

Name	Pos.	Ht.	Wt.	Birthdate	College	Hometown	How Acq.
Barr, Mike (1)	P	6-2	230	12/7/74	Rutgers	Lynchburg, Va.	FA
Baker, Dallas	WR	6-3	206	11/9/78	Florida	New Smyrna Beach, Fla.	D7
Boyd, Cody	TE	6-8	264	10/21/79	Washington State	Bellingham, Wash.	FA
Capizzi, Jason	T	6-9	315	6/18/79	Indiana (Pa.)	Gibsonia, Pa.	FA
Church, Marcello (1)	LB	6-1	230	3/23/78	Florida State	St. Petersburg, Fla.	FA
Davis, Carey (1)	RB	5-10	225	3/26/77	Illinois	St. Louis, Mo.	FA-'06
Dekker, Jon (1)	TE	6-5	250	5/14/79	Princeton	Greenfield, Wis.	FA-'06
Deslauriers, Eric	WR	6-4	207	3/20/77	Eastern Michigan	Gatineau, Quebec, Canada	FA
Fowler, Eric	WR	6-3	198	10/16/80	Grand Valley State	New Haven, Mich.	FA
Gay, William	CB	5-10	190	12/31/80	Louisville	Tallahasee, Fla.	D5b
Hughes, Connor (1)	K	5-10	172	10/3/79	Virginia	Williamsburg, Pa.	FA
Jackson, Chris	WR	6-2	205	7/4/80	Millsaps	Phoenix City, Ala.	FA
Jones, Derrick	DT/DE	6-4	282	1/22/82	Grand Valley State	Barstow, Calif.	FA
Koonce, Richard (1)	LB	6-0	235	6/27/79	East Carolina	Miami, Fla.	FA
Lorello, Mike (1)	S	5-11	208	10/14/80	West Virginia	Powell, Ohio	FA-'06
Mason, Grant (1)	CB	6-0	192	9/17/79	Michigan	Pontiac, Mich.	FA
McBean, Ryan	DE	6-5	290	4/22/80	Oklahoma State	Trinity, Texas	D4b
Mosley, Paul	RB	6-3	235	2/29/80	Baylor	Austin, Texas	FA
Nua, Shaun (1)	DE	6-5	280	5/1/77	Brigham Young	Manu'a, American Samoa	D7a-'05
Paxson, Scott (1)	DT	6-4	292	2/2/79	Penn State	Philadelphia, Pa.	FA-'06
Randall, Bryan (1)	QB	6-0	228	8/15/79	Virginia Tech	Charleston, W. Va.	FA
Rehage, Derek (1)	LB	6-0	242	8/25/78	Miami (Ohio)	Brookville, Ind.	FA
Retkofsky, Jared	LS	6-5	260	3/15/79	Texas Christian	Justin, Texas	FA
Robbins, Aaron	FB	6-4	256	7/15/79	Wyoming	Aurora, Colo.	FA
Russell, Gary	RB	5-11	215	9/7/82	Minnesota	Columbus, Ohio	FA
Sepulveda, Daniel	P	6-3	230	1/11/80	Baylor	Dallas, Texas	D4a
Smith, Harrison (1)	CB	6-2	200	2/27/79	California	Oakland, Calif.	FA
Spaeth, Matt	TE	6-7	270	11/23/80	Minnesota	St. Michael, Minn.	D3
Stapleton, Darnell	G/C	6-3	285	9/20/81	Rutgers	Union, N.J.	FA
Stephenson, Cameron	G	6-4	305	6/17/79	Rutgers	Hawthorne, Calif.	D5a
Timmons, Lawrence	LB	6-1	234	5/13/82	Florida State	Florence, S.C.	D1
Torrey, Brandon (1)	T	6-4	295	5/17/79	Howard	Durham, N.C.	FA-'06
Walker, Gerran (1)	WR	5-10	185	10/1/79	Lehigh	Atlanta, Ga.	FA
Woodley, LaMarr	LB	6-2	265	11/2/80	Michigan	Saginaw, Mich.	D2

The term NFL Rookie is defined as a player who is in his first season of professional football and has not been on the roster of another professional football team for any regular-season or postseason games. A Rookie is designated by an "R" on NFL rosters. Players who have been active in another professional football league or players who have NFL experience, including either preseason training camp or being on an Active List or Inactive List, or on Reserve/Injured or Reserve/Physically Unable to Perform for fewer than six regular-season games, are termed NFL First-Year Players. An NFL First-Year Player is designated by a "1" on NFL rosters. Thereafter, a player is credited with an additional year of experience for each season in which he accumulates six games on the Active List or Inactive List, or on Reserve/Injured or Reserve/Physically Unable to Perform.

Log on to www.steelers.com for an up-to-date roster.

PITTSBURGH STEELERS

COACHING STAFF
Head Coach,
Mike Tomlin

Pro Career: Became the sixteenth head coach in Steelers history when he replaced Bill Cowher on January 22, 2007. The first African-American head coach in Steelers history, Tomlin was the Minnesota Vikings defensive coordinator in 2006 after spending the previous five seasons (2001-05) as defensive backs coach for the Tampa Bay Buccaneers. Tomlin coached one of the top defensive backfields in the NFL for the Buccaneers, culminating with its performance in Super Bowl XXXVII. The secondary recorded four interceptions, returning two for touchdowns to help Tampa Bay capture the franchise's first Super Bowl title. Tomlin served two seasons as the defensive backs coach at the University of Cincinnati (1999-2000) before going to Tampa Bay. Prior to joining the Cincinnati staff, Tomlin had a short stint on the coaching staff at Tennessee-Martin and then spent two seasons at Arkansas State. He spent the 1996 season as a graduate assistant at Memphis. Tomlin began his coaching career in 1995 as wide receivers coach at Virginia Military Institute. Career record: 0-0.

Background: Was a three-year starter at wide receiver at William & Mary (1990-94) and finished his career with 101 receptions for 2,046 yards and a school-record 20 touchdown receptions. A first-team All-Yankee Conference selection in 1994, he established a school record with a 20.2 yards per catch average. Tomlin was a teammate of current Viking Pro Bowl safety Darren Sharper at William and Mary. Graduated in 1994 with a degree in sociology.

Personal: Born in Hampton, Va., on March 15, 1972. He and his wife, Kiya, have two sons, Dino and Mason, and a daughter Harlyn Quinn.

ASSISTANT COACHES

Ken Anderson, quarterbacks; born February 15, 1949, Batavia, Ill. Quarterback Augustana (Ill.) 1967-1970. Pro quarterback Cincinnati Bengals 1971-1986. Pro coach: Cincinnati Bengals 1992-2002, Jacksonville Jaguars 2003-2006, joined Steelers in 2007.

Bruce Arians, offensive coordinator; born October 3, 1952, Paterson, N.J. Quarterback Virginia Tech 1970-74. No pro playing experience. College coach: Virginia Tech 1975-77, Mississippi State 1978-1980, Alabama 1981-82, Temple 1983-88 (head coach), Mississippi State 1993-95, Alabama 1997. Pro coach: Kansas City Chiefs 1989-1992, New Orleans Saints 1996, Indianapolis Colts 1998-2000, Cleveland Browns 2001-03, joined Steelers in 2004.

Keith Butler, linebackers; born May 16, 1956, Anniston, Ala. Linebacker Memphis 1974-77. Pro linebacker Seattle Seahawks 1978-1987. College coach: Memphis 1990-97, Arkansas State 1998. Pro coach: Cleveland Browns 1999-2002, joined Steelers in 2003.

James Daniel, tight ends; born January 17, 1953, Wetumpka, Ala. Guard Alabama State 1970-73. No pro playing experience. College coach: Auburn 1981-1992. Pro coach: New York Giants 1993-96, Atlanta Falcons 1997-2003, joined Steelers in 2004.

Randy Fichtner, wide receivers; born November 7, 1963, Cleveland. Defensive back Purdue 1982-85. No pro playing experience. College coach: Michigan 1986-87, Southern California 1988, Nevada-Las Vegas 1989, Memphis 1990-93, Purdue 1994-96, Arkansas State 1997-2000, Memphis 2001-06. Pro coach: Joined Steelers in 2007.

Ray Horton, defensive backs; born April 12, 1960, Tacoma, Wash. Defensive back Washington 1979-1982. Pro defensive back Cincinnati Bengals 1983-88, Dallas Cowboys 1989-1992. Pro coach: Washington Redskins 1994-96, Cincinnati Bengals 1997-2001, Detroit Lions 2002-03, joined Steelers in 2004.

Amos Jones, asst. special teams; born December 31, 1959, Tallahassee, Fla.. Safety/running back Alabama 1978-1980. No pro playing experience. College coach: Alabama 1981-82, Temple 1983-88, Alabama 1990-91, Pittsburgh 1992, Tulane 1995-96, Cincinnati 1999-2002, James Madison 2003, Mississippi State 2004-06. Pro coach: British Columbia (CFL) 1997, joined Steelers in 2007.

Dick LeBeau, defensive coordinator; born September 9, 1937, London, Ohio. Defensive back Ohio State 1955-58. Pro cornerback Detroit Lions 1959-1972. Pro coach: Philadelphia Eagles 1973-75, Green Bay Packers 1976-79, Cincinnati Bengals 1980-1991, 1997-2002 (head coach 2000-02), Pittsburgh Steelers 1992-96, Buffalo Bills 2003, re-joined Steelers in 2004.

Bob Ligashesky, special teams; born June 2, 1962, Pittsburgh. Linebacker Indiana (Pa.) 1983-84. No pro playing experience. College coach: Wake Forest 1985, Arizona State 1986-89, Kent State 1990, Bowling Green 1991-99, Pittsburgh 2000-03. Pro coach: Jacksonville Jaguars 2004, St. Louis Rams 2005-06, joined Steelers in 2007.

John Mitchell, defensive line; born October 14, 1951, Mobile, Ala. Defensive end Eastern Arizona J.C. 1969-1970, Alabama 1971-72. No pro playing experience. College coach: Alabama 1973-76, Arkansas 1977-1982, Temple 1986, Louisiana State 1987-1990. Pro coach: Birmingham Stallions (USFL) 1983-85, Cleveland Browns 1991-93, joined Steelers in 1994.

Kirby Wilson, running backs; born August 24, 1961, Los Angeles. Running back/wide receiver Pasadena (Calif.) C.C. 1979-1980, Illinois 1981-82. Pro cornerback Winnipeg Blue Bombers (CFL) 1983, Toronto Argonauts (CFL) 1984. College coach: Pasadena (Calif.) C.C. 1989-1990, Southern Illinois 1991-92, Wyoming 1993-94, Iowa State 1995-96, Southern California 2001. Pro coach: New England Patriots 1997-99, Washington Redskins 2000, Tampa Bay Buccaneers 2002-03, Arizona Cardinals 2004-06, joined Steelers in 2007.

Larry Zierlein, offensive line; born July 12, 1945, Norton, Kan. Linebacker/tight end Pratt (Kan.) J.C. 1967-68, linebacker Fort Hays State (Kan.) 1969-1970. No pro playing experience. College coach: Fort Hays State (Kan.) 1970-71, Houston 1978-1986, Tulane 1988-1990, 1995-96, Louisiana State 1993-94, Cincinnati 1997-2000. Pro coach: Washington (AFL) 1987, New York/New JerseyKnights (WLAF) 1991-92, Cleveland Browns 2001-04, Buffalo Bills 2006, joined Steelers in 2007.

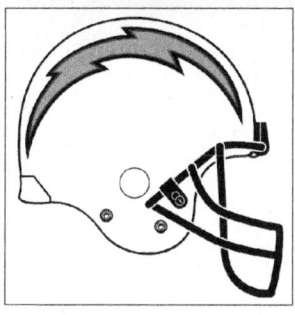

American Football Conference
West Division
Team Colors: Navy Blue, Powder Blue, White, and Gold
P.O. Box 609609
San Diego, California 92160-9609
Telephone: (858) 874-4500

2007 SCHEDULE
PRESEASON
Aug. 12	**Seattle**	5:00
Aug. 18	at St. Louis	7:00
Aug. 25	at Arizona	7:00
Aug. 30	**San Francisco**	7:00

REGULAR SEASON
Sep. 9	**Chicago**	1:15
Sep. 16	at New England	8:15
Sep. 23	at Green Bay	12:00
Sep. 30	**Kansas City**	1:15
Oct. 7	at Denver	2:15
Oct. 14	**Oakland**	1:15
Oct. 21	Open Date	
Oct. 28	**Houston**	1:05
Nov. 4	at Minnesota	12:00
Nov. 11	**Indianapolis**	5:15
Nov. 18	at Jacksonville	1:00
Nov. 25	**Baltimore**	1:15
Dec. 2	at Kansas City	12:00
Dec. 9	at Tennessee	12:00
Dec. 16	**Detroit**	1:15
Dec. 24	**Denver** (Mon.)	5:00
Dec. 30	at Oakland	1:15

Stadium: Qualcomm Stadium
(opened in 1967)
•**Capacity:** 70,000
9449 Friars Road
San Diego, California 92108
Playing Surface: Grass
Training Camp: Chargers Park
4020 Murphy Canyon Rd.
San Diego, CA 92123

CLUB OFFICIALS
Owner: Alex G. Spanos
President/CEO: Dean A. Spanos
Executive Vice President:
Michael A. Spanos
Executive Vice President-General
Manager: A.J. Smith
Executive Vice President-Chief Operating
Officer: Jim Steeg
Executive Vice President:
Jeremiah T. Murphy
Executive Vice President of Football
Operations: Ed McGuire
Executive Vice President-Chief Financial
Officer: Jeanne M. Bonk
Vice President-Chief Marketing Officer:
Ken Derrett
Assistant General Manager-Director of
Player Personnel: Buddy Nix
Director of College Scouting:
Jimmy Raye
Assistant Director of College Scouting:
John Spanos
Director of Pro Scouting:
Dennis Abraham
Head Athletic Trainer: James Collins
Director of Video Operations:
Brian Duddy
Equipment Manager: Bob Wick
Director of Player Development:
Arthur Hightower
Senior Director of Marketing
Partnerships: Dennis O'Leary
Senior Director of Ticket Sales and
Service: Todd Poulsen
Director of Marketing Programs and
Business Development: A.G. Spanos
Director of Business Operations:
John Hinek
Director of Public Relations: Bill Johnston
Director of Public Affairs &
Corporate/Community Relations:
Kimberley Layton
Director of Security: Mike Cash
Director of Player Outreach: Dick Lewis
Director of Stadium/Game Operations &
Events: Sean O'Connor
Controller: Marsha Wells
Director of Ticket Operations:
Michael L. Dougherty

COACHING HISTORY
Los Angeles 1960
(350-367-11)
Records include postseason games
1960-69	Sid Gillman*	83-51-6
1969-1970	Charlie Waller	9-7-3
1971	Sid Gillman**	4-6-0
1971-73	Harland Svare***	7-17-2
1973	Ron Waller	1-5-0
1974-78	Tommy Prothro****	21-39-0
1978-1986	Don Coryell#	72-60-0
1986-88	Al Saunders	17-22-0
1989-1991	Dan Henning	16-32-0
1992-96	Bobby Ross	50-36-0
1997-98	Kevin Gilbride	6-16-0
1998	June Jones	3-7-0
1999-2001	Mike Riley	14-34-0
2002-06	Marty Schottenheimer	47-35-0

*Retired after nine games in 1969
**Resigned after 10 games in 1971
***Resigned after eight games in 1973
****Resigned after four games in 1978
#Resigned after eight games in 1986
##Released after six games in 1998

PAID ATTENDANCE
Home 549,096   Away 541,391
Total 1,090,487
Single-game home record,
69,288 (11/7/99)
Single-season home record,
547,937 (2005)

2007 DRAFT CHOICES
Round	Name	Pos.	College
1	Craig Davis	WR	Louisiana St.
2	Eric Weddle	DB	Utah
3	Anthony Waters	LB	Clemson
4	Scott Chandler	TE	Iowa
5	Legedu Naanee	WR	Boise State
7	Brandon Siler	LB	Florida

QUALCOMM STADIUM

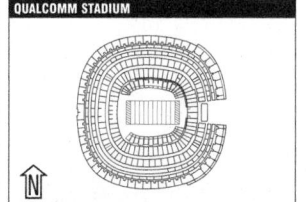

2006 TEAM RECORD

PRESEASON (2-2)

Date	Result	Opponent
8/12	W 17-3	Green Bay
8/18	L 3-24	at Chicago
8/26	W 31-20	Seattle
9/1	L 14-23	at San Francisco

REGULAR SEASON (14-2)

Date	Result	Opponent	Att.
9/11	W 27-0	at Oakland	62,578
9/17	W 40-7	Tennessee	64,344
10/1	L 13-16	at Baltimore	70,743
10/8	W 23-13	Pittsburgh	67,837
10/15	W 48-19	at San Francisco	68,137
10/22	L 27-30	at Kansas City	77,752
10/29	W 38-24	St. Louis	66,598
11/5	W 32-25	Cleveland	65,558
11/12	W 49-41	at Cincinnati	65,917
11/19	W 35-27	at Denver	76,723
11/26	W 21-14	Oakland	66,105
12/3	W 24-21	at Buffalo	63,361
12/10	W 48-20	Denver	67,514
12/17	W 20-9	Kansas City	66,583
12/24	W 20-17	at Seattle	68,174
12/31	W 27-20	Arizona	66,492

POSTSEASON (0-1)

1/14	L 21-24	New England	68,810

SCORE BY PERIODS

Chargers	85	137	94	176	0 —	492
Opponents	66	74	81	82	0 —	303

2006 TEAM STATISTICS

	Chargers	Opp.
Total First Downs	321	285
Rushing	137	87
Passing	169	178
Penalty	15	20
3rd Down: Made/Att	92/213	78/213
3rd Down Pct.	43.2	36.6
4th Down: Made/Att	6/11	6/17
4th Down Pct.	54.5	35.3
Possession Avg.	31:39	28:21
Total Net Yards	5,840	4,825
Avg. Per Game	365.0	301.6
Total Plays	1,016	985
Avg. Per Play	5.7	4.9
Net Yards Rushing	2,578	1,613
Avg. Per Game	161.1	100.8
Total Rushes	522	386
Net Yards Passing	3,262	3,212
Avg. Per Game	203.9	200.8
Sacked/Yards Lost	28/150	61/351
Gross Yards	3,412	3,563
Att./Completions	466/287	538/307
Completion Pct.	61.6	57.1
Had Intercepted	9	16
Punts/Average	69/41.9	88/44.6
Net Punting Avg.	69/38.2	88/38.6
Penalties/Yards	90/791	87/751
Fumbles/Ball Lost	19/6	28/12
Touchdowns	59	33
Rushing	32	13
Passing	24	19
Returns	3	1

2006 INDIVIDUAL STATISTICS

PASSING	Att.	Comp.	Yds.	Pct.	TD	Int.	Tkld.	Rate
Rivers	460	284	3,388	61.7	22	9	27/144	92.0
Tomlinson	3	2	20	66.7	2	0	0/0	125.0
Volek	2	1	4	50.0	0	0	1/6	56.3
Scifres	1	0	—	0.0	0	0	0/0	39.6
Chargers	466	287	3,412	61.6	24	9	28/150	93.0
Opponents	538	307	3,563	57.1	19	16	61/351	76.6

SCORING	TD R	TD P	TD Rt	PAT	FG	Saf	PTS
Tomlinson	28	3	0	0/0	0/0	0	186
Kaeding	0	0	0	58/58	26/29	0	136
Gates	0	9	0	0/0	0/0	0	54
Jackson	0	6	0	0/0	0/0	0	38
Floyd	0	3	0	0/0	0/0	0	18
Manumaleuna	0	3	0	0/0	0/0	0	18
Turner	2	0	0	0/0	0/0	0	12
Dobbins	0	0	1	0/0	0/0	0	6
Harris	0	0	1	0/0	0/0	0	6
McCree	0	0	1	0/0	0/0	0	6
Neal	1	0	0	0/0	0/0	0	6
Whitehurst	1	0	0	0/0	0/0	0	6
Chargers	32	24	3	58/58	26/29	0	492
Opponents	13	19	1	32/33	23/26	2	303

2-Pt. Conversions: Jackson, Chargers 1-1, Opponents 0-0

RUSHING	No.	Yds	Avg	LG	TD
Tomlinson	348	1,815	5.2	85t	28
Turner	80	502	6.3	73	2
Neal	29	140	4.8	43	1
Rivers	48	49	1.0	15	0
Pinnock	4	25	6.3	15	0
Parker	2	19	9.5	18	0
Jackson	3	16	5.3	8	0
Whitehurst	2	13	6.5	14t	1
McCardell	1	8	8.0	8	0
Manumaleuna	1	1	1.0	1	0
Volek	3	-3	-1.0	-1	0
Scifres	1	-7	-7.0	-7	0
Chargers	522	2,578	4.9	85t	32
Opponents	386	1,613	4.2	51	13

RECEIVING	No.	Yds	Avg	LG	TD
Gates	71	924	13.0	57t	9
Tomlinson	56	508	9.1	51t	3
Parker	48	659	13.7	38	0
McCardell	36	437	12.1	28	0
Jackson	27	453	16.8	55	6
Neal	17	83	4.9	21	0
Floyd	15	210	14.0	46t	3
Manumaleuna	14	91	6.5	19	3
Turner	3	47	15.7	30	0
Chargers	287	3,412	11.9	57t	24
Opponents	307	3,563	11.6	74t	19

INTERCEPTIONS	No.	Yds	Avg	LG	TD
Jammer	4	57	14.3	35	0
Hart	3	37	12.3	22	0
Florence	3	24	8.0	23	0
Edwards	3	11	3.7	8	0
Merriman	1	10	10.0	10	0
Castillo	1	1	1.0	1	0
McCree	1	0	0.0	0	0
Chargers	16	140	8.8	35	0
Opponents	9	105	11.7	31t	1

PUNTING	No.	Yds.	Avg.	In 20	LG
Scifres	69	2,893	41.9	35	71
Chargers	69	2,893	41.9	35	71
Opponents	88	3,923	44.6	23	72

PUNT RETURNS	Ret	FC	Yds	Avg	LG	TD
Parker	37	15	331	8.9	50	0
McCardell	5	7	39	7.8	12	0
Gordon	3	1	12	4.0	6	0
Chargers	45	23	382	8.5	50	0
Opponents	27	19	216	8.0	81	0

KICKOFF RETURNS	No.	Yds	Avg	LG	TD
Turner	36	954	26.5	58	0
Cromartie	10	297	29.7	91	0
Neal	3	11	3.7	7	0
Gordon	2	55	27.5	32	0
Parker	2	19	9.5	12	0
Manumaleuna	1	14	14.0	14	0
Withrow	1	0	0.0	0	0
Chargers	55	1,350	24.5	91	0
Opponents	90	1,960	21.8	53	0

FIELD GOALS	1-19	20-29	30-39	40-49	50+
Kaeding	0/0	7/7	11/12	7/9	1/1
Chargers	0/0	7/7	11/12	7/9	1/1
Opponents	0/0	5/5	10/11	6/7	2/3

SACKS	No.
Merriman	17.0
Phillips	11.5
Castillo	7.0
Cesaire	4.0
Godfrey	4.0
Harris	3.0
Cooper	2.5
Edwards	2.5
Polk	2.0
Williams	2.0
Bingham	1.5
Olshansky	1.5
Robinson	1.5
McCree	1.0
Chargers	61.0
Opponents	28.0

RECORD HOLDERS
INDIVIDUAL RECORDS—CAREER

Category	Name	Performance
Rushing (Yds.)	LaDainian Tomlinson, 2001-06	9,176
Passing (Yds.)	Dan Fouts, 1973-1987	43,040
Passing (TDs)	Dan Fouts, 1973-1987	254
Receiving (No.)	Charlie Joiner, 1976-1986	586
Receiving (Yds.)	Lance Alworth, 1962-1970	9,585
Interceptions	Gill Byrd, 1983-1992	42
Punting (Avg.)	Darren Bennett, 1995-2003	43.8
Punt Return (Avg.)	Darrien Gordon, 1993-96	13.6
Kickoff Return (Avg.)	Leslie (Speedy) Duncan, 1964-1970	25.3
Field Goals	John Carney, 1990-2000	261
Touchdowns (Tot.)	LaDainian Tomlinson, 2001-06	111
Points	John Carney, 1990-2000	1,076

INDIVIDUAL RECORDS—SINGLE SEASON

Category	Name	Performance
Rushing (Yds.)	LaDainian Tomlinson, 2006	1,815
Passing (Yds.)	Dan Fouts, 1981	4,802
Passing (TDs)	Dan Fouts, 1981	33
Receiving (No.)	LaDainian Tomlinson, 2003	100
Receiving (Yds.)	Lance Alworth, 1965	1,602
Interceptions	Charlie McNeil, 1961	9
Punting (Avg.)	Darren Bennett, 2000	46.2
Punt Return (Avg.)	Leslie (Speedy) Duncan, 1965	15.5
Kickoff Return (Avg.)	Keith Lincoln, 1962	28.4
Field Goals	John Carney, 1994	34
Touchdowns (Tot.)	LaDainian Tomlinson, 2006	*31
Points	LaDainian Tomlinson, 2006	*186

INDIVIDUAL RECORDS—SINGLE GAME

Category	Name	Performance
Rushing (Yds.)	LaDainian Tomlinson, 12-28-03	243
Passing (Yds.)	Dan Fouts, 10-19-80, 12-11-82	444
Passing (TDs)	Dan Fouts, 11-22-81	6
Receiving (No.)	Kellen Winslow, 10-7-84	15
Receiving (Yds.)	Wes Chandler, 12-20-82	260
Interceptions	Many times	3
	Last time by Dwayne Harper, 11-27-95	
Field Goals	John Carney, 9-5-93, 9-18-93	6
	Greg Davis, 10-5-97	6
Touchdowns (Tot.)	Kellen Winslow, 11-22-81	5
Points	Kellen Winslow, 11-22-81	30

*NFL Record

2007 VETERAN ROSTER

No.	Name	Pos.	Ht.	Wt.	Birthdate	NFL Exp.	College	Hometown	How Acq.	'06 Games/ Starts
97	Bingham, Ryon	DT	6-3	303	6/6/81	3	Nebraska	Sandy, Utah	D7a-'04	16/0
50	Binn, David	LS	6-3	223	2/6/72	14	California	San Mateo, Calif.	FA-'94	16/0
82	Camarillo, Greg	WR	6-1	190	4/18/82	2	Stanford	Menlo Park, Calif.	FA-'05	4/0
93	Castillo, Luis	DE	6-3	290	8/4/83	3	Northwestern	Garfield, N.J.	D1b-'05	10/9
74	Cesaire, Jacques	DE	6-2	295	8/30/80	5	Southern Connecticut State	Gardner, Mass.	FA-'03	16/10
54	Cooper, Stephen	LB	6-1	235	6/19/79	5	Maine	Wareham, Mass.	FA-'03	16/4
	Cottrell, T.J.	TE	6-5	255	5/3/82	2	Buffalo State	Williamsville, N.Y.	FA-'07	0*
31	Cromartie, Antonio	CB	6-2	203	4/15/84	2	Florida State	Tallahassee, Fla.	D1-'06	16/0
68	Dielman, Kris	G	6-4	310	2/3/81	5	Indiana	Troy, Ohio	FA-'03	15/15
51	Dobbins, Tim	LB	6-1	246	10/10/82	2	Iowa State	Nashville, Tenn.	D5-'06	16/0
29	Florence, Drayton	CB	6-0	195	12/19/80	5	Tuskegee	Ocala, Fla.	D2a-'03	16/16
80	Floyd, Malcom	WR	6-5	225	9/8/81	2	Wyoming	Sacramento, Calif.	FA-'04	12/0
85	Gates, Antonio	TE	6-4	260	6/18/80	5	Kent State	Detroit, Mich.	FA-'03	16/16
79	Goff, Mike	G	6-5	311	1/6/76	10	Iowa	Peru, Ill.	UFA(Cin)-'04	16/16
24	Gordon, Cletis	CB	6-1	197	7/17/82	2	Jackson State	Amite City, La.	FA-'06	2/0
28	Gregory, Steve	CB	5-11	185	1/8/83	2	Syracuse	Staten Island, N.Y.	FA-'06	14/0
61	Hardwick, Nick	C	6-4	295	9/2/81	4	Purdue	Indianapolis, Ind.	D3b-'04	16/16
92	Harris, Marques	LB	6-1	231	9/20/81	3	Southern Utah	Grand Junction, Colo.	FA-'05	15/1
42	Hart, Clinton	S	6-0	205	7/20/77	5	Central Florida C.C.	Bushnell, Fla.	W(Phi)-'04	16/1
83	Jackson, Vincent	WR	6-5	241	1/14/83	3	Northern Colorado	Colorado Springs, Colo.	D2-'05	16/7
23	Jammer, Quentin	CB	6-0	204	6/19/79	6	Texas	Angleton, Texas	D1-'02	16/16
27	Jue, Bhawoh	S	6-0	200	5/24/79	7	Penn State	Chantilly, Va.	UFA(GB)-'05	12/2
10	Kaeding, Nate	K	6-0	187	3/26/82	4	Iowa	Coralville, Iowa	D3a-'04	16/0
71	Lekkerkerker, Cory	T	6-7	323	7/25/81	3	California-Davis	Chino, Calif.	FA-'05	15/0
86	Manumaleuna, Brandon	TE	6-2	288	1/4/80	7	Arizona	Torrance, Calif.	T(StL)-'06	16/7
20	McCree, Marlon	S	5-11	202	3/17/77	7	Kentucky	Daytona Beach, Fla.	UFA(Car)-'06	14/14
91	McKinney, Brandon	DT	6-2	324	8/24/83	2	Michigan State	Dayton, Ohio	FA-'06	6/0
73	McNeill, Marcus	T	6-7	336	11/16/83	2	Auburn	Ellenwood, Ga.	D2-'06	16/16
56	Merriman, Shawne	LB	6-4	272	5/25/84	3	Maryland	Upper Marlboro, Md.	D1a-'05	12/12
63	Mruczkowski, Scott	C/G	6-5	318	4/5/82	3	Bowling Green	Garfield Heights, Ohio	D7-'05	7/1
41	Neal, Lorenzo	FB	5-11	255	12/27/70	15	Fresno State	Hanford, Calif.	UFA(Cin)-'03	16/11
72	Oben, Roman	T	6-4	305	10/9/72	12	Louisville	Washington, D.C.	T(TB)-'04	2/0
70	Olivea, Shane	T	6-4	312	10/7/81	4	Ohio State	Long Beach, N.Y.	D7b-'04	16/16
99	Olshansky, Igor	DE	6-6	309	5/3/82	4	Oregon	San Francisco, Calif.	D2-'04	13/13
81	Osgood, Kassim	WR	6-5	220	5/20/80	5	San Diego State	Salinas, Calif.	FA-'03	16/0
88	Parker, Eric	WR	6-0	180	4/14/79	6	Tennessee	Shorewood, Ill.	FA-'02	15/12
95	Phillips, Shaun	LB	6-3	262	5/13/81	4	Purdue	Willingboro, N.J.	D4-'04	14/14
34	Pinnock, Andrew	FB	5-10	250	3/12/80	5	South Carolina	Bloomfield, Conn.	D7-'03	3/0
52	Polk, Carlos	LB	6-2	262	2/22/77	7	Nebraska	Rockford, Ill.	D4-'01	16/4
17	Rivers, Philip	QB	6-5	228	12/8/81	4	North Carolina State	Athens, Ala.	T(NYG)-'04	16/16
98	Robinson, Derreck	DE	6-4	289	3/3/82	3	Iowa	Minneapolis, Minn.	FA-'05	14/0
5	Scifres, Mike	P	6-2	236	10/8/80	5	Western Illinois	Destrehan, La.	D5-'03	16/0
43	Sproles, Darren	RB/KR	5-6	181	6/20/83	3	Kansas State	Olathe, Kan.	D4-'05	0*
21	Tomlinson, LaDainian	RB	5-10	221	6/23/79	7	Texas Christian	Waco, Texas	D1-'01	16/16
33	Turner, Michael	RB	5-10	237	2/13/82	4	Northern Illinois	Chicago, Ill.	D5b-'04	13/0
7	Volek, Billy	QB	6-2	214	4/28/76	8	Fresno State	Fresno, Calif.	T(Tenn)-'06	1/0
6	Whitehurst, Charlie	QB	6-4	227	8/6/82	2	Clemson	Alpharetta, Ga.	D3-'06	2/0
57	Wilhelm, Matt	LB	6-4	245	2/2/81	5	Ohio State	Elyria, Ohio	D4-'03	16/0
76	Williams, Jamal	DT	6-3	348	4/28/76	10	Oklahoma State	Washington, D.C.	D2(Supp)-'98	16/16
65	Withrow, Cory	C/G	6-2	287	4/5/75	8	Washington State	Spokane, Wash.	FA-'06	11/0

* Cottrell missed '05 season with Minnesota because of injury; Sproles missed '06 season because of injury.

Players lost through free agency: (3): LB Donnie Edwards (KC; 16 games in '06); WR Az-Zahir Hakim (Mia; 0); T Leander Jordan (Atl; 0).

* Also played with Chargers in '06—CB Markus Curry (2), LB Akbar Gbaja-Biamila (3), LB Randall Godfrey (13), S Terrence Kiel (15), S Andre Lott (1), WR Keenan McCardell (14),

2007 FIRST-YEAR ROSTER

Name	Pos.	Ht.	Wt.	Birthdate	College	Hometown	How Acq.
Applewhite, Antwan	LB	6-3	246	12/31/85	San Diego State	Torrance, Calif.	FA
Arline, Anthony	CB	6-2	198	10/12/83	Baylor	San Antonio, Texas	FA
Battle, Tra	S	5-11	173	1/5/85	Georgia	Forsyth, Ga.	FA
Bihl, Mark	C	6-4	398	7/18/83	Michigan	Washington Court House, Ohio	FA
Buckley, Eldra	RB	5-9	207	6/23/85	Tennessee-Chattanooga	Charleston, Miss.	FA
Chandler, Scott	TE	6-7	265	7/23/85	Iowa	Southlake, Texas	D4
Clary, Jeromey (1)	T	6-6	306	11/5/83	Kansas State	Mansfield, Texas	D6a-'06
Coleman, Andre	DE	6-3	287	7/26/84	Albany	Buffalo, N.Y.	FA
Cryer, Barry	DE	6-2	287	9/19/84	Nebraska	Marrero, La.	FA
Davis, Craig	WR	6-1	202	10/2/85	Louisiana State	New Orleans, La.	D1
Elliott, Brett (1)	QB	6-3	210	6/11/82	Linfield	Lake Oswego, Ore.	FA
Franklin, Gabe (1)	CB	5-10	185	6/28/82	Boise State	Oakland, Calif.	FA-'06
Grennan, Keith	DE	6-4	298	5/20/84	Eastern Washington	Edmonds, Wash.	FA
Griffeth, Kelly (1)	TE	6-5	298	4/11/82	Fort Hays State	Jewell, Kan.	FA-'06
Gross, Tyronne (1)	RB	5-9	213	5/14/83	Eastern Oregon	Stockton, Calif.	FA-'06
Hicks, Jarrett	WR	6-3	211	4/4/84	Texas Tech	Houston, Texas	FA
Jones, Mike	G	6-5	312	6/25/85	Iowa	Chicago Ridge, Ill.	FA
Jones, Quinton	CB	5-9	182	1/1/84	Boise State	Cerritos, Calif.	FA
Kahui, Kurt (1)	LB	6-1	240	10/18/84	San Diego State	Wailuku, Hawaii	FA-'06
Leonard, Louis	DT	6-4	330	7/16/84	Fresno State	Compton, Calif.	FA
Merrick, Miguel	S	5-10	202	11/1/83	Iowa	Union City, N.J.	FA
Merriweather, Reggie	RB	5-7	218	9/30/83	Clemson	North Augusta, S.C.	FA
Monroe, Brian	P	6-1	205	12/29/84	Miami	Palm Beach Gardens, Fla.	FA
Naanee, Legedu	WR	6-2	226	9/16/83	Boise State	Portland, Ore.	D5
Pape, Tony (1)	T	6-6	302	9/29/81	Michigan	Darien, Ill.	FA
Race, Germaine	RB	5-10	218	4/7/85	Pittsburg State (Kan.)	Warrensburg, Mo.	FA
Roach, Nick	LB	6-0	234	6/16/85	Northwestern	Milwaukee, Wis.	FA
Robertson, Erik	G	6-2	310	10/4/84	California	Apple Valley, Calif.	FA
Schroeder, Chad	WR	6-1	182	6/11/83	Texas A&M	Austin, Texas	FA
Shackelford, Sonny	WR	6-1	188	4/13/85	Washington	Beverly Hills, Calif.	FA
Sheffey, Jeremy	G	6-2	291	4/5/84	West Virginia	Catlettsburg, Ky.	FA
Siler, Brandon	LB	6-2	239	12/5/85	Florida	Orlando, Fla.	D7
Simmons, Mark (1)	WR	5-10	187	1/16/84	Kansas	DeSoto, Texas	FA
Tucker, Jyles	LB	6-3	258	9/18/83	Wake Forest	Dover, N.J.	FA
Warren, Mike (1)	FB	6-1	249	1/6/82	Elon	Fayetteville, N.C.	FA
Waters, Anthony	LB	6-3	238	7/25/84	Clemson	Lake View, S.C.	D3
Weddle, Eric	S	5-11	200	1/4/85	Utah	Alta Loma, Calif.	D2

The term NFL Rookie is defined as a player who is in his first season of professional football and has not been on the roster of another professional football team for any regular-season or postseason games. A Rookie is designated by an "R" on NFL rosters. Players who have been active in another professional football league or players who have NFL experience, including either preseason training camp or being on an Active List or Inactive List, or on Reserve/Injured or Reserve/Physically Unable to Perform for fewer than six regular-season games, are termed NFL First-Year Players. An NFL First-Year Player is designated by a "1" on NFL rosters. Thereafter, a player is credited with an additional year of experience for each season in which he accumulates six games on the Active List or Inactive List, or on Reserve/Injured or Reserve/Physically Unable to Perform.

Log on to www.chargers.com for an up-to-date roster.

COACHING STAFF
Head Coach,
Norv Turner
Pro Career: A veteran coach of 22 NFL seasons, Turner became the 14th head coach in team history on February 19, 2007. A two-time Super Bowl champion as an offensive coordinator with the Dallas Cowboys, Turner's most recent assignment was serving as the offensive coordinator for the San Francisco 49ers in 2006. A Bay Area native from Martinez, California, this is Turner's second stint with the Chargers. He spent the 2001 season as the Bolts' offensive coordinator. Turner's 22 years of coaching experience include nine as a head coach—seven for the Washington Redskins (1994-2000) and two with the Oakland Raiders (2004-05). In 1999, he led the Redskins to a division title. He spent 13 seasons as an NFL assistant coach, including seven as an offensive coordinator with the Dallas Cowboys (1991-93), Chargers (2001), Miami Dolphins (2002-03), and 49ers (2006). Turner also held the title of assistant head coach during his two seasons in Miami. Turner began his NFL coaching career as an assistant with the Los Angeles Rams in 1985. He coached wide receivers from 1985-86 before adding the responsibility of the team's tight ends from 1987-1990. Turner made his coaching mark during his three seasons in Dallas as the Cowboys won back-to-back Super Bowls (XXVII and XXVIII) following the 1992 and 1993 seasons. Career record: 59-83-1.
Background: Turner played quarterback at Oregon, spending two seasons behind former Charger and NFL Hall of Fame quarterback Dan Fouts. Turner coached at Oregon (1975) and Southern California (1976-1984). During his nine-year tenure at USC, the Trojans played in four Rose Bowls, winning all four. One of those was a win over Michigan after the 1978 season that capped a 12-1 season and gave USC the National Championship.
Personal: Born in LeJeune, N.C., May 17, 1952. Turner and his wife, Nancy, have three children—Scott, Stephanie, and Drew.

ASSISTANT COACHES
Clancy Barone, tight ends; born July 26, 1963, San Andreas, Calif. Offensive lineman Cal State-Sacramento 1981-82, Nevada 1985-86. No pro playing experience. College coach: American River (Calif.) J.C. 1987-89, Cal State-Sacramento 1990-92, Texas A&M 1993, Eastern Illinois 1994-96, Wyoming 1997-99, Houston 2000-02, Texas State 2003. Pro coach: Atlanta Falcons 2004-06, joined Chargers in 2007.
Bill Bradley, secondary; born January 24, 1947, Palestine, Texas. Quarterback/defensive back Texas 1966-68. Pro safety/punter/kick returner Philadelphia Eagles 1969-1977, St. Louis Cardinals 1978.

College coach: Texas 1987, Baylor 2004-06. Pro coach: San Antonio Gunslingers (USFL) 1983-84, Memphis Showboats (USFL) 1985, Calgary Stampeders (CFL) 1988-1990, San Antonio Riders (WLAF) 1991-92, Sacramento Gold Miners (CFL) 1994, San Antonio Texans (CFL) 1995, Toronto Argonauts (CFL) 1996-97, Buffalo Bills 1998-2000, New York Jets 2001-03, joined Chargers in 2007.
Ted Cottrell, defensive coordinator; born June 13, 1947, Chester, Pa. Linebacker Delaware Valley College 1966-68. Pro linebacker Atlanta Falcons 1969-1970, Winnipeg Blue Bombers (CFL) 1971. College coach: Rutgers 1973-1980, 1983. Pro coach: Kansas City Chiefs 1981-82, New Jersey Generals (USFL) 1983-84, Buffalo Bills 1986-89, 1995-2000, Arizona Cardinals 1990-94, New York Jets 2001-03, Minnesota Vikings 2004-05, joined Chargers in 2007.
Steve Crosby, special teams; born July 3, 1950, Great Bend, Kan. Running back Fort Hayes State 1970-73. Pro running back New York Giants 1974-76. College coach: Vanderbilt 1998-2001. Pro coach: Miami Dolphins 1979-1982, Atlanta Falcons 1983-84, 1986-89, Cleveland Browns 1985, 1991-95, New England Patriots 1990, joined Chargers in 2002.
John (Jack) Henry, offensive line; born March 14, 1946, Houston, Pa. Linebacker Penn State 1964-65, guard Indiana (Pa.) 1967-68. No pro playing experience. College coach: West Virginia 1970, 1978-79, Edinboro 1973, Louisville 1974, Millersville 1975-76, Southern Illinois 1977, Appalachian State 1980, Wake Forest 1981-85, Indiana (Pa.) 1986-89, Pittsburgh 1993-95. Pro coach: Pittsburgh Steelers 1990-91, San Diego Chargers 1996, Detroit Lions 1997-99, New Orleans Saints 2000-05, re-joined Chargers in 2006.
Hal Hunter, offensive line; born July 8, 1959, Canonsburg, Pa. Linebacker Northwestern 1978. College coach: William & Mary 1982, Pittsburgh 1983-84, Columbia 1985, Indiana (Pa.) 1986, Akron 1987-1990, Vanderbilt 1991-94, Louisiana State 1995-99, Indiana 2000-01, North Carolina 2002-05. Pro coach: Joined Chargers in 2006.
Jeff Hurd, strength and conditioning; born April 24, 1958, Pomona, Calif. No college or pro playing experience. College coach: Fort Hays State 1984, Delta State 1985-86, Clemson 1986-87, Western Michigan 1987-1992, Tulsa 1994. Pro coach: Jacksonville Jaguars 1995-97, Kansas City Chiefs 1998-2006, joined Chargers in 2007.
James Lofton, wide receivers; born July 5, 1956, Fort Ord, Calif. Wide receiver Stanford 1975-77. Pro wide receiver Green Bay Packers 1978-1986, Los Angeles Raiders 1987-88, Buffalo Bills 1989-1992, Los Angeles Rams 1993, Philadelphia Eagles 1993. Pro coach: Joined Chargers in 2002.

Wayne Nunnely, defensive line; born March 29, 1952, Los Angeles. Fullback Nevada-Las Vegas 1972-75. No pro playing experience. College coach: Nevada-Las Vegas 1976, 1982-89 (head coach 1986-89), Cal Poly-Pomona 1977-78, Cal State-Fullerton 1979, Pacific 1980-81, Southern California 1991-92, UCLA 1993-94. Pro coach: New Orleans Saints 1995-96, joined Chargers in 1997.
John Pagano, outside linebackers; born March 30, 1967, Boulder, Colo. Linebacker Mesa State College 1985-88. No pro playing experience. College coach: Mesa State College 1989, Nevada-Las Vegas 1990-91, Louisiana Tech 1994, Mississippi 1995. Pro coach: New Orleans Saints 1996-97, Indianapolis Colts 1998-2001, joined Chargers in 2002.
John Ramsdell, quarterbacks; born August 16, 1954, Lafayette, Ind. Running back Springfield (Mass.) College 1972-75. No pro playing experience. College coach: San Francisco State 1976-77, Long Beach State 1978, Pacific 1979-1982, Oregon 1983-1994. Pro coach: St. Louis Rams 1995-2005, joined Chargers in 2006.
Ron Rivera, inside linebackers; born January 7, 1962, Fort Ord, Calif. Linebacker California 1980-83. Pro linebacker Chicago Bears 1984-1992. Pro coach: Chicago Bears 1997-98, 2004-06, Philadelphia Eagles 1999-2003, joined Chargers in 2007.
Kevin Ross, asst. secondary/quality control; born January 16, 1962, Camden, N.J. Defensive back Temple 1980-83. Pro defensive back Kansas City Chiefs 1984-1993, 1997, Atlanta Falcons 1994-95, San Diego Chargers 1996. Pro coach: Minnesota Vikings 2003-05, joined Chargers in 2007.
Clarence Shelmon, offensive coordinator; born September 17, 1952, Bossier City, La. Running back Houston 1971-75. No pro playing experience. College coach: Army 1978-1980, Indiana 1981-83, Arizona 1984-86, Southern California 1987-1990. Pro coach: Los Angeles Rams 1991, Seattle Seahawks 1992-97, Dallas Cowboys 1998-2001, joined Chargers in 2002.
Matt Simon, running backs; born December 6, 1953, Akron, Ohio. Linebacker Eastern New Mexico 1972-75. No pro playing experience. College coach: Washington 1982-1991, New Mexico 1992-93, North Texas (head coach) 1994-97. Pro coach: Denver Broncos 1998, Baltimore Ravens 1999-2005, joined Chargers in 2007.
Vernon Stephens, asst. strength and conditioning; born November 30, 1974, Jacksonville. No college or pro playing experience. College coach: North Florida 1999-2002, Colorado 2003-06. Pro coach: Jacksonville Jaguars 2002-03, joined Chargers in 2007.

**American Football Conference
South Division
Team Colors:** Navy, Titans Blue, Red, Silver
**460 Great Circle Road
Nashville, Tennessee 37228
Telephone: (615) 565-4000**

2007 SCHEDULE
PRESEASON
Aug. 11 **Washington** 7:00
Aug. 17 at New England 8:00
Aug. 24 at Buffalo 7:00
Aug. 30 **Green Bay**.........................7:00

REGULAR SEASON
Sep. 9 at Jacksonville 1:00
Sep. 16 **Indianapolis** 12:00
Sep. 24 at New Orleans (Mon.) 7:30
Sep. 30 Open Date
Oct. 7 **Atlanta** 12:00
Oct. 14 at Tampa Bay 1:00
Oct. 21 at Houston 12:00
Oct. 28 **Oakland** 12:00
Nov. 4 **Carolina** 12:00
Nov. 11 **Jacksonville** 12:00
Nov. 19 at Denver (Mon.) 6:30
Nov. 25 at Cincinnati 1:00
Dec. 2 **Houston** 12:00
Dec. 9 **San Diego** 12:00
Dec. 16 at Kansas City 12:00
Dec. 23 **N.Y. Jets** 3:15
Dec. 30 at Indianapolis 1:00

Stadium: LP Field
  (opened in 1999)
  •**Capacity:** 69,143
  One Titans Way
  Nashville, Tennessee 37213
Playing Surface: Natural Grass
Training Camp: Baptist Sports Park
  460 Great Circle Road
  Nashville, Tennessee
  37228

LP FIELD

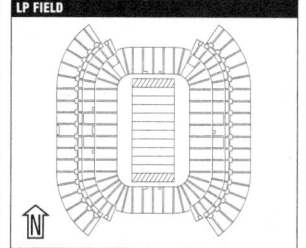

CLUB OFFICIALS
Owner/Chairman of the Board/CEO/
  President: K.S. (Bud) Adams, Jr.
Executive V.P./General Manager:
  Mike Reinfeldt
Executive V.P. of Administration/Facilities:
  Don MacLachlan
Senior Executive V.P./COO:
  Steve Underwood
Vice President/Asst. General Counsel:
  Elza Bullock
Vice President/Finance and CFO:
  Robert McBurnett
Vice President/Community Affairs:
  Bob Hyde
Senior Director of Football
  Administration: Vincent Marino
Director of Player Personnel:
  Rich Snead
Director of College Scouting:
  Mike Ackerley
Senior Director of Sales and Operations:
  Stuart Spears
Operations Manager: Brent Akers
Director of Broadcasting: Mike Keith
Vice President/Marketing:
  Ralph Ockenfels
Controller: Jenneen Kaufman
Director of Information Systems:
  Russ Hudson
Director of Internet
  Operations/Publications: Gary Glenn
Director of Media Relations:
  Robbie Bohren
Asst. Director of Media Relations:
  Dwight Spradlin
Director of Security: Steve Berk
Senior Director of Ticketing:
  Marty Collins
Director of Pro Personnel: Lake Dawson
Director of Player Development:
  Tina Tuggle
Director of Cheerleading: Stacie Kinder
Director of Suite and Club Services:
  Bill Wainwright
Marketing Manager: Brad McClanahan
Head Athletic Trainer: Brad Brown
Assistant Athletic Trainers:
  Don Moseley, Geoff Kaplan
Equipment Manager: Paul Noska
Video Director: Anthony Pastrana
General Manager of LP Field:
  Walter Overton

COACHING HISTORY
**Houston 1960-1996
(354-379-6)**
Records include postseason games
1960-61　Lou Rymkus* 12-7-1
1961　Wally Lemm 10-0-0
1962-63　Frank (Pop) Ivy 17-12-0
1964　Sammy Baugh..............4-10-0
1965　Hugh Taylor 4-10-0
1966-1970　Wally Lemm 28-40-4
1971　Ed Hughes.....................4-9-1
1972-73　Bill Peterson** 1-18-0
1973-74　Sid Gillman...................8-15-0
1975-1980　O.A. (Bum) Phillips 59-38-0
1981-83　Ed Biles***.................8-23-0
1983　Chuck Studley 2-8-0
1984-85　Hugh Campbell****......8-22-0
1985-89　Jerry Glanville.............35-35-0
1990-94　Jack Pardee#.............44-35-0
1994-2006　Jeff Fisher.................110-97-0
  * Released after five games in 1961
  ** Released after five games in 1973
  *** Resigned after six games in 1983
  **** Released after 14 games in 1985
  # Released after 10 games in 1994

PAID ATTENDANCE
Home 535,927　　Away 536,352
Total 1,072,279
Single-game home record,
  69,149, many times (last: 12/18/05)
Single-season home record,
  553,192 (2005)

2007 DRAFT CHOICES
Round	Name	Pos.	College
1	Michael Griffin	DB	Texas
2	Chris Henry	RB	Arizona
3	Paul Williams	WR	Fresno State
4	Leroy Harris	C	North Carolina St.
	Chris Davis	WR	Florida State
5	Antonio Johnson	DT	Mississippi St.
6	Joel Filani	WR	Texas Tech
	Jacob Ford	DE	Central Arkansas
	Ryan Smith	DB	Florida
7	Mike Otto	T	Purdue

2006 TEAM RECORD

PRESEASON (1-3)

Date	Result		Opponent
8/12	L	16-19	New Orleans
8/19	L	10-35	at Denver
8/26	L	6-20	Atlanta
9/1	W	35-21	at Green Bay

REGULAR SEASON (8-8)

Date	Result		Opponent	Att.
9/10	L	16-23	N.Y. Jets	69,143
9/17	L	7-40	at San Diego	64,344
9/24	L	10-13	at Miami	72,733
10/1	L	14-45	Dallas	69,143
10/8	L	13-14	at Indianapolis	57,021
10/15	W	25-22	at Washington	88,550
10/29	W	28-22	Houston	69,143
11/5	L	7-37	at Jacksonville	66,524
11/12	L	26-27	Baltimore	69,143
11/19	W	31-13	at Philadelphia	69,232
11/26	W	24-21	N.Y. Giants	69,143
12/3	W	20-17	Indianapolis	69,143
12/10	W	26-20	at Houston (OT)	70,760
12/17	W	24-17	Jacksonville	69,143
12/24	W	30-29	at Buffalo	54,765
12/31	L	23-40	New England	69,143

SCORE BY PERIODS

Titans	52	87	81	98	6	—	324
Opponents	84	116	85	115	0	—	400

2006 TEAM STATISTICS

	Titans	Opp.
Total First Downs	261	329
Rushing	105	121
Passing	133	181
Penalty	23	27
3rd Down: Made/Att	67/205	90/221
3rd Down Pct.	32.7	40.7
4th Down: Made/Att	7/17	10/17
4th Down Pct.	41.2	58.8
Possession Avg.	27:17	32:43
Total Net Yards	4,810	5,915
Avg. Per Game	300.6	369.7
Total Plays	945	1,062
Avg. Per Play	5.1	5.6
Net Yards Rushing	2,214	2,313
Avg. Per Game	138.4	144.6
Total Rushes	469	506
Net Yards Passing	2,596	3,602
Avg. Per Game	162.3	225.1
Sacked/Yards Lost	29/152	26/148
Gross Yards	2,748	3,750
Att./Completions	447/226	530/335
Completion Pct.	50.6	63.2
Had Intercepted	19	17
Punts/Average	88/42.7	68/42.5
Net Punting Avg.	88/37.3	68/34.4
Penalties/Yards	94/803	102/906
Fumbles/Ball Lost	29/7	19/11
Touchdowns	36	46
Rushing	15	20
Passing	13	24
Returns	8	2

2006 INDIVIDUAL STATISTICS

PASSING	Att.	Comp.	Yds.	Pct.	TD	Int.	Tkld.	Rate
Young	357	184	2,199	51.5	12	13	25/129	66.7
Collins	90	42	549	46.7	1	6	4/23	42.3
Titans	447	226	2,748	50.6	13	19	29/152	61.8
Opponents	530	335	3,750	63.2	24	17	26/148	86.0

SCORING	TD R	TD P	TD Rt	PAT	FG	Saf	PTS
Bironas	0	0	0	32/32	22/28	0	98
Henry	7	0	0	0/0	0/0	0	44
Young	7	0	0	0/0	0/0	0	44
P. Jones	0	0	4	0/0	0/0	0	24
B. Jones	0	4	0	0/0	0/0	0	24
Bennett	0	3	0	0/0	0/0	0	20
Scaife	1	2	0	0/0	0/0	0	18
Troupe	0	2	0	0/0	0/0	0	12
Wade	0	2	0	0/0	0/0	0	12
T. Brown	0	0	1	0/0	0/0	0	6
Bulluck	0	0	1	0/0	0/0	0	6
Finnegan	0	0	1	0/0	0/0	0	6
Hope	0	0	1	0/0	0/0	0	6
Titans	15	13	8	32/32	22/28	2	324
Opponents	20	24	2	41/44	27/33	0	400

2-Pt. Conversions: Bennett, Henry, Young, Titans 3-3, Opponents 1-2.

RUSHING	No.	Yds	Avg	LG	TD
Henry	270	1,211	4.5	70t	7
Young	83	552	6.7	39t	7
L. White	61	244	4.0	26	0
C. Brown	41	156	3.8	21	0
Hall	7	21	3.0	11	0
Scaife	1	13	13.0	13t	1
P. Jones	2	8	4.0	7	0
Givens	1	3	3.0	3	0
B. Jones	1	3	3.0	3	0
Roby	1	3	3.0	3	0
Nickey	1	0	0.0	0	0
Titans	469	2,214	4.7	70t	15
Opponents	506	2,313	4.6	73	20

RECEIVING	No.	Yds	Avg	LG	TD
Bennett	46	737	16.0	39	3
Wade	33	461	14.0	25	2
Scaife	29	370	12.8	34	2
B. Jones	27	384	14.2	53	4
Henry	18	78	4.3	12	0
Hall	15	138	9.2	28	0
L. White	14	60	4.3	13	0
Troupe	13	150	11.5	32	2
Williams	8	121	15.1	20	0
Givens	8	104	13.0	27	0
Hartsock	6	68	11.3	23	0
P. Jones	2	31	15.5	17	0
Roby	2	28	14.0	21	0
Cramer	2	8	4.0	6	0
C. Brown	2	4	2.0	4	0
Wallace	1	6	6.0	6	0
Titans	226	2,748	12.2	53	13
Opponents	335	3,750	11.2	68t	24

INTERCEPTIONS	No.	Yds	Avg	LG	TD
Hope	5	105	21.0	61t	1
P. Jones	4	130	32.5	83t	1
Thompson	3	14	4.7	11	0
Hill	2	20	10.0	11	0
Sirmon	1	13	13.0	13	0
Bulluck	1	0	0.0	0	0
Tulloch	1	0	0.0	0	0
Titans	17	282	16.6	83t	2
Opponents	19	250	13.2	55t	2

PUNTING	No.	Yds.	Avg.	In 20	LG
Hentrich	88	3,760	42.7	32	73
Titans	88	3,760	42.7	32	73
Opponents	68	2,888	42.5	18	61

PUNT RETURNS	Ret	FC	Yds	Avg	LG	TD
P. Jones	34	3	440	12.9	90t	3
Wade	3	3	27	9.0	18	0
Titans	37	6	467	12.6	90t	3
Opponents	33	24	278	8.4	39	0

KICKOFF RETURNS	No.	Yds	Avg	LG	TD
Wade	50	1,194	23.9	48	0
P. Jones	20	521	26.1	70	0
Scaife	4	64	16.0	18	0
Cramer	3	37	12.3	21	0
Hartsock	1	5	5.0	5	0
L. White	1	14	14.0	14	0
Titans	79	1,835	23.2	70	0
Opponents	58	1,263	21.8	52	0

FIELD GOALS	1-19	20-29	30-39	40-49	50+
Bironas	0/0	10/11	7/7	4/8	1/2
Titans	0/0	10/11	7/7	4/8	1/2
Opponents	1/1	10/11	6/10	10/10	0/1

SACKS	No.
Vanden Bosch	6.5
LaBoy	3.5
Starks	3.0
Bulluck	2.5
Finnegan	2.0
Haynesworth	2.0
T. Brown	1.5
Bockwoldt	1.0
P. Jones	1.0
Mahelona	1.0
Odom	0.5
Sirmon	0.5
Smith	0.5
Tulloch	0.5
Titans	26.0
Opponents	29.0

RECORD HOLDERS
INDIVIDUAL RECORDS—CAREER

Category	Name	Performance
Rushing (Yds.)	Eddie George, 1996-2003	10,009
Passing (Yds.)	Warren Moon, 1984-1993	33,685
Passing (TDs)	Warren Moon, 1984-1993	196
Receiving (No.)	Ernest Givins, 1986-1994	542
Receiving (Yds.)	Ernest Givins, 1986-1994	7,935
Interceptions	Jim Norton, 1960-68	45
Punting (Avg.)	Greg Montgomery, 1988-1993	43.6
Punt Return (Avg.)	Billy Johnson, 1974-1980	13.2
Kickoff Return (Avg.)	Bobby Jancik, 1962-67	26.5
Field Goals	Al Del Greco, 1991-2000	246
Touchdowns (Tot.)	Eddie George, 1996-2003	74
Points	Al Del Greco, 1991-2000	1,060

INDIVIDUAL RECORDS—SINGLE SEASON

Category	Name	Performance
Rushing (Yds.)	Earl Campbell, 1980	1,934
Passing (Yds.)	Warren Moon, 1991	4,690
Passing (TDs)	George Blanda, 1961	36
Receiving (No.)	Charley Hennigan, 1964	101
Receiving (Yds.)	Charley Hennigan, 1961	1,746
Interceptions	Fred Glick, 1963	12
	Mike Reinfeldt, 1979	12
Punting (Avg.)	Craig Hentrich, 1998	47.2
Punt Return (Avg.)	Billy Johnson, 1977	15.4
Kickoff Return (Avg.)	Ken Hall, 1960	31.3
Field Goals	Al Del Greco, 1998	36
Touchdowns (Tot.)	Earl Campbell, 1979	19
Points	Al Del Greco, 1998	136

INDIVIDUAL RECORDS—SINGLE GAME

Category	Name	Performance
Rushing (Yds.)	Billy Cannon, 12-10-61	216
	Eddie George, 8-31-97	216
Passing (Yds.)	Warren Moon, 12-16-90	527
Passing (TDs)	George Blanda, 11-19-61	*7
Receiving (No.)	Charley Hennigan, 10-13-61	13
	Haywood Jeffires, 10-13-91	13
	Drew Bennett, 12-19-04	13
Receiving (Yds.)	Charley Hennigan, 10-13-61	272
Interceptions	Many times	3
	Last time by Samari Rolle, 12-26-99	
Field Goals	Roy Gerela, 9-28-69	5
	Al Del Greco, 12-3-00	5
Touchdowns (Tot.)	Billy Cannon, 12-10-61	5
Points	Billy Cannon, 12-10-61	30

*NFL Record

2007 VETERAN ROSTER

No.	Name	Pos.	Ht.	Wt.	Birthdate	NFL Exp.	College	Hometown	How Acq.	'06 Games/ Starts
54	Amano, Eugene	C	6-3	310	3/1/82	4	Southeast Missouri State	San Diego, Calif.	D7-'04	16/1
58	Amato, Ken	LB-LS	6-2	245	5/18/77	5	Montana State	Miami, Fla.	FA-'03	15/0
60	Bell, Jacob	G/T	6-4	295	3/2/81	4	Miami (Ohio)	Cleveland, Ohio	D5-'04	15/15
2	Bironas, Rob	K	6-0	205	1/29/78	3	Georgia Southern	Louisville, Ky.	FA-'05	16/0
29#	Brown, Chris	RB	6-3	220	4/17/81	5	Colorado	Naperville, Ill.	D3-'03	5/3
97	Brown, Tony	DT-DE	6-3	285	9/29/80	3	Memphis	Chattanooga, Tenn.	FA-'06	12/2
53	Bulluck, Keith	LB	6-3	235	4/4/77	8	Syracuse	New City, N.Y.	D1-'00	16/16
5	Collins, Kerry	QB	6-5	245	12/30/72	13	Penn State	Lebanon, Pa.	UFA(Oak)-'06	4/3
77	Conover, Sean	DE	6-5	262	7/31/84	2	Bucknell	Whitman, Mass.	FA-'06	6/2
48	Cramer, Casey	TE	6-2	250	1/5/82	3	Dartmouth	Middleton, Wis.	W(Car)-'06	15/0
31	Finnegan, Cortland	CB	5-10	188	2/2/84	2	Samford	Milton, Fla.	D7a-'06	16/2
52	Fowler, Ryan	LB	6-3	250	5/20/82	4	Duke	Redington Shores, Fla.	RFA(Dall)-'07	16/0*
22	Fuller, Vincent	S	6-1	190	8/3/82	3	Virginia Tech	Baltimore, Md.	D4a-'05	16/0
12	Gage, Justin	WR	6-4	212	1/24/81	5	Missouri	Jefferson City, Mo.	UFA(Chi)-'07	8/0*
73	Geisinger, Justin	C-G	6-3	322	5/24/82	3	Vanderbilt	Pittsburgh, Pa.	FA-'06	2/0
87	Givens, David	WR	6-0	215	8/16/80	6	Notre Dame	Humble, Texas	UFA(NE)-'06	5/5
45	Hall, Ahmard	FB	5-11	242	11/13/79	2	Texas	Angleton, Texas	FA-06'	14/7
20	Harper, Nick	CB	5-10	182	9/10/74	7	Fort Valley State	Baldwin, Ga.	UFA(Ind)-'07	15/15*
88	Hartsock, Ben	TE	6-4	255	7/5/80	4	Ohio State	Chillicothe, Ohio	W(Ind)-'06	6/3
92	Haynesworth, Albert	DT	6-6	320	6/17/81	6	Tennessee	Hartsville, S.C.	D1-'02	11/10
15	Hentrich, Craig	P-K	6-3	213	5/18/71	14	Notre Dame	Alton, Ill.	UFA(GB)-'98	16/0
21	Hill, Reynaldo	CB	5-11	185	8/28/82	3	Florida	Ft. Lauderdale, Fla.	D7-'05	15/14
24	Hope, Chris	S	6-0	208	9/29/80	6	Florida State	Rock Hill, S.C.	UFA(Pitt)-'06	16/16
81	Jones, Brandon	WR	6-1	212	10/6/82	3	Oklahoma	Texarkana, Texas	D3b-'05	16/10
32	Jones, Pacman	CB	5-10	185	9/30/83	3	West Virginia	Atlanta, Ga.	D1-'05	15/15
30	King, Eric	CB	5-10	185	5/10/82	3	Wake Forest	Woodstock, Md.	W(Buff)-'06	11/0
91	LaBoy, Travis	DE	6-3	260	8/20/81	4	Hawaii	San Rafael, Calif.	D2-'04	13/11
99	Long, Rien	DT	6-6	300	8/7/81	5	Washington State	Anacortes, Wash.	D4-'03	0*
70	Loper, Daniel	T	6-6	320	1/15/82	3	Texas Tech	Houston, Texas	D5b-'05	8/0
37	Lowry, Calvin	S	5-11	200	2/13/83	2	Penn State	Fayetteville, N.C.	D4a-'06	16/0
94	Mahelona, Jesse	DT	6-0	311	4/7/83	2	Tennessee	Kailua-Kona, Hawaii	D5b-'06	10/1
68	Mawae, Kevin	C	6-4	289	1/23/71	14	Louisiana State	Leesville, La.	UFA(NYJ)-'06	16/16
23	Nickey, Donnie	S	6-3	210	4/25/80	5	Ohio State	Plain City, Ohio	D5-'03	16/0
98	Odom, Antwan	DE	6-5	274	9/24/81	4	Alabama	Bayou La Batre, Ala.	D2-'04	4/2
69	Ogden, Marques	T	6-5	312	11/15/80	2	Howard	Washington, D.C.	FA-'07	0*
75	Olson, Benji	G	6-4	320	6/5/75	10	Washington	Port Orchard, Wash.	D5-'98	15/15
85	Orr, Jonathan	WR	6-1	193	3/20/83	2	Wisconsin	Detroit, Mich.	D6-'06	0*
6	Rattay, Tim	QB	6-0	200	3/15/77	8	Louisiana Tech	Phoenix, Ariz.	UFA(TB)-'07	4/2*
51	Reynolds, Robert	LB	6-3	247	5/20/81	4	Ohio State	Bowling Green, Ky.	D5-'04	4/0
82	Roby, Courtney	WR	6-0	189	1/10/83	3	Indiana	Indianapolis, Ind.	D3a-'05	12/0
71	Roos, Michael	T	6-7	315	10/5/82	3	Eastern Washington	Vancouver, Wash.	D2-'05	16/16
95	Savage, Josh	DE	6-4	276	9/28/80	3	Utah	Hillcrest, Utah	W(Atl)-'06	5/0
80	Scaife, Bo	TE	6-3	249	1/6/81	3	Texas	Denver, Colo.	D6-'05	14/12
38	Scott, Bryan	S	6-1	219	4/13/81	5	Penn State	Doylestown, Pa.	UFA(NO)-'07	9/0*
59#	Sirmon, Peter	LB	6-2	237	2/18/77	8	Oregon	Walla Walla, Wash.	D4b-'00	16/15
90	Starks, Randy	DT	6-3	312	12/14/83	4	Maryland	Waldorf, Md.	D3-'04	16/8
76	Stewart, David	T	6-7	318	8/28/82	3	Mississippi State	Moulton, Ala.	D4b-'05	14/14
28	Thompson, Lamont	S	6-1	215	7/30/78	6	Washington State	Richmond, Calif.	FA-'03	16/16
50	Thornton, David	LB	6-2	225	11/1/78	6	North Carolina	Goldsboro, N.C.	UFA(Ind)-'06	16/13
84	Troupe, Ben	TE	6-4	270	9/1/82	4	Florida	Augusta, Ga.	D2-'04	10/9
55	Tulloch, Stephen	LB	5-11	235	1/1/85	2	North Carolina State	Miami, Fla.	D4b-'06	16/3
93	Vanden Bosch, Kyle	DE	6-4	278	11/17/78	7	Nebraska	Larchwood, Iowa	UFA(Ariz)-'05	16/16
36	Waddell, Michael	CB	5-10	180	1/9/81	4	North Carolina	Ellerbe, N.C.	D4-'04	0*
64	Wand, Seth	T	6-7	327	8/6/79	5	Northwest Missouri State	Springfield, Mo.	FA-'06	7/0
25	White, LenDale	RB	6-1	235	12/20/84	2	Southern California	Denver, Colo.	D2-'06	13/0
86	Williams, Roydell	WR	6-0	187	3/14/81	3	Tulane	LaPlace, La.	D4c-'05	14/0
49	Woods, LeVar	LB	6-2	241	3/15/78	7	Iowa	Larchwood, Iowa	FA-'06	14/0*
26	Woolfolk, Andre	CB	6-2	197	1/26/80	5	Oklahoma	Denver, Colo.	D1-'03	10/1
10	Young, Vince	QB	6-5	233	5/18/83	2	Texas	Houston, Texas	D1-'06	15/13

* Fowler played 16 games with Dallas in '06; Gage played 8 games with Chicago; Harper played 15 games with Indianapolis; Long missed '06 season because of injury; Ogden last active with Jacksonville in '03; Orr inactive for 15 games; Rattay played 4 games with Tampa Bay; Scott played 9 games with New Orleans; Waddell missed '06 season on reserve/non-football injury list; Woods played 7 games with Detroit and 7 games with Tennessee.

\#   Unrestricted free agent; subject to developments.

Players lost through free agency (3): WR Drew Bennett (StL; 16 games in '06); DT Robaire Smith (Cle; 15); WR Bobby Wade (Minn; 16).

Also played with Titans in '06—LB Colby Bockwoldt (16 games), LS Jon Dorenbos (1), RB Travis Henry (14), G Zach Piller (3), DeQuincy Scott (3).

2007 FIRST-YEAR ROSTER

Name	Pos.	Ht.	Wt.	Birthdate	College	Hometown	How Acq.
Adibi, Nathaniel (1)	DE	6-3	249	1/25/81	Virginia Tech	Hampton, Va.	FA
Allred, Colin (1)	LB	6-1	238	4/15/83	Baylor	Dallas, Texas	FA-'06
Davis, Chris	WR	5-10	181	1/23/84	Florida State	St. Petersburg, Fla.	D4b
Douglas, Cody (1)	G	6-4	312	11/25/83	Tennessee	LaMarque, Texas	FA-'06
Ealy, Biren	WR	6-3	207	7/7/84	Houston	Houston, Texas	FA
Filani, Joel	WR	6-2	211	12/8/83	Texas Tech	Phoenix, Ariz.	D6a
Ford, Jacob	DE	6-4	249	7/20/83	Central Arkansas	Memphis, Tenn.	D6b
Ganther, Quinton (1)	RB	5-9	214	7/15/84	Utah	Richmond, Calif.	D7c-'06
Griffin, Michael	DB	6-0	202	1/4/85	Texas	Austin, Texas	D1
Harris, Charles	T	6-5	326	12/7/82	Washington State	Spokane, Wash.	FA
Harris, Leroy	G/C	6-3	302	6/6/84	North Carolina State	Raleigh, N.C.	D4a
Henry, Chris	RB	5-11	230	6/6/85	Arizona	Oakland, Calif.	D2
Jackson, Jarvis	LB	6-0	225	10/28/84	Georgia	Atlanta, Ga.	FA
Johnson, Antonio	DT	6-3	310	12/8/84	Mississippi State	Leland, Miss.	D5
Keys, Erik	S	5-10	210	12/21/83	Ball State	Indianapolis, Ind.	FA
Koral, David (1)	QB	6-2	212	11/27/82	UCLA	Santa Monia, Calif.	FA
McElveen, Jermaine	DE	6-4	263	8/29/84	Alabama-Birmingham	Atlanta, Ga.	FA
Moore, Dontrell (1)	RB	5-9	208	9/25/82	New Mexico	Hampton, Va.	FA
Nande, Terna (1)	LB	6-0	230	6/17/83	Miami (Ohio)	Grand Rapids, Mich.	D5a-'06
Otto, Mike	T	6-5	308	7/24/83	Purdue	Kokomo, Ind.	D7
Pakulak, Glenn (1)	P	6-3	220	4/9/80	Kentucky	Lapeer, Mich.	FA
Petrowski, Jamie (1)	TE	6-4	250	7/12/82	Indiana State	Terre Haute, Ind.	FA-'06
Pullum, Barron	LB	6-3	225	6/1/85	Mississippi Valley State	Jackson, Miss.	FA
Ross, Richie (1)	WR	6-4	208	9/28/82	Nebraska-Kearney	Lincoln, Neb.	FA-'06
Sharp, Brandon	S	5-10	195	6/25/85	Louisville	Jacksonville, Fla.	FA
Smith, Kent (1)	QB	6-5	215	9/5/83	Central Michigan	Toledo, Ohio	FA
Smith, Ryan	CB	5-10	173	7/17/85	Florida	Diamond Bar, Calif.	D6c
Snell, Isaac (1)	G	6-6	288	11/4/81	North Dakota State	Pipestone, Minn.	FA-'06
Solomon, Clinton (1)	WR	6-3	214	10/21/83	Iowa	Fort Worth, Texas	FA
Stratton, Brock	LB	5-11	231	9/25/81	Texas Tech	San Antonio, Texas	FA
Toone, Spencer (1)	LB	6-2	240	8/25/80	Utah	Blackfoot, Idaho	D7b-'06
Vaughn, John	K	6-0	210	6/15/84	Auburn	Brentwood, Tenn.	FA
Wallace, Cooper (1)	TE	6-3	258	4/26/82	Auburn	Nashville, Tenn.	FA-'06
Ware, Danny	RB	6-0	225	2/18/85	Georgia	Rockmart, Ga.	FA
White, Marcus (1)	DT	6-5	303	11/13/81	Murray State	Theodore, Ala.	FA-'05
Williams, Paul	WR	6-1	205	12/2/83	Fresno State	Avenal, Calif.	D3

The term NFL Rookie is defined as a player who is in his first season of professional football and has not been on the roster of another professional football team for any regular-season or postseason games. A Rookie is designated by an "R" on NFL rosters. Players who have been active in another professional football league or players who have NFL experience, including either preseason training camp or being on an Active List or Inactive List, or on Reserve/Injured or Reserve/Physically Unable to Perform for fewer than six regular-season games, are termed NFL First-Year Players. An NFL First-Year Player is designated by a "1" on NFL rosters. Thereafter, a player is credited with an additional year of experience for each season in which he accumulates six games on the Active List or Inactive List, or on Reserve/Injured or Reserve/Physically Unable to Perform.

Log on to www.titansonline.com for an up-to-date roster.

COACHING STAFF
Head Coach,
Jeff Fisher
Pro Career: Officially became the franchise's fifteenth head coach on January 5, 1995, after closing his first campaign with the Oilers as head coach/defensive coordinator. He replaced Jack Pardee on November 14, 1994, coaching the remaining six games as head coach. Fisher holds the franchise mark for wins with 110 over his 12-year coaching career. In 2006, he became the first coach in franchise history and the 28th head coach in NFL history to reach 200 games. Only 11 other coaches in history have coached 200 games with one team. In 2005, he became the 34th coach in NFL history to reach the 100-win plateau. In 2004, he became the fourth youngest coach (46) since 1960 to reach 90 regular-season victories (John Madden, Don Shula, and Bill Cowher). Over the last eight seasons, Fisher has led the Titans to four playoff appearances, two AFC Championship Games, two division titles and a berth in Super Bowl XXXIV. In 2000, Fisher became only the fifth coach in NFL history to lead his team to consecutive 13-win seasons, joining Mike Holmgren, George Seifert, Marv Levy, and Mike Ditka. Fisher originally joined the Oilers in 1994 as the defensive coordinator, after serving as defensive backs coach for the San Francisco 49ers (1992-93). Prior to heading up the 49ers secondary, Fisher served as the defensive coordinator for the Los Angeles Rams (1991). He began his coaching career with the Philadelphia Eagles in 1986, where he handled defensive backs until becoming the NFL's youngest defensive coordinator in 1988. Drafted by Chicago in seventh round in 1981, he spent five seasons as a cornerback and kick returner for the Bears (1981-85). Assisted defensive coordinator Buddy Ryan in Bears' 1985 Super Bowl championship season after being placed on injured reserve with ankle injury. Career record: 110-97.
Background: Played at Southern California (1977-1980) for John Robinson in a star-studded defensive backfield that included Ronnie Lott, Dennis Smith, and Joey Browner. Member of the USC team that won the national championship in 1978. Also served as the Trojans' backup placekicker and was a Pac-10 All-Academic selection in 1980.
Personal: Born February 25, 1958, in Culver City, Calif. Jeff and his wife, Juli, have three children, sons Brandon and Trenton, and daughter Tara.

ASSISTANT COACHES
Matt Burke, defensive assistant/quality control, born March 25, 1976, Hudson, Mass. Safety Dartmouth 1994-97. No pro playing experience. College coach: Boston College 2000-02, Harvard 2003.

Pro coach: Joined Titans in 2006.
Chuck Cecil, defensive backs; born November 8, 1964, Red Bluff, Calif. Defensive back Arizona 1983-87. Pro safety Green Bay Packers 1988-1992, Phoenix Cardinals 1993, Houston Oilers 1995. Pro coach: Joined Titans in 2001.
Norm Chow, offensive coordinator; born May 3, 1946, Honolulu, Hawaii. Guard Utah 1965-67. No pro playing experience. College coach: Brigham Young 1973-1999, North Carolina State 2000, Southern California 2001-04. Pro coach: Joined Titans in 2005.
Marty Galbraith, asst. special teams; born February 3, 1950, Joplin, Mo. Defensive back Missouri Southern 1971-73. No pro playing experience. College coach: Purdue 1977, Wake Forest 1978-1982, Louisiana State 1987-88, Wake Forest 1989-1990, Pittsburgh 1991, Georgia Tech 1992-93, Marshall 1998-99, North Carolina State 2000-02, Duke 2004. Pro coach: Tampa Bay Bandits (USFL) 1983-84, Kansas City Chiefs 1985, Arizona Outlaws (USFL) 1986, Arizona Cardinals 2003, joined Titans in 2005.
Fred Graves, wide receivers; born March 2, 1950, Los Angeles, Calif. Halfback/split end Utah 1968-1971. Pro halfback California Suns 1973 (World Football League). College coach: Northeast Missouri State 1975-76, Western Illinois 1977-78, New Mexico State 1979-1981, Utah 1982-2000. Pro coach: Buffalo Bills 2001-03, Cleveland Browns 2004, Detroit Lions 2005, joined Titans in 2007.
Craig Johnson, quarterbacks; born March 3, 1960, Rome, N.Y. Quarterback Wyoming 1978-1982. No pro playing experience. College coach: Wyoming 1983, Arkansas 1984, Army 1985, Rutgers 1986-88, Virginia Military Institute 1989-1991, Northwestern 1992-96, Maryland 1997-99. Pro coach: Joined Titans in 2000.
Alan Lowry, special teams; born November 21, 1950, Miami, Okla. Defensive back/quarterback Texas 1970-72. No pro playing experience. College coach: Virginia Tech 1974, Wyoming 1975, Texas 1977-1981. Pro coach: Dallas Cowboys 1982-1990, Tampa Bay Buccaneers 1991, San Francisco 49ers 1992-95, joined Titans/Oilers in 1996.
Dave McGinnis, linebackers; born August 7, 1951, Independence, Kan. Defensive back Texas Christian 1970-72. No pro playing experience. College coach: Texas Christian 1973-74, 1982, Missouri 1975-77, Indiana State 1978, 1980-81, Kansas State 1983-85. Pro coach: Chicago Bears 1986-1995, Arizona Cardinals 1996-2003 (head coach 2000-2003), joined Titans in 2004.
Mike Munchak, offensive line; born March 5, 1960, Scranton, Pa. Guard-tackle Penn State 1979-1981. Pro guard Houston Oilers 1982-1993. Inducted into

Pro Football Hall of Fame 2001. Pro coach: Joined Titans/Oilers in 1994.
Marcus Robertson, asst. secondary; born October 2, 1969, Pasadena, Calif. Defensive back Iowa State 1987-1990. Pro safety Houston Oilers/Tennessee Titans 1991-2000, Seattle Seahawks 2001-02. Pro coach: Joined Titans in 2007.
Jim Schwartz, defensive coordinator; born June 2, 1966, Baltimore. Linebacker Georgetown 1984-88. No pro playing experience. College coach: Maryland 1989, Minnesota 1990, North Carolina Central 1991, Colgate 1992. Pro coach: Cleveland Browns/Baltimore Ravens 1995-98, joined Titans in 1999.
Sherman Smith, asst. head coach/ offense; born November 1, 1954, Youngstown, Ohio. Quarterback Miami (Ohio) 1972-75. Pro running back Seattle Seahawks 1976-1982, San Diego Chargers 1983-84. College coach: Miami (Ohio) 1990-91, Illinois 1992-94. Pro coach: Joined Titans/Oilers in 1995.
Jim Washburn, defensive line; born December 2, 1949, Shelby, N.C. Offensive lineman Gardner-Webb 1969-1973. No pro playing experience. College coach: Southern Methodist 1976, Lees McRae (N.C.) J.C. 1977-78, Livingston 1979, New Mexico 1980-82, South Carolina 1983-88, Purdue 1989, Arkansas 1994-97, Houston 1998. Pro coach: London Monarchs (WLAF) 1991, Charlotte Rage (AFL) 1993, joined Titans in 1999.
Steve Watterson, strength and rehabilitation; born November 27, 1956, Newport, R.I. Attended Rhode Island. No college or pro playing experience. Pro coach: Philadelphia Eagles 1984-85, joined Titans/Oilers in 1986.
John Zernhelt, tight ends, born January 4, 1954, Pottsville, Pa. Offensive lineman Maryland 1974-77. No pro playing experience. College coach: Ferrum 1977-1980, Marshall 1981, East Carolina 1982-86, Maryland 1987-1991, Rice 1992-93, Duke 1994-95, South Carolina 1996-98, James Madison 1999-2002, The Citadel 2003-04. Pro coach: New York Jets 2005, joined Titans in 2006.

The NFC

National Football Conference
West Division
Team Colors: Cardinal Red, Black, and White
P.O. Box 888
Phoenix, Arizona 85001-0888
Telephone: (602) 379-0101

2007 SCHEDULE
PRESEASON
Aug. 11	at Oakland	7:00
Aug. 18	**Houston**	1:00
Aug. 25	**San Diego**	7:00
Aug. 30	at Denver	7:00

REGULAR SEASON
Sep. 10	at San Francisco (Mon.)	7:15
Sep. 16	**Seattle**	1:05
Sep. 23	at Baltimore	1:00
Sep. 30	**Pittsburgh**	1:15
Oct. 7	at St. Louis	12:00
Oct. 14	**Carolina**	1:05
Oct. 21	at Washington	1:00
Oct. 28	Open Date	
Nov. 4	at Tampa Bay	1:00
Nov. 11	**Detroit**	2:15
Nov. 18	at Cincinnati	1:00
Nov. 25	**San Francisco**	2:05
Dec. 2	**Cleveland**	2:05
Dec. 9	at Seattle	1:05
Dec. 16	at New Orleans	12:00
Dec. 23	**Atlanta**	2:05
Dec. 30	**St. Louis**	2:15

Stadium: University of Phoenix Stadium (opened in 2006)
•**Capacity:** 65,000
1 Cardinals Drive
Glendale, Arizona 85305
Playing Surface: Grass
Training Camp: Northern Arizona University Flagstaff, Arizona 86011

UNIVERSITY OF PHOENIX STADIUM

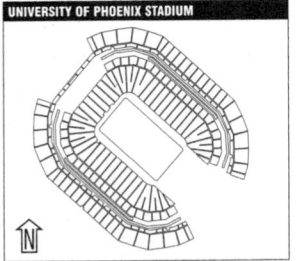

CLUB OFFICIALS
President: William V. Bidwill
Vice President/General Counsel: Michael Bidwill
Vice President: William V. Bidwill, Jr.
Vice President-Football Operations: Rod Graves
Vice President-Sales and Marketing: Ron Minegar
Chief Financial Officer: Adrian Bracy
Video Director: Benny Greenberg
Senior Director of Media Relations: Mark Dalton
Senior Director of Marketing and Promotions: Lisa Manning
Senior Director of Business Development: Steve Ryan
Senior Director of Information Technology: Mark Feller
Senior Director of Security: Rick Knight
Director of College Scouting: Steve Keim
Director of Players Programs: Anthony Edwards
Director of Community Relations: Luis Zendejas
Director of Cardinals Charities: Pat Tankersley
Director of Broadcasting/Executive Producer: Tom Hanny
Director of Ticketing: Steve Bomar
Director of Ticket Sales: Jamie Brandt
Director of Human Resources: Lisa Lutich
Director of Stadium Operations: John Drum
Director of Cheerleading: Heather Shrake
Head Trainer: John Omohundro
Assistant Trainers: Jim Shearer, Jeff Herndon, Freddie Carbajal
Equipment Manager: Mark Ahlemeier
Assistant Equipment Manager: Steve Christensen
Equipment Coordinator: Chris Janczewski

COACHING HISTORY
Chicago 1920-1959, St. Louis 1960-1987 (458-664-39)
Records include postseason games
1920-22	John (Paddy) Driscoll	17-8-4
1923-24	Arnold Horween	13-8-1
1925-26	Norman Barry	16-8-2
1927	Guy Chamberlin	3-7-1
1928	Fred Gillies	1-5-0
1929	Dewey Scanlon	6-6-1
1930	Ernie Nevers	5-6-2
1931	LeRoy Andrews*	0-1-0
1931	Ernie Nevers	5-3-0
1932	Jack Chevigny	2-6-2
1933-34	Paul Schissler	6-15-1
1935-38	Milan Creighton	16-26-4
1939	Ernie Nevers	1-10-0
1940-42	Jimmy Conzelman	8-22-3
1943-45	Phil Handler**	1-29-0
1946-48	Jimmy Conzelman	27-10-0
1949	Phil Handler-Buddy Parker***	2-4-0
1949	Raymond (Buddy) Parker	4-1-1
1950-51	Earl (Curly) Lambeau****	7-15-0
1951	Phil Handler-Cecil Isbell#	1-1-0
1952	Joe Kuharich	4-8-0
1953-54	Joe Stydahar	3-20-1
1955-57	Ray Richards	14-21-1
1958-1961	Frank (Pop) Ivy##	15-31-2
1961	Chuck Drulis-Ray Prochaska-Ray Willsey###	2-0-0
1962-65	Wally Lemm	27-26-3
1966-1970	Charley Winner	35-30-5
1971-72	Bob Hollway	8-18-2
1973-77	Don Coryell	42-29-1
1978-79	Bud Wilkinson####	9-20-0
1979	Larry Wilson	2-1-0
1980-85	Jim Hanifan	39-50-1
1986-89	Gene Stallings@	23-34-1
1989	Hank Kuhlmann	0-5-0
1990-93	Joe Bugel	20-44-0
1994-95	Buddy Ryan	12-20-0
1996-2000	Vince Tobin@@	29-44-0
2000-03	Dave McGinnis	17-40-0
2004-06	Dennis Green	16-32-0

     * Resigned after one game in 1931
    ** Co-coach with Walt Kiesling in Chicago Cardinals-Pittsburgh merger in 1944
  *** Co-coaches for first six games in 1949
 **** Resigned after 10 games in 1951
     # Co-coaches
    ## Resigned after 12 games in 1961
  ### Co-coaches
Released after 13 games in 1979
     @ Released after 11 games in 1989
  @@ Released after seven games in 2000

PAID ATTENDANCE
Home 496,501   Away 521,185
Total 1,017,686
Single-game home record, 73,025* (9/19/93)
Single-season home record, 508,829 (2006)
*Team holds NFL attendance record of 103,467 for home game at Azteca Stadium, Mexico City, Mexico

2007 DRAFT CHOICES
Round	Name	Pos.	College
1	Levi Brown	T	Penn State
2	Alan Branch	DT	Michigan
3	Buster Davis	LB	Florida State
5	Steve Breaston	WR	Michigan
7	Ben Patrick	TE	Delaware

2006 TEAM RECORD
PRESEASON (2-2)

Date	Result	Opponent
8/12	W 21-13	Pittsburgh
8/19	L 3-30	at New England
8/25	W 23-16	at Chicago
8/31	L 23-29	Denver

REGULAR SEASON (5-11)

Date	Result	Opponent	Att.
9/10	W 34-27	San Francisco	63,407
9/17	L 10-21	at Seattle	67,470
9/24	L 14-16	St. Louis	63,278
10/1	L 10-32	at Atlanta	68,981
10/8	L 20-23	Kansas City	63,445
10/16	L 23-24	Chicago	63,977
10/22	L 9-22	at Oakland	61,595
10/29	L 14-31	at Green Bay	70,809
11/12	L 10-27	Dallas	63,926
11/19	W 17-10	Detroit	63,348
11/26	L 26-31	at Minnesota	63,483
12/3	W 34-20	at St. Louis	65,612
12/10	W 27-21	Seattle	63,603
12/17	L 20-37	Denver	63,845
12/24	W 26-20	at San Francisco	67,751
12/31	L 20-27	at San Diego	66,492

SCORE BY PERIODS

Cardinals	104	81	46	83	0 —	314
Opponents	84	100	100	105	0 —	389

2006 TEAM STATISTICS

	Cardinals	Opp.
Total First Downs	298	331
Rushing	84	114
Passing	187	186
Penalty	27	31
3rd Down: Made/Att	83/212	83/201
3rd Down Pct.	39.2	41.3
4th Down: Made/Att	10/15	7/15
4th Down Pct.	66.7	46.7
Possession Avg.	29:59	30:01
Total Net Yards	5000	5591
Avg. Per Game	312.5	349.4
Total Plays	999	1018
Avg. Per Play	5.0	5.5
Net Yards Rushing	1338	1897
Avg. Per Game	83.6	118.6
Total Rushes	419	458
Net Yards Passing	3662	3694
Avg. Per Game	228.9	230.9
Sacked/Yards Lost	35/262	38/238
Gross Yards	3924	3932
Att./Completions	545/322	522/321
Completion Pct.	59.1	61.5
Had Intercepted	17	16
Punts/Average	68/43.6	58/44.8
Net Punting Avg.	68/34.5	58/37.7
Penalties/Yards	117/937	95/815
Fumbles/Ball Lost	31/13	29/17
Touchdowns	33	42
Rushing	12	16
Passing	17	21
Returns	4	5

2006 INDIVIDUAL STATISTICS

PASSING

PASSING	Att.	Comp.	Yds.	Pct.	TD	Int.	Tkld.	Rate
Leinart	377	214	2,547	56.8	11	12	21/158	74.0
Warner	168	108	1,377	64.3	6	5	14/104	89.3
Cardinals	545	322	3,924	59.1	17	17	35/262	78.7
Opponents	522	321	3,932	61.5	21	16	38/238	85.4

SCORING

SCORING	TD R	TD P	TD Rt	PAT	FG	Saf	PTS
Rackers	0	0	0	32/32	28/37	0	116
Fitzgerald	0	6	0	0/0	0/0	0	36
James	6	0	0	0/0	0/0	0	36
Boldin	0	4	0	0/0	0/0	0	24
Bry. Johnson	0	4	0	0/0	0/0	0	24
Shipp	4	0	0	0/0	0/0	0	24
Leinart	2	0	0	0/0	0/0	0	12
Walters	0	2	0	0/0	0/0	0	12
Wilson	0	0	2	0/0	0/0	0	12
Arrington	0	0	1	0/0	0/0	0	6
Bergen	0	1	0	0/0	0/0	0	6
Smith	0	0	1	0/0	0/0	0	6
Cardinals	12	17	4	32/32	28/37	0	314
Opponents	16	21	5	42/42	31/34	1	389

2-Pt. Conversions:
Cardinals 0-1, Opponents 0-0

RUSHING

RUSHING	Att.	Yds.	Avg.	LG	TD
James	337	1159	3.4	18	6
Leinart	22	49	2.2	14	2
Shipp	17	41	2.4	9t	4
Ayanbadejo	9	37	4.1	11	0
Boldin	5	28	5.6	18	0
Arrington	14	19	1.4	9	0
Schable	1	5	5.0	5	0
Warner	13	3	0.2	9	0
Bry. Johnson	1	-3	-3.0	-3	0
Cardinals	419	1338	3.2	18	12
Opponents	458	1897	4.1	78t	16

RECEIVING

RECEIVING	No.	Yds	Avg	LG	TD
Boldin	83	1203	14.5	64	4
Fitzgerald	69	946	13.7	57	6
Bry. Johnson	40	740	18.5	58	4
James	38	217	5.7	14	0
Walters	23	209	9.1	26	2
Ayanbadejo	17	139	8.2	27	0
Pope	16	161	10.1	33	0
Bergen	15	111	7.4	17	1
Arrington	8	58	7.3	19	0
Shipp	6	60	10.0	22	0
Spurlock	4	31	7.8	15	0
Wakefield	2	24	12.0	19	0
Bronson	1	25	25.0	25	0
Cardinals	322	3924	12.2	64	17
Opponents	321	3932	12.2	78	21

INTERCEPTIONS

INTERCEPTIONS	No.	Yds	Avg	LG	TD
Wilson	4	146	36.5	99t	1
Griffith	3	30	10.0	23	0
Hayes	3	24	8.0	24	0
Francisco	2	61	30.5	44	0
Macklin	1	56	56.0	56	0
Rolle	1	23	23.0	23	0
Beisel	1	11	11.0	11	0
Dockett	1	-1	-1.0	-1	0
Cardinals	16	350	21.9	99t	1
Opponents	17	110	6.5	37t	1

PUNTING

PUNTING	No.	Yds.	Avg.	In 20	LG
Player	66	2965	44.9	18	58
Cardinals	68	2965	43.6	18	58
Opponents	58	2596	44.8	18	66

PUNT RETURNS

PUNT RETURNS	Ret	FC	Yds	Avg	LG	TD
Walters	24	12	250	10.4	37	0
Bry. Johnson	1	1	0	0.0	0	0
Cardinals	25	13	250	10.0	37	0
Opponents	44	6	562	12.8	83t	1

KICKOFF RETURNS

KICKOFF RETURNS	No.	Yds	Avg	LG	TD
Arrington	67	1520	22.7	99t	1
Spurlock	3	54	18.0	21	0
Bry. Johnson	2	29	14.5	16	0
Wakefield	1	7	7.0	7	0
Cardinals	73	1610	22.1	99t	1
Opponents	58	1481	25.5	64	0

FIELD GOALS

FIELD GOALS	1-19	20-29	30-39	40-49	50+
Rackers	0/0	11/11	9/9	7/10	1/7
Cardinals	0/0	11/11	9/9	7/10	1/7
Opponents	1/1	9/9	11/13	9/9	1/2

SACKS

SACKS	No.
Okeafor	8.5
Dansby	8.0
Berry	6.0
Wilson	5.0
Smith	2.5
Cooper	2.0
Dockett	2.0
Clancy	1.0
Hayes	1.0
Pace	1.0
Watson	1.0
Cardinals	38.0
Opponents	35.0

RECORD HOLDERS
INDIVIDUAL RECORDS—CAREER

Category	Name	Performance
Rushing (Yds.)	Ottis Anderson, 1979-1986	7,999
Passing (Yds.)	Jim Hart, 1966-1983	34,639
Passing (TDs)	Jim Hart, 1966-1983	209
Receiving (No.)	Larry Centers, 1990-98	535
Receiving (Yds.)	Roy Green, 1979-1990	8,497
Interceptions	Larry Wilson, 1960-1972	52
Punting (Avg.)	Jerry Norton, 1959-1961	44.9
Punt Return (Avg.)	Charley Trippi, 1947-1955	13.7
Kickoff Return (Avg.)	Ollie Matson, 1952, 1954-58	28.5
Field Goals	Jim Bakken, 1962-1978	282
Touchdowns (Tot.)	Roy Green, 1979-1990	70
Points	Jim Bakken, 1962-1978	1,380

INDIVIDUAL RECORDS—SINGLE SEASON

Category	Name	Performance
Rushing (Yds.)	Ottis Anderson, 1979	1,605
Passing (Yds.)	Neil Lomax, 1984	4,614
Passing (TDs)	Charley Johnson, 1963	28
	Neil Lomax, 1984	28
Receiving (No.)	Larry Fitzgerald, 2005	103
Receiving (Yds.)	David Boston, 2001	1,598
Interceptions	Bob Nussbaumer, 1949	12
Punting (Avg.)	Jerry Norton, 1960	45.6
Punt Return (Avg.)	John (Red) Cochran, 1949	20.9
Kickoff Return (Avg.)	Ollie Matson, 1958	35.5
Field Goals	Neil Rackers, 2005	*40
Touchdowns (Tot.)	John David Crow, 1962	17
Points	Neil Rackers, 2005	140

INDIVIDUAL RECORDS—SINGLE GAME

Category	Name	Performance
Rushing (Yds.)	LeShon Johnson, 9-22-96	214
Passing (Yds.)	Boomer Esiason, 11-10-96 (OT)	522
Passing (TDs)	Jim Hardy, 10-2-50	6
	Charley Johnson, 9-26-65, 11-2-69	6
Receiving (No.)	Sonny Randle, 11-4-62	16
Receiving (Yds.)	Sonny Randle, 11-4-62	256
Interceptions	Bob Nussbaumer, 11-13-49	*4
	Jerry Norton, 11-20-60	*4
	Kwamie Lassiter, 12-27-98	*4
Field Goals	Jim Bakken, 9-24-67	*7
Touchdowns (Tot.)	Ernie Nevers, 11-28-29	*6
Points	Ernie Nevers, 11-28-29	*40

*NFL Record

2007 VETERAN ROSTER

No.	Name	Pos.	Ht.	Wt.	Birthdate	NFL Exp.	College	Hometown	How Acq.	'06 Games/ Starts
28	Arrington, J.J.	RB	5-9	218	1/23/83	3	California	Nashville, N.C.	D2-'05	16/0
30	Ayanbadejo, Obafemi	FB	6-2	230	3/5/75	9	San Diego State	Santa Cruz, Calif.	UFA(Mia)-'04	14/0
91	Bailey, Rodney	DE	6-3	305	10/7/79	7	Ohio State	Cleveland, Ohio	UFA(Pitt)-'07	12/0*
52	Beisel, Monty	LB	6-3	240	8/20/78	7	Kansas State	Douglass, Kan.	FA-'06	8/2
92	Berry, Bertrand	DE	6-3	270	8/15/75	10	Notre Dame	Houston, Texas	UFA(Den)-'04	10/10
55	Blackstock, Darryl	LB	6-3	240	5/30/83	3	Virginia	Newport News, Va.	D3b-'05	16/1
81	Boldin, Anquan	WR	6-1	223	10/3/80	5	Florida State	Pahokee, Fla.	D2-'03	16/16
39	Bronson, John	TE	6-3	275	7/8/82	3	Penn State	Kent, Wash.	FA-'05	2/0
61	Brown, Elton	G	6-5	340	5/22/82	3	Virginia	Hampton, Va.	D4-'05	0*
67	Brown, Milford	G	6-5	330	8/15/80	6	Florida State	Montgomery, Ala.	UFA(Hou)-'06	13/12
20	Brown, Ralph	CB	5-10	185	9/16/78	8	Nebraska	LaPuenta, Calif.	UFA(Cle)-'07	16/4*
70	Clancy, Kendrick	DT	6-1	305	9/17/78	8	Mississippi	Tuscaloosa, Ala.	UFA(NYG)-'06	11/11
93	Cooper, Chris	DT/DE	6-5	285	12/27/77	6	Nebraska-Omaha	Rochester, Minn.	FA-'06	13/0
58	Dansby, Karlos	LB	6-4	240	11/3/81	4	Auburn	Birmingham, Ala.	D2-'04	14/10
90	Dockett, Darnell	DT	6-4	290	5/27/81	4	Florida State	Burtonsville, Md.	D3-'04	16/16
11	Fitzgerald, Larry	WR	6-3	226	8/31/83	4	Pittsburgh	Minneapolis, Minn.	D1-'04	13/13
47	Francisco, Aaron	S	6-2	212	7/5/83	3	Brigham Young	Laie, Hawaii	FA-'05	16/2
69	Gandy, Mike	T	6-4	310	1/3/79	7	Notre Dame	Dallas, Texas	UFA(Buff)-'07	16/16*
72	Gorin, Brandon	T	6-6	308	7/17/78	6	Purdue	Muncie, Ind.	T(NE)-'06	0*
25	Green, Eric	CB	5-11	194	3/16/82	3	Virginia Tech	Pahokee, Fla.	D3a-'05	15/8
54	Hayes, Gerald	LB	6-1	253	10/10/80	5	Pittsburgh	Paterson, N.J.	D3-'03	14/14
48	Hodel, Nathan	LS	6-2	242	11/12/77	6	Illinois	Fairview Heights, Ill.	FA-'01	16/0
42	Holt, Terrence	S	6-2	208	3/5/80	5	North Carolina State	Gibsonville, N.C.	UFA(Det)-'07	16/15*
26	Hood, Roderick	CB	5-11	196	10/3/81	5	Auburn	Columbus, Ga.	UFA(Phil)-'07	10/5*
23	Hunter, Darrell	CB	6-1	206	11/29/83	2	Miami (Ohio)	Middletown, Ohio	FA-'06	3/0
32	James, Edgerrin	RB	6-0	220	8/1/78	9	Miami	Immokalee, Fla.	UFA(Ind)-'06	16/16
50	Johnson, Al	C	6-5	311	1/27/79	5	Wisconsin	Brussels, Wis.	UFA(Dall)-'07	16/0*
59	Johnson, Brandon	LB	6-5	224	5/5/83	2	Louisville	Birmingham, Ala.	D5-'06	3/0
80	Johnson, Bryant	WR	6-3	216	3/7/81	5	Penn State	Baltimore, Md.	D1a-'03	16/8
96	Kolodziej, Ross	DT	6-3	292	5/11/78	7	Wisconsin	Plover, Wis.	UFA(Minn)-'07	12/0*
60	Leckey, Nick	C	6-3	291	3/12/82	4	Kansas State	Grapevine, Texas	D6-04	14/11
7	Leinart, Matt	QB	6-5	230	5/11/83	2	Southern California	Santa Ana, Calif.	D1-'06	12/11
95	Lewis, Jonathan	DT	6-1	312	7/12/84	2	Virginia Tech	Richmond, Va.	D6-06	4/0
76	Lutui, Deuce	G	6-4	338	5/5/83	2	Southern California	Mesa, Ariz.	D2-'06	15/9
19	McCoy, LeRon	WR	6-1	219	1/24/82	3	Indiana (Pa.)	Harrisburg, Pa.	D7-'05	0*
86	Merritt, Ahmad	WR	5-10	195	2/5/77	4	Wisconsin	Chicago, Ill.	FA-'07	0*
37	Milligan, Hanik	S	6-3	200	11/3/79	5	Houston	Coconut Creek, Fla.	W(SD)-'06	16/0
73	Mitchell, Qasim	T	6-5	347	12/3/79	5	North Carolina A&T	Jacksonville, N.C.	FA-'07	0*
87	Morey, Sean	WR	5-11	200	2/26/76	6	Brown	Marshfield, Mass.	UFA(Pitt)-'07	16/0*
56	Okeafor, Chike	DE	6-5	265	3/27/76	9	Purdue	Grand Rapids, Mich.	UFA(Sea)-'05	16/15
97	Pace, Calvin	LB	6-4	272	10/28/80	5	Wake Forest	Douglasville, Ga.	D1b-'03	16/5
10	Player, Scott	P	6-1	206	12/17/69	10	Florida State	St. Augustine, Fla.	FA-'98	16/0
82	Pope, Leonard	TE	6-8	265	9/9/83	2	Georgia	Americus, Ga.	D3-'06	16/6
1	Rackers, Neil	K	6-1	212	8/16/76	8	Illinois	St. Louis, Mo.	FA-'03	16/0
21	Rolle, Antrel	CB	6-0	208	12/16/82	3	Miami	Homestead, Fla.	D1-'05	16/16
79	Ross, Oliver	T	6-4	327	9/27/74	9	Iowa State	Los Angeles, Calif.	UFA(Pitt)-'05	11/5
44	Schable, A.J.	FB	6-3	281	5/18/84	2	South Dakota	Ida Grove, Iowa	FA-'06	11/0
31	Shipp, Marcel	RB	5-11	232	8/8/78	7	Massachusetts	Paterson, N.J.	FA-'01	15/0
94	Smith, Antonio	DE	6-4	280	10/21/81	4	Oklahoma State	Oklahoma City, Okla.	D5-'04	16/8
15	Spurlock, Michael	WR	5-10	214	1/31/83	2	Mississippi	Indianola, Miss.	FA-'06	1/0
71	Tafoya, Joe	DE	6-4	265	9/6/78	6	Arizona	Pittsburg, Calif.	UFA(Sea)-'07	13/0*
22	Ware, Matt	CB	6-2	210	12/2/82	4	UCLA	Los Angeles, Calif.	W(Phil)-'06	14/1
13	Warner, Kurt	QB	6-2	222	6/22/71	10	Northern Iowa	Burlington, Iowa	UFA(NYG)-'05	6/5
98	Watson, Gabe	DT	6-3	340	9/24/83	2	Michigan	Southfield, Mich.	D4-'06	12/5
74	Wells, Reggie	G/T	6-4	318	11/3/80	5	Clarion (Pa.)	Library, Pa.	D6a-'03	16/16
24	Wilson, Adrian	S	6-3	230	10/12/79	7	North Carolina State	High Point, N.C.	D3-'01	16/16

* Bailey played 12 games with Pittsburgh in '06; E. Brown inactive for 16 games; R. Brown played 16 games with Cleveland; Gandy played 16 games with Buffalo; Gorin did not play in 2 games; Holt playd 16 games with Detroit; Hood played 10 games with Philadelphia; A. Johnson played 16 games with Dallas; Kolodziej played 12 games with Minnesota; McCoy missed '06 season because of injury; Merritt last active with Chicago in '03; Morey played 16 games with Pittsburgh; Tafoya played 13 games with Seattle.

Players lost through free agency (4): T Leonard Davis (Dall; 16 games in '06), G Chris Liwenski (Mia; 16), CB David Macklin (Wash; 14), TE Fred Wakefield (Oak; 16).

Also played with Cardinals in '06—TE Adam Bergen (14 games), LB James Darling (3), RB Diamond Ferri (3), S Robert Griffith (16), WR Carlyle Holiday (4), LB Orlando Huff (10), DT Langston Moore (3), C Alex Stepanovich (5), CB Robert Tate (9), WR Troy Walters (15).

2007 FIRST-YEAR ROSTER

Name	Pos.	Ht.	Wt.	Birthdate	College	Hometown	How Acq.
Adams, Michael	CB	5-8	178	6/17/85	Louisiana-Lafayette	Dallas, Texas	FA
Bain, Travarous	CB	6-0	175	10/15/83	Hampton	Miami, Fla.	FA
Baylark, Steve	RB	6-0	225	7/28/83	Massachusetts	Apopka, Fla.	FA
Bienemann, Troy (1)	TE	6-5	242	2/18/83	Washington State	Mountain View, Calif.	FA
Blagman, Ray	DT	6-2	321	6/1/84	Connecticut	Roosevelt, N.Y.	FA
Boyd, Shane (1)	QB	6-1	232	9/18/82	Kentucky	Lexington, Ky.	FA-'06
Branch, Alan	DT	6-5	334	12/29/84	Michigan	Rio Rancho, N.M.	D2
Breaston, Steve	WR	6-0	193	8/20/83	Michigan	North Braddock, Pa.	D5
Brown, Levi	T	6-5	323	3/16/84	Penn State	Norfolk, Va.	D1
Castille, Tim	FB	5-11	234	5/29/84	Alabama	Birmingham, Ala.	FA
Davis, Buster	LB	5-9	239	10/20/83	Florida State	Daytona Beach, Fla.	D3
Downing, T.J.	G	6-4	305	3/6/84	Ohio State	Canton, Ohio	FA
Gulley, Will	FS	6-3	220	4/20/84	Houston	Newton, Texas	FA
Hamesiter-Ries, Jon	G	6-6	308	1/26/84	Tulsa	Edmonton, Alberta, Canada	FA
Holloway, David	LB	6-2	230	12/4/83	Maryland	Stephentown, N.Y.	FA
Johnson, Brian	G	6-4	307	3/24/84	Louisiana State	Tallahassee, Fla.	FA
Keeler, Brandon	S	6-3	215	8/17/84	Eastern Washington	Federal Way, Wash.	FA
Korrodi, Toby	QB	6-3	233	9/20/83	Central Missouri	San Antonio, Texas	FA
Lee, Greg (1)	WR	6-1	201	10/19/84	Pittsburgh	Tampa, Fla.	FA-'06
Patrick, Ben	TE	6-3	252	8/23/84	Delaware	Savannah, Ga.	D7
Prall, Evan	WR	5-11	185	12/27/83	East Stroudsburg	Scranton, PA	FA
Schmitt, Ricky	P/K	6-2	192	8/17/85	Shepherd	Virginia Beach, Va.	FA
Sendlein, Lyle	G	6-2	305	3/16/84	Texas	Scottsdale, Ariz.	FA
Shor, Alex (1)	TE	6-7	250	1/29/83	Syracuse	Panama City, Fla.	FA-'06
Snow, BranDon	FB	6-0	242	6/9/83	Penn State	Wilmington, Del.	FA
Togafau, Pago	LB	5-10	250	1/10/84	Idaho State	Long Beach, Calif.	FA
Trannon, Matt	WR	6-6	235	7/7/83	Michigan State	Flint, Mich.	FA
Vallejo, Elliott	T	6-7	315	5/17/84	California-Davis	Salinas, Calif.	FA
Vercher, Roshon	FB	5-11	245	12/15/83	Fresno State	Bakersfield, Calif.	FA
Watkins, Todd (1)	WR	6-2	191	6/22/83	Brigham Young	San Diego, Calif.	D7-'06
Wyatt, Justin (1)	CB	5-9	193	1/27/84	Southern California	Compton, Calif.	FA-'06

The term NFL Rookie is defined as a player who is in his first season of professional football and has not been on the roster of another professional football team for any regular-season or postseason games. A Rookie is designated by an "R" on NFL rosters. Players who have been active in another professional football league or players who have NFL experience, including either preseason training camp or being on an Active List or Inactive List, or on Reserve/Injured or Reserve/Physically Unable to Perform for fewer than six regular-season games, are termed NFL First-Year Players. An NFL First-Year Player is designated by a "1" on NFL rosters. Thereafter, a player is credited with an additional year of experience for each season in which he accumulates six games on the Active List or Inactive List, or on Reserve/Injured or Reserve/Physically Unable to Perform.

Log on to www.azcardinals.com for an up-to-date roster.

COACHING STAFF

Head Coach,
Ken Whisenhunt

Pro Career: Became an NFL head coach for the first time when hired by Arizona on January 14, 2007. Comes to the Cardinals with 10 years of experience as an NFL assistant coach and also played nine seasons in the league as a tight end. Whisenhunt spent the previous six seasons as an assistant on Bill Cowher's staff with the Pittsburgh Steelers, the first three as tight ends coach and the last three as offensive coordinator. Whisenhunt took over as Pittsburgh's offensive coordinator in 2004, the same year the team drafted quarterback Ben Roethlisberger, who went on to set an NFL record with wins in his first 13 career starts en route to Offensive Rookie of the Year honors. The next season he became the youngest quarterback in NFL history to win a Super Bowl and finished third in the league in passer rating (98.6). In Whisenhunt's first year as coordinator, the Steelers rushing attack improved from thirty-first to second and the overall offense ranked sixteenth. His second year ended with an NFL title after the Steelers offense averaged 26.8 points per game in the playoffs. He joined the Steelers in January of 2001 as tight ends coach. Whisenhunt previously coached at the pro level with the New York Jets (tight ends, 2000), Cleveland Browns (special teams, 1999) and Baltimore Ravens (tight ends, 1997-98). He began his coaching career in the collegiate ranks with Vanderbilt for two seasons (1995-96). Whisenhunt was selected in the 12th round of the 1985 NFL Draft by the Atlanta Falcons out of Georgia Tech. He went on to play nine NFL seasons with the Falcons (1985-88), Washington Redskins (1989-90), and New York Jets (1991-93). In 74 career games (37 starts), he caught 62 passes for 601 yards and 6 touchdowns. Career record: 0-0.

Background: After going to Georgia Tech as a walk-on, he played four seasons as a tight end/H-back. He finished his college playing career ranked second on the Yellow Jackets' receiving yardage list (1,264 yards) and fourth in career receptions (82). Whisenhunt was a consensus All-ACC and honorable mention All-America selection as a senior in 1984 when he averaged 19.1 yards-per-catch.

Personal: Born February 28, 1962 in Atlanta. Whisenhunt earned a degree in civil engineering from Georgia Tech. Ken and his wife, Alice, have two children—son, Kenneth, Jr. and daughter, Mary Ashley.

ASSISTANT COACHES

Ron Aiken, defensive line; born August 18, 1955, Moncks Corner, S.C. Guard/center North Carolina A&T 1973-76. No pro playing experience. College coach: Bethany College 1979-1981, Tarkio College 1982-84, Rensselaer Polytechnic Institute 1985, Langston 1986-89, New Mexico 1990-94, Vanderbilt 1995-96, Texas 1997, San Diego State 1998, Iowa 1999-2006. Pro coach: Joined Cardinals in 2007.

Teryl Austin, defensive backs; born March 3, 1965, Sharon, Pa. Defensive back Pittsburgh 1984-87. Pro defensive back Montreal Machine (WLAF) 1991. College coach: Penn State 1991-92, Wake Forest 1993-95, Syracuse 1996-98, Michigan 1999-2002. Pro coach: Seattle Seahawks 2003-06, joined Cardinals in 2007.

Maurice Carthon, running backs; born April 24, 1961, Chicago. Running back Arkansas State 1979-1982. Pro running back New Jersey Generals (USFL) 1983-85, New York Giants 1985-1991, Indianapolis Colts 1992. Pro coach: New England Patriots 1994-96, New York Jets 1997-2000, Detroit Lions 2001-02, Dallas Cowboys 2003-04, Cleveland Browns 2005-06, joined Cardinals in 2007.

Rick Courtright, asst. defensive backs; born January 4, 1961, Miami. Linebacker Wheaton College 1980-83. No pro playing experience. College coach: Washington 1991-92, Minnesota-Morris 1993, Ohio 1994, Idaho State 1995, Idaho 1996-99, Murray State 2000, Western Illinois 2001-03. Pro coach: Joined Cardinals in 2004.

Billy Davis, linebackers; born November 5, 1965, Youngstown, Ohio. Quarterback Cincinnati 1985-88. College coach: Michigan State 1990-91. Pro coach: Pittsburgh Steelers 1992-94, Carolina Panthers 1995-98, Cleveland Browns 1999, Green Bay Packers 2000, Atlanta Falcons 2001-03, New York Giants 2004, San Francisco 49ers 2005-06, joined Cardinals in 2007.

Russ Grimm, asst. head coach/offensive line; born May 2, 1959, Scottdale, Pa. Center Pittsburgh 1977-1980. Pro guard Washington Redskins 1981-1991. Pro coach: Washington Redskins 1992-2000, Pittsburgh Steelers 2001-06, joined Cardinals in 2007.

Todd Haley, offensive coordinator; born February 28, 1967, Atlanta. Attended Florida and Miami. No college or pro playing experience. Pro coach: New York Jets 1997-2000, Chicago Bears 2001-03, Dallas Cowboys 2004-06, joined Cardinals in 2007.

Freddie Kitchens, tight ends; born November 29, 1974, Gadsden, Ala. Quarterback Alabama 1994-97. No pro playing experience. College coach: Glenville State College 1999, Louisiana State 2000, North Texas 2001-03, Mississippi State 2004-05. Pro coach: Dallas Cowboys 2006, joined Cardinals in 2007.

John Lott, strength and conditioning; born May 9, 1964, Denton, Texas. Offensive lineman North Texas 1983-86. Pro offensive lineman Pittsburgh Steelers 1987. College coach: Texas 1988, North Texas 1989-1990, Houston 1991-96. Pro coach: New York Jets 1997-2004, Cleveland Browns 2005-06, joined Cardinals in 2007.

Mike Miller, wide receivers; born April 9, 1970, Plum Borough, Pa. Attended Clarion. No college or pro playing experience. College coach: Robert Morris 1997-98, 2006. Pro coach: Pittsburgh Steelers 1999-2003, Buffalo Bills 2004-05, Berlin Thunder (NFLE) 2006, joined Cardinals in 2007.

Clancy Pendergast, defensive coordinator; born November 29, 1967, Phoenix. Attended Arizona. No college or pro playing experience. College coach: Mississippi State 1991, Southern California 1992, Oklahoma 1993-94, Alabama-Birmingham 1995. Pro coach: Houston Oilers 1995, Dallas Cowboys 1996-2002, Cleveland Browns 2003, joined Cardinals in 2004.

Matt Raich, defensive assistant; born August 16, 1970, Monaca, Pa. Middle linebacker Westminster College 1989-1992. No pro playing experience. College coach: Westminster 1993-94, Robert Morris 1996-98, 2000-02, Glenville State 1999. Pro coach: Pittsburgh Steelers 2004-06, joined Cardinals in 2007.

Jeff Rutledge, quarterbacks; born January 22, 1957, Birmingham, Ala. Quarterback Alabama 1975-78. Pro quarterback Los Angeles Rams 1979-1981, New York Giants 1982-89, Washington Redskins 1990-92. College coach: Vanderbilt 1995-2001. Pro coach: Joined Cardinals in 2007.

Kevin Spencer, special teams; born November 2, 1953, Queens, N.Y. Outside linebacker Springfield College 1971. No pro playing experience. College coach: SUNY-Cortland 1975-76, Cornell 1979-1980, Ithaca 1981-86, Wesleyan 1987-1991. Pro coach: Cleveland Browns 1991-94, Oakland Raiders 1995-97, Indianapolis Colts 1998-2001, Pittsburgh Steelers 2002-06, joined Cardinals in 2007.

Keith Vulgamott, asst. strength and conditioning; born January 15, 1981, Jewell, Iowa. Defensive end Iowa State 1999, linebacker Simpson College 2001-02. No pro playing experience. College coach: Texas Tech 2005. Pro coach: Joined Cardinals in 2006.

Dedric Ward, offensive quality control; born September 29, 1974, Cedar Rapids, Iowa. Wide receiver Northern Iowa 1993-96. Pro wide receiver New York Jets 1997-2000, Miami Dolphins 2001-02, New England Patriots 2003, Dallas Cowboys 2004. College coach: Missouri State 2006. Pro coach: Joined Cardinals in 2007.

National Football Conference
South Division
Team Colors: Black, Red, Silver, and White
4400 Falcon Parkway
Flowery Branch, Georgia 30542
Telephone: (770) 965-3115

2007 SCHEDULE
PRESEASON
Aug. 10 at N.Y. Jets 7:00
Aug. 17 at Buffalo 7:00
Aug. 27 **Cincinnati** 8:00
Aug. 31 **Baltimore**...........................7:30

REGULAR SEASON
Sep. 9   at Minnesota 12:00
Sep. 16 at Jacksonville 1:00
Sep. 23 **Carolina** 4:15
Sep. 30 **Houston** 1:00
Oct. 7   at Tennessee 12:00
Oct. 15 **N.Y. Giants** (Mon.) 8:30
Oct. 21 at New Orleans 12:00
Oct. 28 Open Date
Nov. 4   **San Francisco** 1:00
Nov. 11 at Carolina 1:00
Nov. 18 **Tampa Bay** 1:00
Nov. 22 **Indianapolis** (Thu.) 8:15
Dec. 2   at St. Louis 12:00
Dec. 10 **New Orleans** (Mon.) 8:30
Dec. 16 at Tampa Bay 1:00
Dec. 23 at Arizona 2:05
Dec. 30 **Seattle** 1:00

Stadium: Georgia Dome
(opened in 1992)
• **Capacity:** 71,228
One Georgia Dome Drive
Atlanta, Georgia 30313
Playing Surface: FieldTurf
Training Camp: Atlanta Falcons
4400 Falcon Parkway
Flowery Branch, GA 30542

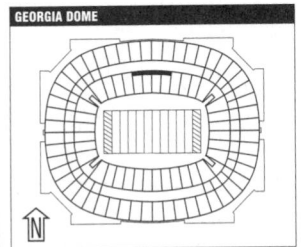

GEORGIA DOME

CLUB OFFICIALS
Owner & CEO: Arthur M. Blank
President-General Manager: Rich McKay
Head Coach: Bobby Petrino
Executive Vice President-Marketing:
Dick Sullivan
Vice President-Human Resources &
Organizational Effectiveness:
Tim Bolton
Vice President & CFO: Greg Beadles
Controller: Rob Geoffroy
Vice President of Football
Communications: Reggie Roberts
Vice President of Information
Technology: Danny Branch
Vice President of Marketing: Jim Smith
Vice President of Sales: Dave Cohen
Senior Director of Media Relations:
Frank Kleha
Senior Director of Player Development:
Kevin Winston
Assistant General Manager: Billy Devaney
Director of Logistics and Facilities:
Spencer Treadwell
Director of Ticket Operations:
Jack Ragsdale
Director of Event Marketing: Roddy White
Director of Football Operations: Nick Polk
Director of Football Administration:
Brian Xanders
Director of Pro Personnel: Les Snead
Director of College Scouting: Phil Emery
Director of Community Relations:
Kendyl Baugh Moss
Coordinator-Program Development/
Player Outreach: Chris Demos
Area Scouts: Matt Berry, Boyd Dowler,
Bob Harrison, Taylor Morton,
Mark Olson, Alex Page,
Bruce Plummer, Chris Vaszily
Pro Scouts: Shepley Heard, DeJuan Polk
Head Athletic Trainer: Ron Medlin
Assistant Athletic Trainers:
Roland Ramirez, Tom Reed
Video Director: Mike Crews
Video Assistants: Rocky Sabbatini,
Keith Phillips Jr., Phil Tieman
Equipment Manager: Brian Boigner
Director of Sponsorship Sales:
Tim Zulawski
Director of Retail: Chris DiPierri
Director of New Media: Dan Levak
Football Communications Manager:
Ted Crews
Football Communications Coordinator:
Matt Conti
Football Communications Coordinator:
Brian Cearns

COACHING HISTORY
(258-374-6)
Records include postseason games
1966-68	Norb Hecker*	4-26-1
1968-1974	Norm Van Brocklin**	37-49-3
1974-76	Marion Campbell***	6-19-0
1976	Pat Peppler	3-6-0
1977-1982	Leeman Bennett	47-44-0
1983-86	Dan Henning	22-41-1
1987-89	Marion Campbell****	11-32-0
1989	Jim Hanifan	0-4-0
1990-93	Jerry Glanville	28-38-0
1994-96	June Jones	19-30-0
1997-2003	Dan Reeves#	52-61-1
2003	Wade Phillips	2-1-0
2004-06	Jim Mora	27-23-0

*Released after three games in 1968
**Released after eight games in 1974
***Released after five games in 1976
****Retired after 12 games in 1989
#Released after 13 games in 2003

PAID ATTENDANCE
Home 551,591   Away 554,552
Total 1,106,143
Single-game home record,
71,079 (10/9/05)
Single-season home record,
553,979 (1992)

2007 DRAFT CHOICES
Round	Name	Pos.	College
1	Jamaal Anderson	DE	Arkansas
2	Justin Blalock	G	Texas
	Chris Houston	DB	Arkansas
3	Laurent Robinson	WR	Illinois State
4	Stephen Nicholas	LB	South Florida
	Martrez Milner	TE	Georgia
6	Trey Lewis	DT	Washburn
	David Irons	DB	Auburn
	Doug Datish	C	Ohio State
	Daren Stone	DB	Maine
7	Jason Snelling	RB	Virginia

2006 TEAM RECORD
PRESEASON (2-2)

Date	Result	Opponent
8/11	W 26-23	New England
8/19	L 10-38	at Green Bay
8/26	W 20-6	at Tennessee
8/31	L 17-20	Jacksonville

REGULAR SEASON (7-9)

Date	Result	Opponent	Att.
9/10	W 20-6	at Carolina	73,522
9/17	W 14-3	Tampa Bay	70,828
9/25	L 3-23	at New Orleans	70,003
10/1	W 32-10	Arizona	68,981
10/15	L 14-27	N.Y. Giants	70,840
10/22	W 41-38	Pittsburgh (OT)	71,151
10/29	W 29-27	at Cincinnati	65,978
11/5	L 14-30	at Detroit	60,987
11/12	L 13-17	Cleveland	70,793
11/19	L 10-24	at Baltimore	70,790
11/26	L 13-31	New Orleans	70,933
12/3	W 24-14	at Washington	86,436
12/10	W 17-6	at Tampa Bay	65,691
12/16	L 28-38	Dallas	71,102
12/24	L 3-10	Carolina	68,834
12/31	L 17-24	at Philadelphia	69,341

(OT) Overtime

SCORE BY PERIODS

Falcons	59	98	96	36	3	—	292
Opponents	102	98	60	68	0	—	328

2006 TEAM STATISTICS

	Falcons	Opp.
Total First Downs	287	313
Rushing	134	97
Passing	133	183
Penalty	20	33
3rd Down: Made/Att	79/220	87/207
3rd Down Pct.	35.9	42.0
4th Down: Made/Att	8/20	4/10
4th Down Pct.	40.0	40.0
Possession Avg.	29:48	30:12
Total Net Yards	5310	5325
Avg. Per Game	331.9	332.8
Total Plays	1000	994
Avg. Per Play	5.3	5.4
Net Yards Rushing	2939	1657
Avg. Per Game	183.7	103.6
Total Rushes	537	442
Net Yards Passing	2371	3668
Avg. Per Game	148.2	229.3
Sacked/Yards Lost	47/311	37/235
Gross Yards	2682	3903
Att./Completions	416/222	515/321
Completion Pct.	53.4	62.3
Had Intercepted	15	12
Punts/Average	78/41.0	77/43.9
Net Punting Avg.	78/35.9	77/38.6
Penalties/Yards	96/877	99/799
Fumbles/Ball Lost	18/5	25/14
Touchdowns	32	37
Rushing	9	14
Passing	21	20
Returns	2	3

2006 INDIVIDUAL STATISTICS

PASSING	Att.	Comp.	Yds.	Pct.	TD	Int.	Tkld.	Rate
Vick	388	204	2,474	52.6	20	13	45/303	75.7
Schaub	27	18	208	66.7	1	2	2/8	71.2
Norwood	1	0	—	0.0	0	0	0/0	39.6
Falcons	416	222	2,682	53.4	21	15	47/311	75.2
Opponents	515	321	3,903	62.3	20	12	37/235	88.8

SCORING	TD R	TD P	TD Rt	PAT	FG	Saf	PTS
Andersen	0	0	0	27/27	20/23	0	87
Crumpler	0	8	0	0/0	0/0	0	48
Jenkins	0	7	0	0/0	0/0	0	42
Dunn	4	1	0	0/0	0/0	0	30
Griffith	1	3	0	0/0	0/0	0	24
Koenen	0	0	0	4/4	3/9	0	13
Norwood	2	0	0	0/0	0/0	0	12
Vick	2	0	0	0/0	0/0	0	12
Hall	0	0	1	0/0	0/0	0	6
Lelie	0	1	0	0/0	0/0	0	6
McCrary	0	1	0	0/0	0/0	0	6
D. Williams	0	0	1	0/0	0/0	0	6
Falcons	9	21	2	31/31	23/32	0	292
Opponents	14	20	3	37/37	23/29	0	328

2-Pt. Conversions:
Falcons 0-1, Opponents 0-0.

RUSHING	Att.	Yds.	Avg.	LG	TD
Dunn	286	1140	4.0	90t	4
Vick	123	1039	8.4	51	2
Norwood	99	633	6.4	78t	2
Griffith	19	106	5.6	21t	1
Schaub	7	21	3.0	19	0
M. Jackson	1	2	2.0	2	0
Jenkins	1	2	2.0	2	0
Jennings	1	-4	-4.0	-4	0
Falcons	537	2939	5.5	90t	9
Opponents	442	1657	3.7	35t	14

RECEIVING	No.	Yds.	Avg.	LG	TD
Crumpler	56	780	13.9	46	8
Jenkins	39	436	11.2	34t	7
White	30	506	16.9	55	0
Lelie	28	430	15.4	51	1
Griffith	23	168	7.3	16	3
Dunn	22	170	7.7	18	1
Norwood	12	102	8.5	32	0
Blakley	6	76	12.7	28	0
McCrary	3	13	4.3	7	1
Vick	1	1	1.0	1	0
Beverly	1	0	0.0	0	0
Hall	1	0	0.0	0	0
Falcons	222	2682	12.1	55	21
Opponents	321	3903	12.2	89t	20

INTERCEPTIONS	No.	Yds	Avg	LG	TD
Hall	4	131	32.8	60	1
Boley	2	44	22.0	40	0
Webster	2	-2	-1.0	3	0
Davis	1	41	41.0	41	0
Crocker	1	28	28.0	28	0
D. Williams	1	9	9.0	9	0
Babineaux	1	6	6.0	6	0
Falcons	12	257	21.4	60	1
Opponents	15	219	14.6	99t	2

PUNTING	No.	Yds.	Avg.	In 20	LG
Koenen	76	3199	42.1	25	65
Falcons	78	3199	41.0	25	65
Opponents	77	3378	43.9	26	58

PUNT RETURNS	No.	FC	Yds.	Avg.	LG	TD
Rossum	37	13	288	7.8	41	0
Falcons	37	13	288	7.8	41	0
Opponents	25	21	279	11.2	65	0

KICKOFF RETURNS	No.	Yds.	Avg.	LG	TD
Rossum	46	1082	23.5	51	0
Norwood	13	320	24.6	37	0
Jennings	7	123	17.6	26	0
McCrary	2	17	8.5	10	0
Falcons	68	1542	22.7	51	0
Opponents	53	1093	20.6	59	0

FIELD GOALS	1-19	20-29	30-39	40-49	50+
Andersen	0/0	7/8	6/6	7/8	0/1
Koenen	0/0	1/1	1/4	0/1	1/3
Falcons	0/0	8/9	7/10	7/9	1/4
Opponents	1/1	10/11	3/3	6/9	3/5

SACKS	No.
Coleman	6.0
Kerney	4.5
Abraham	4.0
Mallard	4.0
Boley	3.0
Carrington	3.0
Brooking	2.5
Milloy	2.0
Babineaux	1.0
Crocker	1.0
Davis	1.0
Hartwell	1.0
T. Jackson	1.0
Mathis	1.0
Shropshire	1.0
D. Williams	1.0
Falcons	37.0
Opponents	47.0

RECORD HOLDERS
INDIVIDUAL RECORDS—CAREER

Category	Name	Performance
Rushing (Yds.)	Gerald Riggs, 1982-88	6,631
Passing (Yds.)	Steve Bartkowski, 1975-1985	23,468
Passing (TDs)	Steve Bartkowski, 1975-1985	154
Receiving (No.)	Terance Mathis, 1994-2001	573
Receiving (Yds.)	Terance Mathis, 1994-2001	7,349
Interceptions	Rolland Lawrence, 1973-1980	39
Punting (Avg.)	Rick Donnelly, 1985-89	42.6
Punt Return (Avg.)	Darrien Gordon, 2001	14.1
Kickoff Return (Avg.)	Darrick Vaughn, 2000-01	25.7
Field Goals	Morten Andersen, 1995-2000, 2006	159
Touchdowns (Tot.)	Terance Mathis, 1994-2001	57
Points	Morten Andersen, 1995-2000, 2006	707

INDIVIDUAL RECORDS—SINGLE SEASON

Category	Name	Performance
Rushing (Yds.)	Jamal Anderson, 1998	1,846
Passing (Yds.)	Jeff George, 1995	4,143
Passing (TDs)	Steve Bartkowski, 1980	31
Receiving (No.)	Terance Mathis, 1994	111
Receiving (Yds.)	Alfred Jenkins, 1981	1,358
Interceptions	Scott Case, 1988	10
Punting (Avg.)	Billy Lothridge, 1968	44.3
Punt Return (Avg.)	Darrien Gordon, 2001	14.1
Kickoff Return (Avg.)	Darrick Vaughn, 2000	27.7
Field Goals	Jay Feely, 2002	32
Touchdowns (Tot.)	Jamal Anderson, 1998	16
Points	Jay Feely, 2002	138

INDIVIDUAL RECORDS—SINGLE GAME

Category	Name	Performance
Rushing (Yds.)	Gerald Riggs, 9-2-84	202
Passing (Yds.)	Steve Bartkowski, 11-15-81	416
Passing (TDs)	Wade Wilson, 12-13-92	5
Receiving (No.)	William Andrews, 11-15-81	15
Receiving (Yds.)	Terance Mathis, 12-13-98	198
Interceptions	Many times	2
	Last time by DeAngelo Hall, 9-17-06	
Field Goals	Norm Johnson, 11-13-94	6
Touchdowns (Tot.)	T.J. Duckett, 12-12-04	4
Points	T.J. Duckett, 12-12-04	24

2007 VETERAN ROSTER

No.	Name	Pos.	Ht.	Wt.	Birthdate	NFL Exp.	College	Hometown	How Acq.	'06 Games/ Starts
55	Abraham, John	DE	6-4	258	5/6/78	8	South Carolina	Timmonsville, S.C.	T(NYJ)-'06	8/7
64	Alexander, P.J.	G	6-4	297	12/23/78	5	Syracuse	Springfield, Mass.	FA-'06	4/4
95	Babineaux, Jonathan	DT	6-2	286	10/12/81	3	Iowa	Port Arthur, Texas	D2-'05	16/1
52	Beck, Jordan	LB	6-2	233	4/18/83	3	Cal Poly	Santa Cruz, Calif.	D3-'05	15/0
85	Blakley, Dwayne	TE	6-4	257	8/10/79	4	Missouri	St. Joseph, Mo.	W(Tenn)-'04	16/4
59	Boley, Michael	LB	6-3	236	8/24/82	3	Southern Miss	Gadsden, Ala.	D5a-'05	16/14
56	Brooking, Keith	LB	6-2	245	10/30/75	10	Georgia Tech	Senoia, Ga.	D1-'98	16/16
97	Bryant, Anthony	DT	6-3	337	11/6/81	2	Alabama	Newbern, Ala.	W(Det)-'07	4/3*
91	Carrington, Paul	DE	6-7	250	11/11/82	2	Central Florida	Guyton, Ga.	FA-'06	15/2
77	Clabo, Tyson	G	6-6	314	10/17/81	2	Wake Forest	Knoxville, Tenn.	FA-'06	10/10
93	Clemons, Nic	DE	6-6	298	2/3/80	2	Georgia	Griffin, Ga.	FA-'07	0*
75	Coleman, Rod	DT	6-2	285	8/16/76	9	East Carolina	Vicksburg, Miss.	UFA(Oak)-'04	15/15
25	Crocker, Chris	S	5-11	192	3/9/80	5	Marshall	Chesapeake, Va.	T(Cle)-'06	16/15
83	Crumpler, Alge	TE	6-2	262	12/23/77	7	North Carolina	Wilmington, N.C.	D2-'01	16/16
4	Cundiff, Billy	K	6-1	207	3/30/80	5	Drake	Valley Center, Calif.	FA-'07	5/0*
92	Davis, Chauncey	DE	6-2	277	1/27/83	3	Florida State	Bartow, Fla.	D4-'05	16/14
28	Dunn, Warrick	RB	5-9	180	1/5/75	11	Florida State	Baton Rouge, La.	UFA(TB)-'02	16/16
2	Elling, Aaron	K	6-2	201	5/31/78	4	Wyoming	Waconia, Minn.	FA-'07	0*
18	Elliott, Jamin	WR	5-11	195	10/5/79	2	Delaware	Portsmouth, Va.	FA-'06	1/0
89	Fells, Daniel	TE	6-4	252	9/23/83	2	Cal-Davis	Anaheim, Calif.	FA-'06	0*
86	Finneran, Brian	WR	6-5	217	1/31/76	9	Villanova	Mission Viejo, Calif.	FA-'00	0*
68	Fonoti, Toniu	G	6-4	350	11/26/81	6	Nebraska	American Samoa	UFA(Mia)-'07	6/0*
65	Forney, Kynan	G	6-3	307	9/8/78	7	Hawaii	Nacogdoches, Texas	D7b-'01	7/7
72	Gandy, Wayne	T	6-5	308	2/10/71	14	Auburn	Haines City, Fla.	T(NO)-'06	16/16
21	Hall, DeAngelo	CB	5-10	197	11/19/83	4	Virginia Tech	Chesapeake, Va.	D1a-'04	16/16
15	Hamilton, Derrick	WR	6-4	203	11/30/81	3	Clemson	Dillon, S.C.	FA-'07	0*
13	Harrington, Joey	QB	6-4	220	10/21/78	6	Oregon	Portland, Ore.	FA-'07	11/11
87	Horn, Joe	WR	6-1	213	1/16/72	12	Itawamba (Miss.) J.C.	New Haven, Conn.	FA-'07	10/9*
90	Jackson, Grady	DT	6-2	345	1/21/73	11	Knoxville	Greensboro, Ala.	FA-'06	16/15
99	Jackson, Tommy	DT	6-1	311	12/12/83	2	Auburn	Opelika, Ala.	FA-'06	5/0
12	Jenkins, Michael	WR	6-4	217	6/18/82	4	Ohio State	Tampa, Fla.	D1b-'04	16/16
81	Jennings, Adam	WR	5-9	181	11/17/82	2	Fresno State	Granite Bay, Calif.	D6-'06	15/0
37	Johnson, Derrick	CB	5-10	186	2/9/82	3	Washington	Riverside, Calif.	FA-'06	2/0
73	Jordan, Leander	T/G	6-4	320	9/15/77	7	Indiana (Pa.)	Pittsburgh, Pa.	UFA(SD)-'07	0*
9	Koenen, Michael	P	5-11	195	7/13/82	3	Western Washington	Ferndale, Wash.	FA-'05	16/0
66	Lacy, Bo	G/T	6-4	300	11/22/80	2	Arkansas	New Port, Ark.	FA-'07	0*
53	Leake, John	LB	6-0	228	8/28/81	3	Clemson	Plano, Texas	UFA(GB)-'06	14/0
26	Lowe, Omare	CB	6-1	195	4/20/78	6	Washington	Seattle, Wash.	W(Sea)-'05	16/0
94	Mallard, Josh	DE	6-2	259	3/21/79	3	Georgia	Savannah, Ga.	FA-'06	14/0
62	McClure, Todd	C	6-1	286	2/16/77	9	Louisiana State	Baton Rouge, La.	D7a-'99	16/16
38	McIntyre, Corey	FB	6-0	244	1/25/79	3	West Virginia	Indiantown, Fla.	FA-'06	4/0
36	Milloy, Lawyer	S	6-0	210	11/14/73	12	Washington	St. Louis, Mo.	FA-'06	16/16
34	Mughelli, Ovie	FB	6-1	255	6/10/80	5	Wake Forest	Boston, Mass.	UFA(Balt)-'07	16/8*
32	Norwood, Jerious	RB	5-11	204	7/29/83	2	Mississippi State	Jackson, Miss.	D3-'06	14/0
76	Ojinnaka, Quinn	T	6-5	292	4/23/84	2	Syracuse	Seabrook, Md.	D5-'06	11/0
70	Omiyale, Frank	T	6-4	310	11/23/82	3	Tennessee Tech	Nashville, Tenn.	D 5b-'05	1/0
8	Redman, Chris	QB	6-3	223	7/7/77	5	Louisville	Louisville, Ky.	FA-'07	0*
42	Robertson, Jamal	RB	5-10	215	1/10/77	5	Ohio Northern	Dayton, Ohio	FA-'06	1/0
20	Rossum, Allen	CB	5-8	178	10/22/75	10	Notre Dame	Dallas, Texas	UFA(GB)-'02	16/1
29	Sanders, Lewis	CB	6-1	210	6/22/78	8	Maryland	Staten Island, N.Y.	UFA(Hou)-'07	9/7*
3	Shockley, D.J.	QB	6-0	214	3/25/83	2	Georgia	College Park, Ga.	D7-'06	0*
71	Shropshire, Darrell	DT	6-2	301	3/18/83	3	South Carolina	Kershaw, S.C.	D7-'05	13/1
47	Stutz, Boone	LS	6-4	260	11/4/82	2	Texas A&M	Arlington, Texas	FA-'06	16/0
27	Turnbull, Nick	S	6-2	222	7/28/81	2	Florida International	Miami, Fla.	W-'07	3/0*
7	Vick, Michael	QB	6-0	215	6/26/80	7	Virginia Tech	Newport News, Va.	D1-'01	16/16
74	Weiner, Todd	T	6-4	297	9/16/75	10	Kansas State	Coral Springs, Fla.	UFA(Sea)-'02	16/16
84	White, Roddy	WR	6-0	208	11/2/81	3	Alabama-Birmingham	James Island, S.C.	D1-'05	16/5
50	Wilkins, Marcus	LB	6-2	231	1/2/80	6	Texas	Austin, Texas	UFA(Cin)-'07	16/0*
51	Williams, Demorrio	LB	6-0	232	7/6/80	4	Nebraska	Beckville, Texas	D4-'04	16/9
24	Williams, Jimmy	CB	6-2	216	3/8/84	2	Virginia Tech	Hampton, Va.	D2-'06	13/5

* Bryant played 4 games with Detroit in '06; Clemons last active with Washington in '05; Cundiff played 5 games with New Orleans; Elling last active with Baltimore in '05; Fells inactive for 16 games; Finneran missed '06 season because of injury; Fonoti played 6 games with Miami; Hamilton played 2 games with San Francisco in '04; Horn played 10 games with New Orleans; Jordan missed '06 season with San Diego because of injury; Lacy inactive for Chicago and Cleveland in '04; Mughelli played 16 games with Baltimore; Redman last played with Baltimore in '03; Sanders played 9 games with Houston; Shockley inactive third quarterback for 16 games; Turnbull played 2 games with Atlanta and 1 with Chicago; Wilkins played 16 games with Cincinnati.

Traded—QB Matt Schaub (16 games in '06) to Houston.

Players lost through free agency (3): FB Justin Griffith (Oak; 16 games in '06), DE Patrick Kerney (Sea; 9), WR Ashley Lelie (SF; 15).

Also played with Falcons in '06—K Morten Andersen (14 games), TE Eric Beverly (16), RB Kevin Dudley (1), LB Edgerton Hartwell (8), C Austin King (14), G Matt Lehr (11), S Kevin Mathis (8), FB Fred McCrary (15), S Cam Newton (3), LB Ike Reese (16), S Lance Schulters (7), CB Jason Webster (8), WR Kevin Youngblood (1).

2007 FIRST-YEAR ROSTER

Name	Pos.	Ht.	Wt.	Birthdate	College	Hometown	How Acq.
Anderson, Adam (1)	P	6-0	190	6/28/81	Western Michigan	Grand Rapids, Mich.	FA
Anderson, Jamaal	DE	6-6	262	2/6/86	Arkansas	Little Rock, Ark.	D1
Bacchus, Allyn	CB/S	6-0	205	9/15/85	Villanova	Hampton, Va.	FA
Blalock, Justin	G	6-4	329	12/20/83	Texas	Dallas, Texas	D2a
Bozeman, Michael (1)	DT	6-2	290	12/9/82	Mississippi	Hawkinsville, Ga.	FA
Burchette, Noland	DE/DT	6-2	263	3/23/83	Virginia Tech	Richmond, Va.	FA
Datish, Doug	C	6-5	295	8/1/83	Ohio State	Warren, Ohio	D6c
Ely-Kelso, Gordon	P	6-2	215	9/29/83	Georgia	Athens, Ga.	FA
Ferentz, Brian (1)	C	6-3	282	3/28/83	Iowa	Iowa City, Iowa	FA
Foster, Renardo	G/T	6-7	327	7/15/84	Louisville	Ripley, Tenn.	FA
Gibson, Fred (1)	WR	6-4	202	10/26/81	Georgia	Waycross, Ga.	FA
Grimes, Brent (1)	CB	5-10	180	7/19/83	Shippensburg	Philadelphia, Pa.	FA
Hamlett, Jon	TE	6-4	255	6/29/84	North Carolina	Lynchburg, Va.	FA
Harris, Antoine (1)	CB	5-10	240	4/8/82	Louisville	Columbus, Ohio	FA
Henderson, Taurean (1)	RB	5-10	210	1/20/83	Texas Tech	Gatesville, Texas	FA
Houston, Chris	CB	5-11	181	10/18/84	Arkansas	Austin, Texas	D2b
Irons, David	CB	5-11	188	10/9/82	Auburn	Dacula, Ga.	D6b
Johnson, Jeramie	CB	5-11	213	10/7/84	Mississippi State	East Point, Ga.	FA
Lewis, Trey	DT	6-3	290	5/23/85	Washburn	Topeka, Kan.	D6a
Marshall, Vincent	WR	5-8	175	11/12/83	Houston	Ennis, Texas	FA
Milner, Martrez	TE	6-4	240	8/8/84	Georgia	Gainesville, Ga.	D4b
Newman, Eric	WR	6-0	190	2/16/83	Louisiana Tech	Oak Grove, La.	FA
Nicholas, Stephen	LB	6-3	225	5/1/83	South Florida	Jacksonville, Fla.	D4a
Palermo, Jason (1)	G/T	6-3	307	10/16/82	Wisconsin	Madison, Wis.	FA
Patterson, David	DE/DT	6-5	285	2/11/85	Ohio State	Warrensville Heights, Ohio	FA
Quarterman, Kurt	G/T	6-5	348	10/5/85	Louisville	Albany, Ga.	FA
Robinson, Laurent	WR	6-2	195	5/20/85	Illinois State	Fort Lewis, Wash.	D3
Sheldon, Dan (1)	WR	5-11	173	5/23/82	Northern Illinois	Elgin, Ill.	FA
Snelling, Jason	RB	5-11	232	12/29/83	Virginia	Chester, Va.	D7
Stone, Daren	CB	6-3	221	8/21/85	Maine	Lockport, N.Y.	D6d
Talavou, Kelly	DE/DT	6-2	319	10/4/84	Utah	Los Angeles, Calif.	FA
Taylor, Tony	LB	6-0	237	7/21/84	Georgia	Watkinsville, Ga.	FA
Vincent, Justin	RB	5-10	219	1/25/83	Louisiana State	Lake Charles, La.	FA
Weems, Eric	WR	5-9	175	7/4/85	Bethune-Cookman	Ormond Beach, Fla.	FA
Williams, Travis (1)	LB	6-1	213	1/20/83	Auburn	Columbia, S.C.	FA

The term NFL Rookie is defined as a player who is in his first season of professional football and has not been on the roster of another professional football team for any regular-season or postseason games. A Rookie is designated by an "R" on NFL rosters. Players who have been active in another professional football league or players who have NFL experience, including either preseason training camp or being on an Active List or Inactive List, or on Reserve/Injured or Reserve/Physically Unable to Perform for fewer than six regular-season games, are termed NFL First-Year Players. An NFL First-Year Player is designated by a "1" on NFL rosters. Thereafter, a player is credited with an additional year of experience for each season in which he accumulates six games on the Active List or Inactive List, or on Reserve/Injured or Reserve/Physically Unable to Perform.

Log on to www.atlantafalcons.com for an up-to-date roster.

COACHING STAFF

Head Coach,
Bobby Petrino

Pro Career: Named Falcons' thirteenth head coach on January 7, 2007. Petrino joined the Falcons after spending the previous four years (2003-06) as the head coach at Louisville. He helped the Cardinals earn bowl appearances in each of his four seasons, while leading them to a combined record of 41-9 during his tenure. Under Petrino, Louisville became one of only two NCAA Division I-A teams to rank in the top 10 nationally in total offense for four consecutive seasons. Of the 50 games Petrino coached at Louisville, the Cardinals scored at least 40 points in more than half of their games (28 of 50). Petrino had his first taste of the NFL as a member of the Jacksonville Jaguars coaching staff, spending two seasons (1999-2000) as the quarterbacks coach and a third (2001) as offensive coordinator. Career record: 0-0.

Background: Petrino graduated with a bachelor's degree in math and physical education from Carroll College, where he was a two-time NAIA All-American quarterback. Petrino started his 23-year coaching career at his alma mater, Carroll College, as a graduate assistant in 1983. He went on to coach collegiately at Weber State (1984, 1987-88), Carroll College (1985-86), Idaho (1989-1991), Arizona State (1992-93), Nevada (1994), Utah State (1995-97), Louisville (1998, 2003-06) and Auburn (2002).

Personal: Born March 10, 1961 in Helena, Mont. Petrino is married to the former Becky Schaff and they have four children—Kelsey, Nick, Bobby, and Katie.

ASSISTANT COACHES

Jonathan Gannon, defensive quality control; born April 4, 1983, Cleveland. Safety Louisville 2002-03. No pro playing experience. Pro coach: Joined Falcons in 2007.

Hue Jackson, offensive coordinator; born October 22, 1965, Los Angeles. Quarterback Pacific 1985-86. No pro playing experience. College coach: Pacific 1987-89, Cal State-Fullerton 1990, Arizona State 1992-95, California 1996, Southern California 1997-2000. Pro coach: London Monarchs (WFL) 1991, Washington Redskins 2001-03, Cincinnati Bengals 2004-06, joined Falcons in 2007.

Billy "White Shoes" Johnson, asst. strength and conditioning; born January 21, 1952, Boothwyn, Pa. Wide receiver Widener 1971-74. Pro wide receiver Houston Oilers 1974-1980, Atlanta Falcons 1982-87, Washington Redskins 1988. Pro coach: Joined Falcons in 2006.

Evan Marcus, head strength and conditioning; born January 2, 1968, Cranford, N.J. Tackle Ithica 1986-1990. No pro playing experience. College coach: Arizona State 1991-92, Rutgers 1993,

Maryland 1994, Texas 1995-97, Louisville 1998-99, Virginia 2003-06. Pro coach: New Orleans Saints 2000-02, joined Falcons in 2007.

Tom McMahon, asst. special teams; born July 12, 1969, Helena, Mont. Quarterback Carroll College 1988-1991. No pro playing experience. College coach: Carroll College 1992, 1994, Utah State, 1995-2005, Louisville 2006. Pro coach: Joined Falcons in 2007.

Bill Musgrave, quarterbacks; born November 11, 1967, Grand Junction, Colo. Quarterback Oregon 1987-1990. Pro quarterback San Francisco 49ers 1991-94, Denver Broncos 1995-96. College coach: Virgnia 2001-02. Pro coach: Oakland Raiders 1997, Philadelphia Eagles 1998, Carolina Panthers 1999-2000, Jacksonville Jaguars 2003-04, Washington Redskins 2005, joined Falcons in 2006.

Derrick Nix, offensive assistant/quality control; born February 22, 1980, Attalla, Ala. Running back Southern Mississippi 1998-2000, 2002. No pro playing experience. College coach: Southern Mississippi 2003-06. Pro coach: Joined Falcons in 2007.

Paul Petrino, wide receivers; born May 25, 1967, Butte, Mont. Quarterback Carroll College 1985-88. No pro playing experience. College coach: Carroll College 1989-1991, Idaho 1992-94, Utah State 1995-97, Louisville 1998-2000, 2003-06, Southern Mississippi 2000-02. Pro coach: Joined Falcons in 2007.

Dave Puloka, asst. strength and conidi-tioning; born January 12, 1979, Arlington, Mass. Linebacker Holy Cross 1997-2000. No pro playing experience. College coach: Stevens Institute of Technology 2005, Virginia 2006. Pro coach: Joined Falcons in 2007.

Jerry Rosburg, special teams coordinator; born Nov. 24, 1955, Fairmont, Minn. Linebacker North Dakota State 1974-77. No pro playing experience. College coach: Northern Michigan 1981-86, Western Michigan 1987-1991, Cincinnati 1992-95, Minnesota 1996, Boston College 1997-98, Notre Dame 1999-2000. Pro coach: Cleveland Browns 2001-06, joined Falcons in 2007.

Keith Rowen, tight ends; born Sept. 2, 1952, New York. Tackle Stanford 1972-74. No pro playing experience. College coach: Stanford 1975-76, Long Beach State 1977-78, Arizona 1979-1982. Pro coach: Boston/New Orleans Breakers (USFL) 1983-84, Cleveland Browns 1984, Indianapolis Colts 1985-88, New England Patriots 1989, Atlanta Falcons 1990-93, Minnesota Vikings 1994-96, Oakland Raiders 1997-98, Kansas City Chiefs 1999-2004, Arizona Cardinals 2005-06, re-joined Falcons in 2007.

Andy Sugarman, offensive assistant; born May 23, 1972, San Francisco. Attended California. No college or pro

playing experience. College coach: California 1990-97. Pro coach: San Francisco 49ers 1998-2002, Detroit Lions 2003-05, joined Falcons in 2007.

Mike Summers, offensive line; born June 16, 1956, Lexington, Kent. Offensive line Georgetown College 1974-78. No pro playing experience. College coach: Kentucky 1979-1981, Texas A&M 1982-84, Northern Illinois 1985-90, Oregon State 1991-95, University of the South 1996-98, Oklahoma State 1999-2000, Ohio 2001-02, Louisville 2003-06. Pro coach: Joined Falcons in 2007.

Emmitt Thomas, defensive backs; born June 3, 1943, Angleton, Texas. Quarterback/receiver Bishop (Texas) College 1963-65. Pro defensive back Kansas City Chiefs 1966-1978. College coach: Central Missouri State 1979-1980. Pro coach: St. Louis Cardinals 1981-85, Washington Redskins 1986-1994, Philadelphia Eagles 1995-98, Green Bay Packers 1999, Minnesota Vikings 2000-01, joined Falcons in 2002.

Brian VanGorder, linebackers; April 17, 1959, Jackson, Mich. Linebacker Wayne State 1979-1980. No pro playing experience. College coach: Grand Valley State 1989-1991, Wayne State 1992-94 (head coach), Central Florida 1995-97, Central Michigan 1998-99, Western Illinois 2000, Georgia 2001-04, Georgia Southern 2006 (head coach). Pro coach: Jacksonville Jaguars 2005, joined Falcons in 2007.

Joe Whitt Jr., asst. defensive backs; born July 19, 1978, Auburn, Ala. Wide receiver Auburn 1997-99. No pro playing experience. College coach: Auburn 2000-01, Citadel 2002, Louisville 2003-06. Pro coach: Joined Falcons in 2007.

Ollie Wilson, running backs; born March 3, 1951, Worcester, Mass. Wide receiver Springfield 1971-73. No pro playing experience. College coach: Springfield 1975, Northeastern 1976-1982, California 1983-1990. Pro coach: Atlanta Falcons 1991-96, San Diego Chargers 1997-2001, re-joined Falcons in 2002.

Kevin Wolthausen, defensive line; born Dec. 27, 1957, Santa Barbara, Calif. Linebacker Santa Barbara City College 1976-77, Humboldt State 1978-79. No pro playing experience. College coach: Cal State-Northridge 1980, Humboldt State 1980-82, Arizona 1983-86, Southern California 1987-92, Oklahoma 1993-94, Arizona State 1995-2000, Eastern Michigan 2002, Louisville 2003-06. Pro coach: Arizona Rattlers (AFL) 2002, joined Falcons in 2007.

Mike Zimmer, defensive coordinator; born June 5, 1956, Peoria, Ill. Quarterback/linebacker Illinois State 1974-76. No pro playing experience. College coach: Missouri 1979-1980, Weber State 1981-88, Washington State 1989-1993, Pro coach: Dallas Cowboys 1994-2006, joined Falcons in 2007.

National Football Conference
South Division
Team Colors: Black, Panther Blue, and
Silver
800 South Mint Street
Charlotte, North Carolina 28202-1502
Telephone: (704) 358-7000

2007 SCHEDULE
PRESEASON
Aug. 11 at N.Y. Giants.....................8:00
Aug. 17 at Philadelphia...................7:00
Aug. 24 **New England** 8:00
Aug. 30 **Pittsburgh**...........................8:00

REGULAR SEASON
Sep. 9 at St. Louis 12:00
Sep. 16 **Houston** 1:00
Sep. 23 at Atlanta 4:15
Sep. 30 **Tampa Bay** 4:05
Oct. 7 at New Orleans 12:00
Oct. 14 at Arizona 1:05
Oct. 21 Open Date
Oct. 28 **Indianapolis** 1:00
Nov. 4 at Tennessee 12:00
Nov. 11 **Atlanta** 1:00
Nov. 18 at Green Bay 12:00
Nov. 25 **New Orleans** 1:00
Dec. 2 **San Francisco** 1:00
Dec. 9 at Jacksonville 1:00
Dec. 16 **Seattle** 1:00
Dec. 22 **Dallas** (Sat.) 8:15
Dec. 30 at Tampa Bay 1:00

Stadium: Bank of America Stadium
(opened in 1996)
• **Capacity:** 73,298
Charlotte, North Carolina
28202-1502
Playing Surface: Grass
Training Camp: Wofford College
Spartanburg,
South Carolina 29303

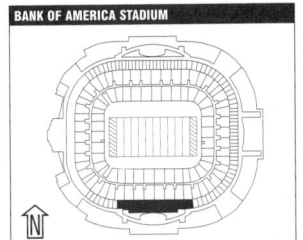

BANK OF AMERICA STADIUM

CLUB OFFICIALS
Owner/Founder: Jerry Richardson
President, Panthers Football LLC:
Mark Richardson
President Panthers Stadium LLC:
Jon Richardson
General Manager: Marty Hurney
General Counsel: Richard Thigpen
Chief Financial Officer: Dave Olsen
Controller: Mike Dudan
Director of Pro Scouting: Mark Koncz
Pro Scouts: Trent Kirchner, Tag Ribary,
Brandon Taylor
Director of College Scouting:
Don Gregory
College Scouts: Brian Adams,
Ryan Cowden, Khary Darlington,
Jeff Morrow, Joe Schoen,
Mike Szabo, Gerald Williams
Director of Communications:
Charlie Dayton
Communications Assistant:
Bruce Speight
Public Relations Assistant: Deedee Mills
Media Relations Assistant:
Steven Drummond
Director of Ticket Operations:
Phil Youtsey
Director of Player Development:
Donnie Shell
Director of Community Relations and
Cheerleader/Mascot Programs:
Riley Fields
Director of Sponsor Sales and Services:
Kyle Caddell
Director of Broadcast Administration:
Henry Thomas
Executive Producer-Television:
Greg Brannon
Executive Producer-Radio: David Langton
Salary Cap Analyst/Negotiatior:
Rob Rogers
Video Director: Mark Hobbs
Assistant Video Director: Jeff Mueller
Head Trainer: Ryan Vermillion
Assistant Trainers: Mark Shermansky,
Reggie Scott
Equipment Manager: Jackie Miles
Assistant Equipment Manager: Don Toner
Director of Security: Gene Brown
Stadium Operations Manager: Scott Paul
Director of Entertainment and
Panthervision: Kyle Ritchie
Facility Manager: Matthew Getz
Head Groundskeeper: Tom Vaughan
Director of Human Resources:
Jackie Jeffries

COACHING HISTORY
(96-105-0)
Records include postseason games
1995-98   Dom Capers 31-35-0
1999-2001 George Seifert 16-32-0
2002-06   John Fox....................49-38-0

PAID ATTENDANCE
Home 579,192   Away 550,494
Total 1,129,686
Single-game home record,
76,136 (12/10/95)
Single-season home record, 579,192
(2006)

2007 DRAFT CHOICES
Round	Name	Pos.	College
1	Jon Beason	LB	Miami
2	Dwayne Jarrett	WR	So. California
	Ryan Kalil	C	So. California
3	Charles Johnson	DE	Georgia
4	Ryne Robinson	WR	Miami (Ohio)
5	Dante Rosario	TE	Oregon
	Tim Shaw	LB	Penn State
7	C.J. Wilson	DB	Baylor

2006 TEAM RECORD
PRESEASON (3-1)
8/12	W 14-13	Buffalo
8/19	W 17-10	at Jacksonville
8/24	W 19-10	Miami
8/31	L 17-21	at Pittsburgh

REGULAR SEASON (8-8)
Date	Result	Opponent	Att.
9/10	L 6-20	Atlanta	73,522
9/17	L 13-16	at Minnesota (OT)	63,623
9/24	W 26-24	at Tampa Bay	65,423
10/1	W 21-18	New Orleans	73,392
10/8	W 20-12	Cleveland	73,520
10/15	W 23-21	at Baltimore	70,762
10/22	L 14-17	at Cincinnati	65,964
10/29	L 14-35	Dallas	73,688
11/13	W 24-10	Tampa Bay	73,573
11/19	W 15-0	St. Louis	73,348
11/26	L 13-17	at Washington	85,450
12/4	L 24-27	at Philadelphia	69,098
12/10	L 13-27	N.Y. Giants	73,702
12/17	L 3-37	Pittsburgh	73,798
12/24	W 10-3	at Atlanta	68,834
12/31	W 31-21	at New Orleans	69,569

(OT) Overtime

SCORE BY PERIODS
Panthers	68	94	53	55	0 —	270
Opponents	29	95	68	110	3 —	305

2006 TEAM STATISTICS
	Panthers	Opp.
Total First Downs	278	267
Rushing	100	96
Passing	158	149
Penalty	20	22
3rd Down: Made/Att	65/209	70/222
3rd Down Pct.	31.1	31.5
4th Down: Made/Att	3/9	11/14
4th Down Pct.	33.3	78.6
Possession Avg.	30:12	29:48
Total Net Yards	4923	4737
Avg. Per Game	307.7	296.1
Total Plays	994	990
Avg. Per Play	5.0	4.8
Net Yards Rushing	1659	1737
Avg. Per Game	103.7	108.6
Total Rushes	423	449
Net Yards Passing	3264	3000
Avg. Per Game	204.0	187.5
Sacked/Yards Lost	32/222	41/265
Gross Yards	3486	3265
Att./Completions	539/325	500/291
Completion Pct.	60.3	58.2
Had Intercepted	17	14
Punts/Average	100/45.1	98/43.8
Net Punting Avg.	100/38.8	98/40.7
Penalties/Yards	103/744	89/735
Fumbles/Ball Lost	21/10	22/8
Touchdowns	28	33
Rushing	7	10
Passing	19	22
Returns	2	1

2006 INDIVIDUAL STATISTICS
PASSING
	Att.	Comp.	Yds.	Pct.	TD	Int.	Tkld.	Rate
Delhomme	431	263	2,805	61.0	17	11	22/167	82.6
Weinke	96	56	625	58.3	2	4	10/55	67.4
Basanez	11	6	56	54.5	0	1	0/0	30.9
K. Johnson	1	0	—	0.0	0	1	0/0	0.0
Panthers	539	325	3,486	60.3	19	17	32/222	77.9
Opponents	500	291	3,265	58.2	22	14	41/265	80.8

SCORING
	TD R	TD P	TD Rt	PAT	FG	Saf	PTS
Kasay	0	0	0	28/28	24/27	0	100
Smith	1	8	0	0/0	0/0	0	54
K. Johnson	1	4	0	0/0	0/0	0	30
Carter	0	3	0	0/0	0/0	0	18
Foster	3	0	0	0/0	0/0	0	18
D. Williams	1	1	0	0/0	0/0	0	12
Gamble	0	0	1	0/0	0/0	0	6
Goings	0	1	0	0/0	0/0	0	6
Hoover	1	0	0	0/0	0/0	0	6
King	0	1	0	0/0	0/0	0	6
Mangum	0	1	0	0/0	0/0	0	6
Marshall	0	0	1	0/0	0/0	0	6
Rucker	0	0	0	0/0	0/0	1	2
Panthers	7	19	2	28/28	24/27	1	270
Opponents	10	22	1	31/31	24/30	0	305

2-Pt. Conversions:
Panthers 0-0, Opponents 2-2

RUSHING
	Att.	Yds.	Avg.	LG	TD
Foster	227	897	4.0	43t	3
D. Williams	121	501	4.1	31	1
Hoover	22	73	3.3	17	1
Smith	8	61	7.6	24t	1
Goings	11	52	4.7	28	0
Shelton	8	23	2.9	9	0
Carter	2	18	9.0	11	0
Weinke	4	16	4.0	13	0
Delhomme	18	12	0.7	12	0
K. Johnson	1	4	4.0	4t	1
Basanez	1	2	2.0	2	0
Panthers	423	1659	3.9	43t	7
Opponents	449	1737	3.9	41t	10

RECEIVING
	No.	Yds.	Avg.	LG	TD
Smith	83	1166	14.0	72t	8
K. Johnson	70	815	11.6	40	4
D. Williams	33	313	9.5	41	1
Foster	32	159	5.0	14	0
Carter	28	357	12.8	42t	3
Mangum	21	170	8.1	19	1
Hoover	20	122	6.1	16	0
Gaines	15	146	9.7	19	0
Goings	10	107	10.7	23	1
Colbert	5	56	11.2	16	0
Biddle	3	37	12.3	22	0
Hankton	3	31	10.3	18	0
Shelton	1	6	6.0	6	0
King	1	1	1.0	1t	1
Panthers	325	3486	10.7	72t	19
Opponents	291	3265	11.2	86t	22

INTERCEPTIONS
	No.	Yds.	Avg.	LG	TD
Marshall	3	59	19.7	30t	1
Gamble	3	31	10.3	18t	1
Lucas	3	13	4.3	13	0
S. Williams	2	1	0.5	1	0
Morton	1	8	8.0	8	0
Minter	1	3	3.0	3	0
Branch	1	0	0.0	0	0
Panthers	14	115	8.2	30t	2
Opponents	17	145	8.5	38	0

PUNTING
	No.	Yds.	Avg.	In 20	LG
Baker	98	4483	45.7	31	70
Kasay	1	25	25.0	0	25
Panthers	100	4508	45.1	31	70
Opponents	98	4290	43.8	40	60

PUNT RETURNS
	No.	FC	Yds.	Avg.	LG	TD
Gamble	36	13	185	5.1	24	0
Smith	9	3	30	3.3	16	0
Biddle	2	1	11	5.5	11	0
Marshall	2	0	-1	-.5	0	0
Panthers	49	17	225	4.6	24	0
Opponents	61	17	390	6.4	65t	1

KICKOFF RETURNS
	No.	Yds.	Avg.	LG	TD
D. Williams	32	623	19.5	39	0
Marshall	14	291	20.8	26	0
Goings	9	218	24.2	33	0
Hoover	3	37	12.3	21	0
Gaines	2	32	16.0	17	0
Smith	2	-1	-0.5	3	0
Panthers	62	1200	19.4	39	0
Opponents	59	1302	22.1	64	0

FIELD GOALS
	1-19	20-29	30-39	40-49	50+
Kasay	2/2	6/6	4/4	8/8	4/7
Panthers	2/2	6/6	4/4	8/8	4/7
Opponents	2/2	12/12	5/6	5/7	0/3

SACKS
	No.
Peppers	13.0
Draft	5.5
Rucker	5.0
Lewis	4.5
Jenkins	3.0
Wallace	3.0
Anderson	2.0
T. Davis	1.5
Gamble	1.0
Marshall	1.0
(group)	1.0
Moorehead	0.5
Panthers	41.0
Opponents	32.0

RECORD HOLDERS
INDIVIDUAL RECORDS—CAREER

Category	Name	Performance
Rushing (Yds.)	Tshimanga Biakabutuka, 1996-2001	2,530
Passing (Yds.)	Jake Delhomme, 2003-06	13,331
Passing (TDs)	Jake Delhomme, 2003-06	89
Receiving (No.)	Muhsin Muhammad, 1996-2004	578
Receiving (Yds.)	Muhsin Muhammad, 1996-2004	7,751
Interceptions	Eric Davis, 1996-2000	25
Punting (Avg.)	Todd Sauerbrun, 2001-04	45.5
Punt Return (Avg.)	Winslow Oliver, 1996-98	10.7
Kickoff Return (Avg.)	Michael Bates, 1996-2000	25.7
Field Goals	John Kasay, 1995-2006	252
Touchdowns (Tot.)	Wesley Walls, 1996-2002	44
	Muhsin Muhammad, 1996-2004	44
Points	John Kasay, 1995-2006	1,063

INDIVIDUAL RECORDS—SINGLE SEASON

Category	Name	Performance
Rushing (Yds.)	Stephen Davis, 2003	1,444
Passing (Yds.)	Steve Beuerlein, 1999	4,436
Passing (TDs)	Steve Beuerlein, 1999	36
Receiving (No.)	Steve Smith, 2005	103
Receiving (Yds.)	Steve Smith, 2005	1,563
Interceptions	Doug Evans, 2001	8
Punting (Avg.)	Todd Sauerbrun, 2001	47.5
Punt Return (Avg.)	Winslow Oliver, 1996	11.5
Kickoff Return (Avg.)	Michael Bates, 1996	30.2
Field Goals	John Kasay, 1996	37
Touchdowns (Tot.)	Muhsin Muhammad, 2004	16
Points	John Kasay, 1996	145

INDIVIDUAL RECORDS—SINGLE GAME

Category	Name	Performance
Rushing (Yds.)	Stephen Davis, 10-26-03	178
Passing (Yds.)	Chris Weinke, 12-10-06	423
Passing (TDs)	Steve Beuerlein, 1-2-00	5
Receiving (No.)	Steve Smith, 11-20-05	14
Receiving (Yds.)	Steve Smith, 10-30-05	201
Interceptions	Deon Grant, 9-22-02	3
Field Goals	John Kasay, 12-5-04	6
Touchdowns (Tot.)	Many times	3
	Last time by Steve Smith, 9-25-05	
Points	Fred Lane, 11-2-97	18
	Tshimanga Biakabutuka, 10-3-99	18
	Muhsin Muhammad, 12-18-99, 11-14-04	18
	Steve Smith, 12-8-02, 9-25-05	18
	Nick Goings, 11-21-04	18
	Stephen Davis, 9-18-05	18

2007 VETERAN ROSTER

No.	Name	Pos.	Ht.	Wt.	Birthdate	NFL Exp.	College	Hometown	How Acq.	'06 Games/ Starts
50	Anderson, James	LB	6-2	232	9/26/83	2	Virginia Tech	Chesapeake, Va.	D3a-'06	16/2
7	Baker, Jason	P	6-2	205	5/17/78	7	Iowa	Fort Wayne, Ind.	T(Den)-'05	16/0
96	Ball, Dave	DE	6-5	277	1/4/81	4	UCLA	Dixon, Calif.	FA-'07	10/0*
14	Basanez, Brett	QB	6-2	210	5/11/83	2	Northwestern	Arlington Heights, Ill.	FA-'06	1/0
76	Batiste, D'Anthony	G	6-4	318	3/29/82	2	Louisiana-Lafayette	Marksville, La.	FA-'06	0*
11	Biddle, Taye	WR	6-1	175	2/27/83	2	Mississippi	Decatur, Ala.	FA-'06	2/0
28#	Branch, Colin	S	5-11	205	3/2/80	5	Stanford	Carlsbad, Calif.	D4-'03	16/4
73	Bridges, Jeremy	T	6-4	326	4/19/80	5	Southern Mississippi	McComb, Miss.	FA-'06	16/4
79	Butler, Rashad	T	6-4	293	2/10/82	2	Miami	Palm Bch Gardens, Fla.	D3b-'06	0*
23	Byrum, Dion	CB	5-10	192	5/18/83	2	Ohio University	Monroe, N.C.	FA-'06	3/0
8	Carr, David	QB	6-3	216	7/21/79	6	Fresno State	Bakersfield, Calif.	FA-'07	16/16*
67	Carstens, Jordan	DT	6-5	300	1/22/81	4	Iowa State	Bagley, Iowa	FA-'04	1/0
18	Carter, Drew	WR	6-3	200	9/5/81	4	Ohio State	Solon, Ohio	D5-'04	14/2
83	Colbert, Keary	WR	6-1	200	5/21/82	4	Southern California	Oxnard, Calif.	D2-'04	12/3
35	Cooper, Deke	S	6-2	210	10/18/77	5	Notre Dame	Evansville, Ind.	UFA(SF)-'07	1/0*
58	Davis, Thomas	LB	6-0	231	3/22/83	3	Georgia	Shellman, Ga.	D1-'05	14/14
17	Delhomme, Jake	QB	6-2	215	1/10/75	9	Louisiana-Lafayette	Lafayette, La.	UFA(NO)-'03	13/13
41	Deloatch, Curtis	CB	6-2	214	10/4/81	4	North Carolina A&T	Ahoskie, N.C.	FA-'07	7/0*
53	Diggs, Na'il	LB	6-4	240	7/8/78	8	Ohio State	Los Angeles, Calif.	FA-'06	15/10
78#	Fordham, Todd	T	6-5	319	10/9/73	10	Florida State	Atlanta, Ga.	T(Pitt)-'04	16/1
26	Foster, DeShaun	RB	6-0	222	1/10/80	6	UCLA	Tustin, Calif.	D2-'02	14/14
84	Gaines, Michael	TE	6-3	280	3/30/80	4	Central Florida	Tallahassee, Fla.	D7-'04	16/9
20	Gamble, Chris	CB	6-1	200	3/11/83	4	Ohio State	Sunrise, Fla.	D1-'04	15/13
36	Garrett, Kevin	CB	5-9	194	7/29/80	3	Southern Methodist	Brazoria, Texas	FA-'07	1/0*
37	Goings, Nick	RB	6-0	225	1/26/78	7	Pittsburgh	Dublin, Ohio	FA-'01	11/0
60	Grigsby, Otis	DE	6-3	260	11/19/80	3	Kentucky	Converse, Texas	FA-'06	0*
69	Gross, Jordan	T	6-4	300	7/20/80	5	Utah	Fruitland, Idaho	D1-'03	16/16
63	Hangartner, Geoff	C	6-5	301	4/22/82	3	Texas A&M	New Braunfels, Texas	D5b-'05	16/15
75	Hartwig, Justin	C	6-4	312	11/21/78	6	Kansas	W. Des Moines, Iowa	UFA(Tenn)-'06	2/1
45	Hoover, Brad	FB	6-0	245	11/11/76	8	Western Carolina	Thomasville, N.C.	FA-'00	16/12
81	Horn, Chris	WR	5-11	195	7/13/77	5	Rocky Mountain	Notus, Idaho	FA-'07	0*
23#	Howard, Reggie	CB	6-0	185	5/17/77	8	Memphis	Memphis, Tenn.	FA-'06	6/0
57	Jamison, Brandon	LB	6-1	205	7/31/81	2	West Georgia	Hopkins, S.C.	W(Atl)-'06	4/0
77	Jenkins, Kris	DT	6-4	335	8/3/79	7	Maryland	Ypsilanti, Mich.	D2-'01	16/16
61#	Kadela, Dave	T	6-6	304	5/6/78	6	Virginia Tech	Deerborn, Mich.	FA-'04	0*
4	Kasay, John	K	5-10	198	10/27/69	17	Georgia	Athens, Ga.	UFA(Sea)-'95	16/0
99	Kemoeatu, Maake	DT	6-5	350	1/10/79	6	Utah	Kahuku, Hawaii	UFA-'06	16/13
87	King, Jeff	TE	6-3	253	2/19/83	2	Virginia Tech	Pulaski, Va.	D5-'06	12/0
56	Kyle, Jason	LB	6-3	242	5/12/72	13	Arizona State	Tempe, Ariz.	UFA(SF)-'01	16/0
91	Lavalais, Chad	DT	6-1	292	4/15/79	3	Louisiana State	Marksville, La.	FA-'07	0*
92	Lewis, Damione	DT	6-2	301	3/1/78	7	Miami	Sulphur Springs, Texas	UFA(StL)-'06	16/3
21	Lucas, Ken	CB	6-0	205	1/23/79	7	Mississippi	Cleveland, Miss.	UFA(Sea)-'05	13/12
31	Marshall, Richard	CB	5-11	189	12/12/84	2	Fresno State	Los Angeles, Calif.	D2-'06	16/8
71	Mathis, Evan	G	6-5	304	11/1/81	3	Alabama	Homewood, Ala.	D3a-'05	15/15
74	McClover, Stanley	DE	6-2	263	12/16/84	2	Auburn	Fort Lauderdale, Fla.	D7b-'06	2/0
54	Melton, Terrence	LB	6-1	235	1/1/77	4	Rice	Houston, Texas	FA-'07	16/0*
30	Minter, Mike	S	5-10	195	1/15/74	11	Nebraska	Lawton, Okla.	D2-'97	16/16
66	Montgomery, Will	C	6-3	312	2/13/83	2	Virginia Tech	Clifton, Va.	D7-'06	6/4
94	Moorehead, Kindal	DT	6-2	285	10/14/78	5	Alabama	Memphis, Tenn.	D5-'03	16/0
55	Morgan, Dan	LB	6-2	245	12/19/78	7	Miami	Coral Springs, Fla.	D1-'01	1/1
25	Morton, Christian	CB	6-0	181	4/28/81	3	Illinois	St. Louis, Mo.	FA-'06	7/2
29	Newton, Cam	S	6-1	203	5/19/82	3	Furman	Bennettsville, S.C.	FA-'06	0*
90	Peppers, Julius	DE	6-7	283	1/18/80	6	North Carolina	Bailey, N.C.	D1-'02	16/16
64#	Peters, Scott	G	6-3	300	11/23/78	4	Arizona State	Pleasanton, Calif.	FA-'05	0*
93	Rucker, Micheal	DE	6-5	275	2/28/75	9	Nebraska	St. Joseph, Mo.	D2b-'99	14/14
33	Salley, Nate	S	6-1	216	2/5/84	2	Ohio State	Ft. Lauderdale, Fla.	D4-'06	8/0
	Sciullo, Steve	G	6-5	325	8/27/80	4	Marshall	Pittsburgh, Pa.	FA-'07	0*
59	Seward, Adam	LB	6-2	248	6/15/82	3	Nevada-Las Vegas	Las Vegas, Nev.	D5a-'05	16/2
32	Shelton, Eric	RB	6-1	246	6/23/83	3	Louisville	Lexington, Ky.	D2-'05	9/0
89	Smith, Steve	WR	5-9	185	5/12/79	7	Utah	Lynwood, Calif.	D3'-01	14/14
22	Strait, Derrick	CB	5-11	189	8/27/80	4	Oklahoma	Austin, Texas	W(Chi)-'06	2/0
68	Wahle, Mike	G	6-6	304	3/29/77	10	Navy	Lake Arrowhead, Calif.	UFA(GB)-'05	13/13
70	Wharton, Travelle	T	6-4	312	5/19/81	4	South Carolina	Simpsonville, S.C.	D3-'04	1/1
34	Williams, DeAngelo	RB	5-9	217	4/25/83	2	Memphis	Wynne, Ark.	D1-'06	13/2
36#	Williams, Shaun	S	6-2	218	10/10/76	10	UCLA	Encino, Calif.	UFA(NYG)-'06	12/12
98	Williams, Stephen	DT	6-2	306	9/21/81	2	Northwest Missouri State	Bolingbrook, IL	FA-'07	11/0*

*   Ball played 10 games with N.Y. Jets in '06; Batiste inactive for 9 games; Butler inactive for 11 games; Carr played 16 games with Houston; Cooper played 1 game with San Francisco; Deloatch played 7 games with New Orleans; Garrett played 1 game with Houston; Grigsby last active with Miami in '03; Horn last active with Kansas City in '05; Kadela inactive for 2 games; Lavalais last active with Atlanta in '05; Melton played 16 games with New Orleans; Newton inactive for 1 game; Peters missed '06 season because of injury; Sciullo last active with Philadelphia in '04; Williams played 11 games with Kansas City.

\#   Unrestricted Free Agent, subject to developments.

Players lost through free agency (3): LB Vinny Ciurciu (Minn; 16 games in '06), LB Chris Draft (StL; 16); TE Mike Seidman (Ind; 3).

Also played with Panthers in '06—DT Tony Brown (1 game), LB Rod Davis (1), WR Karl Hankton (16), WR Keyshawn Johnson (16), S Kevin McCadam (16), DE Al Wallace (16), QB Chris Weinke (3).

2007 FIRST-YEAR ROSTER

Name	Pos.	Ht.	Wt.	Birthdate	College	Hometown	How Acq.
Beason, Jonathan	LB	6-0	237	1/14/85	Miami	Miramar, Fla.	D1
Bell, Dalton	QB	6-3	195	3/9/83	West Texas A&M	Canyon, Texas	FA
Bennett, Nathan	G	6-4	310	1/19/84	Clemson	Dallas, Ga.	FA
Biggs, Rondell	DE	6-2	269	8/5/84	Michigan	Southfield, Mich.	FA
Curvey, Brent	DT	6-0	295	3/15/85	Iowa State	Houston, Texas	FA
Daniels, Jessie	S	5-11	216	1/8/84	Louisiana State	Breaux Bridge, La.	FA
Gilmore, Jahkeen	WR	6-0	211	8/25/83	Indiana	Brooklyn, N.Y.	FA
Graham, Eric	T	6-6	325	4/20/84	East Carolina	Richlands, N.C.	FA
Hall, Jason (1)	DE	6-2	253	10/31/83	Tennessee	Chattanooga, Tenn.	FA
Haynes, Alex (1)	RB	5-10	223	2/13/82	Central Florida	Orlando, Fla.	FA-'05
Jackson, Steven (1)	FB	6-2	260	5/11/84	Clemson	Columbia, S.C.	FA-'06
Jarrett, Dwayne	WR	6-4	219	9/11/86	Southern California	New Brunswick, N.J.	D2a
Johnson, Charles	DE	6-2	270	7/10/86	Georgia	Hawkinsville, Ga.	D3
Kalil, Ryan	C	6-2	291	3/29/85	Southern California	Corona, Calif.	D2b
Latsko, Billy	FB	5-10	233	2/16/84	Florida	Gainesville, Fla.	FA
McClellan, Julius	WR	6-3	246	4/18/83	North Carolina Central	Lakeland, Fla.	FA
McCullum, Justin (1)	WR	6-4	220	10/5/82	Stanford	Mercer Island, Wash.	FA-'06
Pimentel, Mickey	LB	6-2	238	3/29/85	California	San Diego, Calif.	FA
Riley, Rueben	T	6-4	305	9/20/84	Michigan	Grand Rapids, Mich.	FA
Robinson, Ryne	WR	5-9	179	11/4/84	Miami (Ohio)	Toledo, Ohio	D4
Rosario, Dante	FB	6-4	240	10/25/84	Oregon	Dayton, Ore.	D5a
Shaw, Tim	LB	6-1	236	3/27/84	Penn State	Livonia, Mich.	D5b
Teal, Quinton	S	6-1	187	3/8/84	Coastal Carolina	Bennettsville, S.C.	FA
Thornton, Marques	DE/DT	6-1	279	7/25/84	Texas A&M	Houston, Texas	FA
Upshaw, Chad	TE	6-4	246	6/23/84	Buffalo	Southport, Conn.	FA
Watson, Theodric	G/T	6-5	295	7/13/85	South Florida	St. Petersburg, Fla.	FA
Wellock, Andrew	K	5-11	182	12/3/84	Eastern Michigan	Green, Ohio	FA
Wilds, Garnell (1)	CB	5-11	195	6/8/81	Virginia Tech	Tampa, Fla.	FA
Wilson, C.J.	S	6-1	195	4/2/85	Baylor	Terrell, Texas	D7
Youngblood, Kevin (1)	WR	6-2	215	11/22/80	Clemson	Jacksonville, Fla.	FA

The term NFL Rookie is defined as a player who is in his first season of professional football and has not been on the roster of another professional football team for any regular-season or postseason games. A Rookie is designated by an "R" on NFL rosters. Players who have been active in another professional football league or players who have NFL experience, including either preseason training camp or being on an Active List or Inactive List, or on Reserve/Injured or Reserve/Physically Unable to Perform for fewer than six regular-season games, are termed NFL First-Year Players. An NFL First-Year Player is designated by a "1" on NFL rosters. Thereafter, a player is credited with an additional year of experience for each season in which he accumulates six games on the Active List or Inactive List, or on Reserve/Injured or Reserve/Physically Unable to Perform.

Log on to www.panthers.com for an up-to-date roster.

COACHING STAFF

Head Coach,

John Fox

Pro Career: Became third coach in Carolina Panthers history on January 25, 2002. During tenure from 2002-06, 49 overall victories stand as the third-highest total in the NFC and seventh-highest amount in the NFL. Since arrival in 2002, Panthers are one of five teams that have ranked among the NFL's top 10 in total defense in each of the last five seasons. Became the fifth head coach in NFL history to record four career postseason road wins. Equaled an NFL record with four consecutive postseason road wins. In 2004, directed Carolina team that overcame a 1-7 record to end the regular season with mark of 7-9. Of the 28 NFL teams that began season with 1-7 record since 1990, Panthers became only third team to finish season with seven victories. In 2003, guided Panthers to Super Bowl XXXVIII two years after inheriting team that won one game in 2001. Joined Vince Lombardi and Bill Parcells as the only coaches in NFL history to inherit a one-win team and guide it to the playoffs in their second season. In 2002, engineered a six-game turn-around that ranks second for rookie head coaches since 1978. In 2002, the Panthers became the only team since 1970 to improve from thirty-first to second in total defense in one season. Prior to joining Carolina he served as the defensive coordinator for the N.Y. Giants (1997-2001). In 2000, Fox helped the Giants reach Super Bowl XXXV, including posting the first shutout in a conference title game since 1986. Before joining the Giants, Fox was a consultant for the Rams (1996), defensive coordinator for the Raiders (1994-95), defensive backs coach for the Chargers (1992-93) and Steelers (1989-1991), and secondary coach for the USFL's Los Angeles Express (1985). Career record: 49-38.

Background: Defensive back at San Diego State (1976-77). Coached at San Diego State (1978), U.S. International (1979) Boise State (1980), Long Beach State (1981), Utah (1982), Kansas (1983), Iowa State (1984), and Pittsburgh (1986-88). Received bachelor's degree in physical education and earned a teaching credential from San Diego State.

Personal: Born February 8, 1955, in Virginia Beach, Va. He and his wife, Robin, have four children—Mathew, Mark, Cody, and Halle.

ASSISTANT COACHES

Geep Chryst, tight ends/quality control-offense; born June 25, 1962, Madison, Wis. Linebacker Princeton 1981-84. Pro linebacker Orlando Thunder (WFL) 1992. College coach: Wisconsin-Platteville 1987, Wisconsin 1988, Wyoming 1989-1990. Pro coach: Orlando Thunder (WL) 1991, Chicago Bears 1991-95, Arizona Cardinals 1996-98, 2001-03, San Diego Chargers 1999-2000, joined Panthers in 2006.

Danny Crossman, special teams; born January 17, 1967, El Paso, Texas. Defensive back Kansas 1985, Pittsburgh 1987-89. Pro defensive back Washington Redskins 1990, Detroit Lions 1991-92. College coach: U.S. Coast Guard Academy 1993, Western Kentucky 1994-96, Central Florida 1997-98, Georgia Tech 1999-2001, Michigan State 2002. Pro coach: Joined Panthers in 2003.

Jeff Davidson, offensive coordinator; born Oct. 3, 1967, Akron, Ohio. Offensive lineman Ohio State 1986-89. Pro offensive lineman Denver Broncos 1990-92, New Orleans Saints 1994. Pro coach: New Orleans Saints 1995-96, New England Patriots 1997-2004, Cleveland Browns 2005-06, joined Panthers in 2007.

Ken Flajole, linebackers; born October 4, 1954, Seattle. Linebacker Wenatchee Valley (Wash.) C.C. 1973-74, Pacific Lutheran 1975-76. No pro playing experience. College coach: Pacific Lutheran 1977-78, Washington 1979, Montana 1980-85, Texas-El Paso 1986-88, Missouri 1989-1993, Richmond 1994, Hawaii 1995, Nevada 1996-97. Pro coach: Green Bay Packers 1998, Seattle Seahawks 1999-2002, joined Panthers in 2003.

Mike Gillhamer, secondary/safeties; born February 20, 1956, Oakland. Defensive back Carroll College 1972, Wenatchee (Wash.) J.C. 1973, Humboldt State 1974-75. No pro playing experience. College coach: College of the Sequoias 1979-1983, Weber State 1984, Utah 1985-89, San Jose State 1990-93, Nevada 1994-95, Oregon 2001-02, Louisville 2003. Pro coach: New York Giants 1997-2000, joined Panthers in 2004.

Tony Levine, special teams assistant/asst. strength and conditioning; born October 28, 1972, St. Paul, Minn. Wide receiver Minnesota 1991-95. Pro wide receiver Minnesota (AFL) 1996. College coach: Southwest Texas State 1997-99, Aubun 2000-01, Louisiana Tech 2002, Louisville 2003-05. Pro coach: Joined Panthers in 2006.

Tim Lewis, secondary; born December 18, 1961, Quakertown, Pa. Defensive back Pittsburgh 1979-1982. Pro cornerback Green Bay Packers 1983-86. College coach: Texas A&M 1987-88, Southern Methodist 1989-1992, Pittsburgh 1993-94. Pro coach: Pittsburgh Steelers 1995-2003, New York Giants 2004-06, joined Panthers in 2007.

David Magazu, offensive line; born June 10, 1957, Taunton Mass. Defensive tackle Springfield College 1976-79. No pro playing experience. College coach: Ithaca 1980, Western Michigan 1981, Eastern Michigan 1982, Michigan 1983, Northern

Illinois 1984, Ball State 1985-86, Navy 1987-89, Indiana State 1990-91, Colorado State 1992-94, Kentucky 1995-96, Memphis 1997-98, Boston College 1999-2002. Pro coach: Joined Panthers in 2003.

Mike McCoy, quarterbacks; born April 1, 1972, San Francisco. Quarterback Long Beach State 1990-91, Utah 1992-94. Pro quarterback Amsterdam Admirals (NFLE) 1997, Calgary Stampeders (CFL) 1999. Pro coach: Joined Panthers in 2000.

Sam Mills III, quality control/defense; born May 20, 1978, Long Branch, N.J. Cornerback Montclair State 1997-98. No pro playing experience. Pro coach: Joined Panthers in 2006.

Jerry Simmons, strength and conditioning; born June 15, 1954, Elkhart, Kan. Linebacker Fort Hays State 1976-77. No pro playing experience. College coach: Fort Hays State 1978, Clemson 1980, Rice 1981-82, Southern California 1983-87. Pro coach: New England Patriots 1988-1990, Cleveland Browns/Baltimore Ravens 1991-98, joined Panthers in 1999.

Jim Skipper, asst. head coach/running backs; born January 23, 1949, Breaux Bridge, La. Defensive back Whittier College 1971-72. No pro playing experience. College coach: Cal Poly-Pomona 1974-76, San Jose State 1977-78, Pacific 1979, Oregon 1980-82. Pro coach: Philadelphia/Baltimore Stars (USFL) 1983-85, New Orleans Saints 1986-1995, Arizona Cardinals 1996, New York Giants 1997-2000, San Francisco Demons (XFL) 2001 (head coach), joined Panthers in 2002.

Sal Sunseri, defensive line; born August 1, 1959, Pittsburgh. Linebacker Pittsburgh 1979-1981. College coach: Pittsburgh 1985-1992, Iowa Wesleyan 1993, Louisville 1995-97, Alabama A&M 1998-99, Louisiana State 2000, Michigan State 2001. Pro coach: Joined Panthers in 2002.

Mike Trgovac, defensive coordinator; born February 27, 1959, Youngstown, Ohio. Defensive lineman Michigan 1977-1980. No pro playing experience. College coach: Michigan 1984-85, Ball State 1986-88, Navy 1989, Colorado State 1990-91, Notre Dame 1992-94. Pro coach: Philadelphia Eagles 1995-98, Green Bay Packers 1999, Washington Redskins 2000-01, joined Panthers in 2002.

Richard Williamson, wide receivers; born April 13, 1941, Ft. Deposit, Ala. Receiver Alabama 1961-62. No pro playing experience. College coach: Alabama 1963-67, 1970-71, Arkansas 1968-69, 1972-74, Memphis State 1975-1980 (head coach). Pro coach: Kansas City Chiefs 1983-86, Tampa Bay Buccaneers 1987-1991 (interim head coach 1990, head coach 1991), Cincinnati Bengals 1992-94, joined Panthers in 1995.

**National Football Conference
North Division**
Team Colors: Navy Blue, Orange, and
White
Halas Hall at Conway Park
1000 Football Drive
Lake Forest, Illinois 60045
Telephone: (847) 295-6600

2007 SCHEDULE
PRESEASON
Aug. 11 at Houston 7:00
Aug. 20 at Indianapolis 8:00
Aug. 25 **San Francisco** 7:00
Aug. 30 **Cleveland** 7:00

REGULAR SEASON
Sep. 9 at San Diego 1:15
Sep. 16 **Kansas City** 3:15
Sep. 23 **Dallas** 7:15
Sep. 30 at Detroit 1:00
Oct. 7 at Green Bay 7:15
Oct. 14 **Minnesota** 12:00
Oct. 21 at Philadelphia 4:15
Oct. 28 **Detroit** 12:00
Nov. 4 Open Date
Nov. 11 at Oakland 1:15
Nov. 18 at Seattle *5:15
Nov. 25 **Denver** 12:00
Dec. 2 **N.Y. Giants**........................3:15
Dec. 6 at Washington (Thu.)..........8:15
Dec. 17 at Minnesota (Mon.)...........7:30
Dec. 23 **Green Bay** 12:00
Dec. 30 **New Orleans** 12:00
Sunday night games in Weeks 11-17 subject to change

Stadium: Soldier Field
(opened in 1924)
•**Capacity:** 61,500
1410 S. Museum Campus Dr.
Chicago, Illinois 60605
Playing Surface: Natural Grass
Training Camp: Olivet-Nazarene Univ.
Bourbonnais, Illinois
60901

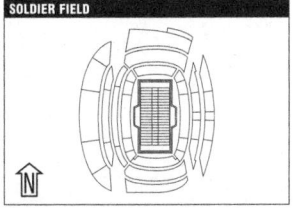
SOLDIER FIELD

CLUB OFFICIALS
Chairman of the Board:
Michael B. McCaskey
Secretary: Virginia H. McCaskey
President and CEO: Ted Phillips
General Manager: Jerry Angelo
Vice President: Tim McCaskey
Senior Director of Special Projects:
Pat McCaskey
Senior Director of Ticket Operations:
George McCaskey
Senior Director of Business Development
& Alumni Relations: Brian McCaskey
Senior Director of Administration:
John Bostrom
Senior Director of Finance & Treasurer:
Karen Murphy
Senior Director of Corporate Sales &
Marketing: Chris Hibbs
Senior Director of Corporate
Communications: Scott Hagel
Director of Pro Personnel: Bobby DePaul
Director of College Scouting:
Greg Gabriel
Senior Director of Football Administration
and General Counsel: Cliff Stein
Assistant Director of Pro Personnel:
Morocco Brown
Director of Player Development:
Isaiah Harris
Director of Community Relations:
Caroline Guip
Director of Broadcasting: Greg Miller
Media Services Manager: Jim Christman
Media Relations Assistant: Mike Corbo
Video Director: Dean Pope
Assistant Video Directors:
Dave Hendrickson, Dan Tuohy
Head Athletic Trainer: Tim Bream
Assistant Trainers: Scott DeGraff,
Chris Hanks
Director of Rehabilitation: Bobby Slater
Head Equipment Manager: Tony Medlin
Assistant Equipment Managers:
Carl Piekarski, John Perkins
Scouts: Chris Ballard, Marty Barrett,
Rex Hogan, Ted Monago,
Mark Sadowski, Jeff Shiver

COACHING HISTORY
**Decatur Staleys 1920,
Chicago Staleys 1921
(686-499-42)**
Records include postseason games

Year	Coach	Record
1920-29	George Halas	84-31-19
1930-32	Ralph Jones	24-10-7
1933-1942	George Halas*	88-24-4
1942-45	Hunk Anderson- Luke Johnsos**	24-12-2
1946-1955	George Halas	76-43-2
1956-57	John (Paddy) Driscoll	14-10-1
1958-1967	George Halas	76-53-6
1968-1971	Jim Dooley	20-36-0
1972-74	Abe Gibron	11-30-1
1975-77	Jack Pardee	20-23-0
1978-1981	Neill Armstrong	30-35-0
1982-1992	Mike Ditka	112-68-0
1993-98	Dave Wannstedt	41-57-0
1999-2003	Dick Jauron	35-46-0
2004-06	Lovie Smith	31-21-0

*Retired after five games to enter U.S. Navy
**Co-coaches

PAID ATTENDANCE
Home 487,280   Away 550,028
Total 1,037,308
Single-game home record,
66,900 (9/5/93)
Single-season home record, 527,769
(1999)

2007 DRAFT CHOICES
Round	Name	Pos.	College
1	Greg Olsen	TE	Miami
2	Dan Bazuin	DE	Central Michigani
3	Garrett Wolfe	RB	Northern Illinois
	Michael Okwo	LB	Stanford
4	Josh Beekman	G	Boston College
5	Kevin Payne	DB	Louisiana-Monroe
	Corey Graham	DB	New Hampshire
7	Trumaine McBride	DB	Mississippi
	Aaron Brant	T	Iowa State

2006 TEAM RECORD
PRESEASON (2-2)

Date	Result	Opponent
8/11	L 14-28	at San Francisco
8/18	W 24-3	San Diego
8/25	L 16-23	Arizona
8/31	W 20-7	at Cleveland

REGULAR SEASON (13-3)

Date	Result	Opponent	Att.
9/10	W 26-0	at Green Bay	70,918
9/17	W 34-7	Detroit	62,181
9/24	W 19-16	at Minnesota	63,754
10/1	W 37-6	Seattle	62,225
10/8	W 40-7	Buffalo	62,206
10/16	W 24-23	at Arizona	63,977
10/29	W 41-10	San Francisco	62,200
11/5	L 13-31	Miami	62,206
11/12	W 38-20	at N.Y. Giants	78,641
11/19	W 10-0	at N.Y. Jets	77,632
11/26	L 13-17	at New England	68,756
12/3	W 23-13	Minnesota	62,221
12/11	W 42-27	at St. Louis	66,234
12/17	W 34-31	Tampa Bay (OT)	62,260
12/24	W 26-21	at Detroit	60,665
12/31	L 7-26	Green Bay	62,287

(OT) Overtime

POSTSEASON (2-1)

1/14	W 27-24	Seattle (OT)	62,184
1/21	W 39-14	New Orleans	61,817
2/4	L 17-29	vs. Indianapolis,	74,512
		at South Florida	

SCORE BY PERIODS

Bears	73	140	101	110	3	—	427
Opponents	47	71	48	89	0	—	255

2006 TEAM STATISTICS

	Bears	Opp.
Total First Downs	300	258
Rushing	103	77
Passing	161	159
Penalty	36	22
3rd Down: Made/Att	85/231	74/239
3rd Down Pct.	36.8	31.0
4th Down: Made/Att	9/13	10/16
4th Down Pct.	69.2	62.5
Possession Avg.	30:34	29:26
Total Net Yards	5199	4706
Avg. Per Game	324.9	294.1
Total Plays	1042	1023
Avg. Per Play	5.0	4.6
Net Yards Rushing	1918	1590
Avg. Per Game	119.9	99.4
Total Rushes	503	402
Net Yards Passing	3281	3116
Avg. Per Game	205.1	194.8
Sacked/Yards Lost	25/165	40/272
Gross Yards	3446	3388
Att./Completions	514/282	581/328
Completion Pct.	54.9	56.5
Had Intercepted	22	24
Punts/Average	77/44.2	100/43.7
Net Punting Avg.	77/37.6	100/35.2
Penalties/Yards	112/923	132/1084
Fumbles/Ball Lost	26/14	32/20
Touchdowns	47	29
Rushing	14	7
Passing	24	18
Returns	9	4

2006 INDIVIDUAL STATISTICS

PASSING

	Att.	Comp.	Yds.	Pct.	TD	Int.	Tkld.	Rate
Grossman	480	262	3,193	54.6	23	20	21/142	73.9
Griese	32	18	220	56.3	1	2	3/22	62.0
Jones	1	1	-4	100.0	0	0	1/1	79.2
Maynard	1	1	37	100.0	0	0	0/0	118.8
Bears	514	282	3,446	54.9	24	22	25/165	73.5
Opponents	581	328	3,388	56.5	18	24	40/272	66.5

SCORING

	TD R	TD P	TD Rt	PAT	FG	Saf	PTS
Gould	0	0	0	47/47	32/36	0	143
Benson	6	0	0	0/0	0/0	0	36
Berrian	0	6	0	0/0	0/0	0	36
Clark	0	6	0	0/0	0/0	0	36
Hester	0	0	6	0/0	0/0	0	36
Jones	6	0	0	0/0	0/0	0	36
Muhammad	0	5	0	0/0	0/0	0	30
Bradley	0	3	0	0/0	0/0	0	18
Davis	0	2	0	0/0	0/0	0	12
Gilmore	0	2	0	0/0	0/0	0	12
Peterson	2	0	0	0/0	0/0	0	12
M. Brown	0	0	1	0/0	0/0	0	6
R. Manning	0	0	1	0/0	0/0	0	6
Tillman	0	0	1	0/0	0/0	0	6
Ta. Johnson	0	0	0	0/0	0/0	1	2
Bears	14	24	9	47/47	32/36	1	427
Opponents	7	18	4	27/28	18/27	0	255

2-Pt. Conversions: Bears 0-0, Opponents 0-1

RUSHING

	Att.	Yds.	Avg.	LG	TD
Jones	296	1210	4.1	30t	6
Benson	157	647	4.1	30	6
Peterson	10	41	4.1	11	2
McKie	8	18	2.3	7	0
Berrian	2	5	2.5	5	0
Grossman	24	2	0.1	22	0
Griese	6	-5	-0.8	0	0
Bears	503	1918	3.8	30t	14
Opponents	402	1590	4.0	53	7

RECEIVING

	No.	Yds.	Avg.	LG	TD
Muhammad	60	863	14.4	40	5
Berrian	51	775	15.2	62	6
Clark	45	626	13.9	33	6
Jones	36	154	4.3	21	0
McKie	25	162	6.5	26	0
Davis	22	303	13.8	31	2
Bradley	14	282	20.1	75t	3
Benson	8	54	6.8	22	0
Peterson	6	88	14.7	37	0
Gilmore	6	38	6.3	18	2
Gage	4	68	17.0	34	0
Reid	4	37	9.3	19	0
Grossman	1	-4	-4.0	-4	0
Bears	282	3446	12.2	75t	24
Opponents	328	3388	10.3	64t	18

INTERCEPTIONS

	No.	Yds.	Avg.	LG	TD
R. Manning	5	113	22.6	54t	1
Tillman	5	32	6.4	13	0
Urlacher	3	38	12.7	36	0
Vasher	3	11	3.7	7	0
D. Manning	2	26	13.0	15	0
A. Brown	2	22	11.0	18	0
C. Harris	2	19	9.5	16	0
Briggs	2	18	9.0	18	0
Bears	24	279	11.6	54t	1
Opponents	22	321	14.6	55t	4

PUNTING

	No.	Yds.	Avg.	In 20	LG
Maynard	77	3404	44.2	24	65
Bears	77	3404	44.2	24	65
Opponents	100	4368	43.7	23	67

PUNT RETURNS

	No.	FC	Yds.	Avg.	LG	TD
Hester	47	12	600	12.8	84t	3
Berrian	2	0	7	3.5	7	0
Wesley	1	0	0	0.0	0	0
Bears	50	12	607	12.1	84t	3
Opponents	38	14	367	9.7	48	0

KICKOFF RETURN

	No.	Yds.	Avg.	LG	TD
Davis	32	753	23.5	42	0
Hester	20	528	26.4	96t	2
Peterson	3	49	16.3	25	0
D. Manning	1	20	20.0	20	0
McKie	1	11	11.0	11	0
McClover	1	9	9.0	9	0
Muhammad	1	3	3.0	3	0
Bears	59	1373	23.3	96t	2
Opponents	83	1730	20.8	35	0

FIELD GOALS

	1-19	20-29	30-39	40-49	50+
Gould	0/0	6/6	14/16	12/14	0/0
Bears	0/0	6/6	14/16	12/14	0/0
Opponents	0/0	9/9	2/5	6/9	1/4

SACKS

	No.
Anderson	12.0
A. Brown	7.0
Ogunleye	6.5
T. Harris	5.0
Ta. Johnson	3.5
Boone	2.0
R. Manning	2.0
Briggs	1.0
Worrell	1.0
Bears	40.0
Opponents	25.0

RECORD HOLDERS
INDIVIDUAL RECORDS—CAREER

Category	Name	Performance
Rushing (Yds.)	Walter Payton, 1975-1987	16,726
Passing (Yds.)	Sid Luckman, 1939-1950	14,686
Passing (TDs)	Sid Luckman, 1939-1950	137
Receiving (No.)	Walter Payton, 1975-1987	492
Receiving (Yds.)	Johnny Morris, 1958-1967	5,059
Interceptions	Gary Fencik, 1976-1987	38
Punting (Avg.)	George Gulyanics, 1947-1952	44.5
Punt Return (Avg.)	George McAfee, 1940-41, 1945-1950	*12.8
Kickoff Return (Avg.)	Gale Sayers, 1965-1971	*30.6
Field Goals	Kevin Butler, 1985-1995	243
Touchdowns (Tot.)	Walter Payton, 1975-1987	125
Points	Kevin Butler, 1985-1995	1,116

INDIVIDUAL RECORDS—SINGLE SEASON

Category	Name	Performance
Rushing (Yds.)	Walter Payton, 1977	1,852
Passing (Yds.)	Erik Kramer, 1995	3,838
Passing (TDs)	Erik Kramer, 1995	29
Receiving (No.)	Marty Booker, 2001	100
Receiving (Yds.)	Marcus Robinson, 1999	1,400
Interceptions	Mark Carrier, 1990	10
Punting (Avg.)	Bobby Joe Green, 1963	46.5
Punt Return (Avg.)	Harry Clark, 1943	15.8
Kickoff Return (Avg.)	Gale Sayers, 1967	37.7
Field Goals	Robbie Gould, 2006	32
Touchdowns (Tot.)	Gale Sayers, 1965	22
Points	Kevin Butler, 1985	144

INDIVIDUAL RECORDS—SINGLE GAME

Category	Name	Performance
Rushing (Yds.)	Walter Payton, 11-20-77	275
Passing (Yds.)	Johnny Lujack, 12-11-49	468
Passing (TDs)	Sid Luckman, 11-14-43	*7
Receiving (No.)	Jim Keane, 10-23-49	14
Receiving (Yds.)	Harlon Hill, 10-31-54	214
Interceptions	Many times	3
	Last time by Mark Carrier, 12-9-90	
Field Goals	Roger LeClerc, 12-3-61	5
	Mac Percival, 10-20-68	5
Touchdowns (Tot.)	Gale Sayers, 12-12-65	*6
Points	Gale Sayers, 12-12-65	36

*NFL Record

2007 VETERAN ROSTER

No.	Name	Pos.	Ht.	Wt.	Birthdate	NFL Exp.	College	Hometown	How Acq.	'06 Games/ Starts
95	Adams, Anthony	DT	6-0	297	6/18/80	5	Penn State	Detroit, Mich.	UFA(SF)-'07	14/5*
97	Anderson, Mark	DE	6-4	255	5/26/83	2	Alabama	Tulsa, Okla.	D5-'06	16/1
86	Angulo, Richard	TE	6-8	260	8/13/80	3	Western New Mexico	Albuquerque, N.M.	W(Minn)-'06	0*
20 t-	Archuleta, Adam	S	6-0	215	11/27/77	7	Arizona State	Chandler; Ariz.	T(Wash)-'07	16/7*
94	Ayanbadejo, Brendon	LB	6-1	228	9/6/76	5	UCLA	Santa Cruz, Calif.	T(Mia)-'05	16/1
32	Benson, Cedric	RB	5-11	220	12/28/82	3	Texas	Midland, Texas	D1-'05	15/0
80	Berrian, Bernard	WR	6-1	185	12/27/80	4	Fresno State	Winton, Calif.	D3-'04	15/14
16	Bradley, Mark	WR	6-2	198	1/29/82	3	Oklahoma	Pine Bluff, Ark.	D2-'05	10/0
55	Briggs, Lance	LB	6-1	240	11/12/80	5	Arizona	Sacramento, Calif.	D3-'03	16/16
96	Brown, Alex	DE	6-3	260	6/4/79	6	Florida	White Springs, Fla.	D4-'02	16/16
30	Brown, Mike	S	5-10	207	2/13/78	8	Nebraska	Scottsdale, Ariz.	D2-'00	6/6
74	Brown, Ruben	G	6-3	300	2/13/72	13	Pittsburgh	Lynchburg, Va.	FA-'04	16/16
88	Clark, Desmond	TE	6-3	249	4/20/77	9	Wake Forest	Lakeland, Fla.	UFA(Mia)-'03	16/16
81	Davis, Rashied	WR	5-9	183	7/24/79	3	San Jose State	Granada Hills, Calif.	FA-'05	16/2
22	Everett, Tyler	S	5-11	202	11/4/83	2	Ohio State	Canton, Ohio	W(Den)-'06	3/0
90	Garay, Antonio	DT	6-3	303	11/30/79	3	Boston College	Rahway, N.J.	FA-'05	4/0
63	Garza, Roberto	G/C	6-2	305	3/26/79	7	Texas A&M-Kingsville	Rio Hondo, Texas	UFA(Atl)-'05	16/16
85	Gilmore, John	TE	6-5	257	9/21/79	6	Penn State	West Lawn, Pa.	FA-'02	16/3
9	Gould, Robbie	K	6-0	183	12/30/81	3	Penn State	Lock Haven, Pa.	FA-'05	16/0
14	Griese, Brian	QB	6-3	214	3/18/75	10	Michigan	Miami, Fla.	FA-'06	6/0
8	Grossman, Rex	QB	6-1	217	8/23/80	5	Florida	Bloomington, Ind.	D1b-'03	16/16
46	Harris, Chris	S	6-0	205	8/6/82	3	Louisiana-Monroe	Little Rock, Ark.	D6-'05	11/7
91	Harris, Tommie	DT	6-3	295	4/29/83	4	Oklahoma	Killeen, Texas	D1-'04	12/11
23	Hester, Devin	KR/PR	5-11	186	11/4/82	2	Miami	Riviera Beach, Fla.	D2b-'06	16/0
92	Hillenmeyer, Hunter	LB	6-4	238	10/28/80	5	Vanderbilt	Nashville, Tenn.	FA-'03	15/13
71	Idonije, Israel	DE/DT	6-6	270	11/17/80	4	Manitoba	Lagos, Nigeria	FA-'03	13/1
53	Joe, Leon	LB	6-1	230	10/26/81	4	Maryland	Fort Washington, Md.	W(Ariz)-'05	9/0
99	Johnson, Tank	DT	6-3	300	12/7/81	4	Washington	Tempe, Ariz.	D2-'04	14/10
57	Kreutz, Olin	C	6-2	292	6/9/77	10	Washington	Honolulu, Hawaii	D3-'98	16/16
65	Mannelly, Patrick	LS	6-5	265	4/18/75	10	Duke	Atlanta, Ga.	D6b-'98	16/0
38	Manning, Danieal	S	5-11	196	8/9/82	2	Abilene Christian	Corsicana, Texas	D2a-'06	16/14
24	Manning, Jr., Ricky	CB	5-9	188	11/18/80	5	UCLA	Fresno, Calif.	FA-'06	15/6
4	Maynard, Brad	P	6-1	186	2/9/74	11	Ball State	Sheridan, Ind.	UFA(NYG)-'01	16/0
58	McClover, Darrell	LB	6-2	226	8/25/81	4	Miami	Coconut Creek, Fla.	W(NYJ)-'06	7/0
36	McGowan, Brandon	S	5-11	196	9/16/83	3	Maine	Jersey City, N.J.	FA-'05	1/0
37	McKie, Jason	FB	5-11	243	5/22/80	6	Temple	Gulf Breeze, Fla.	W(Dall)-'03	15/12
60	Metcalf, Terrence	G	6-3	318	1/28/78	6	Mississippi	Clarksdale, Miss.	D3-'02	16/0
69	Miller, Fred	T	6-7	314	2/6/73	12	Baylor	Aldine, Texas	FA-'05	16/16
87	Muhammad, Muhsin	WR	6-2	215	5/5/73	12	Michigan State	Lansing, Mich.	FA-'05	16/16
1	Novak, Nick	K	6-0	190	8/21/81	4	Maryland	Charlottesville, Va.	W(Wash)-'07	6/6*
17	O'Sullivan, J.T.	QB	6-2	227	8/25/79	6	California-Davis	Carmichael, Calif.	FA-'07	0*
68	Oakley, Anthony	C/G	6-4	298	8/16/81	2	Western Kentucky	Houston, Texas	W(Cle)-'05	0*
93	Ogunleye, Adewale	DE	6-4	260	8/9/77	7	Indiana	Staten Island, N.Y.	T(Mia)-'04	14/14
18	Orton, Kyle	QB	6-4	217	11/14/82	3	Purdue	Runnels, Iowa	D4-'05	0*
29	Peterson, Adrian	RB	5-10	210	7/1/79	6	Georgia Southern	Alachua, Fla.	D6a-'02	16/0
48	Runnels, J.D.	FB	5-11	240	6/19/84	2	Oklahoma	Midwest City, Okla.	D6a-'06	2/0
78	St. Clair, John	T	6-5	315	7/15/77	8	Virginia	Roanoke, Va.	FA-'05	16/2
76	Tait, John	T	6-6	312	1/26/75	9	Brigham Young	Tempe, Ariz.	RFA(KC)-'04	14/14
33	Tillman, Charles	CB	6-1	196	2/23/81	5	Louisiana-Lafayette	Copperas Cove, Texas	D2-'03	14/14
54	Urlacher, Brian	LB	6-4	258	5/25/78	8	New Mexico	Lovington, N.M.	D1-'00	16/16
31	Vasher, Nathan	CB	5-10	180	11/17/81	4	Texas	Texarkana, Texas	D4a-'04	14/13
21	Wesley, Dante	CB	6-1	210	4/5/79	6	Arkansas-Pine Bluff	Pine Bluff, Ark.	UFA(Car)-'06	13/0
52	Williams, Jamar	LB	6-0	234	6/14/84	2	Arizona State	Houston, Texas	D4-'06	3/0
59	Wilson, Rod	LB	6-2	230	11/12/81	2	South Carolina	Cross, S.C.	D7-'05	13/0

* Adams played 14 games with San Francisco in '06; Angulo last active with Minnesota in '05; Archuleta played 16 games with Washington; Novak played 6 games with Washington; O'Sullivan last active with Green Bay in '04; Oakley did not play in 2 games; Orton inactive as third QB for 16 games; Rideau was on practice squad of Chicago in '06.

t- Bears traded for Archuleta (Wash.).

Traded—RB Thomas Jones (16 games in '06) to N.Y. Jets.

Players lost through free agency (5): DT Alfonso Boone (KC; 12 games in '06), WR Justin Gage (Tenn; 8), S Todd Johnson (StL; 12), DT Ian Scott (Phil; 15), S Cameron Worrell (Mia; 16).

Also played with Bears in '06—WR Airese Currie (1 game), CB Marcus Maxey (1), CB Derek Strait (1), S Nick Turnbull (1).

2007 FIRST-YEAR ROSTER

Name	Pos.	Ht.	Wt.	Birthdate	College	Hometown	How Acq.
Allen, Josh	RB	5-11	215	6/11/83	Maryland	Tampa, Fla.	FA
Ball, David	WR	6-0	193	6/6/84	New Hampshire	Orange, Vt.	FA
Bazuin, Dan	DE	6-3	266	7/22/83	Central Michigan	McBain, Mich.	D2
Beekman, Josh	G/C	6-2	313	6/30/83	Boston College	Amsterdam, N.Y.	D4
Brant, Aaron	T	6-7	320	9/16/84	Iowa State	Dubuque, Iowa	D7b
Bryan, Copeland (1)	DE	6-3	253	7/14/83	Arizona	San Jose, Calif.	W(Tenn)-'06
Collins, Tory	DT	6-3	280	12/19/82	Northwestern State	New Orleans, La.	FA
Dvoracek, Dusty (1)	DT	6-3	303	3/3/83	Oklahoma	Lake Dallas, Texas	D3-'06
Fassitt, Greg	CB	5-11	181	4/20/85	Grambling	New Orleans, La.	FA
Filipovic, Filip (1)	P	6-2	216	11/5/77	South Dakota	Belgrade, Yugoslavia	W(Dall)
Frome, Chris	DE	6-5	262	1/21/84	Notre Dame	Saugus, Calif.	FA
Graham, Corey	CB	6-0	195	7/25/84	New Hampshire	Buffalo, N.Y.	D5b
Hass, Mike (1)	WR	6-1	209	1/2/83	Oregon State	Portland, Ore.	W(NO)-'06
James, Drisan	WR	5-11	186	10/6/84	Boise State	Phoenix, Ariz.	FA
Leak, Chris	QB	6-0	207	5/3/85	Florida	Charlotte, N.C.	FA
LeVoir, Mark (1)	T	6-7	310	7/29/82	Notre Dame	Eden Prairie, Minn.	FA-'06
McBride, Trumaine	CB	5-9	185	9/24/85	Mississippi	Clarksdale, Miss.	D7a
McMeans, Tyler (1)	G	6-4	325	4/4/80	Miami	Shippenville, Pa.	FA-'06
Mines, Fontel	TE	6-4	223	2/26/85	Virginia	Richmond, Va.	FA
Mixon, Tim	CB	5-10	184	7/8/84	California	Compton, CA	FA
Okwo, Michael	LB	5-11	232	1/24/85	Stanford	Redondo Beach, Calif.	D3b
Olsen, Greg	TE	6-6	254	3/11/85	Miami	Wayne, N.J.	D1
Payne, Kevin	S	6-0	220	12/5/83	Louisiana-Monroe	Junction City, Ark.	D5a
Reed, Tyler (1)	G	6-4	307	10/6/82	Penn State	Jefferson Borough, Pa.	D6b-'06
Rideau, Brandon (1)	WR	6-3	200	10/18/82	Kansas	Ozen, Texas	W(Cle)-'06
Riggs, Jr., Gerald (1)	RB	5-11	229	9/28/83	Tennessee	Chattanooga, Tenn.	W(Mia)
Shanle, Andrew	S	6-1	210	3/9/83	Nebraska	St. Edward, Neb.	FA
Staggs, Jay	S	6-1	220	9/26/83	Nevada-Las Vegas	Goleta, Calif.	FA
Stelly, Joel (1)	P	5-10	200	1/13/84	Louisiana-Monroe	Cecilia, La.	FA-'06
Swain, Jayson	WR	6-1	205	7/27/84	Tennessee	Huntsville, Ala.	FA
Verdun Wheeler, Danny	LB	6-2	244	3/16/85	Georgia	Thomson; Ga.	FA
Wolfe, Garrett	RB	5-7	186	8/17/84	Northern Illinois	Chicago, Ill.	D3a

The term NFL Rookie is defined as a player who is in his first season of professional football and has not been on the roster of another professional football team for any regular-season or postseason games. A Rookie is designated by an "R" on NFL rosters. Players who have been active in another professional football league or players who have NFL experience, including either preseason training camp or being on an Active List or Inactive List, or on Reserve/Injured or Reserve/Physically Unable to Perform for fewer than six regular-season games, are termed NFL First-Year Players. An NFL First-Year Player is designated by a "1" on NFL rosters. Thereafter, a player is credited with an additional year of experience for each season in which he accumulates six games on the Active List or Inactive List, or on Reserve/Injured or Reserve/Physically Unable to Perform.

Log on to www.chicagobears.com for an up-to-date roster.

COACHING STAFF

Head Coach,
Lovie Smith

Pro Career: Named the thirteenth head coach in Chicago Bears history on January 15, 2004. The first coach in team history to lead the Bears to the postseason in two of his first three seasons while guiding the team to its first Super Bowl in 21 years, Smith is the franchise record-holder for victories over his first three seasons as head coach. Smith's 29-19 (.604) regular season record is the seventh-best in the NFL over the last three years. Chicago rode home-field advantage in the NFC playoffs in 2006 to the team's first conference championship since 1985 with a 13-3 record. In three seasons, Smith has a 12-6 record against NFC North opponents. Smith earned the 2005 AP NFL Coach of the Year Award after turning a 1-3 start to the season into 11 victories, the most by a second-year coach in club annals, and the second seed in the NFC Playoffs. Fueled by an eight-game win streak, Smith led a worst-to-first revival in the NFC North division as the Bears six-win improvement from the previous season was tied for the biggest in the NFL in 2005. In Smith's first season, Chicago posted a 5-11 record. From 2004-06, the Bears had a league-high 13 touchdowns via defensive return—including a franchise-record 6 in 2004. Allowing the fewest points in the NFL in 2005, Chicago ranked second in overall defense before ranking fifth in 2006. Smith came to Chicago from St. Louis (2001-03), where he served as defensive coordinator. In 2001 he helped the Rams return to the Super Bowl after missing the playoffs the previous season. Smith previously coached the linebackers for the Tampa Bay Buccaneers (1996-2000). Career record: 31-21.

Background: Played at Tulsa (1976-79), where he was a linebacker before moving to strong safety and earning two-time All-America and three-time All-Missouri Conference defensive back honors. Began his coaching career at his hometown high school (Big Sandy, Texas) in 1980 before moving to Cascia Hall Prep in Tulsa the following year. Two years later Smith began coaching collegiately at Tulsa (1983-86), Wisconsin (1987), Arizona State (1988-1991), Kentucky (1992), Tennessee (1993-94), and Ohio State (1995).

Personal: Born May 8, 1958, Gladewater, Texas. Lovie and his wife MaryAnne have three sons—Mikal, Matthew and Miles and twin grandsons—Malachi and Noah.

ASSISTANT COACHES

Jim Arthur, strength and conditioning assistant; born July 12, 1978. Attended Springfield (Mass.) College. No college or pro playing experience. College coach: Springfield (Mass.) College 2000, Louisiana Tech 2001, Boston College 2002. Pro coach: Joined Bears in 2005.

Bob Babich, defensive coordinator; born February 20, 1961, Aliquippa, Pa. Linebacker Mesa (Colo.) C.C. 1979-1980, Tulsa 1981-82. No pro playing experience. College coach: Tulsa 1984-87, 1990, Wisconsin 1988-89, Bowling Green 1991, East Carolina 1992-93, Pittsburgh 1994-96, North Dakota State 1997-2002 (head coach). Pro coach: St. Louis Rams 2003, joined Bears in 2004.

Rob Boras, tight ends; born September 30, 1970, Glen Ellyn, Ill. Center DePauw 1988-1991. No pro playing experience. College coach: DePauw 1992-93, Texas 1994-97, Benedictine 1998 (head coach), Nevada-Las Vegas 1999-2003. Pro coach: Joined Bears in 2004.

Luke Butkus, asst. offensive line; born June 26, 1979, Steger, Ill. Center Illinois 1998-2001. Pro center San Diego Chargers 2002-03. College coach: Oregon 2005-06. Pro coach: Joined Bears in 2007.

Gill Byrd, asst. defensive backs; born February 20, 1961, San Francisco. Cornerback San Jose State 1979-1982. Pro cornerback San Diego Chargers 1983-1992. Pro coach: St. Louis Rams 2003-05, joined Bears in 2006.

Darryl Drake, wide receivers; born December 11, 1956, Louisville, Ky. Wide receiver Western Kentucky 1975-78. Pro wide receiver Washington Redskins 1979, Ottawa Rough Riders (CFL) 1981, Cincinnati Bengals 1983. College coach: Western Kentucky 1983-1991, Georgia 1992-96, Baylor 1997, Texas 1998-2003. Pro coach: Joined Bears in 2004.

Brick Haley, defensive line; born May 16, 1966, Gadsen, Ala. Linebacker Alabama A&M 1984-88. No pro playing experience. College coach: Arkansas 1990, Austin Peay 1991-93, Troy State 1994-96, Houston 1997, Clemson 1998, Baylor 1999-2001, Georgia Tech 2002-03, Mississippi State 2004-06. Pro coach: Joined Bears in 2007.

Pep Hamilton, quarterbacks; born September 19, 1974, Charlotte, N.C. Quarterback Howard 1993-96. No pro playing experience. College coach: Howard 1997-2002. Pro coach: New York Jets 2003-05, San Francisco 49ers 2006, joined Bears in 2007.

Harry Hiestand, offensive line; born November 19, 1958, Malvern, Pa. Offensive lineman Springfield College 1978-79, East Stroudsburg 1980. No pro playing experience. College coach: East Stroudsburg 1981-85, Pennsylvania 1986, Southern California 1987, Toledo 1988, Cincinnati 1989-1993, Missouri 1994-96, Illinois 1997-2004. Pro coach: Joined Bears in 2005.

Rusty Jones, strength and conditioning coordinator; born August 14, 1953. Attended Springfield (Mass.) College. No college or pro playing experience. College coach: Springfield (Mass.) College 1979-1982. Pro coach: Buffalo Bills 1985-

2004, joined Bears in 2005.

Lloyd Lee, defensive assistant; born August 10, 1976, Minneapolis. Safety Dartmouth 1994-97. Pro safety San Diego Chargers 1998-99. Pro coach: Tampa Bay Buccaneers (scout) 2001-03, joined Bears in 2004.

Charles London, offensive quality control; born August 12, 1975, Dunwoody, Ga. Running back Duke 1994-96. No pro playing experience. College coach: Duke 2004-06. Pro coach: Joined Bears in 2007.

Hardy Nickerson, linebackers; born September 1, 1965, Compton, Calif. Linebacker Califorinia 1983-86. Pro linebacker Pittsburgh Steelers 1987-1992, Tampa Bay Buccaneers 1993-99, Jacksonville Jaguars 2000-01, Green Bay Packers 2002. Pro coach: Joined Bears in 2007.

Kevin O'Dea, asst. special teams; born June 9, 1960, Williamsport, Pa. Wide receiver/defensive back Lock Haven 1983-85. No pro playing experience. College coach: Lock Haven 1986, Cornell 1987, Virginia 1988-1990, Penn State 1991-93. Pro coach: San Diego Chargers 1994-95, Tampa Bay Buccaneers 1996-2001, Detroit Lions 2002-03, Arizona Cardinals 2004-05, joined Bears in 2006.

Tim Spencer, running backs; born December 10, 1960, Martin Ferry, Ohio. Running back Ohio State 1979-1982. Pro running back Chicago Blitz (USFL) 1983, Arizona Wranglers (USFL) 1984, Memphis Showboats (USFL) 1985, San Diego Chargers 1985-1990. College coach: Ohio State 1994-2003. Pro coach: Joined Bears in 2004.

Dave Toub, special teams coordinator; born June 1, 1962, Ossining, N.Y. Offensive lineman Springfield College 1980-81, Texas-El Paso 1983-84. No pro playing experience. College coach: Texas El-Paso 1987-89, Missouri 1989-2000. Pro coach: Philadelphia Eagles 2001-03, joined Bears in 2004.

Ron Turner, offensive coordinator; born December 5, 1953, Martinez, Calif. Wide receiver Diablo Valley (Calif.) C.C. 1973-74, Pacific 1975-76. No pro playing experience. College coach: Pacific 1977, Arizona 1978-1980, Northwestern 1981-82, Pittsburgh 1983-84, Southern California 1985-87, Texas A&M 1988, Stanford 1989-1991, San Jose State 1992 (head coach), Illinois 1997-2004 (head coach). Pro coach: Chicago Bears 1993-96, re-joined Bears in 2005.

Steven Wilks, defensive backs; born August 8, 1969, Charlotte. Defensive back Appalachian State 1987-1991. Pro defensive back/wide receiver Charlotte Rage (AFL) 1993. College coach: Johnson C. Smith 1995-96, Savannah State 1997-99, Illinois State 2000, Appalachian State 2001, East Tennessee State 2002, Bowling Green State 2003, Notre Dame 2004, Washington 2005. Pro coach: Joined Bears in 2006.

**National Football Conference
East Division
Team Colors:** Royal Blue, Metallic Silver
Blue, and White
**Cowboys Center
One Cowboys Parkway
Irving, Texas 75063
Telephone:** (972) 556-9900

**2007 SCHEDULE
PRESEASON**
Aug. 9   **Indianapolis**......................7:00
Aug. 18 **Denver**...............................7:00
Aug. 25 at Houston 7:00
Aug. 30 at Minnesota 7:00

REGULAR SEASON
Sep. 9   **N.Y. Giants**......................7:15
Sep. 16 at Miami 4:05
Sep. 23 at Chicago 7:15
Sep. 30 **St. Louis** 12:00
Oct. 8   at Buffalo (Mon.) 8:30
Oct. 14 **New England** 3:15
Oct. 21 **Minnesota** 12:00
Oct. 28 Open Date
Nov. 4   at Philadelphia 8:15
Nov. 11 at N.Y. Giants....................4:15
Nov. 18 **Washington** 12:00
Nov. 22 **N.Y. Jets** (Thu.)................3:15
Nov. 29 **Green Bay** (Thu.) 7:15
Dec. 9   at Detroit 1:00
Dec. 16 **Philadelphia** 3:15
Dec. 22 at Carolina (Sat.) 8:15
Dec. 30 at Washington 1:00

Stadium: Texas Stadium (opened in 1971)
•**Capacity:** 65,529
2401 E. Airport Freeway
Irving, Texas 75062
Playing Surface: Sportfield Realgrass
Training Camp: Marriott Riverwalk &
Rivercenter
San Antonio, TX 78205

TEXAS STADIUM

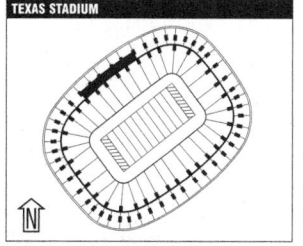

CLUB OFFICIALS
Owner/President/General Manager:
Jerry Jones
Chief Operating Officer/Executive Vice
President/Director of Player Personnel:
Stephen Jones
Vice President/Director of Charities and
Special Events: Charlotte Anderson
Chief Sales and Marketing Officer/Vice
President: Jerry Jones Jr.
CFO: George Mitchell
Vice President of College and Pro
Scouting: Jeff Ireland
Vice President, Sales and Marketing:
Greg McElroy
General Counsel: Alec Scheiner
Director of Public Relations:
Rich Dalrymple
Director of Corporate Communications:
Brett Daniels
Director of Community Relations:
Emily Robbins
Assistant Director of College Scouting:
Tom Ciskowski
Assistant Director of Pro Scouting:
Brian Gaine
Director of Operations: Bruce Mays
Director of Player Development:
Steve Carichoff
Chief Human Resources and Diversity
Officer: Vincent Thompson
Director of Information Technology:
Peter Walsh
Director of Broadcasting: Scott Purcel
Internet Director: Derek Eagleton
Director of Ticket Operations:
Carol Padgett
Head Athletic Trainer: Jim Maurer
Equipment Manager: Mike McCord
Video Director: Robert Blackwell
Cheerleader Director: Kelli Finglass

COACHING HISTORY
(433-322-6)
Records include postseason games
1960-1988 Tom Landry 270-178-6
1989-1993 Jimmy Johnson 51-37-0
1994-97 Barry Switzer 45-26-0
1998-99 Chan Gailey 18-16-0
2000-02 Dave Campo 15-33-0
2003-06 Bill Parcells 34-32-0

PAID ATTENDANCE
Home 500,057   Away 568,012
Total 1,068,069
Single-game home record,
65,180 (11/12/95)
Single-season home record,
518,167 (1995)

2007 DRAFT CHOICES

Round	Name	Pos.	College
1	Anthony Spencer	LB	Purdue
3	James Marten	T	Boston College
4	Isaiah Stanback	WR	Washington
	Doug Free	T	Northern Illinois
6	Nick Folk	K	Arizona
	Deon Anderson	FB	Connecticut
7	Courtney Brown	DB	Cal Poly-SLO
	Alan Ball	DB	Illinois

DALLAS COWBOYS

2006 TEAM RECORD
PRESEASON (3-0-1)
Date	Result		Opponent
8/12	W	13-3	at Seattle
8/21	W	30-7	at New Orleans
8/26	W	17-7	San Francisco
8/31	T	10-10	Minnesota

REGULAR SEASON (9-7)
Date	Result		Opponent	Att.
9/10	L	17-24	at Jacksonville	67,164
9/17	W	27-10	Washington	63,152
10/1	W	45-14	at Tennessee	69,143
10/8	L	24-38	at Philadelphia	69,268
10/15	W	34-6	Houston	63,186
10/23	L	22-36	N.Y. Giants	63,512
10/29	W	35-14	at Carolina	73,688
11/5	L	19-22	at Washington	90,250
11/12	W	27-10	at Arizona	63,926
11/19	W	21-14	Indianapolis	63,706
11/23	W	38-10	Tampa Bay	63,183
12/3	W	23-20	at N.Y. Giants	78,666
12/10	L	17-42	New Orleans	63,722
12/16	W	38-28	at Atlanta	71,102
12/25	L	7-23	Philadelphia	62,839
12/31	L	31-39	Detroit	63,008

POSTSEASON (0-1)
1/6	L	20-21	at Seattle	68,756

SCORE BY PERIODS
Cowboys	65	122	96	142	0	—	425
Opponents	78	111	80	81	0	—	350

2006 TEAM STATISTICS
	Cowboys	Opp.
Total First Downs	336	294
Rushing	107	88
Passing	197	179
Penalty	32	27
3rd Down: Made/Att	100/205	93/212
3rd Down Pct.	48.8	43.9
4th Down: Made/Att	9/19	8/16
4th Down Pct.	47.4	50.0
Possession Avg.	31:02	28:58
Total Net Yards	5772	5165
Avg. Per Game	360.8	322.8
Total Plays	1015	974
Avg. Per Play	5.7	5.3
Net Yards Rushing	1936	1659
Avg. Per Game	121.0	103.7
Total Rushes	472	429
Net Yards Passing	3836	3506
Avg. Per Game	239.8	219.1
Sacked/Yards Lost	37/231	34/223
Gross Yards	4067	3729
Att./Completions	506/310	511/301
Completion Pct.	61.3	58.9
Had Intercepted	21	18
Punts/Average	56/48.2	72/43.1
Net Punting Avg.	56/38.6	72/36.7
Penalties/Yards	100/939	93/895
Fumbles/Ball Lost	21/9	26/13
Touchdowns	52	40
Rushing	21	12
Passing	26	25
Returns	5	3

2006 INDIVIDUAL STATISTICS
PASSING	Att.	Comp.	Yds.	Pct.	TD	Int.	Tkld.	Rate
Romo	337	220	2,903	65.3	19	13	21/124	95.1
Bledsoe	169	90	1,164	53.3	7	8	16/107	69.2
Cowboys	506	310	4,067	61.3	26	21	37/231	86.5
Opponents	511	301	3,729	58.9	25	18	34/223	83.2

SCORING	TD R	TD P	TD Rt	PAT	FG	Saf	PTS
Barber	14	2	0	0/0	0/0	0	96
Owens	0	13	0	0/0	0/0	0	80
Vanderjagt	0	0	0	33/33	13/18	0	72
T. Glenn	0	6	0	0/0	0/0	0	36
Gramatica	0	0	0	14/14	6/8	0	32
Crayton	0	4	0	0/0	0/0	0	24
J. Jones	4	0	0	0/0	0/0	0	24
Bledsoe	2	0	0	0/0	0/0	0	12
Ware	0	0	2	0/0	0/0	0	12
Burnett	0	0	1	0/0	0/0	0	6
James	0	0	1	0/0	0/0	0	6
Newman	0	0	1	0/0	0/0	0	6
Thompson	1	0	0	0/0	0/0	0	6
Witten	0	1	0	0/0	0/0	0	6
Suisham	0	0	0	2/2	1/2	0	5
Romo	0	0	0	0/0	0/0	0	2
Cowboys	21	26	5	49/49	20/28	0	425
Opponents	12	25	3	38/38	22/25	2	350

2-Pt. Conversions: Owens, Romo, Cowboys 2-3, Opponents 1-2.

RUSHING	No.	Yds	Avg	LG	TD
J. Jones	267	1084	4.1	77t	4
Barber	135	654	4.8	25	14
Romo	34	102	3.0	16	0
Thompson	13	30	2.3	7t	1
Bledsoe	8	28	3.5	11	2
Polite	7	18	2.6	4	0
T. Glenn	3	11	3.7	22	0
Kincade	4	9	2.3	7	0
McBriar	1	0	0.0	0	0
Cowboys	472	1936	4.1	77t	21
Opponents	429	1659	3.9	38t	12

RECEIVING	No.	Yds	Avg	LG	TD
Owens	85	1,180	13.9	56t	13
T. Glenn	70	1,047	15.0	54	6
Witten	64	754	11.8	42	1
Crayton	36	516	14.3	53t	4
Barber	23	196	8.5	26	2
Fasano	14	126	9.0	22	0
J. Jones	9	142	15.8	39	0
Hurd	5	75	15.0	33	0
Polite	2	21	10.5	12	0
Hoyte	2	10	5.0	6	0
Cowboys	310	4,067	13.1	56t	26
Opponents	301	3,729	12.4	87t	25

INTERCEPTIONS	No.	Yds	Avg	LG	TD
Williams	5	33	6.6	27	0
Watkins	3	45	15.0	24	0
Henry	2	41	20.5	37	0
A. Ayodele	2	2	1.0	2	0
Ware	1	41	41.0	41t	1
Burnett	1	39	39.0	39t	1
James	1	15	15.0	15t	1
Newman	1	12	12.0	12	0
A. Glenn	1	7	7.0	7	0
Ellis	1	-1	-1.0	-1	0
Cowboys	18	234	13.0	41t	3
Opponents	21	334	15.9	102t	2

PUNTING	No.	Yds.	Avg.	In 20	LG
McBriar	56	2697	48.2	22	75
Cowboys	56	2697	48.2	22	75
Opponents	72	3100	43.1	14	60

PUNT RETURNS	Ret	FC	Yds	Avg	LG	TD
Newman	20	6	202	10.1	56t	1
Crayton	11	7	85	7.7	19	0
Green	5	3	26	5.2	13	0
Rector	4	1	22	5.5	8	0
Cowboys	40	17	335	8.4	56t	1
Opponents	31	12	334	10.8	45	0

KICKOFF RETURNS	No.	Yds	Avg	LG	TD
Austin	29	753	26.0	37	0
Thompson	21	546	26.0	41	0
Elam	4	95	23.8	26	0
A. Glenn	3	24	8.0	14	0
Green	3	59	19.7	21	0
A. Johnson	1	3	3.0	3	0
N. Jones	1	13	13.0	13	0
Ratliff	1	0	0.0	0	0
Watkins	1	0	0.0	0	0
Cowboys	64	1493	23.3	41	0
Opponents	80	1571	19.6	100t	1

FIELD GOALS	1-19	20-29	30-39	40-49	50+
Vanderjagt	0/0	6/7	5/6	1/4	1/1
Gramatica	0/0	1/1	2/2	3/5	0/0
Suisham	0/0	0/0	1/2	0/0	0/0
Cowboys	0/0	7/8	8/10	4/9	1/1
Opponents	1/1	10/10	7/7	4/6	0/1

SACKS	No.
Ware	11.5
Ellis	4.5
K. Coleman	4.0
Ratliff	4.0
Hatcher	2.5
Carpenter	1.5
A. Ayodele	1.0
Bowen	1.0
Burnett	1.0
Canty	1.0
Singleton	1.0
Spears	1.0
Cowboys	34.0
Opponents	37.0

RECORD HOLDERS
INDIVIDUAL RECORDS—CAREER

Category	Name	Performance
Rushing (Yds.)	Emmitt Smith, 1990-2002	*17,162
Passing (Yds.)	Troy Aikman, 1989-2000	32,942
Passing (TDs)	Troy Aikman, 1989-2000	165
Receiving (No.)	Michael Irvin, 1988-1999	750
Receiving (Yds.)	Michael Irvin, 1988-1999	11,904
Interceptions	Mel Renfro, 1964-1977	52
Punting (Avg.)	Toby Gowin, 1997-99, 2003	41.7
Punt Return (Avg.)	Deion Sanders, 1995-99	13.3
Kickoff Return (Avg.)	Mel Renfro, 1964-1977	26.4
Field Goals	Rafael Septien, 1978-1986	162
Touchdowns (Tot.)	Emmitt Smith, 1990-2002	164
Points	Emmitt Smith, 1990-2002	986

INDIVIDUAL RECORDS—SINGLE SEASON

Category	Name	Performance
Rushing (Yds.)	Emmitt Smith, 1995	1,773
Passing (Yds.)	Danny White, 1983	3,980
Passing (TDs)	Danny White, 1983	29
Receiving (No.)	Michael Irvin, 1995	111
Receiving (Yds.)	Michael Irvin, 1995	1,603
Interceptions	Everson Walls, 1981	11
Punting (Avg.)	Mat McBriar, 2006	48.2
Punt Return (Avg.)	Bob Hayes, 1968	20.8
Kickoff Return (Avg.)	Mel Renfro, 1965	30.0
Field Goals	Richie Cunningham, 1997	34
Touchdowns (Tot.)	Emmitt Smith, 1995	25
Points	Emmitt Smith, 1995	150

INDIVIDUAL RECORDS—SINGLE GAME

Category	Name	Performance
Rushing (Yds.)	Emmitt Smith, 10-31-93	237
Passing (Yds.)	Don Meredith, 11-10-63	460
Passing (TDs)	Many times	5
	Last time by Troy Aikman, 9-12-99	
Receiving (No.)	Lance Rentzel, 11-19-67	13
Receiving (Yds.)	Bob Hayes, 11-13-66	246
Interceptions	Many times	3
	Last time by Terance Newman, 12-14-03	
Field Goals	Chris Boniol, 11-18-96	*7
	Billy Cundiff, 9-15-03	*7
Touchdowns (Tot.)	Many times	4
	Last time by Emmitt Smith, 9-4-95	
Points	Many times	24
	Last time by Emmitt Smith, 9-4-95	

*NFL Record

2007 VETERAN ROSTER

No.	Name	Pos.	Ht.	Wt.	Birthdate	NFL Exp.	College	Hometown	How Acq.	'06 Games/ Starts
76	Adams, Flozell	T	6-7	343	5/18/75	10	Michigan State	Bellwood, Ill.	D2-'98	16/16
19	Austin, Miles	WR	6-3	215	6/30/84	2	Monmouth University	Garfield, N.J.	FA-'06	9/0
51	Ayodele, Akin	LB	6-2	250	9/17/79	6	Purdue	Irving, Texas	UFA(Jax)-'06	16/16
24	Barber, Marion	RB	6-0	220	6/10/83	3	Minnesota	Wayzata, Minn.	D4a-'05	16/1
67	Berger, Joe	G	6-5	315	5/25/82	3	Michigan Tech	Newaygo, Mich.	W(Mia)-'06	0*
72	Bowen, Stephen	DE	6-5	300	3/28/84	2	Hofstra	Wheatley Heights, N.Y.	FA-'06	1/0
57	Burnett, Kevin	LB	6-3	240	12/24/82	3	Tennessee	Carson, Calif.	D2-'05	16/0
99	Canty, Chris	DE	6-7	280	11/10/82	3	Virginia	Charlotte, N.C.	D4b-'05	16/16
54	Carpenter, Bobby	LB	6-2	257	8/1/83	2	Ohio State	Lancaster, Ohio	D1-'06	13/1
75	Colombo, Marc	T	6-8	320	10/8/78	6	Boston College	Bridgewater, Mass.	FA-'05	1616
84	Crayton, Patrick	WR	6-0	200	4/7/79	4	Northwestern Oklahoma State	DeSoto, Texas	D7b-'04	16/6
89	Curtis, Tony	TE	6-5	265	2/11/83	3	Portland State	Seaside, Calif.	FA-'06	4/0
66	Darilek, Trey	C	6-5	305	4/23/81	4	Texas El-Paso	San Antonio, Texas	FA-'07	0*
29	Davis, Keith	S	5-10	198	12/30/78	5	Sam Houston	Italy, Texas	FA-'04	15/6
70	Davis, Leonard	T	6-6	366	9/5/78	7	Texas	Wortham, Texas	UFA(Ariz)-'07	16/16*
37	Elam, Abram	S	6-0	210	10/15/81	2	Kent State	Riviera Beach, Fla.	FA-'06	15/0
98	Ellis, Greg	LB	6-6	270	8/14/75	10	North Carolina	Wendell, N.C.	D1-'98	9/9
80	Fasano, Anthony	TE	6-4	258	4/20/84	2	Notre Dame	Verona, N.J.	D2-'06	16/4
95	Ferguson, Jason	DT	6-3	310	11/28/74	11	Georgia	Nettleton, Miss.	UFA(NYJ)-'05	16/16
20	Glenn, Aaron	CB	5-9	185	7/16/72	14	Texas A&M	Humble, Texas	FA-'05	16/1
83	Glenn, Terry	WR	5-11	193	7/23/74	12	Ohio State	Columbus, Ohio	T(GB)-'03	15/14
53	Glymph, Junior	LB	6-6	272	9/2/80	4	Carson-Newman	Newberry, S.C.	FA-'06	3/0
7	Gramatica, Martin	K	5-8	175	11/27/75	8	Kansas State	LaBelle, Fla.	FA-'06	8/0
65	Gurode, Andre	G	6-4	312	3/6/78	6	Colorado	Houston, Texas	D2a-'02	16/16
27	Hamlin, Ken	S	6-2	209	1/20/81	5	Arkansas	Memphis, Tenn.	UFA(Sea)-'07	16/16*
97	Hatcher, Jason	DE	6-6	295	7/13/82	2	Grambling State	Alexandria, La.	D3-'06	14/0
42	Henry, Anthony	CB	6-1	208	11/3/76	7	South Florida	Fort Myers, Fla.	UFA(Cle)-'05	16/16
46	Hoyte, Oliver	FB/LB	6-3	250	10/5/84	2	North Carolina State	Tampa, Fla.	FA-'06	12/6
17	Hurd, Sam	WR	6-2	195	4/24/85	2	Northern Illinois	San Antonio, Texas	FA-'06	15/2
56	James, Bradie	LB	6-2	250	1/17/81	5	Louisiana State	Monroe, La.	D4-'03	16/16
14	Johnson, Brad	QB	6-5	225	9/13/68	16	Florida State	Marietta, Ga.	FA-'07	15/14*
21	Jones, Julius	RB	5-10	211	8/14/81	4	Notre Dame	Big Stone Gap, Va.	D2a-'04	16/16
33	Jones, Nathan	CB	5-10	192	6/13/82	4	Rutgers	Scotch Plains, N.J.	D7a-'04	5/0
63	Kosier, Kyle	G	6-5	305	11/27/78	6	Arizona State	Peoria, Ariz.	UFA(Det)-'06	16/16
91	Ladouceur, Louis-Philippe	LS	6-4	255	3/13/81	3	California	Pointe-Claire, Quebec, Canada	FA-'05	16/0
1	McBriar, Mat	P	6-1	223	7/8/79	4	Hawaii	East Brighton, Australia	FA-'04	16/0
77	McQuistan, Pat	T	6-6	315	4/30/83	2	Weber State	Lebanon, Ore.	D7-'06	1/0
69	Molinaro, Jim	T	6-6	310	4/27/81	4	Notre Dame	Bethlehem, Pa.	FA-'07	1/0*
41	Newman, Terence	CB	5-11	195	9/4/78	5	Kansas State	Salina, Kan.	D1-'03	16/16
81	Owens, Terrell	WR	6-3	224	12/7/73	12	Tennessee-Chattanooga	Alexander City, Ala.	FA-'06	16/15
39	Polite, Lousaka	FB	6-0	248	9/14/81	3	Pittsburgh	Woodland Hills, Pa.	FA-'04	12/0
71	Procter, Cory	G	6-4	305	10/18/82	3	Montana	Gig Harbor, Wash.	FA-'05	0*
90	Ratliff, Jay	DE	6-4	305	8/29/81	3	Auburn	Valdosta, Ga.	FA-'05	15/0
85	Rector, Jamaica	WR	5-10	186	8/10/81	2	Northwest Missouri State	Celeste, Tex.	FA-'05	1/0
35	Reeves, Jacques	CB	5-11	192	10/8/82	4	Purdue	Lancaster, Texas	D7c-'04	13/0
62	Rivera, Marco	G	6-4	309	4/26/72	12	Penn State	Elmont, N.Y.	UFA(GB)-'05	16/16
9	Romo, Tony	QB	6-2	225	4/21/80	5	Eastern Illinois	Burlington, Wis.	FA-'03	16/8
96	Spears, Marcus	DE	6-4	298	3/8/83	3	Louisiana State	Baton Rouge, La.	D1b-'05	16/16
60	Stanley, Montavious	DT	6-2	313	10/10/81	2	Louisville	Albany, Ga.	FA-'06	3/0*
23	Thomas, Joey	CB	6-1	190	8/29/80	3	Montana State	Seattle, Wash.	FA-'07	0*
28	Thompson, Tyson	RB	6-1	215	5/21/81	3	San Jose State	Irving, Texas	FA-'05	7/0
15	Urban, Jerheme	WR	6-3	212	11/26/80	3	Trinity (Texas)	Victoria, Texas	FA-'06	0*
94	Ware, DeMarcus	DE	6-4	257	7/31/82	3	Troy State	Auburn, Ala.	D1a-'05	16/16
25	Watkins, Patrick	S	6-5	211	12/18/82	2	Florida State	Tallahassee, Fla.	D5-'06	14/9
31	Williams, Roy	S	6-0	229	8/14/80	6	Oklahoma	Union City, Calif.	D1-'02	16/16
82	Witten, Jason	TE	6-5	265	5/6/82	5	Tennessee	Elizabethton, Tenn.	D3-'03	16/15

* Berger inactive for 5 games; Darilek last active with Philadelphia in '05; Davis played 16 games with Arizona in '06; Hamlin played in 16 games with Seattle; Johnson played 15 games with Minnesota; Molinaro played 1 game with Washington; Procter inactive for 16 games; Stanley played 3 games with Jacksonville; Thomas last active with New Orleans in '05; Urban last active with Seattle in '05.

Retired—Drew Bledsoe, 14-year quarterback, 6 games with Dallas in '06.

Players lost through free agency (3): DE Kenyon Coleman (NYJ; 16 games in '06), LB Ryan Fowler (Tenn; 16), C Al Johnson (Ariz; 16).

Also played with Cowboys in '06—S Marcus Coleman (3 games), TE Tony Curtis (4), T Jason Fabini (15), RB Skyler Green (2), TE Ryan Hannam (2), RB Keylon Kincade (1); DT J'Vonne Parker (2); S Tony Parrish (1); LB Al Singleton (16); K Shaun Suisham (3); K Mike Vanderjagt (10).

2007 FIRST-YEAR ROSTER

Name	Pos.	Ht.	Wt.	Birthdate	College	Hometown	How Acq.
Anderson, Deon	FB	5-10	236	1/27/83	Connecticut	Providence, R.I.	D6b
Ayodele, Remi (1)	NT	6-2	300	4/22/83	Oklahoma	Grand Prairie, Texas	FA
Baker, Matt (1)	QB	6-2	212	5/11/83	North Carolina	Rochester Hills, Mich.	FA-'06
Ball, Alan	CB	6-1	176	3/29/85	Illinois	Detroit, Mich.	D7b
Battle, Jackie	RB	6-2	238	10/1/83	Houston	Humble, Texas	FA
Bilbo, Damarius (1)	S	6-2	220	12/3/82	Georgia Tech	Moss Point, Miss.	FA-'06
Brown, Courtney	CB	6-1	200	2/10/84	Cal Poly	Berkeley, Calif.	D7a
Butler, Quincy (1)	CB	6-1	190	11/25/81	Texas Christian	San Antonio, Texas	FA-'06
Coleman, Alonzo	RB	5-9	207	1/27/84	Hampton	South Boston, Va.	FA
Dagunduro, Ola	NT	6-2	313	1/6/84	Nebraska	Inglewood, Calif.	FA
Folk, Nick	K	6-1	225	11/5/84	Arizona	Sherman Oaks, Calif.	D6a
Free, Doug	T	6-6	324	1/6/84	Northern Illinois	Manitowoc, Wis.	D4b
Hannah, Rodney	TE	6-6	256	8/9/84	Houston	Roseville, Calif.	FA
Harrington, Dedrick	LB	6-3	248	9/25/83	Missouri	Mexico, Mo.	FA
Jefferson, Mike	WR	6-1	215	12/28/82	Montana State	El Paso, Texas	FA
Johnson, Jasper	S	6-1	210	6/9/85	Central Arkansas	Pine Bluff, Ark.	FA
Marten, James	T	6-7	303	4/18/84	Boston College	Indianapolis, Ind.	D3
Moore, Matt	QB	6-3	192	8/9/84	Oregon State	Van Nuys, Calif.	FA
Obomese, Alex	LB	6-3	248	5/9/84	Texas-El Paso	Houston, Texas	FA
Paulescu, Sam	P	6-0	194	4/18/84	Oregon State	Fullerton, Calif.	FA
Phillips, Blair	LB	6-1	243	3/5/84	Oregon	Oakland, Calif.	FA
Rabb, Jerard	WR	6-2	201	8/19/84	Boise State	El Modena, Calif.	FA
Richardson, Jamel	WR	6-3	220	1/22/82	Victor Valley	Syracuse, N.Y.	FA
Rissler, Steve	G	6-2	300	11/10/84	Florida	Sarasota, Fla.	FA
Saldi, John (1)	LB	6-5	245	6/14/82	Texas Tech	Southlake, Texas	FA
Smith, Marcus	DE	6-4	281	2/7/84	Arizona	San Diego, Calif.	FA
Spencer, Anthony	DE	6-3	265	1/23/84	Purdue	Fort Wayne, Ind.	D1
Stanback, Isaiah	WR	6-2	216	8/16/84	Washington	Seattle, Wash.	D4a
Thorn, Andy (1)	TE	6-5	250	2/4/82	Northern Iowa	Waterford, Mich.	FA-'06

The term NFL Rookie is defined as a player who is in his first season of professional football and has not been on the roster of another professional football team for any regular-season or postseason games. A Rookie is designated by an "R" on NFL rosters. Players who have been active in another professional football league or players who have NFL experience, including either preseason training camp or being on an Active List or Inactive List, or on Reserve/Injured or Reserve/Physically Unable to Perform for fewer than six regular-season games, are termed NFL First-Year Players. An NFL First-Year Player is designated by a "1" on NFL rosters. Thereafter, a player is credited with an additional year of experience for each season in which he accumulates six games on the Active List or Inactive List, or on Reserve/Injured or Reserve/Physically Unable to Perform.

Log on to www.dallascowboys.com for an up-to-date roster.

COACHING STAFF
Head Coach,
Wade Phillips
Pro Career: Named the seventh coach in club history on February 8, 2007, Phillips brings to the Cowboys 30 years of NFL coaching experience, including five as a head coach and 20 as a defensive coordinator. In head coaching stints with Denver and Buffalo, Phillips produced a 45-35 regular-season record and guided his teams to three playoff appearances. He has had only one non-winning season as a head coach. Phillips also served as interim head coach in New Orleans for four games in 1985 (1-3 record) and Atlanta for three games in 2003 (2-1). The last six times Phillips has taken over as a head coach or defensive coordinator, his new team has reached the playoffs in his first season. In all six of those instances he has never joined a team that was coming off a winning record. Over the last 18 years as a head coach or coordinator, he has been a part of only four teams that have had non-winning records. During that time he has worked with a defense that ranked in the NFL's top 10 eight times. For the past three seasons, Phillips served as the defensive coordinator for the San Diego Chargers (2004-06). Phillips directed a unit that improved each season, moving from 18th in total defense in his first season to 13th in 2005 and then 10th in 2006. In 2006, the Chargers led the NFL with 61 sacks, the second most in club history. His 2005 unit led the NFL in run defense (84.3 yards per game), while his 2004 defense allowed 81.7 rushing yards per game to rank third in the NFL. He spent two years as defensive coordinator in Atlanta in 2002-03, finishing the 2003 season as interim head coach. Phillips' defense in Atlanta in 2002 finished with 47 sacks, second-most in team history and had 39 takeaways—second in the league. During the 1998-2000 seasons as head coach in Buffalo, the Bills compiled a regular season record of 29-19. Phillips took the reins after a 6-10 finish in 1997 and reversed the team's fortunes by leading it to a 10-6 record and the playoffs in 1998. It was the most successful campaign of any first-year head coach in Bills history. His 1999 team led the NFL in total defense, went 11-5 and earned another trip to the postseason. Before becoming the Bills head coach in 1998, he was the team's defensive coordinator (1995-97). Phillips had a two-year stint as Denver's head coach (1993-94), after serving as defensive coordinator the previous four seasons. He led the Broncos to a playoff berth in his first season (1993). He was the Philadelphia Eagles defensive coordinator and linebackers coach from 1986-88. His first coordinator's position came with the New Orleans Saints (1981-85). Phillips' professional coaching career began with the

Houston Oilers in 1976 as the linebackers coach under his father, longtime NFL coach Bum Phillips. From 1977-1980 he coached the Oilers' defensive line. Career record: 48-41.
Background: Played linebacker at Houston (1966-68). Served as a college coach at Houston (1969), Oklahoma State (1973-74), and Kansas (1975).
Personal: Born June 21, 1947, in Orange, Texas. He and his wife Laurie, have one son, Wesley, and one daughter, Tracy.

ASSISTANT COACHES
Todd Bowles, secondary; born November 18, 1963, Elizabeth, N.J. Defensive back Temple 1982-85. Pro defensive back Washington Redskins 1986-1990, 1992-93, San Francisco 49ers 1991. College coach: Morehouse College 1997, Grambling State 1998-99. Pro coach: New York Jets 2000, Cleveland Browns 2001-04, joined Cowboys in 2005.
Jason Garrett, offensive coordinator; born March 28, 1966, Abington, Pa. Quarterback Princeton 1987-88. Pro quarterback San Antonio Riders (World League) 1991, Ottawa RoughRiders (CFL) 1991, Dallas Cowboys 1993-99, New York Giants 2000-03, Tampa Bay Buccaneers 2004, Miami Dolphins 2004. College coach: Princeton 1990. Pro coach: Miami Dolphins 2005-06, joined Cowboys in 2007.
John Garrett, tight ends; born March 2, 1965, Danville, Pa. Wide receiver Columbia 1983-85, Princeton 1986-87. Pro wide receiver Cincinnati Bengals 1989, Buffalo Bills 1991, San Antonio Riders (World League) 1991. College coach: Virginia 2004-06. Pro coach: Cincinnati Bengals 1995-98, 2001-02, Arizona Cardinals 1999-2000, joined Cowboys in 2007.
Joe Juraszek, strength and conditioning; born June 8, 1958, Chicago. Linebacker/defensive end New Mexico 1976-1980. No pro playing experience. College coach: Oklahoma 1981-86, 1993-96, Texas Tech 1987-1992. Pro coach: Joined Cowboys in 1997.
Dat Nguyen, asst. linebackers/defensive quality control; born November 25, 1975, Rockport, Texas. Linebacker Texas A&M 1994-1998. Pro linebacker Dallas Cowboys 1999-2005. Pro coach: Joined Cowboys in 2007.
Paul Pasqualoni, linebackers; born August 16, 1949, New Haven, Conn. Linebacker Penn State 1968-1971. No pro playing experience. College coach: Southern Connecticut State 1976-1981, Western Connecticut 1982-86 (head coach), Syracuse 1987-2004 (head coach 1991-2004). Pro coach: Joined Cowboys in 2005.
Skip Peete, running backs; born January 30, 1963, Mesa, Ariz. Wide receiver Arizona 1981-82, Kansas 1984-85. Pro wide receiver New York Jets 1987. College

coach: Pittsburgh 1988-1992, Michigan State 1993-94, Rutgers 1995, UCLA 1996-97. Pro coach: Oakland Raiders 1998-2006, joined Cowboys in 2007.
Wes Phillips, offensive assistant/offensive quality control; born February 17, 1979, Houston. Quarterback Texas-El Paso 1997-2001. Pro quarterback San Diego Riptide (AFL2) 2002-03. College coach: Texas-El Paso 2003, West Texas A&M 2004-05, Baylor 2006. Pro coach: Joined Cowboys in 2007.
Bruce Read, special teams; born January 1, 1962, Santa Rosa, Calif. College coach: Montana 1985-1996, Oregon State 1997-98, 2004-06. Pro coach: San Diego Chargers 1999-2001, New York Giants 2002-03, joined Cowboys in 2007.
Kacy Rodgers, defensive line; born June 24, 1969, Humboldt, Tenn. Linebacker/defensive end Tennessee 1988-1991. Pro linebacker Shreveport Pirates (CFL) 1994. College coach: Tennesse-Martin 1994-97, Louisiana-Monroe 1998, Middle Tennessee State 1999-2001, Arkansas 2002. Pro coach: Joined Cowboys in 2003.
Ray Sherman, wide receivers; born November 27, 1951, Berkeley, Calif. Wide receiver/defensive back Fresno State 1971-72. College coach: San Jose State 1974, California 1975, 1981, Michigan State 1976-77, Wake Forest 1978-1980, Purdue 1982-85, Georgia 1986-87. Pro coach: Houston Oilers 1988-89, Atlanta Falcons 1990, San Francisco 49ers 1991-93, New York Jets 1994, Minnesota Vikings 1995-97, 1999, Pittsburgh Steelers 1998, Green Bay Packers 2000-04, Tennessee Titans 2005-06, joined Cowboys in 2007.
Tony Sparano, asst. head coach/offensive line; born October 7, 1961, West Haven, Conn. Center New Haven 1978-1981. No pro playing experience. College coach: New Haven 1984-87, 1994-98 (head coach 1994-98), Boston University 1988-1993. Pro coach: Cleveland Browns 1999-2000, Washington Redskins 2001, Jacksonville Jaguars 2002, joined Cowboys in 2003.
Brian Stewart, defensive coordinator; born December 4, 1964, San Diego. Cornerback/free safety Northern Arizona 1983, 1986-87, Santa Monica City College 1984-85. College coach: Cal Poly-San Luis Obispo 1993-94, Northern Arizona 1995, Missouri 1996, 1999-2000, San Jose State 1997-98, Syracuse 2001. Pro coach: Houston Texans 2002-03, San Diego Chargers 2004-06, joined Cowboys in 2007.
Wade Wilson, quarterbacks; born February 1, 1959, Commerce, Texas. Quarterback East Texas State 1977-1980. Pro quarterback Minnesota Vikings 1981-1991, Atlanta Falcons 1992, New Orleans Saints 1993-94, Dallas Cowboys 1995-97, Oakland Raiders 1998-99. Pro coach: Dallas Cowboys 2000-02, Chicago Bears 2004-06, re-joined Cowboys in 2007.

National Football Conference
North Division
Team Colors: Honolulu Blue and Silver
Detroit Lions Practice &
Training Facility
222 Republic Drive
Allen Park, Michigan 48101
Telephone: (313) 216-4000

2007 SCHEDULE
PRESEASON
Aug. 9   **Cincinnati** 7:30
Aug. 18   at Cleveland 7:00
Aug. 25   at Indianapolis 7:00
Aug. 30   **Buffalo**..............................7:00

REGULAR SEASON
Sep. 9   at Oakland 1:15
Sep. 16   **Minnesota** 4:05
Sep. 23   at Philadelphia 1:00
Sep. 30   **Chicago** 1:00
Oct. 7   at Washington 1:00
Oct. 14   Open Date
Oct. 21   **Tampa Bay** 1:00
Oct. 28   at Chicago 12:00
Nov. 4   **Denver** 1:00
Nov. 11   at Arizona 2:15
Nov. 18   **N.Y. Giants**......................4:15
Nov. 22   **Green Bay** (Thu.) 12:30
Dec. 2   at Minnesota 12:00
Dec. 9   **Dallas** 1:00
Dec. 16   at San Diego 1:15
Dec. 23   **Kansas City** 1:00
Dec. 30   at Green Bay 12:00

Stadium: Ford Field (opened in 2002)
   •**Capacity:** 64,500
   2000 Brush Street
   Detroit, Michigan 48226
Playing Surface: FieldTurf
Training Camp: 222 Republic Drive
   Allen Park, Michigan
   48101

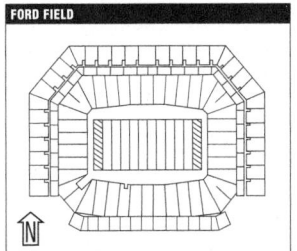

FORD FIELD

CLUB OFFICIALS
Chairman and Owner: William Clay Ford
Vice Chairman: William Clay Ford, Jr.
President and CEO: Matt Millen
Executive Vice President/COO:
   Tom Lewand
Senior Vice President & Assistant GM:
   Martin Mayhew
Senior Vice President: Bill Keenist
Senior Vice President/CFO: Tom Lesnau
Corporate Secretary: David Hempstead
Director of Pro Personnel: Sheldon White
Director of College Scouting:
   Scott McEwen
Scouts: Bob Beers, Chad Henry,
   Dennis Gentry, Silas McKinnie,
   Bob Merrit, Lance Newmark,
   Dave Uyrus, Charlie Sanders
Senior Director of Community Affairs:
   Tim Pendell
Director of Media Relations:
   Matt Barnhart
Director of Broadcasting and Production:
   Bryan Bender
Director of Ticket Operations:
   Mark Graham
Coordinator of Athletic Medicine/
   Athletic Trainer: Dean Kleinschmidt
Head Athletic Trainer: Al Bellamy
Equipment Manager: Tim O'Neill
Video Director: Robert Yanagi

COACHING HISTORY
Portsmouth Spartans 1930-33
(488-554-32)
Records include postseason games
1930   Hal (Tubby) Griffen 5-6-3
1931-36   George (Potsy) Clark ...49-20-6
1937-38   Earl (Dutch) Clark 14-8-0
1939   Elmer (Gus) Henderson ...6-5-0
1940   George (Potsy) Clark 5-5-1
1941-42   Bill Edwards* 4-9-1
1942   John Karcis 0-8-0
1943-47   Charles (Gus) Dorais ...20-31-2
1948-1950   Alvin (Bo) McMillin 12-24-0
1951-56   Raymond (Buddy) Parker..50-24-2
1957-1964   George Wilson........55-45-6
1965-66   Harry Gilmer................10-16-2
1967-1972   Joe Schmidt 43-35-7
1973   Don McCafferty 6-7-1
1974-76   Rick Forzano** 15-17-0
1976-77   Tommy Hudspeth 11-13-0
1978-1984   Monte Clark................43-63-1
1985-88   Darryl Rogers*** 18-40-0
1988-1996   Wayne Fontes............67-71-0
1997-2000   Bobby Ross****.....27-32-0
2000   Gary Moeller....................4-3-0
2001-02   Marty Mornhinweg 5-27-0
2003-05   Steve Mariucci#.......15-28-0
2005   Dick Jauron 1-4-0
2006   Rod Marinelli 3-13-0
   *Released after three games in 1942
  **Resigned after four games in 1976
 ***Released after 11 games in 1988
****Resigned after nine games in 2000
   # Released after 11 games in 2005

PAID ATTENDANCE
Home 487,114   Away 530,112
Total 1,017,226
Single-game home record,
   80,444 (12/20/81)
Single-season home record, 644,904
   (1980)

2007 DRAFT CHOICES
Round	Name	Pos.	College
1	Calvin Johnson	WR	Georgia Tech
2	Drew Stanton	QB	Michgian State
	Ikaika Alama-Francis	DE	Hawaii
	Gerald Alexander	DB	Boise State
4	A.J. Davis	DB	North Carolina St.
	Manuel Ramirez	G	Texas Tech
5	Johnny Baldwin	LB	Alabama A&M
7	Ramzee Robinson	DB	Alabama

DETROIT LIONS

2006 TEAM RECORD

PRESEASON (1-3)

Date	Result	Opponent
8/11	W 20-13	Denver
8/18	L 16-20	at Cleveland
8/25	L 3-21	at Oakland
8/31	L 13-20	Buffalo

REGULAR SEASON (3-13)

Date	Result	Opponent	Att.
9/10	L 6-9	Seattle	60,535
9/17	L 7-34	at Chicago	62,181
9/24	L 24-31	Green Bay	61,095
10/1	L 34-41	at St. Louis	65,563
10/8	L 17-26	at Minnesota	63,906
10/15	W 20-17	Buffalo	60,704
10/22	L 24-31	at N.Y. Jets	76,953
11/5	W 30-14	Atlanta	60,987
11/12	L 13-19	San Francisco	60,707
11/19	L 10-17	at Arizona	63,348
11/23	L 10-27	Miami	61,562
12/3	L 21-28	at New England	68,756
12/10	L 20-30	Minnesota	60,861
12/17	L 9-17	at Green Bay	70,472
12/24	L 21-26	Chicago	60,665
12/31	W 39-31	at Dallas	63,008

SCORE BY PERIODS

Lions	73	75	85	72	0 —	305
Opponents	101	121	61	115	0 —	398

2006 TEAM STATISTICS

	Lions	Opp.
Total First Downs	290	319
Rushing	53	111
Passing	208	183
Penalty	29	25
3rd Down: Made/Att	62/190	90/207
3rd Down Pct.	32.6	43.5
4th Down: Made/Att	9/22	4/5
4th Down Pct.	40.9	80.0
Possession Avg.	27:41	32:19
Total Net Yards	4949	5530
Avg. Per Game	309.3	345.6
Total Plays	963	1033
Avg. Per Play	5.1	5.4
Net Yards Rushing	1129	2010
Avg. Per Game	70.6	125.6
Total Rushes	304	492
Net Yards Passing	3820	3520
Avg. Per Game	238.8	220.0
Sacked/Yards Lost	63/388	30/201
Gross Yards	4208	3721
Att./Completions	596/372	511/339
Completion Pct.	62.4	66.3
Had Intercepted	22	12
Punts/Average	66/45.0	68/44.0
Net Punting Avg.	66/38.2	68/36.4
Penalties/Yards	116/939	102/869
Fumbles/Ball Lost	26/17	29/18
Touchdowns	31	44
Rushing	9	18
Passing	21	22
Returns	1	4

2006 INDIVIDUAL STATISTICS

PASSING	Att.	Comp.	Yds.	Pct.	TD	Int.	Tkld.	Rate
Kitna	596	372	4,208	62.4	21	22	63/388	79.9
Lions	596	372	4,208	62.4	21	22	63/388	79.9
Opponents	511	339	3,721	66.3	22	12	30/201	92.3

SCORING	TD R	TD P	TD Rt	PAT	FG	Saf	PTS
Hanson	0	0	0	30/30	29/33	0	117
Jones	6	2	0	0/0	0/0	0	48
R. Williams	0	7	0	0/0	0/0	0	42
Furrey	0	6	0	0/0	0/0	0	36
Campbell	0	4	0	0/0	0/0	0	24
Kitna	2	0	0	0/0	0/0	0	12
Bryson	0	1	0	0/0	0/0	0	6
Fletcher	0	0	1	0/0	0/0	0	6
A. Harris	1	0	0	0/0	0/0	0	6
M. Williams	0	1	0	0/0	0/0	0	6
DeVries	0	0	0	0/0	0/0	1	2
Lions	9	21	1	30/30	29/33	1	305
Opponents	18	22	4	40/41	30/33	0	398

2-Pt. Conversions: Lions 0-1, Opponents 2-3

RUSHING	No.	Yds	Avg	LG	TD
Jones	181	689	3.8	52	6
A. Harris	49	158	3.2	20	1
Kitna	34	156	4.6	18	2
Cason	24	94	3.9	16	0
Calhoun	7	19	2.7	7	0
Drummond	1	4	4.0	4	0
Ellis	2	3	1.5	12	0
Gordon	1	2	2.0	2	0
R. Williams	2	2	1.0	2	0
Bryson	2	1	0.5	1	0
Hakim	1	1	1.0	1	0
Lions	304	1,129	3.7	52	9
Opponents	492	2,010	4.1	61t	18

RECEIVING	No.	Yds	Avg	LG	TD
Furrey	98	1,086	11.1	31	6
R. Williams	82	1,310	16.0	60t	7
Jones	61	520	8.5	26	2
Campbell	21	308	14.7	30	4
A. Harris	18	132	7.3	20	0
Hakim	17	147	8.6	23	0
Bradford	14	164	11.7	23	0
Pollard	12	100	8.3	22	0
M. Williams	8	99	12.4	21t	1
Bryson	8	98	12.3	37t	1
Schlesinger	8	36	4.5	6	0
Fitzsimmons	7	71	10.1	18	0
Cason	5	26	5.2	14	0
Ellis	4	41	10.3	19	0
McHugh	3	25	8.3	11	0
Calhoun	2	20	10.0	18	0
McCown	2	15	7.5	8	0
Drummond	2	10	5.0	8	0
Lions	372	4,208	11.3	60t	21
Opponents	339	3,721	11.0	75t	22

INTERCEPTIONS	No.	Yds	Avg	LG	TD
Fletcher	3	122	40.7	88t	1
Bly	3	13	4.3	8	0
Holt	3	8	2.7	7	0
Kennedy	2	17	8.5	17	0
Lenon	1	0	0.0	0	0
Lions	12	160	13.3	88t	1
Opponents	22	280	12.7	47	2

PUNTING	No.	Yds.	Avg.	In 20	LG
N. Harris	66	2,967	45.0	18	67
Lions	66	2,967	45.0	18	67
Opponents	68	2,990	44.0	25	66

PUNT RETURNS	Ret	FC	Yds	Avg	LG	TD
Drummond	28	13	296	10.6	40	0
Ellis	4	1	61	15.3	48	0
Bly	3	3	39	13.0	36	0
Hakim	0	1	0	—	—	0
Lions	35	18	396	11.3	48	0
Opponents	38	9	267	7.0	56t	1

KICKOFF RETURNS	No.	Yds	Avg	LG	TD
Drummond	62	1,349	21.8	65	0
Ellis	6	139	23.2	28	0
Cason	4	110	27.5	40	0
Bly	1	27	27.0	27	0
Furrey	1	23	23.0	23	0
Lions	74	1,648	22.3	65	0
Opponents	63	1,444	22.9	72	0

FIELD GOALS	1-19	20-29	30-39	40-49	50+
Hanson	1/1	12/12	6/6	7/8	3/6
Lions	1/1	12/12	6/6	7/8	3/6
Opponents	1/1	11/11	8/8	8/10	2/3

SACKS	
Redding	8.0
Hall	5.0
K Edwards	3.0
Rogers	3.0
Jackson	2.0
C Smith	2.0
(group)	2.0
Bailey	1.0
Bell	1.0
Bullocks	1.0
Kennedy	1.0
Holt	0.5
Sims	0.5
Lions	30.0
Opponents	63.0

RECORD HOLDERS

INDIVIDUAL RECORDS—CAREER

Category	Name	Performance
Rushing (Yds.)	Barry Sanders, 1989-1998	15,269
Passing (Yds.)	Bobby Layne, 1950-58	15,710
Passing (TDs)	Bobby Layne, 1950-58	118
Receiving (No.)	Herman Moore, 1991-2001	670
Receiving (Yds.)	Herman Moore, 1991-2001	9,174
Interceptions	Dick LeBeau, 1959-1972	62
Punting (Avg.)	Yale Lary, 1952-53, 1956-1964	44.3
Punt Return (Avg.)	Jack Christiansen, 1951-58	12.8
Kickoff Return (Avg.)	Pat Studstill, 1961-67	25.7
Field Goals	Jason Hanson, 1992-2006	356
Touchdowns (Tot.)	Barry Sanders, 1989-1998	109
Points	Jason Hanson, 1992-2006	1,537

INDIVIDUAL RECORDS—SINGLE SEASON

Category	Name	Performance
Rushing (Yds.)	Barry Sanders, 1997	2,053
Passing (Yds.)	Scott Mitchell, 1995	4,338
Passing (TDs)	Scott Mitchell, 1995	32
Receiving (No.)	Herman Moore, 1995	123
Receiving (Yds.)	Herman Moore, 1995	1,686
Interceptions	Don Doll, 1950	12
	Jack Christiansen, 1953	12
Punting (Avg.)	Yale Lary, 1963	48.9
Punt Return (Avg.)	Pat Studstill, 1962	15.8
Kickoff Return (Avg.)	Mel Gray, 1994	28.4
Field Goals	Jason Hanson, 1993	34
Touchdowns (Tot.)	Barry Sanders, 1991	17
Points	Jason Hanson, 1995	132

INDIVIDUAL RECORDS—SINGLE GAME

Category	Name	Performance
Rushing (Yds.)	Barry Sanders, 11-13-94	237
Passing (Yds.)	Charlie Batch, 11-18-01	436
Passing (TDs)	Gary Danielson, 12-9-78	5
Receiving (No.)	Herman Moore, 12-4-95	14
Receiving (Yds.)	Cloyce Box, 12-3-50	302
Interceptions	Don Doll, 10-23-49	*4
Field Goals	Garo Yepremian, 11-13-66	6
	Jason Hanson, 10-17-99	6
Touchdowns (Tot.)	Dutch Clark, 10-22-34	4
	Cloyce Box, 12-3-50	4
	Barry Sanders, 11-24-91	4
Points	Dutch Clark, 10-22-34	24
	Cloyce Box, 12-3-50	24
	Barry Sanders, 11-24-91	24

*NFL Record

2007 VETERAN ROSTER

No.	Name	Pos.	Ht.	Wt.	Birthdate	NFL Exp.	College	Hometown	How Acq.	'06 Games/ Starts
76	Backus, Jeff	T	6-5	305	9/21/77	7	Michigan	Norcross, Ga.	D1-'01	16/16
97	Bailey, Boss	LB	6-3	235	10/14/79	5	Georgia	Folkston, Ga.	D2-'03	16/12
44	Bashir, Idrees	S	6-2	198	12/7/78	6	Memphis	Decatur, Ga.	FA-'07	0*
41	Beckham, Tony	CB	6-1	195	10/1/78	5	Wisconsin-Stout	Gainesville, Fla.	FA-'07	0*
28 t-	Bell, Tatum	RB	5-11	213	3/2/1981	4	Memphis	DeSoto, Texas	T(Den)-'07	13/13*
25	Bryant, Fernando	CB	5-11	184	3/26/77	9	Alabama	Murfeesboro, Tenn.	UFA(Jax)-'04	10/10
24	Bryson, Shawn	RB	6-1	230	11/30/76	9	Tennessee	Franklin, N.C.	UFA(Buff)-'03	6/1
27	Bullocks, Daniel	S	6-0	212	2/28/83	2	Nebraska	Chattanooga, Tenn.	D2-'06	15/7
29	Calhoun, Brian	RB	5-10	208	5/8/84	2	Wisconsin	Oak Creek, Wisc.	D3-'06	7/0
89	Campbell, Dan	TE	6-5	265	4/13/76	8	Texas A&M	Glen Rose, Texas	UFA(Dall)-'06	16/11
52	Cannon, Anthony	LB	6-0	228	12/31/84	2	Tulane	Stone Mountain, Ga.	D7b-'06	12/0
36	Cason, Aveion	RB	5-10	204	7/12/79	6	Illinois State	St. Petersburg, Fla.	FA-'06	6/2
47	Charlton, Ike	CB	6-0	205	10/6/77	5	Virginia Tech	Orlando, Fla.	FA-'07	0*
75	Cody, Shaun	DT	6-4	310	1/22/83	3	Southern California	Hacienda Heights, Calif.	D2-'05	6/5
55	Curry, Donté	LB	6-1	240	7/22/78	7	Morris Brown	College Park, Ga.	W(Wash)-'02	16/0
61	Davis, Frank	G	6-3	325	8/22/81	2	South Florida	Panama City, Panama	FA-'06	11/3
95	DeVries, Jared	DE	6-4	275	6/11/76	9	Iowa	Aplington, Iowa	D3-'99	14/9
18	Drummond, Eddie	WR	5-9	190	4/12/80	6	Penn State	Pittsburgh, Pa.	FA-'02	14/0
45	Duckett, T.J.	RB	6-0	254	2/17/81	6	Michigan State	Kalamazoo, Mich.	UFA(Wash)-'07	10/0*
98	Edwards, Kalimba	DE	6-6	265	12/26/79	6	South Carolina	Atlanta, Ga.	D2-'02	16/10
80	Ellis, Devale	WR	5-10	174	4/2/84	2	Hofstra	Brooklyn, N.Y.	FA-'06	9/2
21	Fisher, Travis	CB	5-10	189	9/12/79	6	Central Florida	Tallahassee, Fla.	UFA(StL)-'07	9/9*
82	FitzSimmons, Casey	TE	6-4	258	10/10/80	5	Carroll College (Mont.)	Helena, Mont.	FA-'03	11/2
72	Foster, George	T	6-5	338	6/9/80	5	Georgia	Macon, Ga.	T(Den)-'07	16/13*
87	Furrey, Mike	WR	6-0	195	5/12/77	5	Northern Iowa	Grove City, Ohio	UFA(StL)-'06	16/14
4	Hanson, Jason	K	6-0	190	6/17/70	16	Washington State	Spokane, Wash.	D2b-'92	16/0
2	Harris, Nick	P	6-2	218	7/23/78	7	California	Avondale, Ariz.	W(Cin)-'03	16/0
34	Jones, Kevin	RB	6-0	228	8/21/82	4	Virginia Tech	Chester, Pa.	D1b-'04	12/12
85	Kasper, Kevin	WR	6-1	202	12/23/77	5	Iowa	Hinsdale, Ill.	FA-'07	1/1
26	Kennedy, Kenoy	S	6-1	215	11/15/77	8	Arkansas	Terrell, Texas	UFA(Den)-'05	10/9
8	Kitna, Jon	QB	6-2	220	9/21/72	11	Central Washington	Tacoma, Wash.	UFA(Cin)-'06	16/16
54	Lehman, Teddy	LB	6-1	238	11/18/81	4	Oklahoma	Fort Gibson, Okla.	D2-'04	4/0
53	Lenon, Paris	LB	6-2	235	11/26/77	6	Richmond	Lynchburg, Va.	UFA(GB)-'06	16/16
59	Lewis, Alex	LB	6-0	230	6/11/81	4	Wisconsin	Delran, N.J.	D5-'04	11/2
43	Matthews, Will	FB	6-3	250	4/30/81	2	Texas	Austin, Texas	FA-'05	0*
84	McDonald, Shaun	WR	5-10	183	6/13/81	5	Arizona State	Phoenix, Ariz.	UFA(StL)-'07	16/0*
49	McHugh, Sean	FB/TE	6-5	265	5/27/82	2	Penn State	Springfield, Mass.	FA-'05	6/2
79	Moore, Langston	DT	6-1	305	7/17/81	3	South Carolina	Charleston, S.C.	D3-'06	0*
48	Muhlbach, Don	LS	6-4	265	8/17/81	4	Texas A&M	Lufkin, Texas	FA-'04	16/0
64	Mulitalo, Edwin	G	6-3	345	9/1/74	9	Arizona	Daly City, Calif.	FA-'07	4/4*
63	Noll, Ben	G	6-4	315	11/14/81	3	Pennsylvania	Minneapolis, Minn.	FA-'06	0*
6	Orlovsky, Dan	QB	6-5	230	8/18/83	3	Connecticut	Shelton, Conn.	D5-'05	0*
66	Peterman, Stephen	G	6-4	323	1/11/82	3	Louisiana State	Gulfport, Miss.	FA-'06	3/2
62	Pinkney, Cleveland	DT	6-1	300	9/14/77	4	South Carolina	Sumpter, S.C.	FA-'06	8/0
35	Pruitt, Etric	DB	6-0	318	8/16/81	3	Southern Mississippi	Theodore, Ala.	FA-'06	0*
51	Raiola, Dominic	C	6-1	295	12/30/78	7	Nebraska	Honolulu, Hawaii	D2a-'01	16/16
78	Redding, Cory	DT	6-4	295	11/15/80	5	Texas	Houston, Texas	D3-'03	16/16
86	Robinson, Marcus	WR	6-3	215	2/27/75	10	South Carolina	Fort Valley, Ga.	FA-'07	10/3*
92	Rogers, Shaun	DT	6-4	340	3/12/79	7	Texas	LaPorte, Texas	D2b-'01	6/6
19	Russell, Cliff	WR	5-11	195	2/8/79	5	Utah	Ewa Beach, Hawaii	FA-'07	3/0*
67	Saipaia, Blaine	G	6-3	315	8/25/78	4	Colorado State	Oxnard, Calif.	FA-'06	6/4
83	Sanders, Darnell	TE	6-6	270	3/16/79	4	Ohio State	Warrensville Hts, Ohio	FA-'07	0*
73	Scott, Jonathan	T	6-6	318	1/10/83	2	Texas	Dallas, Texas	D5-'06	13/4
15	Shepherd, Edell	WR	6-1	175	5/18/80	4	San Jose State	Los Angeles, Calif.	FA-'07	7/0*
50	Sims, Ernie	LB	6-0	225	12/23/84	2	Florida State	Tallahassee, Fla.	D1-'06	16/16
93	Smith, Corey	DE	6-2	250	10/2/79	5	North Carolina State	Richmond, Va.	FA-'06	8/1
23	Smith, Keith	CB	5-11	191	3/20/80	4	McNeese State	Leesville, La.	D3-'04	16/0
68	Stokes, Barry	G/T	6-4	310	12/20/73	10	Eastern Michigan	Davison, Mich.	UFA(Atl)-'06	11/11
90	Swancutt, Bill	DE	6-4	265	9/4/82	3	Oregon State	Salem, Ore.	D6a-'05	0*
74	Tucker, Rex	T	6-5	315	12/20/76	9	Texas A&M	Midland, Texas	UFA(StL)-'06	6/5
99	White, Dewayne	DE	6-2	273	10/19/79	5	Louisville	Marbury, Ala.	UFA(TB)-'07	0*
11	Williams, Roy	WR	6-3	211	12/20/81	4	Texas	Odessa, Texas	D1a-'04	16/16
31	Wilson, Stanley	CB	5-11	189	11/5/82	3	Stanford	Carson, Calif.	D3-'05	13/4
65	Woody, Damien	G	6-3	340	11/3/77	9	Boston College	Beaverdam, Va.	UFA(NE)-'04	5/5

* Bashir last active with Carolina in '05; Beckham last active with Tennessee in '05; Bell played 13 games with Denver in '06; Charlton last active with N.Y. Giants in '03; Duckett played 10 games with Washington; Fisher played 9 games with St. Louis; Foster played 16 games with Denver; Matthews missed '06 season because of injury; McDonald played 16 games with St. Louis; Moore inactive for 2 games; Mulitalo played 4 games with Baltimore; Noll last active with St. Louis in '05; Orlovsky inactive as third quarterback for 16 games; Pruitt last active with Seattle in '05; Robinson played 10 games with Minnesota; Russell played 3 games with Miami, Sanders last active with Atlanta in '04; Shepherd played 7 games with Houston; Swancutt missed '06 season because of injury; White played 16 games with Tampa Bay.

t- Lions traded for Bell (Den).

Traded—CB Dre' Bly (16 games in '06) to Denver.

Players lost through free agency (5): G Rick DeMulling (Ind; 14), CB Jamar Fletcher (Tenn; 13), S Terrence Holt (Ariz; 16), S Jon McGraw (KC; 16), FB Cory Schlesinger (Mia; 14).

Also played with Lions in '06—DT Marcus Bell (13 games), CB Dré Bly (16), WR Shaun Bodiford (3), WR Corey Bradford (9), DT Anthony Bryant (5), RB Lamar Gordon (1), WR Az-Zahir Hakim (6), DE James Hall (7), RB Arlen Harris (10), DT Tyoka Jackson (15), QB Josh McCown (2), C Dave Pearson (2), TE Marcus Pollard (15), G Ross Verba (7), WR Mike Williams (8).

2007 FIRST-YEAR ROSTER

Name	Pos.	Ht.	Wt.	Birthdate	College	Hometown	How Acq.
Alama-Francis, Ikaika	DE	6-5	280	12/4/84	Hawaii	Oahu, Hawaii	D2b
Alexander, Gerald	S	6-2	204	6/28/84	Boise State	Rancho Cucamonga, Calif.	D2c
Baldwin, Johnny	LB	6-2	232	1/1/84	Alabama A&M	Bessemer, Ala.	D5
Burgess, Rodney	TE	6-4	230	11/27/84	Coastal Carolina	Irmo, S.C.	FA
Byrd, Kenny	K	6-0	171	6/25/84	New Mexico	Albuquerque, N.M.	FA
Cooper, George	TE	6-5	260	3/19/84	Georgia Tech	Westerville, Ohio	FA
Davis, A.J.	CB	5-10	193	5/29/83	North Carolina State	Durham, N.C.	D4a
Deraney, John	P	6-4	224	9/5/83	North Carolina State	Fayetteville, Ga.	FA
Hardiman, Pinknie	LB	6-3	220	12/3/84	Southeast Louisiana	Grenada, Miss.	FA
Hargrave, James (1)	LB	5-11	224	10/21/83	Connecticut	Montvale, N.J.	FA
Harriott, Claude (1)	DE	6-3	260	4/8/81	Pittsburgh	Belle Glade, Fla.	FA-'06
Hicks, LaMarcus (1)	CB	6-0	189	4/15/83	Iowa State	Clarksdale, Miss.	FA
Horvath, Phil	QB	6-3	197	10/4/83	Northern Illinois	Naperville, Ill.	FA
Johnson, Calvin	WR	6-5	239	9/25/85	Georgia Tech	Tyrone, Ga.	D1
Lewis, Marcus (1)	DT	6-3	295	10/3/80	Urbana	Lithonia, Ga.	FA
McCann, Dee (1)	CB	5-10	200	4/24/83	West Virginia	Greene Co., Miss.	D6-'06
Moss, Terry	WR	5-10	187	11/29/84	Ball State	Huber Heights, Ohio	FA
Parker, Marcus (1)	DT	6-2	273	5/18/83	New Mexico	Garland, Texas	FA
Pearson, Dave (1)	C	6-3	287	3/29/81	Michigan	Brighton, Mich.	FA-'05
Ramirez, Manny	G	6-3	326	2/13/83	Texas Tech	Houston, Texas	D4b
Rice, Matthew (1)	DE	6-4	256	2/12/82	Penn State	Baltimore, Md.	FA-'06
Robinson, Ramzee	CB	5-10	186	2/20/84	Alabama	Huntsville, Ala.	D7
Sherrell, Anthony (1)	RB	5-9	193	8/13/83	Eastern Michigan	Roseville, Mich.	FA
Stanton, Drew	QB	6-3	226	5/7/84	Michigan State	Farmington Hills, Mich.	D2a
Stickdorn, Clint (1)	T	6-5	307	4/30/82	Cincinnati	Toledo, Ohio	FA-'05
Sylvan, Rudy	TE	6-4	274	12/23/84	Ohio	Suisan City, Calif.	FA

The term NFL Rookie is defined as a player who is in his first season of professional football and has not been on the roster of another professional football team for any regular-season or postseason games. A Rookie is designated by an "R" on NFL rosters. Players who have been active in another professional football league or players who have NFL experience, including either preseason training camp or being on an Active List or Inactive List, or on Reserve/Injured or Reserve/Physically Unable to Perform for fewer than six regular-season games, are termed NFL First-Year Players. An NFL First-Year Player is designated by a "1" on NFL rosters. Thereafter, a player is credited with an additional year of experience for each season in which he accumulates six games on the Active List or Inactive List, or on Reserve/Injured or Reserve/Physically Unable to Perform.

Log on to www.detroitlions.com for an up-to-date roster.

COACHING STAFF
Head Coach,
Rod Marinelli
Pro Career: Named Lions' twenty-fourth head coach January 19, 2006. Marinelli joined the Lions after spending 10 previous seasons with Tampa Bay (1996-2005) as defensive line coach and holding the additional duties of assistant head coach for the last four seasons. In Marinelli's 10-year tenure, the Buccaneers recorded 416 sacks, with 328.5 coming courtesy of his defensive line. The 328.5 sacks registered by Marinelli's line ranked first in the NFL among all defensive lines during that span. Additionally, the Buccaneers' defensive front four garnered top 5 rankings in sacks during six of the 10 seasons under Marinelli. Among individual leaders, a Tampa Bay defensive lineman ranked in the league's top 15 in sacks on eight occasions and in the top 10 six times. The defensive line also played a major role in setting an NFL record for consecutive games with a sack (69) from 1999-2003. Career record: 3-13.
Background: Marinelli's college playing career was split due to a one-year tour of duty in Vietnam. In 1968, he played offensive and defensive tackle at Utah. After his service in the military, he attended California Lutheran from 1970-72, earning NAIA All-America honors as an offensive tackle his senior season. He began his coaching career at his high school alma mater, Rosemead (San Gabriel Valley, Calif.) from 1973-75. Collegiately, Marinelli coached defensive line at Utah State (1976), California (1983-91), Arizona State (1992-94), and Southern California (1995).
Personal: Born July 13, 1949, in Rosemead, Calif., He and his wife, Barbara, have two daughters, Chris and Gina. Chris is married to Joe Barry, the Lions' defensive coordinator. Marinelli also has two granddaughters and two grandsons.

ASSISTANT COACHES
Jason Arapoff, strength and conditioning; born July 8, 1965, Weymouth, Mass. Defensive back Springfield College 1985-88. No college or pro playing experience. Pro coach: Washington Redskins 1992-2000, joined Lions in 2001.
Joe Barry, defensive coordinator; born July 5, 1970, Boulder, Colo. Linebacker Southern California 1991-93. No pro playing experience. College coach: Southern California 1994-95, Northern Arizona 1996-98, Nevada-Las Vegas 1999. Pro coach: San Francisco 49ers 2000, Tampa Bay Buccaneers 2001-2006, joined Lions in 2007.
Mike Barry, asst. offensive line; born October 18, 1946, Brooklyn, N.Y. Center Nebraska 1964-65, Southern Illinois 1966-68. No pro playing experience.

College coach: Southern Illinois 1977-79, Arizona 1980-83, Iowa State 1986, Colorado 1987-1992, Southern California 1993-97, Tennessee 1998-2002, North Carolina State 2003-05. Pro coach: San Antonio Gunslingers (USFL) 1984, New Orleans/Portland Breakers (USFL) 1984-85, joined Lions in 2006.
Malcolm Blacken, asst. strength and conditioning; born October 12, 1965, Richmond, Va. Running back Virginia Tech 1984-88. No pro playing experience. College coach: South Carolina 1990-91, George Mason 1992-94, Virginia 1995. Pro coach: Washington Redskins 1996-2000, joined Lions in 2001.
Kippy Brown, wide receivers; born March 6, 1955, Sweetwater, Tenn. Quarterback Memphis State 1974-77. No pro playing experience. College coach: Memphis State 1978-1980, Louisville 1982, Tennessee 1983-89, 1993-94. Pro coach: New York Jets 1990-92, Tampa Bay Buccaneers 1995, Miami Dolphins 1996-99, Green Bay Packers 2000, Memphis Maniax (XFL head coach) 2001, Houston Texans 2002-05, joined Lions in 2006.
Pat Carter, tight ends; born August 1, 1966, Sarasota, Fla. Tight end Florida State 1984-87. Pro tight end Detroit Lions 1988, Los Angeles Rams 1989-1994, Houston Oilers 1995-96, Arizona Cardinals 1997. Pro coach: St. Louis Rams 2005, joined Lions in 2006.
Don Clemons, defensive quality control; born February 15, 1954, Newark, N.J. Defensive end Muhlenberg (Pa.) 1973-76. No pro playing experience. College coach: Kutztown State 1977-78, New Mexico 1979, Arizona State 1980-84. Pro coach: Joined Lions in 1985.
Jim Colletto, offensive line; born October 2, 1944, San Francisco. Fullback/linebacker UCLA 1964-66. No pro playing experience. College coach: UCLA 1967-68, 1980-81, 2006, Brown 1969, Xavier 1970-71, Pacific 1972-74, Cal State Fullerton 1975-79 (head coach), Purdue 1982-84, Arizona State 1985-87, Ohio State 1988-90, Purdue 1991-96 (head coach), Notre Dame 1997-98. Pro coach: Baltimore Ravens 1999-2004, Oakland Raiders 2005, joined Lions in 2007.
Joe Cullen, defensive line; born December 15, 1967, Quincy, Mass. Nose Guard Massachusetts 1986-89. No pro playing experience. College coach: Massachusetts 1990-91, Richmond 1992-98, 2000, Louisiana State 1999, Memphis 2001, Indiana 2002-04, Illinois 2005. Pro coach: Joined Lions in 2006.
Adam Gase, quarterbacks; born March 29, 1978, Ypsilanti, Mich. Attended Michigan State. No college or pro playing experience. College coach: Louisiana State 2000-02. Pro coach: Joined Lions in 2003.
Sam Gash, asst. special teams; born March 7, 1969, Henderson, N.C. Fullback Penn State 1987-1991. Pro fullback New

England Patriots 1992-97, Buffalo Bills 1998-99, 2003, Baltimore Ravens 2000-02. Pro coach: New York Jets 2005-06, joined Lions in 2007.
Shawn Jefferson, offensive assistant; born February 22, 1969, Jacksonville. Wide receiver Central Florida 1988-1990. Pro wide receiver San Diego Chargers 1991-95, New England Patriots 1996-99, Atlanta Falcons 2000-02, Detroit Lions 2003. Pro coach: Joined Lions in 2005.
Stan Kwan, special teams; born November 2, 1967, Phoenix. Attended South Mountain (Ariz.) C.C., San Diego State. No college or pro playing experience. Pro coach: San Diego Chargers 1991-96, Detroit Lions 1997-2000, Arizona Cardinals 2001-2003, re-joined Lions in 2004.
Clayton Lopez, defensive backs; born May 26, 1971, Los Angeles. Safety Nevada 1991-94. No pro playing experience. College coach: Nevada 1995-98. Pro coach: Seattle Seahawks 1999-2003, Oakland Raiders 2004-2005, joined Lions in 2006.
Mike Martz, offensive coordinator; born May 13, 1951, Sioux Falls, S.D. Tight end Fresno State 1972. No pro playing experience. College coach: San Diego Mesa C.C. 1974, 1976-77, San Jose State 1975, Santa Ana College 1978, Fresno State 1979, Pacific 1980-81, Minnesota 1982, Arizona State 1983-1991. Pro coach: St. Louis Rams 1992-96, 1999-2005 (head coach 2000-05), Washington Redskins 1997-98, joined Lions in 2006.
Tim Martz, offensive assistant; born August 30, 1981, Stockton, Calif. Linebacker Colorado State 2000-02, Western Illinois 2003-05. No pro playing experience. Pro coach: Joined Lions in 2007.
Wilbert Montgomery, running backs; born September 16, 1954, Greenville, Miss. Running back Abilene Christian 1973-76. Pro running back Philadelphia Eagles 1977-1984, Detroit Lions 1985. Pro coach: St. Louis Rams 1997-2005, joined Lions in 2006.
Fred Reed, defensive assistant; born July 31, 1967, Meridian, Miss. Safety Mesa State (Colo.) College 1991-92. No pro playing experience. College coach: South Dakota 1994, Nebraska-Omaha 1995, 2000-04, Minnesota Morris 1996, Michigan Tech 1997-99, Ohio 2005. Pro coach: Joined Lions in 2006.
Phil Snow, linebackers; born December 22, 1955, Woodland, Calif. Quarterback Sacremento City College 1974-75, Cal State Hayward 1977-78. No pro playing experience. College coach: Laney (Calif.) College 1979-1981, Boise State 1982-86, California 1987-1991, Arizona State 1992-2000, UCLA 2001-02, Washington 2003-04. Pro coach: Joined Lions in 2005.

National Football Conference
North Division
Team Colors: Dark Green, Gold, and White
Lambeau Field Atrium
1265 Lombardi Avenue
Green Bay, Wisconsin 54304
Telephone: (920) 569-7500

2007 SCHEDULE
PRESEASON
Aug. 11	at Pittsburgh	7:30
Aug. 18	**Seattle**	7:00
Aug. 23	**Jacksonville**	7:00
Aug. 30	at Tennessee	7:00

REGULAR SEASON
Sep. 9	**Philadelphia**	12:00
Sep. 16	at N.Y. Giants	1:00
Sep. 23	**San Diego**	12:00
Sep. 30	at Minnesota	12:00
Oct. 7	**Chicago**	7:15
Oct. 14	**Washington**	12:00
Oct. 21	Open Date	
Oct. 29	at Denver (Mon.)	6:30
Nov. 4	at Kansas City	12:00
Nov. 11	**Minnesota**	12:00
Nov. 18	**Carolina**	12:00
Nov. 22	at Detroit (Thu.)	12:30
Nov. 29	at Dallas (Thu.)	7:15
Dec. 9	**Oakland**	12:00
Dec. 16	at St. Louis	12:00
Dec. 23	at Chicago	12:00
Dec. 30	**Detroit**	12:00

Stadium: Lambeau Field (opened in 1957)
 • **Capacity:** 72,928
  1265 Lombardi Avenue
  Green Bay, Wisconsin 54304
Playing Surface: Grass
Training Camp: St. Norbert College
  De Pere, Wisconsin 54115

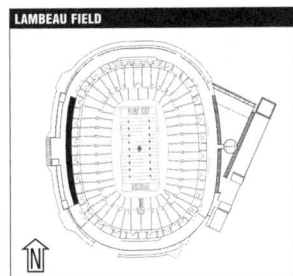

LAMBEAU FIELD

CLUB OFFICIALS
Chairman of the Board: Bob Harlan
President and Chief Operating Officer:
 John Jones
Vice President: John Fabry
Secretary: Peter Platten
Treasurer: Larry Weyers
Executive Vice President/General
 Manager/Director of Football
 Operations: Ted Thompson
Vice President of Player Finance/General
 Counsel: Andrew Brandt
Vice President of Finance:
 Vicki Vannieuwenhoven
Vice President of Administration/
 Corporate Counsel: Jason Wied
Dir. of College Scouting: John Dorsey
Dir. of Pro Personnel: Reggie McKenzie
Personnel Analyst to General Manager:
 John Schneider
Director of Player Development:
 George Koonce
Director of Public Relations: Jeff Blumb
Assistant Director of Public Relations:
 Zak Gilbert
Public Relations Coordinators:
 Sarah Quick, Adam Woullard
Corporate Communications Specialist:
 Aaron Popkey
Ticket Director: Mark Wagner
Director of Marketing and Corporate
 Sales: Craig Benzel
Director of Premium Sales and Guest
 Services: Jennifer Ark
Director of Retail Operations:
 Kate Hogan
Team Historian: Lee Remmel
Director of Administrative Affairs:
 Mark Schiefelbein
Director of Information Technology:
 Wayne Wichlacz
Director of Facility Operations:
 Ted Eisenreich
Director of Corporate Security:
 Jerry Parins
Assistant Director of Security:
 Doug Collins
Manager of Community Relations:
 Cathy Dworak
Assistant Director of College Scouting:
 Shaun Herock
College Scouts: Lee Gissendaner,
 Brian Gutekunst, Alonzo Highsmith,
 Lenny McGill, Sam Seale,
 Jon-Eric Sullivan
Scouting Coordinator: Danny Mock
Pro Personnel Assistants: Tim Terry,
 Eliot Wolf
Director of Research and Development:
 Mike Eayrs
Football Administration Coordinator:
 Matt Klein
Video Director: Bob Eckberg
Head Trainer: Pepper Burruss
Equipment Manager: Gordon (Red) Batty

COACHING HISTORY
(648-514-36)
Records include postseason games
1921-1949	Earl (Curly) Lambeau	.212-106-21
1950-53	Gene Ronzani*	14-31-1
1953	Hugh Devore-	
	Ray (Scooter) McLean**	0-2-0
1954-57	Lisle Blackbourn	17-31-0
1958	Ray (Scooter) McLean	1-10-1
1959-1967	Vince Lombardi	98-30-4
1968-1970	Phil Bengtson	20-21-1
1971-74	Dan Devine	25-28-4
1975-1983	Bart Starr	53-77-3
1984-87	Forrest Gregg	25-37-1
1988-1991	Lindy Infante	24-40-0
1992-98	Mike Holmgren	84-42-0
1999	Ray Rhodes	8-8-0
2000-05	Mike Sherman	59-43-0
2006	Mike McCarthy	8-8-0

*Resigned after 10 games in 1953
**Co-coaches

PAID ATTENDANCE
Home 565,682   Away 531,098
Total 1,096,780
Single-game home record,
 70,918 (9/10/06)
Single-season home record,
 565,682 (2006)

2007 DRAFT CHOICES
Round	Name	Pos.	College
1	Justin Harrell	DT	Tennessee
2	Brandon Jackson	RB	Nebraska
3	James Jones	WR	San Jose State
	Aaron Rouse	DB	Virginia Tech
4	Allen Barbre	T	Missouri Southern
5	David Clowney	WR	Virignia Tech
6	Korey Hall	LB	Boise State
	Desmond Bishop	LB	California
	Mason Crosby	K	Colorado
7	DeShawn Wynn	RB	Florida
	Clark Harris	TE	Rutgers

2006 TEAM RECORD
PRESEASON (1-3)

Date	Result	Opponent
8/12	L 3-17	at San Diego
8/19	W 38-10	Atlanta
8/28	L 17-48	at Cincinnati
9/1	L 21-35	Tennessee

REGULAR SEASON (8-8)

Date	Result	Opponent	Att.
9/10	L 0-26	Chicago	70,918
9/17	L 27-34	New Orleans	70,602
9/24	W 31-24	at Detroit	61,095
10/2	L 9-31	at Philadelphia	69,222
10/8	L 20-23	St. Louis	70,804
10/22	W 34-24	at Miami	73,548
10/29	W 31-14	Arizona	70,809
11/5	L 10-24	at Buffalo	72,205
11/12	W 23-17	at Minnesota	63,924
11/19	L 0-35	New England	70,753
11/27	L 24-34	at Seattle	68,256
12/3	L 10-38	N.Y. Jets	70,527
12/10	W 30-19	at San Francisco	68,539
12/17	W 17-9	Detroit	70,472
12/21	W 9-7	Minnesota	70,864
12/31	W 26-7	at Chicago	62,287

SCORE BY PERIODS

Packers	87	79	62	73	0 —	301
Opponents	64	115	84	103	0 —	366

2006 TEAM STATISTICS

	Packers	Opp.
Total First Downs	301	291
Rushing	93	95
Passing	185	169
Penalty	23	27
3rd Down: Made/Att	94/240	70/215
3rd Down Pct.	39.2	32.6
4th Down: Made/Att	7/17	13/21
4th Down Pct.	41.2	61.9
Possession Avg.	30:45	29:15
Total Net Yards	5458	5134
Avg. Per Game	341.1	320.9
Total Plays	1085	1002
Avg. Per Play	5.0	5.1
Net Yards Rushing	1663	1825
Avg. Per Game	103.9	114.1
Total Rushes	431	441
Net Yards Passing	3795	3309
Avg. Per Game	237.2	206.8
Sacked/Yards Lost	24/152	46/337
Gross Yards	3947	3646
Att./Completions	630/350	515/286
Completion Pct.	55.6	55.5
Had Intercepted	18	23
Punts/Average	84/44.5	83/44.6
Net Punting Avg.	84/35.7	83/37.9
Penalties/Yards	90/689	97/710
Fumbles/Ball Lost	25/15	29/10
Touchdowns	32	41
Rushing	9	12
Passing	18	25
Returns	5	4

2006 INDIVIDUAL STATISTICS

PASSING

	Att.	Comp.	Yds.	Pct.	TD	Int.	Tkld.	Rate
Favre	613	343	3,885	56.0	18	18	21/134	72.7
Rodgers	15	6	46	40.0	0	0	3/18	48.2
Holiday	1	0	—	0.0	0	0	0/0	39.6
Ryan	1	1	16	100.0	0	0	0/0	118.8
Packers	630	350	3,947	55.6	18	18	24/152	72.1
Opponents	515	286	3,646	55.5	25	23	46/337	75.4

SCORING

	TD R	TD P	TD Rt	PAT	FG	Saf	PTS
Rayner	0	0	0	31/32	26/35	0	109
Driver	0	8	0	0/0	0/0	0	48
Green	5	1	0	0/0	0/0	0	36
Herron	1	2	0	0/0	0/0	0	18
Jennings	0	3	0	0/0	0/0	0	18
D. Martin	0	2	0	0/0	0/0	0	12
Morency	2	0	0	0/0	0/0	0	12
Collins	0	0	1	0/0	0/0	0	6
Dendy	0	0	1	0/0	0/0	0	6
Favre	1	0	0	0/0	0/0	0	6
Ferguson	0	1	0	0/0	0/0	0	6
Hodge	0	0	1	0/0	0/0	0	6
Manuel	0	0	1	0/0	0/0	0	6
R. Martin	0	1	0	0/0	0/0	0	6
Woodson	0	0	1	0/0	0/0	0	6
Packers	9	18	5	31/32	26/35	0	301
Opponents	12	25	4	38/38	26/27	0	366

2-Pt. Conversions:
Packers 0-0, Opponents 2-3

RUSHING

	No.	Yds	Avg	LG	TD
Green	266	1,059	4.0	70t	5
Morency	91	421	4.6	39	2
Herron	37	150	4.1	19	1
Favre	23	29	1.3	14	1
Driver	7	16	2.3	16	0
Rodgers	2	11	5.5	6	0
I. Martin	2	-5	-2.5	-2	0
Gado	2	-7	-3.5	-3	0
Ryan	1	-11	-11.0	-11	0
Packers	431	1,663	3.9	70t	9
Opponents	441	1,825	4.1	72	12

RECEIVING

	No.	Yds	Avg	LG	TD
Driver	92	1,295	14.1	82t	8
Green	46	373	8.1	20	1
Jennings	45	632	14.0	75t	3
Herron	29	211	7.3	16	2
Franks	25	232	9.3	19	0
R. Martin	21	358	17.0	36t	1
D. Martin	21	198	9.4	23	2
Morency	16	112	7.0	29	0
Henderson	12	62	5.2	13	0
Lee	10	150	15.0	32	0
Holiday	9	126	14.0	35	0
Miree	9	57	6.3	20	0
Robinson	7	89	12.7	24	0
Ferguson	5	31	6.2	10	1
Francis	2	16	8.0	12	0
Gado	1	5	5.0	5	0
Packers	350	3,947	11.3	82t	18
Opponents	286	3,646	12.7	75t	25

INTERCEPTIONS

	No.	Yds	Avg	LG	TD
Woodson	8	61	7.6	23t	1
Collins	3	68	22.7	55t	1
Harris	3	39	13.0	34	0
Dendy	3	37	12.3	30t	1
Hawk	2	31	15.5	25	0
Barnett	2	3	1.5	3	0
Manuel	1	29	29.0	29t	1
Poppinga	1	21	21.0	21	0
Packers	23	289	12.6	55t	4
Opponents	18	201	11.2	76	2

PUNTING

	No.	Yds.	Avg.	In 20	LG
Ryan	84	3,739	44.5	17	66
Packers	84	3,739	44.5	17	66
Opponents	83	3,704	44.6	22	65

PUNT RETURNS

	Ret	FC	Yds	Avg	LG	TD
Woodson	41	2	363	8.9	40	0
Bodiford	6	1	25	4.2	16	0
Jennings	5	0	29	5.8	10	0
R. Martin	1	0	-2	-2.0	-2	0
Packers	53	3	415	7.8	40	0
Opponents	55	4	503	9.1	84t	1

KICKOFF RETURNS

	No.	Yds	Avg	LG	TD
Morency	31	670	21.6	35	0
Robinson	12	253	21.1	31	0
Herron	8	143	17.9	23	0
Bodiford	5	81	16.2	22	0
Ferguson	5	110	22.0	26	0
Henderson	4	41	10.3	16	0
Gado	3	57	19.0	23	0
Montgomery	1	14	14.0	14	0
Woodson	1	10	10.0	10	0
Packers	70	1,379	19.7	35	0
Opponents	60	1,348	22.5	61	0

FIELD GOALS

	1-19	20-29	30-39	40-49	50+
Rayner	0/0	11/12	6/9	8/11	1/3
Packers	0/0	11/12	6/9	8/11	1/3
Opponents	0/0	8/8	7/7	11/11	0/1

SACKS

	No.
Kampman	15.5
C. Williams	7.0
Jenkins	6.5
Gbaja-Biamila	6.0
Hawk	3.5
Barnett	2.0
Montgomery	1.5
Carroll	1.0
Cole	1.0
Poppinga	1.0
Woodson	1.0
Packers	46.0
Opponents	24.0

RECORD HOLDERS
INDIVIDUAL RECORDS—CAREER

Category	Name	Performance
Rushing (Yds.)	Jim Taylor, 1958-1966	8,207
Passing (Yds.)	Brett Favre, 1992-2006	57,500
Passing (TDs)	Brett Favre, 1992-2006	414
Receiving (No.)	Sterling Sharpe, 1988-1994	595
Receiving (Yds.)	James Lofton, 1978-1986	9,656
Interceptions	Bobby Dillon, 1952-59	52
Punting (Avg.)	Craig Hentrich, 1994-97	42.8
Punt Return (Avg.)	Desmond Howard, 1996, 1999	13.8
Kickoff Return (Avg.)	Travis Williams, 1967-1970	26.7
Field Goals	Ryan Longwell, 1997-2005	226
Touchdowns (Tot.)	Don Hutson, 1935-1945	105
Points	Ryan Longwell, 1997-2005	1,054

INDIVIDUAL RECORDS—SINGLE SEASON

Category	Name	Performance
Rushing (Yds.)	Ahman Green, 2003	1,883
Passing (Yds.)	Lynn Dickey, 1983	4,458
Passing (TDs)	Brett Favre, 1996	39
Receiving (No.)	Sterling Sharpe, 1993	112
Receiving (Yds.)	Robert Brooks, 1995	1,497
Interceptions	Irv Comp, 1943	10
Punting (Avg.)	Craig Hentrich, 1997	45.0
Punt Return (Avg.)	Billy Grimes, 1950	19.1
Kickoff Return (Avg.)	Travis Williams, 1967	*41.1
Field Goals	Chester Marcol, 1972	33
	Ryan Longwell, 2000	33
Touchdowns (Tot.)	Ahman Green, 2003	20
Points	Paul Hornung, 1960	176

INDIVIDUAL RECORDS—SINGLE GAME

Category	Name	Performance
Rushing (Yds.)	Ahman Green, 12-28-03	218
Passing (Yds.)	Lynn Dickey, 10-12-80	418
Passing (TDs)	Many times	5
	Last time by Brett Favre, 9-27-98	
Receiving (No.)	Don Hutson, 11-22-42	14
Receiving (Yds.)	Billy Howton, 10-21-56	257
Interceptions	Bobby Dillon, 11-26-53	*4
	Willie Buchanon, 9-24-78	*4
Field Goals	Chris Jacke, 11-11-90, 10-14-96	5
	Ryan Longwell, 9-24-00	5
Touchdowns (Tot.)	Paul Hornung, 12-12-65	5
Points	Paul Hornung, 10-8-61	33

*NFL Record

2007 VETERAN ROSTER

No.	Name	Pos.	Ht.	Wt.	Birthdate	NFL Exp.	College	Hometown	How Acq.	'06 Games/ Starts
49	Alcorn, Zac	TE	6-4	255	8/24/80	2	Black Hills State	Chadron, Neb.	FA-'06	6/0
56	Barnett, Nick	LB	6-2	232	5/27/81	5	Oregon State	Fontana, Calif.	D1-'03	15/15
71	Barry, Kevin	T	6-4	332	7/20/79	6	Arizona	Racine, Wis.	FA-'02	0*
30	Beach, Arliss	RB	5-10	222	3/28/84	2	Kentucky	Ashland, Ky.	FA-'06	0*
20	Bigby, Atari	S	5-11	211	9/19/81	2	Central Florida	Miami, Fla.	FA-'06	5/0
27	Blackmon, Will	CB	6-1	202	10/27/84	2	Boston College	Warwick, R.I.	D4b-'06	4/0
19	Bodiford, Shaun	WR	5-11	186	5/4/82	2	Portland State	Federal Way, Wash.	W(Det)-'06	3/0
8	#Bouman, Todd	QB	6-2	226	8/1/72	10	St. Cloud State	Tyler, Minn.	FA-'06	0*
67	Bourke, Josh	T	6-7	314	10/16/82	2	Grand Valley State	Orchard Lake, Mich.	FA-'06	0*
24	Bush, Jarrett	CB	6-1	197	5/21/84	2	Utah State	Vacaville, Calif.	W(Car)-'06	16/0
76	Clifton, Chad	T	6-5	320	6/26/76	8	Tennessee	Martin, Tenn.	D2-'00	15/15
90	Cole, Colin	DT	6-1	315	6/24/80	3	Iowa	Ft. Lauderdale, Fla.	FA-'04	15/3
73	Colledge, Daryn	G/T	6-4	305	2/11/82	2	Boise State	North Pole, Alaska	D2a-'06	16/15
36	Collins, Nick	S	5-11	200	8/16/83	3	Bethune-Cookman	Cross City, Fla.	D2a-'05	16/16
62	Coston, Junius	G/T	6-3	313	11/5/83	3	North Carolina A&T	Raleigh, N.C.	D5a-'05	1/0
29	Culver, Tyrone	S	6-1	200	7/6/83	2	Fresno State	Palmdale, Calif.	D6b-'06	14/0
60	Davis, Rob	LS	6-3	284	12/10/68	12	Shippensburg	Greenbelt, Md.	FA-'97	16/0
43	Dendy, Patrick	CB	6-1	190	3/10/82	3	Rice	Austin, Texas	FA-'05	12/3
80	Driver, Donald	WR	6-1	190	2/2/75	9	Alcorn State	Houston, Texas	D7b-'99	16/16
4	Favre, Brett	QB	6-2	222	10/10/69	17	Southern Mississippi	Kiln, Miss.	T(Atl)-'92	16/16
87	Ferguson, Robert	WR	6-1	219	12/17/79	7	Texas A&M	Houston, Texas	D2-'01	4/1
83	Francies, Chris	WR	6-1	193	7/26/82	2	Texas-El Paso	Houston, Texas	FA-'06	7/0
88	Franks, Bubba	TE	6-6	265	1/6/78	8	Miami	Big Spring, Texas	D1-'00	16/4
94	Gbaja-Biamila, Kabeer	DE	6-4	247	9/24/77	8	San Diego State	Los Angeles, Calif.	D5-'00	16/13
31	Harris, Al	CB	6-1	188	12/7/74	10	Texas A&M-Kingsville	Pompano Beach, Fla.	T(Phil)-'03	16/16
50	Hawk, A.J.	LB	6-1	247	1/6/84	2	Ohio State	Centerville, Ohio	D1-'06	16/16
23	Herron, Noah	RB	5-11	218	4/3/82	3	Northwestern	Mattawan, Mich.	FA-'05	16/0
52	Hodge, Abdul	LB	6-1	229	9/9/82	2	Iowa	Lauderdale Lakes, Fla.	D3a-'06	8/1
18	Holiday, Carlyle	WR	6-2	217	10/4/81	2	Notre Dame	San Antonio, Texas	W(Ariz)-'06	4/0
84	Humphrey, Tory	TE	6-2	250	1/20/83	2	Central Michigan	Saginaw, Mich.	FA-'05	7/0
57	Hunter, Jason	DE	6-4	250	8/28/83	2	Appalachian State	Fayetteville, N.C.	FA-'06	14/0
77	Jenkins, Cullen	DE/DT	6-2	295	1/20/81	4	Central Michigan	Belleville, Mich.	FA-'04	14/5
85	Jennings, Greg	WR	5-11	197	9/21/83	2	Western Michigan	Kalamazoo, Mich.	D2b-'06	14/11
93	Jolly, Johnny	DT	6-3	312	2/21/83	2	Texas A&M	Houston, Texas	D6a-'06	6/0
74	Kampman, Aaron	DE	6-4	270	11/30/79	6	Iowa	Parkersburg, Iowa	D5a-'02	16/16
86	Lee, Donald	TE	6-4	248	8/31/80	5	Mississippi State	Maben, Miss.	FA-'05	15/2
22	Manuel, Marquand	S	6-1	209	7/11/79	6	Florida	Miami, Fla.	UFA(Sea)-'06	16/16
7	Martin, Ingle	QB	6-2	220	8/15/82	2	Furman	Nashville, Tenn.	D5a-'06	1/0
82	Martin, Ruvell	WR	6-4	210	8/10/82	2	Saginaw Valley State	Muskegon, Mich.	FA-'06	13/3
40	Miree, Brandon	FB	6-1	236	4/14/81	3	Pittsburgh	Cincinnati, Ohio	FA-'06	10/3
75	Moll, Tony	T/G	6-5	304	8/23/83	2	Nevada	Sonoma, Calif.	D5b-'06	16/10
96	Montgomery, Michael	DE	6-5	265	8/18/83	3	Texas A&M	Center, Texas	D6a-'05	11/0
34	Morency, Vernand	RB	5-10	212	2/4/80	3	Oklahoma State	Miami, Fla.	T(Hou)-'06	13/2
64	Palmer, Tony	G/C	6-2	311	2/23/83	2	Missouri	Midwest City, Okla.	W(StL)-'06	6/0
26	Peprah, Charlie	S	5-11	202	2/24/83	2	Alabama	Plano, Texas	W(NYG)-'06	8/0
79	Pickett, Ryan	DT	6-2	322	10/8/79	7	Ohio State	Zephyrhills, Fla.	UFA(StL)-'06	16/16
28	Pope, P.J.	RB	5-9	212	2/26/84	2	Bowling Green	Wyoming, Ohio	FA-'06	1/0
51	Poppinga, Brady	LB	6-3	245	9/21/79	3	Brigham Young	Evanston, Wyo.	D4b-'05	16/12
16	Rayner, Dave	K	6-2	210	10/26/82	3	Michigan State	Oxford, Mich.	W(Ind)-'06	16/0
12	Rodgers, Aaron	QB	6-2	223	12/2/83	3	California	Chico, Calif.	D1-'05	2/0
9	Ryan, Jon	P	6-1	202	11/26/81	2	Regina (Canada)	Regina, Saskatchewan, Canada	FA-'06	16/0
72	Spitz, Jason	G/C	6-3	300	12/19/82	2	Louisville	Jacksonville, Fla.	D3b-'06	14/13
65	Tauscher, Mark	T	6-3	315	6/17/77	8	Wisconsin	Auburndale, Wis.	D7a-'00	11/11
58#	Taylor, Ben	LB	6-2	232	8/31/78	6	Virginia Tech	Bellaire, Ohio	UFA(Cle)-'06	10/0
25	Underwood, Marviel	S	5-10	200	2/17/82	3	San Diego State	San Leandro, Calif.	D4a-'05	0*
41	Walker, Frank	CB	5-11	196	8/6/81	5	Tuskegee	Tuskegee, Ala.	UFA(NYG)-'07	11/1*
70	Walter, Tyson	T/G	6-4	300	3/17/78	6	Ohio State	Chagrin Falls, Ohio	FA-'06	5/0
63	Wells, Scott	C	6-2	295	1/7/81	4	Tennessee	Brentwood, Tenn.	FA-'04	16/16
59	White, Tracy	LB	6-1	234	4/14/81	5	Howard	St. Stephens, S.C.	FA-'05	14/0
99	Williams, Corey	DT	6-4	313	8/17/80	4	Arkansas State	Camden, Ark.	D6-'04	16/11
21	Woodson, Charles	CB	6-1	200	10/7/76	10	Michigan	Fremont, Ohio	UFA(Oak)-'06	16/16

* Barry missed '06 season because of injury; Beach missed '06 season because of injury; Bouman did not play in 6 games; Bourke missed '06 season because of injury; Underwood missed missed '06 season because of injury; Walker played 11 games with N.Y. Giants in '06.

Players lost through free agency (3): DT Kenderick Allen (Cin; 2 games in '06), RB Ahman Green (Hou; 14), TE David Martin (Mia; 11).

Also played with Packers in '06—CB Ahmad Carroll (4 games), RB Samkon Gado (1), FB William Henderson (14), FB Vonta Leach (1), WR Koren Robinson (4).

2007 FIRST-YEAR ROSTER

Name	Pos.	Ht.	Wt.	Birthdate	College	Hometown	How Acq.
Babb, Jerry	QB	6-2	225	9/20/83	Louisiana Lafayette	Lafayette, La.	FA
Barbre, Allen	T/G	6-4	300	6/22/84	Missouri Southern State	Granby, Mo.	D4
Birdine, Larry	DE	6-4	265	10/6/83	Oklahoma	Lawton, Okla.	FA
Bishop, Desmond	LB	6-2	241	7/24/84	California	Fairfield, Calif.	D6b
Brewster, Carlton (1)	WR	5-11	208	2/12/83	Ferris State	Grand Rapids, Mich.	FA
Clowney, David	WR	6-0	188	7/7/85	Virginia Tech	Delray Beach, Fla.	D5
Crosby, Mason	K	6-1	212	9/3/84	Colorado	Georgetown, Texas	D6c
Goodwell, Tim (1)	LB	6-0	237	1/30/84	Memphis	Tucker, Ga.	FA
Hall, Korey	FB	6-0	236	8/5/83	Boise State	Glenns Ferry, Idaho	D6a
Harrell, Justin	DT	6-4	310	2/14/84	Tennessee	Martin, Tenn.	D1
Harris, Clark	TE	6-5	256	7/10/84	Rutgers	Manahawkin, N.J.	D7b
Havner, Spencer (1)	LB	6-3	244	2/2/83	UCLA	Grass Valley, Calif.	FA
Jackson, Brandon	RB	5-10	212	10/2/85	Nebraska	Horn Lake, Miss.	D2
Johnson, Rory	LB	6-0	237	3/15/86	Mississippi	Vicksburg, Miss.	FA
Jones, James	WR	6-1	207	3/31/84	San Jose State	San Jose, Calif.	D3a
Leffew, Travis (1)	G/T	6-4	292	1/27/83	Louisville	Danville, Ky.	FA
Lonie, David (1)	P	6-5	210	5/6/79	California	Palm Beach, Australia	FA
Malone, Antonio	CB	6-0	188	1/24/84	Toledo	Portsmouth, Ohio	FA
Muir, Daniel	DT	6-2	298	9/12/83	Kent State	Riverdale, Md.	FA
Murray, Pat	G/T	6-3	310	10/31/84	Truman State	Pocahontas, Iowa	FA
Nnabuife, Alvin (1)	S	6-1	212	4/3/83	Southern Methodist	Missouri City, Texas	FA
Powdrell, Ryan	FB	5-11	254	12/20/83	Southern California	Mission Viejo, Calif.	FA
Randall, Marcus (1)	LB	6-1	232	3/14/82	Louisiana State	Baton Rouge, La.	FA
Rouse, Aaron	S	6-4	223	1/8/84	Virginia Tech	Virginia Beach, Va.	D3b
Russell, Calvin (1)	WR	6-0	190	6/14/83	Tuskegee	Fairburn, Ga.	FA
Scandrett, Devarick (1)	DT	6-4	322	1/23/84	Middle Tennessee State	Forsyth, Ga.	FA
Simpson, Juwan	LB	6-2	225	7/8/84	Alabama	Decatur, Ala.	FA
Stenavich, Adam (1)	G/T	6-4	308	3/11/83	Michigan	Marshfield, Wis.	FA
Thompson, Orrin (1)	T	6-6	322	11/11/82	Duke	Charlotte, N.C.	FA
Williams, Tramon (1)	CB	5-11	182	3/16/83	Louisiana Tech	Napoleonville, La.	FA
Wynn, DeShawn	RB	5-10	232	10/9/83	Florida	Cincinnati, Ohio	D7a

The term NFL Rookie is defined as a player who is in his first season of professional football and has not been on the roster of another professional football team for any regular-season or postseason games. A Rookie is designated by an "R" on NFL rosters. Players who have been active in another professional football league or players who have NFL experience, including either preseason training camp or being on an Active List or Inactive List, or on Reserve/Injured or Reserve/Physically Unable to Perform for fewer than six regular-season games, are termed NFL First-Year Players. An NFL First-Year Player is designated by a "1" on NFL rosters. Thereafter, a player is credited with an additional year of experience for each season in which he accumulates six games on the Active List or Inactive List, or on Reserve/Injured or Reserve/Physically Unable to Perform.

Log on to www.packers.com for an up-to-date roster.

COACHING STAFF
Head Coach,
Mike McCarthy
Pro Career: Named the fourteenth head coach in team history January 12, 2006. Guided Packers to 8-8 record in 2006, finishing year with four-game winning streak, and became the first head coach in franchise history to win five road games in his inaugural season. Had returned to Green Bay after serving as the team's quarterbacks coach in 1999. Subsequently was a highly successful offensive coordinator for the New Orleans Saints (2000-04). With McCarthy calling plays, the Saints racked up 10 offensive team records and 26 individual marks. He was named NFC Assistant Coach of the Year by *USA Today* in 2000, and New Orleans led the league with 432 points and 49 touchdowns in 2002. The list of quarterbacks he has coached includes Joe Montana, Elvis Grbac, Rich Gannon, Brett Favre, Matt Hasselbeck, Aaron Brooks, Jake Delhomme and Marc Bulger—a collection that combines for 26 career Pro Bowl selections and eight Super Bowl starts. Career record: 8-8.
Background: Graduated with a degree in business administration from Baker University following a two-year playing career (1985-86). Was an all-conference tight end, helping the school to a NAIA Division II runner-up finish as a senior captain. Coached collegiately at Fort Hays State (1987-88) and Pittsburgh (1989-1992), before moving to the NFL with the Kansas City Chiefs (1993-98), Green Bay Packers (1999), New Orleans Saints (2000-04) and San Francisco 49ers (2005).
Personal: Born November 10, 1963, in Pittsburgh. Has a daughter, Alexandra.

ASSISTANT COACHES
Edgar Bennett, running backs; born February 15, 1969, Jacksonville. Running back Florida State 1987, 1989-1991. Pro running back Green Bay Packers 1992-96, Chicago Bears 1998-99. Pro coach: Joined Packers in 2001.
James Campen, offensive line; born June 11, 1964, Sacramento, Calif. Center Sacramento City (Calif.) J.C. 1982-83, Tulane 1984-85. Pro center New Orleans Saints 1987-88, Green Bay Packers 1989-1993. Pro coach: Joined Packers in 2004.
Tom Clements, quarterbacks; born June 18, 1953, McKees Rocks, Pa. Quarterback Notre Dame 1972-74. Pro quarterback Ottawa Rough Riders (CFL) 1975-78, Hamilton Tiger-Cats (CFL) 1979, 1981-82, Kansas City Chiefs 1980, Winnipeg Blue Bombers (CFL) 1983-87. College coach: Notre Dame 1992-95. Pro coach: New Orleans Saints 1997-99, Kansas City Chiefs 2000, Pittsburgh Steelers 2001-03, Buffalo Bills 2004-05, joined Packers in 2006.
Jerry Fontenot, asst. offensive line; born

November 21, 1966, Lafayette, La. Guard Texas A&M 1985-88. Pro center Chicago Bears 1989-1996, New Orleans Saints 1997-2003, Cincinnati Bengals 2004. Pro coach: Joined Packers in 2006.
Rock Gullickson, strength & conditioning; born April 11, 1955, Moorhead, Minn. Guard Moorhead (Minn.) State 1973-76. No pro playing experience. College coach: Moorhead State 1978, Mayville (N.D.) State 1979-1980, South Dakota State 1981, Montana State 1982-89, Rutgers 1990-92, Texas 1993-97, Louisville 1988-1999. Pro coach: New Orleans Saints 2000-05, joined Packers in 2006.
Carl Hairston, defensive ends; born December 15, 1952, Martinsville, Va. Defensive end Maryland-Eastern Shore 1972-75. Pro defensive end Philadelphia Eagles 1976-1983, Cleveland Browns 1984-89, Phoenix Cardinals 1990. Pro coach: Kansas City Chiefs 1995-96, 2001-05, St. Louis Rams 1997-2000, joined Packers in 2006.
Ty Knott, offensive quality control; born December 9, 1965, Los Angeles. Defensive back Oregon Tech 1988-89. No pro playing experience. College coach: Whittier College 1994-95, Indiana University (Pa.) 1997-99, Mt. San Antonio (Calif.) J.C. 2000, Greenville 2001. Pro coach: Jacksonville Jaguars 2002, New Orleans Saints 2003-05, joined Packers in 2006.
Eric Lewis, defensive quality control; born January 2, 1976, East Lansing, Mich. Defensive back San Diego State 1995-98. No pro playing experience. College coach: Michigan State 2001, Bucknell 2002, Ball State 2003-05. Pro coach: Joined Packers in 2006.
Ben McAdoo, tight ends; born July 7, 1977, Homer City, Pa. Attended Indiana University (Pa.). No college or pro playing experience. College coach: Michigan State 2001, Fairfield 2002, Pittsburgh 2003, Akron 2004, Stanford 2005. Pro coach: New Orleans Saints 2004, San Francisco 49ers 2005, joined Packers in 2006.
Winston Moss, asst. head coach/linebackers; born December 24, 1965, Miami. Linebacker Miami 1983-86. Pro linebacker Tampa Bay Buccaneers 1987-1990, Los Angeles Raiders 1991-94, Seattle Seahawks 1995-97. Pro coach: Seattle Seahawks 1998, New Orleans Saints 2000-05, joined Packers in 2006.
Robert Nunn, defensive tackles; born June 10, 1965, Apache, Okla. Linebacker Oklahoma State 1983-84, 1986-87. No pro playing experience. College coach: Northeastern Oklahoma 1988, Tennessee 1989-1990, Georgia Military College 1991-99 (head coach 1992-99). Pro coach: Miami Dolphins 2000-02, 2004, Washington Redskins 2003, joined Packers in 2005.
Joe Philbin, offensive coordinator; born July 2, 1961, Springfield, Mass. Tight end Washington & Jefferson 1980. No pro playing experience. College coach: Tulane

1984-85, Worcester Tech 1986-87, U.S. Merchant Marine Academy 1988-89, Allegheny 1990-93, Ohio University 1994, Northeastern 1995-96, Harvard 1997-98, Iowa 1999-2002. Pro coach: Joined Packers in 2003.
Jimmy Robinson, wide receivers; born January 3, 1953, Atlanta. Wide receiver Georgia Tech 1972-74. Pro wide receiver New York Giants 1976-79, San Francisco 49ers 1980, Denver Broncos 1981. College coach: Georgia Tech 1987-89. Pro coach: Memphis Showboats (USFL) 1984-85, Atlanta Falcons 1990-93, Indianapolis Colts 1994-97, New York Giants 1998-2003, New Orleans Saints 2004-05, joined Packers in 2006.
Bob Sanders, defensive coordinator; born December 5, 1953, Jacksonville, N.C. Linebacker Davidson College 1973-75. No pro playing experience. College coach: Georgia Tech 1978, East Carolina 1980-82, Richmond 1983-84, Duke 1985-89, Florida 1990-2000. Pro coach: Miami Dolphins 2001-04, joined Packers in 2005.
Kurt Schottenheimer, secondary; born October 1, 1949, McDonald, Pa. Quarterback Coffeyville (Kan.) J.C. 1967-68, defensive back Miami (Fla.) 1969-70. No pro playing experience. College coach: William Paterson 1974, Michigan State 1978-1982, Tulane 1983, Louisiana State 1984-85, Notre Dame 1986. Pro coach: Cleveland Browns 1987-88, Kansas City Chiefs 1989-2000, Washington Redskins 2001, Detroit Lions 2002-03, Green Bay Packers 2004, St. Louis Rams 2005, rejoined Packers in 2006.
Shawn Slocum, asst. special teams; born February 21, 1965, Bryan, Texas. Linebacker Texas A&M 1983-84. No pro playing experience. College coach: Texas A&M 1989, 1991-97, 2000-02, Pittsburgh 1990, Southern California 1998-99, Mississippi 2005. Pro coach: Joined Packers in 2006.
Mike Stock, special teams coordinator; born September 29, 1939, Barberton, Ohio. Fullback Northwestern 1957-1960. Pro running back Saskatchewan Roughriders (CFL) 1961. College coach: Northwestern 1961, Buffalo 1966-67, Navy 1968, Notre Dame 1969-1974, 1983-86, Wisconsin 1975-77, Eastern Michigan 1978-1982 (head coach), Ohio State 1992-94. Pro coach: New Jersey Generals (USFL) 1983, Cincinnati Bengals 1987-1991, Kansas City Chiefs 1995-2000, Washington Redskins 2001-03, St. Louis Rams 2004, joined Packers in 2006.
Lionel Washington, defensive nickel package/cornerbacks; born October 21, 1960, New Orleans. Defensive back Tulane 1979-1982. Pro defensive back St. Louis Cardinals 1983-86, Los Angeles/Oakland Raiders 1987-1994, 1997, Denver Broncos 1995-96. Pro coach: Joined Packers in 1999.

National Football Conference
North Division
Team Colors: Purple, Gold, and White
9520 Viking Drive
Eden Prairie, Minnesota 55344
Telephone: (952) 828-6500

2007 SCHEDULE
PRESEASON
Aug. 10 **St. Louis** 7:00
Aug. 17 at N.Y. Jets 8:00
Aug. 25 at Seattle 6:00
Aug. 30 **Dallas** 7:00

REGULAR SEASON
Sep. 9 **Atlanta** 12:00
Sep. 16 at Detroit 4:05
Sep. 23 at Kansas City 12:00
Sep. 30 **Green Bay** 12:00
Oct. 7 Open Date
Oct. 14 at Chicago 12:00
Oct. 21 at Dallas 12:00
Oct. 28 **Philadelphia** 12:00
Nov. 4 **San Diego** 12:00
Nov. 11 at Green Bay 12:00
Nov. 18 **Oakland** 12:00
Nov. 25 at N.Y. Giants....................1:00
Dec. 2 **Detroit** 12:00
Dec. 9 at San Francisco 1:05
Dec. 17 **Chicago** (Mon.)................7:30
Dec. 23 **Washington** 12:00
Dec. 30 at Denver 2:15

Stadium: Hubert H. Humphrey Metrodome
(opened in 1982)
• **Capacity:** 64,121
500 11th Avenue South
Minneapolis, Minnesota 55415
Playing Surface: FieldTurf
Training Camp: Minnesota State-Mankato
Mankato, Minnesota
56001

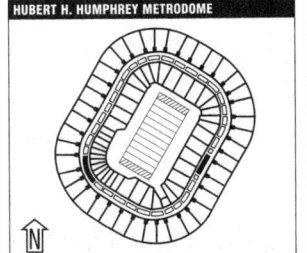

HUBERT H. HUMPHREY METRODOME

CLUB OFFICIALS
Owner/Chairman: Zygi Wilf
Owner/President: Mark Wilf
Owner/Vice Chairman: Leonard Wilf
Ownership Partners: Reggie Fowler,
Alan Landis, David Mandelbaum
Vice President of Public Affairs/Stadium
Development: Lester Bagley
Vice President of Football Operations:
Rob Brzezinski
Vice President of Sales and Marketing:
Steve LaCroix
Vice President of Finance: Steve Poppen
Vice President of Player Personnel:
Rick Spielman
Vice President of Operations and Legal
Counsel: Kevin Warren
Director of College Scouting:
Scott Studwell
Director of Football Administration:
Dave Blando
Director of Public Relations: Bob Hagan
Director of Community Relations:
Brad Madson
Director of Operations/Team Travel:
Luther Hippe
Director of Operations/Stadium and
Logistics: Chad Lundeen
Director of Ticketing and Hospitality:
Phil Huebner
Director of Video: Bob Marcus
Director of Player Development/Legal:
Les Pico
Director of Security: Kim Klawiter
Head Athletic Trainer: Eric Sugarman
Equipment Manager: Dennis Ryan
Director of Marketing & Business
Development: Dannon Hulskotter
Director of Corporate Sales: Mike Slates

COACHING HISTORY
(395-332-9)
Records include postseason games
1961-66   Norm Van Brocklin 29-51-4
1967-1983 Bud Grant 161-99-5
1984   Les Steckel 3-13-0
1985   Bud Grant 7-9-0
1986-1991 Jerry Burns...............55-46-0
1992-2001 Dennis Green* 101-70-0
2001-05   Mike Tice 33-34-0
2006   Brad Childress 6-10-0
*Resigned after 15 games in 2001

PAID ATTENDANCE
Home 496,143   Away 557,964
Total 1,054,107
Single-game home record,
64,482 (11/2/03)
Single-season home record,
510,741 (1998)

2007 DRAFT CHOICES
Round	Name	Pos.	College
1	Adrian Peterson	RB	Oklahoma
2	Sidney Rice	WR	South Carolina
3	Marcus McCauley	DB	Fresno State
4	Brian Robison	DE	Texas
5	Aundrae Allison	WR	East Carolina
6	Rufus Alexander	LB	Oklahoma
7	Tyler Thigpen	QB	Coastal Carolina
	Chandler Williams	WR	Florida International

2006 TEAM RECORD
PRESEASON (2-1-1)

Date	Result	Opponent
8/14	L	13-16 Oakland
8/19	W	17-10 at Pittsburgh
8/25	W	30-7 Baltimore
8/31	T	10-10 at Dallas (OT)

REGULAR SEASON (6-10)

Date	Result	Opponent	Att.
9/11	W	19-16 at Washington	90,608
9/17	W	16-13 Carolina (OT)	63,623
9/24	L	16-19 Chicago	63,754
10/1	L	12-17 at Buffalo	71,972
10/8	W	26-17 Detroit	63,906
10/22	W	31-13 at Seattle	68,118
10/30	L	7-31 New England	63,819
11/5	L	3-9 at San Francisco	68,088
11/12	L	17-23 Green Bay	63,924
11/19	L	20-24 at Miami	73,070
11/26	W	31-26 Arizona	63,483
12/3	L	13-23 at Chicago	62,221
12/10	W	30-20 at Detroit	60,861
12/17	L	13-26 N.Y. Jets	63,677
12/21	L	7-9 at Green Bay	70,864
12/31	L	21-41 St. Louis	63,557

(OT) OVertime

SCORE BY PERIODS

Vikings	66	49	54	110	3	—	282
Opponents	57	129	73	68	0	—	327

2006 TEAM STATISTICS

	Vikings	Opp.
Total First Downs	272	272
Rushing	87	53
Passing	160	192
Penalty	25	27
3rd Down: Made/Att	77/233	74/215
3rd Down Pct.	33.0	34.4
4th Down: Made/Att	15/21	7/13
4th Down Pct.	71.4	53.8
Possession Avg.	31:37	28:23
Total Net Yards	4943	4803
Avg. Per Game	308.9	300.2
Total Plays	1025	977
Avg. Per Play	4.8	4.9
Net Yards Rushing	1820	985
Avg. Per Game	113.8	61.6
Total Rushes	442	348
Net Yards Passing	3123	3818
Avg. Per Game	195.2	238.6
Sacked/Yards Lost	43/279	30/197
Gross Yards	3402	4015
Att./Completions	540/332	599/355
Completion Pct.	61.5	59.3
Had Intercepted	20	21
Punts/Average	94/42.1	79/45.4
Net Punting Avg.	94/35.5	79/37.8
Penalties/Yards	123/903	112/899
Fumbles/Ball Lost	31/12	25/15
Touchdowns	32	32
Rushing	12	9
Passing	13	15
Returns	7	8

2006 INDIVIDUAL STATISTICS

PASSING

	Att.	Comp.	Yds.	Pct.	TD	Int.	Tkld.	Rate
Br. Johnson	439	270	2,750	61.5	9	15	29/200	72.0
Jackson	81	47	475	58.0	2	4	8/37	62.5
Bollinger	18	13	146	72.2	0	1	6/42	72.9
Longwell	1	1	16	100.0	1	0	0/0	158.3
Moore	1	1	15	100.0	1	0	0/0	158.3
Vikings	540	332	3,402	61.5	13	20	43/279	72.2
Opponents	599	355	4,015	59.3	15	21	30/197	73.1

SCORING

	TD R	TD P	TD Rt	PAT	FG	Saf	PTS
Longwell	0	0	0	27/28	21/25	0	90
C. Taylor	6	0	0	0/0	0/0	0	36
Robinson	0	4	0	0/0	0/0	0	24
McMullen	0	2	1	0/0	0/0	0	18
Pinner	3	0	0	0/0	0/0	0	18
T. Taylor	0	3	0	0/0	0/0	0	18
Moore	0	1	1	0/0	0/0	0	12
Dugan	0	1	0	0/0	0/0	0	6
Fason	1	0	0	0/0	0/0	0	6
Henderson	0	0	1	0/0	0/0	0	6
Jackson	1	0	0	0/0	0/0	0	6
Br. Johnson	1	0	0	0/0	0/0	0	6
Leber	0	0	1	0/0	0/0	0	6
Owens	0	1	0	0/0	0/0	0	6
Smoot	0	0	1	0/0	0/0	0	6
Wiggins	0	1	0	0/0	0/0	0	6
K. Williams	0	0	1	0/0	0/0	0	6
Winfield	0	0	1	0/0	0/0	0	6
Vikings	12	13	7	27/28	21/25	0	282
Opponents	9	15	8	31/31	34/40	1	327

2-Pt. Conversions: Vikings 0-4, Opponents 0-1

RUSHING

	No.	Yds	Avg	LG	TD
C. Taylor	303	1,216	4.0	95t	6
Pinner	43	190	4.4	21	3
Moore	24	131	5.5	15	0
Fason	18	99	5.5	15	1
Br. Johnson	29	82	2.8	10	1
Jackson	15	77	5.1	13	1
Richardson	5	12	2.4	3	0
Be. Johnson	4	8	2.0	5	0
T. Taylor	1	5	5.0	5	0
Vikings	442	1,820	4.1	95t	12
Opponents	348	985	2.8	59t	9

RECEIVING

	No.	Yds	Avg	LG	TD
T. Taylor	57	651	11.4	36	3
Moore	46	468	10.2	50	1
Wiggins	46	386	8.4	24	1
C. Taylor	42	288	6.9	24	0
Williamson	37	455	12.3	46	0
Robinson	29	381	13.1	40t	4
McMullen	23	307	13.3	40t	2
Richardson	13	111	8.5	25	0
Be. Johnson	9	156	17.3	40	0
Dugan	8	40	5.0	10	1
Kleinsasser	7	47	6.7	14	0
Owens	6	45	7.5	16t	1
Nance	4	33	8.3	12	0
Fason	3	19	6.3	12	0
Pinner	2	15	7.5	8	0
Vikings	332	3,402	10.2	50	13
Opponents	355	4,015	11.3	82t	15

INTERCEPTIONS

	No.	Yds	Avg	LG	TD
D. Smith	4	81	20.3	47	0
Winfield	4	33	8.3	26	1
Sharper	4	10	2.5	10	0
Harris	3	20	6.7	11	0
Henderson	2	48	24.0	45t	1
Griffin	2	4	2.0	4	0
Smoot	1	47	47.0	47t	1
Leber	1	0	0.0	0	0
Vikings	21	243	11.6	47t	3
Opponents	20	399	20.0	88t	4

PUNTING

	No.	Yds.	Avg.	In 20	LG
Kluwe	93	3,934	42.3	28	68
Longwell	1	27	27.0	1	27
Vikings	94	3,961	42.1	29	68
Opponents	79	3,583	45.4	17	65

PUNT RETURNS

	Ret	FC	Yds	Avg	LG	TD
Moore	36	9	365	10.1	71t	1
Gordon	1	0	1	1.0	1	0
D. Smith	1	0	8	8.0	8	0
Vikings	38	9	374	9.8	71t	1
Opponents	50	21	485	9.7	45t	1

KICKOFF RETURNS

	No.	Yds	Avg	LG	TD
Be. Johnson	45	1,054	23.4	65	0
Williamson	14	324	23.1	44	0
Pinner	4	76	19.0	24	0
Moore	1	25	25.0	25	0
Rosenthal	1	13	13.0	13	0
Owens	1	0	0.0	0	0
Vikings	66	1,492	22.6	65	0
Opponents	59	1,369	23.2	99t	1

FIELD GOALS

	1-19	20-29	30-39	40-49	50+
Longwell	2/2	7/7	8/8	4/6	0/2
Vikings	2/2	7/7	8/8	4/6	0/2
Opponents	0/0	16/16	3/5	9/13	6/6

SACKS

	No.
Scott	5.5
K Williams	5.0
R Edwards	3.0
Henderson	3.0
Leber	3.0
Mitchell	3.0
Harris	2.5
Sharper	1.0
D Smith	1.0
Thomas	1.0
P Williams	1.0
(group)	1.0
Vikings	30.0
Opponents	43.0

RECORD HOLDERS
INDIVIDUAL RECORDS—CAREER

Category	Name	Performance
Rushing (Yds.)	Robert Smith, 1993-2000	6,818
Passing (Yds.)	Fran Tarkenton, 1961-66, 1972-78	33,098
Passing (TDs)	Fran Tarkenton, 1961-66, 1972-78	239
Receiving (No.)	Cris Carter, 1990-2001	1,004
Receiving (Yds.)	Cris Carter, 1990-2001	12,383
Interceptions	Paul Krause, 1968-1979	53
Punting (Avg.)	Harry Newsome, 1990-93	43.8
Punt Return (Avg.)	David Palmer, 1994-2000	9.4
Kickoff Return (Avg.)	Charlie West, 1968-1973	25.5
Field Goals	Fred Cox, 1963-1977	282
Touchdowns (Tot.)	Cris Carter, 1990-2001	110
Points	Fred Cox, 1963-1977	1,365

INDIVIDUAL RECORDS—SINGLE SEASON

Category	Name	Performance
Rushing (Yds.)	Robert Smith, 2000	1,521
Passing (Yds.)	Daunte Culpepper, 2004	4,717
Passing (TDs)	Daunte Culpepper, 2004	39
Receiving (No.)	Cris Carter, 1994, 1995	122
Receiving (Yds.)	Randy Moss, 2003	1,632
Interceptions	Paul Krause, 1975	10
Punting (Avg.)	Bobby Walden, 1964	46.4
Punt Return (Avg.)	David Palmer, 1995	13.2
Kickoff Return (Avg.)	John Gilliam, 1972	26.3
Field Goals	Gary Anderson, 1998	35
Touchdowns (Tot.)	Chuck Foreman, 1975	22
Points	Gary Anderson, 1998	164

INDIVIDUAL RECORDS—SINGLE GAME

Category	Name	Performance
Rushing (Yds.)	Chuck Foreman, 10-24-76	200
Passing (Yds.)	Tommy Kramer, 11-2-86	490
Passing (TDs)	Joe Kapp, 9-28-69	*7
Receiving (No.)	Rickey Young, 12-16-79	15
Receiving (Yds.)	Sammy White, 11-7-76	210
Interceptions	Many Times	3
	Last time by Darren Sharper, 11-13-05	
Field Goals	Rich Karlis, 11-5-89	*7
Touchdowns (Tot.)	Chuck Foreman, 12-20-75	4
	Ahmad Rashad, 9-2-79	4
Points	Chuck Foreman, 12-20-75	24
	Ahmad Rashad, 9-2-79	24

*NFL Record

2007 VETERAN ROSTER

No.	Name	Pos.	Ht.	Wt.	Birthdate	NFL Exp.	College	Hometown	How Acq.	'06 Games/ Starts
78	Birk, Matt	C	6-4	309	7/23/76	10	Harvard	St. Paul, Minn.	D6-'98	16/16
20	Blue, Greg	S	6-2	216	3/12/82	2	Georgia	Atlanta, Ga.	D5-'06	16/2
32	Body, Patrick	CB	6-2	198	1/17/82	2	Toledo	Pittsburgh, Pa.	FA-'06	0*
9	Bollinger, Brooks	QB	6-1	205	11/15/79	5	Wisconsin	Grand Forks, N.D.	T(NYJ)-'06	2/0
11	Carter, Jason	WR	6-0	205	9/15/82	2	Texas A&M	Caldwell, Texas	FA-'06	1/0
50	Ciurciu, Vinny	LB	6-0	235	5/2/80	5	Boston College	Paramus, N.J.	UFA(Car)-'07	16/0*
62	Cook, Ryan	T	6-6	328	5/8/83	2	New Mexico	Albuquerque, N.M.	D2b-'06	6/3
21	Doss, Mike	S	5-10	207	3/24/81	5	Ohio State	Canton, Ohio	UFA(Ind)-'07	6/4*
83	Dugan, Jeff	TE	6-4	258	4/8/81	4	Maryland	Pittsburgh, Pa.	D7-'04	7/7
36	Edwards, Dovonte	CB	6-0	182	10/17/82	3	North Carolina State	Chapel Hill, N.C.	FA-'05	0*
91	Edwards, Ray	DE	6-5	268	1/1/85	2	Purdue	Cincinnati, Ohio	D4-'06	15/2
59	Farwell, Heath	LB	6-0	235	12/31/81	3	San Diego State	Corona, Calif.	FA-'05	16/0
35	Fason, Ciatrick	RB	6-0	207	10/29/82	3	Florida	Jacksonville, Fla.	D4-'05	5/0
55	Glenn, Jason	LB	6-0	231	8/20/79	7	Texas A&M	Humble, Texas	FA-'06	9/0
41	Gordon, Charles	CB	5-11	180	7/18/84	2	Kansas	Santa Monica, Calif.	FA-'06	8/1
69	Green, Howard	DT	6-2	320	1/12/79	3	Louisiana State	Donaldsonville, La.	FA-'07	0*
52	Greenway, Chad	LB	6-3	242	1/12/83	2	Iowa	Mt. Vernon, S.D.	D1-'06	0*
23	Griffin, Cedric	CB	6-0	203	11/11/82	2	Texas	San Antonio, Texas	D2a-'06	14/7
16	Hankton, Cortez	WR	6-0	200	1/20/81	5	Texas Southern	New Orleans, La.	UFA(Jax)-'07	12/1*
37	Hawkins, Mike	CB	6-1	187	7/15/83	3	Oklahoma	Carrollton, Texas	W(Cle)-06	7/0*
56	Henderson, E.J.	LB	6-1	245	8/3/80	5	Maryland	Aberdeen, Md.	D2-'03	16/16
2	Henson, Drew	QB	6-4	235	2/13/80	3	Michigan	Brighton, Mich.	FA-'06	0*
64	Herrera, Anthony	G	6-2	315	6/14/80	4	Tennessee	Naples, Fla.	FA-'04	2/0
79	Hicks, Artis	G	6-4	335	11/28/78	6	Memphis	Jackson, Tenn.	T(Phil)-'06	14/14
76	Hutchinson, Steve	G	6-5	313	11/1/77	7	Michigan	Ft. Lauderdale, Fla.	RFA(Sea)-'06	16/16
85	Hymes, Randy	WR	6-3	211	8/7/79	5	Grambling State	Hitchcock, Texas	FA-'07	0*
7	Jackson, Tarvaris	QB	6-2	232	4/21/83	2	Alabama State	Montgomery, Ala.	D2c-'06	4/2
99	James, Erasmus	DE	6-4	266	11/4/82	3	Wisconsin	Hollywood, Fla.	D1b-'05	0*
72	Johnson, Marcus	T	6-6	321	12/1/81	3	Mississippi	Coffeeville, Miss.	D2-'05	10/10
97	Johnson, Spencer	DT	6-3	286	12/12/81	4	Auburn	Silas, Ala.	FA-'04	14/0
66	Katnik, Norm	C	6-4	295	7/2/81	2	Southern California	Santa Ana, Calif.	FA-'06	3/2*
40	Kleinsasser, Jim	TE	6-3	272	1/31/77	9	North Dakota	Carrington, N.D.	D2-'99	16/12
5	Kluwe, Chris	P	6-4	215	12/24/81	3	UCLA	Los Alamitos, Calif.	W(Sea)-'05	16/0
51	Leber, Ben	LB	6-3	244	12/7/78	6	Kansas State	Vermillion, S.D.	UFA(SD)-'06	15/11
46	Loeffler, Cullen	LS	6-5	241	1/27/81	4	Texas	Ingram, Texas	FA-'04	16/0
8	Longwell, Ryan	K	6-0	200	8/16/74	11	California	Bend, Ore.	UFA(GB)-'06	16/0
44	Maddox, Andre	S	6-1	200	10/8/82	2	North Carolina State	Miami, Fla.	FA-'07	0*
17	Mann, Maurice	WR	6-1	190	9/14/82	2	Nevada	Monterey, Calif.	PS(Sea)-'06	1/0
74	McKinnie, Bryant	T	6-8	335	9/23/79	6	Miami	Woodbury, N.J.	D1-'02	16/16
12	McMullen, Billy	WR	6-4	215	3/8/80	5	Virginia	Richmond, Va.	T(Phil)-'06	16/0
92	Mitchell, Jayme	DE	6-6	285	3/15/84	2	Mississippi	Jackson, Miss.	FA-'06	13/0
30	Moore, Mewelde	RB	5-11	209	7/24/82	4	Tulane	Baton Rouge, La.	D4b-'04	16/0
45	Owens, Richard	TE	6-4	273	11/4/80	4	Louisville	Middleburg, Fla.	FA-'04	16/2
22	Pinner, Artose	RB	5-10	232	1/5/78	5	Kentucky	Hopkinsville, Ky.	W(Det)-'06	12/1
49	Richardson, Tony	FB	6-1	238	12/17/71	13	Auburn	Daleville, Ala.	UFA(KC)-'06	9/7
98	Scott, Darrion	DE	6-3	289	10/25/81	4	Ohio State	Charleston, W. Va.	D3-'04	16/13
42	Sharper, Darren	S	6-2	210	11/3/75	11	William & Mary	Richmond, Va.	FA-'05	16/16
81	Shiancoe, Visanthe	TE	6-4	250	6/18/80	5	Morgan State	Laurel, Md.	UFA(NYG)'-07	16/4*
24	Smith, Dwight	S	5-10	201	8/13/78	7	Akron	Detroit, Mich.	FA-'06	15/14
84	Spach, Stephen	TE	6-4	250	7/18/82	2	Fresno State	Clovis, Calif.	FA-'07	0*
38	Tahi, Naufahu	FB	6-0	254	10/30/81	2	Brigham Young	West Valley City, Utah	W(Cin)-'06	0*
29	Taylor, Chester	RB	5-11	213	9/22/79	6	Toledo	River Rouge, Mich.	UFA(Balt)-'06	15/15
54	Thomas, Dontarrious	LB	6-2	241	9/2/80	4	Auburn	Perry, Ga.	D2-'04	16/3
95	Udeze, Kenechi	DE	6-3	281	3/5/83	4	Southern California	Los Angeles, Calif.	D1-'04	16/15
19	Wade, Bobby	WR	5-10	186	2/25/81	5	Arizona	Phoenix, Ariz.	UFA(Tenn)-'07	16/2*
27	Whitaker, Ronyell	CB	5-9	196	3/19/79	2	Virginia Tech	Norfolk, Va.	FA-'06	16/2
93	Williams, Kevin	DT	6-5	311	8/16/80	5	Oklahoma State	Fordyce, Ark.	D1-'03	16/16
94	Williams, Pat	DT	6-3	317	10/24/72	11	Texas A&M	Monroe, La.	UFA(Buff)-'05	16/16
25	Williams, Tank	S	6-2	223	6/30/80	6	Stanford	Bay St. Louis, Miss.	UFA(Tenn)-'06	0*
82	Williamson, Troy	WR	6-1	203	4/30/83	3	South Carolina	Aiken, S.C.	D1a-'05	14/11
26	Winfield, Antoine	CB	5-9	180	6/24/77	9	Ohio State	Akron, Ohio	UFA(Buff)-'04	16/16
39	Wishom, Jerron	CB	6-0	197	3/1/82	2	Louisiana Tech	Lutcher, La.	FA-'07	0*

* Body last active with Cincinnati in '05; Ciurciu played 16 games with Carolina in '06; Doss played 6 games with Indianapolis; D. Edwards missed '06 season because of injury; Green last active with New Orleans in '04; Greenway missed '06 season because of injury; Hankton played 12 games with Jacksonville; Hawkins played 7 games with Cleveland; Henson last active with Dallas in '04; Hymes last active with Baltimore in '05; James missed '06 season because of injury; Katnik played 3 games with N.Y. Jets; Maddox missed '05 season with N.Y. Jets because of injury; Shiancoe played 16 games with N.Y. Giants; Spach last active with Philadelphia in '05; Tahi inactive for 6 games; Wade played 16 games for Tennessee; T. Williams missed '06 season because of injury; Wishom last active with Green Bay in '05.

Players lost through free agency (4): LB Napoleon Harris (KC; 16 games in '06), WR Bethel Johnson (Phil; 11), DT Ross Kolodziej (Ariz; 12), C Jason Whittle (Buff; 16).

Also played with Vikings in '06—S Rashad Baker (1 game), LB Marquis Cooper (1), LB Rod Davis (9), S Will Hunter (10), QB Brad Johnson (15), WR Marcus Robinson (10), T Mike Rosenthal (15), CB Fred Smoot (14), WR Travis Taylor (16), TE Jermaine Wiggins (16).

2007 FIRST-YEAR ROSTER

Name	Pos.	Ht.	Wt.	Birthdate	College	Hometown	How Acq.
Alexander, Rufus	LB	6-1	232	4/12/83	Oklahoma	Baton Rouge, La.	D6
Allison, Aundrae	WR	6-0	198	4/20/86	East Carolina	Kannapolis, N.C.	D5
Anoai, Joe	DT	6-3	303	5/25/85	Georgia Tech	Pensacola, Fla.	FA
Bolston, Conrad	DT	6-4	300	1/9/85	Maryland	Washington, D.C.	FA
Bradley, Joe	DT	6-4	265	12/11/82	Louisiana-Lafayette	Compton, Calif.	FA
Burnett, Jeremy	S	6-1	198	10/6/83	South Florida	Tampa, Fla.	FA
Cook, Kyle	C/G	6-3	295	7/25/83	Michigan State	Macomb, Mich.	FA
Daniels, Brian	G	6-4	303	10/31/84	Colorado	Denver, Colo.	FA
Day, Josh	T	6-4	304	12/15/83	Colorado State	Aurora, Colo.	FA
Guerrero, Alex (1)	DT	6-1	303	2/16/84	Boise State	Brea, Calif.	FA
Hall, George	LB	6-0	240	8/2/84	Purdue	Groton, Conn.	FA
Herron, David	LB	6-1	239	6/17/84	Michigan State	Warren, Ohio	FA
Johnson, Chase	T	6-8	330	12/16/83	Wyoming	Loveland, Colo.	FA
Jones, Braden	TE	6-3	260	4/20/83	Southern Illinois	Harrisburg, Ill.	FA
Lowber, Todd	WR	6-3	205	1/26/82	Ramapo	Delran, N.J.	FA
Martin, Jimmy (1)	G	6-5	306	10/19/82	Virginia Tech	Chantilly, Va.	FA
Mathis, Wendell (1)	RB	5-11	213	9/28/83	Fresno State	Merced, Calif.	FA
McCauley, Marcus	CB	6-1	203	9/3/83	Fresno State	Sacramento, Calif.	D3
Mozes, Dan	C/G	6-3	293	9/15/83	West Virginia	Washington, Pa.	FA
Nance, Martin (1)	WR	6-3	212	5/26/83	Miami (Ohio)	Maryland Heights, Mo.	FA
Peterson, Adrian	RB	6-1	217	3/21/85	Oklahoma	Palestine, Texas	D1
Reyes, Alex	P	6-1	234	6/18/85	Texas Tech	Allen, Texas	FA
Rice, Sidney	WR	6-4	200	9/1/86	South Carolina	Gaffney, S.C.	D2
Robison, Brian	DE	6-3	259	4/28/83	Texas	Splendora, Texas	D4
Smith, Khreem (1)	DE	6-4	270	7/7/79	Oklahoma State	Miami, Fla.	FA
Surrency, Justin (1)	WR	6-0	182	1/9/85	Northern Iowa	St. Paul, Minn.	FA
Thigpen, Tyler	QB	6-1	226	4/14/84	Coastal Carolina	Winnsboro, S.C.	D7a
Whitlock, Arkee	RB	5-9	203	5/10/84	Southern Illinois	Rock Hill, S.C.	FA
Williams, Chandler	WR	5-11	184	8/9/85	Florida International	Miami, Fla.	D7b

The term NFL Rookie is defined as a player who is in his first season of professional football and has not been on the roster of another professional football team for any regular-season or postseason games. A Rookie is designated by an "R" on NFL rosters. Players who have been active in another professional football league or players who have NFL experience, including either preseason training camp or being on an Active List or Inactive List, or on Reserve/Injured or Reserve/Physically Unable to Perform for fewer than six regular-season games, are termed NFL First-Year Players. An NFL First-Year Player is designated by a "1" on NFL rosters. Thereafter, a player is credited with an additional year of experience for each season in which he accumulates six games on the Active List or Inactive List, or on Reserve/Injured or Reserve/Physically Unable to Perform.

Log on to www.vikings.com for an up-to-date roster.

COACHING STAFF
Head Coach,
Brad Childress
Pro Career: Named the seventh head coach in Vikings' history on January 6, 2006. This marks Childress' 30th season coaching, including his tenth on an NFL sideline, and his second with the Vikings. He became the first coach in Vikings history to win his first two games. The Vikings' eighth-ranked defense was the highest since 1994 and the team sent a pair of offensive linemen and defensive linemen to the Pro Bowl. He joined the Vikings following seven years with the Philadelphia Eagles, including the last four seasons as offensive coordinator, when the Eagles reached Super Bowl XXXIX and played in four straight NFC Championship games. He began his NFL coaching career as the Indianapolis Colts' quarterbacks coach (1985). Career record: 6-10.
Background: Coached at Illinois (1978-1984), Northern Arizona (1986-89), Utah (1990), and Wisconsin (1991-98). Childress briefly played quarterback and wide receiver at Illinois before transferring to Eastern Illinois, where he graduated with a bachelor's degree in psychology.
Personal: Born June 27, 1956 in Aurora, Ill. He and his wife Dru-Ann have four children: Cara, Kyle, Andrew, and Christopher.

ASSISTANT COACHES
Juney Barnett, asst. strength and conditioning; born January 11, 1979, Philadelphia. Defensive back Bloomsburg 1997-2000. College coach: Bloomsburg 2001, Army 2005. Pro coach: Rhein Fire (NFLE) 2004-05, joined Vikings in 2006.
Darrell Bevell, offensive coordinator; born January 6, 1970, Yuma, Ariz. Quarterback Northern Arizona 1989, Wisconsin 1992-95. No pro playing experience. College coach: Westmar 1996, Iowa State 1997, Connecticut 1998-99. Pro coach: Green Bay Packers 2000-05, joined Vikings in 2006.
Eric Bieniemy, running backs; born August 15, 1969, New Orleans. Running back Colorado 1987-1990. Pro running back San Diego Chargers 1991-94, Cincinnati Bengals 1995-98, Philadelphia Eagles 1999. College coach: Colorado 2001-02, UCLA 2003-05. Pro coach: Joined Vikings in 2006.
Brendan Daly, defensive assistant; born September 10, 1975, Chicago. Tight end Drake 1993-96. No pro playing experience. College coach: Drake 1998, Villanova 1999, 2005, Maryland 2000, Oklahoma State 2001-03, Illinois State 2004. Pro coach: Joined Vikings in 2006.
Karl Dunbar, defensive line; born May 18, 1967, Plaisance, La. Defensive lineman Louisiana State 1986-89. Pro defensive lineman Pittsburgh Steelers 1990, New Orleans Saints 1992-93, Arizona Cardinals 1994-95. College coach: Nicholls State 1998-99, Louisiana State 2000-01, 2005, Oklahoma State 2002-03. Pro coach:

Chicago Bears 2004, joined Vikings in 2006.
Paul Ferraro, special teams coordinator; born April 30, 1959, Ridgewood, N.J. Defensive back Springfield College 1980-82. No pro playing experience. College coach: Massachusetts 1982, Syracuse 1983, Villanova 1984-86, Dartmouth 1987, Catholic 1988, Maine 1989, Ohio 1990, Bowling Green 1991-98, Georgia Tech 1999-2000, Rutgers 2001-04. Pro coach: Carolina Panthers 2005, joined Vikings in 2006.
Ryan Ficken, quality control/offense; born February 20, 1980, Aurora, Colo. Wide receiver Arizona State 1998-99. No pro playing experience. College coach: UCLA 2004-06. Pro coach: Joined Vikings in 2007.
Leslie Frazier, defensive coordinator; born April 3, 1959, Columbus, Miss. Defensive back Alcorn State 1977-1980. Pro defensive back Chicago Bears 1981-86. College coach: Trinity (Ill.) College 1988-1996 (head coach), Illinois 1997-98. Pro coach Philadelphia Eagles 1999-2002, Cincinnati Bengals 2003-04, Indianapolis Colts 2005-06, joined Vikings in 2007.
Jim Hueber, asst. offensive line; born August 14, 1948, Philadelphia. Center South Dakota 1966-67. No pro playing experience. College coach: Cincinnati 1974, Dodge City (Kan.) C.C. 1975-78, Wichita State 1979-1980, Temple 1981-82, Memphis State 1983, Minnesota 1984-1991, Wisconsin 1992-2005. Pro coach: Joined Vikings in 2006.
Jeff Imamura, quality control/defense; born May 22, 1974, Lubbock, Texas. Attended Texas Christian. No college or pro playing experience. College coach: Texas Christian 1997-99, Northern Arizona 2000-02, Saginaw Valley State 2003. Pro coach: Joined Vikings in 2006.
Jimmie Johnson, tight ends; born October 6, 1966, Augusta, Ga. Tight end Howard 1985-88. Pro tight end Washington Redskins 1989-1991, Detroit Lions 1992-93, Kansas City Chiefs 1994, Philadelphia Eagles 1995-98. College coach: South Carolina State 2001, Shaw 2002-03, Texas Southern 2004-05. Pro coach: Joined Vikings in 2006.
Tom Kanavy, strength and conditioning; born April 8, 1970, Archibald, Pa. Attended Penn State. No college or pro playing experience. College coach: Miami 1993, Penn State 1993-95. Pro coach: Philadelphia Eagles 1995-2005, joined Vikings in 2006.
Derek Mason, asst. defensive backs; born September 29, 1969, Phoenix. Defensive back Northern Arizona 1987-1991. No pro playing experience. College coach: Mesa C.C. 1994, Weber State 1995-96, Idaho State 1997-98, Bucknell 1999-2001, Utah 2002, St. Mary's (Calif.) 2003, New Mexico State 2004, Ohio 2005-06. Pro coach: Joined Vikings in 2007.
Pat Morris, offensive line; born April 7, 1954, Cleveland. Offensive lineman

Southern California 1972-75. College coach: Southern California 1976-77, 1983-86, Northern Arizona 1978, Minnesota 1979-1982, Michigan State 1987-1994, Stanford 1995-96. Pro coach: San Francisco 49ers 1997-2003, Detroit Lions 2004-05, joined Vikings in 2006.
Brian Murphy, asst. special teams; born July 17, 1969, Elmwood Park, Ill. Defensive lineman Lehigh 1988-1991. No pro playing experience. College coach: Benedictine 1992, Wisconsin 1994-96, 2002-05, Baylor 1997, San Diego 1998, Lehigh 1999. Pro coach: Joined Vikings in 2006.
Chad O'Shea, offensive assistant; born December 18, 1972, Houston. Quarterback Marshall 1991-93, Houston 1994-95. No pro playing experience. College coach: Houston 1996-99, Southern Mississippi 2000-02. Pro coach: Kansas City Chiefs 2004-05, joined Vikings in 2006.
Fred Pagac, linebackers; born April 26, 1952, Richeyville, Pa. Tight end Ohio State 1971-73. Pro tight end Chicago Bears 1974, Tampa Bay Buccaneers 1976. College coach: Ohio State 1978-2000. Pro coach: Oakland Raiders 2001-03, Kansas City Chiefs 2004-05, joined Vikings in 2006.
Kevin Rogers, quarterbacks; born September 7, 1951, Brooklyn, N.Y. Linebacker Massanutten Academy 1969-1970, William & Mary 1971-73. College coach: Ohio State 1977-78, William & Mary 1980-82, Navy 1983-1990, Syracuse 1991-98, Notre Dame 1999-2001, Virginia Tech 2002-05. Pro coach: Joined Vikings in 2006.
Kevin Stefanski, asst. to the head coach; born May 8, 1982, Philadelphia. Safety Pennsylvania 2000-04. College coach: Pennsylvania 2005. Pro coach: Joined Vikings in 2006.
George Stewart, wide receivers; born December 29, 1958, Little Rock, Ark. Guard Arkansas 1977-1980. No pro playing experience. College coach: Minnesota 1984-85, Notre Dame 1986-88. Pro coach: Pittsburgh Steelers 1989-1991, Tampa Bay Buccaneers 1992-95, San Francisco 49ers 1996-2002, Atlanta Falcons 2003-06, joined Vikings in 2007.
Martin Streight, asst. strength and conditioning; born June 20, 1969, Trenton, N.J. Attended Indiana (Penn.). No college or pro playing experience. College coach: Penn State 1994, Princeton 1995-96. Pro coach: Philadelphia Eagles 1995-96, Arizona Cardinals 1997-2003, Scottish Claymores (NFLE) 2003, Berlin Thunder (NFLE) 2004-05, joined Vikings in 2006.
Joe Woods, defensive backs; born June 25, 1970, Natrona Heights, Pa. Safety Illinois State 1988-1991. College coach: Muskingum 1992, Eastern Michigan 1993, Northwestern (La.) State 1994, Grand Valley State 1994-96, Kent State 1997, Hofstra 1998-2000, Western Michigan 2001-03. Pro coach: Tampa Bay Buccaneers 2004-05, joined Vikings in 2006.

National Football Conference
South Division
Team Colors: Old Gold, Black, and White
5800 Airline Drive
Metairie, Louisiana 70003
Telephone: (504) 733-0255

2007 SCHEDULE
PRESEASON
Aug. 6   vs. Pittsburgh at Canton, OH 8:00
Aug. 10 **Buffalo** 7:00
Aug. 18 at Cincinnati 7:30
Aug. 23 at Kansas City 7:30
Aug. 30 **Miami** 7:00

REGULAR SEASON
Sep. 6   at Indianapolis (Thu.)..........8:30
Sep. 16 at Tampa Bay 1:00
Sep. 24 **Tennessee** (Mon.) 7:30
Sep. 30 Open Date
Oct. 7   **Carolina** 12:00
Oct. 14 at Seattle 5:15
Oct. 21 **Atlanta** 12:00
Oct. 28 at San Francisco 1:15
Nov. 4   **Jacksonville** 12:00
Nov. 11 **St. Louis** 12:00
Nov. 18 at Houston 12:00
Nov. 25 at Carolina 1:00
Dec. 2   **Tampa Bay** 12:00
Dec. 10 at Atlanta (Mon.) 8:30
Dec. 16 **Arizona** 12:00
Dec. 23 **Philadelphia** 12:00
Dec. 30 at Chicago 12:00
Stadium: Louisiana Superdome
      (opened in 1975)
      •**Capacity:** 65,000
      1500 Poydras Street
      New Orleans, Louisiana 70112
Playing Surface: Sportexe Momentum
Training Camp: Millsaps College
      Jackson, Mississippi 39210

LOUISIANA SUPERDOME

CLUB OFFICIALS
Owner/President: Tom Benson
Owner/Executive Vice President of
  Administration: Rita Benson LeBlanc
Executive Vice President/
  General Manager: Mickey Loomis
Senior Vice President/Chief Financial
  Officer: Dennis Lauscha
Vice President of Football Administration:
  Russ Ball
Vice President of Player Personnel:
  Rick Mueller
Vice President of Communications:
  Greg Bensel
Vice President of Marketing and
  Business Development: Ben Hales
Vice President/General Counsel:
  Vicky Neumeyer
Vice President of Ticket and Suite Sales:
  Mike Stanfield
Director of Operations: James Nagaoka
Director of College Scouting:
  Rick Reiprish
College Scouting Coordinator:
  Rick Thompson
Pro Scouts: Ryan Pace, Bill Quinter,
  Terry Fontenot
Area Scouts: David Hinson, Jim Monos,
  Dwaune Jones, Barrett Wiley
Combine Scout: Ryan Powell
Scouting Assistant: Josh Lucas
Scouting Administrative Assistant:
  Joseph Laine
Equipment Manager: Dan Simmons
Assistant Equipment Manager:
  Glennon (Silky) Powell
Equipment Assistants: Eddie Falgout,
  John Baumgartner
Head Athletic Trainer: Scottie B. Patton
Assistant Athletic Trainers:
  Duane Brooks, Kevin Mangum
Video Director: Dave Desposito
Coaching Assistants: Joe Alley,
  Josh Constant, Carter Sheridan
Senior Director of New Media:
  Doug Miller
Director of Communications: Ricky Zeller
Media & Public Relations Manager:
  Justin Macione
Communications Assistant:
  David Lawrence
Director of Security: Geoff Santini
Director of Photography:
  Michael C. Hebert
Assistant Director of Community Affairs:
  Nick Karl
Information Technology/Network
  Manager: Jeff Huffman
Facilities Manager: Terry Ashburn

COACHING HISTORY
(249-364-5)
Records include postseason games
1967-70	Tom Fears*	13-34-2
1970-72	J.D. Roberts	7-25-3
1973-75	John North**	11-23-0
1975	Ernie Hefferle	1-7-0
1976-77	Hank Stram	7-21-0
1978-80	Dick Nolan***	15-29-0
1980	Dick Stanfel	1-3-0
1981-85	O.A. (Bum) Phillips****	27-42-0
1985	Wade Phillips	1-3-0
1986-96	Jim Mora#	93-78-0
1996	Rick Venturi	1-7-0
1997-99	Mike Ditka	15-33-0
2000-05	Jim Haslett	46-52-0
2006	Sean Payton	11-7-0

    *Released after seven games in 1970
    **Released after six games in 1975
    ***Released after 12 games in 1980
    ****Resigned after 12 games in 1985
    #Resigned after eight games in 1996

PAID ATTENDANCE
Home 528,382   Away 552,679
Total 1,081,061
Single-game home record,
  70,940 (9/2/79)
Single-season home record,
  548,728 (1992)

2007 DRAFT CHOICES
Round	Name	Pos.	College
1	Robert Meachem	WR	Tennessee
3	Usama Young	DB	Kent State
	Andy Alleman	G	Akron
4	Antonio Pittman	RB	Ohio State
	Jermon Bushrod	T	Towson
5	David Jones	DB	Wingate (NC)
7	Marvin Mitchell	LB	Tennessee

NEW ORLEANS SAINTS

2006 TEAM RECORD
PRESEASON (1-3)

Date	Result	Opponent
8/12	W 19-16	at Tennessee
8/21	L 7-30	Dallas (Shreveport, LA)
8/26	L 14-27	Indianapolis (Jackson, MS)
8/31	L 9-10	at Kansas City

REGULAR SEASON (10-6)

Date	Result	Opponent	Att.
9/10	W 19-14	at Cleveland	72,915
9/17	W 34-27	at Green Bay	70,602
9/25	W 23-3	Atlanta	70,003
10/1	L 18-21	at Carolina	73,392
10/8	W 24-21	Tampa Bay	68,183
10/15	W 27-24	Philadelphia	68,269
10/29	L 22-35	Baltimore	69,152
11/5	W 31-14	at Tampa Bay	65,561
11/12	L 31-38	at Pittsburgh	61,911
11/19	L 16-31	Cincinnati	68,001
11/26	W 31-13	at Atlanta	70,933
12/3	W 34-10	San Francisco	68,241
12/10	W 42-17	at Dallas	63,722
12/17	L 10-16	Washington	69,052
12/24	W 30-7	at N.Y. Giants	78,539
12/31	L 21-31	Carolina	69,569

POSTSEASON (1-1)

Date	Result	Opponent	Att.
1/13	W 27-24	Philadelphia	70,001
1/21	L 14-39	at New Orleans	61,817

SCORE BY PERIODS

Saints	82	136	82	113	0	—	413
Opponents	95	57	80	90	0	—	322

2006 TEAM STATISTICS

	Saints	Opp.
Total First Downs	330	262
Rushing	99	96
Passing	207	148
Penalty	24	18
3rd Down: Made/Att	105/234	69/199
3rd Down Pct.	44.9	34.7
4th Down: Made/Att	12/20	6/13
4th Down Pct.	60.0	46.2
Possession Avg.	31:53	28:07
Total Net Yards	6264	4917
Avg. Per Game	391.5	307.3
Total Plays	1075	930
Avg. Per Play	5.8	5.3
Net Yards Rushing	1761	2063
Avg. Per Game	110.1	128.9
Total Rushes	472	418
Net Yards Passing	4503	2854
Avg. Per Game	281.4	178.4
Sacked/Yards Lost	23/123	38/268
Gross Yards	4626	3122
Att./Completions	580/372	474/267
Completion Pct.	64.1	56.3
Had Intercepted	13	11
Punts/Average	77/43.8	96/43.6
Net Punting Avg.	77/37.5	96/38.0
Penalties/Yards	79/597	89/674
Fumbles/Ball Lost	23/10	22/8
Touchdowns	49	40
Rushing	19	10
Passing	27	26
Returns	3	4

2006 INDIVIDUAL STATISTICS

PASSING

	Att.	Comp.	Yds.	Pct.	TD	Int.	Tkld.	Rate
Brees	554	356	4,418	64.3	26	11	18/105	96.2
Jami. Martin	24	16	208	66.7	1	1	5/18	90.3
Bush	1	0	—	0.0	0	1	0/0	0.0
Horn	1	0	—	0.0	0	0	0/0	39.6
Saints	580	372	4,626	64.1	27	13	23/123	94.9
Opponents	474	267	3,122	56.3	26	11	38/268	85.1

SCORING

	TD R	TD P	TD Rt	PAT	FG	Saf	PTS
Carney	0	0	0	46/47	23/25	0	115
McAllister	10	0	1	0/0	0/0	0	66
Bush	6	2	1	0/0	0/0	0	54
Colston	0	8	0	0/0	0/0	0	48
Henderson	1	5	0	0/0	0/0	0	36
Horn	0	4	0	0/0	0/0	0	26
Copper	0	3	0	0/0	0/0	0	18
Karney	1	2	0	0/0	0/0	0	18
Branch	0	1	0	0/0	0/0	0	6
Conwell	0	1	0	0/0	0/0	0	6
Deloatch	0	0	1	0/0	0/0	0	6
Jones	0	1	0	0/0	0/0	0	6
McAfee	1	0	0	0/0	0/0	0	6
Miller	0	0	0	0/0	0/0	0	2
Cundiff	0	0	0	0/0	0/1	0	0
Saints	19	27	3	46/47	23/26	0	413
Opponents	10	26	4	40/40	14/18	0	322

2-Pt. Conversions: Horn, Miller,
Saints 2-2, Opponents 0-0

RUSHING

	No.	Yds	Avg	LG	TD
McAllister	244	1,057	4.3	57	10
Bush	155	565	3.6	18	6
Karney	11	33	3.0	8	1
Brees	42	32	0.8	16	0
Branch	10	29	2.9	9	0
Henderson	2	14	7.0	11t	1
McAfee	3	12	4.0	6t	1
Stecker	4	11	2.8	4	0
Copper	1	8	8.0	8	0
Saints	472	1,761	3.7	57	19
Opponents	418	2,063	4.9	77t	10

RECEIVING

	No.	Yds	Avg	LG	TD
Bush	88	742	8.4	74	2
Colston	70	1,038	14.8	86t	8
Horn	37	679	18.4	72t	4
Henderson	32	745	23.3	76t	5
McAllister	30	198	6.6	24	0
Copper	23	385	16.7	48t	3
Stecker	19	190	10.0	48	0
Campbell	18	164	9.1	30	0
Karney	15	96	6.4	12	2
Miller	14	129	9.2	22	0
Conwell	8	57	7.1	15	1
Jones	6	108	18.0	41	1
Branch	5	14	2.8	7t	1
Owens	4	44	11.0	25	0
Lawrie	1	17	17.0	17	0
McIntyre	1	10	10.0	10	0
L. Moore	1	10	10.0	10	0
Saints	372	4,626	12.4	86t	27
Opponents	267	3,122	11.7	60t	26

INTERCEPTIONS

	No.	Yds	Avg	LG	TD
M. McKenzie	2	54	27.0	54	0
Fujita	2	19	9.5	19	0
Bullocks	2	14	7.0	14	0
Stoutmire	2	10	5.0	10	0
F. Thomas	1	9	9.0	9	0
Craft	1	0	0.0	0	0
Simoneau	1	0	0.0	0	0
Saints	11	106	9.6	54	0
Opponents	13	180	13.8	52t	4

PUNTING

	No.	Yds.	Avg.	In 20	LG
Weatherford	77	3,369	43.8	19	59
Saints	77	3,369	43.8	19	59
Opponents	96	4,181	43.6	30	65

PUNT RETURNS

	Ret	FC	Yds	Avg	LG	TD
Bush	28	2	216	7.7	65t	1
Lewis	16	10	111	6.9	26	0
L. Moore	6	2	45	7.5	25	0
Bellamy	1	0	0	0.0	0	0
Saints	51	14	372	7.3	65t	1
Opponents	40	17	279	7.0	31	0

KICKOFF RETURNS

	No.	Yds	Avg	LG	TD
Lewis	37	914	24.7	51	0
Stecker	10	216	21.6	31	0
Jones	6	130	21.7	29	0
Copper	4	79	19.8	25	0
McAfee	1	20	20.0	20	0
Karney	1	10	10.0	10	0
Lake	1	8	8.0	8	0
Saints	60	1,377	23.0	51	0
Opponents	72	1,598	22.2	40	0

FIELD GOALS

	1-19	20-29	30-39	40-49	50+
Carney	1/1	9/9	7/8	5/6	1/1
Cundiff	0/0	0/0	0/0	0/0	0/1
Saints	1/1	9/9	7/8	5/6	1/2
Opponents	1/1	7/8	5/6	1/3	0/0

SACKS

	No.
Smith	10.5
Grant	6.0
Young	5.5
Shanle	4.0
Fujita	3.5
H Thomas	3.5
Cooper	1.0
Harper	1.0
Lake	1.0
Simoneau	1.0
Whitehead	1.0
Saints	38.0
Opponents	23.0

RECORD HOLDERS
INDIVIDUAL RECORDS—CAREER

Category	Name	Performance
Rushing (Yds.)	Deuce McAllister, 2001-06	5,586
Passing (Yds.)	Archie Manning, 1971-1982	21,734
Passing (TDs)	Aaron Brooks, 2000-05	120
Receiving (No.)	Eric Martin, 1985-1993	532
Receiving (Yds.)	Eric Martin, 1985-1993	7,854
Interceptions	Dave Waymer, 1980-89	37
Punting (Avg.)	Mark Royals, 1997-98	45.7
Punt Return (Avg.)	Mel Gray, 1986-88	13.4
Kickoff Return (Avg.)	Walter Roberts, 1967	26.3
Field Goals	Morten Andersen, 1982-1994	302
Touchdowns (Tot.)	Dalton Hilliard, 1986-1993	53
Points	Morten Andersen, 1982-1994	1,318

INDIVIDUAL RECORDS—SINGLE SEASON

Category	Name	Performance
Rushing (Yds.)	George Rogers, 1981	1,674
Passing (Yds.)	Drew Brees, 2006	4,418
Passing (TDs)	Aaron Brooks, 2002	27
Receiving (No.)	Joe Horn, 2000, 2004	94
Receiving (Yds.)	Joe Horn, 2004	1,399
Interceptions	Dave Whitsell, 1967	10
Punting (Avg.)	Mark Royals, 1997	45.9
Punt Return (Avg.)	Mel Gray, 1987	14.7
Kickoff Return (Avg.)	Don Shy, 1969	27.9
	Mel Gray, 1986	27.9
Field Goals	Morten Andersen, 1985	31
	John Carney, 2002	31
Touchdowns (Tot.)	Dalton Hilliard, 1989	18
Points	John Carney, 2002	130

INDIVIDUAL RECORDS—SINGLE GAME

Category	Name	Performance
Rushing (Yds.)	George Rogers, 9-4-83	206
Passing (Yds.)	Drew Brees, 11-19-06	510
Passing (TDs)	Billy Kilmer, 11-2-69	6
Receiving (No.)	Tony Galbreath, 9-10-78	14
Receiving (Yds.)	Wes Chandler, 9-2-79	205
Interceptions	Tommy Myers, 9-3-78	5
	Dave Waymer, 10-6-85	5
	Reggie Sutton, 10-18-87	5
	Gene Atkins, 12-22-91	3
	Sammy Knight, 9-9-01	3
Field Goals	Many times	5
	Last time by John Carney, 9-26-04	
Touchdowns (Tot.)	Joe Horn, 12-14-03	4
	Reggie Bush, 12-3-06	4
Points	Joe Horn, 12-14-03	24
	Reggie Bush, 12-3-06	24

2007 VETERAN ROSTER

No.	Name	Pos.	Ht.	Wt.	Birthdate	NFL Exp.	College	Hometown	How Acq.	'06 Games/ Starts
60	Archibald, Ben	T	6-3	320	8/26/78	2	Brigham Young	Gearheart, Ore.	FA-'07	0*
20	Bellamy, Jay	S	5-11	200	7/8/72	13	Rutgers	Aberdeen, N.J.	FA-'06	12/4
9	Brees, Drew	QB	6-0	209	1/15/79	7	Purdue	Austin, Texas	UFA(SD)-'06	16/16
70	Brown, Jammal	T	6-6	313	3/30/81	3	Oklahoma	Lawton, Okla.	D1-'05	15/15
29	Bullocks, Josh	S	6-1	207	2/28/83	3	Nebraska	Chattanooga, Tenn.	D2-'05	16/16
25	Bush, Reggie	RB	6-0	203	3/2/85	2	Southern California	Spring Valley, Calif.	D1-'06	16/7
80	Campbell, Mark	TE	6-6	260	12/6/75	9	Michigan	Clawson, Mich.	FA-'06	14/11
12	Colston, Marques	WR	6-4	231	6/5/83	2	Hofstra	Harrisburg, Pa.	D7b-'06	14/12
97	Cooper, Josh	DE	6-3	265	12/5/80	2	Mississippi	Marietta, Ga.	FA-'06	5/1
18	Copper, Terrance	WR	6-0	207	3/12/82	4	East Carolina	Washington, N.C.	W(Dall)-'06	15/4
21	Craft, Jason	CB	5-10	187	2/13/76	9	Colorado State	Denver, Colo.	T(Jax)-'04	16/5
42	David, Jason	CB	5-8	180	6/12/82	4	Washington State	Covina, Calif.	RFA(Ind)-'07	16/16*
73	Evans, Jahri	G	6-4	318	8/22/83	2	Bloomsburg	Philadelphia, Pa.	D4-'06	16/16
54	Evans, Troy	LB	6-3	238	12/3/77	6	Cincinnati	Cincinnati, Ohio	UFA(Hou)-'07	16/0*
52	Faine, Jeff	C	6-3	291	4/6/81	5	Notre Dame	Sanford, Fla.	T(Cle)-'06	16/16
57	Faulk, Trev	LB	6-3	254	8/6/81	5	Louisiana State	Lafayette, La.	FA-'07	0*
56	Fincher, Alfred	LB	6-1	238	8/15/83	3	Connecticut	Norwood, Mass.	D3-'05	6/0
55	Fujita, Scott	LB	6-5	250	4/28/79	6	California	Oxnard, Calif.	UFA(Dall)-'06	16/16
37	Gleason, Steve	S	5-11	212	3/19/77	7	Washington State	Spokane, Wash.	FA-'01	15/0
76	Goodwin, Jonathan	G/C	6-3	318	12/2/78	6	Michigan	Richland, S.C.	UFA(NYJ)-'06	16/0
94	Grant, Charles	DE	6-3	290	9/3/78	6	Georgia	Colquitt, Ga.	D1b-'02	16/16
28	Groce, DeJuan	CB	5-10	192	2/17/80	5	Nebraska	Garfield Heights, Ohio	W(StL)-'06	12/0
6	Hanson, Chris	P	6-2	202	10/25/76	7	Marshall	Senoia. Ga.	FA-'07	16/0*
41	Harper, Roman	S	6-1	200	12/11/82	2	Alabama	Prattville, Ala.	D2-'06	5/5
19	Henderson, Devery	WR	5-11	200	3/26/82	4	Louisiana State	Opelousas, La.	D2a-'04	13/7
47	Houser, Kevin	LS	6-2	252	8/23/77	8	Ohio State	Westlake, Ohio	D7-'00	16/0
82	Johnson, Eric	TE	6-3	252	9/15/79	7	Yale	Needham, Mass.	UFA(SF)-'07	13/9*
89	Jones, Jamal	WR	5-11	205	4/24/81	2	North Carolina A&T	Washington, D.C.	FA-'06	12/1
43	Kaesviharn, Kevin	S	6-1	196	8/29/76	7	Augustana (S.D.)	Paramount, Calif.	UFA(Cin)-'07	14/7*
44	Karney, Mike	FB	5-11	258	7/6/81	4	Arizona State	Kent, Wash.	D5b-'04	15/7
96	Lake, Antwan	DT	6-4	308	7/10/79	5	West Virginia	Cambridge, Md.	W(Atl)-'06	15/1
77	Leisle, Rodney	DT	6-3	315	2/5/81	4	UCLA	Bakersfield, Calif.	D5a-'04	14/1
84	Lewis, Michael	WR	5-8	173	11/14/71	7	None	New Orleans, La.	FA-'01	10/0
2 t-	Mare, Olindo	K	5-11	190	6/6/73	11	Syracuse	Cooper City, Fla.	T(Mia)-'07	16/0*
10	Martin, Jamie	QB	6-2	205	2/8/70	13	Weber State	Arroyo Grande, Calif.	UFA(StL)-'06	16/0
26	McAllister, Deuce	RB	6-1	232	12/27/78	7	Mississippi	Lena, Miss.	D1-'01	15/13
34	McKenzie, Mike	CB	6-0	194	4/26/76	9	Memphis	Miami, Fla.	T(GB)-'04	16/16
83	Miller, Billy	TE	6-3	252	4/24/77	8	Southern California	Westlake Village, Calif.	FA-'06	10/3
16	Moore, Lance	WR	5-9	177	8/31/83	2	Toledo	Westerville, Ohio	FA-'07	4/0
67	Nesbit, Jamar	G/T	6-4	328	12/17/76	9	South Carolina	Summerville, S.C.	UFA(Jax)-'04	16/16
93	Ninkovich, Rob	DE	6-2	252	2/1/84	2	Purdue	New Lenox, Ill.	D5-'06	3/0
86	Owens, John	TE	6-3	255	1/10/80	5	Notre Dame	Hyattsville, Md.	FA-'06	5/0
81	Patten, David	WR	5-10	190	8/19/74	11	Western Carolina	Columbia, S.C.	FA-'07	5/0*
79	Petitti, Rob	T	6-6	327	5/21/82	2	Pittsburgh	Rumson, N.J.	W(Dall)-'06	1/0
88	Ridgeway, Dante	WR	6-1	200	4/18/84	2	Ball State	Decatur, Ill.	FA-'07	0*
58	Shanle, Scott	LB	6-2	245	11/23/79	5	Nebraska	St. Edward, Neb.	T(Dall)-'06	16/15
51	Simmons, Brian	LB	6-3	244	6/21/75	10	North Carolina	New Bern, N.C.	FA-'07	11/8*
53	Simoneau, Mark	LB	6-0	245	1/16/77	8	Kansas State	Smith Center, Kan.	T(Phil)-'06	16/14
75	Sims, Wes	G	6-4	317	4/8/81	2	Oklahoma	Weatherford, Okla	FA-'07	0*
91	Smith, Will	DE	6-3	282	7/4/81	4	Ohio State	Utica, N.Y.	D1-'04	14/14
27	Stecker, Aaron	RB	5-10	213	11/13/75	8	Western Illinois	Green Bay, Wis.	UFA(TB)-'04	12/1
78	Stinchcomb, Jon	T	6-5	315	8/27/79	5	Georgia	Lilburn, Ga.	D2-'03	16/16
64	Strief, Zach	T	6-7	349	9/22/83	2	Northwestern	Milford, Ohio	D7a-'06	9/1
22	Thomas, Fred	CB	5-9	185	9/11/73	12	Tennessee-Martin	Bruce, Miss.	UFA(Sea)-'00	13/13
99	Thomas, Hollis	DT	6-0	306	1/10/74	12	Northern Illinois	St. Louis, Mo.	T(Phil)-'06	12/12
7	Weatherford, Steve	P	6-3	215	12/17/82	2	Illinois	Terre Haute, Ind.	FA-'06	16/0
98	Whitehead, Willie	DT	6-3	300	1/26/73	9	Auburn	Tuskegee, Ala.	FA-'99	12/3
66	Young, Brian	DT	6-2	298	7/8/77	8	Texas-El Paso	El Paso, Texas	UFA(StL)-'04	16/16
68	Yovanovits, Dave	G	6-3	300	3/6/81	3	Temple	Stanhope, N.J.	FA-'07	0*

* Archibald last active with New Orleans in '05; David played 16 games with Indianapolis in '06; T. Evans played 16 games with Houston; Faulk last active with St. Louis in '05; Hanson played 16 games with Jacksonville; Johnson played 13 games with San Francisco; Kaesviharn played 14 games with Cincinnati; Mare played 16 games with Miami; Patten played 5 games with Washington; Ridgeway last active with N.Y. Jets in '05; Simmons played 11 games with Cincinnati; Sims last active with San Diego in '05; Yovanovits last active with Cleveland in '05.

t- Saints traded for Mare (Mia).

Players lost to free agency (4): LB Danny Clark (Hou; 16 games in '06), G Montrae Holland (Den; 8), S Bryan Scott (Tenn; 9); S Omar Stoutmire (Wash; 13).

Also played with Saints in '06—RB Jamaal Branch (1 game), K John Carney (16), TE Ernie Conwell (7), K Billy Cundiff (5), CB Curtis Deloatch (7), WR Joe Horn (10), DE Trevor Johnson (1), RB Keith Joseph (1), TE Nate Lawrie (7), RB Fred McAfee (4), FB Corey McIntyre (4), LB Terrence Melton (16), DE Eric Moore (4).

2007 FIRST-YEAR ROSTER

Name	Pos.	Ht.	Wt.	Birthdate	College	Hometown	How Acq.
Alleman, Andy	G	6-4	302	11/20/1983	Akron	Greentown, Ohio	D3b
Bergstrom, Brett	K	6-2	220	4/6/1983	Eastern Washington	Bellevue, Wash.	FA
Boykin, McKinley (1)	DT	6-1	289	3/24/1983	Mississippi	Bessemer, Ala.	FA
Branch, Jamaal (1)	RB	5-11	230	1/30/1981	Colgate	New Hampton, N.H.	FA-'06
Bushrod, Jermon	T	6-5	315	8/19/1984	Towson	King George, Va.	D4b
Dudley, Kevin (1)	FB	6-0	238	1/2/1982	Michigan	Oxford, Ohio	FA
Dyakowski, Peter	T	6-5	310	4/19/1984	Louisiana State	Vancouver, B.C.	FA
Evans, Willie (1)	DE	6-1	269	3/5/1984	Mississippi State	Waynesboro, Miss.	FA
Fife, Jason (1)	QB	6-4	225	11/2/1981	Oregon	Lake Elsinore, Calif.	FA
Greer, Keith	FB	6-1	248	7/16/1984	Idaho	Santa Ana, Calif.	FA
Hamm, Jon	DE	6-7	272	2/13/1978	Clark Atlanta	Atlanta, Ga.	FA
Johnson, Robert (1)	TE	6-6	278	6/20/1980	Auburn	Montgomery, Ala.	FA
Jones, David	CB	6-0	196	9/19/1985	Wingate	Greenville, S.C.	D5
Koehl, Wade	LB	6-2	230	9/22/1984	Houston	Midland, Texas	FA
Kuresa, Jake	G	6-4	330	10/2/1983	Brigham Young	Millville, Utah	FA
MacDonald, Pat	LS	6-3	247	2/20/1982	Alberta	Oakville, Ont.	FA
McKnight, Rhema	WR	6-1	211	3/6/1984	Notre Dame	Inglewood, Calif.	FA
Meachem, Robert	WR	6-2	214	9/28/1984	Tennessee	Tulsa, Okla.	D1
Mitchell, Marvin	LB	6-3	249	10/21/1984	Tennessee	Norfolk, Va.	D7
Palko, Tyler	QB	6-1	215	8/9/1983	Pittsburgh	Imperial, Pa.	FA
Phillips, Anwar (1)	CB	6-0	187	10/25/1982	Penn State	St. Petersburg, Fla.	FA
Pittman, Antonio	RB	5-11	207	12/19/1985	Ohio State	Akron, Ohio	D4a
Porter, Joe	CB	6-0	200	11/27/1985	Rutgers	Franklin, N.J.	FA
Powell, Calen (1)	TE	6-5	257	2/16/1981	Duke	Bellevue, Wash.	FA
Reis, Chris (1)	DB	6-1	215	9/19/1983	Georgia Tech	Roswell, Ga.	FA
Thomas, Pierre	RB	5-11	210	12/18/1984	Illinois	Lynwood, Ill.	FA
Villarreal, Brandon (1)	DT	6-2	289	6/1/1983	Purdue	Allen, Texas	FA
Young, Usama	CB	6-0	194	5/8/1985	Kent State	Largo, Md.	D3a

The term NFL Rookie is defined as a player who is in his first season of professional football and has not been on the roster of another professional football team for any regular-season or postseason games. A Rookie is designated by an "R" on NFL rosters. Players who have been active in another professional football league or players who have NFL experience, including either preseason training camp or being on an Active List or Inactive List, or on Reserve/Injured or Reserve/Physically Unable to Perform for fewer than six regular-season games, are termed NFL First-Year Players. An NFL First-Year Player is designated by a "1" on NFL rosters. Thereafter, a player is credited with an additional year of experience for each season in which he accumulates six games on the Active List or Inactive List, or on Reserve/Injured or Reserve/Physically Unable to Perform.

Log on to www.neworleanssaints.com for an up-to-date roster.

COACHING STAFF
Head Coach,
Sean Payton
Pro Career: Named the fourteenth head coach in Saints history on Jan. 18, 2006 and in his opening season led the Saints to the NFC Championship Game for the first time in club history. A unanimous choice for NFL coach of the year honors after also guiding the team to a 10-6 record and the NFC South title following a dramatic roster overhaul. Came to New Orleans following a three-year stint with Dallas Cowboys, serving as the assistant head coach/passing game coordinator in 2005 after spending his first two seasons as assistant head coach/quarterbacks. Considered one of the NFL's brightest offensive minds, he has led a resurgence in his unit's productivity at each career stop, including in New Orleans, where the Saints featured the league's top-ranked offense in 2006. Additional experience includes four years with the New York Giants (1999-2002), the last three seasons as offensive coordinator. Also previously worked for the Philadelphia Eagles (1997-98) as quarterbacks coach. Career record: 11-7.

Background: Earned a degree in communications at Eastern Illinois, where he departed with a school-record 10,665 passing yards, then the third-highest total in NCAA Division I-AA history. A three-time All-American, Payton had brief playing stops with Chicago of the Arena Football League, the Ottawa Rough Riders of the Canadian Football League and the Chicago Bears in 1987. Inducted into the Eastern Illinois Hall of Fame in 2000, Payton entered the NFL after two coaching stints at San Diego State (1988-89, 1992-93) around a stop at Indiana State (1990-91). He also was quarterbacks coach/co-offensive coordinator at Miami (Ohio) from 1994-95.

Personal: Born Dec. 29, 1963 in San Mateo, Calif. and raised in Naperville, Ill, Payton and his wife, Beth, have a daughter, Meghan, and a son, Connor.

ASSISTANT COACHES
Dennis Allen, asst. defensive line; born Sept. 22, 1972, Atlanta. Safety Texas A&M 1992-95. No pro playing experience. College Coach: Texas A&M 1996-99, Tulsa 2000-01. Pro coach: Atlanta Falcons 2002-05, joined Saints in 2006.

Adam Bailey, asst. strength and conditioning; born March 30, 1976, Tyler, Texas. Attended Louisville. No college or pro playing experience. College coach: Texas 1996-1997, Louisville 1998-1999, Auburn 2000-2001, Missouri 2002-2003. Pro coach: New Orleans VooDoo (AFL) 2004-2005, joined Saints in 2005.

John Bonamego, special teams coordinator; born Aug. 14, 1963, Waynesboro, Pa. Wide receiver/quarterback Central Michigan 1985-86. No pro playing experi-

ence. College coach: Maine 1988-1991, Lehigh 1992, Army 1993-98. Pro coach: Jacksonville Jaguars 1999-2002, Green Bay Packers 2003-05, joined Saints in 2006.

Pete Carmichael Jr., quarterbacks/passing game; born October 6, 1971, Farmingham, Mass. Attended Boston College. No college or pro playing experience. College coach: New Hampshire 1994, Louisiana Tech 1995-99. Pro coach: Cleveland Browns 2000, Washington Redskins 2001, San Diego Chargers 2002-05, joined Saints in 2006.

Dan Dalrymple, head strength and conditioning; born Aug. 26, 1965, Cleveland. Offensive lineman Miami (Ohio) 1983-86. No pro playing experience. College coach: Miami (Ohio) 1987-2005. Pro coach: Joined Saints in 2006.

Gary Gibbs, defensive coordinator; born Aug. 13, 1952, Beaumont, Texas. Linebacker Oklahoma 1972-75. No pro playing experience. College coach: Oklahoma 1975-1994 (head coach 1989-1994), Georgia 2000, Louisiana State 2001. Pro coach: Dallas Cowboys 2002-04, joined Saints in 2006.

Tom Hayes, defensive backs; born March 26, 1949, Keokuk, Iowa. Defensive back Iowa 1967-1971. No pro playing experience. College coach: Coe College 1973, Iowa 1977-78, Cal State-Fullerton 1979, UCLA 1980-88, Texas A&M 1989, Oklahoma 1990-94, Kansas 2001 (interim head coach final three games), Stanford 2005. Pro coach: Washington Redskins 1995-2000, joined Saints in 2006.

George Henshaw, senior assistant/running backs; born Jan. 22, 1948, Richmond, Va. Defensive tackle West Virginia 1967-69. No pro playing experience. College coach: West Virginia 1970-75, Florida State 1976-1982, Alabama 1983-86, Tulsa 1987 (head coach). Pro coach: Denver Broncos 1988-1992, New York Giants 1993-96, Tennessee Oilers 1997-98, Tennessee Titans 1999-2005, joined Saints in 2006.

Marion Hobby, defensive line; born November 7, 1966, Birmingham, Ala. Defensive end Tennessee 1985-89. Pro defensive end New England Patriots 1990-92. College coach: Tennessee-Martin 1995, Southwestern Louisiana 1996-97, Tennessee 1998, Mississippi 1999-2004, Clemson 2005. Pro coach: Joined Saints in 2006.

Curtis Johnson, wide receivers; born November 5, 1961, New Orleans. Wide receiver Idaho 1979-1983. No pro playing experience. College coach: Idaho 1987-88, San Diego State 1989-1993, Southern Methodist 1994, California 1995, Miami 1996-2005. Pro coach: Joined Saints in 2006.

Joe Lombardi, offensive assistant; born June 6, 1981, Seattle. Tight end Air Force

1992-94. No pro playing experience. College coach: Dayton 1996-98, Virginia Military Institute 1999, Bucknell 2000, Mercyhurst 2002-05. Pro coach: Atlanta Falcons 2006, joined Saints in 2007.

Terry Malone, tight ends; born February 26, 1960, Buffalo. Tight end Holy Cross 1978-1982. No pro playing experience. College coach: Arizona 1983-84, Holy Cross 1985, Bowling Green 1986-1995, Boston College 1996, Michigan 1997-2005. Pro coach: Joined Saints in 2006.

Doug Marrone, offensive coordinator/offensive line, born July 25, 1964, Bronx, N.Y. Offensive lineman Syracuse 1983-85. Pro offensive lineman Miami Dolphins 1987, New Orleans Saints 1989, London Monarchs (NFLE) 1992. College coach: Cortland College 1992, U.S. Coast Guard Academy 1993, Northeastern 1994, Georgia Tech 1995-99, Georgia 2000, Tennessee 2001. Pro coach: New York Jets 2002-05, joined Saints in 2006.

Greg McMahon, asst. special teams, born Jan. 2, 1960, Rantoul, Ill. Defensive back Eastern Illinois 1978-1981. College coach: Eastern Illinois 1982, Minnesota 1983-84, North Alabama 1985-87, Southern Illinois 1988, Valdosta State 1989, Nevada Las-Vegas 1990-91, Illinois 1992-2004, East Carolina 2005. Pro coach: Joined Saints in 2006.

Tony Oden, defensive assistant/secondary; born June 30, 1973, Cleveland. Linebacker Baldwin-Wallace College 1991-95. No pro playing experience. College coach: Millersville (Penn.) 1996, Boston College 1997, Army 1998-99, East Carolina 2000-02, Eastern Michigan 2003. Pro coach: Houston Texans 2004-05, joined Saints in 2006.

Joe Vitt, asst. head coach/linebackers; born August 23, 1954, Syracuse, N.Y. Linebacker Towson State 1974-78. No pro playing experience. Pro coach: Baltimore Colts 1979-1981, Seattle Seahawks 1982-1991, Los Angeles Rams 1992-94, Philadelphia Eagles 1995-98, Green Bay Packers 1999, Kansas City Chiefs 2000-03, St. Louis Rams 2004-05 (head coach, final 11 games of 2005), joined Saints in 2006.

National Football Conference
East Division
Team Colors: Blue, Red, and White
Giants Stadium
East Rutherford, New Jersey 07073
Telephone: (201) 935-8111

2007 SCHEDULE
PRESEASON
Aug. 11	**Carolina**	8:00
Aug. 19	at Baltimore	8:00
Aug. 25	**N.Y. Jets**	8:00
Aug. 30	at New England	7:30

REGULAR SEASON
Sep. 9	at Dallas	7:15
Sep. 16	**Green Bay**	1:00
Sep. 23	at Washington	4:15
Sep. 30	**Philadelphia**	8:15
Oct. 7	**N.Y. Jets**	1:00
Oct. 15	at Atlanta (Mon.)	8:30
Oct. 21	**San Francisco**	1:00
Oct. 28	at Miami (London)	5:00
Nov. 4	Open Date	
Nov. 11	**Dallas**	4:15
Nov. 18	at Detroit	4:15
Nov. 25	**Minnesota**	1:00
Dec. 2	at Chicago	3:15
Dec. 9	at Philadelphia	1:00
Dec. 16	**Washington**	*8:15
Dec. 23	at Buffalo	1:00
Dec. 29	**New England** (Sat.)	8:15

Sunday night games in Weeks 11-17 subject to change

Stadium: Giants Stadium (opened in 1976)
•**Capacity:** 80,242
East Rutherford, New Jersey 07073
Playing Surface: FieldTurf
Training Camp: University at Albany
1400 Washington Avenue
Albany, New York 12222

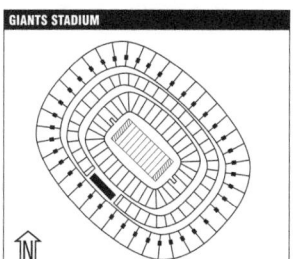

GIANTS STADIUM

CLUB OFFICIALS
President/CEO: John K. Mara
Chairman/EVP: Steve Tisch
Treasurer: Jonathan Tisch
Senior Vice President-General Manager:
Jerry Reese
Senior Vice President and Chief
Marketing Officer: Mike Stevens
Vice President-Player Evalutions:
Chris Mara
Vice President-Chief Financial Officer:
Christine Procops
Vice President-Marketing: Rusty Hawley
Vice President-Medical Services:
Ronnie Barnes
Vice-President-Communications:
Pat Hanlon
Vice President, Media and Partnerships:
Dan Lynch
Vice President and Executive Producer,
Giants Entertainment: Don Sperling
Assistant General Manager:
Kevin Abrams
Director of Player Personnel: TBD
Director of Pro Player Personnel:
David Gettleman
Assistant Director of Pro Player
Personnel: Ken Sternfeld
Director of College Scouting: Jerry Shay
Director of Research and Development:
Raymond J. Walsh, Jr.
Director of Player Development:
Charles Way
Director of Marketing Partnerships:
Glenn Todd
Pro Personnel Assistants: Tom Polifroni,
Matthew Shauger
Director of Promotions: Frank Mara
Ticket Manager: John Gorman
Director of Administration: Jim Phelan
Controller: Steven Hamrahi
Director of Community Relations:
Allison Stangeby
Director of Creative Services:
Doug Murphy
Director of Public Relations:
Peter John-Baptiste
Assistant Director of Communications:
Avis Roper
Head Athletic Trainer: Ronnie Barnes
Assistant Athletic Trainers: John Johnson,
Steve Kennelly, Byron Hansen
Equipment Manager: Ed Wagner, Jr.
Assistant Equipment Managers:
Joseph Skiba, Ed Skiba, Tim Slaman
Video Director: Dave Maltese
Assistant Video Directors:
Carmen Pizzano, Ed Triggs
Assistant Director of Community
Relations: Ethan Medley
Broadcast Production Manager:
Stephen Venditti
Director of Information Technology:
Jon Berger
Director of Marketing Services & Youth
Programs: Beth Roche

COACHING HISTORY
(612-523-33)
Records include postseason games
1925	Bob Folwell	8-4-0
1926	Joe Alexander	8-4-1
1927-28	Earl Potteiger	15-8-3
1929-1930	LeRoy Andrews*	24-5-1
1930	Benny Friedman-Steve Owen	2-0-0
1931-1953	Steve Owen	153-108-17
1954-1960	Jim Lee Howell	55-29-4
1961-68	Allie Sherman	57-54-4
1969-1973	Alex Webster	29-40-1
1974-76	Bill Arnsparger**	7-28-0
1976-78	John McVay	14-23-0
1979-1982	Ray Perkins	24-35-0
1983-1990	Bill Parcells	85-52-1
1991-92	Ray Handley	14-18-0
1993-96	Dan Reeves	32-34-0
1997-2003	Jim Fassel	60-56-1
2004-06	Tom Coughlin	25-25-0

*Released after 15 games in 1930
**Released after seven games in 1976

PAID ATTENDANCE
Home 628,925 — Away 555,653
Total 1,184,578
Single-game home record,
79,378 (1/8/06)
Single-season home record,
629,874 (2004)

2007 DRAFT CHOICES
Round	Name	Pos.	College
1	Aaron Ross	DB	Texas
2	Steve Smith	WR	So. California
3	Jay Alford	DT	Penn State
4	Zak DeOssie	LB	Brown
5	Kevin Boss	TE	Western Oregon
6	Adam Koets	T	Oregon State
7	Michael Johnson	DB	Arizona
	Ahmad Bradshaw	RB	Marshall

2006 TEAM RECORD
PRESEASON (3-1)

Date	Result	Opponent
8/11	W 17-16	at Baltimore
8/17	W 17-0	Kansas City
8/25	W 13-7	at N.Y. Jets
9/1	W 31-23	New England

REGULAR SEASON (8-8)

Date	Result	Opponent	Att.
9/10	L 21-26	Indianapolis	78,622
9/17	W 30-24	at Philadelphia (OT)	69,241
9/24	L 30-42	at Seattle	68,161
10/8	W 19-3	Washington	78,653
10/15	W 27-14	at Atlanta	70,840
10/23	W 36-22	at Dallas	63,512
10/29	W 17-3	Tampa Bay	78,647
11/5	W 14-10	Houston	78,485
11/12	L 20-38	Chicago	78,641
11/20	L 10-26	at Jacksonville	67,164
11/26	L 21-24	at Tennessee	69,143
12/3	L 20-23	Dallas	78,666
12/10	W 27-13	at Carolina	73,702
12/17	L 22-36	Philadelphia	78,657
12/24	L 7-30	New Orleans	78,539
12/30	W 34-28	at Washington	86,141

(OT) Overtime

POSTSEASON (0-1)

Date	Result	Opponent	
1/7	L 20-23	at Philadelphia	69,094

SCORE BY PERIODS

Giants	74	86	79	110	6	—	355
Opponents	64	101	65	132	0	—	362

2006 TEAM STATISTICS

	Giants	Opp.
Total First Downs	304	314
Rushing	120	106
Passing	163	189
Penalty	21	19
3rd Down: Made/Att	77/203	97/226
3rd Down Pct.	37.9	42.9
4th Down: Made/Att	7/15	9/24
4th Down Pct.	46.7	37.5
Possession Avg.	29:35	30:25
Total Net Yards	5214	5479
Avg. Per Game	325.9	342.4
Total Plays	1003	1057
Avg. Per Play	5.2	5.2
Net Yards Rushing	2156	1830
Avg. Per Game	134.8	114.4
Total Rushes	455	458
Net Yards Passing	3058	3649
Avg. Per Game	191.1	228.1
Sacked/Yards Lost	25/186	32/181
Gross Yards	3244	3830
Att./Completions	523/301	567/333
Completion Pct.	57.6	58.7
Had Intercepted	18	17
Punts/Average	77/40.2	69/41.9
Net Punting Avg.	77/37.0	69/35.4
Penalties/Yards	101/881	97/771
Fumbles/Ball Lost	23/10	23/11
Touchdowns	41	42
Rushing	14	19
Passing	24	21
Returns	3	2

2006 INDIVIDUAL STATISTICS

PASSING	Att.	Comp.	Yds.	Pct.	TD	Int.	Tkld.	Rate
Manning	522	301	3,244	57.7	24	18	25/186	77.0
Feagles	1	0	—	0.0	0	0	0/0	39.6
Giants	523	301	3,244	57.6	24	18	25/186	76.8
Opponents	567	333	3,830	58.7	21	17	32/181	79.0

SCORING	TD R	TD P	TD Rt	PAT	FG	Saf	PTS
Feely	0	0	0	38/38	23/27	0	107
Burress	0	10	0	0/0	0/0	0	60
Jacobs	9	0	0	0/0	0/0	0	54
Shockey	0	7	0	0/0	0/0	0	42
Barber	5	0	0	0/0	0/0	0	30
Carter	0	2	1	0/0	0/0	0	18
Toomer	0	3	0	0/0	0/0	0	18
Tyree	0	2	0	0/0	0/0	0	12
Dockery	0	0	1	0/0	0/0	0	6
McQuarters	0	0	1	0/0	0/0	0	6
Arrington	0	0	0	0/0	0/0	1	2
Giants	14	24	3	38/38	23/27	1	355
Opponents	19	21	2	40/40	22/29	0	362

2-Pt. Conversions: Giants 0-2, Opponents 2-2

RUSHING	No.	Yds	Avg	LG	TD
Barber	327	1,662	5.1	55t	5
Jacobs	96	423	4.4	16	9
Morton	1	22	22.0	22	0
Manning	25	21	0.8	9	0
Finn	2	14	7.0	12	0
Jennings	2	12	6.0	21	0
Lorenzen	1	2	2.0	2	0
Toomer	1	0	0.0	0	0
Giants	455	2,156	4.7	55t	14
Opponents	458	1,830	4.0	90t	19

RECEIVING	No.	Yds	Avg	LG	TD
Shockey	66	623	9.4	25	7
Burress	63	988	15.7	55t	10
Barber	58	465	8.0	28	0
Toomer	32	360	11.3	44	3
Carter	22	253	11.5	27	2
Tyree	19	197	10.4	33	2
Shiancoe	12	81	6.8	16	0
Jacobs	11	149	13.5	43	0
Finn	8	54	6.8	11	0
Jennings	5	49	9.8	20	0
Moss	5	25	5.0	10	0
Giants	301	3,244	10.8	55t	24
Opponents	333	3,830	11.5	53t	21

INTERCEPTIONS	No.	Yds	Avg	LG	TD
Dockery	2	100	50.0	96t	1
McQuarters	2	67	33.5	27t	1
Kiwanuka	2	44	22.0	32	0
Demps	2	30	15.0	29	0
Madison	2	28	14.0	24	0
Wilson	2	25	12.5	25	0
Robbins	2	12	6.0	11	0
Pierce	1	6	6.0	6	0
Webster	1	0	0.0	0	0
Bell	1	-7	-7.0	-7	0
Giants	17	305	17.9	96t	2
Opponents	18	216	12.0	37	1

PUNTING	No.	Yds.	Avg.	In 20	LG
Feagles	77	3098	40.2	27	54
Giants	77	3098	40.2	27	54
Opponents	69	2892	41.9	18	59

PUNT RETURNS	Ret	FC	Yds	Avg	LG	TD
Morton	29	13	268	9.2	38	0
McQuarters	4	2	20	5.0	12	0
Giants	33	15	288	8.7	38	0
Opponents	33	13	191	5.8	23	0

KICKOFF RETURNS	No.	Yds	Avg	LG	TD
Morton	31	670	21.6	51	0
Ward	23	466	20.3	36	0
Moss	10	194	19.4	33	0
Jacobs	3	58	19.3	28	0
McQuarters	1	17	17.0	17	0
Blackburn	1	2	2.0	2	0
Ruegamer	1	0	0.0	0	0
Giants	70	1,407	20.1	51	0
Opponents	65	1,455	22.4	64	0

FIELD GOALS	1-19	20-29	30-39	40-49	50+
Feely	0/0	7/7	10/11	6/8	0/1
Giants	0/0	7/7	10/11	6/8	0/1
Opponents	0/0	4/4	9/9	9/15	0/1

SACKS	No.
Umenyiora	6.0
Robbins	5.5
Kiwanuka	4.0
Strahan	3.0
Joseph	2.0
Short	2.0
Cofield	1.5
Arrington	1.0
Awasom	1.0
Demps	1.0
Emmons	1.0
McQuarters	1.0
Pierce	1.0
Torbor	1.0
Webster	1.0
Giants	32.0
Opponents	25.0

RECORD HOLDERS
INDIVIDUAL RECORDS—CAREER

Category	Name	Performance
Rushing (Yds.)	Tiki Barber, 1997-2006	10,449
Passing (Yds.)	Phil Simms, 1979-1993	33,462
Passing (TDs)	Phil Simms, 1979-1993	199
Receiving (No.)	Amani Toomer, 1996-2006	562
Receiving (Yds.)	Amani Toomer, 1996-2006	8,157
Interceptions	Emlen Tunnell, 1948-1958	74
Punting (Avg.)	Don Chandler, 1956-1964	43.8
Punt Return (Avg.)	Ward Cuff, 1941-45	12.1
Kickoff Return (Avg.)	Rocky Thompson, 1971-73	27.2
Field Goals	Pete Gogolak, 1966-1974	126
Touchdowns (Tot.)	Frank Gifford, 1952-1964	78
Points	Pete Gogolak, 1966-1974	646

INDIVIDUAL RECORDS—SINGLE SEASON

Category	Name	Performance
Rushing (Yds.)	Tiki Barber, 2005	1,860
Passing (Yds.)	Kerry Collins, 2002	4,073
Passing (TDs)	Y.A. Tittle, 1963	36
Receiving (No.)	Amani Toomer, 2002	82
Receiving (Yds.)	Amani Toomer, 2002	1,343
Interceptions	Otto Schnellbacher, 1951	11
	Jim Patton, 1958	11
Punting (Avg.)	Don Chandler, 1959	46.6
Punt Return (Avg.)	Merle Hapes, 1942	15.5
Kickoff Return (Avg.)	John Salscheider, 1949	31.6
Field Goals	Ali Haji-Sheikh, 1983	35
	Jay Feely, 2005	35
Touchdowns (Tot.)	Joe Morris, 1985	21
Points	Jay Feely, 2005	148

INDIVIDUAL RECORDS—SINGLE GAME

Category	Name	Performance
Rushing (Yds.)	Tiki Barber, 12-17-05	220
Passing (Yds.)	Phil Simms, 10-13-85	513
Passing (TDs)	Y.A. Tittle, 10-28-62	*7
Receiving (No.)	Tiki Barber, 1-2-00	13
Receiving (Yds.)	Del Shofner, 10-28-62	269
Interceptions	Many times	3
	Last time by Terry Kinard, 9-20-87	
Field Goals	Joe Danelo, 10-18-81	6
Touchdowns (Tot.)	Ron Johnson, 10-2-72	4
	Earnest Gray, 9-7-80	4
	Rodney Hampton, 9-24-95	4
Points	Ron Johnson, 10-2-72	24
	Earnest Gray, 9-7-80	24
	Rodney Hampton, 9-24-95	24

*NFL Record

2007 VETERAN ROSTER

No.	Name	Pos.	Ht.	Wt.	Birthdate	NFL Exp.	College	Hometown	How Acq.	'06 Games/ Starts
95	Awasom, Adrian	DE	6-5	280	10/25/83	3	North Texas	Fort Bend, Texas	FA-'06	10/0
33	Bell, Jason	S	6-0	196	4/1/78	7	UCLA	Long Beach, Calif.	UFA(Hou)-'06	15/1
99	Bell, Marcus	DT	6-2	325	6/1/79	7	Memphis	Memphis, Tenn.	FA-'07	0*
57	Blackburn, Chase	LB	6-3	247	6/10/83	3	Akron	Marysville, Ohio	FA-'05	16/0
17	Burress, Plaxico	WR	6-5	232	8/12/77	8	Michigan State	Virginia Beach, Va.	UFA(Pitt)-'05	15/15
37	Butler, James	S	6-3	215	9/7/82	3	Georgia Tech	Climax, Ga.	FA-'05	14/0
96	Cofield, Barry	DT	6-4	306	3/19/84	2	Northwestern	Cleveland Heights, Ohio	D4a-'06	16/16
52	Davis, James	LB	6-1	240	4/26/79	4	West Virginia	Stuart, Fla.	FA-'07	0*
47	Demps, Will	S	6-0	208	11/7/79	6	San Diego State	Palmdale, Calif.	UFA(Balt)-'06	16/16
66	Diehl, David	G	6-5	319	9/15/80	5	Illinois	Oak Lawn, Ill.	D5-'03	16/16
35	Dockery, Kevin	CB	5-8	188	1/8/84	2	Mississippi State	Hernando, Miss.	FA-'06	14/0
22	t-Droughns, Reuben	RB	5-11	220	8/21/78	8	Oregon	Anaheim, Calif.	T(Cle)-'07	14/12*
18	Feagles, Jeff	P	6-1	215	3/7/66	20	Miami	Phoenix, Ariz.	UFA(Sea)-'03	16/0
20	Finn, Jim	FB	6-0	245	12/9/76	8	Pennsylvania	Fair Lawn, N.J.	UFA(Ind)-'03	16/11
8	Hasselbeck, Tim	QB	6-1	214	4/6/78	6	Boston College	Westwood, Mass.	W(Wash)-'05	0*
27	Jacobs, Brandon	RB	6-4	264	7/6/82	3	So. Illinois	Napoleanville, La.	D4-'05	15/0
15	Jennings, Michael	WR	5-11	181	9/7/79	2	Florida State	Jacksonville, Fla.	FA-'04	8/0
94	Joseph, William	DT	6-5	308	9/3/79	5	Miami	Miami, Fla.	D1-'03	16/3
97	Kiwanuka, Mathias	DE	6-5	265	3/8/83	2	Boston College	Indianapolis, Ind.	D1-'06	16/9
90	Kuehl, Ryan	LS	6-5	276	1/18/72	11	Virginia	Potomac, Md.	UFA(Cle)-'03	16/0
64	Lentz, Matthew	G	6-6	320	11/19/82	2	Michigan	Ortonville, Mich.	FA-'06	0*
12	Lorenzen, Jared	QB	6-4	285	2/14/81	3	Kentucky	Ft. Thomas, Ky.	FA-'04	2/0
29	Madison, Sam	CB	5-11	180	4/23/74	11	Louisville	Tallahassee, Fla.	FA - '06	12/12
10	Manning, Eli	QB	6-4	225	1/3/81	4	Mississippi	New Orleans, La.	T(SD)-'04	16/16
67	McKenzie, Kareem	T	6-6	327	5/24/79	7	Penn State	Willingboro, N.J.	UFA(NYJ)-'05	16/16
25	McQuarters, R.W.	CB	5-10	194	12/21/76	10	Oklahoma State	Tulsa, Okla.	UFA(Det) - '06	16/10
55	Mitchelll, Kawika	LB	6-1	253	10/10/79	5	South Florida	Winter Springs, Fla.	UFA(KC)-'07	16/16*
83	Moss, Sinorice	WR	5-8	185	12/28/83	2	Miami	Miami, Fla.	D2-'06	6/0
60	O'Hara, Shaun	C	6-3	303	6/23/77	8	Rutgers	Hillsborough, N.J.	UFA(Cle)-'04	15/15
58	Pierce, Antonio	LB	6-1	238	10/26/78	7	Arizona	Ontario, Calif.	UFA(Wash)-'05	16/16
98	Robbins, Fred	DT	6-4	317	3/25/77	8	Wake Forest	Pensacola, Fla.	UFA(Minn)-'04	16/16
65	Ruegamer, Grey	G	6-4	299	6/11/76	9	Arizona State	Las Vegas, Nev.	FA-'06	16/1
75	Seawright, Jonas	DT	6-6	335	4/12/82	2	North Carolina	Orangeburg, S.C.	FA-'05	9/0
69	Seubert, Rich	G	6-3	310	3/30/79	7	Western Illinois	Marshfield, Wis.	FA-'01	14/3
80	Shockey, Jeremy	TE	6-5	251	8/18/80	6	Miami	Ada, Okla.	D1-'02	15/15
48	Smith, Tyson	LB	6-2	240	10/9/81	2	Iowa State	Des Moines, Iowa	FA-'06	3/0
76	Snee, Chris	G	6-3	317	1/18/82	4	Boston College	Montrose, Pa.	D2-'04	16/16
44	Stone, Michael	DB	6-0	207	2/13/78	7	Memphis	Southfield, Mich.	UFA(Hou)-'07	2/0*
92	Strahan, Michael	DE	6-5	255	11/21/71	15	Texas Southern	Westbury, Texas	D2-'93	9/9
81	Toomer, Amani	WR	6-3	203	9/8/74	12	Michigan	Berkeley, Calif.	D2-'96	8/8
53	Torbor, Reggie	LB	6-2	250	1/25/81	4	Auburn	Baton Rouge, La.	D4-'04	16/3
91	Tuck, Justin	DE	6-5	274	3/29/83	3	Notre Dame	Kellyton, Ala.	D3-'05	6/0
85	Tyree, David	WR	6-0	206	1/3/80	5	Syracuse	Montclair, N.J.	D6c-'03	16/1
72	Umenyiora, Osi	DE	6-3	261	11/16/81	5	Troy State	Auburn, Ala.	D2-'03	11/11
31	Underwood, E.J.	CB	6-1	185	8/4/83	2	Pikeville	Cincinnatti, Ohio	FA-'06	0*
34	Ward, Derrick	RB	5-11	228	8/30/80	4	Ottawa	Moreno Valley, Calif.	FA-'04	8/0
87	Watts, Darius	WR	6-2	190	12/19/81	3	Marshall	Atlanta, Ga.	FA-'06	0*
23	Webster, Corey	CB	6-0	202	3/2/82	3	Louisiana State	Vacherie, La.	D2-'05	12/10
79	Whimper, Guy	T	6-5	302	5/21/83	2	East Carolina	Havelock, N.C.	D4b-'06	8/0
59	Wilkinson, Gerris	LB	6-3	231	4/5/83	2	Georgia Tech	Oakland, Calif.	D3-'06	16/2
28	Wilson, Gibril	S	6-0	209	11/12/81	4	Tennessee	San Jose, Calif.	D5-'04	15/15
2	Wright, Anthony	QB	6-1	211	2/14/76	9	South Carolina	Vanceboro, N.C.	UFA(Cin)-'07	4/0*

* M. Bell played 13 games with Detroit in '06; Davis last active with Detroit in '05; Droughns played 14 games with Cleveland; Hasselbeck inactive third quarterback for 16 games; Lentz missed '06 season because of injury; Mitchell played 16 games with Kansas City; Stone played 2 games for Houston; Underwood missed '06 season because of injury; Watts inactive for 1 game; Wright played 4 games for Cincinati.

t - Giants traded for Droughns (Cle).

Traded—WR Tim Carter (16 games in '06) to Cleveland.

Retired—Tiki Barber, 10-year running back, 16 games in '06.

Players lost through free agency (3): K Jay Feely (Mia; 16 games in '06); TE Visanthe Shiancoe (Minn; 16), CB Frank Walker (GB; 11).

Also played with Giants in '06—LB LaVar Arrington (6 games), LB Chris Claiborne (4), DE Lance Legree (2), T Luke Petitgout (9), LB Brandon Short (9), RB James Sims (2), T Bob Whitfield (16).

2007 FIRST-YEAR ROSTER

Name	Pos.	Ht.	Wt.	Birthdate	College	Hometown	How Acq.
Adams, Titus	DT	6-4	305	1/28/83	Nebraska	Omaha, Neb.	FA-'06
Alford, Jay	DT	6-3	304	5/28/83	Penn State	Orange, N.J.	D3
Anderson, Sir Henry	DT	6-4	308	10/16/82	Oregon State	Oakland, Calif.	FA
Austin, Rob	T	6-5	272	9/27/82	Troy State	Ft. Payne, Ala.	FA
Birmingham, Decori	RB	5-10	210	11/22/82	Arkansas	Atlanta, Texas	FA
Boss, Kevin	TE	6-6	253	1/11/84	Western Oregon	Philomath, Ore.	D5
Bradshaw, Ahmad	RB	5-9	198	3/19/86	Marshall	Bluefield, Va.	D7b
Clinger, Joel	T	6-6	320	7/12/83	Missouri	Warrenton, Mo.	FA
Cobbs, R.J. (1)	CB	5-11	190	7/26/81	Massachusetts	Parsippany Hills, N.J.	FA-'06
Dahl, Craig	S	6-1	207	6/7/85	North Dakota State	Mankato, Minn.	FA
Davis, Charles	TE	6-6	260	3/13/83	Purdue	Fraser, Mich.	FA
Davis, Tommy (1)	DE	6-2	257	10/18/82	North Carolina	Dudley, N.C.	FA-'06
DeOssie, Zak	LB	6-4	249	5/24/84	Brown	North Andover, N.J.	D4
Douglas, Robert (1)	RB	6-1	230	7/25/82	Memphis	St. Louis, Mo.	FA-'06
Dunn, Jonathan (1)	T	6-7	324	12/12/81	Virginia Tech	Virginia Beach, Va.	FA-'06
Grant, Ryan (1)	RB	6-1	218	12/9/82	Notre Dame	Ramsey, N.J.	FA-'05
Gunn, Marquies	DE	6-4	264	11/22/83	Auburn	Alexander City, Ala.	FA
Hall, Gabe	T	6-4	293	10/1/83	Texas Tech	Lubbock, Texas	FA
Hickok, Marc	K	6-0	211	8/14/80	Connecticut	Gloversville, N.Y.	FA
Humes, Cedric	RB	6-1	228	8/7/83	Virginia Tech	Virginia Beach, Va.	FA
Huston, Josh	K	6-1	200	2/28/82	Ohio State	Findlay, Ohio	FA
Johnson, Darcy (1)	TE	6-5	252	2/11/83	Central Florida	Palatka, Fla.	FA-'06
Johnson, Michael	S	6-2	207	5/9/84	Arizona	Round Rock, Texas	D7a
Johnson, Travonti	CB	6-2	190	5/9/84	Central Florida	Miami, Fla.	FA
Jones, Justin	T	6-6	305	1/5/84	Central Arkansas	Harrison, Ark.	FA
Keenan, Ryan	G	6-5	295	8/18/83	Northwestern	Westlake, Ohio	FA
Koets, Adam	T	6-5	300	1/7/84	Oregon State	Santa Ana, Calif.	D6
London, Brandon	WR	6-4	210	10/16/84	Massachusetts	Charlottesville, Va.	FA
Londot, Todd (1)	G/T	6-5	301	4/4/83	Miami (Ohio)	Utica, Ohio	FA-'06
Matthews, Michael	TE	6-4	270	10/9/83	Georgia Tech	Cincinatti, Ohio	FA
McPherson, Gerrick (1)	CB	5-10	197	12/29/83	Maryland	Columbia, Md.	D7-'06
Mitchell, Jason	LB	6-1	227	5/6/83	Tennessee	Abbeville, La.	FA
Mix, Anthony (1)	WR	6-5	235	1/20/83	Auburn	Bay Minette, Ala.	FA-'06
Myles, Brandon	WR	6-3	185	7/25/83	West Virginia	Goochland, Va.	FA
Ohnesorge, Cory	P	6-4	208	5/22/84	Occidental College	Oceanside, Calif.	FA
Robertson, Barry	LB	6-3	245	11/30/81	Louisiana Tech	Hattiesburgh, Miss.	FA
Ross, Aaron	CB	6-0	197	9/15/82	Texas	Tyler, Texas	D1
Ruegamer, Grey (1)	G	6-4	299	6/11/76	Arizona State	Las Vegas, Nev.	FA-'06
Smith, Steve	WR	5-11	195	5/6/85	Southern California	Woodland Hills, Calif.	D2
Tarullo, Matt (1)	G/T	6-5	312	8/13/82	Syracuse	Albany, N.Y.	FA-'06
Taylor, Charrod	DE	6-2	286	5/20/80	Georgia Southern	Athens, Ga.	FA
Thomas, Marco	WR	6-1	175	11/27/83	Western Illinois	Chicago, Ill.	FA

The term NFL Rookie is defined as a player who is in his first season of professional football and has not been on the roster of another professional football team for any regular-season or postseason games. A Rookie is designated by an "R" on NFL rosters. Players who have been active in another professional football league or players who have NFL experience, including either preseason training camp or being on an Active List or Inactive List, or on Reserve/Injured or Reserve/Physically Unable to Perform for fewer than six regular-season games, are termed NFL First-Year Players. An NFL First-Year Player is designated by a "1" on NFL rosters. Thereafter, a player is credited with an additional year of experience for each season in which he accumulates six games on the Active List or Inactive List, or on Reserve/Injured or Reserve/Physically Unable to Perform.

Log on to www.giants.com for an up-to-date roster.

COACHING STAFF

Head Coach,
Tom Coughlin

Pro Career: Was named the sixteenth head coach in Giants history on January 6, 2004. Coached the Giants to an 11-5 record and the NFC East title in 2005, and guided the club to the playoffs in 2006, his second and third seasons with the team. Coughlin previously spent eight years (1995-2002) with the Jacksonville Jaguars. Under Coughlin, the Jaguars had the most victories of any NFL expansion team in its first seven seasons. They were also the only expansion team in NFL history to advance to the playoffs four times in their first five seasons. Coughlin's team went 9-7 in 1996 and an NFL-best 14-2 in 1999, both times reaching the AFC Championship Game. Coughlin previously coached the Philadelphia Eagles (1984-85), Green Bay Packers (1986-87), and Giants (1988-1990). He was a member of the Giants' Super Bowl XXV champion coaching staff. Career record: 97-89.

Background: Served as head coach at Boston College (1991-93), where he posted a 21-13-1 record, and coached at Syracuse (1969, 1974-1980), Rochester Institute of Technology 1970-73 (head coach), and Boston College (1981-83). Played wingback for Syracuse (1965-67), with Larry Csonka and Floyd Little. Received Syracuse 1967 Orange Key Award as outstanding scholar athlete, and graduated with bachelor's and master's degree.

Personal: Born August 31, 1947, Waterloo, N.Y. Tom and his wife, Judy, have two daughters, Keli and Katie, two sons, Brian and Tim, a daughter-in-law, Andrea (Tim's wife), and two grandchildren, Emma Rose and Dylan.

ASSISTANT COACHES

Andre Curtis, defensive assistant; born December 8, 1976, Richmond, Va. Linebacker Virginia Military Institute 1996-1999. No pro playing experience. College coach: Virginia Military Institute 2002-03, Georgia Southern 2004-05. Pro coach: Joined Giants in 2006.

Dave DeGuglielmo, asst. offensive line; born July 15, 1968, Cambridge, Mass. Attended Boston University. No college or pro playing experience. College coach: Boston College 1991-92, Boston University 1993-96, Connecticut 1997-98, South Carolina 1999-2003. Pro coach: Joined Giants in 2004.

Pat Flaherty, offensive line; born April 27, 1956, Hanover, Pa. Center East Stroudsburg 1974-77. No pro playing experience. College coach: East Stroudsburg 1980-81, Penn State 1982-83, Rutgers 1984-1991, East Carolina 1992, Wake Forest 1993-98, Iowa 1999. Pro coach: Washington Redskins 2000, Chicago Bears 2001-03, joined Giants in 2004.

Kevin Gilbride, offensive coordinator; born August 27, 1951, New Haven, Conn. Quarterback/tight end Southern

Connecticut State 1971-73. No pro playing experience. College coach: Idaho State 1974-75, Tufts 1976-77, American International 1978-79. Southern Connecticut State 1980-84, East Carolina 1987-88. Pro coach: Ottawa Rough Riders (CFL) 1985-86, Houston Oilers 1989-1994, Jacksonville Jaguars 1995-96, San Diego Chargers 1997-98 (head coach), Pittsburgh Steelers 1999-2000, Buffalo Bills 2002-2003, joined Giants in 2004.

Peter Giunta, secondary/corners; born August 11, 1956, Salem, Mass. Running back/defensive back Northeastern 1974-77. No pro playing experience. College coach: Penn State 1981-83, Brown 1984-87, Lehigh 1988-1990. Pro coach: Philadelphia Eagles 1991-94, N.Y. Jets 1995-96, St. Louis Rams 1997-2000, Kansas City Chiefs 2001-2005, joined Giants in 2006.

Jerald Ingram, running backs; born December 24, 1960, Dayton, Ohio. Fullback Michigan 1979-1983. College coach: Michigan 1984, Ball State 1985-1990, Boston College 1991-93. Pro coach: Jacksonville Jaguars 1994-2002, joined Giants in 2004.

Thomas McGaughey, asst. special teams coordinator; born May 8, 1973, Chicago. Safety Houston 1991-95. Pro safety Philadelphia Eagles 1996, Barcelona Dragons (NFLE) 1997. College coach Houston 1997, 2003-04. Pro coach: Scottish Claymores (NFLE) 2002, Kansas City Chiefs 2002, Denver Broncos 2005-06, joined Giants in 2007.

David Merritt Sr., secondary/safeties; born September 8, 1971, Raleigh, N.C. Linebacker North Carolina State 1989-1992. Pro linebacker Miami Dolphins 1993, Arizona Cardinals 1993-96, Rhein Fire (NFLE) 1997. College coach: Chattanooga 1997, Virginia Military Institute 1998-2000. Pro coach: New York Jets 2001-2003, joined Giants in 2004.

Chris Palmer, quarterbacks; born September 23, 1949, Brewster, N.Y. Quarterback Southern Connecticut State 1968-1971. No pro playing experience. College coach: Connecticut 1972-74, Lehigh 1975, Colgate 1976-1982, New Haven 1986-87 (head coach), Boston 1988-89 (head coach). Pro coach: Montreal Concordes (CFL) 1983, New Jersey Generals (USFL) 1984-85, Houston Oilers 1990-92, New England Patriots 1993-96, Jacksonville Jaguars 1997-98, Cleveland Browns 1999-2000 (head coach), Houston Texans 2001-05, Dallas Cowboys 2006, joined Giants in 2007.

Jerry Palmieri, strength and conditioning; born October 30, 1958, Englewood, N.J. Attended Montclair State. No college or pro playing experience. College coach: North Carolina 1982-83, Oklahoma State 1984-86, Kansas State 1987-1992, Boston College 1993-94. Pro coach: Jacksonville Jaguars 1995-2002, New Orleans Saints 2003, joined Giants in 2004.

Marcus Paul, asst. strength and conditioning; born April 1, 1966, Orlando, Fla. Safety Syracuse 1984-88. Pro safety Chicago Bears 1989-1993, Tampa Buccaneers 1993. Pro coach: New Orleans Saints 1998-99, New England Patriots 2000-04, New York Jets 2005-2006, joined Giants in 2007.

Michael Pope, tight ends; born March 15, 1942, Monroe, N.C. Quarterback Lenoir-Rhyne 1962-64. No pro playing experience. College coach: Florida State 1970-74, Texas Tech 1975-77, Mississippi 1978-1982. Pro coach: New York Giants 1983-1991, Cincinnati Bengals 1992-93, New England Patriots 1994-96, Washington Redskins 1997-99, re-joined Giants in 2000.

Tom Quinn, special teams coodinator; born January 27, 1968, Pasadena, Calif. Linebacker Arizona 1986-1990. No pro playing experience. College coach; Davidson College 1991, James Madison 1992-94, Boston 1995, Holy Cross 1996-98, San Jose State 1999-2001, Stanford 2002-05. Pro coach: Joined Giants in 2006.

Sean Ryan, offensive quality control; born May 1, 1972, Glenn Falls, N.Y. Defensive back Hamilton College 1994. No pro playing experience. College coach: Albany 1998-99, Colgate 2000, Boston College 2001-02, Columbia 2003-04, Harvard 2006. Pro coach: Joined Giants in 2007.

Bill Sheridan, linebackers; born January 27, 1959, Detroit. Linebacker Grand Valley State 1979-1982. No pro playing experience. College coach: Michigan 1985-86, Maine 1987-88, Cincinnati 1989-1991, Army 1992-97, Michigan State 1998-2000, Notre Dame 2001, Michigan 2002-04. Pro coach. Joined Giants in 2005.

Steve Spagnuolo, defensive coordinator; born December 21, 1959, Witinville, Mass. Wide receiver Springfield College 1979-1981. No pro playing experience. College coach: Massachusetts 1982-83, Lafayette 1984-86, Connecticut 1987-1991, Maine 1993, Rutgers 1994-95, Bowling Green 1996-97. Pro coach: Barcelona Dragons (World League) 1992, Frankfurt Galaxy (NFLE) 1988, Philadelphia Eagles 1999-2006, joined Giants in 2007.

Mike Sullivan, wide receivers; born January 28, 1967, Santa Maria, Calif. Defensive back Army 1987-88. No pro playing experience. College coach: Mt. San Jacinto (Calif.) J.C. 1993, Humboldt State 1993-94, Army 1995-96, 1999-2000, Youngstown State 1997-98, Ohio 2001. Pro coach: Jacksonville Jaguars 2002-03, joined Giants in 2004.

Mike Waufle, defensive line; born June 27, 1954, Hornell, N.Y. U.S. Marines 1972-75. Defensive lineman Bakersfield (Calif.) J.C. 1975-76, Utah State 1977-78. No pro playing experience. College coach: Alfred 1979, Utah State 1980-84, Fresno State 1985-88, UCLA 1989, Oregon State 1990-91, California 1992-97. Pro coach: Oakland Raiders 1998-2003, joined Giants in 2004.

National Football Conference
East Division
Team Colors: Midnight Green, Silver, Black, and White
NovaCare Complex
One NovaCare Way
Philadelphia, Pennsylvania 19145
Telephone: (215) 463-2500

2007 SCHEDULE
PRESEASON
Aug. 13	at Baltimore	7:00
Aug. 17	**Carolina**	7:00
Aug. 26	at Pittsburgh	8:00
Aug. 30	**N.Y. Jets**	7:30

REGULAR SEASON
Sep. 9	at Green Bay	12:00
Sep. 17	**Washington** (Mon.)	8:30
Sep. 23	**Detroit**	1:00
Sep. 30	at N.Y. Giants	8:15
Oct. 7	Open Date	
Oct. 14	at N.Y. Jets	1:00
Oct. 21	**Chicago**	4:15
Oct. 28	at Minnesota	12:00
Nov. 4	**Dallas**	8:15
Nov. 11	at Washington	1:00
Nov. 18	**Miami**	1:00
Nov. 25	at New England	*8:15
Dec. 2	**Seattle**	1:00
Dec. 9	**N.Y. Giants**	1:00
Dec. 16	at Dallas	3:15
Dec. 23	at New Orleans	12:00
Dec. 30	**Buffalo**	1:00

Sunday night games in Weeks 11-17 subject to change

Stadium: Lincoln Financial Field
(opened in 2003)
• **Capacity:** 68,400
One Lincoln Financial Field Way
Philadelphia, Pennsylvania 19148
Playing Surface: Natural Grass
Training Camp: Lehigh University
Bethlehem, PA 18015

LINCOLN FINANCIAL FIELD

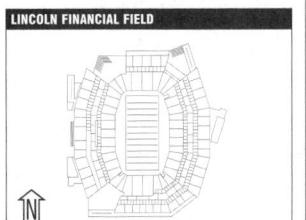

CLUB OFFICIALS
Chairman/Chief Executive Officer:
Jeffrey Lurie
President: Joe Banner
Head Coach/Executive Vice President of
Football Operations: Andy Reid
General Manager: Tom Heckert
Vice President of Player Personnel:
Jason Licht
Senior Vice President of Business
Operations: Mark Donovan
Senior Vice President/Chief Financial
Officer: Don Smolenski
Vice President of Football Administration:
Howie Roseman
Vice President of Sales and Service:
Bill Manning
Executive Director of Eagles Youth
Partnership: Sarah Martinez-Helfman
Director of Pro Personnel: Scott Cohen
Director of Football Media Relations:
Derek Boyko
Assistant Director of Football Media
Services: Bob Lange
Director of Marketing: Mike Malo
Director of Human Resources:
Kristie Pappal
Manager of Community Relations:
Julie Hirshey
Director of Stadium Operations:
Dave Duernberger
Director, Broadcasting: Rob Alberino
Director of Events: Leonard Bonacci
Director of Ticket Operations:
Laini Delawter
Director of Ticket Client Relations:
Leo Carlin
Director of Merchandise:
Steve Strawbridge
Travel Manager: Tracey Detweiler
Director of Team Security:
Anthony (Butch) Buchanico
Director of Facility and Stadium Security:
Victor Cooper
Head Athletic Trainer: Rick Burkholder
Asst. Athletic Trainers: Steve Condon,
Chris Peduzzi
Video Director: Mike Dougherty
Head Equipment Manager: John Hatfield

COACHING HISTORY
(488-533-25)
Records include postseason games
1933-35	Lud Wray	9-21-1
1936-1940	Bert Bell	10-44-2
1941-1950	Earle (Greasy) Neale*	66-44-5
1951	Alvin (Bo) McMillin**	2-0-0
1951	Wayne Millner	2-8-0
1952-55	Jim Trimble	25-20-3
1956-57	Hugh Devore	7-16-1
1958-1960	Lawrence (Buck) Shaw	20-16-1
1961-63	Nick Skorich	15-24-3
1964-68	Joe Kuharich	28-41-1
1969-1971	Jerry Williams***	7-22-2
1971-72	Ed Khayat	8-15-2
1973-75	Mike McCormack	16-25-1
1976-1982	Dick Vermeil	57-51-0
1983-85	Marion Campbell****	17-29-1
1985	Fred Bruney	1-0-0
1986-1990	Buddy Ryan	43-38-1
1991-94	Rich Kotite	37-29-0
1995-98	Ray Rhodes	30-36-1
1999-2006	Andy Reid	88-54-0

*Co-coach with Walt Kiesling in Philadelphia-
Pittsburgh merger in 1943
**Retired after two games in 1951
***Released after three games in 1971
****Released after 15 games in 1985

PAID ATTENDANCE
Home 543,289   Away 546,845
Total 1,090,134
Single-game home record,
72,111 (11/1/81)
Single-season home record,
557,325 (1980)

2007 DRAFT CHOICES
Round	Name	Pos.	College
2	Kevin Kolb	QB	Houston
	Victor Abiamiri	DE	Notre Dame
3	Stewart Bradley	LB	Nebraska
	Tony Hunt	RB	Penn State
5	C.J. Gaddis	DB	Clemson
	Brent Celek	TE	Cincinnati
6	Rashad Barksdale	DB	Albany
7	Nate Ilaoa	RB	Hawaii

PHILADELPHIA EAGLES

2006 TEAM RECORD

PRESEASON (2-3)

Date	Result	Opponent
8/6	L 10-16	vs. Oakland in Canton, OH
8/15	W 20-7	Cleveland
8/17	L 10-20	at Baltimore
8/25	W 16-7	Pittsburgh
9/1	L 17-20	at N.Y. Jets

REGULAR SEASON (10-6)

Date	Result	Opponent	Att.
9/10	W 24-10	at Houston	70,180
9/17	L 24-30	N.Y. Giants (OT)	69,241
9/24	W 38-24	at San Francisco	68,166
10/2	W 31-9	Green Bay	69,222
10/8	W 38-24	Dallas	69,268
10/15	L 24-27	at New Orleans	68,269
10/22	L 21-23	at Tampa Bay	65,808
10/29	L 6-13	Jacksonville	69,249
11/12	W 27-3	Washington	69,143
11/19	L 13-31	Tennessee	69,232
11/26	L 21-45	at Indianapolis	57,296
12/4	W 27-24	Carolina	69,098
12/10	W 21-19	at Washington	84,164
12/17	W 36-22	at N.Y. Giants	78,657
12/25	W 23-7	at Dallas	62,839
12/31	W 24-17	Atlanta	69,341

(OT) Overtime

REGULAR SEASON (1-1)

1/7	W 23-20	N.Y. Giants	69,094
1/13	L 24-27	at New Orleans	69,241

SCORE BY PERIODS

Eagles	75	109	96	118	0	— 398
Opponents	79	86	61	96	6	— 328

2006 TEAM STATISTICS

	Eagles	Opp.
Total First Downs	312	314
Rushing	106	126
Passing	189	154
Penalty	17	34
3rd Down: Made/Att	88/209	83/222
3rd Down Pct.	42.1	37.4
4th Down: Made/Att	5/11	10/21
4th Down Pct.	45.5	47.6
Possession Avg.	28:38	31:22
Total Net Yards	6,103	5,249
Avg. Per Game	381.4	328.1
Total Plays	988	1054
Avg. Per Play	6.2	5.0
Net Yards Rushing	1,984	2,182
Avg. Per Game	124.0	136.4
Total Rushes	416	489
Net Yards Passing	4,119	3,067
Avg. Per Game	257.4	191.7
Sacked/Yards Lost	28/190	40/300
Gross Yards	4,309	3,367
Att./Completions	544/323	525/309
Completion Pct.	59.4	58.9
Had Intercepted	9	19
Punts/Average	78/42.6	82/43.5
Net Punting Avg.	78/34.9	82/37.2
Penalties/Yards	112/983	96/807
Fumbles/Ball Lost	26/15	25/10
Touchdowns	49	36
Rushing	13	12
Passing	31	17
Returns	5	7

2006 INDIVIDUAL STATISTICS

PASSING	Att.	Comp.	Yds.	Pct.	TD	Int.	Tkld.	Rate
McNabb	316	180	2,647	57.0	18	6	21/140	95.5
Garcia	188	116	1,309	61.7	10	2	6/40	95.8
Feeley	38	26	342	68.4	3	0	1/10	122.9
Akers	1	1	11	100.0	0	0	0/0	112.5
Baskett	1	0	—	0.0	0	1	0/0	0.0
Eagles	544	323	4,309	59.4	31	9	28/190	96.7
Opponents	525	309	3,367	58.9	17	19	40/300	73.6

SCORING	TD R	TD P	TD Rt	PAT	FG	Saf	PTS
Akers	0	0	0	48/48	18/23	0	102
Westbrook	7	4	0	0/0	0/0	0	66
R. Brown	1	8	0	0/0	0/0	0	54
Smith	0	5	0	0/0	0/0	0	32
Stallworth	0	5	0	0/0	0/0	0	30
Buckhalter	2	1	0	0/0	0/0	0	18
McNabb	3	0	0	0/0	0/0	0	18
Baskett	0	2	0	0/0	0/0	0	12
G. Lewis	0	2	0	0/0	0/0	0	12
Schobel	0	2	0	0/0	0/0	0	12
Avant	0	1	0	0/0	0/0	0	6
S. Brown	0	0	1	0/0	0/0	0	6
T. Cole	0	0	1	0/0	0/0	0	6
M. Lewis	0	0	1	0/0	0/0	0	6
Patterson	0	0	1	0/0	0/0	0	6
Sheppard	0	0	1	0/0	0/0	0	6
Tapeh	0	1	0	0/0	0/0	0	6
Eagles	13	31	5	48/48	18/23	0	398
Opponents	12	17	7	34/34	26/28	0	328

2-Pt. Conversions: Smith,
Eagles 1-1, Opponents 0-1

RUSHING	No.	Yds	Avg	LG	TD
Westbrook	240	1,217	5.1	71t	7
Buckhalter	83	345	4.2	20	2
McNabb	32	212	6.6	37	3
Garcia	25	87	3.5	12	0
Moats	22	69	3.1	13	0
R. Brown	3	24	8.0	15t	1
Mahe	4	18	4.5	11	0
Tapeh	5	9	1.8	4	0
Feeley	1	3	3.0	3	0
Johnson	1	0	0.0	0	0
Eagles	416	1,984	4.8	71t	13
Opponents	489	2,182	4.5	70t	12

RECEIVING	No.	Yds	Avg	LG	TD
Westbrook	77	699	9.1	52t	4
Smith	50	611	12.2	65	5
R. Brown	46	816	17.7	60t	8
Stallworth	38	725	19.1	84t	5
G. Lewis	24	348	14.5	45t	2
Buckhalter	24	256	10.7	55t	1
Baskett	22	464	21.1	89t	2
Tapeh	16	85	5.3	15	1
Schobel	14	214	15.3	60	2
Avant	7	68	9.7	18	1
Mahe	5	23	4.6	8	0
Eagles	323	4,309	13.3	89t	31
Opponents	309	3,367	10.9	75	17

INTERCEPTIONS	No.	Yds	Avg	LG	TD
Sheppard	6	157	26.2	102t	1
Dawkins	4	38	9.5	38	0
M. Lewis	2	105	52.5	84t	1
S. Brown	1	70	70.0	70t	1
T. Cole	1	19	19.0	19t	1
Trotter	1	17	17.0	17	0
Gaither	1	16	16.0	16	0
Considine	1	12	12.0	12	0
Walker	1	6	6.0	6	0
Ramsey	1	-12	-12.0	-12	0
Eagles	19	428	22.5	102t	4
Opponents	9	250	27.8	66t	2

PUNTING	No.	Yds.	Avg.	In 20	LG
Johnson	78	3,326	42.6	21	60
Eagles	78	3,326	42.6	21	60
Opponents	82	3,566	43.5	25	61

PUNT RETURNS	Ret	FC	Yds	Avg	LG	TD
Mahe	18	12	169	9.4	23	0
Wynn	13	5	131	10.1	22	0
Westbrook	5	3	39	7.8	13	0
Eagles	36	20	339	9.4	23	0
Opponents	41	13	380	9.3	90t	1

KICKOFF RETURNS	No.	Yds	Avg	LG	TD
Mahe	30	667	22.2	64	0
Wynn	18	362	20.1	34	0
Perry	3	57	19.0	24	0
G. Lewis	2	46	23.0	28	0
Moats	2	43	21.5	23	0
Schobel	2	13	6.5	11	0
Sheppard	1	16	16.0	16	0
Eagles	58	1,204	20.8	64	0
Opponents	71	1,647	23.2	41	0

FIELD GOALS	1-19	20-29	30-39	40-49	50+
Akers	0/0	9/10	3/5	6/8	0/0
Eagles	0/0	9/10	3/5	6/8	0/0
Opponents	0/0	4/4	11/11	9/10	2/3

SACKS	No.
T. Cole	8.0
J. Thomas	6.0
Walker	6.0
Howard	5.0
Kearse	3.5
M. Lewis	2.0
M. McCoy	2.0
Considine	1.5
Patterson	1.5
Dawkins	1.0
Gaither	1.0
Hood	1.0
McDougle	1.0
Jones	0.5
Eagles	40.0
Opponents	28.0

RECORD HOLDERS
INDIVIDUAL RECORDS—CAREER

Category	Name	Performance
Rushing (Yds.)	Wilbert Montgomery, 1977-1984	6,538
Passing (Yds.)	Ron Jaworski, 1977-1986	26,963
Passing (TDs)	Ron Jaworski, 1977-1986	175
Receiving (No.)	Harold Carmichael, 1971-1983	589
Receiving (Yds.)	Harold Carmichael, 1971-1983	8,978
Interceptions	Bill Bradley, 1969-1976	34
	Eric Allen, 1988-1994	34
Punting (Avg.)	Joe Muha, 1946-1950	42.9
Punt Return (Avg.)	Ernie Steele, 1942-48	16.8
Kickoff Return (Avg.)	Steve Van Buren, 1944-1951	26.7
Field Goals	David Akers, 1999-2006	173
Touchdowns (Tot.)	Harold Carmichael, 1971-1983	79
Points	Bobby Walston, 1951-1962	881

INDIVIDUAL RECORDS—SINGLE SEASON

Category	Name	Performance
Rushing (Yds.)	Wilbert Montgomery, 1979	1,512
Passing (Yds.)	Donovan McNabb, 2004	3,875
Passing (TDs)	Sonny Jurgensen, 1961	32
Receiving (No.)	Irving Fryar, 1996	88
Receiving (Yds.)	Mike Quick, 1983	1,409
Interceptions	Bill Bradley, 1971	11
Punting (Avg.)	Joe Muha, 1948	47.2
Punt Return (Avg.)	Steve Van Buren, 1944	15.3
Kickoff Return (Avg.)	Al Nelson, 1972	29.1
Field Goals	Paul McFadden, 1984	30
	David Akers, 2002	30
Touchdowns (Tot.)	Steve Van Buren, 1945	18
Points	David Akers, 2002	133

INDIVIDUAL RECORDS—SINGLE GAME

Category	Name	Performance
Rushing (Yds.)	Steve Van Buren, 11-27-49	205
Passing (Yds.)	Donovan McNabb, 12-5-04	464
Passing (TDs)	Adrian Burk, 10-17-54	*7
Receiving (No.)	Don Looney, 12-1-40	14
Receiving (Yds.)	Tommy McDonald, 12-10-60	237
Interceptions	Russ Craft, 9-24-50	*4
Field Goals	Tom Dempsey, 11-12-72	6
Touchdowns (Tot.)	Many times	4
	Last time by Irving Fryar, 10-20-96	
Points	Bobby Walston, 10-17-54	25

*NFL Record

2007 VETERAN ROSTER

No.	Name	Pos.	Ht.	Wt.	Birthdate	NFL Exp.	College	Hometown	How Acq.	'06 Games/ Starts
2	Akers, David	K	5-10	200	12/09/74	9	Louisville	Lexington, Ky.	FA-'99	16/0
73	Andrews, Shawn	G/T	6-4	340	12/25/82	4	Arkansas	Camden, Ark.	D1-'04	16/16
81	Avant, Jason	WR	6-0	212	4/20/83	2	Michigan	Chicago, Ill.	D4b-'06	8/3
88	Bartrum, Mike	TE/LS	6-4	245	6/23/70	14	Marshall	Pomeroy, Ohio	FA-'00	11/0
84	Baskett, Hank	WR	6-4	220	9/04/82	2	New Mexico	Clovis, N.M.	T(Minn)-'06	16/5
11	Bloom, Jeremy	WR	5-9	180	4/02/82	2	Colorado	Loveland, Colo.	D5a-'06	0*
86	Brown, Reggie	WR	6-1	197	1/13/81	3	Georgia	Carrollton, Ga.	D2a-'05	16/15
24	Brown, Sheldon	CB	5-10	200	3/19/79	6	South Carolina	Ft. Lawn, S.C.	D2b-'02	16/16
28	Buckhalter, Correll	RB	6-0	217	10/06/78	7	Nebraska	Collins, Miss.	D4-'01	16/1
97	Bunkley, Brodrick	DT	6-2	306	11/23/83	2	Florida State	Tampa, Fla.	D1-'06	15/0
45	Cain, Jeremy	FB/LS	6-1	240	3/24/80	3	Massachusetts	Tamarac, Fla.	FA-'07	0*
59	Cole, Nick	C	6-0	350	7/28/84	2	New Mexico State	Lawton, Okla.	FA-'06	16/0
58	Cole, Trent	LB/DE	6-3	270	10/05/82	3	Cincinnati	Xenia, Ohio	D5a-'05	16/14
37	Considine, Sean	S	6-0	212	10/28/81	3	Iowa	Byron, Ill.	D4a-'05	16/9
80	Curtis, Kevin	WR	5-11	186	7/17/78	5	Utah State	South Jordan, Utah	FA(StL)-'07	16/1*
56	Daniels, Tank	LB	6-3	248	12/27/81	2	Harding	Clarendon, Ark.	FA-'06	6/0
42	Davis, Jason	FB	5-11	240	11/02/83	2	Illinois	St. Louis, Mo.	FA-'06	0*
20	Dawkins, Brian	S	6-0	210	10/13/73	12	Clemson	Jacksonville, Fla.	D2b-'96	16/16
46	Dorenbos, Jon	LS	6-0	250	7/21/80	5	Texas-El Paso	Garden Grove, Calif.	FA-'06	5/0
14	Feeley, A.J.	QB	6-3	220	5/16/77	7	Oregon	Ontario, Ore.	FA-'06	2/0
25	Fox, Dustin	CB	5-11	200	10/08/82	2	Ohio State	Canton, Ohio	FA-'06	1/0
96	Gaither, Omar	LB	6-1	235	3/18/84	2	Tennessee	Charlotte, N.C.	D5b-'06	16/5
57	Gocong, Chris	LB	6-2	263	11/16/83	2	Cal Poly	Carpinteria, Calif.	D3-'06	0*
22	Hanson, Joselio	CB	5-9	185	8/13/81	3	Texas Tech	Playa del Rey, Calif.	FA-'06	16/1
79	Herremans, Todd	G/T	6-6	321	10/13/82	3	Saginaw Valley State	Ravenna, Mich.	D4b-'05	16/16
10 t-	Holcomb, Kelly	QB	6-2	212	7/09/73	11	Middle Tennessee State	Fayetteville, Tenn.	T(Buff)-'07	0*
90	Howard, Darren	DE	6-3	275	11/19/76	8	Kansas State	St. Petersburg, Fla.	UFA(NO)-'06	16/16
67	Jackson, Jamaal	C	6-4	330	5/08/80	4	Delaware State	Miami, Fla.	FA-'03	16/16
21	James, William	CB	6-0	200	6/15/79	7	Western Illinois	Uniontown, Pa.	FA-'06	3/0
62	Jean-Gilles, Max	G	6-3	358	11/19/83	2	Georgia	Miami, Fla.	D4a-'06	0*
16	Johnson, Bethel	WR	5-10	200	2/11/79	5	Texas A&M	Corsicana, Texas	UFA(Minn)-'07	11/2*
8	Johnson, Dirk	P	6-0	205	6/01/75	5	Northern Colorado	Montrose, Colo.	FA-'03	16/0
74	Justice, Winston	T	6-6	320	9/14/84	2	Southern California	Long Beach, Calif.	D2-'06	0*
93	Kearse, Jevon	DE	6-4	265	9/03/76	9	Florida	Ft. Myers, Fla.	UFA(Tenn)-'04	2/2
83	Lewis, Greg	WR	6-0	180	2/12/80	5	Illinois	Matteson, Ill.	FA-'03	16/3
50	McCoy, Matt	LB	5-11	230	10/14/82	3	San Diego State	Tustin, Calif.	D2b-'05	15/10
68	McCoy, Pat	T	6-5	328	12/14/80	2	West Texas	Fairfield, Calif.	FA-'06	0*
95	McDougle, Jerome	DE	6-2	264	12/15/78	5	Miami	Pompano Beach, Fla.	D1-'03	14/0
5	McNabb, Donovan	QB	6-2	240	11/25/76	9	Syracuse	Chicago, Ill.	D1-'99	10/10
27	Mikell, Quintin	S	5-10	206	9/16/80	5	Boise State	Eugene, Ore.	FA-'03	16/1
23	Moats, Ryan	RB	5-8	210	12/17/82	3	Louisiana Tech	Dallas, Texas	D3-'05	8/0
98	Patterson, Mike	DT	6-0	292	9/01/83	3	Southern California	Los Alamitos, Calif.	D1-'05	16/16
77	Ramsey, LaJuan	DT	6-3	291	3/19/84	2	Southern California	Compton, Calif.	D6-'06	6/0
91	Rayburn, Sam	DT	6-3	303	10/20/80	5	Tulsa	Chickasha, Ok.	FA-'03	11/0
94	Reagor, Montae	DT	6-3	285	6/29/77	9	Texas Tech	Waxahachie, Texas	FA-'07	5/5*
52	Richmond, Greg	LB	6-1	235	7/15/81	2	Oklahoma State	Oklahoma City, Ok.	FA-'04	0*
64	Rodgers, Stefan	T	6-3	304	11/03/81	2	Lambuth	North Little Rock, Ark.	FA-'06	0*
53	Roper, Dedrick	LB	6-2	245	7/31/81	3	Northwood	Milpitas, Calif.	FA-'05	8/0
69	Runyan, Jon	T	6-7	330	11/27/73	12	Michigan	Flint, Mich.	UFA(Tenn)-'00	16/16
89	Schobel, Matt	TE	6-5	255	11/04/78	6	Texas Christian	Columbus, Texas	UFA(Cin)-'06	16/4
	Scott, Ian	DT	6-3	305	11/8/81	5	Florida	Gainesville, Fla.	UFA(Chi)-'07	15/7*
26	Sheppard, Lito	CB	5-10	194	4/08/81	6	Florida	Jacksonville, Fla.	D1-'02	13/13
82	Smith, L.J.	TE	6-3	258	5/13/80	5	Rutgers	Highland Park, NJ	D2-'03	16/15
51 t-	Spikes, Takeo	LB	6-2	242	12/17/76	10	Auburn	Sandersville, Ga.	T(Buff)-'07	12/11*
38	Tapeh, Thomas	FB	6-1	243	3/28/80	4	Minnesota	St. Paul, Minn.	D5-'04	16/8
75	Thomas, Juqua	DE	6-2	250	5/15/78	7	Oklahoma State	Houston, Texas	FA-'05	16/1
72	Thomas, William	T	6-7	335	11/20/74	10	Florida State	Deland, Fla.	D1-'98	16/16
54	Trotter, Jeremiah	LB	6-1	262	1/20/77	10	Stephen F. Austin	Hooks, Texas	FA-'04	16/16
36	Westbrook, Brian	RB	5-10	203	9/02/79	6	Villanova	Ft. Washington, Md.	D3-'02	15/14
71	Young, Scott	G	6-4	312	7/15/81	3	Brigham Young	Salt Lake City, Utah	D5b-'05	12/0

* Bloom missed '06 season because of injury; Cain last active with Chicago in '05; Curtis played 16 games with St. Louis in '06; Davis missed '06 season because of injury; Gocong missed '06 season because of injury; Holcomb inactive for 16 games with Buffalo; Jean-Gilles inactive for 16 games; B. Johnson played 11 games with Minnesota; Justice inactive for 16 games; McCoy inactive for 16 games; Reagor played 5 games with Indianapolis; Richmond missed '05 season because of injury; Rodgers missed '06 season because of injury; Scott played 15 games with Chicago; Spikes played 12 games with Buffalo.

t- Eagles traded for Holcomb (Buff) and Spikes (Buff).

Traded —DT Darwin Walker (16 games in '06) to Buffalo.

Players lost through free agency (5): LB Shawn Barber (Hou; 13 games in '06), QB Jeff Garcia (TB; 8), CB Roderick Hood (Ariz; 10), S Michael Lewis (SF; 14), WR Donte Stallworth (NE; 12).

Also played with Eagles in '06—LB Dhani Jones (16 games), RB Reno Mahe (12), RB Bruce Perry (3), LB Jason Short (12), CB Dexter Wynn (6).

2007 FIRST-YEAR ROSTER

Name	Pos.	Ht.	Wt.	Birthdate	College	Hometown	How Acq.
Abiamiri, Victor	DE	6-4	267	1/14/86	Notre Dame	Baltimore, Md.	D2b
Bagwell, Antoine (1)	RB	5-11	190	9/13/84	California (Pa.)	Lansing, Mich.	FA
Barksdale, Rashad	CB	6-0	208	5/11/84	Albany	Hudson, N.Y.	D6
Bradley, Stewart	LB	6-3	254	11/2/83	Nebraska	Salt Lake City, Utah	D3a
Celek, Brent	TE	6-4	255	1/25/85	Cincinnati	Cincinnati, Ohio	D5b
Clark, Jeremy	DT	6-3	309	9/6/83	Alabama	Daphne, Ala.	FA
Cochrane, E.J. (1)	K	5-11	196	10/31/80	Montana State	Philadelphia, Pa.	FA
Collie, Zac	WR	5-11	187	5/17/82	Brigham Young	El Dorado Hills, Calif.	FA
Faulkner, Dereck	WR	6-3	228	5/6/85	Hampton	Moorestown, N.J.	FA
Gaddis, C.J.	S	5-11	203	8/12/85	Clemson	Raeford, N.C.	D5a
Gasperson, Michael (1)	WR	6-4	220	6/10/82	San Diego	Monterey, Calif.	FA-'05
Graham, Nick	CB	5-10	191	1/19/84	Tulsa	Oklahoma City, Okla.	FA
Harris, Erick (1)	S	5-11	208	12/17/82	Liberty	Crestview, Fla.	FA-'06
Harvey, Jasper (1)	C	6-3	305	4/8/83	San Diego State	New Orleans, La.	FA-'06
Hobbs, Jacob	G	6-3	303	2/17/83	Albany	Schenectady, N.Y.	FA
Hunt, Tony	RB	6-1	233	11/24/85	Penn State	Alexandria, Va.	D3b
Ilaoa, Nate	RB	5-9	245	4/4/83	Hawaii	Stafford, Va.	D7
Jamison, Jermaine (1)	WR	6-2	201	4/9/83	Fresno State	Los Angeles, Calif.	FA
Jordan, Akeem	LB	6-1	226	8/17/85	James Madison	Harrisonburg, Va.	FA
Kobel, Craig (1)	LB	6-2	265	1/26/82	South Florida	Lake Worth, Fla.	FA
Kolb, Kevin	QB	6-3	218	8/24/84	Houston	Stephenville, Texas	D2a
Mroz, Jeff (1)	QB	6-5	225	7/11/83	Yale	Greensburg, Pa.	FA
Murrell, Marques	DE	6-2	246	3/20/85	Appalachian State	Fayetteville, N.C.	FA
Outlaw, J.J. (1)	WR	5-9	187	2/8/84	Villanova	Columbia, Md.	FA
Palmer, Jonathan	T	6-4	336	12/3/83	Auburn	Ellenwood, Ga.	FA
Paschal, Marcus	S	6-0	201	8/31/84	Iowa	Largo, Fla.	FA
Rocca, Saverio	P	6-5	265	11/20/73	None	Lakeside, Australia	FA
Sampy, Bill (1)	WR	5-11	192	5/10/83	Louisiana Lafayette	Carencro, La.	FA-'06
Smith, Chris	S	5-10	215	6/3/85	Florida International	Gainesville, Fla.	FA
Tuiasosopo, Zach (1)	FB	6-2	245	12/19/81	Washington	Woodinville, Wash.	FA-'06
Vickers, Lee (1)	TE	6-6	275	3/13/81	North Alabama	Athens, Ga.	FA-'06
White, Chris	G	6-3	321	11/23/83	South Carolina	Chester, S.C.	FA

The term NFL Rookie is defined as a player who is in his first season of professional football and has not been on the roster of another professional football team for any regular-season or postseason games. A Rookie is designated by an "R" on NFL rosters. Players who have been active in another professional football league or players who have NFL experience, including either preseason training camp or being on an Active List or Inactive List, or on Reserve/Injured or Reserve/Physically Unable to Perform for fewer than six regular-season games, are termed NFL First-Year Players. An NFL First-Year Player is designated by a "1" on NFL rosters. Thereafter, a player is credited with an additional year of experience for each season in which he accumulates six games on the Active List or Inactive List, or on Reserve/Injured or Reserve/Physically Unable to Perform.

Log on to www.philadelphiaeagles.com for an up-to-date roster.

COACHING STAFF

Head Coach/Executive Vice President of Football Operations, Andy Reid

Pro Career: Reid has earned NFL coach of the year honors twice, compiled the highest win total (88), winning percentage (.620), and playoff total (8) in team history. He has captured five division titles and four trips to the NFC Championship game. Since he was hired in 1999, no other franchise has earned more divisional playoff round appearances (6) and championship game appearances (4) than Philadelphia. Among coaches with 100 games under their belt entering 2007, Reid's .620 winning percentage is 11th in NFL history and third among active coaches behind Indianapolis' Tony Dungy (.637) and Washington's Joe Gibbs (.635). In his 15-year NFL coaching career, Reid's teams have made the playoffs 12 times (17-11 record). He has coached in the Super Bowl three times, in the NFC Championship game seven times, and in the Pro Bowl four times. Reid became the twentieth head coach in franchise history on January 11, 1999, and was promoted to head coach/executive vice president of football operations in 2001. He was named NFL coach of the year in 2000 and 2002. He joined the Eagles after a seven-year stint as an assistant coach with Green Bay (1992-98) under Mike Holmgren. With Green Bay, Reid helped the Packers earn a Super Bowl XXXI victory over the New England Patriots. Career record: 88-54.

Background: Coached at Brigham Young (1982), San Francisco State (1983-85), Northern Arizona (1986), Texas-El Paso (1987-88), and Missouri (1989-1991). Reid first met Holmgren, who was a member of BYU's coaching staff, when Reid was an offensive tackle and guard on three Cougar Holiday Bowl teams. Reid graduated with a bachelor's degree in physical education. He also received a master's degree in professional leadership in physical education and athletics.

Personal: Born in Los Angeles on March 19, 1958, Reid and his wife Tammy have five children—Garrett, Britt, Crosby, Drew Ann, and Spencer.

ASSISTANT COACHES

Juan Castillo, offensive line; born October 8, 1959, Port Isabel, Texas. Linebacker Texas A&I (now Texas A&M-Kingsville) 1978-1980. Pro linebacker San Antonio Gunslingers (USFL) 1984-85. College coach: Texas A&I/Texas A&M-Kingsville 1982-85, 1990-94. Pro coach: Joined Eagles in 1995.

David Culley, wide receivers; born September 17, 1955, Sparta, Tenn. Quarterback Vanderbilt 1973-77. No pro playing experience. College coach: Austin Peay 1978, Vanderbilt 1979-1981, Middle Tennessee State 1982, Tennessee-Chattanooga 1983, Western Kentucky 1984, Southwestern Louisiana 1985-88, Texas-El Paso 1989-1990, Texas A&M 1991-93. Pro coach: Tampa Bay Buccaneers 1994-95, Pittsburgh Steelers 1996-1998, joined Eagles in 1999.

John Harbaugh, secondary; born September 23, 1962, Perrysburg, Ohio. Defensive back Miami (Ohio) 1980-83. No pro playing experience. College coach: Western Michigan 1984-86, Pittsburgh 1987, Morehead State 1988, Cincinnati 1989-1996, Indiana 1997. Pro coach: Joined Eagles in 1998.

Pete Jenkins, defensive line; born August 27, 1941, Macon, Ga. Linebacker/nose tackle Western Carolina 1963-64. No pro playing experience. College coach: Troy State 1968-1970, South Carolina 1971-74, Southern Mississippi 1975-77, Oklahoma State 1978, Florida 1979, Louisiana State 1980-1990, 2000-02, Mississippi State 1991-94, Auburn 1995-1999. Pro coach: Joined Eagles in 2006.

Jim Johnson, defensive coordinator; born May 26, 1941, Maywood, Ill. Quarterback Missouri 1959-1962. Pro tight end Buffalo Bills 1963-64. College coach: Missouri Southern 1967-68 (head coach), Drake 1969-1972, Indiana 1973-76, Notre Dame 1977-1980. Pro coach: Oklahoma Outlaws (USFL) 1984, Jacksonville Bulls (USFL) 1985, Phoenix Cardinals 1986-1993, Indianapolis Colts 1994-97, Seattle Seahawks 1998, joined Eagles in 1999.

Sean McDermott, linebackers; born March 21, 1974, Omaha, Neb. Safety William & Mary 1994-97. No pro playing experience. College coach: William & Mary 1998. Pro coach: Joined Eagles in 1998.

Tom Melvin, tight ends; born October 1, 1961, Redwood City, Calif. Offensive lineman San Francisco State 1982-83. No pro playing experience. College coach: San Francisco State 1984-85, Northern Arizona 1986-87, California-Santa Barbara 1988-1990, Occidental College 1991-98. Pro coach: Joined Eagles in 1999.

Marty Mornhinweg, asst. head coach/offensive coordinator; born March 29, 1962, Edmond, Okla. Quarterback Montana 1981-84. Pro quarterback Denver Dynamite (AFL) 1987. College coach: Montana 1985, Texas-El Paso 1986-87, Northern Arizona 1988, 1994, Southeast Missouri State 1989-1990, Missouri 1991-93. Pro coach: Green Bay Packers 1995-96, San Francisco 49ers 1997-2000, Detroit Lions 2001-02 (head coach), joined Eagles in 2003.

Jeff Nixon, special teams quality control; born October 16, 1974, Rochester, Pa. Running back West Virginia 1993-94, Penn State 1996. No pro playing experience. College coach: Penn State 1997, Princeton 1998, Shippensburg 1999-2002, Tennessee-Chattanooga 2003-05, Temple 2006. Pro coach: Joined Eagles in 2007.

Ryan Segrest, special teams coordinator; born May 20, 1973, Waycross, Ga. Tackle Alabama 1991-93. No pro playing experience. College coach: Alabama 1994-97, Auburn 1997-98, Southeast Missouri State 1999-2001, Samford 2002-05. Pro coach: Joined Eagles in 2006.

Bill Shuey, defensive assistant/quality control; born October 5, 1974, Bethlehem, Pa. Attended Slippery Rock. No college or pro playing experience. Pro coach: Joined Eagles in 2003.

Pat Shurmur, quarterbacks; born April 14, 1965, Dearborn Heights, Mich. Center Michigan State 1983-87. No pro playing experience. College coach: Michigan State 1988-1997, Stanford 1998. Pro coach: Joined Eagles in 1999.

James Urban, offensive assistant/quality control; born December 1, 1973, Mechanicsburg, Pa. Wide receiver Washington and Lee 1993-96. No pro playing experience. College coach: Clarion 1997-98, Pennsylvania 1999-2004. Pro coach: Joined Eagles in 2007.

Trent Walters, secondary; born November 20. 1943, Knoxville, Tenn. Defensive back Indiana 1963-65. Pro defensive back Edmonton Eskimos (CFL) 1966-67. College coach: Indiana 1968-1971, Louisville 1972, 1986-1990, Indiana 1973-1980, Washington 1981-83, Pittsburgh 1985, Texas A&M 1991-93, Notre Dame 2002-03. Pro coach: Cincinnati Bengals 1984, Minnesota Vikings 1994-2001, joined Eagles in 2004.

Ted Williams, running backs; born November 17, 1943, Lyons, Texas. Attended Cal Poly-Pomona. No college or pro playing experience. College coach: UCLA 1980-89, Washington State 1991-93, Arizona 1994. Pro coach: Joined Eagles in 1995.

Mike Wolf, strength and conditioning; born May 15, 1965, Allentown, Pa. Center Penn State 1983-87. No pro playing experience. College coach: Vanderbilt 1988-89, Lehigh 1990, Penn State 1991. Pro coach: Minnesota Vikings 1992-94, joined Eagles in 1995.

National Football Conference
West Division
Team Colors: New Century Gold,
Millennium Blue, and White
One Rams Way
St. Louis, Missouri 63045
Telephone: (314) 982-7267

2007 SCHEDULE
PRESEASON

Aug. 10	at Minnesota	7:00
Aug. 18	**San Diego**	7:00
Aug. 25	at Oakland	7:00
Aug. 30	**Kansas City**	7:00

REGULAR SEASON

Sep. 9	**Carolina**	12:00
Sep. 16	**San Francisco**	12:00
Sep. 23	at Tampa Bay	1:00
Sep. 30	at Dallas	12:00
Oct. 7	**Arizona**	12:00
Oct. 14	at Baltimore	1:00
Oct. 21	at Seattle	1:15
Oct. 28	**Cleveland**	12:00
Nov. 4	Open Date	
Nov. 11	at New Orleans	12:00
Nov. 18	at San Francisco	1:15
Nov. 25	**Seattle**	12:00
Dec. 2	**Atlanta**	12:00
Dec. 9	at Cincinnati	1:00
Dec. 16	**Green Bay**	12:00
Dec. 20	**Pittsburgh** (Thu.)	7:15
Dec. 30	at Arizona	2:15

Stadium: Edward Jones Dome
(opened in 1995)
•**Capacity:** 66,000
701 Convention Plaza
St. Louis, Missouri 63101
Playing Surface: FieldTurf
Training Camp: Russell Training Center
1 Rams Way
St. Louis, Missouri 63045

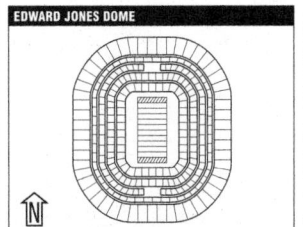

EDWARD JONES DOME

CLUB OFFICIALS
Owner/Chariman: Georgia Frontiere
Owner/Vice Chairman: Stan Kroenke
President: John Shaw
President, Football Operations:
Jay Zygmunt
Executive Vice President and General
Counsel: Bob Wallace
Treasurer: Jeff Brewer
Vice President, Player Personnel:
Tony Softli
Director, Marketing & Sponsorship
Services: Adam Jacobs
Vice President, Business Operation:
Jim McCallum
Vice President, Ticket Operations:
Michael T. Naughton
Vice President, Operations: John Oswald
Vice President, Public Relations:
Rick Smith
Director, Football Administration:
Samir Suleiman
Head Trainer: Jim Anderson
Assistant Trainers: Dake Walden,
James Lomax
Equipment Manager: Todd Hewitt
Scouts: Cary Conklin, Dick Daniels,
Luke Driscoll, Mel Foels, John Mancini

COACHING HISTORY
Cleveland 1937-1945,
Los Angeles 1946-1994
(517-465-20)
Records include postseason games

1937-38	Hugo Bezdek*	1-13-0
1938	Art Lewis	4-4-0
1939-1942	Earl (Dutch) Clark	16-26-2
1944	Aldo (Buff) Donelli	4-6-0
1945-46	Adam Walsh	16-5-1
1947	Bob Snyder	6-6-0
1948-49	Clark Shaughnessy	14-8-3
1950-52	Joe Stydahar**	19-9-0
1952-54	Hamp Pool	23-11-2
1955-59	Sid Gillman	28-32-1
1960-62	Bob Waterfield***	9-24-1
1962-65	Harland Svare	14-31-3
1966-1970	George Allen	49-19-4
1971-72	Tommy Prothro	14-12-2
1973-77	Chuck Knox	57-20-1
1978-1982	Ray Malavasi	43-36-0
1983-1991	John Robinson	79-74-0
1992-94	Chuck Knox	15-33-0
1995-96	Rich Brooks	13-19-0
1997-99	Dick Vermeil	25-26-0
2000-05	Mike Martz****	56-36-0
2005	Joe Vitt	4-7-0
2006	Scott Linehan	8-8-0

* Released after three games in 1938
** Resigned after one game in 1952
*** Resigned after eight games in 1962
**** Took medical leave after five games in 2005

PAID ATTENDANCE
Home 509,010   Away 511,368
Total 1,020,378
Single-game home record,
66,273 (12/10/00)
Single-season home record,
520,926 (1999)

2007 DRAFT CHOICES

Round	Name	Pos.	College
1	Adam Carriker	DE	Nebraska
2	Brian Leonard	RB	Rutgers
3	Jonathan Wade	DB	Tennessee
5	Dustin Fry	C	Clemson
	Clifton Ryan	DT	Michigan State
6	Ken Shackleford	T	Georgia
7	Keith Jackson	DT	Arkansas
	Derek Stanley	WR	Wis.-Whitewater

2006 TEAM RECORD

PRESEASON (1-3)

Date	Result	Opponent
8/10	W 19-17	Indianapolis
8/19	L 20-27	Houston
8/26	L 12-16	at Kansas City
8/31	L 9-29	at Miami

REGULAR SEASON (8-8)

Date	Result	Opponent	Att.
9/10	W 18-10	Denver	65,577
9/17	L 13-20	at San Francisco	67,791
9/24	W 16-14	at Arizona	63,278
10/1	W 41-34	Detroit	65,563
10/8	W 23-20	at Green Bay	70,804
10/15	L 28-30	Seattle	65,592
10/29	L 24-38	at San Diego	66,598
11/5	L 17-31	Kansas City	66,191
11/12	L 22-24	at Seattle	68,175
11/19	L 0-15	at Carolina	73,348
11/26	W 20-17	San Francisco	65,517
12/3	L 20-34	Arizona	65,612
12/11	L 27-42	Chicago	66,234
12/17	W 20-0	at Oakland	50,164
12/24	W 37-31	Washington (OT)	62,324
12/31	W 41-21	at Minnesota	63,557

(OT) Overtime

SCORE BY PERIODS

Rams	53	136	74	98	6 —	367
Opponents	76	106	79	120	0 —	381

2006 TEAM STATISTICS

	Rams	Opp.
Total First Downs	332	313
Rushing	94	121
Passing	212	164
Penalty	26	28
3rd Down: Made/Att	83/222	93/205
3rd Down Pct.	37.4	45.4
4th Down: Made/Att	12/18	2/6
4th Down Pct.	66.7	33.3
Possession Avg.	31:07	28:53
Total Net Yards	5,767	5,362
Avg. Per Game	360.4	335.1
Total Plays	1,065	962
Avg. Per Play	5.4	5.6
Net Yards Rushing	1,805	2,327
Avg. Per Game	112.8	145.4
Total Rushes	424	477
Net Yards Passing	3,962	3,035
Avg. Per Game	247.6	189.7
Sacked/Yards Lost	49/366	34/214
Gross Yards	4,328	3,249
Att./Completions	592/371	451/266
Completion Pct.	62.7	59.0
Had Intercepted	8	17
Punts/Average	76/42.4	67/45.2
Net Punting Avg.	76/37.8	67/39.0
Penalties/Yards	116/960	92/835
Fumbles/Ball Lost	20/10	24/15
Touchdowns	39	46
Rushing	13	21
Passing	24	21
Returns	2	4

2006 INDIVIDUAL STATISTICS

PASSING

	Att.	Comp.	Yds.	Pct.	TD	Int.	Tkld.	Rate
Bulger	588	370	4,301	62.9	24	8	49/366	92.9
Frerotte	3	1	27	33.3	0	0	0/0	67.4
Bruce	1	0	—	0.0	0	0	0/0	39.6
Rams	592	371	4,328	62.7	24	8	49/366	92.7
Opponents	451	266	3,249	59.0	21	17	34/214	81.1

SCORING

	TD R	TD P	TD Rt	PAT	FG	Saf	PTS
Wilkins	0	0	0	35/35	32/37	0	131
Jackson	13	3	0	0/0	0/0	0	96
Holt	0	10	0	0/0	0/0	0	60
Curtis	0	4	0	0/0	0/0	0	24
Bruce	0	3	0	0/0	0/0	0	20
Adeyanju	0	0	1	0/0	0/0	0	6
Bartell	0	0	1	0/0	0/0	0	6
Byrd	0	1	0	0/0	0/0	0	6
Davis	0	1	0	0/0	0/0	0	6
Klopfenstein	0	1	0	0/0	0/0	0	6
McDonald	0	1	0	0/0	0/0	0	6
Rams	13	24	2	35/35	32/37	0	367
Opponents	21	21	4	46/46	19/24	1	381

2-Pt. Conversions: Bruce, Rams 1-3,
Opponents 0-0.

RUSHING

	No.	Yds	Avg	LG	TD
Jackson	346	1,528	4.4	59t	13
Davis	40	177	4.4	16	0
Bulger	18	44	2.4	29	0
Turk	2	19	9.5	16	0
Looker	1	13	13.0	13	0
To. Fisher	6	9	1.5	4	0
Kay-Jay Harris	3	9	3.0	9	0
Curtis	4	4	1.0	7	0
Hedgecock	1	2	2.0	2	0
Fitzpatrick	3	0	0.0	2	0
Rams	424	1,805	4.3	59t	13
Opponents	477	2,327	4.9	51	21

RECEIVING

	No.	Yds	Avg	LG	TD
Holt	93	1,188	12.8	67t	10
Jackson	90	806	9.0	64t	3
Bruce	74	1,098	14.8	45	3
Curtis	40	479	12.0	42	4
Klopfenstein	20	226	11.3	28	1
To. Fisher	14	159	11.4	28	0
McDonald	13	136	10.5	28	1
Davis	12	90	7.5	18	1
Hedgecock	7	29	4.1	7	0
Walker	5	68	13.6	26	0
Byrd	2	39	19.5	27t	1
Kay-Jay Harris	1	10	10.0	10	0
Rams	371	4,328	11.7	67t	24
Opponents	266	3,249	12.2	72t	21

INTERCEPTIONS

	No.	Yds	Avg	LG	TD
Bartell	3	63	21.0	38t	1
Hill	3	20	6.7	14	0
F. Brown	3	17	5.7	20	0
Atogwe	3	8	2.7	7	0
Carter	2	39	19.5	36	0
Coakley	2	0	0.0	0	0
Chavous	1	17	17.0	17	0
Rams	17	164	9.6	38t	1
Opponents	8	118	14.8	56	0

PUNTING

	No.	Yds.	Avg.	In 20	LG
Turk	72	3,132	43.5	26	74
Wilkins	3	91	30.3	3	33
Rams	76	3,223	42.4	29	74
Opponents	67	3,026	45.2	20	66

PUNT RETURNS

	Ret	FC	Yds	Avg	LG	TD
McDonald	23	14	172	7.5	33	0
Looker	7	6	47	6.7	10	0
Ponder	0	0	15	—	15	0
Rams	30	20	234	7.8	33	0
Opponents	27	22	247	9.1	90t	1

KICKOFF RETURNS

	No.	Yds	Avg	LG	TD
Ponder	26	605	23.3	40	0
Reed	17	346	20.4	40	0
Curtis	9	188	20.9	28	0
To. Fisher	8	165	20.6	26	0
Kay-Jay Harris	4	76	19.0	23	0
P. Smith	1	3	3.0	3	0
Rams	65	1,383	21.3	40	0
Opponents	69	1,701	24.7	96t	2

FIELD GOALS

	1-19	20-29	30-39	40-49	50+
Wilkins	1/1	11/11	6/6	11/16	3/3
Rams	1/1	11/11	6/6	11/16	3/3
Opponents	0/0	7/7	5/7	5/8	2/2

SACKS

	No.
Little	13.0
Glover	5.5
Witherspoon	3.0
Chillar	2.0
Tinoisamoa	2.0
R. Smith	1.5
Adeyanju	1.0
Atogwe	1.0
F. Brown	1.0
Chavous	1.0
Kennedy	1.0
Wroten	1.0
Green	0.5
Hargrove	0.5
Rams	34.0
Opponents	49.0

RECORD HOLDERS
INDIVIDUAL RECORDS—CAREER

Category	Name	Performance
Rushing (Yds.)	Eric Dickerson, 1983-87	7,245
Passing (Yds.)	Jim Everett, 1986-1993	23,758
Passing (TDs)	Roman Gabriel, 1962-1972	154
Receiving (No.)	Isaac Bruce, 1994-2006	887
Receiving (Yds.)	Isaac Bruce, 1994-2006	13,376
Interceptions	Ed Meador, 1959-1970	46
Punting (Avg.)	Danny Villanueva, 1960-64	44.3
Punt Return (Avg.)	Az-Zahir Hakim, 1998-2001	11.4
Kickoff Return (Avg.)	Ron Brown, 1984-89, 1991	26.3
Field Goals	Jeff Wilkins, 1997-2006	241
Touchdowns (Tot.)	Marshall Faulk, 1999-2005	85
Points	Jeff Wilkins, 1997-2006	1,126

INDIVIDUAL RECORDS—SINGLE SEASON

Category	Name	Performance
Rushing (Yds.)	Eric Dickerson, 1984	*2,105
Passing (Yds.)	Kurt Warner, 2001	4,830
Passing (TDs)	Kurt Warner, 1999	41
Receiving (No.)	Isaac Bruce, 1995	119
Receiving (Yds.)	Isaac Bruce, 1995	1,781
Interceptions	Dick (Night Train) Lane, 1952	*14
Punting (Avg.)	Danny Villanueva, 1962	45.5
Punt Return (Avg.)	Woodley Lewis, 1952	18.5
Kickoff Return (Avg.)	Verda (Vitamin T) Smith, 1950	33.7
Field Goals	Jeff Wilkins, 2003	39
Touchdowns (Tot.)	Marshall Faulk, 2000	26
Points	Jeff Wilkins, 2003	163

INDIVIDUAL RECORDS—SINGLE GAME

Category	Name	Performance
Rushing (Yds.)	Willie Ellison, 12-5-71	247
Passing (Yds.)	Norm Van Brocklin, 9-28-51	*554
Passing (TDs)	Many times	5
	Last time by Kurt Warner, 10-10-99	
Receiving (No.)	Tom Fears, 12-3-50	18
Receiving (Yds.)	Willie Anderson, 11-26-89	*336
Interceptions	Many times	3
	Last time by Keith Lyle, 12-15-96	
Field Goals	Bob Waterfield, 12-9-51	5
	Jeff Wilkins, 10-1-00	5
Touchdowns (Tot.)	Many times	4
	Last time by Marshall Faulk, 10-20-02	
Points	Many times	24
	Last time by Marshall Faulk, 10-20-02	

*NFL Record

2007 VETERAN ROSTER

No.	Name	Pos.	Ht.	Wt.	Birthdate	NFL Exp.	College	Hometown	How Acq.	'06 Games/ Starts
94	Adeyanju, Victor	DE	6-4	270	2/11/83	2	Indiana	Chicago, Ill.	D4-'06	12/9
32	Alexis, Rich	RB	6-0	213	5/6/81	3	Washington	Coral Springs, Fla.	FA-'06	0*
57	Alston, Jon	LB	6-0	221	6/4/83	2	Stanford	Shreveport, La.	D3b-'06	3/0
49	Anelli, Mark	TE	6-3	265	6/5/79	4	Wisconsin	Addison, Ill.	FA-'06	0*
21	Atogwe, Oshiomogho	S	5-11	210	6/23/81	3	Stanford	Windsor, Ontario, Canada	D3a-'05	16/16
70	Barron, Alex	T	6-7	315	9/28/82	3	Florida State	Orangeburg, S.C.	D1-'05	16/16
24	Bartell, Ron	CB	6-1	200	2/22/82	3	Howard	Detroit, Mich.	D2-'05	16/0
83	Bennett, Drew	WR	6-5	206	8/26/78	7	UCLA	Orinda, Calif.	UFA(Tenn)-'07	16/15*
34	Brown, Fakhir	CB	5-11	192	9/21/77	8	Grambling State	Mansfield, La.	UFA(NO)-'06	14/14
80	Bruce, Isaac	WR	6-0	188	11/10/72	14	Memphis State	Fort Lauderdale, Fla.	D2A-'94	16/13
10	Bulger, Marc	QB	6-3	212	4/5/77	7	West Virginia	Pittsburgh, Pa.	FA-'01	16/16
23	Butler, Jerametrius	CB	5-10	185	11/28/78	7	Kansas State	Dallas, Texas	D5-'01	6/0
86	Byrd, Dominique	TE	6-2	254	2/7/84	2	Southern California	Golden Valley, Minn.	D3c-'06	5/0
42	Carter, Jerome	S	5-11	219	10/25/82	3	Florida State	Lake City, Fla.	D4a-'05	14/0
25	Chavous, Corey	S	6-1	208	1/5/76	10	Vanderbilt	Aiken, S.C.	UFA(Minn)-'06	16/16
54	Chillar, Brandon	LB	6-3	242	10/21/82	4	UCLA	Carlsbad, Calif.	D4-'04	16/15
52	Draft, Chris	LB	5-11	232	2/26/76	9	Stanford	Placentia, Calif.	UFA(Car)-'07	16/16*
28	Faulk, Marshall	RB	5-10	211	2/26/73	14	San Diego State	New Orleans, La.	T(Ind)-'99	0*
11	Fitzpatrick, Ryan	QB	6-2	221	11/24/82	3	Harvard	Gilbert, Ariz.	D7a-'05	1/0
12	Frerotte, Gus	QB	6-3	233	7/31/71	14	Tulsa	Ford City, Pa.	FA-'06	1/0
97	Glover, La'Roi	DT	6-2	290	7/4/74	12	San Diego State	San Diego, Calif.	FA-'06	16/16
72	Goldberg, Adam	G	6-7	310	8/12/80	5	Wyoming	Edina, Minn.	T(Minn)-'06	15/2
82 t-	Hall, Dante	WR	5-8	187	9/20/78	8	Texas A&M	Houston, Texas	T(KC)-'07	15/0*
96 t-	Hall, James	DE	6-2	280	2/4/77	8	Michigan	New Orleans, La.	T(Det)-'07	7/7*
33	Harris, Kay-Jay	RB	6-0	229	3/27/79	2	West Virginia	Tampa, Fla.	FA-'06	7/0
44	Hedgecock, Madison	RB	6-3	266	8/27/81	3	North Carolina	Wallburg, N.C.	D7b-'05	16/9
26	Hill, Tye	CB	5-10	185	6/3/82	2	Clemson	St. George, S.C.	D1-'06	16/10
81	Holt, Torry	WR	6-0	190	6/5/76	9	North Carolina State	Greensboro, N.C.	D1-'99	16/16
68	Incognito, Richie	G	6-3	305	7/5/83	3	Nebraska	Glendale, Ariz.	D3b-'05	16/16
39	Jackson, Steven	RB	6-2	231	7/22/83	4	Oregon State	Las Vegas, Nev.	D1-'04	16/16
35	Johnson, Todd	S	6-1	200	12/18/78	5	Florida	Sarasota, Fla.	UFA(Chi)-'07	12/6*
93	Johnson, Trevor	DE	6-4	260	2/26/81	4	Nebraska	Lincoln, Neb.	W(NO)-'07	1/0*
5	Jones, Donnie	P	6-3	222	7/5/80	4	Louisiana State	Baton Rouge, La.	RFA(Mia)-'07	16/0*
73	Kennedy, Jimmy	DT	6-4	325	11/15/79	5	Penn State	Yonkers, N.Y.	D1-'03	16/16
88	Klopfenstein, Joe	TE	6-5	256	11/9/83	2	Colorado	Aurora, Colo.	D2-'06	16/16
91	Little, Leonard	DE	6-3	263	10/19/74	10	Tennessee	Asheville, N.C.	D3-'98	16/16
89	Looker, Dane	WR	6-0	194	5/5/76	7	Washington	Puyallup, Wash.	FA-'02	16/0
45	Massey, Chris	LS	6-0	245	8/21/79	6	Marshall	Chesapeake, W.Va.	D7-'02	16/0
67	McCollum, Andy	C	6-4	300	6/2/70	14	Toledo	Richfield, Ohio	UFA(NO)-'99	1/1
84	McMichael, Randy	TE	6-3	255	6/28/79	6	Georgia	Fort Valley, Ga.	FA-'07	16/16*
22	Minor, Travis	RB	5-10	203	6/30/79	7	Florida State	Baton Rouge, La.	UFA(Mia)-'07	16/0*
92	Moore, Eric	DE	6-4	268	2/28/81	3	Florida State	Pahokee, Fla.	FA-'06	7/0*
76	Pace, Orlando	T	6-7	325	11/4/75	11	Ohio State	Sandusky, Ohio	D1-'97	8/8
64	Parquet, Jeremy	T	6-6	321	4/11/82	3	Southern Mississippi	Destrehan, La.	FA-'06	0*
65	Romberg, Brett	C	6-2	298	10/10/79	4	Miami	Windsor, Ontario, Canada	FA-'06	10/3
31	Rumph, Mike	CB	6-2	206	11/8/79	6	Miami	Delray Beach, Fla.	FA-'07	7/0*
66	Setterstrom, Mark	G	6-4	314	3/3/84	2	Minnesota	Northfield, Minn.	D7b-'06	7/6
56	Smith, Raonall	LB	6-2	245	10/22/78	6	Washington State	Gig Harbor, Wash.	UFA(Minn)-'06	16/0
79	Steussie, Todd	T	6-6	310	12/1/70	14	California	Agoura, Calif.	UFA(TB)-'06	16/15
75	Terrell, Claude	G	6-2	330	4/20/82	3	New Mexico	LaMarque, Texas	D4b-'05	0*
17	Thompson, Dominique	WR	5-11	205	12/28/82	2	William & Mary	Durham, N.C.	FA-'05	0*
50	Tinoisamoa, Pisa	LB	6-1	235	7/15/81	5	Hawaii	Vista, Calif.	D2-'03	11/11
87	Walker, Aaron	TE	6-6	261	3/14/80	5	Florida	Titusville, Fla.	FA-'05	16/6
27	Walls, Lenny	CB	6-4	192	9/26/79	6	Boston College	San Francisco, Calif.	UFA(KC)-'07	16/2*
14	Wilkins, Jeff	K	6-2	205	4/19/72	14	Youngstown State	Austintown, Ohio	RFA(SF)-'97	16/0
51	Witherspoon, Will	LB	6-1	234	8/19/80	6	Georgia	Panama City, Fla.	UFA(Car)-'06	16/16
99	Wroten, Claude	DT	6-2	295	9/16/83	2	Louisiana State	Bastrop, La.	D3a-'06	15/0

* Alexis inactive for 3 games; Anelli last active with San Francisco in '02; Bennett played 16 games with Tennessee in '06; Draft played 16 games with Carolina; D. Hall played 15 games with Kansas City; J. Hall played 7 games with Detroit; Faulk missed '06 season because of injury; Todd Johnson played 12 games with Chicago; Tr. Johnson played 1 game with New Orleans; Jones played 16 games with Miami; McMichael played 16 games with Miami; Minor played 16 games with Miami; Moore played 4 games with New Orleans and 3 games with St. Louis; Parquet inactive for 3 games; Rumph played 7 games with Washington; Terrell missed '06 season because of injury; Thompson last active with St. Louis in '05; Walls played 16 games with Kansas City.

t- Rams traded for D. Hall (KC) and J. Hall (Det).

Players lost through free agency (5): WR Kevin Curtis (Phil; 16 games in '06), CB Travis Fisher (Det; 9), DE Brandon Green (Sea; 13), WR Shaun McDonald (Det; 16), FB Paul Smith (Den; 10).

Also played with Rams in '06—LB Jamal Brooks (7 games), S Dwaine Carpenter (9), LB Dexter Coakley (16), RB Stephen Davis (15), RB Tony Fisher (8), DT Jason Fisk (16), DE Anthony Hargrove (4), LB Isaiah Kacyvenski (10), WR Willie Ponder (6), CB/S J.R. Reed (6), G Adam Timmerman (13), P Matt Turk (16), G/C Larry Turner (1).

2007 FIRST-YEAR ROSTER

Name	Pos.	Ht.	Wt.	Birthdate	College	Hometown	How Acq.
Barrett, Lamart	WR	6-0	191	8/9/83	North Carolina State	Miami Springs, Fla.	FA
Buches, Steve	TE	6-3	251	3/8/84	Pittsburgh	Pittsburgh, Pa.	FA
Capshaw, Fred (1)	P	5-11	183	12/27/79	Miami	Rock Springs, Wyo.	FA
Carriker, Adam	DE/DT	6-6	296	5/6/84	Nebraska	Kennewick, Wash.	D1
Culberson, Quinton	LB	6-1	236	10/21/85	Mississippi State	Jackson, Miss.	FA
Daniels, Stanley	G	6-3	328	11/30/84	Washington	San Diego, Calif.	FA
Dukes, Jeffery	S	6-1	207	4/24/85	Alabama	Oxford, Miss.	FA
Fry, Dustin	C	6-3	314	10/3/83	Clemson	Summerville, S.C.	D5a
Hagans, Marques (1)	WR	5-10	205	12/29/82	Virginia	Hampton, Va.	D5-'06
Jackson, Keith	DT	6-0	305	2/25/85	Arkansas	Little Rock, Ark.	D7a
James, Anthony	T	6-5	262	6/4/84	Louisiana Tech	Baton Rouge, La.	FA
Kirkland, Andre	S	6-0	204	10/2/84	Kent State	Upper Marlboro, Md.	FA
Lau, Brad	RB	6-0	237	4/17/81	Boise State	Boise, Idaho	FA
Lay, Josh (1)	CB	6-1	197	9/8/82	Pittsburgh	Valley Forge, Pa.	FA-'06
Leonard, Brian	RB	6-1	226	2/3/84	Rutgers	Gouverneur, N.Y.	D2
Lovell, Kevin	K	5-9	155	4/14/84	Cincinnati	Manhattan Beach, Calif.	FA
McGarigle, Tim (1)	LB	6-0	238	10/25/83	Northwestern	Chicago, Ill.	D7a-'06
McLee, Kevin	LB	6-0	244	11/24/83	West Virginia	Uniontown, Pa.	FA
Messner, Chris	T	6-6	282	10/9/83	Oklahoma	Frederick, Okla.	FA
Morton, Nate	WR	6-2	213	9/2/82	Wake Forest	Harlingen, Texas	FA
Pettway, Alton	DE	6-1	242	1/25/84	Albany State (Ga.)	Bay Minette, Ala.	FA
Reaves, Terrance	CB	6-0	207	4/2/85	Villanova	Gibsonton, Fla.	FA
Ryan, Clifton	DT	6-3	310	2/18/84	Michigan State	Saginaw, Mich.	D5b
Sandidge, Tim (1)	DT	6-1	300	6/12/83	Virginia Tech	Madison Heights, Va.	W(KC)
Shackleford, Ken	T	6-5	322	2/2/85	Georgia	Villa Rica, Ga.	D6
Smith, Shaine	WR	6-2	189	12/25/83	Hofstra	Jamaica, N.Y.	FA
Stanley, Derek	WR	5-11	179	8/27/85	Wisconsin-Whitewater	Verona, Wis.	D7b
Strojny, Drew (1)	T	6-7	305	6/30/81	Duke	Westwood, Mass.	FA-'05
Tate, Drew	QB	5-11	200	10/8/84	Iowa	Baytown, Texas	FA
Thompson, David	G	6-2	309	2/22/83	Massachusetts	Virginia Beach, Va.	FA
Vinnett, Darius	CB	5-8	170	9/30/84	Arkansas	Destrehan, La.	FA
Wade, Jonathan	CB	5-10	195	3/27/84	Tennessee	Shreveport, La.	D3
Washington, John David (1)	RB	5-9	208	7/28/84	Morehouse	Toluca Lake, Calif.	FA-'06
White, Markee	WR	6-6	210	10/4/83	Texas State	Long Beach, Calif.	FA
Willis, Ryan	DE	6-3	265	10/5/83	Louisiana State	New Orleans, La.	FA

The term NFL Rookie is defined as a player who is in his first season of professional football and has not been on the roster of another professional football team for any regular-season or postseason games. A Rookie is designated by an "R" on NFL rosters. Players who have been active in another professional football league or players who have NFL experience, including either preseason training camp or being on an Active List or Inactive List, or on Reserve/Injured or Reserve/Physically Unable to Perform for fewer than six regular-season games, are termed NFL First-Year Players. An NFL First-Year Player is designated by a "1" on NFL rosters. Thereafter, a player is credited with an additional year of experience for each season in which he accumulates six games on the Active List or Inactive List, or on Reserve/Injured or Reserve/Physically Unable to Perform.

Log on to www.stlouisrams.com for an up-to-date roster.

COACHING STAFF

Head Coach,
Scott Linehan

Pro Career: Named twenty-second head coach in franchise history by Owner/Chairman Georgia Frontiere on January 19, 2006. Rallied the Rams to 8-8 finish. Quarterback Marc Bulger enjoyed the best season of his career, including 4,301 yards passing and 24 touchdowns. Balancing the offensive attack, Linehan guided Steven Jackson to lead the league with 2,234 combined yards, and set a Rams record for a running back with 90 catches. Prior to joining the Rams Linehan was the offensive coordinator of the Miami Dolphins; the Dolphins improved from 29th in 2004 to 14th in total offense in 2005. Linehan spent three seasons (2002-04) as offensive coordinator for the Minnesota Vikings. In 2004, Daunte Culpepper posted the fourth-highest single season passer rating in NFL history (110.9). A college quarterback, Linehan was a free agent signee with the Dallas Cowboys before a shoulder injury ended his active career. Career record: 8-8.

Background: Linehan was an assistant coach on the collegiate level at Idaho (1989-1990, 1992-93), Nevada-Las Veags (1991), Washington (1994-1998) and Louisville (1999-2001). Played quarterback at Idaho under Dennis Erickson (1982-86). The Vandals won the Big Sky Championship (1985) and made three consecutive playoff appearances (1984-86).

Personal: Born September 17, 1963 in Sunnyside, Wash. He and his wife, Kristen, have three sons: Matthew, Michael, and Marcus.

ASSISTANT COACHES

Brian Baker, defensive line; born June 20, 1962, Baltimore. Linebacker Maryland 1980-83. No pro playing experience. College coach: Maryland 1984-85, Army 1986, Georgia Tech 1987-1995. Pro coach: San Diego Chargers 1996, Detroit Lions 1997-2000, Minnesota Vikings 2001-05, joined Rams in 2006.

Paul Boudreau, offensive line; born December 30, 1949, Arlington, Mass. Offensive lineman Boston College 1971-73. No pro playing experience. College coach: Boston College 1974-75, Maine 1976-78, Dartmouth 1979-1981, Navy 1982. Pro coach: Edmonton Eskimos (CFL) 1983-86, New Orleans Saints 1987-1993, Detroit Lions 1994-96, New England Patriots 1997-98, Miami Dolphins 1999-2000, Carolina Panthers 2001-02, Jacksonville Jaguars 2003-05, joined Rams in 2006.

Jim Chaney, asst. offensive line; born January 12, 1962, Warrensburg, Mo. Guard Central Missouri State 1981-85. No pro playing experience. College coach: Cal State-Fullerton 1985-1992, Wyoming 1993-1996, Purdue 1997-2005. Pro coach: Joined Rams in 2006.

Mike Cox, defensive quality control/asst. defensive line; born March 12, 1965,

Coeur d' Alene, Idaho. Linebacker Idaho 1983-86. No pro playing experience. College coach: Idaho 1987-1994, Utah State 1995-97, Louisville 1998-2002, Michigan State 2002-06. Pro coach: Joined Rams in 2007.

Todd Downing, coaching/special teams assistant; born July 22, 1980, Eden Prairie, Minn. Attended Minnesota. No college or pro playing experience. Pro coach: Minnesota Vikings 2003-05, joined Rams in 2006.

Henry Ellard, wide receivers; born July 21, 1961, Fresno, Calif. Wide receiver Fresno State 1979-1982. Pro wide receiver/punt returner Los Angeles Rams 1983-1993, Washington Redskins 1994-97, New England Patriots 1998, Washington Redskins 1998. College coach: Fresno State 2000. Pro coach: Joined Rams in 2001.

Judd Garrett, tight ends; born June 25, 1967, Abington, Pa. Running back Princeton 1987-89. Pro running back London Monarchs (WLAF) 1991-92, Dallas Cowboys 1993, Las Vegas Posse (CFL) 1994, San Antonio Texans (CFL) 1995. College coach: Princeton 1990. Pro coach: New Orleans Saints 1997-99, Miami Dolphins 2000-05, joined Rams in 2006.

Jim Haslett, defensive coordinator; born December 9, 1955, Pittsburgh. Defensive end Indiana (Pa.) 1975-1978. Pro linebacker Buffalo Bills 1979-1986, N.Y. Jets 1987. College coach: Buffalo 1988-1990, Pittsburgh 1997-99. Pro coach: Sacramento Surge (NFLE) 1991-92, Los Angeles Raiders 1993-94, New Orleans Saints 1995-96, 2000-05 (head coach 2000-05), joined Rams in 2006.

Jeff Horton, special assistant/offense; born July 13, 1957, Tulsa, Okla. Attended Nevada. No college or pro playing experience. College coach: Minnesota 1984, Nevada 1985-89, 1992-93, Nevada-Las Vegas 1990-91, 1994-98 (head coach 1994-98), Wisconsin 1999-2005, Iowa State 2006. Pro coach: Joined Rams in 2006.

Dana LeDuc, strength and conditioning; born March 22, 1953, Tacoma, Wash. Attended Texas. No college or pro playing experience. College coach: Texas 1977-1992, Miami 1993-94. Pro coach: Seattle Seahawks 1995-98, joined Rams in 1999.

Ron Milus, asst. secondary; born November 25, 1963, Tacoma, Wash. Cornerback-punt returner Washington 1982-1985. No pro playing experience. College coach: Washington 1991-98, Texas A&M 1999. Pro coach: Denver Broncos 2000-02, Arizona Cardinals 2003, New York Giants 2004-05, joined Rams in 2006.

Wayne Moses, running backs, born January 11, 1955, New Gulf, Texas. Washington 1975-78. No pro playing experience. College coach: Cal State-Fullerton 1978, Chaffey (Calif) J.C. 1980, Bowling Green 1981-83, Rutgers 1984-1985, San Diego State 1986-88, New Mexico 1989, UCLA 1990-95, 2001, California 1996, Washington 1997-2000,

Stanford 2002-03, 2005. Pro coach: Joined Rams in 2006.

Keith Murphy, offensive quality control; born July 7, 1974, Seattle. Wide receiver Washington 1992-95. No pro playing experience. College coach: Washington 1997-98, Eastern Washington 1999-2006. Pro coach: Joined Rams in 2007.

Doug Nussmeier, quarterbacks, born December 11, 1970, Portland, Ore. Quarterback Idaho 1990-93. Pro quarterback New Orleans Saints 1994-97, Indianapolis Colts 1998, British Columbia Lions (CFL) 2000. College coach: Michigan State 2003-05. Pro coach: British Columbia Lions (CFL) 2001, Ottawa Renegades (CFL) 2002, joined Rams in 2006.

Greg Olson, offensive coordinator; born March 1, 1963, Richland, Wash. Quarterback Central Washington 1983-86. No pro playing experience. College coach: Washington State 1987-89, Central Washington 1990-93, Idaho 1994-96, Purdue 1997-2000, 2002. Pro coach: San Francisco 49ers 2001, Chicago Bears 2003, Lions 2004-05, joined Rams in 2006.

Al Roberts, special teams; born January 6, 1944, Fresno, Calif. Running back Washington 1964-65, Puget Sound. No pro playing experience. College coach: Washington 1977-1982, 1996, Wyoming 1986, Purdue 1987. Pro coach: L.A. Express (USFL) 1983-84, Houston Oilers 1984-85, Philadelphia Eagles 1988-1990, New York Jets 1991-93, Arizona Cardinals 1994-95, Cincinnati Bengals 1997-2002, joined Rams in 2007.

Willy Robinson, secondary; born February 10, 1956, Ft. Carson, Colo. Defensive back Fresno State 1976-77. College coach: Fresno State 1978, 1980-1993, San Jose State 1979, Miami 1994, Oregon State 1999. Pro coach: Seattle Seahawks 1995-98, Pittsburgh Steelers 2000-03, San Francisco 49ers 2004, New Orleans Saints 2005, joined Rams in 2006.

Brad Roll, asst. strength & conditioning; born July 4, 1958, Houston. Center Blinn (Tex.) J.C. 1976-77, Stephen F. Austin 1978-79. No pro playing experience. College coach: Stephen F. Austin 1980, Southwestern Louisiana 1981-86, Kansas 1987-88, Miami 1989-1992. Pro coach: Tampa Bay Buccaneers 1993-95, Miami Dolphins 1996-2003, Buffalo Bills 2004-05, joined Rams in 2006.

Rick Venturi, asst. head coach/linebackers; born February 23, 1946, Taylorville, Ill. Quarterback/defensive back Northwestern 1965-67. No pro playing experience. College coach: Northwestern 1968-1972, 1978-1980 (head coach 1978-1980), Purdue 1973-76, Illinois 1977. Pro coach: Hamilton Tiger-Cats (CFL) 1981, Indianapolis Colts 1982-1993 (interim head coach for final 11 games of 1991), Cleveland Browns 1994-95, Saints 1996-2005 (interim head coach for final eight games of 1996), joined Rams in 2006.

**National Football Conference
West Division**
Team Colors: Metalllic Gold,
Cardinal Red, and Beige
**4949 Centennial Boulevard
Santa Clara, California 95054
Telephone: (408) 562-4949**

2007 SCHEDULE
PRESEASON
Aug. 13 **Denver** 5:00
Aug. 18 **Oakland** 7:00
Aug. 25 at Chicago...........................7:00
Aug. 30 at San Diego.......................7:00

REGULAR SEASON
Sep. 10 **Arizona** (Mon.)...................7:15
Sep. 16 at St. Louis 12:00
Sep. 23 at Pittsburgh 1:00
Sep. 30 **Seattle** 1:05
Oct. 7 **Baltimore** 1:15
Oct. 14 Open Date
Oct. 21 at N.Y. Giants.....................1:00
Oct. 28 **New Orleans** 1:15
Nov. 4 at Atlanta 1:00
Nov. 12 at Seattle (Mon.) 5:30
Nov. 18 **St. Louis** 1:15
Nov. 25 at Arizona 2:05
Dec. 2 at Carolina 1:00
Dec. 9 **Minnesota** 1:05
Dec. 15 **Cincinnati** (Sat).................5:15
Dec. 23 **Tampa Bay** *5:15
Dec. 30 at Cleveland Browns...........1:00
Sunday night games in Weeks 11-17 subject to change

Stadium: Monster Park (opened in 1958)
•**Capacity:** 69,732
San Francisco, California
94124
Playing Surface: Natural Grass
Training Camp: Marie P. DeBartolo
Sports Center
4949 Centennial Boulevard
Santa Clara, CA 95054

MONSTER PARK

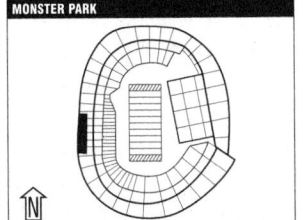

CLUB OFFICIALS
OWNERSHIP
Owner: The DeBartolo Corporation
Owner: Denise DeBartolo York
Owner: Dr. John York
Limited Partner: Franklin Mieuli
Limited Partner: Rick and Carla Morabito
MANAGEMENT
Executive Vice President of Football
Operations: Lal Heneghan
Vice President of Player Personnel:
Scot McCloughan
Vice President/Operations: Murlan Fowell
Vice President Communications:
Lisa Lang
Vice President/CFO: Larry MacNeil
Vice President/Sales And Marketing:
David Peart
Director of Football Operations:
Paraag Marathe
Director of Football Administration:
Terry Tumey
Ticket Manager: Lynn Carrozzi
Director of Security: Fred Formosa
Director of Information Technology:
Alexander Ignacio
Director of Stadium Operations:
Jim Mercurio
Director of Public Relations: Aaron Salkin
Equipment Manager: Steve Urbaniak
Video Operations Director: Keith Yanagi

COACHING HISTORY
(470-385-13)
Records include postseason games
1950-54	Lawrence (Buck) Shaw	33-25-2
1955	Norman (Red) Strader	4-8-0
1956-58	Frankie Albert	19-17-1
1959-1963	Howard (Red) Hickey*	27-27-1
1963-67	Jack Christiansen	26-38-3
1968-1975	Dick Nolan	56-56-5
1976	Monte Clark	8-6-0
1977	Ken Meyer	5-9-0
1978	Pete McCulley**	1-8-0
1978	Fred O'Connor	1-6-0
1979-1988	Bill Walsh	102-63-1
1989-1996	George Seifert	108-35-0
1997-2002	Steve Mariucci	60-43-0
2003-04	Dennis Erickson	9-23-0
2005-06	Mike Nolan	11-21-0

*Resigned after three games in 1963
**Released after nine games in 1978

PAID ATTENDANCE
Home 521,473   Away 531,037
Total 1,052,510
Single-game home record,
69,014 (11/13/94)
Single-season home record,
544,228 (1999)

2007 DRAFT CHOICES
Round	Name	Pos.	College
1	Patrick Willis	LB	Mississippi
	Joe Staley	T	Central Michigan
3	Jason Hill	WR	Washington St.
	Ray McDonald	DE	Florida
4	Jay Moore	LB	Nebraska
	Dashon Goldson	DB	Washington
	Joe Cohen	DT	Florida
5	Tarell Brown	DB	Texas
6	Thomas Clayton	RB	Kansas State

SAN FRANCISCO 49ERS

2006 TEAM RECORD
PRESEASON (2-2)

Date	Result	Opponent
8/11	W 28-14	Chicago
8/20	L 7-23	at Oakland
8/26	L 7-17	at Dallas
9/1	W 23-14	San Diego

REGULAR SEASON (7-9)

Date	Result	Opponent	Att.
9/10	L 27-34	at Arizona	63,407
9/17	W 20-13	St. Louis	67,791
9/24	L 24-38	Philadelphia	68,166
10/1	L 0-41	at Kansas City	77,609
10/8	W 34-20	Oakland	68,368
10/15	L 19-48	San Diego	68,137
10/29	L 10-41	at Chicago	62,200
11/5	W 9-3	Minnesota	68,088
11/12	W 19-13	at Detroit	60,707
11/19	W 20-14	Seattle	68,367
11/26	L 17-20	at St. Louis	65,517
12/3	L 10-34	at New Orleans	68,241
12/10	L 19-30	Green Bay	68,539
12/14	W 24-14	at Seattle	67,650
12/24	L 20-26	Arizona	67,751
12/31	W 26-23	at Denver (OT)	75,555

(OT) Overtime

SCORE BY PERIODS

49ers	46	67	87	95	3 —	298
Opponents	116	145	54	97	0 —	412

2006 TEAM STATISTICS

	49ers	Opp.
Total First Downs	243	326
Rushing	97	107
Passing	132	189
Penalty	14	30
3rd Down: Made/Att	72/209	96/216
3rd Down Pct.	34.4	44.4
4th Down: Made/Att	6/11	7/14
4th Down Pct.	54.5	50.0
Possession Avg.	28:37	31:23
Total Net Yards	4,860	5,507
Avg. Per Game	303.8	344.2
Total Plays	918	1,025
Avg. Per Play	5.3	5.4
Net Yards Rushing	2,172	1,936
Avg. Per Game	135.8	121.0
Total Rushes	439	473
Net Yards Passing	2,688	3,571
Avg. Per Game	168.0	223.2
Sacked/Yards Lost	35/202	34/246
Gross Yards	2,890	3,817
Att./Completions	444/257	518/331
Completion Pct.	57.9	63.9
Had Intercepted	16	14
Punts/Average	81/44.8	66/42.3
Net Punting Avg.	81/36.8	66/36.6
Penalties/Yards	93/818	87/703
Fumbles/Ball Lost	24/16	23/13
Touchdowns	30	46
Rushing	12	18
Passing	16	25
Returns	2	3

2006 INDIVIDUAL STATISTICS

PASSING

	Att.	Comp.	Yds.	Pct.	TD	Int.	Tkld.	Rate
A. Smith	442	257	2,890	58.1	16	16	35/202	74.8
Battle	1	0	—	0.0	0	0	0/0	39.6
Robinson	1	0	—	0.0	0	0	0/0	39.6
49ers	444	257	2,890	57.9	16	16	35/202	74.4
Opponents	518	331	3,817	63.9	25	14	34/246	90.9

SCORING

	TD R	TD P	TD Rt	PAT	FG	Saf	PTS
Nedney	0	0	0	29/29	29/35	0	116
Gore	8	1	0	0/0	0/0	0	54
Battle	0	3	0	0/0	0/0	0	18
Bryant	0	3	0	0/0	0/0	0	18
V. Davis	0	3	0	0/0	0/0	0	18
Johnson	0	2	0	0/0	0/0	0	12
Norris	0	2	0	0/0	0/0	0	12
Robinson	2	0	0	0/0	0/0	0	12
A. Smith	2	0	0	0/0	0/0	0	12
Gilmore	0	1	0	0/0	0/0	0	6
W. Harris	0	0	1	0/0	0/0	0	6
Hicks	0	1	0	0/0	0/0	0	6
Oliver	0	0	1	0/0	0/0	0	6
49ers	12	16	2	29/29	29/35	1	298
Opponents	18	25	3	46/46	30/32	0	412

2-Pt. Conversions: 49ers 0-1, Opponents 0-0

RUSHING

	No.	Yds	Avg	LG	TD
Gore	312	1,695	5.4	72	8
A. Smith	44	147	3.3	22	2
Robinson	38	116	3.1	33	2
Gilmore	7	94	13.4	22	0
Hicks	29	82	2.8	9	0
Battle	5	25	5.0	18	0
Norris	2	8	4.0	4	0
V. Davis	2	5	2.5	9	0
49ers	439	2,172	4.9	72	12
Opponents	473	1,936	4.1	71t	18

RECEIVING

	No.	Yds	Avg	LG	TD
Gore	61	485	8.0	39	1
Battle	59	686	11.6	56	3
Bryant	40	733	18.3	72t	3
Johnson	34	292	8.6	26	2
V. Davis	20	265	13.3	52t	3
Hicks	13	137	10.5	33t	1
Robinson	9	47	5.2	12	0
Gilmore	8	150	18.8	75	1
Norris	5	36	7.2	32t	2
Jacobs	4	29	7.3	10	0
Delanie Walker	2	30	15.0	29	0
Hetherington	2	0	0.0	0	0
49ers	257	2,890	11.2	75	16
Opponents	331	3,817	11.5	74	25

INTERCEPTIONS

	No.	Yds	Avg	LG	TD
W. Harris	8	84	10.5	42	1
Lewis	2	24	12.0	24	0
C. Williams	1	43	43.0	43	0
Roman	1	27	27.0	27	0
Lawson	1	0	0.0	0	0
Spencer	1	0	0.0	0	0
49ers	14	178	12.7	43	1
Opponents	16	213	13.3	70t	1

PUNTING

	No.	Yds.	Avg.	In 20	LG
Lee	81	3,625	44.8	22	66
49ers	81	3,625	44.8	22	66
Opponents	66	2,794	42.3	23	65

PUNT RETURNS

	Ret	FC	Yds	Avg	LG	TD
B. Williams	22	12	147	6.7	25	0
Battle	6	7	90	15.0	60	0
49ers	28	19	237	8.5	60	0
Opponents	35	19	462	13.2	60t	1

KICKOFF RETURNS

	No.	Yds	Avg	LG	TD
Hicks	57	1,428	25.1	64	0
B. Williams	16	380	23.8	44	0
Robinson	4	73	18.3	19	0
Delanie Walker	1	25	25.0	25	0
Norris	1	1	1.0	1	0
49ers	79	1,907	24.1	64	0
Opponents	65	1,373	21.1	47	0

FIELD GOALS

	1-19	20-29	30-39	40-49	50+
Nedney	2/2	11/12	8/10	7/9	1/2
49ers	2/2	11/12	8/10	7/9	1/2
Opponents	1/1	12/12	10/11	6/7	1/1

SACKS

	No.
Moore	6.5
Young	5.5
Green	4.5
Douglas	3.0
Lawson	2.5
C. Williams	2.5
A. Adams	2.0
Spencer	2.0
Sopoaga	1.5
W. Harris	1.0
Lewis	1.0
Oliver	1.0
Roman	1.0
49ers	34.0
Opponents	35.0

RECORD HOLDERS
INDIVIDUAL RECORDS—CAREER

Category	Name	Performance
Rushing (Yds.)	Joe Perry, 1950-1960, 1963	7,344
Passing (Yds.)	Joe Montana, 1979-1992	35,124
Passing (TDs)	Joe Montana, 1979-1992	244
Receiving (No.)	Jerry Rice, 1985-2000	1,281
Receiving (Yds.)	Jerry Rice, 1985-2000	19,247
Interceptions	Ronnie Lott, 1981-1990	51
Punting (Avg.)	Tommy Davis, 1959-1969	44.7
Punt Return (Avg.)	Dana McLemore, 1982-87	10.8
Kickoff Return (Avg.)	Abe Woodson, 1958-1964	29.4
Field Goals	Ray Wersching, 1977-1987	190
Touchdowns (Tot.)	Jerry Rice, 1985-2000	187
Points	Jerry Rice, 1985-2000	1,130

INDIVIDUAL RECORDS—SINGLE SEASON

Category	Name	Performance
Rushing (Yds.)	Garrison Hearst, 1998	1,570
Passing (Yds.)	Jeff Garcia, 2000	4,278
Passing (TDs)	Steve Young, 1998	36
Receiving (No.)	Jerry Rice, 1995	122
Receiving (Yds.)	Jerry Rice, 1995	*1,848
Interceptions	Dave Baker, 1960	10
	Ronnie Lott, 1986	10
Punting (Avg.)	Tommy Davis, 1965	45.8
Punt Return (Avg.)	Dana McLemore, 1982	22.3
Kickoff Return (Avg.)	Joe Arenas, 1953	34.4
Field Goals	Jeff Wilkins, 1996	30
Touchdowns (Tot.)	Jerry Rice, 1987	23
Points	Jerry Rice, 1987	138

INDIVIDUAL RECORDS—SINGLE GAME

Category	Name	Performance
Rushing (Yds.)	Charlie Garner, 9-24-00	201
Passing (Yds.)	Joe Montana, 10-14-90	476
Passing (TDs)	Joe Montana, 10-14-90	6
Receiving (No.)	Terrell Owens, 12-17-00	*20
Receiving (Yds.)	Jerry Rice, 12-18-95	289
Interceptions	Dave Baker, 12-4-60	*4
Field Goals	Ray Wersching, 10-16-83	6
	Jeff Wilkins, 9-29-96	6
Touchdowns (Tot.)	Jerry Rice, 10-14-90	5
Points	Jerry Rice, 10-14-90	30

*NFL Record

2007 VETERAN ROSTER

No.	Name	Pos.	Ht.	Wt.	Birthdate	NFL Exp.	College	Hometown	How Acq.	'06 Games/ Starts
71	Allen, Larry	G	6-4	325	11/28/75	14	Sonoma State	Los Angeles, Calif.	FA-'06	11/11
64	Baas, David	G	6-5	312	9/29/85	3	Michigan	Sarasota, Fla.	D2-'05	16/0
47	Bajema, Billy	TE	6-5	255	11/1/86	3	Oklahoma State	Oklahoma City, Okla.	D7d-'05	16/6
95	Banta-Cain, Tully	LB	6-3	250	8/29/84	5	California	Sunnyvale, Calif.	UFA(NE)-'07	16/5*
83	Battle, Arnaz	WR	6-2	206	2/23/84	5	Notre Dame	Shreveport, La.	D6-'03	16/15
57	Bockwoldt, Colby	LB	6-3	237	4/15/85	4	Brigham Young	Ogden, Utah	FA-'07	16/1*
22	Clements, Nate	CB	6-2	209	12/13/83	7	Ohio State	Shaker Heights, Ohio	UFA(Buff)-'07	16/16*
76	Dahl, Harvey	T	6-6	305	6/25/85	2	Nevada	Fallon, Nev.	FA-'05	4/0
85	Davis, Vernon	TE	6-4	253	2/1/88	2	Maryland	Washington, D.C.	D1-'06	10/8
12	Dilfer, Trent	QB	6-5	234	3/14/76	14	Fresno State	Aptos, Calif	T(Cle)-'06	0*
94	Douglas, Marques	DE	6-3	286	3/16/81	7	Howard	Greensboro, N.C.	UFA(Balt)-'05	16/16
63	Duckett, Damane	T	6-7	300	1/22/85	4	East Carolina	Lexington, N.C.	FA-'06	6/0
78	Estes, Patrick	T	6-8	283	2/5/87	3	Virginia	Richmond, Va.	D7c-'05	1/0
93	Fields, Ronald	DT	6-3	310	9/14/85	3	Mississippi State	Bogalusa, La.	D5a-'05	13/9
92	Franklin, Aubrayo	DT	6-2	320	8/28/84	5	Tennessee	Johnson City, Tenn.	UFA(Balt)-'07	14/0*
84	Gilmore, Bryan	WR	6-2	193	7/22/82	7	Midwestern State	Lufkin, Texas	UFA(Mia)-'06	16/3
21	Gore, Frank	RB	5-10	215	5/15/87	3	Miami	Coral Gables, Fla.	D2-'05	16/16
54	Green, Roderick	LB	6-3	245	4/27/86	4	Central Missouri State	Brenham, Texas	W(Balt)-'06	9/0
98	Haralson, Parys	DE/LB	6-2	250	1/25/88	2	Tennessee	Flora, Miss.	D5-'06	7/0
	Hardy, Jermaine	S	5-11	218	3/21/86	2	Virginia	Roanoke, Va.	FA-'07	0*
77	Harris, Kwame	T	6-8	306	3/16/86	5	Stanford	Newark, Del.	D1-'03	16/16
27	Harris, Walt	CB	5-12	192	8/11/78	12	Mississippi State	LaGrange, Ga.	FA-'06	15/15
66	Heitmann, Eric	C	6-4	307	2/25/84	6	Stanford	Katy, Texas	D7a-'02	14/14
43	Hicks, Maurice	RB	5-12	196	7/23/82	4	North Carolina A&T	Emporia, Va.	FA-'04	16/0
13	Hill, Shaun	QB	6-4	226	1/10/84	6	Maryland	Parsons, Kan.	FA-'06	0*
23	Hudson, Marcus	S	6-3	200	11/16/86	2	North Carolina State	Miami, Fla.	D6b-'06	16/0
t-	Jackson, Darrell	WR	6-2	201	12/7/82	8	Florida	Tampa, Fla.	T(Sea)-'07	13/13*
88	Jacobs, Taylor	WR	6-2	202	5/31/85	5	Florida	Tallahassee, Fla.	W(Wash)-'06	8/0
86	Jennings, Brian	TE/LS	6-5	233	10/14/76	8	Arizona State	Mesa, Ariz.	D7b-'00	16/0
75	Jennings, Jonas	T	6-4	323	11/22/81	7	Georgia	College Park, Ga.	FA-'05	13/13
99	Lawson, Manny	LB	6-5	240	7/4/88	2	North Carolina State	Goldsboro, N.C.	D1b-'06	16/11
4	Lee, Andy	P	6-0	183	8/11/82	4	Pittsburgh	Westminster, S.C.	D6a-'04	16/0
82	Lelie, Ashley	WR	6-3	200	2/16/80	6	Hawaii	Bellflower, Calif.	UFA(Atl)-'07	15/10*
28	Lewis, Keith	S	6-0	210	10/20/81	4	Oregon	Sacramento, Calif.	D6b-'04	16/9
32	Lewis, Michael	S	6-1	222	4/29/80	6	Colorado	Houston, Texas	UFA(Phil)-'07	14/6*
19	Maxwell, Marcus	WR	6-5	205	7/9/87	2	Oregon	Berkeley, Calif.	D7b-'05	0*
56	Moore, Brandon	LB	6-2	246	1/17/83	6	Oklahoma	Baldwin, N.Y.	FA-'02	16/11
55#	Navies, Hannibal	LB	6-4	252	7/20/81	9	Colorado	Berkeley, Calif.	FA-'06	6/3
6	Nedney, Joe	K	6-6	235	3/23/77	11	San Jose State	San Jose, Calif.	FA-'05	16/0
44	Norris, Moran	FB	6-3	250	6/17/82	7	Kansas	Houston, Texas	FA-'06	14/7
96	Oliver, Melvin	DE	6-4	279	7/26/87	2	Louisiana State	Opelika, Ala.	D6c-'06	16/14
24	Robinson, Michael	RB	6-1	218	2/7/87	2	Penn State	Richmond, Va.	D4-'06	16/0
26	Roman, Mark	S	5-11	201	3/27/81	8	Louisiana State	Lafayette, La.	FA-'06	16/11
52#	Slaughter, T.J.	LB	6-2	233	2/21/81	8	Southern Mississippi	Birmingham, Ala.	UFA(NO)-'06	10/1
65	Smiley, Justin	G	6-4	300	11/12/85	4	Alabama	Ellabel, Ga.	D2a-'04	16/16
11	Smith, Alex	QB	6-5	210	5/8/88	3	Utah	San Diego, Calif.	D1-'05	16/16
50	Smith, Derek	LB	6-3	237	1/19/79	11	Arizona State	American Fork, Utah	UFA(Wash)-'01	13/12
68	Snyder, Adam	T/G	6-7	312	1/31/86	3	Oregon	Fullerton, Calif.	D3b-'05	14/6
90	Sopoaga, Isaac	DT	6-3	332	9/5/85	3	Hawaii	Pago Pago, American Samoa	D4a-'04	15/2
36	Spencer, Shawntae	CB	6-2	179	2/23/86	4	Pittsburgh	Rankin, Pa.	D2b-'04	13/13
30	Strickland, Donald	S	5-11	187	11/25/84	5	Colorado	San Francisco, Calif.	FA-'06	3/3
20	Tucker, B.J.	CB	5-11	188	10/13/84	3	Wisconsin	Sierra Leone, West Africa	FA-'05	4/1
53	Ulbrich, Jeff	LB	6-0	240	2/17/77	8	Hawaii	San Jose, Calif.	D3b-'00	16/9
46	Walker, Delanie	TE	6-2	237	8/13/88	2	Central Missouri State	Pomona, Calif.	D6a-'06	7/1
81	Williams, Brandon	WR	5-12	175	2/25/88	2	Wisconsin	St. Louis, Mo.	D3-'06	13/0
69	Wragge, Tony	G	6-5	320	8/15/83	4	New Mexico State	Creighton, Neb.	FA-'05	14/4
97	Young, Bryant	DE	6-3	297	1/27/72	14	Notre Dame	Chicago Heights, Ill.	D1-'94	16/16

* Banta-Cain played 16 games wtih New England in '06; Bockwoldt playd 16 games with Tennessee; Clements played 16 games with Buffalo; Dilfer did not play in 16 games; Franklin played 14 games with Baltimore; Hardy last active with Carolina in '05; Hill inactive for 16 games; Jackson played 13 games with Seattle; Lelie played 15 games with Atlanta; M. Lewis played 14 games with Philadelphia; Maxwell last active with San Francisco in '05.

\# - Unrestriced Free Agent; subject to developments.

t- 49ers traded for Jackson (Sea).

Players lost through free agency (5): DT Anthony Adams (Chi; 14 games in '06), S Deke Cooper (Car; 1), TE Eric Johnson (NO; 13), DE Lance Legree (TB; 2), C Jeremy Newberry (Oak; 0).

Also played with 49ers in '06—S Mike Adams (16 games), WR Antonio Bryant (14), CB Sammy Davis (13), LB Jay Foreman (2), FB Chris Hetherington (3), S Tony Parrish (9), CB Chad Williams (15), LB Renauld Williams (3).

2007 FIRST-YEAR ROSTER

Name	Pos.	Ht.	Wt.	Birthdate	College	Hometown	How Acq.
Brewer, C.J. (1)	WR	6-2	205	5/12/82	Wyoming	Denver, Colo.	FA-'06
Brown, Tarell	CB	5-11	192	1/6/85	Texas	Mesquite, Texas	D5
Clayton, Thomas	RB	6-2	205	4/26/84	Kansas State	Alexandria, Va.	D6
Cohen, Joe	DT	6-2	295	6/6/84	Florida	Melbourne, Fla.	D4c
Goldson, Dashon	S	6-2	205	9/18/84	Washington	Carson, Calif.	D4b
Hill, Jason	WR	6-1	204	1/25/85	Washington State	San Francisco, Calif.	D3a
Kesasy, Zak (1)	FB	6-2	236	3/20/86	Princeton	Lake Orion, Mich.	FA-'06
McDonald, Ray	DE	6-3	276	9/2/84	Florida	Belle Glade, Fla.	D3b
Moore, Jay	DE	6-4	274	8/16/83	Nebraska	Elkhorn, Neb.	D4a
Staley, Joe	T	6-5	306	8/30/84	Central Michigan	Rockford, Mich.	D1b
Steitz, Nick (1)	G	6-2	300	8/19/86	Oregon	Los Banos, Calif.	FA
Syptak, John (1)	DE	6-1	253	3/16/84	Rice	Bellville, Texas	FA
Vaughn, Vickiel (1)	S	6-1	204	10/24/83	Arkansas	Plano, Texas	D7-'06
Washington, Tavares (1)	T	6-3	320	4/20/83	Florida	Greenville, Miss.	FA-'06
Willis, Patrick	LB	6-1	242	1/25/85	Mississippi	Bruceton, Tenn.	D1a

The term NFL Rookie is defined as a player who is in his first season of professional football and has not been on the roster of another professional football team for any regular-season or postseason games. A Rookie is designated by an "R" on NFL rosters. Players who have been active in another professional football league or players who have NFL experience, including either preseason training camp or being on an Active List or Inactive List, or on Reserve/Injured or Reserve/Physically Unable to Perform for fewer than six regular-season games, are termed NFL First-Year Players. An NFL First-Year Player is designated by a "1" on NFL rosters. Thereafter, a player is credited with an additional year of experience for each season in which he accumulates six games on the Active List or Inactive List, or on Reserve/Injured or Reserve/Physically Unable to Perform.

Log on to www.sf49ers.com for an up-to-date roster.

COACHING STAFF
Head Coach,
Mike Nolan
Pro Career: Named the fifteenth head coach in 49ers history on January 19, 2005, Mike Nolan enters his third season as head coach of the San Francisco 49ers. Nolan is in his twentieth year in the league and twenty-sixth year in coaching. Nolan joins San Francisco after an impressive stint as defensive coordinator of the Baltimore Ravens, a position he has held with three other teams: New York Jets (2000), Washington Redskins (1997-99), and New York Giants (1993-96). In Baltimore, Nolan's defense was among the NFL's best, finishing third overall. Baltimore ranked first in the AFC with 17 fumble recoveries and led the NFL in sacks (47) and tied for first in the AFC and second in the NFL with 41 takeaways. Nolan joined the Ravens after a one-year stay as the New York Jets defensive coordinator in 2000. Under Nolan's tutelage, the Jets defense rebounded to tenth overall (tied with the Philadelphia Eagles) in the league—an improvement of 11 spots from the previous year. From 1997-99 Nolan was the defensive coordinator of the Washington Redskins. In 1997, the Redskins allowed the eighth-fewest points in NFL and finished third overall in pass defense. He also spent four seasons as defensive coordinator under then-head coach Dan Reeves for the New York Giants (1993-96). In his first season, the Giants' defense allowed the fewest points in the NFL (205). Nolan also worked on Reeves' staff from 1987-1992 with the Denver Broncos as linebackers coach and as special teams coach/defensive assistant. Career record: 11-21.
Background: Nolan participated in the Broncos' 1981 training camp as a defensive back under Dan Reeves. He joined the Broncos after earning three letters at free safety for the Oregon Ducks (1978-1980). Nolan graduated from Woodside (Calif.) high school. He is the son of former NFL head coach Dick Nolan (San Francisco and New Orleans).
Personal: Born March 7, 1959, Baltimore. He and wife Kathy, have four children: sons, Michael and Christopher, and daughters, Laura and Jennifer.

ASSISTANT COACHES
Duane Carlisle, asst. strength and conditioning; born Nov. 13, 1965, Haverhill, Mass. Attended Maryland. No college or pro playing experience. Pro coach: Speed development consultant for Philadelphia Eagles 2000-04, joined 49ers in 2005.
Frank Cignetti, Jr., quarterbacks; born October 4, 1965, Pittsburgh. Defensive back Indiana (Pa.) 1984-87. No pro playing experience. College coach: Pittsburgh 1989, Indiana (Pa.) 1990-98, Fresno State 2002-05, North Carolina 2006. Pro coach: Kansas City Chiefs 1999, New

Orleans Saints 2000-01, joined 49ers in 2007.
Al Everest, special teams coordinator; born August 22, 1950, Santa Barbara, Calif. Safety Southern Methodist 1970-71. No pro playing experience. College coach: Southern Methodist 1972, North Texas 1973-74, Cameron University 1974-75. Pro coach: Arizona Cardinals 1996-99, New Orleans Saints 2000-05, joined 49ers in 2007.
Bishop Harris, running backs; born November 23, 1941, Phenix City, Ala. Running back/defensive back North Carolina College 1960-63. College coach: Duke 1972-75, North Carolina State 1977-79, Louisiana State 1980-83, Notre Dame 1984-85, Minnesota 1986-1990, North Carolina Central 1991-92 (head coach). Pro coach: Denver Broncos 1993-94, Oakland Raiders 1995-97, Buffalo Bills 1998-99, New York Jets 2001-04, joined 49ers in 2005.
Pete Hoener, tight ends; born June 14, 1954, Peoria, Ill. Tight end/defensive end Bradley 1969-1970. College coach: Missouri 1975-76, Illinois State 1977, Indiana State 1978-1984, Illinois 1986-88, Purdue 1989-1990, Texas Christian 1991-97, Iowa State 1998-99, Texas A&M 2000. Pro coach: St. Louis Cardinals 1985-86, Arizona Cardinals 2003, Chicago Bears 2004, joined 49ers in 2005.
Jim Hostler, offensive coordinator; born November 11, 1966, Pittsburgh. Defensive back Indiana (Pa.) 1986-89. College coach: Indiana (Pa.) 1990-92, 1994-99, Juanita (Pa.) 1993. Pro coach: Kansas City Chiefs 2000, New Orleans Saints 2001-02, New York Jets 2003-04, joined 49ers in 2005.
Vance Joseph, secondary assistant; born September 20, 1972, Marrero, La. Defensive back Colorado 1990-94. Pro defensive back New York Jets 1995, Indianapolis Colts 1996. College coach: Colorado 1999-2001, 2002-03, Wyoming 2002, Bowling Green State 2004. Pro coach: Joined 49ers in 2005.
Johnnie Lynn, secondary; born December 19, 1956, Los Angeles. Defensive back UCLA 1975-78. Pro defensive back New York Jets 1979-1986. College coach: Arizona 1988-1993. Pro coach: Tampa Bay Buccaneers 1994-95, San Francisco 49ers 1996, New York Giants 1997-2003, Baltimore Ravens 2004-05, joined 49ers in 2006.
Greg Manusky, defensive coordinator; born August 12, 1966, Wilkes-Barre, Pa. Linebacker Colgate 1983-87. Pro linebacker Washington Redskins 1988-1990, Minnesota Vikings 1991-93, Kansas City Chiefs 1994-99. Pro coach: Washington Redskins 2001, San Diego Chargers 2002-06, joined 49ers in 2007.
Mark Nori, offensive assistant/line; born January 1, 1974, Philadelphia. Offensive line Boston College 1992-96. Pro offen-

sive lineman Jacksonville Jaguars 1997-98. College coach: Mount Ida College 2001, Pittsburgh 2002, Maine 2003, Akron 2004-06. Pro coach: Joined 49ers in 2007.
Johnny Parker, strength & conditioning; born February 1, 1947, Greenville, S.C. Attended Mississippi. No college or pro playing experience. College coach: South Carolina, 1974-76, Indiana 1977-79, Louisiana State 1980, Mississippi 1981-83. Pro coach: New York Giants 1984-92, New England Patriots 1993-99, Tampa Bay Buccaneers 2002, joined 49ers in 2005.
Jeff Rodgers, special teams assistant; born January 12, 1978, St. Paul, Minn. Linebacker North Texas 1997-2000. No pro playing experience. College coach: Arizona 2001-02. Pro coach: Joined 49ers in 2003.
Mike Singletary, asst. head coach/linebackers; born October 9, 1958, Houston. Linebacker Baylor 1977-1980. Pro linebacker Chicago Bears 1981-1992. Inducted into Pro Football Hall of Fame 1998. Pro coach: Baltimore Ravens 2003-04, joined 49ers in 2005.
Jerry Sullivan, wide receivers; born July 13, 1944, Miami, Fla. Quarterback Florida State 1963-64. No pro playing experience. College coach: Kansas State 1971-72, Texas Tech 1973-75, South Carolina 1976-1982, Indiana 1983, Louisiana State 1984-1990, Ohio State 1991. Pro coach: San Diego Chargers 1992-96, Detroit Lions 1997-2000, Arizona Cardinals 2001-03, Miami Dolphins 2004, joined 49ers in 2005.
Jason Tarver, defensive quality control/defensive assistant; born August 28, 1974, Stanford, Calif. Defensive back West Valley College 1994-95. No pro playing experience. College coach: West Valley College 1996-97, UCLA 1998-2000. Pro coach: Joined 49ers in 2001.
Jim Tomsula, defensive line; born April 14, 1967, Homestead, Pa. Middle Tennessee State 1985-86, Catawba College 1987-1990. No pro playing experience College coach: Charleston Southern 1997. Pro coach: England Monarchs (NFL Europe) 1998, Scottish Claymores (NFL Europe) 1999-2003, Berlin Thunder (NFL Eurpoe) 2004-05, Rhein Fire (NFL Europa head coach) 2006, joined 49ers in 2007.
George Warhop, offensive line; born September 19, 1961, Riverside, Ca. Guard/center Mt. San Jacinto (Calif.) J.C. 1979-1980, Cincinnati 1981-82. College coach: Cincinnati 1983, Kansas 1984-86, Vanderbilt 1987-89, New Mexico 1990, Southern Methodist 1993, Boston College 1994-95. Pro coach: London Monarchs (WL) 1991-92, St. Louis Rams 1996-97, Arizona Cardinals 1998-2002, Dallas Cowboys 2003-04, joined 49ers in 2005.

**National Football Conference
West Division**
Team Colors: Seahawks Blue, Seahawks
Navy, Seahawks Bright Green
11220 N.E. 53ᴿᴰ Street
Kirkland, Washington, 98033
Telephone: (425) 827-9777

2007 SCHEDULE
PRESEASON
Aug. 12	at San Diego	5:00
Aug. 18	at Green Bay	7:00
Aug. 25	**Minnesota**	6:00
Aug. 30	**Oakland**	7:00

REGULAR SEASON
Sep. 9	**Tampa Bay**	1:15
Sep. 16	at Arizona	1:05
Sep. 23	**Cincinnati**	1:05
Sep. 30	at San Francisco	1:05
Oct. 7	at Pittsburgh	1:00
Oct. 14	**New Orleans**	5:15
Oct. 21	**St. Louis**	1:15
Oct. 28	Open Date	
Nov. 4	at Cleveland	4:05
Nov. 12	**San Francisco** (Mon.)	5:30
Nov. 18	**Chicago**	*5:15
Nov. 25	at St. Louis	12:00
Dec. 2	at Philadelphia	1:00
Dec. 9	**Arizona**	1:05
Dec. 16	at Carolina	1:00
Dec. 23	**Baltimore**	1:15
Dec. 30	at Atlanta	1:00

Sunday night games in Weeks 11-17 subject to change

Stadium: Qwest Field
(opened in 2002)
• **Capacity:** 67,000
Playing Surface: FieldTurf
Training Camp: Seahawks Headquarters
Kirkland, WA 98033

QWEST FIELD

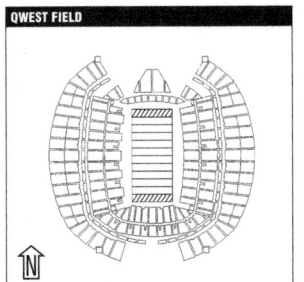

CLUB OFFICIALS
Chairman: Paul Allen
CEO: Tod Leiweke
President of Football Operations:
Tim Ruskell
Executive VP of Football Operations/
Head Coach: Mike Holmgren
Senior VP/CMO: John Rizzardini
Senior VP/CFO: Martha Fuller
VP/Football Administration: John Izdik
VP/Player Personnel: Ruston Webster
VP/Community Outreach: Mike Flood
VP/Corporate Partnership/Legal Affairs:
Lance Lopes
VP/Corporate Sales: Scott Patrick
VP/Administration: Gary Wright
Director of Marketing: Bill Chapin
Director of Corp. Hospitality, Suite Sales
& Service: Amy Sprangers
Director of Pro Personnel: Will Lewis
Director of Communications and
Broadcasting: Dave Pearson
Asst. Director of Communications:
Lane Gammel
Director of Community Outreach:
Sandy Gregory
Director of Ticket Sales/Operations:
Chuck Arnold
Gameday Presentation: Rick Crawford
Video Director Football: Thom Fermstad
Head Athletic Trainer: Sam Ramsden
Equipment Manager: Erik Kennedy
Team Travel: Jeremy Young

COACHING HISTORY
(242-257-0)
Records include postseason games
1976-1982	Jack Patera*	35-59-0
1982	Mike McCormack	4-3-0
1983-1991	Chuck Knox	83-67-0
1992-94	Tom Flores	14-34-0
1995-98	Dennis Erickson	31-33-0
1999-2006	Mike Holmgren	75-61-0

*Released after two games in 1982

PAID ATTENDANCE
Home 532,042   Away 530,395
Total 1,062,437
Single-game home record,
68,681 (12/16/00)
Single-season home record,
522,656 (1999)

2007 DRAFT CHOICES
Round	Name	Pos.	College
2	Josh Wilson	DB	Maryland
3	Brandon Mebane	DT	California
4	Baraka Atkins	DE	Miami
	Mansfield Wrotto	G	Georgia Tech
5	Will Herring	LB	Auburn
6	Courtney Taylor	WR	Auburn
	Jordan Kent	WR	Oregon
7	Steve Vallos	G	Wake Forest

2006 TEAM RECORD
PRESEASON (2-2)

Date	Result	Opponent
8/12	L 3-13	Dallas
8/20	W 30-17	at Indianapolis
8/26	L 20-31	at San Diego
8/31	W 30-7	Oakland

REGULAR SEASON (9-7)

Date	Result	Opponent	Att.
9/10	W 9-6	at Detroit	60,535
9/17	W 21-10	Arizona	67,470
9/24	W 42-30	N.Y. Giants	68,161
10/1	L 6-37	at Chicago	62,225
10/15	W 30-28	at St. Louis	65,592
10/22	L 13-31	Minnesota	68,118
10/29	L 28-35	at Kansas City	77,645
11/6	W 16-0	Oakland	67,816
11/12	W 24-22	St. Louis	68,175
11/19	L 14-20	at San Francisco	68,367
11/27	W 34-24	Green Bay	68,256
12/3	W 23-20	at Denver	76,146
12/10	L 21-27	at Arizona	63,603
12/14	L 14-24	San Francisco	67,650
12/24	L 17-20	San Diego	68,174
12/31	W 23-7	at Tampa Bay	65,660

POSTSEASON (1-1)

Date	Result	Opponent	
1/6	W 21-20	Dallas	68,756
1/14	L 24-27	at Chicago (OT)	62,184

(OT) Overtime

SCORE BY PERIODS

Seahawks	103	73	52	107	0	—	335
Opponents	67	104	54	116	0	—	341

2006 TEAM STATISTICS

	Seahawks	Opp.
Total First Downs	312	277
Rushing	112	102
Passing	167	160
Penalty	33	15
3rd Down: Made/Att	85/224	80/219
3rd Down Pct.	37.9	36.5
4th Down: Made/Att	2/8	6/12
4th Down Pct.	25.0	50.0
Possession Avg.	29:48	30:12
Total Net Yards	4,977	5,285
Avg. Per Game	311.1	330.3
Total Plays	1,045	986
Avg. Per Play	4.8	5.4
Net Yards Rushing	1,923	2,029
Avg. Per Game	120.2	126.8
Total Rushes	484	441
Net Yards Passing	3,054	3,256
Avg. Per Game	190.9	203.5
Sacked/Yards Lost	49/315	41/282
Gross Yards	3,369	3,538
Att./Completions	512/292	504/299
Completion Pct.	57.0	59.3
Had Intercepted	22	12
Punts/Average	86/44.5	88/42.9
Net Punting Avg.	86/37.0	88/36.9
Penalties/Yards	94/700	118/950
Fumbles/Ball Lost	21/12	34/14
Touchdowns	37	39
Rushing	8	12
Passing	26	23
Returns	3	4

2006 INDIVIDUAL STATISTICS

PASSING

	Att.	Comp.	Yds.	Pct.	TD	Int.	Tkld.	Rate
Hasselbeck	371	210	2,442	56.6	18	15	34/229	76.0
Wallace	141	82	927	58.2	8	7	14/83	76.2
Branch	0	0	—	—	0	0	1/3	—
Seahawks	512	292	3,369	57.0	26	22	49/315	76.0
Opponents	504	299	3,538	59.3	23	12	41/282	86.1

SCORING

	TD R	TD P	TD Rt	PAT	FG	Saf	PTS
J. Brown	0	0	0	36/36	25/31	0	111
Jackson	0	10	0	0/0	0/0	0	60
Alexander	7	0	0	0/0	0/0	0	42
Stevens	0	4	0	0/0	0/0	0	26
Branch	0	4	0	0/0	0/0	0	24
Hackett	0	4	0	0/0	0/0	0	24
Burleson	0	2	1	0/0	0/0	0	18
Engram	0	1	0	0/0	0/0	0	6
Heller	0	1	0	0/0	0/0	0	6
Herndon	0	0	1	0/0	0/0	0	6
Strong	1	0	0	0/0	0/0	0	6
Tapp	0	0	1	0/0	0/0	0	6
Seahawks	8	26	3	36/36	25/31	0	335
Opponents	12	23	4	36/36	23/33	0	341

2-Pt. Conversions: Stevens,
Seahawks 1-1, Opponents 1-3.

RUSHING

	No.	Yds	Avg	LG	TD
Alexander	252	896	3.6	33t	7
Morris	161	604	3.8	29	0
Strong	33	149	4.5	17	1
Wallace	12	122	10.2	17	0
Hasselbeck	18	110	6.1	19	0
Branch	4	30	7.5	19	0
Weeks	3	8	2.7	3	0
Engram	1	4	4.0	4	0
Seahawks	484	1,923	4.0	37	8
Opponents	441	2,029	4.6	95t	12

RECEIVING

	No.	Yds	Avg	LG	TD
Jackson	63	956	15.2	72t	10
Branch	53	725	13.7	38t	4
Hackett	45	610	13.6	47	4
Strong	29	159	5.5	13	0
Engram	24	290	12.1	25	1
Stevens	22	231	10.5	26	4
Burleson	18	192	10.7	36	2
Alexander	12	48	4.0	14	0
Morris	11	46	4.2	27	0
Mili	10	69	6.9	15	0
Heller	4	32	8.0	12	1
Parry	1	11	11.0	11	0
Seahawks	292	3,369	11.5	72t	26
Opponents	299	3,538	11.8	71t	23

INTERCEPTIONS

	No.	Yds	Avg	LG	TD
Hamlin	3	63	21.0	37	0
Boulware	2	1	0.5	1	0
Tapp	1	25	25.0	25t	1
Babineaux	1	20	20.0	20	0
Tatupu	1	19	19.0	19	0
Herndon	1	0	0.0	0	0
Jennings	1	0	0.0	0	0
Trufant	1	0	0.0	0	0
Peterson	1	-4	-4.0	-4	0
Seahawks	12	124	10.3	37	1
Opponents	22	141	6.4	39	1

PUNTING

	No.	Yds.	Avg.	In 20	LG
Plackemeier	84	3,778	45.0	25	72
J. Brown	2	49	24.5	1	28
Seahawks	86	3,827	44.5	26	72
Opponents	88	3,773	42.9	25	61

PUNT RETURNS

	Ret	FC	Yds	Avg	LG	TD
Burleson	34	7	322	9.5	90t	1
Williams	14	9	102	7.3	22	0
Trufant	1	0	0	0.0	0	0
Seahawks	49	16	424	8.7	90t	1
Opponents	39	12	343	8.8	40	0

KICKOFF RETURNS

	No.	Yds	Avg	LG	TD
Burleson	26	643	24.7	50	0
Ponder	25	587	23.5	41	0
Scobey	17	315	18.5	33	0
Weeks	1	3	3.0	3	0
Seahawks	69	1,548	22.4	50	0
Opponents	61	1,499	24.6	51	0

FIELD GOALS

	1-19	20-29	30-39	40-49	50+
J. Brown	0/0	10/10	5/7	7/9	3/5
Seahawks	0/0	10/10	5/7	7/9	3/5
Opponents	1/1	1/3	11/12	10/12	0/5

SACKS

	No.
Peterson	10.0
Fisher	4.0
Wistrom	4.0
Bernard	3.5
Darby	3.5
Davis	3.0
Tapp	3.0
Terrill	3.0
Hamlin	2.0
Hill	2.0
Tatupu	1.5
Lewis	1.0
Tubbs	0.5
Seahawks	41.0
Opponents	49.0

RECORD HOLDERS
INDIVIDUAL RECORDS—CAREER

Category	Name	Performance
Rushing (Yds.)	Shaun Alexander, 2000-06	8,713
Passing (Yds.)	Dave Krieg, 1980-1991	26,132
Passing (TDs)	Dave Krieg, 1980-1991	195
Receiving (No.)	Steve Largent, 1976-1989	819
Receiving (Yds.)	Steve Largent, 1976-1989	13,089
Interceptions	Dave Brown, 1976-1986	50
Punting (Avg.)	Rick Tuten, 1991-97	43.8
Punt Return (Avg.)	Charlie Rogers, 1999-2001	12.7
Kickoff Return (Avg.)	Steve Broussard, 1995-98	23.2
Field Goals	Norm Johnson, 1982-1990	159
Touchdowns (Tot.)	Steve Largent, 1976-1989	101
Points	Norm Johnson, 1982-1990	810

INDIVIDUAL RECORDS—SINGLE SEASON

Category	Name	Performance
Rushing (Yds.)	Shaun Alexander, 2005	1,880
Passing (Yds.)	Matt Hasselbeck, 2003	3,841
Passing (TDs)	Dave Krieg, 1984	32
Receiving (No.)	Darrell Jackson, 2004	87
Receiving (Yds.)	Steve Largent, 1985	1,287
Interceptions	John Harris, 1981	10
	Kenny Easley, 1984	10
Punting (Avg.)	Ryan Plackemeier, 2006	45.0
Punt Return (Avg.)	Charlie Rogers, 1999	14.5
Kickoff Return (Avg.)	Charlie Rogers, 2000	24.9
Field Goals	Todd Peterson, 1999	34
Touchdowns (Tot.)	Shaun Alexander, 2005	28
Points	Shaun Alexander, 2005	168

INDIVIDUAL RECORDS—SINGLE GAME

Category	Name	Performance
Rushing (Yds.)	Shaun Alexander, 11-11-01	266
Passing (Yds.)	Matt Hasselbeck, 12-29-02	449
Passing (TDs)	Dave Krieg, 12-2-84, 9-15-85, 11-28-88	5
	Warren Moon, 10-26-97	5
	Matt Hasselbeck, 11-23-03, 9-24-06	5
Receiving (No.)	Steve Largent, 10-18-87	15
Receiving (Yds.)	Steve Largent, 10-18-87	261
Interceptions	Kenny Easley, 9-3-84	3
	Eugene Robinson, 12-6-92	3
	Darryl Williams, 9-21-97	3
Field Goals	Norm Johnson, 9-20-87, 12-18-88	5
Touchdowns (Tot.)	Shaun Alexander, 9-29-02	5
Points	Shaun Alexander, 9-29-02	30

2007 VETERAN ROSTER

No.	Name	Pos.	Ht.	Wt.	Birthdate	NFL Exp.	College	Hometown	How Acq.	'06 Games/ Starts
37	Alexander, Shaun	RB	5-11	225	8/30/77	8	Alabama	Florence, Ky.	D1a-'00	10/10
68	Ashworth, Tom	T	6-6	305	10/10/77	5	Colorado	Centennial, Colo.	UFA(NE)-'06	16/6
27	Babineaux, Jordan	S	6-0	200	8/31/82	4	Southern Arkansas	Port Arthur, Texas	FA-'04	15/8
57	Bentley, Kevin	LB	6-0	245	12/29/79	6	Northwestern	Montclair, Calif.	UFA(Cle)-'05	14/0
99	Bernard, Rocky	DT	6-3	293	4/19/79	6	Texas A&M	Baytown, Texas	D5a-'02	16/16
28	Boulware, Michael	S	6-3	223	9/17/81	4	Florida State	Columbia, S.C.	D2-'04	16/8
83	Branch, Deion	WR	5-9	193	7/18/79	6	Louisville	Albany, Ga.	T(NE)-'06	14/13
3	Brown, Josh	K	6-0	202	4/29/79	5	Nebraska	Foyil, Okla.	D7a-'03	16/0
81	Burleson, Nate	WR	6-0	192	8/19/81	5	Nevada	Seattle, Wash.	RFA(Minn)-'06	16/7
58	Cooper, Marquis	LB	6-3	213	3/11/82	4	Washington	Mesa, Ariz.	FA-'06	1/0
91	Darby, Chuck	DT	6-0	270	10/22/75	7	South Carolina State	North, S.C.	UFA(TB)-'05	16/14
95	Davis, Russell	DT	6-4	306	3/28/75	9	North Carolina	Fayetteville, N.C.	UFA(Ari)-'06	13/0
84	Engram, Bobby	WR	5-10	188	1/7/73	12	Penn State	Camden, S.C.	UFA(Chi)-'01	7/6
94	Fisher, Bryce	DE	6-3	268	5/12/77	7	Air Force	Renton, Wash.	UFA(StL)-'05	16/16
33	Gardner, Rich	CB	5-10	194	2/1/81	4	Penn State	Chicago, Ill.	FA-'06	0*
24	Grant, Deon	S	6-2	210	3/14/79	8	Tennessee	Augusta, Ga.	UFA(Jax)-'07	16/16*
62	Gray, Chris	G	6-4	308	6/19/70	15	Auburn	Birmingham, Ala.	UFA(Chi)-'98	15/15
70	Green, Brandon	DE	6-3	264	9/5/80	5	Rice	Vanderbilt, Texas	UFA(StL)-'07	13/0*
98	Green, Marcus	DT	6-1	307	9/27/83	2	Ohio State	Louisville, Ky.	PS(NYG)-'06	2/0
42	Green, Mike	S	6-0	195	12/6/76	8	Northwestern St. (La.)	Ruston, La.	T(Chi)-'06	0*
11	Greene, David	QB	6-3	226	6/22/82	3	Georgia	Snellville, Ga.	D3a-'05	0*
18	Hackett, D.J.	WR	6-2	199	7/3/81	3	Colorado	Ontario, Calif.	D5-'04	14/5
8	Hasselbeck, Matt	QB	6-4	223	9/25/75	9	Boston College	Westwood, Mass.	T(GB)-'01	12/12
85	Heller, Will	TE	6-6	265	2/28/81	5	Georgia Tech	Dunwoody, Ga.	UFA(TB)-'06	16/0
31	Herndon, Kelly	CB	5-10	180	11/3/76	6	Toledo	Twinsburg, Ohio	RFA(Den)-'05	16/16
56	Hill, Leroy	LB	6-1	229	9/14/82	3	Clemson	Haddock, Ga.	D3b-'05	15/15
29	Hunter, Pete	CB	6-2	208	5/25/80	6	Virginia Union	Atlantic City, N.J.	FA-'06	0*
21	Jennings, Kelly	CB	5-11	178	11/30/82	2	Miami	Live Oak, Fla.	D1-'06	16/2
71	Jones, Walter	T	6-5	315	1/19/74	11	Florida State	Aliceville, Ala.	D1b-'97	16/16
47	Joppru, Ben	TE	6-4	242	1/5/80	5	Michigan	Wayzata, Minn.	PS(Chi)-'06	5/0
97	Kerney, Patrick	DE	6-5	273	12/30/76	9	Virginia	Newtown, Pa.	UFA(Atl)-'07	9/9*
64	King, Austin	C	6-3	288	4/11/81	5	Northwestern	Cincinnati, Ohio	FA-'07	14/0*
34	Kirtman, David	FB	6-0	232	2/12/83	2	Southern California	Mercer Island, Wash.	D5-'06	0*
53	Koutouvides, Niko	LB	6-2	238	3/25/81	4	Purdue	Plainville, Conn.	D4-'04	16/0
50	Laury, Lance	LB	6-2	233	1/17/82	2	South Carolina	Hopkins, S.C.	FA-'06	8/0
75	Locklear, Sean	T	6-4	301	5/29/81	4	North Carolina State	Lumberton, N.C.	D3-'04	10/10
73	Morley, Steve	T	6-7	330	8/18/81	3	St. Mary's (Nova Scotia)	Halifax, Nova Scotia	FA-'07	0*
20	Morris, Maurice	RB	5-11	202	12/1/79	6	Oregon	Chester, S.C.	D2a-'02	16/8
49 t-	Parry, Josh	FB	6-2	250	4/5/78	4	San Jose State	Sonora, Calif.	T(Phil)-'06	8/0*
59	Peterson, Julian	LB	6-3	235	7/28/78	8	Michigan State	Washington, D.C.	UFA(SF)-'06	16/16
1	Plackemeier, Ryan	P	6-3	248	3/5/84	2	Wake Forest	Bonsall, Calif.	D7a-'06	16/0
88	Pollard, Marcus	TE	6-3	250	2/8/72	13	Bradley	Valley, Ala.	FA-'07	15/5*
48	Rackley, Derek	LS	6-4	250	7/18/77	8	Minnesota	Apple Valley, Minn.	FA-'06	15/0
25	Russell, Brian	S	6-2	207	2/5/78	6	San Diego State	West Covina, Calif.	UFA(Cle)-'07	12/12*
67	Sims, Rob	G	6-3	307	12/6/83	2	Ohio State	Macedonia, Ohio	D4-'06	14/3
65	Spencer, Chris	C	6-3	309	3/28/82	3	Mississippi	Madison, Miss.	D1-'05	16/13
89	Stephens, Leonard	TE	6-3	250	7/9/78	3	Howard	Brooklyn, N.Y.	FA-'06	0*
38	Strong, Mack	FB	6-0	245	9/11/71	14	Georgia	Columbus, Ga.	FA-'93	16/10
55	Tapp, Darryl	DE	6-1	265	9/13/84	2	Virginia Tech	Chesapeake, Va.	D2-'06	16/0
51	Tatupu, Lofa	LB	6-0	238	11/15/82	3	Southern California	Wretham, Mass.	D2-'05	16/16
78	Taylor, Eric	DT	6-2	305	12/14/81	2	Memphis	Winchester, Tenn.	FA-'06	0*
93	Terrill, Craig	DT	6-2	294	6/27/80	4	Purdue	Lebanon, Ind.	D6-'04	11/0
23	Trufant, Marcus	CB	5-11	199	12/25/80	5	Washington State	Tacoma, Wash.	D1-'03	15/15
90	Tubbs, Marcus	DT	6-3	324	5/16/81	4	Texas	DeSoto, Texas	D1-'04	5/2
15	Wallace, Seneca	QB	5-11	196	8/6/80	5	Iowa State	Sacramento, Calif.	D4a-'03	8/4
43	Weaver, Leonard	FB	6-0	251	9/23/82	3	Carson-Newman	Melbourne, Fla.	FA-'05	0*
30	Weeks, Marquis	RB	5-10	216	10/2/80	2	Virginia	Norristown, Pa.	FA-'05	10/0
74	Willis, Ray	T	6-6	327	8/13/82	3	Florida State	Angleton, Texas	D4-'05	1/0
77	Womack, Floyd	G	6-4	333	11/15/78	7	Mississippi State	Cleveland, Miss.	D4c-'01	9/9

* Gardner inactive for 1 game in '06; B. Green played 13 games with St. Louis in '06; Mike Green missed '06 season because of injury; Greene did not play in 4 games; Hunter last active with Cleveland in '05; Kerney played 9 games With Atlanta; King played 14 games with Atlanta; Kirtman inactive for 3 games; Morley last active with N.Y. Jets in '05; Pollard played 15 games with Detroit; Russeell played 12 games with Cleveland; Stephens last active with Washington in '02; Taylor last active with Pittsburgh in '05; Weaver missed '06 season because of injury.

Traded—WR Darrell Jackson (13 games in '06) to San Francisco.

Players lost through free agency (6): LB Jean-Philippe Darche (KC; 1 game in '06), S Ken Hamlin (Dall; 16), LB D.D. Lewis (Den; 5), RB Josh Scobey (Buff; 12), TE Jerramy Stevens (TB; 11), DE Joe Tafoya (Ariz; 13).

Also played with Seahawks in '06—LB Isaiah Kacyvenski (3 games), TE Itula Mili (10), DE Robert Pollard (1), WR Willie Ponder (6), C Robbie Tobeck (8), CB Jimmy Williams (16), DE Grant Wistrom (16).

2007 FIRST-YEAR ROSTER

Name	Pos.	Ht.	Wt.	Birthdate	College	Hometown	How Acq.
Atkins, Baraka	DE	6-4	271	9/28/84	Miami	Sarasota, Fla.	D4a
Davis, Dennis (1)	CB	6-0	185	11/24/82	Georgia Tech	Sicklerville, N.J.	FA
Fernandez, Joe	WR	5-10	175	10/25/84	Fresno State	Morgan Hill, Calif.	FA
Gafford, Thomas	LS	6-2	252	1/29/83	Houston	Houston, Texas	FA
Ghee, Patrick	S	6-1	211	5/5/84	Wake Forest	Kingsport, Tenn.	FA
Herring, Will	LB	6-3	221	8/28/83	Auburn	Opelika, Ala.	D5
James, Kenny	RB	5-10	215	4/14/84	Washington	Dos Palos, Calif.	FA
Jensen, Cameron	LB	6-1	248	6/29/82	Brigham Young	Bountiful, Utah	FA
Jones, Chris (1)	WR	6-3	203	7/17/82	Jackson State	Macon, Miss.	FA
Jones, Nick	C	6-3	295	7/5/85	Georgia	Bowdon, Ga.	FA
Kent, Jordan	WR	6-4	217	7/24/84	Oregon	Eugene, Ore.	D6b
Lulay, Travis (1)	QB	6-2	216	9/27/83	Montana State	Aumsville, Ore.	FA
McGruder, Lynn (1)	DT	6-1	307	2/13/82	Oklahoma	Las Vegas, Nev.	FA
Mebane, Brandon	DT	6-1	309	1/15/85	California	Los Angeles, Calif.	D3
Mixon, Tim	CB	5-10	184	7/8/84	California	Compton, Calif.	FA
Murphy, Jason (1)	G	6-2	304	8/7/82	Virginia Tech	Baltimore, Md.	FA-'06
Newton, Joe	TE	6-7	256	10/15/83	Oregon State	Roseburg, Ore.	FA
Obomanu, Ben (1)	WR	6-0	203	10/30/83	Auburn	Selma, Ala.	D7b-'06
Payne, Logan	WR	6-2	205	1/21/85	Minnesota	Lutz, Fla.	FA
Robinson, Tony (1)	LB	6-1	235	9/4/83	Carson-Newman	Winston-Salem, N.C.	FA
Ross, Gerard (1)	CB	6-1	200	12/27/82	Florida State	Jacksonville, Fla.	FA-'06
Ross, Pat (1)	C	6-3	301	3/16/83	Boston College	Reading, Ohio	FA-'06
Stringer, Kyle	P	5-8	194	5/10/85	Boise State	Humble, Texas	FA
Tafisi, Nu'u	DE	6-2	265	6/30/81	California	Salt Lake City, Utah	FA
Taylor, Courtney	WR	6-1	204	4/7/84	Auburn	Carrollton, Ala.	D6a
Vallos, Steve	G	6-3	290	12/28/83	Wake Forest	Boardman, Ohio	D7
Wallace, C.J.	S	6-0	205	4/17/85	Washington	Sacramento, Calif.	FA
Wilson, Josh	CB	5-9	189	3/11/85	Maryland	Upper Marlboro, Md.	D2
Wrotto, Mansfield	G	6-3	310	10/12/84	Georgia Tech	Snellville, Ga.	D4b

The term NFL Rookie is defined as a player who is in his first season of professional football and has not been on the roster of another professional football team for any regular-season or postseason games. A Rookie is designated by an "R" on NFL rosters. Players who have been active in another professional football league or players who have NFL experience, including either preseason training camp or being on an Active List or Inactive List, or on Reserve/Injured or Reserve/Physically Unable to Perform for fewer than six regular-season games, are termed NFL First-Year Players. An NFL First-Year Player is designated by a "1" on NFL rosters. Thereafter, a player is credited with an additional year of experience for each season in which he accumulates six games on the Active List or Inactive List, or on Reserve/Injured or Reserve/Physically Unable to Perform.

Log on to www.seahawks.com for an up-to-date roster.

COACHING STAFF

Executive Vice President of Football Operations/Head Coach,
Mike Holmgren

Pro Career: Named as the Seahawks' sixth head coach on January 8, 1999. In 2006, the Seahawks won their third consecutive NFC West crown and fifth-ever division title. In 2005, led them to a franchise-record 13-3 finish, and their first-ever Super Bowl berth. In 2003, the Seahawks posted their first double-digit victory total since 1986. Holmgren joined Seattle after serving as the head coach of the Packers (1992-98). By winning at least one game in five consecutive postseasons (1993-97) Holmgren joined John Madden (1973-77) as the only coaches in league history to accomplish that feat. In 21 NFL seasons (1999-2006 head coach Seattle, 1992-98 head coach Green Bay, 1986-1991 assistant coach San Francisco) Holmgren's teams have a 218-116-1 (.652) record, posted double-digit win totals 12 times, made the postseason 16 times, won three Super Bowls (XXIII, XXIV, and XXXI), and reached two others (XXXII and XL). Career record: 159-103.

Background: Quarterback at Southern California (1966-69) and was drafted by the St. Louis Cardinals in the eighth round of the 1970 NFL Draft. He served as an assistant coach at San Francisco State (1981) and Brigham Young (1982-85). Earned his bachelor degree in business finance at Southern California.

Personal: Born June 15, 1948, in San Francisco. He and his wife, Kathy, have four daughters—Calla, Jenny, Emily, and Gretchen.

ASSISTANT COACHES

Dwaine Board, defensive line; born November 29, 1956, Rocky Mount, Va. Defensive lineman North Carolina A&T 1974-77. Pro defensive lineman San Francisco 49ers 1979-1987, New Orleans Saints 1988. Pro coach: San Francisco 49ers 1990-2002, joined Seahawks in 2003.

Mike Clark, strength and conditioning; born August 22, 1954, Wichita, Kan. Linebacker Ottawa College 1973-76. No pro playing experience. College coach: Kansas 1977-78, 1982, Wyoming 1981, Oregon 1983-87, Southern California 1988-89, Texas A&M 2000-2003. Pro coach: Joined Seahawks in 2004.

Nolan Cromwell, wide receivers; born January 30, 1955, Smith Center, Kan. Quarterback/safety Kansas 1973-76. Pro defensive back Los Angeles Rams 1977-1987. Pro coach: Los Angeles Rams 1991, Green Bay Packers 1992-98, joined Seahawks in 1999.

Bruce DeHaven, special teams; born September 8, 1948, Trousdale, Kan. Attended Southwestern (Kan.) College. No college or pro playing experience. College coach: Kansas 1979-1981, New Mexico

State 1982. Pro coach: New Jersey Generals (USFL) 1983, Pittsburgh Maulers (USFL) 1984, Orlando Renegades (USFL) 1985, Buffalo Bills 1987-1999, San Francisco 49ers 2000-02, Dallas Cowboys 2003-2006, joined Seahawks in 2007.

Keith Gilbertson, offensive consultant; born May 15, 1948, Snohomish, Wash. Defensive line Central Washington 1967, Columbia Basin (Wash.) J.C. 1968, Hawaii 1969-1970. No pro playing experience. College coach: Idaho State 1971-74, Western Washington 1975, Washington 1976, Utah State 1977-1981, Idaho 1982, 1986-88, Washington 1989-1991, California 1992-95 (head coach), Washington 1999-2004 (head coach 2003-04). Pro coach: L.A. Express (USFL) 1983-85, Seattle Seahawks 1996-98, re-joined Seahawks in 2005.

Gil Haskell, offensive coordinator; born September 24, 1943, San Francisco. Defensive back San Francisco State 1961, 1963-65. No pro playing experience. College coach: Southern California 1978-1982. Pro coach: Los Angeles Rams 1983-1991, Green Bay Packers 1992-97, Carolina Panthers 1998-99, joined Seahawks in 2000.

Tom Headlee, quality control/defense; born November 6, 1976, Bothell, Wash. Attended Washington State. No college or pro playing experience. Pro coach: Joined Seahawks in 2006.

John Jamison, special teams assistant; born May 26, 1948, San Francisco. Wide receiver California 1968. No pro playing experience. Pro coach: Joined Seahawks in 2005.

Darren Krein, asst. strength & conditioning; born July 7, 1971, Aurora, Colo. Linebacker/defensive end Miami 1989-1993. Pro linebacker San Diego Chargers 1994, Barcelona Dragons (NFLE) 1996. Pro coach: Seattle 1997-98, re-joined Seahawks in 2002.

Bill Laveroni, offensive line; born July 20, 1948, San Francisco. Center California 1967-69. No pro playing experience. College coach: California 1970, 1978, 1983-89, San Francisco 1971, Utah State 1979-1982, San Jose State 1990-94, Rutgers 1996-2000, Vanderbilt 2001. Pro coach: San Jose Sabercats (AFL) 1995, joined Seahawks in 2002.

Jim Lind, tight ends; born Novemeber 11, 1947, Isle, Minn. Linebacker Bethel College 1965-66, defensive back Bemidji State 1971-72. No pro playing experience. College coach: St. Cloud State 1977-78, St. John's (Minn.) 1979-1980, Brigham Young 1981-82, Minnesota-Morris 1983-86 (head coach), Wisconsin-Eau Claire 1987-1991 (head coach). Pro coach: Green Bay Packers 1992-98, joined Seahawks in 1999.

Larry Marmie, defensive assistant/secondary; born October 17, 1942, Berea, Kent. Quarterback Eastern Kentucky 1962-65. No pro playing experience. College

coach: Morehead State 1968-1971, Eastern Kentucky 1972-76, Tulsa 1977-78, North Carolina 1979-1982, Tennessee 1983-84, Arizona State 1985-1991 (head coach 1988-1991), Tennessee 1992-94, UCLA 1995. Pro coach: Arizona Cardinals 1996-2003, St. Louis Rams 2004-05, joined Seahawks in 2006.

John Marshall, defensive coordinator; born October 2, 1945, Arroyo Grande, Calif. Linebacker Washington State 1964. No pro playing experience. College coach: Oregon 1970-76, Southern California 1977-79. Pro coach: Green Bay Packers 1980-82, Indianapolis Colts 1986-88, San Francisco 49ers 1989-1998, Carolina Panthers 1999-2001, Detroit Lions 2002, joined Seahawks in 2003.

Stump Mitchell, running backs; born March 15, 1959, St. Mary's, Ga. Tailback The Citadel 1977-1980. Running back St. Louis/Phoenix Cardinals 1981-89. College coach: Morgan State 1995-98 (head coach 1996-98). Pro coach: San Antonio Rough Riders (WLAF) 1991, joined Seahawks in 1999.

Jim Mora, defensive backs; born November 19, 1961, Los Angeles. Defensive back Washington 1980-83. No pro playing experience. College coach: Washington 1984. Pro coach: San Diego Chargers 1986-1991, New Orleans Saints 1992-1996, San Francisco 49ers 1997-2003, Atlanta Falcons 2004-2006 (head coach), joined Seahawks in 2007.

Gary Reynolds, offensive assistant/quality control; born October 15, 1966, Boston. Attended Texas A&M. No college or pro playing experience. College coach: Texas A&M 1991, Tennessee 1992. Pro coach: Green Bay Packers 1996-98, joined Seahawks in 1999.

Ray Rhodes, special projects/defense; born October 20, 1950, Mexia, Texas. Running back Texas Christian 1969-1970, wide receiver/defensive back/kick returner Tulsa 1972-73. Pro wide receiver/defensive back New York Giants 1974-79, San Francisco 49ers 1980. Pro coach: San Francisco 49ers 1981-1991, 1994, Green Bay Packers 1992-93, 1999 (head coach 1999), Philadelphia Eagles 1995-98 (head coach), Washington Redskins 2000, Denver Broncos 2001-02, joined Seahawks in 2003.

Zerick Rollins, linebackers; born June 20, 1975, Houston. Defensive end Texas A&M 1995-97. No pro playing experience. Graduate assistant Texas A&M 1997-2000. Pro coach: Joined Seahawks in 2001.

Jim Zorn, quarterbacks; born May 10, 1953, Whittier, Calif. Quarterback Cal Poly-Pomona 1973-75. Pro quarterback Seattle Seahawks 1975-1984, Green Bay Packers 1985, Winnipeg Blue Bombers (CFL) 1986, Tampa Bay Buccaneers 1987. College coach: Boise State 1989-1991, Utah State 1992-94, Minnesota 1995-96. Pro coach: Seattle Seahawks 1997, Detroit Lions 1998-2000, re-joined Seahawks in 2001.

**National Football Conference
South Division
Team Colors:** Buccaneer Red, Pewter,
Black, and Orange
**One Buccaneer Place
Tampa, Florida 33607
Telephone:** (813) 870-2700

2007 SCHEDULE
PRESEASON
Aug. 10 **New England** 7:30
Aug. 18 at Jacksonville 7:30
Aug. 25 at Miami..........................7:30
Aug. 30 **Houston**............................8:00

REGULAR SEASON
Sep. 9   at Seattle 1:15
Sep. 16 **New Orleans** 1:00
Sep. 23 **St. Louis** 1:00
Sep. 30 at Carolina 4:05
Oct. 7   at Indianapolis 4:05
Oct. 14 **Tennessee** 1:00
Oct. 21 at Detroit 1:00
Oct. 28 **Jacksonville** 4:05
Nov. 4 **Arizona** 1:00
Nov. 11 Open Date
Nov. 18 at Atlanta 1:00
Nov. 25 **Washington** 1:00
Dec. 2 at New Orleans 12:00
Dec. 9 at Houston 12:00
Dec. 16 **Atlanta** 1:00
Dec. 23 at San Francisco *5:15
Dec. 30 **Carolina** 1:00
Sunday night games in Weeks 11-17 subject to change

Stadium: Raymond James Stadium
(opened in 1998)
• **Capacity:** 65,908
Tampa, Florida 33607
Playing Surface: Grass
Training Camp: Disney's Wide World of
Sports
Lake Buena Vista, Florida
92830

RAYMOND JAMES STADIUM

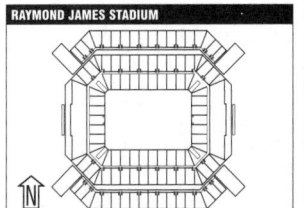

CLUB OFFICIALS
Owner/President: Malcolm Glazer
Executive Vice President: Bryan Glazer
Executive Vice President: Joel Glazer
Executive Vice President: Edward Glazer
General Manager: Bruce Allen
Chief Operating Officer: Eric Land
Director of Football Operations:
  Mark Arteaga
Director of College Scouting:
  Dennis Hickey
Director of Pro Personnel: Mark Dominik
Personnel Executive: Doug Williams
General Counsel: Roxanne Kosarzycki
Director of Player Development:
  Eric Vance
National College Scouts: Jim Abrams,
  Brian Gardner
College Scouts: Reggie Cobb,
  Frank Dorazio, Seth Turner
National Combine Scout: Mike Martin
Director of Accounting: Nick Reader
Director of Game Day and Video
  Production: Chris Kartzmark
Director of Information Technology:
  Scott Burgin
Director of Marketing and Business
  Development: Jeff Ajluni
Director of Public Relations: Jeff Kamis
Director of Sales: Kristin Bold
Director of Security and Facilities:
  Andre Trescastro
Director of Team Services: Tom Szubka
Director of Ticketing and Business
  Administration: Jason Layton
Broadcasting Operations Manager:
  Jeff Ryan
Website Manager: Scott Smith
Public Relations Manager: Jason Wahlers
Trainer: Todd Toriscelli
Director of Rehabilitation:
  Shannon Merrick
Equipment Manager: James Sorenson
Assistant Equipment Manager:
  Larry Hoyt
Video Director: Dave Levy
Assistant Video Director: Chris Bryan

COACHING HISTORY
(193-304-1)
Records include postseason games
1976-1984 John McKay.................45-91-1
1985-86   Leeman Bennett.............4-28-0
1987-1990 Ray Perkins*...............19-41-0
1990-91   Richard Williamson 4-15-0
1992-95   Sam Wyche 23-41-0
1996-2001 Tony Dungy.................56-46-0
2002-06   Jon Gruden 42-42-0
*Released after 13 games in 1990

PAID ATTENDANCE
Home 511,068   Away 539,882
Total 1,050,950
Single-game home record,
  73,523 (12/7/97)
Single-season home record,
  545,980 (1979)

2007 DRAFT CHOICES

Round	Name	Pos.	College
1	Gaines Adams	DE	Clemson
2	Arron Sears	G	Tennessee
	Sabby Piscitelli	DB	Oregon State
3	Quincy Black	LB	New Mexico
4	Tanard Jackson	DB	Syracuse
5	Greg Peterson	DT	No. Carolina Central
6	Adam Hayward	LB	Portland State
7	Chris Denman	T	Fresno State
	Marcus Hamilton	DB	Virginia
	Kenneth Darby	RB	Alabama

2006 TEAM RECORD
PRESEASON (1-3)

Date	Result	Opponent
8/11	W 16-13	N.Y. Jets
8/19	L 10-13	Miami
8/26	L 18-29	at Jacksonville
8/31	L 13-16	at Houston

REGULAR SEASON (4-12)

Date	Result	Opponent	Att.
9/10	L 0-27	Baltimore	65,087
9/17	L 3-14	at Atlanta	70,828
9/24	L 24-26	Carolina	65,423
10/8	L 21-24	at New Orleans	68,183
10/15	W 14-13	Cincinnati	65,732
10/22	W 23-21	Philadelphia	65,808
10/29	L 3-17	at N.Y. Giants	78,647
11/5	L 14-31	New Orleans	65,561
11/13	L 10-24	at Carolina	73,573
11/19	W 20-17	Washington	65,699
11/23	L 10-38	at Dallas	63,183
12/3	L 3-20	at Pittsburgh	59,843
12/10	L 6-17	Atlanta	65,691
12/17	L 31-34	at Chicago (OT)	62,260
12/24	W 22-7	at Cleveland	69,603
12/31	L 7-23	Seattle	65,660

(OT) Overtime

SCORE BY PERIODS

Buccaneers	30	53	58	70	0	— 211
Opponents	82	89	95	84	3	— 353

2006 TEAM STATISTICS

	Buccaneers	Opp.
Total First Downs	237	300
Rushing	82	108
Passing	133	174
Penalty	22	18
3rd Down: Made/Att	82/222	82/217
3rd Down Pct.	36.9	37.8
4th Down: Made/Att	4/16	5/12
4th Down Pct.	25.0	41.7
Possession Avg.	28:06	31:54
Total Net Yards	4,321	5,271
Avg. Per Game	270.1	329.4
Total Plays	972	1,015
Avg. Per Play	4.4	5.2
Net Yards Rushing	1,523	1,917
Avg. Per Game	95.2	119.8
Total Rushes	404	497
Net Yards Passing	2,798	3,354
Avg. Per Game	174.9	209.6
Sacked/Yards Lost	33/196	25/166
Gross Yards	2,994	3,520
Att./Completions	535/296	493/301
Completion Pct.	55.3	61.1
Had Intercepted	18	11
Punts/Average	93/43.5	81/41.6
Net Punting Avg.	93/36.8	81/35.3
Penalties/Yards	87/732	83/658
Fumbles/Ball Lost	27/14	25/9
Touchdowns	23	41
Rushing	6	11
Passing	14	26
Returns	3	4

2006 INDIVIDUAL STATISTICS

PASSING	Att.	Comp.	Yds.	Pct.	TD	Int.	Tkld.	Rate
Gradkowski	328	177	1,661	54.0	9	9	25/146	65.9
Simms	106	58	585	54.7	1	7	4/32	46.3
Rattay	101	61	748	60.4	4	2	4/18	88.2
Buccaneers	535	296	2,994	55.3	14	18	33/196	66.2
Opponents	493	301	3,520	61.1	26	11	25/166	91.0

SCORING	TD R	TD P	TD Rt	PAT	FG	Saf	PTS
M. Bryant	0	0	0	22/23	17/22	0	73
Galloway	0	7	0	0/0	0/0	0	42
Alstott	3	0	0	0/0	0/0	0	18
Smith	0	3	0	0/0	0/0	0	18
Barber	0	0	2	0/0	0/0	0	12
Hilliard	0	2	0	0/0	0/0	0	12
Becht	0	1	0	0/0	0/0	0	6
Brooks	0	0	1	0/0	0/0	0	6
Clayton	0	1	0	0/0	0/0	0	6
Pittman	1	0	0	0/0	0/0	0	6
Simms	1	0	0	0/0	0/0	0	6
C. Williams	1	0	0	0/0	0/0	0	6
Buccaneers	6	14	3	22/23	17/22	0	211
Opponents	11	26	4	41/41	22/30	0	353

2-Pt. Conversions:
Buccaneers 0-0, Opponents 0-0.

RUSHING	No.	Yds	Avg	LG	TD
C. Williams	225	798	3.5	38	1
Pittman	50	245	4.9	32	1
Alstott	60	171	2.9	17	3
Gradkowski	41	161	3.9	14	0
Graham	11	59	5.4	17	0
Clayton	5	41	8.2	27	0
Stovall	2	29	14.5	18	0
Galloway	2	9	4.5	7	0
Simms	4	7	1.8	3	1
Rattay	4	3	0.8	4	0
Buccaneers	404	1,523	3.8	38	6
Opponents	497	1,917	3.9	57	11

RECEIVING	No.	Yds	Avg	LG	TD
Galloway	62	1,057	17.0	64t	7
Pittman	47	405	8.6	25	0
Smith	35	250	7.1	27	3
Hilliard	34	339	10.0	44t	2
Clayton	33	356	10.8	27	1
C. Williams	30	196	6.5	21	0
Alstott	21	85	4.0	18	0
Becht	18	115	6.4	13	1
Stovall	7	102	14.6	27	0
Warren	5	63	12.6	26	0
Moore	1	9	9.0	9	0
Jolley	1	7	7.0	7	0
Sowell	1	6	6.0	6	0
Graham	1	4	4.0	4	0
Buccaneers	296	2,994	10.1	64t	14
Opponents	301	3,520	11.7	52t	26

INTERCEPTIONS	No.	Yds	Avg	LG	TD
Barber	3	103	34.3	66t	2
Brooks	3	51	17.0	21t	1
Phillips	2	45	22.5	29	0
Buchanon	2	0	0.0	0	0
Bolden	1	27	27.0	27	0
Buccaneers	11	226	20.5	66t	3
Opponents	18	280	15.6	60t	1

PUNTING	No.	Yds.	Avg.	In 20	LG
Bidwell	93	4,045	43.5	20	59
Buccaneers	93	4,045	43.5	20	59
Opponents	81	3,373	41.6	25	58

PUNT RETURNS	Ret	FC	Yds	Avg	LG	TD
Hilliard	24	3	163	6.8	16	0
Jones	20	4	155	7.8	18	0
Buchanon	6	2	16	2.7	8	0
Barber	2	0	7	3.5	8	0
Galloway	2	0	3	1.5	2	0
Cox	0	0	9	—	9	0
Buccaneers	54	9	353	6.5	18	0
Opponents	50	16	487	9.7	65t	1

KICKOFF RETURNS	No.	Yds	Avg	LG	TD
Pittman	39	867	22.2	37	0
Cox	18	387	21.5	44	0
Jones	1	29	29.0	29	0
Graham	1	13	13.0	13	0
Sowell	1	11	11.0	11	0
Adams	1	0	0.0	0	0
Buccaneers	61	1,307	21.4	44	0
Opponents	46	846	18.4	34	0

FIELD GOALS	1-19	20-29	30-39	40-49	50+
M. Bryant	0/0	8/8	3/3	5/9	1/2
Buccaneers	0/0	8/8	3/3	5/9	1/2
Opponents	0/0	7/7	6/12	6/7	3/4

SACKS	No.
Spires	5.0
D. White	5.0
Wyms	5.0
Quarles	2.5
Hovan	2.0
Rice	2.0
Nece	1.5
Bolden	1.0
Phillips	1.0
Buccaneers	25.0
Opponents	33.0

RECORD HOLDERS
INDIVIDUAL RECORDS—CAREER

Category	Name	Performance
Rushing (Yds.)	James Wilder, 1981-89	5,957
Passing (Yds.)	Vinny Testaverde, 1987-1992	14,820
Passing (TDs)	Vinny Testaverde, 1987-1992	77
Receiving (No.)	James Wilder, 1981-89	430
Receiving (Yds.)	Mark Carrier, 1987-1992	5,018
Interceptions	Donnie Abraham, 1996-2001	31
Punting (Avg.)	Josh Bidwell, 2004-06	43.8
Punt Return (Avg.)	Jacquez Green, 1998-2001	12.0
Kickoff Return (Avg.)	Aaron Stecker, 2000-03	23.8
Field Goals	Martín Gramatica, 1999-2004	137
Touchdowns (Tot.)	Mike Alstott, 1996-2006	71
Points	Martín Gramatica, 1999-2004	592

INDIVIDUAL RECORDS—SINGLE SEASON

Category	Name	Performance
Rushing (Yds.)	James Wilder, 1984	1,544
Passing (Yds.)	Brad Johnson, 2003	3,811
Passing (TDs)	Brad Johnson, 2003	26
Receiving (No.)	Keyshawn Johnson, 2001	106
Receiving (Yds.)	Mark Carrier, 1989	1,422
Interceptions	Ronde Barber, 2001	10
Punting (Avg.)	Josh Bidwell, 2005	45.6
Punt Return (Avg.)	Karl Williams, 1996	21.1
Kickoff Return (Avg.)	Karl Williams, 1996	27.4
Field Goals	Martín Gramatica, 2002	32
Touchdowns (Tot.)	James Wilder, 1984	13
Points	Martín Gramatica, 2002	128

INDIVIDUAL RECORDS—SINGLE GAME

Category	Name	Performance
Rushing (Yds.)	James Wilder, 11-6-83	219
Passing (Yds.)	Doug Williams, 11-16-80	486
Passing (TDs)	Steve DeBerg, 9-13-87	5
	Brad Johnson, 11-3-02	5
Receiving (No.)	James Wilder, 9-15-85	13
Receiving (Yds.)	Mark Carrier, 12-6-87	212
Interceptions	Ronde Barber, 12-23-01, 12-4-05	3
Field Goals	Martín Gramatica, 12-29-02	5
Touchdowns (Tot.)	Jimmie Giles, 10-20-85	4
Points	Jimmie Giles, 10-20-85	24

2007 VETERAN ROSTER

No.	Name	Pos.	Ht.	Wt.	Birthdate	NFL Exp.	College	Hometown	How Acq.	'06 Games/ Starts
40	Alstott, Mike	FB	6-1	248	12/21/73	12	Purdue	Joliet, Ill.	D2-'96	16/15
35	Askew, B.J.	FB	6-3	233	8/19/80	5	Michigan	Cincinnati, Ohio	UFA(NYJ)-'07	13/5*
20	Barber, Ronde	CB	5-10	184	4/7/75	11	Virginia	Roanoke, Va.	D3b-'97	16/16
88	Becht, Anthony	TE	6-5	272	8/8/77	8	West Virginia	Drexel Hill, Pa.	UFA(NYJ)-'05	16/16
92	Bennett, Charles	DE	6-3	254	4/4/83	2	Clemson	Camden, S.C.	D7a-'06	3/0
9	Bidwell, Josh	P	6-3	220	3/13/76	8	Oregon	Winston, Ore.	UFA(GB)-'04	16/0
11	Boston, David	WR	6-2	228	8/19/78	8	Ohio State	Humble, Texas	FA-'07	0*
98	Bradley, Jon	DT	6-0	301	1/13/81	4	Arkansas State	West Helena, Ark.	FA-'04	7/3
55	Brooks, Derrick	LB	6-0	235	4/18/73	13	Florida State	Pensacola, Fla.	D1b-'95	16/16
3	Bryant, Matt	K	5-9	200	5/29/75	6	Baylor	Orange, Texas	FA-'05	16/0
31	Buchanon, Phillip	CB	5-11	186	9/19/80	6	Miami	Ft. Myers, Fla.	FA-'06	14/4*
72	Buenning, Dan	G	6-4	320	10/26/81	3	Wisconsin	Green Bay, Wis.	D4-'05	10/7
93	Carter, Kevin	DE/DT	6-6	305	9/21/73	13	Florida	Tallahassee, Fla.	FA-'07	16/16*
52	Cash, Antoine	LB	6-1	223	3/5/82	2	Southern Mississippi	Anguilla, Miss.	FA-'05	16/0
54	Chukwurah, Patrick	DE/LB	6-1	250	3/1/79	6	Wyoming	Irving, Texas	UFA(Den)-'07	14/0*
80	Clayton, Michael	WR	6-4	215	10/13/82	4	Louisiana State	Baton Rouge, La.	D1-'04	12/9
61	Colmer, Chris	T	6-5	310	11/21/80	3	North Carolina State	Port Jefferson, N.Y.	D3b-'05	0*
27	Cox, Torrie	CB	5-10	181	10/29/80	5	Pittsburgh	Miami, Fla	D6-'03	16/3
69	Davis, Anthony	T	6-4	322	3/27/80	4	Virginia Tech	Victoria, Va.	FA-'03	16/16
22	Davis, Sammy	CB	6-1	195	4/8/80	5	Texas A&M	Humble, Texas	FA-'07	12/1*
48	Economos, Andrew	LS	6-1	250	6/24/82	2	Georgia Tech	Atlanta, Ga.	FA-'06	3/0
84	Galloway, Joey	WR	5-11	197	11/20/71	13	Ohio State	Bellaire, Ohio	T(Dall)-'04	16/14
7	Garcia, Jeff	QB	6-1	205	2/24/70	9	San Jose State	Gilroy, Calif.	UFA(Phil)-'07	8/6*
28	Gates, Lionel	RB	6-0	223	3/13/82	2	Louisville	Jacksonville, Fla.	FA-'06	0*
5	Gradkowski, Bruce	QB	6-1	220	1/27/83	2	Toledo	Pittsburgh, Pa.	D6a-'06	13/11
34	Graham, Earnest	RB	5-9	225	1/15/80	4	Florida	Ft. Myers, Fla.	FA-'03	16/0
71	Haye, Jovan	DT	6-2	295	6/21/82	3	Vanderbilt	Ft. Lauderdale, Fla.	FA-'06	9/0
87	Heinrich, Keith	TE	6-5	250	3/19/79	5	Sam Houston State	Tomball, Texas	FA-'06	0*
19	Hilliard, Ike	WR	5-11	210	4/5/76	11	Florida	Patterson, La.	FA-'05	16/0
95	Hovan, Chris	DT	6-2	296	5/12/78	8	Boston College	Rocky River, Ohio	FA-'05	16/16
91	Jenkins, Julian	DT/DE	6-3	277	10/25/83	2	Stanford	Atlanta, Ga.	D5-'06	12/0
86	#Jolley, Doug	TE	6-4	250	1/2/79	6	Brigham Young	St. George, Utah	T(NYJ)-'06	11/0
89	Jones, Mark	WR	5-9	185	11/3/80	4	Tennessee	Wallingford, Pa.	FA-'05	7/0
75	Joseph, Davin	G	6-3	313	11/22/83	2	Oklahoma	Hallandale, Fla.	D1-'06	13/12
59	June, Cato	LB	6-0	227	11/18/79	5	Michigan	Washington, D.C.	UFA(Ind)-'07	16/16*
25	Kelly, Brian	CB	5-11	193	1/14/76	10	Southern California	Aurora, Colo.	D2b-'98	2/2
	Legree, Lance	DE	6-1	300	12/22/77	6	Notre Dame	St. Stephens, S.C.	UFA(SF)-'07	0*
73	Lehr, Matt	G	6-2	304	4/25/79	7	Virginia Tech	Woodbridge, Va.	FA-'05	11/1*
54	#Mallard, Wesly	LB	6-1	230	11/21/78	6	Oregon	Columbus, Ga.	FA-'05	16/0
12	McCown, Luke	QB	6-3	212	7/12/81	4	Louisiana Tech	Jacksonville, Texas	T(Cle)-'05	0*
83	#Moore, Dave	TE/LS	6-2	250	11/11/69	16	Pittsburgh	Succasunna, N.J.	FA-'04	13/0
56	Nece, Ryan	LB	6-3	224	2/24/79	6	UCLA	San Bernardino, Calif.	FA-'02	15/11
30	Nicholson, Donte	S	6-1	216	12/18/81	2	Oklahoma	Diamond Bar, Calif.	D5a-'05	1/0
39	Pearson, Kalvin	S	5-10	190	10/22/78	3	Grambling State	Town Creek, Ala.	FA-'04	16/0
70	Penn, Donald	T	6-5	305	4/27/83	2	Utah State	Playa del Rey, Calif.	FA-'06	0*
79	Petitgout, Luke	T	6-6	310	6/16/76	9	Notre Dame	Georgetown, Del.	FA-'07	9/9*
23	Phillips, Jermaine	S	6-1	214	3/27/79	6	Georgia	Roswell, Ga.	D5-'02	16/16
32	Pittman, Michael	RB	6-0	228	8/14/75	10	Fresno State	San Diego, Calif.	UFA(Ariz)-'02	16/3
16	t- Plummer, Jake	QB	6-2	212	12/19/74	11	Arizona State	Boise, Idaho	T(Den)-'07	16/11*
97	Rice, Simeon	DE	6-5	268	2/24/74	12	Illinois	Chicago, Ill.	UFA(Ariz)-'01	8/8
51	Ruud, Barrett	LB	6-2	241	5/20/83	3	Nebraska	Lincoln, Neb.	D2-'05	16/5
2	Simms, Chris	QB	6-4	220	8/29/80	5	Texas	Ramapo, N.J.	D3-'03	3/3
98	t- Sims, Ryan	DT	6-4	315	5/4/80	6	North Carolina	Spartanburg, S.C.	T(KC)-'07	16/0*
81	Smith, Alex	TE	6-4	258	5/22/82	3	Stanford	Denver, Colo.	D3a-'05	14/7
33	#Sowell, Jerald	FB	6-0	237	1/21/74	11	Tulane	Baker, La.	FA-'06	11/0
94	Spires, Greg	DE	6-1	265	8/12/74	10	Florida State	Cape Coral, Fla.	UFA(Cle)-'02	16/16
86	Stevens, Jerramy	TE	6-7	260	11/13/79	6	Washington	Olympia, Wash.	UFA(Sea)-'07	11/6*
85	Stovall, Maurice	WR	6-5	220	2/21/85	2	Notre Dame	Philadelphia, Pa.	D3-'06	9/2
77	Terry, Jeb	G	6-5	311	4/10/81	4	North Carolina	Dallas, Texas	D5-'04	10/1
65	Trueblood, Jeremy	T	6-8	320	5/10/83	2	Boston College	Indianapolis, Ind.	D2-'06	15/13
76	Wade, John	C	6-5	299	1/25/75	10	Marshall	Harrisonburg, Va.	UFA(Jax)-'03	16/16
82	Warren, Paris	WR	6-0	213	9/6/82	3	Utah	Sacramento, Calif.	D7b-'05	8/0
24	Williams, Carnell	RB	5-11	217	4/21/82	3	Auburn	Attalla, Ala.	D1-'05	14/14
45	Williams, T.J.	TE	6-3	258	9/24/82	2	North Carolina State	Tarboro, N.C.	D6b-'06	0*
50	Winborn, Jamie	LB	5-11	242	5/14/79	7	Vanderbilt	Wetumpka, Ala.	UFA(Jax)-'06	14/0

| 96 | Wyms, Ellis | DT | 6-3 | 290 | 4/12/79 | 7 | Mississippi State | Indianola, Miss. | D6b-'01 | 13/8 |
| 29 | Zemaitis, Alan | CB | 6-2 | 200 | 8/24/82 | 2 | Penn State | Rochester, N.Y. | D4-'06 | 0* |

* Askew played 13 games with N.Y. Jets in '06; Boston last active with Miami in '05; Buchanon played 4 games with Houston and 10 with Tampa Bay; Carter played 16 games with Miami; Chukwurah played 14 games with Denver; Colmer inactive for 16 games in '05; S. Davis played 12 games with San Francisco; Garcia played 8 games with Philadelphia; Gates last active with Buffalo in '05; Heinrich last active with Cleveland in '04; June played 16 games with Indianapolis; Legree inactive 2 games with San Francisco in '06; Lehr played 11 games with Atlanta; McCown inactive for 9 games; Penn inactive for 13 games; Petitgout played 9 games with N.Y. Giants; Plummer played 16 games with Denver; Sims played 16 games with Kansas City; Stevens played 11 games with Seattle; T. Williams missed '06 season because of injury; Zemaitis inactive for 15 games.

\# Unrestricted free agent; subject to developments.

t- Buccaneers traded for Plummer (Den), Sims (KC).

Traded—DT Anthony McFarland (Ind; 5 games in '06).

Players lost through free agency (4): T Cornell Green (Oak; 14 games in '06), G Sean Mahan (Pitt; 16), QB Tim Rattay (Tenn; 4), DE Dewayne White (Det; 16).

Also played with Buccaneers '06—S Blue Adams (16 games), CB Juran Bolden (16), DT Anthony McFarland (5), LB Shelton Quarles (12), T Kenyatta Walker (3).

2007 FIRST-YEAR ROSTER

Name	Pos.	Ht.	Wt.	Birthdate	College	Hometown	How Acq.
Adams, Gaines	DE	6-5	258	6/8/83	Clemson	Greenwood, S.C.	D1
Benjamin, Evan (1)	LB	6-0	222	1/29/83	Washington	Redmond, Wash.	FA
Black, Quincy	LB	6-2	240	2/28/84	New Mexico	Chicago, Ill.	D3
Bouknight, Jovon (1)	WR	6-1	191	8/19/78	Wyoming	Denver, Colo.	FA
Campbell, Darrell (1)	DT	6-4	295	7/6/81	Notre Dame	South Holland, Ill.	FA-'06
Clinkscale, Jonathan (1)	G/C	6-2	315	4/17/82	Wisconsin	Altadena, Calif.	FA-'05
Darby, Kenneth	RB	5-10	211	12/26/82	Alabama	Huntsville, Ala.	D7c
Denman, Chris	T	6-7	315	10/7/83	Fresno State	Tehachapi, Calif.	D7a
Eugene, Bruce (1)	QB	6-0	283	6/20/82	Grambling	New Orleans, La.	FA
Frick, Justin	DT	6-3	295	7/31/84	North Dakota State	Yankton, S.D.	FA
Gessner, Chas (1)	WR	6-4	215	8/17/81	Brown	College Park, Md.	FA-'06
Goldsberry, Jon (1)	FB	6-1	246	12/4/81	Purdue	Santa Claus, Ind.	FA-'06
Hamilton, Marcus	CB	6-0	192	2/17/84	Virginia	Centreville, Va.	D7b
Hayward, Adam	LB	6-0	235	6/23/84	Portland State	Westminster, Calif.	D6
Hendricks, Carlos (1)	CB	5-11	190	8/31/83	Alabama-Birmingham	Montgomery, Ala.	FA-'06
Herian, Matt	TE	6-5	245	10/7/83	Nebraska	Pierce, Neb.	FA
Jackson, Tanard	S	6-0	200	7/21/85	Syracuse	Potomac, Md.	D4
Lucas, Chad (1)	WR	6-1	201	11/7/81	Alabama State	Tuskegee, Ala.	FA-'06
Mackey Jerry	LB	6-1	233	9/20/84	Syracuse	Freeport, N.Y.	FA
Mihlhauser, Nick (1)	C	6-3	305	7/6/84	Washington State	Arroyo Grande, Calif.	FA'06
Olajubutu, Sam	LB	5-9	227	11/15/83	Arkansas	LaGrange, Ga.	FA
Owens, Chad (1)	WR	5-7	188	4/3/82	Hawaii	Honolulu, Hawaii	FA
Peterson, Greg	DT	6-5	272	1/21/84	North Carolina Central	East Duplin, N.C.	D5
Piscitelli, Sabby	S	6-3	224	8/24/83	Oregon State	Boca Raton, Fla.	D2b
Rivas, Garrett	K	5-9	216	12/1/85	Michigan	Tampa, Fla.	FA
Roland, Dennis (1)	T	6-9	325	3/10/83	Georgia	Bolivar, Mo.	FA-'06
Scott, Kenny	CB	6-2	185	1/21/85	Georgia Tech	Daytona, Fla.	FA
Sears, Arron	G	6-3	319	10/25/84	Tennessee	Russellville, Ala.	D2a
Smith, Kyle (1)	WR	6-0	170	10/15/84	Youngstown State	Buffalo, N.Y.	FA
Storer, Byron	FB	6-1	219	5/1/84	California	Modesto, Calif.	FA
Taylor, Zac	QB	6-2	210	5/10/83	Nebraska	Norman, Okla.	FA
Williams, Chaz	CB	6-0	190	6/17/84	Louisiana-Monroe	Lake Charles, La.	FA
Wollschlager, Anthony	G	6-4	288	1/6/84	Miami	Ft. Lauderdale, Fla.	FA

The term NFL Rookie is defined as a player who is in his first season of professional football and has not been on the roster of another professional football team for any regular-season or postseason games. A Rookie is designated by an "R" on NFL rosters. Players who have been active in another professional football league or players who have NFL experience, including either preseason training camp or being on an Active List or Inactive List, or on Reserve/Injured or Reserve/Physically Unable to Perform for fewer than six regular-season games, are termed NFL First-Year Players. An NFL First-Year Player is designated by a "1" on NFL rosters. Thereafter, a player is credited with an additional year of experience for each season in which he accumulates six games on the Active List or Inactive List, or on Reserve/Injured or Reserve/Physically Unable to Perform.

Log on to www.buccaneers.com for an up-to-date roster.

COACHING STAFF

**Head Coach,
Jon Gruden**

Pro Career: Gruden was named the seventh head coach in Buccaneers history on February 18, 2002, when he signed a five-year contract. Gruden led Tampa Bay to its first Super Bowl title in his first season as head coach in 2002. Gruden set two NFL records—he became the youngest head coach (39) to win a Super Bowl, and was the first veteran head coach to lead his team to the Super Bowl in his first season with a new team. In 2005, the Buccaneers won the NFC South for the second time in four seasons. Prior to joining the Buccaneers, Gruden guided the Oakland Raiders to division titles in each of his final two seasons. He steered the Raiders to a 40-28 mark in four seasons (1998-2001), with postseason appearances in 2000 and 2001. Under Gruden, the Raiders advanced to the AFC title game in 2000 and in 2001 lost a divisional playoff game to eventual Super Bowl champion New England. Prior to his four seasons in Oakland, Gruden spent 1995-97 as offensive coordinator for the Philadelphia Eagles and three years (1992-94) as wide receivers coach for Green Bay Packers. He worked as offensive assistant for the San Francisco 49ers in 1990. Career record: 82-72.

Background: Quarterback at Dayton (1982-84), graduating with a degree in communications. The Flyers had a 24-7 record in Gruden's three varsity seasons. Coach collegiately at Tennessee (1986-87), Southeast Missouri State (1988), Pacific (1989), and Pittsburgh (1991).

Personal: Born August 17, 1963 in Sandusky, Ohio. Jon and his wife Cindy, have three sons, Jon II, Michael, and Jayson.

ASSISTANT COACHES

Tim Berbenich, offensive quality control; born December 19, 1979, Huntington, N.Y. Wide receiver Hamilton College 1998-2001. No pro playing experience. Pro coach: New York Jets 2003-05, joined Buccaneers in 2006.

Richard Bisaccia, special teams coordinator; born June 3, 1960, Yonkers, N.Y. Defensive back Yankton College 1979-1982, Philadelphia Stars (USFL) 1983. College coach: Wayne State College 1983-87, South Carolina 1988-1993, Clemson 1994-98, Mississippi 1999-2001. Pro coach: Joined Buccaneers in 2002.

Casey Bradley, linebackers; born July 5, 1966, Zumbrota, Minn. Safety/punter North Dakota State 1984-1988. No pro playing experience. College coach: North Dakota State 1990-1991, 1996-2005, Fort Lewis College 1992-1996. Pro coach: Joined Buccaneers in 2006.

Bob Casullo, tight ends; born March 21, 1951, Little Falls, N.Y. Running back

Brockport (N.Y.) State College 1970-73. No pro playing experience. College coach: Syracuse 1985-1994, Georgia Tech 1995-98, Michigan State 1999. Pro coach: Oakland Raiders 2000-03, New York Jets 2004, Seattle Seahawks 2005-06, joined Buccaneers in 2007.

Larry Coyer, asst. head coach/defensive line; born April 19, 1943, Huntington, W. Va. Linebacker Marshall 1962-64. No pro playing experience. College coach: Marshall 1965-67, Iowa 1974-77, Oklahoma State 1978, Iowa State 1979-1983, 1995-96, UCLA 1987-89, Houston 1990, Ohio State 1991-92, East Carolina 1993, Pittsburgh 1997-99. Pro coach: Michigan Panthers (USFL) 1984-85, New York Jets 1994, Denver Broncos 2000-06, joined Buccaneers in 2007.

Jay Gruden, offensive assistant; born March 4, 1967. Quarterback Louisville 1985-88. Pro quarterback Tampa Bay Storm (AFL) 1991-96, Orlando Predators (AFL) 2002-03. Pro coach: Nashville Kats (AFL) 1997, Orlando Predators (AFL) 1998-2001, 2004-06, joined Buccaneers in 2002.

Nathaniel Hackett, offensive quality control; born December 19, 1979, Fullerton, Calif. Linebacker Cal-Davis 1999-2002. No pro playing experience. College coach: Stanford 2003-05. Pro coach: Joined Buccaneers in 2006.

Paul Hackett, quarterbacks; born July 5, 1947, Burlington, Vt. Quarterback Cal-Davis 1965-68. No pro playing experience. College coach: Cal-Davis 1969-1971, California 1972-75, Southern California 1976-1980, 1998-2000 (head coach 1998-2000), Pittsburgh 1989-1992 (head coach 1990-92). Pro coach: Cleveland Browns 1981-82, San Francisco 49ers 1983-85, Dallas Cowboys 1986-88, Kansas City Chiefs 1993-97, New York Jets 2001-04, joined Buccaneers in 2005.

Monte Kiffin, defensive coordinator; born February 29, 1940, Lexington, Neb. Offensive/defensive tackle Nebraska 1959-1963. Pro defensive end Winnipeg Blue Bombers (CFL) 1965. College coach: Nebraska 1966-1976, Arkansas 1977-79, North Carolina State 1980-82 (head coach). Pro coach: Green Bay Packers 1983, Buffalo Bills 1984-85, Minnesota Vikings 1986-89, 1991-94, New York Jets 1990, New Orleans Saints 1995, joined Buccaneers in 1996.

Aaron Kromer, senior assistant/offensive line; born April 30, 1967, Sandusky, Ohio. Offensive tackle Miami (Ohio) 1986-89. No pro playing experience. College coach: Miami (Ohio) 1990-98, Northwestern 1999-2000. Pro coach: Oakland Raiders 2001-04, joined Buccaneers in 2005.

Jimmy Lake, asst. defensive backs; born December 17, 1976, San Francisco. Safety Eastern Washington 1995-98. No pro playing experience. College coach: Eastern Washington 1999-2003,

Washington 2004, Montana State 2005. Pro coach: Joined Buccaneers in 2006.

Richard Mann, wide receivers; born April 20, 1947, Aliquippa, Pa. Wide receiver Arizona State 1966-68. No pro playing experience. College coach: Arizona State 1974-79, Louisville 1980-81. Pro coach: Baltimore/Indianapolis Colts 1982-84, Cleveland Browns 1985-1993, New York Jets 1994-96, Baltimore Ravens 1997-98, Kansas City Chiefs 1999-2000, Washington Redskins 2001, joined Buccaneers in 2002.

Mike Morris, head strength and conditioning; born May 7, 1964, Ayer, Mass. Wide receiver Syracuse 1981-85. No pro playing experience. Pro coach: New England Patriots 1997-99, joined Buccaneers in 2002.

Raheem Morris, defensive backs; born September 3, 1976, Irvington, N.J. Safety Hofstra 1994-97. No pro playing experience. College coach: Hofstra 1998, 2000-2001, Cornell 1999, Kansas State 2006. Pro coach: New York Jets 2001, Tampa Bay Buccaneers 2002-05, re-joined Buccaneers in 2007.

Bill Muir, offensive coordinator/offensive line; born October 26, 1942, Pittsburgh. Tackle Susquehanna 1962-64. No pro playing experience. College coach: Susquehanna 1965, Delaware Valley 1966-67, Rhode Island 1970-71, Idaho State 1972-73, Southern Methodist 1976-77. Pro coach: Orlando (Continental Football League) 1968-69, Houston Shreveport Steamer (WFL) 1975, New England Patriots 1982-88, Indianapolis Colts 1989-1991, Philadelphia Eagles 1992-94, New York Jets 1995-2001, joined Buccaneers in 2002.

Kurt Shultz, asst. strength and conditioning; born March 10, 1972, Baltimore. Attended Maryland. No college or pro playing experience. College coach: Loyola (Md.) 1995-98, Maryland and Johns Hopkins 1999-2002. Pro coach: Cincinnati Bengals 2003, Minnesota Vikings 2004-05, joined Buccaneers in 2006.

Art Valero, asst. head coach/running backs; born May 12, 1958, Whittier, Calif. Offensive lineman Boise State 1979-1980. No pro playing experience. College coach: Boise State 1981-82, Iowa State 1983, Long Beach State 1984-86, New Mexico 1987-89, Idaho 1990-94, Louisville 1998-2001. Pro coach: Kansas City Chiefs 1994, Buffalo Bills 1996, joined Buccaneers in 2002.

Todd Wash, defensive quality control; born July 19, 1968, Miles City, Mont. Linebacker North Dakota State 1988-1991. No pro playing experience. College coach: Fort Lewis College 1996-99, Nebraska-Kearney 2000-01, North Dakota State 2002-03, 2005-06, Missouri Southern State 2004. Pro coach: Joined Buccaneers in 2006.

**National Football Conference
East Division**
Team Colors: Burgundy and Gold
Redskins Park
21300 Redskins Park Drive
Ashburn, Virginia 20147
Telephone: (703) 726-7000

2007 SCHEDULE
PRESEASON
Aug. 11 at Tennessee 7:00
Aug. 18 **Pittsburgh** 8:00
Aug. 25 **Baltimore** 8:00
Aug. 30 at Jacksonville 7:30

REGULAR SEASON
Sep. 9   **Miami** 1:00
Sep. 17 at Philadelphia (Mon.).........8:30
Sep. 23 **N.Y. Giants** 4:15
Sep. 30 Open Date
Oct. 7   **Detroit** 1:00
Oct. 14 at Green Bay 12:00
Oct. 21 **Arizona** 1:00
Oct. 28 at New England 4:15
Nov. 4   at N.Y. Jets 1:00
Nov. 11 **Philadelphia** 1:00
Nov. 18 at Dallas 12:00
Nov. 25 at Tampa Bay 1:00
Dec. 2   **Buffalo** 1:00
Dec. 6   **Chicago** (Thu.)..................8:15
Dec. 16 at N.Y. Giants *8:15
Dec. 23 at Minnesota 12:00
Dec. 30 **Dallas** 1:00
*Sunday night games in Weeks 11-17 subject to change

Stadium: FedExField (opened in 1997)
•**Capacity:** 91,704
1600 FedEx Way
Landover, Maryland 20785
Playing Surface: Natural Grass
Training Camp: Redskins Park
Ashburn, Virginia 20147

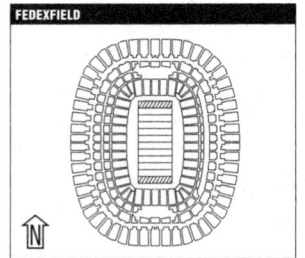

CLUB OFFICIALS
Owner: Daniel M. Snyder
Chief Operating Officer: Mitch Gershman
Chief Financial Officer: Jay Sloan
General Counsel: Dave Donovan
Senior Vice President: Karl Swanson
Senior Vice President, Marketing:
Terry Bateman
Senior Vice President, Stadium
Operations: Michael Dillow
Director of Ticket Operations: Jeff Ritter
Vice President, Football Operations:
Vinny Cerrato
Director of Pro Personnel: Louis Riddick
Director of College Scouting:
Scott Campbell
Pro Scouts: Terry Ray, Donnie Warren
College Scouts: Mike Faulkiner,
Tim Gribble, Shemy Schembechler,
Jim Zeches
National Scout: Russ Bolinger,
Joel Patten
Director of Football Administration:
Eric Schaffer
Director of Player Development:
John "JJ" Jefferson
Vice President, Public Relations:
Chris Helein
Leadership Council/Community Affairs:
Charlene Lefkowitz
Director of Team Administration:
Derrick Crawford
Video Director: Mike Bracken
Video Department: Todd Davis,
George Claiborne
Director of Sports Medicine: Bubba Tyer
Head Athletic Trainer: John Burrell
Assistant Athletic Trainers: Eric Steward,
Larry Hess
Equipment Manager: Brad Berlin
Assistant Equipment Manager:
Anders Beutel, Chris Collins

COACHING HISTORY
Boston 1932-36
(543-495-27)
Records include postseason games
1932   Lud Wray.........................4-4-2
1933-34   William (Lone Star) Dietz11-11-2
1935   Eddie Casey.....................2-8-1
1936-1942 Ray Flaherty 56-23-3
1943   Arthur (Dutch) Bergman.....7-4-1
1944-45   Dudley DeGroot 14-6-1
1946-48   Glen (Turk) Edwards 16-18-1
1949   John Whelchel* 3-3-1
1949-1951 Herman Ball** 4-16-0
1951   Dick Todd 5-4-0
1952-53   Earl (Curly) Lambeau 10-13-1
1954-58   Joe Kuharich.................26-32-2
1959-1960 Mike Nixon......................4-18-2
1961-65   Bill McPeak 21-46-3
1966-68   Otto Graham 17-22-3
1969   Vince Lombardi.................7-5-2
1970   Bill Austin 6-8-0
1971-77   George Allen 69-35-1
1978-1980 Jack Pardee 24-24-0
1981-1992 Joe Gibbs 140-65-0
1993   Richie Petitbon..............4-12-0
1994-2000 Norv Turner***.............50-60-1
2000   Terry Robiskie..................1-2-0
2001   Marty Schottenheimer.......8-8-0
2002-03   Steve Spurrier 12-20-0
2004-06   Joe Gibbs 22-28-0
*Released after seven games in 1949
**Released after three games in 1951
***Released after 13 games in 2000

PAID ATTENDANCE
Home 708,952   Away 523,248
Total 1,240,223
Single-game home record,
88,678 (9/27/04)
Single-season home record,
708,952 (2006)

2007 DRAFT CHOICES
Round	Name	Pos.	College
1	LaRon Landry	DB	Louisiana State
5	Dallas Sartz	LB	So. California
6	H.B. Blades	LB	Pittsburgh
	Jordan Palmer	QB	Texas El-Paso
7	Tyler Ecker	TE	Michigan

2006 TEAM RECORD
PRESEASON (3-1)

Date	Result		Opponent
8/13	L	3-19	at Cincinnati
8/19	L	14-27	N.Y. Jets
8/26	L	0-41	at New England
8/31	L	10-17	Baltimore

REGULAR SEASON (5-11)

Date	Result		Opponent	Att.
9/11	L	16-19	Minnesota	90,608
9/17	L	10-27	at Dallas	63,152
9/24	W	31-15	at Houston	70,069
10/1	W	36-30	Jacksonville (OT)	89,450
10/8	L	3-19	at N.Y. Giants	78,653
10/15	L	22-25	Tennessee	88,550
10/22	L	22-36	at Indianapolis	57,274
11/5	W	22-19	Dallas	90,250
11/12	L	3-27	at Philadelphia	69,143
11/19	L	17-20	at Tampa Bay	65,699
11/26	W	17-13	Carolina	85,450
12/3	L	14-24	Atlanta	86,436
12/10	L	19-21	Philadelphia	84,164
12/17	W	16-10	at New Orleans	69,052
12/24	L	31-37	at St. Louis (OT)	62,324
12/30	L	28-34	N.Y. Giants	86,141

SCORE BY PERIODS

Redskins	76	94	55	76	6 —	307
Opponents	69	126	95	80	6 —	376

2006 TEAM STATISTICS

	Redskins	Opp.
Total First Downs	295	301
Rushing	123	104
Passing	150	169
Penalty	22	28
3rd Down: Made/Att	79/211	97/222
3rd Down Pct.	37.4	43.7
4th Down: Made/Att	6/13	6/9
4th Down Pct.	46.2	66.7
Possession Avg.	29:59	30:01
Total Net Yards	5,243	5,688
Avg. Per Game	327.7	355.5
Total Plays	979	997
Avg. Per Play	5.4	5.7
Net Yards Rushing	2,216	2,197
Avg. Per Game	138.5	137.3
Total Rushes	490	492
Net Yards Passing	3,027	3,491
Avg. Per Game	189.2	218.2
Sacked/Yards Lost	19/147	19/95
Gross Yards	3,174	3,586
Att./Completions	470/274	486/289
Completion Pct.	58.3	59.5
Had Intercepted	10	6
Punts/Average	82/42.3	79/42.0
Net Punting Avg.	82/36.7	79/34.9
Penalties/Yards	106/951	94/856
Fumbles/Ball Lost	20/7	15/6
Touchdowns	34	41
Rushing	13	9
Passing	19	30
Returns	2	2

2006 INDIVIDUAL STATISTICS

PASSING	Att.	Comp.	Yds.	Pct.	TD	Int.	Tkld.	Rate
Brunell	260	162	1,789	62.3	8	4	12/92	86.5
J. Campbell	207	110	1,297	53.1	10	6	7/55	76.5
Randle El	3	2	88	66.7	1	0	0/0	149.3
Redskins	470	274	3,174	58.3	19	10	19/147	83.4
Opponents	486	289	3,586	59.5	30	6	19/95	97.8

SCORING	TD R	TD P	TD Rt	PAT	FG	Saf	PTS
Portis	7	0	0	0/0	0/0	0	42
Cooley	0	6	0	0/0	0/0	0	38
Moss	0	6	0	0/0	0/0	0	38
Hall	0	0	0	9/9	9/11	0	36
Suisham	0	0	0	12/12	8/9	0	36
Betts	4	1	0	0/0	0/0	0	30
Novak	0	0	0	10/10	5/10	0	25
Randle El	0	3	1	0/0	0/0	0	24
Duckett	2	0	0	0/0	0/0	0	12
Cartwright	0	0	1	0/0	0/0	0	6
Sellers	0	1	0	0/0	0/0	0	6
Thrash	0	1	0	0/0	0/0	0	6
Yoder	0	1	0	0/0	0/0	0	6
Marshall	0	0	0	0/0	0/0	1	2
Redskins	13	19	2	31/31	22/30	1	307
Opponents	9	30	2	36/36	30/34	1	376

*2-Pt. Conversions: Cooley, Moss,
Redskins 2-2, Opponents 1-4.*

RUSHING	No.	Yds	Avg	LG	TD
Betts	245	1154	4.7	26	4
Portis	127	523	4.1	38t	7
Duckett	38	132	3.5	19	2
Randle El	19	118	6.2	20	0
J. Campbell	24	107	4.5	15	0
Moss	7	82	11.7	35	0
Sellers	12	51	4.3	13	0
Brunell	13	34	2.6	12	0
Cartwright	5	15	3.0	9	0
Redskins	490	2,216	4.5	38t	13
Opponents	492	2,197	4.5	69t	9

RECEIVING	No.	Yds	Avg	LG	TD
Cooley	57	734	12.9	66t	6
Moss	55	790	14.4	68t	6
Betts	53	445	8.4	34	1
Randle El	32	351	11.0	34t	3
Lloyd	23	365	15.9	52	0
Sellers	18	105	5.8	15	1
Portis	17	170	10.0	74	0
Thrash	12	151	12.6	27	1
Fauria	2	17	8.5	11	0
Duckett	2	16	8.0	19	0
Patten	1	25	25.0	25	0
Yoder	1	4	4.0	4t	1
Kozlowski	1	1	1.0	1	0
Redskins	274	3,174	11.6	74	19
Opponents	289	3,586	12.4	84t	30

INTERCEPTIONS	No.	Yds	Avg	LG	TD
Taylor	1	25	25.0	25	0
Springs	1	4	4.0	4	0
Daniels	1	0	0.0	0	0
Rogers	1	0	0.0	0	0
Wright	1	0	0.0	0	0
Fox	1	-4	-4.0	-4	0
Redskins	6	25	4.2	25	0
Opponents	10	272	27.2	84t	2

PUNTING	No.	Yds.	Avg.	In 20	LG
Frost	81	3,471	42.9	27	60
Redskins	82	3,471	42.3	27	60
Opponents	79	3,316	42.0	19	70

PUNT RETURNS	Ret	FC	Yds	Avg	LG	TD
Randle El	39	11	342	8.8	87t	1
Redskins	39	11	342	8.8	87t	1
Opponents	45	12	319	7.1	33	0

KICKOFF RETURNS	No.	Yds	Avg	LG	TD
Cartwright	64	1,541	24.1	100t	1
Sellers	4	53	13.3	22	0
Betts	2	27	13.5	27	0
Evans	1	0	0.0	0	0
Golston	1	0	0.0	0	0
Thrash	1	10	10.0	10	0
Redskins	73	1,631	22.3	100t	1
Opponents	67	1,396	20.8	44	0

FIELD GOALS	1-19	20-29	30-39	40-49	50+
Hall	0/0	3/3	4/4	2/4	0/0
Suisham	0/0	1/1	5/5	1/1	1/2
Novak	0/0	1/1	1/3	3/6	0/0
Redskins	0/0	5/5	1,0/12	6/11	1/2
Opponents	1/1	6/6	1,3/14	8/10	2/3

SACKS	No.
A. Carter	6.0
Daniels	3.0
Washington	2.5
Evans	2.0
Marshall	1.5
Archuleta	1.0
Griffin	1.0
Holdman	1.0
Golston	0.5
Montgomery	0.5
Redskins	19.0
Opponents	19.0

RECORD HOLDERS
INDIVIDUAL RECORDS—CAREER

Category	Name	Performance
Rushing (Yds.)	John Riggins, 1976-79, 1981-85	7,472
Passing (Yds.)	Joe Theismann, 1974-1985	25,206
Passing (TDs)	Sammy Baugh, 1937-1952	187
Receiving (No.)	Art Monk, 1980-1993	888
Receiving (Yds.)	Art Monk, 1980-1993	12,028
Interceptions	Darrell Green, 1983-2001	54
Punting (Avg.)	Sammy Baugh, 1937-1952	45.1
Punt Return (Avg.)	Johnny Williams, 1952-53	12.8
Kickoff Return (Avg.)	Bobby Mitchell, 1962-68	28.5
Field Goals	Mark Moseley, 1974-1986	263
Touchdowns (Tot.)	Charley Taylor, 1964-1977	90
Points	Mark Moseley, 1974-1986	1,206

INDIVIDUAL RECORDS—SINGLE SEASON

Category	Name	Performance
Rushing (Yds.)	Clinton Portis, 2005	1,516
Passing (Yds.)	Jay Schroeder, 1986	4,109
Passing (TDs)	Sonny Jurgensen, 1967	31
Receiving (No.)	Art Monk, 1984	106
Receiving (Yds.)	Santana Moss, 2005	1,483
Interceptions	Dan Sandifer, 1948	13
Punting (Avg.)	Sammy Baugh, 1940	*51.4
Punt Return (Avg.)	Johnny Williams, 1952	15.3
Kickoff Return (Avg.)	Mike Nelms, 1981	29.7
Field Goals	Mark Moseley, 1983	33
Touchdowns (Tot.)	John Riggins, 1983	24
Points	Mark Moseley, 1983	161

INDIVIDUAL RECORDS—SINGLE GAME

Category	Name	Performance
Rushing (Yds.)	Gerald Riggs, 9-17-89	221
Passing (Yds.)	Sammy Baugh, 10-31-43	446
Passing (TDs)	Sammy Baugh, 10-31-43, 11-23-47	6
	Mark Rypien, 11-10-91	6
Receiving (No.)	Art Monk, 12-15-85, 11-4-90	13
	Kelvin Bryant, 12-7-86	13
Receiving (Yds.)	Anthony Allen, 10-4-87	255
Interceptions	Sammy Baugh, 11-14-43	*4
	Dan Sandifer, 10-31-48	*4
Field Goals	Many times	5
	Last time by Chip Lohmiller, 10-25-92	
Touchdowns (Tot.)	Dick James, 12-17-61	4
	Larry Brown, 12-16-73	4
Points	Dick James, 12-17-61	24
	Larry Brown, 12-16-73	24

*NFL Record

2007 VETERAN ROSTER

No.	Name	Pos.	Ht.	Wt.	Birthdate	NFL Exp.	College	Hometown	How Acq.	'06 Games/ Starts
71	Albright, Ethan	LS	6-5	265	5/1/71	13	North Carolina	Greensboro, N.C.	UFA(Buff)-'01	16/0
75	Armstrong, Calvin	T	6-7	325	3/31/82	2	Washington State	Centralia, Wash.	PS-'06	0*
46	Betts, Ladell	RB	5-10	223	8/27/79	6	Iowa	Blue Springs, Mo.	D2-'02	16/9
73	Boschetti, Ryan	DT	6-4	305	10/7/81	4	UCLA	Belmont, Calif.	FA-'04	2/0
5	Bramlet , Casey	QB	6-4	220	4/2/81	2	Wyoming	Wheatland, Wyo.	FA-'07	0*
8	Brunell, Mark	QB	6-1	217	9/17/70	15	Washington	Santa Maria, Calif.	T(Jax)-'04	10/9
17	Campbell, Jason	QB	6-4	230	12/31/81	3	Auburn	Taylorsville, Miss.	D1-'05	7/7
50	Campbell, Khary	LB	6-3	232	4/4/79	6	Bowling Green	Toledo, Ohio	FA-'03	14/1
99	Carter, Andre	DE	6-4	265	5/12/79	7	California	Denver, Colo.	UFA(SF)-'06	16/16
31	Cartwright, Rock	RB	5-7	215	12/3/79	6	Kansas State	Conroe, Texas	D7-'02	16/0
74	Clauss, Jared	DT	6-4	290	4/7/81	3	Iowa	West Des Moines, Iowa	FA-'07	0*
15	Collins, Todd	QB	6-4	228	11/5/71	13	Michigan	Walpole, Mass.	UFA(KC)-'06	0*
47	Cooley, Chris	TE	6-3	250	7/11/82	4	Utah State	Powell, Utah	D3-'04	16/16
93	Daniels, Phillip	DE	6-3	290	3/4/73	12	Georgia	Donalson, Ga.	UFA(Chi)-'04	16/15
37	Doughty, Reed	S	6-1	210	11/4/82	2	Northern Colorado	Johnstown, Colo.	D6-06	10/0
84	Edwards, Eric	TE	6-5	257	8/4/80	3	Louisiana State	Monroe, La.	FA-'07	0*
92	Evans, Demetric	DE/DT	6-3	285	9/3/79	6	Georgia	Haynesville, La.	FA-'04	16/0
69	Fabini, Jason	T/G	6-7	309	8/25/74	10	Cincinnati	Verona, N.J.	FA-'07	0*
59	Fletcher, London	LB	5-10	245	5/19/75	10	John Carroll	Cleveland, Ohio	UFA(Buff)-'07	15/0*
39	Fox, Vernon	S	5-10	200	10/9/79	6	Fresno State	Las Vegas, Nev.	FA-'06	16/6
4	Frost, Derrick	P	6-2	202	11/25/80	4	Northern Iowa	St. Louis, Mo.	FA-'05	16/0
64	Golston, Kedric	DT	6-4	292	5/30/83	2	Georgia	Tyrone, Ga.	D6-06	16/13
91	Green, Jamal	DE	6-2	258	6/5/80	2	Miami	Camden, N.J.	PS-'06	0*
96	Griffin, Cornelius	DT	6-3	310	12/3/76	8	Alabama	Brundidge, Ala.	FA-'04 (NYG)	14/14
76	Jansen, Jon	T	6-6	308	1/28/76	8	Michigan	Clawson, Mich.	D2-99	15/15
32	Jimoh, Ade	CB	6-1	195	4/18/80	5	Utah State	Woodland Hills, Calif.	FA-'03	16/0
85	Lloyd, Brandon	WR	6-0	192	7/5/81	5	Illinois	Kansas City, Mo.	T(SF)-'06	15/12
38	Macklin, David	CB	5-10	206	7/14/78	8	Penn State	Newport News, Va.	UFA(Ariz)-'07	14/7*
98	Marshall, Lemar	LB	6-2	232	12/17/76	6	Michigan State	Cincinnati, Ohio	FA-'01	15/15
52	McIntosh, Rocky	LB	6-2	231	11/15/82	2	Miami	Gaffney, S.C.	D2-'06	16/2
94	Montgomery, Anthony	DT	6-5	305	3/8/84	2	Minnesota	Cleveland, Ohio	D5-'06	5/1
89	Moss, Santana	WR	5-10	190	6/1/79	7	Miami	Miami, Fla.	T(NYJ)-'05	14/14
26	Portis, Clinton	RB	5-11	212	9/1/81	6	Miami	Gainesville, Fla.	T(Den)-'04	7/6
20	Prioleau, Pierson	S	5-11	185	8/6/77	9	Virginia Tech	Alvin, S.C.	UFA(Buff)-'05	1/0
62	Pucillo, Mike	G/T	6-4	311	7/14/79	5	Auburn	Cleveland, Ohio	UFA(Cle)-'06	12/0
61	Rabach, Casey	C/G	6-4	295	9/24/77	6	Wisconsin	Sturgeon Bay, Wis.	UFA(Balt)-'05	16/16
82	Randle El, Antwaan	WR	5-10	192	8/17/79	6	Indiana	Riverdale, Ill.	UFA(Pitt)-'06	16/16
22	Rogers, Carlos	CB	6-0	195	7/2/81	3	Auburn	Augusta, Ga.	D1-'05	15/15
95	Salave'a, Joe	DT/DE	6-3	317	3/25/75	9	Arizona	Leone, American Samoa	FA-'04	13/4
60	Samuels, Chris	T	6-5	310	7/28/77	8	Alabama	Mobile, Ala.	D1-'00	16/16
45	Sellers, Mike	FB	6-3	278	7/21/75	8	Walla Walla (Wash.) C.C.	North Thurston, Wash.	FA-'04	16/6
27	Smoot, Fred	CB	5-11	178	4/17/79	7	Mississippi State	Jackson, Miss.	FA-'07	14/11*
24	Springs, Shawn	CB	6-0	200	3/11/75	11	Ohio State	Silver Spring, Md.	UFA(Sea)-'04	9/8
23	Stoutmire, Omar	S	5-11	205	7/9/74	11	Fresno State	Long Beach, Calif.	UFA(NO)-'07	13/9*
6	Suisham, Shaun	K	6-0	205	12/29/81	3	Bowling Green	Wallaceburg, Ontario, Canada	FA-'06	8/0*
21	Taylor, Sean	S	6-2	232	4/1/83	4	Miami	Miami, Fla.	D1-'04	16/16
77	Thomas, Randy	G	6-5	310	1/19/76	9	Mississippi State	East Point, Ga.	UFA(NYJ)-'03	16/16
83	Thrash, James	WR	6-0	205	4/28/75	11	Missouri Southern	Wewoka, Okla.	T(Phil)-'04	16/0
29	Torrence, Leigh	CB	6-0	183	1/4/82	3	Stanford	Atlanta, Ga.	FA-'06	0*
68	Tucker, Ross	T/G	6-4	310	3/2/79	6	Princeton	Wyomissing, Pa.	FA-'07	0*
74	Wade, Todd	T/G	6-8	317	10/30/76	8	Mississippi	Jackson, Miss.	FA-'06	3/1
53	Washington, Marcus	LB	6-3	250	10/17/77	8	Auburn	Auburn, Ala.	UFA(Ind)-'04	14/14
72	Whitley, Taylor	T/G	6-4	305	2/21/80	5	Texas A&M	Baytown, Texas	FA-'06	0*
63	Whitticker, William	T/G	6-5	338	8/2/82	3	Michigan State	Evansville, Ind.	FA-'07	0*
97	Wynn, Renaldo	DL	6-3	285	9/3/74	11	Notre Dame	Chicago, Ill.	UFA(Jax)-'02	15/1
87	Yoder, Todd	TE	6-4	262	3/18/78	8	Vanderbilt	New Palestine, Ind.	UFA(Jax)-'06	14/0

* Clauss last active with Tennessee in '05; Collins did not play in 9 games; Edwards last active with Arizona in '05; Fabini played 15 games with Dallas in '06; Green last active with Philadelphia in '04; Macklin played 14 games with Arizona; Smoot played 14 games with Minnesota; Stoutmire played 13 games with New Orleans; Suisham played 5 games for Washington and 3 games for Dallas; Torrence last active with Atlanta in '05; Tucker last active with New England in '05; Whitley last active with Denver in '05; Whitticker last active with Green Bay in '05.

Players lost through free agency (4): G Derrick Dockery (Buff; 16 games in '06), RB TJ Duckett (Det; 10), LB Warrick Holdman (Den; 16), CB Kenny Wright (Cle; 16).

Traded—S Adam Archuleta (16 games in '06) to Chicago.

Also played with Redskins in '06—FB Nehemiah Broughton (2 games), S Curry Burns (2), TE Christian Fauria (9), K John Hall (5), TE Brian Kozlowski (2), K Nick Novak (6), WR David Patten (5), LB Jeff Posey (16), CB Mike Rumph (7), S Troy Vincent (8), G/T Tyson Walter (2).

2007 FIRST-YEAR ROSTER

Name	Pos.	Ht.	Wt.	Birthdate	College	Hometown	How Acq.
Alexander, Lorenzo (1)	DT	6-1	301	5/31/83	California	Berkeley, Calif.	FA
Bell, Brian	TE	6-2	238	4/4/84	Kent State	Kettering, Md.	FA
Blades, H.B.	LB	5-11	236	9/30/84	Pittsburgh	Plantation, Fla.	D6
Bonner, Cedric (1)	WR	5-11	181	12/14/78	Texas A&M-Commerce	Dallas, Texas	FA-'07 (Atl)
Brown, Kyle (1)	WR	6-1	204	12/31/83	Michigan State	West Bloomfield, Mich.	FA-'07 (KC)
Buzbee, Alex	DE	6-3	246	11/27/85	Georgetown	Chester, N.J.	FA
Caulley, Terry	RB	5-7	185	6/22/84	Connecticut	Lusby, Md.	FA
Cox, Chip (1)	CB	5-9	194	6/24/83	Ohio	Columbus, Ohio	FA
Ecker, Tyler	TE	6-6	251	4/18/82	Michigan	El Dorado Hills, Calif.	D7
Espy, Mike (1)	WR	5-11	195	11/29/82	Mississippi	Madison, Miss.	FA
Eubanks, John (1)	CB	5-10	173	7/13/83	Southern Mississippi	Mound Bayou, Miss.	FA
Francis, Daniel	CB	5-11	185	9/9/84	Louisiana State	Port Barre, La.	FA
Fredrickson, Tyler (1)	K	6-3	205	2/26/81	California	Goleta, Calif.	FA-'07 (Dal)
Heyer, Stephon	G/T	6-6	320	1/16/84	Maryland	Lawrenceville, Ga.	FA
Hickman, Justin	DE	6-2	263	7/20/85	UCLA	Glendale, Ariz.	FA
Hoag, Ryan (1)	WR	6-2	200	11/23/79	Gustavus Adolphus	Minneapolis, Minn.	FA
Hollenbach, Sam	QB	6-4	214	9/9/83	Maryland	Sellersville, Pa.	FA
Jones, Kevin	LB	6-1	230	4/4/82	St. Augustine	South Hill, Va.	FA
Landry, LaRon	S	6-0	213	10/14/84	Louisiana State	Ama, La.	D1
Latimer, Zach	LB	6-1	234	10/21/83	Oklahoma	Denver, Colo.	FA
Lefotu, Kili (1)	G/T	6-5	315	11/23/83	Arizona	Riverside, Calif.	FA
Manupuna, Vaka (1)	DT	6-0	300	6/30/82	Colorado	Honolulu, Hawaii	FA
Mason, Marcus	RB	5-9	215	6/23/84	Youngstown State	Potomac, Md.	FA
Melendez, Dan (1)	WR	6-2	179	2/16/84	Maryland	Lancaster, Pa.	FA
Palmer, Jordan	QB	6-5	231	5/30/84	Texas-El Paso	Mission Viejo, Calif.	D6
Register, Brandon	CB/S	5-10	195	8/26/84	Alabama-Birmingham	Donalsonville, Ga.	FA
Rogers, Cornelius	G	6-2	315	4/6/84	Alabama-Birmingham	Birmingham, Ala.	FA
Sartz, Dallas	LB	6-4	235	7/8/83	Southern California	Granite Bay, Calif.	D5
Schmitt, Pete	FB	6-1	248	10/14/84	Wisconsin-Whitewater	Mount Horeb, Wis.	FA
Shaw, Bryant (1)	DE	6-3	287	7/17/78	Mississippi College	Ocean Springs, Miss.	FA-'07 (Det)
Sykes, Joe (1)	DE	6-2	266	10/22/82	Southern A&M	Grenada, Miss.	FA-'06
Trucks, Anthony (1)	LB	6-1	230	12/1/83	Oregon	Martinez, Calif.	FA
Westbrook, Byron	CB/S	5-10	194	12/26/85	Salisbury	Washington, D.C.	FA
Williams, Deyon	WR	6-3	196	9/24/85	Virginia	Upper Marlboro, Md.	FA
Wilson, Chris (1)	DE	6-4	240	7/10/82	Northwood College	Flint, Mich.	FA

The term NFL Rookie is defined as a player who is in his first season of professional football and has not been on the roster of another professional football team for any regular-season or postseason games. A Rookie is designated by an "R" on NFL rosters. Players who have been active in another professional football league or players who have NFL experience, including either preseason training camp or being on an Active List or Inactive List, or on Reserve/Injured or Reserve/Physically Unable to Perform for fewer than six regular-season games, are termed NFL First-Year Players. An NFL First-Year Player is designated by a "1" on NFL rosters. Thereafter, a player is credited with an additional year of experience for each season in which he accumulates six games on the Active List or Inactive List, or on Reserve/Injured or Reserve/Physically Unable to Perform.

Log on to www.redskins.com for an up-to-date roster.

COACHING STAFF
Head Coach,
Joe Gibbs
Pro Career: On January 7, 2004, Joe Gibbs made his return to the Washington Redskins as head coach and team president. The most successful coach in Redskins history, Gibbs, who coached the team from 1981-1992, led the Redskins to four Super Bowls (XVI, XVII, XXII, and XXVI). He is the only coach to win three Super Bowls with three different quarterbacks. His 162 wins ranks 12th in NFL history, and his .635 win percentage is third among all NFL coaches with more than 125 wins. Gibbs coached with the St. Louis Cardinals (1973-1977), Tampa Bay Buccaneers (1978), and San Diego Chargers (1979-1980), before joining the Redskins in 1981. Career record: 162-93.
Background: Played tight end, offensive guard and linebacker at San Diego State. Coached at San Diego State (1964-66), Florida State (1967-1968), USC (1969-1970), and Arkansas (1971-1972).
Personal: Born November 25, 1940 in Mocksville, N.C,. lives in Charlotte, with wife Pat. They have two sons: J.D. and Coy.

ASSISTANT COACHES
Greg Blache, defensive coordinator/defensive line; born March 9, 1949, New Orleans. Attended Notre Dame. No college or pro playing experience. College coach: Notre Dame 1972-75, 1981-83, Tulane 1976-1980, Southern 1986, Kansas 1987. Pro coach: Jacksonville Bulls (USFL) 1984-85, Green Bay Packers 1988-1993, Indianapolis Colts 1994-98, Chicago Bears 1999-2003, joined Redskins in 2004.
Don Breaux, offensive coordinator; born August 3, 1940, Jennings, La. Quarterback McNeese State 1958-1961. Pro quarterback Denver Broncos 1963, San Diego Chargers 1964-65. College coach: Florida State 1966-67, Arkansas 1968-1971, 1977-1980, Florida 1973-74, Texas 1975-76. Pro coach: Houston Oilers 1972, Washington Redskins 1981-1993, New York Jets 1994, Carolina Panthers 1995-2001, re-joined Redskins in 2004.
Joe Bugel, asst. head coach-offense; born March 10, 1940, Pittsburgh. Guard/linebacker Western Kentucky 1960-63. No pro playing experience. College coach: Western Kentucky 1964-1968, Navy 1969-1972, Iowa State 1973, Ohio State 1974. Pro coach: Detroit Lions 1975-76, Houston Oilers 1977-1980, Washington Redskins 1981-89, Phoenix Cardinals 1990-1993 (head coach), Oakland Raiders 1995-97 (head coach 1997), San Diego Chargers 1998-2001, re-joined Redskins in 2004.
Jack Burns, offensive assistant; born January 3, 1949, Tampa. Safety Florida 1967-1970. No pro playing experience.

College coach: Florida 1971-73, 1975, Louisville 1974, 1985-88, Texas 1976, Vanderbilt 1977-78, Auburn 1979-1980. Pro coach: Tampa Bay Bandits (USFL) 1983, Washington Redskins 1989-1991, Minnesota Vikings 1992-93, Atlanta Falcons 1997-2003, re-joined Redskins in 2004.
Earnest Byner, running backs; born September 15, 1962, Milledgeville, Ga. Running back East Carolina 1980-83. Pro running back Cleveland Browns 1984-88, 1994-95, Washington Redskins 1989-1993, Baltimore Ravens 1996-97. Pro coach: Joined Redskins in 2004.
Bobby Crumpler, strength and conditioning; born April 23, 1965, Newton Grove, N.C. Running back North Carolina State 1983-87. No pro playing experience. College coach: North Carolina State 1989, 1992-96, 2000-01, Kansas 2002. Pro coach: Joined Redskins in 2003.
Jerry Gray, secondary-cornerbacks; born December 16, 1962, Lubbock, Texas. Safety Texas 1981-84. Pro defensive back Los Angeles Rams 1985-1991, Houston Oilers 1992, Tampa Bay Buccaneers 1993. College coach: Southern Methodist 1995-96. Pro coach: Tennessee Titans 1997-2000, Buffalo Bills 2001-05, joined Redskins in 2006.
John Hastings, strength and conditioning; born July 5, 1964, Newport News, Va. Attended Ohio University. No college or pro playing experience. Pro coach: San Diego Chargers 1990-2001, joined Redskins in 2002.
Stan Hixon, wide receivers; born July 24, 1957, Lakeland, Fla. Wide receiver Iowa State 1975-78. No pro playing experience. College coach: Morehead State 1980-82, Appalachian State 1983-88, South Carolina 1989-1992, Wake Forest 1993-94, Georgia Tech 1995-99, Louisiana State 2000-03. Pro coach: Joined Redskins in 2004.
Steve Jackson, passing game-safeties; born April 8, 1969, Houston. Defensive back Purdue 1987-1990. Pro defensive back Houston Oilers/Tennessee Titans 1991-1999. Pro coach: Buffalo Bills 2001-03, joined Redskins in 2004.
Bill Khayat, offensive quality control; born March 26, 1973, York, Pa. Tight end Duke 1992-95. Pro tight end Kansas City Chiefs 1996, Carolina Panthers 1997, Barcelona Dragons (NFLE) 1998. College coach: Tennessee State 2000-03. Pro coach: Arizona Cardinals 2004-06, joined Redskins in 2007.
Bill Lazor, quarterbacks; born June 14, 1972, Scranton, Pa. Quarterback Cornell 1991-93. No pro playing experience. College coach: Cornell 1994-2000, Buffalo 2001-02. Pro coach: Atlanta Falcons 2003, joined Redskins in 2004.
Kirk Olivadotti, linebackers; born January 1, 1974, Wilmington, Del. Wide receiver Purdue 1992-1996. No pro playing experience. College coach: Maine Maritime

Academy 1997, Indiana State 1998-99. Pro coach: Joined Redskins in 2000.
Al Saunders, associate head coach-offense; born February 1, 1947, London, England. Wide receiver/defensive back San Jose State 1966-68. No pro playing experience. College coach: Southern California 1970-71, Missouri 1972, Utah State 1973-75, California 1976-1981, Tennessee 1982. Pro coach: San Diego Chargers 1983-88 (head coach 1986-88), Kansas City Chiefs 1989-1998, 2001-05, St. Louis Rams 1999-2000, joined Redskins in 2006.
Bob Saunders, assistant coach/special projects; born November 21, 1976, Walnut Creek, Calif. Wide receiver/defensive back Southern Methodist 1995. No pro playing experience. Pro coach: Kansas City Chiefs 2002-05, joined Redskins in 2006.
Matthew Shea, defensive quality control; born February 10, 1977, Glenwood, Minn. Quarterback, tight end, and linebacker Minnesota-Morris 1996-2000. No pro playing experience. Pro coach: joined Redskins in 2007.
Warren (Rennie) Simmons, tight end; born February 25, 1942, Poughkeepsie, N.Y. Center San Diego State 1961-65. No pro playing experience. College coach: Cal State-Fullerton 1974-78, Cerritos (Calif.) J.C. 1978-1980, Vanderbilt 1995. Pro coach: Washington Redskins 1981-1993, Los Angeles Rams 1994, Houston Oilers 1996, Atlanta Falcons 1997-2003, re-joined Redskins in 2004.
Danny Smith, special teams; born September 7, 1953, Pittsburgh. Defensive back Edinboro State 1972-75. No pro playing experience. College coach: Edinboro State 1976, Clemson 1979, William & Mary 1980-83, The Citadel 1984-86, Georgia Tech 1987-1994. Pro coach: Philadelphia Eagles 1995-98, Detroit Lions 1999-2000, Buffalo Bills 2001-03, joined Redskins in 2004.
Gregg Williams, asst. head coach-defense; born July 15, 1958, Excelsior Springs, Mo. Quarterback Northeast Missouri State 1976-79. No pro playing experience. College coach: Houston Oilers/Tennessee Titans 1990-2000, Buffalo Bills 2001-03 (head coach), joined Redskins in 2004.

2006 Season in Review

2006 TRADES

Wide receiver **Brandon Lloyd** from San Francisco to Washington for the Redskins' third-round selection in 2006 (WR **Brandon Williams**) and an unannounced selection choice. (3/13)

Quarterback **Daunte Culpepper** from Minnesota to Miami for the Dolphins' second-round selection in 2006 (C **Ryan Cook**). (3/15)

Quarterback **Patrick Ramsey** from Washington to New York Jets for the Jets' sixth-round selection in 2006 (DB **Reed Doughty**). (3/17)

Defensive back **Chris Crocker** from Cleveland to Atlanta for the Falcons' fourth-round selection in 2006 (G **Isaac Sowells**). (3/20)

Defensive end **John Abraham** from New York Jets to Atlanta. Atlanta's first-round selection in 2006 (#15) from Atlanta to Denver. Denver's first-round selection in 2006 (C **Nick Mangold**) from Denver to New York Jets. Denver's third-round selection in 2006 (#93) and an unannounced selection from Denver to Atlanta. (3/22)

Defensive back **Bryan Scott** from Atlanta to New Orleans for tackle **Wayne Gandy**. (4/6)

Wide receiver **Eric Moulds** from Buffalo to Houston for the Texans' fifth-round selection in 2006 (DT **Kyle Williams**). (4/6)

Defensive back **Sammy Davis** from San Diego to San Francisco for wide receiver **Rashaun Woods**. (4/13)

Denver's first-round selection in 2006 (DE **Manny Lawson**) from Denver to San Francisco for the 49ers' second-round selection in 2006 (#37) and third-round selection in 2006 (#68). (4/19)

Defensive back **Mike Green** from Chicago to Seattle for the Seahawks' sixth-round selection in 2006 (G **Tyler Reed**). (4/25)

Atlanta's first-round selection in 2006 (DB **Tye Hill**) and San Francisco's third-round selection in 2006 (DT **Claude Wroten**) from Denver to St. Louis for the Rams' first-round selection in 2006 (DT **Jay Cutler**). (4/29)

Baltimore's first-round selection in 2006 (DE **Kamerion Wimbley**) and sixth-round selection in 2006 (DT **Babatunde Oshinowo**) from Baltimore to Cleveland for the Browns' first-round selection in 2006 (DT **Haloti Ngata**). (4/29)

N.Y. Giants' first-round selection in 2006 (WR **Santonio Holmes**) from Giants to Pittsburgh for the Steelers' first-round selection in 2006 (DE **Mathias Kiwanuka**), third-round selection in 2006 (LB **Gerris Wilkinson**), and fourth-round selection in 2006 (T **Guy Whimper**). (4/29)

Buffalo's second-round selection in 2006 (DB **Danieal Manning**) and third-round selection in 2006 (DT **Dusty Dvoracek**) from Buffalo to Chicago for the Bears' first-round selection in 2006 (DT **John McCargo**). (4/29)

Center **Jeff Faine** and the Browns' second-round selection in 2006 (DB **Roman Harper**) from Cleveland to New Orleans for the Saints' second-round selection (LB **D'Qwell Jackson**). (4/29)

N.Y. Jets' second-round selection in 2006 (LB **Rocky McIntosh**) from the Jets to Washington for the Redskins' second-round selection in 2006 (#53), sixth-round selection in 2006 (DB **Drew Coleman**), and second-round selection in 2007. (4/29)

Green Bay's second-round selection in 2006 (WR **Chad Jackson**) from Green Bay to New England for the Redskins' second-round selection in 2006 (WR **Greg Jennings**) and the Ravens' third-round selection in 2006 (G **Jason Spitz**). (4/29)

Wide receiver **Javon Walker** from Green

Bay to Denver for the 49ers' second-round selection in 2006 (#37). (4/29)

Atlanta's second-round selection in 2006 (T **Daryn Colledge**), the Broncos' third-round selection in 2006 (#93), and the Falcons' fifth-round selection in 2006 (QB **Ingle Martin**) from Atlanta to Green Bay for the 49ers' second-round selection in 2006 (DB **Jimmy Williams**) and the Packers' fifth-round selection in 2006 (T **Quinn Ojinnaka**). (4/29)

Philadelphia's second-round selection in 2006 (#45) and the Cowboys' fourth-round selection in 2006 (LB **Stephen Tulloch**) from Philadelphia to Tennessee for the Titans' second-round selection in 2006 (T **Winston Justice**). (4/29)

Baltimore's second-round selection in 2006 (WR **Sinorice Moss**) from Baltimore to the N.Y. Giants for the Giants' second-round selection in 2006 (C **Chris Chester**) and third-round selection in 2006 (DB **David Pittman**). (4/29)

Dallas' second-round selection in 2006 (#49) from Dallas to the N.Y. Jets for the Redskins' second-round selection in 2006 (TE **Anthony Fasano**), the Redskins' sixth-round selection in 2006 (#189), and the Jets' seventh-round selection in 2006 (T **Pat McQuistan**). (4/29)

Minnesota's third-round selection in 2006 (DB **Anthony Smith**) and the Seahawks' third-round selection in 2006 (WR **Willie Reid**) from Minnesota to Pittsburgh for the Steelers' second-round selection in 2006 (QB **Tarvaris Jackson**). (4/29)

N.Y. Jets' third-round selection in 2006 (LB **Chris Gocong**) from the Jets to Philadelphia for the Eagles' third-round selection in 2006 (LB **Anthony Schlegel**) and seventh-round selection in 2006 (DE **Titus Adams**). (4/29)

Dallas' third-round selection in 2006 (LB **Clint Ingram**) from Dallas to Jacksonville for the Jaguars' third-round selection in 2006 (DE **Jason Hatcher**) and fourth-round selection in 2006 (KR **Skyler Green**). (4/29)

Denver's third-round selection in 2006 (TE **Dominique Byrd**) from Green Bay to St. Louis for the Rams' fourth-round selection in 2006 (#109) and sixth-round selection in 2006 (DT **Johnny Jolly**). (4/29)

Defensive tackle **Hollis Thomas** and Philadelphia's fourth-round selection in 2006 (T **Jahri Evans**) from Philadelphia to New Orleans for the Saints' fourth-round selection in 2006 (G **Max Jean-Gilles**). (4/30)

Guard **Artis Hicks** and Indianapolis' fourth-round selection in 2006 (DE **Ray Edwards**) from Philadelphia to Minnesota for the Vikings' fourth-round selection in 2006 (#115) and sixth-round selection in 2006 (#185). (4/30)

Tight end **Brandon Manumaleuna** from St. Louis to San Diego for the Chargers' fourth-round selection in 2006 (DE **Victor Adeyanju**). (4/30)

St. Louis' fourth-round selection in 2006 (WR **Jason Avant**) from Green Bay to Philadelphia for the Vikings' fourth-round selection in 2006 (DB **Will Blackmon**) and the Vikings' sixth-round selection in 2006 (DB **Tyrone Culver**). (4/30)

Dallas' fifth-round selection in 2006 (TE **Jason Pociask**) and the Redskins' sixth-round selection in 2006 (DB **Drew Coleman**) from Dallas to the N.Y. Jets for the Jets' fifth-round selection in 2006 (DB **Pat Watkins**). (4/30)

Jacksonville's sixth-round selection in 2006 (DE **Melvin Oliver**) from Jacksonville to San Francisco for the 49ers' seventh-round selection in 2006 (DE **James Wyche**) and the Jaguars' seventh-round selection in 2006 (DB **Dee Webb**). (4/30)

Indianapolis' sixth-round selection in 2007 (DB **Ryan Smith**) from Indianapolis to Tennessee for the Colts' seventh-round selection in 2006 (DB **T.J. Rushing**). (4/30)

Quarterback **Trent Dilfer** from Cleveland to San Francisco for quarterback **Ken Dorsey** and an unannounced selection. (5/8)

Quarterback **Joey Harrington** from Detroit to Miami for an unannounced selection. (5/15)

Wide receiver **Hank Baskett** from Minnesota to Philadelphia for wide receiver **Billy McMullen**. (5/18)

Wide receiver **Bethel Johnson** from New England to New Orleans for defensive tackle **Johnathan Sullivan**. (6/5)

Tight end **Tim Euhus** from Buffalo to New Orleans for linebacker **Courtney Watson**. (6/7)

Quarterback **Steve McNair** from Tennessee to Baltimore for the Ravens' fourth-round selection in 2007 (WR **Chris Davis**). (6/9)

Defensive back **Gerome Sapp** from Indianapolis to Baltimore for the Ravens' seventh-round selection in 2007. (6/19)

Quarterback **Dave Ragone** from Cincinnati to St. Louis for the Rams' seventh-round selection in 2007. (6/20)

Quarterback **Cody Pickett** from San Francisco to Houston for the Texans' seventh-round selection in 2007. (7/27)

Running Back **Michael Bennett** from New Orleans to Kansas City for the Chiefs' fourth-round selection in 2007. (8/2)

Center **Ross Tucker** from New England to Cleveland for the Browns' seventh-round selection in 2007. (8/8)

Running Back **Lee Suggs** from Cleveland to the New York Jets for defensive back **Derrick Strait**. (8/14)

Defensive back **Mike Rumph** from San Francisco to Washington for wide receiver **Taylor Jacobs**. (8/15)

Wide receiver **Charlie Adams** from Denver to Dallas for the Cowboys' sixth-round selection in 2007. (8/18)

Running Back **Kevan Barlow** from San Francisco to the New York Jets for the Jets' fourth-round selection in 2007. (8/21)

Wide receiver **Carlton Brewster** from Cleveland to Green Bay for defensive back **Therrian Fontenot**. (8/22)

Tackle **Brandon Gorin** from New England to Arizona for the Cardinals' seventh-round selection in 2007. (8/22)

Linebacker **Scott Shanle** from Dallas to New Orleans for the Saints' seventh-round selection in 2007 (DB **Alan Ball**). (8/23)

Running back **T.J. Duckett** from Atlanta to Washington, wide receiver **Ashley Lelie** from Denver to Atlanta, Denver's first-round selection in 2007 (from the Broncos to Washington, and Washington's first-round selection in 2007 from the Redskins to Denver. (8/24)

Center **Lennie Friedman** from Chicago to Cleveland for San Francisco's seventh-round selection in 2007. (8/24)

Wide receiver **Donte' Stallworth** from New Orleans to Philadelphia for linebacker **Mark Simoneau** and the Eagles' fourth-round selection in 2007 (T **Jermon Bushrod**). (8/25)

Tight end **Sean Ryan** from Dallas to the New York Jets for Detroit's seventh-round selection in 2007 (DB **Courtney Brown**). (8/31)

Quarterback **Brooks Bollinger** from the New York Jets to Minnesota for defensive tackle **C.J. Mosley** and the Vikings' seventh-round selection in 2008. (8/31)

Tight end **Doug Jolley** from the New York Jets to Tampa Bay for the Buccaneers' sixth-round selection in 2007 (T **Jacob Bender**). (8/31)

Running back **Patrick Cobbs** from New England to Pittsburgh for the Steelers' seventh-round selection in 2007. (9/1)

Defensive end **Bobby Hamilton** from Oakland to the New York Jets for Minnesota's seventh-round selection in 2008. (9/2)

Running back **Josh Parry** from Philadelphia to Seattle for the Seahawks' seventh-round selection in 2008. (9/2)

Center **Hank Fraley** from Philadelphia to Cleveland for the Browns' seventh-round selection in 2008. (9/2)

Wide receiver **Doug Gabriel** from Oakland to New England for the Patriots' fifth-round selection in 2007 (DB **Eric Frampton**). (9/2)

Guard **Adam Goldberg** from Minnesota to St. Louis for the Rams' seventh-round selection in 2008. (9/2)

Defensive end **Ryan LaCasse** from Baltimore to Indianapolis for the Colts' seventh-round selection in 2008. (9/2)

Wide receiver **Deion Branch** from New England to Seattle for the Seahawks' first-round selection in 2007 (DB **Brandon Meriweather**). (9/11)

Running back **Samkon Gado** from Green Bay to Houston for Running Back **Vernand Morency**. (9/13)

Quarterback **Billy Volek** from Tennessee to San Diego for the Chargers' sixth-round selection in 2007 (DE **Jacob Ford**. (9/19)

Defensive end **Tony Hargrove** from St. Louis to Buffalo for the Bills' fifth-round selection in 2007 (#148). (10/16)

Defensive tackle **Anthony McFarland** from Tampa Bay to Indianapolis for the Colts' second-round selection in 2007 (DB **Sabby Piscitelli**). (10/17)

* *Draft choice number is listed if club later traded the pick.*

2007 TRADES

Running back **Tatum Bell**, tackle **George Foster**, and Broncos' fifth-round selection in 2007 (LB **Johnny Baldwin**) from Denver to Detroit for cornerback **Dre' Bly** and the Lions' sixth-round selection in 2007 (#176). (3/2)

Defensive end **James Hall** from Detroit to St. Louis for the Rams' fifth-round selection in 2007 (#154). (3/2)

Quarterback **Jake Plummer** from Denver to Tampa Bay for an unannounced selection. (3/3)

Wide receiver **Wes Welker** from Miami to New England for the Patriots' second-round selection in 2007 (G **Samson Satele**) and seventh-round selection (DE **Abraham Wright**). (3/5)

Running back **Thomas Jones** and the Bears' second-round selection in 2007 (#63) from Chicago to New York Jets for the Redskins' second-round selection in 2007 (#37). (3/7)

Running back **Willie McGahee** from Buffalo to Baltimore for the Ravens' third-round selection (QB **Trent Edwards**) and seventh-round selection in 2007 (DE **C.J. Ah You**). (3/8)

Wide receiver **Tim Carter** from New York Giants to Cleveland for running back **Reuben Droughns**. (3/9)

Quarterback **Matt Schaub** and the Falcons' first-round selection in 2007 (DT **Amobi Okoye**) from Atlanta to Houston for the Texans' first-round selection (DE **Jamaal Anderson**), second-round selection (G **Justin Blalock**) in 2007, and an unannounced selection choice. (3/22)

Defensive back **Adam Archuleta** from Washington to Chicago for the Bears' sixth-round selection in 2007 (QB **Jordan Palmer**).

(3/22)

Linebacker **Takeo Spikes** and quarterback Kelly Holcomb from Buffalo to Philadelphia for defensive tackle **Darwin Walker** and an unannounced selection choice. (3/28)

Kicker **Olindo Mare** from Miami to New Orleans for the Saints' sixth-round selection in 2007 (C **Drew Mormino**). (4/3)

Carolina's first-round selection (DB **Darrelle Revis**) and sixth-round selection (#191) in 2007 from Carolina to New York Jets for the Jets' first-round selection in 2007 (LB **Jon Beason**), second-round selection in 2007 (C **Ryan Kalil**), and fifth-round selection in 2007 (LB **Tim Shaw**). (4/28)

Jacksonville's first-round selection in 2007 (DE **Jarvis Moss**) from Jacksonville to Denver for the Broncos' first-round selection in 2007 (DB **Reggie Nelson**), third-round selection in 2007 (#86), and sixth-round selection in 2007 (#198). (4/28)

Dallas' first-round selection in 2007 (QB **Brady Quinn**) from Dallas to Cleveland for the Browns' second-round selection in 2007 (#36), and first-round selection in 2008. (4/28)

Philadelphia's first-round selection in 2007 (LB **Anthony Spencer**) from Philadelphia to Dallas for the Browns' second-round selection in 2007 (QB **Kevin Kolb**), and the Cowboys' third-round selection in 2007 (LB **Stewart Bradley**) and fifth-round selection in 2007 (DB **C.J. Gaddis**). (4/28)

New England's first-round selection in 2007 (T **Joe Staley**) from New England to San Francisco for the 49ers' fourth-round selection in 2007 (#110) and first-round selection in 2008. (4/28)

Oakland's second-round selection in 2007 (DT **Alvin Branch**) from Oakland to Arizona for the Cardinals' second-round selection in 2007 (TE **Zach Miller**) and fourth-round selection in 2007 (#105). (4/28)

Detroit's second-round selection in 2007 (LB **Paul Posluszny**) from Detroit to Buffalo for the Bills' second-round selection in 2007 (QB **Drew Stanton**) and third-round selection in 2007 (#74). (4/28)

Washington's second-round selection in 2007 (DB **Eric Weddle**) from Chicago to San Diego for the Chargers' second-round selection in 2007 (DE **Dan Bazuin**), third-round selection in 2007 (RB **Garrett Wolfe**), fifth-round selection in 2007 (DB **Kevin Payne**), and third-round selection in 2008. (4/28)

Minnesota's second-round selection in 2007 (DB **Chris Houston**) from Minnesota to Atlanta for the Falcons' second-round selection in 2007 (WR **Sidney Rice**) and the Broncos' fourth-round selection in 2007 (#121). (4/28)

San Francisco's second-round selection in 2007 (T **Tony Ugoh**) from San Francisco to Indianapolis for the Saints' fourth-round selection in 2007 (DB **Dashon Goldson**) and the Colts' first-round selection in 2008. (4/28)

Green Bay's second-round selection in 2007 (LB **David Harris**) and the Jets' seventh-round selection in 2007 (WR **Chansi Stuckey**) from Green Bay to New York Jets for the Bears' second-round selection in 2007 (RB **Brandon Jackson**), third-round selection in 2007 (DB **Aaron Rouse**), and the Panthers' sixth-round selection in 2007 (LB **Korey Hall**). (4/28)

Quarterback **Josh McCown** and wide receiver Mike Williams from Detroit to Oakland for the Cardinals' fourth-round selection in 2007 (DB **A.J. Davis**). (4/28)

Dallas' second-round selection in 2007 (DB Eric **Wright**) and sixth-round selection in 2007 (#195) from the Dallas to Cleveland for

the Browns' third-round selection in 2007 (T **James Marten**), fourth-round selection in 2007 (QB **Isaiah Stanback**), and sixth-round selection in 2007 (K **Nick Folk**). (4/28)

New Orleans' second-round selection in 2007 (DE **Ikaika Alama-Francis**) from New Orleans to Detroit for the Lions' third-round selection in 2007 (DB **Usama Young**), and the Dolphins' fifth-round selection in 2007 (DB **David Jones**). (4/28)

Baltimore's second-round selection in 2007 (DB **Gerald Alexander**) from Baltimore to Detroit for the Bills' third-round selection in 2007 (WR **Yamon Figurs**) and the Lions' fourth-round selection in 2007 (#101). (4/29)

Denver's third-round selection in 2007 (T **Marshal Yanda**) from Jacksonville to Baltimore for the Lions' fourth-round selection in 2007 (P **Adam Podlesh**), and the Ravens' fifth-round selection in 2007 (DT **Derek Landri**) and sixth-round selection in 2007 (#203). (4/28)

New England's third-round selection in 2007 (T **Mario Henderson**) from New England to Oakland for the Raiders' seventh-round selection in 2007 (LB **Oscar Lua**) and third-round selection in 2008. (4/28)

Wide receiver **Darrell Jackson** from Seattle to San Francisco for the Jets' fourth-round selection in 2007 (G **Mansfield Wrotto**). (4/29)

Tampa Bay's fourth-round selection in 2007 (DE **Brian Robison**) from Tampa Bay to Minnesota for the Vikings' fourth-round selection in 2007 (DB **Tanard Jackson**) and sixth-round selection in 2007 (LB **Adam Hayward**). (4/29)

Wide receiver **Randy Moss** from Oakland to New England for the 49ers' fourth-round selection in 2007 (DB **John Bowie**). (4/29)

Houston's fourth-round selection in 2007 (RB **Antonio Pittman**) from Houston to New Orleans for the Chiefs' fourth-round selection in 2007 (DB **Fred Bennett**) and fifth-round selection in 2007 (T **Brandon Frye**). (4/29)

Green Bay's fourth-round selection in 2007 (P **Daniel Sepulveda**) from Green Bay to Pittsburgh for the Steelers' fourth-round selection in 2007 (T **Allen Barbre**) and sixth-round selection in 2007 (LB **Desmond Bishop**). (4/29)

St. Louis' fourth-round selection in 2007 (G **Manuel Ramirez**) from St. Louis to Detroit for the Lions' fifth-round selection in 2007 (C **Dustin Fry**) and the Rams' fifth-round selection in 2007 (DT **Clifton Ryan**). (4/29)

Denver's fourth-round selection in 2007 (DT **Marcus Thomas**) from Minnesota to Denver for the Lions' sixth-round selection in 2007 (LB **Rufus Alexander**), and the Broncos' seventh-round selection in 2007 (WR **Chandler Williams**) and third-round selection in 2008. (4/29)

Atlanta's fifth-round selection in 2007 (G **Uche Nwaneri**) from Atlanta to Jacksonville for the Jaguars' sixth-round selection in 2007 (DB **David Irons**), the Broncos' sixth-round selection in 2007 (C **Doug Datish**), and the Ravens' sixth-round selection in 2007 (DB **Daren Stone**). (4/29)

Dallas' sixth-round selection in 2007 (RB **Deon Anderson**) from Cleveland to Dallas for the Jets' sixth-round selection in 2007 (DE **Melila Purcell**) and the Cowboys' seventh-round selection in 2007 (WR **Syndric Steptoe**). (4/29)

Defensive tackle **Ryan Sims** from Kansas City to Tampa Bay for an unannounced selection. (5/3)

* *Draft choice number is listed if club later traded the pick.*

PRESEASON STANDINGS
AMERICAN FOOTBALL CONFERENCE
East Division

	W	L	T	Pct.	Pts.	OP
Miami	2	2	0	.500	78	69
New England	2	2	0	.500	117	60
New York Jets	2	2	0	.500	57	60
Buffalo	1	3	0	.250	81	91

North Division

	W	L	T	Pct.	Pts.	OP
Cincinnati	4	0	0	1.000	131	54
Baltimore	2	2	0	.500	60	67
Cleveland	2	2	0	.500	54	73
Pittsburgh	0	4	0	.000	43	69

South Division

	W	L	T	Pct.	Pts.	OP
Houston	3	1	0	.750	81	64
Jacksonville	3	1	0	.750	90	78
Indianapolis	1	3	0	.250	64	83
Tennessee	1	3	0	.250	67	95

West Division

	W	L	T	Pct.	Pts.	OP
Oakland	4	1	0	.800	83	63
Denver	3	1	0	.750	94	67
Kansas City	2	2	0	.500	40	62
San Diego	2	2	0	.500	65	70

AFC PRESEASON RECORDS—TEAM BY TEAM

East Division
BUFFALO (2-2)

13	at Carolina	14
31	Cincinnati	44
17	Cleveland	20
20	at Detroit	13
81		91

MIAMI (2-2)

26	Jacksonville	31
13	at Tampa Bay	10
10	at Carolina	19
29	St. Louis	9
78		69

NEW ENGLAND (2-2)

23	at Atlanta	26
30	Arizona	3
41	Washington	0
23	at New York Giants	31
117		60

N.Y. JETS (2-2)

3	at Tampa Bay	16
27	at Washington	14
7	New York Giants	13
20	Philadelphia	17
57		60

North Division
BALTIMORE (2-2)

16	New York Giants	17
20	Philadelphia	10
7	at Minnesota	30
17	at Washington	10
60		67

CINCINNATI (4-0)

19	Washington	3
44	at Buffalo	31
48	Green Bay	17
20	at Indianapolis	3
131		54

CLEVELAND (2-2)

7	at Philadelphia	20
20	Detroit	16
20	at Buffalo	17
7	Chicago	20
54		73

PITTSBURGH (0-4)

13	at Arizona	21
10	Minnesota	17
7	at Philadelphia	16
13	Carolina	15
43		69

South Division
HOUSTON (3-1)

24	Kansas City	14
27	at St. Louis	20
14	at Denver	17
16	Tampa Bay	13
81		64

INDIANAPOLIS (1-3)

17	at St. Louis	19
17	Seattle	30
27	at New Orleans	14
3	Cincinnati	20
64		83

JACKSONVILLE (3-1)

31	at Miami	26
10	Carolina	17
29	Tampa Bay	18
20	at Atlanta	17
90		78

TENNESSEE (1-3)

16	New Orleans	19
10	at Denver	35
6	Atlanta	20
35	at Green Bay	21
67		95

West Division
DENVER (3-1)

13	at Detroit	20
35	Tennessee	10
17	Houston	14
29	at Arizona	23
94		67

KANSAS CITY (2-2)

14	at Houston	24
0	at New York Giants	17
16	St. Louis	12
10	New Orleans	9
40		62

OAKLAND (4-1)

16	at Philadelphia (a)	10
16	at Minnesota	13
23	San Francisco	7
21	Detroit	3
7	at Seattle	30
83		63

SAN DIEGO (2-2)

17	Green Bay	3
3	at Chicago	24
31	Seattle	20
14	at San Francisco	23
65		70

(a) Pro Football Hall of Fame Game at Canton, Ohio

NFC PRESEASON RECORDS—TEAM BY TEAM

East Division

DALLAS (3-0-1)

13	at Seattle	3
30	at New Orleans	7
17	San Francisco	7
10	Minnesota	10
70		27

N.Y. GIANTS (4-0)

17	at Baltimore	16
17	Kansas City	0
13	at New York Jets	7
31	New England	23
78		46

PHILADELPHIA (2-3)

10	Oakland (a)	16
20	Cleveland	7
10	at Baltimore	20
16	Pittsburgh	7
17	at New York Jets	20
73		70

WASHINGTON (0-4)

3	at Cincinnati	19
14	New York Jets	27
0	at New England	41
10	Baltimore	17
27		104

North Division

CHICAGO (2-2)

14	at San Francisco	28
24	San Diego	3
16	Arizona	23
20	at Cleveland	7
74		61

DETROIT (1-3

20	Denver	13
16	at Cleveland	20
3	at Oakland	21
13	Buffalo	20
52		74

GREEN BAY (3-1)

3	at San Diego	17
38	Atlanta	10
17	at Cincinnati	48
21	Tennessee	35
79		110

MINNESOTA (2-1-1)

13	Oakland	16
17	at Pittsburgh	10
30	Baltimore	7
10	at Dallas	10
70		43

South Division

ATLANTA (2-2)

26	New England	23
10	at Green Bay	38
20	at Tennessee	6
17	Jacksonville	20
73		87

CAROLINA (4-0)

14	Buffalo	13
17	at Jacksonville	10
19	Miami	10
15	at Pittsburgh	13
65		46

NEW ORLEANS (1-3)

19	at Tennessee	16
7	Dallas	30
14	Indianapolis	27
9	at Kansas City	10
49		83

TAMPA BAY (1-3)

16	New York Jets	3
10	Miami	13
18	at Jacksonville	29
13	at Houston	16
57		61

West Division

ARIZONA (2-2)

21	Pittsburgh	13
3	at New England	30
23	at Chicago	16
23	Denver	29
70		88

ST. LOUIS (1-3)

19	Indianapolis	17
20	Houston	27
12	at Kansas City	16
9	at Miami	29
60		89

SAN FRANCISCO (2-2)

28	Chicago	14
7	at Oakland	23
7	at Dallas	17
23	San Diego	14
65		68

SEATTLE (2-2)

3	Dallas	13
30	at Indianapolis	17
20	at San Diego	31
30	Oakland	7
83		68

PRESEASON STANDINGS
NATIONAL FOOTBALL CONFERENCE

East Division

	W	L	T	Pct.	Pts.	OP
New York Giants	4	0	0	1.000	78	46
Dallas	3	0	1	.875	70	27
Philadelphia	2	3	0	.400	73	70
Washington	0	4	0	.000	27	104

North Division

	W	L	T	Pct.	Pts.	OP
Minnesota	2	1	1	.625	70	43
Chicago	2	2	0	.500	74	61
Detroit	1	3	0	.250	52	74
Green Bay	1	3	0	.250	79	110

South Division

	W	L	T	Pct.	Pts.	OP
Carolina	4	0	0	1.000	65	46
Atlanta	2	2	0	.500	73	87
New Orleans	1	3	0	.250	49	83
Tampa Bay	1	3	0	.250	57	61

West Division

	W	L	T	Pct.	Pts.	OP
Arizona	2	2	0	.500	70	88
San Francisco	2	2	0	.500	65	68
Seattle	2	2	0	.500	83	68
St. Louis	1	3	0	.250	60	89

(a) Pro Football Hall of Fame Game at Canton, Ohio

AMERICAN FOOTBALL CONFERENCE

BALTIMORE (13-3)
27	at Tampa Bay	0
28	Oakland	6
15	at Cleveland	14
16	San Diego	13
3	at Denver	13
21	Carolina	23
35	at New Orleans	22
26	Cincinnati	20
27	at Tennessee	26
24	Atlanta	10
27	Pittsburgh	0
7	at Cincinnati	13
20	at Kansas City	10
27	Cleveland	17
31	at Pittsburgh	7
19	Buffalo	7
353		**201**

DENVER (9-7)
10	at St. Louis	18
9	Kansas City (OT)	6
17	at New England	7
13	Baltimore	3
13	Oakland	3
17	at Cleveland	7
31	Indianapolis	34
31	at Pittsburgh	20
17	at Oakland	13
27	San Diego	35
10	at Kansas City	19
20	Seattle	23
20	at San Diego	48
37	at Arizona	20
24	Cincinnati	23
23	San Francisco (OT)	26
319		**305**

KANSAS CITY (9-7)
10	Cincinnati	23
6	at Denver (OT)	9
41	San Francisco	0
23	at Arizona	20
7	at Pittsburgh	45
30	San Diego	27
35	Seattle	28
31	at St. Louis	17
10	at Miami	13
17	Oakland	13
19	Denver	10
28	at Cleveland (OT)	31
10	Baltimore	20
9	at San Diego	20
20	at Oakland	9
35	Jacksonville	30
331		**315**

OAKLAND (2-14)
0	San Diego	27
6	at Baltimore	28
21	Cleveland	24
20	at San Francisco	34
3	at Denver	13
22	Arizona	9
20	Pittsburgh	13
0	at Seattle	16
13	Denver	17
13	at Kansas City	17
14	at San Diego	21
14	Houston	23
10	at Cincinnati	27
0	St. Louis	20
9	Kansas City	20
3	at New York Jets	23
168		**332**

BUFFALO (7-9)
17	at New England	19
16	at Miami	6
20	New York Jets	28
17	Minnesota	12
7	at Chicago	40
17	at Detroit	20
6	New England	28
24	Green Bay	10
16	at Indianapolis	17
24	at Houston	21
27	Jacksonville	24
21	San Diego	24
31	at New York Jets	13
21	Miami	0
29	Tennessee	30
7	at Baltimore	19
300		**311**

HOUSTON (6-10)
10	Philadelphia	24
24	at Indianapolis	43
15	Washington	31
17	Miami	15
6	at Dallas	34
27	Jacksonville	7
22	at Tennessee	28
10	at New York Giants	14
13	at Jacksonville	10
21	Buffalo	24
11	at New York Jets	26
23	at Oakland	14
20	Tennessee (OT)	26
7	at New England	40
27	Indianapolis	24
14	Cleveland	6
267		**366**

MIAMI (6-10)
17	at Pittsburgh	28
6	Buffalo	16
13	Tennessee	10
15	at Houston	17
10	at New England	20
17	at New York Jets	20
24	Green Bay	34
31	at Chicago	13
13	Kansas City	10
24	Minnesota	20
27	at Detroit	10
10	Jacksonville	24
21	New England	0
0	at Buffalo	21
10	New York Jets	13
22	at Indianapolis	27
260		**283**

PITTSBURGH (8-8)
28	Miami	17
0	at Jacksonville	9
20	Cincinnati	28
13	at San Diego	23
45	Kansas City	7
38	at Atlanta (OT)	41
13	at Oakland	20
20	Denver	31
38	New Orleans	31
24	at Cleveland	20
0	at Baltimore	27
20	Tampa Bay	3
27	Cleveland	7
37	at Carolina	3
7	Baltimore	31
23	at Cincinnati (OT)	17
353		**315**

CINCINNATI (8-8)
23	at Kansas City	10
34	Cleveland	17
28	at Pittsburgh	20
13	New England	38
13	at Tampa Bay	14
17	Carolina	14
27	Atlanta	29
20	at Baltimore	26
41	San Diego	49
31	at New Orleans	16
30	at Cleveland	0
13	Baltimore	7
27	Oakland	10
16	at Indianapolis	34
23	at Denver	24
17	Pittsburgh (OT)	23
373		**331**

INDIANAPOLIS (12-4)
26	at New York Giants	21
43	Houston	24
21	Jacksonville	14
31	at New York Jets	28
14	Tennessee	13
36	Washington	22
34	at Denver	31
27	at New England	20
17	Buffalo	16
14	at Dallas	21
45	Philadelphia	21
17	at Tennessee	20
17	at Jacksonville	44
34	Cincinnati	16
24	at Houston	27
27	Miami	22
427		**360**

NEW ENGLAND (12-4)
19	Buffalo	17
24	at New York Jets	17
7	Denver	17
38	at Cincinnati	13
20	Miami	10
28	at Buffalo	6
31	at Minnesota	7
20	Indianapolis	27
14	New York Jets	17
35	at Green Bay	0
17	Chicago	13
28	Detroit	21
0	at Miami	21
40	Houston	7
24	at Jacksonville	21
40	at Tennessee	23
385		**237**

SAN DIEGO (14-2)
27	at Oakland	0
40	Tennessee	7
13	at Baltimore	16
23	Pittsburgh	13
48	at San Francisco	19
27	at Kansas City	30
38	St. Louis	24
32	Cleveland	25
49	at Cincinnati	41
35	at Denver	27
21	Oakland	14
24	at Buffalo	21
48	Denver	20
20	Kansas City	9
20	at Seattle	17
27	Arizona	20
492		**303**

CLEVELAND (4-12)
14	New Orleans	19
17	at Cincinnati	34
14	Baltimore	15
24	at Oakland	21
12	at Carolina	20
7	Denver	17
20	New York Jets	13
25	at San Diego	32
17	at Atlanta	13
20	Pittsburgh	24
0	Cincinnati	30
31	Kansas City (OT)	28
7	at Pittsburgh	27
17	at Baltimore	27
7	Tampa Bay	22
6	at Houston	14
238		**356**

JACKSONVILLE (8-8)
24	Dallas	17
9	Pittsburgh	0
14	at Indianapolis	21
30	at Washington (OT)	36
41	New York Jets	0
7	at Houston	27
13	at Philadelphia	6
37	Tennessee	7
10	Houston	13
26	New York Giants	10
24	at Buffalo	27
24	at Miami	10
44	Indianapolis	17
17	at Tennessee	24
21	New England	24
30	at Kansas City	35
371		**274**

NEW YORK JETS (10-6)
23	at Tennessee	16
17	New England	24
28	at Buffalo	20
28	Indianapolis	31
0	at Jacksonville	41
20	Miami	17
31	Detroit	24
13	at Cleveland	20
17	at New England	14
0	Chicago	10
26	Houston	11
38	at Green Bay	10
13	Buffalo	31
26	at Minnesota	13
13	at Miami	10
23	Oakland	3
316		**295**

TENNESSEE (8-8)
16	New York Jets	23
7	at San Diego	40
10	at Miami	13
14	Dallas	45
13	at Indianapolis	14
25	at Washington	22
28	Houston	22
7	at Jacksonville	37
26	Baltimore	27
31	at Philadelphia	13
24	New York Giants	21
20	Indianapolis	17
26	at Houston (OT)	20
24	Jacksonville	17
30	at Buffalo	29
23	New England	40
324		**400**

NATIONAL FOOTBALL CONFERENCE

ARIZONA (5-11)
34	San Francisco	27
10	at Seattle	21
14	St. Louis	16
10	at Atlanta	32
20	Kansas City	23
23	Chicago	24
9	at Oakland	22
14	at Green Bay	31
10	Dallas	27
17	Detroit	10
26	at Minnesota	31
34	at St. Louis	20
27	Seattle	21
20	Denver	37
26	at San Francisco	20
20	at San Diego	27
314		**389**

ATLANTA (7-9)
20	at Carolina	6
14	Tampa Bay	3
3	at New Orleans	23
32	Arizona	10
14	New York Giants	27
41	Pittsburgh (OT)	38
29	at Cincinnati	27
14	at Detroit	30
13	Cleveland	17
10	at Baltimore	24
13	New Orleans	31
24	at Washington	14
17	at Tampa Bay	6
28	Dallas	38
3	Carolina	10
17	at Philadelphia	24
292		**328**

CAROLINA (8-8)
6	Atlanta	20
13	at Minnesota (OT)	16
26	at Tampa Bay	24
21	New Orleans	18
20	Cleveland	12
23	at Baltimore	21
14	at Cincinnati	17
14	Dallas	35
24	Tampa Bay	10
15	St. Louis	0
13	at Washington	17
24	at Philadelphia	27
13	New York Giants	27
3	Pittsburgh	37
10	at Atlanta	3
31	at New Orleans	21
270		**305**

CHICAGO (13-3)
26	at Green Bay	0
34	Detroit	7
19	at Minnesota	16
37	Seattle	6
40	Buffalo	7
24	at Arizona	23
41	San Francisco	10
13	Miami	31
38	at New York Giants	20
10	at New York Jets	0
13	at New England	17
23	Minnesota	13
42	at St. Louis	27
34	Tampa Bay (OT)	31
26	at Detroit	21
7	Green Bay	26
427		**255**

DALLAS (9-7)
17	at Jacksonville	24
27	Washington	10
45	at Tennessee	14
24	at Philadelphia	38
34	Houston	6
22	New York Giants	36
35	at Carolina	14
19	at Washington	22
27	at Arizona	10
21	Indianapolis	14
38	Tampa Bay	10
23	at New York Giants	20
17	New Orleans	42
38	at Atlanta	28
7	Philadelphia	23
31	Detroit	39
425		**350**

DETROIT (3-13)
6	Seattle	9
7	at Chicago	34
24	Green Bay	31
34	at St. Louis	41
17	at Minnesota	26
20	Buffalo	17
24	at New York Jets	31
30	Atlanta	14
13	San Francisco	19
10	at Arizona	17
10	Miami	27
21	at New England	28
20	Minnesota	30
9	at Green Bay	17
21	Chicago	26
39	at Dallas	31
305		**398**

GREEN BAY (8-8)
0	Chicago	26
27	New Orleans	34
31	at Detroit	24
9	at Philadelphia	31
20	St. Louis	23
34	at Miami	24
31	Arizona	14
10	at Buffalo	24
23	at Minnesota	17
0	New England	35
24	at Seattle	34
10	New York Jets	38
30	at San Francisco	19
17	Detroit	9
9	Minnesota	7
26	at Chicago	7
301		**366**

MINNESOTA (6-10)
19	at Washington	16
16	Carolina (OT)	13
16	Chicago	19
12	at Buffalo	17
26	Detroit	17
31	at Seattle	13
7	New England	31
3	at San Francisco	9
17	Green Bay	23
20	at Miami	24
31	Arizona	26
13	at Chicago	23
30	at Detroit	20
13	New York Jets	26
7	at Green Bay	9
21	St. Louis	41
282		**327**

NEW ORLEANS (10-6)
19	at Cleveland	14
34	at Green Bay	27
23	Atlanta	3
18	at Carolina	21
24	Tampa Bay	21
27	Philadelphia	24
22	Baltimore	35
31	at Tampa Bay	14
31	at Pittsburgh	38
16	Cincinnati	31
31	at Atlanta	13
34	San Francisco	10
42	at Dallas	17
10	Washington	16
30	at New York Giants	7
21	Carolina	31
413		**322**

NEW YORK GIANTS (8-8)
21	Indianapolis	26
30	at Philadelphia (OT)	24
30	at Seattle	42
19	Washington	3
27	at Atlanta	14
36	at Dallas	22
17	Tampa Bay	3
14	Houston	10
20	Chicago	38
10	at Jacksonville	26
21	at Tennessee	24
20	Dallas	23
27	at Carolina	13
22	Philadelphia	36
7	New Orleans	30
34	at Washington	28
355		**362**

PHILADELPHIA (10-6)
24	at Houston	10
24	New York Giants (OT)	30
38	at San Francisco	24
31	Green Bay	9
38	Dallas	24
24	at New Orleans	27
21	at Tampa Bay	23
6	Jacksonville	13
27	Washington	3
13	Tennessee	31
21	at Indianapolis	45
27	Carolina	24
21	at Washington	19
36	at New York Giants	22
23	at Dallas	7
24	Atlanta	17
398		**328**

ST. LOUIS (8-8)
18	Denver	10
13	at San Francisco	20
16	at Arizona	14
41	Detroit	34
23	at Green Bay	20
28	Seattle	30
24	at San Diego	38
17	Kansas City	31
22	at Seattle	24
0	at Carolina	15
20	San Francisco	17
20	Arizona	34
27	Chicago	42
20	at Oakland	0
37	Washington (OT)	31
41	at Minnesota	21
367		**381**

SAN FRANCISCO (7-9)
27	at Arizona	34
20	St. Louis	13
24	Philadelphia	38
0	at Kansas City	41
34	Oakland	20
19	San Diego	48
10	at Chicago	41
9	Minnesota	3
19	at Detroit	13
20	Seattle	14
17	at St. Louis	20
10	at New Orleans	34
19	Green Bay	30
24	at Seattle	14
20	Arizona	26
26	at Denver (OT)	23
298		**412**

SEATTLE (9-7)
9	at Detroit	6
21	Arizona	10
42	New York Giants	30
6	at Chicago	37
30	at St. Louis	28
13	Minnesota	31
28	at Kansas City	35
16	Oakland	0
24	St. Louis	22
14	at San Francisco	20
34	Green Bay	24
23	at Denver	20
21	at Arizona	27
14	San Francisco	24
17	San Diego	20
23	at Tampa Bay	7
335		**341**

TAMPA BAY (4-12)
0	Baltimore	27
3	at Atlanta	14
24	Carolina	26
21	at New Orleans	24
14	Cincinnati	13
23	Philadelphia	21
3	at New York Giants	17
14	New Orleans	31
10	at Carolina	24
20	Washington	17
10	at Dallas	38
3	at Pittsburgh	20
6	Atlanta	17
31	at Chicago (OT)	34
22	at Cleveland	7
7	Seattle	23
211		**353**

WASHINGTON (5-11)
16	Minnesota	19
10	at Dallas	27
31	at Houston	15
36	Jacksonville (OT)	30
3	at New York Giants	19
22	Tennessee	25
22	at Indianapolis	36
22	Dallas	19
3	at Philadelphia	27
17	at Tampa Bay	20
17	Carolina	13
14	Atlanta	24
19	Philadelphia	21
16	at New Orleans	10
31	at St. Louis (OT)	37
28	New York Giants	34
307		**376**

FINAL STANDINGS

AMERICAN FOOTBALL CONFERENCE

East Division

	W	L	T	Pct.	Pts.	OP
New England	12	4	0	.750	385	237
New York Jets	10	6	0	.625	316	295
Buffalo	7	9	0	.438	300	311
Miami	6	10	0	.375	260	283

North Division

	W	L	T	Pct.	Pts.	OP
Baltimore	13	3	0	.813	353	201
Cincinnati	8	8	0	.500	373	331
Pittsburgh	8	8	0	.500	353	315
Cleveland	4	12	0	.250	238	356

South Division

	W	L	T	Pct.	Pts.	OP
Indianapolis	12	4	0	.750	427	360
Tennessee	8	8	0	.500	324	400
Jacksonville	8	8	0	.500	371	274
Houston	6	10	0	.375	267	366

West Division

	W	L	T	Pct.	Pts.	OP
San Diego	14	2	0	.875	492	303
Kansas City	9	7	0	.563	331	315
Denver	9	7	0	.563	319	305
Oakland	2	14	0	.125	168	332

NATIONAL FOOTBALL CONFERENCE

East Division

	W	L	T	Pct.	Pts.	OP
Philadelphia	10	6	0	.625	398	328
Dallas	9	7	0	.563	425	350
New York Giants	8	8	0	.500	355	362
Washington	5	11	0	.313	307	376

North Division

	W	L	T	Pct.	Pts.	OP
Chicago	13	3	0	.813	427	255
Green Bay	8	8	0	.500	301	366
Minnesota	6	10	0	.375	282	327
Detroit	3	13	0	.188	305	398

South Division

	W	L	T	Pct.	Pts.	OP
New Orleans	10	6	0	.625	413	322
Carolina	8	8	0	.500	270	305
Atlanta	7	9	0	.438	292	328
Tampa Bay	4	12	0	.250	211	353

West Division

	W	L	T	Pct.	Pts.	OP
Seattle	9	7	0	.563	335	341
St. Louis	8	8	0	.500	367	381
San Francisco	7	9	0	.438	298	412
Arizona	5	11	0	.313	314	389

* Wild-Card qualifier for playoffs
\# Top playoff seed in conference

* *Indianapolis finished ahead of New England based on head-to-head victory. Cincinnati finished ahead of Pittsburgh based on better division record (4-2 to 3-3). Tennessee finished ahead of Jacksonville based on better division record (4-2 to 2-4). Kansas City finished ahead of Denver based on better division record (4-2 to 3-3). New Orleans finished ahead of Philadelphia based on head-to-head victory. N.Y. Giants and Green Bay finished ahead of Carolina and St. Louis based on better conference record (Giants' 7-5 and Packers' 7-5 to Panthers' 6-6 and Rams' 6-6), and N.Y. Giants finished ahead of Green Bay based on strength of victory (.422 to Packers' .383).*

WILD-CARD PLAYOFFS

AFC
INDIANAPOLIS 23, Kansas City 8
NEW ENGLAND 37, N.Y. Jets 16

NFC
SEATTLE 21, Dallas 20
PHILADELPHIA 23, N.Y. Giants 20

DIVISIONAL PLAYOFFS

AFC
Indianapolis 15, BALTIMORE 6
New England 24, SAN DIEGO 21

NFC
NEW ORLEANS 27, Philadelphia 24
CHICAGO 27, Seattle 24 (OT)

CHAMPIONSHIP GAMES

AFC
INDIANAPOLIS 38, New England 34

NFC
CHICAGO 39, New Orleans 14

SUPER BOWL XLI

Indianapolis (AFC) 29, CHICAGO (NFC) 17
at Dolphin Stadium, South Florida

AFC-NFC PRO BOWL

AFC 31, NFC 28
at Aloha Stadium, Honolulu, Hawaii

Home teams in playoff games are indicated in CAPS.

FIRST WEEK SUMMARIES

American Football Conference

East Division	W	L	T	Pct.	Pts.	OP
New England	1	0	0	1.000	19	17
N.Y. Jets	1	0	0	1.000	23	16
Buffalo	0	1	0	.000	17	19
Miami	0	1	0	.000	17	28

North Division	W	L	T	Pct.	Pts.	OP
Baltimore	1	0	0	1.000	27	0
Cincinnati	1	0	0	1.000	23	10
Pittsburgh	1	0	0	1.000	28	17
Cleveland	0	1	0	.000	14	19

South Division	W	L	T	Pct.	Pts.	OP
Indianapolis	1	0	0	1.000	26	21
Jacksonville	1	0	0	1.000	24	17
Houston	0	1	0	.000	10	24
Tennessee	0	1	0	.000	16	23

West Division	W	L	T	Pct.	Pts.	OP
San Diego	1	0	0	1.000	27	0
Denver	0	1	0	.000	10	18
Kansas City	0	1	0	.000	10	23
Oakland	0	1	0	.000	0	27

National Football Conference

East Division	W	L	T	Pct.	Pts.	OP
Philadelphia	1	0	0	1.000	24	10
Dallas	0	1	0	.000	17	24
N.Y. Giants	0	1	0	.000	21	26
Washington	0	1	0	.000	16	19

North Division	W	L	T	Pct.	Pts.	OP
Chicago	1	0	0	1.000	26	0
Minnesota	1	0	0	1.000	19	16
Detroit	0	1	0	.000	6	9
Green Bay	0	1	0	.000	0	26

South Division	W	L	T	Pct.	Pts.	OP
Atlanta	1	0	0	1.000	20	6
New Orleans	1	0	0	1.000	19	14
Carolina	0	1	0	.000	6	20
Tampa Bay	0	1	0	.000	0	27

West Division	W	L	T	Pct.	Pts.	OP
Arizona	1	0	0	1.000	34	27
St. Louis	1	0	0	1.000	18	10
Seattle	1	0	0	1.000	9	6
San Francisco	0	1	0	.000	27	34

THURSDAY NIGHT, SEPTEMBER 7

PITTSBURGH 28, MIAMI 17—at Heinz Field, attendance 64,927. Charlie Batch passed for 3 touchdowns as the defending Super Bowl-champion Steelers rallied to defeat the Dolphins. Batch, named the starter four days earlier after Ben Roethlisberger's appendectomy, finished a 12-play, 75-yard drive with a 27-yard scoring pass to Nate Washington. Wes Welker's 47-yard punt return midway through the second quarter led to the first of two Ronnie Brown touchdown runs. Brown's second scoring run capped the Dolphins' first drive of the second half to give Miami a 17-14 lead with 6:11 left in the third quarter. The Steelers drove to the Dolphins' 1 early in the fourth quarter, but Batch fumbled the snap and Will Allen recovered. On the first play of the Steelers' next possession, Batch lofted a 20-yard pass to Heath Miller, who outran the Dolphins to the end zone for a 21-17 lead with 6:11 to play. Jeff Reed missed a 44-yard field-goal attempt with 3:09 left, but on the next play Joey Porter intercepted Daunte Culpepper's pass over the middle and raced untouched 42 yards for the game's final points. Batch was 15 of 25 for 209 yards and his first 3-touchdown game since 2001. Willie Parker rushed 29 times for 115 yards. Miller had 3 catches for 101 yards. Culpepper was 18 of 37 for 262 yards, with 2 interceptions.

Miami	0	10	7	0	—	17
Pittsburgh	0	14	0	14	—	28
Pitt	—	Washington 27 pass from Batch (Reed kick)				
Mia	—	Brown 2 run (Mare kick)				
Pitt	—	Ward 7 pass from Batch (Reed kick)				
Mia	—	FG Mare 26				
Mia	—	Brown 5 run (Mare kick)				
Pitt	—	Miller 87 pass from Batch				

(Reed kick)

Pitt	—	Porter 42 interception return				

(Reed kick)

SUNDAY, SEPTEMBER 10

ARIZONA 34, SAN FRANCISCO 27—at Cardinals Stadium, attendance 63,407. Kurt Warner passed for 3 touchdowns as Arizona withstood a late rally to win the first game at Cardinals Stadium. The Cardinals scored touchdowns on their first three possessions, the latter two set up by fumble recoveries at the 49ers' 5 and 41, respectively, to jump to a 21-7 lead. It marked the first time since 1975 that the Cardinals had scored 3 first-quarter touchdowns. In the third quarter, Walt Harris sack and fumble recovery at the Cardinals' 7 led to Frank Gore's touchdown run two plays later to pull the 49ers within 24-21. Warner responded with an 86-yard touchdown drive, capped by Adam Bergen's 7-yard catch, to extend the lead to 31-21. Arnaz Battle's 60-yard punt return set up Joe Nedney's 22-yard field goal with 8:52 remaining, but the Cardinals converted 3 third-down situations on their ensuing drive, capped by Neil Rackers' 30-yard field goal with 1:50 to play. Antonio Bryant's 46-yard catch set up Nedney's 44-yard field goal with 32 seconds left, and Marcus Hudson recovered the ensuing onside kick. From the Cardinals' 36, Alex Smith lofted a Hail Mary pass into the end zone that was batted down as time expired. Warner was 23 of 37 for 301 yards and 3 touchdowns. Fitzgerald had 9 catches for 133 yards. Smith was 23 of 40 for 288 yards and 1 touchdown. Bryant had 4 receptions for 114 yards.

San Francisco	7	7	7	6	—	27
Arizona	21	3	7	3	—	34
SF	—	Davis 31 pass from A. Smith (Nedney kick)				
Ariz	—	Walters 2 pass from Warner (Rackers kick)				
Ariz	—	James 1 run (Rackers kick)				
Ariz	—	Boldin 6 pass from Warner (Rackers kick)				
SF	—	Gore 4 run (Nedney kick)				
Ariz	—	FG Rackers 36				
SF	—	Gore 2 run (Nedney kick)				
Ariz	—	Bergen 7 pass from Warner (Rackers kick)				
SF	—	FG Nedney 22				
Ariz	—	FG Rackers 30				
SF	—	FG Nedney 44				

ATLANTA 20, CAROLINA 6—at Bank of America Stadium, attendance 73,522. Michael Vick passed for 2 touchdowns and Warrick Dunn rushed for 129 yards as the Falcons handed the Panthers their third consecutive home-opening defeat. The Panthers outgained the Falcons 385-215 in total yards and registered 4 sacks. In the first half, Atlanta drove to at least the Panthers' 34 on all five possessions, finishing with 1 touchdown, 2 field goals, and 2 missed field goals. Vick's 14-yard run to the Panthers' 4 set up Alge Crumpler's 1-yard touchdown catch for a 20-6 lead with 35 seconds left in the third quarter. The Panthers did not drive inside the Falcons' 30 in their final five possessions. Vick was 10 of 22 for 140 yards and 2 touchdowns. Dunn had 29 carries for 132 yards. Jake Delhomme was 21 of 39 for 186 yards, with 1 interception.

Atlanta	3	10	7	0	—	20
Carolina	3	0	3	0	—	6
Car	—	FG Kasay 54				
Atl	—	FG Koenen 25				
Atl	—	FG Koenen 32				
Atl	—	Jenkins 34 pass from Vick (Koenen kick)				
Car	—	FG Kasay 46				
Atl	—	Crumpler 1 pass from Vick (Koenen kick)				

NEW ORLEANS 19, CLEVELAND 14—at Cleveland Browns Stadium, attendance 72,915. John Carney kicked 4 field goals and Reggie Bush had 119 yards from scrimmage in his debut as the Saints allowed just 186 yards to win Sean Payton's first game as a head coach. Braylon Edwards caught a 74-yard touchdown pass on the Browns' first offensive play, only to have the play nullified by a penalty. Carney ended three of the Saints first four drives with field goals, the last of which was set up by Scott Fujita's 19-yard interception return, to take a 9-0 lead. Kellen Winslow's first career touchdown capped the opening 67-yard drive of the second half to pull the Browns within 9-7, but late in the quarter Drew Brees completed 3 third-down passes, culminated by rookie Marques Colston's 12-yard touchdown catch, for a 16-7 lead. The Browns responded with a 13-play, 74-yard drive to pull within 16-14 with 11:20 to play, The Saints extended their lead to five points on the ensuing drive, highlighted by Devery Henderson's 19-yard catch on third-and-8, to take a 19-14 lead with 5:42 remaining. Josh Bullocks' interception at the Saints' 30 with 1:36 left capped the victory. Brees, in his first game with the Saints, was 16 of 30 for 170 yards and 1 touchdown, with 1 interception. Charlie Frye was 16 of 27 for 132 yards and 1 touchdown, with 2 interceptions.

New Orleans	3	6	7	3	—	19
Cleveland	0	0	7	7	—	14
NO	—	FG Carney 43				
NO	—	FG Carney 25				
NO	—	FG Carney 21				
Cle	—	Winslow 18 pass from Frye (Dawson kick)				
NO	—	Colston 12 pass from Brees (Carney kick)				
Cle	—	Frye 1 run (Dawson kick)				
NO	—	FG Carney 20				

SEATTLE 9, DETROIT 6—at Ford Field, attendance 60,535. Josh Brown kicked a 42-yard field goal as time expired to give the defending NFC-champion Seahawks a hard-fought victory to spoil Rod Marinelli's coaching debut. Brown had 2 first-half field-goal attempts blocked, by Shaun Rogers and James Hall, but the Seahawks led 6-3 at halftime thanks to Brown's 51-yard field goal as the half expired. Jason Hanson tied the game with a 37-yard field goal with 7:05 to play. After an exchange of punts, the Seahawks began their final drive from their own 20 with 3:13 remaining. Matt Hasselbeck's 14-yard pass to David Hackett gave the Seahawks a first down at the Lions' 41. Maurice Morris' 17-yard run around right end with 16 seconds left set up Brown's winning kick. Hasselbeck was 25 of 30 for 210 yards. Kitna was 21 of 37 for 229 yards.

Seattle	0	6	0	3	—	9
Detroit	3	0	0	3	—	6
Det	—	FG Hanson 44				
Sea	—	FG J. Brown 20				
Sea	—	FG J. Brown 51				
Det	—	FG Hanson 37				
Sea	—	FG J. Brown 42				

CHICAGO 26, GREEN BAY 0—at Lambeau Field, attendance 70,918. The Bears' defense forced 3 turnovers to register the first shutout against a Brett Favre-led team in Mike McCarthy's first game as a head coach. The Bears scored on four of their first five possessions en route to a 16-0 halftime lead. The Packers never drove inside the Bears' 35-yard line, and Charles Tillman and rookie Danieal Manning intercepted Favre in the fourth quarter to thwart any rally. Rex Grossman was 18 of 26 for 262 yards and 1 touchdown, with 1 interception. Muhsin Muhammad had 6 catches for 102 yards. Favre was 15 of 29 for 170 yards, with 2 interceptions. Ahman Green had 20 carries for 110 yards.

Chicago	7	9	3	7	—	26
Green Bay	0	0	0	0	—	0
Chi	—	Berrian 49 pass from Grossman (Gould kick)				
Chi	—	FG Gould 40				
Chi	—	FG Gould 39				
Chi	—	FG Gould 28				
Chi	—	FG Gould 30				

Chi   —   Hester 84 punt return (Gould kick)

PHILADELPHIA 24, HOUSTON 10—at Reliant Stadium, attendance 70,180. Donovan McNabb passed for 314 yards and 3 touchdowns as the Eagles had 200 more yards of offense (441-241) to defeat the Texans. The Texans began Gary Kubiak's coaching career with a 10-play, 77-yard drive, capped by David Carr's 25-yard touchdown pass to Eric Moulds, for a quick 7-0 lead. The Eagles drove 84, 80, and 75 yards on their 3 touchdown drives, capped by Brian Westbrook's 31-yard scoring catch for a 21-10 lead with 11:28 left in the third quarter. David Akers banked in a 42-yard field goal off the right upright to extend the lead to 24-10. The Texans responded by driving to the Eagles' 17, but Carr's fourth-and-4 pass fell incomplete, and the Eagles used 16 plays to run out the final 8:56 off the clock. McNabb was 24 of 35 for 314 yards and 3 touchdowns, with 1 interception. Donte' Stallworth, who had just been traded to the Eagles two weeks earlier, had 6 receptions for 141 yards. Carr was 18 of 27 for 208 yards and 1 touchdown. Andre Johnson had 6 catches for 101 yards.

Philadelphia	0	14	7	3	—	24
Houston	7	3	0	0	—	10

Hou	—	Moulds 25 pass rom Carr (K. Brown kick)
Phil	—	Stallworth 42 pass from McNabb (Akers kick)
Hou	—	FG K. Brown 34
Phil	—	R. Brown 5 pass from McNabb (Akers kick)
Phil	—	Westbrook 31 pass from McNabb (Akers kick)
Phil	—	FG Akers 42

JACKSONVILLE 24, DALLAS 17—at Alltel Stadium, attendance 67,164. Byron Leftwich passed for 1 touchdown and ran for another and the Jaguars' defense forced 3 turnovers to defeat the Cowboys. The Cowboys scored on their first two drives for a 10-0 lead. With 1:43 left in the half, Rashean Mathis intercepted a pass and returned it to the Cowboys' 32 to set up Fred Taylor's 5-yard touchdown catch with seven seconds left in the half to tie the game. Both teams missed third-quarter field goals before Leftwich capped a 74-yard drive, highlighted by Matt Jones' 25- and 22-yard catches, with a 1-yard scoring sneak for a 17-10 lead with 11:27 remaining. Nick Greisen intercepted a pass near midfield later in the quarter to set up Fred Taylor's 5-yard touchdown run for a 24-10 lead. Drew Bledsoe responded with a 51-yard pass to Terry Glenn that led to a 21-yard touchdown catch by Terrell Owens, making his Cowboys' debut, with 1:54 to play. The Cowboys forced a punt with 51 seconds left, but Mike Peterson intercepted Bledsoe in Cowboys' territory with 14 seconds left to preserve the victory. Leftwich was 23 of 34 for 237 yards and 1 touchdown, with 1 interception. Bledsoe was 16 of 33 for 246 yards and 1 touchdown, with 3 interceptions.

Dallas	10	0	0	7	—	17
Jacksonville	0	10	0	14	—	24

Dall	—	J. Jones 23 run (Suisham kick)
Dall	—	FG Suisham 32
Jax	—	FG Scobee 35
Jax	—	R. Williams 6 pass from Leftwich (Scobee kick)
Jax	—	Leftwich 3 run (Scobee kick)
Jax	—	Taylor 5 run (Scobee kick)
Dall	—	Owens 21 pass from Bledsoe (Suisham kick)

CINCINNATI 23, KANSAS CITY 10—at Arrowhead Stadium, attendance 77,956. Rudi Johnson rushed for 96 yards and 1 touchdown and the Bengals' defense forced 3 turnovers to spoil Herm Edwards' first game as the Chiefs' coach. The Bengals trailed 3-0 when Dante Hall muffed a punt and Landon Johnson recovered the ball to set up the first of three consecutive scoring possessions for Cincinnati to take a 17-3 halftime lead. Tony Gonzalez caught a 9-yard scoring pass from

Damon Huard in the fourth quarter to pull within 20-10, and Kansas City forced a punt, but Justin Smith sacked Huard on fourth down in Chiefs' territory with 2:49 remaining to stop their final threat. Carson Palmer was 13 of 19 for 127 yards. Trent Green, making his 81st consecutive start, was 11 of 15 for 90 yards, with 1 interception, before leaving the game in the third quarter with a concussion. Huard replaced him and was 12 of 20 for 140 yards and 1 touchdown.

Cincinnati	0	17	0	6	—	23
Kansas City	3	0	0	7	—	10

KC	—	FG Tynes 29
Cin	—	FG Graham 37
Cin	—	R. Johnson 22 run (Graham kick)
Cin	—	Watson 8 run (Graham kick)
Cin	—	FG Graham 42
KC	—	Gonzalez 9 pass from D. Huard (Tynes kick)
Cin	—	FG Graham 36

NEW ENGLAND 19, BUFFALO 17—at Gillette Stadium, attendance 68,756. Ty Warren sacked J.P. Losman for a safety as the Patriots rallied to defeat the Bills in Dick Jauron's first game as their coach. The Bills scored 12 seconds into the game when London Fletcher-Baker recovered a fumble by Tom Brady and returned it 5 yards for a touchdown. Buffalo added scoring drives of 48 and 73 yards on its first two offensive possessions for a 17-7 lead. Maintaining their 17-7 lead, the Bills drove to the Patriots' 7 on their first possession of the second half, but Willis McGahee was stopped for no gain on fourth-and-1. The Patriots responded with a 12-play, 93-yard touchdown drive and field goal on their next two possessions to tie the game. On third-and-11 from the Bills' 8, Losman dropped back to pass, avoided one defender, and was sacked by Warren for a safety with 8:33 to play. The Patriots regained possession with 6:15 to play and ran out the clock, highlighted by Corey Dillon's 6-yard run on fourth-and-2 from the Bills' 26 with 2:00 to play. Brady was 11 of 23 for 163 yards and 2 touchdowns, with 1 interception. Losman was 15 of 23 for 164 yards.

Buffalo	10	7	0	0	—	17
New England	7	0	5	7	—	19

Buff	—	Fletcher-Baker 5 fumble return (Lindell kick)
NE	—	T. Brown 9 pass from Brady (Gostkowski kick)
Buff	—	FG Lindell 53
Buff	—	Thomas 18 run (Lindell kick)
NE	—	Faulk 17 pass from Brady (Gostkowski kick)
NE	—	FG Gostkowski 32
NE	—	Safety, Warren sacked Losman in end zone

ST. LOUIS 18, DENVER 10—at Edward Jones Dome, attendance 65,577. Jeff Wilkins kicked a club-record 6 field goals as Scott Linehan won his NFL coaching debut. The Rams had 5 field-goal attempts in the first half, with Wilkins making 4, three of which were set up by Broncos' turnovers. Wilkins added a 48-yard field goal to begin the second half and give the Rams a 15-7 lead. Jason Elam kicked a 49-yard field goal to pull within five points with 14:18 to play, and the Broncos' defense forced a punt. However, Corey Chavous intercepted a long pass at the Broncos' 7 with 12:00 to play, and the Rams responded with an 11-play, 82-yard drive capped by Wilkins' sixth field goal with 6:24 remaining. The Broncos drove to the Rams' 28, but Fakhir Brown intercepted Jake Plummer's pass with 2:26 to play. Marc Bulger was 18 of 34 for 217 yards. Steven Jackson added 22 carries for 121 yards. Plummer was 13 of 26 for 138 yards, with 3 interceptions. Tatum Bell rushed 15 times for 103 yards.

Denver	0	7	0	3	—	10
St. Louis	3	9	3	3	—	18

StL	—	FG Wilkins 26
StL	—	FG Wilkins 38
StL	—	FG Wilkins 29
StL	—	FG Wilkins 51

Den	—	M. Bell 1 run (Elam kick)
StL	—	FG Wilkins 48
Den	—	FG Elam 49
StL	—	FG Wilkins 24

BALTIMORE 27, TAMPA BAY 0—at Raymond James Stadium, attendance 65,087. The Ravens' defense allowed just 142 yards and scored a touchdown as Baltimore ended its NFL-long 11-game road losing streak. Steve McNair began his Ravens' career with a 14-play, 80-yard touchdown drive, capped by Jamal Lewis' 4-yard run. Chris McAlister's interception and 60-yard touchdown return down the far sideline early in the second quarter extended the lead to 14-0. The Ravens led 20-0 before the Buccaneers engineered their lone scoring threat by driving to the Ravens' 6, but Chris Simms' fourth-down pass fell incomplete. McNair was 17 of 27 for 181 yards and 1 touchdown. Simms was 17 of 29 for 133 yards, with 3 interceptions.

Baltimore	7	10	3	7	—	27
Tampa Bay	0	0	0	0	—	0

Balt	—	J. Lewis 4 run (Stover kick)
Balt	—	McAlister 60 interception return (Stover kick)
Balt	—	FG Stover 20
Balt	—	FG Stover 42
Balt	—	Wilcox 4 pass from McNair (Stover kick)

N.Y. JETS 23, TENNESSEE 16—at LP Field, attendance 69,143. Chris Baker caught a 12-yard touchdown pass from Chad Pennington with 2:10 to play as the Jets withstood a late rally to win Eric Mangini's coaching debut. Andre Dyson's interception with 1:30 left in the half sparked a 36-yard touchdown drive, capped by Jerricho Cotchery's 8-yard touchdown catch with 17 seconds left in the half for a 13-0 lead. On the first play of the second half, Kerry Rhodes intercepted a pass and returned it 25 yards to the Titans' 22 to set up Mike Nugent's 18-yard field goal for a 16-0 lead. Tennessee cut the lead to 16-8, and Cortland Finnegan sacked Pennington at the Jets' 5 and forced him to fumble. Randy Starks recovered at the 1-yard line and Travis Henry scored on the next play. Collins' 2-point conversion pass to Drew Bennett tied the game with 5:58 remaining. Justin Miller returned the ensuing kickoff 41 yards and Pennington capped the 57-yard drive with his touchdown pass to Baker with 2:10 to play. The Titans drove to the Jets' 8, but Collins' fourth-down pass intended for Bo Scaife fell incomplete with 35 seconds to play. Pennington was 24 of 33 for 319 yards and 2 touchdowns. Laveranues Coles had 8 catches for 153 yards. Collins, who signed 13 days earlier, was 17 of 38 for 223 yards, with 2 interceptions. Bennett had 4 receptions for 106 yards.

N.Y. Jets	0	13	3	7	—	23
Tennessee	0	0	0	16	—	16

NYJ	—	Barlow 1 run (Nugent kick)
NYJ	—	Cotchery 8 pass from Pennington (kick failed)
NYJ	—	FG Nugent 18
Tenn	—	Henry 3 run (Henry run)
Tenn	—	Henry 1 run (Bennett pass from Collins)
NYJ	—	Baker 12 pass from Pennington (Nugent kick)

SUNDAY NIGHT, SEPTEMBER 10
INDIANAPOLIS 26, N.Y. GIANTS 21—at Giants Stadium, attendance 78,622. Peyton Manning passed for 276 yards and 1 touchdown as the Colts won the first game that featured two brothers starting at quarterback. The Colts scored on their first four possessions, with the touchdown set up by Jay Feely's missed 40-yard field goal, to take a 16-7 halftime lead. The Giants began the second half with a 69-yard touchdown drive, capped by Eli Manning's 15-yard touchdown pass to Jeremy Shockey. The Giants had the ball near midfield late in the third quarter when Robert Mathis recovered a mishandled snap. Dominic Rhodes scored eight plays later to give the

Colts a 23-14 lead with 13:13 to play. Tiki Barber had a 22-yard run and 11-yard catch on the next drive to set up Brandon Jacobs' 1-yard run with 8:01 remaining. Nick Harper intercepted a pass with 3:51 to play to set up Adam Vinatieri's 32-yard field goal with 1:12 remaining, and the Giants reached their own 46 as time expired. Peyton Manning was 25 of 41 for 276 yards and 1 touchdown, with 1 interception. Harrison had 9 catches for 113 yards. Eli Manning was 20 of 34 for 247 yards and 2 touchdowns, with 1 interception. Barber had 18 carries for 110 yards.

Indianapolis	3	13	0	10	—	26
N.Y. Giants	0	7	7	7	—	21

Ind	—	FG Vinatieri 26
Ind	—	FG Vinatieri 32
Ind	—	Clark 2 pass from P. Manning (Vinatieri kick)
NYG	—	Burress 34 pass from E. Manning (Feely kick)
Ind	—	FG Vinatieri 48
NYG	—	Shockey 15 pass from E. Manning (Feely kick)
Ind	—	Rhodes 1 run (Vinatieri kick)
NYG	—	Jacobs 1 run (Feely kick)
Ind	—	FG Vinatieri 32

MONDAY NIGHT, SEPTEMBER 11
MINNESOTA 19, WASHINGTON 16—at FedExField, attendance 90,608. Ryan Longwell kicked a 31-yard field goal with 1:00 to play, and John Hall missed a 48-yard attempt with 12 seconds remaining, as the Vikings won Brad Childress' coaching debut. The Vikings began their season on a 10-play, 80-yard touchdown drive, but failed to cross midfield again until Longwell kicked a 46-yard field goal as the half expired to pull within 13-9. Mewelde Moore's 20-yard punt return early in the second half led to Marcus Robinson's 20-yard touchdown pass on third-and-5 to give the Vikings a 16-13 lead. With the score tied with 2:50 to play in the game, Troy Williamson caught a 13-yard pass on third-and-9 for a first down. A 15-yard facemask penalty gave the Vikings the ball at the Redskins' 24, setting up Longwell's field goal. The Redskins drove to the Vikings' 35, but on third-and-6, Antwaan Randle El ran out of bounds just shy of the first-down marker with 17 seconds to play. On fourth-and-1, Hall's 48-yard field-goal attempt sailed wide left. Johnson was 16 of 30 for 223 yards and 1 touchdown. Mark Brunell was 17 of 28 for 163 yards.

Minnesota	6	3	7	3	—	19
Washington	3	10	3	0	—	16

Minn	—	Taylor 4 run (run failed)
Wash	—	FG Hall 27
Wash	—	Portis 5 run (Hall kick)
Wash	—	FG Hall 27
Minn	—	FG Longwell 46
Minn	—	M. Robinson 20 pass from B. Johnson (Longwell kick)
Wash	—	FG Hall 22
Minn	—	FG Longwell 31

SAN DIEGO 27, OAKLAND 0—at McAfee Coliseum, attendance 62,578. The Chargers' defense registered 9 sacks, 3 by Shawne Merriman, to give the franchise its first shutout against the Raiders since 1961. The Chargers outgained the Raiders 302-129 in total yards. San Diego had scoring drives of 51, 66, and 64 yards on its first three possessions. The Raiders punted at the end of their first nine possessions, four of which lost yardage, and their lone scoring chance ended on the game's final play as Drayton Florence knocked Randal Williams out of bounds at the Chargers' 3-yard line. Philip Rivers, making his first start, was 8 of 11 for 108 yards and 1 touchdown. LaDainian Tomlinson rushed 31 times for 131 yards. Aaron Brooks was 6 of 14 for 68 yards, and Andrew Walter was 2 of 5 for 28 yards.

San Diego	3	10	0	14	—	27
Oakland	0	0	0	0	—	0

SD	—	FG Kaeding 47
SD	—	Tomlinson 1 run (Kaeding kick)
SD	—	FG Kaeding 29
SD	—	Gates 4 pass from Rivers (Kaeding kick)
SD	—	Turner 1 run (Kaeding kick)

SECOND WEEK SUMMARIES
American Football Conference

East Division	W	L	T	Pct.	Pts.	OP
New England	2	0	0	1.000	43	34
Buffalo	1	1	0	.500	33	25
N.Y. Jets	1	1	0	.500	40	40
Miami	0	2	0	.000	23	44
North Division	**W**	**L**	**T**	**Pct.**	**Pts.**	**OP**
Cincinnati	2	0	0	1.000	57	27
Baltimore	2	0	0	1.000	55	6
Pittsburgh	1	1	0	.500	28	26
Cleveland	0	2	0	.000	31	53
South Division	**W**	**L**	**T**	**Pct.**	**Pts.**	**OP**
Indianapolis	2	0	0	1.000	69	45
Jacksonville	2	0	0	1.000	33	17
Houston	0	2	0	.000	34	67
Tennessee	0	2	0	.000	23	63
West Division	**W**	**L**	**T**	**Pct.**	**Pts.**	**OP**
San Diego	2	0	0	1.000	67	7
Denver	1	1	0	.500	19	24
Kansas City	0	2	0	.000	16	32
Oakland	0	2	0	.000	6	55

National Football Conference

East Division	W	L	T	Pct.	Pts.	OP
Dallas	1	1	0	.500	44	34
N.Y. Giants	1	1	0	.500	51	50
Philadelphia	1	1	0	.500	48	40
Washington	0	2	0	.000	26	46
North Division	**W**	**L**	**T**	**Pct.**	**Pts.**	**OP**
Chicago	2	0	0	1.000	60	7
Minnesota	2	0	0	1.000	35	29
Detroit	0	2	0	.000	13	43
Green Bay	0	2	0	.000	27	60
South Division	**W**	**L**	**T**	**Pct.**	**Pts.**	**OP**
Atlanta	2	0	0	1.000	34	9
New Orleans	2	0	0	1.000	53	41
Carolina	0	2	0	.000	19	36
Tampa Bay	0	2	0	.000	3	41
West Division	**W**	**L**	**T**	**Pct.**	**Pts.**	**OP**
Seattle	2	0	0	1.000	30	16
Arizona	1	1	0	.500	44	48
St. Louis	1	1	0	.500	31	30
San Francisco	1	1	0	.500	47	47

SUNDAY, SEPTEMBER 17
ATLANTA 14, TAMPA BAY 3—at Georgia Dome, attendance 70,828. Michael Vick passed for 1 touchdown and rushed for 127 yards and a score as the Falcons established a franchise record with 306 rushing yards. Leading 7-0, DeAngelo Hall intercepted a pass and returned it 18 yards to the Buccaneers' 12 to set up Vick's 4-yard touchdown pass to Fred McCrary. Matt Bryant kicked a 22-yard field goal at the end of the first half, and Tampa Bay drove to the Falcons' 3 to begin the second half, but Chris Simms' pass was deflected by Demorrio Williams and Lawyer Milloy and intercepted by Jason Webster near the goal line. The Falcons drove into the Buccaneers' red zone six times, but Michael Koenen missed all 4 of his field-goal attempts. Vick was 10 of 15 for 92 yards and 1 touchdown, with 1 interception. Warrick Dunn carried 21 times for 134 yards, and Vick added 14 carries for 127 yards, his sixth career 100-yard rushing game, which added to his own record. Simms was 28 of 53 for 313 yards, with 3 interceptions. Joey Galloway had 9 receptions for 161 yards.

Tampa Bay	0	3	0	0	—	3
Atlanta	7	7	0	0	—	14

Atl	—	Vick 1 run (Koenen kick)
Atl	—	McCrary 4 pass from Vick (Koenen kick)
TB	—	FG Bryant 22

BALTIMORE 28, OAKLAND 6—at M & T Bank Stadium, attendance 70,744. The Ravens' defense forced 6

turnovers and registered 6 sacks to post its second consecutive game without allowing a touchdown and begin 2-0 for the first time since their Super Bowl-winning 2000 season. The Ravens' defense forced fumbles on Oakland's first two possessions to take a 9-0 lead. The Raiders pulled within 9-3, but the Ravens responded with a 65-yard scoring drive, capped by Todd Heap's 1-yard touchdown catch, for a 16-3 lead. In the third quarter, Adalius Thomas' sack of Andrew Walter resulted in a safety. Later in the quarter, Kelly Gregg returned a fumble 59 yards to set up Matt Stover's fourth field goal for a 21-3 lead. The Raiders pulled within 21-6, and drove to the Ravens' 19 on their next possession, but Walter threw 4 consecutive incompletions with 4:15 to play. Steve McNair was 16 of 33 for 143 yards and 1 touchdown, with 1 interception. Walter, who replaced Aaron Brooks a few plays into the game when Brooks suffered an injury, was 10 of 27 for 162 yards, with 3 interceptions.

Oakland	0	3	0	3	—	6
Baltimore	9	7	2	10	—	28

Balt	—	FG Stover 25
Balt	—	FG Stover 33
Balt	—	FG Stover 37
Oak	—	FG Janikowski 34
Balt	—	Heap 1 pass from McNair (Stover kick)
Balt	—	Safety, Thomas sacked Walter in end zone
Balt	—	FG Stover 23
Oak	—	FG Janikowski 51
Balt	—	Anderson 34 run (Stover kick)

CHICAGO 34, DETROIT 7—at Soldier Field, attendance 62,181. Rex Grossman established career highs with 289 passing yards and 4 touchdowns as the Bears improved to 2-0. The Bears' defense recovered 3 fumbles, including on Detroit's first two possessions, to set up 10 points. The Bears scored on their next two drives as well, capped by Grossman's 31-yard touchdown pass to Desmond Clark for a 24-0 lead with 3:36 left in the half. Detroit drove 86 yards in 10 plays to begin the second half, culminated with Jon Kitna's 1-yard scoring run to pull within 24-7. But Chicago scored on two of its next three drives to extend the lead to 34-7 with 10:03 to play. Grossman was 20 of 27 for 289 yards and 4 touchdowns. Kitna was 23 of 30 for 230 yards.

Detroit	0	0	7	0	—	7
Chicago	10	14	7	3	—	34

Chi	—	Gilmore 3 pass from Grossman (Gould kick)
Chi	—	FG Gould 32
Chi	—	Berrian 41 pass from Grossman (Gould kick)
Chi	—	Clark 31 pass from Grossman (Gould kick)
Det	—	Kitna 1 run (Hanson kick)
Chi	—	Gilmore 5 pass from Grossman (Gould kick)
Chi	—	FG Gould 45

CINCINNATI 34, CLEVELAND 17—at Paul Brown Stadium, attendance 66,072. Carson Palmer passed for 352 yards and 2 touchdowns and Rudi Johnson ran for 145 yards and 2 scores as the Bengals rolled up 481 yards of offense. The Bengals had touchdown drives of 75 and 92 yards in the first half, and led 20-3 early in the fourth quarter. Braylon Edwards caught a 75-yard pass to set up Reuben Droughns' 1-yard touchdown run at 13:06 to play. The Bengals responded with an 80-yard drive, highlighted by runs of 20, 15, and 10 yards by Johnson and culminated with his 1-yard run with 9:50 remaining for a 27-10 lead. Landon Johnson intercepted a pass two plays later to set up Rudi Johnson's final touchdown run. Palmer was 24 of 40 for 352 yards and 2 touchdowns, with 2 interceptions. Rudi Johnson rushed 26 times for 145 yards. Chris Henry had 5 receptions for 113 yards. Charlie Frye was 20 of 33 for 244 yards, with 2 interceptions. Edwards had 4 catches for 110 yards.

Cleveland	3	0	0	14	—	17

Cincinnati		14	3	0	17	—	34

Cin — Washington 22 pass from Palmer (Graham kick)
Cle — FG Dawson 30
Cin — C. Johnson 8 pass from Palmer (Graham kick)
Cin — FG Graham 37
Cin — FG Graham 37
Cle — Droughns 1 run (Dawson kick)
Cin — R. Johnson 1 run (Graham kick)
Cin — R. Johnson 9 run (Graham kick)
Cle — Frye 2 run (Dawson kick)

DENVER 9, KANSAS CITY 6 (OT)—at INVESCO Field at Mile High, attendance 76,786. Jason Elam kicked a 39-yard field goal in overtime as the Broncos rallied for their first victory. The game marked the first time in 93 meetings between the teams that neither scored a touchdown. The Chiefs led 6-0 in the middle of the third quarter and reached the Broncos' 34, but Damon Huard fumbled and Michael Myers recovered. The Broncos responded with a 12-play drive, highlighted by Javon Walker's 16-yard reverse on fourth-and-1, and capped by Elam's 23-yard field goal late in the third quarter. The Broncos' defense forced a punt, and the offense drove 76 yards in 14 plays to tie the game with Elam's 22-yard field goal with 5:54 to play. In overtime, the Broncos won the toss. Tatum Bell had a 20-yard run and Walker caught a 24-yard pass from Jake Plummer to set up Elam's winning kick. Plummer was 16 of 30 for 173 yards, with 1 interception. Huard, playing for the injured Trent Green, was 17 of 23 for 133 yards. Larry Johnson had 27 carries for 126 yards.

Kansas City		0	3	3	0	—	6
Denver		0	0	3	3	3	—	9

KC — FG Tynes 29
KC — FG Tynes 45
Den — FG Elam 23
Den — FG Elam 22
Den — FG Elam 39

NEW ORLEANS 34, GREEN BAY 27—at Lambeau Field, attendance 70,602. Drew Brees passed for 353 yards and 2 touchdowns as the Saints rallied to post their first 2-0 start since 2002. The Packers forced 3 turnovers on the Saints' first three possessions to take a 13-0 lead. The Saints responded with touchdown drives of 58 and 73 yards to end the half with a 14-13 lead. The Packers drove the length of the field to begin the second half, only to have Omar Stoutmire intercept Brett Favre's pass in the end zone for a touchback. With the score 20-20, Marques Colston caught a 35-yard touchdown pass from Brees for a 27-20 lead with 8:20 remaining. On the next play from scrimmage, Charles Grant forced Ahman Green to fumble and Will Smith recovered. Deuce McAllister scored on the ensuing play, a 23-yard run, to give the Saints 14 points in 26 seconds for a 34-20 advantage. The Packers pulled within 34-27 and got the ball back with 3:09 to play, but Favre threw 4 consecutive incompletions from the Saints' 44 with 1:57 remaining. Brees was 26 of 41 for 353 yards and 2 touchdowns, with 1 interception. Favre was 31 of 55 for 340 yards and 3 touchdowns, with 1 interception. Donald Driver had 8 catches for 153 yards.

New Orleans		0	14	6	14	—	34
Green Bay		13	0	0	14	—	27

GB — Jennings 22 pass from Favre (Rayner kick)
GB — FG Rayner 24
GB — FG Rayner 36
NO — McAllister 3 run (Carney kick)
NO — Henderson 26 pass from Brees (Carney kick)
NO — FG Carney 45
NO — FG Carney 47
GB — Ferguson 4 pass from Favre (Rayner kick)
NO — Colston 35 pass from Brees (Carney kick)
NO — McAllister 23 run (Carney kick)

GB — Herron 6 pass from Favre (Rayner kick)

INDIANAPOLIS 43, HOUSTON 24—at RCA Dome, attendance 56,614. Peyton Manning passed for 400 yards and 3 touchdowns as the Colts rolled up 515 yards of offense. The Colts scored on six of their first seven possessions, to take a 30-3 lead with 3:17 left in the third quarter, at which point the Colts had outgained the Texans 364-94 in total yards. Houston drove 80, 68, and 61 yards on its final three possessions, all ending in touchdowns. The Colts converted 9 of 12 third-down situations, and only punted once. Manning was 26 of 38 for 400 yards and 3 touchdowns. Marvin Harrison had 7 catches for 127 yards and Reggie Wayne added 6 receptions for 135 yards. David Carr was 22 of 26 for 219 yards and 3 touchdowns.

Houston		0	3	0	21	—	24
Indianapolis		14	6	10	13	—	43

Ind — Stokley 10 pass from Manning (Vinatieri kick)
Ind — Addai 21 pass from Manning (Vinatieri kick)
Ind — FG Vinatieri 39
Hou — FG K. Brown 43
Ind — FG Vinatieri 43
Ind — Fletcher 15 pass from Manning (Vinatieri kick)
Ind — FG Vinatieri 38
Hou — Daniels 33 pass from Carr (K. Brown kick)
Ind — Rhodes 2 run (Vinatieri kick)
Hou — Bruener 1 pass from Carr (K. Brown kick)
Hou — Carthon 3 run (kick blocked)
Hou — A. Johnson 10 pass from Carr (K. Brown kick)

BUFFALO 16, MIAMI 6—at Dolphin Stadium, attendance 72,797. The Bills' defense forced 5 sacks, including 3 by Ryan Denney, to give the Dolphins just their second 0-2 start since 1970. The Bills accumulated just 171 yards of offense, but led 3-0 at halftime and drove 72 yards on its lone sustained drive to begin the second half, capped by J.P. Losman's 4-yard scoring pass to Josh Reed, for a 10-0 lead. The Bills scored on their next two possessions as well, the second set up by Coy Wire's blocked punt, for a 16-0 lead. Chris Chambers made a diving 23-yard touchdown catch with 1:54 to play, but the 2-point conversion attempt failed and Robert Royal recovered the onside kick to secure the victory. Losman was 11 of 18 for 83 yards and 1 touchdown. Daunte Culpepper was 23 of 32 for 250 yards and 1 touchdown, with 1 interception.

Buffalo		3	0	13	0	—	16
Miami		0	0	0	6	—	6

Buff — FG Lindell 33
Buff — Reed 4 pass from Losman (Lindell kick)
Buff — FG Lindell 45
Buff — FG Lindell 43
Mia — Chambers 23 pass from Culpepper (pass failed)

MINNESOTA 16, CAROLINA 13 (OT)—at Metrodome, attendance 63,623. Ryan Longwell became just the second player in NFL history to pass for a tying touchdown and kick a game-winning field goal as the Vikings improved to 2-0. Longwell matched George Blanda's feat performed in 1970. DeAngelo Williams' 3-yard touchdown run capped a 12-play, 85-yard drive just before halftime to give Carolina a 10-6 lead. Julius Peppers blocked Longwell's 51-yard field-goal attempt in the third quarter to set up John Kasay's 26-yard field goal for a 13-6 lead. In the fourth quarter, Chris Gamble caught a punt but attempted a cross-field lateral. The ball was underthrown and Jason Glenn recovered at the Panthers' 21. Four plays later the Vikings lined up for a field goal. Holder Chris Kluwe received the snap and pitched the ball to

Longwell, who then tossed a pass to Richard Owens, who dove into the end zone for a 16-yard touchdown to tie the game with 7:48 to play. In overtime, the Panthers won the toss but were forced to punt. On third-and-10, Brad Johnson completed a 30-yard pass to Troy Williamson. Two plays later, Chester Taylor broke free for a 33-yard run to the Panthers' 2 to set up Longwell's winning kick with 7:25 left. Johnson was 19 of 31 for 243 yards, with 1 interception. Taylor rushed 24 times for 113 yards. Williamson had 6 catches for 102 yards. Jake Delhomme was 17 of 33 for 181 yards. Keyshawn Johnson had 5 catches for 106 yards.

Carolina		0	10	3	0	0	—	13
Minnesota		3	3	0	7	3	—	16

Minn — FG Longwell 26
Car — FG Kasay 25
Minn — FG Longwell 22
Car — Williams 3 run (Kasay kick)
Car — FG Kasay 26
Minn — Owens 16 pass from Longwell (Longwell kick)
Minn — FG Longwell 19

NEW ENGLAND 24, N.Y. JETS 17—at The Meadowlands, attendance 77,595. Tom Brady passed for 220 yards and 1 touchdown as the Patriots defeated the Jets and Eric Mangini, who had been a New England assistant the previous six seasons. The Patriots had scoring drives of 82 and 87 yards in the first half, and led 17-0 at halftime. The Patriots' defense stopped Kevan Barlow for no gain on fourth-and-1 to begin the second half, and Laurence Maroney scored seven plays later to give New England a 24-0 lead. On the next drive, Jerricho Cotchery seemingly defied gravity when he made a catch down the sideline, rolled off two defenders, regained his feet and continued for a 71-yard touchdown. David Barrett intercepted Brady four plays later to set up Laveranues Coles' 46-yard touchdown catch and cut the deficit to 24-14. Four plays later, Brady was sacked by Kerry Rhodes and fumbled. Bryan Thomas recovered and Mike Nugent's 42-yard field goal cut the lead to 24-17 with 9:20 to play. The Patriots consumed the next 8:15 off the clock, but Jonathan Vilma blocked Stephen Gostkowski's 29-yard field-goal attempt. The Jets reached their own 45-yard line with 15 seconds left, but Tedy Bruschi ended the comeback attempt with an interception. Brady was 15 of 29 for 220 yards and 1 touchdown, with 1 interception. Chad Pennington was 22 of 37 for 306 yards and 2 touchdowns, with 1 interception. Cotchery had 6 receptions for 121 yards and Coles had 6 catches for 100 yards.

New England		7	10	7	0	—	24
N.Y. Jets		0	0	14	3	—	17

NE — Dillon 1 run (Gostkowski kick)
NE — FG Gostkowski 20
NE — Jackson 13 pass from Brady (Gostkowski kick)
NE — Maroney 1 run (Gostkowski kick)
NYJ — Cotchery 71 pass from Pennington (Nugent kick)
NYJ — Coles 46 pass from Pennington (Nugent kick)
NYJ — FG Nugent 42

N.Y. GIANTS 30, PHILADELPHIA 24 (OT)—at Lincoln Financial Field, attendance 69,241. Eli Manning passed for 371 yards and 3 touchdowns, including the game-winning 31-yard pass to Plaxico Burress in overtime, as the Giants overcame a 17-point fourth-quarter deficit to defeat the Eagles. The Eagles outgained the Giants 309-87 in total yards in the first half, and led 24-7 after three quarters. On the third play of the fourth quarter, Plaxico Burress caught a 23-yard pass but fumbled at the Giants' 16. The ball bounced into the end zone where Tim Carter fell on it for a touchdown. The Eagles still led 24-14 with 4:22 to play when Will Demps recovered Brian Westbrook's fumble at the Eagles' 33. Manning fired a 22-yard touchdown pass to Amani Toomer in the back of the end zone with 3:28 remaining. The Giants' defense forced a punt with 58 seconds left. Starting from their own 20, Manning completed 3 consecutive passes to reach the Eagles' 40. An 8-yard pass to Jeremy Shockey, along with a personal foul penalty, set up Jay Feely's game-tying 35-yard field goal with seven seconds left in regulation. In overtime, each team punted once before the Giants drove 85 yards in 13 plays, capped by Manning's game-winning 31-yard pass to Burress, who outleaped Sheldon Brown for the ball, on third-and-11 with 3:11 remaining. Manning, who was sacked 8 times, was 31 of 43 for 371 yards and 3 touchdowns, with 1 interception. Toomer had 12 catches for 137 yards, and Burress added 6 receptions for 114 yards. Donovan McNabb was 27 of 45 for 350 yards and 2 touchdowns. L.J. Smith had 7 catches for 111 yards.

| N.Y. Giants | 7 | 0 | 17 | 6 | — | 30 |
| Philadelphia | 7 | 10 | 7 | 0 | — | 24 |

NYG	—	Toomer 37 pass from E. Manning (Feely kick)
Phil	—	Westbrook 12 run (Akers kick)
Phil	—	Stallworth 20 pass from McNabb (Akers kick)
Phil	—	FG Akers 37
Phil	—	R. Brown 23 pass from McNabb (Akers kick)
NYG	—	Carter fumble recovery in end zone (Feely kick)
NYG	—	Toomer 22 pass from E. Manning (Feely kick)
NYG	—	FG Feely 35
NYG	—	Burress 31 pass from E. Manning

SAN DIEGO 40, TENNESSEE 7—at Qualcomm Stadium, attendance 64,344. The Chargers outgained the Titans 476-218 in total yards and maintained possession for 38 minutes, 35 seconds en route to a commanding victory. At halftime the Chargers led 20-0, had 16 first downs compared to 1 for Tennessee, and had outgained the Titans 250-15 in yards. The Chargers scored on their first three drives of the second half, capped by Vincent Jackson's first career touchdown, a 12-yard catch, for a 33-0 lead. Rookie Vince Young completed his first touchdown pass, an 18-yard toss to Drew Bennett on third-and-9 with 3:09 to play, to spoil what would have been the first back-to-back shutouts in Chargers' history. Philip Rivers was 25 of 35 for 235 yards and 1 touchdown. Michael Turner had 13 carries for 138 yards. Kerry Collins started and was 6 of 19 for 57 yards, with 2 interceptions. Young was 7 of 20 for 106 yards and 1 touchdown.

| Tennessee | 0 | 0 | 0 | 7 | — | 7 |
| San Diego | 3 | 17 | 6 | 14 | — | 40 |

SD	—	FG Kaeding 28
SD	—	Tomlinson 4 run (Kaeding kick)
SD	—	Tomlinson 8 run (Kaeding kick)
SD	—	FG Kaeding 31
SD	—	FG Kaeding 35
SD	—	FG Kaeding 44
SD	—	Jackson 12 pass from Rivers (Kaeding kick)
Tenn	—	Bennett 18 pass from Young (Bironas kick)
SD	—	Whitehurst 14 run (Kaeding kick)

SAN FRANCISCO 20, ST. LOUIS 13—at Monster Park, attendance 67,791. Frank Gore rushed for 127 yards and 1 touchdown as the 49ers rallied to defeat the Rams. The Rams led 10-3 at halftime, but Maurice Hicks returned the second half's opening kickoff 59 yards. Two plays later, Gore scored on a 32-yard run to tie the game. The 49ers forced a punt, and Alex Smith fired a 72-yard touchdown pass to Antonio Bryant down the right sideline for a 17-10 lead 4:17 into the second half. Marques Douglas' sack and Isaac Sopoaga's fumble recovery with 8:03 left set up Joe Nedney's 20-yard field goal for a 20-13 lead. Gore's 10-yard run on second-and-6 with 1:54 to play allowed the 49ers to run out the clock. Smith was 11 of 22 for 233 yards and 1 touchdown. Gore carried 29 times for 127 yards. Bryant had 4 catches for 131 yards. Marc Bulger, who was sacked 6 times, was 19 of 34 for 185

yards and 1 touchdown. Steven Jackson rushed 22 times for 103 yards.

| St. Louis | 0 | 10 | 0 | 3 | — | 13 |
| San Francisco | 3 | 0 | 14 | 3 | — | 20 |

SF	—	FG Nedney 32
StL	—	FG Wilkins 49
StL	—	Holt 3 pass from Bulger (Wilkins kick)
SF	—	Gore 32 run (Nedney kick)
SF	—	Bryant 72 pass from Smith (Nedney kick)
StL	—	FG Wilkins 40
SF	—	FG Nedney 20

SEATTLE 21, ARIZONA 10—at Qwest Field, attendance 67,470. The Seahawks' defense registered 5 sacks as Seattle improved its record to 2-0. The Seahawks drove 80 and 74 yards with their first two possessions to take a 14-0 lead at 4:51 left in the first quarter. The Seahawks played a bend-but-don't-break defense, allowing the Cardinals into their territory seven times but never in the red zone. Bryant Johnson's 40-yard touchdown catch with 11:20 to play cut the deficit to 21-10, and Adrian Wilson intercepted a pass on the next play to give Arizona a chance. But Kelly Herndon forced Adam Bergen to fumble four plays later and Lofa Tatupu recovered to quell the comeback attempt. Matt Hasselbeck was 12 of 27 for 221 yards and 1 touchdown, with 2 interceptions. Darrell Jackson had 5 catches for 127 yards. Kurt Warner was 24 of 38 for 231 yards and 1 touchdown, with 1 interception.

| Arizona | 0 | 0 | 3 | 7 | — | 10 |
| Seattle | 14 | 0 | 0 | 7 | — | 21 |

Sea	—	Alexander 2 run (J. Brown kick)
Sea	—	Jackson 75 pass from Hasselbeck (J. Brown kick)
Ariz	—	FG Rackers 43
Sea	—	Strong 1 run (J. Brown kick)
Ariz	—	Bry. Johnson 40 pass from Warner (Rackers kick)

SUNDAY NIGHT, SEPTEMBER 17
DALLAS 27, WASHINGTON 10—at Texas Stadium, attendance 63,152. Drew Bledsoe passed for 2 touchdowns and the Cowboys' defense registered 6 sacks to defeat their rival. Dallas scored on three of its first four possessions for a 17-3 lead with 8:38 left in the second quarter. Rock Cartwright returned the ensuing kickoff for 100 yards to pull the Redskins within 17-10, and the Redskins' defense forced punts on Dallas' next five possessions, but the offense could not score. Washington's best scoring chance came late in the third quarter, but on third-and-9 from the Cowboys' 21, Roy Williams intercepted Mark Brunell's pass at the 1-yard line. Bledsoe's 26-yard pass to Marion Barber on third-and-10, followed immediately by his 40-yard touchdown pass to Terry Glenn, capped the ensuing 6-play, 99-yard drive and gave the Cowboys a 24-10 lead with 14:53 to play. Bledsoe was 19 of 38 for 237 yards and 2 touchdowns. Brunell was 18 of 32 for 197 yards, with 1 interception.

| Washington | 0 | 10 | 0 | 0 | — | 10 |
| Dallas | 10 | 7 | 0 | 10 | — | 27 |

Dall	—	FG Vanderjagt 26
Dall	—	Crayton 4 pass from Bledsoe (Vanderjagt kick)
Wash	—	FG Hall 39
Dall	—	Barber 1 run (Vanderjagt kick)
Wash	—	Cartwright 100 kickoff return (Hall kick)
Dall	—	Glenn 40 pass from Bledsoe (Vanderjagt kick)
Dall	—	FG Vanderjagt 50

MONDAY NIGHT, SEPTEMBER 18
JACKSONVILLE 9, PITTSBURGH 0—at Alltel Stadium, attendance 67,164. Josh Scobee kicked 3 second-half field goals as the Jaguars won the lowest-scoring game in the 37-year history of *Monday Night Football*. The Jaguars outgained the Super Bowl champions 362-153 in

total yards, maintained possession for 37 minutes, 25 seconds, and allowed just 9 first downs. The Steelers crossed midfield just once, and had to punt following their first eight possessions, the last of which led to Scobee's second field goal for a 6-0 lead. Four plays later, Rashean Mathis intercepted Ben Roethlisberger's pass and returned it 19 yards to the Steelers' 29 to set up Scobee's third field goal with 4:26 left to secure the victory. Byron Leftwich was 26 of 39 for 260 yards, with 1 interception. Roethlisberger, playing just 15 days after an appendectomy, was 17 of 32 for 141 yards, with 2 interceptions.

| Pittsburgh | 0 | 0 | 0 | 0 | — | 0 |
| Jacksonville | 0 | 0 | 3 | 6 | — | 9 |

Jax	—	FG Scobee 31
Jax	—	FG Scobee 32
Jax	—	FG Scobee 42

THIRD WEEK SUMMARIES
American Football Conference

East Division	W	L	T	Pct.	Pts.	OP
New England	2	1	0	.667	50	51
N.Y. Jets	2	1	0	.667	68	60
Buffalo	1	2	0	.333	53	53
Miami	1	2	0	.333	36	54
North Division	**W**	**L**	**T**	**Pct.**	**Pts.**	**OP**
Baltimore	3	0	0	1.000	70	20
Cincinnati	3	0	0	1.000	85	47
Pittsburgh	1	2	0	.333	48	54
Cleveland	0	3	0	.000	45	68
South Division	**W**	**L**	**T**	**Pct.**	**Pts.**	**OP**
Indianapolis	3	0	0	1.000	90	59
Jacksonville	2	1	0	.667	47	38
Houston	0	3	0	.000	49	98
Tennessee	0	3	0	.000	33	76
West Division	**W**	**L**	**T**	**Pct.**	**Pts.**	**OP**
San Diego	2	0	0	1.000	67	7
Denver	2	1	0	.667	36	31
Kansas City	1	2	0	.333	16	32
Oakland	0	2	0	.000	6	55

National Football Conference

East Division	W	L	T	Pct.	Pts.	OP
Philadelphia	2	1	0	.667	86	64
Dallas	1	1	0	.500	44	34
N.Y. Giants	1	2	0	.333	81	92
Washington	1	2	0	.333	57	61
North Division	**W**	**L**	**T**	**Pct.**	**Pts.**	**OP**
Chicago	3	0	0	1.000	79	23
Minnesota	2	1	0	.667	51	48
Green Bay	1	2	0	.333	58	84
Detroit	0	3	0	.000	37	74
South Division	**W**	**L**	**T**	**Pct.**	**Pts.**	**OP**
New Orleans	3	0	0	1.000	76	44
Atlanta	2	1	0	.667	37	32
Carolina	1	2	0	.333	45	60
Tampa Bay	0	3	0	.000	27	62
West Division	**W**	**L**	**T**	**Pct.**	**Pts.**	**OP**
Seattle	3	0	0	1.000	72	46
St. Louis	2	1	0	.667	47	44
Arizona	1	2	0	.333	58	64
San Francisco	1	2	0	.333	71	85

SUNDAY, SEPTEMBER 24
ST. LOUIS 16, ARIZONA 14—at Cardinals Stadium, attendance 63,278. Will Witherspoon recovered Kurt Warner's fumbled snap at the Rams' 18-yard line with 1:41 remaining as St. Louis held off the Cardinals. The Cardinals led 7-3 in the second quarter and were about to score when Oshiomogho Atogwe intercepted a pass to spark a 94-yard drive, capped by Torry Holt's 9-yard touchdown catch. On the next play, Fakhir Brown intercepted Warner's pass to set up Jeff Wilkins' 47-yard field goal as the half expired for a 13-7 Rams' lead. Edgerrin James capped a 16-play, 87-yard drive that consumed 10 minutes, 47 seconds to pull within 16-14 with 4:13 to play. Four plays later, Marc Bulger fumbled and Antonio Smith recovered at the Rams' 30 with 1:58 to play. The Cardinals reached the Rams' 18, but Warner fumbled the snap and Witherspoon recovered the ball to clinch the victory. Bulger was 21 of 31 for 309 yards and 1 touch-

down. Holt had 8 receptions for 120 yards. Warner was 19 of 28 for 256 yards and 1 touchdown, with 3 interceptions. Anquan Boldin had 10 catches for 129 yards.

St. Louis	0	13	3	0	—	16
Arizona	7	0	7	—	14	

Ariz	—	Fitzgerald 12 pass from Warner (Rackers kick)
StL	—	FG Wilkins 26
StL	—	Holt 9 pass from Bulger (Wilkins kick)
StL	—	FG Wilkins 47
StL	—	FG Wilkins 21
Ariz	—	James 6 run (Rackers kick)

N.Y. JETS 28, BUFFALO 20—at Ralph Wilson Stadium, attendance 72,067. Chad Pennington passed for 183 yards and 1 touchdown as the Jets withstood the sometimes 40-mile-per-hour gusty winds and rain to improve their record to 2-1. The Jets won despite being outgained 475-256 total yards. The Jets had just three productive drives, but all led to touchdowns, and Victor Hobson added a 32-yard fumble return, caused by Kerry Rhodes' sack of J.P. Losman, for a touchdown in the third quarter to give the Jets a 21-10 lead. Rian Lindell kicked a 28-yard field goal to pull within 21-13 with 9:14 to play, but the Jets responded with a 9-play, 58-yard drive capped by Cedric Houston's 5-yard run with 3:20 to play. Losman's 12-yard run pulled the Bills within six points with 1:15 remaining, and Andre Davis recovered the onside kick, but Losman's fourth-and-3 pass from their own 45-yard line fell incomplete with 35 seconds left. Pennington was 19 of 29 for 183 yards and 1 touchdown. Laveranues Coles had 10 catches for 78 yards. The Bills became the first home team in history to have a 300-yard passer and 150-yard rusher and lose. Losman was 22 of 38 for 328 yards and 1 touchdown, with 1 interception. McGahee had 26 carries for 150 yards. Evans had 8 catches for 107 yards, and Parrish added 4 receptions for 104 yards.

N.Y. Jets	0	14	7	7	—	28
Buffalo	7	3	0	10	—	20

Buff	—	Parrish 51 pass from Losman (Lindell kick)
NYJ	—	Barlow 3 run (Nugent kick)
Buff	—	FG Lindell 36
NYJ	—	Baker 1 pass from Pennington (Nugent kick)
NYJ	—	Hobson 32 fumble return (Nugent kick)
Buff	—	FG Lindell 28
NYJ	—	Houston 5 run (Nugent kick)
Buff	—	Losman 12 run (Lindell kick)

BALTIMORE 15, CLEVELAND 14—at Cleveland Browns Stadium, attendance 72,474. Chris McAlister made a key interception and Matt Stover kicked 3 field goals, including the game-winner from 52 yards with 20 seconds left, to shock the Browns. For nearly three quarters, the Browns dominated the game, leading 14-3 and having allowed just 8 first downs. Steve McNair responded with a 38-yard pass to Derrick Mason to set up Todd Heap's 3-yard catch to pull within 14-9. Stover's 43-yard field goal on the Ravens' next drive cut the deficit to 14-12 with 10:22 to play. The Browns answered with a 76-yard drive to the Ravens' 4, but McAlister's interception in the end zone on second-and-goal sparked a 12-play drive, including two third-down catches by Mark Clayton, to set up Stover's winning kick. McNair was 23 of 41 for 264 yards and 1 touchdown. Mason had 7 receptions for 132 yards. Charlie Frye was 21 of 33 for 298 yards and 1 touchdown, with 1 interception. Braylon Edwards had 5 catches for 116 yards.

Baltimore	3	0	0	12	—	15
Cleveland	0	14	0	0	—	14

Balt	—	FG Stover 32
Cle	—	Edwards 58 pass from Frye (Dawson kick)
Cle	—	Frye 1 run (Dawson kick)
Balt	—	Heap 3 pass from McNair

		(pass failed)
Balt	—	FG Stover 43
Balt	—	FG Stover 52

GREEN BAY 31, DETROIT 24—at Ford Field, attendance 61,095. Brett Favre passed for 340 yards and 3 touchdowns, giving him 402 for his career, to give Mike McCarthy his first career victory. Favre became the second player (Dan Marino, 420) with 400 career touchdowns when Greg Jennings caught a short pass, spun away from the defenders and broke a tackle down the right sideline for a 75-yard touchdown. In the third quarter, Favre completed 2 key third-down passes on the Packers' opening drive of the second half to take a 24-14 lead. Jason Hanson's 40-yard field goal cut the Lions' deficit to 31-24 with 5:24 to play, and the defense forced a three-and-out. On fourth-and-2 from the Lions' own 39-yard-line, Corey Williams sacked Jon Kitna. The Lions got the ball back when Ahman Green fumbled and recovered by Jamal Fletcher with 54 seconds left. Detroit reached midfield, but Kitna's long pass fell incomplete in the end zone as time expired. Favre was 25 of 36 for 340 yards and 3 touchdowns. Jennings had 3 catches for 101 yards. Kitna was 25 of 40 for 342 yards and 2 touchdowns, with 1 interception. Roy Williams had 7 catches for 138 yards.

Green Bay	14	3	7	7	—	31
Detroit	14	0	7	3	—	24

GB	—	Jennings 75 pass from Favre (Rayner kick)
Det	—	Bryson 37 pass from Kitna (Hanson kick)
GB	—	Manuel 29 interception return (Rayner kick)
Det	—	R. Williams 42 pass from Kitna (Hanson kick)
GB	—	FG Rayner 24
GB	—	Driver 5 pass from Favre
Det	—	K. Jones 5 run (Hanson kick)
GB	—	Green 10 pass from Favre (Rayner kick)
Det	—	FG Hanson 40

WASHINGTON 31, HOUSTON 15—at Reliant Stadium, attendance 70,069. Mark Brunell set an NFL single-game record with 22 consecutive completions as the Redskins posted their first victory. The Redskins outgained the Texans 495-261, and maintained possession for 38 minutes, 27 seconds. The Texans scored on their first possession, but the Redskins answered by scoring touchdowns on four of their next five drives, covering 91, 74, 82, and 70 yards. The 31 unanswered points gave Washington a 31-7 lead with 14:50 to play. Brunell completed his first 22 passes, setting the mark on a short toss for Santana Moss that resulted in 6 yards. His first incompletion came with 23 seconds left in the third quarter, when Travis Johnson knocked away his pass. Brunell was 24 of 27 for 261 yards and 1 touchdown. Ladell Betts had 16 carries for 124 yards. David Carr was 19 of 29 for 208 yards and 2 touchdowns, with 1 interception. Andre Johnson had 11 catches for 152 yards.

Washington	7	14	7	3	—	31
Houston	7	0	0	8	—	15

Hou	—	Bruener 2 pass from Carr (K. Brown kick)
Wash	—	Betts 9 run (Hall kick)
Wash	—	Randle El 23 pass from Brunell (Hall kick)
Wash	—	Portis 30 run (Hall kick)
Wash	—	Portis 1 run (Hall kick)
Wash	—	FG Hall 46
Hou	—	Daniels 2 pass from Carr (Dayne run)

INDIANAPOLIS 21, JACKSONVILLE 14—at RCA Dome, attendance 57,041. Terrence Wilkins sparked the Colts with an 82-yard punt return for a touchdown as the Colts rallied to remain undefeated. The Jaguars outgained the

Colts 185-66 total yards in the first half and had possession for 24 minutes, 31 seconds, but the game was tied 7-7 thanks to Wilkins' punt return. The Colts began the second half with an 80-yard drive, highlighted by Peyton Manning's 38-yard pass to Marvin Harrison, and capped by his 30-yard touchdown pass to a wide open Dallas Clark. Josh Scobee, who missed a 24-yard field goal in the first half, missed from 49 yards late in the third quarter. The Colts extended the lead when Manning hit Reggie Wayne with a 22-yard pass on third-and-10 to reach the Jaguars' 1. Two plays later, Manning scored on a naked bootleg for a 21-7 lead with 8:30 remaining. Maurice Drew-Jones returned the ensuing kickoff 41 yards to set up his own 7-yard scoring catch with 3:32 left, and the Jaguars forced a punt to begin on their own 42-yard line with 1:00 remaining. But Mike Doss intercepted Byron Leftwich's pass two plays later to clinch the victory. Manning was 14 of 31 for 219 yards and 1 touchdown. Leftwich was 16 of 28 for 107 yards, 1 touchdown, with 2 interceptions. Jones-Drew had 13 carries for 103 yards.

Jacksonville	7	0	0	7	—	14
Indianapolis	0	7	7	7	—	21

Jax	—	Leftwich 4 run (Scobee kick)
Ind	—	Wilkins 82 punt return (Gramatica kick)
Ind	—	Clark 30 pass from Manning (Gramatica kick)
Ind	—	Manning 2 run (Gramatica kick)
Jax	—	Jones-Drew 7 pass from Leftwich (Scobee kick)

MIAMI 13, TENNESSEE 10—at Dolphin Stadium, attendance 72,733. Olindo Mare kicked a 39-yard field goal with 3:39 to play as the Dolphins rallied for their first victory. The Dolphins trailed 7-3 at halftime, but drove 80 yards in 11 plays, capped by Daunte Culpepper's 5-yard scramble up the middle. The Dolphins then forced a punt, but Wes Welker fumbled and Cortland Finnegan recovered to set up Rob Bironas' 22-yard field goal to tie the game late in the third quarter. Ronnie Brown's 27-yard run on a draw, followed by Marty Booker's 18-yard reverse, set up Mare's go-ahead 39-yard field goal with 3:39 to play. The Titans reached the Dolphins' 43, but Travis Daniels intercepted Kerry Collins' pass with 1:54 left, and Culpepper completed a 19-yard pass to Welker on third-and-8 with 1:32 remaining to clinch the victory. Culpepper was 17 of 26 for 168 yards, and sacked 6 times. Collins was 19 of 33 for 269 yards and 1 touchdown, with 2 interceptions.

Tennessee	0	7	3	0	—	10
Miami	3	0	7	3	—	13

Mia	—	FG Mare 40
Tenn	—	Scaife 25 pass from Collins (Bironas kick)
Mia	—	Culpepper 5 run (Mare kick)
Tenn	—	FG Bironas 22
Mia	—	FG Mare 39

CHICAGO 19, MINNESOTA 16—at Metrodome, attendance 63,754. Rex Grossman's first career fourth-quarter touchdown pass, a 24-yard strike to Rashied Davis with 1:53 to play, gave the Bears a hard-fought victory in a battle of undefeated teams. The Vikings' defense intercepted 2 passes, the first of which led to Ryan Longwell's second field goal. The second interception, by Antoine Winfield on an ill-advised screen play, was returned 7 yards for a touchdown and 13-9 Vikings' lead with 14:53 to play. The Vikings led 16-12 and had the ball on third-and-8 with 3:31 to play when Chester Taylor fumbled the ball and Adewale Ogunleye recovered at the Vikings' 37. Grossman completed an 11-yard pass to Muhsin Muhammad on third-and-8 to set up Davis' winning catch. The Bears' defense did not allow a first down to clinch the victory. Grossman was 23 of 41 for 278 yards and 1 touchdown, with 2 interceptions. Muhammad had 9 catches for 118 yards. Johnson was 21 of 31 for 194 yards.

Chicago	3	0	6	10	—	19

Minnesota	3	3	0	10	—	16
Minn	—	FG Longwell 31				
Chi	—	FG Gould 41				
Minn	—	FG Longwell 26				
Chi	—	FG Gould 24				
Chi	—	FG Gould 31				
Minn	—	Winfield 7 interception return (Longwell kick)				
Chi	—	FG Gould 49				
Minn	—	FG Longwell 41				
Chi	—	Davis 24 pass from Grossman (Gould kick)				

CINCINNATI 28, PITTSBURGH 20—at Heinz Field, attendance 64,922. Carson Palmer passed for 4 touchdowns and the Bengals' defense forced 5 turnovers to remain undefeated. The Bengals' 4 touchdowns came off 3 turnovers and a missed field goal. Pittsburgh led 7-0 and drove to the Bengals' 6, but Madieu Williams intercepted Ben Roethlisberger's pass in the end zone. Fourteen plays and 97 yards later, the Bengals tied the game, and Chris Henry's 3-yard catch with five seconds left in the half gave Cincinnati a 14-7 lead. The Steelers answered by scoring on their first two drives of the second half for a 17-14 lead, and were in control as they forced a Bengals' punt with 8:16 to play. However, Ricardo Colclough, battling the swirling wind, muffed the punt and Tony Stewart recovered. Palmer fired a 9-yard, play-action, touchdown pass to T.J. Houshmandzadeh on the next play to take a 21-17 lead. Two plays later, Verron Haynes fumbled and Brian Simmons recovered to set up Houshmandzadeh's second touchdown catch in 54 seconds, a leaping 30-yard grab for an 11-point lead with 7:05 remaining. The Steelers cut the deficit to 28-20, forced a punt, and drove to the Bengals' 16-yard line with 10 seconds left when Kevin Kaesviharn intercepted a pass in the end zone to clinch the victory. Palmer was 18 of 26 for 193 yards and 4 touchdowns, with 2 interceptions and was sacked 6 times. Roethlisberger was 18 of 39 for 208 yards, with 3 interceptions. Willie Parker had 31 carries for 133 yards.

Cincinnati	0	14	0	14	—	28
Pittsburgh	7	0	10	3	—	20
Pitt	—	Parker 3 run (Reed kick)				
Cin	—	Henry 16 pass from Palmer (Graham kick)				
Cin	—	Henry 3 pass from Palmer (Graham kick)				
Pitt	—	FG Reed 37				
Pitt	—	Parker 1 run (Reed kick)				
Cin	—	Houshmandzadeh 9 pass from Palmer (Graham kick)				
Cin	—	Houshmandzadeh 30 pass from Palmer (Graham kick)				
Pitt	—	FG Reed 36				

PHILADELPHIA 38, SAN FRANCISCO 24—at Monster Park, attendance 68,166. Brian Westbrook scored 3 touchdowns and Mike Patterson had a club-record 98-yard fumble return as the Eagles rolled past the 49ers. The Eagles outgained the 49ers 337-110 total yards in the first half en route to a 24-3 lead. In the third quarter, the 49ers tried to come back, but Frank Gore fumbled near the goal line. Patterson, listed at 292 pounds, picked up the fumble and started to running. By the time others realized the play was in play, Patterson used two blockers to fend off Alex Smith and score for a 31-3 lead. The 49ers pulled within 31-17 early in the fourth quarter, but Donovan McNabb completed a 60-yard pass to Matt Schobel to set up Westbrook's third touchdown with 12:32 remaining for a 38-17 lead. McNabb was 18 of 33 for 296 yards and 2 touchdowns. Westbrook had 8 carries for 117 yards. Reggie Brown had 5 receptions for 106 yards. Smith was 27 of 46 for 293 yards and 1 touchdown.

Philadelphia	14	10	7	7	—	38
San Francisco	0	3	7	14	—	24
Phil	—	Westbrook 4 pass from McNabb (Akers kick)				
Phil	—	L. Smith 1 pass from McNabb (Akers kick)				
SF	—	FG Nedney 48				
Phil	—	Westbrook 71 run (Akers kick)				
Phil	—	FG Akers 21				
Phil	—	Patterson 98 fumble return (Akers kick)				
SF	—	Robinson 1 run (Nedney kick)				
SF	—	Robinson 1 run (Nedney kick)				
Phil	—	Westbrook 8 run (Akers kick)				
SF	—	E. Johnson 15 pass from A. Smith (Nedney kick)				

SEATTLE 42, N.Y. GIANTS 30—at Qwest Field, attendance 68,161. Matt Hasselbeck passed for 5 touchdowns as the Seahawks jumped to a 42-3 lead and remained undefeated. The Seahawks' defense forced 4 turnovers, all of which resulted in touchdowns, capped by Bobby Engram's 21-yard touchdown catch with 45 seconds left in the half. Leading 35-3 in the third quarter, the Seahawks used their first drive of the second half to march 70 yards in 17 plays to take a 42-3 lead with 3:18 left in the third quarter. Eli Manning engineered 3 consecutive touchdown drives in the fourth quarter, along with R.W. McQuarters' interception return, to cut the deficit to 42-30 with 2:42 remaining. But Jay Feely's onside kick bounced out of bounds, and the Seahawks ran off all but the final 22 seconds. Hasselbeck was 24 of 33 for 227 yards and 5 touchdowns, with 3 interceptions. Ken Hamlin had 2 interceptions. Manning was 24 of 36 for 275 yards and 3 touchdowns, with 3 interceptions.

N.Y. Giants	0	3	0	27	—	30
Seattle	21	14	7	0	—	42
Sea	—	Alexander 2 run (J. Brown kick)				
Sea	—	Burleson 12 pass from Hasselbeck (J. Brown kick)				
Sea	—	Jackson 4 pass from Hasselbeck (J. Brown kick)				
Sea	—	Heller 10 pass from Hasselbeck (J. Brown kick)				
Sea	—	Engram 21 pass from Hasselbeck (J. Brown kick)				
NYG	—	FG Feely 46				
Sea	—	Jackson 12 pass from Hasselbeck (J. Brown kick)				
NYG	—	Toomer 13 pass from Manning (Feely kick)				
NYG	—	Carter 25 pass from Manning (Feely kick)				
NYG	—	McQuarters 27 interception return (Feely kick)				
NYG	—	Tyree 9 pass from Manning (pass failed)				

CAROLINA 26, TAMPA BAY 24—at Raymond James Stadium, attendance 65,423. John Kasay kicked the game-winning 46-yard field goal with two seconds left as the Panthers posted their first victory. Kasay became the first kicker in NFL history to kick 4 field goals of 45 or more yards in a single game. The Panthers scored on three of their first four possessions, sparked by Chris Gamble's interception that led to Keyshawn Johnson's touchdown catch 59 seconds into the game, to take a 17-0 lead. Early in the third quarter, Simeon Rice sacked Jake Delhomme and forced him to fumble. Dewayne White recovered the fumble at the Panthers' 15 and Carnell Williams scored two plays later to pull the Buccaneers within 20-14. Tampa Bay forced a punt, then drove to the Panthers' 2. Faced with fourth-and-1, Chris Simms rolled left and landed head-over-heels in the end zone for a touchdown and a 21-20 lead. Simms then missed a few plays in the fourth quarter, but returned for their final two possessions, including one that went 51 yards and resulted in Matt Bryant's go-ahead field goal with 5:01 to play. It was later discovered Simms suffered a ruptured spleen. The Panthers trailed 24-23 with 1:41 left and drove to the Buccaneers' 29, keyed by Jake Delhomme's 12-yard run on fourth-and-7, to set up Kasay's game-winning kick. Delhomme was 22 of 36 for 272 yards and 1 touchdown.

Steve Smith, who missed the first two games of the season with a hamstring injury, had 7 catches for 112 yards. Simms was 13 of 24 for 139 yards and 1 touchdown, with 1 interception.

Carolina	10	10	3	3	—	26
Tampa Bay	0	7	14	3	—	24
Car	—	K. Johnson 31 pass from Delhomme (Kasay kick)				
Car	—	FG Kasay 51				
Car	—	K. Johnson 4 run (Kasay kick)				
TB	—	Galloway 8 pass from Simms (Bryant kick)				
Car	—	FG Kasay 50				
TB	—	C. Williams 4 run (Bryant kick)				
TB	—	Simms 2 run (Bryant kick)				
Car	—	FG Kasay 49				
TB	—	FG Bryant 38				
Car	—	FG Kasay 46				

SUNDAY NIGHT, SEPTEMBER 24

DENVER 17, NEW ENGLAND 7—at Gillette Stadium, attendance 68,756. Jake Plummer passed for 2 touchdowns and the Broncos' defense became the first to not allow a touchdown in the season's first 11 quarters since the 1942 Chicago Cardinals. Early in the second quarter, the Broncos' defense stopped Laurence Maroney for no gain on fourth-and-1. The change in possession resulted in a 59-yard scoring drive. The Patriots responded by driving to the Broncos' 19, but Dominique Foxworth blocked Stephen Gostkowski's field-goal attempt, and Javon Walker caught a 32-yard touchdown pass from Plummer seven plays later for a 10-0 lead. The Patriots didn't score until trailing 17-0, using a No-Huddle, Shotgun offense that resulted in a 10-play, 80-yard drive capped by Doug Gabriel's 8-yard touchdown catch with 9:13 to play. The Patriots then drove to the Broncos' 20 with 1:07 remaining, but Tom Brady's fourth-and-1 pass fell incomplete. Tatum Bell rushed 27 times for 123 yards. Walker had 3 catches for 130 yards. Brady was 31 of 55 for 320 yards and 1 touchdown.

Denver	0	10	0	7	—	17
New England	0	0	0	7	—	7
Den	—	FG Elam 23				
Den	—	Walker 32 pass from Plummer (Elam kick)				
Den	—	Walker 83 pass from Plummer (Elam kick)				
NE	—	Gabriel 8 pass from Brady (Gostkowski kick)				

MONDAY NIGHT, SEPTEMBER 25

NEW ORLEANS 23, ATLANTA 3—at Louisiana Superdome, attendance 70,003. The Saints, playing their first game in New Orleans since Hurricane Katrina hit the town nearly 13 months earlier, improved their record to 3-0 with an overwhelming performance. The Saints' defense registered 5 sacks and limited the Falcons to 229 total yards. Steve Gleason set the tone by blocking Michael Koenen's punt 1:30 into the game. Curtis Deloatch recovered in the end zone for a touchdown. The Falcons answered with a field goal, a 26-yard kick by 46-year-old Morten Andersen in his first game since 2004, but were only able to drive into the red zone one other time the rest of the game. At that point, the Saints already led 17-3, and Josh Bullocks blocked Andersen's 25-yard attempt. The Saints responded with a 54-yard scoring drive, capped by John Carney's 51-yard field goal as the half ended, for a 20-3 lead. The Falcons lone second half scoring threat was thwarted when Michael Vick's fourth-and-12 pass from the Falcons' 31 fell incomplete with 5:46 to play. Brees was 20 of 28 for 191 yards. Vick was 12 of 31 for 137 yards.

Atlanta	3	0	0	0	—	3
New Orleans	14	6	3	0	—	23
NO	—	Deloatch recovered blocked punt in end zone (Carney kick)				
Atl	—	FG Andersen 26				
NO	—	Henderson 11 run (Carney kick)				

NO — FG Carney 37
NO — FG Carney 51
NO — FG Carney 20

FOURTH WEEK SUMMARIES
American Football Conference

East Division	W	L	T	Pct.	Pts.	OP
New England	3	1	0	.750	88	64
Buffalo	2	2	0	.500	70	65
N.Y. Jets	2	2	0	.500	96	91
Miami	1	3	0	.250	51	71
North Division	**W**	**L**	**T**	**Pct.**	**Pts.**	**OP**
Baltimore	4	0	0	1.000	86	33
Cincinnati	3	1	0	.750	98	85
Pittsburgh	1	2	0	.333	48	54
Cleveland	1	3	0	.250	69	89
South Division	**W**	**L**	**T**	**Pct.**	**Pts.**	**OP**
Indianapolis	4	0	0	1.000	121	87
Jacksonville	2	2	0	.500	77	74
Houston	1	3	0	.250	66	113
Tennessee	0	4	0	.000	47	121
West Division	**W**	**L**	**T**	**Pct.**	**Pts.**	**OP**
Denver	2	1	0	.667	36	31
San Diego	2	1	0	.667	80	23
Kansas City	1	2	0	.333	57	32
Oakland	0	3	0	.000	27	79

National Football Conference

East Division	W	L	T	Pct.	Pts.	OP
Philadelphia	3	1	0	.750	117	73
Dallas	2	1	0	.667	89	48
Washington	2	2	0	.500	93	91
N.Y. Giants	1	2	0	.333	81	92
North Division	**W**	**L**	**T**	**Pct.**	**Pts.**	**OP**
Chicago	4	0	0	1.000	116	29
Minnesota	2	2	0	.500	63	65
Green Bay	1	3	0	.250	67	115
Detroit	0	4	0	.000	71	115
South Division	**W**	**L**	**T**	**Pct.**	**Pts.**	**OP**
Atlanta	3	1	0	.750	69	42
New Orleans	3	1	0	.750	94	65
Carolina	2	2	0	.500	66	78
Tampa Bay	0	3	0	.000	27	67
West Division	**W**	**L**	**T**	**Pct.**	**Pts.**	**OP**
St. Louis	3	1	0	.750	88	78
Seattle	3	1	0	.750	78	83
Arizona	1	3	0	.250	68	96
San Francisco	1	3	0	.250	71	126

SUNDAY, OCTOBER 1

ATLANTA 32, ARIZONA 10—at Georgia Dome, attendance 68,981. Morten Andersen kicked 5 field goals as the Falcons generated 405 yards of offense, and the defense allowed just 187 yards and forced 4 consecutive second-half turnovers en route to victory. In the second quarter, the Falcons led 9-3 and drove to the Cardinals' 3 only to have Adrian Wilson intercept Michael Vick's pass and return it 4 yards for a touchdown to give the Cardinals a 10-9 lead. The Falcons added a field goal just before halftime, and drove 67 yards for a field goal to begin the second half for a 15-10 lead. DeAngelo Hall then returned an interception 37 yards for a touchdown and 22-10 lead. The Cardinals turned the ball over on their next three possessions, as well, as Atlanta pulled away, highlighted by Jerious Norwood's franchise-record 78-yard touchdown run with 13:18 to play. Vick was 13 of 22 for 153 yards, with 1 interception. Norwood rushed 6 times for 106 yards, and Vick carried 11 times for 101 yards. Kurt Warner was 11 of 20 for 128 yards, with 1 interception and 1 lost fumble. Matt Leinart replaced him in the fourth quarter and was 5 of 8 for 49 yards, with 1 interception and 1 lost fumble.

Arizona	3	7	0	0 —	10
Atlanta	6	6	10	10 —	32

Atl	—	FG Andersen 34
Atl	—	FG Andersen 40
Ariz	—	FG Rackers 29
Atl	—	FG Koenen 51
Ariz	—	Wilson 99 interception return (Rackers kick)

Atl	—	FG Andersen 36
Atl	—	FG Andersen 26
Atl	—	Hall 37 interception return (Andersen kick)
Atl	—	Norwood 78 run (Andersen kick)
Atl	—	FG Andersen 28

BALTIMORE 16, SAN DIEGO 13—at M & T Bank Stadium, attendance 70,743. Steve McNair completed a 10-yard touchdown pass to Todd Heap with 34 seconds remaining as the Ravens scored 9 points in the final 3:12 to hand the Chargers their first defeat. The Chargers scored on two of their first three possessions, and added Nate Kaeding's 54-yard field goal just before halftime, for a 13-7 lead. Kaeding missed a 40-yard kick to begin the third quarter and a mishandled hold did not allow him to attempt a 52-yard kick in the fourth quarter. The Ravens' defense allowed just 31 yards in the Chargers' final 23 plays. With 3:31 to play, Mike Scifres boomed a 55-yard punt, but it was nullified by an illegal man downfield penalty. The ball was moved back to the Chargers' 7, and instead of punting, Scifres took an intentional safety to cut the Chargers' lead to 13-9 with 3:12 remaining. Steve McNair completed 4 of 5 passes on the ensuing 60-yard drive, with a 12-yard run mixed in, and capped by Heap's 10-yard catch with 34 seconds left. The Chargers reached midfield on one last play, but Jarret Johnson sacked Philip Rivers as time expired. McNair was 17 of 30 for 158 yards and 2 touchdowns, with 2 interceptions. Rivers was 13 of 22 for 145 yards and 1 touchdown, with 1 interception.

San Diego	7	6	0	0 —	13
Baltimore	7	0	0	9 —	16

SD	—	Floyd 31 pass from Rivers (Kaeding kick)
Balt	—	Wilcox 5 pass from McNair (Stover kick)
SD	—	FG Kaeding 34
SD	—	FG Kaeding 54
Balt	—	Safety, Reed ran Scifres out of end zone
Balt	—	Heap 10 pass from McNair (Stover kick)

BUFFALO 17, MINNESOTA 12—at Ralph Wilson Stadium, attendance 71,972. The Vikings had field goals on their first and last possessions of the first half, but did not have a first down on their four drives in between, and trailed 7-6 at halftime. The Bills opened the second half with an 11-play, 70-yard drive capped by J.P. Losman's 8-yard touchdown pass to Peerless Price for a 14-6 lead. Later in the third quarter, Angelo Crowell intercepted a pass to set up Rian Lindell's 28-yard field goal with 14:05 to play. The Vikings pulled within five points when Brad Johnson capped a 55-yard drive with a touchdown pass to Marcus Robinson, but his two-point conversion pass for Travis Taylor fell incomplete with 3:07 remaining. The Vikings forced a punt and started on their own 17-yard line with 1:39 to play. Johnson completed 5 passes to reach the Bills' 25 with 14 seconds left. Johnson completed a 9-yard pass over the middle to Billy McMullen, who was tackled at the Bills' 16 and time expired before another snap could occur. Losman was 23 of 32 for 222 yards and 1 touchdown. Johnson was 25 of 44 for 267 yards and 1 touchdown, with 2 interceptions.

Minnesota	3	3	0	6 —	12
Buffalo	0	7	7	3 —	17

Minn	—	FG Longwell 37
Buff	—	McGahee 1 run (Lindell kick)
Minn	—	FG Longwell 49
Buff	—	Price 8 pass from Losman (Lindell kick)
Buff	—	FG Lindell 28
Minn	—	M. Robinson 29 pass from B. Johnson (pass failed)

CAROLINA 21, NEW ORLEANS 18—at Bank of America Stadium, attendance 73,392. DeShaun Foster broke free for a 43-yard touchdown run with 1:45 left as the Panthers handed the Saints their first loss. The Panthers had more than 25 yards on just one of their first eight drives, but the Saints did not take the lead until Deuce McAllister capped an 82-yard drive with a 3-yard run with 13:33 to play. The Panthers answered with a 12-play, 91-yard drive, highlighted by 3 catches by Steve Smith, and capped by Drew Carter's 4-yard touchdown grab with 7:15 to play for a 14-10 lead. Carolina forced a punt and drove to the Saints' 43 with 1:56 to play. On third-and-6, DeShaun Foster took a handoff and ran 43 yards around right end for a touchdown and 21-10 lead. Two plays later, Drew Brees fired an 86-yard scoring pass to Marques Colston, and a two-point conversion to Joe Horn, to pull within 21-18 with 1:15 to play. However, Nick Goings recovered the onside kick and the Panthers ran out the clock. Jake Delhomme was 19 of 29 for 169 yards and 2 touchdowns. Foster rushed 16 times for 105 yards. Brees was 28 of 38 for 349 yards and 1 touchdown. Colston had 5 receptions for 132 yards.

New Orleans	0	3	0	15 —	18
Carolina	7	0	0	14 —	21

Car	—	S. Smith 9 pass from Delhomme (Kasay kick)
NO	—	FG Carney 31
NO	—	McAllister 3 run (Carney kick)
Car	—	Carter 4 pass from Delhomme (Kasay kick)
Car	—	Foster 43 run (Kasay kick)
NO	—	Colston 86 pass from Brees (Horn pass from Brees)

NEW ENGLAND 38, CINCINNATI 13—at Paul Brown Stadium, attendance 66,035. Laurence Maroney ran for 2 touchdowns and the Patriots' defense registered 4 sacks and forced 2 fourth-quarter fumbles to win on the road. The Patriots led 14-6 at halftime, but Stephen Gostkowski missed a 48-yard field-goal attempt to begin the third quarter. The Bengals responded with a 62-yard drive, capped by Rudi Johnson's 2-yard run to pull within 14-13. The Patriots responded by driving 75 yards for a touchdown, forced a punt, and then drove 88 yards for a field goal and 24-13 lead with 14:45 to play. Three plays later Jarvis Green sacked Carson Palmer, forced him to fumble, and recovered the ball. Six plays later Corey Dillon scored on fourth-and-goal from the 1-yard line, and after another Palmer fumble, recovered this tim by Ty Warren, Daniel Graham caught a 3-yard touchdown pass for a 38-13 lead with 7:55 to play. Brady was 15 of 26 for 188 yards. Maroney carried 15 times for 125 yards, as the Patriots rushed for 236 yards. Palmer was 20 of 35 for 245 yards.

New England	0	14	7	17 —	38
Cincinnati	6	0	7	0 —	13

Cin	—	FG Graham 40
Cin	—	FG Graham 45
NE	—	Maroney 11 run (Gostkowski kick)
NE	—	Gabriel 25 pass from Brady (Gostkowski kick)
Cin	—	R. Johnson 2 run (Graham kick)
NE	—	Maroney 25 run (Gostkowski kick)
NE	—	FG Gostkowski 24
NE	—	Dillon 1 run (Gostkowski kick)
NE	—	Graham 3 pass from Brady (Gostkowski kick)

HOUSTON 17, MIAMI 15—at Reliant Stadium, attendance 70,071. Rookie Mario Williams tipped away a 2-point conversion pass attempt with 1:39 to play as the Texans posted their first victory. The Texans trailed 6-3 late in the third quarter and were faced with third-and-8, but David Carr fired a 28-yard pass to Eric Moulds to keep alive the drive, and Carr scored on a 1-yard sneak seven plays later to give Houston a 10-6 lead. The Texans' defense forced a three-and-out, and Carr completed a key third-and-6 pass to Andre Johnson for 30 yards to set up Johnson's 3-yard touchdown catch on third-and-goal with 9:49 remaining. Olindo Mare's field goal with 5:41 to play cut the deficit to 17-9, and the Dolphins forced a punt. Beginning from his own 20-yard line with 3:40

remaining, Daunte Culpepper completed a 29-yard pass to Wes Welker on fourth-and-3 to jump start the possession, and capped the drive with a 16-yard touchdown pass to Chris Chambers with 1:39 to play. The Dolphins attempted a halfback option pass on the two-point conversion, and Williams tipped away Ronnie Brown's pass intended for Chambers. Miami's onside kick barely slithered out of bounds, and the Texans did not need to punt to run out the clock. Carr was 22 of 29 for 230 yards and 1 touchdown, with 1 interception. Johnson had 9 receptions for 101 yards. Culpepper was 23 of 39 for 249 yards and 1 touchdown.

Miami	0	3	3	9	—	15
Houston	0	3	0	14	—	17
Mia	—	FG Mare 52				
Hou	—	FG K. Brown 32				
Mia	—	FG Mare 29				
Hou	—	Carr 1 run (K. Brown kick)				
Hou	—	A. Johnson 3 pass from Carr (K. Brown kick)				
Mia	—	FG Mare 22				
Mia	—	Chambers 16 pass from Culpepper (pass failed)				

KANSAS CITY 41, SAN FRANCISCO 0—at Arrowhead Stadium, attendance 77,609. Damon Huard passed for 2 touchdowns and Larry Johnson ran for 2 as the Chiefs posted their first shutout since 2002. The Chiefs outgained the 49ers 333-165 in total yards, and the Chiefs' defense registered 4 sacks and forced 4 turnovers as the 49ers were shutout for just the second time since 1977. Kansas City scored on five of its first six possessions, three of which came on drives of 21, 34, and 20 yards after a turnover, to take a 27-0 lead with 11:47 left in the third quarter. The 49ers had six more possessions, but gained just a total of 52 yards in 22 plays. Dante Hall capped the day with his 60-yard punt return for a touchdown with 5:39 remaining. Huard was 18 of 23 for 208 yards and 2 touchdowns. Johnson had 30 carries for 101 yards. Alex Smith was 13 of 25 for 92 yards, with 2 interceptions.

San Francisco	0	0	0	0	—	0
Kansas City	10	14	3	14	—	41
KC	—	Hall 13 pass from Huard (Tynes kick)				
KC	—	FG Tynes 22				
KC	—	L. Johnson 1 run (Tynes kick)				
KC	—	Kennison 34 pass from Huard (Tynes kick)				
KC	—	FG Tynes 49				
KC	—	L. Johnson 2 run (Tynes kick)				
KC	—	Hall 60 punt return (Tynes kick)				

INDIANAPOLIS 31, N.Y. JETS 28—at The Meadowlands, attendance 77,190. Peyton Manning engineered a 61-yard touchdown drive in the final 2:20 as the Colts held off the Jets. With the score 14-14, the Jets drove to the Colts' 2-yard-line late in the third quarter, but Chad Pennington's fourth-and-goal pass was intercepted by Aaron Moorehead. The Colts responded with their best drive, 15 plays and 78 yards, but had to settle for Martin Gramatica's 20-yard field goal with 12:58 to play. The teams then exchanged time consuming touchdown drives, giving the Colts a 24-21 lead with 2:34 left. Justin Miller responded by returning the ensuing kickoff 103 yards for a touchdown and 28-24 Jets' lead with 2:20 remaining. Manning completed 4 consecutive passes to begin the drive, and his 19-yard pass to Marvin Harrison on third-and-6, along with a 15-yard pass to Reggie Wayne, set up Manning's 1-yard sneak with 50 seconds left for a 31-28 lead. With eight seconds left, from their own 32, the Jets nearly pulled off a historical lateral-filled play. Pennington completed an 8-yard pass to Leon Washington, which led to a play with four laterals and a few intentional fumbles. Finally, center Nick Mangold lost the ball and Jason David recovered at the Colts' 39 with no time on the clock. Manning was 21 of 30 for 217 yards. Pennington was 17 of 23 for 207 yards and 1 touchdown, with 1 interception.

Indianapolis	7	7	0	17	—	31
N.Y. Jets	0	14	0	14	—	28
Ind	—	Rhodes 6 run (M. Gramatica kick)				
NYJ	—	Cotchery 33 pass from Pennington (Nugent kick)				
NYJ	—	Barlow 1 run (Nugent kick)				
Ind	—	Addai 2 run (M. Gramatica kick)				
Ind	—	FG M. Gramatica 20				
NYJ	—	Barlow 5 run (Nugent kick)				
Ind	—	Fletcher 2 run from Manning (M. Gramatica kick)				
NYJ	—	J. Miller 103 kickoff return (Nugent kick)				
Ind	—	P. Manning 1 run (M. Gramatica kick)				

CLEVELAND 24, OAKLAND 21—at McAfee Coliseum, attendance 61,426. Charlie Frye passed for 3 touchdowns as the Browns rallied from an 18-point deficit. LaMont Jordan's 59-yard touchdown run two plays after Phil Dawson's field goal staked the Raiders to a 21-3 lead with 4:08 remaining in the first half. Joshua Cribbs returned the ensuing kickoff 53 yards to set up Frye's first touchdown pass, a 3-yard pass to Darnell Dinkins with just 58 seconds left in the half. The Browns took the second half opening kickoff and drove 69 yards in 14 plays, capped by Frye's 2-yard toss to Kellen Winslow, to to pull within 21-17. A 58-yard punt return by Dennis Northcutt to the Browns' 17 set up Joe Jurevicius' 5-yard touchdown catch with 1:40 left in the third quarter. Orpheus Roye dropped Jordan for a 2-yard loss on fourth-and-1 with 11:17 to play, and Reuben Droughns rushed for 7 yards on third-and-1 with 1:49 remaining to clinch the victory. Frye was 22 of 32 for 192 yards and 3 touchdowns, with 2 interceptions. Droughns rushed 25 times for 100 yards. Andrew Walter, in his first career start, was 9 of 23 for 68 yards and 1 touchdown, with 1 interception. Jordan rushed 20 times for 128 yards.

Cleveland	0	10	14	0	—	24
Oakland	7	14	0	0	—	21
Oak	—	S. Williams 30 fumble return (Janikowski kick)				
Oak	—	Moss 5 pass from Walter (Janikowski kick)				
Cle	—	FG Dawson 28				
Oak	—	Jordan 59 run (Janikowski kick)				
Cle	—	Dinkins 3 pass from Frye (Dawson kick)				
Cle	—	Winslow 2 pass from Frye (Dawson kick)				
Cle	—	Jurevicius 5 pass from Frye (Dawson kick)				

ST. LOUIS 41, DETROIT 34—at Edward Jones Dome, attendance 65,563. Marc Bulger's 5-yard touchdown pass to Isaac Bruce, along with the pair's ensuing 2-point conversion, with 1:56 to play lifted the Rams past the Lions. The Rams scored on three of their first four possessions for a 13-3 lead, but the Lions strung together consecutive touchdown drives for 50 and 82 yards in the second quarter, and then scored on three consecutive second-half possessions to take a 34-30 lead with 11:11 remaining. The Rams responded with Jeff Wilkins' 47-yard field goal to pull within 34-33 with 6:16 to play. The Rams' defense forced a three-and-out, and Bulger's 22-yard pass to Steven Jackson led to Bruce's 5-yard touchdown pass on third-and-4 with 1:56 remaining. Their successful 2-point conversion increased the lead to 41-34. Jerome Carter's interception on the next play gave the Rams a chance to put the game away, but Wilkins missed a 47-yard field-goal attempt wide right with 47 seconds left. The Lions reached the Rams' 37, but Jon Kitna's fourth-and-3 pass fell incomplete. Bulger was 26 of 42 for 328 yards and 3 touchdowns. Bruce had 7 catches for 100 yards, and Torry Holt added 6 receptions for 102 yards. Kitna was 29 of 43 for 280 yards and 2 touchdowns, with 2 interceptions. Roy Williams had 9 receptions for 139 yards.

Detroit	3	14	10	7	—	34

St. Louis	13	3	14	11	—	41
StL	—	FG Wilkins 42				
StL	—	FG Wilkins 19				
Det	—	FG Hanson 29				
StL	—	Klopfenstein 16 pass from Bulger (Wilkins kick)				
Det	—	Furrey 1 pass from Kitna (Hanson kick)				
Det	—	Furrey 10 pass from Kitna (Hanson kick)				
StL	—	FG Wilkins 46				
StL	—	Holt 16 pass from Bulger (Wilkins kick)				
Det	—	FG Hanson 20				
Det	—	K. Jones 35 run (Hanson kick)				
Det	—	S. Jackson 1 run (Wilkins kick)				
Det	—	K. Jones 7 run (Hanson kick)				
StL	—	FG Wilkins 47				
StL	—	Bruce 5 pass from Bulger (Bruce pass from Bulger)				

DALLAS 45, TENNESSEE 14—at LP Field, attendance 69,143. Drew Bledsoe passed for 2 touchdowns as the Cowboys spoiled rookie Vince Young's first career start. On his first drive, Young took advantage of getting the ball at midfield thanks to Chris Hope's interception, and led the Titans 35 yards to Rob Bironas' field goal. However, the Cowboys drove into the Titans' red zone on their next five drives, covering 80, 55, 75, 56, and 44 yards, capped by Marion Barber's 1-yard scoring run with 6:38 left in the third quarter for a 28-6 lead. The Titans responded with Young's 17-yard touchdown pass to Ben Troupe on third-and-7, followed by Young's 2-point conversion run to cut the deficit to 28-14 with 3:40 remaining in the third quarter. Bradie James intercepted a pass and returned it 15 yards for a touchdown with 8:23 remaining to extend the lead to 38-14. Bledsoe was 13 of 20 for 179 yards and 2 touchdowns, with 1 interception. Julius Jones rushed 23 times for 122 yards. Young was 14 of 29 for 155 yards and 1 touchdown, with 2 interceptions.

Dallas	7	7	14	17	—	45
Tennessee	3	3	8	0	—	14
Tenn	—	FG Bironas 33				
Dall	—	Glenn 13 pass from Bledsoe (Vanderjagt kick)				
Dall	—	Glenn 13 pass from Bledsoe (Vanderjagt kick)				
Tenn	—	FG Bironas 39				
Dall	—	J. Jones 5 run (Vanderjagt kick)				
Dall	—	Barber 1 run (Vanderjagt kick)				
Tenn	—	Troupe 17 pass from Young (Young run)				
Dall	—	FG Vanderjagt 43				
Dall	—	James 15 interception return (Vanderjagt kick)				
Dall	—	Thompson 7 run (Vanderjagt kick)				

WASHINGTON 36, JACKSONVILLE 30 (OT)—at FedEx Field, attendance 89,450. Santana Moss caught an 8-yard touchdown pass in overtime, his third scoring grab of the game, as the Redskins outlasted the Jaguars. The Redskins outgained the Jaguars 481-307 in total yards, and scored on consecutive second-half possessions to take a 27-17 lead on Mark Brunell's 8-yard touchdown pass to Moss with 12:24 left. On the next play, Byron Leftwich completed a 35-yard pass to Reggie Williams and the same pair hooked up for a 21-yard touchdown three plays later to trim the deficit to 27-24. Two plays later, Brian Williams forced Brunell to fumble and Deon Grant recovered. Josh Scobee tied the game with 6:40 to play, and again with six seconds left, with a John Hall field goal in between, to force overtime. The Redskins won the toss, on the session's third play, Brunell fired deep down the left sideline to Moss, who caught the pass between two defenders and outran them to the end zone. Brunell was 18 of 30 for 329 yards and 3 touchdowns, with 1 interception. Clinton Portis carried 27 times for 112 yards. Moss had 4 catches for 138 yards. Leftwich was 20 of 34 for 290 yards and 3 touchdowns, with 1 interception.

Jacksonville	10	7	0	13	0	—	30
Washington	7	6	7	10	6	—	36

Jax — FG Scobee 46
Wash — S. Moss 55 pass from Brunell (Hall kick)
Jax — R. Williams 33 pass from Leftwich (Scobee kick)
Wash — FG Hall 44
Jax — Jones-Drew 51 pass from Leftwich (Scobee kick)
Wash — FG Hall 37
Wash — Portis 1 run (Hall kick)
Wash — S. Moss 8 pass from Brunell (Hall kick)
Jax — R. Williams 21 pass from Leftwich (Scobee kick)
Jax — FG Scobee 43
Wash — FG Hall 37
Jax — FG Scobee 41
Wash — S. Moss 68 pass from Brunell

SUNDAY NIGHT, OCTOBER 1
CHICAGO 37, SEATTLE 6—at Soldier Field, attendance 62,225. Rex Grossman passed for 2 touchdowns and Ricky Manning Jr. had 2 interceptions as the Bears posted their best start in 15 years. Both of Manning's interceptions came in the second quarter and led to 10 points for a 20-3 lead. Josh Brown's 24-yard field goal just before halftime cut the deficit to 20-6, but the Bears responded with touchdown drives of 65 and 73 yards in the third quarter, the latter capped by Bernard Berrian's 40-yard touchdown catch deep down the right sideline, for a 34-6 lead. Grossman was 17 of 31 for 232 yards and 2 touchdowns. Berrian had 3 receptions for 108 yards. Hasselbeck was 16 of 35 for 196 yards, with 2 interceptions, as the Seahawks played their first game without injured Shaun Alexander.

Seattle	3	3	0	0	—	6
Chicago	7	13	14	3	—	37

Sea — FG J. Brown 23
Chi — Muhammad 9 pass from Grossman (Gould kick)
Chi — FG Gould 36
Chi — FG Gould 20
Chi — T. Jones 3 run (Gould kick)
Sea — FG J. Brown 24
Chi — T. Jones 1 run (Gould kick)
Chi — Berrian 40 pass from Grossman (Gould kick)
Chi — FG Gould 41

MONDAY NIGHT, OCTOBER 2
PHILADELPHIA 31, GREEN BAY 9—at Lincoln Financial Field, attendance 69,222. Donovan McNabb passed for 2 touchdowns and ran for 2 others as the Eagles scored 24 unanswered points in the second half. The Eagles fumbled twice inside the Packers' 5 in the first half and trailed 9-7 at halftime, thanks in part to Dave Rayner's franchise-record-tying 54-yard field goal. The Eagles responded by scoring on their first four second-half drives. The second score came two plays after Rayner's missed field goal, and the 45-yard touchdown pass to Greg Lewis gave the Eagles a 17-9 lead. Two plays later, rookie LaJuan Ramsey intercepted Brett Favre's bobbled pass to set up Lewis' second touchdown catch in 1:17. Michael Lewis intercepted Favre on the Packers' next possession, and McNabb scrambled in from 15 yards with 12:41 remaining for his first 2-touchdown rushing game. McNabb was 16 of 30 for 288 yards and 2 touchdowns. Favre was 22 of 44 for 205 yards, with 2 interceptions, and Aaron Rodgers played the final drive and was 2 of 3 for 14 yards.

Green Bay	3	6	0	0	—	9
Philadelphia	0	7	17	7	—	31

GB — FG Rayner 23
Phil — McNabb 6 run (Akers kick)
GB — FG Rayner 54
GB — FG Rayner 46
Phil — G Akers 40

Phil — Lewis 45 pass from McNabb (Akers kick)
Phil — Lewis 30 pass from McNabb (Akers kick)
Phil — McNabb 15 run (Akers kick)

FIFTH WEEK SUMMARIES
American Football Conference

East Division	W	L	T	Pct.	Pts.	OP
New England	4	1	0	.800	108	74
Buffalo	2	3	0	.400	77	105
N.Y. Jets	2	3	0	.400	96	132
Miami	1	4	0	.200	61	91
North Division	W	L	T	Pct.	Pts.	OP
Baltimore	4	1	0	.800	89	46
Cincinnati	3	1	0	.750	98	85
Pittsburgh	1	3	0	.250	61	77
Cleveland	1	4	0	.200	81	109
South Division	W	L	T	Pct.	Pts.	OP
Indianapolis	5	0	0	1.000	135	100
Jacksonville	3	2	0	.600	118	74
Houston	1	3	0	.250	66	113
Tennessee	0	5	0	.000	60	135
West Division	W	L	T	Pct.	Pts.	OP
Denver	3	1	0	.750	49	34
San Diego	3	1	0	.750	103	36
Kansas City	2	2	0	.500	80	52
Oakland	0	4	0	.000	47	113

National Football Conference

East Division	W	L	T	Pct.	Pts.	OP
Philadelphia	4	1	0	.800	155	97
Dallas	2	2	0	.500	113	86
N.Y. Giants	2	2	0	.500	100	95
Washington	2	3	0	.400	96	110
North Division	W	L	T	Pct.	Pts.	OP
Chicago	5	0	0	1.000	156	36
Minnesota	3	2	0	.600	89	82
Green Bay	1	4	0	.200	87	138
Detroit	0	5	0	.000	88	141
South Division	W	L	T	Pct.	Pts.	OP
New Orleans	4	1	0	.800	118	86
Atlanta	3	1	0	.750	69	42
Carolina	3	2	0	.600	86	90
Tampa Bay	0	4	0	.000	48	91
West Division	W	L	T	Pct.	Pts.	OP
St. Louis	4	1	0	.800	111	98
Seattle	3	1	0	.750	78	83
San Francisco	2	3	0	.400	105	146
Arizona	1	4	0	.200	88	119

SUNDAY, OCTOBER 8
KANSAS CITY 23, ARIZONA 20—at Cardinals Stadium, attendance 63,445. The Chiefs rallied with 13 unanswered points in the fourth quarter to defeat the Cardinals. Matt Leinart, making his first start, guided the Cardinals to touchdowns on their first two drives for a 14-0 lead less than nine minutes into the game, but Arizona did not run another play in the Chiefs' red zone the rest of the day. The Cardinals led 20-10 after three quarters, but Samie Parker's 15-yard catch of Damon Huard's pass cut the deficit to 20-17 with 9:35 left. Ty Law intercepted a pass at the Cardinals' 22 to set up Lawrence Tynes' game-tying field goal with 5:06 to play. On their next possession, Huard tossed a screen pass to Larry Johnson that resulted in a 78-yard play. Four plays later, Tynes kicked a 19-yard field goal with 1:36 remaining for a 23-20 lead. Leinart drove the Cardinals to the Chiefs' 33 with seven seconds left, but Neil Rackers' 51-yard field-goal attempt sailed wide right. Huard was 26 of 38 for 288 yards and 2 touchdowns. Johnson had 6 catches for 106 yards. Leinart was 22 of 35 for 253 yards and 2 touchdowns, with 1 interception.

Kansas City	0	10	0	13	—	23
Arizona	14	3	3	0	—	20

Ariz — Boldin 49 pass from Leinart (Rackers kick)
Ariz — Fitzgerald 5 pass from Leinart (Rackers kick)
KC — FG Tynes 45

KC — L. Johnson 9 pass from Huard (Tynes kick)
Ariz — FG Rackers 41
Ariz — FG Rackers 45
KC — Parker 15 pass from Huard (Tynes kick)
KC — FG Tynes 40
KC — FG Tynes 19

CAROLINA 20, CLEVELAND 12—at Bank of America Stadium, attendance 73,520. John Kasay kicked 2 field goals and Richard Marshall returned an interception for his first NFL touchdown as the Panthers held off the Browns. John Kasay's 24-yard field goal to cap the Panthers' opening drive of the second half gave Carolina a 17-3 lead. The Browns kicked field goals on two of their next three drives to pull within 17-9. Kasay added a 19-yard field goal with 4:03 remaining for an 11-point lead. The Browns drove to the Panthers' 29, but Mike Minter intercepted Charlie Frye's pass with 1:59 left. The Browns forced a punt and Phil Dawson kicked his fourth field goal with five seconds left to give the Browns a chance, but Steve Smith recovered the onside kick to clinch the victory for Carolina. Jake Delhomme was 20 of 29 for 170 yards and 1 touchdown. Foster had 24 carries for 106 yards. Frye was 26 of 43 for 173 yards, with 2 interceptions.

Cleveland	3	0	3	6	—	12
Carolina	7	7	3	3	—	20

Cle — FG Dawson 41
Car — Marshall 30 interception return (Kasay kick)
Car — K. Johnson 17 pass from Delhomme (Kasay kick)
Car — FG Kasay 24
Cle — FG Dawson 47
Cle — FG Dawson 22
Car — FG Kasay 19
Cle — FG Dawson 32

CHICAGO 40, BUFFALO 7—at Soldier Field, attendance 62,206. The Bears' defense forced 5 turnovers and allowed just 145 yards as the offense posted its biggest point total in 13 years and the Bears had their first 5-0 start in 20 years. On the Bills' first possession, punter Brian Moorman fumbled the snap on a fake punt and Brendon Ayanbadejo recovered at the Bills' 40. That set the tone, as the Bears scored on their first five possessions, two of which were set up by turnovers, to take a 27-0 lead on Rex Grossman's 15-yard touchdown pass to Rashied Davis with 4:22 left in the second quarter. At halftime, the Bears had outgained the Bills 211-59 in total yards, and only Brian Griese's fumbled snap at the Bears' 42 with 2:44 to play set up J.P. Losman's 5-yard touchdown pass to Lee Evans with 1:06 to play to avoid the shutout. Grossman was 15 of 27 for 182 yards and 2 touchdowns. Thomas Jones had 21 carries for 110 yards. Losman was 14 of 24 for 115 yards and 1 touchdown, with 3 interceptions.

Buffalo	0	0	0	7	—	7
Chicago	6	21	3	10	—	40

Chi — FG Gould 42
Chi — FG Gould 43
Chi — Berrian 8 pass from Grossman (Gould kick)
Chi — Benson 1 run (Gould kick)
CHi — Davis 15 pass from Grossman (Gould kick)
Chi — FG Gould 32
Chi — FG Gould 41
Chi — Benson 1 run (Gould kick)
Buff — Evans 5 pass from Losman (Lindell kick)

ST. LOUIS 23, GREEN BAY 20—at Lambeau Field, attendance 70,804. Jerametrius Butler recovered a fumble at the Rams' 13 with 36 seconds left as the Rams remained in first place in the NFC West. Dave Rayner's 32-yard field goal as the half expired cut the Rams' lead to 14-13, but

St. Louis had three consecutive scoring drives in the second half, all set up by punts, resulting in 3 field goals in a span of less than nine minutes, to pull ahead 23-13 with 9:25 to play. Brett Favre connected with Greg Jennings on a 46-yard touchdown pass with 6:42 to play, and the Packers drove to the Rams' 11 in the final minute. On second-and-10, as Jimmy Kennedy was sacking Favre, Leonard Little reached in and forced him to fumble. Butler recovered the ball with 36 seconds remaining to clinch the victory. Favre was 22 of 39 for 220 yards and 1 touchdown. Jennings had 5 catches for 105 yards. Noah Herron had 20 carries for 106 yards. Marc Bulger was 18 of 28 for 220 yards and 2 touchdowns.

St. Louis	7	7	3	6	—	23
Green Bay	7	6	0	7	—	20

StL	—	Holt 6 pass from Bulger (Wilkins kick)
GB	—	Herron 1 run (Rayner kick)
GB	—	FG Rayner 27
StL	—	Curtis 3 pass from Bulger (Wilkins kick)
GB	—	FG Rayner 32
StL	—	FG Wilkins 31
StL	—	FG Wilkins 26
StL	—	FG Wilkins 20
GB	—	Jennings 46 pass from Favre (Rayner kick)

INDIANAPOLIS 14, TENNESSEE 13—at RCA Dome, attendance 57,021. Peyton Manning completed 2 second-half touchdown passes as the Colts had to rally to remain undefeated and beat the winless Titans. The Titans drove 88 yards on their initial drive and led 10-0 at halftime. The Colts drove 12 plays, 90 yards to begin the second half, capped by Manning's 13-yard touchdown pass to Marvin Harrison on third-and-1, to pull within 10-7. The Titans responded with a 47-yard Rob Bironas field goal, and Chris Hope intercepted Manning's pass at the Titans' 4 to stop the next possession. But the Colts forced a punt, Manning completed a key third-and-8 pass to Reggie Wayne for 12 yards, and Wayne caught a 2-yard touchdown pass on third-and-goal with 5:10 remaining to give the Colts their first lead. After an exchange of punts, Young's desperation passed was knocked down near the 10-yard-line as time expired. Manning was 20 of 31 for 166 yards and 2 touchdowns, with 1 interception. Young, making his second start, was 10 of 21 for 63 yards, with 1 interception. Travis Henry had 19 carries for 123 yards, as the Titans rushed for 214 yards.

Tennessee	7	3	3	0	—	13
Indianapolis	0	0	7	7	—	14

Tenn	—	Young 19 run (Bironas kick)
Tenn	—	FG Bironas 22
Ind	—	Harrison 13 pass from Manning (M. Gramatica kick)
Tenn	—	FG Bironas 47
Ind	—	Wayne 2 pass from Manning (M. Gramatica kick)

JACKSONVILLE 41, N.Y. JETS 0—at Alltel Stadium, attendance 66,604. The Jaguars' defense allowed just 177 yards, registered 6 sacks, and forced 4 turnovers to record its second shutout of the season. Jacksonville scored on four of its first five possessions, and led 28-0 with 7:10 left in the first half. Two of those drives covered just 50 and 23 yards because they were set up by turnovers, and a third was an 8-yard drive after a blocked punt by Gerald Sensabaugh. The Jets only threatened once, trailing 38-0 in the fourth quarter, but B.J. Askew and Leon Washington were stopped on consecutive plays on third- and fourth-down at the Jaguars' 1. Leftwich was 9 of 20 for 140 yards and 2 touchdowns. Fred Taylor rushed 21 times for 111 yards. Pennington was 10 of 17 for 71 yards, with 3 interceptions. Washington had 23 carries for 101 yards.

N.Y. Jets	0	0	0	0	—	0
Jacksonville	14	14	10	3	—	41

Jax	—	Jones-Drew 6 run (Scobee kick)
Jax	—	Taylor 13 run (Scobee kick)
Jax	—	Jones-Drew 4 run (Scobee kick)
Jax	—	Wrighster 1 pass from Leftwich (Scobee kick)
Jax	—	FG Scobee 43
Jax	—	R. Williams 16 pass from Leftwich (Scobee kick)
Jax	—	FG Scobee 40

MINNESOTA 26, DETROIT 17—at Metrodome, attendance 63,906. E.J. Henderson returned an interception 45 yards for a touchdown with 1:31 left as the Vikings scored 23 unanswered fourth-quarter points to keep the Lions winless. The Lions scored three times in four possessions, with both touchdowns being set up by Vikings' turnovers, to take a 17-3 lead into the fourth quarter. Two plays into the fourth quarter, Brad Johnson completed a 3-yard touchdown pass on third-and-goal to Travis Taylor. Two plays later, Pat Williams sacked Jon Kitna at the 5-yard-line. Kitna fumbled and Ben Leber recovered the ball in the end zone. Jared DeVries blocked Ryan Longwell's extra-point attempt, so the Lions still led 17-16 at 13:12 to play. Longwell's 20-yard field goal with 3:00 left gave Minnesota the lead, and on fourth-and-10 from midfield with 1:31 left, Kitna was pressured and about to be sacked. He desperately shoveled the ball forward, but it was intercepted by Henderson, who returned it 45 yards for the game-clinching touchdown. Johnson was 26 of 34 for 201 yards and 1 touchdown, with 1 interception. Chester Taylor had 26 carries for 123 yards. Kitna was 23 of 42 for 225 yards and 1 touchdown, with 3 interceptions.

Detroit	0	10	7	0	—	17
Minnesota	3	0	0	23	—	26

Minn	—	FG Longwell 26
Det	—	Kitna 8 run (Hanson kick)
Det	—	FG Hanson 53
Det	—	Campbell 12 pass from Kitna (Hanson kick)
Minn	—	Taylor 3 pass from B. Johnson (Longwell kick)
Minn	—	Leber recovered fumble in end zone (kick blocked)
Minn	—	FG Longwell 20
Minn	—	Henderson 45 interception return (Longwell kick)

NEW ENGLAND 20, MIAMI 10—at Gillette Stadium, attendance 68,756. The Patriots scored on their first three possessions and held off the Dolphins. A fumble recovery by Tedy Bruschi sparked a 20-yard scoring drive to open the game. The Dolphins then drove into field-goal range, only to have Mike Wright block Olindo Mare's 40-yard attempt. Fifteen plays later, Stephen Gostkowski kicked a 31-yard field goal and four plays later Asante Samuel's interception and return to the Dolphins' 10 set up Troy Brown's touchdown catch for a 13-0 lead. The Dolphins scored on their next two drives to pull within 13-10. But Samuel's second interception, at the Dolphins' 24, and a pass interference penalty in the end zone on third down, led to Heath Evans' 1-yard scoring catch with 9:47 to play. Mare's 50-yard kick sailed wide right on their next drive, and the Patriots ran off the final 5:59, highlighted by Brady's 15-yard pass to Ben Watson on fourth-and-3. Brady was 16 of 29 for 140 yards and 2 touchdowns. Joey Harrington, making his first start of the season in place of injured Daunte Culpepper, was 26 of 41 for 232 yards, with 2 interceptions.

Miami	0	10	0	0	—	10
New England	3	10	0	7	—	20

NE	—	FG Gostkowski 35
NE	—	FG Gostkowski 31
NE	—	T. Brown 10 pass from Brady (Gostkowski kick)
Mia	—	R. Brown 2 run (Mare kick)
Mia	—	FG Mare 40
NE	—	Evans 1 pass from Brady (Gostkowski kick)

NEW ORLEANS 24, TAMPA BAY 21—at Louisiana Superdome, attendance 68,183. Reggie Bush returned a punt 65 yards for a touchdown with 4:17 to play as the Saints rallied to move into first place. Leading 10-7, the Saints increased the advantage to 17-7 in the third quarter when Rodney Leisle recovered Bruce Gradkowski's fumble at the Buccaneers' 25 to set up Drew Brees' third-and-goal 9-yard touchdown pass to Ernie Conwell. The Buccaneers answered with Mike Alstott's 1-yard scoring run, keyed by Gradkowski's 52-yard pass to Joey Galloway. In the fourth quarter, a 34-yard run by Carnell Williams set up Gradkowski's third-and-goal 3-yard touchdown pass to Alex Smith for a 21-17 lead with 10:03 to play. At 4:33 to play, Josh Bidwell punted 45 yards down the center of the field. Bush caught the punt, and raced outside to the right sideline for a 65-yard return. The Buccaneers were stopped on downs near midfield with 2:23 to play. Brees was 21 of 33 for 171 yards and 1 touchdown. McAllister had 15 carries for 123 yards. Bush had 11 catches for 63 yards. Gradkowski, making his first NFL start, was 20 of 31 for 225 yards and 2 touchdowns.

Tampa Bay	7	0	7	7	—	21
New Orleans	3	7	7	7	—	24

TB	—	Galloway 18 pass from Gradkowski (Bryant kick)
NO	—	FG Carney 21
NO	—	McAllister 24 run (Carney kick)
NO	—	Conwell 9 pass from Brees (Carney kick)
TB	—	Alstott 1 run (Bryant kick)
TB	—	A. Smith 3 pass from Gradkowski (Bryant kick)
NO	—	Bush 65 punt return (Carney kick)

N.Y. GIANTS 19, WASHINGTON 3—at Giants Stadium, attendance 78,653. The Giants outgained the Redskins 411-164 in total yards. Jay Feely missed a 47-yard field goal on the Giants' opening possession, and the Redskins responded with John Halls' 39-yard field goal. The Giants answered with drives of 50, 52, and 84 yards, which all culminated in Feely field goals, the last one two seconds before halftime, for a 9-3 lead. The Giants then drove 69 yards in 15 plays, capped by Eli Manning's 2-yard scoring toss to Plaxico Burress, for a 16-3 lead. Hall missed a 42-yard field-goal attempt on the Redskins' next possession, and Washington failed to cross midfield on its final three drives. The Giants completed 9 of 16 third-down situations. Manning was 23 of 33 for 256 yards and 1 touchdown. Barber had 23 carries for 123 yards. Brunell was 12 of 22 for 109 yards.

Washington	3	0	0	0	—	3
N.Y. Giants	0	9	7	3	—	19

Wash	—	FG Hall 39
NYG	—	FG Feely 24
NYG	—	FG Feely 34
NYG	—	FG Feely 32
NYG	—	Burress 2 pass from E. Manning (Feely kick)
NYG	—	FG Feely 40

PHILADELPHIA 38, DALLAS 24—at Lincoln Financial Field, attendance 69,268. Lito Sheppard returned an interception 102 yards for a touchdown with 16 seconds to play as the Eagles remained in first place. The Eagles' defense forced 5 turnovers and registered 7 sacks. Trailing 21-17 in the third quarter, Donovan McNabb completed an 87-yard touchdown pass to Hank Baskett. The Cowboys tied the game early in the fourth quarter on Mike Vanderjagt's 39-yard field goal. On the ensuing drive the Eagles used a flea flicker, with McNabb receiving a pitchback from Correll Buckhalter and then completing a 40-yard touchdown pass to Reggie Brown, to take a 31-24 lead. Sheppard intercepted a long pass at the Eagles' 7 with 7:23 to play to thwart one drive, and, with the Cowboys 6 yards from tying the game, he stepped in front of Jason Witten and returned the ball 102 yards for a touchdown with 16 seconds left to clinch the victory. The game marked the return of Terrell Owens, who had 3 catches for 45 yards, to Philadelphia. McNabb was 18 of 33 for 354 yards and 2 touchdowns. Baskett had 3 catches for 112 yards. Bledsoe was 18 of 38 for 223 yards, with 3 interceptions. Julius Jones carried 26 times for 100 yards.

Dallas	7	14	0	3	—	24
Philadelphia	10	7	7	14	—	38

Phil	—	Westbrook 5 run (Akers kick)
Phil	—	FG Akers 27
Dall	—	Barber 2 run (Vanderjagt kick)
Dall	—	Ware 69 fumble return (Vanderjagt kick)
Phil	—	McNabb 1 run (Akers kick)
Dall	—	Bledsoe 7 run (Vanderjagt kick)
Phil	—	Baskett 87 pass from McNabb (Akers kick)
Dall	—	FG Vanderjagt 39
Phil	—	R. brown 40 pass from McNabb (Akers kick)
Phil	—	Sheppard 102 interception return (Akers kick)

SAN FRANCISCO 34, OAKLAND 20—at Monster Park, attendance 68,368. The 49ers' defense forced 5 second-half turnovers en route to a come-from-behind victory. The Raiders led 13-7 at half, thanks to Randy Moss' 100th career touchdown catch, with the defense twice stopping the 49ers on downs inside the red zone. In the third quarter, Manny Lawson blocked Shane Lechler's punt. The 49ers needed just 9 yards to re-take the lead on Alex Smith's second touchdown pass to Arnaz Battle. Walt Harris intercepted a pass for a touchback on the next drive that led to a 33-yard touchdown pass on third-and-12 screen pass from Smith to Maurice Hicks for a 21-13 lead. After Chad Williams' interception set up a field goal, the Raiders trailed 24-13. On their next play, Andrew Walter threw a lateral to LaMont Jordan. The ball fell to the ground, and Melvin Oliver picked up the ball and jogged 12 yards for a touchdown and 31-13 lead with 10:30 to play. Smith was 15 of 19 for 165 yards and 3 touchdowns, with 1 interception. Gore carried 27 times for 134 yards. Walter was 14 of 23 for 164 yards and 1 touchdown, with 2 interceptions. Marques Tuiasosopo replaced Walter in the fourth quarter and was 4 of 9 for 52 yards and 1 touchdown, with 2 interceptions.

Oakland	3	10	0	7	—	20
San Francisco	7	0	14	13	—	34

SF	—	Battle 4 pass from A. Smith (Nedney kick)
Oak	—	FG Janikowski 33
Oak	—	FG Janikowski 36
Oak	—	R. Moss 22 pass from Walter (Janikowski kick)
SF	—	Battle 6 pass from A. Smith (Nedney kick)
SF	—	Hicks 33 pass from A. Smith (Nedney kick)
SF	—	FG Nedney 19
SF	—	Oliver 12 fumble return (Nedney kick)
Oak	—	Anderson 8 pass from Tuiasosopo (Janikowski kick)
SF	—	FG Nedney 39

SUNDAY NIGHT, OCTOBER 8
SAN DIEGO 23, PITTSBURGH 13—at Qualcomm Stadium, attendance 67,837. The Chargers scored on their first four second-half possessions to rally and hand the Steelers their third consecutive loss. The Chargers had consecutive scoring drives of 61, 63, and 54 yards in the first half en route to a 13-7 halftime lead. Michael Turner returned the opening kickoff of the second half 51 yards to set up a field goal. Drayton Florence then intercepted Ben Roethlisberger's pass to spark an 11-play, 91-yard touchdown drive, capped by Philip Rivers' 22-yard scoring toss to Antonio Gates. The Chargers' defense did not allow the Steelers to cross midfield on their next two possessions, while the offense then drove 14 and 11 plays to set up 2 more Nate Kaeding field goals, the latter with

1:05 to play. The Chargers held the ball for 21:07 of the second half. Rivers was 24 of 37 for 242 yards and 2 touchdowns, with 1 interception. Roethlisberger was 20 of 31 for 220 yards, with 2 interceptions.

Pittsburgh	7	6	0	0	—	13
San Diego	0	7	10	6	—	23

Pitt	—	Parker 9 run (Reed kick)
Pitt	—	FG Reed 39
SD	—	Floyd 9 pass from Rivers (Kaeding kick)
Pitt	—	FG Reed 44
SD	—	FG Kaeding 28
SD	—	Gates 22 pass from Rivers (Kaeding kick)
SD	—	FG Kaeding 33
SD	—	FG Kaeding 22

MONDAY NIGHT, OCTOBER 9
DENVER 13, BALTIMORE 3—at INVESCO Field at Mile High, attendance 76,355. The Broncos' defense intercepted 3 passes to hand the Ravens their first defeat. With the temperature at 39 degrees at kickoff, and rain throughout the game, the Ravens took advantage of Tatum Bell's fumble, recovered by Chris McAlister, to get a 24-yard field goal by Matt Stover. With the score 3-3, the Ravens drove to the Broncos' 10 just before halftime, but Champ Bailey intercepted Steve McNair's pass for a touchback. Neither team threatened again until the fourth quarter, when the Broncos took advantage of Sam Koch's 10-yard punt, converted 2 third-down situations, including a 9-yard pass from Jake Plummer to Rod Smith, to set up a Jason Elam 44-yard field goal with 8:03 to play. Four plays later, Darrent Williams intercepted McNair's pass and Bell had a key 12-yard run on third-and-10 to set up Smith's 4-yard touchdown catch with 1:55 to play. Domonique Foxworth intercepted a pass at the Broncos' 20 with 36 seconds left to clinch the victory. Plummer was 13 of 24 for 106 yards and 1 touchdown, with 1 interception. McNair was 20 of 34 for 165 yards, with 3 interceptions.

Baltimore	3	0	0	0	—	3
Denver	0	3	0	10	—	13

Balt	—	FG Stover 24
Den	—	FG Elam 43
Den	—	FG Elam 44
Den	—	R. Smith 4 pass from Plummer (Elam kick)

SIXTH WEEK SUMMARIES
American Football Conference

East Division	W	L	T	Pct.	Pts.	OP
New England	4	1	0	.800	108	74
N.Y. Jets	3	3	0	.500	116	149
Buffalo	2	4	0	.333	94	125
Miami	1	5	0	.167	78	111
North Division	**W**	**L**	**T**	**Pct.**	**Pts.**	**OP**
Baltimore	4	2	0	.667	110	69
Cincinnati	3	2	0	.600	111	99
Pittsburgh	2	3	0	.400	106	84
Cleveland	1	4	0	.200	81	109
South Division	**W**	**L**	**T**	**Pct.**	**Pts.**	**OP**
Indianapolis	5	0	0	1.000	135	100
Jacksonville	3	2	0	.600	118	74
Houston	1	4	0	.200	72	147
Tennessee	1	5	0	.167	85	157
West Division	**W**	**L**	**T**	**Pct.**	**Pts.**	**OP**
Denver	4	1	0	.800	62	37
San Diego	4	1	0	.800	151	55
Kansas City	2	3	0	.400	87	97
Oakland	0	5	0	.000	50	126

National Football Conference

East Division	W	L	T	Pct.	Pts.	OP
Philadelphia	4	2	0	.667	179	124
Dallas	3	2	0	.600	147	92
N.Y. Giants	3	2	0	.600	127	109
Washington	2	4	0	.333	118	135
North Division	**W**	**L**	**T**	**Pct.**	**Pts.**	**OP**
Chicago	6	0	0	1.000	180	59
Minnesota	3	2	0	.600	89	82

Green Bay	1	4	0	.200	87	138
Detroit	1	5	0	.167	108	158
South Division	**W**	**L**	**T**	**Pct.**	**Pts.**	**OP**
New Orleans	5	1	0	.833	145	110
Carolina	4	2	0	.667	109	111
Atlanta	3	2	0	.600	83	69
Tampa Bay	1	4	0	.200	62	104
West Division	**W**	**L**	**T**	**Pct.**	**Pts.**	**OP**
Seattle	4	1	0	.800	108	111
St. Louis	4	2	0	.667	139	128
San Francisco	2	4	0	.333	124	194
Arizona	1	5	0	.167	111	143

SUNDAY, OCTOBER 15
N.Y. GIANTS 27, ATLANTA 14—at Georgia Dome, attendance 70,840. Tiki Barber rushed for 185 yards, including nine runs of at least 12 yards, and the teams combined for 482 rushing yards as the Giants scored 24 second-half points to defeat the Falcons. The Giants dominated the second half by maintaining possession for 21 minutes, 25 seconds of the 30-minute half. On the first play of the third quarter, Warrick Dunn broke free for a franchise-record 90-yard touchdown run and 14-3 lead. The Giants' offense answered by putting together four consecutive scoring drives of 84, 91, 30, and 55 yards. The Falcons went three-and-out on offense in their three possessions during the stretch, meaning the Giants ran 35 of 44 plays to score 24 straight points and take a 27-14 lead on Eli Manning's 4-yard touchdown pass to Jeremy Shockey with 3:45 to play. The Falcons did a get a first down on their next possession, but Barry Cofield sacked Michael Vick on fourth-and-7 from the Giants' 44 with 2:14 to play to clinch the victory. Manning was 17 of 30 for 180 yards and 2 touchdowns, with 2 interceptions. Barber had 26 carries for 185 yards. Vick was 14 of 27 for 154 yards, with 1 interception. Dunn had 14 carries for 146 yards.

N.Y. Giants	0	3	14	10	—	27
Atlanta	0	7	0	7	—	14

NYG	—	FG Feely 21
Atl	—	Vick 22 run (Andersen kick)
Atl	—	Dunn 90 run (Andersen kick)
NYG	—	Jacobs 2 run (Feely kick)
NYG	—	Shockey 2 pass from E. Manning (Feely kick)
NYG	—	FG Feely 39
NYG	—	Shockey 4 pass from E. Manning (Feely kick)

CAROLINA 23, BALTIMORE 21—at M & T Bank Stadium, attendance 70,762. Jake Delhomme passed for 365 yards, 189 of which went to Steve Smith, as the Panthers won their fourth consecutive game. The Ravens' defense forced 3 turnovers, but each time the offense committed a turnover to give the ball right back to Carolina. The Panthers strung together consecutive drives for 77 and 65 yards just before halftime to score 10 points and take a 13-7 halftime lead. Baltimore trailed 16-7 with 4:45 left, but on third-and-13 Mark Clayton caught a tipped pass and outran the secondary for a 62-yard touchdown—his second tipped touchdown-catch of the day. On the next play from scrimmage, Delhomme completed a long pass to a wide open Smith for a 72-yard touchdown and 23-14 advantage with 4:15 to play. Todd Heap scored with 2:13 left, but on third-and-1, Delhomme completed a 4-yard pass to Drew Carter which enabled the Panthers to run out the clock. Delhomme was 24 of 39 for 365 yards and 2 touchdowns, with 2 interceptions. Smith had 8 receptions for 189 yards. Steve McNair was 2 of 4 for 4 yards, with 1 interception, before suffering a concussion and sprained neck in the first quarter. Kyle Boller replaced him and was 17 of 31 for 226 yards and 3 touchdowns, with 1 interception.

Carolina	3	10	0	10	—	23
Baltimore	0	7	0	14	—	21

Car	—	FG Kasay 21
Balt	—	Clayton 14 pass from Boller (Stover kick)
Car	—	D. Carter 42 pass from Delhomme

(Kasay kick)

Car	—	FG Kasay 31
Car	—	FG Kasay 21
Balt	—	Clayton 62 pass from Boller (Stover kick)
Car	—	S. Smith 72 pass from Delhomme (Kasay kick)
Balt	—	Heap 7 pass from Boller (Stover kick)

DALLAS 34, HOUSTON 6—at Texas Stadium, attendance 63,186. Terrell Owens had 3 second-half touchdown catches and the Cowboys' defense forced 3 turnovers, which resulted in 17 points, en route to victory. The Texans drove to the Cowboys' 1 to begin the game, but settled for a field goal. Kris Brown's second field goal as the half expired sent the Texans to the locker room with a 6-3 lead. The Cowboys drove 68 yards for a touchdown to begin the second half to take a 10-6 lead. Later in the quarter, Bradie James tipped David Carr's pass. Greg Ellis intercepted it, and Owens caught his second touchdown, on third-and-8, from 21 yards with 3:41 left in the quarter. Anthony Henry's interception three plays later set up Marion Barber's 1-yard scoring run, and Roy Williams recovered Edell Shepherd's fumbled kickoff seconds later which led to Mike Vanderjagt's field goal and a 27-6 lead with 11:28 to play. Drew Bledsoe was 17 of 28 for 168 yards and 2 touchdowns. Tony Romo played the Cowboys' final series and was 2 for 2, his first NFL passes, for 35 yards and 1 touchdown. Carr was 15 of 27 for 128 yards, with 2 interceptions. Sage Rosenfels played the final series and was 8 of 11 for 70 yards.

Houston	3	3	0	0 —	6
Dallas	0	3	14	17 —	34

Hou	—	FG K. Brown 19
Dall	—	FG Vanderjagt 22
Hou	—	FG K. Brown 48
Dall	—	Owens 3 pass from Bledsoe (Vanderjagt kick)
Dall	—	Owens 21 pass from Bledsoe (Vanderjagt kick)
Dall	—	Barber 1 run (Vanderjagt kick)
Dall	—	FG Vanderjagt 21
Dall	—	Owens 2 pass from Bledsoe (Vanderjagt kick)

DETROIT 20, BUFFALO 17—at Ford Field, attendance 60,704. Jon Kitna passed for 278 yards and a touchdown as the Lions posted their first victory for coach Rod Marinelli. The Lions scored on two of their first three possessions, and despite being stopped on the Bills' 1 on the other drive they took a 10-0 lead. The Lions led 17-10 late in the third quarter when James Hall sacked J.P. Losman and forced him to fumble. Shaun Rogers recovered at the Lions' 38 and Jason Hanson's 29-yard field goal nine plays later stretched the lead to 20-10. The Bills responded with a 74-yard touchdown drive to cut the deficit to 20-17 with 9:23 to play. The Bills got the ball back twice, but never crossed midfield. Kitna was 24 of 36 for 278 yards and 1 touchdown, with 1 interception. Roy Williams had 10 catches for 161 yards, both totals being career highs. Jones rushed 23 times for 127 yards. Losman was 21 of 34 for 207 yards and 2 touchdowns, with 1 interception.

Buffalo	0	10	0	7 —	17
Detroit	10	7	0	3 —	20

Det	—	FG Hanson 43
Det	—	K. Jones 7 run (Hanson kick)
Buff	—	Parrish 44 pass from Losman (Lindell kick)
Det	—	R. Williams 28 pass from Kitna (Hanson kick)
Buff	—	FG Lindell 53
Det	—	FG Hanson 29
Buff	—	Neufeld 4 pass from Losman (Lindell kick)

NEW ORLEANS 27, PHILADELPHIA 24—at Louisiana Superdome, attendance 68,269. John Carney capped a 16-play, 72-yard, 8 minute and 26 second drive with a 31-yard field goal as time expired to propel the Saints to victory. Just before halftime, Dexter Wynn muffed a punt and Terrance Copper recovered at the Eagles' 19. Four plays later, on third-and-goal, Drew Brees completed a 7-yard touchdown pass to Marques Colston for a 17-3 halftime lead. Reggie Brown's 60-yard touchdown catch three plays into the second half trimmed the deficit, and L.J. Smith's 4-yard touchdown pass from Donovan McNabb tied the game with 1:03 left in the third quarter. Darwin Walker intercepted a pass three plays later, and Brown's second touchdown of the half gave the Eagles 14 points in 1:09 and a 24-17 lead with 14:54 to play. The Saints answered with a 5-play, 69-yard drive capped by Joe Horn's 48-yard touchdown pass deep down the right side to tie the game. On fourth-and-11 from their own 46, the Eagles punted with 8:26 to play and never got the ball back. It looked like the Eagles had stopped the Saints when Brees was sacked on third-and-10 at the Eagles' 35 with 3:13 left, but Philadelphia had 12 players on the field. On the next play, Brees completed a 7-yard pass to Mark Campbell for a first down. Deuce McAllister's 5-yard run on third-and-1 moments later, and the fact the Eagles were out of time outs, allowed the Saints to run three kneeldown plays to set up Carney's winning kick. Brees was 27 of 37 for 275 yards and 3 touchdowns, with 2 interceptions. Horn had 6 catches for 110 yards. McNabb was 19 of 32 for 247 yards and 2 touchdowns, with 1 interception. Reggie Brown had 6 catches for 121 yards.

Philadelphia	0	3	14	7 —	24
New Orleans	10	7	0	10 —	27

NO	—	FG Carney 39
NO	—	Horn 14 pass from Brees (Carney kick)
Phil	—	FG Akers 47
NO	—	Colston 7 pass from Brees (Carney kick)
Phil	—	R. Brown 60 pass from McNabb (Akers kick)
Phil	—	L. Smith 4 pass from McNabb (Akers kick)
Phil	—	R. Brown 15 run (Akers kick)
NO	—	Horn 48 pass from Brees (Carney kick)
NO	—	FG Carney 31

N.Y. JETS 20, MIAMI 17—at The Meadowlands, attendance 77,439. The Jets jumped to a 20-3 lead before holding on to defeat the Dolphins. It was a battle of field position for nearly three quarters until Chad Pennington fired a 58-yard touchdown pass to Laveranues Coles for a 13-3 lead. On the next drive, Sammy Morris fumbled and Victor Hobson recovered at the Dolphins' 43. Six plays later, on third-and-1, the Jets went for the end zone and Pennington and Coles hooked up on a 22-yard touchdown for a 20-3 lead with 13:15 to play. The Dolphins went with a no-huddle offense to drive 81 and 74 yards for touchdowns on their next two possessions to pull within 20-17 with 2:56 left. The Dolphins' defense forced a punt, and Joey Harrington completed four passes to drive to the Jets' 32, but Olindo Mare's 51-yard field-goal attempt fell short with 28 seconds remaining. Pennington was 17 of 29 for 175 yards and 2 touchdowns. Coles had 5 catches for 106 yards. Harrington was 27 of 43 for 266 yards and 1 touchdown, with 2 interceptions. Ronnie Brown had 22 carries for 127 yards.

Miami	0	0	3	14 —	17
N.Y. Jets	3	0	10	7 —	20

NYJ	—	FG Nugent 33
NYJ	—	FG Nugent 33
Mia	—	FG Mare 21
NYJ	—	Coles 58 pass from Pennington (Nugent kick)
NYJ	—	Coles 22 pass from Pennington (Nugent kick)
Mia	—	Chambers 2 pass from Harrington (Mare kick)
Mia	—	R. Brown 1 run (Mare kick)

PITTSBURGH 45, KANSAS CITY 7—at Heinz Field, attendance 64,727. The Steelers jumped to a 31-0 lead en route to climbing back into the AFC North race. The Steelers outgained the Chiefs 457-213 total yards. The Chiefs went three-and-out in six of their first seven possessions. By their eighth drive, the Chiefs trailed 31-0. The Steelers had scoring drives in the first half of 73, 58, 80, 65, and 76 yards. Roethlisberger was 16 of 19 for 238 yards and 2 touchdowns. Parker had 21 carries for 109 yards. Huard was 16 of 32 for 162 yards, with 1 interception, and Brodie Croyle was 3 of 7 for 23 yards, with 2 interceptions.

Kansas City	0	0	7	0 —	7
Pittsburgh	14	17	0	14 —	45

Pitt	—	Parker 3 run (Reed kick)
Pitt	—	Washington 47 pass from Roethlisberger (Reed kick)
Pitt	—	Parker 8 run (Reed kick)
Pitt	—	Ward 13 pass from Roethlisberger (Reed kick)
Pitt	—	FG Reed 32
KC	—	L. Johnson 2 run (Tynes kick)
Pitt	—	Davenport 1 run (Reed kick)
Pitt	—	Wallace 30 interception return (Reed kick)

SEATTLE 30, ST. LOUIS 28—at Edward Jones Dome, attendance 65,592. Kris Brown became the first kicker in NFL history with 3 field goals of at least 49 yards in the same quarter, capped by his 54-yard field goal as time expired, to give the Seahawks a stunning come-from-behind victory over a half-game ahead of their divisional rival. Torry Holt caught 2 first-half touchdowns as the Rams scored on three of their first four possessions for a 21-7 lead. Brown's 49-yard field goal two plays into the fourth quarter cut the deficit to 21-17. On the ensuing kickoff, Kevin Curtis fumbled and Kevin Bentley recovered. Matt Hasselbeck's 19-yards touchdown pass to Deion Branch came 48 seconds after Brown's kick and gave the Seahawks a 24-21 lead. The Seahawks led 27-21 when Lofa Tatupu intercepted a pass at the Rams' 17 with 3:09 left. But Maurice Morris fumbled three plays later and Jimmy Kennedy recovered the ball. Five plays later, Holt made a juggling, one-handed catch of a deep pass thrown by Marc Bulger and ran into the end zone for a 67-yard touchdown to give the Rams a 28-27 lead with 1:44 to play. The Seahawks reached the Rams' 31, but an illegal formation penalty pushed Seattle back to the 36-yard line with four seconds left. Brown calmly drilled the 54-yard field goal for the victory. Hasselbeck was 19 of 34 or 268 yards and 3 touchdowns. Bulger was 26 of 39 for 360 yards and 3 touchdowns, with 1 interception. Holt had 8 catches for 154 yards.

Seattle	7	0	7	16 —	30
St. Louis	7	14	0	7 —	28

StL	—	Holt 9 pass from Bulger (Wilkins kick)
Sea	—	Branch 14 pass from Hasselbeck (J. Brown kick)
StL	—	S. Jackson 2 run (Wilkins kick)
StL	—	Holt 10 pass from Bulger (Wilkins kick)
Sea	—	D. Jackson 42 pass from Hasselbeck (J. Brown kick)
Sea	—	FG J. Brown 49
Sea	—	Branch 19 pass from Hasselbeck (J. Brown kick)
Sea	—	FG J. Brown 49
StL	—	Holt 67 pass from Bulger (Wilkins kick)
Sea	—	FG J. Brown 54

SAN DIEGO 48, SAN FRANCISCO 19—at Monster Park, attendance 68,137. LaDainian Tomlinson scored 4 touchdowns as the Chargers outlasted the 49ers. The Chargers outgained the 49ers 421-274 total yards and held the ball for 35:48. The Chargers scored touchdowns on their first four drives to take a 28-10 lead. The 49ers responded with a touchdown and, two plays later, Ronald Fields pressured Philip Rivers, who was flagged for intentional grounding in the end zone for a safety to cut the deficit to 28-19 with 3:12 left in the half. But Luis Castillo intercepted Alex Smith's pass on the first play after the free kick, and Tomlinson scored with 33 seconds left for a 35-19 halftime lead. San Diego scored on three of its first four second-half possessions, and the 49ers did not enter Chargers' territory in the second half until the final minute. Rivers was 29 of 39 for 334 yards and 2 touchdowns. Tomlinson rushed 21 times for 71 yards and 4 touchdowns. Tomlinson's first touchdown, a 5-yard run in the first quarter, gave him a Chargers' record 84 career touchdowns. Smith was 20 of 31 for 214 yards and 2 touchdowns, with 1 interception.

| San Diego | 14 | 21 | 3 | 10 | — | 48 |
| San Francisco | 7 | 12 | 0 | 0 | — | 19 |

SD	—	Gates 57 pass from Rivers (Kaeding kick)
SF	—	Gilmore 15 pass from A. Smith (Nedney kick)
SD	—	Tomlinson 5 run (Kaeding kick)
SF	—	FG Nedney 42
SD	—	V. Jackson 33 pass from Rivers (Kaeding kick)
SD	—	Tomlinson 1 run (Kaeding kick)
SF	—	Norris 2 pass from A. Smith (Nedney kick)
SF	—	Safety, Rivers penalized for intentional grounding in end zone
SD	—	Tomlinson 1 run (Kaeding kick)
SD	—	FG Kaeding 24
SD	—	FG Kaeding 44
SD	—	Tomlinson 6 run (Kaeding kick)

TAMPA BAY 14, CINCINNATI 13—at Raymond James Stadium, attendance 65,732. Michael Clayton lunged across the goal line with an 8-yard touchdown catch with 35 seconds to play as the Buccaneers posted their first victory. Bruce Gradkowski, making his second NFL start in place of injured Chris Simms, trailed 7-0 at halftime, but opened the second half with an 11-play, 80-yard drive to tie the score. The Bengals bounced back with 2 field goals to take a 13-7 lead with 10:34 remaining. An exchange of punts gave the Buccaneers the ball at their own 46-yard-line with 4:21 left. A 15-yard pass to Clayton on third-and-3 and a roughing-the-passer penalty helped move the ball to the Bengals' 8, where on fourth-and-3 Gradkowski hit Clayton going across the middle. Clayton dove for the end zone, with the ball reaching the goal line with 35 seconds to play. The catch was originally ruled incomplete, but was overturned by replay. Shayne Graham missed a 62-yard field-goal attempt as the clock expired. Gradkowski was 25 of 44 for 184 yards and 2 touchdowns, with 1 interception. Carson Palmer was 24 of 37 for 261 yards and 1 touchdown. T.J. Houshmandzadeh had 10 catches for 102 yards.

| Cincinnati | 0 | 7 | 3 | 3 | — | 13 |
| Tampa Bay | 0 | 0 | 7 | 7 | — | 14 |

Cin	—	Houshmandzadeh 33 pass from Palmer (Graham kick)
TB	—	A. Smith 2 pass from Gradkowski (Bryant kick)
Cin	—	FG Graham 37
Cin	—	FG Graham 47
TB	—	Clayton 8 pass from Gradkowski (Bryant kick)

TENNESSEE 25, WASHINGTON 22—at FedExField, attendance 88,550. Travis Henry rushed for 178 yards as Vince Young, making his third start, and the Titans won their first game by rallying to stun the Redskins. The Redskins drove 78 and 70 yards on their first two possessions to take a 14-3 lead. The Titans then scored on three of their next four drives, capped by Henry's 2-yard run to culminate a 74-yard drive to begin the second half, for a 20-14 lead. Three plays later, Casey Cramer blocked Derrick Frost's punt out of the end zone to stake the Titans to an eight-point lead. A 52-yard post pass from Mark Brunell to Brandon Lloyd to the Titans' 4 set up Clinton

Portis' second touchdown. Brunell completed a 2-point conversion pass to Santana Moss to tie the game with 10:57 remaining. Adam Jones' 14-yard punt return later in the quarter sparked a 30-yard drive, 26 of which came on 4 carries by Henry, capped by Ron Bironas' 30-yard field goal with 5:11 to play for a 25-22 lead. After an exchange of punts, the Redskins got the ball on their own 16-yard line with 1:06 to play, but Brunell's first pass was intercepted by Lamont Thompson. Young was 13 of 25 for 161 yards. Henry rushed 32 times for 178 yards. Brunell was 16 of 30 for 180 yards and 1 touchdown, with 1 interception.

| Tennessee | 3 | 10 | 9 | 3 | — | 25 |
| Washington | 7 | 7 | 0 | 8 | — | 22 |

Tenn	—	FG Bironas 32
Wash	—	Portis 10 run (Novak kick)
Wash	—	Cooley 24 pass from Brunell (Novak kick)
Tenn	—	FG Bironas 26
Tenn	—	B. Jones 3 pass from Young (Bironas kick)
Tenn	—	Henry 2 run (Bironas kick)
Tenn	—	Safety, Cramer blocked punt out of end zone
Wash	—	Portis 4 run (S. Moss pass from Brunell)
Tenn	—	FG Bironas 30

SUNDAY NIGHT, OCTOBER 15

DENVER 13, OAKLAND 3—at INVESCO Field at Mile High, attendance 76,691. The Broncos' dominant defense forced 2 turnovers and became the first team since the 1934 Lions to begin a season allowing just one touchdown through five games. The Broncos scored on three successive first-half drives, capped by Jason Elam's 22-yard boot with 3:59 left in the half, for a 13-0 lead. The Raiders pulled within 13-3, but Andrew Walter's fourth-and-6 pass from the Broncos' 43 fell incomplete with 8:40 to play, and LaMont Jordan fumbled and Michael Myers recovered at the Broncos' 23 with 4:24 to play. The Broncos' offense generated 4 first downs in the final possession to run out the clock. Jake Plummer was 11 of 18 for 102 yards. Walter was 13 of 26 for 189 yards, with 1 interception.

| Oakland | 0 | 0 | 3 | 0 | — | 3 |
| Denver | 7 | 6 | 0 | 0 | — | 13 |

Den	—	T. Bell 2 run (Elam kick)
Den	—	FG Elam 51
Den	—	FG Elam 22
Oak	—	FG Janikowski 47

MONDAY NIGHT, OCTOBER 16

CHICAGO 24, ARIZONA 23—at University of Phoenix Stadium, attendance 63,977. The Bears scored 3 second-half touchdowns, none by the offense, to overcome a 20-point deficit and remain undefeated. The Cardinals' defense forced 6 turnovers and allowed just 168 yards. The first turnover, an interception by Aaron Francisco, set up Anquan Boldin's 26-yard touchdown catch to give Arizona a 14-0 first-quarter lead. Rex Grossman fumbled twice in the second quarter, both while being sacked, to set up 2 field goals by Neil Rackers and give the Cardinals a 20-0 halftime lead. Arizona led 23-3 late in the third quarter when unblocked rookie Mark Anderson blindsided Matt Leinart and forced him to fumble. Mike Brown picked up the loose ball and strolled in from 3 yards to pull the Bears within 23-10 with two seconds left in the third quarter. Two more interceptions by the Cardinals' defense gave Arizona the ball at their own 41-yard-line with 5:52 to play. On second down, Edgerrin James had the ball ripped from his hands by Brian Urlacher. Charles Tillman picked up the ball and returned it 40 yards for a touchdown. The Bears then forced a punt, and Devin Hester returned it 83 yards for the go-ahead touchdown with 2:58 to play. Leinart, making his second NFL start, completed 5 of 6 passes to reach the Bears' 24. Two running plays netted 1 yard, and on fourth-and-2 Rackers' 40-yard field-goal attempt sailed wide left. Grossman was 14 of 37 for 144 yards, with 4 interceptions. The Bears'

defense had a record-setting night against Edgerrin James, who had 36 carries for 55 yards. It was the most carries by a player averaging less than 2 yards per attempt. Leinart was 24 of 42 for 232 yards and 2 touchdowns. Boldin had 12 catches for 136 yards.

| Chicago | 0 | 0 | 10 | 14 | — | 24 |
| Arizona | 14 | 6 | 3 | 0 | — | 23 |

Ariz	—	Bry. Johnson 11 pass from Leinart (Rackers kick)
Ariz	—	Boldin 26 pass from Leinart (Rackers kick)
Ariz	—	FG Rackers 41
Ariz	—	FG Rackers 28
Chi	—	FG Gould 23
Ariz	—	FG Rackers 29
Chi	—	M. Brown 3 fumble return (Gould kick)
Chi	—	Tillman 40 fumble return (Gould kick)
Chi	—	Hester 83 punt return (Gould kick)

SEVENTH WEEK SUMMARIES
American Football Conference

East Division	W	L	T	Pct.	Pts.	OP
New England	5	1	0	.833	136	80
N.Y. Jets	4	3	0	.571	147	173
Buffalo	2	5	0	.286	100	153
Miami	1	6	0	.143	102	145
North Division	**W**	**L**	**T**	**Pct.**	**Pts.**	**OP**
Baltimore	4	2	0	.667	110	69
Cincinnati	4	2	0	.667	128	113
Pittsburgh	2	4	0	.333	144	125
Cleveland	1	5	0	.167	88	126
South Division	**W**	**L**	**T**	**Pct.**	**Pts.**	**OP**
Indianapolis	6	0	0	1.000	171	122
Jacksonville	3	3	0	.500	125	101
Houston	2	4	0	.333	99	154
Tennessee	1	5	0	.167	85	157
West Division	**W**	**L**	**T**	**Pct.**	**Pts.**	**OP**
Denver	5	1	0	.833	79	44
San Diego	4	2	0	.667	178	85
Kansas City	3	3	0	.500	117	124
Oakland	1	5	0	.167	72	135

National Football Conference

East Division	W	L	T	Pct.	Pts.	OP
N.Y. Giants	4	2	0	.667	163	131
Philadelphia	4	3	0	.571	200	147
Dallas	3	3	0	.500	169	128
Washington	2	5	0	.286	140	171
North Division	**W**	**L**	**T**	**Pct.**	**Pts.**	**OP**
Chicago	6	0	0	1.000	180	59
Minnesota	4	2	0	.667	120	95
Green Bay	2	4	0	.333	121	162
Detroit	1	6	0	.143	132	189
South Division	**W**	**L**	**T**	**Pct.**	**Pts.**	**OP**
New Orleans	5	1	0	.833	145	110
Atlanta	4	2	0	.667	124	107
Carolina	4	3	0	.571	123	128
Tampa Bay	2	4	0	.333	85	125
West Division	**W**	**L**	**T**	**Pct.**	**Pts.**	**OP**
St. Louis	4	2	0	.667	139	128
Seattle	4	2	0	.667	121	142
San Francisco	2	4	0	.333	124	194
Arizona	1	6	0	.143	120	165

SUNDAY, OCTOBER 22

ATLANTA 41, PITTSBURGH 38 (OT)—at Georgia Dome, attendance 71,151. Morten Andersen kicked a 32-yard field goal 6:56 into overtime as the Falcons broke the first 3-touchdown game of Michael Vick's career to victory. Michael Vick and Ben Roethlisberger each had 3 touchdown passes at halftime, marking just the third time in NFL history that had occurred. For the game, Hines Ward and Alge Crumpler each had 3 touchdown receptions, marking just the third time in history that opposing receivers had each caught a trio of scoring passes. The Steelers scored on their first three possessions and led 17-7. The Falcons cut the lead to 17-14, then Jerrious Norwood recovered an onside kick and Vick completed a

17-yard touchdown pass to Michael Jenkins for a 21-17 lead. With 7:45 left in the third quarter, Roethlisberger suffered a concussion and Charlie Batch replaced him. The Falcons scored on their next two drives, sandwiched around Batch's 70-yard touchdown pass to Ward, to give Atlanta a 35-31 lead with 1:10 left in the third quarter. The Falcons extended the lead to 38-31 on Andersen's 25-yard field goal, but the Steelers needed just 6 plays to drive 79 yards, highlighted by Nate Washington's 49-yard catch, and capped by Ward's 17-yard scoring grab with 3:19 to play to tie the game. With 35 seconds left, Michael Koenen made a 56-yard field-goal attempt, but the Steelers had called timeout. On his second attempt, Koenen missed but a running into the kicker penalty gave Atlanta another chance. Andersen tried a 52-yard attempt, but his kick fell just short. Batch completed a 25-yard pass to Ward to the Falcons' 33 but, with the clock running at eight seconds, the Steelers tried to spike the ball but Washington was flagged for a false start and the 10-second runoff sent the game to overtime. In overtime, the Falcons won the toss and drove 11 plays, 65 yards, keyed by Vick's 26-yard pass to Crumpler on fourth-and-9, and capped by Andersen's 32-yard winning kick. Vick was 18 of 30 for 232 yards and 4 touchdowns, with 2 interceptions. Crumpler had 6 receptions for 117 yards. Roethlisberger was 16 of 22 for 238 yards and 3 touchdowns. Batch was 8 of 13 for 195 yards and 2 touchdowns. Ward had 8 catches for 171 yards.

Pittsburgh	10	14	7	7	0	—	38
Atlanta	7	14	14	3	3	—	41

Atl	—	Crumpler 22 pass from Vick (Andersen kick)
Pitt	—	FG Reed 28
Pitt	—	Ward 11 pass from Roethlisberger (Reed kick)
Pitt	—	Miller 1 pass from Roethlisberger (Reed kick)
Atl	—	Crumpler 3 pass from Vick (Andersen kick)
Atl	—	Jenkins 17 pass from Vick (Andersen kick)
Pitt	—	Washington 10 pass from Roethlisberger (Reed kick)
Atl	—	Dunn 1 run (Andersen kick)
Pitt	—	Ward 70 pass from Batch (Reed kick)
Atl	—	Crumpler 31 pass from Vick (Andersen kick)
Atl	—	FG Andersen 25
Pitt	—	Ward 17 pass from Batch (Reed kick)
Atl	—	FG Andersen 32

NEW ENGLAND 28, BUFFALO 6—at Ralph Wilson Stadium, attendance 72,180. Tom Brady passed for 2 touchdowns as the Patriots won their third consecutive victory. The Patriots scored touchdowns on their first two possessions, the second set up by Laurence Maroney's 74-yard kickoff return, to take a 14-3 first-quarter lead. The Bills reached the Patriots' 23 just before halftime, but Asante Samuel intercepted J.P. Losman's pass to maintain the 11-point margin. Late in the third quarter, Tom Brady completed a key third-and-5 pass to Ben Watson for 20 yards, and on the next play Brady found Chad Jackson deep in the right corner of the end zone for a 35-yard touchdown and 21-3 lead. Rian Lindell's second field goal pulled the Bills to within 21-6 with 11:45 left, but the Patriots dashed any comeback hope by driving 67 yards in eight plays, keyed by another Brady-to-Watson third-down conversion, and capped by Doug Gabriel's 5-yard touchdown catch in the back of the end zone for a 28-6 lead with 7:36 remaining. Brady was 18 of 27 for 195 yards and 2 touchdowns. Losman was 16 of 25 for 192 yards, with 1 interception.

New England	14	0	7	7	—	28
Buffalo	3	0	0	3	—	6

NE	—	Dillon 8 run (Gostkowski kick)
Buff	—	FG Lindell 40
NE	—	Dillon 12 run (Gostkowski kick)

NE	—	Jackson 35 pass from Brady (Gostkowski kick)
Buff	—	FG Lindell 46
NE	—	Gabriel 5 pass from Brady (Gostkowski kick)

CINCINNATI 17, CAROLINA 14—at Paul Brown Stadium, attendance 65,964. Kevin Kaesviharn intercepted a pass in the end zone for a touchback with 3:50 remaining as the Bengals snapped the Panthers' four-game winning streak. The Bengals went three-and-out on their first four possessions before driving 80 yards in 13 plays to tie the game on Reggie Kelly's 16-yard touchdown catch in the second quarter. However, the Panthers responded with a 63-yard drive to pull ahead 14-7 at halftime. Trailing 14-10, the Bengals had fourth-and-1 on the Panthers' 35 with 9:13 to play. Carson Palmer lofted a pass deep down the right sideline and Chad Johnson made a diving catch at the Panthers' 3. Two plays later, Palmer found T.J. Houshmandzadeh in the end zone for a 17-14 lead with 8:07 to play. Later in the fourth quarter, catches of 18 and 23 yards by Steve Smith helped send the Panthers to the Bengals' 10-yard line. On third-and-goal, Jake Delhomme tried to find Keyshawn Johnson in the back of the end zone, but Kaesviharn intercepted the pass. The Bengals got 2 first downs so Carolina did not get the ball back until it were on its own 13-yard line with 16 seconds left. Palmer was 23 of 39 for 240 yards and 2 touchdowns. Rudi Johnson carried 26 times for 101 yards. Delhomme was 20 of 34 for 238 yards and 2 touchdowns, with 1 interception. Smith had 8 catches for 126 yards.

Carolina	7	7	0	0	—	14
Cincinnati	0	7	3	7	—	17

Car	—	Mangum 7 pass from Delhomme (Kasay kick)
Cin	—	Kelly 16 pass from Palmer (Graham kick)
Car	—	Goings 20 pass from Delhomme (Kasay kick)
Cin	—	FG Graham 23
Cin	—	Houshmandzadeh 1 pass from Palmer (Graham kick)

DENVER 17, CLEVELAND 7—at Cleveland Browns Stadium, attendance 73,024. Tatum Bell rushed for 115 yards and 1 touchdown as the Broncos' defense allowed just 165 yards to gain sole possession of first place in the AFC West. The Browns did not run a play inside the Broncos' 40 on their first eight possessions in the first three quarters, by which time they trailed 17-0. Andra Davis intercepted a pass from Jake Plummer and returned it 19 yards to the Broncos' 18. Reuben Droughns had carries for 5 and 7 yards, and on first and goal Charlie Frye tossed a 6-yard touchdown pass to Joe Jurevicius to pull within 17-7 with 11:43 to play. It was just the second touchdown allowed by the Broncos in six games. The Browns got the ball back three more times, but once again failed to cross the Broncos' 40. Plummer was 20 of 41 for 209 yards and 1 touchdown, with 2 interceptions. Javon Walker had 9 receptions for 107 yards. Tatum Bell had 24 carries for 115 yards. Frye was 19 of 33 for 149 yards and 1 touchdown, with 1 interception.

Denver	0	10	7	0	—	17
Cleveland	0	0	0	7	—	7

Den	—	FG Elam 32
Den	—	T. Bell 9 run (Elam kick)
Den	—	Marshall 9 pass from Plummer (Elam kick)
Cle	—	Jurevicius 6 pass from Frye (Dawson kick)

HOUSTON 27, JACKSONVILLE 7—at Reliant Stadium, attendance 70,035. David Carr passed for 2 touchdowns as the Texans posted consecutive home victories for the first time in the franchise's five-year history. The Texans' defense forced Jacksonville to punt at the conclusion of its five first-half possessions, but when Maurice Jones-Drew capped the 70-yard drive to begin the second half with a touchdown, Houston led just 10-7. The Jaguars

drove to the Texans' 22 late in the third quarter when Antwan Peek forced Fred Taylor to fumble. Mario Williams recovered, and Wali Lundy scored his first NFL touchdown eight plays later for a 17-7 lead with 11:32 remaining. On the next play from scrimmage, Ernest Wilford fumbled and Morlon Greenwood recovered at the Jaguars' 26. Three plays later, Owen Daniels caught a 14-yard pass from Carr, to give Houston 14 points in 95 seconds and a 24-7 lead with 9:57 to play. Carr was 25 of 34 for 224 yards and 2 touchdowns. Andre Johnson had 8 catches for 106 yards. Byron Leftwich was 14 of 28 for 125 yards.

Jacksonville	0	0	7	0	—	7
Houston	0	10	0	17	—	27

Hou	—	A. Johnson 35 pass from Carr (K. Brown kick)
Hou	—	FG K. Brown 43
Jax	—	Jones-Drew 1 run (Scobee kick)
Hou	—	Lundy 2 run (K. Brown kick)
Hou	—	Daniels 14 pass from Carr (K. Brown kick)
Hou	—	FG K. Brown 21

INDIANAPOLIS 36, WASHINGTON 22—at RCA Dome, attendance 57,274. Peyton Manning passed for 4 touchdowns as the Colts erased a halftime deficit to remain undefeated. The Colts led 10-7 when Antwaan Randle El returned a punt 87 yards for a touchdown. The Colts responded by scoring on their next five possessions. Adam Vinatieri's 19-yard field goal with eight seconds left in the half cut the deficit to 14-13, and the Colts drove 55, 81, and 66 yards on their second three second half drives, using just a combined 7:14 off the clock, and capped by Manning's 1-yard scoring pass to Marvin Harrison for a 33-14 lead with 2:46 left in the third quarter. His scoring pass to Harrison was the 256th of his career, moving him to tenth place on the all-time touchdown passes list. Mark Brunell was 27 of 37 for 226 yards and 2 touchdowns. Manning was 25 of 35 for 342 yards and 4 touchdowns. Reggie Wayne had 7 receptions for 122 yards.

Washington	0	14	0	8	—	22
Indianapolis	7	6	20	3	—	36

Ind	—	Clark 1 pass from Manning (Vinatieri kick)
Wash	—	Cooley 13 pass from Brunell (Novak kick)
Ind	—	FG Vinatieri 30
Wash	—	Randle El 87 punt return (Novak kick)
Ind	—	FG Vinatieri 19
Ind	—	Harrison 4 pass from Manning (Vinatieri kick)
Ind	—	Wayne 51 pass from Manning (Vinatieri kick)
Ind	—	Harrison 1 pass from Manning (pass failed)
Ind	—	FG Vinatieri 47
Wash	—	Thrash 5 pass from Brunell (Cooley pass from Brunell)

KANSAS CITY 30, SAN DIEGO 27—at Arrowhead Stadium, attendance 77,752. Lawrence Tynes kicked a 53-yard field goal with six seconds remaining as the Chiefs downed the Chargers. San Diego committed turnovers on three of its first four possessions, leading directly to 14 points and a 14-0 Chiefs lead. The Chargers trailed 20-6 at halftime, and scored on their first two possessions of the second half to pull within 27-20 with 13:16 to play. A few drives later, Marques Harris sacked Damon Huard and forced him to fumble. Luis Castillo recovered at the Chiefs' 23 and, five plays later, running back LaDainian Tomlinson lofted a 1-yard touchdown pass to Brandon Manumaleuna to tie the game with 5:10 remaining. With 33 seconds left, the Chargers punted and the Chiefs had the ball on their own 18. Huard completed a 15-yard pass to Larry Johnson, and passes of 19 and 18 yards to Tony Gonzalez to reach the Chargers' 30 with 11 seconds remaining. Tynes made his first game-winning attempt, from 48 yards, but the play was nullified by a false start penalty. Pushed back five yards, Tynes made the 53-yard boot, the longest of his career. Huard was 15 of 27 for 232 yards and 2 touchdowns. Gonzalez had 6 catches for 138 yards. Johnson had 28 carries for 132 yards. Philip Rivers was 25 of 43 for 266 yards and 2 touchdowns, with 1 interception.

San Diego	0	6	7	14	—	27
Kansas City	14	6	7	3	—	30

KC	—	Wilson 11 pass from Huard (Tynes kick)
KC	—	Kennison 21 pass from Huard (Tynes kick)
SD	—	FG Kaeding 39
KC	—	L. Johnson 11 run (kick failed)
SD	—	FG Kaeding 31
SD	—	Gates 1 pass from Rivers (Kaeding kick)
KC	—	L. Johnson 1 run (Tynes kick)
SD	—	Tomlinson 37 pass from Rivers (Kaeding kick)
SD	—	Manumaleuna 1 pass from Tomlinson (Kaeding kick)
KC	—	FG Tynes 53

GREEN BAY 34, MIAMI 24—at Dolphin Stadium, attendance 73,548. Brett Favre passed for 2 touchdowns, and the Packers' defense intercepted 3 passes, as Green Bay defeated the Dolphins in Miami for the first time in seven games. The Dolphins led 10-6 at halftime, with both of Green Bay's field goals having been set up by interceptions. Two plays into the second half, Charles Woodson intercepted Joey Harrington's pass and returned it 23 yards for a touchdown. It was Woodson's first interception return for a touchdown since 1999. The Dolphins did not fold, and eventually pulled within 20-16 early in the fourth quarter. However, on the next play from scrimmage Ahman Green ran 70 yards over left tackle for a touchdown and 27-16 lead with 13:14 remaining. The Dolphins needed just five plays to cut the deficit to three points with 11:56 to play and hand the Packers in a fourth-and-1 situation on the Miami 40-yard-line. The Packers went for the first down, and Donald Driver got it on a 6-yard end around. Four plays later, Favre found David Martin for a touchdown and 34-24 lead with 6:11 left. The Dolphins reached the Packers' 29, but on fourth-and-2 a delay of game penalty pushed Miami back 5 yards. Olindo Mare then tried a 52-yard field-goal attempt, but it hit the left upright with 2:06 to play. Favre was 19 of 35 for 206 yards and 2 touchdowns. Driver had 10 catches for 93 yards. Green carried 18 times for 118 yards. Harrington was 33 of 62, a franchise record for attempts, for 414 yards and 2 touchdowns, with 3 interceptions. Marty Booker had 7 receptions for 110 yards.

Green Bay	0	6	14	14	—	34
Miami	7	3	3	11	—	24

Mia	—	Booker 8 pass from Harrington (Mare kick)
GB	—	FG Rayner 42
GB	—	FG Rayner 34
Mia	—	FG Mare 32
GB	—	Woodson 23 interception return (Rayner kick)
GB	—	Driver 34 pass from Favre (Rayner kick)
Mia	—	FG Mare 40
Mia	—	FG Mare 45
GB	—	Green 70 run (Rayner kick)
Mia	—	Hagan 13 pass from Harrington (Booker pass from Harrington)
GB	—	Martin 13 pass from Favre (Rayner kick)

N.Y. JETS 31, DETROIT 24—at The Meadowlands, attendance 76,953. Rookie Leon Washington rushed for 129 yards and 2 touchdowns, the first of his career, as the Jets matched their 2005 victory total. The Jets scored on three of their first four possessions en route to a 21-7 halftime lead. The teams exchanged field goals, then touchdowns, in the second half, with the Lions pulling to

within 31-24 on Jon Kitna's 18-yard touchdown pass to Mike Furrey with 2:22 to play. Washington ran 9 yards on second-and-5 to get the final first down needed to run out the clock. Chad Pennington was 16 of 22 for 189 yards and 1 touchdown, with 1 interception. Washington had 20 carries for 129 yards. Kitna was 22 of 36 for 269 yards and 3 touchdowns, with 2 interceptions. Furrey had 9 catches for 109 yards.

Detroit	0	7	3	14	—	24
N.Y. Jets	14	7	0	10	—	31

NYJ	—	Washington 5 run (Nugent kick)
NYJ	—	McCareins 44 pass from Pennington (Nugent kick)
Det	—	R. Williams 22 pass from Kitna (Hanson kick)
NYJ	—	Barlow 3 run (Nugent kick)
Det	—	FG Hanson 25
NYJ	—	FG Nugent 33
Det	—	K. Jones 9 pass from Kitna (Hanson kick)
NYJ	—	Washington 16 run (Nugent kick)
Det	—	Furrey 18 pass from Kitna (Hanson kick)

OAKLAND 22, ARIZONA 9—at McAfee Coliseum, attendance 61,595. Andrew Walter passed for 263 yards and 1 touchdown as the Raiders snapped an 11-game losing streak and Art Shell recorded his first coaching victory since 1994. The Raiders' defense allowed just 9 first downs, while the offense, despite committing 5 turnovers, maintained possession for 37:01. Leading 7-0, Derrick Burgess tipped a pass and Terdell Sands intercepted it. On the next play, Walter connected on a 32-yard scoring pass deep down the right side to Randy Moss for a 14-0 lead. Leading 20-3, the Raiders sacked Matt Leinart on consecutive plays for losses of 10 and 9 yards to push the Cardinals back to their own 1-yard line. On third-and-29, Michael Huff tackled Marcel Shipp in the end zone for a safety. Walter was 17 of 30 for 263 yards and 1 touchdown, with 1 interception. Moss had 7 catches for 129 yards. Leinart was 13 of 32 for 203 yards, with 2 interceptions.

Arizona	0	3	3	3	—	9
Oakland	14	3	5	0	—	22

Oak	—	Lee 1 run (Janikowski kick)
Oak	—	Moss 32 pass from Walter (Janikowski kick)
Oak	—	FG Janikowski 31
Ariz	—	FG Rackers 29
Oak	—	FG Janikowski 35
Oak	—	Safety, Huff tackled Shipp in end zone
Ariz	—	FG Rackers 45
Ariz	—	FG Rackers 38

MINNESOTA 31, SEATTLE 13—at Qwest Field, attendance 68,118. Chester Taylor had a franchise-record-long 95-yard touchdown run as the Vikings surprised the Seahawks. With the score 10-10, Matt Hasselbeck injured his knee three plays into the third quarter when a Vikings' pass rusher was pushed into him. The Vikings scored on their next possession when running back Mewelde Moore completed a 15-yard touchdown pass to Jermaine Wiggins. With 5:06 left in the third quarter, leading 17-10, Taylor took a handoff, bounced outside around left end and raced 95 yards for a touchdown. The Seahawks responded with a field goal, and had the ball on their own 9-yard-line with 8:00 left when Ben Leber blindsided Seneca Wallace and forced him to fumble. Kevin Williams recovered the ball in the end zone for a 31-13 lead. Brad Johnson was 15 of 24 for 171 yards and 1 touchdown. Hasselbeck was 7 of 17 for 127 yards and 1 touchdown. Wallace replaced him after the injury and was 14 of 25 for 134 yards, with 2 interceptions. Darrell Jackson had 7 catches for 136 yards.

Minnesota	3	7	14	7	—	31
Seattle	7	3	0	3	—	13

Minn	—	FG Longwell 33
Sea	—	Jackson 72 pass from

	Hasselbeck (J. Brown kick)
Sea	—	FG J. Brown 42
Minn	—	M. Robinson 40 pass from B. Johnson (Longwell kick)
Minn	—	Wiggins 15 pass from Moore (Longwell kick)
Minn	—	Taylor 95 run (Longwell kick)
Sea	—	FG J. Brown 26
Minn	—	K. Williams fumble recovery in end zone (Longwell kick)

TAMPA BAY 23, PHILADELPHIA 21—at Raymond James Stadium, attendance 65,808. Matt Bryant kicked a game-winning 62-yard field goal as time expired, and Ronde Barber returned 2 interceptions for touchdowns, as the Eagles lost on a last-play field goal for the second consecutive week. The Eagles outgained the Buccaneers 506-196 in total yards, but Tampa Bay forced 4 turnovers. The Eagles reached the Buccaneers' 6 just before halftime, but L.J. Smith was tackled at the 2-yard line after catching a short pass and the half ran out with Tampa Bay up 7-0. The Buccaneers increased the lead to 17-0 with 5:19 left in the third quarter on Barber's second scoring return, this one down the right sideline. The Eagles responded with touchdown drives of 79, 72, and 80 yards, the last of which culminated with Brian Westbrook breaking five tackles en route to a 52-yard catch of a screen pass that resulted in a touchdown and 21-20 lead with 33 seconds left. Bruce Gradkowski scrambled 9 yards to get to the Eagles' 44 with 10 seconds left. After an incomplete pass, Bryant trotted onto the field and drilled a 62-yard field goal, the third-longest kick in NFL history. Gradkowski was 13 of 26 for 104 yards. McNabb was 22 of 35 for 302 yards and 3 touchdowns, with 3 interceptions. Westbrook became just the fourth player since 1987 to finish with at 100 receiving yards (7 catches for 113 yards) and rushing yards (13 carries for 101 yards) in the same game.

Philadelphia	0	0	7	14	—	21
Tampa Bay	0	7	10	6	—	23

TB	—	R. Barber 37 interception return (Bryant kick)
TB	—	FG Bryant 30
TB	—	R. Barber 66 interception return (Bryant kick)
Phil	—	Tapeh 12 pass from McNabb (Akers kick)
Phil	—	R. Brown 7 pass from McNabb (Akers kick)
TB	—	FG Bryant 44
Phil	—	Westbrook 52 pass from McNabb (Akers kick)
TB	—	FG Bryant 62

MONDAY NIGHT, OCTOBER 23
N.Y. GIANTS 36, DALLAS 22—at Texas Stadium, attendance 63,512. The Giants' defense registered 6 sacks and intercepted 4 passes which resulted in 17 points, highlighted by Kevin Dockery's 96-yard touchdown return, as New York moved into first place in the NFC East. The Giants led 12-0 in the second quarter, but the Cowboys drove 80 yards for a touchdown and then Bradie James recovered a fumble at the Giants' 14. But on second-and-goal from the 4-yard line just before half-time, Sam Madison intercepted Drew Bledsoe's pass. The Cowboys inserted Tony Romo at quarterback in the second half, and his first pass was tipped by Michael Strahan and intercepted by Antonio Pierce. Three plays later, Jeremey Shockey caught a touchdown pass from Eli Manning for a 19-7 lead. The Cowboys fell behind 26-7, but cut it to 26-15 and got the ball back with 11:19 to play. The Cowboys reached the Giants' 34 but Fred Robbins intercepted Romo's pass. Jay Feely capitalized on the turnover with a 32-yard field goal with 3:54 remaining. In less than one minute the Cowboys drove to the Giants' 11 and had a chance to cut the deficit to seven points, but Dockery stepped in front of a pass intended for Patrick Crayton and raced untouched 96 yards with his first interception to give the Giants a 36-15 lead with 2:33

remaining. Manning was 12 of 26 for 189 yards and 2 touchdowns, with 1 interception. Tiki Barber rushed 27 times for 114 yards. Bledsoe was 7 of 12 for 111 yards, with 1 interception. Romo was 14 of 25 for 227 yards and 2 touchdowns, with 3 interceptions.

N.Y. Giants	9	3	14	10	—	36
Dallas	0	7	0	15	—	22

NYG	—	Burress 50 pass from Manning (Feely kick)
NYG	—	Safety, Arrington sacked Bledsoe in end zone
NYG	—	FG Feely 31
Dall	—	Bledsoe 1 run (Vanderjagt kick)
NYG	—	Shockey 13 pass from Manning (Feely kick)
NYG	—	Jacobs 3 run (Feely kick)
Dall	—	Owens 8 pass from Romo (Romo run)
NYG	—	FG Feely 32
NYG	—	Dockery 96 interception return (Feely kick)
Dall	—	Crayton 53 pass from Romo (Vanderjagt kick)

EIGHTH WEEK SUMMARIES
American Football Conference

East Division	W	L	T	Pct.	Pts.	OP
New England	6	1	0	.857	167	87
N.Y. Jets	4	4	0	.500	160	193
Buffalo	2	5	0	.286	100	153
Miami	1	6	0	.143	102	145
North Division	**W**	**L**	**T**	**Pct.**	**Pts.**	**OP**
Baltimore	5	2	0	.714	145	91
Cincinnati	4	3	0	.571	155	142
Cleveland	5	2	0	.286	108	139
Pittsburgh	2	5	0	.286	157	145
South Division	**W**	**L**	**T**	**Pct.**	**Pts.**	**OP**
Indianapolis	7	0	0	1.000	205	153
Jacksonville	4	3	0	.571	138	107
Houston	2	5	0	.286	121	182
Tennessee	2	5	0	.286	113	179
West Division	**W**	**L**	**T**	**Pct.**	**Pts.**	**OP**
Denver	5	2	0	.714	110	78
San Diego	5	2	0	.714	216	109
Kansas City	4	3	0	.571	152	152
Oakland	2	5	0	.286	92	148

National Football Conference

East Division	W	L	T	Pct.	Pts.	OP
N.Y. Giants	5	2	0	.714	180	134
Dallas	4	3	0	.571	204	142
Philadelphia	4	4	0	.500	206	160
Washington	2	5	0	.286	140	171
North Division	**W**	**L**	**T**	**Pct.**	**Pts.**	**OP**
Chicago	7	0	0	1.000	221	69
Minnesota	4	3	0	.571	127	126
Green Bay	3	4	0	.429	152	176
Detroit	1	6	0	.143	132	189
South Division	**W**	**L**	**T**	**Pct.**	**Pts.**	**OP**
Atlanta	5	2	0	.714	153	134
New Orleans	5	2	0	.714	167	145
Carolina	4	4	0	.500	137	163
Tampa Bay	2	5	0	.286	88	142
West Division	**W**	**L**	**T**	**Pct.**	**Pts.**	**OP**
St. Louis	4	3	0	.571	163	166
Seattle	4	3	0	.571	149	177
San Francisco	2	5	0	.286	134	235
Arizona	1	7	0	.125	134	196

SUNDAY, OCTOBER 29

CHICAGO 41, SAN FRANCISCO 10—at Soldier Field, attendance 62,200. The Bears scored on seven of their eight first-half possessions, and established a club record with 24 first-quarter points, en route to a 41-0 lead and matched their best start (5-0) since 1985. The Bears forced 5 turnovers and the offense held the ball for 37:05. Four of the turnovers occurred in the first half, and all 4 led to touchdowns. At halftime, the Bears had a 289-74 advantage in total yards, and had 17 first downs compared to 2 for the 49ers. The tone was set early, as the

Bears opened the game with a field goal and Maurice Hicks fumbled the ensuing kickoff return. Cameron Worrell recovered and Thomas Jones scored three plays later for a 10-0 lead with 10:39 remaining in the first quarter. The Bears scored 14 points in 53 seconds later in the quarter, with Tommie Harris' fumble recovery coming in between the touchdowns, to take a 24-0 lead. The Bears capped the half by driving 70 yards in four plays, with Rex Grossman's 27-yard touchdown pass to Desmond Clark giving the Bears a 41-0 lead with 10 seconds left in the half. Grossman was 23 of 29 for 252 yards and 3 touchdowns. Jones rushed 23 times for 111 yards. Alex Smith was 14 of 25 for 135 yards and 1 touchdown, with 1 interception. Frank Gore rushed 12 times for 111 yards.

San Francisco	0	0	0	10	—	10
Chicago	24	17	0	0	—	41

Chi	—	FG Gould 43
Chi	—	T. Jones 7 run (Gould kick)
Chi	—	Muhammad 5 pass from Grossman (Gould kick)
Chi	—	Benson 1 run (Gould kick)
Chi	—	Clark 1 pass from Grossman (Gould kick)
Chi	—	FG Gould 36
Chi	—	Clark 27 pass from Grossman (Gould kick)
SF	—	FG Nedney 23
SF	—	Bryant 16 pass from A. Smith (Nedney kick)

ATLANTA 29, CINCINNATI 27—at Paul Brown Stadium, attendance 65,978. Michael Vick passed for 3 touchdowns as the Falcons won their second consecutive game. Not counting a two-play possession at the end of the half, the Falcons scored three consecutive drives, erasing a 14-6 deficit and taking a 26-20 lead with 2:21 left in the third quarter when Vick escaped the pass rush and lofted a 26-yard touchdown pass to Michael Jenkins. After Morten Andersen's 39-yard field goal, and an exchange of punts, Carson Palmer completed a 55-yard post pattern pass to Chris Henry to pull within two points with 3:41 to play. Vick completed a 17-yard pass to Alge Crumpler on second-and-9 for a key first down. The Bengals did not get the ball back until 19 seconds remained at their own 17-yard-line. Vick was 19 of 27 for 291 yards and 3 touchdowns. Palmer was 24 of 36 for 266 yards and 2 touchdowns.

Atlanta	6	7	13	3	—	29
Cincinnati	7	10	3	7	—	27

Atl	—	FG Andersen 42
Cin	—	R. Johnson 1 run (Graham kick)
Atl	—	FG Andersen 40
Cin	—	C. Johnson 12 pass from Palmer (Graham kick)
Atl	—	Crumpler 16 pass from Vick (Andersen kick)
Cin	—	FG Graham 51
Atl	—	Jenkins 26 pass from Vick (Andersen kick)
Cin	—	FG Graham 26
Atl	—	Griffith 8 pass from Vick (pass failed)
Atl	—	FG Andersen 39
Cin	—	Henry 55 pass from Palmer (Graham kick)

CLEVELAND 20, N.Y. JETS 13—at Cleveland Browns Stadium, attendance 72,507. The Browns' defense allowed just 193 yards, 3 turnovers, and no touchdowns as the Browns outlasted the Jets. The Browns scored on their first two drives for a 10-3 lead, and Charlie Frye's 30-yard touchdown pass to Kellen Winslow capped the opening drive of the second half for a 17-3 lead. Later in the quarter, Kamerion Wimbley recovered Leon Washington's fumble at the Jets' 9 to set up Phil Dawson's 21-yard field goal. The Jets answered with Justin Miller's 99-yard kickoff return for a touchdown and, after a punt, Mike Nugent drilled a 47-yard field goal to pull within 20-13 with 12:54 to play. The Jets reached the Browns' 24 with

1:14 left, but Chad Pennington threw 3 consecutive incomplete passes, the last caught just out of the end zone by Chris Baker with 59 seconds left, to end the threat. Frye was 15 of 22 for 141 yards and 1 touchdown, with 1 interception. Droughns rushed 33 times for 125 yards. Pennington was 11 of 28 for 108 yards, with 2 interceptions.

N.Y. Jets	3	0	7	3	—	13
Cleveland	3	7	10	0	—	20

NYJ	—	FG Nugent 27
Cle	—	FG Dawson 47
Cle	—	Droughns 2 run (Dawson kick)
Cle	—	Winslow 30 pass from Frye (Dawson kick)
Cle	—	FG Dawson 21
NYJ	—	Miller 99 kickoff return (Nugent kick)
NYJ	—	FG Nugent 47

INDIANAPOLIS 34, DENVER 31—at INVESCO Field at Mile High, attendance 76,767. Peyton Manning completed 3 touchdown passes to Reggie Wayne and Adam Vinatieri kicked a 37-yard field goal with two seconds remaining as the Colts became the first team to begin consecutive seasons with a 7-0 record since the 1929-1931 Green Bay Packers. The Broncos rushed for 227 yards, but still were outgained 437-396 in total yards. The Colts punted at the end of their first drive, had a one-play kneeldown at halftime, but otherwise scored on their other seven possessions against a team that had allowed just 44 points in its first six games. The Broncos led 14-6 at halftime, and were up 14-13 in the third quarter when Jake Plummer was sacked and fumbled. Raheem Brock recovered at the Broncos' 12, and three plays later Manning connected with Wayne on a 5-yard touchdown pass. The Broncos responded with touchdown drives of 91 and 80 yards, both capped by 1-yard runs by Mike Bell, to take a 28-23 lead with 6:54 remaining. Manning completed 3 passes to Wayne on the ensuing seven-play drive, which culminated with Wayne's third touchdown, and also the two-point conversion, to take a 31-28 lead with 3:35 left. Bell ran for 48 yards on the next play from scrimmage, and Jason Elam's 49-yard field goal tied the game with 1:49 remaining. Manning completed all 5 pass attempts on the final eight-play drive, and Joseph Addai had a 10-yard run to the Broncos' 18, to set up Vinatieri's winning kick. Manning was 32 of 39 for 345 yards and 3 touchdowns. Wayne had 10 receptions for 138 yards. Plummer was 13 of 21 for 174 yards. Bell rushed 15 times for 136 yards.

Indianapolis	3	3	14	14	—	34
Denver	0	14	7	10	—	31

Ind	—	FG Vinatieri 42
Den	—	Plummer 1 run (Elam kick)
Ind	—	FG Vinatieri 30
Den	—	Walker 15 pass from Plummer (Elam kick)
Ind	—	Wayne 12 pass from Manning (Vinatieri kick)
Ind	—	Wayne 5 pass from Manning (Vinatieri kick)
Den	—	M. Bell 1 run (Elam kick)
Ind	—	FG Vinatieri 48
Den	—	M. Bell 1 run (Elam kick)
Ind	—	Wayne 19 pass from Manning (Wayne pass from Manning)
Den	—	FG Elam 49
Ind	—	FG Vinatieri 37

GREEN BAY 31, ARIZONA 14—at Lambeau Field, attendance 70,809. Ahman Green rushed for 2 touchdowns and Brett Favre passed for a touchdown and ran for another as the Cardinals dropped their seventh consecutive game. The Packers scored on four consecutive possessions, not counting a one-play kneeldown at the end of the half, to take a 28-7 lead on Favre's 1-yard rollout, followed by an attempted Lambeau Leap, with 7:41 left in the third quarter. The Packers' 4 touchdown drives covered 88, 70, 87, and 74 yards, and averaged 10 plays. The

Packers' defense allowed just 218 yards and registered 4 sacks. Favre was 17 of 25 for 180 yards and 1 touchdown. Green rushed 21 times for 106 yards, and Vernand Morency had 11 carries for 101 yards. It was the first time since 1985 the Packers had two 100-yard rushers in the same game. Leinart was 14 of 35 for 157 yards and 1 touchdown, with 1 interception.

Arizona	0	7	7	0	—	14
Green Bay	7	14	7	3	—	31

GB — Martin 1 pass from Favre (Rayner kick)
GB — Green 4 run (Rayner kick)
GB — Green 2 run (Rayner kick)
Ariz — James 1 run (Rackers kick)
GB — Favre 1 run (Rayner kick)
Ariz — Walters 17 pass from Leinart (Rackers kick)
GB — FG Rayner 42

KANSAS CITY 35, SEATTLE 28—at Arrowhead Stadium, attendance 77,645. Larry Johnson scored 4 touchdowns and the Chiefs rolled up 499 yards of offense, and had the ball for 42:15, to hand the Seahawks their second consecutive defeat. The Seahawks played without Matt Hasselbeck and Shaun Alexander, both of whom were injured. Seattle needed to drive just 7 yards, thanks to a fumble recovery, to set up its first touchdown. The Chiefs scored on their five of their first six possessions and led 27-14 as they lined up for a field goal late in the third quarter. Holder Dustin Colquitt bobbled the snap and then rolled out and attempted to pass the ball, but it slipped out of his hand and was picked up by Kelly Herndon, who returned it 61 yards for a touchdown to trim the deficit to 27-21. Lawrence Tynes missed a 50-yard field-goal attempt in the middle of the fourth quarter, and Seneca Wallace connected on a 49-yard touchdown pass to a wide open Darrell Jackson to give the Seahawks a 28-27 lead with 6:30 to play. The Chiefs answered with an 80-yard drive, keyed by Eddie Kennison's 51-yard catch, and capped by Johnson's fourth touchdown, with 2:15 to play. The Seahawks drove to the Chiefs' 46, but on fourth-and-15, Wallace threw underneath the coverage to Mack Strong, who gained 8 yards before being gang tackled with 53 seconds left to clinch the victory. Damon Huard was 17 of 25 for 312 yards and 1 touchdown. Johnson carried 39 times for 155 yards. Kennison had 6 catches for 132 yards, and Tony Gonzalez had 6 catches for 116 yards. Wallace, making his first start, was 15 of 30 for 198 yards and 3 touchdowns, with 2 interceptions.

Seattle	7	7	7	7	—	28
Kansas City	10	10	7	8	—	35

KC — FG Tynes 38
Sea — Hackett 8 pass from Wallace (J. Brown kick)
KC — L. Johnson 3 run (Tynes kick)
KC — FG Tynes 32
Sea — Stevens 2 pass from Wallace (J. Brown kick)
KC — L. Johnson 9 pass from Huard (Tynes kick)
KC — L. Johnson 2 run (Tynes kick)
Sea — Herndon 61 fumble return (J. Brown kick)
Sea — D. Jackson 49 pass from Wallace (J. Brown kick)
KC — L. Johnson 3 run (Gonzalez pass from Huard)

BALTIMORE 35, NEW ORLEANS 22—at Louisiana Superdome, attendance 69,152. Steve McNair passed for 2 touchdowns and ran for another as the Ravens scored 2 defensive touchdowns to snap a two-game losing streak. The Saints gained 403 yards, but 262 of those yards came once the Saints fell behind 35-7. The Ravens' defense forced 5 turnovers, 4 of which led to 28 points. Chris McAlister recovered Drew Brees' fumble near midfield to set up the first touchdown. Reggie Bush's halfback option pass was intercepted in the end zone by Ray Lewis that led to the second touchdown. Rookie Ronnie Prude's 12-yard interception return gave the Ravens a 21-0 lead with 6:09 left in the half. It was 28-7 at halftime, and rookie Dawan Landry intercepted Brees' pass and returned it 12 yards for a touchdown and 35-7 lead with 8:05 remaining in the third quarter. McNair was 17 of 23 for 159 yards and 2 touchdowns. Jamal Lewis carried 31 times for 109 yards. Brees was 24 of 45 for 383 yards and 3 touchdowns, with 3 interceptions. Marques Colston had 6 receptions for 163 yards, and Joe Horn had 5 catches for 126 yards.

Baltimore	7	21	7	0	—	35
New Orleans	0	7	0	15	—	22

Balt — McNair 5 run (Stover kick)
Balt — Moore 4 pass from McNair (Stover kick)
Balt — Prude 12 interception return (Stover kick)
NO — Horn 32 pass from Brees (Carney kick)
Balt — Heap 6 pass from McNair (Stover kick)
Balt — Landry 12 interception return (Stover kick)
NO — Colston 47 pass from Brees (Carney kick)
NO — Colston 25 pass from Brees (B. Miller pass from Brees)

N.Y. GIANTS 17, TAMPA BAY 3—at Giants Stadium, attendance 78,647. The Giants' defense allowed just 174 yards and limited the Buccaneers' to 2 of 16 on third-down conversions in a game played in 40 mile-per-hour wind gusts. The Buccaneers did not have a first down until their seventh possession, by which time the Giants led 14-0. The second touchdown was set up by Fred Robbins' recovery of a fumbled pitchout at the Buccaneers' 28. Matt Bryant kicked a field goal just before halftime, but Tampa Bay never ran a play in the Giants' red zone, and were stopped on downs three times, as both teams punted 9 times. Eli Manning was 16 of 31 for 154 yards and 1 touchdown. Bruce Gradkowski was 20 of 48 for 139 yards.

Tampa Bay	0	3	0	0	—	3
N.Y. Giants	7	7	0	3	—	17

NYG — Burress 7 pass from E. Manning (Feely kick)
NYG — Jacobs 1 run (Feely kick)
TB — FG Bryant 43
NYG — FG Feely 31

OAKLAND 20, PITTSBURGH 13—at McAfee Coliseum, attendance 62,385. The Raiders returned 2 interceptions for touchdowns to win their second consecutive game despite gaining just 98 total yards of offense. The Raiders were outgained by the Steelers 360-98 in yards, but Oakland's defense forced 4 turnovers. The Raiders intercepted 2 first-quarter passes, including Nnamdi Asomugha's 24-yard return for a touchdown. The Steelers cut the deficit to 7-6, but Chris Carr returned the ensuing kickoff 50 yards to set up Sebastian Janikowski's 19-yard field goal just before halftime. The Raiders benefited from two unsportsmanlike conduct penalties to begin the second half that led to Janikowski's second field goal. Kirk Morrison intercepted Ben Roethlisberger's pass at the Raiders' 39 to begin the fourth quarter. The Steelers then drove to the Raiders' 7, but Carr intercepted Roethlisberger's third-and-goal pass and returned it untouched 100 yards down the right sideline for a 20-6 lead with 9:32 to play. Pittsburgh answered with Roethlisberger's 25-yard touchdown pass to Willie Parker, and then Joey Porter intercepted a pass with 5:29 remaining. The Steelers drove to the Raiders' 1, but Robert Thomas made two big tackles, and on fourth-and-goal from the Raiders' 3 Morrison knocked down Roethlisberger's pass. Pittsburgh's final possession began with 36 seconds left. From their own 47 with five seconds left, Roethlisberger's Hail Mary pass was caught by Nate Washington at the Raiders' 4, but Carr tackled him to end the game. Walter was 5 of 14 for 51 yards, with 1 interception. Roethlisberger was 25 of 37 for 301 yards and 1 touchdown, with 4 interceptions.

Pittsburgh	0	6	0	7	—	13
Oakland	7	3	3	7	—	20

Oak — Asomugha 24 interception return (Janikowski kick)
Pitt — FG Reed 29
Pitt — FG Reed 39
Oak — FG Janikowski 19
Oak — FG Janikowski 41
Oak — Carr 100 interception return (Janikowski kick)
Pitt — Parker 25 pass from Roethlisberger (Reed kick)

JACKSONVILLE 13, PHILADELPHIA 6—at Lincoln Financial Field, attendance 69,249. The Jaguars' defense limited the NFL's top-ranked offense to 227 yards to hand the Eagles their third consecutive defeat. Fred Taylor capped the Jaguars' first drive with a 15-yard touchdown run up the middle. The drive was kept alive by David Garrard's 13-yard run on fourth-and-3. The Eagles only had 4 first downs in their first eight possessions to fall behind 10-0, but David Akers' 25-yard field goal cut the deficit to 10-3 late in the third quarter. The Jaguars responded with a 62-yard scoring drive, capped by Josh Scobee's 27-yard field goal with 9:28 to play. After an exchange of punts, Akers kicked another field goal with 31 seconds left, but Daryl Smith recovered the onside kick to clinch the victory. Garrard, starting in place of an injured Byron Leftwich, was 10 of 17 for 87 yards. Taylor rushed 15 times for 103 yards. Donovan McNabb was 18 of 34 for 161 yards.

Jacksonville	7	0	3	3	—	13
Philadelphia	0	0	3	3	—	6

Jax — Taylor 15 run (Scobee kick)
Jax — FG Scobee 40
Phil — FG Akers 25
Jax — FG Scobee 27
Phil — FG Akers 28

SAN DIEGO 38, ST. LOUIS 24—at Qualcomm Stadium, attendance 66,598. LaDainian Tomlinson scored 3 touchdowns and Marlon McCree had a key fumble return for a score as the Chargers caught the Broncos in the AFC West standings. There was only 1 turnover in the game, and it occurred in the third quarter when Stephen Davis fumbled. McCree fell on the ball, quickly got to his feet in traffic, found a wedge to get to the right sideline, and raced 79 yards for a touchdown and 21-3 lead. The Rams responded with a field goal, but the Chargers scored on their next two possessions, culminated by Michael Turner's 14-yard run to cap an 84-yard drive and give the Chargers a 31-10 lead with 11:44 to play. The Rams cut the deficit to 31-17, but Tomlinson recovered the onside kick and then five plays later, on third-and-8, caught a 25-yard touchdown pass from Philip Rivers with 3:58 remaining for a 21-point lead. Rivers was 15 of 23 for 206 yards and 1 touchdown. Tomlinson carried 25 times for 183 yards. Marc Bulger was 27 of 40 for 327 yards and 2 touchdowns. Isaac Bruce had 5 catches for 105 yards.

St. Louis	0	7	3	14	—	24
San Diego	14	0	10	14	—	38

SD — Tomlinson 2 run (Kaeding kick)
SD — Tomlinson 38 run (Kaeding kick)
StL — S. Jackson 3 run (Wilkins kick)
SD — McCree 79 fumble return (Kaeding kick)
StL — FG Wilkins 34
SD — FG Kaeding 31
SD — Turner 14 run (Kaeding kick)
StL — McDonald 7 pass from Bulger (Wilkins kick)
SD — Tomlinson 25 pass from Rivers (Kaeding kick)
StL — Curtis 6 pass from Bulger (Wilkins kick)

TENNESSEE 28, HOUSTON 22—at LP Field, attendance 69,143. The Titans were outgained 427-197 in total yards, but forced 5 turnovers and scored a touchdown on defense and special teams to win consecutive games for the first time since the end of 2003, a span of 39 games. The Titans led 7-3 as the first half was winding down. On third-and-13 from his own 46, David Carr dropped back to pass. Kyle Vanden Bosch sacked Carr, forced him to fumble, and Tony Brown picked up the ball and ran 40 yards for a touchdown with eight seconds left in the half for a 14-3 lead. Carr fumbled on the Texans' first drive of the second half and he was replaced by Sage Rosenfels. However, Adam Jones intercepted Rosenfels' first pass attempt, and three plays later Vince Young completed a 20-yard touchdown pass to Bobby Wade for a 21-3 lead. The Texans pulled within 21-10, but Jones bounced the lead back to 18 points with a 53-yard punt return down the left sideline for a touchdown with 10:52 remaining. The Texans scored on their next two drives to cut the deficit to 28-22 with 1:54 left, but Wade recovered the onside kick to clinch the victory. Young was 7 of 15 for 87 yards and 1 touchdown. Carr was 15 of 21 for 113 yards, with 1 interception. Rosenfels was 18 of 25 for 186 yards and 3 touchdowns, with 1 interception. Wali Lundy carried 18 times for 116 yards.

Houston	0	3	7	12	—	22
Tennessee	0	14	7	7	—	28

Tenn	—	Young 20 run (Bironas kick)
Hou	—	FG K. Brown 27
Tenn	—	T. Brown 40 fumble return (Bironas kick)
Tenn	—	Wade 20 pass from Young (Bironas kick)
Hou	—	A. Johnson 10 pass from Rosenfels (K. Brown kick)
Tenn	—	A. Jones 53 punt return (Bironas kick)
Hou	—	Daniels 1 pass from Rosenfels (kick blocked)
Hou	—	Daniels 2 pass from Rosenfels (pass failed)

SUNDAY NIGHT, OCTOBER 29

DALLAS 35, CAROLINA 14—at Bank of America Stadium, attendance 73,682. The Cowboys scored 25 points in a span of 7:15 of the fourth quarter to defeat the Panthers. The Cowboys outgained the Panthers 414-204 in total yards and had a 38:16-21:44 time of possession advantage. The Panthers scored 2 touchdowns within 2:14 of the first quarter to take a 14-0 lead, but did not cross the Cowboys' 37 the rest of the game. Carolina still led 14-10 entering the fourth quarter. The Cowboys cut the deficit to 14-13 with Mike Vanderjagt's field goal with 9:47 left. On the ensuing kickoff, Brad Hoover fumbled and Sam Hurd recovered. On the next play, Julius Jones scored on a 14-yard run. Tony Romo's two-point conversion pass to Terrell Owens extended the lead to 21-14. Roy Williams intercepted a pass later in the quarter and Marion Barber gained 9 yards on third-and-8 to set up his own 3-yard touchdown run with 2:17 left. Greg Ellis sacked Jake Delhomme two plays later, Delhomme fumbled and Jay Ratliff recovered to set up Barber's second touchdown run in 40 seconds, to give Dallas a 35-14 lead with 1:37 to play. Romo, making his first start, was 24 of 36 for 270 yards and 1 touchdown, with 1 interception. Owens had 9 catches for 107 yards. Delhomme was 17 of 31 for 149 yards, with 1 interception.

Dallas	0	10	0	25	—	35
Carolina	14	0	0	0	—	14

Car	—	Foster 1 run (Kasay kick)
Car	—	S. Smith 24 run (Kasay kick)
Dall	—	Witten 3 pass from Romo (Vanderjagt kick)
Dall	—	FG Vanderjagt 38
Dall	—	FG Vanderjagt 24
Dall	—	J. Jones 14 run (Owens pass from Romo)
Dall	—	Barber 3 run (Vanderjagt kick)
Dall	—	Barber 14 run (Vanderjagt kick)

MONDAY NIGHT, OCTOBER 30

NEW ENGLAND 31, MINNESOTA 7—at Metrodome, attendance 63,819. Tom Brady passed for 372 yards and 4 touchdowns as the Patriots rolled past the Vikings. The Patriots outgained the Vikings 430-284 in total yards, with Brady completing passes to 10 different players, and the defense intercepted 4 passes and registered 4 sacks. The Vikings, trailing 7-0, had a scoring chance in the first quarter when Darren Sharper intercepted a pass near midfield, but Rodney Harrison intercepted Brad Johnson's pass in the end zone on third-and-goal to stop the threat. The Patriots drove 93 and 74 yards on two of their next three possessions to take a 17-0 halftime lead. Mewelde Moore gave the Vikings a chance when he returned a punt 71 yards for a touchdown in the third quarter, but Laurence Maroney returned the ensuing kickoff 77 yards and Brady tossed a 7-yard touchdown pass to Troy Brown three plays later to give New England a 24-7 lead. Brady was 29 of 43 for 372 yards and 4 touchdowns, with 1 interception. Johnson was 20 of 33 for 185 yards, with 3 interceptions. Brooks Bollinger played the last three series and was 6 of 9 for 76 yards, with 1 interception.

New England	7	10	14	0	—	31
Minnesota	0	0	7	0	—	7

NE	—	Caldwell 6 pass from Brady (Gostkowski kick)
NE	—	FG Gostkowski 23
NE	—	Watson 9 pass from Brady (Gostkowski kick)
Minn	—	M. Moore 71 punt return (Longwell kick)
NE	—	T. Brown 7 pass from Brady (Gostkowski kick)
NE	—	C. Jackson 10 pass from Brady (Gostkowski kick)

NINTH WEEK SUMMARIES
American Football Conference

East Division	W	L	T	Pct.	Pts.	OP
New England	6	2	0	.750	187	114
N.Y. Jets	4	4	0	.500	160	193
Buffalo	3	5	0	.375	124	163
Miami	2	6	0	.250	133	158
North Division	**W**	**L**	**T**	**Pct.**	**Pts.**	**OP**
Baltimore	6	2	0	.750	171	111
Cincinnati	4	4	0	.500	175	168
Cleveland	2	6	0	.250	133	171
Pittsburgh	2	6	0	.250	177	176
South Division	**W**	**L**	**T**	**Pct.**	**Pts.**	**OP**
Indianapolis	8	0	0	1.000	232	173
Jacksonville	5	3	0	.625	175	114
Houston	2	6	0	.250	131	196
Tennessee	2	6	0	.250	120	216
West Division	**W**	**L**	**T**	**Pct.**	**Pts.**	**OP**
Denver	6	2	0	.750	141	98
San Diego	6	2	0	.750	248	134
Kansas City	5	3	0	.625	183	169
Oakland	2	6	0	.250	92	164

National Football Conference

East Division	W	L	T	Pct.	Pts.	OP
N.Y. Giants	6	2	0	.750	194	144
Dallas	4	4	0	.500	223	164
Philadelphia	4	4	0	.500	206	160
Washington	3	5	0	.375	162	190
North Division	**W**	**L**	**T**	**Pct.**	**Pts.**	**OP**
Chicago	7	1	0	.875	234	100
Minnesota	4	4	0	.500	130	135
Green Bay	3	5	0	.375	162	200
Detroit	2	6	0	.250	162	203
South Division	**W**	**L**	**T**	**Pct.**	**Pts.**	**OP**
New Orleans	6	2	0	.750	198	159
Atlanta	5	3	0	.625	167	164
Carolina	4	4	0	.500	137	163
Tampa Bay	2	6	0	.250	102	173
West Division	**W**	**L**	**T**	**Pct.**	**Pts.**	**OP**
Seattle	5	3	0	.625	165	177
St. Louis	4	4	0	.500	180	197
San Francisco	3	5	0	.375	143	238
Arizona	1	7	0	.125	134	196

SUNDAY, NOVEMBER 5

BALTIMORE 26, CINCINNATI 20—at M&T Bank Stadium, attendance 70,792. The Ravens' defense set up two early touchdowns as Baltimore took a two-game lead in the division. The Bengals fumbled the opening kickoff, which led to a quick touchdown, and moments later Samari Rolle intercepted a pass. Rolle returned it 24 yards, and then lateralled to Ed Reed, who took the ball the remaining 25 yards for a touchdown to give the Ravens a 14-0 less than five minutes into the game. The Ravens continued to move the ball, but had to settle for field goals. Carson Palmer's 71-yard pass to Chris Henry set up Rudi Johnson's 4-yard run to pull the Bengals within 23-17 with 13:31 to play. A 10-yard scramble by Steve McNair on the ensuing drive set up Matt Stover's fourth field goal for a 26-17 lead. Shayne Graham's 31-yard field goal pulled the Bengal to within 26-20 with 4:01 remaining, and the Bengals forced a three-an-out. But Palmer's fourth-down pass fell incomplete with 1:55 left, and Chris McAlister intercepted a Hail Mary pass at the Ravens' 20 with three seconds to play. McNair was 21 of 31 for 245 yards. Palmer was 12 of 26 for 194 yards and 1 touchdown, with 2 interceptions.

Cincinnati	0	7	3	10	—	20
Baltimore	14	3	6	3	—	26

Balt	—	J. Lewis 2 run (Stover kick)
Balt	—	Reed 25 interception return (Stover kick)
Balt	—	FG Stover 43
Cin	—	Houshmandzadeh 26 pass from Palmer (Graham kick)
Balt	—	FG Stover 25
Balt	—	FG Stover 36
Cin	—	FG Graham 51
Cin	—	R. Johnson 4 run (Graham kick)
Balt	—	FG Stover 35
Cin	—	FG Graham 31

BUFFALO 24, GREEN BAY 10—at Ralph Wilson Stadium, attendance 72,205. The Bills' defense forced 4 turnovers as Buffalo snapped a three-game losing streak despite being outgained by 243 yards (427-184 yards). With Willis McGahee injured four minutes into the game, London Fletcher-Baker's 17-yard interception return for a touchdown sparked the Bills and gave the club an early lead. The Packers drove to the Bills' 5 just before halftime, but a poor Shotgun snap was recovered by Aaron Schobel and Buffalo maintained a 10-0 halftime lead. Dave Rayner's 49-yard field goal tied the game with 12:41 to play. On second-and-20 from the Packer's 43 with 8:08 remaining, J.P. Losman completed a pass deep down the left sideline to Lee Evans, who caught the ball at the 5-yard line and reached the end zone to give the Bills a 17-10 lead. The Packers drove to the Bills' 1, but on first-and-goal, Nate Clements tipped Brett Favre' pass and Ko Simpson intercepted it and returned the ball 76 yards. Three players later, Anthony Thomas scored to give Buffalo a 24-10 lead with 3:01 to play. The Bills iced the game as Buffalo's fourth-and-10 pass from the Bills' 39 was overthrown with 1:26 remaining. Losman was 8 of 15 for 102 yards and 1 touchdown. Favre was 28 of 47 for 287 yards and 1 touchdown, with 2 interceptions. Ahman Green carried 23 times for 122 yards.

Green Bay	0	0	7	3	—	10
Buffalo	3	7	0	14	—	24

Buff	—	FG Lindell 28
Buff	—	Fletcher-Baker 17 interception return (Lindell kick)
GB	—	Driver 1 pass from Favre (Rayner kick)
GB	—	FG Rayner 49
Buff	—	Evans 43 pass from Losman (Lindell kick)
Buff	—	Thomas 14 run (Lindell kick)

MIAMI 31, CHICAGO 13—at Soldier Field, attendance 62,206. The Dolphins' defense forced six turnovers as

Miami snapped a four-game losing streak and handed the Bears their first loss of the season. A muffed punt by Devin Hester set up Miami's first touchdown. Fifteen seconds later, Jason Taylor intercepted an errant pass and returned it 20 yards for a touchdown and 14-3 lead. The Bears pulled to within 14-10 late in the first half, and Israel Idonije blocked Olindo Mare's 37-yard field goal attempt as the half expired. But Justin Gage fumbled on the first play of the second half. Andre Goodman recovered the ball and Joey Harrington completed a 6-yard touchdown pass to Wes Welker three plays later for a 21-10 lead. Nathan Vasher intercepted a pass at the Dolphins' 23 late in the third quarter, but the Bears had to settle for a field goal. Renaldo Hill's interception at the Bears' 24 was followed one play later by Chris Chambers' 24-yard touchdown catch for a 28-13 lead with 10:00 remaining. Chicago failed to drive inside the Dolphins' 30 the rest of the game. Harrington was 16 of 32 for 137 yards and 3 touchdowns, with 2 interceptions. Ronnie Brown had 29 carries for 157 yards. Rex Grossman was 18 of 42 for 210 yards and 1 touchdown, with 3 interceptions.

Miami	0	14	7	10	—	31
Chicago	3	7	0	3	—	13

Chi	—	FG Gould 38
Mia	—	Booker 5 pass from Harrington (Mare kick)
Mia	—	Taylor 20 interception return (Mare kick)
Chi	—	Muhammad 30 pass from Grossman (Gould kick)
Mia	—	Welker 6 pass from Harrington (Mare kick)
Chi	—	FG Gould 38
Mia	—	Chambers 24 pass from Harrington (Mare kick)
Mia	—	FG Mare 20

DETROIT 30, ATLANTA 14—at Ford Field, attendance 60,987. The Lions outgained the Falcons 435-319 in total yards and forced 3 turnovers to post their second victory. The Lions moved the ball at will in the first half, scoring 17 quick points and it could have been more, but the Falcons stopped the Lions on downs at the 2-yard line early in the second quarter. Just before halftime, a 33-yard scramble by Michael Vick set up Warrick Dunn's 1-yard run to pull the Falcons to within 17-14. The Lions led 20-14 early in the fourth quarter when Jon Kitna connected with Roy Williams on a 60-yard touchdown pass deep down the right side for a 27-14 lead with 13:09 to play. The Lions' defense forced a punt, and the offense took 6:36 off the clock with a 65-yard drive, capped by Jason Hanson's third field goal, for a 30-14 lead with 2:52 left. Kenoy Kennedy intercepted a pass in the end zone as time expired. Kitna was 20 of 32 for 321 yards and 1 touchdown, with 1 interception. Kevin Jones had 26 carries for 110 yards. Vick was 17 of 32 for 163 yards and 1 touchdown, with 2 interceptions.

Atlanta	7	7	0	0	—	14
Detroit	10	7	3	10	—	30

Det	—	FG Hanson 28
Det	—	K. Jones 35 run (Hanson kick)
Atl	—	Crumpler 19 pass from Vick (Andersen kick)
Det	—	K. Jones 2 run (Hanson kick)
Atl	—	Dunn 1 run (Andersen kick)
Det	—	FG Hanson 19
Det	—	R. Williams 60 pass from Kitna (Hanson kick)
Det	—	FG Hanson 36

JACKSONVILLE 37, TENNESSEE 7—at Alltel Stadium, attendance 66,524. The Jaguars turned 3 interceptions into 17 points as Jacksonville rolled pas the Titans. The Jaguars scored on four of their first five possessions to take a 20-0 lead with 9:10 still remaining in the first half. Rashean Mathis had 2 interceptions to set up 10 of the points. The Jaguars had a 73-yard touchdown drive to begin the second half, and Scott Starks intercepted a pass

moments later and returned it 55 yards for a touchdown and 34-0 lead with 9:34 left in the third quarter. The Titans did not cross the Jaguars' 40 until late in the fourth quarter. David Garrard, playing for an injured Byron Leftwich, was 12 of 22 for 177 yards and 3 touchdowns. Vince Young was 15 of 36 for 163 yards and 1 touchdown, with 3 interceptions.

Tennessee	0	0	0	7	—	7
Jacksonville	14	6	17	0	—	37

Jax	—	Wilford 11 pass from Garrard (Scobee kick)
Jax	—	Wrighster 14 pass from Garrard (Scobee kick)
Jax	—	FG Scobee 47
Jax	—	FG Scobee 21
Jax	—	Wilford 22 pass from Garrard (Scobee kick)
Jax	—	Starks 55 interception return (Scobee kick)
Jax	—	FG Scobee 39
Tenn	—	Bennett 32 pass from Young (Bironas kick)

N.Y. GIANTS 14, HOUSTON 10—at Giants Stadium, attendance 78,485. The Giants maintained their two-game first-place advantage in the NFC East with a come-from-behind victory. The Giants had five drives of at least 4 minutes and 48 seconds, but scored just twice. The Texans had just three second-half possessions. Houston took a 10-7 lead on the strength of n 18-play, 80-yard drive, highlighted by Wali Lundy's 3-yard run on fourth-and-1, and capped by David Carr's 2-yard scramble. In the fourth quarter, Tiki Barber's 7-yard run on third-and-6 to the Texans' 12 set up Eli Manning's 3-yard touchdown pass to Jeremy Shockey for a 14-10 lead with 7:49 to play. On the next drive, Gerris Wilkinson forced Jameel Cook to fumble. Corey Webster recovered the fumble at the Giants' 33 with 5:11 remaining. Manning's 6-yard pass to Amani Toomer gained a key first down, and Barber's 14-yard run for another first down clinched the victory. Manning was 17 of 28 for 179 yards and 1 touchdown, with 1 interception. Barber had 17 carries for 115 yards. Carr was 21 of 30 for 176 yards.

Houston	0	3	7	0	—	10
N.Y. Giants	7	0	0	7	—	14

NYG	—	Barber 16 run (Feely kick)
Hou	—	FG K. Brown 41
Hou	—	Carr 2 run (K. Brown kick)
NYG	—	Shockey 3 pass from E. Manning (Feely kick)

DENVER 31, PITTSBURGH 20—at Heinz Field, attendance 64,661. The Broncos' defense forced 6 turnovers and registered 4 sacks to stifle the Steelers and ruin a career-high passing day for Ben Roethlisberger. The Broncos scored 2 touchdowns in the first 3:55, the second set up by Darrent Williams' recovery of Santonio Holmes' fumbled kickoff, for a 14-0 lead. The Steelers rallied to pull to within 14-10 at halftime, but would have been leading if not for a fumble at the 6-yard line and an interception at the 3-yard line which allowed the Broncos to remain ahead. On the second play of the second half, Javon Walker raced 72 yards around left end on a reverse for a touchdown and 21-10 lead. In the fourth quarter, Plummer connected with Walker on a 10-yard touchdown pass with 11:16 to play for a 28-17 lead, and Walker had a 61-yard catch to set up Jason Elam's field goal. Trailing 31-20, the Steelers drove deep into Broncos territory. Hines Ward caught a short pass at the 1-yard line, but John Lynch forced Ward to fumble and Curome Cox recovered with 1:50 to play. The Steelers got the ball back one last time, but Cox intercepted Roethlisberger's fourth-down desperation pass with nine seconds remaining to clinch the victory. Plummer was 16 of 27 for 227 yards and 3 touchdowns. Walker had 6 receptions for 134 yards. Roethlisberger was 38 of 54 for 433 yards and 1 touchdown, with 3 interceptions. Ward had 7 catches for 127 yards.

Denver	14	0	7	10	—	31

Pittsburgh	0	10	7	3	—	20

Den	—	R. Smith 16 pass from Plummer (Elam kick)
Den	—	Walker 10 pass from Plummer (Elam kick)
Pitt	—	Parker 15 pass from Roethlisberger (Reed kick)
Pitt	—	FG Reed 46
Den	—	Walker 72 run (Elam kick)
Pitt	—	Parker 3 run (Reed kick)
Den	—	Walker 10 pass from Plummer (Elam kick)
Pitt	—	FG Reed 29
Den	—	FG Elam 32

KANSAS CITY 31, ST. LOUIS 17—at Edward Jones Dome, attendance 66,191. The Chiefs scored 17 points in less than seven minutes, set up by a muffed punt and two fumbles, to take a 17-0 lead with the first half. It was 24-7 late in the first half before Jeff Wilkins kicked a field goal as the half expired, and Marcus Bulger capped a 12-play, 80-yard drive in the third quarter with a 2-yard touchdown pass to Kevin Curtis to pull the Rams within 24-17. The Rams forced a punt and drove to the Chiefs' 26, but on second-and-1, consecutive false start penalties on Alex Barron pushed the Rams out of field-goal range. Damon Huard and the Chiefs responded with a 94-yard drive, highlighted by runs of 16 and 15 yards by Johnson, and capped by Huard's 11-yard touchdown pass to Kris Wilson with 6:20 to play. The Rams reached the Chiefs five-yard line with 2:39 to play, but Bulger had 4 consecutive incompletions. Huard was 10 of 15 for 148 yards and 3 touchdowns. Johnson carried 27 times for 172 yards. Bulger was 31 of 42 for 354 yards and 1 touchdown. Steven Jackson had 13 receptions for 133 yards, and 19 carries for 86 yards.

Kansas City	7	17	0	7	—	31
St. Louis	0	10	7	0	—	17

KC	—	L. Johnson 1 run (Tynes kick)
KC	—	Gonzalez 3 pass from Huard (Tynes kick)
KC	—	FG Tynes 42
StL	—	S. Jackson 2 run (Wilkins kick)
KC	—	Gonzalez 25 pass from Huard (Tynes kick)
StL	—	FG Wilkins 41
StL	—	Curtis 2 pass from Bulger (Wilkins kick)
KC	—	Wilson 11 pass from Huard (Tynes kick)

SAN DIEGO 32, CLEVELAND 25—at Qualcomm Stadium, attendance 65,558. LaDainian Tomlinson scored 3 second-half touchdowns to lead the Chargers. The Browns finished in Chargers' territory on 7 of their first 10 possessions, but settled for 4 field goals and led 12-10 late in the second quarter. The Chargers, whose lone touchdown had come earlier when Randall Godfrey sacked Charlie Frye, who fumbled and Marques Harris' recovered in the end zone, took the lead on LaDainian Tomlinson's 41-yard touchdown run. The Browns responded with Phil Dawson's 36-yard field goal, but the Chargers drove 77 yards, capped by Tomlinson's second touchdown, for a 24-15 lead with 9:15 remaining. After Dawson's sixth field goal pulled the Browns to within 24-18, Tomlinson had a 32-yard run to set up his 8-yard touchdown run, his third touchdown in a span of 12 minutes, 19 seconds, for a 32-18 lead with 3:53 remaining. The Browns reached the end zone with 1:11 left, but Tomlinson recovered the onside kick to clinch the victory. Philip Rivers was 19 of 28 for 211 yards. Tomlinson had 18 carries for 172 yards. Frye was 26 of 44 for 241 yards and 1 touchdown, with 1 interception.

Cleveland	3	9	0	13	—	25
San Diego	3	7	15	7	—	32

SD	—	FG Kaeding 29
Cle	—	FG Dawson 37
Cle	—	FG Dawson 20
SD	—	Harris fumble recovery in

end zone (Kaeding kick)

Cle	—	FG Dawson 42
Cle	—	FG Dawson 30
SD	—	Tomlinson 41 run (Kaeding kick)
Cle	—	FG Dawson 36
SD	—	Tomlinson 7 run (Kaeding kick)
Cle	—	FG Dawson 35
SD	—	Tomlinson 8 run
		(Jackson pass from Rivers)
Cle	—	Edwards 4 pass from Frye
		(Dawson kick)

SAN FRANCISCO 9, MINNESOTA 3—at Monster Park, attendance 68,088. The 49ers' had just 8 first downs and gained only 133 yards, but Joe Nedney kicked 3 field goals as San Francisco slipped by the Vikings. With the scored 3-3 in the second quarter, Marques Douglas sacked Brad Johnson and forced him to fumble. Shawntae Spencer recovered at the Vikings' 21 to set up Nedney's second field goal. The Vikings finally drove inside the 49ers' 30 early in the fourth quarter, but Bryant Young forced Johnson to fumble, and Manny Lawson recovered. Nine plays later, Nedney made a 51-yard field goal with 7:15 remaining. The Vikings reached the 49ers' 27 with 1:10 to play, but Brad Johnson's fourth-and-7 pass for Bethel Johnson at the goal line fell incomplete thanks to the efforts of Mark Roman and Spencer. Alex Smith was 13 of 21 for 105 yards, with 1 interception. Johnson was 21 of 31 for 136 yards, with 1 interception.

Minnesota	3	0	0	0	—	3
San Francisco	0	6	0	3	—	9
Minn	—	FG Longwell 21
SF	—	FG Nedney 25
SF	—	FG Nedney 30
SF	—	FG Nedney 51

NEW ORLEANS 31, TAMPA BAY 14—at Raymond James Stadium, attendance 65,561. Drew Brees passed for 314 yards and 3 touchdowns as the Saints improved their record to 6-2, their best start since 2002. The Saints scored on its first three possessions to take a 17-0 lead. The Buccaneers drove 77 and 69 yards on their last two possessions of the first half to pull within 17-14. The Saints responded by scoring twice in the third quarter, capped by Devery Henderson's 45-yard touchdown catch deep down the left side to take a 31-14 lead with 33 seconds left in the third quarter. Tampa Bay did not threaten again. Brees was 24 of 32 for 314 yards and 3 touchdowns. Marques Colston had 11 catches for 123 yard and Devery Henderson added 3 receptions for 111 yards. Bruce Gradkowski was 18 of 31 for 185 yard and 2 touchdowns.

New Orleans	14	3	14	0	—	31
Tampa Bay	0	14	0	0	—	14
NO	—	Colston 15 pass from Brees
		(Carney kick)
NO	—	Henderson 52 pass from Brees
		(Carney kick)
NO	—	FG Carney 46
TB	—	Galloway 44 pass from Gradkowski (Bryant kick)
TB	—	Galloway 17 pass from Gradkowski (Bryant kick)
NO	—	McAllister 3 run (Carney kick)
NO	—	Henderson 45 pass from Brees (Carney kick)

WASHINGTON 22, DALLAS 19—at FedExField, attendance 90,250. Troy Vincent blocked Mike Vanderjagt's game-winning field-goal attempt with time running out, and Nick Novak kicked a 47-yard field goal with time on the clock as the Redskins registered an improbable victory. Trailing 5-0, the Cowboys scored a touchdown early in the second quarter and went for the 2-point conversion. Kenny Wright knocked down Tony Romo's pass, limiting the Cowboys lead to 6-5. Dallas scored on its next three possessions as well to take a 19-12 third-quarter lead. With the score 19-19, Novak had a chance to give the Redskins a lead with 35 seconds left, but his kick

sailed wide right. Romo completed 3 passes to get the Cowboys to the Redskins' 17 with six seconds left. Vanderjagt's 35-yard field-goal attempt was blocked by Vincent, who was coming off the right end. Sean Taylor picked up the bouncing ball and, during his 30-yard return, Dallas' Kyle Kosier was called for a facemask penalty while trying to tackle Taylor. Since the game cannot end on a defensive penalty, the Redskins were given one free play with no time on the clock. Novak made the 47-yard field goal to win the game. Mark Brunell was 14 of 23 for 192 yards and 1 touchdown. Romo was 24 of 36 for 284 yards and 2 touchdowns.

Dallas	0	12	7	0	—	19
Washington	5	7	0	10	—	22
Wash	—	Marshall tackled J. Jones in end zone
Wash	—	FG Novak 28
Dall	—	Glenn 10 pass from Romo (pass failed)
Dall	—	FG Vanderjagt 33
Wash	—	Portis 38 run (Novak kick)
Dall	—	FG Vanderjagt 30
Dall	—	Owens 4 pass from Romo (Vanderjagt kick)
Wash	—	Cooley 18 pass from Brunell (Novak kick)
Wash	—	FG Novak 47

SUNDAY NIGHT, NOVEMBER 5
INDIANAPOLIS 27, NEW ENGLAND 20—at Gillette Stadium, attendance 68,756. Indianapolis scored early and used 2 fourth-quarter interceptions by Cato June to be the NFL's last unbeaten team. The Colts became the first team since the 1929-1931 Green Bay Packers to post back-to-back seasons with a record of at least 8-0. The Colts scored on their first three possessions, and Bob Sanders intercepted Tom Brady's pass at the Colts' 3 just before halftime to allow Indianapolis to maintain a 17-14 lead. Stephen Gostkowski's 49-yard field goal cut the deficit to 24-17, and Terrence Wilkins fumbled the ensuing kickoff. Artrell Hawkins recovered, but Gostkowski missed a 36-yard field goal. The Patriots had the ball near midfield early in the fourth quarter, but June intercepted Brady's pass and Adam Vinatieri, playing against his former team for the first time, made a 31-yard field goal for a 27-17 lead with 10:17 to play. Gostkowski's 26-yard field goal trimmed the deficit to 27-20, and Vinatieri missed a 46-yard field-goal attempt wide right with 1:55 to play. Brady connected with Ben Watson on a 25-yard pass play to reach the Colts' 39, but June's second interception of the fourth quarter iced the victory. Peyton Manning was 20 of 36 for 326 yards and 2 touchdowns, with 1 interception. Marvin Harrison had 8 carries for 145 yards. Brady was 20 of 35 for 201 yards, with 4 interceptions.

Indianapolis	7	10	7	3	—	27
New England	0	14	3	3	—	20
Ind	—	Harrison 5 pass from P. Manning (Vinatieri kick)
NE	—	Dillon 1 run (Gostkowski kick)
Ind	—	Addai 2 run (Vinatieri kick)
NE	—	Dillon 4 run (Gostkowski kick)
Ind	—	FG Vinatieri 23
Ind	—	Harrison 4 pass from P. Manning (Vinatieri kick)
NE	—	FG Gostkowski 49
Ind	—	FG Vinatieri 31
NE	—	FG Gostkowski 26

MONDAY NIGHT, NOVEMBER 6
SEATTLE 16, OAKLAND 0—at Qwest Field, attendance 67,816. In a game played in the rain and wind, the Seahawks' defense allowed just 185 yards and registered 9 sacks en route to their first shutout of the season. The Seahawks scored on their first three possessions for a 13-0 lead. Oakland punted to conclude 10 of their first 11 possessions with a one-play kneeldown at the end of the half serving as the lone exception. The Raiders never drove inside the Seahawks' 3. Josh Brown's third field

goal gave the Seahawks a 16-0 lead with 1:17 to play. Seneca Wallace, starting in place of the injured Matt Hasselbeck, was 18 of 30 for 176 yards and 1 touchdown. Morris, had 30 carries for 138 yards. Andrew Walter was 16 of 35 for 166 yards.

Oakland	0	0	0	0	—	0
Seattle	10	3	3	—	16
Sea	—	Branch 22 pass from S. Wallace (J. Brown kick)
Sea	—	FG J. Brown 20
Sea	—	FG J. Brown 25
Sea	—	FG J. Brown 20

TENTH WEEK SUMMARIES
American Football Conference

East Division	W	L	T	Pct.	Pts.	OP
New England	6	3	0	.667	201	131
N.Y. Jets	5	4	0	.556	177	207
Buffalo	3	6	0	.333	140	180
Miami	3	6	0	.333	146	168
North Division	**W**	**L**	**T**	**Pct.**	**Pts.**	**OP**
Baltimore	7	2	0	.778	198	137
Cincinnati	4	5	0	.444	216	217
Cleveland	3	6	0	.333	150	184
Pittsburgh	3	6	0	.333	215	207
South Division	**W**	**L**	**T**	**Pct.**	**Pts.**	**OP**
Indianapolis	9	0	0	1.000	249	189
Jacksonville	5	4	0	.556	185	127
Houston	3	6	0	.333	144	206
Tennessee	2	7	0	.222	146	243
West Division	**W**	**L**	**T**	**Pct.**	**Pts.**	**OP**
Denver	7	2	0	.778	158	111
San Diego	7	2	0	.778	297	175
Kansas City	5	4	0	.556	193	182
Oakland	2	7	0	.222	105	181

National Football Conference

East Division	W	L	T	Pct.	Pts.	OP
N.Y. Giants	6	3	0	.667	214	182
Dallas	5	4	0	.556	250	174
Philadelphia	5	4	0	.556	233	163
Washington	3	6	0	.333	165	217
North Division	**W**	**L**	**T**	**Pct.**	**Pts.**	**OP**
Chicago	8	1	0	.889	272	120
Green Bay	4	5	0	.444	185	217
Minnesota	4	5	0	.444	185	217
Detroit	2	7	0	.222	175	222
South Division	**W**	**L**	**T**	**Pct.**	**Pts.**	**OP**
New Orleans	6	3	0	.667	229	197
Atlanta	5	4	0	.556	180	181
Carolina	5	4	0	.556	161	173
Tampa Bay	2	7	0	.222	112	197
West Division	**W**	**L**	**T**	**Pct.**	**Pts.**	**OP**
Seattle	6	3	0	.667	189	199
St. Louis	4	5	0	.444	202	221
San Francisco	4	5	0	.444	162	251
Arizona	1	8	0	.111	144	223

SUNDAY, NOVEMBER 12
DALLAS 27, ARIZONA 10—at University of Phoenix Stadium, attendance 63,926. Tony Romo passed for 2 touchdowns as the Cowboys handed the Cardinals their eighth consecutive loss. The Cowboys led 13-3 in the third quarter when Akin Ayodele intercepted Matt Leinart's pass. On the next play, Tony Romo completed a 51-yard touchdown pass to Terrell Owens for a 20-3 lead. Patrick Watkins intercepted Leinart on the Cowboys' next drive, and Marion Barber scored six plays later for a 27-3 lead with 14:17 to play. Romo was 20 of 29 for 308 yards and 2 touchdowns. Crayton had 5 receptions for 104 yards. Leinart was 20 of 38 for 216 yards, with 2 interceptions.

Dallas	3	10	7	7	—	27
Arizona	0	3	0	7	—	10
Dall	—	FG Vanderjagt 28
Dall	—	Crayton 30 pass from Romo (Vanderjagt kick)
Ari	—	FG Rackers 28
Dall	—	FG Vanderjagt 38
Dall	—	Owens 51 pass from Romo

(Vanderjagt kick)
Dall — Barber 5 run (Vanderjagt kick)
Ari — Leinart 3 run (Rackers kick)

CLEVELAND 17, ATLANTA 13—at Georgia Dome, attendance 70,793. The Browns generated just 9 first downs yet had enough to win on the road. Sean Jones intercepted a pass near midfield to set up Braylon Edwards' 19-yard touchdown catch for a 14-0 lead with 11:59 left in the second quarter. Allen Rossum's 37-yard punt return in the third quarter set up Michael Jenkins' 12-yard touchdown catch to pull within 14-10. The Browns led 17-13 with 3:31 left when the Falcons regained possession. Michael Vick completed a 55-yard pass to Roddy White. But two plays later, Vick rolled out, stumbled and fumbled. Jereme Perry recovered the ball for the Browns to clinch the victory. Charlie Frye was 16 of 22 for 165 yards and 1 touchdown. Vick was 16 of 40 for 197 yards and 1 touchdown, with 2 interceptions.

Cleveland	7	7	0	3	—	17
Atlanta	0	3	7	3	—	13

Cle	—	Droughns 1 run (Dawson kick)
Cle	—	Edwards 19 pass from Frye (Dawson kick)
Atl	—	FG Andersen 44
Atl	—	Jenkins 12 pass from Vick (Andersen kick)
Atl	—	FG Andersen 41
Cle	—	FG Dawson 43

SAN DIEGO 49, CINCINNATI 41—at Paul Brown Stadium, attendance 65,917. The Chargers scored 42 second-half points to rally and defeat the Bengals. The teams combined for 975 yards, including 545 yards for the Bengals, but the Chargers, not counting a one-play drive at the end of the first half, scored touchdowns on six consecutive possessions. The Bengals scored on their first three drives for a 21-0 lead. The Chargers scored with 5:27 in the half, but the Bengals used a 14-play, 74-yard drive to take a 28-7 lead on Chris Henry's 7-yard touchdown catch with 16 seconds left in the half. The Chargers responded by scoring 5 touchdowns in a span of 11 minutes, seven seconds. The scoring spree began with a 69-yard drive. The Chargers' defense forced a punt, and on the next play Malcom Floyd caught a 46-yard touchdown to pull the Chargers within 28-21 with 9:08 left in the third quarter. Shayne Graham booted a 21-yard field goal, but the Chargers bounced back with a 9-play, 80-yard drive to pull within 31-28 with 3:08 left in the third quarter. Chad Johnson caught a 74-yard touchdown on the next play for a 38-28 lead, and Michael Turner returned the ensuing kickoff 49 yards to set up LaDainian Tomlinson's 2-yard run on the first play of the fourth quarter. Shaun Phillips sacked Carson Palmer and forced him to fumble. Phillips recovered, and Tomlinson scored on a 9-yard run on the next play for a 42-38 lead with 14:40 remaining. Graham's 44-yard field goal pulled the Bengals to within 42-41 with 7:48 left, but the Chargers strung together a 12-play, 72-yard drive, capped by Rivers' 5-yard shovel pass to Brandon Manumaleuna to take a 49-41 lead with 2:29 left. The Bengals drove to the Chargers' 15, but Palmer's fourth-and-10 pass fell incomplete with 44 seconds left. Rivers was 24 of 36 for 337 yards and 3 touchdowns. Floyd had 5 catches for 109 yards, and Tomlinson had 22 carries for 104 yards. Palmer was 31 of 42 for 440 yards and 3 touchdowns. Chad Johnson had 11 receptions for 260 yards.

San Diego	0	7	21	21	—	49
Cincinnati	21	7	10	3	—	41

Cin	—	J. Johnson 3 run (Graham kick)
Cin	—	R. Johnson 7 run (Graham kick)
Cin	—	C. Johnson 51 pass from Palmer (Graham kick)
SD	—	Tomlinson 9 run (Kaeding kick)
Cin	—	Henry 7 pass from Palmer (Graham kick)
SD	—	Tomlinson 4 run (Kaeding kick)
SD	—	Floyd 46 pass from Rivers (Kaeding kick)
Cin	—	FG Graham 21
SD	—	Manumaleuna 9 pass from Rivers (Kaeding kick)
Cin	—	C. Johnson 74 pass from Palmer (Graham kick)
SD	—	Tomlinson 2 run (Kaeding kick)
SD	—	Tomlinson 9 run (Kaeding kick)
Cin	—	FG Graham 44
SD	—	Manumaleuna 5 pass from Rivers (Kaeding kick)

SAN FRANCISCO 19, DETROIT 13—at Ford Field, attendance 60,707. The 49ers' defense forced 4 turnovers as San Francisco outlasted the Lions. The 49ers scored on three of their first four possessions to take a 13-0 lead. Shawntae Spencer sacked Jon Kitna on the first play of the second half and Marques Douglas recovered to set up Joe Nedney's third field goal and a 16-3 lead. Later in the third quarter, Cory Redding forced Alex Smith to fumble and Jon McGraw recovered to set up Dan Campbell's 8-yard touchdown catch. An exchange of field goals pulled the Lions to within 19-13, and Detroit got the ball back with 4:22 to play and drove to the 49ers' 19, but Kevin Lewis intercepted Kitna's fourth-and-13 pass with 2:31 to play. Smith completed a 7-yard pass to Arnaz Battle on third-and-4 to clinch the victory. Smith was 14 of 20 for 136 yards. Frank Gore had 22 carries for 159 yards. Kitna was 19 of 30 for 202 yards and 1 touchdown, with 1 interception.

San Francisco	10	3	3	3	—	19
Detroit	0	3	7	3	—	13

SF	—	Gore 61 run (Nedney kick)
SF	—	FG Nedney 28
SF	—	FG Nedney 23
Det	—	FG Hanson 25
SF	—	FG Nedney 23
Det	—	Campbell 8 pass from Kitna (Hanson kick)
SF	—	FG Nedney 47
Det	—	FG Hanson 33

INDIANAPOLIS 17, BUFFALO 16—at RCA Dome, attendance 57,306. The Colts outgained the Bills 384-162 in total yards, yet had to hold on for the victory to become the first club in NFL history to begin consecutive seasons with a 9-0 record. The Colts led 10-3 late in the second quarter when Angelo Crowell forced Ben Utecht to fumble. Terrence McGee recovered and returned the ball 68 yards for a game-tying touchdown. The Colts opened the second half with a 74-yard touchdown drive, but McGee returned the ensuing kickoff 88 yards to set up Rian Lindell's 30-yard field goal to pull the Bills within 17-13. Lindell added a 43-yard field goal with 10:35 remaining, and Nate Clements recovered Dominic Rhodes' fumble with 8:49 to play. The Bills drove to the Colts' 17, but Dwight Freeney sacked J.P. Losman on third-and-5. The seven-yard loss resulted in a 41-yard field-goal attempt, and Lindell's kick sailed wide right with 6:22 left. The Colts then ran out the clock, with Joseph Addai gaining 3 key first downs. Peyton Manning was 27 of 39 for 236 yards and 1 touchdown. J.P. Losman was 9 of 13 for 83 yards.

Buffalo	3	7	3	3	—	16
Indianapolis	0	10	7	0	—	17

Buff	—	FG Lindell 22
Ind	—	Wayne 1 pass from Manning (Vinatieri kick)
Ind	—	FG Vinatieri 31
Buff	—	McGee 68 fumble return (Lindell kick)
Ind	—	Addai 5 run (Vinatieri kick)
Buff	—	FG Lindell 30
Buff	—	FG Lindell 43

HOUSTON 13, JACKSONVILLE 10—at Alltel Stadium, attendance 65,918. The Texans scored on their first two possessions and then relied on their defense that registered 4 interceptions to snap a 12-game road losing streak. Anthony Weaver's interception and 21-yard return in the third quarter led to Kris Brown's 28-yard field goal

and a 13-3 lead. The Jaguars pulled within 13-10 with 4:32 to play, and then forced a punt with 2:34 remaining. Three plays later, faced with fourth-and-20, the Jaguars punted. Jacksonville then used all three timeouts and the Texans were faced with fourth-and-1 on their own 41 with 1:40 remaining. Houston went for it, and Samkon Gado got 1-yard to clinch the victory. David Carr was 16 of 32 for 167 yards. David Garrard was 15 of 34 for 214 yards, with 4 interceptions.

Houston	10	0	3	0	—	13
Jacksonville	0	3	0	7	—	10

Hou	—	Lundy 1 run (K. Brown kick)
Hou	—	FG K. Brown 25
Jax	—	FG Scobee 44
Hou	—	FG K. Brown 28
Jax	—	Jones-Drew 3 run (Scobee kick)

MIAMI 13, KANSAS CITY 10—at Dolphin Stadium, attendance 73,132. Miami used a strong defense and just enough offense to snap the Chiefs' three-game winning streak. The Dolphins scored on three of their first four possessions, highlighted by a 46-yard flea-flicker to Chris Chambers to set up a touchdown, and just before the Chiefs had a first down. The Dolphins led 13-3 and had the ball near midfield with 8:11 remaining in the game when Ronnie Brown attempted to hand a reverse to Chambers, who was unable to secure the hand off. Jared Allen scooped up the ball and returned it to the Dolphins' 20. Four plays later, Larry Johnson scored on a 2-yard run to cut the deficit to 13-10 with 7:14 to play. The Chiefs forced a punt, but failed to cross midfield with their final drive. Trent Green was 19 of 35 for 201 yards. Damon Huard was 15 of 38 for 201 yards.

Kansas City	0	0	0	10	—	10
Miami	3	10	0	0	—	13

Mia	—	FG Mare 40
Mia	—	FG Mare 22
Mia	—	R. Brown 1 run (Mare kick)
KC	—	FG Tynes 27
KC	—	L. Johnson 2 run (Tynes kick)

GREEN BAY 23, MINNESOTA 17—at Metrodome, attendance 63,924. Donald Driver had a career high 191 receiving yards and Brett Favre passed for 347 yards as the Packers handed the Vikings their third consecutive defeat. Billy McMullen scored 2 touchdowns in the second quarter, the latter coming when Chester Taylor fumbled at the goal line but McMullen recovered the ball in the end zone. The Vikings led 14-10 and the Packers were pinned on their own 3-yard line following a punt. Three plays later Donald Driver caught an 82-yard touchdown pass with 48 seconds left in the half to give Green Bay a 17-14 halftime lead. In the second half, Driver took a lateral from Greg Jennings and turned a 12-yard pass play into a 42-yard play to set up Dave Rayner's field goal. Rayner added a third field goal with 2:11 remaining for a 23-14 lead. The Vikings kicked a field goal with 58 seconds left, and then recovered the onside kick, but an offside penalty nullified the play. The Vikings attempted another onside kick, but Ryan Longwell's kick bounced out of bounds, and the Packers ran out the clock. Favre was 24 of 42 for 347 yards and 2 touchdowns. Driver had 6 receptions for 191 yards. Johnson was 18 of 30 for 257 yards and 1 touchdown, with 1 interception.

Green Bay	10	7	3	3	—	23
Minnesota	0	14	0	3	—	17

GB	—	FG Rayner 20
GB	—	Herron 5 pass from Favre (Rayner kick)
Minn	—	McMullen 40 pass from B. Johnson (Longwell kick)
Minn	—	McMullen fumble recovery in end zone (Longwell kick)
GB	—	Driver 82 pass from Favre (Rayner kick)
GB	—	FG Rayner 24
GB	—	FG Rayner 29
Minn	—	FG Longwell 34

N.Y. JETS 17, NEW ENGLAND 14—at Gillette Stadium, attendance 68,756. The Jets' defense forced just 2 turnovers, but both were turned into touchdowns as the Jets handed the Patriots consecutive losses for the first time in 57 games. Former Patriots' defensive coordinator Eric Mangini's defense led to 4 sacks and the 2 turnovers in a game played in rain and poor conditions. Kerry Rhodes recovered a Doug Gabriel fumble to spark a 16-play, 81-yard drive, which was highlighted by Chad Pennington's 3-yard run on fourth-and-1, to take a 7-3 lead. The Jets led 10-6 in the fourth quarter when Erik Coleman intercepted Tom Brady's pass at the Patriots' 35. Four plays later, Pennington completed a 22-yard pass to Jerricho Cotchery for a 17-6 lead with 4:45 remaining. The Patriots needed just four plays and 31 seconds to cut the deficit to 17-14, and after a punt New England got the ball back on their own 11-yard line with 1:08 to play. The Patriots reached the Jets' 46, but Shaun Ellis sacked Brady to thwart his Hail Mary pass attempt as time expired. Pennington was 22 of 37 for 168 yards and 1 touchdown, with 1 interception. Brady was 25 of 37 for 255 yards and 1 touchdown, with 1 interception.

N.Y. Jets	0	7	3	7	—	17
New England	0	6	0	8	—	14

NE	—	FG Gostkowski 31
NYJ	—	Barlow 2 run (Nugent kick)
NE	—	FG Gostkowski 21
NYJ	—	FG Nugent 34
NYJ	—	Cotchery 22 pass from Pennington (Nugent kick)
NE	—	Caldwell 15 pass from Brady (Caldwell pass from Brady)

DENVER 17, OAKLAND 13—at McAfee Coliseum, attendance 62,094. The Broncos rallied in the fourth quarter to hand the Raiders their eleventh consecutive loss within the division. The Raiders led 3-7 at halftime and entering the fourth quarter. On fourth-and-goal from the Raiders' 1 with 11:10 to play, the Broncos went for the touchdown and got it when Jake Plummer tossed a 1-yard pass to Kyle Johnson to take a 14-13 lead. Later in the fourth quarter, Kenard Lang sacked Andrew Walter and forced him to fumble. John Engelberger recovered at the Raiders' 12 and Jason Elam kicked a 24-yard field goal with 1:56 remaining to extend the lead to four points. On the next play from scrimmage, Walter mishandled the snap and Elvis Dumervil recovered to clinch the victory. Plummer was 20 of 31 for 210 yards and 2 touchdowns, with 3 interceptions. Walter was 18 of 33 for 214 yards.

Denver	7	0	0	10	—	17
Oakland	7	6	0	0	—	13

Oak	—	Jordan 1 run (Janikowski kick)
Den	—	Walker 39 pass from Plummer (Elam kick)
Oak	—	FG Janikowski 55
Oak	—	FG Janikowski 10
Den	—	K. Johnson 1 pass from Plummer (Elam kick)
Den	—	FG Elam 24

PHILADELPHIA 27, WASHINGTON 3—at Lincoln Financial Field, attendance 69,143. Donovan McNabb completed 2 long touchdown passes as the Eagles downed the Redskins. The Eagles scored on their first three possessions, taking a 17-0 lead thanks to a little luck. McNabb completed a pass to Reggie Brown, who was hit by Shawn Springs. The ball popped into the air and was caught on the run by Correll Buckhalter, who raced down the sideline for a 55-yard touchdown with 10:44 left in the second quarter. The Redskins kicked a field goal before halftime, but did not drive inside the Eagles' 30 in the second half. Sheldon Brown returned an interception 70 yards to finish the scoring. McNabb was 12 of 26 for 257 yards and 2 touchdowns. Stallworth had 6 catches for 139 yards. Brian Westbrook had 22 carries for 113 yards. Mark Brunell was 16 of 31 for 132 yards, with 1 interception, and Clinton Por-

tis suffered a broken hand in the first quarter.

Washington	0	3	0	0	—	3
Philadelphia	10	7	10	0	—	27

Phil	—	FG Akers 37
Phil	—	Stallworth 84 pass from McNabb (Akers kick)
Phil	—	Buckhalter 55 pass from McNabb (Akers kick)
Wash	—	FG Novak 32
Phil	—	FG Akers 25
Phil	—	S. Brown 70 interception return (Akers kick)

PITTSBURGH 38, NEW ORLEANS 31—at Heinz Field, attendance 61,911. Willie Parker rushed for 213 yards as the Steelers outlasted the Saints. The club's gained 984 yards, 517 by the Saints who scored on four consecutive first-half possessions on drives of 52, 78, 71, and 72 yards, to take a 24-17 halftime lead. The Saints still led in the middle of the third quarter when Larry Foote forced Reggie Bush to fumble. Ryan Clark recovered, and on the next play Ben Roethlisberger fired a 38-yard touchdown pass to Cedrick Wilson to tie the game 24-24. The Saints drove into scoring position, but John Carney missed a 32-yard field-goal attempt. Two plays later, Parker raced 72 yards to set up his own 3-yard touchdown run for a 31-24 lead. The Steelers forced a punt, and Parker had a 76-yard run that led to his 4-yard touchdown run with 9:55 to play. The Saints pulled within 38-31 and then drove to the Steers' 45 in the final minute. Drew Brees completed a pass to Terrance Copper at the Steelers'' 25. However, Tyrone Carter forced Copper to fumble and Clark recovered with 39 seconds remaining to clinch the victory. Roethlisberger was 17 of 28 for 264 yards and 3 touchdowns. Parker had 22 carries for 213 yards. Brees was 31 of 47 for 398 yards and 1 touchdown. Marques Colston had 10 receptions for 169 yards.

New Orleans	7	10	7	0	—	31
Pittsburgh	14	3	7	14	—	38

Pitt	—	Ward 37 pass from Roethlisberger (Reed kick)
Pitt	—	Miller 2 pass from Roethlisberger (Reed kick)
NO	—	Copper 3 pass from Brees (Carney kick)
NO	—	FG Carney 20
NO	—	Bush 15 run (Carney kick)
Pitt	—	FG Reed 32
NO	—	McAllister 4 run (Carney kick)
Pitt	—	Wilson 38 pass from Roethlisberger (Reed kick)
Pitt	—	Parker 3 run (Reed kick)
Pitt	—	Parker 4 run (Reed kick)
NO	—	McAllister 4 run (Carney kick)

SEATTLE 24, ST. LOUIS 22—at Qwest Field, attendance 68,175. Playing without injured Matt Hasselbeck and Shaun Alexander, Josh Brown beat the Rams for the second time in a month with a game-winning kick in the final seconds. The Rams had just three first-half possessions, but trailed just 14-13 thanks to Victor Adeyanju's 89-yard fumble return for a touchdown. The Rams led 16-14 and reached the Seahawks' 12, but Marc Bulger's fourth-and-1 pass fell incomplete with 14:22 to play. Nate Burleson then gave the Seahawks a 90-yard punt return for a touchdown and 21-16 lead with 8:19 remaining. The Rams responded with a 69-yard touchdown drive, capped by Steven Jackson's 14-yard run with 2:30 to play. Bulger then completed a 2-point conversion pass to Torry Holt, but it was nullified by a holding penalty. The Rams went for two points again, but the pass was incomplete. A personal foul penalty on Jackson's touchdown forced the Rams to kickoff from the 15-yard line, and Josh Scobey returned the ensuing kickoff to the Rams' 49. Seneca Wallace then completed 2 key passes to set up Brown's winning kick. Wallace was 15 of 23 for 161 yards and 2 touchdowns. Maurice Morris had 21 carries for 124 yards. Bulger was 26 of 40 for 215 yards, with 1 interception.

St. Louis	10	3	3	6	—	22
Seattle	7	7	0	10	—	24

StL	—	Adeyanju 89 fumble return (Wilkins kick)
Sea	—	Jackson 3 pass from Wallace (J. Brown kick)
StL	—	FG Wilkins 40
Sea	—	Stevens 15 pass from Wallace (J. Brown kick)
StL	—	FG Wilkins 42
StL	—	FG Wilkins 35
Sea	—	Burleson 90 punt return (J. Brown kick)
StL	—	Jackson 14 run (pass failed)
Sea	—	FG J. Brown 38

BALTIMORE 27, TENNESSEE 26—at LP Field, attendance 69,143. The Ravens scored the game's final 20 points and Trevor Pryce blocked a field-goal attempt in the final minute to defeat the Titans. Tennessee scored on four of its first five possessions and led 26-7 with 9:51 left in the first half. The Titans had scoring drives of 66, 64, and 53 yards, and the defense registered a safety and Lamont Thompson intercepted a pass to set up Travis Henry's 1-yard run for the 26-7 lead. The Ravens scored on their last two possessions of the half, and Ed Reed's interception set up Matt Stover's 40-yard field goal to pull within 26-20 with 14:06 to play. Later in the quarter, Steve McNair completed a 34-yard pass to Demetrius Williams to set up Derrick Mason's 11-yard scoring grab for a 27-26 lead with 3:35 to play. Vince Young had a 17-yard scramble to put the Titans in position to win the game, but Pryce blocked Rob Bironas' 43-yard field-goal attempt with 33 seconds to play. McNair was 29 of 47 for 373 yards and 3 touchdowns, with 2 interceptions. Mark Clayton had 7 receptions for 125 yards. Young was 13 of 25 for 211 yards, with 1 interception. Drew Bennett had 6 receptions for 115 yards. Travis Henry had 27 carries for 107 yards.

Baltimore	7	10	0	10	—	27
Tennessee	12	14	0	0	—	26

Tenn	—	FG Bironas 21
Balt	—	Clayton 65 pass from McNair (Stover kick)
Tenn	—	Young 2 run (Bironas kick)
Tenn	—	Safety, T. Brown and Bulluck sack McNair out of bounds in end zone
Tenn	—	Scaife 13 run (Bironas kick)
Tenn	—	Henry 1 run (Bironas kick)
Balt	—	Mughelli 30 pass from McNair (Stover kick)
Balt	—	FG Stover 27
Balt	—	FG Stover 30
Balt	—	Mason 11 pass from McNair (Stover kick)

SUNDAY NIGHT, NOVEMBER 12
CHICAGO 38, N.Y. GIANTS 20—at Giants Stadium, attendance 78,641. The Bears scored 4 touchdowns in a span of 15 minutes, highlighted by the record-tying-longest play in NFL history, a 108-yard missed field goal return by Devin Hester, to defeat the Giants. Jay Feely's 40-yard field goal gave the Giants a 13-3 lead at 2:21 left in the second quarter. A 26-yard run by Thomas Jones on third-and-22 set up Rex Grossman's 29-yard touchdown pass to Mark Bradley with 35 seconds left in the half. The Bears took the lead 17-13, and two plays later Eli Manning fumbled and Adewale Ogunleye recovered to set up Desmond Clark's 2-yard touchdown pass for a 24-13 lead with 5:35 left in the third quarter. The Giants cut the deficit to 24-20, and then got the ball back and set up for a 52-yard field-goal attempt. Feely's kick was short, and Hester caught the ball and then stood in the end zone. He lulled the Giants to sleep and then raced 108 yards untouched down the sideline for a touchdown and 31-20 lead with 11:20 to play. Three plays later, Chris Harris intercepted Manning and Jones scored on a 2-yard run with 8:20 remaining for a commanding 38-20 lead. Grossman was 18 of 30 for 246 yards and 3 touch-

downs, with 1 interception. Muhsin Muhammad had 7 receptions for 123 yards. Jones had 30 catches for 113 yards. Manning was 14 of 32 for 121 yards, with 2 interceptions. Tiki Barber had 19 carries for 141 yards.

Chicago	3	7	14	14	—	38
N.Y. Giants	7	6	7	0	—	20

NYG	—	Jacobs 1 run (Feely kick)
Chi	—	FG Gould 49
NYG	—	FG Feely 46
NYG	—	FG Feely 40
Chi	—	Bradley 29 pass from Grossman (Gould kick)
Chi	—	Muhammad 10 pass from Grossman (Gould kick)
Chi	—	Clark 2 pass from Grossman (Gould kick)
NYG	—	Jacobs 8 run (Feely kick)
Chi	—	Hester 108 field goal return (Gould kick)
Chi	—	T. Jones 2 run (Gould kick)

MONDAY NIGHT, NOVEMBER 13
CAROLINA 24, TAMPA BAY 10—at Bank of America Stadium, attendance 73,573. The Panthers turned 2 second-half turnovers into touchdowns to rally and defeat the Buccaneers. Keyshawn Johnson's fumble in the first quarter gave the Buccaneers the ball at the Panthers' 48, and five plays later Bruce Gradkowski completed a 6-yard touchdown pass to Ike Hilliard. The Panthers scored on their first two possessions of the second half, the latter set up by Julius Peppers' fumble recovery, for a 10-7 lead. Mike Minter recovered a fumble at the Buccaneers' 16 later in the quarter that led to Brad Hoover's 5-yard run for a 17-7 lead. The Buccaneers cut the deficit to 17-10 with 8:32 remaining, but the Panthers needed just eight plays and 72 yards on the ensuing drive, capped by Jake Delhomme's 36-yard touchdown pass deep down the left side to Steve Smith with 3:11 to play. Delhomme 22 of 34 for 240 yards and 2 touchdowns, with 1 interception. Smith, who played despite the flu, had 8 catches for 149 yards. Gradkowski was 17 of 32 for 173 yards and 1 touchdown, with 2 interceptions.

Tampa Bay	7	0	0	3	—	10
Carolina	0	0	17	7	—	24

TB	—	Hilliard 6 pass from Gradkowski (Bryant kick)
Car	—	FG Kasay 28
Car	—	K. Johnson 4 pass from Delhomme (Kasay kick)
Car	—	Hoover 5 run (Kasay kick)
TB	—	FG Bryant 28
Car	—	S. Smith 36 pass from Delhomme (Kasay kick)

ELEVENTH WEEK SUMMARIES
American Football Conference

East Division	W	L	T	Pct.	Pts.	OP
New England	7	3	0	.700	236	131
N.Y. Jets	5	5	0	.500	177	217
Buffalo	4	6	0	.400	164	201
Miami	4	6	0	.400	170	188
North Division	**W**	**L**	**T**	**Pct.**	**Pts.**	**OP**
Baltimore	8	2	0	.800	222	147
Cincinnati	5	5	0	.500	247	233
Pittsburgh	4	6	0	.400	239	227
Cleveland	3	7	0	.300	170	208
South Division	**W**	**L**	**T**	**Pct.**	**Pts.**	**OP**
Indianapolis	9	1	0	.900	263	210
Jacksonville	6	4	0	.600	211	137
Houston	3	7	0	.300	165	230
Tennessee	3	7	0	.300	177	256
West Division	**W**	**L**	**T**	**Pct.**	**Pts.**	**OP**
San Diego	8	2	0	.800	332	202
Denver	7	3	0	.700	185	146
Kansas City	6	4	0	.600	210	195
Oakland	2	8	0	.200	118	198

National Football Conference

East Division	W	L	T	Pct.	Pts.	OP
Dallas	6	4	0	.600	271	188

N.Y. Giants	6	4	0	.600	224	208
Philadelphia	5	5	0	.500	246	194
Washington	3	7	0	.300	182	237
North Division	**W**	**L**	**T**	**Pct.**	**Pts.**	**OP**
Detroit	2	8	0	.200	185	239
Minnesota	4	6	0	.400	167	182
Chicago	9	1	0	.900	282	120
Green Bay	4	6	0	.400	185	252
South Division	**W**	**L**	**T**	**Pct.**	**Pts.**	**OP**
Carolina	6	4	0	.600	176	173
New Orleans	6	4	0	.600	245	228
Atlanta	5	5	0	.500	190	205
Tampa Bay	3	7	0	.300	132	214
West Division	**W**	**L**	**T**	**Pct.**	**Pts.**	**OP**
Seattle	6	4	0	.600	203	219
San Francisco	5	5	0	.500	182	265
St. Louis	4	6	0	.400	202	236
Arizona	2	8	0	.200	161	233

SUNDAY, NOVEMBER 19
ARIZONA 17, N.Y. JETS 10—at University of Phoenix Stadium, attendance 63,348. The Cardinals snapped an eight-game losing streak, and in his sixth start Matt Leinart posted his first victory. Aaron Francisco intercepted a pass near the goal line to thwart an early Jets scoring attempt. The Cardinals scored on three consecutive drives, capped by Leinart's 9-yard run to complete a six-play, 86-yard drive to begin the second half, to take a 17-0 lead. The Lions had scoring drives of 77 and 97 yards in the second half to pull within 17-10 with 4:35 to play. Edgerrin James and Marcel Shipp each rushed for a first down in the final moments to secure the victory. Leinart was 19 of 29 for 233 yards and 1 touchdown. Kitna was 23 of 38 for 248 yards, with 1 interception.

Detroit	0	0	3	7	—	10
Arizona	0	10	7	0	—	17

Ariz	—	Bry. Johnson 2 pass from Leinart (Rackers kick)
Ariz	—	FG Rackers 36
Ariz	—	Leinart 9 run (Rackers kick)
Det	—	FG Hanson 32
Det	—	Harris 1 run (Hanson kick)

BALTIMORE 24, ATLANTA 10—at M & T Bank Stadium, attendance 70,790. Jamal Lewis scored 3 touchdowns as the Ravens won their fourth consecutive game. The Ravens' defense allowed just 186 yards, the offense maintained possession for 36 minutes, 43 seconds, and B.J. Sams had 212 combined return yards. The Ravens trailed 7-0 at halftime, but scored on their first four possessions of the second half. The Falcons tied the game 10-10 with 1:58 left in the third quarter, only to watch Sams return the ensuing kickoff 59 yards to set up Lewis' 16-yard touchdown run, his second of the day. The Falcons drove to the Ravens' 19, but on third-and-4, Trevor Pryce and Gerome Sapp combined to sack Michael Vick for a 17-yard loss, taking the Falcons out of field-goal range. After the punt, the Ravens used 15 plays to drive 87 yards, capped by Lewis' 5-yard touchdown run for a 24-10 lead. Steve McNair was 24 of 34 for 236 yards. Vick was 11 of 21 for 127 yards and 1 touchdown.

Atlanta	7	0	3	0	—	10
Baltimore	0	0	17	7	—	24

Atl	—	Jenkins 13 pass from Vick (Andersen kick)
Balt	—	FG Stover 29
Balt	—	J. Lewis 2 run (Stover kick)
Atl	—	FG Andersen 21
Balt	—	J. Lewis 16 run (Stover kick)
Balt	—	J. Lewis 5 run (Stover kick)

CAROLINA 15, ST. LOUIS 0—at Bank of America Stadium, attendance 73,348. The Panthers' defense allowed just 111 total yards, while the offense rolled up 411 yards, as the Rams suffered their first shutout since 1998. The Panthers needed a 62-yard touchdown pass from Jake Delhomme to Steve Smith with 1:31 left in the half to take a 10-0 lead despite outgaining the Rams 261-38 in first-

half yardage. An interception at the Panthers' 15 late in the third quarter by Christian Morton set up John Kasay's 34-yard field goal, and Mike Rucker sacked Marc Bulger in the end zone for a safety with 2:24 to play to finish the scoring. Delhomme was 13 of 25 for 191 yards and 1 touchdown, with 1 interception. DeAngelo Williams had 20 carries for 114 yards. Bulger was 19 of 34 for 142 yards, with 1 interception.

St. Louis	0	0	0	0	—	0
Carolina	0	10	3	2	—	15

Car	—	FG Kasay 40
Car	—	S. Smith 62 pass from Delhomme (Kasay kick)
Car	—	FG Kasay 34
Car	—	Safety, Rucker sacked Bulger in end zone

PITTSBURGH 24, CLEVELAND 20—at Cleveland Browns Stadium, attendance 73,296. The Steelers scored on their final four possessions, capped by Ben Roethlisberger's 4-yard touchdown pass to Willie Parker with 32 seconds remaining, to defeat the Browns. Cleveland's defense intercepted Roethlisberger on there consecutive first-half possessions en route to a 10-0 halftime lead. The rally began late in the third quarter when Casey Hampton forced Jason Wright to fumble. Ryan Clark recovered, and Jeff Reed kicked a field goal five plays later to pull the Steelers within 10-3. Santonio Holmes' 20-yard touchdown catch pulled the Steelers within 13-10 early in the fourth quarter, but Josh Cribbs returned the ensuing kickoff 92 yards for a touchdown 20-10 led with 9:21 remaining. Undaunted, the Steelers drove 79 yards in 17 plays to pull within three points, then forced a three-and-out. Holmes had two key receptions to help set up Parker's 4-yard touchdown catch on second and goal with 32 seconds to play. The Browns drove to the Steelers' 22, but Charlie Frye's pass for Braylon Edwards in the end zone fell incomplete as time expired. Roethlisberger was 25 of 44 for 272 yards and 2 touchdowns, with 3 interceptions. Frye was 17 of 27 for 224 yards. Edwards had 7 catches for 137 yards.

Pittsburgh	0	0	3	21	—	24
Cleveland	0	10	0	10	—	20

Cle	—	Holly 57 interception return (Dawson kick)
Cle	—	FG Dawson 23
Pitt	—	FG Reed 43
Cle	—	FG Dawson 35
Pitt	—	Holmes 20 pass from Roethlisberger (Reed kick)
Cle	—	Cribbs 92 kickoff return (Dawson kick)
Pitt	—	Parker 1 run (reed kick)
Pitt	—	Parker 4 pass from Roethlisberger (Reed kick)

DALLAS 21, INDIANAPOLIS 14—at Texas Stadium, attendance 63,706. Marion Barber scored 2 fourth-quarter touchdowns as the Colts suffered their first defeat of the season. The Colts committed four turnovers in the first 31 minutes, yet led 7-0 and were up 14-7 entering the fourth quarter. Tony Romo gained 1-yard on fourth-and-1 on the opening play of the fourth quarter to sustain a 15-play drive that culminated with Barber's 5-yard touchdown run to tie the game with 11:36 to play. The Cowboys' defense forced a three-and-out, and Romo promptly completed passes of 19 and 33 yards to Terry Glenn to set up Barber's 1-yard scoring run with 6:00 remaining for a 21-14 lead. The Colts drove to the Cowboys' 8, but Manning's third-and-fourth-down passes fell incomplete. Romo completed a 7-yard pas to Glenn on third-and-7 with 2:00 to play that enabled the Cowboys to run out the clock. Romo was 19 of 23 for 226 yards, with 1 interception. Manning was 20 of 39 for 254 yards and 2 touchdowns, with 2 interceptions. Reggie Wayne had 7 receptions for 111 yards.

Indianapolis	0	7	7	0	—	14
Dallas	0	0	7	14	—	21

Ind	—	Wayne 23 pass from Manning

Dall	—	Burnett 39 interception return (Vanderjagt kick)
Ind	—	Clark 4 pass from Manning (Vinatieri kick)
Dall	—	Barber 5 run (Vanderjagt kick)
Dall	—	Barber 1 run (Vanderjagt kick)

NEW ENGLAND 35, GREEN BAY 0—at Lambeau Field, attendance 70,753. The Patriots' defense allowed just 5 first downs and Tom Brady passed for 4 touchdowns as New England snapped its first losing streak in four years. The Patriots outgained the Packers 357-120 total yards, and maintained possession for nearly 40 minutes. Brady's 2-yard touchdown pass to Daniel Graham came on fourth-and-goal and set the tone for the day. Trailing 21-0, Brett Favre was sacked by Tully Banta-Cain and Tedy Bruschi just before halftime and suffered an injured elbow. He did not return, and with Aaron Rodgers running the offense, the Patriots permitted just 53 second-half yards. Brady was 20 of 31 for 244 yards nd 4 touchdowns. Favre was 5 of 15 for 73 yards, and Rodgers was 4 of 12 for 32 yards.

New England	7	14	7	7	—	35
Green Bay	0	0	0	0	—	0

NE	—	Graham 2 pass from Brady (Gostkowski kick)
NE	—	Dillon 1 run (Gostkowski kick)
NE	—	Caldwell 54 pass from Brady (Gostkowski kick)
NE	—	Watson 8 pass from Brady (Gostkowski kick)
NE	—	Maroney 19 pass from Brady (Gostkowski kick)

BUFFALO 24, HOUSTON 21—at Reliant Stadium, attendance 70,125. Lee Evans had a pair of 83-yard touchdown catches in the first quarter, but it was Peerless Price's 15-yard touchdown catch with nine seconds left that won the game for Buffalo. Evans' 2 scoring grabs were on similar passes deep down the left side less than six minutes apart. The Texans scored on their next two drives, with David Carr completing an NFL-record-tying 22 consecutive completions during the game, a streak that ended with an incomplete pass intended for Andre Johnson with 5:44 to play in the game. Dunta Robinson's 9-yard interception return for a touchdown in the third quarter staked the Texans to a 21-17 lead. Carr's third-and-2 pass fell incomplete with 1:57 remaining, forcing the Texans to punt. Beginning on their own 45-yard line, J.P. Losman completed his first five passes before spiking the ball with 15 seconds left. On second-and-10 from the 15-yard line, Losman fired a 15-yard touchdown pass to a diving Price in the back of the end zone with nine seconds remaining. Losman was 26 of 38 for 340 yards and 3 touchdowns, with 1 interception. Evans had 11 catches for 265 yards. Carr was 25 of 30 for 223 yards, with 1 interception.

Buffalo	14	3	0	7	—	24
Houston	7	7	7	0	—	21

Buff	—	Evans 83 pas from Losman (Lindell kick)
Buff	—	Evans 83 pass from Losman (Lindell kick)
Hou	—	Lundy 17 run (K. Brown kick)
Buff	—	FG Lindell 40
Hou	—	Gado 1 run (K. Brown kick)
Hou	—	Robinson 9 interception return (K. Brown kick)
Buff	—	Price 15 pass from Losman (Lindell kick)

KANSAS CITY 17, OAKLAND 13—at Arrowhead Stadium, attendance 78,097. Larry Johnson rushed for 154 yards and 2 touchdowns and Jarrod Page clinched the victory with an interception in the end zone in the final minute. The Raiders strung together three consecutive 11-play scoring drives in the first half en route to a 13-7 lead at intermission. The Chiefs trailed 13-10 when they began with the ball on their own 20 with 4:53 to play. On fourth-and-1, Johnson gained 2 yards, and a 15-yard facemask penalty moved the ball out to near midfield. Later in the drive, Trent Green, making his first appearance in 10 weeks following a concussion, completed a 16-yard pass to Samie Parker on third-and-10 to reach the Raiders' 9. Two plays later, Johnson scored, with 1:32 remaining, for a 17-13 lead. Aaron Brooks completed a 39-yard pass to Ronald Curry to reach the Chiefs' 8 with 32 seconds left. On the next play, Page intercepted Brooks' pass intended for Randy Moss to clinch the victory. Green was 9 of 16 for 102 yards. Johnson carried 31 times for 154 yards. Brooks was 13 of 22 for 179 yards and 1 touchdown, with 1 interception.

Oakland	3	10	0	0	—	13
Kansas City	7	0	3	7	—	17

KC	—	L. Johnson 5 run (Tynes kick)
Oak	—	FG Janikowski 41
Oak	—	FG Janikowski 36
Oak	—	C. Anderson 2 pass from Brooks (Janikowski kick)
KC	—	FG Tynes 37
KC	—	L. Johnson 1 run (Tynes kick)

MIAMI 24, MINNESOTA 20—at Dolphin Stadium, attendance 73,070. The Dolphins' defense scored 2 fourth-quarter touchdowns to overcome an anemic offensive effort. The Vikings' defense allowed just minus-3 rushing yards, making the Dolphins the first team since 1961 to win with such a low rushing total. The Vikings tied the game 10-10 in the third quarter. Olindo Mare then missed a 44-yard field goal and, on the Dolphins' next possession, Antoine Winfield intercepted a pass and returned it 26 yards to the Dolphins' 3. However, the Vikings settled for Ryan Longwell's 19-yard field goal. With 9:27 to play, Matt Roth forced Chester Taylor to fumble. Renaldo Hill recovered and returned it 48 yards for a go-ahead touchdown. With 3:25 remaining, Jason Taylor intercepted Brad Johnson's short pass and returned it 49 yards for a touchdown and 24-13 lead. Chester Taylor scored as time expired. Joey Harrington was 26 of 42 for 254 yards and 1 touchdown, with 1 interception. Johnson was 26 of 44 for 262 yards, with 1 interception.

Minnesota	7	0	3	10	—	20
Miami	0	10	0	14	—	24

Minn	—	C. Taylor 1 run (Longwell kick)
Mia	—	FG Mare 44
Mia	—	Peelle 11 pass from Harrington (Mare kick)
Minn	—	FG Longwell 35
Minn	—	FG Longwell 19
Mia	—	Hill 48 fumble return (Mare kick)
Mia	—	J. Taylor 51 interception return (Mare kick)
Minn	—	C. Taylor 1 run (Longwell kick)

CINCINNATI 31, NEW ORLEANS 16—at Louisiana Superdome, attendance 68,801. Chad Johnson had 190 receiving yards and 3 touchdowns to overshadow Drew Brees' 510 passing yards and snap a three-game losing streak. The Saints outgained the Bengals 595-385 in total yards, but committed 4 turnovers. Two of the turnovers were interceptions near the goal line to thwart first-half scoring opportunities. Marc Simoneau's interception deep in Saints' territory led to John Carney's game-tying 24-yard field goal with 13:39 to play. On the ensuing drive, faced with third-and-2, Carson Palmer threw a pass deep down the left sideline for Johnson for a 60-yard touchdown with 10:23 to play. The Bengals forced a punt, and Johnson caught a 48-yard pass two plays later, followed immediately by his 4-yard scoring grab, for a 24-10 lead with 7:37 to play. Four plays later, Ethan Kilmer intercepted Brees' pass and returned it 52 yards for the Bengals third touchdown in a span of four minutes, nine seconds. Palmer was 14 of 22 for 275 yards and 3 touchdowns, with 1 interception. Rudi Johnson had 27 carries for 111 yards. Brees was 37 of 52 for 510 yards and 2 touchdowns, with 3 interceptions. Devery Henderson had 9 receptions for 169 yards.

Cincinnati	7	3	0	21	—	31
New Orleans	7	0	9	0	—	16

Cin	—	C. Johnson 41 pass from Palmer (Graham kick)
NO	—	Horn 72 pass from Brees (Carney kick)
Cin	—	FG Graham 21
NO	—	FG Carney 24
Cin	—	C. Johnson 60 pass from Palmer (Graham kick)
Cin	—	C. Johnson 4 pass from Palmer (Graham kick)
Cin	—	Kilmer 52 interception return (Graham kick)
NO	—	Copper 27 pass from Brees (kick blocked)

CHICAGO 10, N.Y. JETS 0—at The Meadowlands, attendance 77,632. The Bears posted their second shutout of the season to improve their record to 9-1. The lone scoring threat for either team in the first half was by the Jets, but Brian Urlacher intercepted Chad Pennington's third-and-goal pass in the end zone in the second quarter to quell the opportunity. The Jets opened the second half by attempting an onside kick, but Chris Harris recovered at the Jets' 44. Thomas Jones carried seven consecutive plays to set up Robbie Gould's 20-yard field goal. On the first play of the fourth quarter, Rex Grossman beat the blitz and completed a short pass to Mark Bradley, who made one move and outran the Jets for a 57-yard touchdown. The Jets never drove inside the Bears' 30 thereafter. Grossman was 11 of 22 for 119 yards and 1 touchdown. Jones had 23 carries for 121 yards. Chad Pennington was 19 of 35 for 162 yards, with 2 interceptions.

Chicago	0	0	3	7	—	10
N.Y. Jets	0	0	0	0	—	0

Chi	—	FG Gould 20
Chi	—	Bradley 57 pass from Grossman (Gould kick)

TENNESSEE 31, PHILADELPHIA 13—at Lincoln Financial Field, attendance 69,232. The Titans capitalized on three big plays to defeat the Eagles. In the second quarter, Donovan McNabb suffered a season-ending knee injury while throwing an incomplete pass with 14:48 left in the second quarter. Rob Bironas' 36-yard field goal as the half expired capped a 15-play drive and gave Tennessee a 10-6 lead. On the Titans' first play of the second half, Travis Henry broke free for a 70-yard touchdown. Less than four minutes later, Pacman Jones returned a punt 90 yards for a touchdown and 24-6 lead with 8:55 left in the third quarter. In the game's final minute, Randy Starks recovered a poor Shotgun snap. Starks returned the ball 42 yards, and lateralled to Keith Bulluck, who took the ball the remaining 16 yards for a touchdown. Vince Young was 8 of 22 for 101 yards and 1 touchdown. Henry had 18 carries for 143 yards. McNabb was 6 of 13 for 78 yards, with 1 interception. Jeff Garcia was 26 of 48 for 189 yards and 1 touchdown. Brian Westbrook carried 22 times for 102 yards, and had 12 catches for 46 yards.

Tennessee	7	3	14	7	—	31
Philadelphia	3	3	0	7	—	13

Tenn	—	Troupe 14 pass from Young (Bironas kick)
Phil	—	FG Akers 42
Phil	—	FG Akers 38
Tenn	—	FG Bironas 36
Tenn	—	Henry 70 run (Bironas kick)
Tenn	—	Jones 90 punt return (Bironas kick)
Phil	—	L. Smith 5 pass from Garcia (Akers kick)
Tenn	—	Bulluck 16 fumble return (Bironas kick)

SAN FRANCISCO 20, SEATTLE 14—at Monster Park, attendance 68,367. Frank Gore rushed for a team-record 212 yards as the 49ers held on to defeat the Seahawks.

The 49ers outgained Seattle 256-96 in the first half, and scored on four of their six possessions, capped by Joe Nedney's 18-yard field goal as the half expired, to take a 20-0 lead. The Seahawks pulled within 20-14 on Darrell Jackson's 41-yard touchdown reception with 6:40 remaining, but Bryant Young and the 49ers' defense stopped Shaun Alexander for a 1-yard loss on fourth-and-1 from the Seahawks' 37 with 2:00 remaining. Gore fumbled on the next play, but Walt Harris intercepted Seneca Wallace's pass with 1:18 remaining. Alex Smith was 19 of 25 for 163 yards and 1 touchdown. Gore carried 24 times for 212 yards. Wallace was 19 of 31 for 252 yards and 2 touchdowns, with 3 interceptions. Deion Branch had 7 catches for 113 yards.

Seattle	0	0	7	7	—	14
San Francisco	3	17	0	0	—	20

SF	—	FG Nedney 39
SF	—	Battle 9 pass from Smith (Nedney kick)
SF	—	Smith 1 run (Nedney kick)
SF	—	FG Nedney 18
Sea	—	Branch 38 pass from Wallace (J. Brown kick)
Sea	—	Jackson 41 pass from Wallace (J. Brown kick)

TAMPA BAY 20, WASHINGTON 17—at Raymond James Stadium, attendance 65,699. Carnell Williams ran for 122 yards as the Buccaneers defeated the Redskins in Jason Campbell's first NFL start. The teams each had long touchdown drives to begin the second half, with the Buccaneers tying the game on Anthony Becht's 2-yard touchdown catch. Early in the fourth quarter, Juran Bolden recovered Ladell Betts' fumble, and Bruce Gradkowski fired a 34-yard touchdown pass to Joey Galloway three plays later for a 17-10 lead with 9:35 to play. After a three-and-out, Williams carried six consecutive times, including a 25-yard run, to set up Matt Bryant's 31-yard field goal with 3:50 to play for a 10-point lead. The Redskins scored with 32 seconds left, but Michael Clayton recovered the onside kick to secure the victory. Gradkowski was 14 of 21 for 178 yards and 2 touchdowns, with 1 interception. Williams carried 27 times for 122 yards. Campbell was 19 of 34 for 196 yards and 2 touchdowns.

Washington	3	0	7	7	—	17
Tampa Bay	3	0	7	10	—	20

TB	—	FG Bryant 26
Wash	—	FG Novak 45
Wash	—	Cooley 3 pass from Campbell (Novak kick)
TB	—	Becht 2 pass from Gradkowski (Bryant kick)
TB	—	Galloway 34 pass from Gradkowski (Bryant kick)
TB	—	FG Bryant 31
Wash	—	Yoder 4 pass from Campbell (Novak kick)

SUNDAY NIGHT, NOVEMBER 19
SAN DIEGO 35, DENVER 27—at INVESCO Field at Mile High, attendance 76,723. LaDainian Tomlinson scored 4 touchdowns as the Chargers became the first team in NFL history to rally from 17-point road deficits in consecutive weeks. Darrent Williams intercepted a pass and returned it 31 yards for a touchdown to give the Broncos a 24-7 lead with 9:25 left in the third quarter. The Chargers responded with two touchdowns within the next six minutes, the latter coming on Tomlinson's 51-yard touchdown catch of a short pass, to pull within 24-21. The Broncos took 7:38 off the clock on their next possession, but settled for Jason Elam's 38-yard field goal. Michael Turner's 44-yard kickoff return sparked the ensuing drive, capped by Philip Rivers' 5-yard touchdown pass to Vincent Jackson to give the Chargers a 28-27 lead with 6:45 to play. Drayton Florence intercepted Jake Plummer's fourth-down pass on the ensuing possession to set up Tomlinson's fourth touchdown with 1:14 remaining. The Broncos reached the Chargers' 32, but Shaun Phillips

sacked Plummer as time expired. Rivers was 19 of 26 for 222 yards and 2 touchdowns, with 2 interceptions. Tomlinson had 20 carries for 105 yards, and reached 100 touchdowns faster than any player in NFL history (89 games, compared to 93 for Emmitt Smith and Jim Brown). Tomlinson's 19 touchdowns in a six-game stretch was also an NFL record. Plummer was 13 of 28 for 183 yards, with 1 interception.

San Diego	7	0	14	14	—	35
Denver	0	14	10	3	—	27

SD	—	Tomlinson 3 run (Kaeding kick)
Den	—	M. Bell 3 run (Elam kick)
Den	—	M. Bell 3 run (Elam kick)
Den	—	FG Elam 42
Den	—	Da. Williams 31 interception return (Elam kick)
SD	—	Tomlinson 3 run (Kaeding kick)
SD	—	Tomlinson 51 pass from Rivers (Kaeding kick)
Den	—	FG Elam 38
SD	—	Jackson 5 pass from Rivers (Kaeding kick)
SD	—	Tomlinson 1 run (Kaeding kick)

MONDAY NIGHT, NOVEMBER 20
JACKSONVILLE 26, N.Y. GIANTS 10—at Alltel Stadium, attendance 67,164. The Jaguars' defense limited Tiki Barber to his lowest rushing total in three seasons as Jacksonville improved its record to 6-4. The Jaguars' defense allowed just 3 first-half first downs, and the offense scored on its first four possessions of the second half. The key play was David Garrard's 49-yard pass to Matt Jones on third-and-4 early in the fourth quarter. On the next play, Maurice Jones-Drew scored a 3-yard touchdown to stake the Jaguars to a 23-10 lead. Clint Ingram's interception on the next drive led to Josh Scobee's fourth field goal for a 26-10 lead with 5:39 remaining. Garrard was 19 of 32 for 249 yards. Eli Manning was 19 of 41 for 230 yards and 1 touchdown, with 2 interceptions.

N.Y. Giants	3	0	7	0	—	10
Jacksonville	3	7	6	10	—	26

NYG	—	FG Feely 40
Jax	—	FG Scobee 39
Jax	—	Taylor 10 run (Scobee kick)
Jax	—	FG Scobee 24
NYG	—	Burress 25 pass from Manning (Feely kick)
Jax	—	FG Scobee 23
Jax	—	Jones-Drew 3 run (Scobee kick)
Jax	—	FG Scobee 48

TWELFTH WEEK SUMMARIES
American Football Conference

East Division	W	L	T	Pct.	Pts.	OP
New England	8	3	0	.727	253	144
N.Y. Jets	6	5	0	.545	203	228
Buffalo	5	6	0	.455	191	225
Miami	5	6	0	.455	197	198
North Division	**W**	**L**	**T**	**Pct.**	**Pts.**	**OP**
Baltimore	9	2	0	.818	249	147
Cincinnati	6	5	0	.545	277	233
Pittsburgh	4	7	0	.364	239	254
Cleveland	3	8	0	.273	170	238
South Division	**W**	**L**	**T**	**Pct.**	**Pts.**	**OP**
Indianapolis	10	1	0	.909	308	231
Jacksonville	6	5	0	.545	235	164
Tennessee	4	7	0	.364	201	277
Houston	3	8	0	.273	176	256
West Division	**W**	**L**	**T**	**Pct.**	**Pts.**	**OP**
San Diego	9	2	0	.818	353	216
Denver	7	4	0	.636	195	165
Kansas City	7	4	0	.636	229	205
Oakland	2	9	0	.182	132	219

National Football Conference

East Division	W	L	T	Pct.	Pts.	OP
Dallas	7	4	0	.636	309	198
N.Y. Giants	6	5	0	.545	245	232
Philadelphia	5	6	0	.455	268	239
Washington	4	7	0	.364	199	250
North Division	**W**	**L**	**T**	**Pct.**	**Pts.**	**OP**
Chicago	9	2	0	.818	295	137
Minnesota	5	6	0	.455	198	208
Green Bay	4	7	0	.364	209	286
Detroit	2	9	0	.182	195	266
South Division	**W**	**L**	**T**	**Pct.**	**Pts.**	**OP**
New Orleans	7	4	0	.636	276	241
Carolina	6	5	0	.545	189	190
Atlanta	5	6	0	.455	203	236
Tampa Bay	3	8	0	.273	142	252
West Division	**W**	**L**	**T**	**Pct.**	**Pts.**	**OP**
Seattle	7	4	0	.636	237	243
St. Louis	5	6	0	.455	222	253
San Francisco	5	6	0	.455	199	285
Arizona	2	9	0	.182	187	264

THURSDAY, NOVEMBER 23
MIAMI 27, DETROIT 10—at Ford Field, attendance 61,562. In his return to Detroit, Joey Harrington passed for 2 touchdowns as the Dolphins won their first consecutive game. The Lions scored on their first two possessions, but only generated 8 first downs the remainder of the game. The Lions still led 10-7 late in the first half when Renaldo Hill intercepted Jon Kitna's pass and returned it 21 yards to set up Randy McMichael's 5-yard scoring grab. The Dolphins scored on their first three second-half possessions to take a 27-10 lead, and the Lions never seriously threatened. Harrington was 19 of 29 for 213 yards and 3 touchdowns, with 1 interception. Marty Booker had 7 catches for 115 yards. Kitna was 22 of 40 for 252 yards and 1 touchdown, with 1 interception. Roy Williams had 6 receptions for 126 yards.

Miami	7	7	10	3	—	27
Detroit	10	0	0	0	—	10

Det	—	Campbell 2 pass from Kitna (Hanson kick)
Det	—	FG Hanson 52
Mia	—	Booker 8 pass from Harrington (Mare kick)
Mia	—	McMichael 5 pass from Harrington (Mare kick)
Mia	—	FG Mare 42
Mia	—	Booker 19 pass from Harrington (Mare kick)
Mia	—	FG Mare 28

DALLAS 38, TAMPA BAY 10—at Texas Stadium, attendance 63,183. The Cowboys scored on six of seven possessions during the game to overwhelm the Buccaneers. The Cowboys outgained the Buccaneers 435-211 in total yards, with three of Dallas' touchdown drives being at least 70 yards. Roy Williams sparked the spurt with an interception to set up Tony Romo's go-ahead 2-yard touchdown pass to Terry Glenn for a 14-7 lead. Romo engineered 4-play, 74-yard drive just before halftime to increase the lead to 21-10, and Dallas scored on its first three drives of the second half. Gradkowski was 10 of 20 for 120 yards, with 2 interceptions. Romo was 22 of 29 for 306 yards and 5 touchdowns. Owens had 8 receptions for 107 yards.

Tampa Bay	7	3	0	0	—	10
Dallas	7	14	14	3	—	38

TB	—	Alstott 1 run (Bryant kick)
Dall	—	Glenn 30 pass from Romo (Vanderjagt kick)
Dall	—	Glenn 2 pass from Romo (Vanderjagt kick)
TB	—	FG Bryant 46
Dall	—	Barber 1 pass from Romo (Vanderjagt kick)
Dall	—	Barber 2 pass from Romo (Vanderjagt kick)
Dall	—	Owens 7 pass from Romo (Vanderjagt kick)
Dall	—	FG Vanderjagt 22

THURSDAY NIGHT, NOVEMBER 23
KANSAS CITY 19, DENVER 10—at Arrowhead Stadium, attendance 72,134. In the first-ever game broadcast live

on NFL Network, Lawrence Tynes kicked 4 field goals to cap the NFL's newly-established Thanksgiving tripleheader. Larry Johnson' 1-yard touchdown run late in the first half staked the Chiefs to a 10-0 lead. The Broncos scored on their next two possessions to pull within 13-10, but the Chiefs responded with a pair of field goals to give Kansas City a 19-10 lead with 2:42 to play. Green was 13 of 22 for 161 yards, with 1 interception. Johnson had 34 carries for 157 yards. Plummer was 25 of 39 for 216 yards and 1 touchdown, with 1 interception.

Denver	0	3	7	0	—	10
Kansas City	3	7	3	6	—	19

KC	—	FG Tynes 24
KC	—	L. Johnson 1 run (Tynes kick)
Den	—	FG Elam 31
KC	—	FG Tynes 34
Den	—	Alexander 1 pass from Plummer (Elam kick)
KC	—	FG Tynes 29
KC	—	FG Tynes 21

SUNDAY, NOVEMBER 26

NEW ORLEANS 31, ATLANTA 13—at Georgia Dome, attendance 70,933. Drew Brees passed for 349 yards, marking his fifth straight game of at least 300 yards, as the Falcons dropped their fourth consecutive game. The Saints scored on their first two drives of the game, and expanded their lead to 21-6 when Terrance Copper caught Brees' Hail Mary pass for a touchdown as the half expired. Warrick Dunn's 1-yard scoring run on fourth-and-goal pulled the Falcons to within 21-13. The Saints had scoring drives of 80 and 74 yards in the fourth quarter to pull away. Brees was 21 of 30 for 349 yards and 2 touchdowns. Henderson had 4 receptions for 158 yards. Vick was 9 of 24 for 84 yards, but rushed 12 times for 166 yards.

New Orleans	14	7	0	10	—	31
Atlanta	3	3	7	0	—	13

NO	—	Henderson 76 pass from Brees (Carney kick)
NO	—	McAllister 1 run (Carney kick)
Atl	—	FG Andersen 22
Atl	—	FG Andersen 30
NO	—	Copper 48 pass from Brees (Carney kick)
Atl	—	Dunn 1 run (Andersen kick)
NO	—	FG Carney 25
NO	—	McAllister 9 run (Carney kick)

BALTIMORE 27, PITTSBURGH 0—at M & T Bank Stadium, attendance 70,946. The Ravens' defense allowed just 172 yards, forced 3 turnovers, and registered 9 sacks to hand the Steelers their biggest point-differential defeat since 1997. The Ravens' allowed just 3 first down in the first half en route to a 17-0 halftime lead. The Steelers did not cross midfield until the third quarter, and that drive culminated with Ben Roethlisberger getting sacked by Corey Ivy. Roethlisberger fumbled and Adalius Thomas recovered the ball and raced 57 yards for a touchdown and 24-0 lead. Bart Scott intercepted a pass at the Ravens' 12 in the final minutes to preserve the shutout. Steve McNair was 18 of 24 for 140 yards and 1 touchdown. Roethlisberger, who was knocked from the game for a play after a sack by Scott in the second quarter, was 21 of 41 for 214 yards, with 2 interceptions.

Pittsburgh	0	0	0	0	—	0
Baltimore	7	10	7	3	—	27

Balt	—	Heap 20 pass from McNair (Stover kick)
Balt	—	J. Lewis 1 run (Stover kick)
Balt	—	FG Stover 37
Balt	—	Thomas 57 fumble return (Stover kick)
Balt	—	FG Stover 40

BUFFALO 27, JACKSONVILLE 24—at Ralph Wilson Stadium, attendance 63,608. Roscoe Parrish made two key plays and Rian Lindell kicked a 42-yard field goal as time expired to lift the Bills to victory. The Bills scored on

three consecutive first-half drives to take a 17-7 lead. The Jaguars responded with a 71-yard touchdown drive to cut the deficit to 17-14 at halftime. Late in the third quarter, Roscoe Parrish returned a punt 82 yards for a touchdown for the Bills, zig-zagging his way to the left sideline and then down the field, for a 24-14 lead. The Jaguars responded with a field goal to pull within seven points. David Garrard engineered an 11-play, 62-yard drive, which was highlighted by his 16-yard scramble on fourth-and-14, and capped by Garrard's 3-yard touchdown pass to Matt Jones with 28 seconds remaining. Terrence McGee returned the squib kickoff to the 40-yard line, and J.P. Losman completed a 30-yard pass to Parrish with 10 seconds remaining to set up Lindell's game-winning 42-yard field goal as the time expired. Losman was 21 of 28 for 169 yards, with 1 interception. Garrard was 16 of 22 for 132 yards and 2 touchdowns. Fred Taylor rushed 22 times for 101 yards.

Jacksonville	0	14	0	10	—	24
Buffalo	7	10	7	3	—	27

Buff	—	McGahee 4 run (Lindell kick)
Buff	—	FG Lindell 21
Jax	—	Jones-Drew 14 run (Scobee kick)
Buff	—	McGahee 30 run (Lindell kick)
Jax	—	Lewis 1 pass from Garrard (Scobee kick)
Buff	—	Parrish 82 punt return (Lindell kick)
Jax	—	FG Scobee 27
Jax	—	Jones 3 pass from Garrard (Scobee kick)
Buff	—	FG Lindell 42

CINCINNATI 30, CLEVELAND 0—at Cleveland Browns Stadium, attendance 72,926. The Bengals posted their first shutout since 1989 en route to defeating the Browns for a record fifth consecutive time. The Bengals scored on three of their four first-half possessions to take a 17-0 lead, and then drove 70 yards in 10 plays to begin the second half, capped by Carson Palmer's 6-yard touchdown pass to T.J. Houshmandzadeh, for a 23-0 lead. The Bengals intercepted 4 passes, including 2 by Tory James in the fourth quarter, to preserve the shutout. Palmer was 25 of 32 for 275 yards and 3 touchdowns, with 1 interception. Chad Johnson had 7 catches for 123 yards. Frye was 18 of 29 for 186 yards, with 4 interceptions.

Cincinnati	7	10	6	7	—	30
Cleveland	0	0	0	0	—	0

Cin	—	R. Johnson 1 run (Graham kick)
Cin	—	Henry 7 pass from Palmer (Graham kick)
Cin	—	FG Graham 24
Cin	—	Houshmandzadeh 6 pass from Palmer (kick blocked)
Cin	—	Henry 10 pass from Palmer (Graham kick)

MINNESOTA 31, ARIZONA 26—at Metrodome, attendance 63,483. The Vikings survived two big plays and a Hail Mary Pass as time expired to snap their four-game losing streak. Both teams finished with 412 yards, but the Cardinals had 5 turnovers compared to just 1 miscue by the Vikings. J.J. Arrington opened the game with a 99-yard kickoff return. The Cardinals led 13-7 in the final minute of the first half when Brad Johnson completed a 17-yard touchdown pass to Marcus Robinson to take the lead. The Vikings scored on three of their first four second-half possessions, too, and were about to score a fourth time when Chester Taylor fumbled at the 1-yard line. Adrian Wilson came out of the goal-line pile with the ball and ran 99 yards for a touchdown. The Cardinals went for 2 points trailing by 12 with 10:08 to play, and Matt Leinart's pass for Anquan Boldin fell incomplete. The Cardinals forced a punt and drove to the Vikings' 15, but, needing a touchdown since they went for the 2-point conversion, Leinart's fourth-down pass fell incomplete with 3:17 to play. The Cardinals' defense forced another punt, and Leinart engineered a 53-yard drive, capped by Anquan Boldin 9-yard touchdown catch with 39 seconds

left. Monty Beisel recovered the onside kick of the Cardinals, and Leinart completed a 20-yard pass to Larry Fitzgerald to get the Vikings' 36. But Leinart's Hail Mary pass as time expired was intercepted by Dwight Smith. Johnson was 27 of 41 for 271 yards and 3 touchdowns. Taylor carried 27 times for 136 yards. Leinart was 31 of 51 for 405 yards and 1 touchdown, with 2 interceptions. Fitzgerald had 11 catches for 172 yards and Boldin added 9 receptions for 140 yards.

Arizona	7	6	0	13	—	26
Minnesota	7	7	10	7	—	31

Ariz	—	Arrington 99 kickoff return (Rackers kick)
Minn	—	Taylor 1 run (Longwell kick)
Ariz	—	FG Rackers 21
Ariz	—	FG Rackers 50
Minn	—	M. Robinson 17 pass from B. Johnson (Longwell kick)
Minn	—	McMullen 9 pass from B. Johnson (Longwell kick)
Minn	—	FG Longwell 40
Minn	—	Dugan 3 pass from B. Johnson (Longwell kick)
Ariz	—	Wilson 99 fumble return (pass failed)
Ariz	—	Boldin 9 pass from Leinart (Rackers kick)

NEW ENGLAND 17, CHICAGO 13—at Gillette Stadium, attendance 68,756. Asante Samuel intercepted 3 passes as the Patriots outlasted the Bears. In the first half, Richard Seymour blocked a 45-yard field goal-attempt and recovered Rex Grossman's fumble at the Patriots' 8-yard line to thwart another rally. Steven Gostkowski's career-long 52-yard field goal as the half expired lifted the Patriots to a 10-3 lead. The Bears tied the game early in the fourth quarter, but the Patriots responded with an 11-play, 73-yard drive, capped by Brady's 2-yard touchdown pass to Ben Watson for a 17-10 lead with 8:22 to play. The Bears added a field goal and then Danieal Manning forced Corey Dillon to fumble. Alex Brown recovered the ball at the Bears' 22 with 1:52 left. On the next play, Grossman threw the ball deep down the middle and Samuel intercepted his third pass of the game, this one to clinch the victory. Brady was 22 of 33 for 267 yards and 1 touchdown, with 2 interceptions. Grossman was 15 of 34 for 176 yards, with 3 interceptions. Bernard Berrian had 5 receptions for 104 yards.

Chicago	0	3	0	10	—	13
New England	0	10	0	7	—	17

NE	—	Maroney 1 run (Gostkowski kick)
Chi	—	FG Gould 46
NE	—	FG Gostkowski 52
Chi	—	Benson 2 run (Gould kick)
NE	—	Watson 2 pass from Brady (Gostkowski kick)
Chi	—	FG Gould 32

N.Y. JETS 26, HOUSTON 11—at The Meadowlands, attendance 76,596. Mike Nugent made 4 field goals and the Jets committed zero turnovers and just one penalty en route to victory. The Jets scored on four consecutive possessions, capped by a 91-yard drive that ended with Chad Pennington's 12-yard touchdown pass to Laveranues Coles. Kerry Rhodes intercepted a pass later in the quarter that led to Cedric Houston's 1-yard scoring run to give the Jets a 23-3 lead with 3:33 left in the third quarter. Pennington was 24 of 31 for 286 yards and a 1 touchdown. Coles had 9 catches for 111 yards, and Jerricho Cotchery had 7 receptions for 110 yards. David Carr was 39 of 54 for 321 yards and 1 touchdown, with 1 interception.

Houston	0	3	0	8	—	11
N.Y. Jets	3	6	14	3	—	26

NYJ	—	FG Nugent 23
NYJ	—	FG Nugent 34
Hou	—	FG K. Brown 47
NYJ	—	FG Nugent 54
NYJ	—	Coles 12 pass from Pennington

(Nugent kick)
NYJ — Houston 1 run (Nugent kick)
NYJ — FG Nugent 40
Hou — A. Johnson 3 pass from Carr
(Lundy pass from Carr)

ST. LOUIS 20, SAN FRANCISCO 17—at Edward Jones Dome, attendance 65,517. The 49ers completed 2 third-down situations on a 14-play, 65-yard drive in the third quarter, capped by Alex Smith's 1-yard touchdown pass to Eric Johnson, for a 14-13 49ers lead. On third-and-1 from the Rams' 7-yard line with 4:20 to play, Brandon Chillar and Raonall Smith stopped Michael Robinson for no gain, forcing the 49ers to settle for a field goal and 17-13 lead. Bulger was flawless down the stretch, completing all 9 of his pass attempts on the final drive, capped by his 5-yard touchdown pass to Kevin Curtis with 27 seconds remaining. Oshiomogho Atogwe intercepted Smith's pass at the Rams' 39 as time expired. Bulger was 23 of 34 for 291 yards and 1 touchdown, with 1 interception. Jackson had 23 carries for 121 yards. Smith was 13 of 25 for 148 yards and 1 touchdown, with 2 interceptions.

| San Francisco | 0 | 7 | 7 | 3 | — | 17 |
| St. Louis | 0 | 13 | 0 | 7 | — | 20 |

StL — FG Wilkins 24
StL — Jackson 36 run (Wilkins kick)
SF — Gore 12 run (Nedney kick)
StL — FG Wilkins 51
SF — E. Johnson 1 pass from A. Smith
(Nedney kick)
SF — FG Nedney 24
StL — Curtis 5 pass from Bulger
(Wilkins kick)

SAN DIEGO 21, OAKLAND 14—at Qualcomm Stadium, attendance 66,105. LaDainian Tomlinson rushed for 109 yards, scored a touchdown, and passed for another, as the Chargers rallied to rally in the fourth quarter to defeat the Raiders. The victory was the 200th of Marty Schottenheimer's career, making him the seventh coach in NFL history to reach that plateau. For two and a half quarters, the Raiders moved the ball very well against eh Chargers' defense, missing a 36-yard field goal but scoring 2 touchdowns to take a 14-7 lead with 7:40 left in the third quarter. The Chargers' defense buckled down from that point, holding the Raiders to minus-4 yards and intercepting 2 passes on their final four possessions. One of those interceptions, by Quentin Jammer with 13:26 to play, sparked a 48-yard drive, highlighted by Vincent Jackson's 13-yard catch on fourth-and-2, and punctuated by Tomlinson's 19-yard halfback-option touchdown pass to Antonio Gates to tie the game with 9:46 remaining. It was Tomlinson's sixth career touchdown pass. After a punt, Tomlinson had a 44-yard run to set up his 10-yard touchdown jaunt around left end or a 21-14 lead with 3:39 remaining. Drayton Florence's interception with 1:48 to play clinched the victory. Rivers was 14 of 31 for 133 yards, 1 interception. Tomlinson rushed 19 times for 109 yards. Brooks was 17 of 30 for 187 yards and 1 touchdown, with 2 interceptions.

| Oakland | 0 | 7 | 7 | 0 | — | 14 |
| San Diego | 0 | 7 | 0 | 14 | — | 21 |

Oak — Lee 1 run (Janikowski kick)
SD — Tomlinson 4 run (Kaeding kick)
Oak — Madison 2 pass from Brooks
(Janikowski kick)
SD — Gates 19 pass from Tomlinson
(Kaeding kick)
SD — Tomlinson 10 run (Kaeding kick)

TENNESSEE 24, N.Y. GIANTS 21—at LP Field, attendance 69,143. Rob Bironas kicked a 49-yard field goal with six seconds remaining as the Titans set a club record by overcoming a 21-point fourth-quarter deficit to register their fourth victory in their last six games. The Giants scored touchdowns on three consecutive first-half possessions, two of which were drives of 52 and 29 yards that were set up by fumble recoveries, to take a 21-0 lead

with 8:05 left in the second quarter. The score was still 21-0 as the Titans punted with 13:49 to play. Two plays later, Pacman Jones intercepted Eli Manning's pass and returned it 26 yards to the Giants' 46. An unnecessary roughness call on fourth down kept alive the drive, and Vince Young completed a 4-yard touchdown pass to Bo Scaife with 9:35 to play. The Titans forced a three-and-out, and Jones returned the punt 23 yards to the Giants' 36. Six plays later, Young scored on a 1-yard sneak to pull the Titans to within 21-14 with 5:24 to play. The Giants managed one first down on their next possessions, but punted with 3:07 left. On a drive that began from their own 24-yard line, Young scrambled for 19 yards on fourth-and-10, and had a 16-yard scrambled mixed among 3 completions, capped by a 14-yard touchdown pass to Brandon Jones with 44 seconds left to tie the game. Two plays later, Jones intercepted Manning's pass at the Giants' 49. Young completed two passes, the second to Jones at the Titans' 31, and Bironas drilled the game-winning 49-yard field goal with six seconds remaining. Young was 24 of 35 for 249 yards and 2 touchdowns. Manning was 18 of 28 for 143 yards and 1 touchdown, with 2 interceptions.

| N.Y. Giants | 7 | 14 | 0 | 0 | — | 21 |
| Tennessee | 0 | 0 | 0 | 24 | — | 24 |

NYG — Burress 3 pass from Manning
(Feely kick)
NYG — Jacobs 10 run (Feely kick)
NYG — Jacobs 4 run (Feely kick)
Tenn — Scaife 4 pass from Young
(Bironas kick)
Tenn — Young 1 run (Bironas kick)
Tenn — Jones 14 pass from Young
(Bironas kick)
Tenn — FG Bironas 49

WASHINGTON 17, CAROLINA 13—at FedExField, attendance 85,450. Jason Campbell completed 2 second-half touchdown passes as he engineered a fourth-quarter rally to register his first NFL victory. John Kasay's 51-yard field goal as the first half expired gave the Panthers a 6-3 lead. An 11-yard punt by Jason Baker gave the Redskins the ball at the Panthers' 36 late in the third quarter, and Washington capitalized as Campbell completed a 4-yard touchdown pass to Antwaan Randle El for a 10-6 lead. The Panthers responded with their best drive of the day, marching 74 yards in 15 plays capped by their fourth third-down conversion of the drive, an 8-yard touchdown pass to Steve Smith with 7:55 to play. With 4:37 remaining, faced with third-and-8, Campbell completed a short pass to Chris Cooley who raced 66 yards for a touchdown and 17-13 lead. Sean Taylor intercepted Jake Delhomme's long pass into the end zone with 55 seconds remaining to clinch the victory. Campbell was 11 of 23 for 118 yards and 2 touchdowns, with 1 interception. Ladell Betts had 24 carries for 104 yards. Delhomme was 23 of 38 for 168 yards and 1 touchdown, with 2 interceptions.

| Carolina | 3 | 3 | 0 | 7 | — | 13 |
| Washington | 0 | 3 | 7 | 7 | — | 17 |

Car — FG Kasay 42
Wash — FG Novak 42
Car — FG Kasay 51
Wash — Randle El 4 pass from Campbell
(Novak kick)
Car — Smith 8 pass from Delhomme
(Kasay kick)
Wash — Cooley 66 pass from Campbell
(Novak kick)

SUNDAY NIGHT, NOVEMBER 26
INDIANAPOLIS 45, PHILADELPHIA 21—at RCA Dome, attendance 57,296. Joseph Addai tied an NFL rookie record by rushing for 4 touchdowns as the Colts downed the Eagles. The Colts opened the game with touchdown drives of 79, 74, and 60 yards, all which culminated in touchdown runs by Addai, for a 21-0 lead with 8:58 left in the second quarter. The Colts expanded the lead to 31-7 when Peyton Manning capped a nine-play, 89-yard drive which culminated with Reggie Wayne's 11-yard

touchdown catch. Lito Sheppard's interception and 25-yard return early in the fourth quarter led to Brian Westbrook's 6-yard run with 10:13 to play to pull within 31-21. The Colts answered with a 13-play drive, all rushing plays, capped by Addai's 4-yard run with 3:38 remaining. On the next play from scrimmage, Robert Mathis forced Jeff Garcia to fumble. Kelvin Hayden picked up the ball and returned it 26 yards for a touchdown. Manning was 14 of 20 for 183 yards and 1 touchdown, with 1 interception. Addai had 24 carries for 171 yards. Garcia was 19 of 23 for 140 yards and 2 touchdowns.

| Philadelphia | 0 | 7 | 7 | 7 | — | 21 |
| Indianapolis | 7 | 17 | 7 | 14 | — | 45 |

Ind — Addai 15 run (Vinatieri kick)
Ind — Addai 10 run (Vinatieri kick)
Ind — Addai 15 run (Vinatieri kick)
Phil — L. Smith 1 pass from Garcia
(Akers kick)
Ind — FG Vinatieri 44
Ind — Wayne 11 pass from Manning
(Vinatieri kick)
Phil — R. Brown 3 pass from Garcia
(Akers kick)
Phil — Westbrook 6 run (Akers kick)
Ind — Addai 4 run (Vinatieri kick)
Ind — Hayden 26 fumble return
(Vinatieri kick)

MONDAY NIGHT, NOVEMBER 27
SEATTLE 34, GREEN BAY 24—at Qwest Field, attendance 52.250. Shaun Alexander carried 40 times for 201 yards and Matt Hasselbeck, in his first game back after four weeks off with a sprained knee, passed for 3 touchdowns to lead the Seahawks to victory in the snow. It was the first time Seattle had snow at a home game, and the 34-degree kickoff temperature made it the coldest home game in franchise history. Alexander, who had missed six games with a foot injury before returning the previous week, set a career high for carries. Hasselbeck, threw 3 interceptions on the Seahawks' first four possessions, and later committed a fumble that Abdul Hodge returned for a touchdown as Seattle trailed 14-12 at halftime. Trailing 21-12 in the third quarter, Hasselbeck got hot, engineering drives of 62, 77, and 51 yards that all culminated in touchdown passes. The final touchdown pass, to Jerramy Stevens with 6:13 to play, increased the lead to 34-24. Marcus Trufant and Kelly Jennings each intercepted passes in the final minutes to keep the Packers at bay. Hasselbeck was 17 of 36 for 157 yards and 3 touchdowns, with 3 interceptions. Brett Favre was 22 of 36 for 266 yards and 1 touchdown, with 3 interceptions.

| Green Bay | 7 | 7 | 3 | 7 | — | 24 |
| Seattle | 3 | 9 | 7 | 15 | — | 34 |

GB — Green 5 run (Rayner kick)
Sea — FG J. Brown 45
Sea — FG J. Brown 41
Sea — FG J. Brown 37
GB — Hodge 29 fumble return
(Rayner kick)
Sea — FG J. Brown 28
GB — Driver 48 pass from Favre
(Rayner kick)
Sea — Hackett 23 pass from Hasselbeck
(J. Brown kick)
Sea — Jackson 4 pass from Hasselbeck
(Stevens pass from Hasselbeck)
GB — FG Rayner 34
Sea — Stevens 3 pass from Hasselbeck
(J. Brown kick)

THIRTEENTH WEEK SUMMARIES
American Football Conference

East Division	W	L	T	Pct.	Pts.	OP
New England	9	3	0	.750	281	165
N.Y. Jets	7	5	0	.583	241	238
Buffalo	5	7	0	.417	212	249
Miami	5	7	0	.417	207	222
North Division	**W**	**L**	**T**	**Pct.**	**Pts.**	**OP**
Baltimore	9	3	0	.750	256	160

	W	L	T	Pct.	Pts.	OP
Cincinnati	7	5	0	.583	290	240
Pittsburgh	5	7	0	.417	259	257
Cleveland	4	8	0	.333	201	266
South Division	**W**	**L**	**T**	**Pct.**	**Pts.**	**OP**
Indianapolis	10	2	0	.833	325	251
Jacksonville	7	5	0	.583	259	174
Tennessee	5	7	0	.417	221	294
Houston	4	8	0	.333	199	270
West Division	**W**	**L**	**T**	**Pct.**	**Pts.**	**OP**
San Diego	10	2	0	.833	237	237
Denver	7	5	0	.583	215	188
Kansas City	7	5	0	.583	257	236
Oakland	2	10	0	.167	146	242

National Football Conference

East Division	**W**	**L**	**T**	**Pct.**	**Pts.**	**OP**
Dallas	8	4	0	.667	332	218
N.Y. Giants	6	6	0	.500	265	255
Philadelphia	6	6	0	.500	294	263
Washington	4	8	0	.333	213	274
North Division	**W**	**L**	**T**	**Pct.**	**Pts.**	**OP**
Chicago*	10	2	0	.833	318	150
Minnesota	5	7	0	.417	211	231
Green Bay	4	8	0	.333	219	324
Detroit	2	10	0	.167	216	294
South Division	**W**	**L**	**T**	**Pct.**	**Pts.**	**OP**
New Orleans	8	4	0	.667	310	251
Atlanta	6	6	0	.500	227	250
Carolina	6	6	0	.500	213	217
Tampa Bay	3	9	0	.250	145	272
West Division	**W**	**L**	**T**	**Pct.**	**Pts.**	**OP**
Seattle	8	4	0	.667	260	263
St. Louis	5	7	0	.417	242	287
San Francisco	5	7	0	.417	209	319
Arizona	3	9	0	.250	221	284

*Clinched division title
#Clinched playoff berth

THURSDAY NIGHT, NOVEMBER 30

CINCINNATI 13, BALTIMORE 7—at Paul Brown Stadium, attendance 65,973. The Bengals' defense came within 61 seconds of consecutive shutouts as Cincinnati continued to make a postseason push. The Bengals' defense became the first in franchise history to register seven consecutive scoreless quarters. The Bengals' offense had just three drives of more than 20 yards, with 2 resulting in second-quarter field goals and the other culminating with Carson Palmer's 40-yard touchdown pass to T.J. Houshmandzadeh. With 1:01 to play, McNair completed a 36-yard touchdown pass to Derrick Mason, but Keiwan Ratliff recovered the onside kick to clinch the victory. McNair was 26 of 43 for 227 yards and 1 touchdown. Palmer was 21 of 32 for 234 yards and 1 touchdown. Houshmandzadeh had 10 catches for 106 yards.

Baltimore	0	0	0	7	—	7
Cincinnati	0	6	7	0	—	13

Cin	—	FG Graham 23
Cin	—	FG Graham 27
Cin	—	Houshmandzadeh 40 pass from Palmer (Graham kick)
Balt	—	Mason 36 pass from McNair (Stover kick)

SUNDAY, DECEMBER 3

SAN DIEGO 24, BUFFALO 21—at Ralph Wilson Stadium, attendance 63,361. LaDainian Tomlinson rushed for 178 yards and 2 touchdowns for the Chargers. Philip Rivers' 11-yard touchdown pass to Antonio Gates capped a perfectly executed 43-yard drive and keyed the Chargers to a 17-0 halftime lead. Three plays into the second half, Rivers fumbled and Chris Kelsay recovered to set up a 19-yard touchdown drive. Moments later, Jim Leonhard returned a punt 32 yards to set up a 13-yard drive, capped by Willis McGahee's 2-yard run to pull the Bills within 17-14. In the fourth quarter, Tomlinson carried eight times on a 13-play, 80-yard drive to set up his 2-yard touchdown to give the Chargers a 24-14 lead with 3:26 to play. The Bills added a touchdown with 30 seconds left, but Buffalo illegally touched the ensuing onside kick and the Chargers ran out the clock. Rivers was 17 of

29 for 160 yards and 1 touchdown. Tomlinson had 28 carries for 178 yards. J.P. Losman was 21 of 37 for 184 yards and 2 touchdowns, with 2 interceptions.

San Diego	10	7	0	7	—	24
Buffalo	0	0	14	7	—	21

SD	—	FG Kaeding 42
SD	—	Tomlinson 51 run (Kaeding kick)
SD	—	Gates 11 pass from Rivers (Kaeding kick)
Buff	—	Royal 5 pass from Losman (Lindell kick)
Buff	—	McGahee 2 run (Lindell kick)
SD	—	Tomlinson 2 run (Kaeding kick)
Buff	—	Price 6 pass from Losman (Lindell kick)

CHICAGO 23, MINNESOTA 13—at Soldier Field, attendance 62,221. The Bears overcame a 107-yard, 6-first down output by the offense to clinch the NFC North division title. Devin Hester returned a punt for a touchdown in the second quarter, and Ricky Manning Jr. returned an interception fro a touchdown in the third quarter for a 14-6 lead. On the next play, Brian Urlacher intercepted Brad Johnson' pass to set up Cedric Benson's 24-yard touchdown run, on fourth-and-1, to give the Bears a 21-6 lead. Brooks Bollinger and Tavaris Jackson each played in the fourth quarter, with Bollinger guiding the Vikings to their lone touchdown. Rex Grossman was 6 of 19 for 34 yards. Johnson was 11 of 26 for 73 yards, with 4 interceptions.

Minnesota	0	3	3	7	—	13
Chicago	0	7	14	2	—	23

Chi	—	Hester 45 punt return (Gould kick)
Minn	—	FG Longwell 23
Minn	—	FG Longwell 30
Chi	—	R. Manning 54 interception return (Gould kick)
Chi	—	Benson 24 run (Gould kick)
Chi	—	Safety, Ta. Johnson tackled Fason in end zone
Minn	—	Fason 14 run (Longwell kick)

CLEVELAND 31, KANSAS CITY 28 (OT)—at Cleveland Browns Stadium, 71,927. The Brown rallied from a 14-point fourth-quarter deficit behind backup quarterback Derek Anderson, who was making his first NFL appearance, and won the game on Phil Dawson's 33-yard field goal in overtime. The Chiefs offense scored touchdowns on four of six possessions during the middle of the game, on drives of 85, 80, 77, and 99 yards, to take a 28-14 lead with 12:19 remaining. With Anderson at quarterback, having replaced an injured Charlie Frye in the third quarter, the Browns went 81 yards in eight plays, keyed by a 54-yard pass to Jason Wright on third-and-4, to pull within 28-21 with 8:55 to play. After a punt, the Browns drove 70 yards, capped by Steve Heiden's 3-yard touchdown catch with 35 seconds left, to tie the game. In overtime, the Chiefs won the toss but had to punt. Anderson completed a 26-yard pass to Kellen Winslow and then had a 33-yard scramble to set up Dawson's winning kick. Frye was 11 of 12 for 122 yards and 1 touchdown. Anderson was 12 of 21 for 171 yards and 2 touchdowns, with 1 interception. Trent Green was 24 of 32 for 297 yards and 4 touchdowns, with 1 interception. Larry Johnson carried 28 times for 110 yards.

Kansas City	0	14	7	7	0	—	28
Cleveland	7	7	0	14	3	—	31

Cle	—	Edwards 23 pass from Frye (Dawson kick)
KC	—	Kennison 22 pass from Green (Tynes kick)
KC	—	Gonzalez 9 pass from Green (Tynes kick)
Cle	—	Droughns 1 run (Dawson kick)
KC	—	Wilson 6 pass from Green (Tynes kick)
KC	—	Gonzalez 23 pass from Green (Tynes kick)
Cle	—	Heiden 6 pass from Anderson

	(Dawson kick)
Cle	—	Heiden 3 pass from Anderson (Dawson kick)
Cle	—	FG Dawson 33

N.Y. JETS 38, GREEN BAY 10—at Lambeau Field, attendance 70,527. Cedric Houston rushed for 105 yards and 2 touchdowns as the Jets rolled past the Packers amidst snow flurries on a 19-degree day. The Jets scored on their first five possessions, on drives of 63, 51, 83, 70, and 77 yards to take a 31-0 halftime lead. In the first half, the Jets maintained possession for 21 minutes, 36 seconds and outgained the Packers 340-97 in total yards. Chad Pennington was 25 of 35 for 263 yards and 2 touchdowns, with 2 interceptions. Brett Favre was 24 of 47 for 214 yards and 1 touchdown, with 2 interceptions. Ahman Green carried 14 times for 102 yards.

N.Y. Jets	10	21	0	7	—	38
Green Bay	0	0	10	0	—	10

NYJ	—	FG Nugent 24
NYJ	—	Cotchery 12 pass from Pennington (Nugent kick)
NYJ	—	Houston 3 run (Nugent kick)
NYJ	—	Houston 1 run (Nugent kick)
NYJ	—	Baker 1 pass from Pennington (Nugent kick)
GB	—	FG Rayner 34
GB	—	Driver 20 pass from Favre (Rayner kick)
NYJ	—	Washington 20 run (Nugent kick)

JACKSONVILLE 24, MIAMI 10—at Dolphin Stadium, attendance 73,160. The Dolphins drove 80 yards for a touchdown to open the game, but failed to cross the goal line thereafter. Miami drove to the Jaguars' 5 in the second quarter, but Gerald Sensabaugh intercepted a pass to thwart the drive. Rashean Mathis' interception later in the quarter set up Garrard's 16-yard touchdown pass to George Wrighster to give Jacksonville a 17-7 lead. The Jaguars offense, which had an 11-play, 95-yard drive in the first half, had a 91-yard drive in the second half to take a 24-7 lead. The Dolphins rallied late, kicking a field goal, recovering an onside kick, and driving to the Jaguars' 5, but they were stopped on downs with 1:41 to play. Garrard was 16 of 22 for 229 yards and 2 touchdowns. Matt Jones had 6 catches for 128 yards. Joey Harrington was 27 of 42 for 267 yards and 1 touchdown, with 2 interceptions. Chris Chambers had 8 catches for 121 yards.

Jacksonville	3	14	0	7	—	24
Miami	7	0	0	3	—	10

Mia	—	Booker 17 pass from Harrington (Mare kick)
Jax	—	FG Scobee 48
Jax	—	M. Jones 15 pass from Garrard (Scobee kick)
Jax	—	Wrighster 16 pass from Garrard (Scobee kick)
Jax	—	Jones-Drew 32 run (Scobee kick)
Mia	—	FG Mare 42

NEW ENGLAND 28, DETROIT 21—at Gillette Stadium, attendance 68,756. Corey Dillon scored 2 fourth-quarter touchdowns as the Patriots rallied at home to defeat the Lions. The Patriots led 13-10 at halftime, but the Lions opened the second half with 2 field goals, a safety, which occurred when Tom Brady was sacked by Kenoy Kennedy, fumbled, and Heath Evans fell on the ball in the end zone, and another field goal for a 21-13 Detroit lead with 13:07 to play. The Patriots tied the game with Dillon's touchdown run and Brady's 2-point conversion pass to Troy Brown. Later in the quarter, Rosevelt Colvin sacked Jon Kitna and forced him to fumble. Mike Wright recovered at the Lions' 32, and Dillon scored seven plays later for a 28-21 lead with 2:33 to play. Mike Vrabel's interception three plays later clinched the victory. Brady was 27 of 38 for 305 yards, with 1 interception. Reche Caldwell had 8 catches for 112 yards. Kitna was 22 of 38 for 314 yards and 1 touchdown, with 3 interceptions. Mike Furrey had 9 receptions for 123 yards.

Detroit	0	10	8	3	—	21
New England	3	10	0	15	—	28

NE	—	FG Gostkowski 25
Det	—	Furrey 5 pass from Kitna (Hanson kick)
Det	—	FG Hanson 29
NE	—	Dillon 6 run (Gostkowski kick)
NE	—	FG Gostkowski 27
Det	—	FG Hanson 38
Det	—	FG Hanson 49
Det	—	Safety, DeVries tackled Evans in end zone
Det	—	FG Hanson 26
NE	—	Dillon 2 run (Brown pass from Brady)
NE	—	Dillon 4 run (Gostkowski kick)

NEW ORLEANS 34, SAN FRANCISCO 10—at Louisiana Superdome, attendance 68,001. Reggie Bush scored a career-high 4 touchdowns as the Saints marched past the 49ers. The Saints led 14-3 at halftime, but the 49ers scored early in the second half and then Michael Robinson recovered an onside kick. However, Mike McKenzie intercepted Alex Smith's pass on the next play, and the Saints scored on their next four possessions, with the 49ers' offense posting three consecutive three-and-out's, to take a 34-10 lead with 2:31 to play. Drew Brees was 17 of 28 for 186 yards and 1 touchdown. Deuce McAllister had 26 carries for 136 yards, and Bush had 9 catches for 131 yards. Smith was 14 of 28 for 171 yards and 1 touchdown, with 3 interceptions.

San Francisco	3	0	7	0	—	10
New Orleans	0	14	10	10	—	34

SF	—	FG Nedney 29
NO	—	Bush 1 run (Carney kick)
NO	—	Bush 8 run (Carney kick)
SF	—	Bryant 48 pass from Smith (Nedney kick)
NO	—	FG Carney 19
NO	—	Bush 5 pass from Brees (Carney kick)
NO	—	Bush 10 run (Carney kick)
NO	—	FG Carney 33

DALLAS 23, N.Y. GIANTS 20—at Giants Stadium, attendance 78,666. In a seesaw second half, Martin Gramatica, playing in his first game with the Cowboys, kicked a 46-yard field goal with one second remaining to lift Dallas past the Giants in a key NFC East game. The Giants took possession in the third quarter, with 13:05 left the clock, trailing 10-7. From that point on, neither offense could be stopped. The Giants kicked 2 field goals and Eli Manning's 5-yard touchdown pass to Plaxico Burress tied the game 20-20 with 1:06 to play. On the next play Tony Romo completed a 42-yard pass to Jason Witten to set up Gramatica's 46-yard field goal with one second remaining. Romo was 20 of 34 for 257 yards, with 2 interceptions. Manning was 24 of 36 for 270 yards and 2 touchdowns.

Dallas	7	3	3	10	—	23
N.Y. Giants	7	0	3	10	—	20

NYG	—	Shockey 17 pass from Manning (Feely kick)
Dall	—	Barber 1 run (Gramatica kick)
Dall	—	FG Gramatica 41
NYG	—	FG Feely 23
Dall	—	FG Gramatica 35
NYG	—	FG Feely 22
Dall	—	Barber 7 run (Gramatica kick)
NYG	—	Burress 5 pass from Manning (Feely kick)
Dall	—	FG Gramatica 46

HOUSTON 23, OAKLAND 14—at McAfee Coliseum, attendance 46,276. The Texans defeated the Raiders despite posting minus-5 passing yards for the game. David Carr completed seven passes for 32 yards, but was sacked five times for minus-37 yards. Trailing 14-7 at halftime, Jerome Mathis returned the second half's open-

ing kickoff 87 yards to the Raiders' 3, where Wali Lundy scored on the next play to tie the game. After Sebastian Janikowski bounced field-goal attempts of 29 and 37 yards off the left upright in the third quarter, the Texans took a 17-14 lead with 9:58 to play on Kris Brown's field goal that had been set up by Dexter Wynn's 58-yards punt return to the Raiders' 21. Five plays later, DeMeco Ryans recovered Randal Williams' fumble near midfield to set up Brown's second field goal. On the next play from scrimmage, Williams fumbled again, and Morlon Greenwood recovered at the Raiders' 26 to set up Brown's third field goal with 2:15 to play for a 23-14 lead. Carr was 7 of 14 for 32 yards. Aaron Brooks was 25 of 42 for 238 yards, with 2 interceptions.

Houston	7	0	7	9	—	23
Oakland	0	14	0	0	—	14

Hou	—	Faggins 5 fumble return (K. Brown kick)
Oak	—	Fargas 3 run (Janikowski kick)
Oak	—	Morrison 35 fumble recovery (Janikowski kick)
Hou	—	Lundy 3 run (K. Brown kick)
Hou	—	FG K. Brown 42
Hou	—	FG K. Brown 47
Hou	—	FG K. Brown 39

PITTSBURGH 20, TAMPA BAY 3—at Heinz Field, attendance 59,843. Ben Roethlisberger passed for 2 touchdowns and the Steelers' defense nearly registered a shutout en route to victory. The Steelers led 10-0 at halftime, and the Jaguars did not threaten until late in the third quarter, when they reached the Steelers' 4 only to have Bryant McFadden intercept Bruce Gradkowski's pass in the end zone for a touchback. Five plays later, Roethlisberger completed a 16-yard touchdown pass to Heath Miller for a 17-0 lead. Matt Bryant kicked a 27-yard field goal as time expired to avoid being shutout. Roethlisberger was 12 of 25 for 198 yards and 2 touchdowns, with 1 interception. Gradkowski was 20 of 34 for 175 yards, with 3 interceptions.

Tampa Bay	0	0	0	3	—	3
Pittsburgh	7	3	0	10	—	20

Pitt	—	Turman 2 pass from Roethlisberger (Reed kick)
Pitt	—	FG Reed 50
Pitt	—	Miller 16 pass from Roethlisberger (Reed kick)
Pitt	—	FG Reed 39
TB	—	FG Bryant 27

ARIZONA 34, ST. LOUIS 20—at Edward Jones Dome, attendance 65,612. Marcel Shipp rushed for 3 touchdowns as the Cardinals forced 3 turnovers to surprise the Rams at home. Adrian Wilson's interception and 35-yard return set up Neil Rackers' 23-yard field goal just before halftime to stake the Cardinals to a 17-3 lead. An 88-yard drive, which was aided by a 27-yard pass interference penalty, set up Shipp's second touchdown and gave the Cardinals a 24-10 lead with 2:10 left in the third quarter. David Macklin's fourth-quarter interception and 56-yard return to the Rams' 19 led to Shipp's third touchdown with 8:14 remaining for a 31-13 lead. Matt Leinart was 15 of 24 for 186 yards and 1 touchdown. Edgerrin James rushed 26 times for 115 yards. Marc Bulger was 27 of 45 for 314 yards and 2 touchdowns, with 3 interceptions. Torry Holt had 7 receptions for 115 yards.

Arizona	7	10	7	10	—	34
St. Louis	3	0	7	10	—	20

Ariz	—	Shipp 1 run (Rackers kick)
StL	—	FG Wilkins 27
Ariz	—	Fitzgerald 11 pass from Leinart (Rackers kick)
Ariz	—	FG Rackers 23
StL	—	Holt 15 pass from Bulger (Wilkins kick)
Ariz	—	Shipp 6 run (Rackers kick)
StL	—	FG Wilkins 37
Ariz	—	Shipp 9 run (Rackers kick)
Ariz	—	FG Rackers 20

StL	—	Bruce 1 pass from Bulger (Wilkins kick)

TENNESSEE 20, INDIANAPOLIS 17—at LP Field, attendance 69,143. Rob Bironas kicked a 60-yard field goal with seven seconds remaining as the Titans won for the fifth time in seven games. Indianapolis had scoring drives of 80 and 81 yards to take a 14-0 lead midway through the second quarter. The Titans cut the deficit to 14-3, and then Keith Bulluck intercepted a pass at the Colts' 42 with 31 seconds left in the half. Three plays later, Vince Young completed a 20-yard touchdown pass to Drew Bennett to pull the Titans within 14-10 at halftime. Young had a 15-yard scramble on third down to keep alive a 95-yard drive, capped by Brandon Jones' 9-yard touchdown catch, to give Tennessee a 17-14 lead with 12:24 to play. Adam Vinatieri gave the Colts a 17-14 lead with 2:28 left, and the Titans drove to the Colts' 42. With 12 seconds left, faced with fourth-and-11, Bironas drilled a 60-yard field goal, becoming just the sixth kicker in NFL history to make a field goal of at least 60 yards. Young was 15 of 25 for 163 yards and 2 touchdowns, with 2 interceptions. Peyton Manning was 21 of 28 for 351 yards and 1 touchdown, with 2 interceptions. Marvin Harrison had 7 receptions for 172 yards.

Indianapolis	7	7	0	3	—	17
Tennessee	0	10	0	10	—	20

Ind	—	Harrison 68 pass from Manning (Vinatieri kick)
Ind	—	Rhodes 2 run (Vinatieri kick)
Tenn	—	FG Bironas 25
Tenn	—	Bennett 20 pass from Young (Bironas kick)
Tenn	—	B. Jones 9 pass from Young (Bironas kick)
Ind	—	FG Vinatieri 20
Tenn	—	FG Bironas 60

ATLANTA 24, WASHINGTON 14—at FedExField, attendance 86,436. The Redskins scored on their first two possessions to take a 14-0 lead and drove into Falcons' territory five additional times, but never scored. The Falcons' defense forced a punt, missed field goal, 2 interceptions, and stopped the Redskins on downs. Michael Vick's 16-yard touchdown followed Shaun Suisham's missed 50-yard field-goal attempt. An interception by Lawyer Milloy and 41-yard return early in the second half set up Vick's 22-yard touchdown pass to Michael Jenkins gave Atlanta a 17-14 lead. In the fourth quarter, Jerious Norwood flew around the right end for a 69-yard touchdown run and 24-14 lead. Chris Crocker intercepted a pass at the goal line with 2:31 to play, and Jason Campbell's forth-and-goal pass fell incomplete with 20 seconds remaining to clinch the victory. Vick was 8 of 16 for 122 yards and 2 touchdowns. Norwood carried 9 times for 107 yards. Campbell was 18 of 38 for 217 yards and 1 touchdown, with 2 interceptions. Ladell Betts had 28 carries for 155 yards. Santana Moss had 7 receptions for 123 yards.

Atlanta	0	10	7	7	—	24
Washington	14	0	0	0	—	14

Wash	—	Betts 8 run (Suisham kick)
Wash	—	Moss 42 pass from Campbell (Suisham kick)
Atl	—	FG Andersen 34
Atl	—	Crumpler 16 pass from Vick (Andersen kick)
Atl	—	Jenkins 22 pass from Vick (Andersen kick)
Atl	—	Norwood 69 run (Andersen kick)

SUNDAY NIGHT, DECEMBER 3
SEATTLE 23, DENVER 20—at INVESCO Field at Mile High, attendance 76,146. Josh Brown kicked a 50-yard field goal with five seconds remaining, his NFL-record-tying fourth game-winning kick of the season, as the Seahawks spoiled the starting debut of Jay Cutler. The Seahawks' defense forced 5 turnovers, including 2 interceptions and a fumble by Cuter, that led to 13 points. The

Seahawks offense had just 5 first downs and generated zero points in first 11 possessions. A first half interception return for a touchdown by Darryl Tapp put the Seahawks on the board, and consecutive passes for 27 and 33 yards from Matt Hasselbeck to Darrell Jackson set up Shaun Alexander's 1-yard run for a 14-13 lead with 8:04 to play. Denver fumbled the ensuing kickoff to set up Brown's 44-yard field goal, and on the next play Jordan Babineaux intercepted Cutler. Brown kicked a a 23-yard field goal and Seattle had 13 points in just over five minutes and a 20-13 lead with 2:58 remaining. However, on the next play, Cutler fired a 71-yard touchdown pass to Brandon Marshall to tie the game. Hasselbeck completed 4 of 5 passes to get the Seahawks down field, and then spiked the ball with 10 seconds left to set up Brown's winning kick. Hasselbeck was 16 of 28 for 168 yards, with 1 interception. Cutler was 10 of 21 for 143 yards and 2 touchdowns, with 2 interceptions. Tatum Bell had 23 carries for 133 yards.

Seattle	3	7	0	16 —	23
Denver	3	10	0	7 —	20

Den	—	FG Elam 37
Den	—	Alexander 7 pass from Cutler (Elam kick)
Sea	—	Tapp 25 interception return (J. Brown kick)
Den	—	FG Elam 41
Sea	—	Alexander 1 run (J. Brown kick)
Sea	—	FG J. Brown 44
Sea	—	FG J. Brown 23
Den	—	Marshall 71 pass from Cutler (Elam kick)
Sea	—	FG J. Brown 50

MONDAY NIGHT, DECEMBER 4

PHILADELPHIA 27, CAROLINA 24—at Lincoln Financial Field, attendance 69,098. Two fourth quarter interceptions, the second by Lito Sheppard for a touchback with 24 seconds to play, allowed the Eagles to stay in the playoff hunt. The Eagles trailed 14-7 at halftime, but scored on their first four possessions of the second half, capped by David Akers' 25-yard field goal that was set up by Brian Dawkins' interception, to take a 27-24 lead with 3:13 to play. The Panthers drove to the Eagles' 7 with 28 seconds left, but Sheppard intercepted Jake Delhomme's fade pass, intended for Keyshawn Johnson, to ice the game. Jeff Garcia was 21 of 39 for 312 yards and 3 touchdowns. Donte Stallworth had 4 receptions for 111 yards. Delhomme was 22 of 37 for 269 yards, with 2 interceptions. DeAngelo Williams had 7 receptions for 101 yards.

Carolina	7	7	7	3 —	24
Philadelphia	0	7	13	7 —	27

Car	—	Smith 9 pass from Delhomme (Kasay kick)
Phil	—	Westbrook 8 pass from Garcia (Akers kick)
Car	—	K. Johnson 1 pass from Delhomme (Kasay kick)
Phil	—	Stallworth 30 pass from Garcia (Akers kick)
Car	—	Williams 35 pass from Delhomme (Kasay kick)
Phil	—	FG Akers 28
Car	—	FG Kasay 45
Phil	—	R. Brown 40 pass from Garcia (Akers kick)
Phil	—	FG Akers 25

FOURTEENTH WEEK SUMMARIES
American Football Conference

East Division	W	L	T	Pct.	Pts.	OP
New England	9	4	0	.692	281	186
N.Y. Jets	7	6	0	.538	254	269
Buffalo	6	7	0	.462	243	262
Miami	6	7	0	.462	228	222
North Division	**W**	**L**	**T**	**Pct.**	**Pts.**	**OP**
Baltimore	10	3	0	.769	276	170
Cincinnati	8	5	0	.615	317	250

	W	L	T	Pct.	Pts.	OP
Pittsburgh	6	7	0	.462	286	264
Cleveland	4	9	0	.308	208	293
South Division	**W**	**L**	**T**	**Pct.**	**Pts.**	**OP**
Indianapolis	10	3	0	.769	342	295
Jacksonville	8	5	0	.615	303	191
Tennessee	6	7	0	.462	247	314
Houston	4	9	0	.308	219	296
West Division	**W**	**L**	**T**	**Pct.**	**Pts.**	**OP**
San Diego*	11	2	0	.846	425	257
Denver	7	6	0	.538	235	236
Kansas City	7	6	0	.538	267	256
Oakland	2	11	0	.154	156	269

National Football Conference

East Division	W	L	T	Pct.	Pts.	OP
Dallas	8	5	0	.615	349	260
N.Y. Giants	7	6	0	.538	292	268
Philadelphia	7	6	0	.538	315	282
Washington	4	9	0	.308	232	295
North Division	**W**	**L**	**T**	**Pct.**	**Pts.**	**OP**
Chicago*	11	2	0	.846	360	177
Minnesota	6	7	0	.462	241	251
Green Bay	5	8	0	.385	249	343
Detroit	2	11	0	.154	236	324
South Division	**W**	**L**	**T**	**Pct.**	**Pts.**	**OP**
New Orleans	9	4	0	.692	352	268
Atlanta	7	6	0	.538	244	256
Carolina	6	7	0	.462	226	244
Tampa Bay	3	10	0	.231	151	289
West Division	**W**	**L**	**T**	**Pct.**	**Pts.**	**OP**
Seattle	8	5	0	.615	281	290
St. Louis	5	8	0	.385	269	329
San Francisco	5	8	0	.385	228	349
Arizona	4	9	0	.308	248	305

*Clinched division title
#Clinched playoff berth

THURSDAY NIGHT, DECEMBER 7

PITTSBURGH 27, CLEVELAND 7—at Heinz Field, attendance 55,246. Willie Parker rushed for a club-record 223 yards and 1 touchdown as the Steelers defeated the Browns for the seventh consecutive game. The gametime termperature at 20 degrees with a 7-degree wind chill, and the second half wind chill below zero, the Steelers outgained the Browns 528-294 in total yards, including a 303-18 advantage in rushing yards, and maintained possession for 38 minutes, 47 seconds. The Browns missed a 40-yard field-goal attempt just before halftime, and the Steelers scored on their first three second-half possessions to take a 27-0 lead. with 7:26 to play. Parker set the team record on the first play of the fourth quarter, a 3-yard run, and came out after the second play, a 2-yard run, of the quarter and did not return. Ben Roethlisberger was 11 of 21 for 225 yards and 1 touchdown. Parker rushed 32 times for 223 yards. Derek Anderson was 21 of 37 for 276 yards and 1 touchdown, with 1 interception. Joe Jurevicius had 7 receptions for 111 yards.

Cleveland	0	0	0	7 —	7
Pittsburgh	7	3	14	3 —	27

Pitt	—	Washington 49 pass from Roethlisberger (Reed kick)
Pitt	—	FG Reed 23
Pitt	—	Roethlisberger 2 run (Reed kick)
Pitt	—	Parker 3 run (Reed kick)
Pitt	—	FG Reed 28
Cle	—	Edwards 45 pass from Anderson (Dawson kick)

SUNDAY, DECEMBER 10

ARIZONA 27, SEATTLE 21—at University of Phoenix Stadium, attendance 63,603. Edgerrin James posted his second consecutive 100-yard game and the Cardinals' defense made two key plays in the final minute to defeat the Seahawks. The Seahawks trailed 17-7 but drove 91 yards in eight plays to score a touchdown just before halftime, and then capitalized on a missed field goal by driving 57 yards, capped by Matt Hasselbeck's 2-yard touchdown pass to Darrell Jackson, for a 21-17 lead. The Seahawks' defense then forced a punt, but on the next

play from scrimmage Mack Strong fumbled and Chris Cooper recovered at the Seahawks' 36 to set up Matt Leinart's 5-yard touchdown pass to Larry Fitzgerald on the first play of the fourth quarter. Neil Rackers added a 40-yard field goal with 3:30 to play. The Seahawks drove to the Cardinals' 15, but Chike Okeafor sacked Hasselbeck, and on fourth-and-20 Adrian Wilson knocked down a pass intended for Deion Branch. Leinart was 21 of 34 for 232 yards and 2 touchdowns, with 1 interception. James had 26 carries for 115 yards. Hasselbeck was 20 of 28 for 243 yards. D.J. Hackett had 4 receptions for 104 yards.

Seattle	7	7	7	0 —	21
Arizona	14	3	0	10 —	27

Ariz	—	Bry. Johnson 56 pass from Leinart (Rackers kick)
Ariz	—	James 7 run (Rackers kick)
Sea	—	Hackett 23 pass from Hasselbeck (J. Brown kick)
Ariz	—	FG Rackers 32
Sea	—	Burleson 5 pass from Hasselbeck (J. Brown kick)
Sea	—	Jackson 2 pass from Hasselbeck (J. Brown kick)
Ariz	—	Fitzgerald 5 pass from Leinart (Rackers kick)
Ariz	—	FG Rackers 40

N.Y. GIANTS 27, CAROLINA 13—at Bank of America Stadium, attendance 73,702. Eli Manning passed for 3 touchdowns as the Giants snapped their four-game losing streak. The Giants led 17-10 at halftime, but scored on their first two possessions of the second half, the latter set up by Gibril Wilson's 14-yard interception return to the Panthers' 14, to take a 27-10 lead. Chris Weinke, making his first start in more than four years, passed for a club-record 423 yards. He attempted 43 passes in the second half as the Panthers tried to come back, but he was intercepted twice in the fourth quarter. Manning was 17 of 33 for 172 yards and 3 touchdowns. Tiki Barber carried 20 times for 112 yards. Weinke was 34 of 61 for 423 yards and 1 touchdown, with 3 interceptions. Drew Carter had 8 catches for 144 yards.

N.Y. Giants	3	14	10	0 —	27
Carolina	0	10	0	3 —	13

NYG	—	FG Feely 32
NYG	—	Burress 28 pass from Manning (Feely kick)
Car	—	Carter 36 pass from Weinke (Kasay kick)
Car	—	FG Kasay 37
NYG	—	Shockey 2 pass from Manning (Feely kick)
NYG	—	FG Feely 29
NYG	—	Tyree 3 pass from Manning (Feely kick)
Car	—	FG Kasay 45

CINCINNATI 27, OAKLAND 10—at Paul Brown Stadium, attendance 65,882. Carson Palmer passed for 297 yards and 2 touchdowns as the Bengals won their fourth consecutive game. The Bengals outgained the Raiders 439-223 in total yards, and gained at least 50 yards on six of their nine possessions, not counting a one-play kneeldown at the end of the first half. Rudi Johnson's 6-yard touchdown run capped a 13-play, 88-yard drive to begin the second half and stake the Bengals to a 21-3 lead. ReShard Lee then was stopped for a loss of 3 yards on fourth-and-1 at the Bengals' 46 to set up Palmer's 20-yard touchdown pass to T.J. Houshmandzadeh for a 27-3 lead with 59 seconds left in the third quarter. Palmer was 20 of 28 for 297 yards and 2 touchdowns, with 3 interceptions. Rudi Johnson rushed 30 times for 117 yards. Houshmandzadeh had 8 catches for 118 yards and Chad Johnson added 5 receptions for 101 yards. Aaron Brooks was 23 of 39 for 199 yards and 1 touchdown, with 1 interception.

Oakland	0	3	0	7 —	10
Cincinnati	14	0	13	0 —	27

Cin — Henry 8 pass from Palmer (Graham kick)
Cin — R. Johnson 9 run (Graham kick)
Oak — FG Janikowski 33
Cin — R. Johnson 6 run (Graham kick)
Cin — Houshmandzadeh 20 pass from Palmer (kick failed)
Oak — Curry 5 pass from Brooks (Janikowski kick)

MINNESOTA 30, DETROIT 20—at Ford Field, attendance 60,861. Artose Pinner rushed for 125 yards and 3 touchdowns against his former team as the Vikings remained in the playoff hunt. The Vikings' defense forced 6 turnovers, two of which set up Minnesota's second and third touchdowns en route to a 20-0 lead. The Vikings were about to score again when Jamar Fletcher intercepted a Brad Johnson pass and returned it 88 yards for a touchdown. The Lions pulled to within 30-20 early in the fourth quarter, and drove to the Vikings' 1 on second-and-goal with 5:06 to play. But Kevin Jones suffered a season-ending foot injury on second down, Arlen Harris was stopped for no gain on third down, and Dwight Smith sacked Jon Kitna on fourth down. Johnson was 14 of 22 for 159 yards, with 1 interception. Pinner carried 29 times for 125 yards. Kitna was 28 of 41 for 294 yards and 1 touchdown, with 3 interceptions.

Minnesota	14	6	3	7	—	30	
Detroit	0	10	3	7	—	20	

Minn — Pinner 3 run (Longwell kick)
Minn — Pinner 4 run (Longwell kick)
Minn — B. Johnson 3 run (pass failed)
Det — Fletcher 88 interception return (Hanson kick)
Det — FG Hanson 53
Minn — FG Longwell 30
Det — FG Hanson 45
Minn — Pinner 1 run (Longwell kick)
Det — K. Jones 23 pass from Kitna (Hanson kick)

TENNESSEE 26, HOUSTON 20 (OT)—at Reliant Stadium, attendance 70,760. Vince Young sprinted 39 yards for a touchdown in overtime to give the Titans their fourth consecutive victory, including their third successive comeback win. Demarcus Faggins' interception at the Texans' 42 set up Kris Brown's 49-yard field goal to give Houston a 17-13 lead with 12:00 to play. Young responded with a 15-play, 88-yard drive, highlighted by 3 third-down conversions, including 2 on runs by Young, and capped by Travis Henry's 2-yard touchdown run with 3:53 left for a 20-17 lead. David Carr completed a 21-yard pass to Andre Johnson to set up Brown's game-tying field goal with 2:09 remaining. In overtime, the Titans won the toss and Pacman Jones returned the kickoff 36 yards to the Titans' 43. Five plays later, on third-and-14 from the Texans' 39, Young dropped back to pass and then scrambled up the middle, avoiding defenders and sprinting into the end zone for the game-winning touchdown. Young was 19 of 29 for 218 yards, with 1 interception. Drew Bennett had 6 catches for 113 yards. Carr was 17 of 23 for 140 yards.

Tennessee	3	3	7	7	6	—	26
Houston	0	7	7	6	0	—	20

Tenn — FG Bironas 41
Tenn — FG Bironas 33
Hou — Dayne 1 run (K. Brown kick)
Hou — Dayne 2 run (K. Brown kick)
Tenn — Henry 9 run (Bironas kick)
Tenn — FG K. Brown 49
Tenn — Henry 2 run (Bironas kick)
Hou — FG K. Brown 46
Tenn — Young 39 run

JACKSONVILLE 44, INDIANAPOLIS 17—at Alltel Stadium, attendance 67,164. The Jaguars rushed for 375 yards, tied for the second-most in the NFL since 1970, and averaged 8.9 yards per carry to literally overrun the Colts. Trailing 10-7, the Jaguars scored on five consecu-

tive possessions, posting 27 points on the scoreboard in nine minutes, 38 seconds, including a 93-yard kickoff return for a touchdown by Maurice Jones-Drew to begin the second half, to take a 34-10 lead with 11:07 left in the third quarter. The Colts cut the deficit to 37-17, but the Jaguars responded with an 11-play, 80-yard drive, capped by Alvin Pearman's 6-yard touchdown run with 3:59 to play. David Garrard was 8 of 14 for 79 yards, with 1 interception. Jones-Drew rushed 15 times for 166 yards and Fred Taylor added 9 carries for 131 yards. Peyton Manning was 25 of 50 for 313 yards, with 1 interception. Reggie Wayne had 8 catches for 110 yards, and Marvin Harrison had 6 receptions for 101 yards.

Indianapolis	3	7	0	7	—	17	
Jacksonville	7	17	13	7	—	44	

Jax — Jones-Drew 18 run (Scobee kick)
Ind — FG Vinatieri 41
Ind — Rhodes 1 run (Vinatieri kick)
Jax — Taylor 21 run (Scobee kick)
Jax — Jones-Drew 48 run (Scobee kick)
Jax — FG Scobee 48
Jax — Jones-Drew 93 kickoff return (Scobee kick)
Jax — FG Scobee 34
Jax — FG Scobee 46
Ind — Manning 1 run (Vinatieri kick)
Jax — Pearman 6 run (Scobee kick)

BALTIMORE 20, KANSAS CITY 10—at Arrowhead Stadium, attendance 77,232. The Ravens' defense forced 3 turnovers and registered 4 sacks as Baltimore became the first visiting team to win in Kansas City in December since 1995. The Chiefs committed 3 turnovers in the first half, and missed a 32-yard field goal, to trail 6-0 at halftime. In the second half, Steve McNair connnected on a 87-yard touchdown pass to Mark Clayton to take a 13-0 lead. Leading 13-3, McNair engineered a 16-play, 86-yard drive, which featured five third-down conversions and was capped by Jamal Lewis' 1-yard run with 2:51 to play to take a 20-3 lead. After the Chiefs scored a touchdown, Derrick Mason recovered the onside kick with 1:20 left to secure the victory. McNair was 12 of 27 for 283 yards and 1 touchdown. Mark Clayton had 5 catches for 112 yards. Green was 15 of 27 for 178 yards and 1 touchdown, with 2 interceptions. Larry Johnson had 23 carries for 120 yards.

Baltimore	3	3	7	7	—	20	
Kansas City	0	0	3	7	—	10	

Balt — FG Stover 41
Balt — FG Stover 23
Balt — Clayton 87 pass from McNair (Stover kick)
KC — FG Tynes 49
Balt — J. Lewis 1 run (Stover kick)
KC — D. Hall 5 pass from Green (Tynes kick)

MIAMI 21, NEW ENGLAND 0—at Dolphin Stadium, attendance 74,003. The Dolphins' defense allowed just 189 yards and registered 5 sacks to register their first shutout since 2000. The Patriots never ran a play inside the Dolphins' 30, yet it was just a 6-0 lead late in the third quarter when Sammy Morris gained 2 yards on fourth-and-1 to maintain possession. On the next play, Joey Harrington completed a 32-yard touchdown pass to Marty Booker for a 13-0 lead with 2:51 to play in the third quarter. In the fourth quarter, Yeremiah Bell sacked Tom Brady, forced him to fumble and recovered the ball at the Dolphins' 39. Eight plays later, and keyed by Booker's 26-yard catch, Morris scored on a 3-yard run with 4:56 to play. Harrington was 18 of 30 for 190 yards and 1 touchdown. Morris had 25 carries for 123 yards. Booker had 8 receptions for 103 yards. Brady was 12 of 25 for 78 yards.

New England	0	0	0	0	—	0	
Miami	3	3	7	8	—	21	

Mia — FG Mare 35
Mia — FG Mare 33
Mia — Booker 32 pass from Harrington

(Mare kick)
Mia — Morris 3 run (Booker pass from Harrington)

BUFFALO 31, N.Y. JETS 13—at The Meadowlands, attendance 77,131. The Bills capitalized on two key defensive plays to win for the third time in four games. Trailing 10-7, J.P. Losman connected on a 77-yard touchdown pass to Lee Evans with 4:47 left in the half. Six plays later, Nate Clements intercepted Chad Pennington's pass and returned it 58 yards for a touchdown and 21-10 lead. Late in the third quarter, Aaron Schobel sacked Pennington and forced him to fumble. Ryan Denney recovered and Robert Royal caught a 6-yard touchdown pass four plays later to give the Bills a commanding 28-10 lead. Losman was 10 of 15 for 157 yards and 2 touchdowns. Willis McGahee carried 16 times for 125 yards. Pennington was 22 of 35 for 182 yards and 1 touchdown, with 2 interceptions.

Buffalo	7	14	7	3	—	31	
N.Y. Jets	7	6	0	0	—	13	

Buff — McGahee 57 run (Lindell kick)
NYJ — Coles 10 pass from Pennington (Nugent kick)
NYJ — FG Nugent 30
Buff — Evans 77 pass from Losman (Lindell kick)
Buff — Clements 58 interception return (Lindell kick)
NYJ — FG Nugent 38
Buff — Royal 6 pass from Losman (Lindell kick)
Buff — FG Lindell 34

SAN DIEGO 48, DENVER 20—at Qualcomm Stadium, attendance 67,514. Tomlinson scored 3 touchdowns to set an NFL single-season record with 29 touchdowns as the Chargers rolled past the Broncos. The Chargers scored on four consecutive possessions in the first half to take a 28-3 lead. The Broncos scored on their first three possessions of the second half, aided by a fumbled kickoff return when the score was 28-10, to pull within 28-20 with 1:02 left in the third quarter. The Chargers kicked field goals on their next two possessions to take a 34-20 lead, and Tomlinson added 2 touchdown runs just 47 seconds apart, the latter set up by Shawne Merriman's sack that forced Jay Cutler to fumble, to finish the scoring. The last touchdown, with 3:10 to play, was a 7-yard run around left end and gave Tomlinson the NFL single-season record, surpassing the mark of 28 set the previous year by Shaun Alexander. It was also Tomlinson's 26th touchdown in his last nine games. Rivers was 15 of 23 for 279 yards and 2 touchdowns. Gates had 7 receptions for 104 yards. Tomlinson carried 28 times for 103 yards. Cutler was 17 of 30 for 188 yards and 2 touchdowns. Bell had 17 carries for 116 yards.

Denver	0	3	17	0	—	20	
San Diego	14	14	0	20	—	48	

SD — Gates 12 pass from Rivers (Kaeding kick)
SD — Neal 4 run (Kaeding kick)
Den — FG Elam 34
SD — Tomlinson 1 run (Kaeding kick)
SD — Gates 7 pass from Rivers (Kaeding kick)
Den — Scheffler 28 pass from Cutler (Elam kick)
Den — Scheffler 11 pass from Cutler (Elam kick)
Den — FG Elam 33
SD — FG Kaeding 34
SD — FG Kaeding 35
SD — Tomlinson 6 run (Kaeding kick)
SD — Tomlinson 7 run (Kaeding kick)

GREEN BAY 30, SAN FRANCISCO 19—at Monster Park, attendance 68,539. Brett Favre passed for 293 yards and 2 touchdowns as the Packers snapped a three-game losing streak. The Packers jumped to a 17-3 lead, but when Frank Gore scored to cap the 49ers' opening drive of the second half, the Packers' lead was just 17-13. However, later in the quarter Nick Collins intercepted Alex Smith's pass and two plays later Favre connected on a 68-yard touchdown pass to Donald Driver. The Packers added field goals on their next two possessions to take a 30-13 lead with 8:47 to play. Favre was 22 of 34 for 293 yards and 2 touchdowns. Driver had 9 catches for 160 yards. Smith was 12 of 29 for 201 yards and 1 touchdown, with 2 interceptions. Frank Gore carried 19 times for 130 yards.

| Green Bay | 7 | 10 | 7 | 6 | — | 30 |
| San Francisco | 3 | 3 | 7 | 6 | — | 19 |

SF	—	FG Nedney 24
GB	—	Martin 36 pass from Favre (Rayner kick)
GB	—	FG Rayner 23
GB	—	Green 1 run (Rayner kick)
SF	—	FG Nedney 36
SF	—	Gore 1 run (Nedney kick)
GB	—	Driver 68 pass from Favre (Rayner kick)
GB	—	FG Rayner 44
GB	—	FG Rayner 21
SF	—	Davis 52 pass from Smith (mishandled snap-no attempt)

ATLANTA 17, TAMPA BAY 6—at Raymond James Stadium, attendance 65,691. The Falcons' defense forced 2 turnovers which led to 10 points in the second half as Atlanta rallied to defeat Tampa Bay. The Buccaneers kicked field goals on their first two possessions, and did not cross the Falcons' 30 again until the game's final minute. The Falcons trailed 6-0 at halftime, but got a big boost from their defense when John Abraham sacked Bruce Gradkowski and forced him to fumble. Demorrio Williams returned the fumble 54 yards for a touchdown. The Falcons' defense then forced a punt, and Justin Griffith capped the ensuing drive with a 21-yard touchdown run on third-and-4 for a 14-6 lead. Josh Mallard recovered Carnell Williams' fumble at the Buccaneers' 13 to set up Morten Andersen's 23-yard field goal with 3:14 to play. Michael Vick was 14 of 23 for 155 yards, with 1 interception. Gradkowski was 13 of 24 for 121 yards.

| Atlanta | 0 | 0 | 14 | 3 | — | 17 |
| Tampa Bay | 3 | 3 | 0 | 0 | — | 6 |

TB	—	FG Bryant 42
TB	—	FG Bryant 24
Atl	—	Williams 54 fumble return (Andersen kick)
Atl	—	Griffith 21 run (Andersen kick)
Atl	—	FG Andersen 23

PHILADELPHIA 21, WASHINGTON 19—at FedExField, attendance 84,164. The Eagles jumped to a 21-3 lead and held off the Redskins to remain in a battle for a wild-card berth. Omar Gaither intercepted a pass near midfield to set up Jeff Garcia's 10-yard touchdown pass to L.J. Smith. On the Redskins' next drive, Michael Lewis intercepted Jason Campbell's short pass and returned it 84 yards for a touchdown. The next time Philadelphia had the ball, Garcia completed a 60-yard pass to Reggie Brown to set up his 3-yard scoring pass to Donte Stallworth for a 21-3 lead. The Redskins pulled within 21-16 and had first-and-goal at the Eagles' 3. But T.J. Duckett was stopped for no gain, and after an incomplete pass and five-yard illegal substitution penalty, Brian Dawkins sacked Jason Campbell to force the Redskins to settle for Shaun Suisham's fourth field goal with 4:58 to play. Washington never got the ball back, as Brian Westbrook's 12-yard run on second-and-7 iced the game. Garcia was 15 of 23 for 164 yards and 2 touchdowns. Campbell was 15 of 27 for 182 yards and 1 touchdown, with 2 interceptions. Ladell Betts had 33 carries for 171 yards.

| Philadelphia | 7 | 14 | 0 | 0 | — | 21 |
| Washington | 3 | 3 | 10 | 3 | — | 19 |

Wash	—	FG Suisham 31
Phil	—	L. Smith 10 pass from Garcia (Akers kick)
Phil	—	M. Lewis 84 interception return (Akers kick)
Phil	—	Stallworth 3 pass from Garcia (Akers kick)
Wash	—	FG Suisham 45
Wash	—	FG Suisham 32
Wash	—	Randle El 34 pass from Campbell (Suisham kick)
Wash	—	FG Suisham 35

SUNDAY NIGHT, DECEMBER 10
NEW ORLEANS 42, DALLAS 17—at Texas Stadium, attendance 63,722. Drew Brees passed for 5 touchdowns as the Saints tallied 536 yards of offense to overwhelm the Cowboys. Leading 14-7, the Saints drove 95 yards late in the first half and scored on Brees' 27-yard touchdown pass to Jamal Jones with 44 seconds left in the half. Each team scored twice to begin the second half, with Mike Karney's 6-yard touchdown catch giving the Saints a 35-17 lead. The Saints' Jay Bellamay then recovered an onside kick and Brees completed a 42-yard touchdown pass to Devery Henderson for a 42-17 lead with 3:47 left in the third quarter. Brees was 26 of 38 for 384 yards and 5 touchdowns. Deuce McAllister had 21 carries for 111 yards. Reggie Bush had 6 catches for 125 yards. Tony Romo was 16 of 33 for 249 yards and 1 touchdown, with 2 interceptions. Terry Glenn had 8 receptions for 150 yards.

| New Orleans | 0 | 21 | 21 | 0 | — | 42 |
| Dallas | 7 | 0 | 10 | 0 | — | 17 |

Dall	—	J. Jones 77 run (Gramatica kick)
NO	—	Karney 2 run (Carney kick)
NO	—	Karney 3 pass from Brees (Carney kick)
NO	—	J. Jones 27 pass from Brees (Carney kick)
Dall	—	FG Gramatica 24
NO	—	Bush 61 pass from Brees (Carney kick)
Dall	—	Owens 34 pass from Romo (Gramatica kick)
NO	—	Karney 6 pass from Brees (Carney kick)
NO	—	Henderson 42 pass from Brees (Carney kick)

MONDAY NIGHT, DECEMBER 11
CHICAGO 42, ST. LOUIS 27—at Edward Jones Dome, attendance 66,234. Devin Hester returned 2 kickoffs for touchdowns, giving him an NFL record 6 for the season, as the Bears scored touchdowns on six of their seven possessions during the middle of the game, the first and last being Hester's 94- and 96-yard returns. Ahead 14-13 at halftime, the Bears' defense forced 3 punts to begin the second half, and the offense responded with touchdown drives of 94, 74, and 55 yards. Hester's 96-yard return, with 7:22 to play, gave the Bears a 42-20 lead. Rex Grossman was 13 of 23 for 200 yards and 2 touchdowns. Marc Bulger was 34 of 55 for 356 yards and 3 touchdowns, with 1 interception. Steven Jackson had 10 receptions for 58 yards.

| Chicago | 0 | 14 | 14 | 14 | — | 42 |
| St. Louis | 0 | 13 | 0 | 14 | — | 27 |

StL	—	Holt 1 pass from Bulger (mishandled snap-no attempt)
Chi	—	Hester 94 kickoff return (Gould kick)
StL	—	Jackson 2 run (Wilkins kick)
Chi	—	Berrian 34 pass from Grossman (Gould kick)
Chi	—	T. Jones 30 run (Gould kick)
Chi	—	Muhammad 14 pass from Grossman (Gould kick)
Chi	—	Peterson 1 run (Gould kick)
StL	—	Holt 6 pass from Bulger (Wilkins kick)

| Chi | — | Hester 96 kickoff return (Gould kick) |
| StL | — | Jackson 6 pass from Bulger (Wilkins kick) |

FIFTEENTH WEEK SUMMARIES
American Football Conference

East Division	W	L	T	Pct.	Pts.	OP
New England	10	4	0	.714	321	193
N.Y. Jets	8	6	0	.571	280	282
Buffalo	7	7	0	.500	264	262
Miami	6	8	0	.429	228	243
North Division	**W**	**L**	**T**	**Pct.**	**Pts.**	**OP**
Baltimore*	11	3	0	.786	303	187
Cincinnati	8	6	0	.571	333	284
Pittsburgh	7	7	0	.500	323	267
Cleveland	4	10	0	.286	225	320
South Division	**W**	**L**	**T**	**Pct.**	**Pts.**	**OP**
Indianapolis*	11	3	0	.786	376	311
Jacksonville	8	6	0	.571	320	215
Tennessee	7	7	0	.500	271	331
Houston	4	10	0	.286	226	336
West Division	**W**	**L**	**T**	**Pct.**	**Pts.**	**OP**
San Diego*	12	2	0	.857	445	266
Denver	8	6	0	.571	272	256
Kansas City	7	7	0	.500	276	276
Oakland	2	12	0	.143	156	289

National Football Conference

East Division	W	L	T	Pct.	Pts.	OP
Dallas	9	5	0	.643	387	288
Philadelphia	8	6	0	.571	351	304
N.Y. Giants	7	7	0	.500	314	304
Washington	5	9	0	.357	248	305
North Division	**W**	**L**	**T**	**Pct.**	**Pts.**	**OP**
Chicago*	12	2	0	.857	394	208
Green Bay	6	8	0	.429	266	352
Minnesota	6	8	0	.429	254	277
Detroit	2	12	0	.143	245	341
South Division	**W**	**L**	**T**	**Pct.**	**Pts.**	**OP**
New Orleans*	9	5	0	.643	362	284
Atlanta	7	7	0	.500	272	294
Carolina	6	8	0	.429	229	281
Tampa Bay	3	11	0	.214	182	323
West Division	**W**	**L**	**T**	**Pct.**	**Pts.**	**OP**
Seattle	8	6	0	.571	295	314
St. Louis	6	8	0	.429	289	329
San Francisco	6	8	0	.429	252	363
Arizona	4	10	0	.286	268	342

*Clinched division title
#Clinched playoff berth

THURSDAY NIGHT, DECEMBER 14
SAN FRANCISCO 24, SEATTLE 14—at Qwest Field, attendance 67,650. The 49ers scored 3 fourth-quarter touchdowns to rally on the road and remain in playoff contention. The three touchdown drives covered 90, 73, and 86 yards. Prior to that offensive flurry, the 49ers had gained just 125 yards in nine possessions, with 74 of those yards coming on a drive that resulted in a second-quarter field goal. On the other eight possessions, the 49ers did not even get a first down. Alex Smith passed for 2 touchdowns, and then scrambled from 18 yards with 1:42 to play to clinch the victory. The game was played on a rain-soaked field that endured a severe thunderstorm just before kickoff. Smith was 14 of 25 for 162 yards and 2 touchdowns. Frank Gore rushed 29 times for 144 yards. Matt Hasselbeck was 20 of 37 for 220 yards and 1 touchdown, with 2 interceptions.

| San Francisco | 0 | 3 | 0 | 21 | — | 24 |
| Seattle | 0 | 7 | 0 | 7 | — | 14 |

Sea	—	Alexander 3 run (J. Brown kick)
SF	—	FG Nedney 39
SF	—	V. Davis 8 pass from A. Smith (Nedney kick)
SF	—	Gore 20 pass from A. Smith (Nedney kick)
SF	—	A. Smith 18 run (Nedney kick)
Sea	—	Stevens 22 pass from Hasselbeck (J. Brown kick)

SATURDAY NIGHT, DECEMBER 16

DALLAS 38, ATLANTA 28—at Georgia Dome, attendance 71,102. The Falcons scored touchdowns on four of five possession to take a 28-21 lead with 11:09 left in the third quarter. The Cowboys rallied with a field goal and then Tony Romo engineered touchdown drives of 66 and 80 yards, the latter lasting 11 plays and consuming 6:32 off the clock, to take a 38-28 lead with 2:18 remaining. Marion Barber capped both drives with tough scoring runs. Vick finished the game with 990 rushing yards for the season, breaking Bobby Douglass' mark of 968 set in 1972. Kicker Morten Andersen surpassed Gary Anderson's mark of 2,434 career points. Andersen's second extra point of the night, with 6:30 left in the second quarter, set the NFL record for points. Romo was 22 of 29 for 278 yards and 2 touchdowns, with 1 interception. Vick was 16 of 24 for 237 yards and 4 touchdowns, with 1 interception. Roddy White had 3 catches for 104 yards.

Dallas	7	14	10	7	—	38
Atlanta	0	21	7	0	—	28

Dall	—	Owens 7 pass from Romo (Gramatica kick)
Dall	—	Ware 41 interception return (Gramatica kick)
Atl	—	Griffith 1 pass from Vick (Andersen kick)
Atl	—	Jenkins 9 pass from Vick (Andersen kick)
Dall	—	Owens 51 pass from Romo (Gramatica kick)
Atl	—	Lelie 8 pass from Vick (Andersen kick)
Atl	—	Griffith 5 pass from Vick (Andersen kick)
Dall	—	FG Gramatica 48
Dall	—	Barber 9 run (Gramatica kick)
Dall	—	Barber 3 run (Gramatica kick)

SUNDAY, DECEMBER 17

DENVER 37, ARIZONA 20—at University of Phoenix Stadium, attendance 63,845. Jay Cutler passed for 261 yards and 2 touchdowns as the Broncos snapped their four-game losing streak and kept alive their playoff hopes. The Broncos scored on three consecutive second-half possessions to pull away in Cutler's first road victory. The Broncos dominated the first half, outgaining the Cardinals 240-60, and led just 16-10 at halftime. Mike Bell's 2 fourth-quarter touchdown runs helped put the game out of reach. Cutler was 21 of 31 for 261 yards and 2 touchdowns, with 1 interception. Matt Leinart was 20 of 35 for 214 yards, with 2 interceptions.

Denver	10	6	7	14	—	37
Arizona	0	10	3	7	—	20

Den	—	Walker 54 pass from Cutler (Elam kick)
Den	—	FG Elam 30
Den	—	FG Elam 22
Ariz	—	FG Rackers 48
Ariz	—	A. Smith 4 fumble return (Rackers kick)
Den	—	FG Elam 30
Den	—	R. Smith 10 pass from Cutler (Elam kick)
Ariz	—	FG Rackers 38
Den	—	M. Bell 1 run (Elam kick)
Ariz	—	James 20 run (Rackers kick)
Den	—	M. Bell 1 run (Elam kick)

BALTIMORE 27, CLEVELAND 17—at M & T Bank Stadium, attendance 68,809. Kyle Boller replaced an injured Steve McNair and passed for 2 touchdowns as the Ravens clinched a playoff berth. McNair cut his hand on the second possession, and Boller stepped in to help the Ravens make their first postseason appearance since 2003. The Ravens scored on consecutive first half possessions, and in the third quarter Boller connected on a 77-yard touchdown pass to Demetrius Williams, hitting the big receiver in stride for a long touchdown to put the game away. Boller was 13 of 21 for 238 yards and 2

touchdowns, with 1 interception. Williams had 2 receptions for 100 yards. Derek Anderson was 23 of 32 for 223 yards and 2 touchdowns, with 2 interceptions.

Cleveland	3	7	7	0	—	17
Baltimore	7	10	7	3	—	27

Cle	—	FG Dawson 51
Balt	—	J. Lewis 7 run (Stover kick)
Balt	—	Mughelli 9 pass from Boller (Stover kick)
Balt	—	FG Stover 38
Cle	—	Jurevicius 3 pass from Anderson (Dawson kick)
Cle	—	Edwards 14 pass from Anderson (Dawson kick)
Balt	—	D. Williams 77 pass from Boller (Stover kick).
Balt	—	FG Stover 22

BUFFALO 21, MIAMI 0—at Ralph Wilson Stadium, attendance 71,011. J.P. Losman passed for 3 touchdowns and the Bills' defense recorded its first shutout since 1993 as Buffalo won for the fifth time in its last seven games. The Dolphins fell out of the playoff race, while the victory allowed the Bills to maintain a slim hope of the postseason. The Dolphins' offense did not threaten to score until the end of the game, but the defense knocked down Cleo Lemon's pass to preserve the shutout. Losman was 13 of 19 for 200 yards and 3 touchdowns. Harrington was 5 of 17 for 20 yards, with 2 interception. Cleo Lemon replaced Harrington in the second half and was 9 of 16 for 98 yards.

Miami	0	0	0	0	—	0
Buffalo	0	7	7	7	—	21

Buff	—	Royal 33 pass from Losman (Lindell kick)
Buff	—	Reed 27 pass from Losman (Lindell kick)
Buff	—	Evans 21 pass from Losman (Lindell kick)

PITTSBURGH 37, CAROLINA 3—at Bank of America Stadium, attendance 73,798. Willie Parker rushed for 132 yards and 1 touchdown as the Steelers won their third consecutive game and the Panthers lost their fifth straight game. The Steelers also excelled in special teams, as they blocked a punt and Santonio Holmes returned another punt 65 yards for a touchdown. Roethlisberger was 11 of 18 for 140 yards and 1 touchdown. Parker carried 23 times for 132 yards. Chris Weinke, starting his second consecutive game, in place of injured Jake Delhomme, was 18 of 28 for 170 yards, with 1 interception, and rookie Brett Basanez was 6 of 11 for 56 yards, with 1 interception.

Pittsburgh	0	17	10	10	—	37
Carolina	3	0	0	0	—	3

Pitt	—	Roethlisberger 1 run (Reed kick)
Pitt	—	FG Reed 19
Pitt	—	Davenport 13 pass from Roethlisberger (Reed kick)
Car	—	FG Kasay 37
Pitt	—	FG Reed 45
Pitt	—	Parker 41 run (Reed kick)
Pitt	—	Holmes 65 punt return (Reed kick)
Pitt	—	FG Reed 26

CHICAGO 34, TAMPA BAY 31 (OT)—at Soldier Field, attendance 62,260. Robbie Gould kicked a 25-yard field goal with less than four minutes remaining in overtime as the Bears secured home-field advantage throughout the NFC playoffs. Tim Rattay replaced Bruce Gradkowski in the second quarter and passed for 268 yards and 3 touchdowns to help the Buccaneers rally. The Buccaneers scored 31 points despite getting just 11 first downs, using numerous big plays, including touchdown passes of 64 and 44 yards in the fourth quarter, to tie the game. In overtime, Gould missed a 37-yard field goal before connecting from 25 yards to win the game. Rex Grossman's 28-yard pass to Rashied Davis on third-and-

8 set up the winning kick. Grossman was 29 of 44 for 339 yards and 2 touchdowns. Desmond Clark had 7 receptions for 125 yards and 2 touchdowns. Gradkowski was 5 of 11 for 37 yards. Galloway had 3 receptions for 107 yards.

Tampa Bay	0	3	7	21	0	—	31
Chicago	7	14	3	7	3	—	34

Chi	—	Clark 24 pass from Grossman (Gould kick)
TB	—	FG Bryant 45
Chi	—	T. Jones 5 run (Gould kick)
Chi	—	Clark 12 pass from Grossman (Gould kick)
TB	—	Alstott 14 run (Bryant kick)
TB	—	A. Smith 9 pass from Rattay (Bryant kick)
Chi	—	Benson 4 run (Gould kick)
TB	—	Galloway 64 pass from Rattay (Bryant kick)
TB	—	Hilliard 44 pass from Rattay (Bryant kick)
Chi	—	FG Gould 25

GREEN BAY 17, DETROIT 9—at Lambeau Field, attendance 70,472. Vernand Morency rushed for 2 touchdowns and Brett Favre set an NFL record as the Packers won their second consecutive game and remained in the playoff chase. Just before halftime, Favre completed a 21-yard pass to Carlyle Holiday to register his 4,968th career completion, surpassing Dan Marino's mark. The Packers' defense allowed just 142 total yards. Favre was 20 of 47 for 174 yards, with 3 interceptions. Kitna was 16 of 26 for 135 yards, with 2 interceptions.

Detroit	3	0	3	3	—	9
Green Bay	3	7	0	7	—	17

Det	—	FG Hanson 42
GB	—	FG Rayner 24
GB	—	Morency 14 run (Rayner kick)
Det	—	FG Hanson 42
Det	—	FG Hanson 23
GB	—	Morency 21 run (Rayner kick)

N.Y. JETS 26, MINNESOTA 13—at Metrodome, attendance 63,677. Chad Pennington passed for a career-high 339 yards as the Jets posted their third consecutive road victory. Tarvaris Jackson, who came off the bench to replace Brad Johnson, guided the Vikings, who were still mathematically alive in the postseason chase despite the loss, to a fourth-quarter touchdown. Pennington was 29 of 39 for 339 yards and 1 touchdown, with 1 interception. Laveranues Coles had 12 catches for 144 yards. Johnson was 10 of 17 for 96 yards and 1 touchdown. Jackson was 14 of 23 for 177 yards and 1 touchdown, with 1 interception.

N.Y. Jets	7	16	3	0	—	26
Minnesota	7	0	0	6	—	13

Minn	—	Taylor 30 pass from B. Johnson (Longwell kick)
NYJ	—	Houston 6 run (Nugent kick)
NYJ	—	FG Nugent 25
NYJ	—	Coles 21 pass from Pennington (Nugent kick)
NYJ	—	FG Nugent 52
NYJ	—	FG Nugent 45
NYJ	—	FG Nugent 20
Minn	—	Moore 35 pass from Jackson (pass failed)

NEW ENGLAND 40, HOUSTON 7—at Gillette Stadium, attendance 68,756. The Patriots' defense forced 4 interceptions, which led directly to 16 points, as the Patriots rolled past the Texans. Amazingly, the Patriots outscored the Texans by 33 points (40-7) despite outgaining them by just 32 yards (230-198). The Texans trailed 27-0 before finally scoring, only to then watch Ellis Hobbs return the ensuing kickoff 93 yards for a touchdown. Tom Brady was 16 of 23 for 109 yards and 2 touchdowns. David Carr was 16 of 28 for 127 yards, with 4 interceptions.

Houston	0	0	7	0	—	7
New England	17	10	7	6	—	40

NE — Faulk 11 run (Gostkowski kick)
NE — FG Gostkowski 36
NE — Faulk 43 pass from Brady (Gostkowski kick)
NE — FG Gostkowski 32
NE — Gaffney 6 pass from Brady (Gostkowski kick)
Hou — Dayne 1 run (K. Brown kick)
NE — Hobbs 93 kickoff return (Gostkowski kick)
NE — FG Gostkowski 31
NE — FG Gostkowski 21

WASHINGTON 16, NEW ORLEANS 10—at Louisiana Superdome, attendance 69,052. Jason Campbell passed for a touchdown as the Redskins surprised the Saints. Despite the loss, the Saints clinched the NFC South when Carolina lost to the Steelers during the Saints' game. The Redskins' offense was quiet for the next two quarters, but Campbell engineered a 10-play, 61-yard scoring drive when he needed it most, capped by Shaun Suisham's 22-yard field goal with 4:15 to play to stretch the lead to six points. Drew Brees led the Saints to the Redskins' 16, but his fourth-and-7 pass intended for Terrance Copper fell incomplete with 47 seconds remaining. Campbell was 13 of 28 for 204 yards and 1 touchdown. Ladell Betts had 22 carries for 119 yards. Brees was 21 of 38 for 207 yards, with 1 interception.

Washington	10	3	0	3	—	16
New Orleans	0	7	0	3	—	10

Wash — FG Suisham 37
Wash — Moss 31 pass from Campbell (Suisham kick)
NO — McAlister 1 run (Carney kick)
Wash — FG Suisham 37
NO — FG Carney 41
Wash — FG Suisham 22

PHILADELPHIA 36, N.Y. GIANTS 22—at Giants Stadium, attendance 78,657. The Eagles scored 15 points in ten seconds, capped by Trent Cole's 19-yard interception return for a touchdown with 2:47 to play, to win their third consecutive game. The Eagles rallied with 22 fourth-quarter points to maintain control of their own destiny in the postseason. Trailing 21-16, Will Demps intercepted a pass and the Giants drove 35 yards to take a 22-21 lead on Brandon Jacobs' 1-yard run with 6:59 to play. The Eagles and Jeff Garcia responded with an eight-play, 80-yard drive, capped by Garcia's 19-yard touchdown pass to Reggie Brown. The Eagles then converted the 2-point attempt as Garcia found L.J. Smith. On the first play after the kickoff, Cole intercepted a short pass intended for Tiki Barber and returned it 19 yards for a touchdown. Garcia was 19 of 28 for 237 yards and 1 touchdown, with 1 interception. Manning was 24 of 40 for 282 yards, with 2 interceptions. Plaxico Burress had 6 receptions for 120 yards.

Philadelphia	7	7	0	22	—	36
N.Y. Giants	7	3	3	9	—	22

NYG — Barber 11 run (Feely kick)
Phil — Buckhalter 2 run (Akers kick)
Phil — Westbrook 1 run (Akers kick)
NYG — FG Feely 47
NYG — FG Feely 23
NYG — FG Feely 24
Phil — Westbrook 28 run (Akers kick)
NYG — Jacobs 1 run (run failed)
Phil — Brown 19 pass from Garcia (Smith pass from Garcia)
Phil — Cole 19 interception return (Akers kick)

ST. LOUIS 20, OAKLAND 0—at McAfee Coliseum, attendance 50,164. Steven Jackson scored 2 touchdowns to culminate short drives as the Rams posted their first shutout since 2003. A muffed punt at the Raiders' 24 set up Jackson's first touchdown run, and in the fourth quar-

ter Jackson scored on a 19-yard run one play after Ron Bartell intercepted a pass and returned it 16 yards. Marc Bulger was 11 of 22 for 137 yards. Jackson had 31 carries for 127 yards. Aaron Brooks was 11 of 19 for 98 yards, with 1 interception. Andrew Walter replaced Brooks in the fourth quarter and was 14 of 20 for 131 yards, with 2 interceptions.

St. Louis	0	6	7	7	—	20
Oakland	0	0	0	0	—	0

StL — FG Wilkins 24
StL — FG Wilkins 34
StL — Jackson 4 run (Wilkins kick)
StL — Jackson 19 run (Wilkins kick)

TENNESSEE 24, JACKSONVILLE 17—at LP Field, attendance 69,143. The Titans scored 3 defensive touchdowns to win their fifth consecutive game despite being outgained 396-98 in total yards. Pacman Jones returned an interception 83 yards for a touchdown in the first quarter. The Jaguars threatened to score in the third quarter when Garrard scrambled 16 yards, fumbled, and Cortland Finnegan weaved his way 92 yards with the fumble return for a touchdown and 17-10 Titans' lead. Six plays later, Chris Hope stepped in front of a short pass and raced 61 yards for a touchdown. The Jaguars pulled within 24-17 and regained possession, but Reynaldo Hill intercepted a pass to clinch the win. Young was 8 of 15 for 85 yards. Garrard was 22 of 37 for 233 yards and 1 touchdown, with 3 interceptions. The Jaguars rushed for 202 yards, with four players posting at least 25 yards.

Jacksonville	7	3	0	7	—	17
Tennessee	7	0	17	0	—	24

Tenn — P. Jones 83 interception return (Bironas kick)
Jax — Jones-Drew 12 run (Scobee kick)
Jax — FG Scobee 43
Tenn — FG Bironas 27
Tenn — Finnegan 92 fumble return (Bironas kick)
Tenn — Hope 61 interception return (Bironas kick)
Jax — Jones 3 pass from Garrard (Scobee kick)

SUNDAY NIGHT, DECEMBER 17
SAN DIEGO 20, KANSAS CITY 9—at Qualcomm Stadium, attendance 66,583. LaDainian Tomlinson rushed for 199 yards and 2 touchdowns as the Chargers won their eighth consecutive game. Tomlinson's 85-yard touchdown run came one play after David Binn recovered a Bernard Pollard blocked punt by the Chiefs that Derrick Ross touched beyond the line of scrimmage. Tomlinson' touchdown was the last of his NFL record 31 for the season. it also marked the eighth consecutive game in which he had multiple touchdowns, setting an NFL record. Philip Rivers was 8 of 23 for 97 yards, with 2 interceptions. Tomlinson carried 25 times for 199 yards. Trent Green was 23 of 41 for 185 yards, with 1 interception.

Kansas City	0	3	3	3	—	9
San Diego	7	7	0	6	—	20

SD — Tomlinson 15 run (Kaeding kick)
KC — FG Tynes 45
SD — Tomlinson 85 run (Kaeding kick)
SD — FG Tynes 52
SD — FG Kaeding 30
KC — FG Tynes 24
SD — FG Kaeding 22

MONDAY NIGHT, DECEMBER 18
INDIANAPOLIS 34, CINCINNATI 16—at RCA Dome, attendance 57,292. The Colts, who had clinched the AFC South the previous day when Jacksonville was defeated, used 4 touchdown passes by Peyton Manning to snap the Bengals' four-game winning streak. Marvin Harrison was on the receiving end of 3 of Manning's four scoring passes, as the Colts used consecutive touchdown drives of 75 and 57 yards in the third quarter to break open a 17-13 game and take a 31-13 lead. Manning was 29 of 36 for 282 yards and 4 touchdowns. Carson Palmer was 14 of

28 for 176 yards.

Cincinnati	3	7	3	3	—	16
Indianapolis	3	14	14	3	—	34

Ind — FG Vinatieri 30
Cin — FG Graham 27
Ind — Harrison 4 pass from Manning (Vinatieri kick)
Cin — R. Johnson 12 run (Graham kick)
Ind — Harrison 3 pass from Manning (Vinatieri kick)
Ind — FG Graham 30
Ind — Harrison 1 pass from Manning (Vinatieri kick)
Ind — Wayne 18 pass from Manning (Vinatieri kick)
Cin — FG Graham 28
Ind — FG Vinatieri 44

SIXTEENTH WEEK SUMMARIES
American Football Conference

East Division	W	L	T	Pct.	Pts.	OP
New England*	11	4	0	.733	345	214
N.Y. Jets	9	6	0	.600	293	292
Buffalo	7	8	0	.467	293	292
Miami	6	9	0	.400	238	256

North Division	W	L	T	Pct.	Pts.	OP
Baltimore*	12	3	0	.800	334	194
Cincinnati	8	7	0	.533	356	308
Pittsburgh	7	8	0	.467	330	298
Cleveland	4	11	0	.267	232	342

South Division	W	L	T	Pct.	Pts.	OP
Indianapolis*	11	4	0	.733	400	338
Jacksonville	8	7	0	.533	341	239
Tennessee	8	7	0	.533	301	360
Houston	5	10	0	.333	253	360

West Division	W	L	T	Pct.	Pts.	OP
San Diego*	13	2	0	.867	465	283
Denver	9	6	0	.600	296	279
Kansas City	8	7	0	.533	296	285
Oakland	2	13	0	.133	165	309

National Football Conference

East Division	W	L	T	Pct.	Pts.	OP
Dallas#	9	6	0	.600	394	311
Philadelphia	9	6	0	.600	374	311
N.Y. Giants	7	8	0	.467	321	334
Washington	5	10	0	.333	279	342

North Division	W	L	T	Pct.	Pts.	OP
Chicago*	13	2	0	.867	420	229
Green Bay	7	8	0	.467	275	359
Minnesota	6	9	0	.400	261	286
Detroit	2	13	0	.133	266	367

South Division	W	L	T	Pct.	Pts.	OP
New Orleans*	10	5	0	.667	392	291
Atlanta	7	8	0	.467	239	284
Carolina	7	8	0	.467	275	304
Tampa Bay	4	11	0	.267	204	330

West Division	W	L	T	Pct.	Pts.	OP
Seattle	8	7	0	.533	312	334
St. Louis	7	8	0	.467	326	360
San Francisco	6	9	0	.400	272	389
Arizona	5	10	0	.333	294	362

*Clinched division title
#Clinched playoff berth

THURSDAY NIGHT, DECEMBER 21
GREEN BAY 9, MINNESOTA 7—at Lambeau Field, attendance 70,864. Dave Rayner kicked 3 field goals and Brett Favre engineered a fourth-quarter game-winning drive for Green Bay to keep its playoff hopes alive. The Packers completely dominated the game, outgaining the Vikings 319-104 in total yards, accumulating 19 first down compared to 3 by Minnesota, and maintaining possession for 34:39. Yet, Fred Smoot's 47-yard interception return for a touchdown in the third quarter gave the Vikings a 7-6 lead. With 4:47 to play, Favre engineered a 41-yard drive, keyed by a 36-yard pass to Ruvell Martin, to set up Rayner's 44-yard field goal with 1:34 to play. The Vikings did not get a first down on their final possession. Favre was 26 of 50 for 285 yards, with 2 interceptions. Making

his first NFL start, rookie Tarvaris Jackson was 10 of 29 for 50 yards, with 1 interception.

Minnesota	0	0	7	0	—	7
Green Bay	3	3	0	3	—	9

GB	—	FG Rayner 38
GB	—	FG Rayner 44
Minn	—	Smoot 47 interception return (Longwell kick)
GB	—	FG Rayner 44

SATURDAY NIGHT, DECEMBER 23

KANSAS CITY 20, OAKLAND 9—at McAfee Coliseum, attendance 61,446. Larry Johnson rushed for 135 yards and a touchdown as the Chiefs stayed in the playoff hunt. Late in the second quarter, the Raiders had the ball at midfield when Jared Allen sacked Andrew Walter and forced him to fumble. Allen recovered the ball, and Johnson scored five plays later, with 40 seconds remaining in the half, for a 17-6 lead. Trent Green was 12 of 24 for 148 yards. Johnson rushed 31 times for 135 yards. Walter was 27 of 37 for 226 yards, with 2 interceptions. Ronald Curry had 11 receptions for 106 yards.

Kansas City	10	7	0	3	—	20
Oakland	3	3	3	0	—	9

Oak	—	FG Janikowski 25
KC	—	Kennison 6 pass from Green (Tynes kick)
KC	—	FG Tynes 29
Oak	—	FG Janikowski 37
KC	—	L. Johnson 1 run (Tynes kick)
Oak	—	FG Janikowski 53
KC	—	FG Tynes 28

SUNDAY, DECEMBER 24

CAROLINA 10, ATLANTA 3—at Georgia Dome, attendance 68,834. In a defensive-dominated game in which neither team gained 200 yards, the Panthers outlasted the Falcons to have a leg up in the NFC South and better chance at a playoff berth. The Panthers ran 52 times and passed just 10 times, with Chris Weinke getting sacked on three of those opportunities, to maintain possession a whopping 41 minutes, 47 seconds. Both teams scored on their first possession, but neither team ran a play inside the opponents' 25-yard line thereafter. Weinke was 4 of 7 for 32 yards and 1 touchdown. Michael Vick was 9 of 20 for 109 yards, with 2 interceptions.

Carolina	0	10	0	0	—	10
Atlanta	3	0	0	0	—	3

Atl	—	FG Andersen 40
Car	—	King 1 pass from Weinke (Kasay kick)
Car	—	FG Kasay 42

TENNESSEE 30, BUFFALO 29—at Ralph Wilson Stadium, attendance 54,765. Rob Bironas kicked a 30-yard field goal with 2:10 remaining as the Titans posted yet another fourth-quarter comeback to win their sixth consecutive game. It marked the fourth time in 12 career starts that Young had engineered a fourth-quarter comeback. The defeat eliminated the Bills from the playoff chase. Trailing 29-20, the Titans had a 62-yard drive to pull within 29-27 on Brandon Jones' 29-yard touchdown catch with 11:14 to play. After a punt, the Titans took 7:15 off the clock with 14-play, 75-yard drive, capped by Bironas' field goal. Reynaldo Hill intercepted a pass near the goal line on fourth down in the final minute to secure the victory. Young was 13 of 20 for 183 yards and 2 touchdowns. Brandon Jones had 5 catches for 101 yards, and Travis Henry carried 25 times for 135 yards. J.P. Losman was 19 of 33 for 266 yards and 1 touchdown, with 2 interceptions.

Tennessee	7	13	0	10	—	30
Buffalo	10	9	10	0	—	29

Buff	—	FG Lindell 21
Tenn	—	Wade 22 pass from Young (Bironas kick)
Buff	—	McGahee 1 run (Lindell kick)
Tenn	—	FG Bironas 42
Tenn	—	FG Birnoas 20
Buff	—	FG Lindell 36
Buff	—	FG Lindell 45
Tenn	—	Young 36 run (Bironas kick)
Buff	—	FG Lindell 21
Buff	—	Evans 37 pass from Losman (Lindell kick)
Buff	—	FG Lindell 24
Tenn	—	B. Jones 29 pass from Young (Bironas kick)
Tenn	—	FG Bironas 30

TAMPA BAY 22, CLEVELAND 7—at Cleveland Browns Stadium, attendance 69,603. Derrick Brooks returned an interception for a touchdown to highlight a strong defensive performance by the Buccaneers. With Tim Rattay making his first start at quarterback, the Buccaneers nearly doubled the Browns' offensive output (355-187 in total yards) and maintained possession for 37 minutes, 16 seconds. Leading 6-0, the Buccaneers drove 74 yards for a touchdown to begin the third quarter to take a 12-0 lead, which was never threatened. Rattay was 16 of 26 for 212 yards, with 1 interception. Derek Anderson was 10 of 27 for 123 yards, with 4 interceptions.

Tampa Bay	3	3	6	10	—	22
Cleveland	0	0	0	7	—	7

TB	—	FG Bryant 23
TB	—	FG Bryant 24
TB	—	Pittman 11 run (kick blocked)
TB	—	Brooks 21 interception return (Bryant kick)
Cle	—	Holly 40 fumble return (Dawson kick)
TB	—	FG Bryant 37

DENVER 24, CINCINNATI 23—at INVESCO Field at Mile High, attendance 75,759. On a slightly snowy day, a poor snap on an extra-point with 41 seconds to play denied the Bengals an opportunity to tie the game, and putting their playoff aspirations in doubt. The Broncos would have clinched a postseason berth with a victory. The Broncos took a 21-17 lead in the third quarter when rookie Jay Cutler drove the Broncos 99 yards in 14 plays, capped by Mike Bell's 2-yard run. The Bengals did not threaten again until their final possession, when Carson Palmer engineered a 12-play, 90-yard drive that culminated in a 10-yard touchdown pass to T.J. Houshmandzadeh to pull the Bengals to within one point with 41 seconds left. However, the snap of the extra-point attempt by Brad St. Louis sailed beyond the reach of holder Kyle Larson. The Bengals then recovered the onside kick, but an offensive off-side penalty nullified the play. A second attempt was recovered by Denver's Quincy Morgan to secure the victory. Cutler was 12 of 23 for 179 yards and 2 touchdowns, with 1 interception. Palmer was 21 of 40 for 209 yards and 2 touchdowns, with 2 interceptions. Rudi Johnson had 30 carries for 129 yards.

Cincinnati	7	10	0	6	—	23
Denver	0	14	7	3	—	24

Cin	—	R. Johnson 6 run (Graham kick)
Den	—	Scheffler 1 pass from Cutler (Elam kick)
Den	—	Walker 39 pass from Cutler (Elam kick)
Cin	—	FG Graham 46
Cin	—	Henry 11 pass from Palmer (Graham kick)
Den	—	M. Bell 2 run (Elam kick)
Den	—	FG Elam 24
Cin	—	Houshmandzadeh 10 pass from Palmer (poor snap-no attempt)

CHICAGO 26, DETROIT 21—at Ford Field, attendance 60,665. Trailing 21-17, the Bears rallied with three fourth-quarter field goals by Robbie Gould to defeat the Lions. In the third quarter, Jon Kitna capped an 11-play drive with a 2-yard touchdown pass to Roy Williams. The Bears responded with drives of 58 and 72 yards to take a 23-21 lead. Three plays later, Mark Anderson sacked Kitna and forced him to fumble. Adewale Ogunleye recovered

at the Lions' 32, and Gould connected on a 44-yard kick with 2:50 to play. The Lions drove to the Bears' 22, but Kitna's pass intended for Mike Williams in the end zone fell incomplete as time expired. With home-field advantage throughout the playoffs already secured, Brian Griese played quarterback for the Bears' last two field-goal drives. Rex Grossman was 20 of 36 for 197 yards and 1 touchdown. Kitna was 27 of 45 for 283 yards and 3 touchdowns. Mike Furrey had 10 receptions for 107 yards.

Chicago	3	14	0	9	—	26
Detroit	7	0	14	0	—	21

Chi	—	FG Gould 36
Det	—	Campbell 23 pass from Kitna (Hanson kick)
Chi	—	Berrian 13 pass from Grossman (Gould kick)
Chi	—	Peterson 2 run (Gould kick)
Det	—	Furrey 20 pass from Kitna (Hanson kick)
Det	—	R. Williams 2 pass from Kitna (Hanson kick)
Chi	—	FG Gould 36
Chi	—	FG Gould 39
Chi	—	FG Gould 44

HOUSTON 27, INDIANAPOLIS 24—at Reliant Stadium, attendance 70,132. Kris Brown made a 48-yard field goal as time expired and Ron Dayne rushed for 153 yards and 2 touchdowns as the Texans beat the Colts for the first time in 10 attempts. In a game of long drives for both teams, the Texans scored on five of their seven possessions. Houston had the ball for nearly 36 minutes, and had drives of 15, 14, 10, nine, and eight plays. Marvin Harrison's second touchdown catch tied the game with 2:41 to play, but a 38-yard kickoff return by Dexter Wynn and a 17-yard pass from David Carr to Andre Johnson set up Brown's winning 48-yard field goal. Carr was 16 of 23 for 163 yards and 1 touchdown. Dayne had 32 carries for 153 yards. Manning was 21 of 27 for 205 yards and 3 touchdowns. Harrison had 8 receptions for 112 yards. Addai carried 15 times for 100 yards.

Indianapolis	7	7	3	7	—	24
Houston	14	7	0	6	—	27

Hou	—	Dayne 3 run (K. Brown kick)
Hou	—	Dayne 6 run (K. Brown kick)
Ind	—	Harrison 37 pass from Manning (Vinatieri kick)
Ind	—	Moorehead 9 pass from Manning (Vinatieri kick)
Hou	—	Leach 3 pass from Carr (K. Brown kick)
Ind	—	FG Vinatieri 33
Hou	—	FG K. Brown 42
Ind	—	Harrison 7 pass from Manning (Vinatieri kick)
Hou	—	FG K. Brown 48

NEW ENGLAND 24, JACKSONVILLE 21—at Alltel Stadium, attendance 67,164. Tom Brady passed for 249 yards and Laurence Maroney ran a key 27-yard touchdown run as the Patriots clinched their fourth consecutive AFC East title. David Garrard's 33-yard touchdown pass to Matt Jones with 3:03 pulled the Jaguars to within three points, and Jacksonville forced a punt, but on the next play Jarvis Green sacked Garrard and forced him to fumble. Rodney Harrison recovered near midfield with 1:46 to play to secure the victory. Brady was 28 of 39 for 249 yards and 1 touchdown. Jones-Drew carried 19 times for 131 yards.

New England	0	10	7	7	—	24
Jacksonville	0	7	7	7	—	21

NE	—	FG Gostkowski 48
Jax	—	Jones-Drew 74 run (Scobee kick)
NE	—	Dillon 1 run (Gostkowski kick)
NE	—	Thomas 22 pass from Brady (Gostkowski kick)
Jax	—	Jones-Drew 1 run (Scobee kick)
NE	—	Maroney 27 run (Gostkowski kick)

Jax — M. Jones 33 pass from Garrard (Scobee kick)

NEW ORLEANS 30, N.Y. GIANTS 7—at Giants Stadium, attendance 78,539. The Saints had two 100-yard rushers on offense, and the defense allowed the Giants just 6 first downs and 142 total yards. The Giants, who lost for the sixth time in seven games, scored four plays into the game, on Eli Manning's 55-yard touchdown pass to Plaxico Burress. The Giants did not run a play in Saints' territory the entire game. New Orleans' offense maintained possession for 40 minutes, 34 seconds. Drew Brees was 13 of 32 for 132 yards and 1 touchdown. Reggie Bush carried 20 times for 126 yards. Deuce McAllister had 27 carries for 108 yards. Manning was 9 of 25 for 74 yards and 1 touchdown, with 1 interception.

New Orleans	3	10	7	10	—	30
N.Y. Giants	7	0	0	0	—	7

NYG — Burress 55 pass from Manning (Feely kick)
NO — FG Carney 32
NO — FG Carney 26
NO — Colston 2 pass from Brees (Carney kick)
NO — Bush 1 run (Carney kick)
NO — McAllister 9 run (Carney kick)
NO — FG Carney 38

BALTIMORE 31, PITTSBURGH 7—at Heinz Field, attendance 68,804. Steve McNair passed for 3 touchdowns as the Ravens put themselves in position to get a first-round bye in the playoffs. The game proved to be the last home game for Bill Cowher, who after the season stepped down after 15 years with the Steelers. The Ravens led 14-7 at halftime, drove 69 yards to begin the second half to take a 21-7 lead, and had scoring drives of 8 and 17 yards, after interceptions, in the fourth quarter to pull away. McNair was 21 of 31 for 256 yards and 3 touchdowns, with 2 interceptions. Clayton had 7 catches for 108 yards. Roethlisberger was 15 of 31 for 156 yards and 1 touchdown, with 2 interceptions.

Baltimore	7	7	7	10	—	31
Pittsburgh	0	7	0	0	—	7

Balt — Clayton 35 pass from McNair (Stover kick)
Balt — Wilcox 1 pass from McNair (Stover kick)
Pitt — Miller 1 pass from Roethlisberger (Reed kick)
Balt — Williams 25 pass from McNair (Stover kick)
Balt — FG Stover 26
Balt — J. Lewis 1 run (Stover kick)

ST. LOUIS 37, WASHINGTON 31 (OT)—at Edward Jones Dome, attendance 62,324. Steven Jackson rushed for 150 yards, had 102 receiving yards, and scored 2 touchdowns, including the game-winning 21-yard run in overtime. The Rams generated 579 yards offense, posting four scoring drive of more than 80 yards. Shaun Suisham tied the game with a 52-yard field goal with 3:21 to play. The Rams had a chance to win at the end of regulation play, but Jeff Wilkins' 41-yard kick sailed wide left. In overtime, Shaun McDonald's 33-yard punt return set up Jackson's game-winning run. Marc Bulger was 25 of 38 for 388 yards and 4 touchdowns. Isaac Bruce had 9 receptions for 148 yards. Jackson carried 33 times for 150 yards an had 6 receptions for 102 yards. Jason Campbell was 13 of 26 for 160 yards and 1 touchdown. Ladell Betts carried 29 times for 129 yards.

Washington	7	14	7	3	0	—	31
St. Louis	0	14	14	3	6	—	37

Wash — Duckett 5 run (Suisham kick)
StL — Bruce 10 run from Bulger (Wilkins kick)
StL — Byrd 27 pass from Bulger (Wilkins kick)
Wash — Betts 6 run (Suisham kick)
Wash — Cooley 9 pass from Campbell

(Suisham kick)
Wash — Betts 7 run (Suisham kick)
StL — Jackson 64 pass from Bulger (Wilkins kick)
StL — Davis 10 pass from Bulger (Wilkins kick)
StL — FG Wilkins 21
Wash — FG Suisham 52
StL — Jackson 21 run

ARIZONA 26, SAN FRANCISCO 20—at Monster Park, attendance 67,751. The Cardinals scored on their first four possessions to take a 20-6 halftime lead. The 49ers, who were knocked from postseason contention with the loss, rallied in the second half, and Frank Gore's 1-yard run pulled them within six points with 5:00 to play, but Marcel Shipp gained 5 yards on third-and-4 with 2:00 left to secure the victory. Matt Leinart was 9 of 13 for 162 yards and 1 touchdown before being injured. Kurt Warner was 9 of 13 for 105 yards. Edgerrin James rushed 29 times for 105 yards. Smith was 18 of 29 for 190 yards, with 1 interception.

Arizona	10	10	0	6	—	26
San Francisco	3	3	7	7	—	20

SF — FG Nedney 49
Ariz — FG Rackers 25
Ariz — Shipp run (Rackers kick)
Ariz — Fitzgerald 6 pass from Leinart (Rackers kick)
Ariz — FG Rackers 39
SF — FG Nedney 32
SF — Gore 2 run (Nedney kick)
Ariz — FG Rackers 37
Ariz — FG Rackers 32
SF — Gore 1 run (Nedney kick)

SAN DIEGO 20, SEATTLE 17—at Qwest Field, attendance 68,809. Vincent Jackson got behind the defense and caught a 37-yard touchdown pass from Philip Rivers with 29 seconds remaining to give the Chargers their ninth consecutive victory. The Seahawks, who had clinched the NFC West moments earlier when the 49ers lost at home, lost their third consecutive game. Rivers was 10 of 30 for 181 yards and 2 touchdowns. LaDainian Tomlinson carried 22 times for 123 yards, his ninth consecutive 100-yard game. Matt Hasselbeck was 17 of 37 for 189 yards, with 2 interceptions. Shaun Alexander carried 31 times for 140 yards.

San Diego	0	7	6	7	—	20
Seattle	0	0	7	10	—	17

SD — Jackson 9 pass from Rivers (Kaeding kick)
SD — FG Kaeding 46
Sea — Alexander 33 run (J. Brown kick)
SD — FG Kaeding 40
Sea — Alexander 9 run (J. Brown kick)
Sea — FG J. Brown 33
SD — Jackson 37 pass from Rivers (Kaeding kick)

MONDAY, DECEMBER 25
PHILADELPHIA 23, DALLAS 7—at Texas Stadium, attendance 62,839. Jeff Garcia passed for 238 yards and a touchdown for the Eagles. The Eagles dominated the game statistically, outgaining the Cowboys 426-201 in total yards and maintaining possession for more than 37 minutes. The Eagles scored on four of their first five possessions, including two 89-yard drives and a 77-yard drive, to take a 16-7 lead. Tony Romo was intercepted twice in the second half, and the Eagles held the ball for more than 20 minutes after the break to maintain and expand their lead. Garcia was 15 of 23 for 238 yards and 1 touchdown, with 1 interception. Brian Westbrook carried 26 times for 122 yards. Romo was 14 of 29 for 42 yards and 1 touchdown, with 2 interceptions.

Philadelphia	7	6	3	7	—	23
Dallas	0	7	0	0	—	7

Phil — Schobel 25 pass from Garcia (Akers kick)

Phil — FG Akers 25
Dall — Owens 14 pass from Romo (Gramatica kick)
Phil — FG Akers 45
Phil — FG Akers 21
Phil — Buckhalter 1 run (Akers kick)

MONDAY NIGHT, DECEMBER 25
N.Y. JETS 13, MIAMI 10—at Dolphin Stadium, attendance 73,500. Mike Nugent's 30-yard field goal with 10 seconds left helped the Jets beat the Dolphins. Neither team scored in the first half, before the teams exchanged touchdowns in the second half, with the Jets taking a 10-7 lead on Chad Pennington's 32-yard touchdown pass to Jerricho Cotchery with 8:04 to play. Olindo Mare tied the game with 2:09 remaining, but on the next play Leon Washington took a short pass from Pennington and weaved and raced 64 yards to the Dolphins' 16 to set up Nugent's winning kick. Pennington was 14 of 29 for 237 yards. Cleo Lemon came off the bench and was 11 of 16 for 104 yards and 1 touchdown. Joey Harrington was 7 of 15 for 42 yards. Ronnie Brown had 18 carries for 110 yards.

N.Y. Jets	0	0	3	10	—	13
Miami	0	0	10	0	—	10

NYJ — FG Nugent 22
Mia — McMichael 7 pass from Lemon (Mare kick)
NYJ — Cotchery 32 pass from Pennington (Nugent kick)
Mia — FG Mare 25
NYJ — FG Nugent 30

SEVENTEENTH WEEK SUMMARIES
American Football Conference

East Division	W	L	T	Pct.	Pts.	OP
New England*	12	4	0	.750	385	237
N.Y. Jets#	10	6	0	.625	316	295
Buffalo	7	9	0	.438	300	311
Miami	6	10	0	.375	260	283
North Division	**W**	**L**	**T**	**Pct.**	**Pts.**	**OP**
Baltimore*	13	3	0	.813	353	201
Cincinnati	8	8	0	.500	373	331
Pittsburgh	8	8	0	.500	353	315
Cleveland	4	12	0	.250	238	356
South Division	**W**	**L**	**T**	**Pct.**	**Pts.**	**OP**
Indianapolis*	12	4	0	.750	427	360
Tennessee	8	8	0	.500	324	400
Jacksonville	8	8	0	.500	371	274
Houston	6	10	0	.375	267	366
West Division	**W**	**L**	**T**	**Pct.**	**Pts.**	**OP**
San Diego*	14	2	0	.875	492	303
Kansas City#	9	7	0	.563	331	315
Denver	9	7	0	.563	319	305
Oakland	2	14	0	.125	168	332

National Football Conference

East Division	W	L	T	Pct.	Pts.	OP
Philadelphia*	10	6	0	.625	398	328
Dallas#	9	7	0	.563	425	350
N.Y. Giants#	8	8	0	.500	355	362
Washington	5	11	0	.313	307	376
North Division	**W**	**L**	**T**	**Pct.**	**Pts.**	**OP**
Chicago*	13	3	0	.813	427	255
Green Bay	8	8	0	.500	301	366
Minnesota	6	10	0	.375	282	327
Detroit	3	13	0	.188	305	398
South Division	**W**	**L**	**T**	**Pct.**	**Pts.**	**OP**
New Orleans*	10	6	0	.625	413	322
Carolina	8	8	0	.500	270	305
Atlanta	7	9	0	.438	292	328
Tampa Bay	4	12	0	.250	211	353
West Division	**W**	**L**	**T**	**Pct.**	**Pts.**	**OP**
Seattle*	9	7	0	.563	335	341
St. Louis	8	8	0	.500	367	381
San Francisco	7	9	0	.438	298	412
Arizona	5	11	0	.313	314	389

*Clinched division title
#Clinched playoff berth

SATURDAY NIGHT, DECEMBER 30
N.Y. GIANTS 34, WASHINGTON 28—at FedExField, attendance 86,141. Playing in his final regular season game, Tiki Barber rushed for franchise-record 234 yards and 3 touchdowns as the Giants nearly ensured themselves a playoff berth. Barber's 15-yard touchdown run with 13:15 left in the second quarter gave the Giants 10-7 lead. With 5:44 left in the half, his 55-yard run increased the lead to 17-7, and he capped the night with a 50-yard run for a 34-21 lead with 6:13 remaining. On Sunday, the Giants, who had lost six of seven prior to the he victory over Washington, did indeed earn a wild-card berth. Manning was 12 of 26 for 101 yards and 1 touchdown. Barber carried 23 times for 234 yards. Campbell was 21 of 31 for 220 yards and 2 touchdowns, with 1 interception. Moss had 6 catches for 103 yards.

N.Y. Giants	3	17	7	7	—	34
Washington	7	0	7	14	—	28

NYG	—	FG Feely 34
Wash	—	Moss 48 pass from Randle El (Suisham kick)
NYG	—	Barber 15 run (Feely kick)
NYG	—	Barber 55 run (Feely kick)
NYG	—	FG Feely 31
NYG	—	T. Carter 6 pass from Manning (Feely kick)
Wash	—	Betts 7 pass from Campbell (Suisham kick)
Wash	—	Duckett 1 run (Suisham kick)
NYG	—	Barber 50 run (Feely kick)
Wash	—	Sellers 1 pass from Campbell (Suisham kick)

SUNDAY, DECEMBER 31
BALTIMORE 19, BUFFALO 7—at M & T Bank Stadium, attendance 70,913. Chris McAlister returned an interception for a touchdown as the Ravens secured a first-round bye with a victory over the Bills. The Ravens allowed just 39 rushing yards, and finished the season with four consecutive victories and nine wins in their last ten games. The Bills only drove into the Ravens' red zone once, and Samari Rolle intercepted J.P. Losman's pass with 2:15 remaining to secure the victory. Steve McNair was 23 of 35 for 216 yards, with 1 interception. Losman's was 20 of 35 for 237 yards and 1 touchdown, with 2 interceptions. Lee Evans had 7 catches for 145 yards.

Buffalo	0	0	7	0	—	7
Baltimore	3	3	10	3	—	19

Balt	—	FG Stover 26
Balt	—	FG Stover 37
Balt	—	FG Stover 39
Buff	—	Evans 44 pass from Losman's (Lindell kick)
Balt	—	McAlister 31 interception return (Stover kick)
Balt	—	FG Stover 29

PITTSBURGH 23, CINCINNATI 17 (OT)—at Paul Brown Stadium, attendance 66,049. Ben Roethlisberger completed a 67-yard touchdown pass to Santonio Holmes three plays into overtime as the Steelers knocked the Bengals out of the playoff chase. The game marked the final game of Bill Cowher's 15-year tenure with the Steelers. The Bengals had a chance to win the game. They scored on touchdown drives of 80 and 73 yards in the fourth quarter to take a 17-14 lead Jeff Reed's 35-yard field goal with 1:03 left tied the game, but Carson Palmer completed a 47-yard pass to Chris Henry to set up a potential game-winning, playoff-bound kick, but Shayne Graham's 39-yard kick sailed wide right. In overtime, Holmes caught a short pass and outran the defense to the end zone. Roethlisberger was 19 of 28 for 280 yards and 1 touchdown, with 1 interception. Holmes had 4 receptions for 124 yards. Willie Parker rushed 37 times for 134 yards. Palmer was 20 of 38 for 251 yards. Henry had 4 receptions for 124 yards.

Pittsburgh	0	7	0	10	6	—	23
Cincinnati	0	3	0	14	0	—	17

Pitt	—	Parker 1 run (Reed kick)
Cin	—	FG Graham 34
Cin	—	Henry 66 pass from Palmer (Graham kick)
Pitt	—	Parker 1 run (Reed kick)
Cin	—	Stewart 5 pass from Palmer (Graham kick)
Pitt	—	FG Reed 35
Pitt	—	Holmes 67 pass from Roethlisberger

DETROIT 39, DALLAS 31—at Texas Stadium, attendance 63,008. Jon Kitna passed for 4 touchdowns as the Lions knocked the Cowboys into the wild-card round. The Lions won the game when a host of defenders stuffed Tony Romo as the quarterback attempted to scramble into the end zone on fourth down. Kitna was 28 of 42 for 306 yards and 4 touchdowns, with 1 interception. Mike Furrey had 11 receptions for 102 yards, and Roy Williams added 6 catches for 104 yards. Romo was 23 of 32 for 321 yards and 2 touchdowns, with 1 interception. Terrell Owens had 6 catches for 117 yards and Terry Glenn for 6 receptions for 109 yards.

Detroit	13	7	10	9	—	39
Dallas	0	14	10	7	—	31

Det	—	FG Hanson 33
Det	—	FG Hanson 25
Det	—	R. Williams 20 pass from Kitna
Dall	—	Barber 1 run (Gramatica kick)
Dall	—	Crayton 6 pass from Romo (Gramatica kick)
Det	—	R. Williams 15 pass from Kitna (Hanson kick)
Dall	—	Newman 56 punt return (Gramatica kick)
Det	—	FG Hanson 26
Det	—	Furrey 13 pass from Kitna (Hanson kick)
Dall	—	FG Gramatica 39
Dall	—	Owens 56 pass from Romo (Gramatica kick)
Det	—	M. Williams 21 pass from Kitna (pass failed)
Det	—	FG Hanson 23

SAN FRANCISCO 26, DENVER 23 (OT)—at INVESCO Field at Mile High, attendance 75,555. Joe Nedney kicked a 36-yard field goal with 1:56 left in overtime as the 49ers knocked the Broncos out of the playoffs. A win or a tie would have given the Broncos a playoff berth. Walt Harris had 2 interceptions for the 49ers, including a 28-yard return to give the 49ers a 17-13 lead in the third quarter. Rookie Jay Cutler engineered a game-tying 10-play, 80-yard drive capped by Tony Scheffler's 9-yard touchdown grab with 1:30 left in regulation, to tie the game. In overtime, on the 49ers' second possessions, Brian Gilmore had a 20-yard end-around and a 14-yard catch on third-and-8 to setup Joe Nedney's winning kick with 13:04 gone in overtime. Smith was 17 of 32 for 194 yards and 1 touchdown, with 1 interception. Gore carried 31 times for 153 yards. Cutler was 21 of 32 for 230 yards and 1 touchdown, with 1 interception.

San Francisco	0	3	14	6	3	—	26
Denver	0	10	3	7	0	—	23

Den	—	FG Elam 22
Den	—	FG Elam 21
Den	—	Bailey 70 interception return (Elam kick)
SF	—	FG Nedney 46
SF	—	Norris 32 pass from Smith (Nedney kick)
SF	—	Harris 28 interception return (Nedney kick)
Den	—	FG Elam 22
SF	—	FG Nedney 29
SF	—	FG Nedney 46
Den	—	Scheffler 9 pass from Cutler (Elam kick)
SF	—	FG Nedney 36

HOUSTON 14, CLEVELAND 6—at Reliant Stadium, attendance 70,097. Rookie Chris Taylor rushed for 99 yards and a touchdown as the Texans posted back-to-back victories for the first time since 2004. Taylor's first NFL touchdown, a 5-yard run in the third quarter, gave Houston a 7-3 lead. The Texans increased their lead when defensive tackle Anthony Maddox sack Charlie Frye, stripped him of the ball, picked it up and ran 47 yards for a touchdown. Phil Dawson's second field goal, from 36 yards with 7:08 to play, cut the deficit to 14-6, but the Browns failed to run another play in Texans' territory on their final two possessions. David Carr was 9 of 15 for 86 yards, with 1 interception. Frye, who had missed the previous three games with a wrist injury, was 25 of 34 for 187 yards, with 1 interception. Kellen Winslow had 11 receptions for 93 yards.

Cleveland	0	3	0	3	—	6
Houston	0	0	14	0	—	14

Cle	—	FG Dawson 43
Hou	—	Taylor 5 run (K. Brown kick)
Hou	—	Maddox 47 fumble return (K. Brown kick)
Cle	—	FG Dawson 36

INDIANAPOLIS 27, MIAMI 22—at RCA Dome, attendance 57,310. Peyton Manning passed for 2 touchdowns as the Colts secured a home game and the third seed in the AFC playoffs. The victory gave the Colts their first perfect season at home since 1958, despite being the only team in the NFL to allow at least 100 rushing yards by all 16 opponents. Defensive tackle Dan Klecko caught his first-ever NFL touchdown in the second quarter. Manning was 22 of 37 for 282 yards and 2 touchdowns. Lemon was 18 of 36 for 210 yards and 1 touchdown, with 1 interception. Brown had 21 carries for 115 yards.

Miami	3	3	6	10	—	22
Indianapolis	0	17	3	7	—	27

Mia	—	FG Mare 28
Ind	—	Klecko 2 pass from Manning (Vinatieri kick)
Mia	—	FG Mare 38
Ind	—	Manning 11 run (Vinatieri kick)
Ind	—	FG Vinatieri 46
Mia	—	FG Mare 42
Ind	—	FG Vinatieri 34
Mia	—	FG Mare 27
Mia	—	FG Mare 34
Ind	—	Harrison 27 pass from Manning (Vinatieri kick)
Mia	—	McMichael 6 pass from Lemon (Mare kick)

KANSAS CITY 35, JACKSONVILLE 30—at Arrowhead Stadium, attendance 77,500. Larry Johnson rushed for 3 touchdowns as the Chiefs earned a wild-card berth. At the conclusion of the game, the Chiefs still needed Cincinnati and Denver to lose. The Bengals lost in overtime moments after the Chiefs' victory, and Denver lost later in the day to San Francisco. Tennessee also had to lose for the Chiefs, and the Titans fell to the Patriots. As it turner out, the Jaguars would have made the playoffs with a victory. Ty Law's interception and return to the Jaguars' 2 set up Johnson' third touchdown and gave the Chiefs a 28-10 leads with 12:08 to play in the third quarter. Trent Green was 14 of 21 for 181 yards and 1 touchdown, with 2 interceptions. Johnson had 33 carries for 138 yards. Johnson set an NFL record for carries, 416 in a season, breaking the record of 410 held by Jamal Anderson. David Garrard was 10 of 18 for 140 yards and 1 touchdown, with 1 interception. Quinn Gray replaced Garrard in the third quarter and was 13 of 22 for 166 yards.

Jacksonville	0	10	14	6	—	30
Kansas City	7	14	14	0	—	35

KC	—	Pollard blocked punt recovery in end zone (Tynes kick)
Jax	—	Taylor 26 pass from Garrard (Scobee kick)

Jax — FG Scobee 33
KC — L. Johnson 1 run (Tynes kick)
KC — Kennison 35 pass from Green (Tynes kick)
KC — L. Johnson 2 run (Tynes kick)
Jax — Gray 9 run (Scobee kick)
KC — L. Johnson 12 run (Tynes kick)
Jax — Gray 17 run (Scobee kick)
Jax — Jones-Drew 5 run (run failed)

ST. LOUIS 41, MINNESOTA 21—at Metrodome, attendance 63,557. Steve Jackson scored 4 touchdowns as the Rams downed the Vikings. The Rams, who were knocked out of the playoff hunt by virtue of the Giants' victory on Saturday night, finished the season with three consecutive wins. The Rams scored on four successive drives in the middle of the game, and Jackson capped the day with a 59-yard touchdown run with 11:09 remaining for a 41-7 lead. Bulger was 19 of 30 for 248 yards and 1 touchdowns. Jackson rushed 25 times for 142 yards. Tarvaris Jackson was 20 of 34 for 213 yards and 1 touchdown, with 2 interceptions.

St. Louis	10	14	10	7 —	41
Minnesota	7	0	0	14 —	21

StL — Bartell 38 interception return (Wilkins kick)
StL — FG Wilkins 42
Minn — T. Jackson 1 run (Longwell kick)
StL — S. Jackson 4 run (Wilkins kick)
StL — S. Jackson 10 pass from Bulger (Wilkins kick)
StL — FG Wilkins 53
StL — S. Jackson 2 run (Wilkins kick)
StL — S. Jackson 59 run (Wilkins kick)
Minn — Taylor 1 run (Longwell kick)
Minn — Taylor 3 pass from T. Jackson (Longwell kick)

CAROLINA 31, NEW ORLEANS 21—at Louisiana Superdome, attendance 69,569. Jake Delhomme passed for 2 touchdowns as the Panthers defeated the Saints. New Orleans had already secured a first-round bye, and only used its skill-position starters for the first part of the game. The Panthers took the lead on Chris Gamble's 18-yard interception return, and scored their final touchdown following a fumble recovery by Chris Draft at the Saints' 24. Delhomme was 23 of 27 for 207 yards and 2 touchdowns. Drew Brees was 4 of 5 for 46 yards before coming out. Jamie Martin was 16 of 24 for 208 yards and 1 touchdown, with 1 interception.

Carolina	7	7	14	3 —	31
New Orleans	7	7	7	0 —	21

NO — Bush 1 run (Carney kick)
Car — Smith 22 pass from Delhomme (Kasay kick)
NO — Branch 7 pass from Martin (Carney kick)
Car — Foster 2 run (Kasay kick)
Car — Gamble 18 interception return (Kasay kick)
Car — Smith 15 pass from Delhomme (Kasay kick)
NO — McAfee 6 run (Carney kick)
Car — FG Kasay 19

N.Y. JETS 23, OAKLAND 3—at The Meadowlands, attendance 78,039. Leon Washington had a 15-yard touchdown run to help the Jets clinch a wild-card playoff berth in coach Eric Mangini's first season. The Jets' defense allowed just 209 total yards, and the offense had 2 touchdowns and 3 field goals. Chad Pennington was 22 of 30 for 157 yards and 1 touchdown. Aaron Brooks was 15 of 26 for 136 yards, with 1 interception, for the Raiders who, by virtue of their loss and the Lions' victory, received the first pick in the 2007 NFL Draft.

Oakland	0	3	0	0 —	3
N.Y. Jets	7	3	3	10 —	23

NYJ — Baker 1 pass from Pennington (Nugent kick)
Oak — FG Janikowski 35
NYJ — FG Nugent 35
NYJ — FG Nugent 22
NYJ — Washington 15 run (Nugent kick)
NYJ — FG Nugent 35

PHILADELPHIA 24, ATLANTA 17—at Lincoln Financial Field, attendance 69,341. With the Eagles NFC East title secure, A.J. Feeley came off the sidelines to pass for 321 yards and 3 touchdowns, including a game-winning 89-yard pass to Hank Baskett. The Eagles clinched less than five minutes into the game when Dallas lost to Detroit. It marked the Eagles' fifth division title in six years. Jeff Garcia was then removed from the game and Feeley took over. Feeley was 22 of 33 for 321 yards and 3 touchdowns. Baskett finished with 7 catches for 177 yards. Michael Vick was 8 of 14 for 81 yards and 1 touchdown. Matt Schaub replaced him and was 15 of 21 for 175 yards and 1 touchdown, with 1 interception.

Atlanta	7	3	0	7 —	17
Philadelphia	10	7	0	7 —	24

Phil — FG Akers 41
Atl — Dunn 7 pass from Vick (Andersen kick)
Phil — Schobel 14 pass from Feeley (Akers kick)
Atl — FG Andersen 45
Phil — Avant 5 pass from Feeley (Akers kick)
Atl — Crumpler 9 pass from Schaub (Andersen kick)
Phil — Baskett 89 pass from Feeley (Akers kick)

SAN DIEGO 27, ARIZONA 20—at Qualcomm Stadium, attendance 66,492. Philip Rivers passed for 2 touchdowns as the Chargers won their tenth consecutive game and earned the number-one AFC seed. Tim Dobbins recovered a fumble in the end zone early in the third quarter, followed soon thereafter by Nate Kaeding's second field goal, to give San Diego a 27-7 lead with 6:23 left in the third quarter. Rivers was 19 of 24 for 231 yards and 2 touchdowns, with 1 interception. Kurt Warner, playing for the injured Matt Leinart, was 22 of 32 for 356 yards and 1 touchdown. Anquan Boldin had 4 catches for 112 yards.

Arizona	7	0	3	0 —	20
San Diego	3	14	10	0 —	27

Ariz — James 8 run (Rackers kick)
SD — FG Kaeding 47
SD — Gates 33 pass from Rivers (Kaeding kick)
SD — Jackson 14 pass from Rivers (Kaeding kick)
SD — Dobbins recovered fumble in end zone (Kaeding kick)
SD — FG Kaeding 35
Ariz — FG Rackers 28
Ariz — Fitzgerald 9 pass from Warner (Rackers kick)
Ariz — FG Rackers 20

SEATTLE 23, TAMPA BAY 7—at Raymond James Stadium, attendance 68,809. The Seahawks, riding a three-game losing streak but already having clinched the NFC West, got back on track just in time for the playoffs. Matt Hasselbeck passed for a touchdown, and the Seahawks controlled the ball form more than 37 minutes behind 28 carries for 92 yards by Shaun Alexander. Hasselbeck was 17 of 29 for 216 yards and 1 touchdown. Tim Rattay was 16 of 27 for 185 yards and 1 touchdown. Joey Galloway had 8 receptions for 118 yards.

Seattle	10	7	3	3 —	23
Tampa Bay	0	7	0	0 —	7

Sea — FG J. Brown 35
Sea — Alexander 1 run (J. Brown kick)
TB — Galloway 4 pass from Rattay (Bryant kick)
Sea — Hackett 5 pass from Hasselbeck

(J. Brown kick)
Sea — FG J. Brown 30
Sea — FG J. Brown 23

NEW ENGLAND 40, TENNESSEE 23—at LP Field, attendance 69,143. The Titans five-game winning streak and near improbable playoff-run came to a halt as the Patriots rushed for 3 touchdowns and defeated Tennessee. The Patriots scored on four consecutive first-half possessions, capped by a 91-yard drive that culminated in a 1-yard run by Corey Dillon, to take a 19-10 halftime lead. The Patriots added two fourth-quarter touchdowns, including Vinny Testaverde's 6-yard touchdown pass to Troy Brown with 1:45 left. The scoring toss gave Testaverde an NFL-record 20th season with a touchdown pass. Tom Brady was 15 of 24 for 225 yards and 1 touchdown. Vince Young was 15 of 36 for 227 yards, with 2 interceptions. Travis Henry carried 21 times for 102 yards.

New England	9	10	7	14 —	40
Tennessee	3	7	13	0 —	23

Tenn — FG Bironas 25
NE — FG Gostkowski 28
NE — Dillon 21 run (kick blocked)
NE — FG Gostkowski 26
NE — Dillon 1 run (Gostkowski kick)
Tenn — P. Jones 81 punt return (Bironas kick)
Tenn — FG Bironas 27
NE — Caldwell 62 pas from Brady (Gostkowski kick)
Tenn — FG Bironas 27
Tenn — Young 28 run (Bironas kick)
NE — Maroney 1 run (Gostkowski kick)
NE — Brown 6 pass from Testaverde (Gostkowski kick)

SUNDAY NIGHT, DECEMBER 31
GREEN BAY 26, CHICAGO 7—at Soldier Field, attendance 62,287. Brett Favre passed for 1 touchdown and the Packers' defense registered 5 interceptions to win their fourth consecutive game. With their number-one NFC seed secure, the Chicago Bears played most of the game with their skill-position regulars only in the first half. Many believed the game would be the last one for Favre, but he later announced he would return for the 2007 season. Favre was 21 of 42 for 285 yards and 1 touchdown, with 1 interception. Grossman was 2 of 12 for 33 yards, with 3 interceptions, before being replaced by Brian Griese, who was 5 of 15 for 124 yards and 1 touchdown, with 2 interceptions.

Green Bay	13	10	0	3 —	26
Chicago	0	0	7	0 —	7

GB — Driver 9 pass from Favre (Rayner kick)
GB — Collins 55 interception return (kick failed)
GB — FG Rayner 25
GB — Dendy 30 interception return (Rayner kick)
Chi — Bradley 75 pass from Griese (Gould kick)
GB — FG Rayner 46

2006 PRO FOOTBALL AWARDS

ASSOCIATED PRESS
Most Valuable Player	LaDainian Tomlinson
Offensive Player of the Year	LaDainian Tomlinson
Defensive Player of the Year	Jason Taylor
Offensive Rookie of the Year	Vince Young
Defensive Rookie of the Year	DeMeco Ryans
Coach of the Year	Sean Payton
Comeback Player of the Year	Chad Pennington

THE SPORTING NEWS
Player of the Year	LaDainian Tomlinson
Rookie of the Year	Vince Young
Coach of the Year	Sean Payton

PRO FOOTBALL WEEKLY/PFWA
Executive of the Year	Mickey Loomis
Most Valuable Player	LaDainian Tomlinson
Defensive Most Valuable Player	Jason Taylor
Offensive Rookie of the Year	Vince Young
Defensive Rookie of the Year	DeMeco Ryans
Coach of the Year	Sean Payton
Assistant Coach of the Year	Rex Ryan
Golden Toe	Josh Brown
Comeback Player of the Year	Chad Pennington
Most Improved Player of the Year	Frank Gore

SPORTS ILLUSTRATED
Most Valuable Player	Drew Brees
Rookie of the Year	Vince Young
Coach of the Year	Sean Payton

MAXWELL CLUB PLAYER OF THE YEAR
(Bert Bell Trophy)	LaDainian Tomlinson

MAXWELL CLUB COACH OF THE YEAR
(Earle "Greasy" Neale Trophy)	Sean Payton

DIET PEPSI ROOKIE OF THE YEAR
Rookie of the Year	Vince Young

FEDEX AIR & GROUND NFL PLAYERS OF THE YEAR
FedEx Express NFL Player of the Year	Drew Brees
FedEx Ground NFL Player of the Year	LaDainian Tomlinson

MOTOROLA NFL COACH OF THE YEAR
Motorola Coach of the Year	Sean Payton

WALTER PAYTON/ NFL MAN OF THE YEAR
Man of the Year	Drew Brees
	LaDainian Tomlinson

SUPER BOWL XLI MOST VALUABLE PLAYER
Pete Rozelle Trophy	Peyton Manning

AFC-NFC 2007 PRO BOWL PLAYER OF THE GAME
Dan McGuire Award	Carson Palmer

2006 ALL-PRO TEAMS

2006 PFW/PFWA ALL-PRO TEAM
Selected by *Pro Football Weekly* and the Professional Football Writers of America

Offense:
Drew Brees, New Orleans	Quarterback
LaDainian Tomlinson, San Diego	Running Back
Larry Johnson, Kansas City	Running Back
Antonio Gates, San Diego	Tight End
Marvin Harrison, Indianapolis	Wide Receiver
Chad Johnson, Cincinnati	Wide Receiver
Walter Jones, Seattle	Tackle
Jammal Brown, New Orleans	Tackle
Steve Hutchinson, Seattle	Guard
Alan Faneca, Pittsburgh	Guard
Olin Kreutz, Chicago	Center

Defense:
Jason Taylor, Miami	End
Julius Peppers, Carolina	End
Jamal Williams, San Diego	Tackle
Kevin Williams, Minnesota	Tackle
Shawne Merriman, San Diego	Outside Linebacker
Adalius Thomas, Baltimore	Outside Linebacker
Brian Urlacher, Chicago	Middle Linebacker
Champ Bailey, Denver	Cornerback
Rashean Mathis, Jacksonville	Cornerback
Ed Reed, Baltimore	Safety
Adrian Wilson, Arizona	Safety

Special Teams:
Robbie Gould, Chicago	Kicker
Brian Moorman, Buffalo	Punter
Justin Miller, N.Y. Jets	Kick Returner
Devin Hester, Chicago	Punt Returner
Brandon Ayanbadejo, Chicago	Special Teams Player

2006 ASSOCIATED PRESS ALL-PRO TEAM
Selected by the Associated Press

Offense:
Drew Brees, New Orleans	Quarterback
LaDainian Tomlinson, San Diego	Running Back
Larry Johnson, Kansas City	Running Back
Lorenzo Neal, San Diego	Fullback
Antonio Gates, San Diego	Tight End
Marvin Harrison, Indianapolis	Wide Receiver
Chad Johnson, Cincinnati	Wide Receiver
Jammal Brown, New Orleans	Tackle
Willie Anderson, Cincinnati	Tackle
Shawn Andrews, Philadelphia	Guard
Alan Faneca, Pittsburgh	Guard
Olin Kreutz, Chicago	Center

Defense:
Jason Taylor, Miami	End
Julius Peppers, Carolina	End
Jamal Williams, San Diego	Tackle
Kevin Williams, Minnesota	Tackle
Shawne Merriman, San Diego	Outside Linebacker
Adalius Thomas, Baltimore	Outside Linebacker
Brian Urlacher, Chicago	Inside Linebacker
Zach Thomas, Miami	Inside Linebacker
Champ Bailey, Denver	Cornerback
Rashean Mathis, Jacksonville	Cornerback
Brian Dawkins, Philadelphia	Safety
Ed Reed, Baltimore	Safety

Specialists:
Robbie Gould, Chicago	Kicker
Brian Moorman, Buffalo	Punter

2006 ALL-NFL TEAM
Selected by the *Associated Press, Pro Football Weekly,* and the Professional Football Writers of America
Offense:

Drew Brees, New Orleans (PFW, AP)	Quarterback
LaDainian Tomlinson, San Diego (PFW, AP)	Running Back
Larry Johnson, Kansas City (PFW, AP)	Running Back
Lorenzo Neal, San Diego (AP)	Fullback
Antonio Gates, San Diego (PFW, AP)	Tight End
Marvin Harrison, Indianapolis (PFW, AP)	Wide Receiver
Chad Johnson, Cincinnati (PFW, AP)	Wide Receiver
Jammal Brown, New Orleans (PFW, AP)	Tackle
Walter Jones, Seattle (PFW)	Tackle
Willie Anderson, Cincinnati (AP)	Tackle
Alan Faneca, Pittsburgh (PFW, AP)	Guard
Steve Hutchinson, Minnesota (PFW)	Guard
Shawn Andrews, Philadelphia (AP)	Guard
Olin Kreutz, Chicago (PFW, AP)	Center

Defense:

Jason Taylor, Miami (PFW, AP)	End
Julius Peppers, Carolina (PFW, AP)	End
Jamal Williams, San Diego (PFW, AP)	Tackle
Kevin Williams, Minnesota (PFW, AP)	Tackle
Shawne Merriman, San Diego (PFW, AP)	Outside Linebacker
Adalius Thomas, Baltimore (PFW, AP)	Outside Linebacker
Brian Urlacher, Chicago (PFW, AP)	Inside Linebacker
Zach Thomas, Miami (AP)	Inside Linebacker
Champ Bailey, Denver (PFW, AP)	Cornerback
Rashean Mathis, Jacksonville (PFW, AP)	Cornerback
Ed Reed, Baltimore (PFW, AP)	Safety
Adrian Wilson, Arizona (PFW)	Safety
Brian Dawkins, Philadelphia (AP)	Safety

Specialists:

Robbie Gould, Chicago (PFW, AP)	Kicker
Brian Moorman, Buffalo (PFW, AP)	Punter
Justin Miller, N.Y. Jets (PFW)	Kick Returner
Devin Hester, Chicago (PFW)	Punt Returner
Brandon Ayanbadejo, Chicago (PFW)	Special Teams Player

2006 PFW/PFWA ALL-ROOKIE TEAM
Selected by *Pro Football Weekly* and the Professional Football Writers of America
Offense:

Vince Young, Tennessee	Quarterback
Maurice Jones-Drew, Jacksonville	Running Back
Reggie Bush, New Orleans	Running Back
Owen Daniels, Houston	Tight End
Marques Colston, New Orleans	Wide Receiver
Greg Jennings, Green Bay	Wide Receiver
Marcus McNeill, San Diego	Tackle
D'Brickashaw Ferguson, N.Y. Jets	Tackle
Jahri Evans, New Orleans	Guard
Daryn Colledge, Green Bay	Guard
Nick Mangold, N.Y. Jets	Center

Defense:

Mark Anderson, Chicago	End
Tamba Hali, Kansas City	End
Haloti Ngata, Baltimore	Defensive Tackle
Barry Cofield, N.Y. Giants	Nose Tackle
DeMeco Ryans, Houston	Linebacker
A.J. Hawk, Green Bay	Linebacker
Ernie Sims, Detroit	Linebacker
Richard Marshall, Carolina	Cornerback
Tye Hill, St. Louis	Cornerback
Dawan Landry, Baltimore	Safety
Donte Whitner, Buffalo	Safety

Special Teams:

Stephen Gostkowski, New England	Kicker
Ryan Plackemeier, Seattle	Punter
Devin Hester, Chicago	Kickoff Returner
Devin Hester, Chicago	Punt Returner
Bernard Pollard, Kansas City	Special Teams Player

2006 AFC PLAYERS OF THE WEEK

	Offense		Defense		Special Teams
Week 1	QB Chad Pennington, N.Y. Jets	LB	Ray Lewis, Baltimore	K	Adam Vinatieri, Indianapolis
Week 2	QB Peyton Manning, Indianapolis	CB	Rashean Mathis, Jacksonville	S	Coy Wire, Buffalo
Week 3	WR T.J. Houshmandzadeh, Cincinnati	S	Kerry Rhodes, N.Y. Jets	WR	Terrence Wilkins, Indianapolis
Week 4	WR Andre Johnson, Houston	DE	Jarvis Green, New England	WR	Joshua Cribbs, Cleveland
Week 5	QB Damon Huard, Kansas City	DT	Jamal Williams, San Diego	K	Lawrence Tynes, Kansas City
Week 6	QB Philip Rivers, San Diego	S	Troy Polamalu, Pittsburgh	TE	Casey Cramer, Tennessee
Week 7	QB Peyton Manning, Indianapolis	DE	Derrick Burgess, Oakland	RB	Laurence Maroney, New England
Week 8	RB Larry Johnson, Kansas City	S	Sean Jones, Cleveland	K	Adam Vinatieri, Indianapolis
Week 9	RB LaDainian Tomlinson, San Diego	DE	Jason Taylor, Miami	P	Brian Moorman, Buffalo
Week 10	RB Willie Parker, Pittsburgh	DT	Dewayne Robertson, N.Y. Jets	DE	Trevor Pryce, Baltimore
Week 11	RB LaDainian Tomlinson, San Diego	DE	Jason Taylor, Miami	KR	B.J. Sams, Baltimore
Week 12	RB Joseph Addai, Indianapolis	CB	Asante Samuel, New England	PR	Roscoe Parrish, Buffalo
Week 13	QB David Garrard, Jacksonville	LB	DeMeco Ryans, Houston	K	Rob Bironas, Tennessee
Week 14	RB LaDainian Tomlinson, San Diego	DE	Aaron Schobel, Buffalo	RB	Maurice Jones-Drew, Jacksonville
Week 15	RB LaDainian Tomlinson, San Diego	DE	Dwight Freeney, Indianapolis	P	Brian Moorman, Buffalo
Week 16	QB Vince Young, Tennessee	LB	Shawne Merriman, San Diego	K	Kris Brown, Houston
Week 17	QB Peyton Manning, Indianapolis	CB	Chris McAlister, Baltimore	S	Bernard Pollard, Kansas City

2006 AFC PLAYERS OF THE MONTH

	Offense		Defense		Special Teams
September	WR Laveranues Coles, N.Y. Jets	LB	Bart Scott, Baltimore	K	Matt Stover, Baltimore
October	QB Peyton Manning, Indianapolis	CB	Champ Bailey, Denver	KR	Justin Miller, N.Y. Jets
November	RB LaDainian Tomlinson, San Diego	DE	Jason Taylor, Miami	P	Brian Moorman, Buffalo
December	WR Marvin Harrison, Indianapolis	DE	Ty Warren, New England	K	Mike Nugent, N.Y. Jets

2006 NFC PLAYERS OF THE WEEK

	Offense		Defense		Special Teams
Week 1	QB Kurt Warner, Arizona	DE	John Abraham, Atlanta	K	Jeff Wilkins, St. Louis
Week 2	QB Eli Manning, N.Y. Giants	DT	Tommie Harris, Chicago	K	Ryan Longwell, Minnesota
Week 3	QB Brett Favre, Green Bay	LB	Scott Fujita, New Orleans	K	John Kasay, Carolina
Week 4	WR Santana Moss, Washington	DT	Tommie Harris, Chicago	K	Morten Anderson, Atlanta
Week 5	RB Frank Gore, San Francisco	CB	Lito Sheppard, Philadelphia	RB	Reggie Bush, New Orleans
Week 6	RB Tiki Barber, N.Y. Giants	DE	James Hall, Detroit	K	Josh Brown, Seattle
Week 7	TE Alge Crumpler, Atlanta	CB	Ronde Barber, Tampa Bay	K	Matt Bryant, Tampa Bay
Week 8	QB Michael Vick, Atlanta	DE	Aaron Kampman, Green Bay	WR	Sam Hurd, Dallas
Week 9	QB Drew Brees, New Orleans	LB	Brandon Moore, San Francisco	S	Troy Vincent, Washington
Week 10	QB Tony Romo, Dallas	DE	Julius Peppers, Carolina	PR	Devin Hester, Chicago
Week 11	RB Frank Gore, San Francisco	DE	Mike Rucker, Carolina	P	Mat McBriar, Dallas
Week 12	QB Tony Romo, Dallas	S	Sean Taylor, Washington	K	Josh Brown, Seattle
Week 13	RB Reggie Bush, New Orleans	S	Lawyer Milloy, Atlanta	PR	Devin Hester, Chicago
Week 14	QB Drew Brees, New Orleans	CB	Cedric Griffin, Minnesota	KR	Devin Hester, Chicago
Week 15	QB Rex Grossman, Chicago	S	Brian Dawkins, Philadelphia	P	Matt Turk, St. Louis
Week 16	RB Steven Jackson, St. Louis	DE	Aaron Kampman, Green Bay	K	Robbie Gould, Chicago
Week 17	RB Tiki Barber, N.Y. Giants	CB	Walt Harris, San Francisco	K	Jason Hanson, Detroit

2006 NFC PLAYERS OF THE MONTH

	Offense		Defense		Special Teams
September	QB Rex Grossman, Chicago	S	Ken Hamlin, Seattle	K	John Carney, New Orleans
October	RB Tiki Barber, N.Y. Giants	DE	Julius Peppers, Carolina	K	Robbie Gould, Chicago
November	QB Tony Romo, Dallas	CB	Walt Harris, San Francisco	PR	Nate Burleson, Seattle
December	RB Steven Jackson, St. Louis	S	Brian Dawkins, Philadelphia	KR	Devin Hester, Chicago

2006 NFL ROOKIES OF THE MONTH

	Offense (College)		Defense (College)
September	T Marcus McNeill, San Diego (Auburn)	S	Donte Whitner, Buffalo (Ohio State)
October	WR Marques Colston, New Orleans (Hofstra)	DE	Mark Anderson, Chicago (Alabama)
November	RB Joseph Addai, Indianapolis (Louisiana State)	LB	Clint Ingram, Jacksonville (Oklahoma)
December	RB Reggie Bush, New Orleans (Southern California)	LB	DeMeco Ryans, Houston (Alabama)

TEN BEST RUSHING PERFORMANCES, 2006

	Att.	Yards	TD
1. Tiki Barber	23	234	3
New York Giants vs. Washington, Dec. 30			
2. Willie Parker	32	223	1
Pittsburgh vs. Cleveland, Dec. 7			
3. Willie Parker	22	213	2
Pittsburgh vs. New Orleans, Nov. 12			
4. Frank Gore	24	212	0
San Francisco vs. Seattle, Nov. 19			
5. Shaun Alexander	40	201	0
Seattle vs. Green Bay, Nov. 27			
6. LaDainian Tomlinson	25	199	2
San Diego vs. Kansas City, Dec. 17			
7. Tiki Barber	26	185	0
New York Giants vs. Atlanta, Oct. 15			
8. LaDainian Tomlinson	25	183	2
San Diego vs. St. Louis, Oct. 29			
9. LaDainian Tomlinson	28	178	2
San Diego vs. Buffalo, Dec. 3			
Travis Henry	32	178	1
Tennessee vs. Washington, Oct. 15			

100-YARD RUSHING PERFORMANCES, 2006

First Week
Warrick Dunn, Atlanta — 132 yards vs. Carolina
LaDainian Tomlinson, San Diego — 131 yards vs. Oakland
Steven Jackson, St. Louis — 121 yards vs. Denver
Willie Parker, Pittsburgh — 115 yards vs. Miami
Tiki Barber, New York Giants — 110 yards vs. Indianapolis
Ahman Green, Green Bay — 110 yards vs. Chicago
Tatum Bell, Denver — 103 yards vs. St. Louis

Second Week
Rudi Johnson, Cincinnati — 145 yards vs. Cleveland
Michael Turner, San Diego — 138 yards vs. Tennessee
Warrick Dunn, Atlanta — 134 yards vs. Tampa Bay
Michael Vick, Atlanta — 127 yards vs. Tampa Bay
Frank Gore, San Francisco — 127 yards vs. St. Louis
Larry Johnson, Kansas City — 126 yards vs. Denver
Chester Taylor, Minnesota — 113 yards vs. Carolina
Steven Jackson, St. Louis — 103 yards vs. San Francisco

Third Week
Willis McGahee, Buffalo — 150 yards vs. New York Jets
Willie Parker, Pittsburgh — 133 yards vs. Cincinnati
Ladell Betts, Washington — 124 yards vs. Houston
Tatum Bell, Denver — 123 yards vs. New England
Brian Westbrook, Philadelphia — 117 yards vs. San Francisco
Maurice Jones-Drew, Jacksonville — 103 yards vs. Indianapolis

Fourth Week
LaMont Jordan, Oakland — 128 yards vs. Cleveland
Laurence Maroney, New England — 125 yards vs. Cincinnati
Julius Jones, Dallas — 122 yards vs. Tennessee
Clinton Portis, Washington — 112 yards vs. Jacksonville
Jerious Norwood, Atlanta — 106 yards vs. Arizona
DeShaun Foster, Carolina — 105 yards vs. New Orleans
Michael Vick, Atlanta — 101 yards vs. Arizona
Larry Johnson, Kansas City — 101 yards vs. San Francisco
Reuben Droughns, Cleveland — 100 yards vs. Oakland

Fifth Week
Frank Gore, San Francisco — 134 yards vs. Oakland
Tiki Barber, New York Giants — 123 yards vs. Washington
Travis Henry, Tennessee — 123 yards vs. Indianapolis
Deuce McAllister, New Orleans — 123 yards vs. Tampa Bay
Chester Taylor, Minnesota — 123 yards vs. Detroit
Fred Taylor, Jacksonville — 111 yards vs. New York Jets
Carnell Williams, Tampa Bay — 111 yards vs. New Orleans Saints
Thomas Jones, Chicago — 110 yards vs. Buffalo
Noah Herron, Green Bay — 106 yards vs. St. Louis
DeShaun Foster, Cleveland — 106 yards vs. Cleveland
Leon Washington, New York Jets — 101 yards vs. Jacksonville
Julius Jones, Dallas — 100 yards vs. Philadelphia

Sixth Week
Tiki Barber, New York Giants — 185 yards vs. Atlanta
Travis Henry, Tennessee — 178 yards vs. Washington
Warrick Dunn, Atlanta — 146 yards vs. New York Giants
Kevin Jones, Detroit — 127 yards vs. Buffalo
Ronnie Brown, Miami — 127 yards vs. New York Jets
Willie Parker, Pittsburgh — 109 yards vs. Kansas City
Julius Jones, Dallas — 106 yards vs. Houston

Seventh Week
Chester Taylor, Minnesota — 169 yards vs. Seattle
Larry Johnson, Kansas City — 132 yards vs. San Diego
Leon Washington, New York Jets — 129 yards vs. Detroit
Ahman Green, Green Bay — 118 yards vs. Miami
Tatum Bell, Denver — 115 yards vs. Cleveland
Tiki Barber, New York Giants — 114 yards vs. Dallas
Rudi Johnson, Cincinnati — 101 yards vs. Carolina
Brian Westbrook, Philadelphia — 101 yards vs. Tampa Bay

Eighth Week
LaDainian Tomlinson, San Diego — 183 yards vs. St. Louis
Larry Johnson, Kansas City — 155 yards vs. Seattle
Mike Bell, Denver — 136 yards vs. Indianapolis
Reuben Droughns, Cleveland — 125 yards vs. New York Jets
Wali Lundy, Houston — 116 yards vs. Tennessee
Thomas Jones, Chicago — 111 yards vs. San Francisco
Frank Gore, San Francisco — 111 yards vs. Chicago
Jamal Lewis, Baltimore — 109 yards vs. New Orleans
Ahman Green, Green Bay — 106 yards vs. Arizona
Fred Taylor, Jacksonville — 103 yards vs. Philadelphia
Vernand Morency, Green Bay — 101 yards vs. Arizona

Ninth Week
LaDainian Tomlinson, San Diego — 172 yards vs. Cleveland
Larry Johnson, Kansas City — 172 yards vs. St. Louis
Ronnie Brown, Miami — 157 yards vs. Chicago
Maurice Morris, Seattle — 138 yards vs. Oakland
Ahman Green, Green Bay — 122 yards vs. Buffalo
Tiki Barber, New York Giants — 115 yards vs. Houston
Kevin Jones, Detroit — 110 yards vs. Atlanta

Tenth Week
Willie Parker, Pittsburgh — 213 yards vs. New Orleans
Frank Gore, San Francisco — 159 yards vs. Detroit
Tiki Barber, New York Giants — 141 yards vs. Chicago
Maurice Morris, Seattle — 124 yards vs. St. Louis
Brian Westbrook, Philadelphia — 113 yards vs. Washington
Thomas Jones, Chicago — 113 yards vs. New York Giants
Anthony Thomas, Buffalo — 109 yards vs. Indianapolis
Travis Henry, Tennessee — 107 yards vs. Baltimore
LaDainian Tomlinson, San Diego — 104 yards vs. Cincinnati

Eleventh Week
Frank Gore, San Francisco — 212 yards vs. Seattle
Larry Johnson, Kansas City — 154 yards vs. Oakland
Travis Henry, Tennessee — 143 yards vs. Philadelphia
Carnell Williams, Tampa Bay — 122 yards vs. Washington
Thomas Jones, Chicago — 121 yards vs. New York Jets
DeAngelo Williams, Carolina — 114 yards vs. St. Louis
Rudi Johnson, Cincinnati — 111 yards vs. New Orleans
LaDainian Tomlinson, San Diego — 105 yards vs. Denver
Brian Westbrook, Philadelphia — 102 yards vs. Tennessee

Twelfth Week
Shaun Alexander, Seattle — 201 yards vs. Green Bay
Joseph Addai, Indianapolis — 171 yards vs. Philadelphia
Michael Vick, Atlanta — 166 yards vs. New Orleans
Larry Johnson, Kansas City — 157 yards vs. Denver
Chester Taylor, Minnesota — 136 yards vs. Arizona
Frank Gore, San Francisco — 134 yards vs. St. Louis
Brian Westbrook, Philadelphia — 124 yards vs. Indianapolis
Steven Jackson, St. Louis — 121 yards vs. San Francisco
LaDainian Tomlinson, San Diego — 109 yards vs. Oakland
Ladell Betts, Washington — 104 yards vs. Carolina
Fred Taylor, Jacksonville — 101 yards vs. Buffalo

Thirteenth Week
LaDainian Tomlinson, San Diego — 178 yards vs. Buffalo

Ladell Betts, Washington	155 yards vs. Atlanta
Deuce McAllister, New Orleans	136 yards vs. San Francisco
Tatum Bell, Denver	133 yards vs. Seattle
Edgerrin James, Arizona	115 yards vs. St. Louis
Larry Johnson, Kansas City	110 yards vs. Cleveland
Jerious Norwood, Atlanta	107 yards vs. Washington
Cedric Houston, New York Jets	105 yards vs. Green Bay
Ahman Green, Green Bay	102 yards vs. New York Jets

Fourteenth Week

Willie Parker, Pittsburgh	223 yards vs. Cleveland
Ladell Betts, Washington	171 yards vs. Philadelphia
Maurice Jones-Drew, Jacksonville	166 yards vs. Indianapolis
Fred Taylor, Jacksonville	131 yards vs. Indianapolis
Frank Gore, San Francisco	130 yards vs. Green Bay
Artose Pinner, Minnesota	125 yards vs. Detroit
Willis McGahee, Buffalo	125 yards vs. New York Jets
Sammy Morris, Miami	123 yards vs. New England
Larry Johnson, Kansas City	120 yards vs. Baltimore
Rudi Johnson, Cincinnati	117 yards vs. Oakland
Tatum Bell, Denver	116 yards vs. San Diego
Julius Jones, Dallas	116 yards vs. New Orleans
Edgerrin James, Arizona	115 yards vs. Seattle
Tiki Barber, New York Giants	112 yards vs. Carolina
Deuce McAllister, New Orleans	111 yards vs. Dallas
LaDainian Tomlinson, San Diego	103 yards vs. Denver

Fifteenth Week

LaDainian Tomlinson, San Diego	199 yards vs. Kansas City
Frank Gore, San Francisco	144 yards vs. Seattle
Willie Parker, Pittsburgh	132 yards vs. Carolina
Steven Jackson, St. Louis	127 yards vs. Oakland
Ladell Betts, Washington	119 yards vs. New Orleans
Jamal Lewis, Baltimore	109 yards vs. Cleveland

Sixteenth Week

Ron Dayne, Houston	153 yards vs. Indianapolis
Steven Jackson, St. Louis	150 yards vs. Washington
Shaun Alexander, Seattle	140 yards vs. San Diego
Travis Henry, Tennessee	135 yards vs. Buffalo
Larry Johnson, Kansas City	135 yards vs. Oakland
Maurice Jones-Drew, Jacksonville	131 yards vs. New England
Ladell Betts, Washington	129 yards vs. St. Louis
Rudi Johnson, Cincinnati	129 yards vs. Denver
Reggie Bush, New Orleans	126 yards vs. New York Giants
LaDainian Tomlinson, San Diego	123 yards vs. Seattle
Brian Westbrook, Philadelphia	122 yards vs. Dallas
Ronnie Brown, Miami	110 yards vs. New York Jets
Deuce McAllister, New Orleans	108 yards vs. New York Giants
Edgerrin James, Arizona	105 yards vs. San Francisco
DeShaun Foster, Carolina	102 yards vs. Atlanta
Joseph Addai, Indianapolis	100 yards vs. Houston

Seventeenth Week

Tiki Barber, New York Giants	234 yards vs. Washington
Frank Gore, San Francisco	153 yards vs. Denver
Steven Jackson, St. Louis	142 yards vs. Minnesota
Larry Johnson, Kansas City	138 yards vs. Jacksonville
Willie Parker, Pittsburgh	134 yards vs. Cincinnati
Ronnie Brown, Miami	115 yards vs. Indianapolis
Cedric Benson, Chicago	109 yards vs. Green Bay
Travis Henry, Tennessee	102 yards vs. New England

Times 100 or More (159)

L. Johnson, 11; Tomlinson, 10; Gore, 9; Barber, 8;
Parker 7; Betts, Henry, S. Jackson, Westbrook, 6;
T. Bell, Green, R. Johnson, 5; R. Brown, J. Jones,
T. Jones, McAllister, C. Taylor, F. Taylor, 4; Dunn, Foster,
James, Jones-Drew, Vick, 3; Addai, Alexander, Droughns,
K. Jones, J. Lewis, McGahee, M. Morris, Norwood,
L. Washington, C. Williams, 2.

TEN BEST PASSING PERFORMANCES, 2006

	Att.	Comp.	Yards	TD
1. Drew Brees	37	52	510	2
New Orleans vs. Cincinnati, Nov. 19				
2. Carson Palmer	31	42	440	3
Cincinnati vs. San Diego, Nov. 12				
3. Ben Roethlisberger	38	54	433	1
Pittsburgh vs. Denver, Nov. 5				
4. Chris Weinke	34	61	423	1
Carolina vs. New York Giants, Dec. 10				
5. Joey Harrington	33	62	414	2
Miami vs. Green Bay, Oct 22				
6. Matt Leinart	31	51	405	1
Arizona vs. Minnesota, Nov. 26				
7. Peyton Manning	26	38	400	3
Indianapolis vs. Houston, Sept. 17				
8. Drew Brees	31	47	398	1
New Orleans vs. Pittsburgh, Nov. 12				
9. Marc Bulger	25	38	388	4
St. Louis vs. Washington, Dec. 24				
10. Drew Brees	26	38	384	5
New Orleans vs. Dallas, Dec. 10				

300-YARD PASSING PERFORMANCES, 2006

First Week

Chad Pennington, New York Jets	319 yards vs. Tennessee
Donovan McNabb, Philadelphia	314 yards vs. Houston
Kurt Warner, Arizona	301 yards vs. San Francisco

Second Week

Peyton Manning, Indianapolis	400 yards vs. Houston
Eli Manning, New York Giants	371 yards vs. Philadelphia
Drew Brees, New Orleans	353 yards vs. Green Bay
Carson Palmer, Cincinnati	352 yards vs. Cleveland
Donovan McNabb, Philadelphia	350 yards vs. New York Giants
Brett Favre, Green Bay	340 yards vs. New Orleans
Chris Simms, Tampa Bay	313 yards vs. Atlanta
Chad Pennington, New York Jets	306 yards vs. New England

Third Week

Jon Kitna, Detroit	342 yards vs. Green Bay
Brett Favre, Green Bay	340 yards vs. Detroit
J.P. Losman, Buffalo	328 yards vs. New York Jets
Tom Brady, New England	320 yards vs. Denver
Marc Bulger, St. Louis	309 yards vs. Arizona

Fourth Week

Drew Brees, New Orleans	349 yards vs. Carolina
Mark Brunell, Washington	329 yards vs. Jacksonville
Marc Bulger, St. Louis	328 yards vs. Detroit

Fifth Week

Donovan McNabb, Philadelphia	354 yards vs. Dallas

Sixth Week

Jake Delhomme, Carolina	365 yards vs. Baltimore
Marc Bulger, St. Louis	360 yards vs. Seattle
Philip Rivers, San Diego	334 yards vs. San Francisco

Seventh Week

Joey Harrington, Miami	414 yards vs. Green Bay
Peyton Manning, Indianapolis	342 yards vs. Washington
Donovan McNabb, Philadelphia	302 yards vs. Tampa Bay

Eighth Week

Drew Brees, New Orleans	383 yards vs. Baltimore
Tom Brady, New England	372 yards vs. Minnesota
Peyton Manning, Indianapolis	345 yards vs. Denver
Marc Bulger, St. Louis	327 yards vs. San Diego
Damon Huard, Kansas City	312 yards vs. Seattle
Ben Roethlisberger, Pittsburgh	301 yards vs. Oakland

Ninth Week

Ben Roethlisberger, Pittsburgh	433 yards vs. Denver
Marc Bulger, St. Louis	354 yards vs. Kansas City
Peyton Manning, Indianapolis	326 yards vs. New England
Jon Kitna, Detroit	321 yards vs. Atlanta
Drew Brees, New Orleans	314 yards vs. Tampa Bay

Tenth Week

Carson Palmer, Cincinnati	440 yards vs. San Diego
Drew Brees, New Orleans	398 yards vs. Pittsburgh
Steve McNair, Baltimore	373 yards vs. Tennessee
Brett Favre, Green Bay	347 yards vs. Minnesota
Philip Rivers, San Diego	338 yards vs. Cincinnati
Tony Romo, Dallas	308 yards vs. Arizona

Eleventh Week

Drew Brees, New Orleans	510 yards vs. Cincinnati
J.P. Losman, Buffalo	340 yards vs. Houston

Twelfth Week

Matt Leinart, Arizona	405 yards vs. Minnesota
Drew Brees, New Orleans	349 yards vs. Atlanta
David Carr, Houston	323 yards vs. New York Jets
Tony Romo, Dallas	306 yards vs. Tampa Bay

Thirteenth Week

Peyton Manning, Indianapolis	351 yards vs. Tennessee
Marc Bulger, St. Louis	314 yards vs. Arizona
Jon Kitna, Detroit	314 yards vs. New England
Jeff Garcia, Philadelphia	312 yards vs. Carolina
Tom Brady, New England	305 yards vs. Detroit

Fourteenth Week

Chris Weinke, Carolina	423 yards vs. New York Giants
Drew Brees, New Orleans	384 yards vs. Dallas
Marc Bulger, St. Louis	356 yards vs. Chicago
Peyton Manning, Indianapolis	313 yards vs. Jacksonville

Fifteenth Week

Chad Pennington, New York Jets	339 yards vs. Minnesota
Rex Grossman, Chicago	339 yards vs. Tampa Bay

Sixteenth Week

Marc Bulger, St. Louis	388 yards vs. Washington

Seventeenth Week

Kurt Warner, Arizona	356 yards vs. San Diego
Tony Romo, Dallas	321 yards vs. Detroit
A.J. Feeley, Philadelphia	321 yards vs. Atlanta
Jon Kitna, Detroit	306 yards vs. Dallas

Times 300 or more (65)

Brees, Bulger, 8; P. Manning 6; Kitna, McNabb 4; Brady, Favre, Pennington, Romo, 3; Losman, Palmer, Rivers, Roethlisberger, Warner, 2

TEN BEST RECEIVING PERFORMANCES, 2006

	No.	Yards	TD
1. Lee Evans	11	265	2
Buffalo vs. Houston, Nov. 19			
2. Chad Johnson	11	260	2
Cincinnati vs. San Diego, Nov. 12			
3. Donald Driver	6	191	1
Green Bay vs. Minnesota, Nov. 12			
4. Chad Johnson	6	190	3
Cincinnati vs. New Orleans, Nov. 19			
5. Steve Smith	8	189	1
Carolina vs. Baltimore, Oct. 15			
6. Hank Baskett	7	177	1
Philadelphia vs. Atlanta, Dec. 31			
7. Larry Fitzgerald	11	172	0
Arizona vs. Minnesota, Nov. 26			
8. Marvin Harrison	7	172	1
Indianapolis vs. Tennessee, Dec. 3			
9. Hines Ward	8	171	3
Pittsburgh vs. Atlanta, Oct. 22			
10. Devery Henderson	9	169	0
New Orleans vs. Cincinnati, Nov. 19			
Marques Colston	10	169	0
New Orleans vs. Pittsburgh, Nov. 12			

100-YARD RECEIVING PERFORMANCES, 2006

First Week

Laveranues Coles, New York Jets	153 yards vs. Tennessee
Donte' Stallworth, Philadelphia	141 yards vs. Houston
Larry Fitzgerald, Arizona	133 yards vs. San Francisco
Antonio Bryant, San Francisco	114 yards vs. Arizona
Marvin Harrison, Indianapolis	113 yards vs. New York Giants
Drew Bennett, Tennessee	106 yards vs. New York Jets
Muhsin Muhammad, Chicago	102 yards vs. Green Bay
Heath Miller, Pittsburgh	101 yards vs. Miami
Andre Johnson, Houston	101 yards vs. Philadelphia

Second Week

Joey Galloway, Tampa Bay	161 yards vs. Atlanta
Donald Driver, Green Bay	153 yards vs. New Orleans
Amani Toomer, New York Giants	137 yards vs. Philadelphia
Reggie Wayne, Indianapolis	135 yards vs. Houston
Antonio Bryant, San Francisco	131 yards vs. St. Louis
Darrell Jackson, Seattle	127 yards vs. Arizona
Marvin Harrison, Indianapolis	127 yards vs. Houston
Jerricho Cotchery, New York Jets	121 yards vs. New England
Plaxico Burress, New York Giants	114 yards vs. Philadelphia
Chris Henry, Cincinnati	113 yards vs. Cleveland
L.J. Smith, Philadelphia	111 yards vs. New York Giants
Braylon Edwards, Cleveland	110 yards vs. Cincinnati
Keyshawn Johnson, Carolina	106 yards vs. Minnesota
Troy Williamson, Minnesota	102 yards vs. Carolina
Laveranues Coles, New York Jets	100 yards vs. New England

Third Week

Andre Johnson, Houston	152 yards vs. Washington
Roy Williams, Detroit	138 yards vs. Green Bay
Derrick Mason, Baltimore	132 yards vs. Cleveland
Javon Walker, Denver	130 yards vs. New England
Anquan Boldin, Arizona	129 yards vs. St. Louis
Torry Holt, St. Louis	120 yards vs. Arizona
Muhsin Muhammad, Chicago	118 yards vs. Minnesota
Braylon Edwards, Cleveland	116 yards vs. Baltimore
Steve Smith, Carolina	112 yards vs. Tampa Bay
Lee Evans, Buffalo	107 yards vs. New York Jets
Reggie Brown, Philadelphia	106 yards vs. San Francisco
Roscoe Parrish, Buffalo	104 yards vs. New York Jets
Greg Jennings, Green Bay	101 yards vs. Detroit

Fourth Week

Roy Williams, Detroit	139 yards vs. St. Louis
Santana Moss, Washington	138 yards vs. Jacksonville
Marques Colston, New Orleans	132 yards vs. Carolina
Bernard Berrian, Chicago	108 yards vs. Seattle
Torry Holt, St. Louis	102 yards vs. Detroit
Andre Johnson, Houston	101 yards vs. Miami
Isaac Bruce, St. Louis	100 yards vs. Detroit

Fifth Week

Hank Baskett, Philadelphia	112 yards vs. Dallas
Joey Galloway, Tampa Bay	110 yards vs. New Orleans
Larry Johnson, Kansas City	106 yards vs. Arizona
Greg Jennings, Green Bay	105 yards vs. St. Louis

Sixth Week

Steve Smith, Carolina	189 yards vs. Baltimore
Roy Williams, Detroit	161 yards vs. Buffalo
Torry Holt, St. Louis	154 yards vs. Seattle
Anquan Boldin, Arizona	136 yards vs. Chicago
Reggie Brown, Philadelphia	121 yards vs. New Orleans
Joe Horn, New Orleans	110 yards vs. Philadelphia
Laveranues Coles, New York Jets	106 yards vs. Miami
T.J. Houshmandzadeh, Cincinnati	102 yards vs. Tampa Bay
Mark Clayton, Baltimore	101 yards vs. Carolina

Seventh Week

Hines Ward, Pittsburgh	171 yards vs. Atlanta
Tony Gonzalez, Kansas City	138 yards vs. San Diego
Darrell Jackson, Seattle	136 yards vs. Minnesota
Randy Moss, Oakland	129 yards vs. Arizona

Steve Smith, Carolina	126 yards vs. Cincinnati	Drew Carter, Carolina	144 yards vs. New York Giants
Reggie Wayne, Indianapolis	122 yards vs. Washington	Reggie Bush, New Orleans	125 yards vs. Dallas
Alge Crumpler, Atlanta	117 yards vs. Pittsburgh	T.J. Houshmandzadeh, Cincinnati	118 yards vs. Oakland
Brian Westbrook, Philadelphia	113 yards vs. Tampa Bay	Drew Bennett, Tennessee	113 yards vs. Houston
Marty Booker, Miami	110 yards vs. Green Bay	Mark Clayton, Baltimore	112 yards vs. Kansas City
Mike Furrey, Detroit	109 yards vs. New York Jets	Joe Jurevicius, Cleveland	111 yards vs. Pittsburgh
Javon Walker, Denver	107 yards vs. Cleveland	Reggie Wayne, Indianapolis	110 yards vs. Jacksonville
Andre Johnson, Houston	106 yards vs. Jacksonville	Antonio Gates, San Diego	104 yards vs. Denver

Eighth Week

		D.J. Hackett, Seattle	104 yards vs. Arizona
Marques Colston, New Orleans	163 yards vs. Baltimore	Marty Booker, Miami	103 yards vs. New England
Reggie Wayne, Indianapolis	138 yards vs. Denver	Chad Johnson, Cincinnati	101 yards vs. Oakland
Eddie Kennison, Kansas City	132 yards vs. Seattle	Marvin Harrison, Indianapolis	101 yards vs. Jacksonville
Joe Horn, New Orleans	126 yards vs. Baltimore		

Fifteenth Week

Tony Gonzalez, Kansas City	116 yards vs. Seattle	Laveranues Coles, New York Jets	144 yards vs. Minnesota
Terrell Owens, Dallas	107 yards vs. Carolina	Desmond Clark, Chicago	125 yards vs. Tampa Bay
Isaac Bruce, St. Louis	105 yards vs. San Diego	Plaxico Burress, New York Giants	120 yards vs. Philadelphia
		Joey Galloway, Tampa Bay	107 yards vs. Chicago

Ninth Week

		Roddy White, Atlanta	104 yards vs. Dallas
Marvin Harrison, Indianapolis	145 yards vs. New England	Demetrius Williams, Baltimore	100 yards vs. Cleveland
Roy Williams, Detroit	138 yards vs. Atlanta		

Sixteenth Week

Javon Walker, Denver	134 yards vs. Pittsburgh	Isaac Bruce, St. Louis	148 yards vs. Washington
Steven Jackson, St. Louis	133 yards vs. Kansas City	Marvin Harrison, Indianapolis	112 yards vs. Houston
Hines Ward, Pittsburgh	127 yards vs. Denver	Mark Clayton, Pittsburgh	108 yards vs. Pittsburgh
Marques Colston, New Orleans	123 yards vs. Tampa Bay	Leon Washington, New York Jets	108 yards vs. Miami
Devery Henderson, New Orleans	111 yards vs. Tampa Bay	Mike Furrey, Detroit	107 yards vs. Chicago

Tenth Week

		Ronald Curry, Oakland	106 yards vs. Kansas City
Chad Johnson, Cincinnati	260 yards vs. San Diego	Steven Jackson, St. Louis	102 yards vs. Washington
Donald Driver, Green Bay	191 yards vs. Minnesota	Brandon Jones, Tennessee	101 yards vs. Buffalo
Marques Colston, New Orleans	169 yards vs. Pittsburgh		

Seventeenth Week

Steve Smith, Carolina	149 yards vs. Tampa Bay	Hank Baskett, Philadelphia	177 yards vs. Atlanta
Donte' Stallworth, Philadelphia	139 yards vs. Washington	Lee Evans, Buffalo	145 yards vs. Baltimore
Mark Clayton, Baltimore	125 yards vs. Tennessee	Eddie Kennison, Kansas City	144 yards vs. Jacksonville
Muhsin Muhammad, Chicago	123 yards vs. New York Giants	Reche Caldwell, New England	134 yards vs. Tennessee
Drew Bennett, Tennessee	115 yards vs. Baltimore	Santonio Holmes, Pittsburgh	124 yards vs. Cincinnati
Malcolm Floyd, San Diego	109 yards vs. Cincinnati	Chris Henry, Cincinnati	124 yards vs. Pittsburgh
Patrick Crayton, Dallas	104 yards vs. Arizona	Ruvell Martin, Green Bay	118 yards vs. Chicago

Eleventh Week

		Joey Galloway, Tampa Bay	118 yards vs. Seattle
Lee Evans, Buffalo	265 yards vs. Houston	Terrell Owens, Dallas	117 yards vs. Detroit
Chad Johnson, Cincinnati	190 yards vs. New Orleans	Anquan Boldin, Arizona	112 yards vs. San Diego
Devery Henderson, New Orleans	169 yards vs. Cincinnati	Terry Glenn, Dallas	109 yards vs. Detroit
Braylon Edwards, Cleveland	137 yards vs. Pittsburgh	Roy Williams, Detroit	104 yards vs. Dallas
Deion Branch, Seattle	113 yards vs. San Francisco	Matt Jones, Jacksonville	104 yards vs. Kansas City
Reggie Wayne, Indianapolis	111 yards vs. Dallas	Santana Moss, Washington	103 yards vs. New York Giants

Twelfth Week

		Mike Furrey, Detroit	102 yards vs. Dallas
Larry Fitzgerald, Arizona	172 yards vs. Minnesota		
Devery Henderson, New Orleans	158 yards vs. Atlanta		
Anquan Boldin, Arizona	140 yards vs. Minnesota		
Roy Williams, Detroit	126 yards vs. Miami		
Chad Johnson, Cincinnati	123 yards vs. Cleveland		
Marty Booker, Miami	115 yards vs. Detroit		
Laveranues Coles, New York Jets	111 yards vs. Houston		
Jerricho Cotchery, New York Jets	110 yards vs. Houston		
Terrell Owens, Dallas	107 yards vs. Tampa Bay		
Bernard Berrian, Chicago	104 yards vs. New England		

Thirteenth Week

Marvin Harrison, Indianapolis	172 yards vs. Tennessee
Reggie Bush, New Orleans	131 yards vs. San Francisco
Matt Jones, Jacksonville	128 yards vs. Miami
Santana Moss, Washington	123 yards vs. Atlanta
Mike Furrey, Detroit	123 yards vs. New England
Chris Chambers, Miami	121 yards vs. Jacksonville
Eddie Kennison, Kansas City	117 yards vs. Cleveland
Torry Holt, St. Louis	115 yards vs. Arizona
Reche Caldwell, New England	112 yards vs. Detroit
Donte' Stallworth, Philadelphia	111 yards vs. Carolina
T.J. Houshmandzadeh, Cincinnati	106 yards vs. Baltimore
Tony Gonzalez, Kansas City	105 yards vs. Cleveland
DeAngelo Williams, Carolina	101 yards vs. Philadelphia

Fourteenth Week

Donald Driver, Green Bay	160 yards vs. San Francisco
Terry Glenn, Dallas	150 yards vs. New Orleans

Times 100 or more (165)

Harrison, R. Williams, 6; Coles, Wayne, 5; Boldin, Clayton, Colston, Furrey, Galloway, Holt, A. Johnson, C. Johnson, S. Smith, 4; Bennett, Booker, Bruce, Driver, Edwards, Evans, Gonzalez, Henderson, Houshmandzadeh, Kennison, S. Moss, Muhammad, Owens, Stallworth, Walker, 3; Baskett, Berrian, Bryant, R. Brown, Burress, R. Bush, Caldwell, Cotchery, Fitzgerald, Glenn, Henry, Horn, D. Jackson, S. Jackson, Jennings, M. Jones, Ward, 2.

TOP QUARTERBACK SACK PERFORMANCES, 2006
(3.0 or More Sacks Per Game Needed to Qualify)

First Week
Justin Smith, Cincinnati	3.0 vs. Kansas City
Shawne Merriman, San Diego	3.0 vs. Oakland

Second Week
Aaron Kampman, Green Bay	3.0 vs. New Orleans
Ryan Denney, Buffalo	3.0 vs. Miami
Julius Peppers, Carolina	3.0 vs. Minnesota

Third Week
None

Fourth Week
Jarvis Green, New England	3.0 vs. Cincinnati

Fifth Week
Darwin Walker, Philadelphia	3.0 vs. Dallas

Sixth Week
James Hall, Detroit	3.0 vs. Buffalo

Seventh Week
Elvis Dumervil, Denver	3.0 vs. Cleveland
Bertrand Berry, Arizona	3.0 vs. Oakland

Eighth Week
Shawne Merriman, San Diego	3.0 vs. St. Louis

Ninth Week
Corey Williams, Green Bay	3.0 vs. Buffalo
Craig Terrill, Seattle	3.0 vs. Oakland

Tenth Week
Julius Peppers, Carolina	3.0 vs. Tampa Bay

Eleventh Week
None

Twelfth Week
None

Thirteenth Week
None

Fourteenth Week
Aaron Schobel, Buffalo	3.0 vs. New York Jets

Fifteenth Week
Cullen Jenkins, Green Bay	3.0 vs. Detroit
Dwight Freeney, Indianapolis	3.0 vs. Cincinnati

Sixteenth Week
Shawne Merriman, San Diego	3.5 vs. Seattle
Aaron Kampman, Green Bay	3.0 vs. Minnesota

Seventeenth Week
DeMarcus Ware, Dallas	3.0 vs. Detroit

2007 PLAYER RANKINGS AND PROJECTIONS

The *NFL.com 2007 Fantasy Football Preview*, available at newsstands now, contains 160 pages of fantasy football facts, tips, and projections for the upcoming season. The following eight pages display the projections for the running backs, wide receivers, quarterbacks, tight ends, and kickers for the 2007 season, as devised by the magazine's experts. Page 293 provides the statistical average for each team's defense over the past three seasons, allowing you a comprehensive look at which team defense can consistently help lead your fantasy team to the title. Pick up a copy of the *NFL.com 2007 Fantasy Football Preview* today.

RUNNING BACKS	Rushing Yards	Rushing Touchdowns	Receiving	Receiving Yards	Receiving Touchdowns	Total Touchdowns
1. LaDainian Tomlinson, San Diego	1775	21	61	450	3	24
2. Larry Johnson, Kansas City	1625	16	44	425	2	18
3. Steven Jackson, St. Louis	1400	14	78	725	2	16
4. Frank Gore, San Francisco	1550	9	56	425	0	9
5. Shaun Alexander, Seattle	1375	14	17	100	0	14
6. Willie Parker, Pittsburgh	1375	10	24	200	2	12
7. Brian Wesbrook, Philadelphia	1025	6	68	650	4	10
8. Ruid Johnson, Cincinnati	1350	12	21	150	0	12
9. Clinton Portis, Washington	1275	9	31	275	1	10
10. Joseph Addai, Indianapolis	1125	8	52	425	1	9
11. Laurence Maroney, New England	1300	8	33	275	0	8
12. Reggie Bush, New Orleans	700	6	83	825	3	9
13. Travis Henry, Denver	1350	8	21	150	0	8
14. Wilis McGahee, Baltimore	1300	8	23	175	0	8
15. Chester Taylor, Minnesota	850	5	38	250	1	6
16. Maurice Jones-Drew, Jacksonville	975	8	41	425	1	9
17. Ronnie Brown, Miami	1225	8	31	250	0	8
18. Deuce McAllister, New Orleans	1100	9	32	225	0	9
19. Edgerrin James, Arizona	1225	7	33	225	0	7
20. Cedric Benson, Chicago	1175	7	19	150	0	7
21. Ahman Green, Houston	1025	5	35	325	1	6
22. Thomas Jones, N.Y. Jets	1075	6	28	150	0	6
23. Brandon Jacobs, N.Y. Giants	925	8	17	175	0	8
24. Carnell Williams, Tampa Bay	1025	5	27	225	0	5
25. Jamal Lewis, Cleveland	1050	6	19	125	0	6
26. Marion Barber, Dallas	725	8	27	225	0	8
27. LaMont Jordan, Oakland	825	5	40	325	0	5
28. Fred Taylor, Jacksonville	1000	4	19	200	0	
29. Julius Jones, Dallas	1025	4	14	150	0	4
30. Warrick Dunn, Atlanta	1025	4	20	125	0	4
31. DeAngelo Williams, Carolina	800	4	40	350	0	4
32. Kevin Jones, Detroit	650	5	42	325	2	7
33. LenDale White, Tennessee	775	5	24	175	0	5
34. DeShaun Foster, Carolina	850	3	28	175	0	3
35. Corey Dillon, Free Agent	700	6	12	125	0	6
36. Tatum Bell, Detroit	725	4	18	250	0	4
37. Michael Turner, San Diego	625	4	12	175	0	4
38. Ladell Betts, Washington	575	4	17	175	0	4
39. Jerious Norwood, Atlanta	675	3	21	150	0	3
40. Leon Washington, N.Y. Jets	450	3	28	375	0	3
41. Dominic Rhodes, Oakland	500	4	29	200	0	4
42. Reuben Droughns, N.Y. Giants	650	3	24	175	0	3
43. Vernand Morency, Green Bay	600	4	18	125	0	4
44. Anthony Thomas, Buffalo	525	4	27	175	0	4
45. Mike Bell, Denver	475	4	23	175	0	4
46. Ricky Williams, Miami	525	4	15	75	0	4
47. Correll Buckhalter, Philadelphia	350	3	18	275	0	3
48. Michael Pittman, Tampa Bay	350	1	36	300	1	2
49. Chris Brown, Free Agent	450	3	12	75	0	3
50. Najeh Davenport, Pittsburgh	325	3	18	175	0	3
51. Mewelde Moore, Minnesota	175	0	25	200	1	1
52. Adrain Peterson, Chicago	375	2	12	100	0	2
53. Ron Dayne, Houston	300	3	13	100	0	3
54. Maurice Morris, Seattle	400	1	8	50	0	1
55. Marcel Shipp, Arizona	225	2	10	75	0	2
56. T.J. Duckett, Detroit	175	4	3	25	0	4
57. Kevin Faulk, New England	125	0	30	250	1	1
58. Cedric Houston, N.Y. Jets	225	3	4	25	0	3

	Rushing Yards	Rushing Touchdowns	Receiving	Receiving Yards	Receiving Touchdowns	Total Touchdowns
59. Shawn Bryson, Detroit 200	2	10	45	0	2
60. Marcel Shipp, Arizona 225	2	10	75	0	2
61. Mike Alstott, Tampa Bay 125	2	17	115	0	2
62. Noah Herron, Green Bay 125	1	20	150	1	2
63. Maurice Hicks, San Francisco 200	1	10	125	0	1
64. Wali Lundy, Houston 225	2	5	25	0	2
65. Musa Smith, Baltimore........................175	1	15	125	0	1
66. Shaud Williams, Buffalo.......................145	1	15	125	0	1
67. Michael Bennett, Kansas City 375	2	10	150	0	2
68. Mike Anderson, Baltimore 225	2	7	50	0	2
69. Samkon Gado, Houston 175	1	10	75	0	1
70. Sammy Morris, New England...............250	1	7	50	0	1
71. Justin Fargas, Oakland 175	1	5	65	0	1
72. Michael Robinson, San Francisco........145	1	15	85	0	1
73. Chris Perry, Cincinnati..........................45	0	25	175	1	1
74. Mack Strong, Seattle 75	1	22	140	0	1
75. ReShard Lee, Oakland 125	1	15	85	0	1
76. J.J. Arrington, Arizona.........................175	1	9	75	1	2
77. Travis Minor, St. Louis..........................70	0	15	125	1	1
78. Lorenzo Neal, San Diego 125	1	15	75	0	1
79. Heath Evans, New England....................75	0	12	125	1	1
80. Artose Pinner, MInnesota 125	1	10	75	0	1
81. Nick Goings, Carolina..........................125	0	15	125	0	0
82. Zack Crockett, Oakland.......................125	1	10	55	0	1
83. Eric Shelton, Carolina..........................125	1	5	45	0	1
84. Ciatrick Fason, Minnesota 75	2	5	25	0	2
85. Brad Hoover, Carolina...........................55	1	15	105	0	1
86. Justin Griffith, Oakland 75	1	15	125	0	1
87. James Mungro, Indianapolis...............125	0	10	85	0	0
88. Mike Karney, New Orleans....................25	0	15	95	1	1
89. Chris Taylor, Houston 75	1	5	45	0	1
90. Obafemi Ayanbadejo, Arizona...............55	0	20	110	0	0
91. Mike Sellers, Washington 5	0	10	45	2	2
92. Kenny Watson, Cincinnati......................75	0	15	75	0	0
93. Jerome Harrison, Cleveland...................85	0	12	75	0	0
94. Aveion Cason, Detroit..........................125	0	5	25	0	0
95. Greg Jones, Jacksonville......................125	1	5	25	0	1
96. Jeremi Johnson, Cincinnati 35	1	8	45	0	1
97. Ryan Moats, Philadelphia 55	0	5	20	0	0

ROOKIES

	Rushing Yards	Rushing Touchdowns	Receiving	Receiving Yards	Receiving Touchdowns	Total Touchdowns
A. Adrian Peterson, Minnesota 800	*8*	*25*	*250*	*2*	*10*
B. Marshawn Lynch, Buffalo..................900	*6*	*25*	*175*	*1*	*7*
C. Brandon Jackson, Green Bay 750	*4*	*15*	*225*	*2*	*6*

Players in bold/italics are rookies who could have significantly higher value.

For more in-depth analysis, pick up a copy of the NFL.com 2007 Fantasy Football Preview, *available at newsstands today.*

WIDE RECEIVERS	Receiving	Yards	Touchdowns
1. Steve Smith, Carolina	96	1375	11
2. Chad Johnson, Cincinnati	89	1300	9
3. Torry Holt, St. Louis	97	1250	10
4. Marvin Harrison, Indianapolis	91	1225	10
5. Terrell Owens, Dallas	83	1150	11
6. Larry Fitzgerald, Arizona	95	1275	8
7. Reggie Wayne, Indianapolis	84	1250	8
8. Anquan Boldin, Arizona	87	1225	8
9. Roy Williams, Detroit	84	1250	8
10. Javon Walker, Denver	77	1150	8
11. Marques Colston, New Orleans	81	1200	8
12. Donald Driver, Green Bay	87	1225	7
13. Lee Evans, Buffalo	79	1225	2
14. T.J. Houshmandzadeh, Cincinnati	86	1050	8
15. Andre Johnson, Houston	98	1175	7
16. Darrell Jackson, San Francisco	78	1125	8
17. Hines Ward, Pittsburgh	81	1100	7
18. Plaxico Burress, N.Y. Giants	68	1000	8
19. Reggie Brown, Philadelphia	66	1025	7
20. Laveranues Coles, N.Y. Jets	86	1050	6
21. Mark Clayton, Baltimore	71	1050	6
22. Donte Stallworth, New England	62	975	6
23. Randy Moss, New England	69	1000	7
24. Santana Moss, Washington	66	1000	5
25. Chris Chambers, Miami	68	925	6
26. Joe Horn, Atlanta	67	950	6
27. Terry Glenn, Dallas	64	1000	5
28. Braylon Edwards, Cleveland	68	975	5
29. Jerricho Cotchery, N.Y. Jets	77	975	5
30. Vincent Jackson, San Diego	61	940	6
31. Mike Furrey, Detroit	67	825	4
32. Joey Galloway, Tampa Bay	58	950	5
33. Deion Branch, Seattle	77	1025	6
34. Bernard Berrian, Chicago	57	900	5
35. Matt Jones, Jacksonville	61	800	6
36. Devery Henderson, New Orleans	56	850	5
37. Kevin Curtis, Philadelphia	53	825	5
38. Greg Jennings, Green Bay	61	775	5
39. Santonio Holmes, Pittsburgh	53	825	4
40. Brandon Jones, Tennessee	61	825	
41. Isaac Bruce, St. Louis	62	900	3
42. Muhsin Muhammad, Chicago	62	825	4
43. Keyshawn Johsnon, Free Agent	68	825	4
44. Eddie Kennison, Kansas City	56	800	4
45. Ronald Curry, Oakland	76	975	5
46. Derrick Mason, Baltimore	61	750	4
47. Amani Toomer, N.Y. Giants	58	725	4
48. Reggie Williams, Jacksonville	50	675	4
49. Marty Booker, Miami	52	550	2
50. Arnaz Battle, San Francisco	58	650	4
51. Drew Bennett, St. Louis	44	600	5
52. Michael Jenkins, Atlanta	41	650	4
53. Bryant Johnson, Arizona	42	600	3
54. D.J. Hackett, Seattle	61	900	5
55. Brandon Marshall, Denver	37	550	3
56. Hank Baskett, Philadelphia	40	500	3
57. Joe Jurevicius, Cleveland	42	500	3
58. Wes Welker, New England	35	450	2
59. Ashely Lelie, San Francisco	38	475	3
60. Eric Parker, San Diego	45	525	2
61. Rod Smith, Denver	38	475	3
62. Jerry Porter, Oakland	49	675	4
63. Patrick Crayton, Dallas	33	450	3
64. Ernest Wilford, Jacksonville	31	475	2
65. Reche Caldwell, New England	24	245	1
66. Nate Washington, Pittsburgh	27	485	2
67. Troy Williamson, Minnesota	34	435	2
68. Terrance Copper, New Orleans	34	445	2
69. Greg Lewis, Philadelphia	25	425	2

WIDE RECEIVERS	Receiving	Yards	Touchdowns
70. Chris Henry, Cincinnati	25	360	3
71. Travis Taylor, Minnesota	42	480	1
72. David Givens, Tennessee	38	480	2
73. Malcom Floyd, San Diego	27	425	2
74. Bobby Wade, Minnesota	35	380	2
75. David Tyree, N.Y. Giants	25	405	2
76. Derek Hagan, Miami	28	390	2
77. Michael Clayton, Tampa Bay	25	375	2
78. Roscoe Parrish, Buffalo	30	345	2
79. Robert Ferguson, Green Bay	25	380	2
80. Cedrick Wilson, Pittsburgh	25	385	2
81. Troy Brown, New England	37	388	2
82. Antwaan Randle El, Washington	29	325	2
83. Nate Burleson, Seattle	35	425	1
84. Doug Gabriel, Oakland	25	420	1
85. Jeff Webb, Kansas City	18	350	2
86. Chad Jackson, New England	28	325	2
87. Justin Gage, Tennessee	35	385	1
88. Brian Finneran, Atlanta	27	325	2
89. Brandon Lloyd, Washington	35	380	1
90. Marcus Robinson, Minnesota	25	315	2
91. Bobby Engram, Seattle	30	375	1
92. Mark Bradley, Chicago	27	375	1
93. Rashied Davis, Chicago	25	375	1
94. Ruvell Martin, Green Bay	28	375	1
95. Shaun McDonald, Detroit	25	370	1
96. Peerless Price, Buffalo	42	400	2
97. Josh Reed, Buffalo	25	245	3

Rookies

A. Calvin Johnson, Detroit	*62*	*825*	*5*
B. Dwayne Bowe, Kansas City	*42*	*525*	*3*
C. Ted Ginn, Jr., Miami	*38*	*550*	*4*

Players in bold/italics are rookies who could have significantly higher value.

For more in-depth analysis, pick up a copy of the NFL.com 2007 Fantasy Football Preview, available at newsstands today.

QUARTERBACKS	Passing Yards	Passing Touchdowns	Rushing Yards	Rushing Touchdowns
1. Peyton Manning, Indianapolis	4275	32	50	2
2. Drew Brees, New Orleans	4125	26	50	0
3. Carson Palmer, Cincinnati	4035	28	37	0
4. Marc Bulger, St. Louis	4075	25	75	0
5. Tom Brady, New England	4000	25	50	1
6. Donovan McNabb, Philadelphia	3375	24	275	2
7. Vince Young, Tennessee	2575	17	725	7
8. Michael Vick, Atlanta	2850	19	675	1
9. Matt Hasselbeck, Seatle	3475	24	150	1
10. Philip Rivers, San Diego	3650	24	50	0
11. Tony Romo, Dallas	3600	23	150	0
12. Matt Leinart, Arizona	3525	20	125	2
13. Eli Manning, N.Y. Giants	3425	24	25	0
14. Jay Cutler, Denver	3350	19	75	1
15. Brett Favre, Green Bay	3775	19	25	1
16. Jake Delhomme, Carolina	3250	22	50	0
17. Jon Kitna, Detroit	3925	18	50	1
18. Ben Roethlisberger, Pittsburgh	3325	18	125	1
19. Rex Grossman, Chicago	3225	21	50	0
20. J.P. Losman, Buffalo	3075	18	125	2
21. Jason Campbell, Washington	3025	18	225	0
22. Chad Pennington, N.Y. Jets	3175	18	100	0
23. Alex Smith, San Francisco	3025	18	125	1
24. Trent Green, Kansas City	2875	14	50	0
25. Matt Schaub, Houston	3125	16	125	0
26. Steve McNair, Baltimore	3025	16	100	1
27. Byron Leftwich, Jacksonville	2750	14	100	1
28. Jeff Garcia, Tampa Bay	2625	15	150	0
29. Daunte Culpepper, Miami	2525	15	175	1
30. Damon Huard, Kansas City	3375	17	0	0
31. Charlie Frye, Cleveland	2325	12	225	2
32. Tarvaris Jackson, Minnesota	2100	13	225	2
33. Andrew Walter, Oakland	200	2	0	0
34. Chris Simms, Tampa Bay	290	2	10	1
35. David Garrard, Jacksonville	1200	6	125	1
36. David Carr, Carolina	625	3	25	0
37. Derek Anderson, Cleveland	325	2	25	0
38. Brooks Bollinger, Minnesota	425	2	50	0
39. Kurt Warner, Arizona	450	3	0	0
40. A.J. Feeley, Philadelphia	375	2	50	0
41. Seneca Wallace, Seattle	225	0	50	1
42. Aaron Rodgers, Green Bay	275	2	15	0
43. Gus Frerotte, St. Louis	225	2	0	0
44. Sage Rosenfels, Houston	275	2	5	0
45. Charlie Batch, Pittsburgh	275	2	5	0
46. Kellen Clemens, N.Y. Jets	225	2	5	0
47. Kerry Collins, Tennessee	125	2	5	0
48. Kyle Boller, Baltimore	375	2	25	0
49. Mark Brunell, Washington	250	2	0	0
50. Cleo Lemon, Miami	475	2	75	0
51. Jamie Martin, New Orleans	200	1	0	0
52. Jim Sorgi, Indianapolis	175	1	0	0
53. Bruce Gradkowski, Tampa Bay	125	1	25	0
54. Brian Griese, Chicago	275	2	0	0
55. Brodie Croyle, Kansas City	150	1	25	1
56. Anthony Wright, N.Y. Giants	100	1	15	0
57. Joey Harrington, Atlanta	350	2	25	0
58. Patrick Ramsey, Denver	110	1	5	0
59. Kelly Holcomb, Philadelphia	105	1	0	0
60. Billy Volek, San Diego	75	1	0	0

Rookies

A. *JaMarcus Russell, Oakland*	*3350*	*13*	*150*	*1*
B. *Brady Quinn, Cleveland*	*500*	*4*	*25*	*0*

Players in bold/italics are rookies who could have significantly higher value.

TIGHT ENDS	Receiving	Yards	Touchdowns
1. Antonio Gates, San Diego	78	975	8
2. Tony Gonzalez, Kansas City	74	925	6
3. Todd Heap, Baltimore	77	825	6
4. Jeremy Shockey, N.Y. Giants	68	775	6
5. Kellen Winslow, Cleveland	79	825	5
6. Chris Cooley, Washington	60	750	6
7. Alge Crumpler, Atlanta	58	775	5
8. Benajmin Watson, New England	56	750	5
9. Jason Witten, Dallas	61	725	4
10. Vernon Davis, San Francisco	53	650	5
11. L.J. Smith, Philadelphia	53	600	4
12. Randy McMichael, St. Louis	56	550	4
13. Dallas Clark, Indianapolis	38	475	5
14. Daniel Graham, Denver	38	475	4
15. Desmond Clark, Chicago	41	450	4
16. Heath Miller, Pittsburgh	38	425	4
17. Eric Johnson, New Orleans	44	450	3
18. Marcus Pollard, Seattle	39	425	3
19. David Martin, Miami	43	425	3
20. Ben Troupe, Tennessee	32	375	3
21. Owen Daniels, Houston	36	350	3
22. Tony Scheffler, Denver	27	325	3
23. Chris Baker, N.Y. Jets	29	300	3
24. Jerramy Stevens, Tampa Bay	26	300	3
25. Ben Utecht, Indianapolis	25	295	3
26. Bo Scaife, Tennessee	32	280	2
27. Leonard Pope, Arizona	27	275	2
28. Steve Heiden, Cleveland	40	275	2
29. Bryant Fletcher, Indianapolis	25	275	2
30. Jermaine Wiggins, Jacksonville	38	325	1
31. David Thomas, New England	28	225	2
32. George Wrighster, Jacksonville	25	280	1
33. Alex Smith, Tampa Bay	28	275	1
34. Marcedes Lewis, Jacksonville	20	185	2
35. Dan Campbell, Detroit	15	225	1
36. Doug Jolley, Tampa Bay	25	210	1
37. Justin Peelee, Miami	22	140	2
38. Jeb Putzier, Houston	18	175	1
39. Anthony Fasano, Dallas	22	175	1
40. Reggie Kelly, Cincinnati	18	175	1
41. Bubba Franks, Green Bay	16	175	1
42. Joe Klopfenstein, St. Louis	18	145	1
43. Courtney Anderson, Oakland	18	145	1
44. Daniel Wilcox, Baltimore	17	145	1
45. Brandon Manumaleuna, San Diego	12	75	2
46. Robert Royal, Buffalo	12	75	2
47. Randal Williams, Oakland	25	185	0
48. Stephen Alexander, Denver	15	125	1
49. Visanthe Shiancoe, Minnesota	12	90	1
50. Ernie Conwell, New Orleans	10	85	1

Rookie

A. Greg Olsen, Chicago	*30*	*325*	*3*

Players in bold/italics are rookies who could have significantly higher value.

For more in-depth analysis, pick up a copy of the NFL.com 2007 Fantasy Football Preview, *available at newsstands today.*

KICKERS	PTS	XP/XPA	FG/FGA
1. Nate Kaeding, San Diego	139	52/52	29/33
2. Jeff Wilkins, St. Loius	137	38/38	33/39
3. Adam Vinatieri, Indianapolis	129	42/42	29/33
4. Robbie Gould, Chicago	124	40/40	28/34
5. Neil Rackers, Arizona	124	46/46	26/29
6. Shayne Graham, Cincinnati	119	41/41	26/31
7. Matt Stover, Baltimore	118	31/31	29/33
8. Jason Elam, Denver	117	39/39	26/31
9. Josh Brown, Seattle	117	45/45	24/29
10. Josh Scobee, Jacksonville	117	42/43	25/31
11. Lawrence Tynes, Kansas City	115	46/47	23/27
12. Stphen Gostkowski, New England	115	43/43	24/29
13. David Akers, Philadelphia	114	42/42	24/29
14. John Kasay, Carolina	112	40/41	24/32
15. Oliindo Mare, New Orleans	112	43/43	23/29
16. Jason Hanson, Detroit	109	34/34	25/29
17. Joe Nedney, San Francisco	108	33/33	25/30
18. Dave Rayner, Green Bay	107	32/32	25/32
19. Mike Nugent, N.Y. Jets	106	34/35	24/28
20. Rian Lindell, Buffalo	105	36/37	23/30
21. Jay Feely, Miami	105	27/27	26/30
22. Rob Bironas, Tennessee	102	36/37	22/29
23. Jeff Reed, Pittsburgh	103	40/41	21/25
24. Shaun Suisham, Washington	101	32/33	23/28
25. Ryan Longwell, Minnesota	99	30/30	23/28
26. Martin Gramatica, Dallas	99	33/33	22/27
27. Phil Dawson, Cleveland	97	25/25	24/28
28. Kris Brown, Houston	91	25/25	22/26
29. Sebastian Janikowski, Oakland	87	24/24	21/26
30. Matt Bryant, Tampa Bay	84	30/30	18/24

DEFENSE/ SPECIAL TEAMS*	Yards Per Game	Points Per Game	Takeaways	Sacks	Safeties	Touchdowns DEF/RET
1. Ravens	282.8	16.0	33.3	47.0	0.7	6.0
2. Bears	304.3	16.4	35.7	38.7	1.3	7.3
3. Chargers	315.3	19.3	27.0	45.3	0.3	2.3
4. Patriots	311.8	17.4	29.7	40.7	0.3	2.7
5. Dolphins	304.1	19.9	27.7	44.0	1.3	2.0
6. Broncos	306.0	18.1	28.7	33.7	0.3	2.3
7. Cowboys	307.5	19.4	30.7	43.0	1.7	2.3
8. Eagles	324.4	20.4	28.0	38.7	0.0	3.3
9. Steelers	280.9	17.2	30.3	42.3	0.7	3.7
10. Vikings	330.8	22.2	31.0	34.3	0.0	5.0
11. Jaguars	298.5	17.1	26.7	39.7	0.7	1.7
12. Panthers	325.6	19.5	27.0	38.0	0.3	2.7
13. Packers	320.1	22.7	23.0	40.3	0.0	4.3
14. Seahawks	332.8	20.5	29.7	43.3	0.0	3.0
15. Chiefs	344.8	22.4	24.0	34.0	0.0	3.0
16. Colts	336.7	19.9	31.0	38.7	0.0	3.7
17. 49ers	359.3	27.0	24.7	30.3	0.7	3.7
18. Bills	312.5	20.0	31.0	41.0	0.7	5.7
19. Jets	315.1	19.0	28.7	34.0	0.0	3.7
20. Buccaneers	297.2	19.4	25.7	35.3	0.3	3.3
21. Giants	327.8	24.7	28.0	37.0	0.7	4.7
22. Bengals	343.0	22.0	37.0	33.3	0.0	2.3
23. Raiders	328.9	24.1	20.0	31.7	0.7	2.0
24. Saints	334.4	23.4	23.7	33.3	0.3	2.3
25. Redskins	307.0	19.5	22.0	31.3	0.3	2.7
26. Titans	349.0	26.2	26.0	33.0	1.0	5.0
27. Falcons	327.7	21.0	29.0	40.7	0.3	3.7
28. Cardinals	322.1	22.9	29.7	37.7	0.3	3.0
29. Rams	339.9	25.0	24.7	36.3	0.3	3.0
30. Texans	347.5	23.7	22.7	29.7	0.0	3.3
31. Browns	329.2	21.8	26.0	28.0	0.0	2.7
32. Lions	335.2	22.8	28.3	33.0	1.0	3.3

Defense/Special Team statistics reflect an average of the past three seasons (2004-06); clubs are ranked in projected order.

For more in-depth analysis, pick up a copy of the NFL.com 2007 Fantasy Football Preview, available at newsstands today.

AMERICAN FOOTBALL CONFERENCE OFFENSE

	Balt.	Buff.	Cin.	Cle.	Den.	Hou.	Ind.	Jax.	KC	Mia.	NE	NYJ	Oak.	Pitt.	SD	Tenn.
First Downs	282	234	313	250	285	282	376	293	310	281	330	289	243	327	321	261
Rushing	86	82	88	72	106	106	112	127	105	82	121	99	73	100	137	105
Passing	179	132	200	153	151	156	241	147	184	180	181	161	144	201	169	133
Penalty	17	20	25	25	28	20	23	19	21	19	28	29	26	26	15	23
Rushes	476	420	435	372	488	431	439	513	513	402	499	491	394	469	522	469
Net Yds. Gained	1637	1552	1629	1335	2152	1687	1762	2541	2143	1673	1969	1738	1519	1992	2578	2214
Avg. Gain	3.4	3.7	3.7	3.6	4.4	3.9	4.0	5.0	4.2	4.2	3.9	3.5	3.9	4.2	4.9	4.7
Avg. Yds. per Game	102.3	97.0	101.8	83.4	134.5	105.4	110.1	158.8	133.9	104.6	123.1	108.6	94.9	124.5	161.1	138.4
Passes Attempted	524	431	523	512	454	481	557	446	450	591	527	488	483	523	466	447
Completed	328	268	327	318	256	329	362	266	272	342	326	313	263	312	287	226
% Completed	62.6	62.2	62.5	62.1	56.4	68.4	65.0	59.6	60.4	57.9	61.9	64.1	54.5	59.7	61.6	50.6
Total Yds. Gained	3535	3051	4066	3247	2995	3032	4397	3060	3243	3577	3590	3352	2850	4026	3412	2748
Times Sacked	17	47	36	54	31	43	15	30	41	41	29	34	72	49	28	29
Yds. Lost	100	332	233	349	196	254	89	178	243	290	190	199	430	293	150	152
Net Yds. Gained	3435	2719	3833	2898	2799	2778	4308	2882	3000	3287	3400	3153	2420	3733	3262	2596
Avg. Yds. per Game	214.7	169.9	239.6	181.1	174.9	173.6	269.3	180.1	187.5	205.4	212.5	197.1	151.3	233.3	203.9	162.3
Net Yds. per Pass Play	6.35	5.69	6.86	5.12	5.77	5.30	7.53	6.05	6.11	5.20	6.12	6.04	4.36	6.53	6.60	5.45
Yds. Gained per Comp.	10.78	11.38	12.43	10.21	11.70	9.22	12.15	11.50	11.92	10.46	11.01	10.71	10.84	12.90	11.89	12.16
Combined Net Yds. Gained	5072	4271	5462	4233	4951	4465	6070	5423	5143	4960	5369	4891	3939	5725	5840	4810
% Total Yds. Rushing	32.3	36.3	29.8	31.5	43.5	37.8	29.0	46.9	41.7	33.7	36.7	35.5	38.6	34.8	44.1	46.0
% Total Yds. Passing	67.7	63.7	70.2	68.5	56.5	62.2	71.0	53.1	58.3	66.3	63.3	64.5	61.4	65.2	55.9	54.0
Avg. Yds. per Game	317.0	266.9	341.4	264.6	309.4	279.1	379.4	338.9	321.4	310.0	335.6	305.7	246.2	357.8	365.0	300.6
Ball Control Plays	1017	898	994	938	973	955	1011	989	1004	1034	1055	1013	949	1041	1016	945
Avg. Yds. per Play	5.0	4.8	5.5	4.5	5.1	4.7	6.0	5.5	5.1	4.8	5.1	4.8	4.2	5.5	5.7	5.1
Avg. Time of Poss.	32:49	28:04	28:34	29:21	29:50	29:14	29:32	32:11	30:06	30:01	31:35	31:03	28:13	31:13	31:39	27:17
Third Down Efficiency	41.2	31.7	35.8	33.5	37.0	38.9	56.1	39.2	40.6	37.6	42.5	43.8	36.3	42.9	43.2	32.7
Had Intercepted	14	14	13	25	18	13	9	14	12	19	12	16	24	23	9	19
Yds. Opp Returned	142	198	180	273	292	174	136	222	146	207	72	148	286	441	105	250
Ret. by Opp. for TD	0	2	1	2	2	0	1	2	1	2	0	1	0	3	1	2
Punts	86	92	77	83	80	76	48	73	72	86	69	74	78	65	69	88
Yds. Punted	3695	4012	3428	3621	3338	3161	2085	2920	3178	3640	2847	3211	3660	2687	2893	3760
Avg. Yds. per Punt	43.0	43.6	44.5	43.6	41.7	41.6	43.4	40.0	44.1	42.3	41.3	43.4	46.9	41.3	41.9	42.7
Punt Returns	45	39	36	36	32	23	23	45	33	41	36	29	35	34	45	37
Yds. Returned	351	422	239	371	294	242	207	361	264	378	422	243	216	288	382	467
Avg. Yds. per Return	7.8	10.8	6.6	10.3	9.2	10.5	9.0	8.0	8.0	9.2	11.7	8.4	6.2	8.4	8.5	12.6
Returned for TD	0	1	0	0	0	0	1	0	1	0	0	0	0	1	0	3
Kickoff Returns	45	63	59	71	54	71	58	49	64	52	58	60	73	55	55	79
Yds. Returned	1046	1503	1209	1635	1187	1609	1368	1136	1404	1102	1553	1445	1811	1214	1350	1835
Avg. Yds. per Return	23.2	23.9	20.5	23.0	22.0	22.7	23.6	23.2	21.9	21.2	26.8	24.1	24.8	22.1	24.5	23.2
Returned for TD	0	0	0	1	0	0	0	1	0	0	1	2	0	0	0	0
Fumbles	21	28	25	23	29	28	13	16	25	19	27	21	32	27	19	29
Lost	9	15	11	17	12	12	10	9	14	6	15	9	22	14	6	7
Out of Bounds	1	1	1	0	3	3	2	1	0	1	1	0	1	0	1	2
Own Rec. for TD	0	0	0	0	0	0	0	0	0	0	0	0	0	0	0	0
Opp. Rec. by	12	11	12	9	13	11	11	4	15	19	13	9	5	9	12	11
Opp. Rec. for TD	1	2	0	1	0	2	1	0	0	1	0	1	2	0	3	3
Penalties	109	87	92	74	67	90	86	97	76	90	98	70	111	69	90	94
Yds. Penalized	878	629	717	687	478	761	718	806	577	789	940	560	847	611	791	803
Total Points Scored	353	300	373	238	319	267	427	371	331	260	385	316	168	353	492	324
Total TDs	38	33	43	25	34	30	50	42	37	26	46	35	16	42	59	36
TDs Rushing	11	9	14	7	12	13	17	23	17	7	20	15	5	16	32	15
TDs Passing	21	19	28	15	20	14	31	17	18	16	25	17	7	23	24	13
TDs on Ret. and Rec.	6	5	1	3	2	3	2	2	2	3	1	3	4	3	3	8
Extra Point Kicks	37	33	40	25	34	26	47	41	35	22	43	34	16	41	58	32
Extra Point Kicks Att.	37	33	42	25	34	27	48	41	36	22	44	35	16	41	58	32
2Pt Conversions	0	0	0	0	0	2	1	0	1	2	2	0	0	0	1	3
2Pt Conversions Att.	1	0	1	0	0	3	2	1	4	2	2	0	0	0	1	3
Safeties	2	0	0	0	0	0	0	0	0	0	1	0	1	0	0	2
Field Goals Made	28	23	25	21	27	19	26	26	24	26	20	24	18	20	26	22
Field Goals Attempted	30	25	30	29	29	25	29	32	31	36	26	27	25	27	29	28
% Successful	93.3	92.0	83.3	72.4	93.1	76.0	89.7	81.3	77.4	72.2	76.9	88.9	72.0	74.1	89.7	78.6

AMERICAN FOOTBALL CONFERENCE DEFENSE

	Balt.	Buff.	Cin.	Cle.	Den.	Hou.	Ind.	Jax.	KC	Mia.	NE	NYJ	Oak.	Pitt.	SD	Tenn.
First Downs	236	298	337	303	291	312	325	259	298	267	264	312	267	269	285	329
Rushing	59	117	109	107	97	115	150	94	109	72	67	111	107	72	87	121
Passing	151	168	206	178	183	174	150	143	171	166	164	181	137	176	178	181
Penalty	26	13	22	18	11	23	25	22	18	29	33	20	23	21	20	27
Rushes	367	476	448	514	447	446	519	420	461	461	388	453	542	408	386	506
Net Yds. Gained	1214	2254	1863	2275	1813	1956	2768	1460	1928	1618	1507	2084	2144	1412	1613	2313
Avg. Gain	3.3	4.7	4.2	4.4	4.1	4.4	5.3	3.5	4.2	3.5	3.9	4.6	4.0	3.5	4.2	4.6
Avg. Yds. per Game	75.9	140.9	116.4	142.2	113.3	122.3	173.0	91.3	120.5	101.1	94.2	130.3	134.0	88.3	100.8	144.6
Passes Attempted	509	513	555	499	538	505	415	523	506	497	518	532	410	529	538	530
Completed	279	324	349	283	327	328	266	294	314	279	294	316	245	319	307	335
% Completed	54.8	63.2	62.9	56.7	60.8	65.0	64.1	56.2	62.1	56.1	56.8	59.4	59.8	60.3	57.1	63.2
Total Yds. Gained	3429	3284	4029	3379	3612	3635	2705	3278	3524	3275	3484	3452	2631	3619	3563	3750
Times Sacked	60	40	35	28	35	28	25	35	32	47	44	35	34	39	61	26
Yds. Lost	418	265	211	137	202	191	157	200	190	268	281	230	218	226	351	148
Net Yds. Gained	3011	3019	3818	3242	3410	3444	2548	3078	3334	3007	3203	3222	2413	3393	3212	3602
Avg. Yds. per Game	188.2	188.7	238.6	202.6	213.1	215.3	159.3	192.4	208.4	187.9	200.2	201.4	150.8	212.1	200.8	225.1
Net Yds. per Pass Play	5.29	5.46	6.47	6.15	5.95	6.46	5.79	5.52	6.20	5.53	5.70	5.68	5.43	5.97	5.36	6.48
Yds. Gained per Comp.	12.29	10.14	11.54	11.94	11.05	11.08	10.17	11.15	11.22	11.74	11.85	10.92	10.74	11.34	11.61	11.19
Combined Net Yds. Gained	4225	5273	5681	5517	5223	5400	5316	4538	5262	4625	4710	5306	4557	4805	4825	5915
% Total Yds. Rushing	28.7	42.7	32.8	41.2	34.7	36.2	52.1	32.2	36.6	35.0	32.0	39.3	47.0	29.4	33.4	39.1
% Total Yds. Passing	71.3	57.3	67.2	58.8	65.3	63.8	47.9	67.8	63.4	65.0	68.0	60.7	53.0	70.6	66.6	60.9
Avg. Yds. per Game	264.1	329.6	355.1	344.8	326.4	337.5	332.3	283.6	328.9	289.1	294.4	331.6	284.8	300.3	301.6	369.7
Ball Control Plays	936	1029	1038	1041	1020	979	959	978	999	1005	950	1020	986	976	985	1062
Avg. Yds. per Play	4.5	5.1	5.5	5.3	5.1	5.5	5.5	4.6	5.3	4.6	5.0	5.2	4.6	4.9	4.9	5.6
Avg. Time of Poss.	27:12	31:56	31:26	30:39	30:10	30:46	30:28	27:49	29:54	29:59	28:25	28:57	31:47	28:47	28:21	32:43
Third Down Efficiency	28.8	36.6	41.7	43.9	36.7	44.4	47.1	36.6	39.2	38.0	35.9	36.5	35.7	39.3	36.6	40.7
Intercepted By	28	13	19	18	17	11	15	20	15	8	22	16	18	20	16	17
Yds. Returned By	544	203	248	256	244	78	157	280	124	116	262	56	206	272	140	282
Returned for TD	5	2	1	1	2	1	0	1	0	2	0	0	2	2	0	2
Punts	86	86	72	77	74	65	47	90	75	91	79	74	68	86	88	68
Yds. Punted	3864	3578	3131	3309	3240	2949	2036	3724	3063	3785	3283	3266	2822	3769	3923	2888
Avg. Yds. per Punt	44.9	41.6	43.5	43.0	43.8	45.4	43.3	41.4	40.8	41.6	41.6	44.1	41.5	43.8	44.6	42.5
Punt Returns	44	36	42	43	39	36	25	29	32	49	29	28	34	38	27	33
Yds. Returned	404	265	236	312	268	275	327	343	254	367	322	205	437	219	216	278
Avg. Yds. per Return	9.2	7.4	5.6	7.3	6.9	7.6	13.1	11.8	7.9	7.5	11.1	7.3	12.9	5.8	8.0	8.4
Returned for TD	0	0	0	0	0	1	1	2	0	2	0	0	0	0	0	0
Kickoff Returns	75	60	70	48	55	52	78	60	71	40	68	69	42	70	90	58
Yds. Returned	1636	1279	1472	1053	1480	1215	2029	1262	1646	981	1547	1462	1200	1570	1960	1263
Avg. Yds. per Return	21.8	21.3	21.0	21.9	26.9	23.4	26.0	21.0	23.2	24.5	22.8	21.2	28.6	22.4	21.8	21.8
Returned for TD	0	0	0	1	0	1	2	0	0	0	0	0	0	1	0	0
Fumbles	24	28	24	13	28	16	28	12	29	35	24	17	16	16	28	19
Lost	12	11	12	9	13	11	11	4	15	19	13	9	5	9	12	11
Out of Bounds	1	2	1	0	2	0	1	2	3	0	1	0	0	0	2	1
Own Rec. for TD	0	0	0	0	0	0	0	0	0	0	0	0	1	0	0	0
Opp. Rec. by	9	15	11	17	12	12	10	9	14	6	15	9	22	14	6	7
Opp. Rec. for TD	0	1	0	3	1	2	1	1	1	0	1	0	2	1	0	0
Penalties	79	90	97	84	97	96	86	80	85	91	102	105	85	104	87	102
Yds. Penalized	580	709	836	678	785	792	667	684	709	720	918	843	665	862	751	906
Total Points Scored	201	311	331	356	305	366	360	274	315	283	237	295	332	315	303	400
Total TDs	21	35	40	40	29	42	41	32	34	31	24	34	34	36	33	46
TDs Rushing	5	14	15	14	13	16	20	14	14	7	11	14	15	9	13	20
TDs Passing	16	18	24	20	13	22	16	12	18	22	10	19	17	21	19	24
TDs on Ret. and Rec.	0	3	1	6	3	4	5	6	2	2	3	1	2	6	1	2
Extra Point Kicks	20	33	37	36	27	39	40	31	33	31	23	29	33	36	32	41
Extra Point Kicks Att.	20	33	38	38	27	40	40	31	33	31	23	29	34	36	33	44
2Pt Conversions	1	0	1	1	1	0	1	0	0	0	1	4	0	0	0	1
2Pt Conversions Att.	1	2	1	2	2	1	1	0	1	0	1	5	0	0	0	2
Safeties	1	1	0	0	0	0	0	0	0	0	1	0	1	0	2	0
Field Goals Made	17	22	18	26	34	25	24	17	26	22	22	18	31	21	23	27
Field Goals Attempted	23	26	25	31	42	29	35	24	32	25	30	24	37	27	26	33
% Successful	73.9	84.6	72.0	83.9	81.0	86.2	68.6	70.8	81.3	88.0	73.3	75.0	83.8	77.8	88.5	81.8

NATIONAL FOOTBALL CONFERENCE OFFENSE

	Ariz.	Atl.	Car.	Chi.	Dall.	Det.	GB	Minn.	NO	NYG	Phil.	StL	SF	Sea.	TB	Wash.
First Downs	298	287	278	300	336	290	301	272	330	304	312	332	243	312	237	295
Rushing	84	134	100	103	107	53	93	87	99	120	106	94	97	112	82	123
Passing	187	133	158	161	197	208	185	160	207	163	189	212	132	167	133	150
Penalty	27	20	20	36	32	29	23	25	24	21	17	26	14	33	22	22
Rushes	419	537	423	503	472	304	431	442	472	455	416	424	439	484	404	490
Net Yds. Gained	1338	2939	1659	1918	1936	1129	1663	1820	1761	2156	1984	1805	2172	1923	1523	2216
Avg. Gain	3.2	5.5	3.9	3.8	4.1	3.7	3.9	4.1	3.7	4.7	4.8	4.3	4.9	4.0	3.8	4.5
Avg. Yds. per Game	83.6	183.7	103.7	119.9	121.0	70.6	103.9	113.8	110.1	134.8	124.0	112.8	135.8	120.2	95.2	138.5
Passes Attempted	545	416	539	514	506	596	630	540	580	523	544	592	444	512	535	470
Completed	322	222	325	282	310	372	350	332	372	301	323	371	257	292	296	274
% Completed	59.1	53.4	60.3	54.9	61.3	62.4	55.6	61.5	64.1	57.6	59.4	62.7	57.9	57.0	55.3	58.3
Total Yds. Gained	3924	2682	3486	3446	4067	4208	3947	3402	4626	3244	4309	4328	2890	3369	2994	3174
Times Sacked	35	47	32	25	37	63	24	43	23	25	28	49	35	49	33	19
Yds. Lost	262	311	222	165	231	388	152	279	123	186	190	366	202	315	196	147
Net Yds. Gained	3662	2371	3264	3281	3836	3820	3795	3123	4503	3058	4119	3962	2688	3054	2798	3027
Avg. Yds. per Game	228.9	148.2	204.0	205.1	239.8	238.8	237.2	195.2	281.4	191.1	257.4	247.6	168.0	190.9	174.9	189.2
Net Yds. per Pass Play	6.31	5.12	5.72	6.09	7.06	5.80	5.80	5.36	7.47	5.58	7.20	6.18	5.61	5.44	4.93	6.19
Yds. Gained per Comp.	12.19	12.08	10.73	12.22	13.12	11.31	11.28	10.25	12.44	10.78	13.34	11.67	11.25	11.54	10.11	11.58
Combined Net Yds. Gained	5000	5310	4923	5199	5772	4949	5458	4943	6264	5214	6103	5767	4860	4977	4321	5243
% Total Yds. Rushing	26.8	55.3	33.7	36.9	33.5	22.8	30.5	36.8	28.1	41.4	32.5	31.3	44.7	38.6	35.2	42.3
% Total Yds. Passing	73.2	44.7	66.3	63.1	66.5	77.2	69.5	63.2	71.9	58.6	67.5	68.7	55.3	61.4	64.8	57.7
Avg. Yds. per Game	312.5	331.9	307.7	324.9	360.8	309.3	341.1	308.9	391.5	325.9	381.4	360.4	303.8	311.1	270.1	327.7
Ball Control Plays	999	1000	994	1042	1015	963	1085	1025	1075	1003	988	1065	918	1045	972	979
Avg. Yds. per Play	5.0	5.3	5.0	5.0	5.7	5.1	5.0	4.8	5.8	5.2	6.2	5.4	5.3	4.8	4.4	5.4
Avg. Time of Poss.	29:59	29:48	30:12	30:34	31:02	27:41	30:45	31:37	31:53	29:35	28:38	31:07	28:37	29:48	28:06	29:59
Third Down Efficiency	39.2	35.9	31.1	36.8	48.8	32.6	39.2	33.0	44.9	37.9	42.1	37.4	34.4	37.9	36.9	37.4
Had Intercepted	17	15	17	22	21	22	18	20	13	18	9	8	16	22	18	10
Yds. Opp Returned	110	219	145	321	334	280	201	399	180	216	250	118	213	141	280	272
Ret. by Opp. for TD	1	2	0	4	2	2	2	4	4	1	2	0	1	1	1	2
Punts	68	78	100	77	56	66	84	94	77	77	78	76	81	86	93	82
Yds. Punted	2965	3199	4508	3404	2697	2967	3739	3961	3369	3098	3326	3223	3625	3827	4045	3471
Avg. Yds. per Punt	43.6	41.0	45.1	44.2	48.2	45.0	44.5	42.1	43.8	40.2	42.6	42.4	44.8	44.5	43.5	42.3
Punt Returns	25	37	49	50	40	35	53	38	51	33	36	30	28	49	54	39
Yds. Returned	250	288	225	607	335	396	415	374	372	288	339	234	237	424	353	342
Avg. Yds. per Return	10.0	7.8	4.6	12.1	8.4	11.3	7.8	9.8	7.3	8.7	9.4	7.8	8.5	8.7	6.5	8.8
Returned for TD	0	0	0	3	1	0	0	1	1	0	0	0	0	1	0	1
Kickoff Returns	73	68	62	59	64	74	70	66	60	70	58	65	79	69	61	73
Yds. Returned	1610	1542	1200	1373	1493	1648	1379	1492	1377	1407	1204	1383	1907	1548	1307	1631
Avg. Yds. per Return	22.1	22.7	19.4	23.3	23.3	22.3	19.7	22.6	23.0	20.1	20.8	21.3	24.1	22.4	21.4	22.3
Returned for TD	1	0	0	2	0	0	0	0	0	0	0	0	0	0	0	1
Fumbles	31	18	21	26	21	26	25	31	23	23	26	20	24	21	27	20
Lost	13	5	10	14	9	17	15	12	10	10	15	10	16	12	14	7
Out of Bounds	3	3	2	2	1	1	5	3	2	2	0	2	2	1	2	5
Own Rec. for TD	0	0	0	0	0	0	0	1	1	1	0	0	0	0	0	0
Opp. Rec. by	17	14	8	20	13	18	10	15	8	11	10	15	13	14	9	6
Opp. Rec. for TD	2	1	0	2	1	0	1	2	0	0	1	1	1	1	0	0
Penalties	117	96	103	112	100	116	90	123	79	101	112	116	93	94	87	106
Yds. Penalized	937	877	744	923	939	939	689	903	597	881	983	960	818	700	732	951
Total Points Scored	314	292	270	427	425	305	301	282	413	355	398	367	298	335	211	307
Total TDs	33	32	28	47	52	31	32	32	49	41	49	39	30	37	23	34
TDs Rushing	12	9	7	14	21	9	9	12	19	14	13	13	12	8	6	13
TDs Passing	17	21	19	24	26	21	18	13	27	24	31	24	16	26	14	19
TDs on Ret. and Rec.	4	2	2	9	5	1	5	7	3	3	5	2	2	3	3	2
Extra Point Kicks	32	31	28	47	49	30	31	27	46	38	48	35	29	36	22	31
Extra Point Kicks Att.	32	31	28	47	49	30	32	28	47	38	48	35	29	36	23	31
2Pt Conversions	0	0	0	0	2	0	0	0	2	0	1	1	0	1	0	2
2Pt Conversions Att.	1	1	0	0	3	1	0	4	2	2	1	3	1	1	0	2
Safeties	0	0	1	1	0	1	0	0	0	1	0	0	1	0	0	1
Field Goals Made	28	23	24	32	20	29	26	21	23	23	18	32	29	25	17	22
Field Goals Attempted	37	32	27	36	28	33	35	25	26	27	23	37	35	31	22	30
% Successful	75.7	71.9	88.9	88.9	71.4	87.9	74.3	84.0	88.5	85.2	78.3	86.5	82.9	80.6	77.3	73.3

NATIONAL FOOTBALL CONFERENCE DEFENSE

	Ariz.	Atl.	Car.	Chi.	Dall.	Det.	GB	Minn.	NO	NYG	Phil.	StL	SF	Sea.	TB	Wash.
First Downs	331	313	267	258	294	319	291	272	262	314	314	313	326	277	300	301
Rushing	114	97	96	77	88	111	95	53	96	106	126	121	107	102	108	104
Passing	186	183	149	159	179	183	169	192	148	189	154	164	189	160	174	169
Penalty	31	33	22	22	27	25	27	27	18	19	34	28	30	15	18	28
Rushes	458	442	449	402	429	492	441	348	418	458	489	477	473	441	497	492
Net Yds. Gained	1897	1657	1737	1590	1659	2010	1825	985	2063	1830	2182	2327	1936	2029	1917	2197
Avg. Gain	4.1	3.7	3.9	4.0	3.9	4.1	4.1	2.8	4.9	4.0	4.5	4.9	4.1	4.6	3.9	4.5
Avg. Yds. per Game	118.6	103.6	108.6	99.4	103.7	125.6	114.1	61.6	128.9	114.4	136.4	145.4	121.0	126.8	119.8	137.3
Passes Attempted	522	515	500	581	511	511	515	599	474	567	525	451	518	504	493	486
Completed	321	321	291	328	301	339	286	355	267	333	309	266	331	299	301	289
% Completed	61.5	62.3	58.2	56.5	58.9	66.3	55.5	59.3	56.3	58.7	58.9	59.0	63.9	59.3	61.1	59.5
Total Yds. Gained	3932	3903	3265	3388	3729	3721	3646	4015	3122	3830	3367	3249	3817	3538	3520	3586
Times Sacked	38	37	41	40	34	30	46	30	38	32	40	34	34	41	25	19
Yds. Lost	238	235	265	272	223	201	337	197	268	181	300	214	246	282	166	95
Net Yds. Gained	3694	3668	3000	3116	3506	3520	3309	3818	2854	3649	3067	3035	3571	3256	3354	3491
Avg. Yds. per Game	230.9	229.3	187.5	194.8	219.1	220.0	206.8	238.6	178.4	228.1	191.7	189.7	223.2	203.5	209.6	218.2
Net Yds. per Pass Play	6.60	6.64	5.55	5.02	6.43	6.51	5.90	6.07	5.57	6.09	5.43	6.26	6.47	5.97	6.47	6.91
Yds. Gained per Comp.	12.25	12.16	11.22	10.33	12.39	10.98	12.75	11.31	11.69	11.50	10.90	12.21	11.53	11.83	11.69	12.41
Combined Net Yds. Gained	5591	5325	4737	4706	5165	5530	5134	4803	4917	5479	5249	5362	5507	5285	5271	5688
% Total Yds. Rushing	33.9	31.1	36.7	33.8	32.1	36.3	35.5	20.5	42.0	33.4	41.6	43.4	35.2	38.4	36.4	38.6
% Total Yds. Passing	66.1	68.9	63.3	66.2	67.9	63.7	64.5	79.5	58.0	66.6	58.4	56.6	64.8	61.6	63.6	61.4
Avg. Yds. per Game	349.4	332.8	296.1	294.1	322.8	345.6	320.9	300.2	307.3	342.4	328.1	335.1	344.2	330.3	329.4	355.5
Ball Control Plays	1018	994	990	1023	974	1033	1002	977	930	1057	1054	962	1025	986	1015	997
Avg. Yds. per Play	5.5	5.4	4.8	4.6	5.3	5.4	5.1	4.9	5.3	5.2	5.0	5.6	5.4	5.4	5.2	5.7
Avg. Time of Poss.	30:01	30:12	29:48	29:26	28:58	32:19	29:15	28:23	28:07	30:25	31:22	28:53	31:23	30:12	31:54	30:01
Third Down Efficiency	41.3	42.0	31.5	31.0	43.9	43.5	32.6	34.4	34.7	42.9	37.4	45.4	44.4	36.5	37.8	43.7
Intercepted By	16	12	14	24	18	12	23	21	11	17	19	17	14	12	11	6
Yds. Returned By	350	257	115	279	234	160	289	243	106	305	428	164	178	124	226	25
Returned for TD	1	1	2	1	3	1	4	3	0	2	4	1	1	1	3	0
Punts	58	77	98	100	72	68	83	79	96	69	82	67	66	88	81	79
Yds. Punted	2596	3378	4290	4368	3100	2990	3704	3583	4181	2892	3566	3026	2794	3773	3373	3316
Avg. Yds. per Punt	44.8	43.9	43.8	43.7	43.1	44.0	44.6	45.4	43.6	41.9	43.5	45.2	42.3	42.9	41.6	42.0
Punt Returns	44	25	61	38	31	38	55	50	40	33	41	27	35	39	50	45
Yds. Returned	562	279	390	367	334	267	503	485	279	191	380	247	462	343	487	319
Avg. Yds. per Return	12.8	11.2	6.4	9.7	10.8	7.0	9.1	9.7	7.0	5.8	9.3	9.1	13.2	8.8	9.7	7.1
Returned for TD	1	0	1	0	0	0	1	1	0	0	1	1	1	0	1	0
Kickoff Returns	58	53	59	83	80	63	60	59	72	65	71	69	65	61	46	67
Yds. Returned	1481	1093	1302	1730	1571	1444	1348	1369	1598	1455	1647	1701	1373	1499	846	1396
Avg. Yds. per Return	25.5	20.6	22.1	20.8	19.6	22.9	22.5	23.2	22.2	22.4	23.2	24.7	21.1	24.6	18.4	20.8
Returned for TD	0	0	0	0	1	0	0	1	0	0	0	2	0	0	0	0
Fumbles	29	25	22	32	26	29	29	25	22	23	25	24	23	34	25	15
Lost	17	14	8	20	13	18	10	15	8	11	10	15	13	14	9	6
Out of Bounds	1	2	4	3	3	1	2	4	5	0	3	2	1	0	4	3
Own Rec. for TD	0	0	0	0	0	0	1	0	0	0	1	0	0	0	0	0
Opp. Rec. by	13	5	10	14	9	17	15	12	10	10	15	10	16	12	14	7
Opp. Rec. for TD	3	0	0	0	0	1	0	2	0	0	3	1	1	3	2	0
Penalties	95	99	89	132	93	102	97	112	89	97	96	92	87	118	83	94
Yds. Penalized	815	799	735	1084	895	869	710	899	674	771	807	835	703	950	658	856
Total Points Scored	389	328	305	255	350	398	366	327	322	362	328	381	412	341	353	376
Total TDs	42	37	33	29	40	44	41	32	40	42	36	46	46	39	41	41
TDs Rushing	16	14	10	7	12	18	12	9	10	19	12	21	18	12	11	9
TDs Passing	21	20	22	18	25	22	25	15	26	21	17	21	25	23	26	30
TDs on Ret. and Rec.	5	3	1	4	3	4	4	8	4	2	7	4	3	4	4	2
Extra Point Kicks	42	37	31	27	38	40	38	31	40	40	34	46	46	36	41	36
Extra Point Kicks Att.	42	37	31	28	38	41	38	31	40	40	34	46	46	36	41	36
2Pt Conversions	0	0	2	0	1	2	2	0	0	2	0	0	0	1	0	1
2Pt Conversions Att.	0	0	2	1	2	3	3	1	0	2	1	0	0	3	0	4
Safeties	1	0	0	0	2	0	0	1	0	0	0	1	0	0	0	1
Field Goals Made	31	23	24	18	22	30	26	34	14	22	26	19	30	23	22	30
Field Goals Attempted	34	29	30	27	25	33	27	40	18	29	28	24	32	33	30	34
% Successful	91.2	79.3	80.0	66.7	88.0	90.9	96.3	85.0	77.8	75.9	92.9	79.2	93.8	69.7	73.3	88.2

AFC, NFC, AND NFL SUMMARY

	AFC Offense Total	AFC Offense Average	AFC Defense Total	AFC Defense Average	NFC Offense Total	NFC Offense Average	NFC Defense Total	NFC Defense Average	NFL Total	NFL Average
First Downs	4677	292.3	4652	290.8	4727	295.4	4752	297.0	9404	293.9
Rushing	1601	100.1	1594	99.6	1594	99.6	1601	100.1	3195	99.8
Passing	2712	169.5	2707	169.2	2742	171.4	2747	171.7	5454	170.4
Penalty	364	22.8	351	21.9	391	24.4	404	25.3	755	23.6
Rushes	7333	458.3	7242	452.6	7115	444.7	7206	450.4	14448	451.5
Net Yds. Gained	30121	1882.6	30222	1888.9	29942	1871.4	29841	1865.1	60063	1877.0
Avg. Gain	—	4.1	—	4.2	—	4.2	—	4.1	—	4.2
Avg. Yds. per Game	—	117.7	—	118.1	—	117.0	—	116.6	—	117.3
Passes Attempted	7903	493.9	8117	507.3	8486	530.4	8272	517.0	16389	512.2
Completed	4795	299.7	4859	303.7	5001	312.6	4937	308.6	9796	306.1
% Completed	—	60.7	—	59.9	—	58.9	—	59.7	—	59.8
Total Yds. Gained	54181	3386.3	54649	3415.6	58096	3631.0	57628	3601.8	112277	3508.7
Times Sacked	596	37.3	604	37.8	567	35.4	559	34.9	1163	36.3
Yds. Lost	3678	229.9	3693	230.8	3735	233.4	3720	232.5	7413	231.7
Net Yds. Gained	50503	3156.4	50956	3184.8	54361	3397.6	53908	3369.3	104864	3277.0
Avg. Yds. per Game	—	197.3	—	199.0	—	212.3	—	210.6	—	204.8
Net Yds. per Pass Play	—	5.94	—	5.84	—	6.00	—	6.10	—	5.97
Yds. Gained per Comp.	—	11.30	—	11.25	—	11.62	—	11.67	—	11.46
Combined Net Yds. Gained	80624	5039.0	81178	5073.6	84303	5268.9	83749	5234.3	164927	5154.0
% Total Yds. Rushing	—	37.4	—	37.2	—	35.5	—	35.6	—	36.4
% Total Yds. Passing	—	62.6	—	62.8	—	64.5	—	64.4	—	63.6
Avg. Yds. per Game	—	314.9	—	317.1	—	329.3	—	327.1	—	322.1
Ball Control Plays	15832	989.5	15963	997.7	16168	1010.5	16037	1002.3	32000	1000.0
Avg. Yds. per Play	—	5.1	—	5.1	—	5.2	—	5.2	—	5.2
Third Down Efficiency	—	39.5	—	38.6	—	37.9	—	38.9	—	38.7
Interceptions	254	15.9	273	17.1	266	16.6	247	15.4	520	16.3
Yds. Returned	3272	204.5	3468	216.8	3679	229.9	3483	217.7	6951	217.2
Returned for TD	20	1.3	21	1.3	29	1.8	28	1.8	49	1.5
Punts	1216	76.0	1226	76.6	1273	79.6	1263	78.9	2489	77.8
Yds. Punted	52136	3258.5	52630	3289.4	55424	3464.0	54930	3433.1	107560	3361.3
Avg. Yds. per Punt	—	42.9	—	42.9	—	43.5	—	43.5	—	43.2
Punt Returns	569	35.6	564	35.3	647	40.4	652	40.8	1216	38.0
Yds. Returned	5144	321.5	4728	295.5	5479	342.4	5895	368.4	10623	332.0
Avg. Yds. per Return	—	9.0	—	8.4	—	8.5	—	9.0	—	8.7
Returned for TD	7	0.4	6	0.4	8	0.5	9	0.6	15	0.5
Kickoff Returns	966	60.4	1006	62.9	1071	66.9	1031	64.4	2037	63.7
Yds. Returned	22407	1400.4	23055	1440.9	23501	1468.8	22853	1428.3	45908	1434.6
Avg. Yds. per Return	—	23.2	—	22.9	—	21.9	—	22.2	—	22.5
Returned for TD	5	0.3	5	0.3	4	0.3	4	0.3	9	0.3
Fumbles	382	23.9	357	22.3	383	23.9	408	25.5	765	23.9
Lost	188	11.8	176	11.0	189	11.8	201	12.6	377	11.8
Out of Bounds	18	1.1	16	1.0	36	2.3	38	2.4	54	1.7
Own Rec. for TD	0	0.0	1	0.1	3	0.2	2	0.1	3	0.1
Opp. Rec.	176	11.0	188	11.8	201	12.6	189	11.8	377	11.8
Opp. Rec. for TD	17	1.1	14	0.9	13	0.8	16	1.0	30	0.9
Penalties	1400	87.5	1470	91.9	1645	102.8	1575	98.4	3045	95.2
Yds. Penalized	11592	724.5	12105	756.6	13573	848.3	13060	816.3	25165	786.4
Total Points Scored	5277	329.8	4984	311.5	5300	331.3	5593	349.6	10577	330.5
Total TDs	592	37.0	552	34.5	589	36.8	629	39.3	1181	36.9
TDs Rushing	233	14.6	214	13.4	191	11.9	210	13.1	424	13.3
TDs Passing	308	19.3	291	18.2	340	21.3	357	22.3	648	20.3
TDs on Ret. and Rec.	51	3.2	47	2.9	58	3.6	62	3.9	109	3.4
Extra Point Kicks	564	35.3	521	32.6	560	35.0	603	37.7	1124	35.1
Extra Point Kicks Att.	571	35.7	530	33.1	564	35.3	605	37.8	1135	35.5
2Pt Conversions	12	0.8	10	0.6	9	0.6	11	0.7	21	0.7
2Pt Conversions Att.	19	1.2	19	1.2	22	1.4	22	1.4	41	1.3
Safeties	6	0.4	6	0.4	6	0.4	6	0.4	12	0.4
Field Goals Made	375	23.4	373	23.3	392	24.5	394	24.6	767	24.0
Field Goals Attempted	458	28.6	469	29.3	484	30.3	473	29.6	942	29.4
% Successful	—	81.9	—	79.5	—	81.0	—	83.3	—	81.4

CLUB LEADERS

	Offense	Defense
First Downs	Indianapolis 376	Baltimore 236
Rushing	San Diego 137	Minnesota 53
Passing	Indianapolis 241	Oakland 137
Penalty	Chicago 36	Denver 11
Rushes	Atlanta 537	Minnesota 348
Net Yds. Gained	Atlanta 2939	Minnesota 985
Avg. Gain	Atlanta 5.5	Minnesota 2.8
Passes Attempted	Green Bay 630	Oakland 410
Completed	Detroit & New Orleans 372	Oakland 245
% Completed	Houston 68.4	Baltimore 54.8
Total Yds. Gained	New Orleans 4626	Oakland 2631
Times Sacked	Indianapolis 15	San Diego 61
Yds. Lost	Indianapolis 89	Baltimore 418
Net Yds. Gained	New Orleans 4503	Oakland 2413
Net Yds. per Pass Play	Indianapolis 7.5	Chicago 5.0
Yds. Gained per Comp.	Philadelphia 13.3	Buffalo 10.1
Combined Net Yds. Gained	New Orleans 6264	Baltimore 4225
% Total Yds. Rushing	Atlanta 55.3	Minnesota 20.5
% Total Yds. Passing	Detroit 77.2	Indianapolis 47.9
Ball Control Plays	Green Bay 1085	New Orleans 930
Avg. Yds. per Play	Philadelphia 6.2	Baltimore 4.5
Avg. Time of Poss.	Baltimore 32:48	
Third Down Efficiency	Indianapolis 56.1	Baltimore 28.8
Interceptions	—	Baltimore 28
Yds. Returned	—	Baltimore 544
Returned for TD	—	Baltimore 5
Punts	Carolina 100	—
Yds. Punted	Carolina 4508	—
Avg. Yds. per Punt	Dallas 48.2	—
Punt Returns	Tampa Bay 54	Atlanta & Indianapolis 25
Yds. Returned	Chicago 607	N.Y. Giants 191
Avg. Yds. per Return	Tennessee 12.6	Cincinnati 5.6
Returned for TD	Chicago & Tennessee 3	—
Kickoff Returns	San Francisco & Tennessee 79	Miami 40
Yds. Returned	San Francisco 1907	Tampa Bay 846
Avg. Yds. per Return	New England 26.8	Tampa Bay 18.4
Returned for TD	Chicago & N.Y. Jets 2	—
Total Points Scored	San Diego 492	Baltimore 201
Total TDs	San Diego 59	Baltimore 21
TDs Rushing	San Diego 32	Baltimore 5
TDs Passing	Indianapolis & Philadelphia 31	New England 10
TDs on Ret. and Rec.	Chicago 9	Baltimore 0
Extra Point Kicks	San Diego 58	Baltimore 20
2-Point Conversions	Tennessee 3	—
Safeties	Baltimore & Tennessee 2	—
Field Goals Made	Chicago & St. Louis 32	New Orleans 14
Field Goals Attempted	Arizona & St. Louis 37	New Orleans 18
% Successful	Baltimore 93.3	Chicago 66.7

NFL CLUB RANKINGS BY YARDS

	Offense			Defense		
	Total	Rush	Pass	Total	Rush	Pass
Arizona	18	30	10	29	16	30
Atlanta	12	*1	32	22	9	29
Baltimore	17	25	11	*1	2	6
Buffalo	30	27	28	18	28	7
Carolina	24	24	15	7	11	4
Chicago	15	15	14	5	6	11
Cincinnati	8	26	6	30	15	31T
Cleveland	31	31	23	27	29	15
Dallas	5	13	5	13	10	24
Denver	21	8	25	14	12	21
Detroit	22	32	7	28	21	25
Green Bay	9	23	8	12	13	17
Houston	28	21	27	24	20	22
Indianapolis	3	18	2	21	32	2
Jacksonville	10	3	24	2	4	10
Kansas City	16	9	22	16	18	18
Miami	20	22	13	4	8	5
Minnesota	23	16	18	8	*1	31T
New England	11	12	12	6	5	12
New Orleans	*1	19	*1	11	23	3
New York Giants	14	7	19	25	14	28
New York Jets	25	20	17	20	24	14
Oakland	32	29	31	3	25	*1
Philadelphia	2	11	3	15	26	9
Pittsburgh	7	10	9	9	3	20
St. Louis	6	17	4	23	31	8
San Diego	4	2	16	10	7	13
San Francisco	26	6	29	26	19	26
Seattle	19	14	20	19	22	16
Tampa Bay	29	28	26	17	17	19
Tennessee	27	5	30	32	30	27
Washington	13	4	21	31	27	23

T = Tied for position   * = League Leader

AFC TAKEAWAYS/GIVEAWAYS

	Takeaways			Giveaways			Net
	Int	Fum	Total	Int	Fum	Total	Diff.
Baltimore	28	12	40	14	9	23	+17
San Diego	16	12	28	9	6	15	+13
New England	22	13	35	12	15	27	+8
Cincinnati	19	12	31	13	11	24	+7
Indianapolis	15	11	26	9	10	19	+7
Kansas City	15	15	30	12	14	26	+4
Miami	8	19	27	19	6	25	+2
Tennessee	17	11	28	19	7	26	+2
Jacksonville	20	4	24	14	9	23	+1
Denver	17	13	30	18	12	30	0
N.Y. Jets	16	9	25	16	9	25	0
Houston	11	11	22	13	12	25	-3
Buffalo	13	11	24	14	15	29	-5
Pittsburgh	20	9	29	23	14	37	-8
Cleveland	18	9	27	25	17	42	-15
Oakland	18	5	23	24	22	46	-23
AFC Totals	273	176	449	254	188	442	+7

NFC TAKEAWAYS/GIVEAWAYS

	Takeaways			Giveaways			Net
	Int	Fum	Total	Int	Fum	Total	Diff.
St. Louis	17	15	32	8	10	18	+14
Chicago	24	20	44	22	14	36	+8
Atlanta	12	14	26	15	5	20	+6
Philadelphia	19	10	29	9	15	24	+5
Minnesota	21	15	36	20	12	32	+4
Arizona	16	17	33	17	13	30	+3
Dallas	18	13	31	21	9	30	+1
Green Bay	23	10	33	18	15	33	0
N.Y. Giants	17	11	28	18	10	28	0
New Orleans	11	8	19	13	10	23	-4
Carolina	14	8	22	17	10	27	-5
San Francisco	14	13	27	16	16	32	-5
Washington	6	6	12	10	7	17	-5
Seattle	12	14	26	22	12	34	-8
Detroit	12	18	30	22	17	39	-9
Tampa Bay	11	9	20	18	14	32	-12
NFC Totals	247	201	448	266	189	455	-7

SCORING

POINTS

AFC:	186	LaDainian Tomlinson, San Diego
NFC:	143	Robbie Gould, Chicago

TOUCHDOWNS

AFC:	31	LaDainian Tomlinson, San Diego
NFC:	16	Marion Barber, Dallas
	16	Steven Jackson, St. Louis

EXTRA POINT KICKS

AFC:	58	Nate Kaeding, San Diego
NFC:	48	David Akers, Philadelphia

TWO-POINT EXTRA POINT PLAYS

AFC:	2	Marty Booker, Miami
NFC:	1	Isaac Bruce, St. Louis
	1	Chris Cooley, Washington
	1	Joe Horn, New Orleans
	1	Billy Miller, New Orleans
	1	Santana Moss, Washington
	1	Terrell Owens, Dallas
	1	Tony Romo, Dallas
	1	L.J. Smith, Philadelphia
	1	Jerramy Stevens, Seattle

FIELD GOALS

NFC:	32	Robbie Gould, Chicago
	32	Jeff Wilkins, St. Louis
AFC:	28	Matt Stover, Baltimore

FIELD GOAL ATTEMPTS

NFC:	37	Neil Rackers, Arizona
	37	Jeff Wilkins, St. Louis
AFC:	36	Olindo Mare, Miami

LONGEST FIELD GOAL

NFC:	62	Matt Bryant, Tampa Bay vs. Philadelphia, October 22
AFC:	60	Rob Bironas, Tennessee vs. Indianapolis, December 3

MOST POINTS, GAME

AFC:	24	LaDainian Tomlinson, San Diego at San Francisco, October 15 (4 TD)
	24	Larry Johnson, Kansas City vs. Seattle, October 29 (4 TD)
	24	LaDainian Tomlinson, San Diego at Cincinnati, November 12 (4 TD)
	24	LaDainian Tomlinson, San Diego at Denver, November 19 (4 TD)
	24 *	Joseph Addai, Indianapolis vs. Philadelphia, November 26 (4 TD)
NFC:	24 *	Reggie Bush, New Orleans vs. San Francisco, December 3 (4 TD)
	24	Steven Jackson, St. Louis at Minnesota, December 31 (4 TD)

TEAM LEADERS, POINTS

AFC: BALTIMORE, 121, Matt Stover; BUFFALO, 102, Rian Lindell; CINCINNATI, 115, Shayne Graham; CLEVELAND, 88, Phil Dawson; DENVER, 115, Jason Elam; HOUSTON, 83, Kris Brown; INDIANAPOLIS, 113, Adam Vinatieri; JACKSONVILLE, 119, Josh Scobee; KANSAS CITY, 114, Larry Johnson; MIAMI, 100, Olindo Mare; NEW ENGLAND, 103, *, Stephen Gostkowski; N.Y. JETS, 106, Mike Nugent; OAKLAND, 70, Sebastian Janikowski; PITTSBURGH, 101, Jeff Reed; SAN DIEGO, 186, LaDainian Tomlinson;

TENNESSEE, 98, Rob Bironas.

NFC: ARIZONA, 116, Neil Rackers; ATLANTA, 87, Morten Andersen; CAROLINA, 100, John Kasay; CHICAGO, 143, Robbie Gould; DALLAS, 96, Marion Barber; DETROIT, 117, Jason Hanson; GREEN BAY, 109, Dave Rayner; MINNESOTA, 90, Ryan Longwell; NEW ORLEANS, 115, John Carney; N.Y. GIANTS, 107, Jay Feely; PHILADELPHIA, 102, David Akers; ST. LOUIS, 131, Jeff Wilkins; SAN FRANCISCO, 116, Joe Nedney; SEATTLE, 111, Josh Brown; TAMPA BAY, 73, Matt Bryant; WASHINGTON, 42, Clinton Portis.

TEAM CHAMPION

AFC:	492	San Diego
NFC:	427	Chicago

NFL TOP TEN SCORERS—KICKERS

	XP	XPA	FG	FGA	PTS
Gould, Robbie, Chi.	47	47	32	36	143
Kaeding, Nate, S.D.	58	58	26	29	136
Wilkins, Jeff, St.L	35	35	32	37	131
Stover, Matt, Bal.	37	37	28	30	121
Scobee, Josh, Jac.	41	41	26	32	119
Hanson, Jason, Det.	30	30	29	33	117
Nedney, Joe, S.F.	29	29	29	35	116
Rackers, Neil, Ariz	32	32	28	37	116
Carney, John, N.O.	46	47	23	25	115
Elam, Jason, Den.	34	34	27	29	115
Graham, Shayne, Cin.	40	42	25	30	115

NFL TOP TEN SCORERS—NONKICKERS

	TD	TDR	TDP	TDM	2-PT.	PTS
Tomlinson, LaDainian, S.D.	31	28	3	0	0	186
Johnson, Larry, K.C.	19	17	2	0	0	114
Barber, Marion, Dal.	16	14	2	0	0	96
Jackson, Steven, St.L	16	13	3	0	0	96
Jones-Drew, Maurice, Jac.	16	13	2	1	0	96
Parker, Willie, Pit.	16	13	3	0	0	96
Owens, Terrell, Dal.	13	0	13	0	1	80
Dillon, Corey, N.E.	13	13	0	0	0	78
Harrison, Marvin, Ind.	12	0	12	0	0	72
Johnson, Rudi, Cin.	12	12	0	0	0	72

AFC—INDIVIDUAL SCORERS

KICKERS

	XP	XPA	FG	FGA	PTS
Kaeding, Nate, S.D.	58	58	26	29	136
Stover, Matt, Bal.	37	37	28	30	121
Scobee, Josh, Jac.	41	41	26	32	119
Elam, Jason, Den.	34	34	27	29	115
Graham, Shayne, Cin.	40	42	25	30	115
Vinatieri, Adam, Ind.	38	38	25	28	113
Tynes, Lawrence, K.C.	35	36	24	31	107
Nugent, Mike, NYJ	34	35	24	27	106
* Gostkowski, Stephen, N.E.	43	44	20	26	103
Lindell, Rian, Buf.	33	33	23	25	102
Reed, Jeff, Pit.	41	41	20	27	101
Mare, Olindo, Mia.	22	22	26	36	100
Bironas, Rob, Ten.	32	32	22	28	98
Dawson, Phil, Cle.	25	25	21	29	88
Brown, Kris, Hou.	26	27	19	25	83
Janikowski, Sebastian, Oak.	16	16	18	25	70
Smith, Hunter, Ind.	0	1	0	0	0

NONKICKERS

	TD	TDR	TDP	TDM	2-PT.	PTS
Tomlinson, LaDainian, S.D.	31	28	3	0	0	186
Johnson, Larry, K.C.	19	17	2	0	0	114

	TD	TDR	TDP	TDM	2-PT.	PTS
* Jones-Drew, Maurice, Jac.	16	13	2	1	0	96
Parker, Willie, Pit.	16	13	3	0	0	96
Dillon, Corey, N.E.	13	13	0	0	0	78
Harrison, Marvin, Ind.	12	0	12	0	0	72
Johnson, Rudi, Cin.	12	12	0	0	0	72
Wayne, Reggie, Ind.	9	0	9	0	1	56
Gates, Antonio, S.D.	9	0	9	0	0	54
Henry, Chris, Cin.	9	0	9	0	0	54
Houshmandzadeh, T.J., Cin.	9	0	9	0	0	54
Lewis, Jamal, Bal.	9	9	0	0	0	54
Walker, Javon, Den.	9	1	8	0	0	54
* Addai, Joseph, Ind.	8	7	1	0	0	48
* Bell, Mike, Den.	8	8	0	0	0	48
Evans, Lee, Buf.	8	0	8	0	0	48
Henry, Travis, Ten.	7	7	0	0	1	44
* Young, Vince, Ten.	7	7	0	0	1	44
Johnson, Chad, Cin.	7	0	7	0	0	42
* Maroney, Laurence, N.E.	7	6	1	0	0	42
Booker, Marty, Mia.	6	0	6	0	2	40
Jackson, Vincent, S.D.	6	0	6	0	1	38
Barlow, Kevan, NYJ	6	6	0	0	0	36
Coles, Laveranues, NYJ	6	0	6	0	0	36
Cotchery, Jerricho, NYJ	6	0	6	0	0	36
Edwards, Braylon, Cle.	6	0	6	0	0	36
Heap, Todd, Bal.	6	0	6	0	0	36
McGahee, Willis, Buf.	6	6	0	0	0	36
Taylor, Fred, Jac.	6	5	1	0	0	36
Ward, Hines, Pit.	6	0	6	0	0	36
Dayne, Ron, Hou.	5	5	0	0	1	32
Gonzalez, Tony, K.C.	5	0	5	0	1	32
Brown, Ronnie, Mia.	5	5	0	0	0	30
Clayton, Mark, Bal.	5	0	5	0	0	30
* Daniels, Owen, Hou.	5	0	5	0	0	30
Houston, Cedric, NYJ	5	5	0	0	0	30
Johnson, Andre, Hou.	5	0	5	0	0	30
Kennison, Eddie, K.C.	5	0	5	0	0	30
Miller, Heath, Pit.	5	0	5	0	0	30
Rhodes, Dominic, Ind.	5	5	0	0	0	30
Brown, Troy, N.E.	4	0	4	0	1	26
Caldwell, Reche, N.E.	4	0	4	0	1	26
* Lundy, Wali, Hou.	4	4	0	0	1	26
Baker, Chris, NYJ	4	0	4	0	0	24
Chambers, Chris, Mia.	4	0	4	0	0	24
Clark, Dallas, Ind.	4	0	4	0	0	24
Droughns, Reuben, Cle.	4	4	0	0	0	24
Jones, Pacman, Ten.	4	0	0	4	0	24
Jones, Brandon, Ten.	4	0	4	0	0	24
Jones, Matt, Jac.	4	0	4	0	0	24
Manning, Peyton, Ind.	4	4	0	0	0	24
* Scheffler, Tony, Den.	4	0	4	0	0	24
* Washington, Leon, NYJ	4	4	0	0	0	24
Washington, Nate, Pit.	4	0	4	0	0	24
Williams, Reggie, Jac.	4	0	4	0	0	24
Bennett, Drew, Ten.	3	0	3	0	1	20
Faulk, Kevin, N.E.	3	1	2	0	0	18
Floyd, Malcom, S.D.	3	0	3	0	0	18
Frye, Charlie, Cle.	3	3	0	0	0	18
Gabriel, Doug, N.E.	3	0	3	0	0	18
Hall, Dante, K.C.	3	0	2	1	0	18
* Holmes, Santonio, Pit.	3	0	2	1	0	18
* Jackson, Chad, N.E.	3	0	3	0	0	18
Jurevicius, Joe, Cle.	3	0	3	0	0	18
Manumaleuna, Brandon, S.D.	3	0	3	0	0	18
McMichael, Randy, Mia.	3	0	3	0	0	18
Moss, Randy, Oak.	3	0	3	0	0	18
Parrish, Roscoe, Buf.	3	0	2	1	0	18
Price, Peerless, Buf.	3	0	3	0	0	18
Royal, Robert, Buf.	3	0	3	0	0	18

	TD	TDR	TDP	TDM	2-PT.	PTS
Scaife, Bo, Ten.	3	1	2	0	0	18
Smith, Rod, Den.	3	0	3	0	0	18
Watson, Benjamin, N.E.	3	0	3	0	0	18
Wilcox, Daniel, Bal.	3	0	3	0	0	18
Wilson, Kris, K.C.	3	0	3	0	0	18
Winslow, Kellen, Cle.	3	0	3	0	0	18
Wrighster, George, Jac.	3	0	3	0	0	18
Alexander, Stephen, Den.	2	0	2	0	0	12
Anderson, Courtney, Oak.	2	0	2	0	0	12
Bell, Tatum, Den.	2	2	0	0	0	12
Bruener, Mark, Hou.	2	0	2	0	0	12
Carr, David, Hou.	2	2	0	0	0	12
Davenport, Najeh, Pit.	2	1	1	0	0	12
Fletcher, Bryan, Ind.	2	0	2	0	0	12
Fletcher-Baker, London, Buf.	2	0	0	2	0	12
Graham, Daniel, N.E.	2	0	2	0	0	12
Gray, Quinn, Jac.	2	2	0	0	0	12
Heiden, Steve, Cle.	2	0	2	0	0	12
Holly, Daven, Cle.	2	0	0	2	0	12
Jordan, LaMont, Oak.	2	2	0	0	0	12
Lee, ReShard, Oak.	2	2	0	0	0	12
Leftwich, Byron, Jac.	2	2	0	0	0	12
* Marshall, Brandon, Den.	2	0	2	0	0	12
Mason, Derrick, Bal.	2	0	2	0	0	12
McAlister, Chris, Bal.	2	0	0	2	0	12
Miller, Justin, NYJ	2	0	0	2	0	12
Mughelli, Ovie, Bal.	2	0	2	0	0	12
Reed, Josh, Buf.	2	0	2	0	0	12
Roethlisberger, Ben, Pit.	2	2	0	0	0	12
Taylor, Jason, Mia.	2	0	0	2	0	12
Thomas, Anthony, Buf.	2	2	0	0	0	12
Troupe, Ben, Ten.	2	0	2	0	0	12
Turner, Michael, S.D.	2	2	0	0	0	12
Wade, Bobby, Ten.	2	0	2	0	0	12
Wilford, Ernest, Jac.	2	0	2	0	0	12
* Williams, Demetrius, Bal.	2	0	2	0	0	12
Reed, Ed, Bal.	1	0	0	1	0	^8
Thomas, Adalius, Bal.	1	0	0	1	0	^8
Anderson, Mike, Bal.	1	1	0	0	0	6
Asomugha, Nnamdi, Oak.	1	0	0	1	0	6
Bailey, Champ, Den.	1	0	0	1	0	6
Brown, Tony, Ten.	1	0	0	1	0	6
Bulluck, Keith, Ten.	1	0	0	1	0	6
Carr, Chris, Oak.	1	0	0	1	0	6
Carthon, Ran, Ind.	1	1	0	0	0	6
Clements, Nate, Buf.	1	0	0	1	0	6
Cribbs, Josh, Cle.	1	0	0	1	0	6
Culpepper, Daunte, Mia.	1	1	0	0	0	6
Curry, Ronald, Oak.	1	0	1	0	0	6
Dinkins, Darnell, Cle.	1	0	1	0	0	6
* Dobbins, Tim, S.D.	1	0	0	1	0	6
Evans, Heath, N.E.	1	0	1	0	0	6
Faggins, Demarcus, Hou.	1	0	0	1	0	6
Fargas, Justin, Oak.	1	1	0	0	0	6
* Finnegan, Cortland, Ten.	1	0	0	1	0	6
Gado, Samkon, Hou.	1	1	0	0	0	6
Gaffney, Jabar, N.E.	1	0	1	0	0	6
* Hagan, Derek, Mia.	1	0	1	0	0	6
Harris, Marques, S.D.	1	0	0	1	0	6
Hayden, Kelvin, Ind.	1	0	0	1	0	6
Hill, Renaldo, Mia.	1	0	0	1	0	6
Hobbs, Ellis, N.E.	1	0	0	1	0	6
Hobson, Victor, NYJ	1	0	0	1	0	6
Hope, Chris, Ten.	1	0	0	1	0	6
Johnson, Kyle, Den.	1	0	1	0	0	6
Johnson, Jeremi, Cin.	1	1	0	0	0	6
Kelly, Reggie, Cin.	1	0	1	0	0	6
* Kilmer, Ethan, Cin.	1	0	0	1	0	6

	TD	TDR	TDP	TDM	2-PT	PTS
Klecko, Dan, Ind.	1	0	1	0	0	6
* Landry, Dawan, Bal.	1	0	0	1	0	6
Leach, Vonta, Hou.	1	0	1	0	0	6
* Lewis, Marcedes, Jac.	1	0	1	0	0	6
Losman, J.P., Buf.	1	1	0	0	0	6
Maddox, Anthony, Hou.	1	0	0	1	0	6
* Madsen, John, Oak.	1	0	1	0	0	6
McCareins, Justin, NYJ	1	0	1	0	0	6
McCree, Marlon, S.D.	1	0	0	1	0	6
McGee, Terrence, Buf.	1	0	0	1	0	6
McNair, Steve, Bal.	1	1	0	0	0	6
Moore, Clarence, Bal.	1	0	1	0	0	6
Moorehead, Aaron, Ind.	1	0	1	0	0	6
Morris, Sammy, Mia.	1	1	0	0	0	6
Morrison, Kirk, Oak.	1	0	0	1	0	6
Moulds, Eric, Hou.	1	0	1	0	0	6
Neal, Lorenzo, S.D.	1	1	0	0	0	6
Neufeld, Ryan, Buf.	1	0	1	0	0	6
Parker, Samie, K.C.	1	0	1	0	0	6
Pearman, Alvin, Jac.	1	1	0	0	0	6
Peelle, Justin, Mia.	1	0	1	0	0	6
Plummer, Jake, Den.	1	1	0	0	0	6
* Pollard, Bernard, K.C.	1	0	0	1	0	6
Porter, Joey, Pit.	1	0	0	1	0	6
* Prude, Ronnie, Bal.	1	0	0	1	0	6
Robinson, Dunta, Hou.	1	0	0	1	0	6
Starks, Scott, Jac.	1	0	0	1	0	6
Stewart, Tony, Cin.	1	0	1	0	0	6
Stokley, Brandon, Ind.	1	0	1	0	0	6
* Taylor, Chris, Hou.	1	1	0	0	0	6
* Thomas, David, N.E.	1	0	1	0	0	6
Tuman, Jerame, Pit.	1	0	1	0	0	6
Wallace, Rian, Pit.	1	0	0	1	0	6
Washington, Kelley, Cin.	1	0	1	0	0	6
Watson, Kenny, Cin.	1	1	0	0	0	6
Welker, Wes, Mia.	1	0	1	0	0	6
* Whitehurst, Charlie, S.D.	1	1	0	0	0	6
Wilkins, Terrence, Ind.	1	0	0	1	0	6
Williams, Darrent, Den.	1	0	0	1	0	6
Williams, Sam, Oak.	1	0	0	1	0	6
Wilson, Cedrick, Pit.	1	0	1	0	0	6
* Huff, Michael, Oak.	0	0	0	0	0	^2
Warren, Ty, N.E.	0	0	0	0	0	^2

^ Safety ; Team safety credited to Tennessee
* Player that was a rookie in 2006

NFC - INDIVIDUAL SCORERS
KICKERS

	XP	XPA	FG	FGA	PTS
Gould, Robbie, Chi.	47	47	32	36	143
Wilkins, Jeff, St.L	35	35	32	37	131
Hanson, Jason, Det.	30	30	29	33	117
Nedney, Joe, S.F.	29	29	29	35	116
Rackers, Neil, Ariz	32	32	28	37	116
Carney, John, N.O.	46	47	23	25	115
Brown, Josh, Sea.	36	36	25	31	111
Rayner, Dave, G.B.	31	32	26	35	109
Feely, Jay, NY-G	38	38	23	27	107
Akers, David, Phi.	48	48	18	23	102
Kasay, John, Car.	28	28	24	27	100
Longwell, Ryan, Min.	27	28	21	25	90
Andersen, Morten, Atl.	27	27	20	23	87
Bryant, Matt, T.B.	22	23	17	22	73
Vanderjagt, Mike, Dal.	33	33	13	18	72
Gramatica, Martin, Ind.-Dal.	23	23	7	9	44
Suisham, Shaun, Dal.-Was.	14	14	9	11	41
Hall, John, Was.	9	9	9	11	36

	XP	XPA	FG	FGA	PTS
Novak, Nick, Was.	10	10	5	10	25
Koenen, Michael, Atl.	4	4	3	9	13
Cundiff, Billy, N.O.	0	0	0	1	0

NONKICKERS

	TD	TDR	TDP	TDM	X2G	PTS
Barber, Marion, Dal.	16	14	2	0	0	96
Jackson, Steven, St.L	16	13	3	0	0	96
Owens, Terrell, Dal.	13	0	13	0	1	80
McAllister, Deuce, N.O.	11	10	0	1	0	66
Westbrook, Brian, Phi.	11	7	4	0	0	66
Burress, Plaxico, NY-G	10	0	10	0	0	60
Holt, Torry, St.L	10	0	10	0	0	60
Jackson, Darrell, Sea.	10	0	10	0	0	60
Brown, Reggie, Phi.	9	1	8	0	0	54
* Bush, Reggie, N.O.	9	6	2	1	0	54
Gore, Frank, S.F.	9	8	1	0	0	54
Jacobs, Brandon, NY-G	9	9	0	0	0	54
Smith, Steve, Car.	9	1	8	0	0	54
* Colston, Marques, N.O.	8	0	8	0	0	48
Crumpler, Alge, Atl.	8	0	8	0	0	48
Driver, Donald, G.B.	8	0	8	0	0	48
Jones, Kevin, Det.	8	6	2	0	0	48
Alexander, Shaun, Sea.	7	7	0	0	0	42
Galloway, Joey, T.B.	7	0	7	0	0	42
Jenkins, Michael, Atl.	7	0	7	0	0	42
Portis, Clinton, Was.	7	7	0	0	0	42
Shockey, Jeremy, NY-G	7	0	7	0	0	42
Williams, Roy, Det.	7	0	7	0	0	42
Cooley, Chris, Was.	6	0	6	0	1	38
Moss, Santana, Was.	6	0	6	0	1	38
Benson, Cedric, Chi.	6	6	0	0	0	36
Berrian, Bernard, Chi.	6	0	6	0	0	36
Clark, Desmond, Chi.	6	0	6	0	0	36
Fitzgerald, Larry, Ariz	6	0	6	0	0	36
Furrey, Mike, Det.	6	0	6	0	0	36
Glenn, Terry, Dal.	6	0	6	0	0	36
Green, Ahman, G.B.	6	5	1	0	0	36
Henderson, Devery, N.O.	6	1	5	0	0	36
* Hester, Devin, Chi.	6	0	0	6	0	36
James, Edgerrin, Ariz	6	6	0	0	0	36
Jones, Thomas, Chi.	6	6	0	0	0	36
Taylor, Chester, Min.	6	6	0	0	0	36
Smith, L.J., Phi.	5	0	5	0	1	32
Barber, Tiki, NY-G	5	5	0	0	0	30
Betts, Ladell, Was.	5	4	1	0	0	30
Dunn, Warrick, Atl.	5	4	1	0	0	30
Johnson, Keyshawn, Car.	5	1	4	0	0	30
Muhammad, Muhsin, Chi.	5	0	5	0	0	30
Stallworth, Donte', Phi.	5	0	5	0	0	30
Horn, Joe, N.O.	4	0	4	0	1	26
Stevens, Jerramy, Sea.	4	0	4	0	1	26
Boldin, Anquan, Ariz	4	0	4	0	0	24
Branch, Deion, Sea.	4	0	4	0	0	24
Campbell, Dan, Det.	4	0	4	0	0	24
Crayton, Patrick, Dal.	4	0	4	0	0	24
Curtis, Kevin, St.L	4	0	4	0	0	24
Griffith, Justin, Atl.	4	1	3	0	0	24
Hackett, D.J., Sea.	4	0	4	0	0	24
Johnson, Bryant, Ariz	4	0	4	0	0	24
Jones, Julius, Dal.	4	4	0	0	0	24
Randle El, Antwaan, Was.	4	0	3	1	0	24
Robinson, Marcus, Min.	4	0	4	0	0	24
Shipp, Marcel, Ariz	4	4	0	0	0	24
Bruce, Isaac, St.L	3	0	3	0	1	20
Alstott, Mike, T.B.	3	3	0	0	0	18
Battle, Arnaz, S.F.	3	0	3	0	0	18
Bradley, Mark, Chi.	3	0	3	0	0	18

	TD	TDR	TDP	TDM	2-PT.	PTS
Bryant, Antonio, S.F.	3	0	3	0	0	18
Buckhalter, Correll, Phi.	3	2	1	0	0	18
Burleson, Nate, Sea.	3	0	2	1	0	18
Carter, Drew, Car.	3	0	3	0	0	18
Carter, Tim, NY-G	3	0	2	1	0	18
Copper, Terrance, N.O.	3	0	3	0	0	18
* Davis, Vernon, S.F.	3	0	3	0	0	18
Foster, DeShaun, Car.	3	3	0	0	0	18
Herron, Noah, G.B.	3	1	2	0	0	18
* Jennings, Greg, G.B.	3	0	3	0	0	18
Karney, Mike, N.O.	3	1	2	0	0	18
McMullen, Billy, Min.	3	0	2	1	0	18
McNabb, Donovan, Phi.	3	3	0	0	0	18
Pinner, Artose, Min.	3	3	0	0	0	18
Smith, Alex, T.B.	3	0	3	0	0	18
Taylor, Travis, Min.	3	0	3	0	0	18
Toomer, Amani, NY-G	3	0	3	0	0	18
Barber, Ronde, T.B.	2	0	0	2	0	12
* Baskett, Hank, Phi.	2	0	2	0	0	12
Bledsoe, Drew, Dal.	2	2	0	0	0	12
Davis, Rashied, Chi.	2	0	2	0	0	12
Duckett, T.J., Was.	2	2	0	0	0	12
Gilmore, John, Chi.	2	0	2	0	0	12
Hilliard, Ike, T.B.	2	0	2	0	0	12
Johnson, Eric, S.F.	2	0	2	0	0	12
Kitna, Jon, Det.	2	2	0	0	0	12
* Leinart, Matt, Ariz	2	2	0	0	0	12
Lewis, Greg, Phi.	2	0	2	0	0	12
Martin, David, G.B.	2	0	2	0	0	12
Moore, Mewelde, Min.	2	0	1	1	0	12
Morency, Vernand, G.B.	2	2	0	0	0	12
Norris, Moran, S.F.	2	0	2	0	0	12
* Norwood, Jerious, Atl.	2	2	0	0	0	12
Peterson, Adrian, Chi.	2	2	0	0	0	12
* Robinson, Michael, S.F.	2	2	0	0	0	12
Schobel, Matt, Phi.	2	0	2	0	0	12
Smith, Alex, S.F.	2	2	0	0	0	12
Tyree, David, NY-G	2	0	2	0	0	12
Vick, Michael, Atl.	2	2	0	0	0	12
Walters, Troy, Ariz	2	0	2	0	0	12
Ware, DeMarcus, Dal.	2	0	0	2	0	12
* Williams, DeAngelo, Car.	2	1	1	0	0	12
Wilson, Adrian, Ariz	2	0	0	2	0	12
* Adeyanju, Victor, St.L	1	0	0	1	0	6
Arrington, J.J., Ariz	1	0	0	1	0	6
* Avant, Jason, Phi.	1	0	1	0	0	6
Bartell, Ronald, St.L	1	0	0	1	0	6
Becht, Anthony, T.B.	1	0	1	0	0	6
Bergen, Adam, Ariz	1	0	1	0	0	6
* Branch, Jamaal, N.O.	1	0	1	0	0	6
Brooks, Derrick, T.B.	1	0	0	1	0	6
Brown, Mike, Chi.	1	0	0	1	0	6
Brown, Sheldon, Phi.	1	0	0	1	0	6
Bryson, Shawn, Det.	1	0	1	0	0	6
Burnett, Kevin, Dal.	1	0	0	1	0	6
* Byrd, Dominique, St.L	1	0	1	0	0	6
Cartwright, Rock, Was.	1	0	0	1	0	6
Clayton, Michael, T.B.	1	0	1	0	0	6
Cole, Trent, Phi.	1	0	0	1	0	6
Collins, Nick, G.B.	1	0	0	1	0	6
Conwell, Ernie, N.O.	1	0	1	0	0	6
Davis, Stephen, St.L	1	0	1	0	0	6
Deloatch, Curtis, N.O.	1	0	0	1	0	6
Dendy, Patrick, G.B.	1	0	0	1	0	6
* Dockery, Kevin, NY-G	1	0	0	1	0	6
Dugan, Jeff, Min.	1	0	1	0	0	6
Engram, Bobby, Sea.	1	0	1	0	0	6
Fason, Ciatrick, Min.	1	1	0	0	0	6

	TD	TDR	TDP	TDM	2-PT.	PTS
Favre, Brett, G.B.	1	1	0	0	0	6
Ferguson, Robert, G.B.	1	0	1	0	0	6
Fletcher, Jamar, Det.	1	0	0	1	0	6
Gamble, Chris, Car.	1	0	0	1	0	6
Gilmore, Bryan, S.F.	1	0	1	0	0	6
Goings, Nick, Car.	1	0	1	0	0	6
Hall, DeAngelo, Atl.	1	0	0	1	0	6
Harris, Arlen, Det.	1	1	0	0	0	6
Harris, Walt, S.F.	1	0	0	1	0	6
Heller, Will, Sea.	1	0	1	0	0	6
Henderson, E.J., Min.	1	0	0	1	0	6
Herndon, Kelly, Sea.	1	0	0	1	0	6
Hicks, Maurice, S.F.	1	0	1	0	0	6
* Hodge, Abdul, G.B.	1	0	0	1	0	6
Hoover, Brad, Car.	1	1	0	0	0	6
* Jackson, Tarvaris, Min.	1	1	0	0	0	6
James, Bradie, Dal.	1	0	0	1	0	6
Johnson, Brad, Min.	1	1	0	0	0	6
Jones, Jamal, N.O.	1	0	1	0	0	6
* King, Jeff, Car.	1	0	1	0	0	6
* Klopfenstein, Joe, St.L	1	0	1	0	0	6
Leber, Ben, Min.	1	0	0	1	0	6
Lelie, Ashley, Atl.	1	0	1	0	0	6
Lewis, Michael, Phi.	1	0	0	1	0	6
Mangum, Kris, Car.	1	0	1	0	0	6
Manning, Ricky, Chi.	1	0	0	1	0	6
Manuel, Marquand, G.B.	1	0	0	1	0	6
* Marshall, Richard, Car.	1	0	0	1	0	6
Martin, Ruvell, G.B.	1	0	1	0	0	6
McAfee, Fred, N.O.	1	1	0	0	0	6
McCrary, Fred, Atl.	1	0	1	0	0	6
McDonald, Shaun, St.L	1	0	1	0	0	6
McQuarters, R.W., NY-G	1	0	0	1	0	6
Newman, Terence, Dal.	1	0	0	1	0	6
* Oliver, Melvin, S.F.	1	0	1	0	0	6
Owens, Richard, Min.	1	0	1	0	0	6
Patterson, Mike, Phi.	1	0	0	1	0	6
Pittman, Michael, T.B.	1	1	0	0	0	6
Sellers, Mike, Was.	1	0	1	0	0	6
Sheppard, Lito, Phi.	1	0	0	1	0	6
Simms, Chris, T.B.	1	1	0	0	0	6
Smith, Antonio, Ariz	1	0	0	1	0	6
Smoot, Fred, Min.	1	0	0	1	0	6
Strong, Mack, Sea.	1	1	0	0	0	6
Tapeh, Thomas, Phi.	1	0	1	0	0	6
* Tapp, Darryl, Sea.	1	0	1	0	0	6
Thompson, Tyson, Dal.	1	1	0	0	0	6
Thrash, James, Was.	1	0	1	0	0	6
Tillman, Charles, Chi.	1	0	0	1	0	6
Wiggins, Jermaine, Min.	1	0	1	0	0	6
Williams, Cadillac, T.B.	1	1	0	0	0	6
Williams, Demorrio, Atl.	1	0	0	1	0	6
Williams, Kevin, Min.	1	0	0	1	0	6
Williams, Mike, Det.	1	0	1	0	0	6
Winfield, Antoine, Min.	1	0	0	1	0	6
Witten, Jason, Dal.	1	0	1	0	0	6
Woodson, Charles, G.B.	1	0	0	1	0	6
Yoder, Todd, Was.	1	0	1	0	0	6
Arrington, LaVar, NY-G	0	0	0	0	0	^2
DeVries, Jared, Det.	0	0	0	0	0	^2
Johnson, Tank, Chi.	0	0	0	0	0	^2
Marshall, Lemar, Was.	0	0	0	0	0	^2
Miller, Billy, N.O.	0	0	0	0	1	2
Romo, Tony, Dal.	0	0	0	0	1	2
Rucker, Mike, Car.	0	0	0	0	0	^2

^ *Safety; Team safety credited to San Francisco*
* *Player that was a rookie in 2006*

AMERICAN FOOTBALL CONFERENCE—SCORING

	TD	TDR	TDP	TDM	XKG	XKAtt	X2G	X2Att	FG	FGA	SAF	POINTS
San Diego	59	32	24	3	58	58	1	1	26	29	0	492
Indianapolis	50	17	31	2	47	48	1	2	26	29	0	427
New England	46	20	25	1	43	44	2	2	20	26	1	385
Cincinnati	43	14	28	1	40	42	0	1	25	30	0	373
Jacksonville	42	23	17	2	41	41	0	1	26	32	0	371
Baltimore	38	11	21	6	37	37	0	1	28	30	2	353
Pittsburgh	42	16	23	3	41	41	0	0	20	27	0	353
Kansas City	37	17	18	2	35	36	1	1	24	31	0	331
Tennessee	36	15	13	8	32	32	3	3	22	28	2	324
Denver	34	12	20	2	34	34	0	0	27	29	0	319
N.Y. Jets	35	15	17	3	34	35	0	0	24	27	0	316
Buffalo	33	9	19	5	33	33	0	0	23	25	0	300
Houston	30	13	14	3	26	27	2	3	19	25	0	267
Miami	26	7	16	3	22	22	2	4	26	36	0	260
Cleveland	25	7	15	3	25	25	0	0	21	29	0	238
Oakland	16	5	7	4	16	16	0	0	18	25	1	168
AFC Total	592	233	308	51	564	571	12	19	375	458	6	5277
AFC Average	37.0	14.6	19.3	3.2	35.3	35.7	0.8	1.2	23.4	28.6	0.4	329.8

NATIONAL FOOTBALL CONFERENCE—SCORING

	TD	TDR	TDP	TDM	XKG	XKAtt	X2G	X2Att	FG	FGA	SAF	POINTS
Chicago	47	14	24	9	47	47	0	0	32	36	1	427
Dallas	52	21	26	5	49	49	2	3	20	28	0	425
New Orleans	49	19	27	3	46	47	2	2	23	26	0	413
Philadelphia	49	13	31	5	48	48	1	1	18	23	0	398
St. Louis	39	13	24	2	35	35	1	3	32	37	0	367
N.Y. Giants	41	14	24	3	38	38	0	2	23	27	1	355
Seattle	37	8	26	3	36	36	1	1	25	31	0	335
Arizona	33	12	17	4	32	32	0	1	28	37	0	314
Washington	34	13	19	2	31	31	2	2	22	30	1	307
Detroit	31	9	21	1	30	30	0	1	29	33	1	305
Green Bay	32	9	18	5	31	32	0	0	26	35	0	301
San Francisco	30	12	16	2	29	29	0	1	29	35	1	298
Atlanta	32	9	21	2	31	31	0	1	23	32	0	292
Minnesota	32	12	13	7	27	28	0	4	21	25	0	282
Carolina	28	7	19	2	28	28	0	0	24	27	1	270
Tampa Bay	23	6	14	3	22	23	0	0	17	22	0	211
NFC Total	589	191	340	58	560	564	9	22	392	484	6	5300
NFC Average	36.8	11.9	21.3	3.6	35.0	35.3	0.6	1.4	24.5	30.3	0.4	331.3
NFL Total	1181	424	648	109	1124	1135	21	41	767	942	12	10577
NFL Average	36.9	13.3	20.3	3.4	35.1	35.5	0.7	1.3	24.0	29.4	0.4	330.5

FIELD GOALS

FIELD GOAL PERCENTAGE
AFC: .933 Matt Stover, Baltimore
NFC: .920 John Carney, New Orleans

FIELD GOALS
NFC: 32 Robbie Gould, Chicago
32 Jeff Wilkins, St. Louis
AFC: 28 Matt Stover, Baltimore

FIELD GOAL ATTEMPTS
NFC: 37 Neil Rackers, Arizona
37 Jeff Wilkins, St. Louis
AFC: 36 Olindo Mare, Miami

FIELD GOALS, GAME
AFC: 6 Phil Dawson, Cleveland at San Diego, November 5 (6 attempts)
NFC: 6 Jeff Wilkins, St. Louis vs. Seattle, September 10 (7 attempts)

LONGEST FIELD GOAL
NFC: 62 Matt Bryant, Tampa Bay vs. Philadelphia, October 22
AFC: 60 Rob Bironas, Tennessee vs. Indianapolis, December 3

AVERAGE YARDS MADE
AFC: 37.9 Kris Brown, Houston
NFC: 36.8 John Kasay, Carolina

AMERICAN FOOTBALL CONFERENCE—FIELD GOALS

	FG	FGA	Pct	Long
Baltimore	28	30	.933	52
Denver	27	29	.931	51
Buffalo	23	25	.920	53
Indianapolis	26	29	.897	48
San Diego	26	29	.897	54
N.Y. Jets	24	27	.889	54
Cincinnati	25	30	.833	51
Jacksonville	26	32	.813	48
Tennessee	22	28	.786	60
Kansas City	24	31	.774	53
New England	20	26	.769	52
Houston	19	25	.760	49
Pittsburgh	20	27	.741	50
Cleveland	21	29	.724	51
Miami	26	36	.722	52
Oakland	18	25	.720	55
AFC Total	375	458	—	60
AFC Average	23.4	28.6	.819	—

NATIONAL FOOTBALL CONFERENCE—FIELD GOALS

	FG	FGA	Pct	Long
Carolina	24	27	.889	54
Chicago	32	36	.889	49
New Orleans	23	26	.885	51
Detroit	29	33	.879	53
St. Louis	32	37	.865	53
N.Y. Giants	23	27	.852	47
Minnesota	21	25	.840	49
San Francisco	29	35	.829	51
Seattle	25	31	.806	54
Philadelphia	18	23	.783	47
Tampa Bay	17	22	.773	62
Arizona	28	37	.757	50
Green Bay	26	35	.743	54
Washington	22	30	.733	52
Atlanta	23	32	.719	51
Dallas	20	28	.714	50
NFC Total	392	484	—	62
NFC Average	24.5	30.3	.810	—
League Total	767	942	—	62
League Average	24.0	29.4	.814	—

AFC—INDIVIDUAL FIELD GOALS

	1-19 Yards	20-29 Yards	30-39 Yards	40-49 Yards	50 or Longer	Totals	Avg Yds Att	Avg Yds Made	Avg Yds Miss	Long
Stover, Matt, Bal.	0-0 —	12-13 .923	9-9 1.000	6-7 .857	1-1 1.000	28-30 .933	33.2	33.0	35.5	52
Elam, Jason, Den.	0-0 —	10-10 1.000	10-10 1.000	6-8 .750	1-1 1.000	27-29 .931	33.3	32.6	43.5	51
Lindell, Rian, Buf.	0-0 —	8-8 1.000	5-5 1.000	8-10 .800	2-2 1.000	23-25 .920	35.9	35.3	42.5	53
Kaeding, Nate, S.D.	0-0 —	7-7 1.000	11-12 .917	7-9 .778	1-1 1.000	26-29 .897	35.8	35.2	41.0	54
Vinatieri, Adam, Ind.	1-1 1.000	3-3 1.000	12-13 .923	9-10 .900	0-1 .000	25-28 .893	36.6	35.5	45.3	48
Nugent, Mike, NYJ	1-1 1.000	7-7 1.000	10-12 .833	4-4 1.000	2-3 .667	24-27 .889	33.8	33.2	38.7	54
Graham, Shayne, Cin.	0-0 —	9-9 1.000	8-9 .889	6-8 .750	2-4 .500	25-30 .833	36.9	34.6	48.4	51
Scobee, Josh, Jac.	0-0 —	5-6 .833	7-7 1.000	14-18 .778	0-1 .000	26-32 .813	39.0	37.8	44.2	48
Bironas, Rob, Ten.	0-0 —	10-11 .909	7-7 1.000	4-8 .500	1-2 .500	22-28 .786	34.4	32.5	41.7	60
Tynes, Lawrence, K.C.	1-1 1.000	10-10 1.000	4-6 .667	7-10 .700	2-4 .500	24-31 .774	36.9	35.1	43.1	53
* Gostkowski, Stephen, N.E.	0-0 —	10-11 .909	7-10 .700	2-4 .500	1-1 1.000	20-26 .769	32.7	30.9	38.7	52
Brown, Kris, Hou.	1-1 1.000	4-4 1.000	3-5 .600	11-13 .846	0-2 .000	19-25 .760	39.4	37.9	44.0	49
Reed, Jeff, Pit.	1-1 1.000	6-7 .857	8-11 .727	4-7 .571	1-1 1.000	20-27 .741	35.6	35.0	37.4	50
Dawson, Phil, Cle.	0-0 —	5-6 .833	9-10 .900	6-12 .500	1-1 1.000	21-29 .724	36.7	34.9	41.5	51
Mare, Olindo, Mia.	0-0 —	10-10 1.000	6-8 .750	9-12 .750	1-6 .167	26-36 .722	37.1	34.1	45.1	52
Janikowski, Sebastian, Oak.	1-1 1.000	2-3 .667	9-11 .818	3-3 1.000	3-7 .429	18-25 .720	38.9	36.8	44.4	55
AFC Totals	6-6 1.000	119-126 .944	125-145 .862	106-143 .741	19-38 .500	375-458 .819	36.0	34.6	42.5	60
NFL Totals	15-15 1.000	257-269 .955	239-279 .857	216-294 .735	40-85 .471	767-942 .814	36.0	34.4	43.1	62

* Player that was a rookie in 2006
Leader based on overall percentage, minimum 16 field goals

NFC—INDIVIDUAL FIELD GOALS

	1-19 Yards	20-29 Yards	30-39 Yards	40-49 Yards	50 or Longer	Totals	Avg Yds Att	Avg Yds Made	Avg Yds Miss	Long
Carney, John, N.O.	1-1 1.000	9-9 1.000	7-8 .875	5-6 .833	1-1 1.000	23-25 .920	32.4	32.0	37.5	51
Gould, Robbie, Chi.	0-0 —	6-6 1.000	14-16 .875	12-14 .857	0-0 —	32-36 .889	36.8	36.2	42.0	49
Kasay, John, Car.	2-2 1.000	6-6 1.000	4-4 1.000	8-8 1.000	4-7 .571	24-27 .889	38.9	36.8	56.0	54
Hanson, Jason, Det.	1-1 1.000	12-12 1.000	6-6 1.000	7-8 .875	3-6 .500	29-33 .879	36.3	34.4	50.0	53
Andersen, Morten, Atl.	0-0 —	7-8 .875	6-6 1.000	7-8 .875	0-1 .000	20-23 .870	34.3	33.4	40.0	45
Wilkins, Jeff, St.L	1-1 1.000	11-11 1.000	6-6 1.000	11-16 .688	3-3 1.000	32-37 .865	36.8	35.5	45.2	53
Feely, Jay, NY-G	0-0 —	7-7 1.000	10-11 .909	6-8 .750	0-1 .000	23-27 .852	34.4	32.9	43.0	47
Longwell, Ryan, Min.	2-2 1.000	7-7 1.000	8-8 1.000	4-6 .667	0-2 .000	21-25 .840	33.6	30.4	50.0	49
Nedney, Joe, S.F.	2-2 1.000	11-12 .917	8-10 .800	7-9 .778	1-2 .500	29-35 .829	34.3	33.2	39.5	51
Brown, Josh, Sea.	0-0 —	10-10 1.000	5-7 .714	7-9 .778	3-5 .600	25-31 .806	36.2	34.9	41.8	54
Akers, David, Phi.	0-0 —	9-10 .900	3-5 .600	6-8 .750	0-0 —	18-23 .783	34.3	33.0	39.0	47
Bryant, Matt, T.B.	0-0 —	8-8 1.000	3-3 1.000	5-9 .556	1-2 .500	17-22 .773	36.7	34.2	45.2	62
Rackers, Neil, Ariz	0-0 —	11-11 1.000	9-9 1.000	7-10 .700	1-7 .143	28-37 .757	37.6	34.0	48.9	50
Rayner, Dave, G.B.	0-0 —	11-12 .917	6-9 .667	8-11 .727	1-3 .333	26-35 .743	35.7	34.0	40.9	54
Vanderjagt, Mike, Dal.	0-0 —	6-7 .857	5-6 .833	1-4 .250	1-1 1.000	13-18 .722	34.0	31.8	39.6	50
(Nonqualifiers)										
Hall, John, Was.	0-0 —	3-3 1.000	4-4 1.000	2-4 .500	0-0 —	9-11 .818	37.1	35.3	45.0	46
Suisham, Shaun, Dal.-Was.	0-0 —	1-1 1.000	6-7 .857	1-1 1.000	1-2 .500	9-11 .818	37.2	35.9	43.0	52
Novak, Nick, Was.	0-0 —	1-1 1.000	1-3 .333	3-6 .500	0-0 —	5-10 .500	41.2	38.8	43.6	47
Gramatica, Martin, Ind.-Dal.	0-0 —	2-2 1.000	2-2 1.000	3-5 .600	0-0 —	7-9 .778	37.8	36.1	43.5	48
Koenen, Michael, Atl.	0-0 —	1-1 1.000	1-4 .250	0-1 .000	1-3 .333	3-9 .333	38.2	36.0	39.3	51
Cundiff, Billy, N.O.	0-0 —	0-0 —	0-0 —	0-0 —	0-1 .000	0-1 .000	51.0	—	51.0	0
NFC Totals	9-9 1.000	138-143 .965	114-134 .851	110-151 .728	21-47 .447	392-484 .810	36.0	34.2	43.6	62
NFL Totals	15-15 1.000	257-269 .955	239-279 .857	216-294 .735	40-85 .471	767-942 .814	36.0	34.4	43.1	62

Leader based on overall percentage, minimum 16 field goals

RUSHING

YARDS
AFC: 1815 LaDainian Tomlinson, San Diego
NFC: 1695 Frank Gore, San Francisco

YARDS, GAME
NFC: 234 Tiki Barber, N.Y. Giants at Washington, December 30 (23 attempts, 3 TD)
AFC: 223 Willie Parker, Pittsburgh vs. Cleveland, December 7 (32 attempts, 1 TD)

LONGEST
NFC: 95 Chester Taylor, Minnesota at Seattle, October 22 - TD
AFC: 85 LaDainian Tomlinson, San Diego vs. Kansas City, December 17 - TD

ATTEMPTS
AFC: 416 Larry Johnson, Kansas City
NFC: 346 Steven Jackson, St. Louis

ATTEMPTS, GAME
NFC: 40 Shaun Alexander, Seattle vs. Green Bay, November 27 (201 yards, 0 TD)
AFC: 39 Larry Johnson, Kansas City vs. Seattle, October 29 (155 yards, 3 TD)

YARDS PER ATTEMPT
NFC: 8.4 Michael Vick, Atlanta
AFC: 5.7* Maurice Jones-Drew, Jacksonville

TOUCHDOWNS
AFC: 28 LaDainian Tomlinson, San Diego
NFC: 14 Marion Barber, Dallas

TEAM LEADERS, YARDS
AFC: BALTIMORE, 1132, Jamal Lewis; BUFFALO, 990, Willis McGahee; CINCINNATI, 1309, Rudi Johnson; CLEVELAND, 758, Reuben Droughns; DENVER, 1025, Tatum Bell; HOUSTON, 612, Ron Dayne; INDIANAPOLIS, 1081, *Joseph Addai; JACKSONVILLE, 1146, Fred Taylor; KANSAS CITY, 1789, Larry Johnson; MIAMI, 1008, Ronnie Brown; NEW ENGLAND, 812, Corey Dillon; N.Y. JETS, 650, *Leon Washington, OAKLAND, 659, Justin Fargas; PITTSBURGH, 1494, Willie Parker; SAN DIEGO, 1815, LaDainian Tomlinson; TENNESSEE, 1211, Travis Henry

NFC: ARIZONA, 1159, Edgerrin James; ATLANTA, 1140, Warrick Dunn; CAROLINA, 897, DeShaun Foster; CHICAGO, 1210, Thomas Jones; DALLAS, 1084, Julius Jones; DETROIT, 689, Kevin Jones; GREEN BAY, 1059, Ahman Green; MINNESOTA, 1216, Chester Taylor; NEW ORLEANS, 1057, Deuce McAllister; N.Y. GIANTS, 1662, Tiki Barber; PHILADELPHIA, 1217, Brian Westbrook; ST. LOUIS, 1528, Steven Jackson; SAN FRANCISCO, 1695, Frank Gore; SEATTLE, 896, Shaun Alexander; TAMPA BAY, 798, Cadillac Williams; WASHINGTON, 1154, Ladell Betts

TEAM CHAMPION
NFC: 2939 Atlanta
AFC: 2578 San Diego

*Player that was a rookie in 2006

NFL TOP TEN RUSHERS

	Att	Yards	Avg	Long	TD
Tomlinson, LaDainian, S.D.	348	1815	5.2	85t	28
Johnson, Larry, K.C.	416	1789	4.3	47	17
Gore, Frank, S.F.	312	1695	5.4	72	8
Barber, Tiki, NY-G	327	1662	5.1	55t	5
Jackson, Steven, St.L	346	1528	4.4	59t	13
Parker, Willie, Pit.	337	1494	4.4	76	13
Johnson, Rudi, Cin.	341	1309	3.8	22t	12
Westbrook, Brian, Phi.	240	1217	5.1	71t	7
Taylor, Chester, Min.	303	1216	4.0	95t	6
Henry, Travis, Ten.	270	1211	4.5	70t	7

AFC—INDIVIDUAL RUSHERS

	Att	Yards	Avg	Long	TD
Tomlinson, LaDainian, S.D.	348	1815	5.2	85t	28
Johnson, Larry, K.C.	416	1789	4.3	47	17
Parker, Willie, Pit.	337	1494	4.4	76	13
Johnson, Rudi, Cin.	341	1309	3.8	22t	12
Henry, Travis, Ten.	270	1211	4.5	70t	7
Taylor, Fred, Jac.	231	1146	5.0	76	5
Lewis, Jamal, Bal.	314	1132	3.6	52	9
* Addai, Joseph, Ind.	226	1081	4.8	41	7
Bell, Tatum, Den.	233	1025	4.4	51	2
Brown, Ronnie, Mia.	241	1008	4.2	47	5
McGahee, Willis, Buf.	259	990	3.8	57t	6
* Jones-Drew, Maurice, Jac.	166	941	5.7	74t	13
Dillon, Corey, N.E.	199	812	4.1	50	13
Droughns, Reuben, Cle.	220	758	3.4	22	4
* Maroney, Laurence, N.E.	175	745	4.3	41	6
* Bell, Mike, Den.	157	677	4.3	48	8
Fargas, Justin, Oak.	178	659	3.7	48	1
* Washington, Leon, NYJ	151	650	4.3	23	4
Rhodes, Dominic, Ind.	187	641	3.4	17	5
Dayne, Ron, Hou.	151	612	4.1	19	5
* Young, Vince, Ten.	83	552	6.7	39t	7
Turner, Michael, S.D.	80	502	6.3	73	2
* Lundy, Wali, Hou.	124	476	3.8	35	4
Jordan, LaMont, Oak.	114	434	3.8	59t	2
Morris, Sammy, Mia.	92	400	4.3	55	1
Thomas, Anthony, Buf.	107	378	3.5	19	2
Houston, Cedric, NYJ	113	374	3.3	31	5
Barlow, Kevan, NYJ	131	370	2.8	12	6
Garrard, David, Jac.	47	250	5.3	20	0
* White, LenDale, Ten.	61	244	4.0	26	0
Davenport, Najeh, Pit.	60	221	3.7	48	1
Frye, Charlie, Cle.	47	215	4.6	17	3
Gado, Samkon, G.B.-Hou.	56	210	3.8	34	1
Bennett, Michael, K.C.	36	200	5.6	41	0
Carr, David, Hou.	53	195	3.7	16	2
Wright, Jason, Cle.	62	189	3.0	18	0
Anderson, Mike, Bal.	39	183	4.7	34t	1
Crockett, Zack, Oak.	39	163	4.2	17	0
Brown, Chris, Ten.	41	156	3.8	21	0
Smith, Musa, Bal.	36	153	4.3	30	1
Losman, J.P., Buf.	38	140	3.7	15	1
Neal, Lorenzo, S.D.	29	140	4.8	43	1
Watson, Kenny, Cin.	25	138	5.5	18	1
Brooks, Aaron, Oak.	22	124	5.6	23	0
Faulk, Kevin, N.E.	25	123	4.9	11t	1
* Taylor, Chris, Hou.	28	123	4.4	17	1
Walker, Javon, Den.	9	123	13.7	72t	0
McNair, Steve, Bal.	45	119	2.6	19	1
Evans, Heath, N.E.	27	117	4.3	35	0
Plummer, Jake, Den.	36	112	3.1	19	1
Pennington, Chad, NYJ	35	109	3.1	15	0
* Smith, Brad, NYJ	18	103	5.7	32	0
Brady, Tom, N.E.	49	102	2.1	22	0
Roethlisberger, Ben, Pit.	32	98	3.1	20	2
Chambers, Chris, Mia.	8	95	11.9	39	0

Player	Att	Yards	Avg	Long	TD		Player	Att	Yards	Avg	Long	TD
Pearman, Alvin, Jac.	19	89	4.7	12	1		* Ross, Derrick, K.C.	3	8	2.7	4	0
Sapp, Cecil, Den.	10	80	8.0	28	0		Washington, Nate, Pit.	3	8	2.7	8	0
Haynes, Verron, Pit.	15	78	5.2	13	0		Edwards, Braylon, Cle.	3	7	2.3	8	0
Minor, Travis, Mia.	19	74	3.9	9	0		Lemon, Cleo, Mia.	3	7	2.3	6	0
Lee, ReShard, Oak.	21	72	3.4	13	2		Parker, Samie, K.C.	3	7	2.3	5	0
Nash, Damien, Den.	18	66	3.7	26	0		Houshmandzadeh, T.J., Cin.	3	6	2.0	13	0
* Harrison, Jerome, Cle.	20	60	3.0	15	0		Moulds, Eric, Hou.	1	6	6.0	6	0
Green, Trent, K.C.	19	59	3.1	10	0		Alexis, Rich, Jac.	3	5	1.7	3	0
Perry, Chris, Cin.	10	57	5.7	18	0		Caldwell, Reche, N.E.	1	5	5.0	5	0
Johnson, Jeremi, Cin.	15	56	3.7	15	1		Kreider, Dan, Pit.	1	5	5.0	5	0
Mughelli, Ovie, Bal.	12	50	4.2	12	0		Rosenfels, Sage, Hou.	4	5	1.3	7	0
Rivers, Philip, S.D.	48	49	1.0	15	0		Shepherd, Edell, Hou.	2	5	2.5	6	0
Anderson, Derek, Cle.	4	47	11.8	33	0		Carthon, Ran, Ind.	3	4	1.3	3t	1
Blaylock, Derrick, NYJ	25	44	1.8	6	0		Cassel, Matt, N.E.	2	4	2.0	5	0
Leftwich, Byron, Jac.	25	41	1.6	7	2		Curry, Ronald, Oak.	1	4	4.0	4	0
Palmer, Carson, Cin.	26	37	1.4	11	0		* Page, Jarrad, K.C.	1	4	4.0	4	0
Manning, Peyton, Ind.	23	36	1.6	12	4		Perry, Tab, Cin.	2	4	2.0	2	0
Boller, Kyle, Bal.	22	34	1.5	10	0		Whitted, Alvis, Oak.	1	4	4.0	4	0
Williams, Reggie, Jac.	7	33	4.7	10	0		Givens, David, Ten.	1	3	3.0	3	0
Northcutt, Dennis, Cle.	3	32	10.7	16	0		Jones, Brandon, Ten.	1	3	3.0	3	0
Johnson, Kyle, Den.	5	30	6.0	15	0		Roby, Courtney, Ten.	1	3	3.0	3	0
Walter, Andrew, Oak.	14	30	2.1	12	0		* Scheffler, Tony, Den.	1	3	3.0	3	0
Ward, Hines, Pit.	2	30	15.0	21	0		Walter, Kevin, Hou.	1	3	3.0	3	0
Tuiasosopo, Marques, Oak.	4	29	7.3	11	0		Wimbush, Derrick, Jac.	1	3	3.0	3	0
Dwight, Tim, NYJ	2	28	14.0	28	0		Elam, Jason, Den.	1	2	2.0	2	0
Gray, Quinn, Jac.	2	26	13.0	17t	2		Moorman, Brian, Buf.	2	2	1.0	2	0
Suggs, Lee, Mia.	6	26	4.3	7	0		* Vickers, Lawrence, Cle.	3	2	0.7	2	0
Cotchery, Jerricho, NYJ	5	25	5.0	10	0		Williams, Shaud, Buf.	2	2	1.0	2	0
Pinnock, Andrew, S.D.	4	25	6.3	15	0		Wilson, Quincy, Cin.	2	2	1.0	5	0
Brown, Dee, K.C.	10	24	2.4	7	0		Manumaleuna, Brandon, S.D.	1	1	1.0	1	0
Harrington, Joey, Mia.	19	24	1.3	7	0		Colquitt, Dustin, K.C.	1	0	0.0	0	0
Johnson, Chad, Cin.	6	24	4.0	8	0		Graham, Ben, NYJ	1	0	0.0	0	0
* Jackson, Chad, N.E.	4	22	5.5	14	0		Jones, Donnie, Mia.	1	0	0.0	0	0
Toefield, LaBrandon, Jac.	10	22	2.2	12	0		Nickey, Donnie, Ten.	1	0	0.0	0	0
* Hall, Ahmard, Ten.	7	21	3.0	11	0		Simmons, Jason, Hou.	1	0	0.0	0	0
Pass, Patrick, N.E.	6	21	3.5	6	0		Stanley, Chad, Hou.	1	0	0.0	0	0
Culpepper, Daunte, Mia.	10	20	2.0	7	1		McFadden, Bryant, Pit.	1	-2	-2.0	-2	0
Booker, Marty, Mia.	3	19	6.3	18	0		* Croyle, Brodie, K.C.	3	-3	-1.0	-1	0
Cruz, Ronnie, K.C.	5	19	3.8	7	0		Volek, Billy, S.D.	3	-3	-1.0	-1	0
Parker, Eric, S.D.	2	19	9.5	18	0		Mason, Derrick, Bal.	1	-4	-4.0	-4	0
Brown, Troy, N.E.	2	18	9.0	16	0		Smith, Rod, Den.	1	-5	-5.0	-5	0
Cook, Jameel, Hou.	3	18	6.0	14	0		Scifres, Mike, S.D.	1	-7	-7.0	-7	0
* Cutler, Jay, Den.	12	18	1.5	9	0		Testaverde, Vinny, N.E.	8	-8	-1.0	-1	0
Kuhn, John, Pit.	2	18	9.0	16	0		Royal, Robert, Buf.	1	-9	-9.0	-9	0
Parrish, Roscoe, Buf.	2	18	9.0	11	0		Wright, Anthony, Cin.	4	-12	-3.0	-1	0
Price, Peerless, Buf.	5	18	3.6	9	0		Jones, Matt, Jac.	2	-15	-7.5	-6	0
Jackson, Vincent, S.D.	3	16	5.3	8	0		Clayton, Mark, Bal.	7	-30	-4.3	3	0
Kennison, Eddie, K.C.	4	16	4.0	9	0							
Batch, Charlie, Pit.	13	15	1.2	12	0							
Coles, Laveranues, NYJ	2	14	7.0	15	0							
Johnson, Andre, Hou.	3	14	4.7	18	0							
Smith, Terrelle, Cle.	8	14	1.8	3	0							
Wilson, Cedrick, Pit.	2	14	7.0	14	0							
* Holmes, Santonio, Pit.	1	13	13.0	13	0							
Reed, Josh, Buf.	4	13	3.3	15	0							
Scaife, Bo, Ten.	1	13	13.0	13t	1							
* Whitehurst, Charlie, S.D.	2	13	6.5	14t	1							
* Marshall, Brandon, Den.	2	12	6.0	6	0							
Askew, B.J., NYJ	6	11	1.8	5	0							
Cribbs, Josh, Cle.	2	11	5.5	9	0							
Hall, Dante, K.C.	3	11	3.7	9	0							
* Clemens, Kellen, NYJ	2	10	5.0	8	0							
Cobbs, Cedric, Den.	3	9	3.0	5	0							
Huard, Damon, K.C.	9	9	1.0	8	0							
Jones, Pacman, Ten.	2	8	4.0	7	0							
Kight, Kelvin, N.E.	1	8	8.0	8	0							
McCardell, Keenan, S.D.	1	8	8.0	8	0							
* McNeal, Reggie, Cin.	1	8	8.0	8	0							

t = Touchdown; * Player that was a rookie in 2006
Leader based on most yards gained

NFC—INDIVIDUAL RUSHERS

Player	Att	Yards	Avg	Long	TD
Gore, Frank, S.F.	312	1695	5.4	72	8
Barber, Tiki, NY-G	327	1662	5.1	55t	5
Jackson, Steven, St.L	346	1528	4.4	59t	13
Westbrook, Brian, Phi.	240	1217	5.1	71t	7
Taylor, Chester, Min.	303	1216	4.0	95t	6
Jones, Thomas, Chi.	296	1210	4.1	30t	6
James, Edgerrin, Ariz	337	1159	3.4	18	6
Betts, Ladell, Was.	245	1154	4.7	26	4
Dunn, Warrick, Atl.	286	1140	4.0	90t	4
Jones, Julius, Dal.	267	1084	4.1	77t	4
Green, Ahman, G.B.	266	1059	4.0	70t	5
McAllister, Deuce, N.O.	244	1057	4.3	57	10
Vick, Michael, Atl.	123	1039	8.4	51	2
Foster, DeShaun, Car.	227	897	4.0	43t	3

	Att	Yards	Avg	Long	TD
Alexander, Shaun, Sea.	252	896	3.6	33t	7
Williams, Cadillac, T.B.	225	798	3.5	38	1
Jones, Kevin, Det.	181	689	3.8	52	6
Barber, Marion, Dal.	135	654	4.8	25	14
Benson, Cedric, Chi.	157	647	4.1	30	6
* Norwood, Jerious, Atl.	99	633	6.4	78t	1
Morris, Maurice, Sea.	161	604	3.8	29	0
* Bush, Reggie, N.O.	155	565	3.6	18	6
Portis, Clinton, Was.	127	523	4.1	38t	7
* Williams, DeAngelo, Car.	121	501	4.1	31	1
Morency, Vernand, Hou.-G.B.	96	434	4.5	39	2
Jacobs, Brandon, NY-G	96	423	4.4	16	9
Buckhalter, Correll, Phi.	83	345	4.2	20	2
Pittman, Michael, T.B.	50	245	4.9	32	1
McNabb, Donovan, Phi.	32	212	6.6	37	3
Pinner, Artose, Min.	43	190	4.4	21	3
Davis, Stephen, St.L	40	177	4.4	16	0
Alstott, Mike, T.B.	60	171	2.9	17	3
* Gradkowski, Bruce, T.B.	41	161	3.9	14	0
Harris, Arlen, Det.	49	158	3.2	20	1
Kitna, Jon, Det.	34	156	4.6	18	2
Herron, Noah, G.B.	37	150	4.1	19	1
Strong, Mack, Sea.	33	149	4.5	17	1
Smith, Alex, S.F.	44	147	3.3	22	2
Duckett, T.J., Was.	38	132	3.5	19	2
Moore, Mewelde, Min.	24	131	5.5	15	0
Wallace, Seneca, Sea.	12	122	10.2	37	0
Randle El, Antwaan, Was.	19	118	6.2	20	1
* Robinson, Michael, S.F.	38	116	3.1	33	2
Hasselbeck, Matt, Sea.	18	110	6.1	19	0
Campbell, Jason, Was.	24	107	4.5	15	0
Griffith, Justin, Atl.	19	106	5.6	21t	1
Romo, Tony, Dal.	34	102	3.0	16	0
Fason, Ciatrick, Min.	18	99	5.5	15	1
Cason, Aveion, Det.	24	94	3.9	16	0
Gilmore, Bryan, S.F.	7	94	13.4	22	0
Garcia, Jeff, Phi.	25	87	3.5	12	0
Hicks, Maurice, S.F.	29	82	2.8	9	0
Johnson, Brad, Min.	29	82	2.8	10	1
Moss, Santana, Was.	7	82	11.7	35	0
* Jackson, Tarvaris, Min.	15	77	5.1	13	1
Hoover, Brad, Car.	22	73	3.3	17	1
Moats, Ryan, Phi.	22	69	3.1	13	0
Smith, Steve, Car.	8	61	7.6	24t	1
Graham, Earnest, T.B.	11	59	5.4	17	0
Goings, Nick, Car.	11	52	4.7	28	0
Sellers, Mike, Was.	12	51	4.3	13	0
* Leinart, Matt, Ariz	22	49	2.2	14	2
Bulger, Marc, St.L	18	44	2.4	29	0
Clayton, Michael, T.B.	5	41	8.2	27	0
Peterson, Adrian, Chi.	10	41	4.1	11	2
Shipp, Marcel, Ariz	17	41	2.4	9t	4
Ayanbadejo, Obafemi, Ariz	9	37	4.1	11	0
Brunell, Mark, Was.	13	34	2.6	12	0
Karney, Mike, N.O.	11	33	3.0	8	1
Brees, Drew, N.O.	42	32	0.8	16	0
Branch, Deion, Sea.	4	30	7.5	19	0
Thompson, Tyson, Dal.	13	30	2.3	7t	1
* Branch, Jamaal, N.O.	10	29	2.9	9	0
Favre, Brett, G.B.	23	29	1.3	14	1
* Stovall, Maurice, T.B.	2	29	14.5	18	0
Bledsoe, Drew, Dal.	8	28	3.5	11	2
Boldin, Anquan, Ariz	5	28	5.6	18	0
Battle, Arnaz, S.F.	5	25	5.0	18	0
Brown, Reggie, Phi.	3	24	8.0	15t	1
Shelton, Eric, Car.	8	23	2.9	9	0
Morton, Chad, NY-G	1	22	22.0	22	0
Manning, Eli, NY-G	25	21	0.8	9	0

	Att	Yards	Avg	Long	TD
Schaub, Matt, Atl.	7	21	3.0	19	0
Arrington, J.J., Ariz	14	19	1.4	9	0
* Calhoun, Brian, Det.	7	19	2.7	7	0
Turk, Matt, St.L	2	19	9.5	16	0
Carter, Drew, Car.	2	18	9.0	11	0
Mahe, Reno, Phi.	4	18	4.5	11	0
McKie, Jason, Chi.	8	18	2.3	7	0
Polite, Lousaka, Dal.	7	18	2.6	4	0
Driver, Donald, G.B.	7	16	2.3	16	0
Weinke, Chris, Car.	4	16	4.0	13	0
Cartwright, Rock, Was.	5	15	3.0	9	0
Finn, Jim, NY-G	2	14	7.0	12	0
Henderson, Devery, N.O.	2	14	7.0	11t	1
Looker, Dane, St.L	1	13	13.0	13	0
Delhomme, Jake, Car.	18	12	0.7	12	0
Jennings, Mike, NY-G	2	12	6.0	21	0
McAfee, Fred, N.O.	3	12	4.0	6t	1
Richardson, Tony, Min.	5	12	2.4	3	0
Glenn, Terry, Dal.	3	11	3.7	22	0
Rodgers, Aaron, G.B.	2	11	5.5	6	0
Stecker, Aaron, N.O.	4	11	2.8	4	0
Fisher, Tony, St.L	6	9	1.5	4	0
Galloway, Joey, T.B.	2	9	4.5	7	0
Harris, Kay-Jay, St.L	3	9	3.0	9	0
Kincade, Keylon, Dal.	4	9	2.3	7	0
Tapeh, Thomas, Phi.	5	9	1.8	4	0
Copper, Terrance, N.O.	1	8	8.0	8	0
Johnson, Bethel, Min.	4	8	2.0	5	0
Norris, Moran, S.F.	2	8	4.0	4	0
Weeks, Marquis, Sea.	3	8	2.7	3	0
Simms, Chris, T.B.	4	7	1.8	3	1
Berrian, Bernard, Chi.	2	5	2.5	5	0
* Davis, Vernon, S.F.	2	5	2.5	9	0
* Schable, A.J., Ariz	1	5	5.0	5	0
Taylor, Travis, Min.	1	5	5.0	5	0
Curtis, Kevin, St.L	4	4	1.0	7	0
Drummond, Eddie, Det.	1	4	4.0	4	0
Engram, Bobby, Sea.	1	4	4.0	4	0
Johnson, Keyshawn, Car.	1	4	4.0	4t	1
* Ellis, Devale, Det.	2	3	1.5	12	0
Feeley, A.J., Phi.	1	3	3.0	3	0
Rattay, Tim, T.B.	4	3	0.8	4	0
Warner, Kurt, Ariz	13	3	0.2	9	0
* Basanez, Brett, Car.	1	2	2.0	2	0
Gordon, Lamar, Det.	1	2	2.0	2	0
Grossman, Rex, Chi.	24	2	0.1	22	0
Hedgecock, Madison, St.L	1	2	2.0	2	0
Jackson, Marlion, Atl.	1	2	2.0	2	0
Jenkins, Michael, Atl.	1	2	2.0	2	0
Lorenzen, Jared, NY-G	1	2	2.0	2	0
Williams, Roy, Det.	2	2	1.0	2	0
Bryson, Shawn, Det.	2	1	0.5	1	0
Hakim, Az-Zahir, Det.	1	1	1.0	1	0
Fitzpatrick, Ryan, St.L	3	0	0.0	2	0
Johnson, Dirk, Phi.	1	0	0.0	0	0
McBriar, Mat, Dal.	1	0	0.0	0	0
Toomer, Amani, NY-G	1	0	0.0	0	0
Johnson, Bryant, Ariz	1	-3	-3.0	-3	0
* Jennings, Adam, Atl.	1	-4	-4.0	-4	0
Griese, Brian, Chi.	6	-5	-0.8	9	0
* Martin, Ingle, G.B.	2	-5	-2.5	-2	0
Ryan, Jon, G.B.	1	-11	-11.0	-11	0

t = Touchdown; Leader based on most yards gained
* Player that was a rookie in 2006

AMERICAN FOOTBALL CONFERENCE—RUSHING

	Att	Yards	Avg	Long	TD
San Diego	522	2578	4.9	85t	32
Jacksonville	513	2541	5.0	76	23
Tennessee	469	2214	4.7	70t	15
Denver	488	2152	4.4	72t	12
Kansas City	513	2143	4.2	47	17
Pittsburgh	469	1992	4.2	76	16
New England	499	1969	3.9	50	20
Indianapolis	439	1762	4.0	41	17
N.Y. Jets	491	1738	3.5	32	15
Houston	431	1687	3.9	35	13
Miami	402	1673	4.2	55	7
Baltimore	476	1637	3.4	52	11
Cincinnati	435	1629	3.7	22t	14
Buffalo	420	1552	3.7	57t	9
Oakland	394	1519	3.9	59t	5
Cleveland	372	1335	3.6	33	7
AFC Total	7333	30121	4.1	85t	233
AFC Average	458.3	1882.6	4.1	—	14.6

NATIONAL FOOTBALL CONFERENCE—RUSHING

	Att	Yards	Avg	Long	TD
Atlanta	537	2939	5.5	90t	9
Washington	490	2216	4.5	38t	13
San Francisco	439	2172	4.9	72	12
N.Y. Giants	455	2156	4.7	55t	14
Philadelphia	416	1984	4.8	71t	13
Dallas	472	1936	4.1	77t	21
Seattle	484	1923	4.0	37	8
Chicago	503	1918	3.8	30t	14
Minnesota	442	1820	4.1	95t	12
St. Louis	424	1805	4.3	59t	13
New Orleans	472	1761	3.7	57	19
Green Bay	431	1663	3.9	70t	9
Carolina	423	1659	3.9	43t	7
Tampa Bay	404	1523	3.8	38	6
Arizona	419	1338	3.2	18	12
Detroit	304	1129	3.7	52	9
NFC Total	7115	29942	4.2	95t	191
NFC Average	444.7	1871.4	4.2	—	11.9
League Total	14448	60063	—	95t	424
League Average	451.5	1877.0	4.2	—	13.3

PASSING

HIGHEST RATING
AFC:	101.0	Peyton Manning, Indianapolis
NFC:	96.2	Drew Brees, New Orleans

COMPLETION PERCENTAGE
AFC:	68.3	David Carr, Houston
NFC:	65.3	Tony Romo, Dallas

ATTEMPTS
NFC:	613	Brett Favre, Green Bay
AFC:	557	Peyton Manning, Indianapolis

COMPLETIONS
NFC:	372	Jon Kitna, Detroit
AFC:	362	Peyton Manning, Indianapolis

YARDS
NFC:	4418	Drew Brees, New Orleans
AFC:	4397	Peyton Manning, Indianapolis

YARDS, GAME
NFC:	510	Drew Brees, New Orleans vs. Cincinnati, November 19 (37-52, 2 TD)
AFC:	440	Carson Palmer, Cincinnati vs. San Diego, November 12 (31-42, 3 TD)

LONGEST
NFC:	89	A.J. Feeley (to Hank Baskett*) Philadelphia vs. Atlanta, December 31 - TD
AFC:	87	Charlie Batch (to Heath Miller) Pittsburgh vs. Miami, September 7 - TD
	87	Steve McNair (to Mark Clayton) Baltimore at Kansas City, December 10 - TD

YARDS PER ATTEMPT
NFC:	8.61	Tony Romo, Dallas
AFC:	7.89	Peyton Manning, Indianapolis

TOUCHDOWN PASSES
AFC:	31	Peyton Manning, Indianapolis
NFC:	26	Drew Brees, New Orleans

TOUCHDOWN PASSES, GAME
NFC:	5	Matt Hasselbeck, Seattle vs. N.Y. Giants, September 24 (24-33, 227 yards)
	5	Tony Romo, Dallas vs. Tampa Bay, November 23 (22-29, 306 yards)
	5	Drew Brees, New Orleans at Dallas, December 10 (26-38, 384 yards)
AFC:	4	Carson Palmer, Cincinnati at Pittsburgh, September 24 (18-26, 193 yards)
	4	Peyton Manning, Indianapolis vs. Washington, October 22 (25-35, 342 yards)
	4	Tom Brady, New England at Minnesota, October 30 (29-43, 372 yards)
	4	Tom Brady, New England at Green Bay, November 19 (20-31, 244 yards)
	4	Trent Green, Kansas City at Cleveland, December 3 (24-32, 297 yards) - (OT)
	4	Peyton Manning, Indianapolis vs. Cincinnati, December 18 (29-36, 282 yards)

LOWEST INTERCEPTION PERCENTAGE
NFC:	1.4	Marc Bulger, St. Louis
AFC:	0.4	Damon Huard, Kansas City

TEAM CHAMPION (MOST NET YARDS)
NFC:	4503	New Orleans
AFC:	4308	Indianapolis

NFL TOP TEN PASSERS

	Att	Comp	Pct Comp	Yds	Avg Gain	TD	Pct TD	Long	Int	Pct Int	Sack	Yds Lost	Rating Points
Manning, Peyton, Ind.	557	362	65.0	4397	7.89	31	5.6	68t	9	1.6	14	86	101.0
Huard, Damon, K.C.	244	148	60.7	1878	7.70	11	4.5	78	1	0.4	16	106	98.0
Brees, Drew, N.O.	554	356	64.3	4418	7.97	26	4.7	86t	11	2.0	18	105	96.2
McNabb, Donovan, Phi.	316	180	57.0	2647	8.38	18	5.7	87t	6	1.9	21	140	95.5
Romo, Tony, Dal.	337	220	65.3	2903	8.61	19	5.6	56t	13	3.9	21	124	95.1
Palmer, Carson, Cin.	520	324	62.3	4035	7.76	28	5.4	74t	13	2.5	36	233	93.9
Bulger, Marc, St.L	588	370	62.9	4301	7.31	24	4.1	67t	8	1.4	49	366	92.9
Rivers, Philip, S.D.	460	284	61.7	3388	7.37	22	4.8	57t	9	2.0	27	144	92.0
Brady, Tom, N.E.	516	319	61.8	3529	6.84	24	4.7	62t	12	2.3	26	175	87.9
Brunell, Mark, Was.	260	162	62.3	1789	6.88	8	3.1	74	4	1.5	12	92	86.5

AMERICAN FOOTBALL CONFERENCE—PASSING

	Att	Comp	Pct Comp	Gross Yards	Sacked	Yds Lost	Net Yards	Yds/ Att	Yards/ Comp	TD	Pct TD	Long	Int	Pct Int
Indianapolis	557	362	65.0	4397	15	89	4308	7.89	12.15	31	5.57	68t	9	1.6
Cincinnati	523	327	62.5	4066	36	233	3833	7.77	12.43	28	5.35	74t	13	2.5
Pittsburgh	523	312	59.7	4026	49	293	3733	7.70	12.90	23	4.40	87t	23	4.4
New England	527	326	61.9	3590	29	190	3400	6.81	11.01	25	4.74	62t	12	2.3
Miami	591	342	57.9	3577	41	290	3287	6.05	10.46	16	2.71	52	19	3.2
Baltimore	524	328	62.6	3535	17	100	3435	6.75	10.78	21	4.01	87t	14	2.7
San Diego	466	287	61.6	3412	28	150	3262	7.32	11.89	24	5.15	57t	9	1.9
N.Y. Jets	488	313	64.1	3352	34	199	3153	6.87	10.71	15	3.48	71t	16	3.3
Cleveland	512	318	62.1	3247	54	349	2898	6.34	10.21	15	2.93	75	25	4.9
Kansas City	450	272	60.4	3243	41	243	3000	7.21	11.92	18	4.00	78	12	2.7
Jacksonville	446	266	59.6	3060	30	178	2882	6.86	11.50	17	3.81	51t	14	3.1
Buffalo	431	268	62.2	3051	47	332	2719	7.08	11.38	19	4.41	83t	14	3.2
Houston	481	329	68.4	3032	43	254	2778	6.30	9.22	14	2.91	53	13	2.7
Denver	454	256	56.4	2995	31	196	2799	6.60	11.70	20	4.41	83t	18	4.0
Oakland	483	263	54.5	2850	72	430	2420	5.90	10.84	7	1.45	57	24	5.0
Tennessee	447	226	50.6	2748	29	152	2596	6.15	12.16	13	2.91	53	19	4.3
AFC Total	7903	4795	—	54181	596	3678	50503	—	—	308	—	87t	254	—
AFC Average	493.9	299.7	60.7	3386.3	37.3	229.9	3156.4	6.86	11.30	19.3	3.9	—	15.9	3.2

NATIONAL FOOTBALL CONFERENCE—PASSING

	Att	Comp	Pct Comp	Gross Yards	Sacked	Yds Lost	Net Yards	Yds/ Att	Yards/ Comp	TD	Pct TD	Long	Int	Pct Int
New Orleans	580	372	64.1	4626	23	123	4503	7.98	12.44	27	4.66	86t	13	2.2
St. Louis	592	371	62.7	4328	49	366	3962	7.31	11.67	24	4.05	67t	8	1.4
Philadelphia	544	323	59.4	4309	28	190	4119	7.92	13.34	31	5.70	89t	9	1.7
Detroit	596	372	62.4	4208	63	388	3820	7.06	11.31	21	3.52	60t	22	3.7
Dallas	506	310	61.3	4067	37	231	3836	8.04	13.12	26	5.14	56t	21	4.2
Green Bay	630	350	55.6	3947	24	152	3795	6.27	11.28	18	2.86	82t	18	2.9
Arizona	545	322	59.1	3924	35	262	3662	7.20	12.19	17	3.12	64	17	3.1
Carolina	539	325	60.3	3486	32	222	3264	6.47	10.73	19	3.53	72t	17	3.2
Chicago	514	282	54.9	3446	25	165	3281	6.70	12.22	24	4.67	75t	22	4.3
Minnesota	540	332	61.5	3402	43	279	3123	6.30	10.25	13	2.41	50	20	3.7
Seattle	512	292	57.0	3369	49	315	3054	6.58	11.54	26	5.08	72t	22	4.3
N.Y. Giants	523	301	57.6	3244	25	186	3058	6.20	10.78	24	4.59	55t	18	3.4
Washington	470	274	58.3	3174	19	147	3027	6.75	11.58	19	4.04	74	10	2.1
Tampa Bay	535	296	55.3	2994	33	196	2798	5.60	10.11	14	2.62	64t	18	3.4
San Francisco	444	257	57.9	2890	35	202	2688	6.51	11.25	16	3.60	75	16	3.6
Atlanta	416	222	53.4	2682	47	311	2371	6.45	12.08	21	5.05	55	15	3.6
NFC Total	8486	5001	—	58096	567	3735	54361	—	—	340	—	89t	266	—
NFC Average	530.4	312.6	58.9	3631.0	35.4	233.4	3397.6	6.85	11.62	21.3	4.0	—	16.6	3.1
League Total	16389	9796	—	112277	1163	7413	104864	—	—	648	—	89t	520	—
League Average	512.2	306.1	59.8	3508.7	36.3	231.7	3277.0	6.85	11.46	20.3	4.0	—	16.3	3.2

AFC—INDIVIDUAL PASSERS

	Att	Comp	Pct Comp	Yds	Avg Gain	TD	Pct TD	Long	Int	Pct Int	Sack	Yds Lost	Rating Points
Manning, Peyton, Ind.	557	362	65.0	4397	7.89	31	5.6	68t	9	1.6	14	86	101.0
Huard, Damon, K.C.	244	148	60.7	1878	7.70	11	4.5	78	1	0.4	16	106	98.0
Palmer, Carson, Cin.	520	324	62.3	4035	7.76	28	5.4	74t	13	2.5	36	233	93.9
Rivers, Philip, S.D.	460	284	61.7	3388	7.37	22	4.8	57t	9	2.0	27	144	92.0
Brady, Tom, N.E.	516	319	61.8	3529	6.84	24	4.7	62t	12	2.3	26	175	87.9
Losman, J.P., Buf.	429	268	62.5	3051	7.11	19	4.4	83t	14	3.3	47	332	84.9
Pennington, Chad, NYJ	485	313	64.5	3352	6.91	17	3.5	71t	16	3.3	30	172	82.6
McNair, Steve, Bal.	468	295	63.0	3050	6.52	16	3.4	87t	12	2.6	14	84	82.5
Carr, David, Hou.	442	302	68.3	2767	6.26	11	2.5	53	12	2.7	41	240	82.1
Garrard, David, Jac.	241	145	60.2	1735	7.20	10	4.1	49	9	3.7	20	119	80.5
Roethlisberger, Ben, Pit.	469	280	59.7	3513	7.49	18	3.8	67t	23	4.9	46	280	75.4
Frye, Charlie, Cle.	393	252	64.1	2454	6.24	10	2.5	75	17	4.3	44	262	72.0
Plummer, Jake, Den.	317	175	55.2	1994	6.29	11	3.5	83t	13	4.1	18	111	68.8
Harrington, Joey, Mia.	388	223	57.5	2236	5.76	12	3.1	48	15	3.9	15	116	68.2
* Young, Vince, Ten.	357	184	51.5	2199	6.16	12	3.4	53	13	3.6	25	129	66.7
Walter, Andrew, Oak.	276	147	53.3	1677	6.08	3	1.1	51	13	4.7	46	256	55.8
(Nonqualifiers)													
Batch, Charlie, Pit.	53	31	58.5	492	9.28	5	9.4	87t	0	0.0	3	13	121.0
Boller, Kyle, Bal.	55	33	60.0	485	8.82	5	9.1	77t	2	3.6	3	16	104.0
Rosenfels, Sage, Hou.	39	27	69.2	265	6.79	3	7.7	28	1	2.6	1	5	103.0
* Cutler, Jay, Den.	137	81	59.1	1001	7.31	9	6.6	71t	5	3.6	13	85	88.5
Gray, Quinn, Jac.	22	13	59.1	166	7.55	0	0.0	32	0	0.0	1	11	82.8
Leftwich, Byron, Jac.	183	108	59.0	1159	6.33	7	3.8	51t	5	2.7	9	48	79.0
Lemon, Cleo, Mia.	68	38	55.9	412	6.06	2	2.9	38	1	1.5	5	24	77.6
Culpepper, Daunte, Mia.	134	81	60.4	929	6.93	2	1.5	52	3	2.2	21	150	77.0
Green, Trent, K.C.	198	121	61.1	1342	6.78	7	3.5	39	9	4.5	24	127	74.1
Anderson, Derek, Cle.	117	66	56.4	793	6.78	5	4.3	54	8	6.8	8	66	63.1
Brooks, Aaron, Oak.	192	110	57.3	1105	5.76	3	1.6	57	8	4.2	26	174	61.7
Tuiasosopo, Marques, Oak.	13	6	46.2	68	5.23	1	7.7	29	2	15.4	0	0	48.4
Collins, Kerry, Ten.	90	42	46.7	549	6.10	1	1.1	36	6	6.7	4	23	42.3
(Fewer than 10 attempts)													
* Addai, Joseph, Ind.	0	0	—	0	—	0	—	—	0	—	1	3	—
Brown, Ronnie, Mia.	1	0	0.0	0	0.00	0	0.0	0	0	0.0	0	0	39.6
Cassel, Matt, N.E.	8	5	62.5	32	4.00	0	0.0	10	0	0.0	3	15	70.8
Clayton, Mark, Bal.	1	0	0.0	0	0.00	0	0.0	0	0	0.0	0	0	39.6
* Clemens, Kellen, NYJ	1	0	0.0	0	0.00	0	0.0	0	0	0.0	4	27	39.6
Cribbs, Josh, Cle.	1	0	0.0	0	0.00	0	0.0	0	0	0.0	0	0	39.6
* Croyle, Brodie, K.C.	7	3	42.9	23	3.29	0	0.0	11	2	28.6	1	10	11.9
Curry, Ronald, Oak.	2	0	0.0	0	0.00	0	0.0	0	1	50.0	0	0	0.0
Dorsey, Ken, Cle.	1	0	0.0	0	0.00	0	0.0	0	0	0.0	1	7	39.6
Evans, Lee, Buf.	1	0	0.0	0	0.00	0	0.0	0	0	0.0	0	0	39.6
Graham, Ben, NYJ	1	0	0.0	0	0.00	0	0.0	0	0	0.0	0	0	39.6
Johnson, Larry, K.C.	1	0	0.0	0	0.00	0	0.0	0	0	0.0	0	0	39.6
* Lundy, Wali, Hou.	0	0	—	0	—	0	—	—	0	—	1	9	—
Moorman, Brian, Buf.	1	0	0.0	0	0.00	0	0.0	0	0	0.0	0	0	39.6
Ramsey, Patrick, NYJ	1	0	0.0	0	0.00	0	0.0	0	0	0.0	0	0	39.6
Scifres, Mike, S.D.	1	0	0.0	0	0.00	0	0.0	0	0	0.0	0	0	39.6
Testaverde, Vinny, N.E.	3	2	66.7	29	9.67	1	33.3	23	0	0.0	0	0	137.5
Tomlinson, LaDainian, S.D.	3	2	66.7	20	6.67	2	66.7	19t	0	0.0	0	0	125.0
Volek, Billy, S.D.	2	1	50.0	4	2.00	0	0.0	4	0	0.0	1	6	56.3
Wilson, Cedrick, Pit.	1	1	100.0	21	21.00	0	0.0	21	0	0.0	0	0	118.8
Winslow, Kellen, Cle.	0	0	—	0	—	0	—	—	0	—	1	14	—
Wright, Anthony, Cin.	3	3	100.0	31	10.33	0	0.0	22	0	0.0	0	0	109.7

t = Touchdown; *Player that was a rookie in 2006
Leader based on rating points, minimum 224 attempts

NFC—INDIVIDUAL PASSERS

	Att	Comp	Pct Comp	Yds	Avg Gain	TD	Pct TD	Long	Int	Pct Int	Sack	Yds Lost	Rating Points
Brees, Drew, N.O.	554	356	64.3	4418	7.97	26	4.7	86t	11	2.0	18	105	96.2
McNabb, Donovan, Phi.	316	180	57.0	2647	8.38	18	5.7	87t	6	1.9	21	140	95.5
Romo, Tony, Dal.	337	220	65.3	2903	8.61	19	5.6	56t	13	3.9	21	124	95.1
Bulger, Marc, St.L	588	370	62.9	4301	7.31	24	4.1	67t	8	1.4	49	366	92.9
Brunell, Mark, Was.	260	162	62.3	1789	6.88	8	3.1	74	4	1.5	12	92	86.5
Delhomme, Jake, Car.	431	263	61.0	2805	6.51	17	3.9	72t	11	2.6	22	167	82.6
Kitna, Jon, Det.	596	372	62.4	4208	7.06	21	3.5	60t	22	3.7	63	388	79.9
Manning, Eli, NY-G	522	301	57.7	3244	6.21	24	4.6	55t	18	3.4	25	186	77.0
Hasselbeck, Matt, Sea.	371	210	56.6	2442	6.58	18	4.9	72t	15	4.0	34	229	76.0
Vick, Michael, Atl.	388	204	52.6	2474	6.38	20	5.2	55	13	3.4	45	303	75.7
Smith, Alex, S.F.	442	257	58.1	2890	6.54	16	3.6	75	16	3.6	35	202	74.8
* Leinart, Matt, Ariz	377	214	56.8	2547	6.76	11	2.9	58	12	3.2	21	158	74.0
Grossman, Rex, Chi.	480	262	54.6	3193	6.65	23	4.8	62	20	4.2	21	142	73.9
Favre, Brett, G.B.	613	343	56.0	3885	6.34	18	2.9	82t	18	2.9	21	134	72.7
Johnson, Brad, Min.	439	270	61.5	2750	6.26	9	2.1	46	15	3.4	29	200	72.0
* Gradkowski, Bruce, T.B.	328	177	54.0	1661	5.06	9	2.7	53	9	2.7	25	146	65.9
(Nonqualifiers)													
Feeley, A.J., Phi.	38	26	68.4	342	9.00	3	7.9	89t	0	0.0	1	10	122.9
Garcia, Jeff, Phi.	188	116	61.7	1309	6.96	10	5.3	65	2	1.1	6	40	95.8
Martin, Jamie, N.O.	24	16	66.7	208	8.67	1	4.2	65	1	4.2	5	18	90.3
Warner, Kurt, Ariz	168	108	64.3	1377	8.20	6	3.6	64	5	3.0	14	104	89.3
Rattay, Tim, T.B.	101	61	60.4	748	7.41	4	4.0	64t	2	2.0	4	18	88.2
Campbell, Jason, Was.	207	110	53.1	1297	6.27	10	4.8	66t	6	2.9	7	55	76.5
Wallace, Seneca, Sea.	141	82	58.2	927	6.57	8	5.7	49t	7	5.0	14	83	76.2
Bollinger, Brooks, Min.	18	13	72.2	146	8.11	0	0.0	50	1	5.6	6	42	72.9
Schaub, Matt, Atl.	27	18	66.7	208	7.70	1	3.7	47	2	7.4	2	8	71.2
Bledsoe, Drew, Dal.	169	90	53.3	1164	6.89	7	4.1	51	8	4.7	16	107	69.2
Weinke, Chris, Car.	96	56	58.3	625	6.51	2	2.1	38	4	4.2	10	55	67.4
* Jackson, Tarvaris, Min.	81	47	58.0	475	5.86	2	2.5	50	4	4.9	8	37	62.5
Griese, Brian, Chi.	32	18	56.3	220	6.88	1	3.1	75t	2	6.3	3	22	62.0
Rodgers, Aaron, G.B.	15	6	40.0	46	3.07	0	0.0	16	0	0.0	3	18	48.2
Simms, Chris, T.B.	106	58	54.7	585	5.52	1	0.9	55	7	6.6	4	32	46.3
* Basanez, Brett, Car.	11	6	54.5	56	5.09	0	0.0	18	1	9.1	0	0	30.9
(Fewer than 10 attempts)													
Akers, David, Phi.	1	1	100.0	11	11.00	0	0.0	11	0	0.0	0	0	112.5
* Baskett, Hank, Phi.	1	0	0.0	0	0.0	0	0.0	0	1	100.0	0	0	0.0
Battle, Arnaz, S.F.	1	0	0.0	0	0.00	0	0.0	0	0	0.0	0	0	39.6
Branch, Deion, Sea.	0	0	—	0	—	0	—	—	0	—	1	3	—
Bruce, Isaac, St.L	1	0	0.0	0	0.00	0	0.0	0	0	0.0	0	0	39.6
* Bush, Reggie, N.O.	1	0	0.0	0	0.00	0	0.0	0	1	100.0	0	0	0.0
Feagles, Jeff, NY-G	1	0	0.0	0	0.00	0	0.0	0	0	0.0	0	0	39.6
Frerotte, Gus, St.L	3	1	33.3	27	9.00	0	0.0	27	0	0.0	0	0	67.4
Holiday, Carlyle, G.B.	1	0	0.0	0	0.00	0	0.0	0	0	0.0	0	0	39.6
Horn, Joe, N.O.	1	0	0.0	0	0.00	0	0.0	0	0	0.0	0	0	39.6
Johnson, Keyshawn, Car.	1	0	0.0	0	0.00	0	0.0	0	1	100.0	0	0	0.0
Jones, Thomas, Chi.	1	1	100.0	-4	-4.00	0	0.0	-4	0	0.0	1	1	79.2
Longwell, Ryan, Min.	1	1	100.0	16	16.00	1	100.0	16t	0	0.0	0	0	158.3
Maynard, Brad, Chi.	1	1	100.0	37	37.00	0	0.0	37	0	0.0	0	0	118.8
Moore, Mewelde, Min.	1	1	100.0	15	15.00	1	100.0	15t	0	0.0	0	0	158.3
* Norwood, Jerious, Atl.	1	0	0.0	0	0.00	0	0.0	0	0	0.0	0	0	39.6
Randle El, Antwaan, Was.	3	2	66.7	88	29.33	1	33.3	48t	0	0.0	0	0	149.3
* Robinson, Michael, S.F.	1	0	0.0	0	0.00	0	0.0	0	0	0.0	0	0	39.6
Ryan, Jon, G.B.	1	1	100.0	16	16.00	0	0.0	16	0	0.0	0	0	118.8

*t = Touchdown; * Player that was a rookie in 2006*
Leader based on rating points, minimum 224 attempts

PASS RECEIVING

RECEPTIONS
AFC: 103   Andre Johnson, Houston
NFC: 98   Mike Furrey, Detroit

RECEPTIONS, GAME
NFC: 13   Steven Jackson, St. Louis vs. Kansas City, November 5 (133 yards, 0 TD)
AFC: 12   Laveranues Coles, N.Y. Jets at Minnesota, December 17 (144 yards, 1 TD)

YARDS
AFC: 1369   Chad Johnson, Cincinnati
NFC: 1310   Roy Williams, Detroit

YARDS, GAME
AFC: 265   Lee Evans, Buffalo at Houston, November 19 (11 receptions, 2 TD)
NFC: 191   Donald Driver, Green Bay at Minnesota, November 12 (6 receptions, 1 TD)

LONGEST
NFC: 89   * Hank Baskett (from A.J. Feeley), Philadelphia vs. Atlanta, December 31 - TD
AFC: 87   Heath Miller (from Charlie Batch), Pittsburgh vs. Miami, September 7 - TD
     87   Mark Clayton (from Steve McNair), Baltimore at Kansas City, December 10 - TD

YARDS PER RECEPTION
NFC: 23.3   Devery Henderson, New Orleans
AFC: 17.8   Nate Washington, Pittsburgh

TOUCHDOWNS
NFC: 13   Terrell Owens, Dallas
AFC: 12   Marvin Harrison, Indianapolis

TEAM LEADERS, RECEPTIONS
AFC: BALTIMORE, 73, Todd Heap; BUFFALO, 82, Lee Evans; CINCINNATI, 90, T.J. Houshmandzadeh; CLEVELAND, 89, Kellen Winslow; DENVER, 69, Javon Walker; HOUSTON, 103, Andre Johnson; INDIANAPOLIS, 95, Marvin Harrison; JACKSONVILLE, 52, Reggie Williams; KANSAS CITY, 73, Tony Gonzalez; MIAMI, 67, Wes Welker; NEW ENGLAND, 61, Reche Caldwell; N.Y. JETS, 91, Laveranues Coles; OAKLAND, 62, Ronald Curry; PITTSBURGH, 74, Hines Ward; SAN DIEGO, 71, Antonio Gates; TENNESSEE, 46, Drew Bennett

NFC: ARIZONA, 83, Anquan Boldin; ATLANTA, 56, Alge Crumpler; CAROLINA, 83, Steve Smith; CHICAGO, 60, Muhsin Muhammad; DALLAS, 85, Terrell Owens; DETROIT, 98, Mike Furrey; GREEN BAY, 92, Donald Driver; MINNESOTA, 57, Travis Taylor; NEW ORLEANS, 88, Reggie Bush*; N.Y. GIANTS, 66, Jeremy Shockey; PHILADELPHIA, 77, Brian Westbrook; ST. LOUIS, 93, Torry Holt; SAN FRANCISCO, 61, Frank Gore; SEATTLE, 63, Darrell Jackson; TAMPA BAY, 62, Joey Galloway; WASHINGTON, 57, Chris Cooley

Player that was a rookie in 2006

NFL TOP TEN PASS RECEIVERS

	No	Yards	Avg	Long	TD
Johnson, Andre, Hou.	103	1147	11.1	53	5
Furrey, Mike, Det.	98	1086	11.1	31	6
Harrison, Marvin, Ind.	95	1366	14.4	68t	12
Holt, Torry, St.L	93	1188	12.8	67t	10
Driver, Donald, G.B.	92	1295	14.1	82t	8
Coles, Laveranues, NYJ	91	1098	12.1	58t	6
Houshmandzadeh, T.J., Cin.	90	1081	12.0	40t	9
Jackson, Steven, St.L	90	806	9.0	64t	3
Winslow, Kellen, Cle.	89	875	9.8	40	3
* Bush, Reggie, N.O.	88	742	8.4	74	2

NFL TOP TEN RECEIVERS BY YARDS

	Yards	No	Avg	Long	TD
Johnson, Chad, Cin.	1369	87	15.7	74t	7
Harrison, Marvin, Ind.	1366	95	14.4	68t	12
Wayne, Reggie, Ind.	1310	86	15.2	51t	9
Williams, Roy, Det.	1310	82	16.0	60t	7
Driver, Donald, G.B.	1295	92	14.1	82t	8
Evans, Lee, Buf.	1292	82	15.8	83t	8
Boldin, Anquan, Ariz	1203	83	14.5	64	4
Holt, Torry, St.L	1188	93	12.8	67t	10
Owens, Terrell, Dal.	1180	85	13.9	56t	13
Smith, Steve, Car.	1166	83	14.0	72t	8

AFC—INDIVIDUAL RECEIVERS

	No	Yards	Avg	Long	TD
Johnson, Andre, Hou.	103	1147	11.1	53	5
Harrison, Marvin, Ind.	95	1366	14.4	68t	12
Coles, Laveranues, NYJ	91	1098	12.1	58t	6
Houshmandzadeh, T.J., Cin.	90	1081	12.0	40t	9
Winslow, Kellen, Cle.	89	875	9.8	40	3
Johnson, Chad, Cin.	87	1369	15.7	74t	7
Wayne, Reggie, Ind.	86	1310	15.2	51t	9
Evans, Lee, Buf.	82	1292	15.8	83t	8
Cotchery, Jerricho, NYJ	82	961	11.7	71t	6
Ward, Hines, Pit.	74	975	13.2	70t	6
Gonzalez, Tony, K.C.	73	900	12.3	57	5
Heap, Todd, Bal.	73	765	10.5	30	6
Gates, Antonio, S.D.	71	924	13.0	57t	9
Walker, Javon, Den.	69	1084	15.7	83t	8
Mason, Derrick, Bal.	68	750	11.0	38	2
Clayton, Mark, Bal.	67	939	14.0	87t	5
Welker, Wes, Mia.	67	687	10.3	38	1
Curry, Ronald, Oak.	62	727	11.7	39	1
McMichael, Randy, Mia.	62	640	10.3	24	3
Edwards, Braylon, Cle.	61	884	14.5	75	6
Caldwell, Reche, N.E.	61	760	12.5	62t	4
Chambers, Chris, Mia.	59	677	11.5	46	4
Moulds, Eric, Hou.	57	557	9.8	29	1
Tomlinson, LaDainian, S.D.	56	508	9.1	51t	3
Booker, Marty, Mia.	55	747	13.6	52	6
Kennison, Eddie, K.C.	53	860	16.2	51	5
Williams, Reggie, Jac.	52	616	11.8	48	4
Smith, Rod, Den.	52	512	9.8	20	3
* Holmes, Santonio, Pit.	49	824	16.8	67t	2
Watson, Benjamin, N.E.	49	643	13.1	40	3
Price, Peerless, Buf.	49	402	8.2	25	3
Parker, Eric, S.D.	48	659	13.7	38	0
Bennett, Drew, Ten.	46	737	16.0	39	3
* Jones-Drew, Maurice, Jac.	46	436	9.5	51t	2
Brown, Troy, N.E.	43	384	8.9	23	4
Faulk, Kevin, N.E.	43	356	8.3	43t	2
Moss, Randy, Oak.	42	553	13.2	51	3
Jones, Matt, Jac.	41	643	15.7	49	4
Parker, Samie, K.C.	41	561	13.7	43	1
Johnson, Larry, K.C.	41	410	10.0	78	2
Jurevicius, Joe, Cle.	40	495	12.4	52	3
* Addai, Joseph, Ind.	40	325	8.1	21t	1

Player	No	Yards	Avg	Long	TD
Wrighster, George, Jac.	39	353	9.1	23	3
Wilson, Cedrick, Pit.	37	504	13.6	38t	1
Utecht, Ben, Ind.	37	377	10.2	26	0
Henry, Chris, Cin.	36	605	16.8	71	9
Wilford, Ernest, Jac.	36	524	14.6	41	2
McCardell, Keenan, S.D.	36	437	12.1	28	0
Rhodes, Dominic, Ind.	36	251	7.0	27	0
Heiden, Steve, Cle.	36	249	6.9	13	2
Washington, Nate, Pit.	35	624	17.8	49t	4
Reed, Josh, Buf.	34	410	12.1	52	2
Miller, Heath, Pit.	34	393	11.6	87t	5
* Daniels, Owen, Hou.	34	352	10.4	33t	5
Wade, Bobby, Ten.	33	461	14.0	25	2
Brown, Ronnie, Mia.	33	276	8.4	24	0
* Lundy, Wali, Hou.	33	204	6.2	15	0
Baker, Chris, NYJ	31	300	9.7	28	4
Parker, Willie, Pit.	31	222	7.2	25t	3
Gabriel, Doug, N.E.-Oak.	30	428	14.3	45	3
Clark, Dallas, Ind.	30	367	12.2	40	4
Scaife, Bo, Ten.	29	370	12.8	34	2
Williams, Randal, Oak.	28	293	10.5	28	0
Jackson, Vincent, S.D.	27	453	16.8	55	6
Jones, Brandon, Ten.	27	384	14.2	53	4
Whitted, Alvis, Oak.	27	299	11.1	33	0
Droughns, Reuben, Cle.	27	169	6.3	24	0
Hall, Dante, K.C.	26	204	7.8	19	2
Anderson, Courtney, Oak.	25	285	11.4	35	2
* Washington, Leon, NYJ	25	270	10.8	64	0
Bell, Tatum, Den.	24	115	4.8	16	0
McCareins, Justin, NYJ	23	347	15.1	50	1
Parrish, Roscoe, Buf.	23	320	13.9	51t	2
Taylor, Fred, Jac.	23	242	10.5	36	1
Royal, Robert, Buf.	23	233	10.1	33t	3
Watson, Kenny, Cin.	23	213	9.3	46	0
Johnson, Rudi, Cin.	23	124	5.4	18	0
* Williams, Demetrius, Bal.	22	396	18.0	77t	2
Northcutt, Dennis, Cle.	22	228	10.4	43	0
* Maroney, Laurence, N.E.	22	194	8.8	31	1
Thomas, Anthony, Buf.	22	139	6.3	18	0
Smith, Musa, Bal.	22	135	6.1	30	0
Kelly, Reggie, Cin.	21	254	12.1	32	1
Graham, Daniel, N.E.	21	235	11.2	29	2
* Hagan, Derek, Mia.	21	221	10.5	24	1
Mughelli, Ovie, Bal.	21	182	8.7	30t	2
Morris, Sammy, Mia.	21	162	7.7	44	0
* Marshall, Brandon, Den.	20	309	15.5	71t	2
Wilcox, Daniel, Bal.	20	166	8.3	35	3
* Bell, Mike, Den.	20	158	7.9	24	0
Lee, ReShard, Oak.	20	138	6.9	15	0
* Scheffler, Tony, Den.	18	286	15.9	29	4
Fletcher, Bryan, Ind.	18	202	11.2	26	2
Alexander, Stephen, Den.	18	160	8.9	24	2
McGahee, Willis, Buf.	18	156	8.7	56	0
Lewis, Jamal, Bal.	18	115	6.4	15	0
Cook, Jameel, Hou.	18	107	5.9	15	0
Haynes, Verron, Pit.	18	95	5.3	16	0
Henry, Travis, Ten.	18	78	4.3	12	0
Walter, Kevin, Hou.	17	160	9.4	15	0
Gado, Samkon, G.B.-Hou.	17	85	5.0	19	0
Neal, Lorenzo, S.D.	17	83	4.9	21	0
Peelle, Justin, Mia.	16	116	7.3	25	1
Dwight, Tim, NYJ	16	112	7.0	15	0
Floyd, Malcom, S.D.	15	210	14.0	46t	3
Davenport, Najeh, Pit.	15	193	12.9	32	1
Dillon, Corey, N.E.	15	147	9.8	52	0
* Hall, Ahmard, Ten.	15	138	9.2	28	0
Wilson, Kris, K.C.	15	132	8.8	19	3
Stewart, Tony, Cin.	14	120	8.6	26	1
Manumaleuna, Brandon, S.D.	14	91	6.5	19	3
Dayne, Ron, Hou.	14	77	5.5	13	0
* White, LenDale, Ten.	14	60	4.3	13	0
* Jackson, Chad, N.E.	13	152	11.7	35t	3
Troupe, Ben, Ten.	13	150	11.5	32	2
* Lewis, Marcedes, Jac.	13	126	9.7	31	1
Putzier, Jeb, Hou.	13	125	9.6	26	0
Fargas, Justin, Oak.	13	91	7.0	21	0
* Thomas, David, N.E.	11	159	14.5	36	1
* Madsen, John, Oak.	11	146	13.3	57	1
Gaffney, Jabar, N.E.	11	142	12.9	33	1
Cribbs, Josh, Cle.	10	91	9.1	14	0
Jordan, LaMont, Oak.	10	74	7.4	21	0
Crockett, Zack, Oak.	10	53	5.3	14	0
Kircus, David, Den.	9	187	20.8	45	0
Washington, Kelley, Cin.	9	115	12.8	22t	1
Bennett, Michael, K.C.	9	77	8.6	14	0
Bruener, Mark, Hou.	9	62	6.9	25	2
* Smith, Brad, NYJ	9	61	6.8	19	0
Anderson, Mike, Bal.	9	54	6.0	13	0
Askew, B.J., NYJ	9	50	5.6	12	0
* Harrison, Jerome, Cle.	9	47	5.2	12	0
Perry, Chris, Cin.	9	42	4.7	12	0
Williams, Roydell, Ten.	8	121	15.1	20	0
Givens, David, Ten.	8	104	13.0	27	0
Stokley, Brandon, Ind.	8	85	10.6	23	1
Moorehead, Aaron, Ind.	8	82	10.3	36	1
Kreider, Dan, Pit.	8	62	7.8	15	0
Sapp, Cecil, Den.	8	34	4.3	9	0
Smith, Terrelle, Cle.	8	21	2.6	7	0
Tuman, Jerame, Pit.	7	73	10.4	21	1
Morant, Johnnie, Oak.	7	70	10.0	18	0
Houston, Cedric, NYJ	7	43	6.1	11	0
Johnson, Kyle, Den.	7	37	5.3	20	1
Shelton, Daimon, Buf.	7	35	5.0	14	0
Evans, Heath, N.E.	7	34	4.9	11	1
Barlow, Kevan, NYJ	7	21	3.0	8	0
Wright, Jason, Cle.	6	82	13.7	54	0
Hartsock, Ben, Ten.	6	68	11.3	23	0
Leach, Vonta, Hou.	6	61	10.2	19	1
* Vickers, Lawrence, Cle.	6	60	10.0	29	0
Cieslak, Brad, Buf.	6	46	7.7	13	0
Ryan, Sean, NYJ	6	44	7.3	10	0
Johnson, Jeremi, Cin.	6	37	6.2	17	0
Perry, Tab, Cin.	5	81	16.2	30	0
Jackson, Nate, Den.	5	49	9.8	24	0
Hankton, Cortez, Jac.	5	48	9.6	15	0
Brady, Kyle, Jac.	5	37	7.4	13	0
Blaylock, Derrick, NYJ	5	29	5.8	9	0
Nash, Damien, Den.	4	41	10.3	13	0
Dunn, Jason, K.C.	4	40	10.0	15	0
Wimbush, Derrick, Jac.	4	23	5.8	9	0
Green, Justin, Bal.	4	17	4.3	12	0
Turner, Michael, S.D.	3	47	15.7	30	0
* Taylor, Chris, Hou.	3	40	13.3	24	0
Proehl, Ricky, Ind.	3	30	10.0	13	0
* Webb, Jeff, K.C.	3	23	7.7	11	0
Barnes, Darian, Mia.	3	22	7.3	13	0
Chatman, Antonio, Cin.	3	22	7.3	10	0
Shepherd, Edell, Hou.	3	22	7.3	8	0
Minor, Travis, Mia.	3	2	0.7	4	0
* Wilson, Travis, Cle.	2	32	16.0	16	0
Jones, Pacman, Ten.	2	31	15.5	17	0
Morey, Sean, Pit.	2	29	14.5	15	0
Roby, Courtney, Ten.	2	28	14.0	21	0
Pass, Patrick, N.E.	2	24	12.0	16	0
Mustard, Chad, Den.	2	23	11.5	14	0
Cruz, Ronnie, K.C.	2	20	10.0	11	0

	No	Yards	Avg	Long	TD		No	Yards	Avg	Long	TD
Gardner, Rod, K.C.	2	17	8.5	13	0	Brown, Reggie, Phi.	46	816	17.7	60t	8
* Sypniewski, Quinn, Bal.	2	15	7.5	9	0	Moore, Mewelde, Min.	46	468	10.2	50	1
Dinkins, Darnell, Cle.	2	14	7.0	11	1	Wiggins, Jermaine, Min.	46	386	8.4	24	1
Russell, Cliff, Mia.	2	14	7.0	9	0	Green, Ahman, G.B.	46	373	8.1	20	1
Davis, Andre, Buf.	2	13	6.5	8	0	* Jennings, Greg, G.B.	45	632	14.0	75t	3
Pearman, Alvin, Jac.	2	12	6.0	7	0	Clark, Desmond, Chi.	45	626	13.9	33	6
Hodgins, James, NYJ	2	9	4.5	6	0	Hackett, D.J., Sea.	45	610	13.6	47	4
Cramer, Casey, Ten.	2	8	4.0	6	0	Taylor, Chester, Min.	42	288	6.9	24	0
Childress, Brandon, N.E.	2	7	3.5	5	0	Johnson, Bryant, Ariz	40	740	18.5	58	4
Brown, Chris, Ten.	2	4	2.0	4	0	Bryant, Antonio, S.F.	40	733	18.3	72t	3
Moore, Clarence, Bal.	2	1	0.5	4t	1	Curtis, Kevin, St.L	40	479	12.0	42	4
Huard, Damon, K.C.	2	-6	-3.0	-2	0	Jenkins, Michael, Atl.	39	436	11.2	34t	7
* Anderson, David, Hou.	1	27	27.0	27	0	Stallworth, Donte', Phi.	38	725	19.1	84t	5
Porter, Jerry, Oak.	1	19	19.0	19	0	James, Edgerrin, Ariz	38	217	5.7	14	0
Young, Walter, Pit.	1	17	17.0	17	0	Horn, Joe, N.O.	37	679	18.4	72t	4
Kuhn, John, Pit.	1	15	15.0	15	0	Williamson, Troy, Min.	37	455	12.3	46	0
Adkisson, James, Oak.	1	9	9.0	9	0	Crayton, Patrick, Dal.	36	516	14.3	53t	4
* Buchanon, Will, Oak.	1	9	9.0	9	0	Jones, Thomas, Chi.	36	154	4.3	21	0
Kight, Kelvin, N.E.	1	9	9.0	9	0	Smith, Alex, T.B.	35	250	7.1	27	3
* Wallace, Cooper, Ten.	1	6	6.0	6	0	Hilliard, Ike, T.B.	34	339	10.0	44t	4
Brown, Dee, K.C.	1	5	5.0	5	0	Johnson, Eric, S.F.	34	292	8.6	26	2
Lewis, Derrick, Hou.	1	5	5.0	5	0	Clayton, Michael, T.B.	33	356	10.8	27	1
Neufeld, Ryan, Buf.	1	4	4.0	4t	1	* Williams, DeAngelo, Car.	33	313	9.5	41	1
* Holt, Glenn, Cin.	1	3	3.0	3	0	Henderson, Devery, N.O.	32	745	23.3	76t	5
Klecko, Dan, Ind.	1	2	2.0	2t	1	Toomer, Amani, NY-G	32	360	11.3	44	3
Everett, Kevin, Buf.	1	1	1.0	1	0	Randle El, Antwaan, Was.	32	351	11.0	34t	3
Suggs, Lee, Mia.	0	13	—	13	0	Foster, DeShaun, Car.	32	159	5.0	14	0
Pennington, Chad, NYJ	0	7	—	7	0	White, Roddy, Atl.	30	506	16.9	55	0
						McAllister, Deuce, N.O.	30	198	6.6	24	0
						Williams, Cadillac, T.B.	30	196	6.5	21	0
						Robinson, Marcus, Min.	29	381	13.1	40t	4
						Herron, Noah, G.B.	29	211	7.3	16	2
						Strong, Mack, Sea.	29	159	5.5	13	0

t = Touchdown; * Player that was a rookie in 2006
Leader based on receptions

NFC—INDIVIDUAL RECEIVERS

	No	Yards	Avg	Long	TD		No	Yards	Avg	Long	TD
Furrey, Mike, Det.	98	1086	11.1	31	6	Lelie, Ashley, Atl.	28	430	15.4	51	1
Holt, Torry, St.L	93	1188	12.8	67t	10	Carter, Drew, Car.	28	357	12.8	42t	3
Driver, Donald, G.B.	92	1295	14.1	82t	8	Franks, Bubba, G.B.	25	232	9.3	19	0
Jackson, Steven, St.L	90	806	9.0	64t	3	McKie, Jason, Chi.	25	162	6.5	26	0
* Bush, Reggie, N.O.	88	742	8.4	74	2	Lewis, Greg, Phi.	24	348	14.5	45t	2
Owens, Terrell, Dal.	85	1180	13.9	56t	13	Engram, Bobby, Sea.	24	290	12.1	25	1
Boldin, Anquan, Ariz	83	1203	14.5	64	4	Buckhalter, Correll, Phi.	24	256	10.7	55t	1
Smith, Steve, Car.	83	1166	14.0	72t	8	Copper, Terrance, N.O.	23	385	16.7	48t	3
Williams, Roy, Det.	82	1310	16.0	60t	7	Lloyd, Brandon, Was.	23	365	15.9	52	0
Westbrook, Brian, Phi.	77	699	9.1	52t	4	McMullen, Billy, Min.	23	307	13.3	40t	2
Bruce, Isaac, St.L	74	1098	14.8	45	3	Walters, Troy, Ariz	23	209	9.1	26	2
Glenn, Terry, Dal.	70	1047	15.0	54	6	Barber, Marion, Dal.	23	196	8.5	26	2
* Colston, Marques, N.O.	70	1038	14.8	86t	8	Griffith, Justin, Atl.	23	168	7.3	16	3
Johnson, Keyshawn, Car.	70	815	11.6	40	4	* Baskett, Hank, Phi.	22	464	21.1	89t	2
Fitzgerald, Larry, Ariz	69	946	13.7	57	6	Davis, Rashied, Chi.	22	303	13.8	31	2
Shockey, Jeremy, NY-G	66	623	9.4	25	7	Carter, Tim, NY-G	22	253	11.5	27	2
Witten, Jason, Dal.	64	754	11.8	42	1	Stevens, Jerramy, Sea.	22	231	10.5	26	4
Burress, Plaxico, NY-G	63	988	15.7	55t	10	Dunn, Warrick, Atl.	22	170	7.7	18	1
Jackson, Darrell, Sea.	63	956	15.2	72t	10	Martin, Ruvell, G.B.	21	358	17.0	36t	1
Galloway, Joey, T.B.	62	1057	17.0	64t	7	Campbell, Dan, Det.	21	308	14.7	30	4
Jones, Kevin, Det.	61	520	8.5	26	2	Martin, David, G.B.	21	198	9.4	23	2
Gore, Frank, S.F.	61	485	8.0	39	1	Mangum, Kris, Car.	21	170	8.1	19	1
Muhammad, Muhsin, Chi.	60	863	14.4	40	5	Alstott, Mike, T.B.	21	85	4.0	18	0
Battle, Arnaz, S.F.	59	686	11.6	56	3	* Davis, Vernon, S.F.	20	265	13.3	52t	3
Barber, Tiki, NY-G	58	465	8.0	28	0	* Klopfenstein, Joe, St.L	20	226	11.3	28	1
Cooley, Chris, Was.	57	734	12.9	66t	6	Hoover, Brad, Car.	20	122	6.1	16	0
Taylor, Travis, Min.	57	651	11.4	36	3	Tyree, David, NY-G	19	197	10.4	33	2
Crumpler, Alge, Atl.	56	780	13.9	46	8	Stecker, Aaron, N.O.	19	190	10.0	48	0
Moss, Santana, Was.	55	790	14.4	68t	6	Burleson, Nate, Sea.	18	192	10.7	36	2
Branch, Deion, Sea.	53	725	13.7	38t	4	Campbell, Mark, N.O.	18	164	9.1	33	0
Betts, Ladell, Was.	53	445	8.4	34	1	Harris, Arlen, Det.	18	132	7.3	20	0
Berrian, Bernard, Chi.	51	775	15.2	62	6	Becht, Anthony, T.B.	18	115	6.4	13	1
Smith, L.J., Phi.	50	611	12.2	65	5	Sellers, Mike, Was.	18	105	5.8	15	1
Pittman, Michael, T.B.	47	405	8.6	25	0	Portis, Clinton, Was.	17	170	10.0	74	0
						Hakim, Az-Zahir, Det.	17	147	8.6	23	0

	No	Yards	Avg	Long	TD
Ayanbadejo, Obafemi, Ariz	17	139	8.2	27	0
Morency, Vernand, Hou.-G.B.	17	118	6.9	29	0
* Pope, Leonard, Ariz	16	161	10.1	33	0
Tapeh, Thomas, Phi.	16	85	5.3	15	1
Gaines, Michael, Car.	15	146	9.7	19	0
Bergen, Adam, Ariz	15	111	7.4	17	1
Karney, Mike, N.O.	15	96	6.4	12	2
Bradley, Mark, Chi.	14	282	20.1	75t	3
Schobel, Matt, Phi.	14	214	15.3	60	2
Bradford, Corey, Det.	14	164	11.7	23	0
Fisher, Tony, St.L	14	159	11.4	49	0
Miller, Billy, N.O.	14	129	9.2	22	0
* Fasano, Anthony, Dal.	14	126	9.0	22	0
Hicks, Maurice, S.F.	13	137	10.5	33t	1
McDonald, Shaun, St.L	13	136	10.5	28	1
Richardson, Tony, Min.	13	111	8.5	25	0
Thrash, James, Was.	12	151	12.6	27	1
* Norwood, Jerious, Atl.	12	102	8.5	32	0
Pollard, Marcus, Det.	12	100	8.3	22	0
Davis, Stephen, St.L	12	90	7.5	18	1
Shiancoe, Visanthe, NY-G	12	81	6.8	16	0
Henderson, William, G.B.	12	62	5.2	13	0
Alexander, Shaun, Sea.	12	48	4.0	14	0
Jacobs, Brandon, NY-G	11	149	13.5	43	0
Morris, Maurice, Sea.	11	46	4.2	27	0
Lee, Donald, G.B.	10	150	15.0	32	0
Goings, Nick, Car.	10	107	10.7	23	1
Mili, Itula, Sea.	10	69	6.9	15	0
Johnson, Bethel, Min.	9	156	17.3	40	0
Jones, Julius, Dal.	9	142	15.8	39	0
Holiday, Carlyle, G.B.	9	126	14.0	35	0
Miree, Brandon, G.B.	9	57	6.3	20	0
* Robinson, Michael, S.F.	9	47	5.2	12	0
Gilmore, Bryan, S.F.	8	150	18.8	75	1
Williams, Mike, Det.	8	99	12.4	21t	1
Bryson, Shawn, Det.	8	98	12.3	37t	1
Arrington, J.J., Ariz	8	58	7.3	19	0
Conwell, Ernie, N.O.	8	57	7.1	15	1
Benson, Cedric, Chi.	8	54	6.8	22	0
Finn, Jim, NY-G	8	54	6.8	11	0
Dugan, Jeff, Min.	8	40	5.0	10	1
Schlesinger, Cory, Det.	8	36	4.5	6	0
* Stovall, Maurice, T.B.	7	102	14.6	27	0
Robinson, Koren, G.B.	7	89	12.7	24	0
Fitzsimmons, Casey, Det.	7	71	10.1	18	0
* Avant, Jason, Phi.	7	68	9.7	18	1
Kleinsasser, Jimmy, Min.	7	47	6.7	14	0
Hedgecock, Madison, St.L	7	29	4.1	7	0
Jones, Jamal, N.O.	6	108	18.0	41	1
Peterson, Adrian, Chi.	6	88	14.7	37	0
Blakley, Dwayne, Atl.	6	76	12.7	28	0
Shipp, Marcel, Ariz	6	60	10.0	22	0
Owens, Richard, Min.	6	45	7.5	16t	1
Gilmore, John, Chi.	6	38	6.3	18	2
* Hurd, Sam, Dal.	5	75	15.0	33	0
Walker, Aaron, St.L	5	68	13.6	26	0
Warren, Paris, T.B.	5	63	12.6	26	0
Colbert, Keary, Car.	5	56	11.2	16	0
Jennings, Mike, NY-G	5	49	9.8	20	0
Norris, Moran, S.F.	5	36	7.2	32t	2
Ferguson, Robert, G.B.	5	31	6.2	10	1
Cason, Aveion, Det.	5	26	5.2	14	0
* Moss, Sinorice, NY-G	5	25	5.0	10	0
Mahe, Reno, Phi.	5	23	4.6	8	0
* Branch, Jamaal, N.O.	5	14	2.8	7t	1
Gage, Justin, Chi.	4	68	17.0	34	0
Owens, John, N.O.	4	44	11.0	25	0
* Ellis, Devale, Det.	4	41	10.3	19	0

	No	Yards	Avg	Long	TD
Reid, Gabe, Chi.	4	37	9.3	19	0
* Nance, Martin, Min.	4	33	8.3	12	0
Heller, Will, Sea.	4	32	8.0	12	1
* Spurlock, Michael, Ariz	4	31	7.8	15	0
Jacobs, Taylor, S.F.	4	29	7.3	10	0
* Biddle, Taye, Car.	3	37	12.3	22	0
Hankton, Karl, Car.	3	31	10.3	18	0
McHugh, Sean, Det.	3	25	8.3	11	0
Fason, Ciatrick, Min.	3	19	6.3	12	0
McCrary, Fred, Atl.	3	13	4.3	7	1
* Byrd, Dominique, St.L	2	39	19.5	27t	1
* Walker, Delanie, S.F.	2	30	15.0	29	0
Wakefield, Fred, Ariz	2	24	12.0	19	0
Polite, Lousaka, Dal.	2	21	10.5	12	0
* Calhoun, Brian, Det.	2	20	10.0	18	0
Fauria, Christian, Was.	2	17	8.5	11	0
Duckett, T.J., Was.	2	16	8.0	19	0
* Francies, Chris, G.B.	2	16	8.0	12	0
McCown, Josh, Det.	2	15	7.5	8	0
Pinner, Artose, Min.	2	15	7.5	8	0
Drummond, Eddie, Det.	2	10	5.0	8	0
* Hoyte, Oliver, Dal.	2	10	5.0	6	0
Hetherington, Chris, S.F.	2	0	0.0	0	0
Bronson, John, Ariz	1	25	25.0	25	0
Patten, David, Was.	1	25	25.0	25	0
Lawrie, Nate, N.O.	1	17	17.0	17	0
Parry, Josh, Sea.	1	11	11.0	11	0
Harris, Kay-Jay, St.L	1	10	10.0	10	0
McIntyre, Corey, N.O.	1	10	10.0	10	0
Moore, Lance, N.O.	1	10	10.0	10	0
Moore, Dave, T.B.	1	9	9.0	9	0
Jolley, Doug, T.B.	1	7	7.0	7	0
Shelton, Eric, Car.	1	6	6.0	6	0
Sowell, Jerald, T.B.	1	6	6.0	6	0
Graham, Earnest, T.B.	1	4	4.0	4	0
Yoder, Todd, Was.	1	4	4.0	4t	0
* King, Jeff, Car.	1	1	1.0	1t	1
Kozlowski, Brian, Was.	1	1	1.0	1	0
Vick, Michael, Atl.	1	1	1.0	1	0
Beverly, Eric, Atl.	1	0	0.0	0	0
Hall, DeAngelo, Atl.	1	0	0.0	0	0
Grossman, Rex, Chi.	1	-4	-4.0	-4	0

t = Touchdown; * Player that was a rookie in 2006
Leader based on receptions

INTERCEPTIONS

INTERCEPTIONS
AFC:	10	Champ Bailey, Denver
	10	Asante Samuel, New England
NFC:	8	Walt Harris, San Francisco
	8	Charles Woodson, Green Bay

INTERCEPTIONS, GAME
AFC:	3	Asante Samuel, New England vs. Chicago, November 26 (26 yards, 0 TD)
NFC:	3	Walt Harris, San Francisco vs. Oakland, October 8 (5 yards, 0 TD)

YARDS
AFC:	162	Champ Bailey, Denver
NFC:	157	Lito Sheppard, Philadelphia

LONGEST
NFC:	102	Lito Sheppard, Philadelphia vs. Dallas, October 8 - TD
AFC:	100	Chris Carr, Oakland vs. Pittsburgh, October 29 - TD

TOUCHDOWNS
AFC:	2	Chris McAlister, Baltimore
	2	Jason Taylor, Miami
NFC:	2	Ronde Barber, Tampa Bay

TEAM LEADERS, INTERCEPTIONS

AFC: BALTIMORE, 6, Chris McAlister ; BUFFALO, 4, London Fletcher-Baker ; CINCINNATI, 6, Kevin Kaesviharn ; CLEVELAND, 5, Daven Holly, Sean Jones ; DENVER, 10, Champ Bailey ; HOUSTON, 2, Demarcus Faggins, Dunta Robinson ; INDIANAPO-LIS, 3, Nick Harper, Cato June ; JACKSONVILLE, 8, Rashean Mathis ; KANSAS CITY, 4, Ty Law ; MIAMI, 2, Renaldo Hill, Jason Taylor; NEW ENGLAND, 10, Asante Samuel ; N.Y. JETS, 4, Andre Dyson, Kerry Rhodes; OAKLAND, 8, Nnamdi Asomugha; PITTS-BURGH, 3, Bryant McFadden, Troy Polamalu ; SAN DIEGO, 4, Quentin Jammer ; TENNESSEE, 5, Chris Hope

NFC: ARIZONA, 4, Adrian Wilson; ATLANTA, 4, DeAngelo Hall; CAROLINA, 3, Chris Gamble, Ken Lucas, Richard Marshall*; CHICAGO, 5, Ricky Manning, Charles Tillman; DALLAS, 5, Roy Williams; DETROIT, 3, Dre' Bly, Jamar Fletcher, Terrence Holt; GREEN BAY, 8, Charles Woodson; MINNESOTA, 4, Darren Sharper, Dwight Smith, Antoine Winfield; NEW ORLEANS, 2, Josh Bullocks, Scott Fujita, Mike McKenzie, Omar Stoutmire; N.Y. GIANTS, 2, Will Demps, Kevin Dockery*, Mathias Kiwanuka*, Sam Madison, R.W. McQuarters, Fred Robbins, Gibril Wilson; PHILADELPHIA, 6, Lito Sheppard; ST. LOUIS, 3, O.J. Atogwe, Ronald Bartell, Fakhir Brown, Tye Hill*; SAN FRANCISCO, 8, Walt Harris; SEAT-TLE, 3, Ken Hamlin; TAMPA BAY, 3, Ronde Barber, Derrick Brooks; WASHINGTON, 1, Phillip Daniels, Vernon Fox, Carlos Rogers, Shawn Springs, Sean Taylor, Kenny Wright

TEAM CHAMPION
AFC:	28	Baltimore
NFC:	24	Chicago

NFL TOP TEN INTERCEPTORS
	No	Yards	Avg	Long	TD
Bailey, Champ, Den.	10	162	16.2	70t	1
Samuel, Asante, N.E.	10	120	12.0	33	0
Asomugha, Nnamdi, Oak.	8	59	7.4	24t	1
Harris, Walt, S.F.	8	84	10.5	42	1
Mathis, Rashean, Jac.	8	146	18.3	55	0
Woodson, Charles, G.B.	8	61	7.6	23t	1
Kaesviharn, Kevin, Cin.	6	24	4.0	22	0
McAlister, Chris, Bal.	6	121	20.2	60t	2
Sheppard, Lito, Phi.	6	157	26.2	102t	1
Holly, Daven, Cle.	5	127	25.4	57t	1
Hope, Chris, Ten.	5	105	21.0	61t	1
Jones, Sean, Cle.	5	46	9.2	19	0
* Landry, Dawan, Bal.	5	101	20.2	37	1
Manning, Ricky, Chi.	5	113	22.6	54t	1
Reed, Ed, Bal.	5	70	14.0	37	1
Tillman, Charles, Chi.	5	32	6.4	13	0
Williams, Roy, Dal.	5	33	6.6	27	0

AFC—INDIVIDUAL INTERCEPTORS
	No	Yards	Avg	Long	TD
Bailey, Champ, Den.	10	162	16.2	70t	1
Samuel, Asante, N.E.	10	120	12.0	33	0
Mathis, Rashean, Jac.	8	146	18.3	55	0
Asomugha, Nnamdi, Oak.	8	59	7.4	24t	1
McAlister, Chris, Bal.	6	121	20.2	60t	2
Kaesviharn, Kevin, Cin.	6	24	4.0	22	0
Holly, Daven, Cle.	5	127	25.4	57t	1
Hope, Chris, Ten.	5	105	21.0	61t	1
* Landry, Dawan, Bal.	5	101	20.2	37	1
Reed, Ed, Bal.	5	70	14.0	37	1
Jones, Sean, Cle.	5	46	9.2	19	0
Jones, Pacman, Ten.	4	130	32.5	83t	1
Jammer, Quentin, S.D.	4	57	14.3	35	0
Rhodes, Kerry, NYJ	4	46	11.5	25	0
James, Tory, Cin.	4	44	11.0	28	0
Williams, Darrent, Den.	4	37	9.3	31t	1
Fletcher-Baker, London, Buf.	4	30	7.5	17t	1
Law, Ty, K.C.	4	11	2.8	16	0
Washington, Fabian, Oak.	4	4	1.0	7	0
Dyson, Andre, NYJ	4	-3	-.8	0	0
Clements, Nate, Buf.	3	80	26.7	58t	1
Rolle, Samari, Bal.	3	60	20.0	44	0
Polamalu, Troy, Pit.	3	51	17.0	49	0
McFadden, Bryant, Pit.	3	39	13.0	39	0
Wesley, Greg, K.C.	3	39	13.0	29	0
Hart, Clinton, S.D.	3	37	12.3	22	0
Williams, Madieu, Cin.	3	33	11.0	25	0
* Page, Jarrad, K.C.	3	30	10.0	30	0
Florence, Drayton, S.D.	3	24	8.0	23	0
Harper, Nick, Ind.	3	18	6.0	19	0
June, Cato, Ind.	3	14	4.7	8	0
Thompson, Lamont, Ten.	3	14	4.7	11	0
Edwards, Donnie, S.D.	3	11	3.7	8	0
Barrett, David, NYJ	3	0	0.0	0	0
Vrabel, Mike, N.E.	3	0	0.0	2	0
Hobbs, Ellis, N.E.	2	79	39.5	70	0
* Simpson, Ko, Buf.	2	76	38.0	76	0
Taylor, Jason, Mia.	2	71	35.5	51t	2
* Prude, Ronnie, Bal.	2	66	33.0	54	1
Porter, Joey, Pit.	2	49	24.5	42t	1
Bodden, Leigh, Cle.	2	48	24.0	35	0
Doss, Mike, Ind.	2	47	23.5	31	0
* Smith, Anthony, Pit.	2	40	20.0	20	0
Taylor, Ike, Pit.	2	34	17.0	34	0
Hill, Renaldo, Mia.	2	33	16.5	21	0
Morrison, Kirk, Oak.	2	32	16.0	31	0
Scott, Chad, N.E.	2	32	16.0	32	0
Scott, Bart, Bal.	2	31	15.5	24	0

	No	Yards	Avg	Long	TD
Lewis, Ray, Bal.	2	27	13.5	27	0
Grant, Deon, Jac.	2	25	12.5	24	0
Hill, Reynaldo, Ten.	2	20	10.0	11	0
Davis, Andra, Cle.	2	19	9.5	19	0
David, Jason, Ind.	2	16	8.0	16	0
Robinson, Dunta, Hou.	2	9	4.5	9t	1
Sensabaugh, Gerald, Jac.	2	8	4.0	8	0
Townsend, Deshea, Pit.	2	6	3.0	6	0
Simmons, Brian, Cin.	2	5	2.5	5	0
* Smith, Eric, NYJ	2	1	0.5	1	0
Crowell, Angelo, Buf.	2	0	0.0	0	0
Faggins, Demarcus, Hou.	2	0	0.0	0	0
Carr, Chris, Oak.	1	100	100.0	100t	1
* Ngata, Haloti, Bal.	1	60	60.0	60	0
Starks, Scott, Jac.	1	55	55.0	55t	1
* Kilmer, Ethan, Cin.	1	52	52.0	52t	1
Jackson, Dexter, Cin.	1	46	46.0	46	0
Foxworth, Domonique, Den.	1	45	45.0	45	0
O'Neal, Deltha, Cin.	1	42	42.0	42	0
* Bethea, Antoine, Ind.	1	38	38.0	38	0
Wallace, Rian, Pit.	1	30	30.0	30t	1
Knight, Sammy, K.C.	1	27	27.0	27	0
Jackson, Marlin, Ind.	1	24	24.0	24	0
Mitchell, Kawika, K.C.	1	23	23.0	23	0
Sanders, James, N.E.	1	21	21.0	21	0
Weaver, Anthony, Hou.	1	21	21.0	21	0
McCleon, Dexter, Hou.	1	19	19.0	19	0
Cousin, Terry, Jac.	1	16	16.0	16	0
* Ryans, DeMeco, Hou.	1	16	16.0	16	0
Peterson, Mike, Jac.	1	15	15.0	15	0
Sirmon, Peter, Ten.	1	13	13.0	13	0
Kriewaldt, Clint, Pit.	1	12	12.0	12	0
Allen, Will, Mia.	1	11	11.0	11	0
Foote, Larry, Pit.	1	11	11.0	11	0
Simmons, Jason, Hou.	1	11	11.0	11	0
Baxter, Gary, Cle.	1	10	10.0	10	0
Merriman, Shawne, S.D.	1	10	10.0	10	0
* Whitner, Donte, Buf.	1	10	10.0	10	0
Hobson, Victor, NYJ	1	9	9.0	9	0
Bruschi, Tedy, N.E.	1	8	8.0	8	0
* Allen, Jason, Mia.	1	7	7.0	7	0
* Ellison, Keith, Buf.	1	7	7.0	7	0
Thomas, Adalius, Bal.	1	7	7.0	7	0
Greisen, Nick, Jac.	1	6	6.0	6	0
Routt, Stanford, Oak.	1	6	6.0	6	0
Russell, Brian, Cle.	1	6	6.0	6	0
Sands, Terdell, Oak.	1	5	5.0	5	0
Smith, Daryl, Jac.	1	4	4.0	4	0
Williams, Brian, Jac.	1	4	4.0	4	0
Allen, Jared, K.C.	1	3	3.0	3	0
Coleman, Erik, NYJ	1	3	3.0	3	0
Earl, Glenn, Hou.	1	2	2.0	2	0
Harrison, Rodney, N.E.	1	2	2.0	2	0
Johnson, Landon, Cin.	1	2	2.0	2	0
Castillo, Luis, S.D.	1	1	1.0	1	0
Farrior, James, Pit.	1	1	1.0	1	0
* Webb, Dee, Jac.	1	1	1.0	1	0
Boiman, Rocky, Ind.	1	0	0.0	0	0
Brown, C.C., Hou.	1	0	0.0	0	0
Bulluck, Keith, Ten.	1	0	0.0	0	0
Cox, Curome, Den.	1	0	0.0	0	0
Ferguson, Nick, Den.	1	0	0.0	0	0
Giordano, Matt, Ind.	1	0	0.0	0	0
Greenwood, Morlon, Hou.	1	0	0.0	0	0
Haggans, Clark, Pit.	1	0	0.0	0	0
Hawkins, Artrell, N.E.	1	0	0.0	0	0
* Ingram, Clint, Jac.	1	0	0.0	0	0
Ivy, Corey, Bal.	1	0	0.0	0	0
McCree, Marlon, S.D.	1	0	0.0	0	0

	No	Yards	Avg	Long	TD
McGinest, Willie, Cle.	1	0	0.0	0	0
Pool, Brodney, Cle.	1	0	0.0	0	0
Poole, Tyrone, Oak.	1	0	0.0	0	0
Sanders, Bob, Ind.	1	0	0.0	0	0
Seymour, Richard, N.E.	1	0	0.0	0	0
Surtain, Patrick, K.C.	1	0	0.0	0	0
* Tulloch, Stephen, Ten.	1	0	0.0	0	0
Vilma, Jonathan, NYJ	1	0	0.0	0	0
Clark, Ryan, Pit.	1	-1	-1.0	-1	0
Daniels, Travis, Mia.	1	-2	-2.0	-2	0
Thomas, Zach, Mia.	1	-4	-4.0	-4	0
* Hali, Tamba, K.C.	1	-9	-9.0	-9	0
Sapp, Gerome, Bal.	0	1	—	1	0

*t = Touchdown; * Player that was a rookie in 2006*
Leader based on interceptions

NFC—INDIVIDUAL INTERCEPTORS

	No	Yards	Avg	Long	TD
Harris, Walt, S.F.	8	84	10.5	42	1
Woodson, Charles, G.B.	8	61	7.6	23t	1
Sheppard, Lito, Phi.	6	157	26.2	102t	1
Manning, Ricky, Chi.	5	113	22.6	54t	1
Williams, Roy, Dal.	5	33	6.6	27	0
Tillman, Charles, Chi.	5	32	6.4	13	0
Wilson, Adrian, Ariz	4	146	36.5	99t	1
Hall, DeAngelo, Atl.	4	131	32.8	60	1
Smith, Dwight, Min.	4	81	20.3	47	0
Dawkins, Brian, Phi.	4	38	9.5	38	0
Winfield, Antoine, Min.	4	33	8.3	26	1
Sharper, Darren, Min.	4	10	2.5	10	0
Fletcher, Jamar, Det.	3	122	40.7	88t	1
Barber, Ronde, T.B.	3	103	34.3	66t	2
Collins, Nick, G.B.	3	68	22.7	55t	1
Bartell, Ronald, St.L	3	63	21.0	38t	1
Hamlin, Ken, Sea.	3	63	21.0	37	0
* Marshall, Richard, Car.	3	59	19.7	30t	1
Brooks, Derrick, T.B.	3	51	17.0	21t	1
* Watkins, Pat, Dal.	3	45	15.0	24	0
Harris, Al, G.B.	3	39	13.0	34	0
Urlacher, Brian, Chi.	3	38	12.7	36	0
Dendy, Patrick, G.B.	3	37	12.3	30t	1
Gamble, Chris, Car.	3	31	10.3	18t	1
Griffith, Robert, Ariz	3	30	10.0	23	0
Hayes, Gerald, Ariz	3	24	8.0	24	0
Harris, Napoleon, Min.	3	20	6.7	11	0
* Hill, Tye, St.L	3	20	6.7	14	0
Brown, Fakhir, St.L	3	17	5.7	20	0
Bly, Dre', Det.	3	13	4.3	8	0
Lucas, Ken, Car.	3	13	4.3	13	0
Vasher, Nathan, Chi.	3	11	3.7	7	0
Atogwe, O.J., St.L	3	8	2.7	7	0
Holt, Terrence, Det.	3	8	2.7	7	0
Lewis, Michael, Phi.	2	105	52.5	84t	1
* Dockery, Kevin, NY-G	2	100	50.0	96t	1
McQuarters, R.W., NY-G	2	67	33.5	27t	1
Francisco, Aaron, Ariz	2	61	30.5	44	0
McKenzie, Mike, N.O.	2	54	27.0	54	0
Henderson, E.J., Min.	2	48	24.0	45t	1
Phillips, Jermaine, T.B.	2	45	22.5	29	0
Boley, Michael, Atl.	2	44	22.0	40	0
* Kiwanuka, Mathias, NY-G	2	44	22.0	32	0
Henry, Anthony, Dal.	2	41	20.5	37	0
Carter, Jerome, St.L	2	39	19.5	36	0
* Hawk, A.J., G.B.	2	31	15.5	25	0
Demps, Will, NY-G	2	30	15.0	29	0
Madison, Sam, NY-G	2	28	14.0	24	0
* Manning, Danieal, Chi.	2	26	13.0	15	0
Wilson, Gibril, NY-G	2	25	12.5	25	0

	No	Yards	Avg	Long	TD
Lewis, Keith, S.F.	2	24	12.0	24	0
Brown, Alex, Chi.	2	22	11.0	18	0
Fujita, Scott, N.O.	2	19	9.5	19	0
Harris, Chris, Chi.	2	19	9.5	16	0
Briggs, Lance, Chi.	2	18	9.0	18	0
Kennedy, Kenoy, Det.	2	17	8.5	17	0
Bullocks, Josh, N.O.	2	14	7.0	14	0
Robbins, Fred, NY-G	2	12	6.0	11	0
Stoutmire, Omar, N.O.	2	10	5.0	10	0
* Griffin, Cedric, Min.	2	4	2.0	4	0
Barnett, Nick, G.B.	2	3	1.5	3	0
Ayodele, Akin, Dal.	2	2	1.0	2	0
Boulware, Michael, Sea.	2	1	0.5	1	0
Williams, Shaun, Car.	2	1	0.5	1	0
Buchanon, Phillip, T.B.	2	0	0.0	0	0
Coakley, Dexter, St.L	2	0	0.0	0	0
Webster, Jason, Atl.	2	-2	-1.0	3	0
Brown, Sheldon, Phi.	1	70	70.0	70t	1
Macklin, David, Ariz	1	56	56.0	56	0
Smoot, Fred, Min.	1	47	47.0	47t	1
Williams, Chad, S.F.	1	43	43.0	43	0
Davis, Chauncey, Atl.	1	41	41.0	41	0
Ware, DeMarcus, Dal.	1	41	41.0	41t	1
Burnett, Kevin, Dal.	1	39	39.0	39t	1
Manuel, Marquand, G.B.	1	29	29.0	29t	1
Crocker, Chris, Atl.	1	28	28.0	28	0
Bolden, Juran, T.B.	1	27	27.0	27	0
Roman, Mark, S.F.	1	27	27.0	27	0
* Tapp, Darryl, Sea.	1	25	25.0	25t	1
Taylor, Sean, Was.	1	25	25.0	25	0
Rolle, Antrel, Ariz	1	23	23.0	23	0
Poppinga, Brady, G.B.	1	21	21.0	21	0
Babineaux, Jordan, Sea.	1	20	20.0	20	0
Cole, Trent, Phi.	1	19	19.0	19t	1
Tatupu, Lofa, Sea.	1	19	19.0	19	0
Chavous, Corey, St.L	1	17	17.0	17	0
Trotter, Jeremiah, Phi.	1	17	17.0	17	0
* Gaither, Omar, Phi.	1	16	16.0	16	0
James, Bradie, Dal.	1	15	15.0	15t	1
Considine, Sean, Phi.	1	12	12.0	12	0
Newman, Terence, Dal.	1	12	12.0	12	0
Beisel, Monty, Ariz	1	11	11.0	11	0
Thomas, Fred, N.O.	1	9	9.0	9	0
Williams, Demorrio, Atl.	1	9	9.0	9	0
Morton, Christian, Car.	1	8	8.0	8	0
Glenn, Aaron, Dal.	1	7	7.0	7	0
Babineaux, Jonathan, Atl.	1	6	6.0	6	0
Pierce, Antonio, NY-G	1	6	6.0	6	0
Walker, Darwin, Phi.	1	6	6.0	6	0
Springs, Shawn, Was.	1	4	4.0	4	0
Minter, Mike, Car.	1	3	3.0	3	0
Branch, Colin, Car.	1	0	0.0	0	0
Craft, Jason, N.O.	1	0	0.0	0	0
Daniels, Phillip, Was.	1	0	0.0	0	0
Herndon, Kelly, Sea.	1	0	0.0	0	0
* Jennings, Kelly, Sea.	1	0	0.0	0	0
* Lawson, Manny, S.F.	1	0	0.0	0	0
Leber, Ben, Min.	1	0	0.0	0	0
Lenon, Paris, Det.	1	0	0.0	0	0
Rogers, Carlos, Was.	1	0	0.0	0	0
Simoneau, Mark, N.O.	1	0	0.0	0	0
Spencer, Shawntae, S.F.	1	0	0.0	0	0
Trufant, Marcus, Sea.	1	0	0.0	0	0
Webster, Corey, NY-G	1	0	0.0	0	0
Wright, Kenny, Was.	1	0	0.0	0	0
Dockett, Darnell, Ariz	1	-1	-1.0	-1	0
Ellis, Greg, Dal.	1	-1	-1.0	-1	0
Fox, Vernon, Was.	1	-4	-4.0	-4	0
Peterson, Julian, Sea.	1	-4	-4.0	-4	0

	No	Yards	Avg	Long	TD
Bell, Jason, NY-G	1	-7	-7.0	-7	0
* Ramsey, LaJuan, Phi.	1	-12	-12.0	-12	0

t = Touchdown; * Player that was a rookie in 2006
Leader based on interceptions

AMERICAN FOOTBALL CONFERENCE—INTERCEPTIONS

	No	Yards	Avg	Long	TD
Baltimore	28	544	19.4	60t	5
New England	22	262	11.9	70	0
Jacksonville	20	280	14.0	55t	1
Pittsburgh	20	272	13.6	49	2
Cincinnati	19	248	13.1	52t	1
Cleveland	18	256	14.2	57t	1
Oakland	18	206	11.4	100t	2
Denver	17	244	14.4	70t	2
Tennessee	17	282	16.6	83t	2
N.Y. Jets	16	56	3.5	25	0
San Diego	16	140	8.8	35	0
Indianapolis	15	157	10.5	38	0
Kansas City	15	124	8.3	30	0
Buffalo	13	203	15.6	76	2
Houston	11	78	7.1	21	1
Miami	8	116	14.5	51t	2
AFC Total	273	3468	12.7	100t	21
AFC Average	17.1	216.8	12.7	—	1.3

NATIONAL FOOTBALL CONFERENCE—INTERCEPTIONS

	No	Yards	Avg	Long	TD
Chicago	24	279	11.6	54t	1
Green Bay	23	289	12.6	55t	4
Minnesota	21	243	11.6	47t	3
Philadelphia	19	428	22.5	102t	4
Dallas	18	234	13.0	41t	3
N.Y. Giants	17	305	17.9	96t	2
St. Louis	17	164	9.6	38t	1
Arizona	16	350	21.9	99t	1
Carolina	14	115	8.2	30t	2
San Francisco	14	178	12.7	43	1
Atlanta	12	257	21.4	60	1
Detroit	12	160	13.3	88t	1
Seattle	12	124	10.3	37	1
New Orleans	11	106	9.6	54	0
Tampa Bay	11	226	20.5	66t	3
Washington	6	25	4.2	25	0
NFC Total	247	3483	14.1	102t	28
NFC Average	15.4	217.7	14.1	—	1.8
League Total	520	6951	—	102t	49
League Average	16.3	217.2	13.4	—	1.5

KICKOFF RETURNS

YARDS PER RETURN
- AFC: 28.3 Justin Miller, N.Y. Jets
- NFC: 26.4 *Devin Hester, Chicago

YARDS
- AFC: 1762 Chris Carr, Oakland
- NFC: 1541 Rock Cartwright, Washington

YARDS, GAME
- NFC: 225 * Devin Hester, Chicago at St. Louis, December 11 (4 returns, 2 TD)
- 225 Bethel Johnson, Minnesota vs. St. Louis, December 31 (8 returns, 0 TD)
- AFC: 206 Chris Carr, Oakland at Baltimore, September 17 (7 returns, 0 TD)

LONGEST
- AFC: 103 Justin Miller, N.Y. Jets vs. Indianapolis, October 1 - TD
- NFC: 100 Rock Cartwright, Washington at Dallas, September 17 - TD

RETURNS
- AFC: 69 Chris Carr, Oakland
- NFC: 67 J.J. Arrington, Arizona

RETURNS, GAME
- NFC: 9 Maurice Hicks, San Francisco vs. San Diego, October 15 (195 yards, 0 TD)
- AFC: 8 Justin Miller, N.Y. Jets at Jacksonville, October 8 (172 yards, 0 TD)
- 8 Dexter Wynn, Houston at New England, December 17 (151 yards, 0 TD)

TOUCHDOWNS
- AFC: 2 Justin Miller, N.Y. Jets
- NFC: 2 * Devin Hester, Chicago

TEAM CHAMPION
- AFC: 26.8 New England
- NFC: 24.1 San Francisco

NFL TOP TEN KICKOFF RETURNERS

	No	Yards	Avg	Long	TD
Miller, Justin, NYJ	46	1304	28.3	103t	2
* Maroney, Laurence, N.E.	28	783	28.0	77	0
* Jones-Drew, Maurice, Jac.	31	860	27.7	93t	1
Turner, Michael, S.D.	36	954	26.5	58	0
Hester, Devin, Chi.	20	528	26.4	96t	2
McGee, Terrence, Buf.	52	1355	26.1	88	0
Jones, Pacman, Ten.	20	521	26.1	70	0
Thompson, Tyson, Dal.	21	546	26.0	41	0
* Austin, Miles, Dal.	29	753	26.0	37	0
Sams, B.J., Bal.	30	772	25.7	72	0

AFC—INDIVIDUAL KICKOFF RETURNERS

	No	Yards	Avg	Long	TD
Miller, Justin, NYJ	46	1304	28.3	103t	2
* Maroney, Laurence, N.E.	28	783	28.0	77	0
* Jones-Drew, Maurice, Jac.	31	860	27.7	93t	1
Turner, Michael, S.D.	36	954	26.5	58	0
McGee, Terrence, Buf.	52	1355	26.1	88	0
Jones, Pacman, Ten.	20	521	26.1	70	0
Sams, B.J., Bal.	30	772	25.7	72	0
Carr, Chris, Oak.	69	1762	25.5	50	0
Cribbs, Josh, Cle.	61	1494	24.5	92t	1
Wilkins, Terrence, Ind.	52	1272	24.5	70	0
Wade, Bobby, Ten.	50	1194	23.9	48	0

	No	Yards	Avg	Long	TD
Hall, Dante, K.C.	53	1207	22.8	60	0
* Clark, Brian, Den.	23	512	22.3	36	0
Welker, Wes, Mia.	48	1064	22.2	46	0
Wynn, Dexter, Phi.-Hou.	48	1032	21.5	38	0
Davenport, Najeh, Pit.	21	448	21.3	40	0
Perry, Chris, Cin.	21	412	19.6	36	0
(Nonqualifiers)					
* Holmes, Santonio, Pit.	18	436	24.2	42	0
Morgan, Quincy, Den.	17	423	24.9	64	0
* Holt, Glenn, Cin.	17	419	24.6	38	0
Shepherd, Edell, Hou.	17	395	23.2	42	0
Faulk, Kevin, N.E.	17	364	21.4	31	0
Hobbs, Ellis, N.E.	10	360	36.0	93t	1
* Cromartie, Antonio, S.D.	10f	297	29.7	91	0
Watson, Kenny, Cin.	10	198	19.8	34	0
* Ross, Cory, Bal.	9	194	21.6	28	0
Morey, Sean, Pit.	8	202	25.3	76	0
Wimbush, Derrick, Jac.	8	181	22.6	33	0
Mathis, Jerome, Hou.	7	192	27.4	87	0
* Webb, Jeff, K.C.	7	169	24.1	50	0
Davis, Andre, Buf.	6	99	16.5	27	0
* Washington, Leon, NYJ	6	79	13.2	23	0
Buchanon, Phillip, Hou.	5	106	21.2	28	0
* Bell, Mike, Den.	5	97	19.4	22	0
* Vickers, Lawrence, Cle.	5	84	16.8	22	0
Sapp, Cecil, Den.	4	95	23.8	53	0
Chatman, Antonio, Cin.	4	93	23.3	31	0
Taylor, Ike, Pit.	4	72	18.0	23	0
Perry, Tab, Cin.	4	69	17.3	34	0
* Lundy, Wali, Hou.	4	67	16.8	23	0
Scaife, Bo, Ten.	4	64	16.0	18	0
Lee, ReShard, Oak.	4	49	12.3	17	0
Brady, Kyle, Jac.	4	18	4.5	9	0
* Anderson, David, Hou.	3	90	30.0	38	0
* Green, Skyler, Dal.-Cin.	3	59	19.7	21	0
Gado, Samkon, G.B.-Hou.	3	57	19.0	23	0
Pearman, Alvin, Jac.	3	56	18.7	22	0
Dinkins, Darnell, Cle.	3	44	14.7	20	0
Cramer, Casey, Ten.	3	37	12.3	21	0
Johnson, Jarret, Bal.	3	28	9.3	14	0
Neal, Lorenzo, S.D.	3	11	3.7	7	0
* Rushing, T.J., Ind.	2	67	33.5	47	0
* Gordon, Cletis, S.D.	2	55	27.5	32	0
Kircus, David, Den.	2	38	19.0	20	0
Chatham, Matt, NYJ	2	26	13.0	20	0
Banta-Cain, Tully, N.E.	2	25	12.5	16	0
Bowens, David, Mia.	2	21	10.5	11	0
Carthon, Ran, Ind.	2	21	10.5	21	0
Parker, Eric, S.D.	2	19	9.5	12	0
Minor, Travis, Mia.	2	17	8.5	17	0
Baker, Chris, NYJ	2	15	7.5	11	0
Preston, Duke, Buf.	2	10	5.0	9	0
Kelly, Reggie, Cin.	2	8	4.0	8	0
Haggan, Mario, Buf.	2	4	2.0	5	0
Lewis, Derrick, Hou.	1	27	27.0	27	0
Smith, Musa, Bal.	1	27	27.0	27	0
Colclough, Ricardo, Pit.	1	26	26.0	26	0
* Jackson, Chad, N.E.	1	21	21.0	21	0
Sapp, Benny, K.C.	1	21	21.0	21	0
* Reid, Willie, Pit.	1	19	19.0	19	0
Alexander, Roc, Hou.	1	18	18.0	18	0
Hodgins, James, NYJ	1	17	17.0	17	0
Johnson, Travis, Hou.	1	17	17.0	17	0
Williams, Shaud, Buf.	1	17	17.0	17	0
Ivy, Corey, Bal.	1	14	14.0	14	0
Johnson, Kyle, Den.	1	14	14.0	14	0
Manumaleuna, Brandon, S.D.	1	14	14.0	14	0
* White, LenDale, Ten.	1	14	14.0	14	0

	No	Yards	Avg	Long	TD
Heiden, Steve, Cle.	1	11	11.0	11	0
* Sypniewski, Quinn, Bal.	1	11	11.0	11	0
Wilson, Cedrick, Pit.	1	11	11.0	11	0
Stewart, Tony, Cin.	1	10	10.0	10	0
Toefield, LaBrandon, Jac.	1	9	9.0	9	0
Bruener, Mark, Hou.	1	8	8.0	8	0
* Collier, Richard, Jac.	1	8	8.0	8	0
Cruz, Ronnie, K.C.	1	7	7.0	7	0
Hartsock, Ben, Ten.	1	5	5.0	5	0
* Owens, Montell, Jac.	1	4	4.0	4	0
* Smith, Brad, NYJ	1	4	4.0	4	0
Reid, Darrell, Ind.	1	3	3.0	3	0
Cook, Jameel, Hou.	1	2	2.0	2	0
Friedman, Lennie, Cle.	1	2	2.0	2	0
Mustard, Chad, Den.	1	2	2.0	2	0
Hayden, Kelvin, Ind.	1	1	1.0	1	0
Brown, Dee, K.C.	1	0	0.0	0	0
Cobbs, Cedric, Den.	1	0	0.0	0	0
Coles, Laveranues, NYJ	1	0	0.0	0	0
Kirschke, Travis, Pit.	1	0	0.0	0	0
* Pollard, Bernard, K.C.	1	0	0.0	0	0
Rhodes, Kerry, NYJ	1	0	0.0	0	0
Withrow, Cory, S.D.	1	0	0.0	0	0
Leonhard, Jim, Buf.	0	18	—	18	0
Wong, Kailee, Hou.	0	17	—	17	0
Williams, Darrent, Den.	0	6	—	6	0
* Dorsey, DeDe, Ind.	0	4	—	4	0
Barnes, Darian, Mia.	0f	0	—	—	0

t = Touchdown; * Player that was a rookie in 2006
f = Fair Catch (Barnes 2, Cromartie 1)
Leader based on average return, minimum 20 returns

NFC—INDIVIDUAL KICKOFF RETURNERS

	No	Yards	Avg	Long	TD
* Hester, Devin, Chi.	20	528	26.4	96t	2
Thompson, Tyson, Dal.	21	546	26.0	41	0
* Austin, Miles, Dal.	29	753	26.0	37	0
Hicks, Maurice, S.F.	57	1428	25.1	64	0
Burleson, Nate, Sea.	26	643	24.7	50	0
Lewis, Michael, N.O.	37	914	24.7	51	0
Cartwright, Rock, Was.	64	1541	24.1	100t	1
Davis, Rashied, Chi.	32	753	23.5	42	0
Rossum, Allen, Atl.	46	1082	23.5	51	0
Johnson, Bethel, Min.	45	1054	23.4	65	0
Ponder, Willie, Sea.-St.L	51	1192	23.4	41	0
Arrington, J.J., Ariz	67	1520	22.7	99t	1
Mahe, Reno, Phi.	30	667	22.2	64	0
Pittman, Michael, T.B.	39	867	22.2	37	0
Drummond, Eddie, Det.	62	1349	21.8	65	0
Morency, Vernand, G.B.	31	670	21.6	35	0
Morton, Chad, NY-G	31	670	21.6	51	0
Ward, Derrick, NY-G	23	466	20.3	36	0
* Williams, DeAngelo, Car.	32	623	19.5	39	0
(Nonqualifiers)					
Cox, Torrie, T.B.	18	387	21.5	44	0
Reed, J.R., St.L	17	346	20.4	40	0
Scobey, Josh, Sea.	17	315	18.5	33	0
* Williams, Brandon, S.F.	16	380	23.8	44	0
Williamson, Troy, Min.	14	324	23.1	44	0
* Marshall, Richard, Car.	14	291	20.8	26	0
* Norwood, Jerious, Atl.	13	320	24.6	37	0
Robinson, Koren, G.B.	12	253	21.1	31	0
Stecker, Aaron, N.O.	10	216	21.6	31	0
* Moss, Sinorice, NY-G	10	194	19.4	33	0
Goings, Nick, Car.	9	218	24.2	33	0
Curtis, Kevin, St.L	9	188	20.9	28	0
Fisher, Tony, St.L	8	165	20.6	26	0
Herron, Noah, G.B.	8	143	17.9	23	0

	No	Yards	Avg	Long	TD
* Jennings, Adam, Atl.	7	123	17.6	26	0
* Ellis, Devale, Det.	6	139	23.2	28	0
Jones, Jamal, N.O.	6	130	21.7	29	0
Ferguson, Robert, G.B.	5	110	22.0	26	0
* Bodiford, Shaun, G.B.	5	81	16.2	22	0
Cason, Aveion, Det.	4	110	27.5	40	0
* Elam, Abram, Dal.	4	95	23.8	26	0
Copper, Terrance, N.O.	4	79	19.8	25	0
Harris, Kay-Jay, Mia.-St.L	4	76	19.0	23	0
Pinner, Artose, Min.	4	76	19.0	24	0
* Robinson, Michael, S.F.	4	73	18.3	19	0
Sellers, Mike, Was.	4	53	13.3	22	0
Henderson, William, G.B.	4	41	10.3	16	0
Jacobs, Brandon, NY-G	3	58	19.3	28	0
Perry, Bruce, Phi.	3	57	19.0	24	0
* Spurlock, Michael, Ariz	3	54	18.0	21	0
Peterson, Adrian, Chi.	3	49	16.3	25	0
Hoover, Brad, Car.	3	37	12.3	21	0
Glenn, Aaron, Dal.	3	24	8.0	14	0
Lewis, Greg, Phi.	2	46	23.0	28	0
Moats, Ryan, Phi.	2	43	21.5	23	0
Gaines, Michael, Car.	2	32	16.0	17	0
Johnson, Bryant, Ariz	2	29	14.5	16	0
Betts, Ladell, Was.	2	27	13.5	27	0
McCrary, Fred, Atl.	2	17	8.5	10	0
Schobel, Matt, Phi.	2	13	6.5	11	0
Smith, Steve, Car.	2	-1	-.5	3	0
Jones, Mark, T.B.	1	29	29.0	29	0
Bly, Dre', Det.	1	27	27.0	27	0
Moore, Mewelde, Min.	1	25	25.0	25	0
* Walker, Delanie, S.F.	1	25	25.0	25	0
Furrey, Mike, Det.	1	23	23.0	23	0
* Manning, Danieal, Chi.	1	20	20.0	20	0
McAfee, Fred, N.O.	1	20	20.0	20	0
McQuarters, R.W., NY-G	1	17	17.0	17	0
Sheppard, Lito, Phi.	1	16	16.0	16	0
Montgomery, Mike, G.B.	1	14	14.0	14	0
Graham, Earnest, T.B.	1	13	13.0	13	0
Jones, Nate, Dal.	1	13	13.0	13	0
Rosenthal, Mike, Min.	1	13	13.0	13	0
McKie, Jason, Chi.	1	11	11.0	11	0
Sowell, Jerald, T.B.	1	11	11.0	11	0
Karney, Mike, N.O.	1	10	10.0	10	0
Thrash, James, Was.	1	10	10.0	10	0
Woodson, Charles, G.B.	1	10	10.0	10	0
McClover, Darrell, Chi.	1	9	9.0	9	0
Lake, Antwan, N.O.	1	8	8.0	8	0
Wakefield, Fred, Ariz	1	7	7.0	7	0
Johnson, Al, Dal.	1	3	3.0	3	0
Muhammad, Muhsin, Chi.	1	3	3.0	3	0
Smith, Paul, St.L	1	3	3.0	3	0
Weeks, Marquis, Sea.	1	3	3.0	3	0
Blackburn, Chase, NY-G	1	2	2.0	2	0
Norris, Moran, S.F.	1	1	1.0	1	0
Adams, Blue, T.B.	1	0	0.0	0	0
Evans, Demetric, Was.	1f	0	0.0	0	0
* Golston, Kedric, Was.	1	0	0.0	0	0
Owens, Richard, Min.	1	0	0.0	0	0
Ratliff, Jay, Dal.	1	0	0.0	0	0
Ruegamer, Grey, NY-G	1	0	0.0	0	0
* Watkins, Pat, Dal.	1	0	0.0	0	0
Evans, Demetric, Was.	1f	0	0.0	0	0
Henderson, E.J., Min.	0f	0	—	—	0
* King, Jeff, Car.	0f	0	—	—	0
Ratliff, Keiwan, Cin.	0f	0	—	—	0

t = Touchdown; * Player that was a rookie in 2006
f = Fair Catch
Leader based on average return, minimum 20 returns

AMERICAN FOOTBALL CONFERENCE—KICKOFF RETURNS

	No	Yards	Avg	Long	TD
New England	58	1553	26.8	93t	1
Oakland	73	1811	24.8	50	0
San Diego	55	1350	24.5	91	0
N.Y. Jets	60	1445	24.1	103t	2
Buffalo	63	1503	23.9	88	0
Indianapolis	58	1368	23.6	70	0
Baltimore	45	1046	23.2	72	0
Tennessee	79	1835	23.2	70	0
Jacksonville	49	1136	23.2	93t	1
Cleveland	71	1635	23.0	92t	1
Houston	71	1609	22.7	87	0
Pittsburgh	55	1214	22.1	76	0
Denver	54	1187	22.0	64	0
Kansas City	64	1404	21.9	60	0
Miami	52	1102	21.2	46	0
Cincinnati	59	1209	20.5	38	0
AFC Total	966	22407	23.2	103t	5
AFC Average	60.4	1400.4	23.2	—	0.3

NATIONAL FOOTBALL CONFERENCE—KICKOFF RETURNS

	No	Yards	Avg	Long	TD
San Francisco	79	1907	24.1	64	0
Dallas	64	1493	23.3	41	0
Chicago	59	1373	23.3	96t	2
New Orleans	60	1377	23.0	51	0
Atlanta	68	1542	22.7	51	0
Minnesota	66	1492	22.6	65	0
Seattle	69	1548	22.4	50	0
Washington	73	1631	22.3	100t	1
Detroit	74	1648	22.3	65	0
Arizona	73	1610	22.1	99t	1
Tampa Bay	61	1307	21.4	44	0
St. Louis	65	1383	21.3	40	0
Philadelphia	58	1204	20.8	64	0
N.Y. Giants	70	1407	20.1	51	0
Green Bay	70	1379	19.7	35	0
Carolina	62	1200	19.4	39	0
NFC Total	1071	23501	21.9	100t	4
NFC Average	66.9	1468.8	21.9	—	0.3
League Total	2037	45908	—	103t	9
League Average	63.7	1434.6	22.5	—	0.3

PUNTING

AVERAGE YARDS PER PUNT
NFC: 48.2 Mat McBriar, Dallas
AFC: 47.5 Shane Lechler, Oakland

NET AVERAGE YARDS PER PUNT
AFC: 39.3 Dustin Colquitt, Kansas City
NFC: 39.0 Jason Baker, Carolina

LONGEST
NFC: 75 Mat McBriar, Dallas vs. Houston, October 15
AFC: 73 Craig Hentrich, Tennessee at Jacksonville, November 5

PUNTS
NFC: 98 Jason Baker, Carolina
AFC: 92 Brian Moorman, Buffalo

PUNTS, GAME
NFC: 11 Josh Bidwell, Tampa Bay at Chicago, December 17 (510 yards) - (OT)
AFC: 10 Shane Lechler, Oakland at Seattle, November 6 (450 yards)
10 Dave Zastudil, Cleveland at Atlanta, November 12 (462 yards)
10 Mike Scifres, San Diego at Seattle, December 24 (425 yards)
10 Donnie Jones, Miami vs. N.Y. Jets, December 25 (427 yards)

TEAM CHAMPION
NFC: 48.2 Dallas
AFC: 46.9 Oakland

AMERICAN FOOTBALL CONFERENCE—PUNTING

	Total Punts	Yards	Long	Avg	TB	Blk	Opp Ret	Return Yards	In 20	Net Avg
Oakland	78	3660	67	46.9	19	1	34	437	19	36.4
Cincinnati	77	3428	67	44.5	11	0	42	236	26	38.6
Kansas City	72	3178	72	44.1	5	0	32	254	24	39.2
Cleveland	83	3621	61	43.6	8	0	43	312	29	37.9
Buffalo	92	4012	66	43.6	7	0	36	265	33	39.2
Indianapolis	48	2085	61	43.4	5	1	25	327	14	34.5
N.Y. Jets	74	3211	69	43.4	11	1	28	205	27	37.6
Baltimore	86	3695	61	43.0	3	0	44	404	30	37.6
Tennessee	88	3760	73	42.7	10	0	33	278	32	37.3
Miami	86	3640	64	42.3	10	1	49	367	28	35.7
San Diego	69	2893	71	41.9	2	0	27	216	35	38.2
Denver	80	3338	61	41.7	7	0	39	268	23	36.6
Houston	76	3161	62	41.6	5	0	36	275	15	36.7
Pittsburgh	65	2687	56	41.3	4	0	38	219	11	36.7
New England	69	2847	62	41.3	7	0	29	322	19	34.6
Jacksonville	73	2920	58	40.0	7	1	29	343	20	33.4
AFC Total	1216	52136	73	—	121	5	564	4728	385	—
AFC Average	76.0	3258.5	--	42.9	7.6	0.3	35.3	295.5	24.1	37.0

NATIONAL FOOTBALL CONFERENCE—PUNTING

	Total Punts	Yards	Long	Avg	TB	Blk	Opp Ret	Return Yards	In 20	Net Avg
Dallas	56	2697	75	48.2	10	0	31	334	22	38.6
Carolina	100	4508	70	45.1	12	1	61	390	31	38.8
Detroit	66	2967	67	45.0	9	0	38	267	18	38.2
San Francisco	81	3625	66	44.8	9	0	35	462	22	36.8
Green Bay	84	3739	66	44.5	12	0	55	503	17	35.7
Seattle	86	3827	72	44.5	15	0	39	343	26	37.0
Chicago	77	3404	65	44.2	7	0	38	367	24	37.6
New Orleans	77	3369	59	43.8	10	0	40	279	19	37.5
Arizona	68	2965	58	43.6	3	2	44	562	18	34.5
Tampa Bay	93	4045	59	43.5	7	0	50	487	20	36.8
Philadelphia	78	3326	60	42.6	11	0	41	380	21	34.9
St. Louis	76	3223	74	42.4	5	1	27	247	29	37.8
Washington	82	3471	60	42.3	7	1	45	319	27	36.7
Minnesota	94	3961	68	42.1	7	0	50	485	29	35.5
Atlanta	78	3199	65	41.0	6	2	25	279	25	35.9
N.Y. Giants	77	3098	54	40.2	3	0	33	191	27	37.0
NFC Total	1273	55424	75	—	133	7	652	5895	375	—
NFC Average	79.6	3464.0	--	43.5	8.3	0.4	40.8	368.4	23.4	36.8
NFL Total	2489	107560	75	—	254	12	1216	10623	760	—
NFL Average	77.8	3361.3	--	43.2	7.9	0.4	38.0	332.0	23.8	36.9

NFL TOP TEN PUNTERS

	No	Yards	Long	Avg	Total Punts	TB	Blk	Opp Ret	Return Yards	In 20	Net Avg
McBriar, Mat, Dal.	56	2697	75	48.2	56	10	0	31	334	22	38.6
Lechler, Shane, Oak.	77	3660	67	47.5	78	19	1	34	437	19	36.4
Baker, Jason, Car.	98	4483	70	45.7	99	12	1	60	382	31	39.0
* Plackemeier, Ryan, Sea.	84	3778	72	45.0	84	15	0	38	343	25	37.3
Harris, Nick, Det.	66	2967	67	45.0	66	9	0	38	267	18	38.2
Player, Scott, Ariz	66	2965	58	44.9	68	3	2	44	562	18	34.5
Lee, Andy, S.F.	81	3625	66	44.8	81	9	0	35	462	22	36.8
Larson, Kyle, Cin.	77	3428	67	44.5	77	11	0	42	236	26	38.6
Ryan, Jon, G.B.	84	3739	66	44.5	84	12	0	55	503	17	35.7
Smith, Hunter, Ind.	47	2085	61	44.4	48	5	1	25	327	14	34.5

AFC—INDIVIDUAL PUNTERS

	No	Yards	Long	Avg	Total Punts	TB	Blk	Opp Ret	Return Yards	In 20	Net Avg
Lechler, Shane, Oak.	77	3660	67	47.5	78	19	1	34	437	19	36.4
Larson, Kyle, Cin.	77	3428	67	44.5	77	11	0	42	236	26	38.6
Smith, Hunter, Ind.	47	2085	61	44.4	48	5	1	25	327	14	34.5
Colquitt, Dustin, K.C.	71	3145	72	44.3	71	5	0	32	254	23	39.3
Graham, Ben, NYJ	72	3182	69	44.2	73	11	1	28	205	26	37.8
Zastudil, Dave, Cle.	81	3563	61	44.0	81	7	0	43	312	28	38.4
Moorman, Brian, Buf.	92	4012	66	43.6	92	7	0	36	265	33	39.2
Miller, Josh, N.E.	43	1848	62	43.0	43	7	0	18	169	12	35.8
* Koch, Sam, Bal.	86	3695	61	43.0	86	3	0	44	404	30	37.6
Jones, Donnie, Mia.	85	3640	64	42.8	86	10	1	49	367	28	35.7
Hentrich, Craig, Ten.	88	3760	73	42.7	88	10	0	33	278	32	37.3
Scifres, Mike, S.D.	69	2893	71	41.9	69	2	0	27	216	35	38.2
Ernster, Paul, Den.	80	3338	61	41.7	80	7	0	39	268	23	36.6
Stanley, Chad, Hou.	76	3161	62	41.6	76	5	0	36	275	15	36.7
Gardocki, Chris, Pit.	65	2687	56	41.3	65	4	0	38	219	11	36.7
Hanson, Chris, Jac.	72	2920	58	40.6	73	7	1	29	343	20	33.4
(Nonqualifiers)											
Walter, Ken, N.E.	16	591	47	36.9	16	0	0	7	52	5	33.7
Sauerbrun, Todd, N.E.	10	408	58	40.8	10	0	0	4	101	2	30.7
Dawson, Phil, Cle.	2	58	31	29.0	2	1	0	0	0	1	19.0
Tynes, Lawrence, K.C.	1	33	33	33.0	1	0	0	0	0	1	33.0
Pennington, Chad, NYJ	1	29	29	29.0	1	0	0	0	0	1	29.0

NFC—INDIVIDUAL PUNTERS

	No	Yards	Long	Avg	Total Punts	TB	Blk	Opp Ret	Return Yards	In 20	Net Avg
McBriar, Mat, Dal.	56	2697	75	48.2	56	10	0	31	334	22	38.6
Baker, Jason, Car.	98	4483	70	45.7	99	12	1	60	382	31	39.0
* Plackemeier, Ryan, Sea.	84	3778	72	45.0	84	15	0	38	343	25	37.3
Harris, Nick, Det.	66	2967	67	45.0	66	9	0	38	267	18	38.2
Player, Scott, Ariz	66	2965	58	44.9	68	3	2	44	562	18	34.5
Lee, Andy, S.F.	81	3625	66	44.8	81	9	0	35	462	22	36.8
Ryan, Jon, G.B.	84	3739	66	44.5	84	12	0	55	503	17	35.7
Maynard, Brad, Chi.	77	3404	65	44.2	77	7	0	38	367	24	37.6
* Weatherford, Steven, N.O.	77	3369	59	43.8	77	10	0	40	279	19	37.5
Turk, Matt, St.L	72	3132	74	43.5	73	5	1	26	239	26	38.3
Bidwell, Josh, T.B.	93	4045	59	43.5	93	7	0	50	487	20	36.8
Frost, Derrick, Was.	81	3471	60	42.9	82	7	1	45	319	27	36.7
Johnson, Dirk, Phi.	78	3326	60	42.6	78	11	0	41	380	21	34.9
Kluwe, Chris, Min.	93	3934	68	42.3	93	7	0	50	485	28	35.6
Koenen, Michael, Atl.	76	3199	65	42.1	78	6	2	25	279	25	35.9
Feagles, Jeff, NY-G	77	3098	54	40.2	77	3	0	33	191	27	37.0
(Nonqualifiers)											
Wilkins, Jeff, St.L	3	91	33	30.3	3	0	0	1	8	3	27.7
Brown, Josh, Sea.	2	49	28	24.5	2	0	0	1	0	1	24.5
Longwell, Ryan, Min.	1	27	27	27.0	1	0	0	0	0	1	27.0
Kasay, John, Car.	1	25	25	25.0	1	0	0	1	8	0	17.0

* Player that was a rookie in 2006
Leader based on average, minimum 40 punts

PUNT RETURNS

YARDS PER RETURN
AFC:	12.9	Pacman Jones, Tennessee
NFC:	12.8*	Devin Hester, Chicago

YARDS
NFC:	600	* Devin Hester, Chicago
AFC:	440	Pacman Jones, Tennessee

YARDS, GAME
NFC:	152	* Devin Hester, Chicago at Arizona, October 16 (6 returns, 1 TD)
AFC:	121	B.J. Sams, Baltimore vs. Atlanta, November 19 (3 returns, 0 TD)

LONGEST
AFC:	90	Pacman Jones, Tennessee at Philadelphia, November 19 - TD
NFC:	90	Nate Burleson, Seattle vs. St. Louis, November 12 - TD

RETURNS
NFC:	47	* Devin Hester, Chicago
AFC:	41	Wes Welker, Miami

RETURNS, GAME
AFC:	7	Kevin Faulk, New England at Green Bay, November 19 (55 yards, 0 TD)
NFC:	7	Mark Jones, Tampa Bay at Chicago, December 17 (46 yards, 0 TD) - (OT)
	7	Charles Woodson, Green Bay vs. Minnesota, December 21 (48 yards, 0 TD)

FAIR CATCHES
AFC:	29	Wes Welker, Miami
NFC:	14	Shaun McDonald, St. Louis

TOUCHDOWNS
AFC:	3	Pacman Jones, Tennessee
NFC:	3	* Devin Hester, Chicago

TEAM CHAMPION
AFC:	12.6	Tennessee
NFC:	12.1	Chicago

NFL TOP TEN PUNT RETURNERS

	No	FC	Yards	Avg	Long	TD
Jones, Pacman, Ten.	34	3	440	12.9	90t	3
* Hester, Devin, Chi.	47	12	600	12.8	84t	3
Parrish, Roscoe, Buf.	32	9	364	11.4	82t	1
Northcutt, Dennis, Cle.	28	13	312	11.1	81	0
Wynn, Dexter, Phi.-Hou.	25	14	270	10.8	58	0
Faulk, Kevin, N.E.	31	5	330	10.6	43	0
Sams, B.J., Bal.	29	4	307	10.6	65	0
Drummond, Eddie, Det.	28	13	296	10.6	40	0
Walters, Troy, Ariz	24	12	250	10.4	37	0
* Holmes, Santonio, Pit.	26	21	264	10.2	65t	1

AFC—INDIVIDUAL PUNT RETURNERS

	No	FC	Yards	Avg	Long	TD
Jones, Pacman, Ten.	34	3	440	12.9	90t	3
Parrish, Roscoe, Buf.	32	9	364	11.4	82t	1
Northcutt, Dennis, Cle.	28	13	312	11.1	81	0
Wynn, Dexter, Phi.-Hou.	25	14	270	10.8	58	0
Faulk, Kevin, N.E.	31	5	330	10.6	43	0
Sams, B.J., Bal.	29	4	307	10.6	65	0
* Holmes, Santonio, Pit.	26	21	264	10.2	65t	1
Welker, Wes, Mia.	41	29	378	9.2	47	0
Wilkins, Terrence, Ind.	21	13	193	9.2	82t	1
Parker, Eric, S.D.	37	15	331	8.9	50	0
Hall, Dante, K.C.	27	6	240	8.9	60t	1
Pearman, Alvin, Jac.	32	16	283	8.8	29	0
Williams, Darrent, Den.	25	12	206	8.2	34	0
Ratliff, Keiwan, Cin.	27	9	176	6.5	38	0
Carr, Chris, Oak.	35	12	216	6.2	35	0
(Nonqualifiers)						
Dwight, Tim, NYJ	14	9	146	10.4	18	0
* Washington, Leon, NYJ	13	6	97	7.5	38	0
* Ross, Cory, Bal.	13	3	37	2.8	9	0
Owens, Chad, Jac.	9	5	56	6.2	13	0
Chatman, Antonio, Cin.	8	3	53	6.6	19	0
Leonhard, Jim, Buf.	7	1	58	8.3	32	0
Kircus, David, Den.	6	4	86	14.3	42	0
Cribbs, Josh, Cle.	6	3	51	8.5	34	0
McCardell, Keenan, S.D.	5	7	39	7.8	12	0
Colclough, Ricardo, Pit.	4	0	6	1.5	3	0
* Jackson, Chad, N.E.	3	0	76	25.3	39	0
Wade, Bobby, Ten.	3	3	27	9.0	18	0
Shepherd, Edell, Hou.	3	2	24	8.0	14	0
Kennison, Eddie, K.C.	3	1	18	6.0	11	0
* Gordon, Cletis, S.D.	3	1	12	4.0	6	0
Brown, Troy, N.E.	2	9	16	8.0	12	0
* Rushing, T.J., Ind.	2	2	14	7.0	8	0
Mathis, Rashean, Jac.	2	1	9	4.5	9	0
Ivy, Corey, Bal.	2	0	7	3.5	7	0
Walls, Lenny, K.C.	2	0	6	3.0	6	0
Wilson, Cedrick, Pit.	2	1	4	2.0	3	0
* Jones-Drew, Maurice, Jac.	1	0	13	13.0	13	0
* Reid, Willie, Pit.	1	0	11	11.0	11	0
O'Neal, Deltha, Cin.	1	2	10	10.0	10	0
Jones, Sean, Cle.	1	0	8	8.0	8	0
Smith, Rod, Den.	1	0	2	2.0	2	0
Kassell, Brad, NYJ	1	0	0	0.0	0	0
Oglesby, Evan, Bal.	1	0	0	0.0	0	0
Poteat, Hank, NYJ	1	0	0	0.0	0	0
* Ross, Derrick, K.C.	1	0	0	0.0	0	0
Taylor, Ike, Pit.	1	0	0	0.0	0	0
Toefield, LaBrandon, Jac.	1	0	0	0.0	0	0
Unck, Mason, Cle.	1	0	0	0.0	0	0
Cotchery, Jerricho, NYJ	0	2	0	—	—	0
Hakim, Az-Zahir, Det.-S.D.	0	1	0	—	—	0
Lewis, Derrick, Hou.	0	2	0	—	—	0

*t = Touchdown; * Player that was a rookie in 2006*
Leader based on average return, minimum 20 returns

NFC—INDIVIDUAL PUNT RETURNERS

	No	FC	Yards	Avg	Long	TD
* Hester, Devin, Chi.	47	12	600	12.8	84t	3
Drummond, Eddie, Det.	28	13	296	10.6	40	0
Walters, Troy, Ariz	24	12	250	10.4	37	0
Moore, Mewelde, Min.	36	9	365	10.1	71t	1
Newman, Terence, Dal.	20	6	202	10.1	56t	1
Burleson, Nate, Sea.	34	7	322	9.5	90t	1
Morton, Chad, NY-G	29	13	268	9.2	38	0
Woodson, Charles, G.B.	41	2	363	8.9	40	0
Randle El, Antwaan, Was.	39	11	342	8.8	87t	1
Rossum, Allen, Atl.	37	13	288	7.8	41	0
Jones, Mark, T.B.	20	4	155	7.8	18	0
* Bush, Reggie, N.O.	28	2	216	7.7	65t	1
McDonald, Shaun, St.L	23	14	172	7.5	33	0
Hilliard, Ike, T.B.	24	3	163	6.8	16	0
* Williams, Brandon, S.F.	22	12	147	6.7	25	0
Gamble, Chris, Car.	36	13	185	5.1	24	0
(Nonqualifiers)						
Mahe, Reno, Phi.	18	12	169	9.4	23	0
Lewis, Michael, N.O.	16	10	111	6.9	26	0
Williams, Jimmy, Sea.	14	9	102	7.3	22	0
Buchanon, Phillip, Hou.-T.B.	14	4	95	6.8	45	0
Crayton, Patrick, Dal.	11	7	85	7.7	19	0
Smith, Steve, Car.	9	3	30	3.3	16	0
Looker, Dane, St.L	7	6	47	6.7	10	0
Battle, Arnaz, S.F.	6	7	90	15.0	60	0
Moore, Lance, N.O.	6	2	45	7.5	25	0
* Bodiford, Shaun, G.B.	6	1	25	4.2	16	0
Westbrook, Brian, Phi.	5	3	39	7.8	13	0
* Green, Skyler, Dal.	5	3	26	5.2	13	0
* Jennings, Greg, G.B.	5	0	29	5.8	10	0
* Ellis, Devale, Det.	4	1	61	15.3	48	0
Rector, Jamaica, Dal.	4	1	22	5.5	8	0
McQuarters, R.W., NY-G	4	2	20	5.0	12	0
Bly, Dre', Det.	3	3	39	13.0	36	0
* Biddle, Taye, Car.	2	1	11	5.5	11	0
Barber, Ronde, T.B.	2	0	7	3.5	8	0
Berrian, Bernard, Chi.	2	0	7	3.5	7	0
Galloway, Joey, T.B.	2	0	3	1.5	2	0
* Marshall, Richard, Car.	2	0	-1	-.5	0	0
Smith, Dwight, Min.	1	0	8	8.0	8	0
* Gordon, Charles, Min.	1	0	1	1.0	1	0
Bellamy, Jay, N.O.	1	0	0	0.0	0	0
Johnson, Bryant, Ariz	1	1	0	0.0	0	0
Trufant, Marcus, Sea.	1	0	0	0.0	0	0
Wesley, Dante, Chi.	1	0	0	0.0	0	0
Martin, Ruvell, G.B.	1	0	-2	-2.0	-2	0
Ponder, Willie, St.L	0	0	15	—	15	0
Cox, Torrie, T.B.	0	0	9	—	9	0

*t = Touchdown; * Player that was a rookie in 2006*
Leader based on average return, minimum 20 returns

AMERICAN FOOTBALL CONFERENCE—PUNT RETURNS

	No	FC	Yards	Avg	Long	TD
Tennessee	37	6	467	12.6	90t	3
New England	36	14	422	11.7	43	0
Buffalo	39	10	422	10.8	82t	1
Houston	23	15	242	10.5	58	0
Cleveland	36	16	371	10.3	81	0
Miami	41	29	378	9.2	47	0
Denver	32	16	294	9.2	42	0
Indianapolis	23	15	207	9.0	82t	1
San Diego	45	23	382	8.5	50	0
Pittsburgh	34	22	285	8.4	65t	1
N.Y. Jets	29	17	243	8.4	38	0
Jacksonville	45	22	361	8.0	29	0
Kansas City	33	7	264	8.0	60t	1
Baltimore	45	7	351	7.8	65	0
Cincinnati	36	14	239	6.6	38	0
Oakland	35	12	216	6.2	35	0
AFC Total	569	245	5144	9.0	90t	7
AFC Average	35.6	15.3	321.5	9.0	—	0.4

NATIONAL FOOTBALL CONFERENCE—PUNT RETURNS

	No	FC	Yards	Avg	Long	TD
Chicago	50	12	607	12.1	84t	3
Detroit	35	18	396	11.3	48	0
Arizona	25	13	250	10.0	37	0
Minnesota	38	9	374	9.8	71t	1
Philadelphia	36	20	339	9.4	23	0
Washington	39	11	342	8.8	87t	1
N.Y. Giants	33	15	288	8.7	38	0
Seattle	49	16	424	8.7	90t	1
San Francisco	28	19	237	8.5	60	0
Dallas	40	17	335	8.4	56t	1
Green Bay	53	3	415	7.8	40	0
St. Louis	30	20	234	7.8	33	0
Atlanta	37	13	288	7.8	41	0
New Orleans	51	14	372	7.3	65t	1
Tampa Bay	54	9	353	6.5	18	0
Carolina	49	17	225	4.6	24	0
NFC Total	647	226	5479	8.5	90t	8
NFC Average	40.4	14.1	342.4	8.5	—	0.5
League Total	1216	471	10623	—	90t	15
League Average	38.0	14.7	332.0	8.7	—	0.5

FUMBLES

MOST FUMBLES

AFC: 16 David Carr, Houston
NFC: 11 * Bruce Gradkowski, Tampa Bay
11 Jon Kitna, Detroit

MOST FUMBLES, GAME

AFC: 4 Carson Palmer, Cincinnati at Indianapolis, December 18
NFC: 4 Kurt Warner, Arizona at Seattle, September 17
4 Michael Vick, Atlanta vs. N.Y. Giants, October 15
4 Tony Romo, Dallas vs. Detroit, December 31

OWN FUMBLES RECOVERED

AFC: 5 David Carr, Houston
NFC: 3 * Bruce Gradkowski, Tampa Bay
3 Ike Hilliard, Tampa Bay
3 Julius Jones, Dallas
3 Mewelde Moore, Minnesota
3 Tony Romo, Dallas
3 Kurt Warner, Arizona

OWN FUMBLES RECOVERED, GAME

NFC: 3 Kurt Warner, Arizona at Seattle, September 17 (0 yards, 0 TD)
AFC: 2 J.P. Losman, Buffalo at New England, September 10 (0 yards, 0 TD)
2 Andrew Walter, Oakland at Baltimore, September 17 (0 yards, 0 TD)
2 * Vince Young, Tennessee at San Diego, September 17 (0 yards, 0 TD)
2 Tatum Bell, Denver at San Diego, December 10 (0 yards, 0 TD)

OPPONENTS' FUMBLES RECOVERED

AFC: 6 Jared Allen, Kansas City
NFC: 3 Michael Boley, Atlanta
3 Rod Coleman, Atlanta
3 Kalimba Edwards, Detroit
3 Adewale Ogunleye, Chicago
3 Mike Patterson, Philadelphia
3 Jay Ratliff, Dallas
3 Fred Robbins, N.Y. Giants
3 Dewayne White, Tampa Bay
3 Kevin Williams, Minnesota

OPPONENTS' FUMBLES RECOVERED, GAME

AFC: 2 Kelly Gregg, Baltimore vs. Oakland, September 17 (59 yards, 0 TD)
2 Tony Brown, Tennessee vs. Houston, October 29 (33 yards, 1 TD)
2 Darrent Williams, Denver at Pittsburgh, November 5 (12 yards, 0 TD)
2 Ryan Clark, Pittsburgh vs. New Orleans, November 12 (5 yards, 0 TD)
2 Jared Allen, Kansas City at Oakland, December 23 (4 yards, 0 TD)
NFC: 2 Dewayne White, Tampa Bay vs. Carolina, September 24 (0 yards, 0 TD)
2 Mike Patterson, Philadelphia at San Francisco, September 24 (98 yards, 1 TD)
2 Rod Coleman, Atlanta vs. Arizona, October 1 (0 yards, 0 TD)

YARDS

NFC: 99 Adrian Wilson, Arizona
AFC: 92 * Cortland Finnegan, Tennessee

LONGEST

NFC: 99 Adrian Wilson, Arizona at Minnesota, November 26 - TD
AFC: 92 * Cortland Finnegan, Tennessee vs. Jacksonville, December 17 - TD

AFC—TOUCHDOWNS ON FUMBLE RECOVERIES

Brown, Tony, Ten.	1
Bulluck, Keith, Ten.	1
Dobbins, Tim, S.D.	1
Faggins, Demarcus, Hou.	1
* Finnegan, Cortland, Ten.	1
Fletcher-Baker, London, Buf.	1
Harris, Marques, S.D.	1
Hayden, Kelvin, Ind.	1
Hill, Renaldo, Mia.	1
Hobson, Victor, NYJ	1
Holly, Daven, Cle.	1
Maddox, Anthony, Hou.	1
McCree, Marlon, S.D.	1
McGee, Terrence, Buf.	1
Morrison, Kirk, Oak.	1
Thomas, Adalius, Bal.	1
Williams, Sam, Oak.	1

NFC—TOUCHDOWNS ON FUMBLE RECOVERIES

Adeyanju, Victor, St.L	1
Brown, Mike, Chi.	1
Carter, Tim, NY-G	1
Herndon, Kelly, Sea.	1
* Hodge, Abdul, G.B.	1
Leber, Ben, Min.	1
McAllister, Deuce, N.O.	1
McMullen, Billy, Min.	1
* Oliver, Melvin, S.F.	1
Patterson, Mike, Phi.	1
Smith, Antonio, Ariz	1
Tillman, Charles, Chi.	1
Ware, DeMarcus, Dal.	1
Williams, Demorrio, Atl.	1
Williams, Kevin, Min.	1
Wilson, Adrian, Ariz	1

AFC FUMBLES—INDIVIDUAL

	Fum	Own Rec	Opp Rec	Yards	Tot Rec
* Addai, Joseph, Ind.	2	0	0	-2	0
Aiken, Sam, Buf.	0	1	0	0	1
Alexander, Stephen, Den.	0	1	0	0	1
Allen, Jared, K.C.	1	0	6	24	6
Allen, Will, Mia.	0	0	3	1	3
Amano, Eugene, Ten.	0	1	0	0	1
Anderson, Courtney, Oak.	1	1	0	0	1
Anderson, Derek, Cle.	2	0	0	0	0
Bailey, Champ, Den.	0	0	1	4	1
Baker, Chris, NYJ	0	1	0	0	1
Barlow, Kevan, NYJ	1	1	0	0	1
Batch, Charlie, Pit.	1	0	0	-3	0
Bell, Jacob, Ten.	0	2	0	-8	2
* Bell, Mike, Den.	1	0	0	0	0
Bell, Tatum, Den.	5	2	0	0	2
Bell, Yeremiah, Mia.	0	0	2	0	2
Bennett, Drew, Ten.	2	1	0	0	1
Bennett, Michael, K.C.	1	1	0	0	1
Binn, David, S.D.	0	0	1	0	1
Black, Jordan, K.C.	0	1	0	0	1
Bockwoldt, Colby, Ten.	0	1	0	0	1
Boller, Kyle, Bal.	3	2	0	-12	2
Bowens, David, Mia.	0	0	2	4	2
Brady, Tom, N.E.	12	1	0	-2	1

Player	Fum	Own Rec	Opp Rec	Yards	Tot Rec
Brock, Raheem, Ind.	0	0	3	0	3
Brooks, Aaron, Oak.	5	2	0	-9	2
Brown, Tony, Ten.	1	0	2	33	2
Brown, C.C., Hou.	0	0	1	0	1
Brown, Chris, Ten.	1	1	0	0	1
Brown, Dee, K.C.	1	0	1	0	1
Brown, Ronnie, Mia.	4	0	0	-16	0
Bruschi, Tedy, N.E.	0	0	2	0	2
Bulluck, Keith, Ten.	0	0	1	17	1
Caldwell, Reche, N.E.	2	1	0	8	1
Carey, Vernon, Mia.	0	3	0	0	3
Carlisle, Cooper, Den.	0	2	0	0	2
Carr, Chris, Oak.	2	1	0	0	1
Carr, David, Hou.	16	5	0	-4	5
Carter, Kevin, Mia.	0	0	2	0	2
Carter, Tyrone, Pit.	0	1	0	0	1
Cassel, Matt, N.E.	1	0	0	0	0
Castillo, Luis, S.D.	0	0	1	0	1
Chambers, Chris, Mia.	0	1	0	5	1
* Clark, Brian, Den.	2	0	0	0	0
Clark, Ryan, Pit.	0	0	3	5	3
* Clemens, Kellen, NYJ	1	0	0	0	0
Clements, Nate, Buf.	0	0	2	18	2
Colclough, Ricardo, Pit.	1	0	0	0	0
Coles, Laveranues, NYJ	1	1	0	13	1
Colquitt, Dustin, K.C.	2	1	0	-20	1
Colvin, Rosevelt, N.E.	0	0	1	0	1
Cook, Jameel, Hou.	2	0	0	0	0
Cotchery, Jerricho, NYJ	0	2	0	0	2
Cox, Curome, Den.	0	0	1	11	1
Cramer, Casey, Ten.	0	2	0	0	2
Cribbs, Josh, Cle.	3	1	0	0	1
Crockett, Zack, Oak.	2	0	0	-7	0
* Cromartie, Antonio, S.D.	1	0	0	0	0
Cruz, Ronnie, K.C.	0	1	0	0	1
Culpepper, Daunte, Mia.	3	1	0	0	1
* Cutler, Jay, Den.	8	3	0	-8	3
Davenport, Najeh, Pit.	2	1	0	0	1
David, Jason, Ind.	0	0	1	5	1
Dayne, Ron, Hou.	1	0	0	0	0
Denney, John, Mia.	0	0	1	0	1
Denney, Ryan, Buf.	0	0	1	0	1
Dillon, Corey, N.E.	2	0	0	0	0
Dinkins, Darnell, Cle.	1	0	0	0	0
* Dobbins, Tim, S.D.	0	0	1	0	1
Droughns, Reuben, Cle.	5	1	0	0	1
* Dumervil, Elvis, Den.	0	0	3	13	3
Dunn, Jason, K.C.	0	1	0	0	1
Dwight, Tim, NYJ	1	1	0	0	1
Edwards, Donnie, S.D.	1	0	1	0	1
* Ellison, Keith, Buf.	0	0	1	0	1
Engelberger, John, Den.	0	0	1	0	1
Evans, Heath, N.E.	1	1	0	0	1
Evans, Lee, Buf.	1	0	0	0	0
Faggins, Demarcus, Hou.	0	0	2	58	2
Faneca, Alan, Pit.	0	2	0	0	2
Fargas, Justin, Oak.	1	2	0	-7	2
Farrior, James, Pit.	0	0	1	0	1
Faulk, Kevin, N.E.	2	1	0	0	1
* Finnegan, Cortland, Ten.	0	0	2	92	2
Fletcher-Baker, London, Buf.	0	0	1	5	1
Flynn, Mike, Bal.	0	1	0	0	1
Foote, Larry, Pit.	0	0	1	0	1
Foster, George, Den.	0	1	0	0	1
Fowler, Melvin, Buf.	1	0	1	0	1
Frye, Charlie, Cle.	8	0	0	-6	0
Gabriel, Doug, N.E.	1	0	0	0	0
Gado, Samkon, Hou.	1	0	0	0	0
Garrard, David, Jac.	4	1	0	-16	1
Gates, Antonio, S.D.	0	1	0	4	1
Ghiaciuc, Eric, Cin.	0	2	0	0	2
Glenn, Tarik, Ind.	0	1	0	0	1
Goff, Mike, S.D.	0	1	0	0	1
Gonzalez, Tony, K.C.	1	0	0	0	0
Goodman, Andre', Mia.	0	0	2	64	2
Graham, Ben, NYJ	1	0	0	-8	0
Graham, Daniel, N.E.	1	0	0	0	0
Grant, Deon, Jac.	0	0	1	6	1
Green, Jarvis, N.E.	0	0	1	0	1
Green, Louis, Den.	0	0	1	0	1
Green, Trent, K.C.	5	0	0	-8	0
Greenwood, Morlon, Hou.	0	0	3	15	3
Gregg, Kelly, Bal.	0	0	3	59	3
* Gregory, Steve, S.D.	0	1	0	0	1
Greisen, Nick, Jac.	0	0	1	1	1
Griffin, Kris, K.C.	0	1	0	0	1
Haggans, Clark, Pit.	0	0	1	0	1
* Hali, Tamba, K.C.	0	0	1	0	1
* Hall, Ahmard, Ten.	1	0	0	0	0
Hall, Dante, K.C.	2	0	0	0	0
Hamilton, Bobby, NYJ	0	0	1	0	1
Harrington, Joey, Mia.	4	2	0	-3	2
Harris, Marques, S.D.	0	0	2	0	2
* Harrison, Jerome, Cle.	1	0	0	0	0
Harrison, Marvin, Ind.	1	0	0	0	0
Harrison, Rodney, N.E.	0	0	1	0	1
Hart, Clinton, S.D.	1	0	1	0	1
Hartings, Jeff, Pit.	0	1	0	0	1
Hawkins, Artrell, N.E.	0	0	1	0	1
Hayden, Kelvin, Ind.	0	0	1	26	1
Haynes, Verron, Pit.	1	0	0	0	0
Heiden, Steve, Cle.	0	0	1	0	1
Henry, Travis, Ten.	3	2	0	0	2
Hill, Renaldo, Mia.	0	0	1	48	1
Hobbs, Ellis, N.E.	0	0	1	5	1
Hobson, Victor, NYJ	0	0	2	32	2
Hochstein, Russ, N.E.	0	1	0	0	1
Holliday, Vonnie, Mia.	0	0	1	0	1
Holly, Daven, Cle.	0	0	1	40	1
* Holmes, Santonio, Pit.	5	1	0	0	1
Hope, Chris, Ten.	0	0	1	0	1
Huard, Damon, K.C.	9	1	0	-22	1
Huntley, Kevin, Oak.	0	0	1	0	1
Ivy, Corey, Bal.	1	0	0	0	0
Jackson, Dexter, Cin.	0	0	1	0	1
Jackson, Eddie, Mia.	0	0	1	0	1
Jacox, Kendyl, Mia.	0	1	0	0	1
Jeanty, Rashad, Cin.	0	0	1	0	1
Johnson, Andre, Hou.	1	0	0	0	0
Johnson, Chad, Cin.	1	1	0	0	1
Johnson, Derrick, K.C.	0	0	2	0	2
Johnson, Larry, K.C.	2	1	0	0	1
Johnson, Rudi, Cin.	6	2	0	0	2
Jones, Pacman, Ten.	4	2	0	1	2
Jones, Donnie, Mia.	1	1	0	-10	1
Jones, Matt, Jac.	1	0	0	0	0
Jones, Sean, Cle.	0	0	1	-3	1
* Jones-Drew, Maurice, Jac.	1	0	0	0	0
Jordan, LaMont, Oak.	1	0	0	0	0
* Joseph, Johnathan, Cin.	0	1	1	7	2
June, Cato, Ind.	0	0	1	0	1
Jurevicius, Joe, Cle.	0	1	0	0	1
Kassell, Brad, NYJ	1	0	0	0	0
Keisel, Brett, Pit.	0	0	1	1	1
Kelsay, Chris, Buf.	0	0	1	0	1
Kemoeatu, Chris, Pit.	0	1	0	0	1

2006 INDIVIDUAL STATISTICS—FUMBLES

	Fum	Own Rec	Opp Rec	Yards	Tot Rec		Fum	Own Rec	Opp Rec	Yards	Tot Rec
Kiel, Terrence, S.D.	0	0	1	6	1	Peters, Jason, Buf.	0	1	0	0	1
* Kilmer, Ethan, Cin.	0	0	1	0	1	Phillips, Shaun, S.D.	0	1	1	0	2
Knight, Sammy, K.C.	0	0	0	5	0	Pitts, Chester, Hou.	0	3	0	0	3
Koppen, Dan, N.E.	0	3	0	0	3	Plummer, Jake, Den.	7	1	0	-5	1
Lee, ReShard, Oak.	1	0	0	0	0	* Pollard, Bernard, K.C.	0	0	1	0	1
Leftwich, Byron, Jac.	2	1	0	-5	1	Pool, Brodney, Cle.	0	0	2	0	2
Leonhard, Jim, Buf.	2	1	0	0	1	Poteat, Hank, NYJ	0	0	1	4	1
Lewis, Jamal, Bal.	4	1	0	0	1	Price, Peerless, Buf.	1	0	0	0	0
Lewis, Ray, Bal.	0	0	1	0	1	Ratliff, Keiwan, Cin.	1	0	0	0	0
Light, Matt, N.E.	0	1	0	0	1	Reagor, Montae, Ind.	0	0	1	0	1
Losman, J.P., Buf.	13	4	0	-22	4	Reed, Ed, Bal.	0	0	1	32	1
* Lundy, Wali, Hou.	1	0	0	0	0	Reyes, Tutan, Buf.	0	1	0	0	1
Lynch, John, Den.	0	0	1	7	1	Rhodes, Dominic, Ind.	3	0	0	0	0
Maddox, Anthony, Hou.	0	0	1	47	1	Rhodes, Kerry, NYJ	0	0	1	4	1
* Mangold, Nick, NYJ	1	0	0	-7	0	Rivers, Philip, S.D.	8	4	0	-25	4
Manning, Peyton, Ind.	2	0	0	0	0	Robertson, Dewayne, NYJ	0	0	1	0	1
Manuwai, Vince, Jac.	0	1	0	0	1	Roethlisberger, Ben, Pit.	5	0	0	-1	0
* Maroney, Laurence, N.E.	1	0	0	0	0	* Ross, Cory, Bal.	1	0	0	0	0
* Marshall, Brandon, Den.	1	0	0	0	0	* Ross, Derrick, K.C.	1	0	0	0	0
Mason, Derrick, Bal.	1	1	0	0	1	Roth, Matt, Mia.	0	1	0	0	1
Mathis, Robert, Ind.	0	0	2	0	2	Royal, Robert, Buf.	0	1	1	0	2
Mawae, Kevin, Ten.	1	0	0	-11	0	Ryan, Sean, NYJ	1	0	0	0	0
McAlister, Chris, Bal.	0	0	2	0	2	* Ryans, DeMeco, Hou.	0	0	1	0	1
McCardell, Keenan, S.D.	2	0	0	0	0	Salaam, Ephraim, Hou.	0	1	0	0	1
McCareins, Justin, NYJ	1	0	0	0	0	Sampson, Kevin, K.C.	0	1	0	0	1
McCree, Marlon, S.D.	0	0	1	79	1	Sapp, Cecil, Den.	0	0	1	0	1
McFadden, Bryant, Pit.	0	2	1	0	3	Scaife, Bo, Ten.	1	0	0	0	0
McFarland, Anthony, Ind.	0	0	1	0	1	Schobel, Aaron, Buf.	0	0	1	0	1
McGahee, Willis, Buf.	4	1	0	0	1	Schweigert, Stuart, Oak.	0	0	1	0	1
McGee, Terrence, Buf.	2	0	1	68	1	Scifres, Mike, S.D.	1	1	0	0	1
McGinest, Willie, Cle.	0	0	1	0	1	Sensabaugh, Gerald, Jac.	0	0	1	0	1
McKinney, Steve, Hou.	0	1	0	0	1	Seymour, Richard, N.E.	0	0	1	0	1
McNair, Steve, Bal.	7	3	0	-21	3	Shaffer, Kevin, Cle.	0	1	0	0	1
* McNeill, Marcus, S.D.	0	1	0	0	1	Shepherd, Edell, Hou.	2	0	0	0	0
Meier, Rob, Jac.	0	0	1	0	1	Simmons, Brian, Cin.	0	0	1	0	1
Merriman, Shawne, S.D.	0	0	1	0	1	Smith, Aaron, Pit.	0	0	1	0	1
Miller, Caleb, Cin.	0	0	1	0	1	* Smith, Brad, NYJ	1	2	0	-7	2
Miller, Heath, Pit.	0	1	0	0	1	Smith, Justin, Cin.	0	0	2	0	2
Miller, Justin, NYJ	1	1	1	0	2	Smith, Marvel, Pit.	0	1	0	0	1
Mitchell, Kawika, K.C.	0	0	1	0	1	Smith, Musa, Bal.	1	1	1	0	2
Moorman, Brian, Buf.	1	0	0	-11	0	* Smith, Rob, Cle.	0	0	1	0	1
Morant, Johnnie, Oak.	2	0	0	0	0	Smith, Rod, Den.	2	1	0	0	1
Morey, Sean, Pit.	1	0	0	0	0	Spragan, Donnie, Mia.	0	0	1	0	1
Morris, Sammy, Mia.	4	1	0	0	1	Stanley, Chad, Hou.	1	1	0	-9	1
Morrison, Kirk, Oak.	0	0	1	35	1	Starks, Randy, Ten.	0	0	2	26	2
Moulds, Eric, Hou.	1	0	0	0	0	Steinbach, Eric, Cin.	0	2	0	0	2
Mughelli, Ovie, Bal.	1	0	0	0	0	Stewart, David, Ten.	0	1	0	0	1
Myers, Michael, Den.	0	0	2	11	2	Stewart, Tony, Cin.	0	0	2	0	2
Nash, Damien, Den.	0	1	0	0	1	Stills, Gary, Bal.	0	1	1	0	2
Neal, Lorenzo, S.D.	2	1	0	0	1	Suggs, Terrell, Bal.	0	0	2	0	2
Nickey, Donnie, Ten.	1	0	0	-2	0	Surtain, Patrick, K.C.	0	0	1	19	1
Northcutt, Dennis, Cle.	1	0	0	0	0	* Taylor, Chris, Hou.	0	1	0	0	1
Nugent, Mike, NYJ	0	1	0	-3	1	Taylor, Fred, Jac.	3	0	0	0	0
* O'Callaghan, Ryan, N.E.	0	1	0	0	1	Taylor, Ike, Pit.	0	1	0	0	1
Ogden, Jonathan, Bal.	0	1	0	0	1	Taylor, Jason, Mia.	0	0	2	33	2
Olshansky, Igor, S.D.	0	0	1	0	1	Thomas, Adalius, Bal.	0	0	1	57	1
O'Neal, Deltha, Cin.	0	0	1	0	1	Thomas, Anthony, Buf.	1	0	0	0	1
Orr, Shantee, Hou.	0	0	1	19	1	Thomas, Bryan, NYJ	0	0	1	0	1
* Page, Jarrad, K.C.	0	0	1	0	1	Thomas, Josh, Ind.	0	0	1	0	1
Palmer, Carson, Cin.	15	2	0	-9	2	Thomas, Robert, Oak.	0	0	1	0	1
Parker, Willie, Pit.	7	0	0	0	0	Thompson, Lamont, Ten.	0	1	1	19	2
Parrish, Roscoe, Buf.	2	0	0	0	0	Thornton, John, Cin.	0	0	1	0	1
Pass, Patrick, N.E.	1	0	0	0	0	Tomlinson, LaDainian, S.D.	2	1	0	0	1
Paymah, Karl, Den.	0	1	0	0	1	Tripplett, Larry, Buf.	0	0	1	0	1
Pearman, Alvin, Jac.	2	1	0	0	1	Troupe, Ben, Ten.	0	2	0	0	2
Pennington, Chad, NYJ	7	1	0	-3	1	Tuiasosopo, Marques, Oak.	1	0	0	0	0
* Perry, Jereme, Cle.	0	0	1	1	1	* Tulloch, Stephen, Ten.	0	0	1	0	1
Perry, Chris, Cin.	2	1	0	0	1	Turley, Kyle, K.C.	0	1	0	0	1

	Fum	Own Rec	Opp Rec	Yards	Tot Rec
Utecht, Ben, Ind.	1	0	0	0	0
Vilma, Jonathan, NYJ	0	0	1	12	1
Vrabel, Mike, N.E.	0	0	1	0	1
Wade, Bobby, Ten.	2	0	0	0	0
Walter, Andrew, Oak.	13	3	0	-20	3
Walter, Kevin, Hou.	1	0	0	0	0
Ward, Hines, Pit.	2	0	0	0	0
Warren, Ty, N.E.	0	0	1	0	1
* Washington, Leon, NYJ	3	1	0	0	1
Watson, Benjamin, N.E.	3	1	0	0	1
Watson, Kenny, Cin.	0	2	0	8	2
Wayne, Reggie, Ind.	1	0	0	0	0
Weaver, Anthony, Hou.	0	0	1	0	1
* Webb, Dee, Jac.	1	0	0	0	0
Welker, Wes, Mia.	3	1	0	0	1
Whitted, Alvis, Oak.	1	0	0	0	0
Wiegert, Zach, Hou.	0	1	0	0	1
Wilcox, Daniel, Bal.	2	0	0	0	0
Wilford, Ernest, Jac.	1	0	0	0	0
Wilfork, Vince, N.E.	0	0	1	0	1
Wilkins, Terrence, Ind.	3	0	0	0	0
Williams, Darrent, Den.	3	1	2	12	3
* Williams, Mario, Hou.	0	0	1	0	1
Williams, Randal, Oak.	2	0	0	0	0
Williams, Reggie, Jac.	1	2	0	0	2
Williams, Sam, Oak.	0	0	1	30	1
* Williams, Steve, K.C.	0	0	1	3	1
Wilson, Cedrick, Pit.	2	1	0	-7	1
Wilson, Kris, K.C.	0	1	0	0	1
* Wimbley, Kamerion, Cle.	0	0	3	1	3
Winslow, Kellen, Cle.	1	0	0	0	0
Wire, Coy, Buf.	0	1	0	0	1
Withrow, Cory, S.D.	1	0	0	0	0
Woods, LeVar, Det.-Ten.	0	1	1	1	2
Wright, Jason, Cle.	1	0	0	0	0
Wright, Mike, N.E.	0	0	2	0	2
Wynn, Dexter, Phi.-Hou.	4	1	0	0	1
* Young, Vince, Ten.	12	4	0	-8	4
Zgonina, Jeff, Mia.	0	0	1	0	1

*Player that was a rookie in 2006
Yards includes aborted plays, own recoveries, and opponents' recoveries.

NFC FUMBLES—INDIVIDUAL

	Fum	Own Rec	Opp Rec	Yards	Tot Rec
* Adeyanju, Victor, St.L	0	0	2	89	2
Alexander, Shaun, Sea.	6	2	0	0	2
Alstott, Mike, T.B.	1	0	0	0	0
* Anderson, Mark, Chi.	0	0	1	0	1
Arrington, J.J., Ariz	1	0	0	0	0
Atogwe, O.J., St.L	0	0	1	0	1
* Austin, Miles, Dal.	3	1	0	0	1
* Avant, Jason, Phi.	1	0	0	0	0
Ayanbadejo, Obafemi, Ariz	1	0	0	0	0
Ayanbadejo, Brendon, Chi.	0	1	2	2	3
Ayodele, Akin, Dal.	1	0	2	2	2
Babineaux, Jonathan, Atl.	0	0	1	0	1
Barber, Tiki, NY-G	3	1	0	0	1
Barber, Shawn, Phi.	0	0	1	0	1
Barnett, Nick, G.B.	0	0	1	0	1
Barron, Alex, St.L	0	1	0	0	1
Bartrum, Mike, Phi.	1	0	0	-11	0
Battle, Arnaz, S.F.	2	0	0	0	0
Becht, Anthony, T.B.	1	0	0	0	0
Bell, Marcus, Det.	0	0	1	0	1

	Fum	Own Rec	Opp Rec	Yards	Tot Rec
Bentley, Kevin, Sea.	0	0	1	0	1
Bergen, Adam, Ariz	2	1	0	1	1
Bernard, Rocky, Sea.	0	0	1	0	1
Berrian, Bernard, Chi.	2	0	0	0	0
Berry, Bertrand, Ariz	0	0	1	0	1
Betts, Ladell, Was.	6	0	0	0	0
Birk, Matt, Min.	0	1	0	0	1
Blackstock, Darryl, Ariz	0	0	1	0	1
Bledsoe, Drew, Dal.	3	1	0	0	1
Bly, Dre', Det.	0	0	1	5	1
Bolden, Juran, T.B.	0	0	1	0	1
Boldin, Anquan, Ariz	1	0	0	0	0
Boley, Michael, Atl.	0	0	3	0	3
Boulware, Michael, Sea.	0	0	1	32	1
Bradford, Corey, Det.	1	0	0	0	0
Branch, Deion, Sea.	0	0	1	0	1
Brees, Drew, N.O.	8	1	0	-3	1
Briggs, Lance, Chi.	0	0	1	0	1
Brooking, Keith, Atl.	0	0	1	0	1
Brown, Alex, Chi.	0	0	2	0	2
Brown, Jammal, N.O.	0	1	0	0	1
Brown, Mike, Chi.	0	0	1	3	1
Brown, Milford, Ariz	0	2	0	0	2
Brunell, Mark, Was.	5	1	0	-8	1
Bryant, Anthony, Det.	0	0	1	0	1
Bryant, Fernando, Det.	0	0	1	0	1
Buchanon, Phillip, T.B.	0	0	1	0	1
Buckhalter, Correll, Phi.	2	2	0	0	2
Bulger, Marc, St.L	6	1	0	-6	1
Burleson, Nate, Sea.	2	2	0	0	2
Burress, Plaxico, NY-G	2	0	0	0	0
* Bush, Reggie, N.O.	2	1	0	0	1
Butler, Jerametrius, St.L	0	0	1	0	1
* Calhoun, Brian, Det.	1	1	0	0	1
Campbell, Jason, Was.	1	1	0	0	1
Campbell, Khary, Was.	0	0	1	0	1
Carpenter, Dwaine, St.L	0	0	1	0	1
Carter, Tim, NY-G	1	1	0	0	1
Cartwright, Rock, Was.	1	0	0	0	0
Celestin, Oliver, Sea.	0	1	0	0	1
Chavous, Corey, St.L	0	0	2	0	2
Clayton, Michael, T.B.	2	0	0	0	0
Cole, Trent, Phi.	0	0	1	1	1
Coleman, Rod, Atl.	0	0	3	9	3
Colombo, Marc, Dal.	0	1	0	0	1
Considine, Sean, Phi.	0	0	2	0	2
Cooley, Chris, Was.	0	1	0	0	1
Cooper, Chris, Ariz	0	0	1	0	1
Copper, Terrance, N.O.	2	0	1	0	1
Cox, Torrie, T.B.	0	0	1	0	1
Crayton, Patrick, Dal.	1	0	0	0	0
Crumpler, Alge, Atl.	0	1	0	0	1
Curry, Donte, Det.	0	0	1	0	1
Curtis, Kevin, St.L	1	0	0	0	0
Dansby, Karlos, Ariz	0	0	1	0	1
Davis, Anthony, T.B.	0	1	0	0	1
Davis, Chauncey, Atl.	0	0	1	0	1
Davis, Rashied, Chi.	1	0	0	0	0
Davis, Rod, Min.	0	0	1	0	1
Davis, Russell, Sea.	0	0	1	0	1
Davis, Stephen, St.L	1	0	0	0	0
* Davis, Vernon, S.F.	1	1	0	0	1
Delhomme, Jake, Car.	6	0	0	0	0
Demps, Will, NY-G	0	0	2	0	2
Dockett, Darnell, Ariz	0	0	2	5	2
Douglas, Marques, S.F.	0	0	1	0	1
Draft, Chris, Car.	0	0	2	8	2

	Fum	Own Rec	Opp Rec	Yards	Tot Rec		Fum	Own Rec	Opp Rec	Yards	Tot Rec
Driver, Donald, G.B.	1	1	0	0	1	Incognito, Richie, St.L	1	1	0	-8	1
Drummond, Eddie, Det.	4	2	0	0	2	Jackson, Darrell, Sea.	1	0	0	0	0
Duckett, T.J., Was.	1	0	0	0	0	Jackson, Jamaal, Phi.	1	0	0	-16	0
Dunn, Warrick, Atl.	1	2	0	0	2	Jackson, Steven, St.L	4	2	0	0	2
Edwards, Kalimba, Det.	0	0	3	3	3	* Jackson, Tarvaris, Min.	4	1	0	0	1
* Elam, Abram, Dal.	0	1	0	1	1	Jacobs, Brandon, NY-G	2	0	0	0	0
* Ellis, Devale, Det.	1	0	0	0	0	James, Bradie, Dal.	0	0	2	0	2
* Evans, Jahri, N.O.	0	2	0	1	2	James, Edgerrin, Ariz	3	0	0	0	0
Faine, Jeff, N.O.	1	1	0	0	1	Jenkins, Cullen, G.B.	0	0	2	0	2
Farwell, Heath, Min.	0	0	1	0	1	Jenkins, Michael, Atl.	0	1	0	0	1
Favre, Brett, G.B.	8	2	0	-9	2	* Jennings, Adam, Atl.	0	0	1	0	1
Feeley, A.J., Phi.	1	0	0	0	0	* Jennings, Greg, G.B.	1	0	0	0	0
Finn, Jim, NY-G	0	2	0	0	2	Jimoh, Ade, Was.	0	0	1	0	1
Fisher, Bryce, Sea.	0	0	1	0	1	Johnson, Bethel, Min.	1	0	0	0	0
Fletcher, Jamar, Det.	0	0	1	3	1	Johnson, Bryant, Ariz	1	0	0	0	0
Foster, DeShaun, Car.	4	2	0	2	2	Johnson, Dirk, Phi.	0	1	0	0	1
Franks, Bubba, G.B.	2	0	0	0	0	Johnson, Eric, S.F.	0	1	0	0	1
Furrey, Mike, Det.	1	0	0	0	0	Johnson, Brad, Min.	9	1	0	-9	1
Gage, Justin, Chi.	1	0	0	0	0	Johnson, Keyshawn, Car.	1	0	0	0	0
Galloway, Joey, T.B.	0	1	0	0	1	Johnson, Marcus, Min.	0	1	0	0	1
Gamble, Chris, Car.	2	1	0	0	1	Jones, Jamal, N.O.	0	0	1	0	1
Gandy, Wayne, Atl.	0	1	0	0	1	Jones, Julius, Dal.	1	3	0	0	3
Garcia, Jeff, Phi.	6	2	0	-7	2	Jones, Kevin, Det.	5	1	0	0	1
Garza, Roberto, Chi.	0	1	0	0	1	Jones, Thomas, Chi.	1	0	0	0	0
Gilmore, Bryan, S.F.	1	0	0	0	0	Kampman, Aaron, G.B.	0	0	1	0	1
Glenn, Jason, Min.	0	0	1	0	1	Kennedy, Jimmy, St.L	0	0	2	0	2
Glover, La'Roi, St.L	0	0	1	0	1	Kennedy, Kenoy, Det.	0	0	1	0	1
* Golston, Kedric, Was.	0	0	1	0	1	Kitna, Jon, Det.	11	0	0	-10	0
* Gordon, Charles, Min.	1	2	0	0	2	* Kiwanuka, Mathias, NY-G	1	0	0	0	0
Gore, Frank, S.F.	6	0	0	0	0	Kluwe, Chris, Min.	0	1	0	0	1
* Gradkowski, Bruce, T.B.	11	3	0	-2	3	* Lawson, Manny, S.F.	0	0	2	0	2
Grant, Charles, N.O.	0	0	2	0	2	Leber, Ben, Min.	0	0	2	0	2
Green, Ahman, G.B.	4	1	0	0	1	* Leinart, Matt, Ariz	8	2	0	-13	2
Green, Eric, Ariz	0	0	1	0	1	Leisle, Rodney, N.O.	0	0	1	0	1
Griese, Brian, Chi.	1	0	0	0	0	Lenon, Paris, Det.	0	0	2	10	2
* Griffin, Cedric, Min.	0	0	1	-4	1	Lewis, Greg, Phi.	1	0	0	0	0
Griffith, Justin, Atl.	3	0	0	0	0	Lewis, Keith, S.F.	0	0	1	23	1
Griffith, Robert, Ariz	0	0	1	0	1	Lewis, Michael, N.O.	3	1	0	0	1
Gross, Jordan, Car.	0	1	0	0	1	Liwienski, Chris, Ariz	0	1	0	0	1
Grossman, Rex, Chi.	8	2	0	-4	2	Lloyd, Brandon, Was.	1	0	0	0	0
Gurode, Andre, Dal.	1	0	0	0	0	Loeffler, Cullen, Min.	1	0	0	0	0
Hall, DeAngelo, Atl.	1	0	1	25	1	Looker, Dane, St.L	1	0	0	0	0
Hankton, Karl, Car.	0	0	1	0	1	Lowe, Omare, Atl.	0	1	0	0	1
Harris, Kwame, S.F.	0	1	0	0	1	* Lutui, Deuce, Ariz	0	1	0	0	1
Harris, Tommie, Chi.	0	0	1	17	1	Madison, Sam, NY-G	0	0	1	0	1
Harris, Walt, S.F.	1	0	2	0	2	Mahe, Reno, Phi.	4	0	0	0	0
Hasselbeck, Matt, Sea.	3	2	0	-3	2	Mallard, Josh, Atl.	0	0	1	0	1
* Hawk, A.J., G.B.	0	0	2	0	2	Mallard, Wesly, T.B.	0	0	1	4	1
Hayes, Gerald, Ariz	0	0	2	19	2	* Manning, Danieal, Chi.	0	0	1	0	1
Henderson, E.J., Min.	0	0	2	2	2	Manning, Eli, NY-G	9	1	0	-3	1
Herndon, Kelly, Sea.	0	0	1	61	1	Manning, Ricky, Chi.	0	2	0	0	2
Herron, Noah, G.B.	2	0	0	0	0	Marshall, Lemar, Was.	0	0	1	0	1
* Hester, Devin, Chi.	8	2	0	0	2	* Marshall, Richard, Car.	1	2	2	25	4
Hicks, Maurice, S.F.	2	0	1	0	1	Martin, Jamie, N.O.	3	0	0	0	0
* Hill, Tye, St.L	0	0	1	2	1	Massey, Chris, St.L	0	0	1	0	1
Hill, Leroy, Sea.	0	0	1	4	1	McAllister, Deuce, N.O.	3	2	0	4	2
Hillenmeyer, Hunter, Chi.	0	0	1	0	1	McBriar, Mat, Dal.	1	0	0	-27	0
Hilliard, Ike, T.B.	3	3	0	3	3	McClure, Todd, Atl.	0	1	0	0	1
* Hodge, Abdul, G.B.	0	0	1	29	1	McDonald, Shaun, St.L	2	0	0	0	0
Holt, Terrence, Det.	0	0	1	0	1	McGraw, Jon, Det.	0	0	1	0	1
Holt, Torry, St.L	2	0	0	0	0	McKenzie, Kareem, NY-G	0	2	0	0	2
Hood, Roderick, Phi.	0	0	1	0	1	McMullen, Billy, Min.	0	1	0	0	1
Hoover, Brad, Car.	2	1	0	0	1	McNabb, Donovan, Phi.	3	1	0	-3	1
Hovan, Chris, T.B.	0	0	1	0	1	Melton, Terrence, N.O.	0	1	0	0	1
Howard, Darren, Phi.	0	0	1	0	1	Miller, Billy, N.O.	1	0	0	0	0
* Hudson, Marcus, S.F.	0	0	1	0	1	Minter, Mike, Car.	0	0	1	0	1
* Hurd, Sam, Dal.	0	0	2	0	2	Moats, Ryan, Phi.	0	1	0	0	1
Idonije, Israel, Chi.	0	0	2	0	2	Moore, Dave, T.B.	1	0	0	0	0

	Fum	Own Rec	Opp Rec	Yards	Tot Rec		Fum	Own Rec	Opp Rec	Yards	Tot Rec
Moore, Mewelde, Min.	3	3	0	6	3	Tapeh, Thomas, Phi.	0	2	0	0	2
Morency, Vernand, G.B.	2	0	0	0	0	Tatupu, Lofa, Sea.	0	0	1	0	1
Morris, Maurice, Sea.	1	0	0	0	0	Taylor, Chester, Min.	5	1	0	0	1
Morton, Chad, NY-G	2	0	0	0	0	Taylor, Travis, Min.	2	2	0	-1	2
Moss, Santana, Was.	2	2	0	0	2	Terrill, Craig, Sea.	0	0	1	5	1
Muhammad, Muhsin, Chi.	1	0	0	0	0	Thomas, Hollis, N.O.	0	0	1	0	1
* Nance, Martin, Min.	1	0	0	0	0	Tillman, Charles, Chi.	0	0	1	40	1
Newman, Terence, Dal.	1	0	0	0	0	Tinoisamoa, Pisa, St.L	0	0	1	0	1
Ogunleye, Adewale, Chi.	0	0	3	0	3	* Trueblood, Jeremy, T.B.	0	1	0	0	1
O'Hara, Shaun, NY-G	1	0	0	-9	0	Turk, Matt, St.L	1	1	0	0	1
Okeafor, Chike, Ariz	0	0	2	0	2	Udeze, Kenechi, Min.	0	0	1	0	1
* Oliver, Melvin, S.F.	0	0	1	12	1	Urlacher, Brian, Chi.	0	0	1	0	1
Owens, Richard, Min.	0	1	0	0	1	Vick, Michael, Atl.	9	2	1	-4	3
Pace, Orlando, St.L	0	1	0	0	1	Wakefield, Fred, Ariz	1	1	0	0	1
Patterson, Mike, Phi.	0	0	3	98	3	Wallace, Seneca, Sea.	5	1	0	-2	1
Peppers, Julius, Car.	0	0	2	0	2	Walters, Troy, Ariz	3	1	0	0	1
Peterson, Adrian, Chi.	2	1	0	0	1	Ward, Derrick, NY-G	1	1	0	0	1
Peterson, Julian, Sea.	0	0	1	25	1	Ware, DeMarcus, Dal.	0	0	1	69	1
Petitgout, Luke, NY-G	0	1	0	0	1	Warner, Kurt, Ariz	10	3	0	-12	3
Phillips, Jermaine, T.B.	0	0	1	17	1	Washington, Marcus, Was.	0	0	2	6	2
Pickett, Ryan, G.B.	0	0	1	0	1	* Watkins, Pat, Dal.	0	0	1	53	1
Pierce, Antonio, NY-G	0	0	2	0	2	* Watson, Gabe, Ariz	0	0	1	0	1
Pinner, Artose, Min.	1	0	0	0	0	Webster, Corey, NY-G	0	0	1	4	1
Pittman, Michael, T.B.	2	1	0	0	1	Weinke, Chris, Car.	2	1	0	-2	1
Ponder, Willie, St.L	1	1	0	0	1	Wells, Scott, G.B.	4	0	0	-7	0
Portis, Clinton, Was.	0	2	0	0	2	Wesley, Dante, Chi.	1	0	0	0	0
Raiola, Dominic, Det.	0	1	0	0	1	Westbrook, Brian, Phi.	2	0	0	0	0
Randle El, Antwaan, Was.	2	1	0	0	1	White, Dewayne, T.B.	0	0	3	2	3
Ratliff, Jay, Dal.	0	0	3	0	3	White, Roddy, Atl.	1	0	0	0	0
Rattay, Tim, T.B.	2	1	0	-1	1	Wiggins, Jermaine, Min.	1	1	0	0	1
Redding, Cory, Det.	0	0	1	2	1	* Williams, Brandon, S.F.	1	0	0	0	0
Rivera, Marco, Dal.	0	1	0	0	1	Williams, Cadillac, T.B.	3	0	0	0	0
Robbins, Fred, NY-G	0	0	3	67	3	Williams, Corey, G.B.	0	0	1	0	1
Robinson, Marcus, Min.	2	0	0	0	0	* Williams, DeAngelo, Car.	1	1	0	0	1
Rodgers, Aaron, G.B.	1	0	0	0	0	Williams, Demorrio, Atl.	0	0	1	54	1
Rogers, Shaun, Det.	0	0	1	0	1	Williams, Jimmy, Sea.	0	0	1	0	1
Roman, Mark, S.F.	0	0	1	0	1	Williams, Kevin, Min.	0	0	3	0	3
Romo, Tony, Dal.	9	3	0	-20	3	Williams, Roy, Det.	2	0	0	0	0
Rossum, Allen, Atl.	2	0	0	0	0	Williams, Roy, Dal.	0	0	2	0	2
* Schable, A.J., Ariz	0	1	0	0	1	Wilson, Adrian, Ariz	0	0	2	99	2
Schaub, Matt, Atl.	1	1	0	-11	1	Wilson, Gibril, NY-G	0	0	2	0	2
Schlesinger, Cory, Det.	0	0	1	0	1	Winfield, Antoine, Min.	0	0	1	0	1
Schobel, Matt, Phi.	1	1	0	0	1	Wistrom, Grant, Sea.	0	0	1	0	1
Scott, Ian, Chi.	0	0	1	0	1	Witherspoon, Will, St.L	0	0	1	0	1
Sellers, Mike, Was.	1	0	0	0	0	Woodson, Charles, G.B.	0	0	1	0	1
Sheppard, Lito, Phi.	0	0	1	0	1	Worrell, Cameron, Chi.	0	1	2	0	3
Shiancoe, Visanthe, NY-G	1	1	0	0	1	Young, Brian, N.O.	0	0	1	0	1
Shipp, Marcel, Ariz	0	1	0	0	1						
Shockey, Jeremy, NY-G	0	1	0	0	1	*Player that was a rookie in 2006					
* Sims, Ernie, Det.	0	0	1	0	1	*Yards includes aborted plays, own recoveries, and opponents'*					
Smiley, Justin, S.F.	0	1	0	0	1	*recoveries.*					
Smith, Alex, S.F.	10	2	0	-3	2						
Smith, Antonio, Ariz	0	0	2	4	2						
Smith, Dwight, Min.	0	0	1	5	1						
Smith, Alex, T.B.	1	0	0	0	0						
Smith, Keith, Det.	0	2	0	0	2						
Smith, Raonall, St.L	0	0	1	0	1						
Smith, Steve, Car.	2	0	0	0	0						
Smith, Will, N.O.	0	0	1	0	1						
Smoot, Fred, Min.	0	0	1	29	1						
Sopoaga, Isaac, S.F.	0	0	1	0	1						
Spencer, Shawntae, S.F.	0	0	2	11	2						
* Spitz, Jason, G.B.	0	1	0	0	1						
Stepanovich, Alex, Ariz	0	1	0	0	1						
Stevens, Jerramy, Sea.	1	0	0	0	0						
Stinchcomb, Jonathan, N.O.	0	1	0	0	1						
Strong, Mack, Sea.	2	0	0	0	0						
Tafoya, Joe, Sea.	0	0	1	0	1						

AMERICAN FOOTBALL CONFERENCE—FUMBLES

	Fum	Own Rec	Fum OB	TD	Opp Rec	TD	Fum Yards	Tot Rec
Indianapolis	13	1	2	0	11	1	29	12
Jacksonville	16	6	1	0	4	0	-14	10
Miami	19	12	1	0	19	1	126	31
San Diego	19	12	1	0	12	3	64	24
Baltimore	21	11	1	0	12	1	115	23
N.Y. Jets	21	12	0	0	9	1	37	21
Cleveland	23	6	0	0	9	1	33	15
Cincinnati	25	13	1	0	12	0	6	25
Kansas City	25	11	0	0	15	0	1	26
New England	27	11	1	0	13	0	11	24
Pittsburgh	27	13	0	0	9	0	-5	22
Buffalo	28	12	1	0	11	2	58	23
Houston	28	13	3	0	11	2	126	24
Denver	29	14	3	0	13	0	45	27
Tennessee	29	20	2	0	11	3	160	31
Oakland	32	9	1	0	5	2	22	14
AFC Total	382	176	18	0	176	17	814	352
AFC Average	23.9	11.0	1.1	0.0	11.0	1.1	50.9	22.0

NATIONAL FOOTBALL CONFERENCE—FUMBLES

	Fum	Own Rec	Fum OB	TD	Opp Rec	TD	Fum Yards	Tot Rec
Atlanta	18	10	3	0	14	1	73	24
St. Louis	20	8	2	0	15	1	77	23
Washington	20	8	5	0	6	0	-2	14
Carolina	21	9	2	0	8	0	33	17
Dallas	21	11	1	0	13	1	78	24
Seattle	21	8	1	0	14	1	122	22
New Orleans	23	11	2	1	8	0	2	19
N.Y. Giants	23	11	2	0	11	0	59	22
San Francisco	24	6	2	0	13	1	43	19
Green Bay	25	5	5	0	10	1	13	15
Chicago	26	10	2	0	20	2	58	30
Detroit	26	8	1	0	18	0	13	26
Philadelphia	26	11	0	0	10	1	62	21
Tampa Bay	27	11	2	0	9	0	20	20
Arizona	31	15	3	0	17	2	103	32
Minnesota	31	16	3	1	15	2	28	31
NFC Total	383	158	36	3	201	13	782	359
NFC Average	23.9	9.9	2.3	0.2	12.6	0.8	48.9	22.4
NFL Total	765	334	54	3	377	30	1596	711
NFL Average	23.9	10.4	1.7	0.1	11.8	0.9	49.9	22.2

SACKS

MOST SACKS
- AFC: 17.0 Shawne Merriman, San Diego
- NFC: 15.5 Aaron Kampman, Green Bay

MOST SACKS, GAME
- AFC: 3.5 Shawne Merriman, San Diego at Seattle, December 24
- NFC: 3.0 Aaron Kampman, Green Bay vs. New Orleans, September 17
- 3.0 Julius Peppers, Carolina at Minnesota, September 17 - (OT)
- 3.0 Darwin Walker, Philadelphia vs. Dallas, October 8
- 3.0 James Hall, Detroit vs. Buffalo, October 15
- 3.0 Bertrand Berry, Arizona at Oakland, October 22
- 3.0 Corey Williams, Green Bay at Buffalo, November 5
- 3.0 Craig Terrill, Seattle vs. Oakland, November 6
- 3.0 Julius Peppers, Carolina vs. Tampa Bay, November 13
- 3.0 Cullen Jenkins, Green Bay vs. Detroit, December 17
- 3.0 Aaron Kampman, Green Bay vs. Minnesota, December 21
- 3.0 DeMarcus Ware, Dallas vs. Detroit, December 31

TEAM LEADERS, SACKS
- AFC: BALTIMORE, 13.0, Trevor Pryce; BUFFALO, 14.0, Aaron Schobel; CINCINNATI, 10.5, Robert Geathers; CLEVELAND, 11.0, *Kamerion Wimbley; DENVER, 8.5, *Elvis Dumervil; HOUSTON, 5.0, Jason Babin; INDIANAPOLIS, 9.5, Robert Mathis; JACKSONVILLE, 10.0, Bobby McCray; KANSAS CITY, 8.0, *Tamba Hali; MIAMI, 13.5, Jason Taylor; NEW ENGLAND, 8.5, Rosevelt Colvin; N.Y. JETS, 8.5, Bryan Thomas; OAKLAND, 11.0, Derrick Burgess; PITTSBURGH, 7.0, Joey Porter; SAN DIEGO, 17.0, Shawne Merriman; TENNESSEE, 6.5, Kyle Vanden Bosch

- NFC: ARIZONA, 8.5, Chike Okeafor; ATLANTA, 6.0, Rod Coleman; CAROLINA, 13.0, Julius Peppers; CHICAGO, 12.0, *Mark Anderson; DALLAS, 11.5, DeMarcus Ware; DETROIT, 8.0, Cory Redding; GREEN BAY, 15.5, Aaron Kampman; MINNESOTA, 5.5, Darrion Scott; NEW ORLEANS, 10.5, Will Smith; N.Y. GIANTS, 6.0, Osi Umenyiora; PHILADELPHIA, 8.0, Trent Cole; ST. LOUIS, 13.0, Leonard Little; SAN FRANCISCO, 6.5, Brandon Moore; SEATTLE, 10.0, Julian Peterson; TAMPA BAY, 5.0, Greg Spires, Dewayne White, Ellis Wyms; WASHINGTON, 6.0, Andre Carter

TEAM CHAMPION
- AFC: 61.0 San Diego
- NFC: 46.0 Green Bay

NFL TOP TEN LEADERS—SACKS

	Sacks
Merriman, Shawne, S.D.	17.0
Kampman, Aaron, G.B.	15.5
Schobel, Aaron, Buf.	14.0
Taylor, Jason, Mia.	13.5
Little, Leonard, St.L	13.0
Peppers, Julius, Car.	13.0
Pryce, Trevor, Bal.	13.0
* Anderson, Mark, Chi.	12.0
Phillips, Shaun, S.D.	11.5
Ware, DeMarcus, Dal.	11.5

AMERICAN FOOTBALL CONFERENCE—SACKS

	Sacks	Yards
San Diego	61	351
Baltimore	60	418
Miami	47	268
New England	44	281
Buffalo	40	265
Pittsburgh	39	226
Cincinnati	35	211
Denver	35	202
Jacksonville	35	200
N.Y. Jets	35	230
Oakland	34	218
Kansas City	32	190
Cleveland	28	137
Houston	28	191
Tennessee	26	148
Indianapolis	25	157
AFC Total	604	3693
AFC Average	37.8	230.8

NATIONAL FOOTBALL CONFERENCE—SACKS

	Sacks	Yards
Green Bay	46	337
Carolina	41	265
Seattle	41	282
Chicago	40	272
Philadelphia	40	300
Arizona	38	238
New Orleans	38	268
Atlanta	37	235
Dallas	34	223
St. Louis	34	214
San Francisco	34	246
N.Y. Giants	32	181
Detroit	30	201
Minnesota	30	197
Tampa Bay	25	166
Washington	19	95
NFC Total	559	3720
NFC Average	34.9	232.5
League Total	1163	7413
League Average	36.3	231.7

AFC—INDIVIDUAL SACKS

	Sacks
Merriman, Shawne, S.D.	17.0
Schobel, Aaron, Buf.	14.0
Taylor, Jason, Mia.	13.5
Pryce, Trevor, Bal.	13.0
Phillips, Shaun, S.D.	11.5
Burgess, Derrick, Oak.	11.0
Thomas, Adalius, Bal.	11.0
* Wimbley, Kamerion, Cle.	11.0
Geathers, Robert, Cin.	10.5
McCray, Bobby, Jac.	10.0
Sapp, Warren, Oak.	10.0
Mathis, Robert, Ind.	9.5
Scott, Bart, Bal.	9.5
Suggs, Terrell, Bal.	9.5
Colvin, Rosevelt, N.E.	8.5
* Dumervil, Elvis, Den.	8.5
Thomas, Bryan, NYJ	8.5
* Hali, Tamba, K.C.	8.0
Allen, Jared, K.C.	7.5
Green, Jarvis, N.E.	7.5
Smith, Justin, Cin.	7.5
Warren, Ty, N.E.	7.5
Castillo, Luis, S.D.	7.0
Ekuban, Ebenezer, Den.	7.0
Holliday, Vonnie, Mia.	7.0
Porter, Joey, Pit.	7.0
Vanden Bosch, Kyle, Ten.	6.5
Denney, Ryan, Buf.	6.0
Haggans, Clark, Pit.	6.0
Hobson, Victor, NYJ	6.0
Lang, Kenard, Den.	6.0
Banta-Cain, Tully, N.E.	5.5
Carter, Kevin, Mia.	5.5
Freeney, Dwight, Ind.	5.5
Keisel, Brett, Pit.	5.5
Kelsay, Chris, Buf.	5.5
Babin, Jason, Hou.	5.0
Bowens, David, Mia.	5.0
Ellis, Shaun, NYJ	5.0
Lewis, Ray, Bal.	5.0
Meier, Rob, Jac.	5.0
Rhodes, Kerry, NYJ	5.0
Barton, Eric, NYJ	4.5
Chukwurah, Patrick, Den.	4.5
Fraser, Simon, Cle.	4.5
Johnson, Derrick, K.C.	4.5
Smith, Aaron, Pit.	4.5
Vrabel, Mike, N.E.	4.5
* Williams, Mario, Hou.	4.5
Cesaire, Jacques, S.D.	4.0
Farrior, James, Pit.	4.0
Foote, Larry, Pit.	4.0
Godfrey, Randall, S.D.	4.0
Kaesviharn, Kevin, Cin.	4.0
McGinest, Willie, Cle.	4.0
Seymour, Richard, N.E.	4.0
Traylor, Keith, Mia.	4.0
Gregg, Kelly, Bal.	3.5
Henderson, John, Jac.	3.5
Kelly, Tommy, Oak.	3.5
LaBoy, Travis, Ten.	3.5
Roth, Matt, Mia.	3.5
* Ryans, DeMeco, Hou.	3.5
Brock, Raheem, Ind.	3.0
Harris, Marques, S.D.	3.0
* Landry, Dawan, Bal.	3.0
Robinson, Bryan, Cin.	3.0
Smith, Daryl, Jac.	3.0
Spicer, Paul, Jac.	3.0
Starks, Randy, Ten.	3.0
Thomas, Zach, Mia.	3.0
Bulluck, Keith, Ten.	2.5
Cooper, Stephen, S.D.	2.5
Edwards, Donnie, S.D.	2.5
Edwards, Ron, K.C.	2.5
Huntley, Kevin, Oak.	2.5
McFarland, Anthony, Ind.	2.5
* Peko, Domata, Cin.	2.5
Robertson, Dewayne, NYJ	2.5
Stroud, Marcus, Jac.	2.5
Tripplett, Larry, Buf.	2.5
Warren, Gerard, Den.	2.5
Adams, Sam, Cin.	2.0
Bell, Yeremiah, Mia.	2.0
Carter, Tyrone, Pit.	2.0
Crowell, Angelo, Buf.	2.0
Earl, Glenn, Hou.	2.0
* Finnegan, Cortland, Ten.	2.0
Fletcher-Baker, London, Buf.	2.0
* Hawkins, Brent, Jac.	2.0
Haynesworth, Albert, Ten.	2.0
Ivy, Corey, Bal.	2.0
Johnstone, Lance, Oak.	2.0
Kalu, N. D., Hou.	2.0
Kirschke, Travis, Pit.	2.0
Knight, Sammy, K.C.	2.0
Maddox, Anthony, Hou.	2.0
Myers, Michael, Den.	2.0
Pettway, Kenneth, Jac.	2.0
Polk, Carlos, S.D.	2.0
Thompson, Chaun, Cle.	2.0
Thornton, John, Cin.	2.0
Townsend, Deshea, Pit.	2.0
Williams, Jamal, S.D.	2.0
Bingham, Ryon, S.D.	1.5
Brown, Tony, Ten.	1.5
Bruschi, Tedy, N.E.	1.5
Hargrove, Anthony, St.L-Buf.	1.5
* Ingram, Clint, Jac.	1.5
Johnson, Jarret, Bal.	1.5
Mitchell, Kawika, K.C.	1.5
Olshansky, Igor, S.D.	1.5
Orr, Shantee, Hou.	1.5
Robinson, Derreck, S.D.	1.5
Spragan, Donnie, Mia.	1.5
Veal, Demetrin, Den.	1.5
Allen, Will, Mia.	1.0
Asomugha, Nnamdi, Oak.	1.0
Bell, Kendrell, K.C.	1.0
Bockwoldt, Colby, Ten.	1.0
* Brooks, Ahmad, Cin.	1.0
Brown, C.C., Hou.	1.0
Brown, Chad, Pit.	1.0
* Coleman, Drew, NYJ	1.0
Crowder, Channing, Mia.	1.0
Dalton, Lional, Hou.	1.0
Davis, Andra, Cle.	1.0
* Ellison, Keith, Buf.	1.0
Engelberger, John, Den.	1.0
Faggins, Demarcus, Hou.	1.0
Fox, Keyaron, K.C.	1.0
Gilbert, Tony, Jac.	1.0
Greenwood, Morlon, Hou.	1.0
Harrison, Rodney, N.E.	1.0
Jackson, Dexter, Cin.	1.0
Jones, Pacman, Ten.	1.0
June, Cato, Ind.	1.0

Player	Sacks
Law, Ty, K.C.	1.0
* Mahelona, Jesse, Ten.	1.0
McCree, Marlon, S.D.	1.0
* McDaniel, Tony, Jac.	1.0
McKinley, Alvin, Cle.	1.0
Miller, Caleb, Cin.	1.0
Morrison, Kirk, Oak.	1.0
Mosley, C.J., NYJ	1.0
* Ngata, Haloti, Bal.	1.0
* Page, Jarrad, K.C.	1.0
Payne, Seth, Hou.	1.0
Peek, Antwan, Hou.	1.0
Polamalu, Troy, Pit.	1.0
Pool, Brodney, Cle.	1.0
Poole, Tyrone, Oak.	1.0
Reagor, Montae, Ind.	1.0
Reed, James, K.C.	1.0
Rolle, Samari, Bal.	1.0
Roye, Orpheus, Cle.	1.0
Sanders, James, N.E.	1.0
Sands, Terdell, Oak.	1.0
Seau, Junior, N.E.	1.0
* Simpson, Ko, Buf.	1.0
Spikes, Takeo, Buf.	1.0
Stewart, Matt, Cle.	1.0
Surtain, Patrick, K.C.	1.0
Thomas, Josh, Ind.	1.0
von Oelhoffen, Kimo, NYJ	1.0
Weaver, Anthony, Hou.	1.0
Wilfork, Vince, N.E.	1.0
Williams, D.J., Den.	1.0
* Williams, Leon, Cle.	1.0
Williams, Sam, Oak.	1.0
Wilson, Al, Den.	1.0
Wright, Mike, N.E.	1.0
Johnson, Landon, Cin.	0.5
Jones, Sean, Cle.	0.5
Malone, Alfred, Hou.	0.5
Odom, Antwan, Ten.	0.5
Schobel, Bo, Ind.	0.5
Sirmon, Peter, Ten.	0.5
Smith, Robaire, Ten.	0.5
* Stanley, Montavious, Jac.	0.5
* Tulloch, Stephen, Ten.	0.5
Washington, Rashad, NYJ	0.5

Player that was a rookie in 2006

NFC—INDIVIDUAL SACKS

Player	Sacks
Kampman, Aaron, G.B.	15.5
Little, Leonard, St.L	13.0
Peppers, Julius, Car.	13.0
* Anderson, Mark, Chi.	12.0
Ware, DeMarcus, Dal.	11.5
Smith, Will, N.O.	10.5
Peterson, Julian, Sea.	10.0
Okeafor, Chike, Ariz	8.5
Cole, Trent, Phi.	8.0
Dansby, Karlos, Ariz	8.0
Redding, Cory, Det.	8.0
Brown, Alex, Chi.	7.0
Williams, Corey, G.B.	7.0
Jenkins, Cullen, G.B.	6.5
Moore, Brandon, S.F.	6.5
Ogunleye, Adewale, Chi.	6.5
Berry, Bertrand, Ariz	6.0
Carter, Andre, Was.	6.0
Coleman, Rod, Atl.	6.0
Gbaja-Biamila, Kabeer, G.B.	6.0
Grant, Charles, N.O.	6.0
Thomas, Juqua, Phi.	6.0
Umenyiora, Osi, NY-G	6.0
Walker, Darwin, Phi.	6.0
Draft, Chris, Car.	5.5
Glover, La'Roi, St.L	5.5
Robbins, Fred, NY-G	5.5
Scott, Darrion, Min.	5.5
Young, Bryant, S.F.	5.5
Young, Brian, N.O.	5.5
Hall, James, Det.	5.0
Harris, Tommie, Chi.	5.0
Howard, Darren, Phi.	5.0
Rucker, Mike, Car.	5.0
Spires, Greg, T.B.	5.0
White, Dewayne, T.B.	5.0
Williams, Kevin, Min.	5.0
Wilson, Adrian, Ariz	5.0
Wyms, Ellis, T.B.	5.0
Ellis, Greg, Dal.	4.5
Green, Roderick, S.F.	4.5
Kerney, Patrick, Atl.	4.5
Lewis, Damione, Car.	4.5
Abraham, John, Atl.	4.0
Coleman, Kenyon, Dal.	4.0
Fisher, Bryce, Sea.	4.0
* Kiwanuka, Mathias, NY-G	4.0
Mallard, Josh, Atl.	4.0
Ratliff, Jay, Dal.	4.0
Shanle, Scott, N.O.	4.0
Wistrom, Grant, Sea.	4.0
Bernard, Rocky, Sea.	3.5
Darby, Chartric, Sea.	3.5
Fujita, Scott, N.O.	3.5
* Hawk, A.J., G.B.	3.5
Johnson, Tank, Chi.	3.5
Kearse, Jevon, Phi.	3.5
Thomas, Hollis, N.O.	3.5
Boley, Michael, Atl.	3.0
* Carrington, Paul, Atl.	3.0
Daniels, Phillip, Was.	3.0
Davis, Russell, Sea.	3.0
Douglas, Marques, S.F.	3.0
Edwards, Kalimba, Det.	3.0
* Edwards, Ray, Min.	3.0
Henderson, E.J., Min.	3.0
Jenkins, Kris, Car.	3.0
Leber, Ben, Min.	3.0

Player	Sacks
* Mitchell, Jayme, Min.	3.0
Rogers, Shaun, Det.	3.0
Strahan, Michael, NY-G	3.0
* Tapp, Darryl, Sea.	3.0
Terrill, Craig, Sea.	3.0
Wallace, Al, Car.	3.0
Witherspoon, Will, St.L	3.0
Brooking, Keith, Atl.	2.5
Harris, Napoleon, Min.	2.5
* Hatcher, Jason, Dal.	2.5
* Lawson, Manny, S.F.	2.5
Quarles, Shelton, T.B.	2.5
Smith, Antonio, Ariz	2.5
Washington, Marcus, Was.	2.5
Williams, Chad, S.F.	2.5
Adams, Anthony, S.F.	2.0
* Anderson, James, Car.	2.0
Barnett, Nick, G.B.	2.0
Boone, Alfonso, Chi.	2.0
Chillar, Brandon, St.L	2.0
Cooper, Chris, Ariz	2.0
Dockett, Darnell, Ariz	2.0
Evans, Demetric, Was.	2.0
Hamlin, Ken, Sea.	2.0
Hill, Leroy, Sea.	2.0
Hovan, Chris, T.B.	2.0
Jackson, Tyoka, Det.	2.0
Joseph, William, NY-G	2.0
Lewis, Michael, Phi.	2.0
Manning, Ricky, Chi.	2.0
McCoy, Matt, Phi.	2.0
Milloy, Lawyer, Atl.	2.0
Rice, Simeon, T.B.	2.0
Short, Brandon, NY-G	2.0
Smith, Corey, Det.	2.0
Spencer, Shawntae, S.F.	2.0
Tinoisamoa, Pisa, St.L	2.0
* Carpenter, Bobby, Dal.	1.5
* Cofield, Barry, NY-G	1.5
Considine, Sean, Phi.	1.5
Davis, Thomas, Car.	1.5
Marshall, Lemar, Was.	1.5
Montgomery, Mike, G.B.	1.5
Nece, Ryan, T.B.	1.5
Patterson, Mike, Phi.	1.5
Smith, Raonall, St.L	1.5
Sopoaga, Isaac, S.F.	1.5
Tatupu, Lofa, Sea.	1.5
* Adeyanju, Victor, St.L	1.0
Archuleta, Adam, Was.	1.0
Arrington, LaVar, NY-G	1.0
Atogwe, O.J., St.L	1.0
Awasom, Adrian, NY-G	1.0
Ayodele, Akin, Dal.	1.0
Babineaux, Jonathan, Atl.	1.0
Bailey, Boss, Det.	1.0
Bell, Marcus, Det.	1.0
Bolden, Juran, T.B.	1.0
* Bowen, Stephen, Dal.	1.0
Briggs, Lance, Chi.	1.0
Brown, Fakhir, St.L	1.0
* Bullocks, Daniel, Det.	1.0
Burnett, Kevin, Dal.	1.0
Canty, Chris, Dal.	1.0
Carroll, Ahmad, G.B.	1.0
Chavous, Corey, St.L	1.0
Clancy, Kendrick, Ariz	1.0
Cole, Colin, G.B.	1.0
Cooper, Josh, N.O.	1.0

	Sacks
Crocker, Chris, Atl.	1.0
Davis, Chauncey, Atl.	1.0
Dawkins, Brian, Phi.	1.0
Demps, Will, NY-G	1.0
Emmons, Carlos, NY-G	1.0
* Gaither, Omar, Phi.	1.0
Gamble, Chris, Car.	1.0
Griffin, Cornelius, Was.	1.0
* Harper, Roman, N.O.	1.0
Harris, Walt, S.F.	1.0
Hartwell, Edgerton, Atl.	1.0
Hayes, Gerald, Ariz	1.0
Holdman, Warrick, Was.	1.0
Hood, Roderick, Phi.	1.0
* Jackson, T.J., Atl.	1.0
Kennedy, Jimmy, St.L	1.0
Kennedy, Kenoy, Det.	1.0
Lake, Antwan, N.O.	1.0
Lewis, D.D., Sea.	1.0
Lewis, Keith, S.F.	1.0
* Marshall, Richard, Car.	1.0
Mathis, Kevin, Atl.	1.0
McDougle, Jerome, Phi.	1.0
McQuarters, R.W., NY-G	1.0
* Oliver, Melvin, S.F.	1.0
Pace, Calvin, Ariz	1.0
Phillips, Jermaine, T.B.	1.0
Pierce, Antonio, NY-G	1.0
Poppinga, Brady, G.B.	1.0
Roman, Mark, S.F.	1.0
Sharper, Darren, Min.	1.0
Shropshire, Darrell, Atl.	1.0
Simoneau, Mark, N.O.	1.0
Singleton, Alshermond, Dal.	1.0
Smith, Dwight, Min.	1.0
Spears, Marcus, Dal.	1.0
Thomas, Dontarrious, Min.	1.0
Torbor, Reggie, NY-G	1.0
* Watson, Gabe, Ariz	1.0
Webster, Corey, NY-G	1.0
Whitehead, Willie, N.O.	1.0
Williams, Demorrio, Atl.	1.0
Williams, Pat, Min.	1.0
Woodson, Charles, G.B.	1.0
Worrell, Cameron, Chi.	1.0
* Wroten, Claude, St.L	1.0
* Golston, Kedric, Was.	0.5
Green, Brandon, St.L	0.5
Holt, Terrence, Det.	0.5
Jones, Dhani, Phi.	0.5
* Montgomery, Anthony, Was.	0.5
Moorehead, Kindal, Car.	0.5
* Sims, Ernie, Det.	0.5
Tubbs, Marcus, Sea.	0.5

*Player that was a rookie in 2006

2006 NFL PAID ATTENDANCE BREAKDOWN

	Games	Attendance	Average
NFL Preseason Total	65	4,083,282	62,820
NFL Regular-Season Total	256	17,340,879	67,738
NFL Postseason Total	12	775,551	64,629
NFL All Games	333	22,199,712	66,666

1.1-MILLION CLUB

During the 2006 season, 11 teams drew more than 1.1 million paid attendance home and away during the regular season. For the seventh consecutive year, the Washington Redskins led the league in regular-season paid attendance (1,232,200). The Redskins also set an NFL record for single-season home paid attendance (708,952).

Team	Total Paid Home Attendance	Total Paid Visiting Attendance	Total Paid Attendance
Washington	708,952	523,248	1,232,200
New York Giants	628,925	555,653	1,184,578
New York Jets	618,563	546,796	1,165,359
Kansas City	624,171	530,045	1,154,216
Denver	596,550	543,020	1,139,570
Carolina	579,192	550,494	1,129,686
New England	578,661	548,597	1,127,258
Miami	585,973	530,106	1,116,079
Baltimore	557,707	548,953	1,106,660
Atlanta	551,591	554,552	1,106,143
Cleveland	563,827	536,694	1,100,521

For complete year-by-year attendance records, see pages 614-615.

Inside the Numbers

GREATEST COMEBACKS IN NFL HISTORY
(Most Points Overcome To Win Game)

REGULAR SEASON GAMES

FROM 28 POINTS BEHIND TO WIN:
December 7, 1980, at San Francisco

New Orleans	14	21	0	0	0	—	35
San Francisco	0	7	14	14	3	—	38

- NO — Harris 33 pass from Manning (Ricardo kick)
- NO — Childs 21 pass from Manning (Ricardo kick)
- NO — Holmes 1 run (Ricardo kick)
- SF — Solomon 57 punt return (Wersching kick)
- NO — Holmes 1 run (Ricardo kick)
- NO — Harris 41 pass from Manning (Ricardo kick)
- SF — Montana 1 run (Wersching kick)
- SF — Clark 71 pass from Montana (Wersching kick)
- SF — Solomon 14 pass from Montana (Wersching kick)
- SF — Elliott 7 run (Wersching kick)
- SF — FG Wersching 36

FROM 26 POINTS BEHIND TO WIN:
September 21, 1997, at Buffalo

Indianapolis	14	12	0	9	—	35
Buffalo	0	10	6	21	—	37

- Ind — Bailey 10 pass from Harbaugh (Blanchard kick)
- Ind — Faulk 10 run (Blanchard kick)
- Ind — FG Blanchard 39
- Ind — FG Blanchard 36
- Ind — FG Blanchard 49
- Ind — FG Blanchard 22
- Buff — Johnson 16 pass from Collins (Christie kick)
- Buff — FG Christie 27
- Buff — A. Smith 15 run (2-pt attempt failed)
- Ind — FG Blanchard 25
- Buff — Early 4 pass from Collins (Christie kick)
- Buff — A. Smith 1 run (Christie kick)
- Buff — A. Smith 54 run (Christie kick)
- Ind — Harrison 2 pass from Justin (2-pt attempt failed)

FROM 25 POINTS BEHIND TO WIN:
November 8, 1987, at St. Louis

Tampa Bay	7	7	14	0	—	28
St. Louis	0	3	0	28	—	31

- TB — Carrier 5 pass from DeBerg (Igwebuike kick)
- TB — Carter 3 pass from DeBerg (Igwebuike kick)
- StL — FG Gallery 31
- TB — Smith 34 pass from DeBerg (Igwebuike kick)
- TB — Smith 3 run (Igwebuike kick)
- StL — Awalt 4 pass from Lomax (Gallery kick)
- StL — Noga 23 fumble recovery (Gallery kick)

- StL — J. Smith 11 pass from Lomax (Gallery kick)
- StL — J. Smith 17 pass from Lomax (Gallery kick)

FROM 24 POINTS BEHIND TO WIN:
October 27, 1946, at Washington

Philadelphia	0	0	14	14	—	28
Washington	10	14	0	0	—	24

- Wash — Rosato 2 run (Poillon kick)
- Wash — FG Poillon 28
- Wash — Rosato 4 run (Poillon kick)
- Wash — Lapka recovered fumble in end zone (Poillon kick)
- Phil — Steele 1 run (Lio kick)
- Phil — Pritchard 45 pass from Thompson (Lio kick)
- Phil — Steinke 7 pass from Thompson (Lio kick)
- Phil — Ferrante 30 pass from Thompson (Lio kick)

FROM 24 POINTS BEHIND TO WIN:
October 20, 1957, at Detroit

Baltimore	7	14	6	0	—	27
Detroit	0	3	7	21	—	31

- Balt — Mutscheller 15 pass from Unitas (Rechichar kick)
- Det — FG Martin 47
- Balt — Moore 72 pass from Unitas (Rechichar kick)
- Balt — Mutscheller 52 pass from Unitas (Rechichar kick)
- Balt — Moore 4 pass from Unitas (kick failed)
- Det — Junker 14 pass from Rote (Layne kick)
- Det — Cassady 26 pass from Layne (Layne kick)
- Det — Johnson 1 run (Layne kick)
- Det — Cassady 29 pass from Layne (Layne kick)

FROM 24 POINTS BEHIND TO WIN:
October 25, 1959, at Minneapolis

Philadelphia	0	0	21	7	—	28
Chicago Cardinals	7	10	7	0	—	24

- Cardinals — Crow 10 pass from Roach (Conrad kick)
- Cardinals — J. Hill 77 blocked field goal return (Conrad kick)
- Cardinals — FG Conrad 15
- Cardinals — Lane 37 interception return (Conrad kick)
- Phil — Barnes 1 run (Walston kick)
- Phil — McDonald 29 pass from Van Brocklin (Walston kick)
- Phil — Barnes 2 run (Walston kick)
- Phil — McDonald 22 pass from Van Brocklin (Walston kick)

FROM 24 POINTS BEHIND TO WIN:
October 23, 1960, at Denver

Boston	10	7	0	—	24	
Denver	0	0	14	17	—	31

- Bos — FG Cappelletti 12
- Bos — Colclough 10 pass from Songin (Cappelletti kick)
- Bos — Wells 6 pass from Songin (Cappelletti kick)
- Bos — Miller 47 pass from Songin (Cappelletti kick)
- Den — Carmichael 21 pass from Tripucka (Mingo kick)

- Den — Jessup 19 pass from Tripucka (Mingo kick)
- Den — Carmichael 35 lateral from Taylor, pass from Tripucka (Mingo kick)
- Den — Taylor 8 pass from Tripucka (Mingo kick)
- Den — FG Mingo 9

FROM 24 POINTS BEHIND TO WIN:
December 15, 1974, at Miami

New England	21	3	0	3	—	27
Miami	0	17	7	10	—	34

- NE — Hannah recovered fumble in end zone (J. Smith kick)
- NE — Sanders 23 interception return (J. Smith kick)
- NE — Herron 4 pass from Plunkett (J. Smith kick)
- NE — FG J. Smith 46
- Mia — Nottingham 1 run (Yepremian kick)
- Mia — Baker 37 pass from Morrall (Yepremian kick)
- Mia — FG Yepremian 28
- Mia — Baker 46 pass from Morrall (Yepremian kick)
- NE — FG J. Smith 34
- Mia — Nottingham 2 run (Yepremian kick)
- Mia — FG Yepremian 40

FROM 24 POINTS BEHIND TO WIN:
December 4, 1977, at Minnesota

San Francisco	0	10	14	3	—	27
Minnesota	0	0	7	21	—	28

- SF — Delvin Williams 2 run (Wersching kick)
- SF — FG Wersching 31
- SF — Dave Williams 80 kickoff return (Wersching kick)
- SF — Delvin Williams 5 run (Wersching kick)
- Minn — McClanahan 15 pass from Lee (Cox kick)
- Minn — Rashad 8 pass from Kramer (Cox kick)
- Minn — Tucker 9 pass from Kramer (Cox kick)
- SF — FG Wersching 31
- Minn — S. White 69 pass from Kramer (Cox kick)

FROM 24 POINTS BEHIND TO WIN:
September 23, 1979, at Denver

Seattle	10	10	14	0	—	34
Denver	0	10	21	6	—	37

- Sea — FG Herrera 28
- Sea — Doornik 5 run (Herrera kick)
- Den — FG Turner 27
- Sea — Doornik 5 run (Herrera kick)
- Den — Armstrong 2 run (Turner kick)
- Sea — FG Herrera 22
- Sea — McCullum 13 pass from Zorn (Herrera kick)
- Sea — Smith 1 run (Herrera kick)
- Den — Studdard 2 pass from Morton (Turner kick)
- Den — Moses 11 pass from Morton (Turner kick)
- Den — Upchurch 35 pass from Morton (Turner kick)

Den — Lytle 1 run (kick failed)

FROM 24 POINTS BEHIND TO WIN:
September 23, 1979, at Cincinnati

Houston	0	10	17	0	3	—	30
Cincinnati	14	10	0	3	0	—	27

Cin — Johnson 1 run (Bahr kick)
Cin — Alexander 2 run (Bahr kick)
Cin — Johnson 1 run (Bahr kick)
Cin — FG Bahr 52
Hou — Burrough 35 pass from Pastorini (Fritsch kick)
Hou — FG Fritsch 33
Hou — Campbell 8 run (Fritsch kick)
Hou — Caster 22 pass from Pastorini (Fritsch kick)
Hou — FG Fritsch 47
Cin — FG Bahr 55
Hou — FG Fritsch 29

FROM 24 POINTS BEHIND TO WIN:
November 22, 1982, at Los Angeles

San Diego	10	14	0	0	—	24
L.A. Raiders	0	7	14	7	—	28

SD — FG Benirschke 19
SD — Scales 29 pass from Fouts (Benirschke kick)
SD — Muncie 2 run (Benirschke kick)
SD — Muncie 1 run (Benirschke kick)
Raiders — Christensen 1 pass from Plunkett (Bahr kick)
Raiders — Allen 3 run (Bahr kick)
Raiders — Allen 6 run (Bahr kick)
Raiders — Hawkins 1 run (Bahr kick)

FROM 24 POINTS BEHIND TO WIN:
September 26, 1988, at Denver

L.A. Raiders	0	0	14	13	3	— 30
Denver	7	17	0	3	0	— 27

Den — Dorsett 1 run (Karlis kick)
Den — Dorsett 1 run (Karlis kick)
Den — Sewell 7 pass from Elway (Karlis kick)
Den — FG Karlis 39
Raiders — Smith 40 pass from Schroeder (Bahr kick)
Raiders — Smith 42 pass from Schroeder (Bahr kick)
Raiders — FG Bahr 28
Raiders — Allen 4 run (Bahr kick)
Den — FG Karlis 25
Raiders — FG Bahr 44
Raiders — FG Bahr 35

FROM 24 POINTS BEHIND TO WIN:
December 6, 1992, at Tampa

L.A. Rams	0	3	21	7	—	31
Tampa Bay	6	21	0	0	—	27

TB — FG Murray 34
TB — FG Murray 47
TB — Armstrong 81 pass from Testaverde (Murray kick)
TB — Jones 26 fumble recovery (Murray kick)
Rams — FG Zendejas 18
TB — Carrier 10 pass from Testaverde (Murray kick)
Rams — Anderson 40 pass from Everett (Zendejas kick)
Rams — Chadwick 27 pass from Everett (Zendejas kick)
Rams — Lang 1 run (Zendejas kick)

Rams — Carter 8 pass from Everett (Zendejas kick)

POSTSEASON GAMES

FROM 32 POINTS BEHIND TO WIN:
AFC First-Round Playoff Game
January 3, 1993, at Buffalo

Houston	7	21	7	3	0	— 38
Buffalo	3	0	28	7	3	— 41

Hou — Jeffires 3 pass from Moon (Del Greco kick)
Buff — FG Christie 36
Hou — Slaughter 7 pass from Moon (Del Greco kick)
Hou — Duncan 26 pass from Moon (Del Greco kick)
Hou — Jeffires 27 pass from Moon (Del Greco kick)
Hou — McDowell 58 interception return (Del Greco kick)
Buff — Davis 1 run (Christie kick)
Buff — Beebe 38 pass from Reich (Christie kick)
Buff — Reed 26 pass from Reich (Christie kick)
Buff — Reed 18 pass from Reich (Christie kick)
Buff — Reed 17 pass from Reich (Christie kick)
Hou — FG Del Greco 26
Buff — FG Christie 32

FROM 24 POINTS BEHIND TO WIN:
NFC First-Round Playoff Game
January 5, 2003, at San Francisco

N.Y. Giants	7	21	10	0	— 38
San Francisco	7	7	8	17	— 39

SF — Owens 76 pass from Garcia (Chandler kick)
NYG — Toomer 12 pass from Collins (Bryant kick)
NYG — Shockey 2 pass from Collins (Bryant kick)
SF — Barlow 1 run (Chandler kick)
NYG — Toomer 8 pass from Collins (Bryant kick)
NYG — Toomer 24 pass from Collins (Bryant kick)
NYG — Barber 6 run (Bryant kick)
NYG — FG Bryant 21
SF — Owens 26 pass from Garcia (Owens from Garcia)
SF — Garcia 14 run (Owens from Garcia)
SF — Garcia 14 run (Owens from Garcia)
SF — FG Chandler 25
SF — Streets 13 pass from Garcia (2-pt attempt failed)

FROM 20 POINTS BEHIND TO WIN:
Western Conference Playoff Game
December 22, 1957, at San Francisco

Detroit	0	7	14	10	— 31
San Francisco	14	10	3	0	— 27

SF — Owens 34 pass from Tittle (Soltau kick)
SF — McElhenny 47 pass from Tittle (Soltau kick)
Det — Junker 4 pass from Rote (Martin kick)
SF — Wilson 12 pass from Tittle (Soltau kick)
SF — FG Soltau 25

SF — FG Soltau 10
Det — Tracy 2 run (Martin kick)
Det — Tracy 58 run (Martin kick)
Det — Gedman 3 run (Martin kick)
Det — FG Martin 14

FROM 18 POINTS BEHIND TO WIN:
NFC Divisional Playoff Game
December 23, 1972, at San Francisco

Dallas	3	10	0	17	— 30
San Francisco	7	14	7	0	— 28

SF — Washington 97 kickoff return (Gossett kick)
Dall — FG Fritsch 37
SF — Schreiber 1 run (Gossett kick)
SF — Schreiber 1 run (Gossett kick)
Dall — FG Fritsch 45
Dall — Alworth 28 pass from Morton (Fritsch kick)
SF — Schreiber 1 run (Gossett kick)
Dall — FG Fritsch 27
Dall — Parks 20 pass from Staubach (Fritsch kick)
Dall — Sellers 10 pass from Staubach (Fritsch kick)

FROM 18 POINTS BEHIND TO WIN:
AFC Divisional Playoff Game
January 4, 1986, at Miami

Cleveland	7	7	7	0	— 21
Miami	3	0	14	7	— 24

Mia — FG Reveiz 51
Cle — Newsome 16 pass from Kosar (Bahr kick)
Cle — Byner 21 run (Bahr kick)
Cle — Byner 66 run (Bahr kick)
Mia — Moore 6 pass from Marino (Reveiz kick)
Mia — Davenport 31 run (Reveiz kick)
Mia — Davenport 1 run (Reveiz kick)

FROM 18 POINTS BEHIND TO WIN:
AFC Divisional Playoff Game
January 21, 2007, at Indianapolis

New England	7	14	7	6	— 34
Indianapolis	3	3	15	17	— 38

NE — Mankins 0 fumble recovery (Gostkowski kick)
Ind — FG Vinatieri 42
NE — Dillon 7 run (Gostkowski kick)
NE — Samuel 39 interception return (Gostkowski kick)
Ind — FG Vinatieri 26
Ind — Manning 1 run (Vinatieri kick)
Ind — Klecko 1 pass from Manning (Harrison from Manning)
NE — Gaffney 6 pass from Brady (Gostkowski kick)
Ind — Saturday 0 fumble recovery (Vinatieri kick)
NE — FG Gostkowski 28
Ind — FG Vinatieri 36
NE — FG Gostkowski 43
Ind — Addai 3 run (Vinatieri kick)

RECORDS FOR NFL TEAMS FOR MOST POINTS IN A GAME (REGULAR SEASON ONLY)

Note: When the record has been achieved more than once, only the most recent game is shown; summaries are listed in alphabetical order by conference. Bold face indicates team holding record.

BALTIMORE RAVENS
December 19, 2005, at Baltimore

Green Bay	3	0	0	0	— 3
Baltimore	14	10	10	14	— 48

TD: Balt—Todd Heap 2, Mark Clayton, Randy Hymes, Jamal Lewis, Adalius Thomas. TD Passes: Balt—Kyle Boller 3. FG: Balt—Matt Stover 2; GB—Ryan Longwell.

BUFFALO BILLS
September 18, 1966, at Buffalo

Miami	3	7	0	14	— 24
Buffalo	21	27	3	7	— 58

TD: Buff—Bobby Burnett 2, Butch Byrd 2, Jack Spikes 2, Bobby Crockett, Jack Kemp; Mia—Dave Kocourek, Bo Roberson, John Roderick. TD Passes: Buff—Jack Kemp, Daryle Lamonica; Mia—George Wilson 3. FG: Buff—Booth Lusteg; Mia—Gene Mingo.

CINCINNATI BENGALS
December 17, 1989, at Cincinnati

Houston	0	0	0	7	— 7
Cincinnati	21	10	21	9	— 61

TD: Cin—Eddie Brown 2, Eric Ball, James Brooks, Ira Hillary, Rodney Holman, Tim McGee, Craig Taylor; Hou—Lorenzo White. TD Passes: Cin—Boomer Esiason 4, Erik Wilhelm. FG: Cin—Jim Breech 2.

CLEVELAND BROWNS
November 7, 1954, at Cleveland

Washington	0	3	0	0	— 3
Cleveland	13	14	21	14	— 62

TD: Cle—Darrell Brewster 2, Mo Bassett, Ken Gorgal, Otto Graham, Dub Jones, Dante Lavelli, Curley Morrison. TD Passes: Cle—George Ratterman 3, Otto Graham. FG: Cle—Lou Groza 2; Wash—Vic Janowicz.

DENVER BRONCOS
October 6, 1963, at Denver

San Diego	13	7	0	14	— 34
Denver	3	14	9	24	— 50

TD: Den—Lionel Taylor 2, Goose Gonsoulin, Gene Prebola, Donnie Stone; SD—Keith Lincoln 2, Lance Alworth, Paul Lowe, Jacque MacKinnon. TD Passes: Den—John McCormick 3; SD—Tobin Rote 3, John Hadl 2. FG: Den—Gene Mingo 5.

HOUSTON TEXANS
November 28, 2004 at Houston

Tennessee	14	7	0	0	— 21
Houston	3	7	14	7	— 31

TD: Tenn—Erron Kinney 2, Derrick Mason; Hou—Domanick Davis, Andre Johnson, Billy Miller, Jonathan Wells. TD Passes: Tenn—Steve McNair 3; Hou—David Carr 2. FG: Hou—Kris Brown.

INDIANAPOLIS COLTS
December 12, 1976, at Baltimore

Buffalo	3	3	7	7	— 20
Baltimore Colts	7	13	28	10	— 58

TD: Balt—Roger Carr, Raymond Chester, Glenn Doughty, Roosevelt Leaks, Derrel Luce, Lydell Mitchell, Howard Stevens; Buff—Bob Chandler, O.J. Simpson. TD Passes: Balt—Bert Jones 3; Buff—Gary Marangi. FG: Balt—Toni Linhart 3; Buff—George Jakowenko 2.

JACKSONVILLE JAGUARS
December 3, 2000, at Jacksonville

Cleveland	0	0	0	0	— 0
Jacksonville	3	17	21	7	— 48

TD: Jax—Fred Taylor 3, Keenan McCardell, Mark Brunell, Shyrone Stith. TD Passes: Jax—Mark Brunell. FG: Jax—Mike Hollis 2.

KANSAS CITY CHIEFS
September 7, 1963, at Denver

Kansas City	14	14	21	10	— 59
Denver	0	7	0	0	— 7

TD: KC—Chris Burford 2, Frank Jackson 2, Dave Grayson, Abner Haynes, Sherrill Headrick, Curtis McClinton; Den—Lionel Taylor. TD Passes: KC—Len Dawson 4, Curtis McClinton; Den—Mickey Slaughter. FG: KC—Tommy Brooker.

MIAMI DOLPHINS
November 24, 1977, at St. Louis

Miami	14	14	20	7	— 55
St. Louis Cardinals	7	0	0	7	— 14

TD: Mia—Nat Moore 3, Gary Davis, Duriel Harris, Leroy Harris, Benny Malone, Andre Tillman; StL—Ike Harris, Terry Metcalf. TD Passes: Mia—Bob Griese 6; StL—Jim Hart.

NEW ENGLAND PATRIOTS
September 9, 1979, at New England

New York Jets	3	0	0	0	— 3
New England	14	21	7	14	— 56

TD: NE—Harold Jackson 3, Stanley Morgan 2, Allan Clark, Andy Johnson, Don Westbrook. TD Passes: NE—Steve Grogan 5, Tom Owen. FG: NYJ—Pat Leahy.

NEW YORK JETS
November 17, 1985, at New York

Tampa Bay	14	7	7	0	— 28
New York Jets	17	24	14	7	— 62

TD: NYJ—Mickey Shuler 3, Johnny Hector 2, Tony Paige, Al Toon, Wesley Walker; TB—James Wilder 2, Kevin House, Calvin Magee. TD Passes: NYJ—Ken O'Brien 5; TB—Steve DeBerg 2. FG: NYJ—Pat Leahy 2.

OAKLAND RAIDERS
September 29, 2002 at Oakland

Tennessee	7	0	12	6	— 25
Oakland	21	10	7	14	— 52

TD: Oak—Tim Brown, Phillip Buchanon, Charlie Garner, Terry Kirby, Jerry Porter, Jim Rice, Rod Woodson; Tenn—Drew Bennett, Eddie George, Justin McCareins, John Simon. TD Passes: Oak—Rich Gannon 4; Tenn—Steve McNair 2. FG: Oak—Sebastian Janikowski.

PITTSBURGH STEELERS
November 30, 1952, at Pittsburgh

New York Giants	0	0	7	0	— 7
Pittsburgh	14	14	7	28	— 63

TD: Pitt—Lynn Chandnois 2, Dick Hensley 2, Jack Butler, George Hays, Ray Mathews, Ed Modzelewski, Elbie Nickel; NYG—Bill Stribling. TD Passes: Pitt—Jim Finks 4, Gary Kerkorian; NYG—Tom Landry.

SAN DIEGO CHARGERS
December 22, 1963, at San Diego

Denver	7	10	3	0	— 20
San Diego	10	16	10	22	— 58

TD: SD—Paul Lowe 2, Chuck Allen, Bobby Jackson, Dave Kocourek, Keith Lincoln, Jacque MacKinnon; Den—Billy Joe, Donnie Stone. TD Passes: SD—John Hadl, Tobin Rote; Den—Don Breaux. FG: SD—George Blair 3; Den—Gene Mingo 2.

TENNESSEE TITANS
December 9, 1990, at Houston

Cleveland	0	7	7	0	— 14
Houston Oilers	14	31	7	6	— 58

TD: Hou—Lorenzo White 4, Ernest Givins, Leonard Harris, Tony Jones, Terry Kinard; Cle—Eric Metcalf 2. TD Passes: Hou—Warren Moon 2, Cody Carlson; Cle—Bernie Kosar. FG: Hou—Teddy Garcia.

ARIZONA CARDINALS
November 13, 1949, at New York

Chicago Cardinals	7	31	14	13	— 65
New York Bulldogs	7	0	6	7	— 20

TD: Chi—Red Cochran 2, Pat Harder 2, Bill Dewell, Mel Kutner, Bob Ravensburg, Vic Schwall, Charlie Trippi; NY—Joe Golding, Frank Muehlheuser, Johnny Rauch. TD Passes: Chi—Paul Christman 3, Jim Hardy 3; NY—Bobby Layne. FG: Chi—Pat Harder.

ATLANTA FALCONS
September 16, 1973, at New Orleans

Atlanta	0	24	21	17	— 62
New Orleans	0	0	7	0	— 7

TD: Atl—Ken Burrow 2, Eddie Ray 2, Wes Chesson, Tom Hayes, Art Malone, Joe Profit; NO—Bill Butler. TD Passes: Atl—Dick Shiner 3, Bob Lee; NO—Archie Manning. FG: Atl—Nick Mike-Mayer 2.

Carolina Panthers
December 8, 2002, at Carolina

Cincinnati	7	10	14	0	— 31
Carolina	9	7	21	15	— 52

TD: Car—Steve Smith 3, Dee Brown, Muhsin Muhammad, Al Wallace, Wesley Walls; Cin—Peter Warrick 2, Jon Kitna, Takeo Spikes. TD Passes: Car—Rodney Peete 3; Cin—Jon Kitna 2. FG: Cin—Neil Rackers.

CHICAGO BEARS
December 7, 1980, at Chicago

Green Bay	0	7	0	0	— 7
Chicago	0	28	13	20	— 61

TD: Chi—Walter Payton 3, Brian Baschnagel, Robin Earl, Roland Harper, Willie McClendon, Len Walterscheid, Rickey Watts; GB—James Lofton. TD Passes: Chi—Vince Evans 3; GB—Lynn Dickey.

DALLAS COWBOYS
October 12, 1980, at Dallas

San Francisco	0	7	0	7	— 14
Dallas	14	24	14	7	— 59

TD: Dall—Drew Pearson 3, Ron Springs 2, Tony Dorsett, Billy Joe DuPree, Robert Newhouse; SF—Dwight Clark 2. TD Passes: Dall—Danny White 4; SF—Steve DeBerg 2. FG: Dall—Rafael Septien.

DETROIT LIONS
November 27, 1997, at Detroit

Chicago	14	6	0	0	— 20
Detroit	3	14	17	21	— 55

TD: Det—Herman Moore, Johnnie Morton, Ron Rivers, Barry Sanders 3, Tracy Scroggins; Chi—Raymont Harris, Ricky Proehl. TD Passes: Det—Scott Mitchell 2; Chi—Erik Kramer. FG: Det—Jason Hanson 2; Chi—Jeff Jaeger 2.

GREEN BAY PACKERS
October 7, 1945, at Milwaukee

Detroit	0	7	7	7	— 21
Green Bay	0	41	9	7	— 57

TD: GB—Don Hutson 4, Charley Brock, Irv Comp, Ted Fritsch, Clyde Goodnight; Det—Chuck Fenenbock, John Greene, Bob Westfall. TD Passes: GB—Tex McKay 4, Lou Brock, Irv Comp; Det—Dave Ryan.

MINNESOTA VIKINGS
October 18, 1970, at Minnesota

Dallas	3	3	0	7	— 13
Minnesota	14	20	17	3	— 54

TD: Minn—Clint Jones 2, Ed Sharockman 2, John Beasley, Dave Osborn; Dall—Calvin Hill. TD Pass: Minn—Gary Cuozzo. FG: Minn—Fred Cox 4; Dall—Mike Clark 2.

NEW ORLEANS SAINTS
November 21, 1976, at Seattle

New Orleans	3	17	28	3	— 51
Seattle	6	0	7	14	— 27

TD: NO—Bobby Douglass 2, Tony Galbreath, Chuck Muncie, Tom Myers, Elex Price; Sea—Sherman Smith 2, Steve Largent, Jim Zorn. TD Pass: Sea—Bill Munson. FG: NO—Rich Szaro 3.

NEW YORK GIANTS
November 26, 1972, at New York

Philadelphia	3	7	0	0	— 10
New York Giants	14	24	10	14	— 62

TD: NYG—Don Herrmann 2, Ron Johnson 2, Bob Tucker 2, Randy Johnson; Phil—Harold Jackson. TD Passes: NYG—Norm Snead 3, Randy Johnson 2; Phil—John Reaves. FG: NYG—Pete Gogolak 2; Phil—Tom Dempsey.

PHILADELPHIA EAGLES
November 6, 1934, at Philadelphia

Cincinnati Reds	0	0	0	0	— 0
Philadelphia	26	6	12	20	— 64

TD: Phil—Joe Carter 3, Swede Hanson 3, Marvin Ellstrom, Roger Kirkman, Ed Matesic, Ed Storm, Albert Weiner 2, Marvin Elstrom. TD Passes: Phil—Ed Matesic 2, Albert Weiner 2, Marvin Elstrom.

ST. LOUIS RAMS
October 22, 1950, at Los Angeles

Baltimore	13	0	7	7	— 27
Los Angeles Rams	21	14	14	21	— 70

TD: LA—Bob Boyd 2, Vitamin T. Smith 2, Tom Fears, Elroy (Crazylegs) Hirsch, Dick Hoerner, Ralph Pasquariello, Dan Towler, Bob Waterfield; Balt—Chet Mutryn 2, Adrian Burk, Billy Stone. TD Passes: LA—Norm Van Brocklin 2, Bob Waterfield 2, Glenn Davis; Balt—Adrian Burk 3.

SAN FRANCISCO 49ERS
October 18, 1992, at San Francisco

Atlanta	7	3	0	7	— 17
San Francisco	21	21	14	0	— 56

TD: SF—Jerry Rice 3, Ricky Watters 3, Brent Jones, Tom Rathman; Atl—Michael Haynes, Jason Phillips. TD Passes: SF—Steve Young 3; Atl—Chris Miller, Wade Wilson. FG: Atl—Norm Johnson.

SEATTLE SEAHAWKS
October 30, 1977, at Seattle

Buffalo	3	0	7	7	— 17
Seattle	14	28	7	7	— 56

TD: Sea—Steve Largent 2, Duke Fergerson, Al Hunter, David Sims, Sherman Smith, Don Testerman, Jim Zorn; Buff—Joe Ferguson, John Kimbrough. TD Passes: Sea—Jim Zorn 4; Buff—Joe Ferguson. FG: Buff—Carson Long.

TAMPA BAY BUCCANEERS
December 23, 2001, at Tampa Bay

New Orleans	0	0	7	14	— 21
Tampa Bay	17	13	3	15	— 48

TD: TB—Mike Alstott, Ronde Barber, Warrick Dunn, Dave Moore, Karl Williams; NO—Joe Horn 2, Eddie Williams. TD Passes: TB—Brad Johnson 3; NO—Aaron Brooks 3. FG: TB—Martin Gramatica 4.

WASHINGTON REDSKINS
November 27, 1966, at Washington

New York Giants	0	14	14	13	— 41
Washington	13	21	14	24	— 72

TD: Wash—A.D. Whitfield 3, Brig Owens 2, Charley Taylor 2, Rickie Harris, Joe Don Looney, Bobby Mitchell; NYG—Allen Jacobs, Homer Jones, Dan Lewis, Joe Morrison, Aaron Thomas, Gary Wood. TD Passes: Wash—Sonny Jurgensen 3; NYG—Gary Wood 2, Tom Kennedy. FG: Wash—Charlie Gogolak.

RECORDS OF NFL TEAMS SINCE 1970 AFL-NFL MERGER

AFC	W	L	T	Pct.	Division Titles	Playoff Berths	Postseason Record	Super Bowl Record
Miami	353	213	2	.623	12	21	20-19	2-3
Pittsburgh	341	225	2	.602	17	22	28-17	5-1
Denver	332	230	6	.590	10	17	17-15	2-4
Oakland	319	243	6	.567	12	18	22-15	3-1
Jacksonville**	102	90	0	.531	2	5	4-5	0-0
Baltimore***	91	84	1	.520	2	4	5-3	1-0
Kansas City	288	273	7	.513	5	11	3-11	0-0
New England	287	281	0	.505	9	14	18-11	3-2
Tennessee	270	296	2	.477	4	14	12-14	0-1
Buffalo	269	297	2	.475	7	13	12-13	0-4
Indianapolis	269	297	2	.475	10	15	13-13	2-0
San Diego	257	306	5	.457	7	9	6-9	0-1
Cleveland+	234	283	3	.453	6	11	4-11	0-0
Cincinnati	254	314	0	.447	6	8	5-8	0-2
N.Y. Jets	249	317	2	.440	2	10	6-10	0-0
Houston****	24	56	0	.300	0	0	0-0	0-0

NFC	W	L	T	Pct.	Division Titles	Playoff Berths	Postseason Record	Super Bowl Record
Dallas	334	234	0	.588	15	24	31-19	5-3
San Francisco	325	240	3	.575	17	21	25-16	5-0
Minnesota	325	241	2	.574	14	22	16-22	0-3
Washington	316	250	2	.558	6	15	20-12	3-2
St. Louis	307	257	4	.544	11	19	16-18	1-2
Philadelphia	287	274	7	.511	7	16	13-16	0-2
Green Bay	280	280	8	.500	7	12	12-11	1-1
Chicago	283	284	1	.499	9	13	9-12	1-1
Seattle*	236	248	0	.488	5	9	6-9	0-1
N.Y. Giants	272	293	2	.482	6	12	12-10	2-1
Carolina**	90	102	0	.469	2	3	6-3	0-1
Atlanta	240	323	5	.427	3	8	6-8	0-1
Detroit	239	257	4	.424	3	9	1-9	0-0
New Orleans	235	329	4	.417	3	6	2-6	0-0
Arizona	224	338	6	.399	2	4	1-4	0-0
Tampa Bay*	187	296	1	.387	5	9	6-8	1-0

*Entered NFL in 1976.
**Entered NFL in 1995.
***Entered NFL in 1996.
****Entered NFL in 2002.
+Did not play 1996-98.
Oakland totals include L.A. Raiders, 1982-1994.
Tennessee totals include Houston, 1970-1996.
Indianapolis totals include Baltimore, 1970-1983.
St. Louis totals include L.A. Rams, 1970-1994.
Arizona totals include St. Louis, 1970-1987, and Phoenix, 1988-1993.
Tie games before 1972 are not calculated in won-lost percentage.

HOME RECORDS OF NFL TEAMS SINCE 1970 AFL-NFL MERGER

AFC	W	L	T	Pct.
Miami	203	79	1	.719
Pittsburgh	203	80	1	.717
Denver	202	79	4	.717
Baltimore***	57	30	1	.653
Jacksonville**	61	35	0	.635
Oakland	178	104	2	.631
Kansas City	176	104	3	.628
New England	165	119	0	.581
Buffalo	159	125	1	.560
Tennessee	155	128	1	.548
Cincinnati	155	129	0	.546
San Diego	147	134	2	.523
Indianapolis	144	138	2	.511
Cleveland+	129	128	2	.502
N.Y. Jets	133	149	1	.472
Houston****	14	26	0	.350

NFC	W	L	T	Pct.
Dallas	192	92	0	.676
Minnesota	191	93	1	.672
Washington	180	101	2	.640
San Francisco	175	107	2	.620
St. Louis	170	112	2	.603
Green Bay	168	111	5	.601
Chicago	167	116	1	.590
Seattle*	140	103	0	.576
Philadelphia	161	121	3	.570
Detroit	155	128	1	.548
N.Y. Giants	151	133	1	.532
Carolina**	49	47	0	.510
Atlanta	143	141	1	.504
Tampa Bay*	116	125	1	.481
Arizona	133	147	3	.475
New Orleans	125	158	1	.442

*Entered NFL in 1976.
**Entered NFL in 1995.
***Entered NFL in 1996.
****Entered NFL in 2002.
+Did not play 1996-98.
Oakland totals include L.A. Raiders,
    1982-1994.
Tennessee totals include Houston,
    1970-1996.
Indianapolis totals include Baltimore,
    1970-1983.
St. Louis totals include L.A. Rams,
    1970-1994.
Arizona totals include St. Louis,
    1970-1987, and Phoenix, 1988-1993.
Tie games before 1972 are not
    calculated in won-lost percentage.

ROAD RECORDS OF NFL TEAMS SINCE 1970 AFL-NFL MERGER

AFC	W	L	T	Pct.
Miami	150	134	1	.528
Oakland	141	139	4	.504
Pittsburgh	138	145	1	.488
Denver	130	151	2	.463
Indianapolis	125	159	0	.440
New England	122	162	0	.430
Jacksonville**	41	55	0	.427
N.Y. Jets	116	168	1	.409
Tennessee	115	168	1	.406
Cleveland+	105	155	1	.404
Kansas City	112	169	4	.400
San Diego	110	172	3	.391
Buffalo	110	172	1	.390
Baltimore***	34	54	0	.386
Cincinnati	99	185	0	.349
Houston****	10	30	0	.250

NFC	W	L	T	Pct.
San Francisco	150	133	1	.530
Dallas	142	142	0	.500
St. Louis	137	145	2	.486
Washington	136	149	0	.477
Minnesota	134	148	1	.475
Philadelphia	126	153	4	.452
N.Y. Giants	121	160	2	.431
Carolina**	41	55	0	.427
Chicago	116	168	0	.408
Green Bay	112	169	3	.399
Seattle*	96	145	0	.398
New Orleans	110	171	3	.392
Atlanta	97	182	4	.348
Arizona	91	191	3	.324
Detroit	84	197	3	.300
Tampa Bay*	71	171	0	.293

*Entered NFL in 1976.
**Entered NFL in 1995.
***Entered NFL in 1996.
****Entered NFL in 2002.
+Did not play 1996-98.
Oakland totals include L.A. Raiders, 1982-1994.
Tennessee totals include Houston, 1970-1996.
Indianapolis totals include Baltimore, 1970-1983.
St. Louis totals include L.A. Rams, 1970-1994.
Arizona totals include St. Louis, 1970-1987, and Phoenix, 1988-1993.
Tie games before 1972 are not calculated in won-lost percentage.

RECORDS OF TEAMS ON OPENING DAY

AFC	W	L	T	Pct.	Longest W Strk.	Longest L Strk.	Current Streak
Jacksonville	9	3	0	.750	6	2	W-3
Denver	29	17	1	.630	4	4	L-2
Miami	23	17	1	.575	11	5	L-1
San Diego	27	20	0	.574	6	6	W-1
Kansas City	26	21	0	.553	7	4	L-1
Pittsburgh	36	32	4	.529	4	3	W-4
Indianapolis	32	30	1	.516	8	8	W-2
Oakland	24	23	0	.511	5	5	L-4
Tennessee	24	23	0	.511	4	3	L-2
Cleveland	27	27	0	.500	5	6	L-2
New England	23	24	0	.489	6	3	W-3
Cincinnati	18	21	0	.462	4	4	W-2
N.Y. Jets	20	27	0	.426	3	5	W-1
Buffalo	19	28	0	.404	6	5	L-1
Houston	2	3	0	.400	2	3	L-3
Baltimore	4	7	0	.364	2	4	W-1

NFC	W	L	T	Pct.	Longest W Strk.	Longest L Strk.	Current Streak
Dallas	31	15	1	.674	17	5	L-1
Chicago	49	33	5	.598	9	6	W-1
N.Y. Giants	46	31	5	.597	4	3	L-1
Minnesota	26	19	1	.578	5	3	W-1
Green Bay	47	36	3	.566	5	6	L-2
St. Louis	38	31	0	.551	5	6	W-1
Detroit	41	34	2	.547	10	4	L-1
Atlanta	22	19	0	.537	5	3	W-4
San Francisco	29	27	1	.518	5	3	L-1
Washington	36	35	4	.507	6	5	L-1
Tampa Bay	13	18	0	.419	3	5	L-1
Arizona	34	50	2	.405	6	7	W-1
Philadelphia	29	43	1	.403	5	9	W-1
Carolina	4	8	0	.333	3	4	L-3
New Orleans	13	27	0	.325	2	6	W-2
Seattle	10	21	0	.323	3	8	W-1

Kansas City totals include Dallas Texans, 1960-62.
Oakland totals include L.A. Raiders, 1982-1994.
San Diego totals include L.A. Chargers, 1960.
Indianapolis totals include Baltimore, 1953-1983.
Tennessee totals include Houston, 1960-1996.
New England totals include Boston, 1960-1970.
St. Louis totals include Cleveland, 1937-1942 and 1944-45, and L.A. Rams, 1946-1994.
Detroit totals include Portsmouth, 1930-33.
Arizona totals include Chi. Cardinals, 1920-1959, St. Louis, 1960-1987, and Phoenix, 1988-1993.
Chicago totals include Decatur, 1920.
Washington totals include Boston Braves, 1932 and Boston Redskins, 1933-36.
NOTE: All tied games occurred prior to 1972, when calculation of ties in percentages as half-win, half-loss was begun.

RECORDS OF NFL TEAMS, 1997-2006

AFC	W	L	T	Pct.	Division Titles	Playoff Berths	Postseason Record	Super Bowl Record
New England	102	58	0	.638	6	7	13-4	3-0
Denver	102	58	0	.638	2	6	8-4	2-0
Pittsburgh	96	63	1	.603	4	5	8-4	1-0
Indianapolis	95	65	0	.594	5	7	7-6	1-0
Tennessee	89	71	0	.556	2	4	5-4	0-1
Jacksonville	89	71	0	.556	2	4	2-4	0-0
Kansas City	89	71	0	.556	2	3	0-3	0-0
Miami	88	72	0	.550	1	5	3-5	0-0
Baltimore	87	72	1	.547	2	4	5-3	1-0
N.Y. Jets	87	73	0	.544	2	5	3-5	0-0
Buffalo	73	87	0	.456	0	2	0-2	0-0
San Diego	70	90	0	.438	2	2	0-2	0-0
Oakland	68	92	0	.425	3	3	4-3	0-1
Cincinnati	61	99	0	.381	1	1	0-1	0-0
Cleveland	40	88	0	.313	0	1	0-1	0-0
Houston	24	56	0	.300	0	0	0-0	0-0

Cleveland did not play from 1997-98.
Houston entered the NFL in 2002.

NFC	W	L	T	Pct.	Division Titles	Playoff Berths	Postseason Record	Super Bowl Record
Green Bay	97	63	0	.606	4	6	4-6	0-1
Philadelphia	89	70	1	.559	5	6	8-6	0-1
Minnesota	88	72	0	.550	2	5	5-5	0-0
Seattle	88	72	0	.550	4	5	3-5	0-1
St. Louis	87	73	0	.544	3	5	6-4	1-1
Tampa Bay	87	73	0	.544	3	6	5-5	1-0
N.Y. Giants	83	76	1	.522	3	5	2-5	0-1
Atlanta	77	82	1	.484	2	3	4-3	0-1
San Francisco	77	83	0	.481	2	4	3-4	0-0
Washington	73	86	1	.459	1	2	2-2	0-0
Dallas	73	87	0	.456	1	4	0-4	0-0
Chicago	72	88	0	.450	3	3	2-3	0-1
Carolina	71	89	0	.444	1	2	5-2	0-1
New Orleans	70	90	0	.438	2	2	2-2	0-0
Detroit	55	105	0	.344	0	2	0-2	0-0
Arizona	54	106	0	.338	0	1	1-1	0-0

Seattle was in the AFC from 1997-2001.

HOME RECORDS, 1997-2006

AFC	W - L - T	Pct.
Denver	60-20-0	.750
Kansas City	58-22-0	.725
New England	57-23-0	.713
Baltimore	53-26-1	.669
Indianapolis	53-27-0	.663
Miami	53-27-0	.663
Pittsburgh	52-27-1	.656
Jacksonville	52-28-0	.650
Tennessee	49-31-0	.613
N.Y. Jets	47-33-0	.588
Buffalo	44-36-0	.550
San Diego	41-39-0	.513
Oakland	40-40-0	.500
Cincinnati	36-44-0	.450
Houston	14-26-0	.350
Cleveland	20-44-0	.313

NFC	W - L - T	Pct.
Green Bay	56-24-0	.700
Minnesota	55-25-0	.688
Seattle	53-27-0	.663
Tampa Bay	51-29-0	.638
Philadelphia	50-30-0	.625
St. Louis	50-30-0	.625
San Francisco	49-31-0	.613
Dallas	48-32-0	.600
N.Y. Giants	44-36-0	.550
Washington	43-36-1	.544
Atlanta	42-38-0	.525
Chicago	42-38-0	.525
Detroit	38-42-0	.475
Arizona	36-44-0	.450
Carolina	36-44-0	.450
New Orleans	33-47-0	.413

Cleveland did not play from 1997-98.
Houston entered the NFL in 2002.
Seattle was in the AFC from 1997-2001.

ROAD RECORDS, 1997-2006

AFC	W-L-T	Pct.
New England	45-35-0	.563
Pittsburgh	44-36-0	.550
Denver	42-38-0	.525
Indianapolis	42-38-0	.525
N.Y. Jets	40-40-0	.500
Tennessee	40-40-0	.500
Jacksonville	37-43-0	.463
Miami	35-45-0	.438
Baltimore	34-46-0	.425
Kansas City	31-49-0	.388
Buffalo	29-51-0	.363
San Diego	29-51-0	.363
Oakland	28-52-0	.350
Cincinnati	25-55-0	.313
Cleveland	20-44-0	.313
Houston	10-30-0	.250

NFC	W-L-T	Pct.
Green Bay	41-39-0	.513
N.Y. Giants	39-40-1	.494
Philadelphia	39-40-1	.494
New Orleans	37-43-0	.463
St. Louis	37-43-0	.463
Tampa Bay	36-44-0	.450
Atlanta	35-44-1	.444
Carolina	35-45-0	.438
Seattle	35-45-0	.438
Minnesota	33-47-0	.413
Chicago	30-50-0	.375
Washington	30-50-0	.375
San Francisco	28-52-0	.350
Dallas	25-55-0	.313
Arizona	18-62-0	.225
Detroit	17-63-0	.213

Cleveland did not play from 1997-98.
Houston entered the NFL in 2002.
Seattle was in the AFC from 1997-2001.

RECORDS BY MONTHS, 1997-2006

AFC	Sept. W-L-T	Oct. W-L-T	Nov. W-L-T	Dec. W-L-T	Total W-L-T	Pct.
Denver	26-10-0	25-16-0	27-11-0	24-21-0	102-58-0	.638
New England	21-12-0	24-17-0	26-16-0	31-13-0	102-58-0	.638
Pittsburgh	16-16-0	28-11-0	22-20-1	30-16-0	96-63-1	.603
Indianapolis	20-13-0	23-15-0	25-18-0	27-19-0	95-65-0	.594
Jacksonville	22-12-0	16-23-0	26-15-0	25-21-0	89-71-0	.556
Kansas City	20-15-0	24-15-0	18-23-0	27-18-0	89-71-0	.556
Tennessee	13-20-0	25-16-0	23-16-0	28-19-0	89-71-0	.556
Miami	20-12-0	21-18-0	25-18-0	22-24-0	88-72-0	.550
Baltimore	19-15-0	16-23-0	25-18-1	27-16-0	87-72-1	.547
N.Y. Jets	15-18-0	20-19-0	26-15-0	26-21-0	87-73-0	.544
Buffalo	12-20-0	22-21-0	19-21-0	20-25-0	73-87-0	.456
San Diego	16-18-0	21-20-0	15-25-0	18-27-0	70-90-0	.438
Oakland	18-16-0	19-20-0	17-24-0	14-32-0	68-92-0	.425
Cincinnati	12-22-0	13-27-0	17-25-0	19-25-0	61-99-0	.381
Cleveland	9-18-0	12-21-0	10-21-0	9-28-0	40-88-0	.313
Houston	4-12-0	7-12-0	6-15-0	7-17-0	24-56-0	.300

Cleveland did not play from 1997-98.
Houston entered the NFL in 2002.
September totals include August; December totals include January.

NFC	Sept. W-L-T	Oct. W-L-T	Nov. W-L-T	Dec. W-L-T	Total W-L-T	Pct.
Green Bay	21-15-0	18-17-0	23-19-0	35-12-0	97-63-0	.606
Philadelphia	16-18-0	23-17-0	25-17-1	25-18-0	89-70-1	.559
Minnesota	21-14-0	25-13-0	23-18-0	19-27-0	88-72-0	.550
Seattle	22-13-0	16-20-0	25-18-0	25-21-0	88-72-0	.550
St. Louis	19-16-0	23-15-0	18-23-0	27-19-0	87-73-0	.544
Tampa Bay	20-14-0	17-21-0	24-18-0	26-20-0	87-73-0	.544
N.Y. Giants	19-16-0	25-14-0	13-27-1	26-19-0	83-76-1	.522
Atlanta	15-19-0	20-20-0	21-19-1	21-24-0	77-82-1	.484
San Francisco	16-17-0	19-21-0	20-21-0	22-24-0	77-83-0	.481
Washington	15-18-0	16-24-0	18-23-1	24-21-0	73-86-1	.459
Dallas	17-15-0	20-21-0	20-22-0	16-29-0	73-87-0	.456
Chicago	9-25-0	21-18-0	20-22-0	22-23-0	72-88-0	.450
Carolina	14-18-0	15-27-0	19-22-0	23-22-0	71-89-0	.444
New Orleans	17-16-0	18-24-0	17-22-0	18-28-0	70-90-0	.438
Detroit	14-20-0	13-24-0	17-28-0	11-33-0	55-105-0	.344
Arizona	9-24-0	12-27-0	16-26-0	17-29-0	54-106-0	.338

Seattle was in the AFC from 1997-2001.
September totals include August; December totals include January.

TAKEAWAYS/GIVEAWAYS, 1997-2006

	Takeaways			Giveaways			
AFC	Int.	Fum.	Total	Int.	Fum.	Total	Net.Diff.
Kansas City	174	143	317	146	98	244	73
Jacksonville	154	123	277	118	104	222	55
New England	190	121	311	151	107	258	53
N.Y. Jets	186	107	293	148	95	243	50
Denver	168	128	296	157	90	247	49
Tennessee	155	131	286	145	109	254	32
Pittsburgh	170	136	306	168	109	277	29
Baltimore	203	128	331	169	139	308	23
Miami	182	127	309	180	127	307	2
Indianapolis	136	128	264	159	104	263	1
Cincinnati	153	121	274	165	116	281	-7
Houston	64	47	111	73	57	130	-19
Oakland	156	111	267	153	137	290	-23
Buffalo	146	106	252	164	130	294	-42
Cleveland	133	83	216	158	110	268	-52
San Diego	164	97	261	195	121	316	-55

Cleveland did not play from 1997-98.
Houston entered NFL in 2002.

	Takeaways			Giveaways			
NFC	Int.	Fum.	Total	Int.	Fum.	Total	Net.Diff.
Tampa Bay	194	117	311	153	125	278	33
Philadelphia	165	136	301	143	133	276	25
N.Y. Giants	167	126	293	158	112	270	23
Atlanta	168	134	302	159	123	282	20
San Francisco	177	110	287	150	119	269	18
Seattle	184	125	309	170	123	293	16
Washington	164	113	277	158	125	283	-6
Carolina	182	137	319	184	144	328	-9
Detroit	156	123	279	189	103	292	-13
Minnesota	159	119	278	178	119	297	-19
Green Bay	187	122	309	197	132	329	-20
Chicago	161	142	303	180	150	330	-27
Dallas	148	114	262	172	123	295	-33
New Orleans	159	139	298	195	143	338	-40
St. Louis	182	121	303	197	154	351	-48
Arizona	155	112	267	210	146	356	-89

Seattle was in the AFC from 1997-2001.

BEST TAKEAWAY/GIVEAWAY DIFFERENTIAL, SEASON

+43	Washington, 1983
+26	Kansas City, 1990
+25	N.Y. Giants, 1997

HIGH AND LOW SINGLE-GAME YARDAGE TOTALS, 1997-2006

Most Total Yards, Game
- 645 Pittsburgh vs. Atlanta, Nov. 10, 2002 (OT)
- 614 St. Louis vs. San Diego, Oct. 1, 2000
- 605 Minnesota at New Orleans, Oct. 17, 2004
- 595 New Orleans vs. Cincinnati, Nov. 19, 2006
- 591 Seattle at San Diego, Dec. 29, 2002 (OT)

Fewest Total Yards, Game
- 26 Cleveland at Buffalo, Dec. 12, 2004
- 40 Cleveland vs. Pittsburgh, Sept. 12, 1999
- 47 Houston at Pittsburgh, Dec. 8, 2002
- 53 Cleveland at Jacksonville, Dec. 3, 2000
- 93 Oakland at Kansas City, Dec. 7, 1997

Most Yards Rushing, Game
- 407 Cincinnati vs. Denver, Oct. 22, 2000
- 375 Jacksonville vs. Indianapolis, Dec. 10, 2006
- 343 Baltimore vs. Cleveland, Sept. 14, 2003
- 337 St. Louis vs. Carolina, Nov. 11, 2001
- 328 San Francisco vs. Detroit, Dec. 14, 1998

Fewest Yards Rushing, Game
- -3 Detroit vs. Minnesota, Dec. 10, 2006
- 4 Buffalo at Tennessee, Nov. 23, 1997
  Cincinnati at Baltimore, Sept. 24, 2000

- 5 New England at Pittsburgh, Oct. 31, 2004
- 6 Dallas at New Orleans, Dec. 6, 1998

Most Yards Passing, Game
- 504 New Orleans vs. Cincinnati, Nov. 19, 2006
- 499 Denver vs. Atlanta, Oct. 31, 2004
- 474 Kansas City at Oakland, Nov. 5, 2000
- 473 N.Y. Jets at Baltimore, Dec. 24, 2000
- 472 Indianapolis at Kansas City, Oct. 31, 2004

Fewest Yards Passing, Game
- -19 San Diego at Kansas City, Sept. 20, 1998
- -9 Cleveland at Jacksonville, Dec. 3, 2000
- -5 Houston at Oakland, Dec. 3, 2006
- -3 Cleveland at Buffalo, Dec. 12, 2004
- 0 Oakland at San Diego, Dec. 28, 2003

NFL INDIVIDUAL LEADERS, 1997-2006

Points		Passing Yards	
Jason Elam	1,193	Brett Favre	38,776
Adam Vinatieri	1,151	Peyton Manning	37,586
Ryan Longwell	1,144	Drew Bledsoe	29,969
Matt Stover	1,144	Jake Plummer	29,253
Jeff Wilkins	1,126	Kerry Collins	29,015

Touchdowns		TD Passes	
Marvin Harrison	114	Peyton Manning	275
Terrell Owens	112	Brett Favre	267
LaDainian Tomlinson	111	Drew Bledsoe	171
Shaun Alexander	107	Steve McNair	163
Marshall Faulk	103	Jake Plummer	161

Field Goals		Receptions	
Matt Stover	281	Marvin Harrison	958
Adam Vinatieri	261	Rod Smith	827
Jason Elam	260	Terrell Owens	766
Ryan Longwell	247	Jimmy Smith	757
Olindo Mare	245	Keyshawn Johnson	751

Rushes		Reception Yards	
Curtis Martin	2,834	Marvin Harrison	12,861
Corey Dillon	2,618	Terrell Owens	11,195
Eddie George	2,530	Rod Smith	11,000
Edgerrin James	2,525	Jimmy Smith	10,755
Jerome Bettis	2,363	Randy Moss	10,700

Rushing Yards		Receiving TDs	
Curtis Martin	11,462	Marvin Harrison	114
Corey Dillon	11,241	Terrell Owens	110
Tiki Barber	10,449	Randy Moss	101
Edgerrin James	10,385	Rod Smith	65
Fred Taylor	9,513	Torry Holt	64

Rushing TDs		Interceptions	
LaDainian Tomlinson	100	Darren Sharper	49
Shaun Alexander	96	Ty Law	44
Priest Holmes	86	Champ Bailey	39
Corey Dillon	82	Sammy Knight	38
Marshall Faulk	71	Tory James	37

Pass Attempts		Sacks	
Brett Favre	5,531	Michael Strahan	114.5
Peyton Manning	4,890	Simeon Rice	108.5
Kerry Collins	4,375	Jason Taylor	106.0
Jake Plummer	4,350	Warren Sapp	82.5
Drew Bledsoe	4,338	Kevin Carter	82.0

Completions	
Brett Favre	3,354
Peyton Manning	3,131
Drew Bledsoe	2,529
Jake Plummer	2,484
Steve McNair	2,471

NFL GAMES IN WHICH A TEAM HAS SCORED 60 OR MORE POINTS

(Home team in capitals)

Regular Season

WASHINGTON 72, New York Giants 41	November 27, 1966
LOS ANGELES RAMS 70, Baltimore 27	October 22, 1950
Chicago Cardinals 65, NEW YORK BULLDOGS 20	November 13, 1949
LOS ANGELES RAMS 65, Detroit 24	October 29, 1950
PHILADELPHIA 64, Cincinnati 0	November 6, 1934
CHICAGO CARDINALS 63, New York Giants 35	October 17, 1948
AKRON 62, Oorang 0	October 29, 1922
PITTSBURGH 62, New York Giants 7	November 30, 1952
CLEVELAND 62, New York Giants 14	December 6, 1953
CLEVELAND 62, Washington 3	November 7, 1954
NEW YORK GIANTS 62, Philadelphia 10	November 26, 1972
Atlanta 62, NEW ORLEANS 7	September 16, 1973
NEW YORK JETS 62, Tampa Bay 28	November 17, 1985
CHICAGO 61, San Francisco 20	December 12, 1965
Cincinnati 61, HOUSTON 17	December 17, 1972
CHICAGO 61, Green Bay 7	December 7, 1980
CINCINNATI 61, Houston 7	December 17, 1989
ROCK ISLAND 60, Evansville 0	October 15, 1922
CHICAGO CARDINALS 60, Rochester 0	October 7, 1923

Postseason

Chicago Bears 73, WASHINGTON 0	December 8, 1940
JACKSONVILLE 62, Miami 7	January 15, 2000

YOUNGEST AND OLDEST PLAYERS IN NFL IN 2006

10 Youngest Players	Birthdate	Games	Starts	Position
Donte Whitner, Buffalo	7/24/1985	15	14	DB
Derrick Martin, Baltimore	5/16/1985	8	0	DB
Sam Hurd, Dallas	4/24/1985	15	2	WR
Maurice Jones-Drew, Jacksonville	3/23/1985	16	1	RB
Chad Jackson, New England	3/6/1985	12	1	WR
Reggie Bush, New Orleans	3/2/1985	16	8	RB
Maurice Stovall, Tampa Bay	2/21/1985	9	2	WR
Laurence Maroney, New England	2/5/1985	14	0	RB
Mario Williams, Houston	1/31/1985	16	16	DE
Tony McDaniel, Jacksonville	1/20/1985	11	0	DT

10 Oldest Players	Birthdate	Games	Starts	Position
Morten Andersen, Atlanta	8/19/1960	14	0	K
Vinny Testaverde, New England	11/13/1963	3	0	QB
John Carney, New Orleans	4/20/1964	16	0	K
Jeff Feagles, N.Y. Giants	3/7/1966	16	0	P
Matt Stover, Baltimore	1/27/1968	16	0	K
Ricky Proehl, Indianapolis	3/7/1968	2	1	WR
Ted Washington, Cleveland	4/13/1968	16	16	NT
Matt Turk, St. Louis	6/16/1968	16	0	P
Fred McAfee, New Orleans	6/20/1968	4	0	RB
Brad Johnson, Minnesota	9/13/1968	15	14	QB

YOUNGEST AND OLDEST REGULAR STARTERS BY POSITION IN 2006

Minimum: 8 Games Started

	Youngest		Oldest	
QB	5/7/84	Alex Smith, SF	9/13/68	Brad Johnson, Min.
RB	3/2/85	Reggie Bush, NO	12/27/70	Lorenzo Neal, SD
WR	9/21/83	Greg Jennings, GB	1/6/70	Keenan McCardell, SD
TE	1/31/84	Vernon Davis, SF	1/14/72	Kyle Brady, Jax.
T	12/10/83	D'Brickashaw Ferguson, NYJ	12/1/70	Todd Steussie, St.L.
G	11/22/83	Davin Joseph, TB	6/19/70	Chris Gray, Sea.
C	1/13/84	Nick Mangold, NYJ	3/6/70	Robbie Tobeck, Sea.
DE	1/31/85	Mario Williams, Hou.	11/21/71	Michael Strahan, NYG
DT	3/19/84	Barry Cofield, NYG	4/13/68	Ted Washington, Cle.
LB	12/23/84	Ernie Sims, Det.	1/19/69	Junior Seau, NE
CB	12/12/84	Richard Marshall, Car.	5/18/73	Tory James, Cin.
S	7/24/85	Donte Whitner, Buf.	11/30/70	Robert Griffith, Ari.

OLDEST INDIVIDUAL SINGLE-SEASON OR SINGLE-GAME RECORDS IN NFL RECORD & FACT BOOK

Most Points, Game—40, Ernie Nevers, Chi. Cardinals vs. Chi. Bears, Nov. 28, 1929 (6-td, 4-pat)

Most Touchdowns Rushing, Game—6, Ernie Nevers, Chi. Cardinals vs. Chi. Bears, Nov. 28, 1929

Highest Rushing Average Gain, Season (Qualifiers)—8.44, Beattie Feathers, Chi. Bears, 1934 (119-1,004)

Highest Punting Average, Season (Qualifiers)—51.40, Sammy Baugh, Washington, 1940 (35-1,799)

Highest Punting Average, Rookie, Season (Qualifiers)—45.92, Frank Sinkwich, Detroit, 1943 (12-551)

Highest Punting Average, Game (minimum: 4 punts)—61.75, Bob Cifers, Detroit vs. Chi. Bears, Nov. 24, 1946 (4-247)

Highest Average Gain, Pass Receptions, Season (minimum: 24 receptions)—32.58, Don Currivan, Boston, 1947 (24-782)

Highest Average Gain, Passing, Game (minimum: 20 passes)—18.58, Sammy Baugh, Washington vs. Boston, Oct. 31, 1948 (24-446)

Most Touchdowns, Fumble Recoveries, Game—2, Fred (Dippy) Evans, Chi. Bears vs. Washington, Nov. 28, 1948

Most Yards Gained, Intercepted Passes, Rookie, Season—301, Don Doll, Detroit, 1949

Most Passes Had Intercepted, Game—8, Jim Hardy, Chi. Cardinals vs. Philadelphia, Sept. 24, 1950

Highest Kickoff Return Average, Game (minimum: 3 returns)—73.50, Wally Triplett, Detroit vs. Los Angeles, Oct. 29, 1950 (4-294)

Highest Punt Return Average, Season (Qualifiers)—23.00, Herb Rich, Baltimore, 1950 (12-276)

Highest Punt Return Average, Rookie, Season (Qualifiers)—23.00, Herb Rich, Baltimore, 1950 (12-276)

Most Yards Passing, Game—554, Norm Van Brocklin, Los Angeles vs. N.Y. Yanks, Sept. 28, 1951

Most Touchdowns, Punt Returns, Rookie, Season—4, Jack Christiansen, Detroit, 1951

Most Interceptions By, Season—14, Dick (Night Train) Lane, Los Angeles, 1952

Most Interceptions By, Rookie, Season—14, Dick (Night Train) Lane, Los Angeles, 1952

Highest Average Gain, Passing, Season (Qualifiers)—11.17, Tommy O'Connell, Cleveland, 1957 (110-1,229)

Most Yards Gained, Pass Receptions, Rookie, Season—1,473, Bill Groman, Houston, 1960

NFL INDIVIDUAL LEADERS OVER RECENT SEASONS

Last 2 Seasons		Last 3 Seasons		Last 4 Seasons	
Points					
306	LaDainian Tomlinson	414	LaDainian Tomlinson	516	LaDainian Tomlinson
256	Neil Rackers	368	Shayne Graham	500	Jeff Wilkins
255	Jay Feely	362	Nate Kaeding	485	Matt Stover
248	Nate Kaeding	359	Jason Elam	479	Jason Elam
248	Jeff Wilkins	354	Adam Vinatieri	474	Shayne Graham
Touchdowns					
51	LaDainian Tomlinson	69	LaDainain Tomlinson	86	LaDainain Tomlinson
40	Larry Johnson	55	Shaun Alexander	71	Shaun Alexander
35	Shaun Alexander	51	Larry Johnson	52	Larry Johnson
26	Corey Dillon	39	Corey Dillon	49	Marvin Harrison
26	Steven Jackson	39	Marvin Harrison	49	Priest Holmes
Field Goals					
68	Neil Rackers	90	Neil Rackers	120	Matt Stover
59	Jeff Wilkins	87	Matt Stover	117	Jeff Wilkins
58	Jay Feely	80	Jason Elam	107	Jason Elam
58	Matt Stover	80	Shayne Graham	102	Shayne Graham
55	Joe Nedney	78	Jeff Wilkins	101	Two tied
Rushes					
752	Larry Johnson	1,039	Rudi Johnson	1,341	Edgerrin James
697	Edgerrin James	1,031	Edgerrin James	1,339	LaDainian Tomlinson
687	LaDainian Tomlinson	1,026	LaDainian Tomlinson	1,301	Shaun Alexander
684	Tiki Barber	1,006	Tiki Barber	1,284	Tiki Barber
678	Rudi Johnson	975	Shaun Alexander	1,254	Rudi Johnson
Rushing Yards					
3,539	Larry Johnson	5,040	Tiki Barber	6,257	LaDainian Tomlinson
3,522	Tiki Barber	4,612	LaDainian Tomlinson	6,256	Tiki Barber
3,277	LaDainian Tomlinson	4,472	Shaun Alexander	5,907	Shaun Alexander
2,776	Shaun Alexander	4,221	Rudi Johnson	5,472	Edgerrin James
2,767	Rudi Johnson	4,213	Edgerrin James	5,178	Rudi Johnson
Rushing Touchdowns					
46	LaDainian Tomlinson	63	LaDainian Tomlinson	76	LaDainian Tomlinson
37	Larry Johnson	50	Shaun Alexander	64	Shaun Alexander
34	Shaun Alexander	46	Larry Johnson	47	Priest Holmes
25	Corey Dillon	37	Corey Dillon	47	Larry Johnson
24	Rudi Johnson	36	Rudi Johnson	45	Rudi Johnson
Passes					
1,220	Brett Favre	1,760	Brett Favre	2,231	Brett Favre
1,079	Eli Manning	1,520	Tom Brady	2,073	Peyton Manning
1,054	Drew Brees	1,507	Peyton Manning	2,047	Tom Brady
1,046	Tom Brady	1,461	Carson Palmer	1,892	Marc Bulger
1,029	Carson Palmer	1,454	Drew Brees	1,848	Jake Delhomme
Completions					
715	Brett Favre	1,061	Brett Favre	1,382	Peyton Manning
679	Drew Brees	1,003	Peyton Manning	1,369	Brett Favre
669	Carson Palmer	941	Tom Brady	1,258	Tom Brady
667	Peyton Manning	941	Drew Brees	1,219	Marc Bulger
653	Tom Brady	932	Carson Palmer	1,146	Drew Brees
Passing Yards					
8,144	Peyton Manning	12,701	Peyton Manning	16,968	Peyton Manning
7,994	Drew Brees	11,854	Brett Favre	15,215	Brett Favre
7,871	Carson Palmer	11,331	Tom Brady	14,951	Tom Brady
7,766	Brett Favre	11,153	Drew Brees	14,407	Marc Bulger
7,639	Tom Brady	10,768	Carson Palmer	13,986	Trent Green

Last 2 Seasons
Touchdown Passes
60	Carson Palmer
59	Peyton Manning
50	Tom Brady
50	Drew Brees
48	Eli Manning

Receptions
195	Torry Holt
186	Steve Smith
185	Anquan Boldin
184	Chad Johnson
178	Donald Driver

Receiving Yards
2,801	Chad Johnson
2,729	Steve Smith
2,605	Anquan Boldin
2,519	Torry Holt
2,516	Donald Driver

Receiving Touchdowns
24	Marvin Harrison
20	Steve Smith
19	Antonio Gates
19	Torry Holt
19	Terrell Owens

Interceptions
18	Champ Bailey
14	Ty Law
13	Rashean Mathis
13	Asante Samuel
13	Darren Sharper

Sacks
27.0	Derrick Burgess
27.0	Shawne Merriman
26.0	Aaron Schobel
25.5	Jason Taylor
23.5	Julius Peppers

Last 3 Seasons
Touchdown Passes
108	Peyton Manning
78	Tom Brady
78	Carson Palmer
77	Drew Brees
70	Jake Delhomme

Receptions
289	Torry Holt
279	Chad Johnson
263	Marvin Harrison
262	Donald Driver
254	Laveranues Coles

Receiving Yards
4,075	Chad Johnson
3,891	Torry Holt
3,724	Donald Driver
3,625	Marvin Harrison
3,575	Reggie Wayne

Receiving Touchdowns
39	Marvin Harrison
33	Terrell Owens
32	Antonio Gates
29	Torry Holt
26	Reggie Wayne

Interceptions
21	Champ Bailey
18	Rashean Mathis
17	Tory James
17	Darren Sharper
16	Two tied

Sacks
35.0	Jason Taylor
34.5	Julius Peppers
34.0	Aaron Schobel
32.5	Dwight Freeney
31.5	Robert Mathis

Last 4 Seasons
Touchdown Passes
137	Peyton Manning
101	Tom Brady
100	Brett Favre
90	Matt Hasselbeck
89	Jake Delhomme

Receptions
406	Torry Holt
369	Chad Johnson
357	Marvin Harrison
345	Derrick Mason
342	Anquan Boldin

Receiving Yards
5,587	Torry Holt
5,430	Chad Johnson
4,897	Marvin Harrison
4,605	Anquan Boldin
4,413	Reggie Wayne

Receiving Touchdowns
49	Marvin Harrison
42	Terrell Owens
41	Torry Holt
41	Randy Moss
35	Chad Johnson

Interceptions
23	Champ Bailey
22	Ed Reed
22	Darren Sharper
21	Tory James
21	Ty Law

Sacks
48.0	Jason Taylor
45.5	Aaron Schobel
43.5	Dwight Freeney
43.0	Simeon Rice
42.0	Leonard Little

NFL TEAM LEADERS OVER RECENT SEASONS
Highest Won-Lost Percentage
.813	Indianapolis	.792	Indianapolis	.781	Indianapolis
.750	Chicago	.750	New England	.781	New England
.719	San Diego	.729	San Diego	.656	Denver
.688	Three tied	.708	Pittsburgh	.641	Philadelphia
		.667	Denver	.641	Seattle

Most Points
910	San Diego	1,388	Indianapolis	1,835	Indianapolis
866	Indianapolis	1,356	San Diego	1,701	Kansas City
794	Cincinnati	1,217	Kansas City	1,669	San Diego
787	Seattle	1,201	New England	1,562	Seattle
777	NY Giants	1,168	Cincinnati	1,549	New England

Most Total Yards
11,869	Indianapolis	18,344	Indianapolis	24,218	Indianapolis
11,407	San Diego	18,030	Kansas City	23,940	Kansas City
11,338	St. Louis	17,215	St. Louis	22,731	Green Bay
11,335	Kansas City	17,049	Denver	22,672	St. Louis
11,295	New Orleans	16,949	San Diego	22,647	Denver

Last 2 Seasons	Last 3 Seasons	Last 4 Seasons
Most Rushing Yards		
5,485 Atlanta	8,157 Atlanta	10,106 Atlanta
4,691 Denver	7,024 Denver	9,653 Denver
4,650 San Diego	6,835 San Diego	8,981 San Diego
4,525 Kansas City	6,814 Kansas City	8,743 Kansas City
4,500 Jacksonville	6,679 Pittsburgh	8,484 Seattle
Most Passing Yards		
8,404 Indianapolis	13,027 Indianapolis	17,206 Indianapolis
8,099 Arizona	12,251 St. Louis	16,212 St. Louis
7,998 St. Louis	12,010 Green Bay	15,250 Green Bay
7,846 New Orleans	11,775 Philadelphia	15,197 Kansas City
7,796 Philadelphia	11,433 New Orleans	14,871 New Orleans
Fewest Turnovers		
38 Indianapolis	55 Indianapolis	75 Indianapolis
40 Jacksonville	61 San Diego	92 San Diego
43 San Diego	62 Jacksonville	93 Jacksonville
44 Cincinnati	71 Washington	94 Kansas City
44 Washington	74 Houston	95 NY Jets
Fewest Points Allowed		
457 Chicago	768 Baltimore	1,049 Baltimore
500 Baltimore	788 Chicago	1,073 New England
543 Jacksonville	823 Jacksonville	1,134 Chicago
563 Denver	824 Pittsburgh	1,151 Pittsburgh
564 Carolina	835 New England	1,154 Jacksonville
Fewest Total Yards Allowed		
8,774 Baltimore	13,483 Pittsburgh	17,918 Baltimore
9,193 Jacksonville	13,577 Baltimore	18,266 Pittsburgh
9,215 Chicago	14,267 Tampa Bay	18,733 Tampa Bay
9,259 Carolina	14,327 Jacksonville	18,984 Jacksonville
9,349 Pittsburgh	14,597 Miami	19,121 Denver
Fewest Rushing Yards Allowed		
2,788 Pittsburgh	4,087 Pittsburgh	5,828 Pittsburgh
2,805 Baltimore	4,269 San Diego	6,022 Baltimore
2,826 Minnesota	4,486 Baltimore	6,093 New England
2,962 San Diego	4,659 New England	6,293 Denver
3,087 New England	4,688 Denver	6,352 Jacksonville
Fewest Passing Yards Allowed		
5,656 Oakland	8,862 Tampa Bay	11,572 Tampa Bay
5,699 Indianapolis	8,906 Miami	11,641 Buffalo
5,703 New Orleans	8,934 Buffalo	11,856 Cleveland
5,969 Baltimore	9,010 Cleveland	11,896 Baltimore
5,977 NY Jets	9,091 Baltimore	12,241 Miami
Most Opponents' Turnovers		
78 Chicago	111 Cincinnati	141 Baltimore
75 Cincinnati	107 Chicago	135 Cincinnati
71 Minnesota	102 Carolina	130 New England
66 Baltimore	100 Baltimore	128 Carolina
66 Denver	93 Four tied	128 Minnesota

COREY DILLON'S CAREER RUSHING VS. EACH OPPONENT

Opponent	Games	Rushes	Yards	Yards Per Rush	Yards Per Game	TD
Arizona	4	74	379	5.1	94.8	1
Atlanta	2	41	172	4.2	86.0	0
Baltimore	15	260	907	3.5	60.5	3
Buffalo	8	139	620	4.5	77.5	7
Carolina	3	52	204	3.9	68.0	0
Chicago	2	27	70	2.6	35.0	0
Cincinnati	2	39	155	4.0	77.5	2
Cleveland	11	217	1,111	5.1	101.0	7
Dallas	2	46	221	4.8	110.5	1
Denver	5	81	496	6.1	99.2	2
Detroit	3	53	286	5.4	95.3	6
Green Bay	2	28	59	2.1	29.5	1
Houston	2	42	153	3.6	76.5	0
Indianapolis	7	100	471	4.7	67.3	5
Jacksonville	11	185	655	3.5	59.5	4
Kansas City	2	32	119	3.7	59.5	2
Miami	6	92	449	4.9	74.8	1
Minnesota	2	24	71	3.0	35.5	0
New England	2	52	183	3.5	91.5	1
New Orleans	1	18	126	7.0	126.0	0
N.Y. Giants	1	5	8	1.6	8.0	1
N.Y. Jets	8	155	657	4.2	82.1	6
Oakland	3	55	206	3.7	68.7	3
Philadelphia	2	35	153	4.4	76.5	0
Pittsburgh	14	239	954	4.0	68.1	7
St. Louis	3	47	188	4.0	62.7	1
San Diego	6	87	387	4.4	64.5	2
San Francisco	3	48	273	5.7	91.0	2
Seattle	2	39	186	4.8	93.0	2
Tampa Bay	4	77	256	3.3	64.0	1
Tennessee	12	229	1,066	4.7	88.8	14
Totals	150	2,618	11,241	4.3	74.9	82

LaDAINIAN TOMLINSON'S CAREER RUSHING VS. EACH OPPONENT

Opponent	Games	Rushes	Yards	Yards Per Rush	Yards Per Game	TD
Arizona	3	63	232	3.7	77.3	2
Atlanta	1	23	64	2.8	64.0	1
Baltimore	2	49	203	4.1	101.5	1
Buffalo	4	91	431	4.7	107.8	4
Carolina	1	17	47	2.8	47.0	1
Chicago	1	16	61	3.8	61.0	1
Cincinnati	4	80	420	5.3	105.0	9
Cleveland	4	89	585	6.6	146.3	7
Dallas	2	46	162	3.5	81.0	1
Denver	12	252	1,048	4.2	87.3	14
Detroit	1	25	88	3.5	88.0	0
Green Bay	1	20	51	2.6	51.0	0
Houston	2	53	205	3.9	102.5	1
Indianapolis	2	45	157	3.5	78.5	1
Jacksonville	2	29	94	3.2	47.0	1
Kansas City	11	208	952	4.6	86.5	7
Miami	3	59	182	3.1	60.7	1
Minnesota	1	16	162	10.1	162.0	2
New England	3	76	425	5.6	141.7	5
New Orleans	1	17	36	2.1	36.0	1
N.Y. Giants	1	21	192	9.1	192.0	3
N.Y. Jets	3	56	254	4.5	84.7	5
Oakland	12	317	1,455	4.6	121.3	12
Philadelphia	2	36	58	1.6	29.0	0
Pittsburgh	3	53	189	3.6	63.0	3
St. Louis	2	49	303	6.2	151.5	3
San Francisco	2	45	159	3.5	79.5	4
Seattle	4	77	315	4.1	78.8	1
Tampa Bay	1	25	131	5.2	131.0	1
Tennessee	2	36	218	6.1	109.0	3
Washington	2	61	297	4.9	148.5	5
Totals	95	2,050	9,176	4.5	96.6	100

EDGERRIN JAMES' CAREER RUSHING VS. EACH OPPONENT

Opponent	Games	Rushes	Yards	Yards Per Rush	Yards Per Game	TD
Atlanta	2	40	167	4.2	83.5	0
Baltimore	3	62	200	3.2	66.7	1
Buffalo	6	141	552	3.9	92.0	7
Chicago	3	76	327	4.3	109.0	2
Cincinnati	3	72	201	2.8	67.0	5
Cleveland	4	80	320	4.0	80.0	4
Dallas	3	66	291	4.4	97.0	1
Denver	4	51	187	3.7	46.8	3
Detroit	3	76	340	4.5	113.3	1
Green Bay	3	62	217	3.5	72.3	2
Houston	8	190	879	4.6	109.9	4
Jacksonville	9	199	785	3.9	87.2	2
Kansas City	5	109	440	4.0	88.0	1
Miami	6	159	668	4.2	111.3	3
Minnesota	3	56	266	4.8	88.7	0
New England	9	232	950	4.1	105.6	3
N.Y. Giants	2	26	121	4.7	60.5	0
N.Y. Jets	6	156	627	4.0	104.5	6
Oakland	4	89	377	4.2	94.3	2
Philadelphia	1	22	152	6.9	152.0	2
Pittsburgh	2	49	186	3.8	93.0	0
St. Louis	3	73	352	4.8	117.3	4
San Diego	4	68	223	3.3	55.8	2
San Francisco	3	76	283	3.7	94.3	2
Seattle	4	95	439	4.6	109.8	4
Tennessee	7	164	713	4.3	101.9	8
Washington	2	36	122	3.4	61.0	1
Totals	112	2,525	10,385	4.1	92.7	70

SHAUN ALEXANDER'S CAREER RUSHING VS. EACH OPPONENT

Opponent	Games	Rushes	Yards	Yards Per Rush	Yards Per Game	TD
Arizona	10	198	962	4.9	96.2	15
Atlanta	4	78	356	4.6	89.0	4
Baltimore	1	22	72	3.3	72.0	0
Buffalo	3	43	174	4.0	58.0	1
Carolina	2	33	195	5.9	97.5	1
Chicago	1	21	101	4.8	101.0	2
Cincinnati	1	20	86	4.3	86.0	0
Cleveland	2	31	130	4.2	65.0	1
Dallas	4	72	229	3.2	57.3	5
Denver	6	86	295	3.4	49.2	3
Detroit	2	39	161	4.1	80.5	1
Green Bay	3	80	376	4.7	125.3	2
Houston	1	22	141	6.4	141.0	4
Indianapolis	2	26	159	6.1	79.5	2
Jacksonville	3	48	262	5.5	87.3	2
Kansas City	5	71	442	6.2	88.4	4
Miami	3	54	188	3.5	62.7	5
Minnesota	3	65	307	4.7	102.3	5
New England	1	16	77	4.8	77.0	1
New Orleans	3	57	262	4.6	87.3	3
N.Y. Giants	4	93	290	3.1	72.5	3
N.Y. Jets	1	19	77	4.1	77.0	0
Oakland	5	69	353	5.1	70.6	5
Philadelphia	3	39	178	4.6	59.3	2
Pittsburgh	1	20	48	2.4	48.0	1
St. Louis	9	183	921	5.0	102.3	9
San Diego	6	105	367	3.5	61.2	4
San Francisco	10	214	876	4.1	87.6	10
Tampa Bay	2	45	137	3.0	68.5	1
Tennessee	1	26	172	6.6	172.0	1

Opponent	Games	Rushes	Yards	Yards Per Rush	Yards Per Game	TD
Washington	4	74	319	4.3	79.8	3
Totals	106	1,969	8,713	4.4	82.2	96

MARVIN HARRISON'S CAREER RECEIVING VS. EACH OPPONENT

Opponent	Games	Rec.	Yards	Yards/ Rec.	Yards/ Game	TD
Arizona	2	8	104	13.0	52.0	1
Atlanta	2	12	183	15.3	91.5	2
Baltimore	6	31	436	14.1	72.7	3
Buffalo	14	61	831	13.6	59.4	9
Carolina	1	8	119	14.9	119.0	0
Chicago	2	10	91	9.1	45.5	1
Cincinnati	6	44	597	13.6	99.5	6
Cleveland	4	38	407	10.7	101.8	2
Dallas	4	29	333	11.5	83.3	3
Denver	5	36	391	10.9	78.2	3
Detroit	3	24	266	11.1	88.7	5
Green Bay	3	15	191	12.7	63.7	2
Houston	10	61	805	13.2	80.5	5
Jacksonville	11	47	709	15.1	64.5	8
Kansas City	5	35	528	15.1	105.6	6
Miami	15	84	1,133	13.5	75.5	9
Minnesota	3	25	255	10.2	85.0	4
New England	16	102	1,458	14.3	91.1	14
New Orleans	3	19	308	16.2	102.7	3
N.Y. Giants	3	25	350	14.0	116.7	3
N.Y. Jets	13	73	826	11.3	63.5	5
Oakland	3	21	245	11.7	81.7	3
Philadelphia	4	18	311	17.3	77.8	4
Pittsburgh	3	15	256	17.1	85.3	2
St. Louis	2	9	135	15.0	67.5	1
San Diego	6	37	563	15.2	93.8	2
San Francisco	3	16	243	15.2	81.0	4
Seattle	2	11	172	15.6	86.0	0
Tampa Bay	2	14	233	16.6	116.5	2
Tennessee	10	70	933	13.3	93.3	8
Washington	4	24	285	11.9	71.3	2
Totals	170	1,022	13,697	13.4	80.6	122

ISAAC BRUCE'S CAREER RECEIVING VS. EACH OPPONENT

Opponent	Games	Rec.	Yards	Yards/ Rec.	Yards/ Game	TD
Arizona	12	50	784	15.7	65.3	6
Atlanta	16	71	1,283	18.1	80.2	10
Baltimore	3	21	334	15.9	111.3	2
Buffalo	2	12	194	16.2	97.0	1
Carolina	14	62	796	12.8	56.9	4
Chicago	7	38	518	13.6	74.0	1
Cincinnati	2	10	192	19.2	96.0	0
Cleveland	2	7	75	10.7	37.5	2
Dallas	2	4	60	15.0	30.0	1
Denver	5	16	204	12.8	40.8	0
Detroit	4	15	200	13.3	50.0	1
Green Bay	7	35	485	13.9	69.3	3
Houston	1	4	94	23.5	94.0	1
Indianapolis	2	13	256	19.7	128.0	2
Jacksonville	1	2	30	15.0	30.0	0
Kansas City	5	22	343	15.6	68.6	4
Miami	4	29	416	14.3	104.0	1
Minnesota	5	30	447	14.9	89.4	2
New England	2	11	189	17.2	94.5	1
New Orleans	14	79	1,397	17.7	99.8	11
N.Y. Giants	6	27	381	14.1	63.5	2
N.Y. Jets	4	18	254	14.1	63.5	3
Oakland	3	12	176	14.7	58.7	1
Philadelphia	6	28	382	13.6	63.7	2
Pittsburgh	2	10	181	18.1	90.5	0
San Diego	4	25	448	17.9	112.0	5

Opponent	Games	Rec.	Yards	Yards/ Rec.	Yards/ Game	TD
San Francisco	24	115	1,726	15.0	71.9	10
Seattle	11	53	698	13.2	63.5	2
Tampa Bay	4	11	163	14.8	40.8	0
Tennessee	2	7	64	9.1	32.0	1
Washington	7	50	606	12.1	86.6	1
Totals	183	887	13,376	15.1	73.1	80

KEENAN McCARDELL'S CAREER RECEIVING VS. EACH OPPONENT

Opponent	Games	Rec.	Yards	Yards/ Rec.	Yards/ Game	TD
Arizona	3	6	104	17.3	34.7	1
Atlanta	6	33	404	12.2	67.3	4
Baltimore	14	82	941	11.5	67.2	1
Buffalo	6	29	338	11.7	56.3	1
Carolina	6	28	381	13.6	63.5	3
Chicago	3	18	176	9.8	58.7	1
Cincinnati	18	73	997	13.7	55.4	10
Cleveland	8	43	482	11.2	60.3	2
Dallas	5	25	330	13.2	66.0	3
Denver	7	26	287	11.0	41.0	0
Detroit	3	7	123	17.6	41.0	1
Green Bay	4	19	256	13.5	64.0	1
Houston	1	5	59	11.8	59.0	0
Indianapolis	4	12	260	21.7	65.0	3
Jacksonville	3	16	161	10.1	53.7	0
Kansas City	10	34	484	14.2	48.4	1
Miami	2	10	144	14.4	72.0	3
Minnesota	3	7	58	8.3	19.3	1
New England	6	23	335	14.6	55.8	5
New Orleans	7	44	519	11.8	74.1	3
N.Y. Giants	4	28	365	13.0	91.3	2
N.Y. Jets	4	11	136	12.4	34.0	0
Oakland	7	29	432	14.9	61.7	2
Philadelphia	5	17	215	12.6	43.0	1
Pittsburgh	20	72	885	12.3	44.3	3
St. Louis	4	25	354	14.2	88.5	2
San Diego	1	9	97	10.8	97.0	0
San Francisco	4	17	262	15.4	65.5	1
Seattle	5	19	316	16.6	63.2	1
Tampa Bay	3	11	143	13.0	47.7	2
Tennessee	19	66	863	13.1	45.4	4
Washington	4	17	210	12.4	52.5	0
Totals	199	861	11,117	12.9	55.9	62

St. Louis totals include one game vs. L.A. Rams
Tennessee totals include seven games vs. Houston

ROD SMITH'S CAREER RECEIVING VS. EACH OPPONENT

Opponent	Games	Rec.	Yards	Yards/ Rec.	Yards/ Game	TD
Arizona	4	23	264	11.5	66.0	4
Atlanta	3	19	353	18.6	117.7	3
Baltimore	6	24	296	12.3	49.3	1
Buffalo	4	21	266	12.7	66.5	2
Carolina	2	8	100	12.5	50.0	1
Chicago	2	10	100	10.0	50.0	1
Cincinnati	6	26	307	11.8	51.2	4
Cleveland	3	15	221	14.7	73.7	3
Dallas	4	16	214	13.4	53.5	1
Detroit	2	9	85	9.4	42.5	0
Green Bay	2	5	63	12.6	31.5	0
Houston	1	3	29	9.7	29.0	1
Indianapolis	5	25	311	12.4	62.2	0
Jacksonville	5	22	259	11.8	51.8	1
Kansas City	22	123	1,789	14.5	81.3	4
Miami	5	27	329	12.2	65.8	0
Minnesota	3	10	141	14.1	47.0	0
New England	11	56	829	14.8	75.4	3
New Orleans	2	5	51	10.2	25.5	0

Opponent	Games	Rec.	Yards	Yards/Rec.	Yards/Game	TD
N.Y. Giants	3	16	217	13.6	72.3	1
N.Y. Jets	4	19	319	16.8	79.8	0
Oakland	24	104	1,342	12.9	55.9	10
Philadelphia	3	12	171	14.3	57.0	3
Pittsburgh	3	12	231	19.3	77.0	4
St. Louis	4	15	295	19.7	73.8	4
San Diego	23	113	1,400	12.4	60.9	6
San Francisco	4	21	234	11.1	58.5	0
Seattle	15	69	931	13.5	62.1	6
Tampa Bay	2	6	56	9.3	28.0	0
Tennessee	2	7	82	11.7	41.0	1
Washington	4	8	104	13.0	26.0	2
Totals	183	849	11,389	13.4	62.2	68

Tennessee totals include one game vs. Houston

MORTEN ANDERSEN'S CAREER KICKING VS. EACH OPPONENT

Opponent	Games	FG	FGA	FG%	Long FG	XP	XPA	Pts.
Arizona	16	28	30	93.3	52	45	46	129
Atlanta	25	40	51	78.4	49	56	58	176
Baltimore	3	4	5	80.0	46	4	4	16
Buffalo	6	9	14	64.3	50	14	14	41
Carolina	13	23	29	79.3	51	23	23	92
Chicago	9	8	13	61.5	60	23	23	47
Cincinnati	7	10	14	71.4	49	20	20	50
Cleveland	7	13	14	92.9	53	17	17	56
Dallas	15	22	30	73.3	54	31	31	97
Denver	10	8	14	57.1	55	31	33	55
Detroit	14	12	19	63.2	50	33	33	69
Green Bay	10	15	17	88.2	52	29	29	74
Houston	2	0	0	100.0	0	10	10	10
Indianapolis	4	5	7	71.4	46	13	13	28
Jacksonville	4	6	7	85.7	46	7	7	25
Kansas City	6	11	12	91.7	50	10	10	43
Miami	6	7	9	77.8	50	21	21	42
Minnesota	12	18	23	78.3	51	20	20	74
New England	7	11	13	84.6	54	21	21	54
New Orleans	16	26	34	76.5	55	37	37	115
N.Y. Giants	11	17	21	81.0	45	18	18	69
N.Y. Jets	7	13	14	92.9	53	14	14	53
Oakland	10	13	16	81.3	51	21	21	60
Philadelphia	15	28	34	82.4	56	24	24	108
Pittsburgh	8	9	13	69.2	50	20	21	47
St. Louis	37	53	62	85.5	51	94	96	253
San Diego	7	7	11	63.6	46	20	20	41
San Francisco	38	62	74	83.8	59	60	62	246
Seattle	8	13	14	92.9	48	17	17	56
Tampa Bay	17	25	33	75.8	50	37	37	112
Tennessee	7	11	15	73.3	47	15	15	48
Washington	11	13	19	68.4	50	20	20	59
Totals	368	540	681	79.3	60	825	835	2,445

Arizona totals include five games vs. St. Louis and four games vs. Phoenix
Oakland totals include four games vs. L.A. Raiders
St. Louis totals include 23 games vs. L.A. Rams
Tennessee totals include five games vs. Houston

JOHN CARNEY'S CAREER KICKING VS. EACH OPPONENT

Opponent	Games	FG	FGA	FG%	Long FG	XP	XPA	Pts.
Arizona	4	5	5	100.0	50	9	9	24
Atlanta	15	23	31	74.2	51	36	36	105
Baltimore	4	4	4	100.0	47	8	8	20
Buffalo	5	10	12	83.3	54	9	9	39
Carolina	14	17	21	81.0	48	29	29	80
Chicago	6	7	13	53.8	50	12	12	33
Cincinnati	6	13	14	92.9	48	13	14	52
Cleveland	6	12	14	85.7	48	12	12	48
Dallas	4	4	4	100.0	44	11	11	23
Denver	21	37	43	86.0	50	31	32	142
Detroit	6	8	10	80.0	47	9	9	33
Green Bay	6	7	11	63.6	47	11	11	32
Houston	1	1	1	100.0	39	4	4	7
Indianapolis	9	17	20	85.0	50	23	23	74
Jacksonville	1	2	2	100.0	38	1	2	7
Kansas City	21	21	28	75.0	54	42	42	105
Miami	6	9	12	75.0	49	12	12	39
Minnesota	6	13	14	92.9	50	14	15	53
New England	6	3	8	37.5	46	9	9	18
New Orleans	4	10	10	100.0	49	11	11	41
N.Y. Giants	6	12	14	85.7	46	15	15	51
N.Y. Jets	6	5	6	83.3	53	16	16	31
Oakland	21	34	42	81.0	48	33	34	135
Philadelphia	5	6	7	85.7	39	9	9	27
Pittsburgh	10	15	18	83.3	48	18	18	63
St. Louis	7	16	19	84.2	53	16	16	64
San Diego	1	1	2	50.0	37	2	2	5
San Francisco	7	14	16	87.5	50	14	14	56
Seattle	23	49	57	86.0	54	35	36	182
Tampa Bay	15	19	23	82.6	48	35	36	92
Tennessee	4	9	10	90.0	48	2	2	29
Washington	5	10	14	71.4	41	9	9	39
Totals	261	413	505	81.8	54	510	517	1,749

Arizona totals include one game vs. Phoenix
Oakland totals include two games vs. L.A. Raiders
St. Louis totals include two games vs. L.A. Rams
Tennessee totals include two games vs. Houston

BRETT FAVRE'S CAREER PASSING VS. EACH OPPONENT

Opponent	Games	Att.	Cmp.	Pct.	Yards	Avg. Gain	TD	Int.	Sacked
Arizona	4	123	78	63.4	1,013	8.24	5	2	3/21
Atlanta	5	191	129	67.5	1,395	7.30	8	6	9/68
Baltimore	3	104	63	60.6	741	7.13	5	4	3/14
Buffalo	5	173	102	59.0	1,040	6.01	9	5	9/61
Carolina	8	308	188	61.0	2,167	7.04	20	12	17/130
Chicago	30	1,004	618	61.6	7,185	7.16	52	34	47/312
Cincinnati	4	156	102	65.4	1,181	7.57	7	7	10/70
Cleveland	4	133	93	69.9	914	6.87	9	2	5/28
Dallas	7	269	161	59.9	1,641	6.10	13	4	13/97
Denver	4	114	59	51.8	751	6.59	6	9	4/26
Detroit	30	1,075	669	62.2	7,774	7.23	49	37	55/359
Houston	1	50	33	66.0	383	7.66	1	2	0/0
Indianapolis	3	105	71	67.6	1,024	9.75	9	3	6/52
Jacksonville	3	116	74	63.8	931	8.03	7	4	5/36
Kansas City	3	119	72	60.5	799	6.71	5	5	11/65
Miami	5	182	111	61.0	1,202	6.60	7	3	11/57
Minnesota	29	983	601	61.1	6,684	6.80	49	33	49/329
New England	4	123	70	56.9	753	6.12	7	2	8/57
New Orleans	5	188	118	62.8	1,283	6.82	13	2	11/65
N.Y. Giants	5	150	89	59.3	1,112	7.41	7	4	7/44
N.Y. Jets	4	142	74	52.1	721	5.08	5	4	5/33
Oakland	3	105	64	61.0	922	8.78	9	3	6/31
Philadelphia	11	368	198	53.8	2,332	6.34	12	19	24/160
Pittsburgh	4	125	79	63.2	959	7.67	4	2	8/55
St. Louis	10	317	193	60.9	2,174	6.86	16	11	18/141
San Diego	4	111	70	63.1	828	7.46	10	4	5/56
San Francisco	7	233	144	61.8	1,808	7.76	12	8	10/66
Seattle	5	167	96	57.5	1,099	6.58	9	8	10/50
Tampa Bay	23	774	474	61.2	5,125	6.62	37	23	44/245
Tennessee	4	134	77	57.5	945	7.05	8	5	7/18
Washington	4	81	51	63.0	614	7.58	4	6	4/49
Totals	241	8,223	5,021	61.1	57,500	6.99	414	273	424/2,795

Oakland totals include one game vs. L.A. Raiders
St. Louis totals include four games vs. L.A. Rams
Tennessee totals include one game vs. Houston

PEYTON MANNING'S CAREER PASSING VS. EACH OPPONENT

Opponent	Games	Att.	Cmp.	Pct.	Yards	Avg. Gain	TD	Int.	Sacked
Arizona	1	2	1	50.0	5	2.50	0	0	1/0
Atlanta	3	92	67	72.8	774	8.41	10	3	1/9
Baltimore	5	199	125	62.8	1,454	7.31	9	3	10/87
Buffalo	10	320	195	60.9	2,250	7.03	13	9	9/66
Carolina	2	68	40	58.8	518	7.62	2	3	5/18
Chicago	2	67	43	64.2	513	7.66	6	2	2/21
Cincinnati	5	169	108	63.9	1,365	8.08	14	3	3/12
Cleveland	4	143	93	65.0	992	6.94	2	4	2/10
Dallas	3	111	71	64.0	819	7.38	5	3	3/20
Denver	5	138	88	63.8	917	6.64	5	2	5/30
Detroit	2	61	45	73.8	524	8.59	9	2	1/7
Green Bay	2	84	53	63.1	687	8.18	8	1	4/27
Houston	10	311	222	71.4	2,708	8.71	25	4	12/74
Jacksonville	11	386	234	60.6	2,926	7.58	20	6	8/56
Kansas City	4	139	87	62.6	1,236	8.89	9	3	7/62
Miami	11	378	230	60.8	2,654	7.02	16	18	17/126
Minnesota	2	65	48	73.8	551	8.48	8	1	1/4
New England	12	434	266	61.3	3,189	7.35	25	17	17/113
New Orleans	3	85	57	67.1	885	10.41	8	4	5/26
N.Y. Giants	3	122	75	61.5	878	7.20	6	4	3/20
N.Y. Jets	10	373	233	62.5	2,503	6.71	13	11	13/85
Oakland	3	115	75	65.2	806	7.01	8	5	4/33
Philadelphia	3	69	48	69.6	737	10.68	7	1	1/8
Pittsburgh	2	73	47	64.4	549	7.52	3	4	4/15
St. Louis	2	60	37	61.7	386	6.43	2	1	4/21
San Diego	4	166	94	56.6	1,260	7.59	6	5	8/45
San Francisco	3	112	72	64.3	856	7.64	5	6	3/16

Opponent	Games	Att.	Cmp.	Pct.	Yards	Avg. Gain	TD	Int.	Sacked
Seattle	3	81	52	64.2	732	9.04	2	1	3/6
Tampa Bay	1	47	34	72.3	386	8.21	2	1	1/5
Tennessee	10	316	222	70.3	2,672	8.46	19	9	9/60
Washington	3	104	69	66.3	854	8.21	8	3	4/26
Totals	144	4,890	3,131	64.0	37,586	7.69	275	139	170/1,108

STEVE McNAIR'S CAREER PASSING VS. EACH OPPONENT

Opponent	Games	Att.	Cmp.	Pct.	Yards	Avg. Gain	TD	Int.	Sacked
Arizona	1	17	9	52.9	146	8.59	2	0	2/13
Atlanta	4	84	53	63.1	605	7.20	3	0	5/29
Baltimore	13	437	248	56.8	2,599	5.95	7	11	26/153
Buffalo	4	116	67	57.8	703	6.06	2	2	7/45
Carolina	3	43	24	55.8	285	6.63	1	2	5/40
Chicago	1	29	18	62.1	187	6.45	1	1	4/11
Cincinnati	15	406	246	60.6	3,023	7.45	21	5	17/115
Cleveland	10	230	127	55.2	1,586	6.90	9	6	11/72
Dallas	3	78	46	59.0	495	6.35	3	3	3/24
Denver	1	34	20	58.8	165	4.85	0	3	2/11
Detroit	2	62	31	50.0	419	6.76	2	3	3/25
Green Bay	3	110	69	62.7	752	6.84	7	1	5/28
Houston	8	242	137	56.6	1,811	7.48	13	8	5/23
Indianapolis	7	213	145	68.1	1,405	6.60	6	2	13/104
Jacksonville	16	457	286	62.6	3,359	7.35	20	13	29/167
Kansas City	2	45	32	71.1	376	8.36	1	2	2/5
Miami	6	125	67	53.6	740	5.92	4	7	7/36
Minnesota	3	71	43	60.6	565	7.96	2	0	6/52
New England	3	107	62	57.9	698	6.52	1	4	6/36
New Orleans	2	56	39	69.6	411	7.34	4	0	3/4
N.Y. Giants	3	101	67	66.3	810	8.02	6	1	4/19
N.Y. Jets	4	103	53	51.5	749	7.27	5	2	7/52
Oakland	7	229	139	60.7	1,513	6.61	8	10	19/130
Philadelphia	2	71	47	66.2	479	6.75	2	1	3/13
Pittsburgh	15	382	237	62.0	2,849	7.46	21	13	23/131
St. Louis	2	68	37	54.4	447	6.57	4	2	3/21
San Diego	2	64	37	57.8	351	5.48	3	2	5/27
San Francisco	2	50	28	56.0	388	7.76	3	2	1/10
Seattle	4	118	65	55.1	835	7.08	4	3	5/24
Tampa Bay	3	66	41	62.1	534	8.09	2	1	4/35
Tennessee	1	47	29	61.7	373	7.94	3	2	1/2
Washington	3	78	51	65.4	533	6.83	2	3	7/25
Totals	155	4,339	2,600	59.9	30,191	6.96	172	115	243/1,482

The NFL rates its passers for statistical purposes against a fixed performance standard based on statistical achievements of all qualified pro passers since 1960. The current system replaced one that rated passers in relation to their position in a total group based on various criteria. The current system, which was adopted in 1973, removes inequities that existed in the former method and, at the same time, provides a means of comparing passing performances from one season to the next.

It is important to remember that the system is used to rate passers, not quarterbacks. Statistics do not reflect leadership, play-calling, and other intangible factors that go into making a successful professional quarterback. Four categories are used as a basis for compiling a rating:

—Percentage of completions per attempt
—Average yards gained per attempt
—Percentage of touchdown passes per attempt
—Percentage of interceptions per attempt

The average standard is 1.000. The bottom is .000. To earn a 2.000 rating, a passer must perform at exceptional levels, i.e., 70 percent in completions, 10 percent in touchdowns, 1.5 percent in interceptions, and 11 yards average gain per pass attempt. The maximum a passer can receive in any category is 2.375.

For example, to gain a 2.375 in completion percentage, a passer would have to complete 77.5 percent of his passes. The NFL record is 70.55 by Ken Anderson (Cincinnati, 1982). To earn a 2.375 in percentage of touchdowns, a passer would have to achieve a percentage of 11.9. The record is 13.9 by Sid Luckman (Chicago, 1943). To gain 2.375 in percentage of interceptions, a passer would have to go the entire season without an interception. The 2.375 figure in average yards is 12.50, compared with the NFL record of 11.17 by Tommy O'Connell (Cleveland, 1957).

In order to make the rating more understandable, the point rating is then converted into a scale of 100, with 158.3 being the highest rating a passer can achieve. In cases where statistical performance has been superior, it is possible for a passer to sur-

pass a 100 rating. For example, take Peyton Manning's record-setting season in 2004 when he completed 336 of 497 passes for 4,557 yards, 49 touchdowns, and 10 interceptions. The four calculations would be:

—Percentage of Completions—336 of 497 is 67.60 percent. Subtract 30 from the completion percentage (37.60) and multiply the result by 0.05. The result is a point rating of 1.880.
Note: If the result is less than zero (Comp. Pct. less than 30.0), award zero points. If the results are greater than 2.375 (Comp. Pct. greater than 77.5), award 2.375.

—Average Yards Gained Per Attempt—4,557 yards divided by 497 attempts is 9.17. Subtract three yards from yards-per-attempt (6.17) and multiply the result by 0.25. The result is 1.543.
Note: If the result is less than zero (yards per attempt less than 3.0), award zero points. If the result is greater than 2.375 (yards per attempt greater than 12.5), award 2.375 points.

—Percentage of Touchdown Passes—49 touchdowns in 497 attempts is 9.86 percent. Multiply the touchdown percentage by 0.2. The result is 1.972.
Note: If the result is greater than 2.375 (touchdown percentage greater than 11.875), award 2.375.

—Percentage of Interceptions—10 interceptions in 497 attempts is 2.01 percent. Multiply the interception percentage by 0.25 (0.503) and subtract the number from 2.375. The result is 1.872.
Note: If the result is less than zero (interception percentage greater than 9.5), award zero points.

The sum of the four steps is (1.880 + 1.543 + 1.972 + 1.872) 7.267. The sum is then divided by six (1.211) and multiplied by 100. In this case, the result is 121.1. This same formula can be used to determine a passer rating for any player who attempts at least one pass.

Thirty-nine qualifying passers have had a single-season passer rating of 100 or higher. The following is a list of the Top 25 single-seasons passer ratings among qualifying players:

TOP 25 NFL SINGLE-SEASON PASSER RATINGS (QUALIFYING PLAYERS)

Player, Team	Season	Rating	Att.	Comp.	Pct.	Yds.	TD Avg.	TD	TD Pct.	Int.	Int. Pct.
Peyton Manning, Indianapolis	2004	121.1	497	336	67.6	4,557	9.17	49	9.9	10	2.0
Steve Young, San Francisco	1994	112.8	461	324	70.2	3,969	8.61	35	7.6	10	2.2
Joe Montana, San Francisco	1989	112.4	386	271	70.2	3,521	9.12	26	6.7	8	2.1
Daunte Culpepper, Minnesota	2004	110.9	548	379	69.2	4,717	8.61	39	7.1	11	2.0
Milt Plum, Cleveland	1960	110.4	250	151	60.4	2,297	9.19	21	8.4	5	2.0
Sammy Baugh, Washington	1945	109.9	182	128	70.3	1,669	9.17	11	6.0	4	2.2
Kurt Warner, St. Louis	1999	109.2	499	325	65.1	4,353	8.72	41	8.2	13	2.6
Dan Marino, Miami	1984	108.9	564	362	64.2	5,084	9.01	48	8.5	17	3.0
Sid Luckman, Chicago Bears	1943	107.5	202	110	54.5	2,194	10.86	28	13.9	12	5.9
Steve Young, San Francisco	1992	107.0	402	268	66.7	3,465	8.62	25	6.2	7	1.7
Randall Cunningham, Minnesota	1998	106.0	425	259	60.9	3,704	8.72	34	8.0	10	2.4
Bart Starr, Green Bay	1966	105.0	251	156	62.2	2,257	8.99	14	5.6	3	1.2
Drew Brees, San Diego	2004	104.8	400	262	65.5	3,159	7.90	27	6.8	7	1.8
Roger Staubach, Dallas	1971	104.8	211	126	59.7	1,882	8.92	15	7.1	4	1.9
Y.A. Tittle, N.Y. Giants	1963	104.8	367	221	60.2	3,145	8.57	36	9.8	14	3.8
Donovan McNabb, Philadelphia	2004	104.7	469	300	64.0	3,875	8.06	31	6.6	8	1.7
Steve Young, San Francisco	1997	104.7	356	241	67.7	3,029	8.51	19	5.3	6	1.7
Bart Starr, Green Bay	1968	104.3	171	109	63.7	1,617	9.46	15	8.8	8	4.7
Chad Pennington, N.Y. Jets	2002	104.2	399	275	68.9	3,120	7.82	22	5.5	6	1.5
Peyton Manning, Indianapolis	2005	104.1	453	305	67.3	3,747	8.27	28	6.2	10	2.2
Ken Stabler, Oakland	1976	103.4	291	194	66.7	2,737	9.41	27	9.3	17	5.8
Brian Griese, Denver	2000	102.9	336	216	64.3	2,688	8.00	19	5.7	4	1.2
Joe Montana, San Francisco	1984	102.9	432	279	64.6	3,630	8.40	28	6.5	10	2.3
Charlie Conerly, N.Y. Giants	1959	102.7	194	113	58.2	1,706	8.79	14	7.2	4	2.1
Bert Jones, Baltimore	1976	102.5	343	207	60.3	3,104	9.05	24	7.0	9	2.6

HIGHEST NFL POSTSEASON PASSER RATINGS (MINIMUM: 150 ATTEMPTS)

Player	Games	Att.	Cmp.	Pct.	Yards	Avg. Gain	TD	Int.	Rating
Bart Starr	10	213	130	61.0	1,753	8.23	15	3	104.8
Joe Montana	23	734	460	62.7	5,772	7.86	45	21	95.6
Jake Delhomme	7	192	113	58.9	1,642	8.55	11	5	95.0
Ken Anderson	6	166	110	66.3	1,321	7.96	9	6	93.5
Kurt Warner	7	268	169	63.1	2,221	8.29	15	10	92.3
Joe Theismann	10	211	128	60.7	1,782	8.45	11	7	91.4
Tom Brady	14	486	295	60.7	3,217	6.62	20	9	86.2
Troy Aikman	16	502	320	63.7	3,849	7.67	23	17	88.3
Steve Young	22	471	292	62.0	3,326	7.06	20	13	85.8
Warren Moon	10	403	259	64.3	2,870	7.12	17	14	84.9

HIGHEST NFL POSTSEASON PASSER RATINGS, ACTIVE PLAYERS (MINIMUM: 100 ATTEMPTS)

Player	Games	Att.	Cmp.	Pct.	Yards	Avg. Gain	TD	Int.	Rating
Jake Delhomme	7	192	113	58.9	1,642	8.55	11	5	95.0
Drew Brees	3	123	78	63.4	916	7.45	5	2	92.7
Kurt Warner	7	268	169	63.1	2,221	8.29	15	10	92.3
Ben Roethlisberger	6	147	89	60.5	1,210	8.23	10	8	86.8
Tom Brady	14	486	295	60.7	3,217	6.62	20	9	86.2
Brett Favre	20	663	401	60.5	4,902	7.39	34	26	84.0
Peyton Manning	13	474	290	61.2	3,496	7.38	18	15	83.3
Chad Pennington	5	178	107	60.1	1,166	6.55	7	4	83.2
Daunte Culpepper	4	134	73	54.5	980	7.31	8	5	82.3
Vinny Testaverde	7	189	114	60.3	1,320	6.98	6	5	81.0

ALL-TIME RANKINGS OF PLAYERS IN FOUR CATEGORIES THAT DETERMINE NFL PASSER RATING

Minimum: 1,500 Attempts

COMPLETION PERCENTAGE	Pct.	Att.	Comp.
Kurt Warner	65.59	2,508	1,645
Chad Pennington	65.10	1,659	1,080
Marc Bulger	65.43	2,106	1,357
Steve Young	64.28	4,149	2,667
Daunte Culpepper	64.17	2,741	1,759
Peyton Manning	64.03	4,890	3,131
Joe Montana	63.24	5,391	3,409
Brian Griese	63.02	2,350	1,481
Drew Brees	62.67	2,363	1,481
Tom Brady	61.88	3,064	1,896

TOUCHDOWN PERCENTAGE	Pct.	Att.	TD
Sid Luckman	7.86	1,744	137
Frank Ryan	6.99	2,133	149
Len Dawson	6.39	3,741	239
Daryle Lamonica	6.31	2,601	164
Sammy Baugh	6.24	2,995	187
Charley Conerly	6.11	2,833	173
Bob Waterfield	6.00	1,617	97
Earl Morrall	5.99	2,689	161
Sonny Jurgensen	5.98	4,262	255
Norm Van Brocklin	5.98	2,895	173

AVERAGE YARDS PER PASS	Avg.	Att.	Yards
Otto Graham	8.63	1,565	13,499
Sid Luckman	8.42	1,744	14,686
Kurt Warner	8.21	2,508	20,591
Norm Van Brocklin	8.16	2,895	23,611
Steve Young	7.98	4,149	33,124
Ed Brown	7.85	1,987	15,600
Bart Starr	7.85	3,149	24,718
Johnny Unitas	7.76	5,186	40,239
Earl Morrall	7.74	2,689	20,809
Marc Bulger	7.71	2,106	16,233

INTERCEPTION PERCENTAGE	Pct.	Att.	Int.
Neil O'Donnell	2.11	3,229	68
Donovan McNabb	2.21	3,259	72
Mark Brunell	2.31	4,594	106
Jeff Garcia	2.46	2,973	73
Steve Bono	2.47	1,701	42
Rich Gannon	2.47	4,206	104
Tom Brady	2.55	3,064	78
Joe Montana	2.58	5,391	139
Steve Young	2.58	4,149	107
Bernie Kosar	2.59	3,365	87

STARTING RECORDS OF ACTIVE NFL QUARTERBACKS

Minimum: 10 starts

	W - L - T	Pct.
Philip Rivers	14-2-0	.875
Tom Brady	70-24-0	.745
Rex Grossman	17-6-0	.739
Ben Roethlisberger	29-11-0	.725
Damon Huard	10-4-0	.714
Kyle Orton	10-5-0	.667
Donovan McNabb	65-33-0	.663
Peyton Manning	92-52-0	.639
Brett Favre	147-90-0	.620
Vince Young	8-5-0	.615
Steve McNair	8958-0	.605
Marc Bulger	36-24-0	.600
Tony Romo	6-4-0	.600
Matt Hasselbeck	47-33-0	.588
Chad Pennington	31-22-0	.585
Brad Johnson	71-51-0	.582
Kurt Warner	43-31-0	.581
Jake Delhomme	36-26-0	.581
Michael Vick	38-28-1	.575
David Garrard	10-8-0	.556
Carson Palmer	25-20-0	.556
Byron Leftwich	24-20-0	.545
Brian Griese	39-33-0	.542
Drew Brees	40-34-0	.541
A.J. Feeley	7-6-0	.538
Trent Dilfer	57-50-0	.533
Kyle Boller	18-16-0	.529
Trent Green	56-51-0	.523
Mark Brunell	78-72-0	.520
Eli Manning	20-19-0	.513
Jake Plummer	69-67-0	.507
Shane Matthews	11-11-0	.500
Jeff Garcia	44-48-0	.478
Chris Simms	7-8-0	.467
Daunte Culpepper	39-45-0	.464
Gus Frerotte	36-42-1	.462
Josh McCown	10-12-0	.455
Charlie Batch	22-27-0	.449
Kerry Collins	66-82-0	.446
Vinny Testaverde	88-119-1	.425
Aaron Brooks	38-52-0	.422
Anthony Wright	8-11-0	.421
Patrick Ramsey	10-14-0	.417
Todd Collins	7-10-0	.412
Jon Kitna	39-56-0	.411
Alex Smith	9-14-0	.391
Kelly Holcomb	8-13-0	.381
Matt Leinart	4-7-0	.364
Joey Harrington	23-43-0	.348
Charlie Frye	6-12-0	.333
J.P. Losman	8-16-0	.333
Billy Volek	3-7-0	.300
David Carr	22- 53-0	.293
Tim Rattay	5-13-0	.278
Bruce Gradkowski	3-8-0	.273
Ken Dorsey	2-8-0	.200
Doug Johnson	2-9-0	.182
Chris Weinke	2-17-0	.105

TEAMS THAT FINISHED IN FIRST PLACE IN THEIR DIVISION THE SEASON AFTER FINISHING IN LAST PLACE

Season	Team	Record	Prior Season
1967	Houston	9-4-1	*3-11-0
1968	Minnesota	8-6-0	3- 8-3
1970	Cincinnati	8-6-0	4- 9-1
1970	San Francisco	10-3-1	4- 8-2
1972	Green Bay	10-4-0	4- 8-2
1975	Baltimore	10-4-0	2-12-0

Season	Team	Record	Prior Season
1979	Tampa Bay	10-6-0	5-11-0
1981	Cincinnati	12-4-0	6-10-0
1987	Indianapolis	9-6-0	3-13-0
1988	Cincinnati	12-4-0	4-11-0
1990	Cincinnati	9-7-0	8- 8-0
1991	Denver	12-4-0	5-11-0
1992	San Diego	11-5-0	4-12-0
1993	Detroit	10-6-0	5-11-0
1997	N.Y. Giants	10-5-1	6-10-0
1999	Indianapolis	13-3-0	3-13-0
1999	St. Louis	13-3-0	4-12-0
2000	New Orleans	10-6-0	3-13-0
2001	Chicago	13-3-0	5-11-0
2001	New England	11-5-0	5-11-0
2003	Carolina	11-5-0	7- 9-0
2003	Kansas City	13-3-0	*8- 8-0
2004	Atlanta	11-5-0	5-11-0
2004	San Diego	12-4-0	*4-12-0
2005	Chicago	11-5-0	5-11-0
2005	Tampa Bay	11-5-0	5-11-0
2006	Baltimore	13-3-0	*6-10-0
2006	New Orleans	10-6-0	3-13-0
2006	Philadelphia	10-6-0	6-10-0

tied for last place

LONGEST WINNING STREAKS SINCE 1970

18	New England, 2003-04	(12 in 2003, 6 in 2004)
16	Miami, 1971-73	(1 in 1971, 14 in 1972, 1 in 1973)
16	Miami, 1983-84	(5 in 1983, 11 in 1984)
16	Pittsburgh, 2004-05	(14 in 2004, 2 in 2005)
15	San Francisco, 1989-90	(5 in 1989, 10 in 1990)
14	Oakland, 1976-77	(10 in 1976, 4 in 1977)
14	Denver, 1997-98	(1 in 1997, 13 in 1998)
13	Minnesota, 1974-75	(3 in 1974, 10 in 1975)
13	Chicago, 1984-85	(1 in 1984, 12 in 1985)
13	N.Y. Giants, 1989-90	(3 in 1989, 10 in 1990)
13	Indianapolis, 2005	
12	Washington, 1990-91	(1 in 1990, 11 in 1991)
11	Pittsburgh, 1975	
11	Baltimore, 1975-76	(9 in 1975, 2 in 1976)
11	Chicago, 1986-87	(7 in 1986, 4 in 1987)
11	Houston, 1993	
11	San Francisco, 1997	
11	Jacksonville, 1999	
11	Indianapolis, 1999	
11	Seattle, 2005	
10	Miami, 1973	
10	Pittsburgh, 1976-77	(9 in 1976, 1 in 1977)
10	Denver, 1984	
10	San Francisco, 1994	
10	Minnesota, 1999-00	(3 in 1999, 7 in 2000)
10	Indianapolis, 2005-06	(1 in 2005, 9 in 2006)
10	San Diego, 2006	

NFL PLAYOFF APPEARANCES BY SEASONS

Team	Number of Seasons in Playoffs
Dallas	28
N.Y. Giants	28
St. Louis	27
Chicago	24
Cleveland	24
Minnesota	24
Green Bay	23
Pittsburgh	23
San Francisco	22
Miami	21
Oakland	21
Washington	21
Indianapolis	20
Philadelphia	20
Tennessee	19

Team	Number of Seasons in Playoffs
Buffalo	17
Denver	17
Kansas City	15
New England	15
Detroit	14
San Diego	14
N.Y. Jets	12
Seattle	9
Tampa Bay	9
Atlanta	8
Cincinnati	8
Arizona	6
New Orleans	6
Jacksonville	5
Baltimore	4
Carolina	3

Year	W	L	T	Pct
1987	95	114	1	.455
1988	92	131	1	.413
1989	95	128	1	.426
1990	93	131	0	.415
1991	92	132	0	.411
1992	88	136	0	.393
1993	101	123	0	.451
1994	96	128	0	.429
1995	96	144	0	.400
1996	91	149	0	.379
1997	93	145	2	.392
1998	89	151	0	.371
1999	100	148	0	.403
2000	110	138	0	.444
2001	112	136	0	.452
2002	107	148	1	.420
2003	99	157	0	.387
2004	111	145	0	.434
2005	105	151	0	.410
2006	120	136	0	.469

TEAMS IN SUPER BOWL CONTENTION (1978-2006)

	With 3 Weeks to Play	With 2 Weeks to Play	With 1 Week to Play
2006	25	24	*20
2005	18	17	14
2004	*27	*26	17
2003	22	17	14
2002	21	21	19
2001	23	16	13
2000	19	17	16
1999	23	20	16
1998	22	19	14
1997	22	18	14
1996	23	21	13
1995	*27	21	18
1994	25	22	15
1993	20	18	16
1992	20	16	14
1991	20	18	13
1990	23	20	15
1989	21	18	17
1988	21	18	15
1987	19	19	15
1986	19	17	14
1985	21	18	13
1984	18	14	13
1983	24	19	15
1982	20	17	16
1981	21	20	16
1980	20	14	12
1979	19	15	13
1978	20	17	12

RECORD OF TEAMS ON THE ROAD (1970-2006)

Year	W	L	T	Pct
1970	72	101	9	.420
1971	74	100	8	.429
1972	87	90	5	.492
1973	66	109	7	.382
1974	82	99	1	.453
1975	81	101	0	.445
1976	83	112	1	.426
1977	83	113	0	.423
1978	93	130	1	.417
1979	92	132	0	.411
1980	101	122	1	.453
1981	84	139	1	.377
1982	57	68	1	.456
1983	104	119	1	.467
1984	94	129	1	.422
1985	80	144	0	.357
1986	104	118	2	.469

GAMES DECIDED BY 7 POINTS OR LESS AND 3 POINTS OR LESS (1970-2006)

	Games Decided by 7 Points or Less	Games Decided by 3 Points or Less
1970	59 of 182 (32.4%)	34 of 182 (18.7%)
1971	76 of 182 (41.8%)	35 of 182 (19.2%)
1972	71 of 182 (39.0%)	38 of 182 (20.9%)
1973	60 of 182 (32.9%)	28 of 182 (15.4%)
1974	91 of 182 (50.0%)	37 of 182 (20.3%)
1975	62 of 182 (34.1%)	35 of 182 (19.2%)
1976	73 of 196 (37.2%)	38 of 196 (19.4%)
1977	85 of 196 (43.4%)	36 of 196 (18.4%)
1978	108 of 224 (48.2%)	49 of 224 (21.9%)
1979	104 of 224 (46.4%)	51 of 224 (22.8%)
1980	108 of 224 (48.2%)	58 of 224 (25.9%)
1981	91 of 224 (40.6%)	60 of 224 (26.8%)
1982	61 of 126 (48.4%)	33 of 126 (26.2%)
1983	106 of 224 (47.3%)	54 of 224 (24.1%)
1984	95 of 224 (42.4%)	58 of 224 (25.9%)
1985	87 of 224 (38.8%)	38 of 224 (17.0%)
1986	106 of 224 (47.3%)	48 of 224 (21.4%)
1987	99 of 210 (47.1%)	40 of 210 (19.0%)
1988	113 of 224 (50.4%)	62 of 224 (27.7%)
1989	107 of 224 (47.8%)	55 of 224 (24.6%)
1990	97 of 224 (43.3%)	54 of 224 (24.1%)
1991	112 of 224 (50.0%)	57 of 224 (25.4%)
1992	88 of 224 (39.3%)	48 of 224 (21.4%)
1993	*105 of 224 (46.9%)	53 of 224 (23.7%)
1994	115 of 224 (51.3%)	60 of 224 (26.8%)
1995	115 of 240 (47.9%)	61 of 240 (25.4%)
1996	109 of 240 (45.4%)	47 of 240 (19.6%)
1997	111 of 240 (46.3%)	67 of 240 (27.9%)
1998	113 of 240 (47.1%)	50 of 240 (20.8%)
1999	115 of 248 (46.4%)	**64 of 248 (25.8%)
2000	109 of 248 (44.0%)	61 of 248 (24.6%)
2001	121 of 248 (48.8%)	62 of 248 (25.0%)
2002	126 of 256 (49.2%)	63 of 256 (24.6%)
2003	124 of 256 (48.4%)	60 of 256 (23.4%)
2004	116 of 256 (45.3%)	61 of 256 (23.8%)
2005	114 of 256 (44.5%)	60 of 256 (23.4%)
2006	117 of 256 (45.7%)	61 of 256 (23.8%)

*Week record: Dec. 11-13, 1993 (Week 15), 12 of 14 games (86%) decided by 7 points or less.
**Week record: Oct. 10-11, 1999 (Week 5), 10 of 14 games (71%) decided by 3 points or less.

GAMES DECIDED BY 8 PTS. OR LESS (1994-2006)

1994	121 of 224 (54.0%)	2001	128 of 248 (51.6%)
1995	123 of 240 (51.3%)	2002	137 of 256 (53.5%)
1996	115 of 240 (47.9%)	2003	132 of 256 (51.6%)
1997	120 of 240 (50.0%)	2004	121 of 256 (47.3%)
1998	120 of 240 (50.0%)	2005	123 of 256 (48.0%)
1999	124 of 248 (50.0%)	2006	126 of 256 (49.2%)
2000	119 of 248 (48.0%)		

TWO-POINT CONVERSION RESULTS (1994-2006)

1994	59 of 116 (50.9%)	2001	40 of 90 (44.4%)
1995	40 of 104 (38.5%)	2002	47 of 98 (48.0%)
1996	44 of 92 (47.8%)	2003	29 of 66 (43.9%)
1997	47 of 109 (43.1%)	2004	37 of 76 (48.7%)
1998	41 of 105 (39.1%)	2005	27 of 53 (50.9%)
1999	31 of 84 (36.9%)	2006	21 of 41 (51.2%)
2000	35 of 85 (41.2%)		

RECORDS AFTER BYE WEEKS (1990-2006)

AFC		NFC	
Baltimore	7-4	Arizona	9-9
Buffalo	12-6	Atlanta	9-9
Cincinnati	4-14	Carolina	5-7
Cleveland	4-9	Chicago	11-7
Denver	14-4	Dallas	13-5
Houston	1-4	Detroit	8-10
Indianapolis	9-9	Green Bay	10-8
Jacksonville	6-6	Minnesota	14-4
Kansas City	12-6	New Orleans	8-10
Miami	11-7	N.Y. Giants	4-14
New England	9-9	Philadelphia	14-4
N.Y. Jets	9-9	St. Louis	9-9
Oakland	9-9	San Francisco	8-10
Pittsburgh	10-8	Seattle	5-13
San Diego	8-9	Tampa Bay	6-12
Tennessee	10-8	Washington	10-8

2006 RECORDS OF TEAMS IN CLOSE GAMES

AFC	Overall Record	Decided by 8 Pts. or Less	Decided By 3 Pts. or Less
Baltimore	13- 4	4-2	3-1
Buffalo	7- 9	3-6	2-5
Cincinnati	8- 8	3-6	1-3
Cleveland	4-12	4-6	2-1
Denver	9- 7	3-5	2-3
Houston	6-10	4-4	3-1
Indianapolis	16- 4	9-3	4-2
Jacksonville	8- 8	2-7	0-3
Kansas City	9- 8	5-3	2-3
Miami	6-10	3-4	2-3
New England	14- 5	6-3	3-1
N.Y. Jets	10- 7	6-3	3-1
Oakland	2-14	1-4	0-1
Pittsburgh	8- 8	3-3	0-1
San Diego	14- 3	7-3	2-3
Tennessee	8- 8	7-4	4-3

NFC	Overall Record	Decided by 8 Pts. or Less	Decided By 3 Pts. or Less
Arizona	5-11	4-5	0-3
Atlanta	7- 9	2-3	2-0
Carolina	8- 8	5-4	3-3
Chicago	15- 4	5-1	4-0
Dallas	9- 8	2-4	1-2
Detroit	3-13	2-9	1-1
Green Bay	8- 8	4-2	1-1
Minnesota	6-10	3-6	2-2
New Orleans	11- 7	5-3	3-1
N.Y. Giants	8- 9	3-4	0-3
Philadelphia	11- 7	4-5	3-3

St. Louis	8- 8	6-3	3-2
San Francisco	7- 9	5-3	1-1
Seattle	10- 8	5-5	5-2
Tampa Bay	4-12	3-3	3-3
Washington	5-11	4-6	1-4

SUPER BOWL CHAMPIONS THAT DID NOT MAKE PLAYOFFS THE FOLLOWING YEAR

Pittsburgh—Super Bowl XL champions did not make playoffs in 2006 season.

Tampa Bay—Super Bowl XXXVII champions did not make playoffs in 2003 season.

New England—Super Bowl XXXVI champions did not make playoffs in the 2002 season.

Denver—Super Bowl XXXIII champions did not make playoffs in the 1999 season.

N.Y. Giants—Super Bowl XXV champions did not make playoffs in the 1991 season.

Washington—Super Bowl XXII champions did not make play-offs in the 1988 season.

N.Y. Giants—Super Bowl XXI champions did not make playoffs in the 1987 season.

San Francisco—Super Bowl XVI champions did not make playoffs in the 1982 season.

Oakland—Super Bowl XV champions did not make playoffs in the 1981 season.

Pittsburgh—Super Bowl XIV champions did not make playoffs in the 1980 season.

Kansas City—Super Bowl IV champions did not make playoffs in the 1970 season.

Green Bay—Super Bowl II champions did not make playoffs in the 1968 season.

NON-DIVISION WINNERS THAT PLAYED IN SUPER BOWL

2005	Pittsburgh Steelers ....Super Bowl XL	
	(Defeated Seattle, 21-10)	
2000	Baltimore Ravens ....Super Bowl XXXV	
	(Defeated N.Y. Giants, 34-7)	
1999	Tennessee Titans ....Super Bowl XXXIV	
	(Lost to St. Louis, 23-16)	
1997	Denver Broncos....................................Super Bowl XXXII	
	(Defeated Green Bay, 31-24)	
1992	Buffalo Bills...Super Bowl XXVII	
	(Lost to Dallas, 52-17)	
1985	New England Patriots............................Super Bowl XX	
	(Lost to Chicago, 46-10)	
1980	Oakland Raiders...................................Super Bowl XV	
	(Defeated Philadelphia, 27-10)	
1975	Dallas Cowboys ....Super Bowl X	
	(Lost to Pittsburgh, 21-17)	
1969	Kansas City Chiefs ....Super Bowl IV	
	(Defeated Minnesota, 23-7)	

TEAMS AT OR UNDER .500 IN POSTSEASON PLAY

2006	New York Giants	8-8
2004	Minnesota Vikings	8-8
2004	St. Louis Rams...	8-8
1999	Dallas Cowboys..	8-8
1999	Detroit Lions..	8-8
1991	New York Jets	8-8
1990	New Orleans Saints	8-8
1985	Cleveland Browns	8-8
1982	Cleveland Browns	4-5
1982	Detroit Lions..	4-5
1969	Houston Oilers	6-6-2

COLDEST NFL GAMES ON RECORD

-13 degrees (-48 degree wind chill)—December 31, 1967, Lambeau Field, Green Bay, Wisconsin, NFL Championship (Green Bay 21, Dallas 17)

-9 degrees (-59 degree wind chill)—January 10, 1982, Riverfront Stadium, Cincinnati, Ohio, AFC Championship (Cincinnati 27, San Diego 7)

0 degrees (-32 degree wind chill)—January 15, 1994, Rich Stadium, Orchard Park, New York, AFC Divisional Playoff (Buffalo 29, Los Angeles Raiders 23)

TEAM LEADERS

Offense	Most Scored		Fewest Scored	
1st Quarter	104	Arizona	29	Cleveland
2nd Quarter	140	Chicago	49	Minnesota
3rd Quarter	106	Indianapolis	21	Oakland
4th Quarter	176	San Diego	24	Oakland

Defense	Most Scored		Fewest Scored	
1st Quarter	116	San Francisco	29	Carolina
2nd Quarter	145	San Francisco	57	New Orleans
3rd Quarter	100	Arizona	30	Baltimore
4th Quarter	132	N.Y. Giants	51	New England

2006 NFL SCORE BY QUARTERS

AFC Offense	1	2	3	4	OT	PTS
San Diego	85	137	94	176	0	492
Indianapolis	68	138	106	115	0	427
New England	74	128	73	110	0	385
Cincinnati	86	111	58	118	0	373
Jacksonville	72	112	80	107	0	371
Pittsburgh	66	107	58	116	6	353
Baltimore	84	91	73	105	0	353
Kansas City	71	105	60	95	0	331
Tennessee	52	87	81	98	6	324
Denver	44	110	75	87	3	319
N.Y. Jets	54	107	67	88	0	316
Buffalo	67	84	75	74	0	300
Houston	55	52	59	101	0	267
Miami	33	73	53	101	0	260
Cleveland	29	74	41	91	3	238
Oakland	44	79	21	24	0	168

NFC Offense	1	2	3	4	OT	PTS
Chicago	73	140	101	110	3	427
Dallas	65	122	96	142	0	425
New Orleans	82	136	82	113	0	413
Philadelphia	75	109	96	118	0	398
St. Louis	53	136	74	98	6	367
N.Y. Giants	74	86	79	110	6	355
Seattle	103	73	52	107	0	335
Arizona	104	81	46	83	0	314
Washington	76	94	55	76	6	307
Detroit	73	75	85	72	0	305
Green Bay	87	79	62	73	0	301
San Francisco	46	67	87	95	3	298
Atlanta	59	98	96	36	3	292
Minnesota	66	49	54	110	3	282
Carolina	68	94	53	55	0	270
Tampa Bay	30	53	58	70	0	211

AFC Defense	1	2	3	4	OT	PTS
Baltimore	32	84	30	55	0	201
New England	32	74	80	51	0	237
Jacksonville	61	64	72	71	6	274
Miami	32	85	59	107	0	283
N.Y. Jets	52	74	53	116	0	295
San Diego	66	74	81	82	0	303
Denver	47	82	64	109	3	305
Buffalo	74	105	55	77	0	311
Kansas City	61	113	58	77	6	315
Pittsburgh	49	98	65	100	3	315
Cincinnati	50	76	85	114	6	331
Oakland	88	68	66	110	0	332
Cleveland	64	90	95	107	0	356
Indianapolis	44	127	59	130	0	360
Houston	72	103	86	99	6	366
Tennessee	84	116	85	115	0	400

NFC Defense	1	2	3	4	OT	PTS
Chicago	47	71	48	89	0	255
Carolina	29	95	68	110	3	305
New Orleans	95	57	80	90	0	322
Minnesota	57	129	73	68	0	327
Atlanta	102	98	60	68	0	328
Philadelphia	79	86	61	96	6	328
Seattle	67	104	54	116	0	341
Dallas	78	111	80	81	0	350
Tampa Bay	82	89	95	84	3	353
N.Y. Giants	64	101	65	132	0	362
Green Bay	64	115	84	103	0	366
Washington	69	126	95	80	6	376
St. Louis	76	106	79	120	0	381
Arizona	84	100	100	105	0	389
Detroit	101	121	61	115	0	398
San Francisco	116	145	54	97	0	412
NFL Totals	**2,118**	**3,087**	**2,250**	**3,074**	**48**	**10,577**

LARGEST TRADES IN NFL HISTORY

(Based on number of players or draft choices involved)

18—October 13, 1989—RB Herschel Walker from the Dallas Cowboys to Minnesota. Dallas also traded its third-round choice in 1990, its tenth-round choice in 1990, and its third-round choice in 1991 to Minnesota. Minnesota traded LB Jesse Solomon, LB David Howard, CB Issiac Holt, and DE Alex Stewart along with its first-round choice in 1990, its second-round choice in 1990, its sixth-round choice in 1990, its first-round choice in 1991, its second-round choice in 1991, its first-round choice in 1992, its second-round choice in 1992, and its third-round choice in 1992 to Dallas. Minnesota traded RB Darrin Nelson to Dallas, which traded Nelson to San Diego for the Chargers' fifth-round choice in 1990, which Dallas then sent to Minnesota.

15—March 26, 1953—T Mike McCormack, DT Don Colo, LB Tom Catlin, DB John Petitbon, and G Herschell Forester from Baltimore to Cleveland for DB Don Shula, DB Bert Rechichar, DB Carl Taseff, LB Ed Sharkey, E Gern Nagler, QB Harry Agganis, T Dick Batten, T Stu Sheets, G Art Spinney, and G Elmer Willhoite.

15—January 28, 1971—LB Marlin McKeever, first- and third-round choices in 1971, and third-, fourth-, fifth-, sixth-, and seventh-round choices in 1972 from Washington to the Los Angeles Rams for LB Maxie Baughan, LB Jack Pardee, LB Myron Pottios, RB Jeff Jordan, G John Wilbur, DT Diron Talbert, and a fifth-round choice in 1971.

12—June 13, 1952—Selection rights to Les Richter from the Dallas Texans to the Los Angeles Rams for RB Dick Hoerner, DB Tom Keane, DB George Sims, C Joe Reid, HB Billy Baggett, T Jack Halliday, FB Dick McKissack, LB Vic Vasicek, E Richard Wilkins, C Aubrey Phillips, and RB Dave Anderson.

10—March 23, 1959—HB Ollie Matson from the Chicago Cardinals to the Los Angeles Rams for T Frank Fuller, DE Glenn Holtzman, T Ken Panfil, DT Art Hauser, E John Tracey, FB Larry Hickman, HB Don Brown, the Rams second-round choice in 1960, and a player to be delivered during the 1959 training camp.

10—October 31, 1987—RB Eric Dickerson from the Los Angeles Rams to Indianapolis. The rights to LB Cornelius Bennett from Indianapolis to Buffalo. Indianapolis running back Owen Gill and the Colts' first- and second-round choices in 1988 and second-round choice in 1989, plus Bills running back Greg Bell and Buffalo's first-round choice in 1988 and first- and second-round choices in 1989 to the Rams.

2006 TOP 100 TELEVISION MARKETS
(NFL TEAM MARKETS IN BOLD)

RANK	MARKET	TV HOUSEHOLDS	% of U.S.
1	**New York**	**7,366,950**	**6.616**
2	Los Angeles	5,611,110	5.039
3	**Chicago**	**3,455,020**	**3.103**
4	**Philadelphia**	**2,941,450**	**2.642**
5	**San Francisco-Oak-San Jose**	**2,383,570**	**2.141**
6	**Dallas-Ft. Worth**	**2,378,660**	**2.136**
7	**Boston (Manchester)**	**2,372,030**	**2.130**
8	**Washington, DC (Hagrstwn)**	**2,272,120**	**2.041**
9	**Atlanta**	**2,205,510**	**1.981**
10	**Houston**	**1,982,120**	**1.780**
11	**Detroit**	**1,938,320**	**1.741**
12	**Tampa-St. Pete (Sarasota)**	**1,755,750**	**1.577**
13	**Phoenix (Prescott)**	**1,725,000**	**1.549**
14	**Seattle-Tacoma**	**1,724,450**	**1.549**
15	**Minneapolis-St. Paul**	**1,678,430**	**1.507**
16	**Miami-Ft. Lauderdale**	**1,538,620**	**1.382**
17	**Cleveland-Akron (Canton)**	**1,537,500**	**1.381**
18	**Denver**	**1,431,910**	**1.286**
19	Orlando-Daytona Bch-Melbrn	1,395,830	1.254
20	Sacramnto-Stkton-Modesto	1,368,680	1.229
21	**St. Louis**	**1,228,980**	**1.104**
22	**Pittsburgh**	**1,163,150**	**1.045**
23	Portland, OR	1,117,990	1.004
24	**Baltimore**	**1,097,290**	**0.985**
25	**Indianapolis**	**1,060,550**	**0.952**
26	**Charlotte**	**1,045,240**	**0.939**
27	**San Diego**	**1,030,020**	**0.925**
28	Hartford & New Haven	1,014,630	0.911
29	Raleigh-Durham (Fayetvlle)	1,006,330	0.904
30	**Nashville**	**944,100**	**0.848**
31	**Kansas City**	**913,280**	**0.820**
32	Columbus, OH	898,030	0.807
33	**Cincinnati**	**886,910**	**0.797**
34	Milwaukee	882,990	0.793
35	Salt Lake City	839,170	0.754
36	Greenvll-Spart-Ashevll-And	826,290	0.742
37	San Antonio	774,470	0.696
38	West Palm Beach-Ft. Pierce	772,140	0.693
39	Grand Rapids-Kalmzoo-B.Crk	734,670	0.660
40	Birmingham (Ann, Tusc)	723,210	0.650
41	Harrisburg-Lncstr-Leb-York	713,960	0.641
42	Norfolk-Portsmth-Newpt Nws	712,790	0.640
43	Las Vegas	671,630	0.603
44	Memphis	664,290	0.597
45	Albuquerque-Santa Fe	662,380	0.595
45	Oklahoma City	662,380	0.595
47	Greensboro-H.Point-W.Salem	660,570	0.593
48	Louisville	648,190	0.582
49	**Buffalo**	**639,990**	**0.575**
50	**Jacksonville**	**639,110**	**0.574**

2006 TOP 100 TELEVISION MARKETS
(NFL TEAM MARKETS IN BOLD)

RANK	MARKET	TV HOUSEHOLDS	% of U.S.
51	Providence-New Bedford	633,950	0.569
52	Austin	602,340	0.541
53	Wilkes Barre-Scranton	590,170	0.530
54	**New Orleans**	**566,960**	**0.509**
55	Fresno-Visalia	557,380	0.501
56	Albany-Schenectady-Troy	554,970	0.498
57	Little Rock-Pine Bluff	539,900	0.485
58	Dayton	531,120	0.477
59	Mobile-Pensacola (Ft Walt)	524,200	0.471
60	Knoxville	523,010	0.470
61	Richmond-Petersburg	517,800	0.465
62	Tulsa	513,090	0.461
63	Lexington	483,520	0.434
64	Ft. Myers-Naples	479,130	0.430
65	Charleston-Huntington	477,040	0.428
66	Flint-Saginaw-Bay City	474,430	0.426
67	Wichita-Hutchinson Plus	445,860	0.400
68	Roanoke-Lynchburg	445,840	0.400
69	**Green Bay-Appleton**	**434,760**	**0.390**
70	Tucson (Sierra Vista)	433,310	0.389
71	Toledo	425,820	0.382
72	Honolulu	419,160	0.376
73	Des Moines-Ames	417,900	0.375
74	Portland-Auburn	409,180	0.367
75	Omaha	403,560	0.362
76	Springfield, MO	402,310	0.361
77	Spokane	395,490	0.355
78	Rochester, NY	392,630	0.353
79	Syracuse	386,940	0.348
80	Paducah-Cape Girard-Harsbg	384,510	0.345
81	Shreveport	381,200	0.342
82	Champaign&Sprngfld-Decatur	378,150	0.340
83	Columbia, SC	377,940	0.339
84	Huntsville-Decatur (Flor)	375,270	0.337
85	Madison	369,220	0.332
86	Chattanooga	347,380	0.312
87	Jackson, MS	343,550	0.309
88	South Bend-Elkhart	334,370	0.300
89	Cedar Rapids-Wtrlo-IWC&Dub	333,270	0.299
90	Burlington-Plattsburgh	327,480	0.294
91	Harlingen-Wslco-Brnsvl-McA	327,070	0.294
92	Tri-Cities, TN-VA	326,560	0.293
93	Baton Rouge	322,540	0.290
94	Colorado Springs-Pueblo	316,630	0.284
95	Waco-Temple-Bryan	311,690	0.280
96	Davenport-R.Island-Moline	308,360	0.277
97	Savannah	298,130	0.268
98	Johnstown-Altoona	294,160	0.264
99	El Paso (Las Cruces)	293,700	0.264
100	Charleston, SC	290,110	0.261
	TOTAL NFL MARKETS	**52,337,750**	**47.004**
	TOTAL TOP 100 MARKETS	**95,720,820**	**85.965**
	TOTAL MARKETS	**111,348,110**	**100.000**

RETIRED UNIFORM NUMBERS IN NFL

AFC

Baltimore	None	
Buffalo	Jim Kelly	12
Cincinnati	Bob Johnson	54
Cleveland	Otto Graham	14
	Jim Brown	32
	Ernie Davis	45
	Don Fleming	46
	Lou Groza	76
Denver	John Elway	7
	Frank Tripucka	18
	Floyd Little	44
Houston	None	
Indianapolis	Johnny Unitas	19
	Buddy Young	22
	Lenny Moore	24
	Art Donovan	70
	Jim Parker	77
	Raymond Berry	82
	Gino Marchetti	89
Jacksonville	None	
Kansas City	Jan Stenerud	3
	Len Dawson	16
	Abner Haynes	28
	Stone Johnson	33
	Mack Lee Hill	36
	Willie Lanier	63
	Bobby Bell	78
	Buck Buchanan	86
Miami	Bob Griese	12
	Dan Marino	13
	Larry Csonka	39
New England	Bruce Armstrong	78
	Gino Cappelletti	20
	Mike Haynes	40
	Steve Nelson	57
	John Hannah	73
	Jim Lee Hunt	79
	Bob Dee	89
New York Jets	Joe Namath	12
	Don Maynard	13
	Joe Klecko	73
Oakland	None	
Pittsburgh	Ernie Stautner	70
San Diego	Dan Fouts	14
	Lance Alworth	19
Tennessee	Warren Moon	1
	Earl Campbell	34
	Jim Norton	43
	Mike Munchak	63
	Elvin Bethea	65
	Bruce Matthews	74

NFC

Arizona	Larry Wilson	8
	Pat Tillman	40
	Stan Mauldin	77
	J.V. Cain	88
	Marshall Goldberg	99
Atlanta	Steve Bartkowski	10
	William Andrews	31
	Jeff Van Note	57
	Tommy Nobis	60
Carolina	Sam Mills	51
Chicago	Bronko Nagurski	3
	George McAfee	5
	George Halas	7
	Willie Galimore	28
	Walter Payton	34
	Gale Sayers	40

	Brian Piccolo	41
	Sid Luckman	42
	Dick Butkus	51
	Bill Hewitt	56
	Bill George	61
	Bulldog Turner	66
	Red Grange	77
Dallas	None	
Detroit	Dutch Clark	7
	Bobby Layne	22
	Doak Walker	37
	Joe Schmidt	56
	Chuck Hughes	85
Green Bay	Tony Canadeo	3
	Don Hutson	14
	Bart Starr	15
	Ray Nitschke	66
	Reggie White	92
Minnesota	Fran Tarkenton	10
	Mick Tingelhoff	53
	Jim Marshall	70
	Korey Stringer	77
	Cris Carter	80
	Alan Page	88
New Orleans	Jim Taylor	31
	Doug Atkins	81
New York Giants	Ray Flaherty	1
	Tuffy Leemans	4
	Mel Hein	7
	Phil Simms	11
	Y.A. Tittle	14
	Frank Gifford	16
	Al Blozis	32
	Joe Morrison	40
	Charlie Conerly	42
	Ken Strong	50
	Lawrence Taylor	56
Philadelphia	Steve Van Buren	15
	Tom Brookshier	40
	Pete Retzlaff	44
	Chuck Bednarik	60
	Al Wistert	70
	Reggie White	92
	Jerome Brown	99
St. Louis	Bob Waterfield	7
	Eric Dickerson	29
	Merlin Olsen	74
	Jackie Slater	78
	Jack Youngblood	85
San Francisco	John Brodie	12
	Joe Montana	16
	Joe Perry	34
	Jimmy Johnson	37
	Hugh McElhenny	39
	Ronnie Lott	42
	Charlie Krueger	70
	Leo Nomellini	73
	Bob St. Clair	79
	Dwight Clark	87
Seattle	"Fans/the twelfth man"	12
	Steve Largent	80
Tampa Bay	Lee Roy Selmon	63
Washington	Sammy Baugh	33

ALL-TIME REGULAR-SEASON RECORDS OF CURRENT NFL TEAMS

AFC
BALTIMORE RAVENS

	All Games			Home Games			Road Games		
Season	W	L	T	W	L	T	W	L	T
1996	4	12		4	4		0	8	
1997	6	9	1	3	4	1	3	5	
1998	6	10		4	4		2	6	
1999	8	8		4	4		4	4	
2000	12	4		6	2		6	2	
2001	10	6		6	2		4	4	
2002	7	9		4	4		3	5	
2003	10	6		7	1		3	5	
2004	9	7		6	2		3	5	
2005	6	10		6	2		0	8	
2006	13	3		7	1		6	2	
	91	84	1	57	30	1	34	54	

BUFFALO BILLS

	All Games			Home Games			Road Games		
Season	W	L	T	W	L	T	W	L	T
1960	5	8	1	3	4		2	4	1
1961	6	8		2	5		4	3	
1962	7	6	1	3	3	1	4	3	
1963	7	6	1	4	2	1	3	4	
1964	12	2		6	1		6	1	
1965	10	3	1	5	2		5	1	1
1966	9	4	1	4	2	1	5	2	
1967	4	10		2	5		2	5	
1968	1	12	1	1	6		0	6	1
1969	4	10		4	3		0	7	
1970	3	10	1	1	6		2	4	1
1971	1	13		1	6		0	7	
1972	4	9	1	2	4	1	2	5	
1973	9	5		5	2		4	3	
1974	9	5		5	2		4	3	
1975	8	6		3	4		5	2	
1976	2	12		1	6		1	6	
1977	3	11		1	6		2	5	
1978	5	11		4	4		1	7	
1979	7	9		3	5		4	4	
1980	11	5		6	2		5	3	
1981	10	6		7	1		3	5	
1982	4	5		4	1		0	4	
1983	8	8		3	5		5	3	
1984	2	14		2	6		0	8	
1985	2	14		2	6		0	8	
1986	4	12		3	5		1	7	
1987	7	8		4	4		3	4	
1988	12	4		8	0		4	4	
1989	9	7		6	2		3	5	
1990	13	3		8	0		5	3	
1991	13	3		7	1		6	2	
1992	11	5		6	2		5	3	
1993	12	4		6	2		6	2	
1994	7	9		4	4		3	5	
1995	10	6		6	2		4	4	
1996	10	6		7	1		3	5	
1997	6	10		4	4		2	6	
1998	10	6		6	2		4	4	
1999	11	5		6	2		5	3	
2000	8	8		5	3		3	5	
2001	3	13		1	7		2	6	
2002	8	8		5	3		3	5	
2003	6	10		4	4		2	6	
2004	9	7		5	3		4	4	
2005	5	11		4	4		1	7	
2006	7	9		4	4		3	5	
	334	366	8	193	158	4	141	208	4

CINCINNATI BENGALS

	All Games			Home Games			Road Games		
Season	W	L	T	W	L	T	W	L	T
1968	3	11		2	5		1	6	
1969	4	9	1	4	3		0	6	1
1970	8	6		5	2		3	4	
1971	4	10		3	4		1	6	
1972	8	6		4	3		4	3	
1973	10	4		7	0		3	4	
1974	7	7		4	3		3	4	
1975	11	3		6	1		5	2	
1976	10	4		6	1		4	3	
1977	8	6		5	2		3	4	
1978	4	12		3	5		1	7	
1979	4	12		4	4		0	8	
1980	6	10		3	5		3	5	
1981	12	4		6	2		6	2	
1982	7	2		4	0		3	2	
1983	7	9		4	4		3	5	
1984	8	8		5	3		3	5	
1985	7	9		5	3		2	6	
1986	10	6		6	2		4	4	
1987	4	11		1	7		3	4	
1988	12	4		8	0		4	4	
1989	8	8		5	3		3	5	
1990	9	7		5	3		4	4	
1991	3	13		3	5		0	8	
1992	5	11		3	5		2	6	
1993	3	13		3	5		0	8	
1994	3	13		2	6		1	7	
1995	7	9		3	5		4	4	
1996	8	8		6	2		2	6	
1997	7	9		6	2		1	7	
1998	3	13		1	7		2	6	
1999	4	12		2	6		2	6	
2000	4	12		3	5		1	7	
2001	6	10		4	4		2	6	
2002	2	14		1	7		1	7	
2003	8	8		5	3		3	5	
2004	8	8		5	3		3	5	
2005	11	5		5	3		6	2	
2006	8	8		4	4		4	4	
	261	334	1	161	137		100	197	1

CLEVELAND BROWNS*

	All Games			Home Games			Road Games		
Season	W	L	T	W	L	T	W	L	T
1950	10	2		5	1		5	1	
1951	11	1		6	0		5	1	
1952	8	4		4	2		4	2	
1953	11	1		6	0		5	1	
1954	9	3		5	1		4	2	
1955	9	2	1	5	1		4	1	1
1956	5	7		1	5		4	2	
1957	9	2	1	6	0		3	2	1
1958	9	3		4	2		5	1	
1959	7	5		3	3		4	2	
1960	8	3	1	4	2		4	1	1
1961	8	5	1	4	3		4	2	1
1962	7	6	1	4	2	1	3	4	
1963	10	4		5	2		5	2	
1964	10	3	1	5	1	1	5	2	
1965	11	3		5	2		6	1	
1966	9	5		5	2		4	3	
1967	9	5		6	1		3	4	
1968	10	4		5	2		5	2	
1969	10	3	1	5	1	1	5	2	
1970	7	7		4	3		3	4	
1971	9	5		4	3		5	2	
1972	10	4		4	3		6	1	

Season	All Games W	L	T	Home Games W	L	T	Road Games W	L	T
1973	7	5	2	5	1	1	2	4	1
1974	4	10		3	4		1	6	
1975	3	11		3	4		0	7	
1976	9	5		6	1		3	4	
1977	6	8		2	5		4	3	
1978	8	8		5	3		3	5	
1979	9	7		5	3		4	4	
1980	11	5		6	2		5	3	
1981	5	11		3	5		2	6	
1982	4	5		2	2		2	3	
1983	9	7		6	2		3	5	
1984	5	11		2	6		3	5	
1985	8	8		5	3		3	5	
1986	12	4		6	2		6	2	
1987	10	5		5	2		5	3	
1988	10	6		6	2		4	4	
1989	9	6	1	5	2	1	4	4	
1990	3	13		2	6		1	7	
1991	6	10		3	5		3	5	
1992	7	9		4	4		3	5	
1993	7	9		4	4		3	5	
1994	11	5		6	2		5	3	
1995	5	11		3	5		2	6	
1999	2	14		0	8		2	6	
2000	3	13		2	6		1	7	
2001	7	9		4	4		3	5	
2002	9	7		3	5		6	2	
2003	5	11		2	6		3	5	
2004	4	12		3	5		1	7	
2005	6	10		4	4		2	6	
2006	4	12		2	6		2	6	
	414	354	10	222	161	5	192	193	5

*Did not play from 1996-98.

DENVER BRONCOS

Season	All Games W	L	T	Home Games W	L	T	Road Games W	L	T
1960	4	9	1	2	4	1	2	5	
1961	3	11		2	5		1	6	
1962	7	7		3	4		4	3	
1963	2	11	1	2	5		0	6	1
1964	2	11	1	2	4	1	0	7	
1965	4	10		2	5		2	5	
1966	4	10		3	4		1	6	
1967	3	11		1	6		2	5	
1968	5	9		3	4		2	5	
1969	5	8	1	4	2	1	1	6	
1970	5	8	1	3	3	1	2	5	
1971	4	9	1	2	4	1	2	5	
1972	5	9		3	4		2	5	
1973	7	5	2	3	3	1	4	2	1
1974	7	6	1	3	3	1	4	3	
1975	6	8		5	2		1	6	
1976	9	5		6	1		3	4	
1977	12	2		6	1		6	1	
1978	10	6		6	2		4	4	
1979	10	6		6	2		4	4	
1980	8	8		4	4		4	4	
1981	10	6		8	0		2	6	
1982	2	7		1	4		1	3	
1983	9	7		6	2		3	5	
1984	13	3		7	1		6	2	
1985	11	5		6	2		5	3	
1986	11	5		7	1		4	4	
1987	10	4	1	7	1		3	3	1
1988	8	8		6	2		2	6	
1989	11	5		6	2		5	3	
1990	5	11		4	4		1	7	

Season	All Games W	L	T	Home Games W	L	T	Road Games W	L	T
1991	12	4		7	1		5	3	
1992	8	8		7	1		1	7	
1993	9	7		5	3		4	4	
1994	7	9		4	4		3	5	
1995	8	8		6	2		2	6	
1996	13	3		8	0		5	3	
1997	12	4		8	0		4	4	
1998	14	2		8	0		6	2	
1999	6	10		3	5		3	5	
2000	11	5		6	2		5	3	
2001	8	8		6	2		2	6	
2002	9	7		5	3		4	4	
2003	10	6		6	2		4	4	
2004	10	6		6	2		4	4	
2005	13	3		8	0		5	3	
2006	9	7		4	4		5	3	
	371	327	10	226	122	7	145	205	3

HOUSTON TEXANS

Season	All Games W	L	T	Home Games W	L	T	Road Games W	L	T
2002	4	12		2	6		2	6	
2003	5	11		3	5		2	6	
2004	7	9		3	5		4	4	
2005	2	14		2	6		0	8	
2006	6	10		4	4		2	6	
	24	56		14	26		10	30	

INDIANAPOLIS COLTS*

Season	All Games W	L	T	Home Games W	L	T	Road Games W	L	T
1953	3	9		2	4		1	5	
1954	3	9		2	4		1	5	
1955	5	6	1	4	1	1	1	5	
1956	5	7		4	2		1	5	
1957	7	5		4	2		3	3	
1958	9	3		6	0		3	3	
1959	9	3		4	2		5	1	
1960	6	6		4	2		2	4	
1961	8	6		5	2		3	4	
1962	7	7		3	4		4	3	
1963	8	6		4	3		4	3	
1964	12	2		7	1		5	1	
1965	10	3	1	5	2		5	1	1
1966	9	5		5	2		4	3	
1967	11	1	2	6	0	1	5	1	1
1968	13	1		6	1		7	0	
1969	8	5	1	4	2	1	4	3	
1970	11	2	1	5	1	1	6	1	
1971	10	4		5	2		5	2	
1972	5	9		2	5		3	4	
1973	4	10		3	4		1	6	
1974	2	12		0	7		2	5	
1975	10	4		5	2		5	2	
1976	11	3		6	1		5	2	
1977	10	4		6	1		4	3	
1978	5	11		2	6		3	5	
1979	5	11		3	5		2	6	
1980	7	9		2	6		5	3	
1981	2	14		1	7		1	7	
1982	0	8	1	0	3	1	0	5	
1983	7	9		3	5		4	4	
1984	4	12		2	6		2	6	
1985	5	11		4	4		1	7	
1986	3	13		1	7		2	6	
1987	9	6		4	4		5	2	
1988	9	7		6	2		3	5	
1989	8	8		6	2		2	6	

Season	All Games W	L	T	Home Games W	L	T	Road Games W	L	T
1990	7	9		3	5		4	4	
1991	1	15		0	8		1	7	
1992	9	7		4	4		5	3	
1993	4	12		2	6		2	6	
1994	8	8		5	3		3	5	
1995	9	7		5	3		4	4	
1996	9	7		6	2		3	5	
1997	3	13		2	6		1	7	
1998	3	13		3	5		0	8	
1999	13	3		7	1		6	2	
2000	10	6		6	2		4	4	
2001	6	10		3	5		3	5	
2002	10	6		5	3		5	3	
2003	12	4		5	3		7	1	
2004	12	4		7	1		5	3	
2005	14	2		7	1		7	1	
2006	12	4		8	0		4	4	
	402	381	7	219	172	5	183	209	2

*includes Baltimore Colts (1953-1983).

JACKSONVILLE JAGUARS

Season	All Games W	L	T	Home Games W	L	T	Road Games W	L	T
1995	4	12		2	6		2	6	
1996	9	7		7	1		2	6	
1997	11	5		7	1		4	4	
1998	11	5		7	1		4	4	
1999	14	2		7	1		7	1	
2000	7	9		4	4		3	5	
2001	6	10		3	5		3	5	
2002	6	10		3	5		3	5	
2003	5	11		5	3		0	8	
2004	9	7		4	4		5	3	
2005	12	4		6	2		6	2	
2006	8	8		6	2		2	6	
	102	90		61	35		41	55	

KANSAS CITY CHIEFS*

Season	All Games W	L	T	Home Games W	L	T	Road Games W	L	T
1960	8	6		5	2		3	4	
1961	6	8		4	3		2	5	
1962	11	3		6	1		5	2	
1963	5	7	2	4	3		1	4	2
1964	7	7		4	3		3	4	
1965	7	5	2	5	2		2	3	2
1966	11	2	1	4	2	1	7	0	
1967	9	5		4	3		5	2	
1968	12	2		6	1		6	1	
1969	11	3		6	1		5	2	
1970	7	5	2	4	1	2	3	4	
1971	10	3	1	7	0		3	3	1
1972	8	6		3	4		5	2	
1973	7	5	2	5	1	1	2	4	1
1974	5	9		1	6		4	3	
1975	5	9		3	4		2	5	
1976	5	9		1	6		4	3	
1977	2	12		1	6		1	6	
1978	4	12		3	5		1	7	
1979	7	9		3	5		4	4	
1980	8	8		3	5		5	3	
1981	9	7		5	3		4	4	
1982	3	6		2	2		1	4	
1983	6	10		5	3		1	7	
1984	8	8		5	3		3	5	
1985	6	10		5	3		1	7	
1986	10	6		6	2		4	4	
1987	4	11		3	4		1	7	

Season	All Games W	L	T	Home Games W	L	T	Road Games W	L	T
1988	4	11	1	4	4		0	7	1
1989	8	7	1	5	3		3	4	1
1990	11	5		6	2		5	3	
1991	10	6		6	2		4	4	
1992	10	6		7	1		3	5	
1993	11	5		7	1		4	4	
1994	9	7		5	3		4	4	
1995	13	3		8	0		5	3	
1996	9	7		5	3		4	4	
1997	13	3		8	0		5	3	
1998	7	9		5	3		2	6	
1999	9	7		6	2		3	5	
2000	7	9		5	3		2	6	
2001	6	10		3	5		3	5	
2002	8	8		6	2		2	6	
2003	13	3		8	0		5	3	
2004	7	9		4	4		3	5	
2005	10	6		7	1		3	5	
2006	9	7		6	2		3	5	
	375	321	12	224	125	4	151	196	8

*includes Dallas Texans (1960-62).

MIAMI DOLPHINS

Season	All Games W	L	T	Home Games W	L	T	Road Games W	L	T
1966	3	11		2	5		1	6	
1967	4	10		4	3		0	7	
1968	5	8	1	1	5	1	4	3	
1969	3	10	1	2	4	1	1	6	
1970	10	4		6	1		4	3	
1971	10	3	1	6	1		4	2	1
1972	14	0		7	0		7	0	
1973	12	2		7	0		5	2	
1974	11	3		7	0		4	3	
1975	10	4		5	2		5	2	
1976	6	8		3	4		3	4	
1977	10	4		6	1		4	3	
1978	11	5		7	1		4	4	
1979	10	6		6	2		4	4	
1980	8	8		5	3		3	5	
1981	11	4	1	6	1	1	5	3	
1982	7	2		4	0		3	2	
1983	12	4		7	1		5	3	
1984	14	2		7	1		7	1	
1985	12	4		8	0		4	4	
1986	8	8		4	4		4	4	
1987	8	7		4	3		4	4	
1988	6	10		4	4		2	6	
1989	8	8		4	4		4	4	
1990	12	4		7	1		5	3	
1991	8	8		5	3		3	5	
1992	11	5		6	2		5	3	
1993	9	7		4	4		5	3	
1994	10	6		6	2		4	4	
1995	9	7		5	3		4	4	
1996	8	8		4	4		4	4	
1997	9	7		6	2		3	5	
1998	10	6		7	1		3	5	
1999	9	7		5	3		4	4	
2000	11	5		5	3		6	2	
2001	11	5		7	1		4	4	
2002	9	7		7	1		2	6	
2003	10	6		4	4		6	2	
2004	4	12		3	5		1	7	
2005	9	7		5	3		4	4	
2006	6	10		4	4		2	6	
	368	252	4	212	96	3	156	156	1

NEW ENGLAND PATRIOTS*

Season	All Games W	L	T	Home Games W	L	T	Road Games W	L	T
1960	5	9		3	4		2	5	
1961	9	4	1	4	2	1	5	2	
1962	9	4	1	6	1		3	3	1
1963	7	6	1	5	1	1	2	5	
1964	10	3	1	4	2	1	6	1	
1965	4	8	2	1	4	2	3	4	
1966	8	4	2	4	2	1	4	2	1
1967	3	10	1	2	4		1	6	1
1968	4	10		2	5		2	5	
1969	4	10		2	5		2	5	
1970	2	12		1	6		1	6	
1971	6	8		5	2		1	6	
1972	3	11		2	5		1	6	
1973	5	9		3	4		2	5	
1974	7	7		3	4		4	3	
1975	3	11		2	5		1	6	
1976	11	3		6	1		5	2	
1977	9	5		6	1		3	4	
1978	11	5		5	3		6	2	
1979	9	7		6	2		3	5	
1980	10	6		6	2		4	4	
1981	2	14		2	6		0	8	
1982	5	4		3	1		2	3	
1983	8	8		5	3		3	5	
1984	9	7		5	3		4	4	
1985	11	5		7	1		4	4	
1986	11	5		4	4		7	1	
1987	8	7		5	3		3	4	
1988	9	7		7	1		2	6	
1989	5	11		3	5		2	6	
1990	1	15		0	8		1	7	
1991	6	10		4	4		2	6	
1992	2	14		1	7		1	7	
1993	5	11		3	5		2	6	
1994	10	6		5	3		5	3	
1995	6	10		3	5		3	5	
1996	11	5		6	2		5	3	
1997	10	6		6	2		4	4	
1998	9	7		6	2		3	5	
1999	8	8		5	3		3	5	
2000	5	11		3	5		2	6	
2001	11	5		6	2		5	3	
2002	9	7		5	3		4	4	
2003	14	2		8	0		6	2	
2004	14	2		8	0		6	2	
2005	10	6		5	3		5	3	
2006	12	4		5	3		7	1	
	350	349	9	198	149	6	152	200	3

*includes Boston Patriots (1960-1970).

NEW YORK JETS*

Season	All Games W	L	T	Home Games W	L	T	Road Games W	L	T
1960	7	7		3	4		4	3	
1961	7	7		5	2		2	5	
1962	5	9		2	5		3	4	
1963	5	8	1	4	2	1	1	6	
1964	5	8	1	5	1	1	0	7	
1965	5	8	1	3	3	1	2	5	
1966	6	6	2	4	3		2	3	2
1967	8	5	1	4	2	1	4	3	
1968	11	3		6	1		5	2	
1969	10	4		5	2		5	2	
1970	4	10		2	5		2	5	
1971	6	8		4	3		2	5	
1972	7	7		4	3		3	4	
1973	4	10		2	4		2	6	
1974	7	7		3	4		4	3	
1975	3	11		1	6		2	5	
1976	3	11		2	5		1	6	
1977	3	11		1	6		2	5	
1978	8	8		4	4		4	4	
1979	8	8		6	2		2	6	
1980	4	12		2	6		2	6	
1981	10	5	1	6	2		4	3	1
1982	6	3		3	1		3	2	
1983	7	9		2	6		5	3	
1984	7	9		3	5		4	4	
1985	11	5		7	1		4	4	
1986	10	6		5	3		5	3	
1987	6	9		4	4		2	5	
1988	8	7	1	5	2	1	3	5	
1989	4	12		1	7		3	5	
1990	6	10		3	5		3	5	
1991	8	8		4	4		4	4	
1992	4	12		3	5		1	7	
1993	8	8		3	5		5	3	
1994	6	10		4	4		2	6	
1995	3	13		2	6		1	7	
1996	1	15		0	8		1	7	
1997	9	7		5	3		4	4	
1998	12	4		7	1		5	3	
1999	8	8		4	4		4	4	
2000	9	7		5	3		4	4	
2001	10	6		3	5		7	1	
2002	9	7		5	3		4	4	
2003	6	10		4	4		2	6	
2004	10	6		6	2		4	4	
2005	4	12		4	4		0	8	
2006	10	6		4	4		6	2	
	318	382	8	174	174	5	144	208	3

*includes New York Titans (1960-62).

OAKLAND RAIDERS*

Season	All Games W	L	T	Home Games W	L	T	Road Games W	L	T
1960	6	8		3	4		3	4	
1961	2	12		1	6		1	6	
1962	1	13		1	6		0	7	
1963	10	4		6	1		4	3	
1964	5	7	2	5	2		0	5	2
1965	8	5	1	5	2		3	3	1
1966	8	5	1	3	3	1	5	2	
1967	13	1		7	0		6	1	
1968	12	2		6	1		6	1	
1969	12	1	1	7	0		5	1	1
1970	8	4	2	6	1		2	3	2
1971	8	4	2	5	1	1	3	3	1
1972	10	3	1	5	1	1	5	2	
1973	9	4	1	5	2		4	2	1
1974	12	2		6	1		6	1	
1975	11	3		6	1		5	2	
1976	13	1		7	0		6	1	
1977	11	3		6	1		5	2	
1978	9	7		4	4		5	3	
1979	9	7		6	2		3	5	
1980	11	5		6	2		5	3	
1981	7	9		4	4		3	5	
1982	8	1		4	0		4	1	
1983	12	4		6	2		6	2	
1984	11	5		6	2		5	3	
1985	12	4		7	1		5	3	
1986	8	8		3	5		5	3	
1987	5	10		3	5		2	5	
1988	7	9		3	5		4	4	

Season	All Games W	L	T	Home Games W	L	T	Road Games W	L	T
1989	8	8		7	1		1	7	
1990	12	4		6	2		6	2	
1991	9	7		5	3		4	4	
1992	7	9		5	3		2	6	
1993	10	6		5	3		5	3	
1994	9	7		4	4		5	3	
1995	8	8		4	4		4	4	
1996	7	9		4	4		3	5	
1997	4	12		2	6		2	6	
1998	8	8		4	4		4	4	
1999	8	8		5	3		3	5	
2000	12	4		7	1		5	3	
2001	10	6		5	3		5	3	
2002	11	5		6	2		5	3	
2003	4	12		4	4		0	8	
2004	5	11		3	5		2	6	
2005	4	12		2	6		2	6	
2006	2	14		2	6		0	8	
	396	301	11	222	129	3	174	172	8

*includes Los Angeles Raiders (1982-1994).

PITTSBURGH STEELERS*

Season	All Games W	L	T	Home Games W	L	T	Road Games W	L	T
1933	3	6	2	2	3		1	3	2
1934	2	10		1	5		1	5	
1935	4	8		2	5		2	3	
1936	6	6		4	1		2	5	
1937	4	7		2	4		2	3	
1938	2	9		0	5		2	4	
1939	1	9	1	1	4		0	5	1
1940	2	7	2	1	2	2	1	5	
1941	1	9	1	1	4		0	5	1
1942	7	4		3	2		4	2	
1945	2	8		1	4		1	4	
1946	5	5	1	4	1		1	4	1
1947	8	4		5	1		3	3	
1948	4	8		4	2		0	6	
1949	6	5	1	3	2	1	3	3	
1950	6	6		2	4		4	2	
1951	4	7	1	1	4	1	3	3	
1952	5	7		2	4		3	3	
1953	6	6		3	3		3	3	
1954	5	7		4	2		1	5	
1955	4	8		3	2		1	6	
1956	5	7		3	3		2	4	
1957	6	6		4	2		2	4	
1958	7	4	1	5	1		2	3	1
1959	6	5	1	3	2	1	3	3	
1960	5	6	1	4	2		1	4	1
1961	6	8		4	3		2	5	
1962	9	5		4	3		5	2	
1963	7	4	3	5	0	2	2	4	1
1964	5	9		2	5		3	4	
1965	2	12		1	6		1	6	
1966	5	8	1	3	3	1	2	5	
1967	4	9	1	1	6		3	3	1
1968	2	11	1	1	6		1	5	1
1969	1	13		1	6		0	7	
1970	5	9		4	3		1	6	
1971	6	8		5	2		1	6	
1972	11	3		7	0		4	3	
1973	10	4		7	1		3	3	
1974	10	3	1	5	2		5	1	1
1975	12	2		6	1		6	1	
1976	10	4		6	1		4	3	
1977	9	5		6	1		3	4	
1978	14	2		7	1		7	1	
1979	12	4		8	0		4	4	
1980	9	7		6	2		3	5	
1981	8	8		5	3		3	5	
1982	6	3		4	0		2	3	
1983	10	6		4	4		6	2	
1984	9	7		6	2		3	5	
1985	7	9		5	3		2	6	
1986	6	10		4	4		2	6	
1987	8	7		4	3		4	4	
1988	5	11		4	4		1	7	
1989	9	7		4	4		5	3	
1990	9	7		6	2		3	5	
1991	7	9		5	3		2	6	
1992	11	5		7	1		4	4	
1993	9	7		6	2		3	5	
1994	12	4		7	1		5	3	
1995	11	5		6	2		5	3	
1996	10	6		7	1		3	5	
1997	11	5		7	1		4	4	
1998	7	9		5	3		2	6	
1999	6	10		2	6		4	4	
2000	9	7		4	4		5	3	
2001	13	3		7	1		6	2	
2002	10	5	1	5	2	1	5	3	
2003	6	10		4	4		2	6	
2004	15	1		8	0		7	1	
2005	11	5		5	3		6	2	
2006	8	8		5	3		3	5	
	498	478	20	293	192	9	205	286	11

*includes Pittsburgh Pirates (1933-1940).

SAN DIEGO CHARGERS*

Season	All Games W	L	T	Home Games W	L	T	Road Games W	L	T
1960	10	4		5	2		5	2	
1961	12	2		6	1		6	1	
1962	4	10		3	4		1	6	
1963	11	3		6	1		5	2	
1964	8	5	1	4	3		4	2	1
1965	9	2	3	4	1	2	5	1	1
1966	7	6	1	5	2		2	4	1
1967	8	5	1	5	2	1	3	3	
1968	9	5		4	3		5	2	
1969	8	6		5	2		3	4	
1970	5	6	3	2	3	2	3	3	1
1971	6	8		6	1		0	7	
1972	4	9	1	2	5		2	4	1
1973	2	11	1	2	5		0	6	1
1974	5	9		3	4		2	5	
1975	2	12		1	6		1	6	
1976	6	8		3	4		3	4	
1977	7	7		3	4		4	3	
1978	9	7		5	3		4	4	
1979	12	4		7	1		5	3	
1980	11	5		6	2		5	3	
1981	10	6		5	3		5	3	
1982	6	3		3	1		3	2	
1983	6	10		4	4		2	6	
1984	7	9		4	4		3	5	
1985	8	8		6	2		2	6	
1986	4	12		2	6		2	6	
1987	8	7		4	3		4	4	
1988	6	10		3	5		3	5	
1989	6	10		4	4		2	6	
1990	6	10		3	5		3	5	
1991	4	12		3	5		1	7	
1992	11	5		6	2		5	3	
1993	8	8		4	4		4	4	

Season	All Games W	L	T	Home Games W	L	T	Road Games W	L	T
1994	11	5		5	3		6	2	
1995	9	7		5	3		4	4	
1996	8	8		5	3		3	5	
1997	4	12		2	6		2	6	
1998	5	11		4	4		1	7	
1999	8	8		4	4		4	4	
2000	1	15		1	7		0	8	
2001	5	11		4	4		1	7	
2002	8	8		5	3		3	5	
2003	4	12		2	6		2	6	
2004	12	4		7	1		5	3	
2005	9	7		4	4		5	3	
2006	14	2		8	0		6	2	
	343	354	11	194	155	5	149	199	6

*includes Los Angeles Chargers (1960).

TENNESSEE TITANS*

Season	All Games W	L	T	Home Games W	L	T	Road Games W	L	T
1960	10	4		6	1		4	3	
1961	10	3	1	6	1		4	2	1
1962	11	3		6	1		5	2	
1963	6	8		4	3		2	5	
1964	4	10		3	4		1	6	
1965	4	10		3	4		1	6	
1966	3	11		3	4		0	7	
1967	9	4	1	5	2		4	2	1
1968	7	7		3	4		4	3	
1969	6	6	2	4	2	1	2	4	1
1970	3	10	1	1	6		2	4	1
1971	4	9	1	3	3	1	1	6	
1972	1	13		1	6		0	7	
1973	1	13		0	7		1	6	
1974	7	7		3	4		4	3	
1975	10	4		5	2		5	2	
1976	5	9		3	4		2	5	
1977	8	6		5	2		3	4	
1978	10	6		5	3		5	3	
1979	11	5		6	2		5	3	
1980	11	5		6	2		5	3	
1981	7	9		5	3		2	6	
1982	1	8		1	4		0	4	
1983	2	14		2	6		0	8	
1984	3	13		2	6		1	7	
1985	5	11		4	4		1	7	
1986	5	11		4	4		1	7	
1987	9	6		5	2		4	4	
1988	10	6		7	1		3	5	
1989	9	7		6	2		3	5	
1990	9	7		6	2		3	5	
1991	11	5		7	1		4	4	
1992	10	6		5	3		5	3	
1993	12	4		7	1		5	3	
1994	2	14		2	6		0	8	
1995	7	9		3	5		4	4	
1996	8	8		2	6		6	2	
1997	8	8		6	2		2	6	
1998	8	8		3	5		5	3	
1999	13	3		8	0		5	3	
2000	13	3		7	1		6	2	
2001	7	9		3	5		4	4	
2002	11	5		6	2		5	3	
2003	12	4		7	1		5	3	
2004	5	11		2	6		3	5	
2005	4	12		3	5		1	7	
2006	8	8		4	4		4	4	
	340	362	6	198	154	2	142	208	4

*includes Houston (1960-1996) and Tennessee Oilers (1997-98).

NFC

ARIZONA CARDINALS*

Season	All Games W	L	T	Home Games W	L	T	Road Games W	L	T
1920	6	2	2	5	1	1	1	1	1
1921	3	3	2	3	3	1	0	0	1
1922	8	3		8	3		0	0	
1923	8	4		8	3		0	1	
1924	5	4	1	5	3	1	0	1	
1925	11	2	1	11	2		0	0	1
1926	5	6	1	3	3		2	3	1
1927	3	7	1	2	3	1	1	4	
1928	1	5		1	1		0	4	
1929	6	6	1	3	2		3	4	1
1930	5	6	2	3	2		2	4	2
1931	5	4		3	0		2	4	
1932	2	6	2	1	2	1	1	4	1
1933	1	9	1	0	4	1	1	5	
1934	5	6		2	2		3	4	
1935	6	4	2	2	2		4	2	2
1936	3	8	1	3	1	1	0	7	
1937	5	5	1	1	3		4	2	1
1938	2	9		1	4		1	5	
1939	1	10		0	4		1	6	
1940	2	7	2	2	1	1	0	6	1
1941	3	7	1	0	3	1	3	4	
1942	3	8		2	2		1	6	
1943	0	10		0	3		0	7	
1945	1	9		0	3		1	6	
1946	6	5		2	2		4	3	
1947	9	3		5	0		4	3	
1948	11	1		5	1		6	0	
1949	6	5	1	2	3	1	4	2	
1950	5	7		3	3		2	4	
1951	3	9		1	5		2	4	
1952	4	8		2	4		2	4	
1953	1	10	1	0	5	1	1	5	
1954	2	10		2	4		0	6	
1955	4	7	1	3	2	1	1	5	
1956	7	5		4	2		3	3	
1957	3	9		0	6		3	3	
1958	2	9	1	1	4	1	1	5	
1959	2	10		2	4		0	6	
1960	6	5	1	3	2	1	3	3	
1961	7	7		3	4		4	3	
1962	4	9	1	2	4	1	2	5	
1963	9	5		3	4		6	1	
1964	9	3	2	4	1	1	5	2	1
1965	5	9		2	5		3	4	
1966	8	5	1	5	1	1	3	4	
1967	6	7	1	3	3	1	3	4	
1968	9	4	1	4	2	1	5	2	
1969	4	9	1	3	4		1	5	1
1970	8	5	1	6	1		2	4	1
1971	4	9	1	1	5	1	3	4	
1972	4	9	1	2	5		2	4	1
1973	4	9	1	2	4	1	2	5	
1974	10	4		5	2		5	2	
1975	11	3		6	1		5	2	
1976	10	4		6	1		4	3	
1977	7	7		4	3		3	4	
1978	6	10		3	5		3	5	
1979	5	11		3	5		2	6	
1980	5	11		2	6		3	5	
1981	7	9		5	3		2	6	
1982	5	4		1	3		4	1	
1983	8	7	1	4	3	1	4	4	
1984	9	7		5	3		4	4	
1985	5	11		4	4		1	7	
1986	4	11	1	3	5		1	6	1

Season	All Games W	L	T	Home Games W	L	T	Road Games W	L	T
1987	7	8		4	3		3	5	
1988	7	9		4	4		3	5	
1989	5	11		2	6		3	5	
1990	5	11		3	5		2	6	
1991	4	12		2	6		2	6	
1992	4	12		3	5		1	7	
1993	7	9		4	4		3	5	
1994	8	8		5	3		3	5	
1995	4	12		3	5		1	7	
1996	7	9		5	3		2	6	
1997	4	12		3	5		1	7	
1998	9	7		5	3		4	4	
1999	6	10		4	4		2	6	
2000	3	13		3	5		0	8	
2001	7	9		3	5		4	4	
2002	5	11		3	5		2	6	
2003	4	12		4	4		0	8	
2004	6	10		5	3		1	7	
2005	5	11		3	5		2	6	
2006	5	11		3	5		2	6	
	456	649	39	266	282	22	190	367	17

*includes Chicago Cardinals (1920-1959), St. Louis Cardinals (1960-1987), and Phoenix Cardinals (1988-1993).

ATLANTA FALCONS

Season	All Games W	L	T	Home Games W	L	T	Road Games W	L	T
1966	3	11		1	6		2	5	
1967	1	12	1	1	5	1	0	7	
1968	2	12		1	6		1	6	
1969	6	8		4	3		2	5	
1970	4	8	2	3	4		1	4	2
1971	7	6	1	4	3		3	3	1
1972	7	7		4	3		3	4	
1973	9	5		4	3		5	2	
1974	3	11		2	5		1	6	
1975	4	10		3	4		1	6	
1976	4	10		3	4		1	6	
1977	7	7		4	3		3	4	
1978	9	7		7	1		2	6	
1979	6	10		3	5		3	5	
1980	12	4		6	2		6	2	
1981	7	9		4	4		3	5	
1982	5	4		2	3		3	1	
1983	7	9		4	4		3	5	
1984	4	12		2	6		2	6	
1985	4	12		3	5		1	7	
1986	7	8	1	2	5	1	5	3	
1987	3	12		2	6		1	6	
1988	5	11		2	6		3	5	
1989	3	13		3	5		0	8	
1990	5	11		5	3		0	8	
1991	10	6		6	2		4	4	
1992	6	10		5	3		1	7	
1993	6	10		4	4		2	6	
1994	7	9		5	3		2	6	
1995	9	7		7	1		2	6	
1996	3	13		2	6		1	7	
1997	7	9		3	5		4	4	
1998	14	2		8	0		6	2	
1999	5	11		4	4		1	7	
2000	4	12		3	5		1	7	
2001	7	9		3	5		4	4	
2002	9	6	1	5	3		4	3	1
2003	5	11		2	6		3	5	
2004	11	5		7	1		4	4	
2005	8	8		4	4		4	4	

Season	All Games W	L	T	Home Games W	L	T	Road Games W	L	T
2006	7	9		3	5		4	4	
	252	366	6	150	161	2	102	205	4

CAROLINA PANTHERS

Season	All Games W	L	T	Home Games W	L	T	Road Games W	L	T
1995	7	9		5	3		2	6	
1996	12	4		8	0		4	4	
1997	7	9		2	6		5	3	
1998	4	12		2	6		2	6	
1999	8	8		5	3		3	5	
2000	7	9		5	3		2	6	
2001	1	15		0	8		1	7	
2002	7	9		4	4		3	5	
2003	11	5		6	2		5	3	
2004	7	9		3	5		4	4	
2005	11	5		5	3		6	2	
2006	8	8		4	4		4	4	
	90	102		49	47		41	55	

CHICAGO BEARS*

Season	All Games W	L	T	Home Games W	L	T	Road Games W	L	T
1920	10	1	2	6	0	1	4	1	1
1921	9	1	1	9	1	1	0	0	
1922	9	3		7	1		2	2	
1923	9	2	1	7	1	1	2	1	
1924	6	1	4	5	0	3	1	1	1
1925	9	5	3	7	1	1	2	4	2
1926	12	1	3	10	0	2	2	1	1
1927	9	3	2	7	1	1	2	2	1
1928	7	5	1	6	3		1	2	1
1929	4	9	2	1	5	2	3	4	
1930	9	4	1	5	2	1	4	2	
1931	8	5		6	3		2	2	
1932	7	1	6	6	1	1	1	0	5
1933	10	2	1	6	0		4	2	1
1934	13	0		5	0		8	0	
1935	6	4	2	1	2	2	5	2	
1936	9	3		3	1		6	2	
1937	9	1	1	4	1		5	0	1
1938	6	5		2	3		4	2	
1939	8	3		4	1		4	2	
1940	8	3		5	0		3	3	
1941	10	1		5	1		5	0	
1942	11	0		6	0		5	0	
1943	8	1	1	5	0		3	1	1
1944	6	3	1	4	0	1	2	3	
1945	3	7		2	3		1	4	
1946	8	2	1	4	1	1	4	1	
1947	8	4		4	2		4	2	
1948	10	2		5	1		5	1	
1949	9	3		5	1		4	2	
1950	9	3		6	0		3	3	
1951	7	5		3	3		4	2	
1952	5	7		3	3		2	4	
1953	3	8	1	1	4	1	2	4	
1954	8	4		4	2		4	2	
1955	8	4		5	1		3	3	
1956	9	2	1	6	0		3	2	1
1957	5	7		2	4		3	3	
1958	8	4		5	1		3	3	
1959	8	4		4	2		4	2	
1960	5	6	1	4	2		1	4	1
1961	8	6		5	2		3	4	
1962	9	5		4	3		5	2	
1963	11	1	2	6	0	1	5	1	1
1964	5	9		2	5		3	4	

Season	All Games W	L	T	Home Games W	L	T	Road Games W	L	T
1965	9	5		5	2		4	3	
1966	5	7	2	4	1	2	1	6	
1967	7	6	1	3	3	1	4	3	
1968	7	7		2	5		5	2	
1969	1	13		1	6		0	7	
1970	6	8		3	4		3	4	
1971	6	8		4	3		2	5	
1972	4	9	1	1	5	1	3	4	
1973	3	11		1	6		2	5	
1974	4	10		4	3		0	7	
1975	4	10		3	4		1	6	
1976	7	7		4	3		3	4	
1977	9	5		5	2		4	3	
1978	7	9		4	4		3	5	
1979	10	6		6	2		4	4	
1980	7	9		5	3		2	6	
1981	6	10		4	4		2	6	
1982	3	6		2	2		1	4	
1983	8	8		5	3		3	5	
1984	10	6		6	2		4	4	
1985	15	1		8	0		7	1	
1986	14	2		7	1		7	1	
1987	11	4		6	2		5	2	
1988	12	4		7	1		5	3	
1989	6	10		4	4		2	6	
1990	11	5		7	1		4	4	
1991	11	5		6	2		5	3	
1992	5	11		4	4		1	7	
1993	7	9		3	5		4	4	
1994	9	7		5	3		4	4	
1995	9	7		5	3		4	4	
1996	7	9		6	2		1	7	
1997	4	12		2	6		2	6	
1998	4	12		3	5		1	7	
1999	6	10		3	5		3	5	
2000	5	11		3	5		2	6	
2001	13	3		7	1		6	2	
2002	4	12		3	5		1	7	
2003	7	9		6	2		1	7	
2004	5	11		2	6		3	5	
2005	11	5		7	1		4	4	
2006	13	3		6	2		7	1	
	670	482	42	394	201	24	276	281	18

*includes Decatur Staleys (1920) and Chicago Staleys (1921).

DALLAS COWBOYS

Season	All Games W	L	T	Home Games W	L	T	Road Games W	L	T
1960	0	11	1	0	6		0	5	1
1961	4	9	1	2	4	1	2	5	
1962	5	8	1	2	4	1	3	4	
1963	4	10		3	4		1	6	
1964	5	8	1	2	4	1	3	4	
1965	7	7		5	2		2	5	
1966	10	3	1	6	1		4	2	1
1967	9	5		5	2		4	3	
1968	12	2		5	2		7	0	
1969	11	2	1	6	0	1	5	2	
1970	10	4		6	1		4	3	
1971	11	3		6	1		5	2	
1972	10	4		5	2		5	2	
1973	10	4		6	1		4	3	
1974	8	6		5	2		3	4	
1975	10	4		5	2		5	2	
1976	11	3		6	1		5	2	
1977	12	2		6	1		6	1	
1978	12	4		7	1		5	3	
1979	11	5		6	2		5	3	

Season	All Games W	L	T	Home Games W	L	T	Road Games W	L	T
1980	12	4		8	0		4	4	
1981	12	4		8	0		4	4	
1982	6	3		3	2		3	1	
1983	12	4		6	2		6	2	
1984	9	7		5	3		4	4	
1985	10	6		7	1		3	5	
1986	7	9		3	5		4	4	
1987	7	8		3	4		4	4	
1988	3	13		1	7		2	6	
1989	1	15		0	8		1	7	
1990	7	9		5	3		2	6	
1991	11	5		6	2		5	3	
1992	13	3		7	1		6	2	
1993	12	4		6	2		6	2	
1994	12	4		6	2		6	2	
1995	12	4		6	2		6	2	
1996	10	6		6	2		4	4	
1997	6	10		5	3		1	7	
1998	10	6		6	2		4	4	
1999	8	8		7	1		1	7	
2000	5	11		3	5		2	6	
2001	5	11		4	4		1	7	
2002	5	11		4	4		1	7	
2003	10	6		6	2		4	4	
2004	6	10		4	4		2	6	
2005	9	7		5	3		4	4	
2006	9	7		4	4		5	3	
	401	299	6	228	121	4	173	178	2

DETROIT LIONS*

Season	All Games W	L	T	Home Games W	L	T	Road Games W	L	T
1930	5	6	3	5	1	2	0	5	1
1931	11	3		8	0		3	3	
1932	6	2	4	3	0	2	3	2	2
1933	6	5		4	1		2	4	
1934	10	3		6	2		4	1	
1935	7	3	2	5	0	1	2	3	1
1936	8	4		5	1		3	3	
1937	7	4		4	2		3	2	
1938	7	4		4	3		3	1	
1939	6	5		4	2		2	3	
1940	5	5	1	3	3		2	2	1
1941	4	6	1	3	2		1	4	1
1942	0	11		0	7		0	4	
1943	3	6	1	2	2	1	1	4	
1944	6	3	1	4	2		2	1	1
1945	7	3		4	1		3	2	
1946	1	10		1	5		0	5	
1947	3	9		2	4		1	5	
1948	2	10		2	4		0	6	
1949	4	8		2	4		2	4	
1950	6	6		4	2		2	4	
1951	7	4	1	3	3	1	4	1	
1952	9	3		6	1		3	2	
1953	10	2		5	1		5	1	
1954	9	2	1	5	0	1	4	2	
1955	3	9		3	4		0	5	
1956	9	3		5	1		4	2	
1957	8	4		5	1		3	3	
1958	4	7	1	2	4		2	3	1
1959	3	8	1	2	4		1	4	1
1960	7	5		5	1		2	4	
1961	8	5	1	2	5		6	0	1
1962	11	3		7	0		4	3	
1963	5	8	1	3	3	1	2	5	
1964	7	5	2	3	3	1	4	2	1
1965	6	7	1	2	4	1	4	3	

Season	All Games W	L	T	Home Games W	L	T	Road Games W	L	T
1966	4	9	1	3	4		1	5	1
1967	5	7	2	3	4		2	3	2
1968	4	8	2	1	4	2	3	4	
1969	9	4	1	5	2		4	2	1
1970	10	4		6	1		4	3	
1971	7	6	1	3	4		4	2	1
1972	8	5	1	5	2		3	3	1
1973	6	7	1	4	3		2	4	1
1974	7	7		5	2		2	5	
1975	7	7		4	3		3	4	
1976	6	8		5	2		1	6	
1977	6	8		5	2		1	6	
1978	7	9		5	3		2	6	
1979	2	14		2	6		0	8	
1980	9	7		6	2		3	5	
1981	8	8		7	1		1	7	
1982	4	5		2	3		2	2	
1983	9	7		6	2		3	5	
1984	4	11	1	2	5	1	2	6	
1985	7	9		6	2		1	7	
1986	5	11		1	7		4	4	
1987	4	11		1	6		3	5	
1988	4	12		2	6		2	6	
1989	7	9		4	4		3	5	
1990	6	10		3	5		3	5	
1991	12	4		8	0		4	4	
1992	5	11		3	5		2	6	
1993	10	6		5	3		5	3	
1994	9	7		6	2		3	5	
1995	10	6		7	1		3	5	
1996	5	11		4	4		1	7	
1997	9	7		6	2		3	5	
1998	5	11		4	4		1	7	
1999	8	8		6	2		2	6	
2000	9	7		4	4		5	3	
2001	2	14		2	6		0	8	
2002	3	13		3	5		0	8	
2003	5	11		5	3		0	8	
2004	6	10		3	5		3	5	
2005	5	11		3	5		2	6	
2006	3	13		2	6		1	7	
	481	544	32	300	225	14	181	319	18

*includes Portsmouth Spartans (1930-33).

GREEN BAY PACKERS

Season	All Games W	L	T	Home Games W	L	T	Road Games W	L	T
1921	3	2	1	2	1		1	1	1
1922	4	3	3	4	1	1	0	2	2
1923	7	2	1	4	2	1	3	0	
1924	7	4		5	0		2	4	
1925	8	5		6	0		2	5	
1926	7	3	3	4	1	2	3	2	1
1927	7	2	1	6	1		1	1	1
1928	6	4	3	2	2	2	4	2	1
1929	12	0	1	5	0		7	0	1
1930	10	3	1	6	0		4	3	1
1931	12	2		8	0		4	2	
1932	10	3	1	5	0	1	5	3	
1933	5	7	1	3	2	1	2	5	
1934	7	6		4	2		3	4	
1935	8	4		5	2		3	2	
1936	10	1	1	5	1		5	0	1
1937	7	4		3	2		4	2	
1938	8	3		4	2		4	1	
1939	9	2		4	1		5	1	
1940	6	4	1	4	2		2	2	1
1941	10	1		4	1		6	0	
1942	8	2	1	4	1		4	1	1
1943	7	2	1	2	1	1	5	1	
1944	8	2		5	0		3	2	
1945	6	4		4	1		2	3	
1946	6	5		2	3		4	2	
1947	6	5	1	4	2		2	3	1
1948	3	9		2	4		1	5	
1949	2	10		1	5		1	5	
1950	3	9		3	3		0	6	
1951	3	9		2	4		1	5	
1952	6	6		3	3		3	3	
1953	2	9	1	1	5		1	4	1
1954	4	8		2	4		2	4	
1955	6	6		5	1		1	5	
1956	4	8		2	4		2	4	
1957	3	9		1	5		2	4	
1958	1	10	1	1	4	1	0	6	
1959	7	5		4	2		3	3	
1960	8	4		4	2		4	2	
1961	11	3		6	1		5	2	
1962	13	1		7	0		6	1	
1963	11	2	1	6	1		5	1	1
1964	8	5	1	4	3		4	2	1
1965	10	3	1	6	1		4	2	1
1966	12	2		6	1		6	1	
1967	9	4	1	4	2	1	5	2	
1968	6	7	1	2	5		4	2	1
1969	8	6		5	2		3	4	
1970	6	8		4	3		2	5	
1971	4	8	2	3	3	1	1	5	1
1972	10	4		4	3		6	1	
1973	5	7	2	3	2	2	2	5	
1974	6	8		4	3		2	5	
1975	4	10		3	4		1	6	
1976	5	9		4	3		1	6	
1977	4	10		2	5		2	5	
1978	8	7	1	5	2	1	3	5	
1979	5	11		4	4		1	7	
1980	5	10	1	4	4		1	6	1
1981	8	8		4	4		4	4	
1982	5	3	1	3	1		2	2	1
1983	8	8		5	3		3	5	
1984	8	8		5	3		3	5	
1985	8	8		5	3		3	5	
1986	4	12		1	7		3	5	
1987	5	9	1	2	5	1	3	4	
1988	4	12		2	6		2	6	
1989	10	6		6	2		4	4	
1990	6	10		3	5		3	5	
1991	4	12		2	6		2	6	
1992	9	7		6	2		3	5	
1993	9	7		6	2		3	5	
1994	9	7		7	1		2	6	
1995	11	5		7	1		4	4	
1996	13	3		8	0		5	3	
1997	13	3		8	0		5	3	
1998	11	5		7	1		4	4	
1999	8	8		5	3		3	5	
2000	9	7		6	2		3	5	
2001	12	4		7	1		5	3	
2002	12	4		8	0		4	4	
2003	10	6		5	3		5	3	
2004	10	6		4	4		6	2	
2005	4	12		3	5		1	7	
2006	8	8		3	5		5	3	
	624	500	36	359	204	16	265	296	20

MINNESOTA VIKINGS

Season	All Games W	L	T	Home Games W	L	T	Road Games W	L	T
1961	3	11		3	4		0	7	
1962	2	11	1	1	5	1	1	6	
1963	5	8	1	3	4		2	4	1
1964	8	5	1	4	3		4	2	1
1965	7	7		2	5		5	2	
1966	4	9	1	2	5		2	4	1
1967	3	8	3	1	4	2	2	4	1
1968	8	6		4	3		4	3	
1969	12	2		7	0		5	2	
1970	12	2		7	0		5	2	
1971	11	3		5	2		6	1	
1972	7	7		3	4		4	3	
1973	12	2		7	0		5	2	
1974	10	4		4	3		6	1	
1975	12	2		7	0		5	2	
1976	11	2	1	6	0	1	5	2	
1977	9	5		5	2		4	3	
1978	8	7	1	5	3		3	4	1
1979	7	9		5	3		2	6	
1980	9	7		5	3		4	4	
1981	7	9		5	3		2	6	
1982	5	4		4	1		1	3	
1983	8	8		3	5		5	3	
1984	3	13		2	6		1	7	
1985	7	9		4	4		3	5	
1986	9	7		5	3		4	4	
1987	8	7		5	3		3	4	
1988	11	5		7	1		4	4	
1989	10	6		8	0		2	6	
1990	6	10		4	4		2	6	
1991	8	8		4	4		4	4	
1992	11	5		5	3		6	2	
1993	9	7		4	4		5	3	
1994	10	6		6	2		4	4	
1995	8	8		6	2		2	6	
1996	9	7		5	3		4	4	
1997	9	7		5	3		4	4	
1998	15	1		8	0		7	1	
1999	10	6		6	2		4	4	
2000	11	5		7	1		4	4	
2001	5	11		5	3		0	8	
2002	6	10		4	4		2	6	
2003	9	7		6	2		3	5	
2004	8	8		5	3		3	5	
2005	9	7		6	2		3	5	
2006	6	10		3	5		3	5	
	377	308	9	218	126	4	159	182	5

NEW ORLEANS SAINTS

Season	All Games W	L	T	Home Games W	L	T	Road Games W	L	T
1967	3	11		2	5		1	6	
1968	4	9	1	3	4		1	5	1
1969	5	9		3	4		2	5	
1970	2	11	1	2	5		0	6	1
1971	4	8	2	2	4	1	2	4	1
1972	2	11	1	2	5		0	6	1
1973	5	9		5	2		0	7	
1974	5	9		4	3		1	6	
1975	2	12		2	5		0	7	
1976	4	10		2	5		2	5	
1977	3	11		2	5		1	6	
1978	7	9		3	5		4	4	
1979	8	8		3	5		5	3	
1980	1	15		0	8		1	7	
1981	4	12		2	6		2	6	
1982	4	5		2	3		2	2	

Season	All Games W	L	T	Home Games W	L	T	Road Games W	L	T
1983	8	8		5	3		3	5	
1984	7	9		3	5		4	4	
1985	5	11		3	5		2	6	
1986	7	9		4	4		3	5	
1987	12	3		6	1		6	2	
1988	10	6		5	3		5	3	
1989	9	7		5	3		4	4	
1990	8	8		5	3		3	5	
1991	11	5		6	2		5	3	
1992	12	4		6	2		6	2	
1993	8	8		4	4		4	4	
1994	7	9		3	5		4	4	
1995	7	9		4	4		3	5	
1996	3	13		2	6		1	7	
1997	6	10		3	5		3	5	
1998	6	10		4	4		2	6	
1999	3	13		3	5		0	8	
2000	10	6		3	5		7	1	
2001	7	9		3	5		4	4	
2002	9	7		4	4		5	3	
2003	8	8		5	3		3	5	
2004	8	8		3	5		5	3	
2005	3	13		1	7		2	6	
2006	10	6		4	4		6	2	
	247	358	5	133	171	1	114	187	4

NEW YORK GIANTS

Season	All Games W	L	T	Home Games W	L	T	Road Games W	L	T
1925	8	4		7	2		1	2	
1926	8	4	1	5	2	1	3	2	
1927	11	1	1	7	1		4	0	1
1928	4	7	2	1	2	2	3	5	
1929	13	1	1	7	1		6	0	1
1930	13	4		6	2		7	2	
1931	7	6	1	4	2	1	3	4	
1932	4	6	2	3	2	1	1	4	1
1933	11	3		7	0		4	3	
1934	8	5		5	1		3	4	
1935	9	3		4	2		5	1	
1936	5	6	1	3	3	1	2	3	
1937	6	3	2	4	2	1	2	1	1
1938	8	2	1	6	1		2	1	1
1939	9	1	1	6	0		3	1	1
1940	6	4	1	4	3		2	1	1
1941	8	3		5	2		3	1	
1942	5	5	1	3	2	1	2	3	
1943	6	3	1	4	2		2	1	1
1944	8	1	1	5	1		3	0	1
1945	3	6	1	2	4		1	2	1
1946	7	3	1	5	1	1	2	2	
1947	2	8	2	2	3	1	0	5	1
1948	4	8		2	4		2	4	
1949	6	6		2	4		4	2	
1950	10	2		5	1		5	1	
1951	9	2	1	5	1		4	1	1
1952	7	5		2	4		5	1	
1953	3	9		2	4		1	5	
1954	7	5		4	2		3	3	
1955	6	5	1	4	1	1	2	4	
1956	8	3	1	4	1	1	4	2	
1957	7	5		3	3		4	2	
1958	9	3		5	1		4	2	
1959	10	2		5	1		5	1	
1960	6	4	2	1	3	2	5	1	
1961	10	3	1	4	2	1	6	1	
1962	12	2		6	1		6	1	
1963	11	3		5	2		6	1	

Season	All Games W	L	T	Home Games W	L	T	Road Games W	L	T
1964	2	10	2	2	5		0	5	2
1965	7	7		3	4		4	3	
1966	1	12	1	1	6		0	6	1
1967	7	7		5	2		2	5	
1968	7	7		3	4		4	3	
1969	6	8		5	2		1	6	
1970	9	5		5	2		4	3	
1971	4	10		1	6		3	4	
1972	8	6		4	3		4	3	
1973	2	11	1	2	4	1	0	7	
1974	2	12		0	7		2	5	
1975	5	9		2	5		3	4	
1976	3	11		3	4		0	7	
1977	5	9		3	4		2	5	
1978	6	10		5	3		1	7	
1979	6	10		4	4		2	6	
1980	4	12		2	6		2	6	
1981	9	7		4	4		5	3	
1982	4	5		2	3		2	2	
1983	3	12	1	1	7		2	5	1
1984	9	7		6	2		3	5	
1985	10	6		6	2		4	4	
1986	14	2		8	0		6	2	
1987	6	9		5	3		1	6	
1988	10	6		5	3		5	3	
1989	12	4		7	1		5	3	
1990	13	3		7	1		6	2	
1991	8	8		5	3		3	5	
1992	6	10		4	4		2	6	
1993	11	5		6	2		5	3	
1994	9	7		4	4		5	3	
1995	5	11		3	5		2	6	
1996	6	10		3	5		3	5	
1997	10	5	1	6	2		4	3	1
1998	8	8		5	3		3	5	
1999	7	9		4	4		3	5	
2000	12	4		5	3		7	1	
2001	7	9		5	3		2	6	
2002	10	6		5	3		5	3	
2003	4	12		1	7		3	5	
2004	6	10		3	5		3	5	
2005	11	5		7	1		4	4	
2006	8	8		3	5		5	3	
	596	500	33	334	232	16	262	268	17

PHILADELPHIA EAGLES

Season	All Games W	L	T	Home Games W	L	T	Road Games W	L	T
1933	3	5	1	2	3	1	1	2	
1934	4	7		2	4		2	3	
1935	2	9		0	5		2	4	
1936	1	11		1	6		0	5	
1937	2	8	1	0	5	1	2	3	
1938	5	6		2	3		3	3	
1939	1	9	1	1	3	1	0	6	
1940	1	10		1	4		0	6	
1941	2	8	1	1	4	1	1	4	
1942	2	9		0	5		2	4	
1944	7	1	2	3	1	2	4	0	
1945	7	3		6	0		1	3	
1946	6	5		3	2		3	3	
1947	8	4		6	1		2	3	
1948	9	2	1	6	0		3	2	1
1949	11	1		6	0		5	1	
1950	6	6		2	4		4	2	
1951	4	8		1	5		3	3	
1952	7	5		4	2		3	3	
1953	7	4	1	5	0	1	2	4	

Season	All Games W	L	T	Home Games W	L	T	Road Games W	L	T
1954	7	4	1	5	1		2	3	1
1955	4	7	1	4	2		0	5	1
1956	3	8	1	2	3	1	1	5	
1957	4	8		3	3		1	5	
1958	2	9	1	2	4		0	5	1
1959	7	5		5	1		2	4	
1960	10	2		5	1		5	1	
1961	10	4		5	2		5	2	
1962	3	10	1	2	5		1	5	1
1963	2	10	2	1	5	1	1	5	1
1964	6	8		3	4		3	4	
1965	5	9		2	5		3	4	
1966	9	5		5	2		4	3	
1967	6	7	1	5	2		1	5	1
1968	2	12		1	6		1	6	
1969	4	9	1	2	5		2	4	1
1970	3	10	1	3	3	1	0	7	
1971	6	7	1	3	4		3	3	1
1972	2	11	1	0	6	1	2	5	
1973	5	8	1	4	3		1	5	1
1974	7	7		5	2		2	5	
1975	4	10		2	5		2	5	
1976	4	10		2	5		2	5	
1977	5	9		4	3		1	6	
1978	9	7		5	3		4	4	
1979	11	5		5	3		6	2	
1980	12	4		7	1		5	3	
1981	10	6		6	2		4	4	
1982	3	6		1	4		2	2	
1983	5	11		1	7		4	4	
1984	6	9	1	5	3		1	6	1
1985	7	9		4	4		3	5	
1986	5	10	1	2	5	1	3	5	
1987	7	8		4	4		3	4	
1988	10	6		5	3		5	3	
1989	11	5		6	2		5	3	
1990	10	6		6	2		4	4	
1991	10	6		4	4		6	2	
1992	11	5		8	0		3	5	
1993	8	8		3	5		5	3	
1994	7	9		5	3		2	6	
1995	10	6		6	2		4	4	
1996	10	6		5	3		5	3	
1997	6	9	1	6	2		0	7	1
1998	3	13		3	5		0	8	
1999	5	11		4	4		1	7	
2000	11	5		5	3		6	2	
2001	11	5		4	4		7	1	
2002	12	4		7	1		5	3	
2003	12	4		5	3		7	1	
2004	13	3		7	1		6	2	
2005	6	10		4	4		2	6	
2006	10	6		5	3		5	3	
	466	512	24	265	229	12	201	283	12

ST. LOUIS RAMS*

Season	All Games W	L	T	Home Games W	L	T	Road Games W	L	T
1937	1	10		0	5		1	5	
1938	4	7		2	2		2	5	
1939	5	5	1	3	2	1	2	3	
1940	4	6	1	3	1	1	1	5	
1941	2	9		1	4		1	5	
1942	5	6		3	2		2	4	
1944	4	6		1	2		3	4	
1945	9	1		4	0		5	1	
1946	6	4	1	3	2		3	2	1
1947	6	6		3	3		3	3	

Season	All Games W	L	T	Home Games W	L	T	Road Games W	L	T
1948	6	5	1	3	2	1	3	3	
1949	8	2	2	5	1		3	1	2
1950	9	3		5	1		4	2	
1951	8	4		5	2		3	2	
1952	9	3		5	1		4	2	
1953	8	3	1	5	1		3	2	1
1954	6	5	1	3	2	1	3	3	
1955	8	3	1	5	1		3	2	1
1956	4	8		4	2		0	6	
1957	6	6		5	1		1	5	
1958	8	4		4	2		4	2	
1959	2	10		0	6		2	4	
1960	4	7	1	2	3	1	2	4	
1961	4	10		4	3		0	7	
1962	1	12	1	0	7		1	5	1
1963	5	9		3	4		2	5	
1964	5	7	2	3	2	2	2	5	
1965	4	10		3	4		1	6	
1966	8	6		5	2		3	4	
1967	11	1	2	5	1	1	6	0	1
1968	10	3	1	5	2		5	1	1
1969	11	3		5	2		6	1	
1970	9	4	1	3	3	1	6	1	
1971	8	5	1	4	2	1	4	3	
1972	6	7	1	4	3		2	4	1
1973	12	2		7	0		5	2	
1974	10	4		6	1		4	3	
1975	12	2		6	1		6	1	
1976	10	3	1	5	2		5	1	1
1977	10	4		7	0		3	4	
1978	12	4		6	2		6	2	
1979	9	7		4	4		5	3	
1980	11	5		6	2		5	3	
1981	6	10		4	4		2	6	
1982	2	7		1	4		1	3	
1983	9	7		5	3		4	4	
1984	10	6		5	3		5	3	
1985	11	5		6	2		5	3	
1986	10	6		6	2		4	4	
1987	6	9		3	4		3	5	
1988	10	6		4	4		6	2	
1989	11	5		6	2		5	3	
1990	5	11		2	6		3	5	
1991	3	13		2	6		1	7	
1992	6	10		4	4		2	6	
1993	5	11		3	5		2	6	
1994	4	12		3	5		1	7	
1995	7	9		4	4		3	5	
1996	6	10		4	4		2	6	
1997	5	11		2	6		3	5	
1998	4	12		2	6		2	6	
1999	13	3		8	0		5	3	
2000	10	6		5	3		5	3	
2001	14	2		6	2		8	0	
2002	7	9		6	2		1	7	
2003	12	4		8	0		4	4	
2004	8	8		6	2		2	6	
2005	6	10		3	5		3	5	
2006	8	8		4	4		4	4	
	498	**441**	**20**	**277**	**187**	**10**	**221**	**254**	**10**

*includes Cleveland Rams (1937-1942, 1944-45) and Los Angeles Rams (1946-1994).

SAN FRANCISCO 49ERS

Season	All Games W	L	T	Home Games W	L	T	Road Games W	L	T
1950	3	9		3	3		0	6	
1951	7	4	1	5	1		2	3	1
1952	7	5		3	3		4	2	
1953	9	3		5	1		4	2	
1954	7	4	1	4	2		3	2	1
1955	4	8		2	4		2	4	
1956	5	6	1	3	3		2	3	1
1957	8	4		5	1		3	3	
1958	6	6		4	2		2	4	
1959	7	5		4	2		3	3	
1960	7	5		3	3		4	2	
1961	7	6	1	5	1	1	2	5	
1962	6	8		1	6		5	2	
1963	2	12		2	5		0	7	
1964	4	10		3	4		1	6	
1965	7	6	1	4	2	1	3	4	
1966	6	6	2	4	2	1	2	4	1
1967	7	7		3	4		4	3	
1968	7	6	1	3	3	1	4	3	
1969	4	8	2	3	3	1	1	5	1
1970	10	3	1	5	1	1	5	2	
1971	9	5		4	3		5	2	
1972	8	5	1	4	2	1	4	3	
1973	5	9		3	4		2	5	
1974	6	8		3	4		3	4	
1975	5	9		2	5		3	4	
1976	8	6		4	3		4	3	
1977	5	9		3	4		2	5	
1978	2	14		2	6		0	8	
1979	2	14		2	6		0	8	
1980	6	10		4	4		2	6	
1981	13	3		7	1		6	2	
1982	3	6		0	5		3	1	
1983	10	6		4	4		6	2	
1984	15	1		7	1		8	0	
1985	10	6		5	3		5	3	
1986	10	5	1	6	2		4	3	1
1987	13	2		6	1		7	1	
1988	10	6		4	4		6	2	
1989	14	2		6	2		8	0	
1990	14	2		6	2		8	0	
1991	10	6		7	1		3	5	
1992	14	2		7	1		7	1	
1993	10	6		6	2		4	4	
1994	13	3		7	1		6	2	
1995	11	5		6	2		5	3	
1996	12	4		6	2		6	2	
1997	13	3		8	0		5	3	
1998	12	4		8	0		4	4	
1999	4	12		3	5		1	7	
2000	6	10		4	4		2	6	
2001	12	4		7	1		5	3	
2002	10	6		5	3		5	3	
2003	7	9		6	2		1	7	
2004	2	14		1	7		1	7	
2005	4	12		3	5		1	7	
2006	8	8		4	4		4	4	
	445	**368**	**13**	**244**	**162**	**7**	**201**	**206**	**6**

SEATTLE SEAHAWKS

Season	All Games W	L	T	Home Games W	L	T	Road Games W	L	T
1976	2	12		1	6		1	6	
1977	5	9		3	4		2	5	
1978	9	7		5	3		4	4	
1979	9	7		5	3		4	4	
1980	4	12		0	8		4	4	
1981	6	10		5	3		1	7	
1982	4	5		3	2		1	3	
1983	9	7		5	3		4	4	

Season	All Games W	L	T	Home Games W	L	T	Road Games W	L	T
1984	12	4		7	1		5	3	
1985	8	8		5	3		3	5	
1986	10	6		7	1		3	5	
1987	9	6		6	2		3	4	
1988	9	7		5	3		4	4	
1989	7	9		3	5		4	4	
1990	9	7		5	3		4	4	
1991	7	9		5	3		2	6	
1992	2	14		1	7		1	7	
1993	6	10		4	4		2	6	
1994	6	10		3	5		3	5	
1995	8	8		5	3		3	5	
1996	7	9		4	4		3	5	
1997	8	8		4	4		4	4	
1998	8	8		6	2		2	6	
1999	9	7		5	3		4	4	
2000	6	10		3	5		3	5	
2001	9	7		6	2		3	5	
2002	7	9		3	5		4	4	
2003	10	6		8	0		2	6	
2004	9	7		5	3		4	4	
2005	13	3		8	0		5	3	
2006	9	7		5	3		4	4	
	236	248		140	103		96	145	

TAMPA BAY BUCCANEERS

Season	All Games W	L	T	Home Games W	L	T	Road Games W	L	T
1976	0	14		0	7		0	7	
1977	2	12		1	6		1	6	
1978	5	11		3	5		2	6	
1979	10	6		5	3		5	3	
1980	5	10	1	2	5	1	3	5	
1981	9	7		6	2		3	5	
1982	5	4		4	1		1	3	
1983	2	14		1	7		1	7	
1984	6	10		6	2		0	8	
1985	2	14		2	6		0	8	
1986	2	14		1	7		1	7	
1987	4	11		2	5		2	6	
1988	5	11		3	5		2	6	
1989	5	11		2	6		3	5	
1990	6	10		4	4		2	6	
1991	3	13		3	5		0	8	
1992	5	11		3	5		2	6	
1993	5	11		3	5		2	6	
1994	6	10		4	4		2	6	
1995	7	9		5	3		2	6	
1996	6	10		5	3		1	7	
1997	10	6		5	3		5	3	
1998	8	8		6	2		2	6	
1999	11	5		7	1		4	4	
2000	10	6		6	2		4	4	
2001	9	7		5	3		4	4	
2002	12	4		6	2		6	2	
2003	7	9		3	5		4	4	
2004	5	11		4	4		1	7	
2005	11	5		6	2		5	3	
2006	4	12		3	5		1	7	
	187	296	1	116	125	1	71	171	

WASHINGTON REDSKINS*

Season	All Games W	L	T	Home Games W	L	T	Road Games W	L	T
1932	4	4	2	2	3	1	2	1	1
1933	5	5	2	4	2		1	3	2
1934	6	6		4	3		2	3	
1935	2	8	1	2	5		0	3	1
1936	7	5		4	3		3	2	
1937	8	3		4	2		4	1	
1938	6	3	2	3	1	1	3	2	1
1939	8	2	1	5	0	1	3	2	
1940	9	2		6	0		3	2	
1941	6	5		4	2		2	3	
1942	10	1		5	1		5	0	
1943	6	3	1	4	2		2	1	1
1944	6	3	1	4	2		2	1	1
1945	8	2		6	0		2	2	
1946	5	5	1	3	2	1	2	3	
1947	4	8		4	2		0	6	
1948	7	5		4	2		3	3	
1949	4	7	1	3	3		1	4	1
1950	3	9		1	5		2	4	
1951	5	7		2	4		3	3	
1952	4	8		1	5		3	3	
1953	6	5	1	3	3		3	2	1
1954	3	9		3	3		0	6	
1955	8	4		3	3		5	1	
1956	6	6		4	2		2	4	
1957	5	6	1	2	3	1	3	3	
1958	4	7	1	3	2	1	1	5	
1959	3	9		2	4		1	5	
1960	1	9	2	1	4	1	0	5	1
1961	1	12	1	1	6		0	6	1
1962	5	7	2	3	4		2	3	2
1963	3	11		1	6		2	5	
1964	6	8		4	3		2	5	
1965	6	8		3	4		3	4	
1966	7	7		4	3		3	4	
1967	5	6	3	2	4	1	3	2	2
1968	5	9		3	4		2	5	
1969	7	5	2	4	2	1	3	3	1
1970	6	8		4	3		2	5	
1971	9	4	1	4	2	1	5	2	
1972	11	3		6	1		5	2	
1973	10	4		7	0		3	4	
1974	10	4		6	1		4	3	
1975	8	6		5	2		3	4	
1976	10	4		5	2		5	2	
1977	9	5		5	2		4	3	
1978	8	8		5	3		3	5	
1979	10	6		6	2		4	4	
1980	6	10		4	4		2	6	
1981	8	8		5	3		3	5	
1982	8	1		3	1		5	0	
1983	14	2		7	1		7	1	
1984	11	5		7	1		4	4	
1985	10	6		5	3		5	3	
1986	12	4		7	1		5	3	
1987	11	4		6	1		5	3	
1988	7	9		4	4		3	5	
1989	10	6		4	4		6	2	
1990	10	6		7	1		3	5	
1991	14	2		7	1		7	1	
1992	9	7		6	2		3	5	
1993	4	12		3	5		1	7	
1994	3	13		0	8		3	5	
1995	6	10		4	4		2	6	
1996	9	7		5	3		4	4	
1997	8	7	1	5	2	1	3	5	
1998	6	10		4	4		2	6	
1999	10	6		6	2		4	4	
2000	8	8		4	4		4	4	
2001	8	8		4	4		4	4	
2002	7	9		5	3		2	6	
2003	5	11		3	5		2	6	

Season	All Games W	L	T	Home Games W	L	T	Road Games W	L	T
2004	6	10		3	5		3	5	
2005	10	6		6	2		4	4	
2006	5	11		3	5		2	6	
	520	479	27	301	210	11	219	269	16

includes Boston Braves (1932) and Boston Redskins (1933-36).

ALL-TIME RECORDS OF NFL TEAMS

AFC	W	L	T	Pct.
Miami	368	252	4	.593
Oakland	396	301	11	.568
Cleveland	414	354	10	.539
Kansas City	375	321	12	.539
Denver	371	327	10	.531
Jacksonville	102	90	0	.531
Baltimore	91	84	1	.520
Indianapolis	402	381	7	.513
Pittsburgh	498	478	20	.510
New England	350	349	9	.501
San Diego	343	354	11	.492
Tennessee	340	362	6	.484
Buffalo	334	366	8	.477
N.Y. Jets	318	382	8	.454
Cincinnati	261	334	1	.439
Houston	24	56	0	.300

NFC	W	L	T	Pct.
Chicago	670	482	42	.582
Dallas	401	299	6	.573
Green Bay	624	500	36	.555
Minnesota	377	308	9	.550
San Francisco	445	368	13	.547
N.Y. Giants	596	500	33	.544
St. Louis	498	441	20	.530
Washington	520	479	27	.521
Seattle	236	248	0	.488
Philadelphia	466	512	24	.477
Detroit	481	544	32	.469
Carolina	90	102	0	.469
Arizona	456	649	39	.413
New Orleans	247	358	5	.408
Atlanta	252	366	6	.408
Tampa Bay	187	296	1	.387

From 1920-1971, tie games were not included in win percentage.

History

The Professional Football Hall of Fame is located in Canton, Ohio, site of the organizational meeting on September 17, 1920, from which the National Football League evolved. The NFL recognized Canton as the Hall of Fame site on April 27, 1961. Canton area individuals, foundations, and companies donated almost $400,000 in cash and services to provide funds for the construction of the original two-building complex, which was dedicated on September 7, 1963. Since that time, the Hall added three buildings with major expansion projects in 1971, 1978, and 1995. The Hall's largest-ever expansion, a $9.2 million project, was completed in early fall 1995. With the new fifth building, the Hall's size is now 82,307 square feet, more than four times its original size.

The expanded Hall represents the sport of pro football in many ways—through (1) GameDay Stadium, a dynamic two-part turntable theater featuring NFL action in Cinemascope for the first time, (2) a standard theater showing NFL films hourly, (3) six large exhibition areas where the history of pro football is detailed in memento, picture, and story form, (4) an extensive archive and information center, and (5) a large museum store.

Throughout the years, the Pro Football Hall of Fame has become an extremely popular tourist attraction. Since its opening, the Hall has had nearly eight million visitors.

New members of the Pro Football Hall of Fame are elected annually by a 40-member National Board of Selectors, made up of media representatives from every league city, seven at-large representatives, and a representative of the Pro Football Writers of America. Between three and six new members are elected each year. An affirmative vote of approximately 80 percent is needed for election.

Any fan may nominate any eligible player or contributor simply by writing to the Pro Football Hall of Fame. Players must be retired five years to be eligible, while a coach needs only to be retired with no time limit specified. Contributors (administrators, owners, *et al.*) may be elected while they are still active.

The charter class of 17 enshrinees was elected in 1963 and the honor roll now stands at 241 (150 living as of May 15, 2007) with the election of a six-man class in 2006. That class consists of Gene Hickerson, Michael Irvin, Bruce Matthews, Charlie Sanders, Thurman Thomas, and Roger Wehrli.

ROSTER OF MEMBERS

HERB ADDERLEY
Cornerback. 6-0, 205. Born in Philadelphia, Pennsylvania, June 8, 1939. Michigan State. Inducted in 1980. 1961-69 Green Bay Packers, 1970-72 Dallas Cowboys. **Highlights:** 48 interceptions, 7 touchdowns. Played in four Super Bowls, five Pro Bowls.

TROY AIKMAN
Quarterback. 6-4, 219. Born in West Covina, California, November 21, 1966. Oklahoma, UCLA. Inducted in 2006. 1989-2000 Dallas Cowboys. **Highlights:** His 90 wins in 1990s make him winningest quarterback of any decade. Led Cowboys to three Super Bowl wins. Passed for 32,942 yards, 165 touchdowns. Named to six Pro Bowls.

GEORGE ALLEN
Coach. Born in Detroit, Michigan, April 29, 1918. Died December 31, 1990. Alma College, Eastern Michigan, Marquette, Michigan. Inducted in 2002. 1966-1970 Los Angeles Rams, 1971-77 Washington Redskins. **Highlights:** 118-54-5 overall record. Never suffered a losing season, and ranked tenth in coaching victories at time of retirement.

MARCUS ALLEN
Running back. 6-2, 210. Born in San Diego, California, March 26, 1960. Southern California. Inducted in 2003. 1982-1992 Los Angeles Raiders, 1993-1997 Kansas City Chiefs. **Highlights:** First player in NFL history to tally 10,000 rushing yards and 5,000 receiving yards. MVP, Super Bowl XVIII.

LANCE ALWORTH
Wide receiver. 6-0, 184. Born in Houston, Texas, August 3, 1940. Arkansas. Inducted in 1978. 1962-1970 San Diego Chargers, 1971-72 Dallas Cowboys. **Highlights:** 542 receptions for 10,266 yards, 85 touchdowns. All-AFL seven times, seven All-Star games.

DOUG ATKINS
Defensive end. 6-8, 275. Born in Humboldt, Tennessee, May 8, 1930. Tennessee. Inducted in 1982. 1953-54 Cleveland Browns, 1955-1966 Chicago Bears, 1967-69 New Orleans Saints. **Highlights:** Eight Pro Bowls, All-NFL four times. Played for 17 years, 205 games.

MORRIS (RED) BADGRO
End. 6-0, 190. Born in Orillia, Washington, December 1, 1902. Died July 13, 1998. Southern California. Inducted in 1981. 1927-28 New York Yankees, 1930-35 New York Giants, 1936 Brooklyn Dodgers. **Highlights:** First- or second-team All-NFL four times. Scored first touchdown in NFL Championship Game series.

LEM BARNEY
Cornerback. 6-0, 190. Born in Gulfport, Mississippi, September 8, 1945. Jackson State. Inducted in 1992. 1967-1977 Detroit Lions. **Highlights:** 56 interceptions for 1,077 yards, 11 touchdowns (7 defensive, 4 special teams). Seven Pro Bowls, All-NFL/NFC four times.

CLIFF BATTLES
Halfback. 6-1, 195. Born in Akron, Ohio, May 1, 1910. Died April 28, 1981. West Virginia Wesleyan. Inducted in 1968. 1932 Boston Braves, 1933-36 Boston Redskins, 1937 Washington Redskins. **Highlights:** NFL rushing champion 1932, 1937. First to gain more than 200 yards in a game, 1933.

SAMMY BAUGH
Quarterback. 6-2, 180. Born in Temple, Texas, March 17, 1914. Texas Christian. Inducted in 1963. 1937-1952 Washington Redskins. **Highlights:** Charter enshrinee. Six-time NFL passing leader. NFL passing, punting, interception champ, 1943.

CHUCK BEDNARIK
Center-linebacker. 6-3, 230. Born in Bethlehem, Pennsylvania, May 1, 1925. Pennsylvania. Inducted in 1967. 1949-1962 Philadelphia Eagles. **Highlights:** Eight Pro Bowls. Missed three games in 14 years. Named NFL all-time center, 1969.

BERT BELL
Team owner. Commissioner. Born in Philadelphia, Pennsylvania, February 25, 1895. Died October 11, 1959. Pennsylvania. Inducted in 1963. 1933-1940 Philadelphia Eagles, 1941-42 Pittsburgh Steelers, 1943 Phil-Pitt, 1944 Card-Pitt, 1945-46 Pittsburgh Steelers. Commissioner, 1946-1959. **Highlights:** Charter enshrinee. Built NFL image as commissioner, 1946-1959. Set up long-term television policies.

BOBBY BELL
Linebacker. 6-4, 225. Born in Shelby, North Carolina, June 17, 1940. Minnesota. Inducted in 1983. 1963-1974 Kansas City Chiefs. **Highlights:** 26 interceptions. All-AFL/AFC eight times. Nine career touchdowns, 1 on onside kick return.

RAYMOND BERRY
End. 6-2, 187. Born in Corpus Christi, Texas, February 27, 1933. Southern Methodist. Inducted in 1973. 1955-1967 Baltimore Colts. **Highlights:** 631 receptions for 9,275 yards, 68 touchdowns. Set NFL title game mark with 12 catches for 178 yards, 1958.

ELVIN BETHEA
Defensive end. 6-2, 260. Born in Trenton, New Jersey, March 1, 1946. North Carolina A&T. Inducted in 2003. 1968-1983 Houston Oilers. **Highlights:** Led team in sacks six times. Elected to eight Pro Bowls. Played for 16 years, 210 games.

CHARLES W. BIDWILL SR.
Team owner. Born in Chicago, Illinois, September 16, 1895. Died April 19, 1947. Loyola of Chicago. Inducted in 1967. 1933-1943 Chicago Cardinals, 1944 Card-Pitt, 1945-47 Chicago Cardinals. **Highlights:** Guiding light for NFL during depression years. Built famous "Dream Backfield."

FRED BILETNIKOFF
Wide receiver. 6-1, 190. Born in Erie, Pennsylvania, February 23, 1943. Florida State. Inducted in 1988. 1965-1978 Oakland Raiders. **Highlights:** 589 receptions for 8,974 yards, 76 touchdowns. 40 catches 10 straight years. MVP, Super Bowl XI.

GEORGE BLANDA
Quarterback-kicker. 6-2, 215. Born in Youngwood, Pennsylvania, September 17, 1927. Kentucky. Inducted in 1981. 1949-1958 Chicago Bears, 1950 Baltimore Colts, 1960-66 Houston Oilers, 1967-1975 Oakland Raiders. **Highlights:** 2,002 career points. 26-season, 340-game career longest in NFL history.

MEL BLOUNT
Cornerback. 6-3, 205. Born in Vidalia, Georgia, April 10, 1948. Southern University. Inducted in 1989. 1970-1983 Pittsburgh Steelers. **Highlights:** 57 interceptions for 736 yards. NFL defensive MVP, 1975. Played in five Pro Bowls.

TERRY BRADSHAW
Quarterback. 6-3, 210. Born in Shreveport, Louisiana, September 2, 1948. Louisiana Tech. Inducted in 1989. 1970-1983 Pittsburgh Steelers. **Highlights:** 27,989 yards passing, 212 touchdowns. MVP in Super Bowls XIII, XIV.

BOB (BOOMER) BROWN
Tackle. 6-4, 280. Born in Cleveland, Ohio, December 8, 1941. Nebraska. Inducted in 2004. 1964-68 Philadelphia Eagles, 1969-1970 Los Angeles Rams, 1971-73 Oakland Raiders. **Highlights:** All-NFL seven of 10 seasons, six Pro Bowls. Named to 1960s All-Decade Team.

JIM BROWN
Fullback. 6-2, 228. Born in St. Simons, Georgia, February 17, 1936. Syracuse. Inducted in 1971. 1957-1965 Cleveland Browns. **Highlights:** 12,312 yards rushing, 756 points. Led NFL rushers eight years. Nine consecutive Pro Bowls.

PAUL BROWN
Coach. Born in Norwalk, Ohio, September 7, 1908. Died August 5, 1991. Miami (Ohio). Inducted in 1967. 1946-49 Cleveland Browns (AAFC), 1950-1962 Cleveland Browns. **Highlights:** Built Cleveland dynasty with 167-53-8 record, four AAFC titles, three NFL crowns. Returned to coaching with Cincinnati Bengals after induction, 1968-1975.

ROOSEVELT BROWN
Tackle. 6-3, 255. Born in Charlottesville, Virginia, October 20, 1932. Died June 9, 2004. Morgan State. Inducted in 1975. 1953-1965 New York Giants. **Highlights:** All-NFL eight consecutive years, nine Pro Bowls. NFL's lineman of year, 1956.

WILLIE BROWN
Cornerback. 6-1, 210. Born in Yazoo City, Mississippi, December 2, 1940. Grambling. Inducted in 1984. 1963-66 Denver Broncos, 1967-1978 Oakland Raiders. **Highlights:** 54 interceptions for 472 yards. Scored on 75-yard interception in Super Bowl XI.

BUCK BUCHANAN
Defensive tackle. 6-7, 274. Born in Gainesville, Alabama, September 10, 1940. Died July 16, 1992. Grambling. Inducted in 1990. 1963-1975 Kansas City Chiefs. **Highlights:** Led Chiefs defensive efforts in Super Bowl I, IV. Did not miss a game in 13 years.

NICK BUONICONTI
Linebacker. 5-11, 220. Born in Springfield, Massachusetts, December 15, 1940. Notre Dame. Inducted in 2001. 1962-68 Boston Patriots, 1969-1974, 1976 Miami Dolphins. **Highlights:** All-AFL/AFC eight times. Named to AFL's All-Time Team.

DICK BUTKUS
Linebacker. 6-3, 245. Born in Chicago, Illinois, December 9, 1942. Illinois. Inducted in 1979. 1965-1973 Chicago Bears. **Highlights:** All-NFL six years, eight consecutive Pro Bowls. 27 fumble recoveries.

EARL CAMPBELL
Running back. 5-11, 233. Born in Tyler, Texas, March 29, 1955. Texas. Inducted in 1991. 1978-1984 Houston Oilers, 1984-85 New Orleans Saints. **Highlights:** 9,407 yards rushing, 74 touchdowns. 1,934 yards rushing in 1980, including four games with at least 200 yards.

TONY CANADEO
Halfback. 5-11, 195. Born in Chicago, Illinois, May 5, 1919. Died November 29, 2003. Gonzaga. Inducted in 1974. 1941-44, 1946-1952 Green Bay Packers. **Highlights:** Two-way player. Third player to rush for 1,000 yards in single season, 1949.

JOE CARR
NFL president. Born in Columbus, Ohio, October 23, 1879. Died May 20, 1939. Did not attend college. Inducted in 1963. President, 1921-1939 National Football League. **Highlights:** Charter enshrinee. NFL co-organizer, 1920. Introduced standard player contract.

HARRY CARSON
Linebacker. 6-2, 237. Born in Florence, South Carolina, November 26, 1953. South Carolina State. Inducted in 2006. 1976-1988 New York Giants. **Highlights:** 11 career interceptions. Named to nine Pro Bowls. Named first- or second-team All-NFL six times.

DAVE CASPER
Tight end. 6-4, 240. Born in Bemidji, Minnesota, February 2, 1952. Notre Dame. Inducted in 2002. 1974-1980 Oakland Raiders, 1980-83 Houston Oilers, 1983 Minnesota Vikings, 1984 Los Angeles Raiders. **Highlights:** 378 receptions for 5,216 yards, 52 touchdowns. Five consecutive Pro Bowls.

GUY CHAMBERLIN
End. Coach. 6-2, 196. Born in Blue Springs, Nebraska, January 16, 1894. Died April 4, 1967. Nebraska. Inducted in 1965. 1919 Canton Bulldogs, 1920-21 Decatur Staleys/Chicago Staleys, player-coach 1922-23 Canton Bulldogs, 1924 Cleveland Bulldogs, 1925-26 Frankford Yellowjackets, 1927-28 Chicago Cardinals. **Highlights:** Player-coach of four NFL championship teams. Six-year coaching record of 58-16-7.

JACK CHRISTIANSEN
Safety. 6-1, 185. Born in Sublette, Kansas, December 20, 1928. Died June 29, 1986. Colorado State. Inducted in 1970. 1951-58 Detroit Lions. **Highlights:** 46 interceptions. NFL interception leader, 1953, 1957. Eight punt returns for touchdowns.

EARL (DUTCH) CLARK
Quarterback. 6-0, 185. Born in Fowler, Colorado, October 11, 1906. Died August 5, 1978. Colorado College. Inducted in 1963. 1931-32 Portsmouth Spartans, 1934-38 Detroit Lions. **Highlights:** Charter enshrinee. NFL scoring champion three years. Led Lions to 1935 NFL title.

GEORGE CONNOR
Tackle-linebacker. 6-3, 240. Born in Chicago, Illinois, January 21, 1925. Died March 31, 2003. Holy Cross, Notre Dame. Inducted in 1975. 1948-1955 Chicago Bears. **Highlights:** All-NFL at three positions—T, DT, LB. All-NFL five years. Played in first four Pro Bowls.

PRO FOOTBALL HALL OF FAME

JIMMY CONZELMAN

Quarterback. Coach. Team owner. 6-0, 180. Born in St. Louis, Missouri, March 6, 1898. Died July 31, 1970. Washington of St. Louis. Inducted in 1964. 1920 Decatur Staleys, 1921-22 Rock Island Independents, 1922-24 Milwaukee Badgers; owner-coach 1925-26 Detroit Panthers; player-coach 1927-29, coach 1930 Providence Steam Roller; coach 1940-42, 1946-48 Chicago Cardinals. **Highlights:** Player-coach of four NFL teams in 1920's. Coached Cardinals to 1947 NFL crown.

LOU CREEKMUR

Tackle-guard. 6-4, 255. Born in Hopelawn, New Jersey. January 22, 1927. William & Mary. Inducted in 1996. 1950-59 Detroit Lions. **Highlights:** All-NFL six times, twice at guard and four times at tackle. Selected to eight Pro Bowls and played on three NFL championship teams.

LARRY CSONKA

Running back. 6-3, 235. Born in Stow, Ohio, December 25, 1946. Syracuse. Inducted in 1987. 1968-1974, 1979 Miami Dolphins, 1976-78 New York Giants. **Highlights:** 8,081 yards rushing, 68 touchdowns. MVP Super Bowl VIII. Only 21 fumbles in 1,891 carries and 106 receptions.

AL DAVIS

Team, League Administrator. Born in Brockton, Massachusetts, July 4, 1929. Wittenberg, Syracuse. Inducted in 1992. 1963-1981, 1995-present Oakland Raiders, 1982-1994 Los Angeles Raiders, 1966 American Football League. **Highlights:** Only person to serve in pros as personnel assistant, scout, assistant coach, head coach, general manager, commissioner, team owner/CEO.

WILLIE DAVIS

Defensive end. 6-3, 245. Born in Lisbon, Louisiana, July 24, 1934. Grambling. Inducted in 1981. 1958-59 Cleveland Browns, 1960-69 Green Bay Packers. **Highlights:** All-NFL five seasons, five Pro Bowls. Did not miss game in 12-year career.

LEN DAWSON

Quarterback. 6-0, 190. Born in Alliance, Ohio, June 20, 1935. Purdue. Inducted in 1987. 1957-59 Pittsburgh Steelers, 1960-61 Cleveland Browns, 1962 Dallas Texans, 1963-1975 Kansas City Chiefs. **Highlights:** 28,711 yards passing, 239 touchdowns. Four AFL passing crowns. MVP, Super Bowl IV.

JOE DeLAMIELLEURE

Guard. 6-3, 254. Born in Detroit, Michigan, March 16, 1951. Michigan State. Inducted in 2003. 1973-1979, 1985 Buffalo Bills, 1980-1984 Cleveland Browns. **Highlights:** Selected All-Pro and All-AFC six consecutive times, 1975-1980. Named to six Pro Bowls. Played 13 years, 185 games.

ERIC DICKERSON

Running back. 6-3, 220. Born in Sealy, Texas, September 2, 1960. Southern Methodist. Inducted in 1999. 1983-87 Los Angeles Rams, 1987-1991 Indianapolis Colts, 1992 Los Angeles Raiders, 1993 Atlanta Falcons. **Highlights:** Rushed for 13,259 career yards, including an NFL record 2,105 yards in 1984. All-Pro five times, six Pro Bowls.

DAN DIERDORF

Tackle. 6-3, 290. Born in Canton, Ohio, June 29, 1949. Michigan. Inducted in 1996. 1971-1983 St. Louis Cardinals. **Highlights:** All-Pro five times, played in six Pro Bowls, named NFL's best blocker three times.

MIKE DITKA

Tight end. 6-3, 225. Born in Carnegie, Pennsylvania, October 18, 1939. Pittsburgh. Inducted in 1988. 1961-66 Chicago Bears, 1967-68 Philadelphia Eagles, 1969-1972 Dallas Cowboys. **Highlights:** 427 receptions for 5,812 yards, 43 touchdowns. First tight end selected to Hall of Fame. Five consecutive Pro Bowls.

ART DONOVAN

Defensive tackle. 6-3, 265. Born in Bronx, New York, June 5, 1925. Boston College. Inducted in 1968. 1950 Baltimore Colts, 1951 New York Yanks, 1952 Dallas Texans, 1953-1961 Baltimore Colts. **Highlights:** Five Pro Bowls. Vital part of Baltimore's climb to powerhouse status in 1950s.

TONY DORSETT

Running back. 5-11, 184. Born in Rochester, Pennsylvania, April 7, 1954. Pittsburgh. Inducted in 1994. 1977-1987 Dallas Cowboys, 1988 Denver Broncos. **Highlights:** 12,739 yards rushing, 398 receptions, 91 touchdowns. Ran record 99 yards for touchdown vs. Minnesota, January, 1983.

JOHN (PADDY) DRISCOLL

Quarterback. 5-11, 160. Born in Evanston, Illinois, January 11, 1896. Died June 29, 1968. Northwestern. Inducted in 1965. 1919 Hammond Pros, 1920 Decatur Staleys, 1920-25 Chicago Cardinals, 1926-29 Chicago Bears. **Highlights:** All-NFL seven times. Dropkicked record 4 field goals in one game, 1925.

BILL DUDLEY

Halfback. 5-10, 182. Born in Bluefield, Virginia, December 24, 1921. Virginia. Inducted in 1966. 1942, 1945-46 Pittsburgh Steelers, 1947-49 Detroit Lions, 1950-51, 1953 Washington Redskins. **Highlights:** Won NFL rushing, interception, punt return titles, 1946. All-NFL 1942, 1946, and 1947.

ALBERT GLEN (TURK) EDWARDS

Tackle. 6-2, 260. Born in Mold, Washington, September 28, 1907. Died January 12, 1973. Washington State. Inducted in 1969. 1932 Boston Braves, 1933-36 Boston Redskins, 1937-1940 Washington Redskins. **Highlights:** All-NFL 1932-34, 1936, 1937. Steamrolling blocker, smothering tackler.

CARL ELLER

Defensive end. 6-6, 247. Born in Winston-Salem, North Carolina, January 25, 1942. Minnesota. Inducted in 2004. 1964-1978 Minnesota Vikings, 1979 Seattle Seahawks. **Highlights:** Fixture on Vikings' "Purple People Eaters" defensive line, All-Pro five time, elected to six Pro Bowls.

JOHN ELWAY

Quarterback. 6-3, 215. Born in Port Angeles, Washington, June 28, 1960. Stanford. Inducted in 2004. 1983-1998 Denver Broncos. **Highlights:** Passed for 51,475 yards, 300 touchdowns. Named to nine Pro Bowls. NFL MVP, 1987; MVP, Super Bowl XXXIII.

WEEB EWBANK

Coach. Born in Richmond, Indiana, May 6, 1907. Died November 17, 1998. Miami (Ohio). Inducted in 1978. 1954-1962 Baltimore Colts, 1963-1973 New York Jets. **Highlights:** Only coach to win championships in both NFL, AFL. Led both Colts (1958 and 1959) and Jets (1968) to championships.

TOM FEARS

End. 6-2, 215. Born in Guadalajara, Mexico, December 3, 1922. Died January 4, 2000. Santa Clara, UCLA. Inducted in 1970. 1948-1956 Los Angeles Rams. **Highlights:** 400 receptions for 5,397 yards, 38 touchdowns. Led NFL receivers first three seasons. Had then-record 18 receptions in single game.

JIM FINKS

Administrator. Born in St. Louis, Missouri, August 31, 1927. Died May 8, 1994. Tulsa. Inducted 1995. 1964-1973 Minnesota Vikings, 1974-1982 Chicago Bears, 1986-1993 New Orleans Saints. **Highlights:** Developed Vikings, Bears, Saints—all teams with losing records—into winners.

RAY FLAHERTY
Coach. Born in Spokane, Washington, September 1, 1903. Died July 19, 1994. Gonzaga. Inducted in 1976. 1936-1942 Boston/Washington Redskins, 1946-48 New York Yankees (AAFC), 1949 Chicago Hornets (AAFC). **Highlights:** 82-41-5 coaching record. Introduced screen pass in 1937 title game and platoon system.

LEN FORD
Defensive end. 6-4, 260. Born in Washington, D.C., February 18, 1926. Died March 14, 1972. Morgan State, Michigan. Inducted in 1976. 1948-49 Los Angeles Dons (AAFC), 1950-57 Cleveland Browns, 1958 Green Bay Packers. **Highlights:** All-NFL five times, four Pro Bowls. Recovered 20 opponents' fumbles.

DAN FORTMANN
Guard. 6-0, 210. Born in Pearl River, New York, April 11, 1916. Died May 23, 1995. Colgate. Inducted in 1965. 1936-1943 Chicago Bears. **Highlights:** At 20, became youngest starter in NFL. First- or second-team All-NFL every season of career.

DAN FOUTS
Quarterback. 6-3, 210. Born in San Francisco, California, June 10, 1951. Oregon. Inducted in 1993. 1973-1987 San Diego Chargers. **Highlights:** 43,040 passing yards, 254 touchdowns. Six Pro Bowls, NFL MVP, 1982.

BENNY FRIEDMAN
Quarterback. 5-10, 183. Born in Cleveland, Ohio, March 18, 1905. Died November 23, 1982. Michigan. Inducted in 2005. 1927 Cleveland Bulldogs, 1928 Detroit Wolverines, 1929-1931 New York Giants, 1932-34 Brooklyn Dodgers. **Highlights:** NFL's first great passer. Set league mark for touchdowns with 20 in 1929. Led NFL in touchdown passes each of his first four seasons.

FRANK GATSKI
Center. 6-3, 240. Born in Farmington, West Virginia, March 18, 1919. Marshall, Auburn. Died November 22, 2005. Inducted in 1985. 1946-49 Cleveland Browns (AAFC), 1950-56 Cleveland Browns, 1957 Detroit Lions. **Highlights:** Never missed game in high school, college, or pro football. Played 11 championship games, winning eight.

BILL GEORGE
Linebacker. 6-2, 230. Born in Waynesburg, Pennsylvania, October 27, 1929. Died September 30, 1982. Wake Forest. Inducted in 1974. 1952-1965 Chicago Bears, 1966 Los Angeles Rams. **Highlights:** All-NFL eight years, eight consecutive Pro Bowls. 14 years of service, longest of any Bears player.

JOE GIBBS
Coach. Born in Mocksville, North Carolina, November 25, 1940. Cerritos (Calif.) J.C., San Diego State. Inducted in 1996. 1981-1992 Washington Redskins. **Highlights:** 124-60-0 record in regular season, 16-5 in postseason, including four Super Bowl appearances—winning three. Won 10 or more games eight times.

FRANK GIFFORD
Halfback. 6-1, 195. Born in Santa Monica, California, August 16, 1930. Southern California. Inducted in 1977. 1952-1960, 1962-64 New York Giants. **Highlights:** Starred on both offense and defense. Seven Pro Bowls, 1956 NFL player of the year.

SID GILLMAN
Coach. Born in Minneapolis, Minnesota, October 26, 1911. Died January 3, 2003. Ohio State. Inducted in 1983. 1955-59 Los Angeles Rams, 1960-69, 1971 Los Angeles/San Diego Chargers, 1973-74 Houston Oilers. **Highlights:** 123-104-7 coaching record. First to win division titles in both NFL, AFL.

OTTO GRAHAM
Quarterback. 6-1, 195. Born in Waukegan, Illinois, December 6, 1921. Died December 17, 2003. Northwestern. Inducted in 1965. 1946-49 Cleveland Browns (AAFC), 1950-55 Cleveland Browns. **Highlights:** 23,584 passing yards, 174 touchdowns. Guided Browns to 10 division or league crowns in 10 years.

HAROLD (RED) GRANGE
Halfback. 6-0, 185. Born in Forksville, Pennsylvania, June 13, 1903. Died January 28, 1991. Illinois. Inducted in 1963. 1925 Chicago Bears, 1926 New York Yankees (AFL), 1927 New York Yankees, 1929-1934 Chicago Bears. **Highlights:** Charter enshrinee. Nicknamed "Galloping Ghost." Name produced first huge pro football crowds.

BUD GRANT
Coach. Born in Superior, Wisconsin, May 20, 1927. Minnesota. Inducted in 1994. 1967-1983, 1985 Minnesota Vikings. **Highlights:** 168-108-5 coaching record. Led Vikings to 11 division championships, four Super Bowls.

JOE GREENE
Defensive tackle. 6-4, 260. Born in Temple, Texas, September 24, 1946. North Texas State. Inducted in 1987. 1969-1981 Pittsburgh Steelers. **Highlights:** NFL defensive player of the year, 1972, 1974. Four-time Super Bowl champion, 10 Pro Bowls.

FORREST GREGG
Tackle. 6-4, 250. Born in Birthright, Texas, October 18, 1933. Southern Methodist. Inducted in 1977. 1956, 1958-1970 Green Bay Packers, 1971 Dallas Cowboys. **Highlights:** Played 188 consecutive games. Nine Pro Bowls. Played on six NFL championship teams, three Super Bowl winners.

BOB GRIESE
Quarterback. 6-1, 190. Born in Evansville, Indiana, February 3, 1945. Purdue. Inducted in 1990. 1967-1980 Miami Dolphins. **Highlights:** 25,092 passing yards, 192 touchdowns. Led Miami to three AFC titles, Super Bowl VII, VIII wins.

LOU GROZA
Tackle-kicker. 6-3, 250. Born in Martins Ferry, Ohio, January 25, 1924. Died November 29, 2000. Ohio State. Inducted in 1974. 1946-49 Cleveland Browns (AAFC), 1950-59, 1961-67 Cleveland Browns. **Highlights:** 1,608 points in 21 years. Nine Pro Bowls, All-NFL six years. NFL player of the year, 1954.

JOE GUYON
Halfback. 6-1, 180. Born on White Earth Indian Reservation, Minnesota, November 26, 1892. Died November 27, 1971. Carlisle, Georgia Tech. Inducted in 1966. 1919-1920 Canton Bulldogs, 1921 Cleveland Indians, 1922-23 Oorang Indians, 1924 Rock Island Independents, 1924-25 Kansas City Cowboys, 1927 New York Giants. **Highlights:** Touchdown pass gave Giants victory over Bears to win 1927 championship.

GEORGE HALAS
End. Coach. Team owner. Born in Chicago, Illinois, February 2, 1895. Died October 31, 1983. Illinois. Inducted in 1963. Player-coach 1920 Decatur Staleys, 1921 Chicago Staleys, 1922-29 Chicago Bears; coach 1933-1942, 1946-1955, 1958-1967 Chicago Bears. **Highlights:** Charter enshrinee. 324 coaching wins. Only person associated with NFL throughout first 50 years. Coached Bears 40 seasons, won six NFL titles.

JACK HAM
Linebacker. 6-1, 225. Born in Johnstown, Pennsylvania, December 23, 1948. Penn State. Inducted in 1988. 1971-1982 Pittsburgh Steelers. **Highlights:** Won four Super Bowls, 21 opponents' fumbles recovered, 32 interceptions. Eight consecutive Pro Bowls.

DAN HAMPTON
Defensive tackle-defensive end. 6-5, 264. Born in Oklahoma City, Oklahoma, September 19, 1957. Arkansas. Inducted in 2002. 1979-1990 Chicago Bears. **Highlights:** A versatile player, he earned all-pro honors at both defensive tackle and defensive end. Named to four Pro Bowls.

JOHN HANNAH
Guard. 6-3, 265. Born in Canton, Georgia, April 4, 1951. Alabama. Inducted in 1991. 1973-1985 New England Patriots. **Highlights:** Renowned as premier guard of era. All-Pro 10 years, nine Pro Bowls.

FRANCO HARRIS
Running back. 6-2, 225. Born in Fort Dix, New Jersey, March 7, 1950. Penn State. Inducted in 1990. 1972-1983 Pittsburgh Steelers, 1984 Seattle Seahawks. **Highlights:** 12,120 rushing yards, 100 total touchdowns. 1,556 rushing yards in 19 postseason games. MVP in Super Bowl IX.

MIKE HAYNES
Cornerback. 6-2, 195. Born in Denison, Texas, July 1, 1953. Arizona State. Inducted in 1997. 1976-1982 New England Patriots, 1983-89 Los Angeles Raiders. **Highlights:** Defensive rookie of the year. Selected to nine Pro Bowls and intercepted 46 passes, plus one pick in Super Bowl XVIII.

ED HEALEY
Tackle. 6-3, 220. Born in Indian Orchard, Massachusetts, December 28, 1894. Died December 9, 1978. Dartmouth. Inducted in 1964. 1920-22 Rock Island Independents, 1922-27 Chicago Bears. **Highlights:** Two-way star. Perennial all-pro with Bears.

MEL HEIN
Center. 6-2, 225. Born in Redding, California, August 22, 1909. Died January 31, 1992. Washington State. Inducted in 1963. 1931-1945 New York Giants. **Highlights:** Charter enshrinee. 60-minute regular for 15 years. All-NFL eight consecutive years.

TED HENDRICKS
Linebacker. 6-7, 235. Born in Guatemala City, Guatemala, November 1, 1947. Miami. Inducted in 1990. 1969-1973 Baltimore Colts, 1974 Green Bay Packers, 1975-1981 Oakland Raiders, 1982-83 Los Angeles Raiders. **Highlights:** 25 blocked field goals, extra points, and punts, 26 interceptions. Played in 215 consecutive games.

WILBUR (PETE) HENRY
Tackle. 6-0, 250. Born in Mansfield, Ohio, October 31, 1897. Died February 7, 1952. Washington & Jefferson. Inducted in 1963. 1920-23, 1925-26 Canton Bulldogs, 1927 New York Giants, 1927-28 Pottsville Maroons. **Highlights:** Charter enshrinee. Largest player of his time at 250 pounds. Bulwark of Canton's championship lines.

ARNIE HERBER
Quarterback. 6-0, 200. Born in Green Bay, Wisconsin, April 2, 1910. Died October 14, 1969. Wisconsin, Regis College. Inducted in 1966. 1930-1940 Green Bay Packers, 1944-45 New York Giants. **Highlights:** NFL passing leader 1932, 1934, 1936. Came out of retirement to lead 1944 Giants to NFL Eastern crown.

BILL HEWITT
End. 5-11, 191. Born in Bay City, Michigan, October 8, 1909. Died January 14, 1947. Michigan. Inducted in 1971. 1932-36 Chicago Bears, 1937-39 Philadelphia Eagles, 1943 Phil-Pitt. **Highlights:** First to be named all-NFL with two teams—1933, 1934, 1936 Bears; 1937 Eagles.

GENE HICKERSON
Guard. 6-3, 248. Born in Trenton, Tennessee, February 15, 1935. Mississippi. Inducted in 2007. 1958-1973 Cleveland Browns. **Highlights:** Blocked for three Hall of Fame running backs. Voted to six straight Pro Bowls. Named to NFL's All-Decade Team of the 1960s.

CLARKE HINKLE
Fullback. 5-11, 201. Born in Toronto, Ohio, April 10, 1909. Died November 9, 1988. Bucknell. Inducted in 1964. 1932-1941 Green Bay Packers. **Highlights:** 3,860 yards rushing, 379 points. Fullback on offense, linebacker on defense.

ELROY (CRAZYLEGS) HIRSCH
Halfback-end. 6-2, 190. Born in Wausau, Wisconsin, June 17, 1923. Died January 28, 2004. Wisconsin, Michigan. Inducted in 1968. 1946-48 Chicago Rockets (AAFC), 1949-1957 Los Angeles Rams. **Highlights:** 387 receptions for 7,029 yards, 60 touchdowns. Key part of Rams' revolutionary "three end" offense, 1949.

PAUL HORNUNG
Halfback. 6-2, 220. Born in Louisville, Kentucky, December 23, 1935. Notre Dame. Inducted in 1986. 1957-1962, 1964-66 Green Bay Packers. **Highlights:** 760 points. Led NFL scorers three years, including record 176 points, 1960. Record 19 points scored in 1961 NFL title game.

KEN HOUSTON
Safety. 6-3, 198. Born in Lufkin, Texas, November 12, 1944. Prairie View A&M. Inducted in 1986. 1967-1972 Houston Oilers, 1973-1980 Washington Redskins. **Highlights:** 49 interceptions, 898 yards, 9 touchdowns. NFL's premier strong safety of 1970s. 12 Pro Bowls.

ROBERT (CAL) HUBBARD
Tackle. 6-5, 250. Born in Keytesville, Missouri, October 31, 1900. Died October 17, 1977. Centenary, Geneva. Inducted in 1963. 1927-28 New York Giants, 1929-1933, 1935 Green Bay Packers, 1936 New York Giants, 1936 Pittsburgh Pirates. **Highlights:** Charter enshrinee. Most feared lineman of his time. All-NFL six years, 1931-33.

SAM HUFF
Linebacker. 6-1, 230. Born in Morgantown, West Virginia, October 4, 1934. West Virginia. Inducted in 1982. 1956-1963 New York Giants, 1964-67, 1969 Washington Redskins. **Highlights:** 30 interceptions. Played in six NFL title games, five Pro Bowls. Redskins player-coach, 1969.

LAMAR HUNT
Team owner. Born in El Dorado, Arkansas, August 2, 1932. Died December 13, 2006. Southern Methodist. Inducted in 1972. 1959-present Dallas Texans/Kansas City Chiefs. **Highlights:** Driving force behind organization of AFL. Spearheaded merger negotiations with NFL, 1966.

DON HUTSON
End. 6-1, 180. Born in Pine Bluff, Arkansas, January 31, 1913. Died June 26, 1997. Alabama. Inducted in 1963. 1935-1945 Green Bay Packers. **Highlights:** Charter enshrinee. 488 receptions for 7,991 yards, 99 touchdowns. NFL receiving champion eight years. NFL MVP, 1941, 1942.

MICHAEL IRVIN
Wide Receiver. 6-2, 207. Born in Ft. Lauderdale, Florida, March 5, 1966. Miami. Inducted in 2007. 1988-1999 Dallas Cowboys. **Highlights:** 750 career receptions for 11,904 yards, 65 touchdowns. Had NFL record eleven 100-yard receiving games, 1995.

JIMMY JOHNSON
Cornerback. 6-2, 187. Born in Dallas, Texas, March 31, 1938. UCLA. Inducted in 1994. 1961-1976 San Francisco 49ers. **Highlights:** 47 interceptions for 615 yards. Five Pro Bowls. Opposing passers avoided throwing in his area.

JOHN HENRY JOHNSON
Fullback. 6-2, 225. Born in Waterproof, Louisiana, November 24, 1929. St. Mary's, Arizona State. Inducted in 1987. 1954-56 San Francisco 49ers, 1957-59 Detroit Lions, 1960-65 Pittsburgh Steelers, 1966 Houston Oilers. **Highlights:** 6,803 yards rushing, 55 total touchdowns. Member of San Francisco's "Million-Dollar" backfield.

CHARLIE JOINER
Wide receiver. 5-11, 180. Born in Many, Louisiana, October 14, 1947. Grambling. Inducted in 1996. 1969-1972 Houston Oilers, 1972-75 Cincinnati Bengals, 1976-1986 San Diego Chargers. **Highlights:** 750 receptions for 12,146 yards and 65 touchdowns. Played 18 seasons, 239 games, most ever for wide receiver at time of retirement.

DAVID (DEACON) JONES
Defensive end. 6-5, 260. Born in Eatonville, Florida, December 9, 1938. South Carolina State, Mississippi Vocational. Inducted in 1980. 1961-1971 Los Angeles Rams, 1972-73 San Diego Chargers, 1974 Washington Redskins. **Highlights:** Specialized in quarterback "sacks," a term he invented. Unanimous all-league five consecutive years.

STAN JONES
Guard-defensive tackle. 6-1, 250. Born in Altoona, Pennsylvania, November 24, 1931. Maryland. Inducted in 1991. 1954-1965 Chicago Bears, 1966 Washington Redskins. **Highlights:** Seven consecutive Pro Bowls. First to rely on weightlifting for football preparation.

HENRY JORDAN
Defensive tackle, 6-3, 240. Born in Emporia, Virginia, January 26, 1935. Died February 21, 1977. Virginia. Inducted in 1995. 1957-58 Cleveland Browns, 1959-1969 Green Bay Packers. **Highlights:** Fixture at DT during Packers' dynasty. Played in four Pro Bowls, seven NFL title games, Super Bowls I, II.

SONNY JURGENSEN
Quarterback. 6-0, 203. Born in Wilmington, North Carolina, August 23, 1934. Duke. Inducted in 1983. 1957-1963 Philadelphia Eagles, 1964-1974 Washington Redskins. **Highlights:** 32,224 yards passing, 255 touchdowns, 82.63 passer rating. Surpassed 3,000 yards passing in five seasons.

JIM KELLY
Quarterback. 6-3, 225. Born in Pittsburgh, Pennsylvania, February 14, 1960. Miami. Inducted in 2002. 1986-1996 Buffalo Bills. **Highlights:** Passed for more than 3,000 yards eight times. Mastered the no-huddle offense that propelled Bills to four consecutive Super Bowls.

LEROY KELLY
Running back. 6-0, 205. Born in Philadelphia, Pennsylvania, May 20, 1942. Morgan State. Inducted in 1994. 1964-1973 Cleveland Browns. **Highlights:** 7,274 yards rushing, 90 total touchdowns, 1,000-yard rusher first three years as starter. Punt return champion, 1965.

WALT KIESLING
Guard. Coach. 6-2, 245. Born in St. Paul, Minnesota, March 27, 1903. Died March 2, 1962. St. Thomas (Minnesota). Inducted in 1966. 1926-27 Duluth Eskimos, 1928 Pottsville Maroons, 1929-1933 Chicago Cardinals, 1934 Chicago Bears, 1935-36 Green Bay Packers 1937-38 Pittsburgh Pirates; coach, 1939 Pittsburgh Pirates, 1940-42 Pittsburgh Steelers; co-coach, 1943 Phil-Pitt, 1944 Card-Pitt; coach, 1954-56 Pittsburgh Steelers. **Highlights:** 34-year career as player, assistant coach, head coach. Led Steelers to first winning season, 1942.

FRANK (BRUISER) KINARD
Tackle. 6-1, 210. Born in Pelahatchie, Mississippi, October 23, 1914. Died September 7, 1985. Mississippi. Inducted in 1971. 1938-1943 Brooklyn Dodgers, 1944 Brooklyn Tigers, 1946-47 New York Yankees (AAFC). **Highlights:** First man to earn both All-NFL, All-AAFC honors. Out because of injury only once.

PAUL KRAUSE
Safety. 6-3, 200. Born in Flint, Michigan, February 19, 1942. Iowa. Inducted in 1998. 1964-67 Washington Redskins, 1968-1979 Minnesota Vikings. **Highlights:** NFL all-time leader with 81 interceptions. Played in eight Pro Bowls. Starting safety in four Super Bowls.

EARL (CURLY) LAMBEAU
Coach. Born in Green Bay, Wisconsin, April 9, 1898. Died June 1, 1965. Notre Dame. Inducted in 1963. 1919-1949 Green Bay Packers, 1950-51 Chicago Cardinals, 1952-53 Washington Redskins. **Highlights:** Charter enshrinee. 229-134-22 coaching record with six NFL championships. Founded pre-NFL Packers, 1919.

JACK LAMBERT
Linebacker. 6-4, 220. Born in Mantua, Ohio, July 8, 1952. Kent State. Inducted in 1990. 1974-1984 Pittsburgh Steelers. **Highlights:** Leader of 'Steel Curtain.' NFL defensive player of year in 1976, nine Pro Bowls.

TOM LANDRY
Coach. Born in Mission, Texas, September 11, 1924. Died February 12, 2000. Texas. Inducted in 1990. 1960-1988 Dallas Cowboys. **Highlights:** 270-178-6 coaching record. 20 consecutive winning seasons. Innovator on offense and defense.

DICK (NIGHT TRAIN) LANE
Cornerback. 6-2, 210. Born in Austin, Texas, April 16, 1928. Died January 29, 2002. Scottsbluff Junior College. Inducted in 1974. 1952-53 Los Angeles Rams, 1954-59 Chicago Cardinals, 1960-65 Detroit Lions. **Highlights:** 68 interceptions for 1,207 yards, 5 touchdowns. Record 14 interceptions as rookie. Seven Pro Bowls.

JIM LANGER
Center. 6-2, 255. Born in Little Falls, Minnesota, May 16, 1948. South Dakota State. Inducted in 1987. 1970-79 Miami Dolphins, 1980-81 Minnesota Vikings. **Highlights:** Played every offensive down in Dolphins' perfect 1972 season. Six Pro Bowls.

WILLIE LANIER
Linebacker. 6-1, 245. Born in Clover, Virginia, August 21, 1945. Morgan State. Inducted in 1986. 1967-1977 Kansas City Chiefs. **Highlights:** 27 interceptions. Defensive star in Super Bowl IV upset. Nicknamed 'Contact' for ferocious tackling.

STEVE LARGENT
Wide receiver. 5-11, 191. Born in Tulsa, Oklahoma, September 28, 1954, Tulsa. Inducted in 1995. 1976-1989 Seattle Seahawks. **Highlights:** 819 receptions for 13,089 yards, 100 touchdowns. Receptions in 177 consecutive games.

YALE LARY
Defensive back-punter. 5-11, 189. Born in Fort Worth, Texas, November 24, 1930. Texas A&M. Inducted in 1979. 1952-53, 1956-1964 Detroit Lions. **Highlights:** 50 interceptions. Three NFL punting crowns, three touchdowns on punt returns. Nine Pro Bowls.

DANTE LAVELLI
End. 6-0, 199. Born in Hudson, Ohio, February 23, 1923. Ohio State. Inducted in 1975. 1946-49 Cleveland Browns (AAFC), 1950-56 Cleveland Browns. **Highlights:** 386 receptions for 6,488 yards, 62 touchdowns. 24 catches in six NFL title games.

BOBBY LAYNE
Quarterback. 6-2, 190. Born in Santa Anna, Texas, December 19, 1926. Died December 1, 1986. Texas. Inducted in 1967. 1948 Chicago Bears, 1949 New York Bulldogs, 1950-58 Detroit Lions, 1958-1962 Pittsburgh Steelers. **Highlights:** 26,768 yards passing, 196 touchdowns, 2,451 yards rushing. Late touchdown pass won 1953 NFL title game.

PRO FOOTBALL HALL OF FAME

ALPHONSE (TUFFY) LEEMANS
Fullback. 6-0, 200. Born in Superior, Wisconsin, November 12, 1912. Died January 19, 1979. Oregon, George Washington. Inducted in 1978. 1936-1943 New York Giants. **Highlights:** 3,132 yards rushing, 2,318 yards passing, 422 yards receiving. Led NFL rushers as rookie, 1936.

MARV LEVY
Coach. Born in Chicago, Illinois, August 3, 1925. Wyoming, Coe College, Harvard. Inducted in 2001. 1978-1982 Kansas City Chiefs, 1986-1997 Buffalo Bills. **Highlights:** Led Bills to unprecedented four consecutive Super Bowls. Had 154-120 record. Coaching victories ranked 10th when retired.

BOB LILLY
Defensive tackle. 6-5, 260. Born in Olney, Texas, July 26, 1939. Texas Christian. Inducted in 1980. 1961-1974 Dallas Cowboys. **Highlights:** Eleven Pro Bowls. Played 196 consecutive games. Foundation of great Dallas defensive units.

LARRY LITTLE
Guard. 6-1, 265. Born in Groveland, Georgia, November 2, 1945. Bethune-Cookman. Inducted in 1993. 1967-68 San Diego Chargers, 1969-1980 Miami Dolphins. **Highlights:** Five Pro Bowls, started in three Super Bowls. Epitome of powerful Dolphins rushing game of 1970s.

JAMES LOFTON
Wide receiver. 6-3, 192. Born in Fort Ord, California, July 5, 1956. Stanford. Inducted in 2003. 1978-1986 Green Bay Packers, 1987-88 Los Angeles Raiders, 1989-1992 Buffalo Bills, 1993 Los Angeles Rams, 1993 Philadelphia Eagles. **Highlights:** Played 16 seasons, 233 games. Caught 764 passes for 75 touchdowns and a then-record 14,004 yards. All-Pro four times, eight Pro Bowls.

VINCE LOMBARDI
Coach. Born in Brooklyn, New York, June 11, 1913. Died September 3, 1970. Fordham. Inducted in 1971. 1959-1967 Green Bay Packers, 1969 Washington Redskins. **Highlights:** 105-35-6 coaching record in 10 years, including five NFL titles and victories in Super Bowls I and II.

HOWIE LONG
Defensive end. 6-5, 268. Born in Somerville, Massachusetts, January 6, 1960. Villanova. Inducted in 2000. 1981-1993 Oakland/Los Angeles Raiders. **Highlights:** All-Pro 1983, 1984, 1985. Named All-AFC four times, 1983-1986. Eight Pro Bowls.

RONNIE LOTT
Cornerback-safety. 6-0, 203. Born in Albuquerque, New Mexico, May 8, 1959. Southern California. Inducted in 2000. 1981-1990 San Francisco 49ers, 1991-92 Los Angeles Raiders, 1993-94 New York Jets. **Highlights:** Ten Pro Bowls, 63 career interceptions, and was named to the NFL's 75th Anniversary Team.

SID LUCKMAN
Quarterback. 6-0, 195. Born in Brooklyn, New York, November 21, 1916. Died July 5, 1998. Columbia. Inducted in 1965. 1939-1950 Chicago Bears. **Highlights:** 137 touchdown passes. All-NFL five times. League MVP in 1943.

WILLIAM ROY (LINK) LYMAN
Tackle. 6-2, 252. Born in Table Rock, Nebraska, November 30, 1898. Died December 28, 1972. Nebraska. Inducted in 1964. 1922-23, 1925 Canton Bulldogs, 1924 Cleveland Bulldogs, 1925 Frankford Yellowjackets, 1926-28, 1930-31, 1933-34 Chicago Bears. **Highlights:** Played for four NFL champions. In 16 seasons of college and pro football, played on one losing team.

TOM MACK
Guard. 6-3, 250. Born in Cleveland, Ohio, November 1, 1943. Michigan. Inducted in 1999. 1966-1978 Los Angeles Rams. **Highlights:** Never missed a game in entire 184-game career. Elected to 11 Pro Bowls.

JOHN MACKEY
Tight end. 6-2, 224. Born in New York, New York, September 24, 1941. Syracuse. Inducted in 1992. 1963-1971 Baltimore Colts, 1972 San Diego Chargers. **Highlights:** 331 receptions for 5,236 yards, 38 touchdowns. Second tight end to enter Hall of Fame.

JOHN MADDEN
Coach. Born in Austin, Minnesota, April 10, 1936. San Mateo Junior College, California Polytechnic College at San Luis Obispo. Inducted in 2006. 1969-1978 Oakland Raiders. **Highlights:** Became one of youngest coaches in history when hired at age 32. 112-39-7 overall record. Owns best regular season winning percentage among coaches with 100 wins.

TIM MARA
Team owner. Born in New York, New York, July 29, 1887. Died February 16, 1959. Did not attend college. Inducted in 1963. 1925-1959 New York Giants. **Highlights:** Charter enshrinee. Founder of New York Giants. Built team into powerhouse winning four NFL titles, 10 division titles.

WELLINGTON MARA
Team owner. Born in New York, New York, August 14, 1916. Died October 25, 2005. Fordham. Inducted in 1997. 1937-2005 New York Giants. **Highlights:** Lifetime contributor to NFL and New York Giants. Worked as Giants' ballboy, secretary, vice-president, president and co-CEO. NFC president 1984-present.

GINO MARCHETTI
Defensive end. 6-4, 245. Born in Smithers, West Virginia, January 2, 1927. San Francisco. Inducted in 1972. 1952 Dallas Texans, 1953-1964, 1966 Baltimore Colts. **Highlights:** Named top defensive end of NFL's first 50 years. 10 consecutive Pro Bowls. All-NFL seven times.

DAN MARINO
Quarterback. 6-4, 218. Born in Pittsburgh, Pennsylvania, September 15, 1961. Pittsburgh. Inducted in 2005. 1983-1999 Miami Dolphins. **Highlights:** Holds NFL records for career passing yardage (61,361), completions (4,967), attempts (8,358), and touchdowns (420). Voted to nine Pro Bowls.

GEORGE PRESTON MARSHALL
Team owner. Born in Grafton, West Virginia, October 11, 1896. Died August 9, 1969. Randolph-Macon. Inducted in 1963. 1932 Boston Braves, 1933-36 Boston Redskins, 1937-1969 Washington Redskins. **Highlights:** Charter enshrinee. Sponsored progressive rules changes. Organized first team band, pioneered halftime shows.

OLLIE MATSON
Halfback. 6-2, 220. Born in Trinity, Texas, May 1, 1930. San Francisco. Inducted in 1972. 1952, 1954-58 Chicago Cardinals, 1959-1962 Los Angeles Rams, 1963 Detroit Lions, 1964-66 Philadelphia Eagles. **Highlights:** Nine touchdowns on kickoff, punt returns. Traded for nine players in 1959.

BRUCE MATTHEWS
Guard-tackle-center. 6-5, 289. Born in Raleigh, North Carolina, August 8, 1961. Southern California. Inducted in 2007. 1983-2001 Houston Oilers/Tennessee Oilers/Tennessee Titans. **Highlights:** Played in 296 games, most ever by positional player at time of his retirement. Named to a record-tying 14 straight Pro Bowls. All-Pro nine times, All-AFC 12 times.

DON MAYNARD
Wide receiver. 6-1, 185. Born in Crosbyton, Texas, January 25, 1935. Texas Western. Inducted in 1987. 1958 New York Giants, 1960-62 New York Titans, 1963-1972 New York Jets, 1973 St. Louis Cardinals. **Highlights:** 633 receptions for 11,834 yards, 88 touchdowns. At least 50 catches and 1,000 yards in five different seasons.

GEORGE McAFEE
Halfback. 6-0, 177. Born in Corbin, Kentucky, March 13, 1918. Duke. Inducted in 1966. 1940-41, 1945-1950 Chicago Bears. **Highlights:** Two-way star. 25 interceptions, 234 points. Career punt-return average of 12.78 yards per return.

MIKE McCORMACK
Tackle. 6-4, 250. Born in Chicago, Illinois, June 21, 1930. Kansas. Inducted in 1984. 1951 New York Yanks, 1954-1962 Cleveland Browns. **Highlights:** Excelled as offensive right tackle for eight years. Six Pro Bowls.

TOMMY McDONALD
Wide receiver. 5-9, 175. Born in Roy, New Mexico, July 26, 1934. Oklahoma. Inducted in 1998. 1957-1963 Philadelphia Eagles, 1964 Dallas Cowboys, 1965-66 Los Angeles Rams, 1967 Atlanta Falcons, 1968 Cleveland Browns. **Highlights:** Recorded 495 receptions for 8,410 yards, 84 touchdowns.

HUGH McELHENNY
Halfback. 6-1, 198. Born in Los Angeles, California, December 31, 1928. Washington. Inducted in 1970. 1952-1960 San Francisco 49ers, 1961-62 Minnesota Vikings, 1963 New York Giants, 1964 Detroit Lions. **Highlights:** 5,281 rushing yards, 360 points. Totaled 11,369 yards rushing, receiving, and returning kicks.

JOHNNY (BLOOD) McNALLY
Halfback. 6-0, 185. Born in New Richmond, Wisconsin, November 27, 1903. Died November 28, 1985. Notre Dame, St. John's (Minnesota). Inducted in 1963. 1925-26 Milwaukee Badgers, 1926-27 Duluth Eskimos, 1928 Pottsville Maroons, 1929-1933, 1935-36 Green Bay Packers, 1934 Pittsburgh Pirates; player-coach, 1937-38 Pittsburgh Pirates. **Highlights:** Charter enshrinee. 49 touchdowns, 297 points in 14 seasons with five teams.

MIKE MICHALSKE
Guard. 6-0, 209. Born in Cleveland, Ohio, April 24, 1903. Died October 26, 1983. Penn State. Inducted in 1964. 1926 New York Yankees (AFL), 1927-28 New York Yankees, 1929-1935, 1937 Green Bay Packers. **Highlights:** Anchored Packers' championship lines, 1929-1931. First guard enshrined in Canton.

WAYNE MILLNER
End. 6-0, 191. Born in Roxbury, Massachusetts, January 31, 1913. Died November 19, 1976. Notre Dame. Inducted in 1968. 1936 Boston Redskins, 1937-1941, 1945 Washington Redskins. **Highlights:** Redskins' all-time leader with 124 catches when retired. 55- and 78-yard touchdown receptions in 1937 NFL Championship Game.

BOBBY MITCHELL
Running back-wide receiver. 6-0, 195. Born in Hot Springs, Arkansas, June 6, 1935. Illinois. Inducted in 1983. 1958-1961 Cleveland Browns, 1962-68 Washington Redskins. **Highlights:** 91 touchdowns, including 8 on kickoff and punt returns. 14,078 combined yards.

RON MIX
Tackle. 6-4, 255. Born in Los Angeles, California, March 10, 1938. Southern California. Inducted in 1979. 1960 Los Angeles Chargers, 1961-69 San Diego Chargers, 1971 Oakland Raiders. **Highlights:** All-AFL nine times. Only two holding penalties in 10 years with the Chargers.

JOE MONTANA
Quarterback. 6-2, 200. Born in New Eagle, Pennsylvania, June, 11, 1956. Notre Dame. Inducted in 2000. 1979-1992 San Francisco 49ers, 1993-94 Kansas City Chiefs. **Highlights:** MVP in Super Bowl's XVI, XIX, and XXIV. Eight Pro Bowls and All-NFL three times.

WARREN MOON
Quarterback. 6-3, 212. Born in Los Angeles, California, November 18, 1956. West Los Angeles Junior College, Washington. Inducted in 2006. 1984-1993 Houston Oilers, 1994-1996 Minnesota Vikings, 1997-1998 Seattle Seahawks, 1999-2000 Kansas City Chiefs. **Highlights:** Passed for 49,325 yards and 291 touchdowns in 17 NFL seasons. Elected to nine Pro Bowls including eight straight. Threw for 3,000 yards in nine seasons.

LENNY MOORE
Flanker-running back. 6-1, 198. Born in Reading, Pennsylvania, November 25, 1933. Penn State. Inducted in 1975. 1956-1967 Baltimore Colts. **Highlights:** From 1963-65, scored touchdowns in record 18 consecutive games. 113 career touchdowns, 12,451 combined net yards.

MARION MOTLEY
Fullback. 6-1, 238. Born in Leesburg, Georgia, June 5, 1920. Died June 27, 1999. South Carolina State, Nevada. Inducted in 1968. 1946-49 Cleveland Browns (AAFC), 1950-53 Cleveland Browns, 1955 Pittsburgh Steelers. **Highlights:** AAFC's all-time rushing champion. Led league in rushing in first NFL season.

MIKE MUNCHAK
Guard. 6-3, 281. Born in Scranton, Pennsylvania, March 5, 1960. Penn State. Inducted in 2001. 1982-1993 Houston Oilers. **Highlights:** Devastating blocker, All-AFC seven times, elected to nine Pro Bowls.

ANTHONY MUÑOZ
Tackle. 6-6, 278. Born in Ontario, California, August 19, 1958. Southern California. Inducted in 1998. 1980-1992 Cincinnati Bengals. **Highlights:** All-Pro choice 11 consecutive years, 1981-1991. Selected to 11 straight Pro Bowls.

GEORGE MUSSO
Guard-tackle. 6-2, 270. Born in Collinsville, Illinois. April 8, 1910. Died September 5, 2000. Millikin. Inducted in 1982. 1933-1944 Chicago Bears. **Highlights:** First player to achieve All-NFL status at two positions—tackle in 1935 and guard in 1937.

BRONKO NAGURSKI
Fullback. 6-2, 225. Born in Rainy River, Ontario, Canada, November 3, 1908. Died January 7, 1990. Minnesota. Inducted in 1963. 1930-37, 1943 Chicago Bears. **Highlights:** Charter enshrinee. 2,778 rushing yards in nine seasons. All-NFL five times.

JOE NAMATH
Quarterback. 6-2, 200. Born in Beaver Falls, Pennsylvania, May 31, 1943. Alabama. Inducted in 1985. 1965-1976 New York Jets, 1977 Los Angeles Rams. **Highlights:** First quarterback to pass for more than 4,000 yards in season, 1967. Guaranteed, delivered victory over Colts in Super Bowl III.

EARLE (GREASY) NEALE
Coach. Born in Parkersburg, West Virginia, November 5, 1891. Died November 2, 1973. West Virginia Wesleyan. Inducted in 1969. 1941-42, 1944-1950 Philadelphia Eagles; co-coach, 1943 Phil-Pitt. **Highlights:** Turned Eagles into winners with three consecutive division crowns, NFL championships in 1948 and 1949.

ERNIE NEVERS
Fullback. 6-1, 205. Born in Willow River, Minnesota, June 11, 1903. Died May 3, 1976. Stanford. Inducted in 1963. 1926-27 Duluth Eskimos, 1929-1931 Chicago Cardinals. **Highlights:** Charter enshrinee. Holds NFL's longest-standing record, 40 points in one game in 1929.

OZZIE NEWSOME
Tight end. 6-2, 232. Born in Muscle Shoals, Alabama, March 16, 1956. Alabama. Inducted in 1999. 1978-1990 Cleveland Browns. **Highlights:** Finished career as all-time leader among tight ends with 662 receptions for 7,980 yards.

RAY NITSCHKE
Linebacker. 6-3, 235. Born in Elmwood Park, Illinois, December 29, 1936. Died March 8, 1998. Illinois. Inducted in 1978. 1958-1972 Green Bay Packers. **Highlights:** MVP of 1962 title game. Named NFL's all-time linebacker in 1969.

CHUCK NOLL
Coach. Born in Cleveland, Ohio, January 5, 1932. Dayton. Inducted in 1993. 1969-1991 Pittsburgh Steelers. **Highlights:** Coached for 23 years. Only coach to win four Super Bowl titles (IX, X, XIII, XIV).

LEO NOMELLINI
Defensive tackle. 6-3, 264. Born in Lucca, Italy, June 19, 1924. Died October 17, 2000. Minnesota. Inducted in 1969. 1950-1963 San Francisco 49ers. **Highlights:** Played every 49ers game for 14 seasons. 10 Pro Bowls.

MERLIN OLSEN
Defensive tackle. 6-5, 270. Born in Logan, Utah, September 15, 1940. Utah State. Inducted in 1982. 1962-1976 Los Angeles Rams. **Highlights:** Member of the Fearsome "Foursome. Named" to 14 consecutive Pro Bowls, Rams' all-time team.

JIM OTTO
Center. 6-2, 255. Born in Wausau, Wisconsin, January 5, 1938. Miami. Inducted in 1980. 1960-1974 Oakland Raiders. **Highlights:** Named AFL's all-time center. Played in 210 games, 12 AFL All-Star Games or Pro Bowls, six AFL/AFC title games.

STEVE OWEN
Tackle. Coach. 6-2, 235. Born in Cleo Springs, Oklahoma, April 21, 1898. Died May 17, 1964. Phillips. Inducted in 1966. 1924-25 Kansas City Cowboys, 1925 Cleveland Bulldogs, 1926-1931, 1933 New York Giants; coach, 1930-1953 New York Giants. **Highlights:** Both player and coach. Coached Giants to record of 155-108-17, eight divisional titles, two NFL championships.

ALAN PAGE
Defensive tackle. 6-4, 225. Born in Canton, Ohio, August 7, 1945. Notre Dame. Inducted in 1988. 1967-1978 Minnesota Vikings, 1978-1981 Chicago Bears. **Highlights:** Dominating defensive tackle played in 218 consecutive games, four Super Bowls. Won league MVP honors in 1971.

CLARENCE (ACE) PARKER
Quarterback. 5-11, 168. Born in Portsmouth, Virginia, May 17, 1912. Duke. Inducted in 1972. 1937-1941 Brooklyn Dodgers, 1945 Boston Yanks, 1946 New York Yankees (AAFC). **Highlights:** Two-way threat. Two-time All-NFL performer, league MVP in 1940.

JIM PARKER
Guard-tackle. 6-3, 273. Born in Macon, Georgia, April 3, 1934. Died July 18, 2005. Ohio State. Inducted in 1973. 1957-1967 Baltimore Colts. **Highlights:** First full-time offensive lineman elected to Hall of Fame. All-NFL eight consecutive years, eight Pro Bowls.

WALTER PAYTON
Running back. 5-10, 202. Born in Columbia, Mississippi, July 25, 1954. Died November 1, 1999. Jackson State. Inducted in 1993. 1975-1987 Chicago Bears. **Highlights:** NFL's all-time leading rusher with 16,726 yards and combined net yardage with 21,803 at time of retirement.

JOE PERRY
Fullback. 6-0, 200. Born in Stevens, Arkansas, January 22, 1927. Compton Junior College. Inducted in 1969. 1948-49 San Francisco 49ers (AAFC), 1950-1960, 1963 San Francisco 49ers, 1961-62 Baltimore Colts. **Highlights:** First player in NFL history to gain 1,000 yards two consecutive seasons. 12,532 combined yards.

PETE PIHOS
End. 6-1, 210. Born in Orlando, Florida, October 22, 1923. Indiana. Inducted in 1970. 1947-1955 Philadelphia Eagles. **Highlights:** Three-time NFL receiving champion. Caught winning touchdown in 1949 NFL Championship Game.

FRITZ POLLARD
Halfback-Coach. 5-9, 165. Born in Chicago, Illinois, January 27, 1894. Died May 11, 1986. Brown. Inducted in 2005. 1919-1921, 1925-26 Akron Pros/Indians, 1922 Milwaukee Badgers, 1923, 1925 Hammond Pros, 1925 Providence Steam Roller. **Highlights:** True pioneer as one of two African American players in the NFL in 1920 and helped lead Akron to league title that season. In 1921, became the league's first black head coach.

HUGH (SHORTY) RAY
Supervisor of officials 1938-1952. Born in Highland Park, Illinois, September 21, 1884. Died September 16, 1956. Illinois. Inducted in 1966. **Highlights:** Supervisor of Officials, 1938-1952. Streamlined rules to improve game tempo, player safety.

DAN REEVES
Team owner. Born in New York, New York, June 30, 1912. Died April 15, 1971. Georgetown. Inducted in 1967. 1941-45 Cleveland Rams, 1946-1971 Los Angeles Rams. **Highlights:** Moved Rams to Los Angeles in 1946 and opened up West Coast to pro football. First postwar owner to sign African-American player.

MEL RENFRO
Cornerback-safety. 6-0, 192. Born in Houston, Texas, December 30, 1941. Oregon. Inducted in 1996. 1964-1977 Dallas Cowboys. **Highlights:** 52 interceptions for 626 yards and 3 touchdowns. Also added 842 yards on punt returns, 2,246 yards on kickoff returns. Elected to Pro Bowl first 10 seasons.

JOHN RIGGINS
Running back. 6-2, 240. Born in Seneca, Kansas, August 4, 1949. Kansas. Inducted in 1992. 1971-75 New York Jets, 1976-79, 1981-85 Washington Redskins. **Highlights:** 11,352 rushing yards, 116 total touchdowns. MVP of Super Bowl XVII with 166 rushing yards including game-winning 43-yard touchdown.

JIM RINGO
Center. 6-2, 230. Born in Orange, New Jersey, November 21, 1931. Syracuse. Inducted in 1981. 1953-1963 Green Bay Packers, 1964-67 Philadelphia Eagles. **Highlights:** Ten-time Pro Bowl selection, seven-time All-NFL selection. Started in then-record 182 consecutive games.

ANDY ROBUSTELLI
Defensive end. 6-0, 230. Born in Stamford, Connecticut, December 6, 1925. Arnold College. Inducted in 1971. 1951-55 Los Angeles Rams, 1956-1964 New York Giants. **Highlights:** Anchored defense in eight championship games. Named NFL's top player in 1962.

ART ROONEY

Team owner. Born in Coulterville, Pennsylvania, January 27, 1901. Died August 25, 1988. Georgetown, Duquesne. Inducted in 1964. 1933-39 Pittsburgh Pirates, 1940-42, 1945-1988 Pittsburgh Steelers, 1943 Phil-Pitt, 1944 Card-Pitt. **Highlights:** Founded Pittsburgh Pirates in 1933 and renamed them Steelers in 1940. Team won four Super Bowls in 1970s.

DAN ROONEY

Team owner. Born in Pittsburgh, Pennsylvania, July, 20, 1932. Duquesne. Inducted in 2000. 1955-present Pittsburgh Steelers. **Highlights:** Has been on the board of directors for the NFL Trust Fund, NFL Films, and Scheduling Committee. Played a key role in the labor agreement reached in 1993 between the NFL owners and players.

PETE ROZELLE

Commissioner. Born in South Gate, California, March 1, 1926. Died December 6, 1996. Compton Junior College, San Francisco. Inducted in 1985. Commissioner, 1960-1989. **Highlights:** Negotiated first league-wide television contract in 1962. Generally recognized as premiere commissioner in all of sports. Credited with making NFL the nation's most popular sport.

BOB ST. CLAIR

Tackle. 6-9, 265. Born in San Francisco, California, February 18, 1931. San Francisco, Tulsa. Inducted in 1990. 1953-1963 San Francisco 49ers. **Highlights:** Exceptional offensive lineman. Also played goal-line defense and had 10 blocked field goals, 1956.

BARRY SANDERS

Running back. 5-8, 203. Born in Wichita, Kansas, July 16, 1968. Oklahoma State. Inducted in 2004. 1989-1998 Detroit Lions. **Highlights:** 15,269 rushing yards, 99 touchdowns. Rushed for 1,000 yards in each of 10 seasons. NFL co-MVP, 1997. Selected to 10 Pro Bowls.

CHARLIE SANDERS

Tight end. 6-4, 230. Born in Richlands, North Carolina, August 25, 1946. Minnesota. Inducted in 2007. 1968-1977 Detroit Lions. **Highlights:** 336 career receptions for 4,817 yards and 31 touchdowns. Selected to seven Pro Bowls. Named to the NFL's All-Decade Team of 1970s.

GALE SAYERS

Running back. 6-0, 200. Born in Wichita, Kansas, May 30, 1943. Kansas. Inducted in 1977. 1965-1971 Chicago Bears. **Highlights:** Broke into league by scoring rookie-record 22 touchdowns. Led league in rushing in 1966, 1969. MVP of three Pro Bowls.

JOE SCHMIDT

Linebacker. 6-0, 222. Born in Pittsburgh, Pennsylvania, January 18, 1932. Pittsburgh. Inducted in 1973. 1953-1965 Detroit Lions. **Highlights:** 24 interceptions. Lions' team captain for nine years. Mastered middle linebacker position that evolved in 1950s.

TEX SCHRAMM

Team president-general manager. Born in San Gabriel, California, June 2, 1920. Died July 15, 2003. Texas. Inducted in 1991. 1947-1956 Los Angeles Rams. 1960-1989 Dallas Cowboys. **Highlights:** Played prominent role in AFL-NFL merger. Chairman of Competition Committee from 1966-1988.

LEE ROY SELMON

Defensive end. 6-3, 250. Born in Eufaula, Oklahoma, October 20, 1954. Oklahoma. Inducted in 1995. 1976-1984 Tampa Bay Buccaneers. **Highlights:** 78½ sacks, 380 quarterback pressures, forced 28 fumbles. Six consecutive Pro Bowl selections.

BILLY SHAW

Guard. 6-2, 258. Born in Natchez, Mississippi, December 15, 1938. Georgia Tech. Inducted in 1999. 1961-69 Buffalo Bills. **Highlights:** First player who played entire career in AFL to be elected to Hall of Fame. Named to AFL's all-time team.

ART SHELL

Tackle. 6-5, 285. Born in Charleston, South Carolina, November 26, 1946. Maryland State-Eastern Shore. Inducted in 1989. 1968-82 Oakland/Los Angeles Raiders. **Highlights:** Cornerstone of Raiders' offensive line in 1970s. 207 regular-season games, 23 postseason games, eight Pro Bowls.

DON SHULA

Coach. Born in Grand River, Ohio, January 4, 1930. John Carroll. Inducted in 1997. 1963-69 Baltimore Colts, 1970-1995 Miami Dolphins. **Highlights:** Won more games (347) than any coach in NFL history. Won two Super Bowl titles, including Super Bowl VII when Dolphins recorded NFL's only perfect season (17-0).

O.J. SIMPSON

Running back. 6-1, 212. Born in San Francisco, California, July 9, 1947. City College (San Francisco), Southern California. Inducted in 1985. 1969-1977 Buffalo Bills, 1978-79 San Francisco 49ers. **Highlights:** In 1973, became first player to rush for 2,000 yards in season. Finished career with four rushing titles, 11,236 yards.

MIKE SINGLETARY

Linebacker. 6-0, 230. Born in Houston, Texas, October 9, 1958. Baylor. Inducted in 1998. 1981-1992 Chicago Bears. **Highlights:** All-Pro choice eight times and All-NFC nine consecutive seasons. Selected to 10 Pro Bowls.

JACKIE SLATER

Tackle. 6-4, 277. Born in Jackson, Mississippi, May 27, 1954. Jackson State. Inducted in 2001. 1976-1995 Los Angeles/St. Louis Rams. **Highlights:** Played 20 seasons, 259 games. Blocked for seven different 1,000-yard rushers. Seven Pro Bowls.

JACKIE SMITH

Tight end. 6-4, 232. Born in Columbia, Mississippi, February 23, 1940. Northwestern State (Louisiana). Inducted in 1994. 1963-1977 St. Louis Cardinals, 1978 Dallas Cowboys. **Highlights:** 480 receptions for 7,918 yards, 40 touchdowns. Third tight end to be elected to Hall of Fame.

JOHN STALLWORTH

Wide receiver. 6-2, 191. Born in Tuscaloosa, Alabama, July 15, 1952. Alabama A&M. Inducted in 2002. 1974-1987 Pittsburgh Steelers. **Highlights:** 537 receptions for 8,723 yards, 63 touchdowns. Scored go-ahead touchdown in Super Bowl XIV on 73-yard reception.

BART STARR

Quarterback. 6-1, 200. Born in Montgomery, Alabama, January 9, 1934. Alabama. Inducted in 1977. 1956-1971 Green Bay Packers. **Highlights:** Quarterbacked Packers to six division titles, five NFL titles, and first two Super Bowls in which he was MVP.

ROGER STAUBACH

Quarterback. 6-3, 202. Born in Cincinnati, Ohio, February 5, 1942. New Mexico Military Institute, Navy. Inducted in 1985. 1969-1979 Dallas Cowboys. **Highlights:** Led Cowboys to four NFC titles and victories in Super Bowls VI, XII. When retired, 83.4 career passer rating was best of all time.

ERNIE STAUTNER

Defensive tackle. 6-2, 235. Born in Prinzing-by-Cham, Bavaria, April 20, 1925. Died February 16, 2006. Boston College. Inducted in 1969. 1950-1963 Pittsburgh Steelers. **Highlights:** Played in nine Pro Bowls and won the best lineman award in 1957. Recorded 3 safeties.

JAN STENERUD
Kicker. 6-2, 190. Born in Fetsund, Norway, November 26, 1942. Montana State. Inducted in 1991. 1967-1979 Kansas City Chiefs, 1980-83 Green Bay Packers, 1984-85 Minnesota Vikings. **Highlights:** 1,699 points on 580 extra points, 373 field goals. First pure placekicker to enter Hall of Fame.

DWIGHT STEPHENSON
Center. 6-2, 255. Born in Murfreesboro, North Carolina, November 20, 1957. Alabama. Inducted in 1998. 1980-87 Miami Dolphins. **Highlights:** Recognized as premier center of his time. All-Pro, All-AFC five straight years. Selected to five Pro Bowls.

HANK STRAM
Coach. Born in Chicago, Illinois, January 3, 1923. Died July 4, 2003. Purdue. Inducted in 2003. 1960-1974 Dallas Texans/Kansas City Chiefs, 1976-1977 New Orleans Saints. **Highlights:** Overall record of 136-100-10. Recorded most wins in AFL history. Guided teams to titles in 1962, 1966, and 1969. Led Chiefs to AFL win in Super Bowl IV.

KEN STRONG
Halfback. 5-11, 210. Born in West Haven, Connecticut, April 21, 1906. Died October 5, 1979. New York University. Inducted in 1967. 1929-1932 Staten Island Stapletons, 1933-35, 1939, 1944-47 New York Giants, 1936-37 New York Yanks (AFL). **Highlights:** Scored 17 points to lead Giants to victory in 1934 'Sneakers' game, led NFL with 64 points, 1933.

JOE STYDAHAR
Tackle. 6-4, 230. Born in Kaylor, Pennsylvania, March 17, 1912. Died March 23, 1977. West Virginia. Inducted in 1967. 1936-1942, 1945-46 Chicago Bears. **Highlights:** One of stalwarts of Bears' 'Monsters of the Midway.' Played on five divisional, three NFL championship teams.

LYNN SWANN
Wide receiver. 5-11, 180. Born in Alcoa, Tennessee, March 7, 1952. Southern California. Inducted in 2001. 1974-1982 Pittsburgh Steelers. **Highlights:** All-AFC three times. Selected to three Pro Bowls. MVP, Super Bowl X.

FRAN TARKENTON
Quarterback. 6-0, 185. Born in Richmond, Virginia, February 3, 1940. Georgia. Inducted in 1986. 1961-66, 1972-78 Minnesota Vikings, 1967-1971 New York Giants. **Highlights:** At retirement, held NFL records for attempts (6,467), completions (3,686), yards (47,003), and touchdowns (342). Four touchdown passes in first NFL game.

CHARLEY TAYLOR
Running back-wide receiver. 6-3, 210. Born in Grand Prairie, Texas, September 28, 1941. Arizona State. Inducted in 1984. 1964-1975, 1977 Washington Redskins. **Highlights:** Won rookie of year honors as running back. Switched to wide receiver and won receiving titles in 1966, 1967.

JIM TAYLOR
Fullback. 6-0, 216. Born in Baton Rouge, Louisiana, September 20, 1935. Louisiana State. Inducted in 1976. 1958-1966 Green Bay Packers, 1967 New Orleans Saints. **Highlights:** 8,597 rushing yards, 558 points. In 1962, led league in rushing and scoring with 19 touchdowns.

LAWRENCE TAYLOR
Linebacker. 6-3, 237. Born in Williamsburg, Virginia, February 4, 1959. North Carolina. Inducted in 1999. 1981-1993 New York Giants. **Highlights:** Redefined the position of outside linebacker. All-Pro nine times, 10 Pro Bowls. NFL MVP in 1986.

THURMAN THOMAS
Running back. 5-10, 198. Born in Houston, Texas, May 16, 1966. Oklahoma State. Inducted in 2007. 1988-1999 Buffalo Bills, 2000 Miami Dolphins. **Highlights:** Amassed 16,532 total yards including 12,074 yards rushing. Scored 88 touchdowns. Only player in history to lead league in yards from scrimmage four straight seasons.

JIM THORPE
Halfback. 6-1, 190. Born in Prague, Oklahoma, May 28, 1888. Died March 28, 1953. Carlisle. Inducted in 1963. 1915-17, 1919-1920, 1926 Canton Bulldogs, 1921 Cleveland Indians, 1922-23 Oorang Indians, 1924 Rock Island Independents, 1925 New York Giants, 1928 Chicago Cardinals. **Highlights:** Charter enshrinee. First president of American Professional Football Association, 1920. Played for 12 seasons.

Y.A. TITTLE
Quarterback. 6-0, 200. Born in Marshall, Texas, October 24, 1926. Louisiana State. Inducted in 1971. 1948-49 Baltimore Colts (AAFC), 1950 Baltimore Colts, 1951-1960 San Francisco 49ers, 1961-64 New York Giants. **Highlights:** 33,070 yards, 242 touchdowns. 33 touchdown passes in 1962 and 36 in 1963. Two-time league MVP.

GEORGE TRAFTON
Center. 6-2, 235. Born in Chicago, Illinois, December 6, 1896. Died September 5, 1971. Notre Dame. Inducted in 1964. 1920-1932 Decatur Staleys/Chicago Staleys/Chicago Bears. **Highlights:** First center to snap with one hand. Named top NFL center of 1920s.

CHARLEY TRIPPI
Halfback-quarterback. 6-0, 185. Born in Pittston, Pennsylvania, December 14, 1922. Georgia. Inducted in 1968. 1947-1955 Chicago Cardinals. **Highlights:** One of football's most versatile performers. Played halfback five years, quarterback for two, defense for two.

EMLEN TUNNELL
Safety. 6-1, 200. Born in Bryn Mawr, Pennsylvania, March 29, 1925. Died July 22, 1975. Toledo, Iowa. Inducted in 1967. 1948-1958 New York Giants, 1959-1961 Green Bay Packers. **Highlights:** 79 interceptions. Gained more yards on kickoff, punt, and interception returns (924) in 1952 than that season's NFL rushing leader.

CLYDE (BULLDOG) TURNER
Center. 6-2, 235. Born in Plains, Texas, March 10, 1919. Died October 30, 1998. Hardin-Simmons. Inducted in 1966. 1940-1952 Chicago Bears. **Highlights:** Anchored defense for four NFL championship teams, including 4 interceptions in five title games.

JOHNNY UNITAS
Quarterback. 6-1, 195. Born in Pittsburgh, Pennsylvania, May 7, 1933. Died September 11, 2002. Louisville. Inducted in 1979. 1956-1972 Baltimore Colts, 1973 San Diego Chargers. **Highlights:** 40,239 passing yards, 290 touchdowns. Led Colts to two NFL championships. Passed for at least one touchdown in 47 consecutive games.

GENE UPSHAW
Guard. 6-5, 255. Born in Robstown, Texas, August 15, 1945. Texas A & I. Inducted in 1987. 1967-1981 Oakland Raiders. **Highlights:** Premier guard of his era played in 10 AFL/AFC Championship Games, three Super Bowls, seven Pro Bowls.

NORM VAN BROCKLIN
Quarterback. 6-1, 190. Born in Eagle Butte, South Dakota, March 15, 1926. Died May 2, 1983. Oregon. Inducted in 1971. 1949-1957 Los Angeles Rams, 1958-1960 Philadelphia Eagles. **Highlights:** NFL-record 554 yards passing in 1951 season opener. Guided Eagles to NFL crown as league MVP in 1960.

STEVE VAN BUREN
Halfback. 6-1, 200. Born in La Ceiba, Honduras, December 28, 1920. Louisiana State. Inducted in 1965. 1944-1951 Philadelphia Eagles. **Highlights:** Four-time rushing champion. Won 1944 punt-return title and was 1945 kick-off-return champion.

DOAK WALKER
Halfback. 5-11, 173. Born in Dallas, Texas, January 1, 1927. Died September 27, 1998. Southern Methodist. Inducted in 1986. 1950-55 Detroit Lions. **Highlights:** 534 points. Won two NFL scoring titles. Had winning 67-yard scoring run in 1952 title game.

BILL WALSH
Coach. Born in Los Angeles, California, November 30, 1931. San Jose State. Inducted in 1993. 1979-1988 San Francisco 49ers. **Highlights:** 102-63-1 coaching record. Guided 49ers to three Super Bowl titles (XVI, XIX, XXIII) in 10 years.

PAUL WARFIELD
Wide receiver. 6-0, 188. Born in Warren, Ohio, November 28, 1942. Ohio State. Inducted in 1983. 1964-69, 1976-77 Cleveland Browns, 1970-74 Miami Dolphins. **Highlights:** 8,565 yards receiving, 85 touchdowns. Eight-time Pro Bowl player. Key to both Cleveland and Miami offenses.

BOB WATERFIELD
Quarterback. 6-2, 200. Born in Elmira, New York, July 26, 1920. Died March 25, 1983. UCLA. Inducted in 1965. 1945 Cleveland Rams, 1946-1952 Los Angeles Rams. **Highlights:** NFL MVP as rookie in 1945 and led Rams to NFL title. Grabbed 20 interceptions in limited defensive duties.

MIKE WEBSTER
Center. 6-2, 260. Born in Tomahawk, Wisconsin, March 18, 1952. Died September 24, 2002. Wisconsin. Inducted in 1997. 1974-1988 Pittsburgh Steelers, 1989-1990 Kansas City Chiefs. **Highlights:** Played in 245 games, nine Pro Bowls, and won four Super Bowls during 17-year career.

ROGER WEHRLI
Cornerback. 6-0, 190. Born in New Point, Missouri, November 26, 1947. Missouri. Inducted in 2007. 1969-1982 St. Louis Cardinals. **Highlights:** 40 career interceptions. Named to the NFL's All-Decade Team of 1970s. All-Pro five times, selected to seven Pro Bowls.

ARNIE WEINMEISTER
Defensive tackle. 6-4, 235. Born in Rhein, Saskatchewan, Canada, March 23, 1923. Died June 29, 2000. Washington. Inducted in 1984. 1948-49 New York Yankees (AAFC), 1950-53 New York Giants. **Highlights:** Dominant defensive tackle of his time. Four-time All-NFL selection, four Pro Bowls.

RANDY WHITE
Defensive tackle. 6-4, 265. Born in Pittsburgh, Pennsylvania, January 15, 1953. Maryland. Inducted in 1994. 1975-1988 Dallas Cowboys. **Highlights:** Missed only one game in 14 seasons. Co-MVP of Super Bowl XII. Nine-time Pro Bowl selection.

REGGIE WHITE
Defensive tackle-defensive end. 6-5, 291. Born in Chattanooga, Tennessee, December 19, 1961. Died December 26, 2004. Tennessee. Inducted in 2006. 1985-1992 Philadelphia Eagles, 1993-1998 Green Bay Packers, 2000 Carolina Panthers. **Highlights:** Retired as all-time sack leader with 198. Named All-Pro 13 of 15 seasons including 10 as first-team selection. Named to 13 straight Pro Bowls.

DAVE WILCOX
Linebacker. 6-3, 241. Born in Ontario, Oregon, September, 29, 1942. Boise State, Oregon. Inducted in 2000. 1964-1974 San Francisco 49ers. **Highlights:** Seven Pro Bowls, All-NFL five times. Missed only one game because of injury.

BILL WILLIS
Guard. 6-2, 215. Born in Columbus, Ohio, October 5, 1921. Ohio State. Inducted in 1977. 1946-1953 Cleveland Browns (AAFC/NFL). **Highlights:** Two-way player who excelled on defense. Four-time All-NFL player, played in three Pro Bowls.

LARRY WILSON
Safety. 6-0, 190. Born in Rigby, Idaho, March 24, 1938. Utah. Inducted in 1978. 1960-1972 St. Louis Cardinals. **Highlights:** 52 interceptions. Had interception in seven consecutive games in 1966. Made "safety blitz" famous.

KELLEN WINSLOW
Tight end. 6-5, 250. Born in St. Louis, Missouri, November 5, 1957. Missouri. Inducted in 1995. 1979-1987 San Diego Chargers **Highlights:** 541 receptions for 6,741 yards, 45 touchdowns. 13 catches, blocked field goal in 1981 playoff win over Miami.

ALEX WOJCIECHOWICZ
Center. 6-0, 235. Born in South River, New Jersey, August 12, 1915. Died July 13, 1992. Fordham. Inducted in 1968. 1938-1946 Detroit Lions, 1946-1950 Philadelphia Eagles. **Highlights:** One of league's first iron men. Played both ways for eight years with Lions.

WILLIE WOOD
Safety. 5-10, 190. Born in Washington, D.C., December 23, 1936. Southern California. Inducted in 1989. 1960-1971 Green Bay Packers. **Highlights:** 48 interceptions. Competed in six NFL Championship Games and Super Bowls I and II.

RAYFIELD WRIGHT
Tackle. 6-6, 255. Born in Griffin, Georgia, August 23, 1945. Fort Valley State. Inducted in 2006. 1967-1979 Dallas Cowboys. **Highlights:** Named first- or second-team All-Pro and voted to Pro Bowl six straight seasons, 1971-76. Played in six NFC championship games and five Super Bowls. Named to NFL's All-Decade Team of 1970s.

RON YARY
Tackle. 6-5, 255. Born in Chicago, Illinois, July 16, 1946. Cerritos (Calif.) J.C., Southern California. Inducted in 2001. 1968-1981 Minnesota Vikings, 1982 Los Angeles Rams. **Highlights:** All-Pro six consecutive seasons, All-NFC eight consecutive years. Named to seven Pro Bowls. Started in four Super Bowls and five NFL/NFC Championship Games.

STEVE YOUNG
Quarterback. 6-2, 205. Born in Salt Lake City, Utah, October 11, 1961. Brigham Young. Inducted in 2005. 1985-86 Tampa Bay Buccaneers, 1987-1999 San Francisco 49ers. **Highlights:** Led the NFL in passing a record-tying six times. Passed for more than 33,000 yards and 232 touchdowns in career. MVP of Super Bowl XXIX. Elected to seven Pro Bowls.

JACK YOUNGBLOOD
Defensive end. 6-4, 247. Born in Jacksonville, Florida, January 26, 1950. Florida. Inducted in 2001. 1971-1984 Los Angeles Rams. **Highlights:** Played in club-record 201 consecutive games. Played in five NFC Championship Games, one Super Bowl. Named All-Pro five times, All-NFC seven times. Elected to seven consecutive Pro Bowls.

ENSHRINEES BY YEAR OF INDUCTION
*Deceased
(Date of enshrinement in parentheses)

1963 CHARTER CLASS
(September 7, 1963)
Sammy Baugh
Bert Bell*
Joe Carr*
Earl (Dutch) Clark*
Harold (Red) Grange*
George Halas*
Mel Hein*
Wilbur (Pete) Henry*
Robert (Cal) Hubbard*
Don Hutson*
Earl (Curly) Lambeau*
Tim Mara*
George Preston Marshall*
John (Blood) McNally*
Bronko Nagurski*
Ernie Nevers*
Jim Thorpe*

CLASS OF 1964
(September 6, 1964)
Jimmy Conzelman*
Ed Healey*
Clarke Hinkle*
William Roy (Link) Lyman*
Mike Michalske*
Art Rooney*
George Trafton*

CLASS OF 1965
(September 12, 1965)
Guy Chamberlin*
John (Paddy) Driscoll*
Dan Fortmann*
Otto Graham*
Sid Luckman*
Steve Van Buren
Bob Waterfield*

CLASS OF 1966
(September 17, 1966)
Bill Dudley
Joe Guyon*
Arnie Herber*
Walt Kiesling*
George McAfee
Steve Owen*
Hugh (Shorty) Ray*
Clyde (Bulldog) Turner*

CLASS OF 1967
(August 5, 1967)
Chuck Bednarik
Charles W. Bidwill Sr.*
Paul Brown*
Bobby Layne*
Dan Reeves*
Ken Strong*
Joe Stydahar*
Emlen Tunnell*

CLASS OF 1968
(August 3, 1968)
Cliff Battles*
Art Donovan
Elroy (Crazylegs) Hirsch*
Wayne Millner*
Marion Motley*
Charley Trippi
Alex Wojciechowicz*

CLASS OF 1969
(September 13, 1969)
Albert Glen (Turk) Edwards*
Earle (Greasy) Neale*
Leo Nomellini*
Joe Perry
Ernie Stautner*

CLASS OF 1970
(August 8, 1970)
Jack Christiansen*
Tom Fears*
Hugh McElhenny
Pete Pihos

CLASS OF 1971
(July 31, 1971)
Jim Brown
Bill Hewitt*
Frank (Bruiser) Kinard*
Vince Lombardi*
Andy Robustelli
Y. A. Tittle
Norm Van Brocklin*

CLASS OF 1972
(July 29, 1972)
Lamar Hunt*
Gino Marchetti
Ollie Matson
Clarence (Ace) Parker

CLASS OF 1973
(July 28, 1973)
Raymond Berry
Jim Parker*
Joe Schmidt

CLASS OF 1974
(July 27, 1974)
Tony Canadeo*
Bill George*
Lou Groza*
Dick (Night Train) Lane*

CLASS OF 1975
(August 2, 1975)
Roosevelt Brown*
George Connor*
Dante Lavelli
Lenny Moore

CLASS OF 1976
(July 24, 1976)
Ray Flaherty*
Len Ford*
Jim Taylor

CLASS OF 1977
(July 30, 1977)
Frank Gifford
Forrest Gregg
Gale Sayers
Bart Starr
Bill Willis

CLASS OF 1978
(July 29, 1978)
Lance Alworth
Weeb Ewbank*
Alphonse (Tuffy) Leemans*
Ray Nitschke*
Larry Wilson

CLASS OF 1979
(July 28, 1979)
Dick Butkus
Yale Lary
Ron Mix
Johnny Unitas*

CLASS OF 1980
(August 2, 1980)
Herb Adderley
David (Deacon) Jones
Bob Lilly
Jim Otto

CLASS OF 1981
(August 1, 1981)
Morris (Red) Badgro*
George Blanda
Willie Davis
Jim Ringo

CLASS OF 1982
(August 7, 1982)
Doug Atkins
Sam Huff
George Musso*
Merlin Olsen

CLASS OF 1983
(July 30, 1983)
Bobby Bell
Sid Gillman*
Sonny Jurgensen
Bobby Mitchell
Paul Warfield

CLASS OF 1984
(July 28, 1984)
Willie Brown
Mike McCormack
Charley Taylor
Arnie Weinmeister*

CLASS OF 1985
(August 3, 1985)
Frank Gatski*
Joe Namath
Pete Rozelle*
O. J. Simpson
Roger Staubach

CLASS OF 1986
(August 2, 1986)
Paul Hornung
Ken Houston
Willie Lanier
Fran Tarkenton
Doak Walker*

CLASS OF 1987
(August 8, 1987)
Larry Csonka
Len Dawson
Joe Greene
John Henry Johnson
Jim Langer
Don Maynard
Gene Upshaw

CLASS OF 1988
(July 30, 1988)
Fred Biletnikoff
Mike Ditka
Jack Ham
Alan Page

CLASS OF 1989
(August 5, 1989)
Mel Blount
Terry Bradshaw
Art Shell
Willie Wood

CLASS OF 1990
(August 4, 1990)
Buck Buchanan*
Bob Griese
Franco Harris
Ted Hendricks
Jack Lambert
Tom Landry*
Bob St. Clair

CLASS OF 1991
(July 27, 1991)
Earl Campbell
John Hannah
Stan Jones
Tex Schramm*
Jan Stenerud

CLASS OF 1992
(August 1, 1992)
Lem Barney
Al Davis
John Mackey
John Riggins

CLASS OF 1993
(July 31, 1993)
Dan Fouts
Larry Little
Chuck Noll
Walter Payton*
Bill Walsh

CLASS OF 1994
(July 30, 1994)
Tony Dorsett
Bud Grant
Jimmy Johnson
Leroy Kelly
Jackie Smith
Randy White

CLASS OF 1995
(July 29, 1995)
Jim Finks*
Henry Jordan*
Steve Largent
Lee Roy Selmon
Kellen Winslow

CLASS OF 1996
(July 27, 1996)
Lou Creekmur
Dan Dierdorf
Joe Gibbs
Charlie Joiner
Mel Renfro

CLASS OF 1997
(July 26, 1997)
Mike Haynes
Wellington Mara*
Don Shula
Mike Webster*

CLASS OF 1998
(August 1, 1998)
Paul Krause
Tommy McDonald
Anthony Muñoz
Mike Singletary
Dwight Stephenson

CLASS OF 1999
(August 7, 1999)
Eric Dickerson
Tom Mack
Ozzie Newsome
Billy Shaw
Lawrence Taylor

CLASS OF 2000
(July 29, 2000)
Howie Long
Ronnie Lott
Joe Montana
Dan Rooney
Dave Wilcox

CLASS OF 2001
(August 4, 2001)
Nick Buoniconti
Marv Levy
Mike Munchak
Jackie Slater
Lynn Swann
Ron Yary
Jack Youngblood

CLASS OF 2002
(August 3, 2002)
George Allen*
Dave Casper
Dan Hampton
Jim Kelly
John Stallworth

CLASS OF 2003
(August 3, 2003)
Marcus Allen
Elvin Bethea
Joe DeLamielleure
James Lofton
Hank Stram*

CLASS OF 2004
(August 8, 2004)
Bob (Boomer) Brown
Carl Eller
John Elway
Barry Sanders

CLASS OF 2005
(August 7, 2005)
Benny Friedman*
Dan Marino
Fritz Pollard*
Steve Young

CLASS OF 2006
(August 6, 2006)
Troy Aikman
Harry Carson
John Madden
Warren Moon
Reggie White*
Rayfield Wright

CLASS OF 2007
(August 4, 2007)
Gene Hickerson
Michael Irvin
Bruce Matthews
Charlie Sanders
Thurman Thomas
Roger Wehrli

1869
Rutgers and Princeton played a college soccer football game, the first ever, November 6. The game used modified London Football Association rules. During the next seven years, rugby gained favor with the major eastern schools over soccer, and modern football began to develop from rugby.

1876
At the Massasoit convention, the first rules for American football were written. Walter Camp, who would become known as the father of American football, first became involved with the game.

1892
In an era in which football was a major attraction of local athletic clubs, an intense competition between two Pittsburgh-area clubs, the Allegheny Athletic Association (AAA) and the Pittsburgh Athletic Club (PAC), led to the making of the first professional football player. Former Yale All-America guard William (Pudge) Heffelfinger was paid $500 by the AAA to play in a game against the PAC, becoming the first person to be paid to play football, November 12. The AAA won the game 4-0 when Heffelfinger picked up a PAC fumble and ran 35 yards for a touchdown.

1893
The Pittsburgh Athletic Club signed one of its players, probably halfback Grant Dibert, to the first known pro football contract, which covered all of the PAC's games for the year.

1895
John Brallier became the first football player to openly turn pro, accepting $10 and expenses to play for the Latrobe YMCA against the Jeannette Athletic Club.

1896
The Allegheny Athletic Association team fielded the first completely professional team for its abbreviated two-game season.

1897
The Latrobe Athletic Association football team went entirely professional, becoming the first team to play a full season with only professionals.

1898
A touchdown was changed from four points to five.

1899
Chris O'Brien formed a neighborhood team, which played under the name the Morgan Athletic Club, on the south side of Chicago. The team later became known as the Normals, then the Racine (for a street in Chicago) Cardinals, the Chicago Cardinals, the St. Louis Cardinals, the Phoenix Cardinals, and, in 1994, the Arizona Cardinals. The team remains the oldest continuing operation in pro football.

1900
William C. Temple took over the team payments for the Duquesne Country and Athletic Club, becoming the first known individual club owner.

1902
Baseball's Philadelphia Athletics, managed by Connie Mack, and the Philadelphia Phillies formed professional football teams, joining the Pittsburgh Stars in the first attempt at a pro football league, named the National Football League. The Athletics won the first night football game ever played, 39-0 over Kanaweola AC at Elmira, New York, November 21.

All three teams claimed the pro championship for the year, but the league president, Dave Berry, named the Stars the champions. Pitcher Rube Waddell was with the Athletics, and pitcher Christy Mathewson a fullback for Pittsburgh.

The first World Series of pro football, actually a five-team tournament, was played among a team made up of players from both the Athletics and the Phillies, but simply named New York; the New York Knickerbockers; the Syracuse AC; the Warlow AC; and the Orange (New Jersey) AC at New York's original Madison Square Garden. New York and Syracuse played the first indoor football game before 3,000, December 28. Syracuse, with Glen (Pop) Warner at guard, won 6-0 and

went on to win the tournament.

1903
The Franklin (Pa.) Athletic Club won the second and last World Series of pro football over the Oreos AC of Asbury Park, New Jersey; the Watertown Red and Blacks; and the Orange AC.

Pro football was popularized in Ohio when the Massillon Tigers, a strong amateur team, hired four Pittsburgh pros to play in the season-ending game against Akron. At the same time, pro football declined in the Pittsburgh area, and the emphasis on the pro game moved west from Pennsylvania to Ohio.

1904
A field goal was changed from five points to four.

Ohio had at least seven pro teams, with Massillon winning the Ohio Independent Championship, that is, the pro title. Talk surfaced about forming a state-wide league to end spiraling salaries brought about by constant bidding for players and to write universal rules for the game. The feeble attempt to start the league failed.

Halfback Charles Follis signed a contract with the Shelby (Ohio) AC, making him the first known black pro football player.

1905
The Canton AC, later to become known as the Bulldogs, became a professional team. Massillon again won the Ohio League championship.

1906
The forward pass was legalized. The first authenticated pass completion in a pro game came on October 27, when George (Peggy) Parratt of Massillon threw a completion to Dan (Bullet) Riley in a victory over a combined Benwood-Moundsville team.

Arch-rivals Canton and Massillon, the two best pro teams in America, played twice, with Canton winning the first game but Massillon winning the second and the Ohio League championship. A betting scandal and the financial disaster wrought upon the two clubs by paying huge salaries

caused a temporary decline in interest in pro football in the two cities and, somewhat, throughout Ohio.

1909
A field goal dropped from four points to three.

1912
A touchdown was increased from five points to six.

Jack Cusack revived a strong pro team in Canton.

1913
Jim Thorpe, a former football and track star at the Carlisle Indian School (Pa.) and a double gold medal winner at the 1912 Olympics in Stockholm, played for the Pine Village Pros in Indiana.

1915
Massillon again fielded a major team, reviving the old rivalry with Canton. Cusack signed Thorpe to play for Canton for $250 a game.

1916
With Thorpe and former Carlisle teammate Pete Calac starring, Canton went 9-0-1, won the Ohio League championship, and was acclaimed the pro football champion.

1917
Despite an upset by Massillon, Canton again won the Ohio League championship.

1919
Canton again won the Ohio League championship, despite the team having been turned over from Cusack to Ralph Hay. Thorpe and Calac were joined in the backfield by Joe Guyon.

Earl (Curly) Lambeau and George Calhoun organized the Green Bay Packers. Lambeau's employer at the Indian Packing Company provided $500 for equipment and allowed the team to use the company field for practices. The Packers went 10-1.

1920
Pro football was in a state of confusion due to three major problems: dramatically rising salaries; players continually jumping from one team to another following the highest offer; and the use of college players still enrolled in school.

A league in which all the members would follow the same rules seemed the answer. An organizational meeting, at which the Akron Pros, Canton Bulldogs, Cleveland Indians, and Dayton Triangles were represented, was held at the Jordan and Hupmobile auto showroom in Canton, Ohio, August 20. This meeting resulted in the formation of the American Professional Football Conference.

A second organizational meeting was held in Canton, September 17. The teams were from four states—Akron, Canton, Cleveland, and Dayton from Ohio; the Hammond Pros and Muncie Flyers from Indiana; the Rochester Jeffersons from New York; and the Rock Island Independents, Decatur Staleys, and Racine Cardinals from Illinois. The name of the league was changed to the American Professional Football Association. Hoping to capitalize on his fame, the members elected Thorpe president; Stanley Cofall of Cleveland was elected vice president. A membership fee of $100 per team was charged to give an appearance of respectability, but no team ever paid it. Scheduling was left up to the teams, and there were wide variations, both in the overall number of games played and in the number played against APFA member teams.

Four other teams—the Buffalo All-Americans, Chicago Tigers, Columbus Panhandles, and Detroit Heralds—joined the league sometime during the year. On September 26, the first game featuring an APFA team was played at Rock Island's Douglas Park. A crowd of 800 watched the Independents defeat the St. Paul Ideals 48-0. A week later, October 3, the first game matching two APFA teams was held. At Triangle Park, Dayton defeated Columbus 14-0, with Lou Partlow of Dayton scoring the first touchdown in a game between Association teams. The same day, Rock Island defeated Muncie 45-0.

By the beginning of December, most of the teams in the APFA had abandoned their hopes for a championship, and some of them, including the Chicago Tigers and the Detroit Heralds, had finished their seasons, disbanded, and had their franchises canceled by the Association. Four teams—Akron, Buffalo, Canton, and Decatur—still had championship as-pirations, but a series of late-season games among them left Akron as the only undefeated team in the Association. At one of these games, Akron sold tackle Bob Nash to Buffalo for $300 and five percent of the gate receipts—the first APFA player deal.

1921

At the league meeting in Akron, April 30, the championship of the 1920 season was awarded to the Akron Pros. The APFA was reorganized, with Joe Carr of the Columbus Panhandles named president and Carl Storck of Dayton secretary-treasurer. Carr moved the Association's headquarters to Columbus, drafted a league constitution and by-laws, gave teams territorial rights, restricted player movements, developed membership criteria for the franchises, and issued standings for the first time, so that APFA would have a clear champion.

The Association's membership increased to 22 teams, including the Green Bay Packers, who were awarded to John Clair of the Acme Packing Company.

Thorpe moved from Canton to the Cleveland Indians, but he was hurt early in the season and played very little.

A.E. Staley turned the Decatur Staleys over to player-coach George Halas, who moved the team to Cubs Park in Chicago. Staley paid Halas $5,000 to keep the name Staleys for one more year. Halas made halfback Ed (Dutch) Sternaman his partner.

Player-coach Fritz Pollard of the Akron Pros became the first black head coach.

The Staleys claimed the APFA championship with a 9-1-1 record, as did Buffalo at 9-1-2. Carr ruled in favor of the Staleys, giving Halas his first championship.

1922

After admitting the use of players who had college eligi-bility remaining during the 1921 season, Clair and the Green Bay management withdrew from the APFA, January 28. Curly Lambeau promised to obey league rules and then used $50 of his own money to buy back the franchise. Bad weather and low attendance plagued the Packers, and Lambeau went broke, but local merchants arranged a $2,500 loan for the club. A public non-profit corporation was set up to operate the team, with Lambeau as head coach and manager.

The American Professional Football Association changed its name to the National Football League, June 24. The Chicago Staleys became the Chicago Bears.

The NFL fielded 18 teams, including the new Oorang Indians of Marion, Ohio, an all-Indian team featuring Thorpe, Joe Guyon, and Pete Calac, and sponsored by the Oorang dog kennels.

Canton, led by player-coach Guy Chamberlin and tackles Link Lyman and Wilbur (Pete) Henry, emerged as the league's first true power-house, going 10-0-2.

1923

For the first time, all of the franchises considered to be part of the NFL fielded teams. Thorpe played his second and final season for the Oorang Indians. Against the Bears, Thorpe fumbled, and Halas picked up the ball and returned it 98 yards for a touchdown, a record that would last until 1972.

Canton had its second consecutive undefeated season, going 11-0-1 for the NFL title.

1924

The league had 18 franchises, including new ones in Kansas City, Kenosha, and Frankford, a section of Philadelphia. League champion Canton, successful on the field but not at the box office, was purchased by the owner of the Cleveland franchise, who kept the Canton franchise inactive, while using the best players for his Cleveland team, which he renamed the Bulldogs. Cleveland won the title with a 7-1-1 record.

1925

Five new franchises were admitted to the NFL—the New York Giants, who were awarded to Tim Mara and Billy Gibson for $500; the Detroit Panthers, featuring Jimmy Conzelman as owner, coach, and tailback; the Providence Steam Roller; a new Canton Bulldogs team; and the Pottsville Maroons, who had been perhaps the most successful independent pro team. The NFL established its first player limit, at 16 players.

Late in the season, the NFL made its greatest coup in gaining national recognition. Shortly after the University of Illinois season ended in November, All-America halfback Harold (Red) Grange signed a contract to play with the Chicago Bears. On Thanksgiving Day, a crowd of 36,000—the largest in pro football history—watched Grange and the Bears play the Chicago Cardinals to a score-less tie at Wrigley Field. At the beginning of December, the Bears left on a barnstorming tour that saw them play eight games in 12 days, in St. Louis, Philadelphia, New York City, Washington, Boston, Pittsburgh, Detroit, and Chicago. A crowd of 73,000 watched the game against the Giants at the Polo Grounds, helping assure the future of the troubled NFL franchise in New York. The Bears then played nine more games in the South and West, including a game in Los Angeles, in which 75,000 fans watched them defeat the Los Angeles Tigers in the Los Angeles Memorial Coliseum.

Pottsville and the Chicago Cardinals were the top contenders for the league title, with Pottsville winning a late-season meeting 21-7. Pottsville scheduled a game against a team of former Notre Dame players for Shibe Park in Philadelphia. Frankford lodged a protest not only because the game was in Frankford's protected territory, but because it was being played the same day as a Yellow Jackets home game. Carr gave three different notices forbidding Pottsville to play the game, but Pottsville played anyway, December 12. That day, Carr fined the club, suspended it from all rights and privileges (including the right to play for the NFL championship), and re-turned its franchise to the league. The Cardinals, who ended the season with the best record in the league, were named the 1925 champions.

1926

Grange's manager, C.C. Pyle, told the Bears that Grange wouldn't play for them unless he was paid a five-figure salary and given one-third ownership of the team. The Bears refused. Pyle leased Yankee Stadium in New York City, then petitioned for an NFL franchise. After he was refused, he started the first American Football League. It lasted one season and included Grange's New York Yankees and eight other teams. The AFL champion Philadelphia Quakers played a December game against the New York Giants, seventh in the NFL, and the Giants won 31-0. At the end of the season, the AFL folded.

Halas pushed through a rule that prohibited any team from signing a player whose college class had not graduated.

The NFL grew to 22 teams, including the Duluth Eskimos, who signed All-America fullback Ernie Nevers of Stanford, giving the league a gate attraction to rival Grange. The 15-member Eskimos, dubbed the Iron Men of the North, played 29 exhibition and league games, 28 on the road, and Nevers played in all but 29 minutes of them.

Frankford edged the Bears for the championship, despite Halas having obtained John (Paddy) Driscoll from the Cardinals. On December 4, the Yellow Jackets scored in the final two minutes to defeat the Bears 7-6 and move ahead of them in the standings.

1927

At a special meeting in Cleveland, April 23, Carr decided to secure the NFL's future by eliminating the financially weaker teams and consolidating the quality players onto a limited number of more successful teams. The new-look NFL dropped to 12 teams, and the center of gravity of the league left the Midwest, where

the NFL had started, and began to emerge in the large cities of the East. One of the new teams was Grange's New York Yankees, but Grange suffered a knee injury and the Yankees finished in the middle of the pack. The NFL championship was won by the cross-town rival New York Giants, who posted 10 shutouts in 13 games.

1928

Grange and Nevers both retired from pro football, and Duluth disbanded, as the NFL was reduced to only 10 teams. The Providence Steam Roller of Jimmy Conzelman and Pearce Johnson won the championship, playing in the Cycledrome, a 10,000-seat oval that had been built for bicycle races.

1929

Chris O'Brien sold the Chicago Cardinals to David Jones, July 27.

The NFL added a fourth official, the field judge, July 28.

Grange and Nevers returned to the NFL. Nevers scored six rushing touchdowns and four extra points as the Cardinals beat Grange's Bears 40-6, November 28. The 40 points set a record that remains in NFL's oldest.

Providence became the first NFL team to host a game at night under floodlights, against the Cardinals, November 6.

The Packers added back Johnny Blood (McNally), tackle Cal Hubbard, and guard Mike Michalske, and won their first NFL championship, edging the Giants, who featured quarterback Benny Friedman.

1930

Dayton, the last of the NFL's original franchises, was purchased by William B. Dwyer and John C. Depler, moved to Brooklyn, and renamed the Dodgers. The Portsmouth, Ohio, Spartans entered the league.

The Packers edged the Giants for the title, but the most improved team was the Bears. Halas retired as a player and replaced himself as coach of the Bears with Ralph Jones, who refined the T-formation by introducing wide

ends and a halfback in motion. Jones also introduced rookie All-America fullback-tackle Bronko Nagurski.

The Giants defeated a team of former Notre Dame players coached by Knute Rockne 22-0 before 55,000 at the Polo Grounds, December 14. The proceeds went to the New York Unemployment Fund to help those suffering because of the Great Depression, and the easy victory helped give the NFL credibility with the press and the public.

1931

The NFL decreased to 10 teams, and halfway through the season the Frankford franchise folded. Carr fined the Bears, Packers, and Portsmouth $1,000 each for using players whose college classes had not graduated.

The Packers won an unprecedented third consecutive title, beating out the Spartans, who were led by rookie backs Earl (Dutch) Clark and Glenn Presnell.

1932

George Preston Marshall, Vincent Bendix, Jay O'Brien, and M. Dorland Doyle were awarded a franchise for Boston, July 9. Despite the presence of two rookies—halfback Cliff Battles and tackle Glen (Turk) Edwards—the new team, named the Braves, lost money and Marshall was left as the sole owner at the end of the year.

NFL membership dropped to eight teams, the lowest in history. Official statistics were kept for the first time. The Bears and the Spartans finished the season in the first-ever tie for first place. After the season finale, the league office arranged for an additional regular-season game to determine the league champion. The game was moved indoors to Chicago Stadium because of bitter cold and heavy snow. The arena allowed only an 80-yard field that came right to the walls. The goal posts were moved from the end lines to the goal lines and, for safety, inbounds lines or hashmarks where the ball would be put in play were drawn 10 yards from the walls that butted against the sidelines. The Bears won 9-0, December 18, scoring the

winning touchdown on a two-yard pass from Nagurski to Grange. The Spartans claimed Nagurski's pass was thrown from less than five yards behind the line of scrimmage, violating the existing passing rule, but the play stood.

1933

The NFL, which long had followed the rules of college football, made a number of significant changes from the college game for the first time and began to develop rules serving its needs and the style of play it preferred. The innovations from the 1932 championship game—inbounds line or hashmarks and goal posts on the goal lines—were adopted. Also the forward pass was legalized from anywhere behind the line of scrimmage, February 25.

Marshall and Halas pushed through a proposal that divided the NFL into two divisions, with the winners to meet in an annual championship game, July 8.

Three new franchises joined the league—the Pittsburgh Pirates of Art Rooney, the Philadelphia Eagles of Bert Bell and Lud Wray, and the Cincinnati Reds. The Staten Island Stapletons suspended operations for a year, but never returned to the league.

Halas bought out Sternaman, became sole owner of the Bears, and reinstated himself as head coach. Marshall changed the name of the Boston Braves to the Redskins. David Jones sold the Chicago Cardinals to Charles W. Bidwill.

In the first NFL Championship Game scheduled before the season, the Western Division champion Bears defeated the Eastern Division champion Giants 23-21 at Wrigley Field, December 17.

1934

G.A. (Dick) Richards purchased the Portsmouth Spartans, moved them to Detroit, and renamed them the Lions.

Professional football gained new prestige when the Bears were matched against the best college football players in the first Chicago College All-Star Game, August 31. The game ended in a scoreless tie before 79,432 at Soldier Field.

The Cincinnati Reds lost their first eight games, then were suspended from the league for defaulting on payments. The St. Louis Gunners, an independent team, joined the NFL by buying the Cincinnati franchise and went 1-2 the last three weeks.

Rookie Beattie Feathers of the Bears became the NFL's first 1,000-yard rusher, gaining 1,004 on 101 carries. The Thanksgiving Day game between the Bears and the Lions became the first NFL game broadcast nationally, with Graham McNamee the announcer for NBC radio.

In the championship game, on an extremely cold and icy day at the Polo Grounds, the Giants trailed the Bears 13-3 in the third quarter before changing to basketball shoes for better footing. The Giants won 30-13 in what has come to be known as the Sneakers Game, December 9.

The player waiver rule was adopted, December 10.

1935
The NFL adopted Bert Bell's proposal to hold an annual draft of college players, to begin in 1936, with teams selecting in an inverse order of finish, May 19. The inbounds line or hashmarks were moved nearer the center of the field, 15 yards from the sidelines.

All-America end Don Hutson of Alabama joined Green Bay. The Lions defeated the Giants 26-7 in the NFL Championship Game, December 15.

1936
There were no franchise transactions for the first year since the formation of the NFL. It also was the first year in which all member teams played the same number of games.

The Eagles made University of Chicago halfback and Heisman Trophy winner Jay Berwanger the first player ever selected in the NFL draft, February 8. The Eagles traded his rights to the Bears, but Berwanger never played pro football. The first player selected to actually sign was the number-two pick, Riley Smith of Alabama, who was selected by Boston.

A rival league was formed, and it became the second to

call itself the American Football League. The Boston Shamrocks were its champions.

Because of poor attendance, Marshall, the owner of the host team, moved the Championship Game from Boston to the Polo Grounds in New York. Green Bay defeated the Redskins 21-6, December 13.

1937
Homer Marshman was granted a Cleveland franchise, named the Rams, February 12. Marshall moved the Redskins to Washington, D.C., February 13. The Redskins signed TCU All-America tailback Sammy Baugh, who led them to a 28-21 victory over the Bears in the NFL Championship Game, December 12.

The Los Angeles Bulldogs had an 8-0 record to win the AFL title, but then the 2-year-old league folded.

1938
At the suggestion of Halas, Hugh (Shorty) Ray became a technical advisor on rules and officiating to the NFL. A new rule called for a 15-yard penalty for roughing the passer.

Rookie Byron (Whizzer) White of the Pittsburgh Pirates led the NFL in rushing. The Giants defeated the Packers 23-17 for the NFL title, December 11.

Marshall, *Los Angeles Times* sports editor Bill Henry, and promoter Tom Gallery established the Pro Bowl game between the NFL champion and a team of pro all-stars.

1939
The New York Giants defeated the Pro All-Stars 13-10 in the first Pro Bowl, at Wrigley Field, Los Angeles, January 15.

Carr, NFL president since 1921, died in Columbus, May 20. Carl Storck was named acting president, May 25.

An NFL game was televised for the first time when NBC broadcast the Brooklyn Dodgers-Philadelphia Eagles game from Ebbets Field to the approximately 1,000 sets then in New York, October 22.

Green Bay defeated New York 27-0 in the NFL Championship Game, December 10 at Milwaukee. NFL attendance

exceeded 1 million in a season for the first time, reaching 1,071,200.

1940
A six-team rival league, the third to call itself the American Football League, was formed, and the Columbus Bullies won its championship.

Halas' Bears, with additional coaching by Clark Shaughnessy of Stanford, defeated the Redskins 73-0 in the NFL Championship Game, December 8. The game, which was the most decisive victory in NFL history, popularized the Bears' T-formation with a man-in-motion. It was the first championship carried on network radio, broadcast by Red Barber to 120 stations of the Mutual Broadcasting System, which paid $2,500 for the rights.

Art Rooney sold the Pittsburgh franchise to Alexis Thompson, December 9, then bought part interest in the Philadelphia Eagles.

1941
Elmer Layden was named the first Commissioner of the NFL, March 1; Storck, the acting president, resigned, April 5. NFL headquarters were moved to Chicago.

Bell and Rooney traded the Eagles to Thompson for the Pirates, then re-named their new team the Steelers. Homer Marshman sold the Rams to Daniel F. Reeves and Fred Levy, Jr.

The league by-laws were revised to provide for playoffs in case there were ties in division races, and sudden-death overtimes in case a playoff game was tied after four quarters. An official *NFL Record Manual* was published for the first time.

Columbus again won the championship of the AFL, but the two-year-old league then folded.

The Bears and the Packers finished in a tie for the Western Division championship, setting up the first divisional playoff game in league history. The Bears won 33-14, then defeated the Giants 37-9 for the NFL championship, December 21.

1942
Players departing for service

in World War II depleted the rosters of NFL teams. Halas left the Bears in midseason to join the Navy, and Luke Johnsos and Heartley (Hunk) Anderson served as co-coaches as the Bears went 11-0 in the regular season. The Redskins defeated the Bears 14-6 in the NFL Championship Game, December 13.

1943
The Cleveland Rams, with co-owners Reeves and Levy in the service, were granted permission to suspend operations for one season, April 6. Levy transferred his stock in the team to Reeves, April 16.

The NFL adopted free substitution, April 7. The league also made the wearing of helmets mandatory and approved a 10-game schedule for all teams.

Philadelphia and Pittsburgh were granted permission to merge for one season, June 19. The team, known as Phil-Pitt (and called the Steagles by fans), divided home games between the two cities, and Earle (Greasy) Neale of Philadelphia and Walt Kiesling of Pittsburgh served as co-coaches. The merger automatically dissolved the last day of the season, December 5.

Ted Collins was granted a franchise for Boston, to become active in 1944.

Sammy Baugh led the league in passing, punting, and interceptions. He led the Redskins to a tie with the Giants for the Eastern Division title, and then to a 28-0 victory in a divisional playoff game. The Bears beat the Redskins 41-21 in the NFL Championship Game, December 26.

1944
Collins, who had wanted a franchise in Yankee Stadium in New York, named his new team in Boston the Yanks. Cleveland resumed operations. The Brooklyn Dodgers changed their name to the Tigers.

Coaching from the bench was legalized, April 20.

The Cardinals and the Steelers were granted permission to merge for one year under the name Card-Pitt, April 21. Phil Handler of the Cardinals and Walt Kiesling of the Steelers served as co-coaches. The merger automatically dissolved the last day of the season, December 3.

In the NFL Championship Game, Green Bay defeated the New York Giants 14-7, December 17.

1945

The inbounds lines or hash-marks were moved from 15 yards away from the sidelines to nearer the center of the field—20 yards from the sidelines.

Brooklyn and Boston merged into a team that played home games in both cities and was known simply as The Yanks. The team was coached by former Boston head coach Herb Kopf. In December, the Brooklyn franchise withdrew from the NFL to join the new All-America Football Conference; all the players on its active and reserve lists were assigned to The Yanks, who once again became the Boston Yanks.

Halas rejoined the Bears late in the season after service with the U.S. Navy. Although Halas took over much of the coaching duties, Anderson and Johnsos remained coaches of record throughout the season.

Steve Van Buren of Philadelphia led the NFL in rushing, kickoff returns, and scoring.

After the Japanese surrendered ending World War II, a count showed that the NFL service roster, limited to men who had played in league games, totaled 638, 21 of whom had died in action.

Rookie quarterback Bob Waterfield led Cleveland to a 15-14 victory over Washington in the NFL Championship Game, December 16.

1946

The contract of Commissioner Layden was not renewed, and Bert Bell, the co-owner of the Steelers, replaced him, January 11. Bell moved the league headquarters from Chicago to the Philadelphia suburb of Bala-Cynwyd.

Free substitution was withdrawn and substitutions were limited to no more than three men at a time. Forward passes were made automatically incomplete upon striking the goal posts, January 11.

The NFL took on a truly national appearance for the first time when Reeves was granted permission by the league to move his NFL champion Rams to Los Angeles.

Halfback Kenny Washington (March 21) and end Woody Strode (May 7) signed with the Los Angeles Rams to become the first African-Americans to play in the NFL in the modern era. Guard Bill Willis (August 6) and running back Marion Motley (August 9) joined the AAFC with the Cleveland Browns.

The rival All-America Football Conference began play with eight teams. The Cleveland Browns, coached by Paul Brown, won the AAFC's first championship, defeating the New York Yankees 14-9.

Bill Dudley of the Steelers led the NFL in rushing, interceptions, and punt returns, and won the league's most valuable player award.

Backs Frank Filchock and Merle Hapes of the Giants were questioned about an attempt by a New York man to fix the championship game with the Bears. Bell suspended Hapes but allowed Filchock to play; he played well, but Chicago won 24-14, December 15.

1947

The NFL added a fifth official, the back judge.

A bonus choice was made for the first time in the NFL draft. One team each year would select the special choice before the first round began. The Chicago Bears won a lottery and the rights to the first choice and drafted back Bob Fenimore of Oklahoma A&M.

The Cleveland Browns again won the AAFC title, defeating the New York Yankees 14-3.

Charles Bidwill, Sr., owner of the Cardinals, died April 19, but his wife and sons retained ownership of the team. On December 28, the Cardinals won the NFL Championship Game 28-21 over the Philadelphia Eagles, who had beaten Pittsburgh 21-0 in a playoff.

1948

Plastic helmets were prohibited. A flexible artificial tee was permitted at the kickoff. Officials other than the referee

were equipped with whistles, not horns, January 14.

Fred Mandel sold the Detroit Lions to a syndicate headed by D. Lyle Fife, January 15.

Halfback Fred Gehrke of the Los Angeles Rams painted horns on the Rams' helmets, the first modern helmet emblems in pro football.

The Cleveland Browns won their third straight championship in the AAFC, going 14-0 and then defeating the Buffalo Bills 49-7.

In a blizzard, the Eagles defeated the Cardinals 7-0 in the NFL Championship Game, December 19.

1949

Alexis Thompson sold the champion Eagles to a syndicate headed by James P. Clark, January 15. The Boston Yanks became the New York Bulldogs, sharing the Polo Grounds with the Giants.

Free substitution was adopted for one year, January 20.

The NFL had two 1,000-yard rushers in the same season for the first time—Steve Van Buren of Philadelphia and Tony Canadeo of Green Bay.

The AAFC played its season with a one-division, seven-team format. On December 9, Bell announced a merger agreement in which three AAFC franchises—Cleveland, San Francisco, and Baltimore—would join the NFL in 1950. The Browns won their fourth consecutive AAFC title, defeating the 49ers 21-7, December 11.

In a heavy rain, the Eagles defeated the Rams 14-0 in the NFL Championship Game, December 18.

1950

Unlimited free substitution was restored, opening the way for the era of two platoons and specialization in pro football, January 20.

Curly Lambeau, founder of the franchise and Green Bay's head coach since 1921, resigned under fire, February 1.

The name National Football League was restored after about three months as the National-American Football League. The American and National conferences were created to replace the Eastern

and Western divisions, March 3.

The New York Bulldogs became the Yanks and divided the players of the former AAFC Yankees with the Giants. A special allocation draft was held in which the 13 teams drafted the remaining AAFC players, with special consideration for Baltimore, which received 15 choices compared to 10 for other teams.

The Los Angeles Rams became the first NFL team to have all of its games—both home and away—televised. The Washington Redskins followed the Rams in arranging to televise their games; other teams made deals to put selected games on television.

In the first game of the season, former AAFC champion Cleveland defeated NFL champion Philadelphia 35-10. For the first time, deadlocks occurred in both conferences and playoffs were necessary. The Browns defeated the Giants in the American and the Rams defeated the Bears in the National. Cleveland defeated Los Angeles 30-28 in the NFL Championship Game, December 24.

1951

The Pro Bowl game, dormant since 1942, was revived under a new format matching the all-stars of each conference at the Los Angeles Memorial Coliseum. The American Conference defeated the National Conference 28-27, January 14.

Abraham Watner returned the Baltimore franchise and its player contracts back to the NFL for $50,000. Baltimore's former players were made available for drafting at the same time as college players, January 18.

A rule was passed that no tackle, guard, or center would be eligible to catch a forward pass, January 18.

The Rams reversed their television policy and televised only road games.

The NFL Championship Game was televised coast-to-coast for the first time, December 23. The DuMont Network paid $75,000 for the rights to the game, in which the Rams defeated the Browns 24-17.

1952

Ted Collins sold the New York Yanks' franchise back to the NFL, January 19. A new franchise was awarded to a group in Dallas after it purchased the assets of the Yanks, January 24. The new Texans went 1-11, with the owners turning the franchise back to the league in midseason. For the last five games of the season, the commissioner's office operated the Texans as a road team, using Hershey, Pennsylvania, as a home base. At the end of the season the franchise was canceled, the last time an NFL team failed.

The Pittsburgh Steelers abandoned the Single-Wing for the T-formation, the last pro team to do so.

The Detroit Lions won their first NFL championship in 17 years, defeating the Browns 17-7 in the title game, December 28.

1953

A Baltimore group headed by Carroll Rosenbloom was granted a franchise and was awarded the holdings of the defunct Dallas organization, January 23. The team, named the Colts, put together the largest trade in league history, acquiring 10 players from Cleveland in exchange for five.

The names of the American and National conferences were changed to the Eastern and Western conferences, January 24.

Jim Thorpe died, March 28.

Mickey McBride, founder of the Cleveland Browns, sold the franchise to a syndicate headed by Dave R. Jones, June 10.

The NFL policy of blacking out home games was upheld by Judge Allan K. Grim of the U.S. District Court in Philadelphia, November 12.

The Lions again defeated the Browns in the NFL Championship Game, winning 17-16, December 27.

1954

The Canadian Football League began a series of raids on NFL teams, signing quarterback Eddie LeBaron and defensive end Gene Brito of Washington and defensive tackle Arnie Weinmeister of the Giants, among others.

Fullback Joe Perry of the

49ers became the first player in league history to gain 1,000 yards rushing in consecutive seasons.

Cleveland defeated Detroit 56-10 in the NFL Championship Game, December 26.

1955

The sudden-death overtime rule was used for the first time in a preseason game between the Rams and Giants at Portland, Oregon, August 28. The Rams won 23-17 three minutes into overtime.

A rule change declared the ball dead immediately if the ball carrier touched the ground with any part of his body except his hands or feet while in the grasp of an opponent.

The Baltimore Colts made an 80-cent phone call to Johnny Unitas and signed him as a free agent. Another quarterback, Otto Graham, played his last game as the Browns defeated the Rams 38-14 in the NFL Championship Game, December 26. Graham had quarterbacked the Browns to 10 championship-game appearances in 10 years.

NBC replaced DuMont as the network for the title game, paying a rights fee of $100,000.

1956

The NFL Players Association was founded.

Grabbing an opponent's facemask (other than the ball carrier) was made illegal. Using radio receivers to communicate with players on the field was prohibited. A natural leather ball with white end stripes replaced the white ball with black stripes for night games.

The Giants moved from the Polo Grounds to Yankee Stadium.

Halas retired as coach of the Bears, and was replaced by Paddy Driscoll.

CBS became the first network to broadcast some NFL regular-season games to selected television markets across the nation.

The Giants routed the Bears 47-7 in the NFL Championship Game, December 30.

1957

Pete Rozelle was named general manager of the Rams. Anthony J. Morabito, founder

and co-owner of the 49ers, died of a heart attack during a game against the Bears at Kezar Stadium, October 28. An NFL-record crowd of 102,368 saw the 49ers-Rams game at the Los Angeles Memorial Coliseum, November 10.

The Lions came from 20 points down to post a 31-27 playoff victory over the 49ers, December 22. Detroit defeated Cleveland 59-14 in the NFL Championship Game, December 29.

1958

The bonus selection in the draft was eliminated, January 29. The last selection was quarterback King Hill of Rice by the Chicago Cardinals.

Halas reinstated himself as coach of the Bears.

Jim Brown of Cleveland gained an NFL-record 1,527 yards rushing. In a divisional playoff game, the Giants held Brown to eight yards and defeated Cleveland 10-0.

Baltimore, coached by Weeb Ewbank, defeated the Giants 23-17 in the first sudden-death overtime in an NFL Championship Game, December 28. The game ended when Colts fullback Alan Ameche scored on a one-yard touchdown run after 8:15 of overtime.

1959

Vince Lombardi was named head coach of the Green Bay Packers, January 28. Tim Mara, the co-founder of the Giants, died, February 17.

Lamar Hunt of Dallas announced his intentions to form a second pro football league. The first meeting was held in Chicago, August 14, and consisted of Hunt representing Dallas; Bob Howsam, Denver; K.S. (Bud) Adams, Houston; Barron Hilton, Los Angeles; Max Winter and Bill Boyer, Minneapolis; and Harry Wismer, New York City. They made plans to begin play in 1960.

The new league was named the American Football League, August 22. Buffalo, owned by Ralph Wilson, became the seventh franchise, October 28. Boston, owned by William H. Sullivan, became the eighth team, November 22. The first AFL draft, lasting 33 rounds,

was held, November 22. Joe Foss was named AFL Commissioner, November 30. An additional draft of 20 rounds was held by the AFL, December 2.

NFL Commissioner Bert Bell died of a heart attack suffered at Franklin Field, Philadelphia, during the last two minutes of a game between the Eagles and the Steelers, October 11. Treasurer Austin Gunsel was named president in the office of the commissioner, October 14.

The Colts again defeated the Giants in the NFL Championship Game, 31-16, December 27.

1960

Pete Rozelle was elected NFL Commissioner as a compromise choice on the twenty-third ballot, January 26. Rozelle moved the league offices to New York City.

Hunt was elected AFL president for 1960, January 26. Minneapolis withdrew from the AFL, January 27, and the same ownership was given an NFL franchise for Minnesota (to start in 1961), January 28. Dallas received an NFL franchise for 1960, January 28. Oakland received an AFL franchise, January 30.

The AFL adopted the two-point option on points after touchdown, January 28. A no-tampering verbal pact, relative to players' contracts, was agreed to between the NFL and AFL, February 9.

The NFL owners voted to allow the transfer of the Chicago Cardinals to St. Louis, March 13.

The AFL signed a five-year television contract with ABC, June 9.

The Boston Patriots defeated the Buffalo Bills 28-7 before 16,000 at Buffalo in the first AFL preseason game, July 30. The Denver Broncos defeated the Patriots 13-10 before 21,597 at Boston in the first AFL regular-season game, September 9.

Philadelphia defeated Green Bay 17-13 in the NFL Championship Game, December 26.

1961

The Houston Oilers defeated the Los Angeles Chargers 24-16 before 32,183 in the first AFL Championship Game,

January 1.

Detroit defeated Cleveland 17-16 in the first Playoff Bowl, or Bert Bell Benefit Bowl, between second-place teams in each conference in Miami, January 7.

End Willard Dewveall of the Bears played out his option and joined the Oilers, becoming the first player to play out his contract and jump from the NFL to the AFL, January 14.

Ed McGah, Wayne Valley, and Robert Osborne bought out their partners in the ownership of the Raiders, January 17. The Chargers were transferred to San Diego, February 10. Dave R. Jones sold the Browns to a group headed by Arthur B. Modell, March 22. The Howsam brothers sold the Broncos to a group headed by Calvin Kunz and Gerry Phipps, May 26.

NBC was awarded a two-year contract for radio and television rights to the NFL Championship Game for $615,000 annually, $300,000 of which was to go directly into the NFL Player Benefit Plan, April 5.

Canton, Ohio, where the league that became the NFL was formed in 1920, was chosen as the site of the Pro Football Hall of Fame, April 27. Dick McCann, a former Redskins executive, was named executive director.

A bill legalizing single-network television contracts by professional sports leagues was introduced in Congress by Representative Emanuel Celler. It passed the House and Senate and was signed into law by President John F. Kennedy, September 30.

Houston defeated San Diego 10-3 for the AFL championship, December 24. Green Bay won its first NFL championship since 1944, defeating the New York Giants 37-0, December 31.

1962

The Western Division defeated the Eastern Division 47-27 in the first AFL All-Star Game, played before 20,973 in San Diego, January 7.

Both leagues prohibited grabbing any player's facemask. The AFL voted to make the scoreboard clock the official timer of the game.

The NFL entered into a single-network agreement with CBS for telecasting all regular-season games for $4.65 million annually, January 10.

Judge Roszel Thompson of the U.S. District Court in Baltimore ruled against the AFL in its antitrust suit against the NFL, May 21. The AFL had charged the NFL with monopoly and conspiracy in areas of expansion, television, and player signings. The case lasted two and a half years, the trial two months.

McGah and Valley acquired controlling interest in the Raiders, May 24. The AFL assumed financial responsibility for the New York Titans, November 8. With Commissioner Rozelle as referee, Daniel F. Reeves regained the ownership of the Rams, outbidding his partners in sealed-envelope bidding for the team, November 27.

The Dallas Texans defeated the Oilers 20-17 for the AFL championship at Houston after 17 minutes, 54 seconds of overtime on a 25-yard field goal by Tommy Brooker, December 23. The game lasted a record 77 minutes, 54 seconds.

Judge Edward Weinfeld of the U.S. District Court in New York City upheld the legality of the NFL's television blackout within a 75-mile radius of home games and denied an injunction that would have forced the championship game between the Giants and the Packers to be televised in the New York City area, December 28. The Packers beat the Giants 16-7 for the NFL title, December 30.

1963

The Dallas Texans transferred to Kansas City, becoming the Chiefs, February 8. The New York Titans were sold to a five-man syndicate headed by David (Sonny) Werblin, March 28. Weeb Ewbank became the Titans' new head coach and the team's name was changed to the Jets, April 15. They began play in Shea Stadium.

NFL Properties, Inc., was founded to serve as the licensing arm of the NFL.

Rozelle indefinitely suspended Green Bay halfback Paul Hornung and Detroit defensive tackle Alex Karras for placing bets on their own

teams and on other NFL games; he also fined five other Detroit players $2,000 each for betting on one game in which they did not participate, and the Detroit Lions Football Company $2,000 on each of two counts for failure to report information promptly and for lack of sideline supervision.

Paul Brown, head coach of the Browns since their inception, was fired and replaced by Blanton Collier. Don Shula replaced Weeb Ewbank as head coach of the Colts.

The AFL allowed the Jets and Raiders to select players from other franchises in hopes of giving the league more competitive balance, May 11.

NBC was awarded exclusive network broadcasting rights for the 1963 AFL Championship Game for $926,000, May 23.

The Pro Football Hall of Fame was dedicated at Canton, Ohio, September 7.

The U.S. Fourth Circuit Court of Appeals reaffirmed the lower court's finding for the NFL in the $10-million suit brought by the AFL, ending three and a half years of litigation, November 21.

Jim Brown of Cleveland rushed for an NFL single-season record 1,863 yards.

Boston defeated Buffalo 26-8 in the first divisional playoff game in AFL history, December 28.

The Bears defeated the Giants 14-10 in the NFL Championship Game, a record sixth and last title for Halas in his thirty-sixth season as the Bears' coach, December 29.

1964

The Chargers defeated the Patriots 51-10 in the AFL Championship Game, January 5.

William Clay Ford, the Lions' president since 1961, purchased the team, January 10. A group representing the late James P. Clark sold the Eagles to a group headed by Jerry Wolman, January 21. Carroll Rosenbloom, the majority owner of the Colts since 1953, acquired complete ownership of the team, January 23.

The AFL signed a five-year, $36-million television contract with NBC to begin with the 1965 season, January 29.

Hornung and Karras were reinstated by Rozelle, March 16.

CBS submitted the winning bid of $14.1 million per year for the NFL regular-season television rights for 1964 and 1965, January 24. CBS acquired the rights to the championship games for 1964 and 1965 for $1.8 million per game, April 17.

Pete Gogolak of Cornell signed a contract with Buffalo, becoming the first soccer-style kicker in pro football.

Buffalo defeated San Diego 20-7 in the AFL Championship Game, December 26. Cleveland defeated Baltimore 27-0 in the NFL Championship Game, December 27.

1965

The NFL teams pledged not to sign college seniors until completion of all their games, including bowl games, and empowered the Commissioner to discipline the clubs up to as much as the loss of an entire draft list for a violation of the pledge, February 15.

The NFL added a sixth official, the line judge, February 19. The color of the officials' penalty flags was changed from white to bright gold, April 5.

Commissioner Rozelle negotiated an agreement on behalf of the NFL clubs to purchase Ed Sabol's Blair Motion Pictures, which was renamed NFL Films, April.

Atlanta was awarded an NFL franchise for 1966, with Rankin Smith, Sr., as owner, June 30. Miami was awarded an AFL franchise for 1966, with Joe Robbie and Danny Thomas as owners, August 16.

Field Judge Burl Toler became the first black official in NFL history, September 19.

According to a Harris survey, sports fans chose professional football (41 percent) as their favorite sport, overtaking baseball (38 percent) for the first time, October.

Green Bay defeated Baltimore 13-10 in sudden-death overtime in a Western Conference playoff game. Don Chandler kicked a 25-yard field goal for the Packers after 13 minutes, 39 seconds of overtime, December 26. The Packers then defeated the Browns 23-12 in the NFL Championship Game, January 2.

In the AFL Championship Game, the Bills again defeated the Chargers, 23-0, December 26.

CBS acquired the rights to the NFL regular-season games in 1966 and 1967, with an option for 1968, for $18.8 million per year, December 29.

1966

The AFL-NFL war reached its peak, as the leagues spent a combined $7 million to sign their 1966 draft choices. The NFL signed 75 percent of its 232 draftees, the AFL 46 percent of its 181. Of the 111 common draft choices, 79 signed with the NFL, 28 with the AFL, and 4 went unsigned.

Buddy Young became the first African-American to work in the league office when Commissioner Rozelle named him director of player relations, February 1.

The rights to the 1966 and 1967 NFL Championship Games were sold to CBS for $2 million per game, February 14.

Foss resigned as AFL Commissioner, April 7. Al Davis, the head coach and general manager of the Raiders, was named to replace him, April 8.

Goal posts offset from the goal line, painted bright yellow, and with uprights 20 feet above the cross-bar were made standard in the NFL, May 16.

A series of secret meetings regarding a possible AFL-NFL merger were held in the spring between Hunt of Kansas City and Tex Schramm of Dallas. Rozelle announced the merger, June 8. Under the agreement, the two leagues would combine to form an expanded league with 24 teams, to be increased to 26 in 1968 and to 28 by 1970 or soon thereafter. All existing franchises would be retained, and no franchises would be transferred outside their metropolitan areas. While maintaining separate schedules through 1969, the leagues agreed to play an annual AFL-NFL World Championship Game beginning in January, 1967, and to hold a combined draft, also beginning in 1967. Preseason games would be held between teams of each league starting in 1967. Official regular-sea-

son play would start in 1970 when the two leagues would officially merge to form one league with two conferences. Rozelle was named Commissioner of the expanded league setup.

Davis rejoined the Raiders, and Milt Woodard was named president of the AFL, July 25.

The St. Louis Cardinals moved into newly constructed Busch Memorial Stadium.

Barron Hilton sold the Chargers to a group headed by Eugene Klein and Sam Schulman, August 25.

Congress approved the AFL-NFL merger, passing legislation exempting the agreement itself from antitrust action, October 21.

New Orleans was awarded an NFL franchise to begin play in 1967, November 1. John Mecom, Jr., of Houston was designated majority stockholder and president of the franchise, December 15.

The NFL was realigned for the 1967-69 seasons into the Capitol and Century Divisions in the Eastern Conference and the Central and Coastal Divisions in the Western Conference, December 2. New Orleans and the New York Giants agreed to switch divisions in 1968 and return to the 1967 alignment in 1969.

The rights to the Super Bowl for four years were sold to CBS and NBC for $9.5 million, December 13.

1967

Green Bay earned the right to represent the NFL in the first AFL-NFL World Championship Game by defeating Dallas 34-27, January 1. The same day, Kansas City defeated Buffalo 31-7 to represent the AFL. The Packers defeated the Chiefs 35-10 before 61,946 fans at the Los Angeles Memorial Coliseum in the first game between AFL and NFL teams, January 15. The winning players' share for the Packers was $15,000 each, and the losing players' share for the Chiefs was $7,500 each. The game was televised by both CBS and NBC.

The "sling-shot" goal post and a six-foot-wide border around the field were made standard in the NFL, February 22.

Baltimore made Bubba

Smith, a Michigan State defensive lineman, the first choice in the first combined AFL-NFL draft, March 14.

The AFL awarded a franchise to begin play in 1968 to Cincinnati, May 23. A group with Paul Brown as part owner, general manager, and head coach, was awarded the Cincinnati franchise, September 27.

Arthur B. Modell, the president of the Cleveland Browns, was elected president of the NFL, May 28.

Defensive back Emlen Tunnell of the New York Giants became the first black player to enter the Pro Football Hall of Fame, August 5.

An AFL team defeated an NFL team for the first time, when Denver beat Detroit 13-7 in a preseason game, August 5.

Green Bay defeated Dallas 21-17 for the NFL championship on a last-minute 1-yard quarterback sneak by Bart Starr in 13-below-zero temperature at Green Bay, December 31. The same day, Oakland defeated Houston 40-7 for the AFL championship.

1968

Green Bay defeated Oakland 33-14 in Super Bowl II at Miami, January 14. The game had the first $3-million gate in pro football history.

Vince Lombardi resigned as head coach of the Packers, but remained as general manager, January 28.

Werblin sold his shares in the Jets to his partners Don Lillis, Leon Hess, Townsend Martin, and Phil Iselin, May 21. Lillis assumed the presidency of the club, but then died July 23. Iselin was appointed president, August 6.

Halas retired for the fourth and last time as head coach of the Bears, May 27.

The Oilers left Rice Stadium for the Astrodome and became the first NFL team to play its home games in a domed stadium.

The movie *Heidi* became a footnote in sports history when NBC didn't show the last 50 seconds of the Jets-Raiders game in order to permit the children's special to begin on time. The Raiders scored two touchdowns in the last 42 seconds to win 43-32,

November 17.

Ewbank became the first coach to win titles in both the NFL and AFL when his Jets defeated the Raiders 27-23 for the AFL championship, December 29. The same day, Baltimore defeated Cleveland 34-0.

1969

The AFL established a playoff format for the 1969 season, with the winner in one division playing the runner-up in the other, January 11.

An AFL team won the Super Bowl for the first time, as the Jets defeated the Colts 16-7 at Miami, January 12 in Super Bowl III. The title Super Bowl was recognized by the NFL for the first time.

Vince Lombardi became part owner, executive vice-president, and head coach of the Washington Redskins, February 7.

Wolman sold the Eagles to Leonard Tose, May 1.

Baltimore, Cleveland, and Pittsburgh agreed to join the AFL teams to form the 13-team American Football Conference of the NFL in 1970, May 17. The NFL also agreed on a playoff format that would include one "wild-card" team per conference—the second-place team with the best record.

The NFL announced a three-year agreement with ABC to televise *Monday Night Football*. The new series makes the NFL the first league with a regular series of national telecasts in prime time, May 26.

George Preston Marshall, president emeritus of the Redskins, died at 72, August 9.

The NFL marked its fiftieth year by the wearing of a special patch by each of the 16 teams.

1970

Kansas City defeated Minnesota 23-7 in Super Bowl IV at New Orleans, January 11. The gross receipts of approximately $3.8 million were the largest ever for a one-day sports event.

Four-year television contracts, under which CBS would televise all NFC games and NBC all AFC games (except Monday night games) and the two would divide televising the Super Bowl and

AFC-NFC Pro Bowl games, were announced, January 26.

Art Modell resigned as president of the NFL, March 12. Milt Woodard resigned as president of the AFL, March 13. Lamar Hunt was elected president of the AFC and George Halas was elected president of the NFC, March 19.

The merged 26-team league adopted rules changes putting names on the backs of players' jerseys, making a point after touchdown worth only one point, and making the scoreboard clock the official timing device of the game, March 18.

The Players Negotiating Committee and the NFL Players Association announced a four-year agreement guaranteeing approximately $4,535,000 annually to player pension and insurance benefits, August 3. The owners also agreed to contribute $250,000 annually to improve or implement items such as disability payments, widows' benefits, maternity benefits, and dental benefits. The agreement also provided for increased preseason game and per diem payments, averaging approximately $2.6 million annually.

The Pittsburgh Steelers moved into Three Rivers Stadium. The Cincinnati Bengals moved to Riverfront Stadium.

Vince Lombardi died of cancer at 57, September 3.

The Super Bowl trophy was renamed the Vince Lombardi trophy, September 10.

Tom Dempsey of New Orleans kicked a game-winning NFL-record 63-yard field goal against Detroit, November 8.

1971
Baltimore defeated Dallas 16-13 on Jim O'Brien's 32-yard field goal with five seconds to go in Super Bowl V at Miami, January 17. The NBC telecast was viewed in an estimated 23,980,000 homes, the largest audience ever for a one-day sports event.

The NFC defeated the AFC 27-6 in the first AFC-NFC Pro Bowl at Los Angeles, January 24.

The Boston Patriots changed their name to the New England Patriots, March

25. Their new stadium, Schaefer Stadium, was dedicated in a 20-14 preseason victory over the Giants.

The Philadelphia Eagles left Franklin Field and played their games at the new Veterans Stadium.

The San Francisco 49ers left Kezar Stadium and moved their games to Candlestick Park.

Daniel F. Reeves, the president and general manager of the Rams, died at 58, April 15.

The Dallas Cowboys moved from the Cotton Bowl into their new home, Texas Stadium, October 24.

Miami defeated Kansas City 27-24 in sudden-death overtime in an AFC Divisional Playoff Game, December 25. Garo Yepremian kicked a 37-yard field goal for the Dolphins after 22 minutes, 40 seconds of overtime, as the game lasted 82 minutes, 40 seconds overall, making it the longest game in history.

1972
Dallas defeated Miami 24-3 in Super Bowl VI at New Orleans, January 16. The CBS telecast was viewed in an estimated 27,450,000 homes, the top-rated one-day telecast ever.

The inbounds lines or hashmarks were moved nearer the center of the field, 23 yards, 1 foot, 9 inches from the sidelines, March 23. The method of determining won-lost percentage in standings changed. Tie games, previously not counted in the standings, were made equal to a half-game won and a half-game lost, May 24.

Robert Irsay purchased the Los Angeles Rams and transferred ownership of the club to Carroll Rosenbloom in exchange for the Baltimore Colts, July 13.

William V. Bidwill purchased the stock of his brother Charles (Stormy) Bidwill to become the sole owner of the St. Louis Cardinals, September 2.

The National District Attorneys Association endorsed the position of professional leagues in opposing proposed legalization of gambling on professional team sports, September 28.

Franco Harris' "Immaculate Reception" gave the Steelers

their first postseason win ever, 13-7 over the Raiders, December 23.

1973
Rozelle announced that all Super Bowl VII tickets were sold and that the game would be telecast in Los Angeles, the site of the game, on an experimental basis, January 3.

Miami defeated Washington 14-7 in Super Bowl VII at Los Angeles, completing a 17-0 season, the first perfect-record regular-season and postseason mark in NFL history, January 14. The NBC telecast was viewed by approximately 75 million people.

The AFC defeated the NFC 33-28 in the Pro Bowl in Dallas, the first time since 1942 that the game was played outside Los Angeles, January 21.

A jersey numbering system was adopted, April 5: 1-19 for quarterbacks and specialists, 20-49 for running backs and defensive backs, 50-59 for centers and linebackers, 60-79 for defensive linemen and interior offensive linemen other than centers, and 80-89 for wide receivers and tight ends. Players who had been in the NFL in 1972 could continue to use old numbers.

NFL Charities, a nonprofit organization, was created to derive an income from monies generated from NFL Properties' licensing of NFL trademarks and team names, June 26. NFL Charities was set up to support education and charitable activities and to supply economic support to persons formerly associated with professional football who were no longer able to support themselves.

Congress adopted experimental legislation (for three years) requiring any NFL game that had been declared a sellout 72 hours prior to kickoff to be made available for local televising, September 14. The legislation provided for an annual review to be made by the Federal Communications Commission.

The Buffalo Bills moved their home games from War Memorial Stadium to Rich Stadium in nearby Orchard Park. The Giants tied the Eagles 23-23 in the final game in Yankee Stadium, September 23. The Giants played the rest of

their home games at the Yale Bowl in New Haven, Connecticut.

A rival league, the World Football League, was formed and was reported in operation, October 2. It had plans to start play in 1974.

O.J. Simpson of Buffalo became the first player to rush for more than 2,000 yards in a season, gaining 2,003.

1974
Miami defeated Minnesota 24-7 in Super Bowl VIII at Houston, the second consecutive Super Bowl championship for the Dolphins, January 13. The CBS telecast was viewed by approximately 75 million people.

Rozelle was given a 10-year contract effective January 1, 1973, February 27.

Tampa Bay was awarded the twenty-seventh franchise to begin operation in 1976, April 24.

Sweeping rules changes were adopted to add action and tempo to games: one sudden-death overtime period was added for preseason and regular-season games; the goal posts were moved from the goal line to the end lines; kickoffs were moved from the 40- to the 35-yard line; after missed field goals from beyond the 20, the ball was to be returned to the line of scrimmage; restrictions were placed on members of the punting team to open up return possibilities; roll-blocking and cutting of wide receivers was eliminated; the extent of downfield contact a defender could have with an eligible receiver was restricted; the penalties for offensive holding, illegal use of the hands, and tripping were reduced from 15 to 10 yards; wide receivers blocking back toward the ball within three yards of the line of scrimmage were prevented from blocking below the waist, April 25.

Seattle was awarded the twenty-eighth NFL franchise to begin play in 1976, June 4. Lloyd W. Nordstrom, president of the Seattle Seahawks, and Hugh Culverhouse, president of the Tampa Bay Buccaneers, signed franchise agreements, December 5.

The Birmingham Americans defeated the Florida Blazers

22-21 in the WFL World Bowl, winning the league championship, December 5.

1975

Pittsburgh defeated Minnesota 16-6 in Super Bowl IX at New Orleans, the Steelers' first championship since entering the NFL in 1933. The NBC telecast was viewed by approximately 78 million people.

The Memphis Southmen of the WFL signed Larry Csonka, Jim Kiick, and Paul Warfield of Miami, March 31.

The divisional winners with the highest won-loss percentage were made the home team for the divisional playoffs, and the surviving winners with the highest percentage made home teams for the championship games. Previously, the home sites were pre-determined by division on a rotating basis, June 26.

Referees were equipped with wireless microphones for all preseason, regular-season, and playoff games.

The Lions moved to the new Pontiac Silverdome. The Giants played their home games in Shea Stadium. The Saints moved into the Louisiana Superdome.

The World Football League folded, October 22.

1976

Pittsburgh defeated Dallas 21-17 in Super Bowl X in Miami. The Steelers joined Green Bay and Miami as the only teams to win two Super Bowls; the Cowboys became the first wild-card team to play in the Super Bowl. The CBS telecast was viewed by an estimated 80 million people, the largest television audience in history.

Lloyd Nordstrom, the president of the Seahawks, died at 66, January 20. His brother Elmer succeeded him as majority representative of the team.

The owners awarded Super Bowl XII, to be played on January 15, 1978, to New Orleans. They also adopted the use of two 30-second clocks for all games, visible to both players and fans to note the official time between the ready-for-play signal and snap of the ball, March 16.

A veteran player allocation was held to stock the Seattle and Tampa Bay franchises with 39 players each, March 30-31. In the college draft, Seattle and Tampa Bay each received eight extra choices, April 8-9.

The Giants moved into new Giants Stadium in East Rutherford, New Jersey.

The Steelers defeated the College All-Stars in a storm-shortened Chicago College All-Star Game, the last of the series, July 23. St. Louis defeated San Diego 20-10 in a preseason game before 38,000 in Korakuen Stadium, Tokyo, in the first NFL game outside of North America, August 16.

1977

Oakland defeated Minnesota 32-14 in Super Bowl XI at Pasadena, January 9. The paid attendance was a pro record 103,438. The NBC telecast was viewed by 81.9 million people, the largest ever to view a sports event. The victory was the fifth consecutive for the AFC in the Super Bowl.

The NFL Players Association and the NFL Management Council ratified a collective bargaining agreement extending until 1982, covering five football seasons while continuing the pension plan—including years 1974, 1975, and 1976—with contributions totaling more than $55 million. The total cost of the agreement was estimated at $107 million. The agreement called for a college draft at least through 1986; contained a no-strike, no-suit clause; established a 43-man active player limit; reduced pension vesting to four years; provided for increases in minimum salaries and preseason and postseason pay; improved insurance, medical, and dental benefits; modified previous practices in player movement and control; and reaffirmed the NFL Commissioner's disciplinary authority. Additionally, the agreement called for the NFL member clubs to make payments totaling $16 million the next 10 years to settle various legal disputes, February 25.

The San Francisco 49ers were sold to Edward J. DeBartolo, Jr., March 28.

A 16-game regular season, 4-game preseason was adopted to begin in 1978, March 29. A second wild-card team was adopted for the playoffs beginning in 1978, with the wild-card teams to play each other and the winners advancing to a round of eight postseason series.

The Seahawks were permanently aligned in the AFC Western Division and the Buccaneers in the NFC Central Division, March 31.

The owners awarded Super Bowl XIII, to be played on January 21, 1979, to Miami, to be played in the Orange Bowl; Super Bowl XIV, to be played January 20, 1980, was awarded to Pasadena, to be played in the Rose Bowl, June 14.

Rules changes were adopted to open up the passing game and to cut down on injuries. Defenders were permitted to make contact with eligible receivers only once; the head slap was outlawed; offensive linemen were prohibited from thrusting their hands to an opponent's neck, face, or head; and wide receivers were prohibited from clipping, even in the legal clipping zone.

Rozelle negotiated contracts with the three television networks to televise all NFL regular-season and postseason games, plus selected preseason games, for four years beginning with the 1978 season. ABC was awarded yearly rights to 16 Monday night games, four prime-time games, the AFC-NFC Pro Bowl, and the Hall of Fame games. CBS received the rights to all NFC regular-season and postseason games (except those in the ABC package) and to Super Bowls XIV and XVI. NBC received the rights to all AFC regular-season and postseason games (except those in the ABC package) and to Super Bowls XIII and XV. Industry sources considered it the largest single television package ever negotiated, October 12.

1978

Dallas defeated Denver 27-10 in Super Bowl XII, held indoors for the first time, at the Louisiana Superdome in New Orleans, January 15. The CBS telecast was viewed by more than 102 million people, meaning the game was watched by more viewers than any other show of any kind in the history of television. Dallas' victory was the first for the NFC in six years.

According to a Louis Harris Sports Survey, 70 percent of the nation's sports fans said they followed football, compared to 54 percent who followed baseball. Football increased its lead as the country's favorite, 26 percent to 16 percent for baseball, January 19.

A seventh official, the side judge, was added to the officiating crew, March 14.

The NFL continued a trend toward opening up the game. Rules changes permitted a defender to maintain contact with a receiver within five yards of the line of scrimmage, but restricted contact beyond that point. The pass-blocking rule was interpreted to permit the extending of arms and open hands, March 17.

A study on the use of instant replay as an officiating aid was made during seven nationally televised preseason games.

The NFL played for the first time in Mexico City, with the Saints defeating the Eagles 14-7 in a preseason game, August 5.

Bolstered by the expansion of the regular-season schedule from 14 to 16 weeks, NFL paid attendance exceeded 12 million (12,771,800) for the first time. The per-game average of 57,017 was the third-highest in league history and the most since 1973.

1979

Pittsburgh defeated Dallas 35-31 in Super Bowl XIII at Miami to become the first team ever to win three Super Bowls, January 21. The NBC telecast was viewed in 35,090,000 homes, by an estimated 96.6 million fans.

NFL rules changes emphasized additional player safety. The changes prohibited players on the receiving team from blocking below the waist during kickoffs, punts, and field-goal attempts; prohibited the wearing of torn or altered equipment and exposed pads that could be hazardous; extended the zone in which there could be no crackback blocks; and instructed officials to quickly whistle a play dead when a quarterback was clearly in the grasp of a tackler, March 16.

Carroll Rosenbloom, the president of the Rams, drowned at 72, April 2. His widow, Georgia, assumed control of the club.

1980
Pittsburgh defeated the Los Angeles Rams 31-19 in Super Bowl XIV at Pasadena to become the first team to win four Super Bowls, January 20. The game was viewed in a record 35,330,000 homes.

The AFC-NFC Pro Bowl, won 37-27 by the NFC, was played before 48,060 fans at Aloha Stadium in Honolulu, Hawaii. It was the first time in the 30-year history of the Pro Bowl that the game was played in a non-NFL city.

Rules changes placed greater restrictions on contact in the area of the head, neck, and face. Under the heading of "personal foul," players were prohibited from directly striking, swinging, or clubbing on the head, neck, or face. Starting in 1980, a penalty could be called for such contact whether or not the initial contact was made below the neck area.

CBS, with a record bid of $12 million, won the national radio rights to 26 NFL regular-season games, including Monday Night Football, and all 10 postseason games for the 1980-83 seasons.

The Los Angeles Rams moved their home games to Anaheim Stadium in nearby Orange County, California.

The Oakland Raiders joined the Los Angeles Coliseum Commission's antitrust suit against the NFL. The suit contended the league violated antitrust laws in declining to approve a proposed move by the Raiders from Oakland to Los Angeles.

Television ratings in 1980 were the second-best in NFL history, trailing only the combined ratings of the 1976 season. All three networks posted gains, and NBC's 15.0 rating was its best ever. CBS and ABC had their best ratings since 1977, with 15.3 and 20.8 ratings, respectively. CBS Radio reported a record

audience of 7 million for Monday night and special games.

1981
Oakland defeated Philadelphia 27-10 in Super Bowl XV at the Louisiana Superdome in New Orleans, to become the first wild-card team to win a Super Bowl, January 25.

Edgar F. Kaiser, Jr., purchased the Denver Broncos from Gerald and Allan Phipps, February 26.

The owners adopted a disaster plan for re-stocking a team should the club be involved in a fatal accident, March 20.

A CBS-New York Times poll showed that 48 percent of sports fans preferred football to 31 percent for baseball.

The NFL teams hosted 167 representatives from 44 predominantly black colleges during training camps for a total of 289 days. The program was adopted for renewal during each training camp period.

ABC and CBS set all-time rating highs. ABC finished with a 21.7 rating and CBS with a 17.5 rating. NBC was down slightly to 13.9.

1982
San Francisco defeated Cincinnati 26-21 in Super Bowl XVI at the Pontiac Silverdome, in the first Super Bowl held in the North, January 24. The CBS telecast achieved the highest rating of any televised sports event ever, 49.1 with a 73.0 share. The game was viewed by a record 110.2 million fans. CBS Radio reported a record 14 million listeners for the game.

The NFL signed a five-year contract with the three television networks (ABC, CBS, and NBC) to televise all NFL regular-season and postseason games starting with the 1982 season.

A jury ruled against the NFL in the antitrust trial brought by the Los Angeles Coliseum Commission and the Oakland Raiders, May 7. The verdict cleared the way for the Raiders to move to Los Angeles, where they defeated Green Bay 24-3 in their first preseason game, August 29.

The 1982 season was reduced from a 16-game schedule to nine as the result of a 57-day players' strike.

The strike was called by the NFLPA at midnight on Monday, September 20, following the Green Bay at New York Giants game. Play resumed November 21-22 following ratification of the Collective Bargaining Agreement by NFL owners, November 17 in New York.

Under the Collective Bargaining Agreement, which was to run through the 1986 season, the NFL draft was extended through 1992 and the veteran free-agent system was left basically unchanged. A minimum salary schedule for years of experience was established; training camp and postseason pay were increased; players' medical, insurance, and retirement benefits were increased; and a severance-pay system was introduced to aid in career transition, a first in professional sports.

Despite the players' strike, the average paid attendance in 1982 was 58,472, the fifth-highest in league history.

1983
Because of the shortened season, the NFL adopted a format of 16 teams competing in a Super Bowl Tournament for the 1982 playoffs. The NFC's number-one seed, Washington, defeated the AFC's number-two seed, Miami, 27-17 in Super Bowl XVII at the Rose Bowl in Pasadena, January 30.

Super Bowl XVII was the second-highest rated live television program of all time, giving the NFL a sweep of the top 10 live programs in television history. The game was viewed in more than 40 million homes, the largest ever for a live telecast.

George Halas, the owner of the Bears and the last surviving member of the NFL's second organizational meeting, died at 88, October 31.

1984
The Los Angeles Raiders defeated Washington 38-9 in Super Bowl XVIII at Tampa Stadium, January 22. The game achieved a 46.4 rating and 71.0 share.

An 11-man group headed by H.R. (Bum) Bright purchased the Dallas Cowboys from Clint Murchison, Jr.,

March 20. Club president Tex Schramm was designated as managing general partner.

Wellington Mara was named president of the NFC, March 20.

Patrick Bowlen purchased a majority interest in the Denver Broncos from Edgar Kaiser, Jr., March 21.

The Colts relocated to Indianapolis, March 28. Their new home became the Hoosier Dome.

The New York Jets moved their home games to Giants Stadium in East Rutherford, New Jersey.

Alex G. Spanos purchased a majority interest in the San Diego Chargers from Eugene V. Klein, August 28.

Houston defeated Pittsburgh 23-20 to mark the one-hundredth overtime game in regular-season play since overtime was adopted in 1974, December 2.

On the field, many all-time records were set: Dan Marino of Miami passed for 5,084 yards and 48 touchdowns; Eric Dickerson of the Los Angeles Rams rushed for 2,105 yards; Art Monk of Washington caught 106 passes; and Walter Payton of Chicago broke Jim Brown's career rushing mark, finishing the season with 13,309 yards.

According to a CBS Sports/New York Times survey, 53 percent of the nation's sports fans said they most enjoyed watching football, compared to 18 percent for baseball, December 2-4.

1985
San Francisco defeated Miami 38-16 in Super Bowl XIX at Stanford Stadium in Stanford, California, January 20. The game was viewed on television by more people than any other live event in history. President Ronald Reagan, who took his second oath of office before tossing the coin for the game, was one of 115,936,000 viewers. The game drew a 46.4 rating and a 63.0 share. In addition, 6 million people watched the Super Bowl in the United Kingdom and a similar number in Italy. Super Bowl XIX had a direct economic impact of $113.5 million on the San Francisco Bay area.

NBC Radio and the NFL

entered into a two-year agreement granting NBC the radio rights to a 37-game package in each of the 1985-86 seasons, March 6. The package included 27 regular-season games and 10 postseason games.

Norman Braman, in partnership with Edward Leibowitz, bought the Philadelphia Eagles from Leonard Tose, April 29.

A group headed by Tom Benson, Jr., was approved to purchase the New Orleans Saints from John W. Mecom, Jr., June 3.

The NFL owners adopted a resolution calling for a series of overseas preseason games, beginning in 1986, with one game to be played in England/Europe and/or one game in Japan each year. The game would be a fifth preseason game for the clubs involved and all arrangements and selection of the clubs would be under the control of the Commissioner, May 23.

The league-wide conversion to videotape from movie film for coaching study was approved.

A Louis Harris poll in December revealed that pro football remained the sport most followed by Americans. Fifty-nine percent of those surveyed followed pro football, compared with 54 percent who followed baseball.

The Chicago-Miami Monday game had the highest rating, 29.6, and share, 46.0, of any prime-time game in NFL history, December 2. The game was viewed in more than 25 million homes.

The NFL showed a ratings increase on all three networks for the season, gaining 4 percent on NBC, 10 on CBS, and 16 on ABC.

1986

Chicago defeated New England 46-10 in Super Bowl XX at the Louisiana Superdome, January 26. The Patriots had earned the right to play the Bears by becoming the first wild-card team to win three consecutive games on the road. The NBC telecast replaced the final episode of *M*A*S*H* as the most-viewed television program in history, with an audience of 127 million viewers, according to A.C.

Nielsen figures. In addition to drawing a 48.3 rating and a 70 percent share in the United States, Super Bowl XX was televised to 59 foreign countries and beamed via satellite to the QE II. An estimated 300 million Chinese viewed a tape delay of the game in March. CBS Radio figures indicated an audience of 10 million for the game.

The owners adopted limited use of instant replay as an officiating aid, prohibited players from wearing or otherwise displaying equipment, apparel, or other items that carry commercial names, names of organizations, or personal messages of any type, March 11.

After an 11-week trial, a jury in U.S. District Court in New York awarded the United States Football League one dollar in its $1.7 billion antitrust suit against the NFL. The jury rejected all of the USFL's television-related claims, which were the self-proclaimed heart of the USFL's case. The jury deliberated five days, July 29.

Chicago defeated Dallas 17-6 at Wembley Stadium in London in the first American Bowl. The game drew a sellout crowd of 82,699 and the NBC national telecast in this country produced a 12.4 rating and 36 percent share, making it the highest daytime preseason television audience ever with 10.65-million viewers, August 3.

ABC's *NFL Monday Night Football*, in its seventeenth season, became the longest-running prime-time series in the history of the network.

1987

The New York Giants defeated Denver 39-20 in Super Bowl XXI and captured their first NFL title since 1956. The game, played in Pasadena's Rose Bowl, drew a sellout crowd of 101,063. According to A.C. Nielsen figures, the CBS broadcast of the game was viewed in the U.S. on television by 122.64-million people, making the telecast the second most-watched television show of all-time behind Super Bowl XX. The game was watched live or on tape in 55 foreign countries and NBC Radio's broadcast of the game

was heard by a record 10.1 million people.

New three-year TV contracts with ABC, CBS, and NBC were announced for 1987-89 at the NFL annual meeting in Maui, Hawaii, March 15. Commissioner Rozelle and Broadcast Committee Chairman Art Modell also announced a three-year contract with ESPN to televise 13 prime-time games each season. The ESPN contract was the first with a cable network. However, NFL games on ESPN also were scheduled for regular television in the city of the visiting team and in the home city if the game was sold out 72 hours in advance.

A special payment program was adopted to benefit nearly 1,000 former NFL players who participated in the League before the current Bert Bell NFL Pension Plan was created and made retroactive to the 1959 season. Players covered by the new program spent at least five years in the League and played all or part of their career prior to 1959. Each vested player would receive $60 per month for each year of service in the League for life.

NFL and CBS Radio jointly announced agreement granting CBS the radio rights to a 40-game package in each of the next three NFL seasons, 1987-89, April 7.

Over 400 former NFL players from the pre-1959 era received first payments from NFL owners, July 1.

The NFL's debut on ESPN produced the two highest-rated and most-watched sports programs in basic cable history. The Chicago at Miami game on August 16 drew an 8.9 rating in 3.81 million homes. Those records fell two weeks later when the Los Angeles Raiders at Dallas game achieved a 10.2 cable rating in 4.36 million homes.

The 1987 season was reduced from a 16-game season to 15 as the result of a 24-day players' strike. The strike was called by the NFLPA on Tuesday, September 22, following the New England at New York Jets game. Games scheduled for the third weekend were canceled but the games of weeks four, five, and six were played with replace-

ment teams. Striking players returned for the seventh week of the season, October 25.

In a three-team deal involving 10 players and/or draft choices, the Los Angeles Rams traded running back Eric Dickerson to the Indianapolis Colts for six draft choices and two players. Buffalo obtained the rights to linebacker Cornelius Bennett from Indianapolis, sending Greg Bell and three draft choices to the Rams. The Colts added Owen Gill and three draft choices of their own to complete the deal with the Rams, October 31.

The Chicago at Minnesota game became the highest-rated and most-watched sports program in basic cable history when it drew a 14.4 cable rating in 6.5 million homes, December 6.

1988

Washington defeated Denver 42-10 in Super Bowl XXII to earn its second victory this decade in the NFL Championship Game. The game, played for the first time in San Diego Jack Murphy Stadium, drew a sellout crowd of 73,302. According to A.C. Nielsen figures, the ABC broadcast of the game was viewed in the U.S. on television by 115,000,000 people. The game was seen live or on tape in 60 foreign countries, including the People's Republic of China, and CBS's radio broadcast of the game was heard by 13.7 million people.

In a unanimous 3-0 decision, the 2nd Circuit Court of Appeals in New York upheld the verdict of the jury that in July, 1986, had awarded the United States Football League one dollar in its $1.7 billion antitrust suit against the NFL. In a 91-page opinion, Judge Ralph K. Winter said the USFL sought through court decree the success it failed to gain among football fans, March 10.

By a 23-5 margin, owners voted to continue the instant replay system for the third consecutive season with the Instant Replay Official to be assigned to a regular seven-man, on-the-field crew. At the NFL annual meeting in Phoenix, Arizona, a 45-second clock was also approved to replace the 30-second clock. For a normal sequence of plays, the interval between plays was changed to 45 seconds from the time the ball is signaled dead until it is snapped on the succeeding play.

NFL owners approved the transfer of the Cardinals' franchise from St. Louis to Phoenix; approved two supplemental drafts each year—one prior to training camp and one prior to the regular season; and voted to initiate an annual series of games in Japan/Asia as early as the 1989 preseason, March 14-18.

The NFL Annual Selection Meeting returned to a separate two-day format and for the first time originated on a Sunday. ESPN drew a 3.6 rating during their seven-hour coverage of the draft, which was viewed in 1.6 million homes, April 24-25.

Art Rooney, founder and owner of the Steelers, died at 87, August 25.

Johnny Grier became the first African-American referee in NFL history, September 4.

Commissioner Rozelle announced that two teams would play a preseason game as part of the American Bowl series on August 6, 1989, in the Korakuen Tokyo Dome in Japan, December 16.

1989
San Francisco defeated Cincinnati 20-16 in Super Bowl XXIII. The game, played for the first time at Joe Robbie Stadium in Miami, was attended by a sellout crowd of 75,129. NBC's telecast of the game was watched by an estimated 110,780,000 viewers, according to A.C. Nielsen, making it the sixth most-watched program in television history. The game was seen live or on tape in 60 foreign countries, including an estimated 300 million in China. The CBS Radio broadcast of the game was heard by 11.2 million people.

Commissioner Rozelle announced his retirement, pending the naming of a successor, March 22 at the NFL annual meeting in Palm Desert, California.

Following the announcement, AFC president Lamar Hunt and NFC president

Wellington Mara announced the formation of a six-man search committee composed of Art Modell, Robert Parins, Dan Rooney, and Ralph Wilson. Hunt and Mara served as co-chairmen.

By a 24-4 margin, owners voted to continue the instant replay system for the fourth straight season. A strengthened policy regarding anabolic steroids and masking agents was announced by Commissioner Rozelle. NFL clubs called for strong disciplinary measures in cases of feigned injuries and adopted a joint proposal by the Long-Range Planning and Finance committees regarding player personnel rules, March 19-23.

Two hundred twenty-nine unconditional free agents signed with new teams under management's Plan B system, April 1.

Jerry Jones purchased a majority interest in the Dallas Cowboys from H.R. (Bum) Bright, April 18.

Tex Schramm was named president of the new World League of American Football to work with a six-man committee of Dan Rooney, chairman; Norman Braman, Lamar Hunt, Victor Kiam, Mike Lynn, and Bill Walsh, April 18.

NFL and CBS Radio jointly announced agreement extending CBS's radio rights to an annual 40-game package through the 1994 season, April 18.

As of opening day, September 10, of the 229 Plan B free agents, 111 were active and 23 others were on teams' reserve lists. Ninety-two others were waived and three retired.

Art Shell was named head coach of the Los Angeles Raiders making him the NFL's first black head coach since Fritz Pollard coached the Akron Pros in 1921, October 3.

The site of the New England Patriots at San Francisco 49ers game scheduled for Candlestick Park on October 22 was switched to Stanford Stadium in the aftermath of the Bay Area Earthquake of October 17. The change was announced on October 19.

Paul Tagliabue became the seventh chief executive of the NFL on October 26 when he

was chosen to succeed Commissioner Pete Rozelle on the sixth ballot of a three-day meeting in Cleveland, Ohio.

In all, 12 ballots were required to select Tagliabue. Two were conducted at a meeting in Chicago on July 6, and four at a meeting in Dallas on October 10-11. On the twelfth ballot, with Seattle absent, Tagliabue received more than the 19 affirmative votes required for election from among the 27 clubs present.

The transfer from Commissioner Rozelle to Commissioner Tagliabue took place at 12:01 A.M. on Sunday, November 5.

NFL Charities donated $1 million through United Way to benefit Bay Area earthquake victims, November 6.

1990
San Francisco defeated Denver 55-10 in Super Bowl XXIV at the Louisiana Superdome, January 28. San Francisco joined Pittsburgh as the NFL's only teams to win four Super Bowls.

The NFL announced revisions in its 1990 draft eligibility rules. College juniors became eligible but must renounce their collegiate football eligibility before applying for the NFL Draft, February 16.

Commissioner Tagliabue announced NFL teams will play their 16-game schedule over 17 weeks in 1990 and 1991 and 16 games over 18 weeks in 1992 and 1993, February 27.

The NFL revised its playoff format to include two additional wild-card teams (one per conference), which raised the total to six wild-card teams.

Commissioner Tagliabue and Broadcast Committee Chairman Art Modell announced a four-year contract with Turner Broadcasting to televise nine Sunday-night games.

New four-year TV agreements were ratified for 1990-93 for ABC, CBS, NBC, ESPN, and TNT at the NFL annual meeting in Orlando, Florida, March 12. The contracts totaled $3.6 billion, the largest in TV history.

The NFL announced plans to expand its American Bowl series of preseason games. In

addition to games in London and Tokyo, American Bowl games were scheduled for Berlin, Germany, and Montreal, Canada, in 1990.

For the fifth straight year, NFL owners voted to continue a limited system of Instant Replay. Beginning in 1990, the replay official will have a two-minute time limit to make a decision. The vote was 21-7, March 12.

Commissioner Tagliabue announced the formation of a Committee on Expansion and Realignment, March 13. He also named a Player Advisory Council, comprised of 12 former NFL players, March 14.

One-hundred eighty-four Plan B unconditional free agents signed with new teams, April 2.

Commissioner Tagliabue appointed Dr. John Lombardo as the League's Drug Advisor for Anabolic Steroids, April 25 and named Dr. Lawrence Brown as the League's Advisor for Drugs of Abuse, May 17.

NFL International Week was celebrated with four preseason games in seven days in Tokyo, London, Berlin, and Montreal. More than 200,000 fans on three continents attended the four games, August 4-11.

Commissioner Tagliabue announced the NFL Teacher of the Month program in which the League furnishes grants and scholarships in recognition of teachers who provided a positive influence upon NFL players in elementary and secondary schools, September 20.

For the first time since 1957, every NFL club won at least one of its first four games, October 1.

The Super Bowl Most Valuable Player trophy was renamed the Pete Rozelle trophy, October 8.

1991
The New York Giants defeated Buffalo 20-19 in Super Bowl XXV to capture their second title in five years. The game was played before a sellout crowd of 73,813 at Tampa Stadium and became the first Super Bowl decided by one point, January 26. The ABC broadcast of the game was seen by more than 112-million

people in the United States and was seen live or taped in 60 other countries.

NFL playoff games earned the top television rating spot of the week for each week of the month-long playoffs, January 29.

New York businessman Robert Tisch purchased a 50 percent interest in the New York Giants from Mrs. Helen Mara Nugent and her children, Tim Mara and Maura Mara Concannon, February 2.

NFL clubs voted to continue a limited system of Instant Replay for the sixth consecutive year. The vote was 21-7, March 19.

The NFL launched the World League of American Football, the first sports league to operate on a weekly basis on two separate continents, March 23.

NFL Charities presented a $250,000 donation to the United Service Organization. The donation was the second largest single grant ever by NFL Charities, April 5.

Commissioner Tagliabue named Harold Henderson as Executive Vice President for Labor Relations and Chairman of the NFL Management Council Executive Committee, April 8.

NFL clubs approved a recommendation by the Expansion and Realignment Committee to add two teams for the 1994 season, resulting in six divisions of five teams each, May 22.

"NFL International Week" featured six 1990 playoff teams playing nationally televised games in London, Berlin, and Tokyo on July 28 and August 3-4. The games drew more than 150,000 fans.

Paul Brown, founder of the Cleveland Browns and Cincinnati Bengals, died at age 82, August 5.

NFL clubs approved a resolution establishing an international division. A three-year financial plan for the World League was approved by NFL clubs at a meeting in Dallas, October 23.

1992
The NFL agreed to provide a minimum of $2.5 million in financial support to the NFL Alumni Association and assistance to NFL Alumni-related

programs. The agreement included contributions from NFL Charities to the Pre-59ers and Dire Need Programs for former players, January 25.

The Washington Redskins defeated the Buffalo Bills 37-24 in Super Bowl XXVI to capture their third world championship in 10 years, January 26. The game was played before a sellout crowd of 63,130 at the Hubert H. Humphrey Metrodome in Minneapolis and attracted the second largest television audience in Super Bowl history. The CBS broadcast was seen by more than 123 million people nationally, second only to the 127 million who viewed Super Bowl XX.

The use in officiating of a limited system of Instant Replay was not approved. The vote was 17-11 in favor of approval (21 votes were required). Instant Replay had been used for six consecutive years (1986-1991), March 18.

St. Louis businessman James Orthwein purchased controlling interest in the New England Patriots from Victor Kiam, May 11.

In a Harris Poll taken during the NFL offseason, professional football again was declared the nation's most popular sport. Professional football finished atop similar surveys conducted by Harris in 1985 and 1989, May 23.

NFL clubs accepted the report of the Expansion Committee at a league meeting in Pasadena. The report names five cities as finalists for the two expansion teams—Baltimore, Charlotte, Jacksonville, Memphis, and St. Louis, May 19.

At a league meeting in Dallas, NFL clubs approved a proposal by the World League Board of Directors to restructure the World League and place future emphasis on its international success, September 17.

NFL teams played their 16-game regular-season schedule over 18 weeks for the only time in league history.

1993
The NFL and lawyers for the players announced a settlement of various lawsuits and an agreement on the terms of

a seven-year deal that included a new player system to be in place through the 1999 season, January 6.

Commissioner Tagliabue announced the establishment of the "NFL World Partnership Program" to develop amateur football internationally through a series of clinics conducted by former NFL players and coaches, January 14.

As part of Super Bowl XXVII, the NFL announced the creation of the first NFL Youth Education Town, a facility located in south central Los Angeles for inner city youth, January 25.

The Dallas Cowboys defeated the Buffalo Bills 52-17 in Super Bowl XXVII to capture their first NFL title since 1978. The game was played before a crowd of 98,374 at the Rose Bowl in Pasadena, California. The NBC broadcast of the game was the most watched program in television history and was seen by 133,400,000 people in the United States. The rating for the game was 45.1, the tenth highest for any televised sports event. The game also was seen live or taped in 101 other countries, January 31.

The NFL and the NFL Players Association officially signed a 7-year Collective Bargaining Agreement in Washington, D.C., which guarantees more than $1 billion in pension, health, and post-career benefits for current and retired players—the most extensive benefits plan in pro sports. It was the NFL's first CBA since the 1982 agreement expired in 1987, June 29.

NFL Enterprises, a newly formed division of the NFL responsible for NFL Films, home video, and special domestic and international television programming was announced, August 19.

NFL announced plans to allow fans, for the first time ever, to join players and coaches in selecting the annual AFC and NFC Pro Bowl teams, October 12.

NFL clubs unanimously awarded the league's twenty-ninth franchise to the Carolina Panthers and owner Jerry Richardson at a meeting in Chicago, October 26.

At the same meeting in

Chicago, NFL clubs approved a plan to form a European league with joint venture partners, October 27.

Don Shula became the winningest coach in NFL history when Miami beat Philadelphia to give Shula his 325th victory, one more than George Halas, November 14.

NFL clubs awarded the league's thirtieth franchise to the Jacksonville Jaguars and owner Wayne Weaver at a meeting in Chicago, November 30.

The NFL announced new 4-year television agreements with NBC, ABC, ESPN, TNT, and NFL newcomer FOX, which took over the NFC package from CBS, December 18.

The NFL completed its new TV agreements by announcing that NBC would retain the rights to the AFC package, December 20.

1994
The Dallas Cowboys defeated the Buffalo Bills 30-13 in Super Bowl XXVIII to become the fifth team to win back-to-back Super Bowl titles. The game was viewed by the largest U.S. audience in television history—134.8 million people. The game's 45.5 rating was the highest for a Super Bowl since 1987 and the tenth highest-rated Super Bowl ever, January 30.

NFL clubs unanimously approved the transfer of the New England Patriots from James Orthwein to Robert Kraft at a meeting in Orlando, February 22.

In a move to increase offensive production, NFL clubs at the league's annual meeting in Orlando adopted a package of changes, including modifications in line play, chucking rules, and the roughing-the-passer rule, plus the adoption of the two-point conversion and moving the spot of the kickoff back to the 30-yard line, March 22.

NFL clubs approved the transfer of the majority interest in the Miami Dolphins from the Robbie family to H. Wayne Huizenga, March 23.

The NFL and FOX announced the formation of a joint venture to create a six-team World League to begin play in Europe in April, 1995, March 23.

The Carolina Panthers earned the right to select first in the 1995 NFL draft by winning a coin toss with the Jacksonville Jaguars. The Jaguars received the second selection in the 1995 draft, April 24.

NFL clubs approved the transfer of the Philadelphia Eagles from Norman Braman to Jeffrey Lurie, May 6.

The NFL launched "NFL Sunday Ticket," a new season subscription service for satellite television dish owners, June 1.

An all-time NFL record crowd of 112,376 attended the American Bowl game between Dallas and Houston in Mexico City. It concluded the biggest American Bowl series in NFL history with four games attracting a record 256,666 fans, August 15.

The NFL reached agreement on a new seven-year contract with its game officials, September 22.

The NFL Management Council and the NFL Players Association announced an agreement on the formulation and implementation of the most comprehensive drug and alcohol policy in sports, October 28.

At an NFL meeting in Chicago, Commissioner Tagliabue slotted the two new expansion teams into the AFC Central (Jacksonville Jaguars) and NFC West (Carolina Panthers) for the 1995 season only. He also appointed a special committee on realignment to make recommendations on the 1996 season and beyond, November 2.

1995
The San Francisco 49ers became the first team to win five Super Bowls when they defeated the San Diego Chargers 49-26 in Super Bowl XXIX at Joe Robbie Stadium in Miami, January 29.

Carolina and Jacksonville stocked their expansion rosters with a total of 66 players from other NFL teams in a veteran player allocation draft in New York, February 16.

CBS Radio and the NFL agreed to a new four-year contract for an annual 53-game package of games, continuing a relationship that spanned 15 of the past 17 years, February 22.

NFL clubs approved the transfer of the Tampa Bay Buccaneers from the estate of the late Hugh Culverhouse to South Florida businessman Malcolm Glazer, March 13.

After a two-year hiatus, the World League of American Football returned to action with six teams in Europe, April 8.

The NFL became the first major sports league to establish a site on the Internet system of on-line computer communication, April 10.

The transfer of the Rams from Los Angeles to St. Louis was approved by a vote of the NFL clubs at a meeting in Dallas, April 12.

ABC's *NFL Monday Night Football* finished the 1994-95 television season as the fifth highest-rated show out of 146 with a 17.8 average rating, the highest finish in the 25-year history of the series, April 18.

The Frankfurt Galaxy defeated the Amsterdam Admirals 26-22 to win the 1995 World Bowl before a crowd of 23,847 in Amsterdam's Olympic Stadium, June 23.

The transfer of the Raiders from Los Angeles to Oakland was approved by a vote of the NFL clubs at a meeting in Chicago, July 22.

Jacksonville Municipal Stadium opened in Jacksonville, Florida before a sold-out crowd of more than 70,000 as the St. Louis Rams defeated the Jacksonville Jaguars 27-10 in their first preseason game, August 18.

NFL Charities and 50 NFL players donated $1 million to the United Negro College Fund in honor of the fiftieth anniversity of the UNCF and the integration of the modern NFL, September 15.

The Trans World Dome opened in St. Louis with a sold-out crowd of 65,598 as the Rams defeated the Carolina Panthers 28-17, November 12.

On the field, many significant records and milestones were achieved: Miami's Dan Marino surpassed Pro Football Hall of Famer Fran Tarkenton in four major passing categories—attempts, completions, yards, and touchdowns—to become the NFL's all-time career leader. San Francisco's Jerry Rice became the all-time reception and receiving-yardage leader

with career totals of 942 catches and 15,123 yards.

1996
The Dallas Cowboys won their third Super Bowl title in four years when they defeated the Pittsburgh Steelers 27-17 in Super Bowl XXX at Sun Devil Stadium in Tempe, Arizona. The game was viewed by the largest audience in U.S. television history—138.5 million people, January 28.

An agreement between the NFL and the city of Cleveland regarding the Cleveland Browns' relocation was approved by a vote of the NFL clubs, February 9. According to the agreement, the city of Cleveland retained the Browns' heritage and records, including the name, logo, colors, history, playing records, trophies, and memorabilia, and committed to building a new 72,000-seat stadium for a reactivated Browns' franchise to begin play there no later than 1999. Art Modell received approval to move his franchise to Baltimore and rename it.

The transfer of the Oilers from Houston to Nashville for the 1998 season was approved by a vote of the NFL clubs at a meeting in Atlanta, April 30.

The Scottish Claymores defeated the Frankfurt Galaxy 32-27 to win the 1996 World Bowl in front of 38,982 at Murrayfield Stadium in Edinburgh, Scotland, June 23.

The NFL returned to Baltimore when the new Baltimore Ravens defeated the Philadelphia Eagles 17-9 in a preseason game before a crowd of 63,804 at Memorial Stadium, August 3.

Ericsson Stadium opened in Charlotte, North Carolina with a crowd of 65,350 as the Carolina Panthers defeated the Chicago Bears 30-12 in a preseason game, August 3.

Former NFL Commissioner Pete Rozelle died at his home in Rancho Santa Fe, California. Rozelle, regarded as the premiere commissioner in sports history, led the NFL for 29 years, from 1960-1989, December 6.

1997
Indianapolis Colts owner Robert Irsay died from compli-

cations related to a stroke he suffered in 1995. Irsay acquired the club in 1972 when he traded his Los Angeles Rams to Carrol Rosenbloom for the Colts. He later moved the Colts from Baltimore to Indianapolis in 1984, January 14.

The Green Bay Packers won their first NFL title in 29 years by defeating the New England Patriots 35-21 in Super Bowl XXXI at the Louisiana Superdome in New Orleans. The game was viewed by the fourth-largest audience in U.S. television history—128 million people, January 26.

The rules governing cross-ownership were modified, permitting NFL club owners to also own teams in other sports in their home market or markets without NFL teams. The vote was 24-5 (one abstention) in favor of approval, March 11.

Washington Redskins owner Jack Kent Cooke died at his home in Washington, D.C. Cooke became majority owner in 1974 and the Redskins won three Super Bowls under his leadership, April 6.

The Barcelona Dragons defeated the Rhein Fire 38-24 to win the 1997 World Bowl in front of 31,100 fans at Estadi Olimpic de Montjuic in Barcelona, Spain, June 22.

NFL clubs approved the transfer of the Seattle Seahawks from Ken Behring to Paul Allen, August 19.

Jack Kent Cooke Stadium opened in Raljon, Maryland with a crowd of 78,270 as the Washington Redskins defeated the Arizona Cardinals 19-13 in overtime, September 14.

The 10,000th regular-season game in NFL history was played when the Seattle Seahawks defeated the Tennessee Oilers 16-13 at the Kingdome in Seattle, October 5.

Atlanta Falcons owner Rankin Smith died of heart failure three days prior to his seventy-third birthday. Smith was the founder of the Falcons and was instrumental in bringing Super Bowls XXVIII and XXXIV to Atlanta, October 26.

1998
The NFL reached agreement on record eight-year television contracts with four networks. ABC (*NFL Monday Night Football*) and FOX (NFC) retained

their previous rights, CBS took over the AFC package from NBC, and ESPN won the right to broadcast the entire Sunday night cable package, January 13.

The World League was renamed the NFL Europe League, January 22.

The Denver Broncos won their first Super Bowl by defeating the defending champion Green Bay Packers 31-24 in Super Bowl XXXII at Qualcomm Stadium in San Diego. The game tied Super Bowl XXVII for the third-largest audience in U.S. television history with 133.4 million viewers, January 25.

The NFL clubs approved an extension of the Collective Bargaining Agreement through 2003. The extended CBA also created a $100 million fund for youth football, March 2.

The NFL clubs unanimously approved an expansion team for Cleveland to fulfill the commitment to return the Browns to the field in 1999, March 23.

The Rhein Fire defeated the Frankfurt Galaxy 34-10 to win the 1998 World Bowl in front of 47,846 fans in Frankfurt's Waldstadion—the biggest crowd to witness a World Bowl since 1991, June 14.

NFL clubs approved the transfer of the Minnesota Vikings from a 10-man ownership group to Red McCombs, July 28.

The NFL Stadium at Camden Yards opened in Baltimore, Maryland before a crowd of 65,938 as the Baltimore Ravens defeated the Chicago Bears 19-14 in a preseason game, August 8.

Raymond James Stadium opened in Tampa, Florida before a crowd of 62,410 as the Tampa Bay Buccaneers defeated the Chicago Bears 27-15, September 20.

Tennessee Oilers owner Bud Adams announced the team will change its name to the Tennessee Titans following the 1998 season. The NFL announced that the name Oilers will be retired—a first in league history, November 14.

1999

The Denver Broncos won their second consecutive Super Bowl title by defeating the NFC champion Atlanta Falcons 34-19 in Super Bowl XXXIII at

Pro Player Stadium in Miami. The game was viewed by 127.5 million viewers, the sixth most-watched program in U.S. television history, January 31.

Jim Pyne, a center allocated by the Detroit Lions, was the first selection of the Cleveland Browns in the 1999 NFL Expansion Draft. The Browns eventually selected 37 players, February 9.

CBS Radio/Westwood One agreed to a 3-year extension of their exclusive national radio rights to NFL games, March 11.

By a vote of 28-3, the owners adopted an instant replay system as an officiating aid for the 1999 season, March 17.

New York Jets owner Leon Hess died from complications of a blood disease. Hess had been involved in the ownership of the Jets since 1963 and was sole owner of the club since 1984, May 9.

A group led by Washington area businessman Daniel Snyder is approved by NFL clubs as the new owner of the Washington Redskins at a league meeting in Atlanta, May 25.

The Frankfurt Galaxy became the first team in NFL Europe League history to win a second World Bowl by defeating the Barcelona Dragons 38-24 at Rheinstadion, in Düsseldorf, Germany, June 27.

The Cleveland Browns returned to the field for the first time since 1995 and defeated the Dallas Cowboys 20-17 in overtime in the annual Hall of Fame Game at Canton, Ohio, August 9.

Cleveland Browns Stadium opened in Cleveland, Ohio before a crowd of 71,398 as the Minnesota Vikings defeated the Browns in a preseason game, 24-17, August 21.

Adelphia Coliseum opened in Nashville, Tennessee before a crowd of 65,729 with the Tennessee Titans defeating the Atlanta Falcons 17-3 in a preseason game, August 26.

Houston, Texas and owner Robert McNair were awarded the NFL's thirty-second franchise in a vote of the NFL clubs at a league meeting in Atlanta. The team will begin play in 2002. The NFL clubs also voted to realign into eight

divisions of four teams each for the 2002 season, October 6.

Walter Payton, the NFL's all-time leading rusher, died of liver cancer at the age of 45. Payton played for the Chicago Bears from 1975-1987 and rushed for an NFL-record 16,726 yards, November 1.

Former NFL Commissioner Pete Rozelle, who guided a still-developing league to its position today as America's most popular sport, was named by The Sporting News as the most powerful person in sports in the 20th Century, December 15.

2000

New York businessman Robert Wood Johnson IV was approved by NFL clubs as the new owner of the New York Jets at a league meeting, January 18.

The St. Louis Rams won their first Super Bowl by defeating the AFC champion Tennessee Titans 23-16 in Super Bowl XXXIV at the Georgia Dome in Atlanta. The game was viewed by 130.7 million viewers, the fifth most-watched program in U.S. television history, January 30.

For the first time in league history, paid attendance topped 16 million for the regular season and more than 65,000 per game, an increase of 1,300 per game over 1998. Paid attendance for all NFL games increased in 1999 for the third year in a row and was the highest ever in the 80-year history of the league. It marked the first time in league history that the 20-million paid attendance mark was reached for all games in a season, March 27.

The Rhein Fire won their second World Bowl in three years, defeating the Scottish Claymores 13-10 to win World Bowl 2000 in front of 35,680 at Frankfurt's Waldstadion, June 25.

More than 100 of the 136 living members of the Pro Football Hall of Fame gathered to celebrate Pro Football's Greatest Reunion in Canton, Ohio, July 28-31.

Paul Brown Stadium opened in Cincinnati, Ohio with a crowd of 56,180 as the Cincinnati Bengals defeated the Chicago Bears 24-20 in a

preseason game, August 19.

Minnesota's Gary Anderson converted a 21-yard field goal against Buffalo to pass George Blanda as the NFL's all-time scoring leader with 2,004 points, October 22.

San Francisco's Terrell Owens set a single-game receiving record with 20 receptions (283 yards) against Chicago, surpassing the previous mark of 18 by Tom Fears of the Los Angeles Rams in 1950, December 17.

2001

NFL clubs approved additional league-wide revenue sharing at a special league meeting in Dallas. The teams agreed to pool the visiting team share of gate receipts for all preseason and regular-season games and divide the pool equally starting in 2002, January 17.

The Baltimore Ravens won their first Super Bowl by defeating the NFC champion New York Giants 34-7 in Super Bowl XXXV at Raymond James Stadium in Tampa. The game was witnessed by 131.2 million viewers, the fifth most-watched program in U.S. television history, January 28.

The Sports Business Daily named NFL Commissioner Paul Tagliabue the 2000 Sports Industrialist of the Year, February 28.

NFL owners unanimously approved a realignment plan for the league starting in 2002. With the addition of the Houston Texans, the league's 32 teams will be divided into eight four-team divisions. Seven clubs change divisions, and the Seattle Seahawks change conferences, moving from the AFC to the NFC. A new scheduling format ensures that every team meets every other team in the league at least once every four years, May 22.

The Berlin Thunder won their first World Bowl, defeating the Barcelona Dragons 24-17 to win World Bowl IX in front of 32,116 at Amsterdam ArenA, June 30.

Heinz Field opened in Pittsburgh, Pennsylvania before a crowd of 57,829 with the Pittsburgh Steelers defeating the Detroit Lions 20-7 in a preseason game; and INVESCO Field at Mile High opened in Denver, Colorado before a crowd of 74,063 with the Denver Broncos defeating the New Orleans Saints 31-24 in a preseason game, August 25.

President George W. Bush became the first United States President to be involved in an NFL regular-season pregame coin toss as he helped kick off the 2001 season from the White House. Via satellite, President Bush tossed the coin for the 10 regular-season games that started at 1:00 P.M. ET, September 9.

In the wake of the September 11 terrorist attacks, Commissioner Paul Tagliabue postponed the games scheduled for September 16-17, September 13.

The league's 16-game regular season was retained when the postponed Week 2 games were rescheduled for the weekend of January 6-7, September 18.

The NFL and its game officials agreed to a new six-year Collective Bargaining Agreement, ending a two-week lockout of the regular officials, who returned to work on September 23, September 19.

The NFL announced that the league's prohibition of anabolic steroids and related substances had been strengthened to include supplements containing ephedrine and other high-risk supplements, September 27.

The NFL announced that the Super Bowl would be rescheduled from January 27 to February 3 in order to retain the full playoff format for the 2002 season. It will be the first Super Bowl played in February, October 3.

President Bush designated Super Bowl XXXVI as a "National Special Security Event," allowing all security for the game to be coordinated by the Secret Service, November 26.

2002
The NFL and the NFL Players Association agreed to a fourth extension of the 1993 Collective Bargaining Agreement through 2007, January 7.

In an AFC Wild Card matchup, the Oakland Raiders defeated the New York Jets 38-24 in the NFL's first-ever prime-time playoff game, January 12.

In a special meeting in New Orleans, NFL owners voted unanimously to approve the purchase of the Atlanta Falcons to Home Depot co-founder Arthur Blank, February 2.

The New England Patriots won their first Super Bowl by defeating the NFC champion St. Louis Rams 20-17 in Super Bowl XXXVI at the Louisiana Superdome in New Orleans. The game marked the first time in Super Bowl history that the winning points came on the final play, a 48-yard field goal by Patriots kicker Adam Vinatieri. Super Bowl XXXVI was viewed by 131.7 million viewers, the fifth-most watched program in U.S. television history, February 3.

Tony Boselli, a five-time Pro Bowl tackle allocated by the Jacksonville Jaguars, was the first selection of the Houston Texans in the 2002 NFL Expansion Draft. The Texans selected 19 players, February 18.

The NFL and Westwood One/CBS Radio Sports announced the renewal of a multiyear agreement for Westwood One/CBS Radio Sports to continue as the exclusive network radio home of the NFL, April 9.

NFL Europe kicked off its tenth season with a record 254 players allocated by NFL clubs, April 13-14.

The Berlin Thunder became the first team to win consecutive World Bowls, defeating the Rhein Fire 26-20 to win World Bowl X in front of 53,109 fans at Rheinstadion, June 22.

Seahawks Stadium opened in Seattle, Washington with an attendance of 52,902 fans as the Indianapolis Colts defeated the Seattle Seahawks 28-10 in a preseason game, August 10.

Gillette Stadium opened in Foxboro, Massachusetts with a crowd of 68,436 fans as the New England Patriots defeated the Philadelphia Eagles 16-15 in a preseason game, August 17.

Reliant Stadium opened in Houston, Texas with 69,432 fans in attendance, the largest non-Super Bowl crowd to ever watch an NFL game in Houston as the Miami Dolphins defeated the Houston Texans 24-3 in a preseason game, August 24.

For the first time, the NFL season kicked off on a Thursday night in prime time as the San Francisco 49ers defeated the New York Giants 16-13 at Giants Stadium. The game was preceded by "NFL Kickoff Live From Times Square," presented by New York City and the NFL, a football and music festival honoring the resilient spirit of New York and America, September 5.

Week 1 of the 2002 season produced the highest-scoring and most competitive Kickoff Weekend in NFL history. The 16 games averaged 49.3 points per game. A total of 788 points and 89 touchdowns were scored, the most in league history for an opening weekend. Eleven of the 16 games were decided by one score (eight points or less), a Kickoff Weekend record, September 5-9.

Johnny Unitas, the legendary quarterback for the Baltimore Colts and a Pro Football Hall of Fame member, died of a heart attack at the age of 69, September 11.

Oakland Raiders wide receiver Jerry Rice became the all-time leader in yards from scrimmage, surpassing Pro Football Hall of Fame running back Walter Payton (21,281 yards), September 29.

Cleveland Browns owner Al Lerner, the NFL Finance Committee Chairman and Chairman and CEO of MBNA Corporation, died at the age of 69, October 23.

Dallas Cowboys running back Emmitt Smith became the NFL's all-time rushing leader, surpassing Pro Football Hall of Fame running back Walter Payton (16,726 yards), October 27.

The NFL and NFLPA announced the creation of USA Football, the first national advocacy organization representing all levels of amateur football, December 5.

The 2002 season concluded with 25 overtime games, the most in NFL history, December 30.

2003
The Tampa Bay Buccaneers won their first Super Bowl by defeating the AFC champion Oakland Raiders 48-21 in Super Bowl XXXVII at Qual-

comm Stadium in San Diego. The game was witnessed by 138.9 million viewers, making Super Bowl XXXVII the most-watched program in U.S. television history, January 26.

Chicago Bears chairman emeritus Edward W. McCaskey died at the age of 83, April 8.

The Frankfurt Galaxy became the first team to win three World Bowls, defeating the Rhein Fire 35-16 to win World Bowl XI in front of 28,138 fans at Hampden Park, June 14.

Tex Schramm, the legendary team president and general manager of the Dallas Cowboys and a member of the Pro Football Hall of Fame, died at the age of 83, July 15.

Lincoln Financial Field opened in Philadelphia, Pennsylvania with an attendance of 66,279 fans as the New England Patriots defeated the Philadelphia Eagles 24-12 in a preseason game, August 22.

A renovated Lambeau Field opened in Green Bay, Wisconsin with a crowd of 69,831 fans as the Carolina Panthers defeated the Green Bay Packers 20-7 in a preseason game, August 23.

A renovated Soldier Field opened in Chicago, Illinois with an attendance of 61,500 fans as the Green Bay Packers defeated the Chicago Bears 38-23 in a regular season game on ABC's *NFL Monday Night Football*, September 29.

NFL Network, the first 24-hour, year-round television channel dedicated to the NFL and the sport of football, launched on DirecTV, November 4.

2004
The New England Patriots won their second Super Bowl in three years by defeating the NFC champion Carolina Panthers 32-29 in Super Bowl XXXVIII at Reliant Stadium in Houston. The game was witnessed by 144.4 million viewers, making Super Bowl XXXVIII the most-watched program in U.S. television history, February 1.

By a vote of 29-3, NFL owners extended the instant replay system for another five seasons through 2008, March 30.

Steve Bisciotti took over as

the controlling owner of the Baltimore Ravens, succeeding Art Modell, who operated the franchise for 43 years, April 8.

Former Arizona Cardinals safety Pat Tillman was killed in a firefight while on combat patrol with the U.S. Army Rangers in Afghanistan, April 22.

A federal appeals court formally ruled in favor of the NFL's draft eligibility rule in Maurice Clarett's lawsuit, citing federal labor policy in permitting the NFL and the Players Association to set rules for when players can enter the league, May 24.

The Berlin Thunder defeated the Frankfurt Galaxy 30-24 to win World Bowl XII in front of 35,413 fans at Arena Auf-Schalke, June 12.

The New England Patriots defeated the New York Jets 13-7 for their NFL-record 18th consecutive regular-season victory, October 24.

The NFL reached an agreement on six-year contract extensions with two of its network television partners—CBS and FOX—to run through the 2011 season, November 8.

The NFL and DirecTV announced a five-year extension on the NFL Sunday Ticket subscription television package to run through the 2010 season, November 8.

NFL Europe named the Hamburg Sea Devils as the league's newest team, November 24.

2005
Indianapolis Colts quarterback Peyton Manning set the NFL single-season record with 49 touchdown passes, January 2.

The New England Patriots became the second team in NFL history to win three Super Bowls in four seasons by defeating the Philadelphia Eagles 24-21 in Super Bowl XXXIX at ALLTEL Stadium in Jacksonville. The game was witnessed by 133.7 million viewers, making Super Bowl XXXIX the fifth-most watched program in U.S. television history, February 6.

The Pat Tillman USO Center opened in Afghanistan. The NFL donated $250,000 to the USO to honor the memory of the former Arizona Cardinals

player who died in Afghanistan while serving in the U.S. Army, April 1.

The NFL reached long-term agreements for its Sunday and Monday primetime TV packages. NBC returned to the NFL by acquiring the Sunday night package for six years (2006-2011). ESPN agreed on an eight-year deal to televise *Monday Night Football* from 2006-2013, April 18.

The NFL strengthened its steroids program by adopting the Olympic testosterone testing standard, tripling the number of times a player can be randomly tested during the offseason from two to six, adding substances to the list of banned substances, and putting new language in the policy to allow for testing of designer drugs and other substances that may have evaded detection, April 27.

NFL owners voted unanimously to approve the purchase of the Minnesota Vikings to real-estate developer Zygi Wilf, May 25.

NFL owners awarded Super Bowl XLIII, to be played on February 1, 2009 to Tampa, May 25.

The Amsterdam Admirals defeated the Berlin Thunder 27-21 to win World Bowl XIII in front of 35,134 fans at LTU Arean in Düsseldrof, Germany, June 11.

The NFL designated September 18-19 as "Hurricane Relief Weekend," which concluded with a telethon in conjunction with a Monday Night Football doubleheader on ABC and ESPN. The New York Giants-New Orleans Saints game, originally scheduled for the Louisiana Superdome, was moved to Giants Stadium following Hurricane Katrina. In total, the NFL, its owners, teams, players, and fans contributed $21 million to aid the Hurricane Katrina rebuilding effort, September 19.

An NFL record 103,467 fans attended the Arizona Cardinals' 31-14 victory over the San Francisco 49ers at Mexico City's Azteca Stadium, the first-ever regular-season NFL game played outside the United States, October 2.

NFL owners, by a vote of 31-1, approved the business plan of the NFL Europe League through its 2010 season,

October 6.

Wellington Mara, the New York Giants' president and co-chief executive officer, died at the age of 89, October 25.

Chicago Bears cornerback Nathan Vasher set an NFL record for the longest scoring play with a 108-yard touchdown return of an errant field goal by San Francico kicker Joe Nedney in Chicago, November 13.

Preston Robert Tisch, the Giants' chairman and co-chief executive officer, died at the age of 79, November 15.

2006
The NFL announced that NFL Network would begin airing a "Road To The Playoffs" package of eight primetime regular season NFL games starting in 2006, January 28.

The Pittsburgh Steelers won their fifth Super Bowl, defeating the Seattle Seahawks 21-10 in Super Bowl XL at Ford Field in Detroit, Michigan. The game was witnessed by 141.1 million viewers, making it the second-most watched program in U.S. television history, February 5.

The NFL clubs approved an extension of the Collective Bargaining Agreement through 2012, March 8.

Commissioner Tagliabue announced his decision to retire by the end of July. The NFL enjoyed an era of unrivaled prosperity in the Tagliabue Era, including labor peace throughout his 17-year tenure, March 20.

NFL clubs unanimously decided to return the name of the official game ball to "The Duke" in honor of the late New York Giants owner Wellington Mara, March 27.

The Amsterdam Admirals defeated the Berlin Thunder 22-7 to win World Bowl XIV in front of 36,286 fans at LTU Arena in Düsseldorf, Germany, May 27.

Roger Goodell became the eighth chief executive of the NFL on August 8 when he was chosen to succeed Paul Tagliabue as commissioner by a unanimous vote of the clubs at a three-day meeting in Chicago, Illinois. The transfer from Commissioner Tagliabue to Commissioner Goodell took place at 6:00 A.M. on Friday, September 1.

Cardinals Stadium opened in Glendale, Arizona with a crowd of 63,400 fans on August 12 as the Arizona Cardinals defeated the Pittsburgh Steelers 21-13 in a preseason game. The facility was later renamed University of Phoenix Stadium on September 26.

President George W. Bush signed into law HR 4954, which included the Internet Gambling Prohibition and Enforcement Act. The bill prohibits online gamblers from using credit cards, checks and electronic fund transfers to place and settle bets, strengthening enforcement of federal and state gambling laws that had been evaded by overseas gambling operations using the Internet, October 13.

NFL owners approved a resolution to stage a limited number of international regular-season games—up to two per season—beginning in 2007 and continuing through 2011, October 24.

The NFL Network broadcast its first-ever regular-season game as the Kansas City Chiefs defeated the Denver Broncos 19-10 at Arrowhead Stadium on Thanksgiving night, November 23.

San Diego Chargers running back LaDainian Tomlinson set the NFL single-season record for touchdowns with 29 on December 10. He finished the season with 31 touchdowns and also set a single-season record for points with 186.

Lamar Hunt, founder of the Kansas City Chiefs and the American Football League, died at the age of 74, December 13.

2007
The NFL announced the Miami Dolphins will host the New York Giants at London's Wembley Stadium on October 28, 2007 in the first regular-season game to be played outside of North America, February 2.

The Indianapolis Colts won their second Super Bowl, defeating the Chicago Bears 29-17 in Super Bowl XLI at Dolphin Stadium in South Florida. The game was witnessed by 139.8 million viewers, making it the third-most watched program in U.S. television history, February 4.

The NFL set an all-time paid

attendance record in 2006 for the fifth consecutive season. Attendance for all 2006 games was 22,199,712, an increase of nearly 408,000 over the previous record of 21,792,096 in 2005. The Washington Redskins set an all-time NFL regular-season home paid attendance record with a total of 708,852 for eight games, breaking their own record of 707,920 in 2004.

NFL clubs approved additional league-wide revenue sharing at a league meeting in Phoenix, Arizona. The teams agreed to redistribute up to $430 million over a four-year span, retroactive to 2006, March 26.

The NFL announced changes to its long-standing personal conduct policy and programs for players, coaches, and other team and league employees. The modifications focus on expanded educational and support programs in addition to increased levels of discipline for violations of the policy, April 10.

NFL Europa, featuring a new name and logo, kicked off its 15th season, April 14.

NFL COMMISSIONERS AND PRESIDENTS*

1920 ....Jim Thorpe, President
1921-39....Joe Carr, President
1939-41 .Carl Storck, President
1941-46 ....Elmer Layden,
              Commissioner
1946-1959 ....Bert Bell,
              Commissioner
1960-1989.........Pete Rozelle,
              Commissioner
1989-2006 .....Paul Tagliabue,
              Commissioner
2006-present ..Roger Goodell,
              Commissioner

*NFL treasurer Austin Gunsel served as president in the office of the commissioner following the death of Bert Bell (Oct. 11, 1959) until the election of Pete Rozelle (Jan. 26, 1960).

2006

AMERICAN CONFERENCE

East Division

	W	L	T	Pct.	Pts.	OP
New England	12	4	0	.750	385	237
New York Jets	10	6	0	.625	316	295
Buffalo	7	9	0	.438	300	311
Miami	6	10	0	.375	260	283

North Division

	W	L	T	Pct.	Pts.	OP
Baltimore	13	3	0	.813	353	201
Cincinnati	8	8	0	.500	373	331
Pittsburgh	8	8	0	.500	353	315
Cleveland	4	12	0	.250	238	356

South Division

	W	L	T	Pct.	Pts.	OP
Indianapolis	12	4	0	.750	427	360
Tennessee	8	8	0	.500	324	400
Jacksonville	8	8	0	.500	371	274
Houston	6	10	0	.375	267	366

West Division

	W	L	T	Pct.	Pts.	OP
San Diego	14	2	0	.875	492	303
Kansas City	9	7	0	.563	331	315
Denver	9	7	0	.563	319	305
Oakland	2	14	0	.125	168	332

NATIONAL CONFERENCE

East Division

	W	L	T	Pct.	Pts.	OP
Philadelphia	10	6	0	.625	398	328
Dallas	9	7	0	.563	425	350
New York Giants	8	8	0	.500	355	362
Washington	5	11	0	.313	307	376

North Division

	W	L	T	Pct.	Pts.	OP
Chicago	13	3	0	.813	427	255
Green Bay	8	8	0	.500	301	366
Minnesota	6	10	0	.375	282	327
Detroit	3	13	0	.188	305	398

South Division

	W	L	T	Pct.	Pts.	OP
New Orleans	10	6	0	.625	413	322
Carolina	8	8	0	.500	270	305
Atlanta	7	9	0	.438	292	328
Tampa Bay	4	12	0	.250	211	353

West Division

	W	L	T	Pct.	Pts.	OP
Seattle	9	7	0	.563	335	341
St. Louis	8	8	0	.500	367	381
San Francisco	7	9	0	.438	298	412
Arizona	5	11	0	.313	314	389

**Wild Card qualifier for playoffs; #Top playoff seed in conference*

Indianapolis finished ahead of New England based on head-to-head victory. Cincinnati finished ahead of Pittsburgh based on better division record (4-2 to 3-3). Tennessee finished ahead of Jacksonville based on better division record (4-2 to 2-4). Kansas City finished ahead of Denver based on better division record (4-2 to 3-3). New Orleans finished ahead of Philadelphia based on head-to-head victory. New York Giants finished ahead of Carolina and St. Louis based on better conference record (Giants' 7-5 to Panthers' 6-6 and Rams' 6-6) and ahead of Green Bay based on strength of victory (.422 to Packers' .383).

Wild Card Playoff: INDIANAPOLIS 23, Kansas City 8
NEW ENGLAND 37, N.Y. Jets 16
Divisionial Playoff: Indianapolis 15, BALTIMORE 6
New England 24, SAN DIEGO 21
AFC Championship: INDIANAPOLIS 38, New England 34
Wild Card Playoff: SEATTLE 21, Dallas 20
PHILADELPHIA 23, N.Y. Giants 20
Divisional Playoff: NEW ORLEANS 27, Philadelphia 24
CHICAGO 27, Seattle 24 (OT)
NFC Championship: CHICAGO 39, New Orleans 14
Super Bowl XLI: Indianapolis (AFC) 29, Chicago (NFC) 17
at Dolphin Stadium, Miami, Florida

In Past Standings section, home teams in playoff games are indicated by capital letters.

Playoff Seeds

AFC
1. San Diego
2. Baltimore
3. **Indianapolis**
4. New England
5. N.Y. Jets
6. Kansas City

NFC
1. **Chicago**
2. New Orleans
3. Philadelphia
4. Seattle
5. Dallas
6. N.Y. Giants

2005

AMERICAN CONFERENCE

East Division

	W	L	T	Pct.	Pts.	OP
New England	10	6	0	.625	379	338
Miami	9	7	0	.563	318	317
Buffalo	5	11	0	.313	271	367
N.Y. Jets	4	12	0	.250	240	355

North Division

	W	L	T	Pct.	Pts.	OP
Cincinnati	11	5	0	.688	421	350
Pittsburgh*	11	5	0	.688	389	258
Baltimore	6	10	0	.375	265	299
Cleveland	6	10	0	.375	232	301

South Division

	W	L	T	Pct.	Pts.	OP
Indianapolis#	14	2	0	.875	439	247
Jacksonville*	12	4	0	.750	361	269
Tennessee	4	12	0	.250	299	421
Houston	2	14	0	.125	260	431

West Division

	W	L	T	Pct.	Pts.	OP
Denver	13	3	0	.813	395	258
Kansas City	10	6	0	.625	403	325
San Diego	9	7	0	.563	418	312
Oakland	4	12	0	.250	290	383

NATIONAL CONFERENCE

East Division

	W	L	T	Pct.	Pts.	OP
N.Y. Giants	11	5	0	.688	422	314
Washington*	10	6	0	.625	359	293
Dallas	9	7	0	.563	325	308
Philadelphia	6	10	0	.375	310	388

North Division

	W	L	T	Pct.	Pts.	OP
Chicago	11	5	0	.688	260	202
Minnesota	9	7	0	.563	306	344
Detroit	5	11	0	.313	254	345
Green Bay	4	12	0	.250	298	344

South Division

	W	L	T	Pct.	Pts.	OP
Tampa Bay	11	5	0	.688	300	274
Carolina*	11	5	0	.688	391	259
Atlanta	8	8	0	.500	351	341
New Orleans	3	13	0	.188	235	398

West Division

	W	L	T	Pct.	Pts.	OP
Seattle#	13	3	0	.813	452	271
St. Louis	6	10	0	.375	363	429
Arizona	5	11	0	.313	311	387
San Francisco	4	12	0	.250	239	428

**Wild Card qualifier for playoffs; #Top playoff seed in conference*

Cincinnati finished ahead of Pittsburgh based on better division record (5-1 to 4-2). Baltimore finished ahead of Cleveland based on better division record (2-4 to 1-5). Tampa Bay finished ahead of Carolina based on better division record (5-1 to 4-2). Chicago finished ahead of Tampa Bay, and Tampa Bay finished ahead of the New York Giants, based on better conference record (Bears' 10-2 to Buccaneers' 9-3 to Giants' 8-4).

Wild Card playoff: NEW ENGLAND 28, Jacksonville 3
Pittsburgh 31, CINCINNATI 17
Divisional playoff: DENVER 27, New England 13
Pittsburgh 21, INDIANAPOLIS 18
AFC Championship: Pittsburgh 34, DENVER 17
Wild Card playoffs: Washington 17, TAMPA BAY 10
Carolina 23, NEW YORK GIANTS 0
Divisional playoff: SEATTLE 20, Washington 10
Carolina 29, CHICAGO 21
NFC Championship: SEATTLE 34, Carolina 14
Super Bowl XL: Pittsburgh (AFC) 21, Seattle (NFC) 10
at Ford Field, Detroit, Michigan

Playoff Seeds

AFC
1. Indianapolis
2. Denver
3. Cincinnati
4. New England
5. Jacksonville
6. **Pittsburgh**

NFC
1. **Seattle**
2. Chicago
3. Tampa Bay
4. New York Giants
5. Carolina
6. Washington

2004

AMERICAN CONFERENCE

East Division

	W	L	T	Pct.	Pts.	OP
New England	14	2	0	.875	437	260
N.Y. Jets*	10	6	0	.625	333	261
Buffalo	9	7	0	.563	395	284
Miami	4	12	0	.250	275	354

North Division

	W	L	T	Pct.	Pts.	OP
Pittsburgh#	15	1	0	.938	372	251
Baltimore	9	7	0	.563	317	268
Cincinnati	8	8	0	.500	374	372
Cleveland	4	12	0	.250	276	390

South Division

	W	L	T	Pct.	Pts.	OP
Indianapolis	12	4	0	.750	522	351
Jacksonville	9	7	0	.563	261	280
Houston	7	9	0	.438	309	339
Tennessee	5	11	0	.313	344	439

West Division

	W	L	T	Pct.	Pts.	OP
San Diego	12	4	0	.750	446	313
Denver*	10	6	0	.625	381	304
Kansas City	7	9	0	.438	483	435
Oakland	5	11	0	.313	320	442

NATIONAL CONFERENCE

East Division

	W	L	T	Pct.	Pts.	OP
Philadelphia#	13	3	0	.813	386	260
N.Y. Giants	6	10	0	.375	303	347
Dallas	6	10	0	.375	293	405
Washington	6	10	0	.375	240	265

North Division

	W	L	T	Pct.	Pts.	OP
Green Bay	10	6	0	.625	424	380
Minnesota*	8	8	0	.500	405	395
Detroit	6	10	0	.375	296	350
Chicago	5	11	0	.313	231	331

South Division

	W	L	T	Pct.	Pts.	OP
Atlanta	11	5	0	.688	340	337
New Orleans	8	8	0	.500	348	405
Carolina	7	9	0	.438	355	339
Tampa Bay	5	11	0	.313	301	304

West Division

	W	L	T	Pct.	Pts.	OP
Seattle	9	7	0	.563	371	373
St. Louis*	8	8	0	.500	319	392
Arizona	6	10	0	.375	284	322
San Francisco	2	14	0	.125	259	452

Wild Card qualifier for playoffs; #Top playoff seed in conference
Indianapolis finished ahead of San Diego based on head-to-head victory. N.Y. Jets finished ahead of Denver based on better record vs. common opponents (5-0 to 3-2). St. Louis finished ahead of New Orleans and Minnesota based on best conference record (7-5 to Saints' 6-6 to Vikings' 5-7), and Minnesota finished ahead of New Orleans based on head-to-head victory. N.Y. Giants finished ahead of Dallas and Washington based on better head-to-head record (3-1 to Cowboys' 2-2 to Redskins' 1-3), and Dallas finished ahead of Washington based on head-to-head sweep (2-0).

Wild Card playoffs: N.Y. Jets 20, SAN DIEGO 17 (OT)
  INDIANAPOLIS 49, Denver 24
Divisional playoffs: PITTSBURGH 20, N.Y. Jets 17 (OT)
  NEW ENGLAND 20, Indianapolis 3
AFC Championship: New England 41, PITTSBURGH 27
Wild Card playoffs: St. Louis 27, SEATTLE 20
  Minnesota 31, GREEN BAY 17
Divisional playoffs: ATLANTA 47, St. Louis 17
  PHILADELPHIA 27, Minnesota 14
NFC Championship: PHILADELPHIA 27, Atlanta 10
Super Bowl XXXIX: New England (AFC) 24, Philadelphia (NFC) 21
  at Alltel Stadium, Jacksonville, Florida

Playoff Seeds

AFC	NFC
1. Pittsburgh	**1. Philadelphia**
2. New England	2. Atlanta
3. Indianapolis	3. Green Bay
4. San Diego	4. Seattle
5. N.Y. Jets	5. St. Louis
6. Denver	6. Minnesota

2003

AMERICAN CONFERENCE

East Division

	W	L	T	Pct.	Pts.	OP
New England#	14	2	0	.875	348	238
Miami	10	6	0	.625	311	261
Buffalo	6	10	0	.375	243	279
N.Y. Jets	6	10	0	.375	283	299

North Division

	W	L	T	Pct.	Pts.	OP
Baltimore	10	6	0	.625	391	281
Cincinnati	8	8	0	.500	346	384
Pittsburgh	6	10	0	.375	300	327
Cleveland	5	11	0	.313	254	322

South Division

	W	L	T	Pct.	Pts.	OP
Indianapolis	12	4	0	.750	447	336
Tennessee*	12	4	0	.750	435	324
Jacksonville	5	11	0	.313	276	331
Houston	5	11	0	.313	255	380

West Division

	W	L	T	Pct.	Pts.	OP
Kansas City	13	3	0	.813	484	332
Denver*	10	6	0	.625	381	301
Oakland	4	12	0	.250	270	379
San Diego	4	12	0	.250	313	441

NATIONAL CONFERENCE

East Division

	W	L	T	Pct.	Pts.	OP
Philadelphia#	12	4	0	.750	374	287
Dallas*	10	6	0	.625	289	260
Washington	5	11	0	.313	287	372
N.Y. Giants	4	12	0	.250	243	387

North Division

	W	L	T	Pct.	Pts.	OP
Green Bay	10	6	0	.625	442	307
Minnesota	9	7	0	.563	416	353
Chicago	7	9	0	.438	283	346
Detroit	5	11	0	.313	270	379

South Division

	W	L	T	Pct.	Pts.	OP
Carolina	11	5	0	.688	325	304
New Orleans	8	8	0	.500	340	326
Tampa Bay	7	9	0	.438	301	264
Atlanta	5	11	0	.313	299	422

West Division

	W	L	T	Pct.	Pts.	OP
St. Louis	12	4	0	.750	447	328
Seattle*	10	6	0	.625	404	327
San Francisco	7	9	0	.438	384	337
Arizona	4	12	0	.250	225	452

Wild Card qualifier for playoffs; #Top playoff seed in conference
Buffalo finished ahead of N.Y. Jets based on better division record (2-4 to Jets' 1-5). Indianapolis finished ahead of Tennessee based on head-to-head sweep (2-0). Jacksonville finished ahead of Houston based on better division record (2-4 to Texans' 1-5). Denver finished ahead of Miami based on better conference record (9-3 to Dolphins' 7-5). Oakland finished ahead of San Diego based on better conference record (3-9 to Chargers' 2-10). Philadelphia finished ahead of St. Louis based on better conference record (9-3 to Rams' 8-4). Seattle finished ahead of Dallas based on better strength of victory (65-95 to Cowboys' 62-98).

Wild Card playoffs: Tennessee 20, BALTIMORE 17;
  INDIANAPOLIS 41, Denver 10
Divisional playoffs: NEW ENGLAND 17, Tennessee 14;
  Indianapolis 38, KANSAS CITY 31
AFC Championship: NEW ENGLAND 24, Indianapolis 14
Wild Card playoffs: CAROLINA 29, Dallas 10;
  GREEN BAY 33, Seattle 27 (OT)
Divisional playoffs: Carolina 29, ST. LOUIS 23 (2OT);
  PHILADELPHIA 20, Green Bay 17 (OT)
NFC Championship: Carolina 14, PHILADELPHIA 3
Super Bowl XXXVIII: New England (AFC) 32, Carolina (NFC) 29
  at Reliant Stadium, Houston, Texas

Playoff Seeds

AFC	NFC
1. New England	1. Philadelphia
2. Kansas City	2. St. Louis
3. Indianapolis	**3. Carolina**
4. Baltimore	4. Green Bay
5. Tennessee	5. Seattle
6. Denver	6. Dallas

2002

AMERICAN CONFERENCE

East Division

	W	L	T	Pct.	Pts.	OP
N.Y. Jets	9	7	0	.563	359	336
New England	9	7	0	.563	381	346
Miami	9	7	0	.563	378	301
Buffalo	8	8	0	.500	379	397

North Division

	W	L	T	Pct.	Pts.	OP
Pittsburgh	10	5	1	.656	390	345
Cleveland*	9	7	0	.563	344	320
Baltimore	7	9	0	.438	316	354
Cincinnati	2	14	0	.125	279	456

South Division

	W	L	T	Pct.	Pts.	OP
Tennessee	11	5	0	.688	367	324
Indianapolis*	10	6	0	.625	349	313
Jacksonville	6	10	0	.375	328	315
Houston	4	12	0	.250	213	356

West Division

	W	L	T	Pct.	Pts.	OP
Oakland#	11	5	0	.688	450	304
Denver	9	7	0	.563	392	344
San Diego	8	8	0	.500	333	367
Kansas City	8	8	0	.500	467	399

NATIONAL CONFERENCE

East Division

	W	L	T	Pct.	Pts.	OP
Philadelphia#	12	4	0	.750	415	241
N.Y. Giants*	10	6	0	.625	320	279
Washington	7	9	0	.438	307	365
Dallas	5	11	0	.313	217	329

North Division

	W	L	T	Pct.	Pts.	OP
Green Bay	12	4	0	.750	398	328
Minnesota	6	10	0	.375	390	442
Chicago	4	12	0	.250	281	379
Detroit	3	13	0	.188	306	451

South Division

	W	L	T	Pct.	Pts.	OP
Tampa Bay	12	4	0	.750	346	196
Atlanta*	9	6	1	.594	402	314
New Orleans	9	7	0	.563	432	388
Carolina	7	9	0	.438	258	302

West Division

	W	L	T	Pct.	Pts.	OP
San Francisco	10	6	0	.625	367	351
St. Louis	7	9	0	.438	316	369
Seattle	7	9	0	.438	355	369
Arizona	5	11	0	.313	262	417

*Wild Card qualifier for playoffs; #Top playoff seed in conference
New York Jets finished ahead of New England based on better record in common games (8-4 to Patriots' 7-5) and Miami based on better division record (4-2 to Dolphins' 2-4). New England finished ahead of Miami based on better division record (4-2 to Dolphins' 2-4). Cleveland finished ahead of Denver and New England based on better conference record (7-5 to Broncos' 5-7 and Patriots' 6-6). Oakland finished ahead of Tennessee based on better head-to-head record (1-0). San Diego finished ahead of Kansas City based on better division record (3-3 to Chiefs' 2-4). Philadelphia finished ahead of Green Bay and Tampa Bay based on better conference record (11-1 to Packers' 9-3 and Buccaneers' 9-3). Tampa Bay finished ahead of Green Bay based on better head-to-head record (1-0). St. Louis finished ahead of Seattle based on better division record (4-2 to Seahawks' 2-4).
Wild Card playoffs: N.Y. JETS 41, Indianapolis 0;
  PITTSBURGH 36, Cleveland 33
Divisional playoffs: TENNESSEE 34, Pittsburgh 31 (OT);
  OAKLAND 30, N.Y. Jets 10
AFC Championship: OAKLAND 41, Tennessee 24
Wild Card playoffs: Atlanta 27, GREEN BAY 7;
  SAN FRANCISCO 39, N.Y. Giants 38
Divisional playoffs: PHILADELPHIA 20, Atlanta 6;
  TAMPA BAY 31, San Francisco 6
NFC Championship: Tampa Bay 27, PHILADELPHIA 10
Super Bowl XXXVII: Tampa Bay (NFC) 48, Oakland (AFC) 21
  at Qualcomm Stadium, San Diego, California

Playoff Seeds

AFC	NFC
1. Oakland	1. Philadelphia
2. Tennessee	2. Tampa Bay
3. Pittsburgh	3. Green Bay
4. N.Y. Jets	4. San Francisco
5. Indianapolis	5. N.Y. Giants
6. Cleveland	6. Atlanta

2001

AMERICAN CONFERENCE

Eastern Division

	W	L	T	Pct.	Pts.	OP
New England	11	5	0	.688	371	272
Miami*	11	5	0	.688	344	290
N.Y. Jets*	10	6	0	.625	308	295
Indianapolis	6	10	0	.375	413	486
Buffalo	3	13	0	.188	265	420

Central Division

	W	L	T	Pct.	Pts.	OP
Pittsburgh#	13	3	0	.813	352	212
Baltimore*	10	6	0	.625	303	265
Cleveland	7	9	0	.438	285	319
Tennessee	7	9	0	.438	336	388
Jacksonville	6	10	0	.375	294	286
Cincinnati	6	10	0	.375	226	309

Western Division

	W	L	T	Pct.	Pts.	OP
Oakland	10	6	0	.625	399	327
Seattle	9	7	0	.563	301	324
Denver	8	8	0	.500	340	339
Kansas City	6	10	0	.375	320	344
San Diego	5	11	0	.313	332	321

NATIONAL CONFERENCE

Eastern Division

	W	L	T	Pct.	Pts.	OP
Philadelphia	11	5	0	.688	343	208
Washington	8	8	0	.500	256	303
N.Y. Giants	7	9	0	.438	294	321
Arizona	7	9	0	.438	295	343
Dallas	5	11	0	.313	246	338

Central Division

	W	L	T	Pct.	Pts.	OP
Chicago	13	3	0	.813	338	203
Green Bay*	12	4	0	.750	390	266
Tampa Bay*	9	7	0	.563	324	280
Minnesota	5	11	0	.313	290	390
Detroit	2	14	0	.125	270	424

Western Division

	W	L	T	Pct.	Pts.	OP
St. Louis#	14	2	0	.875	503	273
San Francisco*	12	4	0	.750	409	282
New Orleans	7	9	0	.438	333	409
Atlanta	7	9	0	.438	291	377
Carolina	1	15	0	.063	253	410

*Wild Card qualifier for playoffs; #Top playoff seed in conference
New England finished ahead of Miami based on better division record (6-2 to Dolphins' 5-3). Baltimore was second Wild Card ahead of N.Y. Jets based on better record against common opponents (3-2 to Jets' 2-2). Cleveland finished ahead of Tennessee based on better division record (5-5 to Titans' 3-7). Jacksonville finished ahead of Cincinnati based on head-to-head record (2-0). N.Y. Giants finished ahead of Arizona based on head-to-head record (2-0). Green Bay was first Wild Card ahead of San Francisco based on better conference record (9-3 to 49ers' 8-4). New Orleans finished ahead of Atlanta based on better division record (4-4 to Falcons' 3-5).
Wild Card playoffs: OAKLAND 38, N.Y. Jets 24;
  Baltimore 20, MIAMI 3
Divisional playoffs: NEW ENGLAND 16, Oakland 13 (OT);
  PITTSBURGH 27, Baltimore 10
AFC Championship: New England 24, PITTSBURGH 17
Wild Card playoffs: PHILADELPHIA 31, Tampa Bay 9;
  GREEN BAY 25, San Francisco 15
Divisional playoffs: Philadelphia 33, CHICAGO 19;
  ST. LOUIS 45, Green Bay 17
NFC Championship: ST. LOUIS 29, Philadelphia 24
Super Bowl XXXVI: New England (AFC) 20, St. Louis (NFC) 17
  at Louisiana Superdome, New Orleans, Louisiana

Playoff Seeds

AFC	NFC
1. Pittsburgh	1. St. Louis
2. New England	2. Chicago
3. Oakland	3. Philadelphia
4. Miami	4. Green Bay
5. Baltimore	5. San Francisco
6. N.Y. Jets	6. Tampa Bay

2000

AMERICAN CONFERENCE

Eastern Division

	W	L	T	Pct.	Pts.	OP
Miami	11	5	0	.688	323	226
Indianapolis*	10	6	0	.625	429	326
N.Y. Jets	9	7	0	.563	321	321
Buffalo	8	8	0	.500	315	350
New England	5	11	0	.313	276	338

Central Division

	W	L	T	Pct.	Pts.	OP
Tennessee#	13	3	0	.813	346	191
Baltimore*	12	4	0	.750	333	165
Pittsburgh	9	7	0	.563	321	255
Jacksonville	7	9	0	.438	367	327
Cincinnati	4	12	0	.250	185	359
Cleveland	3	13	0	.188	161	419

Western Division

	W	L	T	Pct.	Pts.	OP
Oakland	12	4	0	.750	479	299
Denver*	11	5	0	.688	485	369
Kansas City	7	9	0	.438	355	354
Seattle	6	10	0	.375	320	405
San Diego	1	15	0	.063	269	440

NATIONAL CONFERENCE

Eastern Division

	W	L	T	Pct.	Pts.	OP
N.Y. Giants#	12	4	0	.750	328	246
Philadelphia*	11	5	0	.688	351	245
Washington	8	8	0	.500	281	269
Dallas	5	11	0	.313	294	361
Arizona	3	13	0	.188	210	443

Central Division

	W	L	T	Pct.	Pts.	OP
Minnesota	11	5	0	.688	397	371
Tampa Bay*	10	6	0	.625	388	269
Green Bay	9	7	0	.563	353	323
Detroit	9	7	0	.563	307	307
Chicago	5	11	0	.313	216	355

Western Division

	W	L	T	Pct.	Pts.	OP
New Orleans	10	6	0	.625	354	305
St. Louis*	10	6	0	.625	540	471
Carolina	7	9	0	.438	310	310
San Francisco	6	10	0	.375	388	422
Atlanta	4	12	0	.250	252	413

*Wild Card qualifier for playoffs; #Top playoff seed in conference
Green Bay finished ahead of Detroit based on better division record (5-3 to Lions' 3-5). New Orleans finished ahead of St. Louis based on better division record (7-1 to Rams' 5-3). Tampa Bay was second Wild Card based on head-to-head victory over St. Louis (1-0).

Wild Card playoffs: MIAMI 23, Indianapolis 17 (OT); BALTIMORE 21, Denver 3
Divisional playoffs: OAKLAND 27, Miami 0; Baltimore 24, TENNESSEE 10
AFC Championship: Baltimore 16, OAKLAND 3
Wild Card playoffs: NEW ORLEANS 31, St. Louis 28; PHILADELPHIA 21, Tampa Bay 3
Divisional playoffs: MINNESOTA 34, New Orleans 16; N.Y. GIANTS 20, Philadelphia 10
NFC Championship: N.Y. GIANTS 41, Minnesota 0
Super Bowl XXXV: Baltimore (AFC) 34, N.Y. Giants (NFC) 7 at Raymond James Stadium, Tampa, Florida

Playoff Seeds

AFC	NFC
1. Tennessee	1. N.Y. Giants
2. Oakland	2. Minnesota
3. Miami	3. New Orleans
4. Baltimore	4. Philadelphia
5. Denver	5. Tampa Bay
6. Indianapolis	6. St. Louis

1999

AMERICAN CONFERENCE

Eastern Division

	W	L	T	Pct.	Pts.	OP
Indianapolis	13	3	0	.813	423	333
Buffalo*	11	5	0	.688	320	229
Miami*	9	7	0	.563	326	336
N.Y. Jets	8	8	0	.500	308	309
New England	8	8	0	.500	299	284

Central Division

	W	L	T	Pct.	Pts.	OP
Jacksonville#	14	2	0	.875	396	217
Tennessee*	13	3	0	.813	392	324
Baltimore	8	8	0	.500	324	277
Pittsburgh	6	10	0	.375	317	320
Cincinnati	4	12	0	.250	283	460
Cleveland	2	14	0	.125	217	437

Western Division

	W	L	T	Pct.	Pts.	OP
Seattle	9	7	0	.563	338	298
Kansas City	9	7	0	.563	390	322
San Diego	8	8	0	.500	269	316
Oakland	8	8	0	.500	390	329
Denver	6	10	0	.375	314	318

NATIONAL CONFERENCE

Eastern Division

	W	L	T	Pct.	Pts.	OP
Washington	10	6	0	.625	443	377
Dallas*	8	8	0	.500	352	276
N.Y. Giants	7	9	0	.438	299	358
Arizona	6	10	0	.375	245	382
Philadelphia	5	11	0	.313	272	357

Central Division

	W	L	T	Pct.	Pts.	OP
Tampa Bay	11	5	0	.688	270	235
Minnesota*	10	6	0	.625	399	335
Detroit*	8	8	0	.500	322	323
Green Bay	8	8	0	.500	357	341
Chicago	6	10	0	.375	272	341

Western Division

	W	L	T	Pct.	Pts.	OP
St. Louis#	13	3	0	.813	526	242
Carolina	8	8	0	.500	421	381
Atlanta	5	11	0	.313	285	380
San Francisco	4	12	0	.250	295	453
New Orleans	3	13	0	.188	260	434

*Wild Card qualifier for playoffs; #Top playoff seed in conference
Miami was third Wild Card ahead of Kansas City based on better record against common opponents (6-1 to Chiefs' 5-3). N.Y. Jets finished ahead of New England based on better division record (4-4 to Patriots' 2-6). Seattle finished ahead of Kansas City based on head-to-head sweep (2-0). San Diego finished ahead of Oakland based on better division record (5-3 to Raiders' 3-5). Dallas was second Wild Card based on better record against common opponents (3-2 to Lions' 3-3) and better conference record than Carolina (7-5 to Panthers' 6-6). Detroit was third Wild Card based on better conference record than Green Bay (7-5 to Packers' 6-6) and better conference record than Carolina (7-5 to Panthers' 6-6).

Wild Card playoffs: TENNESSEE 22, Buffalo 16; Miami 20, SEATTLE 17
Divisional playoffs: JACKSONVILLE 62, Miami 7; Tennessee 19, INDIANAPOLIS 16
AFC Championship: Tennessee 33, JACKSONVILLE 14
Wild Card playoffs: WASHINGTON 27, Detroit 13; MINNESOTA 27, Dallas 10
Divisional playoffs: TAMPA BAY 14, Washington 13; ST. LOUIS 49, Minnesota 37
NFC Championship: ST. LOUIS 11, Tampa Bay 6
Super Bowl XXXIV: St. Louis (NFC) 23, Tennessee (AFC) 16 at Georgia Dome, Atlanta, Georgia

Playoff Seeds

AFC	NFC
1. Jacksonville	1. St. Louis
2. Indianapolis	2. Tampa Bay
3. Seattle	3. Washington
4. Tennessee	4. Minnesota
5. Buffalo	5. Dallas
6. Miami	6. Detroit

1998

AMERICAN CONFERENCE

Eastern Division

	W	L	T	Pct.	Pts.	OP
N.Y. Jets	12	4	0	.750	416	266
Miami*	10	6	0	.625	321	265
Buffalo*	10	6	0	.625	400	333
New England*	9	7	0	.563	337	329
Indianapolis	3	13	0	.188	310	444

Central Division

	W	L	T	Pct.	Pts.	OP
Jacksonville	11	5	0	.688	392	338
Tennessee	8	8	0	.500	330	320
Pittsburgh	7	9	0	.438	263	303
Baltimore	6	10	0	.375	269	335
Cincinnati	3	13	0	.188	268	452

Western Division

	W	L	T	Pct.	Pts.	OP
Denver#	14	2	0	.875	501	309
Oakland	8	8	0	.500	288	356
Seattle	8	8	0	.500	372	310
Kansas City	7	9	0	.438	327	363
San Diego	5	11	0	.313	241	342

NATIONAL CONFERENCE

Eastern Division

	W	L	T	Pct.	Pts.	OP
Dallas	10	6	0	.625	381	275
Arizona*	9	7	0	.563	325	378
N.Y. Giants	8	8	0	.500	287	309
Washington	6	10	0	.375	319	421
Philadelphia	3	13	0	.188	161	344

Central Division

	W	L	T	Pct.	Pts.	OP
Minnesota#	15	1	0	.938	556	296
Green Bay*	11	5	0	.688	408	319
Tampa Bay	8	8	0	.500	314	295
Detroit	5	11	0	.313	306	378
Chicago	4	12	0	.250	276	368

Western Division

	W	L	T	Pct.	Pts.	OP
Atlanta	14	2	0	.875	442	289
San Francisco*	12	4	0	.750	479	328
New Orleans	6	10	0	.375	305	359
Carolina	4	12	0	.250	336	413
St. Louis	4	12	0	.250	285	378

*Wild Card qualifier for playoffs; #Top playoff seed in conference
Miami finished ahead of Buffalo based on better net division points (6 to Bills' 0). Oakland finished ahead of Seattle based on head-to-head sweep (2-0). Carolina finished ahead of St. Louis based on head-to-head sweep (2-0).
Wild Card playoffs: MIAMI 24, Buffalo 17;
JACKSONVILLE 25, New England 10
Divisional playoffs: DENVER 38, Miami 3;
N.Y. JETS 34, Jacksonville 24
AFC Championship: DENVER 23, N.Y. Jets 10
Wild Card playoffs: Arizona 20, DALLAS 7;
SAN FRANCISCO 30, Green Bay 27
Divisional playoffs: ATLANTA 20, San Francisco 18;
MINNESOTA 41, Arizona 21
NFC Championship: Atlanta 30, MINNESOTA 27 (OT)
Super Bowl XXXIII: Denver (AFC) 34, Atlanta (NFC) 19, at Pro Player Stadium, Miami, Florida

Playoff Seeds

AFC	NFC
1. Denver	1. Minnesota
2. N.Y. Jets	**2. Atlanta**
3. Jacksonville	3. Dallas
4. Miami	4. San Francisco
5. Buffalo	5. Green Bay
6. New England	6. Arizona

1997

AMERICAN CONFERENCE

Eastern Division

	W	L	T	Pct.	Pts.	OP
New England	10	6	0	.625	369	289
Miami*	9	7	0	.563	339	327
N.Y. Jets	9	7	0	.563	348	287
Buffalo	6	10	0	.375	255	367
Indianapolis	3	13	0	.188	313	401

Central Division

	W	L	T	Pct.	Pts.	OP
Pittsburgh	11	5	0	.688	372	307
Jacksonville*	11	5	0	.688	394	318
Tennessee	8	8	0	.500	333	310
Cincinnati	7	9	0	.438	355	405
Baltimore	6	9	1	.406	326	345

Western Division

	W	L	T	Pct.	Pts.	OP
Kansas City#	13	3	0	.813	375	232
Denver*	12	4	0	.750	472	287
Seattle	8	8	0	.500	365	362
Oakland	4	12	0	.250	324	419
San Diego	4	12	0	.250	266	425

NATIONAL CONFERENCE

Eastern Division

	W	L	T	Pct.	Pts.	OP
N.Y. Giants	10	5	1	.656	307	265
Washington	8	7	1	.531	327	289
Philadelphia	6	9	1	.406	317	372
Dallas	6	10	0	.375	304	314
Arizona	4	12	0	.250	283	379

Central Division

	W	L	T	Pct.	Pts.	OP
Green Bay	13	3	0	.813	422	282
Tampa Bay*	10	6	0	.625	299	263
Detroit*	9	7	0	.563	379	306
Minnesota*	9	7	0	.563	354	359
Chicago	4	12	0	.250	263	421

Western Division

	W	L	T	Pct.	Pts.	OP
San Francisco#	13	3	0	.813	375	265
Carolina	7	9	0	.438	265	314
Atlanta	7	9	0	.438	320	361
New Orleans	6	10	0	.375	237	327
St. Louis	5	11	0	.313	299	359

*Wild Card qualifier for playoffs; #Top playoff seed in conference
Miami finished ahead of N.Y. Jets based on head-to-head sweep (2-0). Pittsburgh finished ahead of Jacksonville based on better net division points (78 to Jaguars' 23). Oakland finished ahead of San Diego based on better division record (2-6 to Chargers' 1-7). San Francisco was top playoff seed based on better conference record than Green Bay (11-1 to Packers' 10-2). Detroit finished ahead of Minnesota based on head-to-head sweep (2-0). Carolina finished ahead of Atlanta based on head-to-head sweep (2-0).
Wild Card playoffs: DENVER 42, Jacksonville 17;
NEW ENGLAND 17, Miami 3
Divisional playoffs: PITTSBURGH 7, New England 6;
Denver 14, KANSAS CITY 10
AFC Championship: Denver 24, PITTSBURGH 21
Wild Card playoffs: Minnesota 23, N.Y. GIANTS 22;
TAMPA BAY 20, Detroit 10
Divisional playoffs: SAN FRANCISCO 38, Minnesota 22;
GREEN BAY 21, Tampa Bay 7
NFC Championship: Green Bay 23, SAN FRANCISCO 10
Super Bowl XXXII: Denver (AFC) 31, Green Bay (NFC) 24, at Qualcomm Stadium, San Diego, California

Playoff Seeds

AFC	NFC
1. Kansas City	1. San Francisco
2. Pittsburgh	**2. Green Bay**
3. New England	3. N.Y. Giants
4. Denver	4. Tampa Bay
5. Jacksonville	5. Detroit
6. Miami	6. Minnesota

1996

AMERICAN CONFERENCE
Eastern Division

	W	L	T	Pct.	Pts.	OP
New England	11	5	0	.688	418	313
Buffalo*	10	6	0	.625	319	266
Indianapolis*	9	7	0	.563	317	334
Miami	8	8	0	.500	339	325
N.Y. Jets	1	15	0	.063	279	454

Central Division

	W	L	T	Pct.	Pts.	OP
Pittsburgh	10	6	0	.625	344	257
Jacksonville*	9	7	0	.563	325	335
Cincinnati	8	8	0	.500	372	369
Houston	8	8	0	.500	345	319
Baltimore	4	12	0	.250	371	441

Western Division

	W	L	T	Pct.	Pts.	OP
Denver#	13	3	0	.813	391	275
Kansas City	9	7	0	.563	297	300
San Diego	8	8	0	.500	310	376
Oakland	7	9	0	.438	340	293
Seattle	7	9	0	.438	317	376

NATIONAL CONFERENCE
Eastern Division

	W	L	T	Pct.	Pts.	OP
Dallas	10	6	0	.625	286	250
Philadelphia*	10	6	0	.625	363	341
Washington	9	7	0	.563	364	312
Arizona	7	9	0	.438	300	397
N.Y. Giants	6	10	0	.375	242	297

Central Division

	W	L	T	Pct.	Pts.	OP
Green Bay#	13	3	0	.813	456	210
Minnesota*	9	7	0	.563	298	315
Chicago	7	9	0	.438	283	305
Tampa Bay	6	10	0	.375	221	293
Detroit	5	11	0	.313	302	368

Western Division

	W	L	T	Pct.	Pts.	OP
Carolina	12	4	0	.750	367	218
San Francisco*	12	4	0	.750	398	257
St. Louis	6	10	0	.375	303	409
Atlanta	3	13	0	.188	309	461
New Orleans	3	13	0	.188	229	339

Wild Card qualifier for playoffs; #Top playoff seed in conference
Jacksonville was second Wild Card ahead of Indianapolis and Kansas City based on better conference record (7-5 to Colts' 6-6 and Chiefs' 5-7). Indianapolis was third Wild Card based on head-to-head victory over Kansas City (1-0). Cincinnati finished ahead of Houston based on better net division points (19 to Oilers' 11). Oakland finished ahead of Seattle based on better division record (3-5 to Seahawks' 2-6). Dallas finished ahead of Philadelphia based on better record against common opponents (8-5 to Eagles' 7-6). Minnesota was third Wild Card based on better conference record than Washington (8-4 to Redskins' 6-6). Carolina finished ahead of San Francisco based on head-to-head sweep (2-0). Atlanta finished ahead of New Orleans based on head-to-head sweep (2-0).

Wild Card playoffs: Jacksonville 30, BUFFALO 27;
PITTSBURGH 42, Indianapolis 14
Divisional playoffs: Jacksonville 30, DENVER 27;
NEW ENGLAND 28, Pittsburgh 3
AFC Championship: NEW ENGLAND 20, Jacksonville 6
Wild Card playoffs: DALLAS 40, Minnesota 15;
SAN FRANCISCO 14, Philadelphia 0
Divisional playoffs: GREEN BAY 35, San Francisco 14;
CAROLINA 26, Dallas 17
NFC Championship: GREEN BAY 30, Carolina 13
Super Bowl XXXI: Green Bay (NFC) 35, New England (AFC) 21,
at Louisiana Superdome, New Orleans, Louisiana

Playoff Seeds

AFC	NFC
1. Denver	**1. Green Bay**
2. New England	2. Carolina
3. Pittsburgh	3. Dallas
4. Buffalo	4. San Francisco
5. Jacksonville	5. Philadelphia
6. Indianapolis	6. Minnesota

1995

AMERICAN CONFERENCE
Eastern Division

	W	L	T	Pct.	Pts.	OP
Buffalo	10	6	0	.625	350	335
Indianapolis*	9	7	0	.563	331	316
Miami*	9	7	0	.563	398	332
New England	6	10	0	.375	294	377
N.Y. Jets	3	13	0	.188	233	384

Central Division

	W	L	T	Pct.	Pts.	OP
Pittsburgh	11	5	0	.688	407	327
Cincinnati	7	9	0	.438	349	374
Houston	7	9	0	.438	348	324
Cleveland	5	11	0	.313	289	356
Jacksonville	4	12	0	.250	275	404

Western Division

	W	L	T	Pct.	Pts.	OP
Kansas City#	13	3	0	.813	358	241
San Diego*	9	7	0	.563	321	323
Seattle	8	8	0	.500	363	366
Denver	8	8	0	.500	388	345
Oakland	8	8	0	.500	348	332

NATIONAL CONFERENCE
Eastern Division

	W	L	T	Pct.	Pts.	OP
Dallas#	12	4	0	.750	435	291
Philadelphia*	10	6	0	.625	318	338
Washington	6	10	0	.375	326	359
N.Y. Giants	5	11	0	.313	290	340
Arizona	4	12	0	.250	275	422

Central Division

	W	L	T	Pct.	Pts.	OP
Green Bay	11	5	0	.688	404	314
Detroit*	10	6	0	.625	436	336
Chicago	9	7	0	.563	392	360
Minnesota	8	8	0	.500	412	385
Tampa Bay	7	9	0	.438	238	335

Western Division

	W	L	T	Pct.	Pts.	OP
San Francisco#	11	5	0	.688	457	258
Atlanta*	9	7	0	.563	362	349
St. Louis	7	9	0	.438	309	418
Carolina	7	9	0	.438	289	325
New Orleans	7	9	0	.438	319	348

Wild Card qualifier for playoffs; #Top playoff seed in conference
Indianapolis finished ahead of Miami based on head-to-head sweep (2-0). San Diego was first Wild Card based on head-to-head victory over Indianapolis (1-0). Cincinnati finished ahead of Houston based on better division record (4-4 to Oilers' 3-5). Seattle finished ahead of Denver and Oakland based on best head-to-head record (3-1 to Broncos' 2-2 and Raiders' 1-3). Denver finished ahead of Oakland based on head-to-head sweep (2-0). Philadelphia was first Wild Card ahead of Detroit based on better conference record (9-3 to Lions' 7-5). San Francisco was second playoff seed ahead of Green Bay based on better conference record (8-4 to Packers' 7-5). Atlanta was third Wild Card ahead of Chicago based on better record against common opponents (4-2 to Bears' 3-3). St. Louis finished ahead of Carolina and New Orleans based on best head-to-head record (3-1 to Panthers' 1-3 and Saints' 2-2). Carolina finished ahead of New Orleans based on better conference record (4-8 to 3-9).

Wild Card playoffs: BUFFALO 37, Miami 22;
Indianapolis 35, SAN DIEGO 20
Divisional playoffs: PITTSBURGH 40, Buffalo 21;
Indianapolis 10, KANSAS CITY 7
AFC Championship: PITTSBURGH 20, Indianapolis 16
Wild Card playoffs: PHILADELPHIA 58, Detroit 37;
GREEN BAY 37, Atlanta 20
Divisional playoffs: Green Bay 27, SAN FRANCISCO 17;
DALLAS 30, Philadelphia 11
NFC Championship: DALLAS 38, Green Bay 27
Super Bowl XXX: Dallas (NFC) 27, Pittsburgh (AFC) 17,
at Sun Devil Stadium, Tempe, Arizona

Playoff Seeds

AFC	NFC
1. Kansas City	**1. Dallas**
2. Pittsburgh	2. San Francisco
3. Buffalo	3. Green Bay
4. San Diego	4. Philadelphia
5. Indianapolis	5. Detroit
6. Miami	6. Atlanta

1994

AMERICAN CONFERENCE
Eastern Division

	W	L	T	Pct.	Pts.	OP
Miami	10	6	0	.625	389	327
New England*	10	6	0	.625	351	312
Indianapolis	8	8	0	.500	307	320
Buffalo	7	9	0	.438	340	356
N.Y. Jets	6	10	0	.375	264	320

Central Division

	W	L	T	Pct.	Pts.	OP
Pittsburgh#	12	4	0	.750	316	234
Cleveland*	11	5	0	.688	340	204
Cincinnati	3	13	0	.188	276	406
Houston	2	14	0	.125	226	352

Western Division

	W	L	T	Pct.	Pts.	OP
San Diego	11	5	0	.688	381	306
Kansas City*	9	7	0	.563	319	298
L.A. Raiders	9	7	0	.563	303	327
Denver	7	9	0	.438	347	396
Seattle	6	10	0	.375	287	323

NATIONAL CONFERENCE
Eastern Division

	W	L	T	Pct.	Pts.	OP
Dallas	12	4	0	.750	414	248
N.Y. Giants	9	7	0	.563	279	305
Arizona	8	8	0	.500	235	267
Philadelphia	7	9	0	.438	308	308
Washington	3	13	0	.188	320	412

Central Division

	W	L	T	Pct.	Pts.	OP
Minnesota	10	6	0	.625	356	314
Green Bay*	9	7	0	.563	382	287
Detroit*	9	7	0	.563	357	342
Chicago*	9	7	0	.563	271	307
Tampa Bay	6	10	0	.375	251	351

Western Division

	W	L	T	Pct.	Pts.	OP
San Francisco#	13	3	0	.813	505	296
New Orleans	7	9	0	.438	348	407
Atlanta	7	9	0	.438	317	385
L.A. Rams	4	12	0	.250	286	365

*Wild Card qualifier for playoffs; #Top playoff seed in conference
Miami finished ahead of New England based on head-to-head sweep (2-0). Kansas City finished ahead of L.A. Raiders based on head-to-head sweep (2-0). Green Bay was first Wild Card based on best head-to-head record (3-1) vs. Detroit (2-2) and Chicago (1-3) and better conference record (8-4) than N.Y. Giants (6-6). Detroit was second Wild Card based on better division record (4-4) than Chicago (3-5) and head-to-head victory over N.Y. Giants (1-0). Chicago was third Wild Card based on better record against common opponents (4-4) than N.Y. Giants (3-5). New Orleans finished ahead of Atlanta based on head-to-head sweep (2-0).
Wild Card playoffs: MIAMI 27, Kansas City 17; CLEVELAND 20, New England 13
Divisional playoffs: PITTSBURGH 29, Cleveland 9; SAN DIEGO 22, Miami 21
AFC Championship: San Diego 17, PITTSBURGH 13
Wild Card playoffs: GREEN BAY 16, Detroit 12; Chicago 35, MINNESOTA 18
Divisional playoffs: SAN FRANCISCO 44, Chicago 15; DALLAS 35, Green Bay 9
NFC Championship: SAN FRANCISCO 38, Dallas 28
Super Bowl XXIX: San Francisco (NFC) 49, San Diego (AFC) 26, at Joe Robbie Stadium, Miami, Florida

Playoff Seeds

AFC	NFC
1. Pittsburgh	**1. San Francisco**
2. San Diego	2. Dallas
3. Miami	3. Minnesota
4. Cleveland	4. Green Bay
5. New England	5. Detroit
6. Kansas City	6. Chicago

1993

AMERICAN CONFERENCE
Eastern Division

	W	L	T	Pct.	Pts.	OP
Buffalo#	12	4	0	.750	329	242
Miami	9	7	0	.563	349	351
N.Y. Jets	8	8	0	.500	270	247
New England	5	11	0	.313	238	286
Indianapolis	4	12	0	.250	189	378

Central Division

	W	L	T	Pct.	Pts.	OP
Houston	12	4	0	.750	368	238
Pittsburgh*	9	7	0	.563	308	281
Cleveland	7	9	0	.438	304	307
Cincinnati	3	13	0	.188	187	319

Western Division

	W	L	T	Pct.	Pts.	OP
Kansas City	11	5	0	.688	328	291
L.A. Raiders*	10	6	0	.625	306	326
Denver*	9	7	0	.563	373	284
San Diego	8	8	0	.500	322	290
Seattle	6	10	0	.375	280	314

NATIONAL CONFERENCE
Eastern Division

	W	L	T	Pct.	Pts.	OP
Dallas#	12	4	0	.750	376	229
N.Y. Giants*	11	5	0	.688	288	205
Philadelphia	8	8	0	.500	293	315
Phoenix	7	9	0	.438	326	269
Washington	4	12	0	.250	230	345

Central Division

	W	L	T	Pct.	Pts.	OP
Detroit	10	6	0	.625	298	292
Minnesota	9	7	0	.563	277	290
Green Bay*	9	7	0	.563	340	282
Chicago	7	9	0	.438	234	230
Tampa Bay	5	11	0	.313	237	376

Western Division

	W	L	T	Pct.	Pts.	OP
San Francisco	10	6	0	.625	473	295
New Orleans	8	8	0	.500	317	343
Atlanta	6	10	0	.375	316	385
L.A. Rams	5	11	0	.313	221	367

*Wild Card qualifier for playoffs; #Top playoff seed in conference
Buffalo was top playoff seed based on head-to-head victory over Houston (1-0). Denver was second Wild Card, and Pittsburgh was third Wild Card ahead of Miami, based on better conference record (8-4 to Steelers' 7-5 to Dolphins' 6-6). San Francisco was second playoff seed based on head-to-head victory over Detroit (1-0). Minnesota finished ahead of Green Bay based on head-to-head sweep (2-0).
Wild Card playoffs: KANSAS CITY 27, Pittsburgh 24 (OT); L.A. RAIDERS 42, Denver 24
Divisional playoffs: BUFFALO 29, L.A. Raiders 23; Kansas City 28, HOUSTON 20
AFC Championship: BUFFALO 30, Kansas City 13
Wild Card playoffs: Green Bay 28, DETROIT 24; N.Y. GIANTS 17, Minnesota 10
Divisional playoffs: SAN FRANCISCO 44, N.Y. Giants 3; DALLAS 27, Green Bay 17
NFC Championship: DALLAS 38, San Francisco 21
Super Bowl XXVIII: Dallas (NFC) 30, Buffalo (AFC) 13, at Georgia Dome, Atlanta, Georgia

Playoff Seeds

AFC	NFC
1. Buffalo	**1. Dallas**
2. Houston	2. San Francisco
3. Kansas City	3. Detroit
4. L.A. Raiders	4. N.Y. Giants
5. Denver	5. Minnesota
6. Pittsburgh	6. Green Bay

1992

AMERICAN CONFERENCE

Eastern Division

	W	L	T	Pct.	Pts.	OP
Miami	11	5	0	.688	340	281
Buffalo*	11	5	0	.688	381	283
Indianapolis	9	7	0	.563	216	302
N.Y. Jets	4	12	0	.250	220	315
New England	2	14	0	.125	205	363

Central Division

	W	L	T	Pct.	Pts.	OP
Pittsburgh#	11	5	0	.688	299	225
Houston*	10	6	0	.625	352	258
Cleveland	7	9	0	.438	272	275
Cincinnati	5	11	0	.313	274	364

Western Division

	W	L	T	Pct.	Pts.	OP
San Diego	11	5	0	.688	335	241
Kansas City*	10	6	0	.625	348	282
Denver	8	8	0	.500	262	329
L.A. Raiders	7	9	0	.438	249	281
Seattle	2	14	0	.125	140	312

NATIONAL CONFERENCE

Eastern Division

	W	L	T	Pct.	Pts.	OP
Dallas	13	3	0	.813	409	243
Philadelphia*	11	5	0	.688	354	245
Washington*	9	7	0	.563	300	255
N.Y. Giants	6	10	0	.375	306	367
Phoenix	4	12	0	.250	243	332

Central Division

	W	L	T	Pct.	Pts.	OP
Minnesota	11	5	0	.688	374	249
Green Bay	9	7	0	.563	276	296
Tampa Bay	5	11	0	.313	267	365
Chicago	5	11	0	.313	295	361
Detroit	5	11	0	.313	273	332

Western Division

	W	L	T	Pct.	Pts.	OP
San Francisco#	14	2	0	.875	431	236
New Orleans*	12	4	0	.750	330	202
Atlanta	6	10	0	.375	327	414
L.A. Rams	6	10	0	.375	313	383

*Wild Card qualifier for playoffs; #Top playoff seed in conference

Pittsburgh was top playoff seed, and Miami was second playoff seed ahead of San Diego, based on conference record (10-2 to Dolphins' 9-3 to Chargers' 9-5). Miami finished ahead of Buffalo based on better conference record (9-3 to Bills' 7-5). Houston was second Wild Card based on head-to-head victory over Kansas City (1-0). Washington was third Wild Card based on better conference record than Green Bay (7-5 to Packers' 6-6). Tampa Bay finished ahead of Chicago and Detroit based on better conference record (5-9 to Bears' 4-8 and Lions' 3-9). Atlanta finished ahead of L.A. Rams based on better record against common opponents (5-7 to Rams' 4-8).

Wild Card playoffs: SAN DIEGO 17, Kansas City 0; BUFFALO 41, Houston 38 (OT)

Divisional playoffs: Buffalo 24, PITTSBURGH 3; MIAMI 31, San Diego 0

AFC Championship: Buffalo 29, MIAMI 10

Wild Card playoffs: Washington 24, MINNESOTA 7; Philadelphia 36, NEW ORLEANS 20

Divisional playoffs: SAN FRANCISCO 20, Washington 13; DALLAS 34, Philadelphia 10

NFC Championship: Dallas 30, SAN FRANCISCO 20

Super Bowl XXVII: Dallas (NFC) 52, Buffalo (AFC) 17, at Rose Bowl, Pasadena, California

Playoff Seeds

AFC	NFC
1. Pittsburgh	1. San Francisco
2. Miami	**2. Dallas**
3. San Diego	3. Minnesota
4. Buffalo	4. New Orleans
5. Houston	5. Philadelphia
6. Kansas City	6. Washington

1991

AMERICAN CONFERENCE

Eastern Division

	W	L	T	Pct.	Pts.	OP
Buffalo#	13	3	0	.813	458	318
N.Y. Jets*	8	8	0	.500	314	293
Miami	8	8	0	.500	343	349
New England	6	10	0	.375	211	305
Indianapolis	1	15	0	.063	143	381

Central Division

	W	L	T	Pct.	Pts.	OP
Houston	11	5	0	.688	386	251
Pittsburgh	7	9	0	.438	292	344
Cleveland	6	10	0	.375	293	298
Cincinnati	3	13	0	.188	263	435

Western Division

	W	L	T	Pct.	Pts.	OP
Denver	12	4	0	.750	304	235
Kansas City*	10	6	0	.625	322	252
L.A. Raiders*	9	7	0	.563	298	297
Seattle	7	9	0	.438	276	261
San Diego	4	12	0	.250	274	342

NATIONAL CONFERENCE

Eastern Division

	W	L	T	Pct.	Pts.	OP
Washington#	14	2	0	.875	485	224
Dallas*	11	5	0	.688	342	310
Philadelphia	10	6	0	.625	285	244
N.Y. Giants	8	8	0	.500	281	297
Phoenix	4	12	0	.250	196	344

Central Division

	W	L	T	Pct.	Pts.	OP
Detroit	12	4	0	.750	339	295
Chicago*	11	5	0	.688	299	269
Minnesota	8	8	0	.500	301	306
Green Bay	4	12	0	.250	273	313
Tampa Bay	3	13	0	.188	199	365

Western Division

	W	L	T	Pct.	Pts.	OP
New Orleans	11	5	0	.688	341	211
Atlanta*	10	6	0	.625	361	338
San Francisco	10	6	0	.625	393	239
L.A. Rams	3	13	0	.188	234	390

*Wild Card qualifier for playoffs; #Top playoff seed in conference

N.Y. Jets finished ahead of Miami based on head-to-head sweep (2-0). Chicago was first Wild Card based on better conference record than Dallas (9-3 to Cowboys' 8-4). Atlanta finished ahead of San Francisco based on head-to-head sweep (2-0), and was third Wild Card ahead of Philadelphia based on better conference record (7-5 to Eagles' 6-6).

Wild Card playoffs: KANSAS CITY 10, L.A. Raiders 6; HOUSTON 17, N.Y. Jets 10

Divisional playoffs: DENVER 26, Houston 24; BUFFALO 37, Kansas City 14

AFC Championship: BUFFALO 10, Denver 7

Wild Card playoffs: Atlanta 27, NEW ORLEANS 20; Dallas 17, CHICAGO 13

Divisional playoffs: WASHINGTON 24, Atlanta 7; DETROIT 38, Dallas 6

NFC Championship: WASHINGTON 41, Detroit 10

Super Bowl XXVI: Washington (NFC) 37, Buffalo (AFC) 24, at Hubert H. Humphrey Metrodome, Minneapolis, Minnesota

Playoff Seeds

AFC	NFC
1. Buffalo	**1. Washington**
2. Denver	2. Detroit
3. Houston	3. New Orleans
4. Kansas City	4. Chicago
5. L.A. Raiders	5. Dallas
6. N.Y. Jets	6. Atlanta

1990

AMERICAN CONFERENCE
Eastern Division

	W	L	T	Pct.	Pts.	OP
Buffalo#	13	3	0	.813	428	263
Miami*	12	4	0	.750	336	242
Indianapolis	7	9	0	.438	281	353
N.Y. Jets	6	10	0	.375	295	345
New England	1	15	0	.063	181	446

Central Division

	W	L	T	Pct.	Pts.	OP
Cincinnati	9	7	0	.563	360	352
Houston*	9	7	0	.563	405	307
Pittsburgh	9	7	0	.563	292	240
Cleveland	3	13	0	.188	228	462

Western Division

	W	L	T	Pct.	Pts.	OP
L.A. Raiders	12	4	0	.750	337	268
Kansas City*	11	5	0	.688	369	257
Seattle	9	7	0	.563	306	286
San Diego	6	10	0	.375	315	281
Denver	5	11	0	.313	331	374

NATIONAL CONFERENCE
Eastern Division

	W	L	T	Pct.	Pts.	OP
N.Y. Giants	13	3	0	.813	335	211
Philadelphia*	10	6	0	.625	396	299
Washington*	10	6	0	.625	381	301
Dallas	7	9	0	.438	244	308
Phoenix	5	11	0	.313	268	396

Central Division

	W	L	T	Pct.	Pts.	OP
Chicago	11	5	0	.688	348	280
Tampa Bay	6	10	0	.375	264	367
Detroit	6	10	0	.375	373	413
Green Bay	6	10	0	.375	271	347
Minnesota	6	10	0	.375	351	326

Western Division

	W	L	T	Pct.	Pts.	OP
San Francisco#	14	2	0	.875	353	239
New Orleans*	8	8	0	.500	274	275
L.A. Rams	5	11	0	.313	345	412
Atlanta	5	11	0	.313	348	365

*Wild Card qualifier for playoffs; #Top playoff seed in conference
Cincinnati finished ahead of Houston and Pittsburgh based on best head-to-head record (3-1 to Oilers' 2-2 to Steelers' 1-3). Houston was Wild Card based on better conference record (8-4) than Seattle (7-5) and Pittsburgh (6-6). Philadelphia finished ahead of Washington based on better division record (5-3 to Redskins' 4-4). Tampa Bay was second in NFC Central based on best head-to-head record (5-1) against Detroit (2-4), Green Bay (3-3), and Minnesota (2-4). Detroit finished third based on best net division points (minus 8) against Green Bay (minus 40). Green Bay finished ahead of Minnesota based on better conference record (5-7 to Vikings' 4-8). The L.A. Rams finished ahead of Atlanta based on net points in division (plus 1 to Falcons' minus 31).

Wild Card playoffs: MIAMI 17, Kansas City 16;
  CINCINNATI 41, Houston 14
Divisional playoffs: BUFFALO 44, Miami 34;
  L.A. RAIDERS 20, Cincinnati 10
AFC Championship: BUFFALO 51, L.A. Raiders 3
Wild Card playoffs: Washington 20, PHILADELPHIA 6;
  CHICAGO 16, New Orleans 6
Divisional playoffs: SAN FRANCISCO 28, Washington 10;
  N.Y. GIANTS 31, Chicago 3
NFC Championship: N.Y. Giants 15, SAN FRANCISCO 13
Super Bowl XXV: N.Y. Giants (NFC) 20, Buffalo (AFC) 19,
  at Tampa Stadium, Tampa, Florida

Playoff Seeds

AFC	NFC
1. Buffalo	1. San Francisco
2. L.A. Raiders	2. N.Y. Giants
3. Cincinnati	3. Chicago
4. Miami	4. Philadelphia
5. Kansas City	5. Washington
6. Houston	6. New Orleans

1989

AMERICAN CONFERENCE
Eastern Division

	W	L	T	Pct.	Pts.	OP
Buffalo	9	7	0	.563	409	317
Indianapolis	8	8	0	.500	298	301
Miami	8	8	0	.500	331	379
New England	5	11	0	.313	297	391
N.Y. Jets	4	12	0	.250	253	411

Central Division

	W	L	T	Pct.	Pts.	OP
Cleveland	9	6	1	.594	334	254
Houston*	9	7	0	.563	365	412
Pittsburgh*	9	7	0	.563	265	326
Cincinnati	8	8	0	.500	404	285

Western Division

	W	L	T	Pct.	Pts.	OP
Denver#	11	5	0	.688	362	226
Kansas City	8	7	1	.531	318	286
L.A. Raiders	8	8	0	.500	315	297
Seattle	7	9	0	.438	241	327
San Diego	6	10	0	.375	266	290

NATIONAL CONFERENCE
Eastern Division

	W	L	T	Pct.	Pts.	OP
N.Y. Giants	12	4	0	.750	348	252
Philadelphia*	11	5	0	.688	342	274
Washington	10	6	0	.625	386	308
Phoenix	5	11	0	.313	258	377
Dallas	1	15	0	.063	204	393

Central Division

	W	L	T	Pct.	Pts.	OP
Minnesota	10	6	0	.625	351	275
Green Bay	10	6	0	.625	362	356
Detroit	7	9	0	.438	312	364
Chicago	6	10	0	.375	358	377
Tampa Bay	5	11	0	.313	320	419

Western Division

	W	L	T	Pct.	Pts.	OP
San Francisco#	14	2	0	.875	442	253
L.A. Rams*	11	5	0	.688	426	344
New Orleans	9	7	0	.563	386	301
Atlanta	3	13	0	.188	279	437

*Wild Card qualifier for playoffs; #Top playoff seed in conference
Indianapolis finished ahead of Miami based on better conference record (7-5 vs. Dolphins' 6-8). Houston finished ahead of Pittsburgh based on head-to-head sweep (2-0). The L.A. Rams did not play San Francisco in the divisional playoffs because, from 1970-1989, two teams from the same division could not meet prior to the conference championship game. Philadelphia was first Wild Card ahead of L.A. Rams based on better record against common opponents (6-3 to Rams' 5-4). Minnesota finished ahead of Green Bay based on better division record (6-2 vs. Packers' 5-3).

Wild Card playoff: Pittsburgh 26, HOUSTON 23 (OT)
Divisional playoffs: CLEVELAND 34, Buffalo 30;
  DENVER 24, Pittsburgh 23
AFC Championship: DENVER 37, Cleveland 21
Wild Card playoff: L.A. Rams 21, PHILADELPHIA 7
Divisional playoffs: L.A. Rams 19, N.Y. GIANTS 13 (OT);
  SAN FRANCISCO 41, Minnesota 13
NFC Championship: SAN FRANCISCO 30, L.A. Rams 3
Super Bowl XXIV: San Francisco (NFC) 55, Denver (AFC) 10,
  at Louisiana Superdome, New Orleans, Louisiana

1988

AMERICAN CONFERENCE

Eastern Division

	W	L	T	Pct.	Pts.	OP
Buffalo	12	4	0	.750	329	237
Indianapolis	9	7	0	.563	354	315
New England	9	7	0	.563	250	284
N.Y. Jets	8	7	1	.531	372	354
Miami	6	10	0	.375	319	380

Central Division

	W	L	T	Pct.	Pts.	OP
Cincinnati#	12	4	0	.750	448	329
Cleveland*	10	6	0	.625	304	288
Houston*	10	6	0	.625	424	365
Pittsburgh	5	11	0	.313	336	421

Western Division

	W	L	T	Pct.	Pts.	OP
Seattle	9	7	0	.563	339	329
Denver	8	8	0	.500	327	352
L.A. Raiders	7	9	0	.438	325	369
San Diego	6	10	0	.375	231	332
Kansas City	4	11	1	.281	254	320

NATIONAL CONFERENCE

Eastern Division

	W	L	T	Pct.	Pts.	OP
Philadelphia	10	6	0	.625	379	319
N.Y. Giants	10	6	0	.625	359	304
Washington	7	9	0	.438	345	387
Phoenix	7	9	0	.438	344	398
Dallas	3	13	0	.188	265	381

Central Division

	W	L	T	Pct.	Pts.	OP
Chicago#	12	4	0	.750	312	215
Minnesota*	11	5	0	.688	406	233
Tampa Bay	5	11	0	.313	261	350
Detroit	4	12	0	.250	220	313
Green Bay	4	12	0	.250	240	315

Western Division

	W	L	T	Pct.	Pts.	OP
San Francisco	10	6	0	.625	369	294
L.A. Rams*	10	6	0	.625	407	293
New Orleans	10	6	0	.625	312	283
Atlanta	5	11	0	.313	244	315

*Wild Card qualifier for playoffs; #Top playoff seed in conference

Cincinnati was top playoff seed ahead of Buffalo based on head-to-head victory (1-0). Indianapolis finished ahead of New England based on better record against common opponents (7-5 to Patriots' 6-6). Cleveland finished ahead of Houston based on better division record (4-2 to Oilers' 3-3). Houston did not play Cincinnati, and Minnesota did not play Chicago in the divisional playoffs because, from 1970-1989, two teams from the same division could not meet prior to the conference championship game. Philadelphia finished first in NFC East based on head-to-head sweep of N.Y. Giants (2-0). Washington finished third in NFC East based on better division record (4-4) than Phoenix (3-5). Detroit finished fourth in NFC Central based on head-to-head sweep of Green Bay (2-0). San Francisco finished first in NFC West based on better head-to-head record (3-1) against L.A. Rams (2-2) and New Orleans (1-3). L.A. Rams finished second in NFC West based on better division record (4-2) than New Orleans (3-3) and earned Wild-Card position based on better conference record (8-4) than N.Y. Giants (9-5) and New Orleans (6-6).

Wild Card playoff: Houston 24, CLEVELAND 23
Divisional playoffs: CINCINNATI 21, Seattle 13;
   BUFFALO 17, Houston 10
AFC Championship: CINCINNATI 21, Buffalo 10
Wild Card playoff: MINNESOTA 28, L.A. Rams 17
Divisional playoffs: CHICAGO 20, Philadelphia 12;
   SAN FRANCISCO 34, Minnesota 9
NFC Championship: San Francisco 28, CHICAGO 3
Super Bowl XXIII: San Francisco (NFC) 20, Cincinnati (AFC) 16,
   at Joe Robbie Stadium, Miami, Florida

1987

AMERICAN CONFERENCE

Eastern Division

	W	L	T	Pct.	Pts.	OP
Indianapolis	9	6	0	.600	300	238
New England	8	7	0	.533	320	293
Miami	8	7	0	.533	362	335
Buffalo	7	8	0	.467	270	305
N.Y. Jets	6	9	0	.400	334	360

Central Division

	W	L	T	Pct.	Pts.	OP
Cleveland	10	5	0	.667	390	239
Houston*	9	6	0	.600	345	349
Pittsburgh	8	7	0	.533	285	299
Cincinnati	4	11	0	.267	285	370

Western Division

	W	L	T	Pct.	Pts.	OP
Denver#	10	4	1	.700	379	288
Seattle*	9	6	0	.600	371	314
San Diego	8	7	0	.533	253	317
L.A. Raiders	5	10	0	.333	301	289
Kansas City	4	11	0	.267	273	388

NATIONAL CONFERENCE

Eastern Division

	W	L	T	Pct.	Pts.	OP
Washington	11	4	0	.733	379	285
Dallas	7	8	0	.467	340	348
St. Louis	7	8	0	.467	362	368
Philadelphia	7	8	0	.467	337	380
N.Y. Giants	6	9	0	.400	280	312

Central Division

	W	L	T	Pct.	Pts.	OP
Chicago	11	4	0	.733	356	282
Minnesota*	8	7	0	.533	336	335
Green Bay	5	9	1	.367	255	300
Tampa Bay	4	11	0	.267	286	360
Detroit	4	11	0	.267	269	384

Western Division

	W	L	T	Pct.	Pts.	OP
San Francisco#	13	2	0	.867	459	253
New Orleans*	12	3	0	.800	422	283
L.A. Rams	6	9	0	.400	317	361
Atlanta	3	12	0	.200	205	436

*Wild Card qualifier for playoffs; #Top playoff seed in conference

New England finished ahead of Miami based on head-to-head sweep (2-0). Houston was first Wild Card ahead of Seattle based on better conference record (7-4 to Seahawks' 5-6). Chicago was second playoff seed ahead of Washington based on better conference record (9-2 to Redskins' 9-3). Dallas finished ahead of St. Louis and Philadelphia based on better division record (4-4 to Cardinals' 3-5 and Eagles' 3-5). St. Louis finished ahead of Philadelphia based on better conference record (7-7 to Eagles' 4-7). Tampa Bay finished ahead of Detroit based on better division record (3-4 to Lions' 2-5).

Wild Card playoff: HOUSTON 23, Seattle 20 (OT)
Divisional playoffs: CLEVELAND 38, Indianapolis 21;
   DENVER 34, Houston 10
AFC Championship: DENVER 38, Cleveland 33
Wild Card playoff: Minnesota 44, NEW ORLEANS 10
Divisional playoffs: Minnesota 36, SAN FRANCISCO 24;
   Washington 21, CHICAGO 17
NFC Championship: WASHINGTON 17, Minnesota 10
Super Bowl XXII: Washington (NFC) 42, Denver (AFC) 10,
   at San Diego Jack Murphy Stadium, San Diego, California
Note: 1987 regular season was reduced from 16 to 15 games for each team due to players' strike.

1986

AMERICAN CONFERENCE

Eastern Division

	W	L	T	Pct.	Pts.	OP
New England	11	5	0	.688	412	307
N.Y. Jets*	10	6	0	.625	364	386
Miami	8	8	0	.500	430	405
Buffalo	4	12	0	.250	287	348
Indianapolis	3	13	0	.188	229	400

Central Division

	W	L	T	Pct.	Pts.	OP
Cleveland#	12	4	0	.750	391	310
Cincinnati	10	6	0	.625	409	394
Pittsburgh	6	10	0	.375	307	336
Houston	5	11	0	.313	274	329

Western Division

	W	L	T	Pct.	Pts.	OP
Denver	11	5	0	.688	378	327
Kansas City*	10	6	0	.625	358	326
Seattle	10	6	0	.625	366	293
L.A. Raiders	8	8	0	.500	323	346
San Diego	4	12	0	.250	335	396

NATIONAL CONFERENCE

Eastern Division

	W	L	T	Pct.	Pts.	OP
N.Y. Giants#	14	2	0	.875	371	236
Washington*	12	4	0	.750	368	296
Dallas	7	9	0	.438	346	337
Philadelphia	5	10	1	.344	256	312
St. Louis	4	11	1	.281	218	351

Central Division

	W	L	T	Pct.	Pts.	OP
Chicago	14	2	0	.875	352	187
Minnesota	9	7	0	.563	398	273
Detroit	5	11	0	.313	277	326
Green Bay	4	12	0	.250	254	418
Tampa Bay	2	14	0	.125	239	473

Western Division

	W	L	T	Pct.	Pts.	OP
San Francisco	10	5	1	.656	374	247
L.A. Rams*	10	6	0	.625	309	267
Atlanta	7	8	1	.469	280	280
New Orleans	7	9	0	.438	288	287

*Wild Card qualifier for playoffs; #Top playoff seed in conference
Denver was second playoff seed ahead of New England based on
head-to-head victory (1-0). N.Y. Jets were first Wild Card based
on better conference record (8-4) than Kansas City (9-5), Seattle
(7-5), and Cincinnati (7-5). Kansas City was second Wild Card
based on better conference record (9-5) than Seattle (7-5) and
Cincinnati (7-5). N.Y. Giants were top playoff seed based on better conference record than Chicago (11-1 to Bears' 10-2). Washington did not play the N.Y. Giants in the divisional playoffs
because, from 1970-1989, two teams from the same division
could not meet prior to the conference championship game.
Wild Card playoff: N.Y. JETS 35, Kansas City 15
Divisional playoffs: CLEVELAND 23, N.Y. Jets 20 (OT);
    DENVER 22, New England 17
AFC Championship: Denver 23, CLEVELAND 20 (OT)
Wild Card playoff: WASHINGTON 19, L.A. Rams 7
Divisional playoffs: Washington 27, CHICAGO 13
    N.Y. GIANTS 49, San Francisco 3
NFC Championship: N.Y. GIANTS 17, Washington 0
Super Bowl XXI: N.Y. Giants (NFC) 39, Denver (AFC) 20,
    at Rose Bowl, Pasadena, California

1985

AMERICAN CONFERENCE

Eastern Division

	W	L	T	Pct.	Pts.	OP
Miami	12	4	0	.750	428	320
N.Y. Jets*	11	5	0	.688	393	264
New England*	11	5	0	.688	362	290
Indianapolis	5	11	0	.313	320	386
Buffalo	2	14	0	.125	200	381

Central Division

	W	L	T	Pct.	Pts.	OP
Cleveland	8	8	0	.500	287	294
Cincinnati	7	9	0	.438	441	437
Pittsburgh	7	9	0	.438	379	355
Houston	5	11	0	.313	284	412

Western Division

	W	L	T	Pct.	Pts.	OP
L.A. Raiders#	12	4	0	.750	354	308
Denver	11	5	0	.688	380	329
Seattle	8	8	0	.500	349	303
San Diego	8	8	0	.500	467	435
Kansas City	6	10	0	.375	317	360

NATIONAL CONFERENCE

Eastern Division

	W	L	T	Pct.	Pts.	OP
Dallas	10	6	0	.625	357	333
N.Y. Giants*	10	6	0	.625	399	283
Washington*	10	6	0	.625	297	312
Philadelphia	7	9	0	.438	286	310
St. Louis	5	11	0	.313	278	414

Central Division

	W	L	T	Pct.	Pts.	OP
Chicago#	15	1	0	.938	456	198
Green Bay	8	8	0	.500	337	355
Minnesota	7	9	0	.438	346	359
Detroit	7	9	0	.438	307	366
Tampa Bay	2	14	0	.125	294	448

Western Division

	W	L	T	Pct.	Pts.	OP
L.A. Rams	11	5	0	.688	340	277
San Francisco*	10	6	0	.625	411	263
New Orleans	5	11	0	.313	294	401
Atlanta	4	12	0	.250	282	452

*Wild Card qualifier for playoffs; #Top playoff seed in conference
L.A. Raiders were top playoff seed ahead of Miami based on better
record against common opponents (5-1 to 4-2). N.Y. Jets were
first Wild Card based on better conference record (9-3) than New
England (8-4) and Denver (8-4). New England was second Wild
Card ahead of Denver based on better record against common
opponents (4-2 to Broncos' 3-3). Cincinnati finished ahead of
Pittsburgh based on head-to-head sweep (2-0). Seattle finished
ahead of San Diego based on head-to-head sweep (2-0). Dallas
finished ahead of N.Y. Giants and Washington based on better
head-to-head record (4-0 to Giants' 1-3 and Redskins' 1-3). N.Y.
Giants were first Wild Card based on better conference record
(8-4) than San Francisco (7-5) and Washington (6-6). San Fran-
cisco was second Wild Card based on head-to-head victory over
Washington (1-0). Minnesota finished ahead of Detroit based on
better division record (3-5 to Lions' 2-6).
Wild Card playoff: New England 26, N.Y. JETS 14
Divisional playoffs: MIAMI 24, Cleveland 21;
    New England 27, L.A. RAIDERS 20
AFC Championship: New England 31, MIAMI 14
Wild Card playoff: N.Y. GIANTS 17, San Francisco 3
Divisional playoffs: L.A. RAMS 20, Dallas 0;
    CHICAGO 21, N.Y. Giants 0
NFC Championship: CHICAGO 24, L.A. Rams 0
Super Bowl XX: Chicago (NFC) 46, New England (AFC) 10,
    at Louisiana Superdome, New Orleans, Louisiana

1984

AMERICAN CONFERENCE

Eastern Division

	W	L	T	Pct.	Pts.	OP
Miami#	14	2	0	.875	513	298
New England	9	7	0	.563	362	352
N.Y. Jets	7	9	0	.438	332	364
Indianapolis	4	12	0	.250	239	414
Buffalo	2	14	0	.125	250	454

Central Division

	W	L	T	Pct.	Pts.	OP
Pittsburgh	9	7	0	.563	387	310
Cincinnati	8	8	0	.500	339	339
Cleveland	5	11	0	.313	250	297
Houston	3	13	0	.188	240	437

Western Division

	W	L	T	Pct.	Pts.	OP
Denver	13	3	0	.813	353	241
Seattle*	12	4	0	.750	418	282
L.A. Raiders*	11	5	0	.688	368	278
Kansas City	8	8	0	.500	314	324
San Diego	7	9	0	.438	394	413

NATIONAL CONFERENCE

Eastern Division

	W	L	T	Pct.	Pts.	OP
Washington	11	5	0	.688	426	310
N.Y. Giants*	9	7	0	.563	299	301
St. Louis	9	7	0	.563	423	345
Dallas	9	7	0	.563	308	308
Philadelphia	6	9	1	.406	278	320

Central Division

	W	L	T	Pct.	Pts.	OP
Chicago	10	6	0	.625	325	248
Green Bay	8	8	0	.500	390	309
Tampa Bay	6	10	0	.375	335	380
Detroit	4	11	1	.281	283	408
Minnesota	3	13	0	.188	276	484

Western Division

	W	L	T	Pct.	Pts.	OP
San Francisco#	15	1	0	.938	475	227
L.A. Rams*	10	6	0	.625	346	316
New Orleans	7	9	0	.438	298	361
Atlanta	4	12	0	.250	281	382

*Wild Card qualifier for playoffs; #Top playoff seed in conference
N.Y. Giants finished ahead of St. Louis and Dallas based on best
head-to-head record (3-1 to Cardinals' 2-2 and Cowboys' 1-3).
St. Louis finished ahead of Dallas based on better division record
(5-3 to Cowboys' 3-5).
Wild Card playoff: SEATTLE 13, L.A. Raiders 7
Divisional playoffs: MIAMI 31, Seattle 10;
    Pittsburgh 24, DENVER 17
AFC Championship: MIAMI 45, Pittsburgh 28
Wild Card playoff: N.Y. Giants 16, L.A. RAMS 13
Divisional playoffs: SAN FRANCISCO 21, N.Y. Giants 10;
    Chicago 23, WASHINGTON 19
NFC Championship: SAN FRANCISCO 23, Chicago 0
Super Bowl XIX: San Francisco (NFC) 38, Miami (AFC) 16,
    at Stanford Stadium, Stanford, California

1983

AMERICAN CONFERENCE

Eastern Division

	W	L	T	Pct.	Pts.	OP
Miami	12	4	0	.750	389	250
New England	8	8	0	.500	274	289
Buffalo	8	8	0	.500	283	351
Baltimore	7	9	0	.438	264	354
N.Y. Jets	7	9	0	.438	313	331

Central Division

	W	L	T	Pct.	Pts.	OP
Pittsburgh	10	6	0	.625	355	303
Cleveland	9	7	0	.563	356	342
Cincinnati	7	9	0	.438	346	302
Houston	2	14	0	.125	288	460

Western Division

	W	L	T	Pct.	Pts.	OP
L.A. Raiders#	12	4	0	.750	442	338
Seattle*	9	7	0	.563	403	397
Denver*	9	7	0	.563	302	327
San Diego	6	10	0	.375	358	462
Kansas City	6	10	0	.375	386	367

NATIONAL CONFERENCE

Eastern Division

	W	L	T	Pct.	Pts.	OP
Washington#	14	2	0	.875	541	332
Dallas*	12	4	0	.750	479	360
St. Louis	8	7	1	.531	374	428
Philadelphia	5	11	0	.313	233	322
N.Y. Giants	3	12	1	.219	267	347

Central Division

	W	L	T	Pct.	Pts.	OP
Detroit	9	7	0	.563	347	286
Green Bay	8	8	0	.500	429	439
Chicago	8	8	0	.500	311	301
Minnesota	8	8	0	.500	316	348
Tampa Bay	2	14	0	.125	241	380

Western Division

	W	L	T	Pct.	Pts.	OP
San Francisco	10	6	0	.625	432	293
L.A. Rams*	9	7	0	.563	361	344
New Orleans	8	8	0	.500	319	337
Atlanta	7	9	0	.438	370	389

*Wild Card qualifier for playoffs; #Top playoff seed in conference
L.A. Raiders were top playoff seed ahead of Miami based on head-
to-head victory (1-0). Seattle was second Wild Card ahead of
Denver based on better division record (5-3 to Broncos' 3-5)
after Cleveland was eliminated from three-way tie based on head-
to-head record (Seattle and Denver 2-1 to Browns' 0-2). Seattle
did not play the L.A. Raiders in the divisional playoffs because,
from 1970-1989, two teams from the same division could not
meet prior to the conference championship game. New England
finished ahead of Buffalo based on head-to-head sweep (2-0).
Baltimore finished ahead of N.Y. Jets based on better conference
record (5-9 to Jets' 4-8). San Diego finished ahead of Kansas
City based on head-to-head sweep (2-0). Green Bay finished
ahead of Chicago based on better record against common oppo-
nents (5-5 to Bears' 4-6) after Minnesota was eliminated from
three-way tie based on conference record (Chicago 7-7 and
Green Bay 6-6 to Vikings' 4-8).
Wild Card playoff: SEATTLE 31, Denver 7
Divisional playoffs: Seattle 27, MIAMI 20;
    L.A. RAIDERS 38, Pittsburgh 10
AFC Championship: L.A. RAIDERS 30, Seattle 14
Wild Card playoff: L.A. Rams 24, DALLAS 17
Divisional playoffs: SAN FRANCISCO 24, Detroit 23;
    WASHINGTON 51, L.A. Rams 7
NFC Championship: WASHINGTON 24, San Francisco 21
Super Bowl XVIII: L.A. Raiders (AFC) 38, Washington (NFC) 9,
    at Tampa Stadium, Tampa, Florida

1982

AMERICAN CONFERENCE

	W	L	T	Pct.	Pts.	OP
L.A. Raiders#	8	1	0	.889	260	200
Miami	7	2	0	.778	198	131
Cincinnati	7	2	0	.778	232	177
Pittsburgh	6	3	0	.667	204	146
San Diego	6	3	0	.667	288	221
N.Y. Jets	6	3	0	.667	245	166
New England	5	4	0	.556	143	157
Cleveland	4	5	0	.444	140	182
Buffalo	4	5	0	.444	150	154
Seattle	4	5	0	.444	127	147
Kansas City	3	6	0	.333	176	184
Denver	2	7	0	.222	148	226
Houston	1	8	0	.111	136	245
Baltimore	0	8	1	.056	113	236

NATIONAL CONFERENCE

	W	L	T	Pct.	Pts.	OP
Washington#	8	1	0	.889	190	128
Dallas	6	3	0	.667	226	145
Green Bay	5	3	1	.611	226	169
Minnesota	5	4	0	.556	187	198
Atlanta	5	4	0	.556	183	199
St. Louis	5	4	0	.556	135	170
Tampa Bay	5	4	0	.556	158	178
Detroit	4	5	0	.444	181	176
New Orleans	4	5	0	.444	129	160
N.Y. Giants	4	5	0	.444	164	160
San Francisco	3	6	0	.333	209	206
Chicago	3	6	0	.333	141	174
Philadelphia	3	6	0	.333	191	195
L.A. Rams	2	7	0	.222	200	250

As the result of a 57-day players' strike, the 1982 NFL regular season schedule was reduced from 16 weeks to 9. At the conclusion of the regular season, the NFL conducted a 16-team postseason Super Bowl Tournament. Eight teams from each conference were seeded 1-8 based on their records during the season.

#Top playoff seed in conference

Miami finished ahead of Cincinnati based on better conference record (6-1 to Bengals' 6-2). Pittsburgh finished ahead of San Diego based on better record against common opponents (3-1 to Chargers' 2-1) after N.Y. Jets were eliminated from three-way tie based on conference record (Pittsburgh and San Diego 5-3 to Jets' 2-3). Cleveland finished ahead of Buffalo and Seattle based on better conference record (4-3 to Bills' 3-3 to Seahawks' 3-5). Buffalo finished ahead of Seattle based on better conference record (3-3 to Seahawks' 3-5). Minnesota (4-1), Atlanta (4-3), St. Louis (5-4), Tampa Bay (3-3) seeds were determined by best won-lost record in conference games. Detroit finished ahead of New Orleans and the N.Y. Giants based on best conference record (4-4 to Saints' 3-5 to Giants' 3-5). San Francisco finished ahead of Chicago, and Chicago finished ahead of Philadelphia, based on conference record (49ers' 2-3 to Bears' 2-5 to Eagles' 1-5).

First round playoff: MIAMI 28, New England 13;
 L.A. RAIDERS 27, Cleveland 10;
 N.Y. Jets 44, CINCINNATI 17;
 San Diego 31, PITTSBURGH 28
Second round playoff: N.Y. Jets 17, L.A. RAIDERS 14;
 MIAMI 34, San Diego 13
AFC Championship: MIAMI 14, N.Y. Jets 0
First round playoff: WASHINGTON 31, Detroit 7;
 GREEN BAY 41, St. Louis 16;
 MINNESOTA 30, Atlanta 24;
 DALLAS 30, Tampa Bay 17
Second round playoff: WASHINGTON 21, Minnesota 7;
 DALLAS 37, Green Bay 26
NFC Championship: WASHINGTON 31, Dallas 17
Super Bowl XVII: Washington (NFC) 27, Miami (AFC) 17,
 at Rose Bowl, Pasadena, California

1981

AMERICAN CONFERENCE

Eastern Division

	W	L	T	Pct.	Pts.	OP
Miami	11	4	1	.719	345	275
N.Y. Jets*	10	5	1	.656	355	287
Buffalo*	10	6	0	.625	311	276
Baltimore	2	14	0	.125	259	533
New England	2	14	0	.125	322	370

Central Division

	W	L	T	Pct.	Pts.	OP
Cincinnati#	12	4	0	.750	421	304
Pittsburgh	8	8	0	.500	356	297
Houston	7	9	0	.438	281	355
Cleveland	5	11	0	.313	276	375

Western Division

	W	L	T	Pct.	Pts.	OP
San Diego	10	6	0	.625	478	390
Denver	10	6	0	.625	321	289
Kansas City	9	7	0	.563	343	290
Oakland	7	9	0	.438	273	343
Seattle	6	10	0	.375	322	388

NATIONAL CONFERENCE

Eastern Division

	W	L	T	Pct.	Pts.	OP
Dallas	12	4	0	.750	367	277
Philadelphia*	10	6	0	.625	368	221
N.Y. Giants*	9	7	0	.563	295	257
Washington	8	8	0	.500	347	349
St. Louis	7	9	0	.438	315	408

Central Division

	W	L	T	Pct.	Pts.	OP
Tampa Bay	9	7	0	.563	315	268
Detroit	8	8	0	.500	397	322
Green Bay	8	8	0	.500	324	361
Minnesota	7	9	0	.438	325	369
Chicago	6	10	0	.375	253	324

Western Division

	W	L	T	Pct.	Pts.	OP
San Francisco#	13	3	0	.813	357	250
Atlanta	7	9	0	.438	426	355
Los Angeles	6	10	0	.375	303	351
New Orleans	4	12	0	.250	207	378

*Wild Card qualifier for playoffs; #Top playoff seed in conference

Baltimore finished ahead of New England based on head-to-head sweep (2-0). San Diego finished ahead of Denver based on better division record (6-2 to Broncos' 5-3). Buffalo was second Wild Card based on head-to-head victory over Denver (1-0). Detroit finished ahead of Green Bay based on better record against common opponents (5-5 to Packers' 4-6).

Wild Card playoff: Buffalo 31, N.Y. JETS 27
Divisional playoffs: San Diego 41, MIAMI 38 (OT);
 CINCINNATI 28, Buffalo 21
AFC Championship: CINCINNATI 27, San Diego 7
Wild Card playoff: N.Y. Giants 27, PHILADELPHIA 21
Divisional playoffs: DALLAS 38, Tampa Bay 0;
 SAN FRANCISCO 38, N.Y. Giants 24
NFC Championship: SAN FRANCISCO 28, Dallas 27
Super Bowl XVI: San Francisco (NFC) 26, Cincinnati (AFC) 21,
 at Silverdome, Pontiac, Michigan

1980

AMERICAN CONFERENCE

Eastern Division

	W	L	T	Pct.	Pts.	OP
Buffalo	11	5	0	.688	320	260
New England	10	6	0	.625	441	325
Miami	8	8	0	.500	266	305
Baltimore	7	9	0	.438	355	387
N.Y. Jets	4	12	0	.250	302	395

Central Division

	W	L	T	Pct.	Pts.	OP
Cleveland	11	5	0	.688	357	310
Houston*	11	5	0	.688	295	251
Pittsburgh	9	7	0	.563	352	313
Cincinnati	6	10	0	.375	244	312

Western Division

	W	L	T	Pct.	Pts.	OP
San Diego#	11	5	0	.688	418	327
Oakland*	11	5	0	.688	364	306
Kansas City	8	8	0	.500	319	336
Denver	8	8	0	.500	310	323
Seattle	4	12	0	.250	291	408

NATIONAL CONFERENCE

Eastern Division

	W	L	T	Pct.	Pts.	OP
Philadelphia	12	4	0	.750	384	222
Dallas*	12	4	0	.750	454	311
Washington	6	10	0	.375	261	293
St. Louis	5	11	0	.313	299	350
N.Y. Giants	4	12	0	.250	249	425

Central Division

	W	L	T	Pct.	Pts.	OP
Minnesota	9	7	0	.563	317	308
Detroit	9	7	0	.563	334	272
Chicago	7	9	0	.438	304	264
Tampa Bay	5	10	1	.344	271	341
Green Bay	5	10	1	.344	231	371

Western Division

	W	L	T	Pct.	Pts.	OP
Atlanta#	12	4	0	.750	405	272
Los Angeles*	11	5	0	.688	424	289
San Francisco	6	10	0	.375	320	415
New Orleans	1	15	0	.063	291	487

*Wild Card qualifier for playoffs; #Top playoff seed in conference
San Diego was top playoff seed based on better conference record than Cleveland and Buffalo (9-3 to Browns' 8-4 and Bills' 8-4). Cleveland was second playoff seed based on better record against common opponents (5-2 to Bills' 5-3). Cleveland finished ahead of Houston based on better conference record (8-4 to Oilers' 7-5). Oakland was first Wild Card based on better conference record than Houston (9-3 to Oilers' 7-5). San Diego finished ahead of Oakland based on better net points in division games (plus 60 net points to Raiders' plus 37). Oakland did not play San Diego in the divisional playoffs because, from 1970-1989, two teams from the same division could not meet prior to the conference championship game. Kansas City finished ahead of Denver based on head-to-head sweep (2-0). Atlanta was top playoff seed based on head-to-head victory over Philadelphia (1-0). Philadelphia finished ahead of Dallas based on better net points in division games (plus 84 net points to Cowboys' plus 50). Minnesota finished ahead of Detroit based on better conference record (8-4 to Lions' 9-5). Tampa Bay finished ahead of Green Bay based on better head-to-head record (1-0-1 to Packers' 0-1-1).
Wild Card playoff: OAKLAND 27, Houston 7
Divisional playoffs: SAN DIEGO 20, Buffalo 14;
  Oakland 14, CLEVELAND 12
AFC Championship: Oakland 34, SAN DIEGO 27
Wild Card playoff: DALLAS 34, Los Angeles 13
Divisional playoffs: PHILADELPHIA 31, Minnesota 16;
  Dallas 30, ATLANTA 27
NFC Championship: PHILADELPHIA 20, Dallas 7
Super Bowl XV: Oakland (AFC) 27, Philadelphia (NFC) 10,
  at Louisiana Superdome, New Orleans, Louisiana

1979

AMERICAN CONFERENCE

Eastern Division

	W	L	T	Pct.	Pts.	OP
Miami	10	6	0	.625	341	257
New England	9	7	0	.563	411	326
N.Y. Jets	8	8	0	.500	337	383
Buffalo	7	9	0	.438	268	279
Baltimore	5	11	0	.313	271	351

Central Division

	W	L	T	Pct.	Pts.	OP
Pittsburgh	12	4	0	.750	416	262
Houston*	11	5	0	.688	362	331
Cleveland	9	7	0	.563	359	352
Cincinnati	4	12	0	.250	337	421

Western Division

	W	L	T	Pct.	Pts.	OP
San Diego#	12	4	0	.750	411	246
Denver*	10	6	0	.625	289	262
Seattle	9	7	0	.563	378	372
Oakland	9	7	0	.563	365	337
Kansas City	7	9	0	.438	238	262

NATIONAL CONFERENCE

Eastern Division

	W	L	T	Pct.	Pts.	OP
Dallas#	11	5	0	.688	371	313
Philadelphia*	11	5	0	.688	339	282
Washington	10	6	0	.625	348	295
N.Y. Giants	6	10	0	.375	237	323
St. Louis	5	11	0	.313	307	358

Central Division

	W	L	T	Pct.	Pts.	OP
Tampa Bay	10	6	0	.625	273	237
Chicago*	10	6	0	.625	306	249
Minnesota	7	9	0	.438	259	337
Green Bay	5	11	0	.313	246	316
Detroit	2	14	0	.125	219	365

Western Division

	W	L	T	Pct.	Pts.	OP
Los Angeles	9	7	0	.563	323	309
New Orleans	8	8	0	.500	370	360
Atlanta	6	10	0	.375	300	388
San Francisco	2	14	0	.125	308	416

*Wild Card qualifier for playoffs; #Top playoff seed in conference
San Diego was top playoff seed based on head-to-head victory over Pittsburgh (1-0). Seattle finished ahead of Oakland based on head-to-head sweep (2-0). Dallas finished ahead of Philadelphia based on better conference record (10-2 to Eagles' 9-3). Philadelphia did not play Dallas in the divisional playoffs because, from 1970-1989, two teams from the same division could not meet prior to the conference championship game. Tampa Bay finished ahead of Chicago based on a better division record (6-2 to Bears' 5-3). Chicago was second Wild Card ahead of Washington based on better net points in all games (57 to Redskins' 53).
Wild Card playoff: HOUSTON 13, Denver 7
Divisional playoffs: Houston 17, SAN DIEGO 14;
  PITTSBURGH 34, Miami 14
AFC Championship: PITTSBURGH 27, Houston 13
Wild Card playoff: PHILADELPHIA 27, Chicago 17
Divisional playoffs: TAMPA BAY 24, Philadelphia 17;
  Los Angeles 21, DALLAS 19
NFC Championship: Los Angeles 9, TAMPA BAY 0
Super Bowl XIV: Pittsburgh (AFC) 31, Los Angeles (NFC) 19,
  at Rose Bowl, Pasadena, California

1978

AMERICAN CONFERENCE

Eastern Division

	W	L	T	Pct.	Pts.	OP
New England	11	5	0	.688	358	286
Miami*	11	5	0	.688	372	254
N.Y. Jets	8	8	0	.500	359	364
Buffalo	5	11	0	.313	302	354
Baltimore	5	11	0	.313	239	421

Central Division

	W	L	T	Pct.	Pts.	OP
Pittsburgh#	14	2	0	.875	356	195
Houston*	10	6	0	.625	283	298
Cleveland	8	8	0	.500	334	356
Cincinnati	4	12	0	.250	252	284

Western Division

	W	L	T	Pct.	Pts.	OP
Denver	10	6	0	.625	282	198
Oakland	9	7	0	.563	311	283
Seattle	9	7	0	.563	345	358
San Diego	9	7	0	.563	355	309
Kansas City	4	12	0	.250	243	327

NATIONAL CONFERENCE

Eastern Division

	W	L	T	Pct.	Pts.	OP
Dallas	12	4	0	.750	384	208
Philadelphia*	9	7	0	.563	270	250
Washington	8	8	0	.500	273	283
St. Louis	6	10	0	.375	248	296
N.Y. Giants	6	10	0	.375	264	298

Central Division

	W	L	T	Pct.	Pts.	OP
Minnesota	8	7	1	.531	294	306
Green Bay	8	7	1	.531	249	269
Detroit	7	9	0	.438	290	300
Chicago	7	9	0	.438	253	274
Tampa Bay	5	11	0	.313	241	259

Western Division

	W	L	T	Pct.	Pts.	OP
Los Angeles#	12	4	0	.750	316	245
Atlanta*	9	7	0	.563	240	290
New Orleans	7	9	0	.438	281	298
San Francisco	2	14	0	.125	219	350

*Wild Card qualifier for playoffs; #Top playoff seed in conference
New England finished ahead of Miami based on better division record (6-2 to Dolphins' 5-3). Buffalo finished ahead of Baltimore based on head-to-head sweep (2-0). Oakland finished ahead of Seattle and San Diego based on better record against common opponents (6-2 to Seahawks' 5-3 and Chargers' 4-4). Atlanta was first Wild Card based on better conference record than Philadelphia (8-4 to Eagles' 6-6). Houston did not play Pittsburgh, and Atlanta did not play Los Angeles in the divisional playoffs because, from 1970-1989, two teams from the same division could not meet prior to the conference championship game. St. Louis finished ahead of N.Y. Giants based on better division record (3-5 to Giants' 2-6). Minnesota finished ahead of Green Bay based on better head-to-head record (1-0-1). Detroit finished ahead of Chicago based on better division record (4-4 to Bears' 3-5).

Wild Card playoff: Houston 17, MIAMI 9
Divisional playoffs: Houston 31, NEW ENGLAND 14;
   PITTSBURGH 33, Denver 10
AFC Championship: PITTSBURGH 34, Houston 5
Wild Card playoff: ATLANTA 14, Philadelphia 13
Divisional playoffs: DALLAS 27, Atlanta 20;
   LOS ANGELES 34, Minnesota 10
NFC Championship: Dallas 28, LOS ANGELES 0
Super Bowl XIII: Pittsburgh (AFC) 35, Dallas (NFC) 31,
   at Orange Bowl, Miami, Florida

1977

AMERICAN CONFERENCE

Eastern Division

	W	L	T	Pct.	Pts.	OP
Baltimore	10	4	0	.714	295	221
Miami	10	4	0	.714	313	197
New England	9	5	0	.643	278	217
Buffalo	3	11	0	.214	160	313
N.Y. Jets	3	11	0	.214	191	300

Central Division

	W	L	T	Pct.	Pts.	OP
Pittsburgh	9	5	0	.643	283	243
Cincinnati	8	6	0	.571	238	235
Houston	8	6	0	.571	299	230
Cleveland	6	8	0	.429	269	267

Western Division

	W	L	T	Pct.	Pts.	OP
Denver#	12	2	0	.857	274	148
Oakland*	11	3	0	.786	351	230
San Diego	7	7	0	.500	222	205
Seattle	5	9	0	.357	282	373
Kansas City	2	12	0	.143	225	349

NATIONAL CONFERENCE

Eastern Division

	W	L	T	Pct.	Pts.	OP
Dallas#	12	2	0	.857	345	212
Washington	9	5	0	.643	196	189
St. Louis	7	7	0	.500	272	287
Philadelphia	5	9	0	.357	220	207
N.Y. Giants	5	9	0	.357	181	265

Central Division

	W	L	T	Pct.	Pts.	OP
Minnesota	9	5	0	.643	231	227
Chicago*	9	5	0	.643	255	253
Detroit	6	8	0	.429	183	252
Green Bay	4	10	0	.286	134	219
Tampa Bay	2	12	0	.143	103	223

Western Division

	W	L	T	Pct.	Pts.	OP
Los Angeles	10	4	0	.714	302	146
Atlanta	7	7	0	.500	179	129
San Francisco	5	9	0	.357	220	260
New Orleans	3	11	0	.214	232	336

*Wild Card qualifier for playoffs; #Top playoff seed in conference
Baltimore finished ahead of Miami based on better conference record (9-3 to Dolphins' 8-4). Buffalo finished ahead of N.Y. Jets based on better strength of schedule (.582 to Jets' .536). Cincinnati finished ahead of Houston based on better division record (6-3 to Oilers' 5-4). Oakland did not play Denver in the divisional playoffs because, from 1970-1989, two teams from the same division could not meet prior to the conference championship game. Minnesota finished ahead of Chicago based on fewer losses by common opponents (11 losses to 14 losses by the Bears' opponents). Chicago won Wild Card ahead of Washington based on better net points in conference games (48 to Redskins' 4). Philadelphia finished ahead of N.Y. Giants based on head-to-head sweep (2-0).

Divisional playoffs: DENVER 34, Pittsburgh 21;
   Oakland 37, BALTIMORE 31 (OT)
AFC Championship: DENVER 20, Oakland 17
Divisional playoffs: DALLAS 37, Chicago 7;
   Minnesota 14, LOS ANGELES 7
NFC Championship: DALLAS 23, Minnesota 6
Super Bowl XII: Dallas (NFC) 27, Denver (AFC) 10,
   at Louisiana Superdome, New Orleans, Louisiana

1976

AMERICAN CONFERENCE

Eastern Division

	W	L	T	Pct.	Pts.	OP
Baltimore	11	3	0	.786	417	246
New England*	11	3	0	.786	376	236
Miami	6	8	0	.429	263	264
N.Y. Jets	3	11	0	.214	169	383
Buffalo	2	12	0	.143	245	363

Central Division

	W	L	T	Pct.	Pts.	OP
Pittsburgh	10	4	0	.714	342	138
Cincinnati	10	4	0	.714	335	210
Cleveland	9	5	0	.643	267	287
Houston	5	9	0	.357	222	273

Western Division

	W	L	T	Pct.	Pts.	OP
Oakland#	13	1	0	.929	350	237
Denver	9	5	0	.643	315	206
San Diego	6	8	0	.429	248	285
Kansas City	5	9	0	.357	290	376
Tampa Bay	0	14	0	.000	125	412

NATIONAL CONFERENCE

Eastern Division

	W	L	T	Pct.	Pts.	OP
Dallas	11	3	0	.786	296	194
Washington*	10	4	0	.714	291	217
St. Louis	10	4	0	.714	309	267
Philadelphia	4	10	0	.286	165	286
N.Y. Giants	3	11	0	.214	170	250

Central Division

	W	L	T	Pct.	Pts.	OP
Minnesota#	11	2	1	.821	305	176
Chicago	7	7	0	.500	253	216
Detroit	6	8	0	.429	262	220
Green Bay	5	9	0	.357	218	299

Western Division

	W	L	T	Pct.	Pts.	OP
Los Angeles	10	3	1	.750	351	190
San Francisco	8	6	0	.571	270	190
Atlanta	4	10	0	.286	172	312
New Orleans	4	10	0	.286	253	346
Seattle	2	12	0	.143	229	429

*Wild Card qualifier for playoffs; #Top playoff seed in conference
Baltimore finished ahead of New England based on better division record (7-1 to Patriots' 6-2). Pittsburgh finished ahead of Cincinnati based on head-to-head sweep (2-0). Washington finished ahead of St. Louis based on head-to-head sweep (2-0). Atlanta finished ahead of New Orleans based on better division record (2-4 to Saints' 1-5).
Divisional playoffs: OAKLAND 24, New England 21; Pittsburgh 40, BALTIMORE 14
AFC Championship: OAKLAND 24, Pittsburgh 7
Divisional playoffs: MINNESOTA 35, Washington 20; Los Angeles 14, DALLAS 12
NFC Championship: MINNESOTA 24, Los Angeles 13
Super Bowl XI: Oakland (AFC) 32, Minnesota (NFC) 14, at Rose Bowl, Pasadena, California

1975

AMERICAN CONFERENCE

Eastern Division

	W	L	T	Pct.	Pts.	OP
Baltimore	10	4	0	.714	395	269
Miami	10	4	0	.714	357	222
Buffalo	8	6	0	.571	420	355
N.Y. Jets	3	11	0	.214	258	433
New England	3	11	0	.214	258	358

Central Division

	W	L	T	Pct.	Pts.	OP
Pittsburgh#	12	2	0	.857	373	162
Cincinnati*	11	3	0	.786	340	246
Houston	10	4	0	.714	293	226
Cleveland	3	11	0	.214	218	372

Western Division

	W	L	T	Pct.	Pts.	OP
Oakland	11	3	0	.786	375	255
Denver	6	8	0	.429	254	307
Kansas City	5	9	0	.357	282	341
San Diego	2	12	0	.143	189	345

NATIONAL CONFERENCE

Eastern Division

	W	L	T	Pct.	Pts.	OP
St. Louis	11	3	0	.786	356	276
Dallas*	10	4	0	.714	350	268
Washington	8	6	0	.571	325	276
N.Y. Giants	5	9	0	.357	216	306
Philadelphia	4	10	0	.286	225	302

Central Division

	W	L	T	Pct.	Pts.	OP
Minnesota#	12	2	0	.857	377	180
Detroit	7	7	0	.500	245	262
Chicago	4	10	0	.286	191	379
Green Bay	4	10	0	.286	226	285

Western Division

	W	L	T	Pct.	Pts.	OP
Los Angeles	12	2	0	.857	312	135
San Francisco	5	9	0	.357	255	286
Atlanta	4	10	0	.286	240	289
New Orleans	2	12	0	.143	165	360

*Wild Card qualifier for playoffs; #Top playoff seed in conference
Baltimore finished ahead of Miami based on head-to-head sweep (2-0). Cincinnati did not play Pittsburgh in the divisional playoffs because, from 1970-1989, two teams from the same division could not meet prior to the conference championship game. N.Y. Jets finished ahead of New England based on head-to-head sweep (2-0). Minnesota was top playoff seed based on better Point Rating system than Los Angeles (3 to 6). Chicago finished ahead of Green Bay based on better division record (2-4 to Bears' 1-5).
Divisional playoffs: PITTSBURGH 28, Baltimore 10; OAKLAND 31, Cincinnati 28
AFC Championship: PITTSBURGH 16, Oakland 10
Divisional playoffs: LOS ANGELES 35, St. Louis 23; Dallas 17, MINNESOTA 14
NFC Championship: Dallas 37, LOS ANGELES 7
Super Bowl X: Pittsburgh (AFC) 21, Dallas (NFC) 17, at Orange Bowl, Miami, Florida

1974

AMERICAN CONFERENCE

Eastern Division

	W	L	T	Pct.	Pts.	OP
Miami	11	3	0	.786	327	216
Buffalo*	9	5	0	.643	264	244
New England	7	7	0	.500	348	289
N.Y. Jets	7	7	0	.500	279	300
Baltimore	2	12	0	.143	190	329

Central Division

	W	L	T	Pct.	Pts.	OP
Pittsburgh	10	3	1	.750	305	189
Houston	7	7	0	.500	236	282
Cincinnati	7	7	0	.500	283	259
Cleveland	4	10	0	.286	251	344

Western Division

	W	L	T	Pct.	Pts.	OP
Oakland	12	2	0	.857	355	228
Denver	7	6	1	.536	302	294
Kansas City	5	9	0	.357	233	293
San Diego	5	9	0	.357	212	285

NATIONAL CONFERENCE

Eastern Division

	W	L	T	Pct.	Pts.	OP
St. Louis	10	4	0	.714	285	218
Washington*	10	4	0	.714	320	196
Dallas	8	6	0	.571	297	235
Philadelphia	7	7	0	.500	242	217
N.Y. Giants	2	12	0	.143	195	299

Central Division

	W	L	T	Pct.	Pts.	OP
Minnesota	10	4	0	.714	310	195
Detroit	7	7	0	.500	256	270
Green Bay	6	8	0	.429	210	206
Chicago	4	10	0	.286	152	279

Western Division

	W	L	T	Pct.	Pts.	OP
Los Angeles	10	4	0	.714	263	181
San Francisco	6	8	0	.429	226	236
New Orleans	5	9	0	.357	166	263
Atlanta	3	11	0	.214	111	271

Wild Card qualifier for playoffs

New England finished ahead of N.Y. Jets based on better record against common opponents (5-4 to Jets' 4-5). Houston finished ahead of Cincinnati based on head-to-head sweep (2-0). Kansas City finished ahead of San Diego based on better record against common opponents (4-6 to Chargers' 3-7). St. Louis finished ahead of Washington based on head-to-head sweep (2-0).

Divisional playoffs: OAKLAND 28, Miami 26;
 PITTSBURGH 32, Buffalo 14
AFC Championship: Pittsburgh 24, OAKLAND 13
Divisional playoffs: MINNESOTA 30, St. Louis 14;
 LOS ANGELES 19, Washington 10
NFC Championship: MINNESOTA 14, Los Angeles 10
Super Bowl IX: Pittsburgh (AFC) 16, Minnesota (NFC) 6,
 at Tulane Stadium, New Orleans, Louisiana

From 1933-1974, sites for league/conference championship games alternated by division.

1973

AMERICAN CONFERENCE

Eastern Division

	W	L	T	Pct.	Pts.	OP
Miami	12	2	0	.857	343	150
Buffalo	9	5	0	.643	259	230
New England	5	9	0	.357	258	300
N.Y. Jets	4	10	0	.286	240	306
Baltimore	4	10	0	.286	226	341

Central Division

	W	L	T	Pct.	Pts.	OP
Cincinnati	10	4	0	.714	286	231
Pittsburgh*	10	4	0	.714	347	210
Cleveland	7	5	2	.571	234	255
Houston	1	13	0	.071	199	447

Western Division

	W	L	T	Pct.	Pts.	OP
Oakland	9	4	1	.679	292	175
Kansas City	7	5	2	.571	231	192
Denver	7	5	2	.571	354	296
San Diego	2	11	1	.179	188	386

NATIONAL CONFERENCE

Eastern Division

	W	L	T	Pct.	Pts.	OP
Dallas	10	4	0	.714	382	203
Washington*	10	4	0	.714	325	198
Philadelphia	5	8	1	.393	310	393
St. Louis	4	9	1	.321	286	365
N.Y. Giants	2	11	1	.179	226	362

Central Division

	W	L	T	Pct.	Pts.	OP
Minnesota	12	2	0	.857	296	168
Detroit	6	7	1	.464	271	247
Green Bay	5	7	2	.429	202	259
Chicago	3	11	0	.214	195	334

Western Division

	W	L	T	Pct.	Pts.	OP
Los Angeles	12	2	0	.857	388	178
Atlanta	9	5	0	.643	318	224
San Francisco	5	9	0	.357	262	319
New Orleans	5	9	0	.357	163	312

Wild Card qualifier for playoffs

Cincinnati finished ahead of Pittsburgh based on better conference record (8-3 to Steelers' 7-4). N.Y. Jets finished ahead of Baltimore based on head-to-head sweep (2-0). Kansas City finished ahead of Denver based on better division record (4-2 to Broncos' 3-2-1). Dallas finished ahead of Washington based on better point differential in head-to-head games (13 points). San Francisco finished ahead of New Orleans based on better division record (2-4 to Saints' 1-5).

Divisional playoffs: OAKLAND 33, Pittsburgh 14;
 MIAMI 34, Cincinnati 16
AFC Championship: MIAMI 27, Oakland 10
Divisional playoffs: MINNESOTA 27, Washington 20;
 DALLAS 27, Los Angeles 16
NFC Championship: Minnesota 27, DALLAS 10
Super Bowl VIII: Miami (AFC) 24, Minnesota (NFC) 7,
 at Rice Stadium, Houston, Texas

1972

AMERICAN CONFERENCE

Eastern Division

	W	L	T	Pct.	Pts.	OP
Miami	14	0	0	1.000	385	171
N.Y. Jets	7	7	0	.500	367	324
Baltimore	5	9	0	.357	235	252
Buffalo	4	9	1	.321	257	377
New England	3	11	0	.214	192	446

Central Division

	W	L	T	Pct.	Pts.	OP
Pittsburgh	11	3	0	.786	343	175
Cleveland*	10	4	0	.714	268	249
Cincinnati	8	6	0	.571	299	229
Houston	1	13	0	.071	164	380

Western Division

	W	L	T	Pct.	Pts.	OP
Oakland	10	3	1	.750	365	248
Kansas City	8	6	0	.571	287	254
Denver	5	9	0	.357	325	350
San Diego	4	9	1	.321	264	344

NATIONAL CONFERENCE

Eastern Division

	W	L	T	Pct.	Pts.	OP
Washington	11	3	0	.786	336	218
Dallas*	10	4	0	.714	319	240
N.Y. Giants	8	6	0	.571	331	247
St. Louis	4	9	1	.321	193	303
Philadelphia	2	11	1	.179	145	352

Central Division

	W	L	T	Pct.	Pts.	OP
Green Bay	10	4	0	.714	304	226
Detroit	8	5	1	.607	339	290
Minnesota	7	7	0	.500	301	252
Chicago	4	9	1	.321	225	275

Western Division

	W	L	T	Pct.	Pts.	OP
San Francisco	8	5	1	.607	353	249
Atlanta	7	7	0	.500	269	274
Los Angeles	6	7	1	.464	291	286
New Orleans	2	11	1	.179	215	361

Wild Card qualifier for playoffs

Dallas did not play Washington in the divisional playoffs because, from 1970-1989, two teams from the same division could not meet prior to the conference championship game.

Divisional playoffs: PITTSBURGH 13, Oakland 7;
   MIAMI 20, Cleveland 14
AFC Championship: Miami 21, PITTSBURGH 17
Divisional playoffs: Dallas 30, SAN FRANCISCO 28;
   WASHINGTON 16, Green Bay 3
NFC Championship: WASHINGTON 26, Dallas 3
Super Bowl VII: Miami (AFC) 14, Washington (NFC) 7,
   at Memorial Coliseum, Los Angeles, California

1971

AMERICAN CONFERENCE

Eastern Division

	W	L	T	Pct.	Pts.	OP
Miami	10	3	1	.769	315	174
Baltimore*	10	4	0	.714	313	140
New England	6	8	0	.429	238	325
N.Y. Jets	6	8	0	.429	212	299
Buffalo	1	13	0	.071	184	394

Central Division

	W	L	T	Pct.	Pts.	OP
Cleveland	9	5	0	.643	285	273
Pittsburgh	6	8	0	.429	246	292
Houston	4	9	1	.308	251	330
Cincinnati	4	10	0	.286	284	265

Western Division

	W	L	T	Pct.	Pts.	OP
Kansas City	10	3	1	.769	302	208
Oakland	8	4	2	.667	344	278
San Diego	6	8	0	.429	311	341
Denver	4	9	1	.308	203	275

NATIONAL CONFERENCE

Eastern Division

	W	L	T	Pct.	Pts.	OP
Dallas	11	3	0	.786	406	222
Washington*	9	4	1	.692	276	190
Philadelphia	6	7	1	.462	221	302
St. Louis	4	9	1	.308	231	279
N.Y. Giants	4	10	0	.286	228	362

Central Division

	W	L	T	Pct.	Pts.	OP
Minnesota	11	3	0	.786	245	139
Detroit	7	6	1	.538	341	286
Chicago	6	8	0	.429	185	276
Green Bay	4	8	2	.333	274	298

Western Division

	W	L	T	Pct.	Pts.	OP
San Francisco	9	5	0	.643	300	216
Los Angeles	8	5	1	.615	313	260
Atlanta	7	6	1	.538	274	277
New Orleans	4	8	2	.333	266	347

Wild Card qualifier for playoffs

New England finished ahead of N.Y. Jets based on better strength of schedule (.537 to Jets' .510).

Divisional playoffs: Miami 27, KANSAS CITY 24 (OT);
   Baltimore 20, CLEVELAND 3
AFC Championship: MIAMI 21, Baltimore 0
Divisional playoffs: Dallas 20, MINNESOTA 12;
   SAN FRANCISCO 24, Washington 20
NFC Championship: DALLAS 14, San Francisco 3
Super Bowl VI: Dallas (NFC) 24, Miami (AFC) 3,
   at Tulane Stadium, New Orleans, Louisiana

From 1920-1971, tie games were not included in winning percentage.

1970

AMERICAN CONFERENCE

Eastern Division

	W	L	T	Pct.	Pts.	OP
Baltimore	11	2	1	.846	321	234
Miami*	10	4	0	.714	297	228
N.Y. Jets	4	10	0	.286	255	286
Buffalo	3	10	1	.231	204	337
Boston Patriots	2	12	0	.143	149	361

Central Division

	W	L	T	Pct.	Pts.	OP
Cincinnati	8	6	0	.571	312	255
Cleveland	7	7	0	.500	286	265
Pittsburgh	5	9	0	.357	210	272
Houston	3	10	1	.231	217	352

Western Division

	W	L	T	Pct.	Pts.	OP
Oakland	8	4	2	.667	300	293
Kansas City	7	5	2	.583	272	244
San Diego	5	6	3	.455	282	278
Denver	5	8	1	.385	253	264

NATIONAL CONFERENCE

Eastern Division

	W	L	T	Pct.	Pts.	OP
Dallas	10	4	0	.714	299	221
N.Y. Giants	9	5	0	.643	301	270
St. Louis	8	5	1	.615	325	228
Washington	6	8	0	.429	297	314
Philadelphia	3	10	1	.231	241	332

Central Division

	W	L	T	Pct.	Pts.	OP
Minnesota	12	2	0	.857	335	143
Detroit*	10	4	0	.714	347	202
Green Bay	6	8	0	.429	196	293
Chicago	6	8	0	.429	256	261

Western Division

	W	L	T	Pct.	Pts.	OP
San Francisco	10	3	1	.769	352	267
Los Angeles	9	4	1	.692	325	202
Atlanta	4	8	2	.333	206	261
New Orleans	2	11	1	.154	172	347

Wild Card qualifier for playoffs

Miami did not play Baltimore, and Detroit did not play Minnesota, in the divisional playoffs because, from 1970-1989, two teams from the same division could not meet prior to the conference championship game. Green Bay finished ahead of Chicago based on better division record (2-4 to Bears' 1-5).

Divisional playoffs: BALTIMORE 17, Cincinnati 0;
   OAKLAND 21, Miami 14
AFC Championship: BALTIMORE 27, Oakland 17
Divisional playoffs: DALLAS 5, Detroit 0;
   San Francisco 17, MINNESOTA 14
NFC Championship: Dallas 17, SAN FRANCISCO 10
Super Bowl V: Baltimore (AFC) 16, Dallas (NFC) 13,
   at Orange Bowl, Miami, Florida

1969 NFL

EASTERN CONFERENCE

Capitol Division

	W	L	T	Pct.	Pts.	OP
Dallas	11	2	1	.846	369	223
Washington	7	5	2	.583	307	319
New Orleans	5	9	0	.357	311	393
Philadelphia	4	9	1	.308	279	377

Century Division

	W	L	T	Pct.	Pts.	OP
Cleveland	10	3	1	.769	351	300
N.Y. Giants	6	8	0	.429	264	298
St. Louis	4	9	1	.308	314	389
Pittsburgh	1	13	0	.071	218	404

WESTERN CONFERENCE

Coastal Division

	W	L	T	Pct.	Pts.	OP
Los Angeles	11	3	0	.786	320	243
Baltimore	8	5	1	.615	279	268
Atlanta	6	8	0	.429	276	268
San Francisco	4	8	2	.333	277	319

Central Division

	W	L	T	Pct.	Pts.	OP
Minnesota	12	2	0	.857	379	133
Detroit	9	4	1	.692	259	188
Green Bay	8	6	0	.571	269	221
Chicago	1	13	0	.071	210	339

Conference championships: Cleveland 38, DALLAS 14;
   MINNESOTA 23, Los Angeles 20
NFL championship: MINNESOTA 27, Cleveland 7
Super Bowl IV: Kansas City (AFL) 23, Minnesota (NFL) 7,
   at Tulane Stadium, New Orleans, Louisiana

1969 AFL

EASTERN DIVISION

	W	L	T	Pct.	Pts.	OP
N.Y. Jets	10	4	0	.714	353	269
Houston	6	6	2	.500	278	279
Boston Patriots	4	10	0	.286	266	316
Buffalo	4	10	0	.286	230	359
Miami	3	10	1	.231	233	332

WESTERN DIVISION

	W	L	T	Pct.	Pts.	OP
Oakland	12	1	1	.923	377	242
Kansas City	11	3	0	.786	359	177
San Diego	8	6	0	.571	288	276
Denver	5	8	1	.385	297	344
Cincinnati	4	9	1	.308	280	367

Divisional playoffs: Kansas City 13, N.Y. JETS 6;
   OAKLAND 56, Houston 7
AFL championship: Kansas City 17, OAKLAND 7

1968 NFL

EASTERN CONFERENCE

Capitol Division

	W	L	T	Pct.	Pts.	OP
Dallas	12	2	0	.857	431	186
N.Y. Giants	7	7	0	.500	294	325
Washington	5	9	0	.357	249	358
Philadelphia	2	12	0	.143	202	351

Century Division

	W	L	T	Pct.	Pts.	OP
Cleveland	10	4	0	.714	394	273
St. Louis	9	4	1	.692	325	289
New Orleans	4	9	1	.308	246	327
Pittsburgh	2	11	1	.154	244	397

WESTERN CONFERENCE

Coastal Division

	W	L	T	Pct.	Pts.	OP
Baltimore	13	1	0	.929	402	144
Los Angeles	10	3	1	.769	312	200
San Francisco	7	6	1	.538	303	310
Atlanta	2	12	0	.143	170	389

Central Division

	W	L	T	Pct.	Pts.	OP
Minnesota	8	6	0	.571	282	242
Chicago	7	7	0	.500	250	333
Green Bay	6	7	1	.462	281	227
Detroit	4	8	2	.333	207	241

Conference championships: CLEVELAND 31, Dallas 20;
   BALTIMORE 24, Minnesota 14
NFL championship: Baltimore 34, CLEVELAND 0
Super Bowl III: N.Y. Jets (AFL) 16, Baltimore (NFL) 7,
   at Orange Bowl, Miami, Florida

1968 AFL

EASTERN DIVISION

	W	L	T	Pct.	Pts.	OP
N.Y. Jets	11	3	0	.786	419	280
Houston	7	7	0	.500	303	248
Miami	5	8	1	.385	276	355
Boston Patriots	4	10	0	.286	229	406
Buffalo	1	12	1	.077	199	367

WESTERN DIVISION

	W	L	T	Pct.	Pts.	OP
Oakland	12	2	0	.857	453	233
Kansas City	12	2	0	.857	371	170
San Diego	9	5	0	.643	382	310
Denver	5	9	0	.357	255	404
Cincinnati	3	11	0	.214	215	329

Western Division playoff: OAKLAND 41, Kansas City 6
AFL championship: N.Y. JETS 27, Oakland 23

1967 NFL

EASTERN CONFERENCE
Capitol Division

	W	L	T	Pct.	Pts.	OP
Dallas	9	5	0	.643	342	268
Philadelphia	6	7	1	.462	351	409
Washington	5	6	3	.455	347	353
New Orleans	3	11	0	.214	233	379

Century Division

	W	L	T	Pct.	Pts.	OP
Cleveland	9	5	0	.643	334	297
N.Y. Giants	7	7	0	.500	369	379
St. Louis	6	7	1	.462	333	356
Pittsburgh	4	9	1	.308	281	320

WESTERN CONFERENCE
Coastal Division

	W	L	T	Pct.	Pts.	OP
Los Angeles	11	1	2	.917	398	196
Baltimore	11	1	2	.917	394	198
San Francisco	7	7	0	.500	273	337
Atlanta	1	12	1	.077	175	422

Central Division

	W	L	T	Pct.	Pts.	OP
Green Bay	9	4	1	.692	332	209
Chicago	7	6	1	.538	239	218
Detroit	5	7	2	.417	260	259
Minnesota	3	8	3	.273	233	294

Los Angeles finished ahead of Baltimore based on better point differential in head-to-head games (net 24 points).
Conference championships: DALLAS 52, Cleveland 14; GREEN BAY 28, Los Angeles 7
NFL championship: GREEN BAY 21, Dallas 17
Super Bowl II: Green Bay (NFL) 33, Oakland (AFL) 14, at Orange Bowl, Miami, Florida

1967 AFL

EASTERN DIVISION

	W	L	T	Pct.	Pts.	OP
Houston	9	4	1	.692	258	199
N.Y. Jets	8	5	1	.615	371	329
Buffalo	4	10	0	.286	237	285
Miami	4	10	0	.286	219	407
Boston Patriots	3	10	1	.231	280	389

WESTERN DIVISION

	W	L	T	Pct.	Pts.	OP
Oakland	13	1	0	.929	468	233
Kansas City	9	5	0	.643	408	254
San Diego	8	5	1	.615	360	352
Denver	3	11	0	.214	256	409

AFL championship: OAKLAND 40, Houston 7

1966 NFL

EASTERN CONFERENCE

	W	L	T	Pct.	Pts.	OP
Dallas	10	3	1	.769	445	239
Cleveland	9	5	0	.643	403	259
Philadelphia	9	5	0	.643	326	340
St. Louis	8	5	1	.615	264	265
Washington	7	7	0	.500	351	355
Pittsburgh	5	8	1	.385	316	347
Atlanta	3	11	0	.214	204	437
N.Y. Giants	1	12	1	.077	263	501

WESTERN CONFERENCE

	W	L	T	Pct.	Pts.	OP
Green Bay	12	2	0	.857	335	163
Baltimore	9	5	0	.643	314	226
Los Angeles	8	6	0	.571	289	212
San Francisco	6	6	2	.500	320	325
Chicago	5	7	2	.417	234	272
Detroit	4	9	1	.308	206	317
Minnesota	4	9	1	.308	292	304

NFL championship: Green Bay 34, DALLAS 27
Super Bowl I: Green Bay (NFL) 35, Kansas City (AFL) 10, at Memorial Coliseum, Los Angeles, California

1966 AFL

EASTERN DIVISION

	W	L	T	Pct.	Pts.	OP
Buffalo	9	4	1	.692	358	255
Boston Patriots	8	4	2	.677	315	283
N.Y. Jets	6	6	2	.500	322	312
Houston	3	11	0	.214	335	396
Miami	3	11	0	.214	213	362

WESTERN DIVISION

	W	L	T	Pct.	Pts.	OP
Kansas City	11	2	1	.846	448	276
Oakland	8	5	1	.615	315	288
San Diego	7	6	1	.538	335	284
Denver	4	10	0	.286	196	381

AFL championship: Kansas City 31, BUFFALO 7

1965 NFL

EASTERN CONFERENCE

	W	L	T	Pct.	Pts.	OP
Cleveland	11	3	0	.786	363	325
Dallas	7	7	0	.500	325	280
N.Y. Giants	7	7	0	.500	270	338
Washington	6	8	0	.429	257	301
Philadelphia	5	9	0	.357	363	359
St. Louis	5	9	0	.357	296	309
Pittsburgh	2	12	0	.143	202	397

WESTERN CONFERENCE

	W	L	T	Pct.	Pts.	OP
Green Bay	10	3	1	.769	316	224
Baltimore	10	3	1	.769	389	284
Chicago	9	5	0	.643	409	275
San Francisco	7	6	1	.538	421	402
Minnesota	7	7	0	.500	383	403
Detroit	6	7	1	.462	257	295
Los Angeles	4	10	0	.286	269	328

Western Conference playoff: GREEN BAY 13, Baltimore 10 (OT)
NFL championship: GREEN BAY 23, Cleveland 12

1965 AFL

EASTERN DIVISION

	W	L	T	Pct.	Pts.	OP
Buffalo	10	3	1	.769	313	226
N.Y. Jets	5	8	1	.385	285	303
Boston Patriots	4	8	2	.333	244	302
Houston	4	10	0	.286	298	429

WESTERN DIVISION

	W	L	T	Pct.	Pts.	OP
San Diego	9	2	3	.818	340	227
Oakland	8	5	1	.615	298	239
Kansas City	7	5	2	.583	322	285
Denver	4	10	0	.286	303	392

AFL championship: Buffalo 23, SAN DIEGO 0

1964 NFL

EASTERN CONFERENCE

	W	L	T	Pct.	Pts.	OP
Cleveland	10	3	1	.769	415	293
St. Louis	9	3	2	.750	357	331
Philadelphia	6	8	0	.429	312	313
Washington	6	8	0	.429	307	305
Dallas	5	8	1	.385	250	289
Pittsburgh	5	9	0	.357	253	315
N.Y. Giants	2	10	2	.167	241	399

WESTERN CONFERENCE

	W	L	T	Pct.	Pts.	OP
Baltimore	12	2	0	.857	428	225
Green Bay	8	5	1	.615	342	245
Minnesota	8	5	1	.615	355	296
Detroit	7	5	2	.583	280	260
Los Angeles	5	7	2	.417	283	339
Chicago	5	9	0	.357	260	379
San Francisco	4	10	0	.286	236	330

NFL championship: CLEVELAND 27, Baltimore 0

1964 AFL

EASTERN DIVISION

	W	L	T	Pct.	Pts.	OP
Buffalo	12	2	0	.857	400	242
Boston Patriots	10	3	1	.769	365	297
N.Y. Jets	5	8	1	.385	278	315
Houston	4	10	0	.286	310	355

WESTERN DIVISION

	W	L	T	Pct.	Pts.	OP
San Diego	8	5	1	.615	341	300
Kansas City	7	7	0	.500	366	306
Oakland	5	7	2	.417	303	350
Denver	2	11	1	.154	240	438

AFL championship: BUFFALO 20, San Diego 7

1963 NFL

EASTERN CONFERENCE

	W	L	T	Pct.	Pts.	OP
N.Y. Giants	11	3	0	.786	448	280
Cleveland	10	4	0	.714	343	262
St. Louis	9	5	0	.643	341	283
Pittsburgh	7	4	3	.636	321	295
Dallas	4	10	0	.286	305	378
Washington	3	11	0	.214	279	398
Philadelphia	2	10	2	.167	242	381

WESTERN CONFERENCE

	W	L	T	Pct.	Pts.	OP
Chicago	11	1	2	.917	301	144
Green Bay	11	2	1	.846	369	206
Baltimore	8	6	0	.571	316	285
Detroit	5	8	1	.385	326	265
Minnesota	5	8	1	.385	309	390
Los Angeles	5	9	0	.357	210	350
San Francisco	2	12	0	.143	198	391

NFL championship: CHICAGO 14, N.Y. Giants 10

1963 AFL

EASTERN DIVISION

	W	L	T	Pct.	Pts.	OP
Boston Patriots	7	6	1	.538	327	257
Buffalo	7	6	1	.538	304	291
Houston	6	8	0	.429	302	372
N.Y. Jets	5	8	1	.385	249	399

WESTERN DIVISION

	W	L	T	Pct.	Pts.	OP
San Diego	11	3	0	.786	399	255
Oakland	10	4	0	.714	363	282
Kansas City	5	7	2	.417	347	263
Denver	2	11	1	.154	301	473

Eastern Division playoff: Boston 26, BUFFALO 8
AFL championship: SAN DIEGO 51, Boston 10

1962 NFL

EASTERN CONFERENCE	W	L	T	Pct.	Pts.	OP	WESTERN CONFERENCE	W	L	T	Pct.	Pts.	OP
N.Y. Giants	12	2	0	.857	398	283	Green Bay	13	1	0	.929	415	148
Pittsburgh	9	5	0	.643	312	363	Detroit	11	3	0	.786	315	177
Cleveland	7	6	1	.538	291	257	Chicago	9	5	0	.643	321	287
Washington	5	7	2	.417	305	376	Baltimore	7	7	0	.500	293	288
Dallas Cowboys	5	8	1	.385	398	402	San Francisco	6	8	0	.429	282	331
St. Louis	4	9	1	.308	287	361	Minnesota	2	11	1	.154	254	410
Philadelphia	3	10	1	.231	282	356	Los Angeles	1	12	1	.077	220	334

NFL championship: Green Bay 16, N.Y. GIANTS 7

1962 AFL

EASTERN DIVISION	W	L	T	Pct.	Pts.	OP	WESTERN DIVISION	W	L	T	Pct.	Pts.	OP
Houston	11	3	0	.786	387	270	Dallas Texans	11	3	0	.786	389	233
Boston Patriots	9	4	1	.692	346	295	Denver	7	7	0	.500	353	334
Buffalo	7	6	1	.538	309	272	San Diego	4	10	0	.286	314	392
N.Y. Titans	5	9	0	.357	278	423	Oakland	1	13	0	.071	213	370

AFL championship: Dallas Texans 20, HOUSTON 17 (OT)

1961 NFL

EASTERN CONFERENCE	W	L	T	Pct.	Pts.	OP	WESTERN CONFERENCE	W	L	T	Pct.	Pts.	OP
N.Y. Giants	10	3	1	.769	368	220	Green Bay	11	3	0	.786	391	223
Philadelphia	10	4	0	.714	361	297	Detroit	8	5	1	.615	270	258
Cleveland	8	5	1	.615	319	270	Baltimore	8	6	0	.571	302	307
St. Louis	7	7	0	.500	279	267	Chicago	8	6	0	.571	326	302
Pittsburgh	6	8	0	.429	295	287	San Francisco	7	6	1	.538	346	272
Dallas Cowboys	4	9	1	.308	236	380	Los Angeles	4	10	0	.286	263	333
Washington	1	12	1	.077	174	392	Minnesota	3	11	0	.214	285	407

NFL championship: GREEN BAY 37, N.Y. Giants 0

1961 AFL

EASTERN DIVISION	W	L	T	Pct.	Pts.	OP	WESTERN DIVISION	W	L	T	Pct.	Pts.	OP
Houston	10	3	1	.769	513	242	San Diego	12	2	0	.857	396	219
Boston Patriots	9	4	1	.692	413	313	Dallas Texans	6	8	0	.429	334	343
N.Y. Titans	7	7	0	.500	301	390	Denver	3	11	0	.214	251	432
Buffalo	6	8	0	.429	294	342	Oakland	2	12	0	.143	237	458

AFL championship: Houston 10, SAN DIEGO 3

1960 NFL

EASTERN CONFERENCE	W	L	T	Pct.	Pts.	OP	WESTERN CONFERENCE	W	L	T	Pct.	Pts.	OP
Philadelphia	10	2	0	.833	321	246	Green Bay	8	4	0	.667	332	209
Cleveland	8	3	1	.727	362	217	Detroit	7	5	0	.583	239	212
N.Y. Giants	6	4	2	.600	271	261	San Francisco	7	5	0	.583	208	205
St. Louis	6	5	1	.545	288	230	Baltimore	6	6	0	.500	288	234
Pittsburgh	5	6	1	.455	240	275	Chicago	5	6	1	.455	194	299
Washington	1	9	2	.100	178	309	L.A. Rams	4	7	1	.364	265	297
							Dallas Cowboys	0	11	1	.000	177	369

NFL championship: PHILADELPHIA 17, Green Bay 13

1960 AFL

EASTERN CONFERENCE	W	L	T	Pct.	Pts.	OP	WESTERN CONFERENCE	W	L	T	Pct.	Pts.	OP
Houston	10	4	0	.714	379	285	L.A. Chargers	10	4	0	.714	373	336
N.Y. Titans	7	7	0	.500	382	399	Dallas Texans	8	6	0	.571	362	253
Buffalo	5	8	1	.385	296	303	Oakland	6	8	0	.429	319	388
Boston	5	9	0	.357	286	349	Denver	4	9	1	.308	309	393

AFL championship: HOUSTON 24, L.A. Chargers 16

1959

EASTERN CONFERENCE	W	L	T	Pct.	Pts.	OP	WESTERN CONFERENCE	W	L	T	Pct.	Pts.	OP
N.Y. Giants	10	2	0	.833	284	170	Baltimore	9	3	0	.750	374	251
Cleveland	7	5	0	.583	270	214	Chi. Bears	8	4	0	.667	252	196
Philadelphia	7	5	0	.583	268	278	Green Bay	7	5	0	.583	248	246
Pittsburgh	6	5	1	.545	257	216	San Francisco	7	5	0	.583	255	237
Washington	3	9	0	.250	185	350	Detroit	3	8	1	.273	203	275
Chi. Cardinals	2	10	0	.167	234	324	Los Angeles	2	10	0	.167	242	315

NFL championship: BALTIMORE 31, N.Y. Giants 16

1958

EASTERN CONFERENCE	W	L	T	Pct.	Pts.	OP	WESTERN CONFERENCE	W	L	T	Pct.	Pts.	OP
N.Y. Giants	9	3	0	.750	246	183	Baltimore	9	3	0	.750	381	203
Cleveland	9	3	0	.750	302	217	Chi. Bears	8	4	0	.667	298	230
Pittsburgh	7	4	1	.636	261	230	Los Angeles	8	4	0	.667	344	278
Washington	4	7	1	.364	214	268	San Francisco	6	6	0	.500	257	324
Chi. Cardinals	2	9	1	.182	261	356	Detroit	4	7	1	.364	261	276
Philadelphia	2	9	1	.182	235	306	Green Bay	1	10	1	.091	193	382

Eastern Conference playoff: N.Y. GIANTS 10, Cleveland 0
NFL championship: Baltimore 23, N.Y. GIANTS 17 (OT)

1957

EASTERN CONFERENCE	W	L	T	Pct.	Pts.	OP	WESTERN CONFERENCE	W	L	T	Pct.	Pts.	OP
Cleveland	9	2	1	.818	269	172	Detroit	8	4	0	.667	251	231
N.Y. Giants	7	5	0	.583	254	211	San Francisco	8	4	0	.667	260	264
Pittsburgh	6	6	0	.500	161	178	Baltimore	7	5	0	.583	303	235
Washington	5	6	1	.455	251	230	Los Angeles	6	6	0	.500	307	278
Philadelphia	4	8	0	.333	173	230	Chi. Bears	5	7	0	.417	203	211
Chi. Cardinals	3	9	0	.250	200	299	Green Bay	3	9	0	.250	218	311

Western Conference playoff: Detroit 31, SAN FRANCISCO 27
NFL championship: DETROIT 59, Cleveland 14

1956

EASTERN CONFERENCE	W	L	T	Pct.	Pts.	OP	WESTERN CONFERENCE	W	L	T	Pct.	Pts.	OP
N.Y. Giants	8	3	1	.727	264	197	Chi. Bears	9	2	1	.818	363	246
Chi. Cardinals	7	5	0	.583	240	182	Detroit	9	3	0	.750	300	188
Washington	6	6	0	.500	183	225	San Francisco	5	6	1	.455	233	284
Cleveland	5	7	0	.417	167	177	Baltimore	5	7	0	.417	270	322
Pittsburgh	5	7	0	.417	217	250	Green Bay	4	8	0	.333	264	342
Philadelphia	3	8	1	.273	143	215	Los Angeles	4	8	0	.333	291	307

NFL championship: N.Y. GIANTS 47, Chi. Bears 7

1955

EASTERN CONFERENCE	W	L	T	Pct.	Pts.	OP	WESTERN CONFERENCE	W	L	T	Pct.	Pts.	OP
Cleveland	9	2	1	.818	349	218	Los Angeles	8	3	1	.727	260	231
Washington	8	4	0	.667	246	222	Chi. Bears	8	4	0	.667	294	251
N.Y. Giants	6	5	1	.545	267	223	Green Bay	6	6	0	.500	258	276
Chi. Cardinals	4	7	1	.364	224	252	Baltimore	5	6	1	.455	214	239
Philadelphia	4	7	1	.364	248	231	San Francisco	4	8	0	.333	216	298
Pittsburgh	4	8	0	.333	195	285	Detroit	3	9	0	.250	230	275

NFL championship: Cleveland 38, LOS ANGELES 14

1954

EASTERN CONFERENCE	W	L	T	Pct.	Pts.	OP	WESTERN CONFERENCE	W	L	T	Pct.	Pts.	OP
Cleveland	9	3	0	.750	336	162	Detroit	9	2	1	.818	337	189
Philadelphia	7	4	1	.636	284	230	Chi. Bears	8	4	0	.667	301	279
N.Y. Giants	7	5	0	.583	293	184	San Francisco	7	4	1	.636	313	251
Pittsburgh	5	7	0	.417	219	263	Los Angeles	6	5	1	.545	314	285
Washington	3	9	0	.250	207	432	Green Bay	4	8	0	.333	234	251
Chi. Cardinals	2	10	0	.167	183	347	Baltimore	3	9	0	.250	131	279

NFL championship: CLEVELAND 56, Detroit 10

1953

EASTERN CONFERENCE	W	L	T	Pct.	Pts.	OP	WESTERN CONFERENCE	W	L	T	Pct.	Pts.	OP
Cleveland	11	1	0	.917	348	162	Detroit	10	2	0	.833	271	205
Philadelphia	7	4	1	.636	352	215	San Francisco	9	3	0	.750	372	237
Washington	6	5	1	.545	208	215	Los Angeles	8	3	1	.727	366	236
Pittsburgh	6	6	0	.500	211	263	Chi. Bears	3	8	1	.273	218	262
N.Y. Giants	3	9	0	.250	179	277	Baltimore	3	9	0	.250	182	350
Chi. Cardinals	1	10	1	.091	190	337	Green Bay	2	9	1	.182	200	338

NFL championship: DETROIT 17, Cleveland 16

1952

AMERICAN CONFERENCE	W	L	T	Pct.	Pts.	OP	NATIONAL CONFERENCE	W	L	T	Pct.	Pts.	OP
Cleveland	8	4	0	.667	310	213	Detroit	9	3	0	.750	344	192
N.Y. Giants	7	5	0	.583	234	231	Los Angeles	9	3	0	.750	349	234
Philadelphia	7	5	0	.583	252	271	San Francisco	7	5	0	.583	285	221
Pittsburgh	5	7	0	.417	300	273	Green Bay	6	6	0	.500	295	312
Chi. Cardinals	4	8	0	.333	172	221	Chi. Bears	5	7	0	.417	245	326
Washington	4	8	0	.333	240	287	Dallas Texans	1	11	0	.083	182	427

National Conference playoff: DETROIT 31, Los Angeles 21
NFL championship: Detroit 17, CLEVELAND 7

1951

AMERICAN CONFERENCE	W	L	T	Pct.	Pts.	OP	NATIONAL CONFERENCE	W	L	T	Pct.	Pts.	OP
Cleveland	11	1	0	.917	331	152	Los Angeles	8	4	0	.667	392	261
N.Y. Giants	9	2	1	.818	254	161	Detroit	7	4	1	.636	336	259
Washington	5	7	0	.417	183	296	San Francisco	7	4	1	.636	255	205
Pittsburgh	4	7	1	.364	183	235	Chi. Bears	7	5	0	.583	286	282
Philadelphia	4	8	0	.333	234	264	Green Bay	3	9	0	.250	254	375
Chi. Cardinals	3	9	0	.250	210	287	N.Y. Yanks	1	9	2	.100	241	382

NFL championship: LOS ANGELES 24, Cleveland 17

1950

AMERICAN CONFERENCE	W	L	T	Pct.	Pts.	OP	NATIONAL CONFERENCE	W	L	T	Pct.	Pts.	OP
Cleveland	10	2	0	.833	310	144	Los Angeles	9	3	0	.750	466	309
N.Y. Giants	10	2	0	.833	268	150	Chi. Bears	9	3	0	.750	279	207
Philadelphia	6	6	0	.500	254	141	N.Y. Yanks	7	5	0	.583	366	367
Pittsburgh	6	6	0	.500	180	195	Detroit	6	6	0	.500	321	285
Chi. Cardinals	5	7	0	.417	233	287	Green Bay	3	9	0	.250	244	406
Washington	3	9	0	.250	232	326	San Francisco	3	9	0	.250	213	300
							Baltimore	1	11	0	.083	213	462

American Conference playoff: CLEVELAND 8, N.Y. Giants 3
National Conference playoff: LOS ANGELES 24, Chi. Bears 14
NFL championship: CLEVELAND 30, Los Angeles 28

1949

EASTERN DIVISION	W	L	T	Pct.	Pts.	OP	WESTERN DIVISION	W	L	T	Pct.	Pts.	OP
Philadelphia	11	1	0	.917	364	134	Los Angeles	8	2	2	.800	360	239
Pittsburgh	6	5	1	.545	224	214	Chi. Bears	9	3	0	.750	332	218
N.Y. Giants	6	6	0	.500	287	298	Chi. Cardinals	6	5	1	.545	360	301
Washington	4	7	1	.364	268	339	Detroit	4	8	0	.333	237	259
N.Y. Bulldogs	1	10	1	.091	153	368	Green Bay	2	10	0	.167	114	329

NFL championship: Philadelphia 14, LOS ANGELES 0

1948

EASTERN DIVISION	W	L	T	Pct.	Pts.	OP	WESTERN DIVISION	W	L	T	Pct.	Pts.	OP
Philadelphia	9	2	1	.818	376	156	Chi. Cardinals	11	1	0	.917	395	226
Washington	7	5	0	.583	291	287	Chi. Bears	10	2	0	.833	375	151
N.Y. Giants	4	8	0	.333	297	388	Los Angeles	6	5	1	.545	327	269
Pittsburgh	4	8	0	.333	200	243	Green Bay	3	9	0	.250	154	290
Boston	3	9	0	.250	174	372	Detroit	2	10	0	.167	200	407

NFL championship: PHILADELPHIA 7, Chi. Cardinals 0

1947

EASTERN DIVISION	W	L	T	Pct.	Pts.	OP	WESTERN DIVISION	W	L	T	Pct.	Pts.	OP
Philadelphia	8	4	0	.667	308	242	Chi. Cardinals	9	3	0	.750	306	231
Pittsburgh	8	4	0	.667	240	259	Chi. Bears	8	4	0	.667	363	241
Boston	4	7	1	.364	168	256	Green Bay	6	5	1	.545	274	210
Washington	4	8	0	.333	295	367	Los Angeles	6	6	0	.500	259	214
N.Y. Giants	2	8	2	.200	190	309	Detroit	3	9	0	.250	231	305

Eastern Division playoff: Philadelphia 21, PITTSBURGH 0
NFL championship: CHI. CARDINALS 28, Philadelphia 21

1946

EASTERN DIVISION	W	L	T	Pct.	Pts.	OP	WESTERN DIVISION	W	L	T	Pct.	Pts.	OP
N.Y. Giants	7	3	1	.700	236	162	Chi. Bears	8	2	1	.800	289	193
Philadelphia	6	5	0	.545	231	220	Los Angeles	6	4	1	.600	277	257
Washington	5	5	1	.500	171	191	Green Bay	6	5	0	.545	148	158
Pittsburgh	5	5	1	.500	136	117	Chi. Cardinals	6	5	0	.545	260	198
Boston	2	8	1	.200	189	273	Detroit	1	10	0	.091	142	310

NFL championship: Chi. Bears 24, N.Y. GIANTS 14

1945

EASTERN DIVISION	W	L	T	Pct.	Pts.	OP	WESTERN DIVISION	W	L	T	Pct.	Pts.	OP
Washington	8	2	0	.800	209	121	Cleveland	9	1	0	.900	244	136
Philadelphia	7	3	0	.700	272	133	Detroit	7	3	0	.700	195	194
N.Y. Giants	3	6	1	.333	179	198	Green Bay	6	4	0	.600	258	173
Boston	3	6	1	.333	123	211	Chi. Bears	3	7	0	.300	192	235
Pittsburgh	2	8	0	.200	79	220	Chi. Cardinals	1	9	0	.100	98	228

NFL championship: CLEVELAND 15, Washington 14

1944

EASTERN DIVISION	W	L	T	Pct.	Pts.	OP	WESTERN DIVISION	W	L	T	Pct.	Pts.	OP
N.Y. Giants	8	1	1	.889	206	75	Green Bay	8	2	0	.800	238	141
Philadelphia	7	1	2	.875	267	131	Chi. Bears	6	3	1	.667	258	172
Washington	6	3	1	.667	169	180	Detroit	6	3	1	.667	216	151
Boston	2	8	0	.200	82	233	Cleveland	4	6	0	.400	188	224
Brooklyn	0	10	0	.000	69	166	Card-Pitt	0	10	0	.000	108	328

NFL championship: Green Bay 14, N.Y. GIANTS 7

1943

EASTERN DIVISION	W	L	T	Pct.	Pts.	OP	WESTERN DIVISION	W	L	T	Pct.	Pts.	OP
Washington	6	3	1	.667	229	137	Chi. Bears	8	1	1	.889	303	157
N.Y. Giants	6	3	1	.667	197	170	Green Bay	7	2	1	.778	264	172
Phil-Pitt	5	4	1	.556	225	230	Detroit	3	6	1	.333	178	218
Brooklyn	2	8	0	.200	65	234	Chi. Cardinals	0	10	0	.000	95	238

Eastern Division playoff: Washington 28, N.Y. GIANTS 0
NFL championship: CHI. BEARS 41, Washington 21

1942

EASTERN DIVISION	W	L	T	Pct.	Pts.	OP	WESTERN DIVISION	W	L	T	Pct.	Pts.	OP
Washington	10	1	0	.909	227	102	Chi. Bears	11	0	0	1.000	376	84
Pittsburgh	7	4	0	.636	167	119	Green Bay	8	2	1	.800	300	215
N.Y. Giants	5	5	1	.500	155	139	Cleveland	5	6	0	.455	150	207
Brooklyn	3	8	0	.273	100	168	Chi. Cardinals	3	8	0	.273	98	209
Philadelphia	2	9	0	.182	134	239	Detroit	0	11	0	.000	38	263

NFL championship: WASHINGTON 14, Chi. Bears 6

1941

EASTERN DIVISION	W	L	T	Pct.	Pts.	OP	WESTERN DIVISION	W	L	T	Pct.	Pts.	OP
N.Y. Giants	8	3	0	.727	238	114	Chi. Bears	10	1	0	.909	396	147
Brooklyn	7	4	0	.636	158	127	Green Bay	10	1	0	.909	258	120
Washington	6	5	0	.545	176	174	Detroit	4	6	1	.400	121	195
Philadelphia	2	8	1	.200	119	218	Chi. Cardinals	3	7	1	.300	127	197
Pittsburgh	1	9	1	.100	103	276	Cleveland	2	9	0	.182	116	244

Western Division playoff: CHI. BEARS 33, Green Bay 14
NFL championship: CHI. BEARS 37, N.Y. Giants 9

1940

EASTERN DIVISION	W	L	T	Pct.	Pts.	OP	WESTERN DIVISION	W	L	T	Pct.	Pts.	OP
Washington	9	2	0	.818	245	142	Chi. Bears	8	3	0	.727	238	152
Brooklyn	8	3	0	.727	186	120	Green Bay	6	4	1	.600	238	155
N.Y. Giants	6	4	1	.600	131	133	Detroit	5	5	1	.500	138	153
Pittsburgh	2	7	2	.222	60	178	Cleveland	4	6	1	.400	171	191
Philadelphia	1	10	0	.091	111	211	Chi. Cardinals	2	7	2	.222	139	222

NFL championship: Chi. Bears 73, WASHINGTON 0

1939

EASTERN DIVISION	W	L	T	Pct.	Pts.	OP	WESTERN DIVISION	W	L	T	Pct.	Pts.	OP
N.Y. Giants	9	1	1	.900	168	85	Green Bay	9	2	0	.818	233	153
Washington	8	2	1	.800	242	94	Chi. Bears	8	3	0	.727	298	157
Brooklyn	4	6	1	.400	108	219	Detroit	6	5	0	.545	145	150
Philadelphia	1	9	1	.100	105	200	Cleveland	5	5	1	.500	195	164
Pittsburgh	1	9	1	.100	114	216	Chi. Cardinals	1	10	0	.091	84	254

NFL championship: GREEN BAY 27, N.Y. Giants 0

1938

EASTERN DIVISION	W	L	T	Pct.	Pts.	OP	WESTERN DIVISION	W	L	T	Pct.	Pts.	OP
N.Y. Giants	8	2	1	.800	194	79	Green Bay	8	3	0	.727	223	118
Washington	6	3	2	.667	148	154	Detroit	7	4	0	.636	119	108
Brooklyn	4	4	3	.500	131	161	Chi. Bears	6	5	0	.545	194	148
Philadelphia	5	6	0	.455	154	164	Cleveland	4	7	0	.364	131	215
Pittsburgh	2	9	0	.182	79	169	Chi. Cardinals	2	9	0	.182	111	168

NFL championship: N.Y. GIANTS 23, Green Bay 17

1937

EASTERN DIVISION	W	L	T	Pct.	Pts.	OP	WESTERN DIVISION	W	L	T	Pct.	Pts.	OP
Washington	8	3	0	.727	195	120	Chi. Bears	9	1	1	.900	201	100
N.Y. Giants	6	3	2	.667	128	109	Green Bay	7	4	0	.636	220	122
Pittsburgh	4	7	0	.364	122	145	Detroit	7	4	0	.636	180	105
Brooklyn	3	7	1	.300	82	174	Chi. Cardinals	5	5	1	.500	135	165
Philadelphia	2	8	1	.200	86	177	Cleveland	1	10	0	.091	75	207

NFL championship: Washington 28, CHI. BEARS 21

1936

EASTERN DIVISION	W	L	T	Pct.	Pts.	OP	WESTERN DIVISION	W	L	T	Pct.	Pts.	OP
Boston	7	5	0	.583	149	110	Green Bay	10	1	1	.909	248	118
Pittsburgh	6	6	0	.500	98	187	Chi. Bears	9	3	0	.750	222	94
N.Y. Giants	5	6	1	.455	115	163	Detroit	8	4	0	.667	235	102
Brooklyn	3	8	1	.273	92	161	Chi. Cardinals	3	8	1	.273	74	143
Philadelphia	1	11	0	.083	51	206							

NFL championship: Green Bay 21, Boston 6, at Polo Grounds, N.Y.

1935

EASTERN DIVISION	W	L	T	Pct.	Pts.	OP	WESTERN DIVISION	W	L	T	Pct.	Pts.	OP
N.Y. Giants	9	3	0	.750	180	96	Detroit	7	3	2	.700	191	111
Brooklyn	5	6	1	.455	90	141	Green Bay	8	4	0	.667	181	96
Pittsburgh	4	8	0	.333	100	209	Chi. Bears	6	4	2	.600	192	106
Boston	2	8	1	.200	65	123	Chi. Cardinals	6	4	2	.600	99	97
Philadelphia	2	9	0	.182	60	179							

NFL championship: DETROIT 26, N.Y. Giants 7
One game between Boston and Philadelphia was canceled.

1934

EASTERN DIVISION	W	L	T	Pct.	Pts.	OP	WESTERN DIVISION	W	L	T	Pct.	Pts.	OP
N.Y. Giants	8	5	0	.615	147	107	Chi. Bears	13	0	0	1.000	286	86
Boston	6	6	0	.500	107	94	Detroit	10	3	0	.769	238	59
Brooklyn	4	7	0	.364	61	153	Green Bay	7	6	0	.538	156	112
Philadelphia	4	7	0	.364	127	85	Chi. Cardinals	5	6	0	.455	80	84
Pittsburgh	2	10	0	.167	51	206	St. Louis	1	2	0	.333	27	61
							Cincinnati	0	8	0	.000	10	243

NFL championship: N.Y. GIANTS 30, Chi. Bears 13

1933

EASTERN DIVISION	W	L	T	Pct.	Pts.	OP	WESTERN DIVISION	W	L	T	Pct.	Pts.	OP
N.Y. Giants	11	3	0	.786	244	101	Chi. Bears	10	2	1	.833	133	82
Brooklyn	5	4	1	.556	93	54	Portsmouth	6	5	0	.545	128	87
Boston	5	5	2	.500	103	97	Green Bay	5	7	1	.417	170	107
Philadelphia	3	5	1	.375	77	158	Cincinnati	3	6	1	.333	38	110
Pittsburgh	3	6	2	.333	67	208	Chi. Cardinals	1	9	1	.100	52	101

NFL championship: CHI. BEARS 23, N.Y. Giants 21

1932

	W	L	T	Pct.
Chicago Bears	7	1	6	.875
Green Bay Packers	10	3	1	.769
Portsmouth Spartans	6	2	4	.750
Boston Braves	4	4	2	.500
New York Giants	4	6	2	.400
Brooklyn Dodgers	3	9	0	.250
Chicago Cardinals	2	6	2	.250
Staten Island Stapletons	2	7	3	.222

Chicago Bears and Portsmouth finished regularly scheduled games tied for first place. Bears won playoff game, which counted in standings, 9-0.

1931

	W	L	T	Pct.
Green Bay Packers	12	2	0	.857
Portsmouth Spartans	11	3	0	.786
Chicago Bears	8	5	0	.615
Chicago Cardinals	5	4	0	.556
New York Giants	7	6	1	.538
Providence Steam Roller	4	4	3	.500
Staten Island Stapletons	4	6	1	.400
Cleveland Indians	2	8	0	.200
Brooklyn Dodgers	2	12	0	.143
Frankford Yellow Jackets	1	6	1	.143

1930

	W	L	T	Pct.
Green Bay Packers	10	3	1	.769
New York Giants	13	4	0	.765
Chicago Bears	9	4	1	.692
Brooklyn Dodgers	7	4	1	.636
Providence Steam Roller	6	4	1	.600
Staten Island Stapletons	5	5	2	.500
Chicago Cardinals	5	6	2	.455
Portsmouth Spartans	5	6	3	.455
Frankford Yellow Jackets	4	13	1	.222
Minneapolis Red Jackets	1	7	1	.125
Newark Tornadoes	1	10	1	.091

1929

	W	L	T	Pct.
Green Bay Packers	12	0	1	1.000
New York Giants	13	1	1	.929
Frankford Yellow Jackets	10	4	5	.714
Chicago Cardinals	6	6	1	.500
Boston Bulldogs	4	4	0	.500
Staten Island Stapletons	3	4	3	.429
Providence Steam Roller	4	6	2	.400
Orange Tornadoes	3	5	4	.375
Chicago Bears	4	9	2	.308
Buffalo Bisons	1	7	1	.125
Minneapolis Red Jackets	1	9	0	.100
Dayton Triangles	0	6	0	.000

1928

	W	L	T	Pct.
Providence Steam Roller	8	1	2	.889
Frankford Yellow Jackets	11	3	2	.786
Detroit Wolverines	7	2	1	.778
Green Bay Packers	6	4	3	.600
Chicago Bears	7	5	1	.583
New York Giants	4	7	2	.364
New York Yankees	4	8	1	.333
Pottsville Maroons	2	8	0	.200
Chicago Cardinals	1	5	0	.167
Dayton Triangles	0	7	0	.000

1927

	W	L	T	Pct.
New York Giants	11	1	1	.917
Green Bay Packers	7	2	1	.778
Chicago Bears	9	3	2	.750
Cleveland Bulldogs	8	4	1	.667
Providence Steam Roller	8	5	1	.615
New York Yankees	7	8	1	.467
Frankford Yellow Jackets	6	9	3	.400
Pottsville Maroons	5	8	0	.385
Chicago Cardinals	3	7	1	.300
Dayton Triangles	1	6	1	.143
Duluth Eskimos	1	8	0	.111
Buffalo Bisons	0	5	0	.000

1926

	W	L	T	Pct.
Frankford Yellow Jackets	14	1	2	.933
Chicago Bears	12	1	3	.923
Pottsville Maroons	10	2	2	.833
Kansas City Cowboys	8	3	0	.727
Green Bay Packers	7	3	3	.700
Los Angeles Buccaneers	6	3	1	.667
New York Giants	8	4	1	.667
Duluth Eskimos	6	5	3	.545
Buffalo Rangers	4	4	2	.500
Chicago Cardinals	5	6	1	.455
Providence Steam Roller	5	7	1	.417
Detroit Panthers	4	6	2	.400
Hartford Blues	3	7	0	.300
Brooklyn Lions	3	8	0	.273
Milwaukee Badgers	2	7	0	.222
Akron Indians	1	4	3	.200
Dayton Triangles	1	4	1	.200
Racine Tornadoes	1	4	0	.200
Columbus Tigers	1	6	0	.143
Canton Bulldogs	1	9	3	.100
Hammond Pros	0	4	0	.000
Louisville Colonels	0	4	0	.000

1925

	W	L	T	Pct.
Chicago Cardinals	11	2	1	.846
Pottsville Maroons	10	2	0	.833
Detroit Panthers	8	2	2	.800
New York Giants	8	4	0	.667
Akron Indians	4	2	2	.667
Frankford Yellow Jackets	13	7	0	.650
Chicago Bears	9	5	3	.643
Rock Island Independents	5	3	3	.625
Green Bay Packers	8	5	0	.615
Providence Steam Roller	6	5	1	.545
Canton Bulldogs	4	4	0	.500
Cleveland Bulldogs	5	8	1	.385
Kansas City Cowboys	2	5	1	.286
Hammond Pros	1	4	0	.200
Buffalo Bisons	1	6	2	.143
Duluth Kelleys	0	3	0	.000
Rochester Jeffersons	0	6	1	.000
Milwaukee Badgers	0	6	0	.000
Dayton Triangles	0	7	1	.000
Columbus Tigers	0	9	0	.000

1924

	W	L	T	Pct.
Cleveland Bulldogs	7	1	1	.875
Chicago Bears	6	1	4	.857
Frankford Yellow Jackets	11	2	1	.846
Duluth Kelleys	5	1	0	.833
Rock Island Independents	5	2	2	.714
Green Bay Packers	7	4	0	.636
Racine Legion	4	3	3	.571
Chicago Cardinals	5	4	1	.556
Buffalo Bisons	6	5	0	.545
Columbus Tigers	4	4	0	.500
Hammond Pros	2	2	1	.500
Milwaukee Badgers	5	8	0	.385
Akron Indians	2	6	0	.250
Dayton Triangles	2	6	0	.250
Kansas City Blues	2	7	0	.222
Kenosha Maroons	0	4	1	.000
Minneapolis Marines	0	6	0	.000
Rochester Jeffersons	0	7	0	.000

1923

	W	L	T	Pct.
Canton Bulldogs	11	0	1	1.000
Chicago Bears	9	2	1	.818
Green Bay Packers	7	2	1	.778
Milwaukee Badgers	7	2	3	.778
Cleveland Indians	3	1	3	.750
Chicago Cardinals	8	4	0	.667
Duluth Kelleys	4	3	0	.571
Buffalo All-Americans	5	4	3	.556
Columbus Tigers	5	4	1	.556
Racine Legion	4	4	2	.500
Toledo Maroons	3	3	2	.500
Rock Island Independents	2	3	3	.400
Minneapolis Marines	2	5	2	.286
St. Louis All-Stars	1	4	2	.200
Hammond Pros	1	5	1	.167
Dayton Triangles	1	6	1	.143
Akron Indians	1	6	0	.143
Oorang Indians	1	10	0	.091
Louisville Brecks	0	3	0	.000
Rochester Jeffersons	0	4	0	.000

1922

	W	L	T	Pct.
Canton Bulldogs	10	0	2	1.000
Chicago Bears	9	3	0	.750
Chicago Cardinals	8	3	0	.727
Toledo Maroons	5	2	2	.714
Rock Island Independents	4	2	1	.667
Racine Legion	6	4	1	.600
Dayton Triangles	4	3	1	.571
Green Bay Packers	4	3	3	.571
Buffalo All-Americans	5	4	1	.556
Akron Pros	3	5	2	.375
Milwaukee Badgers	2	4	3	.333
Oorang Indians	3	6	0	.333
Minneapolis Marines	1	3	0	.250
Louisville Brecks	1	3	0	.250
Evansville Crimson Giants	0	3	0	.000
Rochester Jeffersons	0	4	1	.000
Hammond Pros	0	5	1	.000
Columbus Panhandles	0	8	0	.000

1921

	W	L	T	Pct.
Chicago Staleys	9	1	1	.900
Buffalo All-Americans	9	1	2	.900
Akron Pros	8	3	1	.727
Canton Bulldogs	5	2	3	.714
Rock Island Independents	4	2	1	.667
Evansville Crimson Giants	3	2	0	.600
Green Bay Packers	3	2	1	.600
Dayton Triangles	4	4	1	.500
Chicago Cardinals	3	3	2	.500
Rochester Jeffersons	2	3	0	.400
Cleveland Indians	3	5	0	.375
Washington Senators	1	2	0	.333
Cincinnati Celts	1	3	0	.250
Hammond Pros	1	3	1	.250
Minneapolis Marines	1	3	0	.250
Detroit Tigers	1	5	1	.167
Columbus Panhandles	1	8	0	.111
Tonawanda Kardex	0	1	0	.000
Muncie Flyers	0	2	0	.000
Louisville Brecks	0	2	0	.000
New York Giants	0	2	0	.000

1920*

	W	L	T	Pct.
Akron Pros	8	0	3	1.000
Decatur Staleys	10	1	2	.909
Buffalo All-Americans	9	1	1	.900
Chicago Cardinals	6	2	2	.750
Rock Island Independents	6	2	2	.750
Dayton Triangles	5	2	2	.714
Rochester Jeffersons	6	3	2	.667
Canton Bulldogs	7	4	2	.636
Detroit Heralds	2	3	3	.400
Cleveland Tigers	2	4	2	.333
Chicago Tigers	2	5	1	.286
Hammond Pros	2	5	0	.286
Columbus Panhandles	2	6	2	.250
Muncie Flyers	0	1	0	.000

No official standings were maintained for the 1920 season, and the championship was awarded to the Akron Pros in a League meeting on April 30, 1921. Clubs played schedules that included games against nonleague opponents.

RS=REGULAR SEASON
PS=POSTSEASON

*ARIZONA vs. ATLANTA
RS: Cardinals lead series, 13-10
1966—Falcons, 16-10 (A)
1968—Cardinals, 17-12 (StL)
1971—Cardinals, 26-9 (A)
1973—Cardinals, 32-10 (A)
1975—Cardinals, 23-20 (StL)
1978—Cardinals, 42-21 (StL)
1980—Falcons, 33-27 (StL) OT
1981—Falcons, 41-20 (A)
1982—Cardinals, 23-20 (A)
1986—Falcons, 33-13 (A)
1987—Cardinals, 34-21 (A)
1989—Cardinals, 34-20 (P)
1990—Cardinals, 24-13 (A)
1991—Cardinals, 16-10 (P)
1992—Falcons, 20-17 (A)
1993—Cardinals, 27-10 (A)
1994—Falcons, 10-6 (Atl)
1995—Cardinals, 40-37 (Ariz) OT
1997—Falcons, 29-26 (Ariz)
1999—Falcons, 37-14 (Atl)
2001—Falcons, 34-14 (Ariz)
2004—Falcons, 6-3 (Atl)
2006—Falcons, 32-10 (Atl)
(RS Pts.—Cardinals 501, Falcons 491)
*Franchise known as Phoenix prior to 1994
and in St. Louis prior to 1988*

*ARIZONA vs. BALTIMORE
RS: Ravens lead series, 2-1
1997—Cardinals, 16-13 (B)
2000—Ravens, 13-7 (A)
2003—Ravens, 26-18 (A)
(RS Pts.—Ravens 52, Cardinals 41)

*ARIZONA vs. BUFFALO
RS: Bills lead series, 5-3
1971—Cardinals, 28-23 (B)
1975—Bills, 32-14 (StL)
1981—Cardinals, 24-0 (StL)
1984—Cardinals, 37-7 (StL)
1986—Bills, 17-10 (B)
1990—Bills, 45-14 (B)
1999—Bills, 31-21 (A)
2004—Bills, 38-14 (B)
(RS Pts.—Bills 193, Cardinals 162)
*Franchise known as Phoenix prior to 1994
and in St. Louis prior to 1988*

ARIZONA vs. CAROLINA
RS: Panthers lead series, 4-2
1995—Panthers, 27-7 (C)
2001—Cardinals, 30-7 (C)
2002—Cardinals, 16-13 (C)
2003—Panthers, 20-17 (A)
2004—Panthers, 35-10 (C)
2005—Panthers, 24-20 (A)
(RS Pts.—Panthers 126, Cardinals 100)

*ARIZONA vs. **CHICAGO
RS: Bears lead series, 55-26-6
(NP denotes Normal Park;
Wr denotes Wrigley Field;
Co denotes Comiskey Park;
So denotes Soldier Field;
all Chicago)
1920—Cardinals, 7-6 (NP)
　　　Staleys, 10-0 (Wr)
1921—Tie, 0-0 (Wr)
1922—Cardinals, 6-0 (Co)
　　　Cardinals, 9-0 (Co)

1923—Bears, 3-0 (Wr)
1924—Bears, 6-0 (Wr)
　　　Bears, 21-0 (Co)
1925—Cardinals, 9-0 (Co)
　　　Tie, 0-0 (Wr)
1926—Bears, 16-0 (Wr)
　　　Bears, 10-0 (So)
　　　Tie, 0-0 (Wr)
1927—Bears, 9-0 (NP)
　　　Cardinals, 3-0 (Wr)
1928—Bears, 15-0 (NP)
　　　Bears, 34-0 (Wr)
1929—Tie, 0-0 (Wr)
　　　Cardinals, 40-6 (Co)
1930—Bears, 32-6 (Co)
　　　Bears, 6-0 (Wr)
1931—Bears, 26-13 (Wr)
　　　Bears, 18-7 (Wr)
1932—Tie, 0-0 (Wr)
　　　Bears, 34-0 (Wr)
1933—Bears, 12-9 (Wr)
　　　Bears, 22-6 (Wr)
1934—Bears, 20-0 (Wr)
　　　Bears, 17-6 (Wr)
1935—Tie, 7-7 (Wr)
　　　Bears, 13-0 (Wr)
1936—Bears, 7-3 (Wr)
　　　Cardinals, 14-7 (Wr)
1937—Bears, 16-7 (Wr)
　　　Bears, 42-28 (Wr)
1938—Bears, 16-13 (So)
　　　Bears, 34-28 (Wr)
1939—Bears, 44-7 (Wr)
　　　Bears, 48-7 (Co)
1940—Cardinals, 21-7 (Co)
　　　Bears, 31-23 (Wr)
1941—Bears, 53-7 (Wr)
　　　Bears, 34-24 (Co)
1942—Bears, 41-14 (Wr)
　　　Bears, 21-7 (Co)
1943—Bears, 20-0 (Wr)
　　　Bears, 35-24 (Co)
1945—Cardinals, 16-7 (Wr)
　　　Bears, 28-20 (Co)
1946—Bears, 34-17 (Co)
　　　Cardinals, 35-28 (Wr)
1947—Cardinals, 31-7 (Co)
　　　Cardinals, 30-21 (Wr)
1948—Bears, 28-17 (Co)
　　　Cardinals, 24-21 (Wr)
1949—Bears, 17-7 (Co)
　　　Bears, 52-21 (Wr)
1950—Bears, 27-6 (Wr)
　　　Cardinals, 20-10 (Co)
1951—Cardinals, 28-14 (Co)
　　　Cardinals, 24-14 (Wr)
1952—Cardinals, 21-10 (Co)
　　　Bears, 10-7 (Wr)
1953—Cardinals, 24-17 (Wr)
1954—Bears, 29-7 (Co)
1955—Cardinals, 53-14 (Co)
1956—Bears, 10-3 (Wr)
1957—Bears, 14-6 (Co)
1958—Bears, 30-14 (Wr)
1959—Bears, 31-7 (So)
1965—Bears, 34-13 (Wr)
1966—Cardinals, 24-17 (StL)
1967—Bears, 30-3 (Wr)
1969—Cardinals, 20-17 (StL)
1972—Bears, 27-10 (StL)

1975—Cardinals, 34-20 (So)
1977—Cardinals, 16-13 (StL)
1978—Bears, 17-10 (So)
1979—Bears, 42-6 (So)
1982—Cardinals, 10-7 (So)
1984—Cardinals, 38-21 (StL)
1990—Bears, 31-21 (P)
1994—Bears, 19-16 (A) OT
1998—Cardinals, 20-7 (A)
2001—Bears, 20-13 (C)
2003—Bears, 28-3 (C)
2006—Bears, 24-23 (A)
(RS Pts.—Bears 1,646, Cardinals 1,073)
*Franchise known as Phoenix prior to
1994, in St. Louis prior to 1988, and in
Chicago prior to 1960
**Franchise in Decatur prior to 1921 and
known as Staleys prior to 1922*

*ARIZONA vs. CINCINNATI
RS: Bengals lead series, 5-3
1973—Bengals, 42-24 (C)
1979—Bengals, 34-28 (C)
1985—Cardinals, 41-27 (StL)
1988—Bengals, 21-14 (C)
1994—Cardinals, 28-7 (A)
1997—Bengals, 24-21 (C)
2000—Bengals, 24-13 (C)
2003—Cardinals, 17-14 (A)
(RS Pts.—Bengals 193, Cardinals 186)
*Franchise known as Phoenix prior to 1994
and in St. Louis prior to 1988*

*ARIZONA vs. CLEVELAND
RS: Browns lead series, 33-11-3
1950—Browns, 34-24 (Cle)
　　　Browns, 10-7 (Chi)
1951—Browns, 34-17 (Chi)
　　　Browns, 49-28 (Cle)
1952—Browns, 28-13 (Cle)
　　　Browns, 10-0 (Chi)
1953—Browns, 27-7 (Chi)
　　　Browns, 27-16 (Cle)
1954—Browns, 31-7 (Cle)
　　　Browns, 35-3 (Chi)
1955—Browns, 26-20 (Chi)
　　　Browns, 35-24 (Cle)
1956—Cardinals, 9-7 (Chi)
　　　Cardinals, 24-7 (Cle)
1957—Browns, 11-7 (Chi)
　　　Browns, 31-0 (Cle)
1958—Browns, 35-28 (Cle)
　　　Browns, 38-24 (Chi)
1959—Browns, 34-7 (Chi)
　　　Browns, 17-7 (Cle)
1960—Browns, 28-27 (Cle)
　　　Tie, 17-17 (StL)
1961—Browns, 20-17 (Cle)
　　　Browns, 21-10 (StL)
1962—Browns, 34-7 (StL)
　　　Browns, 38-14 (Cle)
1963—Cardinals, 20-14 (Cle)
　　　Browns, 24-10 (StL)
1964—Tie, 33-33 (Cle)
　　　Cardinals, 28-19 (StL)
1965—Cardinals, 49-13 (Cle)
　　　Browns, 27-24 (StL)
1966—Cardinals, 34-28 (Cle)
　　　Browns, 38-10 (StL)
1967—Browns, 20-16 (Cle)
　　　Browns, 20-16 (StL)
1968—Cardinals, 27-21 (Cle)

Cardinals, 27-16 (StL)
1969—Tie, 21-21 (Cle)
    Browns, 27-21 (StL)
1974—Cardinals, 29-7 (StL)
1979—Browns, 38-20 (StL)
1985—Cardinals, 27-24 (Cle) OT
1988—Browns, 29-21 (P)
1994—Browns, 32-0 (Cle)
2000—Cardinals, 29-21 (A)
2003—Browns, 44-6 (Cle)
(RS Pts.—Browns 1,206, Cardinals 832)
*Franchise known as Phoenix prior to
1994, in St. Louis prior to 1988,
and in Chicago prior to 1960*
*ARIZONA vs. DALLAS
RS: Cowboys lead series, 55-27-1
PS: Cardinals lead series, 1-0
1960—Cardinals, 12-10 (StL)
1961—Cardinals, 31-17 (D)
    Cardinals, 31-13 (StL)
1962—Cardinals, 28-24 (D)
    Cardinals, 52-20 (StL)
1963—Cardinals, 34-7 (D)
    Cowboys, 28-24 (StL)
1964—Cardinals, 16-6 (D)
    Cowboys, 31-13 (StL)
1965—Cardinals, 20-13 (StL)
    Cowboys, 27-13 (D)
1966—Tie, 10-10 (StL)
    Cowboys, 31-17 (D)
1967—Cowboys, 46-21 (D)
1968—Cowboys, 27-10 (StL)
1969—Cowboys, 24-3 (D)
1970—Cardinals, 20-7 (StL)
    Cardinals, 38-0 (D)
1971—Cowboys, 16-13 (StL)
    Cowboys, 31-12 (D)
1972—Cowboys, 33-24 (D)
    Cowboys, 27-6 (StL)
1973—Cowboys, 45-10 (D)
    Cowboys, 30-3 (StL)
1974—Cardinals, 31-28 (StL)
    Cowboys, 17-14 (D)
1975—Cowboys, 37-31 (D) OT
    Cardinals, 31-17 (StL)
1976—Cardinals, 21-17 (StL)
    Cowboys, 19-14 (D)
1977—Cowboys, 30-24 (StL)
    Cardinals, 24-17 (D)
1978—Cowboys, 21-12 (D)
    Cowboys, 24-21 (StL) OT
1979—Cowboys, 22-21 (StL)
    Cowboys, 22-13 (D)
1980—Cowboys, 27-24 (StL)
    Cowboys, 31-21 (D)
1981—Cowboys, 30-17 (D)
    Cardinals, 20-17 (StL)
1982—Cowboys, 24-7 (StL)
1983—Cowboys, 34-17 (StL)
    Cowboys, 35-17 (D)
1984—Cardinals, 31-20 (D)
    Cowboys, 24-17 (StL)
1985—Cardinals, 21-10 (StL)
    Cowboys, 35-17 (D)
1986—Cowboys, 31-7 (StL)
    Cowboys, 37-6 (D)
1987—Cardinals, 24-13 (StL)
    Cowboys, 21-16 (D)
1988—Cowboys, 17-14 (P)
    Cardinals, 16-10 (D)

1989—Cardinals, 19-10 (D)
    Cardinals, 24-20 (P)
1990—Cardinals, 20-3 (P)
    Cardinals, 41-10 (D)
1991—Cowboys, 17-9 (P)
    Cowboys, 27-7 (D)
1992—Cowboys, 31-20 (D)
    Cowboys, 16-10 (P)
1993—Cowboys, 17-10 (P)
    Cowboys, 20-15 (D)
1994—Cowboys, 38-3 (D)
    Cowboys, 28-21 (A)
1995—Cowboys, 34-20 (D)
    Cowboys, 37-13 (A)
1996—Cowboys, 17-3 (D)
    Cowboys, 10-6 (A)
1997—Cardinals, 25-22 (A) OT
    Cowboys, 24-6 (D)
1998—Cowboys, 38-10 (D)
    Cowboys, 35-28 (A)
    **Cardinals, 20-7 (D)
1999—Cowboys, 35-7 (D)
    Cardinals, 13-9 (A)
2000—Cardinals, 32-31 (A)
    Cowboys, 48-7 (D)
2001—Cowboys, 17-3 (D)
    Cardinals, 17-10 (A)
2002—Cardinals, 9-6 (A) OT
2003—Cowboys, 24-7 (D)
2005—Cowboys, 34-13 (D)
2006—Cowboys, 27-10 (A)
(RS Pts.—Cowboys 1,936, Cardinals 1,407)
(PS Pts.—Cardinals 20, Cowboys 7)
*Franchise known as Phoenix prior to 1994
and in St. Louis prior to 1988*
**NFC First-Round Playoff*
*ARIZONA vs. DENVER
RS: Broncos lead series, 7-0-1
1973—Tie, 17-17 (StL)
1977—Broncos, 7-0 (D)
1989—Broncos, 37-0 (P)
1991—Broncos, 24-19 (D)
1995—Broncos, 38-6 (D)
2001—Broncos, 38-17 (A)
2002—Broncos, 37-7 (D)
2006—Broncos, 37-20 (A)
(RS Pts.—Broncos 235, Cardinals 86)
*Franchise known as Phoenix prior to 1994
and in St. Louis prior to 1988*
*ARIZONA vs. **DETROIT
RS: Lions lead series, 31-22-5
1930—Tie, 0-0 (Port)
    Cardinals, 23-0 (C)
1931—Spartans, 13-3 (Port)
    Cardinals, 20-19 (C)
1932—Tie, 7-7 (Port)
1933—Spartans, 7-6 (Port)
1934—Lions, 6-0 (D)
    Lions, 17-13 (C)
1935—Tie, 10-10 (D)
    Lions, 7-6 (C)
1936—Lions, 39-0 (D)
    Lions, 14-7 (C)
1937—Lions, 16-7 (C)
    Lions, 16-7 (D)
1938—Lions, 10-0 (D)
    Lions, 7-3 (C)
1939—Lions, 21-3 (D)
    Lions, 17-3 (C)
1940—Tie, 0-0 (Buffalo)

    Lions, 43-14 (C)
1941—Tie, 14-14 (C)
    Lions, 21-3 (D)
1942—Cardinals, 13-0 (C)
    Cardinals, 7-0 (D)
1943—Lions, 35-17 (D)
    Lions, 7-0 (Buffalo)
1945—Lions, 10-0 (Milwaukee)
    Lions, 26-0 (D)
1946—Cardinals, 34-14 (C)
    Cardinals, 36-14 (D)
1947—Cardinals, 45-21 (C)
    Cardinals, 17-7 (D)
1948—Cardinals, 56-20 (C)
    Cardinals, 28-14 (D)
1949—Lions, 24-7 (C)
    Cardinals, 42-19 (D)
1959—Lions, 45-21 (D)
1961—Lions, 45-14 (StL)
1967—Cardinals, 38-28 (StL)
1969—Lions, 20-0 (D)
1970—Lions, 16-3 (D)
1973—Lions, 20-16 (StL)
1975—Cardinals, 24-13 (D)
1978—Cardinals, 21-14 (StL)
1980—Lions, 20-7 (D)
    Cardinals, 24-23 (StL)
1989—Cardinals, 16-13 (D)
1993—Lions, 26-20 (D)
    Lions, 21-14 (Phx)
1995—Cardinals, 20-17 (D)
1998—Cardinals, 17-15 (D)
1999—Cardinals, 23-19 (A)
2001—Cardinals, 45-38 (A)
2002—Cardinals, 23-20 (A) OT
2003—Lions, 42-24 (D)
2004—Lions, 26-12 (D)
2005—Lions, 29-21 (D)
2006—Cardinals, 17-10 (A)
(RS Pts.—Lions 1,048, Cardinals 881)
*Franchise known as Phoenix prior to
1994, in St. Louis prior to 1988,
and in Chicago prior to 1960*
**Franchise in Portsmouth prior to 1934
and known as the Spartans*
*ARIZONA vs. GREEN BAY
RS: Packers lead series, 42-22-4
PS: Packers lead series, 1-0
1921—Tie, 3-3 (C)
1922—Cardinals, 16-3 (C)
1924—Cardinals, 3-0 (C)
1925—Cardinals, 9-6 (C)
1926—Cardinals, 13-7 (GB)
    Packers, 3-0 (C)
1927—Packers, 13-0 (GB)
    Tie, 6-6 (C)
1928—Packers, 20-0 (GB)
1929—Packers, 9-2 (GB)
    Packers, 7-6 (C)
    Packers, 12-0 (C)
1930—Packers, 14-0 (GB)
    Cardinals, 13-6 (C)
1931—Packers, 26-7 (GB)
    Cardinals, 21-13 (C)
1932—Packers, 15-7 (GB)
    Packers, 19-9 (C)
1933—Packers, 14-6 (C)
1934—Packers, 15-0 (GB)
    Cardinals, 9-0 (Mil)
    Cardinals, 6-0 (C)

1935—Cardinals, 7-6 (GB)
Cardinals, 3-0 (Mil)
Cardinals, 9-7 (C)
1936—Packers, 10-7 (GB)
Packers, 24-0 (Mil)
Tie, 0-0 (C)
1937—Cardinals, 14-7 (GB)
Packers, 34-13 (Mil)
1938—Packers, 28-7 (Mil)
Packers, 24-22 (Buffalo)
1939—Packers, 14-10 (GB)
Packers, 27-20 (Mil)
1940—Packers, 31-6 (Mil)
Packers, 28-7 (C)
1941—Packers, 14-13 (Mil)
Packers, 17-9 (GB)
1942—Packers, 17-13 (C)
Packers, 55-24 (GB)
1943—Packers, 28-7 (C)
Packers, 35-14 (Mil)
1945—Packers, 33-14 (GB)
1946—Packers, 19-7 (C)
Cardinals, 24-6 (GB)
1947—Cardinals, 14-10 (GB)
Cardinals, 21-20 (C)
1948—Cardinals, 17-7 (Mil)
Cardinals, 42-7 (C)
1949—Cardinals, 39-17 (Mil)
Cardinals, 41-21 (C)
1955—Packers, 31-14 (GB)
1956—Packers, 24-21 (C)
1962—Packers, 17-0 (Mil)
1963—Packers, 30-7 (StL)
1967—Packers, 31-23 (StL)
1969—Packers, 45-28 (GB)
1971—Tie, 16-16 (StL)
1973—Packers, 25-21 (GB)
1976—Cardinals, 29-0 (StL)
1982—**Packers, 41-16 (GB)
1984—Packers, 24-23 (GB)
1985—Cardinals, 43-28 (StL)
1988—Packers, 26-17 (P)
1990—Packers, 24-21 (P)
1999—Packers, 49-24 (GB)
2000—Packers, 29-3 (A)
2003—Cardinals, 20-13 (A)
2006—Packers, 31-14 (GB)
(RS Pts.—Packers 1,200, Cardinals 884)
(PS Pts.—Packers 41, Cardinals 16)
*Franchise known as Phoenix prior to
1994, in St. Louis prior to 1988,
and in Chicago prior to 1960
**NFC First-Round Playoff
ARIZONA vs. HOUSTON
RS: Texans lead series, 1-0
2005—Texans, 30-19 (H)
(RS Pts.—Texans 30, Cardinals 19)
*ARIZONA vs. **INDIANAPOLIS
RS: Colts lead series, 7-6
1961—Colts, 16-0 (B)
1964—Colts, 47-27 (B)
1968—Colts, 27-0 (B)
1972—Cardinals, 10-3 (B)
1976—Cardinals, 24-17 (StL)
1978—Colts, 30-17 (StL)
1980—Cardinals, 17-10 (B)
1981—Cardinals, 35-24 (B)
1984—Cardinals, 34-33 (I)
1990—Cardinals, 20-17 (P)
1992—Colts, 16-13 (I)

1996—Colts, 20-13 (I)
2005—Colts, 17-13 (I)
(RS Pts.—Colts 277, Cardinals 223)
*Franchise known as Phoenix prior to 1994
and in St. Louis prior to 1988
**Franchise in Baltimore prior to 1984
ARIZONA vs. JACKSONVILLE
RS: Jaguars lead series, 2-0
2000—Jaguars, 44-10 (J)
2005—Jaguars, 24-17 (A)
(RS Pts.—Jaguars 68, Cardinals 27)
*ARIZONA vs. KANSAS CITY
RS: Chiefs lead series, 7-2-1
1970—Tie, 6-6 (KC)
1974—Chiefs, 17-13 (StL)
1980—Chiefs, 21-13 (StL)
1983—Chiefs, 38-14 (KC)
1986—Cardinals, 23-14 (StL)
1995—Chiefs, 24-3 (A)
1998—Chiefs, 34-24 (KC)
2001—Cardinals, 24-16 (A)
2002—Chiefs, 49-0 (KC)
2006—Chiefs, 23-20 (A)
(RS Pts.—Chiefs 242, Cardinals 140)
*Franchise known as Phoenix prior to 1994
and in St. Louis prior to 1988
*ARIZONA vs. MIAMI
RS: Dolphins lead series, 8-1
1972—Dolphins, 31-10 (M)
1977—Dolphins, 55-14 (StL)
1978—Dolphins, 24-10 (M)
1981—Dolphins, 20-7 (StL)
1984—Dolphins, 36-28 (StL)
1990—Dolphins, 23-3 (M)
1996—Dolphins, 38-10 (A)
1999—Dolphins, 19-16 (M)
2004—Cardinals, 24-23 (M)
(RS Pts.—Dolphins 269, Cardinals 122)
*Franchise known as Phoenix prior to 1994
and in St. Louis prior to 1988
*ARIZONA vs. MINNESOTA
RS: Series tied, 9-9
PS: Vikings lead series, 2-0
1963—Cardinals, 56-14 (M)
1967—Cardinals, 34-24 (M)
1969—Vikings, 27-10 (StL)
1972—Cardinals, 19-17 (M)
1974—Vikings, 28-24 (StL)
**Vikings, 30-14 (M)
1977—Cardinals, 27-7 (M)
1979—Cardinals, 37-7 (StL)
1981—Cardinals, 30-17 (StL)
1983—Cardinals, 41-31 (StL)
1991—Vikings, 34-7 (M)
Vikings, 28-0 (P)
1994—Cardinals, 17-7 (A)
1995—Vikings, 30-24 (A) OT
1996—Vikings, 41-17 (M)
1997—Vikings, 20-19 (A)
1998—**Vikings, 41-21 (M)
2000—Vikings, 31-14 (M)
2003—Cardinals, 18-17 (A)
2006—Vikings, 31-26 (M)
(RS Pts.—Cardinals 420, Vikings 411)
(PS Pts.—Vikings 71, Cardinals 35)
*Franchise known as Phoenix prior to 1994
and in St. Louis prior to 1988
**NFC Divisional Playoff
*ARIZONA vs. **NEW ENGLAND
RS: Cardinals lead series, 6-5

1970—Cardinals, 31-0 (StL)
1975—Cardinals, 24-17 (StL)
1978—Patriots, 16-6 (StL)
1981—Cardinals, 27-20 (NE)
1984—Cardinals, 33-10 (NE)
1990—Cardinals, 34-14 (P)
1991—Cardinals, 24-10 (P)
1993—Patriots, 23-21 (P)
1996—Patriots, 31-0 (NE)
1999—Patriots, 27-3 (A)
2004—Patriots, 23-12 (A)
(RS Pts.—Cardinals 215, Patriots 191)
*Franchise known as Phoenix prior to 1994
and in St. Louis prior to 1988
**Franchise in Boston prior to 1971
*ARIZONA vs. NEW ORLEANS
RS: Cardinals lead series, 13-11
1967—Cardinals, 31-20 (StL)
1968—Cardinals, 21-20 (NO)
Cardinals, 31-17 (StL)
1969—Saints, 51-42 (StL)
1970—Cardinals, 24-17 (StL)
1974—Saints, 14-0 (NO)
1977—Cardinals, 49-31 (StL)
1980—Cardinals, 40-7 (NO)
1981—Cardinals, 30-3 (StL)
1982—Cardinals, 21-7 (NO)
1983—Saints, 28-17 (NO)
1984—Saints, 34-24 (NO)
1985—Cardinals, 28-16 (StL)
1986—Saints, 16-7 (StL)
1987—Cardinals, 24-19 (StL)
1990—Saints, 28-7 (NO)
1991—Saints, 27-3 (P)
1992—Saints, 30-21 (P)
1993—Saints, 20-17 (P)
1996—Cardinals, 28-14 (NO)
1997—Saints, 27-10 (NO)
1998—Cardinals, 19-17 (A)
2000—Saints, 21-10 (A)
2004—Cardinals, 34-10 (A)
(RS Pts.—Cardinals 538, Saints 494)
*Franchise known as Phoenix prior to 1994
and in St. Louis prior to 1988
*ARIZONA vs. N.Y. GIANTS
RS: Giants lead series, 78-41-2
1926—Giants, 20-0 (NY)
1927—Giants, 28-7 (NY)
1929—Giants, 24-21 (NY)
1930—Giants, 25-12 (NY)
Giants, 13-7 (C)
1935—Cardinals, 14-13 (NY)
1936—Giants, 14-6 (NY)
1938—Giants, 6-0 (NY)
1939—Giants, 17-7 (NY)
1941—Cardinals, 10-7 (NY)
1942—Giants, 21-7 (NY)
1943—Giants, 24-13 (NY)
1946—Giants, 28-24 (NY)
1947—Giants, 35-31 (NY)
1948—Giants, 63-35 (NY)
1949—Giants, 41-38 (C)
1950—Cardinals, 17-3 (C)
Giants, 51-21 (NY)
1951—Cardinals, 28-17 (NY)
Giants, 10-0 (C)
1952—Cardinals, 24-23 (NY)
Giants, 28-6 (C)
1953—Giants, 21-7 (NY)
Giants, 23-20 (C)

1954—Giants, 41-10 (C)
    Giants, 31-17 (NY)
1955—Cardinals, 28-17 (C)
    Giants, 10-0 (NY)
1956—Cardinals, 35-27 (C)
    Giants, 23-10 (NY)
1957—Giants, 27-14 (NY)
    Giants, 28-21 (C)
1958—Giants, 37-7 (Buffalo)
    Cardinals, 23-6 (NY)
1959—Giants, 9-3 (NY)
    Giants, 30-20 (Minn)
1960—Giants, 35-14 (StL)
    Cardinals, 20-13 (NY)
1961—Cardinals, 21-10 (NY)
    Giants, 24-9 (StL)
1962—Giants, 31-14 (StL)
    Giants, 31-28 (NY)
1963—Giants, 38-21 (StL)
    Cardinals, 24-17 (NY)
1964—Giants, 34-17 (NY)
    Tie, 10-10 (StL)
1965—Giants, 14-10 (NY)
    Giants, 28-15 (StL)
1966—Cardinals, 24-19 (StL)
    Cardinals, 20-17 (NY)
1967—Cardinals, 37-20 (StL)
    Giants, 37-14 (NY)
1968—Cardinals, 28-21 (NY)
1969—Cardinals, 42-17 (StL)
    Giants, 49-6 (NY)
1970—Giants, 35-17 (NY)
    Giants, 34-17 (StL)
1971—Giants, 21-20 (StL)
    Cardinals, 24-7 (NY)
1972—Giants, 27-21 (NY)
    Giants, 13-7 (StL)
1973—Cardinals, 35-27 (StL)
    Giants, 24-13 (New Haven)
1974—Cardinals, 23-21 (New Haven)
    Cardinals, 26-14 (StL)
1975—Cardinals, 26-14 (StL)
    Cardinals, 20-13 (NY)
1976—Cardinals, 27-21 (StL)
    Cardinals, 17-14 (NY)
1977—Cardinals, 28-0 (StL)
    Giants, 27-7 (NY)
1978—Cardinals, 20-10 (StL)
    Giants, 17-0 (NY)
1979—Cardinals, 27-14 (NY)
    Cardinals, 29-20 (StL)
1980—Giants, 41-35 (StL)
    Cardinals, 23-7 (NY)
1981—Giants, 34-14 (NY)
    Giants, 20-10 (StL)
1982—Cardinals, 24-21 (StL)
1983—Tie, 20-20 (StL) OT
    Cardinals, 10-6 (NY)
1984—Giants, 16-10 (NY)
    Cardinals, 31-21 (StL)
1985—Giants, 27-17 (NY)
    Giants, 34-3 (StL)
1986—Giants, 13-6 (StL)
    Giants, 27-7 (NY)
1987—Giants, 30-7 (NY)
    Cardinals, 27-24 (StL)
1988—Cardinals, 24-17 (P)
    Giants, 44-7 (NY)
1989—Giants, 35-7 (NY)
    Giants, 20-13 (P)

1990—Giants, 20-19 (NY)
    Giants, 24-21 (P)
1991—Giants, 20-9 (NY)
    Giants, 21-14 (P)
1992—Giants, 31-21 (NY)
    Cardinals, 19-0 (P)
1993—Giants, 19-17 (NY)
    Cardinals, 17-6 (P)
1994—Giants, 20-17 (A)
    Cardinals, 10-9 (NY)
1995—Giants, 27-21 (NY) OT
    Giants, 10-6 (A)
1996—Giants, 16-8 (NY)
    Cardinals, 31-23 (A)
1997—Giants, 27-13 (A)
    Giants, 19-10 (NY)
1998—Giants, 34-7 (NY)
    Giants, 23-19 (A)
1999—Cardinals, 14-3 (A)
    Cardinals, 34-24 (NY)
2000—Giants, 21-16 (NY)
    Giants, 31-7 (A)
2001—Giants, 17-10 (A)
    Giants, 17-13 (NY)
2002—Cardinals, 21-7 (A)
2004—Cardinals, 17-14 (A)
2005—Giants, 42-19 (NY)
(RS Pts.—Giants 2,661, Cardinals 2,046)
*Franchise known as Phoenix prior to
1994, in St. Louis prior to 1988,
and in Chicago prior to 1960
ARIZONA vs. N.Y. JETS
RS: Jets lead series, 4-2
1971—Cardinals, 17-10 (StL)
1975—Cardinals, 37-6 (NY)
1978—Jets, 23-10 (NY)
1996—Jets, 31-21 (A)
1999—Jets, 12-7 (NY)
2004—Jets, 13-3 (A)
(RS Pts.—Cardinals 95, Jets 95)
*Franchise known as Phoenix prior to 1994
and in St. Louis prior to 1988
ARIZONA vs. **OAKLAND
RS: Raiders lead series, 5-2
1973—Raiders, 17-10 (StL)
1983—Cardinals, 34-24 (LA)
1989—Raiders, 16-14 (LA)
1998—Raiders, 23-20 (A)
2001—Cardinals, 34-31 (O) OT
2002—Raiders, 41-20 (A)
2006—Raiders, 22-9 (O)
(RS Pts.— Raiders 174, Cardinals 141)
*Franchise known as Phoenix prior to 1994
and in St. Louis prior to 1988
**Franchise in Los Angeles from
1982-1994
ARIZONA vs. PHILADELPHIA
RS: Cardinals lead series, 53-52-5
PS: Series tied, 1-1
1935—Cardinals, 12-3 (C)
1936—Cardinals, 13-0 (C)
1937—Tie, 6-6 (P)
1938—Eagles, 7-0 (Erie, Pa.)
1941—Eagles, 21-14 (P)
1945—Eagles, 21-6 (P)
1947—Cardinals, 45-21 (P)
    **Cardinals, 28-21 (C)
1948—Cardinals, 21-14 (C)
    **Eagles, 7-0 (P)
1949—Eagles, 28-3 (P)

1950—Eagles, 45-7 (C)
    Cardinals, 14-10 (P)
1951—Eagles, 17-14 (C)
1952—Eagles, 10-7 (P)
    Cardinals, 28-22 (C)
1953—Eagles, 56-17 (C)
    Eagles, 38-0 (P)
1954—Eagles, 35-16 (C)
    Eagles, 30-14 (P)
1955—Tie, 24-24 (C)
    Eagles, 27-3 (P)
1956—Cardinals, 20-6 (P)
    Cardinals, 28-17 (C)
1957—Eagles, 38-21 (C)
    Cardinals, 31-27 (P)
1958—Tie, 21-21 (C)
    Eagles, 49-21 (P)
1959—Eagles, 28-24 (Minn)
    Eagles, 27-17 (P)
1960—Eagles, 31-27 (P)
    Eagles, 20-6 (StL)
1961—Cardinals, 30-27 (P)
    Eagles, 20-7 (StL)
1962—Cardinals, 27-21 (P)
    Cardinals, 45-35 (StL)
1963—Cardinals, 28-24 (P)
    Cardinals, 38-14 (StL)
1964—Cardinals, 38-13 (P)
    Cardinals, 36-34 (StL)
1965—Eagles, 34-27 (P)
    Eagles, 28-24 (StL)
1966—Cardinals, 16-13 (StL)
    Cardinals, 41-10 (P)
1967—Cardinals, 48-14 (StL)
    Cardinals, 45-17 (P)
1969—Eagles, 34-30 (StL)
1970—Cardinals, 35-20 (P)
    Cardinals, 23-14 (StL)
1971—Eagles, 37-20 (StL)
    Eagles, 19-7 (P)
1972—Tie, 6-6 (P)
    Cardinals, 24-23 (StL)
1973—Cardinals, 34-23 (P)
    Eagles, 27-24 (StL)
1974—Cardinals, 7-3 (StL)
    Cardinals, 13-3 (P)
1975—Cardinals, 31-20 (StL)
    Cardinals, 24-23 (P)
1976—Cardinals, 33-14 (StL)
    Cardinals, 17-14 (P)
1977—Cardinals, 21-17 (P)
    Cardinals, 21-16 (StL)
1978—Cardinals, 16-10 (P)
    Eagles, 14-10 (StL)
1979—Eagles, 24-20 (StL)
    Eagles, 16-13 (P)
1980—Cardinals, 24-14 (StL)
    Eagles, 17-3 (P)
1981—Eagles, 52-10 (StL)
    Eagles, 38-0 (P)
1982—Cardinals, 23-20 (P)
1983—Cardinals, 14-11 (P)
    Cardinals, 31-7 (StL)
1984—Cardinals, 34-14 (P)
    Cardinals, 17-16 (StL)
1985—Eagles, 30-7 (P)
    Eagles, 24-14 (StL)
1986—Cardinals, 13-10 (StL)
    Tie, 10-10 (P) OT
1987—Eagles, 28-23 (P)

Cardinals, 31-19 (P)
1988—Eagles, 31-21 (P)
Eagles, 23-17 (Phx)
1989—Eagles, 17-5 (Phx)
Eagles, 31-14 (P)
1990—Cardinals, 23-21 (P)
Eagles, 23-21 (Phx)
1991—Cardinals, 26-10 (P)
Eagles, 34-14 (Phx)
1992—Cardinals, 31-14 (Phx)
Eagles, 7-3 (P)
1993—Eagles, 23-17 (P)
Cardinals, 16-3 (Phx)
1994—Eagles, 17-7 (P)
Cardinals, 12-6 (A)
1995—Eagles, 31-19 (A)
Eagles, 21-20 (P)
1996—Cardinals, 36-30 (A)
Eagles, 29-19 (P)
1997—Eagles, 13-10 (P) OT
Cardinals, 31-21 (A)
1998—Eagles, 17-3 (A)
Cardinals, 20-17 (P) OT
1999—Cardinals, 25-24 (P)
Cardinals, 21-17 (A)
2000—Eagles, 33-14 (A)
Eagles, 34-9 (P)
2001—Cardinals, 21-20 (P)
Eagles, 21-7 (A)
2002—Eagles, 38-14 (P)
2005—Cardinals, 27-21 (A)
(RS Pts.—Eagles 2,340, Cardinals 2,133)
(PS Pts.—Eagles 28, Cardinals 28)
*Franchise known as Phoenix prior to
1994, in St. Louis prior to 1988,
and in Chicago prior to 1960
**NFL Championship
**ARIZONA vs. **PITTSBURGH
RS: Steelers lead series, 31-22-3
1933—Pirates, 14-13 (C)
1935—Pirates, 17-13 (P)
1936—Cardinals, 14-6 (C)
1937—Cardinals, 13-7 (P)
1939—Cardinals, 10-0 (P)
1940—Tie, 7-7 (P)
1942—Steelers, 19-3 (P)
1945—Steelers, 23-0 (P)
1946—Steelers, 14-7 (P)
1948—Cardinals, 24-7 (P)
1950—Steelers, 28-17 (C)
Steelers, 28-7 (P)
1951—Steelers, 28-14 (C)
1952—Steelers, 34-28 (C)
Steelers, 17-14 (P)
1953—Steelers, 31-28 (P)
Steelers, 21-17 (C)
1954—Cardinals, 17-14 (C)
Steelers, 20-17 (P)
1955—Steelers, 14-7 (P)
Cardinals, 27-13 (C)
1956—Steelers, 14-7 (P)
Cardinals, 38-27 (C)
1957—Steelers, 29-20 (P)
Steelers, 27-2 (C)
1958—Steelers, 27-20 (C)
Steelers, 38-21 (P)
1959—Cardinals, 45-24 (C)
Steelers, 35-20 (P)
1960—Steelers, 27-14 (P)
Cardinals, 38-7 (StL)

1961—Steelers, 30-27 (P)
Cardinals, 20-0 (StL)
1962—Steelers, 26-17 (StL)
Steelers, 19-7 (P)
1963—Steelers, 23-10 (P)
Cardinals, 24-23 (StL)
1964—Cardinals, 34-30 (StL)
Cardinals, 21-20 (P)
1965—Cardinals, 20-7 (P)
Cardinals, 21-17 (StL)
1966—Steelers, 30-9 (P)
Cardinals, 6-3 (StL)
1967—Cardinals, 28-14 (P)
Tie, 14-14 (StL)
1968—Tie, 28-28 (StL)
Cardinals, 20-10 (P)
1969—Cardinals, 27-14 (P)
Cardinals, 47-10 (StL)
1972—Steelers, 25-19 (StL)
1979—Steelers, 24-21 (StL)
1985—Steelers, 23-10 (P)
1988—Cardinals, 31-14 (Phx)
1994—Cardinals, 20-17 (A) OT
1997—Steelers, 26-20 (A) OT
2003—Steelers, 28-15 (P)
(RS Pts.—Steelers 1,092, Cardinals 1,038)
*Franchise known as Phoenix prior to
1994, in St. Louis prior to 1988,
and in Chicago prior to 1960
**Steelers known as Pirates prior to 1941
*ARIZONA vs. **ST. LOUIS
RS: Rams lead series, 30-24-2
PS: Rams lead series, 1-0
1937—Cardinals, 6-0 (Clev)
Cardinals, 13-7 (Chi)
1938—Cardinals, 7-6 (Clev)
Cardinals, 31-17 (Chi)
1939—Rams, 24-0 (Chi)
Rams, 14-0 (Clev)
1940—Rams, 26-14 (Clev)
Cardinals, 17-7 (Chi)
1941—Rams, 10-6 (Clev)
Cardinals, 7-0 (Chi)
1942—Cardinals, 7-0 (Buffalo)
Rams, 7-3 (Clev)
1945—Rams, 21-0 (Clev)
Rams, 35-21 (Chi)
1946—Cardinals, 34-10 (Chi)
Rams, 17-14 (LA)
1947—Rams, 27-7 (LA)
Cardinals, 17-10 (Chi)
1948—Cardinals, 27-22 (LA)
Cardinals, 27-24 (Chi)
1949—Tie, 28-28 (Chi)
Cardinals, 31-27 (LA)
1951—Rams, 45-21 (LA)
1953—Tie, 24-24 (Chi)
1954—Rams, 28-17 (LA)
1958—Rams, 20-14 (Chi)
1960—Cardinals, 43-21 (LA)
1965—Rams, 27-3 (StL)
1968—Rams, 24-13 (StL)
1970—Rams, 34-13 (LA)
1972—Cardinals, 24-14 (StL)
1975—***Rams, 35-23 (LA)
1976—Cardinals, 30-28 (LA)
1979—Rams, 21-0 (LA)
1980—Rams, 21-13 (StL)
1984—Rams, 16-13 (StL)
1985—Rams, 46-14 (LA)

1986—Rams, 16-10 (StL)
1987—Rams, 27-24 (StL)
1988—Cardinals, 41-27 (LA)
1989—Rams, 37-14 (LA)
1991—Cardinals, 24-14 (LA)
1992—Cardinals, 20-14 (LA)
1993—Cardinals, 38-10 (P)
1994—Rams, 14-12 (LA)
1996—Cardinals, 31-28 (A) OT
1998—Cardinals, 20-17 (StL)
2002—Rams, 27-14 (A)
Rams, 30-28 (StL)
2003—Rams, 37-13 (StL)
Rams, 30-27 (A) OT
2004—Rams, 17-10 (StL)
Cardinals, 31-7 (A)
2005—Rams, 17-12 (A)
Cardinals, 38-28 (StL)
2006—Rams, 16-14 (A)
Cardinals, 34-20 (StL)
(RS Pts.—Rams 1,141, Cardinals 1,014)
(PS Pts.—Rams 35, Cardinals 23)
*Franchise known as Phoenix prior to
1994, in St. Louis prior to 1988,
and in Chicago prior to 1960
**Franchise in Los Angeles prior to 1995
and in Cleveland prior to 1946
***NFC Divisional Playoff
*ARIZONA vs. SAN DIEGO
RS: Chargers lead series, 8-3
1971—Chargers, 20-17 (SD)
1976—Chargers, 43-24 (SD)
1983—Cardinals, 44-14 (StL)
1987—Chargers, 28-24 (SD)
1989—Chargers, 24-13 (P)
1992—Chargers, 27-21 (P)
1995—Chargers, 28-25 (SD)
1998—Cardinals, 16-13 (A)
2001—Cardinals, 20-17 (SD)
2002—Chargers, 23-15 (A)
2006—Chargers, 27-20 (SD)
(RS Pts.—Chargers 264, Cardinals 239)
*Franchise known as Phoenix prior to
1994, in St. Louis prior to 1988,
*ARIZONA vs. SAN FRANCISCO
RS: 49ers lead series, 17-14
1951—Cardinals, 27-21 (SF)
1957—Cardinals, 20-10 (SF)
1962—49ers, 24-17 (StL)
1964—Cardinals, 23-13 (SF)
1968—49ers, 35-17 (SF)
1971—49ers, 26-14 (StL)
1974—Cardinals, 34-9 (SF)
1976—Cardinals, 23-20 (StL) OT
1978—Cardinals, 16-10 (SF)
1979—Cardinals, 13-10 (StL)
1980—49ers, 24-21 (SF) OT
1982—49ers, 31-20 (StL)
1983—49ers, 42-27 (StL)
1986—49ers, 43-17 (SF)
1987—49ers, 34-28 (SF)
1988—Cardinals, 24-23 (P)
1991—49ers, 14-10 (SF)
1992—Cardinals, 24-14 (P)
1993—49ers, 28-14 (SF)
1999—49ers, 24-10 (A)
2000—49ers, 27-20 (SF)
2002—49ers, 38-28 (SF)
49ers, 17-14 (A)
2003—Cardinals, 16-13 (A) OT

49ers, 50-14 (SF)
2004—49ers, 31-28 (SF) OT
　49ers, 31-28 (A) OT
2005—Cardinals, 31-14 (Mex. City)
　Cardinals, 17-10 (SF)
2006—Cardinals, 34-27 (A)
　Cardinals, 26-20 (SF)
(RS Pts.—49ers 733, Cardinals 655)
*Franchise known as Phoenix prior to
1994, in St. Louis prior to 1988,
and in Chicago prior to 1960*
ARIZONA vs. SEATTLE
RS: Series tied, 8-8
1976—Cardinals, 30-24 (S)
1983—Cardinals, 33-28 (StL)
1989—Cardinals, 34-24 (S)
1993—Cardinals, 30-27 (S) OT
1995—Cardinals, 20-14 (A) OT
1998—Seahawks, 33-14 (S)
2002—Cardinals, 24-13 (S)
　Seahawks, 27-6 (A)
2003—Seahawks, 38-0 (A)
　Seahawks, 28-10 (S)
2004—Cardinals, 25-17 (A)
　Seahawks, 24-21 (S)
2005—Seahawks, 37-12 (S)
　Seahawks, 33-19 (A)
2006—Seahawks, 21-10 (S)
　Cardinals, 27-21 (A)
(RS Pts.—Seahawks 409, Cardinals 315)
*Franchise known as Phoenix prior to 1994
and in St. Louis prior to 1988*
ARIZONA vs. TAMPA BAY
RS: Cardinals lead series, 8-7
1977—Buccaneers, 17-7 (TB)
1981—Buccaneers, 20-10 (TB)
1983—Cardinals, 34-27 (TB)
1985—Buccaneers, 16-0 (TB)
1986—Cardinals, 30-19 (TB)
　Cardinals, 21-17 (StL)
1987—Cardinals, 31-28 (StL)
　Cardinals, 31-14 (TB)
1988—Cardinals, 30-24 (TB)
1989—Buccaneers, 14-13 (P)
1992—Cardinals, 23-7 (TB)
　Buccaneers, 7-3 (P)
1996—Cardinals, 13-9 (A)
1997—Buccaneers, 19-18 (TB)
2004—Cardinals, 12-7 (A)
(RS Pts.—Buccaneers 261, Cardinals 260)
*Franchise known as Phoenix prior to 1994
and in St. Louis prior to 1988*
ARIZONA vs. **TENNESSEE
RS: Cardinals lead series, 5-3
1970—Cardinals, 44-0 (StL)
1974—Cardinals, 31-27 (H)
1979—Cardinals, 24-17 (H)
1985—Oilers, 20-10 (StL)
1988—Oilers, 38-20 (H)
1994—Cardinals, 30-12 (H)
1997—Oilers, 41-14 (A)
2005—Cardinals, 20-10 (A)
(RS Pts.—Cardinals 193, Titans 165)
*Franchise known as Phoenix prior to 1994
and in St. Louis prior to 1988
**Franchise in Houston prior to 1997;
known as Oilers prior to 1999*
ARIZONA vs. **WASHINGTON
RS: Redskins lead series, 71-44-2
1932—Cardinals, 9-0 (B)

Braves, 8-6 (C)
1933—Redskins, 10-0 (C)
　Tie, 0-0 (B)
1934—Redskins, 9-0 (B)
1935—Cardinals, 6-0 (B)
1936—Redskins, 13-10 (B)
1937—Cardinals, 21-14 (W)
1939—Redskins, 28-7 (W)
1940—Redskins, 28-21 (W)
1942—Redskins, 28-0 (W)
1943—Redskins, 13-7 (W)
1945—Redskins, 24-21 (W)
1947—Redskins, 45-21 (W)
1949—Cardinals, 38-7 (C)
1950—Redskins, 38-28 (W)
1951—Redskins, 7-3 (C)
　Redskins, 20-17 (W)
1952—Redskins, 23-7 (C)
　Cardinals, 17-6 (W)
1953—Cardinals, 24-13 (C)
　Redskins, 28-17 (W)
1954—Cardinals, 38-16 (C)
　Redskins, 37-20 (W)
1955—Cardinals, 24-10 (W)
　Redskins, 31-0 (C)
1956—Cardinals, 31-3 (W)
　Redskins, 17-14 (C)
1957—Redskins, 37-14 (C)
　Cardinals, 44-14 (W)
1958—Cardinals, 37-10 (C)
　Redskins, 45-31 (W)
1959—Cardinals, 49-21 (C)
　Redskins, 23-14 (W)
1960—Cardinals, 44-7 (StL)
　Cardinals, 26-14 (W)
1961—Cardinals, 24-0 (W)
　Cardinals, 38-24 (StL)
1962—Redskins, 24-14 (W)
　Tie, 17-17 (StL)
1963—Cardinals, 21-7 (W)
　Cardinals, 24-20 (StL)
1964—Cardinals, 23-17 (W)
　Cardinals, 38-24 (StL)
1965—Cardinals, 37-16 (W)
　Redskins, 24-20 (StL)
1966—Cardinals, 23-7 (StL)
　Redskins, 26-20 (W)
1967—Cardinals, 27-21 (W)
1968—Cardinals, 41-14 (StL)
1969—Redskins, 33-17 (W)
1970—Cardinals, 27-17 (StL)
　Redskins, 28-27 (W)
1971—Redskins, 24-17 (StL)
　Redskins, 20-0 (W)
1972—Redskins, 24-10 (W)
　Redskins, 33-3 (StL)
1973—Cardinals, 34-27 (StL)
　Redskins, 31-13 (W)
1974—Cardinals, 17-10 (W)
　Cardinals, 23-20 (StL)
1975—Redskins, 27-17 (W)
　Cardinals, 20-17 (StL) OT
1976—Redskins, 20-10 (W)
　Redskins, 16-10 (StL)
1977—Redskins, 24-14 (W)
　Redskins, 26-20 (StL)
1978—Redskins, 28-10 (StL)
　Cardinals, 27-17 (W)
1979—Redskins, 17-7 (StL)
　Redskins, 30-28 (W)

1980—Redskins, 23-0 (W)
　Redskins, 31-7 (StL)
1981—Cardinals, 40-30 (StL)
　Redskins, 42-21 (W)
1982—Redskins, 12-7 (StL)
　Redskins, 28-0 (W)
1983—Redskins, 38-14 (StL)
　Redskins, 45-7 (W)
1984—Cardinals, 26-24 (StL)
　Redskins, 29-27 (W)
1985—Redskins, 27-10 (W)
　Redskins, 27-16 (StL)
1986—Redskins, 28-21 (W)
　Redskins, 20-17 (StL)
1987—Redskins, 28-21 (W)
　Redskins, 34-17 (StL)
1988—Cardinals, 30-21 (P)
　Redskins, 33-17 (W)
1989—Redskins, 30-28 (W)
　Redskins, 29-10 (P)
1990—Redskins, 31-0 (W)
　Redskins, 38-10 (P)
1991—Redskins, 34-0 (W)
　Redskins, 20-14 (P)
1992—Cardinals, 27-24 (P)
　Redskins, 41-3 (W)
1993—Cardinals, 17-10 (W)
　Cardinals, 36-6 (P)
1994—Cardinals, 19-16 (W) OT
　Cardinals, 17-15 (A)
1995—Redskins, 27-7 (W)
　Cardinals, 24-20 (A)
1996—Cardinals, 37-34 (W) OT
　Cardinals, 27-26 (A)
1997—Redskins, 19-13 (W) OT
　Redskins, 38-28 (A)
1998—Cardinals, 29-27 (A)
　Cardinals, 45-42 (W)
1999—Redskins, 24-10 (A)
　Redskins, 28-3 (W)
2000—Cardinals, 16-15 (A)
　Redskins, 20-3 (W)
2001—Redskins, 20-10 (A)
　Redskins, 20-17 (W)
2002—Redskins, 31-23 (W)
2005—Redskins, 17-13 (A)
(RS Pts.—Redskins 2,600, Cardinals 2,167)
*Franchise known as Phoenix prior to
1994, in St. Louis prior to 1988,
and in Chicago prior to 1960
**Franchise in Boston prior to 1937 and
known as Braves prior to 1933*

ATLANTA vs. ARIZONA
RS: Cardinals lead series, 13-10;
See Arizona vs. Atlanta
ATLANTA vs. BALTIMORE
RS: Ravens lead series, 2-1
1999—Ravens, 19-13 (A) OT
2002—Falcons, 20-17 (A)
2006—Ravens, 24-10 (B)
(RS Pts.—Ravens 60, Falcons 43)
ATLANTA vs. BUFFALO
RS: Falcons lead series, 5-4
1973—Bills, 17-6 (A)
1977—Bills, 3-0 (B)
1980—Falcons, 30-14 (B)
1983—Falcons, 31-14 (A)
1989—Falcons, 30-28 (A)
1992—Bills, 41-14 (B)

1995—Bills, 23-17 (B)
2001—Falcons, 33-30 (A)
2005—Falcons, 24-16 (B)
(RS Pts.—Bills 186, Falcons 185)
ATLANTA vs. CAROLINA
RS: Falcons lead series, 15-9
1995—Falcons, 23-20 (A) OT
    Panthers, 21-17 (C)
1996—Panthers, 29-6 (C)
    Falcons, 20-17 (A)
1997—Panthers, 9-6 (A)
    Panthers, 21-12 (C)
1998—Falcons, 19-14 (C)
    Falcons, 51-23 (A)
1999—Falcons, 27-20 (A)
    Panthers, 34-28 (C)
2000—Falcons, 15-10 (C)
    Falcons, 13-12 (A)
2001—Falcons, 24-16 (A)
    Falcons, 10-7 (C)
2002—Falcons, 30-0 (A)
    Falcons, 41-0 (C)
2003—Panthers, 23-3 (C)
    Falcons, 20-14 (A) OT
2004—Falcons, 27-10 (C)
    Falcons, 34-31 (A) OT
2005—Panthers, 24-6 (C)
    Panthers, 44-11 (A)
2006—Falcons, 20-6 (C)
    Panthers, 10-3 (A)
(RS Pts.—Falcons 466, Panthers 415)
ATLANTA vs. CHICAGO
RS: Bears lead series, 12-10
1966—Bears, 23-6 (C)
1967—Bears, 23-14 (A)
1968—Falcons, 16-13 (C)
1969—Falcons, 48-31 (A)
1970—Bears, 23-14 (A)
1972—Falcons, 37-21 (C)
1973—Falcons, 46-6 (A)
1974—Falcons, 13-10 (A)
1976—Falcons, 10-0 (C)
1977—Falcons, 16-10 (C)
1978—Bears, 13-7 (C)
1980—Falcons, 28-17 (A)
1983—Falcons, 20-17 (C)
1985—Bears, 36-0 (C)
1986—Bears, 13-10 (A)
1990—Bears, 30-24 (C)
1992—Bears, 41-31 (C)
1993—Bears, 6-0 (C)
1998—Falcons, 20-13 (A)
2001—Bears, 31-3 (A)
2002—Bears, 14-13 (A)
2005—Bears, 16-3 (C)
(RS Pts.—Bears 407, Falcons 379)
ATLANTA vs. CINCINNATI
RS: Bengals lead series, 7-4
1971—Falcons, 9-6 (C)
1975—Bengals, 21-14 (A)
1978—Bengals, 37-7 (C)
1981—Bengals, 30-28 (A)
1984—Bengals, 35-14 (C)
1987—Bengals, 16-10 (A)
1990—Falcons, 38-17 (A)
1993—Bengals, 21-17 (C)
1996—Bengals, 41-31 (C)
2002—Falcons, 30-3 (A)
2006—Falcons, 29-27 (C)
(RS Pts.—Bengals 254, Falcons 227)

ATLANTA vs. CLEVELAND
RS: Browns lead series, 10-2
1966—Browns, 49-17 (A)
1968—Browns, 30-7 (C)
1971—Falcons, 31-14 (C)
1976—Browns, 20-17 (A)
1978—Browns, 24-16 (A)
1981—Browns, 28-17 (C)
1984—Browns, 23-7 (A)
1987—Browns, 38-3 (C)
1990—Browns, 13-10 (C)
1993—Falcons, 17-14 (A)
2002—Browns, 24-16 (C)
2006—Browns, 17-13 (A)
(RS Pts.—Browns 294, Falcons 171)
ATLANTA vs. DALLAS
RS: Cowboys lead series, 13-8
PS: Cowboys lead series, 2-0
1966—Cowboys, 47-14 (A)
1967—Cowboys, 37-7 (D)
1969—Cowboys, 24-17 (A)
1970—Cowboys, 13-0 (D)
1974—Cowboys, 24-0 (A)
1976—Falcons, 17-10 (A)
1978—*Cowboys, 27-20 (D)
1980—*Cowboys, 30-27 (A)
1985—Cowboys, 24-10 (D)
1986—Falcons, 37-35 (D)
1987—Falcons, 21-10 (D)
1988—Cowboys, 26-20 (D)
1989—Falcons 27-21 (A)
1990—Falcons, 26-7 (A)
1991—Cowboys, 31-27 (D)
1992—Cowboys, 41-17 (A)
1993—Falcons, 27-14 (A)
1995—Cowboys, 28-13 (A)
1996—Cowboys, 32-28 (D)
1999—Cowboys, 24-7 (D)
2001—Falcons, 20-13 (A)
2003—Cowboys, 27-13 (D)
2006—Cowboys, 38-28 (A)
(RS Pts.—Cowboys 512, Falcons 390)
(PS Pts.—Cowboys 57, Falcons 47)
*NFC Divisional Playoff
ATLANTA vs. DENVER
RS: Broncos lead series, 7-4
PS: Broncos lead series, 1-0
1970—Broncos, 24-10 (D)
1972—Falcons, 23-20 (A)
1975—Falcons, 35-21 (A)
1979—Broncos, 20-17 (A) OT
1982—Falcons, 34-27 (D)
1985—Broncos, 44-28 (A)
1988—Broncos, 30-14 (D)
1994—Broncos, 32-28 (D)
1997—Broncos, 29-21 (A)
1998—*Broncos, 34-19 (South Florida)
2000—Broncos, 42-14 (D)
2004—Falcons, 41-28 (D)
(RS Pts.—Broncos 317, Falcons 265)
(PS Pts.—Broncos 34, Falcons 19)
*Super Bowl XXXIII
ATLANTA vs. DETROIT
RS: Lions lead series, 23-9
1966—Lions, 28-10 (D)
1967—Lions, 24-3 (D)
1968—Lions, 24-7 (A)
1969—Lions, 27-21 (D)
1971—Lions, 41-38 (D)
1972—Lions, 26-23 (A)

1973—Lions, 31-6 (D)
1975—Lions, 17-14 (A)
1976—Lions, 24-10 (D)
1977—Falcons, 17-6 (A)
1978—Falcons, 14-0 (A)
1979—Lions, 24-23 (D)
1980—Falcons, 43-28 (A)
1983—Falcons, 30-14 (D)
1984—Lions, 27-24 (A) OT
1985—Lions, 28-27 (A)
1986—Falcons, 20-6 (D)
1987—Lions, 30-13 (A)
1988—Lions, 31-17 (D)
1989—Lions, 31-24 (A)
1990—Lions, 21-14 (D)
1993—Lions, 30-13 (D)
1994—Lions, 31-28 (D) OT
1995—Falcons, 34-22 (A)
1996—Lions, 28-24 (D)
1997—Lions, 28-17 (D)
1998—Falcons, 24-17 (D)
2000—Lions, 13-10 (A)
2002—Falcons, 36-15 (A)
2004—Lions, 17-10 (A)
2005—Falcons, 27-7 (D)
2006—Lions, 30-14 (D)
(RS Pts.—Lions 726, Falcons 635)
ATLANTA vs. GREEN BAY
RS: Packers lead series, 12-10
PS: Series tied, 1-1
1966—Packers, 56-3 (Mil)
1967—Packers, 23-0 (Mil)
1968—Packers, 38-7 (A)
1969—Packers, 28-10 (GB)
1970—Packers, 27-24 (GB)
1971—Falcons, 28-21 (A)
1972—Falcons, 10-9 (Mil)
1974—Falcons, 10-3 (A)
1975—Packers, 22-13 (GB)
1976—Packers, 24-20 (A)
1979—Packers, 25-7 (A)
1981—Falcons, 31-17 (GB)
1982—Packers, 38-7 (A)
1983—Falcons, 47-41 (A) OT
1988—Falcons, 20-0 (A)
1989—Packers, 23-21 (Mil)
1991—Falcons, 35-31 (A)
1992—Falcons, 24-10 (A)
1994—Packers, 21-17 (Mil)
1995—*Packers, 37-20 (GB)
2001—Falcons, 23-20 (GB)
2002—Packers, 37-34 (GB) OT
    *Falcons, 27-7 (GB)
2005—Packers, 33-25 (A)
(RS Pts.—Packers 529, Falcons 434)
(PS Pts.—Falcons 47, Packers 44)
*NFC First-Round Playoff
ATLANTA vs. HOUSTON
RS: Texans lead series, 1-0
2003—Texans, 17-13 (H)
(RS Pts.—Texans 17, Falcons 13)
ATLANTA vs. *INDIANAPOLIS
RS: Colts lead series, 12-1
1966—Colts, 19-7 (A)
1967—Colts, 38-31 (B)
    Colts, 49-7 (A)
1968—Colts, 28-20 (A)
    Colts, 44-0 (B)
1969—Colts, 21-14 (A)
    Colts, 13-6 (B)

1974—Colts, 17-7 (A)
1986—Colts, 28-23 (A)
1989—Colts, 13-9 (I)
1998—Falcons, 28-21 (A)
2001—Colts, 41-27 (I)
2003—Colts, 38-7 (I)
(RS Pts.—Colts 370, Falcons 186)
Franchise in Baltimore prior to 1984

ATLANTA vs. JACKSONVILLE
RS: Jaguars lead series, 2-1
1996—Jaguars, 19-17 (J)
1999—Jaguars, 30-7 (A)
2003—Falcons, 21-14 (A)
(RS Pts.—Jaguars 63, Falcons 45)

ATLANTA vs. KANSAS CITY
RS: Chiefs lead series, 5-1
1972—Chiefs, 17-14 (A)
1985—Chiefs, 38-10 (KC)
1991—Chiefs, 14-3 (KC)
1994—Chiefs, 30-10 (A)
2000—Falcons, 29-13 (A)
2004—Chiefs, 56-10 (KC)
(RS Pts.—Chiefs 168, Falcons 76)

ATLANTA vs. MIAMI
RS: Dolphins lead series, 7-3
1970—Dolphins, 20-7 (A)
1974—Dolphins, 42-7 (A)
1980—Dolphins, 20-17 (A)
1983—Dolphins, 31-24 (M)
1986—Falcons, 20-14 (M)
1992—Dolphins, 21-17 (M)
1995—Dolphins, 21-20 (M)
1998—Falcons, 38-16 (A)
2001—Dolphins, 21-14 (M)
2005—Falcons, 17-10 (M)
(RS Pts.—Dolphins 216, Falcons 181)

ATLANTA vs. MINNESOTA
RS: Vikings lead series, 14-8
PS: Series tied, 1-1
1966—Falcons, 20-13 (M)
1967—Falcons, 21-20 (A)
1968—Vikings, 47-7 (M)
1969—Falcons, 10-3 (A)
1970—Falcons, 37-7 (A)
1971—Vikings, 24-7 (M)
1973—Falcons, 20-14 (A)
1974—Vikings, 23-10 (M)
1975—Vikings, 38-0 (M)
1977—Vikings, 14-7 (A)
1980—Vikings, 24-23 (M)
1981—Falcons, 31-30 (A)
1982—*Vikings, 30-24 (M)
1984—Vikings, 27-20 (M)
1985—Falcons, 14-13 (A)
1987—Vikings, 24-13 (M)
1989—Vikings, 43-17 (M)
1991—Vikings, 20-19 (A)
1996—Vikings, 23-17 (A)
1998—**Falcons, 30-27 (M) OT
1999—Vikings, 17-14 (A)
2002—Falcons, 30-24 (M) OT
2003—Vikings, 39-26 (A)
2005—Falcons, 30-10 (A)
(RS Pts.—Vikings 527, Falcons 363)
(PS Pts.—Vikings 57, Falcons 54)
NFC First-Round Playoff
**NFC Championship*

ATLANTA vs. NEW ENGLAND
RS: Falcons lead series, 6-5
1972—Patriots, 21-20 (NE)

1977—Patriots, 16-10 (A)
1980—Falcons, 37-21 (NE)
1983—Falcons, 24-13 (A)
1986—Patriots, 25-17 (NE)
1989—Falcons, 16-15 (A)
1992—Falcons, 34-0 (A)
1995—Falcons, 30-17 (A)
1998—Falcons, 41-10 (NE)
2001—Patriots, 24-10 (A)
2005—Patriots, 31-28 (A)
(RS Pts.—Falcons 267, Patriots 193)

ATLANTA vs. NEW ORLEANS
RS: Falcons lead series, 43-32
PS: Falcons lead series, 1-0
1967—Saints, 27-24 (NO)
1969—Falcons, 45-17 (A)
1970—Falcons, 14-3 (NO)
        Falcons, 32-14 (A)
1971—Falcons, 28-6 (A)
        Falcons, 24-20 (NO)
1972—Falcons, 21-14 (NO)
        Falcons, 36-20 (A)
1973—Falcons, 62-7 (NO)
        Falcons, 14-10 (A)
1974—Saints, 14-13 (NO)
        Saints, 13-3 (A)
1975—Falcons, 14-7 (A)
        Saints, 23-7 (NO)
1976—Saints, 30-0 (NO)
        Falcons, 23-20 (A)
1977—Saints, 21-20 (NO)
        Falcons, 35-7 (A)
1978—Falcons, 20-17 (NO)
        Falcons, 20-17 (A)
1979—Falcons, 40-34 (NO) OT
        Saints, 37-6 (A)
1980—Falcons, 41-14 (NO)
        Falcons, 31-13 (A)
1981—Falcons, 27-0 (A)
        Falcons, 41-10 (NO)
1982—Falcons, 35-0 (A)
        Saints, 35-6 (NO)
1983—Saints, 19-17 (A)
        Saints, 27-10 (NO)
1984—Falcons, 36-28 (NO)
        Saints, 17-13 (A)
1985—Falcons, 31-24 (NO)
        Falcons, 16-10 (NO)
1986—Falcons, 31-10 (NO)
        Saints, 14-9 (A)
1987—Saints, 38-0 (A)
1988—Saints, 29-21 (A)
        Saints, 10-9 (NO)
1989—Saints, 20-13 (NO)
        Saints, 26-17 (A)
1990—Falcons, 28-27 (A)
        Saints, 10-7 (NO)
1991—Saints, 27-6 (A)
        Falcons, 23-20 (NO) OT
        *Falcons, 27-20 (NO)
1992—Falcons, 10-7 (A)
        Saints, 22-14 (NO)
1993—Saints, 34-31 (A)
        Falcons, 26-15 (NO)
1994—Saints, 33-32 (NO)
        Saints, 29-20 (A)
1995—Falcons, 27-24 (NO) OT
        Falcons, 19-14 (A)
1996—Falcons, 17-15 (A)
        Falcons, 31-15 (NO)

1997—Falcons, 23-17 (NO)
        Falcons, 20-3 (A)
1998—Falcons, 31-23 (A)
        Falcons, 27-17 (NO)
1999—Falcons, 20-17 (NO)
        Falcons, 35-12 (A)
2000—Saints, 21-19 (A)
        Saints, 23-7 (NO)
2001—Falcons, 20-13 (NO)
        Saints, 28-10 (A)
2002—Falcons, 37-35 (NO)
        Falcons, 24-17 (A)
2003—Saints, 45-17 (A)
        Saints, 23-20 (NO) OT
2004—Falcons, 24-21 (A)
        Saints, 26-13 (NO)
2005—Falcons, 34-31 (San Antonio)
        Falcons, 36-17 (A)
2006—Saints, 23-3 (NO)
        Saints, 31-13 (A)
(RS Pts.—Falcons 1,626, Saints 1,460)
(PS Pts.—Falcons 27, Saints 20)
NFC First-Round Playoff

ATLANTA vs. N.Y. GIANTS
RS: Falcons lead series, 10-8
1966—Falcons, 27-16 (NY)
1968—Falcons, 24-21 (A)
1971—Giants, 21-17 (A)
1974—Falcons, 14-7 (New Haven)
1977—Falcons, 17-3 (A)
1978—Falcons, 23-20 (A)
1979—Giants, 24-3 (NY)
1981—Giants, 27-24 (A) OT
1982—Falcons, 16-14 (NY)
1983—Giants, 16-13 (A) OT
1984—Giants, 19-7 (A)
1988—Giants, 23-16 (A)
1998—Falcons, 34-20 (NY)
2000—Giants, 13-6 (A)
2002—Falcons, 17-10 (NY)
2003—Falcons, 27-7 (NY)
2004—Falcons, 14-10 (NY)
2006—Giants, 27-14 (A)
(RS Pts.—Falcons 313, Giants 298)

ATLANTA vs. N.Y. JETS
RS: Falcons lead series, 5-4
1973—Falcons, 28-20 (NY)
1980—Jets, 14-7 (A)
1983—Falcons, 27-21 (NY)
1986—Jets, 28-14 (A)
1989—Jets, 27-7 (NY)
1992—Falcons, 20-17 (A)
1995—Falcons, 13-3 (A)
1998—Jets, 28-3 (NY)
2005—Falcons, 27-14 (A)
(RS Pts.—Jets 172, Falcons 146)

ATLANTA vs. *OAKLAND
RS: Raiders lead series, 7-4
1971—Falcons, 24-13 (A)
1975—Raiders, 37-34 (O) OT
1979—Raiders, 50-19 (O)
1982—Raiders, 38-14 (A)
1985—Raiders, 34-24 (A)
1988—Falcons, 12-6 (LA)
1991—Falcons, 21-17 (A)
1994—Raiders, 30-17 (LA)
1997—Raiders, 36-31 (A)
2000—Falcons, 41-14 (O)
2004—Falcons, 35-10 (A)
(RS Pts.—Raiders 312, Falcons 245)

Franchise in Los Angeles from 1982-1994
ATLANTA vs. PHILADELPHIA
RS: Eagles lead series, 12-10-1
PS: Eagles lead series, 2-1
1966—Eagles, 23-10 (P)
1967—Eagles, 38-7 (A)
1969—Falcons, 27-3 (P)
1970—Tie, 13-13 (P)
1973—Falcons, 44-27 (P)
1976—Eagles, 14-13 (A)
1978—*Falcons, 14-13 (A)
1979—Falcons, 14-10 (P)
1980—Falcons, 20-17 (P)
1981—Eagles, 16-13 (P)
1983—Eagles, 28-24 (A)
1984—Falcons, 26-10 (A)
1985—Eagles, 23-17 (P) OT
1986—Eagles, 16-0 (A)
1988—Falcons, 27-24 (P)
1990—Eagles, 24-23 (A)
1994—Falcons, 28-21 (A)
1996—Eagles, 33-18 (A)
1997—Falcons, 20-17 (A)
1998—Falcons, 17-12 (A)
2000—Eagles, 38-10 (P)
2002—**Eagles, 20-6 (P)
2003—Eagles, 23-16 (A)
2004—***Eagles, 27-10 (P)
2005—Falcons, 14-10 (A)
2006—Eagles, 24-17 (P)
(RS Pts.—Eagles 464, Falcons 418)
(PS Pts.—Eagles 60, Falcons 30)
NFC First-Round Playoff
**NFC Divisional Playoff*
***NFC Championship*
ATLANTA vs. PITTSBURGH
RS: Steelers lead series, 11-2-1
1966—Steelers, 57-33 (A)
1968—Steelers, 41-21 (A)
1970—Falcons, 27-16 (A)
1974—Steelers, 24-17 (P)
1978—Steelers, 31-7 (P)
1981—Steelers, 34-20 (A)
1984—Steelers, 35-10 (P)
1987—Steelers, 28-12 (A)
1990—Steelers, 21-9 (P)
1993—Steelers, 45-17 (A)
1996—Steelers, 20-17 (A)
1999—Steelers, 13-9 (P)
2002—Tie, 34-34 (P) OT
2006—Falcons, 41-38 (A) OT
(RS Pts.—Steelers 437, Falcons 274)
ATLANTA vs. *ST. LOUIS
RS: Rams lead series, 46-24-2
PS: Falcons lead series, 1-0
1966—Rams, 19-14 (A)
1967—Rams, 31-3 (A)
　　　Rams, 20-3 (LA)
1968—Rams, 27-14 (LA)
　　　Rams, 17-10 (A)
1969—Rams, 17-7 (LA)
　　　Rams, 38-6 (A)
1970—Tie, 10-10 (A)
　　　Rams, 17-7 (A)
1971—Tie, 20-20 (LA)
　　　Rams, 24-16 (A)
1972—Falcons, 31-3 (A)
　　　Rams, 20-7 (LA)
1973—Rams, 31-0 (LA)
　　　Falcons, 15-13 (A)

1974—Rams, 21-0 (LA)
　　　Rams, 30-7 (A)
1975—Rams, 22-7 (LA)
　　　Rams, 16-7 (A)
1976—Rams, 30-14 (A)
　　　Rams, 59-0 (LA)
1977—Falcons, 17-6 (A)
　　　Rams, 23-7 (LA)
1978—Rams, 10-0 (LA)
　　　Falcons, 15-7 (A)
1979—Rams, 20-14 (LA)
　　　Rams, 34-13 (A)
1980—Falcons, 13-10 (A)
　　　Rams, 20-17 (LA) OT
1981—Rams, 37-35 (A)
　　　Rams, 21-16 (LA)
1982—Falcons, 34-17 (A)
1983—Rams, 27-21 (LA)
　　　Rams, 36-13 (A)
1984—Falcons, 30-28 (LA)
　　　Rams, 24-10 (A)
1985—Rams, 17-6 (LA)
　　　Falcons, 30-14 (A)
1986—Falcons, 26-14 (A)
　　　Rams, 14-7 (LA)
1987—Falcons, 24-20 (A)
　　　Rams, 33-0 (LA)
1988—Rams, 33-0 (A)
　　　Rams, 22-7 (LA)
1989—Rams, 31-21 (A)
　　　Rams, 26-14 (LA)
1990—Rams, 44-24 (LA)
　　　Falcons, 20-13 (A)
1991—Falcons, 31-14 (A)
　　　Falcons, 31-14 (LA)
1992—Falcons, 30-28 (A)
　　　Rams, 38-27 (LA)
1993—Falcons, 30-24 (A)
　　　Falcons, 13-0 (LA)
1994—Falcons, 31-13 (A)
　　　Falcons, 8-5 (LA)
1995—Rams, 21-19 (StL)
　　　Falcons, 31-6 (A)
1996—Rams, 59-16 (StL)
　　　Rams, 34-27 (A)
1997—Falcons, 34-31 (A)
　　　Falcons, 27-21 (StL)
1998—Falcons, 37-15 (A)
　　　Falcons, 21-10 (StL)
1999—Rams, 35-7 (StL)
　　　Rams, 41-13 (A)
2000—Rams, 41-20 (A)
　　　Rams, 45-29 (StL)
2001—Rams, 35-6 (A)
　　　Rams, 31-13 (StL)
2003—Rams, 36-0 (StL)
2004—Falcons, 34-17 (A)
　　　**Falcons, 47-17 (A)
(RS Pts.—Rams 1,700, Falcons 1,167)
(PS Pts.—Falcons 47, Rams 17)
Franchise in Los Angeles prior to 1995
**NFC Divisional Playoff*
ATLANTA vs. SAN DIEGO
RS: Falcons lead series, 6-1
1973—Falcons, 41-0 (SD)
1979—Falcons, 28-26 (SD)
1988—Chargers, 10-7 (A)
1991—Falcons, 13-10 (SD)
1994—Falcons, 10-9 (A)
1997—Falcons, 14-3 (SD)

2004—Falcons, 21-20 (A)
(RS Pts.—Falcons 134, Chargers 78)
ATLANTA vs. SAN FRANCISCO
RS: 49ers lead series, 44-26-1
PS: Falcons lead series, 1-0
1966—49ers, 44-7 (A)
1967—49ers, 38-7 (SF)
　　　49ers, 34-28 (A)
1968—49ers, 28-13 (SF)
　　　49ers, 14-12 (A)
1969—Falcons, 24-12 (A)
　　　Falcons, 21-7 (SF)
1970—Falcons, 21-20 (A)
　　　49ers, 24-20 (SF)
1971—Falcons, 20-17 (A)
　　　49ers, 24-3 (SF)
1972—49ers, 49-14 (A)
　　　49ers, 20-0 (SF)
1973—49ers, 13-9 (A)
　　　Falcons, 17-3 (SF)
1974—49ers, 16-10 (A)
　　　49ers, 27-0 (SF)
1975—Falcons, 17-3 (SF)
　　　Falcons, 31-9 (A)
1976—49ers, 15-0 (SF)
　　　Falcons, 21-16 (A)
1977—Falcons, 7-0 (SF)
　　　49ers, 10-3 (A)
1978—Falcons, 20-17 (SF)
　　　Falcons, 21-10 (A)
1979—49ers, 20-15 (SF)
　　　Falcons, 31-21 (A)
1980—Falcons, 20-17 (SF)
　　　Falcons, 35-10 (A)
1981—Falcons, 34-17 (A)
　　　49ers, 17-14 (SF)
1982—Falcons, 17-7 (SF)
1983—49ers, 24-20 (SF)
　　　Falcons, 28-24 (A)
1984—49ers, 14-5 (SF)
　　　49ers, 35-17 (A)
1985—49ers, 35-16 (SF)
　　　49ers, 38-17 (A)
1986—Tie, 10-10 (A) OT
　　　49ers, 20-0 (SF)
1987—49ers, 25-17 (A)
　　　49ers, 35-7 (SF)
1988—Falcons, 34-17 (SF)
　　　49ers, 13-3 (A)
1989—49ers, 45-3 (SF)
　　　49ers, 23-10 (A)
1990—49ers, 19-13 (SF)
　　　49ers, 45-35 (A)
1991—Falcons, 39-34 (SF)
　　　Falcons, 17-14 (A)
1992—49ers, 56-17 (SF)
　　　49ers, 41-3 (A)
1993—49ers, 37-30 (SF)
　　　Falcons, 27-24 (A)
1994—49ers, 42-3 (A)
　　　49ers, 50-14 (SF)
1995—49ers, 41-10 (SF)
　　　Falcons, 28-27 (A)
1996—49ers, 39-17 (SF)
　　　49ers, 34-10 (A)
1997—49ers, 34-7 (SF)
　　　49ers, 35-28 (A)
1998—49ers, 31-20 (SF)
　　　Falcons, 31-19 (A)
　　　*Falcons, 20-18 (A)

1999—49ers, 26-7 (SF)
　　Falcons, 34-29 (A)
2000—Falcons, 36-28 (A)
　　49ers, 16-6 (SF)
2001—49ers, 16-13 (SF) OT
　　49ers, 37-31 (A) OT
2004—Falcons, 21-19 (SF)
(RS Pts.—49ers 1,730, Falcons 1,196)
(PS Pts.—Falcons 20, 49ers 18)
*NFC Divisional Playoff
ATLANTA vs. SEATTLE
RS: Seahawks lead series, 8-2
1976—Seahawks, 30-13 (S)
1979—Seahawks, 31-28 (A)
1985—Seahawks, 30-26 (S)
1988—Seahawks, 31-20 (A)
1991—Falcons, 26-13 (A)
1997—Falcons, 24-17 (S)
2000—Seahawks, 30-10 (A)
2002—Seahawks, 30-24 (A) OT
2004—Seahawks, 28-26 (S)
2005—Seahawks, 21-18 (S)
(RS Pts.—Seahawks 261, Falcons 215)
ATLANTA vs. TAMPA BAY
RS: Buccaneers lead series, 15-12
1977—Falcons, 17-0 (TB)
1978—Buccaneers, 14-9 (TB)
1979—Falcons, 17-14 (A)
1981—Buccaneers, 24-23 (TB)
1984—Buccaneers, 23-6 (TB)
1986—Falcons, 23-20 (TB) OT
1987—Buccaneers, 48-10 (TB)
1988—Falcons, 17-10 (A)
1990—Buccaneers, 23-17 (TB)
1991—Falcons, 43-7 (A)
1992—Falcons, 35-7 (TB)
1993—Buccaneers, 31-24 (A)
1994—Falcons, 34-13 (A)
1995—Falcons, 24-21 (TB)
1997—Buccaneers, 31-10 (A)
1999—Buccaneers, 19-10 (A)
2000—Buccaneers, 27-14 (A)
2002—Buccaneers, 20-6 (A)
　　Buccaneers, 34-10 (TB)
2003—Buccaneers, 31-10 (A)
　　Falcons, 30-28 (TB)
2004—Falcons, 24-14 (A)
　　Buccaneers, 27-0 (TB)
2005—Buccaneers, 30-27 (A)
　　Buccaneers, 27-24 (TB) OT
2006—Falcons, 14-3 (A)
　　Falcons, 17-6 (TB)
(RS Pts.—Buccaneers 552, Falcons 495)
ATLANTA vs. *TENNESSEE
RS: Titans lead series, 6-5
1972—Falcons, 20-10 (A)
1976—Oilers, 20-14 (H)
1978—Falcons, 20-14 (A)
1981—Falcons, 31-27 (H)
1984—Falcons, 42-10 (A)
1987—Oilers, 37-33 (H)
1990—Falcons, 47-27 (A)
1993—Oilers, 33-17 (H)
1996—Oilers, 23-13 (A)
1999—Titans, 30-17 (T)
2003—Titans, 38-31 (A)
(RS Pts.—Falcons 285, Titans 269)
*Franchise in Houston prior to 1997;
known as Oilers prior to 1999
ATLANTA vs. WASHINGTON

RS: Redskins lead series, 14-5-1
PS: Redskins lead series, 1-0
1966—Redskins, 33-20 (W)
1967—Tie, 20-20 (A)
1969—Redskins, 27-20 (W)
1972—Redskins, 24-13 (W)
1975—Redskins, 30-27 (A)
1977—Redskins, 10-6 (W)
1978—Falcons, 20-17 (A)
1979—Redskins, 16-7 (A)
1980—Falcons, 10-6 (A)
1983—Redskins, 37-21 (W)
1984—Redskins, 27-14 (W)
1985—Redskins, 44-10 (A)
1987—Falcons, 21-20 (A)
1989—Redskins, 31-30 (A)
1991—Redskins, 56-17 (W)
　　*Redskins, 24-7 (W)
1992—Redskins, 24-17 (W)
1993—Redskins, 30-17 (W)
1994—Falcons, 27-20 (W)
2003—Redskins, 33-31 (A)
2006—Falcons, 24-14 (W)
(RS Pts.—Redskins 519, Falcons 372)
(PS Pts.—Redskins 24, Falcons 7)
*NFC Divisional Playoff

BALTIMORE vs. ARIZONA
RS: Ravens lead series, 2-1;
See Arizona vs. Baltimore
BALTIMORE vs. ATLANTA
RS: Rvens lead series, 2-1;
See Atlanta vs. Baltimore
BALTIMORE vs. BUFFALO
RS: Ravens lead series, 2-1
1999—Bills, 13-10 (Balt)
2004—Ravens, 20-6 (Balt)
2006—Ravens, 19-7 (Balt)
(RS Pts.—Ravens 49, Bills 26)
BALTIMORE vs. CAROLINA
RS: Panthers lead series, 3-0
1996—Panthers, 27-16 (C)
2002—Panthers, 10-7 (C)
2006—Panthers, 23-21 (B)
(RS Pts.—Panthers 60, Ravens 44)
BALTIMORE vs. CHICAGO
RS: Bears lead series, 2-1
1998—Bears, 24-3 (C)
2001—Ravens, 17-6 (B)
2005—Bears, 10-6 (C)
(RS Pts.—Bears 40, Ravens 26)
BALTIMORE vs. CINCINNATI
RS: Ravens lead series, 13-9
1996—Bengals, 24-21 (B)
　　Bengals, 21-14 (C)
1997—Ravens, 23-10 (B)
　　Bengals, 16-14 (C)
1998—Ravens, 31-24 (B)
　　Ravens, 20-13 (C)
1999—Ravens, 34-31 (C)
　　Ravens, 22-0 (B)
2000—Ravens, 37-0 (B)
　　Ravens, 27-7 (C)
2001—Bengals, 21-10 (C)
　　Ravens, 16-0 (B)
2002—Ravens, 38-27 (B)
　　Ravens, 27-23 (C)
2003—Bengals, 34-26 (B)
　　Ravens, 31-13 (B)
2004—Ravens, 23-9 (C)

Bengals, 27-26 (B)
2005—Bengals, 21-9 (B)
　　Bengals, 42-29 (C)
2006—Ravens, 26-20 (B)
　　Bengals, 13-7 (C)
(RS Pts.—Ravens 511, Bengals 396)
BALTIMORE vs. CLEVELAND
RS: Ravens lead series, 11-5
1999—Ravens, 17-10 (B)
　　Ravens, 41-9 (C)
2000—Ravens, 12-0 (C)
　　Ravens, 44-7 (B)
2001—Browns, 24-14 (C)
　　Browns, 27-17 (B)
2002—Ravens, 26-21 (C)
　　Browns, 14-13 (B)
2003—Ravens, 33-13 (B)
　　Ravens, 35-0 (C)
2004—Browns, 20-3 (C)
　　Ravens, 27-13 (B)
2005—Ravens, 16-3 (B)
　　Browns, 20-16 (C)
2006—Ravens, 15-14 (C)
　　Ravens, 27-17 (B)
(RS Pts.—Ravens 356, Browns 212)
BALTIMORE vs. DALLAS
RS: Ravens lead series, 2-0
2000—Ravens, 27-0 (B)
2004—Ravens, 30-10 (B)
(RS Pts.—Ravens 57, Cowboys 10)
BALTIMORE vs. DENVER
RS: Series tied, 3-3
PS: Ravens lead series, 1-0
1996—Broncos, 45-34 (D)
2000—*Ravens, 21-3 (B)
2001—Ravens, 20-13 (D)
2002—Ravens, 34-23 (B)
2003—Ravens, 26-6 (B)
2005—Broncos, 12-10 (D)
2006—Broncos, 13-3 (D)
(RS Pts.—Ravens 127, Broncos 112)
(PS Pts.—Ravens 21, Broncos 3)
*AFC First-Round Playoff
BALTIMORE vs. DETROIT
RS: Series tied, 1-1
1998—Ravens, 19-10 (B)
2005—Lions, 35-17 (D)
(RS Pts.—Lions 45, Ravens 36)
BALTIMORE vs. GREEN BAY
RS: Packers lead series, 2-1
1998—Packers, 28-10 (GB)
2001—Packers, 31-23 (GB)
2005—Ravens, 48-3 (B)
(RS Pts.—Ravens 81, Packers 62)
BALTIMORE vs. HOUSTON
RS: Ravens lead series, 2-0
2002—Ravens, 23-19 (H)
2005—Ravens, 16-15 (B)
(RS Pts.—Ravens 39, Texans 34)
BALTIMORE vs. INDIANAPOLIS
RS: Colts lead series, 4-2
PS: Colts lead series, 1-0
1996—Colts, 26-21 (I)
1998—Ravens, 38-31 (B)
2001—Ravens, 39-27 (B)
2002—Colts, 22-20 (I)
2004—Colts, 20-10 (I)
2005—Colts, 24-7 (B)
2006—*Colts, 15-6 (B)
(RS Pts.—Colts 150, Ravens 135)

(PS Pts.—Colts 15, Ravens 6)
AFC Divisional Playoff
BALTIMORE vs. JACKSONVILLE
RS: Jaguars lead series, 9-6
1996—Jaguars, 30-27 (J)
       Jaguars, 28-25 (B) OT
1997—Jaguars, 28-27 (B)
       Jaguars, 29-27 (J)
1998—Jaguars, 24-10 (J)
       Jaguars, 45-19 (B)
1999—Jaguars, 6-3 (J)
       Jaguars, 30-23 (B)
2000—Ravens, 39-36 (B)
       Ravens, 15-10 (J)
2001—Ravens, 18-17 (B)
       Ravens, 24-21 (J)
2002—Ravens, 17-10 (B)
2003—Ravens, 24-17 (B)
2005—Jaguars, 30-3 (J)
(RS Pts.—Jaguars 361, Ravens 301)
BALTIMORE vs. KANSAS CITY
RS: Chiefs lead series, 3-1
1999—Chiefs, 35-8 (B)
2003—Chiefs, 17-10 (B)
2004—Chiefs, 27-24 (B)
2006—Ravens, 20-10 (KC)
(RS Pts.—Chiefs 89, Ravens 62)
BALTIMORE vs. MIAMI
RS: Dolphins lead series, 4-1
PS: Ravens lead series, 1-0
1997—Dolphins, 24-13 (B)
2000—Dolphins, 19-6 (M)
2001—*Ravens, 20-3 (M)
2002—Dolphins, 26-7 (M)
2003—Dolphins, 9-6 (M) OT
2004—Ravens, 30-23 (B)
(RS Pts.—Dolphins 101, Ravens 62)
(PS Pts.—Ravens 20, Dolphins 3)
AFC First-Round Playoff
BALTIMORE vs. MINNESOTA
RS: Ravens lead series, 2-1
1998—Vikings, 38-28 (B)
2001—Ravens, 19-3 (B)
2005—Ravens, 30-23 (B)
(RS Pts.—Ravens 77, Vikings 64)
BALTIMORE vs. NEW ENGLAND
RS: Patriots lead series, 3-0
1996—Patriots, 46-38 (B)
1999—Patriots, 20-3 (NE)
2004—Patriots, 24-3 (NE)
(RS Pts.—Patriots 90, Ravens 44)
BALTIMORE vs. NEW ORLEANS
RS: Ravens lead series, 3-1
1996—Ravens, 17-10 (B)
1999—Ravens, 31-8 (B)
2002—Saints, 37-25 (B)
2006—Ravens, 35-22 (NO)
(RS Pts.—Ravens 108, Saints 77)
BALTIMORE vs. N.Y. GIANTS
RS: Ravens lead series, 2-0
PS: Ravens lead series, 1-0
1997—Ravens, 24-23 (NY)
2000—*Ravens, 34-7 (Tampa)
2004—Ravens, 37-14 (B)
(RS Pts.—Ravens 61, Giants 37)
(PS Pts.—Ravens 34, Giants 7)
Super Bowl XXXV
BALTIMORE vs. N.Y. JETS
RS: Ravens lead series, 4-1
1997—Jets, 19-16 (NY) OT

1998—Ravens, 24-10 (NY)
2000—Ravens, 34-20 (B)
2004—Ravens, 20-17 (NY) OT
2005—Ravens, 13-3 (B)
(RS Pts.—Ravens 107, Jets 69)
BALTIMORE vs. OAKLAND
RS: Ravens lead series, 3-1
PS: Ravens lead series, 1-0
1996—Ravens, 19-14 (B)
1998—Ravens, 13-10 (B)
2000—*Ravens, 16-3 (O)
2003—Raiders, 20-12 (O)
2006—Ravens, 28-6 (B)
(RS Pts.—Ravens 72, Raiders 50)
(PS Pts.—Ravens 16, Raiders 3)
AFC Championship
BALTIMORE vs. PHILADELPHIA
RS: Eagles lead series, 1-0-1
1997—Tie, 10-10 (B) OT
2004—Eagles, 15-10 (P)
(RS Pts.—Eagles 25, Ravens 20)
BALTIMORE vs. PITTSBURGH
RS: Steelers lead series, 13-9
PS: Steelers lead series, 1-0
1996—Steelers, 31-17 (P)
       Ravens, 31-17 (B)
1997—Steelers, 42-34 (B)
       Steelers, 37-0 (P)
1998—Steelers, 20-13 (B)
       Steelers, 16-6 (P)
1999—Steelers, 23-20 (B)
       Ravens, 31-24 (P)
2000—Ravens, 16-0 (P)
       Steelers, 9-6 (B)
2001—Ravens, 13-10 (P)
       Steelers, 26-21 (B)
       *Steelers, 27-10 (P)
2002—Steelers, 31-18 (B)
       Steelers, 34-31 (P)
2003—Steelers, 34-15 (P)
       Ravens, 13-10 (B) OT
2004—Ravens, 30-13 (B)
       Steelers, 20-7 (P)
2005—Steelers, 20-19 (P)
       Ravens, 16-13 (B) OT
2006—Ravens, 27-0 (B)
       Ravens, 31-7 (P)
(RS Pts.—Steelers 437, Ravens 415)
(PS Pts.—Steelers 27, Ravens 10)
AFC Divisional Playoff
BALTIMORE vs. ST. LOUIS
RS: Rams lead series, 2-1
1996—Ravens, 37-31 (B) OT
1999—Rams, 27-10 (StL)
2003—Rams, 33-22 (StL)
(RS Pts.—Rams 91, Ravens 69)
BALTIMORE vs. SAN DIEGO
RS: Ravens lead series, 3-2
1997—Chargers, 21-17 (SD)
1998—Chargers, 14-13 (SD)
2000—Ravens, 24-3 (B)
2003—Ravens, 24-10 (SD)
2006—Ravens, 16-13 (B)
(RS Pts.—Ravens 94, Chargers 61)
BALTIMORE vs. SAN FRANCISCO
RS: Series tied, 1-1
1996—49ers, 38-20 (SF)
2003—Ravens, 44-6 (B)
(RS Pts.—Ravens 64, 49ers 44)
BALTIMORE vs. SEATTLE

RS: Ravens lead series, 2-0
1997—Ravens, 31-24 (B)
2003—Ravens, 44-41 (B) OT
(RS Pts.—Ravens 75, Seahawks 65)
BALTIMORE vs. TAMPA BAY
RS: Buccaneers lead series, 2-1
2001—Buccaneers, 22-10 (TB)
2002—Buccaneers, 25-0 (B)
2006—Ravens, 27-0 (B)
(RS Pts.—Buccaneers 47, Ravens 37)
BALTIMORE vs. *TENNESSEE
RS: Raens lead series, 8-7
PS: Series tied, 1-1
1996—Oilers, 29-13 (H)
       Oilers, 24-21 (B)
1997—Ravens, 36-10 (T)
       Ravens, 21-19 (B)
1998—Oilers, 12-8 (B)
       Oilers, 16-14 (T)
1999—Titans, 14-11 (T)
       Ravens, 41-14 (B)
2000—Titans, 14-6 (B)
       Ravens, 24-23 (T)
       **Ravens, 24-10 (T)
2001—Ravens, 26-7 (B)
       Ravens, 16-10 (T)
2002—Ravens, 13-12 (B)
2003—***Titans, 20-17 (B)
2005—Titans, 25-10 (T)
2006—Ravens, 27-26 (T)
(RS Pts.—Ravens 287, Titans 255)
(PS Pts.—Ravens 41, Titans 30)
*Franchise in Houston prior to 1997;
known as Oilers prior to 1999*
**AFC Divisional Playoff*
***AFC First-Round Playoff*
BALTIMORE vs. WASHINGTON
RS: Ravens lead series, 2-1
1997—Ravens, 20-17 (W)
2000—Redskins, 10-3 (W)
2004—Ravens, 17-10 (W)
(RS Pts.—Ravens 40, Redskins 37)

BUFFALO vs. ARIZONA
RS: Bills lead series, 5-3;
See Arizona vs. Buffalo
BUFFALO vs. ATLANTA
RS: Falcons lead series, 5-4;
See Atlanta vs. Buffalo
BUFFALO vs. BALTIMORE
RS: Ravens lead series, 2-1;
See Baltimore vs. Buffalo
BUFFALO vs. CAROLINA
RS: Bills lead series, 3-1
1995—Bills, 31-9 (B)
1998—Bills, 30-14 (C)
2001—Bills, 25-24 (B)
2005—Panthers, 13-9 (B)
(RS Pts.—Bills 95, Panthers 60)
BUFFALO vs. CHICAGO
RS: Bears lead series, 6-4
1970—Bears, 31-13 (C)
1974—Bills, 16-6 (B)
1979—Bears, 7-0 (B)
1988—Bears, 24-3 (C)
1991—Bills, 35-20 (B)
1994—Bears, 20-13 (C)
1997—Bears, 20-3 (C)
2000—Bills, 20-3 (B)
2002—Bills, 33-27 (B) OT

2006—Bears, 40-7 (C)
(RS Pts.—Bears 198, Bills 143)

BUFFALO vs. CINCINNATI
RS: Bills lead series, 13-9
PS: Bengals lead series, 2-0
1968—Bengals, 34-23 (C)
1969—Bills, 16-13 (B)
1970—Bengals, 43-14 (B)
1973—Bengals, 16-13 (B)
1975—Bengals, 33-24 (C)
1978—Bills, 5-0 (B)
1979—Bills, 51-24 (B)
1980—Bills, 14-0 (C)
1981—Bengals, 27-24 (C) OT
    *Bengals, 28-21 (C)
1983—Bills, 10-6 (C)
1984—Bengals, 52-21 (C)
1985—Bengals, 23-17 (B)
1986—Bengals, 36-33 (C) OT
1988—Bengals, 35-21 (C)
    **Bengals, 21-10 (C)
1989—Bills, 24-7 (B)
1991—Bills, 35-16 (B)
1996—Bills, 31-17 (B)
1998—Bills, 33-20 (C)
2002—Bills, 27-9 (B)
2003—Bills, 22-16 (B) OT
2004—Bills, 33-17 (C)
2005—Bills, 37-27 (C)
(RS Pts.—Bills 528, Bengals 471)
(PS Pts.—Bengals 49, Bills 31)
*AFC Divisional Playoff
**AFC Championship

BUFFALO vs. CLEVELAND
RS: Browns lead series, 7-5
PS: Browns lead series, 1-0
1972—Browns, 27-10 (C)
1974—Bills, 15-10 (C)
1977—Browns, 27-16 (B)
1978—Browns, 41-20 (C)
1981—Bills, 22-13 (B)
1984—Browns, 13-10 (B)
1985—Browns, 17-7 (C)
1986—Browns, 21-17 (B)
1987—Browns, 27-21 (C)
1989—*Browns, 34-30 (C)
1990—Bills, 42-0 (C)
1995—Bills, 22-19 (C)
2004—Bills, 37-7 (B)
(RS Pts.—Bills 239, Browns 222)
(PS Pts.—Browns 34, Bills 30)
*AFC Divisional Playoff

BUFFALO vs. DALLAS
RS: Cowboys lead series, 4-3
PS: Cowboys lead series, 2-0
1971—Cowboys, 49-37 (B)
1976—Cowboys, 17-10 (D)
1981—Cowboys, 27-14 (D)
1984—Bills, 14-3 (B)
1992—*Cowboys, 52-17 (Pasadena)
1993—Bills, 13-10 (D)
    **Cowboys, 30-13 (Atlanta)
1996—Bills, 10-7 (B)
2003—Cowboys, 10-6 (D)
(RS Pts.—Cowboys 123, Bills 104)
(PS Pts.—Cowboys 82, Bills 30)
*Super Bowl XXVII
**Super Bowl XXVIII

BUFFALO vs. DENVER
RS: Bills lead series, 17-14-1

PS: Bills lead series, 1-0
1960—Broncos, 27-21 (B)
    Tie, 38-38 (D)
1961—Broncos, 22-10 (B)
    Bills, 23-10 (D)
1962—Broncos, 23-20 (B)
    Bills, 45-38 (D)
1963—Bills, 30-28 (D)
    Bills, 27-17 (B)
1964—Bills, 30-13 (B)
    Bills, 30-19 (D)
1965—Bills, 30-15 (D)
    Bills, 31-13 (B)
1966—Bills, 38-21 (B)
1967—Bills, 17-16 (D)
    Broncos, 21-20 (B)
1968—Broncos, 34-32 (D)
1969—Bills, 41-28 (B)
1970—Broncos, 25-10 (B)
1975—Bills, 38-14 (B)
1977—Broncos, 26-6 (D)
1979—Broncos, 19-16 (B)
1981—Bills, 9-7 (B)
1984—Broncos, 37-7 (B)
1987—Bills, 21-14 (B)
1989—Broncos, 28-14 (B)
1990—Bills, 29-28 (B)
1991—*Bills, 10-7 (B)
1992—Bills, 27-17 (B)
1994—Bills, 27-20 (B)
1995—Broncos, 22-7 (D)
1997—Broncos, 23-20 (B) OT
2002—Broncos, 28-23 (D)
2005—Broncos, 28-17 (B)
(RS Pts.—Bills 754, Broncos 719)
(PS Pts.—Bills 10, Broncos 7)
*AFC Championship

BUFFALO vs. DETROIT
RS: Lions lead series, 4-3-1
1972—Tie, 21-21 (B)
1976—Lions, 27-14 (D)
1979—Bills, 20-17 (D)
1991—Lions, 17-14 (B) OT
1994—Lions, 35-21 (D)
1997—Bills, 22-13 (B)
2002—Bills, 24-17 (B)
2006—Lions, 20-17 (D)
(RS Pts.—Lions 167, Bills 153)

BUFFALO vs. GREEN BAY
RS: Bills lead series, 7-3
1974—Bills, 27-7 (GB)
1979—Bills, 19-12 (B)
1982—Packers, 33-21 (Mil)
1988—Bills, 28-0 (B)
1991—Bills, 34-24 (Mil)
1994—Bills 29-20 (B)
1997—Packers, 31-21 (GB)
2000—Bills 27-18 (B)
2002—Packers, 10-0 (GB)
2006—Bills, 24-10 (B)
(RS Pts.—Bills 230, Packers 165)

BUFFALO vs. HOUSTON
RS: Bills lead series, 3-1
2002—Bills, 31-24 (H)
2003—Texans, 12-10 (B)
2005—Bills, 22-7 (B)
2006—Bills, 24-21 (H)
(RS Pts.—Bills 87, Texans 64)

BUFFALO vs. *INDIANAPOLIS
RS: Bills lead series, 34-30-1

1970—Tie, 17-17 (Balt)
    Colts, 20-14 (Buff)
1971—Colts, 43-0 (Buff)
    Colts, 24-0 (Balt)
1972—Colts, 17-0 (Buff)
    Colts, 35-7 (Balt)
1973—Bills, 31-13 (Buff)
    Bills, 24-17 (Balt)
1974—Bills, 27-14 (Balt)
    Bills, 6-0 (Buff)
1975—Bills, 38-31 (Balt)
    Colts, 42-35 (Buff)
1976—Colts, 31-13 (Buff)
    Colts, 58-20 (Balt)
1977—Colts, 17-14 (Buff)
    Colts, 31-13 (Buff)
1978—Bills, 24-17 (Buff)
    Bills, 21-14 (Balt)
1979—Bills, 31-13 (Buff)
    Colts, 14-13 (Buff)
1980—Colts, 17-12 (Buff)
    Colts, 28-24 (Balt)
1981—Bills, 35-3 (Balt)
    Bills, 23-17 (Buff)
1982—Bills, 20-0 (Buff)
1983—Bills, 28-23 (Buff)
    Bills, 30-7 (Balt)
1984—Colts, 31-17 (I)
    Bills, 21-15 (Buff)
1985—Colts, 49-17 (I)
    Bills, 21-9 (Buff)
1986—Bills, 24-13 (Buff)
    Colts, 24-14 (I)
1987—Colts, 47-6 (Buff)
    Bills, 27-3 (I)
1988—Bills, 34-23 (Buff)
    Colts, 17-14 (I)
1989—Colts, 37-14 (I)
    Bills, 30-7 (Buff)
1990—Bills, 26-10 (Buff)
    Bills, 31-7 (I)
1991—Bills, 42-6 (Buff)
    Bills, 35-7 (I)
1992—Bills, 38-0 (Buff)
    Colts, 16-13 (I) OT
1993—Bills, 23-9 (Buff)
    Bills, 30-10 (I)
1994—Colts, 27-17 (Buff)
    Colts, 10-9 (I)
1995—Bills, 20-14 (Buff)
    Bills, 16-10 (I)
1996—Bills, 16-13 (Buff) OT
    Colts, 13-10 (I) OT
1997—Bills, 37-35 (B)
    Bills, 9-6 (I)
1998—Bills, 31-24 (I)
    Bills, 34-11 (B)
1999—Colts, 31-14 (I)
    Bills, 31-6 (B)
2000—Colts, 18-16 (B)
    Colts, 44-20 (I)
2001—Colts, 42-26 (I)
    Colts, 30-14 (B)
2003—Colts, 17-14 (B)
2006—Colts, 17-16 (I)
(RS Pts.—Bills 1,347, Colts 1,271)
*Franchise in Baltimore prior to 1984

BUFFALO vs. JACKSONVILLE
RS: Bills lead series, 4-2
PS: Jaguars lead series, 1-0

1996—*Jaguars, 30-27 (B)
1997—Jaguars, 20-14 (B)
1998—Bills, 17-16 (B)
2001—Bills, 13-10 (J)
2003—Bills, 38-17 (J)
2004—Jaguars, 13-10 (B)
2006—Bills, 27-24 (B)
(RS Pts.—Bills 119, Jaguars 100)
(PS Pts.—Jaguars 30, Bills 27)
*AFC First-Round Playoff
BUFFALO vs. *KANSAS CITY
RS: Bills lead series, 19-16-1
PS: Bills lead series, 2-1
1960—Texans, 45-28 (B)
       Texans, 24-7 (D)
1961—Bills, 27-24 (B)
       Bills, 30-20 (D)
1962—Texans, 41-21 (D)
       Bills, 23-14 (B)
1963—Tie, 27-27 (B)
       Bills, 35-26 (KC)
1964—Bills, 34-17 (B)
       Bills, 35-22 (KC)
1965—Bills, 23-7 (KC)
       Bills, 34-25 (B)
1966—Chiefs, 42-20 (B)
       Bills, 29-14 (KC)
       **Chiefs, 31-7 (B)
1967—Chiefs, 23-13 (KC)
1968—Chiefs, 18-7 (B)
1969—Chiefs, 29-7 (B)
       Chiefs, 22-19 (KC)
1971—Chiefs, 22-9 (KC)
1973—Bills, 23-14 (B)
1976—Bills, 50-17 (B)
1978—Bills, 28-13 (B)
       Chiefs, 14-10 (KC)
1982—Bills, 14-9 (B)
1983—Bills, 14-9 (KC)
1986—Chiefs, 20-17 (B)
       Bills, 17-14 (KC)
1991—Chiefs, 33-6 (KC)
       ***Bills, 37-14 (B)
1993—Chiefs, 23-7 (KC)
       ****Bills, 30-13 (B)
1994—Bills, 44-10 (B)
1996—Bills, 20-9 (B)
1997—Chiefs, 22-16 (KC)
2000—Bills, 21-17 (KC)
2002—Chiefs, 17-16 (KC)
2003—Chiefs, 38-5 (KC)
2005—Bills, 14-3 (B)
(RS Pts.—Bills 750, Chiefs 744)
(PS Pts.—Bills 74, Chiefs 58)
*Franchise in Dallas prior to 1963 and
known as Texans
**AFL Championship
***AFC Divisional Playoff
****AFC Championship
BUFFALO vs. MIAMI
RS: Dolphins lead series, 49-32-1
PS: Bills lead series, 3-1
1966—Bills, 58-24 (B)
       Bills, 29-0 (M)
1967—Bills, 35-13 (B)
       Dolphins, 17-14 (M)
1968—Tie, 14-14 (M)
       Dolphins, 21-17 (B)
1969—Dolphins, 24-6 (M)
       Bills, 28-3 (B)

1970—Dolphins, 33-14 (B)
       Dolphins, 45-7 (M)
1971—Dolphins, 29-14 (B)
       Dolphins, 34-0 (M)
1972—Dolphins, 24-23 (M)
       Dolphins, 30-16 (B)
1973—Dolphins, 27-6 (M)
       Dolphins, 17-0 (B)
1974—Dolphins, 24-16 (B)
       Dolphins, 35-28 (M)
1975—Dolphins, 35-30 (B)
       Dolphins, 31-21 (M)
1976—Dolphins, 30-21 (B)
       Dolphins, 45-27 (M)
1977—Dolphins, 13-0 (B)
       Dolphins, 31-14 (M)
1978—Dolphins, 31-24 (M)
       Dolphins, 25-24 (B)
1979—Dolphins, 9-7 (B)
       Dolphins, 17-7 (M)
1980—Bills, 17-7 (B)
       Dolphins, 17-14 (M)
1981—Bills, 31-21 (B)
       Dolphins, 16-6 (M)
1982—Dolphins, 9-7 (B)
       Dolphins, 27-10 (M)
1983—Dolphins, 12-0 (B)
       Bills, 38-35 (M) OT
1984—Dolphins, 21-17 (B)
       Dolphins, 38-7 (M)
1985—Dolphins, 23-14 (B)
       Dolphins, 28-0 (M)
1986—Dolphins, 27-14 (M)
       Dolphins, 34-24 (B)
1987—Bills, 34-31 (M) OT
       Bills, 27-0 (B)
1988—Bills, 9-6 (B)
       Bills, 31-6 (M)
1989—Bills, 27-24 (M)
       Bills, 31-17 (B)
1990—Dolphins, 30-7 (M)
       Bills, 24-14 (B)
       *Bills, 44-34 (B)
1991—Bills, 35-31 (B)
       Bills, 41-27 (M)
1992—Dolphins, 37-10 (B)
       Bills, 26-20 (M)
       **Bills, 29-10 (M)
1993—Dolphins, 22-13 (M)
       Bills, 47-34 (M)
1994—Bills, 21-11 (B)
       Bills, 42-31 (M)
1995—Dolphins, 23-6 (M)
       Bills, 23-20 (B)
       ***Bills, 37-22 (B)
1996—Dolphins, 21-7 (B)
       Dolphins, 16-14 (M)
1997—Bills, 9-6 (B)
       Dolphins, 30-13 (M)
1998—Dolphins, 13-7 (M)
       Bills, 30-24 (B)
       ***Dolphins, 24-17 (M)
1999—Bills, 23-18 (M)
       Bills, 23-3 (B)
2000—Dolphins, 22-13 (M)
       Dolphins, 33-6 (B)
2001—Dolphins, 34-27 (B)
       Dolphins, 34-7 (M)
2002—Bills, 23-10 (M)
       Bills, 38-21 (B)

2003—Dolphins, 17-7 (M)
       Dolphins, 20-3 (B)
2004—Bills, 20-13 (B)
       Bills, 42-32 (M)
2005—Bills, 20-14 (B)
       Dolphins, 24-23 (M)
2006—Bills, 16-6 (M)
       Bills, 21-0 (B)
(RS Pts.—Dolphins 1,791, Bills 1,545)
(PS Pts.—Bills 127, Dolphins 90)
*AFC Divisional Playoff
**AFC Championship
***AFC First-Round Playoff
BUFFALO vs. MINNESOTA
RS: Vikings lead series, 7-4
1971—Vikings, 19-0 (M)
1975—Vikings, 35-13 (B)
1979—Vikings, 10-3 (M)
1982—Bills, 23-22 (B)
1985—Vikings, 27-20 (B)
1988—Bills, 13-10 (B)
1994—Vikings, 21-17 (B)
1997—Vikings, 34-13 (B)
2000—Vikings, 31-27 (M)
2002—Bills, 45-39 (M) OT
2006—Bills, 17-12 (B)
(RS Pts.—Vikings 260, Bills 191)
BUFFALO vs. *NEW ENGLAND
RS: Patriots lead series, 52-40-1
PS: Patriots lead series, 1-0
1960—Bills, 13-0 (Bos)
       Bills, 38-14 (Buff)
1961—Patriots, 23-21 (Buff)
       Patriots, 52-21 (Bos)
1962—Tie, 28-28 (Buff)
       Patriots, 21-10 (Bos)
1963—Bills, 28-21 (Buff)
       Patriots, 17-7 (Bos)
       **Patriots, 26-8 (Buff)
1964—Patriots, 36-28 (Buff)
       Bills, 24-14 (Bos)
1965—Bills, 24-7 (Buff)
       Bills, 23-7 (Bos)
1966—Patriots, 20-10 (Buff)
       Patriots, 14-3 (Bos)
1967—Patriots, 23-0 (Buff)
       Bills, 44-16 (Bos)
1968—Patriots, 16-7 (Buff)
       Patriots, 23-6 (Bos)
1969—Bills, 23-16 (Buff)
       Patriots, 35-21 (Bos)
1970—Bills, 45-10 (Bos)
       Patriots, 14-10 (Buff)
1971—Patriots, 38-33 (NE)
       Bills, 27-20 (Buff)
1972—Bills, 38-14 (Buff)
       Bills, 27-24 (NE)
1973—Bills, 31-13 (NE)
       Bills, 37-13 (Buff)
1974—Bills, 30-28 (Buff)
       Bills, 29-28 (NE)
1975—Bills, 45-31 (Buff)
       Bills, 34-14 (NE)
1976—Patriots, 26-22 (Buff)
       Patriots, 20-10 (NE)
1977—Bills, 24-14 (NE)
       Patriots, 20-7 (Buff)
1978—Patriots, 14-10 (Buff)
       Patriots, 26-24 (NE)
1979—Patriots, 26-6 (Buff)

Bills, 16-13 (NE) OT
1980—Bills, 31-13 (Buff)
Patriots, 24-2 (NE)
1981—Bills, 20-17 (Buff)
Bills, 19-10 (NE)
1982—Patriots, 30-19 (NE)
1983—Patriots, 31-0 (Buff)
Patriots, 21-7 (NE)
1984—Patriots, 21-17 (Buff)
Patriots, 38-10 (NE)
1985—Patriots, 17-14 (Buff)
Patriots, 14-3 (NE)
1986—Patriots, 23-3 (Buff)
Patriots, 22-19 (NE)
1987—Patriots, 14-7 (NE)
Patriots, 13-7 (Buff)
1988—Bills, 16-14 (NE)
Bills, 23-20 (Buff)
1989—Bills, 31-10 (Buff)
Patriots, 33-24 (NE)
1990—Bills, 27-10 (NE)
Bills, 14-0 (Buff)
1991—Bills, 22-17 (Buff)
Patriots, 16-13 (NE)
1992—Bills, 41-7 (NE)
Bills, 16-7 (Buff)
1993—Bills, 38-14 (NE)
Bills, 13-10 (NE) OT
1994—Bills, 38-35 (NE)
Patriots, 41-17 (Buff)
1995—Patriots, 27-14 (NE)
Patriots, 35-25 (Buff)
1996—Bills, 17-10 (Buff)
Patriots, 28-25 (NE)
1997—Patriots, 33-6 (NE)
Patriots, 31-10 (Buff)
1998—Bills, 13-10 (Buff)
Patriots, 25-21 (NE)
1999—Bills, 17-7 (Buff)
Bills, 13-10 (NE) OT
2000—Bills, 16-13 (NE) OT
Patriots, 13-10 (Buff) OT
2001—Patriots, 21-11 (NE)
Patriots, 12-9 (Buff) OT
2002—Patriots, 38-7 (Buff)
Patriots, 27-17 (NE)
2003—Bills, 31-0 (Buff)
Patriots, 31-0 (NE)
2004—Patriots, 31-17 (Buff)
Patriots, 29-6 (NE)
2005—Patriots, 21-16 (NE)
Patriots, 35-7 (Buff)
2006—Patriots, 19-17 (NE)
Patriots, 28-6 (B)
(RS Pts.—Patriots 1,885, Bills 1,726)
(PS Pts.—Patriots 26, Bills 8)
*Franchise in Boston prior to 1971
**Division Playoff
BUFFALO vs. NEW ORLEANS
RS: Series tied, 4-4
1973—Saints, 13-0 (NO)
1980—Bills, 35-26 (NO)
1983—Bills, 27-21 (B)
1989—Saints, 22-19 (B)
1992—Bills, 20-16 (NO)
1998—Bills, 45-33 (NO)
2001—Saints, 24-6 (B)
2005—Saints, 19-7 (San Antonio)
(RS Pts.—Saints 174, Bills 159)
BUFFALO vs. N.Y. GIANTS

RS: Bills lead series, 6-3
PS: Giants lead series, 1-0
1970—Giants, 20-6 (NY)
1975—Giants, 17-14 (B)
1978—Bills, 41-17 (B)
1987—Bills, 6-3 (B) OT
1990—Bills, 17-13 (NY)
*Giants, 20-19 (Tampa)
1993—Bills, 17-14 (B)
1996—Bills, 23-20 (NY) OT
1999—Giants, 19-17 (B)
2003—Bills, 24-7 (NY)
(RS Pts.—Bills 165, Giants 130)
(PS Pts.—Giants 20, Bills 19)
*Super Bowl XXV
BUFFALO vs. *N.Y. JETS
RS: Bills lead series, 50-42
PS: Bills lead series, 1-0
1960—Titans, 27-3 (NY)
Titans, 17-13 (B)
1961—Bills, 41-31 (B)
Titans, 21-14 (NY)
1962—Titans, 17-6 (B)
Bills, 20-3 (NY)
1963—Bills, 45-14 (B)
Bills, 19-10 (NY)
1964—Bills, 34-24 (B)
Bills, 20-7 (NY)
1965—Bills, 33-21 (B)
Jets, 14-12 (NY)
1966—Bills, 33-23 (NY)
Bills, 14-3 (B)
1967—Bills, 20-17 (B)
Jets, 20-10 (NY)
1968—Bills, 37-35 (B)
Jets, 25-21 (NY)
1969—Jets, 33-19 (B)
Jets, 16-6 (NY)
1970—Bills, 34-31 (B)
Bills, 10-6 (NY)
1971—Jets, 28-17 (NY)
Jets, 20-7 (B)
1972—Jets, 41-24 (B)
Jets, 41-3 (NY)
1973—Bills, 9-7 (B)
Bills, 34-14 (NY)
1974—Bills, 16-12 (B)
Jets, 20-10 (NY)
1975—Bills, 42-14 (B)
Bills, 24-23 (NY)
1976—Jets, 17-14 (NY)
Jets, 19-14 (B)
1977—Jets, 24-19 (B)
Bills, 14-10 (NY)
1978—Jets, 21-20 (B)
Jets, 45-14 (NY)
1979—Jets, 46-31 (B)
Bills, 14-12 (NY)
1980—Bills, 20-10 (B)
Bills, 31-24 (NY)
1981—Bills, 31-0 (B)
Jets, 33-14 (NY)
**Bills, 31-27 (NY)
1983—Jets, 34-10 (B)
Bills, 24-17 (NY)
1984—Jets, 28-26 (B)
Jets, 21-17 (NY)
1985—Jets, 42-3 (NY)
Jets, 27-7 (B)
1986—Jets, 28-24 (B)

Jets, 14-13 (NY)
1987—Jets, 31-28 (B)
Bills, 17-14 (NY)
1988—Bills, 37-14 (NY)
Bills, 9-6 (B) OT
1989—Bills, 34-3 (B)
Bills, 37-0 (NY)
1990—Bills, 30-7 (NY)
Bills, 30-27 (B)
1991—Bills, 23-20 (NY)
Bills, 24-13 (B)
1992—Bills, 24-20 (NY)
Jets, 24-17 (B)
1993—Bills, 19-10 (NY)
Bills, 16-14 (B)
1994—Jets, 23-3 (B)
Jets, 22-17 (NY)
1995—Bills, 29-10 (B)
Bills, 28-26 (NY)
1996—Bills, 25-22 (NY)
Bills, 35-10 (B)
1997—Bills, 28-22 (NY)
Bills, 20-10 (B)
1998—Jets, 34-12 (NY)
Jets, 17-10 (B)
1999—Bills, 17-3 (B)
Jets, 17-7 (NY)
2000—Jets, 27-14 (NY)
Bills, 23-20 (B)
2001—Jets, 42-36 (B)
Bills, 14-9 (NY)
2002—Bills, 37-31 (B) OT
Jets, 31-13 (NY)
2003—Jets, 30-3 (NY)
Bills, 17-6 (B)
2004—Bills, 16-14 (NY)
Bills, 22-17 (B)
2005—Bills, 27-17 (B)
Jets, 30-26 (NY)
2006—Jets, 28-20 (B)
Bills, 31-13 (NY)
(RS Pts.—Bills 1,892, Jets 1,834)
(PS Pts.—Bills 31, Jets 27)
*Jets known as Titans prior to 1963
**AFC First-Round Playoff
BUFFALO vs. *OAKLAND
RS: Raiders lead series, 19-15
PS: Bills lead series, 2-0
1960—Bills, 38-9 (B)
Raiders, 20-7 (O)
1961—Raiders, 31-22 (B)
Bills, 26-21 (O)
1962—Bills, 14-6 (B)
Bills, 10-6 (O)
1963—Raiders, 35-17 (O)
Bills, 12-0 (B)
1964—Bills, 23-20 (B)
Raiders, 16-13 (O)
1965—Bills, 17-12 (B)
Bills, 17-14 (O)
1966—Bills, 31-10 (O)
1967—Raiders, 24-20 (B)
Raiders, 28-21 (O)
1968—Raiders, 48-6 (B)
Raiders, 13-10 (O)
1969—Raiders, 50-21 (O)
1972—Raiders, 28-16 (O)
1974—Bills, 21-20 (B)
1977—Raiders, 34-13 (O)
1980—Bills, 24-7 (B)

1983—Raiders, 27-24 (B)
1987—Raiders, 34-21 (LA)
1988—Bills, 37-21 (B)
1990—Bills, 38-24 (B)
   **Bills, 51-3 (B)
1991—Bills, 30-27 (LA) OT
1992—Raiders, 20-3 (LA)
1993—Raiders, 25-24 (B)
   ***Bills, 29-23 (B)
1998—Bills, 44-21 (B)
1999—Raiders, 20-14 (B)
2002—Raiders, 49-31 (B)
2004—Raiders, 13-10 (O)
2005—Raiders, 38-17 (O)
(RS Pts.—Raiders 771, Bills 692)
(PS Pts.—Bills 80, Raiders 26)
*Franchise in Los Angeles from 1982-1994
**AFC Championship
***AFC Divisional Playoff

BUFFALO vs. PHILADELPHIA
RS: Bills lead series, 5-5
1973—Bills, 27-26 (B)
1981—Eagles, 20-14 (B)
1984—Eagles, 27-17 (B)
1985—Eagles, 21-17 (P)
1987—Eagles, 17-7 (P)
1990—Bills, 30-23 (B)
1993—Bills, 10-7 (P)
1996—Bills, 24-17 (P)
1999—Bills, 26-0 (B)
2003—Eagles, 23-13 (B)
(RS Pts.—Bills 185, Eagles 181)

BUFFALO vs. PITTSBURGH
RS: Steelers lead series, 10-8
PS: Steelers lead series, 2-1
1970—Steelers, 23-10 (P)
1972—Steelers, 38-21 (B)
1974—*Steelers, 32-14 (P)
1975—Bills, 30-21 (P)
1978—Steelers, 28-17 (B)
1979—Steelers, 28-0 (P)
1980—Bills, 28-13 (B)
1982—Bills, 13-0 (B)
1985—Steelers, 30-24 (P)
1986—Bills, 16-12 (B)
1988—Bills, 36-28 (B)
1991—Bills, 52-34 (B)
1992—Bills, 28-20 (B)
   *Bills, 24-3 (P)
1993—Steelers, 23-0 (P)
1994—Steelers, 23-10 (P)
1995—*Steelers, 40-21 (P)
1996—Steelers, 24-6 (P)
1999—Bills, 24-21 (B)
2001—Steelers, 20-3 (B)
2004—Steelers, 29-24 (B)
(RS Pts.—Steelers 415, Bills 342)
(PS Pts.—Steelers 75, Bills 59)
*AFC Divisional Playoff

BUFFALO vs. *ST. LOUIS
RS: Bills lead series, 5-4
1970—Rams, 19-0 (B)
1974—Rams, 19-14 (LA)
1980—Bills, 10-7 (B) OT
1983—Rams, 41-17 (LA)
1989—Bills, 23-20 (B)
1992—Bills, 40-7 (B)
1995—Bills, 45-27 (StL)
1998—Rams, 34-33 (B)
2004—Bills, 37-17 (B)

(RS Pts.—Bills 219, Rams 191)
*Franchise in Los Angeles prior to 1995

BUFFALO vs. *SAN DIEGO
RS: Chargers lead series, 20-9-2
PS: Bills lead series, 2-1
1960—Chargers, 24-10 (B)
   Bills, 32-3 (LA)
1961—Chargers, 19-11 (B)
   Chargers, 28-10 (SD)
1962—Bills, 35-10 (B)
   Bills, 40-20 (SD)
1963—Chargers, 14-10 (SD)
   Chargers, 23-13 (B)
1964—Bills, 30-3 (B)
   Bills, 27-24 (SD)
   **Bills, 20-7 (B)
1965—Chargers, 34-3 (B)
   Tie, 20-20 (SD)
   **Bills, 23-0 (SD)
1966—Chargers, 27-7 (SD)
   Tie, 17-17 (B)
1967—Chargers, 37-17 (B)
1968—Chargers, 21-6 (B)
1969—Chargers, 45-6 (SD)
1971—Chargers, 20-3 (SD)
1973—Chargers, 34-7 (SD)
1976—Chargers, 34-13 (B)
1979—Chargers, 27-19 (SD)
1980—Bills, 26-24 (SD)
   ***Chargers, 20-14 (SD)
1981—Bills, 28-27 (SD)
1985—Chargers, 14-9 (B)
   Chargers, 40-7 (SD)
1998—Chargers, 16-14 (SD)
2000—Bills, 27-24 (B) OT
2001—Chargers, 27-24 (SD)
2002—Bills, 20-13 (B)
2005—Chargers, 48-10 (SD)
2006—Chargers, 24-21 (B)
(RS Pts.—Chargers 741, Bills 522)
(PS Pts.—Bills 57, Chargers 27)
*Franchise in Los Angeles prior to 1961
**AFL Championship
***AFC Divisional Playoff

BUFFALO vs. SAN FRANCISCO
RS: Bills lead series, 5-4
1972—Bills, 27-20 (B)
1980—Bills, 18-13 (SF)
1983—49ers, 23-10 (B)
1989—49ers, 21-10 (SF)
1992—Bills, 34-31 (SF)
1995—49ers, 27-17 (SF)
1998—Bills, 26-21 (B)
2001—49ers, 35-0 (SF)
2004—Bills, 41-7 (SF)
(RS Pts.—49ers 198, Bills 183)

BUFFALO vs. SEATTLE
RS: Seahawks lead series, 6-4
1977—Seahawks, 56-17 (S)
1984—Seahawks, 31-28 (S)
1988—Bills, 13-3 (S)
1989—Seahawks, 17-16 (S)
1995—Bills, 27-21 (B)
1996—Seahawks, 26-18 (S)
1999—Seahawks, 26-16 (S)
2000—Bills, 42-23 (S)
2001—Seahawks, 23-20 (B)
2004—Bills, 38-9 (S)
(RS Pts.—Bills 235, Seahawks 235)

BUFFALO vs. TAMPA BAY

RS: Buccaneers lead series, 6-2
1976—Bills, 14-9 (TB)
1978—Buccaneers, 31-10 (TB)
1982—Buccaneers, 24-23 (TB)
1986—Buccaneers, 34-28 (TB)
1988—Buccaneers, 10-5 (TB)
1991—Bills, 17-10 (TB)
2000—Buccaneers, 31-17 (TB)
2005—Buccaneers, 19-3 (TB)
(RS Pts.—Buccaneers 168, Bills 117)

BUFFALO vs. *TENNESSEE
RS: Titans lead series, 24-14
PS: Bills lead series, 2-1
1960—Bills, 25-24 (B)
   Oilers, 31-23 (H)
1961—Bills, 22-12 (H)
   Oilers, 28-16 (B)
1962—Oilers, 28-23 (B)
   Oilers, 17-14 (H)
1963—Oilers, 31-20 (B)
   Oilers, 28-14 (H)
1964—Bills, 48-17 (H)
   Bills, 24-10 (B)
1965—Oilers, 19-17 (B)
   Bills, 29-18 (H)
1966—Bills, 27-20 (B)
   Bills, 42-20 (H)
1967—Oilers, 20-3 (B)
   Oilers, 10-3 (H)
1968—Oilers, 30-7 (B)
   Oilers, 35-6 (H)
1969—Oilers, 17-3 (B)
   Oilers, 28-14 (H)
1971—Oilers, 20-14 (B)
1974—Oilers, 21-9 (B)
1976—Oilers, 13-3 (B)
1978—Oilers, 17-10 (H)
1983—Bills, 30-13 (B)
1985—Bills, 20-0 (B)
1986—Oilers, 16-7 (H)
1987—Bills, 34-30 (B)
1988—**Bills, 17-10 (B)
1989—Bills, 47-41 (H) OT
1990—Oilers, 27-24 (H)
1992—Oilers, 27-3 (H)
   ***Bills, 41-38 (B) OT
1993—Bills, 35-7 (B)
1994—Bills, 15-7 (H)
1995—Oilers, 28-17 (B)
1997—Oilers, 31-14 (T)
1999—***Titans, 22-16 (T)
2000—Bills, 16-13 (B)
2003—Titans, 28-26 (T)
2006—Titans, 30-29 (B)
(RS Pts.—Titans 812, Bills 733)
(PS Pts.—Bills 74, Titans 70)
*Franchise in Houston prior to 1997;
known as Oilers prior to 1999
**AFC Divisional Playoff
***AFC First-Round Playoff

BUFFALO vs. WASHINGTON
RS: Bills lead series, 6-4
PS: Redskins lead series, 1-0
1972—Bills, 24-17 (W)
1977—Redskins, 10-0 (B)
1981—Bills, 21-14 (B)
1984—Redskins, 41-14 (W)
1987—Redskins, 27-7 (B)
1990—Redskins, 29-14 (W)
1991—*Redskins, 37-24 (Minneapolis)

1993—Bills, 24-10 (B)
1996—Bills, 38-13 (B)
1999—Bills, 34-17 (W)
2003—Bills, 24-7 (B)
(RS Pts.—Bills 200, Redskins 185)
(PS Pts.—Redskins 37, Bills 24)
*Super Bowl XXVI

CAROLINA vs. ARIZONA
RS: Panthers lead series, 4-2;
See Arizona vs. Carolina
CAROLINA vs. ATLANTA
RS: Falcons lead series, 15-9;
See Atlanta vs. Carolina
CAROLINA vs. BALTIMORE
RS: Panthers lead series, 3-0;
See Baltimore vs. Carolina
CAROLINA vs. BUFFALO
RS: Bills lead series, 3-1;
See Buffalo vs. Carolina
CAROLINA vs. CHICAGO
RS: Bears lead series, 2-1
PS: Panthers lead series, 1-0
1995—Bears, 31-27 (Chi)
2002—Panthers, 24-14 (Car)
2005—Bears, 13-3 (Chi)
            *Panthers, 29-21 (Chi)
(RS Pts.—Bears 58, Panthers 54)
(PS Pts.—Panthers 29, Bears 21)
*NFC Divisional Playoff
CAROLINA vs. CINCINNATI
RS: Panthers lead series, 2-1
1999—Panthers, 27-3 (Car)
2002—Panthers, 52-31 (Car)
2006—Bengals, 17-14 (Cin)
(RS Pts.—Panthers 93, Bengals 51)
CAROLINA vs. CLEVELAND
RS: Panthers lead series, 3-0
1999—Panthers, 31-17 (Cle)
2002—Panthers, 13-6 (Cle)
2006—Panthers, 20-12 (Car)
(RS Pts.—Panthers 64, Browns 35)
CAROLINA vs. DALLAS
RS: Cowboys lead series, 6-1
PS: Panthers lead series, 2-0
1996—*Panthers, 26-17 (C)
1997—Panthers, 23-13 (D)
1998—Cowboys, 27-20 (D)
2000—Cowboys, 16-13 (C) OT
2002—Cowboys, 14-13 (D)
2003—Cowboys, 24-20 (D)
            **Panthers, 29-10 (C)
2005—Cowboys, 24-20 (C)
2006—Cowboys, 35-14 (C)
(RS Pts.—Cowboys 153, Panthers 123)
(PS Pts.—Panthers 55, Cowboys 27)
*NFC Divisional Playoff
*NFC First-Round Playoff
CAROLINA vs. DENVER
RS: Broncos lead series, 2-0
1997—Broncos, 34-0 (D)
2004—Broncos, 20-17 (D)
(RS Pts.—Broncos 54, Panthers 17)
CAROLINA vs. DETROIT
RS: Panthers lead series, 3-1
1999—Lions, 24-9 (C)
2002—Panthers, 31-7 (C)
2003—Panthers, 20-14 (C)
2005—Panthers, 21-20 (D)
(RS Pts.—Panthers 81, Lions 65)

CAROLINA vs. GREEN BAY
RS: Packers lead series, 5-3
PS: Packers lead series, 1-0
1996—*Packers, 30-13 (GB)
1997—Packers, 31-10 (C)
1998—Packers, 37-30 (C)
1999—Panthers, 33-31 (GB)
2000—Panthers, 31-14 (C)
2001—Packers, 28-7 (C)
2002—Packers, 17-14 (GB)
2004—Packers, 24-14 (C)
2005—Panthers, 32-29 (C)
(RS Pts.—Packers 211, Panthers 171)
(PS Pts.—Packers 30, Panthers 13)
*NFC Championship
CAROLINA vs. HOUSTON
RS: Texans lead series, 1-0
2003—Texans, 14-10 (H)
(RS Pts.—Texans 14, Panthers 10)
CAROLINA vs. INDIANAPOLIS
RS: Panthers lead series, 3-0
1995—Panthers, 13-10 (C)
1998—Panthers, 27-19 (I)
2003—Panthers, 23-20 (I) OT
(RS Pts.—Panthers 63, Colts 49)
CAROLINA vs. JACKSONVILLE
RS: Jaguars lead series, 2-1
1996—Jaguars, 24-14 (J)
1999—Jaguars, 22-20 (C)
2003—Panthers, 24-23 (C)
(RS Pts.—Jaguars 69, Panthers 58)
CAROLINA vs. KANSAS CITY
RS: Chiefs lead series, 2-1
1997—Chiefs, 35-14 (C)
2000—Chiefs, 15-14 (KC)
2004—Panthers, 28-17 (KC)
(RS Pts.—Chiefs 67, Panthers 56)
CAROLINA vs. MIAMI
RS: Dolphins lead series, 3-0
1998—Dolphins, 13-9 (C)
2001—Dolphins, 23-6 (M)
2005—Dolphins, 27-24 (M)
(RS Pts.—Dolphins 63, Panthers 39)
CAROLINA vs. MINNESOTA
RS: Vikings lead series, 4-3
1996—Vikings, 14-12 (M)
1997—Vikings, 21-14 (M)
2000—Vikings, 31-17 (M)
2001—Panthers, 24-13 (M)
2002—Panthers, 21-14 (M)
2005—Panthers, 38-13 (C)
2006—Vikings, 16-13 (M) OT
(RS Pts.—Panthers 139, Vikings 122)
CAROLINA vs. NEW ENGLAND
RS: Panthers lead series, 2-1
PS: Patriots lead series, 1-0
1995—Panthers, 20-17 (NE) OT
2001—Patriots, 38-6 (C)
2003—*Patriots, 32-29 (Houston)
2005—Panthers, 27-17 (C)
(RS Pts.—Patriots 72, Panthers 53)
(PS Pts.—Patriots 32, Panthers 29)
*Super Bowl XXXVIII
CAROLINA vs. NEW ORLEANS
RS: Panthers lead series, 13-11
1995—Panthers, 20-3 (C)
            Saints, 34-26 (NO)
1996—Panthers, 22-20 (NO)
            Panthers, 19-7 (C)
1997—Panthers, 13-0 (NO)

            Saints, 16-13 (C)
1998—Saints, 19-14 (NO)
            Panthers, 31-17 (C)
1999—Saints, 19-10 (NO)
            Panthers, 45-13 (C)
2000—Saints, 24-6 (NO)
            Saints, 20-10 (C)
2001—Saints, 27-25 (C)
            Saints, 27-23 (NO)
2002—Saints, 34-24 (C)
            Panthers, 10-6 (NO)
2003—Panthers, 19-13 (C)
            Panthers, 23-20 (NO) OT
2004—Panthers, 32-21 (NO)
            Saints, 21-18 (C)
2005—Saints, 23-20 (C)
            Panthers, 27-10 (Baton Rouge)
2006—Panthers, 21-18 (C)
            Panthers, 31-21 (NO)
(RS Pts.—Panthers 502, Saints 433)
CAROLINA vs. N.Y. GIANTS
RS: Panthers lead series, 2-1
PS: Panthers lead series, 1-0
1996—Panthers, 27-17 (C)
2003—Panthers, 37-24 (NY)
2005—*Panthers, 23-0 (NY)
2006—Giants, 27-13 (C)
(RS Pts.—Panthers 77, Giants 68)
(PS Pts.—Panthers 23, Giants 0)
*NFC First-Round Playoff
CAROLINA vs. N.Y. JETS
RS: Series tied, 2-2
1995—Panthers, 26-15 (C)
1998—Jets, 48-21 (NY)
2001—Jets, 13-12 (C)
2005—Panthers, 30-3 (C)
(RS Pts.—Panthers 89, Jets 79)
CAROLINA vs. OAKLAND
RS: Raiders lead series, 2-1
1997—Panthers, 38-14 (C)
2000—Raiders, 52-9 (O)
2004—Raiders, 27-24 (C)
(RS Pts.— Raiders 93, Panthers 71)
CAROLINA vs. PHILADELPHIA
RS: Eagles lead series, 4-1
PS: Panthers lead series, 1-0
1996—Eagles, 20-9 (P)
1999—Panthers, 33-7 (C)
2003—Eagles, 25-16 (C)
            *Panthers, 14-3 (P)
2004—Eagles, 30-8 (P)
2006—Eagles, 27-24 (P)
(RS Pts.—Eagles 109, Panthers 90)
(PS Pts.—Panthers 14, Eagles 3)
*NFC Championship
CAROLINA vs. PITTSBURGH
RS: Steelers lead series, 3-1
1996—Panthers, 18-14 (C)
1999—Steelers, 30-20 (P)
2002—Steelers, 30-14 (P)
2006—Steelers, 37-3 (C)
(RS Pts.—Steelers 111, Panthers 55)
CAROLINA vs. ST. LOUIS
RS: Panthers lead series, 9-7
PS: Panthers lead series, 1-0
1995—Rams, 31-10 (C)
            Rams, 28-17 (StL)
1996—Panthers, 45-13 (C)
            Panthers, 20-10 (StL)
1997—Panthers, 16-10 (StL)

Rams, 30-18 (C)
1998—Panthers, 24-20 (StL)
Panthers, 20-13 (C)
1999—Rams, 35-10 (StL)
Rams, 34-21 (C)
2000—Panthers, 27-24 (StL)
Panthers, 16-3 (C)
2001—Rams, 48-14 (StL)
Rams, 38-32 (C)
2003—*Panthers, 29-23 (StL) 2OT
2004—Panthers, 20-7 (C)
2006—Panthers, 15-0 (C)
(RS Pts.—Rams 344, Panthers 325)
(PS Pts.—Panthers 29, Rams 23)
*NFC Divisional Playoff

CAROLINA vs. SAN DIEGO
RS: Panthers lead series, 2-1
1997—Panthers, 26-7 (SD)
2000—Panthers, 30-22 (C)
2004—Chargers, 17-6 (C)
(RS Pts.—Panthers 62, Chargers 46)

CAROLINA vs. SAN FRANCISCO
RS: Panthers lead series, 8-7
1995—Panthers, 13-7 (SF)
49ers, 31-10 (C)
1996—Panthers, 23-7 (C)
Panthers, 30-24 (SF)
1997—49ers, 34-21 (C)
49ers, 27-19 (SF)
1998—49ers, 25-23 (SF)
49ers, 31-28 (C) OT
1999—Panthers, 31-29 (SF)
Panthers, 41-24 (C)
2000—Panthers, 38-22 (SF)
Panthers, 34-16 (C)
2001—49ers, 24-14 (SF)
49ers, 25-22 (C) OT
2004—Panthers, 37-27 (SF)
(RS Pts.—Panthers 384, 49ers 353)

CAROLINA vs. SEATTLE
RS: Series tied, 1-1
PS: Seahawks lead series, 1-0
2000—Panthers, 26-3 (C)
2004—Seahawks, 23-17 (S)
2005—*Seahawks, 34-14 (S)
(RS Pts.—Panthers 43, Seahawks 26)
(PS Pts.—Seahawks 34, Panthers 14)
*NFC Championship

CAROLINA vs. TAMPA BAY
RS: Panthers lead series, 8-5
1995—Buccaneers, 20-13 (C)
1996—Panthers, 24-0 (C)
1998—Buccaneers, 16-13 (TB)
2002—Panthers, 12-9 (C)
Buccaneers, 23-10 (TB)
2003—Panthers, 12-9 (TB) OT
Panthers, 27-24 (C)
2004—Panthers, 21-14 (C)
Panthers, 37-20 (TB)
2005—Panthers, 34-14 (TB)
Buccaneers, 20-10 (C)
2006—Panthers, 26-24 (TB)
Panthers, 24-10 (C)
(RS Pts.—Panthers 260, Buccaneers 206)

CAROLINA vs. *TENNESSEE
RS: Series tied, 1-1
1996—Panthers, 31-6 (H)
2003—Titans, 37-17 (C)
(RS Pts.—Panthers 48, Titans 43)
*Franchise in Houston prior to 1997;

known as Oilers prior to 1999

CAROLINA vs. WASHINGTON
RS: Redskins lead series, 7-1
1995—Redskins, 20-17 (W)
1997—Redskins, 24-10 (C)
1998—Redskins, 28-25 (C)
1999—Redskins, 38-36 (W)
2000—Redskins, 20-17 (W)
2001—Redskins, 17-14 (W) OT
2003—Panthers, 20-17 (C)
2006—Redskins, 17-13 (W)
(RS Pts.—Redskins 181, Panthers 152)

CHICAGO vs. ARIZONA
RS: Bears lead series, 55-26-6;
See Arizona vs. Chicago

CHICAGO vs. ATLANTA
RS: Bears lead series, 12-10;
See Atlanta vs. Chicago

CHICAGO vs. BALTIMORE
RS: Bears lead series, 2-1;
See Baltimore vs. Chicago

CHICAGO vs. BUFFALO
RS: Bears lead series, 6-4;
See Buffalo vs. Chicago

CHICAGO vs. CAROLINA
RS: Bears lead series, 2-1
PS: Panthers lead series, 1-0;
See Carolina vs. Chicago

CHICAGO vs. CINCINNATI
RS: Bengals lead series, 5-3
1972—Bengals, 13-3 (Chi)
1980—Bengals, 17-14 (Chi) OT
1986—Bears, 44-7 (Cin)
1989—Bears, 17-14 (Chi)
1992—Bengals, 31-28 (Chi) OT
1995—Bengals, 16-10 (Cin)
2001—Bears, 24-0 (Cin)
2005—Bengals, 24-7 (Chi)
(RS Pts.—Bears 147, Bengals 122)

CHICAGO vs. CLEVELAND
RS: Browns lead series, 9-4
1951—Browns, 42-21 (Cle)
1954—Browns, 39-10 (Chi)
1960—Browns, 42-0 (Cle)
1961—Bears, 17-14 (Chi)
1967—Browns, 24-0 (Cle)
1969—Browns, 28-24 (Chi)
1972—Bears, 17-0 (Cle)
1980—Browns, 27-21 (Cle)
1986—Bears, 41-31 (Chi)
1989—Browns, 27-7 (Cle)
1992—Browns, 27-14 (Cle)
2001—Bears, 27-21 (Chi) OT
2005—Browns, 20-10 (Cle)
(RS Pts.—Browns 342, Bears 209)

CHICAGO vs. DALLAS
RS: Cowboys lead series, 10-8
PS: Cowboys lead series, 2-0
1960—Bears, 17-7 (C)
1962—Bears, 34-33 (D)
1964—Cowboys, 24-10 (C)
1968—Cowboys, 34-3 (C)
1971—Bears, 23-19 (C)
1973—Cowboys, 20-17 (C)
1976—Cowboys, 31-21 (D)
1977—*Cowboys, 37-7 (D)
1979—Cowboys, 24-20 (D)
1981—Cowboys, 10-9 (D)
1984—Cowboys, 23-14 (C)

1985—Bears, 44-0 (D)
1986—Bears, 24-10 (D)
1988—Bears, 17-7 (C)
1991–**Cowboys, 17-13 (C)
1992—Cowboys, 27-14 (D)
1996—Bears, 22-6 (C)
1997—Cowboys, 27-3 (D)
1998—Bears, 13-12 (C)
2004—Cowboys, 21-7 (D)
(RS Pts.—Cowboys 335, Bears 312)
(PS Pts.—Cowboys 54, Bears 20)
*NFC Divisional Playoff
**NFC First-Round Playoff

CHICAGO vs. DENVER
RS: Series tied, 6-6
1971—Broncos, 6-3 (D)
1973—Bears, 33-14 (D)
1976—Broncos, 28-14 (C)
1978—Broncos, 16-7 (D)
1981—Bears, 35-24 (D)
1983—Bears, 31-14 (C)
1984—Bears, 27-0 (C)
1987—Broncos, 31-29 (D)
1990—Bears, 16-13 (D) OT
1993—Broncos, 13-3 (C)
1996—Broncos, 17-12 (D)
2003—Bears, 19-10 (D)
(RS Pts.—Bears 229, Broncos 186)

CHICAGO vs. *DETROIT
RS: Bears lead series, 87-62-5
1930—Spartans, 7-6 (P)
Bears, 14-6 (C)
1931—Bears, 9-6 (C)
Spartans, 3-0 (P)
1932—Tie, 13-13 (C)
Tie, 7-7 (P)
Bears, 9-0 (C)
1933—Bears, 17-14 (C)
Bears, 17-7 (P)
1934—Bears, 19-16 (D)
Bears, 10-7 (C)
1935—Tie, 20-20 (C)
Lions, 14-2 (D)
1936—Bears, 12-10 (C)
Lions, 13-7 (D)
1937—Bears, 28-20 (C)
Bears, 13-0 (D)
1938—Lions, 13-7 (C)
Lions, 14-7 (D)
1939—Lions, 10-0 (C)
Bears, 23-13 (D)
1940—Bears, 7-0 (C)
Lions, 17-14 (D)
1941—Bears, 49-0 (C)
Bears, 24-7 (D)
1942—Bears, 16-0 (C)
Bears, 42-0 (D)
1943—Bears, 27-21 (D)
Bears, 35-14 (C)
1944—Tie, 21-21 (C)
Lions, 41-21 (D)
1945—Lions, 16-10 (C)
Lions, 35-28 (C)
1946—Bears, 42-6 (C)
Bears, 45-24 (D)
1947—Bears, 33-24 (C)
Bears, 34-14 (C)
1948—Bears, 28-0 (C)
Bears, 42-14 (D)
1949—Bears, 27-24 (C)

Bears, 28-7 (D)
1950—Bears, 35-21 (D)
Bears, 6-3 (C)
1951—Bears, 28-23 (D)
Lions, 41-28 (C)
1952—Lions, 24-23 (C)
Lions, 45-21 (D)
1953—Lions, 20-16 (C)
Lions, 13-7 (D)
1954—Lions, 48-23 (D)
Bears, 28-24 (C)
1955—Bears, 24-14 (D)
Bears, 21-20 (C)
1956—Lions, 42-10 (D)
Bears, 38-21 (C)
1957—Bears, 27-7 (D)
Lions, 21-13 (C)
1958—Bears, 20-7 (D)
Bears, 21-16 (C)
1959—Bears, 24-14 (D)
Bears, 25-14 (C)
1960—Bears, 28-7 (C)
Lions, 36-0 (D)
1961—Bears, 31-17 (D)
Lions, 16-15 (C)
1962—Lions, 11-3 (D)
Bears, 3-0 (C)
1963—Bears, 37-21 (D)
Bears, 24-14 (C)
1964—Lions, 10-0 (C)
Bears, 27-24 (D)
1965—Bears, 38-10 (C)
Bears, 17-10 (D)
1966—Lions, 14-3 (D)
Tie, 10-10 (C)
1967—Bears, 14-3 (C)
Bears, 27-13 (D)
1968—Lions, 42-0 (D)
Lions, 28-10 (C)
1969—Lions, 13-7 (D)
Lions, 20-3 (C)
1970—Lions, 28-14 (D)
Lions, 16-10 (C)
1971—Bears, 28-23 (D)
Lions, 28-3 (C)
1972—Lions, 38-24 (C)
Lions, 14-0 (D)
1973—Lions, 30-7 (C)
Lions, 40-7 (D)
1974—Bears, 17-9 (C)
Lions, 34-17 (D)
1975—Lions, 27-7 (D)
Bears, 25-21 (C)
1976—Bears, 10-3 (C)
Lions, 14-10 (D)
1977—Bears, 30-20 (C)
Bears, 31-14 (D)
1978—Bears, 19-0 (D)
Lions, 21-17 (C)
1979—Bears, 35-7 (C)
Lions, 20-0 (D)
1980—Bears, 24-7 (C)
Bears, 23-17 (D) OT
1981—Lions, 48-17 (D)
Lions, 23-7 (C)
1982—Lions, 17-10 (D)
Bears, 20-17 (C)
1983—Lions, 31-17 (D)
Lions, 38-17 (C)
1984—Bears, 16-14 (C)

Bears, 30-13 (D)
1985—Bears, 24-3 (C)
Bears, 37-17 (D)
1986—Bears, 13-7 (C)
Bears, 16-13 (D)
1987—Bears, 30-10 (C)
1988—Bears, 24-7 (D)
Bears, 13-12 (C)
1989—Bears, 47-27 (D)
Lions, 27-17 (C)
1990—Bears, 23-17 (C) OT
Lions, 38-21 (D)
1991—Bears, 20-10 (C)
Lions, 16-6 (D)
1992—Bears, 27-24 (C)
Lions, 16-3 (D)
1993—Bears, 10-6 (D)
Lions, 20-14 (C)
1994—Lions, 21-16 (D)
Bears, 20-10 (C)
1995—Lions, 24-17 (C)
Lions, 27-7 (D)
1996—Lions, 35-16 (D)
Bears, 31-14 (C)
1997—Lions, 32-7 (C)
Lions, 55-20 (D)
1998—Bears, 31-27 (C)
Lions, 26-3 (D)
1999—Lions, 21-17 (D)
Bears, 28-10 (C)
2000—Lions, 21-14 (C)
Bears, 23-20 (D)
2001—Bears, 13-10 (C)
Bears, 24-0 (D)
2002—Lions, 23-20 (D) OT
Bears, 20-17 (C) OT
2003—Bears, 24-16 (C)
Lions, 12-10 (D)
2004—Lions, 20-16 (C)
Lions, 19-13 (D)
2005—Bears, 38-6 (C)
Bears, 19-13 (D) OT
2006—Bears, 34-7 (C)
Bears, 26-21 (D)
(RS Pts.—Bears 2,893, Lions 2,663)
*Franchise in Portsmouth prior to 1934
and known as the Spartans
CHICAGO vs. GREEN BAY
RS: Bears lead series, 87-79-6
PS: Bears lead series, 1-0
1921—Staleys, 20-0 (C)
1923—Bears, 3-0 (GB)
1924—Bears, 3-0 (C)
1925—Packers, 14-10 (GB)
Bears, 21-0 (C)
1926—Tie, 6-6 (GB)
Bears, 19-13 (C)
Tie, 3-3 (C)
1927—Bears, 7-6 (GB)
Bears, 14-6 (C)
1928—Tie, 12-12 (GB)
Packers, 16-6 (C)
Packers, 6-0 (C)
1929—Packers, 23-0 (GB)
Packers, 14-0 (C)
Packers, 25-0 (C)
1930—Packers, 7-0 (GB)
Packers, 13-12 (C)
Bears, 21-0 (C)
1931—Packers, 7-0 (GB)

Packers, 6-2 (C)
Bears, 7-6 (C)
1932—Tie, 0-0 (GB)
Packers, 2-0 (C)
Bears, 9-0 (C)
1933—Bears, 14-7 (GB)
Bears, 10-7 (C)
Bears, 7-6 (C)
1934—Bears, 24-10 (GB)
Bears, 27-14 (C)
1935—Packers, 7-0 (GB)
Packers, 17-14 (C)
1936—Bears, 30-3 (GB)
Packers, 21-10 (C)
1937—Bears, 14-2 (GB)
Packers, 24-14 (C)
1938—Bears, 2-0 (GB)
Packers, 24-17 (C)
1939—Packers, 21-16 (GB)
Bears, 30-27 (C)
1940—Bears, 41-10 (GB)
Bears, 14-7 (C)
1941—Bears, 25-17 (GB)
Packers, 16-14 (C)
**Bears, 33-14 (C)
1942—Bears, 44-28 (GB)
Bears, 38-7 (C)
1943—Tie, 21-21 (GB)
Bears, 21-7 (C)
1944—Packers, 42-28 (GB)
Bears, 21-0 (C)
1945—Packers, 31-21 (GB)
Bears, 28-24 (C)
1946—Bears, 30-7 (GB)
Bears, 10-7 (C)
1947—Packers, 29-20 (GB)
Bears, 20-17 (C)
1948—Bears, 45-7 (GB)
Bears, 7-6 (C)
1949—Bears, 17-0 (GB)
Bears, 24-3 (C)
1950—Packers, 31-21 (GB)
Bears, 28-14 (C)
1951—Bears, 31-20 (GB)
Bears, 24-13 (C)
1952—Bears, 24-14 (GB)
Packers, 41-28 (C)
1953—Bears, 17-13 (GB)
Tie, 21-21 (C)
1954—Bears, 10-3 (GB)
Bears, 28-23 (C)
1955—Packers, 24-3 (GB)
Bears, 52-31 (C)
1956—Bears, 37-21 (GB)
Bears, 38-14 (C)
1957—Packers, 21-17 (GB)
Bears, 21-14 (C)
1958—Bears, 34-20 (GB)
Bears, 24-10 (C)
1959—Packers, 9-6 (GB)
Bears, 28-17 (C)
1960—Bears, 17-14 (GB)
Packers, 41-13 (C)
1961—Packers, 24-0 (GB)
Packers, 31-28 (C)
1962—Packers, 49-0 (GB)
Packers, 38-7 (C)
1963—Bears, 10-3 (GB)
Bears, 26-7 (C)
1964—Packers, 23-12 (GB)

Packers, 17-3 (C)
1965—Packers, 23-14 (GB)
    Bears, 31-10 (C)
1966—Packers, 17-0 (C)
    Packers, 13-6 (GB)
1967—Packers, 13-10 (GB)
    Packers, 17-13 (C)
1968—Bears, 13-10 (GB)
    Packers, 28-27 (C)
1969—Packers, 17-0 (C)
    Packers, 21-3 (C)
1970—Packers, 20-19 (GB)
    Bears, 35-17 (C)
1971—Packers, 17-14 (C)
    Packers, 31-10 (GB)
1972—Packers, 20-17 (GB)
    Packers, 23-17 (C)
1973—Bears, 31-17 (GB)
    Packers, 21-0 (C)
1974—Bears, 10-9 (C)
    Packers, 20-3 (Mil)
1975—Bears, 27-14 (C)
    Packers, 28-7 (GB)
1976—Bears, 24-13 (C)
    Bears, 16-10 (GB)
1977—Bears, 26-0 (GB)
    Bears, 21-10 (C)
1978—Packers, 24-14 (GB)
    Bears, 14-0 (C)
1979—Bears, 6-3 (C)
    Bears, 15-14 (GB)
1980—Packers, 12-6 (GB) OT
    Bears, 61-7 (C)
1981—Packers, 16-9 (C)
    Packers, 21-17 (GB)
1983—Packers, 31-28 (GB)
    Bears, 23-21 (C)
1984—Bears, 9-7 (GB)
    Packers, 20-14 (C)
1985—Bears, 23-7 (C)
    Bears, 16-10 (GB)
1986—Bears, 25-12 (GB)
    Bears, 12-10 (C)
1987—Bears, 26-24 (GB)
    Bears, 23-10 (C)
1988—Bears, 24-6 (GB)
    Bears, 16-0 (C)
1989—Packers, 14-13 (GB)
    Packers, 40-28 (C)
1990—Bears, 31-13 (GB)
    Bears, 27-13 (C)
1991—Bears, 10-0 (GB)
    Bears, 27-13 (C)
1992—Bears, 30-10 (GB)
    Packers, 17-3 (C)
1993—Packers, 17-3 (GB)
    Bears, 30-17 (C)
1994—Packers, 33-6 (C)
    Packers, 40-3 (GB)
1995—Packers, 27-24 (C)
    Packers, 35-28 (GB)
1996—Packers, 37-6 (C)
    Packers, 28-17 (GB)
1997—Packers, 38-24 (GB)
    Packers, 24-23 (C)
1998—Packers, 26-20 (GB)
    Packers, 16-13 (C)
1999—Bears, 14-13 (GB)
    Packers, 35-19 (C)
2000—Bears, 27-24 (GB)

Packers, 28-6 (C)
2001—Packers, 20-12 (C)
    Packers, 17-7 (GB)
2002—Packers, 34-21 (C)
    Packers, 30-20 (GB)
2003—Packers, 38-23 (C)
    Packers, 34-21 (GB)
2004—Bears, 21-10 (GB)
    Packers, 31-14 (C)
2005—Bears, 19-7 (C)
    Bears, 24-17 (GB)
2006—Bears, 26-0 (GB)
    Packers, 26-7 (C)
(RS Pts.—Bears 2,923, Packers 2,798)
(PS Pts.—Bears 33, Packers 14)
*Bears known as Staleys prior to 1922
**Division Playoff
CHICAGO vs. HOUSTON
RS: Texans lead series, 1-0
2004—Texans, 24-5 (C)
(RS Pts.—Texans 24, Bears 5)
CHICAGO vs. *INDIANAPOLIS
RS: Colts lead series, 22-17
PS: Colts lead seris, 1-0
1953—Colts, 13-9 (B)
    Colts, 16-14 (C)
1954—Bears, 28-9 (C)
    Bears, 28-13 (B)
1955—Colts, 23-17 (B)
    Bears, 38-10 (C)
1956—Colts, 28-21 (B)
    Bears, 58-27 (C)
1957—Colts, 21-10 (B)
    Colts, 29-14 (C)
1958—Colts, 51-38 (B)
    Colts, 17-0 (C)
1959—Bears, 26-21 (B)
    Colts, 21-7 (C)
1960—Colts, 42-7 (B)
    Colts, 24-20 (C)
1961—Bears, 24-10 (C)
    Bears, 21-20 (B)
1962—Bears, 35-15 (C)
    Bears, 57-0 (B)
1963—Bears, 10-3 (C)
    Bears, 17-7 (B)
1964—Colts, 52-0 (B)
    Colts, 40-24 (C)
1965—Colts, 26-21 (C)
    Bears, 13-0 (B)
1966—Bears, 27-17 (C)
    Colts, 21-16 (B)
1967—Colts, 24-3 (C)
1968—Colts, 28-7 (B)
1969—Colts, 24-21 (C)
1970—Colts, 21-20 (B)
1975—Colts, 35-7 (C)
1983—Colts, 22-19 (B) OT
1985—Bears, 17-10 (C)
1988—Bears, 17-13 (I)
1991—Bears, 31-17 (I)
2000—Bears, 27-24 (C)
2004—Colts, 41-10 (C)
2006—**Colts, 29-17 (South Florida)
(RS Pts.—Colts 835, Bears 779)
(PS: Pts.—Colts 29, Bears 17)
*Franchise in Baltimore prior to 1984
**Super Bowl XLI
CHICAGO vs. JACKSONVILLE
RS: Series tied, 2-2

1995—Bears, 30-27 (J)
1998—Jaguars, 24-23 (C)
2001—Bears, 33-13 (C)
2004—Jaguars, 22-3 (J)
(RS Pts.—Bears 89, Jaguars 86)
CHICAGO vs. KANSAS CITY
RS: Bears lead series, 5-4
1973—Chiefs, 19-7 (KC)
1977—Bears, 28-27 (C)
1981—Bears, 16-13 (KC) OT
1987—Bears, 31-28 (C)
1990—Chiefs, 21-10 (C)
1993—Bears, 19-17 (KC)
1996—Chiefs, 14-10 (KC)
1999—Bears, 20-17 (C)
2003—Chiefs, 31-3 (KC)
(RS Pts.—Chiefs 187, Bears 144)
CHICAGO vs. MIAMI
RS: Dolphins lead series, 7-3
1971—Dolphins, 34-3 (M)
1975—Dolphins, 46-13 (C)
1979—Dolphins, 31-16 (M)
1985—Dolphins, 38-24 (M)
1988—Bears, 34-7 (C)
1991—Dolphins, 16-13 (C) OT
1994—Bears, 17-14 (M)
1997—Bears, 36-33 (M) OT
2002—Dolphins, 27-9 (M)
2006—Dolphins, 31-13 (C)
(RS Pts.—Dolphins 277, Bears 178)
CHICAGO vs. MINNESOTA
RS: Vikings lead series, 48-41-2
PS: Bears lead series, 1-0
1961—Vikings, 37-13 (M)
    Bears, 52-35 (C)
1962—Bears, 13-0 (C)
    Bears, 31-30 (C)
1963—Bears, 28-7 (C)
    Tie, 17-17 (C)
1964—Bears, 34-28 (M)
    Vikings, 41-14 (C)
1965—Bears, 45-37 (M)
    Vikings, 24-17 (C)
1966—Bears, 13-10 (M)
    Bears, 41-28 (C)
1967—Bears, 17-7 (M)
    Tie, 10-10 (C)
1968—Bears, 27-17 (M)
    Bears, 26-24 (C)
1969—Vikings, 31-0 (C)
    Vikings, 31-14 (M)
1970—Vikings, 24-0 (C)
    Vikings, 16-13 (M)
1971—Bears, 20-17 (M)
    Vikings, 27-10 (C)
1972—Bears, 13-10 (C)
    Vikings, 23-10 (M)
1973—Vikings, 22-13 (C)
    Vikings, 31-13 (M)
1974—Vikings, 11-7 (M)
    Vikings, 17-0 (C)
1975—Vikings, 28-3 (M)
    Vikings, 13-9 (C)
1976—Vikings, 20-19 (M)
    Bears, 14-13 (C)
1977—Vikings, 22-16 (M) OT
    Bears, 10-7 (C)
1978—Vikings, 24-20 (C)
    Vikings, 17-14 (M)
1979—Bears, 26-7 (C)

Vikings, 30-27 (M)
1980—Vikings, 34-14 (C)
Vikings, 13-7 (M)
1981—Vikings, 24-21 (M)
Bears, 10-9 (C)
1982—Vikings, 35-7 (M)
1983—Vikings, 23-14 (C)
Bears, 19-13 (M)
1984—Bears, 16-7 (C)
Bears, 34-3 (M)
1985—Bears, 33-24 (M)
Bears, 27-9 (C)
1986—Bears, 23-0 (C)
Vikings, 23-7 (M)
1987—Bears, 27-7 (C)
Bears, 30-24 (M)
1988—Vikings, 31-7 (C)
Vikings, 28-27 (M)
1989—Bears, 38-7 (C)
Vikings, 27-16 (M)
1990—Bears, 19-16 (C)
Vikings, 41-13 (M)
1991—Bears, 10-6 (C)
Bears, 34-17 (M)
1992—Vikings, 21-20 (M)
Vikings, 38-10 (C)
1993—Vikings, 10-7 (M)
Vikings, 19-12 (C)
1994—Bears, 42-14 (C)
Vikings, 33-27 (M) OT
*Bears, 35-18 (M)
1995—Bears, 31-14 (C)
Bears, 14-6 (M)
1996—Vikings, 20-14 (C)
Bears, 15-13 (M)
1997—Vikings, 27-24 (C)
Vikings, 29-22 (M)
1998—Vikings, 31-28 (C)
Vikings, 48-22 (M)
1999—Bears, 24-22 (M)
Vikings, 27-24 (C) OT
2000—Vikings, 30-27 (M)
Vikings, 28-16 (C)
2001—Bears, 17-10 (C)
Bears, 13-6 (M)
2002—Bears, 27-23 (C)
Vikings, 25-7 (M)
2003—Vikings, 24-13 (M)
Bears, 13-10 (C)
2004—Vikings, 27-22 (M)
Bears, 24-14 (C)
2005—Bears, 28-3 (C)
Vikings, 34-10 (M)
2006—Bears, 19-16 (M)
Bears, 23-13 (C)
(RS Pts.—Vikings 1,877, Bears 1,689)
(PS Pts.—Bears 35, Vikings 18)
*NFC First-Round Playoff
CHICAGO vs. NEW ENGLAND
RS: Patriots lead series, 7-3
PS: Bears lead series, 1-0
1973—Patriots, 13-10 (C)
1979—Patriots, 27-7 (C)
1982—Bears, 26-13 (C)
1985—Bears, 20-7 (C)
*Bears, 46-10 (New Orleans)
1988—Patriots, 30-7 (NE)
1994—Patriots, 13-3 (C)
1997—Patriots, 31-3 (NE)
2000—Bears, 24-17 (C)

2002—Patriots, 33-30 (C)
2006—Patriots, 17-13 (NE)
(RS Pts.—Patriots 201, Bears 143)
(PS Pts.—Bears 46, Patriots 10)
*Super Bowl XX
CHICAGO vs. NEW ORLEANS
RS: Series tied, 11-11
PS: Bears lead series, 2-0
1968—Bears, 23-17 (NO)
1970—Bears, 24-3 (NO)
1971—Bears, 35-14 (C)
1973—Saints, 21-16 (NO)
1974—Bears, 24-10 (C)
1975—Bears, 42-17 (NO)
1977—Saints, 42-24 (C)
1980—Bears, 22-3 (C)
1982—Saints, 10-0 (C)
1983—Saints, 34-31 (NO) OT
1984—Bears, 20-7 (C)
1987—Saints, 19-17 (C)
1990—*Bears, 16-6 (C)
1991—Bears, 20-17 (NO)
1992—Saints, 28-6 (NO)
1994—Bears, 17-7 (C)
1996—Saints, 27-24 (NO)
1997—Saints, 20-17 (C)
1999—Bears, 14-10 (C)
2000—Saints, 31-10 (C)
2002—Saints, 29-23 (C)
2003—Saints, 20-13 (NO)
2005—Bears, 20-17 (Baton Rouge)
2006—**Bears, 39-14 (C)
(RS Pts.—Bears 442, Saints 403)
(PS Pts.—Bears 55, Saints 20)
*NFC First-Round Playoff
**NFC Championship
CHICAGO vs. N.Y. GIANTS
RS: Bears lead series, 27-17-2
PS: Bears lead series, 5-3
1925—Bears, 19-7 (NY)
Giants, 9-0 (C)
1926—Bears, 7-0 (C)
1927—Giants, 13-7 (NY)
1928—Bears, 13-0 (C)
1929—Giants, 26-14 (C)
Giants, 34-0 (NY)
Giants, 14-9 (C)
1930—Giants, 12-0 (C)
Bears, 12-0 (NY)
1931—Bears, 6-0 (C)
Bears, 12-6 (NY)
Giants, 25-6 (C)
1932—Bears, 28-8 (NY)
Bears, 6-0 (C)
1933—Bears, 14-10 (C)
Giants, 3-0 (NY)
*Bears, 23-21 (C)
1934—Bears, 27-7 (C)
Bears, 10-9 (NY)
*Giants, 30-13 (NY)
1935—Bears, 20-3 (NY)
Giants, 3-0 (C)
1936—Bears, 25-7 (NY)
1937—Tie, 3-3 (NY)
1939—Giants, 16-13 (NY)
1940—Bears, 37-21 (NY)
1941—*Bears, 37-9 (C)
1942—Bears, 26-7 (NY)
1943—Bears, 56-7 (NY)
1946—Giants, 14-0 (NY)

*Bears, 24-14 (NY)
1948—Bears, 35-14 (C)
1949—Giants, 35-28 (NY)
1956—Tie, 17-17 (NY)
*Giants, 47-7 (NY)
1962—Giants, 26-24 (C)
1963—*Bears, 14-10 (C)
1965—Bears, 35-14 (NY)
1967—Bears, 34-7 (C)
1969—Giants, 28-24 (NY)
1970—Bears, 24-16 (NY)
1974—Bears, 16-13 (C)
1977—Bears, 12-9 (NY) OT
1985—**Bears, 21-0 (C)
1987—Bears, 34-19 (C)
1990—**Giants, 31-3 (NY)
1991—Bears, 20-17 (C)
1992—Giants, 27-14 (C)
1993—Giants, 26-20 (C)
1995—Bears, 27-24 (NY)
2000—Giants, 14-7 (C)
2004—Bears, 28-21 (NY)
2006—Bears, 38-20 (NY)
(RS Pts.—Bears 807, Giants 611)
(PS Pts.—Giants 162, Bears 142)
*NFL Championship
**NFC Divisional Playoff
CHICAGO vs. N.Y. JETS
RS: Bears lead series, 6-3
1974—Jets, 23-21 (C)
1979—Bears, 23-13 (C)
1985—Bears, 19-6 (NY)
1991—Bears, 19-13 (C) OT
1994—Bears, 19-7 (NY)
1997—Jets, 23-15 (C)
2000—Jets, 17-10 (NY)
2002—Bears, 20-13 (C)
2006—Bears, 10-0 (NY)
(RS Pts.—Bears 156, Jets 115)
CHICAGO vs. *OAKLAND
RS: Raiders lead series, 6-5
1972—Raiders, 28-21 (O)
1976—Raiders, 28-27 (C)
1978—Raiders, 25-19 (C) OT
1981—Bears, 23-6 (O)
1984—Bears, 17-6 (C)
1987—Bears, 6-3 (LA)
1990—Raiders, 24-10 (LA)
1993—Raiders, 16-14 (C)
1996—Bears, 19-17 (C)
1999—Raiders, 24-17 (O)
2003—Bears, 24-21 (C)
(RS Pts.—Raiders 198, Bears 197)
*Franchise in Los Angeles from 1982-1994
CHICAGO vs. PHILADELPHIA
RS: Bears lead series, 24-8-1
PS: Eagles lead series, 2-1
1933—Tie, 3-3 (P)
1935—Bears, 39-0 (P)
1936—Bears, 17-0 (P)
Bears, 28-7 (P)
1938—Bears, 28-6 (P)
1939—Bears, 27-14 (C)
1941—Bears, 49-14 (P)
1942—Bears, 45-14 (C)
1944—Bears, 28-7 (C)
1946—Bears, 21-14 (C)
1947—Bears, 40-7 (C)
1948—Eagles, 12-7 (P)
1949—Bears, 38-21 (C)

1955—Bears, 17-10 (C)
1961—Eagles, 16-14 (P)
1963—Bears, 16-7 (C)
1968—Bears, 29-16 (P)
1970—Bears, 20-16 (C)
1972—Bears, 21-12 (P)
1975—Bears, 15-13 (C)
1979—*Eagles, 27-17 (P)
1980—Eagles, 17-14 (P)
1983—Bears, 7-6 (P)
　　　Bears, 17-14 (C)
1986—Bears, 13-10 (C) OT
1987—Bears, 35-3 (P)
1988—**Bears, 20-12 (C)
1989—Bears, 27-13 (C)
1993—Bears, 17-6 (P)
1994—Eagles, 30-22 (P)
1995—Bears, 20-14 (C)
1999—Eagles, 20-16 (C)
2000—Eagles, 13-9 (P)
2001—**Eagles, 33-19 (C)
2002—Bears, 19-13 (C)
2004—Eagles, 19-9 (C)
(RS Pts.—Bears 721, Eagles 393)
(PS Pts.—Eagles 72, Bears 56)
*NFC First-Round Playoff
**NFC Divisional Playoff
CHICAGO vs. *PITTSBURGH
RS: Bears lead series, 16-7-1
1934—Bears, 28-0 (P)
1935—Bears, 23-7 (P)
1936—Bears, 27-9 (P)
　　　Bears, 26-6 (C)
1937—Bears, 7-0 (P)
1939—Bears, 32-0 (P)
1941—Bears, 34-7 (C)
1945—Bears, 28-7 (C)
1947—Bears, 49-7 (C)
1949—Bears, 30-21 (C)
1958—Steelers, 24-10 (P)
1959—Bears, 27-21 (C)
1963—Tie, 17-17 (P)
1967—Steelers, 41-13 (P)
1969—Bears, 38-7 (C)
1971—Bears, 17-15 (C)
1975—Steelers, 34-3 (P)
1980—Steelers, 38-3 (P)
1986—Bears, 13-10 (C) OT
1989—Bears, 20-0 (P)
1992—Bears, 30-6 (C)
1995—Steelers, 37-34 (C) OT
1998—Steelers, 17-12 (P)
2005—Steelers, 21-9 (P)
(RS Pts.—Bears 530, Steelers 352)
*Steelers known as Pirates prior to 1941
CHICAGO vs. *ST. LOUIS
RS: Bears lead series, 48-34-3
PS: Series tied, 1-1
1937—Bears, 20-2 (Clev)
　　　Bears, 15-7 (C)
1938—Rams, 14-7 (C)
　　　Rams, 23-21 (Clev)
1939—Bears, 30-21 (Clev)
　　　Bears, 35-21 (C)
1940—Bears, 21-14 (Clev)
　　　Bears, 47-25 (C)
1941—Bears, 48-21 (Clev)
　　　Bears, 31-13 (C)
1942—Bears, 21-7 (Clev)
　　　Bears, 47-0 (C)

1944—Rams, 19-7 (Clev)
　　　Bears, 28-21 (C)
1945—Rams, 17-0 (Clev)
　　　Rams, 41-21 (C)
1946—Tie, 28-28 (C)
　　　Bears, 27-21 (LA)
1947—Bears, 41-21 (LA)
　　　Rams, 17-14 (C)
1948—Bears, 42-21 (C)
　　　Bears, 21-6 (LA)
1949—Rams, 31-16 (C)
　　　Rams, 27-24 (LA)
1950—Bears, 24-20 (LA)
　　　Bears, 24-14 (C)
　　　**Rams, 24-14 (LA)
1951—Rams, 42-17 (C)
1952—Rams, 31-7 (LA)
　　　Rams, 40-24 (C)
1953—Rams, 38-24 (LA)
　　　Bears, 24-21 (C)
1954—Rams, 42-38 (LA)
　　　Bears, 24-13 (C)
1955—Bears, 31-20 (LA)
　　　Bears, 24-3 (C)
1956—Bears, 35-24 (LA)
　　　Bears, 30-21 (C)
1957—Bears, 34-26 (C)
　　　Bears, 16-10 (LA)
1958—Bears, 31-10 (C)
　　　Rams, 41-35 (LA)
1959—Rams, 28-21 (C)
　　　Bears, 26-21 (LA)
1960—Bears, 34-27 (C)
　　　Tie, 24-24 (LA)
1961—Bears, 21-17 (LA)
　　　Bears, 28-24 (C)
1962—Bears, 27-23 (LA)
　　　Bears, 30-14 (C)
1963—Bears, 52-14 (LA)
　　　Bears, 6-0 (C)
1964—Bears, 38-17 (C)
　　　Bears, 34-24 (LA)
1965—Rams, 30-28 (LA)
　　　Bears, 31-6 (C)
1966—Rams, 31-17 (LA)
　　　Bears, 17-10 (C)
1967—Rams, 28-17 (C)
1968—Bears, 17-16 (LA)
1969—Rams, 9-7 (C)
1971—Rams, 17-3 (LA)
1972—Tie, 13-13 (C)
1973—Rams, 26-0 (C)
1975—Rams, 38-10 (LA)
1976—Rams, 20-12 (LA)
1977—Rams, 24-23 (C)
1979—Bears, 27-23 (C)
1981—Rams, 24-7 (C)
1982—Bears, 34-26 (LA)
1983—Rams, 21-14 (LA)
1984—Rams, 29-13 (LA)
1985—***Bears, 24-0 (C)
1986—Rams, 20-17 (C)
1988—Rams, 23-3 (LA)
1989—Bears, 20-10 (C)
1990—Bears, 38-9 (C)
1993—Rams, 20-6 (LA)
1994—Bears, 27-13 (C)
1995—Bears, 34-28 (StL)
1996—Bears, 35-9 (C)
1997—Bears, 13-10 (StL)

1998—Rams, 20-12 (C)
1999—Rams, 34-12 (StL)
2002—Rams, 21-16 (StL)
2003—Rams, 23-21 (C)
2006—Bears, 42-27 (StL)
(RS Pts.—Bears 1,976, Rams 1,750)
(PS Pts.—Bears 38, Rams 24)
*Franchise in Los Angeles prior to 1995
and in Cleveland prior to 1946
**Conference Playoff
***NFC Championship
CHICAGO vs. SAN DIEGO
RS: Bears lead series, 5-4
1970—Chargers, 20-7 (C)
1974—Chargers, 28-21 (SD)
1978—Chargers, 40-7 (SD)
1981—Bears, 20-17 (C) OT
1984—Chargers, 20-7 (SD)
1993—Bears, 16-13 (SD)
1996—Bears, 27-14 (C)
1999—Bears, 23-20 (SD) OT
2003—Bears, 20-7 (C)
(RS Pts.—Chargers 179, Bears 148)
CHICAGO vs. SAN FRANCISCO
RS: Bears lead series, 29-27-1
PS: 49ers lead series, 3-0
1950—Bears, 32-20 (SF)
　　　Bears, 17-0 (C)
1951—Bears, 13-7 (C)
1952—49ers, 40-16 (C)
　　　Bears, 20-17 (SF)
1953—49ers, 35-28 (C)
　　　49ers, 24-14 (SF)
1954—49ers, 31-24 (C)
　　　Bears, 31-27 (SF)
1955—49ers, 20-19 (C)
　　　Bears, 34-23 (SF)
1956—Bears, 31-7 (C)
　　　Bears, 38-21 (SF)
1957—49ers, 21-17 (C)
　　　49ers, 21-17 (SF)
1958—Bears, 28-6 (C)
　　　Bears, 27-14 (SF)
1959—49ers, 20-17 (SF)
　　　Bears, 14-3 (C)
1960—Bears, 27-10 (C)
　　　49ers, 25-7 (SF)
1961—Bears, 31-0 (C)
　　　49ers, 41-31 (SF)
1962—Bears, 30-14 (SF)
　　　49ers, 34-27 (C)
1963—49ers, 20-14 (SF)
　　　Bears, 27-7 (C)
1964—49ers, 31-21 (SF)
　　　Bears, 23-21 (C)
1965—49ers, 52-24 (SF)
　　　Bears, 61-20 (C)
1966—Tie, 30-30 (C)
　　　49ers, 41-14 (SF)
1967—Bears, 28-14 (SF)
1968—Bears, 27-19 (C)
1969—49ers, 42-21 (SF)
1970—49ers, 37-16 (C)
1971—Bears, 13-0 (SF)
1972—49ers, 34-21 (C)
1974—49ers, 34-0 (C)
1975—49ers, 31-3 (SF)
1976—Bears, 19-12 (SF)
1978—Bears, 16-13 (SF)
1979—Bears, 28-27 (SF)

1981—49ers, 28-17 (SF)
1983—Bears, 13-3 (C)
1984—*49ers, 23-0 (SF)
1985—Bears, 26-10 (SF)
1987—49ers, 41-0 (SF)
1988—Bears, 10-9 (C)
    *49ers, 28-3 (C)
1989—49ers, 26-0 (SF)
1991—49ers, 52-14 (SF)
1994—**49ers, 44-15 (SF)
2000—49ers, 17-0 (SF)
2001—Bears, 37-31 (C) OT
2003—49ers, 49-7 (SF)
2004—Bears, 23-13 (C)
2005—Bears, 17-9 (C)
2006—Bears, 41-10 (C)
(RS Pts.—49ers 1,277, Bears 1,188)
(PS Pts.—49ers 95, Bears 18)
*NFC Championship
**NFC Divisional Playoff
CHICAGO vs. SEATTLE
RS: Seahawks lead series, 6-3
PS: Bears lead series, 1-0
1976—Bears, 34-7 (S)
1978—Seahawks, 31-29 (C)
1982—Seahawks, 20-14 (S)
1984—Seahawks, 38-9 (S)
1987—Seahawks, 34-21 (C)
1990—Bears, 17-0 (C)
1999—Seahawks, 14-13 (C)
2003—Seahawks, 24-17 (S)
2006—Bears, 37-6 (C)
    *Bears, 27-24 (C) OT
(RS Pts.—Bears 191, Seahawks 174)
(PS Pts.—Bears 27, Seahawks 24)
*NFC Divisional Playoff
CHICAGO vs. TAMPA BAY
RS: Bears lead series, 35-17
1977—Bears, 10-0 (C)
1978—Buccaneers, 33-19 (TB)
    Bears, 14-3 (C)
1979—Buccaneers, 17-13 (C)
    Bears, 14-0 (TB)
1980—Bears, 23-0 (C)
    Bears, 14-13 (TB)
1981—Bears, 28-17 (C)
    Buccaneers, 20-10 (TB)
1982—Buccaneers, 26-23 (TB) OT
1983—Bears, 17-10 (C)
    Bears, 27-0 (TB)
1984—Bears, 34-14 (C)
    Bears, 44-9 (TB)
1985—Bears, 38-28 (C)
    Bears, 27-19 (TB)
1986—Bears, 23-3 (TB)
    Bears, 48-14 (C)
1987—Bears, 20-3 (C)
    Bears, 27-26 (TB)
1988—Bears, 28-10 (C)
    Bears, 27-15 (TB)
1989—Buccaneers, 42-35 (TB)
    Buccaneers, 32-31 (C)
1990—Bears, 26-6 (TB)
    Bears, 27-14 (C)
1991—Bears, 21-20 (TB)
    Bears, 27-0 (C)
1992—Bears, 31-14 (C)
    Buccaneers, 20-17 (TB)
1993—Bears, 47-17 (C)
    Buccaneers, 13-10 (TB)

1994—Bears, 21-9 (C)
    Bears, 20-6 (TB)
1995—Bears, 25-6 (TB)
    Bears, 31-10 (C)
1996—Bears, 13-10 (C)
    Buccaneers, 34-19 (TB)
1997—Bears, 13-7 (C)
    Buccaneers, 31-15 (TB)
1998—Buccaneers, 27-15 (TB)
    Buccaneers, 31-17 (C)
1999—Buccaneers, 6-3 (TB)
    Buccaneers, 20-6 (C)
2000—Buccaneers, 41-0 (TB)
    Bears, 13-10 (C)
2001—Bears, 27-24 (TB)
    Bears, 27-3 (C)
2002—Buccaneers, 15-0 (C)
2004—Buccaneers, 19-7 (TB)
2005—Bears, 13-10 (TB)
2006—Bears, 34-31 (C) OT
(RS Pts.—Bears 1,119, Buccaneers 808)
CHICAGO vs. TENNESSEE
RS: Bears lead series, 5-4
1973—Bears, 35-14 (C)
1977—Oilers, 47-0 (H)
1980—Oilers, 10-6 (C)
1986—Bears, 20-7 (H)
1989—Oilers, 33-28 (C)
1992—Oilers, 24-7 (H)
1995—Bears, 35-32 (C)
1998—Bears, 23-20 (T)
2004—Bears, 19-17 (T) OT
(RS Pts.—Titans 204, Bears 173)
*Franchise in Houston prior to 1997;
known as Oilers prior to 1999
CHICAGO vs. *WASHINGTON
RS: Bears lead series, 20-17-1
PS: Redskins lead series, 4-3
1932—Tie, 7-7 (B)
1933—Bears, 7-0 (C)
    Redskins, 10-0 (B)
1934—Bears, 21-0 (B)
1935—Bears, 30-14 (B)
1936—Bears, 26-0 (B)
1937—**Redskins, 28-21 (C)
1938—Bears, 31-7 (C)
1940—Redskins, 7-3 (W)
    **Bears, 73-0 (W)
1941—Bears, 35-21 (C)
1942—**Redskins, 14-6 (W)
1943—Redskins, 21-7 (W)
    **Bears, 41-21 (C)
1945—Redskins, 28-21 (W)
1946—Bears, 24-20 (C)
1947—Bears, 56-20 (W)
1948—Bears, 48-13 (C)
1949—Bears, 31-21 (W)
1951—Bears, 27-0 (W)
1953—Bears, 27-24 (W)
1957—Redskins, 14-3 (C)
1964—Redskins, 27-20 (W)
1968—Redskins, 38-28 (C)
1971—Bears, 16-15 (C)
1974—Redskins, 42-0 (W)
1976—Bears, 33-7 (C)
1978—Bears, 14-10 (W)
1980—Bears, 35-21 (W)
1981—Redskins, 24-7 (C)
1984—***Bears, 23-19 (W)
1985—Bears, 45-10 (C)

1986—***Redskins, 27-13 (C)
1987—***Redskins, 21-17 (C)
1988—Bears, 34-14 (W)
1989—Redskins, 38-14 (W)
1990—Redskins, 10-9 (W)
1991—Redskins, 20-7 (C)
1996—Redskins, 10-3 (W)
1997—Redskins, 31-8 (C)
1999—Redskins, 48-22 (W)
2001—Bears, 20-15 (W)
2003—Bears, 27-24 (C)
2004—Redskins, 13-10 (C)
2005—Redskins, 9-7 (W)
(RS Pts.—Bears 763, Redskins 653)
(PS Pts.—Bears 194, Redskins 130)
*Franchise in Boston prior to 1937 and
known as Braves prior to 1933
**NFL Championship
***NFC Championship Playoff

CINCINNATI vs. ARIZONA
RS: Bengals lead series, 5-3;
See Arizona vs. Cincinnati
CINCINNATI vs. ATLANTA
RS: Bengals lead series, 7-4;
See Atlanta vs. Cincinnati
CINCINNATI vs. BALTIMORE
RS: Ravens lead series, 13-9;
See Baltimore vs. Cincinnati
CINCINNATI vs. BUFFALO
RS: Bills lead series, 13-9
PS: Bengals lead series, 2-0;
See Buffalo vs. Cincinnati
CINCINNATI vs. CAROLINA
RS: Panthers lead series, 2-1;
See Carolina vs. Cincinnati
CINCINNATI vs. CHICAGO
RS: Bengals lead series, 5-3;
See Chicago vs. Cincinnati
CINCINNATI vs. CLEVELAND
RS: Bengals lead series, 34-33
1970—Browns, 30-27 (Cle)
    Bengals, 14-10 (Cin)
1971—Browns, 27-24 (Cle)
    Browns, 31-27 (Cle)
1972—Browns, 27-6 (Cle)
    Browns, 27-24 (Cin)
1973—Browns, 17-10 (Cle)
    Bengals, 34-17 (Cin)
1974—Bengals, 33-7 (Cin)
    Bengals, 34-24 (Cle)
1975—Bengals, 24-17 (Cle)
    Browns, 35-23 (Cle)
1976—Bengals, 45-24 (Cle)
    Bengals, 21-6 (Cin)
1977—Browns, 13-3 (Cin)
    Bengals, 10-7 (Cle)
1978—Browns, 13-10 (Cle) OT
    Bengals, 48-16 (Cin)
1979—Browns, 28-27 (Cle)
    Bengals, 16-12 (Cin)
1980—Browns, 31-7 (Cle)
    Browns, 27-24 (Cin)
1981—Browns, 20-17 (Cin)
    Bengals, 41-21 (Cle)
1982—Bengals, 23-10 (Cin)
1983—Browns, 17-7 (Cle)
    Bengals, 28-21 (Cin)
1984—Bengals, 12-9 (Cin)
    Bengals, 20-17 (Cle) OT

1985—Bengals, 27-10 (Cin)
  Browns, 24-6 (Cle)
1986—Bengals, 30-13 (Cle)
  Browns, 34-3 (Cin)
1987—Browns, 34-0 (Cin)
  Browns, 38-24 (Cle)
1988—Bengals, 24-17 (Cin)
  Browns, 23-16 (Cle)
1989—Bengals, 21-14 (Cin)
  Bengals, 21-0 (Cle)
1990—Bengals, 34-13 (Cle)
  Bengals, 21-14 (Cin)
1991—Browns, 14-13 (Cle)
  Bengals, 23-21 (Cin)
1992—Bengals, 30-10 (Cin)
  Browns, 37-21 (Cle)
1993—Browns, 27-14 (Cle)
  Browns, 28-17 (Cin)
1994—Browns, 28-20 (Cin)
  Browns, 37-13 (Cle)
1995—Browns, 29-26 (Cin) OT
  Browns, 26-10 (Cle)
1999—Bengals, 18-17 (Cle)
  Bengals, 44-28 (Cin)
2000—Browns, 24-7 (Cin)
  Bengals, 12-3 (Cle)
2001—Bengals, 24-14 (Cin)
  Browns, 18-0 (Cle)
2002—Browns, 20-7 (Cle)
  Browns, 27-20 (Cin)
2003—Bengals, 21-14 (Cle)
  Browns, 22-14 (Cin)
2004—Browns, 34-17 (Cle)
  Bengals, 58-48 (Cin)
2005—Bengals, 27-13 (Cle)
  Bengals, 23-20 (Cin)
2006—Bengals, 34-17 (Cin)
  Bengals, 30-0 (Cle)
(RS Pts.—Bengals 1,409, Browns 1,371)
CINCINNATI vs. DALLAS
RS: Cowboys lead series, 5-4
1973—Cowboys, 38-10 (D)
1979—Cowboys, 38-13 (D)
1985—Bengals, 50-24 (C)
1988—Bengals, 38-24 (D)
1991—Cowboys, 35-23 (D)
1994—Cowboys, 23-20 (C)
1997—Bengals, 31-24 (C)
2000—Cowboys, 23-6 (D)
2004—Bengals, 26-3 (C)
(RS Pts.—Cowboys 232, Bengals 217)
CINCINNATI vs. DENVER
RS: Broncos lead series, 16-8
1968—Bengals, 24-10 (C)
  Broncos, 10-7 (D)
1969—Broncos, 30-23 (C)
  Broncos, 27-16 (D)
1971—Bengals, 24-10 (D)
1972—Bengals, 21-10 (C)
1973—Broncos, 28-10 (D)
1975—Bengals, 17-16 (D)
1976—Bengals, 17-7 (C)
1977—Broncos, 24-13 (C)
1979—Broncos, 10-0 (D)
1981—Bengals, 38-21 (C)
1983—Broncos, 24-17 (D)
1984—Broncos, 20-17 (D)
1986—Broncos, 34-28 (D)
1991—Broncos, 45-14 (D)
1994—Broncos, 15-13 (D)

1996—Broncos, 14-10 (C)
1997—Broncos, 38-20 (D)
1998—Broncos, 33-26 (C)
2000—Bengals, 31-21 (C)
2003—Broncos, 30-10 (C)
2004—Bengals, 23-10 (C)
2006—Broncos, 24-23 (D)
(RS Pts.—Broncos 511, Bengals 442)
CINCINNATI vs. DETROIT
RS: Bengals lead series, 6-3
1970—Lions, 38-3 (D)
1974—Lions, 23-19 (C)
1983—Bengals, 17-9 (C)
1986—Bengals, 24-17 (D)
1989—Bengals, 42-7 (C)
1992—Lions, 19-13 (C)
1998—Bengals, 34-28 (D) OT
2001—Bengals, 31-27 (D)
2005—Bengals, 41-17 (D)
(RS Pts.—Bengals 224, Lions 185)
CINCINNATI vs. GREEN BAY
RS: Series tied, 5-5
1971—Packers, 20-17 (GB)
1976—Bengals, 28-7 (C)
1977—Bengals, 17-7 (Mil)
1980—Packers, 14-9 (GB)
1983—Bengals, 34-14 (C)
1986—Bengals, 34-28 (Mil)
1992—Packers, 24-23 (GB)
1995—Packers, 24-10 (GB)
1998—Packers, 13-6 (C)
2005—Bengals, 21-14 (C)
(RS Pts.—Bengals 199, Packers 165)
CINCINNATI vs. HOUSTON
RS: Bengals lead series, 3-0
2002—Bengals, 38-3 (H)
2003—Bengals, 34-27 (C)
2005—Bengals, 16-10 (C)
(RS Pts.—Bengals 88, Texans 40)
CINCINNATI vs. *INDIANAPOLIS
RS: Colts lead series, 14-8
PS: Colts lead series, 1-0
1970—**Colts, 17-0 (B)
1972—Colts, 20-19 (C)
1974—Bengals, 24-14 (B)
1976—Colts, 28-27 (B)
1979—Colts, 38-28 (B)
1980—Bengals, 34-33 (C)
1981—Bengals, 41-19 (B)
1982—Bengals, 20-17 (B)
1983—Colts, 34-31 (C)
1987—Bengals, 23-21 (I)
1989—Colts, 23-12 (C)
1990—Colts, 34-20 (C)
1992—Colts, 21-17 (C)
1993—Colts, 9-6 (C)
1994—Colts, 17-13 (C)
1995—Bengals, 24-21 (I) OT
1996—Bengals, 31-24 (C)
1997—Bengals, 28-13 (I)
1998—Colts, 39-26 (I)
1999—Colts, 31-10 (I)
2002—Colts, 28-21 (I)
2005—Colts, 45-37 (C)
2006—Colts, 34-16 (I)
(RS Pts.—Colts 563, Bengals 508)
(PS Pts.—Colts 17, Bengals 0)
*Franchise in Baltimore prior to 1984
**AFC Divisional Playoff
CINCINNATI vs. JACKSONVILLE

RS: Jaguars lead series, 11-5
1995—Bengals, 24-17 (C)
  Bengals, 17-13 (J)
1996—Bengals, 28-21 (C)
  Jaguars, 30-27 (J)
1997—Jaguars, 21-13 (J)
  Bengals, 31-26 (C)
1998—Jaguars, 34-11 (J)
  Jaguars, 34-17 (C)
1999—Jaguars, 41-10 (C)
  Jaguars, 24-7 (J)
2000—Jaguars, 13-0 (J)
  Bengals, 17-14 (C)
2001—Jaguars, 30-13 (J)
  Jaguars, 14-10 (C)
2002—Jaguars, 29-15 (C)
2005—Jaguars, 23-20 (J)
(RS Pts.—Jaguars 374, Bengals 260)
CINCINNATI vs. KANSAS CITY
RS: Chiefs lead series, 12-11
1968—Chiefs, 13-3 (C)
  Chiefs, 16-9 (C)
1969—Bengals, 24-19 (C)
  Chiefs, 42-22 (KC)
1970—Chiefs, 27-19 (C)
1972—Bengals, 23-16 (KC)
1973—Bengals, 14-6 (C)
1974—Bengals, 33-6 (C)
1976—Bengals, 27-24 (KC)
1977—Bengals, 27-7 (KC)
1978—Chiefs, 24-23 (C)
1979—Chiefs, 10-7 (C)
1980—Bengals, 20-6 (KC)
1983—Chiefs, 20-15 (KC)
1984—Chiefs, 27-22 (C)
1986—Chiefs, 24-14 (KC)
1987—Bengals, 30-27 (C) OT
1988—Chiefs, 31-28 (KC)
1989—Bengals, 21-17 (KC)
1993—Chiefs, 17-15 (KC)
2003—Bengals, 24-19 (C)
2005—Chiefs, 37-3 (KC)
2006—Bengals, 23-10 (C)
(RS Pts.—Bengals 446, Chiefs 445)
CINCINNATI vs. MIAMI
RS: Dolphins lead series, 12-4
PS: Dolphins lead series, 1-0
1968—Dolphins, 24-22 (C)
  Bengals, 38-21 (M)
1969—Bengals, 27-21 (C)
1971—Dolphins, 23-13 (C)
1973—*Dolphins, 34-16 (M)
1974—Dolphins, 24-3 (M)
1977—Bengals, 23-17 (C)
1978—Dolphins, 21-0 (M)
1980—Dolphins, 17-16 (M)
1983—Dolphins, 38-14 (M)
1987—Dolphins, 20-14 (C)
1989—Dolphins, 20-13 (C)
1991—Dolphins, 37-13 (M)
1994—Dolphins, 23-7 (C)
1995—Dolphins, 26-23 (C)
2000—Dolphins, 31-16 (C)
2004—Bengals, 16-13 (C)
(RS Pts.—Dolphins 376, Bengals 258)
(PS Pts.—Dolphins 34, Bengals 16)
*AFC Divisional Playoff
CINCINNATI vs. MINNESOTA
RS: Series tied, 5-5
1973—Bengals, 27-0 (C)

1977—Vikings, 42-10 (M)
1980—Bengals, 14-0 (C)
1983—Vikings, 20-14 (M)
1986—Bengals, 24-20 (C)
1989—Vikings, 29-21 (M)
1992—Vikings, 42-7 (C)
1995—Bengals, 27-24 (C)
1998—Vikings, 24-3 (M)
2005—Bengals, 37-8 (C)
(RS Pts.—Vikings 209, Bengals 184)

CINCINNATI vs. *NEW ENGLAND
RS: Patriots lead series, 12-8
1968—Patriots, 33-14 (B)
1969—Patriots, 25-14 (C)
1970—Bengals, 45-7 (C)
1972—Bengals, 31-7 (NE)
1975—Bengals, 27-10 (C)
1978—Patriots, 10-3 (C)
1979—Patriots, 20-14 (C)
1984—Patriots, 20-14 (NE)
1985—Patriots, 34-23 (NE)
1986—Bengals, 31-7 (NE)
1988—Patriots, 27-21 (NE)
1990—Bengals, 41-7 (C)
1991—Bengals, 29-7 (C)
1992—Bengals, 20-10 (C)
1993—Patriots, 7-2 (NE)
1994—Patriots, 31-28 (C)
2000—Patriots, 16-13 (NE)
2001—Bengals, 23-17 (C)
2004—Patriots, 35-28 (NE)
2006—Patriots, 38-13 (C)
(RS Pts.—Bengals 434, Patriots 368)
*Franchise in Boston prior to 1971

CINCINNATI vs. NEW ORLEANS
RS: Bengals lead series, 6-5
1970—Bengals, 26-6 (C)
1975—Bengals, 21-0 (NO)
1978—Saints, 20-18 (C)
1981—Saints, 17-7 (NO)
1984—Bengals, 24-21 (NO)
1987—Saints, 41-24 (C)
1990—Saints, 21-7 (C)
1993—Saints, 20-13 (NO)
1996—Bengals, 30-15 (C)
2002—Bengals, 20-13 (C)
2006—Bengals, 31-16 (NO)
(RS Pts.—Bengals 221, Saints 190)

CINCINNATI vs. N.Y. GIANTS
RS: Bengals lead series, 5-2
1972—Bengals, 13-10 (C)
1977—Bengals, 30-13 (C)
1985—Bengals, 35-30 (C)
1991—Bengals, 27-24 (C)
1994—Giants, 27-20 (NY)
1997—Giants, 29-27 (NY)
2004—Benglas, 23-22 (C)
(RS Pts.—Bengals 175, Giants 155)

CINCINNATI vs. N.Y. JETS
RS: Jets lead series, 12-6
PS: Jets lead series, 1-0
1968—Jets, 27-14 (NY)
1969—Jets, 21-7 (C)
        Jets, 40-7 (NY)
1971—Jets, 35-21 (NY)
1973—Bengals, 20-14 (C)
1976—Bengals, 42-3 (NY)
1981—Bengals, 31-30 (NY)
1982—*Jets, 44-17 (C)
1984—Jets, 43-23 (NY)

1985—Jets, 29-20 (C)
1986—Bengals, 52-21 (C)
1987—Jets, 27-20 (NY)
1988—Bengals, 36-19 (C)
1990—Bengals, 25-20 (C)
1992—Jets, 17-14 (NY)
1993—Jets, 17-12 (NY)
1997—Jets, 31-14 (C)
2001—Jets, 15-14 (NY)
2004—Jets, 31-24 (NY)
(RS Pts.—Jets 440, Bengals 396)
(PS Pts.—Jets 44, Bengals 17)
*AFC First-Round Playoff

CINCINNATI vs. *OAKLAND
RS: Raiders lead series, 17-8
PS: Raiders lead series, 2-0
1968—Raiders, 31-10 (O)
        Raiders, 34-0 (C)
1969—Bengals, 31-17 (C)
        Raiders, 37-17 (O)
1970—Bengals, 31-21 (C)
1971—Raiders, 31-27 (O)
1972—Raiders, 20-14 (C)
1974—Raiders, 30-27 (O)
1975—Bengals, 14-10 (C)
        **Raiders, 31-28 (O)
1976—Raiders, 35-20 (O)
1978—Raiders, 34-21 (C)
1980—Raiders, 28-17 (O)
1982—Bengals, 31-17 (C)
1983—Raiders, 20-10 (C)
1985—Raiders, 13-6 (LA)
1988—Bengals, 45-21 (LA)
1989—Raiders, 28-7 (LA)
1990—Raiders, 24-7 (LA)
        **Raiders, 20-10 (LA)
1991—Raiders, 38-14 (C)
1992—Bengals, 24-21 (C) OT
1993—Bengals, 16-10 (C)
1995—Raiders, 20-17 (C)
1998—Raiders, 27-10 (O)
2003—Raiders, 23-20 (O)
2006—Bengals, 27-10 (C)
(RS Pts.—Raiders 600, Bengals 463)
(PS Pts.—Raiders 51, Bengals 38)
*Franchise in Los Angeles from 1982-1994
**AFC Divisional Playoff

CINCINNATI vs. PHILADELPHIA
RS: Bengals lead series, 7-3
1971—Bengals, 37-14 (C)
1975—Bengals, 31-0 (P)
1979—Bengals, 37-13 (C)
1982—Bengals, 18-14 (P)
1988—Bengals, 28-24 (P)
1991—Eagles, 17-10 (P)
1994—Bengals, 33-30 (C)
1997—Eagles, 44-42 (P)
2000—Eagles, 16-7 (P)
2004—Bengals, 38-10 (P)
(RS Pts.—Bengals 281, Eagles 182)

CINCINNATI vs. PITTSBURGH
RS: Steelers lead series, 43-30
PS: Steelers lead series, 1-0
1970—Steelers, 21-10 (P)
        Bengals, 34-7 (C)
1971—Steelers, 21-10 (P)
        Steelers, 21-13 (C)
1972—Bengals, 15-10 (C)
        Steelers, 40-17 (P)
1973—Bengals, 19-7 (C)

        Steelers, 20-13 (P)
1974—Bengals, 17-10 (C)
        Steelers, 27-3 (P)
1975—Steelers, 30-24 (C)
        Steelers, 35-14 (P)
1976—Steelers, 23-6 (P)
        Steelers, 7-3 (C)
1977—Steelers, 20-14 (C)
        Bengals, 17-10 (C)
1978—Steelers, 28-3 (C)
        Steelers, 7-6 (P)
1979—Bengals, 34-10 (C)
        Steelers, 37-17 (P)
1980—Bengals, 30-28 (C)
        Bengals, 17-16 (P)
1981—Bengals, 34-7 (C)
        Bengals, 17-10 (P)
1982—Steelers, 26-20 (P) OT
1983—Steelers, 24-14 (C)
        Bengals, 23-10 (P)
1984—Steelers, 38-17 (P)
        Bengals, 22-20 (C)
1985—Bengals, 37-24 (P)
        Bengals, 26-21 (C)
1986—Bengals, 24-22 (C)
        Steelers, 30-9 (P)
1987—Steelers, 23-20 (P)
        Steelers, 30-16 (C)
1988—Bengals, 17-12 (P)
        Bengals, 42-7 (C)
1989—Bengals, 41-10 (C)
        Bengals, 26-16 (P)
1990—Bengals, 27-3 (C)
        Bengals, 16-12 (P)
1991—Steelers, 33-27 (C) OT
        Steelers, 17-10 (P)
1992—Steelers, 20-0 (P)
        Steelers, 21-9 (C)
1993—Steelers, 34-7 (P)
        Steelers, 24-16 (C)
1994—Steelers, 14-10 (P)
        Steelers, 38-15 (C)
1995—Bengals, 27-9 (P)
        Steelers, 49-31 (C)
1996—Steelers, 20-10 (C)
        Bengals, 34-24 (C)
1997—Steelers, 26-10 (C)
        Steelers, 20-3 (P)
1998—Bengals, 25-20 (C)
        Bengals, 25-24 (P)
1999—Steelers, 17-3 (C)
        Bengals, 27-20 (P)
2000—Steelers, 15-0 (P)
        Steelers, 48-28 (C)
2001—Steelers, 16-7 (P)
        Bengals, 26-23 (C) OT
2002—Steelers, 34-7 (C)
        Steelers, 29-21 (P)
2003—Steelers, 17-10 (C)
        Bengals, 24-20 (P)
2004—Bengals, 28-17 (P)
        Steelers, 19-14 (C)
2005—Steelers, 27-13 (C)
        Bengals, 38-31 (P)
        *Steelers, 31-17 (C)
2006—Bengals, 28-20 (P)
        Steelers, 23-17 (C) OT
(RS Pts.—Steelers 1,560, Bengals 1,323)
(PS Pts.—Steelers 31, Bengals 17)
*AFC First-Round Playoff

CINCINNATI vs. *ST. LOUIS
RS: Series tied, 5-5
1972—Rams, 15-12 (LA)
1976—Bengals, 20-12 (C)
1978—Bengals, 20-19 (LA)
1981—Bengals, 24-10 (C)
1984—Rams, 24-14 (C)
1990—Bengals, 34-31 (LA) OT
1993—Bengals, 15-3 (C)
1996—Rams, 26-16 (StL)
1999—Rams, 38-10 (C)
2003—Rams, 27-10 (StL)
(RS Pts.—Rams 205, Bengals 175)
*Franchise in Los Angeles prior to 1995
CINCINNATI vs. SAN DIEGO
RS: Chargers lead series, 18-10
PS: Bengals lead series, 1-0
1968—Chargers, 29-13 (SD)
　　　Chargers, 31-10 (C)
1969—Bengals, 34-20 (C)
　　　Chargers, 21-14 (SD)
1970—Bengals, 17-14 (SD)
1971—Bengals, 31-0 (C)
1973—Bengals, 20-13 (SD)
1974—Chargers, 20-17 (C)
1975—Bengals, 47-17 (C)
1977—Chargers, 24-3 (SD)
1978—Chargers, 22-13 (SD)
1979—Chargers, 26-24 (C)
1980—Chargers, 31-14 (C)
1981—Chargers, 40-17 (SD)
　　　*Bengals, 27-7 (C)
1982—Chargers, 50-34 (SD)
1985—Chargers, 44-41 (C)
1987—Chargers, 10-9 (C)
1988—Bengals, 27-10 (C)
1990—Bengals, 21-16 (SD)
1992—Chargers, 27-10 (SD)
1994—Chargers, 27-10 (SD)
1996—Chargers, 27-14 (SD)
1997—Bengals, 38-31 (C)
1999—Chargers, 34-7 (C)
2001—Chargers, 28-14 (SD)
2002—Chargers, 34-6 (C)
2003—Bengals, 34-27 (SD)
2006—Chargers, 49-41 (C)
(RS Pts.—Chargers 699, Bengals 603)
(PS Pts.—Bengals 27, Chargers 7)
*AFC Championship
CINCINNATI vs. SAN FRANCISCO
RS: 49ers lead series, 7-3
PS: 49ers lead series, 2-0
1974—Bengals, 21-3 (SF)
1978—49ers, 28-12 (SF)
1981—49ers, 21-3 (C)
　　　*49ers, 26-21 (Detroit)
1984—49ers, 23-17 (SF)
1987—49ers, 27-26 (C)
1988—**49ers, 20-16 (South Florida)
1990—49ers, 20-17 (C) OT
1993—49ers, 21-8 (SF)
1996—49ers, 28-21 (SF)
1999—Bengals, 44-30 (C)
2003—Bengals, 41-38 (C)
(RS Pts.—49ers 239, Bengals 210)
(PS Pts.—49ers 46, Bengals 37)
*Super Bowl XVI
**Super Bowl XXIII
CINCINNATI vs. SEATTLE
RS: Series tied, 8-8

PS: Bengals lead series, 1-0
1977—Bengals, 42-20 (C)
1981—Bengals, 27-21 (C)
1982—Bengals, 24-10 (C)
1984—Seahawks, 26-6 (C)
1985—Seahawks, 28-24 (C)
1986—Bengals, 34-7 (C)
1987—Bengals, 17-10 (S)
1988—*Bengals, 21-13 (C)
1989—Seahawks, 24-17 (C)
1990—Seahawks, 31-16 (S)
1991—Seahawks, 13-7 (C)
1992—Bengals, 21-3 (S)
1993—Seahawks, 19-10 (C)
1994—Bengals, 20-17 (S) OT
1995—Seahawks, 24-21 (S)
1999—Seahawks, 37-20 (S)
2003—Bengals, 27-24 (C)
(RS Pts.—Bengals 333, Seahawks 314)
(PS Pts.—Bengals 21, Seahawks 13)
*AFC Divisional Playoff
CINCINNATI vs. TAMPA BAY
RS: Buccaneers lead series, 6-3
1976—Bengals, 21-0 (C)
1980—Buccaneers, 17-12 (C)
1983—Bengals, 23-17 (TB)
1989—Bengals, 56-23 (C)
1995—Buccaneers, 19-16 (TB)
1998—Buccaneers, 35-0 (C)
2001—Buccaneers, 16-13 (C) OT
2002—Buccaneers, 35-7 (C)
2006—Buccaneers, 14-13 (TB)
(RS Pts.— Buccaneers 176, Bengals 161)
CINCINNATI vs. *TENNESSEE
RS: Titans lead series, 38-30-1
PS: Bengals lead series, 1-0
1968—Oilers, 27-17 (C)
1969—Tie, 31-31 (H)
1970—Oilers, 20-13 (C)
　　　Bengals, 30-20 (H)
1971—Oilers, 10-6 (H)
　　　Bengals, 28-13 (C)
1972—Bengals, 30-7 (C)
　　　Bengals, 61-17 (H)
1973—Bengals, 24-10 (C)
　　　Bengals, 27-24 (H)
1974—Oilers, 34-21 (C)
　　　Oilers, 20-3 (H)
1975—Bengals, 21-19 (H)
　　　Bengals, 23-19 (C)
1976—Bengals, 27-7 (H)
　　　Bengals, 31-27 (C)
1977—Bengals, 13-10 (C) OT
　　　Oilers, 21-16 (H)
1978—Bengals, 28-13 (C)
　　　Oilers, 17-10 (H)
1979—Oilers, 30-27 (C) OT
　　　Oilers, 42-21 (H)
1980—Oilers, 13-10 (C)
　　　Oilers, 23-3 (H)
1981—Oilers, 17-10 (H)
　　　Bengals, 34-21 (C)
1982—Bengals, 27-6 (C)
　　　Bengals, 35-27 (H)
1983—Bengals, 55-14 (H)
　　　Bengals, 38-10 (C)
1984—Bengals, 13-3 (C)
　　　Bengals, 31-13 (H)
1985—Oilers, 44-27 (H)
　　　Bengals, 45-27 (C)

1986—Bengals, 31-28 (C)
　　　Oilers, 32-28 (H)
1987—Oilers, 31-29 (C)
　　　Oilers, 21-17 (H)
1988—Bengals, 44-21 (C)
　　　Oilers, 41-6 (H)
1989—Oilers, 26-24 (C)
　　　Bengals, 61-7 (C)
1990—Oilers, 48-17 (H)
　　　Bengals, 40-20 (C)
　　　**Bengals, 41-14 (C)
1991—Oilers, 30-7 (C)
　　　Oilers, 35-3 (H)
1992—Oilers, 38-24 (C)
　　　Oilers, 26-10 (H)
1993—Oilers, 28-12 (H)
　　　Oilers, 38-3 (C)
1994—Oilers, 20-13 (H)
　　　Bengals, 34-31 (C)
1995—Oilers, 38-28 (C)
　　　Bengals, 32-25 (H)
1996—Oilers, 30-27 (C) OT
　　　Bengals, 21-13 (H)
1997—Oilers, 30-7 (T)
　　　Bengals, 41-14 (C)
1998—Bengals, 23-14 (C)
　　　Oilers, 44-14 (T)
1999—Titans, 36-35 (T)
　　　Titans, 24-14 (C)
2000—Titans, 23-14 (C)
　　　Titans, 35-3 (T)
2001—Titans, 20-7 (C)
　　　Bengals, 23-21 (T)
2002—Titans, 30-24 (C)
2004—Titans, 27-20 (T)
2005—Bengals, 31-23 (T)
(RS Pts.—Titans 1,633, Bengals 1,594)
(PS Pts.—Bengals 41, Titans 14)
*Franchise in Houston prior to 1997;
known as Oilers prior to 1999
**AFC First-Round Playoff
CINCINNATI vs. WASHINGTON
RS: Redskins lead series, 4-3
1970—Redskins, 20-0 (W)
1974—Bengals, 28-17 (C)
1979—Redskins, 28-14 (W)
1985—Redskins, 27-24 (W)
1988—Bengals, 20-17 (C) OT
1991—Redskins, 34-27 (C)
2004—Bengals, 17-10 (W)
(RS Pts.—Redskins 153, Bengals 130)

CLEVELAND vs. ARIZONA
RS: Browns lead series, 33-11-3;
See Arizona vs. Cleveland
CLEVELAND vs. ATLANTA
RS: Browns lead series, 10-2;
See Atlanta vs. Cleveland
CLEVELAND vs. BALTIMORE
RS: Ravens lead series, 11-5;
See Baltimore vs. Cleveland
CLEVELAND vs. BUFFALO
RS: Browns lead series, 7-5
PS: Browns lead series, 1-0;
See Buffalo vs. Cleveland
CLEVELAND vs. CAROLINA
RS: Panthers lead series, 3-0;
See Carolina vs. Cleveland
CLEVELAND vs. CHICAGO
RS: Browns lead series, 9-4;

See Chicago vs. Cleveland
CLEVELAND vs. CINCINNATI
RS: Bengals lead series, 34-33;
See Cincinnati vs. Cleveland
CLEVELAND vs. DALLAS
RS: Browns lead series, 15-10
PS: Browns lead series, 2-1
1960—Browns, 48-7 (D)
1961—Browns, 25-7 (C)
    Browns, 38-17 (D)
1962—Browns, 19-10 (C)
    Cowboys, 45-21 (D)
1963—Browns, 41-24 (D)
    Browns, 27-17 (D)
1964—Browns, 27-6 (C)
    Browns, 20-16 (D)
1965—Browns, 23-17 (C)
    Browns, 24-17 (D)
1966—Browns, 30-21 (C)
    Cowboys, 26-14 (D)
1967—Cowboys, 21-14 (C)
    *Cowboys, 52-14 (D)
1968—Cowboys, 28-7 (C)
    *Browns, 31-20 (C)
1969—Browns, 42-10 (C)
    *Browns, 38-14 (D)
1970—Cowboys, 6-2 (C)
1974—Cowboys, 41-17 (D)
1979—Browns, 26-7 (C)
1982—Cowboys, 31-14 (D)
1985—Cowboys, 20-7 (D)
1988—Browns, 24-21 (C)
1991—Cowboys, 26-14 (C)
1994—Browns, 19-14 (D)
2004—Cowboys, 19-12 (D)
(RS Pts.—Browns 555, Cowboys 474)
(PS Pts.—Cowboys 86, Browns 83)
*Conference Championship
CLEVELAND vs. DENVER
RS: Broncos lead series, 16-5
PS: Broncos lead series, 3-0
1970—Browns, 27-13 (D)
1971—Broncos, 27-0 (C)
1972—Browns, 27-20 (D)
1974—Browns, 23-21 (C)
1975—Broncos, 16-15 (D)
1976—Broncos, 44-13 (D)
1978—Broncos, 19-7 (C)
1980—Broncos, 19-16 (C)
1981—Broncos, 23-20 (D) OT
1983—Broncos, 27-6 (D)
1984—Broncos, 24-14 (C)
1986—*Broncos, 23-20 (C) OT
1987—*Broncos, 38-33 (D)
1988—Broncos, 30-7 (D)
1989—Browns, 16-13 (C)
    *Broncos, 37-21 (D)
1990—Browns, 30-29 (D)
1991—Broncos, 17-7 (C)
1992—Broncos, 12-0 (C)
1993—Broncos, 29-14 (C)
1994—Broncos, 26-14 (D)
2000—Broncos, 44-10 (D)
2003—Broncos, 23-20 (D) OT
2006—Broncos, 17-7 (C)
(RS Pts.—Broncos 493, Browns 293)
(PS Pts.—Broncos 98, Browns 74)
*AFC Championship
CLEVELAND vs. DETROIT
RS: Lions lead series, 13-4

PS: Lions lead series, 3-1
1952—Lions, 17-6 (D)
    *Lions, 17-7 (C)
1953—*Lions, 17-16 (D)
1954—Lions, 14-10 (C)
    *Browns, 56-10 (C)
1957—Lions, 20-7 (D)
    *Lions, 59-14 (D)
1958—Lions, 30-10 (C)
1963—Lions, 38-10 (D)
1964—Browns, 37-21 (C)
1967—Lions, 31-14 (D)
1969—Lions, 28-21 (C)
1970—Lions, 41-24 (C)
1975—Lions, 21-10 (D)
1983—Browns, 31-26 (D)
1986—Browns, 24-21 (C)
1989—Lions, 13-10 (D)
1992—Lions, 24-14 (D)
1995—Lions, 38-20 (D)
2001—Browns, 24-14 (C)
2005—Lions, 13-10 (C)
(RS Pts.—Lions 410, Browns 282)
(PS Pts.—Lions 103, Browns 93)
*NFL Championship
CLEVELAND vs. GREEN BAY
RS: Packers lead series, 9-7
PS: Packers lead series, 1-0
1953—Browns, 27-0 (Mil)
1955—Browns, 41-10 (C)
1956—Browns, 24-7 (Mil)
1961—Packers, 49-17 (C)
1964—Packers, 28-21 (Mil)
1965—*Packers, 23-12 (GB)
1966—Packers, 21-20 (C)
1967—Packers, 55-7 (Mil)
1969—Browns, 20-7 (C)
1972—Packers, 26-10 (C)
1980—Browns, 26-21 (C)
1983—Packers, 35-21 (Mil)
1986—Packers, 17-14 (C)
1992—Browns, 17-6 (C)
1995—Packers, 31-20 (C)
2001—Packers, 30-7 (GB)
2005—Browns, 26-24 (GB)
(RS Pts.—Packers 367, Browns 318)
(PS Pts.—Packers 23, Browns 12)
*NFL Championship
CLEVELAND vs. HOUSTON
RS: Series tied, 2-2
2002—Browns, 34-17 (C)
2004—Browns, 22-14 (H)
2005—Texans, 19-16 (H)
2006—Texans, 14-6 (H)
(RS Pts.—Browns 78, Texans 64)
CLEVELAND vs. *INDIANAPOLIS
RS: Browns lead series, 13-11
PS: Series tied, 2-2
1956—Colts, 21-7 (C)
1959—Browns, 38-31 (B)
1962—Colts, 36-14 (C)
1964—**Browns, 27-0 (C)
1968—Browns, 30-20 (B)
    **Colts, 34-0 (C)
1971—Browns, 14-13 (B)
    ***Colts, 20-3 (C)
1973—Browns, 24-14 (C)
1975—Colts, 21-7 (B)
1978—Browns, 45-24 (B)
1979—Browns, 13-10 (C)

1980—Browns, 28-27 (B)
1981—Browns, 42-28 (C)
1983—Browns, 41-23 (C)
1986—Browns, 24-9 (I)
1987—Colts, 9-7 (C)
    ***Browns, 38-21 (C)
1988—Browns, 23-17 (C)
1989—Colts, 23-17 (I) OT
1991—Browns, 31-0 (I)
1992—Colts, 14-3 (I)
1993—Colts, 23-10 (I)
1994—Browns, 21-14 (I)
1999—Colts, 29-28 (C)
2002—Colts, 28-23 (I)
2003—Colts, 9-6 (C)
2005—Colts, 13-6 (I)
(RS Pts.—Browns 502, Colts 456)
(PS Pts.—Colts 75, Browns 68)
*Franchise in Baltimore prior to 1984
**NFL Championship
***AFC Divisional Playoff
CLEVELAND vs. JACKSONVILLE
RS: Jaguars lead series, 8-2
1995—Jaguars, 23-15 (C)
    Jaguars, 24-21 (J)
1999—Jaguars, 24-7 (J)
    Jaguars, 24-14 (C)
2000—Jaguars, 27-7 (C)
    Jaguars, 48-0 (J)
2001—Browns, 23-14 (J)
    Jaguars, 15-10 (C)
2002—Browns, 21-20 (J)
2005—Jaguars, 20-14 (C)
(RS Pts.—Jaguars 239, Browns 132)
CLEVELAND vs. KANSAS CITY
RS: Series tied, 9-9-2
1971—Chiefs, 13-7 (KC)
1972—Chiefs, 31-7 (C)
1973—Tie, 20-20 (KC)
1975—Browns, 40-14 (C)
1976—Chiefs, 39-14 (KC)
1977—Browns, 44-7 (C)
1978—Chiefs, 17-3 (KC)
1979—Browns, 27-24 (KC)
1980—Browns, 20-13 (C)
1984—Chiefs, 10-6 (KC)
1986—Browns, 20-7 (C)
1988—Browns, 6-3 (KC)
1989—Tie, 10-10 (C) OT
1990—Chiefs, 34-0 (KC)
1991—Browns, 20-15 (C)
1994—Chiefs, 20-13 (KC)
1995—Browns, 35-17 (C)
2002—Chiefs, 40-39 (C)
2003—Chiefs, 41-20 (KC)
2006—Browns, 31-28 (C) OT
(RS Pts.—Chiefs 403, Browns 382)
CLEVELAND vs. MIAMI
RS: Dolphins lead series, 7-5
PS: Dolphins lead series, 2-0
1970—Browns, 28-0 (M)
1972—*Dolphins, 20-14 (M)
1973—Dolphins, 17-9 (C)
1976—Browns, 17-13 (C)
1979—Browns, 30-24 (C) OT
1985—*Dolphins, 24-21 (M)
1986—Browns, 26-16 (C)
1988—Dolphins, 38-31 (M)
1989—Dolphins, 13-10 (M) OT
1990—Dolphins, 30-13 (C)

1992—Dolphins, 27-23 (C)
1993—Dolphins, 24-14 (C)
2004—Dolphins, 10-7 (M)
2005—Browns, 22-0 (C)
(RS Pts.—Browns 230, Dolphins 212)
(PS Pts.—Dolphins 44, Browns 35)
*AFC Divisional Playoff

CLEVELAND vs. MINNESOTA
RS: Vikings lead series, 9-3
PS: Vikings lead series, 1-0
1965—Vikings, 27-17 (C)
1967—Browns, 14-10 (C)
1969—Vikings, 51-3 (M)
     *Vikings, 27-7 (M)
1973—Vikings, 26-3 (M)
1975—Vikings, 42-10 (C)
1980—Vikings, 28-23 (M)
1983—Vikings, 27-21 (C)
1986—Browns, 23-20 (M)
1989—Browns, 23-17 (C) OT
1992—Vikings, 17-13 (M)
1995—Vikings, 27-11 (M)
2005—Vikings, 24-12 (M)
(RS Pts.—Vikings 316, Browns 173)
(PS Pts.—Vikings 27, Browns 7)
*NFL Championship

CLEVELAND vs. NEW ENGLAND
RS: Browns lead series, 11-8
PS: Browns lead series, 1-0
1971—Browns, 27-7 (C)
1974—Browns, 21-14 (NE)
1977—Browns, 30-27 (C) OT
1980—Patriots, 34-17 (NE)
1982—Browns, 10-7 (C)
1983—Browns, 30-0 (NE)
1984—Patriots, 17-16 (C)
1985—Browns, 24-20 (C)
1987—Browns, 20-10 (NE)
1991—Browns, 20-0 (NE)
1992—Browns, 19-17 (NE)
1993—Patriots, 20-17 (C)
1994—Browns, 13-6 (C)
     *Browns, 20-13 (C)
1995—Patriots, 17-14 (NE)
1999—Patriots, 19-7 (C)
2000—Browns, 19-11 (C)
2001—Patriots, 27-16 (NE)
2003—Patriots, 9-3 (NE)
2004—Patriots, 42-15 (C)
(RS Pts.—Browns 338, Patriots 304)
(PS Pts.—Browns 20, Patriots 13)
*AFC First-Round Playoff

CLEVELAND vs. NEW ORLEANS
RS: Browns lead series, 11-4
1967—Browns, 42-7 (NO)
1968—Browns, 24-10 (NO)
     Browns, 35-17 (C)
1969—Browns, 27-17 (NO)
1971—Browns, 21-17 (NO)
1975—Browns, 17-16 (C)
1978—Browns, 24-16 (NO)
1981—Browns, 20-17 (C)
1984—Saints, 16-14 (C)
1987—Saints, 28-21 (NO)
1990—Saints, 25-20 (NO)
1993—Browns, 17-13 (C)
1999—Browns, 21-16 (NO)
2002—Browns, 24-15 (NO)
2006—Saints, 19-14 (C)
(RS Pts.—Browns 341, Saints 249)

CLEVELAND vs. N.Y. GIANTS
RS: Browns lead series, 25-19-2
PS: Series tied, 1-1
1950—Giants, 6-0 (C)
     Giants, 17-13 (NY)
     *Browns, 8-3 (C)
1951—Browns, 14-13 (C)
     Browns, 10-0 (NY)
1952—Giants, 17-9 (C)
     Giants, 37-34 (NY)
1953—Browns, 7-0 (NY)
     Browns, 62-14 (C)
1954—Browns, 24-14 (C)
     Browns, 16-7 (NY)
1955—Browns, 24-14 (C)
     Tie, 35-35 (NY)
1956—Giants, 21-9 (C)
     Browns, 24-7 (NY)
1957—Browns, 6-3 (C)
     Browns, 34-28 (NY)
1958—Giants, 21-17 (C)
     Giants, 13-10 (NY)
     *Giants, 10-0 (NY)
1959—Giants, 10-6 (C)
     Giants, 48-7 (NY)
1960—Giants, 17-13 (C)
     Browns, 48-34 (NY)
1961—Giants, 37-21 (C)
     Tie, 7-7 (NY)
1962—Browns, 17-7 (C)
     Giants, 17-13 (NY)
1963—Browns, 35-24 (NY)
     Giants, 33-6 (C)
1964—Browns, 42-20 (C)
     Browns, 52-20 (NY)
1965—Browns, 38-14 (NY)
     Browns, 34-21 (C)
1966—Browns, 28-7 (NY)
     Browns, 49-40 (C)
1967—Giants, 38-34 (NY)
     Browns, 24-14 (C)
1968—Browns, 45-10 (NY)
     Browns, 28-17 (C)
1969—Giants, 27-14 (NY)
1973—Browns, 12-10 (C)
1977—Browns, 21-7 (NY)
1985—Browns, 35-33 (NY)
1991—Giants, 13-10 (NY)
1994—Giants, 16-13 (NY)
2000—Giants, 24-3 (C)
2004—Giants, 27-10 (NY)
(RS Pts.—Browns 1,013, Giants 859)
(PS Pts.—Giants 13, Browns 8)
*Conference Playoff

CLEVELAND vs. N.Y. JETS
RS: Browns lead series, 11-7
PS: Browns lead series, 1-0
1970—Browns, 31-21 (C)
1972—Browns, 26-10 (NY)
1976—Browns, 38-17 (C)
1978—Browns, 37-34 (C) OT
1979—Browns, 25-22 (NY) OT
1980—Browns, 17-14 (C)
1981—Jets, 14-13 (C)
1983—Browns, 10-7 (C)
1984—Jets, 24-20 (C)
1985—Jets, 37-10 (NY)
1986—*Browns, 23-20 (C) OT
1988—Jets, 23-3 (C)
1989—Browns, 38-24 (C)

1990—Jets, 24-21 (NY)
1991—Jets, 17-14 (C)
1994—Browns, 27-7 (C)
2002—Browns, 24-21 (NY)
2004—Jets, 10-7 (C)
2006—Browns, 20-13 (C)
(RS Pts.—Browns 381, Jets 339)
(PS Pts.—Browns 23, Jets 20)
*AFC Divisional Playoff

CLEVELAND vs. *OAKLAND
RS: Raiders lead series, 9-7
PS: Raiders lead series, 2-0
1970—Raiders, 23-20 (O)
1971—Raiders, 34-20 (C)
1973—Browns, 7-3 (O)
1974—Raiders, 40-24 (C)
1975—Raiders, 38-17 (O)
1977—Raiders, 26-10 (C)
1979—Raiders, 19-14 (O)
1980—**Raiders, 14-12 (C)
1982—***Raiders, 27-10 (LA)
1985—Raiders, 21-20 (C)
1986—Raiders, 27-14 (LA)
1987—Browns, 24-17 (LA)
1992—Browns, 28-16 (LA)
1993—Browns, 19-16 (LA)
2000—Raiders, 36-10 (O)
2003—Browns, 13-7 (C)
2005—Browns, 9-7 (O)
2006—Browns, 24-21 (O)
(RS Pts.—Raiders 351, Browns 273)
(PS Pts.—Raiders 41, Browns 22)
*Franchise in Los Angeles from 1982-1994
**AFC Divisional Playoff
***AFC First-Round Playoff

CLEVELAND vs. PHILADELPHIA
RS: Browns lead series, 31-14-1
1950—Browns, 35-10 (P)
     Browns, 13-7 (C)
1951—Browns, 20-17 (C)
     Browns, 24-9 (P)
1952—Browns, 49-7 (P)
     Eagles, 28-20 (C)
1953—Browns, 37-13 (C)
     Eagles, 42-27 (P)
1954—Eagles, 28-10 (P)
     Browns, 6-0 (C)
1955—Browns, 21-17 (C)
     Eagles, 33-17 (P)
1956—Browns, 16-0 (C)
     Browns, 17-14 (C)
1957—Browns, 24-7 (C)
     Eagles, 17-7 (P)
1958—Browns, 28-14 (C)
     Browns, 21-14 (P)
1959—Browns, 28-7 (C)
     Browns, 28-21 (P)
1960—Browns, 41-24 (P)
     Eagles, 31-29 (C)
1961—Eagles, 27-20 (P)
     Browns, 45-24 (C)
1962—Eagles, 35-7 (P)
     Tie, 14-14 (C)
1963—Browns, 37-7 (C)
     Browns, 23-17 (P)
1964—Browns, 28-20 (P)
     Browns, 38-24 (C)
1965—Browns, 35-17 (P)
     Browns, 38-34 (C)
1966—Browns, 27-7 (C)

Eagles, 33-21 (P)
1967—Eagles, 28-24 (P)
1968—Browns, 47-13 (C)
1969—Browns, 27-20 (P)
1972—Browns, 27-17 (P)
1976—Browns, 24-3 (C)
1979—Browns, 24-19 (P)
1982—Eagles, 24-21 (C)
1988—Browns, 19-3 (C)
1991—Eagles, 32-30 (C)
1994—Browns, 26-7 (P)
2000—Eagles, 35-24 (C)
2004—Eagles, 34-31 (C) OT
(RS Pts.—Browns 1,175, Eagles 854)

CLEVELAND vs. PITTSBURGH
RS: Browns lead series, 55-53
PS: Steelers lead series, 2-0
1950—Browns, 30-17 (P)
Browns, 45-7 (C)
1951—Browns, 17-0 (C)
Browns, 28-0 (P)
1952—Browns, 21-20 (P)
Browns, 29-28 (C)
1953—Browns, 34-16 (C)
Browns, 20-16 (P)
1954—Steelers, 55-27 (P)
Browns, 42-7 (C)
1955—Browns, 41-14 (C)
Browns, 30-7 (P)
1956—Browns, 14-10 (P)
Steelers, 24-16 (C)
1957—Browns, 23-12 (P)
Browns, 24-0 (C)
1958—Browns, 45-12 (P)
Browns, 27-10 (C)
1959—Steelers, 17-7 (P)
Steelers, 21-20 (C)
1960—Browns, 28-20 (C)
Steelers, 14-10 (P)
1961—Browns, 30-28 (P)
Steelers, 17-13 (C)
1962—Browns, 41-14 (P)
Browns, 35-14 (C)
1963—Browns, 35-23 (C)
Steelers, 9-7 (P)
1964—Steelers, 23-7 (C)
Browns, 30-17 (P)
1965—Browns, 24-19 (C)
Browns, 42-21 (P)
1966—Browns, 41-10 (C)
Steelers, 16-6 (P)
1967—Browns, 21-10 (C)
Browns, 34-14 (P)
1968—Browns, 31-24 (C)
Browns, 45-24 (P)
1969—Browns, 42-31 (C)
Browns, 24-3 (P)
1970—Browns, 15-7 (C)
Steelers, 28-9 (P)
1971—Browns, 27-17 (C)
Steelers, 26-9 (P)
1972—Browns, 26-24 (C)
Steelers, 30-0 (P)
1973—Steelers, 33-6 (P)
Browns, 21-16 (C)
1974—Steelers, 20-16 (P)
Steelers, 26-16 (C)
1975—Steelers, 42-6 (C)
Steelers, 31-17 (P)
1976—Steelers, 31-14 (P)

Browns, 18-16 (C)
1977—Steelers, 28-14 (C)
Steelers, 35-31 (P)
1978—Steelers, 15-9 (P) OT
Steelers, 34-14 (C)
1979—Steelers, 51-35 (C)
Steelers, 33-30 (P) OT
1980—Browns, 27-26 (C)
Steelers, 16-13 (P)
1981—Steelers, 13-7 (P)
Steelers, 32-10 (C)
1982—Browns, 10-9 (C)
Steelers, 37-21 (P)
1983—Steelers, 44-17 (P)
Browns, 30-17 (C)
1984—Browns, 20-10 (C)
Steelers, 23-20 (P)
1985—Browns, 17-7 (C)
Steelers, 10-9 (P)
1986—Browns, 27-24 (P)
Browns, 37-31 (C) OT
1987—Browns, 34-10 (C)
Browns, 19-13 (P)
1988—Browns, 23-9 (P)
Browns, 27-7 (C)
1989—Browns, 51-0 (P)
Steelers, 17-7 (C)
1990—Browns, 13-3 (C)
Steelers, 35-0 (P)
1991—Browns, 17-14 (C)
Steelers, 17-10 (P)
1992—Browns, 17-9 (C)
Steelers, 23-13 (P)
1993—Browns, 28-23 (C)
Steelers, 16-9 (P)
1994—Steelers, 17-10 (C)
Steelers, 17-7 (P)
*Steelers, 29-9 (P)
1995—Steelers, 20-3 (P)
Steelers, 20-17 (C)
1999—Steelers, 43-0 (C)
Browns, 16-15 (P)
2000—Browns, 23-20 (C)
Steelers, 22-0 (P)
2001—Steelers, 15-12 (C) OT
Steelers, 28-7 (P)
2002—Steelers, 16-13 (P) OT
Steelers, 23-20 (C)
**Steelers, 36-33 (P)
2003—Browns, 33-13 (P)
Steelers, 13-6 (C)
2004—Steelers, 34-23 (P)
Steelers, 24-10 (C)
2005—Steelers, 34-21 (P)
Steelers, 41-0 (C)
2005—Steelers, 24-20 (C)
Steelers, 27-7 (P)
(RS Pts.—Browns 2,200, Steelers 2,148)
(PS Pts.—Steelers 65, Browns 42)
*AFC Divisional Playoff
**AFC First-Round Playoff

CLEVELAND vs. *ST. LOUIS
RS: Rams lead series, 9-8
PS: Browns lead series, 2-1
1950—**Browns, 30-28 (C)
1951—Browns, 38-23 (LA)
**Rams, 24-17 (LA)
1952—Browns, 37-7 (C)
1955—**Browns, 38-14 (LA)
1957—Browns, 45-31 (C)

1958—Browns, 30-27 (LA)
1963—Browns, 20-6 (C)
1965—Rams, 42-7 (LA)
1968—Rams, 24-6 (C)
1973—Rams, 30-17 (LA)
1977—Rams, 9-0 (C)
1978—Browns, 30-19 (C)
1981—Rams, 27-16 (LA)
1984—Rams, 20-17 (LA)
1987—Browns, 30-17 (C)
1990—Rams, 38-23 (C)
1993—Browns, 42-14 (LA)
1999—Rams, 34-3 (StL)
2003—Rams, 26-20 (C)
(RS Pts.—Rams 394, Browns 381)
(PS Pts.—Browns 85, Rams 66)
*Franchise in Los Angeles prior to 1995
**NFL Championship

CLEVELAND vs. SAN DIEGO
RS: Chargers lead series, 13-7-1
1970—Chargers, 27-10 (C)
1972—Browns, 21-17 (SD)
1973—Tie, 16-16 (C)
1974—Chargers, 36-35 (SD)
1976—Browns, 21-17 (C)
1977—Chargers, 37-14 (SD)
1981—Chargers, 44-14 (C)
1982—Chargers, 30-13 (C)
1983—Browns, 30-24 (SD) OT
1985—Browns, 21-7 (SD)
1986—Browns, 47-17 (C)
1987—Chargers, 27-24 (SD) OT
1990—Chargers, 24-14 (C)
1991—Browns, 30-24 (SD) OT
1992—Chargers, 14-13 (C)
1995—Chargers, 31-13 (SD)
1999—Chargers, 23-10 (SD)
2001—Browns, 20-16 (C)
2003—Chargers, 26-20 (C)
2004—Chargers, 21-0 (C)
2006—Chargers, 32-25 (SD)
(RS Pts.—Chargers 510, Browns 411)

CLEVELAND vs. SAN FRANCISCO
RS: Browns lead series, 10-6
1950—Browns, 34-14 (C)
1951—49ers, 24-10 (SF)
1953—Browns, 23-21 (C)
1955—Browns, 38-3 (SF)
1959—49ers, 21-20 (C)
1962—Browns, 13-10 (SF)
1968—Browns, 33-21 (SF)
1970—49ers, 34-31 (C)
1974—Browns, 7-0 (C)
1978—Browns, 24-7 (C)
1981—Browns, 15-12 (SF)
1984—49ers, 41-7 (C)
1987—49ers, 38-24 (SF)
1990—49ers, 20-17 (SF)
1993—Browns, 23-13 (C)
2003—Browns, 13-12 (SF)
(RS Pts.—Browns 332, 49ers 291)

CLEVELAND vs. SEATTLE
RS: Seahawks lead series, 11-4
1977—Seahawks, 20-19 (S)
1978—Seahawks, 47-24 (S)
1979—Seahawks, 29-24 (C)
1980—Browns, 27-3 (S)
1981—Seahawks, 42-21 (S)
1982—Browns, 21-7 (S)
1983—Seahawks, 24-9 (C)

1984—Seahawks, 33-0 (S)
1985—Seahawks, 31-13 (S)
1988—Seahawks, 16-10 (C)
1989—Browns, 17-7 (S)
1993—Seahawks, 22-5 (S)
1994—Browns, 35-9 (C)
2001—Seahawks, 9-6 (C)
2003—Seahawks, 34-7 (S)
(RS Pts.—Seahawks 333, Browns 238)

CLEVELAND vs. TAMPA BAY
RS: Browns lead series, 5-2
1976—Browns, 24-7 (TB)
1980—Browns, 34-27 (TB)
1983—Browns, 20-0 (C)
1989—Browns, 42-31 (TB)
1995—Browns, 22-6 (C)
2002—Buccaneers 17-3 (TB)
2006—Buccaneers, 22-7 (C)
(RS Pts.—Browns 152, Buccaneers 110)

CLEVELAND vs. *TENNESSEE
RS: Browns lead series, 33-26
PS: Titans lead series, 1-0
1970—Browns, 28-14 (C)
    Browns, 21-10 (H)
1971—Browns, 31-0 (C)
    Browns, 37-24 (H)
1972—Browns, 23-17 (H)
    Browns, 20-0 (C)
1973—Browns, 42-13 (C)
    Browns, 23-13 (H)
1974—Browns, 20-7 (C)
    Oilers, 28-24 (H)
1975—Oilers, 40-10 (C)
    Oilers, 21-10 (H)
1976—Browns, 21-7 (H)
    Browns, 13-10 (C)
1977—Browns, 24-23 (H)
    Oilers, 19-15 (C)
1978—Oilers, 16-13 (C)
    Oilers, 14-10 (H)
1979—Oilers, 31-10 (H)
    Browns, 14-7 (C)
1980—Oilers, 16-7 (C)
    Browns, 17-14 (H)
1981—Oilers, 9-3 (C)
    Oilers, 17-13 (H)
1982—Browns, 20-14 (H)
1983—Browns, 25-19 (C) OT
    Oilers, 34-27 (H)
1984—Browns, 27-10 (C)
    Browns, 27-20 (H)
1985—Browns, 21-6 (H)
    Browns, 28-21 (C)
1986—Browns, 23-20 (H)
    Browns, 13-10 (C) OT
1987—Oilers, 15-10 (C)
    Browns, 40-7 (H)
1988—Oilers, 24-17 (H)
    Browns, 28-23 (C)
    **Oilers, 24-23 (C)
1989—Browns, 28-17 (C)
    Browns, 24-20 (H)
1990—Oilers, 35-23 (C)
    Oilers, 58-14 (H)
1991—Oilers, 28-24 (H)
    Oilers, 17-14 (C)
1992—Browns, 24-14 (H)
    Oilers, 17-14 (C)
1993—Oilers, 27-20 (C)
    Oilers, 19-17 (H)

1994—Browns, 11-8 (H)
    Browns, 34-10 (C)
1995—Browns, 14-7 (H)
    Oilers, 37-10 (C)
1999—Titans, 26-9 (T)
    Titans, 33-21 (C)
2000—Titans, 24-10 (T)
    Titans, 24-0 (C)
2001—Titans, 31-15 (C)
    Browns, 41-38 (T)
2002—Browns, 31-28 (T) OT
2005—Browns, 20-14 (C)
(RS Pts.—Browns 1,173, Titans 1,125)
(PS Pts.—Titans 24, Browns 23)
*Franchise in Houston prior to 1997;
known as Oilers prior to 1999
**AFC First-Round Playoff

CLEVELAND vs. WASHINGTON
RS: Browns lead series, 33-9-1
1950—Browns, 20-14 (C)
    Browns, 45-21 (W)
1951—Browns, 45-0 (C)
1952—Browns, 19-15 (C)
    Browns, 48-24 (W)
1953—Browns, 30-14 (W)
    Browns, 27-3 (C)
1954—Browns, 62-3 (C)
    Browns, 34-14 (W)
1955—Redskins, 27-17 (C)
    Browns, 24-14 (W)
1956—Redskins, 20-9 (W)
    Redskins, 20-17 (C)
1957—Browns, 21-17 (C)
    Tie, 30-30 (W)
1958—Browns, 20-10 (W)
    Browns, 21-14 (C)
1959—Browns, 34-7 (C)
    Browns, 31-17 (W)
1960—Browns, 31-10 (W)
    Browns, 27-16 (C)
1961—Browns, 31-7 (C)
    Browns, 17-6 (W)
1962—Redskins, 17-16 (C)
    Redskins, 17-9 (W)
1963—Browns, 37-14 (C)
    Browns, 27-20 (W)
1964—Browns, 27-13 (W)
    Browns, 34-24 (C)
1965—Browns, 17-7 (W)
    Browns, 24-16 (C)
1966—Browns, 38-14 (W)
    Browns, 14-3 (C)
1967—Browns, 42-37 (C)
1968—Browns, 24-21 (W)
1969—Browns, 27-23 (C)
1971—Browns, 20-13 (W)
1975—Redskins, 23-7 (C)
1979—Redskins, 13-9 (C)
1985—Redskins, 14-7 (C)
1988—Browns, 17-13 (W)
1991—Redskins, 42-17 (W)
2004—Browns, 17-13 (C)
(RS Pts.—Browns 1,090, Redskins 680)

DALLAS vs. ARIZONA
RS: Cowboys lead series, 55-27-1
PS: Cardinals lead series, 1-0;
See Arizona vs. Dallas
DALLAS vs. ATLANTA
RS: Cowboys lead series, 13-8

PS: Cowboys lead series, 2-0;
See Atlanta vs. Dallas
DALLAS vs. BALTIMORE
RS: Ravens lead series, 2-0;
See Baltimore vs. Dallas
DALLAS vs. BUFFALO
RS: Cowboys lead series, 4-3
PS: Cowboys lead series, 2-0;
See Buffalo vs. Dallas
DALLAS vs. CAROLINA
RS: Cowboys lead series, 6-1
PS: Panthers lead series, 2-0;
See Carolina vs. Dallas
DALLAS vs. CHICAGO
RS: Cowboys lead series, 10-8
PS: Cowboys lead series, 2-0;
See Chicago vs. Dallas
DALLAS vs. CINCINNATI
RS: Cowboys lead series, 5-4;
See Cincinnati vs. Dallas
DALLAS vs. CLEVELAND
RS: Browns lead series, 15-10
PS: Browns lead series, 2-1;
See Cleveland vs. Dallas
DALLAS vs. DENVER
RS: Broncos lead series, 5-4
PS: Cowboys lead series, 1-0
1973—Cowboys, 22-10 (Den)
1977—Cowboys, 14-6 (Dal)
    *Cowboys, 27-10 (New Orleans)
1980—Broncos, 41-20 (Den)
1986—Broncos, 29-14 (Den)
1992—Cowboys, 31-27 (Den)
1995—Cowboys, 31-21 (Dal)
1998—Broncos, 42-23 (Den)
2001—Broncos, 26-24 (Dal)
2005—Broncos, 24-21 (Dal) OT
(RS Pts.—Broncos 226, Cowboys 200)
(PS Pts.—Cowboys 27, Broncos 10)
*Super Bowl XII
DALLAS vs. DETROIT
RS: Cowboys lead series, 10-9
PS: Series tied, 1-1
1960—Lions, 23-14 (Det)
1963—Cowboys, 17-14 (Dal)
1968—Cowboys, 59-13 (Dal)
1970—*Cowboys, 5-0 (Dal)
1972—Cowboys, 28-24 (Det)
1975—Cowboys, 36-10 (Det)
1977—Cowboys, 37-0 (Dal)
1981—Lions, 27-24 (Det)
1985—Lions, 26-21 (Det)
1986—Cowboys, 31-7 (Det)
1987—Lions, 27-17 (Det)
1991—Lions, 34-10 (Det)
    *Lions, 38-6 (Det)
1992—Cowboys, 37-3 (Det)
1994—Lions, 20-17 (Dal) OT
2001—Lions, 15-10 (Det)
2002—Lions, 9-7 (Det)
2003—Cowboys, 38-7 (Det)
2004—Cowboys, 31-21 (Dal)
2005—Cowboys, 20-7 (Dal)
2006—Lions, 39-31 (Dal)
(RS Pts.—Cowboys 485, Lions 326)
(PS Pts.—Lions 38, Cowboys 11)
*NFC Divisional Playoff
DALLAS vs. GREEN BAY
RS: Series tied, 10-10
PS: Cowboys lead series, 4-2

1960—Packers, 41-7 (GB)
1964—Packers, 45-21 (D)
1965—Packers, 13-3 (Mil)
1966—*Packers, 34-27 (D)
1967—*Packers, 21-17 (GB)
1968—Packers, 28-17 (D)
1970—Cowboys, 16-3 (D)
1972—Packers, 16-13 (Mil)
1975—Packers, 19-17 (D)
1978—Cowboys, 42-14 (Mil)
1980—Cowboys, 28-7 (Mil)
1982—**Cowboys, 37-26 (D)
1984—Cowboys, 20-6 (D)
1989—Packers, 31-13 (GB)
      Packers, 20-10 (D)
1991—Cowboys, 20-17 (Mil)
1993—Cowboys, 36-14 (D)
    ***Cowboys, 27-17 (D)
1994—Cowboys, 42-31 (D)
    ***Cowboys, 35-9 (D)
1995—Cowboys, 34-24 (D)
    ****Cowboys, 38-27 (D)
1996—Cowboys, 21-6 (D)
1997—Packers, 45-17 (GB)
1999—Cowboys, 27-13 (D)
2004—Packers, 41-20 (GB)
(RS Pts.—Cowboys 434, Packers 424)
(PS Pts.—Cowboys 181, Packers 134)
*NFL Championship
**NFC Second-Round Playoff
***NFC Divisional Playoff
****NFC Championship

DALLAS vs. HOUSTON
RS: Series tied, 1-1
2002—Texans, 19-10 (H)
2006—Cowboys, 34-6 (D)
(RS Pts.—Cowboys 44, Texans 25)

DALLAS vs. *INDIANAPOLIS
RS: Cowboys lead series, 8-5
PS: Colts lead series, 1-0
1960—Colts, 45-7 (D)
1967—Colts, 23-17 (B)
1969—Cowboys, 27-10 (D)
1970—**Colts, 16-13 (Miami)
1972—Cowboys, 21-0 (B)
1976—Cowboys, 30-27 (D)
1978—Cowboys, 38-0 (D)
1981—Cowboys, 37-13 (B)
1984—Cowboys, 22-3 (D)
1993—Cowboys, 27-3 (I)
1996—Colts, 25-24 (D)
1999—Colts, 34-24 (I)
2002—Colts, 20-3 (I)
2006—Cowboys, 21-14 (D)
(RS Pts.—Cowboys 298, Colts 217)
(PS Pts.—Colts 16, Cowboys 13)
*Franchise in Baltimore prior to 1984
**Super Bowl V

DALLAS vs. JACKSONVILLE
RS: Series tied, 2-2
1997—Cowboys, 26-22 (D)
2000—Jaguars, 23-17 (D) OT
2002—Cowboys, 21-19 (D)
2006—Jaguars, 24-17 (J)
(RS Pts.—Jaguars 88, Cowboys 81)

DALLAS vs. KANSAS CITY
RS: Cowboys lead series, 5-3
1970—Cowboys, 27-16 (KC)
1975—Chiefs, 34-31 (D)
1983—Cowboys, 41-21 (D)

1989—Chiefs, 36-28 (KC)
1992—Cowboys, 17-10 (D)
1995—Cowboys, 24-12 (D)
1998—Chiefs, 20-17 (KC)
2005—Cowboys, 31-28 (D)
(RS Pts.—Cowboys 216, Chiefs 177)

DALLAS vs. MIAMI
RS: Dolphins lead series, 7-3
PS: Cowboys lead series, 1-0
1971—*Cowboys, 24-3 (New Orleans)
1973—Dolphins, 14-7 (D)
1978—Dolphins, 23-16 (M)
1981—Cowboys, 28-27 (D)
1984—Dolphins, 28-21 (M)
1987—Dolphins, 20-14 (D)
1989—Dolphins, 17-14 (D)
1993—Dolphins, 16-14 (D)
1996—Cowboys, 29-10 (M)
1999—Cowboys, 20-0 (D)
2003—Dolphins, 40-21 (D)
(RS Pts.—Dolphins 195, Cowboys 184)
(PS Pts.—Cowboys 24, Dolphins 3)
*Super Bowl VI

DALLAS vs. MINNESOTA
RS: Vikings lead series, 10-9
PS: Cowboys lead series, 4-2
1961—Cowboys, 21-7 (D)
      Cowboys, 28-0 (M)
1966—Cowboys, 28-17 (D)
1968—Cowboys, 20-7 (M)
1970—Vikings, 54-13 (M)
1971—*Cowboys, 20-12 (M)
1973—**Vikings, 27-10 (D)
1974—Vikings, 23-21 (D)
1975—*Cowboys, 17-14 (M)
1977—Cowboys, 16-10 (M) OT
      **Cowboys, 23-6 (D)
1978—Vikings, 21-10 (D)
1979—Cowboys, 36-20 (M)
1982—Vikings, 31-27 (M)
1983—Cowboys, 37-24 (M)
1987—Vikings, 44-38 (D) OT
1988—Vikings, 43-3 (D)
1993—Cowboys, 37-20 (M)
1995—Cowboys, 23-17 (M) OT
1996—***Cowboys, 40-15 (D)
1998—Vikings, 46-36 (D)
1999—Vikings, 27-17 (M)
    ***Vikings, 27-10 (M)
2000—Vikings, 27-15 (D)
2004—Vikings, 35-17 (M)
(RS Pts.—Vikings 473, Cowboys 443)
(PS Pts.—Cowboys 120, Vikings 101)
*NFC Divisional Playoff
**NFC Championship
***NFC First-Round Playoff

DALLAS vs. NEW ENGLAND
RS: Cowboys lead series, 7-2
1971—Cowboys, 44-21 (D)
1975—Cowboys, 34-31 (NE)
1978—Cowboys, 17-10 (D)
1981—Cowboys, 35-21 (NE)
1984—Cowboys, 20-17 (D)
1987—Cowboys, 23-17 (NE) OT
1996—Cowboys, 12-6 (D)
1999—Patriots, 13-6 (NE)
2003—Patriots, 12-0 (NE)
(RS Pts.—Cowboys 191, Patriots 148)

DALLAS vs. NEW ORLEANS
RS: Cowboys lead series, 14-8

1967—Cowboys, 14-10 (D)
      Cowboys, 27-10 (NO)
1968—Cowboys, 17-3 (NO)
1969—Cowboys, 21-17 (NO)
      Cowboys, 33-17 (D)
1971—Saints, 24-14 (NO)
1973—Cowboys, 40-3 (D)
1976—Cowboys, 24-6 (NO)
1978—Cowboys, 27-7 (D)
1982—Cowboys, 21-7 (D)
1983—Cowboys, 21-20 (D)
1984—Cowboys, 30-27 (D) OT
1988—Saints, 20-17 (NO)
1989—Saints, 28-0 (NO)
1990—Cowboys, 17-13 (D)
1991—Cowboys, 23-14 (D)
1994—Cowboys, 24-16 (NO)
1998—Saints, 22-3 (NO)
1999—Saints, 31-24 (NO)
2003—Saints, 13-7 (NO)
2004—Cowboys, 27-13 (D)
2006—Saints, 42-17 (D)
(RS Pts.—Cowboys 434, Saints 377)

DALLAS vs. N.Y. GIANTS
RS: Cowboys lead series, 52-35-2
1960—Tie, 31-31 (NY)
1961—Giants, 31-10 (D)
      Cowboys, 17-16 (NY)
1962—Giants, 41-10 (D)
      Giants, 41-31 (NY)
1963—Giants, 37-21 (NY)
      Giants, 34-27 (D)
1964—Tie, 13-13 (D)
      Cowboys, 31-21 (NY)
1965—Cowboys, 31-2 (D)
      Cowboys, 38-20 (NY)
1966—Cowboys, 52-7 (D)
      Cowboys, 17-7 (NY)
1967—Cowboys, 38-24 (D)
1968—Giants, 27-21 (D)
      Cowboys, 28-10 (NY)
1969—Cowboys, 25-3 (D)
1970—Cowboys, 28-10 (D)
      Giants, 23-20 (NY)
1971—Cowboys, 20-13 (D)
      Cowboys, 42-14 (NY)
1972—Cowboys, 23-14 (NY)
      Giants, 23-3 (D)
1973—Cowboys, 45-28 (D)
      Cowboys, 23-10 (New Haven)
1974—Giants, 14-6 (D)
      Cowboys, 21-7 (New Haven)
1975—Cowboys, 13-7 (NY)
      Cowboys, 14-3 (D)
1976—Cowboys, 24-14 (NY)
      Cowboys, 9-3 (D)
1977—Cowboys, 41-21 (D)
      Cowboys, 24-10 (NY)
1978—Cowboys, 34-24 (NY)
      Cowboys, 24-3 (D)
1979—Cowboys, 16-14 (NY)
      Cowboys, 28-7 (D)
1980—Cowboys, 24-3 (D)
      Giants, 38-35 (NY)
1981—Cowboys, 18-10 (D)
      Giants, 13-10 (NY) OT
1983—Cowboys, 28-13 (D)
      Cowboys, 38-20 (NY)
1984—Giants, 28-7 (NY)
      Giants, 19-7 (D)

1985—Cowboys, 30-29 (NY)
    Cowboys, 28-21 (D)
1986—Cowboys, 31-28 (D)
    Giants, 17-14 (NY)
1987—Cowboys, 16-14 (NY)
    Cowboys, 33-24 (D)
1988—Giants, 12-10 (D)
    Giants, 29-21 (NY)
1989—Cowboys, 30-13 (D)
    Giants, 15-0 (NY)
1990—Giants, 28-7 (D)
    Giants, 31-17 (NY)
1991—Cowboys, 21-16 (D)
    Giants, 22-9 (NY)
1992—Cowboys, 34-28 (NY)
    Cowboys, 30-3 (D)
1993—Cowboys, 31-9 (D)
    Cowboys, 16-13 (NY) OT
1994—Cowboys, 38-10 (D)
    Giants, 15-10 (NY)
1995—Cowboys, 35-0 (NY)
    Cowboys, 21-20 (D)
1996—Cowboys, 27-0 (D)
    Giants, 20-6 (NY)
1997—Giants, 20-17 (NY)
    Giants, 20-7 (D)
1998—Cowboys, 31-7 (NY)
    Cowboys, 16-6 (D)
1999—Giants, 13-10 (NY)
    Cowboys, 26-18 (D)
2000—Giants, 19-14 (NY)
    Giants, 17-13 (D)
2001—Giants, 27-24 (NY) OT
    Cowboys, 20-13 (D)
2002—Giants, 21-17 (D)
    Giants, 37-7 (NY)
2003—Cowboys, 35-32 (NY) OT
    Cowboys, 19-3 (D)
2004—Giants, 26-10 (D)
    Giants, 28-24 (NY)
2005—Cowboys, 16-13 (D) OT
    Giants, 17-10 (NY)
2006—Giants, 36-22 (D)
    Cowboys, 23-20 (NY)
(RS Pts.—Cowboys 1,925, Giants 1,598)

DALLAS vs. N.Y. JETS
RS: Cowboys lead series, 6-2
1971—Cowboys, 52-10 (D)
1975—Cowboys, 31-21 (NY)
1978—Cowboys, 30-7 (NY)
1987—Cowboys, 38-24 (NY)
1990—Jets, 24-9 (NY)
1993—Cowboys, 28-7 (NY)
1999—Jets, 22-21 (D)
2003—Cowboys, 17-6 (NY)
(RS Pts.—Cowboys 226, Jets 121)

DALLAS vs. *OAKLAND
RS: Raiders lead series, 6-3
1974—Raiders, 27-23 (O)
1980—Cowboys, 19-13 (O)
1983—Raiders, 40-38 (D)
1986—Raiders, 17-13 (D)
1992—Cowboys, 28-13 (LA)
1995—Cowboys, 34-21 (O)
1998—Raiders, 13-12 (O)
2001—Raiders, 28-21 (O)
2005—Raiders, 19-13 (O)
(RS Pts.—Cowboys 201, Raiders 191)
Franchise in Los Angeles from 1982-1994

DALLAS vs. PHILADELPHIA

RS: Cowboys lead series, 51-41
PS: Cowboys lead series, 2-1
1960—Eagles, 27-25 (D)
1961—Eagles, 43-7 (D)
    Eagles, 35-13 (P)
1962—Cowboys, 41-19 (D)
    Eagles, 28-14 (P)
1963—Eagles, 24-21 (P)
    Cowboys, 27-20 (D)
1964—Eagles, 17-14 (D)
    Eagles, 24-14 (P)
1965—Eagles, 35-24 (D)
    Cowboys, 21-19 (P)
1966—Cowboys, 56-7 (D)
    Eagles, 24-23 (P)
1967—Eagles, 21-14 (P)
    Cowboys, 38-17 (D)
1968—Cowboys, 45-13 (P)
    Cowboys, 34-14 (D)
1969—Cowboys, 38-7 (P)
    Cowboys, 49-14 (D)
1970—Cowboys, 17-7 (P)
    Cowboys, 21-17 (D)
1971—Cowboys, 42-7 (P)
    Cowboys, 20-7 (D)
1972—Cowboys, 28-6 (D)
    Cowboys, 28-7 (P)
1973—Eagles, 30-16 (P)
    Cowboys, 31-10 (D)
1974—Eagles, 13-10 (D)
    Cowboys, 31-24 (D)
1975—Cowboys, 20-17 (P)
    Cowboys, 27-17 (D)
1976—Cowboys, 27-7 (D)
    Cowboys, 26-7 (P)
1977—Cowboys, 16-10 (P)
    Cowboys, 24-14 (D)
1978—Cowboys, 14-7 (D)
    Cowboys, 31-13 (P)
1979—Eagles, 31-21 (D)
    Cowboys, 24-17 (P)
1980—Eagles, 17-10 (P)
    Cowboys, 35-27 (D)
    *Eagles, 20-7 (P)
1981—Cowboys, 17-14 (P)
    Cowboys, 21-10 (D)
1982—Eagles, 24-20 (D)
1983—Cowboys, 37-7 (D)
    Cowboys, 27-20 (P)
1984—Cowboys, 23-17 (D)
    Cowboys, 26-10 (P)
1985—Eagles, 16-14 (P)
    Cowboys, 34-17 (D)
1986—Cowboys, 17-14 (P)
    Eagles, 23-21 (D)
1987—Cowboys, 41-22 (D)
    Eagles, 37-20 (P)
1988—Eagles, 24-23 (P)
    Eagles, 23-7 (D)
1989—Eagles, 27-0 (D)
    Eagles, 20-10 (P)
1990—Eagles, 21-20 (D)
    Eagles, 17-3 (P)
1991—Eagles, 24-0 (D)
    Cowboys, 25-13 (P)
1992—Eagles, 31-7 (P)
    Cowboys, 20-10 (D)
    **Cowboys, 34-10 (D)
1993—Cowboys, 23-10 (P)
    Cowboys, 23-17 (D)

1994—Cowboys, 24-13 (D)
    Cowboys, 31-19 (P)
1995—Cowboys, 34-12 (D)
    Eagles, 20-17 (P)
    **Cowboys, 30-11 (D)
1996—Cowboys, 23-19 (P)
    Eagles, 31-21 (D)
1997—Cowboys, 21-20 (D)
    Eagles, 13-12 (P)
1998—Cowboys, 34-0 (P)
    Cowboys, 13-9 (D)
1999—Eagles, 13-10 (P)
    Cowboys, 20-10 (D)
2000—Cowboys, 41-14 (D)
    Eagles, 16-13 (P) OT
2001—Eagles, 40-18 (D)
    Eagles, 36-3 (D)
2002—Eagles, 44-13 (P)
    Eagles, 27-3 (D)
2003—Cowboys, 23-21 (D)
    Eagles, 36-10 (P)
2004—Eagles, 49-21 (D)
    Eagles, 12-7 (P)
2005—Cowboys, 33-10 (D)
    Cowboys, 21-20 (P)
2006—Eagles, 38-24 (P)
    Eagles, 23-7 (D)
(RS Pts.—Cowboys 1,986, Eagles 1,780)
(PS Pts.—Cowboys 71, Eagles 41)
NFC Championship
**NFC Divisional Playoff*

DALLAS vs. PITTSBURGH
RS: Cowboys lead series, 14-12
PS: Steelers lead series, 2-1
1960—Steelers, 35-28 (D)
1961—Cowboys, 27-24 (D)
    Steelers, 37-7 (P)
1962—Steelers, 30-28 (D)
    Cowboys, 42-27 (P)
1963—Steelers, 27-21 (P)
    Steelers, 24-19 (D)
1964—Steelers, 23-17 (P)
    Cowboys, 17-14 (D)
1965—Steelers, 22-13 (P)
    Cowboys, 24-17 (D)
1966—Cowboys, 52-21 (D)
    Cowboys, 20-7 (P)
1967—Cowboys, 24-21 (P)
1968—Cowboys, 28-7 (D)
1969—Cowboys, 10-7 (P)
1972—Cowboys, 17-13 (D)
1975—*Steelers, 21-17 (Miami)
1977—Steelers, 28-13 (P)
1978—**Steelers, 35-31 (Miami)
1979—Steelers, 14-3 (P)
1982—Steelers, 36-28 (D)
1985—Cowboys, 27-13 (D)
1988—Steelers, 24-21 (P)
1991—Cowboys, 20-10 (D)
1994—Cowboys, 26-9 (P)
1995—***Cowboys, 27-17 (Tempe)
1997—Cowboys, 37-7 (P)
2004—Steelers, 24-20 (D)
(RS Pts.—Cowboys 589, Steelers 521)
(PS Pts.—Cowboys 75, Steelers 73)
Super Bowl X
**Super Bowl XIII*
***Super Bowl XXX*

DALLAS vs. *ST. LOUIS
RS: Rams lead series, 10-9

PS: Series tied, 4-4
1960—Rams, 38-13 (D)
1962—Cowboys, 27-17 (LA)
1967—Rams, 35-13 (D)
1969—Rams, 24-23 (LA)
1971—Cowboys, 28-21 (D)
1973—Rams, 37-31 (LA)
   **Cowboys, 27-16 (D)
1975—Cowboys, 18-7 (D)
   ***Cowboys, 37-7 (LA)
1976—**Rams, 14-12 (D)
1978—Rams, 27-14 (LA)
   ***Cowboys, 28-0 (LA)
1979—Cowboys, 30-6 (D)
   **Rams, 21-19 (D)
1980—Rams, 38-14 (LA)
   ****Cowboys, 34-13 (D)
1981—Cowboys, 29-17 (D)
1983—****Rams, 24-17 (D)
1984—Cowboys, 20-13 (LA)
1985—**Rams, 20-0 (LA)
1986—Rams, 29-10 (LA)
1987—Cowboys, 29-21 (LA)
1989—Rams, 35-31 (D)
1990—Cowboys, 24-21 (LA)
1992—Rams, 27-23 (D)
2002—Cowboys, 13-10 (StL)
2005—Cowboys, 20-10 (D)
(RS Pts.—Rams 443, Cowboys 400)
(PS Pts.—Cowboys 174, Rams 115)
*Franchise in Los Angeles prior to 1995
**NFC Divisional Playoff
***NFC Championship
****NFC First-Round Playoff

DALLAS vs. SAN DIEGO
RS: Cowboys lead series, 6-2
1972—Cowboys, 34-28 (SD)
1980—Cowboys, 42-31 (D)
1983—Chargers, 24-23 (SD)
1986—Cowboys, 24-21 (SD)
1990—Cowboys, 17-14 (D)
1995—Cowboys, 23-9 (SD)
2001—Chargers, 32-21 (D)
2005—Cowboys, 28-24 (SD)
(RS Pts.—Cowboys 212, Chargers 183)

DALLAS vs. SAN FRANCISCO
RS: 49ers lead series, 14-9-1
PS: Cowboys lead series, 5-2
1960—49ers, 26-14 (D)
1963—49ers, 31-24 (SF)
1965—Cowboys, 39-31 (D)
1967—49ers, 24-16 (SF)
1969—Tie, 24-24 (D)
1970—*Cowboys, 17-10 (SF)
1971—*Cowboys, 14-3 (D)
1972—49ers, 31-10 (D)
   **Cowboys, 30-28 (SF)
1974—Cowboys, 20-14 (D)
1977—Cowboys, 42-35 (SF)
1979—Cowboys, 21-13 (SF)
1980—Cowboys, 59-14 (D)
1981—49ers, 45-14 (SF)
   *49ers, 28-27 (SF)
1983—49ers, 42-17 (SF)
1985—49ers, 31-16 (SF)
1989—49ers, 31-14 (D)
1990—49ers, 24-6 (D)
1992—*Cowboys, 30-20 (SF)
1993—Cowboys, 26-17 (D)
   *Cowboys, 38-21 (D)

1994—49ers, 21-14 (SF)
   *49ers, 38-28 (SF)
1995—49ers, 38-20 (D)
1996—Cowboys, 20-17 (SF) OT
1997—49ers, 17-10 (SF)
2000—49ers, 41-24 (D)
2001—Cowboys, 27-21 (D)
2002—49ers, 31-27 (D)
2005—Cowboys, 34-31 (SF)
(RS Pts.—49ers 650, Cowboys 538)
(PS Pts.—Cowboys 184, 49ers 148)
*NFC Championship
**NFC Divisional Playoff

DALLAS vs. SEATTLE
RS: Cowboys lead series, 6-4
PS: Seahawks lead series, 1-0
1976—Cowboys, 28-13 (S)
1980—Cowboys, 51-7 (D)
1983—Cowboys, 35-10 (S)
1986—Seahawks, 31-14 (D)
1992—Cowboys, 27-0 (D)
1998—Cowboys, 30-22 (D)
2001—Seahawks, 29-3 (S)
2002—Seahawks, 17-14 (D)
2004—Cowboys, 43-39 (S)
2005—Seahawks, 13-10 (S)
2006—*Seahawks, 21-20 (S)
(RS Pts.—Cowboys 255, Seahawks 181)
(PS Pts.—Seahawks 21, Cowboys 20)
*NFC First-Round Playoff

DALLAS vs. TAMPA BAY
RS: Cowboys lead series, 7-3
PS: Cowboys lead series, 2-0
1977—Cowboys, 23-7 (D)
1980—Cowboys, 28-17 (D)
1981—*Cowboys, 38-0 (D)
1982—Cowboys, 14-9 (D)
   **Cowboys, 30-17 (D)
1983—Cowboys, 27-24 (D) OT
1990—Cowboys, 14-10 (D)
   Cowboys, 17-13 (TB)
2000—Buccaneers, 27-7 (TB)
2001—Buccaneers, 10-6 (D)
2003—Buccaneers, 16-0 (TB)
2006—Cowboys, 38-10 (D)
(RS Pts.—Cowboys 174, Buccaneers 143)
(PS Pts.—Cowboys 68, Buccaneers 17)
*NFC Divisional Playoff
**NFC First-Round Playoff

DALLAS vs. *TENNESSEE
RS: Cowboys lead series, 7-5
1970—Cowboys, 52-10 (D)
1974—Cowboys, 10-0 (H)
1979—Oilers, 30-24 (D)
1982—Cowboys, 37-7 (H)
1985—Cowboys, 17-10 (H)
1988—Oilers, 25-17 (D)
1991—Oilers, 26-23 (H) OT
1994—Cowboys, 20-17 (D)
1997—Oilers, 27-14 (D)
2000—Titans, 31-0 (T)
2002—Cowboys, 21-13 (D)
2006—Cowboys, 45-14 (T)
(RS Pts.—Cowboys 280, Titans 210)
*Franchise in Houston prior to 1997;
known as Oilers prior to 1999

DALLAS vs. WASHINGTON
RS: Cowboys lead series, 55-35-2
PS: Redskins lead series, 2-0
1960—Redskins, 26-14 (W)

1961—Tie, 28-28 (D)
   Redskins, 34-24 (W)
1962—Tie, 35-35 (D)
   Cowboys, 38-10 (W)
1963—Redskins, 21-17 (W)
   Cowboys, 35-20 (D)
1964—Cowboys, 24-18 (D)
   Redskins, 28-16 (W)
1965—Cowboys, 27-7 (D)
   Redskins, 34-31 (W)
1966—Cowboys, 31-30 (W)
   Redskins, 34-31 (D)
1967—Cowboys, 17-14 (W)
   Redskins, 27-20 (D)
1968—Cowboys, 44-24 (W)
   Cowboys, 29-20 (D)
1969—Cowboys, 41-28 (W)
   Cowboys, 20-10 (D)
1970—Cowboys, 45-21 (W)
   Cowboys, 34-0 (D)
1971—Redskins, 20-16 (D)
   Cowboys, 13-0 (W)
1972—Redskins, 24-20 (W)
   Redskins, 34-24 (D)
   *Redskins, 26-3 (D)
1973—Redskins, 14-7 (W)
   Cowboys, 27-7 (D)
1974—Redskins, 28-21 (W)
   Cowboys, 24-23 (D)
1975—Redskins, 30-24 (W) OT
   Cowboys, 31-10 (D)
1976—Cowboys, 20-7 (W)
   Redskins, 27-14 (D)
1977—Cowboys, 34-16 (D)
   Cowboys, 14-7 (W)
1978—Redskins, 9-5 (W)
   Cowboys, 37-10 (D)
1979—Redskins, 34-20 (W)
   Cowboys, 35-34 (D)
1980—Cowboys, 17-3 (W)
   Cowboys, 14-10 (D)
1981—Cowboys, 26-10 (W)
   Cowboys, 24-10 (D)
1982—Cowboys, 24-10 (W)
   *Redskins, 31-17 (W)
1983—Cowboys, 31-30 (W)
   Redskins, 31-10 (D)
1984—Cowboys, 34-14 (W)
   Redskins, 30-28 (D)
1985—Cowboys, 44-14 (D)
   Cowboys, 13-7 (W)
1986—Cowboys, 30-6 (D)
   Redskins, 41-14 (W)
1987—Redskins, 13-7 (D)
   Redskins, 24-20 (W)
1988—Redskins, 35-17 (D)
   Cowboys, 24-17 (W)
1989—Redskins, 30-7 (D)
   Cowboys, 13-3 (W)
1990—Redskins, 19-15 (W)
   Cowboys, 27-17 (D)
1991—Redskins, 33-31 (D)
   Cowboys, 24-21 (W)
1992—Cowboys, 23-10 (D)
   Redskins, 20-17 (W)
1993—Redskins, 35-16 (W)
   Cowboys, 38-3 (D)
1994—Cowboys, 34-7 (W)
   Cowboys, 31-7 (D)
1995—Redskins, 27-23 (W)

Redskins, 24-17 (D)
1996—Cowboys, 21-10 (D)
Redskins, 37-10 (W)
1997—Redskins, 21-16 (W)
Cowboys, 17-14 (D)
1998—Cowboys, 31-10 (W)
Cowboys, 23-7 (D)
1999—Cowboys, 41-35 (W) OT
Cowboys, 38-20 (D)
2000—Cowboys, 27-21 (W)
Cowboys, 32-13 (D)
2001—Cowboys, 9-7 (D)
Cowboys, 20-14 (W)
2002—Cowboys, 27-20 (W)
Redskins, 20-14 (W)
2003—Cowboys, 21-14 (D)
Cowboys, 27-0 (W)
2004—Cowboys, 21-18 (W)
Cowboys, 13-10 (D)
2005—Redskins, 14-13 (D)
Redskins, 35-7 (W)
2006—Cowboys, 27-10 (D)
Redskins, 22-19 (W)
(RS Pts.—Cowboys 2,144, Redskins 1,746)
(PS Pts.—Redskins 57, Cowboys 20)
*NFC Championship

DENVER vs. ARIZONA
RS: Broncos lead series, 7-0-1;
See Arizona vs. Denver
DENVER vs. ATLANTA
RS: Broncos lead series, 7-4
PS: Broncos lead series, 1-0;
See Atlanta vs. Denver
DENVER vs. BALTIMORE
RS: Series tied, 3-3
PS: Ravens lead series, 1-0;
See Baltimore vs. Denver
DENVER vs. BUFFALO
RS: Bills lead series, 17-14-1
PS: Bills lead series, 1-0;
See Buffalo vs. Denver
DENVER vs. CAROLINA
RS: Broncos lead series, 2-0;
See Carolina vs. Denver
DENVER vs. CHICAGO
RS: Series tied, 6-6;
See Chicago vs. Denver
DENVER vs. CINCINNATI
RS: Broncos lead series, 16-8;
See Cincinnati vs. Denver
DENVER vs. CLEVELAND
RS: Broncos lead series, 16-5
PS: Broncos lead series, 3-0;
See Cleveland vs. Denver
DENVER vs. DALLAS
RS: Broncos lead series, 5-4
PS: Cowboys lead series, 1-0;
See Dallas vs. Denver
DENVER vs. DETROIT
RS: Broncos lead series, 6-3
1971—Lions, 24-20 (Den)
1974—Broncos, 31-27 (Det)
1978—Lions, 17-14 (Den)
1981—Broncos, 27-21 (Den)
1984—Broncos, 28-7 (Det)
1987—Broncos, 34-0 (Den)
1990—Lions, 40-27 (Det)
1999—Broncos, 17-7 (Det)
2003—Broncos, 20-16 (Den)

(RS Pts.—Broncos 218, Lions 159)
DENVER vs. GREEN BAY
RS: Broncos lead series, 5-4-1
PS: Broncos lead series, 1-0
1971—Packers, 34-13 (Mil)
1975—Broncos, 23-13 (D)
1978—Broncos, 16-3 (D)
1984—Broncos, 17-14 (D)
1987—Tie, 17-17 (Mil) OT
1990—Broncos, 22-13 (D)
1993—Packers, 30-27 (GB)
1996—Packers, 41-6 (GB)
1997—*Broncos, 31-24 (San Diego)
1999—Broncos, 31-10 (D)
2003—Packers, 31-3 (GB)
(RS Pts.—Packers 206, Broncos 175)
(PS Pts.—Broncos 31, Packers 24)
*Super Bowl XXXII
DENVER vs. HOUSTON
RS: Broncos lead series, 1-0
2004—Broncos, 31-13 (D)
(RS Pts.—Broncos 31, Texans 13)
DENVER vs. *INDIANAPOLIS
RS: Broncos lead series, 11-5
PS: Colts lead series, 2-0
1974—Broncos, 17-6 (B)
1977—Broncos, 27-13 (D)
1978—Colts, 7-6 (B)
1981—Broncos, 28-10 (D)
1983—Broncos, 17-10 (B)
Broncos, 21-19 (D)
1985—Broncos, 15-10 (I)
1988—Colts, 55-23 (I)
1989—Broncos, 14-3 (D)
1990—Broncos, 27-17 (I)
1993—Broncos, 35-13 (D)
2001—Colts, 29-10 (I)
2002—Colts, 23-20 (D) OT
2003—Broncos, 31-17 (I)
**Colts, 41-10 (I)
2004—Broncos, 33-14 (D)
**Colts, 49-24 (I)
2006—Colts, 34-31 (D)
(RS Pts.—Broncos 355, Colts 280)
(PS Pts.—Colts 90, Broncos 34)
*Franchise in Baltimore prior to 1984
**AFC First-Round Playoff
DENVER vs. JACKSONVILLE
RS: Broncos lead series, 3-2
PS: Series tied, 1-1
1995—Broncos, 31-23 (D)
1996—*Jaguars, 30-27 (D)
1997—**Broncos, 42-17 (D)
1998—Broncos, 37-24 (D)
1999—Jaguars, 27-24 (J)
2004—Jaguars, 7-6 (J)
2005—Broncos, 20-7 (J)
(RS Pts.—Broncos 118, Jaguars 88)
(PS Pts.—Broncos 69, Jaguars 47)
*AFC Divisional Playoff
**AFC First-Round Playoff
DENVER vs. *KANSAS CITY
RS: Chiefs lead series, 52-41
PS: Broncos lead series, 1-0
1960—Texans, 17-14 (D)
Texans, 34-7 (Dal)
1961—Texans, 19-12 (D)
Texans, 49-21 (Dal)
1962—Texans, 24-3 (D)
Texans, 17-10 (Dal)

1963—Chiefs, 59-7 (D)
Chiefs, 52-21 (KC)
1964—Broncos, 33-27 (D)
Chiefs, 49-39 (KC)
1965—Chiefs, 31-23 (D)
Chiefs, 45-35 (KC)
1966—Chiefs, 37-10 (KC)
Chiefs, 56-10 (D)
1967—Chiefs, 52-9 (KC)
Chiefs, 38-24 (D)
1968—Chiefs, 34-2 (KC)
Chiefs, 30-7 (D)
1969—Chiefs, 26-13 (D)
Chiefs, 31-17 (KC)
1970—Broncos, 26-13 (D)
Chiefs, 16-0 (KC)
1971—Chiefs, 16-3 (D)
Chiefs, 28-10 (KC)
1972—Chiefs, 45-24 (D)
Chiefs, 24-21 (KC)
1973—Chiefs, 16-14 (KC)
Broncos, 14-10 (D)
1974—Broncos, 17-14 (KC)
Chiefs, 42-34 (D)
1975—Broncos, 37-33 (D)
Chiefs, 26-13 (KC)
1976—Broncos, 35-26 (KC)
Broncos, 17-16 (D)
1977—Broncos, 23-7 (D)
Broncos, 14-7 (KC)
1978—Broncos, 23-17 (KC) OT
Broncos, 24-3 (D)
1979—Broncos, 24-10 (KC)
Broncos, 20-3 (D)
1980—Chiefs, 23-17 (D)
Chiefs, 31-14 (KC)
1981—Chiefs, 28-14 (KC)
Broncos, 16-13 (D)
1982—Chiefs, 37-16 (D)
1983—Broncos, 27-24 (D)
Chiefs, 48-17 (KC)
1984—Broncos, 21-0 (D)
Chiefs, 16-13 (KC)
1985—Broncos, 30-10 (KC)
Broncos, 14-13 (D)
1986—Broncos, 38-17 (D)
Chiefs, 37-10 (KC)
1987—Broncos, 26-17 (KC)
Broncos, 20-17 (D)
1988—Chiefs, 20-13 (D)
Broncos, 17-11 (D)
1989—Broncos, 34-20 (D)
Broncos, 16-13 (KC)
1990—Broncos, 24-23 (D)
Chiefs, 31-20 (KC)
1991—Broncos, 19-16 (D)
Broncos, 24-20 (KC)
1992—Broncos, 20-19 (D)
Chiefs, 42-20 (KC)
1993—Chiefs, 15-7 (KC)
Broncos, 27-21 (D)
1994—Chiefs, 31-28 (D)
Broncos, 20-17 (KC) OT
1995—Chiefs, 21-7 (D)
Chiefs, 20-17 (KC)
1996—Chiefs, 17-14 (D)
Broncos, 34-7 (D)
1997—Broncos, 19-3 (D)
Chiefs, 24-22 (KC)
**Broncos, 14-10 (KC)

1998—Broncos, 30-7 (KC)
    Broncos, 35-31 (D)
1999—Chiefs, 26-10 (KC)
    Chiefs, 16-10 (D)
2000—Chiefs, 23-22 (D)
    Chiefs, 20-7 (KC)
2001—Broncos, 20-6 (D)
    Chiefs, 26-23 (KC) OT
2002—Broncos, 37-34 (KC) OT
    Broncos, 31-24 (D)
2003—Chiefs, 24-23 (KC)
    Broncos, 45-27 (D)
2004—Broncos, 34-24 (D)
    Chiefs, 45-17 (KC)
2005—Broncos, 30-10 (D)
    Chiefs, 31-27 (KC)
2006—Broncos, 9-6 (D) OT
    Chiefs, 19-10 (KC)
(RS Pts.—Chiefs 2,220, Broncos 1,825)
(PS Pts.—Broncos 14, Chiefs 10)
*Franchise in Dallas prior to 1963 and known as Texans
**AFC Divisional Playoff
DENVER vs. MIAMI
RS: Dolphins lead series, 10-3-1
PS: Broncos lead series, 1-0
1966—Dolphins, 24-7 (M)
    Broncos, 17-7 (D)
1967—Dolphins, 35-21 (M)
1968—Broncos, 21-14 (D)
1969—Dolphins, 27-24 (M)
1971—Tie, 10-10 (D)
1975—Dolphins, 14-13 (M)
1985—Dolphins, 30-26 (D)
1998—Dolphins, 31-21 (M)
    *Broncos, 38-3 (D)
1999—Dolphins, 38-21 (D)
2001—Dolphins, 21-10 (M)
2002—Dolphins, 24-22 (D)
2004—Broncos, 20-17 (D)
2005—Dolphins, 34-10 (M)
(RS Pts.—Dolphins 326, Broncos 243)
(PS Pts.—Broncos 38, Dolphins 3)
*AFC Divisonal Playoff
DENVER vs. MINNESOTA
RS: Vikings lead series, 7-4
1972—Vikings, 23-20 (D)
1978—Vikings, 12-9 (M) OT
1981—Broncos, 19-17 (D)
1984—Broncos, 42-21 (D)
1987—Vikings, 34-27 (M)
1990—Vikings, 27-22 (M)
1991—Broncos, 13-6 (M)
1993—Vikings, 26-23 (D)
1996—Broncos, 21-17 (M)
1999—Vikings, 23-20 (D)
2003—Vikings, 28-20 (M)
(RS Pts.—Broncos 236, Vikings 234)
DENVER vs. *NEW ENGLAND
RS: Broncos lead series, 24-15
PS: Broncos lead series, 2-0
1960—Broncos, 13-10 (B)
    Broncos, 31-24 (D)
1961—Patriots, 45-17 (B)
    Patriots, 28-24 (D)
1962—Patriots, 41-16 (B)
    Patriots, 33-29 (D)
1963—Broncos, 14-10 (D)
    Patriots, 40-21 (B)
1964—Patriots, 39-10 (D)

Patriots, 12-7 (B)
1965—Broncos, 27-10 (B)
    Patriots, 28-20 (D)
1966—Patriots, 24-10 (D)
    Broncos, 17-10 (B)
1967—Broncos, 26-21 (D)
1968—Patriots, 20-17 (D)
    Broncos, 35-14 (B)
1969—Broncos, 35-7 (D)
1972—Broncos, 45-21 (D)
1976—Patriots, 38-14 (NE)
1979—Broncos, 45-10 (D)
1980—Patriots, 23-14 (NE)
1984—Broncos, 26-19 (D)
1986—Broncos, 27-20 (D)
    **Broncos, 22-17 (D)
1987—Broncos, 31-20 (D)
1988—Broncos, 21-10 (D)
1991—Broncos, 9-6 (NE)
    Broncos, 20-3 (D)
1995—Broncos, 37-3 (NE)
1996—Broncos, 34-8 (NE)
1997—Broncos, 34-13 (D)
1998—Broncos, 27-21 (D)
1999—Patriots, 24-23 (NE)
2000—Patriots, 28-19 (D)
2001—Broncos, 31-20 (D)
2002—Broncos, 24-16 (NE)
2003—Patriots, 30-26 (D)
2005—Broncos, 28-20 (D)
    **Broncos, 27-13 (D)
2006—Broncos, 17-7 (NE)
(RS Pts.—Broncos 921, Patriots 776)
(PS Pts.—Broncos 49, Patriots 34)
*Franchise in Boston prior to 1971
**AFC Divisional Playoff
DENVER vs. NEW ORLEANS
RS: Broncos lead series, 6-2
1970—Broncos, 31-6 (NO)
1974—Broncos, 33-17 (D)
1979—Broncos, 10-3 (D)
1985—Broncos, 34-23 (D)
1988—Saints, 42-0 (NO)
1994—Saints, 30-28 (D)
2000—Broncos, 38-23 (NO)
2004—Broncos, 34-13 (NO)
(RS Pts.—Broncos 208, Saints 157)
DENVER vs. N.Y. GIANTS
RS: Giants lead series, 5-4
PS: Giants lead series, 1-0
1972—Giants, 29-17 (NY)
1976—Broncos, 14-13 (D)
1980—Broncos, 14-9 (NY)
1986—Giants, 19-16 (NY)
    *Giants, 39-20 (Pasadena)
1989—Giants, 14-7 (D)
1992—Broncos, 27-13 (D)
1998—Giants, 20-16 (NY)
2001—Broncos, 31-20 (D)
2005—Giants, 24-23 (NY)
(RS Pts.—Broncos 165, Giants 161)
(PS Pts.—Giants 39, Broncos 20)
*Super Bowl XXI
DENVER vs. *N.Y. JETS
RS: Broncos lead series, 15-14-1
PS: Broncos lead series, 1-0
1960—Titans, 28-24 (NY)
    Titans, 30-27 (D)
1961—Titans, 35-28 (NY)
    Broncos, 27-10 (D)

1962—Broncos, 32-10 (NY)
    Titans, 46-45 (D)
1963—Tie, 35-35 (NY)
    Jets, 14-9 (D)
1964—Jets, 30-6 (NY)
    Broncos, 20-16 (D)
1965—Broncos, 16-13 (D)
    Jets, 45-10 (NY)
1966—Jets, 16-7 (D)
1967—Jets, 38-24 (D)
    Broncos, 33-24 (NY)
1968—Broncos, 21-13 (NY)
1969—Broncos, 21-19 (D)
1973—Broncos, 40-28 (NY)
1976—Broncos, 46-3 (D)
1978—Jets, 31-28 (D)
1980—Broncos, 31-24 (D)
1986—Jets, 22-10 (NY)
1992—Broncos, 27-16 (D)
1993—Broncos, 26-20 (NY)
1994—Jets, 25-22 (NY) OT
1996—Broncos, 31-6 (D)
1998—**Broncos, 23-10 (D)
1999—Jets, 21-13 (D)
2000—Broncos, 30-23 (NY)
2002—Jets, 19-13 (NY)
2005—Broncos, 27-0 (D)
(RS Pts.—Broncos 729, Jets 660)
(PS Pts.—Broncos 23, Jets 10)
*Jets known as Titans prior to 1963
**AFC Championship
DENVER vs. *OAKLAND
RS: Raiders lead series, 53-38-2
PS: Series tied, 1-1
1960—Broncos, 31-14 (D)
    Raiders, 48-10 (O)
1961—Raiders, 33-19 (O)
    Broncos, 27-24 (D)
1962—Broncos, 44-7 (D)
    Broncos, 23-6 (O)
1963—Raiders, 26-10 (D)
    Raiders, 35-31 (O)
1964—Raiders, 40-7 (O)
    Tie, 20-20 (D)
1965—Raiders, 28-20 (D)
    Raiders, 24-13 (O)
1966—Raiders, 17-3 (D)
    Raiders, 28-10 (O)
1967—Raiders, 51-0 (O)
    Raiders, 21-17 (D)
1968—Raiders, 43-7 (O)
    Raiders, 33-27 (D)
1969—Raiders, 24-14 (D)
    Raiders, 41-10 (O)
1970—Raiders, 35-23 (O)
    Raiders, 24-19 (D)
1971—Raiders, 27-16 (D)
    Raiders, 21-13 (O)
1972—Broncos, 30-23 (O)
    Raiders, 37-20 (D)
1973—Tie, 23-23 (D)
    Raiders, 21-17 (O)
1974—Raiders, 28-17 (D)
    Broncos, 20-17 (O)
1975—Raiders, 42-17 (D)
    Raiders, 17-10 (O)
1976—Raiders, 17-10 (D)
    Raiders, 19-6 (O)
1977—Broncos, 30-7 (O)
    Raiders, 24-14 (D)

ALL-TIME TEAM VS. TEAM RESULTS

**Broncos, 20-17 (D)
1978—Broncos, 14-6 (D)
Broncos, 21-6 (O)
1979—Raiders, 27-3 (O)
Raiders, 14-10 (D)
1980—Raiders, 9-3 (O)
Raiders, 24-21 (D)
1981—Broncos, 9-7 (D)
Broncos, 17-0 (O)
1982—Raiders, 27-10 (LA)
1983—Raiders, 22-7 (D)
Raiders, 22-20 (LA)
1984—Broncos, 16-13 (D)
Broncos, 22-19 (LA) OT
1985—Raiders, 31-28 (LA) OT
Raiders, 17-14 (D) OT
1986—Broncos, 38-36 (D)
Broncos, 21-10 (LA)
1987—Broncos, 30-14 (D)
Broncos, 23-17 (LA)
1988—Raiders, 30-27 (D) OT
Raiders, 21-20 (LA)
1989—Broncos, 31-21 (D)
Raiders, 16-13 (LA) OT
1990—Raiders, 14-9 (LA)
Raiders, 23-20 (D)
1991—Raiders, 16-13 (LA)
Raiders, 17-16 (D)
1992—Broncos, 17-13 (D)
Raiders, 24-0 (LA)
1993—Raiders, 23-20 (D)
Raiders, 33-30 (LA) OT
***Raiders, 42-24 (LA)
1994—Raiders, 48-16 (D)
Raiders, 23-13 (LA)
1995—Broncos, 27-0 (D)
Broncos, 31-28 (O)
1996—Broncos, 22-21 (O)
Broncos, 24-19 (D)
1997—Raiders, 28-25 (O)
Broncos, 31-3 (D)
1998—Broncos, 34-17 (O)
Broncos, 40-14 (D)
1999—Broncos, 16-13 (O)
Broncos, 27-21 (D) OT
2000—Broncos, 33-24 (O)
Broncos, 27-24 (D)
2001—Raiders, 38-28 (O)
Broncos, 23-17 (D)
2002—Raiders, 34-10 (D)
Raiders, 28-16 (O)
2003—Broncos, 31-10 (D)
Broncos, 22-8 (O)
2004—Broncos, 31-3 (O)
Raiders, 25-24 (D)
2005—Broncos, 31-17 (O)
Broncos, 22-3 (D)
2006—Broncos, 13-3 (D)
Broncos, 17-13 (O)
(RS Pts.—Raiders 1,999, Broncos 1,805)
(PS Pts.—Raiders 59, Broncos 44)
*Franchise in Los Angeles from 1982-1994
**AFC Championship
***AFC First-Round Playoff
DENVER vs. PHILADELPHIA
RS: Eagles lead series, 6-4
1971—Eagles, 17-16 (P)
1975—Broncos, 25-10 (D)
1980—Eagles, 27-6 (P)
1983—Eagles, 13-10 (D)

1986—Broncos, 33-7 (P)
1989—Eagles, 28-24 (D)
1992—Eagles, 30-0 (P)
1995—Eagles, 31-13 (P)
1998—Broncos, 41-16 (D)
2005—Broncos, 49-21 (D)
(RS Pts.—Broncos 217, Eagles 200)
DENVER vs. PITTSBURGH
RS: Broncos lead series, 12-6-1
PS: Series tied, 3-3
1970—Broncos, 16-13 (D)
1971—Broncos, 22-10 (P)
1973—Broncos, 23-13 (P)
1974—Tie, 35-35 (D) OT
1975—Steelers, 20-9 (P)
1977—Broncos, 21-7 (D)
*Broncos, 34-21 (D)
1978—Steelers, 21-17 (D)
*Steelers, 33-10 (P)
1979—Steelers, 42-7 (P)
1983—Broncos, 14-10 (P)
1984—*Steelers, 24-17 (D)
1985—Broncos, 31-23 (P)
1986—Broncos, 21-10 (P)
1988—Steelers, 39-21 (P)
1989—Broncos, 34-7 (D)
*Broncos, 24-23 (D)
1990—Steelers, 34-17 (D)
1991—Broncos, 20-13 (D)
1993—Broncos, 37-13 (D)
1997—Steelers, 35-24 (P)
**Broncos, 24-21 (P)
2003—Broncos, 17-14 (D)
2005—**Steelers, 34-17 (D)
2006—Broncos, 31-20 (P)
(RS Pts.—Broncos 417, Steelers 379)
(PS Pts.—Steelers 156, Broncos 126)
*AFC Divisional Playoff
**AFC Championship
DENVER vs. *ST. LOUIS
RS: Rams lead series, 6-5
1972—Broncos, 16-10 (LA)
1974—Rams, 17-10 (D)
1979—Rams, 13-9 (D)
1982—Broncos, 27-24 (LA)
1985—Rams, 20-16 (LA)
1988—Broncos, 35-24 (D)
1994—Rams, 27-21 (LA)
1997—Broncos, 35-14 (D)
2000—Rams, 41-36 (StL)
2002—Broncos, 23-16 (D)
2006—Rams, 18-10 (StL)
(RS Pts.—Broncos 238, Rams 224)
*Franchise in Los Angeles prior to 1995
DENVER vs. *SAN DIEGO
RS: Broncos lead series, 52-41-1
1960—Chargers, 23-19 (D)
Chargers, 41-33 (LA)
1961—Chargers, 37-0 (SD)
Chargers, 19-16 (D)
1962—Broncos, 30-21 (D)
Broncos, 23-20 (SD)
1963—Broncos, 50-34 (D)
Chargers, 58-20 (SD)
1964—Chargers, 42-14 (D)
Chargers, 31-20 (D)
1965—Chargers, 34-31 (SD)
Chargers, 33-21 (D)
1966—Chargers, 24-17 (SD)
Broncos, 20-17 (D)

1967—Chargers, 38-21 (D)
Chargers, 24-20 (SD)
1968—Chargers, 55-24 (SD)
Chargers, 47-23 (D)
1969—Broncos, 13-0 (D)
Chargers, 45-24 (SD)
1970—Chargers, 24-21 (SD)
Tie, 17-17 (D)
1971—Broncos, 20-16 (D)
Chargers, 45-17 (SD)
1972—Chargers, 37-14 (SD)
Broncos, 38-13 (D)
1973—Broncos, 30-19 (D)
Broncos, 42-28 (SD)
1974—Broncos, 27-7 (D)
Chargers, 17-0 (SD)
1975—Broncos, 27-17 (SD)
Broncos, 13-10 (D) OT
1976—Broncos, 26-0 (D)
Broncos, 17-0 (SD)
1977—Broncos, 17-14 (SD)
Broncos, 17-9 (D)
1978—Broncos, 27-14 (D)
Chargers, 23-0 (SD)
1979—Broncos, 7-0 (D)
Chargers, 17-7 (SD)
1980—Chargers, 30-13 (D)
Broncos, 20-13 (SD)
1981—Broncos, 42-24 (D)
Chargers, 34-17 (SD)
1982—Chargers, 23-3 (D)
Chargers, 30-20 (SD)
1983—Broncos, 14-6 (D)
Chargers, 31-7 (SD)
1984—Broncos, 16-13 (SD)
Broncos, 16-13 (D)
1985—Chargers, 30-10 (SD)
Broncos, 30-24 (D) OT
1986—Broncos, 31-14 (SD)
Chargers, 9-3 (D)
1987—Broncos, 31-17 (SD)
Broncos, 24-0 (D)
1988—Broncos, 34-3 (D)
Broncos, 12-0 (SD)
1989—Broncos, 16-10 (D)
Chargers, 19-16 (SD)
1990—Chargers, 19-7 (SD)
Broncos, 20-10 (D)
1991—Broncos, 27-19 (D)
Broncos, 17-14 (SD)
1992—Broncos, 21-13 (D)
Chargers, 24-21 (SD)
1993—Broncos, 34-17 (D)
Chargers, 13-10 (SD)
1994—Chargers, 37-34 (D)
Broncos, 20-15 (SD)
1995—Broncos, 17-6 (SD)
Broncos, 30-27 (D)
1996—Broncos, 28-17 (D)
Chargers, 16-10 (SD)
1997—Broncos, 38-28 (SD)
Broncos, 38-3 (D)
1998—Broncos, 27-10 (D)
Broncos, 31-16 (SD)
1999—Broncos, 33-17 (SD)
Chargers, 12-6 (D)
2000—Broncos, 21-7 (SD)
Broncos, 38-37 (D)
2001—Chargers, 27-10 (SD)
Broncos, 26-16 (D)

2007 NFL Record & Fact Book 475

2002—Broncos, 26-9 (D)
    Chargers, 30-27 (SD) OT
2003—Broncos, 37-13 (SD)
    Broncos, 37-8 (D)
2004—Broncos, 23-13 (D)
    Chargers, 20-17 (SD)
2005—Broncos, 20-17 (D)
    Broncos, 23-7 (SD)
2006—Chargers, 35-27 (D)
    Chargers, 48-20 (SD)
(RS Pts.—Broncos 2,008, Chargers 1,946)
Franchise in Los Angeles prior to 1961

DENVER vs. SAN FRANCISCO
RS: Broncos lead series, 6-5
PS: 49ers lead series, 1-0
1970—49ers, 19-14 (SF)
1973—49ers, 36-34 (D)
1979—Broncos, 38-28 (SF)
1982—Broncos, 24-21 (D)
1985—Broncos, 17-16 (D)
1988—Broncos, 16-13 (SF) OT
1989—*49ers, 55-10 (New Orleans)
1994—49ers, 42-19 (SF)
1997—49ers, 34-17 (SF)
2000—Broncos, 38-9 (D)
2002—Broncos, 24-14 (SF)
2006—49ers, 26-23 (D) OT
(RS Pts.—Broncos 264, 49ers 258)
(PS Pts.—49ers 55, Broncos 10)
Super Bowl XXIV

DENVER vs. SEATTLE
RS: Broncos lead series, 33-18
PS: Seahawks lead series, 1-0
1977—Broncos, 24-13 (S)
1978—Broncos, 28-7 (D)
    Broncos, 20-17 (S) OT
1979—Broncos, 37-34 (D)
    Seahawks, 28-23 (S)
1980—Broncos, 36-20 (D)
    Broncos, 25-17 (S)
1981—Seahawks, 13-10 (S)
    Broncos, 23-13 (D)
1982—Seahawks, 17-10 (D)
    Seahawks, 13-11 (S)
1983—Seahawks, 27-19 (S)
    Broncos, 38-27 (D)
    *Seahawks, 31-7 (S)
1984—Seahawks, 27-24 (D)
    Broncos, 31-14 (S)
1985—Broncos, 13-10 (D) OT
    Broncos, 27-24 (S)
1986—Broncos, 20-13 (D)
    Seahawks, 41-16 (S)
1987—Broncos, 40-17 (D)
    Seahawks, 28-21 (S)
1988—Seahawks, 21-14 (D)
    Seahawks, 42-14 (S)
1989—Broncos, 24-21 (S) OT
    Broncos, 41-14 (D)
1990—Broncos, 34-31 (D) OT
    Seahawks, 17-12 (S)
1991—Broncos, 16-10 (D)
    Seahawks, 13-10 (S)
1992—Seahawks, 16-13 (S) OT
    Broncos, 10-6 (D)
1993—Broncos, 28-17 (D)
    Broncos, 17-9 (S)
1994—Broncos, 16-9 (S)
    Broncos, 17-10 (D)
1995—Seahawks, 27-10 (S)

    Seahawks, 31-27 (D)
1996—Broncos, 30-20 (S)
    Broncos, 34-7 (D)
1997—Broncos, 35-14 (S)
    Broncos, 30-27 (D)
1998—Broncos, 21-16 (S)
    Broncos, 28-21 (D)
1999—Seahawks, 20-17 (S)
    Broncos, 36-30 (D) OT
2000—Broncos, 38-31 (S)
    Broncos, 31-24 (D)
2001—Seahawks, 34-21 (S)
    Broncos, 20-7 (D)
2002—Broncos, 31-9 (S)
2006—Seahawks, 23-20 (D)
(RS Pts.—Broncos 1,191, Seahawks 997)
(PS Pts.—Seahawks 31, Broncos 7)
AFC First-Round Playoff

DENVER vs. TAMPA BAY
RS: Broncos lead series, 4-2
1976—Broncos, 48-13 (D)
1981—Broncos, 24-7 (TB)
1993—Buccaneers, 17-10 (D)
1996—Broncos, 27-23 (D)
1999—Buccaneers, 13-10 (TB)
2004—Broncos, 16-13 (TB)
(RS Pts.—Broncos 135, Buccaneers 86)

DENVER vs. *TENNESSEE
RS: Titans lead series, 20-12-1
PS: Broncos lead series, 2-1
1960—Oilers, 45-25 (D)
    Oilers, 20-10 (H)
1961—Oilers, 55-14 (D)
    Oilers, 45-14 (H)
1962—Broncos, 20-10 (D)
    Oilers, 34-17 (H)
1963—Oilers, 20-14 (H)
    Oilers, 33-24 (D)
1964—Oilers, 38-17 (D)
    Oilers, 34-15 (H)
1965—Broncos, 28-17 (D)
    Broncos, 31-21 (H)
1966—Oilers, 45-7 (H)
    Broncos, 40-38 (D)
1967—Oilers, 10-6 (H)
    Oilers, 20-18 (D)
1968—Oilers, 38-17 (H)
1969—Oilers, 24-21 (H)
    Tie, 20-20 (D)
1970—Oilers, 31-21 (H)
1972—Broncos, 30-17 (D)
1973—Broncos, 48-20 (H)
1974—Broncos, 37-14 (D)
1976—Oilers, 17-3 (H)
1977—Broncos, 24-14 (H)
1979—**Oilers, 13-7 (H)
1980—Oilers, 20-16 (D)
1983—Broncos, 26-14 (H)
1985—Broncos, 31-20 (D)
1987—Oilers, 40-10 (D)
    ***Broncos, 34-10 (D)
1991—Oilers, 42-14 (H)
    ***Broncos, 26-24 (D)
1992—Broncos, 27-21 (D)
1995—Oilers, 42-33 (H)
2004—Broncos, 37-16 (T)
(RS Pts.—Titans 895, Broncos 715)
(PS Pts.—Broncos 67, Titans 47)
Franchise in Houston prior to 1997; known as the Oilers prior to 1999

**AFC First-Round Playoff
***AFC Divisional Playoff

DENVER vs. WASHINGTON
RS: Broncos lead series, 6-4
PS: Redskins lead series, 1-0
1970—Redskins, 19-3 (D)
1974—Redskins, 30-3 (W)
1980—Broncos, 20-17 (D)
1986—Broncos, 31-30 (D)
1987—*Redskins, 42-10 (San Diego)
1989—Broncos, 14-10 (W)
1992—Redskins, 34-3 (W)
1995—Broncos, 38-31 (D)
1998—Broncos, 38-16 (W)
2001—Redskins, 17-10 (D)
2005—Broncos, 21-19 (D)
(RS Pts.—Redskins 223, Broncos 181)
(PS Pts.—Redskins 42, Broncos 10)
Super Bowl XXII

DETROIT vs. ARIZONA
RS: Lions lead series, 31-22-5;
See Arizona vs. Detroit
DETROIT vs. ATLANTA
RS: Lions lead series, 23-9;
See Atlanta vs. Detroit
DETROIT vs. BALTIMORE
RS: Series tied, 1-1;
See Baltimore vs. Detroit
DETROIT vs. BUFFALO
RS: Lions lead series, 4-3-1;
See Buffalo vs. Detroit
DETROIT vs. CAROLINA
RS: Panthers lead series, 3-1;
See Carolina vs. Detroit
DETROIT vs. CHICAGO
RS: Bears lead series, 87-62-5;
See Chicago vs. Detroit
DETROIT vs. CINCINNATI
RS: Bengals lead series, 6-3;
See Cincinnati vs. Detroit
DETROIT vs. CLEVELAND
RS: Lions lead series, 13-4
PS: Lions lead series, 3-1;
See Cleveland vs. Detroit
DETROIT vs. DALLAS
RS: Cowboys lead series, 10-9
PS: Series tied, 1-1;
See Dallas vs. Detroit
DETROIT vs. DENVER
RS: Broncos lead series, 6-3;
See Denver vs. Detroit
DETROIT vs. GREEN BAY
RS: Packers lead series, 82-64-7
PS: Packers lead series, 2-0
1930—Packers, 47-13 (GB)
    Tie, 6-6 (P)
1932—Packers, 15-10 (GB)
    Spartans, 19-0 (P)
1933—Packers, 17-0 (GB)
    Spartans, 7-0 (P)
1934—Lions, 3-0 (GB)
    Packers, 3-0 (D)
1935—Packers, 13-9 (Mil)
    Packers, 31-7 (GB)
    Lions, 20-10 (D)
1936—Packers, 20-18 (GB)
    Packers, 26-17 (D)
1937—Packers, 26-6 (GB)
    Packers, 14-13 (D)

1938—Lions, 17-7 (GB)
    Packers, 28-7 (D)
1939—Packers, 26-7 (GB)
    Packers, 12-7 (D)
1940—Lions, 23-14 (GB)
    Packers, 50-7 (D)
1941—Packers, 23-0 (GB)
    Packers, 24-7 (D)
1942—Packers, 38-7 (Mil)
    Packers, 28-7 (D)
1943—Packers, 35-14 (GB)
    Packers, 27-6 (D)
1944—Packers, 27-6 (Mil)
    Packers, 14-0 (D)
1945—Packers, 57-21 (Mil)
    Lions, 14-3 (D)
1946—Packers, 10-7 (Mil)
    Packers, 9-0 (D)
1947—Packers, 34-17 (GB)
    Packers, 35-14 (D)
1948—Packers, 33-21 (GB)
    Lions, 24-20 (D)
1949—Packers, 16-14 (Mil)
    Lions, 21-7 (D)
1950—Lions, 45-7 (GB)
    Lions, 24-21 (D)
1951—Lions, 24-17 (GB)
    Lions, 52-35 (D)
1952—Lions, 52-17 (GB)
    Lions, 48-24 (D)
1953—Lions, 14-7 (GB)
    Lions, 34-15 (D)
1954—Lions, 21-17 (GB)
    Lions, 28-24 (D)
1955—Packers, 20-17 (GB)
    Lions, 24-10 (D)
1956—Lions, 20-16 (GB)
    Packers, 24-20 (D)
1957—Lions, 24-14 (GB)
    Lions, 18-6 (D)
1958—Tie, 13-13 (GB)
    Lions, 24-14 (D)
1959—Packers, 28-10 (GB)
    Packers, 24-17 (D)
1960—Packers, 28-9 (GB)
    Lions, 23-10 (D)
1961—Lions, 17-13 (Mil)
    Packers, 17-9 (D)
1962—Packers, 9-7 (GB)
    Lions, 26-14 (D)
1963—Packers, 31-10 (Mil)
    Tie, 13-13 (D)
1964—Packers, 14-10 (D)
    Packers, 30-7 (GB)
1965—Packers, 31-21 (D)
    Lions, 12-7 (GB)
1966—Packers, 23-14 (GB)
    Packers, 31-7 (D)
1967—Tie, 17-17 (GB)
    Packers, 27-17 (D)
1968—Lions, 23-17 (GB)
    Tie, 14-14 (D)
1969—Packers, 28-17 (D)
    Lions, 16-10 (GB)
1970—Lions, 40-0 (GB)
    Lions, 20-0 (D)
1971—Lions, 31-28 (D)
    Tie, 14-14 (Mil)
1972—Packers, 24-23 (D)
    Packers, 33-7 (GB)

1973—Tie, 13-13 (GB)
    Lions, 34-0 (D)
1974—Packers, 21-19 (Mil)
    Lions, 19-17 (D)
1975—Lions, 30-16 (Mil)
    Lions, 13-10 (D)
1976—Packers, 24-14 (GB)
    Lions, 27-6 (D)
1977—Lions, 10-6 (D)
    Packers, 10-9 (GB)
1978—Packers, 13-7 (D)
    Packers, 35-14 (Mil)
1979—Packers, 24-16 (Mil)
    Packers, 18-13 (D)
1980—Lions, 29-7 (Mil)
    Lions, 24-3 (D)
1981—Lions, 31-27 (D)
    Packers, 31-17 (GB)
1982—Lions, 30-10 (GB)
    Lions, 27-24 (D)
1983—Lions, 38-14 (D)
    Lions, 23-20 (Mil) OT
1984—Packers, 41-9 (GB)
    Lions, 31-28 (D)
1985—Packers, 43-10 (GB)
    Packers, 26-23 (D)
1986—Lions, 21-14 (GB)
    Packers, 44-40 (D)
1987—Lions, 19-16 (GB) OT
    Packers, 34-33 (D)
1988—Lions, 19-9 (Mil)
    Lions, 30-14 (D)
1989—Packers, 23-20 (Mil) OT
    Lions, 31-22 (D)
1990—Packers, 24-21 (D)
    Lions, 24-17 (GB)
1991—Lions, 23-14 (D)
    Lions, 21-17 (GB)
1992—Packers, 27-13 (D)
    Packers, 38-10 (Mil)
1993—Packers, 26-17 (Mil)
    Lions, 30-20 (D)
    **Packers, 28-24 (D)
1994—Packers, 38-30 (Mil)
    Lions, 34-31 (D)
    **Packers, 16-12 (GB)
1995—Packers, 30-21 (GB)
    Lions, 24-16 (D)
1996—Packers, 28-18 (GB)
    Packers, 31-3 (D)
1997—Lions, 26-15 (D)
    Packers, 20-10 (GB)
1998—Packers, 38-19 (GB)
    Lions, 27-20 (D)
1999—Lions, 23-15 (D)
    Packers, 26-17 (GB)
2000—Lions, 31-24 (D)
    Packers, 26-13 (GB)
2001—Packers, 28-6 (GB)
    Packers, 29-27 (D)
2002—Packers, 37-31 (D)
    Packers, 40-14 (GB)
2003—Packers, 31-6 (GB)
    Lions, 22-14 (D)
2004—Packers, 38-10 (D)
    Packers, 16-13 (GB)
2005—Lions, 17-3 (D)
    Packers, 16-13 (GB) OT
2006—Packers, 31-24 (D)
    Packers, 17-9 (GB)

(RS Pts.—Packers 3,145, Lions 2,759)
(PS Pts.—Packers 44, Lions 36)
*Franchise in Portsmouth prior to 1934
and known as the Spartans
**NFC First-Round Playoff
DETROIT vs. HOUSTON
RS: Lions lead series, 1-0
2004—Lions, 28-16 (D)
(RS Pts.—Lions 28, Texans 16)
DETROIT vs. *INDIANAPOLIS
RS: Colts lead series, 19-18-2
1953—Lions, 27-17 (B)
    Lions, 17-7 (D)
1954—Lions, 35-0 (D)
    Lions, 27-3 (B)
1955—Colts, 28-13 (B)
    Lions, 24-14 (D)
1956—Lions, 31-14 (B)
    Lions, 27-3 (D)
1957—Colts, 34-14 (B)
    Lions, 31-27 (D)
1958—Colts, 28-15 (B)
    Colts, 40-14 (D)
1959—Colts, 21-9 (B)
    Colts, 31-24 (D)
1960—Lions, 30-17 (D)
    Lions, 20-15 (B)
1961—Lions, 16-15 (B)
    Colts, 17-14 (D)
1962—Lions, 29-20 (B)
    Lions, 21-14 (D)
1963—Colts, 25-21 (D)
    Colts, 24-21 (B)
1964—Colts, 34-0 (D)
    Lions, 31-14 (B)
1965—Colts, 31-7 (D)
    Tie, 24-24 (D)
1966—Colts, 45-14 (B)
    Lions, 20-14 (D)
1967—Colts, 41-7 (B)
1968—Colts, 27-10 (D)
1969—Tie, 17-17 (B)
1973—Colts, 29-27 (D)
1977—Lions, 13-10 (B)
1980—Colts, 10-9 (D)
1985—Colts, 14-6 (I)
1991—Lions, 33-24 (I)
1997—Lions, 32-10 (D)
2000—Colts, 30-18 (I)
2004—Colts, 41-9 (D)
(RS Pts.—Colts 829, Lions 757)
*Franchise in Baltimore prior to 1984
DETROIT vs. JACKSONVILLE
RS: Jaguars lead series, 2-1
1995—Lions, 44-0 (D)
1998—Jaguars, 37-22 (J)
2004—Jaguars, 23-17 (J) OT
(RS Pts.—Lions 83, Jaguars 60)
DETROIT vs. KANSAS CITY
RS: Chiefs lead series, 7-3
1971—Lions, 32-21 (D)
1975—Chiefs, 24-21 (KC) OT
1980—Chiefs, 20-17 (KC)
1981—Lions, 27-10 (D)
1987—Chiefs, 27-20 (D)
1988—Lions, 7-6 (KC)
1990—Chiefs, 43-24 (KC)
1996—Chiefs, 28-24 (D)
1999—Chiefs, 31-21 (KC)
2003—Chiefs, 45-17 (KC)

(RS Pts.—Chiefs 255, Lions 210)

DETROIT vs. MIAMI
RS: Dolphins lead series, 7-2
1973—Dolphins, 34-7 (M)
1979—Dolphins, 28-10 (D)
1985—Lions, 31-21 (D)
1991—Lions, 17-13 (D)
1994—Dolphins, 27-20 (M)
1997—Dolphins, 33-30 (M)
2000—Dolphins, 23-8 (D)
2002—Dolphins, 49-21 (M)
2006—Dolphins, 27-10 (D)
(RS Pts.—Dolphins 255, Lions 154)

DETROIT vs. MINNESOTA
RS: Vikings lead series, 60-29-2
1961—Lions, 37-10 (M)
Lions, 13-7 (D)
1962—Lions, 17-6 (M)
Lions, 37-23 (D)
1963—Lions, 28-10 (D)
Vikings, 34-31 (M)
1964—Lions, 24-20 (M)
Tie, 23-23 (D)
1965—Lions, 31-29 (M)
Vikings, 29-7 (D)
1966—Lions, 32-31 (M)
Vikings, 28-16 (D)
1967—Tie, 10-10 (M)
Lions, 14-3 (D)
1968—Vikings, 24-10 (M)
Vikings, 13-6 (D)
1969—Vikings, 24-10 (M)
Vikings, 27-0 (D)
1970—Vikings, 30-17 (D)
Vikings, 24-20 (M)
1971—Vikings, 16-13 (D)
Vikings, 29-10 (M)
1972—Vikings, 34-10 (D)
Vikings, 16-14 (M)
1973—Vikings, 23-9 (D)
Vikings, 28-7 (M)
1974—Vikings, 7-6 (D)
Lions, 20-16 (M)
1975—Vikings, 25-19 (M)
Lions, 17-10 (D)
1976—Vikings, 10-9 (D)
Vikings, 31-23 (M)
1977—Vikings, 14-7 (M)
Vikings, 30-21 (D)
1978—Vikings, 17-7 (M)
Lions, 45-14 (D)
1979—Vikings, 13-10 (D)
Vikings, 14-7 (M)
1980—Lions, 27-7 (D)
Vikings, 34-0 (M)
1981—Vikings, 26-24 (M)
Lions, 45-7 (D)
1982—Vikings, 34-31 (D)
1983—Vikings, 20-17 (M)
Lions, 13-2 (D)
1984—Vikings, 29-28 (D)
Lions, 16-14 (M)
1985—Vikings, 16-13 (M)
Lions, 41-21 (D)
1986—Lions, 13-10 (M)
Vikings, 24-10 (D)
1987—Vikings, 34-19 (M)
Vikings, 17-14 (D)
1988—Vikings, 44-17 (M)
Vikings, 23-0 (D)

1989—Vikings, 24-17 (M)
Vikings, 20-7 (D)
1990—Lions, 34-27 (M)
Vikings, 17-7 (D)
1991—Lions, 24-20 (D)
Lions, 34-14 (M)
1992—Lions, 31-17 (D)
Vikings, 31-14 (M)
1993—Lions, 30-27 (M)
Vikings, 13-0 (D)
1994—Vikings, 10-3 (M)
Lions, 41-19 (D)
1995—Vikings, 20-10 (M)
Lions, 44-38 (D)
1996—Vikings, 17-13 (M)
Vikings, 24-22 (D)
1997—Lions, 38-15 (D)
Lions, 14-13 (M)
1998—Vikings, 29-6 (M)
Vikings, 34-13 (D)
1999—Lions, 25-23 (D)
Vikings, 24-17 (M)
2000—Vikings, 31-24 (D)
Vikings, 24-17 (M)
2001—Vikings, 31-26 (M)
Lions, 27-24 (D)
2002—Vikings, 31-24 (M)
Vikings, 38-36 (D)
2003—Vikings, 23-13 (D)
Vikings, 24-14 (M)
2004—Vikings, 22-19 (M)
Vikings, 28-27 (D)
2005—Vikings, 27-14 (M)
Vikings, 21-16 (D)
2006—Vikings, 26-17 (M)
Vikings, 30-20 (D)
(RS Pts.—Vikings 1,970, Lions 1,703)

DETROIT vs. NEW ENGLAND
RS: Patriots lead series, 5-4
1971—Lions, 34-7 (NE)
1976—Lions, 30-10 (D)
1979—Patriots, 24-17 (NE)
1985—Patriots, 23-6 (NE)
1993—Lions, 19-16 (NE) OT
1994—Patriots, 23-17 (D)
2000—Lions, 34-9 (D)
2002—Patriots, 20-12 (D)
2006—Patriots, 28-21 (NE)
(RS Pts.—Lions 190, Patriots 160)

DETROIT vs. NEW ORLEANS
RS: Lions lead series, 9-8-1
1968—Tie, 20-20 (D)
1970—Saints, 19-17 (NO)
1972—Lions, 27-14 (D)
1973—Saints, 20-13 (NO)
1974—Lions, 19-14 (D)
1976—Saints, 17-16 (NO)
1977—Lions, 23-19 (D)
1979—Saints, 17-7 (NO)
1980—Lions, 24-13 (D)
1988—Saints, 22-14 (D)
1989—Lions, 21-14 (D)
1990—Lions, 27-10 (NO)
1992—Saints, 13-7 (D)
1993—Saints, 14-3 (NO)
1997—Saints, 35-17 (NO)
2000—Lions, 14-10 (NO)
2002—Lions, 26-21 (D)
2005—Lions, 13-12 (San Antonio)
(RS Pts.—Lions 308, Saints 304)

***DETROIT vs. N.Y. GIANTS**
RS: Lions lead series, 20-17-1
PS: Lions lead series, 1-0
1930—Giants, 19-6 (P)
1931—Spartans, 14-6 (P)
Giants, 14-0 (NY)
1932—Spartans, 7-0 (P)
Spartans, 6-0 (NY)
1933—Spartans, 17-7 (P)
Giants, 13-10 (NY)
1934—Lions, 9-0 (D)
1935—**Lions, 26-7 (D)
1936—Spartans, 14-7 (NY)
Lions, 38-0 (D)
1937—Lions, 17-0 (NY)
1939—Lions, 18-14 (D)
1941—Giants, 20-13 (NY)
1943—Tie, 0-0 (D)
1945—Giants, 35-14 (D)
1947—Lions, 35-7 (D)
1949—Lions, 45-21 (NY)
1953—Lions, 27-16 (NY)
1955—Giants, 24-19 (D)
1958—Giants, 19-17 (D)
1962—Giants, 17-14 (NY)
1964—Lions, 26-3 (D)
1967—Lions, 30-7 (NY)
1969—Lions, 24-0 (D)
1972—Lions, 30-16 (D)
1974—Lions, 20-19 (D)
1976—Giants, 24-10 (NY)
1982—Giants, 13-6 (D)
1983—Lions, 15-9 (D)
1988—Giants, 30-10 (NY)
Giants, 13-10 (D) OT
1989—Giants, 24-14 (NY)
1990—Giants, 20-0 (NY)
1994—Lions, 28-25 (NY) OT
1996—Giants, 35-7 (D)
1997—Giants, 26-20 (D) OT
2000—Lions, 31-21 (NY)
2004—Lions, 28-13 (NY)
(RS Pts.—Lions 642, Giants 544)
(PS Pts.—Lions 26, Giants 7)
*Franchise in Portsmouth prior to 1934
and known as the Spartans
**NFL Championship

DETROIT vs. N.Y. JETS
RS: Lions lead series, 6-5
1972—Lions, 37-20 (D)
1979—Jets, 31-10 (NY)
1982—Jets, 28-13 (D)
1985—Lions, 31-20 (D)
1988—Jets, 17-10 (D)
1991—Lions, 34-20 (D)
1994—Lions, 18-7 (NY)
1997—Lions, 13-10 (NY)
2000—Lions, 10-7 (NY)
2002—Jets, 31-14 (D)
2006—Jets, 31-24 (NY)
(RS Pts.—Jets 222, Lions 214)

DETROIT vs. *OAKLAND
RS: Raiders lead series, 6-3
1970—Lions, 28-14 (D)
1974—Raiders, 35-13 (O)
1978—Raiders, 29-17 (O)
1981—Lions, 16-0 (D)
1984—Raiders, 24-3 (D)
1987—Raiders, 27-7 (LA)
1990—Raiders, 38-31 (D)

1996—Raiders, 37-21 (O)
2003—Lions, 23-13 (D)
(RS Pts.—Raiders 217, Lions 159)
Franchise in Los Angeles from 1982-1994
DETROIT vs. PHILADELPHIA
RS: Series tied, 12-12-2
PS: Eagles lead series, 1-0
1933—Spartans, 25-0 (P)
1934—Lions, 10-0 (P)
1935—Lions, 35-0 (D)
1936—Lions, 23-0 (P)
1938—Eagles, 21-7 (D)
1940—Lions, 21-0 (P)
1941—Lions, 21-17 (D)
1945—Lions, 28-24 (D)
1948—Eagles, 45-21 (P)
1949—Eagles, 22-14 (D)
1951—Lions, 28-10 (P)
1954—Tie, 13-13 (D)
1957—Lions, 27-16 (P)
1960—Eagles, 28-10 (P)
1961—Eagles, 27-24 (D)
1965—Lions, 35-28 (P)
1968—Eagles, 12-0 (D)
1971—Eagles, 23-20 (D)
1974—Eagles, 28-17 (P)
1977—Lions, 17-13 (D)
1979—Eagles, 44-7 (D)
1984—Tie, 23-23 (D) OT
1986—Lions, 13-11 (P)
1995—**Eagles, 58-37 (P)
1996—Eagles, 24-17 (P)
1998—Eagles, 10-9 (P)
2004—Eagles, 30-13 (D)
(RS Pts.—Lions 478, Eagles 469)
(PS Pts.—Eagles 58, Lions 37)
Franchise in Portsmouth prior to 1934
and known as the Spartans
**NFC First-Round Playoff
DETROIT vs. *PITTSBURGH
RS: Series tied, 14-14-1
1934—Lions, 40-7 (D)
1936—Lions, 28-3 (D)
1937—Lions, 7-3 (D)
1938—Lions, 16-7 (D)
1940—Pirates, 10-7 (D)
1942—Steelers, 35-7 (D)
1946—Lions, 17-7 (D)
1947—Steelers, 17-10 (P)
1948—Lions, 17-14 (D)
1949—Steelers, 14-7 (P)
1950—Lions, 10-7 (P)
1952—Lions, 31-6 (P)
1953—Lions, 38-21 (D)
1955—Lions, 31-28 (P)
1956—Lions, 45-7 (D)
1959—Tie, 10-10 (P)
1962—Lions, 45-7 (D)
1966—Steelers, 17-3 (P)
1967—Steelers, 24-14 (D)
1969—Steelers, 16-13 (P)
1973—Steelers, 24-10 (P)
1983—Lions, 45-3 (D)
1986—Steelers, 27-17 (P)
1989—Steelers, 23-3 (D)
1992—Steelers, 17-14 (P)
1995—Steelers, 23-20 (P)
1998—Lions, 19-16 (D) OT
2001—Steelers, 47-14 (P)
2005—Steelers, 35-21 (P)

(RS Pts.—Lions 559, Steelers 475)
Steelers known as Pirates prior to 1941
DETROIT vs. *ST. LOUIS
RS: Rams lead series, 41-37-1
PS: Lions lead series, 1-0
1937—Lions, 28-0 (C)
    Lions, 27-0 (D)
1938—Rams, 21-17 (C)
    Lions, 6-0 (D)
1939—Lions, 15-7 (D)
    Rams, 14-3 (C)
1940—Lions, 6-0 (D)
    Rams, 24-0 (C)
1941—Lions, 17-7 (D)
    Lions, 14-0 (C)
1942—Rams, 14-0 (D)
    Rams, 27-7 (C)
1944—Rams, 20-17 (D)
    Lions, 26-14 (C)
1945—Rams, 28-21 (D)
1946—Rams, 35-14 (LA)
    Rams, 41-20 (D)
1947—Rams, 27-13 (D)
    Rams, 28-17 (LA)
1948—Rams, 44-7 (LA)
    Rams, 34-27 (D)
1949—Rams, 27-24 (LA)
    Rams, 21-10 (D)
1950—Rams, 30-28 (D)
    Rams, 65-24 (LA)
1951—Rams, 27-21 (D)
    Lions, 24-22 (LA)
1952—Lions, 17-14 (LA)
    Lions, 24-16 (D)
    **Lions, 31-21 (D)
1953—Rams, 31-19 (D)
    Rams, 37-24 (LA)
1954—Lions, 21-3 (D)
    Lions, 27-24 (LA)
1955—Rams, 17-10 (D)
    Rams, 24-13 (LA)
1956—Lions, 24-21 (D)
    Lions, 16-7 (LA)
1957—Lions, 10-7 (D)
    Rams, 35-17 (LA)
1958—Rams, 42-28 (D)
    Lions, 41-24 (LA)
1959—Lions, 17-7 (LA)
    Lions, 23-17 (D)
1960—Rams, 48-35 (LA)
    Lions, 12-10 (D)
1961—Lions, 14-13 (D)
    Lions, 28-10 (LA)
1962—Lions, 13-10 (D)
    Lions, 12-3 (LA)
1963—Lions, 23-2 (LA)
    Rams, 28-21 (D)
1964—Tie, 17-17 (LA)
    Lions, 37-17 (D)
1965—Lions, 20-0 (D)
    Lions, 31-7 (LA)
1966—Lions, 14-7 (D)
    Rams, 23-3 (LA)
1967—Rams, 31-7 (D)
1968—Rams, 10-7 (LA)
1969—Lions, 28-0 (D)
1970—Lions, 28-23 (LA)
1971—Rams, 21-13 (D)
1972—Lions, 34-17 (LA)
1974—Rams, 16-13 (LA)

1975—Rams, 20-0 (D)
1976—Rams, 20-17 (D)
1980—Lions, 41-20 (LA)
1981—Rams, 20-13 (LA)
1982—Lions, 19-14 (LA)
1983—Rams, 21-10 (LA)
1986—Rams, 14-10 (LA)
1987—Rams, 37-16 (D)
1988—Rams, 17-10 (LA)
1991—Lions, 21-10 (D)
1993—Lions, 16-13 (LA)
1999—Lions, 31-27 (D)
2001—Rams, 35-0 (D)
2003—Lions, 30-20 (D)
2006—Rams, 41-34 (StL)
(RS Pts.—Rams 1,559, Lions 1,435)
(PS Pts.—Lions 31, Rams 21)
Franchise in Los Angeles prior to 1995
and in Cleveland prior to 1946
**Conference Playoff
DETROIT vs. SAN DIEGO
RS: Chargers lead series, 5-3
1972—Lions, 34-20 (D)
1977—Lions, 20-0 (D)
1978—Lions, 31-14 (D)
1981—Chargers, 28-23 (SD)
1984—Chargers, 27-24 (SD)
1996—Chargers, 27-21 (SD)
1999—Chargers, 20-10 (D)
2003—Chargers, 14-7 (D)
(RS Pts.—Lions 170, Chargers 150)
DETROIT vs. SAN FRANCISCO
RS: 49ers lead series, 32-26-1
PS: Series tied, 1-1
1950—Lions, 24-7 (D)
    49ers, 28-27 (SF)
1951—49ers, 20-10 (D)
    49ers, 21-17 (SF)
1952—49ers, 17-3 (SF)
    49ers, 28-0 (D)
1953—Lions, 24-21 (D)
    Lions, 14-10 (SF)
1954—49ers, 37-31 (SF)
    Lions, 48-7 (D)
1955—49ers, 27-24 (D)
    49ers, 38-21 (SF)
1956—Lions, 20-17 (D)
    Lions, 17-13 (SF)
1957—49ers, 35-31 (SF)
    Lions, 31-10 (D)
    *Lions, 31-27 (SF)
1958—49ers, 24-21 (SF)
    Lions, 35-21 (D)
1959—49ers, 34-13 (D)
    49ers, 33-7 (SF)
1960—49ers, 14-10 (D)
    Lions, 24-0 (SF)
1961—49ers, 49-0 (D)
    Tie, 20-20 (SF)
1962—Lions, 45-24 (D)
    Lions, 38-24 (SF)
1963—Lions, 26-3 (D)
    Lions, 45-7 (SF)
1964—Lions, 26-17 (SF)
    Lions, 24-7 (D)
1965—49ers, 27-21 (D)
    49ers, 17-14 (SF)
1966—49ers, 27-24 (SF)
    49ers, 41-14 (D)
1967—Lions, 45-3 (SF)

1968—49ers, 14-7 (D)
1969—Lions, 26-14 (SF)
1970—Lions, 28-7 (D)
1971—49ers, 31-27 (SF)
1973—Lions, 30-20 (D)
1974—Lions, 17-13 (D)
1975—Lions, 28-17 (SF)
1977—49ers, 28-7 (SF)
1978—Lions, 33-14 (D)
1980—Lions, 17-13 (D)
1981—Lions, 24-17 (D)
1983—**49ers, 24-23 (SF)
1984—49ers, 30-27 (D)
1985—Lions, 23-21 (D)
1988—49ers, 20-13 (D)
1991—49ers, 35-3 (SF)
1992—49ers, 24-6 (SF)
1993—49ers, 55-17 (D)
1994—49ers, 27-21 (D)
1995—Lions, 27-24 (D)
1996—49ers, 24-14 (SF)
1998—49ers, 35-13 (SF)
2001—49ers, 21-13 (SF)
2003—49ers, 24-17 (SF)
2006—49ers, 19-13 (D)
(RS Pts.—49ers 1,275, Lions 1,245)
(PS Pts.—Lions 54, 49ers 51)
*Conference Playoff
**NFC Divisional Playoff
DETROIT vs. SEATTLE
RS: Seahawks lead series, 6-4
1976—Lions, 41-14 (S)
1978—Seahawks, 28-16 (S)
1984—Seahawks, 38-17 (S)
1987—Seahawks, 37-14 (D)
1990—Seahawks, 30-10 (S)
1993—Lions, 30-10 (D)
1996—Lions, 17-16 (D)
1999—Lions, 28-20 (S)
2003—Seahawks, 35-14 (S)
2006—Seahawks, 9-6 (D)
(RS Pts.—Seahawks 237, Lions 193)
DETROIT vs. TAMPA BAY
RS: Lions lead series, 26-24
PS: Buccaneers lead series, 1-0
1977—Lions, 16-7 (D)
1978—Lions, 15-7 (TB)
      Lions, 34-23 (D)
1979—Buccaneers, 31-16 (TB)
      Buccaneers, 16-14 (D)
1980—Lions, 24-10 (TB)
      Lions, 27-14 (D)
1981—Buccaneers, 28-10 (TB)
      Buccaneers, 20-17 (D)
1982—Buccaneers, 23-21 (TB)
      Lions, 23-20 (D)
1983—Lions, 11-0 (TB)
      Lions, 23-20 (D)
1984—Buccaneers, 21-17 (TB)
      Lions, 13-7 (D) OT
1985—Lions, 30-9 (D)
      Buccaneers, 19-16 (TB) OT
1986—Buccaneers, 24-20 (D)
      Lions, 38-17 (TB)
1987—Buccaneers, 31-27 (D)
      Lions, 20-10 (TB)
1988—Buccaneers, 23-20 (D)
      Buccaneers, 21-10 (TB)
1989—Lions, 17-16 (TB)
      Lions, 33-7 (D)
1990—Buccaneers, 38-21 (D)

Buccaneers, 23-20 (TB)
1991—Lions, 31-3 (D)
      Buccaneers, 30-21 (TB)
1992—Buccaneers, 27-23 (D)
      Lions, 38-7 (TB)
1993—Buccaneers, 27-10 (TB)
      Lions, 23-0 (D)
1994—Buccaneers, 24-14 (TB)
      Lions, 14-9 (D)
1995—Lions, 27-24 (D)
      Lions, 37-10 (TB)
1996—Lions, 21-6 (D)
      Lions, 27-0 (TB)
1997—Buccaneers, 24-17 (D)
      Lions, 27-9 (TB)
      *Buccaneers, 20-10 (TB)
1998—Lions, 27-6 (D)
      Lions, 28-25 (TB)
1999—Lions, 20-3 (D)
      Buccaneers, 23-16 (TB)
2000—Buccaneers, 31-10 (D)
      Lions, 28-14 (TB)
2001—Buccaneers, 20-17 (D)
      Buccaneers, 15-12 (TB)
2002—Buccaneers, 23-20 (D)
2005—Buccaneers, 17-13 (TB)
(RS Pts.—Lions 1,051, Buccaneers 842)
(PS Pts.—Buccaneers 20, Lions 10)
*NFC First-Round Playoff
DETROIT vs. *TENNESSEE
RS: Titans lead series, 6-3
1971—Lions, 31-7 (H)
1975—Oilers, 24-8 (H)
1983—Oilers, 27-17 (H)
1986—Lions, 24-13 (D)
1989—Oilers, 35-31 (H)
1992—Oilers, 24-21 (D)
1995—Lions, 24-17 (H)
2001—Titans, 27-24 (D)
2004—Titans, 24-19 (T)
(RS Pts.—Lions 199, Titans 198)
*Franchise in Houston prior to 1997;
known as Oilers prior to 1999
***DETROIT vs. **WASHINGTON**
RS: Redskins lead series, 25-10
PS: Redskins lead series, 3-0
1932—Spartans, 10-0 (P)
1933—Spartans, 13-0 (B)
1934—Lions, 24-0 (D)
1935—Lions, 17-7 (B)
      Lions, 14-0 (D)
1938—Redskins, 7-5 (D)
1939—Redskins, 31-7 (W)
1940—Redskins, 20-14 (D)
1942—Redskins, 15-3 (D)
1943—Redskins, 42-20 (W)
1946—Redskins, 17-16 (W)
1947—Lions, 38-21 (D)
1948—Redskins, 46-21 (W)
1951—Lions, 35-17 (D)
1956—Redskins, 18-17 (W)
1965—Lions, 14-10 (D)
1968—Redskins, 14-3 (W)
1970—Redskins, 31-10 (W)
1973—Redskins, 20-0 (D)
1976—Redskins, 20-7 (W)
1978—Redskins, 21-19 (D)
1979—Redskins, 27-24 (D)
1981—Redskins, 33-31 (W)
1982—***Redskins, 31-7 (W)

1983—Redskins, 38-17 (W)
1984—Redskins, 28-14 (W)
1985—Redskins, 24-3 (W)
1987—Redskins, 20-13 (W)
1990—Redskins, 41-38 (D) OT
1991—Redskins, 45-0 (W)
      ****Redskins, 41-10 (W)
1992—Redskins, 13-10 (W)
1995—Redskins, 36-30 (W) OT
1997—Redskins, 30-7 (W)
1999—Lions, 33-17 (D)
      ***Redskins, 27-13 (W)
2000—Lions, 15-10 (D)
2004—Redskins, 17-10 (D)
(RS Pts.—Redskins 736, Lions 552)
(PS Pts.—Redskins 99, Lions 30)
*Franchise in Portsmouth prior to 1934
and known as the Spartans.
**Franchise in Boston prior to 1937
***NFC First-Round Playoff
****NFC Championship

GREEN BAY vs. ARIZONA
RS: Packers lead series, 42-22-4
PS: Packers lead series, 1-0;
See Arizona vs. Green Bay
GREEN BAY vs. ATLANTA
RS: Packers lead series, 12-10
PS: Series tied, 1-1;
See Atlanta vs. Green Bay
GREEN BAY vs. BALTIMORE
RS: Packers lead series, 2-1;
See Baltimore vs. Green Bay
GREEN BAY vs. BUFFALO
RS: Bills lead series, 7-3;
See Buffalo vs. Green Bay
GREEN BAY vs. CAROLINA
RS: Packers lead series, 5-3
PS: Packers lead series, 1-0;
See Carolina vs. Green Bay
GREEN BAY vs. CHICAGO
RS: Bears lead series, 87-79-6
PS: Bears lead series, 1-0;
See Chicago vs. Green Bay
GREEN BAY vs. CINCINNATI
RS: Series tied, 5-5;
See Cincinnati vs. Green Bay
GREEN BAY vs. CLEVELAND
RS: Packers lead series, 9-7
PS: Packers lead series, 1-0;
See Cleveland vs. Green Bay
GREEN BAY vs. DALLAS
RS: Series tied, 10-10
PS: Cowboys lead series, 4-2;
See Dallas vs. Green Bay
GREEN BAY vs. DENVER
RS: Broncos lead series, 5-4-1
PS: Broncos lead series, 1-0;
See Denver vs. Green Bay
GREEN BAY vs. DETROIT
RS: Packers lead series, 82-64-7
PS: Packers lead series, 2-0;
See Detroit vs. Green Bay
GREEN BAY vs. HOUSTON
RS: Packers lead series, 1-0
2004—Packers, 16-13 (H)
(RS Pts.—Packers 16, Texans 13)
GREEN BAY vs. *INDIANAPOLIS
RS: Colts lead series, 20-19-1
PS: Packers lead series, 1-0

1953—Packers, 37-14 (GB)
    Packers, 35-24 (B)
1954—Packers, 7-6 (B)
    Packers, 24-13 (Mil)
1955—Colts, 24-20 (Mil)
    Colts, 14-10 (B)
1956—Packers, 38-33 (Mil)
    Colts, 28-21 (B)
1957—Colts, 45-17 (Mil)
    Packers, 24-21 (B)
1958—Colts, 24-17 (Mil)
    Colts, 56-0 (B)
1959—Colts, 38-21 (B)
    Colts, 28-24 (Mil)
1960—Packers, 35-21 (GB)
    Colts, 38-24 (B)
1961—Packers, 45-7 (GB)
    Colts, 45-21 (B)
1962—Packers, 17-6 (B)
    Packers, 17-13 (GB)
1963—Packers, 31-20 (GB)
    Packers, 34-20 (B)
1964—Colts, 21-20 (GB)
    Colts, 24-21 (B)
1965—Packers, 20-17 (Mil)
    Packers, 42-27 (B)
    **Packers, 13-10 (GB) OT
1966—Packers, 24-3 (Mil)
    Packers, 14-10 (B)
1967—Colts, 13-10 (B)
1968—Colts, 16-3 (GB)
1969—Colts, 14-6 (B)
1970—Colts, 13-10 (Mil)
1974—Packers, 20-13 (B)
1982—Tie, 20-20 (B) OT
1985—Colts, 37-10 (I)
1988—Colts, 20-13 (GB)
1991—Packers, 14-10 (Mil)
1997—Colts, 41-38 (I)
2000—Packers, 26-24 (GB)
2004—Colts, 45-31 (I)
(RS Pts.—Colts 906, Packers 861)
(PS Pts.—Packers 13, Colts 10)
*Franchise in Baltimore prior to 1984
**Conference Playoff

GREEN BAY vs. JACKSONVILLE
RS: Packers lead series, 2-1
1995—Packers, 24-14 (J)
2001—Packers, 28-21 (J)
2004—Jaguars, 28-25 (GB)
(RS Pts.—Packers 77, Jaguars 63)

GREEN BAY vs. KANSAS CITY
RS: Chiefs lead series, 6-1-1
PS: Packers lead series, 1-0
1966—*Packers, 35-10 (Los Angeles)
1973—Tie, 10-10 (Mil)
1977—Chiefs, 20-10 (KC)
1987—Packers, 23-3 (KC)
1989—Chiefs, 21-3 (GB)
1990—Chiefs, 17-3 (GB)
1993—Chiefs, 23-16 (KC)
1996—Chiefs, 27-20 (KC)
2003—Chiefs, 40-34 (GB) OT
(RS Pts.—Chiefs 161, Packers 119)
(PS Pts.—Packers 35, Chiefs 10)
*Super Bowl I

GREEN BAY vs. MIAMI
RS: Dolphins lead series, 9-3
1971—Dolphins, 27-6 (Mia)
1975—Dolphins, 31-7 (GB)

1979—Dolphins, 27-7 (Mia)
1985—Dolphins, 34-24 (GB)
1988—Dolphins, 24-17 (Mia)
1989—Dolphins, 23-20 (Mia)
1991—Dolphins, 16-13 (Mia)
1994—Dolphins, 24-14 (Mil)
1997—Packers, 23-18 (GB)
2000—Dolphins, 28-20 (Mia)
2002—Packers, 24-10 (GB)
2006—Packers, 34-24 (M)
(RS Pts.—Dolphins 286, Packers 209)

GREEN BAY vs. MINNESOTA
RS: Packers lead series, 46-44-1
PS: Vikings lead series, 1-0
1961—Packers, 33-7 (Minn)
    Packers, 28-10 (Mil)
1962—Packers, 34-7 (GB)
    Packers, 48-21 (Minn)
1963—Packers, 37-28 (Minn)
    Packers, 28-7 (GB)
1964—Vikings, 24-23 (GB)
    Packers, 42-13 (Minn)
1965—Packers, 38-13 (Minn)
    Packers, 24-19 (GB)
1966—Vikings, 20-17 (GB)
    Packers, 28-16 (Minn)
1967—Vikings, 10-7 (Mil)
    Packers, 30-27 (Minn)
1968—Vikings, 26-13 (Mil)
    Vikings, 14-10 (Minn)
1969—Vikings, 19-7 (Minn)
    Vikings, 9-7 (Mil)
1970—Packers, 13-10 (Mil)
    Vikings, 10-3 (Minn)
1971—Vikings, 24-13 (GB)
    Vikings, 3-0 (Minn)
1972—Vikings, 27-13 (GB)
    Packers, 23-7 (Minn)
1973—Vikings, 11-3 (Minn)
    Vikings, 31-7 (GB)
1974—Vikings, 32-17 (GB)
    Packers, 19-7 (Minn)
1975—Vikings, 28-17 (GB)
    Vikings, 24-3 (Minn)
1976—Vikings, 17-10 (Mil)
    Vikings, 20-9 (Minn)
1977—Vikings, 19-7 (Minn)
    Vikings, 13-6 (GB)
1978—Vikings, 21-7 (Minn)
    Tie, 10-10 (GB) OT
1979—Vikings, 27-21 (Minn) OT
    Packers, 19-7 (Mil)
1980—Packers, 16-3 (GB)
    Packers, 25-13 (Minn)
1981—Vikings, 30-13 (Mil)
    Packers, 35-23 (Minn)
1982—Packers, 26-7 (Mil)
1983—Vikings, 20-17 (GB) OT
    Packers, 29-21 (Minn)
1984—Packers, 45-17 (Mil)
    Packers, 38-14 (Minn)
1985—Packers, 20-17 (Mil)
    Packers, 27-17 (Minn)
1986—Vikings, 42-7 (Minn)
    Vikings, 32-6 (GB)
1987—Packers, 23-16 (Minn)
    Packers, 16-10 (Mil)
1988—Packers, 34-14 (Minn)
    Packers, 18-6 (GB)
1989—Vikings, 26-14 (Minn)

    Packers, 20-19 (Mil)
1990—Packers, 24-10 (Mil)
    Vikings, 23-7 (Minn)
1991—Vikings, 35-21 (GB)
    Packers, 27-7 (Minn)
1992—Vikings, 23-20 (GB) OT
    Vikings, 27-7 (Minn)
1993—Vikings, 15-13 (Minn)
    Vikings, 21-17 (Mil)
1994—Packers, 16-10 (GB)
    Vikings, 13-10 (Minn) OT
1995—Packers, 38-21 (GB)
    Vikings, 27-24 (Minn)
1996—Vikings, 30-21 (Minn)
    Packers, 38-10 (GB)
1997—Packers, 38-32 (GB)
    Packers, 27-11 (Minn)
1998—Vikings, 37-24 (GB)
    Vikings, 28-14 (Minn)
1999—Packers, 23-20 (GB)
    Vikings, 24-20 (Minn)
2000—Packers, 26-20 (GB) OT
    Packers, 33-28 (Minn)
2001—Vikings, 35-13 (Minn)
    Packers, 24-13 (GB)
2002—Vikings, 31-21 (Minn)
    Packers, 26-22 (GB)
2003—Vikings, 30-25 (GB)
    Packers, 30-27 (M)
2004—Packers, 34-31 (GB)
    Packers, 34-31 (M)
    *Vikings, 31-17 (GB)
2005—Vikings, 23-20 (M)
    Vikings, 20-17 (GB)
2006—Packers, 23-17 (M)
    Packers, 9-7 (GB)
(RS Pts.—Packers 1,867, Vikings 1,744)
(PS Pts.—Vikings 31, Packers 17)
*NFC First-Round Playoff

GREEN BAY vs. NEW ENGLAND
RS: Series tied, 4-4
PS: Packers lead series, 1-0
1973—Patriots, 33-24 (NE)
1979—Packers, 27-14 (GB)
1985—Patriots, 26-20 (NE)
1988—Packers, 45-3 (Mil)
1994—Patriots, 17-16 (NE)
1996—*Packers, 35-21 (New Orleans)
1997—Packers, 28-10 (NE)
2002—Packers, 28-10 (NE)
2006—Patriots, 35-0 (GB)
(RS Pts.—Packers 188, Patriots 148)
(PS Pts.—Packers 35, Patriots 21)
*Super Bowl XXXI

GREEN BAY vs. NEW ORLEANS
RS: Packers lead series, 14-6
1968—Packers, 29-7 (Mil)
1971—Saints, 29-21 (Mil)
1972—Packers, 30-20 (NO)
1973—Packers, 30-10 (Mil)
1975—Saints, 20-19 (NO)
1976—Packers, 32-27 (Mil)
1977—Packers, 24-20 (NO)
1978—Packers, 28-17 (Mil)
1979—Packers, 28-19 (Mil)
1981—Packers, 35-7 (NO)
1984—Packers, 23-13 (NO)
1985—Packers, 38-14 (NO)
1986—Saints, 24-10 (NO)
1987—Saints, 33-24 (NO)

1989—Packers, 35-34 (GB)
1993—Packers, 19-17 (NO)
1995—Packers, 34-23 (NO)
2002—Saints, 35-20 (NO)
2005—Packers, 52-3 (GB)
2006—Saints, 34-27 (GB)
(RS Pts.—Packers 558, Saints 406)
GREEN BAY vs. N.Y. GIANTS
RS: Packers lead series, 24-21-2
PS: Packers lead series, 4-1
1928—Giants, 6-0 (GB)
    Packers, 7-0 (NY)
1929—Packers, 20-6 (NY)
1930—Packers, 14-7 (GB)
    Giants, 13-6 (NY)
1931—Packers, 27-7 (GB)
    Packers, 14-10 (NY)
1932—Packers, 13-0 (GB)
    Giants, 6-0 (NY)
1933—Giants, 10-7 (Mil)
    Giants, 17-6 (NY)
1934—Packers, 20-6 (Mil)
    Giants, 17-3 (NY)
1935—Packers, 16-7 (GB)
1936—Packers, 26-14 (NY)
1937—Giants, 10-0 (NY)
1938—Packers, 15-3 (NY)
    *Giants, 23-17 (NY)
1939—*Packers, 27-0 (Mil)
1940—Giants, 7-3 (NY)
1942—Tie, 21-21 (NY)
1943—Packers, 35-21 (NY)
1944—Giants, 24-0 (NY)
    *Packers, 14-7 (NY)
1945—Packers, 23-14 (NY)
1947—Tie, 24-24 (NY)
1948—Giants, 49-3 (Mil)
1949—Giants, 30-10 (GB)
1952—Packers, 17-3 (NY)
1957—Giants, 31-17 (GB)
1959—Giants, 20-3 (NY)
1961—Packers, 20-17 (Mil)
    *Packers, 37-0 (GB)
1962—*Packers, 16-7 (NY)
1967—Packers, 48-21 (NY)
1969—Packers, 20-10 (Mil)
1971—Giants, 42-40 (GB)
1973—Packers, 16-14 (New Haven)
1975—Packers, 40-14 (Mil)
1980—Giants, 27-21 (NY)
1981—Packers, 27-14 (NY)
    Packers, 26-24 (Mil)
1982—Packers, 27-19 (NY)
1983—Giants, 27-3 (NY)
1985—Packers, 23-20 (GB)
1986—Giants, 55-24 (NY)
1987—Giants, 20-10 (NY)
1992—Giants, 27-7 (NY)
1995—Packers, 14-6 (GB)
1998—Packers, 37-3 (NY)
2001—Packers, 34-25 (NY)
2004—Giants, 14-7 (GB)
(RS Pts.—Giants 794, Packers 782)
(PS Pts.—Packers 111, Giants 37)
*NFL Championship
GREEN BAY vs. N.Y. JETS
RS: Jets lead series, 8-2
1973—Packers, 23-7 (Mil)
1979—Jets, 27-22 (GB)
1981—Jets, 28-3 (NY)

1982—Jets, 15-13 (NY)
1985—Jets, 24-3 (Mil)
1991—Jets, 19-16 (NY) OT
1994—Packers, 17-10 (GB)
2000—Jets, 20-16 (GB)
2002—Jets, 42-17 (NY)
2006—Jets, 38-10 (GB)
(RS Pts.—Jets 230, Packers 140)
GREEN BAY vs. *OAKLAND
RS: Raiders lead series, 5-4
PS: Packers lead series, 1-0
1967—**Packers, 33-14 (Miami)
1972—Raiders, 20-14 (GB)
1976—Raiders, 18-14 (O)
1978—Raiders, 28-3 (GB)
1984—Raiders, 28-7 (LA)
1987—Raiders, 20-0 (GB)
1990—Packers, 29-16 (LA)
1993—Packers, 28-0 (GB)
1999—Packers, 28-24 (GB)
2003—Packers, 41-7 (O)
(RS Pts.—Packers 164, Raiders 161)
(PS Pts.—Packers 33, Raiders 14)
*Franchise in Los Angeles from 1982-1994
**Super Bowl II
GREEN BAY vs. PHILADELPHIA
RS: Packers lead series, 22-13
PS: Eagles lead series, 2-0
1933—Packers, 35-9 (GB)
    Packers, 10-0 (P)
1934—Packers, 19-6 (GB)
1935—Packers, 13-6 (P)
1937—Packers, 37-7 (Mil)
1939—Packers, 23-16 (P)
1940—Packers, 27-20 (GB)
1942—Packers, 7-0 (P)
1946—Packers, 19-7 (P)
1947—Eagles, 28-14 (P)
1951—Packers, 37-24 (GB)
1952—Packers, 12-10 (Mil)
1954—Packers, 37-14 (P)
1958—Packers, 38-35 (GB)
1960—*Eagles, 17-13 (P)
1962—Packers, 49-0 (P)
1968—Packers, 30-13 (GB)
1970—Packers, 30-17 (Mil)
1974—Eagles, 36-14 (P)
1976—Packers, 28-13 (GB)
1978—Eagles, 10-3 (P)
1979—Eagles, 21-10 (GB)
1987—Packers, 16-10 (GB) OT
1990—Eagles, 31-0 (P)
1991—Eagles, 20-3 (GB)
1992—Packers, 27-24 (Mil)
1993—Packers, 20-17 (GB)
1994—Eagles, 13-7 (P)
1996—Packers, 39-13 (GB)
1997—Eagles, 10-9 (P)
1998—Packers, 24-16 (GB)
2000—Packers, 6-3 (GB)
2003—Eagles, 17-14 (GB)
    **Eagles, 20-17 (P) OT
2004—Eagles, 47-17 (P)
2005—Eagles, 19-14 (P)
2006—Eagles, 31-9 (P)
(RS Pts.—Packers 694, Eagles 566)
(PS Pts.—Eagles 37, Packers 30)
*NFL Championship
**NFC Divisional Playoff
GREEN BAY vs. *PITTSBURGH

RS: Packers lead series, 18-13
1933—Packers, 47-0 (GB)
1935—Packers, 27-0 (GB)
    Packers, 34-14 (P)
1936—Packers, 42-10 (Mil)
1938—Packers, 20-0 (GB)
1940—Packers, 24-3 (Mil)
1941—Packers, 54-7 (P)
1942—Packers, 24-21 (Mil)
1946—Packers, 17-7 (GB)
1947—Steelers, 18-17 (Mil)
1948—Steelers, 38-7 (P)
1949—Steelers, 30-7 (Mil)
1951—Packers, 35-33 (Mil)
    Steelers, 28-7 (P)
1953—Steelers, 31-14 (P)
1954—Steelers, 21-20 (GB)
1957—Packers, 27-10 (P)
1960—Packers, 19-13 (P)
1963—Packers, 33-14 (Mil)
1965—Packers, 41-9 (P)
1967—Steelers, 24-17 (GB)
1969—Packers, 38-34 (P)
1970—Packers, 20-12 (P)
1975—Steelers, 16-13 (Mil)
1980—Steelers, 22-20 (P)
1983—Steelers, 25-21 (GB)
1986—Steelers, 27-3 (P)
1992—Packers, 17-3 (GB)
1995—Packers, 24-19 (GB)
1998—Steelers, 27-20 (P)
2005—Steelers, 20-10 (GB)
(RS Pts.—Packers 719, Steelers 536)
*Steelers known as Pirates prior to 1941
GREEN BAY vs. *ST. LOUIS
RS: Rams lead series, 45-40-2
PS: Series tied, 1-1
1937—Packers, 35-10 (C)
    Packers, 35-7 (GB)
1938—Packers, 26-17 (GB)
    Packers, 28-7 (C)
1939—Rams, 27-24 (GB)
    Packers, 7-6 (C)
1940—Packers, 31-14 (GB)
    Tie, 13-13 (C)
1941—Packers, 24-7 (Mil)
    Packers, 17-14 (C)
1942—Packers, 45-28 (GB)
    Packers, 30-12 (C)
1944—Packers, 30-21 (GB)
    Packers, 42-7 (C)
1945—Rams, 27-14 (GB)
    Rams, 20-7 (C)
1946—Rams, 21-17 (Mil)
    Rams, 38-17 (LA)
1947—Packers, 17-14 (Mil)
    Packers, 30-10 (LA)
1948—Packers, 16-0 (GB)
    Rams, 24-10 (LA)
1949—Rams, 48-7 (GB)
    Rams, 35-7 (LA)
1950—Rams, 45-14 (Mil)
    Rams, 51-14 (LA)
1951—Rams, 28-0 (Mil)
    Rams, 42-14 (LA)
1952—Rams, 30-28 (Mil)
    Rams, 45-27 (LA)
1953—Rams, 38-20 (Mil)
    Rams, 33-17 (LA)
1954—Packers, 35-17 (Mil)

Rams, 35-27 (LA)
1955—Packers, 30-28 (Mil)
Rams, 31-17 (LA)
1956—Packers, 42-17 (Mil)
Rams, 49-21 (LA)
1957—Rams, 31-27 (Mil)
Rams, 42-17 (LA)
1958—Rams, 20-7 (GB)
Rams, 34-20 (LA)
1959—Rams, 45-6 (Mil)
Packers, 38-20 (LA)
1960—Rams, 33-31 (Mil)
Packers, 35-21 (LA)
1961—Packers, 35-17 (GB)
Packers, 24-17 (LA)
1962—Packers, 41-10 (Mil)
Packers, 20-17 (LA)
1963—Packers, 42-10 (GB)
Packers, 31-14 (LA)
1964—Rams, 27-17 (Mil)
Tie, 24-24 (LA)
1965—Packers, 6-3 (Mil)
Rams, 21-10 (LA)
1966—Packers, 24-13 (GB)
Packers, 27-23 (LA)
1967—Rams, 27-24 (LA)
**Packers, 28-7 (Mil)
1968—Rams, 16-14 (Mil)
1969—Rams, 34-21 (LA)
1970—Rams, 31-21 (GB)
1971—Rams, 30-13 (LA)
1973—Rams, 24-7 (LA)
1974—Packers, 17-6 (Mil)
1975—Rams, 22-5 (LA)
1977—Rams, 24-6 (Mil)
1978—Rams, 31-14 (LA)
1980—Rams, 51-21 (LA)
1981—Rams, 35-23 (LA)
1982—Packers, 35-23 (Mil)
1983—Packers, 27-24 (Mil)
1984—Packers, 31-6 (Mil)
1985—Rams, 34-17 (LA)
1988—Rams, 34-7 (GB)
1989—Rams, 41-38 (LA)
1990—Packers, 36-24 (GB)
1991—Rams, 23-21 (LA)
1992—Packers, 28-13 (GB)
1993—Packers, 36-6 (Mil)
1994—Packers, 24-17 (GB)
1995—Rams, 17-14 (GB)
1996—Packers, 24-9 (StL)
1997—Packers, 17-7 (GB)
2001—***Rams, 45-17 (StL)
2003—Rams, 34-24 (StL)
2004—Packers, 45-17 (GB)
2006—Rams, 23-20 (GB)
(RS Pts.—Rams 2,041, Packers 1,947)
(PS Pts.—Rams 52, Packers 45)
*Franchise in Los Angeles prior to 1995
and in Cleveland prior to 1946
**Conference Championship
***NFC Divisional Playoff

GREEN BAY vs. SAN DIEGO
RS: Packers lead series, 7-1
1970—Packers, 22-20 (SD)
1974—Packers, 34-0 (GB)
1978—Packers, 24-3 (SD)
1984—Chargers, 34-28 (GB)
1993—Packers, 20-13 (SD)
1996—Packers, 42-10 (GB)

1999—Packers, 31-3 (SD)
2003—Packers, 38-21 (SD)
(RS Pts.—Packers 239, Chargers 104)

GREEN BAY vs. SAN FRANCISCO
RS: Packers lead series, 28-25-1
PS: Packers lead series, 4-1
1950—Packers, 25-21 (GB)
49ers, 30-14 (SF)
1951—49ers, 31-19 (SF)
1952—49ers, 24-14 (SF)
1953—49ers, 37-7 (Mil)
49ers, 48-14 (SF)
1954—49ers, 23-17 (Mil)
49ers, 35-0 (SF)
1955—Packers, 27-21 (Mil)
Packers, 28-7 (SF)
1956—49ers, 17-16 (GB)
49ers, 38-20 (SF)
1957—49ers, 24-14 (Mil)
49ers, 27-20 (SF)
1958—49ers, 33-12 (Mil)
49ers, 48-21 (SF)
1959—Packers, 21-20 (GB)
Packers, 36-14 (SF)
1960—Packers, 41-14 (Mil)
Packers, 13-0 (SF)
1961—Packers, 30-10 (GB)
49ers, 22-21 (SF)
1962—Packers, 31-13 (Mil)
Packers, 31-21 (SF)
1963—Packers, 28-10 (Mil)
Packers, 21-17 (SF)
1964—Packers, 24-14 (Mil)
49ers, 24-14 (SF)
1965—Packers, 27-10 (GB)
Tie, 24-24 (SF)
1966—49ers, 21-20 (SF)
Packers, 20-7 (Mil)
1967—Packers, 13-0 (GB)
1968—49ers, 27-20 (SF)
1969—Packers, 14-7 (Mil)
1970—49ers, 26-10 (SF)
1972—Packers, 34-24 (Mil)
1973—49ers, 20-6 (SF)
1974—49ers, 7-6 (SF)
1976—49ers, 26-14 (GB)
1977—Packers, 16-14 (Mil)
1980—Packers, 23-16 (Mil)
1981—49ers, 13-3 (Mil)
1986—49ers, 31-17 (Mil)
1987—49ers, 23-12 (GB)
1989—Packers, 21-17 (SF)
1990—49ers, 24-20 (GB)
1995—*Packers, 27-17 (SF)
1996—Packers, 23-20 (GB) OT
*Packers, 35-14 (GB)
1997—**Packers, 23-10 (SF)
1998—Packers, 36-22 (GB)
***49ers, 30-27 (SF)
1999—Packers, 20-3 (SF)
2000—Packers, 31-28 (GB)
2001—***Packers, 25-15 (GB)
2002—Packers, 20-14 (SF)
2003—Packers, 20-10 (GB)
2006—Packers, 30-19 (SF)
(RS Pts.—49ers 1,096, Packers 1,079)
(PS Pts.—Packers 137, 49ers 86)
*NFC Divisional Playoff
**NFC Championship
***NFC First-Round Playoff

GREEN BAY vs. SEATTLE
RS: Packers lead series, 6-5
PS: Packers lead series, 1-0
1976—Packers, 27-20 (Mil)
1978—Packers, 45-28 (Mil)
1981—Packers, 34-24 (GB)
1984—Seahawks, 30-24 (Mil)
1987—Seahawks, 24-13 (S)
1990—Seahawks, 20-14 (Mil)
1996—Packers, 31-10 (S)
1999—Seahawks, 27-7 (GB)
2003—Packers, 35-13 (GB)
*Packers, 33-27 (GB) OT
2005—Packers, 23-17 (GB)
2006—Seahawks, 34-24 (S)
(RS Pts.—Packers 277, Seahawks 247)
(PS Pts.—Packers 33, Seahawks 27)
*NFC First-Round Playoff

GREEN BAY vs. TAMPA BAY
RS: Packers lead series, 29-19-1
PS: Packers lead series, 1-0
1977—Packers, 13-0 (TB)
1978—Packers, 9-7 (GB)
Packers, 17-7 (TB)
1979—Buccaneers, 21-10 (GB)
Buccaneers, 21-3 (TB)
1980—Tie, 14-14 (TB) OT
Buccaneers, 20-17 (Mil)
1981—Buccaneers, 21-10 (GB)
Buccaneers, 37-3 (TB)
1983—Packers, 55-14 (GB)
Packers, 12-9 (TB) OT
1984—Buccaneers, 30-27 (TB) OT
Packers, 27-14 (GB)
1985—Packers, 21-0 (GB)
Packers, 20-17 (TB)
1986—Packers, 31-7 (Mil)
Packers, 21-7 (TB)
1987—Buccaneers, 23-17 (Mil)
1988—Buccaneers, 13-10 (GB)
Buccaneers, 27-24 (TB)
1989—Buccaneers, 23-21 (GB)
Packers, 17-16 (TB)
1990—Buccaneers, 26-14 (TB)
Packers, 20-10 (Mil)
1991—Packers, 15-13 (GB)
Packers, 27-0 (TB)
1992—Buccaneers, 31-3 (TB)
Packers, 19-14 (Mil)
1993—Packers, 37-14 (TB)
Packers, 13-10 (GB)
1994—Packers, 30-3 (GB)
Packers, 34-19 (TB)
1995—Packers, 35-13 (GB)
Buccaneers, 13-10 (TB) OT
1996—Packers, 34-3 (TB)
Packers, 13-7 (GB)
1997—Packers, 21-16 (GB)
Packers, 17-6 (TB)
*Packers, 21-7 (GB)
1998—Packers, 23-15 (GB)
Buccaneers, 24-22 (TB)
1999—Packers, 26-23 (GB)
Buccaneers, 29-10 (TB)
2000—Buccaneers, 20-15 (TB)
Packers, 17-14 (GB) OT
2001—Buccaneers, 14-10 (TB)
Packers, 21-20 (GB)
2002—Buccaneers, 21-7 (TB)
2003—Packers, 20-13 (TB)

2005—Buccaneers, 17-16 (GB)
(RS Pts.—Packers 928, Buccaneers 756)
(PS Pts.—Packers 21, Buccaneers 7)
NFC Divisional Playoff
GREEN BAY vs. *TENNESSEE
RS: Titans lead series, 5-4
1972—Packers, 23-10 (H)
1977—Oilers, 16-10 (GB)
1980—Oilers, 22-3 (GB)
1983—Packers, 41-38 (H) OT
1986—Oilers, 31-3 (GB)
1992—Packers, 16-14 (H)
1998—Packers, 30-22 (GB)
2001—Titans, 26-20 (T)
2004—Titans, 48-27 (GB)
(RS Pts.—Titans 227, Packers 173)
*Franchise in Houston prior to 1997;
known as Oilers prior to 1999*
GREEN BAY vs. *WASHINGTON
RS: Packers lead series, 16-12-1
PS: Series tied, 1-1
1932—Packers, 21-0 (B)
1933—Tie, 7-7 (GB)
        Redskins, 20-7 (B)
1934—Packers, 10-0 (B)
1936—Packers, 31-2 (GB)
        Packers, 7-3 (B)
        **Packers, 21-6 (New York)
1937—Redskins, 14-6 (W)
1939—Packers, 24-14 (Mil)
1941—Packers, 22-17 (W)
1943—Redskins, 33-7 (Mil)
1946—Packers, 20-7 (W)
1947—Packers, 27-10 (Mil)
1948—Redskins, 23-7 (Mil)
1949—Redskins, 30-0 (W)
1950—Packers, 35-21 (Mil)
1952—Packers, 35-20 (Mil)
1958—Redskins, 37-21 (W)
1959—Packers, 21-0 (GB)
1968—Packers, 27-7 (W)
1972—Redskins, 21-16 (W)
        ***Redskins, 16-3 (W)
1974—Redskins, 17-6 (GB)
1977—Redskins, 10-9 (W)
1979—Redskins, 38-21 (W)
1983—Packers, 48-47 (GB)
1986—Redskins, 16-7 (GB)
1988—Redskins, 20-17 (Mil)
2001—Packers, 37-0 (GB)
2002—Packers, 30-9 (GB)
2004—Packers, 28-14 (W)
(RS Pts.—Packers 554, Redskins 457)
(PS Pts.—Packers 24, Redskins 22)
*Franchise in Boston prior to 1937 and
known as Braves prior to 1933*
**NFL Championship
***NFC Divisional Playoff*

HOUSTON vs. ARIZONA
RS: Texans lead series, 1-0;
See Arizona vs. Houston
HOUSTON vs. ATLANTA
RS: Texans lead series, 1-0;
See Atlanta vs. Houston
HOUSTON vs. BALTIMORE
RS: Ravens lead series, 2-0;
See Baltimore vs. Houston
HOUSTON vs. BUFFALO
RS: Bills lead series, 3-1;

See Buffalo vs. Houston
HOUSTON vs. CAROLINA
RS: Texans lead series, 1-0;
See Carolina vs. Houston
HOUSTON vs. CHICAGO
RS: Texans lead series, 1-0;
See Chicago vs. Houston
HOUSTON vs. CINCINNATI
RS: Bengals lead series, 3-0;
See Cincinnati vs. Houston
HOUSTON vs. CLEVELAND
RS: Series tied, 2-2;
See Cleveland vs. Houston
HOUSTON vs. DALLAS
RS: Series tied, 1-1;
See Dallas vs. Houston
HOUSTON vs. DENVER
RS: Broncos lead series, 1-0;
See Denver vs. Houston
HOUSTON vs. DETROIT
RS: Lions lead series 1-0;
See Detroit vs. Houston
HOUSTON vs. GREEN BAY
RS: Packers lead series, 1-0;
See Green Bay vs. Houston
HOUSTON vs. INDIANAPOLIS
RS: Colts lead series, 9-1
2002—Colts, 23-3 (H)
        Colts, 19-3 (I)
2003—Colts, 30-21 (I)
        Colts, 20-17 (H)
2004—Colts, 49-14 (I)
        Colts, 23-14 (H)
2005—Colts, 38-20 (H)
        Colts, 31-17 (I)
2006—Colts, 43-24 (I)
        Texans, 27-24 (H)
(RS Pts.—Colts 300, Texans 160)
HOUSTON vs. JACKSONVILLE
RS: Texans lead series, 6-4
2002—Texans, 21-19 (J)
        Jaguars, 24-21 (H)
2003—Texans, 24-20 (H)
        Jaguars, 27-0 (J)
2004—Texans, 20-6 (H)
        Texans, 21-0 (J)
2005—Jaguars, 21-14 (J)
        Jaguars, 38-20 (H)
2006—Texans, 27-7 (H)
        Texans, 13-10 (J)
(RS Pts.—Texans 181, Jaguars 172)
HOUSTON vs. KANSAS CITY
RS: Chiefs lead series, 2-1
2003—Chiefs, 42-14 (H)
2004—Texans, 24-21 (KC)
2005—Chiefs, 45-17 (H)
(RS Pts.—Chiefs 108, Texans 55)
HOUSTON vs. MIAMI
RS: Texans lead series, 2-0
2003—Texans, 21-20 (M)
2006—Texans, 17-15 (H)
(RS Pts.—Texans 38, Dolphins 35)
HOUSTON vs. MINNESOTA
RS: Vikings lead series, 1-0
2004—Vikings, 34-28 (H) OT
(RS Pts.—Vikings 34, Texans 28)
HOUSTON vs. NEW ENGLAND
RS: Patriots lead series, 2-0
2003—Patriots, 23-20 (H) OT
2006—Patriots, 40-7 (NE)

(RS Pts.—Patriots 63, Texans 27)
HOUSTON vs. NEW ORLEANS
RS: Saints lead series, 1-0
2003—Saints, 31-10 (NO)
(RS Pts.—Saints 31, Texans 10)
HOUSTON vs. N.Y. GIANTS
RS: Series tied, 1-1
2002—Texans, 16-14 (H)
2006—Giants, 14-10 (NY)
(RS Pts.—Giants 28, Texans 26)
HOUSTON vs. N.Y. JETS
RS: Jets lead series, 3-0
2003—Jets, 19-14 (H)
2004—Jets, 29-7 (NY)
2006—Jets, 26-11 (NY)
(RS Pts.—Jets 74, Texans 32)
HOUSTON vs. OAKLAND
RS: Texans lead series, 2-0
2004—Texans, 30-17 (H)
2006—Texans, 23-14 (O)
(RS Pts.—Texans 53, Raiders 31)
HOUSTON vs. PHILADELPHIA
RS: Eagles lead series, 2-0
2002—Eagles, 35-17 (P)
2006—Eagles, 24-10 (H)
(RS Pts.—Eagles 59, Texans 27)
HOUSTON vs. PITTSBURGH
RS: Series tied, 1-1
2002—Texans, 24-6 (P)
2005—Steelers, 27-7 (H)
(RS Pts.—Steelers 33, Texans 31)
HOUSTON vs. ST. LOUIS
RS: Rams lead series, 1-0
2005—Rams, 33-27 (H) OT
(RS Pts.—Rams 33, Texans 27)
HOUSTON vs. SAN DIEGO
RS: Chargers lead series, 2-0
2002—Chargers, 24-3 (SD)
2004—Chargers, 27-20 (H)
(RS Pts.—Chargers 51, Texans 23)
HOUSTON vs. SAN FRANCISCO
RS: 49ers lead series, 1-0
2005—49ers, 20-17 (SF) OT
(RS Pts.—49ers 20, Texans 17)
HOUSTON vs. SEATTLE
RS: Seahawks lead series, 1-0
2005—Seahawks, 42-10
(RS Pts.—Seahawks 42, Texans 10)
HOUSTON vs. TAMPA BAY
RS: Buccaneers lead series, 1-0
2003—Buccaneers, 16-3 (TB)
(RS Pts.—Buccaneers 16, Texans 3)
HOUSTON vs. TENNESSEE
RS: Titans lead series, 8-2
2002—Titans, 17-10 (T)
        Titans, 13-3 (H)
2003—Titans, 38-17 (T)
        Titans, 27-24 (H)
2004—Texans, 20-10 (T)
        Texans, 31-21 (H)
2005—Titans, 34-20 (H)
        Titans, 13-10 (T)
2006—Titans, 28-22 (T)
        Titans, 26-20 (H) OT
(RS Pts.—Titans 227, Texans 177)
HOUSTON vs. WASHINGTON
RS: Redskins lead series, 2-0
2002—Redskins, 26-10 (W)
2006—Redskins, 31-15 (H)
(RS Pts.—Redskins 57, Texans 25)

INDIANAPOLIS vs. ARIZONA
RS: Colts lead series, 7-6;
See Arizona vs. Indianapolis

INDIANAPOLIS vs. ATLANTA
RS: Colts lead series, 12-1;
See Atlanta vs. Indianapolis

INDIANAPOLIS vs. BALTIMORE
RS: Colts lead series, 4-2
PS: Colts lead series, 1-0;
See Baltimore vs. Indianapolis

INDIANAPOLIS vs. BUFFALO
RS: Bills lead series, 34-30-1;
See Buffalo vs. Indianapolis

INDIANAPOLIS vs. CAROLINA
RS: Panthers lead series, 3-0;
See Carolina vs. Indianapolis

INDIANAPOLIS vs. CHICAGO
RS: Colts lead series, 22-17
PS: Colts lead series, 1-0;
See Chicago vs. Indianapolis

INDIANAPOLIS vs. CINCINNATI
RS: Colts lead series, 14-8
PS: Colts lead series, 1-0;
See Cincinnati vs. Indianapolis

INDIANAPOLIS vs. CLEVELAND
RS: Browns lead series, 13-11
PS: Series tied, 2-2;
See Cleveland vs. Indianapolis

INDIANAPOLIS vs. DALLAS
RS: Cowboys lead series, 8-5
PS: Colts lead series, 1-0;
See Dallas vs. Indianapolis

INDIANAPOLIS vs. DENVER
RS: Broncos lead series, 11-5
PS: Colts lead series, 2-0;
See Denver vs. Indianapolis

INDIANAPOLIS vs. DETROIT
RS: Colts lead series, 19-18-2;
See Detroit vs. Indianapolis

INDIANAPOLIS vs. GREEN BAY
RS: Colts lead series, 20-19-1
PS: Packers lead series, 1-0;
See Green Bay vs. Indianapolis

INDIANAPOLIS vs. HOUSTON
RS: Colts lead series, 9-1;
See Houston vs. Indianapolis

INDIANAPOLIS vs. JACKSONVILLE
RS: Colts lead series, 9-3
1995—Colts, 41-31 (J)
2000—Colts, 43-14 (I)
2002—Colts, 28-25 (J)
　　　 Colts, 20-13 (I)
2003—Colts, 23-13 (I)
　　　 Jaguars, 28-23 (J)
2004—Colts, 24-17 (J)
　　　 Jaguars, 27-24 (I)
2005—Colts, 10-3 (I)
　　　 Colts, 26-18 (J)
2006—Colts, 21-14 (I)
　　　 Jaguars, 44-17 (J)
(RS Pts.—Colts 300, Jaguars 247)

*INDIANAPOLIS vs. KANSAS CITY
RS: Colts lead series, 8-7
PS: Colts lead series, 3-0
1970—Chiefs, 44-24 (B)
1972—Chiefs, 24-10 (KC)
1975—Colts, 28-14 (B)
1977—Colts, 17-6 (KC)
1979—Chiefs, 14-0 (KC)

Chiefs, 10-7 (B)
1980—Colts, 31-24 (KC)
　　　 Chiefs, 38-28 (B)
1985—Chiefs, 20-7 (KC)
1990—Colts, 23-19 (I)
1995—**Colts, 10-7 (KC)
1996—Colts, 24-19 (KC)
1999—Colts, 25-17 (I)
2000—Colts, 27-14 (KC)
2001—Colts, 35-28 (KC)
2003—**Colts, 38-31 (KC)
2004—Chiefs, 45-35 (KC)
2006—***Colts, 23-8 (I)
(RS Pts.—Chiefs 336, Colts 321)
(PS Pts.—Colts 71, Chiefs 46)
*Franchise in Baltimore prior to 1984
**AFC Divisional Playoff
***AFC First-Round Playoff

*INDIANAPOLIS vs. MIAMI
RS: Dolphins lead series, 44-23
PS: Dolphins lead series, 2-0
1970—Colts, 35-0 (B)
　　　 Dolphins, 34-17 (M)
1971—Dolphins, 17-14 (M)
　　　 Colts, 14-3 (B)
　　　 **Dolphins, 21-0 (M)
1972—Dolphins, 23-0 (B)
　　　 Dolphins, 16-0 (M)
1973—Dolphins, 44-0 (M)
　　　 Colts, 16-3 (B)
1974—Dolphins, 17-7 (M)
　　　 Dolphins, 17-16 (B)
1975—Colts, 33-17 (M)
　　　 Colts, 10-7 (B) OT
1976—Colts, 28-14 (B)
　　　 Colts, 17-16 (M)
1977—Colts, 45-28 (B)
　　　 Dolphins, 17-6 (M)
1978—Dolphins, 42-0 (B)
　　　 Dolphins, 26-8 (M)
1979—Dolphins, 19-0 (M)
　　　 Dolphins, 28-24 (B)
1980—Colts, 30-17 (M)
　　　 Dolphins, 24-14 (B)
1981—Dolphins, 31-28 (B)
　　　 Dolphins, 27-10 (M)
1982—Dolphins, 24-20 (M)
　　　 Dolphins, 34-7 (B)
1983—Dolphins, 21-7 (B)
　　　 Dolphins, 37-0 (M)
1984—Dolphins, 44-7 (M)
　　　 Dolphins, 35-17 (I)
1985—Dolphins, 30-13 (M)
　　　 Dolphins, 34-20 (I)
1986—Dolphins, 30-10 (M)
　　　 Dolphins, 17-13 (I)
1987—Dolphins, 23-10 (I)
　　　 Colts, 40-21 (M)
1988—Colts, 15-13 (I)
　　　 Colts, 31-28 (M)
1989—Dolphins, 19-13 (M)
　　　 Colts, 42-13 (I)
1990—Dolphins, 27-7 (I)
　　　 Dolphins, 23-17 (M)
1991—Dolphins, 17-6 (M)
　　　 Dolphins, 10-6 (I)
1992—Colts, 31-20 (M)
　　　 Dolphins, 28-0 (I)
1993—Dolphins, 24-20 (I)
　　　 Dolphins, 41-27 (M)

1994—Dolphins, 22-21 (M)
　　　 Colts, 10-6 (I)
1995—Colts, 27-24 (M) OT
　　　 Colts, 36-28 (I)
1996—Colts, 10-6 (I)
　　　 Dolphins, 37-13 (M)
1997—Dolphins, 16-10 (M)
　　　 Colts, 41-0 (I)
1998—Dolphins, 24-15 (I)
　　　 Dolphins, 27-14 (M)
1999—Dolphins, 34-31 (I)
　　　 Colts, 37-34 (M)
2000—Dolphins, 17-14 (I)
　　　 Colts, 20-13 (M)
　　　 ***Dolphins 23-17 (M) OT
2001—Dolphins, 27-24 (I)
　　　 Dolphins, 41-6 (M)
2002—Dolphins, 21-13 (I)
2003—Colts, 23-17 (M)
2006—Colts, 27-22 (I)
(RS Pts.—Dolphins 1,516, Colts 1,143)
(PS Pts.—Dolphins 44, Colts 17)
*Franchise in Baltimore prior to 1984
**AFC Championship
***AFC First-Round Playoff

*INDIANAPOLIS vs. MINNESOTA
RS: Colts lead series, 13-7-1
PS: Colts lead series, 1-0
1961—Colts, 34-33 (B)
　　　 Vikings, 28-20 (M)
1962—Colts, 34-7 (M)
　　　 Colts, 42-17 (B)
1963—Colts, 37-34 (M)
　　　 Colts, 41-10 (B)
1964—Vikings, 34-24 (M)
　　　 Colts, 17-14 (B)
1965—Colts, 35-16 (B)
　　　 Colts, 41-21 (M)
1966—Colts, 38-23 (M)
　　　 Colts, 20-17 (B)
1967—Tie, 20-20 (M)
1968—Colts, 21-9 (B)
　　　 **Colts, 24-14 (B)
1969—Vikings, 52-14 (M)
1971—Vikings, 10-3 (M)
1982—Vikings, 13-10 (M)
1988—Vikings, 12-3 (M)
1997—Vikings, 39-28 (M)
2000—Colts, 31-10 (I)
2004—Colts, 31-28 (I)
(RS Pts.—Colts 544, Vikings 447)
(PS Pts.—Colts 24, Vikings 14)
*Franchise in Baltimore prior to 1984
**Conference Championship

*INDIANAPOLIS vs. **NEW ENGLAND
RS: Patriots lead series, 41-26
PS: Patriots lead series, 2-1
1970—Colts, 14-6 (Bos)
　　　 Colts, 27-3 (Balt)
1971—Colts, 23-3 (NE)
　　　 Patriots, 21-17 (Balt)
1972—Colts, 24-17 (NE)
　　　 Colts, 31-0 (Balt)
1973—Patriots, 24-16 (NE)
　　　 Colts, 18-13 (Balt)
1974—Patriots, 42-3 (NE)
　　　 Patriots, 27-17 (Balt)
1975—Patriots, 21-10 (NE)
　　　 Colts, 34-21 (Balt)
1976—Colts, 27-13 (NE)

Patriots, 21-14 (Balt)
1977—Patriots, 17-3 (NE)
Colts, 30-24 (Balt)
1978—Colts, 34-27 (NE)
Patriots, 35-14 (Balt)
1979—Colts, 31-26 (Balt)
Patriots, 50-21 (NE)
1980—Patriots, 37-21 (Balt)
Patriots, 47-21 (NE)
1981—Colts, 29-28 (NE)
Colts, 23-21 (Balt)
1982—Patriots, 24-13 (Balt)
1983—Colts, 29-23 (NE) OT
Colts, 12-7 (Balt)
1984—Patriots, 50-17 (I)
Patriots, 16-10 (NE)
1985—Patriots, 34-15 (NE)
Patriots, 38-31 (I)
1986—Patriots, 33-3 (NE)
Patriots, 30-21 (I)
1987—Colts, 30-16 (I)
Patriots, 24-0 (NE)
1988—Patriots, 21-17 (NE)
Colts, 24-21 (I)
1989—Patriots, 23-20 (I) OT
Patriots, 22-16 (NE)
1990—Patriots, 16-14 (I)
Colts, 13-10 (NE)
1991—Patriots, 16-7 (I)
Patriots, 23-17 (NE) OT
1992—Patriots, 37-34 (I) OT
Colts, 6-0 (NE)
1993—Colts, 9-6 (I)
Patriots, 38-0 (NE)
1994—Patriots, 12-10 (I)
Patriots, 28-13 (NE)
1995—Colts, 24-10 (NE)
Colts, 10-7 (I)
1996—Patriots, 27-9 (I)
Patriots, 27-13 (NE)
1997—Patriots, 31-6 (I)
Patriots, 20-17 (NE)
1998—Patriots, 29-6 (NE)
Patriots, 21-16 (I)
1999—Patriots, 31-28 (NE)
Colts, 20-15 (I)
2000—Patriots, 24-16 (NE)
Colts, 30-23 (I)
2001—Patriots, 44-13 (NE)
Patriots, 38-17 (I)
2003—Patriots, 38-34 (I)
***Patriots, 24-14 (NE)
2004—Patriots, 27-24 (NE)
****Patriots, 20-3 (NE)
2005—Colts, 40-21 (NE)
2006—Colts, 27-20 (NE)
***Colts, 38-34 (I)
(RS Pts.—Patriots 1,565, Colts 1,233)
(PS Pts.—Patriots 78, Colts 55)
*Franchise in Baltimore prior to 1984
**Franchise in Boston prior to 1971
***AFC Championship
****AFC Divisional Playoff
*INDIANAPOLIS vs. NEW ORLEANS
RS: Saints lead series, 5-4
1967—Colts, 30-10 (B)
1969—Colts, 30-10 (NO)
1973—Colts, 14-10 (B)
1986—Saints, 17-14 (I)
1989—Saints, 41-6 (NO)

1995—Saints, 17-14 (NO)
1998—Saints, 19-13 (I) OT
2001—Saints, 34-20 (NO)
2003—Colts, 55-21 (NO)
(RS Pts.—Colts 196, Saints 179)
*Franchise in Baltimore prior to 1984
*INDIANAPOLIS vs. N.Y. GIANTS
RS: Colts lead series, 7-6
PS: Colts lead series, 2-0
1954—Colts, 20-14 (B)
1955—Giants, 17-7 (NY)
1958—Giants, 24-21 (NY)
**Colts, 23-17 (NY) OT
1959—**Colts, 31-16 (B)
1963—Giants, 37-28 (B)
1968—Colts, 26-0 (NY)
1971—Colts, 31-7 (NY)
1975—Colts, 21-0 (NY)
1979—Colts, 31-7 (NY)
1990—Giants, 24-7 (I)
1993—Giants, 20-6 (NY)
1999—Colts, 27-19 (NY)
2002—Giants, 44-27 (I)
2006—Colts, 26-21 (NY)
(RS Pts.—Colts 278, Giants 234)
(PS Pts.—Colts 54, Giants 33)
*Franchise in Baltimore prior to 1984
**NFL Championship
*INDIANAPOLIS vs. N.Y. JETS
RS: Colts lead series, 40-25
PS: Jets lead series, 2-0
1968—**Jets 16-7 (Miami)
1970—Colts, 29-22 (NY)
Colts, 35-20 (B)
1971—Colts, 22-0 (B)
Colts, 14-13 (NY)
1972—Jets, 44-34 (B)
Jets, 24-20 (NY)
1973—Jets, 34-10 (B)
Jets, 20-17 (NY)
1974—Colts, 35-20 (NY)
Jets, 45-38 (B)
1975—Colts, 45-28 (NY)
Colts, 52-19 (B)
1976—Colts, 20-0 (NY)
Colts, 33-16 (B)
1977—Colts, 20-12 (NY)
Colts, 33-12 (B)
1978—Jets, 33-10 (B)
Jets, 24-16 (NY)
1979—Colts, 10-8 (B)
Jets, 30-17 (NY)
1980—Colts, 17-14 (NY)
Colts, 35-21 (B)
1981—Jets, 41-14 (B)
Jets, 25-0 (NY)
1982—Jets, 37-0 (NY)
1983—Colts, 17-14 (NY)
Jets, 10-6 (B)
1984—Jets, 23-14 (I)
Colts, 9-5 (NY)
1985—Jets, 25-20 (NY)
Jets, 35-17 (I)
1986—Jets, 26-7 (I)
Jets, 31-16 (NY)
1987—Colts, 6-0 (I)
Colts, 19-14 (NY)
1988—Colts, 38-14 (I)
Jets, 34-16 (NY)
1989—Colts, 17-10 (NY)

Colts, 27-10 (I)
1990—Colts, 17-14 (I)
Colts, 29-21 (NY)
1991—Jets, 17-6 (I)
Colts, 28-27 (NY)
1992—Colts, 6-3 (I) OT
Colts, 10-6 (NY)
1993—Jets, 31-17 (I)
Colts, 9-6 (NY)
1994—Jets, 16-6 (NY)
Colts, 28-25 (I)
1995—Colts, 27-24 (NY) OT
Colts, 17-10 (I)
1996—Colts, 21-7 (NY)
Colts, 34-29 (I)
1997—Jets, 16-12 (I)
Colts, 22-14 (NY)
1998—Jets, 44-6 (NY)
Colts, 24-23 (I)
1999—Colts, 16-13 (NY)
Colts, 13-6 (I)
2000—Colts, 23-15 (I)
Jets, 27-17 (NY)
2001—Colts, 45-24 (NY)
Jets, 29-28 (I)
2002—***Jets, 41-0 (NY)
2003—Colts, 38-31 (I)
2006—Colts, 31-28 (NY)
(RS Pts.—Colts 1,335, Jets 1,319)
(PS Pts.—Jets 57, Colts 7)
*Franchise in Baltimore prior to 1984
**Super Bowl III
***AFC First-Round Playoff
*INDIANAPOLIS vs **OAKLAND
RS: Raiders lead series, 7-3
PS: Series tied, 1-1
1970—***Colts, 27-17 (B)
1971—Colts, 37-14 (O)
1973—Raiders, 34-21 (B)
1975—Raiders, 31-20 (B)
1977—****Raiders, 37-31 (B) OT
1984—Raiders, 21-7 (LA)
1986—Colts, 30-24 (LA)
1991—Raiders, 16-0 (LA)
1995—Raiders, 30-17 (O)
2000—Raiders, 38-31 (I)
2001—Raiders, 23-18 (I)
2004—Colts, 35-14 (I)
(RS Pts.—Raiders 245, Colts 216)
(PS Pts.—Colts 58, Raiders 54)
*Franchise in Baltimore prior to 1984
**Franchise in Los Angeles from 1982-1994
***AFC Championship
****AFC Divisional Playoff
*INDIANAPOLIS vs. PHILADELPHIA
RS: Colts lead series, 10-6
1953—Eagles, 45-14 (P)
1965—Colts, 34-24 (B)
1967—Colts, 38-6 (P)
1969—Colts, 24-20 (B)
1970—Colts, 29-10 (B)
1974—Eagles, 30-10 (P)
1978—Eagles, 17-14 (B)
1981—Eagles, 38-13 (P)
1983—Colts, 22-21 (P)
1984—Eagles, 16-7 (P)
1990—Colts, 24-23 (P)
1993—Eagles, 20-10 (I)
1996—Colts, 37-10 (I)

1999—Colts, 44-17 (P)
2002—Colts, 35-13 (P)
2006—Colts, 45-21 (I)
(RS Pts.—Colts 400, Eagles 331)
Franchise in Baltimore prior to 1984
INDIANAPOLIS vs. PITTSBURGH
RS: Steelers lead series, 13-5
PS: Steelers lead series, 5-0
1957—Steelers, 19-13 (B)
1968—Colts, 41-7 (P)
1971—Colts, 34-21 (B)
1974—Steelers, 30-0 (P)
1975—**Steelers, 28-10 (P)
1976—**Steelers, 40-14 (B)
1977—Colts, 31-21 (B)
1978—Steelers, 35-13 (P)
1979—Steelers, 17-13 (P)
1980—Steelers, 20-17 (B)
1983—Steelers, 24-13 (B)
1984—Colts, 17-16 (I)
1985—Steelers, 45-3 (P)
1987—Steelers, 21-7 (P)
1991—Steelers, 21-3 (I)
1992—Steelers, 30-14 (P)
1994—Steelers, 31-21 (P)
1995—***Steelers, 20-16 (P)
1996—****Steelers, 42-14 (P)
1997—Steelers, 24-22 (P)
2002—Steelers, 28-10 (P)
2005—Colts, 26-7 (I)
　　　**Steelers, 21-18 (I)
(RS Pts.—Steelers 417, Colts 298)
(PS Pts.—Steelers 151, Colts 72)
Franchise in Baltimore prior to 1984
**AFC Divisional Playoff*
***AFC Championship*
****AFC First-Round Playoff*
INDIANAPOLIS vs. **ST. LOUIS
RS: Colts lead series, 22-17-2
1953—Rams, 21-13 (B)
　　　Rams, 45-2 (LA)
1954—Rams, 48-0 (B)
　　　Colts, 22-21 (LA)
1955—Tie, 17-17 (B)
　　　Rams, 20-14 (LA)
1956—Colts, 56-21 (B)
　　　Rams, 31-7 (LA)
1957—Colts, 31-14 (B)
　　　Rams, 37-21 (LA)
1958—Colts, 34-7 (B)
　　　Rams, 30-28 (LA)
1959—Colts, 35-21 (B)
　　　Colts, 45-26 (LA)
1960—Colts, 31-17 (B)
　　　Rams, 10-3 (LA)
1961—Colts, 27-24 (B)
　　　Rams, 34-17 (LA)
1962—Colts, 30-27 (B)
　　　Colts, 14-2 (LA)
1963—Rams, 17-16 (LA)
　　　Colts, 19-16 (B)
1964—Colts, 35-20 (B)
　　　Colts, 24-7 (LA)
1965—Colts, 35-20 (B)
　　　Colts, 20-17 (LA)
1966—Colts, 17-3 (LA)
　　　Rams, 23-7 (B)
1967—Tie, 24-24 (B)
　　　Rams, 34-10 (LA)
1968—Colts, 27-10 (B)

Colts, 28-24 (LA)
1969—Rams, 27-20 (B)
　　　Colts, 13-7 (LA)
1971—Colts, 24-17 (B)
1975—Rams, 24-13 (LA)
1986—Rams, 24-7 (I)
1989—Rams, 31-17 (LA)
1995—Colts, 21-18 (I)
2001—Rams, 42-17 (StL)
2005—Colts, 45-28 (I)
(RS Pts.—Rams 906, Colts 886)
Franchise in Baltimore prior to 1984
**Franchise in Los Angeles prior to 1995*
INDIANAPOLIS vs. SAN DIEGO
RS: Chargers lead series, 13-8
PS: Colts lead series, 1-0
1970—Colts, 16-14 (SD)
1972—Chargers, 23-20 (B)
1976—Colts, 37-21 (SD)
1981—Chargers, 43-14 (B)
1982—Chargers, 44-26 (SD)
1984—Chargers, 38-10 (I)
1986—Chargers, 17-3 (I)
1987—Chargers, 16-13 (I)
　　　Colts, 20-7 (SD)
1988—Colts, 16-0 (SD)
1989—Colts, 10-6 (I)
1992—Chargers, 34-14 (I)
　　　Chargers, 26-0 (SD)
1993—Chargers, 31-0 (I)
1995—Chargers, 27-24 (I)
　　　**Colts, 35-20 (SD)
1996—Chargers, 26-19 (I)
1997—Chargers, 35-19 (SD)
1998—Colts, 17-12 (I)
1999—Colts, 27-19 (SD)
2004—Colts, 34-31 (I) OT
2005—Chargers, 26-17 (I)
(RS Pts.—Chargers 496, Colts 356)
(PS Pts.—Colts 35, Chargers 20)
Franchise in Baltimore prior to 1984
**AFC First-Round Playoff*
INDIANAPOLIS vs. SAN FRANCISCO
RS: Colts lead series, 23-18
1953—49ers, 38-21 (B)
　　　49ers, 45-14 (SF)
1954—Colts, 17-13 (B)
　　　49ers, 10-7 (SF)
1955—Colts, 26-14 (B)
　　　49ers, 35-24 (SF)
1956—49ers, 20-17 (B)
　　　49ers, 30-17 (SF)
1957—Colts, 27-21 (B)
　　　49ers, 17-13 (SF)
1958—Colts, 35-27 (B)
　　　49ers, 21-12 (SF)
1959—Colts, 45-14 (B)
　　　Colts, 34-14 (SF)
1960—49ers, 30-22 (B)
　　　49ers, 34-10 (SF)
1961—Colts, 20-17 (B)
　　　Colts, 27-24 (SF)
1962—49ers, 21-13 (B)
　　　Colts, 22-3 (SF)
1963—Colts, 20-14 (SF)
　　　Colts, 20-3 (B)
1964—Colts, 37-7 (B)
　　　Colts, 14-3 (SF)
1965—Colts, 27-24 (B)
　　　Colts, 34-28 (SF)

1966—Colts, 36-14 (B)
　　　Colts, 30-14 (SF)
1967—Colts, 41-7 (B)
　　　Colts, 26-9 (SF)
1968—Colts, 27-10 (B)
　　　Colts, 42-14 (SF)
1969—49ers, 24-21 (B)
　　　49ers, 20-17 (SF)
1972—49ers, 24-21 (SF)
1986—49ers, 35-14 (SF)
1989—49ers, 30-24 (I)
1995—Colts, 18-17 (I)
1998—49ers, 34-31 (SF)
2001—49ers, 40-21 (I)
2005—Colts, 28-3 (SF)
(RS Pts.—Colts 972, 49ers 822)
Franchise in Baltimore prior to 1984
INDIANAPOLIS vs. SEATTLE
RS: Colts lead series, 5-4
1977—Colts, 29-14 (S)
1978—Colts, 17-14 (S)
1991—Seahawks, 31-3 (S)
1994—Colts, 17-15 (I)
　　　Colts, 31-19 (S)
1997—Seahawks, 31-3 (I)
1998—Seahawks, 27-23 (S)
2000—Colts, 37-24 (S)
2005—Seahawks, 28-13 (S)
(RS Pts.—Seahawks 203, Colts 173)
Franchise in Baltimore prior to 1984
INDIANAPOLIS vs. TAMPA BAY
RS: Colts lead series, 6-4
1976—Colts, 42-17 (B)
1979—Buccaneers, 29-26 (B) OT
1985—Colts, 31-23 (TB)
1987—Colts, 24-6 (I)
1988—Colts, 35-31 (I)
1991—Buccaneers, 17-3 (TB)
1992—Colts, 24-14 (TB)
1994—Buccaneers, 24-10 (TB)
1997—Buccaneers, 31-28 (I)
2003—Colts, 38-35 (TB) OT
(RS Pts.—Colts 261, Buccaneers 227)
Franchise in Baltimore prior to 1984
INDIANAPOLIS vs. **TENNESSEE
RS: Colts lead series, 14-10
PS: Titans lead series, 1-0
1970—Colts, 24-20 (H)
1973—Oilers, 31-27 (B)
1976—Colts, 38-14 (B)
1979—Oilers, 28-16 (B)
1980—Oilers, 21-16 (H)
1983—Colts, 20-10 (B)
1984—Colts, 35-21 (H)
1985—Colts, 34-16 (I)
1986—Oilers, 31-17 (H)
1987—Colts, 51-27 (I)
1988—Oilers, 17-14 (I) OT
1990—Oilers, 24-10 (H)
1992—Oilers, 20-10 (I)
1994—Colts, 45-21 (I)
1999—***Titans, 19-16 (I)
2002—Titans, 23-15 (I)
　　　Titans, 27-17 (T)
2003—Colts, 33-7 (I)
　　　Colts, 29-27 (T)
2004—Colts, 31-17 (T)
　　　Colts, 51-24 (I)
2005—Colts, 31-10 (T)
　　　Colts, 35-3 (I)

2006—Colts, 14-13 (I)
    Titans, 20-17 (T)
(RS Pts.—Colts 630, Titans 472)
(PS Pts.—Titans 19, Colts 16)
*Franchise in Baltimore prior to 1984
**Franchise in Houston prior to 1997;
known as Oilers prior to 1999
***AFC Divisional Playoff

*INDIANAPOLIS vs. WASHINGTON
RS: Colts lead series, 18-10
1953—Colts, 27-17 (B)
1954—Redskins, 24-21 (W)
1955—Redskins, 14-13 (B)
1956—Colts, 19-17 (B)
1957—Colts, 21-17 (W)
1958—Colts, 35-10 (B)
1959—Redskins, 27-24 (W)
1960—Colts, 20-0 (B)
1961—Colts, 27-6 (W)
1962—Colts, 34-21 (B)
1963—Colts, 36-20 (W)
1964—Colts, 45-17 (B)
1965—Colts, 38-7 (W)
1966—Colts, 37-10 (B)
1967—Colts, 17-13 (W)
1969—Colts, 41-17 (B)
1973—Redskins, 22-14 (W)
1977—Colts, 10-3 (B)
1978—Colts, 21-17 (B)
1981—Redskins, 38-14 (W)
1984—Redskins, 35-7 (I)
1990—Colts, 35-28 (I)
1993—Redskins, 30-24 (W)
1994—Redskins, 41-27 (I)
1996—Redskins, 31-16 (W)
1999—Colts, 24-21 (I)
2002—Redskins, 26-21 (W)
2006—Colts, 36-22 (I)
(RS Pts.—Colts 704, Redskins 551)
*Franchise in Baltimore prior to 1984

JACKSONVILLE vs. ARIZONA
RS: Jaguars lead series, 2-0;
See Arizona vs. Jacksonville
JACKSONVILLE vs. ATLANTA
RS: Jaguars lead series, 2-1;
See Atlanta vs. Jacksonville
JACKSONVILLE vs. BALTIMORE
RS: Jaguars lead series, 9-6;
See Baltimore vs. Jacksonville
JACKSONVILLE vs. BUFFALO
RS: Bills lead series, 4-2
PS: Jaguars lead series, 1-0;
See Buffalo vs. Jacksonville
JACKSONVILLE vs. CAROLINA
RS: Jaguars lead series, 2-1;
See Carolina vs. Jacksonville
JACKSONVILLE vs. CHICAGO
RS: Series tied, 2-2;
See Chicago vs. Jacksonville
JACKSONVILLE vs. CINCINNATI
RS: Jaguars lead series, 11-5;
See Cincinnati vs. Jacksonville
JACKSONVILLE vs. CLEVELAND
RS: Jaguars lead series, 8-2;
See Cleveland vs. Jacksonville
JACKSONVILLE vs. DALLAS
RS: Series tied, 2-2;
See Dallas vs. Jacksonville
JACKSONVILLE vs. DENVER

RS: Broncos lead series, 3-2
PS: Series tied, 1-1;
See Denver vs. Jacksonville
JACKSONVILLE vs. DETROIT
RS: Jaguars lead series, 2-1;
See Detroit vs. Jacksonville
JACKSONVILLE vs. GREEN BAY
RS: Packers lead series, 2-1;
See Green Bay vs. Jacksonville
JACKSONVILLE vs. HOUSTON
RS: Texans lead series, 6-4;
See Houston vs. Jacksonville
JACKSONVILLE vs. INDIANAPOLIS
RS: Colts lead series, 9-3;
See Indianapolis vs. Jacksonville
JACKSONVILLE vs. KANSAS CITY
RS: Jaguars lead series, 4-2
1997—Jaguars, 24-10 (J)
1998—Jaguars, 21-16 (J)
2001—Chiefs, 30-26 (J)
2002—Jaguars, 23-16 (KC)
2004—Jaguars, 22-16 (J)
2006—Chiefs, 35-30 (KC)
(RS Pts.—Jaguars 146, Chiefs 123)
JACKSONVILLE vs. MIAMI
RS: Jaguars lead series, 2-1
PS: Jaguars lead series, 1-0
1998—Jaguars, 28-21 (J)
1999—*Jaguars, 62-7 (J)
2003—Dolphins, 24-10 (J)
2006—Jaguars, 24-10 (M)
(RS Pts.—Jaguars 62, Dolphins 55)
(PS Pts.—Jaguars 62, Dolphins 7)
*AFC Divisional Playoff
JACKSONVILLE vs. MINNESOTA
RS: Vikings lead series, 2-1
1998—Vikings, 50-10 (M)
2001—Jaguars, 33-3 (M)
2004—Vikings, 27-16 (M)
(RS Pts.—Vikings 80, Jaguars 59)
JACKSONVILLE vs. NEW ENGLAND
RS: Patriots lead series, 4-0
PS: Patriots lead series, 2-1
1996—Patriots, 28-25 (NE) OT
        *Patriots, 20-6 (NE)
1997—Patriots, 26-20 (J)
1998—**Jaguars, 25-10 (J)
2003—Patriots, 27-13 (NE)
2005—**Patriots, 28-3 (NE)
2006—Patriots, 24-21 (J)
(RS Pts.—Patriots 105, Jaguars 79)
(PS Pts.—Patriots 58, Jaguars 34)
*AFC Championship
**AFC First-Round Playoff
JACKSONVILLE vs. NEW ORLEANS
RS: Jaguars lead series, 2-1
1996—Saints, 17-13 (NO)
1999—Jaguars, 41-23 (J)
2003—Jaguars, 20-19 (J)
(RS Pts.—Jaguars 74, Saints 59)
JACKSONVILLE vs. N.Y. GIANTS
RS: Series tied, 2-2
1997—Jaguars, 40-13 (J)
2000—Giants, 28-25 (NY)
2002—Giants, 24-17 (NY)
2006—Jaguars, 26-10 (J)
(RS Pts.—Jaguars 108, Giants 75)
JACKSONVILLE vs. N.Y. JETS
RS: Jaguars lead series, 5-2
PS: Jets lead series, 1-0

1995—Jets, 27-10 (NY)
1996—Jaguars, 21-17 (J)
1998—*Jets, 34-24 (NY)
1999—Jaguars, 16-6 (NY)
2002—Jaguars, 28-3 (J)
2003—Jets, 13-10 (NY)
2005—Jaguars, 26-20 (NY) OT
2006—Jaguars, 41-0 (J)
(RS Pts.—Jaguars 152, Jets 86)
(PS Pts.—Jets 34, Jaguars 24)
*AFC Divisional Playoff
JACKSONVILLE vs. OAKLAND
RS: Jaguars lead series, 2-1
1996—Raiders, 17-3 (O)
1997—Jaguars, 20-9 (O)
2004—Jaguars, 13-6 (O)
(RS Pts.—Jaguars 36, Raiders 32)
JACKSONVILLE vs. PHILADELPHIA
RS: Jaguars lead series, 3-0
1997—Jaguars, 38-21 (J)
2002—Jaguars, 28-25 (J)
2006—Jaguars, 13-6 (P)
(RS Pts.—Jaguars 79, Eagles 52)
JACKSONVILLE vs. PITTSBURGH
RS: Jaguars lead series, 10-8
1995—Jaguars, 20-16 (J)
        Steelers, 24-7 (P)
1996—Jaguars, 24-9 (J)
        Steelers, 28-3 (P)
1997—Jaguars, 30-21 (J)
        Steelers, 23-17 (P) OT
1998—Steelers, 30-15 (P)
        Jaguars, 21-3 (J)
1999—Jaguars, 17-3 (P)
        Jaguars, 20-6 (J)
2000—Steelers, 24-13 (J)
        Jaguars, 34-24 (P)
2001—Jaguars, 21-3 (J)
        Steelers, 20-7 (P)
2002—Steelers, 25-23 (J)
2004—Steelers, 17-16 (J)
2005—Jaguars, 23-17 (P) OT
2006—Jaguars, 9-0 (J)
(RS Pts.—Jaguars 320, Steelers 293)
JACKSONVILLE vs. ST. LOUIS
RS: Rams lead series, 2-0
1996—Rams, 17-14 (StL)
2005—Rams, 24-21 (StL)
(RS Pts.—Rams 41, Jaguars 35)
JACKSONVILLE vs. SAN DIEGO
RS: Series tied, 1-1
2003—Jaguars, 27-21 (J)
2004—Chargers, 34-21 (SD)
(RS Pts.—Chargers 55, Jaguars 48)
JACKSONVILLE vs. SAN FRANCISCO
RS: Jaguars lead series, 2-0
1999—Jaguars, 41-3 (J)
2005—Jaguars, 10-9 (J)
(RS Pts.—Jaguars 51, 49ers 12)
JACKSONVILLE vs. SEATTLE
RS: Seahawks lead series, 3-2
1995—Seahawks, 47-30 (J)
1996—Jaguars, 20-13 (J)
2000—Seahawks, 28-21 (J)
2001—Seahawks, 24-15 (S)
2005—Jaguars, 26-14 (J)
(RS Pts.—Seahawks 126, Jaguars 112)
JACKSONVILLE vs. TAMPA BAY
RS: Jaguars lead series, 2-1
1995—Buccaneers, 17-16 (TB)

1998—Jaguars, 29-24 (J)
2003—Jaguars, 17-10 (J)
(RS Pts.—Jaguars 62, Buccaneers 51)
JACKSONVILLE vs. *TENNESSEE
RS: Titans lead series, 13-11
PS: Titans lead, 1-0
1995—Oilers, 10-3 (J)
       Jaguars, 17-16 (H)
1996—Oilers, 34-27 (J)
       Jaguars, 23-17 (H)
1997—Jaguars, 30-24 (T)
       Jaguars, 17-9 (J)
1998—Jaguars, 27-22 (T)
       Oilers, 16-13 (J)
1999—Titans, 20-19 (J)
       Titans, 41-14 (T)
       **Titans, 33-14 (J)
2000—Titans, 27-13 (T)
       Jaguars, 16-13 (J)
2001—Jaguars, 13-6 (J)
       Titans, 28-24 (T)
2002—Titans, 23-14 (T)
       Titans, 28-10 (J)
2003—Titans, 30-17 (J)
       Titans, 10-3 (T)
2004—Jaguars, 15-12 (T)
       Titans, 18-15 (J)
2005—Jaguars, 31-28 (T)
       Jaguars, 40-13 (J)
2006—Jaguars, 37-7 (J)
       Titans, 24-17 (T)
(RS Pts.—Titans 476, Jaguars 455)
(PS Pts.—Titans 33, Jaguars 14)
*Franchise in Houston prior to 1997;
known as Oilers prior to 1999
**AFC Championship
JACKSONVILLE vs. WASHINGTON
RS: Redskins lead series, 3-1
1997—Redskins, 24-12 (W)
2000—Redskins, 35-16 (J)
2002—Jaguars, 26-7 (J)
2006—Redskins, 36-30 (W) OT
(RS Pts.—Redskins 102, Jaguars 84)

KANSAS CITY vs. ARIZONA
RS: Chiefs lead series, 7-2-1;
See Arizona vs. Kansas City
KANSAS CITY vs. ATLANTA
RS: Chiefs lead series, 5-1;
See Atlanta vs. Kansas City
KANSAS CITY vs. BALTIMORE
RS: Chiefs lead series, 3-1;
See Baltimore vs. Kansas City
KANSAS CITY vs. BUFFALO
RS: Bills lead series, 19-16-1
PS: Chiefs lead series, 2-1;
See Buffalo vs. Kansas City
KANSAS CITY vs. CAROLINA
RS: Chiefs lead series, 2-1;
See Carolina vs. Kansas City
KANSAS CITY vs. CHICAGO
RS: Bears lead series, 5-4;
See Chicago vs. Kansas City
KANSAS CITY vs. CINCINNATI
RS: Chiefs lead series, 12-11;
See Cincinnati vs. Kansas City
KANSAS CITY vs. CLEVELAND
RS: Series tied, 9-9-2;
See Cleveland vs. Kansas City
KANSAS CITY vs. DALLAS

RS: Cowboys lead series, 5-3;
See Dallas vs. Kansas City
KANSAS CITY vs. DENVER
RS: Chiefs lead series, 52-41
PS: Broncos lead series, 1-0;
See Denver vs. Kansas City
KANSAS CITY vs. DETROIT
RS: Chiefs lead series, 7-3;
See Detroit vs. Kansas City
KANSAS CITY vs. GREEN BAY
RS: Chiefs lead series, 6-1-1
PS: Packers lead series, 1-0;
See Green Bay vs. Kansas City
KANSAS CITY vs. HOUSTON
RS: Chiefs lead series, 2-1;
See Houston vs. Kansas City
KANSAS CITY vs. INDIANAPOLIS
RS: Colts lead series, 8-7
PS: Colts lead series, 3-0;
See Indianapolis vs. Kansas City
KANSAS CITY vs. JACKSONVILLE
RS: Jaguars lead series, 4-2;
See Jacksonville vs. Kansas City
KANSAS CITY vs. MIAMI
RS: Chiefs lead series, 12-11
PS: Dolphins lead series, 3-0
1966—Chiefs, 34-16 (KC)
       Chiefs, 19-18 (M)
1967—Chiefs, 24-0 (M)
       Chiefs, 41-0 (KC)
1968—Chiefs, 48-3 (M)
1969—Chiefs, 17-10 (KC)
1971—*Dolphins, 27-24 (KC) OT
1972—Dolphins, 20-10 (KC)
1974—Dolphins, 9-3 (M)
1976—Chiefs, 20-17 (M) OT
1981—Dolphins, 17-7 (KC)
1983—Dolphins, 14-6 (M)
1985—Dolphins, 31-0 (M)
1987—Dolphins, 42-0 (M)
1989—Chiefs, 26-21 (KC)
       Chiefs, 27-24 (M)
1990—**Dolphins, 17-16 (M)
1991—Chiefs, 42-7 (KC)
1993—Dolphins, 30-10 (M)
1994—Dolphins, 45-28 (M)
       **Dolphins, 27-17 (M)
1995—Dolphins, 13-6 (M)
1997—Dolphins, 17-14 (M)
2002—Chiefs, 48-30 (KC)
2005—Chiefs, 30-20 (M)
2006—Dolphins, 13-10 (M)
(RS Pts.—Chiefs 470, Dolphins 417)
(PS Pts.—Dolphins 71, Chiefs 57)
*AFC Divisional Playoff
**AFC First-Round Playoff
KANSAS CITY vs. MINNESOTA
RS: Series tied, 4-4
PS: Chiefs lead series, 1-0
1969—*Chiefs, 23-7 (New Orleans)
1970—Vikings, 27-10 (M)
1974—Vikings, 35-15 (KC)
1981—Chiefs, 10-6 (M)
1990—Chiefs, 24-21 (KC)
1993—Vikings, 30-10 (M)
1996—Chiefs, 21-6 (M)
1999—Chiefs, 31-28 (KC)
2003—Vikings, 45-20 (M)
(RS Pts.—Vikings 198, Chiefs 141)
(PS Pts.—Chiefs 23, Vikings 7)

*Super Bowl IV
***KANSAS CITY vs. **NEW ENGLAND**
RS: Chiefs lead series, 16-11-3
1960—Patriots, 42-14 (B)
       Texans, 34-0 (D)
1961—Patriots, 18-17 (D)
       Patriots, 28-21 (B)
1962—Texans, 42-28 (D)
       Texans, 27-7 (B)
1963—Tie, 24-24 (B)
       Chiefs, 35-3 (KC)
1964—Patriots, 24-7 (B)
       Patriots, 31-24 (KC)
1965—Chiefs, 27-17 (KC)
       Tie, 10-10 (B)
1966—Chiefs, 43-24 (B)
       Tie, 27-27 (KC)
1967—Chiefs, 33-10 (B)
1968—Chiefs, 31-17 (KC)
1969—Chiefs, 31-0 (B)
1970—Chiefs, 23-10 (KC)
1973—Chiefs, 10-7 (NE)
1977—Patriots, 21-17 (NE)
1981—Patriots, 33-17 (NE)
1990—Chiefs, 37-7 (NE)
1992—Chiefs, 27-20 (KC)
1995—Chiefs, 31-26 (KC)
1998—Patriots, 40-10 (NE)
1999—Chiefs, 16-14 (KC)
2000—Patriots, 30-24 (NE)
2002—Patriots, 41-38 (NE) OT
2004—Patriots, 27-19 (NE)
2005—Chiefs, 26-16 (KC)
(RS Pts.—Chiefs 742, Patriots 602)
*Franchise located in Dallas prior to 1963
and known as Texans
**Franchise in Boston prior to 1971
KANSAS CITY vs. NEW ORLEANS
RS: Series tied, 4-4
1972—Chiefs, 20-17 (NO)
1976—Saints, 27-17 (KC)
1982—Saints, 27-17 (NO)
1985—Chiefs, 47-27 (NO)
1991—Chiefs, 17-10 (KC)
1994—Chiefs, 30-17 (NO)
1997—Chiefs, 25-13 (KC)
2004—Saints, 27-20 (NO)
(RS Pts.—Chiefs 186, Saints 172)
KANSAS CITY vs. N.Y. GIANTS
RS: Giants lead series, 9-2
1974—Giants, 33-27 (KC)
1978—Giants, 26-10 (NY)
1979—Giants, 21-17 (KC)
1983—Chiefs, 38-17 (KC)
1984—Chiefs, 28-27 (NY)
1988—Giants, 28-12 (NY)
1992—Giants, 35-21 (NY)
1995—Chiefs, 20-17 (KC) OT
1998—Giants, 28-7 (NY)
2001—Giants, 13-3 (KC)
2005—Giants, 27-17 (NY)
(RS Pts.—Giants 273, Chiefs 199)
***KANSAS CITY vs. **N.Y. JETS**
RS: Chiefs lead series, 16-14-1
PS: Series tied, 1-1
1960—Titans, 37-35 (D)
       Titans, 41-35 (NY)
1961—Titans, 28-7 (NY)
       Texans, 35-24 (D)
1962—Texans, 20-17 (D)

Texans, 52-31 (NY)
1963—Jets, 17-0 (NY)
Chiefs, 48-0 (KC)
1964—Jets, 27-14 (NY)
Chiefs, 24-7 (KC)
1965—Chiefs, 14-10 (KC)
Jets, 13-10 (KC)
1966—Chiefs, 32-24 (NY)
1967—Chiefs, 42-18 (KC)
Chiefs, 21-7 (NY)
1968—Jets, 20-19 (KC)
1969—Chiefs, 34-16 (NY)
***Chiefs, 13-6 (NY)
1971—Jets, 13-10 (NY)
1974—Chiefs, 24-16 (KC)
1975—Jets, 30-24 (KC)
1982—Chiefs, 37-13 (KC)
1984—Jets, 17-16 (KC)
Jets, 28-7 (NY)
1986—****Jets, 35-15 (NY)
1987—Jets, 16-9 (KC)
1988—Tie, 17-17 (NY)
Chiefs, 38-34 (KC)
1992—Chiefs, 23-7 (NY)
1998—Jets, 20-17 (KC)
2001—Jets, 27-7 (NY)
2002—Chiefs, 29-25 (NY)
2005—Chiefs, 27-7 (KC)
(RS Pts.—Chiefs 727, Jets 607)
(PS Pts.—Jets 41, Chiefs 28)
*Franchise in Dallas prior to 1963 and
known as Texans
**Jets known as Titans prior to 1963
***Inter-Divisional Playoff
****AFC First-Round Playoff
KANSAS CITY vs. **OAKLAND
RS: Chiefs lead series, 49-42-2
PS: Chiefs lead series, 2-1
1960—Texans, 34-16 (O)
Raiders, 20-19 (D)
1961—Texans, 42-35 (O)
Texans, 43-11 (D)
1962—Texans, 26-16 (O)
Texans, 35-7 (D)
1963—Raiders, 10-7 (O)
Raiders, 22-7 (KC)
1964—Chiefs, 21-9 (O)
Chiefs, 42-7 (KC)
1965—Raiders, 37-10 (O)
Chiefs, 14-7 (KC)
1966—Chiefs, 32-10 (O)
Raiders, 34-13 (KC)
1967—Raiders, 23-21 (O)
Raiders, 44-22 (KC)
1968—Chiefs, 24-10 (KC)
Raiders, 38-21 (O)
***Raiders, 41-6 (O)
1969—Raiders, 27-24 (KC)
Raiders, 10-6 (O)
****Chiefs, 17-7 (O)
1970—Tie, 17-17 (KC)
Raiders, 20-6 (O)
1971—Tie, 20-20 (O)
Chiefs, 16-14 (KC)
1972—Chiefs, 27-14 (KC)
Raiders, 26-3 (O)
1973—Chiefs, 16-3 (KC)
Raiders, 37-7 (O)
1974—Raiders, 27-7 (O)
Raiders, 7-6 (KC)

1975—Chiefs, 42-10 (KC)
Raiders, 28-20 (O)
1976—Raiders, 24-21 (KC)
Raiders, 21-10 (O)
1977—Raiders, 37-28 (KC)
Raiders, 21-20 (O)
1978—Raiders, 28-6 (O)
Raiders, 20-10 (KC)
1979—Chiefs, 35-7 (KC)
Chiefs, 24-21 (O)
1980—Raiders, 27-14 (KC)
Chiefs, 31-17 (O)
1981—Chiefs, 27-0 (KC)
Chiefs, 28-17 (O)
1982—Raiders, 21-16 (KC)
1983—Raiders, 21-20 (LA)
Raiders, 28-20 (KC)
1984—Raiders, 22-20 (KC)
Raiders, 17-7 (LA)
1985—Chiefs, 36-20 (KC)
Raiders, 19-10 (LA)
1986—Raiders, 24-17 (KC)
Chiefs, 20-17 (LA)
1987—Raiders, 35-17 (LA)
Chiefs, 16-10 (KC)
1988—Raiders, 27-17 (KC)
Raiders, 17-10 (LA)
1989—Chiefs, 24-19 (KC)
Raiders, 20-14 (LA)
1990—Chiefs, 9-7 (KC)
Chiefs, 27-24 (LA)
1991—Chiefs, 24-21 (KC)
Chiefs, 27-21 (LA)
*****Chiefs, 10-6 (KC)
1992—Chiefs, 27-7 (KC)
Raiders, 28-7 (LA)
1993—Chiefs, 24-9 (KC)
Chiefs, 31-20 (LA)
1994—Chiefs, 13-3 (KC)
Chiefs, 19-9 (LA)
1995—Chiefs, 23-17 (KC) OT
Chiefs, 29-23 (O)
1996—Chiefs, 19-3 (KC)
Raiders, 26-7 (O)
1997—Chiefs, 28-27 (KC)
Chiefs, 30-0 (KC)
1998—Chiefs, 28-8 (O)
Chiefs, 31-24 (O)
1999—Chiefs, 37-34 (O)
Raiders, 41-38 (KC) OT
2000—Raiders, 20-17 (KC)
Raiders, 49-31 (O)
2001—Raiders, 27-24 (KC)
Raiders, 28-26 (O)
2002—Chiefs, 20-10 (KC)
Raiders, 24-0 (O)
2003—Chiefs, 17-10 (O)
Chiefs, 27-24 (KC)
2004—Chiefs, 34-27 (O)
Chiefs, 31-30 (KC)
2005—Chiefs, 23-17 (O)
Chiefs, 27-23 (KC)
2006—Chiefs, 17-13 (KC)
Chiefs, 20-9 (O)
(RS Pts.—Chiefs 1,960, Raiders 1,836)
(PS Pts.—Raiders 54, Chiefs 33)
*Franchise in Dallas prior to 1963 and
known as Texans
**Franchise in Los Angeles from
1982-1994

***Division Playoff
****AFL Championship
*****AFC First-Round Playoff
KANSAS CITY vs. PHILADELPHIA
RS: Eagles lead series, 3-2
1972—Eagles, 21-20 (KC)
1992—Chiefs, 24-17 (KC)
1998—Chiefs, 24-21 (P)
2001—Eagles, 23-10 (KC)
2005—Eagles, 37-31 (KC)
(RS Pts.—Eagles 119, Chiefs 109)
KANSAS CITY vs. PITTSBURGH
RS: Steelers lead series, 17-8
PS: Chiefs lead series, 1-0
1970—Chiefs, 31-14 (P)
1971—Chiefs, 38-16 (KC)
1972—Steelers, 16-7 (P)
1974—Steelers, 34-24 (KC)
1975—Steelers, 28-3 (P)
1976—Steelers, 45-0 (KC)
1978—Steelers, 27-24 (P)
1979—Steelers, 30-3 (KC)
1980—Steelers, 21-16 (P)
1981—Chiefs, 37-33 (P)
1982—Steelers, 35-14 (P)
1984—Chiefs, 37-27 (P)
1985—Steelers, 36-28 (KC)
1986—Chiefs, 24-19 (P)
1987—Steelers, 17-16 (KC)
1988—Steelers, 16-10 (P)
1989—Steelers, 23-17 (P)
1992—Steelers, 27-3 (KC)
1993—*Chiefs, 27-24 (KC) OT
1996—Steelers, 17-7 (KC)
1997—Chiefs, 13-10 (KC)
1998—Steelers, 20-13 (KC)
1999—Chiefs, 35-19 (KC)
2001—Steelers, 20-17 (KC)
2003—Chiefs, 41-20 (KC)
2006—Steelers, 45-7 (P)
(RS Pts.—Steelers 615, Chiefs 465)
(PS Pts.—Chiefs 27, Steelers 24)
*AFC First-Round Playoff
KANSAS CITY vs. *ST. LOUIS
RS: Chiefs lead series, 5-4
1973—Rams, 23-13 (KC)
1982—Rams, 20-14 (LA)
1985—Rams, 16-0 (KC)
1991—Chiefs, 27-20 (LA)
1994—Rams, 16-0 (KC)
1997—Chiefs, 28-20 (StL)
2000—Chiefs, 54-34 (KC)
2002—Chiefs, 49-10 (KC)
2006—Chiefs, 31-17 (StL)
(RS Pts.—Chiefs 216, Rams 176)
*Franchise in Los Angeles prior to 1995
KANSAS CITY vs. **SAN DIEGO
RS: Chiefs lead series, 49-43-1
PS: Chargers lead series, 1-0
1960—Chargers, 21-20 (LA)
Texans, 17-0 (D)
1961—Chargers, 26-10 (D)
Chargers, 24-14 (SD)
1962—Chargers, 32-28 (SD)
Texans, 26-17 (D)
1963—Chargers, 24-10 (SD)
Chargers, 38-17 (KC)
1964—Chargers, 28-14 (KC)
Chiefs, 49-6 (SD)

1965—Tie, 10-10 (SD)
    Chiefs, 31-7 (KC)
1966—Chiefs, 24-14 (KC)
    Chiefs, 27-17 (SD)
1967—Chargers, 45-31 (SD)
    Chargers, 17-16 (KC)
1968—Chiefs, 27-20 (KC)
    Chiefs, 40-3 (SD)
1969—Chiefs, 27-9 (SD)
    Chiefs, 27-3 (KC)
1970—Chiefs, 26-14 (KC)
    Chargers, 31-13 (SD)
1971—Chargers, 21-14 (SD)
    Chiefs, 31-10 (KC)
1972—Chiefs, 26-14 (SD)
    Chargers, 27-17 (KC)
1973—Chiefs, 19-0 (SD)
    Chiefs, 33-6 (KC)
1974—Chiefs, 24-14 (SD)
    Chargers, 14-7 (KC)
1975—Chiefs, 12-10 (SD)
    Chargers, 28-20 (KC)
1976—Chargers, 30-16 (KC)
    Chiefs, 23-20 (SD)
1977—Chargers, 23-7 (KC)
    Chiefs, 21-16 (SD)
1978—Chargers, 29-23 (SD) OT
    Chiefs, 23-0 (KC)
1979—Chargers, 20-14 (KC)
    Chargers, 28-7 (SD)
1980—Chargers, 24-7 (KC)
    Chargers, 20-7 (SD)
1981—Chargers, 42-31 (KC)
    Chargers, 22-20 (SD)
1982—Chiefs, 19-12 (KC)
1983—Chargers, 17-14 (KC)
    Chargers, 41-38 (SD)
1984—Chiefs, 31-13 (KC)
    Chiefs, 42-21 (SD)
1985—Chargers, 31-20 (SD)
    Chiefs, 38-34 (KC)
1986—Chiefs, 42-41 (KC)
    Chiefs, 24-23 (SD)
1987—Chiefs, 20-13 (KC)
    Chargers, 42-21 (SD)
1988—Chargers, 24-23 (KC)
    Chargers, 24-13 (SD)
1989—Chargers, 21-6 (SD)
    Chargers, 20-13 (KC)
1990—Chiefs, 27-10 (KC)
    Chiefs, 24-21 (SD)
1991—Chiefs, 14-13 (SD)
    Chiefs, 20-17 (KC) OT
1992—Chiefs, 24-10 (SD)
    Chiefs, 16-14 (KC)
    ***Chargers, 17-0 (SD)
1993—Chiefs, 17-14 (SD)
    Chiefs, 28-24 (KC)
1994—Chargers, 20-6 (SD)
    Chargers, 14-13 (KC)
1995—Chiefs, 29-23 (KC) OT
    Chiefs, 22-7 (SD)
1996—Chargers, 22-19 (SD)
    Chargers, 28-14 (KC)
1997—Chiefs, 31-3 (KC)
    Chiefs, 29-7 (SD)
1998—Chiefs, 23-7 (KC)
    Chargers, 38-37 (SD)
1999—Chargers, 21-14 (SD)
    Chiefs, 34-0 (KC)

2000—Chiefs, 42-10 (KC)
    Chargers, 17-16 (SD)
2001—Chiefs, 25-20 (SD)
    Chiefs, 20-17 (KC)
2002—Chargers, 35-34 (SD)
    Chiefs, 24-22 (KC)
2003—Chiefs, 27-14 (KC)
    Chiefs, 28-24 (SD)
2004—Chargers, 34-31 (KC)
    Chargers, 24-17 (SD)
2005—Chargers, 28-20 (SD)
    Chiefs, 20-7 (KC)
2006—Chiefs, 30-27 (KC)
    Chargers, 20-9 (SD)
(RS Pts.—Chiefs 2,054, Chargers 1,813)
(PS Pts.—Chargers 17, Chiefs 0)
*Franchise in Dallas prior to 1963 and
known as Texans
**Franchise in Los Angeles prior to 1961
***AFC First-Round Playoff

KANSAS CITY vs. SAN FRANCISCO
RS: 49ers lead series, 6-4
1971—Chiefs, 26-17 (SF)
1975—49ers, 20-3 (KC)
1982—49ers, 26-13 (KC)
1985—49ers, 31-3 (SF)
1991—49ers, 28-14 (SF)
1994—Chiefs, 24-17 (KC)
1997—Chiefs, 44-9 (KC)
2000—49ers, 21-7 (SF)
2002—49ers, 17-13 (SF)
2006—Chiefs, 41-10 (KC)
(PS Pts.—Chiefs 188, 49ers 186)

KANSAS CITY vs. SEATTLE
RS: Chiefs lead series, 31-18
1977—Seahawks, 34-31 (KC)
1978—Seahawks, 13-10 (KC)
    Seahawks, 23-19 (S)
1979—Chiefs, 24-6 (S)
    Chiefs, 37-21 (KC)
1980—Seahawks, 17-16 (KC)
    Chiefs, 31-30 (S)
1981—Chiefs, 20-14 (S)
    Chiefs, 40-13 (KC)
1983—Chiefs, 17-13 (KC)
    Seahawks, 51-48 (S) OT
1984—Seahawks, 45-0 (S)
    Chiefs, 34-7 (KC)
1985—Chiefs, 28-7 (KC)
    Seahawks, 24-6 (S)
1986—Seahawks, 23-17 (S)
    Chiefs, 27-7 (KC)
1987—Seahawks, 43-14 (S)
    Chiefs, 41-20 (KC)
1988—Seahawks, 31-10 (S)
    Chiefs, 27-24 (KC)
1989—Chiefs, 20-16 (S)
    Chiefs, 20-10 (KC)
1990—Seahawks, 19-7 (S)
    Seahawks, 17-16 (KC)
1991—Chiefs, 20-13 (KC)
    Chiefs, 19-6 (S)
1992—Chiefs, 26-7 (KC)
    Chiefs, 24-14 (S)
1993—Chiefs, 31-16 (S)
    Chiefs, 34-24 (KC)
1994—Chiefs, 38-23 (KC)
    Seahawks, 10-9 (S)
1995—Chiefs, 34-10 (S)
    Chiefs, 26-3 (KC)

1996—Chiefs, 35-17 (S)
    Chiefs, 34-16 (KC)
1997—Chiefs, 20-17 (KC) OT
    Chiefs, 19-14 (S)
1998—Chiefs, 17-6 (KC)
    Seahawks, 24-12 (S)
1999—Seahawks, 31-19 (KC)
    Seahawks, 23-14 (S)
2000—Chiefs, 24-17 (KC)
    Chiefs, 24-19 (S)
2001—Chiefs, 19-7 (KC)
    Seahawks, 21-18 (S)
2002—Seahawks, 39-32 (S)
2006—Chiefs, 35-28 (KC)
(RS Pts.—Chiefs 1,143, Seahawks 933)

KANSAS CITY vs. TAMPA BAY
RS: Chiefs lead series, 5-4
1976—Chiefs, 28-19 (TB)
1978—Buccaneers, 30-13 (KC)
1979—Buccaneers, 3-0 (TB)
1981—Chiefs, 19-10 (KC)
1984—Chiefs, 24-20 (KC)
1986—Chiefs, 27-20 (KC)
1993—Chiefs, 27-3 (TB)
1999—Buccaneers, 17-10 (TB)
2004—Buccaneers, 34-31 (TB)
(RS Pts.—Chiefs 179, Buccaneers 156)

*KANSAS CITY vs. **TENNESSEE
RS: Chiefs lead series, 25-18
PS: Chiefs lead series, 2-0
1960—Oilers, 20-10 (H)
    Texans, 24-0 (D)
1961—Texans, 26-21 (D)
    Oilers, 38-7 (H)
1962—Texans, 31-7 (H)
    Oilers, 14-6 (D)
    ***Texans, 20-17 (H) OT
1963—Chiefs, 28-7 (KC)
    Oilers, 28-7 (H)
1964—Chiefs, 28-7 (KC)
    Chiefs, 28-19 (H)
1965—Chiefs, 52-21 (KC)
    Oilers, 38-36 (H)
1966—Chiefs, 48-23 (KC)
1967—Chiefs, 25-20 (H)
    Oilers, 24-19 (KC)
1968—Chiefs, 26-21 (H)
    Chiefs, 24-10 (KC)
1969—Chiefs, 24-0 (KC)
1970—Chiefs, 24-9 (KC)
1971—Chiefs, 20-16 (H)
1973—Chiefs, 38-14 (KC)
1974—Chiefs, 17-7 (H)
1975—Oilers, 17-13 (KC)
1977—Oilers, 34-20 (H)
1978—Oilers, 20-17 (KC)
1979—Oilers, 20-6 (H)
1980—Chiefs, 21-20 (KC)
1981—Chiefs, 23-10 (KC)
1983—Chiefs, 13-10 (H) OT
1984—Oilers, 17-16 (H)
1985—Oilers, 23-20 (H)
1986—Chiefs, 27-13 (KC)
1988—Oilers, 7-6 (H)
1989—Chiefs, 34-0 (KC)
1990—Oilers, 27-10 (KC)
1991—Oilers, 17-7 (H)
1992—Oilers, 23-20 (H) OT
1993—Oilers, 30-0 (H)
    ****Chiefs, 28-20 (H)

1994—Chiefs, 31-9 (KC)
1995—Chiefs, 20-13 (KC)
1996—Chiefs, 20-19 (H)
2000—Titans, 17-14 (T) OT
2004—Chiefs, 49-38 (T)
(RS Pts.—Chiefs 935, Titans 748)
(PS Pts.—Chiefs 48, Titans 37)
*Franchise in Dallas prior to 1963 and
known as Texans
**Franchise in Houston prior to 1997;
known as Oilers prior to 1999
***AFL Championship
****AFC Divisional Playoff

KANSAS CITY vs. WASHINGTON
RS: Chiefs lead series, 6-1
1971—Chiefs, 27-20 (KC)
1976—Chiefs, 33-30 (W)
1983—Redskins, 27-12 (W)
1992—Chiefs, 35-16 (M)
1995—Chiefs, 24-3 (KC)
2001—Chiefs, 45-13 (W)
2005—Chiefs, 28-21, (KC)
(RS Pts.—Chiefs 204, Redskins 130)

MIAMI vs. ARIZONA
RS: Dolphins lead series, 8-1;
See Arizona vs. Miami
MIAMI vs. ATLANTA
RS: Dolphins lead series, 7-3;
See Atlanta vs. Miami
MIAMI vs. BALTIMORE
RS: Dolphins lead series, 4-1
PS: Ravens lead series, 1-0;
See Baltimore vs. Miami
MIAMI vs. BUFFALO
RS: Dolphins lead series, 49-32-1
PS: Bills lead series, 3-1;
See Buffalo vs. Miami
MIAMI vs. CAROLINA
RS: Dolphins lead series, 3-0;
See Carolina vs. Miami
MIAMI vs. CHICAGO
RS: Dolphins lead series, 7-3;
See Chicago vs. Miami
MIAMI vs. CINCINNATI
RS: Dolphins lead series, 12-4
PS: Dolphins lead series, 1-0;
See Cincinnati vs. Miami
MIAMI vs. CLEVELAND
RS: Dolphins lead series, 7-5
PS: Dolphins lead series, 2-0;
See Cleveland vs. Miami
MIAMI vs. DALLAS
RS: Dolphins lead series, 7-3
PS: Cowboys lead series, 1-0;
See Dallas vs. Miami
MIAMI vs. DENVER
RS: Dolphins lead series, 10-3-1
PS: Broncos lead series, 1-0;
See Denver vs. Miami
MIAMI vs. DETROIT
RS: Dolphins lead series, 7-2;
See Detroit vs. Miami
MIAMI vs. GREEN BAY
RS: Dolphins lead series, 9-3;
See Green Bay vs. Miami
MIAMI vs. HOUSTON
RS: Texans lead series, 2-0;
See Houston vs. Miami
MIAMI vs. INDIANAPOLIS

RS: Dolphins lead series, 44-23
PS: Dolphins lead series, 2-0;
See Indianapolis vs. Miami
MIAMI vs. JACKSONVILLE
RS: Jaguars lead series, 2-1
PS: Jaguars lead series, 1-0;
See Jacksonville vs. Miami
MIAMI vs. KANSAS CITY
RS: Chiefs lead series, 12-11
PS: Dolphins lead series, 3-0;
See Kansas City vs. Miami
MIAMI vs. MINNESOTA
RS: Dolphins lead series, 5-4
PS: Dolphins lead series, 1-0
1972—Dolphins, 16-14 (Minn)
1973—*Dolphins, 24-7 (Houston)
1976—Vikings, 29-7 (Mia)
1979—Dolphins, 27-12 (Minn)
1982—Dolphins, 22-14 (Mia)
1988—Dolphins, 24-7 (Mia)
1994—Vikings, 38-35 (Minn)
2000—Vikings, 13-7 (Minn)
2002—Vikings, 20-17 (Minn)
2006—Dolphins, 24-20 (Mia)
(RS Pts.—Dolphins 179, Vikings 167)
(PS Pts.—Dolphins 24, Vikings 7)
*Super Bowl VIII
MIAMI vs. *NEW ENGLAND
RS: Dolphins lead series, 47-33
PS: Patriots lead series, 2-1
1966—Patriots, 20-14 (M)
1967—Patriots, 41-10 (B)
        Dolphins, 41-32 (M)
1968—Dolphins, 34-10 (B)
        Dolphins, 38-7 (M)
1969—Dolphins, 17-16 (B)
        Patriots, 38-23 (Tampa)
1970—Patriots, 27-14 (B)
        Dolphins, 37-20 (M)
1971—Dolphins, 41-3 (M)
        Patriots, 34-13 (NE)
1972—Dolphins, 52-0 (M)
        Dolphins, 37-21 (NE)
1973—Dolphins, 44-23 (M)
        Dolphins, 30-14 (M)
1974—Patriots, 34-24 (NE)
        Dolphins, 34-27 (M)
1975—Dolphins, 22-14 (NE)
        Dolphins, 20-7 (M)
1976—Patriots, 30-14 (NE)
        Dolphins, 10-3 (M)
1977—Dolphins, 17-5 (M)
        Patriots, 14-10 (NE)
1978—Patriots, 33-24 (NE)
        Dolphins, 23-3 (M)
1979—Dolphins, 28-13 (NE)
        Dolphins, 39-24 (M)
1980—Patriots, 34-0 (NE)
        Dolphins, 16-13 (M) OT
1981—Dolphins, 30-27 (NE) OT
        Dolphins, 24-14 (M)
1982—Patriots, 3-0 (NE)
        **Dolphins, 28-13 (M)
1983—Dolphins, 34-24 (M)
        Patriots, 17-6 (NE)
1984—Dolphins, 28-7 (M)
        Dolphins, 44-24 (NE)
1985—Patriots, 17-13 (NE)
        Dolphins, 30-27 (M)
        ***Patriots, 31-14 (M)

1986—Patriots, 34-7 (NE)
        Patriots, 34-27 (M)
1987—Patriots, 28-21 (NE)
        Patriots, 24-10 (M)
1988—Patriots, 21-10 (NE)
        Patriots, 6-3 (M)
1989—Dolphins, 24-10 (NE)
        Dolphins, 31-10 (M)
1990—Dolphins, 27-24 (NE)
        Dolphins, 17-10 (M)
1991—Dolphins, 20-10 (NE)
        Dolphins, 30-20 (M)
1992—Dolphins, 38-17 (M)
        Dolphins, 16-13 (NE) OT
1993—Dolphins, 17-13 (M)
        Patriots, 33-27 (NE) OT
1994—Dolphins, 39-35 (M)
        Dolphins, 23-3 (NE)
1995—Dolphins, 20-3 (NE)
        Patriots, 34-17 (M)
1996—Dolphins, 24-10 (M)
        Patriots, 42-23 (NE)
1997—Patriots, 27-24 (NE)
        Patriots, 14-12 (M)
        **Patriots, 17-3 (NE)
1998—Dolphins, 12-9 (M) OT
        Patriots, 26-23 (NE)
1999—Dolphins, 31-30 (NE)
        Dolphins, 27-17 (M)
2000—Dolphins, 10-3 (M)
        Dolphins, 27-24 (NE)
2001—Dolphins, 30-10 (M)
        Patriots, 20-13 (NE)
2002—Dolphins, 26-13 (M)
        Patriots, 27-24 (NE) OT
2003—Patriots, 19-13 (M) OT
        Patriots, 12-0 (NE)
2004—Patriots, 24-10 (NE)
        Dolphins, 29-28 (M)
2005—Patriots, 23-16 (NE)
        Dolphins, 28-26 (NE)
2006—Patriots, 20-10 (NE)
        Dolphins, 21-0 (M)
(RS Pts.—Dolphins 1,777, Patriots 1,541)
(PS Pts.—Patriots 61, Dolphins 45)
*Franchise in Boston prior to 1971
**AFC First-Round Playoff
***AFC Championship
MIAMI vs. NEW ORLEANS
RS: Dolphins lead series, 6-3
1970—Dolphins, 21-10 (M)
1974—Dolphins, 21-0 (NO)
1980—Dolphins, 21-16 (M)
1983—Saints, 17-7 (NO)
1986—Dolphins, 31-27 (NO)
1992—Saints, 24-13 (NO)
1995—Saints, 33-30 (NO)
1998—Dolphins, 30-10 (M)
2005—Dolphins, 21-6 (Baton Rouge)
(RS Pts.—Dolphins 195, Saints 143)
MIAMI vs. N.Y. GIANTS
RS: Giants lead series, 3-2
1972—Dolphins, 23-13 (NY)
1990—Giants, 20-3 (NY)
1993—Giants, 19-14 (M)
1996—Giants, 17-7 (M)
2003—Dolphins, 23-10 (NY)
(RS Pts.—Giants 79, Dolphins 70)
MIAMI vs. N.Y. JETS
RS: Jets lead series, 43-38-1

PS: Dolphins lead series, 1-0
1966—Jets, 19-14 (M)
　　　Jets, 30-13 (NY)
1967—Jets, 29-7 (NY)
　　　Jets, 33-14 (M)
1968—Jets, 35-17 (NY)
　　　Jets, 31-7 (M)
1969—Jets, 34-31 (NY)
　　　Jets, 27-9 (M)
1970—Dolphins, 20-6 (NY)
　　　Dolphins, 16-10 (M)
1971—Jets, 14-10 (M)
　　　Dolphins, 30-14 (NY)
1972—Dolphins, 27-17 (NY)
　　　Dolphins, 28-24 (M)
1973—Dolphins, 31-3 (M)
　　　Dolphins, 24-14 (NY)
1974—Dolphins, 21-17 (M)
　　　Jets, 17-14 (NY)
1975—Dolphins, 43-0 (NY)
　　　Dolphins, 27-7 (M)
1976—Dolphins, 16-0 (M)
　　　Dolphins, 27-7 (NY)
1977—Dolphins, 21-17 (M)
　　　Dolphins, 14-10 (NY)
1978—Jets, 33-20 (NY)
　　　Jets, 24-13 (M)
1979—Jets, 33-27 (NY)
　　　Jets, 27-24 (M)
1980—Jets, 17-14 (NY)
　　　Jets, 24-17 (M)
1981—Tie, 28-28 (M) OT
　　　Jets, 16-15 (NY)
1982—Dolphins, 45-28 (NY)
　　　Dolphins, 20-19 (M)
　　　*Dolphins, 14-0 (M)
1983—Dolphins, 32-14 (NY)
　　　Dolphins, 34-14 (M)
1984—Dolphins, 31-17 (NY)
　　　Dolphins, 28-17 (M)
1985—Jets, 23-7 (NY)
　　　Dolphins, 21-17 (M)
1986—Jets, 51-45 (NY) OT
　　　Dolphins, 45-3 (M)
1987—Jets, 37-31 (NY) OT
　　　Dolphins, 37-28 (M)
1988—Jets, 44-30 (M)
　　　Jets, 38-34 (NY)
1989—Jets, 40-33 (M)
　　　Dolphins, 31-23 (NY)
1990—Dolphins, 20-16 (M)
　　　Dolphins, 17-3 (NY)
1991—Jets, 41-23 (NY)
　　　Jets, 23-20 (M) OT
1992—Jets, 26-14 (NY)
　　　Dolphins, 19-17 (M)
1993—Jets, 24-14 (M)
　　　Jets, 27-10 (NY)
1994—Dolphins, 28-14 (M)
　　　Dolphins, 28-24 (NY)
1995—Dolphins, 52-14 (M)
　　　Jets, 17-16 (NY)
1996—Dolphins, 36-27 (M)
　　　Dolphins, 31-28 (NY)
1997—Dolphins, 31-20 (NY)
　　　Dolphins, 24-17 (M)
1998—Jets, 20-9 (NY)
　　　Jets, 21-16 (M)
1999—Jets, 28-20 (NY)
　　　Jets, 38-31 (M)

2000—Jets, 40-37 (NY) OT
　　　Jets, 20-3 (M)
2001—Jets, 21-17 (NY)
　　　Jets, 24-0 (M)
2002—Dolphins, 30-3 (M)
　　　Jets, 13-10 (NY)
2003—Dolphins, 21-10 (NY)
　　　Dolphins, 23-21 (M)
2004—Jets, 17-9 (M)
　　　Jets, 41-14 (NY)
2005—Jets, 17-7 (NY)
　　　Dolphins, 24-20 (M)
2006—Jets, 20-7 (NY)
　　　Jets, 13-10 (M)
(RS Pts.—Dolphins 1,824, Jets 1,755)
(PS Pts.—Dolphins 14, Jets 0)
*AFC Championship
MIAMI vs. *OAKLAND
RS: Raiders lead series, 15-11-1
PS: Raiders lead series, 3-1
1966—Raiders, 23-14 (M)
　　　Raiders, 21-10 (O)
1967—Raiders, 31-17 (O)
1968—Raiders, 47-21 (M)
1969—Raiders, 20-17 (O)
　　　Tie, 20-20 (M)
1970—Dolphins, 20-13 (M)
　　　**Raiders, 21-14 (O)
1973—Raiders, 12-7 (O)
　　　***Dolphins, 27-10 (M)
1974—**Raiders, 28-26 (O)
1975—Raiders, 31-21 (M)
1978—Dolphins, 23-6 (M)
1979—Raiders, 13-3 (O)
1980—Raiders, 16-10 (O)
1981—Raiders, 33-17 (M)
1983—Raiders, 27-14 (LA)
1984—Raiders, 45-34 (M)
1986—Raiders, 30-28 (M)
1988—Dolphins, 24-14 (LA)
1990—Raiders, 13-10 (M)
1992—Dolphins, 20-7 (M)
1994—Dolphins, 20-17 (M) OT
1996—Raiders, 17-7 (O)
1997—Dolphins, 34-16 (O)
1998—Dolphins, 27-17 (O)
1999—Dolphins, 16-9 (O)
2000—**Raiders, 27-0 (O)
2001—Dolphins, 18-15 (O)
2002—Dolphins, 23-17 (M)
2005—Dolphins, 33-21 (O)
(RS Pts.—Raiders 551, Dolphins 508)
(PS Pts.—Raiders 86, Dolphins 67)
*Franchise in Los Angeles from 1982-1994
**AFC Divisional Playoff
***AFC Championship
MIAMI vs. PHILADELPHIA
RS: Dolphins lead series, 7-4
1970—Eagles, 24-17 (P)
1975—Dolphins, 24-16 (M)
1978—Eagles, 17-3 (P)
1981—Dolphins, 13-10 (M)
1984—Dolphins, 24-23 (M)
1987—Dolphins, 28-10 (P)
1990—Dolphins, 23-20 (M) OT
1993—Dolphins, 19-14 (P)
1996—Eagles, 35-28 (P)
1999—Dolphins, 16-13 (M)
2003—Eagles, 34-27 (M)
(RS Pts.—Dolphins 222, Eagles 216)

MIAMI vs. PITTSBURGH
RS: Series tied, 9-9
PS: Dolphins lead series, 2-1
1971—Dolphins, 24-21 (M)
1972—*Dolphins, 21-17 (P)
1973—Dolphins, 30-26 (M)
1976—Steelers, 14-3 (P)
1979—**Steelers, 34-14 (P)
1980—Steelers, 23-10 (P)
1981—Dolphins, 30-10 (M)
1984—Dolphins, 31-7 (P)
　　　*Dolphins, 45-28 (M)
1985—Dolphins, 24-20 (M)
1987—Dolphins, 35-24 (M)
1988—Steelers, 40-24 (P)
1989—Steelers, 34-14 (M)
1990—Dolphins, 28-6 (P)
1993—Steelers, 21-20 (M)
1994—Steelers, 16-13 (P) OT
1995—Dolphins, 23-10 (M)
1996—Steelers, 24-17 (M)
1998—Dolphins, 21-0 (M)
2004—Steelers, 13-3 (M)
2006—Steelers, 28-17 (P)
(RS Pts.—Dolphins 367, Steelers 337)
(PS Pts.—Dolphins 80, Steelers 79)
*AFC Championship
**AFC Divisional Playoff
MIAMI vs. *ST. LOUIS
RS: Dolphins lead series, 8-2
1971—Dolphins, 20-14 (LA)
1976—Rams, 31-28 (M)
1980—Dolphins, 35-14 (LA)
1983—Dolphins, 30-14 (M)
1986—Dolphins, 37-31 (LA) OT
1992—Dolphins, 26-10 (M)
1995—Dolphins, 41-22 (StL)
1998—Dolphins, 14-0 (M)
2001—Rams, 42-10 (StL)
2004—Dolphins, 31-14 (M)
(RS Pts.—Dolphins 272, Rams 192)
*Franchise in Los Angeles prior to 1995
MIAMI vs. SAN DIEGO
RS: Dolphins lead series, 11-10
PS: Series tied, 2-2
1966—Chargers, 44-10 (SD)
1967—Chargers, 24-0 (SD)
　　　Dolphins, 41-24 (M)
1968—Chargers, 34-28 (SD)
1969—Chargers, 21-14 (M)
1972—Dolphins, 24-10 (M)
1974—Dolphins, 28-21 (SD)
1977—Chargers, 14-13 (M)
1978—Dolphins, 28-21 (SD)
1980—Chargers, 27-24 (M) OT
1981—*Chargers, 41-38 (M) OT
1982—**Dolphins, 34-13 (M)
1984—Chargers, 34-28 (SD) OT
1986—Chargers, 50-28 (SD)
1988—Dolphins, 31-28 (M)
1991—Chargers, 38-30 (SD)
1992—*Dolphins, 31-0 (M)
1993—Chargers, 45-20 (SD)
1994—*Chargers, 22-21 (SD)
1995—Dolphins, 24-14 (SD)
1999—Dolphins, 12-9 (M)
2000—Dolphins, 17-7 (SD)
2002—Dolphins, 30-3 (M)
2003—Dolphins, 26-10 (Ariz)
2005—Dolphins, 23-21 (SD)

(RS Pts.—Chargers 499, Dolphins 479)
(PS Pts.—Dolphins 124, Chargers 76)
*AFC Divisional Playoff
**AFC Second-Round Playoff
MIAMI vs. SAN FRANCISCO
RS: Dolphins lead series, 5-4
PS: 49ers lead series, 1-0
1973—Dolphins, 21-13 (M)
1977—Dolphins, 19-15 (SF)
1980—Dolphins, 17-13 (M)
1983—Dolphins, 20-17 (SF)
1984—*49ers, 38-16 (Stanford)
1986—49ers, 31-16 (M)
1992—49ers, 27-3 (SF)
1995—49ers, 44-20 (M)
2001—49ers, 21-0 (SF)
2004—Dolphins, 24-17 (SF)
(RS Pts.—49ers 198, Dolphins 140)
(PS Pts.—49ers 38, Dolphins 16)
*Super Bowl XIX
MIAMI vs. SEATTLE
RS: Dolphins lead series, 6-3
PS: Dolphins lead series, 2-1
1977—Dolphins, 31-13 (M)
1979—Dolphins, 19-10 (M)
1983—*Seahawks, 27-20 (M)
1984—*Dolphins, 31-10 (M)
1987—Seahawks, 24-20 (S)
1990—Dolphins, 24-17 (M)
1992—Dolphins, 19-17 (S)
1996—Seahawks, 22-15 (M)
1999—**Dolphins, 20-17 (S)
2000—Dolphins, 23-0 (M)
2001—Dolphins, 24-20 (S)
2004—Seahawks, 24-17 (S)
(RS Pts.—Dolphins 192, Seahawks 147)
(PS Pts.—Dolphins 71, Seahawks 54)
*AFC Divisional Playoff
**AFC First-Round Playoff
MIAMI vs. TAMPA BAY
RS: Series tied, 4-4
1976—Dolphins, 23-20 (TB)
1982—Buccaneers, 23-17 (TB)
1985—Dolphins, 41-38 (M)
1988—Dolphins, 17-14 (TB)
1991—Dolphins, 33-14 (M)
1997—Buccaneers, 31-21 (TB)
2000—Buccaneers, 16-13 (M)
2005—Buccaneers, 27-13 (TB)
(RS Pts.—Buccaneers 183, Dolphins 178)
MIAMI vs. *TENNESSEE
RS: Dolphins lead series, 17-13
PS: Titans lead series, 1-0
1966—Dolphins, 20-13 (H)
Dolphins, 29-28 (M)
1967—Oilers, 17-14 (H)
Oilers, 41-10 (M)
1968—Oilers, 24-10 (M)
Dolphins, 24-7 (H)
1969—Oilers, 22-10 (H)
Oilers, 32-7 (M)
1970—Dolphins, 20-10 (H)
1972—Dolphins, 34-13 (M)
1975—Oilers, 20-19 (H)
1977—Dolphins, 27-7 (M)
1978—Oilers, 35-30 (H)
**Oilers, 17-9 (M)
1979—Oilers, 9-6 (H)
1981—Dolphins, 16-10 (H)
1983—Dolphins, 24-17 (H)

1984—Dolphins, 28-10 (M)
1985—Oilers, 26-23 (H)
1986—Dolphins, 28-7 (M)
1989—Oilers, 39-7 (H)
1991—Oilers, 17-13 (M)
1992—Dolphins, 19-16 (M)
1996—Dolphins, 23-20 (H)
1997—Dolphins, 16-13 (M) OT
1999—Dolphins, 17-0 (M)
2001—Dolphins, 31-23 (T)
2003—Titans, 31-7 (T)
2004—Titans, 17-7 (M)
2005—Dolphins, 24-10 (M)
2006—Dolphins, 13-10 (M)
(RS Pts.—Dolphins 556, Titans 544)
(PS Pts.—Titans 17, Dolphins 9)
*Franchise in Houston prior to 1997;
known as Oilers prior to 1999
**AFC First-Round Playoff
MIAMI vs. WASHINGTON
RS: Dolphins lead series, 6-3
PS: Series tied, 1-1
1972—*Dolphins, 14-7 (Los Angeles)
1974—Redskins, 20-17 (W)
1978—Dolphins, 16-0 (W)
1981—Dolphins, 13-10 (M)
1982—**Redskins, 27-17 (Pasadena)
1984—Dolphins, 35-17 (W)
1987—Dolphins, 23-21 (M)
1990—Redskins, 42-20 (W)
1993—Dolphins, 17-10 (M)
1999—Redskins, 21-10 (W)
2003—Dolphins, 24-23 (M)
(RS Pts.—Dolphins 175, Redskins 164)
(PS Pts.—Redskins 34, Dolphins 31)
*Super Bowl VII
**Super Bowl XVII

MINNESOTA vs. ARIZONA
RS: Series tied, 9-9
PS: Vikings lead series, 2-0;
See Arizona vs. Minnesota
MINNESOTA vs. ATLANTA
RS: Vikings lead series, 14-8
PS: Series tied, 1-1;
See Atlanta vs. Minnesota
MINNESOTA vs. BALTIMORE
RS: Ravens lead series, 2-1;
See Baltimore vs. Minnesota
MINNESOTA vs. BUFFALO
RS: Vikings lead series, 7-4;
See Buffalo vs. Minnesota
MINNESOTA vs. CAROLINA
RS: Vikings lead series, 4-3;
See Carolina vs. Minnesota
MINNESOTA vs. CHICAGO
RS: Vikings lead series, 48-41-2
PS: Bears lead series, 1-0;
See Chicago vs. Minnesota
MINNESOTA vs. CINCINNATI
RS: Series tied, 5-5;
See Cincinnati vs. Minnesota
MINNESOTA vs. CLEVELAND
RS: Vikings lead series, 9-3
PS: Vikings lead series, 1-0;
See Cleveland vs. Minnesota
MINNESOTA vs. DALLAS
RS: Vikings lead series, 10-9
PS: Cowboys lead series, 4-2;
See Dallas vs. Minnesota

MINNESOTA vs. DENVER
RS: Vikings lead series, 7-4;
See Denver vs. Minnesota
MINNESOTA vs. DETROIT
RS: Vikings lead series, 60-29-2;
See Detroit vs. Minnesota
MINNESOTA vs. GREEN BAY
RS: Packers lead series, 46-44-1
PS: Vikings lead series, 1-0;
See Green Bay vs. Minnesota
MINNESOTA vs. HOUSTON
RS: Vikings lead series, 1-0;
See Houston vs. Minnesota
MINNESOTA vs. INDIANAPOLIS
RS: Colts lead series, 13-7-1
PS: Colts lead series, 1-0;
See Indianapolis vs. Minnesota
MINNESOTA vs. JACKSONVILLE
RS: Vikings lead series, 2-1;
See Jacksonville vs. Minnesota
MINNESOTA vs. KANSAS CITY
RS: Series tied, 4-4
PS: Chiefs lead series, 1-0;
See Kansas City vs. Minnesota
MINNESOTA vs. MIAMI
RS: Dolphins lead series, 5-4
PS: Dolphins lead series, 1-0;
See Miami vs. Minnesota
MINNESOTA vs. *NEW ENGLAND
RS: Patriots lead series, 6-4
1970—Vikings, 35-14 (B)
1974—Patriots, 17-14 (M)
1979—Patriots, 27-23 (NE)
1988—Vikings, 36-6 (M)
1991—Patriots, 26-23 (NE) OT
1994—Patriots, 26-20 (NE) OT
1997—Vikings, 23-18 (M)
2000—Vikings, 21-13 (NE)
2002—Patriots, 24-17 (NE)
2006—Patriots, 31-7 (M)
(RS Pts.—Vikings 219, Patriots 202)
*Franchise in Boston prior to 1971
MINNESOTA vs. NEW ORLEANS
RS: Vikings lead series, 17-7
PS: Vikings lead series, 2-0
1968—Saints, 20-17 (NO)
1970—Vikings, 26-0 (M)
1971—Vikings, 23-10 (NO)
1972—Vikings, 37-6 (M)
1974—Vikings, 29-9 (M)
1975—Vikings, 20-7 (NO)
1976—Vikings, 40-9 (NO)
1978—Saints, 31-24 (NO)
1980—Vikings, 23-20 (NO)
1981—Vikings, 20-10 (M)
1983—Saints, 17-16 (NO)
1985—Saints, 30-23 (M)
1986—Vikings, 33-17 (M)
1987—*Vikings, 44-10 (NO)
1988—Vikings, 45-3 (M)
1990—Vikings, 32-3 (M)
1991—Saints, 26-0 (NO)
1993—Saints, 17-14 (M)
1994—Vikings, 21-20 (M)
1995—Vikings, 43-24 (M)
1998—Vikings, 31-24 (M)
2000—**Vikings, 34-16 (M)
2001—Saints, 28-15 (NO)
2002—Vikings, 32-31 (NO)
2004—Vikings, 38-31 (NO)

2005—Vikings, 33-16 (M)
(RS Pts.—Vikings 635, Saints 409)
(PS Pts.—Vikings 78, Saints 26)
*NFC First-Round Playoff
**NFC Divisional Playoff

MINNESOTA vs. N.Y. GIANTS
RS: Vikings lead series, 10-8
PS: Giants lead series, 2-1
1964—Vikings, 30-21 (NY)
1965—Vikings, 40-14 (M)
1967—Vikings, 27-24 (M)
1969—Giants, 24-23 (NY)
1971—Vikings, 17-10 (NY)
1973—Vikings, 31-7 (New Haven)
1976—Vikings, 24-7 (M)
1986—Giants, 22-20 (M)
1989—Giants, 24-14 (NY)
1990—Giants, 23-15 (NY)
1993—*Giants, 17-10 (NY)
1994—Vikings, 27-10 (NY)
1996—Giants, 15-10 (NY)
1997—*Vikings, 23-22 (NY)
1999—Vikings, 34-17 (M)
2000—**Giants, 41-0 (NY)
2001—Vikings, 28-16 (M)
2002—Giants, 27-20 (M)
2003—Giants, 29-17 (M)
2004—Giants, 34-13 (M)
2005—Vikings, 24-21 (NY)
(RS Pts.—Vikings 414, Giants 345)
(PS Pts.—Giants 80, Vikings 33)
*NFC First-Round Playoff
**NFC Championship

MINNESOTA vs. N.Y. JETS
RS: Jets lead series, 7-1
1970—Jets, 20-10 (NY)
1975—Vikings, 29-21 (M)
1979—Jets, 14-7 (NY)
1982—Jets, 42-14 (M)
1994—Jets, 31-21 (M)
1997—Jets, 23-21 (NY)
2002—Jets, 20-7 (NY)
2006—Jets, 26-13 (M)
(RS Pts.—Jets 197, Vikings 122)

MINNESOTA vs. *OAKLAND
RS: Raiders lead series, 8-3
PS: Raiders lead series, 1-0
1973—Vikings, 24-16 (M)
1976—**Raiders, 32-14 (Pasadena)
1977—Raiders, 35-13 (O)
1978—Raiders, 27-20 (O)
1981—Raiders, 36-10 (M)
1984—Raiders, 23-20 (LA)
1987—Vikings, 31-20 (M)
1990—Raiders, 28-24 (M)
1993—Raiders, 24-7 (M)
1996—Vikings, 16-13 (O) OT
1999—Raiders, 22-17 (M)
2003—Raiders, 28-18 (O)
(RS Pts.—Raiders 272, Vikings 200)
(PS Pts.—Raiders 32, Vikings 14)
*Franchise in Los Angeles from 1982-1994
**Super Bowl XI

MINNESOTA vs. PHILADELPHIA
RS: Vikings lead series, 11-8
PS: Eagles lead series, 2-0
1962—Vikings, 31-21 (M)
1963—Vikings, 34-13 (P)
1968—Vikings, 24-17 (P)
1971—Vikings, 13-0 (P)

1973—Vikings, 28-21 (M)
1976—Vikings, 31-12 (P)
1978—Vikings, 28-27 (M)
1980—Eagles, 42-7 (M)
    *Eagles, 31-16 (P)
1981—Vikings, 35-23 (M)
1984—Eagles, 19-17 (P)
1985—Vikings, 28-23 (P)
    Eagles, 37-35 (M)
1988—Vikings, 23-21 (M)
1989—Eagles, 10-9 (P)
1990—Eagles, 32-24 (P)
1992—Eagles, 28-17 (P)
1997—Vikings, 28-19 (M)
2001—Eagles, 48-17 (P)
2004—Eagles, 27-16 (P)
    *Eagles, 27-14 (P)
(RS Pts.—Vikings 445, Eagles 440)
(PS Pts.—Eagles 58, Vikings 30)
*NFC Divisional Playoff

MINNESOTA vs. PITTSBURGH
RS: Vikings lead series, 8-6
PS: Steelers lead series, 1-0
1962—Steelers, 39-31 (P)
1964—Vikings, 30-10 (M)
1967—Vikings, 41-27 (P)
1969—Vikings, 52-14 (M)
1972—Steelers, 23-10 (P)
1974—*Steelers, 16-6 (New Orleans)
1976—Vikings, 17-6 (M)
1980—Steelers, 23-17 (M)
1983—Vikings, 17-14 (P)
1986—Vikings, 31-7 (M)
1989—Steelers, 27-14 (P)
1992—Vikings, 6-3 (P)
1995—Vikings, 44-24 (M)
2001—Steelers, 21-16 (P)
2005—Steelers, 18-3 (M)
(RS Pts.—Vikings 329, Steelers 256)
(PS Pts.—Steelers 16, Vikings 6)
*Super Bowl IX

MINNESOTA vs. *ST. LOUIS
RS: Vikings lead series, 17-14-2
PS: Vikings lead series, 5-2
1961—Rams, 31-17 (LA)
    Vikings, 42-21 (M)
1962—Vikings, 38-14 (LA)
    Tie, 24-24 (M)
1963—Rams, 27-24 (LA)
    Vikings, 21-13 (M)
1964—Rams, 22-13 (LA)
    Vikings, 34-13 (M)
1965—Vikings, 38-35 (LA)
    Vikings, 24-13 (M)
1966—Vikings, 35-7 (M)
    Rams, 21-6 (LA)
1967—Rams, 39-3 (LA)
1968—Rams, 31-3 (M)
1969—Vikings, 20-13 (LA)
    **Vikings, 23-20 (M)
1970—Vikings, 13-3 (M)
1972—Vikings, 45-41 (LA)
1973—Vikings, 10-9 (M)
1974—Rams, 20-17 (LA)
    ***Vikings, 14-10 (M)
1976—Tie, 10-10 (M) OT
    ***Vikings, 24-13 (M)
1977—Rams, 35-3 (LA)
    ****Vikings, 14-7 (LA)
1978—Rams, 34-17 (M)

    ****Rams, 34-10 (LA)
1979—Rams, 27-21 (LA) OT
1985—Rams, 13-10 (LA)
1987—Vikings, 21-16 (LA)
1988—*****Vikings, 28-17 (M)
1989—Vikings, 23-21 (M) OT
1991—Vikings, 20-14 (M)
1992—Vikings, 31-17 (LA)
1998—Vikings, 38-31 (StL)
1999—****Rams, 49-37 (StL)
2000—Rams, 40-29 (StL)
2003—Rams, 48-17 (StL)
2005—Vikings, 27-13 (M)
2006—Rams, 41-21 (M)
(RS Pts.—Rams 757, Vikings 715)
(PS Pts.—Rams 150, Vikings 150)
*Franchise in Los Angeles prior to 1995
**Conference Championship
***NFC Championship
****NFC Divisional Playoff
*****NFC First-Round Playoff

MINNESOTA vs. SAN DIEGO
RS: Chargers lead series, 5-4
1971—Chargers, 30-14 (SD)
1975—Vikings, 28-13 (M)
1978—Chargers, 13-7 (M)
1981—Vikings, 33-31 (SD)
1984—Chargers, 42-13 (M)
1985—Vikings, 21-17 (M)
1993—Chargers, 30-17 (M)
1999—Vikings, 35-27 (M)
2003—Chargers, 42-28 (SD)
(RS Pts.—Chargers 245, Vikings 196)

MINNESOTA vs. SAN FRANCISCO
RS: Series tied, 18-18-1
PS: 49ers lead series, 4-1
1961—49ers, 38-24 (M)
    49ers, 38-28 (SF)
1962—49ers, 21-7 (SF)
    49ers, 35-12 (M)
1963—Vikings, 24-20 (SF)
    Vikings, 45-14 (M)
1964—Vikings, 27-22 (SF)
    Vikings, 24-7 (M)
1965—Vikings, 42-41 (SF)
    49ers, 45-24 (M)
1966—Tie, 20-20 (SF)
    Vikings, 28-3 (SF)
1967—49ers, 27-21 (M)
1968—Vikings, 30-20 (SF)
1969—Vikings, 10-7 (M)
1970—*49ers, 17-14 (M)
1971—49ers, 13-9 (M)
1972—Vikings, 20-17 (SF)
1973—Vikings, 17-13 (SF)
1975—Vikings, 27-17 (M)
1976—49ers, 20-16 (SF)
1977—Vikings, 28-27 (M)
1979—Vikings, 28-22 (M)
1983—49ers, 48-17 (M)
1984—49ers, 51-7 (SF)
1985—Vikings, 28-21 (M)
1986—Vikings, 27-24 (SF) OT
1987—*Vikings, 36-24 (SF)
1988—49ers, 24-21 (SF)
    *49ers, 34-9 (SF)
1989—*49ers, 41-13 (SF)
1990—49ers, 20-17 (M)
1991—Vikings, 17-14 (M)
1992—49ers, 20-17 (M)

1993—49ers, 38-19 (SF)
1994—Vikings, 21-14 (M)
1995—49ers, 37-30 (SF)
1997—49ers, 28-17 (SF)
　　*49ers, 38-22 (SF)
1999—Vikings, 40-16 (M)
2003—Vikings, 35-7 (M)
2006—49ers, 9-3 (SF)
(RS Pts.—49ers 861, Vikings 824)
(PS Pts.—49ers 154, Vikings 94)
*NFC Divisional Playoff

MINNESOTA vs. SEATTLE
RS: Seahawks lead series, 6-4
1976—Vikings, 27-21 (M)
1978—Seahawks, 29-28 (S)
1984—Seahawks, 20-12 (M)
1987—Seahawks, 28-17 (S)
1990—Vikings, 24-21 (S)
1996—Seahawks, 42-23 (S)
2002—Seahawks, 48-23 (S)
2003—Vikings, 34-7 (M)
2004—Seahawks, 27-23 (M)
2006—Vikings, 31-13 (S)
(RS Pts.—Seahawks 256, Vikings 242)

MINNESOTA vs. TAMPA BAY
RS: Vikings lead series, 31-19
1977—Vikings, 9-3 (TB)
1978—Buccaneers, 16-10 (M)
　　Vikings, 24-7 (TB)
1979—Buccaneers, 12-10 (M)
　　Vikings, 23-22 (TB)
1980—Vikings, 38-30 (M)
　　Vikings, 21-10 (TB)
1981—Buccaneers, 21-13 (TB)
　　Vikings, 25-10 (M)
1982—Vikings, 17-10 (M)
1983—Vikings, 19-16 (TB) OT
　　Buccaneers, 17-12 (M)
1984—Buccaneers, 35-31 (TB)
　　Vikings, 27-24 (M)
1985—Vikings, 31-16 (TB)
　　Vikings, 26-7 (M)
1986—Vikings, 23-10 (TB)
　　Vikings, 45-13 (M)
1987—Buccaneers, 20-10 (TB)
　　Vikings, 23-17 (M)
1988—Vikings, 14-13 (M)
　　Vikings, 49-20 (TB)
1989—Vikings, 17-3 (M)
　　Vikings, 24-10 (TB)
1990—Buccaneers, 23-20 (M) OT
　　Buccaneers, 26-13 (TB)
1991—Vikings, 28-13 (M)
　　Vikings, 26-24 (TB)
1992—Vikings, 26-20 (M)
　　Vikings, 35-7 (TB)
1993—Vikings, 15-0 (M)
　　Buccaneers, 23-10 (TB)
1994—Vikings, 36-13 (TB)
　　Buccaneers, 20-17 (M) OT
1995—Buccaneers, 20-17 (TB) OT
　　Vikings, 31-17 (M)
1996—Buccaneers, 24-13 (TB)
　　Vikings, 21-10 (M)
1997—Buccaneers, 28-14 (M)
　　Vikings, 10-6 (TB)
1998—Vikings, 31-7 (M)
　　Buccaneers, 27-24 (TB)
1999—Vikings, 21-14 (M)
　　Buccaneers, 24-17 (TB)

2000—Vikings, 30-23 (M)
　　Buccaneers, 41-13 (TB)
2001—Vikings, 20-16 (M)
　　Buccaneers, 41-14 (TB)
2002—Buccaneers, 38-24 (TB)
2005—Buccaneers, 24-13 (M)
(RS Pts.—Vikings 1,080, Buccaneers 891)

MINNESOTA vs. *TENNESSEE
RS: Vikings lead series, 7-3
1974—Vikings, 51-10 (M)
1980—Oilers, 20-16 (H)
1983—Vikings, 34-14 (M)
1986—Oilers, 23-10 (H)
1989—Vikings, 38-7 (M)
1992—Oilers, 17-13 (M)
1995—Vikings, 23-17 (M) OT
1998—Vikings, 26-16 (T)
2001—Vikings, 42-24 (M)
2004—Vikings, 20-3 (M)
(RS Pts.—Vikings 273, Titans 151)
*Franchise in Houston prior to 1997;
known as Oilers prior to 1999

MINNESOTA vs. WASHINGTON
RS: Redskins lead series, 7-6
PS: Redskins lead series, 3-2
1968—Vikings, 27-14 (M)
1970—Vikings, 19-10 (W)
1972—Redskins, 24-21 (M)
1973—*Vikings, 27-20 (M)
1975—Redskins, 31-30 (W)
1976—*Vikings, 35-20 (M)
1980—Vikings, 39-14 (W)
1982—**Redskins, 21-7 (W)
1984—Redskins, 31-17 (M)
1986—Redskins, 44-38 (W) OT
1987—Redskins, 27-24 (M) OT
　　***Redskins, 17-10 (W)
1992—Redskins, 15-13 (M)
　　****Redskins, 24-7 (M)
1993—Vikings, 14-9 (W)
1998—Vikings, 41-7 (M)
2004—Redskins, 21-18 (W)
2006—Vikings, 19-16 (W)
(RS Pts.—Vikings 320, Redskins 263)
(PS Pts.—Redskins 102, Vikings 86)
*NFC Divisional Playoff
**NFC Second-Round Playoff
***NFC Championship
****NFC First-Round Playoff

NEW ENGLAND vs. ARIZONA
RS: Cardinals lead series, 6-5;
See Arizona vs. New England

NEW ENGLAND vs. ATLANTA
RS: Falcons lead series, 6-5;
See Atlanta vs. New England

NEW ENGLAND vs. BALTIMORE
RS: Patriots lead series, 3-0;
See Baltimore vs. New England

NEW ENGLAND vs. BUFFALO
RS: Patriots lead series, 52-40-1
PS: Patriots lead series, 1-0;
See Buffalo vs. New England

NEW ENGLAND vs. CAROLINA
RS: Panthers lead series, 2-1
PS: Patriots lead series, 1-0;
See Carolina vs. New England

NEW ENGLAND vs. CHICAGO
RS: Patriots lead series, 7-3
PS: Bears lead series, 1-0;

See Chicago vs. New England

NEW ENGLAND vs. CINCINNATI
RS: Patriots lead series, 12-8;
See Cincinnati vs. New England

NEW ENGLAND vs. CLEVELAND
RS: Browns lead series, 11-8
PS: Browns lead series, 1-0;
See Cleveland vs. New England

NEW ENGLAND vs. DALLAS
RS: Cowboys lead series, 7-2;
See Dallas vs. New England

NEW ENGLAND vs. DENVER
RS: Broncos lead series, 24-15
PS: Broncos lead series, 2-0;
See Denver vs. New England

NEW ENGLAND vs. DETROIT
RS: Patriots lead series, 5-4;
See Detroit vs. New England

NEW ENGLAND vs. GREEN BAY
RS: Series tied, 4-4
PS: Packers lead series, 1-0;
See Green Bay vs. New England

NEW ENGLAND vs. HOUSTON
RS: Patriots lead series, 2-0;
See Houston vs. New England

NEW ENGLAND vs. INDIANAPOLIS
RS: Patriots lead series, 41-26
PS: Patriots lead series, 2-1;
See Indianapolis vs. New England

NEW ENGLAND vs. JACKSONVILLE
RS: Patriots lead series, 4-0
PS: Patriots lead series, 2-1;
See Jacksonville vs. New England

NEW ENGLAND vs. KANSAS CITY
RS: Chiefs lead series, 16-11-3;
See Kansas City vs. New England

NEW ENGLAND vs. MIAMI
RS: Dolphins lead series, 47-33
PS: Patriots lead series, 2-1;
See Miami vs. New England

NEW ENGLAND vs. MINNESOTA
RS: Patriots lead series, 6-4;
See Minnesota vs. New England

NEW ENGLAND vs. NEW ORLEANS
RS: Patriots lead series, 8-3
1972—Patriots, 17-10 (NO)
1976—Patriots, 27-6 (NE)
1980—Patriots, 38-27 (NO)
1983—Patriots, 7-0 (NE)
1986—Patriots, 21-20 (NO)
1989—Saints, 28-24 (NE)
1992—Saints, 31-14 (NE)
1995—Saints, 31-17 (NE)
1998—Patriots, 30-27 (NO)
2001—Patriots, 34-17 (NE)
2005—Patriots, 24-17 (NE)
(RS Pts.—Patriots 253, Saints 214)

*NEW ENGLAND vs. N.Y. GIANTS
RS: Patriots lead series, 4-3
1970—Giants, 16-0 (B)
1974—Patriots, 28-20 (New Haven)
1987—Giants, 17-10 (NY)
1990—Giants, 13-10 (NE)
1996—Patriots, 23-22 (NY)
1999—Patriots, 16-14 (NE)
2003—Patriots, 17-6 (NE)
(RS Pts.—Giants 108, Patriots 104)
*Franchise in Boston prior to 1971

*NEW ENGLAND vs. **N.Y. JETS
RS: Jets lead series, 48-44-1

PS: Patriots lead series, 2-0
1960—Patriots, 28-24 (NY)
Patriots, 38-21 (B)
1961—Titans, 21-20 (B)
Titans, 37-30 (NY)
1962—Patriots, 43-14 (NY)
Patriots, 24-17 (B)
1963—Patriots, 38-14 (B)
Jets, 31-24 (NY)
1964—Patriots, 26-10 (B)
Jets, 35-14 (NY)
1965—Jets, 30-20 (B)
Patriots, 27-23 (NY)
1966—Tie, 24-24 (B)
Jets, 38-28 (NY)
1967—Jets, 30-23 (NY)
Jets, 29-24 (B)
1968—Jets, 47-31 (Birmingham)
Jets, 48-14 (NY)
1969—Jets, 23-14 (B)
Jets, 23-17 (NY)
1970—Jets, 31-21 (B)
Jets, 17-3 (NY)
1971—Patriots, 20-0 (NE)
Jets, 13-6 (NY)
1972—Jets, 41-13 (NE)
Jets, 34-10 (NY)
1973—Jets, 9-7 (NE)
Jets, 33-13 (NY)
1974—Patriots, 24-0 (NY)
Jets, 21-16 (NE)
1975—Jets, 36-7 (NY)
Jets, 30-28 (NE)
1976—Patriots, 41-7 (NE)
Patriots, 38-24 (NY)
1977—Jets, 30-27 (NY)
Patriots, 24-13 (NE)
1978—Patriots, 55-21 (NE)
Patriots, 19-17 (NY)
1979—Patriots, 56-3 (NE)
Jets, 27-26 (NY)
1980—Patriots, 21-11 (NY)
Patriots, 34-21 (NE)
1981—Jets, 28-24 (NY)
Jets, 17-6 (NE)
1982—Jets, 31-7 (NE)
1983—Patriots, 23-13 (NE)
Jets, 26-3 (NY)
1984—Patriots, 28-21 (NY)
Patriots, 30-20 (NE)
1985—Patriots, 20-13 (NE)
Jets, 16-13 (NY) OT
***Patriots, 26-14 (NY)
1986—Patriots, 20-6 (NY)
Jets, 31-24 (NE)
1987—Jets, 43-24 (NY)
Patriots, 42-20 (NE)
1988—Patriots, 28-3 (NE)
Patriots, 14-13 (NY)
1989—Patriots, 27-24 (NY)
Jets, 27-26 (NE)
1990—Jets, 37-13 (NE)
Jets, 42-7 (NY)
1991—Jets, 28-21 (NE)
Patriots, 6-3 (NY)
1992—Jets, 30-21 (NY)
Patriots, 24-3 (NE)
1993—Jets, 45-7 (NY)
Jets, 6-0 (NE)
1994—Jets, 24-17 (NY)

Patriots, 24-13 (NE)
1995—Patriots, 20-7 (NY)
Patriots, 31-28 (NE)
1996—Patriots, 31-27 (NY)
Patriots, 34-10 (NE)
1997—Patriots, 27-24 (NE) OT
Jets, 24-19 (NY)
1998—Jets, 24-14 (NE)
Jets, 31-10 (NY)
1999—Patriots, 30-28 (NY)
Jets, 24-17 (NE)
2000—Jets, 20-19 (NY)
Jets, 34-17 (NE)
2001—Jets, 10-3 (NE)
Patriots, 17-16 (NY)
2002—Patriots, 44-7 (NY)
Jets, 30-17 (NE)
2003—Patriots, 23-16 (NE)
Patriots, 21-16 (NY)
2004—Patriots, 13-7 (NE)
Patriots, 23-7 (NY)
2005—Patriots, 16-3 (NE)
Patriots, 31-21 (NY)
2006—Patriots, 24-17 (NY)
Jets, 17-14 (NE)
***Patriots, 37-16 (NE)
(RS Pts.—Patriots 2,030, Jets 2,009)
(PS Pts.—Patriots 63, Jets 30)
*Franchise in Boston prior to 1971
**Jets known as Titans prior to 1963
***AFC First-Round Playoff
**NEW ENGLAND vs. **OAKLAND
RS: Raiders lead series, 14-13-1
PS: Patriots lead series, 2-1
1960—Raiders, 27-14 (O)
Patriots, 34-28 (B)
1961—Patriots, 20-17 (B)
Patriots, 35-21 (O)
1962—Patriots, 26-16 (B)
Raiders, 20-0 (O)
1963—Patriots, 20-14 (O)
Patriots, 20-14 (B)
1964—Patriots, 17-14 (O)
Tie, 43-43 (B)
1965—Raiders, 24-10 (B)
Raiders, 30-21 (O)
1966—Patriots, 24-21 (B)
1967—Raiders, 35-7 (O)
Raiders, 48-14 (B)
1968—Raiders, 41-10 (O)
1969—Raiders, 38-23 (B)
1971—Patriots, 20-6 (NE)
1974—Raiders, 41-26 (O)
1976—Patriots, 48-17 (NE)
***Raiders, 24-21 (O)
1978—Patriots, 21-14 (O)
1981—Raiders, 27-17 (O)
1985—Raiders, 35-20 (NE)
***Patriots, 27-20 (LA)
1987—Patriots, 26-23 (NE)
1989—Raiders, 24-21 (LA)
1994—Raiders, 21-17 (NE)
2001—***Patriots, 16-13 (NE) OT
2002—Raiders, 27-20 (O)
2005—Patriots, 30-20 (NE)
(RS Pts.—Raiders 706, Patriots 604)
(PS Pts.—Patriots 64, Raiders 57)
*Franchise in Boston prior to 1971
**Franchise in Los Angeles from
1982-1994

***AFC Divisional Playoff
NEW ENGLAND vs. PHILADELPHIA
RS: Eagles lead series, 6-3
PS: Patriots lead series, 1-0
1973—Eagles, 24-23 (P)
1977—Patriots, 14-6 (NE)
1978—Patriots, 24-14 (NE)
1981—Eagles, 13-3 (P)
1984—Eagles, 27-17 (P)
1987—Eagles, 34-31 (NE) OT
1990—Eagles, 48-20 (P)
1999—Eagles, 24-9 (P)
2003—Patriots, 31-10 (P)
2004—*Patriots, 24-21 (Jacksonvillle)
(RS Pts.—Eagles 200, Patriots 172)
(PS Pts.—Patriots 24, Eagles 21)
*Super Bowl XXXIX
NEW ENGLAND vs. PITTSBURGH
RS: Steelers lead series, 12-6
PS: Patriots lead series, 3-1
1972—Steelers, 33-3 (P)
1974—Steelers, 21-17 (NE)
1976—Patriots, 30-27 (P)
1979—Steelers, 16-13 (NE) OT
1981—Steelers, 27-21 (P) OT
1982—Steelers, 37-14 (P)
1983—Patriots, 28-23 (P)
1986—Patriots, 34-0 (P)
1989—Steelers, 28-10 (P)
1990—Steelers, 24-3 (P)
1991—Steelers, 20-6 (P)
1993—Steelers, 17-14 (P)
1995—Steelers, 41-27 (P)
1996—*Patriots, 28-3 (NE)
1997—Steelers, 24-21 (NE) OT
*Steelers, 7-6 (P)
1998—Patriots, 23-9 (P)
2001—**Patriots, 24-17 (P)
2002—Patriots, 30-14 (NE)
2004—Steelers, 34-20 (P)
**Patriots, 41-27 (P)
2005—Patriots, 23-20 (P)
(RS Pts.—Steelers 415, Patriots 337)
(PS Pts.—Patriots 99, Steelers 54)
*AFC Divisional Playoff
**AFC Championship
NEW ENGLAND vs. *ST. LOUIS
RS: Rams lead series, 5-4
PS: Patriots lead series, 1-0
1974—Patriots, 20-14 (NE)
1980—Rams, 17-14 (NE)
1983—Patriots, 21-7 (LA)
1986—Patriots, 30-28 (LA)
1989—Rams, 24-20 (NE)
1992—Rams, 14-0 (LA)
1998—Rams, 32-18 (StL)
2001—Rams, 24-17 (NE)
**Patriots, 20-17 (New Orleans)
2004—Patriots, 40-22 (StL)
(RS Pts.—Rams 182, Patriots 180)
(PS Pts.—Patriots 20, Rams 17)
*Franchise in Los Angeles prior to 1995
**Super Bowl XXXVI
*NEW ENGLAND vs. **SAN DIEGO
RS: Patriots lead series, 17-13-2
PS: Series tied, 1-1
1960—Patriots, 35-0 (LA)
Chargers, 45-16 (B)
1961—Chargers, 38-27 (B)
Patriots, 41-0 (SD)

1962—Patriots, 24-20 (B)
    Patriots, 20-14 (SD)
1963—Chargers, 17-13 (SD)
    Chargers, 7-6 (B)
    ***Chargers, 51-10 (SD)
1964—Patriots, 33-28 (SD)
    Chargers, 26-17 (B)
1965—Tie, 10-10 (B)
    Patriots, 22-6 (SD)
1966—Chargers, 24-0 (SD)
    Patriots, 35-17 (B)
1967—Chargers, 28-14 (SD)
    Tie, 31-31 (SD)
1968—Chargers, 27-17 (B)
1969—Chargers, 13-10 (B)
    Chargers, 28-18 (SD)
1970—Chargers, 16-14 (B)
1973—Patriots, 30-14 (NE)
1975—Patriots, 33-19 (SD)
1977—Patriots, 24-20 (SD)
1978—Patriots, 28-23 (NE)
1979—Patriots, 27-21 (NE)
1983—Patriots, 37-21 (NE)
1994—Patriots, 23-17 (NE)
1996—Patriots, 45-7 (SD)
1997—Patriots, 41-7 (NE)
2001—Patriots, 29-26 (NE) OT
2002—Chargers, 21-14 (SD)
2005—Chargers, 41-17 (NE)
2006—****Patriots, 24-21 (SD)
(RS Pts.—Patriots 754, Chargers 635)
(PS Pts.—Chargers 72, Patriots 34)
*Franchise in Boston prior to 1971
**Franchise in Los Angeles prior to 1961
***AFL Championship
****AFC Divisional Playoff

NEW ENGLAND vs. SAN FRANCISCO
RS: 49ers lead series, 7-3
1971—49ers, 27-10 (SF)
1975—Patriots, 24-16 (NE)
1980—49ers, 21-17 (SF)
1983—49ers, 33-13 (NE)
1986—49ers, 29-24 (NE)
1989—49ers, 37-20 (SF)
1992—49ers, 24-12 (NE)
1995—49ers, 28-3 (SF)
1998—Patriots, 24-21 (NE)
2004—Patriots, 21-7 (NE)
(RS Pts.—49ers 243, Patriots 168)
NEW ENGLAND vs. SEATTLE
RS: Series tied, 7-7
1977—Patriots, 31-0 (NE)
1980—Patriots, 37-31 (S)
1982—Patriots, 16-0 (S)
1983—Seahawks, 24-6 (S)
1984—Patriots, 38-23 (NE)
1985—Patriots, 20-13 (S)
1986—Seahawks, 38-31 (NE)
1988—Patriots, 13-7 (NE)
1989—Seahawks, 24-3 (NE)
1990—Seahawks, 33-20 (NE)
1992—Seahawks, 10-6 (NE)
1993—Seahawks, 17-14 (NE)
    Seahawks, 10-9 (S)
2004—Patriots, 30-20 (NE)
(RS Pts.—Patriots 274, Seahawks 250)
NEW ENGLAND vs. TAMPA BAY
RS: Patriots lead series, 4-2
1976—Patriots, 31-14 (TB)
1985—Patriots, 32-14 (TB)

1988—Patriots, 10-7 (NE) OT
1997—Buccaneers, 27-7 (TB)
2000—Buccaneers, 21-16 (NE)
2005—Patriots, 28-0 (NE)
(RS Pts.—Patriots 124, Buccaneers 83)
***NEW ENGLAND vs. **TENNESSEE**
RS: Patriots lead series, 20-15-1
PS: Series tied, 1-1
1960—Oilers, 24-10 (B)
    Oilers, 37-21 (H)
1961—Tie, 31-31 (B)
    Oilers, 27-15 (H)
1962—Patriots, 34-21 (B)
    Oilers, 21-17 (H)
1963—Patriots, 45-3 (B)
    Patriots, 46-28 (H)
1964—Patriots, 25-24 (B)
    Patriots, 34-17 (H)
1965—Oilers, 31-10 (H)
    Patriots, 42-14 (B)
1966—Patriots, 27-21 (B)
    Patriots, 38-14 (H)
1967—Patriots, 18-7 (B)
    Oilers, 27-6 (H)
1968—Oilers, 16-0 (B)
    Oilers, 45-17 (H)
1969—Patriots, 24-0 (B)
    Oilers, 27-23 (H)
1971—Patriots, 28-20 (NE)
1973—Patriots, 32-0 (H)
1975—Oilers, 7-0 (NE)
1978—Oilers, 26-23 (NE)
    ***Oilers, 31-14 (NE)
1980—Oilers, 38-34 (H)
1981—Patriots, 38-10 (NE)
1982—Patriots, 29-21 (NE)
1987—Patriots, 21-7 (H)
1988—Oilers, 31-6 (H)
1989—Patriots, 23-13 (NE)
1991—Patriots, 24-20 (NE)
1993—Oilers, 28-14 (NE)
1998—Patriots, 27-16 (NE)
2002—Titans, 24-7 (T)
2003—Patriots, 38-30 (NE)
    ***Patriots, 17-14 (NE)
2006—Patriots, 40-23 (T)
(RS Pts.—Patriots 867, Titans 749)
(PS Pts.—Titans 45, Patriots 31)
*Franchise in Boston prior to 1971
**Franchise in Houston prior to 1997;
known as Oilers prior to 1999
***AFC Divisional Playoff
NEW ENGLAND vs. WASHINGTON
RS: Redskins lead series, 6-1
1972—Patriots, 24-23 (NE)
1978—Redskins, 16-14 (NE)
1981—Redskins, 24-22 (W)
1984—Redskins, 26-10 (NE)
1990—Redskins, 25-10 (NE)
1996—Redskins, 27-22 (NE)
2003—Redskins, 20-17 (W)
(RS Pts.—Redskins 161, Patriots 119)

NEW ORLEANS vs. ARIZONA
RS: Cardinals lead series, 13-11;
See Arizona vs. New Orleans
NEW ORLEANS vs. ATLANTA
RS: Falcons lead series, 43-32
PS: Falcons lead series, 1-0;
See Atlanta vs. New Orleans

NEW ORLEANS vs. BALTIMORE
RS: Ravens lead series, 3-1;
See Baltimore vs. New Orleans
NEW ORLEANS vs. BUFFALO
RS: Series tied, 4-4;
See Buffalo vs. New Orleans
NEW ORLEANS vs. CAROLINA
RS: Panthers lead series, 13-11;
See Carolina vs. New Orleans
NEW ORLEANS vs. CHICAGO
RS: Series tied, 11-11
PS: Bears lead series, 2-0;
See Chicago vs. New Orleans
NEW ORLEANS vs. CINCINNATI
RS: Bengals lead series, 6-5;
See Cincinnati vs. New Orleans
NEW ORLEANS vs. CLEVELAND
RS: Browns lead series, 11-4;
See Cleveland vs. New Orleans
NEW ORLEANS vs. DALLAS
RS: Cowboys lead series, 14-8;
See Dallas vs. New Orleans
NEW ORLEANS vs. DENVER
RS: Broncos lead series, 6-2;
See Denver vs. New Orleans
NEW ORLEANS vs. DETROIT
RS: Lions lead series, 9-8-1;
See Detroit vs. New Orleans
NEW ORLEANS vs. GREEN BAY
RS: Packers lead series, 14-6;
See Green Bay vs. New Orleans
NEW ORLEANS vs. HOUSTON
RS: Saints lead series, 1-0;
See Houston vs. New Orleans
NEW ORLEANS vs. INDIANAPOLIS
RS: Saints lead series, 5-4;
See Indianapolis vs. New Orleans
NEW ORLEANS vs. JACKSONVILLE
RS: Jaguars lead series, 2-1;
See Jacksonville vs. New Orleans
NEW ORLEANS vs. KANSAS CITY
RS: Series tied, 4-4;
See Kansas City vs. New Orleans
NEW ORLEANS vs. MIAMI
RS: Dolphins lead series, 6-3;
See Miami vs. New Orleans
NEW ORLEANS vs. MINNESOTA
RS: Vikings lead series, 17-7
PS: Vikings lead series, 2-0;
See Minnesota vs. New Orleans
NEW ORLEANS vs. NEW ENGLAND
RS: Patriots lead series, 8-3;
See New England vs. New Orleans
NEW ORLEANS vs. N.Y. GIANTS
RS: Giants lead series, 14-10
1967—Giants, 27-21 (NY)
1968—Giants, 38-21 (NY)
1969—Saints, 25-24 (NY)
1970—Saints, 14-10 (NO)
1972—Giants, 45-21 (NY)
1975—Giants, 28-14 (NY)
1978—Saints, 28-17 (NO)
1979—Saints, 24-14 (NO)
1981—Giants, 20-7 (NY)
1984—Saints, 10-3 (NY)
1985—Giants, 21-13 (NO)
1986—Giants, 20-17 (NY)
1987—Saints, 23-14 (NO)
1988—Giants, 13-12 (NO)
1993—Giants, 24-14 (NO)

1994—Saints, 27-22 (NO)
1995—Giants, 45-29 (NY)
1996—Saints 17-3 (NY)
1997—Giants, 14-9 (NY)
1999—Giants, 31-3 (NY)
2001—Giants, 21-13 (NY)
2003—Saints, 45-7 (NO)
2005—Giants, 27-10 (NY*)
2006—Saints, 30-7 (NY)
(RS Pts.—Giants 495, Saints 447)
*Saints home game

NEW ORLEANS vs. N.Y. JETS
RS: Series tied, 5-5
1972—Jets, 18-17 (NY)
1977—Jets, 16-13 (NO)
1980—Saints, 21-20 (NY)
1983—Jets, 31-28 (NO)
1986—Jets, 28-23 (NY)
1989—Saints, 29-14 (NO)
1992—Saints, 20-0 (NY)
1995—Saints, 12-0 (NY)
2001—Jets, 16-9 (NY)
2005—Saints, 21-19 (NY)
(RS Pts.—Saints 193, Jets 162)

NEW ORLEANS vs. *OAKLAND
RS: Raiders lead series, 5-4-1
1971—Tie, 21-21 (NO)
1975—Raiders, 48-10 (O)
1979—Raiders, 42-35 (NO)
1985—Raiders, 23-13 (LA)
1988—Saints, 20-6 (NO)
1991—Saints, 27-0 (NO)
1994—Raiders, 24-19 (LA)
1997—Saints, 13-10 (O)
2000—Raiders, 31-22 (NO)
2004—Saints, 31-26 (O)
(RS Pts.—Raiders 231, Saints 211)
*Franchise in Los Angeles from 1982-1994

NEW ORLEANS vs. PHILADELPHIA
RS: Eagles lead series, 14-9
PS: Series tied, 1-1
1967—Saints, 31-24 (NO)
       Eagles, 48-21 (P)
1968—Eagles, 29-17 (P)
1969—Eagles, 13-10 (P)
       Saints, 26-17 (NO)
1972—Saints, 21-3 (NO)
1974—Saints, 14-10 (NO)
1977—Eagles, 28-7 (P)
1978—Eagles, 24-17 (NO)
1979—Eagles, 26-14 (NO)
1980—Saints, 34-21 (NO)
1981—Eagles, 31-14 (NO)
1983—Saints, 20-17 (P) OT
1985—Saints, 23-21 (NO)
1987—Eagles, 27-17 (P)
1989—Saints, 30-20 (NO)
1991—Saints, 13-6 (P)
1992—Eagles, 15-13 (P)
       *Eagles, 36-20 (NO)
1993—Eagles, 37-26 (P)
1995—Eagles, 15-10 (NO)
2000—Eagles, 21-7 (NO)
2003—Eagles, 33-20 (P)
2006—Saints, 27-24 (NO)
       **Saints, 27-24 (NO)
(RS Pts.—Eagles 523, Saints 419)
(PS Pts.—Eagles 60, Saints 47)
*NFC First-Round Playoff
**NFC Divisional Playoff

NEW ORLEANS vs. PITTSBURGH
RS: Steelers lead series, 7-6
1967—Steelers, 14-10 (NO)
1968—Saints, 16-12 (P)
       Saints, 24-14 (NO)
1969—Saints, 27-24 (NO)
1974—Steelers, 28-7 (NO)
1978—Steelers, 20-14 (P)
1981—Steelers, 20-6 (NO)
1984—Saints, 27-24 (NO)
1987—Steelers, 20-16 (P)
1990—Steelers, 9-6 (NO)
1993—Steelers, 37-14 (P)
2002—Saints, 32-29 (NO)
2006—Steelers, 38-31 (P)
(RS Pts.—Steelers 285, Saints 234)

NEW ORLEANS vs. *ST. LOUIS
RS: Rams lead series, 37-29
PS: Saints lead series, 1-0
1967—Rams, 27-13 (NO)
1969—Rams, 36-17 (LA)
1970—Rams, 30-17 (NO)
       Rams, 34-16 (LA)
1971—Saints, 24-20 (NO)
       Rams, 45-28 (LA)
1972—Rams, 34-14 (LA)
       Saints, 19-16 (NO)
1973—Rams, 29-7 (LA)
       Rams, 24-13 (NO)
1974—Rams, 24-0 (LA)
       Saints, 20-7 (NO)
1975—Rams, 38-14 (LA)
       Rams, 14-7 (NO)
1976—Rams, 16-10 (NO)
       Rams, 33-14 (LA)
1977—Rams, 14-7 (LA)
       Saints, 27-26 (NO)
1978—Rams, 26-20 (NO)
       Saints, 10-3 (LA)
1979—Rams, 35-17 (NO)
       Saints, 29-14 (LA)
1980—Rams, 45-31 (LA)
       Rams, 27-7 (NO)
1981—Saints, 23-17 (NO)
       Saints, 21-13 (LA)
1983—Rams, 30-27 (LA)
       Rams, 26-24 (NO)
1984—Rams, 28-10 (NO)
       Rams, 34-21 (LA)
1985—Rams, 28-10 (LA)
       Saints, 29-3 (NO)
1986—Saints, 6-0 (NO)
       Rams, 26-13 (LA)
1987—Saints, 37-10 (NO)
       Saints, 31-14 (LA)
1988—Rams, 12-10 (NO)
       Saints, 14-10 (LA)
1989—Saints, 40-21 (LA)
       Rams, 20-17 (NO) OT
1990—Saints, 24-20 (LA)
       Saints, 20-17 (NO)
1991—Saints, 24-7 (NO)
       Saints, 24-17 (LA)
1992—Saints, 13-10 (NO)
       Saints, 37-14 (LA)
1993—Saints, 37-6 (LA)
       Rams, 23-20 (NO)
1994—Saints, 37-34 (NO)
       Saints, 31-15 (LA)
1995—Rams, 17-13 (StL)

       Saints, 19-10 (NO)
1996—Rams, 26-10 (NO)
       Rams, 14-13 (StL)
1997—Rams, 38-24 (StL)
       Rams, 34-27 (NO)
1998—Saints, 24-17 (StL)
       Saints, 24-3 (NO)
1999—Rams, 43-12 (StL)
       Rams, 30-14 (NO)
2000—Saints, 31-24 (StL)
       Rams, 26-21 (NO)
       **Saints, 31-28 (NO)
2001—Saints, 34-31 (StL)
       Rams, 34-21 (NO)
2004—Saints, 28-25 (StL) OT
2005—Rams, 28-17 (StL)
(RS Pts.—Rams 1,472, Saints 1,313)
(PS Pts.—Saints 31, Rams 28)
*Franchise in Los Angeles prior to 1995
**NFC First-Round Playoff

NEW ORLEANS vs. SAN DIEGO
RS: Chargers lead series, 7-2
1973—Chargers, 17-14 (SD)
1977—Chargers, 14-0 (NO)
1979—Chargers, 35-0 (NO)
1988—Saints, 23-17 (SD)
1991—Chargers, 24-21 (SD)
1994—Chargers, 36-22 (NO)
1997—Chargers, 20-6 (NO)
2000—Saints, 28-27 (SD)
2004—Chargers, 43-17 (SD)
(RS Pts.—Chargers 233, Saints 131)

NEW ORLEANS vs. SAN FRANCISCO
RS: 49ers lead series, 45-21-2
1967—49ers, 27-13 (SF)
1969—Saints, 43-38 (NO)
1970—Tie, 20-20 (SF)
       49ers, 38-27 (NO)
1971—49ers, 38-20 (NO)
       Saints, 26-20 (SF)
1972—49ers, 37-2 (NO)
       Tie, 20-20 (SF)
1973—49ers, 40-0 (SF)
       Saints, 16-10 (NO)
1974—49ers, 17-13 (NO)
       49ers, 35-21 (SF)
1975—49ers, 35-21 (SF)
       49ers, 16-6 (NO)
1976—49ers, 33-3 (SF)
       49ers, 27-7 (NO)
1977—49ers, 10-7 (NO) OT
       49ers, 20-17 (SF)
1978—Saints, 14-7 (SF)
       Saints, 24-13 (NO)
1979—Saints, 30-21 (SF)
       Saints, 31-20 (NO)
1980—49ers, 26-23 (NO)
       49ers, 38-35 (SF) OT
1981—49ers, 21-14 (SF)
       49ers, 21-17 (NO)
1982—Saints, 23-20 (NO)
1983—49ers, 32-13 (NO)
       49ers, 27-0 (SF)
1984—49ers, 30-20 (SF)
       49ers, 35-3 (NO)
1985—Saints, 20-17 (SF)
       49ers, 31-19 (NO)
1986—49ers, 26-17 (SF)
       Saints, 23-10 (NO)
1987—49ers, 24-22 (NO)

Saints, 26-24 (SF)
1988—49ers, 34-33 (NO)
49ers, 30-17 (SF)
1989—49ers, 24-20 (NO)
49ers, 31-13 (SF)
1990—49ers, 13-12 (NO)
Saints, 13-10 (SF)
1991—Saints, 10-3 (NO)
49ers, 38-24 (SF)
1992—49ers, 16-10 (NO)
49ers, 21-20 (SF)
1993—Saints, 16-13 (NO)
49ers, 42-7 (SF)
1994—49ers, 24-13 (SF)
49ers, 35-14 (NO)
1995—49ers, 24-22 (NO)
Saints, 11-7 (SF)
1996—49ers, 27-11 (SF)
49ers, 24-17 (NO)
1997—49ers, 33-7 (SF)
49ers, 23-0 (NO)
1998—49ers, 31-0 (NO)
49ers, 31-20 (SF)
1999—49ers, 28-21 (SF)
Saints, 24-6 (NO)
2000—Saints, 31-15 (NO)
Saints, 31-27 (SF)
2001—49ers, 28-27 (SF)
49ers, 38-0 (NO)
2002—Saints, 35-27 (NO)
2004—Saints, 30-27 (NO)
2006—Saints, 34-10 (NO)
(RS Pts.—49ers 1,664, Saints 1,199)

NEW ORLEANS vs. SEATTLE
RS: Seahawks lead series, 5-4
1976—Saints, 51-27 (S)
1979—Seahawks, 38-24 (S)
1985—Seahawks, 27-3 (NO)
1988—Saints, 20-19 (S)
1991—Saints, 27-24 (NO)
1997—Saints, 20-17 (NO) OT
2000—Seahawks, 20-10 (S)
2003—Seahawks, 27-10 (S)
2004—Seahawks, 21-7 (NO)
(RS Pts.—Seahawks 220, Saints 172)

NEW ORLEANS vs. TAMPA BAY
RS: Saints lead series, 19-11
1977—Buccaneers, 33-14 (NO)
1978—Saints, 17-10 (TB)
1979—Saints, 42-14 (TB)
1981—Buccaneers, 31-14 (NO)
1982—Buccaneers, 13-10 (NO)
1983—Saints, 24-21 (TB)
1984—Saints, 17-13 (NO)
1985—Saints, 20-13 (NO)
1986—Saints, 38-7 (NO)
1987—Saints, 44-34 (NO)
1988—Saints, 13-9 (NO)
1989—Buccaneers, 20-10 (TB)
1990—Saints, 35-7 (NO)
1991—Saints, 23-7 (NO)
1992—Saints, 23-21 (NO)
1994—Saints, 9-7 (TB)
1996—Buccaneers, 13-7 (TB)
1998—Saints, 9-3 (NO)
1999—Buccaneers, 31-16 (NO)
2001—Buccaneers, 48-21 (TB)
2002—Saints, 26-20 (TB) OT
Saints, 23-20 (NO)
2003—Saints, 17-14 (TB)

Buccaneers, 14-7 (NO)
2004—Buccaneers, 20-17 (NO)
Saints, 21-17 (TB)
2005—Buccaneers, 10-3 (Baton Rouge)
Buccaneers, 27-13 (TB)
2006—Saints, 24-21 (NO)
Saings, 31-14 (TB)
(RS Pts.—Saints 588, Buccaneers 532)

NEW ORLEANS vs. *TENNESSEE
RS: Titans lead series, 6-4-1
1971—Tie, 13-13 (H)
1976—Oilers, 31-26 (NO)
1978—Oilers, 17-12 (NO)
1981—Saints, 27-24 (H)
1984—Saints, 27-10 (H)
1987—Saints, 24-10 (NO)
1990—Oilers, 23-10 (H)
1993—Saints, 33-21 (NO)
1996—Oilers, 31-14 (NO)
1999—Titans, 24-21 (NO)
2003—Titans, 27-12 (T)
(RS Pts.—Titans 231, Saints 219)
*Franchise in Houston prior to 1997;
known as Oilers prior to 1999*

NEW ORLEANS vs. WASHINGTON
RS: Redskins lead series, 14-7
1967—Redskins, 30-10 (NO)
Saints, 30-14 (W)
1968—Saints, 37-17 (NO)
1969—Redskins, 26-20 (NO)
Redskins, 17-14 (W)
1971—Redskins, 24-14 (W)
1973—Saints, 19-3 (NO)
1975—Redskins, 41-3 (W)
1979—Saints, 14-10 (W)
1980—Redskins, 22-14 (W)
1982—Redskins, 27-10 (NO)
1986—Redskins, 14-6 (NO)
1988—Redskins, 27-24 (W)
1989—Redskins, 16-14 (NO)
1990—Redskins, 31-17 (W)
1992—Saints, 20-3 (NO)
1994—Redskins, 38-24 (NO)
2001—Redskins, 40-10 (NO)
2002—Saints, 43-27 (W)
2003—Saints, 24-20 (W)
2006—Redskins, 16-10 (NO)
(RS Pts.—Redskins 463, Saints 377)

N.Y. GIANTS vs. ARIZONA
RS: Giants lead series, 78-41-2;
See Arizona vs. N.Y. Giants
N.Y. GIANTS vs. ATLANTA
RS: Falcons lead series, 10-8;
See Atlanta vs. N.Y. Giants
N.Y. GIANTS vs. BALTIMORE
RS: Ravens lead series, 2-0
PS: Ravens lead series, 1-0;
See Baltimore vs. N.Y. Giants
N.Y. GIANTS vs. BUFFALO
RS: Bills lead series, 6-3
PS: Giants lead series, 1-0;
See Buffalo vs. N.Y. Giants
N.Y. GIANTS vs. CAROLINA
RS: Panthers lead series, 2-1
PS: Panthers lead series, 1-0;
See Carolina vs. N.Y. Giants
N.Y. GIANTS vs. CHICAGO
RS: Bears lead series, 27-17-2
PS: Bears lead series, 5-3;

See Chicago vs. N.Y. Giants
N.Y. GIANTS vs. CINCINNATI
RS: Bengals lead series, 5-2;
See Cincinnati vs. N.Y. Giants
N.Y. GIANTS vs. CLEVELAND
RS: Browns lead series, 25-19-2
PS: Series tied, 1-1;
See Cleveland vs. N.Y. Giants
N.Y. GIANTS vs. DALLAS
RS: Cowboys lead series, 52-35-2;
See Dallas vs. N.Y. Giants
N.Y. GIANTS vs. DENVER
RS: Giants lead series, 5-4
PS: Giants lead series, 1-0;
See Denver vs. N.Y. Giants
N.Y. GIANTS vs. DETROIT
RS: Lions lead series, 20-17-1
PS: Lions lead series, 1-0;
See Detroit vs. N.Y. Giants
N.Y. GIANTS vs. GREEN BAY
RS: Packers lead series, 24-21-2
PS: Packers lead series, 4-1;
See Green Bay vs. N.Y. Giants
N.Y. GIANTS vs. HOUSTON
RS: Series tied, 1-1;
See Houston vs. N.Y. Giants
N.Y. GIANTS vs. INDIANAPOLIS
RS: Colts lead series, 7-6
PS: Colts lead series, 2-0;
See Indianapolis vs. N.Y. Giants
N.Y. GIANTS vs. JACKSONVILLE
RS: Series tied, 2-2;
See Jacksonville vs. N.Y. Giants
N.Y. GIANTS vs. KANSAS CITY
RS: Giants lead series, 9-2;
See Kansas City vs. N.Y. Giants
N.Y. GIANTS vs. MIAMI
RS: Giants lead series, 3-2;
See Miami vs. N.Y. Giants
N.Y. GIANTS vs. MINNESOTA
RS: Vikings lead series, 10-8
PS: Giants lead series, 2-1;
See Minnesota vs. N.Y. Giants
N.Y. GIANTS vs. NEW ENGLAND
RS: Patriots lead series, 4-3;
See New England vs. N.Y. Giants
N.Y. GIANTS vs. NEW ORLEANS
RS: Giants lead series, 14-10;
See New Orleans vs. N.Y. Giants
N.Y. GIANTS vs. N.Y. JETS
RS: Giants lead series, 6-4
1970—Giants, 22-10 (NYJ)
1974—Jets, 26-20 (New Haven) OT
1981—Jets, 26-7 (NYG)
1984—Giants, 20-10 (NYJ)
1987—Giants, 20-7 (NYG)
1988—Jets, 27-21 (NYJ)
1993—Jets, 10-6 (NYG)
1996—Giants, 13-6 (NYJ)
1999—Giants, 41-28 (NYG)
2003—Giants, 31-28 (NYJ) OT
(RS Pts.—Giants 201, Jets 178)
N.Y. GIANTS vs. *OAKLAND
RS: Raiders lead series, 7-3
1973—Raiders, 42-0 (O)
1980—Raiders, 33-17 (NY)
1983—Raiders, 27-12 (LA)
1986—Giants, 14-9 (LA)
1989—Giants, 34-17 (NY)
1992—Raiders, 13-10 (LA)

1995—Raiders, 17-13 (NY)
1998—Raiders, 20-17 (O)
2001—Raiders, 28-10 (NY)
2005—Giants, 30-21 (O)
(RS Pts.—Raiders 227, Giants 157)
Franchise in Los Angeles from 1982-1994
N.Y. GIANTS vs. PHILADELPHIA
RS: Giants lead series, 76-66-2
PS: Giants lead series, 2-1
1933—Giants, 56-0 (NY)
 Giants, 20-14 (P)
1934—Giants, 17-0 (NY)
 Eagles, 6-0 (P)
1935—Giants, 10-0 (NY)
 Giants, 21-14 (P)
1936—Eagles, 10-7 (P)
 Giants, 21-17 (NY)
1937—Giants, 16-7 (P)
 Giants, 21-0 (NY)
1938—Eagles, 14-10 (P)
 Giants, 17-7 (NY)
1939—Giants, 13-3 (P)
 Giants, 27-10 (NY)
1940—Giants, 20-14 (P)
 Giants, 17-7 (NY)
1941—Giants, 24-0 (P)
 Giants, 16-0 (NY)
1942—Giants, 35-17 (NY)
 Giants, 14-0 (P)
1944—Eagles, 24-17 (NY)
 Tie, 21-21 (P)
1945—Eagles, 38-17 (P)
 Giants, 28-21 (NY)
1946—Eagles, 24-14 (P)
 Giants, 45-17 (NY)
1947—Eagles, 23-0 (P)
 Eagles, 41-24 (NY)
1948—Eagles, 45-0 (P)
 Eagles, 35-14 (NY)
1949—Giants, 24-3 (NY)
 Eagles, 17-3 (P)
1950—Giants, 7-3 (NY)
 Giants, 9-7 (P)
1951—Eagles, 26-24 (NY)
 Giants, 23-7 (P)
1952—Giants, 31-7 (P)
 Eagles, 14-10 (NY)
1953—Eagles, 30-7 (P)
 Giants, 37-28 (NY)
1954—Giants, 27-14 (NY)
 Eagles, 29-14 (P)
1955—Eagles, 27-17 (P)
 Giants, 31-7 (NY)
1956—Giants, 20-3 (NY)
 Giants, 21-7 (P)
1957—Giants, 24-20 (P)
 Giants, 13-0 (NY)
1958—Eagles, 27-24 (P)
 Giants, 24-10 (NY)
1959—Eagles, 49-21 (P)
 Giants, 24-7 (NY)
1960—Eagles, 17-10 (NY)
 Eagles, 31-23 (P)
1961—Giants, 38-21 (NY)
 Giants, 28-24 (P)
1962—Giants, 29-13 (P)
 Giants, 19-14 (NY)
1963—Giants, 37-14 (P)
 Giants, 42-14 (NY)
1964—Eagles, 38-7 (P)

 Eagles, 23-17 (NY)
1965—Giants, 16-14 (P)
 Giants, 35-27 (NY)
1966—Eagles, 35-17 (P)
 Eagles, 31-3 (NY)
1967—Giants, 44-7 (NY)
1968—Giants, 34-25 (P)
 Giants, 7-6 (NY)
1969—Eagles, 23-20 (NY)
1970—Giants, 30-23 (NY)
 Eagles, 23-20 (P)
1971—Eagles, 23-7 (P)
 Eagles, 41-28 (NY)
1972—Giants, 27-12 (P)
 Giants, 62-10 (NY)
1973—Tie, 23-23 (NY)
 Eagles, 20-16 (P)
1974—Eagles, 35-7 (P)
 Eagles, 20-7 (New Haven)
1975—Giants, 23-14 (P)
 Eagles, 13-10 (NY)
1976—Eagles, 20-7 (P)
 Eagles, 10-0 (NY)
1977—Eagles, 28-10 (NY)
 Eagles, 17-14 (P)
1978—Eagles, 19-17 (NY)
 Eagles, 20-3 (P)
1979—Eagles, 23-17 (P)
 Eagles, 17-13 (NY)
1980—Eagles, 35-3 (P)
 Eagles, 31-16 (NY)
1981—Eagles, 24-10 (NY)
 Giants, 20-10 (P)
 *Giants, 27-21 (P)
1982—Giants, 23-7 (NY)
 Giants, 26-24 (P)
1983—Eagles, 17-13 (NY)
 Giants, 23-0 (P)
1984—Giants, 28-27 (NY)
 Eagles, 24-10 (P)
1985—Giants, 21-0 (NY)
 Giants, 16-10 (P) OT
1986—Giants, 35-3 (NY)
 Giants, 17-14 (P)
1987—Giants, 20-17 (P)
 Giants, 23-20 (NY) OT
1988—Eagles, 24-13 (P)
 Eagles, 23-17 (NY) OT
1989—Eagles, 21-19 (P)
 Eagles, 24-17 (NY)
1990—Giants, 27-20 (P)
 Eagles, 31-13 (NY)
1991—Eagles, 30-7 (P)
 Eagles, 19-14 (NY)
1992—Eagles, 47-34 (NY)
 Eagles, 20-10 (P)
1993—Giants, 21-10 (NY)
 Giants, 7-3 (P)
1994—Giants, 28-23 (NY)
 Giants, 16-13 (P)
1995—Eagles, 17-14 (NY)
 Eagles, 28-19 (P)
1996—Eagles, 19-10 (NY)
 Eagles, 24-0 (P)
1997—Giants, 31-17 (NY)
 Giants, 31-21 (P)
1998—Giants, 20-0 (NY)
 Giants, 20-10 (P)
1999—Giants, 16-15 (NY)
 Giants, 23-17 (P) OT

2000—Giants, 33-18 (P)
 Giants, 24-7 (NY)
 **Giants, 20-10 (NY)
2001—Eagles, 10-9 (NY)
 Eagles, 24-21 (P)
2002—Eagles, 17-3 (P)
 Giants, 10-7 (NY) OT
2003—Eagles, 14-10 (NY)
 Eagles, 28-10 (P)
2004—Eagles, 31-17 (P)
 Eagles, 27-6 (NY)
2005—Giants, 27-17 (NY)
 Giants, 26-23 (P) OT
2006—Giants, 30-24 (P) OT
 Eagles, 36-22 (NY)
 *Eagles, 23-20 (P)
(RS Pts.—Giants 2,724, Eagles 2,600)
(PS Pts.—Giants 67, Eagles 54)
NFC First-Round Playoff
**NFC Divisional Playoff*
N.Y. GIANTS vs. *PITTSBURGH
RS: Giants lead series, 43-28-3
1933—Giants, 23-2 (P)
 Giants, 27-3 (NY)
1934—Giants, 14-12 (P)
 Giants, 17-7 (NY)
1935—Giants, 42-7 (P)
 Giants, 13-0 (NY)
1936—Pirates, 10-7 (P)
1937—Giants, 10-7 (P)
 Giants, 17-0 (NY)
1938—Giants, 27-14 (P)
 Pirates, 13-10 (NY)
1939—Giants, 14-7 (P)
 Giants, 23-7 (NY)
1940—Tie, 10-10 (P)
 Giants, 12-0 (NY)
1941—Giants, 37-10 (P)
 Giants, 28-7 (NY)
1942—Steelers, 13-10 (P)
 Steelers, 17-9 (NY)
1945—Giants, 34-6 (P)
 Steelers, 21-7 (NY)
1946—Giants, 17-14 (P)
 Giants, 7-0 (NY)
1947—Steelers, 38-21 (NY)
 Steelers, 24-7 (P)
1948—Giants, 34-27 (NY)
 Steelers, 38-28 (P)
1949—Steelers, 28-7 (P)
 Steelers, 21-17 (NY)
1950—Giants, 18-7 (P)
 Steelers, 17-6 (NY)
1951—Tie, 13-13 (P)
 Giants, 14-0 (NY)
1952—Steelers, 63-7 (P)
1953—Steelers, 24-14 (P)
 Steelers, 14-10 (NY)
1954—Giants, 30-6 (P)
 Giants, 24-3 (NY)
1955—Steelers, 30-23 (P)
 Steelers, 19-17 (NY)
1956—Giants, 38-10 (NY)
 Giants, 17-14 (P)
1957—Giants, 35-0 (NY)
 Steelers, 21-10 (P)
1958—Giants, 17-6 (NY)
 Steelers, 31-10 (P)
1959—Giants, 21-16 (P)
 Steelers, 14-9 (NY)

1960—Giants, 19-17 (P)
Giants, 27-24 (NY)
1961—Giants, 17-14 (P)
Giants, 42-21 (NY)
1962—Giants, 31-27 (P)
Steelers, 20-17 (NY)
1963—Steelers, 31-0 (P)
Giants, 33-17 (NY)
1964—Steelers, 27-24 (P)
Steelers, 44-17 (NY)
1965—Giants, 23-13 (P)
Giants, 35-10 (NY)
1966—Tie, 34-34 (P)
Steelers, 47-28 (NY)
1967—Giants, 27-24 (P)
Giants, 28-20 (NY)
1968—Giants, 34-20 (P)
1969—Giants, 10-7 (NY)
Giants, 21-17 (P)
1971—Steelers, 17-13 (P)
1976—Steelers, 27-0 (NY)
1985—Giants, 28-10 (NY)
1991—Giants, 23-20 (P)
1994—Steelers, 10-6 (NY)
2000—Giants, 30-10 (NY)
2004—Steelers, 33-30 (NY)
(RS Pts.—Giants 1,459, Steelers 1,232)
*Steelers known as Pirates prior to 1941
N.Y. GIANTS vs. *ST. LOUIS
RS: Rams lead series, 25-12
PS: Series tied, 1-1
1938—Giants, 28-0 (NY)
1940—Rams, 13-0 (NY)
1941—Giants, 49-14 (NY)
1945—Rams, 21-17 (NY)
1946—Rams, 31-21 (NY)
1947—Rams, 34-10 (LA)
1948—Rams, 52-37 (NY)
1953—Rams, 21-7 (LA)
1954—Rams, 17-16 (NY)
1959—Giants, 23-21 (LA)
1961—Giants, 24-14 (NY)
1966—Rams, 55-14 (LA)
1968—Rams, 24-21 (LA)
1970—Rams, 31-3 (NY)
1973—Rams, 40-6 (LA)
1976—Rams, 24-10 (LA)
1978—Rams, 20-17 (NY)
1979—Giants, 20-14 (LA)
1980—Rams, 28-7 (NY)
1981—Giants, 10-7 (NY)
1983—Rams, 16-6 (NY)
1984—Rams, 33-12 (LA)
**Giants, 16-13 (LA)
1985—Giants, 24-19 (NY)
1988—Rams, 45-31 (NY)
1989—Rams, 31-10 (LA)
***Rams, 19-13 (NY) OT
1990—Giants, 31-7 (LA)
1991—Rams, 19-13 (NY)
1992—Rams, 38-17 (LA)
1993—Giants, 20-10 (NY)
1994—Rams, 17-10 (LA)
1997—Rams, 13-3 (StL)
1999—Rams, 31-10 (StL)
2000—Rams, 38-24 (NY)
2001—Rams, 15-14 (StL)
2002—Giants, 26-21 (StL)
2003—Giants, 23-13 (NY)
2005—Giants, 44-24 (NY)

(RS Pts.—Rams 871, Giants 658)
(PS Pts.—Rams 32, Giants 29)
*Franchise in Los Angeles prior to 1995
and in Cleveland prior to 1946
**NFC First-Round Playoff
***NFC Divisional Playoff
N.Y. GIANTS vs. SAN DIEGO
RS: Giants lead series, 5-4
1971—Giants, 35-17 (NY)
1975—Giants, 35-24 (NY)
1980—Chargers, 44-7 (SD)
1983—Chargers, 41-34 (NY)
1986—Giants, 20-7 (NY)
1989—Giants, 20-13 (SD)
1995—Chargers, 27-17 (NY)
1998—Giants, 34-16 (SD)
2005—Chargers, 45-23 (SD)
(RS Pts.—Chargers 234, Giants 225)
N.Y. GIANTS vs. SAN FRANCISCO
RS: 49ers lead series, 13-12
PS: 49ers lead series, 4-3
1952—Giants, 23-14 (NY)
1956—Giants, 38-21 (SF)
1957—49ers, 27-17 (NY)
1960—Giants, 21-19 (SF)
1963—Giants, 48-14 (NY)
1968—49ers, 26-10 (NY)
1972—Giants, 23-17 (SF)
1975—Giants, 26-23 (SF)
1977—Giants, 20-17 (NY)
1978—Giants, 27-10 (NY)
1979—Giants, 32-16 (NY)
1980—49ers, 12-0 (SF)
1981—49ers, 17-10 (SF)
*49ers, 38-24 (SF)
1984—49ers, 31-10 (NY)
*49ers, 21-10 (SF)
1985—*Giants, 17-3 (NY)
1986—Giants, 21-17 (SF)
*Giants, 49-3 (NY)
1987—49ers, 41-21 (NY)
1988—49ers, 20-17 (NY)
1989—49ers, 34-24 (SF)
1990—49ers, 7-3 (SF)
***Giants, 15-13 (SF)
1991—Giants, 16-14 (NY)
1992—49ers, 31-14 (NY)
1993—*49ers, 44-3 (SF)
1995—49ers, 20-6 (SF)
1998—49ers, 31-7 (SF)
2002—Giants, 16-13 (NY)
**49ers, 39-38 (SF)
2005—Giants, 24-6 (SF)
(RS Pts.—49ers 501, Giants 471)
(PS Pts.—49ers 161, Giants 156)
*NFC Divisional Playoff
**NFC First-Round Playoff
***NFC Championship
N.Y. GIANTS vs. SEATTLE
RS: Giants lead series, 7-5
1976—Giants, 28-16 (NY)
1980—Giants, 27-21 (S)
1981—Giants, 32-0 (S)
1983—Seahawks, 17-12 (NY)
1986—Seahawks, 17-12 (S)
1989—Giants, 15-3 (NY)
1992—Giants, 23-10 (NY)
1995—Seahawks, 30-28 (S)
2001—Giants, 27-24 (NY)
2002—Giants, 9-6 (NY)

2005—Seahawks, 24-21 (S) OT
2006—Seahawks, 42-30 (S)
(RS Pts.—Giants 264, Seahawks 210)
N.Y. GIANTS vs. TAMPA BAY
RS: Giants lead series, 10-6
1977—Giants, 10-0 (TB)
1978—Giants, 19-13 (TB)
Giants, 17-14 (NY)
1979—Giants, 17-14 (NY)
Buccaneers, 31-3 (TB)
1980—Buccaneers, 30-13 (TB)
1984—Giants, 17-14 (NY)
Buccaneers, 20-17 (TB)
1985—Giants, 22-20 (NY)
1991—Giants, 21-14 (TB)
1993—Giants, 23-7 (TB)
1997—Buccaneers, 20-8 (NY)
1998—Buccaneers, 20-3 (TB)
1999—Giants, 17-13 (TB)
2003—Buccaneers, 19-13 (TB)
2006—Giants, 17-3 (NY)
(RS Pts.—Buccaneers 252, Giants 237)
N.Y. GIANTS vs. *TENNESSEE
RS: Giants lead series, 5-4
1973—Giants, 34-14 (NY)
1982—Giants, 17-14 (NY)
1985—Giants, 35-14 (H)
1991—Giants, 24-20 (NY)
1994—Giants, 13-10 (H)
1997—Oilers, 10-6 (T)
2000—Titans, 28-14 (T)
2002—Titans, 32-29 (NY) OT
2006—Titans, 24-21 (T)
(RS Pts.—Giants 193, Titans 166)
*Franchise in Houston prior to 1997;
known as Oilers prior to 1999
N.Y. GIANTS vs. *WASHINGTON
RS: Giants lead series, 84-60-4
PS: Series tied, 1-1
1932—Braves, 14-6 (B)
Tie, 0-0 (NY)
1933—Redskins, 21-20 (B)
Giants, 7-0 (NY)
1934—Giants, 16-13 (B)
Giants, 3-0 (NY)
1935—Giants, 20-12 (B)
Giants, 17-6 (NY)
1936—Giants, 7-0 (B)
Redskins, 14-0 (NY)
1937—Redskins, 13-3 (W)
Redskins, 49-14 (NY)
1938—Giants, 10-7 (W)
Giants, 36-0 (NY)
1939—Tie, 0-0 (W)
Giants, 9-7 (NY)
1940—Redskins, 21-7 (W)
Giants, 21-7 (NY)
1941—Giants, 17-10 (W)
Giants, 20-13 (NY)
1942—Giants, 14-7 (W)
Redskins, 14-7 (NY)
1943—Giants, 14-10 (NY)
Giants, 31-7 (W)
**Redskins, 28-0 (NY)
1944—Giants, 16-13 (NY)
Giants, 31-0 (W)
1945—Redskins, 24-14 (NY)
Redskins, 17-0 (W)
1946—Redskins, 24-14 (W)
Giants, 31-0 (NY)

1947—Redskins, 28-20 (W)
    Giants, 35-10 (NY)
1948—Redskins, 41-10 (W)
    Redskins, 28-21 (NY)
1949—Giants, 45-35 (W)
    Giants, 23-7 (NY)
1950—Giants, 21-17 (W)
    Giants, 24-21 (NY)
1951—Giants, 35-14 (W)
    Giants, 28-14 (NY)
1952—Giants, 14-10 (W)
    Redskins, 27-17 (NY)
1953—Redskins, 13-9 (W)
    Redskins, 24-21 (NY)
1954—Giants, 51-21 (W)
    Giants, 24-7 (NY)
1955—Giants, 35-7 (NY)
    Giants, 27-20 (W)
1956—Redskins, 33-7 (W)
    Giants, 28-14 (NY)
1957—Giants, 24-20 (W)
    Redskins, 31-14 (NY)
1958—Giants, 21-14 (W)
    Giants, 30-0 (NY)
1959—Giants, 45-14 (NY)
    Giants, 24-10 (W)
1960—Tie, 24-24 (NY)
    Giants, 17-3 (W)
1961—Giants, 24-21 (W)
    Giants, 53-0 (NY)
1962—Giants, 49-34 (NY)
    Giants, 42-24 (W)
1963—Giants, 24-14 (W)
    Giants, 44-14 (NY)
1964—Giants, 13-10 (NY)
    Redskins, 36-21 (W)
1965—Redskins, 23-7 (NY)
    Giants, 27-10 (W)
1966—Giants, 13-10 (NY)
    Redskins, 72-41 (W)
1967—Redskins, 38-34 (W)
1968—Giants, 48-21 (NY)
    Giants, 13-10 (W)
1969—Redskins, 20-14 (W)
1970—Giants, 35-33 (NY)
    Giants, 27-24 (W)
1971—Redskins, 30-3 (NY)
    Redskins, 23-7 (W)
1972—Redskins, 23-16 (NY)
    Redskins, 27-13 (W)
1973—Redskins, 21-3 (New Haven)
    Redskins, 27-24 (W)
1974—Redskins, 13-10 (New Haven)
    Redskins, 24-3 (W)
1975—Redskins, 49-13 (W)
    Redskins, 21-13 (NY)
1976—Redskins, 19-17 (W)
    Giants, 12-9 (NY)
1977—Giants, 20-17 (NY)
    Giants, 17-6 (W)
1978—Giants, 17-6 (NY)
    Redskins, 16-13 (W) OT
1979—Redskins, 27-0 (W)
    Giants, 14-6 (NY)
1980—Redskins, 23-21 (NY)
    Redskins, 16-13 (W)
1981—Giants, 17-7 (W)
    Redskins, 30-27 (NY) OT
1982—Redskins, 27-17 (NY)
    Redskins, 15-14 (W)

1983—Redskins, 33-17 (NY)
    Redskins, 31-22 (W)
1984—Redskins, 30-14 (W)
    Giants, 37-13 (NY)
1985—Giants, 17-3 (NY)
    Redskins, 23-21 (W)
1986—Giants, 27-20 (NY)
    Giants, 24-14 (W)
    ***Giants, 17-0 (NY)
1987—Redskins, 38-12 (NY)
    Redskins, 23-19 (W)
1988—Giants, 27-20 (NY)
    Giants, 24-23 (W)
1989—Giants, 27-24 (W)
    Giants, 20-17 (NY)
1990—Giants, 24-20 (W)
    Giants, 21-10 (NY)
1991—Redskins, 17-13 (NY)
    Redskins, 34-17 (W)
1992—Giants, 24-7 (W)
    Redskins, 28-10 (NY)
1993—Giants, 41-7 (W)
    Giants, 20-6 (NY)
1994—Giants, 31-23 (NY)
    Giants, 21-19 (W)
1995—Giants, 24-15 (W)
    Giants, 20-13 (NY)
1996—Redskins, 31-10 (NY)
    Redskins, 31-21 (W)
1997—Tie, 7-7 (W) OT
    Giants, 30-10 (NY)
1998—Giants, 31-24 (NY)
    Redskins, 21-14 (W)
1999—Redskins, 50-21 (NY)
    Redskins, 23-13 (W)
2000—Redskins, 16-6 (NY)
    Giants, 9-7 (W)
2001—Giants, 23-9 (NY)
    Redskins, 35-21 (W)
2002—Giants, 19-17 (NY)
    Giants, 27-21 (W)
2003—Giants, 24-21 (W) OT
    Redskins, 20-7 (NY)
2004—Giants, 20-14 (NY)
    Redskins, 31-7 (W)
2005—Giants, 36-0 (NY)
    Redskins, 35-20 (W)
2006—Giants, 19-3 (NY)
    Giants, 34-28 (W)
(RS Pts.—Giants 2,945, Redskins 2,691)
(PS Pts.—Redskins 28, Giants 17)
*Franchise in Boston prior to 1937 and
known as Braves prior to 1933
**Division Playoff
***NFC Championship

N.Y. JETS vs. ARIZONA
RS: Jets lead series, 4-2;
See Arizona vs. N.Y. Jets
N.Y. JETS vs. ATLANTA
RS: Falcons lead series, 5-4;
See Atlanta vs. N.Y. Jets
N.Y. JETS vs BALTIMORE
RS: Ravens lead series, 4-1;
See Baltimore vs. N.Y. Jets
N.Y. JETS vs. BUFFALO
RS: Bills lead series, 50-42
PS: Bills lead series, 1-0;
See Buffalo vs. N.Y. Jets
N.Y. JETS vs. CAROLINA

RS: Series tied, 2-2;
See Carolina vs. N.Y. Jets
N.Y. JETS vs. CHICAGO
RS: Bears lead series, 6-3;
See Chicago vs. N.Y. Jets
N.Y. JETS vs. CINCINNATI
RS: Jets lead series, 12-6
PS: Jets lead series, 1-0;
See Cincinnati vs. N.Y. Jets
N.Y. JETS vs. CLEVELAND
RS: Browns lead series, 11-7
PS: Browns lead series, 1-0;
See Cleveland vs. N.Y. Jets
N.Y. JETS vs. DALLAS
RS: Cowboys lead series, 6-2;
See Dallas vs. N.Y. Jets
N.Y. JETS vs. DENVER
RS: Broncos lead series, 15-14-1
PS: Broncos lead series, 1-0;
See Denver vs. N.Y. Jets
N.Y. JETS vs. DETROIT
RS: Lions lead series, 6-5;
See Detroit vs. N.Y. Jets
N.Y. JETS vs. GREEN BAY
RS: Jets lead series, 8-2;
See Green Bay vs. N.Y. Jets
N.Y. JETS vs. HOUSTON
RS: Jets lead series, 3-0;
See Houston vs. N.Y. Jets
N.Y. JETS vs. INDIANAPOLIS
RS: Colts lead series, 40-25
PS: Jets lead series, 2-0;
See Indianapolis vs. N.Y. Jets
N.Y. JETS vs. JACKSONVILLE
RS: Jaguars lead series, 5-2
PS: Jets lead series, 1-0;
See Jacksonville vs. N.Y. Jets
N.Y. JETS vs. KANSAS CITY
RS: Chiefs lead series, 16-14-1
PS: Series tied, 1-1;
See Kansas City vs. N.Y. Jets
N.Y. JETS vs. MIAMI
RS: Jets lead series, 43-38-1
PS: Dolphins lead series, 1-0;
See Miami vs. N.Y. Jets
N.Y. JETS vs. MINNESOTA
RS: Jets lead series, 7-1;
See Minnesota vs. N.Y. Jets
N.Y. JETS vs. NEW ENGLAND
RS: Jets lead series, 48-44-1
PS: Patriots lead series, 2-0;
See New England vs. N.Y. Jets
N.Y. JETS vs. NEW ORLEANS
RS: Series tied, 5-5;
See New Orleans vs. N.Y. Jets
N.Y. JETS vs. N.Y. GIANTS
RS: Giants lead series, 6-4;
See N.Y. Giants vs. N.Y. Jets
*****N.Y. JETS vs. **OAKLAND**
RS: Raiders lead series, 19-14-2
PS: Series tied, 2-2
1960—Raiders, 28-27 (NY)
    Titans, 31-28 (O)
1961—Titans, 14-6 (O)
    Titans, 23-12 (NY)
1962—Titans, 28-17 (O)
    Titans, 31-21 (NY)
1963—Jets, 10-7 (NY)
    Raiders, 49-26 (O)
1964—Jets, 35-13 (NY)

Raiders, 35-26 (O)
1965—Tie, 24-24 (NY)
    Raiders, 24-14 (O)
1966—Raiders, 24-21 (NY)
    Tie, 28-28 (O)
1967—Jets, 27-14 (NY)
    Raiders, 38-29 (O)
1968—Raiders, 43-32 (O)
    ***Jets, 27-23 (NY)
1969—Raiders, 27-14 (NY)
1970—Raiders, 14-13 (NY)
1972—Raiders, 24-16 (O)
1977—Raiders, 28-27 (NY)
1979—Jets, 28-19 (NY)
1982—****Jets, 17-14 (LA)
1985—Raiders, 31-0 (LA)
1989—Raiders, 14-7 (NY)
1993—Raiders, 24-20 (LA)
1995—Raiders, 47-10 (NY)
1996—Raiders, 34-13 (NY)
1997—Jets 23-22 (NY)
1999—Raiders, 24-23 (O)
2000—Raiders, 31-7 (O)
2001—Jets, 24-22 (O)
    *****Raiders, 38-24 (O)
2002—Raiders, 26-20 (O)
    ****Raiders, 30-10 (O)
2003—Jets, 27-24 (O) OT
2005—Jets, 26-10 (NY)
2006—Jets, 23-3 (NY)
(RS Pts.—Raiders 835, Jets 747)
(PS Pts.—Raiders 105, Jets 78)
*Jets known as Titans prior to 1963
**Franchise in Los Angeles from
1982-1994
***AFL Championship
****AFC Second-Round Playoff
*****AFC First-Round Playoff
N.Y. JETS vs. PHILADELPHIA
RS: Eagles lead series, 7-0
1973—Eagles, 24-23 (P)
1977—Eagles, 27-0 (P)
1978—Eagles, 17-9 (P)
1987—Eagles, 38-27 (NY)
1993—Eagles, 35-30 (NY)
1996—Eagles, 21-20 (NY)
2003—Eagles, 24-17 (P)
(RS Pts.—Eagles 186, Jets 126)
N.Y. JETS vs. PITTSBURGH
RS: Steelers lead series, 15-2
PS: Steelers lead series, 1-0
1970—Steelers, 21-17 (P)
1973—Steelers, 26-14 (P)
1975—Steelers, 20-7 (NY)
1977—Steelers, 23-20 (NY)
1978—Steelers, 28-17 (NY)
1981—Steelers, 38-10 (P)
1983—Steelers, 34-7 (NY)
1984—Steelers, 23-17 (NY)
1986—Steelers, 45-24 (NY)
1988—Jets, 24-20 (NY)
1989—Steelers, 13-0 (NY)
1990—Steelers, 24-7 (NY)
1992—Steelers, 27-10 (P)
2000—Steelers, 20-3 (NY)
2001—Steelers, 18-7 (P)
2003—Jets, 6-0 (NY)
2004—Steelers, 17-6 (P)
    *Steelers, 20-17 (P) OT
(RS Pts.—Steelers 397, Jets 196)

(PS Pts.—Steelers 20, Jets 17)
*AFC Divisional Playoff
N.Y. JETS vs. *ST. LOUIS
RS: Rams lead series, 9-2
1970—Jets, 31-20 (LA)
1974—Rams, 20-13 (NY)
1980—Rams, 38-13 (LA)
1983—Jets, 27-24 (NY) OT
1986—Rams, 17-3 (NY)
1989—Rams, 38-14 (LA)
1992—Rams, 18-10 (LA)
1995—Rams, 23-20 (NY)
1998—Rams, 30-10 (StL)
2001—Rams, 34-14 (NY)
2004—Rams, 32-29 (StL) OT
(RS Pts.—Rams 294, Jets 184)
*Franchise in Los Angeles prior to 1995
N.Y. JETS vs. **SAN DIEGO
RS: Chargers lead series, 18-11-1
PS: Jets lead series, 1-0
1960—Chargers, 21-7 (NY)
    Chargers, 50-43 (LA)
1961—Chargers, 25-10 (NY)
    Chargers, 48-13 (SD)
1962—Chargers, 40-14 (SD)
    Titans, 23-3 (NY)
1963—Chargers, 24-20 (SD)
    Chargers, 53-7 (NY)
1964—Tie, 17-17 (NY)
    Chargers, 38-3 (SD)
1965—Chargers, 34-9 (NY)
    Chargers, 38-7 (SD)
1966—Jets, 17-16 (NY)
    Chargers, 42-27 (SD)
1967—Jets, 42-31 (SD)
1968—Jets, 23-20 (NY)
    Jets, 37-15 (SD)
1969—Chargers, 34-27 (SD)
1971—Chargers, 49-21 (SD)
1974—Jets, 27-14 (NY)
1975—Chargers, 24-16 (SD)
1983—Jets, 41-29 (SD)
1989—Jets, 20-17 (SD)
1990—Chargers, 39-3 (NY)
    Chargers, 38-17 (SD)
1991—Jets, 24-3 (NY)
1994—Chargers, 21-6 (NY)
2002—Jets, 44-13 (SD)
2004—Jets, 34-28 (SD)
    ***Jets, 20-17 (SD) OT
2005—Chargers, 31-26 (NY)
(RS Pts.—Chargers 855, Jets 625)
(PS Pts.—Jets 20, Chargers 17)
*Jets known as Titans prior to 1963
**Franchise in Los Angeles prior to 1961
***AFC First-Round Playoff
N.Y. JETS vs. SAN FRANCISCO
RS: 49ers lead series, 8-2
1971—49ers, 24-21 (NY)
1976—49ers, 17-6 (SF)
1980—49ers, 37-27 (NY)
1983—49ers, 27-13 (SF)
1986—49ers, 24-10 (SF)
1989—49ers, 23-10 (NY)
1992—49ers, 31-14 (NY)
1998—49ers, 36-30 (SF) OT
2001—49ers, 19-17 (NY)
2004—Jets, 22-14 (NY)
(RS Pts.—49ers 238, Jets 184)
N.Y. JETS vs. SEATTLE

RS: Series tied, 8-8
1977—Seahawks, 17-0 (NY)
1978—Seahawks, 24-17 (NY)
1979—Seahawks, 30-7 (S)
1980—Seahawks, 27-17 (NY)
1981—Seahawks, 19-3 (NY)
    Seahawks, 27-23 (S)
1983—Seahawks, 17-10 (NY)
1985—Jets, 17-14 (NY)
1986—Jets, 38-7 (S)
1987—Jets, 30-14 (NY)
1991—Seahawks, 20-13 (S)
1995—Jets, 16-10 (S)
1997—Jets, 41-3 (S)
1998—Jets, 32-31 (NY)
1999—Jets, 19-9 (NY)
2004—Jets, 37-14 (NY)
(RS Pts.—Jets 320, Seahawks 283)
N.Y. JETS vs. TAMPA BAY
RS: Jets lead series, 8-1
1976—Jets, 34-0 (NY)
1982—Jets, 32-17 (NY)
1984—Buccaneers, 41-21 (TB)
1985—Jets, 62-28 (NY)
1990—Jets, 16-14 (TB)
1991—Jets, 16-13 (NY)
1997—Jets, 31-0 (NY)
2000—Jets, 21-17 (TB)
2005—Jets, 14-12 (NY)
(RS Pts.—Jets 247, Buccaneers 142)
N.Y. JETS vs. **TENNESSEE
RS: Titans lead series, 20-15-1
PS: Titans lead series, 1-0
1960—Jets, 27-21 (H)
    Oilers, 42-28 (NY)
1961—Oilers, 49-13 (H)
    Oilers, 48-21 (NY)
1962—Oilers, 56-17 (H)
    Oilers, 44-10 (NY)
1963—Jets, 24-17 (NY)
    Oilers, 31-27 (H)
1964—Jets, 24-21 (NY)
    Oilers, 33-17 (H)
1965—Oilers, 27-21 (H)
    Jets, 41-14 (NY)
1966—Jets, 52-13 (NY)
    Oilers, 24-0 (H)
1967—Tie, 28-28 (NY)
1968—Jets, 20-14 (H)
    Jets, 26-7 (H)
1969—Jets, 26-17 (NY)
    Jets, 34-26 (H)
1972—Oilers, 26-20 (H)
1974—Oilers, 27-22 (NY)
1977—Oilers, 20-0 (H)
1979—Oilers, 27-24 (H) OT
1980—Jets, 31-28 (NY) OT
1981—Jets, 33-17 (NY)
1984—Oilers, 31-20 (H)
1988—Jets, 45-3 (NY)
1990—Jets, 17-12 (H)
1991—Oilers, 23-20 (NY)
    ***Oilers, 17-10 (H)
1993—Oilers, 24-0 (H)
1994—Oilers, 24-10 (H)
1995—Oilers, 23-6 (H)
1996—Oilers, 35-10 (NY)
1998—Jets, 24-3 (T)
2003—Jets, 24-17 (NY)
2006—Jets, 23-16 (T)

(RS Pts.—Titans 894, Jets 779)
(PS Pts.—Titans 17, Jets 10)
*Jets known as Titans prior to 1963
**Franchise in Houston prior to 1997;
known as Oilers prior to 1999
***AFC First-Round Playoff

N.Y. JETS vs. WASHINGTON
RS: Redskins lead series, 7-1
1972—Redskins, 35-17 (NY)
1976—Redskins, 37-16 (NY)
1978—Redskins, 23-3 (W)
1987—Redskins, 17-16 (W)
1993—Jets, 3-0 (W)
1996—Redskins, 31-16 (W)
1999—Redskins, 27-20 (NY)
2003—Redskins, 16-13 (W)
(RS Pts.—Redskins 186, Jets 104)

OAKLAND vs. ARIZONA
RS: Raiders lead series, 5-2;
See Arizona vs. Oakland
OAKLAND vs. ATLANTA
RS: Raiders lead series, 7-4;
See Atlanta vs. Oakland
OAKLAND vs. BALTIMORE
RS: Ravens lead series, 3-1
PS: Ravens lead series, 1-0;
See Baltimore vs. Oakland
OAKLAND vs. BUFFALO
RS: Raiders lead series, 19-15
PS: Bills lead series, 2-0;
See Buffalo vs. Oakland
OAKLAND vs CAROLINA
RS: Raiders lead series, 2-1;
See Carolina vs Oakland
OAKLAND vs. CHICAGO
RS: Raiders lead series, 6-5;
See Chicago vs. Oakland
OAKLAND vs. CINCINNATI
RS: Raiders lead series, 17-8
PS: Raiders lead series, 2-0;
See Cincinnati vs. Oakland
OAKLAND vs. CLEVELAND
RS: Raiders lead series, 9-7
PS: Raiders lead series, 2-0;
See Cleveland vs. Oakland
OAKLAND vs. DALLAS
RS: Raiders lead series, 6-3;
See Dallas vs. Oakland
OAKLAND vs. DENVER
RS: Raiders lead series, 53-38-2
PS: Series tied, 1-1;
See Denver vs. Oakland
OAKLAND vs. DETROIT
RS: Raiders lead series, 6-3;
See Detroit vs. Oakland
OAKLAND vs. GREEN BAY
RS: Raiders lead series, 5-4
PS: Packers lead series, 1-0;
See Green Bay vs. Oakland
OAKLAND vs. HOUSTON
RS: Texans lead series, 2-0;
See Houston vs. Oakland
OAKLAND vs. INDIANAPOLIS
RS: Raiders lead series, 7-3
PS: Series tied, 1-1;
See Indianapolis vs. Oakland
OAKLAND vs. JACKSONVILLE
RS: Jaguars lead series, 2-1;
See Jacksonville vs. Oakland

OAKLAND vs. KANSAS CITY
RS: Chiefs lead series, 49-42-2
PS: Chiefs lead series, 2-1;
See Kansas City vs. Oakland
OAKLAND vs. MIAMI
RS: Raiders lead series, 15-11-1
PS: Raiders lead series, 3-1;
See Miami vs. Oakland
OAKLAND vs. MINNESOTA
RS: Raiders lead series, 8-3
PS: Raiders lead series, 1-0;
See Minnesota vs. Oakland
OAKLAND vs. NEW ENGLAND
RS: Raiders lead series, 14-13-1
PS: Patriots lead series, 2-1;
See New England vs. Oakland
OAKLAND vs. NEW ORLEANS
RS: Raiders lead series, 5-4-1;
See New Orleans vs. Oakland
OAKLAND vs. N.Y. GIANTS
RS: Raiders lead series, 7-3;
See N.Y. Giants vs. Oakland
OAKLAND vs. N.Y. JETS
RS: Raiders lead series, 19-14-2
PS: Series tied, 2-2;
See N.Y. Jets vs. Oakland
*OAKLAND vs. PHILADELPHIA
RS: Eagles lead series, 5-4
PS: Raiders lead series, 1-0
1971—Raiders, 34-10 (O)
1976—Raiders, 26-7 (P)
1980—Eagles, 10-7 (P)
    **Raiders, 27-10 (New Orleans)
1986—Eagles, 33-27 (LA) OT
1989—Eagles, 10-7 (P)
1992—Eagles, 31-10 (P)
1995—Raiders, 48-17 (O)
2001—Raiders, 20-10 (P)
2005—Eagles, 23-20 (P)
(RS Pts.—Raiders 199, Eagles 151)
(PS Pts.—Raiders 27, Eagles 10)
*Franchise in Los Angeles from 1982-1994
**Super Bowl XV
*OAKLAND vs. PITTSBURGH
RS: Raiders lead series, 9-8
PS: Series tied, 3-3
1970—Raiders, 31-14 (O)
1972—Steelers, 34-28 (P)
    **Steelers, 13-7 (P)
1973—Steelers, 17-9 (O)
    **Raiders, 33-14 (O)
1974—Raiders, 17-0 (P)
    ***Steelers, 24-13 (O)
1975—***Steelers, 16-10 (P)
1976—Raiders, 31-28 (O)
    ***Raiders, 24-7 (O)
1977—Raiders, 16-7 (P)
1980—Raiders, 45-34 (P)
1981—Raiders, 30-27 (O)
1983—**Raiders, 38-10 (LA)
1984—Steelers, 13-7 (LA)
1990—Raiders, 20-3 (LA)
1994—Steelers, 21-3 (LA)
1995—Steelers, 29-10 (O)
2000—Steelers, 21-20 (P)
2002—Raiders, 30-17 (O)
2003—Steelers, 27-7 (P)
2004—Steelers, 24-21 (P)
2006—Raiders, 20-13 (O)
(RS Pts.—Raiders 345, Steelers 329)

(PS Pts.—Raiders 125, Steelers 84)
*Franchise in Los Angeles from 1982-1994
**AFC Divisional Playoff
***AFC Championship
*OAKLAND vs. **ST. LOUIS
RS: Raiders lead series, 7-4
1972—Raiders, 45-17 (O)
1977—Rams, 20-14 (LA)
1979—Raiders, 24-17 (LA)
1982—Raiders, 37-31 (LA Raiders)
1985—Raiders, 16-6 (LA Rams)
1988—Raiders, 22-17 (LA Raiders)
1991—Raiders, 20-17 (LA Raiders)
1994—Raiders, 20-17 (LA Rams)
1997—Raiders, 35-17 (O)
2002—Rams, 28-13 (StL)
2006—Rams, 20-0 (O)
(RS Pts.—Raiders 241, Rams 212)
*Franchise in Los Angeles from 1982-1994
**Franchise in Los Angeles prior to 1995
*OAKLAND vs. **SAN DIEGO
RS: Raiders lead series, 54-38-2
PS: Raiders lead series, 1-0
1960—Chargers, 52-28 (LA)
    Chargers, 41-17 (O)
1961—Chargers, 44-0 (SD)
    Chargers, 41-10 (O)
1962—Chargers, 42-33 (O)
    Chargers, 31-21 (SD)
1963—Raiders, 34-33 (SD)
    Raiders, 41-27 (O)
1964—Chargers, 31-17 (SD)
    Raiders, 21-20 (O)
1965—Chargers, 17-6 (O)
    Chargers, 24-14 (SD)
1966—Chargers, 29-20 (O)
    Raiders, 41-19 (SD)
1967—Raiders, 51-10 (O)
    Raiders, 41-21 (SD)
1968—Chargers, 23-14 (O)
    Raiders, 34-27 (SD)
1969—Raiders, 24-12 (SD)
    Raiders, 21-16 (O)
1970—Tie, 27-27 (SD)
    Raiders, 20-17 (O)
1971—Raiders, 34-0 (SD)
    Raiders, 34-33 (O)
1972—Tie, 17-17 (O)
    Raiders, 21-19 (SD)
1973—Raiders, 27-17 (SD)
    Raiders, 31-3 (O)
1974—Raiders, 14-10 (SD)
    Raiders, 17-10 (O)
1975—Raiders, 6-0 (SD)
    Raiders, 25-0 (O)
1976—Raiders, 27-17 (SD)
    Raiders, 24-0 (O)
1977—Raiders, 24-0 (O)
    Chargers, 12-7 (SD)
1978—Raiders, 21-20 (SD)
    Chargers, 27-23 (O)
1979—Chargers, 30-10 (SD)
    Raiders, 45-22 (O)
1980—Chargers, 30-24 (SD) OT
    Raiders, 38-24 (O)
    ***Raiders, 34-27 (SD)
1981—Chargers, 55-21 (O)
    Chargers, 23-10 (SD)
1982—Raiders, 28-24 (LA)
    Raiders, 41-34 (SD)

1983—Raiders, 42-10 (SD)
    Raiders, 30-14 (LA)
1984—Raiders, 33-30 (LA)
    Raiders, 44-37 (SD)
1985—Raiders, 34-21 (LA)
    Chargers, 40-34 (SD) OT
1986—Raiders, 17-13 (LA)
    Raiders, 37-31 (SD) OT
1987—Chargers, 23-17 (LA)
    Chargers, 16-14 (SD)
1988—Raiders, 24-13 (LA)
    Raiders, 13-3 (SD)
1989—Raiders, 40-14 (LA)
    Chargers, 14-12 (SD)
1990—Raiders, 24-9 (SD)
    Raiders, 17-12 (LA)
1991—Chargers, 21-13 (LA)
    Raiders, 9-7 (SD)
1992—Chargers, 27-3 (SD)
    Chargers, 36-14 (LA)
1993—Chargers, 30-23 (LA)
    Raiders, 12-7 (SD)
1994—Chargers, 26-24 (LA)
    Raiders, 24-17 (SD)
1995—Raiders, 17-7 (O)
    Chargers, 12-6 (SD)
1996—Chargers, 40-34 (O)
    Raiders, 23-14 (SD)
1997—Chargers, 25-10 (O)
    Raiders, 38-13 (SD)
1998—Raiders, 7-6 (O)
    Raiders, 17-10 (SD)
1999—Raiders, 28-9 (O)
    Chargers, 23-20 (SD)
2000—Raiders, 9-6 (O)
    Raiders, 15-13 (SD)
2001—Raiders, 34-24 (O)
    Raiders, 13-6 (SD)
2002—Chargers, 27-21 (O) OT
    Raiders, 27-7 (SD)
2003—Raiders, 34-31 (O) OT
    Chargers, 21-14 (SD)
2004—Chargers, 42-14 (SD)
    Chargers, 23-17 (O)
2005—Chargers, 27-14 (O)
    Chargers, 34-10 (SD)
2006—Chargers, 27-0 (O)
    Chargers, 21-14 (SD)
(RS Pts.—Raiders 2,094, Chargers 1,970)
(PS Pts.—Raiders 34, Chargers 27)
*Franchise in Los Angeles from 1982-1994
**Franchise in Los Angeles prior to 1961
***AFC Championship
OAKLAND vs. SAN FRANCISCO
RS: Raiders lead series, 6-5
1970—49ers, 38-7 (O)
1974—Raiders, 35-24 (SF)
1979—Raiders, 23-10 (O)
1982—Raiders, 23-17 (SF)
1985—49ers, 34-10 (LA)
1988—Raiders, 9-3 (SF)
1991—Raiders, 12-6 (LA)
1994—49ers, 44-14 (SF)
2000—Raiders, 34-28 (SF) OT
2002—49ers, 23-20 (O) OT
2006—Raiders, 34-20 (SF)
(RS Pts.—49ers 261, Raiders 207)
*Franchise in Los Angeles from 1982-1994
OAKLAND vs. SEATTLE
RS: Raiders lead series, 27-23

PS: Series tied, 1-1
1977—Raiders, 44-7 (O)
1978—Seahawks, 27-7 (S)
    Seahawks, 17-16 (O)
1979—Seahawks, 27-10 (S)
    Seahawks, 29-24 (O)
1980—Raiders, 33-14 (O)
    Raiders, 19-17 (S)
1981—Raiders, 20-10 (O)
    Raiders, 32-31 (S)
1982—Raiders, 28-23 (LA)
1983—Seahawks, 38-36 (S)
    Seahawks, 34-21 (LA)
    **Raiders, 30-14 (LA)
1984—Raiders, 28-14 (LA)
    Seahawks, 17-14 (S)
    ***Seahawks, 13-7 (S)
1985—Seahawks, 33-3 (S)
    Raiders, 13-3 (LA)
1986—Raiders, 14-10 (LA)
    Seahawks, 37-0 (S)
1987—Seahawks, 35-13 (LA)
    Raiders, 37-14 (S)
1988—Seahawks, 35-27 (S)
    Seahawks, 43-37 (LA)
1989—Seahawks, 24-20 (LA)
    Seahawks, 23-17 (S)
1990—Raiders, 17-13 (S)
    Raiders, 24-17 (LA)
1991—Raiders, 23-20 (S) OT
    Raiders, 31-7 (LA)
1992—Raiders, 19-0 (S)
    Raiders, 20-3 (LA)
1993—Raiders, 17-13 (S)
    Raiders, 27-23 (LA)
1994—Seahawks, 38-9 (LA)
    Raiders, 17-16 (S)
1995—Raiders, 34-14 (O)
    Seahawks, 44-10 (S)
1996—Raiders, 27-21 (S)
    Seahawks, 28-21 (O)
1997—Seahawks, 45-34 (S)
    Seahawks, 22-21 (O)
1998—Raiders, 31-18 (S)
    Raiders, 20-17 (O)
1999—Seahawks, 22-21 (S)
    Raiders, 30-21 (O)
2000—Raiders, 31-3 (O)
    Seahawks, 27-24 (S)
2001—Raiders, 38-14 (O)
    Seahawks, 34-27 (S)
2002—Raiders, 31-17 (O)
2006—Seahawks, 16-0 (S)
(RS Pts.—Raiders 1,117, Seahawks 1,075)
(PS Pts.—Raiders 37, Seahawks 27)
*Franchise in Los Angeles from 1982-1994
**AFC Championship
***AFC First-Round Playoff
OAKLAND vs. TAMPA BAY
RS: Raiders lead series, 5-1
PS: Buccaneers lead series, 1-0
1976—Raiders, 49-16 (O)
1981—Raiders, 18-16 (O)
1993—Raiders, 27-20 (LA)
1996—Buccaneers, 20-17 (TB) OT
1999—Raiders, 45-0 (O)
2002—**Buccaneers, 48-21 (San Diego)
2004—Raiders, 30-20 (O)
(RS Pts.—Raiders 186, Buccaneers 92)
(PS Pts.—Buccaneers 48, Raiders 21)

*Franchise in Los Angeles from 1982-1994
**Super Bowl XXXVII
OAKLAND vs. **TENNESSEE
RS: Raiders lead series, 23-17
PS: Raiders lead series, 4-0
1960—Oilers, 37-22 (O)
    Raiders, 14-13 (H)
1961—Oilers, 55-0 (H)
    Oilers, 47-16 (O)
1962—Oilers, 28-20 (O)
    Oilers, 32-17 (H)
1963—Raiders, 24-13 (O)
    Raiders, 52-49 (O)
1964—Oilers, 42-28 (H)
    Raiders, 20-10 (O)
1965—Raiders, 21-17 (O)
    Raiders, 33-21 (H)
1966—Oilers, 31-0 (H)
    Raiders, 38-23 (O)
1967—Raiders, 19-7 (H)
    ***Raiders, 40-7 (O)
1968—Raiders, 24-15 (H)
1969—Raiders, 21-17 (O)
    ****Raiders, 56-7 (O)
1971—Raiders, 41-21 (O)
1972—Raiders, 34-0 (H)
1973—Raiders, 17-6 (H)
1975—Oilers, 27-26 (O)
1976—Raiders, 14-13 (H)
1977—Raiders, 34-29 (O)
1978—Raiders, 21-17 (O)
1979—Oilers, 31-17 (H)
1980—*****Raiders, 27-7 (O)
1981—Oilers, 17-16 (H)
1983—Raiders, 20-6 (LA)
1984—Raiders, 24-14 (H)
1986—Raiders, 28-17 (H)
1988—Oilers, 38-35 (H)
1989—Oilers, 23-7 (H)
1991—Oilers, 47-17 (H)
1994—Oilers, 17-14 (LA)
1997—Oilers, 24-21 (T) OT
1999—Titans, 21-14 (T)
2001—Titans, 13-10 (O)
2002—Raiders, 52-25 (O)
    ******Raiders, 41-24 (O)
2003—Titans, 25-20 (T)
2004—Raiders, 40-35 (O)
2005—Raiders, 34-25 (T)
(RS Pts.—Titans 945, Raiders 928)
(PS Pts.—Raiders 164, Titans 45)
*Franchise in Los Angeles from 1982-1994
**Franchise in Houston prior to 1997; known as Oilers prior to 1999
***AFL Championship
****Inter-Divisional Playoff
*****AFC First-Round Playoff
******AFC Championship
OAKLAND vs. WASHINGTON
RS: Raiders lead series, 7-3
PS: Raiders lead series, 1-0
1970—Raiders, 34-20 (O)
1975—Raiders, 26-23 (W) OT
1980—Raiders, 24-21 (O)
1983—Redskins, 37-35 (W)
    **Raiders, 38-9 (Tampa)
1986—Redskins, 10-6 (W)
1989—Raiders, 37-24 (LA)
1992—Raiders, 21-20 (W)
1995—Raiders, 20-8 (W)

1998—Redskins, 29-19 (O)
2005—Raiders, 16-13 (W)
(RS Pts.—Raiders 238, Redskins 205)
(PS Pts.—Raiders 38, Redskins 9)
*Franchise in Los Angeles from
1982-1994*
**Super Bowl XVIII*

PHILADELPHIA vs. ARIZONA
RS: Cardinals lead series, 53-52-5
PS: Series tied, 1-1;
See Arizona vs. Philadelphia
PHILADELPHIA vs. ATLANTA
RS: Eagles lead series, 12-10-1
PS: Eagles lead series, 2-1;
See Atlanta vs. Philadelphia
PHILADELPHIA vs. BALTIMORE
RS: Eagles lead series, 1-0-1;
See Baltimore vs. Philadelphia
PHILADELPHIA vs. BUFFALO
RS: Series tied, 5-5;
See Buffalo vs. Philadelphia
PHILADELPHIA vs. CAROLINA
RS: Eagles lead series, 4-1
PS: Panthers lead series, 1-0;
See Carolina vs. Philadelphia
PHILADELPHIA vs. CHICAGO
RS: Bears lead series, 24-8-1
PS: Eagles lead series, 2-1;
See Chicago vs. Philadelphia
PHILADELPHIA vs. CINCINNATI
RS: Bengals lead series, 7-3;
See Cincinnati vs. Philadelphia
PHILADELPHIA vs. CLEVELAND
RS: Browns lead series, 31-14-1;
See Cleveland vs. Philadelphia
PHILADELPHIA vs. DALLAS
RS: Cowboys lead series, 51-41
PS: Cowboys lead series, 2-1;
See Dallas vs. Philadelphia
PHILADELPHIA vs. DENVER
RS: Eagles lead series, 6-4;
See Denver vs. Philadelphia
PHILADELPHIA vs. DETROIT
RS: Series tied, 12-12-2
PS: Eagles lead series, 1-0;
See Detroit vs. Philadelphia
PHILADELPHIA vs. GREEN BAY
RS: Packers lead series, 22-13
PS: Eagles lead series, 2-0;
See Green Bay vs. Philadelphia
PHILADELPHIA vs. HOUSTON
RS: Eagles lead series, 2-0;
See Houston vs. Philadelphia
PHILADELPHIA vs. INDIANAPOLIS
RS: Colts lead series, 10-6;
See Indianapolis vs. Philadelphia
PHILADELPHIA vs. JACKSONVILLE
RS: Jaguars lead series, 3-0;
See Jacksonville vs. Philadelphia
PHILADELPHIA vs. KANSAS CITY
RS: Eagles lead series, 3-2;
See Kansas City vs. Philadelphia
PHILADELPHIA vs. MIAMI
RS: Dolphins lead series, 7-4;
See Miami vs. Philadelphia
PHILADELPHIA vs. MINNESOTA
RS: Vikings lead series, 11-8
PS: Eagles lead series, 2-0;
See Minnesota vs. Philadelphia

PHILADELPHIA vs. NEW ENGLAND
RS: Eagles lead series, 6-3
PS: Patriots lead series, 1-0;
See New England vs. Philadelphia
PHILADELPHIA vs. NEW ORLEANS
RS: Eagles lead series, 14-9
PS: Series tied, 1-1;
See New Orleans vs. Philadelphia
PHILADELPHIA vs. N.Y. GIANTS
RS: Giants lead series, 76-66-2
PS: Giants lead series, 2-1;
See N.Y. Giants vs. Philadelphia
PHILADELPHIA vs. N.Y. JETS
RS: Eagles lead series, 7-0;
See N.Y. Jets vs. Philadelphia
PHILADELPHIA vs. OAKLAND
RS: Eagles lead series, 5-4
PS: Raiders lead series, 1-0;
See Oakland vs. Philadelphia
PHILADELPHIA vs. *PITTSBURGH
RS: Eagles lead series, 45-27-3
PS: Eagles lead series, 1-0
1933—Eagles, 25-6 (Phila)
1934—Eagles, 17-0 (Pitt)
    Pirates, 9-7 (Phila)
1935—Pirates, 17-7 (Phila)
    Eagles, 17-6 (Pitt)
1936—Pirates, 17-0 (Pitt)
    Pirates, 6-0 (Johnstown, Pa.)
1937—Pirates, 27-14 (Pitt)
    Pirates, 16-7 (Pitt)
1938—Eagles, 27-7 (Buffalo)
    Eagles, 14-7 (Charleston, W. Va.)
1939—Eagles, 17-14 (Phila)
    Pirates, 24-12 (Pitt)
1940—Pirates, 7-3 (Pitt)
    Eagles, 7-0 (Phila)
1941—Eagles, 10-7 (Pitt)
    Tie, 7-7 (Phila)
1942—Eagles, 24-14 (Pitt)
    Steelers, 14-0 (Phila)
1945—Eagles, 45-3 (Pitt)
    Eagles, 30-6 (Phila)
1946—Steelers, 10-7 (Pitt)
    Eagles, 10-7 (Phila)
1947—Steelers, 35-24 (Pitt)
    Eagles, 21-0 (Phila)
    **Eagles, 21-0 (Pitt)
1948—Eagles, 34-7 (Pitt)
    Eagles, 17-0 (Phila)
1949—Eagles, 38-7 (Pitt)
    Eagles, 34-17 (Phila)
1950—Eagles, 17-10 (Phila)
    Steelers, 9-7 (Phila)
1951—Eagles, 34-13 (Pitt)
    Steelers, 17-13 (Phila)
1952—Eagles, 31-25 (Pitt)
    Eagles, 26-21 (Phila)
1953—Eagles, 23-17 (Phila)
    Eagles, 35-7 (Pitt)
1954—Eagles, 24-22 (Phila)
    Steelers, 17-7 (Pitt)
1955—Steelers, 13-7 (Pitt)
    Eagles, 24-0 (Phila)
1956—Eagles, 35-21 (Pitt)
    Eagles, 14-7 (Phila)
1957—Steelers, 6-0 (Pitt)
    Eagles, 7-6 (Phila)
1958—Steelers, 24-3 (Pitt)
    Steelers, 31-24 (Phila)

1959—Eagles, 28-24 (Phila)
    Steelers, 31-0 (Pitt)
1960—Eagles, 34-7 (Phila)
    Steelers, 27-21 (Pitt)
1961—Eagles, 21-16 (Phila)
    Eagles, 35-24 (Pitt)
1962—Steelers, 13-7 (Pitt)
    Steelers, 26-17 (Phila)
1963—Tie, 21-21 (Phila)
    Tie, 20-20 (Pitt)
1964—Eagles, 21-7 (Phila)
    Eagles, 34-10 (Pitt)
1965—Steelers, 20-14 (Phila)
    Eagles, 47-13 (Pitt)
1966—Eagles, 31-14 (Pitt)
    Eagles, 27-23 (Phila)
1967—Eagles, 34-24 (Phila)
1968—Steelers, 6-3 (Pitt)
1969—Eagles, 41-27 (Phila)
1970—Eagles, 30-20 (Phila)
1974—Steelers, 27-0 (Pitt)
1979—Eagles, 17-14 (Phila)
1988—Eagles, 27-26 (Pitt)
1991—Eagles, 23-14 (Phila)
1994—Steelers, 14-3 (Pitt)
1997—Eagles, 23-20 (Phila)
2000—Eagles, 26-23 (Pitt) OT
2004—Steelers, 27-3 (Pitt)
(RS Pts.—Eagles 1,414, Steelers 1,091)
(PS Pts.—Eagles 21, Steelers 0)
Steelers known as Pirates prior to 1941
**Division Playoff*
PHILADELPHIA vs. *ST. LOUIS
RS: Rams lead series, 17-16-1
PS: Rams lead series, 2-1
1937—Rams, 21-3 (P)
1939—Rams, 35-13 (Colorado Springs)
1940—Rams, 21-13 (C)
1942—Rams, 24-14 (Akron)
1944—Eagles, 26-13 (P)
1945—Eagles, 28-14 (P)
1946—Eagles, 25-14 (LA)
1947—Eagles, 14-7 (P)
1948—Tie, 28-28 (LA)
1949—Eagles, 38-14 (P)
    **Eagles, 14-0 (LA)
1950—Eagles, 56-20 (P)
1955—Rams, 23-21 (P)
1956—Rams, 27-7 (LA)
1957—Rams, 17-13 (LA)
1959—Eagles, 23-20 (P)
1964—Rams, 20-10 (LA)
1967—Rams, 33-17 (LA)
1969—Rams, 23-17 (P)
1972—Rams, 34-3 (P)
1975—Rams, 42-3 (P)
1977—Rams, 20-0 (LA)
1978—Rams, 16-14 (P)
1983—Eagles, 13-9 (P)
1985—Rams, 17-6 (P)
1986—Eagles, 34-20 (P)
1988—Eagles, 30-24 (P)
1989—***Rams, 21-7 (P)
1990—Eagles, 27-21 (LA)
1995—Eagles, 20-9 (P)
1998—Eagles, 17-14 (P)
1999—Eagles, 38-31 (P)
2001—Rams, 20-17 (P) OT
    ****Rams, 29-24 (StL)
2002—Eagles, 10-3 (P)

2004—Rams, 20-7 (StL)
2005—Eagles, 17-16 (StL)
(RS Pts.—Rams 690, Eagles 622)
(PS Pts.—Rams 50, Eagles 45)
*Franchise in Los Angeles prior to 1995
and in Cleveland prior to 1946
**NFL Championship
***NFC First-Round Playoff
****NFC Championship

PHILADELPHIA vs. SAN DIEGO
RS: Chargers lead series, 5-4
1974—Eagles, 13-7 (SD)
1980—Chargers, 22-21 (SD)
1985—Chargers, 20-14 (SD)
1986—Eagles, 23-7 (P)
1989—Chargers, 20-17 (SD)
1995—Chargers, 27-21 (P)
1998—Chargers, 13-10 (SD)
2001—Eagles, 24-14 (P)
2005—Eagles, 20-17 (P)
(RS Pts.—Eagles 163, Chargers 147)

PHILADELPHIA vs. SAN FRANCISCO
RS: 49ers lead series, 16-9-1
PS: 49ers lead series, 1-0
1951—Eagles, 21-14 (P)
1953—49ers, 31-21 (SF)
1956—Tie, 10-10 (P)
1958—49ers, 30-24 (P)
1959—49ers, 24-14 (SF)
1964—49ers, 28-24 (P)
1966—Eagles, 35-34 (SF)
1967—49ers, 28-27 (P)
1969—49ers, 14-13 (SF)
1971—49ers, 31-3 (P)
1973—49ers, 38-28 (SF)
1975—Eagles, 27-17 (P)
1983—Eagles, 22-17 (SF)
1984—49ers, 21-9 (P)
1985—49ers, 24-13 (SF)
1989—49ers, 38-28 (P)
1991—49ers, 23-7 (P)
1992—49ers, 20-14 (SF)
1993—Eagles, 37-34 (SF) OT
1994—Eagles, 40-8 (SF)
1996—*49ers, 14-0 (SF)
1997—49ers, 24-12 (P)
2001—49ers, 13-3 (SF)
2002—Eagles, 38-17 (SF)
2003—49ers, 31-28 (P) OT
2005—Eagles, 42-3 (P)
2006—Eagles, 38-24 (SF)
(RS Pts.—49ers 596, Eagles 578)
(PS Pts.—49ers 14, Eagles 0)
*NFC First-Round Playoff

PHILADELPHIA vs. SEATTLE
RS: Eagles lead series, 6-4
1976—Eagles, 27-10 (P)
1980—Eagles, 27-20 (S)
1986—Seahawks, 24-20 (S)
1989—Eagles, 31-7 (P)
1992—Eagles, 20-17 (S) OT
1995—Seahawks, 26-14 (S)
1998—Seahawks, 38-0 (P)
2001—Eagles, 27-3 (S)
2002—Eagles, 27-20 (S)
2005—Seahawks, 42-0 (P)
(RS Pts.—Seahawks 207, Eagles 193)

PHILADELPHIA vs. TAMPA BAY
RS: Series tied, 5-5
PS: Series tied, 2-2

1977—Eagles, 13-3 (P)
1979—*Buccaneers, 24-17 (TB)
1981—Eagles, 20-10 (P)
1988—Eagles, 41-14 (TB)
1991—Buccaneers, 14-13 (TB)
1995—Eagles, 21-6 (P)
1999—Buccaneers, 19-5 (P)
2000—**Eagles, 21-3 (P)
2001—Eagles, 17-13 (TB)
      **Eagles, 31-9 (P)
2002—Eagles, 20-10 (P)
      ***Buccaneers, 27-10 (P)
2003—Buccaneers, 17-0 (P)
2006—Buccaneers, 23-21 (TB)
(RS Pts.—Eagles 156, Buccaneers 144)
(PS Pts.—Eagles 79, Buccaneers 63)
*NFC Divisional Playoff
**NFC First-Round Playoff
***NFC Championship

PHILADELPHIA vs. *TENNESSEE
RS: Eagles lead series, 6-3
1972—Eagles, 18-17 (H)
1979—Eagles, 26-20 (H)
1982—Eagles, 35-14 (P)
1988—Eagles, 32-23 (H)
1991—Eagles, 13-6 (H)
1994—Eagles, 21-6 (P)
2000—Titans, 15-13 (P)
2002—Titans, 27-24 (T)
2006—Titans, 31-13 (P)
(RS Pts.—Eagles 195, Titans 159)
*Franchise in Houston prior to 1997;
known as Oilers prior to 1999

PHILADELPHIA vs. *WASHINGTON
RS: Redskins lead series, 74-64-5
PS: Redskins lead series, 1-0
1934—Redskins, 6-0 (B)
      Redskins, 14-7 (P)
1935—Eagles, 7-6 (B)
1936—Redskins, 26-3 (P)
      Redskins, 17-7 (B)
1937—Eagles, 14-0 (W)
      Redskins, 10-7 (P)
1938—Redskins, 26-23 (P)
      Redskins, 20-14 (W)
1939—Redskins, 7-0 (P)
      Redskins, 7-6 (W)
1940—Redskins, 34-17 (P)
      Redskins, 13-6 (W)
1941—Redskins, 21-17 (P)
      Redskins, 20-14 (W)
1942—Redskins, 14-10 (P)
      Redskins, 30-27 (W)
1944—Tie, 31-31 (P)
      Eagles, 37-7 (W)
1945—Redskins, 24-14 (W)
      Eagles, 16-0 (P)
1946—Eagles, 28-24 (W)
      Redskins, 27-10 (P)
1947—Eagles, 45-42 (P)
      Eagles, 38-14 (W)
1948—Eagles, 45-0 (W)
      Eagles, 42-21 (P)
1949—Eagles, 49-14 (P)
      Eagles, 44-21 (W)
1950—Eagles, 35-3 (P)
      Eagles, 33-0 (W)
1951—Redskins, 27-23 (P)
      Eagles, 35-21 (W)
1952—Eagles, 38-20 (P)

Redskins, 27-21 (W)
1953—Tie, 21-21 (P)
      Redskins, 10-0 (W)
1954—Eagles, 49-21 (W)
      Eagles, 41-33 (P)
1955—Redskins, 31-30 (P)
      Redskins, 34-21 (W)
1956—Eagles, 13-9 (P)
      Redskins, 19-17 (W)
1957—Eagles, 21-12 (P)
      Redskins, 42-7 (W)
1958—Redskins, 24-14 (P)
      Redskins, 20-0 (W)
1959—Eagles, 30-23 (P)
      Eagles, 34-14 (W)
1960—Eagles, 19-13 (P)
      Eagles, 38-28 (W)
1961—Eagles, 14-7 (P)
      Eagles, 27-24 (W)
1962—Redskins, 27-21 (P)
      Eagles, 37-14 (W)
1963—Eagles, 37-24 (W)
      Redskins, 13-10 (P)
1964—Redskins, 35-20 (W)
      Redskins, 21-10 (P)
1965—Redskins, 23-21 (W)
      Eagles, 21-14 (P)
1966—Redskins, 27-13 (P)
      Eagles, 37-28 (W)
1967—Eagles, 35-24 (P)
      Tie, 35-35 (W)
1968—Redskins, 17-14 (W)
      Redskins, 16-10 (P)
1969—Tie, 28-28 (W)
      Redskins, 34-29 (P)
1970—Redskins, 33-21 (P)
      Redskins, 24-6 (W)
1971—Tie, 7-7 (W)
      Redskins, 20-13 (P)
1972—Redskins, 14-0 (W)
      Redskins, 23-7 (P)
1973—Redskins, 28-7 (P)
      Redskins, 38-20 (W)
1974—Redskins, 27-20 (P)
      Redskins, 26-7 (W)
1975—Eagles, 26-10 (P)
      Eagles, 26-3 (W)
1976—Redskins, 20-17 (P) OT
      Redskins, 24-0 (W)
1977—Redskins, 23-17 (W)
      Redskins, 17-14 (P)
1978—Redskins, 35-30 (W)
      Eagles, 17-10 (P)
1979—Eagles, 28-17 (P)
      Redskins, 17-7 (W)
1980—Eagles, 24-14 (P)
      Eagles, 24-0 (W)
1981—Eagles, 36-13 (P)
      Redskins, 15-13 (W)
1982—Redskins, 37-34 (P) OT
      Redskins, 13-9 (W)
1983—Redskins, 23-13 (P)
      Redskins, 28-24 (W)
1984—Redskins, 20-0 (W)
      Eagles, 16-10 (P)
1985—Eagles, 19-6 (W)
      Redskins, 17-12 (P)
1986—Redskins, 41-14 (W)
      Redskins, 21-14 (P)
1987—Redskins, 34-24 (W)

Eagles, 31-27 (P)
1988—Redskins, 17-10 (W)
Redskins, 20-19 (P)
1989—Eagles, 42-37 (W)
Redskins, 10-3 (P)
1990—Redskins, 13-7 (W)
Eagles, 28-14 (P)
**Redskins, 20-6 (P)
1991—Redskins, 23-0 (W)
Eagles, 24-22 (P)
1992—Redskins, 16-12 (W)
Eagles, 17-13 (P)
1993—Eagles, 34-31 (P)
Eagles, 17-14 (W)
1994—Eagles, 21-17 (P)
Eagles, 31-29 (W)
1995—Eagles, 37-34 (P) OT
Eagles, 14-7 (W)
1996—Eagles, 17-14 (W)
Redskins, 26-21 (P)
1997—Eagles, 24-10 (P)
Redskins, 35-32 (W)
1998—Eagles, 17-12 (P)
Redskins, 28-3 (W)
1999—Eagles, 35-28 (P)
Redskins, 20-17 (W) OT
2000—Redskins, 17-14 (P)
Eagles, 23-20 (W)
2001—Redskins, 13-3 (P)
Eagles, 20-6 (W)
2002—Eagles, 37-7 (W)
Eagles, 34-21 (P)
2003—Eagles, 27-25 (P)
Eagles, 31-7 (W)
2004—Eagles, 28-6 (P)
Eagles, 17-14 (W)
2005—Redskins, 17-10 (W)
Redskins, 31-20 (P)
2006—Eagles, 27-3 (P)
Eagles, 21-19 (W)
(RS Pts.—Eagles 2,928, Redskins 2,790)
(PS Pts.—Redskins 20, Eagles 6)
*Franchise in Boston prior to 1937
**NFC First-Round Playoff

PITTSBURGH vs. ARIZONA
RS: Steelers lead series, 31-22-3;
See Arizona vs. Pittsburgh
PITTSBURGH vs. ATLANTA
RS: Steelers lead series, 11-2-1;
See Atlanta vs. Pittsburgh
PITTSBURGH vs. BALTIMORE
RS: Steelers lead series, 13-9
PS: Steelers lead series, 1-0;
See Baltimore vs. Pittsburgh
PITTSBURGH vs. BUFFALO
RS: Steelers lead series, 10-8
PS: Steelers lead series, 2-1;
See Buffalo vs. Pittsburgh
PITTSBURGH vs. CAROLINA
RS: Steelers lead series, 3-1;
See Carolina vs. Pittsburgh
PITTSBURGH vs. CHICAGO
RS: Bears lead series, 16-7-1;
See Chicago vs. Pittsburgh
PITTSBURGH vs. CINCINNATI
RS: Steelers lead series, 43-30
PS: Steelers lead series, 1-0;
See Cincinnati vs. Pittsburgh
PITTSBURGH vs. CLEVELAND

RS: Browns lead series, 55-53
PS: Steelers lead series, 2-0;
See Cleveland vs. Pittsburgh
PITTSBURGH vs. DALLAS
RS: Cowboys lead series, 14-12
PS: Steelers lead series, 2-1;
See Dallas vs. Pittsburgh
PITTSBURGH vs. DENVER
RS: Broncos lead series, 12-6-1
PS: Series tied, 3-3;
See Denver vs. Pittsburgh
PITTSBURGH vs. DETROIT
RS: Series tied, 14-14-1;
See Detroit vs. Pittsburgh
PITTSBURGH vs. GREEN BAY
RS: Packers lead series, 18-13;
See Green Bay vs. Pittsburgh
PITTSBURGH vs. HOUSTON
RS: Series tied, 1-1;
See Houston vs. Pittsburgh
PITTSBURGH vs. INDIANAPOLIS
RS: Steelers lead series, 13-5
PS: Steelers lead series, 5-0;
See Indianapolis vs. Pittsburgh
PITTSBURGH vs. JACKSONVILLE
RS: Jaguars lead series, 10-8;
See Jacksonville vs. Pittsburgh
PITTSBURGH vs. KANSAS CITY
RS: Steelers lead series, 17-8
PS: Chiefs lead series, 1-0;
See Kansas City vs. Pittsburgh
PITTSBURGH vs. MIAMI
RS: Series tied, 9-9
PS: Dolphins lead series, 2-1;
See Miami vs. Pittsburgh
PITTSBURGH vs. MINNESOTA
RS: Vikings lead series, 8-6
PS: Steelers lead series, 1-0;
See Minnesota vs. Pittsburgh
PITTSBURGH vs. NEW ENGLAND
RS: Steelers lead series, 12-6
PS: Patriots lead series, 3-1;
See New England vs. Pittsburgh
PITTSBURGH vs. NEW ORLEANS
RS: Steelers lead series, 7-6;
See New Orleans vs. Pittsburgh
PITTSBURGH vs. N.Y. GIANTS
RS: Giants lead series, 43-28-3;
See N.Y. Giants vs. Pittsburgh
PITTSBURGH vs. N.Y. JETS
RS: Steelers lead series, 15-2
PS: Steelers lead series, 1-0;
See N.Y. Jets vs. Pittsburgh
PITTSBURGH vs. OAKLAND
RS: Raiders lead series, 9-8
PS: Series tied, 3-3;
See Oakland vs. Pittsburgh
PITTSBURGH vs. PHILADELPHIA
RS: Eagles lead series, 45-27-3
PS: Eagles lead series, 1-0;
See Philadelphia vs. Pittsburgh
***PITTSBURGH vs. **ST. LOUIS**
RS: Rams lead series, 15-5-2
PS: Steelers lead series, 1-0
1938—Rams, 13-7 (New Orleans)
1939—Tie, 14-14 (C)
1941—Rams, 17-14 (Akron)
1947—Rams, 48-7 (P)
1948—Rams, 31-14 (LA)
1949—Tie, 7-7 (P)

1952—Rams, 28-14 (LA)
1955—Rams, 27-26 (LA)
1956—Steelers, 30-13 (P)
1961—Rams, 24-14 (LA)
1964—Rams, 26-14 (P)
1968—Rams, 45-10 (LA)
1971—Rams, 23-14 (P)
1975—Rams, 10-3 (LA)
1978—Rams, 10-7 (LA)
1979—***Steelers, 31-19 (Pasadena)
1981—Steelers, 24-0 (P)
1984—Steelers, 24-14 (P)
1987—Rams, 31-21 (LA)
1990—Steelers, 41-10 (P)
1993—Rams, 27-0 (LA)
1996—Steelers, 42-6 (P)
2003—Rams, 33-21 (P)
(RS Pts.—Rams 457, Steelers 368)
(PS Pts.—Steelers 31, Rams 19)
*Steelers known as Pirates prior to 1941
**Franchise in Los Angeles prior to 1995
and in Cleveland prior to 1946
***Super Bowl XIV
PITTSBURGH vs. SAN DIEGO
RS: Steelers lead series, 19-6
PS: Chargers lead series, 2-0
1971—Steelers, 21-17 (P)
1972—Steelers, 24-2 (SD)
1973—Steelers, 38-21 (P)
1975—Steelers, 37-0 (SD)
1976—Steelers, 23-0 (P)
1977—Steelers, 10-9 (SD)
1979—Chargers, 35-7 (SD)
1980—Chargers, 26-17 (SD)
1982—*Chargers, 31-28 (P)
1983—Steelers, 26-3 (P)
1984—Steelers, 52-24 (P)
1985—Chargers, 54-44 (SD)
1987—Steelers, 20-16 (P)
1988—Chargers, 20-14 (SD)
1989—Steelers, 20-17 (P)
1990—Steelers, 36-14 (P)
1991—Steelers, 26-20 (P)
1992—Steelers, 23-6 (SD)
1993—Steelers,.16-3 (P)
1994—Chargers, 37-34 (SD)
**Chargers, 17-13 (P)
1995—Steelers, 31-16 (P)
1996—Steelers, 16-3 (P)
2000—Steelers, 34-21 (SD)
2003—Steelers, 40-24 (P)
2005—Steelers, 24-22 (SD)
2006—Chargers, 23-13 (SD)
(RS Pts.—Steelers 646, Chargers 433)
(PS Pts.—Chargers 48, Steelers 41)
*AFC First-Round Playoff
**AFC Championship
PITTSBURGH vs. SAN FRANCISCO
RS: 49ers lead series, 10-8
1951—49ers, 28-24 (P)
1952—Steelers, 24-7 (SF)
1954—49ers, 31-3 (SF)
1958—49ers, 23-20 (P)
1961—Steelers, 20-10 (P)
1965—49ers, 27-17 (SF)
1968—49ers, 45-28 (P)
1973—Steelers, 37-14 (SF)
1977—Steelers, 27-0 (P)
1978—Steelers, 24-7 (SF)
1981—49ers, 17-14 (P)

1984—Steelers, 20-17 (SF)
1987—Steelers, 30-17 (P)
1990—49ers, 27-7 (SF)
1993—49ers, 24-13 (P)
1996—49ers, 25-15 (P)
1999—Steelers, 27-6 (SF)
2003—49ers, 30-14 (SF)
(RS Pts.—Steelers 364, 49ers 355)
PITTSBURGH vs. SEATTLE
RS: Seahawks lead series, 8-6
PS: Steelers lead series, 1-0
1977—Steelers, 30-20 (P)
1978—Steelers, 21-10 (P)
1981—Seahawks, 24-21 (S)
1982—Seahawks, 16-0 (S)
1983—Steelers, 27-21 (S)
1986—Seahawks, 30-0 (S)
1987—Steelers, 13-9 (P)
1991—Seahawks, 27-7 (P)
1992—Steelers, 20-14 (P)
1993—Seahawks, 16-6 (S)
1994—Seahawks, 30-13 (S)
1998—Steelers, 13-10 (P)
1999—Seahawks, 29-10 (P)
2003—Seahawks, 23-16 (S)
2005—*Steelers, 21-10 (Detroit)
(RS Pts.—Seahawks 279, Steelers 197)
(PS Pts.—Steelers 21, Seahawks 10)
*Super Bowl XL
PITTSBURGH vs. TAMPA BAY
RS: Steelers lead series, 7-1
1976—Steelers, 42-0 (P)
1980—Steelers, 24-21 (TB)
1983—Steelers, 17-12 (P)
1989—Steelers, 31-22 (TB)
1998—Buccaneers, 16-3 (TB)
2001—Steelers, 17-10 (TB)
2002—Steelers, 17-7 (TB)
2006—Steelers, 20-3 (P)
(RS Pts.—Steelers 171, Buccaneers 91)
PITTSBURGH vs. *TENNESSEE
RS: Steelers lead series, 38-28
PS: Steelers lead series, 3-1
1970—Oilers, 19-7 (P)
      Steelers, 7-3 (H)
1971—Steelers, 23-16 (P)
      Oilers, 29-3 (H)
1972—Steelers, 24-7 (P)
      Steelers, 9-3 (H)
1973—Steelers, 36-7 (H)
      Steelers, 33-7 (P)
1974—Steelers, 13-7 (H)
      Oilers, 13-10 (P)
1975—Steelers, 24-17 (P)
      Steelers, 32-9 (H)
1976—Steelers, 32-16 (P)
      Steelers, 21-0 (H)
1977—Oilers, 27-10 (H)
      Steelers, 27-10 (P)
1978—Oilers, 24-17 (P)
      Steelers, 13-3 (H)
      **Steelers, 34-5 (P)
1979—Steelers, 38-7 (P)
      Oilers, 20-17 (H)
      **Steelers, 27-13 (P)
1980—Steelers, 31-17 (P)
      Oilers, 6-0 (H)
1981—Steelers, 26-13 (P)
      Oilers, 21-20 (H)
1982—Steelers, 24-10 (H)

1983—Steelers, 40-28 (H)
      Steelers, 17-10 (P)
1984—Steelers, 35-7 (P)
      Oilers, 23-20 (H) OT
1985—Steelers, 20-0 (P)
      Steelers, 30-7 (H)
1986—Steelers, 22-16 (H) OT
      Steelers, 21-10 (P)
1987—Oilers, 23-3 (P)
      Oilers, 24-16 (H)
1988—Oilers, 34-14 (P)
      Steelers, 37-34 (H)
1989—Oilers, 27-0 (H)
      Oilers, 23-16 (P)
      ***Steelers, 26-23 (H) OT
1990—Steelers, 20-9 (P)
      Oilers, 34-14 (H)
1991—Steelers, 26-14 (P)
      Oilers, 31-6 (H)
1992—Oilers, 29-24 (H)
      Steelers, 21-20 (P)
1993—Oilers, 23-3 (H)
      Oilers, 26-17 (P)
1994—Steelers, 30-14 (P)
      Steelers, 12-9 (H) OT
1995—Steelers, 34-17 (H)
      Steelers, 21-7 (P)
1996—Steelers, 30-16 (P)
      Oilers, 23-13 (H)
1997—Steelers, 37-24 (P)
      Oilers, 16-6 (T)
1998—Oilers, 41-31 (P)
      Oilers, 23-14 (T)
1999—Titans, 16-10 (T)
      Titans, 47-36 (P)
2000—Titans, 23-20 (P)
      Titans, 9-7 (T)
2001—Steelers, 34-7 (P)
      Steelers, 34-24 (T)
2002—Titans, 31-23 (T)
      ****Titans, 34-31 (T) OT
2003—Titans, 30-13 (P)
2005—Steelers, 34-7 (P)
(RS Pts.—Steelers 1,363, Titans 1,142)
(PS Pts.—Steelers 118, Titans 75)
*Franchise in Houston prior to 1997;
known as Oilers prior to 1999
**AFC Championship
***AFC First-Round Playoff
****AFC Divisional Playoff
*PITTSBURGH vs. **WASHINGTON
RS: Redskins lead series, 42-30-3
1933—Redskins, 21-6 (P)
      Pirates, 16-14 (B)
1934—Redskins, 7-0 (P)
      Redskins, 39-0 (B)
1935—Pirates, 6-0 (P)
      Redskins, 13-3 (B)
1936—Pirates, 10-0 (P)
      Redskins, 30-0 (B)
1937—Redskins, 34-20 (W)
      Pirates, 21-13 (P)
1938—Redskins, 7-0 (P)
      Redskins, 15-0 (W)
1939—Redskins, 44-14 (W)
      Redskins, 21-14 (P)
1940—Redskins, 40-10 (P)
      Redskins, 37-10 (W)
1941—Redskins, 24-20 (P)
      Redskins, 23-3 (W)

1942—Redskins, 28-14 (W)
      Redskins, 14-0 (P)
1945—Redskins, 14-0 (P)
      Redskins, 24-0 (W)
1946—Tie, 14-14 (W)
      Steelers, 14-7 (P)
1947—Redskins, 27-26 (W)
      Steelers, 21-14 (P)
1948—Redskins, 17-14 (W)
      Steelers, 10-7 (P)
1949—Redskins, 27-14 (P)
      Redskins, 27-14 (W)
1950—Steelers, 26-7 (W)
      Redskins, 24-7 (P)
1951—Redskins, 22-7 (P)
      Steelers, 20-10 (W)
1952—Redskins, 28-24 (P)
      Steelers, 24-23 (W)
1953—Redskins, 17-9 (P)
      Steelers, 14-13 (W)
1954—Steelers, 37-7 (P)
      Redskins, 17-14 (W)
1955—Redskins, 23-14 (P)
      Redskins, 28-17 (W)
1956—Steelers, 30-13 (P)
      Steelers, 23-0 (W)
1957—Steelers, 28-7 (P)
      Redskins, 10-3 (W)
1958—Steelers, 24-16 (P)
      Tie, 14-14 (W)
1959—Redskins, 23-17 (P)
      Steelers, 27-6 (W)
1960—Tie, 27-27 (W)
      Steelers, 22-10 (P)
1961—Steelers, 20-0 (P)
      Steelers, 30-14 (W)
1962—Steelers, 23-21 (P)
      Steelers, 27-24 (W)
1963—Steelers, 38-27 (P)
      Steelers, 34-28 (W)
1964—Redskins, 30-0 (P)
      Steelers, 14-7 (W)
1965—Redskins, 31-3 (P)
      Redskins, 35-14 (W)
1966—Redskins, 33-27 (P)
      Redskins, 24-10 (W)
1967—Redskins, 15-10 (P)
1968—Redskins, 16-13 (W)
1969—Redskins, 14-7 (P)
1973—Steelers, 21-16 (P)
1979—Steelers, 38-7 (P)
1985—Redskins, 30-23 (P)
1988—Redskins, 30-29 (W)
1991—Redskins, 41-14 (P)
1997—Steelers, 14-13 (P)
2000—Steelers, 24-3 (P)
2004—Steelers, 16-7 (P)
(RS Pts.—Redskins 1,413, Steelers 1,171)
*Steelers known as Pirates prior to 1941
**Franchise in Boston prior to 1937

ST. LOUIS vs. ARIZONA
RS: Rams lead series, 30-24-2
PS: Rams lead series, 1-0;
See Arizona vs. St. Louis
ST. LOUIS vs. ATLANTA
RS: Rams lead series, 46-24-2
PS: Falcons lead series, 1-0;
See Atlanta vs. St. Louis
ST. LOUIS vs. BALTIMORE

RS: Rams lead series, 2-1;
See Baltimore vs. St. Louis
ST. LOUIS vs. BUFFALO
RS: Bills lead series, 5-4;
See Buffalo vs. St. Louis
ST. LOUIS vs. CAROLINA
RS: Panthers lead series, 9-7
PS: Panthers lead series, 1-0;
See Carolina vs. St. Louis
ST. LOUIS vs. CHICAGO
RS: Bears lead series, 48-34-3
PS: Series tied, 1-1;
See Chicago vs. St. Louis
ST. LOUIS vs. CINCINNATI
RS: Series tied, 5-5;
See Cincinnati vs. St. Louis
ST. LOUIS vs. CLEVELAND
RS: Rams lead series, 9-8
PS: Browns lead series, 2-1;
See Cleveland vs. St. Louis
ST. LOUIS vs. DALLAS
RS: Rams lead series, 10-9
PS: Series tied, 4-4;
See Dallas vs. St. Louis
ST. LOUIS vs. DENVER
RS: Rams lead series, 6-5;
See Denver vs. St. Louis
ST. LOUIS vs. DETROIT
RS: Rams lead series, 41-37-1
PS: Lions lead series, 1-0;
See Detroit vs. St. Louis
ST. LOUIS vs. GREEN BAY
RS: Rams lead series, 45-40-2
PS: Series tied, 1-1;
See Green Bay vs. St. Louis
ST. LOUIS vs. HOUSTON
RS: Rams lead series, 1-0;
See Houston vs. St. Louis
ST. LOUIS vs. INDIANAPOLIS
RS: Colts lead series, 22-17-2;
See Indianapolis vs. St. Louis
ST. LOUIS vs. JACKSONVILLE
RS: Rams lead series, 2-0;
See Jacksonville vs. St. Louis
ST. LOUIS vs. KANSAS CITY
RS: Chiefs lead series; 5-4;
See Kansas City vs. St. Louis
ST. LOUIS vs. MIAMI
RS: Dolphins lead series, 8-2;
See Miami vs. St. Louis
ST. LOUIS vs. MINNESOTA
RS: Vikings lead series, 17-14-2
PS: Vikings lead series, 5-2;
See Minnesota vs. St. Louis
ST. LOUIS vs. NEW ENGLAND
RS: Rams lead series, 5-4
PS: Patriots lead series, 1-0;
See New England vs. St. Louis
ST. LOUIS vs. NEW ORLEANS
RS: Rams lead series, 37-29
PS: Saints lead series, 1-0;
See New Orleans vs. St. Louis
ST. LOUIS vs. N.Y. GIANTS
RS: Rams lead series, 25-12
PS: Series tied, 1-1;
See N.Y. Giants vs. St. Louis
ST. LOUIS vs. N.Y. JETS
RS: Rams lead series, 9-2;
See N.Y. Jets vs. St. Louis
ST. LOUIS vs. OAKLAND

RS: Raiders lead series, 7-4;
See Oakland vs. St. Louis
ST. LOUIS vs. PHILADELPHIA
RS: Rams lead series, 17-16-1
PS: Rams lead series, 2-1;
See Philadelphia vs. St. Louis
ST. LOUIS vs. PITTSBURGH
RS: Rams lead series, 15-5-2
PS: Steelers lead series, 1-0;
See Pittsburgh vs. St. Louis
*ST. LOUIS vs. SAN DIEGO
RS: Rams lead series, 5-4
1970—Rams, 37-10 (LA)
1975—Rams, 13-10 (SD) OT
1979—Chargers, 40-16 (LA)
1988—Chargers, 38-24 (LA)
1991—Rams, 30-24 (LA)
1994—Chargers, 31-17 (SD)
2000—Rams, 57-31 (StL)
2002—Rams, 28-24 (StL)
2006—Chargers, 38-24 (SD)
(RS Pts.—Rams 246, Chargers 246)
Franchise in Los Angeles prior to 1995
*ST. LOUIS vs. SAN FRANCISCO
RS: Rams lead series, 59-53-2
PS: 49ers lead series, 1-0
1950—Rams, 35-14 (SF)
　　　Rams, 28-21 (LA)
1951—49ers, 44-17 (SF)
　　　Rams, 23-16 (LA)
1952—Rams, 35-9 (LA)
　　　Rams, 34-21 (SF)
1953—49ers, 31-30 (SF)
　　　49ers, 31-27 (LA)
1954—Tie, 24-24 (LA)
　　　Rams, 42-34 (SF)
1955—49ers, 23-14 (SF)
　　　Rams, 27-14 (LA)
1956—49ers, 33-30 (SF)
　　　Rams, 30-6 (LA)
1957—49ers, 23-20 (SF)
　　　Rams, 37-24 (LA)
1958—Rams, 33-3 (SF)
　　　Rams, 56-7 (LA)
1959—49ers, 34-0 (SF)
　　　49ers, 24-16 (LA)
1960—49ers, 13-9 (SF)
　　　Rams, 23-7 (LA)
1961—49ers, 35-0 (SF)
　　　Rams, 17-7 (LA)
1962—Rams, 28-14 (SF)
　　　49ers, 24-17 (LA)
1963—Rams, 28-21 (LA)
　　　Rams, 21-17 (SF)
1964—Rams, 42-14 (LA)
　　　49ers, 28-7 (SF)
1965—49ers, 45-21 (LA)
　　　49ers, 30-27 (SF)
1966—Rams, 34-3 (LA)
　　　49ers, 21-13 (SF)
1967—49ers, 27-24 (LA)
　　　Rams, 17-7 (SF)
1968—Rams, 24-10 (LA)
　　　Tie, 20-20 (SF)
1969—Rams, 27-21 (SF)
　　　Rams, 41-30 (LA)
1970—49ers, 20-6 (LA)
　　　Rams, 30-13 (SF)
1971—Rams, 20-13 (SF)
　　　Rams, 17-6 (LA)

1972—Rams, 31-7 (LA)
　　　Rams, 26-16 (SF)
1973—Rams, 40-20 (SF)
　　　Rams, 31-13 (LA)
1974—Rams, 37-14 (LA)
　　　Rams, 15-13 (SF)
1975—Rams, 23-14 (SF)
　　　49ers, 24-23 (LA)
1976—49ers, 16-0 (LA)
　　　Rams, 23-3 (SF)
1977—Rams, 34-14 (LA)
　　　Rams, 23-10 (SF)
1978—Rams, 27-10 (LA)
　　　Rams, 31-28 (SF)
1979—Rams, 27-24 (LA)
　　　Rams, 26-20 (SF)
1980—Rams, 48-26 (LA)
　　　Rams, 31-17 (SF)
1981—49ers, 20-17 (SF)
　　　49ers, 33-31 (LA)
1982—49ers, 30-24 (LA)
　　　Rams, 21-20 (SF)
1983—Rams, 10-7 (SF)
　　　49ers, 45-35 (LA)
1984—49ers, 33-0 (LA)
　　　49ers, 19-16 (SF)
1985—49ers, 28-14 (LA)
　　　Rams, 27-20 (SF)
1986—Rams, 16-13 (LA)
　　　49ers, 24-14 (SF)
1987—49ers, 31-10 (LA)
　　　49ers, 48-0 (SF)
1988—49ers, 24-21 (LA)
　　　Rams, 38-16 (SF)
1989—Rams, 13-12 (LA)
　　　49ers, 30-27 (LA)
　　　**49ers, 30-3 (SF)
1990—Rams, 28-17 (LA)
　　　49ers, 26-10 (LA)
1991—49ers, 27-10 (SF)
　　　49ers, 33-10 (LA)
1992—49ers, 27-24 (SF)
　　　49ers, 27-10 (LA)
1993—49ers, 40-17 (SF)
　　　49ers, 35-10 (LA)
1994—49ers, 34-19 (LA)
　　　49ers, 31-27 (SF)
1995—49ers, 44-10 (StL)
　　　49ers, 41-13 (SF)
1996—49ers, 34-0 (SF)
　　　49ers, 28-11 (StL)
1997—49ers, 15-12 (StL)
　　　49ers, 30-10 (SF)
1998—49ers, 28-10 (StL)
　　　49ers, 38-19 (SF)
1999—Rams, 42-20 (StL)
　　　Rams, 23-7 (SF)
2000—Rams, 41-24 (StL)
　　　Rams, 34-24 (SF)
2001—Rams, 30-26 (SF)
　　　Rams, 27-14 (StL)
2002—49ers, 37-13 (SF)
　　　Rams, 31-20 (StL)
2003—Rams, 27-24 (StL) OT
　　　49ers, 30-10 (SF)
2004—Rams, 24-14 (SF)
　　　Rams, 16-6 (StL)
2005—49ers, 28-25 (SF)
　　　49ers, 24-20 (StL)
2006—49ers, 20-13 (SF)

Rams, 20-17 (StL)
(RS Pts.—Rams 2,540, 49ers 2,521)
(PS Pts.—49ers 30, Rams 3)
*Franchise in Los Angeles prior to 1995
**NFC Championship
ST. LOUIS vs. SEATTLE
RS: Rams lead series, 9-8
PS: Rams lead series, 1-0
1976—Rams, 45-6 (LA)
1979—Rams, 24-0 (S)
1985—Rams, 35-24 (S)
1988—Rams, 31-10 (LA)
1991—Seahawks, 23-9 (S)
1997—Seahawks, 17-9 (StL)
2000—Rams, 37-34 (Sea)
2002—Rams, 37-20 (StL)
        Seahawks, 30-10 (Sea)
2003—Seahawks, 24-23 (Sea)
        Rams, 27-22 (StL)
2004—Rams, 33-27 (Sea) OT
        Rams, 23-12 (StL)
        **Rams, 27-20 (Sea)
2005—Seahawks, 37-31 (StL)
        Seahawks, 31-16 (Sea)
2006—Rams, 30-28 (StL)
        Seahawks, 24-22 (Sea)
(RS Pts.—Rams 440, Seahawks 371)
(PS Pts.—Rams 27, Seahawks 20)
*Franchise in Los Angeles prior to 1995
**NFC First-Round Playoff
ST. LOUIS vs. TAMPA BAY
RS: Rams lead series, 9-6
PS: Rams lead series, 2-0
1977—Rams, 31-0 (LA)
1978—Rams, 26-23 (LA)
1979—Buccaneers, 21-6 (TB)
        **Rams, 9-0 (TB)
1980—Buccaneers, 10-9 (TB)
1984—Rams, 34-33 (TB)
1985—Rams, 31-27 (TB)
1986—Rams, 26-20 (LA) OT
1987—Rams, 35-3 (LA)
1990—Rams, 35-14 (TB)
1992—Rams, 31-27 (TB)
1994—Buccaneers, 24-14 (TB)
1999—**Rams, 11-6 (StL)
2000—Buccaneers, 38-35 (TB)
2001—Buccaneers, 24-17 (StL)
2002—Buccaneers, 26-14 (TB)
2004—Rams, 28-21 (StL)
(RS Pts.—Rams 372, Buccaneers 311)
(PS Pts.—Rams 20, Buccaneers 6)
*Franchise in Los Angeles prior to 1995
**NFC Championship
ST. LOUIS vs. **TENNESSEE
RS: Rams lead series, 6-3
PS: Rams lead series, 1-0
1973—Rams, 31-26 (H)
1978—Rams, 10-6 (H)
1981—Oilers, 27-20 (LA)
1984—Rams, 27-16 (LA)
1987—Oilers, 20-16 (H)
1990—Rams, 17-13 (LA)
1993—Rams, 28-13 (H)
1999—Titans, 24-21 (T)
        ***Rams, 23-16 (Atlanta)
2005—Rams, 31-27 (StL)
(RS Pts.—Rams 201, Titans 172)
(PS Pts.—Rams 23, Titans 16)
*Franchise in Los Angeles prior to 1995

**Franchise in Houston prior to 1997;
known as Oilers prior to 1999
***Super Bowl XXXIV
ST. LOUIS vs. WASHINGTON
RS: Redskins lead series, 20-7-1
PS: Series tied, 2-2
1937—Redskins, 16-7 (C)
1938—Redskins, 37-13 (W)
1941—Redskins, 17-13 (W)
1942—Redskins, 33-14 (W)
1944—Redskins, 14-10 (W)
1945—**Rams, 15-14 (C)
1948—Rams, 41-13 (W)
1949—Rams, 53-27 (LA)
1951—Redskins, 31-21 (W)
1962—Redskins, 20-14 (W)
1963—Redskins, 37-14 (LA)
1967—Tie, 28-28 (LA)
1969—Rams, 24-13 (W)
1971—Redskins, 38-24 (LA)
1974—Redskins, 23-17 (LA)
        ***Rams, 19-10 (LA)
1977—Redskins, 17-14 (W)
1981—Redskins, 30-7 (LA)
1983—Redskins, 42-20 (LA)
        ***Redskins, 51-7 (W)
1986—****Redskins, 19-7 (W)
1987—Rams, 30-26 (W)
1991—Redskins, 27-6 (LA)
1993—Rams, 10-6 (LA)
1994—Redskins, 24-21 (LA)
1995—Redskins, 35-23 (StL)
1996—Redskins, 17-10 (StL)
1997—Rams, 23-20 (W)
2000—Redskins, 33-20 (StL)
2002—Redskins, 20-17 (W)
2005—Redskins, 24-9 (StL)
2006—Rams, 37-31 (StL) OT
(RS Pts.—Redskins 699, Rams 540)
(PS Pts.—Redskins 94, Rams 48)
*Franchise in Los Angeles prior to 1995
and in Cleveland prior to 1946
**NFC Championship
***NFC Divisional Playoff
****NFC First-Round Playoff

SAN DIEGO vs. ARIZONA
RS: Chargers lead series, 8-3;
See Arizona vs. San Diego
SAN DIEGO vs. ATLANTA
RS: Falcons lead series, 6-1;
See Atlanta vs. San Diego
SAN DIEGO vs BALTIMORE
RS: Ravens lead series, 3-2;
See Baltimore vs. San Diego
SAN DIEGO vs. BUFFALO
RS: Chargers lead series, 20-9-2
PS: Bills lead series, 2-1;
See Buffalo vs. San Diego
SAN DIEGO vs. CAROLINA
RS: Panthers lead series, 2-1;
See Carolina vs. San Diego
SAN DIEGO vs. CHICAGO
RS: Bears lead series, 5-4;
See Chicago vs. San Diego
SAN DIEGO vs. CINCINNATI
RS: Chargers lead series, 18-10
PS: Bengals lead series, 1-0;
See Cincinnati vs. San Diego
SAN DIEGO vs. CLEVELAND

RS: Chargers lead series, 13-7-1;
See Cleveland vs. San Diego
SAN DIEGO vs. DALLAS
RS: Cowboys lead series, 6-2;
See Dallas vs. San Diego
SAN DIEGO vs. DENVER
RS: Broncos lead series, 52-41-1;
See Denver vs. San Diego
SAN DIEGO vs. DETROIT
RS: Chargers lead series, 5-3;
See Detroit vs. San Diego
SAN DIEGO vs. GREEN BAY
RS: Packers lead series, 7-1;
See Green Bay vs. San Diego
SAN DIEGO vs. HOUSTON
RS: Chargers lead series, 2-0;
See Houston vs. San Diego
SAN DIEGO vs. INDIANAPOLIS
RS: Chargers lead series, 13-8
PS: Colts lead series, 1-0;
See Indianapolis vs. San Diego
SAN DIEGO vs. JACKSONVILLE
RS: Series tied, 1-1;
See Jacksonville vs. San Diego
SAN DIEGO vs. KANSAS CITY
RS: Chiefs lead series, 49-43-1
PS: Chargers lead series, 1-0;
See Kansas City vs. San Diego
SAN DIEGO vs. MIAMI
RS: Dolphins lead series, 11-10
PS: Series tied, 2-2;
See Miami vs. San Diego
SAN DIEGO vs. MINNESOTA
RS: Chargers lead series, 5-4;
See Minnesota vs. San Diego
SAN DIEGO vs. NEW ENGLAND
RS: Patriots lead series, 17-13-2
PS: Series tied, 1-1;
See New England vs. San Diego
SAN DIEGO vs. NEW ORLEANS
RS: Chargers lead series, 7-2;
See New Orleans vs. San Diego
SAN DIEGO vs. N.Y. GIANTS
RS: Giants lead series, 5-4;
See N.Y. Giants vs. San Diego
SAN DIEGO vs. N.Y. JETS
RS: Chargers lead series, 18-11-1
PS: Jets lead series, 1-0;
See N.Y. Jets vs. San Diego
SAN DIEGO vs. OAKLAND
RS: Raiders lead series, 54-38-2
PS: Raiders lead series, 1-0;
See Oakland vs. San Diego
SAN DIEGO vs. PHILADELPHIA
RS: Chargers lead series, 5-4;
See Philadelphia vs. San Diego
SAN DIEGO vs. PITTSBURGH
RS: Steelers lead series, 19-6
PS: Chargers lead series, 2-0;
See Pittsburgh vs. San Diego
SAN DIEGO vs. ST. LOUIS
RS: Rams lead series, 5-4;
See St. Louis vs. San Diego
SAN DIEGO vs. SAN FRANCISCO
RS: 49ers lead series, 6-5
PS: 49ers lead series, 1-0
1972—49ers, 34-3 (SF)
1976—Chargers, 13-7 (SD) OT
1979—Chargers, 31-9 (SD)
1982—Chargers, 41-37 (SF)

1988—49ers, 48-10 (SD)
1991—49ers, 34-14 (SF)
1994—49ers, 38-15 (SD)
  *49ers, 49-26 (South Florida)
1997—49ers, 17-10 (SF)
2000—49ers, 45-17 (SD)
2002—Chargers, 20-17 (SD) OT
2006—Chargers, 48-19 (SF)
(RS Pts.—49ers 305, Chargers 222)
(PS Pts.—49ers 49, Chargers 26)
*Super Bowl XXIX

SAN DIEGO vs. SEATTLE
RS: Seahawks lead series, 25-23
1977—Chargers, 30-28 (S)
1978—Chargers, 24-20 (S)
  Chargers, 37-10 (SD)
1979—Chargers, 33-16 (S)
  Chargers, 20-10 (SD)
1980—Chargers, 34-13 (S)
  Chargers, 21-14 (SD)
1981—Chargers, 24-10 (S)
  Seahawks, 44-23 (S)
1983—Seahawks, 34-31 (S)
  Chargers, 28-21 (SD)
1984—Seahawks, 31-17 (S)
  Seahawks, 24-0 (SD)
1985—Seahawks, 49-35 (SD)
  Seahawks, 26-21 (S)
1986—Seahawks, 33-7 (S)
  Seahawks, 34-24 (SD)
1987—Seahawks, 34-3 (S)
1988—Chargers, 17-6 (SD)
  Seahawks, 17-14 (S)
1989—Seahawks, 17-16 (SD)
  Seahawks, 10-7 (S)
1990—Chargers, 31-14 (S)
  Seahawks, 13-10 (SD) OT
1991—Seahawks, 20-9 (S)
  Chargers, 17-14 (SD)
1992—Chargers, 17-6 (SD)
  Chargers, 31-14 (S)
1993—Chargers, 18-12 (SD)
  Seahawks, 31-14 (S)
1994—Chargers, 24-10 (S)
  Chargers, 35-15 (SD)
1995—Chargers, 14-10 (S)
  Chargers, 35-25 (S)
1996—Chargers, 29-7 (SD)
  Seahawks, 32-13 (S)
1997—Seahawks, 26-22 (S)
  Seahawks, 37-31 (SD)
1998—Seahawks, 27-20 (SD)
  Seahawks, 38-17 (S)
1999—Seahawks, 13-10 (SD)
  Chargers, 19-16 (S)
2000—Seahawks, 20-12 (SD)
  Seahawks, 17-15 (S)
2001—Seahawks, 13-10 (S) OT
  Seahawks, 25-22 (SD)
2002—Seahawks, 31-28 (SD) OT
2006—Chargers, 20-17 (Sea)
(RS Pts.—Seahawks 1,001, Chargers 992)

SAN DIEGO vs. TAMPA BAY
RS: Chargers lead series, 7-1
1976—Chargers, 23-0 (TB)
1981—Chargers, 24-23 (TB)
1987—Chargers, 17-13 (TB)
1990—Chargers, 41-10 (SD)
1992—Chargers, 29-14 (SD)
1993—Chargers, 32-17 (TB)

1996—Buccaneers, 25-17 (SD)
2004—Chargers, 31-24 (SD)
(RS Pts.—Chargers 214, Buccaneers 126)

*SAN DIEGO vs. **TENNESSEE
RS: Chargers lead series, 21-13-1
PS: Titans lead series, 3-0
1960—Oilers, 38-28 (H)
  Chargers, 24-21 (LA)
  ***Oilers, 24-16 (H)
1961—Chargers, 34-24 (SD)
  Oilers, 33-13 (H)
  ***Oilers, 10-3 (SD)
1962—Chargers, 42-17 (SD)
  Oilers, 33-27 (H)
1963—Chargers, 27-0 (SD)
  Chargers 20-14 (H)
1964—Chargers, 27-21 (SD)
  Chargers, 20-17 (H)
1965—Chargers, 31-14 (SD)
  Chargers, 37-26 (H)
1966—Chargers, 28-22 (H)
1967—Chargers, 13-3 (SD)
  Oilers, 24-17 (H)
1968—Chargers, 30-14 (SD)
1969—Chargers, 21-17 (H)
1970—Tie, 31-31 (SD)
1971—Oilers, 49-33 (H)
1972—Chargers, 34-20 (SD)
1974—Oilers, 21-14 (H)
1975—Oilers, 33-17 (H)
1976—Chargers, 30-27 (SD)
1978—Chargers, 45-24 (H)
1979—****Oilers, 17-14 (SD)
1984—Chargers, 31-14 (SD)
1985—Oilers, 37-35 (H)
1986—Chargers, 27-0 (SD)
1987—Oilers, 33-18 (H)
1989—Oilers, 34-27 (SD)
1990—Oilers, 17-7 (SD)
1992—Oilers, 27-0 (H)
1993—Chargers, 18-17 (SD)
1998—Chargers, 13-7 (T)
2004—Chargers, 38-17 (SD)
2006—Chargers, 40-7 (SD)
(RS Pts.—Chargers 872, Titans 778)
(PS Pts.—Titans 51, Chargers 33)
*Franchise in Los Angeles prior to 1961
**Franchise in Houston prior to 1997; known as Oilers prior to 1999
***AFL Championship
****AFC Divisional Playoff

SAN DIEGO vs. WASHINGTON
RS: Redskins lead series, 6-2
1973—Redskins, 38-0 (W)
1980—Redskins, 40-17 (W)
1983—Redskins, 27-24 (SD)
1986—Redskins, 30-27 (SD)
1989—Redskins, 26-21 (W)
1998—Redskins, 24-20 (W)
2001—Chargers, 30-3 (SD)
2005—Chargers, 23-17 (W) OT
(RS Pts.—Redskins 205, Chargers 162)

SAN FRANCISCO vs. ARIZONA
RS: 49ers lead series, 17-14;
See Arizona vs. San Francisco
SAN FRANCISCO vs. ATLANTA
RS: 49ers lead series, 44-26-1
PS: Falcons lead series, 1-0;
See Atlanta vs. San Francisco

SAN FRANCISCO vs. BALTIMORE
RS: Series tied, 1-1;
See Baltimore vs. San Francisco
SAN FRANCISCO vs. BUFFALO
RS: Bills lead series, 5-4;
See Buffalo vs. San Francisco
SAN FRANCISCO vs. CAROLINA
RS: Panthers lead series, 8-7;
See Carolina vs. San Francisco
SAN FRANCISCO vs. CHICAGO
RS: Bears lead series, 29-27-1
PS: 49ers lead series, 3-0;
See Chicago vs. San Francisco
SAN FRANCISCO vs. CINCINNATI
RS: 49ers lead series, 7-3
PS: 49ers lead series, 2-0;
See Cincinnati vs. San Francisco
SAN FRANCISCO vs. CLEVELAND
RS: Browns lead series, 10-6;
See Cleveland vs. San Francisco
SAN FRANCISCO vs. DALLAS
RS: 49ers lead series, 14-9-1
PS: Cowboys lead series, 5-2;
See Dallas vs. San Francisco
SAN FRANCISCO vs. DENVER
RS: Broncos lead series, 6-5
PS: 49ers lead series, 1-0;
See Denver vs. San Francisco
SAN FRANCISCO vs. DETROIT
RS: 49ers lead series, 32-26-1
PS: Series tied, 1-1;
See Detroit vs. San Francisco
SAN FRANCISCO vs. GREEN BAY
RS: Packers lead series, 28-25-1
PS: Packers lead series, 4-1;
See Green Bay vs. San Francisco
SAN FRANCISCO vs. HOUSTON
RS: 49ers lead series, 1-0;
See Houston vs. San Francisco
SAN FRANCISCO vs. INDIANAPOLIS
RS: Colts lead series, 23-18;
See Indianapolis vs. San Francisco
SAN FRANCISCO vs. JACKSONVILLE
RS: Jaguars lead series, 2-0;
See Jacksonville vs. San Francisco
SAN FRANCISCO vs. KANSAS CITY
RS: 49ers lead series, 6-4;
See Kansas City vs. San Francisco
SAN FRANCISCO vs. MIAMI
RS: Dolphins lead series, 5-4
PS: 49ers lead series, 1-0;
See Miami vs. San Francisco
SAN FRANCISCO vs. MINNESOTA
RS: Series tied, 18-18-1
PS: 49ers lead series, 4-1;
See Minnesota vs. San Francisco
SAN FRANCISCO vs. NEW ENGLAND
RS: 49ers lead series, 7-3;
See New England vs. San Francisco
SAN FRANCISCO vs. NEW ORLEANS
RS: 49ers lead series, 45-21-2;
See New Orleans vs. San Francisco
SAN FRANCISCO vs. N.Y. GIANTS
RS: 49ers lead series, 13-12
PS: 49ers lead series, 4-3;
See N.Y. Giants vs. San Francisco
SAN FRANCISCO vs. N.Y. JETS
RS: 49ers lead series, 8-2;
See N.Y. Jets vs. San Francisco
SAN FRANCISCO vs. OAKLAND

RS: Raiders lead series, 6-5;
See Oakland vs. San Francisco
SAN FRANCISCO vs. PHILADELPHIA
RS: 49ers lead series, 16-9-1
PS: 49ers lead series, 1-0;
See Philadelphia vs. San Francisco
SAN FRANCISCO vs. PITTSBURGH
RS: 49ers lead series, 10-8;
See Pittsburgh vs. San Francisco
SAN FRANCISCO vs. ST. LOUIS
RS: Rams lead series, 59-53-2
PS: 49ers lead series, 1-0;
See St. Louis vs. San Francisco
SAN FRANCISCO vs. SAN DIEGO
RS: 49ers lead series, 6-5
PS: 49ers lead series, 1-0;
See San Diego vs. San Francisco
SAN FRANCISCO vs. SEATTLE
RS: Series tied, 8-8
1976—49ers, 37-21 (Sea)
1979—Seahawks, 35-24 (SF)
1985—49ers, 19-6 (SF)
1988—49ers, 38-7 (Sea)
1991—49ers, 24-22 (Sea)
1997—Seahawks, 38-9 (Sea)
2002—49ers, 28-21 (Sea)
   49ers, 31-24 (SF)
2003—Seahawks, 20-19 (Sea)
   Seahawks, 24-17 (SF)
2004—Seahawks, 34-0 (Sea)
   Seahawks, 42-27 (SF)
2005—Seahawks, 27-25 (SF)
   Seahawks, 41-3 (Sea)
2006—49ers, 20-14 (SF)
   49ers, 24-14 (Sea)
(RS Pts.—Seahawks 390, 49ers 345)
SAN FRANCISCO vs. TAMPA BAY
RS: 49ers lead series, 14-3
PS: Buccaneers lead series, 1-0
1977—49ers, 20-10 (SF)
1978—49ers, 6-3 (SF)
1979—49ers, 23-7 (SF)
1980—Buccaneers, 24-23 (SF)
1983—49ers, 35-21 (SF)
1984—49ers, 24-17 (SF)
1986—49ers, 31-7 (TB)
1987—49ers, 24-10 (TB)
1989—49ers, 20-16 (TB)
1990—49ers, 31-7 (SF)
1992—49ers, 21-14 (SF)
1993—49ers, 45-21 (SF)
1994—49ers, 41-16 (SF)
1997—Buccaneers, 13-6 (TB)
2002—*Buccaneers, 31-6 (TB)
2003—49ers, 24-7 (SF)
2004—Buccaneers, 35-3 (TB)
2005—49ers, 15-10 (SF)
(RS Pts.—49ers 392, Buccaneers 238)
(PS Pts.—Buccaneers 31, 49ers 6)
*NFC Divisional Playoff
SAN FRANCISCO vs. *TENNESSEE
RS: 49ers lead series, 7-4
1970—49ers, 30-20 (H)
1975—Oilers, 27-13 (SF)
1978—Oilers, 20-19 (H)
1981—49ers, 28-6 (SF)
1984—49ers, 34-21 (H)
1987—49ers, 27-20 (SF)
1990—49ers, 24-21 (H)
1993—Oilers, 10-7 (SF)

1996—49ers, 10-9 (H)
1999—49ers, 24-22 (SF)
2005—Titans, 33-22 (T)
(RS Pts.—49ers 238, Titans 209)
*Franchise in Houston prior to 1997;
known as Oilers prior to 1999*
SAN FRANCISCO vs. WASHINGTON
RS: 49ers lead series, 13-9-1
PS: 49ers lead series, 3-1
1952—49ers, 23-17 (W)
1954—49ers, 41-7 (SF)
1955—Redskins, 7-0 (W)
1961—49ers, 35-3 (SF)
1967—Redskins, 31-28 (W)
1969—Tie, 17-17 (SF)
1970—49ers, 26-17 (SF)
1971—*49ers, 24-20 (SF)
1973—Redskins, 33-9 (W)
1976—Redskins, 24-21 (SF)
1978—Redskins, 38-20 (W)
1981—49ers, 30-17 (W)
1983—**Redskins, 24-21 (W)
1984—49ers, 37-31 (SF)
1985—49ers, 35-8 (W)
1986—Redskins, 14-6 (W)
1988—49ers, 37-21 (SF)
1990—49ers, 26-13 (W)
   *49ers, 28-10 (SF)
1992—*49ers, 20-13 (SF)
1994—49ers, 37-22 (W)
1996—49ers, 19-16 (W) OT
1998—49ers, 45-10 (W)
1999—Redskins, 26-20 (SF) OT
2002—49ers, 20-10 (SF)
2004—Redskins, 26-16 (SF)
2005—Redskins, 52-17 (W)
(RS Pts.—49ers 565, Redskins 460)
(PS Pts.—49ers 93, Redskins 67)
*NFC Divisional Playoff
**NFC Championship

SEATTLE vs. ARIZONA
RS: Series tied, 8-8;
See Arizona vs. Seattle
SEATTLE vs. ATLANTA
RS: Seahawks lead series, 8-2;
See Atlanta vs. Seattle
SEATTLE vs. BALTIMORE
RS: Ravens lead series, 2-0;
See Baltimore vs. Seattle
SEATTLE vs. BUFFALO
RS: Seahawks lead series, 6-4;
See Buffalo vs. Seattle
SEATTLE vs. CAROLINA
RS: Series tied, 1-1
PS: Seahawks lead series, 1-0;
See Carolina vs. Seattle
SEATTLE vs. CHICAGO
RS: Seahawks lead series, 6-3
PS: Bears lead series, 1-0;
See Chicago vs. Seattle
SEATTLE vs. CINCINNATI
RS: Series tied, 8-8
PS: Bengals lead series, 1-0;
See Cincinnati vs. Seattle
SEATTLE vs. CLEVELAND
RS: Seahawks lead series, 11-4;
See Cleveland vs. Seattle
SEATTLE vs. DALLAS
RS: Cowboys lead series, 6-4

PS: Seahawks lead series, 1-0;
See Dallas vs. Seattle
SEATTLE vs. DENVER
RS: Broncos lead series, 33-18
PS: Seahawks lead series, 1-0;
See Denver vs. Seattle
SEATTLE vs. DETROIT
RS: Seahawks lead series, 6-4;
See Detroit vs. Seattle
SEATTLE vs. GREEN BAY
RS: Packers lead series, 6-5
PS: Packers lead series, 1-0;
See Green Bay vs. Seattle
SEATTLE vs. HOUSTON
RS: Seahawks lead series, 1-0;
See Houston vs. Seattle
SEATTLE vs. INDIANAPOLIS
RS: Colts lead series, 5-4;
See Indianapolis vs. Seattle
SEATTLE vs. JACKSONVILLE
RS: Seahawks lead series, 3-2;
See Jacksonville vs. Seattle
SEATTLE vs. KANSAS CITY
RS: Chiefs lead series, 31-18;
See Kansas City vs. Seattle
SEATTLE vs. MIAMI
RS: Dolphins lead series, 6-3
PS: Dolphins lead series, 2-1;
See Miami vs. Seattle
SEATTLE vs. MINNESOTA
RS: Seahawks lead series, 6-4;
See Minnesota vs. Seattle
SEATTLE vs. NEW ENGLAND
RS: Series tied, 7-7;
See New England vs. Seattle
SEATTLE vs. NEW ORLEANS
RS: Seahawks lead series, 5-4;
See New Orleans vs. Seattle
SEATTLE vs. N.Y. GIANTS
RS: Giants lead series, 7-5;
See N.Y. Giants vs. Seattle
SEATTLE vs. N.Y. JETS
RS: Series tied, 8-8;
See N.Y. Jets vs. Seattle
SEATTLE vs. OAKLAND
RS: Raiders lead series, 27-23
PS: Series tied, 1-1;
See Oakland vs. Seattle
SEATTLE vs. PHILADELPHIA
RS: Eagles lead series, 6-4;
See Philadelphia vs. Seattle
SEATTLE vs. PITTSBURGH
RS: Seahawks lead series, 8-6
PS: Steelers lead series, 1-0;
See Pittsburgh vs. Seattle
SEATTLE vs. ST. LOUIS
RS: Rams lead series, 9-8
PS: Rams lead series, 1-0;
See St. Louis vs. Seattle
SEATTLE vs. SAN DIEGO
RS: Seahawks lead series, 25-23;
See San Diego vs. Seattle
SEATTLE vs. SAN FRANCISCO
RS: Series tied, 8-8;
See San Francisco vs. Seattle
SEATTLE vs. TAMPA BAY
RS: Seahawks lead series, 6-1
1976—Seahawks, 13-10 (TB)
1977—Seahawks, 30-23 (S)
1994—Seahawks, 22-21 (S)

1996—Seahawks, 17-13 (TB)
1999—Buccaneers, 16-3 (S)
2004—Seahawks, 10-6 (TB)
2006—Seahawks, 23-7 (TB)
(RS Pts.—Seahawks 118, Buccaneers 96)
SEATTLE vs. *TENNESSEE
RS: Seahawks lead series, 9-4
PS: Titans lead series, 1-0
1977—Oilers, 22-10 (S)
1979—Seahawks, 34-14 (S)
1980—Seahawks, 26-7 (H)
1981—Oilers, 35-17 (H)
1982—Oilers, 23-21 (H)
1987—**Oilers, 23-20 (H) OT
1988—Seahawks, 27-24 (S)
1990—Seahawks, 13-10 (S) OT
1993—Oilers, 24-14 (H)
1994—Seahawks, 16-14 (H)
1996—Seahawks, 23-16 (S)
1997—Seahawks, 16-13 (S)
1998—Seahawks, 20-18 (S)
2005—Seahawks, 28-24 (T)
(RS Pts.—Seahawks 265, Titans 244)
(PS Pts.—Titans 23, Seahawks 20)
*Franchise in Houston prior to 1997;
known as Oilers prior to 1999
**AFC First-Round Playoff
SEATTLE vs. WASHINGTON
RS: Redskins lead series, 9-4
PS: Seahawks lead series, 1-0
1976—Redskins, 31-7 (W)
1980—Seahawks, 14-0 (W)
1983—Redskins, 27-17 (S)
1986—Redskins, 19-14 (W)
1989—Redskins, 29-0 (S)
1992—Redskins, 16-3 (S)
1994—Seahawks, 28-7 (W)
1995—Seahawks, 27-20 (W)
1998—Seahawks, 24-14 (S)
2001—Redskins, 27-14 (S)
2002—Redskins, 14-3 (S)
2003—Redskins, 27-20 (W)
2005—Redskins, 20-17 (W) OT
   *Seahawks, 20-10 (S)
(RS Pts.—Redskins 251, Seahawks 188)
(PS Pts.—Seahawks 20, Redskins 10)
*NFC Divisional Playoff

TAMPA BAY vs. ARIZONA
RS: Cardinals lead series, 8-7;
See Arizona vs. Tampa Bay
TAMPA BAY vs. ATLANTA
RS: Buccaneers lead series, 15-12;
See Atlanta vs. Tampa Bay
TAMPA BAY vs. BALTIMORE
RS: Buccaneers lead series, 2-1;
See Baltimore vs. Tampa Bay
TAMPA BAY vs. BUFFALO
RS: Buccaneers lead series, 6-2;
See Buffalo vs. Tampa Bay
TAMPA BAY vs. CAROLINA
RS: Panthers lead series, 8-5;
See Carolina vs. Tampa Bay
TAMPA BAY vs. CHICAGO
RS: Bears lead series, 35-17;
See Chicago vs. Tampa Bay
TAMPA BAY vs. CINCINNATI
RS: Buccaneers lead series, 6-3;
See Cincinnati vs. Tampa Bay
TAMPA BAY vs. CLEVELAND

RS: Browns lead series, 5-2;
See Cleveland vs. Tampa Bay
TAMPA BAY vs. DALLAS
RS: Cowboys lead series, 7-3
PS: Cowboys lead series, 2-0;
See Dallas vs. Tampa Bay
TAMPA BAY vs. DENVER
RS: Broncos lead series, 4-2;
See Denver vs. Tampa Bay
TAMPA BAY vs. DETROIT
RS: Lions lead series, 26-24
PS: Buccaneers lead series, 1-0;
See Detroit vs. Tampa Bay
TAMPA BAY vs. GREEN BAY
RS: Packers lead series, 29-19-1
PS: Packers lead series, 1-0;
See Green Bay vs. Tampa Bay
TAMPA BAY vs. HOUSTON
RS: Buccaneers lead series, 1-0;
See Houston vs. Tampa Bay
TAMPA BAY vs. INDIANAPOLIS
RS: Colts lead series, 6-4;
See Indianapolis vs. Tampa Bay
TAMPA BAY vs. JACKSONVILLE
RS: Jaguars lead series, 2-1;
See Jacksonville vs. Tampa Bay
TAMPA BAY vs. KANSAS CITY
RS: Chiefs lead series, 5-4;
See Kansas City vs. Tampa Bay
TAMPA BAY vs. MIAMI
RS: Series tied, 4-4;
See Miami vs. Tampa Bay
TAMPA BAY vs. MINNESOTA
RS: Vikings lead series, 31-19;
See Minnesota vs. Tampa Bay
TAMPA BAY vs. NEW ENGLAND
RS: Patriots lead series, 4-2;
See New England vs. Tampa Bay
TAMPA BAY vs. NEW ORLEANS
RS: Saints lead series, 19-11;
See New Orleans vs. Tampa Bay
TAMPA BAY vs. N.Y. GIANTS
RS: Giants lead series, 10-6;
See N.Y. Giants vs. Tampa Bay
TAMPA BAY vs. N.Y. JETS
RS: Jets lead series, 8-1;
See N.Y. Jets vs. Tampa Bay
TAMPA BAY vs. OAKLAND
RS: Raiders lead series, 5-1
PS: Buccaneers lead series, 1-0;
See Oakland vs. Tampa Bay
TAMPA BAY vs. PHILADELPHIA
RS: Series tied, 5-5
PS: Series tied, 2-2;
See Philadelphia vs. Tampa Bay
TAMPA BAY vs. PITTSBURGH
RS: Steelers lead series, 7-1;
See Pittsburgh vs. Tampa Bay
TAMPA BAY vs. ST. LOUIS
RS: Rams lead series, 9-6
PS: Rams lead series, 2-0;
See St. Louis vs. Tampa Bay
TAMPA BAY vs. SAN DIEGO
RS: Chargers lead series, 7-1;
See San Diego vs. Tampa Bay
TAMPA BAY vs. SAN FRANCISCO
RS: 49ers lead series, 14-3
PS: Buccaneers lead series, 1-0;
See San Francisco vs. Tampa Bay
TAMPA BAY vs. SEATTLE

RS: Seahawks lead series, 6-1;
See Seattle vs. Tampa Bay
TAMPA BAY vs. *TENNESSEE
RS: Titans lead series, 7-1
1976—Oilers, 20-0 (H)
1980—Oilers, 20-0 (H)
1983—Buccaneers, 33-24 (TB)
1989—Oilers, 20-17 (H)
1995—Oilers, 19-7 (H)
1998—Oilers, 31-22 (TB)
2001—Titans, 31-28 (Tenn) OT
2003—Titans, 33-13 (T)
(RS Pts.—Titans 198, Buccaneers 134)
*Franchise in Houston prior to 1997;
known as Oilers prior to 1999
TAMPA BAY vs. WASHINGTON
RS: Series tied, 7-7
PS: Series tied, 1-1
1977—Redskins, 10-0 (TB)
1982—Redskins, 21-13 (TB)
1989—Redskins, 32-28 (W)
1993—Redskins, 23-17 (TB)
1994—Buccaneers, 26-21 (TB)
   Buccaneers, 17-14 (W)
1995—Buccaneers, 14-6 (TB)
1996—Buccaneers, 24-10 (TB)
1998—Redskins, 20-16 (W)
1999—*Buccaneers, 14-13 (TB)
2000—Redskins, 20-17 (W) OT
2003—Buccaneers, 35-13 (W)
2004—Redskins, 16-10 (W)
2005—Buccaneers, 36-35 (TB)
   **Redskins, 17-10 (TB)
2006—Buccaneers, 20-17 (TB)
(RS Pts.—Buccaneers 273, Redskins 258)
(PS Pts.—Redskins 30, Buccaneers 24)
*NFC Divisional Playoff
**NFC First-Round Playoff

TENNESSEE VS. ARIZONA
RS: Cardinals lead series, 5-3;
See Arizona vs. Tennessee
TENNESSEE vs. ATLANTA
RS: Titans lead series, 6-5;
See Atlanta vs. Tennessee
TENNESSEE vs. BALTIMORE
RS: Ravens lead series, 8-7
PS: Series tied, 1-1;
See Baltimore vs. Tennessee
TENNESSEE vs. BUFFALO
RS: Titans lead series, 24-14
PS: Bills lead series, 2-1;
See Buffalo vs. Tennessee
TENNESSEE vs. CAROLINA
RS: Series tied, 1-1;
See Carolina vs. Tennessee
TENNESSEE vs. CHICAGO
RS: Bears lead series, 5-4;
See Chicago vs. Tennessee
TENNESSEE vs. CINCINNATI
RS: Titans lead series, 38-30-1
PS: Bengals lead series, 1-0;
See Cincinnati vs. Tennessee
TENNESSEE vs. CLEVELAND
RS: Browns lead series, 33-26
PS: Titans lead series, 1-0;
See Cleveland vs. Tennessee
TENNESSEE vs. DALLAS
RS: Cowboys lead series, 7-5;
See Dallas vs. Tennessee

TENNESSEE vs. DENVER
RS: Titans lead series, 20-12-1
PS: Broncos lead series, 2-1;
See Denver vs. Tennessee

TENNESSEE vs. DETROIT
RS: Titans lead series, 6-3;
See Detroit vs. Tennessee

TENNESSEE vs. GREEN BAY
RS: Titans lead series, 5-4;
See Green Bay vs. Tennessee

TENNESSEE vs. HOUSTON
RS: Titans lead series, 8-2;
See Houston vs. Tennessee

TENNESSEE vs. INDIANAPOLIS
RS: Colts lead series, 14-10
PS: Titans lead series, 1-0;
See Indianapolis vs. Tennessee

TENNESSEE vs. JACKSONVILLE
RS: Titans lead series, 13-11
PS: Titans lead series, 1-0;
See Jacksonville vs. Tennessee

TENNESSEE vs. KANSAS CITY
RS: Chiefs lead series, 25-18
PS: Chiefs lead series, 2-0;
See Kansas City vs. Tennessee

TENNESSEE vs. MIAMI
RS: Dolphins lead series, 17-13
PS: Titans lead series, 1-0;
See Miami vs. Tennessee

TENNESSEE vs. MINNESOTA
RS: Vikings lead series, 7-3;
See Minnesota vs. Tennessee

TENNESSEE vs. NEW ENGLAND
RS: Patriots lead series, 20-15-1
PS: Series tied, 1-1;
See New England vs. Tennessee

TENNESSEE vs. NEW ORLEANS
RS: Titans lead series, 6-4-1;
See New Orleans vs. Tennessee

TENNESSEE vs. N.Y. GIANTS
RS: Giants lead series, 5-4;
See N.Y. Giants vs. Tennessee

TENNESSEE vs. N.Y. JETS
RS: Titans lead series, 20-15-1
PS: Titans lead series, 1-0;
See N.Y. Jets vs. Tennessee

TENNESSEE vs. OAKLAND
RS: Raiders lead series, 23-17
PS: Raiders lead series, 4-0;
See Oakland vs. Tennessee

TENNESSEE vs. PHILADELPHIA
RS: Eagles lead series, 6-3;
See Philadelphia vs. Tennessee

TENNESSEE vs. PITTSBURGH
RS: Steelers lead series, 38-28
PS: Steelers lead series, 3-1;
See Pittsburgh vs. Tennessee

TENNESSEE vs. ST. LOUIS
RS: Rams lead series, 6-3
PS: Rams lead series, 1-0;
See St. Louis vs. Tennessee

TENNESSEE vs. SAN DIEGO
RS: Chargers lead series, 21-13-1
PS: Titans lead series, 3-0;
See San Diego vs. Tennessee

TENNESSEE vs. SAN FRANCISCO
RS: 49ers lead series, 7-4;
See San Francisco vs. Tennessee

TENNESSEE vs. SEATTLE
RS: Seahawks lead series, 9-4

PS: Titans lead series, 1-0;
See Seattle vs. Tennessee

TENNESSEE vs. TAMPA BAY
RS: Titans lead series, 7-1;
See Tampa Bay vs. Tennessee

*TENNESSEE vs. WASHINGTON
RS: Titans lead series, 6-4
1971—Redskins, 22-13 (W)
1975—Oilers, 13-10 (H)
1979—Oilers, 29-27 (W)
1985—Redskins, 16-13 (W)
1988—Oilers, 41-17 (H)
1991—Redskins, 16-13 (W) OT
1997—Oilers, 28-14 (T)
2000—Titans, 27-21 (W)
2002—Redskins, 31-14 (T)
2006—Titans, 25-22 (W)
(RS—Titans 216, Redskins 196)
*Franchise in Houston prior to 1997;
known as Oilers prior to 1999*

WASHINGTON vs. ARIZONA
RS: Redskins lead series, 71-44-2;
See Arizona vs. Washington

WASHINGTON vs. ATLANTA
RS: Redskins lead series, 14-5-1
PS: Redskins lead series, 1-0;
See Atlanta vs. Washington

WASHINGTON vs BALTIMORE
RS: Ravens lead series, 2-1;
See Baltimore vs. Washington

WASHINGTON vs. BUFFALO
RS: Bills lead series, 6-4
PS: Redskins lead series, 1-0;
See Buffalo vs. Washington

WASHINGTON vs. CAROLINA
RS: Redskins lead series, 7-1;
See Carolina vs. Washington

WASHINGTON vs. CHICAGO
RS: Bears lead series, 20-17-1
PS: Redskins lead series, 4-3;
See Chicago vs. Washington

WASHINGTON vs. CINCINNATI
RS: Redskins lead series, 4-3;
See Cincinnati vs. Washington

WASHINGTON vs. CLEVELAND
RS: Browns lead series, 33-9-1;
See Cleveland vs. Washington

WASHINGTON vs. DALLAS
RS: Cowboys lead series, 55-35-2
PS: Redskins lead series, 2-0;
See Dallas vs. Washington

WASHINGTON vs. DENVER
RS: Broncos lead series, 6-4
PS: Redskins lead series, 1-0;
See Denver vs. Washington

WASHINGTON vs. DETROIT
RS: Redskins lead series, 25-10
PS: Redskins lead series, 3-0;
See Detroit vs. Washington

WASHINGTON vs. GREEN BAY
RS: Packers lead series, 16-12-1
PS: Series tied, 1-1;
See Green Bay vs. Washington

WASHINGTON vs. HOUSTON
RS: Redskins lead series, 2-0;
See Houston vs. Washington

WASHINGTON vs. INDIANAPOLIS
RS: Colts lead series, 18-10;
See Indianapolis vs. Washington

WASHINGTON vs. JACKSONVILLE
RS: Redskins lead series, 3-1;
See Jacksonville vs. Washington

WASHINGTON vs. KANSAS CITY
RS: Chiefs lead series, 6-1;
See Kansas City vs. Washington

WASHINGTON vs. MIAMI
RS: Dolphins lead series, 6-3
PS: Series tied, 1-1;
See Miami vs. Washington

WASHINGTON vs. MINNESOTA
RS: Redskins lead series, 7-6
PS: Redskins lead series, 3-2;
See Minnesota vs. Washington

WASHINGTON vs. NEW ENGLAND
RS: Redskins lead series, 6-1;
See New England vs. Washington

WASHINGTON vs. NEW ORLEANS
RS: Redskins lead series, 14-7;
See New Orleans vs. Washington

WASHINGTON vs. N.Y. GIANTS
RS: Giants lead series, 84-60-4
PS: Series tied, 1-1;
See N.Y. Giants vs. Washington

WASHINGTON vs. N.Y. JETS
RS: Redskins lead series, 7-1;
See N.Y. Jets vs. Washington

WASHINGTON vs. OAKLAND
RS: Raiders lead series, 7-3
PS: Raiders lead series, 1-0;
See Oakland vs. Washington

WASHINGTON vs. PHILADELPHIA
RS: Redskins lead series, 74-64-5
PS: Redskins lead series, 1-0;
See Philadelphia vs. Washington

WASHINGTON vs. PITTSBURGH
RS: Redskins lead series, 42-30-3;
See Pittsburgh vs. Washington

WASHINGTON vs. ST. LOUIS
RS: Redskins lead series, 20-7-1
PS: Series tied, 2-2;
See St. Louis vs. Washington

WASHINGTON vs. SAN DIEGO
RS: Redskins lead series, 6-2;
See San Diego vs. Washington

WASHINGTON vs. SAN FRANCISCO
RS: 49ers lead series, 13-9-1
PS: 49ers lead series, 3-1;
See San Francisco vs. Washington

WASHINGTON vs. SEATTLE
RS: Redskins lead series, 9-4
PS: Seahawks lead series, 1-0;
See Seattle vs. Washington

WASHINGTON vs. TAMPA BAY
RS: Series tied, 7-7
PS: Series tied, 1-1;
See Tampa Bay vs. Washington

WASHINGTON vs. TENNESSEE
RS: Titans lead series, 6-4;
See Tennessee vs. Washington

SUPER BOWL COMPOSITE STANDINGS

	W	L	Pct.	Pts.	OP
San Francisco 49ers	5	0	1.000	188	89
Baltimore Ravens	1	0	1.000	34	7
New York Jets	1	0	1.000	16	7
Tampa Bay Buccaneers	1	0	1.000	48	21
Pittsburgh Steelers	5	1	.833	141	110
Green Bay Packers	3	1	.750	127	76
Indianapolis/Baltimore Colts	2	1	.667	52	46
New York Giants	2	1	.667	66	73
Dallas Cowboys	5	3	.625	221	132
New England Patriots	3	2	.600	107	148
Oakland/L.A. Raiders	3	2	.600	132	114
Washington Redskins	3	2	.600	122	103
Chicago Bears	1	1	.500	63	39
Kansas City Chiefs	1	1	.500	33	42
Miami Dolphins	2	3	.400	74	103
Denver Broncos	2	4	.333	115	206
St. Louis/L.A. Rams	1	2	.333	59	67
Atlanta Falcons	0	1	.000	19	34
Carolina Panthers	0	1	.000	29	32
San Diego Chargers	0	1	.000	26	49
Seattle Seahawks	0	1	.000	10	21
Tennessee Titans	0	1	.000	16	23
Cincinnati Bengals	0	2	.000	37	46
Philadelphia Eagles	0	2	.000	31	51
Buffalo Bills	0	4	.000	73	139
Minnesota Vikings	0	4	.000	34	95

SUPER BOWL HOST CITIES

Miami/South Florida	9	
New Orleans	9	
Los Angeles	7	(LA Coliseum 2, Rose Bowl 5)
San Diego	3	
Tampa	3	
Atlanta	2	
Detroit	2	
Houston	2	
Jacksonville	1	
Minneapolis	1	
Stanford	1	
Tempe	1	

FUTURE SUPER BOWL SITES

Super Bowl XLII	Feb. 3, 2008	University of Phoenix Stadium, Arizona
Super Bowl XLIII	Feb. 1, 2009	Raymond James Stadium, Tampa, Florida
Super Bowl XLIV	Feb. 7, 2010*	Dolphin Stadium, South Florida

*Tentative Date

PETE ROZELLE TROPHY/SUPER BOWL MVPs*

Super Bowl I	— QB Bart Starr, Green Bay
Super Bowl II	— QB Bart Starr, Green Bay
Super Bowl III	— QB Joe Namath, N.Y. Jets
Super Bowl IV	— QB Len Dawson, Kansas City
Super Bowl V	— LB Chuck Howley, Dallas
Super Bowl VI	— QB Roger Staubach, Dallas
Super Bowl VII	— S Jake Scott, Miami
Super Bowl VIII	— RB Larry Csonka, Miami
Super Bowl IX	— RB Franco Harris, Pittsburgh
Super Bowl X	— WR Lynn Swann, Pittsburgh
Super Bowl XI	— WR Fred Biletnikoff, Oakland
Super Bowl XII	— DT Randy White and DE Harvey Martin, Dallas
Super Bowl XIII	— QB Terry Bradshaw, Pittsburgh
Super Bowl XIV	— QB Terry Bradshaw, Pittsburgh
Super Bowl XV	— QB Jim Plunkett, Oakland
Super Bowl XVI	— QB Joe Montana, San Francisco
Super Bowl XVII	— RB John Riggins, Washington
Super Bowl XVIII	— RB Marcus Allen, L.A. Raiders
Super Bowl XIX	— QB Joe Montana, San Francisco
Super Bowl XX	— DE Richard Dent, Chicago
Super Bowl XXI	— QB Phil Simms, N.Y. Giants
Super Bowl XXII	— QB Doug Williams, Washington
Super Bowl XXIII	— WR Jerry Rice, San Francisco
Super Bowl XXIV	— QB Joe Montana, San Francisco
Super Bowl XXV	— RB Ottis Anderson, N.Y. Giants
Super Bowl XXVI	— QB Mark Rypien, Washington
Super Bowl XXVII	— QB Troy Aikman, Dallas
Super Bowl XXVIII	— RB Emmitt Smith, Dallas
Super Bowl XXIX	— QB Steve Young, San Francisco
Super Bowl XXX	— CB Larry Brown, Dallas
Super Bowl XXXI	— KR-PR Desmond Howard, Green Bay
Super Bowl XXXII	— RB Terrell Davis, Denver
Super Bowl XXXIII	— QB John Elway, Denver
Super Bowl XXXIV	— QB Kurt Warner, St. Louis
Super Bowl XXXV	— LB Ray Lewis, Baltimore
Super Bowl XXXVI	— QB Tom Brady, New England
Super Bowl XXXVII	— S Dexter Jackson, Tampa Bay
Super Bowl XXXVIII	— QB Tom Brady, New England
Super Bowl XXXIX	— WR Deion Branch, New England
Super Bowl XL	— WR Hines Ward, Pittsburgh
Super Bowl XLI	— QB Peyton Manning, Indianapolis

* Award named Pete Rozelle Trophy since Super Bowl XXV.

SUPER BOWL MVP BY POSITION

Quarterback	21
Running Back	7
Wide Receiver	5
Defensive End	2
Linebacker	2
Safety	2
Cornerback	1
Defensive Tackle	1
Kick Returner-Punt Returner	1

A defensive end and defensive tackle shared the Super Bowl XII MVP award.

RESULTS

NFC leads AFC, 21-20

Super Bowl	Date	Winner (Share)	Loser (Share)	Score	Site	Attendance
XLI	2-4-07	Indianapolis ($73,000)	Chicago ($38,000)	29-17	South Florida	74,512
XL	2-5-06	Pittsburgh ($73,000)	Seattle ($38,000)	21-10	Detroit	68,206
XXXIX	2-6-05	New England ($68,000)	Philadelphia ($36,500)	24-21	Jacksonville	78,125
XXXVIII	2-1-04	New England ($68,000)	Carolina ($36,500)	32-29	Houston	71,525
* XXXVII	1-26-03	Tampa Bay ($63,000)	Oakland ($35,000)	48-21	San Diego	67,603
* XXXVI	2-3-02	New England ($63,000)	St. Louis ($34,500)	20-17	New Orleans	72,922
XXXV	1-28-01	Baltimore ($58,000)	N.Y. Giants ($34,500)	34-7	Tampa	71,921
* XXXIV	1-30-00	St. Louis ($58,000)	Tennessee ($33,000)	23-16	Atlanta	72,625
XXXIII	1-31-99	Denver ($53,000)	Atlanta ($32,500)	34-19	South Florida	74,803
XXXII	1-25-98	Denver ($48,000)	Green Bay ($29,000)	31-24	San Diego	68,912
XXXI	1-26-97	Green Bay ($48,000)	New England ($29,000)	35-21	New Orleans	72,301
XXX	1-28-96	Dallas ($42,000)	Pittsburgh ($27,000)	27-17	Tempe	76,347
XXIX	1-29-95	San Francisco ($42,000)	San Diego ($26,000)	49-26	South Florida	74,107
* XXVIII	1-30-94	Dallas ($38,000)	Buffalo ($23,500)	30-13	Atlanta	72,817
XXVII	1-31-93	Dallas ($36,000)	Buffalo ($18,000)	52-17	Pasadena	98,374
XXVI	1-26-92	Washington ($36,000)	Buffalo ($18,000)	37-24	Minneapolis	63,130
* XXV	1-27-91	N.Y. Giants ($36,000)	Buffalo ($18,000)	20-19	Tampa	73,813
XXIV	1-28-90	San Francisco ($36,000)	Denver ($18,000)	55-10	New Orleans	72,919
XXIII	1-22-89	San Francisco ($36,000)	Cincinnati ($18,000)	20-16	South Florida	75,129
XXII	1-31-88	Washington ($36,000)	Denver ($18,000)	42-10	San Diego	73,302
XXI	1-25-87	N.Y. Giants ($36,000)	Denver ($18,000)	39-20	Pasadena	101,063
XX	1-26-86	Chicago ($36,000)	New England ($18,000)	46-10	New Orleans	73,818
XIX	1-20-85	San Francisco ($36,000)	Miami ($18,000)	38-16	Stanford	84,059
XVIII	1-22-84	L.A. Raiders ($36,000)	Washington ($18,000)	38-9	Tampa	72,920
* XVII	1-30-83	Washington ($36,000)	Miami ($18,000)	27-17	Pasadena	103,667
XVI	1-24-82	San Francisco ($18,000)	Cincinnati ($9,000)	26-21	Pontiac	81,270
XV	1-25-81	Oakland ($18,000)	Philadelphia ($9,000)	27-10	New Orleans	76,135
XIV	1-20-80	Pittsburgh ($18,000)	Los Angeles ($9,000)	31-19	Pasadena	103,985
XIII	1-21-79	Pittsburgh ($18,000)	Dallas ($9,000)	35-31	Miami	79,484
XII	1-15-78	Dallas ($18,000)	Denver ($9,000)	27-10	New Orleans	75,583
XI	1-9-77	Oakland ($15,000)	Minnesota ($7,500)	32-14	Pasadena	103,438
X	1-18-76	Pittsburgh ($15,000)	Dallas ($7,500)	21-17	Miami	80,187
IX	1-12-75	Pittsburgh ($15,000)	Minnesota ($7,500)	16-6	New Orleans	80,997
VIII	1-13-74	Miami ($15,000)	Minnesota ($7,500)	24-7	Houston	71,882
VII	1-14-73	Miami ($15,000)	Washington ($7,500)	14-7	Los Angeles	90,182
VI	1-16-72	Dallas ($15,000)	Miami ($7,500)	24-3	New Orleans	81,023
V	1-17-71	Baltimore ($15,000)	Dallas ($7,500)	16-13	Miami	79,204
* IV	1-11-70	Kansas City ($15,000)	Minnesota ($7,500)	23-7	New Orleans	80,562
III	1-12-69	N.Y. Jets ($15,000)	Baltimore ($7,500)	16-7	Miami	75,389
II	1-14-68	Green Bay ($15,000)	Oakland ($7,500)	33-14	Miami	75,546
I	1-15-67	Green Bay ($15,000)	Kansas City ($7,500)	35-10	Los Angeles	61,946

* One week between conference championship games and Super Bowl; all others had two weeks between conference championship games and Super Bowl.

SUPER BOWL XLI

Dolphin Stadium, South Florida
February 4, 2007, Attendance: 74,512
INDIANAPOLIS 29, CHICAGO 17—Peyton Manning passed for 247 yards and 1 touchdown as the Colts won their first Super Bowl in 36 years. The Colts outgained the Bears 430-265 in total yards and maintained a 38:04-21:56 edge in time of possession. Devin Hester opened the game with a 92-yard kickoff return for a touchdown, the first time the Super Bowl began with a touchdown. Two possessions later, on third-and-10, Manning found Reggie Wayne wide open deep down the middle for a 53-yard touchdown to tie the score. A steady rain forced the teams to commit 4 first-quarter turnovers, and Hunter Smith mishandled the snap on the extra point, allowing the Bears to maintain a 7-6 lead. Later in the quarter, Thomas Jones' 52-yard run set up Rex Grossman's short touchdown pass to Muhsin Muhammad for a 14-6 lead. The Colts scored on back-to-back drives to begin the second quarter, capped by Dominic Rhodes' 1-yard run, for a 16-14 lead. To begin the second half, the Colts ran 7:34 off the clock with a 13-play, 56-yard drive that culminated with Adam Vinatieri's 24-yard field goal for a 19-14 lead. The teams then exchanged field goals, and the Bears forced a punt. On first-and-10 from the Bears' 38 with 11:59 to play, Grossman's pass intended for Muhammad was thrown high. Kelvin Hayden intercepted the pass, maneuvered up the far sideline while staying inbounds, and raced 56 yards for a touchdown. It was Hayden's first-ever professional interception. Four plays later, Bob Sanders intercepted Grossman's deep pass. The Bears got the ball back twice, but never ran a play across midfield. Manning, who won the Pete Rozelle MVP award, was 25 of 38 for 247 yards and 1 touchdown, with 1 interception. Rhodes carried 21 times for 113 yards. Joseph Addai had 10 receptions for 66 yards. Grossman was 20 of 28 for 165 yards and 1 touchdown, with 2 interceptions. Jones rushed 15 times for 112 yards.

Indianapolis (29) Offense		Chicago (17)
Reggie Wayne	WR	Muhsin Muhammad
Tarik Glenn	LT	John Tait
Ryan Lilja	LG	Ruben Brown
Jeff Satruday	C	Olin Kreutz
Jake Scott	RG	Roberto Garza
Ryan Diem	RT	Fred Miller
Dallas Clark	TE	Desmond Clark

Marvin Harrison	WR	Bernard Berrian
Peyton Manning	QB	Rex Grossman
Joseph Addai	RB	Thomas Johns
Ben Utecht	H-B/FB	Jason McKie

Defense

Robert Mathis	LDE	Adewale Ogunleye
Anthony McFarland	LDT	Tank Johnson
Raheem Brock	RDT	Ian Scott
Dwight Freeney	RDE	Alex Brown
Cato June	WLB	Lance Briggs
Gary Brackett	MLB	Brian Urlacher
Rob Morris	SLB	Hunter Hillenmeyer
Nick Harper	LCB	Charles Tillman
Jason David	RCB	Nathan Vasher
Antoine Bethea	SS	Chris Harris
Bob Sanders	FS	Danieal Manning

SUBSTITUTIONS

INDIANAPOLIS—Specialists: K—Adam Vinatieri. P—Hunter Smith. Offense: RB—De De Dorsey, Dominic Rhodes. WR—Aaron Moorehead, Terrence Wilkins. TE—Bryan Fletcher, Justin Snow. T—Charlie Johnson. C/G—Dylan Gandy. Defense: DT—Dan Klecko, Darrell Reid. DE—Bo Schobel, Josh Thomas. LB—Rocky Boiman, Tyjuan Hagler, Freddie Keiaho, Keith O'Neil. DB—Matt Giordano, Kelvin Hayden, Marlin Jackson, Dexter Reid. DNP: QB—Jim Sorgi. Not Active: WR—Ricky Proehl, John Standeford. G—Matt Ulrich. T—Daniel Federkeil. DE—Ryan LaCasse. LB—Gilbert Gardner. DB—Tim Jennings, T.J. Rushing.
Chicago—Specialists: K—Robbie Gould. P—Brad Maynard. LS—Patrick Mannelly. Offense: RB—Cedric Benson, Adrian Peterson. WR—Rashied Davis. TE—John Gilmore, Gabe Reid. G—Terrence Metcalf. T—John St. Clair. Defense: DT—Alfonso Boone. DL—Israel Idonije. DE—Mark Anderson. LB—Brendon Ayanbadejo, Leon Joe, Darrell McClover. CB—Devin Hester, Ricky Manning Jr., Dante Wesley. S—Todd Johnson, Cameron Worrell. DNP: QB—Brian Griese. WR—Mark Bradley. Not Active: QB—Kyle Orton. FB—J.D. Runnels. WR—Justin Gage. C/G—Anthony Oakley. DT—Antonio Garay. LB—Rod Wilson. S—Tyler Everett, Nick Turnbull.

OFFICIALS

Referee—Tony Corrente. Umpire—Carl Paganelli. Line Judge—Ron Marinucci. Side Judge—John Parry. Head Linesman—George Hayward. Back Judge—Perry Paganelli. Field Judge—Jim Saracino. Replay Official—Mark Burns.

SCORING

Indianapolis (AFC)	6	10	6	7	— 29
Chicago (NFC)	14	0	3	0	— 17

Chi—	Hester 92 kickoff return (Gould kick) (14:46)	
Ind—	Wayne 53 pass from Manning (mishandled hold) (6:50)	
Chi—	Muhammad 4 pass from Grossman (Gould kick) (4:34)	
Ind—	FG Vinatieri 29 (11:17)	
Ind—	Rhodes 1 run (Vinatieri kick) (6:09)	
Ind—	FG Vinatieri 24 (7:26)	
Ind—	FG Vinatieri 20 (3:16)	
Chi—	FG Gould 44 (1:14)	
Ind—	Hayden 56 interception return (Vinatieri kick) (11:44)	

TEAM STATISTICS

	IND	CHI
Total First Downs	24	11
Rushing	12	3
Passing	11	8
Penalty	1	0
Total Net Yardage	430	265
Total Offensive Plays	81	48
Avg. Gain Per Offensive Play	5.3	5.5
Rushes	42	19
Yards Gained Rushing (Net)	191	111
Avg. Yards per Rush	4.5	5.8
Passes Attempted	38	28
Passes Completed	25	20
Had Intercepted	1	2
Tackled Attempting to Pass	1	1
Yards Lost Attempting to Pass	8	11
Yards Gained Passing (Net)	239	154
Punts	4	5
Avg. Distance	40.5	45.2
Punt Returns	3	1
Punt Return Yardage	42	3
Kickoff Returns	4	6
Kickoff Return Yardage	89	138
Interception Return Yardage	94	6
Total Return Yardage	136	9
Fumbles	2	4
Fumbles Lost	2	3
Own Fumbles Recovered	0	1
Opponent Fumbles Recovered	3	2
Penalties	6	4
Yards Penalized	40	35
Field Goals	3	1
Field Goals Attempted	4	1
Third-Down Efficiency	8/18	3/10
Fourth-Down Efficiency	0/1	0/1
Time of Possession	38:04	21:56

INDIVIDUAL STATISTICS

RUSHING: IND: Rhodes 21-113-1, Addai 19-77-0, Clark 1-1-0, Manning 1-0-0. CHI: Jones 15-112-0, Grossman 2-0-0, Bensoon 2-(1)-0.
PASSING: IND: Manning 38-25-247-1-1. CHI: Grossman 28-20-165-1-2.
RECEIVING: IND: Addai 10-66-0, Harrison 5-59-0, Clark 4-36-0, Wayne 2-61-1, Fletcher 2-9-0, Rhdoes 1-8-0, Utecht 1-8-0. CHI: Clark 6-64-0, Berrian 4-38-0, Jones 4-18-0, Muhammad 3-35-1,McKie 2-8-0, Davis 1-2-0.
KICKOFF RETURNS: IND: Wilkins 4-89-0. CHI: Gilmore 2-12-0, Hester 1-92-1, Davis 1-15-0, Peterson 1-10-0, Reid 1-9-0.
PUNT RETURNS: IND: Wilkins 3-42-0. CHI: Hester 1-3-0.
PUNTING: IND: Smith 4-162-40.5. CHI: Maynard 5-226-45.2.
INTERCEPTIONS: IND: Hayden 1-56-1, Sanders 1-38-0. CHI: C. Harris 1-6-0.
SACKS: IND: McFarland 1. CHI: Anderson 0.5, Ta. Johnson 0.5.

SUPER BOWL XL
Ford Field, Detroit, Michigan
February 5, 2006, Attendance: 68,206
PITTSBURGH 21, SEATTLE 10—at Ford Field, attendance 68,206. The Steelers made three big plays on offense and played a bend-but-don't-break defense to win their record-tying fifth Super Bowl title. The Seahawks lost despite winning the turnover battle (2-1), having more total yards (396-339), and consuming more of the clock (33:02-26:58). The Seahawks crossed midfield on 9 of their 12 possessions, but scored just twice. Late in the first quarter, Darrell Jackson's 16-yard touchdown catch was nullified by pass interference. The Seahawks settled for Josh Brown's 47-yard field goal. With 3:58 left in the second quarter, faced with third-and-28 from the Seahawks' 40, Ben Roethlisberger eluded the rush, rolled left and threw a deep pass across field. Hines Ward outleaped Michael Boulware at the 3-yard line for a 37-yard pass play. Two plays later, on a broken play, Roethlisberger dove over left tackle and reached the goal line for a touchdown. The Seahawks reached the Steelers' 40 with 54 seconds left, but Matt Hasselbeck's third-and-6 pass fell incomplete and Brown's 54-yard field-goal attempt sailed wide right. On the second play of the second half, Willie Parker set a Super Bowl record with his 75-yard touchdown run over right tackle. Brown's 50-yard field-goal attempt sailed wide left on the next possession, and the Steelers drove to the Seahawks' 7. On third-and-6, Roethlisberger's pass to the right flat was intercepted by Kelly Herndon, who returned the ball a Super Bowl-record 76 yards to the Steelers' 20. Three plays later, Jerramy Stevens caught Hasselbeck's 16-yard touchdown pass to cut the deficit to 14-10 with 6:45 left in the third quarter. Early in the fourth quarter, the Seahawks drove to the Steelers' 19. On first down, Stevens caught an 18-yard pass, but a holding penalty nullified the catch and Ike Taylor intercepted Hasselbeck's pass a few plays later. Three plays later, Parker took a handoff and gave the ball to Antwaan Randle El on a reverse. Rolling to his right, Randle El fired a perfect 43-yard touchdown pass to Ward for a 21-10 lead with 8:56 to play. The Seahawks punted and then did not get the ball back until there was 1:51 remaining. Seattle reached the Steelers' 26 with 35 seconds left. From the Steelers' 23, Hasselbeck's fourth-and-7 pass to Stevens fell incomplete at the 2-yard line with three seconds remaining. Roethlisberger, who became the youngest quarterback to win the Super Bowl, was 9 of 21 for 123 yards, with 2 interceptions. Ward had 5 catches for 123 yards to earn the Pete Rozelle Trophy as the game's most valuable player. Hasselbeck was 26 of 49 for 273 yards and 1 touchdown, with 1 interception.

Seattle (NFC)	3 0 7 0	—	10
Pittsburgh (AFC)	0 7 7 7	—	21

Sea— FG J. Brown 47 (0:22)
Pitt— Roethlisberger 1 run (Reed kick) (1:55)
Pitt— Parker 75 run (Reed kick) (14:38)
Sea— Stevens 16 pass from Hasselbeck (J. Brown kick) (6:45)
Pitt— Ward 43 pass from Randle El (Reed kick) (8:56)

SUPER BOWL XXXIX

Alltel Stadium, Jacksonville, Florida
February 6, 2005, Attendance: 78,125
NEW ENGLAND 24, PHILADELPHIA 21—Deion Branch had 11 receptions for 133 yards and the Patriots' defense forced 4 turnovers en route to becoming the eighth team to post consecutive Super Bowl titles. The Patriots matched the Dallas Cowboys (XXVII, XXVIII, and XXX) as the only team with three Super Bowl victories in the span of four seasons. The Eagles threatened first, driving to the Patriots' 8 late in the first quarter. On first down, Mike Vrabel sacked Donovan McNabb for a 16-yard loss and, after a penalty overturned an interception, Rodney Harrison stepped in front of a pass for an interception at the Eagles' 4. Early in the second quarter the Eagles drove 81 yards, keyed by Todd Pinkston's 40-yard catch, and capped by McNabb's 6-yard touchdown pass to L.J. Smith on third-and-goal for a 7-0 lead. The Patriots responded by driving to the Eagles' 4, but Tom Brady fumbled on a fake handoff attempt and Darwin Walker recovered. Later in the quarter, a 29-yard punt by Dirk Johnson allowed the Patriots to drive just 37 yards, keyed by Branch's 7-yard catch on third-and-3, and capped by Brady's pass to David Givens on the right side of the end zone to tie the game with 1:10 left in the half. New England began the second half with a 9-play, 69-yard drive, including 4 receptions, 2 on third down, by Branch, and capped by Vrabel's 2-yard catch. The Eagles put together a 10-play, 74-yard drive later in the third quarter, keyed by Brian Westbrook's 4-yard catch on third-and-3, and followed on the next play by his 10-yard touchdown catch to tie the game. On the ensuing drive, Kevin Faulk caught screen passes of 13 and 14 yards, and had a 12-yard run, and Corey Dillon capped the possession with a 2-yard run with 13:44 remaining for a 21-14 lead. The Patriots' defense forced a three-and-out, and Branch's 19-yard catch set up Adam Vinatieri's 22-yard field goal with 8:40 to play. Tedy Bruschi intercepted McNabb's pass at the Patriots' 24 with 7:20 remaining. The Eagles forced a punt and, beginning at their own 21 with 5:40 to play, needed 13 plays to drive 79 yards, capped by McNabb's 30-yard touchdown pass on a post-pattern to Greg Lewis with

1:48 to play. Christian Fauria recovered the onside kick, but the Eagles' defense forced a punt. Dexter Reid downed Josh Miller's 32-yard punt at the Eagles' 4 with 46 seconds left, and Harrison intercepted McNabb's pass three plays later to clinch the title. Brady was 23 of 33 for 236 yards and 2 touchdowns. Branch earned MVP honors with his Super Bowl-record-tying 11 catches. McNabb was 30 of 51 for 357 yards and 3 touchdowns, with 3 interceptions. Terrell Owens had 9 receptions for 122 yards.

New England (AFC)	0 7 7 10	—	24
Philadelphia (NFC)	0 7 7 7	—	21

Phil— Smith 6 pass from McNabb (Akers kick) (9:55)
NE— Givens 4 pass from Brady (Vinatieri kick) (1:10)
NE— Vrabel 2 pass from Brady (Vinatieri kick) (11:04)
Phil— Westbrook 10 pass from McNabb (Akers kick) (3:35)
NE — Dillon 2 run (Vinatieri kick) (13:44)
NE— FG Vinatieri 22 (8:40)
Phil— G. Lewis 30 pass from McNabb (Akers kick) (1:48)

SUPER BOWL XXXVIII

Reliant Stadium, Houston, Texas
February 1, 2004, Attendance: 71,525
NEW ENGLAND 32, CAROLINA 29—Adam Vinatieri kicked a 41-yard field goal with four seconds remaining as the Patriots won their second Super Bowl in three seasons. While it took a Super Bowl-record 26 minutes and 55 seconds for the first points to be scored, the teams combined for 868 yards (481 for New England) and the game also featured the highest scoring quarter (combined 37 points in the fourth). Vinatieri missed a 31-yard field goal on the Patriots' first possession, and had a 36-yard attempt blocked by Shane Burton with 6:00 left in the second quarter. But three plays later, Mike Vrabel sacked Jake Delhomme and forced him to fumble. Richard Seymour recovered at the Panthers' 20, and a 12-yard scramble by Tom Brady on third-and-7 set up his 5-yard touchdown pass to Deion Branch with 3:05 left in the first half. The Panthers responded with an 8-play, 95-yard drive capped by Delhomme's 39-yard perfectly placed touchdown pass to Steve Smith with 1:07 left in the half. Delhomme beat the blitz by lofting the pass deep down the left sideline. Brady's 52-yard pass to Branch with 37 seconds left in the half set up David Givens' 5-yard touchdown catch with 18 seconds left. New England squibbed the ensuing kickoff and Kris Mangum returned it 12 yards to the Panthers' 47. A 21-yard run by Stephen Davis set up John Kasay's 50-yard field goal as the half expired for a 14-10 New England lead. Neither team scored in the third quarter, but Antowain Smith's 2-yard touchdown run two plays into the final

quarter capped a 71-yard drive and gave the Patriots a 21-10 lead. Undaunted, Carolina scored on its next two possessions. First, Delhomme completed passes of 18 and 22 yards to Smith to set up DeShaun Foster's 33-yard touchdown run to cut the deficit to 21-16 with 12:39 to play. Carolina went for the 2-point conversion, but Delhomme's pass was incomplete. New England marched to the Panthers' 9 with the ensuing kickoff, but Reggie Howard intercepted Brady's third-and-goal pass in the end zone. Two plays later, Delhomme rolled left and fired a Super Bowl-record 85-yard touchdown pass to Muhammad for a 22-21 lead with 6:53 left. Once again, the Panthers went for 2 points and Delhomme's pass was incomplete. New England drove 68 yards on its next possession, with Givens catching a 25-yard pass and 18-yard pass on third-and-9, to set up Brady's 1-yard touchdown pass to Vrabel, who was lined up as a tight end. A direct snap to Kevin Faulk resulted in a 2-point conversion for a 29-22 lead with 2:51 left. Delhomme completed passes of 19 yards to Muhammad and 31 yards to Ricky Proehl before finding Proehl from 12 yards with the tying touchdown with 1:08 remaining. Kasay's ensuing kickoff went out of bounds, giving New England the ball at their own 40. Five plays later, faced with third-and-3 from the Panthers' 40 with 14 seconds left, Brady fired a 17-yard pass to Branch to set up Vinatieri's Super Bowl-winning 41-yard field goal. Brady, who was named the Super Bowl most valuable player for the second time in his career, was 32 of 48 for 354 yards and 3 touchdowns, with 1 interception. Branch had 10 receptions for 143 yards. Delhomme was 16 of 33 for 323 yards and 3 touchdowns, and Muhammad had 4 catches for 140 yards.

Carolina (NFC)	0 10 0 19	—	29
New England (AFC)	0 14 0 18	—	32

NE — Branch 5 pass from Brady (Vinatieri kick) (3:05)
Car— Smith 39 pass from Delhomme (Kasay kick) (1:07)
NE — Givens 5 pass from Brady (Vinatieri kick) (0:18)
Car— FG Kasay 50 (0:00)
NE— Smith 2 run (Vinatieri kick) (14:49)
Car— Foster 33 run (pass failed) (12:39)
Car— Muhammad 85 pass from Delhomme (pass failed) (6:53)
NE — Vrabel 1 pass from Brady (Faulk run) (2:51)
Car— Proehl 12 pass from Delhomme (Kasay kick) (1:08)
NE — FG Vinatieri 41 (0:04)

SUPER BOWL XXXVII

Qualcomm Stadium, San Diego, CA
January 26, 2003, Attendance: 67,603
TAMPA BAY 48, OAKLAND 21—The Buccaneers' defense intercepted 5 passes, 3

of which were returned for touchdowns, and recorded 5 sacks as Tampa Bay scored 34 unanswered points en route to its first Super Bowl victory. Charles Woodson intercepted Brad Johnson three plays into the game to give Oakland the ball at the Buccaneers' 36. But Simeon Rice sacked Rich Gannon on third down to force the Raiders to settle for Sebastian Janikowski's 40-yard field goal. On their next nine possessions, the Raiders registered just 2 first downs and did not run a play inside the Buccaneers' 40 as Tampa Bay scored the next 34 points. The Buccaneers answered Janikowski's field goal with Martin Gramatica's 31-yard boot to tie the game. An interception by Dexter Jackson set up Gramatica's go-ahead field goal early in the second quarter. Midway through the second quarter, a 25-yard punt return by Karl Williams and a 19-yard run by Michael Pittman led to Mike Alstott's 2-yard touchdown run. Late in the half, the Buccaneers drove 77 yards, aided by 3 defensive penalties and pass receptions of 16 and 12 yards by Alstott, to set up Brad Johnson's 5-yard touchdown pass to Keenan McCardell with 30 seconds left in the half, which gave Tampa Bay a 20-3 lead. With their first possession of the second half, the Buccaneers put together a 14-play, 89-yard drive that consumed 7:52 and was culminated by Johnson's 8-yard scoring toss to McCardell. Two plays later, Dwight Smith intercepted Gannon's pass and returned it 44 yards for a touchdown and a 34-3 lead with 4:47 left in the third quarter. Tampa Bay scored 4 touchdowns in a span of 16:37. Jerry Porter's 39-yard touchdown catch in the back of the end zone made it 34-9. Less than three minutes later, Tim Johnson blocked Tom Tupa's punt. Eric Johnson caught the ball and dove into the end zone for a touchdown to cut the deficit to 34-15 with 14:16 remaining. The Buccaneers drove deep downfield again, but Tupa mishandled the snap for a field-goal attempt, allowing the Raiders to regain possession. Gannon hit Jerry Rice with a 48-yard touchdown pass with 6:06 left to trim the lead to 34-21. A 9-yard pass by Johnson to Alstott on third-and-7 allowed Tampa Bay to take another two minutes off the clock before Tupa punted with 2:44 remaining. On third-and-18 from the Raiders' 29, Derrick Brooks intercepted Gannon's pass and raced 44 yards down the left sideline for a touchdown with 1:18 remaining to give Tampa Bay a commanding 41-21 lead. Smith intercepted a tipped pass and returned it 50 yards for a touchdown with two seconds left to finish the scoring. Johnson was 18 of 34 for 215 yards and 2 touchdowns, with 1 interception. Pittman had 29 carries for 124 yards. Gannon was 24 of 44 for 272 yards and 2 touchdowns, with a Super Bowl record 5 interceptions. Jackson,

who had the first 2 interceptions, 1 of which led to the go-ahead field goal, was named the game's most valuable player.

Oakland (AFC)	3	0	6	12	—	21
Tampa Bay (NFC)	3	17	14	14	—	48

Oak — FG Janikowski 40 (10:40)
TB — FG Gramatica 31 (7:51)
TB — FG Gramatica 43 (11:16)
TB — Alstott 2 run (Gramatica kick) (6:24)
TB — McCardell 5 pass from B. Johnson (Gramatica kick) (0:30)
TB — McCardell 8 pass from B. Johnson (Gramatica kick) (5:30)
TB — D. Smith 44 interception return (Gramatica kick) (4:47)
Oak — Porter 39 pass from Gannon (pass failed) (2:14)
Oak — E. Johnson 13 return of blocked punt (pass failed) (14:16)
Oak — Rice 48 pass from Gannon (pass failed) (6:06)
TB — Brooks 44 interception return (Gramatica kick) (1:18)
TB — D. Smith 50 interception return (Gramatica kick) (0:02)

SUPER BOWL XXXVI

Louisiana Superdome, New Orleans, LA
February 3, 2002, Attendance: 72,922
NEW ENGLAND 20, ST. LOUIS 17—Adam Vinatieri's 48-yard field goal as time expired gave the New England Patriots their first Super Bowl title. The Rams outgained the Patriots 427-267 in total yards, but the Patriots forced 3 turnovers, which resulted in 17 points, while committing no turnovers. Jeff Wilkins' 50-yard field goal capped a 10-play, 48-yard drive midway through the first quarter to give the Rams a 3-0 lead. The first turnover came with 8:49 left in the second quarter, when Ty Law stepped in front of an out-pattern pass intended for Isaac Bruce and raced 47 yards untouched down the left sideline into the end zone. Late in the first half, Kurt Warner completed a 15-yard pass to Ricky Proehl to the Patriots' 40, but Antwan Harris forced Proehl to fumble and Terrell Buckley recovered. Five plays later, Tom Brady's 8-yard touchdown pass to David Patten with 31 seconds left in the quarter gave New England a 14-3 halftime lead. Late in the third quarter, Torry Holt slipped coming off the line of scrimmage, and Otis Smith intercepted Warner's pass and returned it 30 yards to the Rams' 33 to set up Vinatieri's 37-yard field goal and a 17-3 lead. The Rams responded by driving to the Patriots' 3. On fourth-and-goal, Warner scrambled, was tackled by Roman Phifer, and fumbled. Tebucky Jones picked up the ball and raced the length of the field for an apparent touchdown, but the play was negated by Willie McGinest's holding penalty. Warner scored two plays later to trim the deficit to 17-10 with 9:31 left. The

Patriots went three and out on their next two possessions, giving the Rams the ball on their 45-yard-line with 1:51 left. Warner completed an 18-yard pass to Az-Zahir Hakim and an 11-yard pass to Yo Murphy before connecting on a 26-yard touchdown pass to Proehl with 1:30 left to tie the game. Operating without any time outs, Brady completed 3 short passes to J.R. Redmond to reach the Patriots' 41 with 33 seconds left. After an incompletion, Brady completed 23- and 16-yard passes to Troy Brown and Jermaine Wiggins, respectively, to reach the Rams' 30, and then spiked the ball with 7 seconds remaining. Vinatieri drilled the 48-yard field-goal attempt, marking the first time in Super Bowl history the game had been won on the final play. Brady, who earned most valuable player honors, was 16 of 27 for 145 yards and 1 touchdown. Warner was 28 of 44 for 365 yards and 1 touchdown, with 2 interceptions.

St. Louis (NFC)	3	0	0	14	—	17
New England (AFC)	0	14	3	3	—	20

StL — FG Wilkins 50 (3:10)
NE — Law 47 interception return (Vinatieri kick) (8:49)
NE — Patten 8 pass from Brady (Vinatieri kick) (0:31)
NE — FG Vinatieri 37 (1:18)
StL — Warner 2 run (Wilkins kick) (9:31)
StL — Proehl 26 pass from Warner (Wilkins kick) (1:30)
NE — FG Vinatieri 48 (0:00)

SUPER BOWL XXXV

Raymond James Stadium, Tampa, Florida
January 28, 2001, Attendance: 71,921
BALTIMORE 34, N.Y. GIANTS 7—The Ravens' defense completed a dominating season by permitting just 152 yards, forcing 5 turnovers, recording 4 sacks, and not allowing an offensive touchdown en route to the franchise's first Super Bowl victory. Jermaine Lewis' punt return into Giants' territory midway through the first quarter was followed two plays later by Trent Dilfer's 38-yard touchdown pass to Brandon Stokley, which gave the Ravens a 7-0 lead. Early in the second quarter, Jessie Armstead intercepted a short pass by Dilfer and returned it 43 yards for a touchdown, but the play was nullified by a penalty. Dilfer's 36-yard pass to Qadry Ismail in the second quarter set up Matt Stover's 47-yard field goal with 1:48 left in the half. Tiki Barber's 27-yard run gave the Giants their deepest penetration of the game, to the Ravens' 29, but Chris McAlister intercepted Kerry Collins' pass on the next play to preserve a 10-0 lead. In the third quarter, Duane Starks stepped in front of Amani Toomer and intercepted Collins' pass. Starks returned it 49 yards untouched for a 17-0 lead. The Giants immediately cut the lead to 10 points when Ron Dixon returned the ensuing kickoff 97 yards for a touchdown. Howev-

er, Jermaine Lewis then matched Dixon's kickoff return as he cut across the field and raced 84 yards for a 24-7 lead with 3:13 left in the third quarter. The 3 touchdowns in 36 seconds were a Super Bowl record. The Giants gained just 1 first down on their final four possessions. Jamal Lewis' 3-yard touchdown run midway through the fourth quarter gave Baltimore a 31-7 lead, and Robert Bailey recovered Dixon's fumble on the ensuing kickoff return to set up Stover's 34-yard field goal with 5:27 remaining to finish the scoring. Dilfer completed 12 of 25 passes for 153 yards and 1 touchdown. Jamal Lewis had 27 carries for 102 yards. Collins was 15 of 39 for 112 yards, with 4 interceptions. Ray Lewis was named Super Bowl most valuable player.

Baltimore (AFC)   7   3   14 10 — 34
N.Y. Giants (NFC)   0   0   7   0 — 7

Balt — Stokley 38 pass from Dilfer (Stover kick) (6:50)
Balt — FG Stover 47 (1:41)
Balt — Starks 49 interception return (Stover kick) (3:49)
NYG — Dixon 97 kickoff return (Daluiso kick) (3:31)
Balt — Je. Lewis 84 kickoff return (Stover kick) (3:13)
Balt — Ja. Lewis 3 run (Stover kick) (8:45)
Balt — FG Stover 34 (5:27)

SUPER BOWL XXXIV
Georgia Dome, Atlanta, Georgia
January 30, 2000, Attendance: 72,625
ST. LOUIS 23, TENNESSEE 16—Mike Jones tackled Kevin Dyson at the 1-yard line as time expired, preserving the Rams' first-ever Super Bowl title. The Rams drove inside the Titans' 20 with each of their first six possessions, but compiled just 3 field goals and a touchdown to take a 16-0 lead. Holder Mike Horan's bobbled snap averted a 35-yard field-goal attempt to conclude the Rams' first drive. The Titans responded with a 42-yard drive, their longest of the half, but Al Del Greco missed a 47-yard attempt. Jeff Wilkins added 3 field goals and missed a 34-yard attempt while the Titans did not threaten the rest of the half, giving the Rams a 9-0 lead at intermission despite outgaining the Titans in total yards (294-89). Tennessee drove 43 yards with the second half's opening kickoff, but Todd Lyght blocked Del Greco's 47-yard attempt to keep the Titans off the board. Kurt Warner's 31-yard pass to Isaac Bruce keyed the ensuing drive that was capped by Warner's 9-yard touchdown pass to Torry Holt with 7:20 left in the third quarter to give the Rams a 16-0 lead. The Titans responded with touchdown drives in excess of seven minutes on each of their next two possessions. Steve McNair's 23-yard scramble set up Eddie George's 1-yard run in the final minute of the third quarter. McNair's 2-point conversion pass to Frank

Wycheck was incomplete, but the Titans' defense forced a punt and the offense drove 79 yards in 13 plays, highlighted by 21-yard passes from McNair to Isaac Byrd and Jackie Harris, and capped by George's 2-yard run to cut the deficit to 16-13 with 7:21 remaining. The Rams once again failed to get a first down, and following a punt, the Titans needed just 28 yards to set up Del Greco's game-tying 43-yard kick with 2:12 left. On the next play from scrimmage, Warner fired a deep pass down the right sideline to Bruce, who caught the ball at the Titans' 38, cut toward the inside, and outran the defense to the end zone to give the Rams a 23-16 lead with 1:54 left. The Titans drove downfield, and McNair avoided a sack and completed a 16-yard pass to Kevin Dyson at the Rams' 10 with six seconds remaining. With no timeouts, McNair attempted a quick pass to a slanting Dyson, who caught the ball in stride at the Rams' 3. However, Jones reacted quickly and stepped up to tackle Dyson at the 1-yard line as time expired. Warner, who was named the game's most valuable player, was 24 of 45 for a Super Bowl-record 414 yards and 2 touchdowns. Bruce had 6 catches for 162 yards, and Holt had 7 for 109 yards. McNair was 22 of 36 for 214 yards. The Titans were the first team in Super Bowl history to come back from a 16-point deficit.

St. Louis (NFC)   3   6   7   7 — 23
Tennessee (AFC)   0   0   6 10 — 16

StL — FG Wilkins 27 (3:00)
StL — FG Wilkins 29 (4:16)
StL — FG Wilkins 28 (0:15)
StL — Holt 9 pass from Warner (Wilkins kick) (3:59)
Tenn — George 1 run (pass failed) (0:14)
Tenn — George 2 run (Del Greco kick) (7:21)
Tenn — FG Del Greco 43 (2:12)
StL — Bruce 73 pass from Warner (Wilkins kick) (1:54)

SUPER BOWL XXXIII
Pro Player Stadium, South Florida
January 31, 1999, Attendance: 74,803
DENVER 34, ATLANTA 19—John Elway, in his last game, passed for 336 yards and ran for a touchdown to earn most valuable player honors as the Broncos became the first AFC team to win consecutive Super Bowls since the Steelers won XIII and XIV. A 25-yard pass interference penalty on Ray Crockett assisted the Falcons' nine-play, 80-yard game-opening drive that was capped by Morten Andersen's 32-yard field goal. Elway's 41-yard pass to Rod Smith kept alive Denver's ensuing drive and led to Howard Griffith's 1-yard touchdown run. Ronnie Bradford's interception and return to the Broncos' 35 late in the first quarter gave Atlanta excellent field position. However, Jamal Anderson was stopped for no gain on third-and-

1 and thrown for a 2-yard loss on fourth down. Denver capitalized on its defensive effort with Jason Elam's 26-yard field goal. The Falcons responded by driving to the Broncos' 8, but Andersen's 26-yard field-goal attempt sailed wide right and on the next play, Elway fired an 80-yard touchdown pass to Smith to turn a possible 10-6 game into a 17-3 Broncos lead. Andersen's 28-yard field goal and 2 misses by Elam on the Broncos' first two second-half possessions gave Atlanta an opportunity to climb back into the game. However, Darrien Gordon dashed the Falcons' hopes with interceptions on consecutive possessions inside the Broncos' 20 to stop drives and set up Broncos touchdowns. Gordon returned the first interception, on a tipped pass, 58 yards to the Falcons' 24 to set up Griffith's second touchdown five plays later, and picked the second pass off at the Broncos' 2 and returned it 50 yards. Terrell Davis turned a short pass into a 39-yard gain, and Elway scored two plays later to give Denver a 31-6 lead. Tim Dwight returned the ensuing kickoff for a touchdown, and, after a field goal by Elam, the Falcons' offense scored with 2:04 remaining on Chandler's 3-yard pass to Terance Mathis. Byron Chamberlain recovered the ensuing onside kick, but Tyrone Braxton recovered Anderson's fumble at the Falcons' 33 with 1:30 remaining to ice the game. The Falcons drove inside the Broncos' 30 seven times, but tallied just 1 touchdown and 2 field goals, throwing 2 interceptions, missing 1 field goal, and turning the ball over 1 time on downs during the other possessions. Elway was 18 of 29 for 336 yards and 1 touchdown, with 1 interception. Davis had 25 carries for 102 yards. Smith had 5 receptions for 152 yards. Chandler was 19 of 35 for 219 yards and 1 touchdown, with 3 interceptions.

Denver (AFC)   7   10   0 17 — 34
Atlanta (NFC)   3   3   0 13 — 19

Atl — FG Andersen 32 (9:35)
Den — Griffith 1 run (Elam kick) (3:55)
Den — FG Elam 26 (9:17)
Den — R. Smith 80 pass from Elway (Elam kick) (4:54)
Atl — FG Andersen 28 (2:25)
Den — Griffith 1 run (Elam kick) (14:56)
Den — Elway 3 run (Elam kick) (11:20)
Atl — Dwight 94 kickoff return (Andersen kick) (11:01)
Den — FG Elam 37 (7:08)
Atl — Mathis 3 pass from Chandler (pass failed) (2:04)

SUPER BOWL XXXII
Qualcomm Stadium, San Diego, California
January 25, 1998, Attendance: 68,912
DENVER 31, GREEN BAY 24—Terrell Davis rushed for 157 yards and a Super Bowl-record 3 touchdowns to lead the

Broncos to their first NFL championship and break the NFC's streak of Super Bowl victories at 13. The defending Super Bowl champion Packers took the opening kickoff and marched 76 yards in just over four minutes, scoring the first points on Brett Favre's 22-yard touchdown pass to Antonio Freeman. The Broncos responded with a 10-play, 58-yard drive capped by Davis' 1-yard run to tie the game. Tyrone Braxton intercepted Favre two plays later, and John Elway scored on a third-and-goal play to begin the second quarter. Steve Atwater forced Favre to fumble three plays later, and Neil Smith recovered at the Packers' 33. Jason Elam converted a 51-yard field goal, the second longest in Super Bowl history, to give the Broncos a 17-7 lead with 12:21 left in the half. After an exchange of punts, the Packers produced a 17-play, 95-yard drive that consumed 7:26 and finished with Favre's 6-yard touchdown pass to Mark Chmura on third-and-5 with 12 seconds left in the half. Tyrone Williams forced and recovered Davis' fumble at the Broncos' 26 on the first play from scrimmage in the second half. However, the Broncos' defense kept the Packers out of the end zone as Ryan Longwell's 27-yard field goal tied the game with 11:59 left in the third quarter. After another exchange of punts, Elway's 36-yard pass to Ed McCaffrey keyed a 13-play, 92-yard drive capped by Davis' 1-yard touchdown run with 34 seconds left in the third quarter. Tim McKyer recovered Freeman's fumble at the Packers' 22 on the ensuing kickoff return, giving the Broncos a golden opportunity, but Eugene Robinson intercepted Elway's pass in the end zone on the next play. Sparked by Robinson's play, the Packers took just four plays, three on passes to Freeman, to score the tying touchdown with 13:32 remaining. Each defense stiffened, forcing two punts, but the Broncos got great field position following Craig Hentrich's 39-yard punt to the Packers' 49 with 3:27 left and the score tied 24-24. Davis rushed for 2 yards on the first play, but Darrius Holland's 15-yard facemask penalty moved the ball to the Packers' 32. Elway threw a 23-yard pass to Howard Griffith two plays later, and after a holding penalty, Davis rushed 17 yards to the Packers' 1 with 1:47 left. After a timeout, Davis waltzed into the end zone to give Denver a 31-24 lead with 1:45 remaining. Freeman returned the kickoff 22 yards to the Broncos' 30, and Favre completed 22- and 13-yard screen passes to Dorsey Levens to reach the Broncos' 35 with 1:04 left. But after a 4-yard pass to Levens and incompletions to Freeman and Brooks, John Mobley knocked away Favre's pass to Chmura with 32 seconds left to give the Broncos the Vince Lombardi Trophy. Elway was 12 of 22 for 123 yards, with 1 interception. Favre was 25 of 42 for 256 yards and 1 touchdown,

with 1 interception. Freeman had 9 receptions for 126 yards. Davis was named the game's most valuable player.

Green Bay (NFC)		7	7	3	7	—	24
Denver (AFC)		7	10	7	7	—	31

GB — Freeman 22 pass from Favre (Longwell kick) (10:58)
Den — Davis 1 run (Elam kick) (5:39)
Den — Elway 1 run (Elam kick) (14:55)
Den — FG Elam 51 (12:21)
GB — Chmura 6 pass from Favre (Longwell kick) (0:12)
GB — FG Longwell 27 (11:59)
Den — Davis 1 run (Elam kick) (0:34)
GB — Freeman 13 pass from Favre (Longwell kick) (13:32)
Den — Davis 1 run (Elam kick) (1:45)

SUPER BOWL XXXI

Louisiana Superdome, New Orleans, LA
January 26, 1997, Attendance: 72,301
GREEN BAY 35, NEW ENGLAND 21—Desmond Howard returned a kickoff 99 yards for a touchdown and Brett Favre passed for 2 touchdowns and ran for a score as the Packers won their first Super Bowl in twenty-nine years. Howard, en route to garnering the MVP trophy, equaled a Super Bowl record with 244 total return yards. It was Favre's arm that struck first, as he hit Andre Rison on a 54-yard touchdown pass on the Packers' second play from scrimmage to take a 7-0 lead. Two plays later Doug Evans made a diving interception of Drew Bledsoe's pass at the 28-yard line, setting up Chris Jacke's field goal and giving the Packers a 10-0 lead just 6:18 into the Super Bowl. The Patriots answered with touchdowns on their next two possessions. Craig Newsome's pass interference penalty set up the first touchdown and a 44-yard completion from Bledsoe to Terry Glenn preceding Ben Coates' touchdown gave New England its first and only lead. The 24 combined first quarter points were the most in Super Bowl history. Green Bay struck again 56 seconds into the second quarter as Favre hit Antonio Freeman with a Super Bowl-record 81-yard touchdown bomb. Jacke booted his second field goal on Green Bay's next possession. After a Mike Prior interception, Favre orchestrated a 74-yard, nearly 6-minute drive that concluded with a diving Favre touching the ball against the pylon to give Green Bay a 27-14 halftime lead. Curtis Martin brought the Patriots to within a score by running in from 18 yards out with 3:27 left in the third quarter. But Howard broke the Patriots' spirit by returning the ensuing kickoff a Super Bowl-record 99 yards. Favre found Mark Chmura for the 2-point conversion to finish the scoring. Bledsoe was intercepted twice in the fourth quarter as the Patriots never crossed midfield in 4 fourth-quarter possessions. Reggie White set a Super Bowl record with 3 sacks. Favre complet-

ed 14 of 27 passes for 246 yards, with no interceptions. Bledsoe completed 11 more passes than Favre, but for just 7 more yards, and threw 4 interceptions.

New England (AFC)		14	0	7	0	—	21
Green Bay (NFC)		10	17	8	0	—	35

GB — Rison 54 pass from Favre (Jacke kick) (11:28)
GB — FG Jacke 37 (8:42)
NE — Byars 1 pass from Bledsoe (Vinatieri kick) (6:35)
NE — Coates 4 pass from Bledsoe (Vinatieri kick) (2:33)
GB — Freeman 81 pass from Favre (Jacke kick) (14:04)
GB — FG Jacke 31 (8:15)
GB — Favre 2 run (Jacke kick) (1:11)
NE — Martin 18 run (Vinatieri kick) (3:27)
GB — Howard 99 kickoff return (Chmura pass from Favre) (3:10)

SUPER BOWL XXX

Sun Devil Stadium, Tempe, Arizona
January 28, 1996, Attendance: 76,347
DALLAS 27, PITTSBURGH 17—Cornerback Larry Brown's 2 interceptions led to 14 second-half points and helped lift the Cowboys to their third Super Bowl victory in the last four seasons and their record-tying fifth title overall. Brown's interceptions foiled the comeback efforts of the Steelers, and earned him the Pete Rozelle Trophy as the game's most valuable player. Dallas scored on each of its first three possessions, taking a 13-0 lead on Troy Aikman's 3-yard touchdown pass to Jay Novacek and a pair of field goals by Chris Boniol. Neil O'Donnell's 6-yard touchdown pass to Yancey Thigpen 13 seconds before halftime pulled Pittsburgh within 6 points, and the Steelers had the ball near midfield midway through the third quarter. But O'Donnell's third-down pass was intercepted by Brown at the Cowboys' 38-yard line, and his 44-yard return carried to Pittsburgh's 18. After Aikman's 17-yard completion to Michael Irvin, Emmitt Smith ran 1 yard for the touchdown that put Dallas ahead again by 13 points. The Steelers rallied, though, behind Norm Johnson's 46-yard field goal, a successful surprise onside kick, and Byron (Bam) Morris' 1-yard touchdown run with 6:36 to play in the game. And when they forced a punt and took possession at their own 32-yard line trailing only 20-17 with 4:15 remaining, it appeared they might have a chance to break the NFC's recent domination in the Super Bowl. But on second down, Brown struck again, intercepting O'Donnell's pass at the 39 and returning it 33 yards to the 6. Two plays later, Smith barreled over from 4 yards out for the clinching touchdown with 3:43 to go. Pittsburgh limited the Cowboys' powerful running game to only 56 yards and enjoyed a whopping 201-61 advantage in total yards

in the second half, but could not overcome the 3 interceptions (another came on the game's final play) thrown by O'Donnell, the NFL's career leader for fewest interceptions per pass attempt. In all, O'Donnell completed 28 of 49 passes for 239 yards. Morris rushed for a game-high 73 yards on 19 carries. For Dallas, Aikman completed 15 of 23 pass attempts for 209 yards. The Cowboys' victory was the twelfth in a row for NFC teams over AFC teams in the Super Bowl.

| Dallas (NFC) | 10 3 7 7 — 27 |
| Pittsburgh (AFC) | 0 7 0 10 — 17 |

Dall — FG Boniol 42 (12:05)
Dall — Novacek 3 pass from Aikman (Boniol kick) (5:23)
Dall — FG Boniol 35 (6:03)
Pitt — Thigpen 6 pass from O'Donnell (N. Johnson kick) (0:13)
Dall — E. Smith 1 run (Boniol kick) (6:42)
Pitt — FG N. Johnson 46 (11:20)
Pitt — Morris 1 run (N. Johnson kick) (6:36)
Dall — E. Smith 4 run (Boniol kick) (3:43)

SUPER BOWL XXIX
Joe Robbie Stadium, South Florida
January 29, 1995, Attendance: 74,107
SAN FRANCISCO 49, SAN DIEGO 26— Steve Young passed for a record 6 touchdowns, and the 49ers became the first team to win five Super Bowls when they routed the Chargers. Young, the game's most valuable player, directed an explosive offense that generated 7 touchdowns, 28 first downs, and 455 total yards. He completed 24 of 36 passes for 325 yards, and broke the record of 5 touchdown passes set by fromer 49ers quarterback Joe Montana in Super Bowl XXIV. San Francisco wasted little time scoring, taking the lead for good on Young's 44-yard touchdown pass to Jerry Rice only three plays and 1:24 into the game. The next time they had the ball, the 49ers marched 79 yards in four plays, taking a 14-0 lead when Young teamed with running back Ricky Watters on a 51-yard touchdown pass with 10:05 still to play in the opening period. San Diego then put together its most impressive possession of the game, a 13-play, 78-yard drive that consumed more than 7 minutes and was capped by Natrone Means' 1-yard touchdown run, to cut its deficit to 14-7 late in the quarter. But San Francisco countered with a 70-yard drive of its own, and Young's 5-yard touchdown pass to fullback William Floyd made it 21-7. Young's fourth touchdown pass of the half, 8 yards to Watters 4:44 before halftime, increased the advantage to 28-7, and the Chargers could get no closer than 18 points after that. Watters, who ran 9 yards for a touchdown in the third quarter, equaled the Super Bowl record with 3

touchdowns. Rice also scored 3 touchdowns (the second time in his career he'd done that in a Super Bowl) while catching 10 passes for 149 yards. He established career records for receptions, yards, and touchdowns in a Super Bowl. Young, who scrambled 21 yards and 15 yards to set up touchdowns in the first half, was the game's leading rusher with 49 yards on 5 carries. San Diego's Means, who rushed for 1,350 yards during the regular season, was limited to 33 yards on 13 attempts. Chargers quarterback Stan Humphries completed 24 of 49 passes for 275 yards. Rookie Andre Coleman became only the third player in Super Bowl history to return a kickoff for a touchdown, going 98 yards in the third quarter. The 75 points scored by the two teams established another record, breaking the previous mark of 69 set in Dallas' 52-17 victory over Buffalo in XXVII. The 49ers' victory was the eleventh straight for NFC teams over AFC teams in the Super Bowl.

| San Diego (AFC) | 7 3 8 8 — 26 |
| San Francisco (NFC) | 14 14 14 7 — 49 |

SF — Rice 44 pass from S. Young (Brien kick) (13:36)
SF — Watters 51 pass from S. Young (Brien kick) (10:05)
SD — Means 1 run (Carney kick) (2:44)
SF — Floyd 5 pass from S. Young (Brien kick) (13:02)
SF — Watters 8 pass from S. Young (Brien kick) (4:44)
SD — FG Carney 31 (1:44)
SF — Watters 9 run (Brien kick) (9:35)
SF — Rice 15 pass from S. Young (Brien kick) (3:18)
SD — Coleman 98 kickoff return (Seay pass from Humphries) (3:01)
SF — Rice 7 pass from S. Young (Brien kick) (13:49)
SD — Martin 30 pass from Humphries (Pupunu pass from Humphries) (2:25)

SUPER BOWL XXVIII
Georgia Dome, Atlanta, Georgia
January 30, 1994, Attendance: 72,817
DALLAS 30, BUFFALO 13—Emmitt Smith rushed for 132 yards and 2 second-half touchdowns to power the Cowboys to their second consecutive NFL title. By winning, Dallas joined San Francisco and Pittsburgh as the only franchises with four Super Bowl victories. The Bills, meanwhile, extended a dubious string by losing in the Super Bowl for the fourth consecutive year. To win, the Cowboys had to rally from a 13-6 halftime deficit. Buffalo had forged the lead on Thurman Thomas' 4-yard touchdown run and a pair of field goals by Steve Christie, including a 54-yard kick, the longest in Super Bowl history. But just 55 seconds into the second half, Thomas was stripped of the ball by

Dallas defensive tackle Leon Lett. Safety James Washington recovered and weaved his way 46 yards for a touchdown to tie the game at 13-13. After forcing the Bills to punt, the Cowboys began their next possession on their 36-yard line and Smith, the game's most valuable player, took over. He carried 7 times for 61 yards on the ensuing 8-play, 64-yard drive, capping the march with a 15-yard touchdown run to give Dallas the lead for good with 8:42 remaining in the third quarter. Early in the fourth quarter, Washington intercepted Jim Kelly's pass and returned it 12 yards to Buffalo's 34. A penalty moved the ball back to the 39, but Smith carried twice for 10 yards and caught a screen pass for 9, and quarterback Troy Aikman completed a 16-yard pass to Alvin Harper to give the Cowboys a first-and-goal at the 6. Smith took it from there, cracking the end zone on fourth-and-goal from the 1 to put Dallas ahead 27-13 with 9:50 remaining. Eddie Murray's third field goal, from 20 yards with 2:50 left, ended any doubt about the game's outcome. Smith had 30 carries in all, with 19 of his attempts and 92 yards coming after intermission. Washington, normally a reserve who played most of the game because the Cowboys used five defensive backs to combat the Bills' No-Huddle offense, had 11 tackles and forced another fumble by Thomas in the first quarter. Aikman completed 19 of 27 passes for 207 yards. Buffalo's Kelly completed a Super Bowl-record 31 passes in 50 attempts for 260 yards. Dallas, the first team in NFL history to begin the regular season 0-2 and go on to win the Super Bowl, also became the fifth to win back-to-back titles, following Green Bay, Miami, Pittsburgh (the Steelers did it twice), and San Francisco. Buffalo became the third team, along with Minnesota and Denver, to lose four Super Bowls. The Cowboys' victory was the tenth in succession for the NFC over the AFC.

| Dallas (NFC) | 6 0 14 10 — 30 |
| Buffalo (AFC) | 3 10 0 0 — 13 |

Dall — FG Murray 41 (12:41)
Buff — FG Christie 54 (10:19)
Dall — FG Murray 24 (3:55)
Buff — Thomas 4 run (Christie kick) (12:26)
Buff — FG Christie 28 (0:00)
Dall — Washington 46 fumble return (Murray kick) (14:05)
Dall — E. Smith 15 run (Murray kick) (8:42)
Dall — E. Smith 1 run (Murray kick) (9:50)
Dall — FG Murray 20 (2:50)

SUPER BOWL XXVII
Rose Bowl, Pasadena, California
January 31, 1993, Attendance: 98,374
DALLAS 52, BUFFALO 17—Troy Aikman passed for 4 touchdowns, Emmitt Smith rushed for 108 yards, and the Cowboys

converted 9 turnovers into 35 points while coasting to the victory. Dallas' win was its third in its record sixth Super Bowl appearance; the Bills became the first team to drop three in succession. Buffalo led 7-0 until the first 2 of its record number of turnovers helped the Cowboys take the lead for good late in the opening quarter. First, Dallas safety James Washington intercepted Jim Kelly's pass and returned it 13 yards to the Bills' 47, setting up Aikman's 23-yard touchdown pass to tight end Jay Novacek with 1:36 remaining in the period. On the next play from scrimmage, Kelly was sacked by Charles Haley and fumbled at the Bills' 2-yard line where the Cowboys' Jimmie Jones picked up the loose ball and ran 2 yards for a touchdown. Dallas, which recovered 5 fumbles and intercepted 4 passes, struck just as quickly late in the first half, when Aikman tossed 19- and 18-yard touchdown passes to Michael Irvin 18 seconds apart to give the Cowboys a 28-10 lead at intermission. The second score was set up when Bills running back Thurman Thomas lost a fumble at his 19-yard line. Buffalo scored for the last time when backup quarterback Frank Reich, playing because Kelly was injured while attempting to pass midway through the second quarter, threw a 40-yard touchdown pass to Don Beebe on the final play of the third period to trim the deficit to 31-17. But Dallas put the game out of reach by scoring three times in a span of 2:33 of the fourth quarter. Aikman, the game's most valuable player, completed 22 of 30 passes for 273 yards. The victory was the ninth in succession for the NFC over the AFC.

Buffalo (AFC)	7	3	7	0 — 17
Dallas (NFC)	14	14	3	21 — 52

Buff — Thomas 2 run (Christie kick) (10:00)
Dall — Novacek 23 pass from Aikman (Elliott kick) (1:36)
Dall — J. Jones 2 fumble recovery return (Elliott kick) (1:21)
Buff — FG Christie 21 (3:24)
Dall — Irvin 19 pass from Aikman (Elliott kick) (1:54)
Dall — Irvin 18 pass from Aikman (Elliott kick) (1:36)
Dall — FG Elliott 20 (8:21)
Buff — Beebe 40 pass from Reich (Christie kick) (0:00)
Dall — Harper 45 pass from Aikman (Elliott kick) (10:04)
Dall — E. Smith 10 run (Elliott kick) (8:12)
Dall — Norton 9 fumble recovery return (Elliott kick) (7:31)

SUPER BOWL XXVI
Metrodome, Minneapolis, Minnesota
January 26, 1992, Attendance: 63,130
WASHINGTON 37, BUFFALO 24—Mark Rypien passed for 292 yards and 2 touchdowns as the Redskins overwhelmed the Bills to win their third Super Bowl in the

past 10 years. Rypien, the game's most valuable player, completed 18 of 33 passes, including a 10-yard scoring strike to Earnest Byner and a 30-yard touchdown to Gary Clark. The latter came late in the third quarter after Buffalo had trimmed a 24-0 deficit to 24-10, and effectively put the game out of reach. Washington went on to lead by as much as 37-10 before the Bills made it close with a pair of touchdowns in the final six minutes. Though the Redskins struggled early, converting their first three drives inside the Bills' 20-yard line into only 3 points, they built a 17-0 halftime lead. And they made it 24-0 just 16 seconds into the second half, after Kurt Gouveia intercepted Buffalo quarterback Jim Kelly's pass on the first play of the third quarter and returned it 23 yards to the Bills' 2. One play later, Gerald Riggs scored his second touchdown of the game to make it 24-0. Kelly, forced to bring Buffalo from behind, completed 28 of a Super Bowl-record 58 passes for 275 yards and 2 touchdowns, but was intercepted 4 times. Bills running back Thurman Thomas, who had an AFC-high 1,407 yards rushing and an NFL-best 2,038 total yards from scrimmage during the regular season, ran for only 13 yards on 10 carries and was limited to 27 yards on 4 receptions. Clark had 7 catches for 114 yards and Art Monk added 7 for 113 for the Redskins, who amassed 417 yards of total offense while limiting the explosive Bills to 283. Washington's Joe Gibbs became only the third head coach to win three Super Bowls.

Washington (NFC)	0	17	14	6 — 37
Buffalo (AFC)	0	0	10	14 — 24

Wash — FG Lohmiller 34 (13:02)
Wash — Byner 10 pass from Rypien (Lohmiller kick) (9:54)
Wash — Riggs 1 run (Lohmiller kick) (7:17)
Wash — Riggs 2 run (Lohmiller kick) (14:44)
Buff — FG Norwood 21 (11:59)
Buff — Thomas 1 run (Norwood kick) (5:58)
Wash — Clark 30 pass from Rypien (Lohmiller kick) (1:24)
Wash — FG Lohmiller 25 (14:54)
Wash — FG Lohmiller 39 (11:36)
Buff — Metzelaars 2 pass from Kelly (Norwood kick) (5:59)
Buff — Beebe 4 pass from Kelly (Norwood kick) (3:55)

SUPER BOWL XXV
Tampa Stadium, Tampa, Florida
January 27, 1991, Attendance: 73,813
NEW YORK GIANTS 20, BUFFALO 19—The NFC champion New York Giants won their second Super Bowl in five years with a 20-19 victory over AFC titlist Buffalo. New York, employing its ball-control offense, had possession for 40 minutes, 33 seconds, a Super Bowl record. The Bills, who scored 95 points in their previ-

ous two playoff games leading to Super Bowl XXV, had the ball for less than eight minutes in the second half and just 19:27 for the game. Fourteen of New York's 73 plays came on its initial drive of the third quarter, which covered 75 yards and consumed a Super Bowl-record 9:29 before running back Ottis Anderson ran 1 yard for a touchdown. Giants quarterback Jeff Hostetler kept the long drive going by converting three third-down plays—an 11-yard pass to running back David Meggett on third-and-eight, a 14-yard toss to wide receiver Mark Ingram on third-and-13, and a 9-yard pass to Howard Cross on third-and-four—to give New York a 17-12 lead in the third quarter. Buffalo jumped to a 12-3 lead midway through the second quarter before Hostetler completed a 14-yard scoring strike to wide receiver Stephen Baker to close the score to 12-10 at halftime. Buffalo's Thurman Thomas ran 31 yards for a touchdown on the opening play of the fourth quarter to help Buffalo recapture the lead 19-17. Matt Bahr's 21-yard field goal gave the Giants a 20-19 lead, but Buffalo's Scott Norwood had a chance to win the game with seconds remaining before his 47-yard field-goal attempt sailed wide right. Hostetler completed 20 of 32 passes for 222 yards and 1 touchdown. Anderson rushed 21 times for 102 yards and 1 touchdown to capture most-valuable-player honors. Thomas totaled 190 scrimmage yards, rushing 15 times for 135 yards and catching 5 passes for 55 yards.

Buffalo (AFC)	3	9	0	7 — 19
N.Y. Giants (NFC)	3	7	7	3 — 20

NYG — FG Bahr 28 (7:14)
Buff — FG Norwood 23 (5:51)
Buff — D. Smith 1 run (Norwood kick) (12:30)
Buff — Safety, B. Smith tackled Hostetler in end zone (8:27)
NYG — Baker 14 pass from Hostetler (Bahr kick) (0:25)
NYG — Anderson 1 run (Bahr kick) (5:31)
Buff — Thomas 31 run (Norwood kick) (14:52)
NYG — FG Bahr 21 (7:20)

SUPER BOWL XXIV
Louisiana Superdome, New Orleans, LA
January 28, 1990, Attendance: 72,919
SAN FRANCISCO 55, DENVER 10—NFC titlist San Francisco won its fourth Super Bowl championship with a 55-10 victory over AFC champion Denver. The 49ers, who also won Super Bowls XVI, XIX, and XXIII, tied the Pittsburgh Steelers for most Super Bowl victories. The Steelers captured Super Bowls IX, X, XIII, and XIV. San Francisco's 55 points broke the previous Super Bowl scoring mark of 46 points by Chicago in Super Bowl XX. San Francisco scored touchdowns on four of its six first-half possessions to hold a 27-3 lead at halftime. Interceptions by Michael Walter

and Chet Brooks ended the Broncos' first two possessions of the second half. San Francisco quarterback Joe Montana was named the Super Bowl most valuable player for a record third time. Montana completed 22 of 29 passes for 297 yards and a Super Bowl-record 5 touchdowns. Jerry Rice, Super Bowl XXIII most valuable player, caught 7 passes for 148 yards and 3 touchdowns. The 49ers' domination included first downs (28 to 12), net yards (461 to 167), and time of possession (39:31 to 20:29).

| San Francisco (NFC) | 13 14 14 14 — 55 |
| Denver (AFC) | 3 0 7 0 — 10 |

SF	—	Rice 20 pass from Montana (Cofer kick) (10:06)
Den	—	FG Treadwell 42 (6:47)
SF	—	Jones 7 pass from Montana (kick failed) (0:03)
SF	—	Rathman 1 run (Cofer kick) (7:15)
SF	—	Rice 38 pass from Montana (Cofer kick) (0:34)
SF	—	Rice 28 pass from Montana (Cofer kick) (12:48)
SF	—	Taylor 35 pass from Montana (Cofer kick) (9:44)
Den	—	Elway 3 run (Treadwell kick) (6:53)
SF	—	Rathman 3 run (Cofer kick) (14:57)
SF	—	Craig 1 run (Cofer kick) (13:47)

SUPER BOWL XXIII

Joe Robbie Stadium, South Florida
January 22, 1989, Attendance: 75,129
SAN FRANCISCO 20, CINCINNATI 16—NFC champion San Francisco captured its third Super Bowl of the 1980s by defeating AFC champion Cincinnati 20-16. The 49ers, who also won Super Bowls XVI and XIX, became the first NFC team to win three Super Bowls. Pittsburgh, with four Super Bowl titles (IX, X, XIII, and XIV), and the Oakland/Los Angeles Raiders, with three (XI, XV, and XVIII), lead AFC franchises. Even though San Francisco held an advantage in total net yards (453 to 229), the 49ers found themselves trailing the Bengals late in the game. With the score 13-13, Cincinnati took a 16-13 lead on Jim Breech's 40-yard field goal with 3:20 remaining. It was Breech's third field goal of the day, following earlier successes from 34 and 43 yards. The 49ers started their winning drive at their 8-yard line. Over the next 11 plays, San Francisco covered 92 yards with the decisive score coming on a 10-yard pass from quarterback Joe Montana to wide receiver John Taylor with 34 seconds remaining. At halftime, the score was 3-3, the first time in Super Bowl history the game was tied at intermission. After the teams traded third-period field goals, the Bengals jumped ahead 13-6 on Stanford Jennings' 93-yard kickoff return for a touchdown with 34 seconds remaining in the quarter. The

49ers didn't waste any time coming back as they covered 85 yards in four plays, concluding with Montana's 14-yard scoring pass to Jerry Rice 57 seconds into the final stanza. Rice was named the game's most valuable player after compiling 11 catches for a Super Bowl-record 215 yards. Montana completed 23 of 36 passes for a Super Bowl-record 357 yards and 2 touchdowns.

| Cincinnati (AFC) | 0 3 10 3 — 16 |
| San Francisco (NFC) | 3 0 3 14 — 20 |

SF	—	FG Cofer 41 (3:14)
Cin	—	FG Breech 34 (1:15)
Cin	—	FG Breech 43 (5:39)
SF	—	FG Cofer 32 (0:50)
Cin	—	Jennings 93 kickoff return (Breech kick) (0:34)
SF	—	Rice 14 pass from Montana (Cofer kick) (14:03)
Cin	—	FG Breech 40 (3:20)
SF	—	Taylor 10 pass from Montana (Cofer kick) (0:34)

SUPER BOWL XXII

San Diego Jack Murphy Stadium, San Diego, CA
January 31, 1988, Attendance: 73,302
WASHINGTON 42, DENVER 10—NFC champion Washington won Super Bowl XXII and its second NFL championship of the 1980s with a 42-10 decision over AFC champion Denver. The Redskins, who also won Super Bowl XVII, enjoyed a record-setting second quarter en route to the victory. The Broncos broke in front 10-0 when quarterback John Elway threw a 56-yard touchdown pass to wide receiver Ricky Nattiel on the Broncos' first play from scrimmage. Following a Washington punt, Denver's Rich Karlis kicked a 24-yard field goal to cap a seven-play, 61-yard scoring drive. The Redskins then erupted for 35 points on five straight possessions in the second period and coasted thereafter. The 35 points established an NFL postseason mark for most points in a period. Redskins quarterback Doug Williams led the second-period explosion by passing for a Super Bowl record-tying 4 touchdowns, including 80- and 50-yard passes to wide receiver Ricky Sanders, a 27-yard toss to wide receiver Gary Clark, and an 8-yard pass to tight end Clint Didier. Washington scored 5 touchdowns in 18 plays with total time of possession of only 5:47. Overall, Williams completed 18 of 29 passes for 340 yards and was named the game's most valuable player. His pass-yardage total eclipsed the Super Bowl record of 331 yards by Joe Montana of San Francisco in Super Bowl XIX. Sanders ended with 193 yards on 9 catches, breaking the previous Super Bowl yardage record of 161 yards by Lynn Swann of Pittsburgh in Game X. Rookie running back Timmy Smith was the game's leading rusher with 22 carries for a Super Bowl-record 204 yards, breaking the previous mark of 191 yards by Marcus Allen of the Raiders in Game

XVIII. Smith also scored twice on runs of 58 and 4 yards. Washington's 6 touchdowns and 602 total yards gained also set Super Bowl records. Redskins cornerback Barry Wilburn had 2 of the team's 3 interceptions, and strong safety Alvin Walton had 2 of Washington's 5 sacks.

| Washington (NFC) | 0 35 0 7 — 42 |
| Denver (AFC) | 10 0 0 0 — 10 |

Den	—	Nattiel 56 pass from Elway (Karlis kick) (13:03)
Den	—	FG Karlis 24 (9:09)
Wash	—	Sanders 80 pass from Williams (Haji-Sheikh kick) (14:07)
Wash	—	Clark 27 pass from Williams (Haji-Sheikh kick) (10:15)
Wash	—	Smith 58 run (Haji-Sheikh kick) (6:27)
Wash	—	Sanders 50 pass from Williams (Haji-Sheikh kick) (3:42)
Wash	—	Didier 8 pass from Williams (Haji-Sheikh kick) (1:04)
Wash	—	Smith 4 run (Haji-Sheikh kick) (13:09)

SUPER BOWL XXI

Rose Bowl, Pasadena, California
January 25, 1987, Attendance: 101,063
NEW YORK GIANTS 39, DENVER 20—The NFC champion New York Giants captured their first NFL title since 1956 when they downed the AFC champion Denver Broncos 39-20 in Super Bowl XXI. The victory marked the NFC's fifth NFL title in the past six seasons. The Broncos, behind the passing of quarterback John Elway, who was 13 of 20 for 187 yards in the first half, held a 10-9 lead at intermission, the narrowest halftime margin in Super Bowl history. Denver's Rich Karlis opened the scoring with a Super Bowl record-tying 48-yard field goal. New York drove 78 yards in nine plays on the next series to take a 7-3 lead on quarterback Phil Simms' 6-yard touchdown pass to tight end Zeke Mowatt. The Broncos came right back with a 58-yard scoring drive on six plays capped by Elway's 4-yard touchdown run. The only scoring in the second period was the sack of Elway in the end zone by defensive end George Martin for a New York safety. The Giants produced a key defensive stand early in the second quarter when the Broncos had a first down at the New York 1-yard line, but failed to score on three running plays and Karlis' 23-yard missed field-goal attempt. The Giants took command of the game in the third period en route to a 30-point second half, the most ever scored in one half of Super Bowl play. New York took the lead for good on tight end Mark Bavaro's 13-yard touchdown catch 4:52 into the third period. The nine-play, 63-yard scoring drive included the successful conversion of a fourth-and-1 play on the New York 46-yard line. Denver was limited to only 2 net yards on 10 offensive plays in

the third period. Simms set Super Bowl records for most consecutive completions (10) and highest completion percentage (88 percent on 22 completions in 25 attempts). He also passed for 268 yards and 3 touchdowns and was named the game's most valuable player. New York running back Joe Morris was the game's leading rusher with 20 carries for 67 yards. Denver wide receiver Vance Johnson led all receivers with 5 catches for 121 yards.

Denver (AFC)	10 0 0 10 — 20	
N.Y. Giants (NFC)	7 2 17 13 — 39	

Den — FG Karlis 48 (10:51)
NYG — Mowatt 6 pass from Simms (Allegre kick) (5:27)
Den — Elway 4 run (Karlis kick) (2:06)
NYG — Safety, Martin tackled Elway in end zone (2:46)
NYG — Bavaro 13 pass from Simms (Allegre kick) (10:08)
NYG — FG Allegre 21 (3:54)
NYG — Morris 1 run (Allegre kick) (0:24)
NYG — McConkey 6 pass from Simms (Allegre kick) (10:56)
Den — FG Karlis 28 (6:01)
NYG — Anderson 2 run (kick failed) (4:18)
Den — V. Johnson 47 pass from Elway (Karlis kick) (2:06)

SUPER BOWL XX

Louisiana Superdome, New Orleans, LA
January 26, 1986, Attendance: 73,818
CHICAGO 46, NEW ENGLAND 10—The NFC champion Chicago Bears, seeking their first NFL title since 1963, scored a Super Bowl-record 46 points in downing AFC champion New England 46-10 in Super Bowl XX. The previous record for most points in a Super Bowl was 38, shared by San Francisco in XIX and the Los Angeles Raiders in XVIII. The Bears' league-leading defense tied the Super Bowl record for sacks (7) and limited the Patriots to a record-low 7 rushing yards. New England took the quickest lead in Super Bowl history when Tony Franklin kicked a 36-yard field goal with 1:19 elapsed in the first period. The score came about because of Larry McGrew's fumble recovery at the Chicago 19-yard line. However, the Bears rebounded for a 23-3 first-half lead, while building a yardage advantage of 236 total yards to New England's minus 19. Running back Matt Suhey rushed 8 times for 37 yards, including an 11-yard touchdown run, and caught 1 pass for 24 yards in the first half. After the Patriot's first drive of the second half ended with a punt to the Bears' 4-yard line, Chicago marched 96 yards in nine plays with quarterback Jim McMahon's 1-yard scoring run capping the drive. McMahon became the first quarterback in Super Bowl history to rush for a pair of touchdowns. The Bears completed their

scoring via a 28-yard interception return by reserve cornerback Reggie Phillips, a 1-yard run by defensive tackle/fullback William Perry, and a safety when defensive end Henry Waechter tackled Patriots quarterback Steve Grogan in the end zone. Bears defensive end Richard Dent became the fourth defender to be named the game's most valuable player after contributing 1.5 sacks. The Bears' victory margin of 36 points was the largest in Super Bowl history, bettering the previous mark of 29 by the Los Angeles Raiders when they topped Washington 38-9 in Game XVIII. McMahon completed 12 of 20 passes for 256 yards before leaving the game in the fourth period with a wrist injury. The NFL's all-time leading rusher, Bears running back Walter Payton, carried 22 times for 61 yards. Wide receiver Willie Gault caught 4 passes for 129 yards, the fourth-most receiving yards in a Super Bowl. Chicago coach Mike Ditka became the second man (Tom Flores of Raiders was the other) to win a Super Bowl ring as a player and as a coach.

Chicago (NFC)	13 10 21 2 — 46	
New England (AFC)	3 0 0 7 — 10	

NE — FG Franklin 36 (13:41)
Chi — FG Butler 28 (9:20)
Chi — FG Butler 24 (1:26)
Chi — Suhey 11 run (Butler kick) (0:23)
Chi — McMahon 2 run (Butler kick) (7:24)
Chi — FG Butler 24 (0:00)
Chi — McMahon 1 run (Butler kick) (7:22)
Chi — Phillips 28 interception return (Butler kick) (6:16)
Chi — Perry 1 run (Butler kick) (3:22)
NE — Fryar 8 pass from Grogan (Franklin kick) (13:14)
Chi — Safety, Waechter tackled Grogan in end zone (5:36)

SUPER BOWL XIX

Stanford Stadium, Stanford, California
January 20, 1985, Attendance: 84,059
SAN FRANCISCO 38, MIAMI 16—The San Francisco 49ers captured their second Super Bowl title with a dominating offense and a defense that tamed Miami's explosive passing attack. The Dolphins held a 10-7 lead at the end of the first period, which represented the most points scored by two teams in an opening quarter of a Super Bowl. However, the 49ers used excellent field position in the second period to build a 28-16 halftime lead. Running back Roger Craig set a Super Bowl record by scoring 3 touchdowns on pass receptions of 8 and 16 yards and a run of 2 yards. San Francisco's Joe Montana was voted the game's most valuable player. He joined Green Bay's Bart Starr and Pittsburgh's Terry Bradshaw as the only two-time Super Bowl most valuable players. Montana completed 24 of 35 passes

for a Super Bowl-record 331 yards and 3 touchdowns, and rushed 5 times for 59 yards, including a 6-yard touchdown. Craig had 58 yards on 15 carries and caught 7 passes for 77 yards. Wendell Tyler rushed 13 times for 65 yards and had 4 catches for 70 yards. Dwight Clark had 6 receptions for 77 yards, while Russ Francis had 5 for 60. San Francisco's 537 total net yards bettered the previous Super Bowl record of 429 yards by Oakland in Super Bowl XI. The 49ers also held a time of possession advantage over the Dolphins of 37:11 to 22:49.

Miami (AFC)	10 6 0 0 — 16	
San Francisco (NFC)	7 21 10 0 — 38	

Mia — FG von Schamann 37 (7:24)
SF — Monroe 33 pass from Montana (Wersching kick) (3:12)
Mia — D. Johnson 2 pass from Marino (von Schamann kick) (0:45)
SF — Craig 8 pass from Montana (Wersching kick) (11:34)
SF — Montana 6 run (Wersching kick) (6:58)
SF — Craig 2 run (Wersching kick) (2:05)
Mia — FG von Schamann 31 (0:12)
Mia — FG von Schamann 30 (0:00)
SF — FG Wersching 27 (10:12)
SF — Craig 16 pass from Montana (Wersching kick) (6:18)

SUPER BOWL XVIII

Tampa Stadium, Tampa, Florida
January 22, 1984, Attendance: 72,920
LOS ANGELES RAIDERS 38, WASHINGTON 9—The Los Angeles Raiders dominated the Washington Redskins from the beginning in Super Bowl XVIII and achieved the most lopsided victory in Super Bowl history, surpassing Green Bay's 35-10 win over Kansas City in Super Bowl I. The Raiders took a 7-0 lead 4:52 into the game when Derrick Jensen blocked Jeff Hayes' punt and recovered it in the end zone for a touchdown. With 9:14 remaining in the first half, Raiders quarterback Jim Plunkett fired a 12-yard touchdown pass to wide receiver Cliff Branch to complete a three-play, 65-yard drive. Washington cut the Raiders' lead to 14-3 on a 24-yard field goal by Mark Moseley. With seven seconds left in the first half, Raiders linebacker Jack Squirek intercepted Joe Theismann's pass at the Redskins' 5-yard line and ran it in for a touchdown to give Los Angeles a 21-3 halftime lead. In the third period, running back Marcus Allen, who rushed for a Super Bowl-record 191 yards on 20 carries, increased the Raiders' lead to 35-9 on touchdown runs of 5 and 74 yards, the latter erasing the Super Bowl record of 58 yards set by Baltimore's Tom Matte in Game III. Allen was named the game's most valuable player. The victory over Washington raised Raiders coach Tom

Flores' playoff record to 8-1, including a 27-10 win against Philadelphia in Super Bowl XV. The 38 points scored by the Raiders were the highest total by a Super Bowl team. The previous high was 35 points by Green Bay in Game I.

Washington (NFC)	0 3 6 0	—	9
L.A. Raiders (AFC)	7 14 14 3	—	38

Raiders — Jensen recovered blocked punt in end zone (Bahr kick) (10:08)
Raiders — Branch 12 pass from Plunkett (Bahr kick) (9:14)
Wash — FG Moseley 24 (3:05)
Raiders — Squirek 5 interception return (Bahr kick) (0:07)
Wash — Riggins 1 run (kick blocked) (10:52)
Raiders — Allen 5 run (Bahr kick) (7:06)
Raiders — Allen 74 run (Bahr kick) (0:00)
Raiders — FG Bahr 21 (2:24)

SUPER BOWL XVII

Rose Bowl, Pasadena, California
January 30, 1983, Attendance: 103,667
WASHINGTON 27, MIAMI 17—Fullback John Riggins ran for a Super Bowl-record 166 yards on 38 carries to spark Washington to a 27-17 victory over AFC champion Miami. It was Riggins' fourth straight 100-yard rushing game during the playoffs, also a record. The win marked Washington's first NFL title since 1942, and was only the second time in Super Bowl history NFL/NFC teams scored consecutive victories (Green Bay did it in Super Bowls I and II and San Francisco won Super Bowl XVI). The Redskins, under second-year head coach Joe Gibbs, used a balanced offense that accounted for 400 total yards (a Super Bowl-record 276 yards rushing and 124 passing), second in Super Bowl history to 429 yards by Oakland in Super Bowl XI. The Dolphins built a 17-10 halftime lead on a 76-yard touchdown pass from quarterback David Woodley to wide receiver Jimmy Cefalo 6:49 into the first period, a 20-yard field goal by Uwe von Schamann with 6:00 left in the half, and a Super Bowl-record 98-yard kickoff return by Fulton Walker with 1:38 remaining. Washington had tied the score at 10-10 with 1:51 left on a 4-yard touchdown pass from Joe Theismann to wide receiver Alvin Garrett. Mark Moseley started the Redskins' scoring with a 31-yard field goal late in the first period, and added a 20-yard kick midway through the third period to cut the Dolphins' lead to 17-13. Riggins, who was voted the game's most valuable player, gave Washington its first lead of the game with 10:01 left when he ran 43 yards off left tackle for a touchdown in a fourth-and-1 situation. Wide receiver Charlie Brown caught a 6-yard scoring pass from Theismann with 1:55 left to complete the scoring. The Dolphins managed only 176 yards (142 in

first half). Theismann completed 15 of 23 passes for 143 yards, with 2 touchdowns and 2 interceptions. For Miami, Woodley was 4 of 14 for 97 yards, with 1 touchdown, and 1 interception. Don Strock was 0 for 3 in relief.

Miami (AFC)	7 10 0 0	—	17
Washington (NFC)	0 10 3 14	—	27

Mia — Cefalo 76 pass from Woodley (von Schamann kick) (8:11)
Wash — FG Moseley 31 (0:39)
Mia — FG von Schamann 20 (6:00)
Wash — Garrett 4 pass from Theismann (Moseley kick) (1:51)
Mia — Walker 98 kickoff return (von Schamann kick) (1:38)
Wash — FG Moseley 20 (8:09)
Wash — Riggins 43 run (Moseley kick) (10:01)
Wash — Brown 6 pass from Theismann (Moseley kick) (1:55)

SUPER BOWL XVI

Pontiac Silverdome, Pontiac, Michigan
January 24, 1982, Attendance: 81,270
SAN FRANCISCO 26, CINCINNATI 21—Ray Wersching's Super Bowl record-tying 4 field goals and Joe Montana's controlled passing helped lift the San Francisco 49ers to their first NFL championship with a 26-21 victory over Cincinnati. The 49ers built a game-record 20-0 halftime lead via Montana's 1-yard touchdown run, which capped an 11-play, 68-yard drive; fullback Earl Cooper's 11-yard scoring pass from Montana, which climaxed a Super Bowl record 92-yard drive on 12 plays; and Wersching's 22- and 26-yard field goals. The Bengals rebounded in the second half, closing the gap to 20-14 on quarterback Ken Anderson's 5-yard run and Dan Ross' 4-yard reception from Anderson, who established Super Bowl passing records for completions (25) and completion percentage (73.5 percent on 25 of 34). Wersching added early fourth-period field goals of 40 and 23 yards to increase the 49ers' lead to 26-14. The Bengals managed to score on an Anderson-to-Ross 3-yard pass with only 16 seconds remaining. Ross set a Super Bowl record with 11 receptions for 104 yards. Montana, the game's most valuable player, completed 14 of 22 passes for 157 yards. Cincinnati compiled 356 yards to San Francisco's 275, which marked the first time in Super Bowl history that the team that gained the most yards from scrimmage lost the game.

San Francisco (NFC)	7 13 0 6	—	26
Cincinnati (AFC)	0 0 7 14	—	21

SF — Montana 1 run (Wersching kick) (5:52)
SF — Cooper 11 pass from Montana (Wersching kick) (6:53)
SF — FG Wersching 22 (0:15)
SF — FG Wersching 26 (0:02)
Cin — Anderson 5 run (Breech kick) (11:25)

Cin — Ross 4 pass from Anderson (Breech kick) (10:06)
SF — FG Wersching 40 (5:25)
SF — FG Wersching 23 (1:57)
Cin — Ross 3 pass from Anderson (Breech kick) (0:16)

SUPER BOWL XV

Louisiana Superdome, New Orleans, LA
January 25, 1981, Attendance: 76,135
OAKLAND 27, PHILADELPHIA 10—Jim Plunkett passed for 3 touchdowns, including an 80-yard strike to Kenny King, as the Raiders became the first wild-card team to win the Super Bowl. Plunkett's touchdown bomb to King—the longest play in Super Bowl history—gave Oakland a decisive 14-0 lead with nine seconds left in the first period. Linebacker Rod Martin had set up Oakland's first touchdown with a 2-yard reception by Cliff Branch, with a 17-yard interception return to the Eagles' 30-yard line. The Eagles never recovered from that early deficit, managing only Tony Franklin's field goal (30 yards) and an 8-yard touchdown pass from Ron Jaworski to Keith Krepfle. Plunkett, who became a starter in the sixth game of the season, completed 13 of 21 for 261 yards and was named the game's most valuable player. Oakland won 9 of 11 games with Plunkett starting, but that was good enough only for second place in the AFC West, although they tied division winner San Diego with an 11-5 record. The Raiders, who had previously won Super Bowl XI over Minnesota, had to win three playoff games to get to the championship game. Oakland defeated Houston 27-7 at home followed by road victories over Cleveland (14-12) and San Diego (34-27). Oakland's Mark van Eeghen was the game's leading rusher with 75 yards on 18 carries. Philadelphia's Wilbert Montgomery led all receivers with 6 receptions for 91 yards. Branch had 5 for 67 and Harold Carmichael of Philadelphia 5 for 83. Martin finished the game with 3 interceptions, a Super Bowl record.

Oakland (AFC)	14 0 10 3	—	27
Philadelphia (NFC)	0 3 0 7	—	10

Oak — Branch 2 pass from Plunkett (Bahr kick) (8:56)
Oak — King 80 pass from Plunkett (Bahr kick) (0:09)
Phil — FG Franklin 30 (10:28)
Oak — Branch 29 pass from Plunkett (Bahr kick) (12:24)
Oak — FG Bahr 46 (4:35)
Phil — Krepfle 8 pass from Jaworski (Franklin kick) (13:59)
Oak — FG Bahr 35 (8:29)

SUPER BOWL XIV

Rose Bowl, Pasadena, California
January 20, 1980, Attendance: 103,985
PITTSBURGH 31, LOS ANGELES 19—Terry Bradshaw completed 14 of 21 passes for 309 yards and set two passing records as the Steelers became the first

team to win four Super Bowls. Despite 3 interceptions by the Rams, Bradshaw kept his poise and brought the Steelers from behind twice in the second half. Trailing 13-10 at halftime, Pittsburgh went ahead 17-13 when Bradshaw hit Lynn Swann with a 47-yard touchdown pass after 2:48 of the third quarter. On the Rams' next possession Vince Ferragamo, who was 15 of 25 for 212 yards, responded with a 50-yard pass to Billy Waddy that moved Los Angeles from its 26 to the Steelers' 24. On the following play, Lawrence McCutcheon connected with Ron Smith on a halfback option pass that gave the Rams a 19-17 lead. On Pittsburgh's initial possession of the final period, Bradshaw lofted a 73-yard scoring pass to John Stallworth to put the Steelers in front to stay 24-19. Franco Harris scored on a 1-yard run later in the quarter to seal the verdict. A 45-yard pass from Bradshaw to Stallworth was the key play in the drive to Harris' score. Bradshaw, the game's most valuable player for the second straight year, set career Super Bowl records for most touchdown passes (9) and most passing yards (932). Larry Anderson gave the Steelers excellent field position throughout the game with 5 kickoff returns for a record 162 yards.

Los Angeles (NFC)		7 6 6 0 — 19	
Pittsburgh (AFC)		3 7 7 14 — 31	
Pitt	—	FG Bahr 41 (7:31)	
LA	—	Bryant 1 run (Corral kick) (2:44)	
Pitt	—	Harris 1 run (Bahr kick) (12:52)	
LA	—	FG Corral 31 (7:21)	
LA	—	FG Corral 45 (0:14)	
Pitt	—	Swann 47 pass from Bradshaw (Bahr kick) (12:12)	
LA	—	Smith 24 pass from McCutcheon (kick failed) (10:15)	
Pitt	—	Stallworth 73 pass from Bradshaw (Bahr kick) (12:04)	
Pitt	—	Harris 1 run (Bahr kick) (1:49)	

SUPER BOWL XIII
Orange Bowl, Miami, Florida
January 21, 1979, Attendance: 79,484
PITTSBURGH 35, DALLAS 31—Terry Bradshaw passed for a record 4 touchdowns to lead the Steelers to victory. The Steelers became the first team to win three Super Bowls, mostly because of Bradshaw's accurate arm. Bradshaw, voted the game's most valuable player, completed 17 of 30 passes for 318 yards, a personal high. Four of those passes went for touchdowns—2 to John Stallworth and the third, with 26 seconds remaining in the second period, to Rocky Bleier for a 21-14 halftime lead. The Cowboys scored twice before intermission on Roger Staubach's 39-yard pass to Tony Hill and a 37-yard fumble return by linebacker Mike Hegman, who stole the ball from Bradshaw. The Steelers broke open

the contest with 2 touchdowns in a span of 19 seconds midway through the final period. Franco Harris rambled 22 yards up the middle to give the Steelers a 28-17 lead with 7:10 left. Pittsburgh got the ball right back when Randy White fumbled the kickoff and Dennis Winston recovered for the Steelers. On first down, Bradshaw fired his fourth touchdown pass, an 18-yard pass to Lynn Swann to boost the Steelers' lead to 35-17 with 6:51 to play. The Cowboys refused to let the Steelers run away with the contest. Staubach connected with Billy Joe DuPree on a 7-yard scoring pass with 2:23 left. Then the Cowboys recovered an onside kick and Staubach took them in for another score, passing 4 yards to Butch Johnson with 22 seconds remaining. Bleier recovered another onside kick with 17 seconds left to seal the victory for the Steelers.

Pittsburgh (AFC)		7 14 0 14 — 35	
Dallas (NFC)		7 7 3 14 — 31	
Pitt	—	Stallworth 28 pass from Bradshaw (Gerela kick) (9:47)	
Dall	—	Hill 39 pass from Staubach (Septien kick) (0:00)	
Dall	—	Hegman 37 fumble recovery return (Septien kick) (12:08)	
Pitt	—	Stallworth 75 pass from Bradshaw (Gerela kick) (10:25)	
Pitt	—	Bleier 7 pass from Bradshaw (Gerela kick) (0:26)	
Dall	—	FG Septien 27 (2:36)	
Pitt	—	Harris 22 run (Gerela kick) (7:10)	
Pitt	—	Swann 18 pass from Bradshaw (Gerela kick) (6:51)	
Dall	—	DuPree 7 pass from Staubach (Septien kick) (2:23)	
Dall	—	B. Johnson 4 pass from Staubach (Septien kick) (0:22)	

SUPER BOWL XII
Louisiana Superdome, New Orleans, LA
January 15, 1978, Attendance: 75,583
DALLAS 27, DENVER 10—The Cowboys evened their Super Bowl record to 2-2 by defeating Denver before a sellout crowd plus 102,010,000 television viewers, the largest audience ever to watch a sporting event. Dallas converted 2 interceptions into 10 points and Efren Herrera added a 35-yard field goal for a 13-0 halftime advantage. In the third period Craig Morton engineered a drive to the Cowboys' 30 and Jim Turner's 47-yard field goal made the score 13-3. After an exchange of punts, Butch Johnson made a spectacular diving catch in the end zone to complete a 45-yard pass from Roger Staubach and put the Cowboys ahead 20-3. Following Rick Upchurch's 67-yard kickoff return, Norris Weese guided the Broncos to a touchdown to cut the deficit to 20-10. Dallas clinched the victory when running back Robert Newhouse tossed a 29-yard touchdown pass to Golden Richards with 7:04 left in the game. It was the first pass

thrown by Newhouse since 1975. Harvey Martin and Randy White, who were named co-most valuable players, led the Cowboys' defense, which recovered 4 fumbles and intercepted 4 passes.

Dallas (NFC)		10 3 7 7 — 27	
Denver (AFC)		0 0 10 0 — 10	
Dall	—	Dorsett 3 run (Herrera kick) (4:29)	
Dall	—	FG Herrera 35 (1:31)	
Dall	—	FG Herrera 43 (11:16)	
Den	—	FG Turner 47 (12:32)	
Dall	—	Johnson 45 pass from Staubach (Herrera kick) (6:59)	
Den	—	Lytle 1 run (Turner kick) (5:39)	
Dall	—	Richards 29 pass from Newhouse (Herrera kick) (7:04)	

SUPER BOWL XI
Rose Bowl, Pasadena, California
January 9, 1977, Attendance: 103,438
OAKLAND 32, MINNESOTA 14—The Raiders won their first NFL championship before a record Super Bowl crowd plus 81 million television viewers, the largest audience ever to watch a sporting event. The Raiders gained a record-breaking 429 yards, including running back Clarence Davis' 137 rushing yards. Wide receiver Fred Biletnikoff made 4 key receptions, which earned him the game's most valuable player trophy. Oakland scored on three successive possessions in the second quarter to build a 16-0 halftime lead. Errol Mann's 24-yard field goal opened the scoring, then the AFC champions put together drives of 64 and 35 yards, scoring on a 1-yard pass from Ken Stabler to Dave Casper and a 1-yard run by Pete Banaszak. The Raiders increased their lead to 19-0 on a 40-yard field goal in the third quarter, but Minnesota responded with a 12-play, 58-yard drive late in the period, with Fran Tarkenton passing 8 yards to wide receiver Sammy White to cut the deficit to 19-7. Two fourth-quarter interceptions clinched the title for the Raiders. One set up Banaszak's second touchdown run, the other resulted in cornerback Willie Brown's Super Bowl-record 75-yard interception return.

Oakland (AFC)		0 16 3 13 — 32	
Minnesota (NFC)		0 0 7 7 — 14	
Oak	—	FG Mann 24 (14:12)	
Oak	—	Casper 1 pass from Stabler (Mann kick) (7:10)	
Oak	—	Banaszak 1 run (kick failed) (3:33)	
Oak	—	FG Mann 40 (5:16)	
Minn	—	S. White 8 pass from Tarkenton (Cox kick) (0:47)	
Oak	—	Banaszak 2 run (Mann kick) (7:39)	
Oak	—	Brown 75 interception return (kick failed) (5:43)	
Minn	—	Voigt 13 pass from Lee (Cox kick) (0:25)	

SUPER BOWL X
Orange Bowl, Miami, Florida
January 18, 1976, Attendance: 80,187
PITTSBURGH 21, DALLAS 17—The Steelers won the Super Bowl for the second year in a row on Terry Bradshaw's 64-yard touchdown pass to Lynn Swann and an aggressive defense that snuffed out a late rally by the Cowboys with an end-zone interception on the final play of the game. In the fourth quarter, Pittsburgh ran on fourth down and gave up the ball on the Cowboys' 39 with 1:22 to play. Roger Staubach ran and passed for 2 first downs but his last desperation pass was picked off by Glen Edwards. Dallas' scoring was the result of 2 touchdown passes by Staubach, one to Drew Pearson for 29 yards and the other to Percy Howard for 34 yards. Howard's reception was the only catch of his NFL career. Toni Fritsch had a 36-yard field goal. The Steelers scored on 2 touchdown passes by Bradshaw, 1 to Randy Grossman for 7 yards and the long bomb to Swann. Roy Gerela had 36- and 18-yard field goals. Reggie Harrison blocked a punt through the end zone for a safety. Swann set a Super Bowl record by gaining 161 yards on his 4 receptions.

Dallas (NFC)	7 3 0 7	— 17
Pittsburgh (AFC)	7 0 0 14	— 21

Dall — D. Pearson 29 pass from Staubach (Fritsch kick) (10:24)
Pitt — Grossman 7 pass from Bradshaw (Gerela kick) (5:57)
Dall — FG Fritsch 36 (14:45)
Pitt — Safety, Harrison blocked Hoopes' punt through end zone (11:28)
Pitt — FG Gerela 36 (8:41)
Pitt — FG Gerela 18 (6:37)
Pitt — Swann 64 pass from Bradshaw (kick failed) (3:02)
Dall — P. Howard 34 pass from Staubach (Fritsch kick) (1:48)

SUPER BOWL IX
Tulane Stadium, New Orleans, Louisiana
January 12, 1975, Attendance: 80,997
PITTSBURGH 16, MINNESOTA 6—AFC champion Pittsburgh, in its initial Super Bowl appearance, and NFC champion Minnesota, making a third bid for its first Super Bowl title, struggled through a first half in which the only score was produced by the Steelers' defense when Dwight White downed Vikings' quarterback Fran Tarkenton in the end zone for a safety 7:49 into the second period. The Steelers forced another break and took advantage on the second-half kickoff when Minnesota's Bill Brown fumbled and Marv Kellum recovered for Pittsburgh on the Vikings' 30. After Rocky Bleier failed to gain on first down, Franco Harris carried 3 consecutive times for 24 yards, a loss of 3, and a 9-yard touchdown and a 9-0 lead. Though its offense was completely stymied by Pittsburgh's defense, Minnesota managed to move into a threatening position after 4:27 of the final period when Matt Blair blocked Bobby Walden's punt and Terry Brown recovered the ball in the end zone for a touchdown. Fred Cox's kick failed and the Steelers led 9-6. Pittsburgh wasted no time putting the victory away. The Steelers took the ensuing kickoff and marched 66 yards in 11 plays, climaxed by Terry Bradshaw's 4-yard scoring pass to Larry Brown with 3:31 left. Pittsburgh's defense permitted Minnesota only 119 yards total offense, including a Super Bowl low of 17 rushing yards. The Steelers, meanwhile, gained 333 yards, including Harris' record 158 yards on 34 carries.

Pittsburgh (AFC)	0 2 7 7	— 16
Minnesota (NFC)	0 0 0 6	— 6

Pitt — Safety, White downed Tarkenton in end zone (7:11)
Pitt — Harris 9 run (Gerela kick) (13:25)
Minn — T. Brown recovered blocked punt in end zone (kick failed) (10:33)
Pitt — L. Brown 4 pass from Bradshaw (Gerela kick) (3:31)

SUPER BOWL VIII
Rice Stadium, Houston, Texas
January 13, 1974, Attendance: 71,882
MIAMI 24, MINNESOTA 7—The defending NFL champion Dolphins, representing the AFC for the third straight year, scored the first two times they had possession on marches of 62 and 56 yards while the Miami defense limited the Vikings to only seven plays in the first period. Larry Csonka climaxed the initial 10-play drive with a 5-yard touchdown bolt through right guard after 5:27 had elapsed. Four plays later, Miami began another 10-play scoring drive, which ended with Jim Kiick bursting 1 yard through the middle for another touchdown after 13:38 of the period. Garo Yepremian added a 28-yard field goal midway in the second period for a 17-0 Miami lead. Minnesota then drove from its 20 to a second-and-2 situation on the Miami 7 yard line with 1:18 left in the half. But on two plays, Miami limited Oscar Reed to 1 yard. On fourth-and-1 from the 6, Reed went over right tackle, but Dolphins middle linebacker Nick Buoniconti jarred the ball loose and Jake Scott recovered for Miami to halt the Minnesota threat. The Vikings were unable to muster enough offense in the second half to threaten the Dolphins. Csonka rushed 33 times for a Super Bowl-record 145 yards. Bob Griese of Miami completed 6 of 7 passes for 73 yards.

Minnesota (NFC)	0 0 0 7	— 7
Miami (AFC)	14 3 7 0	— 24

Mia — Csonka 5 run (Yepremian kick) (5:27)
Mia — Kiick 1 run (Yepremian kick) (1:22)
Mia — FG Yepremian 28 (6:02)
Mia — Csonka 2 run (Yepremian kick) (8:44)
Minn — Tarkenton 4 run (Cox kick) (13:25)

SUPER BOWL VII
Memorial Coliseum, Los Angeles, CA
January 14, 1973, Attendance: 90,182
MIAMI 14, WASHINGTON 7—The Dolphins played virtually perfect football in the first half as their defense permitted the Redskins to cross midfield only once and their offense turned good field position into 2 touchdowns. On its third possession, Miami opened its first scoring drive from the Dolphins' 37 yard line. An 18-yard pass from Bob Griese to Paul Warfield preceded by three plays Griese's 28-yard touchdown pass to Howard Twilley. After Washington moved from its 17 to the Miami 48 with two minutes remaining in the first half, Dolphins linebacker Nick Buoniconti intercepted Billy Kilmer's pass at the Miami 41 and returned it to the Washington 27. Jim Kiick ran for 3 yards, Larry Csonka for 3, Griese passed to Jim Mandich for 19, and Kiick gained 1 to the 1-yard line. With 18 seconds left until intermission, Kiick scored from the 1. Washington's only touchdown came with 2:07 left in the game and resulted from a misplayed field-goal attempt and fumble by Garo Yepremian, with the Redskins' Mike Bass picking the ball out of the air and running 49 yards for the score. Dolphins safety Jake Scott, who had 2 interceptions, including 1 in the end zone to kill a Redskins' drive, was voted the game's most valuable player.

Miami (AFC)	7 7 0 0	— 14
Washington (NFC)	0 0 0 7	— 7

Mia — Twilley 28 pass from Griese (Yepremian kick) (0:01)
Mia — Kiick 1 run (Yepremian kick) (0:18)
Wash — Bass 49 fumble recovery return (Knight kick) (2:07)

SUPER BOWL VI
Tulane Stadium, New Orleans, Louisiana
January 16, 1972, Attendance: 81,023
DALLAS 24, MIAMI 3—The Cowboys rushed for a record 252 yards and their defense limited the Dolphins to a low of 185 yards while not permitting a touchdown for the first time in Super Bowl history. Dallas converted Chuck Howley's recovery of Larry Csonka's first fumble of the season into a 3-0 advantage and led at halftime 10-3. After Dallas received the second-half kickoff, Duane Thomas led a 71-yard march in eight plays for a 17-3 margin. Howley intercepted Bob Griese's pass at the 50 and returned it to the Miami 9 early in the fourth period, and three plays later Roger Staubach passed 7 yards to Mike Ditka for the final touchdown. Thomas rushed for 95 yards and Walt Garrison gained 74. Staubach, voted

the game's most valuable player, completed 12 of 19 passes for 119 yards and 2 touchdowns.

Dallas (NFC)	3 7 7 7 — 24
Miami (AFC)	0 3 0 0 — 3

Dall — FG Clark 9 (1:23)
Dall — Alworth 7 pass from Staubach (Clark kick) (1:15)
Mia — FG Yepremian 31 (0:04)
Dall — D. Thomas 3 run (Clark kick) (9:43)
Dall — Ditka 7 pass from Staubach (Clark kick) (11:42)

SUPER BOWL V

Orange Bowl, Miami, Florida
January 17, 1971, Attendance: 79,204
BALTIMORE 16, DALLAS 13—A 32-yard field goal by rookie kicker Jim O'Brien brought the Baltimore Colts a victory over the Dallas Cowboys in the final five seconds of Super Bowl V. The game between the champions of the AFC and NFC was played on artificial turf for the first time. Dallas led 13-6 at the half but interceptions by Rick Volk and Mike Curtis set up a Baltimore touchdown and O'Brien's decisive kick in the fourth period. Earl Morrall relieved an injured Johnny Unitas late in the first half, although Unitas completed the Colts' only scoring pass. It caromed off receiver Eddie Hinton's fingertips, off Dallas defensive back Mel Renfro, and finally settled into the grasp of John Mackey, who went 45 yards to score on a 75-yard play.

Baltimore (AFC)	0 6 0 10 — 16
Dallas (NFC)	3 10 0 0 — 13

Dall — FG Clark 14 (5:32)
Dall — FG Clark 30 (14:52)
Balt — Mackey 75 pass from Unitas (kick blocked) (14:55)
Dall — Thomas 7 pass from Morton (Clark kick) (7:53)
Balt — Nowatzke 2 run (O'Brien kick) (7:35)
Balt — FG O'Brien 32 (0:05)

SUPER BOWL IV

Tulane Stadium, New Orleans, Louisiana
January 11, 1970, Attendance: 80,562
KANSAS CITY 23, MINNESOTA 7—The AFL squared the Super Bowl at two games apiece with the NFL, building a 16-0 halftime lead behind Len Dawson's superb quarterbacking and a powerful defense. Dawson, the fourth consecutive quarterback to be chosen the Super Bowl's top player, called an almost flawless game, completing 12 of 17 passes and hitting Otis Taylor on a 46-yard play for the final Chiefs touchdown. The Kansas City defense limited Minnesota's strong rushing game to 67 yards and had 3 interceptions and 2 fumble recoveries. The crowd of 80,562 set a Super Bowl record, as did the gross receipts of $3,817,872.69.

Minnesota (NFL)	0 0 7 0 — 7
Kansas City (AFL)	3 13 7 0 — 23

KC — FG Stenerud 48 (6:52)
KC — FG Stenerud 32 (13:20)
KC — FG Stenerud 25 (7:52)
KC — Garrett 5 run (Stenerud kick) (5:34)
Minn — Osborn 4 run (Cox kick) (4:32)
KC — Taylor 46 pass from Dawson (Stenerud kick) (1:22)

SUPER BOWL III

Orange Bowl, Miami, Florida
January 12, 1969, Attendance: 75,389
NEW YORK JETS 16, BALTIMORE 7—Jets quarterback Joe Namath "guaranteed" victory on the Thursday before the game, then went out and led the AFL to its first Super Bowl victory over a Baltimore team that had lost only once in 16 games all season. Namath, chosen the outstanding player, completed 17 of 28 passes for 206 yards and directed a steady attack that dominated the NFL champions after the Jets' defense had intercepted Colts quarterback Earl Morrall 3 times in the first half. The Jets had 337 total yards, including 121 rushing yards by Matt Snell. Johnny Unitas, who had missed most of the season with a sore elbow, came off the bench and led Baltimore to its only touchdown late in the fourth quarter after New York led 16-0.

New York Jets (AFL)	0 7 6 3 — 16
Baltimore (NFL)	0 0 0 7 — 7

NYJ — Snell 4 run (Turner kick) (9:03)
NYJ — FG Turner 32 (10:08)
NYJ — FG Turner 30 (3:58)
NYJ — FG Turner 9 (13:26)
Balt — Hill 1 run (Michaels kick) (3:19)

SUPER BOWL II

Orange Bowl, Miami, Florida
January 14, 1968, Attendance: 75,546
GREEN BAY 33, OAKLAND 14—Green Bay, after winning its third consecutive NFL championship, won the Super Bowl title for the second straight year, defeating the AFL champion Raiders in a game that drew the first $3-million gate in football history. Bart Starr again was chosen the game's most valuable player as he completed 13 of 24 passes for 202 yards and 1 touchdown and directed a Packers' attack that was in control all the way after building a 16-7 halftime lead. Don Chandler kicked 4 field goals and all-pro cornerback Herb Adderley capped the Green Bay scoring with a 60-yard interception return. The game marked the last for Vince Lombardi as Packers coach, ending nine years at Green Bay in which he won six Western Conference championships, five NFL championships, and two Super Bowls.

Green Bay (NFL)	3 13 10 7 — 33
Oakland (AFL)	0 7 0 7 — 14

GB — FG Chandler 39 (9:53)
GB — FG Chandler 20 (11:52)
GB — Dowler 62 pass from Starr (Chandler kick) (10:50)
Oak — Miller 23 pass from Lamonica (Blanda kick) (6:15)
GB — FG Chandler 43 (0:01)
GB — Anderson 2 run (Chandler kick) (5:54)
GB — FG Chandler 31 (0:02)
GB — Adderley 60 interception return (Chandler kick) (11:03)
Oak — Miller 23 pass from Lamonica (Blanda kick) (9:13)

SUPER BOWL I

Memorial Coliseum, Los Angeles, CA
January 15, 1967, Attendance: 61,946
GREEN BAY 35, KANSAS CITY 10—The Green Bay Packers opened the Super Bowl series by defeating the AFL champion Chiefs behind the passing of Bart Starr, the receiving of Max McGee, and a key interception by all-pro safety Willie Wood. Green Bay broke open the game with 3 second-half touchdowns, the first of which was set up by Wood's 50-yard return of an interception. McGee, filling in for ailing Boyd Dowler after having caught only 4 passes all season, caught 7 from Starr for 138 yards and 2 touchdowns. Elijah Pitts ran for 2 other scores. The Chiefs' 10 points came in the second quarter, the only touchdown on a 7-yard pass from Len Dawson to Curtis McClinton. Starr completed 16 of 23 passes for 250 yards and 2 touchdowns and was chosen the most valuable player. The Packers collected $15,000 per man and the Chiefs $7,500—the largest single-game shares in the history of team sports.

Kansas City (AFL)	0 10 0 0 — 10
Green Bay (NFL)	7 7 14 7 — 35

GB — McGee 37 pass from Starr (Chandler kick) (6:04)
KC — McClinton 7 pass from Dawson (Mercer kick) (10:40)
GB — Taylor 14 run (Chandler kick) (4:37)
KC — FG Mercer 31 (0:54)
GB — Pitts 5 run (Chandler kick) (12:33)
GB — McGee 13 pass from Starr (Chandler kick) (0:51)
GB — Pitts 1 run (Chandler kick) (6:35)

AFC CHAMPIONSHIP GAME RESULTS
Includes AFL Championship Games (1960-69)

Season	Date	Winner (Share)	Loser (Share)	Score	Site	Attendance
2006	Jan. 21	Indianapolis ($37,000)	New England ($37,000)	38-34	Indianapolis	57,433
2005	Jan. 22	Pittsburgh ($37,000)	Denver ($37,000)	34-17	Denver	76,775
2004	Jan. 23	New England ($36,500)	Pittsburgh ($36,500)	41-27	Pittsburgh	65,242
2003	Jan. 18	New England ($36,500)	Indianapolis ($36,500)	24-14	Foxborough	68,436
2002	Jan. 19	Oakland ($35,000)	Tennessee ($35,000)	41-24	Oakland	62,544
2001	Jan. 27	New England ($34,500)	Pittsburgh ($34,500)	24-17	Pittsburgh	64,704
2000	Jan. 14	Baltimore ($34,500)	Oakland ($34,500)	16-3	Oakland	62,784
1999	Jan. 23	Tennessee ($33,000)	Jacksonville ($33,000)	33-14	Jacksonville	75,206
1998	Jan. 17	Denver ($32,500)	N.Y. Jets ($32,500)	23-10	Denver	75,482
1997	Jan. 11	Denver ($30,000)	Pittsburgh ($30,000)	24-21	Pittsburgh	61,382
1996	Jan. 12	New England ($29,000)	Jacksonville ($29,000)	20-6	Foxborough	60,190
1995	Jan. 14	Pittsburgh ($27,000)	Indianapolis ($27,000)	20-16	Pittsburgh	61,062
1994	Jan. 15	San Diego ($26,000)	Pittsburgh ($26,000)	17-13	Pittsburgh	61,545
1993	Jan. 23	Buffalo ($23,500)	Kansas City ($23,500)	30-13	Buffalo	76,642
1992	Jan. 17	Buffalo ($18,000)	Miami ($18,000)	29-10	Miami	72,703
1991	Jan. 12	Buffalo ($18,000)	Denver ($18,000)	10-7	Buffalo	80,272
1990	Jan. 20	Buffalo ($18,000)	L.A. Raiders ($18,000)	51-3	Buffalo	80,325
1989	Jan. 14	Denver ($18,000)	Cleveland ($18,000)	37-21	Denver	76,046
1988	Jan. 8	Cincinnati ($18,000)	Buffalo ($18,000)	21-10	Cincinnati	59,747
1987	Jan. 17	Denver ($18,000)	Cleveland ($18,000)	38-33	Denver	76,197
1986	Jan. 11	Denver ($18,000)	Cleveland ($18,000)	23-20*	Cleveland	79,973
1985	Jan. 12	New England ($18,000)	Miami ($18,000)	31-14	Miami	75,662
1984	Jan. 6	Miami ($18,000)	Pittsburgh ($18,000)	45-28	Miami	76,029
1983	Jan. 8	L.A. Raiders ($18,000)	Seattle ($18,000)	30-14	Los Angeles	91,445
1982	Jan. 23	Miami ($18,000)	N.Y. Jets ($18,000)	14-0	Miami	67,396
1981	Jan. 10	Cincinnati ($9,000)	San Diego ($9,000)	27-7	Cincinnati	46,302
1980	Jan. 11	Oakland ($9,000)	San Diego ($9,000)	34-27	San Diego	52,675
1979	Jan. 6	Pittsburgh ($9,000)	Houston ($9,000)	27-13	Pittsburgh	50,475
1978	Jan. 7	Pittsburgh ($9,000)	Houston ($9,000)	34-5	Pittsburgh	50,725
1977	Jan. 1	Denver ($9,000)	Oakland ($9,000)	20-17	Denver	75,044
1976	Dec. 26	Oakland ($8,500)	Pittsburgh ($5,500)	24-7	Oakland	53,821
1975	Jan. 4	Pittsburgh ($8,500)	Oakland ($5,500)	16-10	Pittsburgh	50,609
1974	Dec. 29	Pittsburgh ($8,500)	Oakland ($5,500)	24-13	Oakland	53,800
1973	Dec. 30	Miami ($8,500)	Oakland ($5,500)	27-10	Miami	79,325
1972	Dec. 31	Miami ($8,500)	Pittsburgh ($5,500)	21-17	Pittsburgh	50,845
1971	Jan. 2	Miami ($8,500)	Baltimore ($5,500)	21-0	Miami	76,622
1970	Jan. 3	Baltimore ($8,500)	Oakland ($5,500)	27-17	Baltimore	54,799
1969	Jan. 4	Kansas City ($7,755)	Oakland ($6,252)	17-7	Oakland	53,564
1968	Dec. 29	N.Y. Jets ($7,007)	Oakland ($5,349)	27-23	New York	62,627
1967	Dec. 31	Oakland ($6,321)	Houston ($4,996)	40-7	Oakland	53,330
1966	Jan. 1	Kansas City ($5,309)	Buffalo ($3,799)	31-7	Buffalo	42,080
1965	Dec. 26	Buffalo ($5,189)	San Diego ($3,447)	23-0	San Diego	30,361
1964	Dec. 26	Buffalo ($2,668)	San Diego ($1,738)	20-7	Buffalo	40,242
1963	Jan. 5	San Diego ($2,498)	Boston ($1,596)	51-10	San Diego	30,127
1962	Dec. 23	Dallas ($2,206)	Houston ($1,471)	20-17*	Houston	37,981
1961	Dec. 24	Houston ($1,792)	San Diego ($1,111)	10-3	San Diego	29,556
1960	Jan. 1	Houston ($1,025)	L.A. Chargers ($718)	24-16	Houston	32,183

Sudden death overtime

AFC CHAMPIONSHIP GAME COMPOSITE STANDINGS

	W	L	Pct.	Pts.	OP
Cincinnati Bengals	2	0	1.000	48	17
Baltimore Ravens	1	0	1.000	16	3
Buffalo Bills	6	2	.750	180	92
Denver Broncos	6	2	.750	189	166
Kansas City Chiefs*	3	1	.750	81	61
Miami Dolphins	5	2	.714	152	115
New England Patriots**	5	2	.714	184	167
Pittsburgh Steelers	6	7	.462	285	270
Indianapolis Colts#	2	3	.400	95	116
Tennessee Titans##	3	5	.375	133	195
Oakland Raiders###	5	9	.357	272	304
New York Jets	2	4	.333	37	60
San Diego Chargers***	2	6	.250	128	161
Seattle Seahawks	0	1	.000	14	30
Jacksonville Jaguars	0	2	.000	20	53
Cleveland Browns	0	3	.000	74	98

* One game played when franchise was in Dallas (Texans)
    (Won 20-17)
** One game played when franchise was in Boston (Lost 51-10)
*** One game played when franchise was in Los Angeles
    (Lost 24-16)
\# Two games played when franchise was in Baltimore
    (Won 27-17, lost 21-0)
\#\# Six games played when franchise was in Houston and
    known as Oilers (Won 2, lost 4)
\#\#\# Two games played when franchise was in Los Angeles
    (Won 30-14, lost 51-3)

2006 AFC CHAMPIONSHIP GAME
RCA Dome, Indianapolis, Indiana
January 21, 2007, Attendance: 57,433
INDIANAPOLIS 38, NEW ENGLAND 34—Joseph Addai's 3-yard touchdown run with 1:00 left, and Marlin Jackson's interception with 16 seconds remaining, capped the Colts' 18-point comeback and led the franchise to its first AFC title since 1970. In the

second half, the Colts outgained the Patriots 311-149 in total yards to rally from a 21-6 deficit. The Patriots had scored on touchdown drives of 75 and 72 yards for a 14-3 lead. Two plays later, Asante Samuel intercepted a pass and returned it 39 yards for a touchdown and 21-3 lead with 9:25 left in the second quarter. The Colts drove 80 yards just before halftime to set up Adam Vinatieri's field goal to pull within 21-6. The Colts then had consecutive 76-yard touchdown drives to begin the second half, capped by Dan Klecko's tackle-eligible 1-yard touchdown catch and Marvin Harrison's 2-point conversion grab, to tie the game 21-21. Ellis Hobbs returned the ensuing kickoff 80 yards, and Tom Brady's 6-yard touchdown pass to Jabar Gaffney gave the Patriots a 28-21 lead. The Colts drove to the Patriots' 2. On second-and-goal, Dominic Rhodes fumbled but center Jeff Saturday recovered the ball in the end zone to tie the game 21-21. New England left guard Logan Mankins had also recovered a fumble for a touchdown in the first quarter, in addition to Klecko's scoring grab, it meant three offensive lineman scored a touchdown in the game. Stephen Gostkowski's 28-yard field goal with 7:42 to play gave the Patriots a 31-28 lead, but Manning quickly completed a 52-yard pas to Dallas Clark to set up Adam Vinatieri's 36-yard field goal with 5:31 left. Gostkowski's 43-yard field goal with 3:49 remaining gave New England a 34-31 lead, and the Patriots' defense forced a punt. Brady's third-and-4 pass fell incomplete, and the Colts forced a punt and got the ball on their own 20 with 2:17 to play. Manning completed an 11-yard pass to Reggie Wayne. After an incompletion, he hit Bryan Fletcher for a 32-yard pass. On the next play, Manning completed a 14-yard pass to Wayne, and with a roughing the passer penalty tacked on, the Colts got the ball on the Patriots' 11 with 1:53 to play. On third-and-2 from the 3-yard line, Addai scored up the middle for a 38-34 lead with 1:00 left. The Patriots reached the Colts' 45 with 24 seconds left, and still had a timeout, but Jackson intercepted Brady's pass to clinch the victory. Manning was 27 of 47 for 349 yards and 1 touchdown, with 1 interception. Clark had 6 catches for 137 yards. Brady was 21 of 34 for 232 yards and 1 touchdown, with 1 interception.

New England (34)	Offense	Indianapolis (38)
Reche Caldwell	WR	Reggie Wayne
Matt Light	LT	Tarik Glenn
Logan Mankins	LG	Ryan Lilja
Dan Koppen	C	Jeff Saturday
Stephen Neal	RG	Jake Scott
Nick Kaczur	RT	Ryan Diem
Daniel Graham	TE	Dallas Clark
Jabar Gaffney	WR	Marvin Harrison
Tom Brady	QB	Peyton Manningr
Corey Dillon	RB	Jospeh Addai
Ben Watson	TE/H-B	Ben Utecht
	Defense	
Ty Warren	LE	Robert Mathis
Vince Wilfork	NT-LT	Anthony McFarland
Richard Seymour	RE-RT	Raheem Brock
Rosevelt Colvin	OLB-RE	Dwight Freeney
Tedy Bruschi	ILB-SLB	Rob Morris
Eric Alexander	ILB-MLB	Gary Brackett
Mike Vrabel	OLB-WLB	Cato June
Asante Samuel	LCB	Nick Harper
Ellis Hobbs	RCB	Jason David
James Sanders	SS	Antoine Bethea
Artrell Hawkins	FS	Bob Sanders

SUBSTITUTIONS

New England—Specialists: K—Stephen Gostkowski. P—Todd Sauerbrun. LS—Lonie Paxton. Offense: QB—Matt Cassel. RB—Heath Evans, Kevin Faulk, Laurence Maroney. WR—Troy Brown, Chad Jackson. TE—David Thomas. G/C—Russ Hochstein. Defense: DT/DE—Jarvis Green, Mike Wright. LB—Tully Banta-Cain, Larry Izzo, Corey Mays, Pierre Woods. CB—Chad Scott, Antwain Spann. DB—Willie Andrews, Ray Mickens. S—Rashad Baker. DNP: T—Ryan O'Callaghan. Not Active: QB—Vinny Tes-

taverde. WR—Bam Childress, Kelvin Kight. T—Wesley Britt. G/C—Gene Mruczkowski. DL—Le Kevin Smith. DE—Marquise Hill. S—Rodney Harrison.
Indianapolis—Specialists: K—Adam Vinatieri. P—Hunter Smith. Offense: RB—De De Dorsey, Dominic Rhodes. WR—Aaron Moorehead, Terrence Wilkins. TE—Bryan Fletcher, Justin Snow. T—Charlie Johnson. C/G—Dylan Gandy. Defense: DT—Dan Klecko, Darrell Reid. DE—Josh Thomas. LB—Rocky Boiman, Tyjuan Hagler, Freddie Keiaho, Keith O'Neil. DB—Matt Giordano, Kelvin Hayden, Marlin Jackson, Dexter Reid. DNP: QB—Jim Sorgi. DE—Bo Schobel. Not Active: WR—Ricky Proehl, John Standeford. G—Matt Ulrich. T—Daniel Federkeil. DE—Ryan LaCasse. LB—Gilbert Gardner. DB—Tim Jennings, T.J. Rushing.

OFFICIALS

Referee—Bill Carollo. Umpire—Tony Michalek. Line Judge—Byron Boston Side Judge—Larry Rose. Head Linesman—Gary Slaughter. Back Judge—Scott Helverson. Field Judge—Rob Vernatchi.

SCORING

New England	7	14	7	6	—	34
Indianapolis	3	3	15	17	—	38

NE — Mankins fumble recovery in end zone (Gostkowski kick)
Ind — FG Vinatieri 42
NE — Dillon 7 run (Gostkowski kick)
NE — Samuel 39 interception return (Gostkowski kick)
Ind — FG Vinatieri 26
Ind — Manning 1 run (Vinatieri kick)
Ind — Klecko 1 pass from Manning (Harrison pass from Manning)
NE — Gaffney 6 pass from Brady (Gostkowski kick)
Ind — Saturday fumble recovery in end zone (Vinatieri kick)
NE — FG Gostkowski 28
Ind — FG Vinatieri 36
NE — FG Gostkowski 43
Ind — Addai 3 run (Vinatieri kick)

TEAM STATISTICS	NE	IND
Total First Downs	17	32
Rushing	6	9
Passing	11	20
Penalty	0	3
Total Net Yardage	319	455
Total Offensive Plays	59	80
Average Gain Per Offensive Play	5.4	5.7
Rushes	24	30
Yards Gained Rushing (Net)	93	125
Average Yards per Rush	3.9	4.2
Passes Attempted	34	47
Passes Completed	21	27
Had Intercepted	1	1
Tackled Attempting to Pass	1	3
Yards Lost Attempting to Pass	6	19
Yards Gained Passing (Net)	226	330
Punts	5	4
Average Distance	51.4	52.8
Punt Returns	3	3
Punt Return Yardage	39	40
Kickoff Returns	8	5
Kickoff Return Yardage	231	92
Interception Return Yardage	39	6
Total Return Yardage	78	46
Fumbles	1	2
Fumbles Lost	0	0
Own Fumbles Recovered	1	2
Opponent Fumbles Recovered	0	0
Penalties	8	4
Yards Penalized	63	32
Field Goals	2	3
Field Goals Attempted	2	3
Third-Down Efficiency	5/14	8/15

Fourth-Down Efficiency	2/2	0/0
Time of Possession	28:45	31:15

INDIVIDUAL STATISTICS
RUSHING: NE: Dillon 7-48-1, Fulk 4-27-0, Maroney 8-13-0, Evans 1-4-0, Brady 4-1-0. IND: Rhodes 14-69-0, Addai 14-56-1, Manning 2-0-1.
PASSING: NE: Brady 34-21-232-1-1. IND: Manning 47-27-349-1-1.
RECEIVING: NE: Watson 5-48-0, Caldwell 4-46-0, Evans 4-33-0, Gaffney 3-37-1, Brown 2-32-0, Graham 1-25-0, Maroney 1-6-0, Faulk 1-5-0. IND: Clark 6-137-0, Wayne 5-68-0, Harrison

4-41-0, Rhodes 4-38-0, Moorehead 3-23-0, Addai 2-4-0, Fletcher 1-32-0, Utecht 1-5-0, Klecko 1-1-1.
KICKOFF RETURNS: NE: Hobbs 6-220-0, Maroney 1-11-0, Brown 1-0-0. IND: Wilkins 4-80-0, Johnson 1-12-0.
PUNT RETURNS: NE: Brown 3-39-0, Faulk 0-0-0. IND: Wilkins 3-40-0.
PUNTING: NE: Sauerbrun 5-257-51.4. IND: Smith 4-211-52.8.
INTERCEPTIONS: NE: Samuel 1-39-1. IND: Jackson 1-6-0.
SACKS: NE: Alexander, Colvin, Vrabel. IND: Brock.

NFC CHAMPIONSHIP GAME RESULTS
Includes NFL Championship Games (1933-1969)

Season	Date	Winner (Share)	Loser (Share)	Score	Site	Attendance
2006	Jan. 21	Chicago ($37,000)	New Orleans ($37,000)	39-14	Chicago	61,817
2005	Jan. 22	Seattle ($37,000)	Carolina ($37,000)	34-14	Seattle	67,837
2004	Jan. 23	Philadelphia ($36,500)	Atlanta ($36,500)	27-10	Philadelphia	67,717
2003	Jan. 18	Carolina ($36,500)	Philadelphia ($36,500)	14-3	Philadelphia	67,862
2002	Jan. 19	Tampa Bay ($35,000)	Philadelphia ($35,000)	27-10	Philadelphia	66,713
2001	Jan. 27	St. Louis ($34,500)	Philadelphia ($34,500)	29-24	St. Louis	66,502
2000	Jan. 14	N.Y. Giants ($34,500)	Minnesota ($34,500)	41-0	East Rutherford	79,310
1999	Jan. 23	St. Louis ($33,000)	Tampa Bay ($33,000)	11-6	St. Louis	66,396
1998	Jan. 17	Atlanta ($32,500)	Minnesota ($32,500)	30-27*	Minneapolis	64,060
1997	Jan. 11	Green Bay ($30,000)	San Francisco ($30,000)	23-10	San Francisco	68,987
1996	Jan. 12	Green Bay ($29,000)	Carolina ($29,000)	30-13	Green Bay	60,216
1995	Jan. 14	Dallas ($27,000)	Green Bay ($27,000)	38-27	Dallas	65,135
1994	Jan. 15	San Francisco ($26,000)	Dallas ($26,000)	38-28	San Francisco	69,125
1993	Jan. 23	Dallas ($23,500)	San Francisco ($23,500)	38-21	Dallas	64,902
1992	Jan. 17	Dallas ($18,000)	San Francisco ($18,000)	30-20	San Francisco	64,920
1991	Jan. 12	Washington ($18,000)	Detroit ($18,000)	41-10	Washington	55,585
1990	Jan. 20	N.Y. Giants ($18,000)	San Francisco ($18,000)	15-13	San Francisco	65,750
1989	Jan. 14	San Francisco ($18,000)	L.A. Rams ($18,000)	30-3	San Francisco	65,634
1988	Jan. 8	San Francisco ($18,000)	Chicago ($18,000)	28-3	Chicago	66,946
1987	Jan. 17	Washington ($18,000)	Minnesota ($18,000)	17-10	Washington	55,212
1986	Jan. 11	New York Giants ($18,000)	Washington ($18,000)	17-0	East Rutherford	76,891
1985	Jan. 12	Chicago ($18,000)	L.A. Rams ($18,000)	24-0	Chicago	66,030
1984	Jan. 6	San Francisco ($18,000)	Chicago ($18,000)	23-0	San Francisco	61,336
1983	Jan. 8	Washington ($18,000)	San Francisco ($18,000)	24-21	Washington	55,363
1982	Jan. 22	Washington ($18,000)	Dallas ($18,000)	31-17	Washington	55,045
1981	Jan. 10	San Francisco ($9,000)	Dallas ($9,000)	28-27	San Francisco	60,525
1980	Jan. 11	Philadelphia ($9,000)	Dallas ($9,000)	20-7	Philadelphia	71,522
1979	Jan. 6	Los Angeles ($9,000)	Tampa Bay ($9,000)	9-0	Tampa	72,033
1978	Jan. 7	Dallas ($9,000)	Los Angeles ($9,000)	28-0	Los Angeles	71,086
1977	Jan. 1	Dallas ($9,000)	Minnesota ($9,000)	23-6	Dallas	64,293
1976	Dec. 26	Minnesota ($8,500)	Los Angeles ($5,500)	24-13	Minneapolis	48,379
1975	Jan. 4	Dallas ($8,500)	Los Angeles ($5,500)	37-7	Los Angeles	88,919
1974	Dec. 29	Minnesota ($8,500)	Los Angeles ($5,500)	14-10	Minneapolis	48,444
1973	Dec. 30	Minnesota ($8,500)	Dallas ($5,500)	27-10	Dallas	64,422
1972	Dec. 31	Washington ($8,500)	Dallas ($5,500)	26-3	Washington	53,129
1971	Jan. 2	Dallas ($8,500)	San Francisco ($5,500)	14-3	Dallas	63,409
1970	Jan. 3	Dallas ($8,500)	San Francisco ($5,500)	17-10	San Francisco	59,364
1969	Jan. 4	Minnesota ($7,930)	Cleveland ($5,118)	27-7	Minneapolis	46,503
1968	Dec. 29	Baltimore ($9,306)	Cleveland ($5,963)	34-0	Cleveland	78,410
1967	Dec. 31	Green Bay ($7,950)	Dallas ($5,299)	21-17	Green Bay	50,861
1966	Jan. 1	Green Bay ($9,813)	Dallas ($6,527)	34-27	Dallas	74,152
1965	Jan. 2	Green Bay ($7,819)	Cleveland ($5,288)	23-12	Green Bay	50,777
1964	Dec. 27	Cleveland ($8,052)	Baltimore ($5,571)	27-0	Cleveland	79,544
1963	Dec. 29	Chicago ($5,899)	New York ($4,218)	14-10	Chicago	45,801
1962	Dec. 30	Green Bay ($5,888)	New York ($4,166)	16-7	New York	64,892
1961	Dec. 31	Green Bay ($5,195)	New York ($3,339)	37-0	Green Bay	39,029
1960	Dec. 26	Philadelphia ($5,116)	Green Bay ($3,105)	17-13	Philadelphia	67,325
1959	Dec. 27	Baltimore ($4,674)	New York ($3,083)	31-16	Baltimore	57,545
1958	Dec. 28	Baltimore ($4,718)	New York ($3,111)	23-17*	New York	64,185
1957	Dec. 29	Detroit ($4,295)	Cleveland ($2,750)	59-14	Detroit	55,263
1956	Dec. 30	New York ($3,779)	Chi. Bears ($2,485)	47-7	New York	56,836
1955	Dec. 26	Cleveland ($3,508)	Los Angeles ($2,316)	38-14	Los Angeles	85,693
1954	Dec. 26	Cleveland ($2,478)	Detroit ($1,585)	56-10	Cleveland	43,827
1953	Dec. 27	Detroit ($2,424)	Cleveland ($1,654)	17-16	Detroit	54,577
1952	Dec. 28	Detroit ($2,274)	Cleveland ($1,712)	17-7	Cleveland	50,934
1951	Dec. 23	Los Angeles ($2,108)	Cleveland ($1,483)	24-17	Los Angeles	57,522
1950	Dec. 24	Cleveland ($1,113)	Los Angeles ($686)	30-28	Cleveland	29,751

Season	Date	Winner (Share)	Loser (Share)	Score	Site	Attendance
1949	Dec. 18	Philadelphia ($1,094)	Los Angeles ($739)	14-0	Los Angeles	27,980
1948	Dec. 19	Philadelphia ($1,540)	Chi. Cardinals ($874)	7-0	Philadelphia	36,309
1947	Dec. 28	Chi. Cardinals ($1,132)	Philadelphia ($754)	28-21	Chicago	30,759
1946	Dec. 15	Chi. Bears ($1,975)	New York ($1,295)	24-14	New York	58,346
1945	Dec. 16	Cleveland ($1,469)	Washington ($902)	15-14	Cleveland	32,178
1944	Dec. 17	Green Bay ($1,449)	New York ($814)	14-7	New York	46,016
1943	Dec. 26	Chi. Bears ($1,146)	Washington ($765)	41-21	Chicago	34,320
1942	Dec. 13	Washington ($965)	Chi. Bears ($637)	14-6	Washington	36,006
1941	Dec. 21	Chi. Bears ($430)	New York ($288)	37-9	Chicago	13,341
1940	Dec. 8	Chi. Bears ($873)	Washington ($606)	73-0	Washington	36,034
1939	Dec. 10	Green Bay ($703.97)	New York ($455.57)	27-0	Milwaukee	32,279
1938	Dec. 11	New York ($504.45)	Green Bay ($368.81)	23-17	New York	48,120
1937	Dec. 12	Washington ($225.90)	Chi. Bears ($127.78)	28-21	Chicago	15,870
1936	Dec. 13	Green Bay ($250)	Boston ($180)	21-6	New York	29,545
1935	Dec. 15	Detroit ($313.35)	New York ($200.20)	26-7	Detroit	15,000
1934	Dec. 9	New York ($621)	Chi. Bears ($414.02)	30-13	New York	35,059
1933	Dec. 17	Chi. Bears ($210.34)	New York ($140.22)	23-21	Chicago	26,000

*Sudden death overtime

NFC CHAMPIONSHIP GAME COMPOSITE STANDINGS

	W	L	Pct.	Pts.	OP
Seattle Seahawks	1	0	1.000	34	14
Green Bay Packers	10	3	.769	303	177
Baltimore Colts	3	1	.750	88	60
Detroit Lions	4	2	.667	139	141
Washington Redskins*	7	5	.583	222	255
Chicago Bears	8	6	.571	325	259
Philadelphia Eagles	5	4	.556	143	128
Dallas Cowboys	8	8	.500	361	319
Minnesota Vikings	4	4	.500	135	151
Arizona Cardinals**	1	1	.500	28	28
Atlanta Falcons	1	1	.500	40	54
San Francisco 49ers	5	7	.417	245	222
Cleveland Browns	4	7	.364	224	253
St. Louis Rams***	5	9	.357	163	300
New York Giants	6	11	.353	281	322
Carolina Panthers	1	2	.333	41	67
Tampa Bay Buccaneers	1	2	.333	33	30
New Orleans Saints	0	1	.000	14	39

*One game played when franchise was in Boston (Lost 21-6)
**Both games played when franchise was in Chicago (Won 28-21, lost 7-0)
***One game played when franchise was in Cleveland (Won 15-14), and 11 games when franchise was in Los Angeles (Won 2, lost 9, scored 108 points, allowed 256 points).

2006 NFC CHAMPIONSHIP GAME

Soldier Field, Chicago, Illinois
January 21, 2007, Attendance: 61,817

CHICAGO 39, NEW ORLEANS 14—Thomas Jones rushed for 2 touchdowns and the Bears' defense forced 4 turnovers in the windy, cold, wet conditions en route to Chicago's first NFC title since 1985. The game-time temperature was 28 degrees, with a wind chill of 13 degrees. A pair of first-quarter fumbles led to field goals and gave a 6-0 Chicago lead. With the score 9-0, Jones carried the ball all 8 plays of a 69-yard drive, capped by his 2-yard run, for a 16-0 lead with 1:56 left in the half. The Saints drove 73 yards in 1:10 to pull within 16-7 just before halftime. Then, on the Saints' second play of the third quarter, Drew Brees lofted a pass down the left sideline to Reggie Bush, who cut across field and raced 88 yards for a touchdown to pull within 16-14. The Saints had a chance to take the lead during their next possession, but long-distance kicker Billy Cundiff's 47-yard field-goal attempt was short. The Saints forced another punt, but Brad Maynard's punt went out of bounds at the 5-yard line. Two plays later, Brees was pressured in the end zone and tossed a pass out into the flat, but with no receiver in the area he was flagged for intentional grounding, resulting in a safety. Two plays into the fourth quarter, Rex Grossman completed a 33-yard touchdown pass to leaping Bernard Berrian for a 25-14 lead. Adewale Ogunleye forced Brees to fumble two plays later, leading to Cedric Benson's 12-yard scoring run. Later in the quarter, following Brees' fourth-down incomplete pass, Jones added a 15-yard touchdown with 4:19 to play. Grossman was 11 of 26 for 144 yards and 1 touchdown. Jones rushed 19 times for 123 yards. Brees was 27 of 49 for 354 yards and 2 touchdowns, with 1 interception. Bush had 7 catches for 132 yards.

New Orleans (14)	Offense	Chicago (39)
Marques Colston	WR	Muhsin Muhammad
Jammal Brown	LT	John Tait
Jamar Nesbit	LG	Ruben Brown
Jeff Faine	C	Olin Kreutz
Jahri Evans	RG	Roberto Garza
Jon Stinchcomb	RT	Fred Miller
Mark Campbell	TE	Desmond Clark
Terrance Copper	WR	Bernard Berrian
Drew Brees	QB	Rex Grossman
Deuce McAllister	RB	Thomas Jones
Reggie Brown	RB/FB	Jason McKie
	Defense	
Charles Grant	LE	Adewale Ogunleye
Hollis Thomas	LT/DT	Tank Johnson
Brian Young	RT/NT	Ian Scott
Will Smith	RE	Alex Brown
Scott Fujita	SLB/WLB	Lance Briggs
Dan Morgan	MLB	Brian Urlacher
Will Witherspoon	WLB/DB	Ricky Manning
Chris Gamble	LCB	Charles Tillman
Ken Lucas	RCB	Nathan Vasher
Marlon McCree	SS	Chris Harris
Mike Minter	FS	Daniel Manning

SUBSTITUTIONS

New Orleans—Specialists: K—John Carney, Billy Cundiff. P—Steve Weatherford. LS—Kevin Houser. Offense: FB—Mike Karney. RB—Aaron Stecker. WR—Devery Henderson, Jamal Jones, Michael Lewis. TE—Billy MIller, John Owens. T—Zach Strief. G/C—Jonathan Goodwin. Defense: DT—Antwan Lake, Willie Whitehead. DE—Josh Cooper. LB—Danny Clark, Terrence Melton. CB—Jason Craft. S—Steve Gleason, Bryan Scott. DNP: CB—Dejuan Groce. Not Active: RB—Jamaal Branch. WR—Joe Horn. G—Montrae Holland. T—Rob Petitti. DT—Rodney Leisle. LB—Alfred Fincher. CB—Curtis Deloatch. S—Omar Stoutmire.

Chicago—Specialists: K—Robbie Gould. P—Brad Maynard. LS—Patrick Mannelly. Offense: RB—Cedric Benson, Adrian Peterson. WR—Rashied Davis, Justin Gage. TE—John Gilmore, Gabe Reid. G—Terrence Metcalf. Defense: DT—Alfonso Boone. DL—Israel Idonije. DE—Mark Anderson. LB—Brendon Ayanbadejo, Hunter Hillenmeyer, Darrell McClover, Rod Wilson. CB—Devin Hester, Dante Wesley. S—Todd Johnson, Cameron Worrell. DNP: QB—Brian Griese. Not Active: QB—Kyle Orton. FB—J.D. Runnels. WR—Mark Bradley. C/G—Anthony Oakley. DT—Antonio Garay. LB—Leon Joe. S—Tyler Everett, Nick Turnbull.

OFFICIALS
Referee—Terry McAulay. Umpire—Richard Hall. Line Judge—Michael Spanier. Side Judge—Don Carlsen. Head Linesman—Kent Payne. Back Judge—Gregory Steed. Field Judge—Greg Gautreaux.

SCORING

New Orleans	0	7	7	0	—	14
Chicago	3	13	2	21	—	39

Chi— FG Gould 19
Chi— FG Gould 43
Chi— FG Gould 24
Chi— Jones 2 run (Gould kick)
NO— Colston 13 pass from Brees (Carney kick)
NO— Bush 88 pass from Brees (Carney kick)
Chi— Safety, Brees flagged for intentional grounding in end zone
Car— Berrian 33 pass from Grossman (Gould kick)
Chi— Benson 12 run (Gould kick)
Chi— Jones 15 run (Gould kick)

TEAM STATISTICS

	NO	CHI
Total First Downs	15	18
Rushing	3	12
Passing	12	6
Penalty	0	0
Total Net Yardage	375	340
Total Offensive Plays	64	72
Average Gain Per Offensive Play	4.7	4.3
Rushes	12	46
Yards Gained Rushing (Net)	56	196
Average Yards per Rush	4.7	4.3
Passes Attempted	49	26
Passes Completed	27	11
Had Intercepted	1	0
Tackled Attempting to Pass	3	0
Yards Lost Attempting to Pass	35	0
Yards Gained Passing (Net)	319	144
Punts	5	7
Average Distance	38.8	47.4
Punt Returns	4	2
Punt Return Yardage	15	24
Kickoff Returns	7	3
Kickoff Return Yardage	132	39
Interception Return Yardage	0	0
Total Return Yardage	15	24
Fumbles	4	1
Fumbles Lost	3	0
Own Fumbles Recovered	0	0
Opponent Fumbles Recovered	0	3
Penalties	7	1
Yards Penalized	47	5
Field Goals	0	2
Field Goals Attempted	0	3
Third-Down Efficiency	1/9	8/18
Fourth-Down Efficiency	0/2	2/2
Time of Possession	24:45	35:15

INDIVIDUAL STATISTCS
RUSHING: NO: Bush 4-19-0, McAllister 6-18-0, Karney 1-11-0, Brees 1-8-0. CHI: Jones 19-123-2, Benson 24-60-1, Davis 1-16-0, Grossman 2-(-3)-0.
PASSING: NO: Brees 49-27-354-2-1. CHI: Grossman 26-11-144-1-0.
RECEIVING: NO: Bush 7-132-1, Colston 5-63-1, Miller 4-31-0, Copper 3-29-0, McAllister 3-27-0. Henderson 2-57-0, Campbell 2-6-0, Karney 1-9-0. CHI: Berrian 5-85-1, Clark 1-30-0, Muhammad 1-20-0, McKie 3-6-0, Gilmore 1-3-0.
KICKOFF RETURNS: NO: Lewis 7-132-0. CHI: Hester 3-39-0.
PUNT RETURNS: NO: Bush 3-10-0, Lewis 1-5-0. CHI: Hester 2-24-0.
PUNTING: NO: Weatherford 5-194-38.8. CHI: Maynard 7-332-47.4.
INTERCEPTIONS: NO: None. CHI: Vasher.
SACKS: NO: None. CHI: Anderson, Idonije, Ogunleye.

AFC DIVISIONAL PLAYOFFS RESULTS
Includes Second-Round Playoff Games (1982), AFC Inter-Divisional Games (1969), and special playoff games to break ties for AFL Division Championships (1963, 1968)

Season	Date	Winner (Share)	Loser (Share)	Score	Site	Attendance
2006	Jan. 14	New England ($19,000)	San Diego ($19,000)	24-21	San Diego	68,810
	Jan. 13	Indianapolis ($19,000)	Baltimore ($19,000)	15-6	Baltimore	71,162
2005	Jan. 15	Pittsburgh ($19,000)	Indianapolis ($19,000)	21-18	Indianapolis	57,449
	Jan. 14	Denver ($19,000)	New England ($19,000)	27-13	Denver	76,238
2004	Jan. 16	New England ($18,000)	Indianapolis ($18,000)	20-3	Foxborough	68,756
	Jan. 15	Pittsburgh ($18,000)	N.Y. Jets ($18,000)	20-17*	Pittsburgh	64,915
2003	Jan. 11	Indianapolis ($18,000)	Kansas City ($18,000)	38-31	Kansas City	79,159
	Jan. 10	New England ($18,000)	Tennessee ($18,000)	17-14	Foxborough	68,436
2002	Jan. 12	Oakland ($17,000)	N.Y. Jets ($17,000)	30-10	Oakland	62,207
	Jan. 11	Tennessee ($17,000)	Pittsburgh ($17,000)	34-31*	Nashville	68,809
2001	Jan. 20	Pittsburgh ($17,000)	Baltimore ($17,000)	27-10	Pittsburgh	63,976
	Jan. 19	New England ($17,000)	Oakland ($17,000)	16-13*	Foxborough	60,292
2000	Jan. 7	Baltimore ($16,000)	Tennessee ($16,000)	24-10	Nashville	68,527
	Jan. 6	Oakland ($16,000)	Miami ($16,000)	27-0	Oakland	61,998
1999	Jan. 16	Tennessee ($16,000)	Indianapolis ($16,000)	19-16	Indianapolis	57,097
	Jan. 15	Jacksonville ($16,000)	Miami ($16,000)	62-7	Jacksonville	75,173
1998	Jan. 10	N.Y. Jets ($15,000)	Jacksonville ($15,000)	34-24	East Rutherford	78,817
	Jan. 9	Denver ($15,000)	Miami ($15,000)	38-3	Denver	75,729
1997	Jan. 4	Denver ($15,000)	Kansas City ($15,000)	14-10	Kansas City	76,965
	Jan. 3	Pittsburgh ($15,000)	New England ($15,000)	7-6	Pittsburgh	61,228
1996	Jan. 5	New England ($14,000)	Pittsburgh ($14,000)	28-3	Foxborough	60,188
	Jan. 4	Jacksonville ($14,000)	Denver ($14,000)	30-27	Denver	75,678
1995	Jan. 7	Indianapolis ($13,000)	Kansas City ($13,000)	10-7	Kansas City	77,594
	Jan. 6	Pittsburgh ($13,000)	Buffalo ($13,000)	40-21	Pittsburgh	59,072
1994	Jan. 8	San Diego ($12,000)	Miami ($12,000)	22-21	San Diego	63,381
	Jan. 7	Pittsburgh ($12,000)	Cleveland ($12,000)	29-9	Pittsburgh	58,185
1993	Jan. 16	Kansas City ($12,000)	Houston ($12,000)	28-20	Houston	64,011
	Jan. 15	Buffalo ($12,000)	L.A. Raiders ($12,000)	29-23	Buffalo	61,923

Season	Date	Winner (Share)	Loser (Share)	Score	Site	Attendance
1992	Jan. 10	Miami ($10,000)	San Diego ($10,000)	31-0	Miami	71,224
	Jan. 9	Buffalo ($10,000)	Pittsburgh ($10,000)	24-3	Pittsburgh	60,407
1991	Jan. 5	Buffalo ($10,000)	Kansas City ($10,000)	37-14	Buffalo	80,182
	Jan. 4	Denver ($10,000)	Houston ($10,000)	26-24	Denver	75,301
1990	Jan. 13	L.A. Raiders ($10,000)	Cincinnati ($10,000)	20-10	Los Angeles	92,045
	Jan. 12	Buffalo ($10,000)	Miami ($10,000)	44-34	Buffalo	77,087
1989	Jan. 7	Denver ($10,000)	Pittsburgh ($10,000)	24-23	Denver	75,477
	Jan. 6	Cleveland ($10,000)	Buffalo ($10,000)	34-30	Cleveland	78,921
1988	Jan. 1	Buffalo ($10,000)	Houston ($10,000)	17-10	Buffalo	79,532
	Dec. 31	Cincinnati ($10,000)	Seattle ($10,000)	21-13	Cincinnati	58,560
1987	Jan. 10	Denver ($10,000)	Houston ($10,000)	34-10	Denver	75,440
	Jan. 9	Cleveland ($10,000)	Indianapolis ($10,000)	38-21	Cleveland	79,372
1986	Jan. 4	Denver ($10,000)	New England ($10,000)	22-17	Denver	75,262
	Jan. 3	Cleveland ($10,000)	N.Y. Jets ($10,000)	23-20*	Cleveland	79,720
1985	Jan. 5	New England ($10,000)	L.A. Raiders ($10,000)	27-20	Los Angeles	87,163
	Jan. 4	Miami ($10,000)	Cleveland ($10,000)	24-21	Miami	74,667
1984	Dec. 30	Pittsburgh ($10,000)	Denver ($10,000)	24-17	Denver	74,981
	Dec. 29	Miami ($10,000)	Seattle ($10,000)	31-10	Miami	73,469
1983	Jan. 1	L.A. Raiders ($10,000)	Pittsburgh ($10,000)	38-10	Los Angeles	90,380
	Dec. 31	Seattle ($10,000)	Miami ($10,000)	27-20	Miami	74,136
1982	Jan. 16	Miami ($10,000)	San Diego ($10,000)	34-13	Miami	71,383
	Jan. 15	N.Y. Jets ($10,000)	L.A. Raiders ($10,000)	17-14	Los Angeles	90,038
1981	Jan. 3	Cincinnati ($5,000)	Buffalo ($5,000)	28-21	Cincinnati	55,420
	Jan. 2	San Diego ($5,000)	Miami ($5,000)	41-38*	Miami	73,735
1980	Jan. 4	Oakland ($5,000)	Cleveland ($5,000)	14-12	Cleveland	78,245
	Jan. 3	San Diego ($5,000)	Buffalo ($5,000)	20-14	San Diego	52,253
1979	Dec. 30	Pittsburgh ($5,000)	Miami ($5,000)	34-14	Pittsburgh	50,214
	Dec. 29	Houston ($5,000)	San Diego ($5,000)	17-14	San Diego	51,192
1978	Dec. 31	Houston ($5,000)	New England ($5,000)	31-14	Foxborough	60,735
	Dec. 30	Pittsburgh ($5,000)	Denver ($5,000)	33-10	Pittsburgh	50,230
1977	Dec. 24	Oakland ($5,000)	Baltimore ($5,000)	37-31*	Baltimore	59,925
	Dec. 24	Denver ($5,000)	Pittsburgh ($5,000)	34-21	Denver	75,059
1976	Dec. 19	Pittsburgh [$]	Baltimore [$]	40-14	Baltimore	59,296
	Dec. 18	Oakland [$]	New England [$]	24-21	Oakland	53,050
1975	Dec. 28	Oakland [$]	Cincinnati [$]	31-28	Oakland	53,030
	Dec. 27	Pittsburgh [$]	Baltimore [$]	28-10	Pittsburgh	49,557
1974	Dec. 22	Pittsburgh [$]	Buffalo [$]	32-14	Pittsburgh	49,841
	Dec. 21	Oakland [$]	Miami [$]	28-26	Oakland	53,023
1973	Dec. 23	Miami [$]	Cincinnati [$]	34-16	Miami	78,928
	Dec. 22	Oakland [$]	Pittsburgh [$]	33-14	Oakland	52,646
1972	Dec. 24	Miami [$]	Cleveland [$]	20-14	Miami	78,916
	Dec. 23	Pittsburgh [$]	Oakland [$]	13-7	Pittsburgh	50,327
1971	Dec. 26	Baltimore [$]	Cleveland [$]	20-3	Cleveland	70,734
	Dec. 25	Miami [$]	Kansas City [$]	27-24*	Kansas City	50,374
1970	Dec. 27	Oakland [$]	Miami [$]	21-14	Oakland	52,594
	Dec. 26	Baltimore [$]	Cincinnati [$]	17-0	Baltimore	49,694
1969	Dec. 21	Oakland [$]	Houston [$]	56-7	Oakland	53,539
	Dec. 20	Kansas City [$]	N.Y. Jets [$]	13-6	New York	62,977
1968	Dec. 22	Oakland [$]	Kansas City [$]	41-6	Oakland	53,605
1963	Dec. 28	Boston [$]	Buffalo [$]	26-8	Buffalo	33,044

*Sudden death overtime
$ Players received 1/14 of annual salary for playoff appearances.

2006 AFC DIVISIONAL PLAYOFF GAME

Qualcomm Stadium, San Diego, California
January 14, 2007, Attendance: 68,810
NEW ENGLAND 24, SAN DIEGO 21—Stephen Gostkowsi's 31-yard field goal with 1:10 remaining, and three key plays in the final seven minutes by Reche Caldwell, lifted the Patriots to an improbable victory. Michael Turner's 6-yard touchdown run with 2:04 left in the first half, which was set up by Philip Rivers' 58-yard pass to LaDainian Tomlinson on the previous play, gave the Chargers a 14-3 lead. At that point, the Chargers had outgained the Patriots 198-62, but the Patriots drove 72 yards in 11 plays in 1:56, capped by Tom Brady's 6-yard touchdown pass to Jabar Gaffney, to pull within 14-10 with eight seconds left in the half. Eric Parker's muffed punt, recovered by David Thomas, set up Stephen Gostkowski's second field goal to pull the Patriots' within 14-13. Rivers' 31-yard pass to Vincent Jackson set up Tomlinson's 3-yard run for a 21-13 lead with 8:35 to play. On fourth-and-5 from the Chargers' 41 with 6:16 to play, Marlon McCree intercepted Brady's pass. Troy Brown immediately ripped the ball from McCree, and Caldwell recovered the fumble at the Chargers' 32. Five plays later, Caldwell caught a 4-yard touchdown pass from Brady, and Kevin Faulk ran up the middle for the 2-point conversion, to tie the game with 4:36 remaining. The Patriots' defense forced a three-and-out and on third-and-10 Brady connected deep down the right sideline to Caldwell for a 49-yard pass play to set up Gostkowski's 31-yard go-ahead field goal with 1:10 to play. The Chargers had a chance to tie, but Nate Kaeding's 54-yard field-goal attempt fell short. Brady was 27 of 51 for 280 yards and 2 touchdowns, with 3 interceptions. Gaffney had 10 catches for 103 yards. Rivers was 14 of 32 for 230 yards, with 1 interception. Tomlinson carried 23 times for 123 yards.

New England	3	7	3	11	—	24
San Diego	0	14	0	7	—	21

NE — FG Gostkowski 50
SD — Tomlinson 2 run (Kaeding kick)
SD — Turner 6 run (Kaeding kick)
NE — Gaffney 6 pass from Brady (Gostkowski kick)

NE — FG Gostkowski 34
SD — Tomlinson 3 run (Kaeding kick)
NE — Caldwell 4 pass from Brady (Faulk run)
NE — FG Gostkowski 31

M & T Bank Stadium, Baltimore, Maryland
January 13, 2007, Attendance: 71,162
INDIANAPOLIS 15, BALTIMORE 6—Adam Vinatieri kicked 5 field goals and the Colts' defense forced 4 turnovers as Indianapolis advanced to the AFC title game. The Colts kicked field goals on their first two possessions, the latter set up by Gary Brackett's recovery of Todd Heap's fumble, to take a 6-0 lead. Trailing 6-3 in the second quarter, Ed Reed intercepted a pass and the Ravens drove to the Colts' 4. On third-and-goal, Alvin Bethea intercepted Steve McNair's pass to thwart the rally. The Colts converted two third downs on the ensuing 65-yard drive, capped by Vinatieri's 51-yard field goal, which hit the crossbar and bounced over, for a 9-3 halftime lead. Trailing 12-3 early in the fourth quarter, Matt Stover kicked a 51-yard field goal, and three plays later Reed intercepted a pass at the Ravens' 39. But six plays later, Nick Harper intercpeted McNair's pass at the Colts' 23. With 7:39 to play, the Colts began a drive on their own 36-yard line. Dominic Rhodes carried 11 times on the 13-play drive, which had 3 third-down conversions, and was capped by Vinatieri's 35-yard field goal with 23 seconds to play. Manning was 15 of 30 for 170 yards, with 2 interceptions. McNair was 18 of 29 for 173 yards, with 2 interceptions.

Indianapolis	6	3	3	3	— 15
Baltimore	0	3	0	3	— 6

Ind— FG Vinatieri 23
Ind— FG Vinatieri 42
Balt— FG Stover 40
Ind— FG Vinatieri 51
Ind— FG Vinatieri 48
Balt— FG Stover 51
Ind— FG Vinatieri 35

NFC DIVISIONAL PLAYOFFS RESULTS

Includes Second-Round Playoff Games (1982), NFL Conference Championship Games (1967-69), and special playoff games to break ties for NFL Division or Conference Championships (1941, 1943, 1947, 1950, 1952, 1957, 1958, 1965)

Season	Date	Winner (Share)	Loser (Share)	Score	Site	Attendance
2006	Jan. 14	Chicago ($19,000)	Seattle ($19,000)	27-24*	Chicago	62,184
	Jan. 13	New Orleans ($19,000)	Philadelphia ($19,000)	27-24	New Orleans	70,001
2005	Jan. 15	Carolina ($19,000)	Chicago ($19,000)	29-21	Chicago	62,209
	Jan. 14	Seattle ($19,000)	Washington ($19,000)	20-10	Seattle	67,551
2004	Jan. 16	Philadelphia ($18,000)	Minnesota ($18,000)	27-14	Philadelphia	67,722
	Jan. 15	Atlanta ($18,000)	St. Louis ($18,000)	47-17	Atlanta	70,709
2003	Jan. 11	Philadelphia ($18,000)	Green Bay ($18,000)	20-17*	Philadelphia	67,707
	Jan. 10	Carolina ($18,000)	St. Louis ($18,000)	29-23*	St. Louis	66,165
2002	Jan. 12	Tampa Bay ($17,000)	San Francisco ($17,000)	31-6	Tampa	65,599
	Jan. 11	Philadelphia ($17,000)	Atlanta ($17,000)	20-6	Philadelphia	66,452
2001	Jan. 20	St. Louis ($17,000)	Green Bay ($17,000)	45-17	St. Louis	66,338
	Jan. 19	Philadelphia ($17,000)	Chicago ($17,000)	33-19	Chicago	66,944
2000	Jan. 7	N.Y. Giants ($16,000)	Philadelphia ($16,000)	20-10	East Rutherford	78,765
	Jan. 6	Minnesota ($16,000)	New Orleans ($16,000)	34-16	Minneapolis	63,881
1999	Jan. 16	St. Louis ($16,000)	Minnesota ($16,000)	49-37	St. Louis	66,194
	Jan. 15	Tampa Bay ($16,000)	Washington ($16,000)	14-13	Tampa	65,835
1998	Jan. 10	Minnesota ($15,000)	Arizona ($15,000)	41-21	Minneapolis	63,760
	Jan. 9	Atlanta ($15,000)	San Francisco ($15,000)	20-18	Atlanta	70,262
1997	Jan. 4	Green Bay ($15,000)	Tampa Bay ($15,000)	21-7	Green Bay	60,327
	Jan. 3	San Francisco ($15,000)	Minnesota ($15,000)	38-22	San Francisco	65,018
1996	Jan. 5	Carolina ($14,000)	Dallas ($14,000)	26-17	Charlotte	72,808
	Jan. 4	Green Bay ($14,000)	San Francisco ($14,000)	35-14	Green Bay	60,787
1995	Jan. 7	Dallas ($13,000)	Philadelphia ($13,000)	30-11	Dallas	64,371
	Jan. 6	Green Bay ($13,000)	San Francisco ($13,000)	27-17	San Francisco	69,311
1994	Jan. 8	Dallas ($12,000)	Green Bay ($12,000)	35-9	Dallas	64,745
	Jan. 7	San Francisco ($12,000)	Chicago ($12,000)	44-15	San Francisco	64,644
1993	Jan. 16	Dallas ($12,000)	Green Bay ($12,000)	27-17	Dallas	64,790
	Jan. 15	San Francisco ($12,000)	N.Y. Giants ($12,000)	44-3	San Francisco	67,143
1992	Jan. 10	Dallas ($10,000)	Philadelphia ($10,000)	34-10	Dallas	63,721
	Jan. 9	San Francisco ($10,000)	Washington ($10,000)	20-13	San Francisco	64,991
1991	Jan. 5	Detroit ($10,000)	Dallas ($10,000)	38-6	Detroit	78,290
	Jan. 4	Washington ($10,000)	Atlanta ($10,000)	24-7	Washington	55,181
1990	Jan. 13	N.Y. Giants ($10,000)	Chicago ($10,000)	31-3	East Rutherford	77,025
	Jan. 12	San Francisco ($10,000)	Washington ($10,000)	28-10	San Francisco	65,292
1989	Jan. 7	L.A. Rams ($10,000)	N.Y. Giants ($10,000)	19-13*	East Rutherford	76,526
	Jan. 6	San Francisco ($10,000)	Minnesota ($10,000)	41-13	San Francisco	64,918
1988	Jan. 1	San Francisco ($10,000)	Minnesota ($10,000)	34-9	San Francisco	61,848
	Dec. 31	Chicago ($10,000)	Philadelphia ($10,000)	20-12	Chicago	65,534
1987	Jan. 10	Washington ($10,000)	Chicago ($10,000)	21-17	Chicago	65,268
	Jan. 9	Minnesota ($10,000)	San Francisco ($10,000)	36-24	San Francisco	63,008
1986	Jan. 4	N.Y. Giants ($10,000)	San Francisco ($10,000)	49-3	East Rutherford	75,691
	Jan. 3	Washington ($10,000)	Chicago ($10,000)	27-13	Chicago	65,524
1985	Jan. 5	Chicago ($10,000)	N.Y. Giants ($10,000)	21-0	Chicago	65,670
	Jan. 4	L.A. Rams ($10,000)	Dallas ($10,000)	20-0	Anaheim	66,581
1984	Dec. 30	Chicago ($10,000)	Washington ($10,000)	23-19	Washington	55,431
	Dec. 29	San Francisco ($10,000)	N.Y. Giants ($10,000)	21-10	San Francisco	60,303
1983	Jan. 1	Washington ($10,000)	L.A. Rams ($10,000)	51-7	Washington	54,440
	Dec. 31	San Francisco ($10,000)	Detroit ($10,000)	24-23	San Francisco	59,979

Season	Date	Winner (Share)	Loser (Share)	Score	Site	Attendance
1982	Jan. 16	Dallas ($10,000)	Green Bay ($10,000)	37-26	Dallas	63,972
	Jan. 15	Washington ($10,000)	Minnesota ($10,000)	21-7	Washington	54,593
1981	Jan. 3	San Francisco ($5,000)	N.Y. Giants ($5,000)	38-24	San Francisco	58,360
	Jan. 2	Dallas ($5,000)	Tampa Bay ($5,000)	38-0	Dallas	64,848
1980	Jan. 4	Dallas ($5,000)	Atlanta ($5,000)	30-27	Atlanta	59,793
	Jan. 3	Philadelphia ($5,000)	Minnesota ($5,000)	31-16	Philadelphia	70,178
1979	Dec. 30	Los Angeles ($5,000)	Dallas ($5,000)	21-19	Dallas	64,792
	Dec. 29	Tampa Bay ($5,000)	Philadelphia ($5,000)	24-17	Tampa	71,402
1978	Dec. 31	Los Angeles ($5,000)	Minnesota ($5,000)	34-10	Los Angeles	70,436
	Dec. 30	Dallas ($5,000)	Atlanta ($5,000)	27-20	Dallas	63,406
1977	Dec. 26	Dallas ($5,000)	Chicago ($5,000)	37-7	Dallas	63,260
	Dec. 26	Minnesota ($5,000)	Los Angeles ($5,000)	14-7	Los Angeles	70,203
1976	Dec. 19	Los Angeles [$]	Dallas [$]	14-12	Dallas	63,283
	Dec. 18	Minnesota [$]	Washington [$]	35-20	Minneapolis	47,466
1975	Dec. 28	Dallas [$]	Minnesota [$]	17-14	Minneapolis	48,050
	Dec. 27	Los Angeles [$]	St. Louis [$]	35-23	Los Angeles	73,459
1974	Dec. 22	Los Angeles [$]	Washington [$]	19-10	Los Angeles	77,925
	Dec. 21	Minnesota [$]	St. Louis [$]	30-14	Minneapolis	48,150
1973	Dec. 23	Dallas [$]	Los Angeles [$]	27-16	Dallas	63,272
	Dec. 22	Minnesota [$]	Washington [$]	27-20	Minneapolis	48,040
1972	Dec. 24	Washington [$]	Green Bay [$]	16-3	Washington	52,321
	Dec. 23	Dallas [$]	San Francisco [$]	30-28	San Francisco	59,746
1971	Dec. 26	San Francisco [$]	Washington [$]	24-20	San Francisco	45,327
	Dec. 25	Dallas [$]	Minnesota [$]	20-12	Minneapolis	47,307
1970	Dec. 27	San Francisco [$]	Minnesota [$]	17-14	Minneapolis	45,103
	Dec. 26	Dallas [$]	Detroit [$]	5-0	Dallas	69,613
1969	Dec. 28	Cleveland [$]	Dallas [$]	38-14	Dallas	69,321
	Dec. 27	Minnesota [$]	Los Angeles [$]	23-20	Minneapolis	47,900
1968	Dec. 22	Baltimore [$]	Minnesota [$]	24-14	Baltimore	60,238
	Dec. 21	Cleveland [$]	Dallas [$]	31-20	Cleveland	81,497
1967	Dec. 24	Dallas [$]	Cleveland [$]	52-14	Dallas	70,786
	Dec. 23	Green Bay [$]	Los Angeles [$]	28-7	Milwaukee	49,861
1965	Dec. 26	Green Bay [$]	Baltimore [$]	13-10*	Green Bay	50,484
1958	Dec. 21	N.Y. Giants (#)	Cleveland (#)	10-0	New York	61,274
1957	Dec. 22	Detroit (#)	San Francisco (#)	31-27	San Francisco	60,118
1952	Dec. 21	Detroit (#)	Los Angeles (#)	31-21	Detroit	47,645
1950	Dec. 17	Los Angeles (#)	Chicago Bears (#)	24-14	Los Angeles	83,501
	Dec. 17	Cleveland (#)	N.Y. Giants (#)	8-3	Cleveland	33,054
1947	Dec. 21	Philadelphia (#)	Pittsburgh (#)	21-0	Pittsburgh	35,729
1943	Dec. 19	Washington (¢)	N.Y. Giants (¢)	28-0	New York	42,800
1941	Dec. 14	Chicago Bears (¢)	Green Bay (¢)	33-14	Chicago	43,425

*Sudden death overtime
$ Players received 1/14 of annual salary for playoff appearances.
# Players received 1/12 of annual salary for playoff appearances.
¢ Players received 1/10 of annual salary for playoff appearances.

2006 NFC DIVISIONAL PLAYOFF GAMES

Soldier Field, Chicago, Illinois
January 14, 2007, Attendance: 62,184

CHICAGO 27, SEATTLE 24 (OT)—Robbie Gould kicked a 49-yard field goal 4:58 into overtime as the Bears advanced to the NFC Championship Game for the first time since 1988. The Seahawks tied the score 7-7 early in the second quarter, but on the next play Rex Grossman connected with Bernard Berrian deep down the middle for 68-yard touchdown pass and a 14-7 lead. Shaun Alexander's 4-yard touchdown run, on fourth-and-1, was set up Chuck Darby's recovery of a Grossman fumble forced by Julian Peterson and tied the score 14-14. The Bears responded with their own touchdown on fourth-and-1, a 7-yard run by Thomas Jones with 48 seconds left in the half for a 21-14 halftime lead. The Seahawks scored on their first two possessions of the second half to take a 24-21 lead, and Pete Hunter intercepted Grossman near the goal line to thwart a rally with 13:31 to play. Later in the quarter, Devin Hester's 66-yard punt return for a touchdown was nullified by a penalty, but the Bears did drive 48 yards and Gould made a 41-yard field goal with 4:24 to play to tie the game. In overtime, the Seahawks were forced to punt, and Ryan Plackemeier's kick went 18 yards and out of bounds at the Bears' 34. Grossman's 30-yard pass to Rashied Davis on third-and-10 set up Gould's game-winning 49-yard kick. Grossman was 21 of 38 for 282 yards and 1 touchdown, with 1 interception. Berrian had 5 receptions for 105 yards. Matt Hasselbeck was 18 of 33 for 195 yards and 1 touchdown, with 1 interception.

Seattle	0	14	10	0	0	—29
Chicago	7	14	0	3	3	—21

Chi— T. Jones 9 run (Gould kick)
Sea— Burleson 16 pass from Hasselbeck (J. Brown kick)
Chi— Berrian 68 pass from Grossman (Gould kick)
Sea— Alexander 4 run (J. Brown kick)
Chi— T. Jones 7 run (Gould kick)
Sea— FG J. Brown 40
Sea— Alexander 13 run (J. Brown kick)
Chi— FG Gould 41
Chi— FG Gould 49

Louisiana Superdome, New Orleans, Louisiana
January 13, 2007, Attendance: 70,001

NEW ORLEANS 27, PHILADELPHIA 24—Deuce McAllister rushed for 143 yards and scored twice as the Saints won thier first playoff game since 2000. Brees was 20 of 32 for 243 yards and 1 touchdown. The Eagles used two big plays, a 75-yard touchdown pass from Jeff Garcia to Donte' Stallworth, and a 62-yard touchdown run by Brian Westbrook three plays into the second half, to take a 21-13 lead. The Saints came right back, keyed by Billy Miller's 29-yard catch, and capped by McAllister's 5-yard touchdown run, to pull within 21-20. The Saints' defense then forced a punt, and the offense drove 84 yards, highlighted by a 23-yard run by McAllister, and capped by Drew Brees' 11-yard touchdown pass to McAllister, for a 27-21 lead with 1:05 left in the third quarter. The Eagles drove to the Saints' 4, but on third-and-1 Garcia's short pass to Thomas Tapeh resulted in a 2-yard loss, forcing the Eagles to settle for David Akers' 24-yard field goal to pull within 27-24 with 11:08 remaining. On third-and-1 with 1:37 to play, McAllister gained 5 yards and the Saints ran out the clock. McAllister carried 21 times for 143 yards. Garcia was 15 of 30 for 240 yards and 1 touchdown. Westbrook carried 13 times for 116 yards, and Stallworth had 3 receptions for 100 yards.

Philadelphia	0	14	7	3	—	24
New Orleans	3	10	14	0	—	27

NO— FG Carney 33
NO— FG Carney 23
Phil— Stallworth 75 pass from Garcia (Akers kick)
NO— Bush 4 run (Carney kick)
Phil— Westbrook 1 run (Akers kick)
Phil— Westbrook 62 run (Akers kick)
NO— McAllister 5 run (Carney kick)
NO— McAllister 11 pass from Brees (Carney kick)
Phil— FG Akers 24

AFC WILD CARD PLAYOFF GAMES RESULTS

Season	Date	Winner (Share)	Loser (Share)	Score	Site	Attendance
2006	Jan. 7	New England ($19,000)	N.Y. Jets ($17,000)	37-16	Foxborough	68,756
	Jan. 6	Indianapolis ($19,000)	Kansas City ($17,000)	23-8	Indianapolis	57,215
2005	Jan. 8	Pittsburgh ($17,000)	Cincinnati ($19,000)	31-17	Cincinnati	65,870
	Jan. 7	New England ($19,000)	Jacksonville ($17,000)	28-3	Foxborough	68,756
2004	Jan. 9	Indianapolis ($18,000)	Denver ($15,000)	49-24	Indianapolis	56,609
	Jan. 8	N.Y. Jets ($15,000)	San Diego ($18,000)	20-17*	San Diego	67,536
2003	Jan. 4	Indianapolis ($18,000)	Denver ($15,000)	41-10	Indianapolis	56,586
	Jan. 3	Tennessee ($15,000)	Baltimore ($18,000)	20-17	Baltimore	69,452
2002	Jan. 5	Pittsburgh ($17,000)	Cleveland ($12,500)	36-33	Pittsburgh	62,595
	Jan. 4	N.Y. Jets ($17,000)	Indianapolis ($12,500)	41-0	East Rutherford	78,524
2001	Jan. 13	Baltimore ($12,500)	Miami ($12,500)	20-3	Miami	72,251
	Jan. 12	Oakland ($17,000)	N.Y. Jets ($12,500)	38-24	Oakland	61,503
2000	Dec. 31	Baltimore (12,500)	Denver ($12,500)	21-3	Baltimore	69,638
	Dec. 30	Miami ($16,000)	Indianapolis ($12,500)	23-17*	Miami	73,193
1999	Jan. 9	Miami ($10,000)	Seattle ($16,000)	20-17	Seattle	66,170
	Jan. 8	Tennessee ($10,000)	Buffalo ($10,000)	22-16	Nashville	66,672
1998	Jan. 3	Jacksonville ($15,000)	New England ($10,000)	25-10	Jacksonville	71,139
	Jan. 2	Miami ($10,000)	Buffalo ($10,000)	24-17	Miami	72,698
1997	Dec. 28	New England ($15,000)	Miami ($10,000)	17-3	Foxborough	60,041
	Dec. 27	Denver ($10,000)	Jacksonville ($10,000)	42-17	Denver	74,481
1996	Dec. 29	Pittsburgh ($14,000)	Indianapolis ($10,000)	42-14	Pittsburgh	58,078
	Dec. 28	Jacksonville ($10,000)	Buffalo ($10,000)	30-27	Buffalo	70,213
1995	Dec. 31	Indianapolis ($7,500)	San Diego ($7,500)	35-20	San Diego	61,182
	Dec. 30	Buffalo ($13,000)	Miami ($7,500)	37-22	Buffalo	73,103
1994	Jan. 1	Cleveland ($7,500)	New England ($7,500)	20-13	Cleveland	77,452
	Dec. 31	Miami ($12,000)	Kansas City ($7,500)	27-17	Miami	67,487
1993	Jan. 9	L.A. Raiders ($7,500)	Denver ($7,500)	42-24	Los Angeles	65,314
	Jan. 8	Kansas City ($12,000)	Pittsburgh ($7,500)	27-24*	Kansas City	74,515
1992	Jan. 3	Buffalo ($6,000)	Houston ($6,000)	41-38*	Buffalo	75,141
	Jan. 2	San Diego ($10,000)	Kansas City ($6,000)	17-0	San Diego	58,278
1991	Dec. 29	Houston ($10,000)	N.Y. Jets ($6,000)	17-10	Houston	61,485
	Dec. 28	Kansas City ($6,000)	L.A. Raiders ($6,000)	10-6	Kansas City	75,827
1990	Jan. 6	Cincinnati ($10,000)	Houston ($6,000)	41-14	Cincinnati	60,012
	Jan. 5	Miami ($6,000)	Kansas City ($6,000)	17-16	Miami	67,276
1989	Dec. 31	Pittsburgh ($6,000)	Houston ($6,000)	26-23*	Houston	59,406
1988	Dec. 26	Houston ($6,000)	Cleveland ($6,000)	24-23	Cleveland	75,896
1987	Jan. 3	Houston ($6,000)	Seattle ($6,000)	23-20*	Houston	50,519
1986	Dec. 28	N.Y. Jets ($6,000)	Kansas City ($6,000)	35-15	East Rutherford	75,210
1985	Dec. 28	New England ($6,000)	N.Y. Jets ($6,000)	26-14	East Rutherford	75,945
1984	Dec. 22	Seattle ($6,000)	L.A. Raiders ($6,000)	13-7	Seattle	62,049
1983	Dec. 24	Seattle ($6,000)	Denver ($6,000)	31-7	Seattle	64,275
1982	Jan. 9	N.Y. Jets ($6,000)	Cincinnati ($6,000)	44-17	Cincinnati	57,560
	Jan. 9	San Diego ($6,000)	Pittsburgh ($6,000)	31-28	Pittsburgh	53,546
	Jan. 8	L.A. Raiders ($6,000)	Cleveland ($6,000)	27-10	Los Angeles	56,555
	Jan. 8	Miami ($6,000)	New England ($6,000)	28-13	Miami	68,842
1981	Dec. 27	Buffalo ($3,000)	N.Y. Jets ($3,000)	31-27	New York	57,050
1980	Dec. 28	Oakland ($3,000)	Houston ($3,000)	27-7	Oakland	53,333
1979	Dec. 23	Houston ($3,000)	Denver ($3,000)	13-7	Houston	48,776
1978	Dec. 24	Houston ($3,000)	Miami ($3,000)	17-9	Miami	72,445

*Sudden death overtime

2006 AFC WILD CARD PLAYOFF GAMES

Gillette Stadium, Foxborough, Massachusetts
January 7, 2007, Attendance: 68,756

NEW ENGLAND 37, N.Y. JETS 16—Tom Brady passed for 2 touchdowns as the Patriots held off the Jets' squad led by first-year coach, and former Patriots' defensive coordinator, Eric Mangini. Chad Pennington's 77-yard touchdown pass to Jerricho Cotchery gave the Jets a 10-7 lead early in the second quarter. The Patriots responded by scoring on their next five possessions. Brady's 1-yard touchdown pass to Daniel Graham with 11 seconds left in the half capped a 15-play, 80-yard drive and gave the Patriots a 17-10 halftime lead. The Jets trailed just 20-13 late in the third quarter when Pennington threw a backward pass that was knocked down by Rosevelt Colvin, resulting in a fumble. Vince Wilfork picked up the loose ball and returned it 31 yards, setting up Stephen Gostkowksi's 28-yard field goal. The Jets responded with Mike Nugent's third field goal and trailed just 23-16 with 11:39 remaining. Brady answered with a 13-play, 63-yard drive, capped by Brady's 7-yard touchdown pass to Kevin Faulk on third-and-goal with 5:16 remaining. Two plays later, Asante Samuel intercepted Pennington's pass and returned it 36 yards for the final touchdown. Brady was 22 of 34 for 212 yards and 2 touchdowns. Jabar Gaffney had 8 catches for 104 yards. Pennington was 23 of 40 for 300 yards and 1 touchdown, with 1 interception. Cotchery had 4 receptions for 100 yards.

N.Y. Jets	3	7	3	3 —	16
New England	7	10	6	14 —	37

NE — Dillon 11 run (Gostkowski kick)
NYJ— FG Nugent 28
NYJ— Cotchery 77 pass from Pennington (Nugent kick)
NE — FG Gostkowski 20
NE — Graham 1 pass from Brady (Gostkowski kick)
NYJ— FG Nugent 21
NE — FG Gostkowski 40
NE — FG Gostkowski 28
NYJ— FG Nugent 37

NE — Faulk 7 pass from Brady(Gostkowski kick)
NE — Samuel 36 interception return (Gostkowski kick)

RCA Dome, Indianapolis, Indiana
January 6, 2007, Attendance: 57,215

INDIANAPOLIS 23, KANSAS CITY 8—Joseph Addai rushed for 122 yards, and the Colts' defense did not allow a first down until the third quarter en route to a wild-card victory. For the game, the Colts outgained the Chiefs 435-126 in total yards, had a 28-7 advantage in first downs, and a 39:23-20:37 edge in time of possession. At halftime, the Chiefs had been outgained 255-16 in total yards, but trailed just 9-0. A 12-play, 89-yard drive in the third quarter, capped by Addai's 6-yard run, increased the lead to 16-0. With 3:38 left in the third quarter, Trent Green's 6-yard pass to Tony Gonzalez resulted in the Chiefs' initial first down. Six plays later, the pair hooked up on a similar pass to score, and Green added a 2-point conversion pass to Kris Wilson to cut the deficit to 16-8. But Peyton Manning engineered a 9-play, 71-yard drive on the next possession, capped by Reggie Wayne's 5-yard touchdown catch, for a 23-8 lead lead with 10:16 to play. The Chiefs had one good scoring opportunity, but Robert Mathis and Bo Schobel sacked Green and forced him to fumble. Josh Thomas recovered at the Colts' 30 with 3:55 to play. Manning was 30 of 38 for 268 yards and 1 touchdown, with 3 interceptions. Addai carried 25 times for 122 yards. Dallas Clark had 9 receptions for 103 yards. Green was 14 of 24 for 107 yards and 1 touchdown, with 2 interceptions.

Kansas City	0	0	8	0 —	8
Indianapolis	6	3	7	7 —	23

Ind— FG Vinatieri 48
Ind— FG Vinatieri 19
Ind— FG Vinatieri 50
Ind— Addai 6 run (Vinatieri kick)
KC — Gonzalez 6 pass from T. Green
　　　(K. Wilson pass from T. Green)
Ind— Wayne 5 pass from Manning (Vinatieri kick)

NFC WILD CARD PLAYOFF GAMES RESULTS

Season	Date	Winner (Share)	Loser (Share)	Score	Site	Attendance
2006	Jan. 7	Philadelphia ($19,000)	N.Y. Giants ($17,000)	23-20	Philadelphia	69,094
	Jan. 6	Seattle ($19,000)	Dallas ($17,000)	21-20	Seattle	68,058
2005	Jan. 8	Carolina ($17,000)	N.Y. Giants ($19,000)	23-0	East Rutherford	79,378
	Jan. 7	Washington ($17,000)	Tampa Bay ($19,000)	17-10	Tampa	65,514
2004	Jan. 9	Minnesota ($15,000)	Green Bay ($18,000)	31-17	Green Bay	71,075
	Jan. 8	St. Louis ($15,000)	Seattle ($18,000)	27-20	Seattle	65,397
2003	Jan. 4	Green Bay ($18,000)	Seattle ($15,000)	33-27*	Green Bay	71,457
	Jan. 3	Carolina ($18,000)	Dallas ($15,000)	29-10	Charlotte	73,014
2002	Jan. 5	San Francisco ($17,000)	N.Y. Giants ($12,500)	39-38	San Francisco	66,318
	Jan. 4	Atlanta ($12,500)	Green Bay ($17,000)	27-7	Green Bay	65,358
2001	Jan. 13	Green Bay ($12,500)	San Francisco ($12,500)	25-15	Green Bay	59,825
	Jan. 12	Philadelphia ($17,000)	Tampa Bay ($12,500)	31-9	Philadelphia	65,847
2000	Dec. 31	Philadelphia ($12,500)	Tampa Bay ($12,500)	21-3	Philadelphia	65,813
	Dec. 30	New Orleans ($16,000)	St. Louis ($12,500)	31-28	New Orleans	64,900
1999	Jan. 9	Minnesota ($10,000)	Dallas ($10,000)	27-10	Minneapolis	64,056
	Jan. 8	Washington ($16,000)	Detroit ($10,000)	27-13	Washington	79,411
1998	Jan. 3	San Francisco ($10,000)	Green Bay ($10,000)	30-27	San Francisco	66,506
	Jan. 2	Arizona ($10,000)	Dallas ($15,000)	20-7	Dallas	62,969
1997	Dec. 28	Tampa Bay ($10,000)	Detroit ($10,000)	20-10	Tampa	73,361
	Dec. 27	Minnesota ($10,000)	N.Y. Giants ($15,000)	23-22	East Rutherford	77,497
1996	Dec. 29	San Francisco ($10,000)	Philadelphia ($10,000)	14-0	San Francisco	56,460
	Dec. 28	Dallas ($14,000)	Minnesota ($10,000)	40-15	Dallas	64,682
1995	Dec. 31	Green Bay ($13,000)	Atlanta ($7,500)	37-20	Green Bay	60,453
	Dec. 30	Philadelphia ($7,500)	Detroit ($7,500)	58-37	Philadelphia	66,099
1994	Jan. 1	Chicago ($7,500)	Minnesota ($12,000)	35-18	Minnesota	60,347
	Dec. 31	Green Bay ($7,500)	Detroit ($7,500)	16-12	Green Bay	58,125
1993	Jan. 9	N.Y. Giants ($7,500)	Minnesota ($7,500)	17-10	East Rutherford	75,089
	Jan. 8	Green Bay ($7,500)	Detroit ($12,000)	28-24	Detroit	68,479
1992	Jan. 3	Philadelphia ($6,000)	New Orleans ($6,000)	36-20	New Orleans	68,893
	Jan. 2	Washington ($6,000)	Minnesota ($10,000)	24-7	Minnesota	57,353

Season	Date	Winner (Share)	Loser (Share)	Score	Site	Attendance
1991	Dec. 29	Dallas ($6,000)	Chicago ($6,000)	17-13	Chicago	62,594
	Dec. 28	Atlanta ($6,000)	New Orleans ($10,000)	27-20	New Orleans	68,794
1990	Jan. 6	Chicago ($10,000)	New Orleans ($6,000)	16-6	Chicago	60,767
	Jan. 5	Washington ($6,000)	Philadelphia ($6,000)	20-6	Philadelphia	65,287
1989	Dec. 31	L.A. Rams ($6,000)	Philadelphia ($6,000)	21-7	Philadelphia	65,479
1988	Dec. 26	Minnesota ($6,000)	L.A. Rams ($6,000)	28-17	Minnesota	61,204
1987	Jan. 3	Minnesota ($6,000)	New Orleans ($6,000)	44-10	New Orleans	68,546
1986	Dec. 28	Washington ($6,000)	L.A. Rams ($6,000)	19-7	Washington	54,567
1985	Dec. 29	N.Y. Giants ($6,000)	San Francisco ($6,000)	17-3	East Rutherford	75,131
1984	Dec. 23	N.Y. Giants ($6,000)	L.A. Rams ($6,000)	16-13	Anaheim	67,037
1983	Dec. 26	L.A. Rams ($6,000)	Dallas ($6,000)	24-17	Dallas	62,118
1982	Jan. 9	Dallas ($6,000)	Tampa Bay ($6,000)	30-17	Dallas	65,042
	Jan. 9	Minnesota ($6,000)	Atlanta ($6,000)	30-24	Minnesota	60,560
	Jan. 8	Green Bay ($6,000)	St. Louis ($6,000)	41-16	Green Bay	54,282
	Jan. 8	Washington ($6,000)	Detroit ($6,000)	31-7	Washington	55,045
1981	Dec. 27	N.Y. Giants ($3,000)	Philadelphia ($3,000)	27-21	Philadelphia	71,611
1980	Dec. 28	Dallas ($3,000)	Los Angeles ($3,000)	34-13	Dallas	63,052
1979	Dec. 23	Philadelphia ($3,000)	Chicago ($3,000)	27-17	Philadelphia	69,397
1978	Dec. 24	Atlanta ($3,000)	Philadelphia ($3,000)	14-13	Atlanta	59,403

Sudden death overtime

2006 NFC WILD CARD PLAYOFF GAMES

Lincoln Financial Field, Philadelphia, Pennsylvania
January 7, 2007, Attendance: 69,094

PHILADELPHIA 23, N.Y. GIANTS 20—David Akers kicked a 38-yard field goal as time expired to give the Eagles a hard-fought playoff victory. The Giants scored on their first drive, highlighted by Jared Lorenzen's 2-yard sneak on third-and-1, and capped two plays later by Eli Manning's 17-yard touchdown pass to Plaxico Burress. The Eagles answered in the second quarter with three consecutive scoring drives. The 84- and 80-yard touchdowns drives had a short field-goal drive in the middle, which was set up by Sheldon Brown's interception, and the Eagles led 17-10 at halftime. The Giants, trailing 20-13 with 12:13 to play, converted 3 third-down situations on the ensuing 80-yard drive, capped by Burress' 11-yard touchdown catch with 5:04 remaining to tie the game. The Eagles used runs of 11 and 13 yards by Brian Westbrook to get into position to set up Akers' game-winning 38-yard kick. Jeff Garcia was 17 of 31 for 153 yards and 1 touchdown. Westbrook had 20 carries for 141 yards. Manning was 16 of 27 for 161 yards and 2 touchdowns, with 1 interception. Tiki Barber, playing in his final game, rushed 26 times for 137 yards.

N.Y. Giants	7	3	0	10	—	20
Philadelphia	0	17	3	3	—	23

NYG— Burress 17 pass from E. Manning (Feely kick)
Phil— Westbrook 49 run (Akers kick)
Phil— FG Akers 19
NYG— FG Feely 20
Phil— Stallworth 28 pass from Garcia (Akers kick)
Phil— FG Akers 48
NYG— FG Feely 24
NYG— Burress 11 pass from E. Manning (Feely kick)
Phil— FG Akers 38

Qwest Field, Seattle, Washington
January 6, 2007, Attendance: 68,058

SEATTLE 21, DALLAS 20—Jordan Babineaux tackled Tony Romo at the 2-yard line in the final minute after Romo mishandled the snap for the potential game-winning field goal, giving the Seahawks an improbable victory. The Seahawks trailed 10-6 at halftime, but drove 62 yards in 12 plays to begin the second half. Shaun Alexander's 4-yard run on fourth-and-1 was the key play of the drive, and Jerramy Stevens capped it with a 15-yard touchdown catch to give Seattle a 13-10 lead. However, Miles Austin returned the ensuing kickoff 93 yards for a touchdown and the Cowboys regained the lead. Early in the fourth quarter, Terence Newman tipped a pass to Roy Williams and Williams intercepted it, leading to Martin Gramatica's second field goal and a 20-13 lead. The Seahawks drove to the Cowboys' 1, but Alexander lost 7 yards on the first play of the series, and Matt Hasselbeck's fourth-down pass fell incomplete. On the next play, from the 2-yard line, Terry Glenn caught a quick pass from Romo. Glenn was stripped by Kelly Jennings and a mad scramble ensued for the football, which eventually went out of the end zone for a safety with 6:32 to play. On the fourth play after the free kick, Matt Hasselbeck completed a 37-yard touchdown pass to a wide-open Stevens and the Seahawks led 21-20 with 4:24 remaining. Julius Jones' 35-yard run helped get the Cowboys deep into Seahawks' territory. Faced with fourth-and-1 from the 2-yard line with 1:19 to play, the Cowboys lined up for a field-goal attempt. However, Romo, the holder, dropped the snap. Romo picked up the ball and ran left. He had a clear path to the end zone, but Babineaux, who had been coming hard off the right end, never stopped pursuing Romo and tackled him from behind at the 2-yard line with 1:14 to play. The Cowboys forced a punt and had the ball at midfield with two seconds remaining, but Romo's Hail Mary pass fell incomplete in the end zone. Hasselbeck was 18 of 36 for 240 yards and 2 touchdowns, with 2 interceptions. Romo was 17 of 29 for 189 yards and 1 touchdowns. Jones rushed 22 times for 112 yards.

Dallas	3	7	7	3	—	20
Seattle	3	3	7	8	—	21

Sea— FG J. Brown 23
Dall— FG M. Gramatica 50
Sea— FG J. Brown 30
Dall— Crayton 13 pass from Romo (M. Gramatica kick)
Sea— Stevens 15 pass from Hasselbeck (J. Brown kick)
Dall— Austin 93 kickoff return (M. Gramatica kick)
Dall— FG M. Gramatica 29
Sea— Safety, Glenn fumbled out of end zone
Sea— Stevens 37 pass from Hasselbeck (pass failed)

AFC-NFC PRO BOWL RESULTS (1971-2007)
AFC leads NFC, 19-18

Year	Date	Winner (Share)	Loser (Share)	Score	Site	Attendance
2007	Feb. 10	AFC ($40,000)	NFC ($20,000)	31-28	Honolulu	50,410
2006	Feb. 12	NFC ($40,000)	AFC ($20,000)	23-17	Honolulu	50,190
2005	Feb. 13	AFC ($35,000)	NFC ($17,500)	38-27	Honolulu	50,225
2004	Feb. 8	NFC ($35,000)	AFC ($17,500)	55-52	Honolulu	50,127
2003	Feb. 2	AFC ($30,000)	NFC ($15,000)	45-20	Honolulu	50,125
2002	Feb. 9	AFC ($30,000)	NFC ($15,000)	38-30	Honolulu	50,301
2001	Feb. 4	AFC ($30,000)	NFC ($15,000)	38-17	Honolulu	50,128
2000	Feb. 6	NFC ($25,000)	AFC ($12,500)	51-31	Honolulu	50,112
1999	Feb. 7	AFC ($25,000)	NFC ($12,500)	23-10	Honolulu	50,075
1998	Feb. 1	AFC ($25,000)	NFC ($12,500)	29-24	Honolulu	49,995
1997	Feb. 2	AFC ($20,000)	NFC ($10,000)	26-23 (OT)	Honolulu	50,031
1996	Feb. 4	NFC ($20,000)	AFC ($10,000)	20-13	Honolulu	50,034
1995	Feb. 5	AFC ($20,000)	NFC ($10,000)	41-13	Honolulu	50,529
1994	Feb. 6	NFC ($20,000)	AFC ($10,000)	17-3	Honolulu	50,026
1993	Feb. 7	AFC ($10,000)	NFC ($5,000)	23-20 (OT)	Honolulu	50,007
1992	Feb. 2	NFC ($10,000)	AFC ($5,000)	21-15	Honolulu	50,209
1991	Feb. 3	AFC ($10,000)	NFC ($5,000)	23-21	Honolulu	50,345
1990	Feb. 4	NFC ($10,000)	AFC ($5,000)	27-21	Honolulu	50,445
1989	Jan. 29	NFC ($10,000)	AFC ($5,000)	34-3	Honolulu	50,113
1988	Feb. 7	AFC ($10,000)	NFC ($5,000)	15-6	Honolulu	50,113
1987	Feb. 1	AFC ($10,000)	NFC ($5,000)	10-6	Honolulu	50,101
1986	Feb. 2	NFC ($10,000)	AFC ($5,000)	28-24	Honolulu	50,101
1985	Jan. 27	AFC ($10,000)	NFC ($5,000)	22-14	Honolulu	50,385
1984	Jan. 29	NFC ($10,000)	AFC ($5,000)	45-3	Honolulu	50,445
1983	Feb. 6	NFC ($10,000)	AFC ($5,000)	20-19	Honolulu	49,883
1982	Jan. 31	AFC ($5,000)	NFC ($2,500)	16-13	Honolulu	50,402
1981	Feb. 1	NFC ($5,000)	AFC ($2,500)	21-7	Honolulu	50,360
1980	Jan. 27	NFC ($5,000)	AFC ($2,500)	37-27	Honolulu	49,800
1979	Jan. 29	NFC ($5,000)	AFC ($2,500)	13-7	Los Angeles	46,281
1978	Jan. 23	NFC ($5,000)	AFC ($2,500)	14-13	Tampa	51,337
1977	Jan. 17	AFC ($2,000)	NFC ($1,500)	24-14	Seattle	64,752
1976	Jan. 26	NFC ($2,000)	AFC ($1,500)	23-20	New Orleans	30,546
1975	Jan. 20	NFC ($2,000)	AFC ($1,500)	17-10	Miami	26,484
1974	Jan. 20	AFC ($2,000)	NFC ($1,500)	15-13	Kansas City	66,918
1973	Jan. 21	AFC ($2,000)	NFC ($1,500)	33-28	Dallas	37,091
1972	Jan. 23	AFC ($2,000)	NFC ($1,500)	26-13	Los Angeles	53,647
1971	Jan. 24	NFC ($2,000)	AFC ($1,500)	27-6	Los Angeles	48,222

2007 AFC-NFC PRO BOWL

Aloha Stadium, Honolulu, Hawaii
February 10, 2007, Attendance: 50,410

AFC 31, NFC 28—The NFC scored two touchdowns within 66 seconds to tie the score with 1:48 remaining, but Nate Kaeding made a 21-yard field goal with no time left as the AFC held off the NFC. With the score 7-7, Adalius Thomas recovered Marc Bulger's fumble and returned it 70 yards for a touchdown to give the AFC a 14-7 lead with 7:42 remaining in the first half. The NFC responded with Frank Gore's 1-yard touchdown run to tie the game. To open the second half, LaDainian Tomlinson ran six times on a nine-play drive, capped by Tomlinson's 3-yard scoring run, to give the AFC a 21-14 lead. Antonio Pierce intercepted a pass at the NFC 6-yard-line to stop a drive late in the third quarter, but on the AFC's next possession Carson Palmer completed a 42-yard touchdown pass to teammate Chad Johnson to give the AFC a 28-14 lead. The NFC drove into the AFC red zone on its next two possessions, but Derrick Burgess' fourth-down sack ended one drive and Romo was stopped for no gain on fourth-and-goal from the 1-yard-line on the second possession with 5:00 left. However, Vince Young fumbled three plays later and Sean Taylor recovered at the AFC 11-yard-line. Four plays later, on fourth-and-3, Steven Jackson scored on a 4-yard run with 2:54 left. A bad snap on the extra-point attempt, however, forced holder Romo to throw an incomplete pass, leaving the NFC trailing by eight points. The NFC then attempted an onside kick and Ronde Barber recovered. Four plays later, Romo fired a 47-yard touchdown pass to Anquan Boldin, and a 2-point conversion pass to Steve Smith, to tie the game with 1:48 to play. After Palmer converted a fourth-and-1 with a sneak, he attempted a deep pass for Johnson. Defensive pass interference was called when Adrian Wilson, mistakenly thinking the ball had been tipped, hit Johnson before the ball arrived, and the AFC got the ball at the NFC 2-yard-line. Kaeding made the 21-yard field goal as time expired. Palmer, who was selected the game's outstanding player, was 8 of 17 for 190 yards and 2 touchdowns to lead the AFC. Reggie Wayne had 6 receptions for 137 yards. Ed Reed had 2 interceptions. Romo was 11 of 19 for 156 yards and 1 touchdown, with 1 interception, and Bulger was 8 of 15 for 133 yards.

NFC (28)	Offense	AFC (31)
Donald Driver (Green Bay)	WR	Andre Johnson (Houston)
Walter Jones (Seattle)	LT	Tarik Glenn (Indianapolis)
Larry Allen (San Francisco)	LG	Alan Faneca (Pittsburgh)
Matt Birk (Minnesota)	C	Jeff Saturday (Indianapolis)
Steve Hutchinson (Minnesota)	RG	Will Shields (Kansas City)
Flozell Adams (Dallas)	RT	Marcus McNeill (San Diego)
Alge Crumpler (Atlanta)	TE	Tony Gonzalez (Kansas City)
Steve Smith (Carolina)	WR	Chad Johnson (Cincinnati)
Drew Brees (New Orleans)	QB	Peyton Manning (Indianapolis)

Mack Strong (Seattle)	FB	Lorenzo Neal (San Diego)	
Frank Gore (San Francisco)	RB	LaDainian Tomlinson (San Diego)	

Defense

Julius Peppers (Carolina)	DE	Jason Taylor (Miami)	
Kris Jenkins (Carolina)	DT	Casey Hampton (Pittsburgh)	
Kevin Williams (Minnesota)	DT	Jamal Williams (San Diego)	
Will Smith (New Orleans)	DE	Aaron Schobel (Buffalo)	
Julian Peterson (Seattle)	OLB	Shawne Merriman (San Diego)	
Lofa Tatupu (Seattle)	ILB	Zach Thomas (Miami)	
DeMarcus Ware (Dallas)	OLB	Adalius Thomas (Baltimore)	
Ronde Barber (Tampa Bay)	CB	Champ Baileyr (Denver)	
DeAngelo Hall (Atlanta)	CB	Rashean Mathis (Jacksonville)	
Adrian Wilson (Arizona)	SS	Troy Polamalu (Pittsburgh)	
Roy Williams (Dallas)	FS	Ed Reed (Baltimore)	

SUBSTITUTIONS

NFC—Specialists: K—Robbie Gould (Chicago). P—Mat McBriar (Dallas). KR—Devin Hester (Chicago). LS—Dave Moore (Tampa Bay). ST—Brendon Ayanbadejo (Chicago). Offense: QB—Marc Bulger (St. Louis), Tony Romo (Dallas). RB—Tiki Barber (N.Y. Giants), Steven Jackson (St. Louis). WR—Anquan Boldin (Arizona), Roy Williams (Detroit). TE—Jason Witten (Dallas). G—Ruben Brown (Chicago). C—Andre Gurode (Dallas). Defense: DL—Pat Williams (Minnesota). DE—Aaron Kampman (Green Bay). LB—Derrick Brooks (Tampa Bay), Antonio Pierce (Washington). CB—Walt Harris (San Francisco). S—Sean Taylor (Washington). Did Not Play: T—Chris Samuels (Washington). Not Active: WR—Torry Holt (St. Louis). C—Olin Kreutz (Chicago). G—Shawn Andrews (Philadelphia). T—Jammal Brown (New Orleans). TE—Jeremy Shockey (N.Y. Giants). DL—Tommie Harris (Chicago). LB—Lance Briggs (Chicago), Brian Urlacher (Chicago). CB—Lito Sheppard (Philadelphia).

AFC—Specialists: K—Nate Kaeding (San Diego). P—Brian Moorman (Buffalo). KR—Justin Miller (N.Y. Jets). LS—David Binn (San Diego). ST—Kassim Osgood (San Diego). Offense: QB—Carson Palmer (Cincinnati), Vince Young (Tennessee). RB—Larry Johnson (Kansas City), Willie Parker (Pittsburgh). WR—Reggie Wayne (Indianapolis). TE—Antonio Gates (San Diego). G—Brian Waters (Kansas City). C—Nick Hardwick (San Diego). Defense: DL—John Henderson (Jacksonville). DE—Derrick Burgess (Oakland). LB—Bart Scott (Baltimore), Terrell Suggs (Baltimore). CB—Chris McAlister (Baltimore). S—John Lynch

(Denver). Did Not Play: WR—Marvin Harrison (Indianapolis). Not Active: QB—Philip Rivers (San Diego). T—Willie Anderson (Cincinnati), Jonathan Ogden (Baltimore). DL—Richard Seymour (New England). LB—Al Wilson (Denver).

HEAD COACHES

AFC—Bill Belichick (New England)
NFC—Sean Payton (New Orleans)

OFFICIALS

Referee—Larry Nemmers. Umpire—Chad Brown. Side Judge—Doug Toole. Head Linesman—Ron Phares. Back Judge—Richard Reels. Field Judge—Tom Sifferman. Line Judge—Tom Barnes.

NFC	0	14	0	14	— 28
AFC	0	14	7	10	— 31

NFC— T. Barber 1 run (Gould kick)
AFC— Wayne 72 pass from Palmer (Kaeding kick)
AFC— A. Thomas 70 fumble return (Kaeding kick)
NFC— Gore 1 run (Gould kick)
AFC— Tomlinson 3 run (Kaeding kick)
AFC— C. Johnson 42 pass from Palmer (Kaeding kick)
NFC— S. Jackson 4 run (pass failed)
NFC— Boldin 47 pass from Romo (S. Smith pass from Romo)
AFC— FG Kaeding 21

TEAM STATISTICS

	NFC	AFC
Total First Downs	20	21
Rushing	8	9
Passing	10	11
Penalty	2	1
Total Net Yardage	362	445
Total Offensive Plays	74	70
Avg. Gain Per Offensive Play	4.9	6.4
Rushes	27	30
Yards Gained Rushing (Net)	71	120
Avg. Yards per Rush	2.6	4.0
Passes Attempted	42	39
Passes Completed	21	17
Had Intercepted	2	1
Tackled Attempting to Pass	5	1
Yards Lost Attempting to Pass	21	3
Yards Gained Passing (Net)	291	325
Punts	4	1
Avg. Distance	51.0	64.0
Punt Returns	1	4
Punt Return Yardage	63	37
Kickoff Returns	5	4
Kickoff Return Yardage	102	113
Interception Return Yardage	3	46
Total Return Yardage	66	83
Fumbles	3	4
Fumbles Lost	1	1
Own Fumbles Recovered	2	3
Opponent Fumbles Recovered	1	1
Penalties	2	5
Yards Penalized	44	37
Field Goals	3	1
Field Goals Attempted	5	4
Third-Down Efficiency	9/18	5/15
Fourth-Down Efficiency	1/4	1/5
Time of Possession	31:25	28:35

INDIVIDUAL STATISTICS

RUSHING: NFC: Jackson 7-26-1, Gore 6-26-1, Romo 2-7-0, Smith 1-5-0, T. Barber 7-4-1, Strong 2-3-0, Bulger 1-0-0, Driver 1-0-0. AFC: Tomlinson 10-51-1, L. Johnson 6-33-0, Parker 8-19-0, Young 3-15-0, Wayne 1-2-0, Palmer 1-1-0, Moorman 1-(1)-0.

PASSING: NFC: Romo 19-11-156-1-1, Bulger 15-8-133-0-0, Brees 7-2-23-0-0, T. Barber 1-0-0-0-(1). AFC: Palmer 17-8-190-2-0, Manning 12-5-67-0-0, Young 10-4-71-0-1.

RECEIVING: NFC: Boldin 5-86-1, Smith 4-62-0, R. Williams 3-58-0, Driver 3-38-0, Crumpler 2-50-0, Jackson 2-10-0, T. Barber 1-8-0, Witten 1-0-0. AFC: Wayne 6-137-1, A. Johnson 3-73-0, C. Johnson 3-70-1, Gonzalez 3-35-0, Gates 1-9-0, L. Johnson 1-4-0

KICKOFF RETURNS: NFC: Hester 4-97-0, Hutchinson 1-5-0. AFC: Miller 4-113-0.

PUNT RETURNS: NFC: Hester 1-63-0. AFC: Miller 4-37-0.

PUNTING: NFC: McBriar 4-204-51.0. AFC: Moorman 1-64-64.0.

INTERCEPTIONS: NFC: Pierce 1-3-0. AFC: Reed 2-46-0

SACKS: NFC: Peppers 1. AFC: Burress 1, Schobel 1, Suggs 1, J. Williams 1, TEAM 1.

2006 AFC-NFC PRO BOWL

Aloha Stadium, Honolulu, Hawaii
February 12, 2006, Attendance: 50,190
NFC 23, AFC 17—Derrick Brooks returned an interception 59 yards for a touchdown, and Neil Rackers added 3 field goals, as the NFC held off the AFC. The series is now tied 18-18. The defenses dominated, as the game featured 7 sacks and 10 turnovers. John Lynch's interception and 40-yard return to the NFC 45-yard line set up Peyton Manning's 16-yard touchdown pass to Chris Chambers. With the ball at midfield and holding a 10-3 lead and 48 seconds left in the half, Manning was intercepted for the third time. Roy Williams picked off the pass at the NFC 12, ran 11 yards, handed off to DeAngelo Hall, who raced 57 yards to the AFC 20-yard line. Three plays later, Michael Vick completed a 14-yard touchdown pass to Alge Crumpler to tie the game with two seconds left in the half. In the middle of the third quarter, Brooks intercepted Trent Green's short pass intended for Antonio Gates and returned it 59 yards for a touchdown. Champ Bailey recovered Santana Moss' fumble to spark a 10-play, 68-yard drive capped by Green's 1-yard run to tie the game 17-17 with 12:47 to play. Matt Hasselbeck engineered a 13-play, 59-yard drive on the ensuing possession to set up Rackers' 22-yard field goal for a 20-17 lead with 6:29 to play. Jeremiah Trotter recovered Steve McNair's fumbled snap at the AFC 18-yard line with 3:42 to play, and Rackers added a 20-yard field goal with 1:10 remaining. The AFC reached the NFC

49-yard line with 29 seconds left, but McNair threw 3 consecutive incompletions and Michael Strahan ended the game with a sack. Brooks was selected the game's outstanding player.

AFC	7	3	0	7	—	17
NFC	0	10	7	6	—	23

AFC — Chambers 16 pass from Manning (Graham kick)
NFC — FG Rackers 32
AFC — FG Graham 31
NFC — Crumpler 14 pass from Vick (Rackers kick)
NFC — D. Brooks 59 interception return (Rackers kick)
AFC — T. Green 1 run (Graham kick)
NFC — FG Rackers 22
NFC — FG Rackers 20

2005 AFC-NFC PRO BOWL
Aloha Stadium, Honolulu, Hawaii
February 13, 2005, Attendance: 50,225
AFC 38, NFC 27—Peyton Manning passed for 130 yards and 3 touchdowns as the AFC won for the fourth time in five years. The NFC outgained the AFC 492-343, but committed 3 turnovers and allowed an onside kick for a touchdown. David Akers missed a 43-yard field goal in the first quarter, and the AFC responded with touchdowns on its next four possessions. Manning completed 3 touchdown passes in the stretch, and Hines Ward registered the first onside kick returned for a touchdown in Pro Bowl history. Manning's final scoring pass, a 12-yard toss to Antonio Gates, was set up by Takeo Spikes' interception near midfield, to take a 28-7 lead with 5:50 left in the half. Michael Vick began the second half for the NFC, and engineered a 73-yard drive, capped by Torry Holt's 27-yard touchdown catch. Lito Sheppard intercepted Tom Brady's pass four plays later, and Vick culminated a 69-yard drive with a 3-yard run to cut the deficit to 28-24 with 3:53 left in the third quarter. An exchange of field goals made the score 31-27 with 9:04 remaining, but Drew Brees connected on a 33-yard pass to Gates on a flea-flicker, and LaDainian Tomlinson scored on third-and-goal from the NFC's 4 with 5:15 to play. Nate Clements' interception of Vick's pass with 2:00 remaining clinched the victory. Manning was 6 of 10 for 130 yards and 3 touchdowns to earn the game's most valuable player award. Brady was 4 of 9 for 48 yards, with 1 interception, and Brees was 2 of 2 for 58 yards. Donovan McNabb was 1 of 8 for 24 yards, with 1 interception. Daunte Culpepper was 9 of 15 for 124 yards, with 1 interception. Vick was 14 of 24 for 205 yards and 1 touchdown, with 1 interception, and became the first player to pass and run for a touchdown in the same Pro Bowl game.

NFC	0	10	14	3	—	27
AFC	14	14	0	10	—	38

AFC — Harrison 62 pass from Manning (Vinatieri kick)
AFC — Ward 41 pass from Manning (Vinatieri kick)
NFC — Westbrook 12 run (Akers kick)
AFC — Ward 39 kickoff return (Vinatieri kick)
AFC — Gates 12 pass from Manning (Vinatieri kick)
NFC — FG Akers 33
NFC — Holt 27 pass from Vick (Akers kick)
NFC — Vick 3 run (Akers kick)
AFC — FG Vinatieri 44
NFC — FG Akers 29
AFC — Tomlinson 4 run (Vinatieri kick)

2004 AFC-NFC PRO BOWL
Aloha Stadium, Honolulu, Hawaii
February 8, 2004, Attendance: 50,127
NFC 55, AFC 52—Marc Bulger passed for a Pro Bowl-record 4 touchdowns as the NFC rallied from a 25-point deficit to win the highest scoring game in Pro Bowl history. The AFC set a record with 626 yards, but committed 6 turnovers which led to 35 points. Steve McNair fired a 90-yard touchdown pass to Chad Johnson on the AFC's first play, and Ed Reed blocked Todd Sauerbrun's punt and returned it 23 yards for a touchdown for a 14-0 lead 3:58 into the game. The AFC led 17-13 in the second quarter when Peyton Manning fired a 50-yard touchdown pass to Marvin Harrison, and his 9-yard scoring pass to Tony Gonzalez on the next possession gave the AFC a 31-13 lead. Jamal Lewis' 22-yard touchdown run gave the AFC a 38-13 lead with 11:08 left in the third quarter. The comeback started when Trent Green fumbled and Leonard Little recovered. Bulger completed a 12-yard touchdown pass to Torry Holt two plays later with 8:08 left in the third quarter. Two plays later, Derrick Mason fumbled and Jerry Azumah returned it 36 yards to the AFC's 7 to set up Bulger's 2-yard touchdown toss to Keenan McCardell. But following an exchange of punts, Green completed a 23-yard touchdown pass to Clinton Portis to give the AFC a 45-27 lead with 13:14 left. The NFC scored 28 points in the next 9:42, set up by Azumah's 60-yard kickoff return, Champ Bailey's interception of a pass by Harrison, and interception returns by Dre' Bly, 32 yards for a touchdown, and Corey Chavous, 39 yards to set up Shaun Alexander's 2-yard touchdown run with 3:32 left, for a 55-45 NFC lead. Manning's 10-yard touchdown pass to Hines Ward with 1:54 left pulled the AFC within three points, and Bulger was intercepted by Brock Marion on fourth-and-10 from AFC's 28-yard line with 1:15 left. The AFC drove to the NFC 21, but Kris Jenkins sacked Manning for a 12-yard loss, forcing Vanderjagt, who was 37-for-37 on the season but missed from 52 yards just

before halftime, to attempt a 51-yard field goal as time expired. But the kick sailed wide right and the NFC prevailed. Bulger was 12 of 21 for 152 yards and 4 touchdowns, with 1 interception, and was selected as the player of the game. Holt had 7 receptions for 128 yards. Manning was 22 of 41 for 342 yards and 3 touchdowns, with 2 interceptions. Mason had 6 catches for 113 yards, and Johnson had 5 receptions for 156 yards.

AFC	17	14	7	14	—	52
NFC	10	3	14	28	—	55

AFC — C. Johnson 90 pass from McNair (Vanderjagt kick)
AFC — Reed 23 return of blocked punt (Vanderjagt kick)
NFC — Alexander 12 run (Wilkins kick)
NFC — FG Wilkins 28
AFC — FG Vanderjagt 27
NFC — FG Wilkins 38
AFC — Harrison 50 pass from Manning (Vanderjagt kick)
AFC — Gonzalez 9 pass from Manning (Vanderjagt kick)
AFC — J. Lewis 22 run (Vanderjagt kick)
NFC — Holt 12 pass from Bulger (Wilkins kick)
NFC — McCardell 2 pass from Bulger (Wilkins kick)
AFC — Portis 23 pass from Green (Vanderjagt kick)
NFC — Crumpler 33 pass from Bulger (Wilkins kick)
NFC — Alexander 5 pass from Bulger (pass failed)
NFC — Bly 32 interception return (Green run)
NFC — Alexander 2 run (Wilkins kick)
AFC — Ward 10 pass from Manning (Vanderjagt kick)

2003 AFC-NFC PRO BOWL
Aloha Stadium, Honolulu, Hawaii
February 2, 2003, Attendance: 50,125
AFC 45, NFC 20—Ricky Williams rushed for a game-high 56 yards, scored 2 touchdowns, and forced a fumble on special teams to earn player of the game honors. The AFC, which led by as many as 39 points, won for the third consecutive time. Jason Taylor's interception three plays into the game set up Williams' first touchdown run, and Rich Gannon's 11-yard touchdown pass to Tony Gonzalez capped a 71-yard drive on the AFC's next possession to take a 14-3 lead. Rod Woodson's interception early in the second quarter led to Gannon's 13-yard touchdown pass to Travis Henry, and Williams capped another 71-yard drive with a 1-yard run with 47 seconds left in the half to give the AFC a 28-6 lead. Brad Johnson entered the game in the fourth quarter, and Ty Law intercepted a pass and returned it 43 yards for a touchdown on his first possession, and Sam Madison intercepted Johnson during his second drive to set up

Peyton Manning's 32-yard touchdown pass to Hines Ward, which gave the AFC a 45-6 lead with 7:31 left. Johnson guided the NFC to touchdowns on its next two possessions, with the help of Julian Peterson's onside kick recovery, for the game's final points. All three AFC quarterbacks passed for at least 100 yards, led by Drew Bledsoe's 9 of 18 for 122-yard performance. Gonzalez had 5 receptions for 98 yards to lead all receivers. The AFC's defense had 6 interceptions, 3 of which were thrown by NFC starter Jeff Garcia.

NFC	3	3	0	14	—	20
AFC	14	14	3	14	—	45

AFC — R. Williams 1 run (Vinatieri kick)
NFC — FG Akers 45
AFC — Gonzalez 11 pass from Gannon (Vinatieri kick)
AFC — Henry 13 pass from Gannon (Vinatieri kick)
NFC — FG Akers 53
AFC — R. Williams 1 run (Vinatieri kick)
AFC — FG Vinatieri 20
AFC — Law 43 interception return (Vinatieri kick)
AFC — Ward 32 pass from Manning (Vinatieri kick)
NFC — Horn 12 pass from B. Johnson (Akers kick)
NFC — Alstott 4 pass from B. Johnson (Akers kick)

2002 AFC-NFC PRO BOWL

Aloha Stadium, Honolulu, Hawaii
February 9, 2002, Attendance: 50,301
AFC 38, NFC 30—Rich Gannon passed for 137 yards and 2 touchdowns to become the first player to earn back-to-back Pro Bowl player of the game honors. The game had an inauspicious beginning for Gannon, who fumbled the game's first snap. Hugh Douglas recovered the fumble and returned the ball to the AFC's 2-yard line to set up Ahman Green's touchdown 27 seconds into the game. After a three-and-out series, Kurt Warner's 23-yard pass to David Boston set up David Akers' 29-yard field goal to give the NFC a 10-0 lead. Gannon responded two plays later with a 55-yard touchdown pass to Marvin Harrison. Deltha O'Neal's 24-yard interception return to the NFC's 6-yard line moments later set up Curtis Martin's 4-yard touchdown run and gave the AFC a 14-10 lead. After the NFC went three-and-out, the AFC needed just five plays, keyed by Gannon's 30-yard pass to Troy Brown, and capped by Priest Holmes' 39-yard touchdown run to give the AFC its third touchdown in less than six minutes and a 21-10 lead. A 10-play NFC drive led to Akers' second field goal, but Jermaine Lewis' 54-yard kickoff return set up Gannon's 18-yard touchdown pass to Ken Dilger and gave the AFC a 28-10 lead with 12:03 left in the first half. The NFC overcame Shane Lechler's Pro Bowl-record 73-yard punt with Akers' 49-yard

field goal just before halftime to cut the deficit to 28-16. Junior Seau's interception at the AFC's 5-yard line early in the fourth quarter thrwarted one NFC rally, but Champ Bailey's interception led to Donovan McNabb's 8-yard touchdown pass to Terrell Owens to cut the deficit to 28-23 with 8:12 left. Runs of 29 and 16 yards by Corey Dillon led to Jason Elam's 38-yard field goal and, two plays later, Ty Law intercepted McNabb at the NFC 44-yard line, returned the ball to the NFC 13 before lateralling to Ray Lewis, who dragged three players into the end zone for a 38-23 lead with 2:49 remaining. McNabb's 15-yard touchdown pass to Garrison Hearst with 1:32 left cut the deficit to 38-30, but Rod Woodson recovered the ensuing onside kick to clinch the victory. Gannon was 8 of 10 for 137 yards and 2 touchdowns. McNabb was 12 of 25 for 149 yards and 2 touchdowns, with 2 interceptions, to lead the NFC. Owens had 8 receptions for 122 yards and 1 touchdown.

AFC	21	7	0	10	—	38
NFC	13	3	0	14	—	30

NFC — Green 2 run (Akers kick)
NFC — FG Akers 29
AFC — Harrison 55 pass from Gannon (Elam kick)
AFC — Martin 4 run (Elam kick)
AFC — Holmes 39 run (Elam kick)
NFC — FG Akers 41
AFC — Dilger 18 pass from Gannon (Elam kick)
NFC — FG Akers 49
NFC — Owens 8 pass from McNabb (Akers kick)
AFC — FG Elam 38
AFC — R. Lewis 13 lateral from Law (Elam kick)
NFC — Hearst 15 pass from McNabb (Akers kick)

2001 AFC-NFC PRO BOWL

Aloha Stadium, Honolulu, Hawaii
February 4, 2001, Attendance: 50,128
AFC 38, NFC 17—Rich Gannon completed 12 of 14 passes for 160 yards during the game's first two possessions to win player of the game honors and lead the AFC to victory. Gannon's touchdown passes capped 87- and 90-yard drives and staked the AFC to a 14-0 lead. Gannon, who was still recovering from a separated non-throwing shoulder suffered in the AFC Championship Game, was replaced by Peyton Manning. The Colts' quarterback engineered a scoring drive, capped by Matt Stover's field goal, to give the AFC a 17-0 lead early in the second quarter. At that point, the AFC had 14 first downs and 231 yards of offense while limiting the NFC to no first downs and 6 yards. Jimmy Smith caught a 2-yard touchdown pass 54 seconds before halftime to give the AFC a 24-3 lead. Fourth-quarter touchdown passes by Donovan McNabb and Daunte Culpepper trimmed the AFC's lead to 31-17, but Jason Taylor

batted down Culpepper's fourth-and-1 pass early in the fourth quarter, and Edgerrin James' 20-yard touchdown run a few plays later iced the game. The NFC attempted a Pro Bowl record 56 pass attempts, and the two teams combined for a Pro Bowl record 98 pass attempts. Tony Gonzalez had 6 receptions for 108 yards, all in the first half, for the AFC. Torry Holt had 7 receptions for 103 yards. Smith's touchdown reception gives him 5 for his career, an AFC-NFC Pro Bowl record.

NFC	0	3	14	0	—	17
AFC	14	10	7	7	—	38

AFC — Gonzalez 8 pass from Gannon (Stover kick)
AFC — Harrison 16 pass from Gannon (Stover kick)
AFC — FG Stover 29
NFC — FG Gramatica 48
AFC — J. Smith 2 pass from Manning (Stover kick)
NFC — Owens 17 pass from McNabb (Gramatica kick)
AFC — Harrison 24 pass from Manning (Stover kick)
NFC — Holt 20 pass from Culpepper (Gramatica kick)
AFC — James 20 run (Stover kick)

2000 AFC-NFC PRO BOWL

Aloha Stadium, Honolulu, Hawaii
February 6, 2000, Attendance: 50,112
NFC 51, AFC 31—Randy Moss earned player of the game honors by setting records with 9 receptions for 212 yards as the NFC defeated the AFC in the highest-scoring Pro Bowl ever. Aeneas Williams intercepted Peyton Manning's pass and raced 62 yards down the left sideline to give the NFC an early 7-0 lead. Kurt Warner's 48-yard pass to Moss on the NFC's first possession set up Jason Hanson's first field goal. Mike Alstott and Jimmy Smith each scored twice in the first half, and Michael Bates' 66-yard kickoff return led to Hanson's Pro Bowl-record tying 51-yard field goal as the half expired to give the NFC a 27-21 lead. Alstott's third touchdown increased the NFC's lead to 37-21, and Derrick Brooks' interception of Mark Brunell and 20-yard return staked the NFC to a 44-24 lead with 11:12 left. The AFC responded with Manning's 52-yard touchdown pass to Smith with 6:30 remaining, but Steve Beuerlein found Moss with a 25-yard scoring pass with 1:05 left to finish the scoring. Warner led the three NFC quarterbacks by completing 8 of 11 passes for 123 yards. Alstott led all rushers with 13 carries for 67 yards. The NFC forced 6 turnovers. Manning was 17 of 23 for 270 yards and 2 touchdowns, with 2 interceptions. Smith had 8 receptions for 119 yards. The previous record, 64 points, was set in 1980.

AFC	7	14	0	10	—	31
NFC	10	17	10	14	—	51

NFC — A. Williams 62 interception return (Hanson kick)

NFC — FG Hanson 21
AFC — J. Smith 5 pass from Brunell (Mare kick)
NFC — Alstott 1 run (Hanson kick)
AFC — Gonzalez 10 pass from Gannon (Mare kick)
NFC — Alstott 3 run (Hanson kick)
AFC — J. Smith 21 pass from Manning (Mare kick)
NFC — FG Hanson 51
NFC — Alstott 1 run (Hanson kick)
NFC — FG Hanson 23
AFC — FG Mare 33
NFC — Brooks 20 interception return (Hanson kick)
AFC — J. Smith 52 pass from Manning (Mare kick)
NFC — Moss 25 pass from Beuerlein (Hanson kick)

1999 AFC-NFC PRO BOWL

Aloha Stadium, Honolulu, Hawaii
February 7, 1999, Attendance: 50,075
AFC 23, NFC 10—John Elway, appearing in uniform on a football field for the final time, drove the AFC to its initial touchdown and then watched a strong defensive effort as the AFC won the Pro Bowl for the third consecutive season. Elway capped a game-opening 61-yard drive with a touchdown pass to Sam Gash. The AFC led 10-3 late in the first half when Deion Sanders intercepted a Vinny Testaverde pass at the NFC's 10 and raced downfield, only to be caught by Ed McCaffrey at the AFC 3-yard line as the half expired. The NFC drove into AFC territory early in the second half, but Ty Law thwarted the NFC's spirits with a 67-yard interception return for a touchdown to give the AFC a 17-3 lead with 9:42 left in the third quarter. The NFC reached the end zone three minutes later as Emmitt Smith scored, but the AFC responded with a field goal on its ensuing possession. Jason Elam's third field goal with 1:02 remaining finished the scoring. Elway played just one drive and was 4 of 5 for 55 yards and 1 touchdown. Keyshawn Johnson had 7 catches for 87 yards and shared player of the game honors with Law. Chandler completed 9 of 25 passes for 133 yards en route to leading the NFC to its only touchdown. Randy Moss had 7 catches for 108 yards.

NFC	3	0	7	0	—	10
AFC	7	3	10	3	—	23

AFC — Gash 3 pass from Elway (Elam kick)
NFC — FG Anderson 23
AFC — FG Elam 23
AFC — Law 67 interception return (Elam kick)
NFC — E. Smith 3 run (Anderson kick)
AFC — FG Elam 46
AFC — FG Elam 26

1998 AFC-NFC PRO BOWL

Aloha Stadium, Honolulu, Hawaii
February 1, 1998, Attendance: 49,995
AFC 29, NFC 24—Warren Moon guided the AFC to points on all three of his drives, including the winning touchdown from 1 yard with 1:49 left as the AFC scored the game's final 15 points to beat the NFC. Steve Young threw a 22-yard touchdown pass to Herman Moore to cap the game's opening drive and give the NFC a 7-0 lead. Late in the first quarter, Mark Brunell threw a 17-yard touchdown pass to Andre Rison to tie the game. Both touchdown passes came on third-and-8. The NFC responded with a 7-play, 71-yard drive capped by Young's 36-yard touchdown pass to Rob Moore. Trent Dilfer guided the NFC to its third touchdown, keyed by a 21-yard pass to Irving Fryar and 23-yard pass to Mike Alstott, and capped by Dorsey Levens' 12-yard touchdown run with 1:36 left in the half to give the NFC a 21-7 lead. The NFC had a chance to pad its lead on its first possession of the second half, but Jason Hanson missed a 44-yard field goal. The AFC bounced back with a 10-play, 65-yard drive that culminated with Drew Bledsoe's 14-yard touchdown pass to Jimmy Smith late in the third quarter. After Hanson's 35-yard field goal gave the NFC a 24-14 lead with 13:42 left, Moon entered the game and drove the AFC into field-goal range, where Mike Hollis drilled a 48-yard attempt on 8:51 left. Attempting to grind out the clock, Warrick Dunn fumbled, and Darryl Williams recovered at the AFC's 49 with 3:03 remaining. After a holding penalty moved the AFC back 10 yards, Moon fired a 57-yard pass to Tim Brown to set up Eddie George's 4-yard run with 2:31 left. The AFC went for the lead instead of a tie, but Moon's pass to Rison fell incomplete. However, the AFC got the ball back when Chris Chandler fumbled the snap on the NFC's first play, and Michael Sinclair recovered at the NFC's 16 with 2:19 left. Three runs by George set up Moon's winning sneak with 1:49 remaining. Moon's 2-point conversion pass to Brown was incomplete, keeping the AFC's lead at 29-24. The NFC was unable to move beyond its own 31-yard line in the final moments, and the AFC prevailed. Tim Brown had 5 receptions for 129 yards. Moon, who was 4 of 8 for 89 yards, earned player of the game honors.

AFC	7	0	7	15	—	29
NFC	7	14	0	3	—	24

NFC — H. Moore 22 pass from Young (Hanson kick)
AFC — Rison 17 pass from Brunell (Hollis kick)
NFC — R. Moore 36 pass from Young (Hanson kick)
NFC — Levens 12 run (Hanson kick)
AFC — J. Smith 14 pass from Bledsoe (Hollis kick)
NFC — FG Hanson 35

AFC — FG Hollis 48
AFC — George 4 run (pass failed)
AFC — Moon 1 run (pass failed)

1997 AFC-NFC PRO BOWL

Aloha Stadium, Honolulu, Hawaii
February 2, 1997, Attendance: 50,031
AFC 26, NFC 23 (OT)—Cary Blanchard's 37-yard field goal 8:16 into overtime gave the AFC a 26-23 victory. The field goal was an ironic ending to a game that saw Blanchard and NFC kicker John Kasay, who each broke the previous single-season record of 35 field goals, combine to miss 5 of 8 field-goal attempts. The NFC scored on its first two possessions, with Vikings guard Randall McDaniel, who lined up as a fullback, scoring his first professional touchdown to give the NFC a 9-0 lead. However, the follies of the kicking unit began as holder Matt Turk muffed the snap on the extra point attempt. Blanchard booted a 28-yard field goal with 27 seconds left in the half to cut the NFC's lead to 9-3. In the third quarter, Barry Sanders scored from 6 yards out, but Kerry Collins was sacked on the 2-point attempt. A 41-yard pass from Drew Bledsoe to Tony Martin led to Curtis Martin's 3-yard run, and after Ashley Ambrose ran an interception back 54 yards for a touchdown 11 seconds into the fourth quarter, the AFC found itself with a 16-15 lead. The NFC drove for more than six minutes, only to have Kasay miss a 40-yard field goal attempt. After an AFC punt, Cris Carter caught a 47-yard touchdown bomb from Gus Frerotte to put the NFC ahead 23-16. After each team punted, the AFC got the ball on its own 20-yard line with 55 seconds left. Mark Brunell hit Tim Brown with an 80-yard bomb down the right sideline to tie the game with 44 seconds left. Wesley Walls caught a 33-yard pass to give the NFC a chance to win in regulation, but Kasay missed a 39-yard attempt and the game went to overtime. The AFC won the overtime toss, but Blanchard missed a 41-yard field goal attempt. The NFC had to punt after three plays, and Brunell hit Ben Coates with a 43-yard pass on the AFC's first play. After three running plays failed to gain a first down, Blanchard trotted onto the field and made the game-winning kick. The teams combined for a Pro Bowl record 962 total yards. Brunell, who completed 12 of 22 pass attempts for 236 yards, was selected as the player of the game.

AFC	0	3	7	13	3	—	26
NFC	9	0	6	8	0	—	23

NFC — FG Kasay 20
NFC — R. McDaniel 5 pass from Favre (muffed snap)
AFC — FG Blanchard 28
NFC — Sanders 6 run (pass failed)
AFC — Martin 3 run (Blanchard kick)
AFC — Ambrose 54 interception return (pass failed)

NFC — Carter 53 pass from Frerotte (Walls pass from Frerotte)
AFC — T. Brown 80 pass from Brunell (Blanchard kick)
AFC — FG Blanchard 37

1996 AFC-NFC PRO BOWL

Aloha Stadium, Honolulu, Hawaii
February 4, 1996, Attendance: 50,034
NFC 20, AFC 13—Jerry Rice had 6 receptions for 82 yards and 1 touchdown to earn player of the game honors in the NFC's victory. The 49ers' wide receiver, who was named to the Pro Bowl for the tenth consecutive year, caught a 1-yard touchdown pass from Packers quarterback Brett Favre 1:41 into the second quarter to cap an 80-yard drive and give the NFC the lead for good at 10-7. The AFC had taken a 7-0 lead 2:26 into the game when Bengals quarterback Jeff Blake connected with Steelers wide receiver Yancey Thigpen on a Pro Bowl-record 93-yard touchdown pass. The NFC increased its advantage to 20-7 at halftime on Redskins linebacker Ken Harvey's 36-yard interception return for a touchdown and Falcons kicker Morten Andersen's 24-yard field goal. The AFC trimmed its deficit to 20-13 when Colts quarterback Jim Harbaugh teamed with Patriots running back Curtis Martin on a 17-yard touchdown pass in the final minute of the third quarter, but its bid to win or tie was rebuffed twice in the final minutes of the fourth quarter. First, 49ers safety Tim McDonald intercepted Harbaugh's pass in the end zone with 1:50 remaining. Then, after the AFC forced a punt and got the ball back near midfield, Harbaugh drove his team to the NFC's 9-yard line in the closing seconds. But he spiked the ball once to stop the clock and threw 3 consecutive incompletions as time ran out. The AFC outgained the NFC 390 total yards to 287, but its quarterbacks suffered 4 interceptions, including 3 off Harbaugh, the NFL's leading passer during the regular season. The NFC raised its edge to 15-11 in Pro Bowl games since the AFL-NFL merger in 1970.

NFC	3	17	0	0	—	20
AFC	7	0	6	0	—	13

AFC — Thigpen 93 pass from Blake (Elam kick)
NFC — FG Andersen 36
NFC — Rice 1 pass from Favre (Andersen kick)
NFC — Harvey 36 interception return (Andersen kick)
NFC — FG Andersen 24
AFC — Martin 17 pass from Harbaugh (kick failed)

1995 AFC-NFC PRO BOWL

Aloha Stadium, Honolulu, Hawaii
February 5, 1995, Attendance: 50,529
AFC 41, NFC 13—Colts rookie Marshal Faulk rushed for a Pro Bowl-record 180 yards to key the AFC's rout of the NFC.

Faulk, who earned the Dan McGuire Trophy as the player of the game, averaged nearly 14 yards on his 13 carries and shattered the previous rushing mark of 112 yards set by O.J. Simpson in the 1973 game. Faulk's 49-yard touchdown run from punt formation in the fourth quarter was the longest in Pro Bowl history. The Seahawks' Chris Warren added 127 yards on 14 carries as the AFC amassed records for rushing yards (400) and total yards (552). Steelers tight end Eric Green caught 2 touchdown passes for the victors. The NFC managed only 196 total yards, a large chunk coming when 49ers quarterback Steve Young and Vikings wide receiver Cris Carter teamed on a 51-yard touchdown pass in the first quarter. That gave the NFC a 10-0 advantage, but the AFC rallied in the second quarter and took the lead for good when the Browns' Leroy Hoard scored on a 4-yard touchdown run 2:07 before halftime.

AFC	0	17	3	21	—	41
NFC	10	0	3	0	—	13

NFC — FG Reveiz 28
NFC — Carter 51 pass from Young (Reveiz kick)
AFC — Green 22 pass from Elway (Carney kick)
AFC — FG Carney 22
AFC — Hoard 4 run (Carney kick)
NFC — FG Reveiz 49
AFC — FG Carney 23
AFC — Warren 11 run (Carney kick)
AFC — Green 16 pass from Hostetler (Carney kick)
AFC — Faulk 49 run (Carney kick)

1994 AFC-NFC PRO BOWL

Aloha Stadium, Honolulu, Hawaii
February 6, 1994, Attendance: 50,026
NFC 17, AFC 3—The NFC converted a blocked punt and a fumble recovery into touchdowns just 2:20 apart in the second half of its victory over the AFC. With the score tied 3-3 late in the third quarter, Saints linebacker Renaldo Turnbull deflected a punt by the Oilers' Greg Montgomery, and the NFC took possession at the AFC's 48-yard line. A 32-yard pass from Bobby Hebert to Falcons teammate Andre Rison positioned Rams running back Jerome Bettis for a 4-yard touchdown run with 1:27 left in the third quarter. Moments later, Rams defensive tackle Sean Gilbert recovered a fumble by Oilers quarterback Warren Moon at the AFC's 19. Hebert then teamed with the Vikings' Cris Carter on a 15-yard touchdown pass 53 seconds into the fourth period. The NFC kept the AFC out of the end zone by maintaining possession for more than 38 minutes and forcing 6 turnovers. Rison earned the Dan McGuire Trophy as the player of the game by catching 6 passes for 86 yards. The victory was the fourth in the last six years for the NFC, which leads the series 14-10.

NFC	3	0	7	7	—	17
AFC	0	3	0	0	—	3

NFC — FG Johnson 35
AFC — FG Anderson 25
NFC — Bettis 4 run (Johnson kick)
NFC — Carter 15 pass from Hebert (Johnson kick)

1993 AFC-NFC PRO BOWL

Aloha Stadium, Honolulu, Hawaii
February 7, 1993, Attendance: 50,007
AFC 23, NFC 20—Nick Lowery's 33-yard field goal 4:09 into overtime gave the American Conference all-stars an unlikely 23-20 victory over the National Conference. Despite being overwhelmed by the NFC in first downs (30-9), and total yards (471-114), the AFC won because it forced 6 turnovers, blocked a pair of field goals (1 of which was returned for a touchdown), and returned an interception for a score. Special-teams star Steve Tasker of the Bills earned the Dan McGuire Trophy as the player of the game for making 4 tackles, forcing a fumble, and blocking a field goal. The block came with eight minutes left in regulation and the game tied at 13-13. The Raiders' Terry McDaniel picked up the loose ball and ran 28 yards for a touchdown and a 20-13 AFC lead. The NFC rallied behind 49ers quarterback Steve Young, whose fourth-down, 23-yard touchdown pass to Giants running back Rodney Hampton tied the game at 20-20 with 10 seconds left in regulation. Young completed 18 of 32 passes for 196 yards but was intercepted 3 times and lost a fumble when sacked in overtime. Raiders defensive end Howie Long fell on that fumble at the NFC 28-yard line, and five plays later, Lowery converted the winning field goal.

AFC	0	10	3	7	3	—	23
NFC	3	10	0	7	0	—	20

NFC — FG Andersen 27
AFC — Seau 31 interception return (Lowery kick)
NFC — FG Andersen 37
NFC — Irvin 9 pass from Aikman (Andersen kick)
AFC — FG Lowery 42
AFC — FG Lowery 29
AFC — McDaniel 28 blocked field goal return (Lowery kick)
NFC — Hampton 23 pass from Young (Andersen kick)
AFC — FG Lowery 33

1992 AFC-NFC PRO BOWL

Aloha Stadium, Honolulu, Hawaii
February 2, 1992, Attendance: 50,209
NFC 21, AFC 15—Atlanta's Chris Miller threw an 11-yard touchdown pass to San Francisco's Jerry Rice with 4:04 remaining in the game to lift the NFC over the AFC. It was the NFC's thirteenth win in the 22-game series. The AFC had taken a 15-14 lead when the Raiders' Jeff Jaeger kicked a 27-yard field goal 1:49 into the fourth quarter. But the NFC, aided by a key

roughing-the-passer penalty on a third-down incompletion from the AFC 24-yard line, drove 85 yards for the winning score. The Cowboys' Michael Irvin, playing in his first Pro Bowl, caught 8 passes for 125 yards, including a 13-yard touchdown in the first quarter, and was named the player of the game. Rice had 7 catches for 77 yards. Mark Rypien of Washington, the Super Bowl most valuable player one week earlier, completed 11 of 18 passes for 165 yards and 2 touchdowns for the NFC, including a 35-yard pass to Redskins teammate Gary Clark just 26 seconds before halftime. Miller completed 7 of his 10 attempts for 85 yards.

NFC	7	7	0	7	—	21
AFC	7	5	0	3	—	15

AFC — Clayton 4 pass from Kelly (Jaeger kick)
NFC — Irvin 13 pass from Rypien (Lohmiller kick)
AFC — Safety, Townsend tackled Byner in end zone
AFC — FG Jaeger 48
NFC — Clark 35 pass from Rypien (Lohmiller kick)
AFC — FG Jaeger 27
NFC — Rice 11 pass from Miller (Lohmiller kick)

1991 AFC-NFC PRO BOWL
Aloha Stadium, Honolulu, Hawaii
February 3, 1991, Attendance: 50,345
AFC 23, NFC 21—Buffalo's Jim Kelly and Houston's Ernest Givins combined for a 13-yard scoring pass late in the fourth quarter to rally the AFC over the NFC. Phoenix rookie Johnny Johnson scored on runs of 1 and 9 yards to put the NFC ahead 14-3 in the third quarter. Buffalo's Andre Reed, who led all receivers with 4 catches for 80 yards, caught a 20-yard scoring reception from Kelly early in the fourth quarter to move the AFC to within 1 point. Barry Sanders ran 22 yards for a touchdown to increase the NFC's lead to 21-13. Miami's Jeff Cross blocked a 46-yard field-goal attempt by New Orleans' Morten Andersen with seven seconds remaining to preserve the win. Buffalo's Bruce Smith recorded 3 sacks and also had a blocked field goal. Kelly, who completed 13 of 19 passes for 210 yards and 2 touchdowns, was presented the Dan McGuire Award as player of the game. The AFC's victory narrowed the NFC's Pro Bowl series lead to 12-9.

AFC	3	0	3	17	—	23
NFC	0	7	7	7	—	21

AFC — FG Lowery 26
NFC — J. Johnson 1 run (Andersen kick)
AFC — FG Lowery 43
NFC — J. Johnson 9 run (Andersen kick)
AFC — Reed 20 pass from Kelly (Lowery kick)
NFC — Sanders 22 run (Andersen kick)

AFC — FG Lowery 34
AFC — Givins 13 pass from Kelly (Lowery kick)

1990 AFC-NFC PRO BOWL
Aloha Stadium, Honolulu, Hawaii
February 4, 1990, Attendance: 50,445
NFC 27, AFC 21—The NFC captured its second straight Pro Bowl as the defense accounted for a pair of touchdowns and forced 5 turnovers before the eleventh consecutive sellout crowd at Aloha Stadium. The AFC held a 7-6 halftime edge on a 1-yard scoring run by Christian Okoye of the Chiefs. The NFC then rallied with 21 unanswered points in the third quarter. David Meggett of the Giants began the comeback with an 11-yard touchdown reception from Philadelphia's Randall Cunningham. The Rams' Jerry Gray followed with a 51-yard interception return for a score and the Vikings' Keith Millard added an 8-yard fumble return for a touchdown four minutes later to give the NFC a commanding 27-7 lead. Seattle's Dave Krieg rallied the AFC with a 5-yard touchdown pass to Miami's Ferrell Edmunds. Cleveland's Mike Johnson then returned an interception 22 yards for a score to pull the AFC to within 27-21. Gray, who was credited with 7 tackles, was given the Dan McGuire Award as player of the game. Krieg led all quarterbacks by completing 15 of 23 for 148 yards and 1 touchdown. Buffalo's Thurman Thomas topped all receivers with 5 catches for 47 yards, while Indianapolis' Eric Dickerson led all rushers with 46 yards on 15 carries. The win gave the NFC a 12-8 advantage in Pro Bowl games since 1971.

NFC	3	3	21	0	—	27
AFC	0	7	0	14	—	21

NFC — FG Murray 23
NFC — FG Murray 41
AFC — Okoye 1 run (Treadwell kick)
NFC — Meggett 11 pass from Cunningham (Murray kick)
NFC — Gray 51 interception return (Murray kick)
NFC — Millard 8 fumble recovery return (Murray kick)
AFC — Edmunds 5 pass from Krieg (Treadwell kick)
AFC — M. Johnson 22 interception return (Treadwell kick)

1989 AFC-NFC PRO BOWL
Aloha Stadium, Honolulu, Hawaii
January 29, 1989, Attendance: 50,113
NFC 34, AFC 3—The NFC scored 34 unanswered points to snap a two-game losing streak to the AFC before the tenth straight sellout crowd in Honolulu's Aloha Stadium. Bills kicker Scott Norwood provided the AFC's only points on a 38-yard field goal 6:23 into the game. Touchdown runs by Dallas' Herschel Walker (4 yards) and Atlanta's John Settle (1) brought the NFC a 14-3 halftime lead. Walker added a

7-yard scoring run, the Saints' Morten Andersen kicked field goals of 27 and 51 yards, and Los Angeles Rams' wide receiver Henry Ellard caught an 8-yard scoring pass from Minnesota quarterback Wade Wilson in the second half to complete the scoring. Chicago running back Neal Anderson and Philadelphia quarterback Randall Cunningham, who were both appearing in their first Pro Bowl, also played major roles in the NFC's victory. Anderson rushed 13 times for 85 yards and had 2 receptions for 17. Cunningham, who was voted the game's outstanding player, completed 10 of 14 passes for 63 yards and rushed for 49 yards. The NFC, which had 5 takeaways, outgained the AFC 355 yards to 167 and held a time-of-possession advantage of 35:18 to 24:42. Houston quarterback Warren Moon completed 13 of 20 passes for 134 yards for the AFC. The win gave the NFC an 11-8 advantage in Pro Bowl games.

AFC	3	0	0	0	—	3
NFC	7	7	10	10	—	34

AFC — FG Norwood 38
NFC — Walker 4 run (Andersen kick)
NFC — Settle 1 run (Andersen kick)
NFC — FG Andersen 27
NFC — Walker 7 run (Andersen kick)
NFC — FG Andersen 51
NFC — Ellard 8 pass from Wilson (Andersen kick)

1988 AFC-NFC PRO BOWL
Aloha Stadium, Honolulu, Hawaii
February 7, 1988, Attendance: 50,113
AFC 15, NFC 6—Led by a tenacious pass rush, the AFC defeated the NFC for the second consecutive year before the ninth straight sellout crowd in Honolulu's Aloha Stadium. Buffalo quarterback Jim Kelly scored the game's lone touchdown on a 1-yard run for a 7-6 halftime lead. Colts kicker Dean Biasucci added field goals from 37 and 30 yards to complete the AFC's scoring. Saints kicker Morten Andersen had 25- and 36-yard field goals to account for the NFC's points. AFC defenders held the NFC to 213 yards and recorded 8 sacks. Bills defensive end Bruce Smith, who had 2 sacks among his 5 tackles, was voted the game's outstanding player. Oilers running back Mike Rozier led all rushers with 49 yards on 9 carries. Jets wide receiver Al Toon had 5 receptions for 75 yards. The AFC generated 341 yards total offense and held a time-of-possession advantage of 34:14 to 25:46. By winning, the AFC cut the NFC's lead in the Pro Bowl series to 10-8.

NFC	0	6	0	0	—	6
AFC	0	7	6	2	—	15

NFC — FG Andersen 25
AFC — Kelly 1 run (Biasucci kick)
NFC — FG Andersen 36
AFC — FG Biasucci 37
AFC — FG Biasucci 30
AFC — Safety, Montana forced out of end zone

1987 AFC-NFC PRO BOWL
Aloha Stadium, Honolulu, Hawaii
February 1, 1987, Attendance: 50,101
AFC 10, NFC 6—The AFC defeated the NFC in the lowest-scoring game in AFC-NFC Pro Bowl history. The AFC took a 10-0 halftime lead on Broncos quarterback John Elway's 10-yard touchdown pass to Raiders tight end Todd Christensen and Patriots kicker Tony Franklin's 26-yard field goal. The AFC defense made the lead stand by forcing the NFC to settle for a pair of field goals from 38 and 19 yards by Saints kicker Morten Andersen after the NFC had first downs at the AFC 31-, 7-, 16-, 15-, 5-, and 7-yard lines. Both AFC scores were set up by fumble recoveries by Seahawks linebacker Fredd Young and Dolphins linebacker John Offerdahl, respectively. Eagles defensive end Reggie White, who tied a Pro Bowl record with 4 sacks among his 7 solo tackles, was voted the game's outstanding player. The AFC victory cut the NFC's lead in the Pro Bowl series to 10-7.

AFC	7	3	0	0 —	10
NFC	0	0	3	3 —	6

AFC — Christensen 10 pass from Elway (Franklin kick)
AFC — FG Franklin 26
NFC — FG Andersen 38
NFC — FG Andersen 19

1986 AFC-NFC PRO BOWL
Aloha Stadium, Honolulu, Hawaii
February 2, 1986, Attendance: 50,101
NFC 28, AFC 24—New York Giants quarterback Phil Simms brought the NFC back from a 24-7 halftime deficit to defeat the AFC. Simms, who completed 15 of 27 passes for 212 yards and 3 touchdowns, was named the most valuable player of the game. The AFC had taken its first-half lead on a 2-yard run by Los Angeles Raiders running back Marcus Allen, who also threw a 51-yard scoring pass to San Diego wide receiver Wes Chandler, an 11-yard touchdown catch by Pittsburgh wide receiver Louis Lipps, and a 34-yard field goal by Steelers kicker Gary Anderson. Minnesota's Joey Browner accounted for the NFC's only score before halftime on a 48-yard interception return. After intermission, the NFC blanked the AFC while scoring 3 touchdowns via a 15-yard catch by Washington wide receiver Art Monk, a 2-yard reception by Dallas tight end Doug Cosbie, and a 15-yard catch by Tampa Bay tight end Jimmie Giles with 2:47 remaining in the game. The victory gave the NFC a 10-6 Pro Bowl record against the AFC.

NFC	0	7	7	14 —	28
AFC	7	17	0	0 —	24

AFC — Allen 2 run (Anderson kick)
NFC — Browner 48 interception return (Andersen kick)
AFC — Chandler 51 pass from Allen (Anderson kick)
AFC — FG Anderson 34

AFC — Lipps 11 pass from O'Brien (Anderson kick)
NFC — Monk 15 pass from Simms (Andersen kick)
NFC — Cosbie 2 pass from Simms (Andersen kick)
NFC — Giles 15 pass from Simms (Andersen kick)

1985 AFC-NFC PRO BOWL
Aloha Stadium, Honolulu, Hawaii
January 27, 1985, Attendance: 50,385
AFC 22, NFC 14—Defensive end Art Still of the Kansas City Chiefs recovered a fumble and returned it 83 yards for a touchdown to clinch the AFC's victory over the NFC. Still's touchdown came in the fourth period with the AFC trailing 14-12 and was one of several outstanding defensive plays in a Pro Bowl dominated by two record-breaking defenses. The teams combined for a Pro Bowl-record 17 sacks, including 4 by New York Jets defensive end Mark Gastineau, who was named the game's outstanding player. The AFC's first score came on a safety when Gastineau tackled running back Eric Dickerson of the Los Angeles Rams in the end zone. The AFC's second score, a 6-yard pass from Miami's Dan Marino to Los Angeles Raiders running back Marcus Allen, was set up by a partial block of a punt by Seahawks linebacker Fredd Young. The NFC leads the series 9-6.

AFC	0	9	0	13 —	22
NFC	0	0	7	7 —	14

AFC — Safety, Gastineau tackled Dickerson in end zone
AFC — Allen 6 pass from Marino (Johnson kick)
NFC — Lofton 13 pass from Montana (Stenerud kick)
NFC — Payton 1 run (Stenerud kick)
AFC — FG Johnson 33
AFC — Still 83 fumble recovery return (Johnson kick)
AFC — FG Johnson 22

1984 AFC-NFC PRO BOWL
Aloha Stadium, Honolulu, Hawaii
January 29, 1984, Attendance: 50,445
NFC 45, AFC 3—The NFC won its sixth Pro Bowl in the last seven seasons by routing the AFC. The NFC was led by the passing of most valuable player Joe Theismann of Washington, who completed 21 of 27 passes for 242 yards and 3 touchdowns. Theismann set Pro Bowl records for completions and touchdown passes. The NFC established Pro Bowl marks for most points scored and fewest points allowed. Running back William Andrews of Atlanta had 6 carries for 43 yards and caught 4 passes for 49 yards, including scoring receptions of 16 and 2 yards. Los Angeles Rams rookie Eric Dickerson gained 46 yards on 11 carries, including a 14-yard touchdown run, and had 45 yards on 5 catches. Rams safety Nolan Cromwell had a 44-yard intercep-

tion return for a touchdown early in the third period to give the NFC a commanding 24-3 lead. Green Bay wide receiver James Lofton caught an 8-yard touchdown pass, while tight end teammate Paul Coffman had a 6-yard scoring catch.

NFC	3	14	14	14 —	45
AFC	0	3	0	0 —	3

NFC — FG Haji-Sheikh 23
NFC — Andrews 16 pass from Theismann (Haji-Sheikh kick)
NFC — Andrews 2 pass from Montana (Haji-Sheikh kick)
AFC — FG Anderson 43
NFC — Cromwell 44 interception return (Haji-Sheikh kick)
NFC — Lofton 8 pass from Theismann (Haji-Sheikh kick)
NFC — Coffman 6 pass from Theismann (Haji-Sheikh kick)
NFC — Dickerson 14 run (Haji-Sheikh kick)

1983 AFC-NFC PRO BOWL
Aloha Stadium, Honolulu, Hawaii
February 6, 1983, Attendance: 49,883
NFC 20, AFC 19—Dallas' Danny White threw an 11-yard touchdown pass to the Packers' John Jefferson with 35 seconds remaining to rally the NFC over the AFC. White, who completed 14 of 26 passes for 162 yards, kept the winning 65-yard drive alive with a 14-yard completion to Jefferson on a fourth-and-7 play at the AFC 25. The AFC was ahead 12-10 at halftime and increased the lead to 19-10 in the third period, when Marcus Allen scored on a 1-yard run. San Diego's Dan Fouts, who attempted 30 passes, set Pro Bowl records for most completions (17) and yards (274). Pittsburgh's John Stallworth was the AFC's leading receiver with 7 catches for 67 yards. William Andrews topped the NFC with 5 receptions for 48 yards. Fouts and Jefferson were co-winners of the player of the game award.

AFC	9	3	7	0 —	19
NFC	0	10	0	10 —	20

AFC — Walker 34 pass from Fouts (Benirschke kick)
AFC — Safety, Still tackled Theismann in end zone
NFC — Andrews 3 run (Moseley kick)
NFC — FG Moseley 35
AFC — FG Benirschke 29
AFC — Allen 1 run (Benirschke kick)
NFC — FG Moseley 41
NFC — Jefferson 11 pass from D. White (Moseley kick)

1982 AFC-NFC PRO BOWL
Aloha Stadium, Honolulu, Hawaii
January 31, 1982, Attendance: 50,402
AFC 16, NFC 13—Nick Lowery of Kansas City kicked a 23-yard field goal with three seconds remaining to give the AFC a last-second victory over the NFC. Lowery's kick climaxed a 69-yard drive directed by quarterback Dan Fouts. The NFC gained a 13-13 tie with 2:43 to go when Dallas'

Tony Dorsett ran 4 yards for a touchdown. In the drive to the winning field goal, Fouts completed 3 passes, including a 23-yard toss to San Diego teammate Kellen Winslow that put the ball on the NFC's 5-yard line. Two plays later, Lowery kicked the field goal. Winslow, who caught 6 passes for 86 yards, was named co-player of the game along with Tampa Bay defensive end Lee Roy Selmon.

NFC	0	6	0	7	— 13
AFC	0	0	13	3	— 16

NFC — Giles 4 pass from Montana (kick blocked)
AFC — Muncie 2 run (kick failed)
AFC — Campbell 1 run (Lowery kick)
NFC — Dorsett 4 run (Septien kick)
AFC — FG Lowery 23

1981 AFC-NFC PRO BOWL
Aloha Stadium, Honolulu, Hawaii
February 1, 1981, Attendance: 50,360
NFC 21, AFC 7—Eddie Murray kicked 4 field goals and Steve Bartkowski fired a 55-yard scoring pass to Alfred Jenkins to lead the NFC to its fourth straight victory over the AFC and a 7-4 edge in the series. Murray was named the game's most valuable player and missed tying Garo Yepremian's Pro Bowl record of 5 field goals when a 37-yard attempt hit the crossbar with 22 seconds left. The AFC's only score came on a 9-yard pass from Brian Sipe to Stanley Morgan. Bartkowski completed 9 of 21 passes for 173 yards, while Sipe connected on 10 of 15 for 142 yards. Ottis Anderson led all rushers with 70 yards on 10 carries. Earl Campbell, the NFL's leading rusher in 1980, was limited to 24 yards on 8 attempts.

AFC	0	7	0	0	— 7
NFC	3	6	0	12	— 21

NFC — FG Murray 31
AFC — Morgan 9 pass from Sipe (J. Smith kick)
NFC — FG Murray 31
NFC — FG Murray 34
NFC — Jenkins 55 pass from Bartkowski (Murray kick)
NFC — FG Murray 36
NFC — Safety, Shell called for holding in end zone

1980 AFC-NFC PRO BOWL
Aloha Stadium, Honolulu, Hawaii
January 27, 1980, Attendance: 49,800
NFC 37, AFC 27—Chuck Muncie ran for 2 touchdowns and threw a 25-yard option pass for another score to give the NFC its third consecutive victory over the AFC. The Saints' Muncie, who was selected the game's most valuable player, snapped a 3-3 tie on a 1-yard touchdown run at 1:41 of the second quarter, then scored on an 11-yard run in the fourth quarter for the NFC's final touchdown. Two scoring records were set in the game—37 points by the NFC, eclipsing the 33 by the AFC in 1973, and the 64 points by both teams, surpassing the 61 scored in 1973.

NFC	3	20	7	7	— 37
AFC	3	7	10	7	— 27

NFC — FG Moseley 37
AFC — FG Fritsch 19
NFC — Muncie 1 run (Moseley kick)
AFC — Pruitt 1 pass from Bradshaw (Fritsch kick)
NFC — D. Hill 13 pass from Manning (kick failed)
NFC — T. Hill 25 pass from Muncie (Moseley kick)
NFC — Henry 86 punt return (Moseley kick)
AFC — Campbell 2 run (Fritsch kick)
AFC — FG Fritsch 29
NFC — Muncie 11 run (Moseley kick)
AFC — Campbell 1 run (Fritsch kick)

1979 AFC-NFC PRO BOWL
Memorial Coliseum, Los Angeles, CA
January 29, 1979, Attendance: 46,281
NFC 13, AFC 7—Roger Staubach completed 9 of 15 passes for 125 yards, including the winning touchdown on a 19-yard strike to Dallas Cowboys teammate Tony Hill in the third period. The winning drive began at the AFC's 45-yard line after a shanked punt. Staubach hit Ahmad Rashad with passes of 15 and 17 yards to set up Hill's decisive catch. The victory gave the NFC a 5-4 advantage in Pro Bowl games. Rashad, who accounted for 89 yards on 5 receptions, was named the player of the game. The AFC led 7-6 at halftime on Bob Griese's 8-yard scoring toss to Steve Largent late in the second quarter. Largent had 5 receptions for 75 yards. The NFC scored first as Archie Manning marched his team 70 yards in 11 plays, capped by Wilbert Montgomery's 2-yard touchdown run. The AFC's Earl Campbell was the game's leading rusher with 66 yards on 12 carries.

AFC	0	7	0	0	— 7
NFC	0	6	7	0	— 13

NFC — Montgomery 2 run (kick failed)
AFC — Largent 8 pass from Griese (Yepremian kick)
NFC — T. Hill 19 pass from Staubach (Corral kick)

1978 AFC-NFC PRO BOWL
Tampa Stadium, Tampa, Florida
January 23, 1978, Attendance: 51,337
NFC 14, AFC 13—Walter Payton, the NFL's leading rusher in 1977, sparked a second-half comeback to give the NFC the win and tie the series between the two conferences at four victories each. Payton, who was the game's most valuable player, gained 77 yards on 13 carries and scored the tying touchdown on a 1-yard burst with 7:37 left in the game. Efren Herrera kicked the winning extra point. The AFC dominated the first half of the game, taking a 13-0 lead on field goals of 21 and 39 yards by Toni Linhart and a 10-yard touchdown pass from Ken Stabler to Oakland teammate Cliff Branch. On the

NFC's first possession of the second half, Pat Haden put together the first touchdown drive after Eddie Brown returned a punt to the AFC 46-yard line. Haden connected on all 4 of his passes on that drive, finally hitting Terry Metcalf with a 4-yard scoring toss. The NFC continued to rally and, with Jim Hart at quarterback, moved 63 yards in 12 plays for the go-ahead score. During the winning drive, Hart completed 5 of 6 passes for 38 yards and Payton picked up 20 more on the ground.

AFC	3	10	0	0	— 13
NFC	0	0	7	7	— 14

AFC — FG Linhart 21
AFC — Branch 10 pass from Stabler (Linhart kick)
AFC — FG Linhart 39
NFC — Metcalf 4 pass from Haden (Herrera kick)
NFC — Payton 1 run (Herrera kick)

1977 AFC-NFC PRO BOWL
Kingdome, Seattle, Washington
January 17, 1977, Attendance: 64,752
AFC 24, NFC 14—O.J. Simpson's 3-yard touchdown burst at 7:03 of the first quarter gave the AFC a lead it would not surrender, breaking a two-game NFC win streak and giving the AFC stars a 4-3 series lead. The AFC took a 17-7 lead midway through the second period on the first of 2 Ken Anderson touchdown passes, a 12-yard toss to Charlie Joiner. But the NFC mounted a 73-yard drive capped by Lawrence McCutcheon's 1-yard touchdown plunge to pull within 17-14 at the half. Following a scoreless third quarter, player of the game Mel Blount thwarted a possible NFC score when he intercepted Jim Hart's pass in the end zone. Less than three minutes later, Blount again picked off a Hart pass. That set up Anderson's 27-yard touchdown strike to Cliff Branch for the final score.

NFC	0	14	0	0	— 14
AFC	10	7	0	7	— 24

AFC — Simpson 3 run (Linhart kick)
AFC — FG Linhart 31
NFC — Thomas 15 run (Bakken kick)
AFC — Joiner 12 pass from Anderson (Linhart kick)
NFC — McCutcheon 1 run (Bakken kick)
AFC — Branch 27 pass from Anderson (Linhart kick)

1976 AFC-NFC PRO BOWL
Superdome, New Orleans, Louisiana
January 26, 1976, Attendance: 30,546
NFC 23, AFC 20—Mike Boryla, a late substitute who did not enter the game until 5:39 remained, lifted the National Football Conference to the victory over the American Football Conference with 2 touchdown passes in the final minutes. It was the second straight NFC win, squaring the series at 3-3. Until Boryla started firing the ball the AFC was in control, leading 13-0 at the half. Boryla entered the game after

Billy Johnson had raced 90 yards with a punt to give the AFC a 20-9 lead. He floated a 14-yard touchdown pass to Terry Metcalf and later fired an 8-yard scoring pass to Mel Gray for the winner.

AFC	0	13	0	7	—	20
NFC	0	0	9	14	—	23

AFC — FG Stenerud 20
AFC — FG Stenerud 35
AFC — Burrough 64 pass from Pastorini (Stenerud kick)
NFC — FG Bakken 42
NFC — Foreman 4 pass from Hart (kick blocked)
AFC — Johnson 90 punt return (Stenerud kick)
NFC — Metcalf 14 pass from Boryla (Bakken kick)
NFC — Gray 8 pass from Boryla (Bakken kick)

1975 AFC-NFC PRO BOWL
Orange Bowl, Miami, Florida
January 20, 1975, Attendance: 26,484
NFC 17, AFC 10—Los Angeles quarterback James Harris, who took over the NFC offense after Jim Hart of St. Louis suffered a laceration above his right eye in the second period, threw 2 touchdown passes early in the fourth period to pace the NFC to its second victory in the five-game Pro Bowl series. The NFC win snapped a three-game AFC victory string. Harris, who was named the player of the game, connected with St. Louis' Mel Gray for an 8-yard touchdown 2:03 into the final period. One minute and 24 seconds later, following a fumble recovery by Washington's Ken Houston, Harris tossed another 8-yard scoring pass to Washington's Charley Taylor for the decisive points.

NFC	0	3	0	14	—	17
AFC	0	0	10	0	—	10

NFC — FG Marcol 33
AFC — Warfield 32 pass from Griese (Gerela kick)
AFC — FG Gerela 33
NFC — Gray 8 pass from J. Harris (Marcol kick)
NFC — Taylor 8 pass from J. Harris (Marcol kick)

1974 AFC-NFC PRO BOWL
Arrowhead Stadium, Kansas City, MO
January 20, 1974, Attendance: 66,918
AFC 15, NFC 13—Miami's Garo Yepremian's fifth field goal—a 42-yard kick with 21 seconds remaining—gave the AFC its third straight victory since the NFC won the inaugural game following the 1970 season. The field goal by Yepremian, who was voted the game's outstanding player, offset a 21-yard field goal by Atlanta's Nick Mike-Mayer that had given the NFC a 13-12 advantage with 1:41 remaining. The only touchdown in the game was scored by the NFC on a 14-yard pass from Philadelphia's Roman Gabriel to the Rams' Lawrence McCutcheon.

NFC	0	10	0	3	—	13
AFC	3	3	3	6	—	15

AFC — FG Yepremian 16
NFC — FG Mike-Mayer 27
NFC — McCutcheon 14 pass from Gabriel (Mike-Mayer kick)
AFC — FG Yepremian 37
AFC — FG Yepremian 27
AFC — FG Yepremian 41
NFC — FG Mike-Mayer 21
AFC — FG Yepremian 42

1973 AFC-NFC PRO BOWL
Texas Stadium, Irving, Texas
January 21, 1973, Attendance: 37,091
AFC 33, NFC 28—Paced by the rushing and receiving of player of the game O.J. Simpson, the AFC erased a 14-0 first period deficit and built a commanding 33-14 lead midway through the fourth period before the NFC managed 2 touchdowns in the final minute of play. Simpson rushed for 112 yards and caught 3 passes for 58 more to gain unanimous recognition in the balloting for player of the game. Green Bay Packers running back John Brockington scored 3 touchdowns for the NFC.

AFC	0	10	10	13	—	33
NFC	14	0	0	14	—	28

NFC — Brockington 1 run (Marcol kick)
NFC — Brockington 3 pass from Kilmer (Marcol kick)
AFC — Simpson 7 run (Gerela kick)
AFC — FG Gerela 18
AFC — FG Gerela 22
AFC — Hubbard 11 run (Gerela kick)
AFC — O. Taylor 5 pass from Lamonica (kick failed)
AFC — Bell 12 interception return (Gerela kick)
NFC — Brockington 1 run (Marcol kick)
NFC — Kwalick 12 pass from Snead (Marcol kick)

1972 AFC-NFC PRO BOWL
Memorial Coliseum, Los Angeles, CA
January 23, 1972, Attendance: 53,647
AFC 26, NFC 13—Kansas City's Jan Stenerud kicked 4 field goals to lead the AFC from a 6-0 deficit to victory. The AFC defense picked off 3 passes. Stenerud was selected as the outstanding offensive player and his Kansas City teammate, linebacker Willie Lanier, was the game's outstanding defensive player.

AFC	0	3	13	10	—	26
NFC	0	6	0	7	—	13

NFC — Grim 50 pass from Landry (kick failed)
AFC — FG Stenerud 25
AFC — FG Stenerud 23
AFC — FG Stenerud 48
AFC — Morin 5 pass from Dawson (Stenerud kick)
AFC — FG Stenerud 42
NFC — V. Washington 2 run (Knight kick)
AFC — F. Little 6 run (Stenerud kick)

1971 AFC-NFC PRO BOWL
Memorial Coliseum, Los Angeles, CA
January 24, 1971, Attendance: 48,222
NFC 27, AFC 6—Mel Renfro of Dallas broke open the first meeting between the American Football Conference and National Football Conference all-star teams as he returned a pair of punts 82 and 56 yards for touchdowns in the final period to clinch the NFC victory over the AFC. Renfro was voted the game's outstanding back and linebacker Fred Carr of Green Bay the outstanding lineman.

AFC	0	3	3	0	—	6
NFC	0	3	10	14	—	27

AFC — FG Stenerud 37
NFC — FG Cox 13
NFC — Osborn 23 pass from Brodie (Cox kick)
NFC — FG Cox 35
AFC — FG Stenerud 16
NFC — Renfro 82 punt return (Cox kick)
NFC — Renfro 56 punt return (Cox kick)

Includes AFL All-Star Game played after the 1961-69 seasons.

Date	Result/Honored players	Site (attendance)
Jan. 15, 1939	New York Giants 13, Pro All-Stars 10	Wrigley Field, Los Angeles (20,000)
Jan. 14, 1940	Green Bay 16, NFL All-Stars 7	Gilmore Stadium, Los Angeles (18,000)
Dec. 29, 1940	Chicago Bears 28, NFL All-Stars 14	Gilmore Stadium, Los Angeles (21,624)
Jan. 4, 1942	Chicago Bears 35, NFL All-Stars 24	Polo Grounds, New York (17,725)
Dec. 27, 1942	NFL All-Stars 17, Washington 14	Shibe Park, Philadelphia (18,671)
Jan. 14, 1951	American Conf. 28, National Conf. 27	Los Angeles Memorial Coliseum (53,676)
	Otto Graham, Cleveland, player of the game	
Jan. 12, 1952	National Conf. 30, American Conf. 13	Los Angeles Memorial Coliseum (19,400)
	Dan Towler, Los Angeles, player of the game	
Jan. 10, 1953	National Conf. 27, American Conf. 7	Los Angeles Memorial Coliseum (34,208)
	Don Doll, Detroit, player of the game	
Jan. 17, 1954	East 20, West 9	Los Angeles Memorial Coliseum (44,214)
	Chuck Bednarik, Philadelphia, player of the game	
Jan. 16, 1955	West 26, East 19	Los Angeles Memorial Coliseum (43,972)
	Billy Wilson, San Francisco, player of the game	
Jan. 15, 1956	East 31, West 30	Los Angeles Memorial Coliseum (37,867)
	Ollie Matson, Chi. Cardinals, player of the game	
Jan. 13, 1957	West 19, East 10	Los Angeles Memorial Coliseum (44,177)
	Bert Rechichar, Baltimore, outstanding back	
	Ernie Stautner, Pittsburgh, outstanding lineman	
Jan. 12, 1958	West 26, East 7	Los Angeles Memorial Coliseum (66,634)
	Hugh McElhenny, San Francisco, outstanding back	
	Gene Brito, Washington, outstanding lineman	
Jan. 11, 1959	East 28, West 21	Los Angeles Memorial Coliseum (72,250)
	Frank Gifford, N.Y. Giants, outstanding back	
	Doug Atkins, Chi. Bears, outstanding lineman	
Jan. 17, 1960	West 38, East 21	Los Angeles Memorial Coliseum (56,876)
	Johnny Unitas, Baltimore, outstanding back	
	Gene (Big Daddy) Lipscomb, Baltimore, outstanding lineman	
Jan. 15, 1961	West 35, East 31	Los Angeles Memorial Coliseum (62,971)
	Johnny Unitas, Baltimore, outstanding back	
	Sam Huff, N.Y. Giants, outstanding lineman	
Jan. 7, 1962	AFL West 47, East 27	Balboa Stadium, San Diego (20,973)
	Cotton Davidson, Dallas Texans, player of the game	
Jan. 14, 1962	NFL West 31, East 30	Los Angeles Memorial Coliseum (57,409)
	Jim Brown, Cleveland, outstanding back	
	Henry Jordan, Green Bay, outstanding lineman	
Jan. 13, 1963	AFL West 21, East 14	Balboa Stadium, San Diego (27,641)
	Curtis McClinton, Dallas Texans, outstanding offensive player	
	Earl Faison, San Diego, outstanding defensive player	
Jan. 13, 1963	NFL East 30, West 20	Los Angeles Memorial Coliseum (61,374)
	Jim Brown, Cleveland, outstanding back	
	Gene (Big Daddy) Lipscomb, Pittsburgh, outstanding lineman	
Jan. 12, 1964	NFL West 31, East 17	Los Angeles Memorial Coliseum (67,242)
	Johnny Unitas, Baltimore, player of the game	
	Gino Marchetti, Baltimore, outstanding lineman	
Jan. 19, 1964	AFL West 27, East 24	Balboa Stadium, San Diego (20,016)
	Keith Lincoln, San Diego, outstanding offensive player	
	Archie Matsos, Oakland, outstanding defensive player	
Jan. 10, 1965	NFL West 34, East 14	Los Angeles Memorial Coliseum (60,598)
	Fran Tarkenton, Minnesota, outstanding back	
	Terry Barr, Detroit, outstanding lineman	
Jan. 16, 1965	AFL West 38, East 14	Jeppesen Stadium, Houston (15,446)
	Keith Lincoln, San Diego, outstanding offensive player	
	Willie Brown, Denver, outstanding defensive player	
Jan. 15, 1966	AFL All-Stars 30, Buffalo 19	Rice Stadium, Houston (35,572)
	Joe Namath, N.Y. Jets, most valuable player, offense	
	Frank Buncom, San Diego, most valuable player, defense	
Jan. 15, 1966	NFL East 36, West 7	Los Angeles Memorial Coliseum (60,124)
	Jim Brown, Cleveland, outstanding back	
	Dale Meinert, St. Louis, outstanding lineman	
Jan. 21, 1967	AFL East 30, West 23	Oakland-Alameda County Coliseum (18,876)
	Babe Parilli, Boston, outstanding offensive player	
	Verlon Biggs, N.Y. Jets, outstanding defensive player	
Jan. 22, 1967	NFL East 20, West 10	Los Angeles Memorial Coliseum (15,062)
	Gale Sayers, Chicago, outstanding back	
	Floyd Peters, Philadelphia, outstanding lineman	

Jan. 21, 1968   AFL East 25, West 24 ....Gator Bowl, Jacksonville, Fla. (40,103)
       Joe Namath and Don Maynard, N.Y. Jets, out. off. players
       Leslie (Speedy) Duncan, San Diego, out. def. player

Jan. 21, 1968   NFL West 38, East 20 ....Los Angeles Memorial Coliseum (53,289)
       Gale Sayers, Chicago, outstanding back
       Dave Robinson, Green Bay, outstanding lineman

Jan. 19, 1969   AFL West 38, East 25 ....Gator Bowl, Jacksonville, Fla. (41,058)
       Len Dawson, Kansas City, outstanding offensive player
       George Webster, Houston, outstanding defensive player

Jan. 19, 1969   NFL West 10, East 7 ....Los Angeles Memorial Coliseum (32,050)
       Roman Gabriel, Los Angeles, outstanding back
       Merlin Olsen, Los Angeles, outstanding lineman

Jan. 17, 1970   AFL West 26, East 3 ....Astrodome, Houston (30,170)
       John Hadl, San Diego, player of the game

Jan. 18, 1970   NFL West 16, East 13 ....Los Angeles Memorial Coliseum (57,786)
       Gale Sayers, Chicago, outstanding back
       George Andrie, Dallas, outstanding lineman

Jan. 24, 1971   NFC 27, AFC 6 ....Los Angeles Memorial Coliseum (48,222)
       Mel Renfro, Dallas, outstanding back
       Fred Carr, Green Bay, outstanding lineman

Jan. 23, 1972   AFC 26, NFC 13 ....Los Angeles Memorial Coliseum (53,647)
       Jan Stenerud, Kansas City, outstanding offensive player
       Willie Lanier, Kansas City, outstanding defensive player

Jan. 21, 1973   AFC 33, NFC 28 ....Texas Stadium, Irving (37,091)
       O.J. Simpson, Buffalo, player of the game

Jan. 20, 1974   AFC 15, NFC 13 ....Arrowhead Stadium, Kansas City (66,918)
       Garo Yepremian, Miami, player of the game

Jan. 20, 1975   NFC 17, AFC 10 ....Orange Bowl, Miami (26,484)
       James Harris, Los Angeles, player of the game

Jan. 26, 1976   NFC 23, AFC 20 ....Louisiana Superdome, New Orleans (30,546)
       Billy Johnson, Houston, player of the game

Jan. 17, 1977   AFC 24, NFC 14 ....Kingdome, Seattle (64,752)
       Mel Blount, Pittsburgh, player of the game

Jan. 23, 1978   NFC 14, AFC 13 ....Tampa Stadium (51,337)
       Walter Payton, Chicago, player of the game

Jan. 29, 1979   NFC 13, AFC 7 ....Los Angeles Memorial Coliseum (46,281)
       Ahmad Rashad, Minnesota, player of the game

Jan. 27, 1980   NFC 37, AFC 27 ....Aloha Stadium, Honolulu (49,800)
       Chuck Muncie, New Orleans, player of the game

Feb. 1, 1981   NFC 21, AFC 7 ....Aloha Stadium, Honolulu (50,360)
       Eddie Murray, Detroit, player of the game

Jan. 31, 1982   AFC 16, NFC 13 ....Aloha Stadium, Honolulu (50,402)
       Kellen Winslow, San Diego, and Lee Roy Selmon, Tampa Bay, players of the game

Feb. 6, 1983   NFC 20, AFC 19 ....Aloha Stadium, Honolulu (49,883)
       Dan Fouts, San Diego, and John Jefferson, Green Bay, players of the game

Jan. 29, 1984   NFC 45, AFC 3 ....Aloha Stadium, Honolulu (50,445)
       Joe Theismann, Washington, player of the game

Jan. 27, 1985   AFC 22, NFC 14 ....Aloha Stadium, Honolulu (50,385)
       Mark Gastineau, N.Y. Jets, player of the game

Feb. 2, 1986   NFC 28, AFC 24 ....Aloha Stadium, Honolulu (50,101)
       Phil Simms, N.Y. Giants, player of the game

Feb. 1, 1987   AFC 10, NFC 6 ....Aloha Stadium, Honolulu (50,101)
       Reggie White, Philadelphia, player of the game

Feb. 7, 1988   AFC 15, NFC 6 ....Aloha Stadium, Honolulu (50,113)
       Bruce Smith, Buffalo, player of the game

Jan. 29, 1989   NFC 34, AFC 3 ....Aloha Stadium, Honolulu (50,113)
       Randall Cunningham, Philadelphia, player of the game

Feb. 4, 1990   NFC 27, AFC 21 ....Aloha Stadium, Honolulu (50,445)
       Jerry Gray, L.A. Rams, player of the game

Feb. 3, 1991   AFC 23, NFC 21 ....Aloha Stadium, Honolulu (50,345)
       Jim Kelly, Buffalo, player of the game

Feb. 2, 1992   NFC 21, AFC 15 ....Aloha Stadium, Honolulu (50,209)
       Michael Irvin, Dallas, player of the game

Feb. 7, 1993   AFC 23, NFC 20 (OT) ....Aloha Stadium, Honolulu (50,007)
       Steve Tasker, Buffalo, player of the game

Feb. 6, 1994   NFC 17, AFC 3 ....Aloha Stadium, Honolulu (50,026)
       Andre Rison, Atlanta, player of the game

Feb. 5, 1995   AFC 41, NFC 13 ....Aloha Stadium, Honolulu (50,529)
       Marshall Faulk, Indianapolis, player of the game

Feb. 4, 1996	NFC 20, AFC 13	Aloha Stadium, Honolulu (50,034)
	Jerry Rice, San Francisco, player of the game	
Feb. 2, 1997	AFC 26, NFC 23 (OT)	Aloha Stadium, Honolulu (50,031)
	Mark Brunell, Jacksonville, player of the game	
Feb. 1, 1998	AFC 29, NFC 24	Aloha Stadium, Honolulu (49,995)
	Warren Moon, Seattle, player of the game	
Feb. 7, 1999	AFC 23, NFC 10	Aloha Stadium, Honolulu (50,075)
	Keyshawn Johnson, N.Y. Jets and Ty Law, New England, co-players of the game	
Feb. 6, 2000	NFC 51, AFC 31	Aloha Stadium, Honolulu (50,112)
	Randy Moss, Minnesota, player of the game	
Feb. 4, 2001	AFC 38, NFC 17	Aloha Stadium, Honolulu (50,128)
	Rich Gannon, Oakland, player of the game	
Feb. 9, 2002	AFC 38, NFC 30	Aloha Stadium, Honolulu (50,301)
	Rich Gannon, Oakland, player of the game	
Feb. 2, 2003	AFC 45, NFC 20	Aloha Stadium, Honolulu (50,125)
	Ricky Williams, Miami, player of the game	
Feb. 8, 2004	NFC 55, AFC 52	Aloha Stadium, Honolulu (50,127)
	Marc Bulger, St. Louis, player of the game	
Feb. 13, 2005	NFC 38, NFC 27	Aloha Stadium, Honolulu (50,225)
	Peyton Manning, Indianapolis, player of the game	
Feb. 12, 2006	NFC 23, AFC 17	Aloha Stadium, Honolulu (50,190)
	Derrick Brooks, Tampa Bay, player of the game	
Feb. 10, 2007	AFC 31, NFC 28	Aloha Stadium, Honolulu (50,410)
	Carson Palmer, Cincinnati, player of the game	

Compiled by Elias Sports Bureau
*NFL record.

MONDAY NIGHT RECORDS

SCORING
TOUCHDOWNS
Most Touchdowns, Career
- 36 Jerry Rice, San Francisco, 1985-2000; Oakland, 2001-04; Seattle 2004
- 24 Emmitt Smith, Dallas, 1990-2002; Arizona 2003-04
- 19 Marcus Allen, L.A. Raiders, 1982-1992; Kansas City, 1993-97

Most Touchdowns, Game
- 4 Ron Johnson, N.Y. Giants at Philadelphia, Oct. 2, 1972
  Earl Campbell, Houston vs. Miami, Nov. 20, 1978
  Marcus Allen, L.A. Raiders vs. San Diego, Sept. 24, 1984
  Eric Dickerson, Indianapolis vs. Denver, Oct. 31, 1988
  Emmitt Smith, Dallas at N.Y. Giants, Sept. 4, 1995
  Marshall Faulk, St. Louis at Tampa Bay, Dec. 18, 2000

FIELD GOALS
Most Field Goals, Career
- 51 Gary Anderson, Pittsburgh, 1982-1994; Philadelphia, 1995-96; San Francisco, 1997; Minnesota, 1998-2002; Tennessee, 2003-04
- 43 Jason Elam, Denver, 1993-2006
- 35 Morten Andersen, New Orleans 1982-1994; Atlanta, 1995-2000; N.Y. Giants, 2001; Kansas City, 2002-03; Minnesota, 2004; Atlanta, 2006

Most Field Goals, Game
- 7 Chris Boniol, Dallas vs. Green Bay, Nov. 18, 1996*
  Billy Cundiff, Dallas at N.Y. Giants, Sept. 15, 2003 (OT)*
- 5 Tim Mazzetti, Atlanta vs. Los Angeles, Oct. 30, 1978
  Roger Ruzek, Dallas at L.A. Rams, Dec. 21, 1987
  Rich Karlis, Minnesota vs. Cincinnati, Dec. 25, 1989
  Nick Lowery, Kansas City vs. Denver, Sept. 20, 1993
  Chris Jacke, Green Bay vs. San Francisco, Oct. 14, 1996 (OT)
  Richie Cunningham, Dallas vs. Philadelphia, Sept. 15, 1997

RUSHING
YARDS GAINED
Most Yards Gained, Career
- 2,434 Emmitt Smith, Dallas, 1990-2002; Arizona, 2003-04
- 1,897 Tony Dorsett, Dallas, 1977-1987; Denver, 1988
- 1,769 Thurman Thomas, Buffalo, 1988-1999; Miami, 2000

Most Yards Gained, Game
- 221 Bo Jackson, L.A. Raiders at Seattle, Nov. 30, 1987
- 216 Ricky Williams, Miami vs. Chicago, Dec. 9, 2002
- 214 Thurman Thomas, Buffalo at N.Y. Jets, Sept. 24, 1990

Longest Run From Scrimmage, Game
- 99 Tony Dorsett, Dallas at Minnesota, Jan. 3, 1983 (TD)*
- 91 Bo Jackson, L.A. Raiders at Seattle, Nov. 30, 1987 (TD)
- 83 James Lofton, Green Bay at N.Y. Giants, Sept. 20, 1982 (TD)

TOUCHDOWNS
Most Rushing Touchdowns, Career
- 23 Emmitt Smith, Dallas, 1990-2002; Arizona, 2003-04
- 17 Marcus Allen, L.A. Raiders, 1982-1992; Kansas City, 1993-97
- 14 Eric Dickerson, L.A. Rams, 1983-87; Indianapolis, 1987-1991; L.A. Raiders, 1992; Atlanta, 1993

Most Rushing Touchdowns, Game
- 4 Earl Campbell, Houston vs. Miami, Nov. 20, 1978
  Eric Dickerson, Indianapolis vs. Denver, Oct. 31, 1988
  Emmitt Smith, Dallas at N.Y. Giants, Sept. 4, 1995

PASSING
YARDS GAINED
Most Yards Gained, Career
- 9,654 Dan Marino, Miami, 1983-1999
- 7,547 Brett Favre, Atlanta, 1991; Green Bay, 1992-2006
- 5,148 Joe Montana, San Francisco, 1979-1992; Kansas City, 1993-94

Most Yards Gained, Game
- 458 Joe Montana, San Francisco at L.A. Rams, Dec. 11, 1989
- 448 Marc Bulger, St. Louis at Green Bay, Nov. 29, 2004
- 447 Ken Anderson, Cincinnati vs. Buffalo, Nov. 17, 1975

Longest Pass Play
- 99 Brett Favre to Robert Brooks, Green Bay at Chicago, Sept. 11, 1995 (TD)*
- 97 Bernie Kosar to Webster Slaughter, Cleveland vs. Chicago, Oct. 23, 1989 (TD)
- 95 Joe Montana to John Taylor, San Francisco at L.A. Rams, Dec. 11, 1989 (TD)

TOUCHDOWNS
Most Touchdown Passes, Career
- 74 Dan Marino, Miami, 1983-1999
- 55 Brett Favre, Atlanta, 1991; Green Bay, 1992-2006
- 42 Steve Young, Tampa Bay, 1985-86; San Francisco, 1987-1999

Most Touchdown Passes, Game
- 5 Dave Krieg, Seattle vs. L.A. Raiders, Nov. 28, 1988
  Jim Kelly, Buffalo vs. Cincinnati, Oct. 21, 1991
  Vinny Testaverde, N.Y. Jets vs. Miami, Oct. 23, 2000 (OT)

RECEIVING
PASS RECEPTIONS
Most Pass Receptions, Career
- 254 Jerry Rice, San Francisco, 1985-2000; Oakland, 2001-04; Seattle, 2004
- 124 Andre Reed, Buffalo, 1985-1999; Washington, 2000
- 123 Cris Carter, Philadelphia, 1987-89; Minnesota, 1990-2001; Miami, 2002

Most Pass Receptions, Game
- 14 Herman Moore, Detroit vs. Chicago, Dec. 4, 1995
  Jerry Rice, San Francisco vs. Minnesota, Dec. 18, 1995
- 13 Andre Reed, Buffalo vs. Denver, Sept. 18, 1989
  Terrell Owens, San Francisco vs. Philadelphia, Nov. 25, 2002

YARDS GAINED
Most Yards Gained, Career
- 4,029 Jerry Rice, San Francisco, 1985-2000; Oakland, 2001-04; Seattle, 2004
- 1,783 Andre Reed, Buffalo, 1985-1999; Washington, 2000
- 1,537 Art Monk, Washington 1980-1993; N.Y. Jets, 1994; Philadelphia, 1995

Most Yards Gained, Game
- 289 Jerry Rice, San Francisco vs. Minnesota, Dec. 18, 1995
- 286 John Taylor, San Francisco at L.A. Rams, Dec. 11, 1989
- 260 Wes Chandler, San Diego vs. Cincinnati, Dec. 20, 1982

TOUCHDOWNS

Most Receiving Touchdowns, Career
- 34 Jerry Rice, San Francisco, 1985-2000; Oakland, 2001-04; Seattle, 2004
- 16 Terrell Owens, San Francisco, 1996-2003; Philadelphia, 2004-05; Dallas, 2006
- 15 Mark Clayton, Miami 1983-1992; Green Bay, 1993

Most Receiving Touchdowns, Game
- 3 Ron Johnson, N.Y. Giants at Philadelphia, Oct. 2, 1972
  - Wesley Walker, N.Y. Jets at Detroit, Dec. 6, 1982
  - Steve Largent, Seattle at San Diego, Oct. 29, 1984
  - Mark Clayton, Miami vs. Dallas, Dec. 17, 1984
  - Jerry Rice, San Francisco vs. Chicago, Dec. 14, 1987
  - Jerry Rice, San Francisco vs. Minnesota, Dec. 18, 1995
  - Lamar Thomas, Miami vs. Denver, Dec. 21, 1998
  - Ed McCaffrey, Denver vs. Miami, Sept. 13, 1999
  - Randy Moss, Minnesota vs. N.Y. Giants, Nov. 19, 2001
  - Isaac Bruce, St. Louis at New Orleans, Dec. 17, 2001
  - Terrell Owens, Philadelphia at Dallas, Nov. 15, 2004
  - Drew Bennett, Tennessee vs. Kansas City, Dec. 13, 2004
  - Marvin Harrison, Indianapolis vs. Cincinnati, Dec. 18, 2006

YARDS FROM SCRIMMAGE

Most Scrimmage Yards, Career
- 4,116 Jerry Rice, San Francisco, 1985-2000; Oakland, 2001-04; Seattle, 2004
- 2,836 Emmitt Smith, Dallas, 1990-2002; Arizona, 2003-04
- 2,567 Tony Dorsett, Dallas, 1977-1987; Denver, 1988

INTERCEPTIONS BY

Most Interceptions, Career
- 11 Everson Walls, Dallas, 1981-89; N.Y. Giants, 1990-92; Cleveland, 1992-93
- 9 Merton Hanks, San Francisco, 1991-98; Seattle, 1999
- 8 Emmitt Thomas, Kansas City, 1966-1978

Most Interceptions, Game
- 4 Dick Anderson, Miami vs. Pittsburgh, Dec. 3, 1973*
- 3 Johnny Robinson, Kansas City at Baltimore, Sept. 28, 1970
  - Charlie Babb, Miami vs. Oakland, Sept. 22, 1975
  - Charles Phillips, Oakland vs. Denver, Dec. 8, 1975
  - Mark Murphy, Washington at San Diego, Oct. 31, 1983
  - Ken Easley, Seattle at San Diego, Oct. 29, 1984
  - Dwayne Harper, San Diego vs. Oakland, Nov. 27, 1995
  - Marcus Coleman, N.Y. Jets vs. Miami, Oct. 23, 2000 (OT)

Longest Interception Return
- 102 Eddie Anderson, L.A. Raiders at Miami, Dec. 14, 1992 (TD)
- 101 Lito Sheppard, Philadelphia at Dallas, Nov. 15, 2004 (TD)
- 98 Marcus Coleman, N.Y. Jets vs. Miami, Dec. 27, 1999 (TD)
  - Rod Woodson, Oakland at Denver, Nov. 11, 2002 (TD)

SACKS

Most Sacks, Career
- 24.5 Bruce Smith, Buffalo, 1985-1999; Washington, 2000-03
- 20.0 Richard Dent, Chicago, 1983-1993, 1995; San Francisco, 1994; Indianapolis, 1996; Philadelphia, 1997
- 18.0 Kevin Greene, L.A. Rams, 1985-1992; Pittsburgh, 1993-95; Carolina, 1996, 1998-99; San Francisco, 1997

PUNTING

Highest Punt Average, Career (Minimum: 25 Punts)
- 46.7 Shane Lechler, Oakland, 2000-06
- 45.5 Hunter Smith, Indianapolis, 1999-2006
- 44.5 Tom Tupa, Phoenix, 1988-1991; Indianapolis, 1992; Cleveland, 1994-95; New England, 1996-98; N.Y. Jets, 1999-2001; Tampa Bay, 2002-03; Washington, 2004

Longest Punt
- 90 Rodney Williams, N.Y. Giants at Denver, Sept. 10, 2001
- 83 Bryan Barker, Jacksonville vs. N.Y. Jets, Oct. 11, 1999
- 74 Craig Colquitt, Pittsburgh vs. Oakland, Dec. 7, 1981

PUNT RETURNS

Longest Punt Return
- 95 John Taylor, San Francisco vs. Washington, Nov. 21, 1988 (TD)
- 94 Dennis McKinnon, Chicago vs. N.Y. Giants, Sept. 14, 1987 (TD)
- 91 JoJo Townsell, N.Y. Jets vs. Seattle, Nov. 9, 1987 (TD)
  - Nate Burleson, Minnesota at Indianapolis, Nov. 8, 2004 (TD)

KICKOFF RETURNS

Longest Kickoff Return
- 105 Terry Fair, Detroit vs. Tampa Bay, Sept. 28, 1998 (TD)
- 102 Harold Hart, Oakland at Miami, Sept. 22, 1975 (TD)
- 101 Roell Preston, Green Bay vs. Minnesota, Oct. 5, 1998 (TD)

FUMBLES

Longest Fumble Return
- 99 Don Griffin, San Francisco vs. Chicago, Dec. 23, 1991 (TD)
- 96 Joe Lavender, Philadelphia vs. Dallas, Sept. 23, 1974 (TD)
- 93 Adam Archuleta, St. Louis vs. Tampa Bay, Oct. 18, 2004 (TD)

MONDAY NIGHT FOOTBALL, 1970-2006

(Home Team in capitals, games listed in chronological order.)

2006

Minnesota 19, WASHINGTON 16
San Diego 27, OAKLAND 0
JACKSONVILLE 9, Pittsburgh 0
NEW ORLEANS 23, Atlanta 3
PHILADELPHIA 31, Green Bay 9
DENVER 13, Baltimore 3
Chicago 24, ARIZONA 23
New York Giants 36, DALLAS 22
New England 31, MINNESOTA 7
SEATTLE 16, Oakland 0
CAROLINA 24, Tampa Bay 10
JACKSONVILLE 26, New York Giants 10
SEATTLE 34, Green Bay 24
PHILADELPHIA 27, Carolina 24
Chicago 42, ST. LOUIS 27
INDIANAPOLIS 34, Cincinnati 16
New York Jets 13, MIAMI 10

2005

ATLANTA 14, Philadelphia 10
New York Giants 27, NEW ORLEANS 10
Washington 14, DALLAS 13
DENVER 30, Kansas City 10
CAROLINA 32, Green Bay 29
Pittsburgh 24, SAN DIEGO 22
INDIANAPOLIS 45, St. Louis 28
ATLANTA 27, New York Jets 14
PITTSBURGH 20, Baltimore 19
Indianapolis 40, NEW ENGLAND 21
Dallas 21, PHILADELPHIA 20
Minnesota 20, GREEN BAY 17
INDIANAPOLIS 26, Pittsburgh 7
Seattle 42, PHILADELPHIA 0
ATLANTA 36, New Orleans 17
BALTIMORE 48, Green Bay 3
New England 31, NEW YORK JETS 21

2004

Green Bay 24, CAROLINA 14
PHILADELPHIA 27, Minnesota 16
Dallas 21, WASHINGTON 18
Kansas City 27, BALTIMORE 24
Tennessee 48, GREEN BAY 27
ST. LOUIS 28, Tampa Bay 21
CINCINNATI 23, Denver 10
NEW YORK JETS 41, Miami 14
INDIANAPOLIS 31, Minnesota 28
Philadelphia 49, DALLAS 21
New England 27, KANSAS CITY 19
GREEN BAY 45, St. Louis 17
Dallas 43, SEATTLE 39
Kansas City 49, TENNESSEE 38
MIAMI 29, New England 28
ST. LOUIS 20, Philadelphia 7

2003

Tampa Bay 17, Philadelphia 0
Dallas 35, NEW YORK GIANTS 32 (OT)
DENVER 31, Oakland 10
Green Bay 38, CHICAGO 23
Indianapolis 38, TAMPA BAY 35 (OT)
ST. LOUIS 36, Atlanta 0
Kansas City 17, OAKLAND 10
Miami 26, SAN DIEGO 10
New England 30, DENVER 26
Philadelphia 17, GREEN BAY 14
SAN FRANCISCO 30, Pittsburgh 14
TAMPA BAY 19, New York Giants 13
NEW YORK JETS 24, Tennessee 17
St. Louis 26, CLEVELAND 20
Philadelphia 34, MIAMI 27
Green Bay 41, OAKLAND 7

2002

NEW ENGLAND 30, Pittsburgh 14
Philadelphia 37, WASHINGTON 7
TAMPA BAY 26, St. Louis 14
BALTIMORE 34, Denver 23
Green Bay 34, CHICAGO 21
San Francisco 28, SEATTLE 21
PITTSBURGH 28, Indianapolis 10
PHILADELPHIA 17, New York Giants 3
GREEN BAY 24, Miami 10
Oakland 34, DENVER 10
ST. LOUIS 21, Chicago 16
Philadelphia 38, SAN FRANCISCO 17
OAKLAND 26, New York Jets 20
MIAMI 27, Chicago 9
TENNESSEE 24, New England 7
Pittsburgh 17, TAMPA BAY 7
ST. LOUIS 31, San Francisco 20

2001

DENVER 31, New York Giants 20
GREEN BAY 37, Washington 0
San Francisco 19, NEW YORK JETS 17
St. Louis 35, DETROIT 0
DALLAS 9, Washington 7
Philadelphia 10, NEW YORK GIANTS 9
PITTSBURGH 34, Tennessee 7
OAKLAND 38, Denver 28
Baltimore 16, TENNESSEE 10
MINNESOTA 28, New York Giants 16
Tampa Bay 24, ST. LOUIS 17
Green Bay 28, JACKSONVILLE 21
MIAMI 41, Indianapolis 6
St. Louis 34, NEW ORLEANS 21
BALTIMORE 19, Minnesota 3

2000

ST. LOUIS 41, Denver 36
NEW YORK JETS 20, New England 19
Dallas 27, WASHINGTON 21
INDIANAPOLIS 43, Jacksonville 14
KANSAS CITY 24, Seattle 17
MINNESOTA 30, Tampa Bay 23
TENNESSEE 27, Jacksonville 13
NEW YORK JETS 40, Miami 37 (OT)
Tennessee 27, WASHINGTON 21
GREEN BAY 26, Minnesota 20 (OT)
DENVER 27, Oakland 24
Washington 33, ST. LOUIS 20
CAROLINA 31, Green Bay 14
NEW ENGLAND 30, Kansas City 24
INDIANAPOLIS 44, Buffalo 20
TAMPA BAY 38, St. Louis 35
TENNESSEE 31, Dallas 0

1999

Miami 38, DENVER 21
DALLAS 24, Atlanta 7
San Francisco 24, ARIZONA 10
Buffalo 23, MIAMI 18
Jacksonville 16, NEW YORK JETS 6
NEW YORK GIANTS 13, Dallas 10
PITTSBURGH 13, Atlanta 9
Seattle 27, GREEN BAY 7
MINNESOTA 27, Dallas 17
New York Jets 24, NEW ENGLAND 17
DENVER 27, Oakland 21 (OT)
Green Bay 20, SAN FRANCISCO 3
TAMPA BAY 24, Minnesota 17
JACKSONVILLE 27, Denver 24
MINNESOTA 24, Green Bay 20
New York Jets 38, MIAMI 31
ATLANTA 34, San Francisco 29

1998

DENVER 27, New England 21
San Francisco 45, WASHINGTON 10
Dallas 31, NEW YORK GIANTS 7
DETROIT 27, Tampa Bay 6
Minnesota 37, GREEN BAY 24
JACKSONVILLE 28, Miami 21
New York Jets 24, NEW ENGLAND 14
Pittsburgh 20, KANSAS CITY 13
Dallas 34, PHILADELPHIA 0
PITTSBURGH 27, Green Bay 20
Denver 30, KANSAS CITY 7
NEW ENGLAND 26, Miami 23
SAN FRANCISCO 31, New York Giants 7
TAMPA BAY 24, Green Bay 22
SAN FRANCISCO 35, Detroit 13
MIAMI 31, Denver 21
JACKSONVILLE 21, Pittsburgh 3

1997
GREEN BAY 38, Chicago 24
Kansas City 28, OAKLAND 27
DALLAS 21, Philadelphia 20
JACKSONVILLE 30, Pittsburgh 21
San Francisco 34, CAROLINA 21
DENVER 34, New England 13
WASHINGTON 21, Dallas 16
Buffalo 9, INDIANAPOLIS 6
Green Bay 28, NEW ENGLAND 10
Chicago 36, MIAMI 33 (OT)
KANSAS CITY 13, Pittsburgh 10
San Francisco 24, PHILADELPHIA 12
MIAMI 30, Buffalo 13
DENVER 31, Oakland 3
Green Bay 27, MINNESOTA 11
Carolina 23, DALLAS 13
SAN FRANCISCO 34, Denver 17
New England 14, MIAMI 12

1996
CHICAGO 22, Dallas 6
GREEN BAY 39, Philadelphia 13
PITTSBURGH 24, Buffalo 6
INDIANAPOLIS 10, Miami 6
Dallas 23, PHILADELPHIA 19
Pittsburgh 17, KANSAS CITY 7
GREEN BAY 23, San Francisco 20 (OT)
Oakland 23, SAN DIEGO 14
Chicago 15, MINNESOTA 13
Denver 22, OAKLAND 21
SAN DIEGO 27, Detroit 21
DALLAS 21, Green Bay 6
Pittsburgh 24, MIAMI 17
San Francisco 34, ATLANTA 10
OAKLAND 26, Kansas City 7
MIAMI 16, Buffalo 14
SAN FRANCISCO 24, Detroit 14

1995
Dallas 35, NEW YORK GIANTS 0
Green Bay 27, CHICAGO 24
MIAMI 23, Pittsburgh 10
DETROIT 27, San Francisco 24
Buffalo 22, CLEVELAND 19
KANSAS CITY 29, San Diego 23 (OT)
DENVER 27, Oakland 0
NEW ENGLAND 27, Buffalo 14
Chicago 14, MINNESOTA 6
DALLAS 34, Philadelphia 12
PITTSBURGH 20, Cleveland 3
San Francisco 44, MIAMI 20
SAN DIEGO 12, Oakland 6
DETROIT 27, Chicago 7
MIAMI 13, Kansas City 6
SAN FRANCISCO 37, Minnesota 30
Dallas 37, ARIZONA 13

1994
SAN FRANCISCO 44, L.A. Raiders 14
PHILADELPHIA 30, Chicago 22
Detroit 20, DALLAS 17 (OT)
BUFFALO 27, Denver 20
PITTSBURGH 30, Houston 14
Minnesota 27, NEW YORK GIANTS 10
Kansas City 31, DENVER 28
PHILADELPHIA 21, Houston 6
Green Bay 33, CHICAGO 6
DALLAS 38, New York Giants 10
PITTSBURGH 23, Buffalo 10
New York Giants 13, HOUSTON 10
San Francisco 35, NEW ORLEANS 14
L.A. Raiders 24, SAN DIEGO 17
MIAMI 45, Kansas City 28
Dallas 24, NEW ORLEANS 16
MINNESOTA 21, San Francisco 14

1993
WASHINGTON 35, Dallas 16
CLEVELAND 23, San Francisco 13
KANSAS CITY 15, Denver 7
Pittsburgh 45, ATLANTA 17
MIAMI 17, Washington 10
BUFFALO 35, Houston 7
L.A. Raiders 23, DENVER 20
Minnesota 19, CHICAGO 12
BUFFALO 24, Washington 10
KANSAS CITY 23, Green Bay 16
PITTSBURGH 23, Buffalo 0
SAN FRANCISCO 42, New Orleans 7
San Diego 31, INDIANAPOLIS 0
DALLAS 23, Philadelphia 17
Pittsburgh 21, MIAMI 20
New York Giants 24, NEW ORLEANS 14
SAN DIEGO 45, Miami 20
Philadelphia 37, SAN FRANCISCO 34 (OT)

1992
DALLAS 23, Washington 10
Miami 27, CLEVELAND 23
New York Giants 27, CHICAGO 14
KANSAS CITY 27, L.A. Raiders 7
PHILADELPHIA 31, Dallas 7
WASHINGTON 34, Denver 3
PITTSBURGH 20, Cincinnati 0
Buffalo 24, NEW YORK JETS 20
Minnesota 38, CHICAGO 10
San Francisco 41, ATLANTA 3
Buffalo 26, MIAMI 20
NEW ORLEANS 20, Washington 3
SEATTLE 16, Denver 13 (OT)
HOUSTON 24, Chicago 7
MIAMI 20, L.A. Raiders 7
Dallas 41, ATLANTA 17
SAN FRANCISCO 24, Detroit 6

1991
NEW YORK GIANTS 16, San Francisco 14
Washington 33, DALLAS 31
HOUSTON 17, Kansas City 7
CHICAGO 19, New York Jets 13 (OT)
WASHINGTON 23, Philadelphia 0
KANSAS CITY 33, Buffalo 6
New York Giants 23, PITTSBURGH 20
BUFFALO 35, Cincinnati 16
KANSAS CITY 24, L.A. Raiders 21
PHILADELPHIA 30, New York Giants 7
Chicago 34, MINNESOTA 17
Buffalo 41, MIAMI 27
San Francisco 33, L.A. RAMS 10
Philadelphia 13, HOUSTON 6
MIAMI 37, Cincinnati 13
NEW ORLEANS 27, L.A. Raiders 0
SAN FRANCISCO 52, Chicago 14

1990
San Francisco 13, NEW ORLEANS 12
DENVER 24, Kansas City 23
Buffalo 30, NEW YORK JETS 7
SEATTLE 31, Cincinnati 16
Cleveland 30, DENVER 29
PHILADELPHIA 32, Minnesota 24
Cincinnati 34, CLEVELAND 13
PITTSBURGH 41, L.A. Rams 10
New York Giants 24, INDIANAPOLIS 7
PHILADELPHIA 28, Washington 14
L.A. Raiders 13, MIAMI 10
HOUSTON 27, Buffalo 24
SAN FRANCISCO 7, New York Giants 3
L.A. Raiders 38, DETROIT 31
San Francisco 26, L.A. RAMS 10
NEW ORLEANS 20, L.A. Rams 17

1989
New York Giants 27, WASHINGTON 24
Denver 28, BUFFALO 14
CINCINNATI 21, Cleveland 14
CHICAGO 27, Philadelphia 13
L.A. Raiders 14, NEW YORK JETS 7
BUFFALO 23, L.A. Rams 20
CLEVELAND 27, Chicago 7
NEW YORK GIANTS 24, Minnesota 14
SAN FRANCISCO 31, New Orleans 13
HOUSTON 26, Cincinnati 24
Denver 14, WASHINGTON 10
SAN FRANCISCO 34, New York Giants 24
SEATTLE 17, Buffalo 16
San Francisco 30, L.A. RAMS 27
NEW ORLEANS 30, Philadelphia 20
MINNESOTA 29, Cincinnati 21

1988
NEW YORK GIANTS 27, Washington 20
Dallas 17, PHOENIX 14
CLEVELAND 23, Indianapolis 17
L.A. Raiders 30, DENVER 27 (OT)
NEW ORLEANS 20, Dallas 17
PHILADELPHIA 24, New York Giants 13
Buffalo 37, NEW YORK JETS 14
CHICAGO 10, San Francisco 9
INDIANAPOLIS 55, Denver 23
HOUSTON 24, Cleveland 17
Buffalo 31, MIAMI 6
SAN FRANCISCO 37, Washington 21
SEATTLE 35, L.A. Raiders 27
L.A. RAMS 23, Chicago 3
MIAMI 38, Cleveland 31
MINNESOTA 28, Chicago 27

1987
CHICAGO 34, New York Giants 19
NEW YORK JETS 43, New England 24
San Francisco 41, NEW YORK GIANTS 21
DENVER 30, L.A. Raiders 14
Washington 13, DALLAS 7
CLEVELAND 30, L.A. Rams 17
MINNESOTA 34, Denver 27
DALLAS 33, New York Giants 24
NEW YORK JETS 30, Seattle 14
DENVER 31, Chicago 29
L.A. Rams 30, WASHINGTON 26
L.A. Raiders 37, SEATTLE 14
MIAMI 37, New York Jets 28
SAN FRANCISCO 41, Chicago 0
Dallas 29, L.A. RAMS 21
New England 24, MIAMI 10

1986
DALLAS 31, New York Giants 28
Denver 21, PITTSBURGH 10
Chicago 25, GREEN BAY 12
Dallas 31, ST. LOUIS 7
SEATTLE 33, San Diego 7
CINCINNATI 24, Pittsburgh 22
NEW YORK JETS 22, Denver 10
NEW YORK GIANTS 27, Washington 20
L.A. Rams 20, CHICAGO 17
CLEVELAND 26, Miami 16
WASHINGTON 14, San Francisco 6
MIAMI 45, New York Jets 3
New York Giants 21, SAN FRANCISCO 17
SEATTLE 37, L.A. Raiders 0
Chicago 16, DETROIT 13
New England 34, MIAMI 27

1985
DALLAS 44, Washington 14
CLEVELAND 17, Pittsburgh 7
L.A. Rams 35, SEATTLE 24
Cincinnati 37, PITTSBURGH 24
WASHINGTON 27, St. Louis 10
NEW YORK JETS 23, Miami 7
CHICAGO 23, Green Bay 7
L.A. RAIDERS 34, San Diego 21
ST. LOUIS 21, Dallas 10
DENVER 17, San Francisco 16
WASHINGTON 23, New York Giants 21
SAN FRANCISCO 19, Seattle 6
MIAMI 38, Chicago 24
L.A. Rams 27, SAN FRANCISCO 20
MIAMI 30, New England 27
L.A. Raiders 16, L.A. RAMS 6

1984
Dallas 20, L.A. RAMS 13
SAN FRANCISCO 37, Washington 31
Miami 21, BUFFALO 17
L.A. RAIDERS 33, San Diego 30
PITTSBURGH 38, Cincinnati 17
San Francisco 31, NEW YORK GIANTS 10
DENVER 17, Green Bay 14
L.A. Rams 24, ATLANTA 10
Seattle 24, SAN DIEGO 0
WASHINGTON 27, Atlanta 14
SEATTLE 17, L.A. Raiders 14
NEW ORLEANS 27, Pittsburgh 24
MIAMI 28, New York Jets 17
SAN DIEGO 20, Chicago 7
L.A. Raiders 24, DETROIT 3
MIAMI 28, Dallas 21

1983
Dallas 31, WASHINGTON 30
San Diego 17, KANSAS CITY 14
L.A. RAIDERS 27, Miami 14
NEW YORK GIANTS 27, Green Bay 3
New York Jets 34, BUFFALO 10
Pittsburgh 24, CINCINNATI 14
GREEN BAY 48, Washington 47
ST. LOUIS 20, NEW YORK Giants 20 (OT)
Washington 27, SAN DIEGO 24
DETROIT 15, New York Giants 9
L.A. Rams 36, ATLANTA 13
New York Jets 31, NEW ORLEANS 28
MIAMI 38, Cincinnati 14
DETROIT 13, Minnesota 2
Green Bay 12, TAMPA BAY 9 (OT)
SAN FRANCISCO 42, Dallas 17

1982
Pittsburgh 36, DALLAS 28
Green Bay 27, NEW YORK GIANTS 19
L.A. RAIDERS 28, San Diego 24
TAMPA BAY 23, Miami 17
New York Jets 28, DETROIT 13
Dallas 37, HOUSTON 7
SAN DIEGO 50, Cincinnati 34
MIAMI 27, Buffalo 10
MINNESOTA 31, Dallas 27

1981
San Diego 44, CLEVELAND 14
Oakland 36, MINNESOTA 10
Dallas 35, NEW ENGLAND 21
Los Angeles 24, CHICAGO 7
PHILADELPHIA 16, Atlanta 13
BUFFALO 31, Miami 21
DETROIT 48, Chicago 17
PITTSBURGH 26, Houston 13
DENVER 19, Minnesota 17
DALLAS 27, Buffalo 14
SEATTLE 44, San Diego 23
ATLANTA 31, Minnesota 30
MIAMI 13, Philadelphia 10
OAKLAND 30, Pittsburgh 27
LOS ANGELES 21, Atlanta 16
SAN DIEGO 23, Oakland 10

1980
Dallas 17, WASHINGTON 3
Houston 16, CLEVELAND 7
PHILADELPHIA 35, New York Giants 3
NEW ENGLAND 23, Denver 14
CHICAGO 23, Tampa Bay 0
DENVER 20, Washington 17
Oakland 45, PITTSBURGH 34
NEW YORK JETS 17, Miami 14
CLEVELAND 27, Chicago 21
HOUSTON 38, New England 34
Oakland 19, SEATTLE 17
Los Angeles 27, NEW ORLEANS 7
OAKLAND 9, Denver 3
MIAMI 16, New England 13 (OT)
LOS ANGELES 38, Dallas 14
SAN DIEGO 26, Pittsburgh 17

1979
Pittsburgh 16, NEW ENGLAND 13 (OT)
Atlanta 14, PHILADELPHIA 10
WASHINGTON 27, New York Giants 0
CLEVELAND 26, Dallas 7
GREEN BAY 27, New England 14
OAKLAND 13, Miami 3
NEW YORK JETS 14, Minnesota 7
PITTSBURGH 42, Denver 7
Seattle 31, ATLANTA 28
Houston 9, MIAMI 6
Philadelphia 31, DALLAS 21
LOS ANGELES 20, Atlanta 14
SEATTLE 30, New York Jets 7
Oakland 42, NEW ORLEANS 35
HOUSTON 20, Pittsburgh 17
SAN DIEGO 17, Denver 7

1978
DALLAS 38, Baltimore 0
MINNESOTA 12, Denver 9 (OT)
Baltimore 34, NEW ENGLAND 27
Minnesota 24, CHICAGO 20
WASHINGTON 9, Dallas 5
MIAMI 21, Cincinnati 0
DENVER 16, Chicago 7
Houston 24, PITTSBURGH 17
ATLANTA 15, Los Angeles 7
BALTIMORE 21, Washington 17
Oakland 34, CINCINNATI 21
HOUSTON 35, Miami 30
Pittsburgh 24, SAN FRANCISCO 7
SAN DIEGO 40, Chicago 7
Cincinnati 20, LOS ANGELES 19
MIAMI 23, New England 3

1977
PITTSBURGH 27, San Francisco 0
CLEVELAND 30, New England 27 (OT)
Oakland 37, KANSAS CITY 28
CHICAGO 24, Los Angeles 23
PITTSBURGH 20, Cincinnati 14
LOS ANGELES 35, Minnesota 3
ST. LOUIS 28, New York Giants 0
BALTIMORE 10, Washington 3
St. Louis 24, DALLAS 17
WASHINGTON 10, Green Bay 9
OAKLAND 34, Buffalo 13
MIAMI 17, Baltimore 6
Dallas 42, SAN FRANCISCO 35

1976
Miami 30, BUFFALO 21
Oakland 24, KANSAS CITY 21
Washington 20, PHILADELPHIA 17 (OT)
MINNESOTA 17, Pittsburgh 6
San Francisco 16, LOS ANGELES 0
NEW ENGLAND 41, New York Jets 7
WASHINGTON 20, St. Louis 10
BALTIMORE 38, Houston 14
CINCINNATI 20, Los Angeles 12
DALLAS 17, Buffalo 10
Baltimore 17, MIAMI 16
SAN FRANCISCO 20, Minnesota 16
OAKLAND 35, Cincinnati 20

1975
Oakland 31, MIAMI 21
DENVER 23, Green Bay 13
Dallas 36, DETROIT 10
WASHINGTON 27, St. Louis 17
New York Giants 17, BUFFALO 14
Minnesota 13, CHICAGO 9
Los Angeles 42, PHILADELPHIA 3
Kansas City 34, DALLAS 31
CINCINNATI 33, Buffalo 24
Pittsburgh 32, HOUSTON 9
MIAMI 20, New England 7
OAKLAND 17, Denver 10
SAN DIEGO 24, New York Jets 16

1974
BUFFALO 21, Oakland 20
PHILADELPHIA 13, Dallas 10
WASHINGTON 30, Denver 3
MIAMI 21, New York Jets 17
DETROIT 17, San Francisco 13
CHICAGO 10, Green Bay 9
PITTSBURGH 24, Atlanta 17
Los Angeles 15, SAN FRANCISCO 13
Minnesota 28, ST. LOUIS 24
Kansas City 42, DENVER 34
Pittsburgh 28, NEW ORLEANS 7
MIAMI 24, Cincinnati 3
Washington 23, LOS ANGELES 17

1973
GREEN BAY 23, New York Jets 7
DALLAS 40, New Orleans 3
DETROIT 31, Atlanta 6
WASHINGTON 14, Dallas 7
Miami 17, CLEVELAND 9
DENVER 23, Oakland 23
BUFFALO 23, Kansas City 14
PITTSBURGH 21, Washington 16
KANSAS CITY 19, Chicago 7
ATLANTA 20, Minnesota 14
SAN FRANCISCO 20, Green Bay 6
MIAMI 30, Pittsburgh 26
LOS ANGELES 40, New York Giants 6

1972
Washington 24, MINNESOTA 21
Kansas City 20, NEW ORLEANS 17
New York Giants 27, PHILADELPHIA 12
Oakland 34, HOUSTON 0
Green Bay 24, DETROIT 23
CHICAGO 13, Minnesota 10
DALLAS 28, Detroit 24
Baltimore 24, NEW ENGLAND 17
Cleveland 21, SAN DIEGO 17
WASHINGTON 24, Atlanta 13
MIAMI 31, St. Louis 10
Los Angeles 26, SAN FRANCISCO 16
OAKLAND 24, New York Jets 16

1971
Minnesota 16, DETROIT 13
ST. LOUIS 17, New York Jets 10
Oakland 34, CLEVELAND 20
DALLAS 20, New York Giants 13
KANSAS CITY 38, Pittsburgh 16
MINNESOTA 10, Baltimore 3
GREEN BAY 14, Detroit 14
BALTIMORE 24, Los Angeles 17
SAN DIEGO 20, St. Louis 17
ATLANTA 28, Green Bay 21
MIAMI 34, Chicago 3
Kansas City 26, SAN FRANCISCO 17
Washington 38, LOS ANGELES 24

1970
CLEVELAND 31, New York Jets 21
Kansas City 44, BALTIMORE 24
DETROIT 28, Chicago 14
Green Bay 22, SAN DIEGO 20
OAKLAND 34, Washington 20
MINNESOTA 13, Los Angeles 3
PITTSBURGH 21, Cincinnati 10
Baltimore 13, GREEN BAY 10
St. Louis 38, DALLAS 0
PHILADELPHIA 23, New York Giants 20
Miami 20, ATLANTA 7
Cleveland 21, HOUSTON 10
Detroit 28, LOS ANGELES 23

MONDAY NIGHT WON-LOST RECORDS, 1970-2006
AMERICAN FOOTBALL CONFERENCE

	Balt.	Buff.	Cin.	Cle.	Den.	Hou.	Ind.	Jax.	K.C.	Mia.	N.E.	N.Y.J.	Oak.	Pitt.	S.D.	Tenn.
Total	4-3	17-20	8-17	13-12	24-29-1	0-0	18-10	7-3	20-15	39-33	13-21	17-21	36-23-1	33-22	15-14	16-15
2006	0-1	0-1		1-0			1-0	2-0	0-1	0-1	1-0	1-0	0-2	0-1	1-0	
2005	1-1			1-0			3-0			0-1	1-1	0-2		2-1	0-1	
2004	0-1	1-0		0-1	1-0		2-1		1-1	1-1	1-0					1-1
2003			0-1	1-1	1-0		1-0		1-1	1-0	1-0		0-3	0-1	0-1	0-1
2002	1-0			0-2	0-1				1-1	1-1	0-1		2-0	2-1		1-0
2001	2-0			1-1			0-1	0-1		1-0		0-1	1-0	1-0		0-2
2000		0-1		1-1			2-0	0-2	1-1	0-1	1-1	2-0	0-1			3-0
1999		1-0		1-2			2-0			1-2	0-1	2-1	0-1	1-0		
1998				2-1			2-0	0-2	1-2	1-2	1-0			2-1		
1997		1-1		2-1	0-1		1-0		2-0	1-2	1-2		0-2	0-2		
1996		0-2		1-0	1-0				0-2	1-2			2-1	3-0	1-1	
1995		1-1	0-2	1-0					1-1	2-1	1-0		0-2	1-1	1-1	
1994		1-1		0-2					1-1	1-0		1-1	2-0	0-1	0-3	
1993		2-1		1-0	0-2		0-1		2-0	1-2			1-0	3-0	2-0	0-1
1992		2-0	0-1	0-1	0-2				1-0	2-1		0-1	0-2	1-0		1-0
1991		2-1	0-2						2-1	1-1		0-1	0-2	0-1		1-1
1990		1-1	1-1	1-1	1-1		0-1		0-1	0-1		0-1	2-0	1-0		1-0
1989		1-2	1-2	1-1	2-0							0-1	1-0			1-0
1988		2-0		1-2	0-2		1-1		1-1			0-1	1-1			1-0
1987				1-0	2-1				1-1		1-1	2-1	1-1			
1986		1-0	1-0	1-1					1-2	1-0	1-1	0-1		0-2	0-1	
1985		1-0	1-0	1-0					2-1	0-1	1-0		2-0	0-2	0-1	
1984		0-1	0-1		1-0				3-0		0-1		2-1	1-1	1-2	
1983		0-1	0-2				0-1				2-0		1-0	1-0	1-1	
1982		0-1	0-1						1-1		1-0		1-0	1-0	1-1	0-1
1981		1-1	0-1	1-0					1-1	0-1			2-1	1-1	2-1	0-1
1980			1-1	1-2					1-1	1-2	1-0		3-0	0-2	1-0	2-0
1979			1-0	0-2					0-2	0-2	1-1		2-0	2-1	1-0	2-0
1978		1-2		1-1			2-1			2-1	0-2		1-0	1-1	1-0	2-0
1977		0-1	0-1	1-0			1-1		0-1	1-0	0-1		2-0	2-0		
1976		0-2	1-1				2-0		0-1	1-1	1-0	0-1	2-0	0-1		0-1
1975		0-2	1-0		1-1				1-0	1-1	0-1	0-1	2-0	1-0	1-0	0-1
1974		1-0	0-1		0-2				1-0	2-0		0-1	0-1	2-0		
1973		1-0		0-1	0-0-1				1-1	2-0		0-1	0-0-1	1-1		
1972			1-0				1-0		1-0	1-0	0-1	0-1	2-0			0-1	0-1
1971		0-1					1-1		2-0	1-0		0-1	1-0	0-1	1-0	
1970			0-1	2-0			1-1		1-0	1-0		0-1	1-0	1-0	0-1	0-1

MONDAY NIGHT FOOTBALL ALL-TIME STANDINGS
AMERICAN FOOTBALL CONFERENCE

East	W	L	T	Pct.
Miami	39	33	0	.542
Buffalo	17	20	0	.459
New York Jets	17	21	0	.447
New England	13	21	0	.382

North	W	L	T	Pct.
Pittsburgh	33	22	0	.600
Baltimore	4	3	0	.571
Cleveland	13	12	0	.520
Cincinnati	8	17	0	.320

South	W	L	T	Pct.
Jacksonville	7	3	0	.700
Indianapolis	18	10	0	.643
Tennessee	16	15	0	.516
Houston	0	0	0	.000

West	W	L	T	Pct.
Oakland	36	23	1	.608
Kansas City	20	15	0	.571
San Diego	15	14	0	.517
Denver	24	29	1	.454

From 1970-71, tie games were not included in winning percentage.

MONDAY NIGHT WON-LOST RECORDS, 1970-2006
NATIONAL FOOTBALL CONFERENCE

	Ariz.	Atl.	Car.	Chi.	Dall.	Det.	G.B.	Minn.	N.O.	N.Y.G.	Phil.	St.L.	S.F.	Sea.	T.B.	Wash.
Total	5-11-1	9-19	4-3	18-32	39-29	11-13-1	24-25-1	23-23	7-15	17-30-1	24-20	26-27	37-22	15-8	8-8	25-29
2006	0-1	0-1	1-1	2-0	0-1		0-2	1-1	1-0	1-1	2-0	0-1		2-0	0-1	0-1
2005		3-0	1-0	1-1			0-3	1-0	0-2	1-0	0-3	0-1		1-0		1-0
2004			0-1	2-1			2-1	0-2				2-1	2-1	0-1	0-1	0-1
2003		0-1	0-1	1-0			2-1			0-2		2-1	2-0	1-0	2-1	
2002				0-3			2-0			0-1	3-0	2-1	1-2	0-1	1-1	0-1
2001				1-0	0-1		2-0	1-1	0-1	0-3	1-0	2-1	1-0		1-0	0-2
2000		1-0		1-1			1-1	1-1				1-2		0-1	1-1	1-2
1999	0-1	1-2		1-2			1-2	2-1		1-0			1-2	1-0	1-0	
1998				2-0	1-1		0-3	1-0		0-2	0-1		3-0		1-1	0-1
1997				1-1	1-1	1-2	3-0	0-1			0-2		3-0			1-0
1996		0-1	2-0	2-1	0-2		2-1	0-1			0-2		2-1			
1995	0-1			1-2	3-0	2-0	1-0	0-2		0-1	0-1		2-1			
1994		0-2		2-1	1-0	1-0	2-0	0-2	1-2	2-0			2-1			
1993		0-1		0-1	1-1	0-1	1-0	0-2	1-0	1-1			1-2			1-2
1992		0-2		0-3	2-1	0-1	1-0	1-0	1-0	1-0			2-0		1-0	1-2
1991				2-1	0-1		0-1	1-0	2-1	2-1		0-1	2-1			2-0
1990						0-1	0-1	1-1	1-1	2-0		0-3	3-0	1-0		0-1
1989				1-1			1-1	1-1	2-1		0-2	0-2	3-0	1-0		0-2
1988	0-1			1-2	1-1		1-0	1-0	1-1	1-0	1-0	1-0	1-1	1-0		0-2
1987				1-2	2-1		1-0			0-3		1-2	2-0	0-2		1-1
1986	0-1			2-1	2-0	0-1	0-1		2-1			1-0	0-2	2-0		1-1
1985	1-1			1-1	1-1		0-1			0-1		2-1	1-2	0-2		2-1
1984		0-2		0-1	1-1	0-1	0-1		1-0	0-1		1-1	2-0	2-0		1-1
1983	0-0-1	0-1		1-1	2-0	2-1	0-1		0-1	1-1-1		1-0	1-0		0-1	1-2
1982				1-2	0-1	1-0	1-0			0-1					1-0	
1981		1-2		0-2	2-0	1-0	0-3					1-1	2-0	1-0		
1980				1-1	1-1				0-1	0-1	1-0	2-0		0-1	0-1	0-2
1979		1-2		0-2			1-0	0-1	0-1	0-1	1-1	1-0		2-0		1-0
1978		1-0		0-3	1-1		2-0					0-2	0-1			1-1
1977	2-0			1-0	1-1	0-1	0-1			0-1		1-1	0-2			1-1
1976	0-1			1-0			1-1				0-1	0-2	2-0			2-0
1975	0-1			0-1	1-1	0-1	0-1	1-0		1-0	0-1	1-0				1-0
1974	0-1	0-1		1-0	0-1	1-0	0-1	1-0	0-1		1-0	1-1	0-2			2-0
1973		1-1		0-1	1-1	1-0	1-1	0-1	0-1	0-1		1-0	1-0			1-1
1972	0-1	0-1		1-0	1-0	0-2	1-0	0-2	0-1	1-0	0-1	1-0	0-1			2-0
1971	1-1	1-0		0-1	1-0	0-1-1	0-1-1	2-0		0-1		0-2	0-1			1-0
1970	1-0	0-1		0-1	0-1	2-0	1-1	1-0		0-1	1-0	0-2				0-1

MONDAY NIGHT FOOTBALL ALL-TIME STANDINGS
NATIONAL FOOTBALL CONFERENCE

East	W	L	T	Pct.	South	W	L	T	Pct.
Dallas	39	29	0	.574	Carolina	4	3	0	.571
Philadelphia	24	20	0	.545	Tampa Bay	8	8	0	.500
Washington	25	29	0	.463	Atlanta	9	19	0	.321
New York Giants	17	30	1	.365	New Orleans	7	15	0	.318

North	W	L	T	Pct.	West	W	L	T	Pct.
Minnesota	23	23	0	.500	Seattle	15	8	0	.652
Green Bay	24	25	1	.490	San Francisco	37	22	0	.627
Detroit	11	13	1	.458	St. Louis	26	27	0	.491
Chicago	18	32	0	.360	Arizona	5	11	1	.324

From 1970-71, tie games were not included in winning percentage.

SUNDAY NIGHT FOOTBALL, 1978-2006

(Home Team in capitals, games listed in chronological order.)

2006
Indianapolis 26, NEW YORK GIANTS 21
DALLAS 27, Washington 10
Denver 17, NEW ENGLAND 7
CHICAGO 37, Seattle 6
SAN DIEGO 23, Pittsburgh 13
DENVER 13, Oakland 3
Dallas 35, CAROLINA 14
Indianapolis 27, NEW ENGLAND 20
Chicago 38, NEW YORK GIANTS 20
San Diego 35, DENVER 27
INDIANAPOLIS 45, Philadelphia 21
Seattle 23, DENVER 20
New Orleans 42, DALLAS 17
SAN DIEGO 20, Kansas City 9
Green Bay 26, CHICAGO 7

2005
Indianapolis 24, BALTIMORE 7
Kansas City 23, OAKLAND 17
SAN DIEGO 45, New York Giants 23
ARIZONA 31, San Francisco 14
JACKSONVILLE 23, Cincinnati 20
SEATTLE 42, Houston 10
NEW ENGLAND 21, Buffalo 16
WASHINGTON 17, Philadelphia 10
PITTSBURGH 34, Cleveland 21
Kansas City 45, HOUSTON 17
New Orleans 21, NEW YORK JETS 19
SAN DIEGO 34, Oakland 10
GREEN BAY 16, Detroit 13
CHICAGO 16, Atlanta 3
BALTIMORE 30, Minnesota 23
St. Louis 20, DALLAS 10

2004
DENVER 34, Kansas City 24
CINCINNATI 16, Miami 13
OAKLAND 30, Tampa Bay 20
Pittsburgh 13, MIAMI 3
St. Louis 24, SAN FRANCISCO 14
Baltimore 17, WASHINGTON 10
Minnesota 38, NEW ORLEANS 31
CHICAGO 23, San Francisco 13
BALTIMORE 27, Cleveland 13
NEW ENGLAND 29, Buffalo 6
Green Bay 16, HOUSTON 13
Oakland 25, DENVER 24
Pittsburgh 17, JACKSONVILLE 16
Philadelphia 17, WASHINGTON 14
INDIANAPOLIS 20, Baltimore 10
MIAMI 10, Cleveland 7
NEW YORK GIANTS 28, Dallas 24

2003
TENNESSEE 25, Oakland 20
MINNESOTA 24, Chicago 13
MIAMI 17, Buffalo 7
Indianapolis 55, NEW ORLEANS 21
Cleveland 33, PITTSBURGH 13
SEATTLE 20, San Francisco 19
KANSAS CITY 38, Buffalo 5
Green Bay 30, MINNESOTA 27
ST. LOUIS 33, Baltimore 22
NEW ENGLAND 12, Dallas 0
MIAMI 24, Washington 23
JACKSONVILLE 17, Tampa Bay 10
ATLANTA 20, Carolina 14 (OT)
NEW ORLEANS 45, New York Giants 7
Denver 31, INDIANAPOLIS 17
BALTIMORE 13, Pittsburgh 10 (OT)

2002
HOUSTON 19, Dallas 10
Oakland 30, PITTSBURGH 17
ATLANTA 30, Cincinnati 3
SEATTLE 48, Minnesota 23
Baltimore 26, CLEVELAND 21
Miami 24, DENVER 22
WASHINGTON 26, Indianapolis 21
NEW YORK GIANTS 24, Jacksonville 17
NEW YORK JETS 13, Miami 10
OAKLAND 27, New England 20
Indianapolis 23, DENVER 20 (OT)
NEW ORLEANS 23, Tampa Bay 20
GREEN BAY 26, Minnesota 22
ST. LOUIS 30, Arizona 28
New York Jets 30, NEW ENGLAND 17
Tampa Bay 15, CHICAGO 0

2001
Miami 31, TENNESSEE 23
Denver 38, ARIZONA 17
PHILADELPHIA 40, Dallas 18
SAN FRANCISCO 24, Carolina 14
Oakland 23, INDIANAPOLIS 18
New York Jets 16, NEW ORLEANS 9
SEATTLE 34, Oakland 27
St. Louis 24, NEW ENGLAND 17
Chicago 13, MINNESOTA 6
SAN FRANCISCO 35, Buffalo 0
DENVER 20, Seattle 7
Pittsburgh 26, BALTIMORE 21
New York Jets 29, INDIANAPOLIS 28
Washington 40, NEW ORLEANS 10
Philadelphia 17, TAMPA BAY 13

2000
BUFFALO 16, Tennessee 13
ARIZONA 32, Dallas 31
MIAMI 19, Baltimore 6
Washington 16, NEW YORK GIANTS 6
PHILADELPHIA 38, Atlanta 10
Baltimore 15, JACKSONVILLE 10
Minnesota 28, CHICAGO 16
Oakland 15, SAN DIEGO 13
Carolina 27, ST. LOUIS 24
INDIANAPOLIS 23, New York Jets 15
Jacksonville 34, PITTSBURGH 24
New York Giants 31, ARIZONA 7
Green Bay 28, CHICAGO 6
OAKLAND 31, New York Jets 7
New York Giants 17, DALLAS 13

1999
Pittsburgh 43, CLEVELAND 0
BUFFALO 17, New York Jets 3
NEW ENGLAND 16, New York Giants 14
SEATTLE 22, Oakland 21
GREEN BAY 26, Tampa Bay 23
Washington 24, ARIZONA 10
DETROIT 20, Tampa Bay 3
MIAMI 17, Tennessee 0
SEATTLE 20, Denver 17
JACKSONVILLE 41, New Orleans 23
CAROLINA 34, Atlanta 28
NEW ENGLAND 13, Dallas 6
KANSAS CITY 31, Minnesota 28
Buffalo 31, ARIZONA 21
Washington 26, SAN FRANCISCO 20 (OT)

1998
KANSAS CITY 28, Oakland 8
NEW ENGLAND 29, Indianapolis 6
ARIZONA 17, Philadelphia 3
BALTIMORE 31, Cincinnati 24
KANSAS CITY 17, Seattle 6
Atlanta 34, NEW YORK GIANTS 20
Buffalo 30, CAROLINA 14
Oakland 31, SEATTLE 18
Tennessee 31, TAMPA BAY 22
DETROIT 26, Chicago 3
SAN FRANCISCO 31, New Orleans 20
Denver 31, SAN DIEGO 16
MINNESOTA 48, Chicago 22
New York Jets 21, MIAMI 16
MINNESOTA 50, Jacksonville 10
DALLAS 23, Washington 7

1997
Washington 24, CAROLINA 10
ARIZONA 25, Dallas 22 (OT)
NEW ENGLAND 27, New York Jets 24 (OT)
TAMPA BAY 31, Miami 21
MINNESOTA 28, Philadelphia 19
New Orleans 20, CHICAGO 17
PITTSBURGH 24, Indianapolis 22
CAROLINA 21, Atlanta 12
GREEN BAY 20, Detroit 10
PITTSBURGH 37, Baltimore 0
Oakland 38, SAN DIEGO 13
WASHINGTON 7, New York Giants 7 (OT)
Denver 38, SAN DIEGO 28
MIAMI 33, Detroit 30
Chicago 13, ST. LOUIS 10
SEATTLE 38, San Francisco 9

1996
Buffalo 23, NEW YORK GIANTS 20 (OT)
Miami 38, ARIZONA 10
DENVER 27, Tampa Bay 23
Philadelphia 33, ATLANTA 18
WASHINGTON 31, New York Jets 16
Houston 30, CINCINNATI 27 (OT)
INDIANAPOLIS 26, Baltimore 21
NEW ENGLAND 28, Buffalo 25
San Francisco 24, NEW ORLEANS 17
CAROLINA 27, New York Giants 17
Minnesota 16, OAKLAND 13 (OT)
Green Bay 24, ST. LOUIS 9
New England 45, SAN DIEGO 7
Minnesota 24, DETROIT 22
JACKSONVILLE 20, Seattle 13
SAN DIEGO 16, Denver 10

1995
DENVER 22, Buffalo 7
Philadelphia 31, ARIZONA 19
Dallas 23, MINNESOTA 17 (OT)
Green Bay 24, JACKSONVILLE 14
Oakland 47, NEW YORK JETS 10
Denver 37, NEW ENGLAND 3
New York Giants 24, WASHINGTON 15
Miami 24, SAN DIEGO 14
PHILADELPHIA 31, Denver 13
KANSAS CITY 20, Houston 13
NEW ORLEANS 34, Carolina 26
SAN FRANCISCO 27, Buffalo 17
TAMPA BAY 13, Green Bay 10 (OT)
SEATTLE 44, Oakland 10

1994
San Diego 17, DENVER 34
New York Giants 20, ARIZONA 17
Kansas City 30, ATLANTA 10
Chicago 19, NEW YORK JETS 7
Miami 24, CINCINNATI 7
PHILADELPHIA 21, Washington 17
ARIZONA 20, Pittsburgh 17 (OT)
KANSAS CITY 13, Los Angeles Raiders 3
DETROIT 14, Tampa Bay 9
SAN FRANCISCO 31, Los Angeles Rams 27
New England 12, INDIANAPOLIS 10
Buffalo 42, MIAMI 31
New Orleans 29, ATLANTA 20
Los Angeles Raiders 17, SEATTLE 16
MIAMI 27, Detroit 20

1993
NEW ORLEANS 33, Houston 21
Los Angeles Raiders 17, SEATTLE 13
Dallas 17, PHOENIX 10
NEW YORK JETS 45, New England 7
BUFFALO 17, New York Giants 14
GREEN BAY 30, Denver 27
MIAMI 41, Indianapolis 27
Detroit 30, MINNESOTA 27
WASHINGTON 30, Indianapolis 24
Chicago 16, SAN DIEGO 13
TAMPA BAY 23, Minnesota 10
HOUSTON 23, Pittsburgh 3
SAN FRANCISCO 21, Cincinnati 8
Green Bay 20, SAN DIEGO 13
Philadelphia 20, INDIANAPOLIS 10
MINNESOTA 30, Kansas City 10
HOUSTON 24, New York Jets 0

1992
DENVER 17, Los Angeles Raiders 13
Philadelphia 31, PHOENIX 14
BUFFALO 38, Indianapolis 0
San Francisco 16, NEW ORLEANS 10
NEW YORK JETS 30, New England 21
NEW ORLEANS 13, Los Angeles Rams 10
Pittsburgh 27, KANSAS CITY 3
New York Giants 24, WASHINGTON 7
Cincinnati 31, CHICAGO 28 (OT)
DENVER 27, New York Giants 13
Kansas City 24, SEATTLE 14
SAN DIEGO 27, Los Angeles Raiders 3
Los Angeles Rams 31, TAMPA BAY 27
Green Bay 16, HOUSTON 14
MIAMI 19, New York Jets 17
HOUSTON 27, Buffalo 3

1991
WASHINGTON 45, Detroit 0
Houston 30, CINCINNATI 7
NEW ORLEANS 24, Los Angeles Rams 7
Dallas 17, PHOENIX 9
Denver 13, MINNESOTA 6
Pittsburgh 21, INDIANAPOLIS 3
Los Angeles Raiders 23, SEATTLE 20
Washington 17, NEW YORK GIANTS 13
DENVER 20, Pittsburgh 13
MIAMI 30, New England 20
HOUSTON 28, Cleveland 24
Atlanta 23, NEW ORLEANS 20 (OT)
Los Angeles Raiders 9, SAN DIEGO 7
Minnesota 26, TAMPA BAY 24
Buffalo 35, INDIANAPOLIS 7
SEATTLE 23, Los Angeles Rams 9

1990
NEW YORK GIANTS 27, Philadelphia 20
PITTSBURGH 20, Houston 9
TAMPA BAY 23, Detroit 20
Washington 38, PHOENIX 10
BUFFALO 38, Los Angeles Raiders 24
CHICAGO 38, Los Angeles Rams 9
ATLANTA 38, Cincinnati 17
MINNESOTA 27, Denver 22
San Francisco 24, DALLAS 6
CINCINNATI 27, Pittsburgh 3
Seattle 13, SAN DIEGO 10
MINNESOTA 23, Green Bay 7
MIAMI 23, Philadelphia 20
DETROIT 38, Chicago 21
SEATTLE 17, Denver 12
HOUSTON 34, Pittsburgh 14

1989
Dallas 13, WASHINGTON 3
SAN DIEGO 14, Los Angeles Raiders 12
INDIANAPOLIS 27, New York Jets 10
Los Angeles Rams 20, NEW ORLEANS 17
MINNESOTA 27, Chicago 16
MIAMI 31, New England 10
SEATTLE 23, Los Angeles Raiders 17

1988
HOUSTON 41, Washington 17
Los Angeles Raiders 13, SAN DIEGO 3
Minnesota 43, DALLAS 3
New England 6, MIAMI 3
New York Giants 13, NEW ORLEANS 12
Pittsburgh 37, HOUSTON 34
SEATTLE 42, Denver 14
Los Angeles Rams 38, SAN FRANCISCO 16

1987
NEW YORK GIANTS 17, New England 10
SAN DIEGO 16, Los Angeles Raiders 14
Miami 20, DALLAS 14
SAN FRANCISCO 38, Cleveland 24
Chicago 30, MINNESOTA 24
SEATTLE 28, Denver 21
MIAMI 23, Washington 21
SAN FRANCISCO 48, Los Angeles Rams 0

1986
LOS ANGELES RAMS 29, Dallas 10

1985
Dallas 30, NEW YORK GIANTS 29
SAN DIEGO 54, Pittsburgh 44

1984
Denver 24, CLEVELAND 14
DALLAS 30, New Orleans 27

1983
Los Angeles Raiders 40, DALLAS 38

1982
ATLANTA 17, San Francisco 7

1981
DALLAS 29, Los Angeles 17

1980
DALLAS 42, San Diego 31

1979
DALLAS 30, Los Angeles 6

1978
New England 21, OAKLAND 14
LOS ANGELES 10, Pittsburgh 7
Denver 21, OAKLAND 6

THURSDAY-SATURDAY NIGHT FOOTBALL, 1974-2006

2006
PITTSBURGH 28, Miami 17 (Thurs.)
KANSAS CITY 19, Denver 10 (Thurs.)
CINCINNATI 13, Baltimore 7 (Thurs.)
PITTSBURGH 27, Cleveland 7 (Thurs.)
San Francisco 24, SEATTLE 14 (Thurs.)
Dallas 38, ATLANTA 28 (Sat.)
GREEN BAY 9, Minnesota 7 (Thurs.)
Kansas City 20, OAKLAND 9 (Sat.)
New York Giants 34, WASHINGTON 28 (Sat.)

2005
NEW ENGLAND 30, Oakland 20 (Thurs.)
Kansas City 30, MIAMI 20 (Fri.)
Denver 28, BUFFALO 17 (Sat.)
New York Giants 30, OAKLAND 21 (Sat.)

2004
NEW ENGLAND 27, Indianapolis 24 (Thurs.)
ATLANTA 34, Carolina 31 (OT) (Sat.)
Denver 37, TENNESSEE 16 (Sat.)

2003
WASHINGTON 16, New York Jets 13 (Thurs.)
New England 21, NEW YORK JETS 16 (Sat.)
Philadelphia 31, WASHINGTON 7 (Sat.)

2002
San Francisco 16, NEW YORK GIANTS 13 (Thurs.)
Philadelphia 27, DALLAS 3 (Sat.)

2001
Buffalo 13, JACKSONVILLE 10 (Thurs.)
Indianapolis 35, KANSAS CITY 28 (Thurs.)
Tennessee 13, OAKLAND 10 (Sat.)
TAMPA BAY 22, Baltimore 10 (Sat.)

2000
Detroit 28, TAMPA BAY 14 (Thurs.)
MINNESOTA 24, Detroit 17 (Thurs.)
Buffalo 42, SEATTLE 23 (Sat.)

1999
Kansas City 35, BALTIMORE 8 (Thurs.)
JACKSONVILLE 20, Pittsburgh 6 (Thurs.)
TENNESSEE 21, Oakland 14 (Thurs.)

1998
DETROIT 27, Green Bay 20 (Thurs.)
PHILADELPHIA 17, St. Louis 14 (Thurs.)

1997
KANSAS CITY 31, San Diego 3 (Thurs.)
CINCINNATI 41, Tennessee 14 (Thurs.)

1996
KANSAS CITY 34, Seattle 16 (Thurs.)
INDIANAPOLIS 37, Philadelphia 10 (Thurs.)

1995
ST. LOUIS 21, Atlanta 19 (Thurs.)
Cincinnati 27, PITTSBURGH 9 (Thurs.)
New York Giants 10, ARIZONA 6 (Thurs.)
Indianapolis 10, New England 7 (Sat.)

1994
Cleveland 11, HOUSTON 8 (Thurs.)
MINNESOTA 13, Green Bay 10 (OT) (Thurs.)
MINNESOTA 33, Chicago 27 (OT) (Thurs.)

1993
ATLANTA 30, Los Angeles Rams 24 (Thurs.)

1992
MINNESOTA 31, Detroit 14 (Thurs.)
NEW ORLEANS 22, Atlanta 14 (Thurs.)

1991
Chicago 10, GREEN BAY 0 (Thurs.)

1990
MIAMI 17, New England 10 (Thurs.)
INDIANAPOLIS 35, Washington 28 (Sat.)

1989
Cleveland 24, HOUSTON 20 (Sat.)

1987-88
None

1986
New England 20, NEW YORK JETS 6 (Thurs.)
Cincinnati 30, CLEVELAND 13 (Thurs.)
Los Angeles Raiders 37, SAN DIEGO 31 (OT) (Thurs.)
SAN FRANCISCO 24, Los Angeles Rams 14 (Fri.)

1985
KANSAS CITY 36, Los Angeles Raiders 20 (Thurs.)
Chicago 33, MINNESOTA 24 (Thurs.)
Denver 27, SEATTLE 24 (Fri.)

1984
Pittsburgh 23, NEW YORK JETS 17 (Thurs.)
Washington 31, MINNESOTA 17 (Thurs.)
SAN FRANCISCO 19, Los Angeles Rams 16 (Fri.)

1983
San Francisco 48, MINNESOTA 17 (Thurs.)
CLEVELAND 17, Cincinnati 7 (Thurs.)
Los Angeles Raiders 42, SAN DIEGO 10 (Thurs.)
MIAMI 34, New York Jets 14 (Fri.)

1982
BUFFALO 23, Minnesota 22 (Thurs.)
SAN FRANCISCO 30, Los Angeles Rams 24 (Thurs.)

1981
MIAMI 30, Pittsburgh 10 (Thurs.)
Philadelphia 20, BUFFALO 14 (Thurs.)
HOUSTON 17, Cleveland 13 (Thurs.

1980
TAMPA BAY 10, Los Angeles 9 (Thurs.)
San Diego 27, MIAMI 24 (OT) (Thurs.)
HOUSTON 6, Pittsburgh 0 (Thurs.)

1979
Los Angeles 13, DENVER 9 (Thurs.)
OAKLAND 45, San Diego 22 (Thurs.)
MIAMI 39, New England 24 (Thurs.)

1978
Minnesota 21, DALLAS 10 (Thurs.)

1977
Minnesota 30, DETROIT 21 (Sat.)

1976
Los Angeles 20, DETROIT 17 (Sat.)

1975
LOS ANGELES 10, Pittsburgh 3 (Sat.)

1974
OAKLAND 27, Dallas 23 (Sat.)

THANKSGIVING DAY FOOTBALL, 1920-2006
(Home Team in capitals, games listed in chronological order.)
(AFL)-American Football League, 1960-69.

Nov. 25, 1920   AKRON PROS 7, Canton Bulldogs 0
Decatur Staleys 6, CHICAGO TIGERS 0
ELYRIA (OH) ATHLETICS* 0, Columbus Panhandles 0
DAYTON TRIANGLES 28, Detroit Heralds 0
CHICAGO BOOSTERS* 27, Hammond Pros 0
All-Tonawanda (NY) 14, ROCHESTER JEFFERSONS 3
* Non league team. Games between league teams and non league teams counted in standings in 1920.

Nov. 24, 1921   Canton Bulldogs 14, AKRON PROS 0
Buffalo All-Americans 7, CHICAGO STALEYS 6

Nov. 30, 1922   Buffalo All-Americans 21, ROCHESTER JEFFERSONS 0
CHICAGO CARDINALS 6, Chicago Bears 0
RACINE LEGION 3, Milwaukee Badgers 0
Oorang Indians 18, COLUMBUS PANHANDLES 6
CANTON BULLDOGS 14, Akron Pros 0

Nov. 29, 1923   CANTON BULLDOGS 28, Toledo Maroons 0
CHICAGO BEARS 3, Chicago Cardinals 0
GREEN BAY PACKERS 19, Hammond Pros 0
Milwaukee Badgers 16, RACINE LEGION 0
AKRON PROS 2, Buffalo All-Americans 0

Nov. 27, 1924   AKRON PROS 22, Buffalo Bisons 0
Chicago Bears 21, CHICAGO CARDINALS 0
FRANKFORD YELLOWJACKETS 32, Dayton Triangles 7
CLEVELAND BULLDOGS 53, Milwaukee Badgers 10 (at Canton, Ohio)
Green Bay Packers 17, KANSAS CITY BLUES 6

Nov. 26, 1925   CHICAGO BEARS 0, Chicago Cardinals 0
Kansas City Cowboys 17, CLEVELAND BULLDOGS 0 (at Hartford, Connecticut)
Rock Island Independents 6, DETROIT PANTHERS 3
POTTSVILLE MAROONS 31, Green Bay Packers 0

Nov. 25, 1926   New York Giants 17, BROOKLYN LIONS 0
Los Angeles Buccaneers 9, DETROIT PANTHERS 6
CHICAGO BEARS 0, Chicago Cardinals 0
FRANKFORD YELLOWJACKETS 20, Green Bay Packers 14
POTTSVILLE MAROONS 8, Providence Steam Roller 0
CANTON BULLDOGS 0, Akron Pros 0

Nov. 24, 1927   Chicago Cardinals 3, CHICAGO BEARS 0
POTTSVILLE MAROONS 6, Providence Steam Roller 0
Green Bay Packers 17, FRANKFORD YELLOWJACKETS 9
Cleveland Bulldogs 30, NEW YORK YANKEES 19

Nov. 29, 1928   Providence Steam Roller 7, POTTSVILLE MAROONS 0
DETROIT WOLVERINES 33, Dayton Triangles 0
FRANKFORD YELLOWJACKETS 2, Green Bay Packers 0
CHICAGO BEARS 34, Chicago Cardinals 0

Nov. 28, 1929   New York Giants 21, STATEN ISLAND STAPLETONS 7
FRANKFORD YELLOWJACKETS 0, Green Bay Packers 0
Chicago Cardinals 40, CHICAGO BEARS 6

Nov. 27, 1930   STATEN ISLAND STAPLETONS 7, New York Giants 6
BROOKLYN DODGERS 33, Providence Steam Roller 12
Green Bay Packers 25, FRANKFORD YELLOWJACKETS 7
CHICAGO BEARS 6, Chicago Cardinals 0

Nov. 26, 1931   Green Bay Packers 38, PROVIDENCE STEAM ROLLER 7
STATEN ISLAND STAPLETONS 9, New York Giants 6
CHICAGO BEARS 18, Chicago Cardinals 7

Nov. 24, 1932   CHICAGO BEARS 34, Chicago Cardinals 0
Green Bay Packers 7, BROOKLYN DODGERS 0
STATEN ISLAND STAPLETONS 13, New York Giants 13

Nov. 30, 1933   Chicago Bears 22, CHICAGO CARDINALS 6
New York Giants 10, BROOKLYN DODGERS 0

Nov. 29, 1934	CHICAGO CARDINALS 6, Green Bay Packers 0
	Chicago Bears 19, DETROIT LIONS 16
	New York Giants 27, BROOKLYN DODGERS 0
Nov. 28, 1935	New York Giants 21, BROOKLYN DODGERS 0
	CHICAGO CARDINALS 9, Green Bay Packers 7
	DETROIT LIONS 14, Chicago Bears 2
Nov. 26, 1936	DETROIT LIONS 13, Chicago Bears 7
	New York Giants 14, BROOKLYN DODGERS 0
Nov. 25, 1937	Chicago Bears 13, DETROIT LIONS 0
	BROOKLYN DODGERS 13, New York Giants 13
Nov. 24, 1938	DETROIT LIONS 14, Chicago Bears 7
	BROOKLYN DODGERS 7, New York Giants 7
Nov. 23, 1939#	PHILADELPHIA EAGLES 17, Pittsburgh Steelers 14
Nov. 28, 1940#	Pittsburgh Steelers 7, PHILADELPHIA EAGLES 0

In 1939 and 1940, President Roosevelt moved Thanksgiving one week earlier. Various states celebrated on the date declared by the President, while other states recognized the traditional fourth Thursday of the month. In 1941, Thanksgiving was sanctioned by Congress to be celebrated on the fourth Thursday of November, which it has been ever since.

Nov. 22, 1945	Cleveland Rams 28, DETROIT LIONS 21
Nov. 28, 1946	Boston Yanks 34, DETROIT LIONS 10
Nov. 27, 1947	Chicago Bears 34, DETROIT LIONS 14
Nov. 25, 1948	Chicago Cardinals 28, DETROIT LIONS 14
Nov. 24, 1949	Chicago Bears 28, DETROIT LIONS 7
Nov. 23, 1950	DETROIT LIONS 49, New York Yanks 14
	Pittsburgh Steelers 28, CHICAGO CARDINALS 17
Nov. 22, 1951	DETROIT LIONS 52, Green Bay Packers 35
Nov. 27, 1952	DETROIT LIONS 48, Green Bay Packers 24
	DALLAS TEXANS 27, Chicago Bears 23 (at Akron, Ohio)
Nov. 26, 1953	DETROIT LIONS 34, Green Bay Packers 15
Nov. 25, 1954	DETROIT LIONS 28, Green Bay Packers 24
Nov. 24, 1955	DETROIT LIONS 24, Green Bay Packers 10
Nov. 22, 1956	Green Bay Packers 24, DETROIT LIONS 20
Nov. 28, 1957	DETROIT LIONS 18, Green Bay Packers 6
Nov. 27, 1958	DETROIT LIONS 24, Green Bay Packers 14
Nov. 26, 1959	Green Bay Packers 24, DETROIT LIONS 17
Nov. 24, 1960	DETROIT LIONS 23, Green Bay Packers 10
	(AFL) - NEW YORK TITANS 41, Dallas Texans 35
Nov. 23, 1961	Green Bay Packers 17, DETROIT LIONS 9
	(AFL) - NEW YORK TITANS 21, Buffalo Bills 14
Nov. 22, 1962	DETROIT LIONS 26, Green Bay Packers 14
	(AFL) - New York Titans 46, DENVER BRONCOS 45
Nov. 28, 1963	DETROIT LIONS 13, Green Bay Packers 13
	(AFL) - Oakland Raiders 26, DENVER BRONCOS 10
Nov. 26, 1964	Chicago Bears 27, DETROIT LIONS 24
	(AFL) - Buffalo Bills 27, SAN DIEGO CHARGERS 24
Nov. 25, 1965	DETROIT LIONS 24, Baltimore Colts 24
	(AFL) - SAN DIEGO CHARGERS 20, Buffalo Bills 20
Nov. 24, 1966	San Francisco 49ers 41, DETROIT LIONS 14
	DALLAS COWBOYS 26, Cleveland Browns 14
	(AFL) - Buffalo Bills 31, OAKLAND RAIDERS 10

Nov. 23, 1967	Los Angeles Rams 31, DETROIT LIONS 7 DALLAS COWBOYS 46, St. Louis Cardinals 21 (AFL) - Oakland Raiders 44, KANSAS CITY CHIEFS 22 (AFL) - SAN DIEGO CHARGERS 24, Denver Broncos 20
Nov. 28, 1968	Philadelphia Eagles 12, DETROIT LIONS 0 DALLAS COWBOYS 29, Washington Redskins 20 (AFL) - OAKLAND RAIDERS 13, Buffalo Bills 10 (AFL) - KANSAS CITY CHIEFS 24, Houston Oilers 10
Nov. 27, 1969	Minnesota Vikings 27, DETROIT LIONS 0 DALLAS COWBOYS 24, San Francisco 49ers 24 (AFL) - KANSAS CITY CHIEFS 31, Denver Broncos 17 (AFL) - San Diego Chargers 21, HOUSTON OILERS 17
Nov. 26, 1970	DETROIT LIONS 28, Oakland Raiders 14 DALLAS COWBOYS 16, Green Bay Packers 3
Nov. 25, 1971	DETROIT LIONS 32, Kansas City Chiefs 21 DALLAS COWBOYS 28, Los Angeles Rams 21
Nov. 23, 1972	DETROIT LIONS 37, New York Jets 20 San Francisco 49ers 31, DALLAS COWBOYS 10
Nov. 22, 1973	Washington Redskins 20, DETROIT LIONS 0 Miami Dolphins 14, DALLAS COWBOYS 7
Nov. 28, 1974	Denver Broncos 31, DETROIT LIONS 27 DALLAS COWBOYS 24, Washington Redskins 23
Nov. 27, 1975	Los Angeles Rams 20, DETROIT LIONS 0 Buffalo Bills 32, ST. LOUIS CARDINALS 14
Nov. 25, 1976	DETROIT LIONS 27, Buffalo Bills 14 DALLAS COWBOYS 19, St. Louis Cardinals 14
Nov. 24, 1977	Chicago Bears 31, DETROIT LIONS 14 Miami Dolphins 55, ST. LOUIS CARDINALS 14
Nov. 23, 1978	DETROIT LIONS 17, Denver Broncos 14 DALLAS COWBOYS 37, Washington Redskins 10
Nov. 22, 1979	DETROIT LIONS 20, Chicago Bears 0 Houston Oilers 30, DALLAS COWBOYS 24
Nov. 27, 1980	Chicago Bears 23, DETROIT LIONS 17 (OT) DALLAS COWBOYS 51, Seattle Seahawks 7
Nov. 26, 1981	DETROIT LIONS 27, Kansas City Chiefs 10 DALLAS COWBOYS 10, Chicago Bears 9
Nov. 25, 1982	New York Giants 13, DETROIT LIONS 6 DALLAS COWBOYS 31, Cleveland Browns 14
Nov. 24, 1983	DETROIT LIONS 45, Pittsburgh Steelers 3 DALLAS COWBOYS 35, St. Louis Cardinals 17
Nov. 22, 1984	DETROIT LIONS 31, Green Bay Packers 28 DALLAS COWBOYS 20, New England Patriots 17
Nov. 28, 1985	DETROIT LIONS 31, New York Jets 20 DALLAS COWBOYS 35, St. Louis Cardinals 17
Nov. 27, 1986	Green Bay Packers 44, DETROIT LIONS 40 Seattle Seahawks 31, DALLAS COWBOYS 14
Nov. 26, 1987	Kansas City Chiefs 27, DETROIT LIONS 20 Minnesota Vikings 44, DALLAS COWBOYS 38 (OT)
Nov. 24, 1988	Minnesota Vikings 23, DETROIT LIONS 0 Houston Oilers 25, DALLAS COWBOYS 17
Nov. 23, 1989	DETROIT LIONS 13, Cleveland Browns 10 Philadelphia Eagles 27, DALLAS COWBOYS 0
Nov. 22, 1990	DETROIT LIONS 40, Denver Broncos 27 DALLAS COWBOYS 27, Washington Redskins 17

Nov. 28, 1991	DETROIT LIONS 16, Chicago Bears 6 DALLAS COWBOYS 20, Pittsburgh Steelers 10
Nov. 26, 1992	Houston Oilers 24, DETROIT LIONS 21 DALLAS COWBOYS 30, New York Giants 3
Nov. 25, 1993	Chicago Bears 10, DETROIT LIONS 6 Miami Dolphins 16, DALLAS COWBOYS 14
Nov. 24, 1994	DETROIT LIONS 35, Buffalo Bills 21 DALLAS COWBOYS 42, Green Bay Packers 31
Nov. 23, 1995	DETROIT LIONS 44, Minnesota Vikings 38 DALLAS COWBOYS 24, Kansas City Chiefs 12
Nov. 28, 1996	Kansas City Chiefs 28, DETROIT LIONS 24 DALLAS COWBOYS 21, Washington Redskins 10
Nov. 27, 1997	DETROIT LIONS 55, Chicago Bears 20 Tennessee Titans 27, DALLAS COWBOYS 14
Nov. 26, 1998	DETROIT LIONS 19, Pittsburgh Steelers 16 (OT) Minnesota Vikings 46, DALLAS COWBOYS 36
Nov. 25, 1999	DETROIT LIONS 21, Chicago Bears 17 DALLAS COWBOYS 20, Miami Dolphins 0
Nov. 23, 2000	DETROIT LIONS 34, New England Patriots 9 Minnesota Vikings 27, DALLAS COWBOYS 15
Nov. 22, 2001	Green Bay Packers 29, DETROIT LIONS 27 Denver Broncos 26, DALLAS COWBOYS 24
Nov. 28, 2002	New England Patriots 20, DETROIT LIONS 12 DALLAS COWBOYS 27, Washington Redskins 20
Nov. 27, 2003	DETROIT LIONS 22, Green Bay Packers 14 Miami Dolphins 40, DALLAS COWBOYS 21
Nov. 25, 2004	Indianapolis Colts 41, DETROIT LIONS 9 DALLAS COWBOYS 21, Chicago Bears 7
Nov. 24, 2005	Atlanta Falcons 27, DETROIT LIONS 7 Denver Broncos 24, DALLAS COWBOYS 21
Nov. 23, 2006	Miami Dolphins 27, DETROIT LIONS 10 DALLAS COWBOYS 38, Tampa Bay Buccaneers 10 KANSAS CITY CHIEFS 19, Denver Broncos 10

THANKSGIVING DAY RECORDS
*NFL record; stats compiled by Elias Sports Bureau.

SCORING / Most Touchdowns, Game
6   Ernie Nevers, Chi. Cardinals vs. Chi. Bears,
     Nov. 28, 1929*
4   Sterling Sharpe, Green Bay at Dallas, Nov. 24, 1994
3   By many players

RUSHING / Most Yards Rushing, Game
273   O.J. Simpson, Buffalo at Detroit, Nov. 25, 1976
198   Bob Hoernschemeyer, Detroit vs. N.Y. Yankees,
     Nov. 23, 1950
195   Earl Campbell, Houston at Dallas, Nov. 22, 1979

PASSING / Most Yards Passing, Game
455   Troy Aikman, Dallas vs. Minnesota, Nov. 26, 1998
410   Scott Mitchell, Detroit vs. Minnesota, Nov. 23, 1995
384   Warren Moon, Minnesota at Detroit, Nov. 23, 1995

PASS RECEIVING
RECEPTIONS / Most Pass Receptions, Game
12   Brett Perriman, Detroit vs. Minnesota, Nov. 23, 1995
     Marvin Harrison, Indianapolis at Detroit, Nov. 25, 2004
11   Daryl Johnston, Dallas vs. Miami, Nov. 25, 1993
     Michael Irvin, Dallas vs. Kansas City, Nov. 23, 1995

YARDS GAINED / Most Yards on Pass Receptions, Game
303   Jim Benton, Cleveland at Detroit, Nov. 22, 1945
185   Lance Alworth, San Diego vs. Buffalo, Nov. 26, 1964
184   Anthony Carter, Minnesota at Dallas, Nov. 26, 1987 (OT)

INTERCONFERENCE GAMES

AFC VS. NFC (REGULAR SEASON), 1970-2006

	Balt	Buff	Cin	Cle	Den	Hou	Ind	Jax	KC	Mia
1970		0-3	1-2	0-3	2-2		3-0		0-2-1	2-1
1971		0-3	1-2	2-1	1-3		2-1		2-1	3-0
1972		2-0-1	2-1	1-2	1-3		0-3		2-1	3-0
1973		2-1	2-1	1-2	0-3-1		2-1		1-1-1	3-0
1974		2-1	2-1	1-2	2-2		1-2		1-2	2-1
1975		1-2	3-0	1-3	2-1		2-1		2-1	3-0
1976		0-2	2-0	2-0	2-0		0-2		1-1	0-2
1977		1-1	2-1	1-1	1-1		1-1		1-1	2-0
1978		1-1	2-2	4-0	2-2		2-2		0-2	3-1
1979		2-2	2-2	3-1	3-1		1-1		0-2	4-0
1980		3-1	2-2	3-1	3-1		1-1		2-0	4-0
1981		1-3	2-2	3-1	3-1		0-4		2-2	3-1
1982		1-2	1-0	0-2	2-1		0-1-1		0-3	1-1
1983		1-3	3-1	2-2	0-2		2-0		2-2	3-1
1984		1-3	2-2	1-3	3-1		0-4		1-1	4-0
1985		0-2	2-2	1-3	3-1		3-1		2-2	3-1
1986		1-1	3-1	2-2	3-1		1-3		1-1	2-2
1987		1-2	1-2	2-2	2-1-1		1-0		1-2	3-0
1988		2-2	4-0	4-0	3-1		2-2		0-2	3-1
1989		1-3	2-2	3-1	2-2		1-3		2-0	2-0
1990		3-1	1-3	1-3	1-3		2-2		4-0	2-2
1991		3-1	1-3	0-4	2-0		0-4		2-2	3-1
1992		4-0	1-3	2-2	1-3		2-0		2-2	2-2
1993		4-0	2-2	3-1	1-3		0-4		2-2	3-1
1994		1-3	1-3	3-1	1-3		0-2		3-1	2-2
1995		3-1	2-2	1-3	2-2		2-2	0-4	3-1	2-2
1996	2-2	4-0	2-2		3-1		3-1	2-2	4-0	1-3
1997	2-1-1	1-3	2-2		3-1		1-3	2-2	4-0	1-3
1998	1-3	3-1	1-3		3-1		0-4	3-1	3-1	3-1
1999	2-1	3-1	1-2	1-2	2-2		4-0	4-0	2-2	2-2
2000	2-1	2-2	1-2	0-3	3-1		2-2	2-2	2-2	2-2
2001	2-2	1-3	1-2	1-2	3-1		1-3	1-2	1-3	2-2
2002	0-4	3-1	1-3	2-2	4-0	2-2	2-2	2-2	2-2	2-2
2003	3-1	2-2	2-2	2-2	1-3	2-2	3-1	2-2	3-1	3-1
2004	3-1	4-0	4-0	1-3	3-1	1-3	4-0	3-1	1-3	2-2
2005	2-2	0-4	4-0	2-2	3-1	1-3	3-1	3-1	1-3	2-2
2006	3-1	2-2	2-2	1-3	1-3	0-4	3-1	3-1	4-0	3-1
Total	**22-19-1**	**66-63-1**	**70-62**	**57-65**	**77-59-2**	**6-14**	**57-65-1**	**27-20**	**66-54-2**	**90-43**

	NE	NYJ	Oak	Pitt	SD	Sea	TB	Tenn	TOTALS
1970	0-3	2-1	1-2	0-3	1-2			0-3	12-27-1
1971	0-3	0-3	1-1-1	1-2	2-1			0-2-1	15-23-2
1972	3-0	1-2	3-0	2-1	0-3			0-3	20-19-1
1973	2-1	0-3	2-1	3-0	1-2			0-3	19-19-2
1974	3-0	2-1	3-0	3-0	1-2			0-3	23-17
1975	1-2	0-3	3-0	2-1	0-3			3-0	23-17
1976	1-1	0-2	3-0	1-1	2-0		0-1	2-0	16-12
1977	2-0	1-1	1-1	2-0	1-1	1-0		2-0	19-9
1978	2-2	1-3	4-0	3-1	2-2	3-1		2-2	31-21
1979	3-1	3-1	4-0	3-1	3-1	3-1		2-2	36-16
1980	1-3	1-3	2-2	4-0	2-2	1-3		4-0	33-19
1981	0-4	2-0	2-2	3-1	2-2	0-2		1-3	24-28
1982	0-1	4-0	3-0	1-0	1-0	1-0		0-3	15-14-1
1983	2-2	3-1	2-2	2-2	2-2	1-3		1-3	26-26
1984	0-4	0-2	3-1	3-1	4-0	4-0		0-4	26-26
1985	3-1	2-2	3-1	1-3	1-1	2-2		1-3	27-25
1986	3-1	2-2	1-3	2-2	0-4	3-1		2-2	26-26
1987	0-3	0-4	2-2	2-2	2-0	4-0		2-2	23-22-1
1988	2-2	2-0	1-3	1-3	2-2	1-3		3-1	30-22
1989	0-4	1-3	2-2	3-1	2-2	0-4		3-1	24-28
1990	0-4	2-0	3-1	3-1	1-1	2-2		1-3	26-26
1991	1-1	2-2	2-2	0-4	1-3	1-3		1-3	19-33
1992	0-4	0-4	2-2	1-3	2-0	0-4		3-1	22-30
1993	1-1	2-2	3-1	2-2	2-2	0-2		2-2	27-25
1994	4-0	1-3	3-1	2-2	2-2	2-0		0-4	25-27
1995	0-4	0-4	3-1	2-2	3-1	3-1		1-3	27-33
1996	2-2	1-3	1-3	2-2	1-3	2-2		2-2	32-28
1997	1-3	3-1	2-2	2-2	1-3	2-2		4-0	31-28-1
1998	2-2	2-2	3-1	2-2	1-3	3-1		1-3	31-29
1999	3-1	2-2	3-1	3-0	1-3	2-2		3-1	38-22
2000	0-4	3-1	4-0	1-2	0-4	2-2		4-0	30-30
2001	3-1	2-2	3-1	3-0	2-2	1-3		3-1	30-30
2002	3-1	3-1	2-2	2-1-1	2-2			2-2	34-29-1
2003	3-1	0-4	1-3	1-3	2-2			4-0	34-30
2004	4-0	3-1	2-2	4-0	3-1			2-2	44-20
2005	3-1	1-3	2-2	4-0	2-2			1-3	34-30
2006	4-0	3-1	1-3	3-1	4-0			3-1	40-24
Total	**62-68**	**57-73**	**86-51-1**	**79-52-1**	**61-66**	**44-44**	**0-1**	**65-71-1**	**992-890-10**

NFC VS. AFC (REGULAR SEASON), 1970-2006

Year	Ariz	Atl	Car	Chi	Dall	Det	GB	Minn	NO
1970	2-0-1	1-2		1-2	3-0	3-0	2-1	2-1	0-3
1971	2-1	3-0		1-2	3-0	4-0	2-1	2-1	0-1-2
1972	1-2	2-2		1-2	3-0	2-0-1	1-2	1-2	0-3
1973	0-2-1	2-1		2-2	2-1	0-3	1-1-1	2-1	1-2
1974	2-1	0-3		0-3	2-1	1-2	2-1	2-1	0-3
1975	2-1	1-2		0-3	2-1	1-2	0-3	4-0	0-3
1976	1-1	0-2		0-2	2-0	2-0	0-2	2-0	1-2
1977	0-2	0-2		1-1	1-1	2-0	0-3	1-1	0-2
1978	0-4	1-3		0-4	3-1	2-2	2-2	1-3	1-3
1979	1-3	1-3		2-2	1-3	0-4	1-3	1-3	0-4
1980	1-1	2-2		0-4	3-1	0-2	1-3	1-3	1-3
1981	3-1	1-3		4-0	4-0	2-2	1-1	1-3	2-2
1982		1-1		1-1	2-1	0-1	1-1-1	1-3	1-0
1983	3-1	3-1		1-1	2-2	1-3	2-2	4-0	1-3
1984	3-1	1-3		2-2	2-2	0-4	0-4	0-4	3-1
1985	2-2	0-4		3-1	3-1	2-2	0-4	2-0	0-4
1986	1-1	1-3		4-0	1-3	1-3	1-3	1-3	1-3
1987	0-1	0-4		2-2	2-1	0-4	1-2-1	2-1	4-0
1988	1-3	1-3		3-1	0-4	1-1	1-3	2-2	4-0
1989	1-3	2-2		2-2	0-2	1-3	0-2	2-2	4-0
1990	2-2	2-2		2-2	1-1	1-3	1-3	2-2	2-2
1991	1-1	3-1		2-2	3-1	4-0	1-3	0-2	3-1
1992	0-2	2-2		1-3	4-0	2-2	3-1	3-1	3-1
1993	1-1	1-3		2-2	2-2	2-0	3-1	2-2	2-2
1994	3-1	1-3		3-1	3-1	2-2	1-3	2-2	1-3
1995	1-3	2-2	3-1	2-2	4-0	3-1	4-0	3-1	4-0
1996	0-4	0-4	3-1	2-2	2-2	1-3	3-1	1-3	1-3
1997	1-3	2-2	2-2	2-2	2-2	2-2	3-1	3-1	2-2
1998	1-3	3-1	1-3	2-2	1-3	1-3	3-1	4-0	1-3
1999	0-4	0-4	2-2	2-2	1-3	1-3	2-2	2-2	0-4
2000	1-3	1-3	2-2	2-2	1-3	2-2	1-3	3-1	1-3
2001	3-1	1-3	0-4	3-1	0-4	0-4	3-1	1-3	2-2
2002	0-4	2-1-1	3-1	1-3	2-2	0-4	3-1	1-3	2-2
2003	1-3	1-3	2-2	3-1	2-2	1-3	3-1	2-2	1-3
2004	1-3	3-1	1-3	1-3	1-3	1-3	1-3	3-1	2-2
2005	1-3	3-1	3-1	1-3	2-2	2-2	0-4	1-3	2-2
2006	0-4	2-2	2-2	2-2	3-1	1-3	1-3	0-4	1-3
Total	**43-76-2**	**52-84-1**	**24-24**	**63-72**	**75-57**	**51-78-1**	**56-75-3**	**67-67**	**54-80-2**

Year	NYG	Phil	StL	SF	Sea	TB	Wash	TOTALS
1970	3-0	2-1	2-1	4-0			2-1	27-12-1
1971	1-2	1-2	1-2	2-1			1-2	23-15-2
1972	1-2	2-1	1-2	2-1			1-2	19-20-1
1973	1-2	2-1	3-0	1-2			2-1	19-19-2
1974	1-2	2-1	3-1	0-3			2-1	17-23
1975	2-1	0-3	3-0	1-2			1-2	17-23
1976	0-2	0-2	1-1	1-1	1-0		1-1	12-16
1977	0-2	1-1	2-0	0-2		0-1	1-1	9-19
1978	1-1	3-1	2-2	1-3		2-0	2-2	21-31
1979	1-1	2-2	2-2	0-4		2-0	2-2	16-36
1980	1-3	3-1	2-2	2-2		1-3	1-3	19-33
1981	1-1	3-1	1-3	3-1		0-4	2-2	28-24
1982	1-0	2-1	1-2	1-3		2-1		14-15-1
1983	0-4	1-1	1-3	2-2		1-3	4-0	26-26
1984	2-0	3-1	3-1	3-1		1-1	3-1	26-26
1985	2-2	1-1	3-1	3-1		0-4	4-0	25-27
1986	3-1	2-2	2-2	4-0		1-1	3-1	26-26
1987	2-1	3-1	1-2	3-1		0-2	2-1	22-23-1
1988	1-1	2-2	2-2	2-2		1-3	1-3	22-30
1989	4-0	3-1	3-1	4-0		0-4	2-2	28-24
1990	3-1	1-3	2-2	4-0		0-2	3-1	26-26
1991	3-1	4-0	1-3	3-1		1-3	4-0	33-19
1992	2-2	3-1	2-2	3-1		0-2	2-2	30-22
1993	2-2	2-2	2-2	2-2		1-3	1-3	25-27
1994	3-1	1-3	2-2	3-1		1-1	1-1	27-25
1995	0-4	1-3	1-3	3-1		2-2	0-4	33-27
1996	2-2	2-2	2-2	4-0		2-2	3-1	28-32
1997	1-3	2-1-1	0-4	2-2		3-1	1-3	28-31-1
1998	3-1	0-4	3-1	2-2		2-2	2-2	29-31
1999	2-2	1-3	3-1	1-3		3-1	2-2	22-38
2000	3-1	3-1	3-1	2-2		3-1	2-2	30-30
2001	2-2	3-1	4-0	4-0		2-2	2-2	30-30
2002	2-2	1-3	2-2	2-2	2-2	3-1	3-1	29-34-1
2003	1-3	3-1	4-0	1-3	2-2	1-3	2-2	30-34
2004	1-3	2-2	1-3	0-4	1-3	1-3	0-4	20-44
2005	3-1	3-1	3-1	1-3	3-1	2-2	0-4	30-34
2006	1-3	1-3	2-2	2-2	2-2	2-2	2-2	24-40
Total	**62-62**	**71-61-1**	**76-61**	**78-61**	**11-10**	**40-60**	**67-64**	**890-992-10**

2006 INTERCONFERENCE GAMES
(Home Team in capital letters)
AFC 40, NFC 24
AFC Victories
Baltimore 27, TAMPA BAY 0
JACKSONVILLE 24, Dallas 17
Indianapolis 26, NEW YORK GIANTS 21
BUFFALO 17, Minnesota 12
KANSAS CITY 41, San Francisco 0
Kansas City 23, ARIZONA 20
Tennessee 25, WASHINGTON 22
San Diego 48, SAN FRANCISCO 19
CINCINNATI 17, Carolina 14
NEW YORK JETS 31, Detroit 24
INDIANAPOLIS 36, Washington 22
OAKLAND 22, Arizona 9
KANSAS CITY 35, Seattle 28
Baltimore 35, NEW ORLEANS 22
Jacksonville 13, PHILADELPHIA 6
SAN DIEGO 38, St. Louis 24
New England 31, MINNESOTA 7
BUFFALO 24, Green Bay 10
Miami 31, CHICAGO 13
Kansas City 31, ST. LOUIS 17
Cleveland 17, ATLANTA 13
PITTSBURGH 38, New Orleans 31
BALTIMORE 24, Atlanta 10
New England 35, GREEN BAY 0
MIAMI 24, Minnesota 15
Cincinnati 31, NEW ORLEANS 16
Tennessee 31, PHILADELPHIA 13
JACKSONVILLE 26, New York Giants 10
Miami 27, DETROIT 10
NEW ENGLAND 17, Chicago 13
TENNESSEE 24, New York Giants 21
INDIANAPOLIS 45, Philadelphia 21
New York Jets 38, GREEN BAY 10
NEW ENGLAND 28, Detroit 21
PITTSBURGH 20, Tampa Bay 3
Pittsburgh 37, CAROLINA 3
New York Jets 26, MINNESOTA 13
Denver 37, ARIZONA 20
San Diego 20, SEATTLE 17
SAN DIEGO 27, Arizona 20
NFC Victories
New Orleans 19, CLEVELAND 14
Philadelphia 24, HOUSTON 10
ST. LOUIS 18, Denver 10
Washington 31, HOUSTON 15
Dallas 45, TENNESSEE 14
WASHINGTON 36, Jacksonville 30 (OT)
CAROLINA 20, Cleveland 12
CHICAGO 40, Buffalo 7
SAN FRANCISCO 34, Oakland 20
Carolina 23, BALTIMORE 21
DALLAS 34, Houston 6
DETROIT 20, Buffalo 17
TAMPA BAY 14, Cincinnati 13
ATLANTA 41, Pittsburgh 38 (OT)
Green Bay 34, MIAMI 24
Atlanta 29, CINCINNATI 27
SEATTLE 16, Oakland 0
New York GIANTS 14, Houston 10
Chicago 10, NEW YORK JETS 0
DALLAS 21, Indianapolis 14
Seattle 23, DENVER 20
St. Louis 20, OAKLAND 0
Tampa Bay 22, CLEVELAND 7
San Francisco 26, DENVER 23 (OT)

REGULAR SEASON INTERCONFERENCE RECORDS, 1970-2006

AMERICAN FOOTBALL CONFERENCE

East	W	L	T	Pct.
Miami	90	43	0	.677
Buffalo	66	63	1	.512
New England	62	68	0	.477
New York Jets	57	73	0	.438
North	**W**	**L**	**T**	**Pct.**
Pittsburgh	79	52	1	.602
Baltimore	22	19	1	.536
Cincinnati	70	62	0	.530
Cleveland	57	65	0	.467
South	**W**	**L**	**T**	**Pct.**
Jacksonville	27	20	0	.574
Tennessee	65	71	1	.478
Indianapolis	57	65	1	.467
Houston	6	14	0	.300
West	**W**	**L**	**T**	**Pct.**
Oakland	86	51	1	.628
Denver	77	59	2	.565
Kansas City	66	54	2	.550
San Diego	61	66	0	.480

NATIONAL FOOTBALL CONFERENCE

East	W	L	T	Pct.
Dallas	75	57	0	.568
Philadelphia	71	61	1	.538
Washington	67	64	0	.511
New York Giants	62	62	0	.500
North	**W**	**L**	**T**	**Pct.**
Minnesota	67	67	0	.500
Chicago	63	72	0	.467
Green Bay	56	75	3	.429
Detroit	51	78	1	.396
South	**W**	**L**	**T**	**Pct.**
Carolina	24	24	0	.500
New Orleans	54	80	2	.403
Tampa Bay*	40	61	0	.396
Atlanta	52	84	1	.383
West	**W**	**L**	**T**	**Pct.**
San Francisco	78	61	0	.561
St. Louis	76	61	0	.555
Seattle* #	55	54	0	.505
Arizona	43	76	2	.363

* Records include one game played between Seattle and Tampa Bay, won by the Seahawks 13-10, in their inaugural season (1976) when Seattle competed in the NFC and Tampa Bay in the AFC.

\# Seattle was a member of the AFC from 1977-2001.

From 1970-71, tie games were not included in winning percentage.

INTERCONFERENCE VICTORIES, 1970-2006

REGULAR SEASON				PRESEASON			
	AFC	NFC	Tie		AFC	NFC	Tie
1970	12	27	1	1970	21	28	1
1971	15	23	2	1971	28	28	3
1972	20	19	1	1972	27	25	4
1973	19	19	2	1973	23	35	2
1974	23	17	0	1974	35	25	0
1975	23	17	0	1975	30	26	1
1976	16	12	0	1976	30	31	0
1977	19	9	0	1977	38	25	0
1978	31	21	0	1978	20	19	0
1979	36	16	0	1979	25	18	0
1980	33	19	0	1980	22	20	1
1981	24	28	0	1981	18	19	0
1982	15	14	1	1982	25	16	0
1983	26	26	0	1983	15	24	0
1984	26	26	0	1984	16	19	0
1985	27	25	0	1985	10	22	1
1986	26	26	0	1986	22	17	0
1987	23	22	1	1987	22	22	0
1988	30	22	0	1988	23	16	1
1989	24	28	0	1989	16	27	0
1990	26	26	0	1990	15	29	0
1991	19	33	0	1991	19	27	0
1992	22	30	0	1992	30	22	0
1993	27	25	0	1993	17	22	0
1994	25	27	0	1994	22	16	0
1995	27	33	0	1995	19	26	0
1996	32	28	0	1996	27	19	0
1997	31	28	1	1997	26	17	0
1998	31	29	0	1998	34	16	0
1999	38	22	0	1999	22	25	0
2000	30	30	0	2000	34	17	0
2001	30	30	0	2001	28	23	0
2002	34	29	1	2002	25	24	0
2003	34	30	0	2003	25	21	0
2004	44	20	0	2004	21	18	0
2005	34	30	0	2005	21	29	0
2006	40	24	0	2006	27	24	0
Total	992	890	10	Total	878	837	14

PRO FOOTBALL HALL OF FAME GAME (44)

Date	Winner	Loser	Attendance
August 11, 1962	New York Giants 21 (tie)	St. Louis Cardinals 21 (tie)	14,000
September 8, 1963	Pittsburgh Steelers 16	Cleveland Browns 7	18,462
September 6, 1964	Baltimore Colts 48	Pittsburgh Steelers 17	11,479
September 12, 1965	Washington Redskins 20	Detroit Lions 3	14,416
1966	No game was played		
August 5, 1967	Philadelphia Eagles 28	Cleveland Browns 13	17,304
August 3, 1968	Chicago Bears 30	Dallas Cowboys 24	14,578
September 13, 1969	Green Bay Packers 38	Atlanta Falcons 24	17,411
August 8, 1970	New Orleans Saints 14	Minnesota Vikings 13	17,932
July 31, 1971	Los Angeles Rams (NFC) 17	Houston Oilers (AFC) 6	19,384
July 29, 1972	Kansas City Chiefs (AFC) 23	New York Giants (NFC) 17	19,304
July 28, 1973	San Francisco 49ers (NFC) 20	New England Patriots (AFC) 7	19,685
July 27, 1974	St. Louis Cardinals (NFC) 21	Buffalo Bills (AFC) 13	17,286
August 2, 1975	Washington Redskins (NFC) 17	Cincinnati Bengals (AFC) 9	19,360
July 24, 1976	Denver Broncos (AFC) 10	Detroit Lions (NFC) 7	17,639
July 30, 1977	Chicago Bears (NFC) 20	New York Jets (AFC) 6	19,057
July 29, 1978	Philadelphia Eagles (NFC) 17	Miami Dolphins (AFC) 3	19,255
July 28, 1979	Oakland Raiders (AFC) 20	Dallas Cowboys (NFC) 13	20,648
August 2, 1980*	San Diego Chargers (AFC) 0	Green Bay Packers (NFC) 0	19,972
August 1, 1981	Cleveland Browns (AFC) 24	Atlanta Falcons (NFC) 10	23,921
August 7, 1982	Minnesota Vikings (NFC) 30	Baltimore Colts (AFC) 14	23,379
July 30, 1983	Pittsburgh Steelers (AFC) 27	New Orleans Saints (NFC) 14	23,909
July 28, 1984	Seattle Seahawks (AFC) 38	Tampa Bay Buccaneers (NFC) 0	22,250
August 3, 1985	New York Giants (NFC) 21	Houston Oilers (AFC) 20	23,940
August 2, 1986	New England Patriots (AFC) 21	St. Louis Cardinals (NFC) 16	22,739
August 8, 1987	San Francisco 49ers (NFC) 20	Kansas City Chiefs (AFC) 7	23,826
July 30, 1988	Cincinnati Bengals (AFC) 14	Los Angeles Rams (NFC) 7	23,801
August 5, 1989	Washington Redskins (NFC) 31	Buffalo Bills (AFC) 6	23,948
August 4, 1990	Chicago Bears (NFC) 13	Cleveland Browns (AFC) 0	23,952
July 27, 1991	Detroit Lions (NFC) 14	Denver Broncos (AFC) 3	23,815
August 1, 1992	New York Jets (AFC) 41	Philadelphia Eagles (NFC) 14	23,853
July 31, 1993	Los Angeles Raiders (AFC) 19	Green Bay Packers (NFC) 3	23,863
July 30, 1994	Atlanta Falcons (NFC) 21	San Diego Chargers (AFC) 17	23,185
July 29, 1995	Carolina Panthers (NFC) 20	Jacksonville Jaguars (AFC) 14	24,625
July 27, 1996	Indianapolis Colts (AFC) 10	New Orleans Saints (NFC) 3	23,376
July 26, 1997	Minnesota Vikings (NFC) 28	Seattle Seahawks (AFC) 26	23,846
August 1, 1998	Tampa Bay Buccaneers (NFC) 30	Pittsburgh Steelers (AFC) 6	23,875
August 9, 1999	Cleveland Browns (AFC) 20	Dallas Cowboys (NFC) 17 (OT)	25,156
July 31, 2000	New England Patriots (AFC) 20	San Francisco 49ers (NFC) 0	22,840
August 6, 2001	St. Louis Rams (NFC) 17	Miami Dolphins (AFC) 10	22,736
August 5, 2002	New York Giants (NFC) 34	Houston Texans (AFC) 17	22,461
August 4, 2003**	Kansas City Chiefs (AFC) 9	Green Bay Packers (NFC) 0	22,385
August 9, 2004	Washington Redskins (NFC) 20	Denver Broncos (AFC) 17	22,177
August 8, 2005	Chicago Bears (NFC) 27	Miami Dolphins (AFC) 24	22,292
August 6, 2006	Oakland Raiders (NFC) 16	Philadelphia Eagles (NFC) 10	22,200

Game called with 5:29 remaining because of severe thunder and lightning.
**Game called with 5:49 remaining in the third quarter because of lightning and torrential rain.*

INTERNATIONAL GAMES

NFL INTERNATIONAL GAMES (57)

Date	Site	Teams
August 12, 1950	Ottawa, Canada	N.Y. Giants 27, Ottawa Rough Riders 6
August 11, 1951	Ottawa, Canada	N.Y. Giants 41, Ottawa Rough Riders 18
August 5, 1959	Toronto, Canada	Chi. Cardinals 55, Tor. Argonauts 26
August 3, 1960	Toronto, Canada	Pittsburgh 43, Toronto Argonauts 16
August 15, 1960	Toronto, Canada	Chicago 16, N.Y. Giants 7
August 2, 1961	Toronto, Canada	St. Louis 36, Toronto Argonauts 7
August 5, 1961	Montreal, Canada	Chicago 34, Montreal Allouettes 16
August 8, 1961	Hamilton, Canada	Hamilton Tiger-Cats 38, Buffalo 21
August 25, 1969	Montreal, Canada	Detroit 22, Boston 9
September 11, 1969	Montreal, Canada	Pittsburgh 17, N.Y. Giants 13
August 16, 1976	Tokyo, Japan	St. Louis 20, San Diego 10
August 5, 1978	Mexico City, Mexico	New Orleans 14, Philadelphia 7
August 6, 1983	London, England	Minnesota 28, St. Louis 10
* August 3, 1986	London, England	Chicago 17, Dallas 6
* August 9, 1987	London, England	L.A. Rams 28, Denver 27
* July 31, 1988	London, England	Miami 27, San Francisco 21
August 14, 1988	Goteborg, Sweden	Minnesota 28, Chicago 21
August 18, 1988	Montreal, Canada	N.Y. Jets 11, Cleveland 7
* August 5, 1989	Tokyo, Japan	L.A. Rams 16, San Francisco 13 (OT)
* August 6, 1989	London, England	Philadelphia 17, Cleveland 13
* August 4, 1990	Tokyo, Japan	Denver 10, Seattle 7
* August 5, 1990	London, England	New Orleans 17, L.A. Raiders 10
* August 9, 1990	Montreal, Canada	Pittsburgh 30, New England 14
* August 11, 1990	Berlin, Germany	L.A. Rams 19, Kansas City 3
* July 28, 1991	London, England	Buffalo 17, Philadelphia 13
* August 3, 1991	Berlin, Germany	San Francisco 21, Chicago 7
* August 3, 1991	Tokyo, Japan	Miami 19, L.A. Raiders 17
* August 1, 1992	Tokyo, Japan	Houston 34, Dallas 23
* August 15, 1992	Berlin, Germany	Miami 31, Denver 27
* August 16, 1992	London, England	San Francisco 17, Washington 15
* July 31, 1993	Tokyo, Japan	New Orleans 28, Philadelphia 16
* August 1, 1993	Barcelona, Spain	San Francisco 21, Pittsburgh 14
* August 7, 1993	Berlin, Germany	Minnesota 20, Buffalo 6
* August 8, 1993	London, England	Dallas 13, Detroit 13 (OT)
August 14, 1993	Toronto, Canada	Cleveland 12, New England 9
* July 31, 1994	Barcelona, Spain	L.A. Raiders 25, Denver 22
* August 6, 1994	Tokyo, Japan	Minnesota 17, Kansas City 9
* August 13, 1994	Berlin, Germany	N.Y. Giants 28, San Diego 20
* August 15, 1994	Mexico City, Mexico	Houston 6, Dallas 0
* August 5, 1995	Tokyo, Japan	Denver 24, San Francisco 10
* August 12, 1995	Toronto, Canada	Buffalo 9, Dallas 7
* July 27, 1996	Tokyo, Japan	San Diego 20, Pittsburgh 10
* August 5, 1996	Monterrey, Mexico	Kansas City 32, Dallas 6
* July 27, 1997	Dublin, Ireland	Pittsburgh 30, Chicago 17
* August 4, 1997	Mexico City, Mexico	Miami 38, Denver 19
* August 16, 1997	Toronto, Canada	Green Bay 35, Buffalo 3
* August 1, 1998	Tokyo, Japan	Green Bay 27, Kansas City 24 (OT)
* August 15, 1998	Vancouver, Canada	San Francisco 24, Seattle 21
* August 17, 1998	Mexico City, Mexico	New England 21, Dallas 3
* August 7, 1999	Sydney, Australia	Denver 20, San Diego 17
* August 5, 2000	Tokyo, Japan	Atlanta 20, Dallas 9
* August 19, 2000	Mexico City, Mexico	Indianapolis 24, Pittsburgh 23
* August 27, 2001	Mexico City, Mexico	Dallas 21, Oakland 6
* August 3, 2002	Osaka, Japan	Washington 38, San Francisco 7
* August 2, 2003	Tokyo, Japan	Tampa Bay 30, N.Y. Jets 14
* August 6, 2005	Tokyo, Japan	Atlanta 27, Indianapolis 21
** October 2, 2005	Mexico City, Mexico	Arizona 31, San Francisco 14

* *American Bowl Game*
** *Regular-season Game*

CHICAGO ALL-STAR GAME

Pro teams won 31, lost 9, and tied 2. The game was discontinued after 1976.

Date	Winner	Loser	Attendance
August 31, 1934	Chicago Bears 0	All-Stars 0 (tie)	79,432
August 29, 1935	Chicago Bears 5	All-Stars 0	77,450
September 3, 1936	Detroit Lions 7	All-Stars 7 (tie)	76,000
September 1, 1937	All-Stars 6	Green Bay Packers 0	84,560
August 31, 1938	All-Stars 28	Washington Redskins 16	74,250
August 30, 1939	N.Y. Giants 9	All-Stars 0	81,456
August 29, 1940	Green Bay Packers 45	All-Stars 28	84,567
August 28, 1941	Chicago Bears 37	All-Stars 13	98,203
August 28, 1942	Chicago Bears 21	All-Stars 0	101,100
August 25, 1943	All-Stars 27	Washington Redskins 7	48,471
August 30, 1944	Chicago Bears 24	All-Stars 21	48,769
August 30, 1945	Green Bay Packers 19	All-Stars 7	92,753
August 23, 1946	All-Stars 16	Los Angeles Rams 0	97,380
August 22, 1947	All-Stars 16	Chicago Bears 0	105,840
August 20, 1948	Chicago Cardinals 28	All-Stars 0	101,220
August 12, 1949	Philadelphia Eagles 38	All-Stars 0	93,780
August 11, 1950	All-Stars 17	Philadelphia Eagles 7	88,885
August 17, 1951	Cleveland Browns 33	All-Stars 0	92,180
August 15, 1952	Los Angeles Rams 10	All-Stars 7	88,316
August 14, 1953	Detroit Lions 24	All-Stars 10	93,818
August 13, 1954	Detroit Lions 31	All-Stars 6	93,470
August 12, 1955	All-Stars 30	Cleveland Browns 27	75,000
August 10, 1956	Cleveland Browns 26	All-Stars 0	75,000
August 9, 1957	N.Y. Giants 22	All-Stars 12	75,000
August 15, 1958	All-Stars 35	Detroit Lions 19	70,000
August 14, 1959	Baltimore Colts 29	All-Stars 0	70,000
August 12, 1960	Baltimore Colts 32	All-Stars 7	70,000
August 4, 1961	Philadelphia Eagles 28	All-Stars 14	66,000
August 3, 1962	Green Bay Packers 42	All-Stars 20	65,000
August 2, 1963	All-Stars 20	Green Bay Packers 17	65,000
August 7, 1964	Chicago Bears 28	All-Stars 17	65,000
August 6, 1965	Cleveland Browns 24	All-Stars 16	68,000
August 5, 1966	Green Bay Packers 38	All-Stars 0	72,000
August 4, 1967	Green Bay Packers 27	All-Stars 0	70,934
August 2, 1968	Green Bay Packers 34	All-Stars 17	69,917
August 1, 1969	N.Y. Jets 26	All-Stars 24	74,208
July 31, 1970	Kansas City Chiefs 24	All-Stars 3	69,940
July 30, 1971	Baltimore Colts 24	All-Stars 17	52,289
July 28, 1972	Dallas Cowboys 20	All-Stars 7	54,162
July 27, 1973	Miami Dolphins 14	All-Stars 3	54,103
1974	No game was played		
August 1, 1975	Pittsburgh Steelers 21	All-Stars 14	54,103
July 23, 1976*	Pittsburgh Steelers 24	All-Stars 0	52,895

*Game shortened because of thunderstorms.

NFL PLAYOFF BOWL

Consolation game that matched conference runners-up.
Western Conference won 8, Eastern Conference won 2.
All games played at Miami's Orange Bowl.

January 7, 1961	Detroit Lions 17, Cleveland Browns 16
January 6, 1962	Detroit Lions 38, Philadelphia Eagles 10
January 6, 1963	Detroit Lions 17, Pittsburgh Steelers 10
January 5, 1964	Green Bay Packers 40, Cleveland Browns 23
January 3, 1965	St. Louis Cardinals 24, Green Bay Packers 17
January 9, 1966	Baltimore Colts 35, Dallas Cowboys 3
January 8, 1967	Baltimore Colts 20, Philadelphia Eagles 14
January 7, 1968	Los Angeles Rams 30, Cleveland Browns 6
January 5, 1969	Dallas Cowboys 17, Minnesota Vikings 13
January 3, 1970	Los Angeles Rams 31, Dallas Cowboys 0

HISTORY OF OVERTIME GAMES

PRESEASON

Aug. 28, 1955	Los Angeles 23, New York Giants 17, at Portland, Oregon
Aug. 24, 1962	Denver 27, Dallas Texans 24, at Fort Worth, Texas
Aug. 10, 1974	San Diego 20, New York Jets 14, at San Diego
Aug. 17, 1974	Pittsburgh 33, Philadelphia 30, at Philadelphia
Aug. 17, 1974	Dallas 19, Houston 13, at Dallas
Aug. 17, 1974	Cincinnati 13, Atlanta 7, at Atlanta
Sept. 6, 1974	Buffalo 23, New York Giants 17, at Buffalo
Aug. 9, 1975	Baltimore 23, Denver 20, at Denver
Aug. 30, 1975	New England 20, Green Bay 17, at Milwaukee
Sept. 13, 1975	Minnesota 14, San Diego 14, at San Diego
Aug. 1, 1976	New England 13, New York Giants 7, at New England
Aug. 2, 1976	Kansas City 9, Houston 3, at Kansas City
Aug. 20, 1976	New Orleans 26, Baltimore 20, at Baltimore
Sept. 4, 1976	Dallas 26, Houston 20, at Dallas
Aug. 13, 1977	Seattle 23, Dallas 17, at Seattle
Aug. 28, 1977	New England 13, Pittsburgh 10, at New England
Aug. 28, 1977	New York Giants 24, Buffalo 21, at East Rutherford, N.J.
Aug. 2, 1979	Seattle 12, Minnesota 9, at Minnesota
Aug. 4, 1979	Los Angeles 20, Oakland 14, at Los Angeles
Aug. 24, 1979	Denver 20, New England 17, at Denver
Aug. 23, 1980	Tampa Bay 20, Cincinnati 14, at Tampa Bay
Aug. 5, 1981	San Francisco 27, Seattle 24, at Seattle
Aug. 29, 1981	New Orleans 20, Detroit 17, at New Orleans
Aug. 28, 1982	Miami 17, Kansas City 17, at Kansas City
Sept. 3, 1982	Miami 16, New York Giants 13, at Miami
Aug. 6, 1983	L.A. Raiders 26, San Francisco 23, at Los Angeles
Aug. 6, 1983	Atlanta 13, Washington 10, at Atlanta
Aug. 13, 1983	St. Louis 27, Chicago 24, at St. Louis
Aug. 18, 1983	New York Jets 20, Cincinnati 17, at Cincinnati
Aug. 27, 1983	Chicago 20, Kansas City 17, at Chicago
Aug. 11, 1984	Pittsburgh 20, Philadelphia 17, at Pittsburgh
Aug. 9, 1985	Buffalo 10, Detroit 10, at Pontiac, Mich.
Aug. 10, 1985	Minnesota 16, Miami 13, at Miami
Aug. 17, 1985	Dallas 27, San Diego 24, at San Diego
Aug. 24, 1985	N.Y. Giants 34, N.Y. Jets 31, at East Rutherford, N.J.
Aug. 15, 1986	Washington 27, Pittsburgh 24, at Washington
Aug. 15, 1986	Detroit 30, Seattle 27, at Detroit
Aug. 23, 1986	Los Angeles Rams 20, San Diego 17, at Anaheim
Aug. 30, 1986	Minnesota 23, Indianapolis 20, at Indianapolis
Aug. 23, 1987	Philadelphia 19, New England 13, at New England
Sept. 5, 1987	Cleveland 30, Green Bay 24, at Milwaukee
Sept. 6, 1987	Kansas City 13, St. Louis 10, at Memphis, Tenn.
Aug. 11, 1988	Seattle 16, Detroit 13, at Detroit
Aug. 19, 1988	Miami 16, Denver 13, at Miami
Aug. 19, 1988	Green Bay 21, Kansas City 21, at Milwaukee
Aug. 20, 1988	Houston 20, Los Angeles Rams 17, at Anaheim
Aug. 21, 1988	Minnesota 19, Phoenix 16, at Phoenix
Aug. 5, 1989	Los Angeles Rams 16, San Francisco 13, at Tokyo, Japan
Aug. 26, 1989	Denver 24, Dallas 21, at Denver
Sept. 1, 1989	N.Y. Jets 15, Kansas City 13, at Kansas City
Aug. 24, 1990	Cincinnati 13, New England 10, at New England
Aug. 16, 1991	Cleveland 24, Washington 21, at Washington
Aug. 17, 1991	Cincinnati 27, Minnesota 24, at Cincinnati
Aug. 23, 1991	Dallas 20, Atlanta 17, at Dallas
Aug. 24, 1991	Cincinnati 19, Green Bay 16, at Green Bay
Aug. 22, 1992	Los Angeles Rams 16, Green Bay 13, at Anaheim
Aug. 8, 1993	Dallas 13, Detroit 13, at London, England
Aug. 12, 1995	Washington 16, Houston 13, at Knoxville, Tenn.
Aug. 19, 1995	Indianapolis 20, Green Bay 17, at Green Bay
Aug. 3, 1996	Minnesota 23, San Diego 20, at Minnesota
Aug. 10, 1996	San Francisco 16, San Diego 13, at San Francisco
Aug. 1, 1998	Green Bay 27, Kansas City 24, at Tokyo, Japan
Aug. 7, 1998	Detroit 13, Arizona 10, at Pontiac, Mich.
Aug. 22, 1998	Minnesota 25, Carolina 22, at Charlotte, N.C.
Aug. 9, 1999	Cleveland 20, Dallas 17, at Canton, Ohio
Aug. 4, 2001	Chicago 16, Cincinnati 13, at Chicago
Aug. 18, 2001	San Diego 23, Miami 20, at Miami
Aug. 18, 2001	Arizona 16, Seattle 13, at Seattle
Aug. 25, 2001	San Diego 13, St. Louis 10, at San Diego
Aug. 10, 2002	Kansas City 17, San Francisco 14, at San Francisco
Aug. 31, 2006	Dallas 10, Minnesota 10, at Dallas

* indicates Monday-night game
 # indicates Thursday/Saturday/Sunday-night game
+ indicates Thanksgiving Day game

REGULAR SEASON

Sept. 22, 1974—Pittsburgh 35, Denver 35, at Denver; Steelers win toss. Gilliam's pass intercepted and returned by Rowser to Denver's 42. Turner misses 41-yard field goal. Walden punts and Greer returns to Broncos' 39. Van Heusen punts and Edwards returns to Steelers' 16. Game ends with Steelers on own 26.

Nov. 10, 1974—New York Jets 26, New York Giants 20, at New Haven, Conn.; Giants win toss. Gogolak misses 42-yard field goal. Namath passes to Boozer for five yards and touchdown at 6:53.

Sept. 28, 1975—Dallas 37, St. Louis 31, at Dallas; Cardinals win toss. Hart's pass intercepted and returned by Jordan to Cardinals' 37. Staubach passes to DuPree for three yards and touchdown at 7:53.

Oct. 12, 1975—Los Angeles 13, San Diego 10, at San Diego; Chargers win toss. Partee punts to Rams' 14. Dempsey kicks 22-yard field goal at 9:27.

Nov. 2, 1975—Washington 30, Dallas 24, at Washington; Cowboys win toss. Staubach's pass intercepted and returned by Houston to Cowboys' 35. Kilmer runs one yard for touchdown at 6:34.

Nov. 16, 1975—St. Louis 20, Washington 17, at St. Louis; Cardinals win toss. Bakken kicks 37-yard field goal at 7:00.

Nov. 23, 1975—Kansas City 24, Detroit 21, at Kansas City; Lions win toss. Chiefs take over on downs at own 38. Stenerud kicks 26-yard field goal at 6:44.

Nov. 23, 1975—Oakland 26, Washington 23, at Washington; Redskins win toss. Bragg punts to Raiders' 42. Blanda kicks 27-yard field goal at 7:13.

Nov. 30, 1975—Denver 13, San Diego 10, at Denver; Broncos win toss. Turner kicks 25-yard field goal at 4:13.

Nov. 30, 1975—Oakland 37, Atlanta 34, at Oakland; Falcons win toss. James punts to Raiders' 16. Guy punts and Herron returns to Falcons' 41. Nick Mike-Mayer misses 45-yard field goal. Guy punts into Falcons' end zone. James punts to Raiders' 39. Blanda kicks 36-yard field goal at 15:00.

Dec. 14, 1975—Baltimore 10, Miami 7, at Baltimore; Dolphins win toss. Seiple punts to Colts' 4. Linhart kicks 31-yard field goal at 12:44.

Sept. 19, 1976—Minnesota 10, Los Angeles 10, at Minnesota; Vikings win toss. Tarkenton's pass intercepted by Monte Jackson and returned to Minnesota 16. Allen blocks Dempsey's 30-yard field goal attempt, ball rolls into end zone for touchback. Clabo punts and Scribner returns to Rams' 20. Rusty Jackson punts to Vikings' 35. Tarkenton's pass intercepted by Kay at Rams' 1, no return. Game ends with Rams on own 3.

* Sept. 27, 1976—Washington 20, Philadelphia 17, at Philadelphia; Eagles win toss. Jones punts and E. Brown loses one yard on return to Redskins' 40. Bragg punts 51 yards into end zone for touchback. Jones punts and E. Brown returns to Redskins' 42. Bragg punts and Marshall returns to Eagles' 41. Boryla's pass intercepted by Dusek at Redskins' 37, no return. Bragg punts and Bradley returns. Philadelphia holding penalty moves ball back to Eagles' 8. Boryla pass intercepted by E. Brown and returned to Eagles' 22. Moseley kicks 29-yard field goal at 12:49.

Oct. 17, 1976—Kansas City 20, Miami 17, at Miami; Chiefs win toss. Wilson punts into end zone for touchback. Bulaich fumbles into Kansas City end zone, Collier recovers for touchback. Stenerud kicks 34-yard field goal at 14:48.

Oct. 31, 1976—St. Louis 23, San Francisco 20, at St. Louis; Cardinals win toss. Joyce punts and Leonard fumbles on return, Jones recovers at 49ers' 43. Bakken kicks 21-yard field goal at 6:42.

Dec. 5, 1976—San Diego 13, San Francisco 7, at San Diego; Chargers win toss. Morris runs 13 yards for touchdown at 5:12.

Sept. 18, 1977—Dallas 16, Minnesota 10, at Minnesota; Vikings win toss. Dallas starts on Vikings' 47 after a punt early in the overtime period. Staubach scores seven plays later on a four-yard run at 6:14.

* Sept. 26, 1977—Cleveland 30, New England 27, at Cleveland; Browns win toss. Sipe throws a 22-yard pass to Logan at Patriots' 19. Cockroft kicks 35-yard field goal at 4:45.

Oct. 16, 1977—Minnesota 22, Chicago 16, at Minnesota; Bears win toss. Parsons punts 53 yards to Vikings' 18. Minnesota drives to Bears' 11. On a first-and-10, Vikings fake a field goal and holder Krause hits Voigt with a touchdown pass at 6:45.

Oct. 30, 1977—Cincinnati 13, Houston 10, at Cincinnati; Bengals win toss. Bahr kicks a 22-yard field goal at 5:51.

Nov. 13, 1977—San Francisco 10, New Orleans 7, at New Orleans; Saints win toss. Saints fail to move ball and Blanchard punts to 49ers' 41. Wersching kicks a 33-yard field goal at 6:33.

Dec. 18, 1977—Chicago 12, New York Giants 9, at East Rutherford, N.J.; Giants win toss. The ball changes hands eight times before Thomas kicks a 28-yard field goal at 14:51.

Sept. 10, 1978—Cleveland 13, Cincinnati 10, at Cleveland; Browns win toss. Collins returns kickoff 41 yards to Browns' 47. Cockroft kicks 27-yard field goal at 4:30.

* Sept. 11, 1978—Minnesota 12, Denver 9, at Minnesota; Vikings win toss. Danmeier kicks 44-yard field goal at 2:56.

Sept. 24, 1978—Pittsburgh 15, Cleveland 9, at Pittsburgh; Steelers win toss. Cunningham scores on a 37-yard "gadget" pass from Bradshaw at 3:43. Steelers start winning drive on their 21.

Sept. 24, 1978—Denver 23, Kansas City 17, at Kansas City; Broncos win toss. Dilts punts to Kansas City. Chiefs advance to Broncos' 40 where Reed fails to make first down on fourth-and-one situation. Broncos march downfield. Preston scores two-yard touchdown at 10:28.

Oct. 1, 1978—Oakland 25, Chicago 19, at Chicago; Bears win toss. Both teams punt on first possession. On Chicago's second offensive series, Colzie intercepts Avellini's pass and returns it to Bears' 3. Three plays later, Whittington runs two yards for a touchdown at 5:19.

Oct. 15, 1978—Dallas 24, St. Louis 21, at St. Louis; Cowboys win toss. Dallas drives from its 23 into field goal range. Septien kicks 27-yard field goal at 3:28.

Oct. 29, 1978—Denver 20, Seattle 17, at Seattle; Broncos win toss. Ball changes hands four times before Turner kicks 18-yard field goal at 12:59.

Nov. 12, 1978—San Diego 29, Kansas City 23, at San Diego; Chiefs win toss. Fouts hits Jefferson for decisive 14-yard touchdown pass on the last play (15:00) of overtime period.

Nov. 12, 1978—Washington 16, New York Giants 13, at Washington; Redskins win toss. Moseley kicks winning 45-yard field goal at 8:32 after missing first down field goal attempt of 35 yards at 4:50.

Nov. 26, 1978—Green Bay 10, Minnesota 10, at Green Bay; Packers win toss. Both teams have possession of the ball four times.

Dec. 9, 1978—Cleveland 37, New York Jets 34, at Cleveland; Browns win toss. Cockroft kicks 22-yard field goal at 3:07.

Sept. 2, 1979—Atlanta 40, New Orleans 34, at New Orleans; Falcons win toss. Bartkowski's pass intercepted by Myers and returned to Falcons' 46. Erxleben punts to Falcons' 4. James punts to Chandler on Saints' 43. Erxleben punts and Ryckman returns to Falcons' 28. James punts and Chandler returns to Saints' 36. Erxleben retrieves punt snap on Saints' 1 and attempts pass. Mayberry intercepts and returns six yards for touchdown at 8:22.

Sept. 2, 1979—Cleveland 25, New York Jets 22, at New York;

Jets win toss. Leahy's 43-yard field goal attempt goes wide right at 4:41. Evans's punt blocked by Dykes is recovered by Newton. Ramsey punts into end zone for touchback. Evans punts and Harper returns to Jets' 24. Robinson's pass intercepted by Davis and returned 33 yards to Jets' 31. Cockroft kicks 27-yard field goal at 14:45.

* **Sept. 3, 1979—Pittsburgh 16, New England 13,** at Foxboro; Patriots win toss. Hare punts to Swann at Steelers' 31. Bahr kicks 41-yard field goal at 5:10.

Sept. 9, 1979—Tampa Bay 29, Baltimore 26, at Baltimore; Colts win toss. Landry fumbles, recovered by Kollar at Colts' 14. O'Donoghue kicks 31-yard, first-down field goal at 1:41.

Sept. 16, 1979—Denver 20, Atlanta 17, at Atlanta; Broncos win toss. Broncos march 65 yards to Falcons' 7. Turner kicks 24-yard field goal at 6:15.

Sept. 23, 1979—Houston 30, Cincinnati 27, at Cincinnati; Oilers win toss. Parsley punts and Lusby returns to Bengals' 33. Bahr's 32-yard field goal attempt is wide right at 8:05. Parsley's punt downed on Bengals' 5. McInally punts and Ellender returns to Bengals' 42. Fritsch's third down, 29-yard field goal attempt hits left upright and bounces through at 14:28.

Sept. 23, 1979—Minnesota 27, Green Bay 21, at Minnesota; Vikings win toss. Kramer throws 50-yard touchdown pass to Rashad at 3:18.

Oct. 28, 1979—Houston 27, New York Jets 24, at Houston; Oilers win toss. Oilers march 58 yards to Jets' 18. Fritsch kicks 35-yard field goal at 5:10.

Nov. 18, 1979—Cleveland 30, Miami 24, at Cleveland; Browns win toss. Sipe passes 39 yards to Rucker for touchdown at 1:59.

Nov. 25, 1979—Pittsburgh 33, Cleveland 30, at Pittsburgh; Browns win toss. Sipe's pass intercepted by Blount on Steelers' 4. Bradshaw pass intercepted by Bolton on Browns' 12. Evans punts and Bell returns to Steelers' 17. Bahr kicks 37-yard field goal at 14:51.

Nov. 25, 1979—Buffalo 16, New England 13, at Foxboro; Patriots win toss. Hare's punt downed on Bills' 38. Jackson punts and Morgan returns to Patriots' 20. Grogan's pass intercepted by Haslett and returned to Bills' 42. Ferguson's 51-yard pass to Butler sets up N. Mike-Mayer's 29-yard field goal at 9:15.

Dec. 2, 1979—Los Angeles 27, Minnesota 21, at Los Angeles; Rams win toss. Clark punts and Miller returns to Vikings' 25. Kramer's pass intercepted by Brown and returned to Rams' 40. Cromwell, holding for 22-yard field goal attempt, runs and ends left end untouched for winning score at 6:53.

Sept. 7, 1980—Green Bay 12, Chicago 6, at Green Bay; Bears win toss. Parsons punts and Nixon returns 16 yards. Five plays later, Marcol returns own blocked field goal attempt 24 yards for touchdown at 6:00.

Sept. 14, 1980—San Diego 30, Oakland 24, at San Diego; Raiders win toss. Pastorini's first-down pass intercepted by Edwards. Millen intercepts Fouts' first-down pass and returns to San Diego 46. Bahr's 50-yard field goal attempt partially blocked by Williams and recovered on Chargers' 32. Eight plays later, Fouts throws 24-yard touchdown pass to Jefferson at 8:09.

Sept. 14, 1980—San Francisco 24, St. Louis 21, at San Francisco; Cardinals win toss. Swider punts and Robinson returns to 49ers' 32. San Francisco drives 52 yards to St. Louis 16, where Wersching kicks 33-yard field goal at 4:12.

Oct. 12, 1980—Green Bay 14, Tampa Bay 14, at Tampa Bay; Packers win toss. Teams trade punts twice. Lee returns second Tampa Bay punt to Green Bay 42. Dickey completes three passes to Buccaneers' 18, where Birney's 36-yard field goal attempt is wide right as time expires.

Nov. 9, 1980—Atlanta 33, St. Louis 27, at St. Louis; Falcons win toss. Strong runs 21 yards for touchdown at 4:20.

\# **Nov. 20, 1980—San Diego 27, Miami 24,** at Miami; Chargers win toss. Partridge punts into end zone, Dolphins take over on their own 20. Woodley's pass for Nathan intercepted by Lowe

and returned 28 yards to Dolphins' 12. Benirschke kicks 28-yard field goal at 7:14.

Nov. 23, 1980—New York Jets 31, Houston 28, at New York; Jets win toss. Leahy kicks 38-yard field goal at 3:58.

+ **Nov. 27, 1980—Chicago 23, Detroit 17,** at Detroit; Bears win toss. Williams returns kickoff 95 yards for touchdown at 0:21.

Dec. 7, 1980—Buffalo 10, Los Angeles 7, at Buffalo; Rams win toss. Corral punts and Hooks returns to Bills' 34. Ferguson's 30-yard pass to Lewis sets up N. Mike-Mayer's 30-yard field goal at 5:14.

Dec. 7, 1980—San Francisco 38, New Orleans 35, at San Francisco; Saints win toss. Erxleben's punt downed by Hardy on 49ers' 27. Wersching kicks 36-yard field goal at 7:40.

* **Dec. 8, 1980—Miami 16, New England 13,** at Miami; Dolphins win toss. Von Schamann kicks 23-yard field goal at 3:20.

Dec. 14, 1980—Cincinnati 17, Chicago 14, at Chicago; Bengals win toss. Breech kicks 28-yard field goal at 4:23.

Dec. 21, 1980—Los Angeles 20, Atlanta 17, at Los Angeles; Rams win toss. Corral's punt downed at Rams' 37. James punts into end zone for touchback. Corral's punt downed on Falcons' 17. Bartkowski fumbles when hit by Harris, recovered by Delaney. Corral kicks 23-yard field goal on first play of possession at 7:00.

Sept. 27, 1981—Cincinnati 27, Buffalo 24, at Cincinnati; Bills win toss. Cater punts into end zone for touchback. Bengals drive to the Bills' 10 where Breech kicks 28-yard field goal at 9:33.

Sept. 27, 1981—Pittsburgh 27, New England 21, at Pittsburgh; Patriots win toss. Hubach punts and Smith returns five yards to midfield. Four plays later Bradshaw throws 24-yard touchdown pass to Swann at 3:19.

Oct. 4, 1981—Miami 28, New York Jets 28, at Miami; Jets win toss. Teams trade punts twice. Leahy's 48-yard field goal attempt is wide right as time expires.

Oct. 25, 1981—New York Giants 27, Atlanta 24, at Atlanta; Giants win toss. Jennings' punt goes out of bounds at New York 47. Bright returns Atlanta punt to Giants' 14. Woerner fair catches punt at own 28. Andrews fumbles on first play, recovered by Van Pelt. Danelo kicks 40-yard field goal four plays later at 9:20.

Oct. 25, 1981—Chicago 20, San Diego 17, at Chicago; Bears win toss. Teams trade punts. Bears' second punt returned by Brooks to Chargers' 33. Fouts pass intercepted by Fencik and returned 32 yards to San Diego 27. Roveto kicks 27-yard field goal seven plays later at 9:30.

Nov. 8, 1981—Chicago 16, Kansas City 13, at Kansas City; Bears win toss. Teams trade punts. Kansas City takes over on downs on its own 38. Fuller's fumble recovered by Harris on Chicago 36. Roveto's 37-yard field goal wide, but Chiefs penalized for leverage. Roveto's 22-yard field goal attempt three plays later is good at 13:07.

Nov. 8, 1981—Denver 23, Cleveland 20, at Denver; Browns win toss. D. Smith recovers Hill's fumble at Denver 48. Morton's 33-yard pass to Upchurch and 6-yard run by Preston set up Steinfort's 30-yard field goal at 4:10.

Nov. 8, 1981—Miami 30, New England 27, at New England; Dolphins win toss. Orosz punts and Morgan returns six yards to New England 26. Grogan's pass intercepted by Brudzinski who returns 19 yards to Patriots' 26. Von Schamann kicks 30-yard field goal on first down at 7:09.

Nov. 15, 1981—Washington 30, New York Giants 27, at New York; Giants win toss. Nelms returns Giants' punt 26 yards to New York 47. Five plays later Moseley kicks 48-yard field goal at 3:44.

Dec. 20, 1981—New York Giants 13, Dallas 10, at New York; Cowboys win toss and kick off. Jennings punts to Dallas 40. Taylor recovers Dorsett's fumble on second down. Danelo's 33-yard field goal attempt hits right upright and bounces back. White's pass for Pearson intercepted by Hunt and returned seven yards to Dallas 24. Four plays later Danelo kicks 35-yard field goal at 6:19.

Sept. 12, 1982—Washington 37, Philadelphia 34, at Philadelphia; Redskins win toss. Theismann completes five passes for 63 yards to set up Moseley's 26-yard field goal at 4:47.

Sept. 19, 1982—Pittsburgh 26, Cincinnati 20, at Pittsburgh; Bengals win toss. Anderson's pass intended for Kreider intercepted by Woodruff and returned 30 yards to Cincinnati 2. Bradshaw completes two-yard touchdown pass to Stallworth on first down at 1:08.

Dec. 19, 1982—Baltimore 20, Green Bay 20, at Baltimore; Packers win toss. K. Anderson intercepts Dickey's first-down pass and returns to Packers' 42. Miller's 44-yard field goal attempt blocked by G. Lewis. Teams trade punts before Stenerud's 47-yard field goal attempt is wide right. Teams trade punts again before time expires in Colts possession.

Jan. 2, 1983—Tampa Bay 26, Chicago 23, at Tampa; Bears win toss. Parsons punts to T. Bell at Buccaneers' 40. Capece kicks 33-yard field goal at 3:14.

Sept. 4, 1983—Baltimore 29, New England 23, at New England; Patriots win toss. Cooks runs 52 yards with fumble recovery three plays into overtime at 0:30.

Sept. 4, 1983—Green Bay 41, Houston 38, at Houston; Packers win toss. Stenerud kicks 42-yard field goal at 5:55.

Sept. 11, 1983—New York Giants 16, Atlanta 13, at Atlanta; Giants win toss. Dennis returns kickoff 54 yards to Atlanta 41. Haji-Sheikh kicks 30-yard field goal at 3:38.

Sept. 18, 1983—New Orleans 34, Chicago 31, at New Orleans; Bears win toss. Parsons punts and Groth returns five yards to New Orleans 34. Stabler pass intercepted by Schmidt at Chicago 47. Parsons punt downed by Gentry at New Orleans 2. Stabler gains 36 yards in four passes; Wilson 38 on six carries. Andersen kicks 41-yard field goal at 10:57.

Sept. 18, 1983—Minnesota 19, Tampa Bay 16, at Tampa; Vikings win toss. Coleman punts and Bell returns eight yards to Tampa Bay 47. Capece's 33-yard field goal attempt sails wide at 7:26. Dils and Young combine for 48-yard gain to Tampa Bay 27. Ricardo kicks 42-yard field goal at 9:27.

Sept. 25, 1983—Baltimore 22, Chicago 19, at Baltimore; Colts win toss. Allegre kicks 33-yard field goal nine plays later at 4:51.

Sept. 25, 1983—Cleveland 30, San Diego 24, at San Diego; Browns win toss. Walker returns kickoff 33 yards to Cleveland 37. Sipe completes 48-yard touchdown pass to Holt four plays later at 1:53.

Sept. 25, 1983—New York Jets 27, Los Angeles Rams 24, at New York; Jets win toss. Ramsey punts to Irvin who returns to 25 but penalty puts Rams on own 13. Holmes 30-yard interception return sets up Leahy's 26-yard field goal at 3:22.

Oct. 9, 1983—Buffalo 38, Miami 35, at Miami; Dolphins win toss. Von Schamann's 52-yard field goal attempt goes wide at 12:36. Cater punts to Clayton who loses 11 to own 13. Von Schamann's 43-yard field goal attempt sails wide at 5:15. Danelo kicks 36-yard field goal nine plays later at 13:58.

Oct. 9, 1983—Dallas 27, Tampa Bay 24, at Dallas; Cowboys win toss. Septien's 51-yard field-goal attempt goes wide but Buccaneers penalized for roughing kicker. Septien kicks 42-yard field goal at 4:38.

Oct. 23, 1983—Kansas City 13, Houston 10, at Houston; Chiefs win toss. Lowery kicks 41-yard field goal 13 plays later at 7:41.

Oct. 23, 1983—Minnesota 20, Green Bay 17, at Green Bay; Packers win toss. Scribner's punt downed on Vikings' 42. Ricardo kicks 32-yard field goal eight plays later at 5:05.

* **Oct. 24, 1983—New York Giants 20, St. Louis 20**, at St. Louis; Cardinals win toss. Teams trade punts before O'Donoghue's 44-yard field goal attempt is wide left. Jennings' punt returned by Bird to St. Louis 21. Lomax pass intercepted by Haynes who loses six yards to New York 33. Jennings' punt downed on St. Louis 17. O'Donoghue's 19-yard field goal

attempt is wide right. Rutledge's pass intercepted by L. Washington who returns 25 yards to New York 25. O'Donoghue's 42-yard field goal attempt is wide right. Rutledge's pass intercepted by W. Smith at St. Louis 33 to end game.

Oct. 30, 1983—Cleveland 25, Houston 19, at Cleveland; Oilers win toss. Teams trade punts. Nielsen's pass intercepted by Whitwell who returns to Houston 20. Green runs 20 yards for touchdown on first down at 6:34.

Nov. 20, 1983—Detroit 23, Green Bay 20, at Milwaukee; Packers win toss. Scribner punts and Jenkins returns 14 yards to Green Bay 45. Murray's 33-yard field goal attempt is wide left at 9:32. Whitehurst's pass intercepted by Watkins and returned to Green Bay 27. Murray kicks 37-yard field goal four plays later at 8:30.

Nov. 27, 1983—Atlanta 47, Green Bay 41, at Atlanta; Packers win toss. K. Johnson returns interception 31 yards for touchdown at 2:13.

Nov. 27, 1983—Seattle 51, Kansas City 48, at Seattle; Seahawks win toss. Dixon's 47-yard kickoff return sets up N. Johnson's 42-yard field goal at 1:36.

Dec. 11, 1983—New Orleans 20, Philadelphia 17, at Philadelphia; Eagles win toss. Runager punts to Groth who fair catches on New Orleans 32. Stabler completes two passes for 36 yards to Goodlow to set up Andersen's 50-yard field goal at 5:30.

* **Dec. 12, 1983—Green Bay 12, Tampa Bay 9**, at Tampa; Packers win toss. Stenerud kicks 23-yard field goal 11 plays later at 4:07.

Sept. 9, 1984—Detroit 27, Atlanta 24, at Atlanta; Lions win toss. Murray kicks 48-yard field goal nine plays later at 5:06.

Sept. 30, 1984—Tampa Bay 30, Green Bay 27, at Tampa; Packers win toss. Scribner punts 44 yards to Tampa Bay 2. Epps returns Garcia's punt three yards to Green Bay 27. Scribner's punt downed on Buccaneers' 33. Ariri kicks 46-yard field goal 11 plays later at 10:32.

Oct. 14, 1984—Detroit 13, Tampa Bay 7, at Detroit; Buccaneers win toss. Tampa Bay drives to Lions' 39 before Wilder fumbles. Five plays later Danielson hits Thompson with 37-yard touchdown pass at 4:34.

Oct. 21, 1984—Dallas 30, New Orleans 27, at Dallas; Cowboys win toss. Septien kicks 41-yard field goal eight plays later at 3:42.

Oct. 28, 1984—Denver 22, Los Angeles Raiders 19, at Los Angeles; Raiders win toss. Hawkins fumble recovered by Foley at Denver 7. Teams trade punts. Karlis's 42-yard field goal attempt is wide left. Teams trade punts. Wilson pass intercepted by R. Jackson at Los Angeles 45, returned 23 yards to Los Angeles 22. Karlis kicks 35-yard field goal two plays later at 15:00.

Nov. 4, 1984—Philadelphia 23, Detroit 23, at Detroit; Lions win toss. Lions drive to Eagles' 3 in eight plays. Murray's 21-yard field goal attempt hits right upright and bounces back. Jaworski's pass intercepted by Watkins at Detroit 5. Teams trade punts. Cooper returns Black's punt five yards to Eagles' 14. Time expires four plays later with Eagles on own 21.

Nov. 18, 1984—San Diego 34, Miami 28, at San Diego; Chargers win toss. McGee scores eight plays later on a 25-yard run at 3:17.

Dec. 2, 1984—Cincinnati 20, Cleveland 17, at Cleveland; Browns win toss. Simmons returns Cox's punt 30 yards to Cleveland 35. Breech kicks 35-yard field goal seven plays later at 4:34.

Dec. 2, 1984—Houston 23, Pittsburgh 20, at Houston; Oilers win toss. Cooper kicks 30-yard field goal 16 plays later at 5:53.

Sept. 8, 1985—St. Louis 27, Cleveland 24, at Cleveland; Cardinals win toss. O'Donoghue kicks 35-yard field goal nine plays later at 5:27.

Sept. 29, 1985—New York Giants 16, Philadelphia 10, at Philadelphia; Eagles win toss. Jaworski's pass tipped by Quick and intercepted by Patterson who returns 29 yards for touchdown at 0:55.

Oct. 20, 1985—Denver 13, Seattle 10, at Denver; Seahawks win toss. Teams trade punts twice. Krieg's pass intercepted by Hunter and returned to Seahawks' 15. Karlis kicks 24-yard field goal four plays later at 9:19.

Nov. 10, 1985—Philadelphia 23, Atlanta 17, at Philadelphia; Falcons win toss. Donnelly's 62-yard punt goes out of bounds at Eagles' 1. Jaworski completes 99-yard touchdown pass to Quick two plays later at 1:49.

Nov. 10, 1985—San Diego 40, Los Angeles Raiders 34, at San Diego; Chargers win toss. James scores on 17-yard run seven plays later at 3:44.

Nov. 17, 1985—Denver 30, San Diego 24, at Denver; Chargers win toss. Thomas' 40-yard field goal attempt blocked by Smith and returned 60 yards by Wright for touchdown at 4:45.

Nov. 24, 1985—New York Jets 16, New England 13, at New York; Jets win toss. Teams trade punts twice. Patriots' second punt returned 46 yards by Sohn to Patriots' 15. Leahy kicks 32-yard field goal one play later at 10:05.

Nov. 24, 1985—Tampa Bay 19, Detroit 16, at Tampa; Lions win toss. Teams trade punts. Lions' punt downed on Buccaneers' 38. Igwebuike kicks 24-yard field goal 11 plays later at 12:31.

Nov. 24, 1985—Los Angeles Raiders 31, Denver 28, at Los Angeles; Raiders win toss. Bahr kicks 32-yard field goal six plays later at 2:42.

Dec. 8, 1985—Los Angeles Raiders 17, Denver 14, at Denver; Broncos win toss. Teams trade punts twice. Elway's fumble recovered by Townsend at Broncos' 8. Bahr kicks 26-yard field goal one play later at 4:55.

Sept. 14, 1986—Chicago 13, Philadelphia 10, at Chicago; Eagles win toss. Crawford's fumble of kickoff recovered by Jackson at Eagles' 35. Butler kicks 23-yard field goal 10 plays later at 5:56.

Sept. 14, 1986—Cincinnati 36, Buffalo 33, at Cincinnati; Bills win toss. Zander intercepts Kelly's first-down pass and returns it to Bills' 17. Breech kicks 20-yard field goal two plays later at 0:56.

Sept. 21, 1986—New York Jets 51, Miami 45, at New York; Jets win toss. O'Brien completes 43-yard touchdown pass to Walker five plays later at 2:35.

Sept. 28, 1986—Pittsburgh 22, Houston 16, at Houston; Oilers win toss. Johnson's punt returned 41 yards by Woods to Oilers' 15. Abercrombie scores on three-yard run three plays later at 2:35.

Sept. 28, 1986—Atlanta 23, Tampa Bay 20, at Tampa; Falcons win toss. Teams trade punts. Luckhurst kicks 34-yard field goal 10 plays later at 12:35.

Oct. 5, 1986—Los Angeles Rams 26, Tampa Bay 20, at Anaheim; Rams win toss. Dickerson scores four plays later on 42-yard run at 2:16.

Oct. 12, 1986—Minnesota 27, San Francisco 24, at San Francisco; Vikings win toss. C. Nelson kicks 28-yard field goal nine plays later at 4:27.

Oct. 19, 1986—San Francisco 10, Atlanta 10, at Atlanta; Falcons win toss. Teams trade punts twice. Donnelly punts to 49ers' 27. The following play Wilson recovers Rice's fumble at 49ers' 46 as time expires.

Nov. 2, 1986—Washington 44, Minnesota 38, at Washington; Redskins win toss. Schroeder completes 38-yard touchdown pass to Clark four plays later at 1:46.

#Nov. 20, 1986—Los Angeles Raiders 37, San Diego 31, at San Diego; Raiders win toss. Teams trade punts. Allen scores five plays later on 28-yard run at 8:33.

Nov. 23, 1986—Cleveland 37, Pittsburgh 31, at Cleveland; Browns win toss. Teams trade punts. Six plays later Kosar hits Slaughter with 36-yard touchdown pass at 6:37.

Nov. 30, 1986—Chicago 13, Pittsburgh 10, at Chicago; Bears win toss and kick off. Newsome's punt returned by Barnes to Chicago 49. Butler kicks 42-yard field goal five plays later at

3:55.

Nov. 30, 1986—Philadelphia 33, Los Angeles Raiders 27, at Los Angeles; Eagles win toss. Teams trade punts. Long recovers Cunningham's fumble at Philadelphia 42. Waters returns Allen's fumble 81 yards to Los Angeles 4. Cunningham scores on one-yard run two plays later at 6:53.

Nov. 30, 1986—Cleveland 13, Houston 10, at Cleveland; Oilers win toss and kick off. Gossett punts to Houston 39. Luck's pass intercepted by Minnifield at Cleveland 21. Gossett punts to Houston 34. Luck's pass intercepted by Minnifield at Cleveland 43 who returns 20 yards to Houston 37. Moseley kicks 29-yard field goal nine plays later at 14:44.

Dec. 7, 1986—St. Louis 10, Philadelphia 10, at Philadelphia; Cardinals win toss. White blocks Schubert's 40-yard field goal attempt. Teams trade punts. McFadden's 43-yard field goal attempt is wide left. Schubert's 37-yard field goal attempt is wide right. Cavanaugh's pass intercepted by Carter and returned to Eagles' 48 to end game.

Dec. 14, 1986—Miami 37, Los Angeles Rams 31, at Anaheim; Dolphins win toss. Marino completes 20-yard touchdown pass to Duper six plays later at 3:04.

Sept. 20, 1987—Denver 17, Green Bay 17, at Milwaukee; Packers win toss. Del Greco's 47-yard field goal attempt is short. Teams trade punts. Elway intercepted by Noble who returns 10 yards to Green Bay 34. Davis fumbles on next play and Smith recovers. Two plays later, Karlis' 40-yard field goal attempt is wide left. Time expires two plays later with Packers on own 23.

Oct. 11, 1987—Detroit 19, Green Bay 16, at Green Bay; Lions win toss. Prindle's 42-yard field goal attempt is wide left. Packers punt downed on Detroit 17. Prindle kicks 31-yard field goal 16 plays later at 12:26.

Oct. 18, 1987—New York Jets 37, Miami 31, at New York; Jets win toss. Teams trade punts. Ryan intercepted by Hooper at Jets' 47 who returns 11 yards. Mackey intercepted by Haslett at Jets' 37 who returns 9 yards. Jets punt. Mackey intercepted by Radachowsky who returns 45 yards to Miami 24. Ryan completes eight-yard touchdown pass to Hunter five plays later at 14:26.

Oct. 18, 1987—Green Bay 16, Philadelphia 10, at Green Bay; Packers win toss. Hargrove scores on seven-yard run 10 plays later at 5:04.

Oct. 18, 1987—Buffalo 6, New York Giants 3, at Buffalo; Bills win toss. Schlopy's 28-yard field goal attempt is wide left. Teams trade punts. Rutledge intercepted by Clark who returns 23 yards to Buffalo 40. Schlopy kicks 27-yard field goal nine plays later at 14:41.

Oct. 25, 1987—Buffalo 34, Miami 31, at Miami; Bills win toss. Norwood kicks 27-yard field goal seven plays later at 4:12.

Nov. 1, 1987—San Diego 27, Cleveland 24, at San Diego; Browns win toss. Kosar intercepted by Glenn who returns 20 yards to Browns' 25. Abbott kicks 33-yard field goal three plays later at 2:16.

Nov. 15, 1987—Dallas 23, New England 17, at New England; Cowboys win toss. Walker scores on 60-yard run four plays later at 1:50.

+Nov. 26, 1987—Minnesota 44, Dallas 38, at Dallas; Vikings win toss. Coleman's punt downed by Hilton at Cowboys' 37. White intercepted by Studwell who returns 12 yards to Vikings' 37. D. Nelson scores on 24-yard run seven plays later at 7:51.

Nov. 29, 1987—Philadelphia 34, New England 31, at New England; Patriots win toss. Ramsey intercepted by Joyner who returns 29 yards to Eagles' 32. Fryar fair catches Teltschik's punt at Patriots' 13. Franklin's 46-yard field-goal attempt is short. McFadden's 39-yard field goal attempt is wide left. Tatupu fumbles on next play and Cobb recovers. McFadden kicks 38-yard field goal four plays later at 12:16.

Dec. 6, 1987—New York Giants 23, Philadelphia 20, at New York; Giants win toss and kick off. Teams trade punts twice.

Teltschik's punt is returned 16 yards by McConkey to Eagles' 33. Three plays later, Allegre's 50-yard field goal attempt is blocked by Joyner and returned 25 yards by Hoage to Eagles' 30. McConkey returns Teltschik's punt four yards to Giants' 44. Allegre kicks 28-yard field goal four plays later at 10:42.

Dec. 6, 1987—Cincinnati 30, Kansas City 27, at Cincinnati; Bengals win toss. Teams trade punts. Breech kicks 32-yard field goal 16 plays later at 9:44.

Dec. 26, 1987—Washington 27, Minnesota 24, at Minnesota; Redskins win toss. Haji-Sheikh kicks 26-yard field goal six plays later at 2:09.

Sept. 4, 1988—Houston 17, Indianapolis 14, at Indianapolis; Colts win toss. Dickerson fumble recovered by Lyles who returns six yards to Colts' 42. Zendejas kicks 35-yard field goal six plays later at 3:51.

* **Sept. 26, 1988—Los Angeles Raiders 30, Denver 27,** at Denver; Broncos win toss. Teams trade punts twice. Elway intercepted by Lee who returns 20 yards to Broncos' 31. Bahr kicks 35-yard field goal four plays later at 12:35.

Oct. 2, 1988—New York Jets 17, Kansas City 17, at New York; Chiefs win toss. Chiefs punt goes into end zone for touchback. Leahy's 44-yard field goal attempt is wide right. Chiefs punt is returned by Townsell to Jets' 26. Burruss recovers McNeil's fumble at Chiefs' 11. DeBerg intercepted by Humphery at Jets' 49. Three plays later, time expires.

Oct. 9, 1988—Denver 16, San Francisco 13, at San Francisco; Broncos win toss and kick off. Young intercepted by Haynes at Broncos' 32. Denver punt downed at 49ers' 5. Young intercepted by Wilson who returns seven yards to 49ers' 5. Karlis kicks 22-yard field goal two plays later at 8:11.

Oct. 30, 1988—New York Giants 13, Detroit 10, at Detroit; Lions win toss. James's fumble recovered by Taylor at Lions' 22. Three plays later, McFadden kicks 33-yard field goal at 1:13.

Nov. 20, 1988—Buffalo 9, New York Jets 6, at Buffalo; Jets win toss. Vick's fumble recovered by Bennett at Bills' 32. Norwood kicks 30-yard field goal five plays later at 3:47.

Nov. 20, 1988—Philadelphia 23, New York Giants 17, at New York; Eagles win toss. Philadelphia's punt goes into end zone for touchback. Hostetler intercepted by Hoage who returns 11 yards to Giants' 41. Six plays later, Zendejas's 30-yard field-goal attempt is blocked and ball is recovered behind line of scrimmage by Eagles' Simmons, who runs 15 yards for touchdown at 3:09.

Dec. 11, 1988—New England 10, Tampa Bay 7, at New England; Buccaneers win toss and kick off. Staurovsky kicks 27-yard field goal six plays later at 3:08.

Dec. 17, 1988—Cincinnati 20, Washington 17, at Cincinnati; Bengals win toss. Cincinnati's punt returned by Oliphant to Redskins' 16. Grant recovers Williams's fumble at Redskins' 17. Breech kicks 20-yard field goal three plays later at 7:01.

Sept. 24, 1989—Buffalo 47, Houston 41, at Houston; Oilers win toss. Johnson returns Brady's kickoff 17 yards to Oilers' 19. Oilers drive to Buffalo 25, Zendejas's 37-yard field goal blocked, but Bills offsides and Zendejas's second attempt is wide left. Bills' ball and Kelly completes series of passes, including 28-yard game-winner to Andre Reed, at 8:42.

Oct. 8, 1989—Miami 13, Cleveland 10, at Miami; Browns win toss. Metcalf returns Stoyanovich's kickoff 20 yards to Browns' 28. Browns drive ball 46 yards in eight plays; Bahr wide left on 44-yard field goal attempt. Dolphins ball. Browns called for pass interference on Marino pass to Banks at Cleveland 47. Two plays later, Banks's 20-yard reception at Browns' 23 sets up winning 35-yard field goal by Stoyanovich at 6:23.

Oct. 22, 1989—Denver 24, Seattle 21, at Seattle; Seahawks win toss. Treadwell's 56-yard kickoff returned 18 yards by Jefferson to Seahawks' 27. Seahawks drive to Broncos' 22 in 10 plays, but Johnson's 40-yard field goal attempt wide left. Smith intercepts a Krieg pass and returns it 28 yards to Seahawks' 10. Treadwell kicks winning 27-yard field goal at 7:46.

Oct. 29, 1989—New England 23, Indianapolis 20, at Indi-anapolis; Patriots win toss. Biasucci kickoff returned 13 yards to Patriots' 23 by Martin. Holding penalty brings ball back to Patriots' 13. After six plays, Feagles punt returned 11 yards by Verdin to Colts' 28. Six plays later, Colts punt to Martin at Patriots' 12. Grogan completes three straight passes to Patriots' 44. Five consecutive runs put New England on Colts' 33. Davis kicks a 51-yard winning field goal for Patriots at 9:46.

Oct. 29, 1989—Green Bay 23, Detroit 20, at Milwaukee; Lions win toss. Sanders touchback on Jacke kickoff. On first play, Murphy intercepts Lions' Peete and returns it three yards to Lions' 26. Fullwood gains five yards on three plays to set up Jacke's 38-yard field goal at 2:14.

Nov. 5, 1989—Minnesota 23, Los Angeles Rams 21, at Minneapolis; Rams win toss. Karlis's kick returned 18 yards by Delpino to Rams' 19. Drive stops at Rams' 28. Merriweather blocks Hatcher's punt at 12. Ball rolls out of end zone for safety.

Nov. 19, 1989—Cleveland 10, Kansas City 10, at Cleveland; Browns win toss. Browns punt three times; Chiefs twice; before Kansas City's Lowery misses 47-yard field goal with 17 seconds remaining in overtime. Kosar's pass intercepted as time expired.

Nov. 26, 1989—Los Angeles Rams 20, New Orleans 17, at New Orleans; Saints win toss. Lansford's kickoff returned 27 yards to Saints' 30. After four plays, Barnhardt punts to Rams' 15. Saints penalized 35 yards for interference on Rams' 43. Three plays later, Everett hits Anderson with 14-yard pass to Saints' 40, then 26-yarder to put Rams in field goal position. Lansford kicks 31-yard field goal at 6:38.

Dec. 3, 1989—Los Angeles Raiders 16, Denver 13, at Los Angeles; Broncos win toss. Bell returns Jaeger kickoff 14 yards to Broncos' 18. Broncos' penalized for illegal block to Broncos' 9. Elway completes three passes for two first downs. On third and eight Elway sacked for 10-yard loss. Horan punts, Adams calls for fair catch at Raiders' 29. Dyal's 26-yard reception moves Raiders to Denver 43. Raiders move ball 34 yards in three plays to set up Jaeger's 26-yard field goal at 7:02.

Dec. 10, 1989—Indianapolis 23, Cleveland 17, at Indianapolis; Browns win toss. Teams trade punts. McNeil returns Colts' punt 42 yards to 42. Seven plays later, Bahr misses 35-yard field goal attempt. Three plays later, Stark punts and McNeil returns ball to 50-yard line. Two plays later, Prior intercepts Kosar's pass at Colts' 42 and returns it 58 yards for touchdown at 10:54.

Dec. 17, 1989—Cleveland 23, Minnesota 17, at Cleveland; Browns win toss. Browns punt to Vikings' 18. Six plays later, Vikings punt to Browns' 22. Nine plays later, Bahr lines up to attempt 31-yard field goal. Holder Pagel takes snap and passes 14 yards to Waiters for touchdown at 9:30.

Sept. 23, 1990—Denver 34, Seattle 31, at Denver; Seahawks win toss. Loville returns kickoff 19 yards to Seahawks' 27. Seahawks drive to Broncos' 26, where Johnson misses 44-yard field goal wide right. Broncos take over and Elway completes series of passes to set up Treadwell's 25-yard field goal at 9:14.

Sept. 30, 1990—Tampa Bay 23, Minnesota 20, at Minnesota; Vikings win toss. Vikings drive to Buccaneers' 31; Igwebuike's 48-yard field goal attempt wide left. Buccaneers drive to Vikings' 43 and punt. Gannon's pass is intercepted at Vikings' 26 by Wayne Haddix. Buccaneers drive to Vikings' 19 to set up Christie's 36-yard field goal at 9:11.

Oct. 7, 1990—Cincinnati 34, Los Angeles Rams 31, at Anaheim; Rams win toss. Berry returns kickoff to Rams' 21. After 3 plays, English punts and Green downs ball at Bengals' 25. After 3 plays, Johnson punts and Sutton downs ball at Rams' 29-yard line. After 3 plays, English punts and Price signals fair catch at Bengals' 47. Esiason completes series of passes to 26-yard line to set up Breech's 44-yard field goal at 11:56.

Nov. 4, 1990—Washington 41, Detroit 38, at Detroit; Redskins win toss. Howard downs kickoff on Redskins' 15. After 3 plays, Mojsiejenko punts to Redskins' 45. After 3 plays, Arnold punts to Redskins' 10. Rutledge completes series of passes to set up

Lohmiller's 34-yard field goal at 9:10.

Nov. 18, 1990—Chicago 16, Denver 13, at Denver; Broncos win toss. Ezor returns kickoff to Broncos' 12. Both teams have ball twice and have to punt after each possession. Broncos punt after third possession of overtime and Bailey returns 20 yards to Broncos' 34. Harbaugh completes 10-yard pass to Thornton to set up Butler's 44-yard field goal at 13:14.

Nov. 25, 1990—Seattle 13, San Diego 10, at San Diego; Chargers win toss. Lewis returns kickoff to Chargers' 22. After 2 plays, Cox fumbles and ball is recovered by Porter at Chargers' 23. After two plays, Johnson kicks 40-yard field goal at 3:01.

Dec. 2, 1990—Chicago 23, Detroit 17, at Chicago; Lions win toss. Gray returns kickoff to Lions' 35. After 10 plays, Murray misses 35-yard field goal. Bears take possession at Chicago 20. Harbaugh completes 50-yard game-winning pass to Anderson at 10:57.

Dec. 2, 1990—Seattle 13, Houston 10, at Seattle; Seahawks win toss. Warren returns kickoff to Seahawks' 13. After 5 plays, Donnelly punts to Oilers' 23-yard line. Ford's fumble recovered by Wyman. Seahawks take possession at Oilers' 27. After 2 plays, Johnson kicks 42-yard field goal at 4:25.

Dec. 9, 1990—Miami 23, Philadelphia 20, at Miami; Eagles win toss. After 11 plays, Feagles punts to Dolphins' 26. After 6 plays, Roby punts to Eagles' 14 and Harris returns to 25. After 3 plays, Feagles punts to Dolphins' 43. Marino completes series of passes to Eagles' 22. Stoyanovich kicks 39-yard field goal at 12:32.

Dec. 9, 1990—San Francisco 20, Cincinnati 17, at Cincinnati; 49ers win toss. Carter returns kickoff to 49ers' 19. After 10 plays, Cofer kicks 23-yard field goal at 6:12.

* **Sept. 23, 1991—Chicago 19, New York Jets 13,** at Chicago; Jets win toss. Mathis returns kickoff seven yards to New York's 12. Jets drive to New York 26; Bailey returns punt to Chicago 39. Bears drive to Jets' 44-yard line and punt into the end zone. Jets drive to Bears' 11 where Leahy's 28-yard field goal attempt is wide left. Bears drive from 20 to Jets' 1 where Harbaugh runs for touchdown at 14:42.

Oct. 13, 1991—Los Angeles Raiders 23, Seattle 20, at Seattle; Seahawks win toss. Seahawks begin on 20. After 5 plays, Tuten punts and Brown signals fair catch at Raiders' 24. After 3 plays, Gossett punts and Land downs ball at Seattle 9. After 1 play, Lott intercepts at Seahawks' 19 to set up Jaeger's game-winning 37-yard field goal at 6:37.

Oct. 20, 1991—Cleveland 30, San Diego 24, at San Diego; Chargers win toss. After kickoff, Chargers drive to Browns' 45 and punt to Browns' 6 where Hendrickson downs ball. Browns drive to 38 and punt; Taylor fair catches on Chargers' 14. After 3 plays, Brandon intercepts at Chargers' 30 and scores at 5:58.

Oct. 20, 1991—New England 26, Minnesota 23, at New England; Patriots win toss. Martin returns kickoff 18 yards to New England 22. Patriots drive to Minnesota 19. Staurovsky's 36-yard field goal attempt is wide left. Minnesota drives to the 50 where Newsome punts into end zone. On first play, McMillian intercepts at the 40 for Minnesota. After 2 plays, Marion causes Jordan fumble and Pool recovers at New England 20. New England drives to Minnesota 24 where Staurovsky kicks 42-yard field goal as time expires.

Nov. 3, 1991—New York Jets 19, Green Bay 16, at New York; Packers win toss. Thompson returns kickoff 30 yards to Packers' 39. Green Bay drives to New York 24 where Jacke's 42-yard field-goal attempt is wide right. Jets drive to 50. Aguiar's punt is fumbled by Sikahema and recovered by New York at Packers' 23. After 2 plays, Leahy kicks 37-yard field goal at 9:40.

Nov. 3, 1991—Washington 16, Houston 13, at Washington; Redskins win toss. Mitchell returns kickoff 9 yards to Washington 14. After 4 plays, Goodburn punts and Givins returns to Houston 31. After 1 play, Moon's pass is intercepted by Green at Oilers' 35. After 3 plays, Lohmiller kicks 41-yard field goal at 4:01.

Nov. 10, 1991—Houston 26, Dallas 23, at Houston; Oilers win

toss. Pinkett returns kickoff 20 yards to Houston 24. After 6 plays, Montgomery punts and Martin returns to Dallas 24. Cowboys drive to Oilers' 24 where Smith fumbles and McDowell recovers at Oilers' 15. Houston drives to Dallas 5 where Del Greco kicks 23-yard field goal at 14:31.

Nov. 10, 1991—Pittsburgh 33, Cincinnati 27, at Cincinnati; Steelers win toss. Woodson downs kickoff for touchback. After 3 plays, Stryzinski punts and Barber returns 7 yards to Cincinnati 38. Bengals drive to Pittsburgh 37 where Woods fumbles and Lloyd returns recovery to Cincinnati 44. After 2 plays, O'Donnell passes to Green for 26-yard touchdown at 6:32.

#**Nov. 24, 1991—Atlanta 23, New Orleans 20,** at New Orleans; Falcons wins toss. Falcons begin at 20. After 3 plays, Fulhage punts and Fenerty signals fair catch at New Orleans 43. After 3 plays, Barnhardt punts and Thompson downs ball at Atlanta 23. After 3 plays, Fulhage punts and Fenerty fair catches at New Orleans 25. Saints drive to Atlanta 38 where Andersen misses 55-yard field-goal attempt. After 1 play, Rozier fumbles and Martin recovers on 50. Saints drive to Atlanta 38 where Barnhardt punts to Falcons' 2. Atlanta drives to New Orleans 33 where Johnson kicks 50-yard field goal at 13:03.

Nov. 24, 1991—Miami 16, Chicago 13, at Chicago; Dolphins wins toss. Butler kicks to Miami 20 where Paige returns kickoff 15 yards to 35. Miami drives to Chicago 9 where Stoyanovich kicks 27-yard field goal at 4:11.

Dec. 8, 1991—Buffalo 30, Los Angeles Raiders 27, at Los Angeles; Raiders win toss. Daluiso kicks into end zone for touchback. On third play, Kelso intercepts for Buffalo and returns ball to Bills' 36. Bills drive to Los Angeles 24 where Norwood kicks 42-yard field goal at 2:34.

Dec. 8, 1991—Kansas City 20, San Diego 17, at Kansas City; Chiefs win toss. Carney kicks to Kansas City 10 where Stradford returns 23 yards to 33. After 3 plays, Barker punts to San Diego 4. Chargers drive to 40 where Kidd punts 60 yards into end zone for touchback. Kansas City drives to San Diego 39 where Barker punts 38 yards to 1. After 3 plays, Kidd punts 41 yards to San Diego 42 where Stradford returns 12 yards to 30. Chiefs drive to San Diego 1 where Lowery kicks 18-yard field goal at 11:26.

Dec. 8, 1991—New England 23, Indianapolis 17, at New England; Colts wins toss. Baumann kicks off to Indianapolis 2 where Martin returns 23 yards to 25. After 3 downs, Stark punts to New England 17 where Henderson returns 8 yards to 25. New England drives to 50 where McCarthy punts and Prior signals fair catch at Indianapolis 15. After 3 plays, Stark punts to New England 40 where Henderson returns 7 yards to 47. After 2 plays, Millen passes to Timpson for 45-yard touchdown at 8:55.

Dec. 22, 1991—Detroit 17, Buffalo 14, at Buffalo; Lions wins toss. Daluiso kicks off to Detroit 20 where Dozier returns 15 yards to Lions 35. Lions drive to Bills' 3 where Murray kicks 21-yard field goal at 4:23.

Dec. 22, 1991—New York Jets 23, Miami 20, at Miami; Jets win toss. Aguiar kicks to Miami's 30 where Logan returns 3 yards to the 33. After 4 downs, Stoyanovich punts to Jets' 15 where Baty returns 8 yards to 23. Jets drive to Miami 12 where Allegre kicks 30-yard field goal at 6:33.

Sept. 6, 1992—Minnesota 23, Green Bay 20, at Green Bay; Vikings win toss. Nelson returns kickoff 14 yards to the Minnesota 23. After 5 plays, Newsome punts 49 yards to Green Bay 21 where Brooks returns 12 yards to the 33. After 2 plays, Glenn intercepts pass at the Vikings' 48. On first play, Allen fumbles and Billups recovers at Green Bay 35. After 3 plays, McJulien punts 33 yards to Vikings' 35. Vikings drive to Minnesota 48 where Newsome punts 52 yards for touchback. After 3 plays, McJulien punts and Parker returns 10 yards to Green Bay 48. Vikings drive to Packers' 9 where Reveiz kicks 26-yard field goal at 10:20.

Sept. 13, 1992—Cincinnati 24, Los Angeles Raiders 21, at Cincinnati; Raiders win toss. Land returns kickoff 13 yards but fumbles at Los Angeles' 20; ball recovered by Bengals' Bennett at Raiders' 21. After 1 play, Breech kicks 34-yard field goal at

1:01.

Sept. 20, 1992—Houston 23, Kansas City 20, at Houston; Chiefs win toss. Carter returns kickoff 25 yards to Kansas City 28. On third play of drive, Birden fumbles at Kansas City 34; ball recovered by Houston's D. Smith at Chiefs' 23. After one play, Del Greco kicks 39-yard field goal at 1:55.

Oct. 11, 1992—Indianapolis 6, New York Jets 3, at Indianapolis; Colts win toss. Verdin returns kickoff 33 yards to Colts' 36. Colts drive to Jets' 30 where Biasucci kicks 47-yard field goal at 3:01.

#Nov. 8, 1992—Cincinnati 31, Chicago 28, at Chicago; Bears win toss. Lewis returns kickoff 22 yards to Chicago's 29. Bears drive to Chicago's 46 where Gardocki punts; fair catch by Wright at the Cincinnati 11. Bengals drive to Bears' 18 where Breech kicks 36-yard field goal at 8:39.

Nov. 15, 1992—New England 37, Indianapolis 34, at Indianapolis; Colts win toss. Verdin returns kickoff 10 yards to Colts' 20; holding penalty brings ball back to Colts' 10. After two plays, Henderson intercepts pass at Colts' 38 and returns it 9 yards to the 29. In three plays, Patriots drive to 1 where Baumann kicks 18-yard field goal at 3:25.

Nov. 29, 1992—Indianapolis 16, Buffalo 13, at Indianapolis; Colts win toss. Verdin returns kickoff 24 yards to Colts' 34. Colts drive to Buffalo 22 where Biasucci kicks 40-yard field goal at 3:51.

* Nov. 30, 1992—Seattle 16, Denver 13, at Seattle; Seahawks win toss. Daluiso kicks through end zone for touchback. After three plays, Tuten punts 53 yards to Denver 18 where Marshall returns for no gain. After three plays, Rodriguez punts 29 yards to Seattle 45 where Warren signals fair catch. Seahawks drive to Denver 15 where Kasay's 33-yard field goal attempt misses. Broncos take over at Denver 20. After three plays, Rodriguez punts 43 yards to Seattle 38 where Warren signals for fair catch. After four plays, Tuten punts 39 yards to Denver 4 where Daniels downs punt. After three plays, Rodriguez punts 46 yards to Denver 48 where Warren returns 10 yards to the 38. Seahawks drive to Denver 14 where Kasay kicks 32-yard field goal at 11:10.

Dec. 13, 1992—Philadelphia 20, Seattle 17, at Seattle; Eagles win toss. Sydner returns kick 12 yards to Eagles' 16; illegal block penalty brings ball back to 8. Eagles drive to Philadelphia 45 where Feagles punts for a touchback. After 6 plays, Tuten punts 45 yards to Philadelphia 22 where Sydner returns 7 yards to 29. After 6 plays, Feagles punts 44 yards to Seattle 26 where Warren returns 5 yards to 31. After 5 plays, Tuten punts 32 yards to Philadelphia 20 where Sydner signals for fair catch. Eagles drive to Seattle 27 where Ruzek kicks 44-yard field goal with no time remaining.

Dec. 27, 1992—Miami 16, New England 13, at New England; Patriots win toss. Lockwood returns kickoff 15 yards to Patriots' 21. After three plays, McCarthy punts 39 yards to Miami 33 where Miller returns 2 yards to the 35. Miami drives to New England 18 where Stoyanovich kicks 35-yard field goal at 8:17.

Sept. 12, 1993—Detroit 19, New England 16, at New England; Patriots win toss. Patriots begin at 20. After 3 plays, Saxon punts 42 yards to Detroit 29 where Gray returns 12 yards to the 41. After 3 plays, Arnold punts 41 yards to New England 12 where Brown returns 16 yards to the 28. Patriots drive to Detroit 44 where Saxon punts into the end zone for a touchback. Detroit drives to New England 20 where Hanson kicks 38-yard field goal at 11:04.

Nov. 7, 1993—Buffalo 13, New England 10, at New England; Patriots win toss. T. Brown returns kickoff 27 yards to Patriots 30. Patriots drive to Buffalo 48 where Bills take over on downs. Bills drive to New England 25 where Metzelaars fumbles, and C. Brown recovers. After 3 plays, Saxon punts 46 yards to Buffalo 24 where Copeland returns 11 yards to the 35. Bills drive to New England 14 where Christie kicks 32-yard field goal at 9:22.

Dec. 19, 1993—Phoenix 30, Seattle 27, at Seattle; Cardinals win toss. Bailey returns kickoff 14 yards to Cardinals 20. Cardinals drive to Seattle 23 where Davis kicks 41-yard field goal at

6:45.

Jan. 2, 1994—Dallas 16, New York Giants 13, at New York; Giants win toss. Meggett returns kickoff 19 yards to Giants 19. After 6 plays, Horan punts 45 yards to Cowboys 25 where Widmer downs punt. Cowboys drive to Giants' 23 where Murray kicks 41-yard field goal at 10:44.

Jan. 2, 1994—New England 33, Miami 27, at New England; Dolphins win toss. McDuffie returns kickoff 21 yards to Miami 27. After 3 plays, Hatcher punts 43 yards to New England 29 where Harris returns 6 yards to the 35. After 2 plays, Brown intercepts pass from Bledsoe and returns 3 yards to Miami 49. After 3 plays, Hatcher punts 37 yards to New England 14 where Harris returns 18 yards to the 32. After 2 plays, Bledsoe passes 36 yards to Timpson for touchdown at 4:44.

Jan. 2, 1994—Los Angeles Raiders 33, Denver 30, at Los Angeles; Broncos win toss. Delpino returns kickoff 12 yards to Denver 25. Broncos drive to Los Angeles 22 where Elam's 40-yard field goal attempt is wide left. Raiders drive to Denver 29 where Jaeger kicks 47-yard field goal at 7:10.

* Jan. 3, 1994—Philadelphia 37, San Francisco 34, at San Francisco; 49ers win toss. Walker returns kickoff, 19 yards to San Francisco 27. 49ers drive to Philadelphia 19 where Cofer misses 32-yard field goal. Eagles start at their 20-yard line, and, after 3 plays, Feagles punts 48 yards to San Francisco 36 where Carter fumbles and 49ers recover. After 7 plays, Wilmsmeyer punts 57 yards to Philadelphia 6 where Sikahema returns 16 yards to the 22. Eagles drive to San Francisco 10 where Ruzek kicks 28-yard field goal with no time remaining.

Sept. 4, 1994—Detroit 31, Atlanta 28, at Detroit; Falcons win toss. Falcons start at their own 16 after holding penalty on kickoff. After 3 plays, Alexander punts 43 yards to Detroit 39 where Clay returns 12 yards to Atlanta 49. Detroit drives to Atlanta 20 where Hanson kicks 37-yard field goal at 5:14.

Sept. 11, 1994—New York Jets 25, Denver 22, at New York; Jets win toss. Murrell returns kickoff 24 yards to New York 33. Jets drive to Denver 22 where Lowery kicks 39-yard field goal at 3:57.

* Sept. 19, 1994—Detroit 20, Dallas 17, at Dallas; Lions win toss. Gray returns kickoff 24 yards to Detroit 32. Lions drive to Dallas 34 where Hanson's 51-yard field-goal attempt is blocked by Lett. Cowboys take possession at Dallas 42. Cowboys drive to Detroit 37 where Kennard fumbles and Swilling recovers. Lions take possession at Detroit 45. After 6 plays, Montgomery punts 31 yards to Dallas 16. Cowboys drive to Dallas 49 where Aikman fumbles and Thomas recovers at Dallas 43. Lions drive to Dallas 26 where Hanson kicks 44-yard field goal at 14:33.

Oct. 16, 1994—Arizona 19, Washington 16, at Washington; Redskins win toss. Mitchell returns kickoff 27 yards to Washington 41. Redskins drive to Arizona 34 where Lohmiller's 51-yard field-goal attempt is blocked by Joyner and recovered by Williams who returns it to the Washington 37. After 5 plays, Peterson's 45-yard field-goal attempt is wide right. Redskins take possession at the Washington 36. After 3 plays, Roby punts 36 yards to the Arizona 37 where Robinson returns 3 yards to the 40. After 3 plays, Feagles punts 51 yards for a touchback. After 1 play, Shuler's pass is intercepted by Hoage who returns it to the Washington 12. Peterson kicks 29-yard field goal at 10:00.

Oct. 16, 1994—Miami 20, Los Angeles Raiders 17, at Miami; Dolphins win toss. McDuffie returns kickoff 19 yards to Miami 23. Dolphins drive to Los Angeles 12 where Stoyanovich kicks 29-yard field goal at 5:46.

 # Oct. 20, 1994—Minnesota 13, Green Bay 10, at Minnesota; Vikings win toss. Ismail returns kickoff 22 yards to Minnesota 29. Vikings drive to Green Bay 9 where Fuad Reveiz kicks 27-yard field goal at 4:26.

Oct. 30, 1994—Detroit 28, New York Giants 25, at New York; Giants win toss. Lewis returns kickoff 16 yards to New York 27. After 3 plays, Horan punts 42 yards to Detroit 24 where Gray calls for fair catch. Detroit drives to New York 6 where Hanson kicks 24-yard field goal at 6:43.

#**Oct. 30, 1994—Arizona 20, Pittsburgh 17,** at Arizona; Steelers win toss. Johnson returns kickoff 24 yards to Pittsburgh 30 where he fumbles and Arizona's Merritt recovers at Pittsburgh 32. After 3 plays, Davis kicks 51-yard field goal at 1:40.

Nov. 6, 1994—Cincinnati 20, Seattle 17, at Seattle; Seahawks win toss. Warren returns kickoff 32 yards to Seattle 33. After 3 plays, Tuten punts 37 yards to Cincinnati 28 where Sawyer calls for fair catch. After 3 plays, Johnson punts 64 yards to Seattle 2 where Truitt downs ball. Seahawks drive to Seattle 38 where Tuten punts 50 yards to Cincinnati 12 and Sawyer returns 5 yards to 17. Blake passes to Scott for 76 yards to Seattle 7. Pelfrey kicks 26-yard field goal at 8:14.

Nov. 6, 1994—Pittsburgh 12, Houston 9, at Houston; Steelers win toss. Stone returns kickoff 15 yards to Pittsburgh 28. After 3 plays, Royals punts 53 yards to Houston 13 where Givins downs ball. After 3 plays, Camarillo punts 57 yards to Pittsburgh 31 where Woodson returns 20 yards to Houston 49. After 3 plays, Royals punts 43 yards to Houston 15 where Coleman returns 3 yards to 18. After 5 plays, Camarillo punts 57 yards to Pittsburgh 12 where Hastings returns 12 yards to 24. Steelers drive to Houston 41 where Royals punts 29 yards to Houston 12, and Coleman calls for fair catch. Brown fumbles on first play and Jones recovers at Houston 22. After 1 play, Anderson kicks 40-yard field goal at 11:24.

Nov. 13, 1994—New England 26, Minnesota 20, at New England; Patriots win toss. Thompson returns kickoff 27 yards to New England 33. Patriots drive to Minnesota 14 where Bledsoe passes 14 yards to Turner for touchdown at 4:10.

Nov. 20, 1994—Pittsburgh 16, Miami 13, at Pittsburgh; Steelers win toss. Stone returns kickoff 15 yards to Pittsburgh 16. Steelers drive to Miami 39 where they lose possession on downs. Dolphins drive to Pittsburgh 47 where Arnold punts 35 yards to Pittsburgh 12 and Oliver downs ball. Steelers drive to Miami 21 where Anderson kicks 39-yard field goal at 10:19.

Nov. 27, 1994—Chicago 19, Arizona 16, at Arizona; Cardinals win toss. Levy returns kickoff 31 yards to Arizona 45. After 5 plays, Feagles punts 38 yards to the end zone for a touchback. Bears drive to Arizona 10 where Butler kicks 27-yard field goal at 8:11.

Nov. 27, 1994—Tampa Bay 20, Minnesota 17, at Minnesota; Buccaneers win toss. Harris returns kickoff 12 yards to Tampa Bay 38. After 6 plays, Stryzinski punts 40 yards to Minnesota 4 where Guliford muffs punt and Buccaneers' Brady recovers. Husted kicks 22-yard field goal at 2:08.

Dec. 1, 1994—Minnesota 33, Chicago 27, at Minnesota; Bears win toss. Lewis returns kickoff 23 yards to Chicago 33. Bears drive to Minnesota 22 where Butler's 40-yard field goal attempt is wide left. After 1 play, Moon passes 65 yards to Carter for touchdown at 5:46.

Dec. 4, 1994—Denver 20, Kansas City 17, at Kansas City; Broncos win toss. Milburn returns kickoff 24 yards to Denver 29. After 3 plays, Millen fumbles and Phillips recovers at Denver 35. After 4 plays, Allen fumbles and Smith recovers at Denver 27. After 6 plays, Rouen punts 45 yards to Kansas City 25 where Hughes calls for fair catch. After 3 plays, Aguiar punts 33 yards to Denver 42 where Chiefs down ball. Broncos drive to Kansas City 17 where Elam kicks 34-yard field goal at 12:12.

Sept. 3, 1995—Cincinnati 24, Indianapolis 21, at Indianapolis; Bengals win toss. Dunn returns kickoff 15 yards to Bengals' 17. Cincinnati drives to Indianapolis 29 where Pelfrey kicks 47-yard field goal at 2:36.

Sept. 3, 1995—Atlanta 23, Carolina 20, at Atlanta; Panthers win toss. Baldwin downs kickoff for touchback. Panthers drive to Carolina 42 where Reich fumbles and ball is recovered by Archambeau at Carolina 31. Falcons drive to Panthers' 16 where Andersen kicks 35-yard field goal at 6:17.

Sept. 10, 1995—Indianapolis 27, New York Jets 24, at New York; Jets win toss. Carter downs kickoff for touchback. Jets punt downed at Colts' 37. Colts drive to Jets' 35 where Cofer

kicks 52-yard field goal at 4:27.

Sept. 10, 1995—Kansas City 20, New York Giants 17, at Kansas City; Chiefs win toss. Vanover returns kickoff 30 yards to Chiefs' 28. Aguiar punts to Giants' 3. Horan punts to Chiefs' 49. Chiefs drive to Giants' 6 where Elliott kicks 23-yard field goal at 7:49.

Sept. 17, 1995—Kansas City 23, Oakland 17, at Kansas City; Chiefs win toss. Vanover returns kickoff 28 yards to Chiefs' 41. M. Allen fumbles, ball recovered by Robbins at Raiders' 38. Hasty intercepts pass at Chiefs' 36 and returns it 64 yards for touchdown at 4:27.

Sept. 17, 1995—Atlanta 27, New Orleans 24, at Atlanta; Saints win toss. Hughes returns kickoff 21 yards to Saints' 17. Metcalf returns Wilmsmeyer's punt 18 yards to Saints' 39. Stryzinski punts, fair catch by Hughes at Saints' 14. Wilmsmeyer punt downed at Falcons' 6. Falcons drive to Saints' 3 where Andersen kicks 21-yard field goal at 7:58.

#**Sept. 17, 1995—Dallas 23, Minnesota 17,** at Minnesota; Cowboys win toss. K. Williams returns kickoff 23 yards to Cowboys' 27. E. Smith scores on 31-yard run at 2:26.

Oct. 8, 1995—Indianapolis 27, Miami 24, at Miami; Colts win toss. Warren returns kickoff 25 yards to Colts' 33. Colts drive to Dolphins' 10 where Blanchard kicks 27-yard field goal at 4:58.

Oct. 8, 1995—New York Giants 27, Arizona 21, at New York; Cardinals win toss. Terry returns kickoff 20 yards to Cardinals' 23. Hamilton recovers Krieg's fumble at Cardinals' 36. Lynch recovers Brown's fumble at Cardinals' 38. Armstead intercepts pass at Giants' 42 and returns it 58 yards for touchdown at 4:05.

Oct. 8, 1995—Minnesota 23, Houston 17, at Minnesota; Vikings win toss. Palmer returns kickoff 10 yards to Vikings' 15. Saxon's punt downed at Oilers' 8. Washington intercepts pass at Vikings' 47 and returns it 25 yards to Oilers' 28. R. Smith scores on 20-yard run at 7:10.

Oct. 8, 1995—Philadelphia 37, Washington 34, at Philadelphia; Redskins win toss. Redskins take possession at their 20 after touchback. Turk punt out of bounds at Eagles' 9. Eagles drive to Redskins' 18 where Anderson kicks 35-yard field goal at 10:06.

* **Oct. 9, 1995—Kansas City 29, San Diego 23,** at Kansas City; Chargers win toss. Coleman returns kickoff 24 yards to Chargers' 28. Vanover makes fair catch of Bennett's punt at Chiefs' 15. Coleman makes fair catch of Aguiar's punt at Chargers' 43. Vanover returns Bennett's punt 86 yards for a touchdown at 7:27.

Oct. 15, 1995—Tampa Bay 20, Minnesota 17, at Tampa Bay; Buccaneers win toss. Edmonds returns kickoff 19 yards to Buccaneers' 22. A. Lee returns Roby's punt to Vikings' 48. Vikings drive to Tampa Bays' 35 where Reveiz's 53-yard field-goal attempt is wide right. Buccaneers take over at own 43 and drive to Vikings' 33 where Husted kicks 51-yard field goal at 6:23.

Oct. 22, 1995—Washington 36, Detroit 30, at Washington; Redskins win toss. B. Mitchell returns kickoff 16 yards to Redskins' 27. Turk's punt downed at Lions' 4. D. Green intercepts S. Mitchell's pass and returns it 7 yards for touchdown at 3:41.

Oct. 29, 1995—Carolina 20, New England 17, at New England; Panthers win toss. Baldwin returns kickoff 22 yards to Panthers' 25. Meggett makes fair catch of Barnhardt's punt at Patriots' 9. Guliford returns O'Neill's punt 9 yards to Patriots' 32. Panthers drive to Patriots' 12 where Kasay kicks 29-yard field goal at 7:08.

Oct. 29, 1995—Cleveland 29, Cincinnati 26, at Cincinnati; Browns win toss. Hunter returns kickoff 31 yards to Browns' 31. Bieniemy returns Tupa's punt 9 yards to Bengals' 37. McCardell makes fair catch of Johnson's punt at Browns' 12. Bieniemy returns Tupa's punt 0 yards to Bengals' 38. Hall intercepts Blake's pass and returns it 5 yards to Bengals' 45. Browns drive to Bengals' 11 where Stover kicks 28-yard field goal at 6:30.

Oct. 29, 1995—Arizona 20, Seattle 14, at Arizona; Cardinals win toss. Dowdell returns kickoff 16 yards to Cardinals' 25. Cardinals drive to Seahawks' 10 where G. Davis' 27-yard field goal attempt is blocked. L. Lynch intercepts Friesz's pass at Cardinals' 28 and returns it 72 yards for a touchdown at 11:16.

Nov. 5, 1995—Pittsburgh 37, Chicago 34, at Chicago; Bears win toss. Timpson returns kickoff 23 yards to Bears' 33. Hastings returns Sauerbrun's punt 2 yards to Steelers' 31. Steelers drive to Bears' 6 where N. Johnson kicks 24-yard field goal at 8:19.

Nov. 12, 1995—Minnesota 30, Arizona 24, at Arizona; Vikings win toss. A. Lee returns kickoff 20 yards to Vikings' 25. Moon throws 50-yard touchdown pass to Ismail at 2:16.

Nov. 26, 1995—Arizona 40, Atlanta 37, at Arizona; Falcons win toss. J. Anderson returns kickoff 20 yards to Falcons' 20. Stryzinski fumbles punt snap. Recovered by England at Falcons' 10 where G. Davis kicks 28-yard field goal at 1:43.

#Dec. 10, 1995—Tampa Bay 13, Green Bay 10, at Tampa Bay; Buccaneers win toss. Edmonds returns kickoff 24 yards to Buccaneers' 23. Tampa Bay drives to Packers' 29 where Husted kicks 47-yard field goal at 3:46.

#Sept. 1, 1996—Buffalo 23, New York Giants 20, at New York; Bills win toss. Daluiso kick is a touchback. Bills drive to Buffalo 46. Toomer returns Mohr's punt 5 yards to Giants' 16. Dave Brown's fumble recovered by Spielman at Giants' 33. Bills drive to Giants' 16 where Christie kicks 34-yard field goal at 9:08.

Sept. 22, 1996—New England 28, Jacksonville 25, at New England; Patriots win toss. T. Brown returns kickoff 18 yards to Patriots' 29. Patriots drive to Jaguars' 22 where Vinatieri kicks 40-yard field goal at 2:36.

Sept. 29, 1996—Arizona 31, St. Louis 28, at Arizona; Cardinals win toss. Lohmiller kick is a touchback. Cardinals drive to Rams' 7 where G. Davis kicks 24-yard field goal at 1:54.

Oct. 6, 1996—Buffalo 16, Indianapolis 13, at Buffalo; Colts win toss. Christie kick is a touchback. Colts drive to Indianapolis 32. Burris returns Gardocki's punt to Bills' 35. Bills drive to Colts' 48. Mohr punts out of bounds at Colts' 14. Colts drive to Indianapolis 9. Burris returns Gardocki's punt to Colts' 48. Bills drive to Colts' 22 where Christie kicks 39-yard field goal at 9:22.

#Oct. 6, 1996—Houston 30, Cincinnati 27, at Cincinnati; Bengals win toss. Dunn returns kickoff 23 yards to Bengals' 34. Bengals drive to Cincinnati 36. Floyd returns L. Johnson's punt to Oilers' 18. Oilers drive to Bengals' 31 where Del Greco kicks 49-yard field goal at 7:07.

* Oct. 14, 1996—Green Bay 23, San Francisco 20, at Green Bay; 49ers win toss. D. Carter returns kickoff 23 yards to 49ers' 22. 49ers' drive to San Francisco 25. Howard makes fair catch of Thompson's punt at Packers' 44. Packers drive to 49ers' 35 where Jacke kicks 53-yard field goal at 3:41.

Oct. 27, 1996—Baltimore 37, St. Louis 31, at Baltimore; Rams win toss. J. Thomas returns kickoff 17 yard to Rams' 17. Rams drive to Ravens' 15. F. Miller fumble in field goal formation recovered by S. Moore at Ravens' 17. Ravens drive to Baltimore 49 and turn ball over on downs. Rams drive to Ravens' 40 and turn ball over on downs. Testaverde throws 22-yard scoring pass to M. Jackson at 14:50.

Nov. 10, 1996—Dallas 20, San Francisco 17, at San Francisco; Cowboys win toss. H. Walker returns kickoff 10 yards to Cowboys' 23. Cowboys drive to 49ers' 11 where Boniol kicks 29-yard field goal at 6:17.

Nov. 10, 1996—Arizona 37, Washington 34, at Washington; Cardinals win toss. Blanton's kickoff is a touchback. Cardinals drive to Redskins' 15 where Butler misses 32-yard field goal. Redskins drive to Cardinals' 43 where Turk punts for touchback. L. Johnson fumble returned by Morrison to Cardinals' 27. Redskins drive to Cardinals' 31 where Blanton misses 48-yard field goal. Cardinals drive to Redskins' 15 where Butler kicks 32-yard field goal at 14:27.

Nov. 10, 1996—Tampa Bay 20, Oakland 17, at Tampa Bay; Buccaneers win toss. M. Marshall returns kickoff 15 yards to Bucs' 17. Bucs drive to Tampa Bay 36. T. Brown returns Barnhardt's punt four yards to Raiders' 22. Raiders drive to Oakland

25. M. Marshall returns Gossett's punt nine yards to Bucs' 39. Bucs drive to Raiders' 4 where Husted kicks 23-yard field goal at 11:56.

#Nov. 17, 1996—Minnesota 16, Oakland 13, at Oakland; Raiders win toss. Kaufman returns kickoff 32 yards to Raiders' 27. Raiders drive to Oakland 46 where Gossett punts to Vikings' 17. Vikings drive to Raiders' 12 where Sisson kicks 31-yard field goal at 11:53.

Nov. 24, 1996—Jacksonville 28, Baltimore 25, at Baltimore; Jaguars win toss. Jordon returns kickoff 16 yards to Jaguars' 30. Jaguars drive to Jacksonville 37. Barker's punt is downed at Ravens' 6. Ravens drive to Jaguars' 37 where Pritchett recovers Byner's fumble. Jaguars drive to Ravens' 15 where Hollis kicks 34-yard field goal at 9:06.

Nov. 24, 1996—San Francisco 19, Washington 16, at Washington; 49ers win toss. D. Carter returns kickoff 20 yards to 49ers' 32. 49ers drive to Redskins' 20 where Wilkins kicks 38-yard field goal at 3:24.

Dec. 1, 1996—Indianapolis 13, Buffalo 10, at Indianapolis; Bills win toss. Moulds returns kickoff 26 yards to Bills' 25. Bills drive to Buffalo 49. Stock returns Mohr's punt one yard to Colts' 16. Colts drive to Bills' 32 where Blanchard kicks 49-yard field goal at 10:46.

Aug. 31, 1997—Tennessee 24, Oakland 21, at Tennessee; Oilers win toss. Gray returns kickoff 32 yards to Tennessee 33. Oilers drive to Tennessee 38. Roby's punt is downed at the Oakland 33. Raiders drive to Oakland 32. Gray returns Araguz punt to Tennessee 35. Oilers drive to Oakland 15 where Del Greco kicks 33-yard field goal at 6:57.

Sept. 7, 1997—Miami 16, Tennessee 13, at Miami; Dolphins win toss. Spikes returns kickoff 48 yards to Tennessee 45. Dolphins drive to Tennessee 11 where Mare kicks 29-yard field goal at 2:15.

#Sept. 7, 1997— Arizona 25, Dallas 22, at Arizona; Cowboys win toss. Walker returns kickoff 21 yards to Dallas 25. Cowboys drive to Arizona 43. Gowin punts 43 yards for a touchback. Cardinals drive to Dallas 44. Graham fumbles. Cowboys drive to Arizona 42. Williams fumbles. Cardinals drive to Dallas 3 where Butler kicks 20-yard field goal at 8:30.

Sept. 14, 1997—Washington 19, Arizona 13, at Washington; Cardinals win toss. K. Williams returns kickoff 27 yards to Arizona 34. Cardinals drive to Arizona 40. McElroy fumbles. Redskins drive to Arizona 40. Westbrook catches 40-yard touchdown pass from Frerotte at 1:36.

#Sept. 14, 1997—New England 27, New York Jets 24, at New England; Patriots win toss. Hall's kickoff is a touchback. Patriots drive to New England 15. Bledsoe pass intercepted by O. Smith. Jets drive to New York 46. Hansen punts 47 yards. Meggett returns to New England 21. Patriots drive to New York 17 where Vinatieri kicks 34-yard field goal at 8:03.

Sept. 28, 1997—Kansas City 20, Seattle 17, at Kansas City; Seahawks win toss. Broussard returns kickoff 12 yards to Seattle 14. Seahawks drive to Seattle 17. Vanover returns Tuten punt 8 yards to Kansas City 26. Chiefs drive to Seattle 44. Aguiar punt downed at Seattle 11. Seahawks drive to Seattle 26. Moon pass intercepted by Woods and returned 13 yards to 50. Chiefs drive to Seattle 23 where Stoyanovich kicks 41-yard field goal at 13:04.

Oct. 19, 1997—Philadelphia 13, Arizona 10, at Philadelphia; Cardinals win toss. K. Williams returns kickoff 28 yards to Arizona 42. Cardinals drive to Philadelphia 48. Feagles punts 48 yards for touchback. Eagles drive to Arizona 7 where Boniol kicks 24-yard field goal at 4:02.

Oct. 19, 1997—New York Giants 26, Detroit 20, at Detroit; Giants win toss. Pegram returns kickoff 16 yards to New York 18. Giants drive to New York 32. Calloway catches 68-yard touchdown pass from Kanell at 1:40.

Oct. 26, 1997—Denver 23, Buffalo 20, at Buffalo; Broncos win toss and elects to kickoff. Holmes returns kickoff 20 yards to Buffalo 25. Bills drive to Buffalo 23. Mohr punt downed at

Denver 40. Broncos drive to Buffalo 48. Rouen punt downed at Buffalo 1. Bills drive to Buffalo 20. Gordon returns Mohr punt to Denver 42. Broncos drive to Buffalo 15 where Elam kicks 33-yard field goal at 13:04.

Oct. 26, 1997—Pittsburgh 23, Jacksonville 17, at Pittsburgh; Steelers win toss. Coleman returns kickoff 23 yards to Pittsburgh 23. Steelers drive to Jacksonville 17. Bettis catches 17-yard touchdown pass from Stewart at 3:47.

* **Oct. 27, 1997—Chicago 36, Miami 33**, at Miami; Dolphins win toss. McPhail returns kickoff 23 yards to Miami 27. Dolphins drive to Miami 36. Kidd punts out of bounds at Chicago 10. Bears drive to the Chicago 39. Sauerbrun punt out of bounds at Miami 27. Reeves recovers Marino fumble at Miami 17. Bears drive to Miami 17 where Jaeger kicks 35-yard field goal at 9:25.

Nov. 2, 1997—New York Jets 19, Baltimore 16, at New York; Jets win toss. Stover's kickoff is a touchback. Jets drive to Baltimore 20 where Hall kicks 37-yard field goal at 4:58.

Nov. 16, 1997—Philadelphia 10, Baltimore 10, at Baltimore; Eagles win toss. Stover's kickoff is a touchback. Eagles drive to Philadelphia 19. Hutton punts 36 yards to Baltimore 45. Ravens drive to Baltimore 36 where Eagles take over on downs. Eagles drive to Baltimore 33 where Ravens take over on downs. Ravens drive to Baltimore 37. Montgomery punts 55 yards, and Solomon returns to Philadelphia 22. Eagles drive to Philadelphia 16. Hutton punts 41 yards, and Roe returns to Baltimore 46. Ravens drive to Philadelphia 35 where Stover's 53-yard field-goal attempt is no good. Eagles drive to Baltimore 22 where Boniol's 40-yard field-goal is no good as time expires.

Nov. 16, 1997—New Orleans 20, Seattle 17, at New Orleans; Seahawks win toss. Brien's kickoff is a touchback. Seahawks start at Seattle 20 where Moon's pass intercepted by Tubbs who returns 15 yards to Seattle 20. Saints Brien kicks 38-yard field goal at 17 seconds.

\#**Nov. 23, 1997—New York Giants 7, Washington 7**, at Washington; Redskins win toss. Davis returns kickoff 28 yards to Washington 39. Redskins drive to Washington 36 where Hostetler's pass intercepted by Sehorn who returns minus–2 yards before lateralling to Wooten who returns 5 yards to New York 41. Giants drive to New York 26 where Maynard punts 37 yards to Washington 37. Redskins drive to New York 39 where Hostetler fumble is recovered by Harris at New York 40. Giants drive to New York 43 where Maynard punts 57 yards for a touchback. Washington drives to New York 41. Giants take over on downs at New York 40. Giants drive to Washington 36 where Daluiso's 54-yard field goal attempt is no good. Redskins drive to Washington 45 where Hostetler's pass intercepted by Sparks at New York 49. Giants drive to Washington 36 where Maynard punts 36 yards for a touchback. Redskins drive to New York 36 where Blanton's 54-yard field-goal attempt is no good. Giants drive to New York 45 where Kanell's pass intercepted by Patton who laterals to Pounds who returns 11 yards to Washington 24 as time expires.

Nov. 30, 1997—Pittsburgh 26, Arizona 20, at Arizona; Cardinals win toss. K. Williams returns kickoff 11 yards to Arizona 23. Cardinals drive to Arizona 18 where Feagles punts 43 yards. Hawkins returns punt 9 yards to Pittsburgh 48. Steelers drive to Arizona 10 where Bettis scores on a 10-yard touchdown run at 5:34.

Dec. 13, 1997—Pittsburgh 24, New England 21, at New England; Steelers win toss. Coleman returns kickoff 19 yards to Pittsburgh 26. Steelers drive to New England 13 where Johnson kicks a 31-yard field goal at 4:43.

Sept. 6, 1998—San Francisco 36, New York Jets 30, at San Francisco; Jets win toss. Richey's kickoff is a touchback. Jets drive to New York 11. Gallery punts 48 yards. McQuarters returns to New York 43. 49ers drive to New York 44. Howard punts 23 yards to New York 21. Johnson calls fair catch. Jets drive to New York 47. Gallery's 49-yard punt downed at San

Francisco 4. Hearst runs for a 96-yard touchdown at 4:08.

Sept. 13, 1998—Cincinnati 34, Detroit 28, at Detroit; Lions win toss. Johnson's kickoff is a touchback. Lions drive to Detroit 47 where Mitchell's pass is intercepted by Sawyer and returned for a 58-yard touchdown at 2:06.

Sept. 27, 1998—New Orleans 19, Indianapolis 13, at Indianapolis; Saints win toss. Gardocki's kickoff is returned by Ismail to New Orleans 28. Saints drive to New Orleans 30. Royals punts 64 yards. Poole returns to Indianapolis 12. Colts drive to Indianapolis 20. Gardocki punts 58 yards. Hastings returns to New Orleans 29. Saints drive to New Orleans 32. Royals punts 59 yards. Punt downed at Indianapolis 9. Colts drive to Indianapolis 44 where Manning's pass is intercepted by Drakeford and returned to Indianapolis 36. Saints drive to Indianapolis 33. Wuerffel throws 33-yard touchdown pass to Cleeland at 6:10.

Oct. 25, 1998—Miami 12, New England 9, at Miami; Dolphins win toss. Vinatieri's kickoff is returned by Avery to Miami 15. Dolphins drive to New England 26 where Mare kicks 43-yard field goal at 4:36.

+**Nov. 26, 1998—Detroit 19, Pittsburgh 16**, at Detroit; Lions win toss. Johnson's kickoff is returned by Fair to Detroit 35. Lions drive to Pittsburgh 24 where Hanson kicks 42-yard field goal at 2:52.

Dec. 6, 1998—San Francisco 31, Carolina 28, at Carolina; Panthers win toss. Richey's kickoff is returned by Floyd to Carolina 36. Panthers drive to Carolina 38 where Beuerlein's fumble is recovered by Doleman at Carolina 30. 49ers drive to Carolina 5 where Richey kicks 23-yard field goal at 4:16.

Dec. 13, 1998—Arizona 20, Philadelphia 17, at Philadelphia; Cardinals win toss. Boniol's kickoff is returned by Metcalf to Arizona 28. Cardinals drive to Philadelphia 15 where Jacke kicks 32-yard field goal at 4:30.

Sept. 12, 1999—Dallas 41, Washington 35, at Washington; Redskins win toss. Gowin's kickoff is returned by B. Mitchell to Washington 24. Redskins drive to Washington 47. M. Turk punts 48 yards. Punt downed at Dallas 5. Cowboys drive to Dallas 24. Aikman passes 76-yard touchdown to R. Ismail at 4:09.

Oct. 3, 1999—Baltimore 19, Atlanta 13, at Atlanta; Falcons win toss. Stover's kickoff is returned by Oliver to Atlanta 18. Falcons drive to Atlanta 23. Stryzinski punts 41 yards, out of bounds at Baltimore 36. Baltimore drive to Baltimore 46. Case passes 54-yard touchdown to Armour at 2:29.

Oct. 31, 1999—New York Giants 23, Philadelphia 17, at Philadelphia; Giants win toss. Akers' kickoff is returned by Levingston to New York 27. New York drives to Giants 31. Maynard punts 43 yards to Philadelphia 26. Rossum returns to Eagles 28. Pederson drives to New York 45. Pederson's pass is intercepted by Strahan at Philadelphia 44. Giants' Peter batted ball up in the air as Pederson backpedaled. Strahan for 44 yards and touchdown at 4:24.

Nov. 14, 1999—Minnesota 27, Chicago 24, at Chicago; Vikings win toss. Boniol kicks to Minnesota 2, Williams touchback. Minnesota starts on own 20. George's pass is intercepted by Harris at Minnesota 29 for -1 yard. Chicago starts at Minnesota 29 and moves to Minnesota 23. Boniol's 41-yard field goal is no good. Minnesota starts from own 31 and drives to Chicago 20. Anderson kicks 38-yard field goal at 9:02.

Nov. 21, 1999—Chicago 23, San Diego 20, at San Diego; Bears win toss. Chicago starts from own 22. Miller completes four consecutive passes and Bears drive to San Diego 22. Enis rushes twice to San Diego 19. Boniol kicks 36-yard field goal at 4:58.

* **Nov. 22, 1999—Denver 27, Oakland 21**, at Denver; Broncos win toss. Denver starts from own 33 and drives to Broncos' 35. Rouen punts 46 yards to Oakland 19. Oakland starts at own 19 and drives to Raiders' 25. Gannon fumbles and Broncos' Pryce recovers at Oakland 25. Denver running back Gary scores on 24-yard run at 2:40.

Nov. 28, 1999—Washington 20, Philadelphia 17, at Washington; Redskins win toss. Akers' kickoff is returned by Thrash for 48 yards to Philadelphia 46. Johnson completes 20-yard pass to Connell to Philadelphia 26. Johnson completes 9-yard pass to Mitchell to Philadelphia 9. Mitchell runs for seven yards to Philadelphia 2. On third down, Washington attempts field goal from Philadelphia 2. Johnson fumbles and recovers at Philadelphia 9. Conway kicks 27-yard field goal at 4:34.

Dec. 19, 1999—Denver 36, Seattle 30, at Denver; Broncos win toss. Peterson kicks to Denver 8. Watson returns kick to Denver 27 for 19 yards. Broncos do not convert a first down. Rouen punts 46 yards, out of bounds at Seattle 25. Kitna passes to Dawkins for 17 yards at Seattle 47. Watters runs for 6 yards to Denver 47. Kitna sacked for 11-yard loss by Crockett. Kitna fumbles, forced by Crockett, recovered by Cadrez at Seattle 37. Cadrez for 37 yards and touchdown at 2:34.

Dec. 26, 1999—Buffalo 13, New England 10, at New England; Patriots win toss. New England's Vinatieri misses 44-yard field goal from Buffalo 26. Buffalo takes over at Bills 34. Flutie passes to Moulds to New England 21 for 17 yards. Moulds fumbles, recovered by Bruschi at Patriots 21. New England drives to own 34. Johnson punts from New England 34 to Buffalo 42. Flutie passes to Price for 7 yards to New England 44. Flutie passes to Moulds for 11 yards to New England 27. Thomas runs for 9 yards to New England 6. Christie kicks 23-yard field goal at 13:12.

#Dec. 26, 1999—Washington 26, San Francisco 20, at San Francisco; Redskins win toss. Richey kicks to Washington 9, Thrash returns 13 yards to Washington 22. Johnson passes to Hicks for 25 yards to Washington 47. Centers runs for 12 yards to San Francisco 33. Johnson passes to Centers for 33 yards and touchdown at 2:00.

Jan. 2, 2000—Oakland 41, Kansas City 38, at Kansas City; Raiders win toss. Baker kicks 69 yards from Kansas City 30 to Oakland 1 and out of bounds. Oakland starts at Raiders 40. Gannon passes to Dudley for 21 yards to Kansas City 40. Gannon passes to Brown at Kansas City 16 for 24 yards. Crockett runs to Kansas City 15 for 1 yard. Nedney kicks 33-yard field goal at 3:13.

Sept. 10, 2000—Tennessee 17, Kansas City 14, at Tennessee; Titans win toss. Mason returns kickoff 28 yards to Tennessee 29. Face-mask penalty on Kansas City, 5 yards, enforced at 29. Titans drive to Kansas City 18 where Del Greco kicks 36-yard field goal at 2:58.

Oct. 1, 2000—Dallas 16, Carolina 13, at Carolina; Cowboys win toss. Tucker returns kickoff 20 yards to Dallas 26. Dallas drives to Carolina 6 where Seder kicks 24-yard field goal at 3:52.

Oct. 1, 2000—Washington 20, Tampa Bay 17, at Washington; Redskins win toss. Thrash returns kickoff 32 yards to Washington 30. Washington gains five yards where Barnhardt punts 52 yards to Tampa Bay 13. Green returns for one yard to Tampa Bay 14. Buccaneers gain one yard to Tampa Bay 15 where Royals punts 50 yards to Washington 35. Sanders returns punt 57 yards to Tampa Bay 8. Davis rushes three times and gets to Tampa Bay 2 where Husted kicks 20-yard field goal at 4:09.

Oct. 8, 2000—Oakland 34, San Francisco 28, at San Francisco; Raiders win toss. Dunn returns kickoff 20 yards to Oakland 19. Raiders drive to San Francisco 17 where Janikowski misses 35-yard field-goal attempt wide right. San Francisco drives to Oakland 11 where Richey's 29-yard field-goal attempt is blocked by Dorsett. Raiders recover at Oakland 16. Oakland drives to San Francisco 31 where Gannon passes to Brown for 31-yard touchdown at 10:15.

Oct. 15, 2000—Buffalo 27, San Diego 24, at Buffalo; Bills win toss. Bills drive to Buffalo 47. Mohr punts 42 yards to San Diego 11. Chargers drive to San Diego 38 where Harbaugh is intercepted at Buffalo 41. Flutie in for injured Johnson. Bills drive to San Diego 28. Christie kicks 46-yard field goal at 8:26.

* **Oct. 23, 2000—New York Jets 40, Miami 37,** at New York; Dolphins win toss. Marion returns kickoff 31 yards to Miami 37. Fielder is intercepted at Miami 46 by Coleman, who returns ball to 39 where he fumbles. Gadsden recovers ball for Dolphins and runs out of bounds at Miami 34. Dolphins drive to New York 43 where Fiedler is intercepted again by Coleman at the Jets 34. Jets drive to Miami 23 where Hall kicks 40-yard field goal at 6:47.

Oct. 29, 2000—Jacksonville 23, Dallas 17, at Dallas; Jaguars win toss. Stith returns kickoff 24 yards to Jacksonville 34. Jaguars drive to Dallas 37 where Brunell passes to Whitted for a 37-yard touchdown at 3:02.

Nov. 5, 2000—Buffalo 16, New England 13, at New England; Patriots win toss. Faulk returns kickoff 38 yards to New England 43. Penalty on New England for offensive holding, 10 yards, enforced at New England 33. Patriots lose one yard on three plays. Johnson punts 43 yards to Buffalo 35. Bills drive to New England 13 where Christie kicks 32-yard field goal at 4:21.

Nov. 5, 2000—Philadelphia 16, Dallas 13, at Philadelphia; Eagles win toss. Mitchell returns kickoff 30 yards to Philadelphia 34. Eagles drive to Dallas 36 where McNabb is intercepted by Wortham at Dallas 30. Wortham returns interception to Dallas 31. Cowboys drive to Dallas 48 where Thomas fumbles. Recovered by Hauck at Dallas 48. Eagles drive to Dallas 13 where Akers kicks 32-yard field goal at 7:52.

* **Nov. 6, 2000—Green Bay 26, Minnesota 20,** at Green Bay; Packers win toss. Rossum returns kickoff 13 yards to Green Bay 18. Packers drive to Minnesota 43 where Favre passes to Freeman for a 43-yard touchdown at 3:27.

Nov. 12, 2000—Philadelphia 26, Pittsburgh 23, at Pittsburgh; Eagles win toss. Mitchell returns kickoff 24 yards to Philadelphia 37. Eagles drive to Pittsburgh 24 where Akers kicks 42-yard field goal at 4:09.

Dec. 17, 2000—New England 13, Buffalo 10, at Buffalo; Bills win toss and elect to defend the South goal. Patriots elect to receive. Jackson returns kickoff 38 yards to New England 48. Patriots drive to Buffalo 31 where they turn the ball over on downs. Bills drive to New England 12 where Christie's 30-yard field goal attempt is blocked by Eaton. Patriots recover at New England 11. Patriots drive to Buffalo 6 where Vinatieri kicks 24-yard field goal at 14:37.

Dec. 24, 2000—Green Bay 17, Tampa Bay 14, at Green Bay; Packers win toss. Rossum returns kickoff 29 yards to Green Bay 38. Packers drive to Tampa Bay 4 where Longwell kicks 22-yard field goal at 6:28.

Sept. 9, 2001—St. Louis 20, Philadelphia 17, at Philadelphia; Eagles win toss. Wilkins' kickoff is a touchback. Eagles drive to Philadelphia 30. Landeta punts 34 yards to St. Louis 36. Rams drive to Philadelphia 8. Wilkins kicks 26-yard field goal at 7:56.

Sept. 9, 2001—San Francisco 16, Atlanta 13, at San Francisco; 49ers win toss. Feely's kickoff is a touchback. 49ers drive to Atlanta 6. Cortez kicks 24-yard field goal at 4:04.

Oct. 14, 2001—New England 29, San Diego 26, at New England; Chargers win toss. Jenkins returns kickoff 39 yards to San Diego 40. Chargers drive to San Diego 45. Bennett punts 32 yards to New England 23. Patriots drive to San Diego 26. Vinatieri kicks 44-yard field goal at 4:00.

Oct. 14, 2001—San Francisco 37, Atlanta 31, at Atlanta; 49ers win toss. Sutherland returns kickoff 24 yards to San Francisco 24. 49ers drive to Atlanta 14. Garcia fumbles, Hall recovers at Atlanta 16. Falcons drive to Atlanta 23. Mohr punts 44 yards to San Francisco 33. Garcia throws 52-yard touchdown to Owens at 8:34.

Oct. 14, 2001—Tennessee 31, Tampa Bay 28, at Tennessee; Buccaneers win toss. D. Smith returns kickoff 17 yards to Tampa Bay 18. Buccaneers forced back to Tampa Bay 9. Royals punts 45 yards to Tennessee 46. Titans drive to Tampa Bay 32. Nedney kicks 49-yard field goal at 1:52.

Oct. 21, 2001—Washington 17, Carolina 14, at Washington; Redskins win toss. Bates returns kickoff 17 yards to Washington 14. Redskins drive to Carolina 5. Conway kicks 23-yard field goal at 1:47.

Oct. 28, 2001—Chicago 37, San Francisco 31, at Chicago; 49ers win toss. Edinger's kickoff is a touchback. M. Brown intercepts Garcia pass and returns it 33 yards for touchdown at 16 seconds.

Nov. 4, 2001—Chicago 27, Cleveland 21, at Chicago; Bears win toss. L. Johnson returns kickoff 31 yards to Chicago 32. Bears drive to Chicago 40. Maynard punts 52 yards to Cleveland 8. M. Brown intercepts Couch pass and returns it 16 yards for touchdown at 2:50.

Nov. 4, 2001—New York Giants 27, Dallas 24, at New York; Cowboys win toss. Swinton returns kickoff 21 yards to Dallas 29. Cowboys drive to New York 48. Knorr punts 33 yards to New York 15. Giants drive to Dallas 24. Andersen kicks 42-yard field goal at 7:12.

Nov. 11, 2001—Pittsburgh 15, Cleveland 12, at Cleveland; Steelers win toss. T. Edwards returns kickoff 21 yards to Pittsburgh 28. Steelers drive to Cleveland 14. Brown kicks 32-yard field goal at 5:22.

Nov. 18, 2001—San Francisco 25, Carolina 22, at Carolina; 49ers win toss. Sutherland returns kickoff 24 yards to San Francisco 26. 49ers drive to Carolina 8. Cortez kicks 26-yard field goal at 4:41.

Dec. 2, 2001—Arizona 34, Oakland 31, at Oakland; Raiders win toss. Gramatica's kickoff is a touchback. Raiders drive to Oakland 40. Lechler punts 37 yards to Arizona 23. Cardinals drive to Arizona 48. Stanley punts 29 yards to Oakland 23. Woods recovers Dunn fumble on Oakland 25. Arizona drives to Oakland 18. Gramatica kicks 36-yard field goal at 7:29.

Dec. 2, 2001—Seattle 13, San Diego 10, at Seattle; Seahawks win toss. Rogers returns kickoff 33 yards to Seattle 32. Seahawks drive to San Diego 6. Lindell kicks 24-yard field goal at 6:23.

Dec. 2, 2001—Tampa Bay 16, Cincinnati 13, at Cincinnati; Buccaneers win toss. F. Murphy returns kickoff 20 yards to Tampa Bay 38. Buccaneers drive to Cincinnati 35. Royals punts 31 yards to Cincinnati 4. Lynch recovers Dillon fumble on Cincinnati 3. Gramatica kicks 21-yard field goal at 5:06.

Dec. 16, 2001—Kansas City 26, Denver 23, at Kansas City; Broncos win toss. Carter returns kickoff 24 yards to Denver 41. Broncos drive to Denver 35. Rouen punts 35 yards to Kansas City 30. Chiefs drive to Denver 23. T. Peterson misses 41-yard field-goal attempt. Broncos drive to Denver 32. Rouen punts 38 yards to Kansas City 30. Chiefs drive to Denver 14. T. Peterson kicks 32-yard field goal at 9:04.

Dec. 16, 2001—New England 12, Buffalo 9, at Buffalo; Bills win toss. Bryson returns kickoff 23 yards to Buffalo 28. Bills drive to Buffalo 48. Moorman punts 52 yards to end zone. Patriots drive to Buffalo 5. Vinatieri kicks 23-yard field goal at 5:45.

Dec. 30, 2001—Cincinnati 26, Pittsburgh 23, at Cincinnati; Steelers win toss. Geason returns kickoff and laterals to Logan who carries ball 9 yards to Pittsburgh 38. Steelers drive to Cincinnati 39. Miller punts 38 yards to Cincinnati 1. Bengals drive to Pittsburgh 13. Rackers kicks 31-yard field goal at 10:52.

Sept. 8, 2002—New York Jets 37, Buffalo 31, at Buffalo; Jets win toss. Morton returns kickoff 96 yards for touchdown at 14 seconds.

Sept. 8, 2002—Green Bay 37, Atlanta 34, at Green Bay; Packers win toss. J. Walker returns kickoff 26 yards to Green Bay 34. Packers drive to Atlanta 39. Bidwell punts 27 yards to Atlanta 12. Falcons drive to Atlanta 14. Mohr punts 46 yards to Green Bay 40. Packers drive to Atlanta 19. Longwell kicks 34-yard field goal at 9:40.

Sept. 8, 2002—New Orleans 26, Tampa Bay 20, at Tampa Bay; Tampa Bay wins toss. Stecker returns kickoff 31 yards to

Tampa Bay 42. Buccaneers drive to New Orleans 39. Tupa punts 39 yards into end zone. Saints drive to New Orleans 20. Williams returns Johnson's punt 4 yards to Tampa Bay 46. Buccaneers drive to Tampa Bay 48. Tupa punts 52 yards into end zone. Saints drive to New Orleans 41. Williams returns Johnson's punt -4 yards to Tampa Bay 6. Buccaneers drive to Tampa Bay 5. Tupa pass intercepted by Allen in Tampa Bay end zone at 12:01.

Sept. 15, 2002—Buffalo 45, Minnesota 39, at Minnesota; Buffalo wins toss. Rodgers returns kickoff 22 yards to Buffalo 22. Bills drive to Buffalo 48. Moorman punts 27 yards, downed at Minnesota 25. Vikings drive to Minnesota 32. Richardson punts 45 yards. Downed at Buffalo 23. Bills drive to Minnesota 26. Hollis' 44-yard field-goal attempt is no good. Vikings take over on Minnesota 35. Drive to Minnesota 41. Richardson punts 52 yards. Returned by Rogers 16 yards to Buffalo 24. Bills drive to Minnesota 48. Bledsoe throws 48-yard pass to Price for touchdown at 10:12.

Sept. 22, 2002—Cleveland 31, Tennessee 28, at Tennessee; Cleveland wins toss. White returns kickoff 6 yards to Cleveland 26. Browns drive to Tennessee 15. Dawson kicks 33-yard field goal at 4:09.

Sept. 22, 2002—New England 41, Kansas City 38, at New England; New England wins toss. Branch returns kickoff 30 yards to New England 30. Patriots drive to Kansas City 17. Vinatieri kicks 35-yard field goal at 4:36.

Sept. 29, 2002—Buffalo 33, Chicago 27, at Buffalo; Chicago wins toss. Johnson returns kickoff 19 yards to Chicago 20. Bears drive to Chicago 25. Maynard punts 31 yards to Buffalo 44. Fair catch by Mannelly. Buffalo drives to Chicago 26. Bledsoe throws 26-yard pass to Henry for touchdown at 2:48.

Sept. 29, 2002—Pittsburgh 16, Cleveland 13, at Pittsburgh; Pittsburgh wins toss. Mays returns kickoff 32 yards to Pittsburgh 32. Maddox's pass intercepted by Davis at Pittsburgh 34, returned for no gain. Cleveland drives to Pittsburgh 27. Dawson's 45-yard field-goal attempt no good, tipped at line of scrimmage by Flowers. Steelers take over at Pittsburgh 35. Steelers drive to Cleveland 6, and 24-yard field-goal attempt by Peterson blocked by McKinley, recovered by Peterson, fumbles, recovered by Fiala. Peterson's 31-yard field goal is good at 6:58.

Oct. 20, 2002—Denver 37, Kansas City 34, at Denver; Denver wins toss. Kasper returns kickoff 15 yards to Denver 24. Broncos drive to Denver 33. Rouen punts 43 yards to Kansas City 24. Hall returns punt 13 yards to Kansas City 37. Chiefs drive to Kansas City 43. Stryzinski's punt is blocked and recovered by Burns at Kansas City 32. Denver drives to Kansas City 7. Elam's 25-yard field goal is good at 2:52.

Oct. 20, 2002—Detroit 23, Chicago 20, at Detroit; Detroit wins toss. Edinger's kickoff goes out of bounds at Detroit 2. Lions take over at Detroit 40. Lions drive to Chicago 30. Hanson's 48-yard field goal is good at 4:42.

Oct. 20, 2002—San Diego 27, Oakland 21, at Oakland; San Diego wins toss. Chargers start at San Diego 20 after touchback. Chargers drive to Oakland 19. Tomlinson runs 19 yards for touchdown at 3:33.

Oct. 20, 2002—Arizona 9, Dallas 6, at Arizona; Dallas wins toss. Swinton returns kickoff 26 yards to Dallas 24. Cowboys drive to Dallas 29. Knorr punts 45 yards to Arizona 26. Jackson returns 5 yards to Arizona 31. Cardinals drive to Dallas 38. Player punts 38 yards into end zone. Cowboys take over at Dallas 20. Cowboys drive to Arizona 49. Knorr punts 31 yards to Arizona 18. Fair catch by Jackson. Cardinals drive to Dallas 22. Gramatica's 40-yard field goal is good at 11:45.

Nov. 3, 2002—San Francisco 23, Oakland 20, at Oakland; San Francisco wins toss. Janikowski's kickoff returned to SF 22 by J. Williams. 49ers drive to Oakland 5. Cortez's 23-yard field goal at 8:41.

Nov. 10, 2002—Atlanta 34, Pittsburgh 34, at Pittsburgh; Pittsburgh wins toss. Touchback on Feely kickoff. Pittsburgh starts at own 20, drives to Atlanta 30. Peterson's 48-yard field-goal attempt blocked by Finneran. Atlanta takes over at own 47, drives to Atlanta 33. Mohr punts 47 yards to Randle El, who returns to Pittsburgh 18. Steelers drive to Atlanta 33. Miller punts 22 yards to Atlanta 12, no return. Falcons drive to Atlanta 23. Mohr punts 52 yards. Randle El returns 1 yard to Pittsburgh 26. Steelers drive to Pittsburgh 44. Maddox intercepted by Mathis at Atlanta 43. Mathis returns to Pittsburgh 44. Atlanta drives to Pittsburgh 37. Feely's 56-yard field-goal attempt blocked by Farrior. Pittsburgh takes over on own 49. Maddox pass to Burress downed at Atlanta 1 as time expires.

Nov. 17, 2002—San Diego 20, San Francisco 17, at San Diego; San Diego wins toss. Jenkins returns Cortez kickoff 39 yards to San Diego 38. Chargers drive to San Diego 38. Bennett punts 47 yards to San Francisco 15. Williams returns 9 yards to San Francisco 24. 49ers drive to San Diego 23. Cortez's 41-yard field-goal attempt is no good. San Diego takes over on San Diego 31. Chargers drive to San Francisco 22. Christie's 40-yard field goal is good at 10:49.

Nov. 24, 2002—Chicago 20, Detroit 17, at Chicago; Detroit wins toss. Elects to defend the north goal. Hanson kicks 72 yards. Kick returned 37 yards to Chicago 35. Chicago drives to Detroit 22. Edinger's 40-yard field-goal attempt is good at 6:02.

#Nov. 24, 2002—Indianapolis 23, Denver 20, at Denver; Indianapolis wins toss. Knorr kicks 66 yards. Returned by Walters 28 yards to Indianapolis 20. Colts drive to Denver 33. Vanderjagt's 51-yard field-goal attempt is good at 5:38.

Dec. 1, 2002—Atlanta 30, Minnesota 24, at Minnesota; Minnesota wins toss. Feely kicks 60 yards. Returned by Carter 10 yards to Minnesota 20. Vikings drive to Minnesota 11. Richardson punts 47 yards to Atlanta 42. Returned by Rossum 10 yards to Minnesota 48. Falcons drive to Minnesota 46. Vick runs 46 yards for touchdown at 2:25.

Dec. 1, 2002—Tennessee 28, New York Giants 29, at New York; New York wins toss. Nedney kicks 68 yards. Returned by Joyce 38 yards to New York 40. Giants drive to New York 46. Allen punts 34 yards to Tennessee 20. Fair catch by O'Leary. Titans drive to New York 20. Nedney's 38-yard field goal good at 5:00.

Dec. 1, 2002—San Diego 30, Denver 27, at San Diego; Denver wins toss. Christie kicks 65 yards. Droughns returns 27 yards to Denver 32. Broncos drive to Denver 23. Knorr punts 36 yards to San Diego 41. Fair catch by Dwight. Chargers drive to Denver 19. Christie's 38-yard field-goal attempt blocked. Denver takes over on own 27. Broncos drive to San Diego 34. Elam's 53-yard field-goal attempt is no good. San Diego takes over on own 43. Chargers drive to Denver 9. Christie's field goal is good from 27 yards at 11:59.

Dec. 8, 2002—Arizona 23, Detroit 20, at Arizona; Arizona wins toss. Hanson kicks 64 yards. Kasper returns 19 yards to Arizona 30. Cardinals drive to Detroit 24. Gramatica's 42-yard field-goal attempt is good at 4:12.

Dec. 15, 2002—Seattle 30, Atlanta 24, at Atlanta; Atlanta wins toss. Lindell kicks 69 yards. Returned 17 yards to Atlanta 18 by Rossum. Atlanta drives to Seattle 18. Feely's 36-yard field-goal attempt wide right. Seattle takes over at own 36. Seahawks drive to Atlanta 27. Alexander runs 27 yards for a touchdown at 10:36.

Dec. 29, 2002—New York Giants 10, Philadelphia 7, at N.Y. Giants; Philadelphia wins toss. Bryant kicks 57 yards. Returned by Mitchell 32 yards to Philadelphia 45. Eagles drive to mid-field. Feeley's pass intercepted by Williams at New York 37, returned for no gain. Giants drive to Philadelphia 22. Bryant's 39-yard field-goal attempt is good at 5:10.

Dec. 29, 2002—New England 27, Miami 24, at New England; New England wins toss. Mare kicks 68 yards out of bounds. Patriots begin at own 40. New England drives to Miami 17. Vinatieri's 35-yard field goal is good at 2:03.

Dec. 29, 2002—Seattle 31, San Diego 28, at San Diego;

Seattle wins toss. Christie kicks 64 yards. Returned by Williams 26 yards to Seattle 32. Seahawks drive to San Diego 28. Hasselbeck's pass is intercepted by Molden at San Diego 20 and returned 1 yard to the 21. Chargers drive to San Diego 12. Bennett punts 48 yards to Seattle 40. Returned by Engram 8 yards to Seattle 48. Seahawks drive to San Diego 6. Lindell's 24-yard field goal is good at 9:58.

Sept. 14, 2003—St. Louis 27, San Francisco 24, at St. Louis; Rams win the toss. Harris returns kick 42 yards to St. Louis 48. Rams drive to San Francisco 10. Wilkins kicks 28-yard field goal at 1:56.

Sept. 14, 2003—Carolina 12, Tampa Bay 9, at Tampa Bay; Panthers win toss. Touchback. Carolina starts at own 20, drives to own 37. Sauerbrun punts 45 yards to Tampa Bay 18. Buccaneers drive to Carolina 42. Tupa punts 34 yards to Carolina 8. Smith returns punt 52 yards to Tampa Bay 40. Panthers drive to Tampa Bay 29. Kasay kicks 47-yard field goal at 11:26.

* Sept. 15, 2003—Dallas 35, New York Giants 32, at New York; Cowboys win toss. Smith returns kickoff 21 yards to Dallas 29. Cowboys drive to Dallas 48. Gowin punts 32 yards to Giants 20. Giants drive to New York 15. Feagles punts 42 yards to Dallas 43. Cowboys drive to New York 6. Cundiff kicks 25-yard field goal at 9:04.

Sept. 21, 2003—New York Giants 24, Washington 21, at Washington; Giants win toss. Begin drive on New York 6 due to penalty on kickoff return. Giants drive to Washington 11. Bryant kicks 29-yard field goal at 4:15.

Sept. 28, 2003—Oakland 34, San Diego 31, at Oakland; Chargers win toss. Johnson returns kickoff to San Diego 24. Chargers drive to San Diego 36. Bennett punts 46 yards to Oakland 18. Raiders drive to Oakland 8. Lechler punts 49 yards to San Diego 43. Chargers drive to San Diego 39. Bennett punts to Oakland 8. Raiders drive to San Diego 28. Janikowski kicks 46-yard field goal at 9:59.

Oct. 5, 2003—Buffalo 22, Cincinnati 16, at Buffalo; Bengals win toss. Begin drive on Cincinnati 20 after touchback. Bengals drive to Cincinnati 28. Harris punts 29 yards to Buffalo 43. Bills drive to Cincinnati 2. Henry scores on 2-yard touchdown run at 3:53.

* Oct. 6, 2003—Indianapolis 38, Tampa Bay 35, at Tampa Bay; Buccaneers win toss. Barlow returns kickoff 30 yards to Tampa Bay 30. Buccaneers drive to Indianapolis 41. Tupa punts to Indianapolis 13. Colts drive to Tampa Bay 11. Vanderjagt kicks 29-yard field goal at 11:13.

Oct. 12, 2003—Carolina 23, Indianapolis 20, at Indianapolis; Panthers win toss. Smart returns kickoff to Carolina 27. Panthers drive to Indianapolis 30. Kasay kicks 47-yard field goal at 5:39.

Oct. 12, 2003—Kansas City 40, Green Bay 34, at Green Bay; Chiefs win toss. Hall returns kick to Kansas City 29. Chiefs drive to Green Bay 30. Andersen misses 48-yard field goal (ball tipped at line). Packers take over possession at Green Bay 39. A. Green fumbles after eight-yard run. Chiefs recover at Kansas City 49. T. Green throws 51-yard touchdown pass to Kennison at 6:18.

Oct. 19, 2003—New England 19, Miami 13, at Miami; Dolphins win toss. Rogers returns kickoff 24 yards to Miami 26. Dolphins drive to New England 17. Mare's 35-yard field-goal attempt no good. Patriots take over on New England 26. Patriots drive to New England 40. Walter punts to Miami 21. Returned by Rogers to Miami 30. Dolphins drive to Miami 45. Fiedler pass intercepted by Poole at New England 18. Brady passes 82 yards to Brown for touchdown at 9:15.

Oct. 26, 2003—Carolina 23, New Orleans 20, at New Orleans; Saints win toss. Lewis returns kickoff 53 yards to Carolina 46. Saints drive to Carolina 37. McAllister fumbles on fourth-and-one. Panthers take over at Carolina 38 and drive to New Orleans 12. Kasay kicks 31-yard field goal at 4:36.

Oct. 26, 2003—Arizona 16, San Francisco 13, at Arizona; Cardinals win toss. 49ers' Pochman kicks out of bounds. Cardinals take possession at Arizona 40 and drive to San Francisco 22. Duncan kicks 39-yard field goal at 4:59.

Nov. 2, 2003—New York Giants 31, New York Jets 28, at New York Jets; Giants win toss. Mitchell returns kick 26 yards to Giants 34. Giants drive to Jets 21. Conway misses 39-yard field-goal attempt. Jets take over on own 30. Drive to Giants 49. Stryzinski's punt returned by Mitchell two yards to Giants 18. Giants drive to own 35. Feagles' punt returned six yards by Moss to Jets 29. Jets drive to Giants 32. Brien's 51-yard field goal attempt is blocked by Allen. Giants take over on own 36, drive to Jets 11. Conway kicks 29-yard field goal at 14:56.

Nov. 9, 2003—New York Jets 27, Oakland 24, at Oakland; Jets win toss. Jordan returns kick 12 yards to New York 25. Jets drive to Oakland 21. Brien kicks 38-yard field goal at 5:56.

Nov. 16, 2003—Miami 9, Baltimore 6, at Miami; Dolphins win toss. Dolphins start at Miami 20 after touchback, drive to Baltimore 45. Turk punts 36 yards to Baltimore 9. Ravens drive to Baltimore 36. Lewis fumbles, recovered by Dolphins' Thomas. Dolphins drive to Baltimore 25. Mare kicks 43-yard field goal at 6:12.

Nov. 16, 2003—New Orleans 23, Atlanta 20, at New Orleans; Saints win toss. Lewis returns kick 39 yards to New Orleans 38. Saints drive to New Orleans 40. McAllister fumbles on Atlanta 2 after 58-yard run. Ball recovered by Falcons' Stewart for touchdown. Falcons drive to New Orleans 37. Feely's 54-yard field-goal attempt no good. Saints take over on New Orleans 45. Drive to Atlanta 18. Carney kicks 36-yard field goal at 3:59.

Nov. 23, 2003—New England 23, Houston 20, at Houston; Texans win toss, take over possession at own 13 after penalty on Hollings' return. Patriots intercept Texans at Houston 23. Patriots drive to Houston 19. Vinatieri's 37-yard field-goal attempt blocked. Texans take over at own 27, drive to New England 40. Stanley punts 31 yards to New England 9. Patriots drive to New England 4. Walter punts 31 yards to New England 35. Texans drive to New England 40. Stanley punts 26 yards to New England 14. Patriots drive to Houston 10. Vinatieri kicks 28-yard field goal at 14:19.

Nov. 23, 2003—Baltimore 44, Seattle 41, at Baltimore; Seahawks win toss. Morris returns kick to Seattle 27. Seahawks drive to Seattle 30. Rouen punts 50 yards to Baltimore 20, returned 1 yard by Brightful to Baltimore 21. Ravens drive to Seattle 24. Stover kicks 42-yard field goal at 8:28.

Nov. 23, 2003—St. Louis 30, Arizona 27, at Arizona; Rams win toss. Harris returns kick to St. Louis 14. Rams drive to Arizona 31. Wilkins kicks 49-yard field goal at 3:38.

 # Dec. 7, 2003—Atlanta 20, Carolina 14, at Atlanta; Panthers win toss. Smart returns kickoff 19 yards to Carolina 22. Panthers drive to Carolina 29. Delhomme's pass intercepted by Mathis at Carolina 32 and returned for touchdown at 1:19.

Dec. 14, 2003—Denver 23, Cleveland 20, at Cleveland; Browns win toss, start on Cleveland 20 after touchback. Browns drive to Cleveland 17. Gardocki punts 42 yards, returned by O'Neal 6 yards to Denver 47. Broncos drive to Cleveland 7. Elam kicks 25-yard field goal at 5:10.

Dec. 21, 2003—San Francisco 31, Philadelphia 28, at Philadelphia; Eagles win toss, start on Philadelphia 21 after penalty on Thrash's return. McNabb's pass intercepted by 49ers' Parrish and returned 29 yards to Philadelphia 4. On second down, Peterson kicks 22-yard field goal at 1:05.

 # Dec. 28, 2003—Baltimore 13, Pittsburgh 10, at Baltimore; Steelers win toss. Mays returns kick to Pittsburgh 20. Steelers drive to Pittsburgh 27. Miller punts 43 yards, returned 6 yards by Brightful to Baltimore 36. Ravens drive to Pittsburgh 29. Stover kicks 47-yard field goal at 3:28.

Sept. 26, 2004—New Orleans 28, St. Louis 25, at St. Louis; Rams win the toss. Furrey returns kick 23 yards to St. Louis 32. Rams drive to own 41. Landeta punts 41 yards to New Orleans 18. Lewis returns punt 15 yards to New Orleans 33. Saints drive to St. Louis 13. Carney kicks 31-yard field goal at 7:04.

Oct. 10, 2004—Minnesota 34, Houston 28, at Houston; Vikings win the toss. Burleson returns kick 29 yards to Minnesota 30. Vikings drive to own 35. Bennett punts 47 yards to Houston 18. Houston drives to own 38. Stanley punts 43 yards to Minnesota 19. Minnesota drives to the 50. Culpepper passes to Robinson for 50-yard touchdown at 7:55.

Oct. 10, 2004—St. Louis 33, Seattle 27, at Seattle; Rams win the toss. Harris returns kick 17 yards to St. Louis 29. Rams drive to own 48. Bulger passes to McDonald for 52-yard touchdown at 3:02.

Oct. 10, 2004—San Francisco 31, Arizona 28, at San Francisco; 49ers win the toss. Jackson returns kick 14 yards to San Francisco 39. 49ers drive to Arizona 14. Peterson kicks 32-yard field goal at 3:23.

Oct. 24, 2004—Philadelphia 34, Cleveland 31, at Cleveland; Eagles win the toss. Reed returns kick 27 yards to Philadelphia 30. Eagles drive to Cleveland 37. Johnson punts 47 yards for touchback. Cleveland drives to own 47. Frost punts 30 yards to Eagles 22. Philadelphia drives to Cleveland 32. Akers kicks 50-yard field goal at 9:58.

Nov. 14, 2004—Jacksonville 23, Detroit 17, at Jacksonville; Jaguars win the toss. Lewis returns kick 17 yards to the Jacksonville 24. Jaguars drive to the Detroit 38. Garrard passes to Smith for 38-yard touchdown at 5:28.

Nov. 14, 2004—Chicago 19, Tennessee 17, at Tennessee; Bears win the toss. Azumarh returns kick 22 yards to Chicago 26. Bears drive to own 48. Maynard punts 43 yards to Tennessee. Fair catch by Mason. Volek sacked at Tennessee 0 and fumble is recovered by Miller who is tackled in the end zone for safety at 3:17.

Nov. 14, 2004—Baltimore 20, New York Jets 17, at New York; Jets win the toss. Touchback. Jets drive to own 24. Gowin punts to Baltimore 35. Sams returns punt 9 yards to Baltimore 44. Ravens drive to own 49. Stewart punts 42 yards and ball is downed at the New York 9. Jets drive to own 16. Gowin punts 43 yards to Baltimore 41. Sams returns punt to Baltimore 44. Baltimore drives to New York 24. Stover kicks 42-yard field goal at 7:25.

Dec. 12, 2004—San Francisco 31, Arizona 28, at Arizona; 49ers win the toss. Touchback. 49ers drive to Arizona 37. Lee punts to 34 yards and is downed at Arizona 3. Cardinals drive to own 7. Player punts 51 yards and is returned to Arizona 49. 49ers drive to own 13. Peterson kicks 31-yard field goal at 6:22.

 # Dec. 18, 2004—Atlanta 34, Carolina 31, at Atlanta; Panthers win the toss. Broussard returns kick 16 yards to Carolina 19. Delhomme intercepted by Beasley returns pass 30 yards to Carolina 23. Atlanta drives to Carolina 20. Feely kicks 38-yard field goal at 2:25.

Dec. 26, 2004—Indianapolis 34, San Diego 31, at Indianapolis; Colts win the toss. Rhodes returns kick 17 yards to Indianpolis 27. Colts drive to San Diego 17. Vanderjagt kicks 30-yard field goal at 2:47.

Jan. 2, 2005—St. Louis 32, New York Jets 29, at St. Louis; Rams win the toss. Cason returns kick to St. Louis 24. Rams drive to New York 44. Stemke punts into endzone for touchback. Jets drive to own 44. Gowin punts 33 yards. Fair catch at St. Louis 23. Rams drive to own 31. Stemke punts to New York 27 and returned by McCareins two yards. Jets drive to St. Louis 35. Brien misses 53-yard field goal wide right. Rams begin drive from own 43. Rams drive to Jets 13. Wilkins kicks 31-yard field goal at 11:58.

Sept. 25, 2005—Jacksonville 26, New York Jets 20, at New York; Jets win the toss. Miller returns kick for 29 yards to Jets 21. Mathis intercepts Pennington pass and returns to Jets 46. Rhodes intercepts Leftwich pass at Jets 12 for no return. Jets drive ends at own 1. Graham punts 44 yards. Pearman returns punt 11 yards to Jets 34. Leftwich passes to Smith for 36-yard touchdown at 6:05.

Oct. 2, 2005—Washington 20, Seattle 17, at Washington; Redskins win the toss. Betts returns kick for 24 yards to Washington 23. Redskins drive to Seattle 22. Novak kicks a 39-yard field goal at 5:31.

Oct. 16, 2005—Jacksonville 23, Pittsburgh 17, at Pittsburgh; Steelers win the toss. Morgan returns kick for 74 yards to Jacksonville 26. Maddox fumbles and ball is recovered by Jaguars on own 36. Jaguars drive ends on own 16. Hanson punts 48 yards. Randel El returns punt 2 yards to Pittsburgh 35. Mathis intercepts Maddox pass and returned 41 yards for a touchdown at 3:36.

Oct. 16, 2005—Dallas 16, New York Giants 13, at Dallas; Cowboys win the toss. Thompson returns kick 23 yards to Dallas 23. Cowboys drive to Giants 26. Cortez kicks a 45-yard field goal at 3:47.

Oct. 30, 2005—Chicago 19, Detroit 13, at Detroit; Lions win the toss. Drummond returns kick 15 yards to Detroit 22. Lions drive to own 28. Harris punts 45 yards. Wade returns to Chicago 23 for no gain. Bears drive to own 48. Maynard punts 39 yards. Fair catch by Drummond at Detroit 13. Garcia pass intercepted by Tillman and returned 22 yards for a touchdown at 6:17.

Nov. 20, 2005—Baltimore 16, Pittsburgh 13, at Baltimore; Steelers win the toss. Colclough returns kick 16 yards to Pittsburgh 18. Steelers drive ends at own 36. Gardocki punts 27 yards. Ball downed at Baltimore 37. Ravens drive to own 39. Zastudil punts 26 yards. Ball downed at Pittsburgh 35. Steelers drive ends at own 33. Gardocki punts 37 yards. Sams returns punt 14 yards to Baltimore 44. Ravens drive to Pittsburgh 26. Stover kicks 44-yard field goal at 10:51.

Nov. 24, 2005—Denver 24, Dallas 21, at Dallas; Broncos win the toss. Da. Williams returns kick 27 yards to own 32. Broncos drive to Dallas 7. Elam kicks 24-yard field goal at 1:11.

Nov. 27, 2005—St. Louis 33, Houston 27, at Houston; Texans win the toss. Touchback. Drive begins at Houston 20. Texans drive to St. Louis 47. Stanley punts 47 yards. Touchback. Drive begins at St. Louis 20. Fitzpatrick passes to Curtis for 56-yard touchdown at 6:14.

Nov. 27, 2005—San Diego 23, Washington 17, at Washington; Chargers win the toss. Sproles returns kick 22 yards to San Diego 35. Tomlinson runs 41 yards for a touchdown at 34 seconds.

Nov. 27, 2005—Seattle 24, New York Giants 21, at Seattle; Seahawks win the toss. Scobey returns kick 24 yards to Seattle 22. Seahawks drive ends at own 13. Rouen punts 40 yards. Morton returns punt 2 yards to Giants 49. Giants drive to Seattle 36. Feely misses 54-yard field goal. Seahawks drive begins at own 44. Drive ends at Giants 46. Rouen punts 46 yards. Touchback. Drive begins at Giants 20. Seahawks drive to own 27. Feely misses 45-yard field goal. Drive begins at Seattle 35. Seahawks drive to Giants 18. Brown kicks 36-yard field goal at 12:15.

Dec. 11, 2005—Green Bay 16, Detroit 13, at Green Bay; Packers win the toss. Chatman returns kick 33 yards to Green Bay 35. Packers drive to Lions 11. Longwell kicks 28-yard field goal at 5:17.

Dec. 11, 2005—New York Giants 26, Philadelphia 23, at Philadelphia; Eagles win the toss. Hood returns kick 27 yards to Philadelphia 33. Eagles drive ends on own 33. Landeta punts 41 yards. Morton returns punt 7 yards to Giants 33. Manning pass intercepted by Dawkins at Philadelphia 37 and returned for no gain. McMahon fumbles and ball recovered by K. Allen. Fumble returned 2 yards. Giants drive begins on Philadelphia 37. Giants drive to Philadelphia 18. Feely kicks 36-yard field goal at 11:05.

Dec. 24, 2005—Tampa Bay 27, Falcons 24, at Tampa Bay; Buccaneers win the toss. Shepherd returns kick 18 yards and fumbles. Ball is recovered by Falcons' Heard at Tampa Bay 18. Falcons drive to Tampa Bay 10. Peterson field goal blocked by White. Ball recovered by Kelley and returned 9 yards to Tampa Bay 31. Buccaneers drive to Atlanta 9. Bryant misses 27-yard field goal. Falcons begin drive at own 20. Falcons drive to own

46. Koenen punts 49 yards. Jones returns punt 4 yards to Tampa Bay 9. Buccaneers drive to own 47. Bidwell punts 37 yards out of bounds at Atlanta 16. Falcons drive to Atlanta 24. Koenen punts 53 yards. Jones returns punt 28 yards to Atlanta 49. Buccaneers drive to Atlanta 23. Bryant kicks 41-yard field goal at 14:45.

Jan. 1, 2006—San Francisco 20, Houston 17, at San Francisco; 49ers win the toss. Amey returns kick 15 yards to San Francisco 21. 49ers drive to own 30. Lee punts 39 yards. Ball downed at Houston 31. Texans drive to San Francisco 44. Stanley punts 39 yards. Ball downed at San Francisco 5. 49ers drive to own 49. Lee punts 47 yards. Ball downed at Houston 4. Banks pass intercepted by Adams and laterals to Emanuel. Ball returned 35 yards to Houston 21. 49ers drive to Houston 15. Nedney kicks 31-yard field goal at 11:08.

Sept. 17, 2006—Minnesota 16, Carolina 13, at Minnesota; Panthers win toss. D. Williams returns kick for 19 yards. Drive begins at Panthers 18. Drive ends on Panthers 33. Baker punts 57 yards. M. Moore returns kick 11 yards. Drive begins at Vikings 21. Longwell kicks 19-yard field goal at 7:25.

Sept. 17, 2006—New York Giants 30, Philadelphia 24, at Philadelphia; Giants win toss. Morton returns kick 23 yards. Drive begins at Giants 20. Drive ends at Giants 32. Feagles punts 38 yards. Wynn returns kick 14 yards. Drive begins at Eagles 44. Drive ends at Eagles 36. D. Johnson punts for 49 yards. Morton fair catch. Drive begins at Giants 15. Manning completes 31-yard touchdown pass to Burress at 3:11.

Sept. 17, 2006—Denver 9, Kansas City 6, at Denver; Broncos win toss. Cobbs muffs kick and recovers for no gain. Drive begins at Broncos 16. Elam kicks 39-yard field goal at 9:50.

Oct. 1, 2006—Washington 36, Jacksonville 30, at Washington; Redskins win toss. Cartwright returns kick for 22 yards. Drive begins at Redskins 20. Brunell completes 68-yard touchdown pass to Moss at 13:11.

Oct. 22, 2006—Atlanta 41, Pittsburgh 38, at Atlanta; Falcons win toss. Rossum returns kick for 23 yards. Drive begins at Falcons 21. Andersen kicks 32-yard field goal at 8:04.

Dec. 3, 2006—Cleveland 31, Kansas City 28, at Cleveland; Chiefs win toss. Hall returns kick for 21 yards. Drive begins at Chiefs 20. Drive ends at Chiefs 41. Colquitt punts 42 yards. Northcutt returns punt 5 yards. Drive begins at Browns 22. Dawson kicks 33-yard field goal at 7:25.

Dec. 10, 2006—Tennessee 26, Houston 20, at Houston; Titans win toss. Jones returns kick 36 yards. Drive begins at Texans 43. Young runs for 39-yard touchdown at 11:14.

Dec. 17, 2006—Chicago 34, Tampa Bay 31, at Chicago; Buccaneers win toss. Touchback. Drive begins at Buccaneers 20. Rattay fumbles. Bears recover at Buccaneers 22. Gould misses 37-yard field goal. Drive begins at Buccaneers 27. Bidwell punts 45 yards. Hester returns punt 8 yards and fumbles out of bounds. Drive begins at Bears 29. Maynard punts 47 yards. Drive begins at Buccaneers 2. Bidwell punts 48 yards. Hester returns punt 4 yards. Drive begins at 50-yard line. Gould kicks 25-yard field goal at 3:37.

Dec. 24, 2006—St. Louis 37, Washington 31, at St. Louis; Rams win toss. Ponder returns kickoff 20 yards. Drive begins at Rams 20. Turk punts 44 yards. Drive begins at Redskins 6. Frost punts 57 yards. McDonald returns punt 33 yards. Drive begins at Redskins 39. Jackson runs for 21-yard touchdown at 8:27.

Dec. 31, 2006—Pittsburgh 23, Cincinnati 17, at Cincinnati; Steelers win toss. Holmes returns kickoff 24 yards. Drive begins at Steelers 22. Roethlisberger completes 67-yard touchdown to Holmes at 13:27.

Dec. 31, 2006—San Francisco 26, Denver 23, at Denver; Broncos win the toss. Morgan returns kickoff 28 yards. Drive begins at Broncos 27. Ernster punts 46 yards. Leach fair catch. Drive begins at 49ers 12. Lee punts 33 yards. Kircus fair catch. Drive begins at Broncos 11. Ernster punts 54 yards. B. Williams returns punt 12 yards. Drive begins at 49ers 39. Nedney kicks 36-yard field goal at 1:56.

POSTSEASON

Dec. 28, 1958—Baltimore 23, New York Giants 17, at New York in NFL Championship Game; Giants win toss. Maynard returns kickoff to Giants' 20. Chandler punts and Taseff returns one yard to Colts' 20. Ameche scores on 1-yard run at 8:15.

Dec. 23, 1962—Dallas Texans 20, Houston Oilers 17, at Houston in AFL Championship Game; Texans win toss and kick off. Jancik returns kickoff to Oilers' 33. Norton punts and Jackson makes fair catch on Texans' 22. Wilson punts and Jancik makes fair catch on Oilers' 45. Robinson intercepts Blanda's pass and returns 13 yards to Oilers' 47. Wilson's punt rolls dead at Oilers' 12. Hull intercepts Blanda's pass and returns 23 yards to midfield. Brooker kicks 25-yard field goal at 17:54.

Dec. 26, 1965—Green Bay 13, Baltimore 10, at Green Bay in NFL Divisional Playoff Game; Packers win toss. Moore returns kickoff to Packers' 22. Chandler punts and Haymond returns nine yards to Colts' 41. Gilburg punts and Wood makes fair catch at Packers' 21. Chandler punts and Haymond returns one yard to Colts' 41. Michaels misses 47-yard field goal. Chandler kicks 25-yard field goal at 13:39.

Dec. 25, 1971—Miami 27, Kansas City 24, at Kansas City in AFC Divisional Playoff Game; Chiefs win toss. Podolak, after a lateral from Buchanan, returns kickoff to Chiefs' 46. Stenerud's 42-yard field goal is blocked. Seiple punts and Podolak makes fair catch at Chiefs' 17. Wilson punts and Scott returns 18 yards to Dolphins' 39. Yepremian misses 62-yard field goal. Scott intercepts Dawson's pass and returns 13 yards to Dolphins' 46. Seiple punts and Podolak loses one yard to Chiefs' 15. Wilson punts and Scott makes fair catch on Dolphins' 30. Yepremian kicks 37-yard field goal at 22:40.

Dec. 24, 1977—Oakland 37, Baltimore 31, at Baltimore in AFC Divisional Playoff Game; Colts win toss. Raiders start on own 42 following a punt late in the first overtime. Oakland works way into field-goal range on Stabler's 19-yard pass to Branch at Colts' 26. Four plays later, on the second play of the second overtime, Stabler hits Casper with a 10-yard touchdown pass at 15:43.

Jan. 2, 1982—San Diego 41, Miami 38, at Miami in AFC Divisional Playoff Game; Chargers win toss. San Diego drives from its 13 to Miami 8. On second-and-goal, Benirschke misses 27-yard field goal attempt wide left at 9:15. Miami has the ball twice and San Diego twice more before the Dolphins get their third possession. Miami drives from the San Diego 46 to Chargers' 17 and on fourth-and-two, von Schamann's 34-yard field goal attempt is blocked by San Diego's Winslow after 11:27. Fouts then completes four of five passes, including a 39-yarder to Joiner that puts the ball on Dolphins' 10. On first down, Benirschke kicks a 29-yard field goal at 13:52.

Jan. 3, 1987—Cleveland 23, New York Jets 20, at Cleveland in AFC Divisional Playoff Game; Jets win toss. Jets' punt downed at Browns' 26. Moseley's 23-yard field goal attempt is wide right. Teams trade punts. Jets' second punt downed at Browns' 31. First overtime period expires eight plays later with Browns in possession at Jets' 42. Moseley kicks 27-yard field goal four plays into second overtime at 17:02.

Jan. 11, 1987—Denver 23, Cleveland 20, at Cleveland in AFC Championship Game; Browns win toss. Broncos hold Browns on four downs. Browns' punt returned four yards to Denver's 25. Elway completes 22- and 28-yard passes to set up Karlis's 33-yard field goal nine plays into overtime at 5:38.

Jan. 3, 1988—Houston 23, Seattle 20, at Houston in AFC Wild Card Game; Seahawks win toss. Rodriguez punts to K. Johnson who returns one yard to Houston 15. Zendejas kicks 32-yard field goal 12 plays later at 8:05.

Dec. 31, 1989—Pittsburgh 26, Houston 23, at Houston in AFC Wild Card Playoff Game; Steelers win toss. Steelers punt to Oilers. Oilers' fumble recovered by Woodson and returned

three yards. Four plays and 13 yards later, Anderson kicks a 50-yard field goal at 3:26.

Jan. 7, 1990—Los Angeles Rams 19, New York Giants 13, at New York in NFC Divisional Game; Rams win toss. Everett completes two passes to move ball to Giants' 48. White called for pass interference; ball spotted on Giants' 25. Everett hits Anderson with a 30-yard touchdown pass at 1:06.

Jan. 3, 1993—Buffalo 41, Houston 38, at Buffalo in AFC Wild Card Game; Oilers win toss. Oilers begin at 20. After 2 plays, Moon's pass is intercepted by Odomes who returns ball 2 yards to Houston 35. After 2 plays, Christie kicks 32-yard field goal at 3:06.

Jan. 8, 1994—Kansas City 27, Pittsburgh 24, at Kansas City in AFC Wild Card Game; Chiefs win toss. Hughes returns kickoff 20 yards to Kansas City 25. After 3 plays, Barker punts 48 yards to Pittsburgh 18 where Woodson returns 8 yards to the 26. After 6 plays, Royals punts 30 yards to Kansas City 20. Kansas City drives to Pittsburgh 14 where Lowery kicks 32-yard field goal at 11:03.

Jan. 17, 1999—Atlanta 30, Minnesota 27, at Minnesota in NFC Championship Game; Vikings win toss. Palmer returns kickoff 30 yards to Minnesota 29. After four plays, Berger punts 51 yards to Atlanta 7 where Dwight returns 8 yards to Atlanta 15. Falcons drive to Atlanta 36. Stryzinski punts 37 yards to Vikings' 27. Palmer calls fair catch. Vikings drive to Minnesota 39. Berger punts 52 yards to Atlanta 9. Downed by Vikings. Atlanta drives to Minnesota 21 where Andersen kicks 38-yard field goal at 11:52.

Dec. 30, 2000—Miami 23, Indianapolis 17, at Miami in AFC Wild Card Game; Dolphins win toss. Williams returns kickoff 18 yards to Miami 20. Offensive holding penalty on Freeman, 10 yards, ball spotted on Miami 10. Dolphins drive to Miami 29 where Turk punts 53 yards to Indianapolis 18. Colts drive to Miami 31 where Vanderjagt misses 49-yard field-goal attempt wide right. Dolphins drive to Indianapolis 17 where Smith rushes for a 17-yard touchdown at 11:16.

Jan. 19, 2002—New England 16, Oakland 13, at New England in AFC Divisional Playoff Game; Patriots win toss. Pass returns kickoff 24 yards to New England 34. Patriots drive to Oakland 5. Vinatieri kicks 23-yard field goal at 8:29.

Jan. 11, 2003—Tennessee 34, Pittsburgh 31, at Tennessee in AFC Divisional Playoff Game; Tennessee wins toss. Reed kicks 60 yards. Returned by Simon 21 yards to Tennessee 31. Titans drive to Pittsburgh 8. Nedney's 26-yard field goal is good at 2:15.

Jan. 4, 2004—Green Bay 33, Seattle 27, at Green Bay in NFC Wild Card Game; Seahawks win toss. Morris returns kick to Seattle 33. Seahawks drive to Seattle 42. Rouen's 44-yard punt returned by Chatman to Green Bay 26. Packers drive to Green Bay 31. Bidwell punts 35 yards to Seattle 34. Seahawks drive to Seattle 45. Hasselbeck's pass to Bannister intercepted by Packers' Harris and returned 52 yards for touchdown at 4:25.

Jan. 10, 2004—Carolina 29, St. Louis 23, at St. Louis in NFC Divisional Game; Panthers win toss. Smart returns kick to Carolina 32. Panthers drive to St. Louis 27. Kasay's 45-yard field-goal attempt no good. Rams take over at own 36 and drive to Carolina 35. Wilkins' 53-yard field-goal attempt no good. Panthers take over at Carolina 43, drive to Carolina 47. Sauerbrun punts 40 yards to St. Louis 13. Rams drive to Carolina 38. Bulger's pass intercepted by Manning at Carolina 35. Panthers drive to Carolina 31. First overtime ends. On first play of second overtime, Delhomme passes to Smith for 69-yard touchdown at 15:10.

Jan. 11, 2004—Philadelphia 20, Green Bay 17, at Philadelphia in NFC Divisional Game; Eagles win toss. Thrash returns kick to Philadelphia 28. Eagles drive to Philadelphia 24. Johnson punts 49 yards and Packers start at own 32 after holding penalty. Favre's pass intercepted by Dawkins at Philadelphia 31 and returned to Green Bay 34. Eagles drive to Green Bay 13. Akers kicks 31-yard field goal at 4:48.

Jan. 8, 2005—New York Jets 20, San Diego 17, at San Diego in AFC Wild Card Game; Chargers win toss. Dwight returns kick to San Diego 26. Chargers drive to San Diego 35. Scifres punts 39 yards and ball is downed at the New York 26. Jets gain no yards. Gowin punts 41 yards. Parker loses 3 yards on return. San Diego starts on own 30. Chargers drive to New York 22. Kaeding's 40-yard field-goal attempt no good. Jets drive to San Diego 10. Brien kicks 33-yard field goal at 14:55.

Jan. 15, 2005—Pittsburgh 20, New York Jets 17, at Pittsburgh in AFC Divisional Game; Jets win toss. Cotchery returns kick to New York 31. Jets drive to New York 41. Gowin punts 54 yards. Randle El returns 8 yards to Pittsburgh 13. Steelers drive to New York 15. Reed kicks 33-yard field goal at 11:04.

Jan. 14, 2007—Chicago 27, Seattle 24, at Chicago in NFC Divisional Playoff Game; Seahawks win the toss. Burleson returns kickoff 25. Drive begins at Seahawks 30. Plackemeier punts 18 yards. Drive begins at Bears 34. Gould kicks 49-yard field goal at 4:53.

NFL POSTSEASON OVERTIME GAMES
(BY LENGTH OF GAME)

Dec. 25, 1971	Miami 27, KANSAS CITY 24	82:40
Dec. 23, 1962	Dallas Texans 20, HOUSTON 17	77:54
Jan. 3 1987	CLEVELAND 23, N.Y. Jets 20	77:02
Dec. 24, 1977	Oakland 37, BALTIMORE 31	75:43
Jan. 10, 2004	Carolina 29, ST. LOUIS 23	75:10
Jan. 8, 2005	New York Jets 20, SAN DIEGO 17	74:55
Jan 2, 1982	San Diego 41, MIAMI 38	73:52
Dec. 26, 1965	GREEN BAY 13, Baltimore 10	73:39
Jan 17, 1999	Atlanta 30, MINNESOTA 27	71:52
Dec. 30, 2000	MIAMI 23, Indianapolis 17	71:16
Jan. 15, 2005	PITTSBURGH 20, New York Jets 17	71:04
Jan 8, 1994	KANSAS CITY 27, Pittsburgh 24	71:03
Jan. 19, 2002	NEW ENGLAND 16, Oakland 13	68:29
Dec. 28, 1958	Baltimore 23, N.Y. GIANTS 17	68:15
Jan. 3, 1988	HOUSTON 23, Seattle 20	68:05
Jan. 11, 1987	Denver 23, CLEVELAND 20	65:38
Jan. 14, 2007	CHICAGO 27, Seattle 24	64:53
Jan. 11, 2004	PHILADELPHIA 20, Green Bay 17	64:48
Jan. 4, 2004	GREEN BAY 33, Seattle 27	64:25
Dec. 31, 1989	Pittsburgh 26, HOUSTON 23	63:26
Jan. 3, 1993	BUFFALO 41, Houston 38	63:06
Jan. 11, 2003	TENNESSEE 34, Pittsburgh 31	62:15
Jan. 7, 1990	L.A. Rams 19, N.Y. GIANTS 13	61:06

Home team in CAPS

There have been 23 overtime postseason games dating back to 1958. In 20 cases, both teams have had at least one possession. Last time: 1/14/07, CHICAGO 27, Seattle 24.

OVERTIME GAMES BY YEAR
(REGULAR SEASON)

2006-11	1997-17	1988- 9	1979-12
2005-14	1996-14	1987-13	1978-11
2004-12	1995-21	1986-16	1977-6
2003-23	1994-16	1985-10	1976-5
2002-25*	1993-7	1984- 9	1975-9
2001-17	1992-10	1983-19	1974-2
2000-13	1991-15	1982- 4	
1999-11	1990-10	1981-10	
1998-7	1989-11	1980-13	

*Record

OVERTIME WON-LOST RECORDS, 1974-2006
(REGULAR SEASON)

Team	Win	Loss	Tie	Pct.
AFC				
Baltimore	6	3	1	.650
Buffalo	17	9	0	.654
Cincinnati	14	10	0	.583
Cleveland	14	13	1	.518
Denver	19	13	2	.588
Houston	0	5	0	.000
Indianapolis	12	9	1	.568
Jacksonville	5	3	0	.625
Kansas City	10	13	2	.440
Miami	11	17	1	.397
New England	16	18	0	.470
N.Y. Jets	13	13	2	.500
Oakland	13	16	0	.448
Pittsburgh	16	11	2	.586
San Diego	11	17	0	.393
Tennessee	12	15	0	.444
NFC				
Arizona	16	13	2	.548
Atlanta	11	16	2	.414
Carolina	4	8	0	.333
Chicago	18	14	0	.563
Dallas	13	11	0	.542
Detroit	11	15	1	.426
Green Bay	10	11	4	.480
Minnesota	17	14	2	.529
New Orleans	7	8	0	.466
N.Y. Giants	15	14	2	.516
Philadelphia	11	16	3	.417
St. Louis	12	8	1	.595
San Francisco	16	13	1	.550
Seattle	8	15	0	.348
Tampa Bay	11	14	1	.442
Washington	17	11	1	.603

OVERTIME GAME SUMMARY—1974-2006

There have been 402 overtime games in regular season play since the rule was adopted in 1974 (11 in 2006 season). Breakdown follows:

RESULTS

213 (7) times the team which won the toss won the game (53.0%)

173 (4) times the team which lost the toss won the game (43.0%)

16 (0) games ended tied (4.0%). Last time: Nov. 10, 2002, Atlanta 34 at Pittsburgh 34.

POSSESSIONS

285 (6) times both teams had at least one possession (70.9%)

117 (5) times the team which won the toss drove for winning score (83 FG, 34 TD) (29.1%)

Of the 402 overtime games, there were 12 miscellaneous situations in which non-standard possessions took place:

8 (0) times the defense or special teams won without registering an official possession (5 interceptions, 1 fumble recovery, 1 blocked punt, 1 blocked field goal) (2.0%)

1 (0) times the special teams forced a fumble on the opening kickoff and drove for the winning score (0.25%)

1 (0) times the punting team recovered a muffed punt and drove for winning score with team muffing punt having no official possessions (0.25%)

2 (0) times the team that won the toss elected to kick and the team receiving the ball drove for winning score (0.50%)

OVERTIME GAMES

SCORING

278 (6) games were decided by a field goal (69.2%)
106 (5) games were decided by a touchdown (26.4%)
2 (0) games were decided by a safety (0.50%)
16 (0) games ended tied (4.0%). Last time: Nov. 10, 2002, Atlanta 34 at Pittsburgh 34.

COIN TOSS

393(11) times the team which won the toss elected to receive (97.8%)
9 (0) times the team which won the toss elected to kick off (4 wins) (2.2%)

Note: The number in parentheses is the 2006 Season Total.

MOST OVERTIME GAMES, SEASON

5	Green Bay Packers, 1983
4	Denver Broncos, 1985
	Cleveland Browns, 1989
	Minnesota Vikings, 1994
	Arizona Cardinals, 1995
	Minnesota Vikings, 1995
	Arizona Cardinals, 1997
	San Francisco 49ers, 2001
	Atlanta Falcons, 2002
	San Diego Chargers, 2002
	Carolina Panthers, 2003

LONGEST CONSECUTIVE GAME STREAKS
WITHOUT OVERTIME (Current)

59   Buffalo Bills (Last OT Game, 10/5/03 vs. Cincinnati Bengals)

(Record: 110, St. Louis/Phoenix Cardinals, 12/7/86-12/19/93)

SHORTEST OVERTIME GAMES

0:14	New York Jets 37, BUFFALO 31; 9/8/02
0:16	CHICAGO 37, San Francisco 31; 10/28/01
0:17	NEW ORLEANS 20, Seattle 17; 11/16/97
0:21	Chicago 23, DETROIT 17; 11/27/80
0:30	Baltimore 29, NEW ENGLAND 23; 9/4/83
0:34	San Diego 23, WASHINGTON 17; 11/27/05
0:55	New York Giants 16, PHILADELPHIA 10; 9/29/85

LONGEST OVERTIME GAMES
(ALL POSTSEASON GAMES)

22:40	Miami 27, KANSAS CITY 24; 12/25/71
17:54	Dallas Texans 20, HOUSTON 17; 12/23/62
17:02	CLEVELAND 23, New York Jets 20; 1/3/87
15:43	Oakland 37, BALTIMORE 31; 12/24/77
15:10	Carolina 29, ST. LOUIS 23; 1/10/04

Home team in CAPS
There have been 23 overtime postseason games dating back to 1958. In 20 cases, both teams have had at least one possession. Last time: 1/14/07, CHICAGO 27, Seattle 24.

OVERTIME SCORING SUMMARY

278   were decided by a field goal
49   were decided by a touchdown pass
29   were decided by a touchdown run
17   were decided by an interception (Atlanta 40, New Orleans 34, 9/2/79; Atlanta 47, Green Bay 41, 11/27/83; New York Giants 23, Philadelphia 10, 9/29/85; Indianapolis 23, Cleveland 17, 12/10/89; Cleveland 30, San Diego 24, 10/20/91; Kansas City 23, Oakland 17, 9/17/95; New York Giants 27, Arizona 21, 10/8/95; Washington 36, Detroit 30, 10/22/95; Arizona 20, Seattle 14, 10/29/95; Cincinnati 34, Detroit 28, 9/13/98; New York Giants 23, Philadelphia 17,

10/31/99; Chicago 37, San Francisco 31, 10/28/01; Chicago 27, Cleveland 21, 11/4/01; New Orleans 26, Tampa Bay 20, 9/8/02; Atlanta 20, Carolina 14, 12/7/03; Jacksonville 23, Pittsburgh 17, 10/16/05; Chicago 19, Detroit 13, 10/30/05)

2   were decided on a fake field goal/touchdown pass (Minnesota 22, Chicago 16, 10/16/77; Cleveland 23, Minnesota 17, 12/17/89)

2   were decided by a fumble recovery (Baltimore 29, New England 23, 9/4/83; Denver 36, Seattle 30, 12/19/99)

2   were decided by a kickoff return (Chicago 23, Detroit 17, 11/27/80; New York Jets 37, Buffalo 31, 9/8/02)

2   was decided by a safety (Minnesota 23, Los Angeles Rams 21, 11/5/89; Chicago 19, Tennessee 17, 11/14/04)

1   was decided by a punt return (Kansas City 29, San Diego 23, 10/9/95)

1   was decided on a fake field goal/touchdown run (Los Angeles Rams 27, Minnesota 21, 12/2/79)

1   was decided on a blocked field goal (Denver 30, San Diego 24, 11/17/85)

1   was decided on a blocked field goal/recovery by kicker (Green Bay 12, Chicago 6, 9/7/80)

1   was decided on a blocked field goal/recovery by kicking team (Philadelphia 23, New York Giants 17, 11/20/88)

16   ended tied

OVERTIME RECORDS

Longest Touchdown Pass
99 Yards — Ron Jaworski to Mike Quick, Philadelphia 23, Atlanta 17 (11/10/85)
82 Yards — Tom Brady to Troy Brown, New England 19, Miami 13 (10/19/03)
76 Yards — Troy Aikman to Raghib Ismail, Dallas 41, Washington 35 (9/12/99)

Longest Touchdown Run
96 Yards — Garrison Hearst, San Francisco 36, New York Jets 30 (9/6/98)
60 Yards — Herschel Walker, Dallas 23, New England 17 (11/15/87)
46 Yards — Michael Vick, Atlanta 30, Minnesota 24 (12/1/02)

Longest Field Goal
53 Yards — Chris Jacke, Green Bay 23, San Francisco 20 (10/4/96)
52 Yards — Mike Cofer, Indianapolis 27, New York Jets 24 (9/10/95)
51 Yards — Greg Davis, New England 23, Indianapolis 20 (10/29/89); Greg Davis, Arizona 20, Pittsburgh 17 (10/30/94); Michael Husted, Tampa Bay 20, Minnesota 17 (10/15/95); Mike Vanderjagt, Indianapolis 23, Denver 20 (11/24/02)

Longest Touchdown Plays
99 Yards — (Pass) Ron Jaworski to Mike Quick, Philadelphia 23, Atlanta 17 (11/10/85)
96 Yards — (Run) Garrison Hearst, San Francisco 36, New York Jets 30 (9/6/98)
96 Yards — (Kickoff return) Chad Morton, New York Jets 37, Buffalo 31 (9/8/02)
95 Yards — (Kickoff return) Dave Williams, Chicago 23, Detroit 17 (11/27/80)
86 Yards — (Punt return) Tamarick Vanover, Kansas City 29, San Diego 23 (10/9/95)

FIRST-ROUND SELECTIONS

If club had no first-round selection, first player drafted is listed with round in parentheses.

ARIZONA CARDINALS
Year Player, College, Position
1936 Jim Lawrence, Texas Christian, B
1937 Ray Buivid, Marquette, B
1938 Jack Robbins, Arkansas, B
1939 Charles (Ki) Aldrich, TCU, C
1940 George Cafego, Tennessee, B
1941 John Kimbrough, Texas A&M, B
1942 Steve Lach, Duke, B
1943 Glenn Dobbs, Tulsa, B
1944 Pat Harder, Wisconsin, B
1945 Charley Trippi, Georgia, B
1946 Dub Jones, Louisiana State, B
1947 DeWitt (Tex) Coulter, Army, T
1948 Jim Spavital, Oklahoma A&M, B
1949 Bill Fischer, Notre Dame, G
1950 Jack Jennings, Ohio State, T (2)
1951 Jerry Groom, Notre Dame, C
1952 Ollie Matson, San Francisco, B
1953 Johnny Olszewski, California, B
1954 Lamar McHan, Arkansas, B
1955 Max Boydston, Oklahoma, E
1956 Joe Childress, Auburn, B
1957 Jerry Tubbs, Oklahoma, C
1958 King Hill, Rice, B
       John David Crow, Texas A&M, B
1959 Bill Stacy, Mississippi State, B
1960 George Izo, Notre Dame, QB
1961 Ken Rice, Auburn, T
1962 Fate Echols, Northwestern, DT
       Irv Goode, Kentucky, C
1963 Jerry Stovall, Louisiana State, S
       Don Brumm, Purdue, DE
1964 Ken Kortas, Louisville, DT
1965 Joe Namath, Alabama, QB
1966 Carl McAdams, Oklahoma, LB
1967 Dave Williams, Washington, WR
1968 MacArthur Lane, Utah State, RB
1969 Roger Wehrli, Missouri, DB
1970 Larry Stegent, Texas A&M, RB
1971 Norm Thompson, Utah, CB
1972 Bobby Moore, Oregon, RB-WR
1973 Dave Butz, Purdue, DT
1974 J.V. Cain, Colorado, TE
1975 Tim Gray, Texas A&M, DB
1976 Mike Dawson, Arizona, DT
1977 Steve Pisarkiewicz, Missouri, QB
1978 Steve Little, Arkansas, K
       Ken Greene, Washington State, DB
1979 Ottis Anderson, Miami, RB
1980 Curtis Greer, Michigan, DE
1981 E.J. Junior, Alabama, LB
1982 Luis Sharpe, UCLA, T
1983 Leonard Smith, McNeese St., DB
1984 Clyde Duncan, Tennessee, WR
1985 Freddie Joe Nunn, Mississippi, LB
1986 Anthony Bell, Michigan State, LB
1987 Kelly Stouffer, Colorado State, QB
1988 Ken Harvey, California, LB
1989 Eric Hill, Louisiana State, LB
       Joe Wolf, Boston College, G
1990 Anthony Thompson, Indiana, RB (2)
1991 Eric Swann, No College, DE
1992 Tony Sacca, Penn State, QB (2)

1993 Garrison Hearst, Georgia, RB
       Ernest Dye, South Carolina, T
1994 Jamir Miller, UCLA, LB
1995 Frank Sanders, Auburn, WR (2)
1996 Simeon Rice, Illinois, DE
1997 Tom Knight, Iowa, DB
1998 Andre Wadsworth, Florida St., DE
1999 David Boston, Ohio State, WR
       L.J. Shelton, Eastern Michigan, T
2000 Thomas Jones, Virginia, RB
2001 Leonard Davis, Texas, T
2002 Wendell Bryant, Wisconsin, DT
2003 Bryant Johnson, Penn State, WR
       Calvin Pace, Wake Forest, DE
2004 Larry Fitzgerald, Pittsburgh, WR
2005 Antrel Rolle, Miami, DB
2006 Matt Leinart, So. California, QB
2007 Levi Brown, Penn State, T

ATLANTA FALCONS
Year Player, College, Position
1966 Tommy Nobis, Texas, LB
       Randy Johnson, Texas A&I, QB
1967 Leo Carroll, San Diego St., DE (2)
1968 Claude Humphrey, Tennessee St., DE
1969 George Kunz, Notre Dame, T
1970 John Small, Citadel, LB
1971 Joe Profit, Northeast Louisiana, RB
1972 Clarence Ellis, Notre Dame, DB
1973 Greg Marx, Notre Dame, DT (2)
1974 Gerald Tinker, Kent State, WR (2)
1975 Steve Bartkowski, California, QB
1976 Bubba Bean, Texas A&M, RB
1977 Warren Bryant, Kentucky, T
       Wilson Faumuina, San Jose St., DT
1978 Mike Kenn, Michigan, T
1979 Don Smith, Miami, DE
1980 Junior Miller, Nebraska, TE
1981 Bobby Butler, Florida State, DB
1982 Gerald Riggs, Arizona State, RB
1983 Mike Pitts, Alabama, DE
1984 Rick Bryan, Oklahoma, DT
1985 Bill Fralic, Pittsburgh, T
1986 Tony Casillas, Oklahoma, NT
       Tim Green, Syracuse, LB
1987 Chris Miller, Oregon, QB
1988 Aundray Bruce, Auburn, LB
1989 Deion Sanders, Florida State, DB
       Shawn Collins, No. Arizona, WR
1990 Steve Broussard, Washington St., RB
1991 Bruce Pickens, Nebraska, DB
       Mike Pritchard, Colorado, WR
1992 Bob Whitfield, Stanford, T
       Tony Smith, So. Mississippi, RB
1993 Lincoln Kennedy, Washington, T
1994 Bert Emanuel, Rice, WR (2)
1995 Devin Bush, Florida State, DB
1996 Shannon Brown, Alabama, DT (3)
1997 Michael Booker, Nebraska, DB
1998 Keith Brooking, Georgia Tech, LB
1999 Patrick Kerney, Virginia, DE
2000 Travis Claridge, So. California, T (2)
2001 Michael Vick, Virginia Tech, QB
2002 T.J. Duckett, Michigan State, RB
2003 Bryan Scott, Penn State, DB (2)
2004 DeAngelo Hall, Virginia Tech, DB
       Michael Jenkins, Ohio State, WR
2005 Roddy White, Ala.-Birmingham, WR
2006 Jimmy Williams, Virginia Tech, DB (2)
2007 Jamaal Anderson, Arkansas, DE

BALTIMORE RAVENS
Year Player, College, Position
1996 Jonathan Ogden, UCLA, T
       Ray Lewis, Miami, LB
1997 Peter Boulware, Florida State, DE
1998 Duane Starks, Miami, DB
1999 Chris McAlister, Arizona, DB
2000 Jamal Lewis, Tennessee, RB
       Travis Taylor, Florida, WR
2001 Todd Heap, Arizona State, TE
2002 Ed Reed, Miami, DB
2003 Terrell Suggs, Arizona State, DE
       Kyle Boller, California, QB
2004 Dwan Edwards, Oregon St., DT (2)
2005 Mark Clayton, Oklahoma, WR
2006 Haloti Ngata, Oregon, DT
2007 Ben Grubbs, Auburn, G

BUFFALO BILLS
Year Player, College, Position
1960 Richie Lucas, Penn State, QB
1961 Ken Rice, Auburn, T
1962 Ernie Davis, Syracuse, RB
1963 Dave Behrman, Michigan State, C
1964 Carl Eller, Minnesota, DE
1965 Jim Davidson, Ohio State, T
1966 Mike Dennis, Mississippi, RB
1967 John Pitts, Arizona State, S
1968 Haven Moses, San Diego St., WR
1969 O.J. Simpson, So. California, RB
1970 Al Cowlings, So. California, DE
1971 J.D. Hill, Arizona State, WR
1972 Walt Patulski, Notre Dame, DE
1973 Paul Seymour, Michigan, TE
       Joe DeLamielleure, Michigan St., G
1974 Reuben Gant, Oklahoma State, TE
1975 Tom Ruud, Nebraska, LB
1976 Mario Clark, Oregon, DB
1977 Phil Dokes, Oklahoma State, DT
1978 Terry Miller, Oklahoma State, RB
1979 Tom Cousineau, Ohio State, LB
       Jerry Butler, Clemson, WR
1980 Jim Ritcher, North Carolina St., C
1981 Booker Moore, Penn State, RB
1982 Perry Tuttle, Clemson, WR
1983 Tony Hunter, Notre Dame, TE
       Jim Kelly, Miami, QB
1984 Greg Bell, Notre Dame, RB
1985 Bruce Smith, Virginia Tech, DE
       Derrick Burroughs, Memphis St., DB
1986 Ronnie Harmon, Iowa, RB
       Will Wolford, Vanderbilt, T
1987 Shane Conlan, Penn State, LB
1988 Thurman Thomas, Oklahoma St., RB (2)
1989 Don Beebe, Chadron, Neb., WR (3)
1990 James Williams, Fresno State, DB
1991 Henry Jones, Illinois, DB
1992 John Fina, Arizona, T
1993 Thomas Smith, North Carolina, DB
1994 Jeff Burris, Notre Dame, DB
1995 Ruben Brown, Pittsburgh, G
1996 Eric Moulds, Mississippi St., WR
1997 Antowain Smith, Houston, RB
1998 Sam Cowart, Florida State, LB (2)
1999 Antoine Winfield, Ohio State, DB
2000 Erik Flowers, Arizona State, DE
2001 Nate Clements, Ohio State, DB
2002 Mike Williams, Texas, T
2003 Willis McGahee, Miami, RB

2004 Lee Evans, Wisconsin, WR
J.P. Losman, Tulane, QB
2005 Roscoe Parrish, Miami, WR (2)
2006 Donte' Whitner, Ohio State, DB
John McCargo, North Carolina St., DT
2007 Marshawn Lynch, California, RB

CAROLINA PANTHERS
Year Player, College, Position
1995 Kerry Collins, Penn State, QB
Tyrone Poole, Ft. Valley State, DB
Blake Brockermeyer, Texas, T
1996 Tim Biakabutuka, Michigan, RB
1997 Rae Carruth, Colorado, WR
1998 Jason Peter, Nebraska, DT
1999 Chris Terry, Georgia, T (2)
2000 Rashard Anderson, Jackson St., DB
2001 Dan Morgan, Miami, LB
2002 Julius Peppers, North Carolina, DE
2003 Jordan Gross, Utah, T
2004 Chris Gamble, Ohio State, DB
2005 Thomas Davis, Georgia, DB
2006 DeAngelo Williams, Memphis, RB
2007 Jon Beason, Miami, LB

CHICAGO BEARS
Year Player, College, Position
1936 Joe Stydahar, West Virginia, T
1937 Les McDonald, Nebraska, E
1938 Joe Gray, Oregon State, B
1939 Sid Luckman, Columbia, QB
Bill Osmanski, Holy Cross, B
1940 Clyde (Bulldog) Turner, Hardin-Simmons, C
1941 Tom Harmon, Michigan, B
Norm Standlee, Stanford, B
Don Scott, Ohio State, B
1942 Frankie Albert, Stanford, B
1943 Bob Steber, Missouri, B
1944 Ray Evans, Kansas, B
1945 Don Lund, Michigan, B
1946 Johnny Lujack, Notre Dame, QB
1947 Bob Fenimore, Oklahoma State, B
Don Kindt, Wisconsin, B
1948 Bobby Layne, Texas, QB
Max Bumgardner, Texas, E
1949 Dick Harris, Texas, C
1950 Chuck Hunsinger, Florida, B
Fred Morrison, Ohio State, B
1951 Bob Williams, Notre Dame, B
Billy Stone, Bradley, B
Gene Schroeder, Virginia, E
1952 Jim Dooley, Miami, B
1953 Billy Anderson, Compton (Calif.) J.C., B
1954 Stan Wallace, Illinois, B
1955 Ron Drzewiecki, Marquette, B
1956 Menan (Tex) Schriewer, Texas, E
1957 Earl Leggett, Louisiana State, T
1958 Chuck Howley, West Virginia, G
1959 Don Clark, Ohio State, B
1960 Roger Davis, Syracuse, G
1961 Mike Ditka, Pittsburgh, E
1962 Ronnie Bull, Baylor, RB
1963 Dave Behrman, Michigan State, C
1964 Dick Evey, Tennessee, DT
1965 Dick Butkus, Illinois, LB
Gale Sayers, Kansas, RB
Steve DeLong, Tennessee, T
1966 George Rice, Louisiana State, DT
1967 Loyd Phillips, Arkansas, DE
1968 Mike Hull, Southern California, RB

1969 Rufus Mayes, Ohio State, T
1970 George Farmer, UCLA, WR (3)
1971 Joe Moore, Missouri, RB
1972 Lionel Antoine, Southern Illinois, T
Craig Clemons, Iowa, DB
1973 Wally Chambers, Eastern Kentucky, DE
1974 Waymond Bryant, Tennessee St., LB
Dave Gallagher, Michigan, DT
1975 Walter Payton, Jackson State, RB
1976 Dennis Lick, Wisconsin, T
1977 Ted Albrecht, California, T
1978 Brad Shearer, Texas, DT (3)
1979 Dan Hampton, Arkansas, DT
Al Harris, Arizona State, DE
1980 Otis Wilson, Louisville, LB
1981 Keith Van Horne, So. California, T
1982 Jim McMahon, Brigham Young, QB
1983 Jim Covert, Pittsburgh, T
Willie Gault, Tennessee, WR
1984 Wilber Marshall, Florida, LB
1985 William Perry, Clemson, DT
1986 Neal Anderson, Florida, RB
1987 Jim Harbaugh, Michigan, QB
1988 Brad Muster, Stanford, RB
Wendell Davis, Louisiana St., WR
1989 Donnell Woolford, Clemson, DB
Trace Armstrong, Florida, DE
1990 Mark Carrier, So. California, DB
1991 Stan Thomas, Texas, T
1992 Alonzo Spellman, Ohio State, DE
1993 Curtis Conway, So. California, WR
1994 John Thierry, Alcorn State, DE
1995 Rashaan Salaam, Colorado, RB
1996 Walt Harris, Mississippi State, DB
1997 John Allred, So. California, TE (2)
1998 Curtis Enis, Penn State, RB
1999 Cade McNown, UCLA, QB
2000 Brian Urlacher, New Mexico, LB
2001 David Terrell, Michigan, WR
2002 Marc Colombo, Boston College, T
2003 Michael Haynes, Penn State, DE
Rex Grossman, Florida, QB
2004 Tommie Harris, Oklahoma, DT
2005 Cedric Benson, Texas, RB
2006 Danieal Manning, Abilene Christian, DB (2)
2007 Greg Olsen, Miami, TE

CINCINNATI BENGALS
Year Player, College, Position
1968 Bob Johnson, Tennessee, C
1969 Greg Cook, Cincinnati, QB
1970 Mike Reid, Penn State, DT
1971 Vernon Holland, Tennessee St., T
1972 Sherman White, California, DE
1973 Isaac Curtis, San Diego State, WR
1974 Bill Kollar, Montana State, DT
1975 Glenn Cameron, Florida, LB
1976 Billy Brooks, Oklahoma, WR
Archie Griffin, Ohio State, RB
1977 Eddie Edwards, Miami, DT
Wilson Whitley, Houston, DT
Mike Cobb, Michigan State, TE
1978 Ross Browner, Notre Dame, DT
Blair Bush, Washington, C
1979 Jack Thompson, Washington St., QB
Charles Alexander, Louisiana St., RB
1980 Anthony Muñoz, So. California, T
1981 David Verser, Kansas, WR
1982 Glen Collins, Mississippi State, DE
1983 Dave Rimington, Nebraska, C

1984 Ricky Hunley, Arizona, LB
Pete Koch, Maryland, DE
Brian Blados, North Carolina, T
1985 Eddie Brown, Miami, WR
Emanuel King, Alabama, LB
1986 Joe Kelly, Washington, LB
Tim McGee, Tennessee, WR
1987 Jason Buck, Brigham Young, DE
1988 Rickey Dixon, Oklahoma, DB
1989 Eric Ball, UCLA, RB (2)
1990 James Francis, Baylor, LB
1991 Alfred Williams, Colorado, LB
1992 David Klingler, Houston, QB
Darryl Williams, Miami, DB
1993 John Copeland, Alabama, DE
1994 Dan Wilkinson, Ohio State, DT
1995 Ki-Jana Carter, Penn State, RB
1996 Willie Anderson, Auburn, T
1997 Reinard Wilson, Florida State, LB
1998 Takeo Spikes, Auburn, LB
Brian Simmons, North Carolina, LB
1999 Akili Smith, Oregon, QB
2000 Peter Warrick, Florida State, WR
2001 Justin Smith, Missouri, DE
2002 Levi Jones, Arizona State, T
2003 Carson Palmer, Southern California, QB
2004 Chris Perry, Michigan, RB
2005 David Pollack, Georgia, LB
2006 Johnathan Joseph, South Carolina, DB
2007 Leon Hall, Michigan, DB

CLEVELAND BROWNS
Year Player, College, Position
1950 Ken Carpenter, Oregon State, B
1951 Ken Konz, Louisiana State, B
1952 Bert Rechichar, Tennessee, DB
Harry Agganis, Boston U., QB
1953 Doug Atkins, Tennessee, DE
1954 Bobby Garrett, Stanford, QB
John Bauer, Illinois, G
1955 Kurt Burris, Oklahoma, C
1956 Preston Carpenter, Arkansas, B
1957 Jim Brown, Syracuse, RB
1958 Jim Shofner, Texas Christian, DB
1959 Rich Kreitling, Illinois, DE
1960 Jim Houston, Ohio State, DE
1961 Bobby Crespino, Mississippi, TE
1962 Gary Collins, Maryland, WR
Leroy Jackson, Western Illinois, RB
1963 Tom Hutchinson, Kentucky, WR
1964 Paul Warfield, Ohio State, WR
1965 James Garcia, Purdue, T (2)
1966 Milt Morin, Massachusetts, TE
1967 Bob Matheson, Duke, LB
1968 Marvin Upshaw, Trinity, Tex., DT-DE
1969 Ron Johnson, Michigan, RB
1970 Mike Phipps, Purdue, QB
Bob McKay, Texas, T
1971 Clarence Scott, Kansas State, CB
1972 Thom Darden, Michigan, DB
1973 Steve Holden, Arizona State, WR
Pete Adams, Southern California, T
1974 Billy Corbett, Johnson C. Smith, T (2)
1975 Mack Mitchell, Houston, DE
1976 Mike Pruitt, Purdue, RB
1977 Robert Jackson, Texas A&M, LB
1978 Clay Matthews, So. California, LB
Ozzie Newsome, Alabama, TE
1979 Willis Adams, Houston, WR
1980 Charles White, So. California, RB

1981 Hanford Dixon, So. Mississippi, DB
1982 Chip Banks, So. California, LB
1983 Ron Brown, Arizona State, WR (2)
1984 Don Rogers, UCLA, DB
1985 Greg Allen, Florida State, RB (2)
1986 Webster Slaughter, San Diego St., WR (2)
1987 Mike Junkin, Duke, LB
1988 Clifford Charlton, Florida, LB
1989 Eric Metcalf, Texas, RB
1990 Leroy Hoard, Michigan, RB (2)
1991 Eric Turner, UCLA, DB
1992 Tommy Vardell, Stanford, RB
1993 Steve Everitt, Michigan, C
1994 Antonio Langham, Alabama, DB
     Derrick Alexander, Michigan, WR
1995 Craig Powell, Ohio State, LB
1999 Tim Couch, Kentucky, QB
2000 Courtney Brown, Penn State, DE
2001 Gerard Warren, Florida, DT
2002 William Green, Boston College, RB
2003 Jeff Faine, Norte Dame, C
2004 Kellen Winslow, Miami, TE
2005 Braylon Edwards, Michigan, WR
2006 Kamerion Wimbley, Florida St., DE
2007 Joe Thomas, Wisconsin, T
     Brady Quinn, Notre Dame, QB

DALLAS COWBOYS
Year Player, College, Position
1960 None
1961 Bob Lilly, Texas Christian, DT
1962 Sonny Gibbs, TCU, QB (2)
1963 Lee Roy Jordan, Alabama, LB
1964 Scott Appleton, Texas, DT
1965 Craig Morton, California, QB
1966 John Niland, Iowa, G
1967 Phil Clark, Northwestern, DB (3)
1968 Dennis Homan, Alabama, WR
1969 Calvin Hill, Yale, RB
1970 Duane Thomas, West Texas St., RB
1971 Tody Smith, So. California, DE
1972 Bill Thomas, Boston College, RB
1973 Billy Joe DuPree, Michigan St., TE
1974 Ed (Too Tall) Jones, Tennessee St., DE
     Charley Young, North Carolina St., RB
1975 Randy White, Maryland, LB
     Thomas Henderson, Langston, LB
1976 Aaron Kyle, Wyoming, DB
1977 Tony Dorsett, Pittsburgh, RB
1978 Larry Bethea, Michigan State, DE
1979 Robert Shaw, Tennessee, C
1980 Bill Roe, Colorado, LB (3)
1981 Howard Richards, Missouri, T
1982 Rod Hill, Kentucky State, DB
1983 Jim Jeffcoat, Arizona State, DE
1984 Billy Cannon, Jr., Texas A&M, LB
1985 Kevin Brooks, Michigan, DE
1986 Mike Sherrard, UCLA, WR
1987 Danny Noonan, Nebraska, DT
1988 Michael Irvin, Miami, WR
1989 Troy Aikman, UCLA, QB
1990 Emmitt Smith, Florida, RB
1991 Russell Maryland, Miami, DT
     Alvin Harper, Tennessee, WR
     Kelvin Pritchett, Mississippi, DT
1992 Kevin Smith, Texas A&M, DB
     Robert Jones, East Carolina, LB
1993 Kevin Williams, Miami, WR (2)
1994 Shante Carver, Arizona State, DE
1995 Sherman Williams, Alabama, RB (2)

1996 Kavika Pittman, McNeese St., DE (2)
1997 David LaFleur, Louisiana State, TE
1998 Greg Ellis, North Carolina, DE
1999 Ebenezer Ekuban, North Carolina, DE
2000 Dwayne Goodrich, Tennessee, DB (2)
2001 Quincy Carter, Georgia, QB (2)
2002 Roy Williams, Oklahoma, DB
2003 Terence Newman, Kansas State, DB
2004 Julius Jones, Notre Dame, RB (2)
2005 Demarcus Ware, Troy, DE
     Marcus Spears, Louisiana St., DE
2006 Bobby Carpenter, Ohio State, LB
2007 Anthony Spencer, Purdue, LB

DENVER BRONCOS
Year Player, College, Position
1960 Roger LeClerc, Trinity, Conn., C
1961 Bob Gaiters, New Mexico St., RB
1962 Merlin Olsen, Utah State, DT
1963 Kermit Alexander, UCLA, CB
1964 Bob Brown, Nebraska, T
1965 Dick Butkus, Illinois, LB (2)
1966 Jerry Shay, Purdue, DT
1967 Floyd Little, Syracuse, RB
1968 Curley Culp, Arizona State, DE (2)
1969 Grady Cavness, Texas-El Paso, DB (2)
1970 Bob Anderson, Colorado, RB
1971 Marv Montgomery, So. California, T
1972 Riley Odoms, Houston, TE
1973 Otis Armstrong, Purdue, RB
1974 Randy Gradishar, Ohio State, LB
1975 Louis Wright, San Jose State, DB
1976 Tom Glassic, Virginia, G
1977 Steve Schindler, Boston College, G
1978 Don Latimer, Miami, DT
1979 Kelvin Clark, Nebraska, T
1980 Rulon Jones, Utah State, DE (2)
1981 Dennis Smith, So. California, DB
1982 Gerald Willhite, San Jose St., RB
1983 Chris Hinton, Northwestern, G
1984 Andre Townsend, Mississippi, DE (2)
1985 Steve Sewell, Oklahoma, RB
1986 Jim Juriga, Illinois, T (4)
1987 Ricky Nattiel, Florida, WR
1988 Ted Gregory, Syracuse, NT
1989 Steve Atwater, Arkansas, DB
1990 Alton Montgomery, Houston, DB (2)
1991 Mike Croel, Nebraska, LB
1992 Tommy Maddox, UCLA, QB
1993 Dan Williams, Toledo, DE
1994 Allen Aldridge, Houston, LB (2)
1995 Jamie Brown, Florida A&M, T (4)
1996 John Mobley, Kutztown, LB
1997 Trevor Pryce, Clemson, DT
1998 Marcus Nash, Tennessee, WR
1999 Al Wilson, Tennessee, LB
2000 Deltha O'Neal, California, DB
2001 Willie Middlebrooks, Minnesota, DB
2002 Ashley Lelie, Hawaii, WR
2003 George Foster, Georgia, T
2004 D.J. Williams, Miami, LB
2005 Darrent Wiliams, Oklahoma St., DB (2)
2006 Jay Cutler, Vanderbilt, QB
2007 Jarvis Moss, Florida, DE

DETROIT LIONS
Year Player, College, Position
1936 Sid Wagner, Michigan State, G
1937 Lloyd Cardwell, Nebraska, B
1938 Alex Wojciechowicz, Fordham, C

1939 John Pingel, Michigan State, B
1940 Doyle Nave, Southern California, B
1941 Jim Thomason, Texas A&M, B
1942 Bob Westfall, Michigan, B
1943 Frank Sinkwich, Georgia, B
1944 Otto Graham, Northwestern, B
1945 Frank Szymanski, Notre Dame, C
1946 Bill Dellastatious, Missouri, B
1947 Glenn Davis, Army, B
1948 Y.A. Tittle, Louisiana State, B
1949 John Rauch, Georgia, B
1950 Leon Hart, Notre Dame, E
     Joe Watson, Rice, C
1951 Dick Stanfel, San Francisco, G (2)
1952 Yale Lary, Texas A&M, B (3)
1953 Harley Sewell, Texas, G
1954 Dick Chapman, Rice, T
1955 Dave Middleton, Auburn, B
1956 Hopalong Cassady, Ohio State, B
1957 Bill Glass, Baylor, G
1958 Alex Karras, Iowa, T
1959 Nick Pietrosante, Notre Dame, B
1960 John Robinson, Louisiana State, S
1961 Danny LaRose, Missouri, T (2)
1962 John Hadl, Kansas, QB
1963 Daryl Sanders, Ohio State, T
1964 Pete Beathard, So. California, QB
1965 Tom Nowatzke, Indiana, RB
1966 Nick Eddy, Notre Dame, RB (2)
1967 Mel Farr, UCLA, RB
1968 Greg Landry, Massachusetts, QB
     Earl McCullouch, So. California, WR
1969 Altie Taylor, Utah State, RB (2)
1970 Steve Owens, Oklahoma, RB
1971 Bob Bell, Cincinnati, DT
1972 Herb Orvis, Colorado, DE
1973 Ernie Price, Texas A&I, DE
1974 Ed O'Neil, Penn State, LB
1975 Lynn Boden, South Dakota St., G
1976 James Hunter, Grambling, DB
     Lawrence Gaines, Wyoming, RB
1977 Walt Williams, New Mexico St., DB (2)
1978 Luther Bradley, Notre Dame, DB
1979 Keith Dorney, Penn State, T
1980 Billy Sims, Oklahoma, RB
1981 Mark Nichols, San Jose State, WR
1982 Jimmy Williams, Nebraska, LB
1983 James Jones, Florida, RB
1984 David Lewis, California, TE
1985 Lomas Brown, Florida, T
1986 Chuck Long, Iowa, QB
1987 Reggie Rogers, Washington, DE
1988 Bennie Blades, Miami, DB
1989 Barry Sanders, Oklahoma St., RB
1990 Andre Ware, Houston, QB
1991 Herman Moore, Virginia, WR
1992 Robert Porcher, South Carolina St., DE
1993 Ryan McNeil, Miami, DB (2)
1994 Johnnie Morton, So. California, WR
1995 Luther Elliss, Utah, DT
1996 Reggie Brown, Texas A&M, LB
     Jeff Hartings, Penn State, G
1997 Bryant Westbrook, Texas, DB
1998 Terry Fair, Tennessee, DB
1999 Chris Claiborne, So. California, LB
     Aaron Gibson, Wisconsin, T
2000 Stockar McDougle, Oklahoma, T
2001 Jeff Backus, Michigan, T
2002 Joey Harrington, Oregon, QB
2003 Charles Rogers, Michigan State, WR

2004 Roy Williams, Texas, WR
      Kevin Jones, Virginia Tech, RB
2005 Mike Wiliams, So. California, WR
2006 Ernie Sims, Florida State, LB
2007 Calvin Johnson, Georgia Tech, WR

GREEN BAY PACKERS
Year Player, College, Position
1936 Russ Letlow, San Francisco, G
1937 Eddie Jankowski, Wisconsin, B
1938 Cecil Isbell, Purdue, B
1939 Larry Buhler, Minnesota, B
1940 Harold Van Every, Minnesota, B
1941 George Paskvan, Wisconsin, B
1942 Urban Odson, Minnesota, T
1943 Dick Wildung, Minnesota, T
1944 Merv Pregulman, Michigan, G
1945 Walt Schlinkman, Texas Tech, B
1946 Johnny Strzykalski, Marquette, B
1947 Ernie Case, UCLA, B
1948 Earl (Jug) Girard, Wisconsin, B
1949 Stan Heath, Nevada, B
1950 Clayton Tonnemaker, Minnesota, C
1951 Bob Gain, Kentucky, T
1952 Babe Parilli, Kentucky, QB
1953 Al Carmichael, So. California, B
1954 Art Hunter, Notre Dame, T
      Veryl Switzer, Kansas State, B
1955 Tom Bettis, Purdue, G
1956 Jack Losch, Miami, B
1957 Paul Hornung, Notre Dame, B
      Ron Kramer, Michigan, E
1958 Dan Currie, Michigan State, C
1959 Randy Duncan, Iowa, B
1960 Tom Moore, Vanderbilt, RB
1961 Herb Adderley, Michigan State, CB
1962 Earl Gros, Louisiana State, RB
1963 Dave Robinson, Penn State, LB
1964 Lloyd Voss, Nebraska, DT
1965 Donny Anderson, Texas Tech, RB
      Lawrence Elkins, Baylor, E
1966 Jim Grabowski, Illinois, RB
      Gale Gillingham, Minnesota, T
1967 Bob Hyland, Boston College, C
      Don Horn, San Diego State, QB
1968 Fred Carr, Texas-El Paso, LB
      Bill Lueck, Arizona, G
1969 Rich Moore, Villanova, DT
1970 Mike McCoy, Notre Dame, DT
      Rich McGeorge, Elon, TE
1971 John Brockington, Ohio State, RB
1972 Willie Buchanon, San Diego St., DB
      Jerry Tagge, Nebraska, QB
1973 Barry Smith, Florida State, WR
1974 Barty Smith, Richmond, RB
1975 Bill Bain, So. California, G (2)
1976 Mark Koncar, Colorado, T
1977 Mike Butler, Kansas, DE
      Ezra Johnson, Morris Brown, DE
1978 James Lofton, Stanford, WR
      John Anderson, Michigan, LB
1979 Eddie Lee Ivery, Georgia Tech, RB
1980 Bruce Clark, Penn State, DE
      George Cumby, Oklahoma, LB
1981 Rich Campbell, California, QB
1982 Ron Hallstrom, Iowa, G
1983 Tim Lewis, Pittsburgh, DB
1984 Alphonso Carreker, Florida St., DE
1985 Ken Ruettgers, So. California, T
1986 Kenneth Davis, TCU, RB (2)

1987 Brent Fullwood, Auburn, RB
1988 Sterling Sharpe, South Carolina, WR
1989 Tony Mandarich, Michigan State, T
1990 Tony Bennett, Mississippi, LB
      Darrell Thompson, Minnesota, RB
1991 Vinnie Clark, Ohio State, DB
1992 Terrell Buckley, Florida State, DB
1993 Wayne Simmons, Clemson, LB
      George Teague, Alabama, DB
1994 Aaron Taylor, Notre Dame, T
1995 Craig Newsome, Arizona State, DB
1996 John Michels, Southern California, T
1997 Ross Verba, Iowa, T
1998 Vonnie Holliday, North Carolina, DT
1999 Antuan Edwards, Clemson, DB
2000 Bubba Franks, Miami, TE
2001 Jamal Reynolds, Florida State, DE
2002 Javon Walker, Florida State, WR
2003 Nick Barnett, Oregon State, LB
2004 Ahmad Carroll, Arkansas, DB
2005 Aaron Rodgers, California, QB
2006 A.J. Hawk, Ohio State, LB
2007 Justin Harrell, Tennessee, DT

HOUSTON TEXANS
Year Player, College, Position
2002 David Carr, Fresno State, QB
2003 Andre Johnson, Miami, WR
2004 Dunta Robinson, South Carolina, DB
      Jason Babin, Western Michigan, LB
2005 Travis Johnson, Florida State, DE
2006 Mario Williams, North Carolina St., DE
2007 Amobi Okoye, Louisville, DT

INDIANAPOLIS COLTS
Year Player, College, Position
1953 Billy Vessels, Oklahoma, B
1954 Cotton Davidson, Baylor, B
1955 George Shaw, Oregon, B
      Alan Ameche, Wisconsin, FB
1956 Lenny Moore, Penn State, B
1957 Jim Parker, Ohio State, G
1958 Lenny Lyles, Louisville, B
1959 Jackie Burkett, Auburn, C
1960 Ron Mix, Southern California, T
1961 Tom Matte, Ohio State, RB
1962 Wendell Harris, Louisiana State, S
1963 Bob Vogel, Ohio State, T
1964 Marv Woodson, Indiana, CB
1965 Mike Curtis, Duke, LB
1966 Sam Ball, Kentucky, T
1967 Bubba Smith, Michigan State, DT
      Jim Detwiler, Michigan, RB
1968 John Williams, Minnesota, G
1969 Eddie Hinton, Oklahoma, WR
1970 Norman Bulaich, Texas Christian, RB
1971 Don McCauley, North Carolina, RB
      Leonard Dunlap, North Texas St., DB
1972 Tom Drougas, Oregon, T
1973 Bert Jones, Louisiana State, QB
      Joe Ehrmann, Syracuse, DT
1974 John Dutton, Nebraska, DE
      Roger Carr, Louisiana Tech, WR
1975 Ken Huff, North Carolina, G
1976 Ken Novak, Purdue, DT
1977 Randy Burke, Kentucky, WR
1978 Reese McCall, Auburn, TE
1979 Barry Krauss, Alabama, LB
1980 Curtis Dickey, Texas A&M, RB
      Derrick Hatchett, Texas, DB

1981 Randy McMillan, Pittsburgh, RB
      Donnell Thompson, North Carolina, DT
1982 Johnie Cooks, Mississippi St., LB
      Art Schlichter, Ohio State, QB
1983 John Elway, Stanford, QB
1984 Leonard Coleman, Vanderbilt, DB
      Ron Solt, Maryland, G
1985 Duane Bickett, So. California, LB
1986 Jon Hand, Alabama, DE
1987 Cornelius Bennett, Alabama, LB
1988 Chris Chandler, Washington, QB (3)
1989 Andre Rison, Michigan State, WR
1990 Jeff George, Illinois, QB
1991 Shane Curry, Miami, DE (2)
1992 Steve Emtman, Washington, DT
      Quentin Coryatt, Texas A&M, LB
1993 Sean Dawkins, California, WR
1994 Marshall Faulk, San Diego St., RB
      Trev Alberts, Nebraska, LB
1995 Ellis Johnson, Florida, DT
1996 Marvin Harrison, Syracuse, WR
1997 Tarik Glenn, California, T
1998 Peyton Manning, Tennessee, QB
1999 Edgerrin James, Miami, RB
2000 Rob Morris, Brigham Young, LB
2001 Reggie Wayne, Miami, WR
2002 Dwight Freeney, Syracuse, DE
2003 Dallas Clark, Iowa, TE
2004 Bob Sanders, Iowa, DB (2)
2005 Marlin Jackson, Michigan, DB
2006 Joseph Addai, Louisiana State, RB
2007 Anthony Gonzalez, Ohio State, WR

JACKSONVILLE JAGUARS
Year Player, College, Position
1995 Tony Boselli, Southern California, T
      James Stewart, Tennessee, RB
1996 Kevin Hardy, Illinois, LB
1997 Renaldo Wynn, Notre Dame, DT
1998 Fred Taylor, Florida, RB
      Donovin Darius, Syracuse, DB
1999 Fernando Bryant, Alabama, DB
2000 R. Jay Soward, So. California, WR
2001 Marcus Stroud, Georgia, DT
2002 John Henderson, Tennessee, DT
2003 Byron Leftwich, Marshall, QB
2004 Reggie Williams, Washington, WR
2005 Matt Jones, Arkansas, WR
2006 Marcedes Lewis, UCLA, TE
2007 Reggie Nelson, Florida, DB

KANSAS CITY CHIEFS
Year Player, College, Position
1960 Don Meredith, So. Methodist, QB
1961 E.J. Holub, Texas Tech, C
1962 Ronnie Bull, Baylor, RB
1963 Buck Buchanan, Grambling, DT
      Ed Budde, Michigan State, G
1964 Pete Beathard, So. California, QB
1965 Gale Sayers, Kansas, RB
1966 Aaron Brown, Minnesota, DE
1967 Gene Trosch, Miami, DE-DT
1968 Mo Moorman, Texas A&M, G
      George Daney, Texas-El Paso, G
1969 Jim Marsalis, Tennessee State, CB
1970 Sid Smith, Southern California, T
1971 Elmo Wright, Houston, WR
1972 Jeff Kinney, Nebraska, RB
1973 Gary Butler, Rice, TE (2)
1974 Woody Green, Arizona State, RB

1975 Elmore Stephens, Kentucky, TE (2)
1976 Rod Walters, Iowa, G
1977 Gary Green, Baylor, DB
1978 Art Still, Kentucky, DE
1979 Mike Bell, Colorado State, DE
      Steve Fuller, Clemson, QB
1980 Brad Budde, Southern California, G
1981 Willie Scott, South Carolina, TE
1982 Anthony Hancock, Tennessee, WR
1983 Todd Blackledge, Penn State, QB
1984 Bill Maas, Pittsburgh, DT
      John Alt, Iowa, T
1985 Ethan Horton, North Carolina, RB
1986 Brian Jozwiak, West Virginia, T
1987 Paul Palmer, Temple, RB
1988 Neil Smith, Nebraska, DE
1989 Derrick Thomas, Alabama, LB
1990 Percy Snow, Michigan State, LB
1991 Harvey Williams, Louisiana St., RB
1992 Dale Carter, Tennessee, DB
1993 Will Shields, Nebraska, G (3)
1994 Greg Hill, Texas A&M, RB
1995 Trezelle Jenkins, Michigan, T
1996 Jerome Woods, Memphis, DB
1997 Tony Gonzalez, California, TE
1998 Victor Riley, Auburn, T
1999 John Tait, Brigham Young, T
2000 Sylvester Morris, Jackson St., WR
2001 Eric Downing, Syracuse, DT (3)
2002 Ryan Sims, North Carolina, DT
2003 Larry Johnson, Penn State, RB
2004 Junior Siavii, Oregon, DT (2)
2005 Derrick Johnson, Texas, LB
2006 Tamba Hali, Penn State, DE
2007 Dwayne Bowe, Louisiana State, WR

MIAMI DOLPHINS
Year Player, College, Position
1966 Jim Grabowski, Illinois, RB
      Rick Norton, Kentucky, QB
1967 Bob Griese, Purdue, QB
1968 Larry Csonka, Syracuse, RB
      Doug Crusan, Indiana, T
1969 Bill Stanfill, Georgia, DE
1970 Jim Mandich, Michigan, TE (2)
1971 Otto Stowe, Iowa State, WR (2)
1972 Mike Kadish, Notre Dame, DT
1973 Chuck Bradley, Oregon, C (2)
1974 Donald Reese, Jackson State, DE
1975 Darryl Carlton, Tampa, T
1976 Larry Gordon, Arizona State, LB
      Kim Bokamper, San Jose State, LB
1977 A.J. Duhe, Louisiana State, DT
1978 Guy Benjamin, Stanford, QB (2)
1979 Jon Giesler, Michigan, T
1980 Don McNeal, Alabama, DB
1981 David Overstreet, Oklahoma, RB
1982 Roy Foster, Southern California, G
1983 Dan Marino, Pittsburgh, QB
1984 Jackie Shipp, Oklahoma, LB
1985 Lorenzo Hampton, Florida, RB
1986 John Offerdahl, Western Michigan, LB (2)
1987 John Bosa, Boston College, DE
1988 Eric Kumerow, Ohio State, DE
1989 Sammie Smith, Florida State, RB
      Louis Oliver, Florida, DB
1990 Richmond Webb, Texas A&M, T
1991 Randal Hill, Miami, WR
1992 Troy Vincent, Wisconsin, DB
      Marco Coleman, Georgia Tech, LB

1993 O.J. McDuffie, Penn State, WR
1994 Tim Bowens, Mississippi, DT
1995 Billy Milner, Houston, T
1996 Daryl Gardener, Baylor, DT
1997 Yatil Green, Miami, WR
1998 John Avery, Mississippi, RB
1999 J.J. Johnson, Mississippi St., RB (2)
2000 Todd Wade, Mississippi, T (2)
2001 Jamar Fletcher, Wisconsin, DB
2002 Seth McKinney, Texas A&M, C (3)
2003 Eddie Moore, Tennessee, LB (2)
2004 Vernon Carey, Miami, T
2005 Ronnie Brown, Auburn, RB
2006 Jason Allen, Tennessee, DB
2007 Ted Ginn, Ohio State, WR

MINNESOTA VIKINGS
Year Player, College, Position
1961 Tommy Mason, Tulane, RB
1962 Bill Miller, Miami, WR (3)
1963 Jim Dunaway, Mississippi, T
1964 Carl Eller, Minnesota, DE
1965 Jack Snow, Notre Dame, WR
1966 Jerry Shay, Purdue, DT
1967 Clint Jones, Michigan State, RB
      Gene Washington, Michigan St., WR
      Alan Page, Notre Dame, DT
1968 Ron Yary, Southern California, T
1969 Ed White, California, G (2)
1970 John Ward, Oklahoma State, DT
1971 Leo Hayden, Ohio State, RB
1972 Jeff Siemon, Stanford, LB
1973 Chuck Foreman, Miami, RB
1974 Fred McNeill, UCLA, LB
      Steve Riley, Southern California, T
1975 Mark Mullaney, Colorado State, DE
1976 James White, Oklahoma State, DT
1977 Tommy Kramer, Rice, QB
1978 Randy Holloway, Pittsburgh, DE
1979 Ted Brown, North Carolina St., RB
1980 Doug Martin, Washington, DT
1981 Mardye McDole, Mississippi St., WR (2)
1982 Darrin Nelson, Stanford, RB
1983 Joey Browner, So. California, DB
1984 Keith Millard, Washington St., DE
1985 Chris Doleman, Pittsburgh, LB
1986 Gerald Robinson, Auburn, DE
1987 D.J. Dozier, Penn State, RB
1988 Randall McDaniel, Arizona State, G
1989 David Braxton, Wake Forest, LB (2)
1990 Mike Jones, Texas A&M, TE (3)
1991 Carlos Jenkins, Michigan St., LB (3)
1992 Robert Harris, Southern Univ., DE (2)
1993 Robert Smith, Ohio State, RB
1994 DeWayne Washington, N. Carolina St., DB
      Todd Steussie, California, T
1995 Derrick Alexander, Florida St., DE
      Korey Stringer, Ohio State, T
1996 Duane Clemons, California, DE
1997 Dwayne Rudd, Alabama, LB
1998 Randy Moss, Marshall, WR
1999 Daunte Culpepper, Central Florida, QB
      Dimitrius Underwood, Michigan St., DE
2000 Chris Hovan, Boston College, DT
2001 Michael Bennett, Wisconsin, RB
2002 Bryant McKinnie, Miami, T
2003 Kevin Williams, Oklahoma State, DT
2004 Kenechi Udeze, Southern California, DE
2005 Troy Williamson, South Carolina, WR
      Erasmus James, Wisconsin, DE

2006 Chad Greenway, Iowa, LB
2007 Adrian Peterson, Oklahoma, RB

NEW ENGLAND PATRIOTS
Year Player, College, Position
1960 Ron Burton, Northwestern, RB
1961 Tommy Mason, Tulane, RB
1962 Gary Collins, Maryland, WR
1963 Art Graham, Boston College, WR
1964 Jack Concannon, Boston College, QB
1965 Jerry Rush, Michigan State, DE
1966 Karl Singer, Purdue, T
1967 John Charles, Purdue, S
1968 Dennis Byrd, North Carolina St., DE
1969 Ron Sellers, Florida State, WR
1970 Phil Olsen, Utah State, DE
1971 Jim Plunkett, Stanford, QB
1972 Tom Reynolds, San Diego St., WR (2)
1973 John Hannah, Alabama, G
      Sam Cunningham, So. California, RB
      Darryl Stingley, Purdue, WR
1974 Steve Corbett, Boston College, G (2)
1975 Russ Francis, Oregon, TE
1976 Mike Haynes, Arizona State, DB
      Pete Brock, Colorado, C
      Tim Fox, Ohio State, DB
1977 Raymond Clayborn, Texas, DB
      Stanley Morgan, Tennessee, WR
1978 Bob Cryder, Alabama, G
1979 Rick Sanford, South Carolina, DB
1980 Roland James, Tennessee, DB
      Vagas Ferguson, Notre Dame, RB
1981 Brian Holloway, Stanford, T
1982 Kenneth Sims, Texas, DT
      Lester Williams, Miami, DT
1983 Tony Eason, Illinois, QB
1984 Irving Fryar, Nebraska, WR
1985 Trevor Matich, Brigham Young, C
1986 Reggie Dupard, So. Methodist, RB
1987 Bruce Armstrong, Louisville, T
1988 John Stephens, Northwestern St., La., RB
1989 Hart Lee Dykes, Oklahoma St., WR
1990 Chris Singleton, Arizona, LB
      Ray Agnew, North Carolina St., DE
1991 Pat Harlow, Southern California, T
      Leonard Russell, Arizona St., RB
1992 Eugene Chung, Virginia Tech, T
1993 Drew Bledsoe, Washington St., QB
1994 Willie McGinest, So. California, DE
1995 Ty Law, Michigan, DB
1996 Terry Glenn, Ohio State, WR
1997 Chris Canty, Kansas State, DB
1998 Robert Edwards, Georgia, RB
      Tebucky Jones, Syracuse, DB
1999 Damien Woody, Boston College, C
      Andy Katzenmoyer, Ohio State, LB
2000 Adrian Klemm, Hawaii, T (2)
2001 Richard Seymour, Georgia, DT
2002 Daniel Graham, Colorado, TE
2003 Ty Warren, Texas A&M, DT
2004 Vince Wilfork, Miami, DT
      Ben Watson, Georgia, TE
2005 Logan Mankins, Fresno State, G
2006 Laurence Maroney, Minnesota, RB
2007 Brandon Meriweather, Miami, DB

NEW ORLEANS SAINTS
Year Player, College, Position
1967 Les Kelley, Alabama, RB
1968 Kevin Hardy, Notre Dame, DE

1969 John Shinners, Xavier, G
1970 Ken Burrough, Texas Southern, WR
1971 Archie Manning, Mississippi, QB
1972 Royce Smith, Georgia, G
1973 Derland Moore, Oklahoma, DE (2)
1974 Rick Middleton, Ohio State, LB
1975 Larry Burton, Purdue, WR
    Kurt Schumacher, Ohio State, T
1976 Chuck Muncie, California, RB
1977 Joe Campbell, Maryland, DE
1978 Wes Chandler, Florida, WR
1979 Russell Erxleben, Texas, P-K
1980 Stan Brock, Colorado, T
1981 George Rogers, South Carolina, RB
1982 Lindsay Scott, Georgia, WR
1983 Steve Korte, Arkansas, G (2)
1984 James Geathers, Wichita State, DE
1985 Alvin Toles, Tennessee, LB
1986 Jim Dombrowski, Virginia, T
1987 Shawn Knight, Brigham Young, DT
1988 Craig Heyward, Pittsburgh, RB
1989 Wayne Martin, Arkansas, DE
1990 Renaldo Turnbull, West Virginia, DE
1991 Wesley Carroll, Miami, WR (2)
1992 Vaughn Dunbar, Indiana, RB
1993 Willie Roaf, Louisiana Tech, T
    Irv Smith, Notre Dame, TE
1994 Joe Johnson, Louisville, DE
1995 Mark Fields, Washington State, LB
1996 Alex Molden, Oregon, DB
1997 Chris Naeole, Colorado, G
1998 Kyle Turley, San Diego State, T
1999 Ricky Williams, Texas, RB
2000 Darren Howard, Kansas St., DE (2)
2001 Deuce McAllister, Mississippi, RB
2002 Donte' Stallworth, Tennessee, WR
    Charles Grant, Georgia, DE
2003 Johnathan Sullivan, Georgia, DT
2004 Will Smith, Ohio State, DE
2005 Jammal Brown, Oklahoma, T
2006 Reggie Bush, So. California, RB
2007 Robert Meachem, Tennessee, WR

NEW YORK GIANTS
Year Player, College, Position
1936 Art Lewis, Ohio U., T
1937 Ed Widseth, Minnesota, T
1938 George Karamatic, Gonzaga, B
1939 Walt Neilson, Arizona, B
1940 Grenville Lansdell, So. California, B
1941 George Franck, Minnesota, B
1942 Merle Hapes, Mississippi, B
1943 Steve Filipowicz, Fordham, B
1944 Billy Hillenbrand, Indiana, B
1945 Elmer Barbour, Wake Forest, B
1946 George Connor, Notre Dame, T
1947 Vic Schwall, Northwestern, B
1948 Tony Minisi, Pennsylvania, B
1949 Paul Page, Southern Methodist, B
1950 Travis Tidwell, Auburn, B
1951 Kyle Rote, Southern Methodist, B
    Jim Spavital, Oklahoma A&M, B
1952 Frank Gifford, Southern California, B
1953 Bobby Marlow, Alabama, B
1954 Ken Buck, Pacific, C (2)
1955 Joe Heap, Notre Dame, B
1956 Henry Moore, Arkansas, B (2)
1957 Sam DeLuca, South Carolina, T (2)
1958 Phil King, Vanderbilt, B
1959 Lee Grosscup, Utah, B

1960 Lou Cordileone, Clemson, G
1961 Bruce Tarbox, Syracuse, G (2)
1962 Jerry Hillebrand, Colorado, LB
1963 Frank Lasky, Florida, T (2)
1964 Joe Don Looney, Oklahoma, RB
1965 Tucker Frederickson, Auburn, RB
1966 Francis Peay, Missouri, T
1967 Louis Thompson, Alabama, DT (4)
1968 Dick Buzin, Penn State, T (2)
1969 Fred Dryer, San Diego State, DE
1970 Jim Files, Oklahoma, LB
1971 Rocky Thompson, West Texas St., WR
1972 Eldridge Small, Texas A&I, DB
    Larry Jacobson, Nebraska, DE
1973 Brad Van Pelt, Michigan St., LB (2)
1974 John Hicks, Ohio State, G
1975 Al Simpson, Colorado State, T (2)
1976 Troy Archer, Colorado, DE
1977 Gary Jeter, Southern California, DT
1978 Gordon King, Stanford, T
1979 Phil Simms, Morehead State, QB
1980 Mark Haynes, Colorado, DB
1981 Lawrence Taylor, North Carolina, LB
1982 Butch Woolfolk, Michigan, RB
1983 Terry Kinard, Clemson, DB
1984 Carl Banks, Michigan State, LB
    William Roberts, Ohio State, T
1985 George Adams, Kentucky, RB
1986 Eric Dorsey, Notre Dame, DE
1987 Mark Ingram, Michigan State, WR
1988 Eric Moore, Indiana, T
1989 Brian Williams, Minnesota, C-G
1990 Rodney Hampton, Georgia, RB
1991 Jarrod Bunch, Michigan, RB
1992 Derek Brown, Notre Dame, TE
1993 Michael Strahan, Texas Southern, DE (2)
1994 Thomas Lewis, Indiana, WR
1995 Tyrone Wheatley, Michigan, RB
1996 Cedric Jones, Oklahoma, DE
1997 Ike Hilliard, Florida, WR
1998 Shaun Williams, UCLA, DB
1999 Luke Petitgout, Notre Dame, T
2000 Ron Dayne, Wisconsin, RB
2001 Will Allen, Syracuse, DB
2002 Jeremy Shockey, Miami, TE
2003 William Joseph, Miami, DT
2004 Philip Rivers, North Carolina St., QB
2005 Corey Webster, Louisiana St., DB (2)
2006 Mathias Kiwanuka, Boston College, DE
2007 Aaron Ross, Texas, DB

NEW YORK JETS
Year Player, College, Position
1960 George Izo, Notre Dame, QB
1961 Tom Brown, Minnesota, G
1962 Sandy Stephens, Minnesota, QB
1963 Jerry Stovall, Louisiana State, S
1964 Matt Snell, Ohio State, RB
1965 Joe Namath, Alabama, QB
    Tom Nowatzke, Indiana, RB
1966 Bill Yearby, Michigan, DT
1967 Paul Seiler, Notre Dame, T
1968 Lee White, Weber State, RB
1969 Dave Foley, Ohio State, T
1970 Steve Tannen, Florida, CB
1971 John Riggins, Kansas, RB
1972 Jerome Barkum, Jackson St., WR
    Mike Taylor, Michigan, LB
1973 Burgess Owens, Miami, DB
1974 Carl Barzilauskas, Indiana, DT

1975 Anthony Davis, So. California, RB (2)
1976 Richard Todd, Alabama, QB
1977 Marvin Powell, So. California, T
1978 Chris Ward, Ohio State, T
1979 Marty Lyons, Alabama, DE
1980 Johnny (Lam) Jones, Texas, WR
1981 Freeman McNeil, UCLA, RB
1982 Bob Crable, Notre Dame, LB
1983 Ken O'Brien, Cal-Davis, QB
1984 Russell Carter, So. Methodist, DB
    Ron Faurot, Arkansas, DE
1985 Al Toon, Wisconsin, WR
1986 Mike Haight, Iowa, T
1987 Roger Vick, Texas A&M, RB
1988 Dave Cadigan, So. California, T
1989 Jeff Lageman, Virginia, LB
1990 Blair Thomas, Penn State, RB
1991 Browning Nagle, Louisville, QB (2)
1992 Johnny Mitchell, Nebraska, TE
1993 Marvin Jones, Florida State, LB
1994 Aaron Glenn, Texas A&M, DB
1995 Kyle Brady, Penn State, TE
    Hugh Douglas, Central St., Ohio, DE
1996 Keyshawn Johnson, So. California, WR
1997 James Farrior, Virginia, LB
1998 Dorian Boose, Washington St., DE (2)
1999 Randy Thomas, Mississippi St., G (2)
2000 Shaun Ellis, Tennessee, DE
    John Abraham, South Carolina, LB
    Chad Pennington, Marshall, QB
    Anthony Becht, West Virginia, TE
2001 Santana Moss, Miami, WR
2002 Bryan Thomas, Ala.-Birmingham, DE
2003 Dewayne Robertson, Kentucky, DT
2004 Jonathan Vilma, Miami, LB
2005 Mike Nugent, Ohio State, K (2)
2006 D'Brickashaw Ferguson, Virginia, T
    Nick Mangold, Ohio State, C
2007 Darrelle Revis, Pittsburgh, DB

OAKLAND RAIDERS
Year Player, College, Position
1960 Dale Hackbart, Wisconsin, CB
1961 Joe Rutgens, Illinois, DT
1962 Roman Gabriel, North Carolina St., QB
1963 George Wilson, Alabama, RB (6)
1964 Tony Lorick, Arizona State, RB
1965 Harry Schuh, Memphis State, T
1966 Rodger Bird, Kentucky, S
1967 Gene Upshaw, Texas A&I, G
1968 Eldridge Dickey, Tennessee St., QB
1969 Art Thoms, Syracuse, DT
1970 Raymond Chester, Morgan St., TE
1971 Jack Tatum, Ohio State, S
1972 Mike Siani, Villanova, WR
1973 Ray Guy, Southern Mississippi, P
1974 Henry Lawrence, Florida A&M, T
1975 Neal Colzie, Ohio State, DB
1976 Charles Philyaw, Texas Southern, DT (2)
1977 Mike Davis, Colorado, DB (2)
1978 Dave Browning, Washington, DE (2)
1979 Willie Jones, Florida State, DE (2)
1980 Marc Wilson, Brigham Young, QB
1981 Ted Watts, Texas Tech, DB
    Curt Marsh, Washington, T
1982 Marcus Allen, So. California, RB
1983 Don Mosebar, So. California, T
1984 Sean Jones, Northeastern, DE (2)
1985 Jessie Hester, Florida State, WR
1986 Bob Buczkowski, Pittsburgh, DE

1987	John Clay, Missouri, T
1988	Tim Brown, Notre Dame, WR
	Terry McDaniel, Tennessee, DB
	Scott Davis, Illinois, DE
1989	Jeff Francis, Tennessee, QB (6)
1990	Anthony Smith, Arizona, DE
1991	Todd Marinovich, So. California, QB
1992	Chester McGlockton, Clemson, DE
1993	Patrick Bates, Texas A&M, DB
1994	Rob Fredrickson, Michigan St., LB
1995	Napoleon Kaufman, Washington, RB
1996	Rickey Dudley, Ohio State, TE
1997	Darrell Russell, Southern California, DT
1998	Charles Woodson, Michigan, DB
	Mo Collins, Florida, T
1999	Matt Stinchcomb, Georgia, T
2000	Sebastian Janikowski, Florida St., K
2001	Derrick Gibson, Florida State, DB
2002	Phillip Buchanon, Miami, DB
	Napoleon Harris, Northwestern, LB
2003	Nnamdi Asomugha, California, DB
	Tyler Brayton, Colorado, DE
2004	Robert Gallery, Iowa, T
2005	Fabian Washington, Nebraska, DB
2006	Michael Huff, Texas, DB
2007	JaMarcus Russell, Louisiana State, QB

PHILADELPHIA EAGLES
Year Player, College, Position

1936	Jay Berwanger, Chicago, B
1937	Sam Francis, Nebraska, B
1938	Jim McDonald, Ohio State, B
1939	Davey O'Brien, Texas Christian, B
1940	George McAfee, Duke, B
1941	Art Jones, Richmond, B (2)
1942	Pete Kmetovic, Stanford, B
1943	Joe Muha, Virginia Military, B
1944	Steve Van Buren, Louisiana St., B
1945	John Yonaker, Notre Dame, E
1946	Leo Riggs, Southern California, B
1947	Neill Armstrong, Oklahoma A&M, E
1948	Clyde (Smackover) Scott, Arkansas, B
1949	Chuck Bednarik, Pennsylvania, C
	Frank Tripucka, Notre Dame, B
1950	Harry (Bud) Grant, Minnesota, E
1951	Ebert Van Buren, Louisiana St., B
	Chet Mutryn, Xavier, B
1952	Johnny Bright, Drake, B
1953	Al Conway, Army, B (2)
1954	Neil Worden, Notre Dame, B
1955	Dick Bielski, Maryland, B
1956	Bob Pellegrini, Maryland, C
1957	Clarence Peaks, Michigan State, B
1958	Walt Kowalczyk, Michigan State, B
1959	J.D. Smith, Rice, T (2)
1960	Ron Burton, Northwestern, RB
1961	Art Baker, Syracuse, RB
1962	Pete Case, Georgia, G (2)
1963	Ed Budde, Michigan State, G
1964	Bob Brown, Nebraska, T
1965	Ray Rissmiller, Georgia, T (2)
1966	Randy Beisler, Indiana, DE
1967	Harry Jones, Arkansas, RB
1968	Tim Rossovich, So. California, DE
1969	Leroy Keyes, Purdue, RB
1970	Steve Zabel, Oklahoma, TE
1971	Richard Harris, Grambling, DE
1972	John Reaves, Florida, QB

1973	Jerry Sisemore, Texas, T
	Charle Young, So. California, TE
1974	Mitch Sutton, Kansas, DT (3)
1975	Bill Capraun, Miami, T (7)
1976	Mike Smith, Florida, DE (4)
1977	Skip Sharp, Kansas, DB (5)
1978	Reggie Wilkes, Georgia Tech, LB (3)
1979	Jerry Robinson, UCLA, LB
1980	Roynell Young, Alcorn State, DB
1981	Leonard Mitchell, Houston, DE
1982	Mike Quick, North Carolina St., WR
1983	Michael Haddix, Mississippi St., RB
1984	Kenny Jackson, Penn State, WR
1985	Kevin Allen, Indiana, T
1986	Keith Byars, Ohio State, RB
1987	Jerome Brown, Miami, DT
1988	Keith Jackson, Oklahoma, TE
1989	Jessie Small, Eastern Kentucky, LB (2)
1990	Ben Smith, Georgia, DB
1991	Antone Davis, Tennessee, T
1992	Siran Stacy, Alabama, RB (2)
1993	Lester Holmes, Jackson State, T
	Leonard Renfro, Colorado, DT
1994	Bernard Williams, Georgia, T
1995	Mike Mamula, Boston College, DE
1996	Jermane Mayberry, Texas A&M-Kingsville, T
1997	Jon Harris, Virginia, DE
1998	Tra Thomas, Florida State, T
1999	Donovan McNabb, Syracuse, QB
2000	Corey Simon, Florida State, DT
2001	Freddie Mitchell, UCLA, WR
2002	Lito Sheppard, Florida, DB
2003	Jerome McDougle, Miami, DE
2004	Shawn Andrews, Arkansas, T
2005	Mike Patterson, So. California, DT
2006	Brodrick Bunkley, Florida State, DT
2007	Kevin Kolb, Houston, QB (2)

PITTSBURGH STEELERS
Year Player, College, Position

1936	Bill Shakespeare, Notre Dame, B
1937	Mike Basrak, Duquesne, C
1938	Byron (Whizzer) White, Colorado, B
1939	Bill Patterson, Baylor, B (3)
1940	Kay Eakin, Arkansas, B
1941	Chet Gladchuk, Boston College, C (2)
1942	Bill Dudley, Virginia, B
1943	Bill Daley, Minnesota, B
1944	Johnny Podesto, St. Mary's, Calif., B
1945	Paul Duhart, Florida, B
1946	Felix (Doc) Blanchard, Army, B
1947	Hub Bechtol, Texas, E
1948	Dan Edwards, Georgia, E
1949	Bobby Gage, Clemson, B
1950	Lynn Chandnois, Michigan St., B
1951	Butch Avinger, Alabama, B
1952	Ed Modzelewski, Maryland, B
1953	Ted Marchibroda, St. Bonaventure, B
1954	Johnny Lattner, Notre Dame, B
1955	Frank Varrichione, Notre Dame, T
1956	Gary Glick, Colorado A&M, B
	Art Davis, Mississippi State, B
1957	Len Dawson, Purdue, B
1958	Larry Krutko, West Virginia, B (2)
1959	Tom Barnett, Purdue, B (8)
1960	Jack Spikes, Texas Christian, RB
1961	Myron Pottios, Notre Dame, LB (2)
1962	Bob Ferguson, Ohio State, RB
1963	Frank Atkinson, Stanford, T (8)
1964	Paul Martha, Pittsburgh, S

1965	Roy Jefferson, Utah, WR (2)
1966	Dick Leftridge, West Virginia, RB
1967	Don Shy, San Diego State, RB (2)
1968	Mike Taylor, Southern California, T
1969	Joe Greene, North Texas State, DT
1970	Terry Bradshaw, Louisiana Tech, QB
1971	Frank Lewis, Grambling, WR
1972	Franco Harris, Penn State, RB
1973	J.T. Thomas, Florida State, DB
1974	Lynn Swann, So. California, WR
1975	Dave Brown, Michigan, DB
1976	Bennie Cunningham, Clemson, TE
1977	Robin Cole, New Mexico, LB
1978	Ron Johnson, Eastern Michigan, DB
1979	Greg Hawthorne, Baylor, RB
1980	Mark Malone, Arizona State, QB
1981	Keith Gary, Oklahoma, DE
1982	Walter Abercrombie, Baylor, RB
1983	Gabriel Rivera, Texas Tech, DT
1984	Louis Lipps, So. Mississippi, WR
1985	Darryl Sims, Wisconsin, DE
1986	John Rienstra, Temple, G
1987	Rod Woodson, Purdue, DB
1988	Aaron Jones, Eastern Kentucky, DE
1989	Tim Worley, Georgia, RB
	Tom Ricketts, Pittsburgh, T
1990	Eric Green, Liberty, TE
1991	Huey Richardson, Florida, DE
1992	Leon Searcy, Miami, T
1993	Deon Figures, Colorado, DB
1994	Charles Johnson, Colorado, WR
1995	Mark Bruener, Washington, TE
1996	Jamain Stephens, North Carolina A&T, T
1997	Chad Scott, Maryland, DB
1998	Alan Faneca, Louisiana State, G
1999	Troy Edwards, Lousiana Tech, WR
2000	Plaxico Burress, Michigan St., WR
2001	Casey Hampton, Texas, DT
2002	Kendall Simmons, Auburn, G
2003	Troy Polamalu, Southern California, DB
2004	Ben Roethlisberger, Miami (OH), QB
2005	Heath Miller, Virginia, TE
2006	Santonio Holmes, Ohio State, WR
2007	Lawrence Timmons, Florida State, LB

ST. LOUIS RAMS
Year Player, College, Position

1937	Johnny Drake, Purdue, B
1938	Corbett Davis, Indiana, B
1939	Parker Hall, Mississippi, B
1940	Ollie Cordill, Rice, B
1941	Rudy Mucha, Washington, C
1942	Jack Wilson, Baylor, B
1943	Mike Holovak, Boston College, B
1944	Tony Butkovich, Illinois, B
1945	Elroy (Crazylegs) Hirsch, Wisconsin, B
1946	Emil Sitko, Notre Dame, B
1947	Herman Wedemeyer, St. Mary's, Calif., B
1948	Tom Keane, West Virginia, B (2)
1949	Bobby Thomason, Virginia Military, B
1950	Ralph Pasquariello, Villanova, B
	Stan West, Oklahoma, G
1951	Bud McFadin, Texas, G
1952	Bill Wade, Vanderbilt, QB
	Bob Carey, Michigan State, E
1953	Donn Moomaw, UCLA, C
	Ed Barker, Washington State, E
1954	Ed Beatty, Cincinnati, C
1955	Larry Morris, Georgia Tech, C
1956	Joe Marconi, West Virginia, B

Charles Horton, Vanderbilt, B
1957 Jon Arnett, Southern California, B
Del Shofner, Baylor, E
1958 Lou Michaels, Kentucky, T
Jim Phillips, Auburn, E
1959 Dick Bass, Pacific, B
Paul Dickson, Baylor, T
1960 Billy Cannon, Louisiana State, RB
1961 Marlin McKeever, So. California, E-LB
1962 Roman Gabriel, North Carolina St., QB
Merlin Olsen, Utah State, DT
1963 Terry Baker, Oregon State, QB
Rufus Guthrie, Georgia Tech, G
1964 Bill Munson, Utah State, QB
1965 Clancy Williams, Washington St., CB
1966 Tom Mack, Michigan, G
1967 Willie Ellison, Texas Southern, RB (2)
1968 Gary Beban, UCLA, QB (2)
1969 Larry Smith, Florida, RB
Jim Seymour, Notre Dame, WR
Bob Klein, Southern California, TE
1970 Jack Reynolds, Tennessee, LB
1971 Isiah Robertson, Southern, LB
Jack Youngblood, Florida, DE
1972 Jim Bertelsen, Texas, RB (2)
1973 Cullen Bryant, Colorado, DB (2)
1974 John Cappelletti, Penn State, RB
1975 Mike Fanning, Notre Dame, DT
Dennis Harrah, Miami, T
Doug France, Ohio State, T
1976 Kevin McLain, Colorado State, LB
1977 Bob Brudzinski, Ohio State, LB
1978 Elvis Peacock, Oklahoma, RB
1979 George Andrews, Nebraska, LB
Kent Hill, Georgia Tech, T
1980 Johnnie Johnson, Texas, DB
1981 Mel Owens, Michigan, LB
1982 Barry Redden, Richmond, RB
1983 Eric Dickerson, So. Methodist, RB
1984 Hal Stephens, East Carolina, DE (5)
1985 Jerry Gray, Texas, DB
1986 Mike Schad, Queen's Univ., Canada, T
1987 Donald Evans, Winston-Salem, DE (2)
1988 Gaston Green, UCLA, RB
Aaron Cox, Arizona State, WR
1989 Bill Hawkins, Miami, DE
Cleveland Gary, Miami, RB
1990 Bern Brostek, Washington, C
1991 Todd Lyght, Notre Dame, DB
1992 Sean Gilbert, Pittsburgh, DE
1993 Jerome Bettis, Notre Dame, RB
1994 Wayne Gandy, Auburn, T
1995 Kevin Carter, Florida, DE
1996 Lawrence Phillips, Nebraska, RB
Eddie Kennison, Louisiana St., WR
1997 Orlando Pace, Ohio State, T
1998 Grant Wistrom, Nebraska, DE
1999 Torry Holt, North Carolina St., WR
2000 Trung Canidate, Arizona, RB
2001 Damione Lewis, Miami, DT
Adam Archuleta, Arizona State, DB
Ryan Pickett, Ohio State, DT
2002 Robert Thomas, UCLA, LB
2003 Jimmy Kennedy, Penn State, DT
2004 Steven Jackson, Oregon State, RB
2005 Alex Barron, Florida State, T
2006 Tye Hill, Clemson, DB
2007 Adam Carriker, Nebraska, DE

SAN DIEGO CHARGERS

Year Player, College, Position
1960 Monty Stickles, Notre Dame, E
1961 Earl Faison, Indiana, DE
1962 Bob Ferguson, Ohio State, RB
1963 Walt Sweeney, Syracuse, G
1964 Ted Davis, Georgia Tech, LB
1965 Steve DeLong, Tennessee, DE
1966 Don Davis, Cal St.-Los Angeles, DT
1967 Ron Billingsley, Wyoming, DE
1968 Russ Washington, Missouri, DT
Jimmy Hill, Texas A&I, DB
1969 Marty Domres, Columbia, QB
Bob Babich, Miami, Ohio, LB
1970 Walker Gillette, Richmond, WR
1971 Leon Burns, Long Beach State, RB
1972 Pete Lazetich, Stanford, DE (2)
1973 Johnny Rodgers, Nebraska, WR
1974 Bo Matthews, Colorado, RB
Don Goode, Kansas, LB
1975 Gary Johnson, Grambling, DT
Mike Williams, Louisiana State, DB
1976 Joe Washington, Oklahoma, RB
1977 Bob Rush, Memphis State, C
1978 John Jefferson, Arizona State, WR
1979 Kellen Winslow, Missouri, TE
1980 Ed Luther, San Jose State, QB (4)
1981 James Brooks, Auburn, RB
1982 Hollis Hall, Clemson, DB (7)
1983 Billy Ray Smith, Arkansas, LB
Gary Anderson, Arkansas, WR
Gill Byrd, San Jose State, DB
1984 Mossy Cade, Texas, DB
1985 Jim Lachey, Ohio State, G
1986 Leslie O'Neal, Oklahoma State, DE
James FitzPatrick, So. California, T
1987 Rod Bernstine, Texas A&M, TE
1988 Anthony Miller, Tennessee, WR
1989 Burt Grossman, Pittsburgh, DE
1990 Junior Seau, So. California, LB
1991 Stanley Richard, Texas, DB
1992 Chris Mims, Tennessee, DE
1993 Darrien Gordon, Stanford, DB
1994 Isaac Davis, Arkansas, G (2)
1995 Terrance Shaw, Stephen F. Austin, DB (2)
1996 Bryan Still, Virginia Tech, WR (2)
1997 Freddie Jones, North Carolina, TE (2)
1998 Ryan Leaf, Washington State, QB
1999 Jermaine Fazande, Oklahoma, RB (2)
2000 Rogers Beckett, Marshall, DB (2)
2001 LaDainian Tomlinson, TCU, RB
2002 Quentin Jammer, Texas, DB
2003 Sammy Davis, Texas A&M, DB
2004 Eli Manning, Mississippi, QB
2005 Shawne Merriman, Maryland, LB
Luis Castillo, Northwestern, DT
2006 Antonio Cromartie, Florida State, DB
2007 Craig Davis, Louisiana State, WR

SAN FRANCISCO 49ERS
Year Player, College, Position
1950 Leo Nomellini, Minnesota, T
1951 Y.A. Tittle, Louisiana State, B
1952 Hugh McElhenny, Washington, B
1953 Harry Babcock, Georgia, E
Tom Stolhandske, Texas, E
1954 Bernie Faloney, Maryland, B
1955 Dickie Moegle, Rice, B
1956 Earl Morrall, Michigan State, B
1957 John Brodie, Stanford, B
1958 Jim Pace, Michigan, B

Charlie Krueger, Texas A&M, T
1959 Dave Baker, Oklahoma, B
Dan James, Ohio State, C
1960 Monty Stickles, Notre Dame, E
1961 Jimmy Johnson, UCLA, CB
Bernie Casey, Bowling Green, WR
Bill Kilmer, UCLA, QB
1962 Lance Alworth, Arkansas, WR
1963 Kermit Alexander, UCLA, CB
1964 Dave Parks, Texas Tech, WR
1965 Ken Willard, North Carolina, RB
George Donnelly, Illinois, DB
1966 Stan Hindman, Mississippi, DE
1967 Steve Spurrier, Florida, QB
Cas Banaszek, Northwestern, T
1968 Forrest Blue, Auburn, C
1969 Ted Kwalick, Penn State, TE
Gene Washington, Stanford, WR
1970 Cedrick Hardman, North Texas St., DE
Bruce Taylor, Boston U., DB
1971 Tim Anderson, Ohio State, DB
1972 Terry Beasley, Auburn, WR
1973 Mike Holmes, Texas Southern, DB
1974 Wilbur Jackson, Alabama, RB
Bill Sandifer, UCLA, DT
1975 Jimmy Webb, Mississippi St., DT
1976 Randy Cross, UCLA, C (2)
1977 Elmo Boyd, Eastern Kentucky, WR (3)
1978 Ken MacAfee, Notre Dame, TE
Dan Bunz, Cal St.-Long Beach, LB
1979 James Owens, UCLA, WR (2)
1980 Earl Cooper, Rice, RB
Jim Stuckey, Clemson, DT
1981 Ronnie Lott, So. California, DB
1982 Bubba Paris, Michigan, T (2)
1983 Roger Craig, Nebraska, RB (2)
1984 Todd Shell, Brigham Young, LB
1985 Jerry Rice, Mississippi Valley St., WR
1986 Larry Roberts, Alabama, DE (2)
1987 Harris Barton, North Carolina, T
Terrence Flagler, Clemson, RB
1988 Danny Stubbs, Miami, DE (2)
1989 Keith DeLong, Tennessee, LB
1990 Dexter Carter, Florida State, RB
1991 Ted Washington, Louisville, DT
1992 Dana Hall, Washington, DB
1993 Dana Stubblefield, Kansas, DT
Todd Kelly, Tennessee, DE
1994 Bryant Young, Notre Dame, DT
William Floyd, Florida State, RB
1995 J.J. Stokes, UCLA, WR
1996 Israel Ifeanyi, So.California, DE (2)
1997 Jim Druckenmiller, Virginia Tech, QB
1998 R.W. McQuarters, Oklahoma St., DB
1999 Reggie McGrew, Florida, DT
2000 Julian Peterson, Michigan St., LB
Ahmed Plummer, Ohio State, DB
2001 Andre Carter, California, DE
2002 Mike Rumph, Miami, DB
2003 Kwame Harris, Stanford, T
2004 Rashaun Woods, Oklahoma St., WR
2005 Alex Smith, Utah, QB
2006 Vernon Davis, Maryland, TE
Manny Lawson, North Carolina St., DE
2007 Patrick Willis, Mississippi, LB
Joe Staley, Central Michigan, T

SEATTLE SEAHAWKS
Year Player, College, Position
1976 Steve Niehaus, Notre Dame, DT

1977 Steve August, Tulsa, G	2005 Carnell Williams, Auburn, RB	1944 Mike Micka, Colgate, B
1978 Keith Simpson, Memphis St., DB	2006 Davin Joseph, Oklahoma, G	1945 Jim Hardy, Southern California, B
1979 Manu Tuiasosopo, UCLA, DT	2007 Gaines Adams, Clemson, DE	1946 Cal Rossi, UCLA, B*
1980 Jacob Green, Texas A&M, DE		1947 Cal Rossi, UCLA, B
1981 Ken Easley, UCLA, DB	**TENNESSEE TITANS**	1948 Harry Gilmer, Alabama, B
1982 Jeff Bryant, Clemson, DE	**Year Player, College, Position**	Lowell Tew, Alabama, B
1983 Curt Warner, Penn State, RB	1960 Billy Cannon, Louisiana State, RB	1949 Rob Goode, Texas A&M, B
1984 Terry Taylor, Southern Illinois, DB	1961 Mike Ditka, Pittsburgh, E	1950 George Thomas, Oklahoma, B
1985 Owen Gill, Iowa, RB (2)	1962 Ray Jacobs, Howard Payne, DT	1951 Leon Heath, Oklahoma, B
1986 John L. Williams, Florida, RB	1963 Danny Brabham, Arkansas, LB	1952 Larry Isbell, Baylor, B
1987 Tony Woods, Pittsburgh, LB	1964 Scott Appleton, Texas, DT	1953 Jack Scarbath, Maryland, B
1988 Brian Blades, Miami, WR (2)	1965 Lawrence Elkins, Baylor, WR	1954 Steve Meilinger, Kentucky, E
1989 Andy Heck, Notre Dame, T	1966 Tommy Nobis, Texas, LB	1955 Ralph Guglielmi, Notre Dame, B
1990 Cortez Kennedy, Miami, DT	1967 George Webster, Michigan St., LB	1956 Ed Vereb, Maryland, B
1991 Dan McGwire, San Diego St., QB	Tom Regner, Notre Dame, G	1957 Don Bosseler, Miami, B
1992 Ray Roberts, Virginia, T	1968 Mac Haik, Mississippi, WR (2)	1958 Mike Sommer, George
1993 Rick Mirer, Notre Dame, QB	1969 Ron Pritchard, Arizona State, LB	Washington, B (2)
1994 Sam Adams, Texas A&M, DT	1970 Doug Wilkerson, N. Carolina Central, G	1959 Don Allard, Boston College, B
1995 Joey Galloway, Ohio State, WR	1971 Dan Pastorini, Santa Clara, QB	1960 Richie Lucas, Penn State, QB
1996 Pete Kendall, Boston College, T	1972 Greg Sampson, Stanford, DT	1961 Norman Snead, Wake Forest, QB
1997 Shawn Springs, Ohio State, DB	1973 John Matuszak, Tampa, DE	Joe Rutgens, Illinois, DT
Walter Jones, Florida State, T	George Amundson, Iowa State, RB	1962 Ernie Davis, Syracuse, RB
1998 Anthony Simmons, Clemson, LB	1974 Steve Manstedt, Nebraska, LB (4)	1963 Pat Richter, Wisconsin, TE
1999 Lamar King, Saginaw Valley St., DE	1975 Robert Brazile, Jackson State, LB	1964 Charley Taylor, Arizona St., RB-WR
2000 Shaun Alexander, Alabama, RB	Don Hardeman, Texas A&I, RB	1965 Bob Breitenstein, Tulsa, T (2)
Chris McIntosh, Wisconsin, T	1976 Mike Barber, Louisiana Tech, TE (2)	1966 Charlie Gogolak, Princeton, K
2001 Koren Robinson, North Carolina St., WR	1977 Morris Towns, Missouri, T	1967 Ray McDonald, Idaho, RB
Steve Hutchinson, Michigan, G	1978 Earl Campbell, Texas, RB	1968 Jim Smith, Oregon, DB
2002 Jerramy Stevens, Washington, TE	1979 Mike Stensrud, Iowa State, DE (2)	1969 Eugene Epps, Texas-El Paso, DB (2)
2003 Marcus Trufant, Washington State, DB	1980 Angelo Fields, Michigan St., T (2)	1970 Bill Bundige, Colorado, DT (2)
2004 Marcus Tubbs, Texas, DT	1981 Michael Holston, Morgan St., WR (3)	1971 Cotton Speyrer, Texas, WR (2)
2005 Chris Spencer, Mississippi, C	1982 Mike Munchak, Penn State, G	1972 Moses Denson, Maryland St., RB (8)
2006 Kelly Jennings, Miami, DB	1983 Bruce Matthews, So. California, T	1973 Charles Cantrell, Lamar, G (5)
2007 Josh Wilson, Maryland, DB (2)	1984 Dean Steinkuhler, Nebraska, T	1974 Jon Keyworth, Colorado, TE (6)
	1985 Ray Childress, Texas A&M, DE	1975 Mike Thomas, Nevada-Las Vegas, RB (6)
	Richard Johnson, Wisconsin, DB	1976 Mike Hughes, Baylor, G (5)
TAMPA BAY BUCCANEERS	1986 Jim Everett, Purdue, QB	1977 Duncan McColl, Stanford, DE (4)
Year Player, College, Position	1987 Alonzo Highsmith, Miami, RB	1978 Tony Green, Florida, RB (6)
1976 Lee Roy Selmon, Oklahoma, DT	Haywood Jeffires, North Carolina St., WR	1979 Don Warren, San Diego St., TE (4)
1977 Ricky Bell, Southern California, RB	1988 Lorenzo White, Michigan State, RB	1980 Art Monk, Syracuse, WR
1978 Doug Williams, Grambling, QB	1989 David Williams, Florida, T	1981 Mark May, Pittsburgh, T
1979 Greg Roberts, Oklahoma, G (2)	1990 Lamar Lathon, Houston, LB	1982 Vernon Dean, San Diego St., DB (2)
1980 Ray Snell, Wisconsin, G	1991 Mike Dumas, Indiana, DB (2)	1983 Darrell Green, Texas A&I, DB
1981 Hugh Green, Pittsburgh, LB	1992 Eddie Robinson, Alabama St., LB (2)	1984 Bob Slater, Oklahoma, DT (2)
1982 Sean Farrell, Penn State, G	1993 Brad Hopkins, Illinois, T	1985 Tory Nixon, San Diego St., DB (2)
1983 Randy Grimes, Baylor, C (2)	1994 Henry Ford, Arkansas, DE	1986 Markus Koch, Boise State, DE (2)
1984 Keith Browner, So. California, LB (2)	1995 Steve McNair, Alcorn State, QB	1987 Brian Davis, Nebraska, DB (2)
1985 Ron Holmes, Washington, DE	1996 Eddie George, Ohio State, RB	1988 Chip Lohmiller, Minnesota, K (2)
1986 Bo Jackson, Auburn, RB	1997 Kenny Holmes, Miami, DE	1989 Tracy Rocker, Auburn, DT (3)
Roderick Jones, So. Methodist, DB	1998 Kevin Dyson, Utah, WR	1990 Andre Collins, Penn State, LB (2)
1987 Vinny Testaverde, Miami, QB	1999 Jevon Kearse, Florida, DE	1991 Bobby Wilson, Michigan State, DT
1988 Paul Gruber, Wisconsin, T	2000 Keith Bulluck, Syracuse, LB	1992 Desmond Howard, Michigan, WR
1989 Broderick Thomas, Nebraska, LB	2001 Andre Dyson, Utah, DB (2)	1993 Tom Carter, Notre Dame, DB
1990 Keith McCants, Alabama, LB	2002 Albert Haynesworth, Tennessee, DT	1994 Heath Shuler, Tennessee, QB
1991 Charles McRae, Tennessee, T	2003 Andre Woolfolk, Oklahoma, DB	1995 Michael Westbrook, Colorado, WR
1992 Courtney Hawkins, Michigan St., WR (2)	2004 Ben Troupe, Florida, TE (2)	1996 Andre Johnson, Penn State, T
1993 Eric Curry, Alabama, DE	2005 Adam Jones, West Virginia, DB	1997 Kenard Lang, Miami, DE
1994 Trent Dilfer, Fresno State, QB	2006 Vince Young, Texas, QB	1998 Stephen Alexander, Oklahoma, TE (2)
1995 Warren Sapp, Miami, DT	2007 Michael Griffin, Texas, DB	1999 Champ Bailey, Georgia, DB
Derrick Brooks, Florida State, LB		2000 LaVar Arrington, Penn State, LB
1996 Regan Upshaw, California, DE	**WASHINGTON REDSKINS**	Chris Samuels, Alabama, T
Marcus Jones, North Carolina, DT	**Year Player, College, Position**	2001 Rod Gardner, Clemson, WR
1997 Warrick Dunn, Florida State, RB	1936 Riley Smith, Alabama, B	2002 Patrick Ramsey, Tulane, QB
Reidel Anthony, Florida, WR	1937 Sammy Baugh, Texas Christian, B	2003 Taylor Jacobs, Florida, WR (2)
1998 Jacquez Green, Florida, WR (2)	1938 Andy Farkas, Detroit, B	2004 Sean Taylor, Miami, DB
1999 Anthony McFarland, Louisiana St., DT	1939 I.B. Hale, Texas Christian, T	2005 Carlos Rogers, Auburn, DB
2000 Cosey Coleman, Tennessee, G (2)	1940 Ed Boell, New York U., B	Jason Campbell, Auburn, QB
2001 Kenyatta Walker, Florida, T	1941 Forest Evashevski, Michigan, B	2006 Rocky McIntosh, Miami, LB (2)
2002 Marquise Walker, Michigan, WR (3)	1942 Orban (Spec) Sanders, Texas, B	2007 LaRon Landry, Louisiana State, DB
2003 Dewayne White, Louisville, DE (2)	1943 Jack Jenkins, Missouri, B	*Choice lost because of ineligibility*
2004 Michael Clayton, Louisiana St., WR		

NUMBER-ONE DRAFT CHOICES

Season	Date	Team	Player	Position	College
2007	April 28-29	Oakland	JaMarcus Russell	QB	Louisiana State
2006	April 29-30	Houston	Mario Williams	DE	North Carolina State
2005	April 23-24	San Francisco	Alex Smith	QB	Utah
2004	April 24-25	San Diego	Eli Manning	QB	Mississippi
2003	April 26-27	Cincinnati	Carson Palmer	QB	Southern California
2002	April 20-21	Houston	David Carr	QB	Fresno State
2001	April 21-22	Atlanta	Michael Vick	QB	Virginia Tech
2000	April 15-16	Cleveland	Courtney Brown	DE	Penn State
1999	April 17-18	Cleveland	Tim Couch	QB	Kentucky
1998	April 18-19	Indianapolis	Peyton Manning	QB	Tennessee
1997	April 19-20	St. Louis	Orlando Pace	T	Ohio State
1996	April 20-21	New York Jets	Keyshawn Johnson	WR	Southern California
1995	April 22-23	Cincinnati	Ki-Jana Carter	RB	Penn State
1994	April 24-25	Cincinnati	Dan Wilkinson	DT	Ohio State
1993	April 25-26	New England	Drew Bledsoe	QB	Washington State
1992	April 26-27	Indianapolis	Steve Emtman	DT	Washington
1991	April 21-22	Dallas	Russell Maryland	DT	Miami
1990	April 22-23	Indianapolis	Jeff George	QB	Illinois
1989	April 23-24	Dallas	Troy Aikman	QB	UCLA
1988	April 24-25	Atlanta	Aundray Bruce	LB	Auburn
1987	April 28-29	Tampa Bay	Vinny Testaverde	QB	Miami
1986	April 29-30	Tampa Bay	Bo Jackson	RB	Auburn
1985	April 30-May 1	Buffalo	Bruce Smith	DE	Virginia Tech
1984	May 1-2	New England	Irving Fryar	WR	Nebraska
1983	April 26-27	Baltimore	John Elway	QB	Stanford
1982	April 27-28	New England	Kenneth Sims	DT	Texas
1981	April 28-29	New Orleans	George Rogers	RB	South Carolina
1980	April 29-30	Detroit	Billy Sims	RB	Oklahoma
1979	May 3-4	Buffalo	Tom Cousineau	LB	Ohio State
1978	May 2-3	Houston	Earl Campbell	RB	Texas
1977	May 3-4	Tampa Bay	Ricky Bell	RB	Southern California
1976	April 8-9	Tampa Bay	Lee Roy Selmon	DE	Oklahoma
1975	January 28-29	Atlanta	Steve Bartkowski	QB	California
1974	January 29-30	Dallas	Ed Jones	DE	Tennessee State
1973	January 30-31	Houston	John Matuszak	DE	Tampa
1972	February 1-2	Buffalo	Walt Patulski	DE	Notre Dame
1971	January 28-29	New England	Jim Plunkett	QB	Stanford
1970	January 27-28	Pittsburgh	Terry Bradshaw	QB	Louisiana Tech
1969	January 28-29	Buffalo (AFL)	O.J. Simpson	RB	Southern California
1968	January 30-31	Minnesota	Ron Yary	T	Southern California
1967	March 14	Baltimore	Bubba Smith	DT	Michigan State
1966	November 27, 1965	Atlanta	Tommy Nobis	LB	Texas
	November 28, 1965	Miami (AFL)	Jim Grabowski	RB	Illinois
1965	November 28, 1964	New York Giants	Tucker Frederickson	RB	Auburn
	November 28, 1964	Houston (AFL)	Lawrence Elkins	E	Baylor
1964	December 2, 1963	San Francisco	Dave Parks	E	Texas Tech
	November 30, 1963	Boston (AFL)	Jack Concannon	QB	Boston College
1963	December 3, 1962	Los Angeles	Terry Baker	QB	Oregon State
	December 1, 1962	Kansas City (AFL)	Buck Buchanan	DT	Grambling
1962	December 4, 1961	Washington	Ernie Davis	RB	Syracuse
	December 2, 1961	Oakland (AFL)	Roman Gabriel	QB	North Carolina State
1961	December 27-28, 1960	Minnesota	Tommy Mason	RB	Tulane
	November 23, 1960	Buffalo (AFL)	Ken Rice	G	Auburn
1960	Secret Draft	Los Angeles	Billy Cannon	RB	Louisiana State
	November 22, December 2, 1959	(AFL had no formal first pick)			
1959	December 2, 1958	Green Bay	Randy Duncan	QB	Iowa
1958	December 2, 1957	Chicago Cardinals	King Hill	QB	Rice
1957	November 27, 1956	Green Bay	Paul Hornung	HB	Notre Dame
1956	November 29, 1955	Pittsburgh	Gary Glick	DB	Colorado A&M
1955	January 27-28	Baltimore	George Shaw	QB	Oregon
1954	January 28	Cleveland	Bobby Garrett	QB	Stanford

Season	Date	Team	Player	Position	College
1953	January 22	San Francisco	Harry Babcock	E	Georgia
1952	January 17	Los Angeles	Bill Wade	QB	Vanderbilt
1951	January 18-19	New York Giants	Kyle Rote	HB	Southern Methodist
1950	January 21-22	Detroit	Leon Hart	E	Notre Dame
1949	December 21, 1948	Philadelphia	Chuck Bednarik	C	Pennsylvania
1948	December 19, 1947	Washington	Harry Gilmer	QB	Alabama
1947	December 16, 1946	Chicago Bears	Bob Fenimore	HB	Oklahoma A&M
1946	January 14	Boston	Frank Dancewicz	QB	Notre Dame
1945	April 6	Chicago Cardinals	Charley Trippi	HB	Georgia
1944	April 19	Boston	Angelo Bertelli	QB	Notre Dame
1943	April 8	Detroit	Frank Sinkwich	HB	Georgia
1942	December 22, 1941	Pittsburgh	Bill Dudley	HB	Virginia
1941	December 10, 1940	Chicago Bears	Tom Harmon	HB	Michigan
1940	December 9, 1939	Chicago Cardinals	George Cafego	HB	Tennessee
1939	December 8, 1938	Chicago Cardinals	Ki Aldrich	C	Texas Christian
1938	December 12, 1937	Cleveland	Corbett Davis	FB	Indiana
1937	December 12, 1936	Philadelphia	Sam Francis	FB	Nebraska
1936	February 8	Philadelphia	Jay Berwanger	HB	Chicago

Note: From 1947 through 1958, the first selection in the draft was a Bonus pick, awarded to the winner of a random draw. That club, in turn, forfeited its last-round draft choice. The winner of the Bonus choice was eliminated from future draws. The system was abolished after 1958, by which time all clubs had received a Bonus choice.

NUMBER-ONE DRAFT CHOICES BY POSITION

Quarterbacks:	27
Running Backs:	23
Defenisve Linemen:	13
Wide Receivers:	6
Offensive Linemen:	5
Linebackers:	3
Defensive Backs:	1

THE FOLLOWING AWARDS WERE NAMED BY *ASSOCIATED PRESS* IN BALLOTING BY A NATIONWIDE PANEL OF MEDIA.

NFL MOST VALUABLE PLAYER AWARD

YEAR	PLAYER	POS.	TEAM	ACCOMPLISHMENTS
1957	Jim Brown	RB	Cleveland Browns	Rushed for league-leading 942 yards and added 9 touchdowns as a rookie.
1958	Gino Marchetti	DE	Baltimore Colts	Leader of defense that permitted league-low 1,291 rushing yards and division-low 203 points.
1959	Charley Conerly	QB	New York Giants	Passed for 14 touchdowns and only 4 interceptions. Led offense to division-leading 284 points.
1960*	Norm Van Brocklin	QB	Philadelphia Eagles	Guided Eagles to first division title since 1949. Passed for 2,471 yards and 24 touchdowns.
	Joe Schmidt	LB	Detroit Lions	After 0-3 start, team went 7-2 when he returned from injury. Scored 2 defensive touchdowns.
1961	Paul Hornung	RB	Green Bay Packers	Led league in scoring for second straight season with 146 points (10 TD, 15 FG, 41 PAT).
1962	Jim Taylor	RB	Green Bay Packers	League rushing champion with 1,474 yards. Scored all-time record 19 touchdowns.
1963	Y.A. Tittle	QB	New York Giants	Set all-time season record with 36 touchdown passes. Guided league's top offense (5,024 yards).
1964	Johnny Unitas	QB	Baltimore Colts	Guided Colts to NFL's best record (12-2) and league's top offensive attack (4,779 yards).
1965	Jim Brown	RB	Cleveland Browns	Leader of NFL's top rushing attack. Led league with 1,544 yards, added 21 total touchdowns.
1966	Bart Starr	QB	Green Bay Packers	Passed for 14 touchdowns and only 3 interceptions. Led Packers to league-best 12-2 record.
1967	Johnny Unitas	QB	Baltimore Colts	Passed for 3,428 yards and 20 touchdowns. Led Colts to 11-1-2 record.
1968	Earl Morrall	QB	Baltimore Colts	Guided Colts to NFL-best 13-1 record. Led league with 26 touchdown passes.
1969	Roman Gabriel	QB	Los Angeles Rams	Led NFL with 24 touchdown passes. Guided Rams to 11-3 record.
1970	John Brodie	QB	San Francisco 49ers	Took 49ers to first division title. Threw NFL-best 24 touchdown passes.
1971	Alan Page	DT	Minnesota Vikings	Led defense that allowed NFL-low 139 points. Vikings won fourth straight NFC Central title.
1972	Larry Brown	RB	Washington Redskins	Led conference with 1,216 rushing yards. Redskins had NFC-best 11-3 record.
1973	O.J. Simpson	RB	Buffalo Bills	Rushed for all-time record 2,003 yards, including three 200-yard performances.
1974	Ken Stabler	QB	Oakland Raiders	Led league with 26 touchdown passes and only 12 interceptions. Raiders had NFL-best 12-2 record.
1975	Fran Tarkenton	QB	Minnesota Vikings	Tied for league-best 12-2 record. Led NFC with 91.7 passer rating.
1976	Bert Jones	QB	Baltimore Colts	Threw 24 touchdowns and only 9 interceptions for 102.5 passer rating.
1977	Walter Payton	RB	Chicago Bears	Rushed for league-leading 1,852 yards and 16 total touchdowns.
1978	Terry Bradshaw	QB	Pittsburgh Steelers	Led Steelers to league-leading 14-2 mark. Set club record with 28 touchdown passes.
1979	Earl Campbell	RB	Houston Oilers	Led league with 1,697 rushing yards and 19 touchdowns.
1980	Brian Sipe	QB	Cleveland Browns	NFL-best 91.4 passer rating. Set Browns' records with 30 touchdown passes and 4,132 yards.
1981	Ken Anderson	QB	Cincinnati Bengals	Led Bengals to first division title since 1973. NFL-high 98.5 passer rating.
1982	Mark Moseley	K	Washington Redskins	Converted 20 of 21 FGs. Set consecutive field-goal record at 23 (including last three in '81).
1983	Joe Theismann	QB	Washington Redskins	Leader of offense that scored NFL record 541 points. Redskins had NFL-best 14-2 record.
1984	Dan Marino	QB	Miami Dolphins	Set NFL records with 5,084 yards and 48 touchdown passes. Led Dolphins to AFC-best 14-2 mark.
1985	Marcus Allen	RB	Los Angeles Raiders	Rushed for league-leading 1,759 yards. Tied for AFC lead with 11 rushing touchdowns.
1986	Lawrence Taylor	LB	New York Giants	Recorded league-high 20.5 sacks, and led Giants' second-ranked defense (297.3).
1987	John Elway	QB	Denver Broncos	In 12 games, passed for 19 touchdowns and 3,198 yards, including four 300-yard games.
1988	Boomer Esiason	QB	Cincinnati Bengals	Led NFL with 97.4 passer rating. Tied for AFC lead with 28 TD passes.
1989	Joe Montana	QB	San Francisco 49ers	Set NFL record with 112.4 passer rating, including 70.2 completion percentage.
1990	Joe Montana	QB	San Francisco 49ers	Led 49ers to league-best 14-2 record. Completed NFC-high 61.7 percent of passes.
1991	Thurman Thomas	RB	Buffalo Bills	Recorded league-high 2,038 yards from scrimmage (1,407 rushing, 631 receiving).

ASSOCIATED PRESS NFL MOST VALUABLE PLAYERS

Year	Player	Pos	Team	Notes
1992	Steve Young	QB	San Francisco 49ers	NFL's top passer with 107.0 rating. Led 49ers to league-best 14-2 record.
1993	Emmitt Smith	RB	Dallas Cowboys	Led league in rushing (1,486 yards) for third straight year despite missing first two games.
1994	Steve Young	QB	San Francisco 49ers	Compiled NFL all-time best 112.8 passer rating. Completed more than 70 percent of his passes.
1995	Brett Favre	QB	Green Bay Packers	Led league with 38 touchdown passes and NFC with 99.5 passer rating.
1996	Brett Favre	QB	Green Bay Packers	Led Packers to top conference record (13-3). Threw NFL-best 39 touchdown passes.
1997*	Brett Favre	QB	Green Bay Packers	Led league with 35 touchdown passes. Led NFC with 3,867 passing yards.
	Barry Sanders	RB	Detroit Lions	Rushed for all-time second-best 2,053 yards, including record 14 straight 100-yard games.
1998	Terrell Davis	RB	Denver Broncos	Rushed for 2,008 yards and scored league-best 23 total touchdowns.
1999	Kurt Warner	QB	St. Louis Rams	Became the second QB in history to have 40 touchdown passes in a season (41).
2000	Marshall Faulk	RB	St. Louis Rams	Set NFL record with 26 touchdowns and led NFC with 2,189 yards from scrimmage.
2001	Kurt Warner	QB	St. Louis Rams	Led NFL with 4,830 passing yards, 36 touchdowns, 68.7 completion percentage, and 101.4 passer rating.
2002	Rich Gannon	QB	Oakland Raiders	Set single-season records with 10 300-yard passing games and 418 completions, and led NFL with 4,689 passing yards.
2003*	Peyton Manning	QB	Indianapolis Colts	Led NFL with 4,267 passing yards, had AFC-best 29 touchdown passes, and posted 99.0 passer rating.
	Steve McNair	QB	Tennessee Titans	Posted NFL-best 100.4 passer rating, passing for 3,215 yards with 24 touchdowns against 7 interceptions.
2004	Peyton Manning	QB	Indianapolis Colts	Set NFL records with 49 touchdown passes and 121.1 passer rating while passing for 4,557 yards.
2005	Shaun Alexander	RB	Seattle Seahawks	Set NFL record with 28 touchdowns and led league with 1,880 rushing yards.
2006	LaDainian Tomlinson	RB	San Diego Chargers	Set NFL record for touchdowns (31) and points scored (186). Rushed for team-record 1,815 yards.

Total *Associated Press* NFL MVPs: 53
Two-time Winners: Jim Brown, Brett Favre (3), Peyton Manning, Joe Montana, Johnny Unitas, Kurt Warner, Steve Young
* The award was shared in 1960, 1997, and 2003.

ASSOCIATED PRESS MVPs WHO WON SUPER BOWL/NFL CHAMPIONSHIP IN SAME SEASON: 15

Year	Player	Team
1958	Gino Marchetti	Baltimore Colts
1960	Norm Van Brocklin	Philadelphia Eagles
1961	Paul Hornung	Green Bay Packers
1962	Jim Taylor	Green Bay Packers
1966	Bart Starr	Green Bay Packers
1968	Earl Morrall	Baltimore Colts
1978	Terry Bradshaw	Pittsburgh Steelers
1982	Mark Moseley	Washington Redskins
1986	Lawrence Taylor	New York Giants
1989	Joe Montana	San Francisco 49ers
1993	Emmitt Smith	Dallas Cowboys
1994	Steve Young	San Francisco 49ers
1996	Brett Favre	Green Bay Packers
1998	Terrell Davis	Denver Broncos
1999	Kurt Warner	St. Louis Rams

ASSOCIATED PRESS NFL MVP BY POSITION

Quarterback:	32	Defensive End:	1
Running Back:	16	Defensive Tackle:	1
Linebacker:	2	Kicker:	1

ASSOCIATED PRESS MVPs BY TEAM

7 Indianapolis/Baltimore Colts
6 Green Bay Packers
5 San Francisco 49ers
4 St. Louis/Los Angeles Rams
3 Cleveland Browns
New York Giants
Oakland/Los Angeles Raiders
Washington Redskins
2 Buffalo Bills
Cincinnati Bengals
Denver Broncos
Detroit Lions
Minnesota Vikings

1 Chicago Bears
Dallas Cowboys
Houston Oilers
Miami Dolphins
Philadelphia Eagles
Pittsburgh Steelers
San Diego Chargers
Seattle Seahawks
Tennessee Titans

AP OFFENSIVE PLAYER OF THE YEAR

Year	Player	Pos	Team
1973	O.J. Simpson	RB	Buffalo Bills
1974	Ken Stabler	QB	Oakland Raiders
1975	Fran Tarkenton	QB	Minnesota Vikings
1976	Bert Jones	QB	Baltimore Colts
1977	Walter Payton	RB	Chicago Bears
1978	Earl Campbell	RB	Houston Oilers
1979	Earl Campbell	RB	Houston Oilers
1980	Earl Campbell	RB	Houston Oilers
1981	Ken Anderson	QB	Cincinnati Bengals
1982	Dan Fouts	QB	San Diego Chargers
1983	Joe Theismann	QB	Washington Redskins
1984	Dan Marino	QB	Miami Dolphins
1985	Marcus Allen	RB	Los Angeles Raiders
1986	Eric Dickerson	RB	Los Angeles Rams
1987	Jerry Rice	WR	San Francisco 49ers
1988	Roger Craig	RB	San Francisco 49ers
1989	Joe Montana	QB	San Francisco 49ers
1990	Warren Moon	QB	Houston Oilers
1991	Thurman Thomas	RB	Buffalo Bills
1992	Steve Young	QB	San Francisco 49ers
1993	Jerry Rice	WR	San Francisco 49ers
1994	Barry Sanders	RB	Detroit Lions
1995	Brett Favre	QB	Green Bay Packers
1996	Terrell Davis	RB	Denver Broncos
1997	Barry Sanders	RB	Detroit Lions
1998	Terrell Davis	RB	Denver Broncos
1999	Marshall Faulk	RB	St. Louis Rams
2000	Marshall Faulk	RB	St. Louis Rams
2001	Marshall Faulk	RB	St. Louis Rams
2002	Priest Holmes	RB	Kansas City Chiefs
2003	Jamal Lewis	RB	Baltimore Ravens
2004	Peyton Manning	QB	Indianapolis Colts
2005	Shaun Alexander	RB	Seattle Seahawks
2006	LaDainian Tomlinson	RB	San Diego Chargers

AP OFFENSIVE ROOKIE OF THE YEAR

Year	Player	Pos	Team
1957	Jim Brown	RB	Cleveland Browns
1958	Jimmy Orr	WR	Pittsburgh Steelers
1959	Nick Pietrosante	RB	Detroit Lions
1960	Gail Cogdill	WR	Detroit Lions
1961	Mike Ditka	TE	Chicago Bears
1962	Ron Bull	RB	Chicago Bears
1963	Paul Flatley	WR	Minnesota Vikings
1964	Charley Taylor	WR	Washington Redskins
1965	Gale Sayers	RB	Chicago Bears
1966	Johnny Roland	RB	St. Louis Cardinals
1967	Mel Farr	RB	Detroit Lions
1968	Earl McCullouch	WR	Detroit Lions
1969	Calvin Hill	RB	Dallas Cowboys
1970	Duane Thomas	RB	Dallas Cowboys
1971	John Brockington	RB	Green Bay Packers
1972	Franco Harris	RB	Pittsburgh Steelers
1973	Chuck Foreman	RB	Minnesota Vikings
1974	Don Woods	RB	San Diego Chargers
1975	Mike Thomas	RB	Washington Redskins
1976	Sammy White	WR	Minnesota Vikings
1977	Tony Dorsett	RB	Dallas Cowboys
1978	Earl Campbell	RB	Houston Oilers
1979	Ottis Anderson	RB	St. Louis Cardinals
1980	Billy Sims	RB	Detroit Lions
1981	George Rogers	RB	New Orleans Saints
1982	Marcus Allen	RB	Los Angeles Raiders
1983	Eric Dickerson	RB	Los Angeles Rams
1984	Louis Lipps	WR	Pittsburgh Steelers
1985	Eddie Brown	WR	Cincinnati Bengals
1986	Rueben Mayes	RB	New Orleans Saints
1987	Troy Stradford	RB	Miami Dolphins
1988	John Stephens	RB	New England Patriots
1989	Barry Sanders	RB	Detroit Lions
1990	Emmitt Smith	RB	Dallas Cowboys
1991	Leonard Russell	RB	New England Patriots
1992	Carl Pickens	WR	Cincinnati Bengals
1993	Jerome Bettis	RB	Los Angeles Rams
1994	Marshall Faulk	RB	Indianapolis Colts
1995	Curtis Martin	RB	New England Patriots
1996	Eddie George	RB	Houston Oilers
1997	Warrick Dunn	RB	Tampa Bay Buccaneers
1998	Randy Moss	WR	Minnesota Vikings
1999	Edgerrin James	RB	Indianapolis Colts
2000	Mike Anderson	RB	Denver Broncos
2001	Anthony Thomas	RB	Chicago Bears
2002	Clinton Portis	RB	Denver Broncos
2003	Anquan Boldin	WR	Arizona Cardinals
2004	Ben Roethlisberger	QB	Pittsburgh Steelers
2005	Carnell Williams	RB	Tampa Bay Buccaneers
2006	Vince Young	QB	Tennessee Titans

AP DEFENSIVE PLAYER OF THE YEAR

Year	Player	Pos	Team
1971	Alan Page	DT	Minnesota Vikings
1972	Joe Greene	DT	Pittsburgh Steelers
1973	Dick Anderson	S	Miami Dolphins
1974	Joe Greene	DT	Pittsburgh Steelers
1975	Mel Blount	CB	Pittsburgh Steelers
1976	Jack Lambert	LB	Pittsburgh Steelers
1977	Harvey Martin	DE	Dallas Cowboys
1978	Randy Gradishar	LB	Denver Broncos
1979	Lee Roy Selmon	DE	Tampa Bay Buccaneers
1980	Lester Hayes	CB	Oakland Raiders
1981	Lawrence Taylor	LB	New York Giants
1982	Lawrence Taylor	LB	New York Giants
1983	Doug Betters	DE	Miami Dolphins
1984	Kenny Easley	S	Seattle Seahawks
1985	Mike Singletary	LB	Chicago Bears
1986	Lawrence Taylor	LB	New York Giants
1987	Reggie White	DT	Philadelphia Eagles
1988	Mike Singletary	LB	Chicago Bears
1989	Keith Millard	DT	Minnesota Vikings
1990	Bruce Smith	DE	Buffalo Bills
1991	Pat Swilling	LB	New Orleans Saints
1992	Cortez Kennedy	DT	Seattle Seahawks
1993	Rod Woodson	CB	Pittsburgh Steelers
1994	Deion Sanders	CB	San Francisco 49ers
1995	Bryce Paup	LB	Buffalo Bills
1996	Bruce Smith	DE	Buffalo Bills
1997	Dana Stubblefield	DT	San Francisco 49ers
1998	Reggie White	DE	Green Bay Packers
1999	Warren Sapp	DT	Tampa Bay Buccaneers
2000	Ray Lewis	LB	Baltimore Ravens
2001	Michael Strahan	DE	New York Giants
2002	Derrick Brooks	LB	Tampa Bay Buccaneers
2003	Ray Lewis	LB	Baltimore Ravens
2004	Ed Reed	S	Baltimore Ravens
2005	Brian Urlacher	LB	Chicago Bears
2006	Jason Taylor	DE	Miami Dolphins

AP DEFENSIVE ROOKIE OF THE YEAR

Year	Player	Pos	Team
1967	Lem Barney	CB	Detroit Lions
1968	Claude Humphrey	DE	Atlanta Falcons
1969	Joe Greene	DT	Pittsburgh Steelers
1970	Bruce Taylor	CB	San Franicsco 49ers
1971	Isiah Robertson	LB	Los Angeles Rams
1972	Willie Buchanon	CB	Green Bay Packers
1973	Wally Chambers	DT	Chicago Bears
1974	Jack Lambert	LB	Pittsburgh Steelers
1975	Robert Brazile	LB	Houston Oilers

1976	Mike Haynes	S	New England Patriots
1977	A.J. Duhe	DT	Miami Dolphins
1978	Al Baker	DE	Detroit Lions
1979	Jim Haslett	LB	Buffalo Bills
1980*	Buddy Curry	LB	Atlanta Falcons
	Al Richardson	LB	Atlanta Falcons
1981	Lawrence Taylor	LB	New York Giants
1982	Chip Banks	LB	Cleveland Browns
1983	Vernon Maxwell	LB	Baltimore Colts
1984	Bill Maas	NT	Kansas City Chiefs
1985	Duane Bickett	LB	Indianapolis Colts
1986	John Offerdahl	LB	Miami Dolphins
1987	Shane Conlan	LB	Buffalo Bills
1988	Erik McMillan	S	New York Jets
1989	Derrick Thomas	LB	Kansas City Chiefs
1990	Mark Carrier	S	Chicago Bears
1991	Mike Croel	LB	Denver Broncos
1992	Dale Carter	CB	Kansas City Chiefs
1993	Dana Stubblefield	DT	San Francisco 49ers
1994	Tim Bowens	DT	Miami Dolphins
1995	Hugh Douglas	DE	New York Jets
1996	Simeon Rice	DE	Arizona Cardinals
1997	Peter Boulware	LB	Baltimore Ravens
1998	Charles Woodson	CB	Oakland Raiders
1999	Jevon Kearse	DE	Tennessee Titans
2000	Brian Urlacher	LB	Chicago Bears
2001	Kendrell Bell	LB	Pittsburgh Steelers
2002	Julius Peppers	DE	Carolina Panthers
2003	Terrell Suggs	LB	Baltimore Ravens
2004	Jonathan Vilma	LB	New York Jets
2005	Shawne Merriman	LB	San Diego Chargers
2006	DeMeco Ryans	LB	Houston Texans

*The award was shared in 1980.

1976	Forrest Gregg	Cleveland Browns
1977	Red Miller	Denver Broncos
1978	Jack Patera	Seattle Seahawks
1979	Jack Pardee	Washington Redskins
1980	Chuck Knox	Buffalo Bills
1981	Bill Walsh	San Francisco 49ers
1982	Joe Gibbs	Washington Redskins
1983	Joe Gibbs	Washington Redskins
1984	Chuck Knox	Seattle Seahawks
1985	Mike Ditka	Chicago Bears
1986	Bill Parcells	New York Giants
1987	Jim Mora	New Orleans Saints
1988	Mike Ditka	Chicago Bears
1989	Lindy Infante	Green Bay Packers
1990	Jimmy Johnson	Dallas Cowboys
1991	Wayne Fontes	Detroit Lions
1992	Bill Cowher	Pittsburgh Steelers
1993	Dan Reeves	New York Giants
1994	Bill Parcells	New England Patriots
1995	Ray Rhodes	Philadelphia Eagles
1996	Dom Capers	Carolina Panthers
1997	Jim Fassel	New York Giants
1998	Dan Reeves	Atlanta Falcons
1999	Dick Vermeil	St. Louis Rams
2000	Jim Haslett	New Orleans Saints
2001	Dick Jauron	Chicago Bears
2002	Andy Reid	Philadelphia Eagles
2003	Bill Belichick	New England Patriots
2004	Marty Schottenheimer	San Diego Chargers
2005	Lovie Smith	Chicago Bears
2006	Sean Payton	New Orleans Saints

*The award was shared in 1967.

AP COMEBACK PLAYER OF THE YEAR

1998	Doug Flutie	QB	Buffalo Bills
1999	Bryant Young	DT	San Francisco 49ers
2000	Joe Johnson	DE	New Orleans Saints
2001	Garrison Hearst	RB	San Francisco 49ers
2002	Tommy Maddox	QB	Pittsburgh Steelers
2003	Jon Kitna	QB	Cincinnati Bengals
2004	Drew Brees	QB	San Diego Chargers
2005*	Steve Smith	WR	Carolina Panthers
	Tedy Bruschi	LB	New England Patriots
2006	Chad Pennington	QB	New York Jets

*The award was shared in 2005.

AP COACH OF THE YEAR

1957	George Wilson	Detroit Lions
1958	Weeb Ewbank	Baltimore Colts
1959	Vince Lombardi	Green Bay Packers
1960	Buck Shaw	Philadelphia Eagles
1961	Allie Sherman	New York Giants
1962	Allie Sherman	New York Giants
1963	George Halas	Chicago Bears
1964	Don Shula	Baltimore Colts
1965	George Halas	Chicago Bears
1966	Tom Landry	Dallas Cowboys
1967*	George Allen	Los Angeles Rams
	Don Shula	Baltimore Colts
1968	Don Shula	Baltimore Colts
1969	Bud Grant	Minnesota Vikings
1970	Paul Brown	Cincinnati Bengals
1971	George Allen	Washington Redskins
1972	Don Shula	Miami Dolphins
1973	Chuck Knox	Los Angeles Rams
1974	Don Coryell	St. Louis Cardinals
1975	Ted Marchibroda	Baltimore Colts

WALTER PAYTON NFL MAN OF THE YEAR

The Walter Payton NFL Man of the Year Award is the only NFL award that recognizes a player for his community service activities as well as his excellence on the field. Renamed in 1999 for the legendary Chicago Bears Pro Football Hall of Fame running back, the Walter Payton NFL Man of the Year Award has been given annually since 1970.

YEAR	PLAYER	POS.	TEAM
1970	Johnny Unitas	QB	Baltimore Colts
1971	John Hadl	QB	San Diego Chargers
1972	Willie Lanier	LB	Kansas City Chiefs
1973	Len Dawson	QB	Kansas City Chiefs
1974	George Blanda	QB	Oakland Raiders
1975	Ken Anderson	QB	Cincinnati Bengals
1976	Franco Harris	RB	Pittsburgh Steelers
1977	Walter Payton	RB	Chicago Bears
1978	Roger Staubach	QB	Dallas Cowboys
1979	Joe Greene	DT	Pittsburgh Steelers
1980	Harold Carmichael	WR	Philadelphia Eagles
1981	Lynn Swann	WR	Pittsburgh Steelers
1982	Joe Theismann	QB	Washington Redskins
1983	Rolf Benirschke	K	San Diego Chargers
1984	Marty Lyons	T	New York Jets
1985	Dwight Stephenson	C	Miami Dolphins
1986	Reggie Williams	LB	Cincinnati Bengals
1987	Dave Duerson	S	Chicago Bears
1988	Steve Largent	WR	Seattle Seahawks
1989	Warren Moon	QB	Houston Oilers
1990	Mike Singletary	LB	Chicago Bears
1991	Anthony Muñoz	T	Cincinnati Bengals
1992	John Elway	QB	Denver Broncos
1993	Derrick Thomas	LB	Kansas City Chiefs
1994	Junior Seau	LB	San Diego Chargers
1995	Boomer Esiason	QB	New York Jets
1996	Darrell Green	CB	Washington Redskins
1997	Troy Aikman	QB	Dallas Cowboys
1998	Dan Marino	QB	Miami Dolphins
1999	Cris Carter	WR	Minnesota Vikings
2000*	Derrick Brooks	LB	Tampa Bay Buccaneers
	Jim Flanigan	DT	Chicago Bears
2001	Jerome Bettis	RB	Pittsburgh Steelers
2002	Troy Vincent	CB	Philadelphia Eagles
2003	Will Shields	G	Kansas City Chiefs
2004	Warrick Dunn	RB	Atlanta Falcons
2005	Peyton Manning	QB	Indianapolis Colts
2006*	Drew Brees	QB	New Orleans Saints
	LaDainian Tomlinson	RB	San Diego Chargers

* The award was shared in 2000 and 2006.

NFL'S 10 HIGHEST SCORING WEEKENDS

Point Total	Date	Weekend
788	December 5-6, 2004	13th
788	September 5, 8-9, 2002	1st
762	November 10-11, 1996	11th
761	October 16-17, 1983	7th
753	December 8-9, 2002	14th
748	December 18-20, 2004	15th
740	November 29-30, 1998	13th
739	November 23, 26-27, 1995	13th
736	October 25-26, 1987	7th
735	December 30-31, 2006	17th

TOP 10 TELEVISED SPORTS EVENTS OF ALL-TIME

(Based on A.C. Nielsen Figures)

Program	Date	Network	Share	Rating
Super Bowl XVI	1/24/82	CBS	73%	49.1
Super Bowl XVII	1/30/83	NBC	69%	48.6
Winter Olympics	2/23/94	CBS	64%	48.5
Super Bowl XX	1/26/86	NBC	70%	48.3
Super Bowl XII	1/15/78	CBS	67%	47.2
Super Bowl XIII	1/21/79	NBC	74%	47.1
Super Bowl XVIII	1/22/84	CBS	71%	46.4
Super Bowl XIX	1/20/85	ABC	63%	46.4
Super Bowl XIV	1/20/80	CBS	67%	46.3
Super Bowl XXX	1/28/96	NBC	68%	46.0

TEN MOST WATCHED TV PROGRAMS & ESTIMATED TOTAL NUMBER OF VIEWERS

(Based on A.C. Nielsen Figures)

Program	Date	Network	*Total Viewers
Super Bowl XXXVIII	Feb. 1, 2004	CBS	144,400,000
Super Bowl XL	Feb. 5, 2006	ABC	141,400,000
Super Bowl XLI	Feb. 4, 2007	CBS	139,800,000
Super Bowl XXXVII	Jan. 26, 2003	ABC	138,900,000
Super Bowl XXX	Jan. 28, 1996	NBC	138,488,000
Super Bowl XXVIII	Jan. 30, 1994	NBC	134,800,000
Super Bowl XXXIX	Feb. 6, 2005	FOX	133,700,000
Super Bowl XXXII	Jan. 25, 1998	NBC	133,400,000
Super Bowl XXVII	Jan. 31, 1993	NBC	133,400,000
Super Bowl XXXVI	Feb. 3, 2002	FOX	131,700,000

Watched some portion of the broadcast

NFL'S TOP FIVE PAID ATTENDANCE TOTALS FOR ALL GAMES

Year	Preseason	Regular Season	Postseason	All Games
2006	4,083,282	17,340,879	775,551	22,199,712
2005	3,977,388	17,012,453	802,255	21,792,096
2004	3,918,848	17,000,811	788,965	21,708,624
2003	3,919,910	16,913,584	805,546	21,639,040
2002	3,889,884	16,833,310	781,944	21,505,138

TEN HIGHEST-RATED *NFL MONDAY NIGHT FOOTBALL* GAMES OF ALL-TIME

(Based on A.C. Nielsen Figures)

Game	Date	Share	Rating
Chicago at Miami	12/2/85	46%	29.6
N.Y. Giants at San Francisco	12/3/90	42%	26.9
Dallas at Washington	10/2/78	43%	26.8
Pittsburgh at San Diego	12/22/80	40%	25.3
Philadelphia at Miami	11/30/81	40%	25.3
Pittsburgh at Houston	12/10/79	40%	25.1
Dallas at Miami	12/17/84	40%	25.1
Pittsburgh at Dallas	9/13/82	42%	24.9
Cincinnati at Oakland	12/6/76	40%	24.7
Dallas at Washington	10/8/73	40%	24.6
Minnesota at Atlanta	11/19/73	40%	24.6

NFL'S 10 BIGGEST SINGLE-GAME ATTENDANCE TOTALS

Date	Site	Game	Teams	Attendance
August 15, 1994	Azteca Stadium	American Bowl (Mexico City)	Cowboys vs. Oilers	112,376
August 17, 1998	Azteca Stadium	American Bowl (Mexico City)	Cowboys vs. Patriots	106,424
August 22, 1947	Soldier Field	College All-Star	Bears vs. All-Stars	105,840
August 4, 1997	Estadio Guillermo Canedo	American Bowl (Mexico City)	Broncos vs. Dolphins	104,629
January 20, 1980	Rose Bowl	Super Bowl XIV	Steelers vs. Rams	103,985
January 30, 1983	Rose Bowl	Super Bowl XVII	Redskins vs. Dolphins	103,667
October 2, 2005	Azteca Stadium	Regular Season	49ers at Cardinals	103,467
January 9, 1977	Rose Bowl	Super Bowl XI	Raiders vs. Vikings	103,438
November 10, 1957	L.A. Coliseum	Regular Season	49ers at Rams	102,368
January 25, 1987	Rose Bowl	Super Bowl XXI	Giants vs. Broncos	101,643

PAID ATTENDANCE

NFL'S TOP 10 PAID ATTENDANCE WEEKENDS

Weekend	Games	Attendance
September 8, 11-12, 2005	16	1,115,018
November 20-21, 2005	16	1,112,555
December 27-28, 2003	16	1,106,818
November 19-20, 2006	16	1,106,739
December 24-26, 2005	16	1,102,701
September 7, 10-11, 2006	16	1,102,102
September 9, 12-13, 2004	16	1,101,332
December 7, 10-11, 2006	16	1,099,794
November 23, 26-27, 2006	16	1,096,873
December 30-31, 2006	16	1,096,541

NFL'S TOP 10 TEAM SINGLE-SEASON HOME PAID ATTENDANCE TOTALS

Year	Club	Games	Attendance
2006	Washington Redskins	8	708,952
2004	Washington Redskins	8	707,920
2005	Washington Redskins	8	707,614
2003	Washington Redskins	8	667,033
2002	Washington Redskins	8	663,536
2001	Washington Redskins	8	661,970
2000	Washington Redskins	8	656,599
1980	Detroit Lions	8	634,204
1988	Buffalo Bills	8	631,818
1991	Buffalo Bills	8	631,786

NFL PAID ATTENDANCE

For detailed 2006 attendance, see page 340.

Year	Regular Season			Average	Postseason	Total
2006	#17,340,879	(256 games)		#67,738	775,551 (12)	#18,116,430
2005	17,012,453	(256 games)		66,455	802,255 (12)	17,814,708
2004	17,000,811	(256 games)		66,409	788,965 (12)	17,789,776
2003	16,913,584	(255 games***)		66,328	805,546 (12)	17,719,130
2002	16,833,310	(256 games)		65,755	781,944 (12)	17,615,254
2001	16,166,258	(248 games)		65,187	766,905 (12)	16,933,163
2000	16,387,289	(248 games)		66,078	809,132 (12)	17,196,421
1999	16,206,640	(248 games)		65,349	793,759 (12)	17,000,399
1998	15,364,873	(240 games)		64,020	822,885 (12)	16,187,758
1997	14,967,314	(240 games)		62,364	801,879 (12)	15,769,193
1996	14,612,417	(240 games)		60,885	769,310 (12)	15,381,727
1995	15,043,562	(240 games)		62,682	790,906 (12)	15,834,468
1994	14,030,435	(224 games)		62,636	779,738 (12)	14,810,173
1993	13,966,843	(224 games)		62,352	814,607 (12)	14,781,450
1992	13,828,887	(224 games)		61,736	815,910 (12)	14,644,797
1991	13,841,459	(224 games)		61,792	813,247 (12)	14,654,706
1990	13,959,896	(224 games)		62,321	847,543 (12)	14,807,439
1989	13,625,662	(224 games)		60,829	685,771 (10)	14,311,433
1988	13,539,848	(224 games)		60,446	658,317 (10)	14,198,165
1987	11,406,166	(210 games**)		54,315	656,977 (10)	12,063,143
1986	13,588,551	(224 games)		60,663	734,002 (10)	14,322,553
1985	13,345,047	(224 games)		59,567	710,768 (10)	14,055,815
1984	13,398,112	(224 games)		59,813	665,194 (10)	14,063,306
1983	13,277,222	(224 games)		59,273	675,513 (10)	13,952,735
1982	7,367,438	(126 games*)		58,472	#1,033,153 (16)	8,400,591
1981	13,606,990	(224 games)		60,745	637,763 (10)	14,244,753
1980	13,392,230	(224 games)		59,787	624,430 (10)	14,016,660
1979	13,182,039	(224 games)		58,848	630,326 (10)	13,812,365
1978	12,771,800	(224 games)		57,017	624,388 (10)	13,396,188
1977	11,018,632	(196 games)		56,218	534,925 (8)	11,553,557
1976	11,070,543	(196 games)		56,482	492,884 (8)	11,563,427
1975	10,213,193	(182 games)		56,116	475,919 (8)	10,689,112
1974	10,236,322	(182 games)		56,244	438,664 (8)	10,674,986
1973	10,730,933	(182 games)		58,961	525,433 (8)	11,256,366
1972	10,445,827	(182 games)		57,395	483,345 (8)	10,929,172
1971	10,076,035	(182 games)		55,363	483,891 (8)	10,559,926
1970	9,533,333	(182 games)		52,381	458,493 (8)	9,991,826
1969	6,096,127	(112 games)	NFL	54,430	162,279 (3)	6,258,406
	2,843,373	(70 games)	AFL	40,620	167,088 (3)	3,010,461
1968	5,882,313	(112 games)	NFL	52,521	215,902 (3)	6,098,215
	2,635,004	(70 games)	AFL	37,643	114,438 (2)	2,749,442
1967	5,938,924	(112 games)	NFL	53,026	166,208 (3)	6,105,132
	2,295,697	(63 games)	AFL	36,439	53,330 (1)	2,349,027
1966	5,337,044	(105 games)	NFL	50,829	74,152 (1)	5,411,196
	2,160,369	(63 games)	AFL	34,291	42,080 (1)	2,202,449
1965	4,634,021	(98 games)	NFL	47,286	100,304 (2)	4,734,325
	1,782,384	(56 games)	AFL	31,828	30,361 (1)	1,812,745
1964	4,563,049	(98 games)	NFL	46,562	79,544 (1)	4,642,593
	1,447,875	(56 games)	AFL	25,855	40,242 (1)	1,488,117
1963	4,163,643	(98 games)	NFL	42,486	45,801 (1)	4,209,444
	1,208,697	(56 games)	AFL	21,584	63,171 (2)	1,271,868

Year	Regular Season			Average	Postseason	Total
1962	4,003,421	(98 games)	NFL	40,851	64,892 (1)	4,068,313
	1,147,302	(56 games)	AFL	20,487	37,981 (1)	1,185,283
1961	3,986,159	(98 games)	NFL	40,675	39,029 (1)	4,025,188
	1,002,657	(56 games)	AFL	17,904	29,556 (1)	1,032,213
1960	3,128,296	(78 games)	NFL	40,106	67,325 (1)	3,195,621
	926,156	(56 games)	AFL	16,538	32,183 (1)	958,339
1959	3,140,000	(72 games)		43,617	57,545 (1)	3,197,545
1958	3,006,124	(72 games)		41,752	123,659 (2)	3,129,783
1957	2,836,318	(72 games)		39,393	119,579 (2)	2,955,897
1956	2,551,263	(72 games)		35,434	56,836 (1)	2,608,099
1955	2,521,836	(72 games)		35,026	85,693 (1)	2,607,529
1954	2,190,571	(72 games)		30,425	43,827 (1)	2,234,398
1953	2,164,585	(72 games)		30,064	54,577 (1)	2,219,162
1952	2,052,126	(72 games)		28,502	97,507 (2)	2,149,633
1951	1,913,019	(72 games)		26,570	57,522 (1)	1,970,541
1950	1,977,753	(78 games)		25,356	136,647 (3)	2,114,400
1949	1,391,735	(60 games)		23,196	27,980 (1)	1,419,715
1948	1,525,243	(60 games)		25,421	36,309 (1)	1,561,552
1947	1,837,437	(60 games)		30,624	66,268 (2)	1,903,705
1946	1,732,135	(55 games)		31,493	58,346 (1)	1,790,481
1945	1,270,401	(50 games)		25,408	32,178 (1)	1,302,579
1944	1,019,649	(50 games)		20,393	46,016 (1)	1,065,665
1943	969,128	(40 games)		24,228	71,315 (2)	1,040,443
1942	887,920	(55 games)		16,144	36,006 (1)	923,926
1941	1,108,615	(55 games)		20,157	55,870 (2)	1,164,485
1940	1,063,025	(55 games)		19,328	36,034 (1)	1,099,059
1939	1,071,200	(55 games)		19,476	32,279 (1)	1,103,479
1938	937,197	(55 games)		17,040	48,120 (1)	985,317
1937	963,039	(55 games)		17,510	15,878 (1)	978,917
1936	816,007	(54 games)		15,111	29,545 (1)	845,552
1935	638,178	(53 games)		12,041	15,000 (1)	653,178
1934	492,684	(60 games)		8,211	35,059 (1)	527,743

Record
 *Players' 57-day strike reduced 224-game schedule to 126 games.
**Players' 24-day strike reduced 224-game schedule to 210 games.
***The Week 8 Miami at San Diego game is not included. The game was moved to Arizona due to the San Diego wildfires and tickets were distributed at no charge.

75TH ANNIVERSARY ALL-TIME TEAM

Chosen by a selection committee of media and league personnel in 1994.

Position	Name	Team(s)	Ht.	Wt.	College
OFFENSE					
QB	Sammy Baugh	Washington Redskins (1937-52)	6-2	180	Texas Christian
QB	Otto Graham	Cleveland Browns (1946-55)	6-1	195	Northwestern
QB	Joe Montana	San Francisco 49ers (1979-92), Kansas City Chiefs (1993-94)	6-2	195	Notre Dame
QB	Johnny Unitas	Baltimore Colts (1956-72), San Diego Chargers (1973)	6-1	195	Louisville
RB	Jim Brown	Cleveland Browns (1957-65)	6-2	232	Syracuse
RB	Marion Motley	Cleveland Browns (1946-53), Pittsburgh Steelers (1955)	6-1	238	Nevada-Reno
RB	Bronko Nagurski	Chicago Bears (1930-37, 1943)	6-2	225	Minnesota
RB	Walter Payton	Chicago Bears (1975-87)	5-10	202	Jackson State
RB	Gale Sayers	Chicago Bears (1965-71)	6-0	200	Kansas
RB	O.J. Simpson	Buffalo Bills (1969-77), San Francisco 49ers (1978-79)	6-1	212	Southern California
RB	Steve Van Buren	Philadelphia Eagles (1944-51)	6-1	200	Louisiana State
WR	Lance Alworth	San Diego Chargers (1962-70), Dallas Cowboys (1971-72)	6-0	184	Arkansas
WR	Raymond Berry	Baltimore Colts (1955-67)	6-2	187	Southern Methodist
WR	Don Hutson	Green Bay Packers (1935-45)	6-1	180	Alabama
WR	Jerry Rice	San Francisco 49ers (1985-2000), Oakland Raiders (2001-04), Seattle Seahawks (2004)	6-2	200	Miss. Valley State
TE	Mike Ditka	Chicago Bears (1961-66), Philadelphia Eagles (1967-68), Dallas Cowboys (1969-72)	6-3	225	Pittsburgh
TE	Kellen Winslow	San Diego Chargers (1979-87)	6-5	250	Missouri
T	Roosevelt Brown	New York Giants (1953-65)	6-3	255	Morgan State
T	Forrest Gregg	Green Bay Packers (1956, 1958-70)	6-4	250	Southern Methodist
T	Anthony Muñoz	Cincinnati Bengals (1980-92)	6-6	285	Southern California
G	John Hannah	New England Patriots (1973-85)	6-3	265	Alabama
G	Jim Parker	Baltimore Colts (1957-67)	6-3	273	Ohio State
G	Gene Upshaw	Oakland Raiders (1967-81)	6-5	255	Texas A&I
C	Mel Hein	New York Giants (1931-45)	6-2	225	Washington State
C	Mike Webster	Pittsburgh Steelers (1974-88), Kansas City Chiefs (1989-90)	6-2	250	Wisconsin
DEFENSE					
DE	David (Deacon) Jones	Los Angeles Rams (1961-71), San Diego Chargers (1972-73), Washington Redskins (1974)	6-5	250	Miss. Vocational-South Carolina St.
DE	Gino Marchetti	Dallas Texans (1952), Baltimore Colts (1953-64, 1966)	6-4	245	San Francisco
DE	Reggie White	Philadelphia Eagles (1985-92), Green Bay Packers (1993-1998), Carolina Panthers (2000)	6-5	290	Tennessee
DT	Joe Greene	Pittsburgh Steelers (1969-81)	6-4	260	North Texas State
DT	Bob Lilly	Dallas Cowboys (1961-74)	6-5	260	Texas Christian
DT	Merlin Olsen	Los Angeles Rams (1962-76)	6-5	270	Utah State
LB	Dick Butkus	Chicago Bears (1965-73)	6-3	245	Illinois
LB	Jack Ham	Pittsburgh Steelers (1971-82)	6-1	225	Penn State
LB	Ted Hendricks	Baltimore Colts (1969-73), Green Bay Packers (1974), Oakland/L.A. Raiders (1975-83)	6-7	235	Miami
LB	Jack Lambert	Pittsburgh Steelers (1974-84)	6-4	220	Kent State
LB	Willie Lanier	Kansas City Chiefs (1967-77)	6-1	245	Morgan State
LB	Ray Nitschke	Green Bay Packers (1958-72)	6-3	235	Illinois
LB	Lawrence Taylor	New York Giants (1981-93)	6-3	243	North Carolina
CB	Mel Blount	Pittsburgh Steelers (1970-83)	6-3	205	Southern
CB	Mike Haynes	New England Patriots (1976-82), Los Angeles Raiders (1983-89)	6-2	190	Arizona State
CB	Dick (Night Train) Lane	Los Angeles Rams (1952-53), Chicago Cardinals (1954-59), Detroit Lions (1960-65)	6-2	210	Scottsbluff JC
CB	Rod Woodson	Pittsburgh Steelers (1987-96), San Francisco 49ers (1997), Baltimore Ravens (1998-2001), Oakland Raiders (2002-2003)	6-0	200	Purdue
S	Ken Houston	Houston Oilers (1967-72), Washington Redskins (1973-80)	6-3	198	Prairie View A&M
S	Ronnie Lott	San Francisco 49ers (1981-90), Los Angeles Raiders (1991-92), New York Jets (1993-94)	6-0	200	Southern California
S	Larry Wilson	St. Louis Cardinals (1960-72)	6-0	190	Utah
SPECIAL TEAMS					
P	Ray Guy	Oakland/L.A. Raiders (1973-86)	6-3	190	Southern Mississippi
K	Jan Stenerud	Kansas City Chiefs (1967-79), Green Bay Packers (1980-83), Minnesota Vikings (1984-85)	6-2	190	Montana State
PR	Billy (White Shoes) Johnson	Houston Oilers (1974-80), Atlanta Falcons (1982-87), Washington Redskins (1988)	5-9	170	Widener
KR	Gale Sayers	Chicago Bears (1965-71)	6-0	200	Kansas

75TH ANNIVERSARY ALL-TWO-WAY TEAM
Positions

Quarterback, Defensive Halfback, Punter	Sammy Baugh
Center, Linebacker	Chuck Bednarik
Quarterback, Defensive Halfback, Punter	Earl (Dutch) Clark
Tackle, Defensive Tackle	George Connor
Guard, Defensive Tackle	Danny Fortmann
Center, Defensive Tackle	Mel Hein
Tackle, Defensive Tackle, Punter	Wilbur (Pete) Henry
Back, Defensive Halfback	Bill Hewitt
Fullback, Linebacker, Kicker	Clarke Hinkle
Tackle, Defensive Tackle	Cal Hubbard
End, Defensive Halfback	Don Hutson
Back, Defensive Back	George McAfee
Fullback, Linebacker	Marion Motley
Guard-Tackle, Defensive Tackle	George Musso
Fullback, Linebacker	Bronko Nagurski
Halfback, Defensive Halfback	Ernie Nevers
End, Defensive Back	Pete Pihos
Tackle, Defensive Tackle	Joe Stydahar
Running Back, Defensive Back	Steve Van Buren

50TH ANNIVERSARY TEAM
Chosen by the Hall of Fame Selection Committee in 1969.
Offense

Split End	Don Hutson
Tight End	John Mackey
Tackle	Cal Hubbard
Guard	Jerry Kramer
Center	Chuck Bednarik
Flanker	Elroy Hirsch
Quarterback	Johnny Unitas
Halfback	Jim Thorpe
Halfback	Gale Sayers
Fullback	Jim Brown
Kicker	Lou Groza

Defense

End	Gino Marchetti
Tackle	Leo Nomellini
Linebacker	Ray Nitschke
Cornerback	Dick (Night Train) Lane
Safety	Emlen Tunnell

SUPER BOWL SILVER ANNIVERSARY TEAM
Chosen by the fans in 1990 prior to Super Bowl XXV.

Head Coach	Vince Lombardi

Offense

Quarterback	Joe Montana
Running Back	Franco Harris
Running Back	Larry Csonka
Wide Receiver	Lynn Swann
Wide Receiver	Jerry Rice
Tight End	Dave Casper
Tackle	Art Shell
Tackle	Forrest Gregg
Guard	Gene Upshaw
Guard	Jerry Kramer
Center	Mike Webster

Defense

Defensive End	L.C. Greenwood
Defensive End	Ed (Too Tall) Jones
Defensive Tackle	Joe Greene
Defensive Tackle	Randy White
Inside Linebacker	Jack Lambert
Inside Linebacker	Mike Singletary
Outside Linebacker	Jack Ham
Outside Linebacker	Ted Hendricks
Cornerback	Ronnie Lott
Cornerback	Mel Blount
Safety	Donnie Shell
Safety	Willie Wood

Special Teams

Punter	Ray Guy
Kicker	Jan Stenerud
Kick Returner	John Taylor

All-Decade teams chosen by the Hall of Fame Selection Committee members.

1920s ALL-DECADE TEAM

End	Guy Chamberlin
End	Lavern Dilweg
End	George Halas
Tackle	Ed Healey
Tackle	Wilbur (Pete) Henry
Tackle	Cal Hubbard
Tackle	Steve Owen
Guard	Hunk Anderson
Guard	Walt Kiesling
Guard	Mike Michalske
Center	George Trafton
Quarterback	Jimmy Conzelman
Quarterback	John (Paddy) Driscoll
Halfback	Harold (Red) Grange
Halfback	Joe Guyon
Halfback	Earl (Curly) Lambeau
Halfback	Jim Thorpe
Fullback	Ernie Nevers

1930s ALL-DECADE TEAM

End	Bill Hewitt
End	Don Hutson
End	Wayne Millner
End	Gaynell Tinsley
Tackle	George Christensen
Tackle	Frank Cope
Tackle	Glen (Turk) Edwards
Tackle	Bill Lee
Tackle	Joe Stydahar
Guard	Grover (Ox) Emerson
Guard	Dan Fortmann
Guard	Charles (Buckets) Goldenberg
Guard	Russ Letlow
Center	Mel Hein
Center	George Svendsen
Quarterback	Earl (Dutch) Clark
Quarterback	Arnie Herber
Quarterback	Cecil Isbell
Halfback	Cliff Battles
Halfback	Johnny (Blood) McNally
Halfback	Beattie Feathers
Halfback	Alphonse (Tuffy) Leemans
Halfback	Ken Strong
Fullback	Clarke Hinkle
Fullback	Bronko Nagurski

1940s ALL-DECADE TEAM

End	Jim Benton
End	Jack Ferrante
End	Ken Kavanaugh
End	Dante Lavelli
End	Pete Pihos
End	Mac Speedie
End	Ed Sprinkle
Tackle	Al Blozis
Tackle	George Connor
Tackle	Frank (Bucko) Kilroy
Tackle	Buford (Baby) Ray
Tackle	Vic Sears
Tackle	Al Wistert
Guard	Bruno Banducci
Guard	Bill Edwards
Guard	Garrard (Buster) Ramsey
Guard	Bill Willis
Guard	Len Younce
Center	Charley Brock
Center	Clyde (Bulldog) Turner
Center	Alex Wojciechowicz
Quarterback	Sammy Baugh
Quarterback	Sid Luckman
Quarterback	Bob Waterfield
Halfback	Tony Canadeo
Halfback	Bill Dudley
Halfback	George McAfee
Halfback	Charley Trippi
Halfback	Steve Van Buren
Halfback	Byron (Whizzer) White
Fullback	Pat Harder
Fullback	Marion Motley
Fullback	Bill Osmanski

1950s ALL-DECADE TEAM

Offense

End	Raymond Berry
End	Tom Fears
End	Bobby Walston
Halfback-End	Elroy (Crazylegs) Hirsch
Tackle	Roosevelt Brown
Tackle	Bob St. Clair
Guard	Dick Barwegan
Guard	Jim Parker
Guard	Dick Stanfel
Center	Chuck Bednarik
Quarterback	Otto Graham
Quarterback	Bobby Layne
Quarterback	Norm Van Brocklin
Halfback	Frank Gifford
Halfback	Ollie Matson
Halfback	Hugh McElhenny
Halfback	Lenny Moore
Fullback	Alan Ameche
Fullback	Joe Perry
Kicker	Lou Groza

Defense

End	Len Ford
End	Gino Marchetti
Tackle	Art Donovan
Tackle	Leo Nomellini
Tackle	Ernie Stautner
Linebacker	Joe Fortunato
Linebacker	Bill George
Linebacker	Sam Huff
Linebacker	Joe Schmidt
Halfback	Jack Butler
Halfback	Dick (Night Train) Lane
Safety	Jack Christiansen
Safety	Yale Lary
Safety	Emlen Tunnell

1960s ALL-DECADE TEAM

Offense

Split End	Del Shofner
Split End	Charley Taylor
Flanker	Gary Collins
Flanker	Boyd Dowler
Tight End	John Mackey
Tackle	Bob Brown
Tackle	Forrest Gregg
Tackle	Ralph Neely
Guard	Gene Hickerson
Guard	Jerry Kramer
Guard	Howard Mudd
Center	Jim Ringo
Quarterback	Sonny Jurgensen
Quarterback	Bart Starr
Quarterback	Johnny Unitas
Halfback	John David Crow
Halfback	Paul Hornung
Halfback	Leroy Kelly
Halfback	Gale Sayers
Fullback	Jim Brown
Fullback	Jim Taylor
Kicker	Jim Bakken

Defense

End	Doug Atkins
End	Willie Davis
End	David (Deacon) Jones
Tackle	Alex Karras
Tackle	Bob Lilly
Tackle	Merlin Olsen
Linebacker	Dick Butkus
Linebacker	Larry Morris
Linebacker	Ray Nitschke
Linebacker	Tommy Nobis
Linebacker	Dave Robinson
Cornerback	Herb Adderley
Cornerback	Lem Barney
Cornerback	Bobby Boyd
Safety	Eddie Meador
Safety	Larry Wilson
Safety	Willie Wood
Punter	Don Chandler

1970s ALL-DECADE TEAM
Offense
Wide Receiver	Harold Carmichael
Wide Receiver	Drew Pearson
Wide Receiver	Lynn Swann
Wide Receiver	Paul Warfield
Tight End	Dave Casper
Tight End	Charlie Sanders
Tackle	Dan Dierdorf
Tackle	Art Shell
Tackle	Rayfield Wright
Tackle	Ron Yary
Guard	Joe DeLamielleure
Guard	John Hannah
Guard	Larry Little
Guard	Gene Upshaw
Center	Jim Langer
Center	Mike Webster
Quarterback	Terry Bradshaw
Quarterback	Ken Stabler
Quarterback	Roger Staubach
Running Back	Earl Campbell
Running Back	Franco Harris
Running Back	Walter Payton
Running Back	O.J. Simpson
Kicker	Garo Yepremian

Defense
End	Carl Eller
End	L.C. Greenwood
End	Harvey Martin
End	Jack Youngblood
Tackle	Joe Greene
Tackle	Bob Lilly
Tackle	Merlin Olsen
Tackle	Alan Page
Linebacker	Bobby Bell
Linebacker	Robert Brazile
Linebacker	Dick Butkus
Linebacker	Jack Ham
Linebacker	Ted Hendricks
Linebacker	Jack Lambert
Cornerback	Willie Brown
Cornerback	Jimmy Johnson
Cornerback	Roger Wehrli
Cornerback	Louis Wright
Safety	Dick Anderson
Safety	Cliff Harris
Safety	Ken Houston
Safety	Larry Wilson
Punter	Ray Guy

1980s ALL-DECADE TEAM
Offense
Wide Receiver	Jerry Rice
Wide Receiver	Steve Largent
Wide Receiver	James Lofton
Wide Receiver	Art Monk
Tight End	Kellen Winslow
Tight End	Ozzie Newsome
Tackle	Anthony Munoz
Tackle	Jim Covert
Tackle	Gary Zimmerman
Tackle	Joe Jacoby
Guard	John Hannah
Guard	Russ Grimm
Guard	Bill Fralic
Guard	Mike Munchak
Center	Dwight Stephenson
Center	Mike Webster
Quarterback	Joe Montana
Quarterback	Dan Fouts
Running Back	Walter Payton
Running Back	Eric Dickerson
Running Back	Roger Craig
Running Back	John Riggins

Defense
End	Reggie White
End	Howie Long
End	Lee Roy Selmon
End	Bruce Smith
Tackle	Randy White
Tackle	Dan Hampton
Tackle	Keith Millard
Tackle	Dave Butz
Linebacker	Mike Singletary
Linebacker	Lawrence Taylor
Linebacker	Ted Hendricks
Linebacker	Jack Lambert
Linebacker	Andre Tippett
Linebacker	John Anderson
Linebacker	Carl Banks
Cornerback	Mike Haynes
Cornerback	Mel Blount
Cornerback	Frank Minnifield
Cornerback	Lester Hayes
Safety	Ronnie Lott
Safety	Kenny Easley
Safety	Deron Cherry
Safety	Joey Browner
Safety	Nolan Cromwell

Specialists
Punter	Sean Landeta
Punter	Reggie Roby
Kicker	Morten Andersen
Kicker	Gary Anderson
Kicker	Eddie Murray
Punt Returner	Billy (White Shoes) Johnson
Punt Returner	John Taylor
Kick Returner	Mike Nelms
Kick Returner	Rick Upchurch
Coach	Bill Walsh
Coach	Chuck Noll

1990s ALL-DECADE TEAM
Offense
Wide Receiver	Cris Carter
Wide Receiver	Jerry Rice
Wide Receiver	Tim Brown
Wide Receiver	Michael Irvin
Tight End	Shannon Sharpe
Tight End	Ben Coates
Tackle	William Roaf
Tackle	Gary Zimmerman
Tackle	Tony Boselli
Tackle	Richmond Webb
Guard	Bruce Matthews
Guard	Randall McDaniel
Guard	Larry Allen
Guard	Steve Wisniewski
Center	Dermontti Dawson
Center	Mark Stepnoski
Quarterback	John Elway
Quarterback	Brett Favre
Running Back	Barry Sanders
Running Back	Emmitt Smith
Running Back	Terrell Davis
Running Back	Thurman Thomas

Defense
End	Bruce Smith
End	Reggie White
End	Chris Doleman
End	Neil Smith
Tackle	Cortez Kennedy
Tackle	John Randle
Tackle	Warren Sapp
Tackle	Bryant Young
Linebacker	Kevin Greene
Linebacker	Junior Seau
Linebacker	Derrick Thomas
Linebacker	Cornelius Bennett
Linebacker	Hardy Nickerson
Linebacker	Levon Kirkland
Cornerback	Deion Sanders
Cornerback	Rod Woodson
Cornerback	Darrell Green
Cornerback	Aeneas Williams
Safety	Steve Atwater
Safety	LeRoy Butler
Safety	Carnell Lake
Safety	Ronnie Lott

Specialists
Punter	Darren Bennett
Punter	Sean Landeta
Kicker	Morten Andersen
Kicker	Gary Anderson
Punt Returner	Deion Sanders
Punt Returner	Mel Gray
Kick Returner	Michael Bates
Kick Returner	Mel Gray
Coach	Bill Parcells
Coach	Marv Levy

ALL-TIME AFL TEAM

Chosen by 1969 AFL Hall of Fame Selection Committee members.

Offense

Flanker	Lance Alworth
End	Don Maynard
Tight End	Fred Arbanas
Tackle	Ron Mix
Tackle	Jim Tyrer
Guard	Ed Budde
Guard	Billy Shaw
Center	Jim Otto
Quarterback	Joe Namath
Running Back	Clem Daniels
Running Back	Paul Lowe

Defense

End	Jerry Mays
End	Gerry Philbin
Tackle	Houston Antwine
Tackle	Tom Sestak
Linebacker	Bobby Bell
Linebacker	George Webster
Linebacker	Nick Buoniconti
Cornerback	Willie Brown
Cornerback	Dave Grayson
Safety	Johnny Robinson
Safety	George Saimes

Special Teams

Kicker	George Blanda
Punter	Jerrel Wilson

ALL-TIME NFL TEAM

Chosen by members of the Hall of Fame Selection Committee in 2000 for the book NFL's Greatest.

Offense

Wide Receiver	Don Hutson
Wide Receiver	Jerry Rice
Tight End	John Mackey
Tackle	Roosevelt Brown
Tackle	Anthony Muñoz
Guard	John Hannah
Guard	Jim Parker
Center	Mike Webster
Quarterback	Johnny Unitas
Running Back	Jim Brown
Running Back	Walter Payton

Defense

End	Deacon Jones
End	Reggie White
Tackle	Joe Greene
Tackle	Bob Lilly
Middle Linebacker	Dick Butkus
Outside Linebacker	Jack Ham
Outside Linebacker	Lawrence Taylor
Cornerback	Mel Blount
Cornerback	Dick (Night Train) Lane
Safety	Ronnie Lott
Safety	Larry Wilson

Special Teams

Kicker	Jan Stenerud
Punter	Ray Guy
Kick Returner	Gale Sayers
Punt Returner	Deion Sanders
Special Teams	Steve Tasker

AFL-NFL 1960-1984 ALL-STAR TEAM

Chosen by the Hall of Fame Selection Committee in 1985.

Offense

Quarterback	Johnny Unitas
Running Back	Jim Brown
Running Back	O.J. Simpson
Wide Receiver	Lance Alworth
Wide Receiver	Raymond Berry
Tight End	Kellen Winslow
Tackle	Forrest Gregg
Tackle	Ron Mix
Guard	Jim Parker
Guard	John Hannah
Center	Jim Otto

Defense

End	Gino Marchetti
End	Willie Davis
Tackle	Bob Lilly
Tackle	Merlin Olsen
Linebacker	Dick Butkus
Linebacker	Jack Lambert
Linebacker	Ray Nitschke
Cornerback	Willie Brown
Cornerback	Dick (Night Train) Lane
Safety	Larry Wilson
Safety	Yale Lary

Special Teams

Punter	Ray Guy
Kicker	Jan Stenerud
Kick Returner	Gale Sayers
Kick Returner	Rick Upchurch
Coach	Don Shula
Coach	Vince Lombardi

Records

.Compiled by Elias Sports Bureau

The following records reflect all available official information on the National Football League from its formation in 1920 to date. Also included are all applicable records from the American Football League, 1960-69.

Individuals eligible for Rookie records are players who were in their first season of professional football and had not been on the roster of another professional football team, including teams in other leagues, for any regular-season or postseason games in a previous season. Eligible players, therefore, include those who were under contract to a National Football League club for a previous season but were terminated prior to their club's first regular-season game and not re-signed, or who were placed on Reserve/Injured (or another category of the Reserve List) prior to their club's first regular-season game and were not activated during the rest of the regular season or postseason.

INDIVIDUAL RECORDS

SERVICE

Most Seasons

26   George Blanda, Chi. Bears, 1949, 1950-58; Baltimore, 1950; Houston, 1960-66; Oakland, 1967-1975

24   Morten Andersen, New Orleans, 1982-1994; Atlanta, 1995-2000; N.Y. Giants, 2001; Kansas City, 2002-03; Minnesota, 2004; Atlanta, 2006

23   Gary Anderson, Pittsburgh, 1982-1994; Philadelphia, 1995-96; San Francisco, 1997; Minnesota, 1998-2002; Tennessee, 2003-04

Most Seasons, One Club

20   Jackie Slater, L.A. Rams, 1976-1994; St. Louis, 1995
Darrell Green, Washington, 1983-2002

19   Jim Marshall, Minnesota, 1961-1979
Bruce Matthews, Houston, 1983-1996; Tennessee, 1997-2001

18   Jim Hart, St. Louis, 1966-1983
Jeff Van Note, Atlanta, 1969-1986
Pat Leahy, N.Y. Jets, 1974-1991

Most Games Played, Career

368   Morten Andersen, New Orleans, 1982-1994; Atlanta, 1995-2000; N.Y. Giants, 2001; Kansas City, 2002-03; Minnesota, 2004; Atlanta, 2006

353   Gary Anderson, Pittsburgh, 1982-1994; Philadelphia, 1995-96; San Francisco, 1997; Minnesota, 1998-2002; Tennessee, 2003-04

340   George Blanda, Chi. Bears, 1949, 1950-58; Baltimore, 1950; Houston, 1960-66; Oakland, 1967-1975

Most Consecutive Games Played, Career

304   Jeff Feagles, New England, 1988-89; Philadelphia, 1990-93; Arizona, 1994-97; Seattle, 1998-2002; N.Y. Giants, 2003-06 (current)

282   Jim Marshall, Cleveland, 1960; Minnesota, 1961-1979

248   Morten Andersen, New Orleans, 1987-1994; Atlanta, 1995-2000; N.Y. Giants, 2001; Kansas City, 2002

SCORING

Most Seasons Leading League

5   Don Hutson, Green Bay, 1940-44
Gino Cappelletti, Boston, 1961, 1963-66

3   Earl (Dutch) Clark, Portsmouth, 1932; Detroit, 1935-36
Pat Harder, Chi. Cardinals, 1947-49
Paul Hornung, Green Bay, 1959-1961

2   Jack Manders, Chi. Bears, 1934, 1937
Gordy Soltau, San Francisco, 1952-53
Doak Walker, Detroit, 1950, 1955
Gene Mingo, Denver, 1960, 1962
Jim Turner, N.Y. Jets, 1968-69

Fred Cox, Minnesota, 1969-1970
Chester Marcol, Green Bay, 1972, 1974
John Smith, New England, 1979-1980
Marshall Faulk, St. Louis, 2000-01

Most Consecutive Seasons Leading League

5   Don Hutson, Green Bay, 1940-44

4   Gino Cappelletti, Boston, 1963-66

3   Pat Harder, Chi. Cardinals, 1947-49
Paul Hornung, Green Bay, 1959-1961

POINTS

Most Points, Career

2,445   Morten Andersen, New Orleans, 1982-1994; Atlanta, 1995-2000; N.Y. Giants, 2001; Kansas City, 2002-03; Minnesota, 2004; Atlanta, 2006 (825-pat, 540-fg)

2,434   Gary Anderson, Pittsburgh, 1982-1994; Philadelphia, 1995-96; San Francisco, 1997; Minnesota, 1998-2002; Tennessee, 2003-04 (820-pat, 538-fg)

2,002   George Blanda, Chi. Bears, 1949, 1950-58; Baltimore, 1950; Houston, 1960-66; Oakland, 1967-1975 (9-td, 943-pat, 335-fg)

Most Points, Season

186   LaDainian Tomlinson, San Diego, 2006 (31-td)

176   Paul Hornung, Green Bay, 1960 (15-td, 41-pat, 15-fg)

168   Shaun Alexander, Seattle, 2005 (28-td)

Most Points, No Touchdowns, Season

164   Gary Anderson, Minnesota, 1998 (59-pat, 35-fg)

163   Jeff Wilkins, St. Louis, 2003 (46-pat, 39-fg)

161   Mark Moseley, Washington, 1983 (62-pat, 33-fg)

Most Seasons, 100 or More Points

14   Gary Anderson, Pittsburgh, 1983-85, 1988, 1991-94; Philadelphia 1996; San Francisco, 1997; Minnesota, 1998-2000; Tennessee, 2003
Morten Andersen, New Orleans, 1985-89, 1991-94; Atlanta, 1995, 1997-98; Kansas City, 2002-03
Jason Elam, Denver, 1993-2006

11   Nick Lowery, Kansas City, 1981, 1983-86, 1988-1993
Adam Vinatieri, New England, 1996-2005; Indianapolis, 2006

10   John Carney, San Diego, 1992-94, 1996, 1999; New Orleans, 2001-04, 2006
Matt Stover, Cleveland, 1994-95; Baltimiore, 1997, 1999-2001, 2003-06

Most Points, Rookie, Season

144   Kevin Butler, Chicago, 1985 (51-pat, 31-fg)

132   Gale Sayers, Chicago, 1965 (22-td)

128   Doak Walker, Detroit, 1950 (11-td, 38-pat, 8-fg)
Chester Marcol, Green Bay, 1972 (29-pat, 33-fg)

Most Points, Game

40   Ernie Nevers, Chi. Cardinals vs. Chi. Bears, Nov. 28, 1929 (6-td, 4-pat)

36   Dub Jones, Cleveland vs. Chi. Bears, Nov. 25, 1951 (6-td)
Gale Sayers, Chicago vs. San Francisco, Dec. 12, 1965 (6-td)

33   Paul Hornung, Green Bay vs. Baltimore, Oct. 8, 1961 (4-td, 6-pat, 1-fg)

Most Consecutive Games Scoring

346   Morten Andersen, New Orleans, 1983-1994; Atlanta, 1995-2000; N.Y. Giants, 2001; Kansas City, 2002-03; Minnesota, 2004; Atlanta, 2006 (current)

220   Jason Elam, Denver, 1993-2006 (current)

186   Jim Breech, Oakland, 1979; Cincinnati, 1980-1992

TOUCHDOWNS

Most Seasons Leading League

8   Don Hutson, Green Bay, 1935-38, 1941-44

3   Jim Brown, Cleveland, 1958-59, 1963
     Lance Alworth, San Diego, 1964-66
     Emmitt Smith, Dallas, 1992, 1994-95
2   By many players

Most Consecutive Seasons Leading League
4   Don Hutson, Green Bay, 1935-38, 1941-44
3   Lance Alworth, San Diego, 1964-66
2   By many players

Most Touchdowns, Career
208   Jerry Rice, San Francisco, 1985-2000;
      Oakland, 2001-04; Seattle, 2004
      (10-r, 197-p, 1-ret)
175   Emmitt Smith, Dallas, 1990-2002; Arizona, 2003-04
      (164-r, 11-p)
145   Marcus Allen, L.A. Raiders, 1982-1992; Kansas City,
      1993-97 (123-r, 21-p, 1-ret)

Most Touchdowns, Season
31   LaDainian Tomlinson, San Diego, 2006 (28-r, 3-p)
28   Shaun Alexander, Seattle, 2005 (27-r, 1-p)
27   Priest Holmes, Kansas City, 2003 (27-r)

Most Touchdowns, Rookie, Season
22   Gale Sayers, Chicago, 1965 (14-r, 6-p, 2-ret)
20   Eric Dickerson, L.A. Rams, 1983 (18-r, 2-p)
17   Randy Moss, Minnesota, 1998 (17-p)
     Fred Taylor, Jacksonville, 1998 (14-r, 3-p)
     Edgerrin James, Indianapolis, 1999 (13-r, 4-p)
     Clinton Portis, Denver, 2002 (15-r, 2-p)

Most Touchdowns, Game
6   Ernie Nevers, Chi. Cardinals vs. Chi. Bears,
    Nov. 28, 1929 (6-r)
    Dub Jones, Cleveland vs. Chi. Bears, Nov. 25, 1951
    (4-r, 2-p)
    Gale Sayers, Chicago vs. San Francisco, Dec. 12, 1965
    (4-r, 1-p, 1-ret)
5   Jimmy Conzelman, Rhode Island vs. Evansville,
    Oct. 15, 1922 (5-r)
    Bob Shaw, Chi. Cardinals vs. Baltimore, Oct. 2, 1950
    (5-p)
    Jim Brown, Cleveland vs. Baltimore, Nov. 1, 1959 (5-r)
    Abner Haynes, Dall. Texans vs. Oakland,
    Nov. 26, 1961 (4-r, 1-p)
    Billy Cannon, Houston vs. N.Y. Titans, Dec. 10, 1961
    (3-r, 2-p)
    Cookie Gilchrist, Buffalo vs. N.Y. Jets, Dec. 8, 1963 (5-r)
    Paul Hornung, Green Bay vs. Baltimore,
    Dec. 12, 1965 (3-r, 2-p)
    Kellen Winslow, San Diego vs. Oakland,
    Nov. 22, 1981 (5-p)
    Jerry Rice, San Francisco vs. Atlanta, Oct. 14, 1990
    (5-p)
    James Stewart, Jacksonville vs. Philadelphia,
    Oct. 12, 1997 (5-r)
    Shaun Alexander, Seattle vs. Minnesota,
    Sept. 29, 2002 (4-r, 1-p)
    Clinton Portis, Denver vs. Kansas City, Dec. 7, 2003
    (5-r)
4   By many players. Last time: Steven Jackson,
    St. Louis vs. Minnesota, Dec. 31, 2006

Most Consecutive Games Scoring Touchdowns
18   Lenny Moore, Baltimore, 1963-65
     LaDainian Tomlinson, San Diego, 2004-05
14   O.J. Simpson, Buffalo, 1975
13   John Riggins, Washington, 1982-83
     George Rogers, Washington, 1985-86
     Jerry Rice, San Francisco, 1986-87

POINTS AFTER TOUCHDOWN
Most Seasons Leading League
8   George Blanda, Chi. Bears, 1956; Houston,
    1961-62; Oakland, 1967-69, 1972, 1974

4   Bob Waterfield, Cleveland, 1945; Los Angeles, 1946,
    1950, 1952
3   Earl (Dutch) Clark, Portsmouth, 1932; Detroit,
    1935-36 Jack Manders, Chi. Bears, 1933-35
    Don Hutson, Green Bay, 1941-42, 1945

Most (Kicking) Points After Touchdown Attempted, Career
959   George Blanda, Chi. Bears, 1949, 1950-58; Baltimore,
     1950; Houston, 1960-66; Oakland, 1967-1975
835   Morten Andersen, New Orleans, 1982-1994;
     Atlanta, 1995-2000; N.Y. Giants, 2001;
     Kansas City, 2002-03; Minnesota, 2004;
     Atlanta, 2006
827   Gary Anderson, Pittsburgh, 1982-1994; Philadelphia
     1995-96; San Francisco, 1997; Minnesota,
     1998-2002; Tennessee, 2003-04

Most (Kicking) Points After Touchdown Attempted, Season
70   Uwe von Schamann, Miami, 1984
65   George Blanda, Houston, 1961
64   Jeff Wilkins, St. Louis, 1999

Most (Kicking) Points After Touchdown Attempted, Game
10   Charlie Gogolak, Washington vs. N.Y. Giants,
     Nov. 27, 1966
9   Pat Harder, Chi. Cardinals vs. N.Y. Giants,
    Oct. 17, 1948; vs. N.Y. Bulldogs, Nov. 13, 1949
    Bob Waterfield, Los Angeles vs. Baltimore,
    Oct. 22, 1950
    Bob Thomas, Chicago vs. Green Bay, Dec. 7, 1980
8   By many players

Most (One-Point) Points After Touchdown, Career
943   George Blanda, Chi. Bears, 1949, 1950-58; Baltimore;
     1950; Houston, 1960-66; Oakland, 1967-1975
825   Morten Andersen, New Orleans, 1982-1994;
     Atlanta, 1995-2000; N.Y. Giants, 2001;
     Kansas City, 2002-03; Minnesota, 2004,
     Atlanta, 2006
820   Gary Anderson, Pittsburgh, 1982-1994; Philadelphia
     1995-96; San Francisco, 1997; Minnesota,
     1998-2002; Tennessee, 2003-04

Most (One-Point) Points After Touchdown, Season
66   Uwe von Schamann, Miami, 1984
64   George Blanda, Houston, 1961
     Jeff Wilkins, St. Louis, 1999
62   Mark Moseley, Washington, 1983

Most (One-Point) Points After Touchdown, Game
9   Pat Harder, Chi. Cardinals vs. N.Y. Giants,
    Oct. 17, 1948
    Bob Waterfield, Los Angeles vs. Baltimore,
    Oct. 22, 1950
    Charlie Gogolak, Washington vs. N.Y. Giants,
    Nov. 27, 1966
8   By many players

Most Consecutive (Kicking) Points After Touchdown
371   Jason Elam, Denver, 1993-2002
346   Jeff Wilkins, St. Louis, 1999-2006 (current)
322   Matt Stover, Baltimore, 1996-2006 (current)

Highest (Kicking) Points After Touchdown Percentage, Career
(200 points after touchdown)
100.000   Rian Lindell, Seattle, 2000-02; Buffalo, 2003-06
        (224-224)
99.475   Jason Elam, Denver, 1993-2006 (568-571)
99.472   Mike Vanderjagt, Indianapolis, 1998-2005;
       Dallas, 2006 (377-379)

Most (Kicking) Points After Touchdown, No Misses, Season
64   Jeff Wilkins, St. Louis, 1999
59   Gary Anderson, Minnesota, 1998
58   Jason Elam, Denver, 1998
     Jeff Wilkins, St. Louis, 2001
     Nate Kaeding, San Diego, 2006

Most (Kicking) Points After Touchdown, No Misses, Game
- 9 Pat Harder, Chi. Cardinals vs. N.Y. Giants,
  Oct. 17, 1948
  Bob Waterfield, Los Angeles vs. Baltimore,
  Oct. 22, 1950
- 8 By many players

Most Two-Point Conversions, Career
Two-point conversions include AFL (1960-69) and NFL (since 1994).
- 7 Marshall Faulk, Indianapolis, 1994-98; St. Louis,
  1999-2005
- 6 Terance Mathis, Atlanta, 1994-2001; Pittsburgh, 2002
- 5 Cris Carter, Minnesota, 1994-2001; Miami, 2002
  Rob Moore, N.Y. Jets, 1994; Arizona, 1995-99
  Willie Jackson, Jacksonville, 1995-97; Cincinnati,
  1998-99; New Orleans, 2000-01; Washington,
  2002
  Keenan McCardell, Cleveland, 1994-95; Jacksonville,
  1996-2001; Tampa Bay, 2002-03; San Diego,
  2004-06
  Marvin Harrison, Indianapolis, 1996-2006
  Marcus Pollard, Indianapolis, 1995-2004; Detroit,
  2005-06
  Todd Heap, Baltimore, 2001-06

Most Two-Point Conversions, Season
- 4 Todd Heap, Baltimore, 2003
- 3 Gino Cappelletti, Boston, 1960
  Richie Lucas, Buffalo, 1961
  Ronnie Harmon, San Diego, 1994
  Haywood Jeffires, Houston, 1994
  Tom Tupa, Cleveland, 1994
  Terance Mathis, Atlanta, 1995
  Lamar Smith, Seattle, 1996
  Cris Carter, Minnesota, 1997
  Terrell Davis, Denver, 1997
  James Stewart, Detroit, 2000
  Hines Ward, Pittsburgh, 2002
  Brian Finneran, Atlanta, 2005
- 2 By many players

Most Two-Point Conversions, Game
- 2 Brett Perriman, Detroit vs. Green Bay, Nov. 6, 1994
  Michael Jackson, Baltimore vs. New England,
  Oct. 6, 1996
  Terrell Davis, Denver vs. Atlanta, Sept. 28, 1997
  Charles Johnson, Pittsburgh vs. Tennessee,
  Nov. 1, 1998
  Marshall Faulk, St. Louis vs. Atlanta, Oct. 15, 2000
  Todd Heap, Baltimore vs. Cincinnati, Oct. 19, 2003

FIELD GOALS
Most Seasons Leading League
- 5 Lou Groza, Cleveland, 1950, 1952-54, 1957
- 4 Jack Manders, Chi. Bears, 1933-34, 1936-37
  Ward Cuff, N.Y. Giants, 1938-39, 1943; Green Bay,
  1947
  Mark Moseley, Washington, 1976-77, 1979, 1982
- 3 Bob Waterfield, Los Angeles, 1947, 1949, 1951
  Gino Cappelletti, Boston, 1961, 1963-64
  Fred Cox, Minnesota, 1965, 1969-1970
  Jan Stenerud, Kansas City, 1967, 1970, 1975

Most Consecutive Seasons Leading League
- 3 Lou Groza, Cleveland, 1952-54
- 2 Jack Manders, Chi. Bears, 1933-34
  Armand Niccolai, Pittsburgh, 1935-36
  Jack Manders, Chi. Bears, 1936-37
  Ward Cuff, N.Y. Giants, 1938-39
  Clark Hinkle, Green Bay, 1940-41
  Cliff Patton, Philadelphia, 1948-49
  Gino Cappelletti, Boston, 1963-64
  Jim Turner, N.Y. Jets, 1968-69
  Fred Cox, Minnesota, 1969-1970

     Mark Moseley, Washington, 1976-77
     Chip Lohmiller, Washington, 1991-92
     Pete Stoyanovich, Miami, 1991-92

Most Field Goals Attempted, Career
- 681 Morten Andersen, New Orleans, 1982-1994;
  Atlanta, 1995-2000; N.Y. Giants, 2001;
  Kansas City, 2002-03; Minnesota, 2004;
  Atlanta, 2006
- 672 Gary Anderson, Pittsburgh, 1982-1994; Philadelphia
  1995-96; San Francisco, 1997; Minnesota,
  1998-2002; Tennessee, 2003-04
- 637 George Blanda, Chi. Bears, 1949, 1950-58; Baltimore,
  1950; Houston, 1960-66; Oakland, 1967-1975

Most Field Goals Attempted, Season
- 49 Bruce Gossett, Los Angeles, 1966
  Curt Knight, Washington, 1971
- 48 Chester Marcol, Green Bay, 1972
- 47 Jim Turner, N.Y. Jets, 1969
  David Ray, Los Angeles, 1973
  Mark Moseley, Washington, 1983

Most Field Goals Attempted, Game
- 9 Jim Bakken, St. Louis vs. Pittsburgh, Sept. 24, 1967
- 8 Lou Michaels, Pittsburgh vs. St. Louis, Dec. 2, 1962
  Garo Yepremian, Detroit vs. Minnesota, Nov. 13, 1966
  Jim Turner, N.Y. Jets vs. Buffalo, Nov. 3, 1968
  Billy Cundiff, Dallas vs. N.Y. Giants, Sept. 15, 2003 (OT)
- 7 By many players

Most Field Goals, Career
- 540 Morten Andersen, New Orleans, 1982-1994;
  Atlanta, 1995-2000; N.Y. Giants, 2001;
  Kansas City, 2002-03; Minnesota, 2004;
  Atlanta, 2006
- 538 Gary Anderson, Pittsburgh, 1982-1994; Philadelphia,
  1995-96; San Francisco, 1997; Minnesota,
  1998-2002; Tennessee, 2003-04
- 413 John Carney, Tampa Bay, 1988-89; L.A. Rams,
  1990; San Diego, 1990-2000; New Orleans,
  2001-06

Most Field Goals, Season
- 40 Neil Rackers, Arizona, 2005
- 39 Olindo Mare, Miami, 1999
  Jeff Wilkins, St. Louis, 2003
- 37 John Kasay, Carolina, 1996
  Mike Vanderjagt, Indianapolis, 2003

Most Field Goals, Rookie, Season
- 35 Ali Haji-Sheikh, N.Y. Giants, 1983
- 34 Richie Cunningham, Dallas, 1997
- 33 Chester Marcol, Green Bay, 1972

Most Field Goals, Game
- 7 Jim Bakken, St. Louis vs. Pittsburgh, Sept. 24, 1967
  Rich Karlis, Minnesota vs. L.A. Rams, Nov. 5, 1989
  (OT)
  Chris Boniol, Dallas vs. Green Bay, Nov. 18, 1996
  Billy Cundiff, Dallas vs. N.Y. Giants, Sept. 15, 2003 (OT)
- 6 Gino Cappelletti, Boston vs. Denver, Oct. 4, 1964
  Garo Yepremian, Detroit vs. Minnesota, Nov. 13, 1966
  Jim Turner, N.Y. Jets vs. Buffalo, Nov. 3, 1968
  Tom Dempsey, Philadelphia vs. Houston,
  Nov. 12, 1972
  Bobby Howfield, N.Y. Jets vs. New Orleans,
  Dec. 3, 1972
  Jim Bakken, St. Louis vs. Atlanta, Dec. 9, 1973
  Joe Danelo, N.Y. Giants vs. Seattle, Oct. 18, 1981
  Ray Wersching, San Francisco vs. New Orleans,
  Oct. 16, 1983
  Gary Anderson, Pittsburgh vs. Denver, Oct. 23, 1988
  John Carney, San Diego vs. Seattle, Sept. 5, 1993
  John Carney, San Diego vs. Houston, Sept. 19, 1993
  Doug Pelfrey, Cincinnati vs. Seattle, Nov. 6, 1994 (OT)
  Norm Johnson, Atlanta vs. New Orleans, Nov. 13, 1994

Jeff Wilkins, San Francisco vs. Atlanta, Sept. 29, 1996
Steve Christie, Buffalo vs. N.Y. Jets, Oct. 20, 1996
Greg Davis, San Diego vs. Oakland, Oct. 5, 1997
Gary Anderson, Minnesota vs. Baltimore,
    Dec. 13, 1998
Olindo Mare, Miami vs. New England, Oct. 17, 1999
Jason Hanson, Detroit vs. Minnesota, Oct. 17, 1999
Jeff Reed, Pittsburgh vs. Jacksonville, Dec. 1, 2002
John Kasay, Carolina vs. New Orleans, Dec. 5, 2004
Neil Rackers, Arizona vs. San Francisco,
    Oct. 2, 2008
Jeff Wilkins, St. Louis vs. Denver, Sept. 10, 2006
Phil Dawson, Cleveland vs. San Diego, Nov. 5, 2006
5 By many players

Most Field Goals, One Quarter
4 Garo Yepremian, Detroit vs. Minnesota, Nov. 13, 1966
    (second quarter)
   Curt Knight, Washington vs. N.Y. Giants, Nov. 15, 1970
    (second quarter)
   Roger Ruzek, Dallas vs. N.Y. Giants, Nov. 2, 1987
    (fourth quarter)
   Cary Blanchard, Indianapolis vs. Buffalo,
    Sept. 21 1997 (second quarter)
   Sebastian Janikowski, Oakland vs. Chicago,
    Oct. 5, 2003 (second quarter)
   Jeff Wilkins, St. Louis vs. Baltimore, Nov. 9, 2003
    (fourth quarter)
   Lawrence Tynes, Kansas City vs. New England,
    Nov. 27, 2005 (second quarter)
3 By many players

Most Consecutive Games Scoring Field Goals
38 Matt Stover, Baltimore, 1999-2001
31 Fred Cox, Minnesota, 1968-1970
28 Jim Turner, N.Y. Jets, 1970; Denver, 1971-72
    Chip Lohmiller, Washington, 1988-1990

Most Consecutive Field Goals
42 Mike Vanderjagt, Indianapolis, 2002-04
40 Gary Anderson, San Francisco, 1997; Minnesota,
    1998
36 Matt Stover, Baltimore, 2005-06

Longest Field Goal
63 Tom Dempsey, New Orleans vs. Detroit, Nov. 8, 1970
    Jason Elam, Denver vs. Jacksonville, Oct. 25, 1998
62 Matt Bryant, Tampa Bay vs. Philadelphia,
    Oct. 22, 2006
60 Steve Cox, Cleveland vs. Cincinnati, Oct. 21, 1984
    Morten Andersen, New Orleans vs. Chicago,
    Oct. 27, 1991
    Rob Bironas, Tennessee vs. Indianapolis,
    Dec. 3, 2006

Highest Field Goal Percentage, Career (100 field goals)
86.47 Mike Vanderjagt, Indianapolis, 1998-2005;
       Dallas, 2006 (230-266)
84.03 Shayne Graham, Buffalo, 2001; Carolina, 2002;
       Cincinnati, 2003-06 (121-144)
83.78 Matt Stover, Cleveland, 1991-95; Baltimore,
       1996-2006 (408-487)

Highest Field Goal Percentage, Season (Qualifiers)
100.00 Tony Zendejas, L.A. Rams, 1991 (17-17)
        Gary Anderson, Minnesota, 1998 (35-35)
        Jeff Wilkins, St. Louis, 2000 (17-17)
        Mike Vanderjagt, Indianapolis, 2003 (37-37)
96.43   Chris Boniol, Dallas, 1995 (28-27)
96.30   Norm Johnson, Atlanta, 1993 (27-26)
        Pete Stoyanovich, Kansas City, 1997 (27-26)

Most Field Goals, No Misses, Game
7 Rich Karlis, Minnesota vs. L.A. Rams, Nov. 5, 1989
    (OT)
   Chris Boniol, Dallas vs. Green Bay, Nov. 18, 1996
6 Gino Cappelletti, Boston vs. Denver, Oct. 4, 1964

Joe Danelo, N.Y. Giants vs. Seattle, Oct. 18, 1981
Ray Wersching, San Francisco vs. New Orleans,
    Oct. 16, 1983
Gary Anderson, Pittsburgh vs. Denver, Oct. 23, 1988
John Carney, San Diego vs. Seattle, Sept. 5, 1993
John Carney, San Diego vs. Houston, Sept. 19, 1993
Doug Pelfrey, Cincinnati vs. Seattle, Nov. 6, 1994 (OT)
Norm Johnson, Atlanta vs. New Orleans,
    Nov. 13, 1994
Jeff Wilkins, San Francisco vs. Atlanta,
    Sept. 29, 1996
Greg Davis, San Diego vs. Oakland, Oct. 5, 1997
Gary Anderson, Minnesota vs. Baltimore,
    Dec. 13, 1998
Olindo Mare, Miami vs. New England, Oct. 17, 1999
Jeff Reed, Pittsburgh vs. Jacksonville, Dec. 1, 2002
John Kasay, Carolina vs. New Orleans, Dec. 5, 2004
Neil Rackers, Arizona vs. San Francisco,
    Oct. 2, 2005
Phil Dawson, Cleveland vs. San Diego, Nov. 5, 2006
5 By many players

Most Field Goals, 50 or More Yards, Career
40 Morten Andersen, New Orleans, 1982-1994;
    Atlanta, 1995-2000; N.Y. Giants, 2001;
    Kansas City, 2002-03; Minnesota, 2004;
    Atlanta, 2006
36 Jason Elam, Denver, 1993-2006
33 John Kasay, Seattle, 1991-94; Carolina, 1995-2006

Most Field Goals, 50 or More Yards, Season
8 Morten Andersen, Atlanta, 1995
6 Dean Biasucci, Indianapolis, 1988
   Chris Jacke, Green Bay, 1993
   Tony Zendejas, L.A. Rams, 1993
   Mike Vanderjagt, Indianapolis, 1998
   Neil Rackers, Arizona, 2005
5 Fred Steinfort, Denver, 1980
   Norm Johnson, Seattle, 1986
   Kevin Butler, Chicago, 1993
   Jason Elam, Denver, 1995
   Cary Blanchard, Indianapolis, 1996
   Jason Elam, Denver, 1999
   Martín Gramatica, Tampa Bay, 2000, 2002
   Paul Edinger, Chicago, 2002
   Neil Rackers, Arizona, 2004
   Josh Brown, Seattle, 2005

Most Field Goals, 50 or More Yards, Game
3 Morten Andersen, Atlanta vs. New Orleans,
    Dec. 10, 1995
   Neil Rackers, Arizona vs. Seattle, Oct. 24, 2004
2 By many players. Last time: John Kasay,
    Carolina vs. Tampa Bay, Sept. 24, 2006

SAFETIES
Most Safeties, Career
4 Ted Hendricks, Baltimore, 1969-1973; Green Bay,
    1974; Oakland, 1975-1981; L.A. Raiders, 1982-83
   Doug English, Detroit, 1975-79, 1981-85
3 Bill McPeak, Pittsburgh, 1949-1957
   Charlie Krueger, San Francisco, 1959-1973
   Ernie Stautner, Pittsburgh, 1950-1963
   Jim Katcavage, N.Y. Giants, 1956-1968
   Roger Brown, Detroit, 1960-66; Los Angeles,
    1967-69
   Bruce Maher, Detroit, 1960-67; N.Y. Giants, 1968-69
   Ron McDole, St. Louis, 1961; Houston, 1962;
    Buffalo, 1963-1970; Washington, 1971-78
   Alan Page, Minnesota, 1967-1978; Chicago,
    1979-1981
   Lyle Alzado, Denver, 1971-78; Cleveland,
    1979-1981; L.A. Raiders, 1982-85

Rulon Jones, Denver, 1980-88
Steve McMichael, New England, 1980; Chicago, 1981-1993; Green Bay, 1994
Kevin Greene, L.A. Rams, 1985-1992; Pittsburgh, 1993-95; Carolina, 1996, 1998-99; San Francisco, 1997
Burt Grossman, San Diego, 1989-1993; Philadelphia, 1994
Eric Swann, Phoenix, 1991-93; Arizona, 1994-99; Carolina, 2000
Dan Saleaumua, Detroit, 1987-88; Kansas City, 1989-1996; Seattle, 1997-98
Derrick Thomas, Kansas City, 1989-1999
Bryant Young, San Francisco, 1994-2006
2 By many players

Most Safeties, Season
2 Tom Nash, Green Bay, 1932
Roger Brown, Detroit, 1962
Ron McDole, Buffalo, 1964
Alan Page, Minnesota, 1971
Fred Dryer, Los Angeles, 1973
Benny Barnes, Dallas, 1973
James Young, Houston, 1977
Doug English, Detroit, 1983
Don Blackmon, New England, 1985
Tim Harris, Green Bay, 1988
Brian Jordan, Atlanta, 1991
Burt Grossman, San Diego, 1992
Rod Stephens, Seattle, 1993
Bryant Young, San Francisco, 1996

Most Safeties, Game
2 Fred Dryer, Los Angeles vs. Green Bay, Oct. 21, 1973

RUSHING

Most Seasons Leading League
8 Jim Brown, Cleveland, 1957-1961, 1963-65
4 Steve Van Buren, Philadelphia, 1945, 1947-49
O.J. Simpson, Buffalo, 1972-73, 1975-76
Eric Dickerson, L.A. Rams, 1983-84, 1986; Indianapolis, 1988
Emmitt Smith, Dallas, 1991-93, 1995
Barry Sanders, Detroit, 1990, 1994, 1996-97
3 Earl Campbell, Houston, 1978-1980

Most Consecutive Seasons Leading League
5 Jim Brown, Cleveland, 1957-1961
3 Steve Van Buren, Philadelphia, 1947-49
Jim Brown, Cleveland, 1963-65
Earl Campbell, Houston, 1978-1980
Emmitt Smith, Dallas, 1991-93
2 Bill Paschal, N.Y. Giants, 1943-44
Joe Perry, San Francisco, 1953-54
Jim Nance, Boston, 1966-67
Leroy Kelly, Cleveland, 1967-68
O.J. Simpson, Buffalo, 1972-73; 1975-76
Eric Dickerson, L.A. Rams, 1983-84
Barry Sanders, Detroit, 1996-97
Edgerrin James, Indianapolis, 1999-2000

ATTEMPTS

Most Seasons Leading League
6 Jim Brown, Cleveland, 1958-59, 1961, 1963-65
4 Steve Van Buren, Philadelphia, 1947-1950
Walter Payton, Chicago, 1976-79
3 Cookie Gilchrist, Buffalo, 1963-64; Denver, 1965
Jim Nance, Boston, 1966-67, 1969
O.J. Simpson, Buffalo, 1973-75
Eric Dickerson, L.A. Rams, 1983, 1986; Indianapolis, 1988
Emmitt Smith, Dallas, 1991, 1994-95

Most Consecutive Seasons Leading League
4 Steve Van Buren, Philadelphia, 1947-1950
Walter Payton, Chicago, 1976-79
3 Jim Brown, Cleveland, 1963-65
Cookie Gilchrist, Buffalo, 1963-64; Denver, 1965
O.J. Simpson, Buffalo, 1973-75
2 By many players

Most Attempts, Career
4,409 Emmitt Smith, Dallas, 1990-2002; Arizona, 2003-04
3,838 Walter Payton, Chicago, 1975-1987
3,518 Curtis Martin, New England, 1995-97; N.Y. Jets, 1998-2005

Most Attempts, Season
416 Larry Johnson, Kansas City, 2006
410 Jamal Anderson, Atlanta, 1998
407 James Wilder, Tampa Bay, 1984

Most Attempts, Rookie, Season
390 Eric Dickerson, L.A. Rams, 1983
378 George Rogers, New Orleans, 1981
369 Edgerrin James, Indianapolis, 1999

Most Attempts, Game
45 Jamie Morris, Washington vs. Cincinnati, Dec. 17, 1988 (OT)
43 Butch Woolfolk, N.Y. Giants vs. Philadelphia, Nov. 20, 1983
James Wilder, Tampa Bay vs. Green Bay, Sept. 30, 1984 (OT)
Rudi Johnson, Cincinnati vs. Houston, Nov. 9, 2003
42 James Wilder, Tampa Bay vs. Pittsburgh, Oct. 30, 1983
Terrell Davis, Denver vs. Buffalo, Oct. 26, 1997 (OT)
Ricky Williams, Miami vs. Buffalo, Sept. 21, 2003

YARDS GAINED

Most Yards Gained, Career
18,355 Emmitt Smith, Dallas, 1990-2002; Arizona, 2003-04
16,726 Walter Payton, Chicago, 1975-1987
15,269 Barry Sanders, Detroit, 1989-1998

Most Seasons, 1,000 or More Yards Rushing
11 Emmitt Smith, Dallas, 1991-2001
10 Walter Payton, Chicago, 1976-1981, 1983-86
Barry Sanders, Detroit, 1989-1998
Curtis Martin, New England, 1995-97; N.Y. Jets, 1998-2004
8 Franco Harris, Pittsburgh, 1972, 1974-79, 1983
Tony Dorsett, Dallas, 1977-1981, 1983-85
Thurman Thomas, Buffalo, 1989-1996
Jerome Bettis, L.A. Rams, 1993-94; Pittsburgh, 1996-2001

Most Consecutive Seasons, 1,000 or More Yards Rushing
11 Emmitt Smith, Dallas, 1991-2001
10 Barry Sanders, Detroit, 1989-1998
Curtis Martin, New England, 1995-97; N.Y. Jets, 1998-2004
8 Thurman Thomas, Buffalo, 1989-1996

Most Yards Gained, Season
2,105 Eric Dickerson, L.A. Rams, 1984
2,066 Jamal Lewis, Baltimore, 2003
2,053 Barry Sanders, Detroit, 1997

Most Yards Gained, Rookie, Season
1,808 Eric Dickerson, L.A. Rams, 1983
1,674 George Rogers, New Orleans, 1981
1,605 Ottis Anderson, St. Louis, 1979

Most Yards Gained, Game
295 Jamal Lewis, Baltimore vs. Cleveland, Sept. 14, 2003
278 Corey Dillon, Cincinnati vs. Denver, Oct. 22, 2000
275 Walter Payton, Chicago vs. Minnesota, Nov. 20, 1977

Most Games, 200 or More Yards Rushing, Career
- 6　O.J. Simpson, Buffalo, 1969-1977; San Francisco, 1978-79
- 5　Tiki Barber, N.Y. Giants, 1997-2006
- 4　Jim Brown, Cleveland, 1957-1965
  - Earl Campbell, Houston, 1978-1984; New Orleans, 1984-85
  - Barry Sanders, Detroit, 1989-1998
  - LaDainian Tomlinson, San Diego, 2001-06

Most Games, 200 or More Yards Rushing, Season
- 4　Earl Campbell, Houston, 1980
- 3　O.J. Simpson, Buffalo, 1973
  - Tiki Barber, N.Y. Giants, 2005
- 2　Jim Brown, Cleveland, 1963
  - O.J. Simpson, Buffalo, 1976
  - Walter Payton, Chicago, 1977
  - Eric Dickerson, L.A. Rams, 1984
  - Greg Bell, L.A. Rams, 1989
  - Terrell Davis, Denver, 1997
  - Barry Sanders, Detroit, 1997
  - Corey Dillon, Cincinnati, 2000
  - Marshall Faulk, St. Louis, 2000
  - LaDainian Tomlinson, San Diego, 2002
  - Ricky Williams, Miami, 2002
  - Jamal Lewis, Baltimore, 2003
  - LaDainian Tomlinson, San Diego, 2003
  - Larry Johnson, Kansas City, 2005
  - Willie Parker, Pittsburgh, 2006

Most Consecutive Games, 200 or More Yards Rushing
- 2　O.J. Simpson, Buffalo, 1973, 1976
  - Earl Campbell, Houston, 1980
  - Ricky Williams, Miami, 2002

Most Games, 100 or More Yards Rushing, Career
- 78　Emmitt Smith, Dallas, 1990-2002; Arizona, 2003-04
- 77　Walter Payton, Chicago, 1975-1987
- 76　Barry Sanders, Detroit, 1989-1998

Most Games, 100 or More Yards Rushing, Season
- 14　Barry Sanders, Detroit, 1997
- 12　Eric Dickerson, L.A. Rams, 1984
  - Barry Foster, Pittsburgh, 1992
  - Jamal Anderson, Atlanta, 1998
  - Jamal Lewis, Baltimore, 2003
- 11　O.J. Simpson, Buffalo, 1973
  - Earl Campbell, Houston, 1979
  - Marcus Allen, L.A. Raiders, 1985
  - Eric Dickerson, L.A. Rams, 1986
  - Emmitt Smith, Dallas, 1995
  - Terrell Davis, Denver, 1998
  - Shaun Alexander, Seattle, 2005
  - Larry Johnson, Kansas City, 2006

Most Consecutive Games, 100 or More Yards Rushing
- 14　Barry Sanders, Detroit, 1997
- 11　Marcus Allen, L.A. Raiders, 1985-86
- 9　Walter Payton, Chicago, 1985
  - Fred Taylor, Jacksonville, 2000
  - Deuce McAllister, New Orleans, 2003
  - Larry Johnson, Kansas City, 2005
  - LaDainian Tomlinson, San Diego, 2006

Longest Run From Scrimmage
- 99　Tony Dorsett, Dallas vs. Minnesota, Jan. 3, 1983 (TD)
- 98　Ahman Green, Green Bay vs. Denver, Dec. 28, 2003 (TD)
- 97　Andy Uram, Green Bay vs. Chi. Cardinals, Oct. 8, 1939 (TD)
  - Bob Gage, Pittsburgh vs. Chi. Bears, Dec. 4, 1949 (TD)

AVERAGE GAIN

Highest Average Gain, Career (750 attempts)
- 6.36　Randall Cunningham, Philadelphia, 1985-1995; Minnesota, 1997-99; Dallas, 2000; Baltimore, 2001 (775-4,928)
- 5.22　Jim Brown, Cleveland, 1957-1965 (2,359-12,312)
- 5.14　Eugene (Mercury) Morris, Miami, 1969-1975; San Diego, 1976 (804-4,133)

Highest Average Gain, Season (Qualifiers)
- 8.45　Michael Vick, Atlanta, 2006 (123-1,039)
- 8.44　Beattie Feathers, Chi. Bears, 1934 (119-1,004)
- 7.98　Randall Cunningham, Philadelphia, 1990 (118-942)

Highest Average Gain, Game (10 attempts)
- 17.30　Michael Vick, Atlanta vs. Minnesota, Dec. 1, 2002 (OT) (10-173)
- 17.09　Marion Motley, Cleveland vs. Pittsburgh, Oct. 29, 1950 (11-188)
- 16.70　Bill Grimes, Green Bay vs. N.Y. Yanks, Oct. 8, 1950 (10-167)

TOUCHDOWNS

Most Seasons Leading League
- 5　Jim Brown, Cleveland, 1957-59, 1963, 1965
- 4　Steve Van Buren, Philadelphia, 1945, 1947-49
- 3　Abner Haynes, Dall. Texans, 1960-62
  - Cookie Gilchrist, Buffalo, 1962-64
  - Paul Lowe, L.A. Chargers, 1960; San Diego, 1961, 1965
  - Leroy Kelly, Cleveland, 1966-68
  - Emmitt Smith, Dallas, 1992, 1994-95

Most Consecutive Seasons Leading League
- 3　Steve Van Buren, Philadelphia, 1947-49
  - Jim Brown, Cleveland, 1957-59
  - Abner Haynes, Dall. Texans, 1960-62
  - Cookie Gilchrist, Buffalo, 1962-64
  - Leroy Kelly, Cleveland, 1966-68

Most Touchdowns, Career
- 164　Emmitt Smith, Dallas, 1990-2002; Arizona, 2003-04
- 123　Marcus Allen, L.A. Raiders, 1982-1992; Kansas City, 1993-97
- 110　Walter Payton, Chicago, 1975-1987

Most Touchdowns, Season
- 28　LaDainian Tomlinson, San Diego, 2006
- 27　Priest Holmes, Kansas City, 2003
  - Shaun Alexander, Seattle, 2005
- 25　Emmitt Smith, Dallas, 1995

Most Touchdowns, Rookie, Season
- 18　Eric Dickerson, L.A. Rams, 1983
- 15　Ickey Woods, Cincinnati, 1988
  - Mike Anderson, Denver, 2000
  - Clinton Portis, Denver, 2002
- 14　Gale Sayers, Chicago, 1965
  - Barry Sanders, Detroit, 1989
  - Curtis Martin, New England, 1995
  - Fred Taylor, Jacksonville, 1998

Most Touchdowns, Game
- 6　Ernie Nevers, Chi. Cardinals vs. Chi. Bears, Nov. 28, 1929
- 5　Jimmy Conzelman, Rhode Island vs. Evansville, Oct. 15, 1922
  - Jim Brown, Cleveland vs. Baltimore, Nov. 1, 1959
  - Cookie Gilchrist, Buffalo vs. N.Y. Jets, Dec. 8, 1963
  - James Stewart, Jacksonville vs. Philadelphia, Oct. 12, 1997
  - Clinton Portis, Denver vs. Kansas City, Dec. 7, 2003
- 4　By many players

Most Consecutive Games Rushing for Touchdowns
- 18　LaDainian Tomlinson, San Diego, 2004-05
- 13　John Riggins, Washington, 1982-83
  - George Rogers, Washington, 1985-86

11   Lenny Moore, Baltimore, 1963-64
      Emmitt Smith, Dallas, 1994-95
      Emmitt Smith, Dallas, 1995
      Priest Holmes, Kansas City, 2002

PASSING

Most Seasons Leading League
6   Sammy Baugh, Washington, 1937, 1940, 1943,
      1945, 1947, 1949
      Steve Young San Francisco, 1991-94, 1996-97
4   Len Dawson, Dall. Texans; 1962; Kansas City, 1964,
      1966, 1968
      Roger Staubach, Dallas, 1971, 1973, 1978-79
      Ken Anderson, Cincinnati, 1974-75, 1981-82
3   Arnie Herber, Green Bay, 1932, 1934, 1936
      Norm Van Brocklin, Los Angeles, 1950, 1952, 1954
      Bart Starr, Green Bay, 1962, 1964, 1966
      Peyton Manning, Indianapolis, 2004-06

Most Consecutive Seasons Leading League
4   Steve Young, San Francisco, 1991-94
3   Peyton Manning, Indianapolis, 2004-06
2   Cecil Isbell, Green Bay, 1941-42
      Milt Plum, Cleveland, 1960-61
      Ken Anderson, Cincinnati, 1974-75, 1981-82
      Roger Staubach, Dallas, 1978-79
      Steve Young, San Francisco, 1996-97

PASSER RATING

Highest Passer Rating, Career (1,500 attempts)
96.8   Steve Young, Tampa Bay, 1985-86; San Francisco,
      1987-1999
94.4   Peyton Manning, Indianapolis, 1998-2006
93.8   Kurt Warner, St. Louis, 1998-2003; N.Y. Giants,
      2004; Arizona, 2005-06

Highest Passer Rating, Season (Qualifiers)
121.1   Peyton Manning, Indianapolis, 2004
112.8   Steve Young, San Francisco, 1994
112.4   Joe Montana, San Francisco, 1989

Highest Passer Rating, Rookie, Season (Qualifiers)
98.1   Ben Roethlisberger, Pittsburgh, 2004
96.0   Dan Marino, Miami, 1983
88.2   Greg Cook, Cincinnati, 1969

ATTEMPTS

Most Seasons Leading League
5   Dan Marino, Miami, 1984, 1986, 1988, 1992, 1997
4   Sammy Baugh, Washington, 1937, 1943, 1947-48
      Johnny Unitas, Baltimore, 1957, 1959-1961
      George Blanda, Chi. Bears, 1953; Houston, 1963-65
3   Arnie Herber, Green Bay, 1932, 1934, 1936
      Sonny Jurgensen, Washington, 1966-67, 1969
      Drew Bledsoe, New England, 1994-96
      Brett Favre, Green Bay, 1999, 2005-06

Most Consecutive Seasons Leading League
3   Johnny Unitas, Baltimore, 1959-1961
      George Blanda, Houston, 1963-65
      Drew Bledsoe, New England, 1994-96
2   By many players

Most Passes Attempted, Career
8,358   Dan Marino, Miami, 1983-1999
8,223   Brett Favre, Atlanta, 1991; Green Bay, 1992-2006
7,250   John Elway, Denver, 1983-1998

Most Passes Attempted, Season
691   Drew Bledsoe, New England, 1994
655   Warren Moon, Houston, 1991
636   Drew Bledsoe, New England, 1995

Most Passes Attempted, Rookie, Season
575   Peyton Manning, Indianapolis, 1998
540   Chris Weinke, Carolina, 2001
486   Rick Mirer, Seattle, 1993

Most Passes Attempted, Game
70   Drew Bledsoe, New England vs. Minnesota, Nov. 13,
      1994 (OT)
69   Vinny Testaverde, N.Y. Jets vs. Baltimore, Dec. 24,
      2000
68   George Blanda, Houston vs. Buffalo, Nov. 1, 1964
      Jon Kitna, Cincinnati vs. Pittsburgh, Dec. 30, 2001
      (OT)

COMPLETIONS

Most Seasons Leading League
6   Dan Marino, Miami, 1984-86, 1988, 1992, 1997
5   Sammy Baugh, Washington, 1937, 1943, 1945,
      1947-48
4   George Blanda, Chi. Bears, 1953; Houston, 1963-65
      Sonny Jurgensen, Philadelphia, 1961; Washington,
      1966-67, 1969

Most Consecutive Seasons Leading League
3   George Blanda, Houston, 1963-65
      Dan Marino, Miami, 1984-86
2   By many players

Most Passes Completed, Career
5,021   Brett Favre, Atlanta, 1991; Green Bay, 1992-2006
4,967   Dan Marino, Miami, 1983-1999
4,123   John Elway, Denver, 1983-1998

Most Passes Completed, Season
418   Rich Gannon, Oakland, 2002
404   Warren Moon, Houston, 1991
400   Drew Bledsoe, New England, 1994

Most Passes Completed, Rookie, Season
326   Peyton Manning, Indianapolis, 1998
293   Chris Weinke, Carolina, 2001
274   Rick Mirer, Seattle, 1993

Most Passes Completed, Game
45   Drew Bledsoe, New England vs. Minnesota,
      Nov. 13, 1994 (OT)
43   Rich Gannon, Oakland vs. Pittsburgh, Sept. 15, 2002
42   Richard Todd, N.Y. Jets vs. San Francisco,
      Sept. 21, 1980
      Vinny Testaverde, N.Y. Jets vs. Seattle, Dec. 6, 1998

Most Consecutive Passes Completed
24   Donovan McNabb, Philadelphia vs. N.Y. Giants (10),
      Nov. 28, 2004; vs. Green Bay (14),
      Dec. 5, 2004
22   Joe Montana, San Francisco vs. Cleveland (5),
      Nov. 29, 1987; vs. Green Bay (17), Dec. 6, 1987
      Mark Brunell, Washington vs. Houston,
      Sept. 24, 2006
      David Carr, Houston vs. Buffalo, Nov. 19, 2006
21   Rich Gannon, Oakland vs. Denver, Nov. 11, 2002

COMPLETION PERCENTAGE

Most Seasons Leading League
8   Len Dawson, Dall. Texans, 1962; Kansas City,
      1964-69, 1975
7   Sammy Baugh, Washington, 1940, 1942-43, 1945,
      1947-49
5   Joe Montana, San Francisco, 1980-81, 1985, 1987,
      1989
      Steve Young, San Francisco, 1992, 1994-97

Most Consecutive Seasons Leading League
6   Len Dawson, Kansas City, 1964-69
4   Steve Young, San Francisco, 1994-97
3   Sammy Baugh, Washington, 1947-49
      Otto Graham, Cleveland, 1953-55
      Milt Plum, Cleveland, 1959-1961
      Kurt Warner, St. Louis, 1999-2001

Highest Completion Percentage, Career (1,500 attempts)
65.59   Kurt Warner, St. Louis, 1998-2003; N.Y. Giants, 2004; Arizona, 2005-06 (2,508-1,645)
65.10   Chad Pennington, N.Y. Jets, 2000-06 (1,659-1,080)
64.43   Marc Bulger, St. Louis, 2002-06 (2,106-1,357)

Highest Completion Percentage, Season (Qualifiers)
70.55   Ken Anderson, Cincinnati, 1982 (309-218)
70.33   Sammy Baugh, Washington, 1945 (182-128)
70.28   Steve Young, San Francisco, 1994 (461-324)

Highest Completion Percentage, Rookie, Season (Qualifiers)
66.44   Ben Roethlisberger, Pittsburgh, 2004 (295-196)
58.45   Dan Marino, Miami, 1983 (296-173)
57.18   Byron Leftwich, Jacksonville, 2003 (418-239)

Highest Completion Percentage, Game (20 attempts)
91.30   Vinny Testaverde, Cleveland vs. L.A. Rams, Dec. 26, 1993 (23-21)
90.91   Ken Anderson, Cincinnati vs. Pittsburgh, Nov. 10, 1974 (22-20)
90.48   Lynn Dickey, Green Bay vs. New Orleans, Dec. 13, 1981 (21-19)

YARDS GAINED

Most Seasons Leading League
5   Sonny Jurgensen, Philadelphia, 1961-62; Washington, 1966-67, 1969
   Dan Marino, Miami, 1984-86, 1988, 1992
4   Sammy Baugh, Washington, 1937, 1940, 1947-48
   Johnny Unitas, Baltimore, 1957, 1959-1960, 1963
   Dan Fouts, San Diego, 1979-1982
3   Arnie Herber, Green Bay, 1932, 1934, 1936
   Sid Luckman, Chi. Bears, 1943, 1945-46
   John Brodie, San Francisco, 1965, 1968, 1970
   John Hadl, San Diego, 1965, 1968, 1971
   Joe Namath, N.Y. Jets, 1966-67, 1972

Most Consecutive Seasons Leading League
4   Dan Fouts, San Diego, 1979-1982
3   Dan Marino, Miami, 1984-86
2   By many players

Most Yards Gained, Career
61,361   Dan Marino, Miami, 1983-1999
57,500   Brett Favre, Atlanta, 1991; Green Bay, 1992-2006
51,475   John Elway, Denver, 1983-1998

Most Seasons, 3,000 or More Yards Passing
15   Brett Favre, Green Bay, 1992-2006
13   Dan Marino, Miami, 1984-1992, 1994-95, 1997-98
12   John Elway, Denver, 1985-1991, 1993-97

Most Yards Gained, Season
5,084   Dan Marino, Miami, 1984
4,830   Kurt Warner, St. Louis, 2001
4,802   Dan Fouts, San Diego, 1981

Most Yards Gained, Rookie, Season
3,739   Peyton Manning, Indianapolis, 1998
2,931   Chris Weinke, Carolina, 2001
2,833   Rick Mirer, Seattle, 1993

Most Yards Gained, Game
554   Norm Van Brocklin, Los Angeles vs. N.Y. Yanks, Sept. 28, 1951
527   Warren Moon, Houston vs. Kansas City, Dec. 16, 1990
522   Boomer Esiason, Arizona vs. Washington, Nov. 10, 1996

Most Games, 400 or More Yards Passing, Career
13   Dan Marino, Miami, 1983-1999
7   Joe Montana, San Francisco, 1979-1990, 1992; Kansas City, 1993-94
   Warren Moon, Houston, 1984-1993; Minnesota, 1994-96; Seattle, 1997-98; Kansas City, 1999-2000
   Peyton Manning, Indianapolis, 1998-2006
6   Dan Fouts, San Diego, 1973-1987

   Drew Bledsoe, New England, 1993-2001; Buffalo, 2002-03

Most Games, 400 or More Yards Passing, Season
4   Dan Marino, Miami, 1984
3   Dan Marino, Miami, 1986
2   By many players

Most Consecutive Games, 400 or More Yards Passing
2   Dan Fouts, San Diego, 1982
   Dan Marino, Miami, 1984
   Phil Simms, N.Y. Giants, 1985
   Billy Volek, Tennessee, 2004

Most Games, 300 or More Yards Passing, Career
63   Dan Marino, Miami, 1983-1999
51   Dan Fouts, San Diego, 1973-1987
49   Warren Moon, Houston, 1984-1993; Minnesota, 1994-96; Seattle, 1997-98; Kansas City, 1999-2000

Most Games, 300 or More Yards Passing, Season
10   Rich Gannon, Oakland, 2002
9   Dan Marino, Miami, 1984
   Warren Moon, Houston, 1990
   Kurt Warner, St. Louis, 1999
   Kurt Warner, St. Louis, 2001
8   Dan Fouts, San Diego, 1980
   Kurt Warner, St. Louis, 2000
   Trent Green, Kansas City, 2004
   Marc Bulger, St. Louis, 2006
   Drew Brees, New Orleans, 2006

Most Consecutive Games, 300 or More Yards Passing
6   Steve Young, San Francisco, 1998
   Kurt Warner, St. Louis, 2000
   Rich Gannon, Oakland, 2002
5   Joe Montana, San Francisco, 1982
   Kerry Collins, N.Y. Giants, 2001-02
   Drew Brees, New Orleans, 2006
4   Dan Fouts, San Diego, 1979
   Dan Fouts, San Diego, 1980-81
   Bill Kenney, Kansas City, 1983
   Joe Montana, San Francisco, 1985-86
   Joe Montana, San Francisco, 1990
   Warren Moon, Houston, 1990
   Drew Bledsoe, New England, 1993-94
   Kurt Warner, St. Louis, 1999
   Brian Griese, Denver, 2002
   Daunte Culpepper, Minnesota, 2004
   Trent Green, Kansas City, 2004

Longest Pass Completion (All TDs except as noted)
99   Frank Filchock (to Farkas), Washington vs. Pittsburgh, Oct. 15, 1939
   George Izo (to Mitchell), Washington vs. Cleveland, Sept. 15, 1963
   Karl Sweetan (to Studstill), Detroit vs. Baltimore, Oct. 16, 1966
   Sonny Jurgensen (to Allen), Washington vs. Chicago, Sept. 15, 1968
   Jim Plunkett (to Branch), L.A. Raiders vs. Washington, Oct. 2, 1983
   Ron Jaworski (to Quick), Philadelphia vs. Atlanta, Nov. 10, 1985
   Stan Humphries (to Martin), San Diego vs. Seattle, Sept. 18, 1994
   Brett Favre (to Brooks), Green Bay vs. Chicago, Sept. 11, 1995
   Trent Green (to Boerigter), Kansas City vs. San Diego, Dec. 22, 2002
   Jeff Garcia, (to Davis), Cleveland vs. Cincinnati, Oct. 17, 2004
98   Doug Russell (to Tinsley), Chi. Cardinals vs. Cleveland, Nov. 27, 1938

Ogden Compton (to Lane), Chi. Cardinals vs.
Green Bay, Nov. 13, 1955

Bill Wade (to Farrington), Chicago Bears vs. Detroit,
Oct. 8, 1961

Jacky Lee (to Dewveall), Houston vs. San Diego,
Nov. 25, 1962

Earl Morrall (to Jones), N.Y. Giants vs. Pittsburgh,
Sept. 11, 1966

Jim Hart (to Moore), St. Louis vs. Los Angeles,
Dec. 10, 1972 (no TD)

Bobby Hebert (to Haynes), Atlanta vs. New Orleans,
Sept. 12, 1993

Charlie Batch (to Morton), Detroit vs. Chicago,
Oct. 4, 1998

97 Pat Coffee (to Tinsley), Chi. Cardinals vs. Chi. Bears,
Dec. 5, 1937

Bobby Layne (to Box), Detroit vs. Green Bay,
Nov. 26, 1953

George Shaw (to Tarr), Denver vs. Boston,
Sept. 21, 1962

Bernie Kosar (to Slaughter), Cleveland vs. Chicago,
Oct. 23, 1989

Steve Young (to Taylor), San Francisco vs. Atlanta,
Nov. 3, 1991

AVERAGE GAIN
Most Seasons Leading League
7 Sid Luckman, Chi. Bears, 1939-1943, 1946-47
5 Steve Young, San Francisco, 1991-94, 1997
3 Arnie Herber, Green Bay, 1932, 1934, 1936
   Norm Van Brocklin, Los Angeles, 1950, 1952, 1954
   Len Dawson, Dall. Texans, 1962; Kansas City, 1966,
   1968
   Bart Starr, Green Bay, 1966-68
   Kurt Warner, St. Louis, 1999-2001
Most Consecutive Seasons Leading League
5 Sid Luckman, Chi. Bears, 1939-1943
4 Steve Young, San Francisco, 1991-94
3 Bart Starr, Green Bay, 1966-68
   Kurt Warner, St. Louis, 1999-2001
Highest Average Gain, Career (1,500 attempts)
8.63 Otto Graham, Cleveland, 1950-55 (1,565-13,499)
8.42 Sid Luckman, Chi. Bears, 1939-1950
      (1,744-14,686)
8.21 Kurt Warner, St. Louis, 1998-2003; N.Y. Giants,
      2004; Arizona, 2005-06 (2,508-20,591)
Highest Average Gain, Season (Qualifiers)
11.17 Tommy O'Connell, Cleveland, 1957 (110-1,229)
10.86 Sid Luckman, Chi. Bears, 1943 (202-2,194)
10.55 Otto Graham, Cleveland, 1953 (258-2,722)
Highest Average Gain, Rookie, Season (Qualifiers)
9.411 Greg Cook, Cincinnati, 1969 (197-1,854)
9.409 Bob Waterfield, Cleveland, 1945 (171-1,609)
8.88 Ben Roethlisberger, Pittsburgh, 2004 (295-2,621)
Highest Average Gain, Game (20 attempts)
18.58 Sammy Baugh, Washington vs. Boston,
       Oct. 31, 1948 (24-446)
18.50 Johnny Unitas, Baltimore vs. Atlanta, Nov. 12, 1967
       (20-370)
17.71 Joe Namath, N.Y. Jets vs. Baltimore, Sept. 24, 1972
       (28-496)

TOUCHDOWNS
Most Seasons Leading League
4 Johnny Unitas, Baltimore, 1957-1960
   Len Dawson, Dall. Texans, 1962; Kansas City, 1963,
   1965-66
   Steve Young, San Francisco, 1992-94, 1998
   Brett Favre, Green Bay, 1995-97, 2003
3 Arnie Herber, Green Bay, 1932, 1934, 1936

Sid Luckman, Chi. Bears, 1943, 1945-46
Y.A. Tittle, San Francisco, 1955; N.Y. Giants, 1962-63
Dan Marino, Miami, 1984-86
Peyton Manning, Indianapolis, 2000, 2004, 2006
2 By many players
Most Consecutive Seasons Leading League
4 Johnny Unitas, Baltimore, 1957-1960
3 Dan Marino, Miami, 1984-86
   Steve Young, San Francisco, 1992-94
   Brett Favre, Green Bay, 1995-97
2 By many players
Most Touchdown Passes, Career
420 Dan Marino, Miami, 1983-1999
414 Brett Favre, Atlanta, 1991; Green Bay, 1992-2006
342 Fran Tarkenton, Minnesota, 1961-66, 1972-78;
     N.Y. Giants, 1967-1971
Most Touchdown Passes, Season
49 Peyton Manning, Indianapolis, 2004
48 Dan Marino, Miami, 1984
44 Dan Marino, Miami, 1986
Most Touchdown Passes, Rookie, Season
26 Peyton Manning, Indianapolis, 1998
22 Charlie Conerly, N.Y. Giants, 1948
20 Dan Marino, Miami, 1983
Most Touchdown Passes, Game
7 Sid Luckman, Chi. Bears vs. N.Y. Giants,
   Nov. 14, 1943
   Adrian Burk, Philadelphia vs. Washington,
   Oct. 17, 1954
   George Blanda, Houston vs. N.Y. Titans,
   Nov. 19, 1961
   Y.A. Tittle, N.Y. Giants vs. Washington, Oct. 28, 1962
   Joe Kapp, Minnesota vs. Baltimore, Sept. 28, 1969
6 By many players. Last time:
   Peyton Manning, Indianapolis vs. Detroit,
   Nov. 25, 2004
Most Games, Four or More Touchdown Passes, Career
21 Dan Marino, Miami, 1983-1999
19 Brett Favre, Atlanta, 1991; Green Bay, 1992-2006
17 Johnny Unitas, Baltimore, 1956-1972; San Diego,
    1973
Most Games, Four or More Touchdown Passes, Season
6 Dan Marino, Miami, 1984
   Peyton Manning, Indianapolis, 2004
5 Dan Marino, Miami, 1986
   Brett Favre, Green Bay, 1996
   Donovan McNabb, Philadelphia, 2004
4 George Blanda, Houston, 1961
   Vince Ferragamo, Los Angeles, 1980
   Steve Young, San Francisco, 1994
   Randall Cunningham, Minnesota, 1998
   Daunte Culpepper, Minnesota, 2004
Most Consecutive Games, Four or More Touchdown Passes
5 Peyton Manning, Indianapolis, 2004
4 Dan Marino, Miami, 1984
2 By many players
Most Consecutive Games, Touchdown Passes
47 Johnny Unitas, Baltimore, 1956-1960
36 Brett Favre, Green Bay, 2002-2004
30 Dan Marino, Miami, 1985-87

HAD INTERCEPTED
Most Consecutive Passes Attempted, None Intercepted
308 Bernie Kosar, Cleveland, 1990-91
294 Bart Starr, Green Bay, 1964-65
279 Jeff George, Indianapolis, 1993; Atlanta, 1994
Most Passes Had Intercepted, Career
277 George Blanda, Chi. Bears, 1949, 1950-58; Baltimore,
     1950; Houston, 1960-66; Oakland, 1967-1975

273   Brett Favre, Atlanta, 1991; Green Bay, 1992-2006
268   John Hadl, San Diego, 1962-1972; Los Angeles, 1973-74; Green Bay, 1974-75; Houston, 1976-77

Most Passes Had Intercepted, Season

42   George Blanda, Houston, 1962
35   Vinny Testaverde, Tampa Bay, 1988
34   Frank Tripucka, Denver, 1960

Most Passes Had Intercepted, Game

8   Jim Hardy, Chi. Cardinals vs. Philadelphia, Sept. 24, 1950
7   Parker Hall, Cleveland vs. Green Bay, Nov. 8, 1942
    Frank Sinkwich, Detroit vs. Green Bay, Oct. 24, 1943
    Bob Waterfield, Los Angeles vs. Green Bay, Oct. 17, 1948
    Zeke Bratkowski, Chicago vs. Baltimore, Oct. 2, 1960
    Tommy Wade, Pittsburgh vs. Philadelphia, Dec. 12, 1965
    Ken Stabler, Oakland vs. Denver, Oct. 16, 1977
    Steve DeBerg, Tampa Bay vs. San Francisco, Sept. 7, 1986
    Ty Detmer, Detroit vs. Cleveland, Sept. 23, 2001
6   By many players

Most Attempts, No Interceptions, Game

70   Drew Bledsoe, New England vs. Minnesota, Nov. 13, 1994 (OT)
63   Rich Gannon, Minnesota vs. New England, Oct. 20, 1991 (OT)
60   Davey O'Brien, Philadelphia vs. Washington, Dec. 1, 1940

LOWEST PERCENTAGE, PASSES HAD INTERCEPTED

Most Seasons Leading League, Lowest Percentage, Passes Had Intercepted

5   Sammy Baugh, Washington, 1940, 1942, 1944-45, 1947
3   Charlie Conerly, N.Y. Giants, 1950, 1956, 1959
    Bart Starr, Green Bay, 1962, 1964, 1966
    Roger Staubach, Dallas, 1971, 1977, 1979
    Ken Anderson, Cincinnati, 1972, 1981-82
    Ken O'Brien, N.Y. Jets, 1985, 1987-88
2   By many players

Lowest Percentage, Passes Had Intercepted, Career (1,500 attempts)

2.11   Neil O'Donnell, Pittsburgh, 1991-95; N.Y. Jets, 1996-97; Cincinnati, 1998; Tennessee, 1999-2003 (3,229-68)
2.21   Donovan McNabb, Philadelphia, 1999-2006 (3,259-72)
2.31   Mark Brunell, Green Bay, 1994; Jacksonville, 1995-2003; Washington, 2004-06 (4,594-106)

Lowest Percentage, Passes Had Intercepted, Season (Qualifiers)

0.41   Damon Huard, Kansas City, 2006 (244-1)
0.66   Joe Ferguson, Buffalo, 1976 (151-1)
0.90   Steve DeBerg, Kansas City, 1990 (444-4)

Lowest Percentage, Passes Had Intercepted, Rookie, Season (Qualifiers)

1.98   Charlie Batch, Detroit, 1998 (303-6)
2.03   Dan Marino, Miami, 1983 (296-6)
2.10   Gary Wood, N.Y. Giants, 1964 (143-3)

TIMES SACKED

Times Sacked has been compiled since 1963.

Most Times Sacked, Career

516   John Elway, Denver, 1983-1998
494   Dave Krieg, Seattle, 1980-1991; Kansas City, 1992-93; Detroit, 1994; Arizona, 1995; Chicago, 1996; Tennessee, 1997-98

484   Randall Cunningham, Philadelphia, 1985-1995; Minnesota, 1997-99; Dallas, 2000; Baltimore, 2001

Most Times Sacked, Season

76   David Carr, Houston, 2002
72   Randall Cunningham, Philadelphia, 1986
68   David Carr, Houston, 2005

Most Times Sacked, Game

12   Bert Jones, Baltimore vs. St. Louis, Oct. 26, 1980
    Warren Moon, Houston vs. Dallas, Sept. 29, 1985
11   Charley Johnson, St. Louis vs. N.Y. Giants, Nov. 1, 1964
    Bart Starr, Green Bay vs. Detroit, Nov. 7, 1965
    Jack Kemp, Buffalo vs. Oakland, Oct. 15, 1967
    Bob Berry, Atlanta vs. St. Louis, Nov. 24, 1968
    Greg Landry, Detroit vs. Dallas, Oct. 6, 1975
    Ron Jaworski, Philadelphia vs. St. Louis, Dec. 18, 1983
    Paul McDonald, Cleveland vs. Kansas City, Sept. 30, 1984
    Archie Manning, Minnesota vs. Chicago, Oct. 28, 1984
    Steve Pelluer, Dallas vs. San Diego, Nov. 16, 1986
    Randall Cunningham, Philadelphia vs. L.A. Raiders, Nov. 30, 1986 (OT)
    David Norrie, N.Y. Jets vs. Dallas, Oct. 4, 1987
    Troy Aikman, Dallas vs. Philadelphia, Sept. 15, 1991
    Bernie Kosar, Cleveland vs. Indianapolis, Sept. 6, 1992
10   By many players

RECEIVING

Most Seasons Leading League

8   Don Hutson, Green Bay, 1936-37, 1939, 1941-45
5   Lionel Taylor, Denver, 1960-63, 1965
3   Tom Fears, Los Angeles, 1948-1950
    Pete Pihos, Philadelphia, 1953-55
    Billy Wilson, San Francisco, 1954, 1956-57
    Raymond Berry, Baltimore, 1958-1960
    Lance Alworth, San Diego, 1966, 1968-69
    Sterling Sharpe, Green Bay, 1989, 1992-93

Most Consecutive Seasons Leading League

5   Don Hutson, Green Bay, 1941-45
4   Lionel Taylor, Denver, 1960-63
3   Tom Fears, Los Angeles, 1948-1950
    Pete Pihos, Philadelphia, 1953-55
    Raymond Berry, Baltimore, 1958-1960

Most Pass Receptions, Career

1,549   Jerry Rice, San Francisco, 1985-2000; Oakland, 2001-04; Seattle, 2004
1,101   Cris Carter, Philadelphia, 1987-89; Minnesota, 1990-2001; Miami, 2002
1,094   Tim Brown, L.A. Raiders, 1988-1994; Oakland, 1995-2003; Tampa Bay, 2004

Most Seasons, 50 or More Pass Receptions

17   Jerry Rice, San Francisco, 1986-1996, 1998-2000; Oakland, 2001-03
13   Andre Reed, Buffalo, 1986-1994, 1996-99
11   Cris Carter, Minnesota, 1991-2001
    Tim Brown, L.A. Raiders, 1993-1994; Oakland, 1995-2003
    Shannon Sharpe, Denver 1992-98; Baltimore, 2000-01; Denver, 2002-03
    Marvin Harrison, Indianapolis, 1996-2006

Most Pass Receptions, Season

143   Marvin Harrison, Indianapolis, 2002
123   Herman Moore, Detroit, 1995
122   Cris Carter, Minnesota, 1994
    Cris Carter, Minnesota, 1995
    Jerry Rice, San Francisco, 1995

Most Pass Receptions, Rookie, Season
- 101   Anquan Boldin, Arizona, 2003
- 90   Terry Glenn, New England, 1996
- 88   Reggie Bush, New Orleans, 2006

Most Pass Receptions, Game
- 20   Terrell Owens, San Francisco vs. Chicago, Dec. 17, 2000
- 18   Tom Fears, Los Angeles vs. Green Bay, Dec. 3, 1950
- 17   Clark Gaines, N.Y. Jets vs. San Francisco, Sept. 21, 1980

Most Consecutive Games, Pass Receptions
- 274   Jerry Rice, San Francisco, 1985-2000; Oakland, 2001-04
- 183   Art Monk, Washington, 1983-1993; N.Y. Jets, 1994; Philadelphia, 1995
- 179   Tim Brown, L.A. Raiders, 1993-94; Oakland, 1995-2003; Tampa Bay, 2004

YARDS GAINED

Most Seasons Leading League
- 7   Don Hutson, Green Bay, 1936, 1938-39, 1941-44
- 6   Jerry Rice, San Francisco, 1986, 1989-1990, 1993-95
- 3   Raymond Berry, Baltimore, 1957, 1959-1960
  - Lance Alworth, San Diego, 1965-66, 1968

Most Consecutive Seasons Leading League
- 4   Don Hutson, Green Bay, 1941-44
- 3   Jerry Rice, San Francisco, 1993-95
- 2   By many players

Most Yards Gained, Career
- 22,895   Jerry Rice, San Francisco, 1985-2000; Oakland, 2001-04; Seattle, 2004
- 14,934   Tim Brown, L.A. Raiders, 1988-1994; Oakland, 1995-2003; Tampa Bay, 2004
- 14,004   James Lofton, Green Bay, 1978-1986; L.A. Raiders, 1987-88; Buffalo, 1989-1992; L.A. Rams, 1993; Philadelphia, 1993

Most Seasons, 1,000 or More Yards, Pass Receiving
- 14   Jerry Rice, San Francisco, 1986-1996, 1998; Oakland, 2001-02
- 9   Tim Brown, L.A. Raiders, 1993-94; Oakland, 1995-2001
  - Jimmy Smith, Jacksonville, 1996-2002, 2004-05
- 8   Steve Largent, Seattle, 1978-1981, 1983-86
  - Cris Carter, Minnesota, 1993-2000
  - Rod Smith, Denver, 1997-2002, 2004-05
  - Isaac Bruce, St. Louis, 1995-96, 1999-2002, 2004, 2006
  - Marvin Harrison, Indianapolis, 1999-2006

Most Yards Gained, Season
- 1,848   Jerry Rice, San Francisco, 1995
- 1,781   Isaac Bruce, St. Louis, 1995
- 1,746   Charley Hennigan, Houston, 1961

Most Yards Gained, Rookie, Season
- 1,473   Bill Groman, Houston, 1960
- 1,377   Anquan Boldin, Arizona, 2003
- 1,313   Randy Moss, Minnesota, 1998

Most Yards Gained, Game
- 336   Willie Anderson, L.A. Rams vs. New Orleans, Nov. 26, 1989 (OT)
- 309   Stephone Paige, Kansas City vs. San Diego, Dec. 22, 1985
- 303   Jim Benton, Cleveland vs. Detroit, Nov. 22, 1945

Most Games, 200 or More Yards Pass Receiving, Career
- 5   Lance Alworth, San Diego, 1962-1970; Dallas, 1971-72
- 4   Don Hutson, Green Bay, 1935-45
  - Charley Hennigan, Houston, 1960-66
  - Jerry Rice, San Francisco, 1985-2000; Oakland, 2001-04; Seattle, 2004

- 3   Don Maynard, N.Y. Giants, 1958; N.Y. Jets, 1960-1972; St. Louis, 1973
  - Wes Chandler, New Orleans, 1978-1981; San Diego, 1981-87; San Francisco, 1988
  - Isaac Bruce, L.A. Rams, 1994; St. Louis, 1995-2006

Most Games, 200 or More Yards Pass Receiving, Season
- 3   Charley Hennigan, Houston, 1961
- 2   Don Hutson, Green Bay, 1942
  - Gene Roberts, N.Y. Giants, 1949
  - Lance Alworth, San Diego, 1963
  - Don Maynard, N.Y. Jets, 1968

Most Games, 100 or More Yards Pass Receiving, Career
- 76   Jerry Rice, San Francisco, 1985-2000; Oakland, 2001-04; Seattle, 2004
- 59   Marvin Harrison, Indianapolis, 1996-2006
- 50   Don Maynard, N.Y. Giants, 1958; N.Y. Jets, 1960-1972; St. Louis, 1973

Most Games, 100 or More Yards Pass Receiving, Season
- 11   Michael Irvin, Dallas, 1995
- 10   Charley Hennigan, Houston, 1961
  - Herman Moore, Detroit, 1995
  - Marvin Harrison, Indianapolis, 2002
  - Torry Holt, St. Louis, 2003
- 9   Elroy (Crazylegs) Hirsch, Los Angeles, 1951
  - Bill Groman, Houston, 1960
  - Lance Alworth, San Diego, 1965
  - Don Maynard, N.Y. Jets, 1967
  - Stanley Morgan, New England, 1986
  - Mark Carrier, Tampa Bay, 1989
  - Robert Brooks, Green Bay, 1995
  - Isaac Bruce, St. Louis, 1995
  - Jerry Rice, San Francisco, 1995
  - Marvin Harrison, Indianapolis, 1999
  - Jimmy Smith, Jacksonville, 1999
  - David Boston, Arizona, 2001
  - Steve Smith, Carolina, 2005

Most Consecutive Games, 100 or More Yards Pass Receiving
- 7   Charley Hennigan, Houston, 1961
  - Michael Irvin, Dallas, 1995
- 6   Raymond Berry, Baltimore, 1960
  - Bill Groman, Houston, 1961
  - Pat Studstill, Detroit, 1966
  - Isaac Bruce, St. Louis, 1995
- 5   Elroy (Crazylegs) Hirsch, Los Angeles, 1951
  - Bob Boyd, Los Angeles, 1954
  - Terry Barr, Detroit, 1963
  - Lance Alworth, San Diego, 1966
  - Don Maynard, N.Y. Jets, 1968-69
  - Harold Jackson, Philadelphia, 1971-72
  - Patrick Jeffers, Carolina, 1999
  - Terrell Owens, Philadelphia, 2004
  - Anquan Boldin, Arizona, 2005

Longest Pass Reception (All TDs except as noted)
- 99   Andy Farkas (from Filchock), Washington vs. Pittsburgh, Oct. 15, 1939
  - Bobby Mitchell (from Izo), Washington vs. Cleveland, Sept. 15, 1963
  - Pat Studstill (from Sweetan), Detroit vs. Baltimore, Oct. 16, 1966
  - Gerry Allen (from Jurgensen), Washington vs. Chicago, Sept. 15, 1968
  - Cliff Branch (from Plunkett), L.A. Raiders vs. Washington, Oct. 2, 1983
  - Mike Quick (from Jaworski), Philadelphia vs. Atlanta, Nov. 10, 1985
  - Tony Martin (from Humphries), San Diego vs. Seattle, Sept. 18, 1994
  - Robert Brooks (from Favre), Green Bay vs. Chicago, Sept. 11, 1995

Marc Boerigter (from Green), Kansas City vs. San Diego, Dec. 22, 2002

Andre Davis (from Garcia), Cleveland vs. Cincinnati, Oct. 17, 2004

98 Gaynell Tinsley (from Russell), Chi. Cardinals vs. Cleveland, Nov. 17, 1938

Dick (Night Train) Lane (from Compton), Chi. Cardinals vs. Green Bay, Nov. 13, 1955

John Farrington (from Wade), Chicago vs. Detroit, Oct. 8, 1961

Willard Dewveall (from Lee), Houston vs. San Diego, Nov. 25, 1962

Homer Jones (from Morrall), N.Y. Giants vs. Pittsburgh, Sept. 11, 1966

Bobby Moore (from Hart), St. Louis vs. Los Angeles, Dec. 10, 1972 (no TD)

Michael Haynes (from Hebert), Atlanta vs. New Orleans, Sept. 12, 1993

Johnnie Morton (from Batch), Detroit vs. Chicago, Oct. 4, 1998

97 Gaynell Tinsley (from Coffee), Chi. Cardinals vs. Chi. Bears, Dec. 5, 1937

Cloyce Box (from Layne), Detroit vs. Green Bay, Nov. 26, 1953

Jerry Tarr (from Shaw), Denver vs. Boston, Sept. 21, 1962

Webster Slaughter (from Kosar), Cleveland vs. Chicago, Oct. 23, 1989

John Taylor (from Young), San Francisco vs. Atlanta, Nov. 3, 1991

AVERAGE GAIN
Highest Average Gain, Career (200 receptions)
22.26 Homer Jones, N.Y. Giants, 1964-69; Cleveland, 1970 (224-4,986)

20.83 Buddy Dial, Pittsburgh, 1959-1963; Dallas, 1964-66 (261-5,436)

20.24 Harlon Hill, Chi. Bears, 1954-1961; Pittsburgh, 1962; Detroit, 1962 (233-4,717)

Highest Average Gain, Season (24 receptions)
32.58 Don Currivan, Boston, 1947 (24-782)

31.44 Bucky Pope, Los Angeles, 1964 (25-786)

28.60 Bobby Duckworth, San Diego, 1984 (25-715)

Highest Average Gain, Game (3 receptions)
63.00 Torry Holt, St. Louis vs. Atlanta, Sept. 24, 2000 (3-189)

60.67 Bill Groman, Houston vs. Denver, Nov. 20, 1960 (3-182)

Homer Jones, N.Y. Giants vs. Washington, Dec. 12, 1965 (3-182)

60.33 Don Currivan, Boston vs. Washington, Nov. 30, 1947 (3-181)

TOUCHDOWNS
Most Seasons Leading League
9 Don Hutson, Green Bay, 1935-38, 1940-44

6 Jerry Rice, San Francisco, 1986-87, 1989-1991, 1993

3 Lance Alworth, San Diego, 1964-66
   Cris Carter, Minnesota, 1995, 1997, 1999
   Randy Moss, Minnesota, 1998, 2000, 2003
   Terrell Owens, San Francisco, 2001-02; Dallas, 2006

Most Consecutive Seasons Leading League
5 Don Hutson, Green Bay, 1940-44

4 Don Hutson, Green Bay, 1935-38

3 Lance Alworth, San Diego, 1964-66
   Jerry Rice, San Francisco, 1989-1991

Most Touchdowns, Career
197 Jerry Rice, San Francisco, 1985-2000; Oakland, 2001-04; Seattle, 2004

130 Cris Carter, Philadelphia, 1987-89; Minnesota, 1990-2001; Miami, 2002

122 Marvin Harrison, Indianapolis, 1996-2006

Most Touchdowns, Season
22 Jerry Rice, San Francisco, 1987

18 Mark Clayton, Miami, 1984
   Sterling Sharpe, Green Bay, 1994

17 Don Hutson, Green Bay, 1942
   Elroy (Crazylegs) Hirsch, Los Angeles, 1951
   Bill Groman, Houston, 1961
   Jerry Rice, San Francisco, 1989
   Cris Carter, Minnesota, 1995
   Carl Pickens, Cincinnati, 1995
   Randy Moss, Minnesota, 1998
   Randy Moss, Minnesota, 2003

Most Touchdowns, Rookie, Season
17 Randy Moss, Minnesota, 1998

13 Bill Howton, Green Bay, 1952
   John Jefferson, San Diego, 1978

12 Harlon Hill, Chi. Bears, 1954
   Bill Groman, Houston, 1960
   Mike Ditka, Chicago, 1961
   Bob Hayes, Dallas, 1965

Most Touchdowns, Game
5 Bob Shaw, Chi. Cardinals vs. Baltimore, Oct. 2, 1950
   Kellen Winslow, San Diego vs. Oakland, Nov. 22, 1981
   Jerry Rice, San Francisco vs. Atlanta, Oct. 14, 1990

4 By many players. Last time: Joe Horn, New Orleans vs. N.Y. Giants, Dec. 14, 2003

Most Consecutive Games, Touchdowns
13 Jerry Rice, San Francisco, 1986-87

11 Elroy (Crazylegs) Hirsch, Los Angeles, 1950-51
   Buddy Dial, Pittsburgh, 1959-1960

10 Carl Pickens, Cincinnati, 1994-95
   Randy Moss, Minnesota, 2003-04

YARDS FROM SCRIMMAGE
Most Scrimmage Yards, Career
23,540 Jerry Rice, San Francisco 1985-2000; Oakland, 2001-04; Seattle, 2004

21,579 Emmitt Smith, Dallas, 1990-2002; Arizona, 2003-04

21,264 Walter Payton, Chicago, 1975-1987

Most Scrimmage Yards, Season
2,429 Marshall Faulk, St. Louis, 1999 (1,381 rush., 1,048 rec.)

2,390 Tiki Barber, N.Y. Giants, 2005 (1,860 rush., 530 rec.)

2,370 LaDainian Tomlinson, San Diego, 2003 (1,645 rush., 725 rec.)

Most Scrimmage Yards, Rookie, Season
2,212 Eric Dickerson, L.A. Rams, 1983 (1,808 rush., 404 rec.)

2,139 Edgerrin James, Indianapolis, 1999 (1,553 rush., 586 rec.)

1,924 Billy Sims, Detroit, 1980 (1,303 rush., 621 rec.)

Most Scrimmage Yards, Game
336 Flipper Anderson, L.A. Rams vs. New Orleans, Nov. 26, 1989 (OT) (336 rec.)

330 Billy Cannon, Houston vs. N.Y. Titans, Dec. 10, 1961 (216 rush., 114 rec.)

309 Stephone Paige, Kansas City vs. San Diego, Dec. 22, 1985 (309 rec.)

INTERCEPTIONS BY
Most Seasons Leading League
3 Everson Walls, Dallas, 1981-82, 1985

2 Dick (Night Train) Lane, Los Angeles, 1952; Chi. Cardinals, 1954
   Jack Christiansen, Detroit, 1953, 1957
   Milt Davis, Baltimore, 1957, 1959
   Dick Lynch, N.Y. Giants, 1961, 1963

Johnny Robinson, Kansas City, 1966, 1970
Bill Bradley, Philadelphia, 1971-72
Emmitt Thomas, Kansas City, 1969, 1974
Ronnie Lott, San Francisco, 1986; L.A. Raiders, 1991
Rod Woodson, Baltimore, 1999; Oakland, 2002
Ty Law, New England, 1998; N.Y. Jets, 2005

Most Interceptions By, Career
81   Paul Krause, Washington, 1964-67; Minnesota, 1968-1979
79   Emlen Tunnell, N.Y. Giants, 1948-1958; Green Bay, 1959-1961
71   Rod Woodson, Pittsburgh, 1987-1996; San Francisco, 1997; Baltimore, 1998-2001; Oakland, 2002-03

Most Interceptions By, Season
14   Dick (Night Train) Lane, Los Angeles, 1952
13   Dan Sandifer, Washington, 1948
     Orban (Spec) Sanders, N.Y. Yanks, 1950
     Lester Hayes, Oakland, 1980
12   By nine players

Most Interceptions By, Rookie, Season
14   Dick (Night Train) Lane, Los Angeles, 1952
13   Dan Sandifer, Washington, 1948
12   Woodley Lewis, Los Angeles, 1950
     Paul Krause, Washington, 1964

Most Interceptions By, Game
4   Sammy Baugh, Washington vs. Detroit, Nov. 14, 1943
    Dan Sandifer, Washington vs. Boston, Oct. 31, 1948
    Don Doll, Detroit vs. Chi. Cardinals, Oct. 23, 1949
    Bob Nussbaumer, Chi. Cardinals vs. N.Y. Bulldogs, Nov. 13, 1949
    Russ Craft, Philadelphia vs. Chi. Cardinals, Sept. 24, 1950
    Bobby Dillon, Green Bay vs. Detroit, Nov. 26, 1953
    Jack Butler, Pittsburgh vs. Washington, Dec. 13, 1953
    Austin (Goose) Gonsoulin, Denver vs. Buffalo, Sept. 18, 1960
    Jerry Norton, St. Louis vs. Washington, Nov. 20, 1960; vs. Pittsburgh, Nov. 26, 1961
    Dave Baker, San Francisco vs. L.A. Rams, Dec. 4, 1960
    Bobby Ply, Dall. Texans vs. San Diego, Dec. 16, 1962
    Bobby Hunt, Kansas City vs. Houston, Oct. 4, 1964
    Willie Brown, Denver vs. N.Y. Jets, Nov. 15, 1964
    Dick Anderson, Miami vs. Pittsburgh, Dec. 3, 1973
    Willie Buchanon, Green Bay vs. San Diego, Sept. 24, 1978
    Deron Cherry, Kansas City vs. Seattle, Sept. 29, 1985
    Kwamie Lassiter, Arizona vs. San Diego, Dec. 27, 1998
    Deltha O'Neal, Denver vs. Kansas City, Oct. 7, 2001

Most Consecutive Games, Passes Intercepted By
8   Tom Morrow, Oakland, 1962-63
7   Tom Landry, N.Y. Giants, 1950-51
   Paul Krause, Washington, 1964
   Larry Wilson, St. Louis, 1966
   Ben Davis, Cleveland, 1968
6   By many players.
     Last time: Brian Russell, Minnesota, 2003

YARDS GAINED
Most Seasons Leading League
2   Dick (Night Train) Lane, Los Angeles, 1952; Chi. Cardinals, 1954
   Herb Adderley, Green Bay, 1965, 1969
   Dick Anderson, Miami, 1968, 1970
   Darren Sharper, Green Bay, 2002; Minnesota, 2005

Most Yards Gained, Career
1,483   Rod Woodson, Pittsburgh, 1987-1996; San Francisco, 1997; Baltimore, 1998-2001; Oakland, 2002-03

1,331   Deion Sanders, Atlanta, 1989-1993; San Francisco, 1994; Dallas, 1995-99; Washington, 2000; Baltimore, 2004-05
1,282   Emlen Tunnell, N.Y. Giants, 1948-1958; Green Bay, 1959-1961

Most Yards Gained, Season
358   Ed Reed, Baltimore, 2004
349   Charlie McNeil, San Diego, 1961
303   Deion Sanders, San Francisco, 1994

Most Yards Gained, Rookie, Season
301   Don Doll, Detroit, 1949
298   Dick (Night Train) Lane, Los Angeles, 1952
275   Woodley Lewis, Los Angeles, 1950

Most Yards Gained, Game
177   Charlie McNeil, San Diego vs. Houston, Sept. 24, 1961
170   Louis Oliver, Miami vs. Buffalo, Oct. 4, 1992
167   Dick Jauron, Detroit vs. Chicago, Nov. 18, 1973

Longest Return (All TDs)
106   Ed Reed, Baltimore vs. Cleveland, Nov. 7, 2004
103   Vencie Glenn, San Diego vs. Denver, Nov. 29, 1987
     Louis Oliver, Miami vs. Buffalo, Oct. 4, 1992
102   Bob Smith, Detroit vs. Chi. Bears, Nov. 24, 1949
     Erich Barnes, N.Y. Giants vs. Dall. Cowboys, Oct. 15, 1961
     Gary Barbaro, Kansas City vs. Seattle, Dec. 11, 1977
     Louis Breeden, Cincinnati vs. San Diego, Nov. 8, 1981
     Eddie Anderson, L.A. Raiders vs. Miami, Dec. 14, 1992
     Donald Frank, San Diego vs. L.A. Raiders, Oct. 31, 1993
     Artrell Hawkins, Cincinnati vs. Houston, Nov. 3, 2002
     Marcus Coleman, Houston vs. Kansas City, Sept. 26, 2004
     Lito Sheppard, Philadelphia vs. Dallas, Oct. 8, 2006

TOUCHDOWNS
Most Touchdowns, Career
12   Rod Woodson, Pittsburgh, 1987-1996; San Francisco, 1997; Baltimore, 1998-2001; Oakland, 2002-03
9   Ken Houston, Houston, 1967-1972; Washington, 1973-1980
   Aeneas Williams, Phoenix, 1991-93; Arizona, 1994-2000; St. Louis, 2001-04
   Deion Sanders, Atlanta, 1989-1993; San Francisco, 1994; Dallas, 1995-99; Washington, 2000; Baltimore, 2004-05
8   Eric Allen, Philadelphia, 1988-1994; New Orleans, 1995-97; Oakland, 1998-2001

Most Touchdowns, Season
4   Ken Houston, Houston, 1971
   Jim Kearney, Kansas City, 1972
   Eric Allen, Philadelphia, 1993
3   Dick Harris, San Diego, 1961
   Dick Lynch, N.Y. Giants, 1963
   Herb Adderley, Green Bay, 1965
   Lem Barney, Detroit, 1967
   Miller Farr, Houston, 1967
   Monte Jackson, Los Angeles, 1976
   Rod Perry, Los Angeles, 1978
   Ronnie Lott, San Francisco, 1981
   Lloyd Burruss, Kansas City, 1986
   Wayne Haddix, Tampa Bay, 1990
   Robert Massey, Phoenix, 1992
   Ray Buchanan, Indianapolis, 1994
   Deion Sanders, San Francisco, 1994
   Mark McMillian, Kansas City, 1997
   Otis Smith, N.Y. Jets, 1997
   Jimmy Hitchcock, Minnesota, 1998
   Eric Allen, Oakland, 2000
   Derrick Brooks, Tampa Bay, 2002

2 By many players

Most Touchdowns, Rookie, Season
- 3 Lem Barney, Detroit, 1967
- Ronnie Lott, San Francisco, 1981
- 2 By many players

Most Touchdowns, Game
- 2 Bill Blackburn, Chi. Cardinals vs. Boston, Oct. 24, 1948
- Dan Sandifer, Washington vs. Boston, Oct. 31, 1948
- Bob Franklin, Cleveland vs. Chicago, Dec. 11, 1960
- Bill Stacy, St. Louis vs. Dall. Cowboys, Nov. 5, 1961
- Jerry Norton, St. Louis vs. Pittsburgh, Nov. 26, 1961
- Miller Farr, Houston vs. Buffalo, Dec. 7, 1968
- Ken Houston, Houston vs. San Diego, Dec. 19, 1971
- Jim Kearney, Kansas City vs. Denver, Oct. 1, 1972
- Lemar Parrish, Cincinnati vs. Houston, Dec. 17, 1972
- Dick Anderson, Miami vs. Pittsburgh, Dec. 3, 1973
- Prentice McCray, New England vs. N.Y. Jets, Nov. 21, 1976
- Kenny Johnson, Atlanta vs. Green Bay, Nov. 27, 1983 (OT)
- Mike Kozlowski, Miami vs. N.Y. Jets, Dec. 16, 1983
- Dave Brown, Seattle vs. Kansas City, Nov. 4, 1984
- Lloyd Burruss, Kansas City vs. San Diego, Oct. 19, 1986
- Henry Jones, Buffalo vs. Indianapolis, Sept. 20, 1992
- Robert Massey, Phoenix vs. Washington, Oct. 4, 1992
- Eric Allen, Philadelphia vs. New Orleans, Dec. 26, 1993
- Ken Norton, San Francisco vs. St. Louis, Oct. 22, 1995
- Otis Smith, N.Y. Jets vs. Tampa Bay, Dec. 14, 1997
- Dewayne Washington, Pittsburgh vs. Jacksonville, Nov. 22, 1998
- Aaron Glenn, Houston vs. Pittsburgh, Dec. 8, 2002
- Ronde Barber, Tampa Bay vs. Philadelphia, Oct. 22, 2006

PUNTING

Most Seasons Leading League
- 4 Sammy Baugh, Washington, 1940-43
- Jerrel Wilson, Kansas City, 1965, 1968, 1972-73
- 3 Yale Lary, Detroit, 1959, 1961, 1963
- Jim Fraser, Denver, 1962-64
- Ray Guy, Oakland, 1974-75, 1977
- Rohn Stark, Baltimore, 1983; Indianapolis, 1985-86
- 2 By many players

Most Consecutive Seasons Leading League
- 4 Sammy Baugh, Washington, 1940-43
- 3 Jim Fraser, Denver, 1962-64
- 2 By many players

PUNTS

Most Punts, Career
- 1,514 Jeff Feagles, New England, 1988-89; Philadelphia, 1990-93; Arizona, 1994-97; Seattle, 1998-2002; N.Y. Giants, 2003-06
- 1,401 Sean Landeta, N.Y. Giants, 1985-1993; L.A. Rams, 1993-94; St. Louis, 1995-96; Tampa Bay, 1997; Green Bay, 1998; Philadelphia, 1999-2002; St. Louis, 2003-04; Philadelphia, 2005
- 1,226 Lee Johnson, Houston, 1985-87; Cleveland, 1987-88; Cincinnati, 1988-1998; New England, 1999-2001; Minnesota, 2001; Philadelphia, 2002

Most Punts, Season
- 114 Bob Parsons, Chicago, 1981
- Chad Stanley, Houston, 2002
- 111 Brad Maynard, N.Y. Giants, 1997
- 109 John James, Atlanta, 1978

Most Punts, Rookie, Season
- 111 Brad Maynard, N.Y. Giants, 1997
- 108 John Teltschik, Philadelphia, 1986
- 101 Daniel Pope, Kansas City, 1999

Most Punts, Game
- 16 Leo Araguz, Oakland vs. San Diego, Oct. 11, 1998
- 15 John Teltschik, Philadelphia vs. N.Y. Giants, Dec. 6, 1987 (OT)
- 14 Dick Nesbitt, Chi. Cardinals vs. Chi. Bears, Nov. 30, 1933
- Keith Molesworth, Chi. Bears vs. Green Bay, Dec. 10, 1933
- Sammy Baugh, Washington vs. Philadelphia, Nov. 5, 1939
- Carl Kinscherf, N.Y. Giants vs. Detroit, Nov. 7, 1943
- George Taliaferro, N.Y. Yanks vs. Los Angeles, Sept. 28, 1951

Longest Punt
- 98 Steve O'Neal, N.Y. Jets vs. Denver, Sept. 21, 1969
- 94 Joe Lintzenich, Chi. Bears vs. N.Y. Giants, Nov. 16, 1931
- 93 Shawn McCarthy, New England vs. Buffalo, Nov. 3, 1991

AVERAGE YARDAGE

Highest Average, Punting, Career (250 punts)
- 46.10 Shane Lechler, Oakland, 2000-06 (519-23,926)
- 45.10 Sammy Baugh, Washington, 1937-1952 (338-15,245)
- 44.68 Tommy Davis, San Francisco, 1959-1969 (511-22,833)

Highest Average, Punting, Season (Qualifiers)
- 51.40 Sammy Baugh, Washington, 1940 (35-1,799)
- 48.94 Yale Lary, Detroit, 1963 (35-1,713)
- 48.73 Sammy Baugh, Washington, 1941 (30-1,462)

Highest Average, Punting, Rookie, Season (Qualifiers)
- 45.92 Frank Sinkwich, Detroit, 1943 (12-551)
- 45.91 Shane Lechler, Oakland, 2000 (65-2,984)
- 45.66 Tommy Davis, San Francisco, 1959 (59-2,694)

Highest Average, Punting, Game (4 punts)
- 61.75 Bob Cifers, Detroit vs. Chi. Bears, Nov. 24, 1946 (4-247)
- 61.60 Roy McKay, Green Bay vs. Chi. Cardinals, Oct. 28, 1945 (5-308)
- 59.50 Darren Bennett, San Diego vs. Pittsburgh, Oct. 1, 1995 (4-238)

PUNTS HAD BLOCKED

Most Consecutive Punts, None Blocked
- 1,177 Chris Gardocki, Chicago, 1992-94; Indianapolis, 1995-98; Cleveland, 1999-2003; Pittsburgh, 2004-06 (current)
- 878 Bryan Barker, Kansas City, 1993; Philadelphia, 1994; Jacksonville, 1995-2000; Washington, 2001-03; Green Bay, 2004; St. Louis, 2005
- 638 Tom Tupa, New England, 1997-98; N.Y. Jets, 1999-2001; Tampa Bay, 2002-03; Washington, 2004

Most Punts Had Blocked, Career
- 14 Herman Weaver, Detroit, 1970-76; Seattle, 1977-1980 Harry Newsome, Pittsburgh, 1985-89; Minnesota, 1990-93
- 12 Jerrel Wilson, Kansas City, 1963-1977; New England, 1978
- Tom Blanchard, N.Y. Giants, 1971-73; New Orleans, 1974-78; Tampa Bay, 1979-1981
- 11 David Lee, Baltimore, 1966-1978
- Jeff Feagles, New England, 1988-89; Philadelphia, 1990-93; Arizona, 1994-97; Seattle, 1998-2002; N.Y. Giants, 2003-06

Most Punts Had Blocked, Season
- 6 Harry Newsome, Pittsburgh, 1988
- 4 Bryan Wagner, Cleveland, 1990
- 3 By many players

PUNTS INSIDE THE 20
Punts Inside the 20 have been compiled since 1976.

Most Punts Inside the 20, Career
- 483 Jeff Feagles, New England, 1988-89; Philadelphia, 1990-93; Arizona, 1994-97; Seattle, 1998-2002; N.Y. Giants, 2003-06
- 381 Sean Landeta, N.Y. Giants, 1985-1993; L.A. Rams, 1993-94; St. Louis, 1995-96; Tampa Bay, 1997; Green Bay, 1998; Philadelphia, 1999-2002; St. Louis, 2003-04; Philadelphia, 2005
- 345 Craig Hentrich, Green Bay, 1994-97; Tennessee, 1998-2006

Most Punts Inside the 20, Season
- 39 Kyle Richardson, Baltimore, 1999
- 36 Brad Maynard, Chicago, 2001
  Chad Stanley, Houston, 2002
  Chad Stanley, Houston, 2003
- 35 Rich Camarillo, Houston, 1994
  Mark Royals, Pittsburgh, 1994
  Craig Hentrich, Tennessee, 1999
  Kyle Richardson, Baltimore, 2000
  Todd Sauerbrun, Carolina, 2001
  Mike Scifres, San Diego, 2006

Most Punts Inside the 20, Game
- 8 Mark Royals, Pittsburgh vs. Houston, Nov. 6, 1994 (OT)
  Bryan Barker, Jacksonville vs. Baltimore, Nov. 14, 1999
- 7 Josh Miller, Pittsburgh vs. Cincinnati, Dec. 20, 1998
- 6 By many players

PUNT RETURNS
Most Seasons Leading League
- 3 Les (Speedy) Duncan, San Diego, 1965-66; Washington, 1971
  Rick Upchurch, Denver, 1976, 1978, 1982
- 2 Dick Christy, N.Y. Titans, 1961-62
  Claude Gibson, Oakland, 1963-64
  Billy (White Shoes) Johnson, Houston, 1975, 1977
  Mel Gray, New Orleans, 1987; Detroit, 1991
  Jermaine Lewis, Baltimore, 1997, 2000

PUNT RETURNS
Most Punt Returns, Career
- 463 Brian Mitchell, Washington, 1990-99; Philadelphia, 2000-02; N.Y. Giants, 2003
- 351 Eric Metcalf, Cleveland, 1989-1994; Atlanta, 1995-96; San Diego, 1997; Arizona, 1998; Carolina, 1999; Washington, 2001; Green Bay, 2002
- 349 David Meggett, N.Y. Giants, 1989-1994; New England, 1995-97; N.Y. Jets, 1998

Most Punt Returns, Season
- 70 Danny Reece, Tampa Bay, 1979
- 62 Fulton Walker, Miami-L.A. Raiders, 1985
- 58 J.T. Smith, Kansas City, 1979
  Greg Pruitt, L.A. Raiders, 1983
  Leo Lewis, Minnesota, 1988
  Desmond Howard, Green Bay, 1996

Most Punt Returns, Rookie, Season
- 57 Lew Barnes, Chicago, 1986
- 55 B.J. Sams, Baltimore, 2004
- 54 James Jones, Dallas, 1980

Most Punt Returns, Game
- 11 Eddie Brown, Washington vs. Tampa Bay, Oct. 9, 1977

- 10 Theo Bell, Pittsburgh vs. Buffalo, Dec. 16, 1979
  Mike Nelms, Washington vs. New Orleans, Dec. 26, 1982
  Ronnie Harris, New England vs. Pittsburgh, Dec. 5, 1993
- 9 Rodger Bird, Oakland vs. Denver, Sept. 10, 1967
  Ralph McGill, San Francisco vs. Atlanta, Oct. 29, 1972
  Ed Podolak, Kansas City vs. San Diego, Nov. 10, 1974
  Anthony Leonard, San Francisco vs. New Orleans, Oct. 17, 1976
  Butch Johnson, Dallas vs. Buffalo, Nov. 15, 1976
  Larry Marshall, Philadelphia vs. Tampa Bay, Sept. 18, 1977
  Nesby Glasgow, Baltimore vs. Kansas City, Sept. 2, 1979
  Mike Nelms, Washington vs. St. Louis, Dec. 21, 1980
  Leon Bright, N.Y. Giants vs. Philadelphia, Dec. 11, 1982
  Pete Shaw, N.Y. Giants vs. Philadelphia, Nov. 20, 1983
  Cleotha Montgomery, L.A. Raiders vs. Detroit, Dec. 10, 1984
  Phil McConkey, N.Y. Giants vs. Philadelphia, Dec. 6, 1987 (OT)
  Andre Hastings, Pittsburgh vs. Cleveland, Nov. 13, 1995
  Steve Smith, Carolina vs. Detroit, Sept. 15, 2002
  Reggie Swinton, Arizona vs. Philadelphia, Dec. 24, 2005

FAIR CATCHES
Most Fair Catches, Career
- 231 Brian Mitchell, Washington, 1990-99; Philadelphia, 2000-02; N.Y. Giants, 2003
- 162 Tim Brown, L.A. Raiders, 1988-1994; Oakland, 1995-2003; Tampa Bay, 2004
- 144 Glyn Milburn, Denver, 1993-95; Detroit, 1996-97; Chicago, 1998-2001; San Diego, 2001

Most Fair Catches, Season
- 33 Brian Mitchell, Philadelphia, 2000
- 29 Wes Welker, Miami, 2006
- 27 Leo Lewis, Minnesota, 1989
  Antonio Chatman, Green Bay, 2004

Most Fair Catches, Game
- 7 Bake Turner, N.Y. Jets vs. Miami, Nov. 20, 1966
  Lem Barney, Detroit vs. Chicago, Nov. 21, 1976
  Bobby Morse, Philadelphia vs. Buffalo, Dec. 27, 1987
- 6 Jake Scott, Miami vs. Buffalo, Dec. 20, 1970
  Greg Pruitt, L.A. Raiders vs. Seattle, Oct. 7, 1984
  Phil McConkey, San Diego vs. Kansas City, Dec. 17, 1989
  Gerald McNeil, Houston vs. Pittsburgh, Sept. 16, 1990
  Bobby Engram, Chicago vs. Minnesota, Sept. 15, 1996
  Eddie Kennison, New Orleans vs. Baltimore, Dec. 19, 1999
- 5 By many players

YARDS GAINED
Most Seasons Leading League
- 3 Alvin Haymond, Baltimore, 1965-66; Los Angeles, 1969
- 2 Bill Dudley, Pittsburgh, 1942, 1946
  Emlen Tunnell, N.Y. Giants, 1951-52
  Dick Christy, N.Y. Titans, 1961-62
  Claude Gibson, Oakland, 1963-64
  Rodger Bird, Oakland, 1966-67

J.T. Smith, Kansas City, 1979-1980
Vai Sikahema, St. Louis, 1986-87
David Meggett, N.Y. Giants, 1989-1990
Tamarick Vanover, Kansas City, 1995, 1999

Most Yards Gained, Career
4,999   Brian Mitchell, Washington, 1990-99; Philadelphia, 2000-02; N.Y. Giants, 2003
3,708   David Meggett, N.Y. Giants, 1989-1994; New England, 1995-97; N.Y. Jets, 1998
3,601   Darrien Gordon, San Diego, 1993-94, 1996; Denver, 1997-98; Oakland, 1999-2000; Atlanta, 2001; Green Bay, 2002

Most Yards Gained, Season
875   Desmond Howard, Green Bay, 1996
692   Fulton Walker, Miami-L.A. Raiders, 1985
666   Greg Pruitt, L.A. Raiders, 1983

Most Yards Gained, Rookie, Season
656   Louis Lipps, Pittsburgh, 1984
655   Neal Colzie, Oakland, 1975
619   Leon Johnson, N.Y. Jets, 1997

Most Yards Gained, Game
207   LeRoy Irvin, Los Angeles vs. Atlanta, Oct. 11, 1981
205   George Atkinson, Oakland vs. Buffalo, Sept. 15, 1968
199   Eddie Drummond, Detroit vs. Jacksonville, Nov. 14, 2004 (OT)

Longest Punt Return (All TDs)
103   Robert Bailey, L.A. Rams vs. New Orleans, Oct. 23, 1994
98   Gil LeFebvre, Cincinnati vs. Brooklyn, Dec. 3, 1933
    Charlie West, Minnesota vs. Washington, Nov. 3, 1968
    Dennis Morgan, Dallas vs. St. Louis, Oct. 13, 1974
    Terance Mathis, N.Y. Jets vs. Dallas, Nov. 4, 1990
97   Greg Pruitt, L.A. Raiders vs. Washington, Oct. 2, 1983

AVERAGE YARDAGE
Highest Average, Career (75 returns)
12.78   George McAfee, Chi. Bears, 1940-41, 1945-1950 (112-1,431)
12.75   Jack Christiansen, Detroit, 1951-58 (85-1,084)
12.55   Claude Gibson, San Diego, 1961-62; Oakland, 1963-65 (110-1,381)

Highest Average, Season (Qualifiers)
23.00   Herb Rich, Baltimore, 1950 (12-276)
21.47   Jack Christiansen, Detroit, 1952 (15-322)
21.28   Dick Christy, N.Y. Titans, 1961 (18-383)

Highest Average, Rookie, Season (Qualifiers)
23.00   Herb Rich, Baltimore, 1950 (12-276)
20.88   Jerry Davis, Chi. Cardinals, 1948 (16-334)
20.73   Frank Sinkwich, Detroit, 1943 (11-228)

Highest Average, Game (3 returns)
51.00   Steve Smith, Carolina vs. Cincinnati, Dec. 8, 2002 (3-153)
47.67   Chuck Latourette, St. Louis vs. New Orleans, Sept. 29, 1968 (3-143)
47.33   Johnny Roland, St. Louis vs. Philadelphia, Oct. 2, 1966 (3-142)

TOUCHDOWNS
Most Touchdowns, Career
10   Eric Metcalf, Cleveland, 1989-1994; Atlanta, 1995-96; San Diego, 1997; Arizona, 1998; Carolina, 1999; Washington, 2001; Green Bay, 2002
9   Brian Mitchell, Washington, 1990-99; Philadelphia 2000-02; N.Y. Giants, 2003
8   Jack Christiansen, Detroit, 1951-58
    Rick Upchurch, Denver, 1975-1983
    Desmond Howard, Washington, 1992-94; Jacksonville, 1995; Green Bay, 1996, 1999; Oakland, 1997-98; Detroit, 1999-2002

Most Touchdowns, Season
4   Jack Christiansen, Detroit, 1951
    Rick Upchurch, Denver, 1976
3   Emlen Tunnell, N.Y. Giants, 1951
    Billy (White Shoes) Johnson, Houston, 1975
    LeRoy Irvin, Los Angeles, 1981
    Desmond Howard, Green Bay, 1996
    Darrien Gordon, Denver, 1997
    Eric Metcalf, San Diego, 1997
    Devin Hester, Chicago, 2006
    Pacman Jones, Tennessee, 2006
2   By many players

Most Touchdowns, Rookie, Season
4   Jack Christiansen, Detroit, 1951
3   Devin Hester, Chicago, 2006
2   By many players

Most Touchdowns, Game
2   Jack Christiansen, Detroit vs. Los Angeles, Oct. 14, 1951; vs. Green Bay, Nov. 22, 1951
    Dick Christy, N.Y. Titans vs. Denver, Sept. 24, 1961
    Rick Upchurch, Denver vs. Cleveland, Sept. 26, 1976
    LeRoy Irvin, Los Angeles vs. Atlanta, Oct. 11, 1981
    Vai Sikahema, St. Louis vs. Tampa Bay, Dec. 21, 1986
    Todd Kinchen, L.A. Rams vs. Atlanta, Dec. 27, 1992
    Eric Metcalf, Cleveland vs. Pittsburgh, Oct. 24, 1993; San Diego vs. Cincinnati, Nov. 2, 1997
    Darrien Gordon, Denver vs. Carolina, Nov. 9, 1997
    Jermaine Lewis, Baltimore vs. Seattle, Dec. 7, 1997; Baltimore vs. N.Y. Jets, Dec. 24, 2000
    Steve Smith, Carolina vs. Cincinnati, Dec. 8, 2002
    Eddie Drummond, Detroit vs. Jacksonville, Nov. 14, 2004 (OT)

KICKOFF RETURNS
Most Seasons Leading League
3   Abe Woodson, San Francisco, 1959, 1962-63
2   Lynn Chandnois, Pittsburgh, 1951-52
    Bobby Jancik, Houston, 1962-63
    Travis Williams, Green Bay, 1967; Los Angeles, 1971
    Mel Gray, Detroit, 1991, 1994
    Michael Bates, Carolina, 1996-97

KICKOFF RETURNS
Most Kickoff Returns, Career
607   Brian Mitchell, Washington, 1990-99; Philadelphia 2000-02; N.Y. Giants, 2003
421   Mel Gray, New Orleans, 1986-88; Detroit, 1989-1994; Houston, 1995-96; Tennessee, 1997; Philadelphia, 1997
    Allen Rossum, Philadelphia, 1998-99; Green Bay, 2000-01; Atlanta, 2002-06
407   Glyn Milburn, Denver, 1993-95; Detroit, 1996-97; Chicago, 1998-2001; San Diego, 2001

Most Kickoff Returns, Season
82   MarTay Jenkins, Arizona, 2000
73   Josh Scobey, Arizona, 2003
    Chris Carr, Oakland, 2005
70   Tyrone Hughes, New Orleans, 1996
    Michael Lewis, New Orleans, 2002

Most Kickoff Returns, Rookie, Season
73   Josh Scobey, Arizona, 2003
    Chris Carr, Oakland, 2005
67   Ronney Jenkins, San Diego, 2000
64   Tab Perry, Cincinnati, 2005

Most Kickoff Returns, Game
10   Desmond Howard, Oakland vs. Seattle, Oct. 26, 1997
    Richard Alston, Cleveland vs. Cincinnati, Nov. 28, 2004
9   Noland Smith, Kansas City vs. Oakland, Nov. 23, 1967

Dino Hall, Cleveland vs. Pittsburgh, Oct. 7, 1979
Paul Palmer, Kansas City vs. Seattle, Sept. 20, 1987
Eric Metcalf, Atlanta vs. San Francisco,
   Sept. 29, 1996; vs. St. Louis, Nov. 10, 1996
Michael Bates, Carolina vs. Atlanta, Oct. 4, 1998
Nate Jacquet, Minnesota vs. Philadelphia,
   Nov. 11, 2001
Ahmad Merritt, Chicago vs. San Francisco,
   Sept. 7, 2003
Josh Scobey, Arizona vs. Cleveland, Nov. 16, 2003
Maurice Hicks, San Francisco vs. San Diego,
   Oct. 15, 2006
  8 By many players

YARDS GAINED
Most Seasons Leading League
  3 Bruce Harper, N.Y. Jets, 1977-79
     Tyrone Hughes, New Orleans, 1994-96
  2 Marshall Goldberg, Chi. Cardinals, 1941-42
     Woodley Lewis, Los Angeles, 1953-54
     Al Carmichael, Green Bay, 1956-57
     Timmy Brown, Philadelphia, 1961, 1963
     Bobby Jancik, Houston, 1963, 1966
     Ron Smith, Atlanta, 1966-67
     Chris Carr, Oakland, 2005-06
Most Yards Gained, Career
14,014 Brian Mitchell, Washington, 1990-99; Philadelphia, 2000-02; N.Y. Giants, 2003
10,250 Mel Gray, New Orleans, 1986-88; Detroit, 1989-1994; Houston, 1995-96; Tennessee, 1997; Philadelphia, 1997
 9,788 Glyn Milburn, Denver, 1993-95; Detroit, 1996-97; Chicago, 1998-2001; San Diego, 2001
Most Yards Gained, Season
2,186 MarTay Jenkins, Arizona, 2000
1,807 Michael Lewis, New Orleans, 2002
1,791 Tyrone Hughes, New Orleans, 1996
Most Yards Gained, Rookie, Season
1,752 Chris Carr, Oakland, 2005
1,684 Josh Scobey, Arizona, 2003
1,577 Justin Miller, N.Y. Jets, 2005
Most Yards Gained, Game
 304 Tyrone Hughes, New Orleans vs. L.A. Rams, Oct. 23, 1994
 294 Wally Triplett, Detroit vs. Los Angeles, Oct. 29, 1950
 278 Chad Morton, N.Y. Jets vs. Buffalo, Sept. 8, 2002 (OT)
Longest Kickoff Return (All TDs)
 106 Al Carmichael, Green Bay vs. Chi. Bears, Oct. 7, 1956
      Noland Smith, Kansas City vs. Denver, Dec. 17, 1967
      Roy Green, St. Louis vs. Dallas, Oct. 21, 1979
 105 Frank Seno, Chi. Cardinals vs. N.Y. Giants, Oct. 20, 1946
      Ollie Matson, Chi. Cardinals vs. Washington, Oct. 14, 1956
      Abe Woodson, San Francisco vs. Los Angeles, Nov. 8, 1959
      Timmy Brown, Philadelphia vs. Cleveland, Sept. 17, 1961
      Jon Arnett, Los Angeles vs. Detroit, Oct. 29, 1961
      Eugene (Mercury) Morris, Miami vs. Cincinnati, Sept. 14, 1969
      Travis Williams, Los Angeles vs. New Orleans, Dec. 5, 1971
      Terry Fair, Detroit vs. Tampa Bay, Sept. 28, 1998
 104 By many players

AVERAGE YARDAGE
Highest Average, Career (75 returns)
30.56 Gale Sayers, Chicago, 1965-1971 (91-2,781)

29.57 Lynn Chandnois, Pittsburgh, 1950-56 (92-2,720)
28.69 Abe Woodson, San Francisco, 1958-1964; St. Louis, 1965-66 (193-5,538)
Highest Average, Season (Qualifiers)
41.06 Travis Williams, Green Bay, 1967 (18-739)
37.69 Gale Sayers, Chicago, 1967 (16-603)
35.50 Ollie Matson, Chi. Cardinals, 1958 (14-497)
Highest Average, Rookie, Season (Qualifiers)
41.06 Travis Williams, Green Bay, 1967 (18-739)
33.08 Tom Moore, Green Bay, 1960 (12-397)
32.88 Duriel Harris, Miami, 1976 (17-559)
Highest Average, Game (3 returns)
73.50 Wally Triplett, Detroit vs. Los Angeles, Oct. 29, 1950 (4-294)
67.33 Lenny Lyles, San Francisco vs. Baltimore, Dec. 18, 1960 (3-202)
65.33 Ken Hall, Houston vs. N.Y. Titans, Oct. 23, 1960 (3-196)

TOUCHDOWNS
Most Touchdowns, Career
  6 Ollie Matson, Chi. Cardinals, 1952, 1954-58; L.A. Rams, 1959-1962; Detroit, 1963; Philadelphia, 1964
     Gale Sayers, Chicago, 1965-1971
     Travis Williams, Green Bay, 1967-1970; Los Angeles, 1971
     Mel Gray, New Orleans, 1986-88; Detroit, 1989-1994; Houston, 1995-96; Tennessee, 1997; Philadelphia, 1997
     Dante Hall, Kansas City, 2000-06
  5 Bobby Mitchell, Cleveland, 1958-1961; Washington, 1962-68
     Abe Woodson, San Francisco, 1958-1964; St. Louis, 1965-66
     Timmy Brown, Green Bay, 1959; Philadelphia, 1960-67; Baltimore, 1968
     Michael Bates, Seattle, 1993-94; Cleveland, 1995; Carolina, 1996-2000, 2002; Washington, 2001; N.Y. Jets, 2003; Dallas, 2003
  4 Cecil Turner, Chicago, 1968-1973
     Ron Brown, L.A. Rams, 1984-89, 1991; L.A. Raiders, 1990
     Jon Vaughn, New England, 1991-92; Seattle, 1993-94; Kansas City, 1994
     Andre Coleman, San Diego, 1994-96; Seattle, 1997; Pittsburgh, 1997-98
     Tamarick Vanover, Kansas City, 1995-99, San Diego, 2002
     Tony Horne, St. Louis, 1998-2000
     Brian Mitchell, Washington, 1990-99; Philadelphia, 2000-02; N.Y. Giants, 2003
     Darrick Vaughn, Atlanta, 2000-01; Houston, 2003
     Terrence McGee, Buffalo, 2003-06
Most Touchdowns, Season
  4 Travis Williams, Green Bay, 1967
     Cecil Turner, Chicago, 1970
  3 Verda (Vitamin T) Smith, Los Angeles, 1950
     Abe Woodson, San Francisco, 1963
     Gale Sayers, Chicago, 1967
     Raymond Clayborn, New England, 1977
     Ron Brown, L.A. Rams, 1985
     Mel Gray, Detroit, 1994
     Darrick Vaughn, Atlanta, 2000
     Terrence McGee, Buffalo, 2004
  2 By many players
Most Touchdowns, Rookie, Season
  4 Travis Williams, Green Bay, 1967
  3 Raymond Clayborn, New England, 1977
     Darrick Vaughn, Atlanta, 2000

2 By many players

Most Touchdowns, Game

2 Timmy Brown, Philadelphia vs. Dallas, Nov. 6, 1966
Travis Williams, Green Bay vs. Cleveland,
Nov. 12, 1967
Ron Brown, L.A. Rams vs. Green Bay, Nov. 24, 1985
Tyrone Hughes, New Orleans vs. L.A. Rams,
Oct. 23, 1994
Chad Morton, N.Y. Jets vs. Buffalo, Sept. 8, 2002 (OT)
Devin Hester, Chicago vs. St. Louis, Dec. 11, 2006

COMBINED KICK RETURNS

Most Combined Kick Returns, Career

1,070 Brian Mitchell, Washington, 1990-99; Philadelphia,
2000-02; N.Y. Giants, 2003 (p-463, k-607)
711 Glyn Milburn, Denver, 1993-95; Detroit, 1996-97;
Chicago, 1998-2001; San Diego, 2001 (p-304,
k-407)
673 Mel Gray, New Orleans, 1986-88; Detroit,
1989-1994; Houston, 1995-96; Tennessee,
1997; Philadelphia, 1997 (p-252, k-421)

Most Combined Kick Returns, Season

114 Michael Lewis, New Orleans, 2002 (p-44, k-70)
B.J. Sams, Baltimore, 2004 (p-55, k-59)
107 Chris Carr, Oakland, 2005 (p-34, k-73)
Dante Hall, Kansas City, 2005 (p-42, k-65)
105 Reggie Swinton, Arizona, 2005 (p-42, k-63)

Most Combined Kick Returns, Game

13 Stump Mitchell, St. Louis vs. Atlanta, Oct. 18, 1981
(p-6, k-7)
Ronnie Harris, New England vs. Pittsburgh,
Dec. 5, 1993 (p-10, k-3)
12 Mel Renfro, Dallas vs. Green Bay, Nov. 29, 1964
(p-4, k-8)
Larry Jones, Washington vs. Dallas, Dec. 13, 1975
(p-6, k-6)
Eddie Brown, Washington vs. Tampa Bay,
Oct. 9, 1977 (p-11, k-1)
Nesby Glasgow, Baltimore vs. Denver, Sept. 2, 1979
(p-9, k-3)
Tim Dwight, Atlanta vs. Detroit, Nov. 12, 2000
(p-8, k-4)
Wes Welker, Miami vs. Buffalo, Dec. 5, 2004
(p-6, k-6)
Reggie Swinton, Arizona vs. Philadelphia,
Dec. 24, 2005 (p-9, k-3)
11 By many players

YARDS GAINED

Most Yards Returned, Career

19,013 Brian Mitchell, Washington, 1990-99; Philadelphia,
2000-02; N.Y. Giants, 2003 (p-4,999; k-14,014)
13,003 Mel Gray, New Orleans, 1986-88; Detroit,
1989-1994; Houston, 1995-96; Tennessee,
1997; Philadelphia, 1997 (p-2,753; k-10,250)
12,772 Glyn Milburn, Denver, 1993-95; Detroit, 1996-97;
Chicago, 1998-2001; San Diego, 2001
(p-2,984; k-9,788)

Most Yards Returned, Season

2,432 Michael Lewis, New Orleans, 2002 (p-625, k-1,807)
2,187 MarTay Jenkins, Arizona, 2000 (p-1, k-2,186)
1,992 Charlie Rogers, Seattle, 2000 (p-363, k-1,629)

Most Yards Returned, Game

347 Tyrone Hughes, New Orleans vs. L.A. Rams,
Oct. 23, 1994 (p-43, k-304)

294 Wally Triplett, Detroit vs. Los Angeles, Oct. 29, 1950
(k-294)
Woodley Lewis, Los Angeles vs. Detroit,
Oct. 18, 1953 (p-120, k-174)

289 Eddie Payton, Detroit vs. Minnesota, Dec. 17, 1977
(p-105, k-184)

TOUCHDOWNS

Most Touchdowns, Career

13 Brian Mitchell, Washington, 1990-99; Philadelphia,
2000-02; N.Y. Giants, 2003 (p-9, k-4)
12 Eric Metcalf, Cleveland, 1989-1994; Atlanta,
1995-96; San Diego, 1997; Arizona, 1998;
Carolina, 1999; Washington, 2001; Green Bay,
2002 (p-10, k-2)
11 Dante Hall, Kansas City, 2000-06 (p-5, k-6)

Most Touchdowns, Season

5 Devin Hester, Chicago, 2006 (p-3, k-2)
4 Jack Christiansen, Detroit, 1951 (p-4)
Emlen Tunnell, N.Y. Giants, 1951 (p-3, k-1)
Gale Sayers, Chicago, 1967 (p-1, k-3)
Travis Williams, Green Bay, 1967 (k-4)
Cecil Turner, Chicago, 1970 (k-4)
Billy Johnson, Houston, 1975 (p-3, k-1)
Rick Upchurch, Denver, 1976 (p-4)
Dante Hall, Kansas City, 2003 (p-2, r-2)
Eddie Drummond, Detroit, 2004 (p-2, k-2)
3 By many players

Most Touchdowns, Game

2 Jack Christiansen, Detroit vs. Los Angeles,
Oct. 14, 1951 (p-2); vs. Green Bay,
Nov. 22, 1951 (p-2)
Jim Patton, N.Y. Giants vs. Washington,
Oct. 30, 1955 (p-1, k-1)
Bobby Mitchell, Cleveland vs. Philadelphia,
Nov. 23, 1958 (p-1, k-1)
Dick Christy, N.Y. Titans vs. Denver, Sept. 24, 1961
(p-2)
Al Frazier, Denver vs. Boston, Dec. 3, 1961 (p-1, k-1)
Timmy Brown, Philadelphia vs. Dallas, Nov. 6, 1966
(k-2)
Travis Williams, Green Bay vs. Cleveland,
Nov. 12, 1967 (k-2); vs. Pittsburgh,
Nov. 2, 1969 (p-1, k-1)
Gale Sayers, Chicago vs. San Francisco,
Dec. 3, 1967 (p-1, k-1)
Rick Upchurch, Denver vs. Cleveland,
Sept. 26, 1976 (p-2)
Eddie Payton, Detroit vs. Minnesota, Dec. 17, 1977
(p-1, k-1)
LeRoy Irvin, Los Angeles vs. Atlanta, Oct. 11, 1981
(p-2)
Ron Brown, L.A. Rams vs. Green Bay,
Nov. 24, 1985 (k-2)
Vai Sikahema, St. Louis vs. Tampa Bay,
Dec. 21, 1986 (p-2)
Todd Kinchen, L.A. Rams vs. Atlanta, Dec. 27, 1992
(p-2)
Eric Metcalf, Cleveland vs. Pittsburgh, Oct. 24, 1993
(p-2); San Diego vs. Cincinnati, Nov. 2, 1997
(p-2)
Tyrone Hughes, New Orleans vs. L.A. Rams,
Oct. 23, 1994 (k-2)
Darrien Gordon, Denver vs. Carolina, Nov. 9, 1997
(p-2)
Jermaine Lewis, Baltimore vs. Seattle, Dec. 7, 1997
(p-2); Baltimore vs. N.Y. Jets, Dec. 24, 2000
(p-2)
Chad Morton, N.Y. Jets vs. Buffalo, Sept. 8, 2002
(OT) (k-2)
Michael Lewis, New Orleans vs. Washington,
Oct. 13, 2002 (p-1, k-1)
Dante Hall, Kansas City vs. St. Louis, Dec. 8, 2002
(p-1, k-1)

Steve Smith, Carolina vs. Cincinnati, Dec. 8, 2002
(p-2
Eddie Drummond, Detroit vs. Jacksonville,
Nov. 14, 2004 (OT) (p-2)
Devin Hester, Chicago vs. St. Louis, Dec. 11, 2006
(k-2)

FUMBLES

Most Fumbles, Career
161   Warren Moon, Houston, 1984-1993; Minnesota,
1994-96; Seattle, 1997-98; Kansas City,
1999-2000
153   Dave Krieg, Seattle, 1980-1991; Kansas City,
1992-93; Detroit, 1994; Arizona, 1995;
Chicago, 1996; Tennessee, 1997-98
138   Brett Favre, Atlanta, 1992; Green Bay, 1992-2006

Most Fumbles, Season
23   Kerry Collins, N.Y. Giants, 2001
Daunte Culpepper, Minnesota, 2002
21   Tony Banks, St. Louis, 1996
David Carr, Houston, 2002
18   Dave Krieg, Seattle, 1989
Warren Moon, Houston, 1990

Most Fumbles, Game
7   Len Dawson, Kansas City vs. San Diego,
Nov. 15, 1964
6   Sam Etcheverry, St. Louis vs. N.Y. Giants,
Sept, 17, 1961
Dave Krieg, Seattle vs. Kansas City, Nov. 5, 1989
Brett Favre, Green Bay vs. Tampa Bay, Dec. 7, 1998
Kurt Warner, St. Louis vs. N.Y. Giants, Sept. 7, 2003
Chad Pennington, N.Y. Jets vs. Kansas City,
Sept. 11, 2005
5   Paul Christman, Chi. Cardinals vs. Green Bay,
Nov. 10, 1946
Charlie Conerly, N.Y. Giants vs. San Francisco,
Dec. 1, 1957
Jack Kemp, Buffalo vs. Houston, Oct. 29, 1967
Roman Gabriel, Philadelphia vs. Oakland,
Nov. 21, 1976
Randall Cunningham, Philadelphia vs. L.A. Raiders,
Nov. 30, 1986 (OT)
Willie Totten, Buffalo vs. Indianapolis, Oct. 4, 1987
Dave Walter, Cincinnati vs. Seattle, Oct. 11, 1987
Dave Krieg, Seattle vs. San Diego, Nov. 25, 1990 (OT)
Andre Ware, Detroit vs. Green Bay, Dec. 6, 1992
Steve Beuerlein, Carolina vs. San Francisco,
Nov. 8, 1998
Patrick Ramsey, Washington vs. Green Bay,
Oct. 20, 2002

FUMBLES RECOVERED

Most Fumbles Recovered, Career, Own and Opponents'
56   Warren Moon, Houston, 1984-1993; Minnesota,
1994-96; Seattle, 1997-98; Kansas City,
1999-2000 (56 own)
47   Dave Krieg, Seattle, 1980-1991; Kansas City,
1992-93; Detroit, 1994; Arizona, 1995; Chicago, 1996; Tennessee, 1997-98 (47 own)
45   Boomer Esiason, Cincinnati, 1984-1992, 1997;
N.Y. Jets, 1993-95; Arizona, 1996 (45 own)

Most Fumbles Recovered, Season, Own and Opponents'
12   David Carr, Houston, 2002 (12 own)
9   Don Hultz, Minnesota, 1963 (9 opp)
Dave Krieg, Seattle, 1989 (9 own)
Brian Griese, Denver, 1999 (9 own)
Jon Kitna, Seattle, 2000 (9 own)
8   Paul Christman, Chi. Cardinals, 1945 (8 own)
Joe Schmidt, Detroit, 1955 (8 opp)
Bill Butler, Minnesota, 1963 (8 own)

Kermit Alexander, San Francisco, 1965
(4 own, 4 opp)
Jack Lambert, Pittsburgh, 1976 (1 own, 7 opp)
Danny White, Dallas, 1981 (8 own)
Dan Marino, Miami, 1988 (7 own, 1 opp)
Tony Banks, St. Louis, 1998 (8 own)

Most Fumbles Recovered, Game, Own and Opponents'
4   Otto Graham, Cleveland vs. N.Y. Giants,
Oct. 25, 1953 (4 own)
Sam Etcheverry, St. Louis vs. N.Y. Giants,
Sept. 17, 1961 (4 own)
Roman Gabriel, Los Angeles vs. San Francisco,
Oct. 12, 1969 (4 own)
Joe Ferguson, Buffalo vs. Miami, Sept. 18, 1977
(4 own)
Randall Cunningham, Philadelphia vs. L.A. Raiders,
Nov. 30, 1986 (OT) (4 own)
3   By many players

OWN FUMBLES RECOVERED

Most Own Fumbles Recovered, Career
56   Warren Moon, Houston, 1984-1993; Minnesota,
1994-96; Seattle, 1997-98; Kansas City,
1999-2000
47   Dave Krieg, Seattle, 1980-1991; Kansas City,
1992-93; Detroit, 1994; Arizona, 1995;
Chicago, 1996; Tennessee, 1997-98
45   Boomer Esiason, Cincinnati, 1984-1992, 1997;
N.Y. Jets, 1993-95; Arizona, 1996

Most Own Fumbles Recovered, Season
12   David Carr, Houston, 2002
9   Dave Krieg, Seattle, 1989
Brian Griese, Denver, 1999
Jon Kitna, Seattle, 2000
8   Paul Christman, Chi. Cardinals, 1945
Bill Butler, Minnesota, 1963
Danny White, Dallas, 1981
Tony Banks, St. Louis, 1998

Most Own Fumbles Recovered, Game
4   Otto Graham, Cleveland vs. N.Y. Giants, Oct. 25, 1953
Sam Etcheverry, St. Louis vs. N.Y. Giants,
Sept. 17, 1961
Roman Gabriel, Los Angeles vs. San Francisco,
Oct. 12, 1969
Joe Ferguson, Buffalo vs. Miami, Sept. 18, 1977
Randall Cunningham, Philadelphia vs. L.A. Raiders,
Nov. 30, 1986 (OT)
3   By many players

OPPONENTS' FUMBLES RECOVERED

Most Opponents' Fumbles Recovered, Career
29   Jim Marshall, Cleveland, 1960; Minnesota, 1961-1979
28   Rickey Jackson, New Orleans, 1981-1993;
San Francisco, 1994-95
26   Kevin Greene, L.A. Rams, 1985-1992; Pittsburgh,
1993-95; Carolina, 1996, 1998-99;
San Francisco, 1997
Cornelius Bennett, Buffalo, 1987-1995; Atlanta,
1996-98; Indianapolis, 1999-2000

Most Opponents' Fumbles Recovered, Season
9   Don Hultz, Minnesota, 1963
8   Joe Schmidt, Detroit, 1955
7   Alan Page, Minnesota, 1970
Jack Lambert, Pittsburgh, 1976
Ray Childress, Houston, 1988
Rickey Jackson, New Orleans, 1990

Most Opponents' Fumbles Recovered, Game
3   Corwin Clatt, Chi. Cardinals vs. Detroit, Nov. 6, 1949
Vic Sears, Philadelphia vs. Green Bay, Nov. 2, 1952

Ed Beatty, San Francisco vs. Los Angeles,
Oct. 7, 1956
Ron Carroll, Houston vs. Cincinnati, Oct. 27, 1974
Maurice Spencer, New Orleans vs. Atlanta,
Oct. 10, 1976
Steve Nelson, New England vs. Philadelphia,
Oct. 8, 1978
Charles Jackson, Kansas City vs. Pittsburgh,
Sept. 6, 1981
Willie Buchanon, San Diego vs. Denver,
Sept. 27, 1981
Joey Browner, Minnesota vs. San Francisco,
Sept. 8, 1985
Ray Childress, Houston vs. Washington, Oct. 30, 1988
John Thierry, Chicago vs. Houston, Oct. 22, 1995
Stephen Boyd, Detroit vs. Chicago, Oct. 4, 1998
Darryl Williams, Seattle vs. Kansas City, Oct. 4, 1998
Rod Woodson, Oakland vs. Pittsburgh, Sept. 15, 2002
Brian Young, St. Louis vs. Baltimore, Nov. 9, 2003
  2 By many players

YARDS RETURNING FUMBLES
Longest Fumble Run (All TDs)
 104 Jack Tatum, Oakland vs. Green Bay, Sept. 24, 1972
      Aeneas Williams, Arizona vs. Washington,
      Nov. 5, 2000
 102 Travis Davis, Pittsburgh vs. Carolina, Dec. 26, 1999
 100 Chris Martin, Kansas City vs. Miami, Oct. 13, 1991

TOUCHDOWNS
Most Touchdowns, Career (Total)
  5 Jessie Tuggle, Atlanta, 1987-2000
     Jason Taylor, Miami, 1997-2006
  4 Bill Thompson, Denver, 1969-1981
     Derrick Thomas, Kansas City, 1989-1999
     Keith Bulluck, Tennessee, 2000-06
  3 By many players
Most Touchdowns, Season (Total)
  2 Harold McPhail, Boston, 1934
     Harry Ebding, Detroit, 1937
     John Morelli, Boston, 1944
     Frank Maznicki, Boston, 1947
     Fred (Dippy) Evans, Chi. Bears, 1948
     Ralph Heywood, Boston, 1948
     Art Tait, N.Y. Yanks, 1951
     John Dwyer, Los Angeles, 1952
     Leo Sugar, Chi. Cardinals, 1957
     Doug Cline, Houston, 1961
     Jim Bradshaw, Pittsburgh, 1964
     Royce Berry, Cincinnati, 1970
     Ahmad Rashad, Buffalo, 1974
     Tim Gray, Kansas City, 1977
     Charles Phillips, Oakland, 1978
     Kenny Johnson, Atlanta, 1981
     George Martin, N.Y. Giants, 1981
     Del Rodgers, Green Bay, 1982
     Mike Douglass, Green Bay, 1983
     Shelton Robinson, Seattle, 1983
     Erik McMillan, N.Y. Jets, 1989
     Les Miller, San Diego, 1990
     Seth Joyner, Philadelphia, 1991
     Robert Goff, New Orleans, 1992
     Willie Clay, Detroit, 1993
     Tyrone Hughes, New Orleans, 1994
     Chad Brown, Seattle, 1997
     Marcus Robertson, Tennessee, 1997
     Dwayne Rudd, Minnesota, 1998
     Keith McKenzie, Green Bay, 1999
     Ronde Barber, Tampa Bay, 2004
     Leonard Little, St. Louis, 2004

Antwan Odom, Tennessee, 2005
Adalius Thomas, Baltimore, 2005
Most Touchdowns, Career (Own recovered)
  2 Ken Kavanaugh, Chi. Bears, 1940-41, 1945-1950
     Mike Ditka, Chicago, 1961-66; Philadelphia,
     1967-68; Dallas, 1969-1972
     Gail Cogdill, Detroit, 1960-68; Baltimore, 1968;
     Atlanta, 1969-1970
     Ahmad Rashad, St. Louis, 1972-73; Buffalo, 1974;
     Minnesota, 1976-1982
     Jim Mitchell, Atlanta, 1969-1979
     Drew Pearson, Dallas, 1973-1983
     Del Rodgers, Green Bay, 1982, 1984; San Francisco,
     1987-88
     Alan Ricard, Baltimore, 2001-05
Most Touchdowns, Season (Own recovered)
  2 Ahmad Rashad, Buffalo, 1974
     Del Rodgers, Green Bay, 1982
  1 By many players
Most Touchdowns, Career (Opponents' recovered)
  5 Jessie Tuggle, Atlanta, 1987-2000
     Jason Taylor, Miami, 1997-2006
  4 Derrick Thomas, Kansas City, 1989-1999
     Keith Bulluck, Tennessee, 2000-06
  3 By many players
Most Touchdowns, Season (Opponents' recovered)
  2 Harold McPhail, Boston, 1934
     Harry Ebding, Detroit, 1937
     John Morelli, Boston, 1944
     Frank Maznicki, Boston, 1947
     Fred (Dippy) Evans, Chi. Bears, 1948
     Ralph Heywood, Boston, 1948
     Art Tait, N.Y. Yanks, 1951
     John Dwyer, Los Angeles, 1952
     Leo Sugar, Chi. Cardinals, 1957
     Doug Cline, Houston, 1961
     Jim Bradshaw, Pittsburgh, 1964
     Royce Berry, Cincinnati, 1970
     Tim Gray, Kansas City, 1977
     Charles Phillips, Oakland, 1978
     Kenny Johnson, Atlanta, 1981
     George Martin, N.Y. Giants, 1981
     Mike Douglass, Green Bay, 1983
     Shelton Robinson, Seattle, 1983
     Erik McMillan, N.Y. Jets, 1989
     Les Miller, San Diego, 1990
     Seth Joyner, Philadelphia, 1991
     Robert Goff, New Orleans, 1992
     Willie Clay, Detroit, 1993
     Tyrone Hughes, New Orleans, 1994
     Chad Brown, Seattle, 1997
     Marcus Robertson, Tennessee, 1997
     Dwayne Rudd, Minnesota, 1998
     Keith McKenzie, Green Bay, 1999
     Ronde Barber, Tampa Bay, 2004
     Leonard Little, St. Louis, 2004
     Antwan Odom, Tennessee, 2005
     Adalius Thomas, Baltimore, 2005
Most Touchdowns, Game (Opponents' recovered)
  2 Fred (Dippy) Evans, Chi. Bears vs. Washington,
     Nov. 28, 1948

COMBINED NET YARDS GAINED
Rushing, receiving, interception returns, punt returns, kickoff
returns, and fumble returns
Most Seasons Leading League
  5 Jim Brown, Cleveland, 1958-1961, 1964
  4 Brian Mitchell, Washington, 1994-96, 1998
  3 Cliff Battles, Boston, 1932-33; Washington, 1937
     Gale Sayers, Chicago, 1965-67

Eric Dickerson, L.A. Rams, 1983-84, 1986
Thurman Thomas, Buffalo, 1989, 1991-92

Most Consecutive Seasons Leading League

4   Jim Brown, Cleveland, 1958-1961

3   Gale Sayers, Chicago, 1965-67
    Brian Mitchell, Washington, 1994-96

2   Cliff Battles, Boston, 1932-33
    Charley Trippi, Chi. Cardinals, 1948-49
    Timmy Brown, Philadelphia, 1962-63
    Floyd Little, Denver, 1967-68
    James Brooks, San Diego, 1981-82
    Eric Dickerson, L.A. Rams, 1983-84
    Thurman Thomas, Buffalo, 1991-92
    Dante Hall, Kansas City, 2003-04

ATTEMPTS

Most Attempts, Career

4,939   Emmitt Smith, Dallas, 1990-2002; Arizona, 2003-04
4,368   Walter Payton, Chicago, 1975-1987
4,016   Curtis Martin, New England, 1995-97; N.Y. Jets, 1998-2005

Most Attempts, Season

496   James Wilder, Tampa Bay, 1984
458   Larry Johnson, Kansas City, 2006
455   Eddie George, Tennessee, 2000

Most Attempts, Rookie, Season

442   Eric Dickerson, L.A. Rams, 1983
433   Edgerrin James, Indianapolis, 1999
401   Curtis Martin, New England, 1995

Most Attempts, Game

48   James Wilder, Tampa Bay vs. Pittsburgh, Oct. 30, 1983
    LaDainian Tomlinson, San Diego vs. Denver, Dec. 1, 2002 (OT)
47   James Wilder, Tampa Bay vs. Green Bay, Sept. 30, 1984 (OT)
    Terrell Davis, Denver vs. Buffalo, Oct. 26, 1997 (OT)
46   Gerald Riggs, Atlanta vs. L.A. Rams, Nov. 17, 1985

YARDS GAINED

Most Yards Gained, Career

23,546   Jerry Rice, San Francisco, 1985-2000; Oakland, 2001-04; Seattle, 2004
23,330   Brian Mitchell, Washington, 1990-99; Philadelphia, 2000-02; N.Y. Giants, 2003
21,803   Walter Payton, Chicago, 1975-1987

Most Yards Gained, Season

2,690   Derrick Mason, Tennessee, 2000
2,647   Michael Lewis, New Orleans, 2002
2,535   Lionel James, San Diego, 1985

Most Yards Gained, Rookie, Season

2,317   Tim Brown, L.A. Raiders, 1988
2,272   Gale Sayers, Chicago, 1965
2,250   Maurice Jones-Drew, Jacksonville, 2006

Most Yards Gained, Game

404   Glyn Milburn, Denver vs. Seattle, Dec. 10, 1995
373   Billy Cannon, Houston vs. N.Y. Titans, Dec. 10, 1961
356   Michael Lewis, New Orleans vs. Washington, Oct. 13, 2002

SACKS

Sacks have been compiled since 1982.

Most Seasons Leading League

2   Mark Gastineau, N.Y. Jets, 1983-84
    Reggie White, Philadelphia, 1987-88
    Kevin Greene, Pittsburgh, 1994; Carolina, 1996
    Michael Strahan, N.Y. Giants, 2001, 2003

Most Sacks, Career

200.0   Bruce Smith, Buffalo, 1985-1999; Washington, 2000-03
198.0   Reggie White, Philadelphia, 1985-1992; Green Bay,

1993-98; Carolina, 2000
160.0   Kevin Greene, L.A. Rams, 1985-1992; Pittsburgh, 1993-95; Carolina, 1996, 1998-99; San Francisco, 1997

Most Sacks, Season

22.5   Michael Strahan, N.Y. Giants, 2001
22.0   Mark Gastineau, N.Y. Jets, 1984
21.0   Reggie White, Philadelphia, 1987
    Chris Doleman, Minnesota, 1989

Most Sacks, Rookie, Season

14.5   Jevon Kearse, Tennessee, 1999
13.0   Dwight Freeney, Indianapolis, 2002
12.5   Leslie O'Neal, San Diego, 1986
    Simeon Rice, Arizona, 1996

Most Sacks, Game

7.0   Derrick Thomas, Kansas City vs. Seattle, Nov. 11, 1990
6.0   Fred Dean, San Francisco vs. New Orleans, Nov. 13, 1983
    Derrick Thomas, Kansas City vs. Oakland, Sept. 6, 1998
5.5   William Gay, Detroit vs. Tampa Bay, Sept. 4, 1983

Most Seasons, 10 or More Sacks

13   Bruce Smith, Buffalo, 1986-1990, 1992-98; Washington, 2000
12   Reggie White, Philadelphia, 1985-1992; Green Bay, 1993, 1995, 1997-98
10   Kevin Greene, L.A. Rams, 1988-1990, 1992; Pittsburgh, 1993-94; Carolina, 1996, 1998-99; San Francisco, 1997

Most Consecutive Seasons, 10 or More Sacks

9   Reggie White, Philadelphia, 1985-1992; Green Bay, 1993
8   John Randle, Minnesota, 1992-99
7   Lawrence Taylor, N.Y. Giants, 1984-1990
    Bruce Smith, Buffalo, 1992-98

Most Consecutive Games, Sack

10   Simon Fletcher, Denver, Nov. 15, 1992-Sept. 20, 1993
9   Bruce Smith, Buffalo, Nov. 16, 1986-Oct. 25, 1987
    Kevin Greene, San Francisco-Carolina, Dec. 7, 1997-Oct. 18, 1998
8   By many players

MISCELLANEOUS

Longest Return of Missed Field Goal (All TDs)

108   Nathan Vasher, Chicago vs. San Francisco, Nov. 13, 2005
    Devin Hester, Chicago vs. N.Y. Giants, Nov. 12, 2006
107   Chris McAlister, Baltimore vs. Denver, Sept. 30, 2002
104   Aaron Glenn, N.Y. Jets vs. Indianapolis, Nov. 15, 1998

TEAM RECORDS

CHAMPIONSHIPS

Most Seasons League Champion

12   Green Bay, 1929-1931, 1936, 1939, 1944, 1961-62, 1965-67, 1996
9   Chi. Bears, 1921, 1932-33, 1940-41, 1943, 1946, 1963, 1985
6   N.Y. Giants, 1927, 1934, 1938, 1956, 1986, 1990

Most Consecutive Seasons League Champion

3   Green Bay, 1929-1931
    Green Bay, 1965-67
2   Canton, 1922-23
    Chi. Bears, 1932-33
    Chi. Bears, 1940-41
    Philadelphia, 1948-49
    Detroit, 1952-53
    Cleveland, 1954-55
    Baltimore, 1958-59

Houston, 1960-61
Green Bay, 1961-62
Buffalo, 1964-65
Miami, 1972-73
Pittsburgh, 1974-75
Pittsburgh, 1978-79
San Francisco, 1988-89
Dallas, 1992-93
Denver, 1997-98
New England, 2003-04

Most Times Finishing First, Regular Season

21   N.Y. Giants, 1927, 1933-35, 1938-39, 1941, 1944,
      1946, 1956, 1958-59, 1961-63, 1986,
      1989-1990, 1997, 2000, 2005
     Chi. Bears, 1921, 1932-34, 1937, 1940-43, 1946,
      1956, 1963, 1984-88, 1990, 2001, 2005-06

20   Green Bay, 1929-1931, 1936, 1938-39, 1944,
      1960-62, 1965-67, 1972, 1995-97, 2002-04

19   Dallas, 1966-1971, 1973, 1976-79, 1981, 1985,
      1992-96, 1998

Most Consecutive Times Finishing First, Regular Season

7   Los Angeles, 1973-79
6   Cleveland, 1950-55
   Dallas, 1966-1971
   Minnesota, 1973-78
   Pittsburgh, 1974-79
5   Oakland, 1972-76
   Chicago, 1984-88
   San Francisco, 1986-1990
   Dallas, 1992-96

GAMES WON

Most Consecutive Games Won

18   New England, 2003-04
17   Chi. Bears, 1933-34
16   Chi. Bears, 1941-42
    Miami, 1971-73
    Miami, 1983-84
    Pittsburgh, 2004-05

Most Consecutive Games Without Defeat

25   Canton, 1921-23 (won 22, tied 3)
24   Chi. Bears, 1941-43 (won 23, tied 1)
23   Green Bay, 1928-1930 (won 21, tied 2)

Most Games Won, Season

15   San Francisco, 1984
    Chicago, 1985
    Minnesota, 1998
    Pittsburgh, 2004
14   Frankford, 1926
    Miami, 1972
    Pittsburgh, 1978
    Washington, 1983
    Miami, 1984
    Chicago, 1986
    N.Y. Giants, 1986
    San Francisco, 1989
    San Francisco, 1990
    Washington, 1991
    San Francisco, 1992
    Atlanta, 1998
    Denver, 1998
    Jacksonville, 1999
    St. Louis, 2001
    New England, 2003
    New England, 2004
    Indianapolis, 2005
    San Diego, 2006
13   By many teams

Most Consecutive Games Won, Season

14   Miami, 1972

Pittsburgh, 2004
13   Chi. Bears, 1934
    Denver, 1998
    Indianapolis, 2005
12   Minnesota, 1969
    Chicago, 1985
    New England, 2003

Most Consecutive Games Won, Start of Season

14   Miami, 1972, entire season
13   Chi. Bears, 1934, entire season
    Denver, 1998
    Indianapolis, 2005
12   Chicago, 1985

Most Consecutive Games Won, End of Season

14   Miami, 1972, entire season
    Pittsburgh, 2004
13   Chi. Bears, 1934, entire season
12   New England, 2003

Most Consecutive Games Without Defeat, Season

14   Miami, 1972 (won 14)
    Pittsburgh, 2004 (won 14)
13   Chi. Bears, 1926 (won 11, tied 2)
    Green Bay, 1929 (won 12, tied 1)
    Chi. Bears, 1934 (won 13)
    Baltimore, 1967 (won 11, tied 2)
    Denver, 1998 (won 13)
    Indianapolis, 2005 (won 13)
12   Canton, 1922 (won 10, tied 2)
    Canton, 1923 (won 11, tied 1)
    Minnesota, 1969 (won 12)
    Chicago, 1985 (won 12)
    New England, 2003 (won 12)

Most Consecutive Games Without Defeat, Start of Season

14   Miami, 1972 (won 14), entire season
13   Chi. Bears, 1926 (won 11, tied 2)
    Green Bay, 1929 (won 12, tied 1), entire season
    Chi. Bears, 1934 (won 13), entire season
    Baltimore, 1967 (won 11, tied 2)
    Denver, 1998 (won 13)
    Indianapolis, 2005 (won 13)
12   Canton, 1922 (won 10, tied 2), entire season
    Canton, 1923 (won 11, tied 1), entire season
    Chicago, 1985 (won 12)

Most Consecutive Games Without Defeat, End of Season

14   Miami, 1972 (won 14), entire season
    Pittsburgh, 2004 (won 14)
13   Green Bay, 1929 (won 12, tied 1), entire season
    Chi. Bears, 1934 (won 13), entire season
12   Canton, 1922 (won 10, tied 2), entire season
    Canton, 1923 (won 11, tied 1), entire season
    New England, 2003 (won 12)

Most Consecutive Home Games Won

27   Miami, 1971-74
25   Green Bay, 1995-98
24   Denver, 1996-98

Most Consecutive Home Games Without Defeat

30   Green Bay, 1928-1933 (won 27, tied 3)
27   Miami, 1971-74 (won 27)
25   Chi. Bears, 1923-25 (won 19, tied 6)
    Green Bay, 1995-98 (won 25)

Most Consecutive Road Games Won

18   San Francisco, 1988-1990
11   L.A. Chargers/San Diego, 1960-61
    San Francisco, 1987-88
    Pittsburgh, 2004-05
10   Chi. Bears, 1941-42
    Dallas, 1968-69
    New Orleans, 1987-88

Most Consecutive Road Games Without Defeat

18   San Francisco, 1988-1990 (won 18)

13 Chi. Bears, 1941-43 (won 12, tied 1)
12 Green Bay, 1928-1930 (won 10, tied 2)

Most Shutout Games Won or Tied, Season
10 Pottsville, 1926 (won 9, tied 1)
    N.Y. Giants, 1927 (won 9, tied 1)
 9 Akron, 1921 (won 8, tied 1)
    Canton, 1922 (won 7, tied 2)
    Frankford, 1926 (won 9)
    Frankford, 1929 (won 6, tied 3)
 8 By many teams

Most Consecutive Shutout Games Won or Tied
13 Akron, 1920-21 (won 10, tied 3)
 7 Pottsville, 1926 (won 6, tied 1)
    Detroit, 1934 (won 7)
 6 Buffalo, 1920-21 (won 5, tied 1)
    Frankford, 1926 (won 6)
    Detroit, 1926 (won 4, tied 2)
    N.Y. Giants, 1926-27 (won 5, tied 1)

GAMES LOST
Most Consecutive Games Lost
26 Tampa Bay, 1976-1977
19 Chi. Cardinals, 1942-43, 1945
    Oakland, 1961-62
18 Houston, 1972-73

Most Consecutive Games Without Victory
26 Tampa Bay, 1976-77 (lost 26)
23 Rochester, 1922-25 (lost 21, tied 2)
    Washington, 1960-61 (lost 20, tied 3)
19 Dayton, 1927-29 (lost 18, tied 1)
    Chi. Cardinals, 1942-43, 1945 (lost 19)
    Oakland, 1961-62 (lost 19)

Most Games Lost, Season
15 New Orleans, 1980
    Dallas, 1989
    New England, 1990
    Indianapolis, 1991
    N.Y. Jets, 1996
    San Diego, 2000
    Carolina, 2001
14 By many teams

Most Consecutive Games Lost, Season
15 Carolina, 2001
14 Tampa Bay, 1976
    New Orleans, 1980
    Baltimore, 1981
    New England, 1990
13 Oakland, 1962
    Pittsburgh, 1969
    Indianapolis, 1986

Most Consecutive Games Lost, Start of Season
14 Tampa Bay, 1976, entire season
    New Orleans, 1980
13 Oakland, 1962
    Indianapolis, 1986
12 Tampa Bay, 1977
    Detroit, 2001

Most Consecutive Games Lost, End of Season
15 Carolina, 2001
14 Tampa Bay, 1976, entire season
    New England, 1990
13 Pittsburgh, 1969

Most Consecutive Games Without Victory, Season
15 Carolina, 2001 (lost 15)
14 Tampa Bay, 1976 (lost 14), entire season
    New Orleans, 1980 (lost 14)
    Baltimore, 1981 (lost 14)
    New England, 1990 (lost 14)
13 Washington, 1961 (lost 12, tied 1)
    Oakland, 1962 (lost 13)

Pittsburgh, 1969 (lost 13)
    Indianapolis, 1986 (lost 13)

Most Consecutive Games Without Victory, Start of Season
14 Tampa Bay, 1976 (lost 14), entire season
    New Orleans, 1980 (lost 14)
13 Washington, 1961 (lost 12, tied 1)
    Oakland, 1962 (lost 13)
    Indianapolis, 1986 (lost 13)
12 Dall. Cowboys, 1960 (lost 11, tied 1), entire season
    Tampa Bay, 1977 (lost 12)
    Detroit, 2001 (lost 12)

Most Consecutive Games Without Victory, End of Season
15 Carolina, 2001
14 Tampa Bay, 1976, (lost 14), entire season
    New England, 1990 (lost 14)
13 Pittsburgh, 1969 (lost 13)

Most Consecutive Home Games Lost
14 Dallas, 1988-89
13 Houston, 1972-73
    Tampa Bay, 1976-77
    N.Y. Jets, 1995-97
11 Oakland, 1961-62
    Los Angeles, 1961-63
    Cincinnati, 1998-99

Most Consecutive Home Games Without Victory
14 Dallas, 1988-89 (lost 14)
13 Houston, 1972-73 (lost 13)
    Tampa Bay, 1976-77 (lost 13)
    N.Y. Jets, 1995-97 (lost 13)
    Philadelphia, 1936-38 (lost 12, tied 1)

Most Consecutive Road Games Lost
24 Detroit, 2001-03
23 Houston, 1981-84
22 Buffalo, 1983-86

Most Consecutive Road Games Without Victory
24 Detroit, 2001-03 (lost 24)
23 Houston, 1981-84 (lost 23)
22 Buffalo, 1983-86 (lost 22)

Most Shutout Games Lost or Tied, Season
 8 Frankford, 1927 (lost 6, tied 2)
    Brooklyn, 1931 (lost 8)
 7 Dayton, 1925 (lost 6, tied 1)
    Orange, 1929 (lost 4, tied 3)
    Frankford, 1931 (lost 6, tied 1)
 6 By many teams

Most Consecutive Shutout Games Lost or Tied
 8 Rochester, 1922-24 (lost 8)
 7 Hammond, 1922-23 (lost 6, tied 1)
 6 Providence, 1926-27 (lost 5, tied 1)
    Brooklyn, 1942-43 (lost 6)

TIE GAMES
Most Tie Games, Season
 6 Chi. Bears, 1932
 5 Frankford, 1929
 4 Chi. Bears, 1924
    Orange, 1929
    Portsmouth, 1932

Most Consecutive Tie Games
 3 Chi. Bears, 1932
 2 By many teams

SCORING
Most Seasons Leading League
10 Chi. Bears, 1932, 1934-35, 1939, 1941-43,
    1946-47, 1956
 9 San Francisco, 1953, 1965, 1970, 1987, 1989,
    1992-95
    L.A./St. Louis Rams, 1950-52, 1957, 1967, 1973,
    1999-2001

7   Green Bay, 1931, 1936-38, 1961-62, 1996

Most Consecutive Seasons Leading League
- 4   San Francisco, 1992-1995
- 3   Green Bay, 1936-38
      Chi. Bears, 1941-43
      Los Angeles, 1950-52
      Oakland, 1967-69
      St. Louis, 1999-2001
- 2   By many teams

POINTS

Most Points, Season
- 556   Minnesota, 1998
- 541   Washington, 1983
- 540   St. Louis, 2000

Fewest Points, Season (Since 1932)
- 37   Cincinnati/St. Louis, 1934
- 38   Cincinnati, 1933
      Detroit, 1942
- 51   Pittsburgh, 1934
      Philadelphia, 1936

Most Points, Game
- 72   Washington vs. N.Y. Giants, Nov. 27, 1966
- 70   Los Angeles vs. Baltimore, Oct. 22, 1950
- 66   Rochester vs. *Fort Porter, Oct. 10, 1920
      *Not a member of the American Professional Football Association

Most Points, Both Teams, Game
- 113   Washington (72) vs. N.Y. Giants (41), Nov. 27, 1966
- 106   Cincinnati (58) vs. Cleveland (48), Nov. 28, 2004
- 101   Oakland (52) vs. Houston (49), Dec. 22, 1963

Fewest Points, Both Teams, Game
- 0   In many games. Last time: N.Y. Giants vs. Detroit, Nov. 7, 1943

Most Points, Shutout Victory, Game
- 66   Rochester vs. *Fort Porter, Oct. 10, 1920
      *Not a member of the American Professional Football Association
- 64   Philadelphia vs. Cincinnati, Nov. 6, 1934
- 62   Akron vs. Oorang, Oct. 29, 1922

Fewest Points, Shutout Victory, Game
- 2   Akron vs. Buffalo, Nov. 29, 1923
      Kansas City vs. Buffalo, Nov. 21, 1926
      Frankford vs. Green Bay, Nov. 29, 1928
      Green Bay vs. Chi. Bears, Oct. 16, 1932
      Chi. Bears vs. Green Bay, Sept. 18, 1938

Most Points Overcome to Win Game
- 28   San Francisco vs. New Orleans, Dec. 7, 1980 (OT) (trailed 7-35, won 38-35)
- 26   Buffalo vs. Indianapolis, Sept., 21, 1997 (trailed 0-26, won 37-35)
- 25   St. Louis vs. Tampa Bay, Nov. 8, 1987 (trailed 3-28, won 31-28)

Most Points Overcome to Tie Game
- 31   Denver vs. Buffalo, Nov. 27, 1960 (trailed 7-38, tied 38-38)
- 28   Los Angeles vs. Philadelphia, Oct. 3, 1948 (trailed 0-28, tied 28-28)

Most Points, Each Half
- 1st: 49   Green Bay vs. Tampa Bay, Oct. 2, 1983
-      48   Buffalo vs. Miami, Sept. 18, 1966
-      45   Green Bay vs. Cleveland, Nov. 12, 1967
           Indianapolis vs. Denver, Oct. 31, 1988
           Houston vs. Cleveland, Dec. 9, 1990
           Seattle vs. Minnesota, Sept. 29, 2002
- 2nd: 49   Chi. Bears vs. Philadelphia, Nov. 30, 1941
-      48   Chi. Cardinals vs. Baltimore, Oct. 2, 1950
           N.Y. Giants vs. Baltimore, Nov. 19, 1950
-      45   Cincinnati vs. Houston, Dec. 17, 1972

Most Points, Both Teams, Each Half
- 1st: 70   Houston (35) vs. Oakland (35), Dec. 22, 1963
-      62   N.Y. Jets (41) vs. Tampa Bay (21), Nov. 17, 1985
           Indianapolis (35) vs. Cincinnati (27), Nov. 20, 2005
-      59   St. Louis (31) vs. Philadelphia (28), Dec. 16, 1962
- 2nd: 66   Cleveland (35) vs. Cincinnati (31), Nov. 28, 2004
-      65   Washington (38) vs. N.Y. Giants (27), Nov. 27, 1966
-      62   L.A. Raiders (31) vs. San Diego (31), Jan. 2, 1983
           Baltimore (38) vs. Seattle (24), Nov. 23, 2003

Most Points, One Quarter
- 41   Green Bay vs. Detroit, Oct. 7, 1945 (second quarter)
      Los Angeles vs. Detroit, Oct. 29, 1950 (third quarter)
- 37   Los Angeles vs. Green Bay, Sept. 21, 1980 (second quarter)
- 35   Chi. Cardinals vs. Boston, Oct. 24, 1948 (third quarter)
      Green Bay vs. Cleveland, Nov. 12, 1967 (first quarter)
      Green Bay vs. Tampa Bay, Oct. 2, 1983 (second quarter)

Most Points, Both Teams, One Quarter
- 49   Oakland (28) vs. Houston (21), Dec. 22, 1963 (second quarter)
- 48   Green Bay (41) vs. Detroit (7), Oct. 7, 1945 (second quarter)
      Los Angeles (41) vs. Detroit (7), Oct. 29, 1950 (third quarter)
- 47   St. Louis (27) vs. Philadelphia (20), Dec. 13, 1964 (second quarter)

Most Points, Each Quarter
- 1st: 35   Green Bay vs. Cleveland, Nov. 12, 1967
-      31   Buffalo vs. Kansas City, Sept. 13, 1964
-      28   By eight teams
- 2nd: 41   Green Bay vs. Detroit, Oct. 7, 1945
-      37   Los Angeles vs. Green Bay, Sept. 21, 1980
-      35   Green Bay vs. Tampa Bay, Oct. 2, 1983
- 3rd: 41   Los Angeles vs. Detroit, Oct. 29, 1950
-      35   Chi. Cardinals vs. Boston, Oct. 24, 1948
-      28   By 10 teams
- 4th: 31   Oakland vs. Denver, Dec. 17, 1960
           Oakland vs. San Diego, Dec. 8, 1963
           Atlanta vs. Green Bay, Sept. 13, 1981
-      30   N.Y. Jets vs. Miami, Oct. 23, 2000
-      28   By many teams

Most Points, Both Teams, Each Quarter
- 1st: 42   Green Bay (35) vs. Cleveland (7), Nov. 12, 1967
-      41   Tennessee (24) vs. Indianapolis (17), Dec. 5, 2004
-      35   Dall. Texans (21) vs. N.Y. Titans (14), Nov. 11, 1962
           Dallas (28) vs. Philadelphia (7), Oct. 19, 1969
           Kansas City (21) vs. Seattle (14), Dec. 11, 1977
           Detroit (21) vs. L.A. Raiders (14), Dec. 10, 1990
           Dallas (21) vs. Atlanta (14), Dec. 22, 1991
           Indianapolis (21) vs. Green Bay (14), Sept 26, 2004
           Miami (21) vs. Buffalo (14), Dec. 5, 2004
- 2nd: 49   Oakland (28) vs. Houston (21), Dec. 22, 1963
-      48   Green Bay (41) vs. Detroit (7), Oct. 7, 1945
-      47   St. Louis (27) vs. Philadelphia (20), Dec. 13, 1964
- 3rd: 48   Los Angeles (41) vs. Detroit (7), Oct. 29, 1950
-      42   Washington (28) vs. Philadelphia (14), Oct. 1, 1955
-      41   Green Bay (21) vs. N.Y. Yanks (20), Oct. 8, 1950
- 4th: 42   Chi. Cardinals (28) vs. Philadelphia (14), Dec. 7, 1947
           Green Bay (28) vs. Chi. Bears (14), Nov. 6, 1955
           N.Y. Jets (28) vs. Boston (14), Oct. 27, 1968
           Pittsburgh (21) vs. Cleveland (21), Oct. 18, 1969
           New England (21) vs. Kansas City (21), Sept. 22, 2002
-      41   Baltimore (27) vs. New England (14), Sept. 18, 1978
           New England (27) vs. Baltimore (14), Nov. 23, 1980
-      40   Chicago (21) vs. Tampa Bay (19), Nov. 19, 1989

Most Consecutive Games Scoring
- 420   San Francisco, 1977-2004
- 274   Cleveland, 1950-1971
- 252   Minnesota, 1991-2006 (current)

TOUCHDOWNS
Most Seasons Leading League, Touchdowns
- 13   Chi. Bears, 1932, 1934-35, 1939, 1941-44, 1946-48, 1956, 1965
- 7   Dallas, 1966, 1968, 1971, 1973, 1977-78, 1980
  San Francisco, 1953, 1970, 1987, 1992-95
  L.A./St. Louis Rams, 1949-1952, 1999-2001
  San Diego, 1963, 1965, 1979, 1981-82, 1985, 2006
- 6   Oakland, 1967-69, 1972, 1974, 1977
  Green Bay, 1932, 1937-38, 1961-62, 1996
  Baltimore/Indianapolis Colts, 1957-59, 1964, 1976, 2004

Most Consecutive Seasons Leading League, Touchdowns
- 4   Chi. Bears, 1941-44
  Los Angeles, 1949-1952
  San Francisco, 1992-95
- 3   Chi. Bears, 1946-48
  Baltimore, 1957-59
  Oakland, 1967-69
  St. Louis, 1999-2001
- 2   By many teams

Most Touchdowns, Season
- 70   Miami, 1984
- 67   St. Louis, 2000
- 66   Houston, 1961
  San Francisco, 1994
  St. Louis, 1999
  Indianapolis, 2004

Fewest Touchdowns, Season (Since 1932)
- 3   Cincinnati, 1933
- 4   Cincinnati/St. Louis, 1934
- 5   Detroit, 1942

Most Touchdowns, Game
- 10   Rochester vs. *Fort Porter, Oct. 10, 1920
  *Not a member of the American Professional Football Association
  Philadelphia vs. Cincinnati, Nov. 6, 1934
  Los Angeles vs. Baltimore, Oct. 22, 1950
  Washington vs. N.Y. Giants, Nov. 27, 1966
- 9   Rock Island vs. Evansville, Oct. 15, 1922
  Akron vs. Oorang, Oct. 29, 1922
  Racine vs. Louisville, Nov. 5, 1922
  Chi. Cardinals vs. Rochester, Oct. 7, 1923
  Chi. Cardinals vs. Milwaukee, Dec. 10, 1925
  Chi. Cardinals vs. N.Y. Giants, Oct. 17, 1948
  Chi. Cardinals vs. N.Y. Bulldogs, Nov. 13, 1949
  Los Angeles vs. Detroit, Oct. 29, 1950
  Pittsburgh vs. N.Y. Giants, Nov. 30, 1952
  Chicago vs. San Francisco, Dec. 12, 1965
  Chicago vs. Green Bay, Dec. 7, 1980
- 8   By many teams

Most Touchdowns, Both Teams, Game
- 16   Washington (10) vs. N.Y. Giants (6), Nov. 27, 1966
- 14   Chi. Cardinals (9) vs. N.Y. Giants (5), Oct. 17, 1948
  Los Angeles (10) vs. Baltimore (4), Oct. 22, 1950
  Houston (7) vs. Oakland (7), Dec. 22, 1963
- 13   New Orleans (7) vs. St. Louis (6), Nov. 2, 1969
  Kansas City (7) vs. Seattle (6), Nov. 27, 1983 (OT)
  San Diego (8) vs. Pittsburgh (5), Dec. 8, 1985
  N.Y. Jets (7) vs. Miami (6), Sept. 21, 1986 (OT)
  Cincinnati (7) vs. Cleveland (6), Nov. 28, 2004

Most Consecutive Games Scoring Touchdowns
- 166   Cleveland, 1957-1969
- 97   Oakland, 1966-1973

Minnesota, 1995-2001
- 96   Kansas City, 1963-1970

POINTS AFTER TOUCHDOWN
Most (One-Point) Points After Touchdown, Season
- 66   Miami, 1984
- 65   Houston, 1961
- 64   St. Louis, 1999
  Indianapolis, 2004

Fewest (One-Point) Points After Touchdown, Season
- 2   Chi. Cardinals, 1933
- 3   Cincinnati, 1933
  Pittsburgh, 1934
- 4   Cincinnati/St. Louis, 1934

Most (One-Point) Points After Touchdown, Game
- 10   Los Angeles vs. Baltimore, Oct. 22, 1950
- 9   Chi. Cardinals vs. N.Y. Giants, Oct. 17, 1948
  Pittsburgh vs. N.Y. Giants, Nov. 30, 1952
  Washington vs. N.Y. Giants, Nov. 27, 1966
- 8   By many teams

Most (One-Point) Points After Touchdown, Both Teams, Game
- 14   Chi. Cardinals (9) vs. N.Y. Giants (5), Oct. 17, 1948
  Houston (7) vs. Oakland (7), Dec. 22, 1963
  Washington (9) vs. N.Y. Giants (5), Nov. 27, 1966
- 13   Los Angeles (10) vs. Baltimore (3), Oct. 22, 1950
  Cincinnati (7) vs. Cleveland (6), Nov. 28, 2004
- 12   In many games

Most Two-Point Conversions, Season
- 6   Miami, 1994
  Minnesota, 1997
- 5   Arizona, 1995
  Baltimore, 1996
  Jacksonville, 1996
  Chicago, 1997
  San Francisco, 1998
  Pittsburgh, 2002
- 4   By many teams

Most Two-Point Conversions, Game
- 4   St. Louis vs. Atlanta, Oct. 15, 2000
- 3   Baltimore vs. New England, Oct. 6, 1996
  Pittsburgh vs. Tennessee, Nov. 1, 1998
- 2   By many teams

Most Two-Point Conversions, Both Teams, Game
- 5   Baltimore (3) vs. New England (2), Oct. 6, 1996
  St. Louis (4) vs. Atlanta (1), Oct. 15, 2000
- 3   Seattle (2) vs. Kansas City (1), Oct. 23, 1994
  Minnesota (2) vs. Seattle (1), Nov. 10, 1996
  Pittsburgh (3) vs. Tennessee (0), Nov. 1, 1998
- 2   In many games

FIELD GOALS
Most Seasons Leading League, Field Goals
- 11   Green Bay, 1935-36, 1940-43, 1946-47, 1955, 1972, 1974
- 8   Washington, 1945, 1956, 1971, 1976-77, 1979, 1982, 1992
  L.A./St. Louis Rams, 1949, 1951, 1958, 1966, 1973, 1978, 2003, 2006
- 7   N.Y. Giants, 1933, 1937, 1939, 1941, 1944, 1959, 1983

Most Consecutive Seasons Leading League, Field Goals
- 4   Green Bay, 1940-43
- 3   Cleveland, 1952-54
- 2   By many teams

Most Field Goals Attempted, Season
- 49   Los Angeles, 1966
  Washington, 1971
- 48   Green Bay, 1972
- 47   N.Y. Jets, 1969
  Los Angeles, 1973

Washington, 1983

Fewest Field Goals Attempted, Season (Since 1938)
- 0 Chi. Bears, 1944
- 2 Cleveland, 1939
      Card-Pitt, 1944
      Boston, 1946
      Chi. Bears, 1947
- 3 Chi. Bears, 1945
      Cleveland, 1945

Most Field Goals Attempted, Game
- 9 St. Louis vs. Pittsburgh, Sept. 24, 1967
- 8 Pittsburgh vs. St. Louis, Dec. 2, 1962
      Detroit vs. Minnesota, Nov. 13, 1966
      N.Y. Jets vs. Buffalo, Nov. 3, 1968
      Dallas vs. N.Y. Giants, Sept. 15, 2003 (OT)
- 7 By many teams

Most Field Goals Attempted, Both Teams, Game
- 11 St. Louis (6) vs. Pittsburgh (5), Nov. 13, 1966
       Washington (6) vs. Chicago (5), Nov. 14, 1971
       Green Bay (6) vs. Detroit (5), Sept. 29, 1974
       Washington (6) vs. N.Y. Giants (5), Nov. 14, 1976
- 10 In many games

Most Field Goals, Season
- 43 Arizona, 2005
- 39 Miami, 1999
       St. Louis, 2003
- 37 Carolina, 1996
       Indianapolis, 2003

Fewest Field Goals, Season (Since 1932)
- 0 Boston, 1932, 1935
      Chi. Cardinals, 1932, 1945
      Green Bay, 1932, 1944
      N.Y. Giants, 1932
      Brooklyn, 1944
      Card-Pitt, 1944
      Chi. Bears, 1944, 1947
      Boston, 1946
      Baltimore, 1950
      Dallas, 1952

Most Field Goals, Game
- 7 St. Louis vs. Pittsburgh, Sept. 24, 1967
      Minnesota vs. L.A. Rams, Nov. 5, 1989 (OT)
      Dallas vs. Green Bay, Nov. 18, 1996
      Dallas vs. N.Y. Giants, Sept. 15, 2003 (OT)
- 6 Boston vs. Denver, Oct. 4, 1964
      Detroit vs. Minnesota, Nov. 13, 1966
      N.Y. Jets vs. Buffalo, Nov. 3, 1968
      Philadelphia vs. Houston, Nov. 12, 1972
      N.Y. Jets vs. New Orleans, Dec. 3, 1972
      St. Louis vs. Atlanta, Dec. 9, 1973
      N.Y. Giants vs. Seattle, Oct. 18, 1981
      San Francisco vs. New Orleans, Oct. 16, 1983
      Pittsburgh vs. Denver, Oct. 23, 1988
      San Diego vs. Seattle, Sept. 5, 1993
      San Diego vs. Houston, Sept. 19, 1993
      Cincinnati vs. Seattle, Nov. 6, 1994
      Atlanta vs. New Orleans, Nov. 13, 1994
      San Francisco vs. Atlanta, Sept. 29, 1996
      Buffalo vs. N.Y. Jets, Oct. 20, 1996
      San Diego vs. Oakland, Oct. 5, 1997
      Minnesota vs. Baltimore, Dec. 13, 1998
      Detroit vs. Minnesota, Oct. 17, 1999
      Miami vs. New England, Oct. 17, 1999
      Pittsburgh vs. Jacksonville, Dec. 1, 2002
      Carolina vs. New Orleans, Dec. 5, 2004
      Arizona vs. San Francisco, Oct. 2, 2005
      St. Louis vs. Denver, Sept. 10, 2006
      Atlanta vs. Arizona, Oct. 1, 2006
      Cleveland vs. San Diego, Nov. 5, 2006
- 5 By many teams

Most Field Goals, Both Teams, Game
- 9 San Diego (5) vs. Kansas City (4), Sept. 29, 1996
      Miami (6) vs. New England (3), Oct. 17, 1999
- 8 Cleveland (4) vs. St. Louis (4), Sept. 20, 1964
      Chicago (5) vs. Philadelphia (3), Oct. 20, 1968
      Washington (5) vs. Chicago (3), Nov. 14, 1971
      Kansas City (5) vs. Buffalo (3), Dec. 19, 1971
      Detroit (4) vs. Green Bay (4), Sept. 29, 1974
      Cleveland (5) vs. Denver (3), Oct. 19, 1975
      New England (4) vs. San Diego (4), Nov. 9, 1975
      San Francisco (6) vs. New Orleans (2), Oct. 16, 1983
      Seattle (5) vs. L.A. Raiders (3), Dec. 18, 1988
      Atlanta (6) vs. New Orleans (2), Nov. 13, 1994
      Indianapolis (4) vs. San Diego (4), Nov. 3, 1996
      Dallas (7) vs. N.Y. Giants (1), Sept. 15, 2003 (OT)
      Oakland (5) vs. Chicago (3), Oct. 5, 2003
      Buffalo (5) vs. Tennessee (3), Dec. 24, 2006
- 7 In many games

Most Consecutive Games Scoring Field Goals
- 38 Baltimore, 1999-2001
- 31 Minnesota, 1968-1970
- 28 Washington, 1988-1990

SAFETIES

Most Safeties, Season
- 4 Cleveland, 1927
      Detroit, 1962
      Seattle, 1993
      San Francisco, 1996
      Tennessee, 1999
- 3 By many teams

Most Safeties, Game
- 3 L.A. Rams vs. N.Y. Giants, Sept. 30, 1984
- 2 N.Y. Giants vs. Pottsville, Oct. 30, 1927
      Chi. Bears vs. Pottsville, Nov. 13, 1927
      Detroit vs. Brooklyn, Dec. 1, 1935
      N.Y. Giants vs. Pittsburgh, Sept. 17, 1950
      N.Y. Giants vs. Washington, Nov. 5, 1961
      Chicago vs. Pittsburgh, Nov. 9, 1969
      Dallas vs. Philadelphia, Nov. 19, 1972
      Los Angeles vs. Green Bay, Oct. 21, 1973
      Oakland vs. San Diego, Oct. 26, 1975
      Denver vs. Seattle, Jan. 2, 1983
      New Orleans vs. Cleveland, Sept. 13, 1987
      Buffalo vs. Denver, Nov. 8, 1987
      San Francisco vs. St. Louis, Sept. 8, 1996
      Jacksonville vs. Pittsburgh, Oct. 3, 1999
      Minnesota vs. Atlanta, Oct. 5, 2003
      Dallas vs. Arizona, Oct. 5, 2003
      Buffalo vs. Houston, Nov. 16, 2003

Most Safeties, Both Teams, Game
- 3 L.A. Rams (3) vs. N.Y. Giants (0), Sept. 30, 1984
- 2 Chi. Cardinals (1) vs. Frankford (1), Nov. 19, 1927
      Chi. Cardinals (1) vs. Cincinnati (1), Nov. 12, 1933
      Chi. Bears (1) vs. San Francisco (1), Oct. 19, 1952
      Cincinnati (1) vs. Los Angeles (1), Oct. 22, 1972
      Chi. Bears (1) vs. San Francisco (1), Sept. 19, 1976
      Baltimore (1) vs. Miami (1), Oct. 29, 1978
      Atlanta (1) vs. Detroit (1), Oct. 5, 1980
      Houston (1) vs. Philadelphia (1), Oct. 2, 1988
      Cleveland (1) vs. Seattle (1), Nov. 14, 1993
      Arizona (1) vs. Houston (1), Dec. 4, 1994
      (Also see previous record)

FIRST DOWNS

Most Seasons Leading League
- 9 Chi. Bears, 1935, 1939, 1941, 1943, 1945,
       1947-49, 1955
- 7 San Diego, 1965, 1969, 1980-83, 1985

L.A./St. Louis Rams, 1946, 1950-51, 1954, 1957, 1973, 2001

6   San Francisco, 1965, 1987, 1989, 1993-94, 1998
    Baltimore/Indianapolis Colts, 1958-59, 1967, 2003, 2005-06

Most Consecutive Seasons Leading League
4   San Diego, 1980-83
3   Chi. Bears, 1947-49
2   By many teams

Most First Downs, Season
398   Kansas City, 2004
387   Miami, 1984
383   Denver, 2000

Fewest First Downs, Season
51   Cincinnati, 1933
64   Pittsburgh, 1935
67   Philadelphia, 1937

Most First Downs, Game
39   N.Y. Jets vs. Miami, Nov. 27, 1988
     Washington vs. Detroit, Nov. 4, 1990 (OT)
38   Los Angeles vs. N.Y. Giants, Nov. 13, 1966
37   Green Bay vs. Philadelphia, Nov. 11, 1962

Fewest First Downs, Game
0   N.Y. Giants vs. Green Bay, Oct. 1, 1933
    Pittsburgh vs. Boston, Oct. 29, 1933
    Philadelphia vs. Detroit, Sept. 20, 1935
    N.Y. Giants vs. Washington, Sept. 27, 1942
    Denver vs. Houston, Sept. 3, 1966

Most First Downs, Both Teams, Game
64   Seattle (32) vs. Kansas City (32), Nov. 24, 2002
62   San Diego (32) vs. Seattle (30), Dec. 15, 1985
     Oakland (31) vs. Kansas City (31), Nov. 5, 2000
59   Miami (31) vs. Buffalo (28), Oct. 9, 1983 (OT)
     Seattle (33) vs. Kansas City (26), Nov. 27, 1983 (OT)
     N.Y. Jets (32) vs. Miami (27), Sept. 21, 1986 (OT)
     N.Y. Jets (39) vs. Miami (20), Nov. 27, 1988
     Oakland (31) vs. San Francisco (28), Oct. 8, 2000 (OT)

Fewest First Downs, Both Teams, Game
7   Chi. Cardinals (2) vs. Detroit (5), Sept. 15, 1940
9   Pittsburgh (1) vs. Boston (8), Oct. 27, 1935
    Boston (4) vs. Brooklyn (5), Nov. 24, 1935
    N.Y. Giants (3) vs. Detroit (6), Nov. 7, 1943
    Pittsburgh (4) vs. Chi. Cardinals (5), Nov. 11, 1945
    N.Y. Bulldogs (1) vs. Philadelphia (8), Sept. 22, 1949
10   Philadelphia (4) vs. Brooklyn (6), Nov. 5, 1944
     N.Y. Giants (4) vs. Washington (6), Dec. 11, 1960

Most First Downs, Rushing, Season
181   New England, 1978
177   Los Angeles, 1973
176   Chicago, 1985

Fewest First Downs, Rushing, Season
36   Cleveland, 1942
     Boston, 1944
39   Brooklyn, 1943
40   Philadelphia, 1940
     Detroit, 1945

Most First Downs, Rushing, Game
25   Philadelphia vs. Washington, Dec. 2, 1951
23   St. Louis vs. New Orleans, Oct. 5, 1980
21   Cleveland vs. Philadelphia, Dec. 13, 1959
     Green Bay vs. Philadelphia, Nov. 11, 1962
     Los Angeles vs. New Orleans, Nov. 25, 1973
     Pittsburgh vs. Kansas City, Nov. 7, 1976
     New England vs. Denver, Nov. 28, 1976
     Oakland vs. Green Bay, Sept. 17, 1978
     Buffalo vs. Washington, Nov. 3, 1996
     San Francisco vs. Detroit, Dec. 14, 1998
     Kansas City vs. Atlanta, Oct. 24, 2004

Fewest First Downs, Rushing, Game
0   By many teams. Last time:
    Detroit vs. Minnesota, Dec. 10, 2006
    Oakland vs. Cincinnati, Dec. 10, 2006

Most First Downs, Rushing, Both Teams, Game
36   Philadelphia (25) vs. Washington (11), Dec. 2, 1951
31   Detroit (18) vs. Washington (13), Sept. 30, 1951
30   Los Angeles (17) vs. Minnesota (13), Nov. 5, 1961
     New Orleans (17) vs. Green Bay (13), Sept. 9, 1979
     New Orleans (16) vs. San Francisco (14), Nov. 11, 1979
     New England (16) vs. Kansas City (14), Oct. 4, 1981

Fewest First Downs, Rushing, Both Teams, Game
1   Oakland (0) vs. Tennessee (1), Sept. 7, 2003
    Carolina (0) vs. Detroit (1), Oct. 16, 2005
2   Houston (0) vs. Denver (2), Dec. 2, 1962
    N.Y. Jets, (1) vs. St. Louis (1), Dec. 3, 1995
    Miami (1) vs. San Diego (1), Dec. 19, 1999
    New Orleans (0) vs. Baltimore (2), Dec. 19, 1999
    Baltimore (0) vs. Tennessee (2), Sept. 18, 2005
3   In many games

Most First Downs, Passing, Season
259   San Diego, 1985
251   Houston, 1990
250   Miami, 1986

Fewest First Downs, Passing, Season
18   Pittsburgh, 1941
23   Brooklyn, 1942
     N.Y. Giants, 1944
24   N.Y. Giants, 1943

Most First Downs, Passing, Game
29   N.Y. Giants vs. Cincinnati, Oct. 13, 1985
28   Tennessee vs. Oakland, Dec. 19, 2004
27   San Diego vs. Seattle, Sept. 15, 1985

Fewest First Downs, Passing, Game
0   By many teams. Last time: Cleveland vs.
    Jacksonville, Dec. 3, 2000

Most First Downs, Passing, Both Teams, Game
43   San Diego (23) vs. Cincinnati (20), Dec. 20, 1982
     Miami (24) vs. N.Y. Jets (19), Sept. 21, 1986 (OT)
     Tennessee (28) vs. Oakland (15), Dec. 19, 2004
42   San Francisco (22) vs. San Diego (20), Dec. 11, 1982
41   San Diego (27) vs. Seattle (14), Sept. 15, 1985
     Miami (26) vs. Cleveland (15), Dec. 12, 1988
     Kansas City (23) vs. Oakland (18), Nov. 5, 2000

Fewest First Downs, Passing, Both Teams, Game
0   Brooklyn vs. Pittsburgh, Nov. 29, 1942
1   Green Bay (0) vs. Cleveland (1), Sept. 21, 1941
    Pittsburgh (0) vs. Brooklyn (1), Oct. 11, 1942
    N.Y. Giants (0) vs. Detroit (1), Nov. 7, 1943
    Pittsburgh (0) vs. Chi. Cardinals (1), Nov. 11, 1945
    N.Y. Bulldogs (0) vs. Philadelphia (1), Sept. 22, 1949
    Chicago (0) vs. Buffalo (1), Oct. 7, 1979
2   In many games

Most First Downs, Penalty, Season
47   Buffalo, 2002
     Indianapolis, 2004
44   Dallas, 2005
43   Denver, 1994

Fewest First Downs, Penalty, Season
2   Brooklyn, 1940
4   Chi. Cardinals, 1940
    N.Y. Giants, 1942, 1944
    Washington, 1944
    Cleveland, 1952
    Kansas City, 1969
5   Brooklyn, 1939
    Chi. Bears, 1939
    Detroit, 1953
    Los Angeles, 1953
    Houston, 1982

Most First Downs, Penalty, Game
- 11 Denver vs. Houston, Oct. 6, 1985
- 9   Chi. Bears vs. Cleveland, Nov. 25, 1951
     Baltimore vs. Pittsburgh, Oct. 30, 1977
     N.Y. Jets vs. Houston, Sept. 18, 1988
     Dallas vs. Detroit, Nov. 20, 2005
- 8   Philadelphia vs. Detroit, Dec. 2, 1979
     Cincinnati vs. N.Y. Jets, Oct. 6, 1985
     Buffalo vs. Houston, Sept. 20, 1987
     Houston vs. Atlanta, Sept. 9, 1990
     Kansas City vs. L.A. Raiders, Oct. 3, 1993
     San Francisco vs. New Orleans, Oct. 11, 1998
     Oakland vs. San Francisco, Oct. 8, 2000 (OT)
     Philadelphia vs. Chicago, Nov. 3, 2002
     Detroit vs. Baltimore, Oct. 9, 2005

Most First Downs, Penalty, Both Teams, Game
- 12 Buffalo (7) vs. San Francisco (5), Oct. 4, 1998
     Detroit (8) vs. Baltimore (4), Oct. 9, 2005
- 11 Chi. Bears (9) vs. Cleveland (2), Nov. 25, 1951
     Cincinnati (8) vs. N.Y. Jets (3), Oct. 6, 1985
     Denver (11) vs. Houston (0), Oct. 6, 1985
     Detroit (6) vs. Dallas (5), Nov. 8, 1987
     N.Y. Jets (9) vs. Houston (2), Sept. 18, 1988
     Kansas City (8) vs. L.A. Raiders (3), Oct. 3, 1993
     Detroit (6) vs. San Diego (5), Nov. 11, 1996
     Philadelphia (8) vs. Chicago (3), Nov. 3, 2002
     Arizona (6) vs. St. Louis (5), Dec. 3, 2006
- 10 In many games

NET YARDS GAINED RUSHING AND PASSING

Most Seasons Leading League
- 12 Chi. Bears, 1932, 1934-35, 1939, 1941-44, 1947, 1949, 1955-56
- 9   L.A./St. Louis Rams, 1946, 1950-51, 1954, 1957, 1973, 1999-2001
- 7   San Diego, 1963, 1965, 1980-83, 1985

Most Consecutive Seasons Leading League
- 4   Chi. Bears, 1941-44
     San Diego, 1980-83
- 3   Baltimore, 1958-1960
     Houston, 1960-62
     Oakland, 1968-1970
     St. Louis, 1999-2001
- 2   By many teams

Most Yards Gained, Season
- 7,075 St. Louis, 2000
- 6,936 Miami, 1984
- 6,800 San Francisco, 1998

Fewest Yards Gained, Season
- 1,150 Cincinnati, 1933
- 1,443 Chi. Cardinals, 1934
- 1,486 Chi. Cardinals, 1933

Most Yards Gained, Game
- 735 Los Angeles vs. N.Y. Yanks, Sept. 28, 1951
- 683 Pittsburgh vs. Chi. Cardinals, Dec. 13, 1958
- 682 Chi. Bears vs. N.Y. Giants, Nov. 14, 1943

Fewest Yards Gained, Game
- −7 Seattle vs. Los Angeles, Nov. 4, 1979
- −5 Denver vs. Oakland, Sept. 10, 1967
- 14 Chi. Cardinals vs. Detroit, Sept. 15, 1940

Most Yards Gained, Both Teams, Game
- 1,133 Los Angeles (636) vs. N.Y. Yanks (497), Nov. 19, 1950
- 1,102 San Diego (661) vs. Cincinnati (441), Dec. 20, 1982
- 1,095 Kansas City (590) vs. Indianapolis (505), Oct. 31, 2004

Fewest Yards Gained, Both Teams, Game
- 30 Chi. Cardinals (14) vs. Detroit (16), Sept. 15, 1940
- 136 Chi. Cardinals (50) vs. Green Bay (86), Nov. 18, 1934
- 154 N.Y. Giants (51) vs. Washington (103), Dec. 11, 1960

Most Consecutive Games, 400 or More Yards Gained
- 11 San Diego, 1982-83
- 8   St. Louis, 1999-2000
- 6   Houston, 1961-62
     San Diego, 1981
     San Francisco, 1987

Most Consecutive Games, 300 or More Yards Gained
- 36 Minnesota, 2002-04
- 30 Minnesota, 1999-2000
     St. Louis, 2000-02
- 29 Los Angeles, 1949-1951

RUSHING

Most Seasons Leading League
- 16 Chi. Bears, 1932, 1934-35, 1939-1942, 1951, 1955-56, 1968, 1977, 1983-86
- 7   Buffalo, 1962, 1964, 1973, 1975, 1982, 1991-92
- 6   Cleveland, 1958-59, 1963, 1965-67
     San Francisco, 1952-54, 1987, 1998-99

Most Consecutive Seasons Leading League
- 4   Chi. Bears, 1939-1942
     Chi. Bears, 1983-86
- 3   Detroit, 1936-38
     San Francisco, 1952-54
     Cleveland, 1965-67
     Atlanta, 2004-06
- 2   By many teams

ATTEMPTS

Most Rushing Attempts, Season
- 681 Oakland, 1977
- 674 Chicago, 1984
- 671 New England, 1978

Fewest Rushing Attempts, Season
- 211 Philadelphia, 1982
- 219 San Francisco, 1982
- 225 Houston, 1982

Most Rushing Attempts, Game
- 72 Chi. Bears vs. Brooklyn, Oct. 20, 1935
- 70 Chi. Cardinals vs. Green Bay, Dec. 5, 1948
- 69 Chi. Cardinals vs. Green Bay, Dec. 6, 1936
     Kansas City vs. Cincinnati, Sept. 3, 1978

Fewest Rushing Attempts, Game
- 6   Chi. Cardinals vs. Boston, Oct. 29, 1933
     New England vs. Pittsburgh, Oct. 31, 2004
     Arizona vs. Minnesota, Nov. 26, 2006
- 7   Oakland vs. Buffalo, Oct. 5, 1963
     Houston vs. N.Y. Giants, Dec. 8, 1985
     Seattle vs. L.A. Raiders, Nov. 17, 1991
     Green Bay vs. Miami, Sept. 11, 1994
- 8   Denver vs. Oakland, Dec. 17, 1960
     Buffalo vs. St. Louis, Sept. 9, 1984
     Detroit vs. San Francisco, Oct. 20, 1991
     Atlanta vs. Detroit, Sept. 5, 1993
     St. Louis vs. San Francisco, Nov. 2, 2003
     N.Y. Jets vs. Denver, Nov. 20, 2005
     St. Louis vs. Carolina, Nov. 19, 2006

Most Rushing Attempts, Both Teams, Game
- 108 Chi. Cardinals (70) vs. Green Bay (38), Dec. 5, 1948
- 105 Oakland (62) vs. Atlanta (43), Nov. 30, 1975 (OT)
- 104 Chi. Bears (64) vs. Pittsburgh (40), Oct. 18, 1936

Fewest Rushing Attempts, Both Teams, Game
- 16 Chi. Cardinals (6) vs. Boston (10), Oct. 22, 1933
- 30 Minnesota (15) vs. New England (15), Oct. 30, 2006
- 34 Atlanta (12) vs. Houston (22), Dec. 5, 1993
     Atlanta (15) vs. San Francisco (19), Dec. 24, 1995
     Philadelphia (14) vs. San Diego (20), Oct. 23, 2005

YARDS GAINED

Most Yards Gained Rushing, Season
- 3,165   New England, 1978
- 3,088   Buffalo, 1973
- 2,986   Kansas City, 1978

Fewest Yards Gained Rushing, Season
- 298   Philadelphia, 1940
- 467   Detroit, 1946
- 471   Boston, 1944

Most Yards Gained Rushing, Game
- 426   Detroit vs. Pittsburgh, Nov. 4, 1934
- 423   N.Y. Giants vs. Baltimore, Nov. 19, 1950
- 420   Boston vs. N.Y. Giants, Oct. 8, 1933

Fewest Yards Gained Rushing, Game
- –53   Detroit vs. Chi. Cardinals, Oct. 17, 1943
- –36   Philadelphia vs. Chi. Bears, Nov. 19, 1939
- –33   Brooklyn vs. Phil-Pitt, Oct. 2, 1943

Most Yards Gained Rushing, Both Teams, Game
- 595   Los Angeles (371) vs. N.Y. Yanks (224), Nov. 18, 1951
- 574   Chi. Bears (396) vs. Pittsburgh (178), Oct. 10, 1934
- 558   Boston (420) vs. N.Y. Giants (138), Oct. 8, 1933

Fewest Yards Gained Rushing, Both Teams, Game
- –15   Detroit (–53) vs. Chi. Cardinals (38), Oct. 17, 1943
- 4   Detroit (–10) vs. Chi. Cardinals (14), Sept. 15, 1940
- 45   San Diego (21) vs. Philadelphia (24), Oct. 23, 2005

AVERAGE GAIN

Highest Average Gain, Rushing, Season
- 5.74   Cleveland, 1963
- 5.65   San Francisco, 1954
- 5.56   San Diego, 1963

Lowest Average Gain, Rushing, Season
- 0.94   Philadelphia, 1940
- 1.45   Boston, 1944
- 1.55   Pittsburgh, 1935

TOUCHDOWNS

Most Touchdowns, Rushing, Season
- 36   Green Bay, 1962
- 33   Pittsburgh, 1976
- 32   Kansas City, 2003
-      San Diego, 2006

Fewest Touchdowns, Rushing, Season
- 1   Brooklyn, 1934
- 2   Chi. Cardinals, 1933
-    Cincinnati, 1933
-    Pittsburgh, 1934
-    Philadelphia, 1935
-    Philadelphia, 1936
-    Philadelphia, 1937
-    Philadelphia, 1938
-    Pittsburgh, 1940
-    Philadelphia, 1972
-    N.Y. Jets, 1995
-    Arizona, 2005
- 3   By many teams

Most Touchdowns, Rushing, Game
- 9   Rock Island vs. Evansville, Oct. 15, 1922
-    Racine vs. Louisville, Nov. 5, 1922
- 8   Chi. Cardinals vs. Rochester, Oct. 7, 1923
-    Kansas City vs. Atlanta, Oct. 24, 2004
- 7   By many teams

Most Touchdowns, Rushing, Both Teams, Game
- 9   Rock Island (9) vs. Evansville (0), Oct. 15, 1922
-    Racine (9) vs. Louisville (0), Nov. 5, 1922
- 8   Chi. Cardinals (8) vs. Rochester (0), Oct. 7, 1923
-    Canton (7) vs. Cleveland (1), Nov. 25, 1923
-    Los Angeles (6) vs. N.Y. Yanks (2), Nov. 18, 1951
-    Chi. Bears (5) vs. Green Bay (3), Nov. 6, 1955

-    Denver (5) vs. Kansas City (3), Dec. 7, 2003
-    Kansas City (8) vs. Atlanta (0), Oct. 24, 2004
- 7   In many games

PASSING

ATTEMPTS

Most Passes Attempted, Season
- 709   Minnesota, 1981
- 699   New England, 1994
- 686   New England, 1995

Fewest Passes Attempted, Season
- 102   Cincinnati, 1933
- 106   Boston, 1933
- 120   Detroit, 1937

Most Passes Attempted, Game
- 70   New England vs. Minnesota, Nov. 13, 1994 (OT)
- 69   N.Y. Jets vs. Baltimore, Dec. 24, 2000
- 68   Houston vs. Buffalo, Nov 1, 1964
-    Cincinnati vs. Pittsburgh, Dec. 30, 2001 (OT)

Fewest Passes Attempted, Game
- 0   Green Bay vs. Portsmouth, Oct. 8, 1933
-    Detroit vs. Cleveland, Sept. 10, 1937
-    Pittsburgh vs. Brooklyn, Nov. 16, 1941
-    Pittsburgh vs. Los Angeles, Nov. 13, 1949
-    Cleveland vs. Philadelphia, Dec. 3, 1950

Most Passes Attempted, Both Teams, Game
- 112   New England (70) vs. Minnesota (42), Nov. 13, 1994
- 104   Miami (55) vs. N.Y. Jets (49), Oct. 18, 1987 (OT)
-    N.Y. Jets (58) vs. San Francisco (46), Sept. 6, 1998 (OT)
- 103   Cincinnati (68) vs. Pittsburgh (35), Dec. 30, 2001 (OT)
-    Seattle (53) vs. San Diego (50), Dec. 29, 2002 (OT)

Fewest Passes Attempted, Both Teams, Game
- 4   Chi. Cardinals (1) vs. Detroit (3), Nov. 3, 1935
-    Detroit (0) vs. Cleveland (4), Sept. 10, 1937
- 6   Chi. Cardinals (2) vs. Detroit (4), Sept. 15, 1940
- 8   Brooklyn (2) vs. Philadelphia (6), Oct. 1, 1939

COMPLETIONS

Most Passes Completed, Season
- 432   San Francisco, 1995
- 419   Arizona, 2005
- 418   Oakland, 2002

Fewest Passes Completed, Season
- 25   Cincinnati, 1933
- 33   Boston, 1933
- 34   Chi. Cardinals, 1934

Most Passes Completed, Game
- 45   New England vs. Minnesota, Nov. 13, 1994 (OT)
- 43   Washington vs. Detroit, Nov. 4, 1990 (OT)
-    Oakland vs. Pittsburgh, Sept. 15, 2002
- 42   N.Y. Jets vs. San Francisco, Sept. 21, 1980
-    N.Y. Jets vs. Seattle, Dec. 6, 1998

Fewest Passes Completed, Game
- 0   By many teams. Last time: Buffalo vs. N.Y. Jets, Sept. 29, 1974

Most Passes Completed, Both Teams, Game
- 71   New England (45) vs. Minnesota (26), Nov. 13, 1994
- 68   San Francisco (37) vs. Atlanta (31), Oct. 6, 1985
-    Denver (34) vs. Oakland (34), Nov. 11, 2002
- 66   Cincinnati (40) vs. San Diego (26), Dec. 20, 1982

Fewest Passes Completed, Both Teams, Game
- 1   Chi. Cardinals (0) vs. Philadelphia (1), Nov. 8, 1936
-    Detroit (0) vs. Cleveland (1), Sept. 10, 1937
-    Chi. Cardinals (0) vs. Detroit (1), Sept. 15, 1940
-    Brooklyn (0) vs. Pittsburgh (1), Nov. 29, 1942
- 2   Chi. Cardinals (0) vs. Detroit (2), Nov. 3, 1935
-    Buffalo (0) vs. N.Y. Jets (2), Sept. 29, 1974
-    Chi. Cardinals (0) vs. Green Bay (2), Nov. 18, 1934
- 3   In seven games

YARDS GAINED

Most Seasons Leading League, Passing Yardage
- 10 San Diego, 1965, 1968, 1971, 1978-1983, 1985
- 8 Chi. Bears, 1932, 1939, 1941, 1943, 1945, 1949, 1954, 1964
   Washington, 1938, 1940, 1944, 1947-48, 1967, 1974, 1989
- 7 Houston, 1960-61, 1963-64, 1990-92
   L.A./St. Louis Rams, 1946, 1950-51, 1956, 1999-2001
   Balt./Indianapolis, 1957, 1959, 1960, 1963, 1976, 2003-04

Most Consecutive Seasons Leading League, Passing Yardage
- 6 San Diego, 1978-1983
- 4 Green Bay, 1934-37
- 3 Miami, 1986-88
   Houston, 1990-92
   St. Louis, 1999-2001

Most Yards Gained, Passing, Season
- 5,232 St. Louis, 2000
- 5,018 Miami, 1984
- 4,870 San Diego, 1985

Fewest Yards Gained, Passing, Season
- 302 Chi. Cardinals, 1934
- 357 Cincinnati, 1933
- 459 Boston, 1934

Most Yards Gained, Passing, Game
- 554 Los Angeles vs. N.Y. Yanks, Sept. 28, 1951
- 530 Minnesota vs. Baltimore, Sept. 28, 1969
- 521 Miami vs. N.Y. Jets, Oct. 23, 1988

Fewest Yards Gained, Passing, Game
- –53 Denver vs. Oakland, Sept. 10, 1967
- –52 Cincinnati vs. Houston, Oct. 31, 1971
- –39 Atlanta vs. San Francisco, Oct. 23, 1976

Most Yards Gained, Passing, Both Teams, Game
- 884 N.Y. Jets (449) vs. Miami (435), Sept. 21, 1986 (OT)
- 883 San Diego (486) vs. Cincinnati (397), Dec. 20, 1982
- 874 Miami (456) vs. New England (418), Sept. 4, 1994

Fewest Yards Gained, Passing, Both Teams, Game
- –11 Green Bay (–10) vs. Dallas (–1), Oct. 24, 1965
- 1 Chi. Cardinals (0) vs. Philadelphia (1), Nov. 8, 1936
- 7 Brooklyn (0) vs. Pittsburgh (7), Nov. 29, 1942

TIMES SACKED

Most Seasons Leading League, Fewest Times Sacked
- 10 Miami, 1973, 1982-1990
- 5 N.Y. Jets, 1965-66, 1968, 1993, 2000
   Indianapolis, 1999-2000, 2004-06
- 4 San Diego, 1963-64, 1967-68
   San Francisco, 1964-65, 1970-71

Most Consecutive Seasons Leading League, Fewest Times Sacked
- 9 Miami, 1982-1990
- 3 St. Louis, 1974-76
   Indianapolis, 2004-06
- 2 By many teams

Most Times Sacked, Season
- 104 Philadelphia, 1986
- 78 Arizona, 1997
- 76 Houston, 2002

Fewest Times Sacked, Season
- 7 Miami, 1988
- 8 San Francisco, 1970
   St. Louis, 1975
- 9 N.Y. Jets, 1966
   Washington, 1991

Most Times Sacked, Game
- 12 Pittsburgh vs. Dallas, Nov. 20, 1966
   Baltimore vs. St. Louis, Oct. 26, 1980
   Detroit vs. Chicago, Dec. 16, 1984
   Houston vs. Dallas, Sept. 29, 1985

- 11 St. Louis vs. N.Y. Giants, Nov. 1, 1964
   Los Angeles vs. Baltimore, Nov. 22, 1964
   Denver vs. Buffalo, Dec. 13, 1964
   Green Bay vs. Detroit, Nov. 7, 1965
   Buffalo vs. Oakland, Oct. 15, 1967
   Denver vs. Oakland, Nov. 5, 1967
   Atlanta vs. St. Louis, Nov. 24, 1968
   Detroit vs. Dallas, Oct. 6, 1975
   Philadelphia vs. St. Louis, Dec. 18, 1983
   Cleveland vs. Kansas City, Sept. 30, 1984
   Minnesota vs. Chicago, Oct. 28, 1984
   Atlanta vs. Cleveland, Nov. 18, 1984
   Dallas vs. San Diego, Nov. 16, 1986
   Philadelphia vs. Detroit, Nov. 16, 1986
   Philadelphia vs. L.A. Raiders, Nov. 30, 1986 (OT)
   L.A. Raiders vs. Seattle, Dec. 8, 1986
   N.Y. Jets vs. Dallas, Oct. 4, 1987
   Philadelphia vs. Chicago, Oct. 4, 1987
   Dallas vs. Philadelphia, Sept. 15, 1991
   Cleveland vs. Indianapolis, Sept. 6, 1992
- 10 By many teams

Most Times Sacked, Both Teams, Game
- 18 Green Bay (10) vs. San Diego (8), Sept. 24, 1978
- 17 Buffalo (10) vs. N.Y. Titans (7), Nov. 23, 1961
   Pittsburgh (12) vs. Dallas (5), Nov. 20, 1966
   Atlanta (9) vs. Philadelphia (8), Dec. 16, 1984
   Philadelphia (11) vs. L.A. Raiders (6), Nov. 30, 1986 (OT)
- 16 Los Angeles (11) vs. Baltimore (5), Nov. 22, 1964
   Buffalo (11) vs. Oakland (5), Oct. 15, 1967

COMPLETION PERCENTAGE

Most Seasons Leading League, Completion Percentage
- 14 San Francisco, 1952, 1957-58, 1965, 1981, 1983, 1987, 1989, 1992-97
- 11 Washington, 1937, 1939-1940, 1942-45, 1947-48, 1969-1970
- 8 Green Bay, 1936, 1941, 1961-62, 1964, 1966, 1968, 1998

Most Consecutive Seasons Leading League, Completion Percentage
- 6 San Francisco, 1992-97
- 4 Washington, 1942-45
   Kansas City, 1966-69
- 3 Cleveland, 1953-55
   St. Louis, 1999-2001

Highest Completion Percentage, Season
- 70.65 Cincinnati, 1982 (310-219)
- 70.25 San Francisco, 1994 (511-359)
- 70.19 San Francisco, 1989 (483-339)

Lowest Completion Percentage, Season
- 22.9 Philadelphia, 1936 (170-39)
- 24.5 Cincinnati, 1933 (102-25)
- 25.0 Pittsburgh, 1941 (168-42)

TOUCHDOWNS

Most Touchdowns, Passing, Season
- 51 Indianapolis, 2004
- 49 Miami, 1984
- 48 Houston, 1961

Fewest Touchdowns, Passing, Season
- 0 Cincinnati, 1933
   Pittsburgh, 1945
- 1 Boston, 1932
   Boston, 1933
   Chi. Cardinals, 1934
   Cincinnati/St. Louis, 1934
   Detroit, 1942
- 2 Chi. Cardinals, 1932
   Stapleton, 1932
   Chi. Cardinals, 1935

Brooklyn, 1936
Pittsburgh, 1942

Most Touchdowns, Passing, Game
- 7   Chi. Bears vs. N.Y. Giants, Nov. 14, 1943
  - Philadelphia vs. Washington, Oct. 17, 1954
  - Houston vs. N.Y. Titans, Nov. 19, 1961
  - Houston vs. N.Y. Titans, Oct. 14, 1962
  - N.Y. Giants vs. Washington, Oct. 28, 1962
  - Minnesota vs. Baltimore, Sept. 28, 1969
  - San Diego vs. Oakland, Nov. 22, 1981
- 6   By many teams

Most Touchdowns, Passing, Both Teams, Game
- 12   New Orleans (6) vs. St. Louis (6), Nov. 2, 1969
- 11   N.Y. Giants (7) vs. Washington (4), Oct. 28, 1962
  - Oakland (6) vs. Houston (5), Dec. 22, 1963
- 10   San Diego (5) vs. Seattle (5), Sept. 15, 1985
  - Miami (6) vs. N.Y. Jets (4), Sept. 21, 1986 (OT)
  - San Francisco (6) vs. Atlanta (4), Oct. 14, 1990

PASSES HAD INTERCEPTED

Most Passes Had Intercepted, Season
- 48   Houston, 1962
- 45   Denver, 1961
- 41   Card-Pitt, 1944

Fewest Passes Had Intercepted, Season
- 5   Cleveland, 1960
  - Green Bay, 1966
  - Kansas City, 1990
  - N.Y. Giants, 1990
- 6   Green Bay, 1964
  - St. Louis, 1982
  - Dallas, 1993
  - Jacksonville, 2005
- 7   Los Angeles, 1969
  - Denver, 2005

Most Passes Had Intercepted, Game
- 9   Detroit vs. Green Bay, Oct. 24, 1943
  - Pittsburgh vs. Philadelphia, Dec. 12, 1965
- 8   Green Bay vs. N.Y. Giants, Nov. 21, 1948
  - Chi. Cardinals vs. Philadelphia, Sept. 24, 1950
  - N.Y. Yanks vs. N.Y. Giants, Dec. 16, 1951
  - Denver vs. Houston, Dec. 2, 1962
  - Chi. Bears vs. Detroit, Sept. 22, 1968
  - Baltimore vs. N.Y. Jets, Sept. 23, 1973
- 7   By many teams. Last time: Detroit vs. Cleveland, Sept. 23, 2001

Most Passes Had Intercepted, Both Teams, Game
- 13   Denver (8) vs. Houston (5), Dec. 2, 1962
- 11   Philadelphia (7) vs. Boston (4), Nov. 3, 1935
  - Boston (6) vs. Pittsburgh (5), Dec. 1, 1935
  - Cleveland (7) vs. Green Bay (4), Oct. 30, 1938
  - Green Bay (7) vs. Detroit (4), Oct. 20, 1940
  - Detroit (7) vs. Chi. Bears (4), Nov. 22, 1942
  - Detroit (7) vs. Cleveland (4), Nov. 26, 1944
  - Chi. Cardinals (8) vs. Philadelphia (3), Sept. 24, 1950
  - Washington (7) vs. N.Y. Giants (4), Dec. 8, 1963
  - Pittsburgh (9) vs. Philadelphia (2), Dec 12, 1965
- 10   In many games

PUNTING

Most Seasons Leading League (Average Distance)
- 7   Denver 1962-64, 1966-67, 1982, 1999
- 6   Washington, 1940-43, 1945, 1958
  - Kansas City, 1968, 1971-73, 1979, 1984
  - Oakland, 1974-75, 1977-78, 2003-04
- 5   L.A. Rams, 1946, 1949, 1955-56, 1994

Most Consecutive Seasons Leading League (Average Distance)
- 4   Washington, 1940-43
- 3   Cleveland, 1950-52

Denver, 1962-64
Kansas City, 1971-73

Most Punts, Season
- 116   Houston, 2002
- 114   Chicago, 1981
- 113   Boston, 1934
  - Brooklyn, 1934
  - Dallas, 2002

Fewest Punts, Season
- 23   San Diego, 1982
- 31   Cincinnati, 1982
- 32   Chi. Bears, 1941

Most Punts, Game
- 17   Chi. Bears vs. Green Bay, Oct. 22, 1933
  - Cincinnati vs. Pittsburgh, Oct. 22, 1933
- 16   Cincinnati vs. Portsmouth, Sept. 17, 1933
  - Chi. Cardinals vs. Chi. Bears, Nov. 30, 1933
  - Chi. Cardinals vs. Detroit, Sept. 15, 1940
  - Oakland vs. San Diego, Oct. 11, 1998
- 15   Chi. Cardinals vs. Cincinnati, Nov. 12, 1933
  - N.Y. Giants vs. Chi. Bears, Nov. 17, 1935
  - Philadelphia vs. N.Y. Giants, Dec. 6, 1987 (OT)

Fewest Punts, Game
- 0   By many teams. Last time:
  - Cincinnati vs. Oakland, Dec. 10, 2006

Most Punts, Both Teams, Game
- 31   Chi. Bears (17) vs. Green Bay (14), Oct. 22, 1933
  - Cincinnati (17) vs. Pittsburgh (14), Oct. 22, 1933
- 29   Chi. Cardinals (15) vs. Cincinnati (14), Nov. 12, 1933
  - Chi. Cardinals (16) vs. Chi. Bears (13), Nov. 30, 1933
  - Chi. Cardinals (16) vs. Detroit (13), Sept. 15, 1940
- 28   Philadelphia (14) vs. Washington (14), Nov. 5, 1939

Fewest Punts, Both Teams, Game
- 0   Buffalo vs. San Francisco, Sept. 13, 1992
- 1   Baltimore (0) vs. Cleveland (1), Nov. 1, 1959
  - Dall. Cowboys (0) vs. Cleveland (1), Dec. 3, 1961
  - Chicago (0) vs. Detroit (1), Oct. 1, 1972
  - San Francisco (0) vs. N.Y. Giants (1), Oct. 15, 1972
  - Green Bay (0) vs. Buffalo (1), Dec. 5, 1982
  - Miami (0) vs. Buffalo (1), Oct. 12, 1986
  - Green Bay (0) vs. Chicago (1), Dec. 17, 1989
  - Oakland (0) vs. Seattle (1), Dec. 5, 1999
  - Tampa Bay (0) vs. Minnesota (1), Oct. 29, 2000
  - New Orleans (0) vs. San Francisco (1), Oct. 20, 2002
- 2   In many games

AVERAGE YARDAGE

Highest Average Distance, Punting, Season
- 48.2   Dallas, 2006 (56-2,697)
- 47.6   Detroit, 1961 (56-2,664)
- 47.2   Tennessee, 1998 (69-3,258)

Lowest Average Distance, Punting, Season
- 32.7   Card-Pitt, 1944 (60-1,964)
- 33.8   Cincinnati, 1986 (59-1,996)
- 33.9   Detroit, 1969 (74-2,510)

PUNT RETURNS

Most Seasons Leading League (Average Return)
- 9   Detroit, 1943-45, 1951-52, 1962, 1966, 1969, 1991
- 7   Chi. Cardinals/St. Louis, 1948-49, 1955-56, 1959, 1986-87
- 6   Green Bay, 1950, 1953-54, 1961, 1972, 1996
  - Dallas/Kansas City, 1960, 1968, 1970, 1979-1980, 2003

Most Consecutive Seasons Leading League (Average Return)
- 3   Detroit, 1943-45
- 2   By many teams

Most Punt Returns, Season
- 71   Pittsburgh, 1976
  - Tampa Bay, 1979

L.A. Raiders, 1985
67　Pittsburgh, 1974
　　Los Angeles, 1978
　　L.A. Raiders, 1984
65　San Francisco, 1976
Fewest Punt Returns, Season
12　Baltimore, 1981
　　San Diego, 1982
14　Los Angeles, 1961
　　Philadelphia, 1962
　　Baltimore, 1982
15　Houston, 1960
　　Washington, 1960
　　Oakland, 1961
　　N.Y. Giants, 1969
　　Philadelphia, 1973
　　Kansas City, 1982
Most Punt Returns, Game
12　Philadelphia vs. Cleveland, Dec. 3, 1950
11　Chi. Bears vs. Chi. Cardinals, Oct. 8, 1950
　　Washington vs. Tampa Bay, Oct. 9, 1977
10　Philadelphia vs. N.Y. Giants, Nov. 26, 1950
　　Philadelphia vs. Tampa Bay, Sept. 18, 1977
　　Pittsburgh vs. Buffalo, Dec. 16, 1979
　　Washington vs. New Orleans, Dec. 26, 1982
　　Philadelphia vs. Seattle, Dec. 13, 1992 (OT)
　　New England vs. Pittsburgh, Dec. 5, 1993
Most Punt Returns, Both Teams, Game
17　Philadelphia (12) vs. Cleveland (5), Dec. 3, 1950
16　N.Y. Giants (9) vs. Philadelphia (7), Dec. 12, 1954
　　Washington (11) vs. Tampa Bay (5), Oct. 9, 1977
　　Oakland (8) vs. San Diego (8), Oct. 11, 1998
15　Detroit (8) vs. Cleveland (7), Sept. 27, 1942
　　Los Angeles (8) vs. Baltimore (7), Nov. 27, 1966
　　Pittsburgh (8) vs. Houston (7), Dec. 1, 1974
　　Philadelphia (10) vs. Tampa Bay (5), Sept. 18, 1977
　　Baltimore (9) vs. Kansas City (6), Sept. 2, 1979
　　Washington (10) vs. New Orleans (5), Dec. 26, 1982
　　L.A. Raiders (8) vs. Cleveland (7), Nov. 16, 1986

FAIR CATCHES
Most Fair Catches, Season
34　Baltimore, 1971
33　Philadelphia, 2000
32　San Diego, 1969
　　Oakland, 2001
Fewest Fair Catches, Season
0　San Diego, 1975
　　New England, 1976
　　Tampa Bay, 1976
　　Pittsburgh, 1977
　　Dallas, 1982
1　Cleveland, 1974
　　San Francisco, 1975
　　Kansas City, 1976
　　St. Louis, 1976
　　San Diego, 1976
　　L.A. Rams, 1982
　　St. Louis, 1982
　　Tampa Bay, 1982
　　Arizona, 2001
2　By many teams
Most Fair Catches, Game
7　Minnesota vs. Dallas, Sept. 25, 1966
　　N.Y. Jets vs. Miami, Nov. 20, 1966
　　Detroit vs. Chicago, Nov. 21, 1976
　　Philadelphia vs. Buffalo, Dec. 27, 1987
6　By many teams

YARDS GAINED
Most Yards, Punt Returns, Season
875　Green Bay, 1996
785　L.A. Raiders, 1985
781　Chi. Bears, 1948
Fewest Yards, Punt Returns, Season
27　St. Louis, 1965
35　N.Y. Giants, 1965
37　New England, 1972
Most Yards, Punt Returns, Game
231　Detroit vs. San Francisco, Oct. 6, 1963
225　Oakland vs. Buffalo, Sept. 15, 1968
219　Los Angeles vs. Atlanta, Oct. 11, 1981
Fewest Yards, Punt Returns, Game
-28　Washington vs. Dallas, Dec. 11, 1966
-23　N.Y. Giants vs. Buffalo, Oct. 20, 1975
　　Pittsburgh vs. Houston, Sept. 20, 1970
-20　New Orleans vs. Pittsburgh, Oct. 20, 1968
Most Yards, Punt Returns, Both Teams, Game
282　Los Angeles (219) vs. Atlanta (63), Oct. 11, 1981
245　Detroit (231) vs. San Francisco (14), Oct. 6, 1963
244　Oakland (225) vs. Buffalo (19), Sept. 15, 1968
Fewest Yards, Punt Returns, Both Teams, Game
-18　Buffalo (-18) vs. Pittsburgh (0), Oct. 29, 1972
-14　Miami (-14) vs. Boston (0), Nov. 30, 1969
　　Tennessee (-14) vs. New Orleans (0),
　　　Sept. 21, 2003
-13　N.Y. Giants (-13) vs. Cleveland (0), Nov. 14, 1965

AVERAGE YARDS RETURNING PUNTS
Highest Average, Punt Returns, Season
20.2　Chi. Bears, 1941 (27-546)
19.1　Chi. Cardinals, 1948 (35-669)
18.2　Chi. Cardinals, 1949 (30-546)
Lowest Average, Punt Returns, Season
1.2　St. Louis, 1965 (23-27)
1.5　N.Y. Giants, 1965 (24-35)
1.7　Washington, 1970 (27-45)

TOUCHDOWNS RETURNING PUNTS
Most Touchdowns, Punt Returns, Season
5　Chi. Cardinals, 1959
4　Chi. Cardinals, 1948
　　Detroit, 1951
　　N.Y. Giants, 1951
　　Denver, 1976
3　Washington, 1941
　　Detroit, 1952
　　Pittsburgh, 1952
　　Houston, 1975
　　Los Angeles, 1981
　　Cleveland, 1993
　　Green Bay, 1996
　　Denver, 1997
　　San Diego, 1997
　　Chicago, 2006
　　Tennessee, 2006
Most Touchdowns, Punt Returns, Game
2　Detroit vs. Los Angeles, Oct. 14, 1951
　　Detroit vs. Green Bay, Nov. 22, 1951
　　Chi. Cardinals vs. Pittsburgh, Nov. 1, 1959
　　Chi. Cardinals vs. N.Y. Giants, Nov. 22, 1959
　　N.Y. Titans vs. Denver, Sept. 24, 1961
　　Denver vs. Cleveland, Sept. 26, 1976
　　Los Angeles vs. Atlanta, Oct. 11, 1981
　　St. Louis vs. Tampa Bay, Dec. 21, 1986
　　L.A. Rams vs. Atlanta, Dec. 27, 1992
　　Cleveland vs. Pittsburgh, Oct. 24, 1993
　　San Diego vs. Cincinnati, Nov. 2, 1997
　　Denver vs. Carolina, Nov. 9, 1997

Baltimore vs. Seattle, Dec. 7, 1997
Baltimore vs. N.Y. Jets, Dec. 24, 2000
Oakland vs. Tennessee, Sept. 29, 2002
Carolina vs. Cincinnati, Dec. 8, 2002
Detroit at Jacksonville, Nov. 14, 2004 (OT)

Most Touchdowns, Punt Returns, Both Teams, Game
2 Philadelphia (1) vs. Washington (1), Nov. 9, 1952
Kansas City (1) vs. Buffalo (1), Sept. 11, 1966
Baltimore (1) vs. New England (1), Nov. 18, 1979
L.A. Raiders (1) vs. Philadelphia (1),
  Nov. 30, 1986 (OT)
Cincinnati (1) vs. Green Bay (1), Sept. 20, 1992
Oakland (1) vs. Seattle (1), Nov. 15, 1998
Atlanta (1) vs. Tennessee (1), Nov. 23, 2003
(Also see previous record)

KICKOFF RETURNS

Most Seasons Leading League (Average Return)
8 Washington, 1942, 1947, 1962-63, 1973-74, 1981,
  1995
6 Chicago Bears, 1943, 1948, 1958, 1966, 1972, 1985
  N.Y. Giants, 1944, 1946, 1949, 1951, 1953, 2004
5 Green Bay, 1954, 1964, 1967, 1993, 1998
  New England, 1977, 1980, 1982, 1997, 2006

Most Consecutive Seasons Leading League (Average Return)
3 Denver, 1965-67
2 By many teams

Most Kickoff Returns, Season
89 Cleveland, 1999
88 New Orleans, 1980
87 Atlanta, 1996
  New Orleans, 2001

Fewest Kickoff Returns, Season
17 N.Y. Giants, 1944
20 N.Y. Giants, 1941, 1943
  Chi. Bears, 1942
23 Washington, 1942

Most Kickoff Returns, Game
12 N.Y. Giants vs. Washington, Nov. 27, 1966
10 By many teams

Most Kickoff Returns, Both Teams, Game
19 N.Y. Giants (12) vs. Washington (7), Nov. 27, 1966
  Cleveland (10) vs. Cincinnati (9), Nov. 28, 2004
18 Houston (10) vs. Oakland (8), Dec. 22, 1968
17 Washington (9) vs. Green Bay (8), Oct. 17, 1983
  San Diego (9) vs. Pittsburgh (8), Dec. 8, 1985
  Detroit (9) vs. Green Bay (8), Nov. 27, 1986
  L.A. Raiders (9) vs. Seattle (8), Dec. 18, 1988
  Oakland (10) vs. Seattle (7), Oct. 26, 1997
  Buffalo (9) vs. Minnesota (8), Sept. 15, 2002 (OT)

YARDS GAINED

Most Yards, Kickoff Returns, Season
2,296 Arizona, 2000
2,173 Houston, 2005
2,039 Detroit, 2002

Fewest Yards, Kickoff Returns, Season
282 N.Y. Giants, 1940
381 Green Bay, 1940
424 Chicago, 1963

Most Yards, Kickoff Returns, Game
367 Baltimore vs. Minnesota, Dec. 13, 1998
362 Detroit vs. Los Angeles, Oct. 29, 1950
304 Chi. Bears vs. Green Bay, Nov. 9, 1952
  New Orleans vs. L.A. Rams, Oct. 23, 1994

Most Yards, Kickoff Returns, Both Teams, Game
560 Detroit (362) vs. Los Angeles (198), Oct. 29, 1950
511 Baltimore (367) vs. Minnesota (144), Dec. 13, 1998
501 New Orleans (304) vs. L.A. Rams (197), Oct. 23, 1994

AVERAGE YARDAGE

Highest Average, Kickoff Returns, Season
29.4 Chicago, 1972 (52-1,528)
28.9 Pittsburgh, 1952 (39-1,128)
28.2 Washington, 1962 (61-1,720)

Lowest Average, Kickoff Returns, Season
14.7 N.Y. Jets, 1993 (46-675)
15.8 N.Y. Giants, 1993 (32-507)
15.9 Tampa Bay, 1993 (58-922)

TOUCHDOWNS

Most Touchdowns, Kickoff Returns, Season
4 Green Bay, 1967
  Chicago, 1970
  Detroit, 1994
3 Los Angeles, 1950
  Chi. Cardinals, 1954
  San Francisco, 1963
  Denver, 1966
  Chicago, 1967
  New England, 1977
  L.A. Rams, 1985
  Atlanta, 2000
  Buffalo, 2004
2 By many teams

Most Touchdowns, Kickoff Returns, Game
2 Chi. Bears vs. Green Bay, Sept. 22, 1940
  Chi. Bears vs. Green Bay, Nov. 9, 1952
  Philadelphia vs. Dallas, Nov. 6, 1966
  Green Bay vs. Cleveland, Nov. 12, 1967
  L.A. Rams vs. Green Bay, Nov. 24, 1985
  New Orleans vs. L.A. Rams, Oct. 23, 1994
  Baltimore vs. Minnesota, Dec. 13, 1998
  N.Y. Jets vs. Buffalo, Sept. 8, 2002 (OT)
  Chicago vs. St. Louis, Dec. 11, 2006

Most Touchdowns, Kickoff Returns, Both Teams, Game
3 Baltimore (2) vs. Minnesota (1), Dec. 13, 1998
2 In many games

FUMBLES

Most Fumbles, Season
56 Chi. Bears, 1938
  San Francisco, 1978
54 Philadelphia, 1946
51 New England, 1973

Fewest Fumbles, Season
7 Kansas City, 2002
8 Cleveland, 1959
10 Indianapolis, 1998
  Minnesota, 1998

Most Fumbles, Game
10 Phil-Pitt vs. N.Y. Giants, Oct. 9, 1943
  Detroit vs. Minnesota, Nov. 12, 1967
  Kansas City vs. Houston, Oct. 12, 1969
  San Francisco vs. Detroit, Dec. 17, 1978
9 Philadelphia vs. Green Bay, Oct. 13, 1946
  Boston at Oakland, Dec. 16, 1962
  Kansas City vs. San Diego, Nov. 15, 1964
  N.Y. Giants vs. Buffalo, Oct. 20, 1975
  St. Louis vs. Washington, Oct. 25, 1976
  San Diego vs. Green Bay, Sept. 24, 1978
  Pittsburgh vs. Cincinnati, Oct. 14, 1979
  Cleveland vs. Seattle, Dec. 20, 1981
  Cleveland vs. Pittsburgh, Dec. 23, 1990
  Oakland vs. Seattle, Dec. 22, 1996
8 By many teams

Most Fumbles, Both Teams, Game
14 Washington (8) vs. Pittsburgh (6), Nov. 14, 1937
  Chi. Bears (7) vs. Cleveland (7), Nov. 24, 1940
  St. Louis (8) vs. N.Y. Giants (6), Sept. 17, 1961

Kansas City (10) vs. Houston (4), Oct. 12, 1969
13 Washington (8) vs. Pittsburgh (5), Nov. 14, 1937
Philadelphia (7) vs. Boston (6), Dec. 8, 1946
N.Y. Giants (7) vs. Washington (6), Nov. 5, 1950
Kansas City (9) vs. San Diego (4), Nov. 15, 1964
Buffalo (7) vs. Denver (6), Dec. 13, 1964
N.Y. Jets (7) vs. Houston (6), Sept. 12, 1965
Cleveland (7) vs. New Orleans (6), Dec. 12, 1971
Houston (8) vs. Pittsburgh (5), Dec. 9, 1973
St. Louis (9) vs. Washington (4), Oct. 25, 1976
Cleveland (9) vs. Seattle (4), Dec. 20, 1981
Green Bay (7) vs. Detroit (6), Oct. 6, 1985
12 In many games

FUMBLES LOST
Most Fumbles Lost, Season
36 Chi. Cardinals, 1959
31 Green Bay, 1952
29 Chi. Cardinals, 1946
Pittsburgh, 1950
Cleveland, 1978
Fewest Fumbles Lost, Season
2 Kansas City, 2002
3 Philadelphia, 1938
Minnesota, 1980
4 San Francisco, 1960
Kansas City, 1982
Minnesota, 1998
Detroit, 2003
Most Fumbles Lost, Game
8 St. Louis vs. Washington, Oct. 25, 1976
Cleveland vs. Pittsburgh, Dec. 23, 1990
7 Cincinnati vs. Buffalo, Nov. 30, 1969
Pittsburgh vs. Cincinnati, Oct. 14, 1979
Cleveland vs. Seattle, Dec. 20, 1981
6 By many teams

FUMBLES RECOVERED
Most Fumbles Recovered, Season, Own and Opponents'
58 Minnesota, 1963 (27 own, 31 opp)
51 Chi. Bears, 1938 (37 own, 14 opp)
San Francisco, 1978 (24 own, 27 opp)
50 Philadelphia, 1987 (23 own, 27 opp)
Fewest Fumbles Recovered, Season, Own and Opponents'
9 San Francisco, 1982 (5 own, 4 opp)
10 Jacksonville, 2006 (6 own, 4 opp)
11 Cincinnati, 1982 (5 own, 6 opp)
Most Fumbles Recovered, Game, Own and Opponents'
10 Denver vs. Buffalo, Dec. 13, 1964 (5 own, 5 opp)
Pittsburgh vs. Houston, Dec. 9, 1973 (5 own, 5 opp)
Washington vs. St. Louis, Oct. 25, 1976
(2 own, 8 opp)
9 St. Louis vs. N.Y. Giants, Sept. 17, 1961
(6 own, 3 opp)
Houston vs. Cincinnati, Oct. 27, 1974 (4 own, 5 opp)
Kansas City vs. Dallas, Nov. 10, 1975 (4 own, 5 opp)
Green Bay vs. Detroit, Oct. 6, 1985 (5 own, 4 opp)
Pittsburgh vs. Cleveland, Dec. 23, 1990
(1 own, 8 opp)
8 By many teams
Most Own Fumbles Recovered, Season
37 Chi. Bears, 1938
28 Pittsburgh, 1987
27 Philadelphia, 1946
Minnesota, 1963
Fewest Own Fumbles Recovered, Season
1 Indianapolis, 2006
2 Washington, 1958
Miami, 2000
3 Detroit, 1956

Cleveland, 1959
Houston, 1982
New Orleans, 2005
Most Opponents' Fumbles Recovered, Season
31 Minnesota, 1963
29 Cleveland, 1951
28 Green Bay, 1946
Houston, 1977
Seattle, 1983
Fewest Opponents' Fumbles Recovered, Season
3 Los Angeles, 1974
Green Bay, 1995
4 Philadelphia, 1944
San Francisco, 1982
Jacksonville, 2006
5 Baltimore, 1982
Arizona, 1997
Baltimore, 1998
Chicago, 2003
Oakland, 2006
Most Opponents' Fumbles Recovered, Game
8 Washington vs. St. Louis, Oct. 25, 1976
Pittsburgh vs. Cleveland, Dec. 23, 1990
7 Buffalo vs. Cincinnati, Nov. 30, 1969
Cincinnati vs. Pittsburgh, Oct. 14, 1979
Seattle vs. Cleveland, Dec. 20, 1981
6 By many teams

TOUCHDOWNS
Most Touchdowns, Fumbles Recovered, Season, Own and Opponents'
5 Chi. Bears, 1942 (1 own, 4 opp)
Los Angeles, 1952 (1 own, 4 opp)
San Francisco, 1965 (1 own, 4 opp)
Oakland, 1978 (2 own, 3 opp)
4 Chi. Bears, 1948 (1 own, 3 opp)
Boston, 1948 (4 opp)
Denver, 1979 (1 own, 3 opp)
Atlanta, 1981 (1 own, 3 opp)
Denver, 1984 (4 opp)
St. Louis, 1987 (4 opp)
Minnesota, 1989 (4 opp)
Atlanta, 1991 (4 opp)
Philadelphia, 1995 (4 opp)
Atlanta, 1998 (4 opp)
New Orleans, 1998 (4 opp)
Kansas City, 1999 (4 opp)
3 By many teams
Most Touchdowns, Own Fumbles Recovered, Season
2 Chi. Bears, 1953
New England, 1973
Buffalo, 1974
Denver, 1975
Oakland, 1978
Green Bay, 1982
New Orleans, 1983
Cleveland, 1986
Green Bay, 1989
Miami, 1996
Buffalo, 2000
Most Touchdowns, Opponents' Fumbles Recovered, Season
4 Detroit, 1937
Chi. Bears, 1942
Boston, 1948
Los Angeles, 1952
San Francisco, 1965
Denver, 1984
St. Louis, 1987
Minnesota, 1989
Atlanta, 1991

Philadelphia, 1995
Atlanta, 1998
New Orleans, 1998
Kansas City, 1999
3 By many teams

**Most Touchdowns, Fumbles Recovered, Game,
Own and Opponents'**
2 By many teams

**Most Touchdowns, Fumbles Recovered, Game, Both Teams,
Own and Opponents'**
3 Detroit (2) vs. Minnesota (1), Dec. 9, 1962
    (2 own, 1 opp)
    Green Bay (2) vs. Dallas (1), Nov. 29, 1964 (3 opp)
    Oakland (2) vs. Buffalo (1), Dec. 24, 1967 (3 opp)
    Oakland (2) vs. Philadelphia (1), Sept. 24, 1995
    (3 opp)
    Tennessee (2) vs. Pittsburgh (1), Jan. 2, 2000
    (3 opp)

Most Touchdowns, Own Fumbles Recovered, Game
2 Miami vs. New England, Sept.1, 1996

Most Touchdowns, Opponents' Fumbles Recovered, Game
2 Many times. Last time:
    Chicago vs. Arizona, Oct. 16, 2006

**Most Touchdowns, Opponents' Fumbles Recovered, Game,
Both Teams**
3 Green Bay (2) vs. Dallas (1), Nov. 29, 1964
    Oakland (2) vs. Buffalo (1), Dec. 24, 1967
    Oakland (2) vs. Philadelphia (1), Sept. 24, 1995
    Tennessee (2) vs. Pittsburgh (1), Jan. 2, 2000

TURNOVERS

(Number of times losing the ball on interceptions and fumbles.)

Most Turnovers, Season
65 Denver, 1961
63 San Francisco, 1978
58 Chi. Bears, 1947
    Pittsburgh, 1950
    N.Y. Giants, 1983

Fewest Turnovers, Season
12 Kansas City, 1982
14 N.Y. Giants, 1943
    Cleveland, 1959
    N.Y. Giants, 1990
15 Dallas, 1998
    Jacksonville, 2002
    Kansas City, 2002
    San Diego, 2006

Most Turnovers, Game
12 Detroit vs. Chi. Bears, Nov. 22, 1942
    Chi. Cardinals vs. Philadelphia, Sept. 24, 1950
    Pittsburgh vs. Philadelphia, Dec. 12, 1965
11 San Diego vs. Green Bay, Sept. 24, 1978
10 Washington vs. N.Y. Giants, Dec. 4, 1938
    Pittsburgh vs. Green Bay, Nov. 23, 1941
    Detroit vs. Green Bay, Oct. 24, 1943
    Chi. Cardinals vs. Green Bay, Nov. 10, 1946
    Chi. Cardinals vs. N.Y. Giants, Nov. 2, 1952
    Minnesota vs. Detroit, Dec. 9, 1962
    Houston vs. Oakland, Sept. 7, 1963
    Washington vs. N.Y. Giants, Dec. 8, 1963
    Chicago vs. Detroit, Sept. 22, 1968
    St. Louis vs. Washington, Oct. 25, 1976
    N.Y. Jets vs. New England, Nov. 21, 1976
    San Francisco vs. Dallas, Oct. 12, 1980
    Cleveland vs. Seattle, Dec. 20, 1981
    Detroit vs. Denver, Oct. 7, 1984

Most Turnovers, Both Teams, Game
17 Detroit (12) vs. Chi. Bears (5), Nov. 22, 1942
    Boston (9) vs. Philadelphia (8), Dec. 8, 1946
16 Chi. Cardinals (12) vs. Philadelphia (4),

Sept. 24, 1950
Chi. Cardinals (8) vs. Chi. Bears (8), Dec. 7, 1958
Minnesota (10) vs. Detroit (6), Dec. 9, 1962
Houston (9) vs. Kansas City (7), Oct. 12, 1969
15 Philadelphia (8) vs. Chi. Cardinals (7), Oct. 3, 1954
    Denver (9) vs. Houston (6), Dec. 2, 1962
    Washington (10) vs. N.Y. Giants (5), Dec. 8, 1963
    St. Louis (9) vs. Kansas City (6), Oct. 2, 1983

PENALTIES

Most Seasons Leading League, Fewest Penalties
13 Miami, 1968, 1976-1984, 1986, 1990-91
9 Pittsburgh, 1946-47, 1950-52, 1954, 1963, 1965,
    1968
7 Boston/New England, 1962, 1964-65, 1973, 1987,
    1989, 1993

Most Consecutive Seasons Leading League, Fewest Penalties
9 Miami, 1976-1984
3 Pittsburgh, 1950-52
2 By many teams

Most Seasons Leading League, Most Penalties
16 Chi. Bears, 1941-44, 1946-49, 1951, 1959-1961,
    1963, 1965, 1968, 1976
15 Oakland/L.A. Raiders, 1963, 1966, 1968-69, 1975,
    1982, 1984, 1991, 1993-96, 2003-05
7 L.A./St. Louis Rams, 1950, 1952, 1962, 1969,
    1978, 1980, 1997

Most Consecutive Seasons Leading League, Most Penalties
4 Chi. Bears, 1941-44, 1946-49
    Oakland/L.A. Raiders, 1993-96
3 Chi. Cardinals, 1954-56
    Chi. Bears, 1959-1961
    Oakland, 2003-05

Fewest Penalties, Season
19 Detroit, 1937
21 Boston, 1935
24 Philadelphia, 1936

Most Penalties, Season
158 Kansas City, 1998
156 L.A. Raiders, 1994
     Oakland, 1996
149 Houston, 1989

Fewest Penalties, Game
0 By many teams. Last time:
    Denver vs. Kansas City, Sept. 17, 2006 (OT)

Most Penalties, Game
22 Brooklyn vs. Green Bay, Sept. 17, 1944
    Chi. Bears vs. Philadelphia, Nov. 26, 1944
    San Francisco vs. Buffalo, Oct. 4, 1998
21 Cleveland vs. Chi. Bears, Nov. 25, 1951
    Baltimore vs. Detroit, Oct. 9, 2005
20 Tampa Bay vs. Seattle, Oct. 17, 1976
    Oakland vs. Denver, Dec. 15, 1996

Fewest Penalties, Both Teams, Game
0 Brooklyn vs. Pittsburgh, Oct. 28, 1934
    Brooklyn vs. Boston, Sept. 28, 1936
    Cleveland vs. Chi. Bears, Oct. 9, 1938
    Pittsburgh vs. Philadelphia, Nov. 10, 1940

Most Penalties, Both Teams, Game
37 Cleveland (21) vs. Chi. Bears (16), Nov. 25, 1951
35 Tampa Bay (20) vs. Seattle (15), Oct. 17, 1976
34 San Francisco (22) vs. Buffalo (12), Oct. 4, 1998

YARDS PENALIZED

Most Seasons Leading League, Fewest Yards Penalized
13 Miami, 1967-68, 1973, 1977-1984, 1990-91
10 Boston/Washington, 1935, 1953-54, 1956-58,
    1970, 1985, 1995, 1997
7 Pittsburgh, 1946-47, 1950, 1952, 1962, 1965, 1968
    Boston/New England, 1962, 1964-66, 1987, 1989,

1993

Most Consecutive Seasons Leading League, Fewest Yards Penalized

8   Miami, 1977-1984
3   Washington, 1956-58
    Boston, 1964-66
2   By many teams

Most Seasons Leading League, Most Yards Penalized

15   Chi. Bears, 1935, 1937, 1939-1944, 1946-47,
      1949, 1951, 1961-62, 1968
12   Oakland/L.A. Raiders, 1963-64, 1968-69, 1975,
      1982, 1984, 1991, 1993-94, 1996, 2003
6   Buffalo, 1962, 1967, 1970, 1972, 1981, 1983
    Houston, 1961, 1985-86, 1988-1990

Most Consecutive Seasons Leading League, Most Yards Penalized

6   Chi. Bears, 1939-1944
3   Houston, 1988-1990
2   By many teams

Fewest Yards Penalized, Season

139   Detroit, 1937
146   Philadelphia, 1937
159   Philadelphia, 1936

Most Yards Penalized, Season

1,304   Kansas City, 1998
1,274   Oakland, 1969
1,266   Oakland, 1996

Fewest Yards Penalized, Game

0   By many teams. Last time:
      Denver vs. Kansas City, Sept. 17, 2006 (OT)

Most Yards Penalized, Game

212   Tennessee vs. Baltimore, Oct. 10, 1999
209   Cleveland vs. Chi. Bears, Nov. 25, 1951
191   Philadelphia vs. Seattle, Dec. 13, 1992 (OT)

Fewest Yards Penalized, Both Teams, Game

0   Brooklyn vs. Pittsburgh, Oct. 28, 1934
    Brooklyn vs. Boston, Sept. 28, 1936
    Cleveland vs. Chi. Bears, Oct. 9, 1938
    Pittsburgh vs. Philadelphia, Nov. 10, 1940

Most Yards Penalized, Both Teams, Game

374   Cleveland (209) vs. Chi. Bears (165), Nov. 25, 1951
310   Tampa Bay (190) vs. Seattle (120), Oct. 17, 1976
309   Green Bay (184) vs. Boston (125), Oct. 21, 1945

DEFENSE

SCORING

Most Seasons Leading League, Fewest Points Allowed

11   N.Y. Giants, 1927, 1935, 1938-39, 1941, 1944,
      1958-59, 1961, 1990, 1993
    Chi. Bears, 1932, 1936-37, 1942, 1948, 1963,
      1985-86, 1988, 2001, 2005
7   Cleveland, 1951, 1953-57, 1994
    Green Bay, 1929, 1935, 1947, 1962, 1965-66, 1996
6   Dallas/Kansas City, 1960, 1962, 1968-69, 1995,
      1997

Most Consecutive Seasons Leading League, Fewest Points Allowed

5   Cleveland, 1953-57
3   Buffalo, 1964-66
    Minnesota, 1969-1971
2   By many teams

Fewest Points Allowed, Season (Since 1932)

44   Chi. Bears, 1932
54   Brooklyn, 1933
59   Detroit, 1934

Most Points Allowed, Season

533   Baltimore, 1981
501   N.Y. Giants, 1966
487   New Orleans, 1980

Fewest Touchdowns Allowed, Season (Since 1932)

6   Chi. Bears, 1932
    Brooklyn, 1933
7   Detroit, 1934
8   Green Bay, 1932

Most Touchdowns Allowed, Season

68   Baltimore, 1981
66   N.Y. Giants, 1966
63   Baltimore, 1950

FIRST DOWNS

Fewest First Downs Allowed Season

77   Detroit, 1935
79   Boston, 1935
82   Washington, 1937

Most First Downs Allowed, Season

406   Baltimore, 1981
371   Seattle, 1981
368   Cleveland, 1999

Fewest First Downs Allowed, Rushing, Season

35   Chi. Bears, 1942
40   Green Bay, 1939
41   Brooklyn, 1944

Most First Downs Allowed, Rushing, Season

179   Detroit, 1985
178   New Orleans, 1980
175   Seattle, 1981

Fewest First Downs Allowed, Passing, Season

33   Chi. Bears, 1943
34   Pittsburgh, 1941
    Washington, 1943
35   Detroit, 1940
    Philadelphia, 1940, 1944

Most First Downs Allowed, Passing, Season

230   Atlanta, 1995
227   Kansas City, 2002
221   Detroit, 2002

Fewest First Downs Allowed, Penalty, Season

1   Boston, 1944
3   Philadelphia, 1940
    Pittsburgh, 1945
    Washington, 1957
4   Cleveland, 1940
    Green Bay, 1943
    N.Y. Giants, 1943

Most First Downs Allowed, Penalty, Season

56   Kansas City, 1998
48   Houston, 1985
46   Houston, 1986

NET YARDS ALLOWED RUSHING AND PASSING

Most Seasons Leading League, Fewest Yards Allowed

8   Chi. Bears, 1942-43, 1948, 1958, 1963, 1984-86
6   N.Y. Giants, 1938, 1940-41, 1951, 1956, 1959
    Philadelphia, 1944-45, 1949, 1953, 1981, 1991
    Minnesota, 1969-1970, 1975, 1988-89, 1993
    Pittsburgh, 1957, 1974, 1976, 1990, 2001, 2004
5   Boston/Washington, 1935-37, 1939, 1946

Most Consecutive Seasons Leading League, Fewest Yards Allowed

3   Boston/Washington, 1935-37
    Chicago, 1984-86
2   By many teams

Fewest Yards Allowed, Season

1,539   Chi. Cardinals, 1934
1,703   Chi. Bears, 1942
1,789   Brooklyn, 1933

Most Yards Allowed, Season

6,793   Baltimore, 1981
6,403   Green Bay, 1983

6,391 Seattle, 2000

RUSHING
Most Seasons Leading League, Fewest Yards Allowed
- 10 Chi. Bears, 1937, 1939, 1942, 1946, 1949, 1963, 1984-85, 1987-88
- 7 Detroit, 1938, 1950, 1952, 1962, 1970, 1980-81
  Philadelphia, 1944-45, 1947-48, 1953, 1990-91
  Dallas, 1966-69, 1972, 1978, 1992
  Pittsburgh, 1961, 1976, 1982, 1997, 2001-02, 2004
- 5 N.Y. Giants, 1940, 1951, 1956, 1959, 1986
  L.A./St. Louis Rams, 1964-65, 1973-74, 1999

Most Consecutive Seasons Leading League, Fewest Yards Allowed
- 4 Dallas, 1966-69
- 2 By many teams

Fewest Yards Allowed, Rushing, Season
- 519 Chi. Bears, 1942
- 558 Philadelphia, 1944
- 762 Pittsburgh, 1982

Most Yards Allowed, Rushing, Season
- 3,228 Buffalo, 1978
- 3,106 New Orleans, 1980
- 3,010 Baltimore, 1978

Fewest Touchdowns Allowed, Rushing, Season
- 2 Detroit, 1934
  N.Y. Giants, 1944
  Dallas, 1968
  Minnesota, 1971
- 3 By many teams

Most Touchdowns Allowed, Rushing, Season
- 36 Oakland, 1961
- 31 N.Y. Giants, 1980
  Tampa Bay, 1986
- 30 Baltimore, 1981

PASSING
Most Seasons Leading League, Fewest Yards Allowed
- 10 Green Bay, 1947-48, 1962, 1964-68, 1996, 2005
- 7 Washington, 1939, 1942, 1945, 1952-53, 1980, 1985
  Philadelphia 1934, 1936, 1940, 1949, 1981, 1991, 1998
- 6 Chi. Bears, 1938, 1943-44, 1958, 1960, 1963
  Minnesota, 1969-1970, 1972, 1975-76, 1989
  Pittsburgh, 1941, 1946, 1951, 1955, 1974, 1990

Most Consecutive Seasons Leading League, Fewest Yards Allowed
- 5 Green Bay, 1964-68
- 2 By many teams

Fewest Yards Allowed, Passing, Season
- 545 Philadelphia, 1934
- 558 Portsmouth, 1933
- 585 Chi. Cardinals, 1934

Most Yards Allowed, Passing, Season
- 4,541 Atlanta, 1995
- 4,427 San Francisco, 2005
- 4,389 N.Y. Jets, 1986

Fewest Touchdowns Allowed, Passing, Season
- 1 Portsmouth, 1932
  Philadelphia, 1934
- 2 Brooklyn, 1933
  Chi. Bears, 1934
- 3 Chi. Bears, 1932
  Green Bay, 1932
  Green Bay, 1934
  Chi. Bears, 1936
  New York, 1939
  New York, 1944

Most Touchdowns Allowed, Passing, Season

- 40 Denver, 1963
- 38 St. Louis, 1969
- 37 Washington, 1961
  Baltimore, 1981

SACKS
Most Seasons Leading League
- 5 Oakland/L.A. Raiders, 1966-68, 1982, 1986
- 4 New England/Boston, 1961, 1963, 1977, 1979
  Dallas, 1966, 1968-69, 1978
  Dallas/Kansas City, 1960, 1965, 1969, 1990
  L.A./St. Louis Rams, 1968, 1970, 1988, 1999
- 3 San Francisco, 1967, 1972, 1976
  N.Y. Giants, 1963, 1985, 1998
  New Orleans, 1992, 1997, 2000
  Pittsburgh, 1974, 1994, 2001
  San Diego, 1962, 1980, 2006

Most Consecutive Seasons Leading League
- 3 Oakland, 1966-68
- 2 Dallas, 1968-69

Most Sacks, Season
- 72 Chicago, 1984
- 71 Minnesota, 1989
- 70 Chicago, 1987

Fewest Sacks, Season
- 11 Baltimore, 1982
- 12 Buffalo, 1982
- 13 Baltimore, 1981

Most Sacks, Game
- 12 Dallas vs. Pittsburgh, Nov. 20, 1966
  St. Louis vs. Baltimore, Oct. 26, 1980
  Chicago vs. Detroit, Dec. 16, 1984
  Dallas vs. Houston, Sept. 29, 1985
- 11 N.Y. Giants vs. St. Louis, Nov. 1, 1964
  Baltimore vs. Los Angeles, Nov. 22, 1964
  Buffalo vs. Denver, Dec. 13, 1964
  Detroit vs. Green Bay, Nov. 7, 1965
  Oakland vs. Buffalo, Oct. 15, 1967
  Oakland vs. Denver, Nov. 5, 1967
  St. Louis vs. Atlanta, Nov. 24, 1968
  Dallas vs. Detroit, Oct. 6, 1975
  St. Louis vs. Philadelphia, Dec. 18, 1983
  Kansas City vs. Cleveland, Sept. 30, 1984
  Chicago vs. Minnesota, Oct. 28, 1984
  Cleveland vs. Atlanta, Nov. 18, 1984
  Detroit vs. Philadelphia, Nov. 16, 1986
  San Diego vs. Dallas, Nov. 16, 1986
  L.A. Raiders vs. Philadelphia, Nov. 30, 1986 (OT)
  Seattle vs. L.A. Raiders, Dec. 8, 1986
  Chicago vs. Philadelphia, Oct. 4, 1987
  Dallas vs. N.Y. Jets, Oct. 4, 1987
  Philadelphia vs. Dallas, Sept. 15, 1991
  Indianapolis vs. Cleveland, Sept. 6, 1992
- 10 By many teams

Most Opponents Yards Lost Attempting to Pass, Season
- 666 Oakland, 1967
- 583 Chicago, 1984
- 573 San Francisco, 1976

Fewest Opponents Yards Lost Attempting to Pass, Season
- 72 Jacksonville, 1995
- 75 Green Bay, 1956
- 77 N.Y. Bulldogs, 1949

INTERCEPTIONS BY
Most Seasons Leading League
- 10 N.Y. Giants, 1933, 1937-39, 1944, 1948, 1951, 1954, 1961, 1997
- 8 Green Bay, 1940, 1942-43, 1947, 1955, 1957, 1962, 1965
  Chi. Bears, 1935-36, 1941-42, 1946, 1963, 1985,

1990
  6 Kansas City, 1966-1970, 1974
Most Consecutive Seasons Leading League
  5 Kansas City, 1966-1970
  3 N.Y. Giants, 1937-39
  2 By many teams
Most Passes Intercepted By, Season
 49 San Diego, 1961
 42 Green Bay, 1943
 41 N.Y. Giants, 1951
Fewest Passes Intercepted By, Season
  3 Houston, 1982
  5 Baltimore, 1982
     Oakland, 2005
  6 Houston, 1972
     St. Louis, 1982
     Atlanta, 1996
     St. Louis, 2004
     Washington, 2006
Most Passes Intercepted By, Game
  9 Green Bay vs. Detroit, Oct. 24, 1943
     Philadelphia vs. Pittsburgh, Dec. 12, 1965
  8 N.Y. Giants vs. Green Bay, Nov. 21, 1948
     Philadelphia vs. Chi. Cardinals, Sept. 24, 1950
     N.Y. Giants vs. N.Y. Yanks, Dec. 16, 1951
     Houston vs. Denver, Dec. 2, 1962
     Detroit vs. Chicago, Sept. 22, 1968
     N.Y. Jets vs. Baltimore, Sept. 23, 1973
  7 By many teams. Last time:
       Cleveland vs. Detroit, Sept. 23, 2001
Most Consecutive Games, One or More Interceptions By
 46 L.A. Chargers/San Diego, 1960-63
 37 Detroit, 1960-63
 36 Boston, 1944-47
Most Yards Returning Interceptions, Season
 929 San Diego, 1961
 712 Los Angeles, 1952
 700 Baltimore, 2004
Fewest Yards Returning Interceptions, Season
  5 Los Angeles, 1959
 25 Washington, 2006
 37 Dallas, 1989
Most Yards Returning Interceptions, Game
 325 Seattle vs. Kansas City, Nov. 4, 1984
 314 Los Angeles vs. San Francisco, Oct. 18, 1964
 245 Houston vs. N.Y. Jets, Oct. 15, 1967
Most Yards Returning Interceptions, Both Teams, Game
 356 Seattle (325) vs. Kansas City (31), Nov. 4, 1984
 338 Los Angeles (314) vs. San Francisco (24),
       Oct. 18, 1964
 308 Dallas (182) vs. Los Angeles (126), Nov. 2, 1952
Most Touchdowns, Returning Interceptions, Season
  9 San Diego, 1961
  8 Seattle, 1998
  7 Seattle, 1984
     St. Louis, 1999
Most Touchdowns Returning Interceptions, Game
  4 Seattle vs. Kansas City, Nov. 4, 1984
  3 Baltimore vs. Green Bay, Nov. 5, 1950
     Cleveland vs. Chicago, Dec. 11, 1960
     Philadelphia vs. Pittsburgh, Dec. 12, 1965
     Baltimore vs. Pittsburgh, Sept. 29, 1968
     Buffalo vs. N.Y. Jets, Sept. 29, 1968
     Houston vs. San Diego, Dec. 19, 1971
     Cincinnati vs. Houston, Dec. 17, 1972
     Tampa Bay vs. New Orleans, Dec. 11, 1977
  2 By many teams
Most Touchdown Returning Interceptions, Both Teams, Game
  4 Philadelphia (3) vs. Pittsburgh (1), Dec. 12, 1965
     Seattle (4) vs. Kansas City (0), Nov. 4, 1984

  3 Los Angeles (2) vs. Detroit (1), Nov. 1, 1953
     Cleveland (2) vs. N.Y. Giants (1), Dec. 18, 1960
     Pittsburgh (2) vs. Cincinnati (1), Oct. 10, 1983
     Kansas City (2) vs. San Diego (1), Oct. 19, 1986
     (Also see previous record)

PUNT RETURNS
Fewest Opponents Punt Returns, Season
  7 Washington, 1962
     San Diego, 1982
 10 Buffalo, 1982
 11 Boston, 1962
Most Opponents Punt Returns, Season
 71 Tampa Bay, 1976, 1977
 69 N.Y. Giants, 1953
     Cleveland, 2000
 68 Cleveland, 1974
     Cleveland, 1999
Fewest Yards Allowed, Punt Returns, Season
 22 Green Bay, 1967
 30 Buffalo, 1982
 34 Washington, 1962
Most Yards Allowed, Punt Returns, Season
 932 Green Bay, 1949
 913 Boston, 1947
 906 New Orleans, 1974
Lowest Average Allowed, Punt Returns, Season
 1.20 Chi. Cardinals, 1954 (46-55)
 1.22 Cleveland, 1959 (32-39)
 1.55 Chi. Cardinals, 1953 (44-68)
Highest Average Allowed, Punt Returns, Season
 18.6 Green Bay, 1949 (50-932)
 18.0 Cleveland, 1977 (31-558)
 17.9 Boston, 1960 (20-357)
Most Touchdowns Allowed, Punt Returns, Season
  4 New York, 1959
     Atlanta, 1992
  3 Green Bay, 1949
     Chi. Cardinals, 1951
     L.A. Rams, 1951, 1994
     Washington, 1952
     Dallas, 1952
     Pittsburgh, 1959, 1993
     N.Y. Jets, 1968
     Cleveland, 1977
     Atlanta, 1986
     Tampa Bay, 1986
     Arizona, 2002
     Cincinnati, 2002
     Tennessee, 2002
  2 By many teams

KICKOFF RETURNS
Fewest Opponents Kickoff Returns, Season
 10 Brooklyn, 1943
 13 Denver, 1992
 15 Detroit, 1942
     Brooklyn, 1944
Most Opponents Kickoff Returns, Season
 93 Indianapolis, 2003
 92 Indianapolis, 2004
 91 Washington, 1983
Fewest Yards Allowed, Kickoff Returns, Season
 225 Brooklyn, 1943
 254 Denver, 1992
 293 Brooklyn, 1944
Most Yards Allowed, Kickoff Returns, Season
 2,194 St. Louis, 2001
 2,115 St. Louis, 1999
 2,053 Kansas City, 2005

Lowest Average Allowed, Kickoff Returns, Season
14.3 Cleveland, 1980 (71-1,018)
14.9 Indianapolis, 1993 (37-551)
15.0 Seattle, 1982 (24-361)

Highest Average Allowed, Kickoff Returns, Season
29.5 N.Y. Jets, 1972 (47-1,386)
29.4 Los Angeles, 1950 (48-1,411)
29.1 New England, 1971 (49-1,427)

Most Touchdowns Allowed, Kickoff Returns, Season
4 Minnesota, 1998
3 Minnesota, 1963, 1970
   Dallas, 1966
   Detroit, 1980
   Pittsburgh, 1986
   Buffalo, 1997
   Atlanta, 2000
   Arizona, 2005
2 By many teams

FUMBLES

Fewest Opponents Fumbles, Season
11 Cleveland, 1956
   Baltimore, 1982
   Tennessee, 1998
12 Green Bay, 1995
   Cincinnati, 1998
   Jacksonville, 2006
13 Los Angeles, 1956
   Chicago, 1960
   Cleveland, 1963
   Cleveland, 1965
   Detroit, 1967
   San Diego, 1969
   New England, 2005
   Cleveland, 2006

Most Opponents Fumbles, Season
50 Minnesota, 1963
   San Francisco, 1978
48 N.Y. Giants, 1980
   N.Y. Jets, 1986
47 N.Y. Giants, 1977
   Seattle, 1984

TURNOVERS
(Number of times losing the ball on interceptions and fumbles.)

Fewest Opponents Turnovers, Season
11 Baltimore, 1982
12 Washington, 2006
13 San Francisco, 1982

Most Opponents Turnovers, Season
66 San Diego, 1961
63 Seattle, 1984
61 Washington, 1983

Most Opponents Turnovers, Game
12 Chi. Bears vs. Detroit, Nov. 22, 1942
   Philadelphia vs. Chi. Cardinals, Sept. 24, 1950
   Philadelphia vs. Pittsburgh, Dec. 12, 1965
11 Green Bay vs. San Diego, Sept. 24, 1978
10 By 14 teams

ANNUAL SCORING LEADERS

Year	Player, Team	TD	FG	PAT	TP
2006	LaDainian Tomlinson, AFC	31	0	0	186
	Robbie Gould, Chicago, NFC	0	32	47	143
2005	Shaun Alexander, Seattle, NFC	28	0	0	168
	Shayne Graham, Cincinnati, AFC	0	28	47	131
2004	Adam Vinatieri, New England, AFC	0	31	48	141
	David Akers, Philadelphia, NFC	0	27	41	122
2003	Jeff Wilkins, St. Louis, NFC	0	39	46	163
	Priest Holmes, Kansas City, AFC	27	0	0	162
2002	Priest Holmes, Kansas City, AFC	24	0	0	144
	Jay Feely, Atlanta, NFC	0	32	42	138
2001	Marshall Faulk, St. Louis, NFC	21	0	0	#128
	Mike Vanderjagt, Indianapolis, AFC	0	28	41	125
2000	Marshall Faulk, St. Louis, NFC	26	0	0	##160
	Matt Stover, Baltimore, AFC	0	35	30	135
1999	Mike Vanderjagt, Indianapolis, AFC	0	34	43	145
	Jeff Wilkins, St. Louis, NFC	0	20	64	124
1998	Gary Anderson, Minnesota, NFC	0	35	59	164
	Steve Christie, Buffalo, AFC	0	33	41	140
1997	Mike Hollis, Jacksonville, AFC	0	31	41	134
	Richie Cunningham, Dallas, NFC	0	34	24	126
1996	John Kasay, Carolina, NFC	0	37	34	145
	Cary Blanchard, Indianapolis, AFC	0	36	27	135
1995	Emmitt Smith, Dallas, NFC	25	0	0	150
	Norm Johnson, Pittsburgh, AFC	0	34	39	141
1994	John Carney, San Diego, AFC	0	34	33	135
	Fuad Reveiz, Minnesota, NFC	0	34	30	132
1993	Jeff Jaeger, L.A. Raiders, AFC	0	35	27	132
	Jason Hanson, Detroit, NFC	0	34	28	130
1992	Pete Stoyanovich, Miami, AFC	0	30	34	124
	Morten Andersen, New Orleans, NFC	0	29	33	120
	Chip Lohmiller, Washington, NFC	0	30	30	120
1991	Chip Lohmiller, Washington, NFC	0	31	56	149
	Pete Stoyanovich, Miami, AFC	0	31	28	121
1990	Nick Lowery, Kansas City, AFC	0	34	37	139
	Chip Lohmiller, Washington, NFC	0	30	41	131
1989	Mike Cofer, San Francisco, NFC	0	29	49	136
	*David Treadwell, Denver, AFC	0	27	39	120
1988	Scott Norwood, Buffalo, AFC	0	32	33	129
	Mike Cofer, San Francisco, NFC	0	27	40	121
1987	Jerry Rice, San Francisco, NFC	23	0	0	138
	Jim Breech, Cincinnati, AFC	0	24	25	97
1986	Tony Franklin, New England, AFC	0	32	44	140
	Kevin Butler, Chicago, NFC	0	28	36	120
1985	*Kevin Butler, Chicago, NFC	0	31	51	144
	Gary Anderson, Pittsburgh, AFC	0	33	40	139
1984	Ray Wersching, San Francisco, NFC	0	25	56	131
	Gary Anderson, Pittsburgh, AFC	0	24	45	117
1983	Mark Moseley, Washington, NFC	0	33	62	161
	Gary Anderson, Pittsburgh, AFC	0	27	38	119
1982	*Marcus Allen, L.A. Raiders, AFC	14	0	0	84
	Wendell Tyler, L.A. Rams, NFC	13	0	0	78
1981	Ed Murray, Detroit, NFC	0	25	46	121
	Rafael Septien, Dallas, NFC	0	27	40	121
	Jim Breech, Cincinnati, AFC	0	22	49	115
	Nick Lowery, Kansas City, AFC	0	26	37	115
1980	John Smith, New England, AFC	0	26	51	129
	*Ed Murray, Detroit, NFC	0	27	35	116
1979	John Smith, New England, AFC	0	23	46	115
	Mark Moseley, Washington, NFC	0	25	39	114
1978	*Frank Corral, Los Angeles, NFC	0	29	31	118
	Pat Leahy, N.Y. Jets, AFC	0	22	41	107
1977	Errol Mann, Oakland, AFC	0	20	39	99
	Walter Payton, Chicago, NFC	16	0	0	96
1976	Toni Linhart, Baltimore, AFC	0	20	49	109
	Mark Moseley, Washington, NFC	0	22	31	97
1975	O.J. Simpson, Buffalo, AFC	23	0	0	138
	Chuck Foreman, Minnesota, NFC	22	0	0	132

Year	Player, Team	TD	FG	PAT	TP
1974	Chester Marcol, Green Bay, NFC	0	25	19	94
	Roy Gerela, Pittsburgh, AFC	0	20	33	93
1973	David Ray, Los Angeles, NFC	0	30	40	130
	Roy Gerela, Pittsburgh, AFC	0	29	36	123
1972	*Chester Marcol, Green Bay, NFC	0	33	29	128
	Bobby Howfield, N.Y. Jets, AFC	0	27	40	121
1971	Garo Yepremian, Miami, AFC	0	28	33	117
	Curt Knight, Washington, NFC	0	29	27	114
1970	Fred Cox, Minnesota, NFC	0	30	35	125
	Jan Stenerud, Kansas City, AFC	0	30	26	116
1969	Jim Turner, N.Y. Jets, AFL	0	32	33	129
	Fred Cox, Minnesota, NFL	0	26	43	121
1968	Jim Turner, N.Y. Jets, AFL	0	34	43	145
	Leroy Kelly, Cleveland, NFL	20	0	0	120
1967	Jim Bakken, St. Louis, NFL	0	27	36	117
	George Blanda, Oakland, AFL	0	20	56	116
1966	Gino Cappelletti, Boston, AFL	6	16	35	119
	Bruce Gossett, Los Angeles, NFL	0	28	29	113
1965	*Gale Sayers, Chicago, NFL	22	0	0	132
	Gino Cappelletti, Boston, AFL	9	17	27	132
1964	Gino Cappelletti, Boston, AFL	7	25	36	#155
	Lenny Moore, Baltimore, NFL	20	0	0	120
1963	Gino Cappelletti, Boston, AFL	2	22	35	113
	Don Chandler, N.Y. Giants, NFL	0	18	52	106
1962	Gene Mingo, Denver, AFL	4	27	32	137
	Jim Taylor, Green Bay, NFL	19	0	0	114
1961	Gino Cappelletti, Boston, AFL	8	17	48	147
	Paul Hornung, Green Bay, NFL	10	15	41	146
1960	Paul Hornung, Green Bay, NFL	15	15	41	176
	*Gene Mingo, Denver, AFL	6	18	33	123
1959	Paul Hornung, Green Bay	7	7	31	94
1958	Jim Brown, Cleveland	18	0	0	108
1957	Sam Baker, Washington	1	14	29	77
	Lou Groza, Cleveland	0	15	32	77
1956	Bobby Layne, Detroit	5	12	33	99
1955	Doak Walker, Detroit	7	9	27	96
1954	Bobby Walston, Philadelphia	11	4	36	114
1953	Gordy Soltau, San Francisco	6	10	48	114
1952	Gordy Soltau, San Francisco	7	6	34	94
1951	Elroy (Crazylegs) Hirsch, Los Angeles	17	0	0	102
1950	*Doak Walker, Detroit	11	8	38	128
1949	Pat Harder, Chi. Cardinals	8	3	45	102
	Gene Roberts, N.Y. Giants	17	0	0	102
1948	Pat Harder, Chi. Cardinals	6	7	53	110
1947	Pat Harder, Chi. Cardinals	7	7	39	102
1946	Ted Fritsch, Green Bay	10	9	13	100
1945	Steve Van Buren, Philadelphia	18	0	2	110
1944	Don Hutson, Green Bay	9	0	31	85
1943	Don Hutson, Green Bay	12	3	36	117
1942	Don Hutson, Green Bay	17	1	33	138
1941	Don Hutson, Green Bay	12	1	20	95
1940	Don Hutson, Green Bay	7	0	15	57
1939	Andy Farkas, Washington	11	0	2	68
1938	Clarke Hinkle, Green Bay	7	3	7	58
1937	Jack Manders, Chi. Bears	5	8	15	69
1936	Earl (Dutch) Clark, Detroit	7	4	19	73
1935	Earl (Dutch) Clark, Detroit	6	1	16	55
1934	Jack Manders, Chi. Bears	3	10	31	79
1933	Ken Strong, N.Y. Giants	6	5	13	64
	Glenn Presnell, Portsmouth	6	6	10	64
1932	Earl (Dutch) Clark, Portsmouth	6	3	10	55

*First season of professional football.
#Cappelletti's total and Faulk's total in 2001 include a two-point conversion.
##Faulk's total in 2000 includes 2 two-point conversions.

ANNUAL TOUCHDOWN LEADERS

Year	Player, Team	TD	Rush	Pass	Ret.
2006	LaDainian Tomlinson, San Diego, AFC	31	28	3	0
	Marion Barber, Dallas, NFC	16	14	2	0
	Steven Jackson, St. Louis, NFC	16	13	3	0
2005	Shaun Alexander, Seattle, NFC	28	27	1	0
	Larry Johnson, Kansas City, AFC	21	20	1	0
2004	Shaun Alexander, Seattle, NFC	20	16	4	0
	LaDainian Tomlinson, San Diego, AFC	18	17	1	0
2003	Priest Holmes, Kansas City, AFC	27	27	0	0
	Ahman Green, Green Bay, NFC	20	15	5	0
2002	Priest Holmes, Kansas City, AFC	24	21	3	0
	Shaun Alexander, Seattle, NFC	18	16	2	0
2001	Marshall Faulk, St. Louis, NFC	21	12	9	0
	Shaun Alexander, Seattle, AFC	16	14	2	0
2000	Marshall Faulk, St. Louis, NFC	26	18	8	0
	Edgerrin James, Indianapolis, AFC	18	13	5	0
1999	Stephen Davis, Washington, NFC	17	17	0	0
	*Edgerrin James, Indianapolis, AFC	17	13	4	0
1998	Terrell Davis, Denver, AFC	23	21	2	0
	*Randy Moss, Minnesota, NFC	17	0	17	0
1997	Karim Abdul-Jabbar, Miami, AFC	16	15	1	0
	Barry Sanders, Detroit, NFC	14	11	3	0
1996	Terry Allen, Washington, NFC	21	21	0	0
	Curtis Martin, New England, AFC	17	14	3	0
1995	Emmitt Smith, Dallas, NFC	25	25	0	0
	Carl Pickens, Cincinnati, AFC	17	0	17	0
1994	Emmitt Smith, Dallas, NFC	22	21	1	0
	*Marshall Faulk, Indianapolis, AFC	12	11	1	0
	Natrone Means, San Diego, AFC	12	12	0	0
1993	Jerry Rice, San Francisco, NFC	16	1	15	0
	Marcus Allen, Kansas City, AFC	15	12	3	0
1992	Emmitt Smith, Dallas, NFC	19	18	1	0
	Thurman Thomas, Buffalo, AFC	12	9	3	0
1991	Barry Sanders, Detroit, NFC	17	16	1	0
	Mark Clayton, Miami, AFC	12	0	12	0
	Thurman Thomas, Buffalo, AFC	12	7	5	0
1990	Barry Sanders, Detroit, NFC	16	13	3	0
	Derrick Fenner, Seattle, AFC	15	14	1	0
1989	Dalton Hilliard, New Orleans, NFC	18	13	5	0
	Christian Okoye, Kansas City, AFC	12	12	0	0
	Thurman Thomas, Buffalo, AFC	12	6	6	0
1988	Greg Bell, L.A. Rams, NFC	18	16	2	0
	Eric Dickerson, Indianapolis, AFC	15	14	1	0
	*Ickey Woods, Cincinnati, AFC	15	15	0	0
1987	Jerry Rice, San Francisco, NFC	23	1	22	0
	Johnny Hector, N.Y. Jets, AFC	11	11	0	0
1986	George Rogers, Washington, NFC	18	18	0	0
	Sammy Winder, Denver, AFC	14	9	5	0
1985	Joe Morris, N.Y. Giants, NFC	21	21	0	0
	Louis Lipps, Pittsburgh, AFC	15	1	12	2
1984	Marcus Allen, L.A. Raiders, AFC	18	13	5	0
	Mark Clayton, Miami, AFC	18	0	18	0
	Eric Dickerson, L.A. Rams, NFC	14	14	0	0
	John Riggins, Washington, NFC	14	14	0	0
1983	John Riggins, Washington, NFC	24	24	0	0
	Pete Johnson, Cincinnati, AFC	14	14	0	0
	*Curt Warner, Seattle, AFC	14	13	1	0
1982	*Marcus Allen, L.A. Raiders, AFC	14	11	3	0
	Wendell Tyler, L.A. Rams, NFC	13	9	4	0
1981	Chuck Muncie, San Diego, AFC	19	19	0	0
	Wendell Tyler, Los Angeles, NFC	17	12	5	0
1980	*Billy Sims, Detroit, NFC	16	13	3	0
	Earl Campbell, Houston, AFC	13	13	0	0
	*Curtis Dickey, Baltimore, AFC	13	11	2	0
	John Jefferson, San Diego, AFC	13	0	13	0
1979	Earl Campbell, Houston, AFC	19	19	0	0
	Walter Payton, Chicago, NFC	16	14	2	0
1978	David Sims, Seattle, AFC	15	14	1	0
	Terdell Middleton, Green Bay, NFC	12	11	1	0

Year	Player, Team	TD	Rush	Pass	Ret.
1977	Walter Payton, Chicago, NFC	16	14	2	0
	Nat Moore, Miami, AFC	13	1	12	0
1976	Chuck Foreman, Minnesota, NFC	14	13	1	0
	Franco Harris, Pittsburgh, AFC	14	14	0	0
1975	O.J. Simpson, Buffalo, AFC	23	16	7	0
	Chuck Foreman, Minnesota, NFC	22	13	9	0
1974	Chuck Foreman, Minnesota, NFC	15	9	6	0
	Cliff Branch, Oakland, AFC	13	0	13	0
1973	Larry Brown, Washington, NFC	14	8	6	0
	Floyd Little, Denver, AFC	13	12	1	0
1972	Emerson Boozer, N.Y. Jets, AFC	14	11	3	0
	Ron Johnson, N.Y. Giants, NFC	14	9	5	0
1971	Duane Thomas, Dallas, NFC	13	11	2	0
	Leroy Kelly, Cleveland, AFC	12	10	2	0
1970	Dick Gordon, Chicago, NFC	13	0	13	0
	MacArthur Lane, St. Louis, NFC	13	11	2	0
	Gary Garrison, San Diego, AFC	12	0	12	0
1969	Warren Wells, Oakland, AFL	14	0	14	0
	Tom Matte, Baltimore, NFL	13	11	2	0
	Lance Rentzel, Dallas, NFL	13	0	12	1
1968	Leroy Kelly, Cleveland, NFL	20	16	4	0
	Warren Wells, Oakland, AFL	12	1	11	0
1967	Homer Jones, N.Y. Giants, NFL	14	1	13	0
	Emerson Boozer, N.Y. Jets, AFL	13	10	3	0
1966	Leroy Kelly, Cleveland, NFL	16	15	1	0
	Dan Reeves, Dallas, NFL	16	8	8	0
	Lance Alworth, San Diego, AFL	13	0	13	0
1965	*Gale Sayers, Chicago, NFL	22	14	6	2
	Lance Alworth, San Diego, AFL	14	0	14	0
	Don Maynard, N.Y. Jets, AFL	14	0	14	0
1964	Lenny Moore, Baltimore, NFL	20	16	3	1
	Lance Alworth, San Diego, AFL	15	2	13	0
1963	Art Powell, Oakland, AFL	16	0	16	0
	Jim Brown, Cleveland, NFL	15	12	3	0
1962	Abner Haynes, Dallas, AFL	19	13	6	0
	Jim Taylor, Green Bay, NFL	19	19	0	0
1961	Bill Groman, Houston, AFL	18	1	17	0
	Jim Taylor, Green Bay, NFL	16	15	1	0
1960	Paul Hornung, Green Bay, NFL	15	13	2	0
	Sonny Randle, St. Louis, NFL	15	0	15	0
	Art Powell, N.Y. Titans, AFL	14	0	14	0
1959	Raymond Berry, Baltimore	14	0	14	0
	Jim Brown, Cleveland	14	14	0	0
1958	Jim Brown, Cleveland	18	17	1	0
1957	Lenny Moore, Baltimore	11	3	7	1
1956	Rick Casares, Chi. Bears	14	12	2	0
1955	*Alan Ameche, Baltimore	9	9	0	0
	Harlon Hill, Chi. Bears	9	0	9	0
1954	*Harlon Hill, Chi. Bears	12	0	12	0
1953	Joseph Perry, San Francisco	13	10	3	0
1952	Cloyce Box, Detroit	15	0	15	0
1951	Elroy (Crazylegs) Hirsch, Los Angeles	17	0	17	0
1950	Bob Shaw, Chi. Cardinals	12	0	12	0
1949	Gene Roberts, N.Y. Giants	17	9	8	0
1948	Mal Kutner, Chi. Cardinals	15	1	14	0
1947	Steve Van Buren, Philadelphia	14	13	0	1
1946	Ted Fritsch, Green Bay	10	9	1	0
1945	Steve Van Buren, Philadelphia	18	15	2	1
1944	Don Hutson, Green Bay	9	0	9	0
	Bill Paschal, N.Y. Giants	9	9	0	0
1943	Don Hutson, Green Bay	12	0	11	1
	*Bill Paschal, N.Y. Giants	12	10	2	0
1942	Don Hutson, Green Bay	17	0	17	0
1941	Don Hutson, Green Bay	12	2	10	0
	George McAfee, Chi. Bears	12	6	3	3
1940	John Drake, Cleveland	9	9	0	0
	Richard Todd, Washington	9	4	4	1
1939	Andrew Farkas, Washington	11	5	5	1
1938	Don Hutson, Green Bay	9	0	9	0

Year	Player, Team	TD	Rush	Pass	Ret.
1937	Cliff Battles, Washington 7		5	1	1
	Clarke Hinkle, Green Bay 7		5	2	0
	Don Hutson, Green Bay 7		0	7	0
1936	Don Hutson, Green Bay 9		0	8	1
1935	*Don Hutson, Green Bay 7		0	6	1
1934	*Beattie Feathers, Chi. Bears 9		8	1	0
1933	*Charlie (Buckets) Goldenberg, Green Bay 7		4	1	2
	John (Shipwreck) Kelly, Brooklyn 7		2	3	2
	*Elvin (Kink) Richards, N.Y. Giants 7		4	3	0
1932	Earl (Dutch) Clark, Portsmouth 6		3	3	0
	Red Grange, Chi. Bears 6		3	3	0

First season of professional football.

ANNUAL LEADERS—MOST FIELD GOALS MADE

Year	Player, Team	Att.	Made	Pct.
2006	Robbie Gould, Chicago, NFC 36		32	88.9
	Jeff Wilkins, St. Louis, NFC 37		32	86.5
	Matt Stover, Baltimore, AFC 30		28	93.3
2005	Neil Rackers, Arizona, NFC 42		40	95.2
	Matt Stover, Baltimore, AFC 34		30	88.2
2004	Adam Vinatieri, New England, AFC 33		31	93.9
	David Akers, Philadelphia, NFC 32		27	84.4
2003	Jeff Wilkins, St. Louis, NFC 42		39	92.9
	Mike Vanderjagt, Indianapolis, AFC 37		37	100.0
2002	Jay Feely, Atlanta, NFC 40		32	80.0
	Martín Gramatica, Tampa Bay, NFC 39		32	82.1
	Adam Vinatieri, New England, AFC 30		27	90.0
2001	Jason Elam, Denver, AFC 36		31	86.1
	*Jay Feely, Atlanta, NFC 37		29	78.4
2000	Matt Stover, Baltimore, AFC 39		35	89.7
	Ryan Longwell, Green Bay, NFC 38		33	86.8
1999	Olindo Mare, Miami, AFC 46		39	84.8
	*Martín Gramatica, Tampa Bay, NFC 32		27	84.4
1998	Al Del Greco, Tennessee, AFC 39		36	92.3
	Gary Anderson, Minnesota, NFC 35		35	100.0
1997	Richie Cunningham, Dallas, NFC 37		34	91.9
	Cary Blanchard, Indianapolis, AFC 41		32	78.1
1996	John Kasay, Carolina, NFC 45		37	82.2
	Cary Blanchard, Indianapolis, AFC 40		36	90.0
1995	Norm Johnson, Pittsburgh, AFC 41		34	82.9
	Morten Andersen, Atlanta, NFC 37		31	83.8
1994	John Carney, San Diego, AFC 38		34	89.5
	Fuad Reveiz, Minnesota, NFC 39		34	87.2
1993	Jeff Jaeger, L.A. Raiders, AFC 44		35	79.5
	Jason Hanson, Detroit, NFC 43		34	79.1
1992	Pete Stoyanovich, Miami, AFC 37		30	81.1
	Chip Lohmiller, Washington, NFC 40		30	75.0
1991	Pete Stoyanovich, Miami, AFC 37		31	83.8
	Chip Lohmiller, Washington, NFC 43		31	72.1
1990	Nick Lowery, Kansas City, AFC 37		34	91.9
	Chip Lohmiller, Washington, NFC 40		30	75.0
1989	Rich Karlis, Minnesota, NFC 39		31	79.5
	*David Treadwell, Denver, AFC 33		27	81.8
1988	Scott Norwood, Buffalo, AFC 37		32	86.5
	Mike Cofer, San Francisco, NFC 38		27	71.1
1987	Morten Andersen, New Orleans, NFC 36		28	77.8
	Dean Biasucci, Indianpolis, AFC 27		24	88.9
	Jim Breech, Cincinnati, AFC 30		24	80.0
1986	Tony Franklin, New England, AFC 41		32	78.0
	Kevin Butler, Chicago, NFC 41		28	68.3
1985	Gary Anderson, Pittsburgh, AFC 42		33	78.6
	Morten Andersen, New Orleans, NFC 35		31	88.6
	*Kevin Butler, Chicago, NFC 37		31	83.8
1984	*Paul McFadden, Philadelphia, NFC 37		30	81.1
	Gary Anderson, Pittsburgh, AFC 32		24	75.0
	Matt Bahr, Cleveland, AFC 32		24	75.0
1983	*Ali-Haji-Sheikh, N.Y. Giants, NFC 42		35	83.3
	*Raul Allegre, Baltimore, AFC 35		30	85.7

Year	Player, Team	Att.	Made	Pct.
1982	Mark Moseley, Washington, NFC	21	20	95.2
	Nick Lowery, Kansas City, AFC	24	19	79.2
1981	Rafael Septien, Dallas, NFC	35	27	77.1
	Nick Lowery, Kansas City, AFC	36	26	72.2
1980	*Ed Murray, Detroit, NFC	42	27	64.3
	John Smith, New England, AFC	34	26	76.5
	Fred Steinfort, Denver, AFC	34	26	76.5
1979	Mark Moseley, Washington, NFC	33	25	75.8
	John Smith, New England, AFC	33	23	69.7
1978	*Frank Corral, Los Angeles, NFC	43	29	67.4
	Pat Leahy, N.Y. Jets, AFC	30	22	73.3
1977	Mark Moseley, Washington, NFC	37	21	56.8
	Errol Mann, Oakland, AFC	28	20	71.4
1976	Mark Moseley, Washington, NFC	34	22	64.7
	Jan Stenerud, Kansas City, AFC	38	21	55.3
1975	Jan Stenerud, Kansas City, AFC	32	22	68.8
	Toni Fritsch, Dallas, NFC	35	22	62.9
1974	Chester Marcol, Green Bay, NFC	39	25	64.1
	Roy Gerela, Pittsburgh, AFC	29	20	69.0
1973	David Ray, Los Angeles, NFC	47	30	63.8
	Roy Gerela, Pittsburgh, AFC	43	29	67.4
1972	*Chester Marcol, Green Bay, NFC	48	33	68.8
	Roy Gerela, Pittsburgh, AFC	41	28	68.3
1971	Curt Knight, Washington, NFC	49	29	59.2
	Garo Yepremian, Miami, AFC	40	28	70.0
1970	Jan Stenerud, Kansas City, AFC	42	30	71.4
	Fred Cox, Minnesota, NFC	46	30	65.2
1969	Jim Turner, N.Y. Jets, AFL	47	32	68.1
	Fred Cox, Minnesota, NFL	37	26	70.3
1968	Jim Turner, N.Y. Jets, AFL	46	34	73.9
	Mac Percival, Chicago, NFL	36	25	69.4
1967	Jim Bakken, St. Louis, NFL	39	27	69.2
	Jan Stenerud, Kansas City, AFL	36	21	58.3
1966	Bruce Gossett, Los Angeles, NFL	49	28	57.1
	Mike Mercer, Oakland-Kansas City, AFL	30	21	70.0
1965	Pete Gogolak, Buffalo, AFL	46	28	60.9
	Fred Cox, Minnesota, NFL	35	23	65.7
1964	Jim Bakken, St. Louis, NFL	38	25	65.8
	Gino Cappelletti, Boston, AFL	39	25	64.1
1963	Jim Martin, Baltimore, NFL	39	24	61.5
	Gino Cappelletti, Boston, AFL	38	22	57.9
1962	Gene Mingo, Denver, AFL	39	27	69.2
	Lou Michaels, Pittsburgh, NFL	42	26	61.9
1961	Steve Myhra, Baltimore, NFL	39	21	53.8
	Gino Cappelletti, Boston, AFL	32	17	53.1
1960	Tommy Davis, San Francisco, NFL	32	19	59.4
	*Gene Mingo, Denver, AFL	28	18	64.3
1959	Pat Summerall, N.Y. Giants	29	20	69.0
1958	Paige Cothren, Los Angeles	25	14	56.0
	*Tom Miner, Pittsburgh	28	14	50.0
1957	Lou Groza, Cleveland	22	15	68.2
1956	Sam Baker, Washington	25	17	68.0
1955	Fred Cone, Green Bay	24	16	66.7
1954	Lou Groza, Cleveland	24	16	66.7
1953	Lou Groza, Cleveland	26	23	88.5
1952	Lou Groza, Cleveland	33	19	57.6
1951	Bob Waterfield, Los Angeles	23	13	56.5
1950	Lou Groza, Cleveland	19	13	68.4
1949	Cliff Patton, Philadelphia	18	9	50.0
	Bob Waterfield, Los Angeles	16	9	56.3
1948	Cliff Patton, Philadelphia	12	8	66.7
1947	Ward Cuff, Green Bay	16	7	43.8
	Pat Harder, Chi. Cardinals	10	7	70.0
	Bob Waterfield, Los Angeles	16	7	43.8
1946	Ted Fritsch, Green Bay	17	9	52.9
1945	Joe Aguirre, Washington	13	7	53.8
1944	Ken Strong, N.Y. Giants	12	6	50.0
1943	Ward Cuff, N.Y. Giants	9	3	33.3
	Don Hutson, Green Bay	5	3	60.0

Year	Player, Team	Att.	Made	Pct.
1942	Bill Daddio, Chi. Cardinals	10	5	50.0
1941	Clarke Hinkle, Green Bay	14	6	42.9
1940	Clarke Hinkle, Green Bay	14	9	64.3
1939	Ward Cuff, N.Y. Giants	16	7	43.8
1938	Ward Cuff, N.Y. Giants	9	5	55.6
	Ralph Kercheval, Brooklyn	13	5	38.5
1937	Jack Manders, Chi. Bears		8	
1936	Jack Manders, Chi. Bears		7	
	Armand Niccolai, Pittsburgh		7	
1935	Armand Niccolai, Pittsburgh		6	
	Bill Smith, Chi. Cardinals		6	
1934	Jack Manders, Chi. Bears		10	
1933	*Jack Manders, Chi. Bears		6	
	Glenn Presnell, Portsmouth		6	
1932	Earl (Dutch) Clark, Portsmouth		3	

First season of professional football.

ANNUAL RUSHING LEADERS

Year	Player, Team	Att.	Yards	Avg.	TD
2006	LaDainian Tomlinson, San Diego, AFC	348	1,815	5.2	28
	Frank Gore, San Francisco, NFC	312	1,695	5.4	8
2005	Shaun Alexander, Seattle, NFC	370	1,880	5.1	27
	Larry Johnson, Kansas City, AFC	336	1,750	5.2	20
2004	Curtis Martin, N.Y. Jets, AFC	371	1,697	4.6	12
	Shaun Alexander, Seattle, NFC	353	1,696	4.8	16
2003	Jamal Lewis, Baltimore, AFC	387	2,066	5.3	14
	Ahman Green, Green Bay, NFC	355	1,883	5.3	15
2002	Ricky Williams, Miami, AFC	383	1,853	4.8	16
	Deuce McAllister, New Orleans, NFC	325	1,388	4.3	13
2001	Priest Holmes, Kansas City, AFC	327	1,555	4.8	8
	Stephen Davis, Washington, NFC	356	1,432	4.0	5
2000	Edgerrin James, Indianapolis, AFC	387	1,709	4.4	13
	Robert Smith, Minnesota, NFC	295	1,521	5.2	7
1999	*Edgerrin James, Indianapolis, AFC	369	1,553	4.2	13
	Stephen Davis, Washington, NFC	290	1,405	4.8	17
1998	Terrell Davis, Denver, AFC	392	2,008	5.1	21
	Jamal Anderson, Atlanta, NFC	410	1,846	4.5	14
1997	Barry Sanders, Detroit, NFC	335	2,053	6.1	11
	Terrell Davis, Denver, AFC	369	1,750	4.7	15
1996	Barry Sanders, Detroit, NFC	307	1,553	5.1	11
	Terrell Davis, Denver, AFC	345	1,538	4.5	13
1995	Emmitt Smith, Dallas, NFC	377	1,773	4.7	25
	*Curtis Martin, New England, AFC	368	1,487	4.0	14
1994	Barry Sanders, Detroit, NFC	331	1,883	5.7	7
	Chris Warren, Seattle, AFC	333	1,545	4.6	9
1993	Emmitt Smith, Dallas, NFC	283	1,486	5.3	9
	Thurman Thomas, Buffalo, AFC	355	1,315	3.7	6
1992	Emmitt Smith, Dallas, NFC	373	1,713	4.6	18
	Barry Foster, Pittsburgh, AFC	390	1,690	4.3	11
1991	Emmitt Smith, Dallas, NFC	365	1,563	4.3	12
	Thurman Thomas, Buffalo, AFC	288	1,407	4.9	7
1990	Barry Sanders, Detroit, NFC	255	1,304	5.1	13
	Thurman Thomas, Buffalo, AFC	271	1,297	4.8	11
1989	Christian Okoye, Kansas City, AFC	370	1,480	4.0	12
	*Barry Sanders, Detroit, NFC	280	1,470	5.3	14
1988	Eric Dickerson, Indianapolis, AFC	388	1,659	4.3	14
	Herschel Walker, Dallas, NFC	361	1,514	4.2	5
1987	Charles White, L.A. Rams, NFC	324	1,374	4.2	11
	Eric Dickerson, Indianapolis, AFC	223	1,011	4.5	5
1986	Eric Dickerson, L.A. Rams, NFC	404	1,821	4.5	11
	Curt Warner, Seattle, AFC	319	1,481	4.6	13
1985	Marcus Allen, L.A. Raiders, AFC	380	1,759	4.6	11
	Gerald Riggs, Atlanta, NFC	397	1,719	4.3	10
1984	Eric Dickerson, L.A. Rams, NFC	379	2,105	5.6	14
	Earnest Jackson, San Diego, AFC	296	1,179	4.0	8
1983	*Eric Dickerson, L.A. Rams, NFC	390	1,808	4.6	18
	*Curt Warner, Seattle, AFC	335	1,449	4.3	13

Year	Player, Team	Att.	Yards	Avg.	TD
1982	Freeman McNeil, N.Y. Jets, AFC	151	786	5.2	6
	Tony Dorsett, Dallas, NFC	177	745	4.2	5
1981	*George Rogers, New Orleans, NFC	378	1,674	4.4	13
	Earl Campbell, Houston, AFC	361	1,376	3.8	10
1980	Earl Campbell, Houston, AFC	373	1,934	5.2	13
	Walter Payton, Chicago, NFC	317	1,460	4.6	6
1979	Earl Campbell, Houston, AFC	368	1,697	4.6	19
	Walter Payton, Chicago, NFC	369	1,610	4.4	14
1978	*Earl Campbell, Houston, AFC	302	1,450	4.8	13
	Walter Payton, Chicago, NFC	333	1,395	4.2	11
1977	Walter Payton, Chicago, NFC	339	1,852	5.5	14
	Mark van Eeghen, Oakland, AFC	324	1,273	3.9	7
1976	O.J. Simpson, Buffalo, AFC	290	1,503	5.2	8
	Walter Payton, Chicago, NFC	311	1,390	4.5	13
1975	O.J. Simpson, Buffalo, AFC	329	1,817	5.5	16
	Jim Otis, St. Louis, NFC	269	1,076	4.0	5
1974	Otis Armstrong, Denver, AFC	263	1,407	5.3	9
	Lawrence McCutcheon, Los Angeles, NFC	236	1,109	4.7	3
1973	O.J. Simpson, Buffalo, AFC	332	2,003	6.0	12
	John Brockington, Green Bay, NFC	265	1,144	4.3	3
1972	O.J. Simpson, Buffalo, AFC	292	1,251	4.3	6
	Larry Brown, Washington, NFC	285	1,216	4.3	8
1971	Floyd Little, Denver, AFC	284	1,133	4.0	6
	*John Brockington, Green Bay, NFC	216	1,105	5.1	4
1970	Larry Brown, Washington, NFC	237	1,125	4.7	5
	Floyd Little, Denver, AFC	209	901	4.3	3
1969	Gale Sayers, Chicago, NFL	236	1,032	4.4	8
	Dickie Post, San Diego, AFL	182	873	4.8	6
1968	Leroy Kelly, Cleveland, NFL	248	1,239	5.0	16
	*Paul Robinson, Cincinnati, AFL	238	1,023	4.3	8
1967	Jim Nance, Boston, AFL	269	1,216	4.5	7
	Leroy Kelly, Cleveland, NFL	235	1,205	5.1	11
1966	Jim Nance, Boston, AFL	299	1,458	4.9	11
	Gale Sayers, Chicago, NFL	229	1,231	5.4	8
1965	Jim Brown, Cleveland, NFL	289	1,544	5.3	17
	Paul Lowe, San Diego, AFL	222	1,121	5.0	7
1964	Jim Brown, Cleveland, NFL	280	1,446	5.2	7
	Cookie Gilchrist, Buffalo, AFL	230	981	4.3	6
1963	Jim Brown, Cleveland, NFL	291	1,863	6.4	12
	Clem Daniels, Oakland, AFL	215	1,099	5.1	3
1962	Jim Taylor, Green Bay, NFL	272	1,474	5.4	19
	Cookie Gilchrist, Buffalo, AFL	214	1,096	5.1	13
1961	Jim Brown, Cleveland, NFL	305	1,408	4.6	8
	Billy Cannon, Houston, AFL	200	948	4.7	6
1960	Jim Brown, Cleveland, NFL	215	1,257	5.8	9
	*Abner Haynes, Dall. Texans, AFL	156	875	5.6	9
1959	Jim Brown, Cleveland	290	1,329	4.6	14
1958	Jim Brown, Cleveland	257	1,527	5.9	17
1957	*Jim Brown, Cleveland	202	942	4.7	9
1956	Rick Casares, Chi. Bears	234	1,126	4.8	12
1955	*Alan Ameche, Baltimore	213	961	4.5	9
1954	Joe Perry, San Francisco	173	1,049	6.1	8
1953	Joe Perry, San Francisco	192	1,018	5.3	10
1952	Dan Towler, Los Angeles	156	894	5.7	10
1951	Eddie Price, N.Y. Giants	271	971	3.6	7
1950	Marion Motley, Cleveland	140	810	5.8	3
1949	Steve Van Buren, Philadelphia	263	1,146	4.4	11
1948	Steve Van Buren, Philadelphia	201	945	4.7	10
1947	Steve Van Buren, Philadelphia	217	1,008	4.6	13
1946	Bill Dudley, Pittsburgh	146	604	4.1	3
1945	Steve Van Buren, Philadelphia	143	832	5.8	15
1944	Bill Paschal, N.Y. Giants	196	737	3.8	9
1943	*Bill Paschal, N.Y. Giants	147	572	3.9	10
1942	*Bill Dudley, Pittsburgh	162	696	4.3	5
1941	Clarence (Pug) Manders, Brooklyn	111	486	4.4	5
1940	Byron (Whizzer) White, Detroit	146	514	3.5	5
1939	*Bill Osmanski, Chicago	121	699	5.8	7
1938	*Byron (Whizzer) White, Pittsburgh	152	567	3.7	4
1937	Cliff Battles, Washington	216	874	4.0	5

Year	Player, Team	Att.	Yards	Avg.	TD
1936	*Alphonse (Tuffy) Leemans, N.Y. Giants	206	830	4.0	2
1935	Doug Russell, Chi. Cardinals	140	499	3.6	0
1934	*Beattie Feathers, Chi. Bears	119	1,004	8.4	8
1933	Jim Musick, Boston	173	809	4.7	5
1932	*Cliff Battles, Boston	148	576	3.9	3

*First season of professional football.

ANNUAL PASSING LEADERS

(Current rating system implemented in 1973)

Year	Player, Team	Att.	Comp.	Yards	TD	Int.	Rating
2006	Peyton Manning, Indianapolis, AFC	557	362	4,397	31	9	101.0
	Drew Brees, New Orleans, NFC	554	356	4,418	26	11	96.2
2005	Peyton Manning, Indianapolis, AFC	453	305	3,747	28	10	104.1
	Matt Hasselbeck, Seattle, NFC	449	294	3,459	24	9	98.2
2004	Peyton Manning, Indianapolis, AFC	497	336	4,557	49	10	121.1
	Daunte Culpepper, Minnesota, NFC	548	379	4,717	39	11	110.9
2003	Steve McNair, Tennessee, AFC	400	250	3,215	24	7	100.4
	Daunte Culpepper, Minnesota, NFC	454	295	3,479	25	11	96.4
2002	Chad Pennington, N.Y. Jets, AFC	399	275	3,120	22	6	104.2
	Brad Johnson, Tampa Bay, NFC	451	281	3,049	22	6	92.9
2001	Kurt Warner, St. Louis, NFC	546	375	4,830	36	22	101.4
	Rich Gannon, Oakland, AFC	549	361	3,828	27	9	95.5
2000	Brian Griese, Denver, AFC	336	216	2,688	19	4	102.9
	Trent Green, St. Louis, NFC	240	145	2,063	16	5	101.8
1999	Kurt Warner, St. Louis, NFC	499	325	4,353	41	13	109.2
	Peyton Manning, Indianapolis, AFC	533	331	4,135	26	15	90.7
1998	Randall Cunningham, Minnesota, NFC	425	259	3,704	34	10	106.0
	Vinny Testaverde, N.Y. Jets, AFC	421	259	3,256	29	7	101.6
1997	Steve Young, San Francisco, NFC	356	241	3,029	19	6	104.7
	Mark Brunell, Jacksonville, AFC	435	264	3,281	18	7	91.2
1996	Steve Young, San Francisco NFC	316	214	2,410	14	6	97.2
	John Elway, Denver, AFC	466	287	3,328	26	14	89.2
1995	Jim Harbaugh, Indianapolis, AFC	314	200	2,575	17	5	100.7
	Brett Favre, Green Bay, NFC	570	359	4,413	38	13	99.5
1994	Steve Young, San Francisco, NFC	461	324	3,969	35	10	112.8
	Dan Marino, Miami, AFC	615	385	4,453	30	17	89.2
1993	Steve Young, San Francisco, NFC	462	314	4,023	29	16	101.5
	John Elway, Denver, AFC	551	348	4,030	25	10	92.8
1992	Steve Young, San Francisco, NFC	402	268	3,465	25	7	107.0
	Warren Moon, Houston, AFC	346	224	2,521	18	12	89.3
1991	Steve Young, San Francisco, NFC	279	180	2,517	17	8	101.8
	Jim Kelly, Buffalo, AFC	474	304	3,844	33	17	97.6
1990	Jim Kelly, Buffalo, AFC	346	219	2,829	24	9	101.2
	Phil Simms, N.Y. Giants, NFC	311	184	2,284	15	4	92.7
1989	Joe Montana, San Francisco, NFC	386	271	3,521	26	8	112.4
	Boomer Esiason, Cincinnati, AFC	455	258	3,525	28	11	92.1
1988	Boomer Esiason, Cincinnati, AFC	388	223	3,572	28	14	97.4
	Wade Wilson, Minnesota, NFC	332	204	2,746	15	9	91.5
1987	Joe Montana, San Francisco, NFC	398	266	3,054	31	13	102.1
	Bernie Kosar, Cleveland, AFC	389	241	3,033	22	9	95.4
1986	Tommy Kramer, Minnesota, NFC	372	208	3,000	24	10	92.6
	Dan Marino, Miami, AFC	623	378	4,746	44	23	92.5
1985	Ken O'Brien, N.Y. Jets, AFC	488	297	3,888	25	8	96.2
	Joe Montana, San Francisco, NFC	494	303	3,653	27	13	91.3
1984	Dan Marino, Miami, AFC	564	362	5,084	48	17	108.9
	Joe Montana, San Francisco, NFC	432	279	3,630	28	10	102.9
1983	Steve Bartkowski, Atlanta, NFC	432	274	3,167	22	5	97.6
	*Dan Marino, Miami, AFC	296	173	2,210	20	6	96.0
1982	Ken Anderson, Cincinnati, AFC	309	218	2,495	12	9	95.3
	Joe Theismann, Washington, NFC	252	161	2,033	13	9	91.3
1981	Ken Anderson, Cincinnati, AFC	479	300	3,754	29	10	98.4
	Joe Montana, San Francisco, NFC	488	311	3,565	19	12	88.4
1980	Brian Sipe, Cleveland, AFC	554	337	4,132	30	14	91.4
	Ron Jaworski, Philadelphia, NFC	451	257	3,529	27	12	91.0
1979	Roger Staubach, Dallas, NFC	461	267	3,586	27	11	92.3
	Dan Fouts, San Diego, AFC	530	332	4,082	24	24	82.6
1978	Roger Staubach, Dallas, NFC	413	231	3,190	25	16	84.9
	Terry Bradshaw, Pittsburgh, AFC	368	207	2,915	28	20	84.7

Year	Player, Team	Att.	Comp.	Yards	TD	Int.	Rating
1977	Bob Griese, Miami, AFC	307	180	2,252	22	13	87.8
	Roger Staubach, Dallas, NFC	361	210	2,620	18	9	87.0
1976	Ken Stabler, Oakland, AFC	291	194	2,737	27	17	103.4
	James Harris, Los Angeles, NFC	158	91	1,460	8	6	89.6
1975	Ken Anderson, Cincinnati, AFC	377	228	3,169	21	11	93.9
	Fran Tarkenton, Minnesota, NFC	425	273	2,994	25	13	91.8
1974	Ken Anderson, Cincinnati, AFC	328	213	2,667	18	10	95.7
	Sonny Jurgensen, Washington, NFC	167	107	1,185	11	5	94.5
1973	Roger Staubach, Dallas, NFC	286	179	2,428	23	15	94.6
	Ken Stabler, Oakland, AFC	260	163	1,997	14	10	88.3
1972	Norm Snead, N.Y. Giants, NFC	325	196	2,307	17	12	
	Earl Morrall, Miami, AFC	150	83	1,360	11	7	
1971	Roger Staubach, Dallas, NFC	211	126	1,882	15	4	
	Bob Griese, Miami, AFC	263	145	2,089	19	9	
1970	John Brodie, San Francisco, NFC	378	223	2,941	24	10	
	Daryle Lamonica, Oakland, AFC	356	179	2,516	22	15	
1969	Sonny Jurgensen, Washington, NFL	442	274	3,102	22	15	
	*Greg Cook, Cincinnati, AFL	197	106	1,854	15	11	
1968	Len Dawson, Kansas City, AFL	224	131	2,109	17	9	
	Earl Morrall, Baltimore, NFL	317	182	2,909	26	17	
1967	Sonny Jurgensen, Washington, NFL	508	288	3,747	31	16	
	Daryle Lamonica, Oakland, AFL	425	220	3,228	30	20	
1966	Bart Starr, Green Bay, NFL	251	156	2,257	14	3	
	Len Dawson, Kansas City, AFL	284	159	2,527	26	10	
1965	Rudy Bukich, Chicago, NFL	312	176	2,641	20	9	
	John Hadl, San Diego, AFL	348	174	2,798	20	21	
1964	Len Dawson, Kansas City, AFL	354	199	2,879	30	18	
	Bart Starr, Green Bay, NFL	272	163	2,144	15	4	
1963	Y.A. Tittle, N.Y. Giants, NFL	367	221	3,145	36	14	
	Tobin Rote, San Diego, AFL	286	170	2,510	20	17	
1962	Len Dawson, Dallas Texans, AFL	310	189	2,759	29	17	
	Bart Starr, Green Bay, NFL	285	178	2,438	12	9	
1961	George Blanda, Houston, AFL	362	187	3,330	36	22	
	Milt Plum, Cleveland, NFL	302	177	2,416	18	10	
1960	Milt Plum, Cleveland, NFL	250	151	2,297	21	5	
	Jack Kemp, L.A. Chargers, AFL	406	211	3,018	20	25	
1959	Charlie Conerly, N.Y. Giants	194	113	1,706	14	4	
1958	Eddie LeBaron, Washington	145	79	1,365	11	10	
1957	Tommy O'Connell, Cleveland	110	63	1,229	9	8	
1956	Ed Brown, Chicago Bears	168	96	1,667	11	12	
1955	Otto Graham, Cleveland	185	98	1,721	15	8	
1954	Norm Van Brocklin, Los Angeles	260	139	2,637	13	21	
1953	Otto Graham, Cleveland	258	167	2,722	11	9	
1952	Norm Van Brocklin, Los Angeles	205	113	1,736	14	17	
1951	Bob Waterfield, Los Angeles	176	88	1,566	13	10	
1950	Norm Van Brocklin, Los Angeles	233	127	2,061	18	14	
1949	Sammy Baugh, Washington	255	145	1,903	18	14	
1948	Tommy Thompson, Philadelphia	246	141	1,965	25	11	
1947	Sammy Baugh, Washington	354	210	2,938	25	15	
1946	Bob Waterfield, Los Angeles	251	127	1,747	18	17	
1945	Sammy Baugh, Washington	182	128	1,669	11	4	
	Sid Luckman, Chicago Bears	217	117	1,725	14	10	
1944	Frank Filchock, Washington	147	84	1,139	13	9	
1943	Sammy Baugh, Washington	239	133	1,754	23	19	
1942	Cecil Isbell, Green Bay	268	146	2,021	24	14	
1941	Cecil Isbell, Green Bay	206	117	1,479	15	11	
1940	Sammy Baugh, Washington	177	111	1,367	12	10	
1939	*Parker Hall, Cleveland	208	106	1,227	9	13	
1938	Ed Danowski, N.Y. Giants	129	70	848	7	8	
1937	*Sammy Baugh, Washington	171	81	1,127	8	14	
1936	Arnie Herber, Green Bay	173	77	1,239	11	13	
1935	Ed Danowski, N.Y. Giants	113	57	794	10	9	
1934	Arnie Herber, Green Bay	115	42	799	8	12	
1933	*Harry Newman, N.Y. Giants	136	53	973	11	17	
1932	Arnie Herber, Green Bay	101	37	639	9	9	

*First season of professional football.

ANNUAL PASSING TOUCHDOWN LEADERS

Year	Player, Team	TD
2006	Peyton Manning, Indianapolis, AFC	31
	Drew Brees, New Orleans, NFC	26
2005	Carson Palmer, Cincinnati, AFC	32
	Jake Delhomme, Carolina, NFC	24
	Matt Hasselbeck, Seattle, NFC	24
	Eli Manning, N.Y. Giants, NFC	24
2004	Peyton Manning, Indianapolis, AFC	49
	Daunte Culpepper, Minnesota, NFC	39
2003	Brett Favre, Green Bay, NFC	32
	Peyton Manning, Indianapolis, AFC	29
2002	Tom Brady, New England, AFC	28
	Aaron Brooks, New Orleans, NFC	27
	Brett Favre, Green Bay, NFC	27
2001	Kurt Warner, St. Louis, NFC	36
	Rich Gannon, Oakland, AFC	27
2000	Daunte Culpepper, Minnesota, NFC	33
	Peyton Manning, Indianapolis, AFC	33
1999	Kurt Warner, St. Louis, NFC	41
	Peyton Manning, Indianapolis, AFC	26
1998	Steve Young, San Francisco, NFC	36
	Vinny Testaverde, N.Y. Jets, AFC	29
1997	Brett Favre, Green Bay, NFC	35
	Jeff George, Oakland, AFC	29
1996	Brett Favre, Green Bay, NFC	39
	Vinny Testaverde, Baltimore, AFC	33
1995	Brett Favre, Green Bay, NFC	38
	Jeff Blake, Cincinnati, AFC	28
1994	Steve Young, San Francisco, NFC	35
	Dan Marino, Miami, AFC	30
1993	Steve Young, San Francisco, NFC	29
	John Elway, Denver, AFC	25
1992	Steve Young, San Francisco, NFC	25
	Dan Marino, Miami, AFC	24
1991	Jim Kelly, Buffalo, AFC	33
	Mark Rypien, Washington, NFC	28
1990	Warren Moon, Houston, AFC	33
	Randall Cunningham, Philadelphia, NFC	30
1989	Jim Everett, L.A. Rams, NFC	29
	Boomer Esiason, Cincinnati, AFC	28
1988	Jim Everett, L.A. Rams, NFC	31
	Boomer Esiason, Cincinnati, AFC	28
	Dan Marino, Miami, AFC	28
1987	Joe Montana, San Francisco, NFC	31
	Dan Marino, Miami, AFC	26
1986	Dan Marino, Miami, AFC	44
	Tommy Kramer, Minnesota, NFC	24
1985	Dan Marino, Miami, AFC	30
	Joe Montana, San Francisco, NFC	27
1984	Dan Marino, Miami, AFC	48
	Neil Lomax, St. Louis, NFC	28
	Joe Montana, San Francisco, NFC	28
1983	Lynn Dickey, Green Bay, NFC	32
	Joe Ferguson, Buffalo, AFC	26
	Brian Sipe, Cleveland, AFC	26
1982	Terry Bradshaw, Pittsburgh, AFC	17
	Dan Fouts, San Diego, AFC	17
	Joe Montana, San Francisco, NFC	17
1981	Dan Fouts, San Diego, AFC	33
	Steve Bartkowski, Atlanta, NFC	30
1980	Steve Bartkowski, Atlanta, NFC	31
	Dan Fouts, San Diego, AFC	30
	Brian Sipe, Cleveland, AFC	30
1979	Steve Grogan, New England, AFC	28
	Brian Sipe, Cleveland, AFC	28
	Roger Staubach, Dallas, NFC	27
1978	Terry Bradshaw, Pittsburgh, AFC	28
	Roger Staubach, Dallas, NFC	25
	Fran Tarkenton, Minnesota, NFC	25
1977	Bob Griese, Miami, AFC	22
	Ron Jaworski, Philadelphia, NFC	18
	Roger Staubach, Dallas, NFC	18

Year	Player, Team	TD
1976	Ken Stabler, Oakland, AFC	27
	Jim Hart, St. Louis, NFC	18
1975	Joe Ferguson, Buffalo, AFC	25
	Fran Tarkenton, Minnesota, NFC	25
1974	Ken Stabler, Oakland, AFC	26
	Jim Hart, St. Louis, NFC	20
1973	Roman Gabriel, Philadelphia, NFC	23
	Roger Staubach, Dallas, NFC	23
	Charley Johnson, Denver, AFC	20
1972	Billy Kilmer, Washington, NFC	19
	Joe Namath, N.Y. Jets, AFC	19
1971	John Hadl, San Diego, AFC	21
	John Brodie, San Francisco, NFC	18
1970	John Brodie, San Francisco, NFC	24
	John Hadl, San Diego, AFC	22
	Daryle Lamonica, Oakland, AFC	22
1969	Daryle Lamonica, Oakland, AFL	34
	Roman Gabriel, Los Angeles, NFL	24
1968	John Hadl, San Diego, AFL	27
	Earl Morrall, Baltimore, NFL	26
1967	Sonny Jurgensen, Washington, NFL	31
	Daryle Lamonica, Oakland, AFL	30
1966	Frank Ryan, Cleveland, NFL	29
	Len Dawson, Kansas City, AFL	26
1965	John Brodie, San Francisco, NFL	30
	Len Dawson, Kansas City, AFL	21
1964	Babe Parilli, Boston, AFL	31
	Frank Ryan, Cleveland, NFL	25
1963	Y.A. Tittle, N.Y. Giants, NFL	36
	Len Dawson, Kansas City, AFL	26
1962	Y.A. Tittle, N.Y. Giants, NFL	33
	Len Dawson, Dallas, AFL	29
1961	George Blanda, Houston, AFL	36
	Sonny Jurgensen, Philadelphia, NFL	32
1960	Al Dorow, N.Y. Titans, AFL	26
	Johnny Unitas, Baltimore, NFL	25
1959	Johnny Unitas, Baltimore	32
1958	Johnny Unitas, Baltimore	19
1957	Johnny Unitas, Baltimore	24
1956	Tobin Rote, Green Bay	18
1955	Tobin Rote, Green Bay	17
	Y.A. Tittle, San Francisco	17
1954	Adrian Burk, Philadelphia	23
1953	Robert Thomason, Philadelphia	21
1952	Jim Finks, Pittsburgh	20
	Otto Graham, Cleveland	20
1951	Bobby Layne, Detroit	26
1950	George Ratterman, N.Y. Yanks	22
1949	Johnny Lujack, Chi. Bears	23
1948	Tommy Thompson, Philadelphia	25
1947	Sammy Baugh, Washington	25
1946	Sid Luckman, Chi. Bears	17
	Bob Waterfield, Los Angeles	17
1945	Sid Luckman, Chi. Bears	14
	*Bob Waterfield, Cleveland	14
1944	Frank Filchock, Washington	13
1943	Sid Luckman, Chi. Bears	28
1942	Cecil Isbell, Green Bay	24
1941	Cecil Isbell, Green Bay	15
1940	Sammy Baugh, Washington	12
1939	Frank Filchock, Washington	11
1938	Bob Monnett, Green Bay	9
1937	Bernie Masterson, Chi. Bears	9
1936	Arnie Herber, Green Bay	11
1935	Ed Danowski, N.Y. Giants	10
1934	Arnie Herber, Green Bay	8
1933	*Harry Newman, N.Y. Giants	11
1932	Arnie Herber, Green Bay	9

*First season of professional football.

ANNUAL PASS RECEIVING LEADERS

Year	Player, Team	No.	Yards	Avg.	TD
2006	Andre Johnson, Houston, AFC	103	1,147	11.1	5
	Mike Furrey, Detroit, NFC	98	1,086	11.1	6
2005	Steve Smith, Carolina, NFC	103	1,563	15.2	12
	Larry Fitzgerald, Arizona, NFC	103	1,409	13.7	10
	Chad Johnson, Cincinnati, AFC	97	1,432	14.8	9
2004	Tony Gonzalez, Kansas City, AFC	102	1,258	12.3	7
	Joe Horn, New Orleans, NFC	94	1,399	14.9	11
	Torry Holt, St. Louis, NFC	94	1,372	14.6	10
2003	Torry Holt, St. Louis, NFC	117	1,696	14.5	12
	LaDainian Tomlinson, San Diego, AFC	100	725	7.3	4
2002	Marvin Harrison, Indianapolis, AFC	143	1,722	12.0	11
	Randy Moss, Minnesota, NFC	106	1,347	12.7	7
2001	Rod Smith, Denver, AFC	113	1,343	11.9	11
	Keyshawn Johnson, Tampa Bay, NFC	106	1,266	11.9	1
2000	Marvin Harrison, Indianapolis, AFC	102	1,413	13.9	14
	Muhsin Muhammad, Carolina, NFC	102	1,183	11.6	6
1999	Jimmy Smith, Jacksonville, AFC	116	1,636	14.1	6
	Muhsin Muhammad, Carolina, NFC	96	1,253	13.1	8
1998	O.J. McDuffie, Miami, AFC	90	1,050	11.7	7
	Frank Sanders, Arizona, NFC	89	1,145	12.9	3
1997	Tim Brown, Oakland, AFC	104	1,408	13.5	5
	Herman Moore, Detroit, NFC	104	1,293	12.4	8
1996	Jerry Rice, San Francisco, NFC	108	1,254	11.6	8
	Carl Pickens, Cincinnati, AFC	100	1,180	11.8	12
1995	Herman Moore, Detroit, NFC	123	1,686	13.7	14
	Carl Pickens, Cincinnati, AFC	99	1,234	12.5	17
1994	Cris Carter, Minnesota, NFC	122	1,256	10.3	7
	Ben Coates, New England, AFC	96	1,174	12.2	7
1993	Sterling Sharpe, Green Bay, NFC	112	1,274	11.4	11
	Reggie Langhorne, Indianapolis, AFC	85	1,038	12.2	3
1992	Sterling Sharpe, Green Bay, NFC	108	1,461	13.5	13
	Haywood Jeffires, Houston, AFC	90	913	10.1	9
1991	Haywood Jeffires, Houston, AFC	100	1,181	11.8	7
	Michael Irvin, Dallas, NFC	93	1,523	16.4	8
1990	Jerry Rice, San Francisco, NFC	100	1,502	15.0	13
	Haywood Jeffires, Houston, AFC	74	1,048	14.2	8
	Drew Hill, Houston, AFC	74	1,019	13.8	5
1989	Sterling Sharpe, Green Bay, NFC	90	1,423	15.8	12
	Andre Reed, Buffalo, AFC	88	1,312	14.9	9
1988	Al Toon, N.Y. Jets, AFC	93	1,067	11.5	5
	Henry Ellard, L.A. Rams, NFC	86	1,414	16.4	10
1987	J.T. Smith, St. Louis, NFC	91	1,117	12.3	8
	Al Toon, N.Y. Jets, AFC	68	976	14.4	5
1986	Todd Christensen, L.A. Raiders, AFC	95	1,153	12.1	8
	Jerry Rice, San Francisco, NFC	86	1,570	18.3	15
1985	Roger Craig, San Francisco, NFC	92	1,016	11.0	6
	Lionel James, San Diego, AFC	86	1,027	11.9	6
1984	Art Monk, Washington, NFC	106	1,372	12.9	7
	Ozzie Newsome, Cleveland, AFC	89	1,001	11.2	5
1983	Todd Christensen, L.A. Raiders, AFC	92	1,247	13.6	12
	Roy Green, St. Louis, NFC	78	1,227	15.7	14
	Charlie Brown, Washington, NFC	78	1,225	15.7	8
	Earnest Gray, N.Y. Giants, NFC	78	1,139	14.6	5
1982	Dwight Clark, San Francisco, NFC	60	913	15.2	5
	Kellen Winslow, San Diego, AFC	54	721	13.4	6
1981	Kellen Winslow, San Diego, AFC	88	1,075	12.2	10
	Dwight Clark, San Francisco, NFC	85	1,105	13.0	4
1980	Kellen Winslow, San Diego, AFC	89	1,290	14.5	9
	*Earl Cooper, San Francisco, NFC	83	567	6.8	4
1979	Joe Washington, Baltimore, AFC	82	750	9.1	3
	Ahmad Rashad, Minnesota, NFC	80	1,156	14.5	9
1978	Rickey Young, Minnesota, NFC	88	704	8.0	5
	Steve Largent, Seattle, AFC	71	1,168	16.5	8
1977	Lydell Mitchell, Baltimore, AFC	71	620	8.7	4
	Ahmad Rashad, Minnesota, NFC	51	681	13.4	2
1976	MacArthur Lane, Kansas City, AFC	66	686	10.4	1
	Drew Pearson, Dallas, NFC	58	806	13.9	6

Year	Player, Team	No.	Yards	Avg.	TD
1975	Chuck Foreman, Minnesota, NFC	73	691	9.5	9
	Reggie Rucker, Cleveland, AFC	60	770	12.8	3
	Lydell Mitchell, Baltimore, AFC	60	544	9.1	4
1974	Lydell Mitchell, Baltimore, AFC	72	544	7.6	2
	Charles Young, Philadelphia, NFC	63	696	11.0	3
1973	Harold Carmichael, Philadelphia, NFC	67	1,116	16.7	9
	Fred Willis, Houston, AFC	57	371	6.5	1
1972	Harold Jackson, Philadelphia, NFC	62	1,048	16.9	4
	Fred Biletnikoff, Oakland, AFC	58	802	13.8	7
1971	Fred Biletnikoff, Oakland, AFC	61	929	15.2	9
	Bob Tucker, N.Y. Giants, NFC	59	791	13.4	4
1970	Dick Gordon, Chicago, NFC	71	1,026	14.5	13
	Marlin Briscoe, Buffalo, AFC	57	1,036	18.2	8
1969	Dan Abramowicz, New Orleans, NFL	73	1,015	13.9	7
	Lance Alworth, San Diego, AFL	64	1,003	15.7	4
1968	Clifton McNeil, San Francisco, NFL	71	994	14.0	7
	Lance Alworth, San Diego, AFL	68	1,312	19.3	10
1967	George Sauer, N.Y. Jets, AFL	75	1,189	15.9	6
	Charley Taylor, Washington, NFL	70	990	14.1	9
1966	Lance Alworth, San Diego, AFL	73	1,383	18.9	13
	Charley Taylor, Washington, NFL	72	1,119	15.5	12
1965	Lionel Taylor, Denver, AFL	85	1,131	13.3	6
	Dave Parks, San Francisco, NFL	80	1,344	16.8	12
1964	Charley Hennigan, Houston, AFL	101	1,546	15.3	8
	Johnny Morris, Chicago, NFL	93	1,200	12.9	10
1963	Lionel Taylor, Denver, AFL	78	1,101	14.1	10
	Bobby Joe Conrad, St. Louis, NFL	73	967	13.2	10
1962	Lionel Taylor, Denver, AFL	77	908	11.8	4
	Bobby Mitchell, Washington, NFL	72	1,384	19.2	11
1961	Lionel Taylor, Denver, AFL	100	1,176	11.8	4
	Jim (Red) Phillips, Los Angeles, NFL	78	1,092	14.0	5
1960	Lionel Taylor, Denver, AFL	92	1,235	13.4	12
	Raymond Berry, Baltimore, NFL	74	1,298	17.5	10
1959	Raymond Berry, Baltimore	66	959	14.5	14
1958	Raymond Berry, Baltimore	56	794	14.2	9
	Pete Retzlaff, Philadelphia	56	766	13.7	2
1957	Billy Wilson, San Francisco	52	757	14.6	6
1956	Billy Wilson, San Francisco	60	889	14.8	5
1955	Pete Pihos, Philadelphia	62	864	13.9	7
1954	Pete Pihos, Philadelphia	60	872	14.5	10
	Billy Wilson, San Francisco	60	830	13.8	5
1953	Pete Pihos, Philadelphia	63	1,049	16.7	10
1952	Mac Speedie, Cleveland	62	911	14.7	5
1951	Elroy (Crazylegs) Hirsch, Los Angeles	66	1,495	22.7	17
1950	Tom Fears, Los Angeles	84	1,116	13.3	7
1949	Tom Fears, Los Angeles	77	1,013	13.2	9
1948	*Tom Fears, Los Angeles	51	698	13.7	4
1947	Jim Keane, Chi. Bears	64	910	14.2	10
1946	Jim Benton, Los Angeles	63	981	15.6	6
1945	Don Hutson, Green Bay	47	834	17.7	9
1944	Don Hutson, Green Bay	58	866	14.9	9
1943	Don Hutson, Green Bay	47	776	16.5	11
1942	Don Hutson, Green Bay	74	1,211	16.4	17
1941	Don Hutson, Green Bay	58	738	12.7	10
1940	*Don Looney, Philadelphia	58	707	12.2	4
1939	Don Hutson, Green Bay	34	846	24.9	6
1938	Gaynell Tinsley, Chi. Cardinals	41	516	12.6	1
1937	Don Hutson, Green Bay	41	552	13.5	7
1936	Don Hutson, Green Bay	34	536	15.8	8
1935	*Tod Goodwin, N.Y. Giants	26	432	16.6	4
1934	Joe Carter, Philadelphia	16	238	14.9	4
	Morris (Red) Badgro, N.Y. Giants	16	206	12.9	1
1933	John (Shipwreck) Kelly, Brooklyn	22	246	11.2	3
1932	Ray Flaherty, N.Y. Giants	21	350	16.7	3

*First season of professional football.

ANNUAL PASS RECEIVING LEADERS (YARDS)

Year	Player, Team	No.	Yards	Avg.	TD
2006	Chad Johnson, Cincinnati, AFC	87	1,369	15.7	7
	Roy Williams, Detroit, NFC	82	1,310	16.0	7
2005	Steve Smith, Carolina, NFC	103	1,563	15.2	12
	Chad Johnson, Cincinnati, AFC	97	1,432	14.8	9
2004	Muhsin Muhammad, Carolina, NFC	93	1,405	15.1	16
	Chad Johnson, Cincinnati, AFC	95	1,274	13.4	9
2003	Torry Holt, St. Louis, NFC	117	1,696	14.5	12
	Chad Johnson, Cincinnati, AFC	90	1,355	15.1	10
2002	Marvin Harrison, Indianapolis, AFC	143	1,722	12.0	11
	Randy Moss, Minnesota, NFC	106	1,347	12.7	7
2001	David Boston, Arizona, NFC	98	1,598	16.3	8
	Marvin Harrison, Indianapolis, AFC	109	1,524	14.0	15
2000	Torry Holt, St. Louis, NFC	82	1,635	19.9	6
	Rod Smith, Denver, AFC	100	1,602	16.0	8
1999	Marvin Harrison, Indianapolis, AFC	115	1,663	14.5	12
	Randy Moss, Minnesota, NFC	80	1,413	17.7	11
1998	Antonio Freeman, Green Bay, NFC	84	1,424	17.0	14
	Eric Moulds, Buffalo, AFC	67	1,368	20.4	9
1997	Rob Moore, Arizona, NFC	97	1,584	16.3	8
	Tim Brown, Oakland, AFC	104	1,408	13.5	5
1996	Isaac Bruce, St. Louis, NFC	84	1,338	15.9	7
	Jimmy Smith, Jacksonville, AFC	83	1,244	15.0	7
1995	Jerry Rice, San Francisco, NFC	122	1,848	15.1	15
	Tim Brown, Oakland, AFC	89	1,342	15.1	10
1994	Jerry Rice, San Francisco, NFC	112	1,499	13.4	13
	Tim Brown, L.A. Raiders, AFC	89	1,309	14.7	9
1993	Jerry Rice, San Francisco, NFC	98	1,503	15.3	15
	Tim Brown, L.A. Raiders, AFC	80	1,180	14.8	7
1992	Sterling Sharpe, Green Bay, NFC	108	1,461	13.5	13
	Anthony Miller, San Diego, AFC	72	1,060	14.7	7
1991	Michael Irvin, Dallas, NFC	93	1,523	16.4	8
	Haywood Jeffires, Houston, AFC	100	1,181	11.8	7
1990	Jerry Rice, San Francisco, NFC	100	1,502	15.0	13
	Haywood Jeffires, Houston, AFC	74	1,048	14.2	8
1989	Jerry Rice, San Francisco, NFC	82	1,483	18.1	17
	Andre Reed, Buffalo, AFC	88	1,312	14.9	9
1988	Henry Ellard, L.A. Rams, NFC	86	1,414	16.4	10
	Eddie Brown, Cincinnati, AFC	53	1,273	24.0	9
1987	J.T. Smith, St. Louis, NFC	91	1,117	12.3	8
	Carlos Carson, Kansas City, AFC	55	1,044	19.0	7
1986	Jerry Rice, San Francisco, NFC	86	1,570	18.3	15
	Stanley Morgan, New England, AFC	84	1,491	17.8	10
1985	Steve Largent, Seattle, AFC	79	1,287	16.3	6
	Mike Quick, Philadelphia, NFC	73	1,247	17.1	11
1984	Roy Green, St. Louis, NFC	78	1,555	19.9	12
	John Stallworth, Pittsburgh, AFC	80	1,395	17.4	11
1983	Mike Quick, Philadelphia, NFC	69	1,409	20.4	13
	Carlos Carson, Kansas City, AFC	80	1,351	16.9	7
1982	Wes Chandler, San Diego, AFC	49	1,032	21.1	9
	Dwight Clark, San Francisco, NFC	60	913	15.2	5
1981	Alfred Jenkins, Atlanta, NFC	70	1,358	19.4	13
	Frank Lewis, Buffalo, AFC	70	1,244	17.8	4
	Steve Watson, Denver, AFC	60	1,244	20.7	13
1980	John Jefferson, San Diego, AFC	82	1,340	16.3	13
	James Lofton, Green Bay, NFC	71	1,226	17.3	4
1979	Steve Largent, Seattle, AFC	66	1,237	18.7	9
	Ahmad Rashad, Minnesota, NFC	80	1,156	14.5	9
1978	Wesley Walker, N.Y. Jets, AFC	48	1,169	24.4	8
	Harold Carmichael, Philadelphia, NFC	55	1,072	19.5	8
1977	Drew Pearson, Dallas, NFC	48	870	18.1	2
	Ken Burrough, Houston, AFC	43	816	19.0	8
1976	Roger Carr, Baltimore, AFC	43	1,112	25.9	11
	*Sammy White, Minnesota, NFC	51	906	17.8	10
1975	Ken Burrough, Houston, AFC	53	1,063	20.1	8
	Mel Gray, St. Louis, NFC	48	926	19.3	11
1974	Cliff Branch, Oakland, AFC	60	1,092	18.2	13
	Drew Pearson, Dallas, NFC	62	1,087	17.5	2

Year	Player, Team	No.	Yards	Avg.	TD
1973	Harold Carmichael, Philadelphia, NFC	67	1,116	16.7	9
	*Isaac Curtis, Cincinnati, AFC	45	843	18.7	9
1972	Harold Jackson, Philadelphia, NFC	62	1,048	16.9	4
	Rich Caster, N.Y. Jets, AFC	39	833	21.4	10
1971	Otis Taylor, Kansas City, AFC	57	1,110	19.5	7
	Gene Washington, San Francisco, NFC	46	884	19.2	4
1970	Gene Washington, San Francisco, NFC	53	1,100	20.8	12
	Marlin Briscoe, Buffalo, AFC	57	1,036	18.2	8
1969	Warren Wells, Oakland, AFL	47	1,260	26.8	14
	Harold Jackson, Philadelphia, NFL	65	1,116	17.2	9
1968	Lance Alworth, San Diego, AFL	68	1,312	19.3	10
	Roy Jefferson, Pittsburgh, NFL	58	1,074	18.5	11
1967	Don Maynard, N.Y. Jets, AFL	71	1,434	20.3	10
	Ben Hawkins, Philadelphia, NFL	59	1,265	21.4	10
1966	Lance Alworth, San Diego, AFL	73	1,383	18.9	13
	Pat Studstill, Detroit, NFL	67	1,266	18.9	5
1965	Lance Alworth, San Diego, AFL	69	1,602	23.2	14
	Dave Parks, San Francisco, NFL	80	1,344	16.8	12
1964	Charley Hennigan, Houston, AFL	101	1,546	15.3	8
	Johnny Morris, Chicago, NFL	93	1,200	12.9	10
1963	Bobby Mitchell, Washington, NFL	69	1,436	20.8	7
	Art Powell, Oakland, AFL	73	1,304	17.8	16
1962	Bobby Mitchell, Washington, NFL	72	1,384	19.2	11
	Art Powell, N.Y. Titans, AFL	64	1,130	17.6	8
1961	Charley Hennigan, Houston, AFL	82	1,746	21.3	12
	Tommy McDonald, Philadelphia, NFL	64	1,144	17.9	13
1960	*Bill Groman, Houston, AFL	72	1,473	20.5	12
	Raymond Berry, Baltimore, NFL	74	1,298	17.5	10
1959	Raymond Berry, Baltimore	66	959	14.5	14
1958	Del Shofner, Los Angeles	51	1,097	21.5	8
1957	Raymond Berry, Baltimore	47	800	17.0	6
1956	Billy Howton, Green Bay	55	1,188	21.6	12
1955	Pete Pihos, Philadelphia	62	864	13.9	7
1954	Bob Boyd, Los Angeles	53	1,212	22.9	6
1953	Pete Pihos, Philadelphia	63	1,049	16.7	10
1952	*Bill Howton, Green Bay	53	1,231	23.2	13
1951	Elroy (Crazylegs) Hirsch, Los Angeles	66	1,495	22.7	17
1950	Tom Fears, Los Angeles	84	1,116	13.3	7
1949	Bob Mann, Detroit	66	1,014	15.4	4
1948	Mal Kutner, Chi. Cardinals	41	943	23.0	14
1947	Mal Kutner, Chi. Cardinals	43	944	21.9	7
1946	Jim Benton, Los Angeles	63	981	15.5	6
1945	Jim Benton, Cleveland	45	1,067	23.7	8
1944	Don Hutson, Green Bay	58	866	14.6	9
1943	Don Hutson, Green Bay	47	776	16.5	11
1942	Don Hutson, Green Bay	74	1,211	16.4	17
1941	Don Hutson, Green Bay	58	738	12.7	10
1940	*Don Looney, Philadelphia	58	707	12.2	4
1939	Don Hutson, Green Bay	34	846	24.9	6
1938	Don Hutson, Green Bay	32	548	17.1	9
1937	*Gaynell Tinsley, Chi. Cardinals	36	675	18.8	5
1936	Don Hutson, Green Bay	34	526	15.5	8
1935	Charley Malone, Boston	22	433	19.7	2
1934	Harry Ebding, Detroit	9	257	28.6	2
1933	*Paul Moss, Pittsburgh	18	383	21.3	2
1932	Johnny (Blood) McNally, Green Bay	19	326	17.2	3

First season of professional football.

ANNUAL PUNT RETURN LEADERS

Year	Player, Team	No.	Yards	Avg.	Long	TD
2006	Pacman Jones, Tennessee, AFC	34	440	12.9	90	3
	*Devin Hester, Chicago, NFC	47	600	12.8	84	3
2005	Reno Mahe, Philadelphia, NFC	21	269	12.8	44	0
	B.J. Sams, Baltimore, AFC	33	401	12.2	51	0
2004	Eddie Drummond, Detroit, NFC	24	316	13.2	83	2
	Dennis Northcutt, Cleveland, AFC	36	432	12.0	44	0
2003	Dante Hall, Kansas City, AFC	29	472	16.3	93	2
	Brian Westbrook, Philadelphia, NFC	20	306	15.3	84	2

Year	Player, Team	No.	Yards	Avg.	Long	TD
2002	Jimmy Williams, San Francisco, NFC	20	336	16.8	89	1
	Santana Moss, N.Y. Jets, AFC	25	413	16.5	63	2
2001	Troy Brown, New England, AFC	29	413	14.2	85	2
	Darrien Gordon, Atlanta, NFC	31	437	14.1	74	0
2000	Jermaine Lewis, Baltimore, AFC	36	578	16.1	89	0
	Az-Zahir Hakim, St. Louis, NFC	32	489	15.3	86	1
1999	*Charlie Rogers, Seattle, AFC	22	318	14.5	94	1
	*Mac Cody, Arizona, NFC	32	373	11.7	31	0
1998	Deion Sanders, Dallas, NFC	24	375	15.6	69	2
	Reggie Barlow, Jacksonville, AFC	43	555	12.9	85	1
1997	Jermaine Lewis, Baltimore, AFC	28	437	15.6	89	2
	David Palmer, Minnesota, NFC	34	444	13.1	57	0
1996	Desmond Howard, Green Bay, NFC	58	875	15.1	92	3
	Darrien Gordon, San Diego, AFC	36	537	14.9	81	1
1995	David Palmer, Minnesota, NFC	26	342	13.2	74	1
	Andre Coleman, San Diego, AFC	28	326	11.6	88	1
1994	Brian Mitchell, Washington, NFC	32	452	14.1	78	2
	Darrien Gordon, San Diego, AFC	36	475	13.2	90	2
1993	*Tyrone Hughes, New Orleans, NFC	37	503	13.6	83	2
	Eric Metcalf, Cleveland, AFC	36	464	12.9	91	2
1992	Johnny Bailey, Phoenix, NFC	20	263	13.2	65	0
	Rod Woodson, Pittsburgh, AFC	32	364	11.4	80	1
1991	Mel Gray, Detroit, NFC	25	385	15.4	78	1
	Rod Woodson, Pittsburgh, AFC	28	320	11.4	40	0
1990	Clarence Verdin, Indianapolis, AFC	31	396	12.8	36	0
	*Johnny Bailey, Chicago, NFC	36	399	11.1	95	1
1989	Walter Stanley, Detroit, NFC	36	496	13.8	74	0
	Clarence Verdin, Indianapolis, AFC	23	296	12.9	49	1
1988	John Taylor, San Francisco, NFC	44	556	12.6	95	2
	JoJo Townsell, N.Y. Jets, AFC	35	409	11.7	59	1
1987	Mel Gray, New Orleans, NFC	24	352	14.7	80	0
	Bobby Joe Edmonds, Seattle, AFC	20	251	12.6	40	0
1986	*Bobby Joe Edmonds, Seattle, AFC	34	419	12.3	75	1
	*Vai Sikahema, St. Louis, NFC	43	522	12.1	71	2
1985	Irving Fryar, New England, AFC	37	520	14.1	85	2
	Henry Ellard, L.A. Rams, NFC	37	501	13.5	80	1
1984	Mike Martin, Cincinnati, AFC	24	376	15.7	55	0
	Henry Ellard, L.A. Rams, NFC	30	403	13.4	83	2
1983	*Henry Ellard, L.A. Rams, NFC	16	217	13.6	72	1
	Kirk Springs, N.Y. Jets, AFC	23	287	12.5	76	1
1982	Rick Upchurch, Denver, AFC	15	242	16.1	78	2
	Billy Johnson, Atlanta, NFC	24	273	11.4	71	0
1981	LeRoy Irvin, Los Angeles, NFC	46	615	13.4	84	3
	*James Brooks, San Diego, AFC	22	290	13.2	42	0
1980	J.T. Smith, Kansas City, AFC	40	581	14.5	75	2
	*Kenny Johnson, Atlanta, NFC	23	281	12.2	56	0
1979	John Sciarra, Philadelphia, NFC	16	182	11.4	38	0
	*Tony Nathan, Miami, AFC	28	306	10.9	86	1
1978	Rick Upchurch, Denver, AFC	36	493	13.7	75	1
	Jackie Wallace, Los Angeles, NFC	52	618	11.9	58	0
1977	Billy Johnson, Houston, AFC	35	539	15.4	87	2
	Larry Marshall, Philadelphia, NFC	46	489	10.6	48	0
1976	Rick Upchurch, Denver, AFC	39	536	13.7	92	4
	Eddie Brown, Washington, NFC	48	646	13.5	71	1
1975	Billy Johnson, Houston, AFC	40	612	15.3	83	3
	Terry Metcalf, St. Louis, NFC	23	285	12.4	69	1
1974	Lemar Parrish, Cincinnati, AFC	18	338	18.8	90	2
	Dick Jauron, Detroit, NFC	17	286	16.8	58	0
1973	Bruce Taylor, San Francisco, NFC	15	207	13.8	61	0
	Ron Smith, San Diego, AFC	27	352	13.0	84	2
1972	Ken Ellis, Green Bay, NFC	14	215	15.4	80	1
	Chris Farasopoulos, N.Y. Jets, AFC	17	179	10.5	65	1
1971	Les (Speedy) Duncan, Washington, NFC	22	233	10.6	33	0
	Leroy Kelly, Cleveland, AFC	30	292	9.7	74	0
1970	Ed Podolak, Kansas City, AFC	23	311	13.5	60	0
	*Bruce Taylor, San Francisco, NFC	43	516	12.0	76	0
1969	Alvin Haymond, Los Angeles, NFL	33	435	13.2	52	0
	*Bill Thompson, Denver, AFL	25	288	11.5	40	0

Year	Player, Team	No.	Yards	Avg.	Long	TD
1968	Bob Hayes, Dallas, NFL	15	312	20.8	90	2
	Noland Smith, Kansas City, AFL	18	270	15.0	80	1
1967	Floyd Little, Denver, AFL	16	270	16.9	72	1
	Ben Davis, Cleveland, NFL	18	229	12.7	52	1
1966	Les (Speedy) Duncan, San Diego, AFL	18	238	13.2	81	1
	Johnny Roland, St. Louis, NFL	20	221	11.1	86	1
1965	Leroy Kelly, Cleveland, NFL	17	265	15.6	67	2
	Les (Speedy) Duncan, San Diego, AFL	30	464	15.5	66	2
1964	Bobby Jancik, Houston, AFL	12	220	18.3	82	1
	Tommy Watkins, Detroit, NFL	16	238	14.9	68	2
1963	Dick James, Washington, NFL	16	214	13.4	39	0
	Claude (Hoot) Gibson, Oakland, AFL	26	307	11.8	85	2
1962	Dick Christy, N.Y. Titans, AFL	15	250	16.7	73	2
	Pat Studstill, Detroit, NFL	29	457	15.8	44	0
1961	Dick Christy, N.Y. Titans, AFL	18	383	21.3	70	2
	Willie Wood, Green Bay, NFL	14	225	16.1	72	2
1960	*Abner Haynes, Dall. Texans, AFL	14	215	15.4	46	0
	Abe Woodson, San Francisco, NFL	13	174	13.4	48	0
1959	Johnny Morris, Chi. Bears	14	171	12.2	78	1
1958	Jon Arnett, Los Angeles	18	223	12.4	58	0
1957	Bert Zagers, Washington	14	217	15.5	76	2
1956	Ken Konz, Cleveland	13	187	14.4	65	1
1955	Ollie Matson, Chi. Cardinals	13	245	18.8	78	2
1954	*Veryl Switzer, Green Bay	24	306	12.8	93	1
1953	Charley Trippi, Chi. Cardinals	21	239	11.4	38	0
1952	Jack Christiansen, Detroit	15	322	21.5	79	2
1951	Claude (Buddy) Young, N.Y. Yanks	12	231	19.3	79	1
1950	*Herb Rich, Baltimore	12	276	23.0	86	1
1949	Verda (Vitamin T) Smith, Los Angeles	27	427	15.8	85	1
1948	George McAfee, Chi. Bears	30	417	13.9	60	1
1947	*Walt Slater, Pittsburgh	28	435	15.5	33	0
1946	Bill Dudley, Pittsburgh	27	385	14.3	52	0
1945	*Dave Ryan, Detroit	15	220	14.7	56	0
1944	*Steve Van Buren, Philadelphia	15	230	15.3	55	1
1943	Andy Farkas, Washington	15	168	11.2	33	0
1942	Merlyn Condit, Brooklyn	21	210	10.0	23	0
1941	Byron (Whizzer) White, Detroit	19	262	13.8	64	0

First season of professional football.

ANNUAL KICKOFF RETURN LEADERS

Year	Player, Team	No.	Yards	Avg.	Long	TD
2006	Justin Miller, N.Y. Jets, AFC	46	1,304	28.3	103	2
	*Devin Hester, Chicago, NFC	20	528	26.4	96	2
2005	Terrence McGee, Buffalo, AFC	46	1,391	30.2	99	1
	Koren Robinson, Minnesota, NFC	47	1,221	26.0	86	1
2004	Willie Ponder, N.Y. Giants, NFC	36	967	26.9	91	1
	Terrence McGee, Buffalo, AFC	52	1,370	26.3	104	3
2003	Jerry Azumah, Chicago, NFC	41	1,191	29.0	89	2
	*Bethel Johnson, New England, AFC	30	847	28.2	92	1
2002	MarTay Jenkins, Arizona, NFC	20	559	28.0	95	1
	Kevin Faulk, New England, AFC	26	725	27.9	87	2
2001	Ronney Jenkins, San Diego, AFC	58	1,541	26.6	93	2
	*Steve Smith, Carolina, NFC	56	1,431	25.6	99	2
2000	*Darrick Vaughn, Atlanta, NFC	39	1,082	27.7	100	3
	Derrick Mason, Tennessee, AFC	42	1,132	27.0	66	0
1999	Tony Horne, St. Louis, NFC	30	892	29.7	101	2
	Tremain Mack, Cincinnati, AFC	51	1,382	27.1	99	1
1998	*Terry Fair, Detroit, NFC	51	1,428	28.0	105	2
	Corey Harris, Baltimore, AFC	35	965	27.6	95	1
1997	Michael Bates, Carolina, NFC	47	1,281	27.3	56	0
	Aaron Glenn, N.Y. Jets, AFC	28	741	26.5	96	1
1996	Michael Bates, Carolina, NFC	33	998	30.2	93	1
	Tamarick Vanover, Kansas City, AFC	33	854	25.9	97	1
1995	Ron Carpenter, N.Y. Jets, AFC	20	553	27.7	58	0
	Brian Mitchell, Washington, NFC	55	1,408	25.6	59	0
1994	Mel Gray, Detroit, NFC	45	1,276	28.4	102	3
	Randy Baldwin, Cleveland, AFC	28	753	26.9	85	1
1993	Robert Brooks, Green Bay, NFC	23	611	26.6	95	1
	*Raghib Ismail, L.A. Raiders, AFC	25	605	24.2	66	0

Year	Player, Team	No.	Yards	Avg.	Long	TD
1992	Jon Vaughn, New England, AFC	20	564	28.2	100	1
	Deion Sanders, Atlanta, NFC	40	1,067	26.7	99	2
1991	Mel Gray, Detroit, NFC	36	929	25.8	71	0
	Nate Lewis, San Diego, AFC	23	578	25.1	95	1
1990	Kevin Clark, Denver, AFC	20	505	25.3	75	0
	David Meggett, N.Y. Giants, NFC	21	492	23.4	58	0
1989	Rod Woodson, Pittsburgh, AFC	36	982	27.3	84	1
	Mel Gray, Detroit, NFC	24	640	26.7	57	0
1988	*Tim Brown, L.A. Raiders, AFC	41	1,098	26.8	97	1
	Donnie Elder, Tampa Bay, NFC	34	772	22.7	51	0
1987	Sylvester Stamps, Atlanta, NFC	24	660	27.5	97	1
	Paul Palmer, Kansas City, AFC	38	923	24.3	95	2
1986	Dennis Gentry, Chicago, NFC	20	576	28.8	91	1
	Lupe Sanchez, Pittsburgh, AFC	25	591	23.6	64	0
1985	Ron Brown, L.A. Rams, NFC	28	918	32.8	98	3
	Glen Young, Cleveland, AFC	35	898	25.7	63	0
1984	*Bobby Humphery, N.Y. Jets, AFC	22	675	30.7	97	1
	Barry Redden, L.A. Rams, NFC	23	530	23.0	40	0
1983	Fulton Walker, Miami, AFC	36	962	26.7	78	0
	Darrin Nelson, Minnesota, NFC	18	445	24.7	50	0
1982	*Mike Mosley, Buffalo, AFC	18	487	27.1	66	0
	Alvin Hall, Detroit, NFC	16	426	26.6	96	1
1981	Mike Nelms, Washington, NFC	37	1,099	29.7	84	0
	Carl Roaches, Houston, AFC	28	769	27.5	96	1
1980	Horace Ivory, New England, AFC	36	992	27.6	98	1
	Rich Mauti, New Orleans, NFC	31	798	25.7	52	0
1979	Larry Brunson, Oakland, AFC	17	441	25.9	89	0
	Jimmy Edwards, Minnesota, NFC	44	1,103	25.1	83	0
1978	Steve Odom, Green Bay, NFC	25	677	27.1	95	1
	*Keith Wright, Cleveland, AFC	30	789	26.3	86	0
1977	*Raymond Clayborn, New England, AFC	28	869	31.0	101	3
	*Wilbert Montgomery, Philadelphia, NFC	23	619	26.9	99	1
1976	*Duriel Harris, Miami, AFC	17	559	32.9	69	0
	Cullen Bryant, Los Angeles, NFC	16	459	28.7	90	1
1975	*Walter Payton, Chicago, NFC	14	444	31.7	70	0
	Harold Hart, Oakland, AFC	17	518	30.5	102	1
1974	Terry Metcalf, St. Louis, NFC	20	623	31.2	94	1
	Greg Pruitt, Cleveland, AFC	22	606	27.5	88	1
1973	Carl Garrett, Chicago, NFC	16	486	30.4	67	0
	*Wallace Francis, Buffalo, AFC	23	687	29.9	101	2
1972	Ron Smith, Chicago, NFC	30	924	30.8	94	1
	*Bruce Laird, Baltimore, AFC	29	843	29.1	73	0
1971	Travis Williams, Los Angeles, NFC	25	743	29.7	105	1
	Eugene (Mercury) Morris, Miami, AFC	15	423	28.2	94	1
1970	Jim Duncan, Baltimore, AFC	20	707	35.4	99	1
	Cecil Turner, Chicago, NFC	23	752	32.7	96	4
1969	Bobby Williams, Detroit, NFL	17	563	33.1	96	1
	*Bill Thompson, Denver, AFL	18	513	28.5	63	0
1968	Preston Pearson, Baltimore, NFL	15	527	35.1	102	2
	*George Atkinson, Oakland, AFL	32	802	25.1	60	0
1967	*Travis Williams, Green Bay, NFL	18	739	41.1	104	4
	*Zeke Moore, Houston, AFL	14	405	28.9	92	1
1966	Gale Sayers, Chicago, NFL	23	718	31.2	93	2
	*Goldie Sellers, Denver, AFL	19	541	28.5	100	2
1965	Tommy Watkins, Detroit, NFL	17	584	34.4	94	0
	Abner Haynes, Denver, AFL	34	901	26.5	60	0
1964	*Clarence Childs, N.Y. Giants, NFL	34	987	29.0	100	1
	Bo Roberson, Oakland, AFL	36	975	27.1	59	0
1963	Abe Woodson, San Francisco, NFL	29	935	32.2	103	3
	Bobby Jancik, Houston, AFL	45	1,317	29.3	53	0
1962	Abe Woodson, San Francisco, NFL	37	1,157	31.3	79	0
	*Bobby Jancik, Houston, AFL	24	826	30.3	61	0
1961	Dick Bass, Los Angeles, NFL	23	698	30.3	64	0
	*Dave Grayson, Dall. Texans, AFL	16	453	28.3	73	0
1960	*Tom Moore, Green Bay, NFL	12	397	33.1	84	0
	Ken Hall, Houston, AFL	19	594	31.3	104	1
1959	Abe Woodson, San Francisco, NFL	13	382	29.4	105	1
1958	Ollie Matson, Chi. Cardinals	14	497	35.5	101	2
1957	*Jon Arnett, Los Angeles	18	504	28.0	98	1

Year	Player, Team	No.	Yards	Avg.	Long	TD
1956	*Tom Wilson, Los Angeles	15	477	31.8	103	1
1955	Al Carmichael, Green Bay	14	418	29.9	100	1
1954	Billy Reynolds, Cleveland	14	413	29.5	51	0
1953	Joe Arenas, San Francisco	16	551	34.4	82	0
1952	Lynn Chandnois, Pittsburgh	17	599	35.2	93	2
1951	Lynn Chandnois, Pittsburgh	12	390	32.5	55	0
1950	Verda (Vitamin T) Smith, Los Angeles	22	742	33.7	97	3
1949	*Don Doll, Detroit	21	536	25.5	56	0
1948	*Joe Scott, N.Y. Giants	20	569	28.5	99	1
1947	Eddie Saenz, Washington	29	797	27.5	94	2
1946	Abe Karnofsky, Boston	21	599	28.5	97	1
1945	Steve Van Buren, Philadelphia	13	373	28.7	98	1
1944	Bob Thurbon, Card.-Pitt.	12	291	24.3	55	0
1943	Ken Heineman, Brooklyn	16	444	27.8	69	0
1942	Marshall Goldberg, Chi. Cardinals	15	393	26.2	95	1
1941	Marshall Goldberg, Chi. Cardinals	12	290	24.2	41	0

*First season of professional football.

ANNUAL INTERCEPTION LEADERS

Year	Player, Team	No.	Yards	TD
2006	Champ Bailey, Denver, AFC	10	162	1
	Asante Samuel, New England, AFC	10	120	0
	Walt Harris, San Francisco, NFC	8	84	1
	Charles Woodson, Green Bay, NFC	8	61	1
2005	Ty Law, N.Y. Jets, AFC	10	195	1
	Deltha O'Neal, Cincinnati, AFC	10	103	0
	Darren Sharper, Minnesota, NFC	9	276	2
2004	Ed Reed, Baltimore, AFC	9	358	1
	Ken Lucas, Seattle, AFC	6	46	1
	*Chris Gamble, Carolina, NFC	6	15	0
2003	Tony Parrish, San Francisco, NFC	9	202	0
	Brian Russell, Minnesota, NFC	9	185	0
	Ed Reed, Baltimore, AFC	7	132	1
	Marcus Coleman, Houston, AFC	7	95	0
	Patrick Surtain, Miami, AFC	7	59	0
2002	Rod Woodson, Oakland, AFC	8	225	2
	Brian Kelly, Tampa Bay, NFC	8	68	0
2001	*Anthony Henry, Cleveland, AFC	10	177	1
	Ronde Barber, Tampa Bay, NFC	10	86	1
2000	Darren Sharper, Green Bay, NFC	9	109	0
	Samari Rolle, Tennessee, AFC	7	140	1
	Brian Walker, Miami, AFC	7	80	0
1999	Rod Woodson, Baltimore, AFC	7	195	2
	Sam Madison, Miami, AFC	7	164	1
	James Hasty, Kansas City, AFC	7	98	2
	Donnie Abraham, Tampa Bay, NFC	7	115	2
	Troy Vincent, Philadelphia, NFC	7	91	0
1998	Ty Law, New England, AFC	9	133	1
	Kwamie Lassiter, Arizona, NFC	8	80	0
1997	Ryan McNeil, St. Louis, NFC	9	127	1
	Mark McMillian, Kansas City, AFC	8	274	3
	Darryl Williams, Seattle, AFC	8	172	1
1996	Tyrone Braxton, Denver, AFC	9	128	1
	Keith Lyle, St. Louis, NFC	9	152	0
1995	*Orlando Thomas, Minnesota, NFC	9	108	1
	Willie Williams, Pittsburgh, AFC	7	122	1
1994	Eric Turner, Cleveland, AFC	9	199	1
	Aeneas Williams, Arizona, NFC	9	89	0
1993	Eugene Robinson, Seattle, AFC	9	80	1
	Nate Odomes, Buffalo, AFC	9	65	0
	Deion Sanders, Atlanta, NFC	7	91	0
1992	Henry Jones, Buffalo, AFC	8	263	2
	Audray McMillian, Minnesota, NFC	8	157	2
1991	Ronnie Lott, L.A. Raiders, AFC	8	52	0
	Ray Crockett, Detroit, NFC	6	141	1
	Deion Sanders, Atlanta, NFC	6	119	1
	*Aeneas Williams, Phoenix, NFC	6	60	0
	Tim McKyer, Atlanta, NFC	6	24	0

Year	Player, Team	No.	Yards	TD
1990	*Mark Carrier, Chicago, NFC	10	39	0
	Richard Johnson, Houston, AFC	8	100	1
1989	Felix Wright, Cleveland, AFC	9	91	1
	Eric Allen, Philadelphia, NFC	8	38	0
1988	Scott Case, Atlanta, NFC	10	47	0
	Erik McMillan, N.Y. Jets, AFC	8	168	2
1987	Barry Wilburn, Washington, NFC	9	135	1
	Mike Prior, Indianapolis, AFC	6	57	0
	Mark Kelso, Buffalo, AFC	6	25	0
	Keith Bostic, Houston, AFC	6	-14	0
1986	Ronnie Lott, San Francisco, NFC	10	134	1
	Deron Cherry, Kansas City, AFC	9	150	0
1985	Everson Walls, Dallas, NFC	9	31	0
	Albert Lewis, Kansas City, AFC	8	59	0
	Eugene Daniel, Indianapolis, AFC	8	53	0
1984	Ken Easley, Seattle, AFC	10	126	2
	*Tom Flynn, Green Bay, NFC	9	106	0
1983	Mark Murphy, Washington, NFC	9	127	0
	Ken Riley, Cincinnati, AFC	8	89	2
	Vann McElroy, L.A. Raiders, AFC	8	68	0
1982	Everson Walls, Dallas, NFC	7	61	0
	Ken Riley, Cincinnati, AFC	5	88	1
	Bobby Jackson, N.Y. Jets, AFC	5	84	1
	Dwayne Woodruff, Pittsburgh, AFC	5	53	0
	Donnie Shell, Pittsburgh, AFC	5	27	0
1981	*Everson Walls, Dallas, NFC	11	133	0
	John Harris, Seattle, AFC	10	155	2
1980	Lester Hayes, Oakland, AFC	13	273	1
	Nolan Cromwell, Los Angeles, NFC	8	140	1
1979	Mike Reinfeldt, Houston, AFC	12	205	0
	Lemar Parrish, Washiongton, NFC	9	65	0
1978	Thom Darden, Cleveland, AFC	10	200	0
	Ken Stone, St. Louis, NFC	9	139	0
	Willie Buchanon, Green Bay, NFC	9	93	1
1977	Lyle Blackwood, Baltimore, AFC	10	163	0
	Rolland Lawrence, Atlanta, NFC	7	138	0
1976	Monte Jackson, Los Angeles, NFC	10	173	3
	Ken Riley, Cincinnati, AFC	9	141	1
1975	Mel Blount, Pittsburgh, AFC	11	121	0
	Paul Krause, Minnesota, NFC	10	201	0
1974	Emmitt Thomas, Kansas City, AFC	12	214	2
	Ray Brown, Atlanta, NFC	8	164	1
1973	Dick Anderson, Miami, AFC	8	163	2
	Mike Wagner, Pittsburgh, AFC	8	134	0
	Bobby Bryant, Minnesota, NFC	7	105	1
1972	Bill Bradley, Philadelphia, NFC	9	73	0
	Mike Sensibaugh, Kansas City, AFC	8	65	0
1971	Bill Bradley, Philadelphia, NFC	11	248	0
	Ken Houston, Houston, AFC	9	220	4

Year	Player, Team	No.	Yards	TD
1970	Johnny Robinson, Kansas City, AFC	10	155	0
	Dick LeBeau, Detroit, NFC	9	96	0
1969	Mel Renfro, Dallas, NFL	10	118	0
	Emmitt Thomas, Kansas City, AFL	9	146	1
1968	Dave Grayson, Oakland, AFL	10	195	1
	Willie Williams, N.Y. Giants, NFL	10	103	0
1967	Miller Farr, Houston, AFL	10	264	3
	*Lem Barney, Detroit, NFL	10	232	3
	Tom Janik, Buffalo, AFL	10	222	2
	Dave Whitsell, New Orleans, NFL	10	178	2
	Dick Westmoreland, Miami, AFL	10	127	1
1966	Larry Wilson, St. Louis, NFL	10	180	2
	Johnny Robinson, Kansas City, AFL	10	136	1
	Bobby Hunt, Kansas City, AFL	10	113	0
1965	W.K. Hicks, Houston, AFL	9	156	1
	Bobby Boyd, Baltimore, NFL	9	78	1
1964	Dainard Paulson, N.Y. Jets, AFL	12	157	1
	*Paul Krause, Washington, NFL	12	140	1
1963	Fred Glick, Houston, AFL	12	180	1
	Dick Lynch, N.Y. Giants, NFL	9	251	3
	Roosevelt Taylor, Chicago, NFL	9	172	1
1962	Lee Riley, N.Y. Titans, AFL	11	122	0
	Willie Wood, Green Bay, NFL	9	132	0
1961	Billy Atkins, Buffalo, AFL	10	158	0
	Dick Lynch, N.Y. Giants, NFL	9	60	0
1960	*Austin (Goose) Gonsoulin, Denver, AFL	11	98	0
	Dave Baker, San Francisco, NFL	10	96	0
	Jerry Norton, St. Louis, NFL	10	96	0
1959	Dean Derby, Pittsburgh	7	127	0
	Milt Davis, Baltimore	7	119	1
	Don Shinnick, Baltimore	7	70	0
1958	Jim Patton, N.Y. Giants	11	183	0
1957	Milt Davis, Baltimore	10	219	2
	Jack Christiansen, Detroit	10	137	1
	Jack Butler, Pittsburgh	10	85	0
1956	Linden Crow, Chi. Cardinals	11	170	0
1955	Will Sherman, Los Angeles	11	101	0
1954	Dick (Night Train) Lane, Chi. Cardinals	10	181	0
1953	Jack Christiansen, Detroit	12	238	1
1952	*Dick (Night Train) Lane, Los Angeles	14	298	2
1951	Otto Schnellbacher, N.Y. Giants	11	194	2
1950	Orban (Spec) Sanders, N.Y. Yanks	13	199	0
1949	Bob Nussbaumer, Chi. Cardinals	12	157	0
1948	*Dan Sandifer, Washington	13	258	2
1947	Frank Reagan, N.Y. Giants	10	203	0
	Frank Seno, Boston	10	100	0
1946	Bill Dudley, Pittsburgh	10	242	1
1945	Roy Zimmerman, Philadelphia	7	90	0
1944	*Howard Livingston, N.Y. Giants	9	172	1
1943	Sammy Baugh, Washington	11	112	0
1942	Clyde (Bulldog) Turner, Chi. Bears	8	96	1
1941	Marshall Goldberg, Chi. Cardinals	7	54	0
	*Art Jones, Pittsburgh	7	35	0
1940	Clarence (Ace) Parker, Brooklyn	6	146	1
	Kent Ryan, Detroit	6	65	0
	Don Hutson, Green Bay	6	24	0

*First season of professional football.

ANNUAL PUNTING LEADERS

Year	Player, Team	No.	Avg.	Long
2006	Mat McBriar, Dallas, NFC	56	48.2	75
	Shane Lechler, Oakland, AFC	77	47.5	67
2005	Brian Moorman, Buffalo, AFC	71	45.7	68
	Josh Bidwell, Tampa Bay, NFC	90	45.6	61
2004	Shane Lechler, Oakland, AFC	73	46.7	67
	Tom Tupa, Washington, NFC	103	44.1	61
2003	Shane Lechler, Oakland, AFC	96	46.9	73
	Todd Sauerbrun, Carolina, NFC	77	44.6	64
2002	Todd Sauerbrun, Carolina, NFC	104	45.5	67
	Chris Hanson, Jacksonville, AFC	81	44.2	64
2001	Todd Sauerbrun, Carolina, NFC	93	47.5	73
	Shane Lechler, Oakland, AFC	73	46.2	65
2000	Darren Bennett, San Diego, AFC	92	46.2	66
	Mitch Berger, Minnesota, NFC	62	44.7	60
1999	Tom Rouen, Denver, AFC	84	46.5	65
	Mitch Berger, Minnesota, NFC	61	45.4	75
1998	Craig Hentrich, Tennessee, AFC	69	47.2	71
	Mark Royals, New Orleans, NFL	88	45.6	64
1997	Mark Royals, New Orleans, NFC	88	45.9	66
	Tom Tupa, New England, AFC	78	45.8	73
1996	John Kidd, Miami, AFC	78	46.3	63
	Matt Turk, Washington, NFC	75	45.1	63
1995	Rick Tuten, Seattle, AFC	83	45.0	73
	Sean Landeta, St. Louis, NFC	83	44.3	63
1994	Sean Landeta, L.A. Rams, NFC	78	44.8	62
	Jeff Gossett, L.A. Raiders, AFC	77	43.9	65
1993	Greg Montgomery, Houston, AFC	54	45.6	77
	Jim Arnold, Detroit, NFC	72	44.5	68
1992	Greg Montgomery, Houston, AFC	53	46.9	66
	Harry Newsome, Minnesota, NFC	72	45.0	84
1991	Reggie Roby, Miami, AFC	54	45.7	64
	Harry Newsome, Minnesota, AFC	68	45.5	65
1990	Mike Horan, Denver, AFC	58	44.4	67
	Sean Landeta, N.Y. Giants, NFC	75	44.1	67
1989	Rich Camarillo, Phoenix, NFC	76	43.4	58
	Greg Montgomery, Houston, AFC	56	43.3	63
1988	Harry Newsome, Pittsburgh, AFC	65	45.4	62
	Jim Arnold, Detroit, NFC	97	42.4	69
1987	Rick Donnelly, Atlanta, NFC	61	44.0	62
	Ralf Mojsiejenko, San Diego, AFC	67	42.9	57
1986	Rohn Stark, Indianapolis, AFC	76	45.2	63
	Sean Landeta, N.Y. Giants, NFC	79	44.8	61
1985	Rohn Stark, Indianapolis, AFC	78	45.9	68
	*Rick Donnelly, Atlanta, NFC	59	43.6	68
1984	Jim Arnold, Kansas City, AFC	98	44.9	63
	*Brian Hansen, New Orleans, NFC	69	43.8	66
1983	Rohn Stark, Baltimore, AFC	91	45.3	68
	Frank Garcia, Tampa Bay, NFC	95	42.2	64
1982	Luke Prestridge, Denver, AFC	45	45.0	65
	Carl Birdsong, St. Louis, NFC	54	43.8	65
1981	Pat McInally, Cincinnati, AFC	72	45.4	62
	Tom Skladany, Detroit, NFC	64	43.5	74
1980	Dave Jennings, N.Y. Giants, NFC	94	44.8	63
	Luke Prestridge, Denver, AFC	70	43.9	57
1979	*Bob Grupp, Kansas City, AFC	89	43.6	74
	Dave Jennings, N.Y. Giants, NFC	104	42.7	72
1978	Pat McInally, Cincinnati, AFC	91	43.1	65
	*Tom Skladany, Detroit, NFC	86	42.5	63
1977	Ray Guy, Oakland, AFC	59	43.3	74
	Tom Blanchard, New Orleans, NFC	82	42.4	66
1976	Marv Bateman, Buffalo, AFC	86	42.8	78
	John James, Atlanta, NFC	101	42.1	67
1975	Ray Guy, Oakland, AFC	68	43.8	64
	Herman Weaver, Detroit, NFC	80	42.0	61
1974	Ray Guy, Oakland, AFC	74	42.2	66
	Tom Blanchard, New Orleans, NFC	88	42.1	71
1973	Jerrel Wilson, Kansas City, AFC	80	45.5	68
	*Tom Wittum, San Francisco, NFC	79	43.7	62
1972	Jerrel Wilson, Kansas City, AFC	66	44.8	69
	Dave Chapple, Los Angeles, NFC	53	44.2	70
1971	Dave Lewis, Cincinnati, AFC	72	44.8	56
	Tom McNeill, Philadelphia, NFC	73	42.0	64
1970	Dave Lewis, Cincinnati, AFC	79	46.2	63
	*Julian Fagan, New Orleans, NFC	77	42.5	64
1969	David Lee, Baltimore, NFL	57	45.3	66
	Dennis Partee, San Diego, AFL	71	44.6	62

Year	Player, Team	No.	Avg.	Long
1968	Jerrel Wilson, Kansas City, AFL	63	45.1	70
	Billy Lothridge, Atlanta, NFL	75	44.3	70
1967	Bob Scarpitto, Denver, AFL	105	44.9	73
	Billy Lothridge, Atlanta, NFL	87	43.7	62
1966	Bob Scarpitto, Denver, AFL	76	45.8	70
	*David Lee, Baltimore, NFL	49	45.6	64
1965	Gary Collins, Cleveland, NFL	65	46.7	71
	Jerrel Wilson, Kansas City, AFL	69	45.4	64
1964	Bobby Walden, Minnesota, NFL	72	46.4	73
	Jim Fraser, Denver, AFL	73	44.2	67
1963	Yale Lary, Detroit, NFL	35	48.9	73
	Jim Fraser, Denver, AFL	81	44.4	66
1962	Tommy Davis, San Francisco, NFL	48	45.6	82
	Jim Fraser, Denver, AFL	55	43.6	75
1961	Yale Lary, Detroit, NFL	52	48.4	71
	Billy Atkins, Buffalo, AFL	85	44.5	70
1960	Jerry Norton, St. Louis, NFL	39	45.6	62
	*Paul Maguire, L.A. Chargers, AFL	43	40.5	61
1959	Yale Lary, Detroit	45	47.1	67
1958	Sam Baker, Washington	48	45.4	64
1957	Don Chandler, N.Y. Giants	60	44.6	61
1956	Norm Van Brocklin, Los Angeles	48	43.1	72
1955	Norm Van Brocklin, Los Angeles	60	44.6	61
1954	Pat Brady, Pittsburgh	66	43.2	72
1953	Pat Brady, Pittsburgh	80	46.9	64
1952	Horace Gillom, Cleveland	61	45.7	73
1951	Horace Gillom, Cleveland	73	45.5	66
1950	*Fred (Curly) Morrison, Chi. Bears	57	43.3	65
1949	*Mike Boyda, N.Y. Bulldogs	56	44.2	61
1948	Joe Muha, Philadelphia	57	47.3	82
1947	Jack Jacobs, Green Bay	57	43.5	74
1946	Roy McKay, Green Bay	64	42.7	64
1945	Roy McKay, Green Bay	44	41.2	73
1944	Frank Sinkwich, Detroit	45	41.0	73
1943	Sammy Baugh, Washington	50	45.9	81
1942	Sammy Baugh, Washington	37	48.2	74
1941	Sammy Baugh, Washington	30	48.7	75
1940	Sammy Baugh, Washington	35	51.4	85
1939	*Parker Hall, Cleveland	58	40.8	80

*First season of professional football.

ANNUAL LEADERS IN SACKS (SINCE 1982)

Year	Player, Team	Sacks
2006	Shawne Merriman, San Diego, AFC	17.0
	Aaron Kampman, Green Bay, NFC	15.5
2005	Derrick Burgess, Oakland, AFC	16.0
	Osi Umenyiora, N.Y. Giants, NFC	14.5
2004	Dwight Freeney, Indianapolis, AFC	16.0
	Bertrand Berry, Arizona, NFC	14.5
2003	Michael Strahan, N.Y. Giants, NFC	18.5
	Adewale Ogunleye, Miami, AFC	15.0
2002	Jason Taylor, Miami, AFC	18.5
	Simeon Rice, Tampa Bay, NFC	15.5
2001	Michael Strahan, N.Y. Giants, NFC	22.5
	Peter Boulware, Baltimore, AFC	15.0
2000	La'Roi Glover, New Orleans, NFC	17.0
	Trace Armstrong, Miami, AFC	16.5
1999	Kevin Carter, St. Louis, NFC	17.0
	*Jevon Kearse, Tennessee, AFC	14.5
1998	Michael Sinclair, Seattle, AFC	16.5
	Reggie White, Green Bay, NFC	16.0
1997	John Randle, Minnesota, NFC	15.5
	Bruce Smith, Buffalo, AFC	14.0
1996	Kevin Greene, Carolina, NFC	14.5
	Michael McCrary, Seattle, AFC	13.5
	Bruce Smith, Buffalo, AFC	13.5
1995	Bryce Paup, Buffalo, AFC	17.5
	William Fuller, Philadelphia, NFC	13.0

Year	Team	Points
	Wayne Martin, New Orleans, NFC	13.0
1994	Kevin Greene, Pittsburgh, AFC	14.0
	Ken Harvey, Washington, NFC	13.5
	John Randle, Minnesota, NFC	13.5
1993	Neil Smith, Kansas City, AFC	15.0
	Renaldo Turnbull, New Orleans, NFC	13.0
	Reggie White, Green Bay, NFC	13.0
1992	Clyde Simmons, Philadelphia, NFC	19.0
	Leslie O'Neal, San Diego, AFC	17.0
1991	Pat Swilling, New Orleans, NFC	17.0
	William Fuller, Houston, AFC	15.0
1990	Derrick Thomas, Kansas City, AFC	20.0
	Charles Haley, San Francisco, NFC	16.0
1989	Chris Doleman, Minnesota, NFC	21.0
	Lee Williams, San Diego, AFC	14.0
1988	Reggie White, Philadelphia, NFC	18.0
	Greg Townsend, L.A. Raiders, AFC	11.5
1987	Reggie White, Philadelphia, NFC	21.0
	Andre Tippett, New England, AFC	12.5
1986	Lawrence Taylor, N.Y. Giants, NFC	20.5
	Sean Jones, L.A. Raiders, AFC	15.5
1985	Richard Dent, Chicago, NFC	17.0
	Andre Tippett, New England, AFC	16.5
1984	Mark Gastineau, N.Y. Jets, AFC	22.0
	Richard Dent, Chicago, NFC	17.5
1983	Mark Gastineau, N.Y. Jets, AFC	19.0
	Fred Dean, San Francisco, NFC	17.5
1982	Doug Martin, Minnesota, NFC	11.5
	Jesse Baker, Houston, AFC	7.5

*First season of professional football.

POINTS SCORED

Year	Team	Points
2006	San Diego, AFC	492
	Chicago, NFC	427
2005	Seattle, NFC	452
	Indianapolis, AFC	439
2004	Indianapolis, AFC	522
	Green Bay, NFC	424
2003	Kansas City, AFC	484
	St. Louis, NFC	447
2002	Kansas City, AFC	467
	New Orleans, NFC	432
2001	St. Louis, NFC	503
	Indianapolis, AFC	413
2000	St. Louis, NFC	540
	Denver, AFC	485
1999	St. Louis, NFC	526
	Indianapolis, AFC	423
1998	Minnesota, NFC	556
	Denver, AFC	501
1997	Denver, AFC	472
	Green Bay, NFC	422
1996	Green Bay, NFC	456
	New England, AFC	418
1995	San Francisco, NFC	457
	Pittsburgh, AFC	407
1994	San Francisco, NFC	505
	Miami, AFC	389
1993	San Francisco, NFC	473
	Denver, AFC	373
1992	San Francisco, NFC	431
	Buffalo, AFC	381
1991	Washington, NFC	485
	Buffalo, AFC	458
1990	Buffalo, AFC	428
	Philadelphia, NFC	396
1989	San Francisco, NFC	442
	Buffalo, AFC	409

Year	Team	Points
1988	Cincinnati, AFC	448
	L.A. Rams, NFC	407
1987	San Francisco, NFC	459
	Cleveland, AFC	390
1986	Miami, AFC	430
	Minnesota, NFC	398
1985	San Diego, AFC	467
	Chicago, NFC	456
1984	Miami, AFC	513
	San Francisco, NFC	475
1983	Washington, NFC	541
	L.A. Raiders, AFC	442
1982	San Diego, AFC	288
	Dallas, NFC	226
	Green Bay, NFC	226
1981	San Diego, AFC	478
	Atlanta, NFC	426
1980	Dallas, NFC	454
	New England, AFC	441
1979	Pittsburgh, AFC	416
	Dallas, NFC	371
1978	Dallas, NFC	384
	Miami, AFC	372
1977	Oakland, AFC	351
	Dallas, NFC	345
1976	Baltimore, AFC	417
	Los Angeles, NFC	351
1975	Buffalo, AFC	420
	Minnesota, NFC	377
1974	Oakland, AFC	355
	Washington, NFC	320
1973	Los Angeles, NFC	388
	Denver, AFC	354
1972	Miami, AFC	385
	San Francisco, NFC	353
1971	Dallas, NFC	406
	Oakland, AFC	344
1970	San Francisco, NFC	352
	Baltimore, AFC	321
1969	Minnesota, NFL	379
	Oakland, AFL	377
1968	Oakland, AFL	453
	Dallas, NFL	431
1967	Oakland, AFL	468
	Los Angeles, NFL	398
1966	Kansas City, AFL	448
	Dallas, NFL	445
1965	San Francisco, NFL	421
	San Diego, AFL	340
1964	Baltimore, NFL	428
	Buffalo, AFL	400
1963	N.Y. Giants, NFL	448
	San Diego, AFL	399
1962	Green Bay, NFL	415
	Dall. Texans, AFL	389
1961	Houston, AFL	513
	Green Bay, NFL	391
1960	N.Y. Titans, AFL	382
	Cleveland, NFL	362
1959	Baltimore	374
1958	Baltimore	381
1957	Los Angeles	307
1956	Chi. Bears	363
1955	Cleveland	349
1954	Detroit	337
1953	San Francisco	372
1952	Los Angeles	349
1951	Los Angeles	392
1950	Los Angeles	466

Year	Team	Points
1949	Philadelphia	364
1948	Chi. Cardinals	395
1947	Chi. Bears	363
1946	Chi. Bears	289
1945	Philadelphia	272
1944	Philadelphia	267
1943	Chi. Bears	303
1942	Chi. Bears	376
1941	Chi. Bears	396
1940	Washington	245
1939	Chi. Bears	298
1938	Green Bay	223
1937	Green Bay	220
1936	Green Bay	248
1935	Chi. Bears	192
1934	Chi. Bears	286
1933	N.Y. Giants	244
1932	Chi. Bears	160

TOTAL YARDS GAINED

Year	Team	Yards
2006	New Orleans, NFC	6,264
	Indianapolis, AFC	6,070
2005	Kansas City, AFC	6,192
	Seattle, NFC	5,915
2004	Kansas City, AFC	6,695
	Green Bay, NFC	6,357
2003	Minnesota, NFC	6,294
	Kansas City, AFC	5,910
2002	Oakland, AFC	6,237
	Minnesota, NFC	6,192
2001	St. Louis, NFC	6,690
	Indianapolis, AFC	5,955
2000	St. Louis, NFC	7,075
	Denver, AFC	6,554
1999	St. Louis, NFC	6,412
	Indianapolis, AFC	5,726
1998	San Francisco, NFC	6,800
	Denver, AFC	6,092
1997	Denver, AFC	5,872
	Detroit, NFC	5,798
1996	Denver, AFC	5,791
	Philadelphia, NFC	5,627
1995	Detroit, NFC	6,113
	Denver, AFC	6,040
1994	Miami, AFC	6,078
	San Francisco, NFC	6,060
1993	San Francisco, NFC	6,435
	Miami, AFC	5,812
1992	San Francisco, NFC	6,195
	Buffalo, AFC	5,893
1991	Buffalo, AFC	6,252
	San Francisco, NFC	5,858
1990	Houston, AFC	6,222
	San Francisco, NFC	5,895
1989	San Francisco, NFC	6,268
	Cincinnati, AFC	6,101
1988	Cincinnati, AFC	6,057
	San Francisco, NFC	5,900
1987	San Francisco, NFC	5,987
	Denver, AFC	5,624
1986	Cincinnati, AFC	6,490
	San Francisco, NFC	6,082
1985	San Diego, AFC	6,535
	San Francisco, NFC	5,920
1984	Miami, AFC	6,936
	San Francisco, NFC	6,366
1983	San Diego, AFC	6,197
	Green Bay, NFC	6,172

Year	Team	Yards
1982	San Diego, AFC	4,048
	San Francisco, NFC	3,242
1981	San Diego, AFC	6,744
	Detroit, NFC	5,933
1980	San Diego, AFC	6,410
	Los Angeles, NFC	6,006
1979	Pittsburgh, AFC	6,258
	Dallas, NFC	5,968
1978	New England, AFC	5,965
	Dallas, NFC	5,959
1977	Dallas, NFC	4,812
	Oakland, AFC	4,736
1976	Baltimore, AFC	5,236
	St. Louis, NFC	5,136
1975	Buffalo, AFC	5,467
	Dallas, NFC	5,025
1974	Dallas, NFC	4,983
	Oakland, AFC	4,718
1973	Los Angeles, NFC	4,906
	Oakland, AFC	4,773
1972	Miami, AFC	5,036
	N.Y. Giants, NFC	4,483
1971	Dallas, NFC	5,035
	San Diego, AFC	4,738
1970	Oakland, AFC	4,829
	San Francisco, NFC	4,503
1969	Dallas, NFL	5,122
	Oakland, AFL	5,036
1968	Oakland, AFL	5,696
	Dallas, NFL	5,117
1967	N.Y. Jets, AFL	5,152
	Baltimore, NFL	5,008
1966	Dallas, NFL	5,145
	Kansas City, AFL	5,114
1965	San Francisco, NFL	5,270
	San Diego, AFL	5,188
1964	Buffalo, AFL	5,206
	Baltimore, NFL	4,779
1963	San Diego, AFL	5,153
	N.Y. Giants, NFL	5,024
1962	N.Y. Giants, NFL	5,005
	Houston, AFL	4,971
1961	Houston, AFL	6,288
	Philadelphia, NFL	5,112
1960	Houston, AFL	4,936
	Baltimore, NFL	4,245
1959	Baltimore	4,458
1958	Baltimore	4,539
1957	Los Angeles	4,143
1956	Chi. Bears	4,537
1955	Chi. Bears	4,316
1954	Los Angeles	5,187
1953	Philadelphia	4,811
1952	Cleveland	4,352
1951	Los Angeles	5,506
1950	Los Angeles	5,420
1949	Chi. Bears	4,873
1948	Chi. Cardinals	4,705
1947	Chi. Bears	5,053
1946	Los Angeles	3,793
1945	Washington	3,549
1944	Chi. Bears	3,239
1943	Chi. Bears	4,045
1942	Chi. Bears	3,900
1941	Chi. Bears	4,265
1940	Green Bay	3,400
1939	Chi. Bears	3,988
1938	Green Bay	3,037
1937	Green Bay	3,201

Year	Team	Yards
1936	Detroit	3,703
1935	Chi. Bears	3,454
1934	Chi. Bears	3,900
1933	N.Y. Giants	2,973
1932	Chi. Bears	2,755

YARDS RUSHING

Year	Team	Yards
2006	Atlanta, NFC	2,939
	San Diego, AFC	2,578
2005	Atlanta, NFC	2,546
	Denver, AFC	2,539
2004	Atlanta, NFC	2,672
	Pittsburgh, AFC	2,464
2003	Baltimore, AFC	2,674
	Green Bay, NFC	2,558
2002	Minnesota, NFC	2,507
	Miami, AFC	2,502
2001	Pittsburgh, AFC	2,774
	San Francisco, NFC	2,244
2000	Oakland, AFC	2,470
	Minnesota, NFC	2,129
1999	San Francisco, NFC	2,095
	Jacksonville, AFC	2,091
1998	San Francisco, NFC	2,544
	Denver, AFC	2,468
1997	Pittsburgh, AFC	2,479
	Detroit, NFC	2,464
1996	Denver, AFC	2,362
	Washington, NFC	1,910
1995	Kansas City, AFC	2,222
	Dallas, NFC	2,201
1994	Pittsburgh, AFC	2,180
	Detroit, NFC	2,080
1993	N.Y. Giants, NFC	2,210
	Seattle, AFC	2,015
1992	Buffalo, AFC	2,436
	Philadelphia, NFC	2,388
1991	Buffalo, AFC	2,381
	Minnesota, NFC	2,201
1990	Philadelphia, NFC	2,556
	San Diego, AFC	2,257
1989	Cincinnati, AFC	2,483
	Chicago, NFC	2,287
1988	Cincinnati, AFC	2,710
	San Francisco, NFC	2,523
1987	San Francisco, NFC	2,237
	L.A. Raiders, AFC	2,197
1986	Chicago, NFC	2,700
	Cincinnati, AFC	2,533
1985	Chicago, NFC	2,761
	Indianapolis, AFC	2,439
1984	Chicago, NFC	2,974
	N.Y. Jets, AFC	2,189
1983	Chicago, NFC	2,727
	Baltimore, AFC	2,695
1982	Buffalo, AFC	1,371
	Dallas, NFC	1,313
1981	Detroit, NFC	2,795
	Kansas City, AFC	2,633
1980	Los Angeles, NFC	2,799
	Houston, AFC	2,635
1979	N.Y. Jets, AFC	2,646
	St. Louis, NFC	2,582
1978	New England, AFC	3,165
	Dallas, NFC	2,783
1977	Chicago, NFC	2,811
	Oakland, AFC	2,627

Year	Team	Yards
1976	Pittsburgh, AFC	2,971
	Los Angeles, NFC	2,528
1975	Buffalo, AFC	2,974
	Dallas, NFC	2,432
1974	Dallas, NFC	2,454
	Pittsburgh, AFC	2,417
1973	Buffalo, AFC	3,088
	Los Angeles, NFC	2,925
1972	Miami, AFC	2,960
	Chicago, NFC	2,360
1971	Miami, AFC	2,429
	Detroit, NFC	2,376
1970	Dallas, NFC	2,300
	Miami, AFC	2,082
1969	Dallas, NFL	2,276
	Kansas City, AFL	2,220
1968	Chicago, NFL	2,377
	Kansas City, AFL	2,227
1967	Cleveland, NFL	2,139
	Houston, AFL	2,122
1966	Kansas City, AFL	2,274
	Cleveland, NFL	2,166
1965	Cleveland, NFL	2,331
	San Diego, AFL	2,085
1964	Green Bay, NFL	2,276
	Buffalo, AFL	2,040
1963	Cleveland, NFL	2,639
	San Diego, AFL	2,203
1962	Buffalo, AFL	2,480
	Green Bay, NFL	2,460
1961	Green Bay, NFL	2,350
	Dall. Texans, AFL	2,189
1960	St. Louis, NFL	2,356
	Oakland, AFL	2,056
1959	Cleveland	2,149
1958	Cleveland	2,526
1957	Los Angeles	2,142
1956	Chi. Bears	2,468
1955	Chi. Bears	2,388
1954	San Francisco	2,498
1953	San Francisco	2,230
1952	San Francisco	1,905
1951	Chi. Bears	2,408
1950	N.Y. Giants	2,336
1949	Philadelphia	2,607
1948	Chi. Cardinals	2,560
1947	Los Angeles	2,171
1946	Green Bay	1,765
1945	Cleveland	1,714
1944	Philadelphia	1,661
1943	Phil-Pitt	1,730
1942	Chi. Bears	1,881
1941	Chi. Bears	2,263
1940	Chi. Bears	1,818
1939	Chi. Bears	2,043
1938	Detroit	1,893
1937	Detroit	2,074
1936	Detroit	2,885
1935	Chi. Bears	2,096
1934	Chi. Bears	2,847
1933	Boston	2,260
1932	Chi. Bears	1,770

YARDS PASSING

Leadership in this category has been based on net yards since 1952.

Year	Team	Yards
2006	New Orleans, NFC	4,503
	Indianapolis, AFC	4,308

Year	Team	Yards
2005	Arizona, NFC	4,437
	New England, AFC	4,120
2004	Indianapolis, AFC	4,623
	Minnesota, NFC	4,516
2003	Indianapolis, AFC	4,179
	St. Louis, NFC	3,961
2002	Oakland, AFC	4,475
	St. Louis, NFC	4,154
2001	St. Louis, NFC	4,663
	Indianapolis, AFC	3,989
2000	St. Louis, NFC	5,232
	Indianapolis, AFC	4,282
1999	St. Louis, NFC	4,353
	Indianapolis, AFC	4,066
1998	Minnesota, NFC	4,328
	N.Y. Jets, AFC	3,836
1997	Seattle, AFC	3,959
	Green Bay, NFC	3,705
1996	Jacksonville, AFC	4,110
	Philadelphia, NFC	3,745
1995	San Francisco, NFC	4,608
	Miami, AFC	4,210
1994	New England, AFC	4,444
	Minnesota, NFC	4,324
1993	Miami, AFC	4,353
	San Francisco, NFC	4,302
1992	Houston, AFC	4,029
	San Francisco, NFC	3,880
1991	Houston, AFC	4,621
	San Francisco, NFC	3,997
1990	Houston, AFC	4,805
	San Francisco, NFC	4,177
1989	Washington, NFC	4,349
	Miami, AFC	4,216
1988	Miami, AFC	4,516
	Washington, NFC	4,136
1987	Miami, AFC	3,876
	San Francisco, NFC	3,750
1986	Miami, AFC	4,779
	San Francisco, NFC	4,096
1985	San Diego, AFC	4,870
	Dallas, NFC	3,861
1984	Miami, AFC	5,018
	St. Louis, NFC	4,257
1983	San Diego, AFC	4,661
	Green Bay, NFC	4,365
1982	San Diego, AFC	2,927
	San Francisco, NFC	2,502
1981	San Diego, AFC	4,739
	Minnesota, NFC	4,333
1980	San Diego, AFC	4,531
	Minnesota, NFC	3,688
1979	San Diego, AFC	3,915
	San Francisco, NFC	3,641
1978	San Diego, AFC	3,375
	Minnesota, NFC	3,243
1977	Buffalo, AFC	2,530
	St. Louis, NFC	2,499
1976	Baltimore, AFC	2,933
	Minnesota, NFC	2,855
1975	Cincinnati, AFC	3,241
	Washington, NFC	2,917
1974	Washington, NFC	2,978
	Cincinnati, AFC	2,804
1973	Philadelphia, NFC	2,998
	Denver, AFC	2,519
1972	N.Y. Jets, AFC	2,777
	San Francisco, NFC	2,735
1971	San Diego, AFC	3,134

Year	Team	Yards
	Dallas, NFC	2,786
1970	San Francisco, NFC	2,923
	Oakland, AFC	2,865
1969	Oakland, AFL	3,271
	San Francisco, NFL	3,158
1968	San Diego, AFL	3,623
	Dallas, NFL	3,026
1967	N.Y. Jets, AFL	3,845
	Washington, NFL	3,730
1966	N.Y. Jets, AFL	3,464
	Dallas, NFL	3,023
1965	San Francisco, NFL	3,487
	San Diego, AFL	3,103
1964	Houston, AFL	3,527
	Chicago, NFL	2,841
1963	Baltimore, NFL	3,296
	Houston, AFL	3,222
1962	Denver, AFL	3,404
	Philadelphia, NFL	3,385
1961	Houston, AFL	4,392
	Philadelphia, NFL	3,605
1960	Houston, AFL	3,203
	Baltimore, NFL	2,956
1959	Baltimore	2,753
1958	Pittsburgh	2,752
1957	Baltimore	2,388
1956	Los Angeles	2,419
1955	Philadelphia	2,472
1954	Chi. Bears	3,104
1953	Philadelphia	3,089
1952	Cleveland	2,566
1951	Los Angeles	3,296
1950	Los Angeles	3,709
1949	Chi. Bears	3,055
1948	Washington	2,861
1947	Washington	3,336
1946	Los Angeles	2,080
1945	Chi. Bears	1,857
1944	Washington	2,021
1943	Chi. Bears	2,310
1942	Green Bay	2,407
1941	Chi. Bears	2,002
1940	Washington	1,887
1939	Chi. Bears	1,965
1938	Washington	1,536
1937	Green Bay	1,398
1936	Green Bay	1,629
1935	Green Bay	1,449
1934	Green Bay	1,165
1933	N.Y. Giants	1,348
1932	Chi. Bears	1,013

FEWEST POINTS ALLOWED

Year	Team	Points
2006	Baltimore, AFC	201
	Chicago, NFC	255
2005	Chicago, NFC	202
	Indianapolis, AFC	247
2004	Pittsburgh, AFC	251
	Philadelphia, NFC	260
2003	New England, AFC	238
	Dallas, NFC	260
2002	Tampa Bay, NFC	196
	Miami, AFC	301
2001	Chicago, NFC	203
	Pittsburgh, AFC	212
2000	Baltimore, AFC	165
	Philadelphia, NFC	245
1999	Jacksonville, AFC	217

Year	Team	Points
	Tampa Bay, NFC	235
1998	Miami, AFC	265
	Dallas, NFC	275
1997	Kansas City, AFC	232
	Tampa Bay, NFC	263
1996	Green Bay, NFC	210
	Pittsburgh, AFC	257
1995	Kansas City, AFC	241
	San Francisco, NFC	258
1994	Cleveland, AFC	204
	Dallas, NFC	248
1993	N.Y. Giants, NFC	205
	Houston, AFC	238
1992	New Orleans, NFC	202
	Pittsburgh, AFC	225
1991	New Orleans, NFC	211
	Denver, AFC	235
1990	N.Y. Giants, NFC	211
	Pittsburgh, AFC	240
1989	Denver, AFC	226
	N.Y. Giants, NFC	252
1988	Chicago, NFC	215
	Buffalo, AFC	237
1987	Indianapolis, AFC	238
	San Francisco, NFC	253
1986	Chicago, NFC	187
	Seattle, AFC	293
1985	Chicago, NFC	198
	N.Y. Jets, AFC	264
1984	San Francisco, NFC	227
	Denver, AFC	241
1983	Miami, AFC	250
	Detroit, NFC	286
1982	Washington, NFC	128
	Miami, AFC	131
1981	Philadelphia, NFC	221
	Miami, AFC	275
1980	Philadelphia, NFC	222
	Houston, AFC	251
1979	Tampa Bay, NFC	237
	San Diego, AFC	246
1978	Pittsburgh, AFC	195
	Dallas, NFC	208
1977	Atlanta, NFC	129
	Denver, AFC	148
1976	Pittsburgh, AFC	138
	Minnesota, NFC	176
1975	Los Angeles, NFC	135
	Pittsburgh, AFC	162
1974	Los Angeles, NFC	181
	Pittsburgh, AFC	189
1973	Miami, AFC	150
	Minnesota, NFC	168
1972	Miami, AFC	171
	Washington, NFC	218
1971	Minnesota, NFC	139
	Baltimore, AFC	140
1970	Minnesota, NFC	143
	Miami, AFC	228
1969	Minnesota, NFL	133
	Kansas City, AFL	177
1968	Baltimore, NFL	144
	Kansas City, AFL	170
1967	Los Angeles, NFL	196
	Houston, AFL	199
1966	Green Bay, NFL	163
	Buffalo, AFL	255
1965	Green Bay, NFL	224
	Buffalo, AFL	226

Year	Team	Yards
1964	Baltimore, NFL	225
	Buffalo, AFL	242
1963	Chicago, NFL	144
	San Diego, AFL	255
1962	Green Bay, NFL	148
	Dall. Texans, AFL	233
1961	San Diego, AFL	219
	N.Y. Giants, NFL	220
1960	San Francisco, NFL	205
	Dall. Texans, AFL	253
1959	N.Y. Giants	170
1958	N.Y. Giants	183
1957	Cleveland	172
1956	Cleveland	177
1955	Cleveland	218
1954	Cleveland	162
1953	Cleveland	162
1952	Detroit	192
1951	Cleveland	152
1950	Philadelphia	141
1949	Philadelphia	134
1948	Chi. Bears	151
1947	Green Bay	210
1946	Pittsburgh	117
1945	Washington	121
1944	N.Y. Giants	75
1943	Washington	137
1942	Chi. Bears	84
1941	N.Y. Giants	114
1940	Brooklyn	120
1939	N.Y. Giants	85
1938	N.Y. Giants	79
1937	Chi. Bears	100
1936	Chi. Bears	94
1935	Green Bay	96
	N.Y. Giants	96
1934	Detroit	59
1933	Brooklyn	54
1932	Chi. Bears	44

FEWEST TOTAL YARDS ALLOWED

Year	Team	Yards
2006	Baltimore, AFC	4,225
	Chicago, NFC	4,706
2005	Tampa Bay, NFC	4,444
	Pittsburgh, AFC	4,544
2004	Pittsburgh, AFC	4,134
	Washington, NFC	4,281
2003	Dallas, NFC	4,056
	Buffalo, AFC	4,313
2002	Tampa Bay, NFC	4,044
	Miami, AFC	4,656
2001	Pittsburgh, AFC	4,137
	St. Louis, NFC	4,471
2000	Tennessee, AFC	3,813
	Washington, NFC	4,474
1999	Buffalo, AFC	4,045
	Tampa Bay, NFC	4,280
1998	San Diego, AFC	4,208
	Tampa Bay, NFC	4,345
1997	San Francisco, NFC	4,013
	Denver, AFC	4,671
1996	Green Bay, NFC	4,156
	Pittsburgh, AFC	4,362
1995	San Francisco, NFC	4,398
	Kansas City, AFC	4,549
1994	Dallas, NFC	4,313
	Pittsburgh, AFC	4,326
1993	Minnesota, NFC	4,406

Year	Team	Yards
	Pittsburgh, AFC	4,531
1992	Dallas, NFC	3,931
	Houston, AFC	4,211
1991	Philadelphia, NFC	3,549
	Denver, AFC	4,549
1990	Pittsburgh, AFC	4,115
	N.Y. Giants, NFC	4,206
1989	Minnesota, NFC	4,184
	Kansas City, AFC	4,293
1988	Minnesota, NFC	4,091
	Buffalo, AFC	4,578
1987	San Francisco, NFC	4,095
	Cleveland, AFC	4,264
1986	Chicago, NFC	4,130
	L.A. Raiders, AFC	4,804
1985	Chicago, NFC	4,135
	L.A. Raiders, AFC	4,603
1984	Chicago, NFC	3,863
	Cleveland, AFC	4,641
1983	Cincinnati, AFC	4,327
	New Orleans, NFC	4,691
1982	Miami, AFC	2,312
	Tampa Bay, NFC	2,442
1981	Philadelphia, NFC	4,447
	N.Y. Jets, AFC	4,871
1980	Buffalo, AFC	4,101
	Philadelphia, NFC	4,443
1979	Tampa Bay, NFC	3,949
	Pittsburgh, AFC	4,270
1978	Los Angeles, NFC	3,893
	Pittsburgh, AFC	4,168
1977	Dallas, NFC	3,213
	New England, AFC	3,638
1976	Pittsburgh, AFC	3,323
	San Francisco, NFC	3,562
1975	Minnesota, NFC	3,153
	Oakland, AFC	3,629
1974	Pittsburgh, AFC	3,074
	Washington, NFC	3,285
1973	Los Angeles, NFC	2,951
	Oakland, AFC	3,160
1972	Miami, AFC	3,297
	Green Bay, NFC	3,474
1971	Baltimore, AFC	2,852
	Minnesota, NFC	3,406
1970	Minnesota, NFC	2,803
	N.Y. Jets, AFC	3,655
1969	Minnesota, NFL	2,720
	Kansas City, AFL	3,163
1968	Los Angeles, NFL	3,118
	N.Y. Jets, AFL	3,363
1967	Oakland, AFL	3,294
	Green Bay, NFL	3,300
1966	St. Louis, NFL	3,492
	Oakland, AFL	3,910
1965	San Diego, AFL	3,262
	Detroit, NFL	3,557
1964	Green Bay, NFL	3,179
	Buffalo, AFL	3,878
1963	Chicago, NFL	3,176
	Boston, AFL	3,834
1962	Detroit, NFL	3,217
	Dall. Texans, AFL	3,951
1961	San Diego, AFL	3,726
	Baltimore, NFL	3,782
1960	St. Louis, NFL	3,029
	Buffalo, AFL	3,866
1959	N.Y. Giants	2,843
1958	Chi. Bears	3,066

Year	Team	Yards
1957	Pittsburgh	2,791
1956	N.Y. Giants	3,081
1955	Cleveland	2,841
1954	Cleveland	2,658
1953	Philadelphia	2,998
1952	Cleveland	3,075
1951	N.Y. Giants	3,250
1950	Cleveland	3,154
1949	Philadelphia	2,831
1948	Chi. Bears	2,931
1947	Green Bay	3,396
1946	Washington	2,451
1945	Philadelphia	2,073
1944	Philadelphia	1,943
1943	Chi. Bears	2,262
1942	Chi. Bears	1,703
1941	N.Y. Giants	2,368
1940	N.Y. Giants	2,219
1939	Washington	2,116
1938	N.Y. Giants	2,029
1937	Washington	2,123
1936	Boston	2,181
1935	Boston	1,996
1934	Chi. Cardinals	1,539
1933	Brooklyn	1,789

FEWEST RUSHING YARDS ALLOWED

Year	Team	Yards
2006	Minnesota, NFC	985
	Baltimore, AFC	1,214
2005	San Diego, AFC	1,349
	Carolina, NFC	1,465
2004	Pittsburgh, AFC	1,299
	Washington, NFC	1,304
2003	Tennessee, AFC	1,295
	Dallas, NFC	1,425
2002	Pittsburgh, AFC	1,375
	Tampa Bay, NFC	1,554
2001	Pittsburgh, AFC	1,195
	Chicago, NFC	1,313
2000	Baltimore, AFC	970
	N.Y. Giants, NFC	1,156
1999	St. Louis, NFC	1,189
	Baltimore, AFC	1,231
1998	San Diego, AFC	1,140
	Atlanta, NFC	1,203
1997	Pittsburgh, AFC	1,318
	San Francisco, NFC	1,366
1996	Denver, AFC	1,331
	Green Bay, NFC	1,416
1995	San Francisco, NFC	1,061
	Pittsburgh, AFC	1,321
1994	Minnesota, NFC	1,090
	San Diego, AFC	1,404
1993	Houston, AFC	1,273
	Minnesota, NFC	1,536
1992	Dallas, NFC	1,244
	Buffalo, AFC	1,395
	San Diego, AFC	1,395
1991	Philadelphia, NFC	1,136
	N.Y. Jets, AFC	1,442
1990	Philadelphia, NFC	1,169
	San Diego, AFC	1,515
1989	New Orleans, NFC	1,326
	Denver, AFC	1,580
1988	Chicago, NFC	1,326
	Houston, AFC	1,592
1987	Chicago, NFC	1,413
	Cleveland, AFC	1,433

Year	Team	Yards
1986	N.Y. Giants, NFC	1,284
	Denver, AFC	1,651
1985	Chicago, NFC	1,319
	N.Y. Jets, AFC	1,516
1984	Chicago, NFC	1,377
	Pittsburgh, AFC	1,617
1983	Washington, NFC	1,289
	Cincinnati, AFC	1,499
1982	Pittsburgh, AFC	762
	Detroit, NFC	854
1981	Detroit, NFC	1,623
	Kansas City, AFC	1,747
1980	Detroit, NFC	1,599
	Cincinnati, AFC	1,680
1979	Denver, AFC	1,693
	Tampa Bay, NFC	1,873
1978	Dallas, NFC	1,721
	Pittsburgh, AFC	1,774
1977	Denver, AFC	1,531
	Dallas, NFC	1,651
1976	Pittsburgh, AFC	1,457
	Los Angeles, NFC	1,564
1975	Minnesota, NFC	1,532
	Houston, AFC	1,680
1974	Los Angeles, NFC	1,302
	New England, AFC	1,587
1973	Los Angeles, NFC	1,270
	Oakland, AFC	1,470
1972	Dallas, NFC	1,515
	Miami, AFC	1,548
1971	Baltimore, AFC	1,113
	Dallas, NFC	1,144
1970	Detroit, NFC	1,152
	N.Y. Jets, AFC	1,283
1969	Dallas, NFL	1,050
	Kansas City, AFL	1,091
1968	Dallas, NFL	1,195
	N.Y. Jets, AFL	1,195
1967	Dallas, NFL	1,081
	Oakland, AFL	1,129
1966	Buffalo, AFL	1,051
	Dallas, NFL	1,176
1965	San Diego, AFL	1,094
	Los Angeles, NFL	1,409
1964	Buffalo, AFL	913
	Los Angeles, NFL	1,501
1963	Boston, AFL	1,107
	Chicago, NFL	1,442
1962	Detroit, NFL	1,231
	Dall. Texans, AFL	1,250
1961	Boston, AFL	1,041
	Pittsburgh, NFL	1,463
1960	St. Louis, NFL	1,212
	Dall. Texans, AFL	1,338
1959	N.Y. Giants	1,261
1958	Baltimore	1,291
1957	Baltimore	1,174
1956	N.Y. Giants	1,443
1955	Cleveland	1,189
1954	Cleveland	1,050
1953	Philadelphia	1,117
1952	Detroit	1,145
1951	N.Y. Giants	913
1950	Detroit	1,367
1949	Chi. Bears	1,196
1948	Philadelphia	1,209
1947	Philadelphia	1,329
1946	Chi. Bears	1,060
1945	Philadelphia	817

Year	Team	Yards
1944	Philadelphia	558
1943	Phil-Pitt	793
1942	Chi. Bears	519
1941	Washington	1,042
1940	N.Y. Giants	977
1939	Chi. Bears	812
1938	Detroit	1,081
1937	Chi. Bears	933
1936	Boston	1,148
1935	Boston	998
1934	Chi. Cardinals	954
1933	Brooklyn	964

FEWEST PASSING YARDS ALLOWED

Leadership in this category has been based on net yards since 1952.

Year	Team	Yards
2006	Oakland, AFC	2,413
	New Orleans, NFC	2,854
2005	Green Bay, NFC	2,680
	N.Y. Jets, AFC	2,755
2004	Tampa Bay, NFC	2,579
	Miami, AFC	2,592
2003	Dallas, NFC	2,631
	Buffalo, AFC	2,707
2002	Tampa Bay, NFC	2,490
	Indianapolis, AFC	2,917
2001	Miami, AFC	2,829
	Philadelphia, NFC	2,864
2000	Tennessee, AFC	2,423
	Washington, NFC	2,621
1999	Buffalo, AFC	2,675
	Tampa Bay, NFC	2,873
1998	Philadelphia, NFC	2,720
	Oakland, AFC	2,876
1997	Dallas, NFC	2,522
	Indianapolis, AFC	2,820
1996	Green Bay, NFC	2,740
	Pittsburgh, AFC	2,947
1995	N.Y. Jets, AFC	2,740
	Philadelphia, NFC	2,816
1994	Dallas, NFC	2,752
	Houston, AFC	2,795
1993	New Orleans, NFC	2,606
	Cincinnati, AFC	2,798
1992	New Orleans, NFC	2,470
	Kansas City, AFC	2,537
1991	Philadelphia, NFC	2,413
	Denver, AFC	2,755
1990	Pittsburgh, AFC	2,500
	Dallas, NFC	2,639
1989	Minnesota, NFC	2,501
	Kansas City, AFC	2,527
1988	Kansas City, AFC	2,434
	Minnesota, NFC	2,489
1987	San Francisco, NFC	2,484
	L.A. Raiders, AFC	2,727
1986	St. Louis, NFC	2,637
	New England, AFC	2,978
1985	Washington, NFC	2,746
	Pittsburgh, AFC	2,783
1984	New Orleans, NFC	2,453
	Cleveland, AFC	2,696
1983	New Orleans, NFC	2,691
	Cincinnati, AFC	2,828
1982	Miami, AFC	1,027
	Tampa Bay, NFC	1,384
1981	Philadelphia, NFC	2,696
	Buffalo, AFC	2,870

Year	Team	Yards
1980	Washington, NFC	2,171
	Buffalo, AFC	2,282
1979	Tampa Bay, NFC	2,076
	Buffalo, AFC	2,530
1978	Buffalo, AFC	1,960
	Los Angeles, NFC	2,048
1977	Atlanta, NFC	1,384
	San Diego, AFC	1,725
1976	Minnesota, NFC	1,575
	Cincinnati, AFC	1,758
1975	Minnesota, NFC	1,621
	Cincinnati, AFC	1,729
1974	Pittsburgh, AFC	1,466
	Atlanta, NFC	1,572
1973	Miami, AFC	1,290
	Atlanta, NFC	1,430
1972	Minnesota, NFC	1,699
	Cleveland, AFC	1,736
1971	Atlanta, NFC	1,638
	Baltimore, AFC	1,739
1970	Minnesota, NFC	1,438
	Kansas City, AFC	2,010
1969	Minnesota, NFL	1,631
	Kansas City, AFL	2,072
1968	Houston, AFL	1,671
	Green Bay, NFL	1,796
1967	Green Bay, NFL	1,377
	Buffalo, AFL	1,825
1966	Green Bay, NFL	1,959
	Oakland, AFL	2,118
1965	Green Bay, NFL	1,981
	San Diego, AFL	2,168
1964	Green Bay, NFL	1,647
	San Diego, AFL	2,518
1963	Chicago, NFL	1,734
	Oakland, AFL	2,589
1962	Green Bay, NFL	1,746
	Oakland, AFL	2,306
1961	Baltimore, NFL	1,913
	San Diego, AFL	2,363
1960	Chicago, NFL	1,388
	Buffalo, AFL	2,124
1959	N.Y. Giants	1,582
1958	Chi. Bears	1,769
1957	Cleveland	1,300
1956	Cleveland	1,103
1955	Pittsburgh	1,295
1954	Cleveland	1,608
1953	Washington	1,751
1952	Washington	1,580
1951	Pittsburgh	1,687
1950	Cleveland	1,581
1949	Philadelphia	1,607
1948	Green Bay	1,626
1947	Green Bay	1,790
1946	Pittsburgh	939
1945	Washington	1,121
1944	Chi. Bears	1,052
1943	Chi. Bears	980
1942	Washington	1,093
1941	Pittsburgh	1,168
1940	Philadelphia	1,012
1939	Washington	1,116
1938	Chi. Bears	897
1937	Detroit	804
1936	Philadelphia	853
1935	Chi. Cardinals	793
1934	Philadelphia	545
1933	Portsmouth	558

1,000 YARDS RUSHING IN A SEASON

Year	Player, Team	Att.	Yards	Avg.	Long	TD
2006	LaDainian Tomlinson, San Diego[6]	348	1,815	5.22	85	28
	Larry Johnson, Kansas City[2]	416	1,789	4.30	47	17
	Frank Gore, San Francisco	312	1,695	5.43	72	8
	Tiki Barber, N.Y. Giants[6]	327	1,662	5.08	55	5
	Steven Jackson, St. Louis[2]	346	1,528	4.42	59	13
	Willie Parker, Pittsburgh[2]	337	1,494	4.43	76	13
	Rudi Johnson, Cincinnati[3]	341	1,309	3.84	22	12
	Brian Westbrook, Philadelphia	240	1,217	5.07	71	7
	Chester Taylor, Minnesota	303	1,216	4.01	95	6
	Travis Henry, Tennessee[3]	270	1,211	4.49	70	7
	Thomas Jones, Chicago[2]	296	1,210	4.09	30	6
	Edgerrin James, Arizona[6]	337	1,159	3.44	18	6
	Ladell Betts, Washington	245	1,154	4.71	26	4
	Fred Taylor, Jacksonville[6]	231	1,146	4.96	76	5
	Warrick Dunn, Atlanta[5]	286	1,140	3.99	90	4
	Jamal Lewis, Baltimore[5]	314	1,132	3.61	52	9
	Julius Jones, Dallas	267	1,084	4.06	77	4
	*Joseph Addai, Indianapolis	226	1,081	4.78	41	7
	Ahman Green, Green Bay[6]	266	1,059	3.98	70	5
	Deuce McAllister, New Orleans[4]	244	1,057	4.33	57	10
	Michael Vick, Atlanta	123	1,039	8.45	51	2
	Tatum Bell, Denver	233	1,025	4.40	51	2
	Ronnie Brown, Miami	241	1,008	4.18	47	5
2005	Shaun Alexander, Seattle[5]	370	1,880	5.1	88	27
	Tiki Barber, N.Y. Giants[5]	357	1,860	5.2	95	9
	Larry Johnson, Kansas City	336	1,750	5.2	49	20
	Clinton Portis, Washington[4]	352	1,516	4.3	47	11
	Edgerrin James, Indianapolis[5]	360	1,506	4.2	33	13
	LaDainian Tomlinson, San Diego[5]	339	1,462	4.3	62	18
	Rudi Johnson, Cincinnati[2]	337	1,458	4.3	33	12
	Warrick Dunn, Atlanta[4]	280	1,416	5.1	65	3
	Thomas Jones, Chicago	314	1,335	4.3	42	9
	Willis McGahee, Buffalo[2]	325	1,247	3.8	27	5
	Reuben Droughns, Cleveland[2]	309	1,232	4.0	75	2
	Willie Parker, Pittsburg	255	1,202	4.7	80	4
	*Carnell Williams, Tampa Bay	290	1,178	4.1	71	6
	Steven Jackson, St. Louis	254	1,046	4.1	51	8
	LaMont Jordan, Oakland	272	1,025	3.8	26	9
	Mike Anderson, Denver[2]	239	1,014	4.2	44	12
2004	Curtis Martin, N.Y. Jets[10]	371	1,697	4.6	25	12
	Shaun Alexander, Seattle[4]	353	1,696	4.8	44	16
	Corey Dillon, New England[7]	345	1,635	4.7	44	12
	Edgerrin James, Indianapolis[4]	334	1,548	4.6	40	9
	Tiki Barber, N.Y. Giants[4]	322	1,518	4.7	72	13
	Rudi Johnson, Cincinnati	361	1,454	4.0	52	12
	LaDainian Tomlinson, San Diego[4]	339	1,335	3.9	42	17
	Clinton Portis, Washington[3]	343	1,315	3.8	64	5
	Reuben Droughns, Denver	275	1,240	4.5	51	6
	Fred Taylor, Jacksonville[5]	260	1,224	4.7	46	2
	Domanick Davis, Houston[2]	302	1,188	3.9	44	13
	Ahman Green, Green Bay[5]	259	1,163	4.5	90	7
	*Kevin Jones, Detroit	241	1,133	4.7	74	5
	Willis McGahee, Buffalo	284	1,128	4.0	41	13
	Warrick Dunn, Atlanta[3]	265	1,106	4.2	60	9
	Deuce McAllister, New Orleans[3]	269	1,074	4.0	71	9
	Chris Brown, Tennessee	220	1,067	4.9	52	6
	Jamal Lewis, Baltimore[4]	235	1,006	4.3	75	7
2003	Jamal Lewis, Baltimore[3]	387	2,066	5.3	82	14
	Ahman Green, Green Bay[4]	355	1,883	5.3	98	15
	LaDainian Tomlinson, San Diego[3]	313	1,645	5.3	73	13
	Deuce McAllister, New Orleans[2]	351	1,641	4.7	76	8
	Clinton Portis, Denver[2]	290	1,591	5.5	65	14
	Fred Taylor, Jacksonville[4]	345	1,572	4.6	62	6
	Stephen Davis, Carolina[4]	318	1,444	4.5	40	8
	Shaun Alexander, Seattle[3]	326	1,435	4.4	55	14
	Priest Holmes, Kansas City[4]	320	1,420	4.4	31	27
	Ricky Williams, Miami[4]	392	1,372	3.5	45	9
	Travis Henry, Buffalo[2]	331	1,356	4.1	64	10

Year	Player, Team	Att.	Yards	Avg.	Long	TD
	Curtis Martin, N.Y. Jets[9]	323	1,308	4.1	56	2
	Edgerrin James, Indianapolis[3]	310	1,259	4.1	43	11
	Tiki Barber, N.Y. Giants[3]	278	1,216	4.4	27	2
	*Domanick Davis, Houston	238	1,031	4.3	51	8
	Eddie George, Tennessee[7]	312	1,031	3.3	27	5
	Kevan Barlow, San Francisco	201	1,024	5.1	78	6
	Anthony Thomas, Chicago[2]	244	1,024	4.2	67	6
2002	Ricky Williams, Miami[3]	383	1,853	4.8	63	16
	LaDainian Tomlinson, San Diego[2]	372	1,683	4.5	76	14
	Priest Holmes, Kansas City[3]	313	1,615	5.2	56	21
	*Clinton Portis, Denver	273	1,508	5.5	59	15
	Travis Henry, Buffalo	325	1,438	4.4	34	13
	Deuce McAllister, New Orleans	325	1,388	4.3	62	13
	Tiki Barber, N.Y. Giants[2]	304	1,387	4.6	70	11
	Jamal Lewis, Baltimore[2]	308	1,327	4.3	75	6
	Fred Taylor, Jacksonville[3]	287	1,314	4.6	63	8
	Corey Dillon, Cincinnati[6]	314	1,311	4.2	67	7
	Michael Bennett, Minnesota	255	1,296	5.1	85	5
	Ahman Green, Green Bay[3]	286	1,240	4.3	43	7
	Shaun Alexander, Seattle[2]	295	1,175	4.0	58	16
	Eddie George, Tennessee[6]	343	1,165	3.4	35	12
	Curtis Martin, N.Y. Jets[8]	261	1,094	4.2	35	7
	Duce Staley, Philadelphia[3]	269	1,029	3.8	57	5
	James Stewart, Detroit[2]	231	1,021	4.4	56	4
2001	Priest Holmes, Kansas City[2]	327	1,555	4.8	41	8
	Curtis Martin, N.Y. Jets[7]	333	1,513	4.5	47	10
	Stephen Davis, Washington[3]	356	1,432	4.0	32	5
	Ahman Green, Green Bay[2]	304	1,387	4.6	83	9
	Marshall Faulk, St. Louis[7]	260	1,382	5.3	71	12
	Shaun Alexander, Seattle	309	1,318	4.3	88	14
	Corey Dillon, Cincinnati[5]	340	1,315	3.9	96	10
	Ricky Williams, New Orleans[2]	313	1,245	4.0	46	6
	*LaDainian Tomlinson, San Diego	339	1,236	3.6	54	10
	Garrison Hearst, San Francisco[4]	252	1,206	4.8	43	4
	*Anthony Thomas, Chicago	278	1,183	4.3	46	7
	Antowain Smith, New England[2]	287	1,157	4.0	44	12
	*Dominic Rhodes, Indianapolis	233	1,104	4.7	77	9
	Jerome Bettis, Pittsburgh[8]	225	1,072	4.8	48	4
	Emmitt Smith, Dallas[11]	261	1,021	3.9	44	3
2000	Edgerrin James, Indianapolis[2]	387	1,709	4.4	30	13
	Robert Smith, Minnesota[4]	295	1,521	5.2	72	7
	Eddie George, Tennessee[5]	403	1,509	3.7	35	14
	*Mike Anderson, Denver	297	1,487	5.0	80	15
	Corey Dillon, Cincinnati[4]	315	1,435	4.6	80	7
	Fred Taylor, Jacksonville[2]	292	1,399	4.8	71	12
	*Jamal Lewis, Baltimore	309	1,364	4.4	45	6
	Marshall Faulk, St. Louis[6]	253	1,359	5.4	36	18
	Jerome Bettis, Pittsburgh[7]	355	1,341	3.8	30	8
	Stephen Davis, Washington[2]	332	1,318	4.0	50	11
	Ricky Watters, Seattle[7]	278	1,242	4.5	55	7
	Curtis Martin, N.Y. Jets[6]	316	1,204	3.8	55	9
	Emmitt Smith, Dallas[10]	294	1,203	4.1	52	9
	James Stewart, Detroit	339	1,184	3.5	34	10
	Ahman Green, Green Bay	263	1,175	4.5	39	10
	Charlie Garner, San Francisco[2]	258	1,142	4.4	42	7
	Lamar Smith, Miami	309	1,139	3.7	68	14
	Warrick Dunn, Tampa Bay[2]	248	1,133	4.6	70	8
	James Allen, Chicago	290	1,120	3.9	29	2
	Tyrone Wheatley, Oakland	232	1,046	4.5	80	9
	Jamal Anderson, Atlanta[4]	282	1,024	3.6	42	6
	Tiki Barber, N.Y. Giants	213	1,006	4.7	78	8
	Ricky Williams, New Orleans	248	1,000	4.0	26	8
1999	*Edgerrin James, Indianapolis	369	1,553	4.2	72	13
	Curtis Martin, N.Y. Jets[5]	367	1,464	4.0	50	5
	Stephen Davis, Washington	290	1,405	4.8	76	17
	Emmitt Smith, Dallas[9]	329	1,397	4.3	63	11
	Marshall Faulk, St. Louis[5]	253	1,381	5.5	58	7
	Eddie George, Tennessee[4]	320	1,304	4.1	40	9
	Duce Staley, Philadelphia[2]	325	1,273	3.9	29	4

Year	Player, Team	Att.	Yards	Avg.	Long	TD
	Charlie Garner, San Francisco	241	1,229	5.1	53	4
	Ricky Watters, Seattle[6]	325	1,210	3.7	45	5
	Corey Dillon, Cincinnati[3]	263	1,200	4.6	50	5
	*Olandis Gary, Denver	276	1,159	4.2	71	7
	Jerome Bettis, Pittsburgh[6]	299	1,091	3.7	35	7
	Dorsey Levens, Green Bay[2]	279	1,034	3.7	36	9
	Robert Smith, Minnesota[3]	221	1,015	4.6	70	2
1998	Terrell Davis, Denver[4]	392	2,008	5.1	70	21
	Jamal Anderson, Atlanta[3]	410	1,846	4.5	48	14
	Garrison Hearst, San Francisco[3]	310	1,570	5.1	96	7
	Barry Sanders, Detroit[10]	343	1,491	4.3	73	4
	Emmitt Smith, Dallas[8]	319	1,332	4.2	32	13
	Marshall Faulk, Indianapolis[4]	324	1,319	4.1	68	6
	Eddie George, Tennessee[3]	348	1,294	3.7	37	5
	Curtis Martin, N.Y. Jets[4]	369	1,287	3.5	60	8
	Ricky Watters, Seattle[5]	319	1,239	3.9	39	9
	*Fred Taylor, Jacksonville	264	1,223	4.6	77	14
	Robert Smith, Minnesota[2]	249	1,187	4.8	74	6
	Jerome Bettis, Pittsburgh[5]	316	1,185	3.8	42	3
	Corey Dillon, Cincinnati[2]	262	1,130	4.3	66	4
	Antowain Smith, Buffalo	300	1,124	3.7	30	8
	*Robert Edwards, New England	291	1,115	3.8	53	9
	Duce Staley, Philadelphia	258	1,065	4.1	64	5
	Gary Brown, N.Y. Giants[2]	247	1,063	4.3	45	5
	Adrian Murrell, Arizona[3]	274	1,042	3.8	32	8
	Warrick Dunn, Tampa Bay	245	1,026	4.2	50	2
	Priest Holmes, Baltimore	233	1,008	4.3	56	7
1997	Barry Sanders, Detroit[9]	335	2,053	6.1	82	11
	Terrell Davis, Denver[3]	369	1,750	4.7	50	15
	Jerome Bettis, Pittsburgh[4]	375	1,665	4.4	34	7
	Dorsey Levens, Green Bay	329	1,435	4.4	52	7
	Eddie George, Tennessee[2]	357	1,399	3.9	30	6
	Napoleon Kaufman, Oakland	272	1,294	4.8	83	6
	Robert Smith, Minnesota	232	1,266	5.5	78	6
	Curtis Martin, New England[3]	274	1,160	4.2	70	4
	*Corey Dillon, Cincinnati	233	1,129	4.8	71	10
	Ricky Watters, Philadelphia[4]	285	1,110	3.9	28	7
	Adrian Murrell, N.Y. Jets[2]	300	1,086	3.6	43	7
	Emmitt Smith, Dallas[7]	261	1,074	4.1	44	4
	Marshall Faulk, Indianapolis[3]	264	1,054	4.0	45	7
	Raymont Harris, Chicago	275	1,033	3.8	68	10
	Garrison Hearst, San Francisco[2]	234	1,019	4.4	51	4
	Jamal Anderson, Atlanta[2]	290	1,002	3.5	39	7
1996	Barry Sanders, Detroit[8]	307	1,553	5.1	54	11
	Terrell Davis, Denver[2]	345	1,538	4.5	71	13
	Jerome Bettis, Pittsburgh[3]	320	1,431	4.5	50	11
	Ricky Watters, Philadelphia[3]	353	1,411	4.0	56	13
	*Eddie George, Houston	335	1,368	4.1	76	8
	Terry Allen, Washington[4]	347	1,353	3.9	49	21
	Adrian Murrell, N.Y. Jets	301	1,249	4.1	78	6
	Emmitt Smith, Dallas[6]	327	1,204	3.7	42	12
	Curtis Martin, New England[2]	316	1,152	3.6	57	14
	Anthony Johnson, Carolina	300	1,120	3.7	29	6
	*Karim Abdul-Jabbar, Miami	307	1,116	3.6	29	11
	Jamal Anderson, Atlanta	232	1,055	4.5	32	5
	Thurman Thomas, Buffalo[8]	281	1,033	3.7	36	8
1995	Emmitt Smith, Dallas[5]	377	1,773	4.7	60	25
	Barry Sanders, Detroit[7]	314	1,500	4.8	75	11
	*Curtis Martin, New England	368	1,487	4.0	49	14
	Chris Warren, Seattle[4]	310	1,346	4.3	52	15
	Terry Allen, Washington[3]	338	1,309	3.9	28	10
	Ricky Watters, Philadelphia[2]	337	1,273	3.8	57	11
	Errict Rhett, Tampa Bay[2]	332	1,207	3.6	21	11
	Rodney Hampton, N.Y. Giants[5]	306	1,182	3.9	32	10
	*Terrell Davis, Denver	237	1,117	4.7	60	7
	Harvey Williams, Oakland	255	1,114	4.4	60	9
	Craig Heyward, Atlanta	236	1,083	4.6	31	6
	Marshall Faulk, Indianapolis[2]	289	1,078	3.7	40	11
	*Rashaan Salaam, Chicago	296	1,074	3.6	42	10

Year	Player, Team	Att.	Yards	Avg.	Long	TD
	Garrison Hearst, Arizona	284	1,070	3.8	38	1
	Edgar Bennett, Green Bay	316	1,067	3.4	23	3
	Thurman Thomas, Buffalo[7]	267	1,005	3.8	49	6
1994	Barry Sanders, Detroit[6]	331	1,883	5.7	85	7
	Chris Warren, Seattle[3]	333	1,545	4.6	41	9
	Emmitt Smith, Dallas[4]	368	1,484	4.0	46	21
	Natrone Means, San Diego	343	1,350	3.9	25	12
	*Marshall Faulk, Indianapolis	314	1,282	4.1	52	11
	Thurman Thomas, Buffalo[8]	287	1,093	3.8	29	7
	Rodney Hampton, N.Y. Giants[4]	327	1,075	3.3	27	6
	Terry Allen, Minnesota[2]	255	1,031	4.0	45	8
	Jerome Bettis, L.A. Rams[2]	319	1,025	3.2	19	3
	*Errict Rhett, Tampa Bay	284	1,011	3.6	27	7
1993	Emmitt Smith, Dallas[3]	283	1,486	5.3	62	9
	*Jerome Bettis, L.A. Rams	294	1,429	4.9	71	7
	Thurman Thomas, Buffalo[5]	355	1,315	3.7	27	6
	Erric Pegram, Atlanta	292	1,185	4.1	29	3
	Barry Sanders, Detroit[5]	243	1,115	4.6	42	3
	Leonard Russell, New England	300	1,088	3.6	21	7
	Rodney Hampton, N.Y. Giants[3]	292	1,077	3.7	20	5
	Chris Warren, Seattle[2]	273	1,072	3.9	45	7
	*Reggie Brooks, Washington	223	1,063	4.8	85	3
	*Ron Moore, Phoenix	263	1,018	3.9	20	9
	Gary Brown, Houston	195	1,002	5.1	26	6
1992	Emmitt Smith, Dallas[2]	373	1,713	4.6	68	18
	Barry Foster, Pittsburgh	390	1,690	4.3	69	11
	Thurman Thomas, Buffalo[4]	312	1,487	4.8	44	9
	Barry Sanders, Detroit[4]	312	1,352	4.3	55	9
	Lorenzo White, Houston	265	1,226	4.6	44	7
	Terry Allen, Minnesota	266	1,201	4.5	51	13
	Reggie Cobb, Tampa Bay	310	1,171	3.8	25	9
	Harold Green, Cincinnati	265	1,170	4.4	53	2
	Rodney Hampton, N.Y. Giants[2]	257	1,141	4.4	63	14
	Cleveland Gary, L.A. Rams	279	1,125	4.0	63	7
	Herschel Walker, Philadelphia[2]	267	1,070	4.0	38	8
	Chris Warren, Seattle	223	1,017	4.6	52	3
	Ricky Watters, San Francisco	206	1,013	4.9	43	9
1991	Emmitt Smith, Dallas	365	1,563	4.3	75	12
	Barry Sanders, Detroit[3]	342	1,548	4.5	69	16
	Thurman Thomas, Buffalo[3]	288	1,407	4.9	33	7
	Rodney Hampton, N.Y. Giants	256	1,059	4.1	44	10
	Earnest Byner, Washington[3]	274	1,048	3.8	32	5
	Gaston Green, Denver	261	1,037	4.0	63	4
	Christian Okoye, Kansas City[2]	225	1,031	4.6	48	9
1990	Barry Sanders, Detroit[2]	255	1,304	5.1	45	13
	Thurman Thomas, Buffalo[2]	271	1,297	4.8	80	11
	Marion Butts, San Diego	265	1,225	4.6	52	8
	Earnest Byner, Washington[2]	297	1,219	4.1	22	6
	Bobby Humphrey, Denver[2]	288	1,202	4.2	37	7
	Neal Anderson, Chicago[3]	260	1,078	4.1	52	10
	Barry Word, Kansas City	204	1,015	5.0	53	4
	James Brooks, Cincinnati[3]	195	1,004	5.1	56	5
1989	Christian Okoye, Kansas City	370	1,480	4.0	59	12
	*Barry Sanders, Detroit	280	1,470	5.3	34	14
	Eric Dickerson, Indianapolis[7]	314	1,311	4.2	21	7
	Neal Anderson, Chicago[2]	274	1,275	4.7	73	11
	Dalton Hilliard, New Orleans	344	1,262	3.7	40	13
	Thurman Thomas, Buffalo	298	1,244	4.2	38	6
	James Brooks, Cincinnati[2]	221	1,239	5.6	65	7
	*Bobby Humphrey, Denver	294	1,151	3.9	40	7
	Greg Bell, L.A. Rams[3]	272	1,137	4.2	47	15
	Roger Craig, San Francisco[3]	271	1,054	3.9	27	6
	Ottis Anderson, N.Y. Giants[6]	325	1,023	3.1	36	14
1988	Eric Dickerson, Indianapolis[6]	388	1,659	4.3	41	14
	Herschel Walker, Dallas	361	1,514	4.2	38	5
	Roger Craig, San Francisco[2]	310	1,502	4.8	46	9
	Greg Bell, L.A. Rams[2]	288	1,212	4.2	44	16
	*John Stephens, New England	297	1,168	3.9	52	4
	Gary Anderson, San Diego	225	1,119	5.0	36	3

Year	Player, Team	Att.	Yards	Avg.	Long	TD
	Neal Anderson, Chicago	249	1,106	4.4	80	12
	Joe Morris, N.Y. Giants[3]	307	1,083	3.5	27	5
	*Ickey Woods, Cincinnati	203	1,066	5.3	56	15
	Curt Warner, Seattle[4]	266	1,025	3.9	29	10
	John Settle, Atlanta	232	1,024	4.4	62	7
	Mike Rozier, Houston	251	1,002	4.0	28	10
1987	Charles White, L.A. Rams	324	1,374	4.2	58	11
	Eric Dickerson, L.A. Rams-Indianapolis[5]	283	1,288	4.6	57	6
1986	Eric Dickerson, L.A. Rams[4]	404	1,821	4.5	42	11
	Joe Morris, N.Y. Giants[2]	341	1,516	4.4	54	14
	Curt Warner, Seattle[3]	319	1,481	4.6	60	13
	*Rueben Mayes, New Orleans	286	1,353	4.7	50	8
	Walter Payton, Chicago[10]	321	1,333	4.2	41	8
	Gerald Riggs, Atlanta[3]	343	1,327	3.9	31	9
	George Rogers, Washington[4]	303	1,203	4.0	42	18
	James Brooks, Cincinnati	205	1,087	5.3	56	5
1985	Marcus Allen, L.A. Raiders[3]	390	1,759	4.6	61	11
	Gerald Riggs, Atlanta[2]	397	1,719	4.3	50	10
	Walter Payton, Chicago[9]	324	1,551	4.8	40	9
	Joe Morris, N.Y. Giants	294	1,336	4.5	65	21
	Freeman McNeil, N.Y. Jets[2]	294	1,331	4.5	69	3
	Tony Dorsett, Dallas[8]	305	1,307	4.3	60	7
	James Wilder, Tampa Bay[2]	365	1,300	3.6	28	10
	Eric Dickerson, L.A. Rams[3]	292	1,234	4.2	43	12
	Craig James, New England	263	1,227	4.7	65	5
	Kevin Mack, Cleveland	222	1,104	5.0	61	7
	Curt Warner, Seattle[2]	291	1,094	3.8	38	8
	George Rogers, Washington[3]	231	1,093	4.7	35	7
	Roger Craig, San Francisco	214	1,050	4.9	62	9
	Earnest Jackson, Philadelphia[2]	282	1,028	3.6	59	5
	Stump Mitchell, St. Louis	183	1,006	5.5	64	7
	Earnest Byner, Cleveland	244	1,002	4.1	36	8
1984	Eric Dickerson, L.A. Rams[2]	379	2,105	5.6	66	14
	Walter Payton, Chicago[8]	381	1,684	4.4	72	11
	James Wilder, Tampa Bay	407	1,544	3.8	37	13
	Gerald Riggs, Atlanta	353	1,486	4.2	57	13
	Wendell Tyler, San Francisco[3]	246	1,262	5.1	40	7
	John Riggins, Washington[5]	327	1,239	3.8	24	14
	Tony Dorsett, Dallas[7]	302	1,189	3.9	31	6
	Earnest Jackson, San Diego	296	1,179	4.0	32	8
	Ottis Anderson, St. Louis[5]	289	1,174	4.1	24	6
	Marcus Allen, L.A. Raiders[2]	275	1,168	4.2	52	13
	Sammy Winder, Denver	296	1,153	3.9	24	4
	*Greg Bell, Buffalo	262	1,100	4.2	85	7
	Freeman McNeil, N.Y. Jets	229	1,070	4.7	53	5
1983	*Eric Dickerson, L.A. Rams	390	1,808	4.6	85	18
	William Andrews, Atlanta[4]	331	1,567	4.7	27	7
	*Curt Warner, Seattle	335	1,449	4.3	60	13
	Walter Payton, Chicago[7]	314	1,421	4.5	49	6
	John Riggins, Washington[4]	375	1,347	3.6	44	24
	Tony Dorsett, Dallas[6]	289	1,321	4.6	77	8
	Earl Campbell, Houston[5]	322	1,301	4.0	42	12
	Ottis Anderson, St. Louis[4]	296	1,270	4.3	43	5
	Mike Pruitt, Cleveland[4]	293	1,184	4.0	27	10
	George Rogers, New Orleans[2]	256	1,144	4.5	76	5
	Joe Cribbs, Buffalo[3]	263	1,131	4.3	45	3
	Curtis Dickey, Baltimore	254	1,122	4.4	56	4
	Tony Collins, New England	219	1,049	4.8	50	10
	Billy Sims, Detroit[3]	220	1,040	4.7	41	7
	Marcus Allen, L.A. Raiders	266	1,014	3.8	19	9
	Franco Harris, Pittsburgh[8]	279	1,007	3.6	19	5
1981	*George Rogers, New Orleans	378	1,674	4.4	79	13
	Tony Dorsett, Dallas[5]	342	1,646	4.8	75	4
	Billy Sims, Detroit[2]	296	1,437	4.9	51	13
	Wilbert Montgomery, Philadelphia[3]	286	1,402	4.9	41	8
	Ottis Anderson, St. Louis[2]	328	1,376	4.2	28	9
	Earl Campbell, Houston[4]	361	1,376	3.8	43	10
	William Andrews, Atlanta[3]	289	1,301	4.5	29	10
	Walter Payton, Chicago[6]	339	1,222	3.6	39	6

Year	Player, Team	Att.	Yards	Avg.	Long	TD
	Chuck Muncie, San Diego[2]	251	1,144	4.6	73	19
	*Joe Delaney, Kansas City	234	1,121	4.8	82	3
	Mike Pruitt, Cleveland[3]	247	1,103	4.5	21	7
	Joe Cribbs, Buffalo[2]	257	1,097	4.3	35	3
	Pete Johnson, Cincinnati	274	1,077	3.9	39	12
	Wendell Tyler, Los Angeles[2]	260	1,074	4.1	69	12
	Ted Brown, Minnesota	274	1,063	3.9	34	6
1980	Earl Campbell, Houston[3]	373	1,934	5.2	55	13
	Walter Payton, Chicago[5]	317	1,460	4.6	69	6
	Ottis Anderson, St. Louis[2]	301	1,352	4.5	52	9
	William Andrews, Atlanta[2]	265	1,308	4.9	33	4
	*Billy Sims, Detroit	313	1,303	4.2	52	13
	Tony Dorsett, Dallas[4]	278	1,185	4.3	56	11
	*Joe Cribbs, Buffalo	306	1,185	3.9	48	11
	Mike Pruitt, Cleveland[2]	249	1,034	4.2	56	6
1979	Earl Campbell, Houston[2]	368	1,697	4.6	61	19
	Walter Payton, Chicago[4]	369	1,610	4.4	43	14
	*Ottis Anderson, St. Louis	331	1,605	4.8	76	8
	Wilbert Montgomery, Philadelphia[2]	338	1,512	4.5	62	9
	Mike Pruitt, Cleveland	264	1,294	4.9	77	9
	Ricky Bell, Tampa Bay	283	1,263	4.5	49	7
	Chuck Muncie, New Orleans	238	1,198	5.0	69	11
	Franco Harris, Pittsburgh[7]	267	1,186	4.4	71	11
	John Riggins, Washington[3]	260	1,153	4.4	66	9
	Wendell Tyler, Los Angeles	218	1,109	5.1	63	9
	Tony Dorsett, Dallas[3]	250	1,107	4.4	41	6
	*William Andrews, Atlanta	239	1,023	4.3	23	3
1978	*Earl Campbell, Houston	302	1,450	4.8	81	13
	Walter Payton, Chicago[3]	333	1,395	4.2	76	11
	Tony Dorsett, Dallas[2]	290	1,325	4.6	63	7
	Delvin Williams, Miami[2]	272	1,258	4.6	58	8
	Wilbert Montgomery, Philadelphia	259	1,220	4.7	47	9
	Terdell Middleton, Green Bay	284	1,116	3.9	76	11
	Franco Harris, Pittsburgh[6]	310	1,082	3.5	37	8
	Mark van Eeghen, Oakland[3]	270	1,080	4.0	34	9
	*Terry Miller, Buffalo	238	1,060	4.5	60	7
	Tony Reed, Kansas City	206	1,053	5.1	62	5
	John Riggins, Washington[2]	248	1,014	4.1	31	5
1977	Walter Payton, Chicago[2]	339	1,852	5.5	73	14
	Mark van Eeghen, Oakland[2]	324	1,273	3.9	27	7
	Lawrence McCutcheon, Los Angeles[4]	294	1,238	4.2	48	7
	Franco Harris, Pittsburgh[5]	300	1,162	3.9	61	11
	Lydell Mitchell, Baltimore[3]	301	1,159	3.9	64	3
	Chuck Foreman, Minnesota[3]	270	1,112	4.1	51	6
	Greg Pruitt, Cleveland[3]	236	1,086	4.6	78	3
	Sam Cunningham, New England	270	1,015	3.8	31	4
	*Tony Dorsett, Dallas	208	1,007	4.8	84	12
1976	O.J. Simpson, Buffalo[5]	290	1,503	5.2	75	8
	Walter Payton, Chicago	311	1,390	4.5	60	13
	Delvin Williams, San Francisco	248	1,203	4.9	80	7
	Lydell Mitchell, Baltimore[2]	289	1,200	4.2	43	5
	Lawrence McCutcheon, Los Angeles[3]	291	1,168	4.0	40	9
	Chuck Foreman, Minnesota[2]	278	1,155	4.2	46	13
	Franco Harris, Pittsburgh[4]	289	1,128	3.9	30	14
	Mike Thomas, Washington	254	1,101	4.3	28	5
	Rocky Bleier, Pittsburgh	220	1,036	4.7	28	5
	Mark van Eeghen, Oakland	233	1,012	4.3	21	3
	Otis Armstrong, Denver[2]	247	1,008	4.1	31	5
	Greg Pruitt, Cleveland[2]	209	1,000	4.8	64	4
1975	O.J. Simpson, Buffalo[4]	329	1,817	5.5	88	16
	Franco Harris, Pittsburgh[3]	262	1,246	4.8	36	10
	Lydell Mitchell, Baltimore	289	1,193	4.1	70	11
	Jim Otis, St. Louis	269	1,076	4.0	30	5
	Chuck Foreman, Minnesota	280	1,070	3.8	31	13
	Greg Pruitt, Cleveland	217	1,067	4.9	50	8
	John Riggins, N.Y. Jets	238	1,005	4.2	42	8
	Dave Hampton, Atlanta	250	1,002	4.0	22	5
1974	Otis Armstrong, Denver	263	1,407	5.3	43	9
	*Don Woods, San Diego	227	1,162	5.1	56	7

Year	Player, Team	Att.	Yards	Avg.	Long	TD
	O.J. Simpson, Buffalo[3]	270	1,125	4.2	41	3
	Lawrence McCutcheon, Los Angeles[2]	236	1,109	4.7	23	3
	Franco Harris, Pittsburgh[2]	208	1,006	4.8	54	5
1973	O.J. Simpson, Buffalo[2]	332	2,003	6.0	80	12
	John Brockington, Green Bay[3]	265	1,144	4.3	53	3
	Calvin Hill, Dallas[2]	273	1,142	4.2	21	6
	Lawrence McCutcheon, Los Angeles	210	1,097	5.2	37	2
	Larry Csonka, Miami[3]	219	1,003	4.6	25	5
1972	O.J. Simpson, Buffalo	292	1,251	4.3	94	6
	Larry Brown, Washington[2]	285	1,216	4.3	38	8
	Ron Johnson, N.Y. Giants[2]	298	1,182	4.0	35	9
	Larry Csonka, Miami[2]	213	1,117	5.2	45	6
	Marv Hubbard, Oakland	219	1,100	5.0	39	4
	*Franco Harris, Pittsburgh	188	1,055	5.6	75	10
	Calvin Hill, Dallas	245	1,036	4.2	26	6
	Mike Garrett, San Diego[2]	272	1,031	3.8	41	6
	John Brockington, Green Bay[2]	274	1,027	3.7	30	8
	Eugene (Mercury) Morris, Miami	190	1,000	5.3	33	12
1971	Floyd Little, Denver	284	1,133	4.0	40	6
	*John Brockington, Green Bay	216	1,105	5.1	52	4
	Larry Csonka, Miami	195	1,051	5.4	28	7
	Steve Owens, Detroit	246	1,035	4.2	23	8
	Willie Ellison, Los Angeles	211	1,000	4.7	80	4
1970	Larry Brown, Washington	237	1,125	4.7	75	5
	Ron Johnson, N.Y. Giants	263	1,027	3.9	68	8
1969	Gale Sayers, Chicago[2]	236	1,032	4.4	28	8
1968	Leroy Kelly, Cleveland[3]	248	1,239	5.0	65	16
	*Paul Robinson, Cincinnati	238	1,023	4.3	87	8
1967	Jim Nance, Boston[2]	269	1,216	4.5	53	7
	Leroy Kelly, Cleveland[2]	235	1,205	5.1	42	11
	Hoyle Granger, Houston	236	1,194	5.1	67	6
	Mike Garrett, Kansas City	236	1,087	4.6	58	9
1966	Jim Nance, Boston	299	1,458	4.9	65	11
	Gale Sayers, Chicago	229	1,231	5.4	58	8
	Leroy Kelly, Cleveland	209	1,141	5.5	70	15
	Dick Bass, Los Angeles[2]	248	1,090	4.4	50	8
1965	Jim Brown, Cleveland[7]	289	1,544	5.3	67	17
	Paul Lowe, San Diego[2]	222	1,121	5.0	59	7
1964	Jim Brown, Cleveland[6]	280	1,446	5.2	71	7
	Jim Taylor, Green Bay[5]	235	1,169	5.0	84	12
	John Henry Johnson, Pittsburgh[2]	235	1,048	4.5	45	7
1963	Jim Brown, Cleveland[5]	291	1,863	6.4	80	12
	Clem Daniels, Oakland	215	1,099	5.1	74	3
	Jim Taylor, Green Bay[4]	248	1,018	4.1	40	9
	Paul Lowe, San Diego	177	1,010	5.7	66	8
1962	Jim Taylor, Green Bay[3]	272	1,474	5.4	51	19
	John Henry Johnson, Pittsburgh	251	1,141	4.5	40	7
	Cookie Gilchrist, Buffalo	214	1,096	5.1	44	13
	Abner Haynes, Dall. Texans	221	1,049	4.7	71	13
	Dick Bass, Los Angeles	196	1,033	5.3	57	6
	Charlie Tolar, Houston	244	1,012	4.1	25	7
1961	Jim Brown, Cleveland[4]	305	1,408	4.6	38	8
	Jim Taylor, Green Bay[2]	243	1,307	5.4	53	15
1960	Jim Brown, Cleveland[3]	215	1,257	5.8	71	9
	Jim Taylor, Green Bay	230	1,101	4.8	32	11
	John David Crow, St. Louis	183	1,071	5.9	57	6
1959	Jim Brown, Cleveland[2]	290	1,329	4.6	70	14
	J.D. Smith, San Francisco	207	1,036	5.0	73	10
1958	Jim Brown, Cleveland	257	1,527	5.9	65	17
1956	Rick Casares, Chi. Bears	234	1,126	4.8	68	12
1954	Joe Perry, San Francisco[2]	173	1,049	6.1	58	8
1953	Joe Perry, San Francisco	192	1,018	5.3	51	10
1949	Steve Van Buren, Philadelphia[2]	263	1,146	4.4	41	11
	Tony Canadeo, Green Bay	208	1,052	5.1	54	4
1947	Steve Van Buren, Philadelphia	217	1,008	4.6	45	13
1934	*Beattie Feathers, Chi. Bears	119	1,004	8.4	82	8

First season of professional football.

200 YARDS RUSHING IN A GAME

Date	Player, Team, Opponent	Att.	Yards	TD
Dec. 30, 2006	Tiki Barber, N.Y. Giants vs. Washington	23	234	3
Dec. 7, 2006	Willie Parker, Pittsburgh vs. Cleveland	32	223	1
Nov. 27, 2006	Shaun Alexander, Seattle vs. Green Bay	40	201	0
Nov. 19, 2006	Frank Gore, San Francisco vs. Seattle	24	212	0
Nov. 12, 2006	Willie Parker, Pittsburgh vs. New Orleans	22	213	2
Jan. 1, 2006	Larry Johnson, Kansas City vs. Cincinnati	26	201	3
Dec. 31, 2005	Tiki Barber, N.Y. Giants vs. Oakland	28	203	1
Dec. 17, 2005	Tiki Barber, N.Y. Giants vs. Kansas City	29	220	2
Nov. 20, 2005	Larry Johnson, Kansas City vs. Houston	36	211	2
Oct. 30, 2005	Tiki Barber, N.Y. Giants vs. Washington	24	206	1
Nov. 28, 2004	Rudi Johnson, Cincinnati vs. Cleveland	26	202	2
Nov. 21, 2004	Edgerrin James, Indianapolis vs. Chicago	23	204	1
Dec. 28, 2003	Ahman Green, Green Bay vs. Denver	20	218	2
Dec. 28, 2003	LaDainian Tomlinson, San Diego vs. Oakland	31	243	2
Dec. 21, 2003	Jamal Lewis, Baltimore vs. Cleveland	22	205	2
Dec. 7, 2003	Clinton Portis, Denver vs. Kansas City	22	218	5
Oct. 19, 2003	LaDainian Tomlinson, San Diego vs. Cleveland	26	200	1
Sept. 14, 2003	Jamal Lewis, Baltimore vs. Cleveland	30	295	2
Dec. 29, 2002	*Clinton Portis, Denver vs. Arizona	24	228	2
Dec. 28, 2002	Tiki Barber, N.Y. Giants vs. Philadelphia	32	203	0
Dec. 9, 2002	Ricky Williams, Miami vs. Chicago	31	216	2
Dec. 1, 2002	LaDainian Tomlinson, San Diego vs. Denver	37	220	3
Dec. 1, 2002	Ricky Williams, Miami vs. Buffalo	27	228	2
Sept. 29, 2002	LaDainian Tomlinson, San Diego vs. New England	27	217	2
Dec. 23, 2001	Marshall Faulk, St. Louis vs. Carolina	30	202	2
Nov. 11, 2001	Shaun Alexander, Seattle vs. Oakland	35	266	3
Dec. 24, 2000	Marshall Faulk, St. Louis vs. New Orleans	32	220	2
Dec. 3, 2000	Corey Dillon, Cincinnati vs. Arizona	35	216	1
Dec. 3, 2000	Warrick Dunn, Tampa Bay vs. Dallas	22	210	2
Dec. 3, 2000	*Mike Anderson, Denver vs. New Orleans	37	251	4
Dec. 3, 2000	Curtis Martin, N.Y. Jets vs. Indianapolis	30	203	1
Nov. 19, 2000	Fred Taylor, Jacksonville vs. Pittsburgh	30	234	3
Oct. 22, 2000	Corey Dillon, Cincinnati vs. Denver	22	278	2
Oct. 15, 2000	Marshall Faulk, St. Louis vs. Atlanta	25	208	1
Oct. 15, 2000	Edgerrin James, Indianapolis vs. Seattle	38	219	3
Sept. 24, 2000	Charlie Garner, San Francisco vs. Dallas	36	201	1
Sept. 3, 2000	Duce Staley, Philadelphia vs. Dallas	26	201	1
Nov. 22, 1998	Priest Holmes, Baltimore vs. Cincinnati	36	227	1
Oct. 11, 1998	Terrell Davis, Denver vs Seattle	30	208	1
Dec. 4, 1997	*Corey Dillon, Cincinnati vs. Tennessee	39	246	4
Nov. 23, 1997	Barry Sanders, Detroit vs. Indianapolis	24	216	2
Oct. 26, 1997	Terrell Davis, Denver vs. Buffalo (OT)	42	207	1
Oct. 19, 1997	Napoleon Kaufman, Oakland vs. Denver	28	227	1
Oct. 12, 1997	Barry Sanders, Detroit vs. Tampa Bay	24	215	2
Sept. 21, 1997	Terrell Davis, Denver vs. Cincinnati	27	215	1
Aug. 31, 1997	Eddie George, Tennessee vs. Oakland (OT)	35	216	1
Sept. 22, 1996	LeShon Johnson, Arizona vs. New Orleans	21	214	2
Nov. 13, 1994	Barry Sanders, Detroit vs. Tampa Bay	26	237	0
Dec. 12, 1993	*Jerome Bettis, L.A. Rams vs. New Orleans	28	212	1
Oct. 31, 1993	Emmitt Smith, Dallas vs. Philadelphia	30	237	1
Nov. 24, 1991	Barry Sanders, Detroit vs. Minnesota	23	220	4
Dec. 23, 1990	James Brooks, Cincinnati vs. Houston	20	201	1
Oct. 14, 1990	Barry Word, Kansas City vs. Detroit	18	200	2
Sept. 24, 1990	Thurman Thomas, Buffalo vs. N.Y. Jets	18	214	0
Dec. 24, 1989	Greg Bell, L.A. Rams vs. New England	26	210	1
Sept. 24, 1989	Greg Bell, L.A. Rams vs. Green Bay	28	221	2
Sept. 17, 1989	Gerald Riggs, Washington vs. Philadelphia	29	221	1
Dec. 18, 1988	Gary Anderson, San Diego vs. Kansas City	34	217	1
Nov. 30, 1987	*Bo Jackson, L.A. Raiders vs. Seattle	18	221	2
Nov. 15, 1987	Charles White, L.A. Rams vs. St. Louis	34	213	1
Dec. 7, 1986	Rueben Mayes, New Orleans vs. Miami	28	203	2
Oct. 5, 1986	Eric Dickerson, L.A. Rams vs. Tampa Bay (OT)	30	207	2
Dec. 21, 1985	George Rogers, Washington vs. St. Louis	34	206	1
Dec. 21, 1985	Joe Morris, N.Y. Giants vs. Pittsburgh	36	202	3
Dec. 9, 1984	Eric Dickerson, L.A. Rams vs. Houston	27	215	2
Nov. 18, 1984	*Greg Bell, Buffalo vs. Dallas	27	206	1
Nov. 4, 1984	Eric Dickerson, L.A. Rams vs. St. Louis	21	208	0
Sept. 2, 1984	Gerald Riggs, Atlanta vs. New Orleans	35	202	2
Nov. 27, 1983	*Curt Warner, Seattle vs. Kansas City (OT)	32	207	3
Nov. 6, 1983	James Wilder, Tampa Bay vs. Minnesota	31	219	1

Date	Player, Team, Opponent	Att.	Yards	TD
Sept. 18, 1983	Tony Collins, New England vs. N.Y. Jets	23	212	3
Sept. 4, 1983	George Rogers, New Orleans vs. St. Louis	24	206	2
Dec. 21, 1980	Earl Campbell, Houston vs. Minnesota	29	203	1
Nov. 16, 1980	Earl Campbell, Houston vs. Chicago	31	206	0
Oct. 26, 1980	Earl Campbell, Houston vs. Cincinnati	27	202	2
Oct. 19, 1980	Earl Campbell, Houston vs. Tampa Bay	33	203	0
Nov. 26, 1978	*Terry Miller, Buffalo vs. N.Y. Giants	21	208	2
Dec. 4, 1977	*Tony Dorsett, Dallas vs. Philadelphia	23	206	2
Nov. 20, 1977	Walter Payton, Chicago vs. Minnesota	40	275	1
Oct. 30, 1977	Walter Payton, Chicago vs. Green Bay	23	205	2
Dec. 5, 1976	O.J. Simpson, Buffalo vs. Miami	24	203	1
Nov. 25, 1976	O.J. Simpson, Buffalo vs. Detroit	29	273	2
Oct. 24, 1976	Chuck Foreman, Minnesota vs. Philadelphia	28	200	2
Dec. 14, 1975	Greg Pruitt, Cleveland vs. Kansas City	26	214	3
Sept. 28, 1975	O.J. Simpson, Buffalo vs. Pittsburgh	28	227	1
Dec. 16, 1973	O.J. Simpson, Buffalo vs. N.Y. Jets	34	200	1
Dec. 9, 1973	O.J. Simpson, Buffalo vs. New England	22	219	1
Sept. 16, 1973	O.J. Simpson, Buffalo vs. New England	29	250	2
Dec. 5, 1971	Willie Ellison, Los Angeles vs. New Orleans	26	247	1
Dec. 20, 1970	John (Frenchy) Fuqua, Pittsburgh vs. Philadelphia	20	218	2
Nov. 3, 1968	Gale Sayers, Chicago vs. Green Bay	24	205	0
Oct. 30, 1966	Jim Nance, Boston vs. Oakland	38	208	2
Oct. 10, 1964	John Henry Johnson, Pittsburgh vs. Cleveland	30	200	3
Dec. 8, 1963	Cookie Gilchrist, Buffalo vs. N.Y. Jets	36	243	5
Nov. 3, 1963	Jim Brown, Cleveland vs. Philadelphia	28	223	1
Oct. 20, 1963	Clem Daniels, Oakland vs. N.Y. Jets	27	200	2
Sept. 22, 1963	Jim Brown, Cleveland vs. Dallas	20	232	2
Dec. 10, 1961	Billy Cannon, Houston vs. N.Y. Titans	25	216	3
Nov. 19, 1961	Jim Brown, Cleveland vs. Philadelphia	34	237	4
Dec. 18, 1960	John David Crow, St. Louis vs. Pittsburgh	24	203	0
Nov. 15, 1959	Bobby Mitchell, Cleveland vs. Washington	14	232	3
Nov. 24, 1957	*Jim Brown, Cleveland vs. Los Angeles	31	237	4
Dec. 16, 1956	*Tom Wilson, Los Angeles vs. Green Bay	23	223	0
Nov. 22, 1953	Dan Towler, Los Angeles vs. Baltimore	14	205	1
Nov. 12, 1950	Gene Roberts, N.Y. Giants vs. Chi. Cardinals	26	218	2
Nov. 27, 1949	Steve Van Buren, Philadelphia vs. Pittsburgh	27	205	0
Oct. 8, 1933	Cliff Battles, Boston vs. N.Y. Giants	16	215	1

*First season of professional football.

TIMES 200 OR MORE

107 times by 66 players...Simpson 6; Barber 5; Brown, Campbell, Sanders, Tomlinson 4; Bell, Davis, Dickerson, Dillon, Faulk 3; Alexander, James, Johnson, Lewis, Parker, Payton, Portis, Riggs, Rogers, Williams 2.

4,000 YARDS PASSING IN A SEASON

Year	Player, Team	Att.	Comp.	Pct.	Yards	TD	Int.
2006	Drew Brees, New Orleans	554	356	64.3	4,418	26	11
	Petyon Manning, Indianapolis[7]	557	362	65.0	4,397	31	9
	Marc Bulger, St. Louis	588	370	62.9	4,301	24	8
	Jon Kitna, Detroit	596	372	62.4	4,208	21	22
	Carson Palmer, Cincinnati	520	324	62.3	4,035	28	13
2005	Tom Brady, New England	530	334	63.0	4,110	26	14
	Trent Green, Kansas City[3]	507	317	62.5	4,014	17	10
2004	Daunte Culpepper, Minnesota	548	379	69.2	4,717	39	11
	Trent Green, Kansas City[2]	556	369	66.4	4,591	27	17
	Peyton Manning, Indianapolis[6]	497	336	67.6	4,557	49	10
	Jake Plummer, Denver	521	303	58.2	4,089	27	20
	Brett Favre, Green Bay[4]	540	346	64.1	4,088	30	17
2003	Peyton Manning, Indianapolis[5]	566	379	67.0	4,267	29	10
	Trent Green, Kansas City	523	330	63.1	4,039	24	12
2002	Rich Gannon, Oakland	618	418	67.6	4,689	26	10
	Drew Bledsoe, Buffalo[3]	610	375	61.5	4,359	24	15
	Peyton Manning, Indianapolis[4]	591	392	66.3	4,200	27	19
	Kerry Collins, N.Y. Giants	545	335	61.5	4,073	19	14
2001	Kurt Warner, St. Louis[2]	546	375	68.7	4,830	36	22
	Peyton Manning, Indianapolis[3]	547	343	62.7	4,131	26	23
2000	Peyton Manning, Indianapolis[2]	571	357	62.5	4,413	33	15
	Jeff Garcia, San Francisco	561	355	63.3	4,278	31	10
	Elvis Grbac, Kansas City	547	326	59.6	4,169	28	14
1999	Steve Beuerlein, Carolina	571	343	60.1	4,436	36	15

Year	Player, Team	Att.	Comp.	Pct.	Yards	TD	Int.
	Kurt Warner, St. Louis	499	325	65.1	4,353	41	13
	Peyton Manning, Indianapolis	533	331	62.1	4,135	26	15
	Brett Favre, Green Bay[3]	595	341	57.3	4,091	22	23
	Brad Johnson, Washington	519	316	60.9	4,005	24	13
1998	Brett Favre, Green Bay[2]	551	347	63.0	4,212	31	23
	Steve Young, San Francisco[2]	517	322	62.3	4,170	36	12
1996	Mark Brunell, Jacksonville	557	353	63.4	4,367	19	20
	Vinny Testaverde, Baltimore	549	325	59.2	4,177	33	19
	Drew Bledsoe, New England[2]	623	373	59.9	4,086	27	15
1995	Brett Favre, Green Bay	570	359	63.0	4,413	38	13
	Scott Mitchell, Detroit	583	346	59.3	4,338	32	12
	Warren Moon, Minnesota[4]	606	377	62.2	4,228	33	14
	Jeff George, Atlanta	557	336	60.3	4,143	24	11
1994	Drew Bledsoe, New England[6]	691	400	57.9	4,555	25	27
	Dan Marino, Miami[6]	615	385	62.6	4,453	30	17
	Warren Moon, Minnesota[3]	601	371	61.7	4,264	18	19
1993	John Elway, Denver	551	348	63.2	4,030	25	10
	Steve Young, San Francisco	462	314	68.0	4,023	29	16
1992	Dan Marino, Miami[5]	554	330	59.6	4,116	24	16
1991	Warren Moon, Houston[2]	655	404	61.7	4,690	23	21
1990	Warren Moon, Houston	584	362	62.0	4,689	33	13
1989	Don Majkowski, Green Bay	599	353	58.9	4,318	27	20
	Jim Everett, L.A. Rams	518	304	58.7	4,310	29	17
1988	Dan Marino, Miami[4]	606	354	58.4	4,434	28	23
1986	Dan Marino, Miami[3]	623	378	60.7	4,746	44	23
	Jay Schroeder, Washington	541	276	51.0	4,109	22	22
1985	Dan Marino, Miami[2]	567	336	59.3	4,137	30	21
1984	Dan Marino, Miami	564	362	64.2	5,084	48	17
	Neil Lomax, St. Louis	560	345	61.6	4,614	28	16
	Phil Simms, N.Y. Giants	533	286	53.7	4,044	22	18
1983	Lynn Dickey, Green Bay	484	289	59.7	4,458	32	29
	Bill Kenney, Kansas City	603	346	57.4	4,348	24	18
1981	Dan Fouts, San Diego[3]	609	360	59.1	4,802	33	17
1980	Dan Fouts, San Diego[2]	589	348	59.1	4,715	30	24
	Brian Sipe, Cleveland	554	337	60.8	4,132	30	14
1979	Dan Fouts, San Diego	530	332	62.6	4,082	24	24
1967	Joe Namath, N.Y. Jets	491	258	52.5	4,007	26	28

400 YARDS PASSING IN A GAME

Date	Player, Team, Opponent	Att.	Comp.	Yards	TD
Dec. 10, 2006	Chris Wenke, Carolina vs. N.Y. Giants	61	34	423	1
Nov. 26, 2006	Matt Leinart, Arizona vs. Minnesota	51	31	405	1
Nov. 19, 2006	Drew Brees, New Orleans vs. Cincinnati	52	37	510	2
Nov. 12, 2006	Carson Palmer, Cincinnati vs. San Diego	42	31	440	3
Nov. 5, 2006	Ben Roethlisberger, Pittsburgh vs. Denver	54	38	433	1
Oct. 22, 2006	Joey Harrington, Miami vs. Green Bay	62	33	414	2
Sept. 17, 2006	Peyton Manning, Indianapolis vs. Houston	38	26	400	3
Oct. 2, 2005	Marc Bulger, St. Louis vs. N.Y. Giants	62	40	442	2
Jan. 2, 2005	Marc Bulger, St. Louis vs. N.Y. Jets (OT)	39	29	450	3
Dec. 19, 2004	Daunte Culpepper, Minnesota vs. Detroit	35	25	404	3
Dec. 19, 2004	Billy Volek, Tennessee vs. Oakland	60	40	492	4
Dec. 13, 2004	Billy Volek, Tennessee vs. Kansas City	43	29	426	4
Dec. 6, 2004	Matt Hasselbeck, Seattle vs. Dallas	40	28	414	3
Dec. 5, 2004	Peyton Manning, Indianapolis vs. Tennessee	33	25	425	3
Dec. 5, 2004	Donovan McNabb, Philadelphia vs. Green Bay	43	32	464	5
Nov. 29, 2004	Marc Bulger, St. Louis vs. Green Bay	53	35	448	2
Nov. 28, 2004	Kelly Holcomb, Cleveland vs. Cincinnati	39	30	413	5
Oct. 31, 2004	Peyton Manning, Indianapolis vs. Kansas City	44	25	472	5
Oct. 31, 2004	Jake Plummer, Denver vs. Atlanta	55	31	499	4
Oct. 17, 2004	Daunte Culpepper, Minnesota vs. New Orleans	37	26	425	5
Oct. 10. 2004	Tim Rattay, San Francisco vs. Arizona (OT)	57	38	417	2
Nov. 16, 2003	Peyton Manning, Indianapolis vs. N.Y. Jets	36	27	401	1
Oct. 12, 2003	Trent Green, Kansas City vs. Green Bay (OT)	45	27	400	3
Oct. 12, 2003	Steve McNair, Tennessee vs. Houston	27	18	421	3
Dec. 29, 2002	Matt Hasselbeck, Seattle vs. San Diego (OT)	53	36	449	2
Dec. 1, 2002	Matt Hasselbeck, Seattle vs. San Francisco	55	30	427	3
Nov. 10, 2002	Marc Bulger, St. Louis vs. San Diego	48	36	453	4
Nov. 10, 2002	Tommy Maddox, Pittsburgh vs. Atlanta (OT)	41	28	473	4
Oct. 6, 2002	Drew Bledsoe, Buffalo vs. Oakland	53	32	417	2

Date	Player, Team, Opponent	Att.	Comp.	Yards	TD
Sept. 22, 2002	Tom Brady, New England vs. Kansas City (OT)	54	39	410	4
Sept. 15, 2002	Drew Bledsoe, Buffalo vs. Minnesota (OT)	49	35	463	3
Sept. 15, 2002	Rich Gannon, Oakland vs. Pittsburgh	64	43	403	1
Dec. 30, 2001	Jon Kitna, Cincinnati vs. Pittsburgh	68	35	411	2
Dec. 23, 2001	Chris Chandler, Atlanta vs. Buffalo	40	28	431	2
Nov. 18, 2001	Charlie Batch, Detroit vs. Arizona	62	36	436	3
Nov. 18, 2001	Kurt Warner, St. Louis vs. New England	42	30	401	3
Sept. 23, 2001	Peyton Manning, Indianapolis vs. Buffalo	29	23	421	4
Dec. 24, 2000	Vinny Testaverde, N.Y. Jets vs. Baltimore	69	36	481	2
Dec. 17, 2000	Jeff Garcia, San Francisco vs. Chicago	44	36	402	2
Dec. 3, 2000	Aaron Brooks, New Orleans vs. Denver	48	30	441	2
Nov. 19, 2000	Gus Frerotte, Denver vs. San Diego	58	36	462	5
Nov. 5, 2000	Elvis Grbac, Kansas City vs. Oakland	53	39	504	2
Nov. 5, 2000	Trent Green, St. Louis vs. Carolina	42	29	431	2
Sept. 25, 2000	Peyton Manning, Indianapolis vs. Jacksonville	36	23	440	4
Sept. 4, 2000	Kurt Warner, St. Louis vs. Denver	35	25	441	3
Dec. 26, 1999	Brad Johnson, Washington vs. San Francisco (OT)	47	32	471	2
Dec. 5, 1999	Jeff Garcia, San Francisco vs. Cincinnati	49	33	437	2
Nov. 28, 1999	Jim Harbaugh, San Diego vs. Minnesota	39	25	404	1
Nov. 14, 1999	Jim Miller, Chicago vs. Minnesota (OT)	48	34	422	3
Sept. 26, 1999	Peyton Manning, Indianapolis vs. San Diego	54	29	404	2
Dec. 6, 1998	Vinny Testaverde, N.Y. Jets vs. Seattle	63	42	418	2
Dec. 6, 1998	John Elway, Denver vs. Kansas City	32	22	400	2
Nov. 26, 1998	Troy Aikman, Dallas vs. Minnesota	57	34	455	1
Nov. 23, 1998	Drew Bledsoe, New England vs. Miami	54	28	423	2
Nov. 15, 1998	Jake Plummer, Arizona vs. Dallas	56	31	465	3
Oct. 5, 1998	Randall Cunningham, Minnesota vs. Green Bay	32	20	442	4
Sept. 6, 1998	Glenn Foley, N.Y. Jets vs. San Francisco (OT)	58	30	415	3
Nov. 2, 1997	Tony Banks, St. Louis vs. Atlanta	34	23	401	2
Oct. 26, 1997	Warren Moon, Seattle vs. Oakland	44	28	409	5
Nov. 10, 1996	Boomer Esiason, Arizona vs. Washington (OT)	59	35	522	3
Nov. 3, 1996	Drew Bledsoe, New England vs. Miami	41	30	419	3
Oct. 27, 1996	Vinny Testaverde, Baltimore vs. St. Louis (OT)	51	31	429	3
Oct. 20, 1996	Mark Brunell, Jacksonville vs. St. Louis	52	37	421	0
Sept. 22, 1996	Mark Brunell, Jacksonville vs. New England (OT)	39	23	432	3
Dec. 18, 1995	Steve Young, San Francisco vs. Minnesota	49	30	425	3
Nov. 26, 1995	Dave Krieg, Arizona vs. Atlanta (OT)	43	27	413	4
Nov. 23, 1995	Scott Mitchell, Detroit vs. Minnesota	45	30	410	4
Oct. 1, 1995	Dan Marino, Miami vs. Cincinnati	48	33	450	2
Nov. 20, 1994	Warren Moon, Minnesota vs. N.Y. Jets	50	33	400	2
Nov. 13, 1994	Drew Bledsoe, New England vs. Minnesota (OT)	70	45	426	3
Nov. 6, 1994	Warren Moon, Minnesota vs. New Orleans	57	33	420	3
Sept. 25, 1994	Dan Marino, Miami vs. Minnesota	54	29	431	3
Sept. 4, 1994	Dan Marino, Miami vs. New England (OT)	42	23	473	5
Sept. 4, 1994	Drew Bledsoe, New England vs. Miami (OT)	51	32	421	4
Dec. 19, 1993	Steve Beuerlein, Phoenix vs. Seattle	53	34	431	3
Dec. 5, 1993	Brett Favre, Green Bay vs. Chicago	54	36	402	2
Nov. 28, 1993	Steve Young, San Francisco vs. L.A. Rams	32	26	462	4
Oct. 31, 1993	Jeff Hostetler, L.A. Raiders vs. San Diego	32	20	424	2
Sept. 13, 1992	Steve Young, San Francisco vs. Buffalo	37	26	449	3
Sept. 13, 1992	Jim Kelly, Buffalo vs. San Francisco	33	22	403	3
Nov. 10, 1991	Warren Moon, Houston vs. Dallas (OT)	56	41	432	0
Nov. 10, 1991	Mark Rypien, Washington vs. Atlanta	31	16	442	6
Oct. 13, 1991	Warren Moon, Houston vs. N.Y. Jets	50	35	423	2
Dec. 16, 1990	Warren Moon, Houston vs. Kansas City	45	27	527	3
Nov. 4, 1990	Joe Montana, San Francisco vs. Green Bay	40	25	411	3
Oct. 14, 1990	Joe Montana, San Francisco vs. Atlanta	49	32	476	6
Oct. 7, 1990	Boomer Esiason, Cincinnati vs. L.A. Rams (OT)	45	31	490	3
Dec. 23, 1989	Warren Moon, Houston vs. Cleveland	51	32	414	2
Dec. 11, 1989	Joe Montana, San Francisco vs. L.A. Rams	42	30	458	3
Nov. 26, 1989	Jim Everett, L.A. Rams vs. New Orleans (OT)	51	29	454	1
Nov. 26, 1989	Mark Rypien, Washington vs. Chicago	47	30	401	4
Oct. 2, 1989	Randall Cunningham, Philadelphia vs. Chicago	62	32	401	1
Sept. 24, 1989	Joe Montana, San Francisco vs. Philadelphia	34	25	428	5
Sept. 24, 1989	Dan Marino, Miami vs. N.Y. Jets	55	33	427	3
Sept. 17, 1989	Randall Cunningham, Philadelphia vs. Washington	46	34	447	5
Dec. 18, 1988	Dave Krieg, Seattle vs. L.A. Raiders	32	19	410	4
Dec. 12, 1988	Dan Marino, Miami vs. Cleveland	50	30	404	4
Oct. 23, 1988	Dan Marino, Miami vs. N.Y. Jets	60	35	521	3

Date	Player, Team, Opponent	Att.	Comp.	Yards	TD
Oct. 16, 1988	Vinny Testaverde, Tampa Bay vs. Indianapolis	42	25	469	2
Sept. 11, 1988	Doug Williams, Washington vs. Pittsburgh	52	30	430	2
Nov. 29, 1987	Tom Ramsey, New England vs. Philadelphia	53	34	402	3
Nov. 22, 1987	Boomer Esiason, Cincinnati vs. Pittsburgh	53	30	409	0
Sept. 20, 1987	Neil Lomax, St. Louis vs. San Diego	61	32	457	3
Dec. 21, 1986	Boomer Esiason, Cincinnati vs. N.Y. Jets	30	23	425	5
Dec. 14, 1986	Dan Marino, Miami vs. L.A. Rams (OT)	46	29	403	5
Nov. 23, 1986	Bernie Kosar, Cleveland vs. Pittsburgh (OT)	46	28	414	2
Nov. 17, 1986	Joe Montana, San Francisco vs. Washington	60	33	441	0
Nov. 16, 1986	Dan Marino, Miami vs. Buffalo	54	39	404	4
Nov. 10, 1986	Bernie Kosar, Cleveland vs. Miami	50	32	401	0
Nov. 2, 1986	Tommy Kramer, Minnesota vs. Washington (OT)	35	20	490	4
Nov. 2, 1986	Ken O'Brien, N.Y. Jets vs. Seattle	32	26	431	4
Oct. 27, 1986	Jay Schroeder, Washington vs. N.Y. Giants	40	22	420	1
Oct. 12, 1986	Steve Grogan, New England vs. N.Y. Jets	42	23	401	3
Sept. 21, 1986	Ken O'Brien, N.Y. Jets vs. Miami (OT)	43	29	479	4
Sept. 21, 1986	Dan Marino, Miami vs. N.Y. Jets (OT)	50	30	448	6
Sept. 21, 1986	Tony Eason, New England vs. Seattle	45	26	414	3
Dec. 20, 1985	John Elway, Denver vs. Seattle	42	24	432	1
Nov. 10, 1985	Dan Fouts, San Diego vs. L.A. Raiders (OT)	41	26	436	4
Oct. 13, 1985	Phil Simms, N.Y. Giants vs. Cincinnati	62	40	513	1
Oct. 13, 1985	Dave Krieg, Seattle vs. Atlanta	51	33	405	4
Oct. 6, 1985	Phil Simms, N.Y. Giants vs. Dallas	36	18	432	3
Oct. 6, 1985	Joe Montana, San Francisco vs. Atlanta	57	37	429	5
Sept. 19, 1985	Tommy Kramer, Minnesota vs. Chicago	55	28	436	3
Sept. 15, 1985	Dan Fouts, San Diego vs. Seattle	43	29	440	4
Dec. 16, 1984	Neil Lomax, St. Louis vs. Washington	46	37	468	2
Dec. 9, 1984	Dan Marino, Miami vs. Indianapolis	41	29	404	4
Dec. 2, 1984	Dan Marino, Miami vs. L.A. Raiders	57	35	470	4
Nov. 25, 1984	Dave Krieg, Seattle vs. Denver	44	30	406	3
Nov. 4, 1984	Dan Marino, Miami vs. N.Y. Jets	42	23	422	2
Oct. 21, 1984	Dan Fouts, San Diego vs. L.A. Raiders	45	24	410	3
Sept. 30, 1984	Dan Marino, Miami vs. St. Louis	36	24	429	3
Sept. 2, 1984	Phil Simms, N.Y. Giants vs. Philadelphia	30	23	409	4
Dec. 11, 1983	Bill Kenney, Kansas City vs. San Diego	41	31	411	4
Nov. 20, 1983	Dave Krieg, Seattle vs. Denver	42	31	418	3
Oct. 9, 1983	Joe Ferguson, Buffalo vs. Miami (OT)	55	38	419	5
Oct. 2, 1983	Joe Theismann, Washington vs. L.A. Raiders	39	23	417	3
Sept. 25, 1983	Richard Todd, N.Y. Jets vs. L.A. Rams (OT)	50	37	446	2
Dec. 26, 1982	Vince Ferragamo, L.A. Rams vs. Chicago	46	30	509	3
Dec. 20, 1982	Dan Fouts, San Diego vs. Cincinnati	40	25	435	1
Dec. 20, 1982	Ken Anderson, Cincinnati vs. San Diego	56	40	416	2
Dec. 11, 1982	Dan Fouts, San Diego vs. San Francisco	48	33	444	5
Nov. 21, 1982	Joe Montana, San Francisco vs. St. Louis	39	26	408	3
Nov. 15, 1981	Steve Bartkowski, Atlanta vs. Pittsburgh	50	33	416	2
Oct. 25, 1981	Brian Sipe, Cleveland vs. Baltimore	41	30	444	4
Oct. 25, 1981	David Woodley, Miami vs. Dallas	37	21	408	3
Oct. 11, 1981	Tommy Kramer, Minnesota vs. San Diego	43	27	444	4
Dec. 14, 1980	Tommy Kramer, Minnesota vs. Cleveland	49	38	456	4
Nov. 16, 1980	Doug Williams, Tampa Bay vs. Minnesota	55	30	486	4
Oct. 19, 1980	Dan Fouts, San Diego vs. N.Y. Giants	41	26	444	3
Oct. 12, 1980	Lynn Dickey, Green Bay vs. Tampa Bay (OT)	51	35	418	1
Sept. 21, 1980	Richard Todd, N.Y. Jets vs. San Francisco	60	42	447	3
Oct. 3, 1976	James Harris, Los Angeles vs. Miami	29	17	436	2
Nov. 17, 1975	Ken Anderson, Cincinnati vs. Buffalo	46	30	447	2
Nov. 18, 1974	Charley Johnson, Denver vs. Kansas City	42	28	445	2
Dec. 11, 1972	Joe Namath, N.Y. Jets vs. Oakland	46	25	403	1
Sept. 24, 1972	Joe Namath, N.Y. Jets vs. Baltimore	28	15	496	6
Dec. 21, 1969	Don Horn, Green Bay vs. St. Louis	31	22	410	5
Sept. 28, 1969	Joe Kapp, Minnesota vs. Baltimore	43	28	449	7
Sept. 9, 1968	Pete Beathard, Houston vs. Kansas City	48	23	413	2
Nov. 26, 1967	Sonny Jurgensen, Washington vs. Cleveland	50	32	418	3
Oct. 1, 1967	Joe Namath, N.Y. Jets vs. Miami	39	23	415	3
Sept. 17, 1967	Johnny Unitas, Baltimore vs. Atlanta	32	22	401	2
Nov. 13, 1966	Don Meredith, Dallas vs. Washington	29	21	406	2
Nov. 28, 1965	Sonny Jurgensen, Washington vs. Dallas	43	26	411	3
Oct. 24, 1965	Fran Tarkenton, Minnesota vs. San Francisco	35	21	407	3
Nov. 1, 1964	Len Dawson, Kansas City vs. Denver	38	23	435	6

Date	Player, Team, Opponent	Att.	Comp.	Yards	TD
Oct. 25, 1964	Cotton Davidson, Oakland vs. Denver	36	23	427	5
Oct. 16, 1964	Babe Parilli, Boston vs. Oakland	47	25	422	4
Dec. 22, 1963	Tom Flores, Oakland vs. Houston	29	17	407	6
Nov. 17, 1963	Norm Snead, Washington vs. Pittsburgh	40	23	424	2
Nov. 10, 1963	Don Meredith, Dallas vs. San Francisco	48	30	460	3
Oct. 13, 1963	Charley Johnson, St. Louis vs. Pittsburgh	41	20	428	2
Dec. 16, 1962	Sonny Jurgensen, Philadelphia vs. St. Louis	34	15	419	5
Nov. 18, 1962	Bill Wade, Chicago vs. Dall. Cowboys	46	28	466	2
Oct. 28, 1962	Y.A. Tittle, N.Y. Giants vs. Washington	39	27	505	7
Sept. 15, 1962	Frank Tripucka, Denver vs. Buffalo	56	29	447	2
Dec. 17, 1961	Sonny Jurgensen, Philadelphia vs. Detroit	42	27	403	3
Nov. 19, 1961	George Blanda, Houston vs. N.Y. Titans	32	20	418	7
Oct. 29, 1961	George Blanda, Houston vs. Buffalo	32	18	464	4
Oct. 29, 1961	Sonny Jurgensen, Philadelphia vs. Washington	41	27	436	3
Oct. 13, 1961	Jacky Lee, Houston vs. Boston	41	27	457	2
Dec. 13, 1958	Bobby Layne, Pittsburgh vs. Chi. Cardinals	49	23	409	2
Nov. 8, 1953	Bobby Thomason, Philadelphia vs. N.Y. Giants	44	22	437	4
Oct. 4, 1952	Otto Graham, Cleveland vs. Pittsburgh	49	21	401	3
Sept. 28, 1951	Norm Van Brocklin, Los Angeles vs. N.Y. Yanks	41	27	554	5
Dec. 11, 1949	Johnny Lujack, Chi. Bears vs. Chi. Cardinals	39	24	468	6
Oct. 31, 1948	Sammy Baugh, Washington vs. Boston	24	17	446	4
Oct. 31, 1948	Jim Hardy, Los Angeles vs. Chi. Cardinals	53	28	406	3
Nov. 14, 1943	Sid Luckman, Chi. Bears vs. N.Y. Giants	32	21	433	7

TIMES 400 OR MORE

189 times by 101 players...Marino 13; Manning, Montana, Moon 7; Bledsoe, Fouts 6; Jurgensen, Krieg 5; Bulger, Esiason, Kramer, Testaverde 4; Cunningham, Hasselbeck, Namath, Simms, Young 3; Anderson, Blanda, Brunell, Culpepper, Elway, Garcia, Green, Johnson, Kosar, Lomax, Meredith, O'Brien, Plummer, Rypien, Todd, Volek, Warner, Williams 2.

100 PASS RECEPTIONS IN A SEASON

Year	Player, Team	No.	Yards	Avg.	Long	TD
2006	Andre Johnson, Houston	103	1,147	11.1	53	5
2005	Larry Fitzgerald, Arizona	103	1,409	13.7	47	10
	Steve Smith, Carolina	103	1,563	15.2	80	12
	Anquan Boldin, Arizona[2]	102	1,402	13.7	54	7
	Torry Holt, St. Louis[2]	102	1,331	13.0	44	9
2004	Tony Gonzalez, Kansas City	102	1,258	12.3	32	7
2003	Torry Holt, St. Louis	117	1,696	14.5	48	12
	Randy Moss, Minnesota[2]	111	1,632	14.7	72	17
	*Anquan Boldin, Arizona	101	1,377	13.6	71	8
	LaDainian Tomlinson, San Diego	100	725	7.3	73	4
2002	Marvin Harrison, Indianapolis[4]	143	1,722	12.0	69	11
	Hines Ward, Pittsburgh	112	1,329	11.9	72	12
	Randy Moss, Minnesota	106	1,347	12.7	60	7
	Eric Moulds, Buffalo	100	1,292	12.9	70	10
	Terrell Owens, San Francisco	100	1,300	13.0	76	13
2001	Rod Smith, Denver[2]	113	1,343	11.9	65	11
	Jimmy Smith, Jacksonville[2]	112	1,373	12.3	35	8
	Marvin Harrison, Indianapolis[3]	109	1,524	14.0	68	15
	Keyshawn Johnson, Tampa Bay	106	1,266	11.9	47	1
	Troy Brown, New England	101	1,199	11.9	60	5
	Marty Booker, Chicago	100	1,071	10.7	66	8
2000	Marvin Harrison, Indianapolis[2]	102	1,413	13.9	78	14
	Muhsin Muhammad, Carolina	102	1,183	11.6	36	6
	Ed McCaffrey, Denver	101	1,317	13.0	61	9
	Rod Smith, Denver	100	1,602	16.0	49	8
1999	Jimmy Smith, Jacksonville	116	1,636	14.1	62	6
	Marvin Harrison, Indianapolis	115	1,663	14.5	57	12
1997	Tim Brown, Oakland	104	1,408	13.5	59	5
	Herman Moore, Detroit[3]	104	1,293	12.4	79	8
1996	Jerry Rice, San Francisco[4]	108	1,254	11.6	39	8
	Herman Moore, Detroit[2]	106	1,296	12.2	50	9
	Carl Pickens, Cincinnati	100	1,180	11.8	61	12
1995	Herman Moore, Detroit	123	1,686	13.7	69	14
	Jerry Rice, San Francisco[3]	122	1,848	15.1	81	15
	Cris Carter, Minnesota[2]	122	1,371	11.2	60	17

Year	Player, Team	No.	Yards	Avg.	Long	TD
	Isaac Bruce, St. Louis	119	1,781	15.0	72	13
	Michael Irvin, Dallas	111	1,603	14.4	50	10
	Brett Perriman, Detroit	108	1,488	13.8	91	9
	Eric Metcalf, Atlanta	104	1,189	11.4	62	8
	Robert Brooks, Green Bay	102	1,497	14.7	99	13
	Larry Centers, Arizona	101	962	9.5	32	2
1994	Cris Carter, Minnesota	122	1,256	10.3	65	7
	Jerry Rice, San Francisco[2]	112	1,499	13.4	69	13
	Terance Mathis, Atlanta	111	1,342	12.1	81	11
1993	Sterling Sharpe, Green Bay[2]	112	1,274	11.4	54	11
1992	Sterling Sharpe, Green Bay	108	1,461	13.5	76	13
1991	Haywood Jeffires, Houston	100	1,181	11.8	44	7
1990	Jerry Rice, San Francisco	100	1,502	15.0	64	13
1984	Art Monk, Washington	106	1,372	12.9	72	7
1964	Charley Hennigan, Houston	101	1,546	15.3	53	8
1961	Lionel Taylor, Denver	100	1,176	11.8	52	4

1,000 YARDS PASS RECEIVING IN A SEASON

Year	Player, Team	No.	Yards	Avg.	Long	TD
2006	Chad Johnson, Cincinnati[5]	87	1,369	15.7	74	7
	Marvin Harrison, Indianapolis[8]	95	1,366	14.4	68	12
	Reggie Wayne, Indianapolis[3]	86	1,310	15.2	51	9
	Roy Williams, Detroit	82	1,310	16.0	60	7
	Donald Driver, Green Bay[4]	92	1,295	14.1	82	8
	Lee Evans, Buffalo	82	1,292	15.8	83	8
	Anquan Boldin, Arizona[3]	83	1,203	14.5	64	4
	Torry Holt, St. Louis[7]	93	1,188	12.8	67	10
	Terrell Owens, Dallas[7]	85	1,180	13.9	56	13
	Steve Smith, Carolina[3]	83	1,166	14.1	72	8
	Andre Johnson, Houston[2]	103	1,147	11.1	53	5
	Isaac Bruce, St. Louis[6]	74	1,098	14.8	45	3
	Laveranues Coles, N.Y. Jets[2]	91	1,098	12.1	58	6
	Mike Furrey, Detroit	98	1,086	11.1	31	6
	Javon Walker, Denver[2]	69	1,084	15.7	83	8
	T.J. Houshmanzadeh, Cincinnati	90	1,081	12.0	40	9
	Joey Galloway, Tampa Bay[5]	62	1,057	17.1	64	7
	Terry Glenn, Dallas[4]	70	1,047	15.0	54	6
	*Marques Colston, New Orleans	70	1,038	14.8	86	8
2005	Steve Smith, Carolina[2]	103	1,563	15.2	80	12
	Santana Moss, Washington[2]	84	1,483	17.7	78	9
	Chad Johnson, Cincinnati[4]	97	1,432	14.8	70	9
	Larry Fitzgerald, Arizona	103	1,409	13.7	47	10
	Anquan Boldin, Arizona[2]	102	1,402	13.7	54	7
	Torry Holt, St. Louis[6]	102	1,331	13.0	44	9
	Joey Galloway, Tampa Bay[4]	83	1,287	15.5	80	10
	Donald Driver, Green Bay[3]	86	1,221	14.2	59	5
	Plaxico Burress, N.Y. Giants[3]	76	1,214	16.0	78	7
	Marvin Harrison, Indianapolis[7]	82	1,146	14.0	80	12
	Terry Glenn, Dallas[3]	62	1,136	18.3	71	7
	Chris Chambers, Miami	82	1,118	13.6	77	11
	Rod Smith, Denver[6]	85	1,105	13.0	72	6
	Eddie Kennison, Kansas City[2]	68	1,102	16.2	55	5
	Antonio Gates, San Diego	89	1,101	12.4	38	10
	Derrick Mason, Baltimore[5]	86	1,073	12.5	39	3
	Reggie Wayne, Indianapolis[2]	83	1,055	12.7	66	5
	Jimmy Smith, Jacksonville[9]	70	1,023	14.6	45	6
	Antonio Bryant, Cleveland	69	1,009	14.6	54	4
	Randy Moss, Oakland[7]	60	1,005	16.8	79	8
2004	Muhsin Muhammad, Carolina[3]	93	1,405	15.1	51	16
	Joe Horn, New Orleans[4]	94	1,399	14.9	57	11
	Javon Walker, Green Bay	89	1,382	15.5	79	12
	Torry Holt, St. Louis[5]	94	1,372	14.6	75	10
	Isaac Bruce, St. Louis[7]	89	1,292	14.5	56	6
	Chad Johnson, Cincinnati[3]	95	1,274	13.4	53	9
	Tony Gonzalez, Kansas City[2]	102	1,258	12.3	32	7
	Drew Bennett, Tennessee	80	1,247	15.6	48	11
	Reggie Wayne, Indianapolis	77	1,210	15.7	71	12
	Donald Driver, Green Bay[2]	84	1,208	14.4	50	9
	Terrell Owens, Philadelphia[6]	77	1,200	15.6	59	14

Year	Player, Team	No.	Yards	Avg.	Long	TD
	Darrell Jackson, Seattle[3]	87	1,199	13.8	56	7
	*Michael Clayton, Tampa Bay	80	1,193	14.9	75	7
	Jimmy Smith, Jacksonville[8]	74	1,172	15.8	65	6
	Derrick Mason, Tennessee[4]	96	1,168	12.2	37	7
	Rod Smith, Denver[7]	79	1,144	14.5	85	7
	Andre Johnson, Houston	79	1,142	14.5	54	6
	Marvin Harrison, Indianapolis[6]	86	1,113	12.9	59	15
	Eddie Kennison, Kansas City	62	1,086	17.5	70	8
	Ashley Lelie, Denver	54	1,084	20.1	58	7
	Brandon Stokley, Indianapolis	68	1,077	15.8	69	10
	Eric Moulds, Buffalo[4]	88	1,043	11.9	49	5
	Nate Burleson, Minnesota	68	1,006	14.8	68	9
	Hines Ward, Pittsburgh[4]	80	1,004	12.6	58	4
2003	Torry Holt, St. Louis[4]	117	1,696	14.5	48	12
	Randy Moss, Minnesota[6]	111	1,632	14.7	72	17
	*Anquan Boldin, Arizona	101	1,377	13.6	71	8
	Chad Johnson, Cincinnati[2]	90	1,355	15.1	82	10
	Derrick Mason, Tennessee[3]	95	1,303	13.7	50	8
	Marvin Harrison, Indianapolis[5]	94	1,272	13.5	79	10
	Laveranues Coles, Washington[2]	82	1,204	14.7	64	6
	Keenan McCardell, Tampa Bay[6]	84	1,174	14.0	76	8
	Hines Ward, Pittsburgh[3]	95	1,163	12.2	50	10
	Darrell Jackson, Seattle[2]	68	1,137	16.7	80	9
	Steve Smith, Carolina	88	1,110	12.6	67	7
	Santana Moss, N.Y. Jets	74	1,105	14.9	65	10
	Terrell Owens, San Francisco[5]	80	1,102	13.8	75	9
	Amani Toomer, N.Y. Giants[5]	63	1,057	16.8	77	5
2002	Marvin Harrison, Indianapolis[4]	143	1,722	12.0	69	11
	Randy Moss, Minnesota[5]	106	1,347	12.7	60	7
	Amani Toomer, N.Y. Giants[4]	82	1,343	16.4	82	8
	Hines Ward, Pittsburgh[2]	112	1,329	11.9	72	12
	Plaxico Burress, Pittsburgh[2]	78	1,325	17.0	62	7
	Joe Horn, New Orleans[3]	88	1,312	14.9	63	7
	Torry Holt, St. Louis[3]	91	1,302	14.3	58	4
	Terrell Owens, San Francisco[4]	100	1,300	13.0	76	13
	Eric Moulds, Buffalo[3]	100	1,292	12.9	70	10
	Laveranues Coles, N.Y. Jets	89	1,264	14.2	43	5
	Peerless Price, Buffalo	94	1,252	13.3	73	9
	Koren Robinson, Seattle	78	1,240	15.9	83	5
	Jerry Rice, Oakland[14]	92	1,211	13.2	75	7
	Marty Booker, Chicago[2]	97	1,189	12.3	54	6
	Chad Johnson, Cincinnati	69	1,166	16.9	72	5
	Keyshawn Johnson, Tampa Bay[4]	76	1,088	14.3	76	5
	Isaac Bruce, St. Louis[6]	79	1,075	13.6	34	7
	Donald Driver, Green Bay	70	1,064	15.2	85	9
	Jimmy Smith, Jacksonville[7]	80	1,027	12.8	47	7
	Rod Smith, Denver[6]	89	1,027	11.5	46	5
	Derrick Mason, Tennessee[2]	79	1,012	12.8	40	5
	Rod Gardner, Washington	71	1,006	14.2	43	8
2001	David Boston, Arizona[2]	98	1,598	16.3	61	8
	Marvin Harrison, Indianapolis[3]	109	1,524	14.0	68	15
	Terrell Owens, San Francisco[3]	93	1,412	15.2	60	16
	Jimmy Smith, Jacksonville[6]	112	1,373	12.3	35	8
	Torry Holt, St. Louis[2]	81	1,363	16.8	51	7
	Rod Smith, Denver[5]	113	1,343	11.9	65	11
	Keyshawn Johnson, Tampa Bay[3]	106	1,266	11.9	47	1
	Joe Horn, New Orleans[2]	83	1,265	15.2	56	9
	Randy Moss, Minnesota[4]	82	1,233	15.0	73	10
	Troy Brown, New England	101	1,199	11.9	60	5
	Tim Brown, Oakland[9]	91	1,165	12.8	46	9
	Johnnie Morton, Detroit[4]	77	1,154	15.0	76	4
	Jerry Rice, Oakland[13]	83	1,139	13.7	40	9
	Derrick Mason, Tennessee	73	1,128	15.5	71	9
	Curtis Conway, San Diego[3]	71	1,125	15.8	72	6
	Keenan McCardell, Jacksonville[4]	93	1,110	11.9	45	6
	Isaac Bruce, St. Louis[5]	64	1,106	17.3	51	6
	Kevin Johnson, Cleveland	84	1,097	13.1	55	9
	Darrell Jackson, Seattle	70	1,081	15.4	64	8
	Marty Booker, Chicago	100	1,071	10.7	66	8

Year	Player, Team	No.	Yards	Avg.	Long	TD
	Qadry Ismail, Baltimore[2]	74	1,059	14.3	77	7
	Amani Toomer, N.Y. Giants[3]	72	1,054	14.6	60	5
	Willie Jackson, New Orleans	81	1,046	12.9	63	5
	Plaxico Burress, Pittsburgh	66	1,008	15.3	43	6
	Hines Ward, Pittsburgh	94	1,003	10.7	34	4
2000	Torry Holt, St. Louis	82	1,635	19.9	85	6
	Rod Smith, Denver[4]	100	1,602	16.0	49	8
	Isaac Bruce, St. Louis[4]	87	1,471	16.9	78	9
	Terrell Owens, San Francisco[2]	97	1,451	15.0	69	13
	Randy Moss, Minnesota[3]	77	1,437	18.7	78	15
	Marvin Harrison, Indianapolis[2]	102	1,413	13.9	78	14
	Derrick Alexander, Kansas City[3]	78	1,391	17.8	81	10
	Joe Horn, New Orleans	94	1,340	14.3	52	8
	Eric Moulds, Buffalo[2]	94	1,326	14.1	52	5
	Ed McCaffrey, Denver[3]	101	1,317	13.0	61	9
	Cris Carter, Minnesota[8]	96	1,274	13.3	53	9
	Jimmy Smith, Jacksonville[5]	91	1,213	13.3	65	8
	Keenan McCardell, Jacksonville[3]	94	1,207	12.8	67	5
	Tony Gonzalez, Kansas City	93	1,203	12.9	39	9
	Muhsin Muhammad, Carolina[2]	102	1,183	11.6	36	6
	David Boston, Arizona	71	1,156	16.3	70	7
	Tim Brown, Oakland[8]	76	1,128	14.8	45	11
	Amani Toomer, N.Y. Giants[2]	78	1,094	14.0	54	7
1999	Marvin Harrison, Indianapolis	115	1,663	14.5	57	12
	Jimmy Smith, Jacksonville[4]	116	1,636	14.1	62	6
	Randy Moss, Minnesota[2]	80	1,413	17.7	67	11
	Marcus Robinson, Chicago	84	1,400	16.7	80	9
	Tim Brown, Oakland[7]	90	1,344	14.9	47	6
	Germane Crowell, Detroit	81	1,338	16.5	77	7
	Muhsin Muhammad, Carolina	96	1,253	13.1	60	8
	Cris Carter, Minnesota[7]	90	1,241	13.8	68	13
	Michael Westbrook, Washington	65	1,191	18.3	65	9
	Amani Toomer, N.Y. Giants	79	1,183	15.0	80	6
	Keyshawn Johnson, N.Y. Jets[2]	89	1,170	13.2	65	8
	Isaac Bruce, St. Louis[3]	77	1,165	15.1	60	12
	Terry Glenn, New England[2]	69	1,147	16.6	67	4
	Albert Connell, Washington	62	1,132	18.3	62	7
	Johnnie Morton, Detroit[3]	80	1,129	14.1	48	5
	Qadry Ismail, Baltimore	68	1,105	16.3	76	6
	Raghib Ismail, Dallas[2]	80	1,097	13.7	76	6
	Patrick Jeffers, Carolina	63	1,082	17.2	88	12
	Antonio Freeman, Green Bay[3]	74	1,074	14.5	51	6
	Bill Schroeder, Green Bay	74	1,051	14.2	51	5
	Marshall Faulk, St. Louis	87	1,048	12.1	57	5
	Tony Martin, Miami[4]	67	1,037	15.5	69	5
	Darnay Scott, Cincinnati	68	1,022	15.0	76	7
	Rod Smith, Denver[3]	79	1,020	12.9	71	4
	Ed McCaffrey, Denver[2]	71	1,018	14.3	78	7
	Terance Mathis, Atlanta[4]	81	1,016	12.5	52	6
1998	Antonio Freeman, Green Bay[2]	84	1,424	17.0	84	14
	Eric Moulds, Buffalo	67	1,368	20.4	84	9
	*Randy Moss, Minnesota	69	1,313	19.0	61	17
	Rod Smith, Denver[2]	86	1,222	14.2	58	6
	Jimmy Smith, Jacksonville[3]	78	1,182	15.2	72	8
	Tony Martin, Atlanta[3]	66	1,181	17.9	62	6
	Jerry Rice, San Francisco[12]	82	1,157	14.1	75	9
	Frank Sanders, Arizona[2]	89	1,145	12.9	42	3
	Terance Mathis, Atlanta[3]	64	1,136	17.8	78	11
	Keyshawn Johnson, N.Y. Jets	83	1,131	13.6	41	10
	Terrell Owens, San Francisco	67	1,097	16.4	79	14
	Wayne Chrebet, N.Y. Jets	75	1,083	14.4	63	8
	Michael Irvin, Dallas[7]	74	1,057	14.3	51	1
	Ed McCaffrey, Denver	64	1,053	16.5	48	10
	O.J. McDuffie, Miami	90	1,050	11.7	61	7
	Joey Galloway, Seattle[3]	65	1,047	16.1	81	10
	Johnnie Morton, Detroit[2]	69	1,028	14.9	98	2
	Raghib Ismail, Carolina	69	1,024	14.8	62	8
	Carl Pickens, Cincinnati[4]	82	1,023	12.5	67	5
	Tim Brown, Oakland[6]	81	1,012	12.5	49	9

Year	Player, Team	No.	Yards	Avg.	Long	TD
	Cris Carter, Minnesota[6]	78	1,011	13.0	54	12
1997	Rob Moore, Arizona[3]	97	1,584	16.3	47	8
	Tim Brown, Oakland[5]	104	1,408	13.5	59	5
	Yancey Thigpen, Pittsburgh[2]	79	1,398	17.7	69	7
	Jimmy Smith, Jacksonville[2]	82	1,324	16.1	75	4
	Irving Fryar, Philadelphia[5]	86	1,316	15.3	72	6
	Herman Moore, Detroit[4]	104	1,293	12.4	79	8
	Antonio Freeman, Green Bay	81	1,243	15.3	58	12
	Michael Irvin, Dallas[6]	75	1,180	15.7	55	9
	Rod Smith, Denver	70	1,180	16.9	78	12
	Keenan McCardell, Jacksonville[2]	85	1,164	13.7	60	5
	Jake Reed, Minnesota[4]	68	1,138	16.7	56	6
	Shannon Sharpe, Denver[3]	72	1,107	15.4	68	3
	Andre Rison, Kansas City[5]	72	1,092	15.2	45	7
	Cris Carter, Minnesota[5]	89	1,069	12.0	43	13
	Johnnie Morton, Detroit	80	1,057	13.2	73	6
	Joey Galloway, Seattle[2]	72	1,049	14.6	53	12
	Frank Sanders, Arizona	75	1,017	13.6	70	4
	Robert Brooks, Green Bay[2]	60	1,010	16.8	48	7
	Derrick Alexander, Baltimore[2]	65	1,009	15.5	92	9
1996	Isaac Bruce, St. Louis[2]	84	1,338	15.9	70	7
	Jake Reed, Minnesota[3]	72	1,320	18.3	82	7
	Herman Moore, Detroit[3]	106	1,296	12.2	50	9
	Jerry Rice, San Francisco[11]	108	1,254	11.6	39	8
	Jimmy Smith, Jacksonville	83	1,244	15.0	62	7
	Michael Jackson, Baltimore	76	1,201	15.8	86	14
	Irving Fryar, Philadelphia[4]	88	1,195	13.6	42	11
	Carl Pickens, Cincinnati[3]	100	1,180	11.8	61	12
	Tony Martin, San Diego[2]	85	1,171	13.8	55	14
	Cris Carter, Minnesota[4]	96	1,163	12.1	43	10
	*Terry Glenn, New England	90	1,132	12.6	37	6
	Keenan McCardell, Jacksonville	85	1,129	13.3	52	3
	Tim Brown, Oakland[4]	90	1,104	12.3	42	9
	Derrick Alexander, Baltimore	62	1,099	17.7	64	9
	Shannon Sharpe, Denver[2]	80	1,062	13.3	51	10
	Curtis Conway, Chicago[2]	81	1,049	13.0	58	7
	Andre Reed, Buffalo[4]	66	1,036	15.7	67	6
	Brett Perriman, Detroit[2]	94	1,021	10.9	44	5
	Rob Moore, Arizona[2]	58	1,016	17.5	69	4
	Henry Ellard, Washington[7]	52	1,014	19.5	51	2
	Charles Johnson, Pittsburgh	60	1,008	16.8	70	3
1995	Jerry Rice, San Francisco[10]	122	1,848	15.1	81	15
	Isaac Bruce, St. Louis	119	1,781	15.0	72	13
	Herman Moore, Detroit[2]	123	1,686	13.7	69	14
	Michael Irvin, Dallas[5]	111	1,603	14.4	50	10
	Robert Brooks, Green Bay	102	1,497	14.7	99	13
	Brett Perriman, Detroit	108	1,488	13.8	91	9
	Cris Carter, Minnesota[3]	122	1,371	11.2	60	17
	Tim Brown, Oakland[3]	89	1,342	15.1	80	10
	Yancey Thigpen, Pittsburgh	85	1,307	15.4	43	5
	Jeff Graham, Chicago	82	1,301	15.9	51	4
	Carl Pickens, Cincinnati[2]	99	1,234	12.5	68	17
	Tony Martin, San Diego	90	1,224	13.6	51	6
	Eric Metcalf, Atlanta	104	1,189	11.4	62	8
	Jake Reed, Minnesota[2]	72	1,167	16.2	55	9
	Quinn Early, New Orleans	81	1,087	13.4	70	8
	Anthony Miller, Denver[5]	59	1,079	18.3	62	14
	Bert Emanuel, Atlanta	74	1,039	14.0	52	5
	*Joey Galloway, Seattle	67	1,039	15.5	59	7
	Terance Mathis, Atlanta[2]	78	1,039	13.3	54	9
	Curtis Conway, Chicago	62	1,037	16.7	76	12
	Henry Ellard, Washington[6]	56	1,005	17.9	59	5
	Mark Carrier, Carolina[2]	66	1,002	15.2	66	3
	Brian Blades, Seattle[4]	77	1,001	13.0	49	4
1994	Jerry Rice, San Francisco[9]	112	1,499	13.4	69	13
	Henry Ellard, Washington[5]	74	1,397	18.9	73	6
	Terance Mathis, Atlanta	111	1,342	12.1	81	11
	Tim Brown, L.A. Raiders[2]	89	1,309	14.7	77	9
	Andre Reed, Buffalo[2]	90	1,303	14.5	83	8

Year	Player, Team	No.	Yards	Avg.	Long	TD
	Irving Fryar, Miami[3]	73	1,270	17.4	54	7
	Cris Carter, Minnesota[2]	122	1,256	10.3	65	7
	Michael Irvin, Dallas[4]	79	1,241	15.7	65	6
	Jake Reed, Minnesota	85	1,175	13.8	59	4
	Ben Coates, New England	96	1,174	12.2	62	7
	Herman Moore, Detroit	72	1,173	16.3	51	11
	Fred Barnett, Philadelphia[2]	78	1,127	14.4	54	5
	Carl Pickens, Cincinnati	71	1,127	15.9	70	11
	Sterling Sharpe, Green Bay[4]	94	1,119	11.9	49	18
	Anthony Miller, Denver[4]	60	1,107	18.5	76	5
	Andre Rison, Atlanta[3]	81	1,088	13.4	69	8
	Brian Blades, Seattle[3]	81	1,088	13.4	45	4
	Rob Moore, N.Y. Jets	78	1,010	12.9	41	6
	Shannon Sharpe, Denver	87	1,010	11.6	44	4
1993	Jerry Rice, San Francisco[6]	98	1,503	15.3	80	15
	Michael Irvin, Dallas[3]	88	1,330	15.1	61	7
	Sterling Sharpe, Green Bay[4]	112	1,274	11.4	54	11
	Andre Rison, Atlanta[3]	86	1,242	14.4	53	15
	Tim Brown, L.A. Raiders	80	1,180	14.8	71	7
	Anthony Miller, San Diego[3]	84	1,162	13.8	66	7
	Cris Carter, Minnesota	86	1,071	12.5	58	9
	Reggie Langhorne, Indianapolis	85	1,038	12.2	72	3
	Irving Fryar, Miami[2]	64	1,010	15.8	65	5
1992	Sterling Sharpe, Green Bay[3]	108	1,461	13.5	76	13
	Michael Irvin, Dallas[2]	78	1,396	17.9	87	7
	Jerry Rice, San Francisco[7]	84	1,201	14.3	80	10
	Andre Rison, Atlanta[2]	93	1,119	12.0	71	11
	Fred Barnett, Philadelphia	67	1,083	16.2	71	6
	Anthony Miller, San Diego[2]	72	1,060	14.7	67	7
	Eric Martin, New Orleans[3]	68	1,041	15.3	52	5
1991	Michael Irvin, Dallas	93	1,523	16.4	66	8
	Gary Clark, Washington[5]	70	1,340	19.1	82	10
	Jerry Rice, San Francisco[6]	80	1,206	15.1	73	14
	Haywood Jeffires, Houston[2]	100	1,181	11.8	44	7
	Michael Haynes, Atlanta	50	1,122	22.4	80	11
	Andre Reed, Buffalo[2]	81	1,113	13.7	55	10
	Drew Hill, Houston[5]	90	1,109	12.3	61	4
	Mark Duper, Miami[4]	70	1,085	15.5	43	5
	James Lofton, Buffalo[6]	57	1,072	18.8	77	8
	Mark Clayton, Miami[5]	70	1,053	15.0	43	12
	Henry Ellard, L.A. Rams[4]	64	1,052	16.4	38	3
	Art Monk, Washington[5]	71	1,049	14.8	64	8
	Irving Fryar, New England	68	1,014	14.9	56	3
	John Taylor, San Francisco[2]	64	1,011	15.8	97	9
	Brian Blades, Seattle[2]	70	1,003	14.3	52	2
1990	Jerry Rice, San Francisco[5]	100	1,502	15.0	64	13
	Henry Ellard, L.A. Rams[3]	76	1,294	17.0	50	4
	Andre Rison, Atlanta	82	1,208	14.7	75	10
	Gary Clark, Washington[4]	75	1,112	14.8	53	8
	Sterling Sharpe, Green Bay[2]	67	1,105	16.5	76	6
	Willie Anderson, L.A. Rams[2]	51	1,097	21.5	55	4
	Haywood Jeffires, Houston	74	1,048	14.2	87	8
	Stephone Paige, Kansas City	65	1,021	15.7	86	5
	Drew Hill, Houston[4]	74	1,019	13.8	57	5
	Anthony Carter, Minnesota[3]	70	1,008	14.4	56	8
1989	Jerry Rice, San Francisco[4]	82	1,483	18.1	68	17
	Sterling Sharpe, Green Bay	90	1,423	15.8	79	12
	Mark Carrier, Tampa Bay	86	1,422	16.5	78	9
	Henry Ellard, L.A. Rams[2]	70	1,382	19.7	53	8
	Andre Reed, Buffalo	88	1,312	14.9	78	9
	Anthony Miller, San Diego	75	1,252	16.7	69	10
	Webster Slaughter, Cleveland	65	1,236	19.0	97	6
	Gary Clark, Washington[3]	79	1,229	15.6	80	9
	Tim McGee, Cincinnati	65	1,211	18.6	74	8
	Art Monk, Washington[4]	86	1,186	13.8	60	8
	Willie Anderson, L.A. Rams	44	1,146	26.0	78	5
	Ricky Sanders, Washington[2]	80	1,138	14.2	68	4
	Vance Johnson, Denver	76	1,095	14.4	69	7
	Richard Johnson, Detroit	70	1,091	15.6	75	8

Year	Player, Team	No.	Yards	Avg.	Long	TD
	Eric Martin, New Orleans[2]	68	1,090	16.0	53	8
	John Taylor, San Francisco	60	1,077	18.0	95	10
	Mervyn Fernandez, L.A. Raiders	57	1,069	18.8	75	9
	Anthony Carter, Minnesota[2]	65	1,066	16.4	50	4
	Brian Blades, Seattle	77	1,063	13.8	60	5
	Mark Clayton, Miami[4]	64	1,011	15.8	78	9
1988	Henry Ellard, L.A. Rams	86	1,414	16.4	68	10
	Jerry Rice, San Francisco[3]	64	1,306	20.4	96	9
	Eddie Brown, Cincinnati	53	1,273	24.0	86	9
	Anthony Carter, Minnesota	72	1,225	17.0	67	6
	Ricky Sanders, Washington	73	1,148	15.7	55	12
	Drew Hill, Houston[3]	72	1,141	15.8	57	10
	Mark Clayton, Miami[3]	86	1,129	13.1	45	14
	Roy Green, Phoenix[3]	68	1,097	16.1	52	7
	Eric Martin, New Orleans	85	1,083	12.7	40	7
	Al Toon, N.Y. Jets[2]	93	1,067	11.5	42	5
	Bruce Hill, Tampa Bay	58	1,040	17.9	42	9
	Lionel Manuel, N.Y. Giants	65	1,029	15.8	46	4
1987	J.T. Smith, St. Louis[2]	91	1,117	12.3	38	8
	Jerry Rice, San Francisco[2]	65	1,078	16.6	57	22
	Gary Clark, Washington[2]	56	1,066	19.0	84	7
	Carlos Carson, Kansas City[3]	55	1,044	19.0	81	7
1986	Jerry Rice, San Francisco	86	1,570	18.3	66	15
	Stanley Morgan, New England[3]	84	1,491	17.8	44	10
	Mark Duper, Miami[3]	67	1,313	19.6	85	11
	Gary Clark, Washington	74	1,265	17.1	55	7
	Al Toon, N.Y. Jets	85	1,176	13.8	62	8
	Todd Christensen, L.A. Raiders[3]	95	1,153	12.1	35	8
	Mark Clayton, Miami[2]	60	1,150	19.2	68	10
	*Bill Brooks, Indianapolis	65	1,131	17.4	84	8
	Drew Hill, Houston[2]	65	1,112	17.1	81	5
	Steve Largent, Seattle[8]	70	1,070	15.3	38	9
	Art Monk, Washington[3]	73	1,068	14.6	69	4
	*Ernest Givins, Houston	61	1,062	17.4	60	3
	Cris Collinsworth, Cincinnati[4]	62	1,024	16.5	46	10
	Wesley Walker, N.Y. Jets[2]	49	1,016	20.7	83	12
	J.T. Smith, St. Louis	80	1,014	12.7	45	6
	Mark Bavaro, N.Y. Giants	66	1,001	15.2	41	4
1985	Steve Largent, Seattle[7]	79	1,287	16.3	43	6
	Mike Quick, Philadelphia[3]	73	1,247	17.1	99	11
	Art Monk, Washington[2]	91	1,226	13.5	53	2
	Wes Chandler, San Diego[4]	67	1,199	17.9	75	10
	Drew Hill, Houston	64	1,169	18.3	57	9
	James Lofton, Green Bay[5]	69	1,153	16.7	56	4
	Louis Lipps, Pittsburgh	59	1,134	19.2	51	12
	Cris Collinsworth, Cincinnati[3]	65	1,125	17.3	71	5
	Tony Hill, Dallas[3]	74	1,113	15.0	53	7
	Lionel James, San Diego	86	1,027	11.9	67	6
	Roger Craig, San Francisco	92	1,016	11.0	73	6
1984	Roy Green, St. Louis[2]	78	1,555	19.9	83	12
	John Stallworth, Pittsburgh[3]	80	1,395	17.4	51	11
	Mark Clayton, Miami	73	1,389	19.0	65	18
	Art Monk, Washington	106	1,372	12.9	72	7
	James Lofton, Green Bay[4]	62	1,361	22.0	79	7
	Mark Duper, Miami[2]	71	1,306	18.4	80	8
	Steve Watson, Denver[3]	69	1,170	17.0	73	7
	Steve Largent, Seattle[6]	74	1,164	15.7	65	12
	Tim Smith, Houston[2]	69	1,141	16.5	75	4
	Stacey Bailey, Atlanta	67	1,138	17.0	61	6
	Carlos Carson, Kansas City[2]	57	1,078	18.9	57	4
	Mike Quick, Philadelphia[2]	61	1,052	17.2	90	9
	Todd Christensen, L.A. Raiders[2]	80	1,007	12.6	38	7
	Kevin House, Tampa Bay[2]	76	1,005	13.2	55	5
	Ozzie Newsome, Cleveland[2]	89	1,001	11.2	52	5
1983	Mike Quick, Philadelphia	69	1,409	20.4	83	13
	Carlos Carson, Kansas City	80	1,351	16.9	50	7
	James Lofton, Green Bay[3]	58	1,300	22.4	74	8
	Todd Christensen, L.A. Raiders	92	1,247	13.6	45	12
	Roy Green, St. Louis	78	1,227	15.7	71	14

Year	Player, Team	No.	Yards	Avg.	Long	TD
	Charlie Brown, Washington	78	1,225	15.7	75	8
	Tim Smith, Houston	83	1,176	14.2	47	6
	Kellen Winslow, San Diego[3]	88	1,172	13.3	46	8
	Earnest Gray, N.Y. Giants	78	1,139	14.6	62	5
	Steve Watson, Denver[2]	59	1,133	19.2	78	5
	Cris Collinsworth, Cincinnati[2]	66	1,130	17.1	63	5
	Steve Largent, Seattle[5]	72	1,074	14.9	46	11
	Mark Duper, Miami	51	1,003	19.7	85	10
1982	Wes Chandler, San Diego[3]	49	1,032	21.1	66	9
1981	Alfred Jenkins, Atlanta[2]	70	1,358	19.4	67	13
	James Lofton, Green Bay[2]	71	1,294	18.2	75	8
	Steve Watson, Denver	60	1,244	20.7	95	13
	Frank Lewis, Buffalo[2]	70	1,244	17.8	33	4
	Steve Largent, Seattle[4]	75	1,224	16.3	57	9
	Charlie Joiner, San Diego[4]	70	1,188	17.0	57	7
	Kevin House, Tampa Bay	56	1,176	21.0	84	9
	Wes Chandler, N.O.-San Diego[2]	69	1,142	16.6	51	6
	Dwight Clark, San Francisco	85	1,105	13.0	78	4
	John Stallworth, Pittsburgh[2]	63	1,098	17.4	55	5
	Kellen Winslow, San Diego[2]	88	1,075	12.2	67	10
	Pat Tilley, St. Louis	66	1,040	15.8	75	3
	Stanley Morgan, New England[2]	44	1,029	23.4	76	6
	Harold Carmichael, Philadelphia[3]	61	1,028	16.9	85	6
	Freddie Scott, Detroit	53	1,022	19.3	48	5
	*Cris Collinsworth, Cincinnati	67	1,009	15.1	74	8
	Joe Senser, Minnesota	79	1,004	12.7	53	8
	Ozzie Newsome, Cleveland	69	1,002	14.5	62	6
	Sammy White, Minnesota	66	1,001	15.2	53	3
1980	John Jefferson, San Diego[3]	82	1,340	16.3	58	13
	Kellen Winslow, San Diego	89	1,290	14.5	65	9
	James Lofton, Green Bay	71	1,226	17.3	47	4
	Charlie Joiner, San Diego[3]	71	1,132	15.9	51	4
	Ahmad Rashad, Minnesota[2]	69	1,095	15.9	76	5
	Steve Largent, Seattle[3]	66	1,064	16.1	67	6
	Tony Hill, Dallas[2]	60	1,055	17.6	58	8
	Alfred Jenkins, Atlanta	57	1,026	18.0	57	6
1979	Steve Largent, Seattle[2]	66	1,237	18.7	55	9
	John Stallworth, Pittsburgh	70	1,183	16.9	65	8
	Ahmad Rashad, Minnesota	80	1,156	14.5	52	9
	John Jefferson, San Diego[2]	61	1,090	17.9	65	10
	Frank Lewis, Buffalo	54	1,082	20.0	55	2
	Wes Chandler, New Orleans	65	1,069	16.4	85	6
	Tony Hill, Dallas	60	1,062	17.7	75	10
	Drew Pearson, Dallas[2]	55	1,026	18.7	56	8
	Wallace Francis, Atlanta	74	1,013	13.7	42	8
	Harold Jackson, New England[3]	45	1,013	22.5	59	7
	Charlie Joiner, San Diego[2]	72	1,008	14.0	39	4
	Stanley Morgan, New England	44	1,002	22.8	63	12
1978	Wesley Walker, N.Y. Jets	48	1,169	24.4	77	8
	Steve Largent, Seattle	71	1,168	16.5	57	8
	Harold Carmichael, Philadelphia[2]	55	1,072	19.5	56	8
	*John Jefferson, San Diego	56	1,001	17.9	46	13
1976	Roger Carr, Baltimore	43	1,112	25.9	79	11
	Cliff Branch, Oakland[2]	46	1,111	24.2	88	12
	Charlie Joiner, San Diego	50	1,056	21.1	81	7
1975	Ken Burrough, Houston	53	1,063	20.1	77	8
1974	Cliff Branch, Oakland	60	1,092	18.2	67	13
	Drew Pearson, Dallas	62	1,087	17.5	50	2
1973	Harold Carmichael, Philadelphia	67	1,116	16.7	73	9
1972	Harold Jackson, Philadelphia[2]	62	1,048	16.9	77	4
	John Gilliam, Minnesota	47	1,035	22.0	66	7
1971	Otis Taylor, Kansas City[2]	57	1,110	19.5	82	7
1970	Gene Washington, San Francisco	53	1,100	20.8	79	12
	Marlin Briscoe, Buffalo	57	1,036	18.2	48	8
	Dick Gordon, Chicago	71	1,026	14.5	69	13
	Gary Garrison, San Diego[2]	44	1,006	22.9	67	12
1969	Warren Wells, Oakland[2]	47	1,260	26.8	80	14
	Harold Jackson, Philadelphia	65	1,116	17.2	65	9
	Roy Jefferson, Pittsburgh[2]	67	1,079	16.1	63	9

Year	Player, Team	No.	Yards	Avg.	Long	TD
	Dan Abramowicz, New Orleans	73	1,015	13.9	49	7
	Lance Alworth, San Diego[7]	64	1,003	15.7	76	4
1968	Lance Alworth, San Diego[6]	68	1,312	19.3	80	10
	Don Maynard, N.Y. Jets[5]	57	1,297	22.8	87	10
	George Sauer, N.Y. Jets[3]	66	1,141	17.3	43	3
	Warren Wells, Oakland	53	1,137	21.5	94	11
	Gary Garrison, San Diego	52	1,103	21.2	84	10
	Roy Jefferson, Pittsburgh	58	1,074	18.5	62	11
	Paul Warfield, Cleveland	50	1,067	21.3	65	12
	Homer Jones, N.Y. Giants[3]	45	1,057	23.5	84	7
	Fred Biletnikoff, Oakland	61	1,037	17.0	82	6
	Lance Rentzel, Dallas	54	1,009	18.7	65	6
1967	Don Maynard, N.Y. Jets[4]	71	1,434	20.2	75	10
	Ben Hawkins, Philadelphia	59	1,265	21.4	87	10
	Homer Jones, N.Y. Giants[2]	49	1,209	24.7	70	13
	Jackie Smith, St. Louis	56	1,205	21.5	76	9
	George Sauer, N.Y. Jets[2]	75	1,189	15.9	61	6
	Lance Alworth, San Diego[5]	52	1,010	19.4	71	9
1966	Lance Alworth, San Diego[4]	73	1,383	18.9	78	13
	Otis Taylor, Kansas City	58	1,297	22.4	89	8
	Pat Studstill, Detroit	67	1,266	18.9	99	5
	Bob Hayes, Dallas[2]	64	1,232	19.3	95	13
	Charlie Frazier, Houston	57	1,129	19.8	79	12
	Charley Taylor, Washington	72	1,119	15.5	86	12
	George Sauer, N.Y. Jets	63	1,081	17.2	77	5
	Homer Jones, N.Y. Giants	48	1,044	21.8	98	8
	Art Powell, Oakland[5]	53	1,026	19.4	46	11
1965	Lance Alworth, San Diego[3]	69	1,602	23.2	85	14
	Dave Parks, San Francisco	80	1,344	16.8	53	12
	Don Maynard, N.Y. Jets[3]	68	1,218	17.9	56	14
	Pete Retzlaff, Philadelphia	66	1,190	18.0	78	10
	Lionel Taylor, Denver[4]	85	1,131	13.3	63	6
	Tommy McDonald, Los Angeles[3]	67	1,036	15.5	51	9
	*Bob Hayes, Dallas	46	1,003	21.8	82	12
1964	Charlie Hennigan, Houston[3]	101	1,546	15.3	53	8
	Art Powell, Oakland[4]	76	1,361	17.9	77	11
	Lance Alworth, San Diego[2]	61	1,235	20.2	82	13
	Johnny Morris, Chicago	93	1,200	12.9	63	10
	Elbert Dubenion, Buffalo	42	1,139	27.1	72	10
	Terry Barr, Detroit[2]	57	1,030	18.1	58	9
1963	Bobby Mitchell, Washington[2]	69	1,436	20.8	99	7
	Art Powell, Oakland[3]	73	1,304	17.9	85	16
	Buddy Dial, Pittsburgh[2]	60	1,295	21.6	83	9
	Lance Alworth, San Diego	61	1,205	19.8	85	11
	Del Shofner, N.Y. Giants[4]	64	1,181	18.5	70	9
	Lionel Taylor, Denver[3]	78	1,101	14.1	72	10
	Terry Barr, Detroit	66	1,086	16.5	75	13
	Charley Hennigan, Houston[2]	61	1,051	17.2	83	10
	Sonny Randle, St. Louis[2]	51	1,014	19.9	68	12
	Bake Turner, N.Y. Jets	71	1,009	14.2	53	6
1962	Bobby Mitchell, Washington	72	1,384	19.2	81	11
	Sonny Randle, St. Louis	63	1,158	18.4	86	7
	Tommy McDonald, Philadelphia[2]	58	1,146	19.8	60	10
	Del Shofner, N.Y. Giants[3]	53	1,133	21.4	69	12
	Art Powell, N.Y. Titans[2]	64	1,130	17.7	80	8
	Frank Clarke, Dall. Cowboys	47	1,043	22.2	66	14
	Don Maynard, N.Y. Titans[2]	56	1,041	18.6	86	8
1961	Charley Hennigan, Houston	82	1,746	21.3	80	12
	Lionel Taylor, Denver[2]	100	1,176	11.8	52	4
	Bill Groman, Houston[2]	50	1,175	23.5	80	17
	Tommy McDonald, Philadelphia	64	1,144	17.9	66	13
	Del Shofner, N.Y. Giants[2]	68	1,125	16.5	46	11
	Jim Phillips, Los Angeles	78	1,092	14.0	69	5
	*Mike Ditka, Chicago	56	1,076	19.2	76	12
	Dave Kocourek, San Diego	55	1,055	19.2	76	4
	Buddy Dial, Pittsburgh	53	1,047	19.8	88	12
	R.C. Owens, San Francisco	55	1,032	18.8	54	5
1960	*Bill Groman, Houston	72	1,473	20.5	92	12

Year	Player, Team	No.	Yards	Avg.	Long	TD
	Raymond Berry, Baltimore	74	1,298	17.5	70	10
	Don Maynard, N.Y. Titans	72	1,265	17.6	65	6
	Lionel Taylor, Denver	92	1,235	13.4	80	12
	Art Powell, N.Y. Titans	69	1,167	16.9	76	14
1958	Del Shofner, Los Angeles	51	1,097	21.5	92	8
1956	Bill Howton, Green Bay[2]	55	1,188	21.6	66	12
	Harlon Hill, Chi. Bears[2]	47	1,128	24.0	79	11
1954	Bob Boyd, Los Angeles	53	1,212	22.9	80	6
	*Harlon Hill, Chi. Bears	45	1,124	25.0	76	12
1953	Pete Pihos, Philadelphia	63	1,049	16.7	59	10
1952	*Bill Howton, Green Bay	53	1,231	23.2	90	13
1951	Elroy (Crazylegs) Hirsch, Los Angeles	66	1,495	22.7	91	17
1950	Tom Fears, Los Angeles[2]	84	1,116	13.3	53	7
	Cloyce Box, Detroit	50	1,009	20.2	82	11
1949	Bob Mann, Detroit	66	1,014	15.4	64	4
	Tom Fears, Los Angeles	77	1,013	13.2	51	9
1945	Jim Benton, Cleveland	45	1,067	23.7	84	8
1942	Don Hutson, Green Bay	74	1,211	16.4	73	17

*First season of professional football.

250 YARDS PASS RECEIVING IN A GAME

Date	Player, Team, Opponent	No.	Yards	TD
Nov. 19, 2006	Lee Evans, Buffalo vs. Houston	11	265	2
Nov. 12, 2006	Chad Johnson, Cincinnati vs. San Diego	11	260	2
Nov. 10, 2002	Plaxico Burress, Pittsburgh vs. Atlanta (OT)	9	253	2
Dec. 17, 2000	Terrell Owens, San Francisco vs. Chicago	20	283	1
Sept. 10, 2000	Jimmy Smith, Jacksonville vs. Baltimore	15	291	3
Dec. 12, 1999	Qadry Ismail, Baltimore vs. Pittsburgh	6	258	3
Dec. 18, 1995	Jerry Rice, San Francisco vs. Minnesota	14	289	3
Dec. 11, 1989	John Taylor, San Francisco vs. L.A. Rams	11	286	2
Nov. 26, 1989	Willie Anderson, L.A. Rams vs. New Orleans (OT)	15	336	1
Oct. 18, 1987	Steve Largent, Seattle vs. Detroit	15	261	3
Oct. 4, 1987	Anthony Allen, Washington vs. St. Louis	7	255	3
Dec. 22, 1985	Stephone Paige, Kansas City vs. San Diego	8	309	2
Dec. 20, 1982	Wes Chandler, San Diego vs. Cincinnati	10	260	2
Sept. 23, 1979	*Jerry Butler, Buffalo vs. N.Y. Jets	10	255	4
Nov. 4, 1962	Sonny Randle, St. Louis vs. N.Y. Giants	16	256	1
Oct. 28, 1962	Del Shofner, N.Y. Giants vs. Washington	11	269	1
Oct. 13, 1961	Charley Hennigan, Houston vs. Boston	13	272	1
Oct. 21, 1956	Billy Howton, Green Bay vs. Los Angeles	7	257	2
Dec. 3, 1950	Cloyce Box, Detroit vs. Baltimore	12	302	4
Nov. 22, 1945	Jim Benton, Cleveland vs. Detroit	10	303	1

*First season of professional football.

2,000 COMBINED NET YARDS GAINED IN A SEASON

Year	Player, Team	Rushing Att.-Yds.	Pass Rec.	Punt Ret.	Kickoff Ret.	Fum. Ret.	Total Yds.
2006	Steven Jackson, St. Louis	346-1,528	90,806	0-0	0-0	2-0	438-2,334
	LaDainian Tomlinson, San Diego[3]	348-1,815	56-508	0-0	0-0	1-0	405-2,323
	*Maurice Jones-Drew, Jacksonville	166-941	46-436	1-13	31-860	0-0	244-2,250
	Larry Johnson, Kansas City[2]	416-1,789	41-410	0-0	0-0	1-0	458-2,199
	Frank Gore, San Francisco	312-1,695	61-485	0-0	0-0	0-0	373-2,180
	Wes Welker, Miami[2]	0-0	67-687	41-378	48-1,064	1-0	157-2,129
	Tiki Barber, N.Y. Giants[4]	327-1,662	58-465	0-0	0-0	1-0	386-2,127
	Chris Carr, Oakland	0-0	0-0	35-216	69-1,762	1-0	106-2,078
2005	Tiki Barber, N.Y. Giants[3]	357-1,860	54-530	0-0	0-0	1-0	412-2,390
	Dante Hall, Kansas City[4]	7-11	34-436	42-276	65-1,560	2-0	150-2,283
	Wes Welker, Miami	1-5	29-434	43-390	61-1,379	4-0	138-2,208
	Larry Johnson, Kansas City	336-1,750	33-343	0-0	0-0	3-0	372-2,093
2004	Dante Hall, Kansas City[3]	8-56	25-230	23-232	68-1,718	0-0	124-2,236
	Tiki Barber, N.Y. Giants[2]	322-1,518	52-578	0-0	0-0	2-0	376-2,096
	Edgerrin James, Indianapolis[3]	334-1,548	51-483	0-0	0-0	1-0	386-2,031
2003	Dante Hall, Kansas City[2]	16-73	40-423	29-472	57-1,478	0-0	142-2,446
	LaDainian Tomlinson, San Diego[2]	313-1,645	100-725	0-0	0-0	2-0	415-2,370
	Jamal Lewis, Baltimore	387-2,066	26-205	0-0	0-0	1-0	414-2,271
	Ahman Green, Green Bay	355-1,883	50-367	0-0	0-0	2-0	407-2,250
	Deuce McAllister, New Orleans	351-1,641	69-516	0-0	0-0	3-(-3)	423-2,154
	Priest Holmes, Kansas City[3]	320-1,420	74-690	0-0	0-0	0-0	394-2,110

Year	Player, Team	Rushing Att.-Yds.	Pass Rec.	Punt Ret.	Kickoff Ret.	Fum. Ret.	Total Yds.
2002	Michael Lewis, New Orleans	1-15	8-200	44-625	70-1,807	2-0	125-2,647
	Priest Holmes, Kansas City[2]	313-1,615	70-672	0-0	0-0	0-0	383-2,287
	Ricky Williams, Miami	383-1,853	47-363	0-0	0-0	1-0	431-2,216
	LaDainian Tomlinson, San Diego	372-1,683	79-489	0-0	0-0	0-0	451-2,172
	Dante Hall, Kansas City	11-54	20-322	29-390	57-1,354	1-0	118-2,120
2001	Priest Holmes, Kansas City	327-1,555	62-614	0-0	0-0	0-0	389-2,169
	Marshall Faulk, St. Louis[4]	260-1,382	83-765	0-0	0-0	2-0	345-2,147
	Derrick Mason, Tennessee[2]	0-0	73-1,128	20-128	34-748	1-0	128-2,004
2000	Derrick Mason, Tennessee	1-1	63-895	51-662	42-1,132	1-0	158-2,690
	MarTay Jenkins, Arizona	1-(-4)	17-219	1-1	82-2,186	0-0	101-2,402
	Edgerrin James, Indianapolis[2]	387-1,709	63-594	0-0	0-0	0-0	450-2,303
	Marshall Faulk, St. Louis[3]	253-1,359	81-830	0-0	1-18	2-0	337-2,207
	Tiki Barber, N.Y. Giants	213-1,006	70-719	39-332	1-28	5-0	328-2,085
1999	Marshall Faulk, St. Louis[2]	253-1,381	87-1,048	0-0	0-0	0-0	340-2,429
	*Edgerrin James, Indianapolis	369-1,553	62-586	0-0	0-0	2-0	433-2,139
	*Terrence Wilkins, Indianapolis	1-2	42-565	41-388	51-1,134	1-0	136-2,089
	Glyn Milburn, Chicago[2]	16-102	20-151	30-346	61-1,426	2-0	129-2,025
1998	Brian Mitchell, Washington[4]	39-208	44-306	44-506	59-1,337	0-0	186-2,357
	Marshall Faulk, Indianapolis	324-1,319	86-908	0-0	0-0	2-13	412-2,240
	Terrell Davis, Denver[2]	392-2,008	25-217	0-0	0-0	1-0	418-2,225
	Jamal Anderson, Atlanta	410-1,846	27-319	0-0	0-0	1-0	438-2,165
	Garrison Hearst, San Francisco	310-1,570	39-535	0-0	0-0	1-0	350-2,105
1997	Barry Sanders, Detroit[2]	335-2,053	33-305	0-0	0-0	1-0	369-2,358
	Kevin Williams, Arizona	1-(-2)	20-273	40-462	59-1,458	1-0	121-2,191
	Brian Mitchell, Washington[3]	23-107	36-438	38-442	47-1,094	0-0	144-2,081
	Terrell Davis, Denver	369-1,750	42-287	0-0	0-0	2-(-7)	413-2,030
	Jermaine Lewis, Baltimore	3-35	42-648	28-437	41-905	2-0	116-2,025
1995	Brian Mitchell, Washington[2]	46-301	38-324	25-315	55-1,408	0-0	164-2,348
	Emmitt Smith, Dallas[2]	377-1,773	62-375	0-0	0-0	0-0	439-2,148
	Glyn Milburn, Denver	49-266	22-191	31-354	47-1,269	0-0	149-2,080
	Ernie Mills, Pittsburgh	5-39	39-679	0-0	54-1,306	0-0	98-2,024
1994	Brian Mitchell, Washington	78-311	26-236	32-452	58-1,478	0-0	194-2,477
	Barry Sanders, Detroit	331-1,883	44-283	0-0	0-0	0-0	375-2,166
1992	Thurman Thomas, Buffalo[2]	312-1,487	58-626	0-0	0-0	1-0	371-2,113
	Emmitt Smith, Dallas	373-1,713	59-335	0-0	0-0	1-0	433-2,048
	Barry Foster, Pittsburgh	390-1,690	36-344	0-0	0-0	2-(-20)	428-2,014
1991	Thurman Thomas, Buffalo	288-1,407	62-631	0-0	0-0	0-0	350-2,038
1990	Herschel Walker, Minnesota[2]	184-770	35-315	0-0	44-966	4-0	267-2,051
1988	*Tim Brown, L.A. Raiders	14-50	43-725	49-444	41-1,098	7-0	154-2,317
	Roger Craig, San Francisco[2]	310-1,502	76-534	0-0	2-32	2-0	390-2,068
	Eric Dickerson, Indianapolis[4]	388-1,659	36-377	0-0	0-0	1-0	425-2,036
	Herschel Walker, Dallas	361-1,514	53-505	0-0	0-0	3-0	417-2,019
1986	Eric Dickerson, L.A. Rams[3]	404-1,821	26-205	0-0	0-0	2-0	432-2,026
	Gary Anderson, San Diego	127-442	80-871	25-227	24-482	2-0	258-2,022
1985	Lionel James, San Diego	105-516	86-1,027	25-213	36-779	1-0	253-2,535
	Marcus Allen, L.A. Raiders	380-1,759	67-555	0-0	0-0	2-(-6)	449-2,308
	Roger Craig, San Francisco	214-1,050	92-1,016	0-0	0-0	0-0	306-2,066
	Walter Payton, Chicago[4]	324-1,551	49-483	0-0	0-0	1-0	374-2,034
1984	Eric Dickerson, L.A. Rams[2]	379-2,105	21-139	0-0	0-0	4-15	404-2,259
	James Wilder, Tampa Bay	407-1,544	85-685	0-0	0-0	4-0	496-2,229
	Walter Payton, Chicago[3]	381-1,684	45-368	0-0	0-0	1-0	427-2,052
1983	*Eric Dickerson, L.A. Rams	390-1,808	51-404	0-0	0-0	1-0	442-2,212
	William Andrews, Atlanta[2]	331-1,567	59-609	0-0	0-0	2-0	392-2,176
	Walter Payton, Chicago[2]	314-1,421	53-607	0-0	0-0	2-0	369-2,028
1981	*James Brooks, San Diego	109-525	46-329	22-290	40-949	2-0	219-2,093
	William Andrews, Atlanta	289-1,301	81-735	0-0	0-0	0-0	370-2,036
1980	Bruce Harper, N.Y. Jets[2]	45-126	50-634	28-242	49-1,070	3-0	175-2,072
1979	Wilbert Montgomery, Philadelphia	338-1,512	41-494	0-0	1-6	2-0	382-2,012
1978	Bruce Harper, N.Y. Jets	58-303	13-196	30-378	55-1,280	1-0	157-2,157
1977	Walter Payton, Chicago	339-1,852	27-269	0-0	2-95	5-0	373-2,216
	Terry Metcalf, St. Louis[3]	149-739	34-403	14-108	32-772	1-0	230-2,022
1975	Terry Metcalf, St. Louis[2]	165-816	43-378	23-285	35-960	2-23	268-2,462
	O.J. Simpson, Buffalo[2]	329-1,817	28-426	0-0	0-0	1-0	358-2,243
1974	Mack Herron, New England	231-824	38-474	35-517	28-629	3-0	335-2,444
	Otis Armstrong, Denver	263-1,407	38-405	0-0	16-386	1-0	318-2,198
	Terry Metcalf, St. Louis	152-718	50-377	26-340	20-623	7-0	255-2,058
1973	O.J. Simpson, Buffalo	332-2,003	6-70	0-0	0-0	0-0	338-2,073
1966	Gale Sayers, Chicago[2]	229-1,231	34-447	6-44	23-718	3-0	295-2,440

Year	Player, Team	Rushing Att.-Yds.	Pass Rec.	Punt Ret.	Kickoff Ret.	Fum. Ret.	Total Yds.
	Leroy Kelly, Cleveland	209-1,141	32-366	13-104	19-403	0-0	273-2,014
1965	*Gale Sayers, Chicago	166-867	29-507	16-238	21-660	4-0	236-2,272
1963	Timmy Brown, Philadelphia[2]	192-841	36-487	16-152	33-945	2-3	279-2,428
	Jim Brown, Cleveland	291-1,863	24-268	0-0	0-0	0-0	315-2,131
1962	Timmy Brown, Philadelphia	137-545	52-849	6-81	30-831	4-0	229-2,306
	Dick Christy, N.Y. Titans	114-535	62-538	15-250	38-824	2-0	231-2,147
1961	Billy Cannon, Houston	200-948	43-586	9-70	18-439	2-0	272-2,043
1960	*Abner Haynes, Dallas Texans	156-875	55-576	14-215	19-434	4-0	248-2,100

*First season of professional football.

300 COMBINED NET YARDS GAINED IN A GAME

Date	Player, Team, Opponent	No.	Yards	TD
Dec. 10, 2006	*Maurice Jones-Drew, Jacksonville vs. Indianapolis	19	303	3
Dec. 14, 2003	Derrick Mason, Tennessee vs. Buffalo	21	302	0
Nov. 16, 2003	Jonathan Carter, N.Y. Jets vs. Indianapolis	7	304	2
Dec. 8, 2002	Steve Smith, Carolina vs. Cincinnati	9	313	3
Nov. 24, 2002	Priest Holmes, Kansas City vs. Seattle	30	307	3
Oct. 13, 2002	Michael Lewis, New Orleans vs. Washington	8	356	2
Dec. 24, 1999	Jason Tucker, Dallas vs. New Orleans	13	331	1
Dec. 7, 1997	Jermaine Lewis, Baltimore vs. Seattle	10	308	3
Dec. 25, 1995	Kevin Williams, Dallas vs. Arizona	16	307	2
Dec. 10, 1995	Glyn Milburn, Denver vs. Seattle	33	404	0
Oct. 23, 1994	Tyrone Hughes, New Orleans vs. L.A. Rams	11	347	2
Dec. 11, 1989	John Taylor, San Francisco vs. L.A. Rams	14	321	2
Nov. 26, 1989	Willie Anderson, L.A. Rams vs. New Orleans (OT)	15	336	1
Nov. 28, 1988	*Tim Brown, L.A. Raiders vs. Seattle	12	308	1
Dec. 22, 1985	Stephone Paige, Kansas City vs. San Diego	8	309	2
Nov. 10, 1985	Lionel James, San Diego vs. L.A. Raiders (OT)	23	345	0
Sept. 22, 1985	Lionel James, San Diego vs. Cincinnati	20	316	2
Dec. 21, 1975	*Walter Payton, Chicago vs. New Orleans	32	300	1
Nov. 23, 1975	Greg Pruitt, Cleveland vs. Cincinnati	28	304	2
Nov. 1, 1970	Eugene (Mercury) Morris, Miami vs. Baltimore	17	302	0
Oct. 4, 1970	O.J. Simpson, Buffalo vs. N.Y. Jets	26	303	2
Dec. 6, 1969	Jerry LeVias, Houston vs. N.Y. Jets	18	329	1
Nov. 2, 1969	Travis Williams, Green Bay vs. Pittsburgh	11	314	3
Dec. 18, 1966	Gale Sayers, Chicago vs. Minnesota	20	339	2
Dec. 12, 1965	*Gale Sayers, Chicago vs. San Francisco	17	336	6
Nov. 17, 1963	Gary Ballman, Pittsburgh vs. Washington	12	320	2
Dec. 16, 1962	Timmy Brown, Philadelphia vs. St. Louis	19	341	2
Dec. 10, 1961	Billy Cannon, Houston vs. N.Y. Titans	32	373	5
Nov. 19, 1961	Jim Brown, Cleveland vs. Philadelphia	38	313	4
Dec. 3, 1950	Cloyce Box, Detroit vs. Baltimore	13	302	4
Oct. 29, 1950	Wally Triplett, Detroit vs. Los Angeles	11	331	1
Nov. 22, 1945	Jim Benton, Cleveland vs. Detroit	10	303	1

*First season of professional football.

2,000 SCRIMMAGE YARDS GAINED IN A SEASON

Year	Player, Team	Att.	Rushing Yards	Receptions	Receiving Yards	Scrimm. Yards
2006	Steven Jackson, St. Louis	346	1,528	90	806	2,334
	LaDainian Tomlinson, San Diego[3]	348	1,815	56	508	2,323
	Larry Johnson, Kansas City[2]	416	1,789	41	410	2,199
	Frank Gore, San Francisco	312	1,695	61	485	2,180
	Tiki Barber, N.Y. Giants[3]	327	1,662	58	465	2,127[3]
2005	Tiki Barber, N.Y. Giants[2]	357	1,860	54	530	2,390
	Larry Johnson, Kansas City	336	1,750	33	343	2,093
2004	Tiki Barber, N.Y. Giants	322	1.518	52	578	2,096
	Edgerrin James, Indianapolis[3]	334	1,548	51	483	2,031
2003	LaDainian Tomlinson, San Diego[2]	313	1,645	100	725	2,370
	Jamal Lewis, Baltimore	387	2,066	26	205	2,271
	Ahman Green, Green Bay	355	1,883	50	367	2,250
	Deuce McAllister, New Orleans	351	1,641	69	516	2,157
	Priest Holmes, Kansas City[3]	320	1,420	74	690	2,110
2002	Priest Holmes, Kansas City[2]	313	1,615	70	672	2,287
	Ricky Williams, Miami	383	1,853	47	363	2,216
	LaDainian Tomlinson, San Diego	372	1,683	79	489	2,172
2001	Priest Holmes, Kansas City	327	1,555	62	614	2,169
	Marshall Faulk, St. Louis[4]	260	1,382	83	765	2,147
2000	Edgerrin James, Indianapolis[2]	387	1,709	63	594	2,303

Year	Player, Team	Att.	Rushing Yards	Receptions	Receiving Yards	Scrimm. Yards
	Marshall Faulk, St. Louis[3]	253	1,359	81	830	2,189
1999	Marshall Faulk, St. Louis[2]	253	1,381	87	1,048	2,429
	*Edgerrin James, Indianapolis	369	1,553	62	586	2,139
1998	Marshall Faulk, Indianapolis	324	1,319	86	908	2,227
	Terrell Davis, Denver[2]	392	2,008	25	217	2,225
	Jamal Anderson, Atlanta	410	1,846	27	319	2,165
	Garrison Hearst, San Francisco	310	1,570	39	535	2,105
1997	Barry Sanders, Detroit[2]	335	2,053	33	305	2,358
	Terrell Davis, Denver	369	1,750	42	287	2,037
1995	Emmitt Smith, Dallas[2]	377	1,773	62	375	2,148
1994	Barry Sanders, Detroit	331	1,883	44	283	2,166
1992	Thurman Thomas, Buffalo[2]	312	1,487	58	626	2,113
	Emmitt Smith, Dallas	373	1,713	59	335	2,048
	Barry Foster, Pittsburgh	390	1,690	36	344	2,034
1991	Thurman Thomas, Buffalo	288	1,407	62	631	2,038
1988	Roger Craig, San Francisco[2]	310	1,502	76	534	2,036
	Eric Dickerson, Indianapolis[4]	388	1,659	36	377	2,036
	Herschel Walker, Dallas	361	1,514	53	505	2,019
1986	Eric Dickerson, L.A. Rams[3]	404	1,821	26	205	2,026
1985	Marcus Allen, L.A. Raiders	380	1,759	67	555	2,314
	Roger Craig, San Francisco	214	1,050	92	1,016	2,066
	Walter Payton, Chicago[4]	324	1,551	49	483	2,034
1984	Eric Dickerson, L. A. Rams[2]	379	2,105	21	139	2,244
	James Wilder, Tampa Bay	407	1,544	85	685	2,229
	Walter Payton, Chicago[3]	381	1,684	45	368	2,052
1983	*Eric Dickerson, L.A. Rams	390	1,808	51	404	2,212
	William Andrews, Atlanta[2]	331	1,567	59	609	2,176
	Walter Payton, Chicago[2]	314	1,421	53	607	2,028
1981	William Andrews, Atlanta	289	1,301	81	735	2,036
1979	Wilbert Montgomery, Philadelphia	338	1,512	41	494	2,006
1977	Walter Payton, Chicago	339	1,852	27	269	2,121
1975	O.J. Simpson, Buffalo[2]	329	1,817	28	426	2,243
1973	O.J. Simpson, Buffalo	332	2,003	6	70	2,073
1963	Jim Brown, Cleveland	91	1,863	24	268	2,131

First season of professional football.

300 SCRIMMAGE YARDS GAINED IN A GAME

Date	Player, Team, Opponent	Att.	Yards	TD
Nov. 24, 2002	Priest Holmes, Kansas City vs. Seattle	30	307	3
Nov. 26, 1989	Flipper Anderson, L.A. Rams vs. New Orleans (OT)	15	336	1
Dec. 22, 1985	Stephone Paige, Kansas City vs. San Diego	8	309	2
Dec. 10, 1961	Billy Cannon, Houston vs. N.Y. Titans	30	330	5
Dec. 3, 1950	Cloyce Box, Detroit vs. Baltimore	12	302	4
Nov. 22, 1945	Jim Benton, Cleveland vs. Detroit	10	303	1

TOP 20 SCORERS

Player	Years	TD	FG	PAT	TP
Morten Andersen	24	0	540	825	2,445
Gary Anderson	23	0	538	820	2,434
George Blanda	26	9	335	942	2,002
John Carney	19	0	413	510	1,749
Norm Johnson	18	0	366	638	1,736
Matt Stover	16	0	408	491	1,715
Nick Lowery	18	0	383	562	1,711
Jan Stenerud	19	0	373	580	1,699
Jason Elam	14	0	368	568	1,672
Eddie Murray	19	0	352	538	1,594
Al Del Greco	17	0	347	543	1,584
Jason Hanson	15	0	356	469	1,537
Steve Christie	15	0	336	468	1,476
Pat Leahy	18	0	304	558	1,470
Jim Turner	16	1	304	521	1,439
Matt Bahr	17	0	300	522	1,422
John Kasay	15	0	334	403	1,405
Mark Moseley	16	0	300	482	1,382
Jim Bakken	17	0	282	534	1,380
Fred Cox	15	0	282	519	1,365

TOP 20 TOUCHDOWN SCORERS

Player	Years	Rush	Rec.	Total Returns	TD
Jerry Rice	20	10	197	1	208
Emmitt Smith	15	164	11	0	175
Marcus Allen	16	123	21	1	145
Marshall Faulk	12	100	36	0	136
Cris Carter	16	0	130	1	131
Jim Brown	9	106	20	0	126
Walter Payton	13	110	15	0	125
Marvin Harrison	11	0	122	0	122
Terrell Owens	11	2	114	0	116
John Riggins	14	104	12	0	116
Lenny Moore	12	63	48	2	113
LaDainian Tomlinson	6	100	11	0	111
Barry Sanders	10	99	10	0	109
Shaun Alexander	7	96	11	0	107
Tim Brown	17	1	100	4	105
Don Hutson	11	3	99	3	105
Randy Moss	9	0	101	1	102
Steve Largent	14	1	100	0	101
Franco Harris	13	91	9	0	100
Curtis Martin	11	90	10	0	100

TOP 20 RUSHERS

Player	Years	Att.	Yards	Avg.	Long	TD
Emmitt Smith	15	4,409	18,355	4.2	75	164
Walter Payton	13	3,838	16,726	4.4	76	110
Barry Sanders	10	3,062	15,269	5.0	85	99
Curtis Martin	11	3,518	14,101	4.0	70	90
Jerome Bettis	13	3,479	13,662	3.9	71	91
Eric Dickerson	11	2,996	13,259	4.4	85	90
Tony Dorsett	12	2,936	12,739	4.3	99	77
Jim Brown	9	2,359	12,312	5.2	80	106
Marshall Faulk	12	2,836	12,279	4.3	71	100
Marcus Allen	16	3,022	12,243	4.1	61	123
Franco Harris	13	2,949	12,120	4.1	75	91
Thurman Thomas	13	2,877	12,074	4.2	80	65
John Riggins	14	2,916	11,352	3.9	66	104
Corey Dillon	10	2,618	11,241	4.3	96	82
O.J. Simpson	11	2,404	11,236	4.7	94	61
Ricky Watters	10	2,622	10,643	4.1	57	78
Tiki Barber	10	2,217	10,449	4.7	95	55
Eddie George	9	2,865	10,441	3.6	76	68
Edgerrin James	8	2,525	10,385	4.1	72	70
Ottis Anderson	14	2,562	10,273	4.0	76	81

TOP 20 COMBINED YARDS GAINED

Player	Years	Tot.	Rush.	Rec.	Int. Ret.	Punt Ret.	Kickoff Ret.	Fumble Ret.
Jerry Rice	20	23,546	645	22,895	0	0	6	0
Brian Mitchell	14	23,330	1,967	2,336	0	4,999	14,014	14
Walter Payton	13	21,803	16,726	4,538	0	0	539	0
Emmitt Smith	15	21,564	18,355	3,224	0	0	0	-15
Tim Brown	17	19,682	190	14,934	0	3,320	1,235	3
Marshall Faulk	12	19,190	12,279	6,875	0	0	18	18
Barry Sanders	10	18,308	15,269	2,921	0	0	118	0
Herschel Walker	12	18,168	8,225	4,859	0	0	5,084	0
Marcus Allen	16	17,648	12,243	5,411	0	0	0	-6
Curtis Martin	11	17,421	14,101	3,329	0	0	0	-9
Tiki Barber	10	17,359	10,449	5,183	0	1,181	544	2
Eric Metcalf	13	17,230	2,392	5,572	0	3,453	5,813	0
Thurman Thomas	13	16,532	12,074	4,458	0	0	0	0
Tony Dorsett	12	16,326	12,739	3,554	0	0	0	54
Henry Ellard	16	15,718	50	13,777	0	1,527	364	0
Irving Fryar	17	15,594	242	12,785	0	2,055	505	7
Jim Brown	9	15,459	12,312	2,499	0	0	648	0
Eric Dickerson	11	15,411	13,259	2,137	0	0	0	15
Jerome Bettis	13	15,113	13,662	1,449	0	0	0	2
Glyn Milburn	9	14,911	817	1,322	0	2,984	9,788	0

TOP 20 YARDS FROM SCRIMMAGE

Player	Years	Scrimmage Yards	Rushing Yards	Receiving Yards
Jerry Rice	20	23,540	645	22,895
Emmitt Smith	15	21,579	18,355	3,224
Walter Payton	13	21,264	16,726	4,538
Marshall Faulk	12	19,154	12,279	6,875
Barry Sanders	10	18,190	15,269	2,921
Marcus Allen	16	17,654	12,243	5,411
Curtis Martin	11	17,430	14,101	3,329
Thurman Thomas	13	16,532	12,074	4,458
Tony Dorsett	12	16,293	12,739	3,554
Tiki Barber	10	15,632	10,449	5,183
Eric Dickerson	11	15,396	13,259	2,137
Tim Brown	17	15,124	190	14,934
Jerome Bettis	13	15,111	13,662	1,449
Ricky Watters	10	14,891	10,643	4,248
Jim Brown	9	14,811	12,312	2,499
Franco Harris	13	14,407	12,120	2,287
James Lofton	16	14,250	246	14,004
Cris Carter	16	13,940	41	13,899
Henry Ellard	16	13,827	50	13,777
Marvin Harrison	11	13,725	28	13,697

TOP 20 PASSERS

Player	Years	Att.	Comp.	Pct. Comp.	Yards	Avg. Gain	TD	Pct. TD	Int.	Pct. Int.	Rating
Steve Young	15	4,149	2,667	64.3	33,124	7.98	232	5.6	107	2.6	96.8
Peyton Manning	9	4,890	3,131	64.0	37,586	7.69	275	5.6	139	2.8	94.4
Kurt Warner	9	2,508	1,645	65.6	20,591	8.21	125	5.0	83	3.3	93.8
Joe Montana	15	5,391	3,409	63.2	40,551	7.52	273	5.1	139	2.6	92.3
Marc Bulger	5	2,106	1,357	64.4	16,233	7.71	95	4.5	59	2.8	91.3
Daunte Culpepper	8	2,741	1,759	64.2	21,091	7.69	137	5.0	89	3.2	90.8
Chad Pennington	7	1,659	1,080	65.1	11,973	7.22	72	4.3	46	2.8	89.3
Tom Brady	7	3,064	1,896	61.9	21,564	7.04	147	4.8	78	2.5	88.4
Drew Brees	6	2,363	1,481	62.7	16,766	7.10	106	4.5	64	2.7	87.5
Trent Green	9	3,527	2,143	60.8	26,963	7.64	157	4.5	101	2.9	87.5
Jeff Garcia	8	2,973	1,811	60.9	20,385	6.86	136	4.6	73	2.5	86.4
Dan Marino	17	8,358	4,967	59.4	61,361	7.34	420	5.0	252	3.0	86.4
Donovan McNabb	8	3,259	1,898	58.2	22,080	6.78	152	4.7	72	2.2	85.2
Matt Hasselbeck	8	2,576	1,552	60.3	18,367	7.13	114	4.4	72	2.8	85.1
Brett Favre	16	8,223	5,021	61.1	57,500	6.99	414	5.0	273	3.3	85.1
Rich Gannon	16	4,206	2,533	60.2	28,743	6.83	180	4.3	104	2.5	84.7
Brian Griese	9	2,350	1,481	63.0	16,564	7.05	104	4.4	80	3.4	84.5
Jim Kelly	11	4,779	2,874	60.1	35,467	7.42	237	5.0	175	3.7	84.4
Mark Brunell	13	4,594	2,738	59.6	31,826	6.93	182	4.0	106	2.3	84.2
Jake Delhomme	6	1,936	1,151	59.5	13,965	7.22	92	4.8	63	3.3	84.0

1,500 or more attempts. The passing ratings are based on performance standards established for completion percentage, interception percentage, touchdown percentage, and average gain. Please consult page 364 for more information.

OUTSTANDING PERFORMERS

TOP 20 LEADERS IN PASSES COMPLETED
Brett Favre 5,021
Dan Marino 4,967
John Elway 4,123
Warren Moon 3,988
Drew Bledsoe..3,839
Vinny Testaverde 3,693
Fran Tarkenton 3,686
Joe Montana 3,409
Dan Fouts 3,297
Peyton Manning 3,131
Dave Krieg 3,105
Boomer Esiason...2,969
Troy Aikman..2,898
Steve DeBerg 2,874
Jim Kelly...2,874
Kerry Collins 2,868
Jim Everett..2,841
Johnny Unitas 2,830
Mark Brunell 2,738
Steve Young..2,667

TOP 20 LEADERS IN PASSING YARDS
Dan Marino 61,361
Brett Favre 57,500
John Elway 51,475
Warren Moon 49,325
Fran Tarkenton 47,003
Vinny Testaverde 45,281
Drew Bledsoe...44,611
Dan Fouts 43,040
Joe Montana 40,551
Johnny Unitas 40,239
Dave Krieg 38,147
Boomer Esiason..37,920
Peyton Manning 37,586
Jim Kelly..35,467
Jim Everett...34,837
Jim Hart...34,665
Steve DeBerg 34,241
Kerry Collins 34,186
John Hadl 33,503
Phil Simms 33,462

TOP 20 LEADERS IN TOUCHDOWN PASSES
Dan Marino 420
Brett Favre 414
Fran Tarkenton 342
John Elway 300
Warren Moon 291
Johnny Unitas 290
Peyton Manning 275
Joe Montana 273
Vinny Testaverde 270
Dave Krieg 261
Sonny Jurgensen 255
Dan Fouts 254
Drew Bledsoe...251
Boomer Esiason..247
John Hadl 244
Len Dawson..239
Jim Kelly..237
George Blanda 236
Steve Young..232
John Brodie 214

TOP 20 LEADERS IN RECEPTION YARDS
Jerry Rice 22,895
Tim Brown 14,934
James Lofton 14,004
Cris Carter 13,899
Henry Ellard 13,777
Marvin Harrison 13,697
Isaac Bruce..13,376
Andre Reed 13,198
Steve Largent...13,089
Irving Fryar 12,785
Art Monk..12,721
Jimmy Smith...12,287
Charlie Joiner 12,146
Michael Irvin 11,904
Don Maynard 11,834
Terrell Owens 11,715
Rod Smith...11,389
Keenan McCardell 11,117
Gary Clark..10,856
Stanley Morgan...10,716

TOP 20 PASS RECEIVERS

Player	Years	No.	Yards	Avg.	Long	TD
Jerry Rice	20	1,549	22,895	14.8	96	197
Cris Carter	16	1,101	13,899	12.6	80	130
Tim Brown	17	1,094	14,934	13.7	80	100
Marvin Harrison	11	1,022	13,697	13.4	80	122
Andre Reed	16	951	13,198	13.9	83	87
Art Monk	16	940	12,721	13.5	79	68
Isaac Bruce	13	887	13,376	15.1	80	80
Jimmy Smith	12	862	12,287	14.3	75	67
Keenan McCardell	15	861	11,117	12.9	76	62
Irving Fryar	17	851	12,785	15.0	80	84
Rod Smith	12	849	11,389	13.4	85	68
Larry Centers	14	827	6,797	8.2	54	28
Steve Largent	14	819	13,089	16.0	74	100
Shannon Sharpe	14	815	10,060	12.3	82	62
Henry Ellard	16	814	13,777	16.9	81	65
Keyshawn Johnson	11	814	10,571	13.0	76	64
Terrell Owens	11	801	11,715	14.6	91	114
Marshall Faulk	12	767	6,875	9.0	85	36
James Lofton	16	764	14,004	18.3	80	75
Michael Irvin	12	750	11,904	15.9	87	65
Charlie Joiner	18	750	12,146	16.2	87	65

TOP 20 INTERCEPTORS

Player	Years	No.	Yards	Avg.	Long	TD
Paul Krause	16	81	1,185	14.6	81	3
Emlen Tunnell	14	79	1,282	16.2	55	4
Rod Woodson	17	71	1,483	20.9	98	12
Dick (Night Train) Lane	14	68	1,207	17.8	80	5
Ken Riley	15	65	596	9.2	66	5
Ronnie Lott	14	63	730	11.6	83	5
Dave Brown	15	62	698	11.3	90	5
Dick LeBeau	14	62	762	12.3	70	3
Emmitt Thomas	13	58	937	16.2	73	5
Mel Blount	14	57	736	12.9	52	2
Bobby Boyd	9	57	994	17.4	74	4
Eugene Robinson	16	57	762	13.4	49	1
Johnny Robinson	12	57	741	13.0	57	1
Everson Walls	13	57	504	8.8	40	1
Lem Barney	11	56	1,077	19.2	71	7
Pat Fischer	17	56	941	16.8	69	4
Aeneas Williams	14	55	807	14.7	65	9
Eric Allen	14	54	826	15.3	94	8
Willie Brown	16	54	472	8.7	45	2
Darrell Green	20	54	621	11.5	83	6

TOP 20 PUNTERS (MINIMUM 250 PUNTS)

Player	Years	No.	Yards	Avg.	Long	Blk.
Shane Lechler	7	519	23,926	46.1	73	3
Sammy Baugh	16	338	15,245	45.1	85	9
Tommy Davis	11	511	22,833	44.7	82	2
Yale Lary	11	503	22,279	44.3	74	4
Todd Sauerbrun	12	842	37,008	44.0	73	7
Bob Scarpitto	8	283	12,408	43.8	87	4
Horace Gillom	7	385	16,872	43.8	80	5
Jerry Norton	11	358	15,671	43.8	78	5
Dave Lewis	4	285	12,447	43.7	63	0
Greg Montgomery	9	524	22,831	43.6	77	8
Brian Moorman	6	471	20,473	43.5	84	1
Hunter Smith	8	472	20,514	43.5	69	5
Don Chandler	12	660	28,678	43.5	90	4
Tom Rouen	12	810	35,189	43.4	76	9
Rick Tuten	11	741	32,190	43.4	73	2
Darren Bennett	11	836	36,316	43.4	66	3
Tom Tupa	17	873	37,862	43.4	73	2
Rohn Stark	16	1,141	49,471	43.4	72	7
Sean Landeta	21	1,401	60,707	43.3	74	6
Reggie Roby	16	992	42,951	43.3	77	5

TOP 20 KICKOFF RETURNERS (MINIMUM 75 RETURNS)

Player	Years	No.	Yards	Avg.	Long	TD
Gale Sayers	7	91	2,781	30.6	103	6
Lynn Chandnois	7	92	2,720	29.6	93	3
Abe Woodson	9	193	5,538	28.7	105	5
Buddy Young	6	90	2,514	27.9	104	2
Travis Williams	5	102	2,801	27.5	105	6
Joe Arenas	7	139	3,798	27.3	96	1
Justin Miller	2	106	2,881	27.2	103	3
Clarence Davis	8	79	2,140	27.1	76	0
Terrence McGee	4	158	4,276	27.1	104	4
Steve Van Buren	8	76	2,030	26.7	98	3
Lenny Lyles	12	81	2,161	26.7	103	3
Mercury Morris	8	111	2,947	26.5	105	3
Bobby Jancik	6	158	4,185	26.5	61	0
Mel Renfro	14	85	2,246	26.4	100	2
Bobby Mitchell	14	102	2,690	26.4	98	5
Ollie Matson	14	143	3,746	26.2	105	6
Alvin Haymond	10	170	4,438	26.1	98	2
Noland Smith	3	82	2,137	26.1	106	1
Al Nelson	9	101	2,625	26.0	78	0
Timmy Brown	11	184	4,781	26.0	105	5

TOP 20 PUNT RETURNERS (MINIMUM 75 RETURNS)

Player	Years	No.	Yards	Avg.	Long	TD
George McAfee	8	112	1,431	12.8	74	2
Jack Christiansen	8	85	1,084	12.8	89	8
Claude Gibson	5	110	1,381	12.6	85	3
Bill Dudley	9	124	1,515	12.2	96	3
Rick Upchurch	9	248	3,008	12.1	92	8
Desmond Howard	11	244	2,895	11.9	95	8
Billy Johnson	14	282	3,317	11.8	87	6
Mack Herron	3	84	982	11.7	66	0
Billy Thompson	13	157	1,814	11.6	60	0
Santana Moss	6	95	1,092	11.5	63	2
Darrien Gordon	9	314	3,601	11.5	94	6
Henry Ellard	16	135	1,527	11.3	83	4
Rodger Bird	3	94	1,063	11.3	78	0
Bosh Pritchard	6	95	1,072	11.3	81	2
Terry Metcalf	6	84	936	11.1	69	1
Bob Hayes	11	104	1,158	11.1	90	3
Jermaine Lewis	9	295	3,282	11.1	89	6
Floyd Little	9	81	893	11.0	72	2
Louis Lipps	9	112	1,234	11.0	76	3
Bobby Joe Edmonds	5	134	1,471	11.0	75	1

TOP 20 LEADERS IN SACKS

Player	*Years	No.
Bruce Smith	19	200.0
Reggie White	15	198.0
Kevin Greene	15	160.0
Chris Doleman	15	150.5
Richard Dent	15	137.5
John Randle	14	137.5
Leslie O'Neal	13	132.5
Michael Strahan	14	132.5
Lawrence Taylor	12	132.5
Rickey Jackson	14	128.0
Derrick Thomas	11	126.5
Clyde Simmons	15	121.5
Simeon Rice	11	121.0
Sean Jones	13	113.0
Greg Townsend	13	109.5
Pat Swilling	12	107.5
Trace Armstrong	15	106.0
Jason Taylor	10	106.0
Neil Smith	13	104.5
Jim Jeffcoat	15	102.5

*Years played since 1982 when sacks became an official statistic.

POSTSEASON LEADERS

TOP 10 POSTSEASON RUSHERS

Player	Att.	Yards	Avg.	Long	TD
Emmitt Smith	349	1,586	4.5	65	19
Franco Harris	400	1,556	3.9	50	16
Thurman Thomas	339	1,442	4.3	40	16
Tony Dorsett	302	1,383	4.6	53	9
Marcus Allen	267	1,347	5.0	74	11
Terrell Davis	204	1,140	5.6	62	12
John Riggins	251	996	4.0	43	12
Larry Csonka	225	891	4.0	49	9
Chuck Foreman	229	860	3.8	62	7
Roger Craig	208	841	4.0	80	7

TOP 10 POSTSEASON PASSERS

Player	Att.	Comp.	Pct. Comp.	Yards	Avg. Gain	TD	Pct. TD	Int.	Pct. Int.	Rating
Bart Starr	213	130	61.0	1,753	8.23	15	7.0	3	1.4	104.8
Joe Montana	734	460	62.7	5,772	7.86	45	6.1	21	2.9	95.6
Jake Delhomme	192	113	58.9	1,642	8.55	11	5.7	5	2.6	95.0
Ken Anderson	166	110	66.3	1,321	7.96	9	5.4	6	3.6	93.5
Kurt Warner	268	169	63.1	2,221	8.29	15	5.6	10	3.7	92.3
Joe Theismann	211	128	60.7	1,782	8.45	11	5.2	7	3.3	91.4
Troy Aikman	502	320	63.7	3,849	7.67	23	4.6	17	3.4	88.3
Tom Brady	486	295	60.7	3,217	6.62	20	4.1	9	1.9	86.2
Steve Young	471	292	62.0	3,326	7.06	20	4.2	13	2.8	85.8
Warren Moon	403	259	64.3	2,870	7.12	17	4.2	14	3.5	84.9

TOP 10 POSTSEASON PASS RECEIVERS

Player	No.	Yards	Avg.	Long	TD
Jerry Rice	151	2,245	14.9	72	22
Micahel Irvin	87	1,315	15.1	53	8
Andre Reed	85	1,229	14.5	72	9
Thurman Thomas	76	672	8.8	27	5
Cliff Branch	73	1,289	17.7	72	5
Fred Biletnikoff	70	1,167	16.7	57	10
Art Monk	69	1,062	15.4	48	7
Drew Pearson	67	1,105	16.5	83	8
Tony Nathan	65	649	10.0	39	2
Cris Carter	63	870	13.8	66	8
Roger Craig	63	606	9.6	40	2

TOP 10 POSTSEASON INTERCEPTION LEADERS

Player	Interceptions
Ronnie Lott	9
Bill Simpson	9
Charlie Waters	9
Lester Hayes	8
Willie Brown	7
Dennis Thurman	7
Bobby Bryant	6
Eric Davis	6
Glen Edwards	6
Darrell Green	6
Cliff Harris	6
Rodney Harrison	6
Ty Law	6
Vernon Perry	6
Aeneas Williams	6

TOP 10 POSTSEASON SACK LEADERS

Player	Sacks
Willie McGinest	16.0
Bruce Smith	14.5
Reggie White	12.0
Charles Haley	11.0
Richard Dent	10.5
Trace Armstrong	10.0
Charles Mann	10.0
Tony Tolbert	10.0
Neil Smith	9.5
Jeff Wright	9.0

Sacks became an official statistic in 1982.

Compiled by Elias Sports Bureau

Super Bowl I, 1/15/67	Super Bowl XXII, 1/31/88
Super Bowl II, 1/14/68	Super Bowl XXIII, 1/22/89
Super Bowl III, 1/12/69	Super Bowl XXIV, 1/28/90
Super Bowl IV, 1/11/70	Super Bowl XXV, 1/27/91
Super Bowl V, 1/17/71	Super Bowl XXVI, 1/26/92
Super Bowl VI, 1/16/72	Super Bowl XXVII, 1/31/93
Super Bowl VII, 1/14/73	Super Bowl XXVIII, 1/30/94
Super Bowl VIII, 1/13/74	Super Bowl XXIX, 1/29/95
Super Bowl IX, 1/12/75	Super Bowl XXX, 1/28/96
Super Bowl X, 1/18/76	Super Bowl XXXI, 1/26/97
Super Bowl XI, 1/9/77	Super Bowl XXXII, 1/25/98
Super Bowl XII, 1/15/78	Super Bowl XXXIII, 1/31/99
Super Bowl XIII, 1/21/79	Super Bowl XXXIV, 1/30/00
Super Bowl XIV, 1/20/80	Super Bowl XXXV, 1/28/01
Super Bowl XV, 1/25/81	Super Bowl XXXVI, 2/3/02
Super Bowl XVI, 1/24/82	Super Bowl XXXVII, 1/26/03
Super Bowl XVII, 1/30/83	Super Bowl XXXVIII, 2/1/04
Super Bowl XVIII, 1/22/84	Super Bowl XXXIX, 2/6/05
Super Bowl XIX, 1/20/85	Super Bowl XL, 2/5/06
Super Bowl XX, 1/26/86	Super Bowl XLI, 2/4/07
Super Bowl XXI, 1/25/87	

INDIVIDUAL RECORDS

SERVICE
Most Games
- 6 Mike Lodish, Buffalo, XXV-XXVIII; Denver, XXXII-XXXIII
- 5 Marv Fleming, Green Bay, I-II; Miami, VI-VIII
  Larry Cole, Dallas, V-VI, X, XII-XIII
  Cliff Harris, Dallas, V-VI, X, XII-XIII
  Charles Haley, San Francisco, XXIII-XXIV; Dallas, XXVII-XXVIII, XXX
  D.D. Lewis, Dallas, V-VI, X, XII-XIII
  Preston Pearson, Baltimore, III; Pittsburgh, IX; Dallas, X, XII-XIII
  Charlie Waters, Dallas, V-VI, X, XII-XIII
  Rayfield Wright, Dallas, V-VI, X, XII-XIII
  Cornelius Bennett, Buffalo, XXV-XXVIII; Atlanta, XXXIII
  John Elway, Denver, XXI-XXII, XXIV, XXXII-XXXIII
  Glenn Parker, Buffalo, XXV-XXVIII; N.Y. Giants, XXXV
  Bill Romanowski, San Francisco, XXIII-XXIV; Denver, XXXII-XXXIII; Oakland, XXXVII
  Adam Vinatieri, New England, XXXI, XXXVI, XXXVIII, XXXIX; Indianapolis, XLI
- 4 By many players

Most Games, Winning Team
- 5 Charles Haley, San Francisco, XXIII-XXIV; Dallas, XXVII-XXVIII, XXX
- 4 By many players

Most Games, Coach
- 6 Don Shula, Baltimore, III; Miami, VI-VIII, XVII, XIX
- 5 Tom Landry, Dallas, V-VI, X, XII-XIII
- 4 Bud Grant, Minnesota, IV, VIII-IX, XI
  Chuck Noll, Pittsburgh, IX-X, XIII-XIV
  Joe Gibbs, Washington, XVII-XVIII, XXII, XXVI
  Marv Levy, Buffalo, XXV-XXVIII
  Dan Reeves, Denver, XXI-XXII, XXIV; Atlanta, XXXIII

Most Games, Winning Team, Coach
- 4 Chuck Noll, Pittsburgh, IX-X, XIII-XIV
- 3 Bill Walsh, San Francisco, XVI, XIX, XXIII
  Joe Gibbs, Washington, XVII, XXII, XXVI
  Bill Belichick, New England, XXXVI, XXXVIII-XXXIX
- 2 Vince Lombardi, Green Bay, I-II
  Tom Landry, Dallas, VI, XII
  Don Shula, Miami, VII-VIII
  Tom Flores, Oakland, XV; L.A. Raiders, XVIII
  Bill Parcells, N.Y. Giants, XXI, XXV
  Jimmy Johnson, Dallas, XXVII-XXVIII
  George Seifert, San Francisco, XXIV, XXIX

Mike Shanahan, Denver, XXXII-XXXIII

Most Games, Losing Team, Coach
- 4 Bud Grant, Minnesota, IV, VIII-IX, XI
  Don Shula, Baltimore, III; Miami, VI, XVII, XIX
  Marv Levy, Buffalo, XXV-XXVIII
  Dan Reeves, Denver, XXI-XXII, XXIV; Atlanta, XXXIII
- 3 Tom Landry, Dallas, V, X, XIII

SCORING
POINTS
Most Points, Career
- 48 Jerry Rice, San Francisco-Oakland, 4 games (8-td)
- 34 Adam Vinatieri, New England-Indianapolis, 5 games (7-fg, 13-xp)
- 30 Emmitt Smith, Dallas, 3 games (5-td)

Most Points, Game
- 18 Roger Craig, San Francisco vs. Miami, XIX (3-td)
  Jerry Rice, San Francisco vs. Denver, XXIV (3-td); vs. San Diego, XXIX (3-td)
  Ricky Watters, San Francisco vs. San Diego, XXIX (3-td)
  Terrell Davis, Denver vs. Green Bay, XXXII (3-td)
- 15 Don Chandler, Green Bay vs. Oakland, II (3-pat, 4-fg)
- 14 Ray Wersching, San Francisco vs. Cincinnati, XVI (2-pat, 4-fg)
  Kevin Butler, Chicago vs. New England, XX (5-pat, 3-fg)

TOUCHDOWNS
Most Touchdowns, Career
- 8 Jerry Rice, San Francisco-Oakland, 4 games (8-p)
- 5 Emmitt Smith, Dallas, 3 games (5-r)
- 4 Franco Harris, Pittsburgh, 4 games (4-r)
  Roger Craig, San Francisco, 3 games (2-r, 2-p)
  Thurman Thomas, Buffalo, 4 games (4-r)
  John Elway, Denver, 5 games (4-r)

Most Touchdowns, Game
- 3 Roger Craig, San Francisco vs. Miami, XIX (1-r, 2-p)
  Jerry Rice, San Francisco. vs. Denver, XXIV (3-p); vs. San Diego, XXIX (3-p)
  Ricky Watters, San Francisco vs. San Diego, XXIX (1-r, 2-p)
  Terrell Davis, Denver vs. Green Bay, XXXII (3-r)
- 2 Max McGee, Green Bay vs. Kansas City, I (2-p)
  Elijah Pitts, Green Bay vs. Kansas City, I (2-r)
  Bill Miller, Oakland vs. Green Bay, II (2-p)
  Larry Csonka, Miami vs. Minnesota, VIII (2-r)
  Pete Banaszak, Oakland vs. Minnesota, XI (2-r)
  John Stallworth, Pittsburgh vs. Dallas, XIII (2-p)
  Franco Harris, Pittsburgh vs. Los Angeles, XIV (2-r)
  Cliff Branch, Oakland vs. Philadelphia, XV (2-p)
  Dan Ross, Cincinnati vs. San Francisco, XVI (2-p)
  Marcus Allen, L.A. Raiders vs. Washington, XVIII (2-r)
  Jim McMahon, Chicago vs. New England, XX (2-r)
  Ricky Sanders, Washington vs. Denver, XXII (2-p)
  Timmy Smith, Washington vs. Denver, XXII (2-r)
  Tom Rathman, San Francisco vs. Denver, XXIV (2-r)
  Gerald Riggs, Washington vs. Buffalo, XXVI (2-r)
  Michael Irvin, Dallas vs. Buffalo, XXVII (2-p)
  Emmitt Smith, Dallas vs. Buffalo, XXVIII (2-r)
  Emmitt Smith, Dallas vs. Pittsburgh, XXX (2-r)
  Antonio Freeman, Green Bay vs. Denver, XXXII (2-p)
  Howard Griffith, Denver vs. Atlanta, XXXIII (2-r)
  Eddie George, Tennessee vs. St. Louis, XXXIV (2-r)
  Keenan McCardell, Tampa Bay vs. Oakland, XXXVII (2-r)
  Dwight Smith, Tampa Bay vs. Oakland, XXXVII (2-ret)

POINTS AFTER TOUCHDOWN

Most (One-Point) Points After Touchdown, Career
- 13   Adam Vinatieri, New England-Indianapolis, 5 games (13 att)
- 9   Mike Cofer, San Francisco, 2 games (10 att)
- 8   Don Chandler, Green Bay, 2 games (8 att)
-     Roy Gerela, Pittsburgh, 3 games (9 att)
-     Chris Bahr, Oakland-L.A. Raiders, 2 games (8 att)
-     Jason Elam, Denver, 2 games (8 att)

Most (One-Point) Points After Touchdown, Game
- 7   Mike Cofer, San Francisco vs. Denver, XXIV (8 att)
-     Lin Elliott, Dallas vs. Buffalo, XXVII (7 att)
-     Doug Brien, San Francisco vs. San Diego, XXIX (7 att)
- 6   Ali Haji-Sheikh, Washington vs. Denver, XXII (6 att)
-     Martín Gramatica, Tampa Bay vs. Oakland, XXXVII (6 att)
- 5   Don Chandler, Green Bay vs. Kansas City, I (5 att)
-     Roy Gerela, Pittsburgh vs. Dallas, XIII (5 att)
-     Chris Bahr, L.A. Raiders vs. Washington, XVIII (5 att)
-     Ray Wersching, San Francisco vs. Miami, XIX (5 att)
-     Kevin Butler, Chicago vs. New England, XX (5 att)

Most Two-Point Conversions, Game
- 1   Mark Seay, San Diego vs. San Francisco, XXIX
-     Alfred Pupunu, San Diego vs. San Francisco, XXIX
-     Mark Chmura, Green Bay vs. New England, XXXI
-     Kevin Faulk, New England vs. Carolina, XXXVIII

FIELD GOALS

Field Goals Attempted, Career
- 10   Adam Vinatieri, New England-Indianapolis, 5 games
- 6   Jim Turner, N.Y. Jets-Denver, 2 games
-     Roy Gerela, Pittsburgh, 3 games
-     Rich Karlis, Denver, 2 games
-     Jeff Wilkins, St. Louis, 2 games
- 5   Efren Herrera, Dallas, 1 game
-     Ray Wersching, San Francisco, 2 games
-     Jason Elam, Denver, 2 games

Most Field Goals Attempted, Game
- 5   Jim Turner, N.Y. Jets vs. Baltimore, III
-     Efren Herrera, Dallas vs. Denver, XII
- 4   Don Chandler, Green Bay vs. Oakland, II
-     Roy Gerela, Pittsburgh vs. Dallas, X
-     Ray Wersching, San Francisco vs. Cincinnati, XVI
-     Rich Karlis, Denver vs. N.Y. Giants, XXI
-     Mike Cofer, San Francisco vs. Cincinnati, XXIII
-     Jason Elam, Denver vs. Atlanta, XXXIII
-     Jeff Wilkins, St. Louis vs. Tennessee, XXXIV
-     Adam Vinatieri, Indianapolis vs. Chicago, XLI

Most Field Goals, Career
- 7   Adam Vinatieri, New England-Indianapolis, 5 games (10 att)
- 5   Ray Wersching, San Francisco, 2 games (5 att)
- 4   Don Chandler, Green Bay, 2 games (4 att)
-     Jim Turner, N.Y. Jets-Denver, 2 games (6 att)
-     Uwe von Schamann, Miami, 2 games (4 att)
-     Jeff Wilkins, St. Louis, 2 games (6 att)

Most Field Goals, Game
- 4   Don Chandler, Green Bay vs. Oakland, II
-     Ray Wersching, San Francisco vs. Cincinnati, XVI
- 3   Jim Turner, N.Y. Jets vs. Baltimore, III
-     Jan Stenerud, Kansas City vs. Minnesota, IV
-     Uwe von Schamann, Miami vs. San Francisco, XIX
-     Kevin Butler, Chicago vs. New England, XX
-     Jim Breech, Cincinnati vs. San Francisco, XXIII
-     Chip Lohmiller, Washington vs. Buffalo, XXVI
-     Eddie Murray, Dallas vs. Buffalo, XXVIII
-     Jeff Wilkins, St. Louis vs. Tennessee, XXXIV
-     Adam Vinatieri, Indianapolis vs. Chicago, XLI

Longest Field Goal
- 54   Steve Christie, Buffalo vs. Dallas, XXVIII
- 51   Jason Elam, Denver vs. Green Bay, XXXII
- 50   Jeff Wilkins, St. Louis vs. New England, XXXVI
-     John Kasay, Carolina vs. New England, XXXVIII

SAFETIES

Most Safeties, Game
- 1   Dwight White, Pittsburgh vs. Minnesota, IX
-     Reggie Harrison, Pittsburgh vs. Dallas, X
-     Henry Waechter, Chicago vs. New England, XX
-     George Martin, N.Y. Giants vs. Denver, XXI
-     Bruce Smith, Buffalo vs. N.Y. Giants, XXV

RUSHING

ATTEMPTS

Most Attempts, Career
- 101   Franco Harris, Pittsburgh, 4 games
- 70   Emmitt Smith, Dallas, 3 games
- 64   John Riggins, Washington, 2 games

Most Attempts, Game
- 38   John Riggins, Washington vs. Miami, XVII
- 34   Franco Harris, Pittsburgh vs. Minnesota, IX
- 33   Larry Csonka, Miami vs. Minnesota, VIII

YARDS GAINED

Most Yards Gained, Career
- 354   Franco Harris, Pittsburgh, 4 games
- 297   Larry Csonka, Miami, 3 games
- 289   Emmitt Smith, Dallas, 3 games

Most Yards Gained, Game
- 204   Timmy Smith, Washington vs. Denver, XXII
- 191   Marcus Allen, L.A. Raiders vs. Washington, XVIII
- 166   John Riggins, Washington vs. Miami, XVII

Longest Run From Scrimmage
- 75   Willie Parker, Pittsburgh vs. Seattle, XL (TD)
- 74   Marcus Allen, L.A. Raiders vs. Washington, XVIII (TD)
- 58   Tom Matte, Baltimore vs. N.Y. Jets, III
-     Timmy Smith, Washington vs. Denver, XXII (TD)

AVERAGE GAIN

Highest Average Gain, Career (20 attempts)
- 9.6   Marcus Allen, L.A. Raiders, 1 game (20-191)
- 9.3   Timmy Smith, Washington, 1 game (22-204)
- 5.4   Dominic Rhodes, Indianapolis, 1 game (21-113)

Highest Average Gain, Game (10 attempts)
- 10.5   Tom Matte, Baltimore vs. N.Y. Jets, III (11-116)
- 9.6   Marcus Allen, L.A. Raiders vs. Washington, XVIII (20-191)
- 9.3   Willie Parker, Pittsburgh vs. Seattle, XL (10-93)

TOUCHDOWNS

Most Touchdowns, Career
- 5   Emmitt Smith, Dallas, 3 games
- 4   Franco Harris, Pittsburgh, 4 games
-     Thurman Thomas, Buffalo, 4 games
-     John Elway, Denver, 5 games
- 3   Terrell Davis, Denver, 2 games

Most Touchdowns, Game
- 3   Terrell Davis, Denver vs. Green Bay, XXXII
- 2   Elijah Pitts, Green Bay vs. Kansas City, I
-     Larry Csonka, Miami vs. Minnesota, VIII
-     Pete Banaszak, Oakland vs. Minnesota, XI
-     Franco Harris, Pittsburgh vs. Los Angeles, XIV
-     Marcus Allen, L.A. Raiders vs. Washington, XVIII
-     Jim McMahon, Chicago vs. New England, XX
-     Timmy Smith, Washington vs. Denver, XXII
-     Tom Rathman, San Francisco vs. Denver, XXIV
-     Gerald Riggs, Washington vs. Buffalo, XXVI
-     Emmitt Smith, Dallas vs. Buffalo, XXVIII
-     Emmitt Smith, Dallas vs. Pittsburgh, XXX
-     Howard Griffith, Denver vs. Atlanta, XXXIII

Eddie George, Tennessee vs. St. Louis, XXXIV

PASSING
PASSER RATING
Highest Passer Rating, Career (40 attempts)
- 127.8 Joe Montana, San Francisco, 4 games
- 122.8 Jim Plunkett, Oakland-L.A. Raiders, 2 games
- 112.8 Terry Bradshaw, Pittsburgh, 4 games

ATTEMPTS
Most Passes Attempted, Career
- 152 John Elway, Denver, 5 games
- 145 Jim Kelly, Buffalo, 4 games
- 122 Joe Montana, San Francisco, 4 games

Most Passes Attempted, Game
- 58 Jim Kelly, Buffalo vs. Washington, XXVI
- 51 Donovan McNabb, Philadelphia vs. New England, XXXIX
- 50 Dan Marino, Miami vs. San Francisco, XIX
      Jim Kelly, Buffalo vs. Dallas, XXVIII

COMPLETIONS
Most Passes Completed, Career
- 83 Joe Montana, San Francisco, 4 games
- 81 Jim Kelly, Buffalo, 4 games
- 76 John Elway, Denver, 5 games

Most Passes Completed, Game
- 32 Tom Brady, New England vs. Carolina, XXXVIII
- 31 Jim Kelly, Buffalo vs. Dallas, XXVIII
- 30 Donovan McNabb, Philadelphia vs. New England, XXXIX

Most Consecutive Completions, Game
- 13 Joe Montana, San Francisco vs. Denver, XXIV
- 10 Phil Simms, N.Y. Giants vs. Denver, XXI
      Troy Aikman, Dallas vs. Pittsburgh, XXX
- 9   Jim Kelly, Buffalo vs. Dallas, XXVIII
      Neil O'Donnell, Pittsburgh vs. Dallas, XXX
      Steve McNair, Tennessee vs. St. Louis, XXXIV
      Peyton Manning, Indianapolis vs. Chicago, XLI

COMPLETION PERCENTAGE
Highest Completion Percentage, Career (40 attempts)
- 70.0 Troy Aikman, Dallas, 3 games, (80-56)
- 68.0 Joe Montana, San Francisco, 4 games (122-83)
- 65.7 Tom Brady, New England, 3 games (108-71)

Highest Completion Percentage, Game (20 attempts)
- 88.0 Phil Simms, N.Y. Giants vs. Denver, XXI (25-22)
- 75.9 Joe Montana, San Francisco vs. Denver, XXIV (29-22)
- 73.5 Ken Anderson, Cincinnati vs. San Francisco, XVI (34-25)

YARDS GAINED
Most Yards Gained, Career
- 1,142 Joe Montana, San Francisco, 4 games
- 1,128 John Elway, Denver, 5 games
- 932   Terry Bradshaw, Pittsburgh, 4 games

Most Yards Gained, Game
- 414 Kurt Warner, St. Louis vs. Tennessee, XXXIV
- 365 Kurt Warner, St. Louis vs. New England, XXXVI
- 357 Joe Montana, San Francisco vs. Cincinnati, XXIII
      Donovan McNabb, Philadelphia vs. New England, XXXIX

Longest Pass Completion
- 85 Jake Delhomme (to Muhammad), Carolina vs. New England, XXXVIII (TD)
- 81 Brett Favre (to Freeman), Green Bay vs. New England, XXXI (TD)
- 80 Jim Plunkett (to King), Oakland vs. Philadelphia, XV (TD)

Doug Williams (to Sanders), Washington vs. Denver, XXII (TD)
John Elway (to R. Smith), Denver vs. Atlanta, XXXIII (TD)

AVERAGE GAIN
Highest Average Gain, Career (40 attempts)
- 11.10 Terry Bradshaw, Pittsburgh, 4 games (84-932)
- 9.62   Bart Starr, Green Bay, 2 games (47-452)
- 9.41   Jim Plunkett, Oakland-L.A. Raiders, 2 games (46-433)

Highest Average Gain, Game (20 attempts)
- 14.71 Terry Bradshaw, Pittsburgh vs. Los Angeles, XIV (21-309)
- 12.80 Jim McMahon, Chicago vs. New England, XX (20-256)
- 12.43 Jim Plunkett, Oakland vs. Philadelphia, XV (21-261)

TOUCHDOWNS
Most Touchdown Passes, Career
- 11 Joe Montana, San Francisco, 4 games
- 9   Terry Bradshaw, Pittsburgh, 4 games
- 8   Roger Staubach, Dallas, 4 games

Most Touchdown Passes, Game
- 6 Steve Young, San Francisco vs. San Diego, XXIX
- 5 Joe Montana, San Francisco vs. Denver, XXIV
- 4 Terry Bradshaw, Pittsburgh vs. Dallas, XIII
     Doug Williams, Washington vs. Denver, XXII
     Troy Aikman, Dallas vs. Buffalo, XXVII

HAD INTERCEPTED
Lowest Percentage, Passes Had Intercepted, Career (40 attempts)
- 0.00 Jim Plunkett, Oakland-L.A. Raiders, 2 games (46-0)
        Joe Montana, San Francisco, 4 games (122-0)
- 0.93 Tom Brady, New England, 3 games (108-1)
- 1.25 Troy Aikman, Dallas, 3 games (80-1)

Most Attempts, Without Interception, Game
- 45 Kurt Warner, St. Louis vs. Tennessee, XXXIV
- 36 Joe Montana, San Francisco vs. Cincinnati, XXIII
      Steve Young, San Francisco vs. San Diego, XXIX
      Steve McNair, Tennessee vs. St. Louis, XXXIV
- 35 Joe Montana, San Francisco vs. Miami, XIX

Most Passes Had Intercepted, Career
- 8 John Elway, Denver, 5 games
- 7 Craig Morton, Dallas-Denver, 2 games
     Jim Kelly, Buffalo, 4 games
- 6 Fran Tarkenton, Minnesota, 3 games

Most Passes Had Intercepted, Game
- 5 Rich Gannon, Oakland vs. Tampa Bay, XXXVII
- 4 Craig Morton, Denver vs. Dallas, XII
     Jim Kelly, Buffalo vs. Washington, XXVI
     Drew Bledsoe, New England vs. Green Bay, XXXI
     Kerry Collins, N.Y. Giants vs. Baltimore, XXXV
- 3 By 11 players

PASS RECEIVING
RECEPTIONS
Most Receptions, Career
- 33 Jerry Rice, San Francisco-Oakland, 4 games
- 27 Andre Reed, Buffalo, 4 games
- 21 Deion Branch, New England, 2 games

Most Receptions, Game
- 11 Dan Ross, Cincinnati vs. San Francisco, XVI
      Jerry Rice, San Francisco vs. Cincinnati, XXIII
      Deion Branch, New England vs. Philadelphia, XXXIX
- 10 Tony Nathan, Miami vs. San Francisco, XIX
      Jerry Rice, San Francisco vs. San Diego, XXIX
      Andre Hastings, Pittsburgh vs. Dallas, XXX
      Deion Branch, New England vs. Carolina, XXXVIII
      Joseph Addai, Indianapolis vs. Chicago, XLI

    9 Ricky Sanders, Washington vs. Denver, XXII
       Antonio Freeman, Green Bay vs. Denver, XXXII
       Terrell Owens, Philadelphia vs. New England, XXXIX

YARDS GAINED
Most Yards Gained, Career
  589 Jerry Rice, San Francisco-Oakland, 4 games
  364 Lynn Swann, Pittsburgh, 4 games
  323 Andre Reed, Buffalo, 4 games
Most Yards Gained, Game
  215 Jerry Rice, San Francisco vs. Cincinnati, XXIII
  193 Ricky Sanders, Washington vs. Denver, XXII
  162 Isaac Bruce, St. Louis vs. Tennessee, XXXIV
Longest Reception
   85 Muhsin Muhammad (from Delhomme), Carolina vs.
      New England, XXXVIII
   81 Antonio Freeman (from Favre), Green Bay vs.
      New England, XXXI (TD)
   80 Kenny King (from Plunkett), Oakland vs.
      Philadelphia, XV (TD)
      Ricky Sanders (from Williams), Washington vs.
      Denver, XXII (TD)
      Rod Smith (from Elway), Denver vs. Atlanta, XXXIII

AVERAGE GAIN
Highest Average Gain, Career (8 receptions)
  24.4 John Stallworth, Pittsburgh, 4 games (11-268)
  23.4 Ricky Sanders, Washington, 2 games (10-234)
  22.8 Lynn Swann, Pittsburgh, 4 games (16-364)
Highest Average Gain, Game (3 receptions)
  40.33 John Stallworth, Pittsburgh vs. Los Angeles, XIV
      (3-121)
  40.25 Lynn Swann, Pittsburgh vs. Dallas, X (4-161)
  38.33 John Stallworth, Pittsburgh vs. Dallas, XIII (3-115)

TOUCHDOWNS
Most Touchdowns, Career
    8 Jerry Rice, San Francisco-Oakland, 4 games
    3 John Stallworth, Pittsburgh, 4 games
      Lynn Swann, Pittsburgh, 4 games
      Cliff Branch, Oakland-L.A. Raiders, 3 games
      Antonio Freeman, Green Bay, 2 games
    2 Max McGee, Green Bay, 2 games
      Bill Miller, Oakland, 1 game
      Butch Johnson, Dallas, 2 games
      Dan Ross, Cincinnati, 1 game
      Roger Craig, San Francisco, 3 games
      Ricky Sanders, Washington, 2 games
      John Taylor, San Francisco, 3 games
      Gary Clark, Washington, 2 games
      Don Beebe, Buffalo-Green Bay, 4 games
      Michael Irvin, Dallas, 3 games
      Ricky Watters, San Francisco, 1 game
      Jay Novacek, Dallas, 3 games
      Keenan McCardell, Tampa Bay, 1 game
      Ricky Proehl, St. Louis-Carolina, 3 games
      David Givens, New England, 2 games
      Mike Vrabel, New England, 3 games
      Muhsin Muhammad, Carolina-Chicago, 2 games
Most Touchdowns, Game
    3 Jerry Rice, San Francisco vs. Denver, XXIV; vs.
      San Diego, XXIX
    2 Max McGee, Green Bay vs. Kansas City, I
      Bill Miller, Oakland vs. Green Bay, II
      John Stallworth, Pittsburgh vs. Dallas, XIII
      Cliff Branch, Oakland vs. Philadelphia, XV
      Dan Ross, Cincinnati vs. San Francisco, XVI
      Roger Craig, San Francisco vs. Miami, XIX
      Ricky Sanders, Washington vs. Denver, XXII
      Michael Irvin, Dallas vs. Buffalo, XXVII

      Ricky Watters, San Francisco vs. San Diego, XXIX
      Antonio Freeman, Green Bay vs. Denver, XXXII
      Keenan McCardell, Tampa Bay vs. Oakland, XXXVII

INTERCEPTIONS BY
Most Interceptions By, Career
    3 Chuck Howley, Dallas, 2 games
      Rod Martin, Oakland-L.A. Raiders, 2 games
      Larry Brown, Dallas, 3 games
    2 Randy Beverly, N.Y. Jets, 1 game
      Jake Scott, Miami, 3 games
      Mike Wagner, Pittsburgh, 3 games
      Mel Blount, Pittsburgh, 4 games
      Eric Wright, San Francisco, 4 games
      Barry Wilburn, Washington, 1 game
      Brad Edwards, Washington, 1 game
      Thomas Everett, Dallas, 2 games
      James Washington, Dallas, 2 games
      Darrien Gordon, San Diego-Denver-Oakland,
        4 games
      Dexter Jackson, Tampa Bay, 1 game
      Dwight Smith, Tampa Bay, 1 game
      Rodney Harrison, San Diego-New England, 3 games
Most Interceptions By, Game
    3 Rod Martin, Oakland vs. Philadelphia, XV
    2 Randy Beverly, N.Y. Jets vs. Baltimore, III
      Chuck Howley, Dallas vs. Baltimore, V
      Jake Scott, Miami vs. Washington, VII
      Barry Wilburn, Washington vs. Denver, XXII
      Brad Edwards, Washington vs. Buffalo, XXVI
      Thomas Everett, Dallas vs. Buffalo, XXVII
      Larry Brown, Dallas vs. Pittsburgh, XXX
      Darrien Gordon, Denver vs. Atlanta, XXXIII
      Dexter Jackson, Tampa Bay vs. Oakland, XXXVII
      Dwight Smith, Tampa Bay vs. Oakland, XXXVII
      Rodney Harrison, New England vs. Philadelphia,
        XXXIX

YARDS GAINED
Most Yards Gained, Career
  108 Darrien Gordon, San Diego-Denver-Oakland,
      4 games
   94 Dwight Smith, Tampa Bay, 1 game
   77 Larry Brown, Dallas, 3 games
Most Yards Gained, Game
  108 Darrien Gordon, Denver vs. Atlanta, XXXIII
   94 Dwight Smith, Tampa Bay vs. Oakland, XXXVII
   77 Larry Brown, Dallas vs. Pittsburgh, XXX
Longest Return
   76 Kelly Herndon, Seattle vs. Pittsburgh, XL
   75 Willie Brown, Oakland vs. Minnesota, XI (TD)
   60 Herb Adderley, Green Bay vs. Oakland, II (TD)

TOUCHDOWNS
Most Touchdowns, Game
    2 Dwight Smith, Tampa Bay vs. Oakland, XXXVII
    1 Herb Adderley, Green Bay vs. Oakland, II
      Willie Brown, Oakland vs. Minnesota, XI
      Jack Squirek, L.A. Raiders vs. Washington, XVIII
      Reggie Phillips, Chicago vs. New England, XX
      Duane Starks, Baltimore vs. N.Y. Giants, XXXV
      Ty Law, New England vs. St. Louis, XXXVI
      Derrick Brooks, Tampa Bay vs. Oakland, XXXVII
      Kelvin Hayden, Indianapolis vs. Chicago, XLI

PUNTING
Most Punts, Career
   17 Mike Eischeid, Oakland-Minnesota, 3 games
      Mike Horan, Denver-St. Louis, 4 games
   16 Brad Maynard, N.Y. Giants-Chicago, 2 games

15 Larry Seiple, Miami, 3 games

Most Punts, Game
11 Brad Maynard, N.Y. Giants vs. Baltimore, XXXV
10 Kyle Richardson, Baltimore vs. N.Y. Giants, XXXV
9 Ron Widby, Dallas vs. Baltimore, V

Longest Punt
63 Lee Johnson, Cincinnati vs. San Francisco, XXIII
62 Rich Camarillo, New England vs. Chicago, XX
61 Jerrel Wilson, Kansas City vs. Green Bay, I

AVERAGE YARDAGE
Highest Average, Punting, Career (10 punts)
46.5 Jerrel Wilson, Kansas City, 2 games (11-511)
43.8 Tom Rouen, Denver-Seattle, 3 games (11-482)
43.0 Kyle Richardson, Baltimore, 1 game (10-430)
      Tom Tupa, New England-Tampa Bay, 2 games
      (12-516)

Highest Average, Punting, Game (4 punts)
50.2 Tom Rouen, Seattle vs. Pittsburgh, XL (6-301)
48.8 Bryan Wagner, San Diego vs. San Francisco, XXIX
      (4-195)
48.7 Chris Gardocki, Pittsburgh vs. Seattle, XL (6-292)

PUNT RETURNS
Most Punt Returns, Career
8 Troy Brown, New England, 3 games
6 Willie Wood, Green Bay, 2 games
  Jake Scott, Miami, 3 games
  Theo Bell, Pittsburgh, 2 games
  Mike Nelms, Washington, 1 game
  John Taylor, San Francisco, 3 games
  Desmond Howard, Green Bay, 1 game
  David Meggett, N.Y. Giants-New England, 2 games
  Darrien Gordon, San Diego-Denver-Oakland,
    4 games
5 Dana McLemore, San Francisco, 1 game

Most Punt Returns, Game
6 Mike Nelms, Washington vs. Miami, XVII
  Desmond Howard, Green Bay vs. New England, XXXI
5 Willie Wood, Green Bay vs. Oakland, II
  Dana McLemore, San Francisco vs. Miami, XIX
4 By nine players

Most Fair Catches, Game
4 Jermaine Lewis, Baltimore vs. N.Y. Giants, XXXV
  Karl Williams, Tampa Bay vs. Oakland, XXXVII
3 Ron Gardin, Baltimore vs. Dallas, V
  Golden Richards, Dallas vs. Pittsburgh, X
  Greg Pruitt, L.A. Raiders vs. Washington, XVIII
  Al Edwards, Buffalo vs. N.Y. Giants, XXV
  David Meggett, N.Y. Giants vs. Buffalo, XXV

YARDS GAINED
Most Yards Gained, Career
94 John Taylor, San Francisco, 3 games
90 Desmond Howard, Green Bay, 1 game
67 David Meggett, N.Y. Giants-New England, 2 games

Most Yards Gained, Game
90 Desmond Howard, Green Bay vs. New England, XXXI
56 John Taylor, San Francisco vs. Cincinnati, XXIII
52 Mike Nelms, Washington vs. Miami, XXII

Longest Return
45 John Taylor, San Francisco vs. Cincinnati, XXIII
34 Darrell Green, Washington vs. L.A. Raiders, XVIII
   Desmond Howard, Green Bay vs. New England, XXXI
   Jermaine Lewis, Baltimore vs. N.Y. Giants, XXXV
32 Desmond Howard, Green Bay vs. New England, XXXI

AVERAGE YARDAGE
Highest Average, Career (4 returns)
15.7 John Taylor, San Francisco, 3 games (6-94)
15.0 Desmond Howard, Green Bay, 1 game (6-90)
11.2 David Meggett, N.Y. Giants-New England, 2 games
     (6-67)

Highest Average, Game (3 returns)
18.7 John Taylor, San Francisco vs. Cincinnati, XXIII (3-56)
15.0 Desmond Howard, Green Bay vs. New England, XXXI
     (6-90)
14.0 Terrence Wilkins, Indianapolis vs. Chicago, XLI
     (3-42)

TOUCHDOWNS
Most Touchdowns, Game
None

KICKOFF RETURNS
Most Kickoff Returns, Career
10 Ken Bell, Denver, 3 games
8 Larry Anderson, Pittsburgh, 2 games
  Fulton Walker, Miami, 2 games
  Andre Coleman, San Diego, 1 game
  Marcus Knight, Oakland, 1 game
7 Preston Pearson, Baltimore-Pittsburgh-Dallas, 5 games
  Stephen Starring, New England, 1 game
  David Meggett, N.Y. Giants-New England, 2 games

Most Kickoff Returns, Game
8 Andre Coleman, San Diego vs. San Francisco, XXIX
  Marcus Knight, Oakland vs. Tampa Bay, XXXVII
7 Stephen Starring, New England vs. Chicago, XX
6 Darren Carrington, Denver vs. San Francisco, XXIV
  Antonio Freeman, Green Bay vs. Denver, XXXII
  Ron Dixon, N.Y. Giants vs. Baltimore, XXXV

YARDS GAINED
Most Yards Gained, Career
283 Fulton Walker, Miami, 2 games
244 Andre Coleman, San Diego, 1 game
210 Tim Dwight, Atlanta, 1 game

Most Yards Gained, Game
244 Andre Coleman, San Diego vs. San Francisco, XXIX
210 Tim Dwight, Atlanta vs. Denver, XXXIII
190 Fulton Walker, Miami vs. Washington, XVII

Longest Return
99 Desmond Howard, Green Bay vs. New England, XXXI
   (TD)
98 Fulton Walker, Miami vs. Washington, XVII (TD)
   Andre Coleman, San Diego vs. San Francisco, XXIX
   (TD)
97 Ron Dixon, N.Y. Giants vs. Baltimore, XXXV (TD)

AVERAGE YARDAGE
Highest Average, Career (4 returns)
42.0 Tim Dwight, Atlanta, 1 game (5-210)
38.5 Desmond Howard, Green Bay, 1 game (4-154)
35.4 Fulton Walker, Miami, 2 games (8-283)

Highest Average, Game (3 returns)
47.5 Fulton Walker, Miami vs. Washington, XVII (4-190)
42.0 Tim Dwight, Atlanta vs. Denver, XXXIII (5-210)
38.5 Desmond Howard, Green Bay vs. New England, XXXI
     (4-154)

TOUCHDOWNS
Most Touchdowns, Game
1 Fulton Walker, Miami vs. Washington, XVII
  Stanford Jennings, Cincinnati vs. San Francisco, XXIII
  Andre Coleman, San Diego vs. San Francisco, XXIX
  Desmond Howard, Green Bay vs. New England, XXXI
  Tim Dwight, Atlanta vs. Denver, XXXIII

Ron Dixon, N.Y. Giants vs. Baltimore, XXXV
Jermaine Lewis, Baltimore vs. N.Y. Giants, XXXV
Devin Hester, Chicago vs. Indianapolis, XLI

FUMBLES
Most Fumbles, Career
5   Roger Staubach, Dallas, 4 games
4   Jim Kelly, Buffalo, 4 games
3   Franco Harris, Pittsburgh, 4 games
    Terry Bradshaw, Pittsburgh, 4 games
    John Elway, Denver, 5 games
    Frank Reich, Buffalo, 4 games
    Thurman Thomas, Buffalo, 4 games
Most Fumbles, Game
3   Roger Staubach, Dallas vs. Pittsburgh, X
    Jim Kelly, Buffalo vs. Washington, XXVI
    Frank Reich, Buffalo vs. Dallas, XXVII
2   Franco Harris, Pittsburgh vs. Minnesota, IX
    Butch Johnson, Dallas vs. Denver, XII
    Terry Bradshaw, Pittsburgh vs. Dallas, XIII
    Joe Montana, San Francisco vs. Cincinnati, XXIII
    John Elway, Denver vs. San Francisco, XXIV
    Thurman Thomas, Buffalo vs. Dallas, XXVIII
    Rex Grossman, Chicago vs. Indianapolis, XLI

RECOVERIES
Most Fumbles Recovered, Career
2   Jake Scott, Miami, 3 games (1 own, 1 opp)
    Fran Tarkenton, Minnesota, 3 games (2 own)
    Franco Harris, Pittsburgh, 4 games (2 own)
    Roger Staubach, Dallas, 4 games (2 own)
    Bobby Walden, Pittsburgh, 2 games (2 own)
    John Fitzgerald, Dallas, 4 games (2 own)
    Randy Hughes, Dallas, 3 games (2 opp)
    Butch Johnson, Dallas, 2 games (2 own)
    Mike Singletary, Chicago, 1 game (2 opp)
    John Elway, Denver, 5 games (2 own)
    Jimmie Jones, Dallas, 2 games (2 opp)
    Kenneth Davis, Buffalo, 4 games (2 own)
    Kurt Warner, St. Louis, 2 games (2 own)
Most Fumbles Recovered, Game
2   Jake Scott, Miami vs. Minnesota, VIII (1 own, 1 opp)
    Roger Staubach, Dallas vs. Pittsburgh, X (2 own)
    Randy Hughes, Dallas vs. Denver, XII (2 opp)
    Butch Johnson, Dallas vs. Denver, XII (2 own)
    Mike Singletary, Chicago vs. New England, XX (2 opp)
    Jimmie Jones, Dallas vs. Buffalo, XXVII (2 opp)

YARDS GAINED
Most Yards Gained, Game
64   Leon Lett, Dallas vs. Buffalo, XXVII (opp)
49   Mike Bass, Washington vs. Miami, VII (opp)
46   James Washington, Dallas vs. Buffalo, XXVIII (opp)
Longest Return
64   Leon Lett, Dallas vs. Buffalo, XXVII
49   Mike Bass, Washington vs. Miami, VII (TD)
46   James Washington, Dallas vs. Buffalo, XXVIII (TD)

TOUCHDOWNS
Most Touchdowns, Game
1   Mike Bass, Washington vs. Miami, VII (opp 49 yds)
    Mike Hegman, Dallas vs. Pittsburgh, XIII (opp 37 yds)
    Jimmie Jones, Dallas vs. Buffalo, XXVII (opp 2 yds)
    Ken Norton, Dallas vs. Buffalo, XXVII (opp 9 yds)
    James Washington, Dallas vs. Buffalo, XXVIII
      (opp 46 yds)

COMBINED NET YARDS GAINED
(Rushing, receiving, interception returns, punt returns, kickoff returns, and fumble returns)
ATTEMPTS
Most Attempts, Career
108   Franco Harris, Pittsburgh, 4 games
81   Emmitt Smith, Dallas, 3 games
72   Roger Craig, San Francisco, 3 games
    Thurman Thomas, Buffalo, 4 games
Most Attempts, Game
39   John Riggins, Washington vs. Miami, XVII
35   Franco Harris, Pittsburgh vs. Minnesota, IX
34   Matt Snell, N.Y. Jets vs. Baltimore, III
    Emmitt Smith, Dallas vs. Buffalo, XXVIII

YARDS GAINED
Most Yards Gained, Career
604   Jerry Rice, San Francisco-Oakland, 4 games
468   Franco Harris, Pittsburgh, 4 games
410   Roger Craig, San Francisco, 3 games
Most Yards Gained, Game
244   Andre Coleman, San Diego vs. San Francisco, XXIX
    Desmond Howard, Green Bay vs. New England, XXXI
235   Ricky Sanders, Washington vs. Denver, XXII
230   Antonio Freeman, Green Bay vs. Denver, XXXII

SACKS
Sacks have been compiled since XVII.
Most Sacks, Career
4.5   Charles Haley, San Francisco-Dallas, 5 games
3.0   Danny Stubbs, San Francisco, 2 games
    Leonard Marshall, N.Y. Giants, 2 games
    Jeff Wright, Buffalo, 4 games
    Reggie White, Green Bay, 2 games
    Willie McGinest, New England, 4 games
    Tedy Bruschi, New England, 4 games
    Mike Vrabel, New England, 3 games
2.5   Dexter Manley, Washington, 3 games
Most Sacks, Game
3.0   Reggie White, Green Bay vs. New England, XXXI
2.0   Dwaine Board, San Francisco vs. Miami, XIX
    Dennis Owens, New England vs. Chicago, XX
    Otis Wilson, Chicago vs. New England, XX
    Leonard Marshall, N.Y. Giants vs. Denver, XXI
    Alvin Walton, Washington vs. Denver, XXII
    Charles Haley, San Francisco vs. Cincinnati, XXIII
    Danny Stubbs, San Francisco vs. Denver, XXIV
    Jeff Wright, Buffalo vs. Dallas, XXVIII
    Raylee Johnson, San Diego vs. San Francisco, XXIX
    Chad Hennings, Dallas vs. Pittsburgh, XXX
    Tedy Bruschi, New England vs. Green Bay, XXXI
    Michael McCrary, Baltimore vs. N.Y. Giants, XXXV
    Simeon Rice, Tampa Bay vs. Oakland, XXXVII
    Mike Vrabel, New England vs. Carolina, XXXVIII

TEAM RECORDS

GAMES, VICTORIES, DEFEATS
Most Games
8   Dallas, V-VI, X, XII-XIII, XXVII-XXVIII, XXX
6   Denver, XII, XXI-XXII, XXIV, XXXII-XXXIII
    Pittsburgh, IX-X, XIII-XIV, XXX, XL
5   Miami, VI-VIII, XVII, XIX
    Washington, VII, XVII-XVIII, XXII, XXVI
    San Francisco, XVI, XIX, XXIII-XXIV, XXIX
    Oakland/L.A. Raiders, II, XI, XV, XVIII, XXXVII
    New England, XX, XXXI, XXXVI, XXXVIII-XXXIX
Most Consecutive Games
4   Buffalo, XXV-XXVIII

3   Miami, VI-VIII
2   Green Bay, I-II; XXXI-XXXII
    Dallas, V-VI; XII-XIII; XXVII-XXVIII
    Minnesota, VIII-IX
    Pittsburgh, IX-X; XIII-XIV
    Washington, XVII-XVIII
    Denver, XXI-XXII; XXXII-XXXIII
    San Francisco, XXIII-XXIV
    New England, XXXVIII-XXXIX

Most Games Won
5   San Francisco, XVI, XIX, XXIII-XXIV, XXIX
    Dallas, VI, XII, XXVII-XXVIII, XXX
    Pittsburgh, IX-X, XIII-XIV, XL
3   Oakland/L.A. Raiders, XI, XV, XVIII
    Washington, XVII, XXII, XXVI
    Green Bay, I-II, XXXI
    New England, XXXVI, XXXVIII-XXXIX
2   Miami, VII-VIII
    N.Y. Giants, XXI, XXV
    Denver, XXXII, XXXIII
    Baltimore/Indianapolis, V, XLI

Most Consecutive Games Won
2   Green Bay, I-II
    Miami, VII-VIII
    Pittsburgh, IX-X, XIII-XIV
    San Francisco, XXIII-XXIV
    Dallas, XXVII-XXVIII
    Denver, XXXII-XXXIII
    New England, XXXVIII-XXXIX

Most Games Lost
4   Minnesota, IV, VIII-IX, XI
    Denver, XII, XXI-XXII, XXIV
    Buffalo, XXV-XXVIII
3   Dallas, V, X, XIII
    Miami, VI, XVII, XIX
2   Washington, VII, XVIII
    Cincinnati, XVI, XXIII
    New England, XX, XXXI
    L.A./St. Louis Rams, XIV, XXXVI
    Oakland/L.A. Raiders, II, XXXVII
    Philadelphia, XV, XXXIX

Most Consecutive Games Lost
4   Buffalo, XXV-XXVIII
2   Minnesota, VIII-IX
    Denver, XXI-XXII

SCORING
Most Points, Game
55   San Francisco vs. Denver, XXIV
52   Dallas vs. Buffalo, XXVII
49   San Francisco vs. San Diego, XXIX
Fewest Points, Game
3   Miami vs. Dallas, VI
6   Minnesota vs. Pittsburgh, IX
7   By five teams
Most Points, Both Teams, Game
75   San Francisco (49) vs. San Diego (26), XXIX
69   Dallas (52) vs. Buffalo (17), XXVII
    Tampa Bay (48) vs. Oakland (21), XXXVII
66   Pittsburgh (35) vs. Dallas (31), XIII
Fewest Points, Both Teams, Game
21   Washington (7) vs. Miami (14), VII
22   Minnesota (6) vs. Pittsburgh (16), IX
23   Baltimore (7) vs. N.Y. Jets (16), III
Largest Margin of Victory, Game
45   San Francisco vs. Denver, XXIV (55-10)
36   Chicago vs. New England, XX (46-10)
35   Dallas vs. Buffalo, XXVII (52-17)
Most Points, Each Half
1st: 35   Washington vs. Denver, XXII

2nd: 30   N.Y. Giants vs. Denver, XXI
Most Points, Each Quarter
1st: 14   Miami vs. Minnesota, VIII
        Oakland vs. Philadelphia, XV
        Dallas vs. Buffalo, XXVII
        San Francisco vs. San Diego, XXIX
        New England vs. Green Bay, XXXI
        Chicago vs. Indianapolis, XLI
2nd: 35   Washington vs. Denver, XXII
3rd: 21   Chicago vs. New England, XX
4th: 21   Dallas vs. Buffalo, XXVII
Most Points, Both Teams, Each Half
1st: 45   Washington (35) vs. Denver (10), XXII
2nd: 46   Tampa Bay (28) vs. Oakland (18), XXXVII
Fewest Points, Both Teams, Each Half
1st: 2   Minnesota (0) vs. Pittsburgh (2), IX
2nd: 7   Miami (0) vs. Washington (7), VII
        Denver (0) vs. Washington (7), XXII
Most Points, Both Teams, Each Quarter
1st: 24   New England (14) vs. Green Bay (10), XXXI
2nd: 35   Washington (35) vs. Denver (0), XXII
3rd: 24   Washington (14) vs. Buffalo (10), XXVI
4th: 37   Carolina (19) vs. New England (18), XXXVIII

TOUCHDOWNS
Most Touchdowns, Game
8   San Francisco vs. Denver, XXIV
7   Dallas vs. Buffalo, XXVII
    San Francisco vs. San Diego, XXIX
6   Washington vs. Denver, XXII
    Tampa Bay vs. Oakland, XXXVII
Fewest Touchdowns, Game
0   Miami vs. Dallas, VI
1   By 19 teams
Most Touchdowns, Both Teams, Game
10   San Francisco (7) vs. San Diego (3), XXIX
9   Pittsburgh (5) vs. Dallas (4), XIII
    San Francisco (8) vs. Denver (1), XXIV
    Dallas (7) vs. Buffalo (2), XXVII
    Tampa Bay (6) vs. Oakland (3), XXXVII
8   Carolina (4) vs. New England (4), XXXVIII
Fewest Touchdowns, Both Teams, Game
2   Baltimore (1) vs. N.Y. Jets (1), III
3   In six games

POINTS AFTER TOUCHDOWN
Most (One-Point) Points After Touchdown, Game
7   San Francisco vs. Denver, XXIV
    Dallas vs. Buffalo, XXVII
    San Francisco vs. San Diego, XXIX
6   Washington vs. Denver, XXII
    Tampa Bay vs. Oakland, XXXVII
5   Green Bay vs. Kansas City, I
    Pittsburgh vs. Dallas, XIII
    L.A. Raiders vs. Washington, XVIII
    San Francisco vs. Miami, XIX
    Chicago vs. New England, XX
Most (One-Point) Points After Touchdown, Both Teams, Game
9   Pittsburgh (5) vs. Dallas (4), XIII
    Dallas (7) vs. Buffalo (2), XXVII
8   San Francisco (7) vs. Denver (1), XXIV
    San Francisco (7) vs. San Diego (1), XXIX
7   Washington (6) vs. Denver (1), XXII
    Washington (4) vs. Buffalo (3), XXVI
    Denver (4) vs. Green Bay (3), XXXII
Fewest (One-Point) Points After Touchdown, Both Teams, Game
2   Baltimore (1) vs. N.Y. Jets (1), III
    Baltimore (1) vs. Dallas (1), V
    Minnesota (0) vs. Pittsburgh (2), IX

Most Two-Point Conversions, Game
2 San Diego vs. San Francisco, XXIX
Most Two-Point Conversions, Both Teams, Game
2 San Diego (2) vs. San Francisco (0), XXIX

FIELD GOALS
Most Field Goals Attempted, Game
5 N.Y. Jets vs. Baltimore, III
Dallas vs. Denver, XII
4 Green Bay vs. Oakland, II
Pittsburgh vs. Dallas, XX
San Francisco vs. Cincinnati, XVI; XXIII
Denver vs. N.Y. Giants, XXI
Denver vs. Atlanta, XXXIII
St. Louis vs. Tennessee, XXXIV
Indianapolis vs. Chicago, XLI
Most Field Goals Attempted, Both Teams, Game
7 N.Y. Jets (5) vs. Baltimore (2), III
San Francisco (4) vs. Cincinnati (3), XXIII
St. Louis (4) vs. Tennessee (3), XXXIV
Denver (4) vs. Atlanta (3), XXXIII
6 Dallas (5) vs. Denver (1), XII
5 Green Bay (4) vs. Oakland (1), II
Pittsburgh (4) vs. Dallas (1), X
Oakland (3) vs. Philadelphia (2), XV
Denver (4) vs. N.Y. Giants (1), XXI
Dallas (3) vs. Buffalo (2), XXVIII
Indianapolis (4) vs. Chicago (1), XLI
Fewest Field Goals Attempted, Both Teams, Game
1 Minnesota (0) vs. Miami (1), VIII
San Francisco (0) vs. Denver (1), XXIV
Philadelphia (0) vs. New England (1), XXXIX
2 Green Bay (0) vs. Kansas City (2), I
Miami (1) vs. Washington (1), VII
Minnesota (1) vs. Pittsburgh (1), IX
Dallas (1) vs. Pittsburgh (1), XIII
Dallas (1) vs. Buffalo (1), XXVII
San Diego (1) vs. San Francisco (1), XXIX
Denver (1) vs. Green Bay (1), XXXII
Most Field Goals, Game
4 Green Bay vs. Oakland, II
San Francisco vs. Cincinnati, XVI
3 N.Y. Jets vs. Baltimore, III
Kansas City vs. Minnesota, IV
Miami vs. San Francisco, XIX
Chicago vs. New England, XX
Cincinnati vs. San Francisco, XXIII
Washington vs. Buffalo, XXVI
Dallas vs. Buffalo, XXVIII
St. Louis vs. Tennessee, XXXIV
Indianapolis vs. Chicago, XLI
Most Field Goals, Both Teams, Game
5 Cincinnati (3) vs. San Francisco (2), XXIII
Dallas (3) vs. Buffalo (2), XXVIII
4 Green Bay (4) vs. Oakland (0), II
San Francisco (4) vs. Cincinnati (0), XVI
Miami (3) vs. San Francisco (1), XIX
Chicago (3) vs. New England (1), XX
Washington (3) vs. Buffalo (1), XXVI
Atlanta (2) vs. Denver (2), XXXIII
St. Louis (3) vs. Tennessee (1), XXXIV
Indianapolis (3) vs. Chicago (1), XLI
3 In 13 games
Fewest Field Goals, Both Teams, Game
0 Miami vs. Washington, VII
Pittsburgh vs. Minnesota, IX
1 Green Bay (0) vs. Kansas City (1), I
Minnesota (0) vs. Miami (1), VIII
Pittsburgh (0) vs. Dallas (1), XIII
Washington (0) vs. Denver (1), XXII

San Francisco (0) vs. Denver (1), XXIV
San Francisco (0) vs. San Diego (1), XXIX
Philadelphia (0) vs. New England (1), XXXIX
Pittsburgh (0) vs. Seattle (1), XL

SAFETIES
Most Safeties, Game
1 Pittsburgh vs. Minnesota, IX; vs. Dallas, X
Chicago vs. New England, XX
N.Y. Giants vs. Denver, XXI
Buffalo vs. N.Y. Giants, XXV

FIRST DOWNS
Most First Downs, Game
31 San Francisco vs. Miami, XIX
29 New England vs. Carolina, XXXVIII
28 San Francisco vs. Denver, XXIV
San Francisco vs. San Diego, XXIX
Fewest First Downs, Game
9 Minnesota vs. Pittsburgh, IX
Miami vs. Washington, XVII
10 Dallas vs. Baltimore, V
Miami vs. Dallas, VI
11 Denver vs. Dallas, XII
N.Y. Giants vs. Baltimore, XXXV
Oakland vs. Tampa Bay, XXXVII
Chicago vs. Indianapolis, XLI
Most First Downs, Both Teams, Game
50 San Francisco (31) vs. Miami (19), XIX
Tennessee (27) vs. St. Louis (23), XXXIV
49 Buffalo (25) vs. Washington (24), XXVI
48 San Francisco (28) vs. San Diego (20), XXIX
Fewest First Downs, Both Teams, Game
24 Dallas (10) vs. Baltimore (14), V
N.Y. Giants (11) vs. Baltimore (13), XXXV
26 Minnesota (9) vs. Pittsburgh (17), IX
27 Pittsburgh (13) vs. Dallas (14), X

RUSHING
Most First Downs, Rushing, Game
16 San Francisco vs. Miami, XIX
15 Dallas vs. Miami, VI
14 Washington vs. Miami, XVII
San Francisco vs. Denver, XXIV
Denver vs. Green Bay, XXXII
Fewest First Downs, Rushing, Game
1 New England vs. Chicago, XX
St. Louis vs. Tennessee, XXXIV
Oakland vs. Tampa Bay, XXXVII
2 Minnesota vs. Kansas City, IV; vs. Pittsburgh, IX;
vs. Oakland, XI
Pittsburgh vs. Dallas, XIII
Miami vs. San Francisco, XIX
N.Y. Giants vs. Baltimore, XXXV
3 Miami vs. Dallas, VI
Philadelphia vs. Oakland, XV
New England vs. Green Bay, XXXI
Carolina vs. New England, XXXVIII
Chicago vs. Indianapolis, XLI
Most First Downs, Rushing, Both Teams, Game
21 Washington (14) vs. Miami (7), XVII
19 Washington (13) vs. Denver (6), XXII
San Francisco (14) vs. Denver (5), XXIV
18 Dallas (15) vs. Miami (3), VI
Miami (13) vs. Minnesota (5), VIII
San Francisco (16) vs. Miami (2), XIX
N.Y. Giants (10) vs. Buffalo (8), XXV
Denver (14) vs. Green Bay (4), XXXII
Fewest First Downs, Rushing, Both Teams, Game
7 Oakland (1) vs. Tampa Bay (6), XXXVII

8 Baltimore (4) vs. Dallas (4), V
    Pittsburgh (2) vs. Dallas (6), XIII
    N.Y. Giants (2) vs. Baltimore (6), XXXV
9 Philadelphia (3) vs. Oakland (6), XV

PASSING

Most First Downs, Passing, Game
19 New England vs. Carolina, XXXVIII
18 Buffalo vs. Washington, XXVI
    St. Louis vs. Tennessee, XXXIV
    Philadelphia vs. New England, XXXIX
17 Miami vs. San Francisco, XIX
    San Francisco vs. San Diego, XXIX

Fewest First Downs, Passing, Game
1 Denver vs. Dallas, XII
2 Miami vs. Washington, XVII
4 Miami vs. Minnesota, VIII

Most First Downs, Passing, Both Teams, Game
32 Miami (17) vs. San Francisco (15), XIX
    Philadelphia (18) vs. New England (14), XXXIX
31 San Francisco (17) vs. San Diego (14), XXIX
    St. Louis (18) vs. Tennessee (13), XXXIV
    New England (19) vs. Carolina (12), XXXVIII
30 Buffalo (18) vs. Washington (12), XXVI

Fewest First Downs, Passing, Both Teams, Game
9 Denver (1) vs. Dallas (8), XII
10 Minnesota (5) vs. Pittsburgh (5), IX
11 Dallas (5) vs. Baltimore (6), V
    Miami (2) vs. Washington (9), XVII

PENALTY

Most First Downs, Penalty, Game
4 Baltimore vs. Dallas, V
    Miami vs. Minnesota, VIII
    Cincinnati vs. San Francisco, XVI
    Buffalo vs. Dallas, XXVII
    St. Louis vs. Tennessee, XXXIV
3 Kansas City vs. Minnesota, IV
    Minnesota vs. Oakland, XI
    Buffalo vs. Washington, XXVI
    Green Bay vs. Denver, XXXII
    N.Y. Giants vs. Baltimore, XXXV
    St. Louis vs. New England, XXXVI
    Tampa Bay vs. Oakland, XXXVII
    New England vs. Carolina, XXXVIII

Most First Downs, Penalty, Both Teams, Game
6 Cincinnati (4) vs. San Francisco (2), XVI
    St. Louis (4) vs. Tennessee (2), XXXIV
5 Baltimore (4) vs. Dallas (1), V
    Miami (4) vs. Minnesota (1), VIII
    Buffalo (3) vs. Washington (2), XXVI
    Green Bay (3) vs. Denver (2), XXXII
    New England (3) vs. Carolina (2), XXXVIII
4 Kansas City (3) vs. Minnesota (1), IV
    Buffalo (4) vs. Dallas (0), XXVII
    N.Y. Giants (3) vs. Baltimore (1), XXXV
    St. Louis (3) vs. New England (1), XXXVI
    Tampa Bay (3) vs Oakland (1), XXXVII

Fewest First Downs, Penalty, Both Teams, Game
0 Dallas vs. Miami, VI
    Miami vs. Washington, VII
    Dallas vs. Pittsburgh, X
    Miami vs. San Francisco, XIX
    Pittsburgh vs. Seattle, XL
1 Green Bay (0) vs. Kansas City (1), I
    Miami (0) vs. Washington (1), XVII
    Cincinnati (0) vs. San Francisco (1), XXIII
    San Francisco (0) vs. Denver (1), XXIV
    Dallas (0) vs. Buffalo (1), XXVIII
    Dallas (0) vs. Pittsburgh (1), XXX

    Denver (0) vs. Atlanta (1), XXXIII
    Chicago (0) vs. Indianapolis (1), XLI

NET YARDS GAINED RUSHING AND PASSING

Most Yards Gained, Game
602 Washington vs. Denver, XXII
537 San Francisco vs. Miami, XIX
481 New England vs. Carolina, XXXVIII

Fewest Yards Gained, Game
119 Minnesota vs. Pittsburgh, IX
123 New England vs. Chicago, XX
152 N.Y. Giants vs. Baltimore, XXXV

Most Yards Gained, Both Teams, Game
929 Washington (602) vs. Denver (327), XXII
868 New England (481) vs. Carolina (387), XXXVIII
851 San Francisco (537) vs. Miami (314), XIX

Fewest Yards Gained, Both Teams, Game
396 N.Y. Giants (152) vs. Baltimore (244), XXXV
452 Minnesota (119) vs. Pittsburgh (333), IX
481 Washington (228) vs. Miami (253), VII
    Denver (156) vs. Dallas (325), XII

RUSHING
ATTEMPTS

Most Attempts, Game
57 Pittsburgh vs. Minnesota, IX
53 Miami vs. Minnesota, VIII
52 Oakland vs. Minnesota, XI
    Washington vs. Miami, XVII

Fewest Attempts, Game
9 Miami vs. San Francisco, XIX
11 New England vs. Chicago, XX
    Oakland vs. Tampa Bay, XXXVII
13 New England vs. Green Bay, XXXI
    St. Louis vs. Tennessee, XXXIV

Most Attempts, Both Teams, Game
81 Washington (52) vs. Miami (29), XVII
78 Pittsburgh (57) vs. Minnesota (21), IX
    Oakland (52) vs. Minnesota (26), XI
77 Miami (53) vs. Minnesota (24), VIII
    Pittsburgh (46) vs. Dallas (31), X

Fewest Attempts, Both Teams, Game
45 Philadelphia (17) vs. New England (28), XXXIX
47 St. Louis (22) vs. New England (25), XXXVI
49 Miami (9) vs. San Francisco (40), XIX
    New England (13) vs. Green Bay (36), XXXI
    St. Louis (13) vs. Tennessee (36), XXXIV
    N.Y. Giants (16) vs. Baltimore (33), XXXV

YARDS GAINED

Most Yards Gained, Game
280 Washington vs. Denver, XXII
276 Washington vs. Miami, XVII
266 Oakland vs. Minnesota, XI

Fewest Yards Gained, Game
7 New England vs. Chicago, XX
17 Minnesota vs. Pittsburgh, IX
19 Oakland vs. Tampa Bay, XXXVII

Most Yards Gained, Both Teams, Game
377 Washington (280) vs. Denver (97), XXII
372 Washington (276) vs. Miami (96), XVII
338 N.Y. Giants (172) vs. Buffalo (166), XXV

Fewest Yards Gained, Both Teams, Game
157 Philadelphia (45) vs. New England (112), XXXIX
158 New England (43) vs. Green Bay (115), XXXI
159 Dallas (56) vs. Pittsburgh (103), XXX

AVERAGE GAIN
Highest Average Gain, Game
- 7.00   L.A. Raiders vs. Washington, XVIII (33-231)
-         Washington vs. Denver, XXII (40-280)
- 6.64   Buffalo vs. N.Y. Giants, XXV (25-166)
- 6.22   Baltimore vs. N.Y. Jets, III (23-143)

Lowest Average Gain, Game
- 0.64   New England vs. Chicago, XX (11-7)
- 0.81   Minnesota vs. Pittsburgh, IX (21-17)
- 1.73   Oakland vs. Tampa Bay, XXXVII (11-19)

TOUCHDOWNS
Most Touchdowns, Game
- 4   Chicago vs. New England, XX
-     Denver vs. Green Bay, XXXII
- 3   Green Bay vs. Kansas City, I
-     Miami vs. Minnesota, VIII
-     San Francisco vs. Denver, XXIV
-     Denver vs. Atlanta, XXXIII
- 2   Oakland vs. Minnesota, XI
-     Pittsburgh vs. Los Angeles, XIV
-     L.A. Raiders vs. Washington, XVIII
-     San Francisco vs. Miami, XIX
-     N.Y. Giants vs. Denver, XXI
-     Washington vs. Denver, XXII; vs. Buffalo, XXVI
-     Buffalo vs. N.Y. Giants, XXV
-     Dallas vs. Buffalo, XXVIII; vs. Pittsburgh, XXX
-     Tennessee vs. St. Louis, XXXIV
-     Pittsburgh vs. Seattle, XL

Fewest Touchdowns, Game
- 0   By 27 teams

Most Touchdowns, Both Teams, Game
- 4   Miami (3) vs. Minnesota (1), VIII
-     Chicago (4) vs. New England (0), XX
-     San Francisco (3) vs. Denver (1), XXIV
-     Denver (4) vs. Green Bay (0), XXXII
- 3   In nine games

Fewest Touchdowns, Both Teams, Game
- 0   Pittsburgh vs. Dallas, X
-     Oakland vs. Philadelphia, XV
-     Cincinnati vs. San Francisco, XXIII
- 1   In 12 games

PASSING
ATTEMPTS
Most Passes Attempted, Game
- 59   Buffalo vs. Washington, XXVI
- 55   San Diego vs. San Francisco, XXIX
- 51   Philadelphia vs. New England, XXXIX

Fewest Passes Attempted, Game
- 7   Miami vs. Minnesota, VIII
- 11   Miami vs. Washington, VII
- 14   Pittsburgh vs. Minnesota, IX

Most Passes Attempted, Both Teams, Game
- 93   San Diego (55) vs. San Francisco (38), XXIX
- 92   Buffalo (59) vs. Washington (33), XXVI
- 85   Miami (50) vs. San Francisco (35), XIX

Fewest Passes Attempted, Both Teams, Game
- 35   Miami (7) vs. Minnesota (28), VIII
- 39   Miami (11) vs. Washington (28), VII
- 40   Pittsburgh (14) vs. Minnesota (26), IX
-     Miami (17) vs. Washington (23), XVII

COMPLETIONS
Most Passes Completed, Game
- 32   New England vs. Carolina, XXXVIII
- 31   Buffalo vs. Dallas, XXVIII
- 30   Philadelphia vs. New England, XXXIX

Fewest Passes Completed, Game
- 4   Miami vs. Washington, XVII

- 6   Miami vs. Minnesota, VIII
- 8   Miami vs. Washington, VII
-     Denver vs. Dallas, XII

Most Passes Completed, Both Teams, Game
- 53   Miami (29) vs. San Francisco (24), XIX
-     Philadelphia (30) vs. New England (23), XXXIX
- 52   San Diego (27) vs. San Francisco (25), XXIX
- 50   Buffalo (31) vs. Dallas (19), XXVIII

Fewest Passes Completed, Both Teams, Game
- 19   Miami (4) vs. Washington (15), XVII
- 20   Pittsburgh (9) vs. Minnesota (11), IX
- 22   Miami (8) vs. Washington (14), VII

COMPLETION PERCENTAGE
Highest Completion Percentage, Game (20 attempts)
- 88.0   N.Y. Giants vs. Denver, XXI (25-22)
- 75.0   San Francisco vs. Denver, XXIV (32-24)
- 73.5   Cincinnati vs. San Francisco, XVI (34-25)

Lowest Completion Percentage, Game (20 attempts)
- 32.0   Denver vs. Dallas, XII (25-8)
- 37.9   Denver vs. San Francisco, XXIV (29-11)
- 38.5   Denver vs. Washington, XXII (39-15)
-       N.Y. Giants vs. Baltimore, XXXV (39-15)

YARDS GAINED
Most Yards Gained, Game
- 407   St. Louis vs. Tennessee, XXXIV
- 354   New England vs. Carolina, XXXVIII
- 341   San Francisco vs. Cincinnati, XXIII

Fewest Yards Gained, Game
- 35   Denver vs. Dallas, XII
- 63   Miami vs. Minnesota, VIII
- 69   Miami vs. Washington, VII

Most Yards Gained, Both Teams, Game
- 649   New England (354) vs. Carolina (295), XXXVIII
- 615   San Francisco (326) vs. Miami (289), XIX
-       St. Louis (407) vs. Tennessee (208), XXXIV
- 603   San Francisco (316) vs. San Diego (287), XXIX

Fewest Yards Gained, Both Teams, Game
- 156   Miami (69) vs. Washington (87), VII
- 186   Pittsburgh (84) vs. Minnesota (102), IX
- 204   Miami (80) vs. Washington (124), XVII

TIMES SACKED
Most Times Sacked, Game
- 7   Dallas vs. Pittsburgh, X
-     New England vs. Chicago, XX
- 6   Kansas City vs. Green Bay, I
-     Washington vs. L.A. Raiders, XVIII
-     Denver vs. San Francisco, XXIV
- 5   Dallas vs. Denver, XII; vs. Pittsburgh, XIII
-     Cincinnati vs. San Francisco, XVI; XXIII
-     Denver vs. Washington, XXII
-     Buffalo vs. Washington, XXVI
-     Green Bay vs. New England, XXXI
-     New England vs. Green Bay, XXXI
-     Oakland vs. Tampa Bay, XXXVII

Fewest Times Sacked, Game
- 0   Baltimore vs. N.Y. Jets, III; vs. Dallas, V
-     Minnesota vs. Pittsburgh, IX
-     Pittsburgh vs. Los Angeles, XIV
-     Philadelphia vs. Oakland, XV
-     Washington vs. Buffalo, XXVI
-     Denver vs. Green Bay, XXXII; vs. Atlanta, XXXIII
-     Tampa Bay vs. Oakland, XXXVII
-     New England vs. Carolina, XXXVIII
- 1   By 16 teams

Most Times Sacked, Both Teams, Game
- 10   New England (7) vs. Chicago (3), XX
-       Green Bay (5) vs. New England (5), XXXI

9   Kansas City (6) vs. Green Bay (3), I
    Dallas (7) vs. Pittsburgh (2), X
    Dallas (5) vs. Denver (4), XII
    Dallas (5) vs. Pittsburgh (4), XIII
    Cincinnati (5) vs. San Francisco (4), XXIII
8   Washington (6) vs. L.A. Raiders (2), XVIII

Fewest Times Sacked, Both Teams, Game
1   Philadelphia (0) vs. Oakland (1), XV
    Denver (0) vs. Green Bay (1), XXXII
2   Baltimore (0) vs. N.Y. Jets (2), III
    Baltimore (0) vs. Dallas (2), V
    Minnesota (0) vs. Pittsburgh (2), IX
    Denver (0) vs. Atlanta (2), XXXIII
    Chicago (1) vs. Indianapolis (1), XLI
3   In five games

TOUCHDOWNS
Most Touchdowns, Game
6   San Francisco vs. San Diego, XXIX
5   San Francisco vs. Denver, XXIV
4   Pittsburgh vs. Dallas, XIII
    Washington vs. Denver, XXII
    Dallas vs. Buffalo, XXVII
Fewest Touchdowns, Game
0   By 19 teams
Most Touchdowns, Both Teams, Game
7   Pittsburgh (4) vs. Dallas (3), XIII
    San Francisco (6) vs. San Diego (1), XXIX
6   Carolina (3) vs. New England (3), XXXVIII
5   Washington (4) vs. Denver (1), XXII
    San Francisco (5) vs. Denver (0), XXIV
    Dallas (4) vs. Buffalo (1), XXVII
    Philadelphia (3) vs. New England (2), XXXIX
Fewest Touchdowns, Both Teams, Game
0   N.Y. Jets vs. Baltimore, III
    Miami vs. Minnesota, VIII
    Buffalo vs. Dallas, XXVIII
1   In seven games

INTERCEPTIONS BY
Most Interceptions By, Game
5   Tampa Bay vs. Oakland, XXXVII
4   N.Y. Jets vs. Baltimore, III
    Dallas vs. Denver, XII
    Washington vs. Buffalo, XXVI
    Dallas vs. Buffalo, XXVII
    Green Bay vs. New England, XXXI
    Baltimore vs. N.Y. Giants, XXXV
3   By 13 teams
Most Interceptions By, Both Teams, Game
6   Baltimore (3) vs. Dallas (3), V
    Tampa Bay (5) vs. Oakland (1), XXXVII
5   Washington (4) vs. Buffalo (1), XXVI
4   In 10 games
Fewest Interceptions By, Both Teams, Game
0   Buffalo vs. N.Y. Giants, XXV
    St. Louis vs. Tennessee, XXXIV
1   Oakland (0) vs. Green Bay (1), II
    Miami (0) vs. Dallas (1), VI
    Minnesota (0) vs. Miami (1), VIII
    N.Y. Giants (0) vs. Denver (1), XXI
    Cincinnati (0) vs. San Francisco (1), XXIII
    New England (0) vs. Carolina (1), XXXVIII

YARDS GAINED
Most Yards Gained, Game
172 Tampa Bay vs. Oakland, XXXVII
136 Denver vs. Atlanta, XXXIII
95   Miami vs. Washington, VII

Most Yards Gained, Both Teams, Game
184 Tampa Bay (172) vs. Oakland (12), XXXVII
137 Denver (136) vs. Atlanta (1), XXXIII
100 Seattle (76) vs. Pittsburgh (24), XL
     Indianapolis (94) vs. Chicago (6), XLI

TOUCHDOWNS
Most Touchdowns, Game
3   Tampa Bay vs. Oakland, XXXVII
1   Green Bay vs. Oakland, II
    Oakland vs. Minnesota, XI
    L.A. Raiders vs. Washington, XVIII
    Chicago vs. New England, XX
    Baltimore vs. N.Y. Giants, XXXV
    New England vs. St. Louis, XXXVI
    Indianapolis vs. Chicago, XLI

PUNTING
Most Punts, Game
11 N.Y. Giants vs. Baltimore, XXXV
10 Baltimore vs. N.Y. Giants, XXXV
9   Dallas vs. Baltimore, V
Fewest Punts, Game
1   Atlanta vs. Denver, XXXIII
    Denver vs. Atlanta, XXXIII
2   Pittsburgh vs. Los Angeles, XIV
    Denver vs. N.Y. Giants, XXI
    St. Louis vs. Tennessee, XXXIV
3   By 11 teams
Most Punts, Both Teams, Game
21 N.Y. Giants (11) vs. Baltimore (10), XXXV
15 Washington (8) vs. L.A. Raiders (7), XVIII
    New England (8) vs. Green Bay (7), XXXI
13 Dallas (9) vs. Baltimore (4), V
    Pittsburgh (7) vs. Minnesota (6), IX
Fewest Punts, Both Teams, Game
2   Atlanta (1) vs. Denver (1), XXXIII
5   Denver (2) vs. N.Y. Giants (3), XXI
    St. Louis (2) vs. Tennessee (3), XXXIV
6   Oakland (3) vs. Philadelphia (3), XV

AVERAGE YARDAGE
Highest Average, Game (4 punts)
50.17 Seattle vs. Pittsburgh, XL (6-301)
48.75 San Diego vs. San Francisco, XXIX (4-195)
48.67 Pittsburgh vs. Seattle, XL (6-292)
Lowest Average, Game (4 punts)
31.00 Tampa Bay vs. Oakland, XXXVII (5-155)
31.20 Washington vs. Miami, VII (5-156)
32.38 Washington vs. L.A. Raiders, XVIII (8-259)

PUNT RETURNS
Most Punt Returns, Game
6   Washington vs. Miami, XVII
    Green Bay vs. New England, XXXI
5   By seven teams
Fewest Punt Returns, Game
0   Minnesota vs. Miami, VIII
    Buffalo vs. N.Y. Giants, XXV
    Washington vs. Buffalo, XXVI
    Denver vs. Green Bay, XXXII
    Green Bay vs. Denver, XXXII
    Atlanta vs. Denver, XXXIII
    Denver vs. Atlanta, XXXIII
1   By 20 teams
Most Punt Returns, Both Teams, Game
10 Green Bay (6) vs. New England (4), XXXI
9   Pittsburgh (5) vs. Minnesota (4), IX
8   Green Bay (5) vs. Oakland (3), II
    Baltimore (5) vs. Dallas (3), V

Washington (6) vs. Miami (2), XVII
N.Y. Giants (5) vs. Baltimore (3), XXXV

Fewest Punt Returns, Both Teams, Game
- 0 Denver vs. Green Bay, XXXII
  Atlanta vs. Denver, XXXIII
- 2 Dallas (1) vs. Miami (1), VI
  Denver (1) vs. N.Y. Giants (1), XXI
  Buffalo (0) vs. N.Y. Giants (2), XXV
  Buffalo (1) vs. Dallas (1), XXVIII
- 3 Kansas City (1) vs. Minnesota (2), IV
  Minnesota (0) vs. Miami (3), VIII
  Washington (1) vs. Denver (2), XXII
  Washington (0) vs. Buffalo (3), XXVI
  Dallas (1) vs. Pittsburgh (2), XXX
  Tennessee (1) vs. St. Louis (2), XXXIV

YARDS GAINED
Most Yards Gained, Game
- 90 Green Bay vs. New England, XXXI
- 56 San Francisco vs. Cincinnati, XXIII
- 52 Washington vs. Miami, XVII

Fewest Yards Gained, Game
- −1 Dallas vs. Miami, VI
  Tennessee vs. St. Louis, XXXIV
- 0 By 12 teams

Most Yards Gained, Both Teams, Game
- 120 Green Bay (90) vs. New England (30), XXXI
- 80 N.Y. Giants (46) vs. Baltimore (34), XXXV
- 74 Washington (52) vs. Miami (22), XVII

Fewest Yards Gained, Both Teams, Game
- 0 Denver vs. Green Bay, XXXII
  Atlanta vs. Denver, XXXIII
- 7 Tennessee (-1) vs. St. Louis (8), XXXIV
- 9 Washington (0) vs. Buffalo (9), XXVI

AVERAGE RETURN
Highest Average, Game (3 returns)
- 18.7 San Francisco vs. Cincinnati, XXIII (3-56)
- 15.0 Green Bay vs. New England, XXXI (6-90)
- 14.0 Indianapolis vs. Chicago, XLI (3-42)

TOUCHDOWNS
Most Touchdowns, Game
  None

KICKOFF RETURNS
Most Kickoff Returns, Game
- 9 Denver vs. San Francisco, XXIV
  Oakland vs. Tampa Bay, XXXVII
- 8 San Diego vs. San Francisco, XXIX
- 7 By eight teams

Fewest Kickoff Returns, Game
- 1 N.Y. Jets vs. Baltimore, III
  L.A. Raiders vs. Washington, XVIII
  Washington vs. Buffalo, XXVI
- 2 By nine teams

Most Kickoff Returns, Both Teams, Game
- 13 Oakland (9) vs. Tampa Bay (4), XXXVII
- 12 Denver (9) vs. San Francisco (3), XXIV
  San Diego (8) vs. San Francisco (4), XXIX
- 11 Los Angeles (6) vs. Pittsburgh (5), XIV
  Miami (7) vs. San Francisco (4), XIX
  New England (7) vs. Chicago (4), XX
  Green Bay (6) vs. Denver (5), XXXII

Fewest Kickoff Returns, Both Teams, Game
- 5 N.Y. Jets (1) vs. Baltimore (4), III
  Miami (2) vs. Washington (3), VII
  Washington (1) vs. Buffalo (4), XXVI
- 6 In four games

YARDS GAINED
Most Yards Gained, Game
- 244 San Diego vs. San Francisco, XXIX
- 227 Atlanta vs. Denver, XXXIII
- 222 Miami vs. Washington, XVII

Fewest Yards Gained, Game
- 16 Washington vs. Buffalo, XXVI
- 17 L.A. Raiders vs. Washington, XVIII
- 25 N.Y. Jets vs. Baltimore, III

Most Yards Gained, Both Teams, Game
- 292 San Diego (244) vs. San Francisco (48), XXIX
- 289 Green Bay (154) vs. New England (135), XXXI
- 281 N.Y. Giants (170) vs. Baltimore (111), XXXV

Fewest Yards Gained, Both Teams, Game
- 78 Miami (33) vs. Washington (45), VII
- 82 Pittsburgh (32) vs. Minnesota (50), IX
- 92 San Francisco (40) vs. Cincinnati (52), XVI

AVERAGE GAIN
Highest Average, Game (3 returns)
- 44.0 Cincinnati vs. San Francisco, XXIII (3-132)
- 38.5 Green Bay vs. New England, XXXI (4-154)
- 37.0 Miami vs. Washington, XVII (6-222)

TOUCHDOWNS
Most Touchdowns, Game
- 1 Miami vs. Washington, XVII
  Cincinnati vs. San Francisco, XXIII
  San Diego vs. San Francisco, XXIX
  Green Bay vs. New England, XXXI
  Atlanta vs. Denver, XXXIII
  Baltimore vs. N.Y. Giants, XXXV
  N.Y. Giants vs. Baltimore, XXXV
  Chicago vs. Indianapolis, XLI

Most Touchdowns, Both Teams, Game
- 2 Baltimore (1) vs. N.Y. Giants (1), XXXV

PENALTIES
Most Penalties, Game
- 12 Dallas vs. Denver, XII
  Carolina vs. New England, XXXVIII
- 10 Dallas vs. Baltimore, V
- 9 Dallas vs. Pittsburgh, XIII
  Green Bay vs. Denver, XXXII
  Baltimore vs. N.Y. Giants, XXXV

Fewest Penalties, Game
- 0 Miami vs. Dallas, VI
  Pittsburgh vs. Dallas, X
  Denver vs. San Francisco, XXIV
  Atlanta vs. Denver, XXXIII
- 1 Green Bay vs. Oakland, II
  Miami vs. Minnesota, VIII; vs. San Francisco, XIX
  Buffalo vs. Dallas, XXVIII
- 2 By six teams

Most Penalties, Both Teams, Game
- 20 Dallas (12) vs. Denver (8), XII
  Carolina (12) vs. New England (8), XXXVIII
- 16 Cincinnati (8) vs. San Francisco (8), XVI
  Green Bay (9) vs. Denver (7), XXXII
- 15 St. Louis (8) vs. Tennessee (7), XXXIV
  Baltimore (9) vs. N.Y. Giants (6), XXXV

Fewest Penalties, Both Teams, Game
- 2 Pittsburgh (0) vs. Dallas (2), X
- 3 Miami (0) vs. Dallas (3), VI
  Miami (1) vs. San Francisco (2), XIX
- 4 Denver (0) vs. San Francisco (4), XXIV
  Atlanta (0) vs. Denver (4), XXXIII

YARDS PENALIZED
Most Yards Penalized, Game
- 133 Dallas vs. Baltimore, X
- 122 Pittsburgh vs. Minnesota, IX
- 94 Dallas vs. Denver, XII

Fewest Yards Penalized, Game
- 0 Miami vs. Dallas, VI
   Pittsburgh vs. Dallas, X
   Denver vs. San Francisco, XXIV
   Atlanta vs. Denver, XXXIII
- 4 Miami vs. Minnesota, VIII
- 10 Miami vs. San Francisco, XIX
   San Francisco vs. Miami, XIX
   Buffalo vs. Dallas, XXVIII

Most Yards Penalized, Both Teams, Game
- 164 Dallas (133) vs. Baltimore (31), V
- 154 Dallas (94) vs. Denver (60), XII
- 140 Pittsburgh (122) vs. Minnesota (18), IX

Fewest Yards Penalized, Both Teams, Game
- 15 Miami (0) vs. Dallas (15), VI
- 20 Pittsburgh (0) vs. Dallas (20), X
   Miami (10) vs. San Francisco (10), XIX
- 38 Denver (0) vs. San Francisco (38), XXIV

FUMBLES
Most Fumbles, Game
- 8 Buffalo vs. Dallas, XXVII
- 6 Dallas vs. Denver, XII
   Buffalo vs. Washington, XXVI
- 5 Baltimore vs. Dallas, V

Fewest Fumbles, Game
- 0 By 19 teams

Most Fumbles, Both Teams, Game
- 12 Buffalo (8) vs. Dallas (4), XXVII
- 10 Dallas (6) vs. Denver (4), XII
- 8 Dallas (4) vs. Pittsburgh (4), X

Fewest Fumbles, Both Teams, Game
- 0 Los Angeles vs. Pittsburgh, XIV
   Green Bay vs. New England, XXXI
   Pittsburgh vs. Seattle, XL
- 1 Oakland (0) vs. Minnesota (1), XI
   Oakland (0) vs. Philadelphia (1), XV
   Denver (0) vs. Washington (1), XXII
   N.Y. Giants (0) vs. Buffalo (1), XXV
   Denver (0) vs. Atlanta (1), XXXIII
- 2 In eight games

Most Fumbles Lost, Game
- 5 Buffalo vs. Dallas, XXVII
- 4 Baltimore vs. Dallas, V
   Denver vs. Dallas, XII
   New England vs. Chicago, XX
- 3 Chicago vs. Indianapolis, XLI

Most Fumbles Lost, Both Teams, Game
- 7 Buffalo (5) vs. Dallas (2), XXVII
- 6 Denver (4) vs. Dallas (2), XII
   New England (4) vs. Chicago (2), XX
- 5 Baltimore (4) vs. Dallas (1), V
   Chicago (3) vs. Indianapolis (2), XLI

Fewest Fumbles Lost, Both Teams, Game
- 0 Green Bay vs. Kansas City, I
   Dallas vs. Pittsburgh, X
   Los Angeles vs. Pittsburgh, XIV
   Denver vs. N.Y. Giants, XXI; vs. Washington, XXII
   Buffalo vs. N.Y. Giants, XXV
   San Diego vs. San Francisco, XXIX
   Dallas vs. Pittsburgh, XXX
   Green Bay vs. New England, XXXI
   St. Louis vs. Tennessee, XXXIV
   Oakland vs. Tampa Bay, XXXVII
   Pittsburgh vs. Seattle, XL

Most Fumbles Recovered, Game
- 8 Dallas vs. Denver, XII (4 own, 4 opp.)
- 6 Dallas vs. Buffalo, XXVII (1 own, 5 opp.)
- 5 Chicago vs. New England, XX (1 own, 4 opp.)

TURNOVERS
(Number of times losing the ball on interceptions and fumbles.)
Most Turnovers, Game
- 9 Buffalo vs. Dallas, XXVII
- 8 Denver vs. Dallas, XII
- 7 Baltimore vs. Dallas, V

Fewest Turnovers, Game
- 0 Green Bay vs. Oakland, II
   Miami vs. Minnesota, VIII
   Pittsburgh vs. Dallas, X
   Oakland vs. Minnesota, XI; vs. Philadelphia, XV
   N.Y. Giants vs. Denver, XXI; vs. Buffalo, XXV
   San Francisco vs. Denver, XXIV; vs. San Diego, XXIX
   Buffalo vs. N.Y. Giants, XXV
   Dallas vs. Pittsburgh, XXX
   Green Bay vs. New England, XXXI
   St. Louis vs. Tennessee, XXXIV
   Tennessee vs. St. Louis, XXXIV
   Baltimore vs. N.Y. Giants, XXXV
   New England vs. St. Louis, XXXVI
- 1 By many teams

Most Turnovers, Both Teams, Game
- 11 Baltimore (7) vs. Dallas (4), V
   Buffalo (9) vs. Dallas (2), XXVII
- 10 Denver (8) vs. Dallas (2), XII
- 8 New England (6) vs. Chicago (2), XX
   Chicago (5) vs. Indianapolis (3), XLI

Fewest Turnovers, Both Teams, Game
- 0 Buffalo vs. N.Y. Giants, XXV
   St. Louis vs. Tennessee, XXXIV
- 1 N.Y. Giants (0) vs. Denver (1), XXI
- 2 Green Bay (1) vs. Kansas City (1), I
   Miami (0) vs. Minnesota (2), VIII
   Cincinnati (1) vs. San Francisco (1), XXIII
   Carolina (1) vs. New England (1), XXXVIII

Compiled by Elias Sports Bureau

Throughout this all-time postseason record section, the following abbreviations are used to indicate various levels of postseason games:

SB	Super Bowl (1966 to date)
AFC	AFC Championship Game (1970 to date) or AFL Championship Game (1960-69)
NFC	NFC Championship Game (1970 to date) or NFL Championship Game (1933-69)
AFC-D	AFC Divisional Playoff Game (1970 to date), AFC Second-Round Playoff Game (1982), AFL Inter-Divisional Playoff Game (1969), or special playoff game to break tie for AFL Division Championship (1963, 1968)
NFC-D	NFC Divisional Playoff Game (1970 to date), NFC Second-Round Playoff Game (1982), NFL Conference Championship Game (1967-69), or special playoff game to break tie for NFL Division or Conference Championship (1941, 1943, 1947, 1950, 1952, 1957, 1958, 1965)
AFC-FR	AFC First-Round Playoff Game (1978 to date)
NFC-FR	NFC First-Round Playoff Game (1978 to date)

Year indicates season in which game took place and does not necessarily reflect calendar year.

POSTSEASON GAME COMPOSITE STANDINGS

	W	L	PCT.	PTS.	OP
Carolina Panthers	6	3	.667	206	170
Green Bay Packers	24	14	.632	888	723
Baltimore Ravens	5	3	.625	148	88
New England Patriots#	19	12	.613	664	617
Pittsburgh Steelers	28	18	.609	1,066	928
San Francisco 49ers	25	17	.595	1,044	853
Washington Redskins*	23	16	.590	805	672
Dallas Cowboys	32	23	.582	1,301	1,029
Oakland Raiders**	25	18	.581	1,028	797
Denver Broncos	17	15	.531	694	794
Indianapolis Colts***	17	16	.515	661	667
Miami Dolphins	20	19	.513	780	848
Philadelphia Eagles	17	17	.500	653	608
Chicago Bears	16	17	.485	702	681
Buffalo Bills	14	15	.483	681	658
Tennessee Titans†	14	17	.452	563	732
Jacksonville Jaguars	4	5	.444	211	228
St. Louis Rams††	19	24	.442	770	944
Atlanta Falcons	6	8	.429	298	331
Minnesota Vikings	18	24	.429	824	957
Tampa Bay Buccaneers	6	8	.429	216	255
New York Jets	8	11	.421	388	389
Detroit Lions	7	10	.412	365	404
New York Giants	16	23	.410	667	745
Seattle Seahawks	6	9	.400	301	311
Cincinnati Bengals	5	8	.385	263	288
Kansas City Chiefs****	8	13	.381	340	445
Cleveland Browns	11	20	.355	629	728
San Diego Chargers†††	7	13	.350	370	472
Arizona Cardinals††††	2	5	.286	122	182
New Orleans Saints	2	6	.250	144	248

    *   *One game played when franchise was in Boston (lost 21-6).*

   ** *12 games played when franchise was in Los Angeles (won 6, lost 6, 268 points scored, 224 points allowed).*

 *** *15 games played when franchise was in Baltimore (won 8, lost 7, 264 points scored, 262 points allowed).*

*** * *One game played when franchise was Dallas Texans (won 20-17).*

   # *Two games played when franchise was in Boston (won 26-8, lost 51-10).*

   † *22 games played when franchise was in Houston and known as the Oilers (won 9, lost 13, 371 points scored, 533 points allowed).*

  †† *One game played when franchise was in Cleveland (won 15-14), 32 games played when franchise was in Los*

Angeles (won 12, lost 20, 486 points scored, 683 points allowed).

 ††† *One game played when franchise was in Los Angeles (lost 24-16).*

†††† *Two games played when franchise was in Chicago (won 28-21, lost 7-0), three games played when franchise was in St. Louis (lost 30-14, lost 35-23, lost 41-16).*

INDIVIDUAL RECORDS

SERVICE

Most Games, Career

29	Jerry Rice, San Francisco-Oakland-Seattle (SB 4, NFC 6, AFC 1, NFC-D 11, AFC-D 2, NFC-FR 4, AFC-FR 1)
27	D.D. Lewis, Dallas (SB 5, NFC 9, NFC-D 12, NFC-FR 1)
26	Larry Cole, Dallas (SB 5, NFC 8, NFC-D 12, NFC-FR 1)
	Bill Romanowski, San Francisco-Philadelphia-Denver-Oakland (SB 5, NFC 5, AFC 3, NFC-D 6, AFC-D 4, NFC-FR 1, AFC-FR 2)

Most Games, Head Coach

36	Tom Landry, Dallas
	Don Shula, Baltimore-Miami
24	Chuck Noll, Pittsburgh
23	Joe Gibbs, Washington

Most Championships Won, Head Coach"

6	George Halas, Chicago
	Curly Lambeau, Green Bay
5	Vince Lombardi, Green Bay
4	Guy Chamberlin, Canton Bulldogs-Cleveland Bulldogs-Frankford Yellow Jackets
	Chuck Noll, Pittsburgh

Most Games Won, Head Coach

20	Tom Landry, Dallas
19	Don Shula, Baltimore-Miami
17	Joe Gibbs, Washington

Most Games Lost, Head Coach

17	Don Shula, Baltimore-Miami
16	Tom Landry, Dallas
13	Marty Schottenheimer, Cleveland-Kansas City-San Diego

SCORING

POINTS

Most Points, Career

166	Adam Vinatieri, New England-Indianapolis, 21 games (46-pat, 40-fg)
153	Gary Anderson, Pittsburgh-Philadelphia-San Francisco-Minnesota-Tennessee, 22 games (57-pat, 32-fg)
132	Jerry Rice, San Francisco-Oakland-Seattle, 29 games (22-td)

Most Points, Game

30	Ricky Watters, NFC-D: San Francisco vs. N.Y. Giants, 1993 (5-td)
19	Pat Harder, NFC-D: Detroit vs. Los Angeles, 1952 (2-td, 4-pat, 1-fg)
	Paul Hornung, NFC: Green Bay vs. N.Y. Giants, 1961 (1-td, 4-pat, 3-fg)
18	By many players

Most Consecutive Games Scoring

21	Adam Vinatieri, New England, 1996-2006 (current)
19	George Blanda, Chi. Bears-Houston-Oakland, 1956-1975
16	Norm Johnson, Seattle-Atlanta-Pittsburgh, 1983-1997

TOUCHDOWNS

Most Touchdowns, Career

22	Jerry Rice, San Francisco-Oakland-Seattle, 29 games (22-p)
21	Thurman Thomas, Buffalo, 21 games (16-r, 5-p)
	Emmitt Smith, Dallas, 17 games (19-r, 2-p)
17	Franco Harris, Pittsburgh, 19 games (16-r, 1-p)

Most Touchdowns, Game

5 Ricky Watters, NFC-D: San Francisco vs. N.Y. Giants, 1993 (5-r)
3 Andy Farkas, NFC-D: Washington vs. N.Y. Giants, 1943 (3-r)
   Tom Fears, NFC-D: Los Angeles vs. Chi. Bears, 1950 (3-p)
   Otto Graham, NFC: Cleveland vs. Detroit, 1954 (3-r)
   Gary Collins, NFC: Cleveland vs. Baltimore, 1964 (3-p)
   Craig Baynham, NFC-D: Dallas vs. Cleveland, 1967 (2-r, 1-p)
   Fred Biletnikoff, AFC-D: Oakland vs. Kansas City, 1968 (3-p)
   Tom Matte, NFC: Baltimore vs. Cleveland, 1968 (3-r)
   Larry Schreiber, NFC-D: San Francisco vs. Dallas, 1972 (3-r)
   Larry Csonka, AFC: Miami vs. Oakland, 1973 (3-r)
   Franco Harris, AFC-D: Pittsburgh vs. Buffalo, 1974 (3-r)
   Preston Pearson, NFC: Dallas vs. Los Angeles, 1975 (3-p)
   Dave Casper, AFC-D: Oakland vs. Baltimore, 1977 (OT) (3-p)
   Alvin Garrett, NFC-FR: Washington vs. Detroit, 1982 (3-p)
   John Riggins, NFC-D: Washington vs. L.A. Rams, 1983 (3-r)
   Roger Craig, SB: San Francisco vs. Miami, 1984 (1-r, 2-p)
   Jerry Rice, NFC-D: San Francisco vs. Minnesota, 1988 (3-r)
   Jerry Rice, SB: San Francisco vs. Denver, 1989 (3-p)
   Kenneth Davis, AFC: Buffalo vs. L.A. Raiders, 1990 (3-r)
   Andre Reed, AFC-FR: Buffalo vs. Houston, 1992 (OT) (3-p)
   Sterling Sharpe, NFC-FR: Green Bay vs. Detroit, 1993 (3-p)
   Napoleon McCallum, AFC-FR: L.A. Raiders vs. Denver, 1993 (3-r)
   Thurman Thomas, AFC: Buffalo vs. Kansas City, 1993 (3-r)
   William Floyd, NFC-D: San Francisco vs. Chicago, 1994 (3-r)
   Ricky Watters, SB: San Francisco vs. San Diego, 1994 (1-r, 2-p)
   Jerry Rice, SB: San Francisco vs. San Diego, 1994 (3-p)
   Emmitt Smith, NFC: Dallas vs. Green Bay, 1995 (3-r)
   Curtis Martin, AFC-D: New England vs. Pittsburgh, 1996 (3-r)
   Terrell Davis, SB: Denver vs. Green Bay, 1997 (3-r)
   Mario Bates, NFC-D: Arizona vs. Minnesota, 1998 (3-r)
   Leroy Hoard, NFC-D: Minnesota vs. Arizona, 1998 (2-r, 1-p)
   Willie Jackson, NFC-FR: New Orleans vs. St. Louis, 2000 (3-p)
   Amani Toomer, NFC-FR: N.Y. Giants vs. San Francisco, 2002 (3-p)
   Shaun Alexander, NFC-FR: Seattle vs. Green Bay, 2003 (OT) (3-r)

Most Consecutive Games Scoring Touchdowns

9 Thurman Thomas, Buffalo, 1992-98
8 John Stallworth, Pittsburgh, 1978-1983
   Emmitt Smith, Dallas, 1993-96
7 John Riggins, Washington, 1982-84
   Marcus Allen, L.A. Raiders, 1982-85
   Terrell Davis, Denver, 1996-98
   David Givens, New England, 2003-05 (current)

POINTS AFTER TOUCHDOWN

Most (One-Point) Points After Touchdown, Career

57 Gary Anderson, Pittsburgh-Philadelphia-San Francisco-Minnesota-Tennessee, 22 games (57 att)
49 George Blanda, Chi. Bears-Houston-Oakland, 19 games (49 att)
46 Adam Vinatieri, New England-Indianapolis, 21 games (46 att)

Most (One-Point) Points After Touchdown, Game

8 Lou Groza, NFC: Cleveland vs. Detroit, 1954 (8 att)
   Jim Martin, NFC: Detroit vs. Cleveland, 1957 (8 att)
   George Blanda, AFC-D: Oakland vs. Houston, 1969 (8 att)
   Mike Hollis, AFC-D: Jacksonville vs. Miami, 1999 (8 att)
7 Danny Villanueva, NFC-D: Dallas vs. Cleveland, 1967 (7 att)
   Raul Allegre, NFC-D: N.Y. Giants vs. San Francisco, 1986 (7 att)
   Mike Cofer, SB: San Francisco vs. Denver, 1989 (8 att)

   Lin Elliott, SB: Dallas vs. Buffalo, 1992 (7 att)
   Doug Brien, SB: San Francisco vs. San Diego, 1994 (7 att)
   Gary Anderson, NFC-FR: Philadelphia vs. Detroit, 1995 (7 att)
   Jeff Wilkins, NFC-D: St. Louis vs. Minnesota, 1999 (7 att)
   Mike Vanderjagt, AFC-FR: Indianapolis vs. Denver, 2004 (7 att)
6 George Blair, AFC: San Diego vs. Boston, 1963 (6 att)
   Mark Moseley, NFC-D: Washington vs. L.A. Rams, 1983 (6 att)
   Uwe von Schamann, AFC: Miami vs. Pittsburgh, 1984 (6 att)
   Ali Haji-Sheikh, SB: Washington vs. Denver, 1987 (6 att)
   Scott Norwood, AFC: Buffalo vs. L.A. Raiders, 1990 (7 att)
   Jeff Jaeger, AFC-FR: L.A. Raiders vs. Denver, 1993 (6 att)
   Jason Elam, AFC-FR: Denver vs. Jacksonville, 1997 (6 att)
   Jeff Wilkins, NFC-D: St. Louis vs. Green Bay, 2001 (6 att)
   Martín Gramatica, SB: Tampa Bay vs. Oakland, 2002 (6 att)
   Jay Feely, NFC-D: Atlanta vs. St. Louis, 2004 (6 att)

Most (Kicking) Points After Touchdown, No Misses, Career

57 Gary Anderson, Pittsburgh-Philadelphia-San Francisco-Minnesota-Tennessee, 22 games
49 George Blanda, Chi. Bears-Houston-Oakland, 19 games
46 Adam Vinatieri, New England-Indianapolis, 21 games

Most Two-Point Conversions, Career

2 Terrell Owens, San Francisco-Philadelphia, 10 games
   Kevin Faulk, New England, 14 games

Most Two-Point Conversions, Game

2 Terrell Owens, NFC-FR: San Francisco vs. N.Y. Giants, 2002

FIELD GOALS

Most Field Goals Attempted, Career

49 Adam Vinatieri, New England-Indianapolis, 21 games
40 Gary Anderson, Pittsburgh-Philadelphia-San Francisco-Minnesota-Tennessee, 22 games
39 George Blanda, Chi. Bears-Houston-Oakland, 19 games

Most Field Goals Attempted, Game

6 George Blanda, AFC: Oakland vs. Houston, 1967
   David Ray, NFC-D: Los Angeles vs. Dallas, 1973
   Mark Moseley, AFC-D: Cleveland vs. N.Y. Jets, 1986 (OT)
   Matt Bahr, NFC: N.Y. Giants vs. San Francisco, 1990
   Steve Christie, AFC: Buffalo vs. Miami, 1992
   Jeff Wilkins, NFC-D: St. Louis vs. Carolina, 2003 (2 OT)
5 By many players

Most Field Goals, Career

40 Adam Vinatieri, New England-Indianapolis, 21 games
32 Gary Anderson, Pittsburgh-Philadelphia-San Francisco-Minnesota-Tennessee, 22 games
22 George Blanda, Chi. Bears-Houston-Oakland, 19 games
   Steve Christie, Buffalo, 12 games

Most Field Goals, Game

5 Chuck Nelson, NFC-D: Minnesota vs. San Francisco, 1987
   Matt Bahr, NFC: N.Y. Giants vs. San Francisco, 1990
   Steve Christie, AFC: Buffalo vs. Miami, 1992
   Brad Daluiso, NFC-FR: N.Y. Giants vs. Minnesota, 1997
   John Kasay, NFC-FR: Carolina vs. Dallas, 2003
   Jeff Wilkins, NFC-D: St. Louis vs. Carolina, 2003 (2 OT)
   Adam Vinatieri, AFC: New England vs. Indianapolis, 2003
   Adam Vinatieri, AFC-D: Indianapolis vs. Baltimore, 2006
4 Gino Cappelletti, AFC-D: Boston vs. Buffalo, 1963
   George Blanda, AFC: Oakland vs. Houston, 1967
   Don Chandler, SB: Green Bay vs. Oakland, 1967
   Curt Knight, NFC: Washington vs. Dallas, 1972
   George Blanda, AFC-D: Oakland vs. Pittsburgh, 1973
   Ray Wersching, SB: San Francisco vs. Cincinnati, 1981
   Tony Franklin, AFC-FR: New England vs. N.Y. Jets, 1985
   Jess Atkinson, NFC-FR: Washington vs. L.A. Rams, 1986
   Luis Zendejas, NFC-D: Philadelphia vs. Chicago, 1988
   Gary Anderson, AFC-D: Pittsburgh vs. Houston, 1989 (OT)
   Norm Johnson, AFC-D: Pittsburgh vs. Buffalo, 1995
   Chris Boniol, NFC-FR: Dallas vs. Minnesota, 1996
   John Kasay, NFC-D: Carolina vs. Dallas, 1996

Mike Hollis, AFC-D: Jacksonville vs. New England, 1998
Al Del Greco, AFC-D: Tennessee vs. Indianapolis, 1999
David Akers, NFC-D: Philadelphia vs. Chicago, 2001
3　By many players

Most Consecutive Games Scoring Field Goals
13　Toni Fritsch, Dallas-Houston, 1972-79
12　Adam Vinatieri, New England, 1997-2004
10　David Akers, Philadelphia, 2000-04
　　Morten Andersen, New Orleans-Atlanta-Kansas City-Minnesota, 1987-2004
　　Jason Elam, Denver, 1997-2000, 2003-05 (current)

Most Consecutive Field Goals
16　Gary Anderson, Pittsburgh-Philadelphia, 1989-1995
15　Rafael Septien, Dallas, 1978-1982
14　Mike Hollis, Jacksonville, 1996-99
　　John Kasay, Carolina, 1996-2003

Longest Field Goal
58　Pete Stoyanovich, AFC-FR: Miami vs. Kansas City, 1990
55　Jeff Wilkins, NFC-D: St. Louis vs. Atlanta, 2004
54　Ed Murray, NFC-D: Detroit vs. San Francisco, 1983
　　Steve Christie, SB: Buffalo vs. Dallas, 1993
　　John Carney, AFC-FR: San Diego vs. Indianapolis, 1995

Highest Field Goal Percentage, Career (10 field goals)
92.9　Martin Gramatica, Tampa Bay-Indianapolis-Dallas, 9 games (14-13)
91.3　John Kasay, Carolina, 9 games (23-21)
90.9　Chuck Nelson, L.A. Rams-Minnesota, 6 games (11-10)

SAFETIES
Most Safeties, Game
1　Bill Willis, NFC-D: Cleveland vs. N.Y. Giants, 1950
　　Carl Eller, NFC-D: Minnesota vs. Los Angeles, 1969
　　George Andrie, NFC-D: Dallas vs. Detroit, 1970
　　Alan Page, NFC-D: Minnesota vs. Dallas, 1971
　　Dwight White, SB: Pittsburgh vs. Minnesota, 1974
　　Reggie Harrison, SB: Pittsburgh vs. Dallas, 1975
　　Jim Jensen, NFC-D: Dallas vs. Los Angeles, 1976
　　Ted Washington, AFC: Houston vs. Pittsburgh, 1978
　　Randy White, NFC-D: Dallas vs. Los Angeles, 1979
　　Henry Waechter, SB: Chicago vs. New England, 1985
　　Rulon Jones, AFC-FR: Denver vs. New England, 1986
　　George Martin, SB: N.Y. Giants vs. Denver, 1986
　　D.D. Hoggard, AFC: Cleveland vs. Denver, 1987
　　Bruce Smith, SB: Buffalo vs. N.Y. Giants, 1990
　　Reggie White, NFC-D: Philadelphia vs. New Orleans, 1992
　　Willie Clay, NFC-FR: Detroit vs. Green Bay, 1994
　　Carnell Lake, AFC-D: Pittsburgh vs. Cleveland, 1994
　　Reuben Davis, AFC-D: San Diego vs. Miami, 1994
　　Jevon Kearse, AFC-FR: Tennessee vs. Buffalo, 1999
　　Brady Smith, NFC-D: Atlanta vs. St. Louis, 2004

RUSHING
ATTEMPTS
Most Attempts, Career
400　Franco Harris, Pittsburgh, 19 games
349　Emmitt Smith, Dallas, 17 games
339　Thurman Thomas, Buffalo, 21 games

Most Attempts, Game
40　Lamar Smith, AFC-FR: Miami vs. Indianapolis, 2000 (OT)
38　Ricky Bell, NFC-D: Tampa Bay vs. Philadelphia, 1979
　　John Riggins, SB: Washington vs. Miami, 1982
37　Lawrence McCutcheon, NFC-D: Los Angeles vs. St. Louis, 1975
　　John Riggins, NFC-D: Washington vs. Minnesota, 1982

YARDS GAINED
Most Yards Gained, Career
1,586　Emmitt Smith, Dallas, 17 games
1,556　Franco Harris, Pittsburgh, 19 games
1,442　Thurman Thomas, Buffalo, 21 games

Most Yards Gained, Game
248　Eric Dickerson, NFC-D: L.A. Rams vs. Dallas, 1985
209　Lamar Smith, AFC-FR: Miami vs. Indianapolis, 2000 (OT)
206　Keith Lincoln, AFC: San Diego vs. Boston, 1963

Most Games, 100 or More Yards Rushing, Career
7　Emmitt Smith, Dallas, 17 games
　　Terrell Davis, Denver, 8 games
6　John Riggins, Washington, 9 games
　　Thurman Thomas, Buffalo, 21 games
5　Franco Harris, Pittsburgh, 19 games
　　Marcus Allen, L.A. Raiders-Kansas City, 16 games

Most Consecutive Games, 100 or More Yards Rushing
7　Terrell Davis, Denver, 1997-98
6　John Riggins, Washington, 1982-83
4　Thurman Thomas, Buffalo, 1990-91

Longest Run From Scrimmage
90　Fred Taylor, AFC-D: Jacksonville vs. Miami, 1999 (TD)
80　Roger Craig, NFC-D: San Francisco vs. Minnesota, 1988 (TD)
　　Charlie Garner, AFC-FR: Oakland vs. N.Y. Jets, 2001 (TD)
78　Curtis Martin, AFC-D: New England vs. Pittsburgh, 1996 (TD)

AVERAGE GAIN
Highest Average Gain, Career (100 attempts)
5.59　Terrell Davis, Denver, 8 games (204-1,140)
5.04　Marcus Allen, L.A. Raiders-Kansas City, 16 games (267-1,347)
4.89　Eric Dickerson, L.A. Rams-Indianapolis, 7 games (148-724)

Highest Average Gain, Game (10 attempts)
15.90　Elmer Angsman, NFC: Chi. Cardinals vs. Philadelphia, 1947 (10-159)
15.85　Keith Lincoln, AFC: San Diego vs. Boston, 1963 (13-206)
11.31　Zack Crockett, AFC-FR: Indianapolis vs. San Diego, 1995 (13-147)

TOUCHDOWNS
Most Touchdowns, Career
19　Emmitt Smith, Dallas, 17 games
16　Franco Harris, Pittsburgh, 19 games
　　Thurman Thomas, Buffalo, 21 games
12　John Riggins, Washington, 9 games
　　Terrell Davis, Denver, 8 games

Most Touchdowns, Game
5　Ricky Watters, NFC-D: San Francisco vs. N.Y. Giants, 1993
3　Andy Farkas, NFC-D: Washington vs. N.Y. Giants, 1943
　　Otto Graham, NFC: Cleveland vs. Detroit, 1954
　　Tom Matte, NFC: Baltimore vs. Cleveland, 1968
　　Larry Schreiber, NFC-D: San Francisco vs. Dallas, 1972
　　Larry Csonka, AFC: Miami vs. Oakland, 1973
　　Franco Harris, AFC-D: Pittsburgh vs. Buffalo, 1974
　　John Riggins, NFC-D: Washington vs. L.A. Rams, 1983
　　Kenneth Davis, AFC: Buffalo vs. L.A. Raiders, 1990
　　Napoleon McCallum, AFC-FR: L.A. Raiders vs. Denver, 1993
　　Thurman Thomas, AFC: Buffalo vs. Kansas City, 1993
　　William Floyd, NFC-D: San Francisco vs. Chicago, 1994
　　Emmitt Smith, NFC: Dallas vs. Green Bay, 1995
　　Curtis Martin, AFC-D: New England vs. Pittsburgh, 1996
　　Terrell Davis, SB: Denver vs. Green Bay, 1997
　　Mario Bates, NFC-D: Arizona vs. Minnesota, 1998
　　Shaun Alexander, NFC-FR: Seattle vs. Green Bay, 2003 (OT)

Most Consecutive Games Rushing for Touchdowns
8　Emmitt Smith, Dallas, 1993-96
　　Thurman Thomas, Buffalo, 1992-98
7　John Riggins, Washington, 1982-84
　　Terrell Davis, Denver, 1996-98
5　Franco Harris, Pittsburgh, 1974-75
　　Franco Harris, Pittsburgh, 1977-79
　　Curtis Martin, New England-N.Y. Jets, 1996-98
　　Jerome Bettis, Pittsburgh, 2004-05

PASSING

PASSER RATING

Highest Passer Rating, Career (150 attempts)

- 104.8 Bart Starr, Green Bay, 10 games
- 95.6 Joe Montana, San Francisco-Kansas City, 23 games
- 95.0 Jake Delhomme, Carolina, 7 games

ATTEMPTS

Most Passes Attempted, Career

- 734 Joe Montana, San Francisco-Kansas City, 23 games
- 687 Dan Marino, Miami, 18 games
- 663 Brett Favre, Green Bay, 20 games

Most Passes Attempted, Game

- 65 Steve Young, NFC-D: San Francisco vs. Green Bay, 1995
- 64 Bernie Kosar, AFC-D: Cleveland vs. N.Y. Jets, 1986 (OT)
  Dan Marino, AFC-FR: Miami vs. Buffalo, 1995
- 58 Jim Kelly, SB: Buffalo vs. Washington, 1991

COMPLETIONS

Most Passes Completed, Career

- 460 Joe Montana, San Francisco-Kansas City, 23 games
- 401 Brett Favre, Green Bay, 20 games
- 385 Dan Marino, Miami, 18 games

Most Passes Completed, Game

- 36 Warren Moon, AFC-FR: Houston vs. Buffalo, 1992 (OT)
- 33 Dan Fouts, AFC-D: San Diego vs. Miami, 1981 (OT)
  Bernie Kosar, AFC-D: Cleveland vs. N.Y. Jets, 1986 (OT)
  Dan Marino, AFC-FR: Miami vs. Buffalo, 1995
- 32 Neil Lomax, NFC-FR: St. Louis vs. Green Bay, 1982
  Danny White, NFC-FR: Dallas vs. L.A. Rams, 1983
  Warren Moon, AFC-D: Houston vs. Kansas City, 1993
  Neil O'Donnell, AFC: Pittsburgh vs. San Diego, 1994
  Steve Young, NFC-D: San Francisco vs. Green Bay, 1995
  Tom Brady, AFC-D: New England vs. Oakland, 2001 (OT)
  Tom Brady, SB: New England vs. Carolina, 2003

COMPLETION PERCENTAGE

Highest Completion Percentage, Career (150 attempts)

- 66.3 Ken Anderson, Cincinnati, 6 games (166-110)
- 64.3 Warren Moon, Houston-Minnesota, 10 games (403-259)
- 64.2 Rich Gannon, Minnesota-Kansas City-Oakland, 10 games (240-154)

Highest Completion Percentage, Game (15 completions)

- 88.0 Phil Simms, SB: N.Y. Giants vs. Denver, 1986 (25-22)
- 86.7 Joe Montana, NFC: San Francisco vs. L.A. Rams, 1989 (30-26)
- 84.6 Peyton Manning, AFC-FR: Indianapolis vs. Denver, 2003 (26-22)

YARDS GAINED

Most Yards Gained, Career

- 5,772 Joe Montana, San Francisco-Kansas City, 23 games
- 4,964 John Elway, Denver, 22 games
- 4,902 Brett Favre, Green Bay, 20 games

Most Yards Gained, Game

- 489 Bernie Kosar, AFC-D: Cleveland vs. N.Y. Jets, 1986 (OT)
- 458 Peyton Manning, AFC-FR: Indianapolis vs. Denver, 2004
- 433 Dan Fouts, AFC-D: San Diego vs. Miami, 1981 (OT)

Most Games, 300 or More Yards Passing, Career

- 6 Joe Montana, San Francisco-Kansas City, 23 games
- 5 Dan Fouts, San Diego, 7 games
- 4 Warren Moon, Houston-Minnesota, 10 games
  Troy Aikman, Dallas, 16 games
  Dan Marino, Miami, 18 games
  John Elway, Denver, 22 games
  Kurt Warner, St. Louis, 7 games
  Peyton Manning, Indianapolis, 13 games

Most Consecutive Games, 300 or More Yards Passing

- 4 Dan Fouts, San Diego, 1979-1981

- 3 Jim Kelly, Buffalo, 1989-1990
  Warren Moon, Houston, 1991-93
- 2 Daryle Lamonica, Oakland, 1968
  Ken Anderson, Cincinnati, 1981-82
  Terry Bradshaw, Pittsburgh, 1979-1982
  Joe Montana, San Francisco, 1983-84
  Dan Marino, Miami, 1984
  Troy Aikman, Dallas, 1994
  Steve Young, San Francisco, 1994-95
  Kurt Warner, St. Louis, 1999-2000
  Peyton Manning, Indianapolis, 2003
  Marc Bulger, St. Louis, 2003-04
  Matt Hasselbeck, Seattle, 2003-04

Longest Pass Completion

- 96 Trent Dilfer (to Sharpe), AFC: Baltimore vs. Oakland, 2000 (TD)
- 94 Troy Aikman (to Harper), NFC-D: Dallas vs. Green Bay, 1994 (TD)
- 93 Daryle Lamonica (to Dubenion), AFC-D: Buffalo vs. Boston, 1963 (TD)

AVERAGE GAIN

Highest Average Gain, Career (150 attempts)

- 8.55 Jake Delhomme, Carolina, 7 games (192-1,642)
- 8.45 Joe Theismann, Washington, 10 games (211-1,782)
- 8.43 Jim Plunkett, Oakland/L.A.Raiders, 10 games (272-2,293)

Highest Average Gain, Game (20 attempts)

- 14.71 Terry Bradshaw, SB: Pittsburgh vs. Los Angeles, 1979 (21-309)
- 14.50 Peyton Manning, AFC-FR: Indianapolis vs. Denver, 2003 (26-377)
- 13.88 Peyton Manning, AFC-FR: Indianapolis vs. Denver, 2004 (33-458)

TOUCHDOWNS

Most Touchdown Passes, Career

- 45 Joe Montana, San Francisco-Kansas City, 23 games
- 34 Brett Favre, Green Bay, 20 games
- 32 Dan Marino, Miami, 18 games

Most Touchdown Passes, Game

- 6 Daryle Lamonica, AFC-D: Oakland vs. Houston, 1969
  Steve Young, SB: San Francisco vs. San Diego, 1994
- 5 Sid Luckman, NFC: Chi. Bears vs. Washington, 1943
  Daryle Lamonica, AFC-D: Oakland vs. Kansas City, 1968
  Joe Montana, SB: San Francisco vs. Denver, 1989
  Kurt Warner, NFC-D: St. Louis vs. Minnesota, 1999
  Kerry Collins, NFC: N.Y. Giants vs. Minnesota, 2000
  Peyton Manning, AFC-FR: Indianapolis vs. Denver, 2003
- 4 Otto Graham, NFC: Cleveland vs. Los Angeles, 1950
  Tobin Rote, NFC: Detroit vs. Cleveland, 1957
  Bart Starr, NFC: Green Bay vs. Dallas, 1966
  Ken Stabler, AFC-D: Oakland vs. Miami, 1974
  Roger Staubach, NFC: Dallas vs. Los Angeles, 1975
  Terry Bradshaw, SB: Pittsburgh vs. Dallas, 1978
  Don Strock, AFC-D: Miami vs. San Diego, 1981 (OT)
  Lynn Dickey, NFC-FR: Green Bay vs. St. Louis, 1982
  Dan Marino, AFC: Miami vs. Pittsburgh, 1984
  Phil Simms, NFC-D: N.Y. Giants vs. San Francisco, 1986
  Doug Williams, SB: Washington vs. Denver, 1987
  Jim Kelly, AFC-D: Buffalo vs. Cleveland, 1989
  Joe Montana, NFC-D: San Francisco vs. Minnesota, 1989
  Warren Moon, AFC-FR: Houston vs. Buffalo, 1992 (OT)
  Frank Reich, AFC-FR: Buffalo vs. Houston, 1992 (OT)
  Troy Aikman, SB: Dallas vs. Buffalo, 1992
  Jeff George, NFC-D: Minnesota vs. St. Louis, 1999
  Aaron Brooks, NFC-FR: New Orleans vs. St. Louis, 2000
  Kerry Collins, NFC-FR: N.Y. Giants vs. San Francisco, 2002
  Peyton Manning, AFC: Indianapolis vs. Denver, 2004
  Daunte Culpepper, NFC-FR: Minnesota vs. Green Bay, 2004

Most Consecutive Games, Touchdown Passes

- 16 Brett Favre, Green Bay, 1995-2004 (current)
- 13 Dan Marino, Miami, 1983-1995

12   Tom Brady, New England, 2001-06 (current)

HAD INTERCEPTED
Lowest Percentage, Passes Had Intercepted, Career (150 attempts)
1.41   Bart Starr, Green Bay, 10 games (213-3)
1.85   Tom Brady, New England, 14 games (486-9)
2.15   Phil Simms, N.Y. Giants, 10 games (279-6)
Most Attempts Without Interception, Game
54   Neil O'Donnell, AFC: Pittsburgh vs. San Diego, 1994
48   Warren Moon, AFC-FR: Houston vs. Pittsburgh, 1989 (OT)
      Randall Cunningham, NFC: Minnesota vs. Atlanta, 1998 (OT)
47   Daryle Lamonica, AFC: Oakland vs. N.Y. Jets, 1968
Most Passes Had Intercepted, Career
28   Jim Kelly, Buffalo, 17 games
26   Terry Bradshaw, Pittsburgh, 19 games
      Brett Favre, Green Bay, 20 games
24   Dan Marino, Miami, 18 games
Most Passes Had Intercepted, Game
6   Frank Filchock, NFC: N.Y. Giants vs. Chi. Bears, 1946
    Bobby Layne, NFC: Detroit vs. Cleveland, 1954
    Norm Van Brocklin, NFC: Los Angeles vs. Cleveland, 1955
    Brett Favre, NFC-D: Green Bay vs. St. Louis, 2001
5   Frank Filchock, NFC: Washington vs. Chi. Bears, 1940
    George Blanda, AFC: Houston vs. San Diego, 1961
    George Blanda, AFC: Houston vs. Dall. Texans, 1962 (OT)
    Y.A. Tittle, NFC: N.Y. Giants vs. Chicago, 1963
    Mike Phipps, AFC-D: Cleveland vs. Miami, 1972
    Dan Pastorini, AFC: Houston vs. Pittsburgh, 1978
    Dan Fouts, AFC-D: San Diego vs. Houston, 1979
    Tommy Kramer, NFC-D: Minnesota vs. Philadelphia, 1980
    Dan Fouts, AFC-D: San Diego vs. Miami, 1982
    Richard Todd, AFC: N.Y. Jets vs Miami, 1982
    Gary Danielson, NFC-D: Detroit vs. San Francisco, 1983
    Jay Schroeder, AFC: L.A. Raiders vs. Buffalo, 1990
    Rich Gannon, SB: Oakland vs. Tampa Bay, 2002
4   By many players

PASS RECEIVING
RECEPTIONS
Most Receptions, Career
151   Jerry Rice, San Francisco-Oakland-Seattle, 29 games
87   Michael Irvin, Dallas, 16 games
85   Andre Reed, Buffalo, 21 games
Most Receptions, Game
13   Kellen Winslow, AFC-D: San Diego vs. Miami, 1981 (OT)
    Thurman Thomas, AFC-D: Buffalo vs. Cleveland, 1989
    Shannon Sharpe, AFC-FR: Denver vs. L.A. Raiders, 1993
    Chad Morton, NFC-D: New Orleans vs. Minnesota, 2000
12   Raymond Berry, NFC: Baltimore vs. N.Y. Giants, 1958
    Michael Irvin, NFC: Dallas vs. San Francisco, 1994
    Darrell Jackson, NFC-FR: Seattle vs. St. Louis, 2004
    Steve Smith, NFC-D: Carolina vs. Chicago, 2005
11   Dante Lavelli, NFC: Cleveland vs. Los Angeles, 1950
    Dan Ross, SB: Cincinnati vs. San Francisco, 1981
    Franco Harris, AFC-FR: Pittsburgh vs. San Diego, 1982
    Steve Watson, AFC-D: Denver vs. Pittsburgh, 1984
    John L. Williams, AFC-D: Seattle vs. Cincinnati, 1988
    Jerry Rice, SB: San Francisco vs. Cincinnati, 1988
    Ernest Givins, AFC-FR: Houston vs. Pittsburgh, 1989 (OT)
    Amp Lee, NFC-D: Minnesota vs. Chicago, 1994
    Jay Novacek, NFC-D: Dallas vs. Green Bay, 1994
    O.J. McDuffie, AFC-FR: Miami vs. Buffalo, 1995
    Jerry Rice, NFC-D: San Francisco vs. Green Bay, 1995
    Hines Ward, AFC-FR: Pittsburgh vs. Cleveland, 2002
    Deion Branch, SB: New England vs. Philadelphia, 2004
Most Consecutive Games, Pass Receptions
28   Jerry Rice, San Francisco-Oakland, 1985-2002
22   Drew Pearson, Dallas, 1973-1983
18   Paul Warfield, Cleveland-Miami, 1964-1974
    Cliff Branch, Oakland/L.A. Raiders, 1974-1983

Thurman Thomas, Buffalo, 1989-1998
Shannon Sharpe, Denver-Baltimore-Denver, 1991-2003

YARDS GAINED
Most Yards Gained, Career
2,245   Jerry Rice, San Francisco-Oakland-Seattle, 29 games
1,315   Michael Irvin, Dallas, 16 games
1,289   Cliff Branch, Oakland/L.A. Raiders, 22 games
Most Yards Gained, Game
240   Eric Moulds, AFC-FR: Buffalo vs. Miami, 1998
227   Anthony Carter, NFC-D: Minnesota vs. San Francisco, 1987
221   Reggie Wayne, AFC-FR: Indianapolis vs. Denver, 2004
Most Games, 100 or More Yards Receiving, Career
8   Jerry Rice, San Francisco-Oakland-Seattle, 29 games
6   Michael Irvin, Dallas, 16 games
5   John Stallworth, Pittsburgh, 18 games
   Andre Reed, Buffalo, 21 games
Most Consecutive Games, 100 or More Yards Receiving, Career
3   Tom Fears, Los Angeles, 1950-51
   Jerry Rice, San Francisco, 1988-89
   Randy Moss, Minnesota, 1999-2000
2   By many players
Longest Reception
96   Shannon Sharpe (from Dilfer), AFC: Baltimore vs. Oakland, 2000 (TD)
94   Alvin Harper (from Aikman), NFC-D: Dallas vs. Green Bay, 1994 (TD)
93   Elbert Dubenion (from Lamonica), AFC-D: Buffalo vs. Boston, 1963 (TD)

AVERAGE GAIN
Highest Average Gain, Career (20 receptions)
27.3   Alvin Harper, Dallas, 10 games (24-655)
23.7   Willie Gault, Chicago-L.A. Raiders, 12 games (21-497)
22.8   Harold Jackson, L.A. Rams-New England-Minnesota-Seattle, 14 games (24-548)
Highest Average Gain, Game (3 receptions)
46.3   Harold Jackson, NFC: Los Angeles vs. Minnesota, 1974 (3-139)
42.7   Billy Cannon, AFC: Houston vs. L.A. Chargers, 1960 (3-128)
42.0   Lenny Moore, NFC: Baltimore vs. N.Y. Giants, 1959 (3-126)

TOUCHDOWNS
Most Touchdowns, Career
22   Jerry Rice, San Francisco-Oakland-Seattle, 29 games
12   John Stallworth, Pittsburgh, 18 games
10   Fred Biletnikoff, Oakland, 19 games
    Antonio Freeman, Green Bay-Philadelphia-Green Bay, 16 games
Most Touchdowns, Game
3   Tom Fears, NFC-D: Los Angeles vs. Chi. Bears, 1950
   Gary Collins, NFC: Cleveland vs. Baltimore, 1964
   Fred Biletnikoff, AFC-D: Oakland vs. Kansas City, 1968
   Preston Pearson, NFC: Dallas vs. Los Angeles, 1975
   Dave Casper, AFC-D: Oakland vs. Baltimore, 1977 (OT)
   Alvin Garrett, NFC-FR: Washington vs. Detroit, 1982
   Jerry Rice, NFC-D: San Francisco vs. Minnesota, 1988
   Jerry Rice, SB: San Francisco vs. Denver, 1989
   Andre Reed, AFC-FR: Buffalo vs. Houston, 1992 (OT)
   Sterling Sharpe, NFC-FR: Green Bay vs. Detroit, 1993
   Jerry Rice, SB: San Francisco vs. San Diego, 1994
   Willie Jackson, NFC-FR: New Orleans vs. St. Louis, 2000
   Amani Toomer, NFC-FR: N.Y. Giants vs. San Francisco, 2002
Most Consecutive Games, Touchdown Passes Caught
8   John Stallworth, Pittsburgh, 1978-1983
7   David Givens, New England, 2003-05 (current)
5   James Lofton, Green Bay-Buffalo, 1982-1990
   Randy Moss, Minnesota, 1998-2000
   Antonio Freeman, Green Bay, 1997-2001
   Hines Ward, Pittsburgh, 2002-05

INTERCEPTIONS BY

Most Interceptions, Career
9   Charlie Waters, Dallas, 25 games
    Bill Simpson, Los Angeles-Buffalo, 11 games
    Ronnie Lott, San Francisco-L.A. Raiders, 20 games
8   Lester Hayes, Oakland/L.A. Raiders, 13 games
7   Willie Brown, Oakland, 17 games
    Dennis Thurman, Dallas, 14 games

Most Interceptions, Game
4   Vernon Perry, AFC-D: Houston vs. San Diego, 1979
3   Joe Laws, NFC: Green Bay vs. N.Y. Giants, 1944
    Charlie Waters, NFC-D: Dallas vs. Chicago, 1977
    Rod Martin, SB: Oakland vs. Philadelphia, 1980
    Dennis Thurman, NFC-D: Dallas vs. Green Bay, 1982
    A.J. Duhe, AFC: Miami vs. N.Y. Jets, 1982
    Ty Law, AFC: New England vs. Indianapolis, 2003
    Ricky Manning Jr., NFC: Carolina vs. Philadelphia, 2003
2   By many players

Most Consecutive Games, Interceptions
4   Aeneas Williams, Arizona-St. Louis, 1998-2001
3   By many players. Last time:
      Asante Samuel, New England, 2005-06

YARDS GAINED

Most Yards Gained, Career
196   Willie Brown, Oakland, 17 games
187   Ronnie Lott, San Francisco-L.A.-Raiders, 20 games
160   George Teague, Green Bay-Dallas-Miami-Dallas, 12 games

Most Yards Gained, Game
108   Darrien Gordon, SB: Denver vs. Atlanta, 1998
101   George Teague, NFC-FR: Green Bay vs. Detroit, 1993
100   Champ Bailey, AFC-D: Denver vs. New England, 2005

Longest Return
101   George Teague, NFC-FR: Green Bay vs. Detroit, 1993 (TD)
100   Champ Bailey, AFC-D: Denver vs. New England, 2005
98   Darrol Ray, AFC-FR: N.Y. Jets vs. Cincinnati, 1982 (TD)

TOUCHDOWNS

Most Touchdowns, Career
3   Willie Brown, Oakland, 17 games
    Asante Samuel, New England, 11 games
2   Lester Hayes, Oakland/L.A. Raiders, 13 games
    Ronnie Lott, San Francisco-L.A. Raiders, 20 games
    Darrell Green, Washington, 18 games
    Melvin Jenkins, Seattle-Detroit, 5 games
    George Teague, Green Bay-Dallas-Miami-Dallas, 12 games
    Aeneas Williams, Arizona-St. Louis, 6 games
    Dwight Smith, Tampa Bay, 4 games

Most Touchdowns, Game
2   Aeneas Williams, NFC-D: St. Louis vs. Green Bay, 2001
    Dwight Smith, SB: Tampa Bay vs. Oakland, 2002
1   By many players

PUNTING

Most Punts, Career
111   Ray Guy, Oakland/L.A. Raiders, 22 games
92   Craig Hentrich, Green Bay-Tennessee, 20 games
84   Danny White, Dallas, 18 games
    Sean Landeta, N.Y. Giants-Tampa Bay-Green Bay-
      Philadelphia-St. Louis, 18 games

Most Punts, Game
14   Dave Jennings, AFC-D: N.Y. Jets vs. Cleveland, 1986 (OT)
12   David Lee, AFC-D: Baltimore vs. Oakland, 1977 (OT)
11   Ken Strong, NFC: N.Y. Giants vs. Chi. Bears, 1933
    Jim Norton, AFC: Houston vs. Oakland, 1967
    Ode Burrell, AFC-D: Houston vs. Oakland, 1969
    Dale Hatcher, NFC: L.A. Rams vs. Chicago, 1985
    Brad Maynard, SB: N.Y. Giants vs. Baltimore, 2000

Longest Punt
76   Ed Danowski, NFC: N.Y. Giants vs. Detroit, 1935
    Mike Horan, AFC: Denver vs. Buffalo, 1991
72   Charlie Conerly, NFC-D: N.Y. Giants vs. Cleveland, 1950
    Yale Lary, NFC: Detroit vs. Cleveland, 1953
71   Ray Guy, AFC: Oakland vs. San Diego, 1980

AVERAGE YARDAGE

Highest Average, Career (25 punts)
44.5   Rich Camarillo, New England, 6 games (35-1,559)
44.4   Todd Sauerbrun, Carolina-Denver-New England, 9 games
      (43-1,911)
43.5   Hunter Smith, Indianapolis, 13 games (45-1,958)

Highest Average, Game (4 punts)
56.0   Ray Guy, AFC: Oakland vs. San Diego, 1980 (4-224)
52.8   Hunter Smith, AFC: Indianapolis vs. New England, 2006
      (4-211)
52.5   Sammy Baugh, NFC: Washington vs. Chi. Bears, 1942
      (6-315)

PUNT RETURNS

Most Punt Returns, Career
34   David Meggett, N.Y. Giants-New England-N.Y. Jets,
    13 games
    Brian Mitchell, Washington-Philadelphia, 16 games
33   Troy Brown, New England, 20 games
25   Theo Bell, Pittsburgh-Tampa Bay, 10 games

Most Punt Returns, Game
7   Ron Gardin, AFC-D: Baltimore vs. Cincinnati, 1970
    Carl Roaches, AFC-FR: Houston vs. Oakland, 1980
    Gerald McNeil, AFC-D: Cleveland vs. N.Y. Jets, 1986 (OT)
    Phil McConkey, NFC-D: N.Y. Giants vs. San Francisco,
      1986
    David Meggett, AFC-D: New England vs. Pittsburgh, 1996
    Reggie Barlow, AFC-FR: Jacksonville vs. New England,
      1998
6   George McAfee, NFC-D: Chi. Bears vs. Los Angeles, 1950
    Eddie Brown, NFC-D: Washington vs. Minnesota, 1976
    Theo Bell, AFC: Pittsburgh vs. Houston, 1978
    Eddie Brown, NFC: Los Angeles vs. Tampa Bay, 1979
    John Sciarra, NFC: Philadelphia vs. Dallas, 1980
    Kurt Sohn, AFC: N.Y. Jets vs. Miami, 1982
    Mike Nelms, SB: Washington vs. Miami, 1982
    Anthony Carter, NFC-FR: Minnesota vs. New Orleans,
      1987
    Desmond Howard, SB: Green Bay vs. New England, 1996
    Nate Jacquet, AFC-FR: Miami vs. Seattle, 1999
    Derrick Mason, AFC-FR: Tennessee vs. Baltimore, 2003
    Antonio Chatman, AFC-D: Green Bay vs. Philadelphia,
      2003
5   By many players

YARDS GAINED

Most Yards Gained, Career
339   Brian Mitchell, Washington-Philadelphia, 16 games
315   Troy Brown, New England, 20 games
312   David Meggett, N.Y. Giants-New England-N.Y. Jets,
     13 games

Most Yards Gained, Game
152   Allen Rossum, NFC-D: Atlanta vs. St. Louis, 2004
143   Anthony Carter, NFC-FR: Minnesota vs. New Orleans,
     1987
141   Bob Hayes, NFC-D: Dallas vs. Cleveland, 1967

Longest Return
88   Jermaine Lewis, AFC-D: Baltimore vs. Pittsburgh, 2001
    (TD)
84   Anthony Carter, NFC-FR: Minnesota vs. New Orleans, 1987
    (TD)
81   Hugh Gallarneau, NFC-D: Chi. Bears vs. Green Bay, 1941
    (TD)

AVERAGE YARDAGE

Highest Average, Career (10 returns)

- 23.9 Allen Rossum, Green Bay-Atlanta, 6 games (10-239)
- 15.3 Robert Brooks, Green Bay, 11 games (14-214)
- 15.2 Anthony Carter, Minnesota-Detroit, 9 games (17-259)

Highest Average Gain, Game (3 returns)

- 50.7 Allen Rossum, NFC-D: Atlanta vs. St. Louis, 2004 (3-152)
- 47.0 Bob Hayes, NFC-D: Dallas vs. Cleveland, 1967 (3-141)
- 33.0 Jermaine Lewis, AFC-D: Baltimore vs. Pittsburgh, 2001 (3-99)

TOUCHDOWNS

Most Touchdowns

- 1 Hugh Gallarneau, NFC-D: Chicago Bears vs. Green Bay, 1941
   - Bosh Pritchard, NFC-D: Philadelphia vs. Pittsburgh, 1947
   - Charley Trippi, NFC: Chicago Cardinals vs. Philadelphia, 1947
   - Verda (Vitamin T) Smith, NFC-D: Los Angeles vs. Detroit, 1952
   - George (Butch) Byrd, AFC: Buffalo vs. San Diego, 1965
   - Golden Richards, NFC: Dallas vs. Minnesota, 1973
   - Wes Chandler, AFC-D: San Diego vs. Miami, 1981 (OT)
   - Shaun Gayle, NFC-D: Chicago vs. N.Y. Giants, 1985
   - Anthony Carter, NFC-FR: Minnesota vs. New Orleans, 1987
   - Darrell Green, NFC-D: Washington vs. Chicago, 1987
   - Antonio Freeman, NFC-FR: Green Bay vs. Atlanta, 1995
   - Desmond Howard, NFC-D: Green Bay vs. San Francisco, 1996
   - Jermaine Lewis, AFC-D: Baltimore vs. Pittsburgh, 2001
   - Troy Brown, AFC: New England vs. Pittsburgh, 2001
   - Antwaan Randle El, AFC-FR: Pittsburgh vs. Cleveland, 2002
   - Santana Moss, AFC-D: N.Y. Jets vs. Pittsburgh, 2004 (OT)
   - Allen Rossum, NFC-D: Atlanta vs. St. Louis, 2004
   - Steve Smith, NFC: Carolina vs. Seattle, 2005

KICKOFF RETURNS

Most Kickoff Returns, Career

- 36 Brian Mitchell, Washington-Philadelphia, 16 games
- 31 Kevin Williams, Dallas-Buffalo, 12 games
- 29 Fulton Walker, Miami-L.A. Raiders, 10 games

Most Kickoff Returns, Game

- 8 Marc Logan, AFC-D: Miami vs. Buffalo, 1990
   - Andre Coleman, SB: San Diego vs. San Francisco, 1994
   - Marcus Knight, SB: Oakland vs. Tampa Bay, 2002
- 7 Don Bingham, NFC: Chi. Bears vs. N.Y. Giants, 1956
   - Reggie Brown, NFC-FR: Atlanta vs. Minnesota, 1982
   - David Verser, AFC-FR: Cincinnati vs. N.Y. Jets, 1982
   - Del Rodgers, NFC-D: Green Bay vs. Dallas, 1982
   - Henry Ellard, NFC-D: L.A. Rams vs. Washington, 1983
   - Stephen Starring, SB: New England vs. Chicago, 1985
   - Darick Holmes, AFC-D: Buffalo vs. Pittsburgh, 1995
   - Antonio Freeman, NFC: Green Bay vs. Dallas, 1995
   - Roell Preston, NFC-FR: Green Bay vs. San Francisco, 1998
   - Robert Tate, NFC-D: Minnesota vs. St. Louis, 1999
   - Fred McAfee, NFC-D: New Orleans vs. Minnesota, 2000
   - Michael Bates, NFC-FR: Dallas vs. Carolina, 2003
   - Dante Hall, AFC-D: Kansas City vs. Indianapolis, 2003
   - Michael Lewis, NFC: New Orleans vs. Chicago, 2006
- 6 By many players

YARDS GAINED

Most Yards Gained, Career

- 875 Brian Mitchell, Washington-Philadelphia, 16 games
- 677 Fulton Walker, Miami-L.A. Raiders, 10 games
- 632 Kevin Williams, Dallas-Buffalo, 12 games

Most Yards Gained, Game

- 244 Andre Coleman, SB: San Diego vs. San Francisco, 1994
- 220 Ellis Hobbs, AFC: New England vs. Indianapolis, 2006
- 210 Tim Dwight, SB: Atlanta vs. Denver, 1998

Longest Return

- 100 Brian Mitchell, NFC-D: Washington vs. Tampa Bay, 1999 (TD)
- 99 Desmond Howard, SB: Green Bay vs. New England, 1996 (TD)
- 98 Fulton Walker, SB: Miami vs. Washington, 1982 (TD)
   - Andre Coleman, SB: San Diego vs. San Francisco, 1994 (TD)

AVERAGE YARDAGE

Highest Average, Career (10 returns)

- 30.1 Carl Garrett, Oakland, 5 games (16-481)
- 30.0 Reggie Barlow, Jacksonville, 8 games (12-360)
- 29.2 Chad Morton, New Orleans-N.Y. Jets-N.Y. Giants, 6 games (14-409)

Highest Average, Game (3 returns)

- 56.7 Les (Speedy) Duncan, NFC-D: Washington vs. San Francisco, 1971 (3-170)
- 51.3 Ed Podolak, AFC-D: Kansas City vs. Miami, 1971 (OT) (3-154)
- 49.0 Les (Speedy) Duncan, AFC: San Diego vs. Buffalo, 1964 (3-147)

TOUCHDOWNS

Most Touchdowns, Career

- 2 Ron Dixon, N.Y. Giants, 4 games
- 1 By many players

Most Touchdowns, Game

- 1 Vic Washington, NFC-D: San Francisco vs. Dallas, 1972
   - Nat Moore, AFC-D: Miami vs. Oakland, 1974
   - Marshall Johnson, AFC-D: Baltimore vs. Oakland, 1977 (OT)
   - Fulton Walker, SB: Miami vs. Washington, 1982
   - Stanford Jennings, SB: Cincinnati vs. San Francisco, 1988
   - Eric Metcalf, AFC-D: Cleveland vs. Buffalo, 1989
   - Andre Coleman, SB: San Diego vs. San Francisco, 1994
   - Desmond Howard, SB: Green Bay vs. New England, 1996
   - Chuck Levy, NFC: San Francisco vs. Green Bay, 1997
   - Tim Dwight, SB: Atlanta vs. Denver, 1998
   - Kevin Dyson, AFC-FR: Tennessee vs. Buffalo, 1999
   - Charlie Rogers, AFC-FR: Seattle vs. Miami, 1999
   - Brian Mitchell, NFC-D: Washington vs. Tampa Bay, 1999
   - Tony Horne, NFC-D: St. Louis vs. Minnesota, 1999
   - Derrick Mason, AFC: Tennessee vs. Jacksonville, 1999
   - Ron Dixon, NFC-D: N.Y. Giants vs. Philadelphia, 2000; SB: N.Y. Giants vs. Baltimore, 2000
   - Jermaine Lewis, SB: Baltimore vs. N.Y. Giants, 2000
   - Dante Hall, AFC-D: Kansas City vs. Indianapolis, 2003
   - Miles Austin, NFC-FR: Dallas vs. Seattle, 2006
   - Devin Hester, SB: Chicago vs. Indianapolis, 2006

FUMBLES

Most Fumbles, Career

- 16 Warren Moon, Houston-Minnesota, 10 games
- 14 John Elway, Denver, 22 games
- 13 Tony Dorsett, Dallas, 17 games

Most Fumbles, Game

- 5 Warren Moon, AFC-D: Houston vs. Kansas City, 1993
- 4 Brian Sipe, AFC-D: Cleveland vs. Oakland, 1980
   - Randall Cunningham, NFC-FR: Minnesota vs. N.Y. Giants, 1997
- 3 By many players

RECOVERIES

Most Own Fumbles Recovered, Career

- 8 Warren Moon, Houston-Minnesota, 10 games

7 John Elway, Denver, 22 games
6 Jim Kelly, Buffalo, 17 games

Most Opponents' Fumbles Recovered, Career
4 Cliff Harris, Dallas, 21 games
Harvey Martin, Dallas, 22 games
Ted Hendricks, Baltimore-Oakland/L.A. Raiders, 21 games
Alvin Walton, Washington, 9 games
Monte Coleman, Washington, 21 games
Dave Thomas, Dallas-Jacksonville-N.Y. Giants, 13 games
3 Paul Krause, Minnesota, 19 games
Jack Lambert, Pittsburgh, 18 games
Fred Dryer, Los Angeles, 14 games
Charlie Waters, Dallas, 25 games
Jack Ham, Pittsburgh, 16 games
Mike Hegman, Dallas, 16 games
Tom Jackson, Denver, 10 games
Rich Milot, Washington, 13 games
Mike Singletary, Chicago, 12 games
Darryl Grant, Washington, 16 games
Wes Hopkins, Philadelphia, 3 games
Wilber Marshall, Chicago-Washington, 15 games
Tyrone Braxton, Denver-Miami-Denver, 19 games
Neil Smith, Kansas City-Denver, 16 games
Tony Brackens, Jacksonville, 7 games
Phil Hansen, Buffalo, 14 games
Carnell Lake, Pittsburgh-Jacksonville-Baltimore, 17 games
Jason Gildon, Pittsburgh, 13 games
Tedy Bruschi, New England, 19 games
2 By many players

Most Fumbles Recovered, Game, Own and Opponents'
3 Jack Lambert, AFC: Pittsburgh vs. Oakland, 1975 (3 opp)
Ron Jaworski, NFC-FR: Philadelphia vs. N.Y. Giants, 1981 (3 own)
Devin Hester, NFC-D: Chicago vs. Seattle, 2006 (3-own)
2 By many players

YARDS GAINED
Longest Return
93 Andy Russell, AFC-D: Pittsburgh vs. Baltimore, 1975 (opp, TD)
79 Neil Smith, AFC-D: Denver vs. Miami, 1998 (opp, TD)
64 Leon Lett, SB: Dallas vs. Buffalo, 1992 (opp)

TOUCHDOWNS
Most Touchdowns
1 By many players

COMBINED NET YARDS GAINED
Rushing, receiving, interception returns, punt returns, kickoff returns, and fumble returns.
ATTEMPTS
Most Attempts, Career
454 Franco Harris, Pittsburgh, 19 games
417 Thurman Thomas, Buffalo, 21 games
397 Emmitt Smith, Dallas, 17 games
Most Attempts, Game
43 Lamar Smith, AFC-FR: Miami vs. Indianapolis, 2000 (OT)
42 Curtis Martin, AFC-D: N.Y. Jets vs. Jacksonville, 1998
40 Lawrence McCutcheon, NFC-D: Los Angeles vs. St. Louis, 1975

YARDS GAINED
Most Yards Gained, Career
2,289 Jerry Rice, San Francisco-Oakland-Seattle, 29 games
2,124 Thurman Thomas, Buffalo, 21 games
2,060 Franco Harris, Pittsburgh, 19 games
Most Yards Gained, Game
350 Ed Podolak, AFC-D: Kansas City vs. Miami, 1971 (OT)
329 Keith Lincoln, AFC: San Diego vs. Boston, 1963
285 Bob Hayes, NFC-D: Dallas vs. Cleveland, 1967

SACKS
Sacks have been compiled since 1982.
Most Sacks, Career
16.0 Willie McGinest, New England, 18 games
14.5 Bruce Smith, Buffalo, 20 games
12.0 Reggie White, Philadelphia-Green Bay, 19 games
Most Sacks, Game
4.5 Willie McGinest, AFC-FR: New England vs. Jacksonville, 2005
3.5 Rich Milot, NFC-D: Washington vs. Chicago, 1984
Richard Dent, NFC-D: Chicago vs. N.Y. Giants, 1985
3.0 Richard Dent, NFC-D: Chicago vs. Washington, 1984
Garin Veris, AFC-FR: New England vs. N.Y. Jets, 1985
Gary Jeter, NFC-D: L.A. Rams vs. Dallas, 1985
Carl Hairston, AFC-D: Cleveland vs. N.Y. Jets, 1986 (OT)
Charles Mann, NFC-D: Washington vs. Chicago, 1987
Kevin Greene, NFC-FR: L.A. Rams vs. Minnesota, 1988
Greg Townsend, AFC-D: L.A. Raiders vs. Cincinnati, 1990
Wilber Marshall, NFC: Washington vs. Detroit, 1991
Fred Stokes, NFC-FR: Washington vs. Minnesota, 1992
Pierce Holt, NFC-D: San Francisco vs. Washington, 1992
Tony Casillas, NFC: Dallas vs. San Francisco, 1992
Gerald Williams, AFC-FR: Pittsburgh vs. Kansas City, 1993
Chad Brown, AFC-FR: Pittsburgh vs. Indianapolis, 1996
Reggie White, SB: Green Bay vs. New England, 1996
Warren Sapp, NFC-D: Tampa Bay vs. Green Bay, 1997
Trace Armstrong, AFC-FR: Miami vs. Seattle, 1999
Michael McCrary, AFC-FR: Baltimore vs. Denver, 2000
Willie McGinest, AFC-D: New England vs. Tennessee, 2003

TEAM RECORDS

GAMES, VICTORIES, DEFEATS
Most Seasons Participating in Postseason Games
28 Dallas, 1966-1973, 1975-1983, 1985, 1991-96, 1998-99, 2003, 2006
N.Y. Giants, 1933-35, 1938-39, 1941, 1943-44, 1946, 1950, 1956, 1958-59, 1961-63, 1981, 1984-86, 1989-1990, 1993, 1997, 2000, 2002, 2005-06
27 Cleveland/L.A./St. Louis Rams, 1945, 1949-1952, 1955, 1967, 1969, 1973-1980, 1983-86, 1988-89, 1999-2001, 2003-04
24 Cleveland, 1950-55, 1957-58, 1964-65, 1967-69, 1971-72, 1980, 1982, 1985-89, 1994, 2002
Minnesota, 1968-1971, 1973-78, 1980, 1982, 1987-89, 1992-94, 1996-2000, 2004
Chi. Bears, 1933-34, 1937, 1940-43, 1946, 1950, 1956, 1963, 1977, 1979, 1984-88, 1990-91, 1994, 2001, 2005-06

Most Consecutive Seasons Participating in Postseason Games
9 Dallas, 1975-1983
8 Dallas, 1966-1973
Pittsburgh, 1972-79
Los Angeles, 1973-1980
San Francisco, 1983-1990
7 Houston, 1987-1993
San Francisco, 1992-98

Most Games
55 Dallas, 1966-1973, 1975-1983, 1985, 1991-96, 1998-99, 2003, 2006
46 Pittsburgh, 1947, 1972-79, 1982-84, 1989, 1992-97, 2001-02, 2004-05
43 Oakland/L.A. Raiders, 1967-1970, 1972-77, 1980, 1982-85, 1990-91, 1993, 2000-02
Cleveland/L.A./St. Louis Rams, 1945, 1949-1952, 1955, 1967, 1969, 1973-1980, 1983-86, 1988-89, 1999-2001, 2003-04

Most Games Won
- 32 Dallas, 1967, 1970-73, 1975, 1977-78, 1980-82, 1991-96
- 28 Pittsburgh, 1972, 1974-76, 1978-79, 1984, 1989, 1994-97, 2001-02, 2004-05
- 25 Oakland/L.A. Raiders, 1967-1970, 1973-77, 1980, 1982-83, 1990, 1993, 2000-02

   San Francisco, 1970-71, 1981, 1983-84, 1988-1990, 1992-94, 1996-98, 2002

Most Consecutive Games Won
- 10 New England, 2001, 2003-05
- 9 Green Bay, 1961-62, 1965-67
- 7 Pittsburgh, 1974-76
   San Francisco, 1988-1990
   Dallas, 1992-94
   Denver, 1997-98

Most Games Lost
- 24 Minnesota, 1968-1971, 1973-78, 1980, 1982, 1987-89, 1992-94, 1996-2000, 2004
   L.A./St. Louis Rams, 1949-1950, 1952, 1955, 1967, 1969, 1973-1980, 1983-86, 1988-89, 2000-01, 2003-04
- 23 Dallas, 1966-1970, 1972-73, 1975-76, 1978-1983, 1985, 1991, 1994, 1996, 1998-99, 2003, 2006
   N.Y. Giants, 1933, 1935, 1939, 1941, 1943-44, 1946, 1950, 1958-59, 1961-63, 1981, 1984-85, 1989, 1993, 1997, 2000, 2002, 2005-06
- 20 Cleveland, 1951-53, 1957-58, 1965, 1967-69, 1971-72, 1980, 1982, 1985-89, 1994, 2002

Most Consecutive Games Lost
- 6 N.Y. Giants, 1939, 1941, 1943-44, 1946, 1950
   Cleveland, 1969, 1971-72, 1980, 1982, 1985
   Minnesota, 1988-89, 1992-94, 1996
   Detroit, 1991, 1993-95, 1997, 1999 (current)
   Seattle, 1984, 1987-88, 1999, 2003-04
   Kansas City, 1993-95, 1997, 2003, 2006 (current)
- 5 N.Y. Giants, 1958-59, 1961-63
   Los Angeles, 1952, 1955, 1967, 1969, 1973
   Denver, 1977-79, 1983-84
   Baltimore/Indianapolis, 1971, 1975-77, 1987
   Philadelphia, 1980-81, 1988-1990
   Indianapolis, 1995-96, 1999-2000, 2002)
   Dallas, 1996, 1998-99, 2003, 2006 (current)
- 4 Washington, 1972-74, 1976
   Miami, 1974, 1978-79, 1981
   Chi. Cardinals/St. Louis, 1948, 1974-75, 1982
   Boston/New England, 1963, 1976, 1978, 1982
   New Orleans, 1987, 1990-92
   Buffalo, 1995-96, 1998-99 (current)
   N.Y. Giants, 2000, 2002, 2005-06 (current)
   San Diego, 1994-95, 2004, 2006 (current)

SCORING
Most Points, Game
- 73 NFC: Chi. Bears vs. Washington, 1940
- 62 AFC-D: Jacksonville vs. Miami, 1999
- 59 NFC: Detroit vs. Cleveland, 1957

Most Points, Both Teams, Game
- 95 NFC-FR: Philadelphia (58) vs. Detroit (37), 1995
- 86 NFC-D: St. Louis (49) vs. Minnesota (37), 1999
- 79 AFC-D: San Diego (41) vs. Miami (38), 1981 (OT)
   AFC-FR: Buffalo (41) vs. Houston (38), 1992 (OT)

Fewest Points, Both Teams, Game
- 5 NFC-D: Detroit (0) vs. Dallas (5), 1970
- 7 NFC: Chi. Cardinals (0) vs. Philadelphia (7), 1948
- 9 NFC: Tampa Bay (0) vs. Los Angeles (9), 1979

Largest Margin of Victory, Game
- 73 NFC: Chi. Bears vs. Washington, 1940 (73-0)
- 55 AFC-D: Jacksonville vs. Miami, 1999 (62-7)

- 49 AFC-D: Oakland vs. Houston, 1969 (56-7)

Most Points, Shutout Victory, Game
- 73 NFC: Chi. Bears vs. Washington, 1940
- 41 NFC: N.Y. Giants vs. Minnesota, 2000
   AFC-FR: N.Y. Jets vs. Indianapolis, 2002
- 38 NFC-D: Dallas vs. Tampa Bay, 1981

Most Points Overcome to Win Game
- 32 AFC-FR: Buffalo vs. Houston, 1992 (trailed 3-35, won 41-38) (OT)
- 24 NFC-FR: San Francisco vs. N.Y. Giants, 2002 (trailed 14-38, won 39-38)
- 20 NFC-D: Detroit vs. San Francisco, 1957 (trailed 7-27, won 31-27)

Most Points, Each Half
1st:	41	AFC: Buffalo vs. L.A. Raiders, 1990
		AFC-D: Jacksonville vs. Miami, 1999
	38	NFC-D: Washington vs. L.A. Rams, 1983
		NFC-FR: Philadelphia vs. Detroit, 1995
	35	NFC: Cleveland vs. Detroit, 1954
		AFC-D: Oakland vs. Houston, 1969
		SB: Washington vs. Denver, 1987
		AFC-FR: Indianapolis vs. Denver, 2004
2nd:	45	NFC: Chi. Bears vs. Washington, 1940
	35	AFC-FR: Buffalo vs. Houston, 1992
		NFC-D: St. Louis vs. Minnesota, 1999
	32	AFC: Indianapolis vs. New England, 2006

Most Points, Each Quarter
1st:	28	AFC-D: Oakland vs. Houston, 1969
	24	AFC-D: San Diego vs. Miami, 1981
		AFC-D: Jacksonville vs. Miami, 1999
	21	NFC: Chi. Bears vs. Washington, 1940
		AFC: San Diego vs. Boston, 1963
		AFC-D: Oakland vs. Kansas City, 1968
		AFC: Oakland vs. San Diego, 1980
		AFC: Buffalo vs. L.A. Raiders, 1990
		NFC: San Francisco vs. Dallas, 1994
2nd:	35	SB: Washington vs. Denver, 1987
	31	NFC-FR: Philadelphia vs. Detroit, 1995
	26	NFC-D: Pittsburgh vs. Buffalo, 1974
3rd:	28	AFC-FR: Buffalo vs. Houston, 1992
	26	NFC: Chi. Bears vs. Washington, 1940
	21	NFC-D: Dallas vs. Cleveland, 1967
		NFC-D: Dallas vs. Tampa Bay, 1981
		AFC-D: L.A. Raiders vs. Pittsburgh, 1983
		SB: Chicago vs. New England, 1985
		NFC-D: N.Y. Giants vs. San Francisco, 1986
		AFC: Cleveland vs. Denver, 1987
		AFC: Cleveland vs. Denver, 1989
		NFC-D: St. Louis vs. Minnesota, 1999
4th:	27	NFC: N.Y. Giants vs. Chi. Bears, 1934
	26	NFC-FR: Philadelphia vs. New Orleans, 1992
	24	NFC: Baltimore vs. N.Y. Giants, 1959
OT:	6	NFC: Baltimore vs. N.Y. Giants, 1958
		AFC-D: Oakland vs. Baltimore, 1977
		NFC-D: L.A. Rams vs. N.Y. Giants, 1989
		AFC-FR: Miami vs. Indianapolis, 2000
		NFC-FR: Green Bay vs. Seattle, 2003
		NFC-D: Carolina vs. St. Louis, 2003

TOUCHDOWNS
Most Touchdowns, Game
- 11 NFC: Chi. Bears vs. Washington, 1940
- 8 NFC: Cleveland vs. Detroit, 1954
   NFC: Detroit vs. Cleveland, 1957
   AFC-D: Oakland vs. Houston, 1969
   SB: San Francisco vs. Denver, 1989
   AFC-D: Jacksonville vs. Miami, 1999
- 7 AFC: San Diego vs. Boston, 1963
   NFC-D: Dallas vs. Cleveland, 1967
   NFC-D: N.Y. Giants vs. San Francisco, 1986

AFC: Buffalo vs. L.A. Raiders, 1990
SB: Dallas vs. Buffalo, 1992
SB: San Francisco vs. San Diego, 1994
NFC-FR: Philadelphia vs. Detroit, 1995
NFC-D: St. Louis vs. Minnesota, 1999
AFC-FR: Indianapolis vs. Denver, 2004

Most Touchdowns, Both Teams, Game
12 NFC-FR: Philadelphia (7) vs. Detroit (5), 1995
NFC-D: St. Louis (7) vs. Minnesota (5), 1999
11 NFC: Chi. Bears (11) vs. Washington (0), 1940
10 NFC: Detroit (8) vs. Cleveland (2), 1957
AFC-D: Miami (5) vs. San Diego (5), 1981 (OT)
AFC: Miami (6) vs. Pittsburgh (4), 1984
AFC-FR: Buffalo (5) vs. Houston (5), 1992 (OT)
SB: San Francisco (7) vs. San Diego (3), 1994
NFC-FR: San Francisco (5) vs. N.Y. Giants (5), 2002
AFC-FR: Indianapolis (7) vs. Denver (3), 2004

Fewest Touchdowns, Both Teams, Game
0 NFC-D: N.Y. Giants vs. Cleveland, 1950
NFC-D: Dallas vs. Detroit, 1970
NFC: Los Angeles vs. Tampa Bay, 1979
AFC-D: Baltimore vs. Indianapolis, 2006
1 NFC: Chi. Cardinals (0) vs. Philadelphia (1), 1948
NFC-D: Cleveland (0) vs. N.Y. Giants (1), 1958
AFC: San Diego (0) vs. Houston (1), 1961
AFC-D: N.Y. Jets (0) vs. Kansas City (1), 1969
NFC-D: Green Bay (0) vs. Washington (1), 1972
NFC-FR: New Orleans (0) vs. Chicago (1), 1990
NFC: N.Y. Giants (0) vs. San Francisco (1), 1990
AFC-FR: L.A. Raiders (0) vs. Kansas City (1), 1991
AFC-D: New England (0) vs. Pittsburgh (1), 1997
NFC: Tampa Bay (0) vs. St. Louis (1), 1999
AFC: Oakland (0) vs. Baltimore (1), 2000
2 In many games

POINTS AFTER TOUCHDOWN

Most (One-Point) Points After Touchdown, Game
8 NFC: Cleveland vs. Detroit, 1954
NFC: Detroit vs. Cleveland, 1957
AFC-D: Oakland vs. Houston, 1969
AFC-D: Jacksonville vs. Miami, 1999
7 NFC: Chi. Bears vs. Washington, 1940
NFC-D: Dallas vs. Cleveland, 1967
NFC-D: N.Y. Giants vs. San Francisco, 1986
SB: San Francisco vs. Denver, 1989
SB: Dallas vs. Buffalo, 1992
SB: San Francisco vs. San Diego, 1994
NFC-FR: Philadelphia vs. Detroit, 1995
NFC-D: St. Louis vs. Minnesota, 1999
AFC-FR: Indianapolis vs. Denver, 2004
6 AFC: San Diego vs. Boston, 1963
NFC-D: Washington vs. L.A. Rams, 1983
AFC: Miami vs. Pittsburgh, 1984
SB: Washington vs. Denver, 1987
AFC: Buffalo vs. L.A. Raiders, 1990
AFC-FR: L.A. Raiders vs. Denver, 1993
AFC-FR: Denver vs. Jacksonville, 1997
NFC-D: St. Louis vs. Green Bay, 2001
SB: Tampa Bay vs. Oakland, 2002
NFC-D: Atlanta vs. St. Louis, 2004

Most (One-Point) Points After Touchdown, Both Teams, Game
10 NFC: Detroit (8) vs. Cleveland (2), 1957
AFC-D: Miami (5) vs. San Diego (5), 1981 (OT)
AFC: Miami (6) vs. Pittsburgh (4), 1984
AFC-FR: Buffalo (5) vs. Houston (5), 1992 (OT)
NFC-FR: Philadelphia (7) vs. Detroit (3), 1995
AFC-FR: Indianapolis (7) vs. Denver (3), 2004
9 In many games

Fewest (One-Point) Points After Touchdown, Both Teams, Game
0 NFC-D: N.Y. Giants vs. Cleveland, 1950
NFC-D: Dallas vs. Detroit, 1970
NFC: Los Angeles vs. Tampa Bay, 1979
NFC: St. Louis vs. Tampa Bay, 1999
AFC-D: Baltimore vs. Indianapolis, 2006

Most Two-Point Conversions, Game
2 SB: San Diego vs. San Francisco, 1994
NFC-FR: Detroit vs. Philadelphia, 1995
NFC-FR: San Francisco vs.. N.Y. Giants, 2002
1 By many teams

FIELD GOALS

Most Field Goals, Game
5 NFC-D: Minnesota vs. San Francisco, 1987
NFC: N.Y. Giants vs. San Francisco, 1990
AFC: Buffalo vs. Miami, 1992
NFC-FR: N.Y. Giants vs. Minnesota, 1997
NFC-FR: Carolina vs. Dallas, 2003
NFC-D: St. Louis vs. Carolina, 2003 (2 OT)
AFC: New England vs. Indianapolis, 2003
AFC-D: Indianapolis vs. Baltimore, 2006
4 AFC-D: Boston vs. Buffalo, 1963
AFC: Oakland vs. Houston, 1967
SB: Green Bay vs. Oakland, 1967
NFC: Washington vs. Dallas, 1972
AFC-D: Oakland vs. Pittsburgh, 1973
SB: San Francisco vs. Cincinnati, 1981
AFC-FR: New England vs. N.Y. Jets, 1985
NFC-FR: Washington vs. L.A. Rams, 1986
NFC-D: Philadelphia vs. Chicago, 1988
AFC-FR: Pittsburgh vs. Houston, 1989 (OT)
AFC-D: Pittsburgh vs. Buffalo, 1995
NFC-FR: Dallas vs. Minnesota, 1996
NFC-D: Carolina vs. Dallas, 1996
AFC-FR: Jacksonville vs. New England, 1998
AFC-D: Tennessee vs. Indianapolis, 1999
NFC-D: Philadelphia vs. Chicago, 2001
3 By many teams

Most Field Goals, Both Teams, Game
8 NFC-FR: N.Y. Giants (5) vs. Minnesota (3), 1997
NFC-D: St. Louis (5) vs. Carolina (3), 2003 (2 OT)
7 AFC-FR: Pittsburgh (4) vs. Houston (3), 1989 (OT)
NFC: N.Y. Giants (5) vs. San Francisco (2), 1990
NFC-D: Carolina (4) vs. Dallas (3), 1996
AFC-D: Tennessee (4) vs. Indianapolis (3), 1999
AFC-D: Indianapolis (5) vs. Baltimore (2), 2006
6 NFC-D: Minnesota (5) vs. San Francisco (1), 1987
NFC-D: Philadelphia (4) vs. Chicago (2), 1988
AFC: Buffalo (5) vs. Miami (1), 1992
NFC-FR: Carolina (5) vs. Dallas (1), 2003
AFC-FR: New England (3) vs. N.Y. Jets (3), 2006

Most Field Goals Attempted, Game
6 AFC: Oakland vs. Houston, 1967
NFC-D: Los Angeles vs. Dallas, 1973
AFC-D: Cleveland vs. N.Y. Jets, 1986 (OT)
NFC: N.Y. Giants vs. San Francisco, 1990
AFC: Buffalo vs. Miami, 1992
NFC-D: St. Louis vs. Carolina, 2003 (2 OT)
5 By many teams

Most Field Goals Attempted, Both Teams, Game
11 NFC-D: St. Louis (6) vs. Carolina (5), 2003 (2 OT)
9 NFC-D: Philadelphia (5) vs. Chicago (4), 1988
NFC-FR: N.Y. Giants (5) vs. Minnesota (4), 1997
8 NFC-D: Los Angeles (6) vs. Dallas (2), 1973
NFC-D: Detroit (5) vs. San Francisco (3), 1983
AFC-D: Cleveland (6) vs. N.Y. Jets (2), 1986 (OT)
NFC-D: Minnesota (5) vs. San Francisco (3), 1987
AFC-FR: Houston (4) vs. Pittsburgh (4), 1989 (OT)
NFC-FR: Chicago (4) vs. New Orleans (4), 1990
NFC: N.Y. Giants (6) vs. San Francisco (2), 1990

SAFETIES
Most Safeties, Game
  1 By many teams
Most Safeties, Both Teams, Game
  1 In many games

FIRST DOWNS
Most First Downs, Game
  34 AFC-D: San Diego vs. Miami, 1981 (OT)
  33 AFC-D: Cleveland vs. N.Y. Jets, 1986 (OT)
  32 AFC: Indianapolis vs. New England, 2006
Fewest First Downs, Game
  6 NFC: N.Y. Giants vs. Green Bay, 1961
     AFC-D: Baltimore vs. Tennessee, 2000
  7 NFC: Green Bay vs. Boston, 1936
     NFC-D: Pittsburgh vs. Philadelphia, 1947
     NFC: Chi. Cardinals vs. Philadelphia, 1948
     NFC: Los Angeles vs. Philadelphia, 1949
     NFC-D: Cleveland vs. N.Y. Giants, 1958
     AFC-D: Cincinnati vs. Baltimore, 1970
     NFC-D: Detroit vs. Dallas, 1970
     NFC: Tampa Bay vs. Los Angeles, 1979
     AFC-D: Baltimore vs. Pittsburgh, 2001
     AFC-FR: Kansas City vs. Indianapolis, 2006
  8 By many teams
Most First Downs, Both Teams, Game
  59 AFC-D: San Diego (34) vs. Miami (25), 1981 (OT)
  55 AFC-FR: San Diego (29) vs. Pittsburgh (26), 1982
  54 AFC-FR: Buffalo (28) vs. Miami (26), 1995
Fewest First Downs, Both Teams, Game
  15 NFC: Green Bay (7) vs. Boston (8), 1936
  19 NFC: N.Y. Giants (9) vs. Green Bay (10), 1939
     NFC: Washington (9) vs. Chi. Bears (10), 1942
  20 NFC-D: Cleveland (9) vs. N.Y. Giants (11), 1950

RUSHING
Most First Downs, Rushing, Game
  19 NFC-FR: Dallas vs. Los Angeles, 1980
  18 AFC-D: Miami vs. Cincinnati, 1973
     AFC: Miami vs. Oakland, 1973
     AFC-D: Pittsburgh vs. Buffalo, 1974
     AFC-FR: Buffalo vs. Miami, 1995
     AFC-FR: Denver vs. Jacksonville, 1997
  17 AFC-D: Cincinnati vs. Seattle, 1988
     AFC: Buffalo vs. Kansas City, 1993
Fewest First Downs, Rushing, Game
  0 NFC: Los Angeles vs. Philadelphia, 1949
     AFC-D: Buffalo vs. Boston, 1963
     AFC: Oakland vs. Pittsburgh, 1974
     NFC-FR: New Orleans vs. Minnesota, 1987
     NFC: L.A. Rams vs. San Francisco, 1989
     NFC-D: Chicago vs. N.Y. Giants, 1990
     AFC-FR: Indianapolis vs. Pittsburgh, 1996
     AFC-FR: Seattle vs. Miami, 1999
     AFC-D: Miami vs. Jacksonville, 1999
     AFC-D: Miami vs. Oakland, 2000
     AFC-D: Baltimore vs. Pittsburgh, 2001
     AFC-D: Indianapolis vs. New England, 2004
  1 By many teams
Most First Downs, Rushing, Both Teams, Game
  26 AFC: Buffalo (14) vs. L.A. Raiders (12), 1990
  25 NFC-FR: Dallas (19) vs. Los Angeles (6), 1980
  23 NFC: Cleveland (15) vs. Detroit (8), 1952
     AFC-D: Miami (18) vs. Cincinnati (5), 1973
     AFC-D: Pittsburgh (18) vs. Buffalo (5), 1974
     AFC-FR: Buffalo (18) vs. Miami (5), 1995
Fewest First Downs, Rushing, Both Teams, Game
  2 NFC-FR: New Orleans (1) vs. St. Louis (1), 2000
  5 AFC-D: Buffalo (0) vs. Boston (5), 1963
     NFC-D: Washington (1) vs. Tampa Bay (4), 1999

AFC-FR: Cleveland (2) vs. Pittsburgh (3), 2002
  6 NFC: Green Bay (2) vs. Boston (4), 1936
     NFC-D: Baltimore (2) vs. Minnesota (4), 1968
     AFC-D: Houston (1) vs. Oakland (5), 1969
     AFC-FR: N.Y. Jets (1) vs. Houston (5), 1991
     AFC-FR: Denver (1) vs. Baltimore (5), 2000

PASSING
Most First Downs, Passing, Game
  24 AFC-FR: Pittsburgh vs. Cleveland, 2002
  21 AFC-D: Miami vs. San Diego, 1981 (OT)
     AFC-D: San Diego vs. Miami, 1981 (OT)
     AFC-D: Cleveland vs. N.Y. Jets, 1986 (OT)
     NFC-D: Philadelphia vs. Chicago, 1988
  20 NFC-FR: Dallas vs. L.A. Rams, 1983
     AFC-D: Buffalo vs. Cleveland, 1989
     AFC-FR: Miami vs. Buffalo, 1995
     NFC-FR: Detroit vs. Philadelphia, 1995
     AFC-FR: San Diego vs. Indianapolis, 1995
     NFC-D: Minnesota vs. St. Louis, 1999
     AFC: Indianapolis vs. New England, 2006
Fewest First Downs, Passing, Game
  0 NFC: Philadelphia vs. Chi. Cardinals, 1948
  1 NFC-D: N.Y. Giants vs. Washington, 1943
     NFC: Cleveland vs. Detroit, 1953
     SB: Denver vs. Dallas, 1977
  2 By many teams
Most First Downs, Passing, Both Teams, Game
  42 AFC-D: Miami (21) vs. San Diego (21), 1981 (OT)
     AFC-FR: Pittsburgh (24) vs. Cleveland (18), 2002
  38 AFC-FR: Pittsburgh (19) vs. San Diego (19), 1982
     NFC-D: Minnesota (20) vs. St. Louis (18), 1999
  36 NFC: Minnesota (19) vs. Atlanta (17), 1998 (OT)
Fewest First Downs, Passing, Both Teams, Game
  2 NFC: Philadelphia (0) vs. Chi. Cardinals (2), 1948
  4 NFC-D: Cleveland (2) vs. N.Y. Giants (2), 1950
  5 NFC: Detroit (2) vs. N.Y. Giants (3), 1935
     NFC: Green Bay (2) vs. N.Y. Giants (3), 1939

PENALTY
Most First Downs, Penalty, Game
  7 AFC-D: New England vs. Oakland, 1976
     AFC: Tennessee vs. Oakland, 2002
  6 AFC-D: Cleveland vs. N.Y. Jets, 1986 (OT)
     NFC-D: Chicago vs. Carolina, 2005
  5 AFC-FR: Cleveland vs. L. A. Raiders, 1982
     NFC-D: San Francisco vs. Minnesota, 1997
     AFC-FR: Miami vs. Buffalo, 1998
     NFC-D: Arizona vs. Minnesota, 1998
     AFC: Pittsburgh vs. New England, 2001
     AFC-D: Pittsburgh vs. Tennessee, 2002 (OT)
Most First Downs, Penalty, Both Teams, Game
  10 AFC: Tennessee (7) vs. Oakland (3), 2002
  9 AFC-D: New England (7) vs. Oakland (2), 1976
  8 NFC-FR: Atlanta (4) vs. Minnesota (4), 1982
     AFC-FR: Miami (5) vs. Buffalo (3), 1998

NET YARDS GAINED RUSHING AND PASSING
Most Yards Gained, Game
  610 AFC: San Diego vs. Boston, 1963
  602 SB: Washington vs. Denver, 1987
  569 AFC: Miami vs. Pittsburgh, 1984
Fewest Yards Gained, Game
  86 NFC-D: Cleveland vs. N.Y. Giants, 1958
  99 NFC: Chi. Cardinals vs. Philadelphia, 1948
  114 NFC-D: N.Y. Giants vs. Washington, 1943
     NFC: Minnesota vs. N.Y. Giants, 2000
Most Yards Gained, Both Teams, Game
  1,038 AFC-FR: Buffalo (536) vs. Miami (502), 1995
  1,036 AFC-D: San Diego (564) vs. Miami (472), 1981 (OT)

1,024   AFC: Miami (569) vs. Pittsburgh (455), 1984
Fewest Yards Gained, Both Teams, Game
  331   NFC: Chi. Cardinals (99) vs. Philadelphia (232), 1948
  332   NFC-D: N.Y. Giants (150) vs. Cleveland (182), 1950
  336   NFC: Boston (116) vs. Green Bay (220), 1936

RUSHING
ATTEMPTS
Most Attempts, Game
  65   NFC: Detroit vs. N.Y. Giants, 1935
  61   NFC: Philadelphia vs. Los Angeles, 1949
  59   AFC: New England vs. Miami, 1985
Fewest Attempts, Game
  8   AFC-D: Miami vs. San Diego, 1994
  9   SB: Miami vs. San Francisco, 1984
      NFC: Minnesota vs. N.Y. Giants, 2000
  10   NFC: L.A. Rams vs. San Francisco, 1989
      NFC-FR: Atlanta vs. Green Bay, 1995
      NFC-FR: Detroit vs. Washington, 1999
Most Attempts, Both Teams, Game
  109   NFC: Detroit (65) vs. N.Y. Giants (44), 1935
  97   AFC-D: Baltimore (50) vs. Oakland (47), 1977 (OT)
  91   NFC: Philadelphia (57) vs. Chi. Cardinals (34), 1948
Fewest Attempts, Both Teams, Game
  32   AFC-D: Houston (14) vs. Kansas City (18), 1993
  38   NFC-D: Detroit (16) vs. Dallas (22), 1991
  39   NFC-FR: Atlanta (10) vs. Green Bay (29), 1995

YARDS GAINED
Most Yards Gained, Game
  382   NFC: Chi. Bears vs. Washington, 1940
  341   AFC-FR: Buffalo vs. Miami, 1995
  338   NFC-FR: Dallas vs. Los Angeles, 1980
Fewest Yards Gained, Game
  – 4   NFC-FR: Detroit vs. Green Bay, 1994
  7   AFC-D: Buffalo vs. Boston, 1963
      SB: New England vs. Chicago, 1985
  14   AFC-D: Miami vs. Denver, 1998
      AFC: N.Y. Jets vs. Denver, 1998
Most Yards Gained, Both Teams, Game
  430   NFC-FR: Dallas (338) vs. Los Angeles (92), 1980
  426   NFC: Cleveland (227) vs. Detroit (199), 1952
  411   AFC-FR: Buffalo (341) vs. Miami (70), 1995
Fewest Yards Gained, Both Teams, Game
  77   NFC-FR: Detroit (–4) vs. Green Bay (81), 1994
  84   NFC-FR: St. Louis (34) vs. New Orleans (50), 2000
  90   AFC-D: Buffalo (7) vs. Boston (83), 1963
      NFC-D: Tampa Bay (44) vs. Washington (46), 1999

AVERAGE GAIN
Highest Average Gain, Game
  9.94   AFC: San Diego vs. Boston, 1963 (32-318)
  9.29   NFC-D: Green Bay vs. Dallas, 1982 (17-158)
  8.18   NFC-D: Atlanta vs. St. Louis, 2004 (40-327)
Lowest Average Gain, Game
  – 0.27   NFC-FR: Detroit vs. Green Bay, 1994 (15-(– 4))
  0.58   AFC-D: Buffalo vs. Boston, 1963 (12-7)
  0.64   SB: New England vs. Chicago, 1985 (11-7)

TOUCHDOWNS
Most Touchdowns, Game
  7   NFC: Chi. Bears vs. Washington, 1940
  6   NFC-D: San Francisco vs. N.Y. Giants, 1993
  5   NFC: Cleveland vs. Detroit, 1954
      NFC-D: San Francisco vs. Chicago, 1994
      AFC-FR: Pittsburgh vs. Indianapolis, 1996
      AFC-FR: Denver vs. Jacksonville, 1997
Most Touchdowns, Both Teams, Game
  7   NFC: Chi. Bears (7) vs. Washington (0), 1940
  6   NFC: Cleveland (5) vs. Detroit (1), 1954

      NFC-D: San Francisco (6) vs. N.Y. Giants (0), 1993
      NFC-D: San Francisco (5) vs. Chicago (1), 1994
      AFC-FR: Denver (5) vs. Jacksonville (1), 1997
  5   NFC: Chi. Cardinals (3) vs. Philadelphia (2), 1947
      AFC: San Diego (4) vs. Boston (1), 1963
      AFC-D: Cincinnati (3) vs. Buffalo (2), 1981
      AFC-FR: Pittsburgh (5) vs. Indianapolis (0), 1996
      NFC-D: Arizona (3) vs. Minnesota (2), 1998
      NFC-FR: Seattle (3) vs. Green Bay (2), 2003 (OT)

PASSING
ATTEMPTS
Most Attempts, Game
  66   AFC-FR: Miami vs. Buffalo, 1995
  65   AFC-D: Cleveland vs. N.Y. Jets, 1986 (OT)
      NFC-D: San Francisco vs. Green Bay, 1995
  61   NFC-FR: Minnesota vs. Chicago, 1994
Fewest Attempts, Game
  5   NFC: Detroit vs. N.Y. Giants, 1935
  6   AFC: Miami vs. Oakland, 1973
  7   SB: Miami vs. Minnesota, 1973
Most Attempts, Both Teams, Game
  102   AFC-D: San Diego (54) vs. Miami (48), 1981 (OT)
  96   AFC: N.Y. Jets (49) vs. Oakland (47), 1968
  95   AFC-D: Cleveland (65) vs. N.Y. Jets (30), 1986 (OT)
Fewest Attempts, Both Teams, Game
  18   NFC: Detroit (5) vs. N.Y. Giants (13), 1935
  23   NFC: Chi. Cardinals (11) vs. Philadelphia (12), 1948
  24   NFC-D: Cleveland (9) vs. N.Y. Giants (15), 1950

COMPLETIONS
Most Completions, Game
  36   AFC-FR: Houston vs. Buffalo, 1992 (OT)
  34   AFC-D: Cleveland vs. N.Y. Jets, 1986 (OT)
      AFC-FR: Miami vs. Buffalo, 1995
  33   AFC-D: San Diego vs. Miami, 1981 (OT)
      NFC-FR: Minnesota vs. Chicago, 1994
Fewest Completions, Game
  2   NFC: Detroit vs. N.Y. Giants, 1935
      NFC: Philadelphia vs. Chi. Cardinals, 1948
  3   NFC: N.Y. Giants vs. Chi. Bears, 1941
      NFC: Green Bay vs. N.Y. Giants, 1944
      NFC: Chi. Cardinals vs. Philadelphia, 1947
      NFC: Chi. Cardinals vs. Philadelphia, 1948
      NFC-D: Cleveland vs. N.Y. Giants, 1950
      NFC: N.Y. Giants vs. Cleveland, 1950
      NFC: Cleveland vs. Detroit, 1953
      AFC: Miami vs. Oakland, 1973
  4   NFC: N.Y. Giants vs. Detroit, 1935
      NFC-D: N.Y. Giants vs. Washington, 1943
      NFC-D: Pittsburgh vs. Philadelphia, 1947
      NFC-D: Dallas vs. Detroit, 1970
      AFC: Miami vs. Baltimore, 1971
      SB: Miami vs. Washington, 1982
      AFC-FR: Seattle vs. L.A. Raiders, 1984
Most Completions, Both Teams, Game
  64   AFC-D: San Diego (33) vs. Miami (31), 1981 (OT)
  57   AFC-FR: Houston (36) vs. Buffalo (21), 1992 (OT)
      NFC-FR: N.Y. Giants (29) vs. San Francisco (28), 2002
  56   NFC-D: Dallas (28) vs. Green Bay (28), 1993
      NFC: Minnesota (29) vs. Atlanta (27), 1998 (OT)
      NFC-D: Minnesota (29) vs. St. Louis (27), 1999
      AFC-FR: Pittsburgh (30) vs. Cleveland (26), 2002
Fewest Completions, Both Teams, Game
  5   NFC: Philadelphia (2) vs. Chi. Cardinals (3), 1948
  6   NFC: Detroit (2) vs. N.Y. Giants (4), 1935
      NFC-D: Cleveland (3) vs. N.Y. Giants (3), 1950
  11   NFC: Green Bay (3) vs. N.Y. Giants (8), 1944
      NFC-D: Dallas (4) vs. Detroit (7), 1970

COMPLETION PERCENTAGE
Highest Completion Percentage, Game (20 attempts)
- 88.0 SB: N.Y. Giants vs. Denver, 1986 (25-22)
- 87.1 NFC: San Francisco vs. L.A. Rams, 1989 (31-27)
- 83.9 AFC-FR: Indianapolis vs. Denver, 2003

Lowest Completion Percentage, Game (20 attempts)
- 18.5 NFC: Tampa Bay vs. Los Angeles, 1979 (27-5)
- 20.0 NFC-D: N.Y. Giants vs. Washington, 1943 (20-4)
- 25.8 NFC: Chi. Bears vs. Washington, 1937 (31-8)

YARDS GAINED
Most Yards Gained, Game
- 483 AFC-D: Cleveland vs. N.Y. Jets, 1986 (OT)
- 454 AFC-FR: Indianapolis vs. Denver, 2004
- 435 AFC: Miami vs. Pittsburgh, 1984

Fewest Yards Gained, Game
- 3 NFC: Chi. Cardinals vs. Philadelphia, 1948
- 7 NFC: Philadelphia vs. Chi. Cardinals, 1948
- 9 NFC-D: N.Y. Giants vs. Cleveland, 1950
- NFC: Cleveland vs. Detroit, 1953

Most Yards Gained, Both Teams, Game
- 809 AFC-D: San Diego (415) vs. Miami (394), 1981 (OT)
- 762 NFC-D: Minnesota (388) vs. St. Louis (374), 1999
- 752 AFC-FR: Cleveland (409) vs. Pittsburgh (343), 2002

Fewest Yards Gained, Both Teams, Game
- 10 NFC: Chi. Cardinals (3) vs. Philadelphia (7), 1948
- 38 NFC-D: N.Y. Giants (9) vs. Cleveland (29), 1950
- 102 NFC-D: Dallas (22) vs. Detroit (80), 1970

TIMES SACKED
Most Times Sacked, Game
- 9 AFC: Kansas City vs. Buffalo, 1966
- NFC: Chicago vs. San Francisco, 1984
- AFC-D: N.Y. Jets vs. Cleveland, 1986 (OT)
- AFC-D: Houston vs. Kansas City, 1993
- 8 NFC: Green Bay vs. Dallas, 1967
- NFC: Minnesota vs. Washington, 1987
- NFC-D: Philadelphia vs. Green Bay, 2003 (OT)
- 7 NFC-D: Dallas vs. Los Angeles, 1973
- SB: Dallas vs. Pittsburgh, 1975
- AFC-FR: Houston vs. Oakland, 1980
- NFC-D: Washington vs. Chicago, 1984
- SB: New England vs. Chicago, 1985
- AFC-FR: Kansas City vs. San Diego, 1992
- AFC-D: Pittsburgh vs. Buffalo, 1992

Most Times Sacked, Both Teams, Game
- 13 AFC: Kansas City (9) vs. Buffalo (4), 1966
- AFC-D: N.Y. Jets (9) vs. Cleveland (4), 1986 (OT)
- 12 NFC-D: Dallas (7) vs. Los Angeles (5), 1973
- NFC-D: Washington (7) vs. Chicago (5), 1984
- NFC: Chicago (9) vs. San Francisco (3), 1984
- AFC-FR: Kansas City (7) vs. San Diego (5), 1992
- 11 AFC-D: Houston (9) vs. Kansas City (2), 1993

Fewest Times Sacked, Both Teams, Game
- 0 AFC-D: Buffalo vs. Pittsburgh, 1974
- AFC-FR: Pittsburgh vs. San Diego, 1982
- AFC: Miami vs. Pittsburgh, 1984
- AFC-D: Buffalo vs. Miami, 1990
- AFC-D: Denver vs. Houston, 1991
- AFC-FR: Buffalo vs. Miami, 1995
- AFC-D: Indianapolis vs. Tennessee, 1999
- 1 In many games

TOUCHDOWNS
Most Touchdowns, Game
- 6 AFC-D: Oakland vs. Houston, 1969
- SB: San Francisco vs. San Diego, 1994
- 5 NFC: Chi. Bears vs. Washington, 1943
- NFC: Detroit vs. Cleveland, 1957
- AFC-D: Oakland vs. Kansas City, 1968
- SB: San Francisco vs. Denver, 1989
- NFC-D: St. Louis vs. Minnesota, 1999
- NFC: N.Y. Giants vs. Minnesota, 2000
- AFC-FR: Indianapolis vs. Denver, 2003
- 4 By many teams

Most Touchdowns, Both Teams, Game
- 9 NFC-D: St. Louis (5) vs. Minnesota (4), 1999
- 8 AFC-FR: Buffalo (4) vs. Houston (4), 1992 (OT)
- 7 NFC: Chi. Bears (5) vs. Washington (2), 1943
- AFC-D: Oakland (6) vs. Houston, 1969
- SB: Pittsburgh (4) vs. Dallas (3), 1978
- AFC-D: Miami (4) vs. San Diego (3), 1981 (OT)
- AFC: Miami (4) vs. Pittsburgh (3), 1984
- AFC-D: Buffalo (4) vs. Cleveland (3), 1989
- SB: San Francisco (5) vs. San Diego (1), 1994
- NFC-FR: Detroit (4) vs. Philadelphia (3), 1995
- NFC-FR: New Orleans (4) vs. St. Louis (3), 2000
- NFC-FR: N.Y. Giants (4) vs. San Francisco (3), 2002

INTERCEPTIONS BY
Most Interceptions By, Game
- 8 NFC: Chi. Bears vs. Washington, 1940
- 7 NFC: Cleveland vs. Los Angeles, 1955
- 6 NFC: Green Bay vs. N.Y. Giants, 1939
- NFC: Chi. Bears vs. N.Y. Giants, 1946
- NFC: Cleveland vs. Detroit, 1954
- AFC: San Diego vs. Houston, 1961
- AFC: Buffalo vs. L.A. Raiders, 1990
- NFC-FR: Philadelphia vs. Detroit, 1995
- NFC-D: St. Louis vs. Green Bay, 2001

Most Interceptions By, Both Teams, Game
- 10 NFC: Cleveland (7) vs. Los Angeles (3), 1955
- AFC: San Diego (6) vs. Houston (4), 1961
- 9 NFC: Green Bay (6) vs. N.Y. Giants (3), 1939
- 8 NFC: Chi. Bears (8) vs. Washington (0), 1940
- NFC: Chi. Bears (6) vs. N.Y. Giants (2), 1946
- NFC: Cleveland (6) vs. Detroit (2), 1954
- AFC-FR: Buffalo (4) vs. N.Y. Jets (4), 1981
- AFC: Miami (5) vs. N.Y. Jets (3), 1982

YARDS GAINED
Most Yards Gained, Game
- 172 SB: Tampa Bay vs. Oakland, 2002
- 161 NFC-D: St. Louis vs. Green Bay, 2001
- 138 AFC-FR: N.Y. Jets vs. Cincinnati, 1982

Most Yards Gained, Both Teams, Game
- 184 SB: Tampa Bay (172) vs. Oakland (12), 2002
- 161 NFC-D: St. Louis (161) vs. Green Bay (0), 2001
- 156 NFC: Green Bay (123) vs. N.Y. Giants (33), 1939

TOUCHDOWNS
Most Touchdowns, Game
- 3 NFC: Chi. Bears vs. Washington, 1940
- NFC-D: St. Louis vs. Green Bay, 2001
- SB: Tampa Bay vs. Oakland, 2002
- 2 NFC-D: Los Angeles vs. St. Louis, 1975
- NFC-FR: Philadelphia vs. Detroit, 1995
- 1 In many games

Most Touchdowns, Both Teams, Game
- 3 NFC: Chi. Bears (3) vs. Washington (0), 1940
- NFC-D: St. Louis (3) vs. Green Bay (0), 2001
- SB: Tampa Bay (3) vs. Oakland (0), 2002
- 2 NFC-D: Los Angeles (2) vs. St. Louis (0), 1975
- NFC-D: Dallas (1) vs. Green Bay (1), 1982
- NFC-D: Minnesota (1) vs. San Francisco (1), 1987
- NFC-FR: Detroit (1) vs. Green Bay (1), 1993
- NFC-FR: Philadelphia (2) vs. Detroit (0), 1995
- AFC-FR: Buffalo (1) vs. Jacksonville (1), 1996
- 1 In many games

PUNTING

Most Punts, Game

- 14 AFC-D: N.Y. Jets vs. Cleveland, 1986 (OT)
- 13 NFC: N.Y. Giants vs. Chi. Bears, 1933
- AFC-D: Baltimore vs. Oakland, 1977 (OT)
- 11 AFC: Houston vs. Oakland, 1967
- AFC-D: Houston vs. Oakland, 1969
- NFC: L.A. Rams vs. Chicago, 1985
- SB: N.Y. Giants vs. Baltimore, 2000

Fewest Punts, Game

- 0 NFC-FR: St. Louis vs. Green Bay, 1982
- AFC-FR: N.Y. Jets vs. Cincinnati, 1982
- AFC-FR: Indianapolis vs. Denver, 2003
- AFC-D: Kansas City vs. Indianapolis, 2003
- AFC-D: Indianapolis vs. Kansas City, 2003
- 1 By many teams

Most Punts, Both Teams, Game

- 23 NFC: N.Y. Giants (13) vs. Chi. Bears (10), 1933
- 22 AFC-D: N.Y. Jets (14) vs. Cleveland (8), 1986 (OT)
- 21 AFC-D: Baltimore (13) vs. Oakland (8), 1977 (OT)
- NFC: L.A. Rams (11) vs. Chicago (10), 1985
- SB: N.Y. Giants (11) vs. Baltimore (10), 2000

Fewest Punts, Both Teams, Game

- 0 AFC-D: Kansas City vs. Indianapolis, 2003
- 1 NFC-FR: St. Louis (0) vs. Green Bay (1), 1982
- 2 AFC-FR: N.Y. Jets (0) vs. Cincinnati (2), 1982
- SB: Atlanta (1) vs. Denver (1), 1998
- AFC-FR: Indianapolis (0) vs. Denver (2), 2003

AVERAGE YARDAGE

Highest Average, Punting, Game (4 punts)

- 56.0 AFC: Oakland vs. San Diego, 1980
- 52.8 AFC: Indianapolis vs. New England, 2006
- 52.5 NFC: Washington vs. Chi. Bears, 1942

Lowest Average, Punting, Game (4 punts)

- 24.9 NFC: Washington vs. Chi. Bears, 1937
- 25.3 AFC-FR: Pittsburgh vs. Houston, 1989
- 25.5 NFC: Green Bay vs. N.Y. Giants, 1962

PUNT RETURNS

Most Punt Returns, Game

- 8 NFC: Green Bay vs. N.Y. Giants, 1944
- 7 By many teams

Most Punt Returns, Both Teams, Game

- 13 AFC-FR: Houston (7) vs. Oakland (6), 1980
- 12 AFC-D: New England (7) vs. Pittsburgh (5), 1996
- 11 NFC: Green Bay (8) vs. N.Y. Giants (3), 1944
- NFC-D: Green Bay (6) vs. Baltimore (5), 1965
- AFC-FR: Jacksonville (7) vs. New England (4), 1998

Fewest Punt Returns, Both Teams, Game

- 0 NFC: Chi. Bears vs. N.Y. Giants, 1941
- AFC: Boston vs. San Diego, 1963
- NFC-FR: Green Bay vs. St. Louis, 1982
- AFC-FR: Houston vs. N.Y. Jets, 1991
- AFC-D: Denver vs. Houston, 1991
- NFC-D: San Francisco vs. Washington, 1992
- SB: Denver vs. Green Bay, 1997
- SB: Atlanta vs. Denver, 1998
- AFC-FR: Oakland vs. N.Y. Jets, 2001
- AFC-D: N.Y. Jets vs. Oakland, 2002
- AFC-FR: Denver vs. Indianapolis, 2003
- NFC-D: Carolina vs. St. Louis, 2003
- AFC-D: Indianapolis vs. Kansas City, 2003
- 1 In many games

YARDS GAINED

Most Yards Gained, Game

- 155 NFC-D: Dallas vs. Cleveland, 1967
- 152 NFC-D: Atlanta vs. St. Louis, 2004

- 150 NFC: Chi. Cardinals vs. Philadelphia, 1947

Fewest Yards Gained, Game

- −10 NFC: Green Bay vs. Cleveland, 1965
- −9 NFC: Dallas vs. Green Bay, 1966
- AFC-D: Kansas City vs. Oakland, 1968
- −7 NFC-D: San Francisco vs. Atlanta, 1998

Most Yards Gained, Both Teams, Game

- 166 NFC-D: Dallas (155) vs. Cleveland (11), 1967
- AFC-D: Baltimore (99) vs. Pittsburgh (67), 2001
- 160 NFC: Chi. Cardinals (150) vs. Philadelphia (10), 1947
- 152 NFC-D: Atlanta (152) vs. St. Louis (0), 2004

Fewest Yards Gained, Both Teams, Game

- −9 NFC: Dallas (−9) vs. Green Bay (0), 1966
- −6 AFC-D: Miami (−5) vs. Oakland (−1), 1970
- −3 NFC-D: San Francisco (−5) vs. Dallas (2), 1972

TOUCHDOWNS

Most Touchdowns, Game

- 1 By 18 teams

KICKOFF RETURNS

Most Kickoff Returns, Game

- 10 NFC-D: L.A. Rams vs. Washington, 1983
- NFC-FR: Detroit vs. Philadelphia, 1995
- 9 NFC: Chi. Bears vs. N.Y. Giants, 1956
- AFC: Boston vs. San Diego, 1963
- AFC: Houston vs. Oakland, 1967
- SB: Denver vs. San Francisco, 1989
- AFC-D: Miami vs. Buffalo, 1990
- AFC: L.A. Raiders vs. Buffalo, 1990
- AFC-D: Miami vs. Jacksonville, 1999
- SB: Oakland vs. Tampa Bay, 2002
- 8 By many teams

Most Kickoff Returns, Both Teams, Game

- 15 AFC-D: Miami (9) vs. Buffalo (6), 1990
- 14 NFC-FR: Detroit (10) vs. Philadelphia (4), 1995
- 13 NFC-D: Green Bay (7) vs. Dallas (6), 1982
- NFC-FR: Green Bay (7) vs. San Francisco (6), 1998
- AFC-FR: N.Y. Jets (8) vs. Oakland (5), 2001
- NFC-FR: San Francisco (7) vs. N.Y. Giants (6), 2002
- AFC-D: Tennessee (7) vs. Pittsburgh (6), 2002
- SB: Oakland (9) vs. Tampa Bay (4), 2002
- NFC-FR: Seattle (7) vs. Green Bay (6), 2003 (OT)
- AFC-D: Kansas City (7) vs. Indianapolis (6), 2003
- AFC: Pittsburgh (8) vs. New England (5), 2004
- AFC: New England (8) vs. Indianapolis (5), 2006

Fewest Kickoff Returns, Both Teams, Game

- 1 NFC: Green Bay (0) vs. Boston (1), 1936
- AFC-FR: San Diego (0) vs. Kansas City (1), 1992
- 2 NFC-D: Los Angeles (0) vs. Chi. Bears (2), 1950
- AFC: Houston (0) vs. San Diego (2), 1961
- AFC-D: Oakland (1) vs. Pittsburgh (1), 1972
- AFC: N.Y. Jets (0) vs. L.A. Raiders (2), 1982
- AFC: Miami (1) vs. N.Y. Jets (1), 1982
- NFC: N.Y. Giants (0) vs. Washington (2), 1986
- 3 In many games

YARDS GAINED

Most Yards Gained, Game

- 244 SB: San Diego vs. San Francisco, 1994
- 231 AFC: New England vs. Indianapolis, 2006
- 227 SB: Atlanta vs. Denver, 1998

Most Yards Gained, Both Teams, Game

- 379 AFC-D: Baltimore (193) vs. Oakland (186), 1977 (OT)
- 348 NFC-D: Minnesota (174) vs. St. Louis (174), 1999
- 323 NFC-D: New England (231) vs. Indianapolis (92), 2006

Fewest Yards Gained, Both Teams, Game

- 5 AFC-FR: San Diego (0) vs. Kansas City (5), 1992
- 15 NFC: N.Y. Giants (0) vs. Washington (15), 1986
- 31 NFC-D: Los Angeles (0) vs. Chi. Bears (31), 1950

TOUCHDOWNS

Most Touchdowns, Game

1 NFC-D: San Francisco vs. Dallas, 1972
AFC-D: Miami vs. Oakland, 1974
AFC-D: Baltimore vs. Oakland, 1977 (OT)
SB: Miami vs. Washington, 1982
SB: Cincinnati vs. San Francisco, 1988
AFC-D: Cleveland vs. Buffalo, 1989
SB: San Diego vs. San Francisco, 1994
SB: Green Bay vs. New England, 1996
NFC: San Francisco vs. Green Bay, 1997
SB: Atlanta vs. Denver, 1998
AFC-FR: Tennessee vs. Buffalo, 1999
AFC-FR: Seattle vs. Miami, 1999
NFC-D: Washington vs. Tampa Bay, 1999
NFC-D: St. Louis vs. Minnesota, 1999
AFC: Tennessee vs. Jacksonville, 1999
NFC-D: N.Y. Giants vs. Philadelphia, 2000
SB: Baltimore vs. N.Y. Giants, 2000
SB: N.Y. Giants vs. Baltimore, 2000
AFC-D: Kansas City vs. Indianapolis, 2003
NFC-FR: Dallas vs. Seattle, 2006
SB: Chicago vs. Indianapolis, 2006

Most Touchdowns, Both Teams, Game

2 SB: Baltimore (1) vs. N.Y. Giants (1), 2000

PENALTIES

Most Penalties, Game

17 AFC-FR: L.A. Raiders vs. Denver, 1993
14 AFC-FR: Oakland vs. Houston, 1980
NFC-D: San Francisco vs. N.Y. Giants, 1981
AFC: Oakland vs. Tennessee, 2002
13 AFC-FR: Houston vs. Cleveland, 1988
AFC-D: Houston vs. Denver, 1991
NFC-D: Arizona vs. Minnesota, 1998
NFC-D: Carolina vs. St. Louis, 2003 (2 OT)

Fewest Penalties, Game

0 NFC: Philadelphia vs. Green Bay, 1960
NFC-D: Detroit vs. Dallas, 1970
AFC-D: Miami vs. Oakland, 1970
SB: Miami vs. Dallas, 1971
NFC-D: Washington vs. Minnesota, 1973
SB: Pittsburgh vs. Dallas, 1975
NFC: San Francisco vs. Chicago, 1988
SB: Denver vs. San Francisco, 1989
AFC-D: L.A. Raiders vs. Cincinnati, 1990
AFC-D: Miami vs. San Diego, 1992
SB: Atlanta vs. Denver, 1998
AFC-FR: N.Y. Jets vs. Oakland, 2001
NFC-FR: Carolina vs. Dallas, 2003
1 By many teams

Most Penalties, Both Teams, Game

27 AFC-FR: L.A. Raiders (17) vs. Denver (10), 1993
22 AFC-FR: Oakland (14) vs. Houston (8), 1980
NFC-D: San Francisco (14) vs. N.Y. Giants (8), 1981
AFC-FR: Houston (13) vs. Cleveland (9), 1988
NFC-D: Arizona (13) vs. Minnesota (9), 1998
21 AFC-D: Oakland (11) vs. New England (10), 1976
AFC: Oakland (14) vs. Tennessee (7), 2002

Fewest Penalties, Both Teams, Game

1 AFC-D: L.A. Raiders (0) vs. Cincinnati (1), 1990
2 NFC: Washington (1) vs. Chi. Bears (1), 1937
NFC-D: Washington (0) vs. Minnesota (2), 1973
SB: Pittsburgh (0) vs. Dallas (2), 1975
NFC-FR: Carolina (0) vs. Dallas (2), 2003
3 AFC: Miami (1) vs. Baltimore (2), 1971
NFC: San Francisco (1) vs. Dallas (2), 1971
SB: Miami (0) vs. Dallas (3), 1971
AFC-D: Pittsburgh (1) vs. Oakland (2), 1972
AFC-D: Miami (1) vs. Cincinnati (2), 1973

SB: Miami (1) vs. San Francisco (2), 1984
NFC: San Francisco (0) vs. Chicago (3), 1988
AFC: New England (1) vs. Pittsburgh (2), 2004

YARDS PENALIZED

Most Yards Penalized, Game

145 NFC-D: San Francisco vs. N.Y. Giants, 1981
133 SB: Dallas vs. Baltimore, 1970
130 AFC-FR: L.A. Raiders vs. Denver, 1993

Fewest Yards Penalized, Game

0 By many teams

Most Yards Penalized, Both Teams, Game

227 AFC-FR: L.A. Raiders (130) vs. Denver (97), 1993
206 NFC-D: San Francisco (145) vs. N.Y. Giants (61), 1981
201 NFC-FR: Detroit (126) vs. Washington (75), 1999

Fewest Yards Penalized, Both Teams, Game

5 AFC-D: L.A. Raiders (0) vs. Cincinnati (5), 1990
9 NFC-D: Washington (0) vs. Minnesota (9), 1973
11 NFC-FR: Carolina (0) vs. Dallas (11), 2003

FUMBLES

Most Fumbles, Game

8 SB: Buffalo vs. Dallas, 1992
7 AFC-D: Houston vs. Kansas City, 1993
6 By 12 teams

Most Fumbles, Both Teams, Game

12 AFC: Houston (6) vs. Pittsburgh (6), 1978
SB: Buffalo (8) vs. Dallas (4), 1992
10 NFC: Chi. Bears (5) vs. N.Y. Giants (5), 1934
SB: Dallas (6) vs. Denver (4), 1977
AFC: Jacksonville (5) vs. Tennessee (5), 1999
9 NFC-D: San Francisco (6) vs. Detroit (3), 1957
NFC-D: San Francisco (5) vs. Dallas (4), 1972
NFC: Dallas (5) vs. Philadelphia (4), 1980

Most Fumbles Lost, Game

5 SB: Buffalo vs. Dallas, 1992
AFC-D: Miami vs. Jacksonville, 1999
4 NFC: N.Y. Giants vs. Baltimore, 1958 (OT)
AFC: Kansas City vs. Oakland, 1969
SB: Baltimore vs. Dallas, 1970
AFC: Pittsburgh vs. Oakland, 1975
SB: Denver vs. Dallas, 1977
AFC: Houston vs. Pittsburgh, 1978
AFC: Miami vs. New England, 1985
SB: New England vs. Chicago, 1985
NFC-FR: L.A. Rams vs. Washington, 1986
NFC-FR: Minnesota vs. Dallas, 1996
AFC-FR: Buffalo vs. Miami, 1998
AFC: N.Y. Jets vs. Denver, 1998
AFC: Jacksonville vs. Tennessee, 1999
3 By many teams

Fewest Fumbles, Both Teams, Game

0 NFC: Green Bay vs. Cleveland, 1965
AFC-D: Houston vs. San Diego, 1979
NFC-D: Dallas vs. Los Angeles, 1979
SB: Los Angeles vs. Pittsburgh, 1979
AFC-D: Buffalo vs. Cincinnati, 1981
NFC: Minnesota vs. Washington, 1987
NFC-D: San Francisco vs. Washington, 1990
NFC: Dallas vs. Green Bay, 1995
AFC-D: New England vs. Pittsburgh, 1996
SB: Green Bay vs. New England, 1996
AFC-FR: Miami vs. Seattle, 1999
AFC-FR: Miami vs. Indianapolis, 2000 (OT)
AFC-D: Baltimore vs. Tennessee, 2000
SB: Pittsburgh vs. Seattle, 2005
1 In many games

RECOVERIES

Most Total Fumbles Recovered, Game

- 8 SB: Dallas vs. Denver, 1977 (4 own, 4 opp)
- 7 NFC: Chi. Bears vs. N.Y. Giants, 1934 (5 own, 2 opp)
  - NFC-D: San Francisco vs. Detroit, 1957 (4 own, 3 opp)
  - NFC-D: San Francisco vs. Dallas, 1972 (4 own, 3 opp)
  - AFC: Pittsburgh vs. Houston, 1978 (3 own, 4 opp)
- 6 AFC: Houston vs. San Diego, 1961 (4 own, 2 opp)
  - AFC-D: Cleveland vs. Baltimore, 1971 (4 own, 2 opp)
  - AFC-D: Cleveland vs. Oakland, 1980 (5 own, 1 opp)
  - NFC: Philadelphia vs. Dallas, 1980 (3 own, 3 opp)
  - SB: Dallas vs. Buffalo, 1992 (1 own, 5 opp)
  - NFC-D: Green Bay vs. San Francisco, 1996
    (4 own, 2 opp)
  - AFC: Denver vs. N.Y. Jets, 1998 (2 own, 4 opp)
  - AFC: Tennessee vs. Jacksonville, 1999 (2 own, 4 opp)

Most Own Fumbles Recovered, Game

- 5 NFC: Chi. Bears vs. N.Y. Giants, 1934
  - AFC-D: Cleveland vs. Oakland, 1980
- 4 By many teams

TOUCHDOWNS

Most Touchdowns, Game

- 2 SB: Dallas vs. Buffalo, 1992

TURNOVERS

Numbers of times losing the ball on interceptions and fumbles.

Most Turnovers, Game

- 9 NFC: Washington vs. Chi. Bears, 1940
  - NFC: Detroit vs. Cleveland, 1954
  - AFC: Houston vs. Pittsburgh, 1978
  - SB: Buffalo vs. Dallas, 1992
- 8 NFC: N.Y. Giants vs. Chi. Bears, 1946
  - NFC: Los Angeles vs. Cleveland, 1955
  - NFC: Cleveland vs. Detroit, 1957
  - SB: Denver vs. Dallas, 1977
  - NFC-D: Minnesota vs. Philadelphia, 1980
  - NFC-D: Green Bay vs. St. Louis, 2001
- 7 In many games

Fewest Turnovers, Game

- 0 By many teams

Most Turnovers, Both Teams, Game

- 14 AFC: Houston (9) vs. Pittsburgh (5), 1978
- 13 NFC: Detroit (9) vs. Cleveland (4), 1954
  - AFC: Houston (7) vs. San Diego (6), 1961
- 12 AFC: Pittsburgh (7) vs. Oakland (5), 1975

Fewest Turnovers, Both Teams, Game

- 0 SB: Buffalo vs. N.Y. Giants, 1990
  - AFC-FR: Kansas City vs Pittsburgh, 1993 (OT)
  - NFC-FR: Detroit vs. Green Bay, 1994
  - AFC-FR: Denver vs. Jacksonville, 1996
  - SB: St. Louis vs. Tennessee, 1999
- 1 AFC-D: Baltimore (0) vs. Cincinnati (1), 1970
  - AFC-D: Pittsburgh (0) vs. Buffalo (1), 1974
  - AFC: Oakland (0) vs. Pittsburgh (1), 1976
  - NFC-D: Minnesota (0) vs. Washington (1), 1982
  - NFC-D: Chicago (0) vs. N.Y. Giants (1), 1985
  - SB: N.Y. Giants (0) vs. Denver (1), 1986
  - NFC: Washington (0) vs. Minnesota (1), 1987
  - AFC-D: Cincinnati (0) vs. L.A. Raiders (1), 1990
  - NFC: N.Y. Giants (0) vs. San Francisco (1), 1990
  - NFC-FR: N.Y. Giants (0) vs. Minnesota (1), 1993
  - AFC-FR: L.A. Raiders (0) vs. Denver (1), 1993
  - NFC: Dallas (0) vs. San Francisco (1), 1993
  - AFC: Indianapolis (0) vs. Pittsburgh (1), 1995
  - NFC-D: San Francisco (0) vs. Minnesota (1), 1997
  - AFC-D: Indianapolis (0) vs. Tennessee (1), 1999
  - AFC-FR: Baltimore (0) vs. Denver (1), 2000
  - AFC-D: Baltimore (0) vs. Tennessee (1), 2000
  - AFC-D: Oakland (0) vs. New England (1), 2001

- NFC-FR: Green Bay (0) vs. Seattle (1), 2003 (OT)
- AFC-D: Indianapolis (0) vs. Kansas City (1), 2003
- AFC-FR: N.Y. Jets (0) vs. San Diego (1), 2004 (OT)
- NFC: Philadelphia (0) vs. Atlanta (1), 2003
- NFC-FR: Philadelphia (0) vs. N.Y. Giants (1), 2006
- NFC-D: Philadelphia (0) vs. New Orleans (1), 2006
- 2 In many games

Includes records of AFC-NFC Pro Bowls, 1971-2006
Compiled by Elias Sports Bureau

INDIVIDUAL RECORDS

SERVICE
Most Games

12   Randall McDaniel, Minnesota 1990-2000;
     Tampa Bay 2001
     Will Shields, Kansas City, 1996-2007

11   *Reggie White, Philadelphia, 1987-1993; Green Bay,
     1994, 1996-97, 1999
     Junior Seau, San Diego, 1992-2002
     Rod Woodson, Pittsburgh, 1990-95, 1997;
     Baltimore, 2000-02; Oakland, 2003

10   Lawrence Taylor, N.Y. Giants, 1982-1991
     Ronnie Lott, San Francisco, 1982-85, 1987-1991;
     L.A. Raiders 1992
     Mike Singletary, Chicago, 1984-1993
     **Bruce Matthews, Houston, 1989-1995, 1997;
     Tennessee, 2000, 2002
     ***Jerry Rice, San Francisco, 1987-88, 1990-94,
     1996, 1999; Oakland, 2003

*Also selected, but did not play, in two additional games
**Also selected, but did not play, in four additional games
***Also selected but did not play, in three additional games

SCORING
POINTS
Most Points, Career

45   Morten Andersen, New Orleans, 1986-89, 1991,
     1993; Atlanta, 1996 (15-pat, 10-fg)

30   Jan Stenerud, Kansas City, 1971-72, 1976;
     Minnesota, 1985 (6-pat, 8-fg)
     Jimmy Smith, Jacksonville, 1998-2001 (5-td)
     Marvin Harrison, Indianapolis, 2000-06 (5-td)

29   David Akers, Philadelphia, 2002-03, 2005
     (8-pat, 7-fg)

Most Points, Game

18   John Brockington, Green Bay, 1973 (3-td)
     Mike Alstott, Tampa Bay, 2000 (3-td)
     Jimmy Smith, Jacksonville, 2000 (3-td)
     Shaun Alexander, Seattle, 2004 (3-td)

15   Garo Yepremian, Miami, 1974 (5-fg)
     Jason Hanson, Detroit, 2000 (6-pat, 3-fg)

14   Jan Stenerud, Kansas City, 1972 (2-pat, 4-fg)

TOUCHDOWNS
Most Touchdowns, Career

5   Jimmy Smith, Jacksonville, 1998-2001 (5-p)
    Marvin Harrison, Indianapolis, 2000-06 (5-p)

4   Mike Alstott, Tampa Bay, 1998-2003 (3-r, 1-p)
    Tony Gonzalez, Kansas City, 2000-01, 2003-07 (4-p)
    Hines Ward, Pittsburgh, 2002-05 (3-p, 1-ret)

3   John Brockington, Green Bay, 1972-74 (2-r, 1-p)
    Earl Campbell, Houston, 1979-1982, 1984 (3-r)
    Chuck Muncie, New Orleans, 1980; San Diego,
    1982-83 (3-r)
    William Andrews, Atlanta, 1981-84 (1-r, 2-p)
    Marcus Allen, L.A. Raiders, 1983, 1985-86, 1988;
    Kansas City, 1994 (2-r, 1-p)
    Cris Carter, Minnesota, 1994-2001 (3-p)
    Curtis Martin, New England, 1996-97; N.Y. Jets,
    1999, 2002 (2-r, 1-p)
    Shaun Alexander, Seattle, 2004 (2-r, 1-p)
    Torry Holt, St. Louis, 2001-02, 2004-06 (3-p)

Most Touchdowns, Game

3   John Brockington, Green Bay, 1973 (2-r, 1-p)
    Mike Alstott, Tampa Bay, 2000 (3-r)

    Jimmy Smith, Jacksonville, 2000 (3-p)
    Shaun Alexander, Seattle, 2004 (2-r, 1-p)

2   Mel Renfro, Dallas, 1971 (2-ret)
    Earl Campbell, Houston, 1980 (2-r)
    Chuck Muncie, New Orleans, 1980 (2-r)
    William Andrews, Atlanta, 1984 (2-p)
    Herschel Walker, Dallas, 1989 (2-r)
    Johnny Johnson, Phoenix, 1991 (2-r)
    Eric Green, Pittsburgh, 1995 (2-p)
    Marvin Harrison, Indianapolis, 2001 (2-p)
    Ricky Williiams, Miami, 2003 (2-r)
    Hines Ward, Pittsburgh, 2005 (1-p, 1-ret)

POINTS AFTER TOUCHDOWN
Most Points After Touchdown, Career

15   Morten Andersen, New Orleans, 1986-89, 1991,
     1993; Atlanta, 1996 (15 att)

11   Adam Vinatieri, New England, 2003, 2005 (11 att)

9   Jason Hanson, Detroit, 1998, 2000 (9 att)

Most Points After Touchdown, Game

7   Mike Vanderjagt, Indianapolis, 2004 (7 att)

6   Ali Haji-Sheikh, N.Y. Giants, 1984 (6 att)
    Jason Hanson, Detroit, 2000 (6 att)
    Adam Vinatieri, New England, 2003 (6 att)

5   John Carney, San Diego, 1995 (5 att)
    Matt Stover, Baltimore, 2001 (5 att)
    Jason Elam, Denver, 2002 (5 att)
    Jeff Wilkins, St. Louis, 2004 (5 att)
    Adam Vinatieri, New England, 2005 (5 att)

FIELD GOALS
Most Field Goals Attempted, Career

18   Morten Andersen, New Orleans, 1986-89, 1991,
     1993; Atlanta, 1996

15   Jan Stenerud, Kansas City, 1971-72, 1976;
     Minnesota, 1985

10   Nick Lowery, Kansas City, 1982, 1991, 1993

Most Field Goals Attempted, Game

6   Jan Stenerud, Kansas City, 1972
    Eddie Murray, Detroit, 1981
    Mark Moseley, Washington, 1983

5   Garo Yepremian, Miami, 1974

4   Jan Stenerud, Kansas City, 1976
    Nick Lowery, Kansas City, 1991, 1993
    Morten Andersen, New Orleans, 1993
    Cary Blanchard, Indianapolis, 1997
    John Kasay, Carolina, 1997
    David Akers, Philadelphia, 2002
    Jeff Wilkins, St. Louis, 2004

Most Field Goals, Career

10   Morten Andersen, New Orleans, 1986-89, 1991,
     1993; Atlanta, 1996

8   Jan Stenerud, Kansas City, 1971-72, 1976;
    Minnesota, 1985

7   Nick Lowery, Kansas City, 1982, 1991, 1993
    David Akers, Philadelphia, 2002-03, 2005

Most Field Goals, Game

5   Garo Yepremian, Miami, 1974 (5 att)

4   Jan Stenerud, Kansas City, 1972 (6 att)
    Eddie Murray, Detroit, 1981 (6 att)

3   Nick Lowery, Kansas City, 1991 (4 att)
    Nick Lowery, Kansas City, 1993 (4 att)
    Jason Elam, Denver, 1999 (3 att)
    Jason Hanson, Detroit, 2000 (3 att)
    David Akers, Philadelphia, 2002 (4 att)
    Neil Rackers, Arizona, 2006 (3 att)

Longest Field Goal

53   David Akers, Philadelphia, 2003

51   Morten Andersen, New Orleans, 1989
    Jason Hanson, Detroit, 2000

49 Fuad Reveiz, Minnesota, 1995
    David Akers, Philadelphia, 2002

SAFETIES
Most Safeties, Game
1 Art Still, Kansas City, 1983
   Mark Gastineau, N.Y. Jets, 1985
   Greg Townsend, L.A. Raiders, 1992

RUSHING
ATTEMPTS
Most Attempts, Career
81 Walter Payton, Chicago, 1977-1981, 1984-87
68 O.J. Simpson, Buffalo, 1973-77
66 Barry Sanders, Detroit, 1990-93, 1995-98
Most Attempts, Game
19 O.J. Simpson, Buffalo, 1974
17 Marv Hubbard, Oakland, 1974
16 O.J. Simpson, Buffalo, 1973
    Marcus Allen, L.A. Raiders, 1986

YARDS GAINED
Most Yards Gained, Career
368 Walter Payton, Chicago, 1977-1981, 1984-87
356 O.J. Simpson, Buffalo, 1973-77
271 Marshall Faulk, Indianapolis, 1995-96, 1999;
     St. Louis, 2000, 2002-03
Most Yards Gained, Game
180 Marshall Faulk, Indianapolis, 1995
127 Chris Warren, Seattle, 1995
112 O. J. Simpson, Buffalo, 1973
Longest Run From Scrimmage
49 Marshall Faulk, Indianapolis, 1995 (TD)
41 Lawrence McCutcheon, Los Angeles, 1976
    Natrone Means, San Diego, 1995
    Marshall Faulk, Indianapolis, 1995
39 Chris Warren, Seattle, 1994
    Priest Holmes, Kansas City, 2002

AVERAGE GAIN
Highest Average Gain, Career (20 attempts)
9.36 Chris Warren, Seattle, 1994-96, (25-234)
6.45 Marshall Faulk, Indianapolis, 1995-96, 1999;
      St. Louis, 2000, 2002-03 (42-271)
5.81 Marv Hubbard, Oakland, 1972-74 (36-209)
Highest Average Gain, Game (10 attempts)
13.85 Marshall Faulk, Indianapolis, 1995 (13-180)
9.07 Chris Warren, Seattle, 1995 (14-127)
7.00 O.J. Simpson, Buffalo, 1973 (16-112)
      Ottis Anderson, St. Louis, 1981 (10-70)

TOUCHDOWNS
Most Touchdowns, Career
3 Earl Campbell, Houston, 1979-1982, 1984
   Chuck Muncie, New Orleans, 1980; San Diego,
   1982-83
   Mike Alstott, Tampa Bay, 1998-2003
2 John Brockington, Green Bay, 1972-74
   O.J. Simpson, Buffalo, 1973-77
   Walter Payton, Chicago, 1977-1981, 1984-87
   Marcus Allen, L.A. Raiders, 1983, 1985-86, 1988;
   Kansas City, 1994
   Herschel Walker, Dallas, 1988-89
   Johnny Johnson, Phoenix, 1991
   Barry Sanders, Detroit, 1990-93, 1995-98
   Curtis Martin, New England, 1996-97; N.Y. Jets,
   1999, 2002
   Ricky Williams, Miami, 2003
   Shaun Alexander, Seattle, 200
   LaDainian Tomlinson, San Diego, 2003, 2005-07

Most Touchdowns, Game
3 Mike Alstott, Tampa Bay, 2000
2 John Brockington, Green Bay, 1973
   Earl Campbell, Houston, 1980
   Chuck Muncie, New Orleans, 1980
   Herschel Walker, Dallas, 1989
   Johnny Johnson, Phoenix, 1991
   Ricky Williams, Miami, 2003
   Shaun Alexander, Seattle, 2004

PASSING
ATTEMPTS
Most Attempts, Career
146 Peyton Manning, Indianapolis, 2000-01, 2003-07
120 Dan Fouts, San Diego, 1980-84, 1986
101 Steve Young, San Francisco, 1993-96, 1998-99
Most Attempts, Game
41 Peyton Manning, Indianapolis, 2004
32 Bill Kenney, Kansas City, 1984
    Steve Young, San Francisco, 1993
30 Dan Fouts, San Diego, 1983

COMPLETIONS
Most Completions, Career
84 Peyton Manning, Indianapolis, 2000-01, 2003-07
63 Dan Fouts, San Diego, 1980-84, 1986
48 Steve Young, San Francisco, 1993-96, 1998-99
Most Completions, Game
22 Peyton Manning, Indianapolis, 2004
21 Joe Theismann, Washington, 1984
18 Steve Young, San Francisco, 1993

COMPLETION PERCENTAGE
Highest Completion Percentage, Career (40 attempts)
68.9 Joe Theismann, Washington, 1983-84 (45-31)
67.9 Rich Gannon, Oakland, 2000-03 (53-36)
64.4 Jim Kelly, Buffalo, 1988, 1991-92 (45-29)
Highest Completion Percentage, Game (10 attempts)
90.0 Archie Manning, New Orleans, 1980 (10-9)
85.7 Rich Gannon, Oakland, 2001 (14-12)
80.0 Rich Gannon, Oakland, 2002 (10-8)

YARDS GAINED
Most Yards Gained, Career
1,198 Peyton Manning, Indianapolis, 2000-01, 2003-07
890 Dan Fouts, San Diego, 1980-84, 1986
614 Steve Young, San Francisco, 1993-96, 1998-99
Most Yards Gained, Game
342 Peyton Manning, Indianapolis, 2004
274 Dan Fouts, San Diego, 1983
270 Peyton Manning, Indianapolis, 2000
Longest Completion
93 Jeff Blake, Cincinnati (to Thigpen, Pittsburgh),
    1996 (TD)
90 Steve McNair, Tennessee (to Johnson, Cincinnati),
    2004 (TD)
80 Mark Brunell, Jacksonville (to Brown, Oakland),
    1997 (TD)

AVERAGE GAIN
Highest Average Gain, Career (40 attempts)
8.21 Peyton Manning, Indianapolis, 2000-01,
      2003-07 (146-1,198)
8.19 Rich Gannon, Oakland, 2000-03 (53-434)
8.12 Brett Favre, Green Bay, 1993-94, 1996-97 (57-463)
Highest Average Gain, Game (10 attempts)
15.27 Randall Cunningham, Philadelphia, 1991 (11-168)
13.70 Rich Gannon, Oakland, 2002 (10-137)

13.00   Brett Favre, Green Bay, 1997 (11-143)
       Peyton Manning, Indianapolis, 2005 (10-130)

TOUCHDOWNS

Most Touchdowns, Career
- 12   Peyton Manning, Indianapolis, 2000-01, 2003-07
- 7   Rich Gannon, Oakland, 2000-03
- 4   Steve Young, San Francisco, 1993-96, 1998-99
-     Marc Bulger, St. Louis, 2004, 2007

Most Touchdowns, Game
- 4   Marc Bulger, St. Louis, 2004
- 3   Joe Theismann, Washington, 1984
-     Phil Simms, N.Y. Giants, 1986
-     Peyton Manning, Indianapolis, 2004
-     Peyton Manning, Indianapolis, 2005
- 2   James Harris, Los Angeles, 1975
-     Mike Boryla, Philadelphia, 1976
-     Ken Anderson, Cincinnati, 1977
-     Jim Kelly, Buffalo, 1991
-     Mark Rypien, Washington, 1992
-     Steve Young, San Francisco, 1998
-     Peyton Manning, Indianapolis, 2000
-     Rich Gannon, Oakland, 2001
-     Peyton Manning, Indianapolis, 2001
-     Rich Gannon, Oakland, 2002
-     Donovan McNabb, Philadelphia, 2002
-     Rich Gannon, Oakland, 2003
-     Brad Johnson, Tampa Bay, 2003
-     Carson Palmer, Cincinnati, 2007

HAD INTERCEPTED

Most Passes Had Intercepted, Career
- 8   Dan Fouts, San Diego, 1980-84, 1986
-     Peyton Manning, Indianapolis, 2000-01, 2003-07
- 6   Jim Hart, St. Louis, 1975-78
- 5   Ken Stabler, Oakland, 1974-75, 1978
-     Donovan McNabb, Philadelphia, 2001-03, 2005

Most Passes Had Intercepted, Game
- 5   Jim Hart, St. Louis, 1977
- 4   Ken Stabler, Oakland, 1974
- 3   Dan Fouts, San Diego, 1986
-     Mark Rypien, Washington, 1990
-     Steve Young, San Francisco, 1993
-     Jim Harbaugh, Indianapolis, 1996
-     Vinny Testaverde, N.Y. Jets, 1999
-     Jeff Garcia, San Francisco, 2003
-     Peyton Manning, Indianapolis, 2006

Most Attempts, Without Interception, Game
- 27   Joe Theismann, Washington, 1984
-     Phil Simms, N.Y. Giants, 1986
- 26   John Brodie, San Francisco, 1971
-     Danny White, Dallas, 1983
- 23   Dave Krieg, Seattle, 1990

PERCENTAGE, PASSES HAD INTERCEPTED

**Lowest Percentage, Passes Had Intercepted, Career
(40 attempts)**
- 0.00   Joe Theismann, Washington, 1983-84 (45-0)
- 1.89   Rich Gannon, Oakland, 2000-03 (53-1)
- 2.13   Dave Krieg, Seattle, 1985, 1989-1990 (47-1)

PASS RECEIVING
RECEPTIONS

Most Receptions, Career
- 37   Jerry Rice, San Francisco, 1987-88, 1990-94, 1996, 1999; Oakland, 2003
- 30   Marvin Harrison, Indianapolis, 2000-06
- 29   Tony Gonzalez, Kansas City, 2000-01, 2003-07

Most Receptions, Game
- 9   Randy Moss, Minnesota, 2000

- 8   Steve Largent, Seattle, 1986
-     Michael Irvin, Dallas, 1992
-     Andre Rison, Atlanta, 1993
-     Jimmy Smith, Jacksonville, 2000
-     Marvin Harrison, Indianapolis, 2001
-     Terrell Owens, San Francisco, 2002
-     Steve Smith, Carolina, 2006
- 7   John Stallworth, Pittsburgh, 1983
-     Jerry Rice, San Francisco, 1992
-     Isaac Bruce, St. Louis, 1997
-     Keyshawn Johnson, N.Y. Jets, 1999
-     Randy Moss, Minnesota, 1999
-     Warrick Dunn, Tampa Bay, 2001
-     Torry Holt, St. Louis, 2001
-     Torry Holt, St. Louis, 2004

YARDS GAINED

Most Yards Gained, Career
- 495   Jerry Rice, San Francisco, 1987-88, 1990-94, 1996, 1999; Oakland, 2003
- 462   Marvin Harrison, Indianapolis, 2000-06
- 413   Tony Gonzalez, Kansas City, 2000-01, 2003-07

Most Yards Gained, Game
- 212   Randy Moss, Minnesota, 2000
- 156   Chad Johnson, Cincinnati, 2004
- 137   Tim Brown, Oakland, 1997
-      Reggie Wayne, Indianapolis, 2007

Longest Reception
- 93   Yancey Thigpen, Pittsburgh (from Blake, Cincinnati), 1996 (TD)
- 90   Chad Johnson, Cincinnati (from McNair, Tennessee), 2004 (TD)
- 80   Tim Brown, Oakland (from Brunell, Jacksonville), 1997 (TD)

TOUCHDOWNS

Most Touchdowns, Career
- 5   Jimmy Smith, Jacksonville, 1998-2001
-    Marvin Harrison, Indianapolis, 2000-06
- 4   Tony Gonzalez, Kansas City, 2000-01, 2003-07
- 3   Cris Carter, Minnesota, 1994-2001
-    Torry Holt, St. Louis, 2001-02, 2004-06
-    Hines Ward, Pittsburgh, 2002-05

Most Touchdowns, Game
- 3   Jimmy Smith, Jacksonville, 2000
- 2   William Andrews, Atlanta, 1984
-    Eric Green, Pittsburgh, 1995
-    Marvin Harrison, Indianapolis, 2001

INTERCEPTIONS BY

Most Interceptions By, Career
- 4   Everson Walls, Dallas, 1982-84, 1986
-    Deion Sanders, Atlanta, 1992-94; San Francisco, 1995; Dallas, 1999
-    Champ Bailey, Washington, 2001-04; Denver, 2005-07
- 3   Ken Houston, Houston, 1971-73; Washington, 1974-79
-    Jack Lambert, Pittsburgh, 1976-1984
-    Ted Hendricks, Baltimore, 1972-74; Green Bay, 1975; Oakland, 1981-82; L.A. Raiders, 1983-84
-    Mike Haynes, New England, 1978-1981, 1983; L.A. Raiders, 1985-87
-    Ty Law, New England, 1999, 2002-04; N.Y. Jets, 2006
- 2   By 19 players

Most Interceptions By, Game
- 2   Mel Blount, Pittsburgh, 1977
-    Everson Walls, Dallas, 1982, 1983
-    LeRoy Irvin, L.A. Rams, 1986

David Fulcher, Cincinnati, 1990
Brian Dawkins, Philadelphia, 2000
Rod Woodson, Oakland, 2003
Ed Reed, Baltimore, 2007

YARDS GAINED
Most Yards Gained, Career
147 Ty Law, New England, 1999, 2002-04;
     N.Y. Jets, 2006
103 Deion Sanders, Atlanta, 1992-94; San Francisco,
     1995; Dallas, 1999
  88 Rod Woodson, Pittsburgh, 1990-95, 1997;
     Baltimore, 2000-02; Oakland, 2003
Most Yards Gained, Game
  87 Deion Sanders, Dallas, 1999
  73 Rod Woodson, Pittsburgh, 1994
  67 Ty Law, New England, 1999
Longest Gain
  87 Deion Sanders, Dallas, 1999
  73 Rod Woodson, Pittsburgh, 1994 (lateral)
  67 Ty Law, New England, 1999 (TD)

TOUCHDOWNS
Most Touchdowns, Career
   2 Ty Law, New England, 1999, 2002-04;
     N.Y. Jets, 2006
     Derrick Brooks, Tampa Bay, 1998-2001, 2003,
     2006-07
   1 By many
Most Touchdowns, Game
   1 Bobby Bell, Kansas City, 1973
     Nolan Cromwell, L.A. Rams, 1984
     Joey Browner, Minnesota, 1986
     Jerry Gray, L.A. Rams, 1990
     Mike Johnson, Cleveland, 1990
     Junior Seau, San Diego, 1993
     Ken Harvey, Washington, 1996
     Ashley Ambrose, Cincinnati, 1997
     Ty Law, New England, 1999
     Derrick Brooks, Tampa Bay, 2000
     Aeneas Williams, Arizona, 2000
     Ray Lewis, Baltimore, 2002
     Ty Law, New England, 2003
     Dre' Bly, Detroit, 2004
     Derrick Brooks, Tampa Bay, 2006

PUNTING
Most Punts, Career
  33 Ray Guy, Oakland, 1974-79, 1981
  23 Rohn Stark, Indianapolis, 1986-87, 1991, 1993
  22 Reggie Roby, Miami, 1985, 1990; Washington, 1995
Most Punts, Game
  10 Reggie Roby, Miami, 1985
   9 Tom Wittum, San Francisco, 1974
     Rohn Stark, Indianapolis, 1987
   8 Jerrel Wilson, Kansas City, 1971
     Tom Skladany, Detroit, 1982
     Reggie Roby, Washington, 1995
Longest Punt
  73 Shane Lechler, Oakland, 2002
  70 Shane Lechler, Oakland, 2002
  64 Tom Wittum, San Francisco, 1974
     Darren Bennett, San Diego, 1996
     Brian Moorman, Buffalo, 2007

AVERAGE YARDAGE
Highest Average, Career (10 punts)
46.73 Reggie Roby, Miami, 1985, 1990; Washington, 1995
     (22-1,028)
45.27 Matt Turk, Washington, 1997-99 (15-679)

45.25 Jerrel Wilson, Kansas City, 1971-73 (16-724)
Highest Average, Game (4 punts)
60.75 Shane Lechler, Oakland, 2002 (4-243)
55.50 Darren Bennett, San Diego, 1996 (4-222)
52.00 Matt Turk, Washington, 1999 (4-208)

PUNT RETURNS
Most Punt Returns, Career
  13 Rick Upchurch, Denver, 1977, 1979-1980, 1983
  11 Vai Sikahema, St. Louis, 1987-88
     Eric Metcalf, Cleveland 1994-95; San Diego 1998
  10 Mike Nelms, Washington, 1981-83
Most Punt Returns, Game
   7 Vai Sikahema, St. Louis, 1987
   6 Henry Ellard, L.A. Rams, 1985
     Gerald McNeil, Cleveland, 1988
     Eric Metcalf, Cleveland, 1995
   5 Rick Upchurch, Denver, 1980
     Mike Nelms, Washington, 1981
     Carl Roaches, Houston, 1982
     Johnny Bailey, Phoenix, 1993
Most Fair Catches, Game
   2 Jerry Logan, Baltimore, 1971
     Dick Anderson, Miami, 1974
     Henry Ellard, L.A. Rams, 1985
     Isaac Bruce, St. Louis, 1997
     Desmond Howard, Detroit, 2001

YARDS GAINED
Most Yards Gained, Career
183 Billy Johnson, Houston, 1976, 1978; Atlanta, 1984
138 Mel Renfro, Dallas, 1971-72, 1974
     Rick Upchurch, Denver, 1977, 1979-1980, 1983
135 Eric Metcalf, Cleveland, 1994-95; San Diego 1998
Most Yards Gained, Game
159 Billy Johnson, Houston, 1976
138 Mel Renfro, Dallas, 1971
117 Wally Henry, Philadelphia, 1980
Longest Punt Return
  90 Billy Johnson, Houston, 1976 (TD)
  86 Wally Henry, Philadelphia, 1980 (TD)
  82 Mel Renfro, Dallas, 1971 (TD)

AVERAGE YARDAGE
Highest Average, Career (4 returns)
22.88 Billy Johnson, Houston, 1976, 1978; Atlanta, 1984
     (8-183)
21.50 Tony Green, Washington, 1979 (4-86)
15.67 David Meggett, N.Y. Giants, 1990; New England, 1997
Highest Average, Game (3 returns)
39.75 Billy Johnson, Houston, 1976 (4-159)
39.00 Wally Henry, Philadelphia, 1980 (3-117)
21.50 Tony Green, Washington, 1979 (4-86)

TOUCHDOWNS
Most Touchdowns, Game
   2 Mel Renfro, Dallas, 1971
   1 Billy Johnson, Houston, 1976
     Wally Henry, Philadelphia, 1980

KICKOFF RETURNS
Most Kickoff Returns, Career
  17 Michael Bates, Carolina, 1997-2001
  14 Mel Gray, Detroit, 1991-92, 1995
  11 Eric Metcalf, Cleveland, 1994-95; San Diego, 1998
     Derrick Mason, Tennessee, 2001, 2004
Most Kickoff Returns, Game
   8 Derrick Mason, Tennessee, 2004
   7 Mel Gray, Detroit, 1995
     Jerry Azumah, Chicago, 2004

6   Greg Pruitt, L.A. Raiders, 1984
    David Meggett, New England, 1997
    Michael Bates, Carolina, 1998
    Steve Smith, Carolina, 2002

YARDS GAINED
Most Yards Gained, Career
488   Michael Bates, Carolina, 1997-2001
309   Greg Pruitt, Cleveland, 1974-75, 1977-78;
      L.A. Raiders, 1984
294   Mel Gray, Detroit, 1991-92, 1995
Most Yards Gained, Game
228   Jerry Azumah, Chicago, 2004
217   Michael Lewis, New Orleans, 2003
192   Greg Pruitt, L.A. Raiders, 1984
Longest Kickoff Return
66   Michael Bates, Carolina, 2000
62   Greg Pruitt, L.A. Raiders, 1984
61   Eugene (Mercury) Morris, Miami, 1972

AVERAGE YARDAGE
Highest Average, Career (4 returns)
43.40   Michael Lewis, New Orleans, 2003 (5-217)
35.00   Les (Speedy) Duncan, Washington, 1972 (5-175)
32.57   Jerry Azumah, Chicago, 2004 (7-228)
Highest Average, Game (3 returns)
43.40   Michael Lewis, New Orleans, 2003 (5-217)
42.00   Michael Bates, Carolina, 2000 (4-168)
35.00   Les (Speedy) Duncan, Washington, 1972 (5-175)

TOUCHDOWNS
Most Touchdowns, Game
1   Hines Ward, Pittsburgh, 2005

FUMBLES
Most Fumbles, Career
6   Dan Fouts, San Diego, 1980-84, 1986
4   Lawrence McCutcheon, Los Angeles, 1974-78
    Franco Harris, Pittsburgh, 1973-76, 1978-1981
    Jay Schroeder, Washington, 1987
    Vai Sikahema, St. Louis, 1987-88
    Trent Green, Kansas City, 2004, 2006
3   O.J. Simpson, Buffalo, 1973-77
    William Andrews, Atlanta, 1981-84
    Joe Montana, San Francisco, 1982, 1984-85, 1988
    Walter Payton, Chicago, 1977-1981, 1984-87
    Neil Lomax, St. Louis, 1985, 1988
    Jim Kelly, Buffalo, 1988, 1991-92
    Chris Chandler, Atlanta, 1998-99
    Peyton Manning, Indianapolis, 2000-01, 2003-07
    Marc Bulger, St. Louis, 2004, 2007
Most Fumbles, Game
4   Jay Schroeder, Washington, 1987
    Trent Green, Kansas City, 2004
3   Dan Fouts, San Diego, 1982
    Vai Sikahema, St. Louis, 1987
2   By 17 players

RECOVERIES
Most Fumbles Recovered, Career
3   Harold Jackson, Philadelphia, 1973; Los Angeles,
      1974, 1976, 1978 (3-own)
    Dan Fouts, San Diego, 1980-84, 1986 (3-own)
    Randy White, Dallas, 1978, 1980-86 (3-opp)
    Trent Green, Kansas City, 2004, 2006 (3-own)
2   By many players
Most Fumbles Recovered, Game
3   Trent Green, Kansas City, 2004 (3-own)
2   Dick Anderson, Miami, 1974 (1-own, 1-opp)
    Harold Jackson, Los Angeles, 1974 (2-own)

    Dan Fouts, San Diego, 1982 (2-own)
    Joey Browner, Minnesota, 1990 (2-opp)
    Jessie Armstead, N.Y. Giants, 1999 (1-own, 1-opp)
    Steve Beuerlein, Carolina, 2000 (2-own)

YARDAGE
Longest Fumble Return
83   Art Still, Kansas City, 1985 (TD, opp)
70   Adalius Thomas, Baltimore, 2007 (TD, opp)
51   Phil Villapiano, Oakland, 1974 (opp)

TOUCHDOWNS
Most Touchdowns, Game
1   Art Still, Kansas City, 1985
    Keith Millard, Minnesota, 1990
    Adalius Thomas, Baltimore, 2007

SACKS
Sacks have been compiled since 1983.
Most Sacks, Career
9.5   Reggie White, Philadelphia, 1987-1993; Green Bay,
      1994, 1996-97, 1999
9.0   Howie Long, L.A. Raiders, 1984-88, 1990, 1993-1994
7.5   Bruce Smith, Buffalo, 1988-1991, 1995-96, 1998-99
Most Sacks, Game
4   Mark Gastineau, N.Y. Jets, 1985
    Reggie White, Philadelphia, 1987
3   Richard Dent, Chicago, 1985
    Bruce Smith, Buffalo, 1991
2.5   Bruce Smith, Buffalo, 1998

TEAM RECORDS

SCORING
Most Points, Game
55   NFC, 2004
Fewest Points, Game
3   AFC, 1984, 1989, 1994
Most Points, Both Teams, Game
107   NFC (55) vs. AFC (52), 2004
Fewest Points, Both Teams, Game
16   NFC (6) vs. AFC (10), 1987

TOUCHDOWNS
Most Touchdowns, Game
7   AFC, 2004
   NFC, 2004
Fewest Touchdowns, Game
0   AFC, 1971, 1974, 1984, 1989, 1994
   NFC, 1987, 1988
Most Touchdowns, Both Teams, Game
14   AFC (7) vs. NFC (7), 2004
Fewest Touchdowns, Both Teams, Game
1   AFC (0) vs. NFC (1), 1974
   NFC (0) vs. AFC (1), 1987
   NFC (0) vs. AFC (1), 1988

POINTS AFTER TOUCHDOWN
Most Points After Touchdown, Game
7   AFC, 2004
Most Points After Touchdown, Both Teams, Game
12   AFC (7) vs. NFC (5), 2004

FIELD GOALS
Most Field Goals Attempted, Game
6   AFC, 1972
   NFC, 1981, 1983
Most Field Goals Attempted, Both Teams, Game
9   NFC (6) vs. AFC (3), 1983

Most Field Goals, Game
5   AFC, 1974
Most Field Goals, Both Teams, Game
7   AFC (5) vs. NFC (2), 1974

NET YARDS GAINED RUSHING AND PASSING
Most Yards Gained, Game
626   AFC, 2004
Fewest Yards Gained, Game
114   AFC, 1993
Most Yards Gained, Both Teams, Game
1,022   AFC (626) vs. NFC (396), 2004
Fewest Yards Gained, Both Teams, Game
424   AFC (202) vs. NFC (222), 1987

RUSHING
ATTEMPTS
Most Attempts, Game
50   AFC, 1974
Fewest Attempts, Game
9   NFC, 2001
Most Attempts, Both Teams, Game
80   AFC (50) vs. NFC (30), 1974
Fewest Attempts, Both Teams, Game
32   NFC (9) vs. AFC (23), 2001

YARDS GAINED
Most Yards Gained, Game
400   AFC, 1995
Fewest Yards Gained, Game
28   NFC, 1992
Most Yards Gained, Both Teams, Game
441   AFC (400) vs. NFC (41), 1995
Fewest Yards Gained, Both Teams, Game
119   NFC (36) vs. AFC (83), 2001

TOUCHDOWNS
Most Touchdowns, Game
3   NFC, 1989, 1991, 2000, 2007
    AFC, 1995
Most Touchdowns, Both Teams, Game
4   AFC (2) vs. NFC (2), 1973
    AFC (2) vs. NFC (2), 1980
    NFC (3) vs. AFC (1), 2007

PASSING
ATTEMPTS
Most Attempts, Game
58   NFC, 2002
Fewest Attempts, Game
17   NFC, 1972
Most Attempts, Both Teams, Game
101   NFC (54) vs. AFC (47), 2003
Fewest Attempts, Both Teams, Game
42   NFC (17) vs. AFC (25), 1972

COMPLETIONS
Most Completions, Game
32   NFC, 1993
    AFC, 2001
Fewest Completions, Game
7   NFC, 1972, 1982
Most Completions, Both Teams, Game
60   AFC (32) vs. NFC (28), 2001
Fewest Completions, Both Teams, Game
18   NFC (7) vs. AFC (11), 1972

YARDS GAINED
Most Yards Gained, Game
515   AFC, 2004

Fewest Yards Gained, Game
42   NFC, 1982
Most Yards Gained, Both Teams, Game
775   AFC (515) vs. NFC (260), 2004
Fewest Yards Gained, Both Teams, Game
215   NFC (89) vs. AFC (126), 1972

TIMES SACKED
Most Times Sacked, Game
9   NFC, 1985
Fewest Times Sacked, Game
0   AFC, 1998, 1999, 2000, 2003
    NFC, 1971, 1997, 2001
Most Times Sacked, Both Teams, Game
17   NFC (9) vs. AFC (8), 1985
Fewest Times Sacked, Both Teams, Game
1   NFC (0) vs. AFC (1), 1997

TOUCHDOWNS
Most Touchdowns, Game
5   AFC, 2004
Most Touchdowns, Both Teams, Game
9   AFC (5) vs. NFC (4), 2004

INTERCEPTIONS BY
Most Interceptions By, Game
6   AFC, 1977, 2003
Most Interceptions By, Both Teams, Game
8   AFC (6) vs. NFC (2), 2003

YARDS GAINED
Most Yards Gained, Game
192   NFC, 2006
Most Yards Gained, Both Teams, Game
265   NFC (192) vs. AFC (73), 2006

TOUCHDOWNS
Most Touchdowns, Game
2   NFC, 2000

PUNTING
Most Punts, Game
10   AFC, 1985
Fewest Punts, Game
0   NFC, 1989
Most Punts, Both Teams, Game
16   AFC (10) vs. NFC (6), 1985
Fewest Punts, Both Teams, Game
3   NFC (1) vs. AFC (2), 2005

PUNT RETURNS
Most Punt Returns, Game
7   NFC, 1985, 1987
    AFC, 1995
Fewest Punt Returns, Game
0   AFC, 1984, 1989
    NFC, 2005
Most Punt Returns, Both Teams, Game
11   NFC (7) vs. AFC (4), 1985
Fewest Punt Returns, Both Teams, Game
1   NFC (0) vs. AFC (1), 2005

YARDS GAINED
Most Yards Gained, Game
177   AFC, 1976
Fewest Yards Gained, Game
−1   NFC, 1991
Most Yards Gained, Both Teams, Game
263   AFC (177) vs. NFC (86), 1976

Fewest Yards Gained, Both Teams, Game
   7 NFC (0) vs. AFC (7), 2005

TOUCHDOWNS
Most Touchdowns, Game
   2 NFC, 1971

KICKOFF RETURNS
Most Kickoff Returns, Game
  10 AFC, 2004
Fewest Kickoff Returns, Game
   1 NFC, 1971, 1984, 1994
      AFC, 1988, 1991
Most Kickoff Returns, Both Teams, Game
  18 AFC (10) vs. NFC (8), 2004
Fewest Kickoff Returns, Both Teams, Game
   5 NFC (2) vs. AFC (3), 1979
      AFC (1) vs. NFC (4), 1988
      NFC (2) vs. AFC (3), 1992
      NFC (1) vs. AFC (4), 1994

YARDS GAINED
Most Yards Gained, Game
 247 NFC, 2004
Fewest Yards Gained, Game
   6 NFC, 1971
Most Yards Gained, Both Teams, Game
 461 NFC (247) vs. AFC (214), 2004
Fewest Yards Gained, Both Teams, Game
  99 NFC (48) vs. AFC (51), 1987

TOUCHDOWNS
Most Touchdowns, Game
   1 AFC, 2005

FUMBLES
Most Fumbles, Game
  10 NFC, 1974
Most Fumbles, Both Teams, Game
  15 NFC (10) vs. AFC (5), 1974

RECOVERIES
Most Fumbles Recovered, Game
  10 NFC, 1974 (6 own, 4 opp)
Most Fumbles Lost, Game
   4 AFC, 1974, 1988
      NFC, 1974

YARDS GAINED
Most Yards Gained, Game
  87 AFC, 1985

TOUCHDOWNS
Most Touchdowns, Game
   1 AFC, 1985, 2007
      NFC, 1990

TURNOVERS
(Number of times losing the ball on interceptions and fumbles.)
Most Turnovers, Game
   8 AFC, 1974
Fewest Turnovers, Game
   0 AFC, 1991, 1997
      NFC, 1991, 1995, 1996, 2001
Most Turnovers, Both Teams, Game
  12 AFC (8) vs. NFC (4), 1974
Fewest Turnovers, Both Teams, Game
   0 AFC vs. NFC, 1991

Rules

2007 NFL ROSTER OF OFFICIALS

Mike Pereira, Vice President of Officiating
Larry Upson, Director of Officiating Operations
Jim Daopoulos, Supervisor of Officials

Ron Baynes, Supervisor of Officials
Neely Dunn, Supervisor of Officials
Johnny Grier, Supervisor of Officials

No.	Name	Position	College
86	Anderson, Barry	Side Judge	North Carolina State
66	Anderson, Walt	Referee	Texas
108	Arthur, Gary	Line Judge	Wright State
34	Austin, Gerald	Referee	Western Carolina
26	Baltz, Mark	Head Linesman	Ohio University
72	Banks, Michael	Side Judge	Illinois State
55	Barnes, Tom	Line Judge	Minnesota
32	Bergman, Jeff	Line Judge	Robert Morris
91	Bergman, Jerry	Head Linesman	Robert Morris
7	Blum, Ron	Line Judge	Marin College
109	Boger, Jerome	Referee	Morehouse College
18	Boston, Byron	Line Judge	Austin
74	Bowers, Derick	Line Judge	Oklahoma
31	Brown, Chad	Umpire	East Texas State
134	Camp, Ed	Head Linesman	William Paterson
126	Carey, Don	Back Judge	UC Riverside
94	Carey, Mike	Referee	Santa Clara
39	Carlsen, Don	Side Judge	Cal State-Chico
63	Carollo, Bill	Referee	Wisconsin-Milwaukee
11	Carroll, Duke	Field Judge	Ithaca
60	Cavaletto, Gary	Field Judge	Hancock
41	Cheek, Boris	Field Judge	Morgan State
51	Cheffers, Carl	Side Judge	UC Irvine
95	Coleman, James	Side Judge	Arkansas
65	Coleman, Walt	Referee	Arkansas
99	Corrente, Tony	Referee	Cal State-Fullerton
71	Coukart, Ed	Umpire	Northwestern
70	Dawson, Scott	Umpire	Virginia Tech
53	DeFelice, Garth	Umpire	San Diego State
6	Dornan, Kirk	Back Judge	Central Washington
27	Dyer, Lee	Field Judge	Tennessee-Chattanooga
3	Edwards, Scott	Field Judge	Alabama
81	Ellison, Roy	Umpire	Savannah State
61	Ferguson, Keith	Back Judge	San Jose State
64	Ferrell, Dan	Umpire	Cal State-Fullerton
47	Fincken, Tom	Side Judge	Kansas State
133	Freeman, Steve	Back Judge	Mississippi State
80	Gautreaux, Greg	Field Judge	Southwestern Louisiana
19	Green, Scott	Referee	Delaware
49	Hall, Rich	Umpire	Arizona
40	Hannah, Butch	Umpire	Middle Tennessee State
125	Hayes, Laird	Side Judge	Princeton
54	Hayward, George	Head Linesman	Missouri Western
93	Helverson, Scott	Back Judge	Iowa
97	Hill, Tom	Side Judge	Carson-Newman
28	Hittner, Mark	Head Linesman	Pittsburg State
85	Hochuli, Ed	Referee	Texas-El Paso
82	Horton, Buddy	Field Judge	Oregon State
37	Howey, Jim	Back Judge	Erskine College
35	Hussey, John	Line Judge	Idaho State
76	Jenkins, Darrell	Umpire	San Jose State
101	Johnson, Carl	Line Judge	Nicholls State
103	Lamberth, Jeff	Side Judge	Texas A&M
73	Larrew, Joe	Side Judge	St. Louis University
17	Lawing, Bob	Back Judge	North Carolina State
127	Leavy, Bill	Referee	San Jose State
130	Lewis, Darryll	Line Judge	Dartmouth
98	Lovett, Bill	Field Judge	Maryland

No.	Name	Position	College
106	Mackie, Wayne	Head Linesman	Colgate
92	Madsen, Carl	Umpire	Washington
107	Marinucci, Ron	Head Linesman	Glassboro State
77	McAulay, Terry	Referee	Louisiana State
120	McGrath, John	Head Linesman	Kentucky
110	McKinnely, Phil	Head Linesman	UCLA
48	Mello, Jim	Head Linesman	Northeastern
78	Meyer, Greg	Side Judge	TCU
115	Michalek, Tony	Umpire	Indiana
135	Morelli, Pete	Referee	St. Mary's College
20	Nemmers, Larry	Referee	Upper Iowa
124	Paganelli, Carl	Umpire	Michigan State
46	Paganelli, Perry	Back Judge	Hope College
132	Parry, John	Side Judge	Purdue
15	Patterson, Rick	Side Judge	Wofford
79	Payne, Kent	Head Linesman	Nebraska-Wesleyan
9	Perlman, Mark	Line Judge	Salem
10	Phares, Ron	Line Judge	Virginia Tech
38	Powers, Eddy	Field Judge	Tennessee
5	Quirk, Jim	Umpire	Delaware
83	Reels, Richard	Back Judge	Chicago State
44	Rice, Jeff	Umpire	Northwestern
57	Riveron, Alberto	Side Judge	Miami
128	Rose, Larry	Side Judge	Florida
67	Rosenbaum, Doug	Field Judge	Illinois Wesleyan
58	Saracino, Jim	Field Judge	Northern Colorado
21	Schleyer, John	Head Linesman	Millersville
122	Schmitz, Bill	Back Judge	Colorado State
129	Schuster, Blll	Umpire	Alfred
45	Seeman, Jeff	Line Judge	Minnesota
118	Sifferman, Tom	Field Judge	Seattle
30	Slaughter, Gary	Head Linesman	East Texas State
2	Smith, Billy	Back Judge	East Carolina
90	Spanier, Michael	Line Judge	St. Cloud State
24	Stabile, Tom	Head Linesman	Slippery Rock
12	Steed, Greg	Back Judge	Howard
88	Steenson, Scott	Field Judge	North Texas
84	Steinkerchner, Mark	Line Judge	Akron
22	Stelljes, Steve	Head Linesman	Friends University
68	Stephan, Tom	Line Judge	Pittsburg State
114	Steratore, Gene	Referee	Kent State
112	Steratore, Tony	Back Judge	California (Penn.)
62	Stewart, Charles	Line Judge	Long Beach State
42	Triplette, Jeff	Referee	Wake Forest
75	Vernatchi, Rob	Side Judge	UC Riverside
36	Veteri, Tony	Head Linesman	Manhattan College
52	Vinovich, Bill	Referee	San Diego
25	Waggoner, Bob	Back Judge	Juniata College
96	Wash, Undrey	Umpire	Texas-Arlington
116	Weatherford, Mike	Side Judge	Oklahoma State
87	Weidner, Paul	Head Linesman	Cincinnati
50	Weir, Mike	Field Judge	Missouri
29	Wilson, Steve	Umpire	Whitworth College
14	Winter, Ron	Referee	Michigan State
4	Wrolstad, Craig	Field Judge	Washington
16	Wyant, David	Side Judge	Virginia
33	Zimmer, Steve	Field Judge	Hofstra

Roster as of May 2007

NUMERICAL ROSTER

No.	Name	Position
2	Billy Smith	BJ
3	Scott Edwards	FJ
4	Craig Wrolstad	FJ
5	Jim Quirk	U
6	Kirk Dornan	BJ
7	Ron Blum	LJ
9	Mark Perlman	LJ
10	Ron Phares	LJ
11	Duke Carroll	FJ
12	Greg Steed	BJ
14	Ron Winter	R
15	Rick Patterson	SJ
16	David Wyant	SJ
17	Bob Lawing	BJ
18	Byron Boston	LJ
19	Scott Green	R
20	Larry Nemmers	R
21	John Schleyer	HL
22	Steve Stelljes	HL
24	Tom Stabile	HL
25	Bob Waggoner	BJ
26	Mark Baltz	HL
27	Lee Dyer	FJ
28	Mark Hittner	HL
29	Steve Wilson	U
30	Gary Slaughter	HL
31	Chad Brown	U
32	Jeff Bergman	LJ
33	Steve Zimmer	FJ
34	Gerry Austin	R
35	John Hussey	LJ
36	Tony Veteri	HL
37	Jim Howey	BJ
38	Eddy Powers	FJ
39	Don Carlsen	SJ
40	Butch Hannah	U
41	Boris Cheek	FJ
42	Jeff Triplette	R
44	Jeff Rice	U
45	Jeff Seeman	LJ
46	Perry Paganelli	BJ
47	Tom Fincken	SJ
48	Jim Mello	HL
49	Rich Hall	U
50	Mike Weir	FJ
51	Carl Cheffers	SJ
52	Bill Vinovich	R
53	Garth DeFelice	U
54	George Hayward	HL
55	Tom Barnes	LJ
57	Alberto Riveron	SJ
58	Jim Saracino	FJ
60	Gary Cavaletto	FJ
61	Keith Ferguson	BJ
62	Charles Stewart	LJ
63	Bill Carollo	R
64	Dan Ferrell	U
65	Walt Coleman	R
66	Walt Anderson	R
67	Doug Rosenbaum	FJ
68	Tom Stephan	LJ
70	Scott Dawson	U
71	Ed Coukart	U
72	Michael Banks	SJ
73	Joe Larrew	SJ
74	Derick Bowers	LJ
75	Rob Vernatchi	SJ
76	Darrell Jenkins	U
77	Terry McAulay	R
78	Greg Meyer	SJ
79	Kent Payne	HL
80	Greg Gautreaux	FJ
81	Roy Ellison	U
82	Buddy Horton	FJ
83	Richard Reels	BJ
84	Mark Steinkerchner	LJ
85	Ed Hochuli	R
86	Barry Anderson	SJ
87	Paul Weidner	HL
88	Scott Steenson	FJ
90	Michael Spanier	LJ
91	Jerry Bergman	HL
92	Carl Madsen	U
93	Scott Helverson	BJ
94	Mike Carey	R
95	James Coleman	SJ
96	Undrey Wash	U
97	Tom Hill	SJ
98	Bill Lovett	FJ
99	Tony Corrente	R
101	Carl Johnson	LJ
103	Jeff Lamberth	SJ
106	Wayne Mackie	HL
107	Ron Marinucci	HL
108	Gary Arthur	LJ
109	Jerome Boger	R
110	Phil McKinnely	HL
112	Tony Steratore	BJ
114	Gene Steratore	R
115	Tony Michalek	U
116	Mike Weatherford	SJ
118	Tom Sifferman	FJ
120	John McGrath	HL
122	Bill Schmitz	BJ
124	Carl Paganelli	U
125	Laird Hayes	SJ
126	Don Carey	BJ
127	Bill Leavy	R
128	Larry Rose	SJ
129	Bill Schuster	U
130	Darryll Lewis	LJ
132	John Parry	SJ
133	Steve Freeman	BJ
134	Ed Camp	HL
135	Pete Morelli	R

Roster as of May 2007

OFFICIALS

2007 OFFICIALS AT A GLANCE

REFEREES

Walt Anderson, No. **66,** Texas, college officiating coordinator, 12th year.

Gerry Austin, No. **34,** Western Carolina, president, leadership development group, 26th year.

Jerome Boger, No. **109,** Morehouse College, commercial insurance underwriter, 4th year.

Mike Carey, No. **94,** Santa Clara, owner, skiing accessories, 18th year.

Bill Carollo, No. **63,** Wisconsin-Milwaukee, marketing executive, 19th year.

Walt Coleman, No. **65,** Arkansas, manager, dairy processor, 19th year.

Tony Corrente, No. **99,** Cal State-Fullerton, educator, 13th year.

Scott Green, No. **19,** Delaware, vice-president, government relations, 17th year.

Ed Hochuli, No. **85,** Texas-El Paso, attorney, 18th year.

Bill Leavy, No. **127,** San Jose State, retired firefighter, 13th year.

Terry McAulay, No. **77,** Louisiana State, senior computer scientist, 10th year.

Pete Morelli, No. **135,** St. Mary's, high school principal, 11th year.

Larry Nemmers, No. **20,** Upper Iowa, motivational speaker, 23rd year.

Gene Steratore, No. **114,** Kent State, co-owner, supply company, 5th year.

Jeff Triplette, No. **42,** Wake Forest, vice president, world-wide energy company, 12th year.

Bill Vinovich, No. **52,** San Diego, certified public accountant, 7th year.

Ron Winter, No. **14,** Michigan State, university professor, 13th year.

UMPIRES

Chad Brown, No. **31,** East Texas State, manager, intramural/sports clubs, 16th year.

Ed Coukart, No. **71,** Northwestern, vice-president, commercial bank, 19th year.

Scott Dawson, No. **70,** Virginia Tech, president/owner, commercial construction company, 13th year.

Garth DeFelice, No. **53,** San Diego State, director of distributing, beverage company, 10th year.

Roy Ellison, No. **81,** Savannah State, technical staff member, 5th year.

Dan Ferrell, No. **64,** Cal State-Fullerton, regional manager, parts distribution and logistics, 5th year.

Rich Hall, No. **49,** Arizona, custom cabinetry, 4th year.

Butch Hannah, No. **40,** Middle Tennessee State, federal probation officer, 9th year.

Darrell Jenkins, No. **76,** San Jose State, retired, 6th year.

Carl Madsen, No. **92,** Washington, partner/owner, office furniture dealership, 11th year.

Tony Michalek, No. **115,** Indiana, eurodollar future trader, 6th year.

Carl Paganelli, No. **124,** Michigan State, federal probation officer, 9th year.

Jim Quirk, No. **5,** Delaware, consultant, 20th year.

Jeff Rice, No. **44,** Northwestern, attorney, 13th year.

Bill Schuster, No. **129,** Alfred, insurance broker, 8th year.

Undrey Wash, No. **96,** Texas-Arlington, claims manager, 8th year.

Steve Wilson, No. **29,** Whitworth College, pastor, 9th year.

HEAD LINESMEN

Mark Baltz, No. **26,** Ohio University, sales consultant, 19th year.

Jerry Bergman, No. **91,** Robert Morris, sales executive, 6th year.

Ed Camp, No. **134,** William Paterson, teacher, 8th year.

George Hayward, No. **54,** Missouri Western, vice-president and manager, warehouse company, 17th year.

Mark Hittner, No. **28,** Pittsburg State, investment banker, 11th year.

Wayne Mackie, No. **106,** Colgate, director of housing, 1st year.

Ron Marinucci, No. **107,** Glassboro State, novelty cone company, 10th year.

John McGrath, No. **120,** Kentucky, senior account executive, 6th year.

Phil McKinnely, No. **110,** UCLA, inventory control, former NFL player, 5th year.

Jim Mello, No. **48,** Northeastern, facilities management, 4th year.

Kent Payne, No. **79,** Nebrasksa-Wesleyan, 4th year.

John Schleyer, No. **21,** Millersville, medical sales, 18th year.

Gary Slaughter, No. **30,** East Texas State, general manager, 12th year.

Tom Stabile, No. **24,** Slippery Rock, secondary educational administrator, 13th year.

Steve Stelljes, No. **22,** Friends University, business planning manager, 6th year.

Tony Veteri, No. **36,** Manhattan, director of athletics, 16th year.

Paul Weidner, No. **87,** Cincinnati, marketing manager, 22nd year.

LINE JUDGES

Gary Arthur, No. **108,** Wright State, president, commercial printing company, 11th year.

Tom Barnes, No. **55,** Minnesota, manufacturing representative, 22nd year.

Jeff Bergman, No. **32,** Robert Morris, president and chief executive officer, medical services, 16th year.

Ron Blum, No. **7,** Marin College, professional golfer, 23rd year.

Byron Boston, No. **18,** Austin, tax consultant, 5th year.

Derick Bowers, No. **74,** East Central University, purchasing supervisor, 5th year.

John Hussey, No. **35,** Idaho State, sales representative, retail logistics group, 6th year.

Carl Johnson, No. **101,** Nicholls State, district sales manager, 7th year.

Darryll Lewis, No. **130,** Dartmouth, associate professor, 9th year.

Ron Phares, No. **10,** Virginia Tech, president, construction company, 23rd year.

Mark Perlman, No. **9,** Salem, teacher, 7th year.

Jeff Seeman, No. **45,** Minnesota, brokerage sales, 6th year.

Mike Spanier, No. **90,** St. Cloud State, middle school principal, 9th year.

Mark Steinkerchner, No. **84,** Akron, vice-president, 14th year.

Tom Stephan, No. **68,** Pittsburg State, business broker, 9th year.

Charles Stewart, No. **62,** Long Beach State, retired human services administrator, 16th year.

Roster as of May 2007

FIELD JUDGES

Duke Carroll, No. **11,** Ithaca, insurance sales, 13th year.
Gary Cavaletto, No. **60,** Hancock, general manager, agricultural operations, 5th year.
Boris Cheek, No. **41,** Morgan State, director of operations and management, 12th year.
Lee Dyer, No. **27,** Tennessee-Chattanooga, sales manager, 5th year.
Scott Edwards, No. **3,** Alabama, environmental engineer, 9th year.
Greg Gautreaux, No. **80,** Southwestern Louisiana, athletic programs manager, 6th year.
Buddy Horton, No. **82,** Oregon State, water service worker, 9th year.
Bill Lovett, No. **98,** Maryland, managing partner, financial sales, 18th year.
Eddy Powers, No. **38,** Tennessee, sales/design office supply, 6th year.
Doug Rosenbaum, No. **67,** Illinois Wesleyan, financial advisor, 7th year.
Jim Saracino, No. **58,** Northern Colorado, secondary educator, 13th year.
Tom Sifferman, No. **118,** Seattle, manufacturer's representative, 22nd year.
Scott Steenson, No. **88,** North Texas, commercial real estate broker, 17th year.
Mike Weir, No. **50,** Missouri, owner, sporting goods store, 6th year.
Craig Wrolstad, No. **4,** Washington, education, 5th year.
Steve Zimmer, No. **33,** Hofstra, attorney, 11th year.

SIDE JUDGES

Barry Anderson, No. **86,** North Carolina State, developer/builder, 1st year.
Michael Banks, No. **72,** Illinois State, carpenter foreman, 6th year.
Don Carlsen, No. **39,** Cal State-Chico, retired county school superintendent, 19th year.
Carl Cheffers, No. **51,** UC Irvine, sales manager, 8th year.
James Coleman, No. **95,** Arkansas, 3rd year.
Tom Fincken, No. **47,** Emporia State, retired educational administrator, 24th year.
Laird Hayes, No. **125,** Princeton, professor, physical education & athletics, 13th year.
Tom Hill, No. **97,** Carson Newman, teacher, 9th year.
Jeff Lamberth, No. **103,** Texas A&M, attorney, 6th year.
Joe Larrew, No. **73,** St. Louis University, attorney, 6th year.
Greg Meyer, No. **78,** TCU, banker, 6th year.
John Parry, No. **132,** Purdue, corporate pilot, 8th year.
Rick Patterson, No. **15,** Wofford, banker, 12th year.
Alberto Riveron, No. **57,** Miami, commercial restaurant equipment, 4th year.
Larry Rose, No. **128,** Florida, financial planner, 11th year.
Rob Vernatchi, No. **75,** UC Riverside, enforcement investigator, 4th year.
Mike Weatherford, No. **116,** Oklahoma State, energy trader, 6th year.
David Wyant, No. **16,** Virginia, consulting engineer, 17th year.

BACK JUDGES

Don Carey, No. **126,** UC Riverside, contract manager, 13th year.
Kirk Dornan, No. **6,** Central Washington, purchasing manager, 14th year.
Keith Ferguson, No. **61,** San Jose State, sales, 8th year.
Steve Freeman, No. **133,** Mississippi State, custom home builder, 7th year.
Scott Helverson, No. **93,** Iowa, sales, printing and promotions, 5th year.
Jim Howey, No. **37,** Erskine College, director of adult education, 9th year.
Bob Lawing, No. **17,** North Carolina State, real estate management, 11th year.
Perry Paganelli, No. **46,** Hope College, high school administrator, 10th year.
Richard Reels, No. **83,** Chicago State, director of security, court services, 15th year.
Bill Schmitz, No. **122,** Colorado State, general sales manager, 19th year.
Billy Smith, No. **2,** East Carolina, federal government, 13th year.
Greg Steed, No. **12,** Howard, computer systems analyst, 5th year.
Tony Steratore, No. **112,** California (Penn.), co-owner, supply company, 8th year.
Bob Waggoner, No. **25,** Juniata College, probation officer, 11th year.

Roster as of May 2007

1

**TOUCHDOWN, FIELD GOAL,
or SUCCESSFUL TRY**
Both arms extended above head.

2

SAFETY
Palms together above head.

3

FIRST DOWN
Arm pointed toward defensive
team's goal.

4

**CROWD NOISE,
DEAD BALL, or NEUTRAL
ZONE ESTABLISHED**
One arm above head
with an open hand.
With fist closed: **Fourth Down.**

5

**BALL ILLEGALLY
TOUCHED, KICKED,
or BATTED**
Fingertips tap both shoulders.

6

TIME OUT
Hands crisscrossed above head.
Same signal followed by placing one
hand on top of cap: **Referee's Time Out.**
Same signal followed by arm swung at
side: **Touchback.**

7

**NO TIME OUT or
TIME IN WITH WHISTLE**
Full arm circled to
simulate moving clock.

8

**DELAY OF GAME
or EXCESS TIME OUT**
Folded arms.

9

**FALSE START,
ILLEGAL FORMATION, or
KICKOFF or SAFETY KICK
OUT OF BOUNDS or
KICKING TEAM PLAYER
VOLUNTARILY OUT OF BOUNDS
DURING A PUNT**
Forearms rotated over and over
in front of body.

10

PERSONAL FOUL
One wrist striking the other above head.
Same signal followed by swinging leg:
Roughing the Kicker.
Same signal followed by raised arm
swinging forward:
Roughing the Passer.
Same signal followed by grasping
facemask: **Major Facemask.**

11

HOLDING
Grasping one wrist,
the fist clenched,
in front of chest.

12

**ILLEGAL USE OF HANDS,
ARMS, or BODY**
Grasping one wrist,
the hand open and facing
forward, in front of chest.

13

**PENALTY REFUSED,
INCOMPLETE
PASS, PLAY OVER, or
MISSED FIELD GOAL or
EXTRA POINT**
Hands shifted in horizontal plane.

14

**PASS JUGGLED INBOUNDS AND
CAUGHT OUT OF BOUNDS**
Hands up and down in front of chest
(following incomplete pass signal).

15

ILLEGAL FORWARD PASS
One hand waved behind back
followed by loss of down
signal (23), when appropriate.

16

**INTENTIONAL
GROUNDING OF PASS**
Parallel arms waved in a diagonal
plane across body. Followed by loss of
down signal (23).

17

**INTERFERENCE WITH FORWARD
PASS or FAIR CATCH**
Hands open
and extended forward from
shoulders with hands vertical.

18

INVALID FAIR-CATCH SIGNAL
One hand waved above head.

19

**INELIGIBLE RECEIVER
or INELIGIBLE
MEMBER OF KICKING TEAM
DOWNFIELD**
Right hand touching top of cap.

20

ILLEGAL CONTACT
One open hand extended forward.

21

**OFFSIDE, ENCROACHMENT, or
NEUTRAL ZONE INFRACTION**
Hands on hips.

22

ILLEGAL MOTION AT SNAP
Horizontal arc with one hand.

23

LOSS OF DOWN
Both hands held behind head.

24

**INTERLOCKING
INTERFERENCE, PUSHING, or
HELPING RUNNER**
Pushing movement of hands
to front with arms downward.

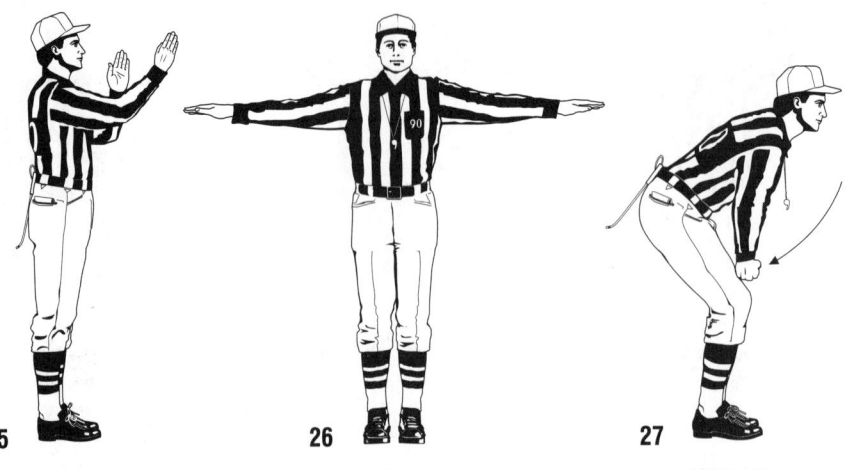

25

**TOUCHING A FORWARD
PASS or SCRIMMAGE KICK**
Diagonal motion of
one hand across another.

26

**UNSPORTSMANLIKE
CONDUCT**
Arms outstretched,
palms down.

27

ILLEGAL CUT
Hand striking front of thigh.
ILLEGAL BLOCK BELOW THE WAIST
One hand striking front of thigh
preceded by personal-foul signal (10).
CHOP BLOCK
Both hands striking side of thighs
preceded by personal-foul signal (10).
CLIPPING
One hand striking back of calf
preceded by personal-foul signal (10).

28

ILLEGAL CRACKBACK
Strike of an
open right hand
against the right mid-thigh
preceded by personal foul
signal (10).

29

PLAYER DISQUALIFIED
Ejection signal.

30

TRIPPING
Repeated action of right foot
in back of left heel.

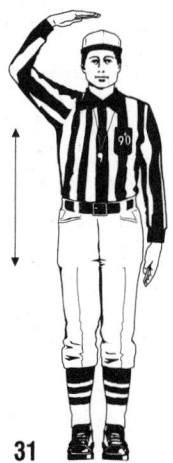

31

**UNCATCHABLE
FORWARD PASS**
Palm of right hand held
parallel to ground above head
and moved back and forth.

32

**TWELVE MEN IN OFFENSIVE HUDDLE
or TOO MANY MEN
ON THE FIELD**
Both hands on top of head.

33

FACEMASK
Grasping facemask with one
hand.

34

ILLEGAL SHIFT
Horizontal arcs with two hands.

35

**RESET PLAY CLOCK–
25 SECONDS**
Pump one arm vertically.

36

**RESET PLAY CLOCK–
40 SECONDS**
Pump two arms vertically.

NFL DIGEST OF RULES

This Digest of Rules of the National Football League has been prepared to aid players, fans, and members of the press, radio, and television media in their understanding of the game.

It is not meant to be a substitute for the official rule book. In any case of conflict between these explanations and the official rules, the rules always have precedence.

In order to make it easier to coordinate the information in this digest, the topics discussed generally follow the order of the rule book.

OFFICIALS' JURISDICTIONS, POSITIONS, AND DUTIES

Referee—General oversight and control of game. Gives signals for all fouls and is final authority for rule interpretations. Takes a position in backfield 10 to 12 yards behind line of scrimmage, favors right side (if quarterback is right-handed passer). Determines legality of snap, observes deep back(s) for legal motion. On running plays, observes quarterback during and after handoff, remains with him until action has cleared away, then proceeds downfield, checking on runner and contact behind him. When runner is downed, Referee determines forward progress from wing official and, if necessary, adjusts final position of ball.

On pass plays, drops back as quarterback begins to fade back, picks up legality of tackle on Head Linesman's side. Changes to complete concentration on quarterback as defenders approach. Primarily responsible to rule on possible roughing action on passer and if ball becomes loose, rules whether ball is free on a fumble or dead on an incomplete pass. Shares responsibility with Umpire, Linesman, and Line Judge on intentional grounding.

During kicking situations, Referee has primary responsibility to rule on kicker's actions and whether or not any subsequent contact by a defender is legal. During punt plays, Referee's position is parallel to kicker and wide. The Referee will announce on the microphone when each period is ended, penalties, a charged team time out, and when the two-minute warning for each half is reached.

Umpire—Primary responsibilities are to rule on players' conduct and actions on scrimmage line, as well as check on their equipment. Lines up approximately four to five yards downfield, varying position from the outside shoulder of one guard to outside shoulder of opposite guard. Looks for possible false start by offensive linemen. Observes legality of contact by both offensive linemen while blocking and by defensive players while they attempt to ward off blockers. Is prepared to call infractions if they occur on offense or defense. Moves forward to line of scrimmage when pass play develops in order to insure that interior linemen do not move illegally downfield. If offensive linemen indicate screen pass is to be attempted, Umpire shifts his attention toward screen side, picks up potential receiver in order to insure that he will legally be permitted to run his pattern and continues to rule on action of blockers. Umpire is to assist in ruling on incomplete or trapped passes when ball is thrown overhead or short. On field goal and try-kick attempts, he will become a second umpire with the Side Judge.

Head Linesman—Primarily responsible for ruling on offside, encroachment, and actions pertaining to scrimmage line prior to or at snap. Takes a position straddling the line of scrimmage. Keys on closest setback on his side of the field. On pass plays, Linesman is responsible to clear his receiver approximately seven yards downfield as he moves to a point five yards beyond the line. Linesman's secondary responsibility is to rule on any illegal action taken by defenders on any delay receiver moving downfield. Has full responsibility for ruling on sideline plays on his side, e.g., pass receiver or runner in or out of bounds. Together with Referee, Linesman is responsible for keeping track of number of downs and is in charge of mechanics of his chain crew in connection with its duties.

Linesman must be prepared to assist in determining forward progress by a runner on play directed toward middle or into his side zone. He, in turn, is to signal Referee or Umpire what forward

point ball has reached. Linesman is also responsible to rule on legality of action involving any receiver who approaches his side zone. He is to call pass interference when the infraction occurs and is to rule on legality of blockers and defenders on plays involving ball carriers, whether it is entirely a running play, a combination pass and run, or a play involving a kick. Also assists referee with intentional grounding.

Line Judge—Straddles line of scrimmage on side of field opposite Linesman. Keeps time of game as a backup for official clock operator. However, should official clock malfunction or be operated improperly, the time kept by the Line Judge is official. Along with Linesman is responsible for offside, encroachment, and actions pertaining to scrimmage line prior to or at snap. Line Judge keys on closest setback on his side of field. Line Judge is to observe his receiver until he moves at least seven yards downfield. He then moves toward backfield side, being especially alert to rule on any back in motion and on flight of ball when pass is made (he must rule whether forward or backward). Line Judge has primary responsibility to rule whether or not passer is behind or beyond line of scrimmage when pass is made. He also assists in observing actions by blockers and defenders who are on his side of field. After pass is thrown, Line Judge directs attention toward activities that occur in back of Umpire. During punting situations, Line Judge remains at line of scrimmage to be sure that only the end men move downfield until kick has been made. He also rules whether or not the kick crossed line and then observes action by members of the kicking team who are moving downfield to cover the kick. The Line Judge will advise the Referee when time has expired at the end of each period.

Field Judge—Operates on same side of field as Line Judge, 20 yards deep. Keys on widest receiver on his side. Concentrates on path of end or back, observing legality of his potential block(s) or of actions taken against him. Is prepared to rule from deep position on holding or illegal use of hands by end or back or on defensive infractions committed by player guarding him. Has primary responsibility to make decisions involving sideline on his side of field, e.g., pass receiver or runner in or out of bounds.

Field Judge makes decisions involving catching, recovery, or illegal touching of a loose ball beyond line of scrimmage. Rules on plays involving pass receiver, including legality of catch or pass interference. Assists in covering actions of runner, including blocks by teammates and that of defenders. Rules on blocking during punt returns and, together with Back Judge, rules whether or not field goal and try-kick attempts are successful.

Side Judge—Operates on same side of field as Linesman, 20 yards deep. Keys on widest receiver on his side. Concentrates on path of this receiver, observing legality of his potential block(s) or of actions taken against him. Is prepared to rule from deep position on holding or illegal use of hands by the receiver or on defensive infractions committed by player defending him. Has primary responsibility to make decisions involving sideline on his side of field, e.g., pass receiver or runner in or out of bounds.

Side Judge makes decisions involving catching, recovery, or illegal touching of a loose ball beyond line of scrimmage. Rules on plays involving pass receiver, including legality of catch or pass interference. Assists in covering actions of runner, including blocks by teammates and that of defenders and rules on blocking during punt returns. On field goals and try-kick attempts, he becomes a second umpire.

Back Judge—Takes a position 25 yards downfield. In general, favors the tight end's side of the field. Usually keys on tight end, concentrates on his path and observes legality of tight end's potential block(s) or of actions taken against him. Is prepared to rule from deep position on holding or illegal use of hands by end or back or on defensive infractions committed by player defending him.

Back Judge times interval between plays on 40/25-second clock plus intermission between two periods of each half. Makes decisions involving catching, recovery, or illegal touching of a loose ball beyond line of scrimmage. Is responsible to rule on plays involving end line. Calls pass interference, fair-catch infractions, and blocking during kick returns and, together with Field Judge, rules whether or not field goal and try-kick attempts are successful.

DEFINITIONS

1. **Chucking:** Warding off an opponent who is in front of a defender by contacting him with a quick extension of arm or arms, followed by the return of arm(s) to a flexed position, thereby breaking the original contact.
2. **Clipping:** Throwing the body across the back of an opponent's leg or hitting him from the back below the waist while moving up from behind unless the opponent is a runner or the contact is above the knee in close line play.
3. **Close Line Play:** The area between the positions normally occupied by the offensive tackles, extending three yards on each side of the line of scrimmage. It is legal to clip above the knee.
4. **Crackback:** Eligible receivers who take or move to a position more than two yards outside the tackle or a player in a backfielf position may not block an opponent below the waist toward the ball at the snap and within five yards of the line of scrimmage.
5. **Dead Ball:** Ball not in play.
6. **Double Foul:** A foul by each team during the same down.
7. **Down:** The period of action that starts when the ball is put in play and ends when it is dead.
8. **Encroachment:** When a defensive player enters the neutral zone and makes contact with an opponent before the ball is snapped.
9. **Fair Catch:** An unhindered catch of a kick by a member of the receiving team who must raise one arm a full length above his head and wave his arm from side to side while the kick is in flight.
10. **Foul:** Any violation of a playing rule.
11. **Free Kick:** A kickoff or safety kick. It may be a placekick, dropkick, or punt, except a punt may not be used on a kickoff following a touchdown, successful field goal, or to begin each half or overtime period. A tee cannot be used on a fair-catch or safety kick.
12. **Fumble:** The unintentional loss of player possession of the ball.
13. **Game Clock:** Scoreboard game clock.
14. **Impetus:** The action of a player that gives momentum to the ball and sends it into the end zone.
15. **Live Ball:** A ball legally free-kicked or snapped. It continues in play until the down ends.
16. **Loose Ball:** A live ball not in possession of any player.
17. **Muff:** The touching of a loose ball by a player in an unsuccessful attempt to obtain possession.
18. **Neutral Zone:** The space the length of a ball between the two scrimmage lines. The offensive team and defensive team must remain behind their end of the ball.
    Exception: The offensive player who snaps the ball.
19. **Offside:** A player is offside when any part of his body is beyond his scrimmage or free kick line when the ball is snapped or kicked. Exception: Snapper, holder of placekick or kicker.
20. **Own Goal:** The goal a team is defending.
21. **Play Clock:** 40/25 second clock.
22. **Pocket Area:** Applies from a point two yards outside of either offensive tackle and includes the tight end if he drops off the line of scrimmage to pass protect. Pocket extends longitudinally behind the line back to offensive team's own end line. For purposes of intentional grounding, the pocket is considered tackle to tackle.
23. **Possession of a Pass:** When a player controls the ball throughout the act of clearly touching both feet, or any other part of his body other than his hand(s), to the ground inbounds.

24. **Post-Possession Foul:** A foul by the receiving team that occurs after a ball is legally kicked from scrimmage prior to possession changing. The ball must cross the line of scrimmage and the receiving team must retain the kicked ball unless it is part of a double foul.
25. **Punt:** A kick made when a player drops the ball and kicks it while it is in flight.
26. **Safety:** The situation in which the ball is dead on or behind a team's own goal if the impetus comes from a player on that team. Two points are scored for the opposing team.
27. **Shift:** The movement of two or more offensive players at the same time before the snap.
28. **Striking:** The act of swinging, clubbing, or propelling the arm or forearm in contacting an opponent.
29. **Sudden Death:** The continuation of a tied game into sudden death overtime in which the team scoring first (by safety, field goal, or touchdown) wins.
30. **Touchback:** When a ball is dead on or behind a team's own goal line, provided the impetus came from an opponent and provided it is not a touchdown or a missed field goal attempt when the ball was kicked outside the 20-yard line.
31. **Touchdown:** When any part of the ball, legally in possession of a player inbounds, breaks the plane of the opponent's goal line, provided it is not a touchback.
32. **Unsportsmanlike Conduct:** Any act contrary to the generally understood principles of sportsmanship.

SUMMARY OF PENALTIES
Automatic First Down
1. Awarded to offensive team on all <u>defensive fouls</u> with these exceptions:
   (a) Offside.
   (b) Encroachment.
   (c) Delay of game.
   (d) Illegal substitution.
   (e) Excessive time out(s).
   (f) Incidental grasp of facemask.
   (g) Neutral zone infraction.
   (h) Running into the kicker.
   (i) More than 11 players on the field at the snap for either team.

Five Yards
1. Defensive holding or illegal use of hands (automatic first down).
2. Delay of game on offense or defense.
3. Delay of kickoff.
4. Encroachment.
5. Excessive time out(s).
6. False start.
7. Illegal formation.
8. Illegal shift.
9. Illegal motion.
10. Illegal substitution.
11. First onside kickoff out of bounds between goal lines and untouched or last touched by kickers.
12. Invalid fair catch signal.
13. More than 11 players on the field at snap for either team.
14. Less than seven men on offensive line at snap.
15. Offside.
16. Failure to pause one second after shift or huddle.
17. Running into kicker.
18. More than one man in motion at snap.
19. Grasping facemask of the ball carrier or quarterback.
20. Player out of bounds at snap.
21. Ineligible member(s) of kicking team going beyond line of scrimmage before ball is kicked.
22. Illegal return.
23. Failure to report change of eligibility.
24. Neutral zone infraction.

DIGEST OF RULES

25. Loss of team time out(s) or five-yard penalty on the defense for excessive crowd noise. Offensive team's quarterback can be penalized if he does not make every effort to put the ball in play.
26. Ineligible player downfield during passing down.
27. Second forward pass behind the line.
28. Forward pass is first touched by eligible receiver who has gone out of bounds and returned.
29. Forward pass touches or is caught by an ineligible receiver on or behind line.
30. Forward pass thrown from behind line of scrimmage after ball once crossed the line.
31. Kicking team player voluntarily out of bounds during a punt.
32. Twelve (12) men in the huddle.

Ten Yards
1. Offensive pass interference.
2. Holding, illegal use of hands, arms, or body by offense.
3. Tripping by a member of either team.
4. Helping the runner.
5. Deliberately batting or punching a loose ball.
6. Deliberately kicking a loose ball.
7. Illegal block above the waist.

Fifteen Yards
1. Chop block.
2. Clipping below the waist.
3. Fair catch interference.
4. Illegal crackback block by offense.
5. Piling on.
6. Roughing the kicker.
7. Roughing the passer.
8. Twisting, turning, or pulling an opponent by the facemask.
9. Unnecessary roughness.
10. Unsportsmanlike conduct.
11. Delay of game at start of either half.
12. Illegal low block.
13. A tackler using his helmet to butt, spear, or ram an opponent.
14. Any player who uses the top of his helmet unnecessarily.
15. A punter, placekicker, or holder who simulates being roughed by a defensive player.
16. Leaping.
17. Leverage.
18. Any player who removes his helmet after a play while on the field.
19. Taunting.

Five Yards and Loss of Down (Combination Penalty)
1. Forward pass thrown from beyond line of scrimmage.

Ten Yards and Loss of Down (Combination Penalty)
1. Intentional grounding of forward pass (safety if passer is in own end zone). If foul occurs more than 10 yards behind line, play results in loss of down at spot of foul.

Fifteen Yards and Loss of Coin Toss Option
1. Team's late arrival on the field prior to scheduled kickoff.
2. Captains not appearing for coin toss.

Fifteen Yards (and disqualification if flagrant)
1. Striking opponent with fist.
2. Kicking or kneeing opponent.
3. Striking opponent on head or neck with forearm, elbow, or hands whether or not the initial contact is made below the neck area.
4. Roughing kicker.
5. Roughing passer.
6. Malicious unnecessary roughness.
7. Unsportsmanlike conduct.
8. Palpably unfair act. (Distance penalty determined by the Referee after consultation with other officials.)

Fifteen Yards and Automatic Disqualification
1. Using a helmet (not worn) as a weapon.
2. Striking or purposely shoving a game official.

Suspension From Game For One Down
1. Illegal equipment. (Player may return after one down when legally equipped.)

Touchdown Awarded (Palpably Unfair Act)
1. When Referee determines a palpably unfair act deprived a team of a touchdown. (Example: Player comes off bench and tackles runner apparently en route to touchdown.)

FIELD
1. Sidelines and end lines are out of bounds. The goal line is actually in the end zone. A player with the ball in his possession scores a touchdown when the ball is on, above, or over the goal line.
2. The field is rimmed by a white border, six feet wide, along the sidelines. All of this is out of bounds.
3. The hashmarks (inbound lines) are 70 feet, 9 inches from each sideline.
4. Goal posts must be single-standard type, offset from the end line and painted bright gold. The goal posts must be 18 feet, 6 inches wide and the top face of the crossbar must be 10 feet above the ground. Vertical posts extend at least 30 feet above the crossbar. A ribbon 4 inches by 42 inches long is to be attached to the top of each post. The actual goal is the plane extending indefinitely above the crossbar and between the outer edges of the posts.
5. The field is 360 feet long and 160 feet wide. The end zones are 30 feet deep. The line used in try-for-point plays is two yards out from the goal line.
6. Chain crew members and ball boys must be uniformly identifiable.
7. All clubs must use standardized sideline markers. Pylons must be used for goal line and end line markings.
8. End zone markings and club identification at 50 yard line must be approved by the Commissioner to avoid any confusion as to delineation of goal lines, sidelines, and end lines.

BALL
1. The home club shall have 36 balls for outdoor games and 24 for indoor games available for testing with a pressure gauge by the referee two hours prior to the starting time of the game to meet with League requirements. Twelve (12) new footballs, sealed in a special box and shipped by the manufacturer, will be opened in the officials' locker room two hours prior to the starting time of the game. These balls are to be specially marked with the letter "k" and used exclusively for the kicking game.

COIN TOSS
1. The toss of coin will take place within three minutes of kickoff in center of field. The toss will be called by the visiting captain before the coin is flipped. The winner may choose one of two privileges and the loser gets the other:
(a) Receive or kick
(b) Goal his team will defend
2. Immediately prior to the start of the second half, the captains of both teams must inform the officials of their respective choices. The loser of the original coin toss gets first choice.

TIMING
1. The stadium game clock is official. In case it stops or is operating incorrectly, the Line Judge takes over the official timing on the field.
2. Each period is 15 minutes. The intermission between the periods is two minutes. Halftime is 12 minutes, unless otherwise specified.
3. On charged team time outs, the Back Judge starts watch and blows whistle after 1 minute 50 seconds, unless television does not utilize the time for commercial. In this case the length of the time out is reduced to 30 seconds.

4. The Referee will allow necessary time to attend to an injured player, or repair a legal player's equipment.
5. Each team is allowed three time outs each half.
6. Time between plays will be 40 seconds from the end of a given play until the snap of the ball for the next play, or a 25-second interval after certain administrative stoppages and game delays.
7. Clock will start running when ball is snapped following all changes of team possession.
8. With the exception of the last two minutes of the first half and the last five minutes of the second half, the game clock will be restarted following a player going out of bounds on a play from scrimmage, or after declined penalties when appropriate on the referee's signal.
9. Consecutive team time outs can be taken by opposing teams but the length of the second time out will be reduced to 30 seconds.
10. On kickoff, clock does not start until the ball has been legally touched by player of either team in the field of play.

SUDDEN DEATH
1. The sudden death system of determining the winner shall prevail when score is tied at the end of the regulation playing time of all NFL games. The team scoring first during overtime play shall be the winner and the game automatically ends upon any score (by safety, field goal, or touchdown) or when a score is awarded by Referee for a palpably unfair act.
2. At the end of regulation time the Referee will immediately toss coin at center of field in accordance with rules pertaining to the usual pregame toss. The captain of the visiting team will call the toss prior to the coin being flipped.
3. Following a three-minute intermission after the end of the regulation game, play will be continued in 15-minute periods or until there is a score. There is a two-minute intermission between subsequent periods. The teams change goals at the start of each period. Each team has three time outs per half and all general timing provisions apply as during a regular game. Disqualified players are not allowed to return.
   Exception: In preseason and regular season games there shall be a maximum of 15 minutes of sudden death with two time outs instead of three. General provisions that apply for the fourth quarter will prevail. Try not attempted if touchdown scored.

TIMING IN FINAL TWO MINUTES OF EACH HALF
1. A team cannot buy an excess time out for a penalty. However, a fourth time out is allowed without penalty for an injured player, who must be removed immediately. A fifth time out or more is allowed for an injury and a five-yard penalty is assessed.
2. If the defensive team is behind in the score and commits a foul when it has no time outs left in the final 40 seconds of either half, the offensive team can decline the penalty for the foul and have the time on the clock expire.
3. Fouls that occur in the last five minutes of the fourth quarter as well as the last two minutes of the first half will result in the clock starting on the snap.

TRY
1. After a touchdown, the scoring team is allowed a try during one scrimmage down. The ball may be spotted anywhere between the inbounds lines, two or more yards from the goal line. The successful conversion counts one point by kick; two points for a successful conversion by touchdown; or one point for a safety.
2. The defensive team never can score on a try. As soon as defense gets possession or the kick is blocked or a touchdown is not scored, the try is over.
3. Any distance penalty for fouls committed by the defense that prevent the try from being attempted can be enforced on the succeeding try or succeeding kickoff. Any foul committed on a successful try will result in a distance penalty being assessed on the ensuing kickoff.
4. Only the fumbling player can recover and advance a fumble during a try.

PLAYERS-SUBSTITUTIONS
1. Each team is permitted 11 men on the field at the snap.
2. Unlimited substitution is permitted. However, players may enter the field only when the ball is dead. Players who have been substituted for are not permitted to linger on the field. Such lingering will be interpreted as unsportsmanlike conduct.
3. Players leaving the game must be out of bounds on their own side, clearing the field between the end lines, before a snap or free kick. If player crosses end line leaving field, it is a delay of game (five-yard penalty).
4. Offensive substitutes who remain in the game must move onto the field as far as the inside of the field numerals before moving to a wide position.
5. With the exception of the last two minutes of either half, the offensive team, while in the process of substitution or simulated substitution, is prohibited from rushing quickly to the line and snapping the ball with the obvious attempt to cause a defensive foul; i.e., too many men on the field.
6. There never can be 12 or more players in the offensive huddle.

KICKOFF
1. The kickoff shall be from the kicking team's 30-yard line at the start of each half and after a field goal and try. A kickoff is one type of free kick.
2. A one-inch tee may be used (no tee permitted for field goal, safety kick, or try attempt) on a kickoff. The ball is put in play by a placekick.
3. A kickoff may not score a field goal.
4. A kickoff is illegal unless it travels 10 yards OR is touched by the receiving team. Once the ball is touched by the receiving team or has gone 10 yards, it is a free ball. Receivers may recover and advance. Kicking team may recover but NOT advance UNLESS receiver had possession and lost the ball.
5. When a kickoff goes out of bounds between the goal lines without being touched by the receiving team, the ball belongs to the receivers 30 yards from the spot of the kick or at the out-of-bounds spot unless the ball went out-of-bounds the first time an onside kick was attempted. In this case, the kicking team is penalized five yards and the ball must be kicked again.
6. When a kickoff goes out of bounds between the goal lines and is touched last by receiving team, it is receiver's ball at out-of-bounds spot.
7. If the kicking team either illegally kicks off out of bounds or is guilty of a short free kick on two or more consecutive onside kicks, receivers may take possession of the ball at the dead ball spot, out-of-bounds spot, or spot of illegal touch.

SAFETY
1. In addition to a kickoff, the other free kick is a kick after a safety (safety kick). A punt may be used (a punt may not be used on a kickoff).
2. On a safety kick, the team scored upon puts ball in play by a punt, dropkick, or placekick without tee. No score can be made on a free kick following a safety, even if a series of penalties places team in position. (A field goal can be scored only on a play from scrimmage or a free kick after a fair catch.)

FAIR CATCH KICK
1. After a fair catch, the receiving team has the option to put the ball in play by a snap or a fair catch kick (field goal attempt),

with fair catch kick lines established ten yards apart. All general rules apply as for a field goal attempt from scrimmage. The clock starts when the ball is kicked. (No tee permitted.)

FIELD GOAL

1. All field goals attempted (kicker) and missed from beyond the 20-yard line will result in the defensive team taking possession of the ball at the spot of the kick. On any field goal attempted and missed where the spot of the kick is on or inside the 20-yard line, ball will revert to defensive team at the 20-yard line.

SAFETY

1. The important factor in a safety is impetus. Two points are scored for the opposing team when the ball is dead on or behind a team's own goal line if the impetus came from a player on that team.

Examples of Safety:

(a) Blocked punt goes out of kicking team's end zone. Impetus was provided by punting team. The block only changes direction of ball, not impetus.

(b) Ball carrier retreats from field of play into his own end zone and is downed. Ball carrier provides impetus.

(c) Offensive team commits a foul and spot of enforcement is behind its own goal line.

(d) Player on receiving team muffs punt and, trying to get ball, forces or illegally kicks (creating new impetus) it into end zone where it goes out of the end zone or is recovered by a member of the receiving team in the end zone.

Examples of Non-Safety:

(a) Player intercepts a pass with both feet inbounds in the field of play and his momentum carries him into his own end zone. Ball is put in play at spot of interception.

(b) Player intercepts a pass in his own end zone and is downed in the end zone, even after recovering in the end zone. Impetus came from passing team, not from defense. (Touchback)

(c) Player passes from behind his own goal line. Opponent bats down ball in end zone. (Incomplete pass)

MEASURING

1. The forward point of the ball is used when measuring.

POSITION OF PLAYERS AT SNAP

1. Offensive team must have at least seven players on line.

2. Offensive players, not on line, must be at least one yard back at snap.
   (Exception: player who takes snap.)

3. No interior lineman may move abruptly after taking or simulating a three-point stance.

4. No player of either team may enter neutral zone before snap.

5. No player of offensive team may charge or move abruptly, after assuming set position, in such manner as to lead defense to believe snap has started. No player of the defensive team within one yard of the line of scrimmage may make an abrupt movement in an attempt to cause the offense to false start.

6. If a player changes his eligibility, the Referee must alert the defensive captain after player has reported to him.

7. All players of offensive team must be stationary at snap, except one back who may be in motion parallel to scrimmage line or backward (not forward).

8. After a shift or huddle all players on offensive team must come to an absolute stop for at least one second with no movement of hands, feet, head, or swaying of body.

9. Quarterbacks can be called for a false start penalty (five yards) if their actions are judged to be an obvious attempt to draw an opponent offside.

10. Offensive linemen are permitted to interlock legs.

USE OF HANDS, ARMS, AND BODY

1. No player on offense may assist a runner except by blocking for him. There shall be no interlocking interference.

2. A runner may ward off opponents with his hands and arms but no other player on offense may use hands or arms to obstruct an opponent by grasping with hands, pushing, or encircling any part of his body during a block. Hands (open or closed) can be thrust forward to initially contact an opponent on or outside the opponent's frame, but the blocker immediately must work to bring his hands on or inside the frame.
   Note: Pass blocking: Hand(s) thrust forward that slip outside the body of the defender will be legal if blocker immediately worked to bring them back inside. Hand(s) or arm(s) that encircle a defender—i.e., hook an opponent—are to be considered illegal and officials are to call a foul for holding. Blocker cannot use his hands or arms to push from behind, hang onto, or encircle an opponent in a manner that restricts his movement as the play develops.

3. Hands cannot be thrust forward above the frame to contact an opponent on the neck, face or head.
   Note: The frame is defined as the part of the opponent's body below the neck that is presented to the blocker.

4. A defensive player may not tackle or hold an opponent other than a runner. Otherwise, he may use his hands, arms, or body only:

   (a) To defend or protect himself against an obstructing opponent.
   Exception: An eligible receiver is considered to be an obstructing opponent ONLY to a point five yards beyond the line of scrimmage unless the player who receives the snap clearly demonstrates no further intention to pass the ball. Within this five-yard zone, a defensive player may chuck an eligible player in front of him. A defensive player is allowed to maintain continuous and unbroken contact within the five-yard zone until a point when the receiver is even with the defender. The defensive player cannot use his hands or arms to push from behind, hang onto, or encircle an eligible receiver in a manner that restricts movement as the play develops. Beyond this five-yard limitation, a defender may use his hands or arms ONLY to defend or protect himself against impending contact caused by a receiver. In such reaction, the defender may not contact a receiver who attempts to take a path to evade him.

   (b) To push or pull opponent out of the way on line of scrimmage.

   (c) In actual attempt to get at or tackle runner.

   (d) To push or pull opponent out of the way in a legal attempt to recover a loose ball.

   (e) During a legal block on an opponent who is not an eligible pass receiver.

   (f) When legally blocking an eligible pass receiver above the waist.
   Exception: Eligible receivers lined up within two yards of the tackle, whether on or immediately behind the line, may be blocked below the waist at or behind the line of scrimmage. NO eligible receiver may be blocked below the waist after he goes beyond the line. (Illegal cut)
   Note: Once the quarterback hands off or pitches the ball to a back, or if the quarterback leaves the pocket area, the restrictions (illegal chuck, illegal cut) on the defensive team relative to the offensive receivers will end, provided the ball is not in the air.

5. A defensive player may not contact an opponent above the shoulders with the palm of his hand except to ward him off on the line. This exception is permitted only if it is not a repeated

act against the same opponent during any one contact. In all other cases the palms may be used on head, neck, or face only to ward off or push an opponent in legal attempt to get at the ball.

6. Any offensive player who pretends to possess the ball or to whom a teammate pretends to give the ball may be tackled provided he is crossing his scrimmage line between the ends of a normal tight offensive line.

7. An offensive player who lines up more than two yards outside his own tackle or a player who, at the snap, is in a backfield position and subsequently takes a position more than two yards outside a tackle may not clip an opponent anywhere nor may he contact an opponent below the waist if the blocker is moving toward the ball and if contact is made within an area five yards on either side of the line. (crackback)

8. A player of either team may block at any time provided it is not pass interference, fair catch interference, or unnecessary roughness.

9. A player may not bat or punch:
   (a) A loose ball (in field of play) toward his opponent's goal line or in any direction in either end zone.
   (b) A ball in player possession.
   Note: If there is any question as to whether a defender is stripping or batting a ball in player possession, the official(s) will rule the action as a legal act (stripping the ball).
   Exception: A forward or backward pass may be batted, tipped, or deflected in any direction at any time by either the offense or the defense.
   Note: A pass in flight that is controlled or caught may only be thrown backward, if it is thrown forward it is considered an illegal bat.

10. No player may deliberately kick any ball except as a punt, dropkick, or placekick.

FORWARD PASS

1. A forward pass may be touched or caught by any eligible receiver. All members of the defensive team are eligible. Eligible receivers on the offensive team are players on either end of line (other than center, guard, or tackle) or players at least one yard behind the line at the snap. A T-formation quarterback is not eligible to receive a forward pass during a play from scrimmage.
   Exception: T-formation quarterback becomes eligible if pass is previously touched by an eligible receiver.

2. An offensive team may make only one forward pass during each play from scrimmage (Loss of 5 yards).

3. The passer must be behind his line of scrimmage (Loss of down and five yards, enforced from the spot of pass).

4. Any eligible offensive player may catch a forward pass. If a pass is touched by one eligible offensive player and touched or caught by a second offensive player, pass completion is legal. Further, all offensive players become eligible once a pass is touched by an eligible receiver or any defensive player.

5. The rules concerning a forward pass and ineligible receivers:
   (a) If ball is touched accidentally by an ineligible receiver on or behind his line: loss of five yards.
   (b) If ineligible receiver is illegally downfield: loss of five yards.
   (c) If touched or caught (intentionally or accidentally) by ineligible receiver beyond the line: loss of 5 yards.

6. The player who first controls and continues to maintain control of a pass will be awarded the ball even though his opponent later establishes joint control of the ball.

7. Any forward pass becomes incomplete and ball is dead if:
   (a) Pass hits the ground or goes out of bounds.
   (b) Pass hits the goal post or the crossbar of either team.

8. A forward pass is complete when a receiver clearly possesses the pass and touches the ground with both feet inbounds while in possession of the ball. If a receiver would have landed inbounds with both feet but is carried or pushed out of bounds while maintaining possession of the ball, pass is complete at the out-of-bounds spot.

9. If a personal foul is committed by the defense prior to the completion of a pass, the penalty is 15 yards from the spot where ball becomes dead.

10. If a personal foul is committed by the offense prior to the completion of a pass, the penalty is 15 yards from the previous line of scrimmage.

INTENTIONAL GROUNDING OF FORWARD PASS

1. Intentional grounding of a forward pass is a foul: loss of down and 10 yards from previous spot if passer is in the field of play or loss of down at the spot of the foul if it occurs more than 10 yards behind the line or safety if passer is in his own end zone when ball is released.

2. Intentional grounding will be called when a passer, facing an imminent loss of yardage due to pressure from the defense, throws a forward pass without a realistic chance of completion.

3. Intentional grounding will not be called when a passer, while out of the pocket and facing an imminent loss of yardage, throws a pass that lands at or beyond the line of scrimmage, even if no offensive player(s) have a realistic chance to catch the ball (including if the ball lands out of bounds over the sideline or end line).

PROTECTION OF PASSER

1. By interpretation, a pass begins when the passer—with possession of ball—starts to bring his hand forward. If ball strikes ground after this action has begun, play is ruled an incomplete pass. If passer loses control of ball prior to his bringing his hand forward, play is ruled a fumble.

2. When a passer is holding the ball to pass it forward, any intentional movement forward of his hand starts a forward pass. If a defensive player contacts the passer or the ball after forward movement begins, and the ball leaves the passer's hand, a forward pass is ruled, regardless of where the ball strikes the ground or a player.

3. No defensive player may run into a passer of a legal forward pass after the ball has left his hand (15 yards). The Referee must determine whether opponent had a reasonable chance to stop his momentum during an attempt to block the pass or tackle the passer while he still had the ball.

4. No defensive player who has an unrestricted path to the quarterback may hit him flagrantly in the area of the knee(s) or below when approaching in any direction.

5. Officials are to blow the play dead as soon as the quarterback is clearly in the grasp and control of any tackler, and his safety is in jeopardy.

6. No defensive player may hit the quarterback in the head, face, or neck.

PASS INTERFERENCE

1. There shall be no interference with a forward pass thrown from behind the line. The restriction for the passing team starts with the snap. The restriction on the defensive team starts when the ball leaves the passer's hand. Both restrictions end when the ball is touched by anyone.

2. The penalty for defensive pass interference is an automatic first down at the spot of the foul. If interference is in the end zone, it is first down for the offense on the defense's 1-yard line. If previous spot was inside the defense's 1-yard line, penalty is half the distance to the goal line.

3. The penalty for offensive pass interference is 10 yards from the previous spot.

4. It is pass interference by either team when any player movement beyond the line of scrimmage significantly hinders the progress of an eligible player of such player's opportunity

to catch the ball. Offensive pass interference rules apply from the time the ball is snapped until the ball is touched. Defensive pass interference rules apply from the time the ball is thrown until the ball is touched.

Actions that constitute defensive pass interference include but are not limited to:

(a) Contact by a defender who is not playing the ball and such contact restricts the receiver's opportunity to make the catch.

(b) Playing through the back of a receiver in an attempt to make a play on the ball.

(c) Grabbing a receiver's arm(s) in such a manner that restricts his opportunity to catch a pass.

(d) Extending an arm across the body of a receiver thus restricting his ability to catch a pass, regardless of whether the defender is playing the ball.

(e) Cutting off the path of a receiver by making contact with him without playing the ball.

(f) Hooking a receiver in an attempt to get to the ball in such a manner that it causes the receiver's body to turn prior to the ball arriving.

Actions that do not constitute pass interference include but are not limited to:

(a) Incidental contact by a defender's hands, arms, or body when both players are competing for the ball, or neither player is looking for the ball. If there is any question whether contact is incidental, the ruling shall be no interference.

(b) Inadvertent tangling of feet when both players are playing the ball or neither player is playing the ball.

(c) Contact that would normally be considered pass interference, but the ball is clearly uncatchable by the involved players.

(d) Laying a hand on a receiver that does not restrict the receiver in an attempt to make a play on the ball.

(e) Contact by a defender who has gained position on a receiver in an attempt to catch the ball.

Actions that constitute offensive pass interference include but are not limited to:

(a) Blocking downfield by an offensive player prior to the ball being touched.

(b) Initiating contact with a defender by shoving or pushing off thus creating a separation in an attempt to catch a pass.

(c) Driving through a defender who has established a position on the field.

Actions that do not constitute offensive pass interference include but are not limited to:

(a) Incidental contact by a receiver's hands, arms, or body when both players are competing for the ball or neither player is looking for the ball.

(b) Inadvertent touching of feet when both players are playing the ball or neither player is playing the ball.

(c) Contact that would normally be considered pass interference, but the ball is clearly uncatchable by involved players.

Note 1: If there is any question whether player contact is incidental, the ruling should be no interference.

Note 2: Defensive players have as much right to the path of the ball as eligible offensive players.

Note 3: Pass interference for both teams ends when the pass is touched.

Note 4: There can be no pass interference at or behind the line of scrimmage, but defensive actions such as tackling a receiver can still result in a 5-yard penalty for defensive holding, if accepted.

Note 5: Whenever a team presents an apparent punting formation, defensive pass interference is not to be called for action on the end man on the line of scrimmage, or an eligible receiver behind the line of scrimmage who is aligned or in motion more than one yard outside the end man on the line. Defensive holding, such as tackling a receiver, still can be called and result in a 5-yard penalty and automatic first down from the previous spot, if accepted. Offensive pass interference rules still apply.

BACKWARD PASS

1. Any pass not forward is regarded as a backward pass. A pass parallel to the line is a backward pass. A runner may pass backward at any time.

2. A backward pass that strikes the ground can be recovered and advanced by either team.

3. A backward pass caught in the air can be advanced by either team.

4. A backward pass in flight may not be batted forward by an offensive player.

FUMBLE

1. The distinction between a fumble and a muff should be kept in mind in considering rules about fumbles. A fumble is the loss of player possession of the ball. A muff is the touching of a loose ball by a player in an unsuccessful attempt to obtain possession.

2. A fumble may be advanced by any player on either team regardless of whether recovered before or after ball hits the ground.

3. A fumble that goes forward and out of bounds will return to the fumbling team at the spot of the fumble unless the ball goes out of bounds in the opponent's end zone. In this case, it is a touchback.

4. On a play from scrimmage, if an offensive player fumbles anywhere on the field during fourth down, only the fumbling player is permitted to recover and/or advance the ball. If any player fumbles after the two-minute warning in a half, only the fumbling player is permitted to recover and/or advance the ball. If recovered by any other offensive player, the ball is dead at the spot of the fumble unless it is recovered behind the spot of the fumble. In that case, the ball is dead at the spot of recovery. Any defensive player may recover and/or advance any fumble at any time.

5. A muffed hand-to-hand snap from center is treated as a fumble.

KICKS FROM SCRIMMAGE

1. Any kick from scrimmage must be made from behind the line to be legal.

2. Any punt or missed field goal that touches a goal post is dead.

3. During a kick from scrimmage, only the end men, as eligible receivers on the line of scrimmage at the time of the snap, are permitted to go beyond the line before the ball is kicked.
   Exception: An eligible receiver who, at the snap, is aligned or in motion behind the line and more than one yard outside the end man on his side of the line, clearly making him the outside receiver, replaces that end man as the player eligible to go downfield after the snap. All other members of the kicking team must remain at the line of scrimmage until the ball has been kicked.

4. Any punt that is blocked and does not cross the line of scrimmage can be recovered and advanced by either team. However, if offensive team recovers it must make the yardage necessary for its first down to retain possession if punt was on fourth down.

5. The kicking team may never advance its own kick even though legal recovery is made beyond the line of scrimmage. Possession only.

6. A member of the receiving team may not run into or rough a kicker who kicks from behind his line unless contact is:
   (a) Incidental to and after he had touched ball in flight.
   (b) Caused by kicker's own motions.

(c) Occurs during a quick kick, or a kick made after a run behind the line, or after kicker recovers a loose ball on the ground. Ball is loose when kicker muffs snap or snap hits ground.

(d) Defender is blocked into kicker.

The penalty for running into the kicker is 5 yards. For roughing the kicker: 15 yards, an automatic first down and disqualification if flagrant.

7. If a member of the kicking team attempting to down the ball on or inside opponent's 5-yard line carries the ball into the end zone, it is a touchback.

8. Fouls during a punt are enforced from the previous spot (line of scrimmage).
Exception: Illegal touching, fair-catch interference, invalid fair-catch signal, or personal foul (blocking after a fair-catch signal).

9. While the ball is in the air or rolling on the ground following a punt or field-goal attempt and receiving team commits a foul only before or after gaining possession, receiving team will retain possession and will be penalized for its foul.

10. It will be illegal for a defensive player to jump or stand on any player, or be picked up by a teammate or to use a hand or hands on a teammate to gain additional height in an attempt to block a kick (Penalty: 15 yards, unsportsmanlike conduct).

11. A punted ball remains a kicked ball until it is declared dead or in possession of either team.

12. Any member of the punting team may down the ball anywhere in the field of play. However, it is illegal touching (Official's time out and receiver's ball at spot of illegal touching). This foul does not offset any foul by receivers during the down.

13. Defensive team may advance all kicks from scrimmage (including unsuccessful field goal) whether or not ball crosses defensive team's goal line. Rules pertaining to kicks from scrimmage apply until defensive team gains possession.

14. When a team presents a punt formation, defensive pass interference is not to be called for actions on the widest player eligible to go beyond line. Defensive holding may be called.

FAIR CATCH

1. The member of the receiving team must raise one arm a full length above his head and wave it from side to side while kick is in flight. (Failure to give proper sign: receivers' ball five yards behind spot of signal.) **Note:** It is legal for the receiver to shield his eyes from the sun by raising one hand no higher than the helmet.

2. No opponent may interfere with the fair catcher, the ball, or his path to the ball. Penalty: 15 yards from spot of foul and fair catch is awarded.

3. A player who signals for a fair catch is not required to catch the ball. However, if a player signals for a fair catch, he may not block or initiate contact with any player on the kicking team until the ball touches a player. Penalty: snap 15 yards.

4. If ball is touched by member of kicking team in flight, fair catch signal is off and all rules for a kicked ball apply.

5. Any undue advance by a fair catch receiver is delay of game. No specific distance is specified for undue advance as ball is dead at spot of catch. If player comes to a reasonable stop, no penalty. For penalty, five yards.

6. If time expires while ball is in play and a fair catch is awarded, receiving team may choose to extend the period with one fair catch kick down. However, placekicker may not use tee.

FOUL ON LAST PLAY OF HALF OR GAME

1. On a foul by defense on last play of half or game, the down is replayed if penalty is accepted.

2. On a foul by the offense on last play of half or game, the down is not replayed and the play in which the foul is committed is nullified.
Exception: Fair catch interference, foul following change of possession, illegal touching. No score by offense counts.

SPOT OF ENFORCEMENT OF FOUL

1. There are four basic spots at which a penalty for a foul is enforced:
   (a) Spot of foul: The spot where the foul is committed.
   (b) Previous spot: The spot where the ball was put in play.
   (c) Spot of snap, backward pass or fumble: The spot where the foul occurred or the spot where the penalty is to be enforced.
   (d) Succeeding spot: The spot where the ball next would be put in play if no distance penalty were to be enforced.
   Exception: If foul occurs after a touchdown and before the whistle for a try, succeeding spot is spot of next kickoff.

2. All fouls committed by offensive team behind the line of scrimmage (except in the end zone) shall be penalized from the previous spot. If the foul is in the end zone, it is a safety.

3. When spot of enforcement for fouls involving defensive holding or illegal use of hands by the defense is behind the line of scrimmage, any penalty yardage to be assessed on that play shall be measured from the line if the foul occurred beyond the line.

DOUBLE FOUL

1. If there is a double foul during a down in which there is a change of possession, the team last gaining possession may keep the ball unless its foul was committed prior to the change of possession.

2. If double foul occurs after a change of possession, the defensive team retains the ball at the spot of its foul or dead ball spot.

3. If one of the fouls of a double foul involves disqualification, that player must be removed, but no penalty yardage is to be assessed.

4. If the kickers foul during a kickoff, punt, safety kick, or field-goal attempt before possession changes, the receivers will have the option of replaying the down at the previous spot (offsetting fouls), or keeping the ball after enforcement for its fouls.

PENALTY ENFORCED ON FOLLOWING KICKOFF

1. When a team scores by touchdown, field goal, extra point, or safety and either team commits a personal foul, unsportsmanlike conduct, or obvious unfair act during the down, the penalty will be assessed on the following kickoff.

EMERGENCIES AND UNFAIR ACTS
Emergencies—Policy

The National Football League requires all League personnel, including game officials, League office employees, players, coaches, and other club employees to use best effort to see that each game—preseason, regular season, and postseason—is played to its conclusion. The League recognizes, however, that emergencies may arise that make a game's completion impossible or inadvisable. Such circumstances may include, but are not limited to, severely inclement weather, natural or manmade disaster, power failure, and spectator interference. Games should be suspended, cancelled, postponed, or terminated when circumstances exist such that comencement or continuation of play would pose a threat to the safety of participants or spectators.

Authority of Commissioner's Office

1. Authority to cancel, postpone, or terminate games is vested only in the Commissioner and the League President (other League office representatives and referees may suspend play temporarily; see point No. 3 under this section and point No. 1 under "Authority of Referee" below). The following definitions apply:

- **Cancel.** To cancel a game is to nullify it either before or after it begins and to make no provision for rescheduling it or for including its score or other performance statistics in League records.
- **Postpone.** To postpone a game is (a) to defer its starting time to a later date, or (b) to suspend it after play has begun and to make provision to resume at a later date with all scores and other performance statistics up to the point of postponement added to those achieved in the resumed portion of the game.
- **Terminate.** To terminate a game is to end it short of a full 60 minutes of play, to record it officially as a completed game, and to make no provision to resume it at a later date. The Commissioner or League President may terminate a game in an emergency if, in his opinion, it is reasonable to project that its resumption (a) would not change its ultimate result or (b) would not adversely affect any other interteam competitive issue.
- **Forfeit.** The Commissioner, (except in cases of disciplinary action; see last section on "Removing Team from Field"), League President, and their representatives, including referees, are not authorized unilaterally to declare forfeits. A forfeit occurs only when a game is not played because of the failure or refusal of *one* team to participate. In that event, the other team, if ready and willing to play, is the winner by a score of 2-0.

2. If an emergency arises that may require cancellation, postponement, or termination (see above), the highest ranking representative from the Commissioner's office working the game in a "control" capacity will consult with the Commissioner, League President, or game-day duty officer designated by the League (by telephone, if that person is not in attendance) concerning such decision. If circumstances warrant, the League representative should also attempt to consult with the weather bureau and with appropriate security personnel of the League, club, stadium, and local authorities. If no representative from the Commissioner's office is working the game in a "control" capacity, the referee will be in charge (see "Authority of Referee" below).

3. In circumstances where safety is of immediate concern, the Commissioner's office representative may, after consulting with the referee, authorize a temporary suspension in play and, if warranted, removal of the participants from the playing field. The representative should be mindful of the safety of spectators, players, game officials, nonplayer personnel in the bench areas, and other field-level personnel such as photographers and cheerleaders.

4. If possible, the League-office representative should consult with authorized representatives of the two participating clubs before any decision involving cancellation, postponement, or termination is made by the Commissioner or League President.

5. If the Commissioner or League President decides to cancel, postpone, or terminate a game, his representative at the game or the game-day duty officer will then determine the method(s) for announcing such decision, e.g., by public-address announcement over referee's wireless microphone, by public-address announcement by home club, or by communication to radio, television, and other news media.

Authority of Referee

1. If a referee determines that an emergency warrants immediate removal of participants from the playing field for safety reasons, he may do so on his own authority. If, however, circumstances allow him the time, he must reach the highest ranking full-time League office representative working at the game in a "control" capacity or the game-day duty officer designated by the League (by telephone, if that person is not in attendance) and discuss the actual or potential emergency with such representative or duty officer. That representative or duty officer then will make the final decision on removal of participants from the field or obtain a decision from the Commissioner or League President.

2. If a referee removes participants from the playing field under No. 1 above, he may order them to their respective bench areas or to their locker rooms, whichever is appropriate in the circumstances.

3. After appropriate consultation under No. 1 above, the referee must advise the two participating head coaches of the nature of the emergency and the action contemplated (if the decision has not yet been reached) or of the final decision.

4. The referee must *not*, before a decision is reached, make an announcement on his microphone concerning the possibility of a cancellation, postponement, or termination unless instructed to do so by an appropriate representative of the Commissioner's office.

5. The referee must *not* discuss a forfeit with head coaches or club personnel and must *not* use that term over the referee's microphone (see definition of *forfeit* under No. 1 of "Authority of Commissioner's Office" above).

6. The referee must *not* assess an unsportsmanlike-conduct penalty on the home team for actions of fans that cause or contribute to an emergency.

7. The referee should be mindful of the safety of not only players and officials, but also of the spectators and other nonparticipants.

8. If an emergency involves spectator interference (for example, nonparticipants on the field or thrown objects), the referee immediately should contact the appropriate club or League representative for additional security assistance, including, if applicable, involvement of the League's security representative(s) assigned to the game.

9. The referee may order the resumption of play when he deems conditions safe for all concerned and, if circumstances warrant, after consultation with appropriate representatives of the Commissioner's office.

10. Under no circumstances is the referee authorized to cancel, postpone, terminate, or declare forfeiture of a game unilaterally.

Procedures for Starting and Resuming Games

Subject to the points of authority listed above, League personnel and referees will be guided by the following procedures for starting and resuming games that are affected by emergencies.

1. If, because of an emergency, a regular-season or postseason game is not started at its scheduled time and cannot be played at any later time that same day, the game nevertheless must be played on a subsequent date to be determined by the Commissioner.

2. If an emergency threatens to occur during the playing of a game (for example, an incoming tropical storm), the starting time of the game will not be moved to an earlier time unless there is clearly sufficient time to make an orderly change.

3. All games that are suspended temporarily and resumed on the same day, and all suspended games that are postponed to a later date, will be resumed at the point of suspension. On suspension, the referee will call timeout and make a record of the following: team possessing the ball, direction in which its offense was headed, position of the ball on the field, down, distance, period, time remaining in the period, and any other pertinent information required for an orderly and equitable resumption of play.

4. For regular-season postponements, the Commissioner will make every effort to set the game for no later than two days after its originally scheduled date and at the same site. If unable to schedule at the same site, he will select an appropriate alternative site. If it is impossible to schedule the game within two days after its original date, the Commissioner will attempt to schedule it on the Tuesday of the next calendar week. The Commissioner will keep in mind the potential for competitive inequities if one or both of the involved clubs has already been scheduled for a game close

to the Tuesday of that week (for example, a Thursday game).

5. For postseason postponements, the Commissioner will make every effort to set the game as soon as possible after its originally scheduled date and at the same site. If unable to schedule at the same site, he will select an appropriate alternative site.

6. Whenever postponement is attributable to negligence by a club, the negligent club is responsible for all home club costs and expenses, including, subject to approval by the Commissioner, gate receipts and television-contract income. [See Section 19.11 (C) of the NFL Constitution and Bylaws.]

7. Each home club is strictly responsible for having the playing surface of its stadium well maintained and suitable for NFL play.

UNFAIR ACTS

Commissioner's Authority

The Commissioner has sole authority to investigate and to take appropriate disciplinary or corrective measures if any club action, nonparticipant interference, or emergency occurs in an NFL game which he deems so unfair or outside the accepted tactics encountered in professional football that such action has a major effect on the result of a game.

No Club Protests

The authority and measures provided for in this section (UNFAIR ACTS) do not constitute a protest machinery for NFL clubs to dispute the result of a game. The Commissioner will conduct an investigation under this section only to review an act or occurrence that he deems so unfair that the result of the game in question may be inequitable to one of the participating teams. The Commissioner will not apply his authority under this section when a club registers a complaint concerning judgmental errors or routine errors of omission by game officials. Games involving such complaints will continue to stand as completed.

Penalties for Unfair Acts

The Commissioner's powers under this section (UNFAIR ACTS) include the imposition of monetary fines and draft choice forfeitures, suspension of persons involved, and, if appropriate, the reversal of a game's result or the rescheduling of a game, either from the beginning or from the point at which the extraordinary act occurred. In the event of rescheduling a game, the Commissioner will be guided by the procedures specified above ("Procedures for Starting and Resuming Games" under EMERGENCIES). In all cases, the Commissioner will conduct a full investigation, including the opportunity for hearings, use of game videotape, and any other procedures he deems appropriate.

REMOVING TEAM FROM FIELD

No player, coach, or other person affiliated with a club may remove that club's team from the field during the playing of any game, including preseason, except at the direction of the referee. Any club violating this rule will be subject to disciplinary action by the Commissioner, including possible game forfeiture and sole liability for financial losses suffered by the opposing club and any other affected member clubs of the League. [See Section 9.1 (E) of the NFL Constitution and Bylaws.]

General Information

AMERICAN FOOTBALL CONFERENCE

BALTIMORE RAVENS
1 Winning Drive
Owings Mills, MD 21117
410/701-4000

BUFFALO BILLS
One Bills Drive
Orchard Park, NY 14127
716/648-1800

CINCINNATI BENGALS
One Paul Brown Stadium
Cincinnati, OH 45202
513/621-3550

CLEVELAND BROWNS
76 Lou Groza Boulevard
Berea, OH 44017
440/891-5000

DENVER BRONCOS
13655 Broncos Parkway
Englewood, CO 80112
303/649-9000

HOUSTON TEXANS
Two Reliant Park
Houston, TX 77054
832/667-2000

INDIANAPOLIS COLTS
P.O. Box 535000
Indianapolis, IN 46253
317/297-2658

JACKSONVILLE JAGUARS
Jacksonville Municipal Stadium
One Stadium Place
Jacksonville, FL 32202
904/633-6000

KANSAS CITY CHIEFS
One Arrowhead Drive
Kansas City, MO 64129
816/920-9300

MIAMI DOLPHINS
7500 S.W. 30th Street
Davie, FL 33314
954/452-7000

NEW ENGLAND PATRIOTS
Gillette Stadium
One Patriot Place
Foxborough, MA 02035
508/543-8200

NEW YORK JETS
1000 Fulton Avenue
Hempstead, NY 11550
516/560-8100

OAKLAND RAIDERS
1220 Harbor Bay Parkway
Alameda, CA 94502
510/864-5000

PITTSBURGH STEELERS
3400 South Water Street
Pittsburgh, PA 15203
412/432-7800

SAN DIEGO CHARGERS
P.O. Box 609609
San Diego, CA 92160
858/874-4500

TENNESSEE TITANS
460 Great Circle Road
Nashville, TN 37228
615/565-4000

NATIONAL FOOTBALL CONFERENCE

ARIZONA CARDINALS
P.O. Box 888
Phoenix, AZ 85001
602/379-0101

ATLANTA FALCONS
4400 Falcon Parkway
Flowery Branch, GA 30542
770/965-3115

CAROLINA PANTHERS
800 South Mint Street
Charlotte, NC 28202
704/358-7000

CHICAGO BEARS
Halas Hall at Conway Park
1000 Football Drive
Lake Forest, IL 60045
847/295-6600

DALLAS COWBOYS
Cowboys Center
One Cowboys Parkway
Irving, TX 75063
972/556-9900

DETROIT LIONS
Detroit Lions Practice & Training Facility
222 Republic Drive
Allen Park, MI 48101
313/216-4000

GREEN BAY PACKERS
Lambeau Field Atrium
1265 Lombardi Avenue
Green Bay, WI 54304
920/569-7500

MINNESOTA VIKINGS
9520 Viking Drive
Eden Prairie, MN 55344
952/828-6500

NEW ORLEANS SAINTS
5800 Airline Drive
Metairie, LA 70003
504/733-0255

NEW YORK GIANTS
Giants Stadium
East Rutherford, NJ 07073
201/935-8111

PHILADELPHIA EAGLES
NovaCare Complex
One NovaCare Way
Philadelphia, PA 19145
215/463-2500

ST. LOUIS RAMS
One Rams Way
St. Louis, MO 63045
314/982-7267

SAN FRANCISCO 49ERS
4949 Centennial Boulevard
Santa Clara, CA 95054
408/562-4949

SEATTLE SEAHAWKS
11220 N.E. 53rd Street
Kirkland, WA 98033
425/827-9777

TAMPA BAY BUCCANEERS
One Buccaneer Place
Tampa, FL 33607
813/870-2700

WASHINGTON REDSKINS
Redskins Park
21300 Redskin Park Drive
Ashburn, VA 20147
703/726-7000

AMERICAN FOOTBALL CONFERENCE

BALTIMORE RAVENS
Stadium: M&T Bank Stadium
(opened in 1998)
•**Capacity:** 70,107
1101 Russell Street
Baltimore, MD 21230
Playing Surface: Sportexe Momentum

BUFFALO BILLS
Stadium: Ralph Wilson Stadium
(opened in 1973)
•**Capacity:** 73,967
One Bills Drive
Orchard Park, NY 14127
Playing Surface: AstroPlay

CINCINNATI BENGALS
Stadium: Paul Brown Stadium
(opened in 2000)
•**Capacity:** 65,515
One Paul Brown Stadium
Cincinnati, OH 45202
Playing Surface: Synthetic

CLEVELAND BROWNS
Stadium: Cleveland Browns Stadium
(opened in 1999)
•**Capacity:** 73,300
100 Alfred Lerner Way
Cleveland, OH 44114
Playing Surface: Grass

DENVER BRONCOS
Stadium: INVESCO Field at Mile High
(opened in 2001)
•**Capacity:** 76,125
1701 Bryant Street
Denver, CO 80204
Playing Surface: DD Grassmaster

HOUSTON TEXANS
Stadium: Reliant Stadium
(opened in 2002)
•**Capacity:** 71,054
Houston, TX 77054
Playing Surface: Grass

INDIANAPOLIS COLTS
Stadium: RCA Dome
(opened in 1983)
•**Capacity:** 55,531
100 South Capitol Avenue
Indianapolis, IN 46225
Playing Surface: FieldTurf

JACKSONVILLE JAGUARS
Stadium: Jacksonville Municipal Stadium
(opened in 1995)
•**Capacity:** 67,164
One Stadium Place
Jacksonville, FL 32202
Playing Surface: Grass

KANSAS CITY CHIEFS
Stadium: Arrowhead Stadium
(opened in 1972)
•**Capacity:** 79,451
One Arrowhead Drive
Kansas City, MO 64129
Playing Surface: Grass

MIAMI DOLPHINS
Stadium: Dolphin Stadium
(opened in 1987)
•**Capacity:** 75,192
2269 Dan Marino Blvd.
Miami Gardens, FL 33056
Playing Surface: Grass (PAT)

NEW ENGLAND PATRIOTS
Stadium: Gillette Stadium
(opened in 2002)
•**Capacity:** 68,756
One Patriot Place
Foxborough, MA 02035
Playing Surface: Grass

NEW YORK JETS
Stadium: Meadowlands
(opened in 1976)
•**Capacity:** 80,062
East Rutherford, NJ 07073
Playing Surface: FieldTurf

OAKLAND RAIDERS
Stadium: McAfee Coliseum
(opened in 1966)
•**Capacity:** 63,132
7000 Coliseum Way
Oakland, CA 94621
Playing Surface: Grass

PITTSBURGH STEELERS
Stadium: Heinz Field
(opened in 2001)
•**Capacity:** 65,050
100 Art Rooney Avenue
Pittsburgh, PA 15212
Playing Surface: DD GrassMaster

SAN DIEGO CHARGERS
Stadium: Qualcomm Stadium
(opened in 1967)
•**Capacity:** 70,000
9449 Friars Road
San Diego, CA 92108
Playing Surface: Grass

TENNESSEE TITANS
Stadium: LP Field
(opened in 1999)
•**Capacity:** 69,143
One Titans Way
Nashville, TN 37213
Playing Surface: Natural Grass

NATIONAL FOOTBALL CONFERENCE

ARIZONA CARDINALS
Stadium: University of Phoenix Stadium
(opened in 2006)
•**Capacity:** 65,000
1 Cardinals Drive
Glendale, AZ 85305
Playing Surface: Grass

ATLANTA FALCONS
Stadium: Georgia Dome
(opened in 1992)
•**Capacity:** 71,228
One Georgia Dome Drive
Atlanta, GA 30313
Playing Surface: FieldTurf

CAROLINA PANTHERS
Stadium: Bank of America Stadium
(opened in 1996)
•**Capacity:** 73,298
Charlotte, NC 28202
Playing Surface: Grass

CHICAGO BEARS
Stadium: Soldier Field
(opened in 1924)
•**Capacity:** 61,500
1410 S. Museum Campus Dr.
Chicago, IL 60605
Playing Surface: Natural Grass

DALLAS COWBOYS
Stadium: Texas Stadium
(opened in 1971)
•**Capacity:** 65,529
2401 E. Airport Freeway
Irving, TX 75062
Playing Surface: Sportfield Realgrass

DETROIT LIONS
Stadium: Ford Field
(opened in 2002)
•**Capacity:** 64,500
2000 Brush Street
Detroit, MI 48226
Playing Surface: FieldTurf

GREEN BAY PACKERS
Stadium: Lambeau Field
(opened in 1957)
•**Capacity:** 72,928
1265 Lombardi Avenue
Green Bay, WI 54304
Playing Surface: Grass

MINNESOTA VIKINGS
Stadium: Hubert H. Humphrey Metrodome
(opened in 1982)
•**Capacity:** 64,121
500 11th Avenue South
Minneapolis, MN 55415
Playing Surface: FieldTurf

NEW ORLEANS SAINTS
Stadium: Louisiana Superdome
(opened in 1975)
•**Capacity:** 65,000
1500 Poydras Street
New Orleans, LA 70112
Playing Surface: Sportexe Momentum

NEW YORK GIANTS
Stadium: Giants Stadium
(opened in 1976)
•**Capacity:** 80,242
East Rutherford, NJ 07073
Playing Surface: FieldTurf

PHILADELPHIA EAGLES
Stadium: Lincoln Financial Field
(opened in 2003)
•**Capacity:** 68,400
One Lincoln Financial Field Way
Philadelphia, PA 19148
Playing Surface: Natural Grass

ST. LOUIS RAMS
Stadium: Edward Jones Dome
(opened in 1995)
•**Capacity:** 66,000
701 Convention Plaza
St. Louis, MO 63101
Playing Surface: FieldTurf

SAN FRANCISCO 49ERS
Stadium: Monster Park
(opened in 1958)
•**Capacity:** 69,732
San Francisco, CA 94124
Playing Surface: Natural Grass

SEATTLE SEAHAWKS
Stadium: Qwest Field
(opened in 2002)
•**Capacity:** 67,000
800 Occidental Ave South, #200
Seattle, WA 98134
Playing Surface: FieldTurf

TAMPA BAY BUCCANEERS
Stadium: Raymond James Stadium
(opened in 1998)
•**Capacity:** 65,908
Tampa, FL 33607
Playing Surface: Grass

WASHINGTON REDSKINS
Stadium: FedExField
(opened in 1997)
•**Capacity:** 91,704
1600 FedEx Way
Landover, MD 20785
Playing Surface: Natural Grass

280 Park Avenue, New York, New York 10017 (212) 450-2000

NFL Internet Network: www.NFL.com

Commissioner: Roger Goodell

Executive Vice President/Football Operations: Ray Anderson

**Executive Vice President of Media/President and
Chief Executive Officer of NFL Network:** Steve Bornstein

Executive Vice President of Communications and Public Affairs: Joe Browne

Executive Vice President of Finance and Strategic Transactions: Eric Grubman

Executive Vice President of Labor Relations/Chairman NFLMC: Harold Henderson

Executive Vice President/Chief Administrative Officer-Counsel: Jeff Pash